C0-AJV-580

# THE OLD TESTAMENT STUDY BIBLE

# PSALMS

*The Complete*

# BIBLICAL LIBRARY

**The Complete Biblical Library: The Old Testament.** Volume 10: STUDY BIBLE, PSALMS.  Published by World Library Press Inc., Springfield, Missouri, U.S.A.
 Printed in the United States of America.
International Standard Book Number
1-884642-34-9—vol. 10
1-884642-49-7—Set

**Library of Congress Cataloging in Publication Data**
The Old Testament Study Bible.
The Complete Biblical Library.
The Old Testament; volumes 1–15.
Includes Bibliographic references.
Contents: [1] Genesis—[2] Exodus—[3] Leviticus, Numbers—[4] Deuteronomy—[5] Joshua, Judges, Ruth—[6] 1 & 2 Samuel—[7] 1 & 2 Kings—[8] 1 & 2 Chronicles—[9] Ezra, Nehemiah, Esther, Job—[10] Psalms—[11] Proverbs, Ecclesiastes, Song of Songs—[12] Isaiah—[13] Jeremiah, Lamentations—[14] Ezekiel, Daniel—[15] Hosea–Malachi
ISBN: 1-884642-34-9
1. Bible. O.T.—Study and Teaching.
I. Series: Complete Biblical Library (Series). Old Testament; 15 volumes
BS1193.05 1995
221.6'1—dc20 95-49455 CIP

**THE NEW TESTAMENT**
Study Bible, Greek-English Dictionary,
Harmony of the Gospels

**THE OLD TESTAMENT**
Study Bible, Hebrew-English Dictionary,
Harmony of the Historical Accounts

**THE BIBLE ENCYCLOPEDIA**

---



---

INTERNATIONAL AND
INTERDENOMINATIONAL
BIBLE STUDY SYSTEM

# THE OLD TESTAMENT STUDY BIBLE

---

# PSALMS

**WORLD LIBRARY PRESS INC.**
Springfield, Missouri, U.S.A.

## VERSE-BY-VERSE COMMENTARY

Alexander MacLaren, D.D.

## VARIOUS VERSIONS

Rev. Gary L. Sherman
Rev. Paul D. Sherman
Verna M. Sherman, A.S.
Craig M. Froman, M.A.
Todd C. Harder, B.A.
Lattis R. Campbell, B.S.
Robert D. Grant, B.S.

## REVIEW BOARD

Gleason L. Archer, Jr., Ph.D.
Roger D. Cotton, Th.D.
Stanley M. Horton, Th.D.
W. E. Nunnally, Ph.D.
Samuel J. Schultz, Th.D.

## ASSISTANT EDITOR

Brian D. Rogers, M.Div.

## TECHNICAL ASSISTANCE

**Editorial Team:** Faye Faucett (editorial assistant); Jess L. Leeper, B.A., James E. Talkington, B.A., Dennis E. Waldrop, M.Div. (Hebrew assistance); Jill M. Canaday, B.A., Caryn S. Daugherty, Chuck J. Goldberg, M.Div., Christy L. Hunsaker, Scott A. Kirby, Edel Kolbe, Wade W. Pettenger, B.S.

**Computer Consultant:** Martin D. Crossland, Ph.D.

**Art Director:** Terry Van Someren, B.F.A.

# Table of Contents

# Introduction

This volume of the *Old Testament Study Bible* is part of a set entitled *The Complete Biblical Library: Old Testament.* It is designed to provide the information needed for a basic understanding of the Old Testament—useful for scholars but also for students and laypeople.

*The Complete Biblical Library: Old Testament* series consists of a fifteen-volume *Study Bible* and a seven-volume *Hebrew-English Dictionary,* which are closely linked. Information about the *Study Bible's* features are found below. The *Hebrew-English Dictionary* (HED) lists all the Hebrew words of the Old Testament in alphabetical order, with an article explaining the background, significance and meaning of the words. The HED also provides a concordance showing each place the words appear in the Old Testament, a list of synonyms and related words, and many other features for a full understanding of each word.

## FEATURES OF THE STUDY BIBLE

The *Study Bible* is a combination of study materials which will help both scholar and layperson achieve a better understanding of the Old Testament and its language. Most of these helps are available in various forms elsewhere, but bringing them together in combination will save many hours of research. Many scholars do not have in their personal libraries all the volumes necessary to provide the information so readily available here.

*The Complete Biblical Library* accomplishes an unusual task: to help scholars in their research and to make available to laypersons the tools to acquire knowledge which, up to this time, has been available only to scholars. Following are the major divisions of the *Study Bible:*

### Overview

Each volume contains an encyclopedic survey of the Old Testament Book. It provides a general outline, discusses matters about which there may be a difference of opinion and provides background information regarding the history, cultures, literature and philosophy of the era covered by the Book.

### Interlinear

Following the principle of providing help for both the scholar and layperson, a unique interlinear has been supplied. Most interlinears, if not all, give the Hebrew text and meanings of the words. This interlinear contains five parts:

1. *Hebrew Text.* This is the original language of the Old Testament as we have it today.

2. *Grammatical Forms.* These are shown above each Hebrew word, beneath its assigned number. Each word's part of speech is identified (constructs being italicized). This information is repeated, along with the Hebrew word, in the *Hebrew-English Dictionary* where more details may be found.

3. *Transliteration.* No other interlinears provide this. Its purpose is to familiarize laypersons with the proper pronunciation of Hebrew words so they will feel comfortable when using them in teaching situations. Information on pronunciation is found on page 10, which shows the Hebrew alphabet.

4. *Translation.* The basic meaning of each Hebrew word is found beneath it. Rather than merely compiling past interlinears, a fresh translation has been made.

5. *Assigned Numbers.* The unique numbering system of *The Complete Biblical Library* makes cross-reference study between the *Study Bible* and the *Hebrew-English Dictionary* the ultimate in simplicity. Each Hebrew word has been assigned a number.

The *Hebrew-English Dictionary* then follows the same cross-referencing plan with each word listed in alphabetical sequence and labeled with the proper number. If further study on a certain word is desired, information can be found by locating its number in the *Dictionary*.

**Various Versions**

The various versions section contains a vast comparison of the Old Testament versions. The King James Version is shown in boldface type; then from more than thirty other versions, various ways the Hebrew phrase may be translated can be found. The Hebrew language of ancient times is such a rich language that, to obtain the full meaning of words, several synonyms may be needed.

**Verse-by-Verse Commentary**

Many scholars have combined their knowledge and skills to provide a reliable commentary. Providing a basic understanding of every verse in the Old Testament, the commentary opens up the nuances of the Hebrew Old Testament.

## HEBREW TRANSLATION

No word-for-word translation can be fully "literal" and still express all the nuances of the original language. Rather, the purpose is to help the reader find the English word which most correctly expresses the original Hebrew word in that particular context. The Hebrew language is so rich in meaning that the same word may have a slightly different meaning in another context.

Language idioms offer a special translation problem. Idioms are expressions that have a meaning which cannot be derived from the conjoined meanings of its elements. The Hebrew language abounds in such phrases which, when translated literally, provide insight, and even humor, to the English reader of the pictorial nature of Hebrew.

## LITERARY AND BIBLICAL STANDARDS

Hundreds of qualified scholars and specialists in particular fields have participated in producing *The Complete Biblical Library.* Great care has been taken to maintain high standards of scholarship and ethics, involving scholars in Review Boards for the *Study Bible* and the *Hebrew-English Dictionary.* There has been particular concern about giving proper credit for citations from other works, and writers have been instructed to show care in this regard. Any deviation from this principle has been inadvertent and unintentional.

Obviously, with writers coming from widely differing backgrounds, there are differences of opinion as to how to interpret certain passages. But, the focus of *The Complete Biblical Library* is always from a conservative and evangelical standpoint, upholding Scripture as the inspired Word of God. When there are strong differences in the interpretations of a particular passage, we have felt it best to present the contrasting viewpoints.

## STUDY HELPS

As you come to the Scripture section of this volume, you will find correlated pages for your study. The facing pages are designed to complement each other, so you will have a better understanding of the Word of God. Each two-page spread will deal with a group of verses.

First is the interlinear with its fivefold helps: (1) the Hebrew text in which the Old Testament was written; (2) the transliteration, showing how to pronounce each word; (3) the translation of each word; (4) an assigned number (you will need this number to learn more about the word in the *Hebrew-English Dictionary*, companion to the *Study Bible*); and (5) the grammatical form.

The second part of each two-page spread contains two features. The various versions section provides an expanded understanding of the various ways Hebrew words or phrases can be translated. The phrase from the King James Version appears in boldface print, then other meaningful ways the Hebrew language has been translated follow. This feature will bring you the riches of the language of the Old Testament.

The verse-by-verse commentary refers to each verse giving a sufficient basic explanation. Significant viewpoints are discussed in addition to the author's.

## THE HEBREW ALPHABET

| | | |
|---|---|---|
| א | aleph | ’ (glottal stop) |
| ב | beth | b, v |
| ג | gimel | g, gh |
| ד | daleth | d, dh |
| ה | he | h |
| ו | waw | w, v |
| ז | zayin | z |
| ח | heth | ch |
| ט | teth | t̲ (hardened) |
| י | yodh | y |
| כ, ךְ, ך | kaph | k, kh |
| ל | lamedh | l |
| מ, ם | mem | m |
| נ, ן | nun | n |
| ס | samekh | s̲ (hardened) |
| ע | ayin | ‘ (aspiration) |
| פ, ף | pe | p, ph |
| צ, ץ | tsade | ts |
| ק | qoph | q |
| ר | resh | r |
| שׂ | sin | s |
| שׁ | shin | sh |
| ת | taw | t, th |

## INTERLINEAR COMPONENTS

### A & B: Number

The first line of each record of the interlinear is a numeral which refers to the *Hebrew-English Dictionary*. The numbers should be referenced *only* by the digits before the decimal. Most words have an ordinary numeral. Only the verbs have the extended system.

The digits after the decimal refer to the standard verb chart found in Hebrew grammars. The first digit after the decimal refers to the “mood” of the verb (simple, passive, causative, intensive, reflexive); the second refers to the “tense” (perfect, imperfect, jussive, imperative, infinitive or participle); the third refers to the person, gender and number (such as 3rd masculine singular).

### C: Location or Grammar

The second line of the interlinear is the description of the grammatical construction of the Hebrew word. Describing a Hebrew word in this manner is called locating the word. You will notice there is often more than one word written as a single Hebrew word. This is because related words are often joined. A full listing of abbreviations and a brief explanation may be found at the end of the book.

### D: Hebrew

This is the original language of the Old Testament as we have it today. The Hebrew text of the interlinear is a comparative text, provided by The Original Word Publishers of Roswell, Georgia.

### E: Transliteration

This is the key to pronouncing the word. The transliteration matches that which is found in the Septuagint research of the *New Testament Greek-English Dictionary* of *The Complete Biblical Library.*

### F: Translation

This is a fresh translation prepared by the executive editor and the commentary writer.

## THE FIRST BOOK OF MOSES CALLED

# GENESIS בְּרֵאשִׁית

| 1:1 904, 7519 | 1282.111 | 435 | 881 | 8452 | 881 | 800 |
|---|---|---|---|---|---|---|
| prep, art, n fs | v Qal pf 3ms | n mp | do | art, n md | cj, do | art, n fs |
| בְּרֵאשִׁית | בָּרָא | אֱלֹהִים | אֵת | הַשָּׁמַיִם | וְאֵת | הָאָרֶץ |
| b$^e$rē'shîth | bārā' | 'ělōhîm | 'ēth | hashshāmayim | w$^e$'ēth | hā'ārets |
| in the beginning | created | God | | the heavens | and | the earth |

A

| 2. 800 | 2030.112 | 8744 | 958 | 2932 | 6142, 6686 |
|---|---|---|---|---|---|
| cj, art, n fs | v Qal pf 3fs | n ms | cj, n ms | cj, n ms | prep, *n mp* |
| וְהָאָרֶץ | הָיְתָה | תֹהוּ | וָבֹהוּ | וְחֹשֶׁךְ | עַל־פְּנֵי |
| w$^e$hā'ārets | hāy$^e$thāh | thōhû | wāvōhû | w$^e$chōshekh | 'al-p$^e$nê |
| and the earth | it was | formless | and empty | and darkness | over the surface of |

B

| 8745 | 7593 | 435 | 7646.353 | 6142, 6686 | 4448 |
|---|---|---|---|---|---|
| n fs | cj, *n fs* | n mp | v Piel ptc fs | prep, *n mp* | art, n md |
| תְהוֹם | וְרוּחַ | אֱלֹהִים | מְרַחֶפֶת | עַל־פְּנֵי | הַמָּיִם |
| th$^e$hôm | w$^e$rûach | 'ělōhîm | m$^e$rachepheth | 'al-p$^e$nê | hammāyim |
| the deep | and the Spirit of | God | hovering | over the surface of | the waters |

C

| 3. 569.121 | 435 | 2030.121 | 214 | 2030.121, 214 | 4. 7495.121 |
|---|---|---|---|---|---|
| cj, v Qal impf 3ms | n mp | v Qal juss 3ms | n ms | cj, v Qal impf 3ms, n ms | cj, v Qal impf 3ms |
| וַיֹּאמֶר | אֱלֹהִים | יְהִי | אוֹר | וַיְהִי־אוֹר | וַיַּרְא |
| wayyō'mer | 'ělōhîm | y$^e$hî | 'ôr | wayhî-'ôr | wayyar$^e$' |
| and He said | God | let there be | light | and there was light | and He saw |

| 435 | 881, 214 | 3706, 3005 | 950.521 | 435 | 1033 | 214 |
|---|---|---|---|---|---|---|
| n mp | do, art, n ms | prep, adj | cj, v Hiphil impf 3ms | n mp | prep | art, n ms |
| אֱלֹהִים | אֶת־הָאוֹר | כִּי־טוֹב | וַיַּבְדֵּל | אֱלֹהִים | בֵּין | הָאוֹר |
| 'ělōhîm | 'eth-hā'ôr | kî-ṭôv | wayyavdēl | 'ělōhîm | bên | hā'ôr |
| God | the light | that good | and He separated | God | between | the light |

D

| 1033 | 2932 | 5. 7410.121 | 435 | 3937, 214 | 3219 | 3937, 2932 |
|---|---|---|---|---|---|---|
| cj, prep | art, n ms | cj, v Qal impf 3ms | n mp | prep, art, n ms | n ms | cj, prep, art, n ms |
| וּבֵין | הַחֹשֶׁךְ | וַיִּקְרָא | אֱלֹהִים | לָאוֹר | יוֹם | וְלַחֹשֶׁךְ |
| ûvên | hachōshekh | wayyiqrā' | 'ělōhîm | lā'ôr | yôm | w$^e$lachōshekh |
| and between | the darkness | and He named | God | the light | day | and the darkness |

| 7410.111 | 4050 | 2030.121, 6394 | 2030.121, 1269 | 3219 | 259 |
|---|---|---|---|---|---|
| v Qal pf 3ms | n ms | cj, v Qal impf 3ms, n ms | cj, v Qal impf 3ms, n ms | n ms | num |
| קָרָא | לָיְלָה | וַיְהִי־עֶרֶב | וַיְהִי־בֹקֶר | יוֹם | אֶחָד |
| qārā' | lāy$^e$lāh | wayhî-'erev | wayhî-vōqer | yôm | 'echādh |
| He named | night | and it was evening | and it was morning | day | one |

E

| 6. 569.121 | 435 | 2030.121 | 7842 | 904, 8761 | 4448 |
|---|---|---|---|---|---|
| cj, v Qal impf 3ms | n mp | v Qal juss 3ms | n ms | prep, *n ms* | art, n md |
| וַיֹּאמֶר | אֱלֹהִים | יְהִי | רָקִיעַ | בְּתוֹךְ | הַמָּיִם |
| wayyō'mer | 'ělōhîm | y$^e$hî | rāqîa' | b$^e$thôkh | hammāyim |
| and He said | God | let there be | expanse | in the middle of | the waters |

F

| 2030.121 | 950.551 | 1033 | 4448 | 3937, 4448 | 7. 6449.121 |
|---|---|---|---|---|---|
| cj, v Qal juss 3ms | v Hiphil ptc ms | prep | n md | prep, art, n md | cj, v Qal impf 3ms |
| וִיהִי | מַבְדִּיל | בֵּין | מַיִם | לָמָיִם | וַיַּעַשׂ |
| wîhî | mavdîl | bên | mayim | lāmāyim | wayya'as |
| and let it be | what separates | between | waters | from the waters | and He made |

# THE BOOK OF

# PSALMS

---

*Expanded Interlinear*
*Various Versions*
*Verse-by-Verse Commentary*

---

THE BOOK OF

# PSALMS תְּהִלִּים

**1:1**

| 869 | 382 | 866 | 3940 | 2050.111 | 904, 6332 | 7857 |
|---|---|---|---|---|---|---|
| *n ms* | art, n ms | rel pron | neg part | v Qal pf 3ms | prep, *n fs* | n mp |
| אַשְׁרֵי | הָאִישׁ | אֲשֶׁר | לֹא | הָלַךְ | בַּעֲצַת | רְשָׁעִים |
| 'ashrê | hā'îsh | 'ăsher | lō' | hālakh | ba'ătsath | reshā'îm |
| blessed | the man | who | not | he has walked | by the counsel of | the wicked |

| 904, 1932 | 2491 | 3940 | 6198.111 | 904, 4319 | 4054.152 | 3940 |
|---|---|---|---|---|---|---|
| cj, prep, *n ms* | n mp | neg part | v Qal pf 3ms | cj, prep, *n ms* | v Qal act ptc mp | neg part |
| וּבְדֶרֶךְ | חַטָּאִים | לֹא | עָמָד | וּבְמוֹשַׁב | לֵצִים | לֹא |
| ûvedherekh | chattā'îm | lō' | 'āmādh | ûvemôshav | lētsîm | lō' |
| or on the way of | sinners | not | he has stood | or on the seat of | those who scorn | not |

| 3553.111 | | 3706 | 524 | 904, 8784 | 3176 | 2761 | 904, 8784 | 1965.121 |
|---|---|---|---|---|---|---|---|---|
| v Qal pf 3ms | **2.** | cj | cj | prep, *n fs* | pn | n ms, ps 3ms | cj, prep, n fs, ps 3ms | v Qal impf 3ms |
| יָשָׁב | | כִּי | אִם | בְּתוֹרַת | יְהוָה | חֶפְצוֹ | וּבְתוֹרָתוֹ | יֶהְגֶּה |
| yāshāv | | kî | 'im | bethôrath | yehwāh | chephtsô | ûvethôrāthô | yehgeh |
| he has sat | | but | rather | in the law of | Yahweh | his delight | and about his law | he meditates |

| 3221 | 4050 | | 2030.111 | 3626, 6320 | 8694.155 | 6142, 6631 | 4448 |
|---|---|---|---|---|---|---|---|
| adv | cj, n ms | **3.** | cj, v Qal pf 3ms | prep, n ms | v Qal pass ptc ms | prep, *n mp* | n mp |
| יוֹמָם | וָלָיְלָה | | וְהָיָה | כְּעֵץ | שָׁתוּל | עַל־פַּלְגֵי | מָיִם |
| yômām | wālāyelāh | | wehāyāh | ke'ēts | shāthûl | 'al-palghê | māyim |
| by day | and by night | | then he will be | like a tree | planted | beside the streams of | water |

| 866 | 6780 | 5598.121 | 904, 6496 | 6149 | 3940, 5209.121 | 3725 |
|---|---|---|---|---|---|---|
| rel part | n ms, ps 3ms | v Qal impf 3ms | prep, n fs, ps 3ms | cj, n ms, ps 3ms | neg part, v Qal impf 3ms | cj, n ms |
| אֲשֶׁר | פִּרְיוֹ | יִתֵּן | בְּעִתּוֹ | וְעָלֵהוּ | לֹא־יִבּוֹל | וְכֹל |
| 'ăsher | piryô | yittēn | be'ittô | we'ālēhû | lō'-yibbôl | wekhōl |
| which | its fruit | he will give | in its season | and its leaf | it will not wither | and all |

**1:1. Blessed is the man:** ... Oh, the joys, *Berkeley* ... Happy are those, *Good News* ... O the happiness of that one, *Young.*

**that walketh not:** ... who has not entered, *Anchor.*

**in the counsel of the ungodly:** ... beneath the sinners' groves, *Fenton* ... rejects the advice of the wicked, *JB* ... does not guide his steps by ill counsel, *Knox* ... who don't listen to, *NCV* ... of the wicked, *Anchor.*

**nor standeth in the way of sinners:** ... on the path of vice, *Fenton* ... or turn aside where sinners walk, *Knox* ... hang around with sinners, *LIVB* ... never takes the sinners' road, *Moffatt* ... don't go where sinners go, *NCV.*

**nor sitteth in the seat of the scornful:** ... where scornful souls gather, sit down to rest, *Knox* ... in the company of the insolent, *NAB* ... don't do what evil people do, *NCV* ... join those who have no use for God, *Good News* ... mockers, *NIV* ... cynics, *JB.*

**2. But his delight:** ... they find joy, *Good News* ... They love the LORD's teachings, *NCV.*

**is in the law of the LORD:** ... everything God wants them to, *LIVB* ... in the Eternal's law, *Moffatt* ... Yahweh, *Anchor.*

**and in his law doth he meditate day and night:** ... recites, *Anchor* ... murmurs his law, *JB* ... poring over it, *Moffatt* ... talk with himself, *Rotherham* ... seeks His rules, *Fenton.*

**3. And he shall be like a tree:** ... stands firm as a tree, *Knox* ... They are strong, like a tree, *NCV.*

**planted by the rivers of water:** ... transplanted near streams, *Anchor* ... brooks, *Darby* ... running water, *Knox* ... beside a watercourse, *NEB* ... water channels, *REB.*

**that bringeth forth his fruit in his season:** ... at the right time, *Good News* ... without fail, *LIVB.*

**his leaf also shall not wither:** ... fadeth not, *Darby* ... dry up, *Good News* ... leaves don't die, *NCV* ... its foliage never fades, *REB.*

*The Psalter may be regarded as the heart's echo to the speech of God, the manifold music of its wind-swept strings as God's breath sweeps across them. Law and prophecy are the two main elements of that speech, and the first two Psalms, as a double prelude to the Book, answer to these, the former setting forth the blessedness of loving and keeping the Law and the latter celebrating the enthronement of the Messiah. Jewish tradition says that the two Psalms were originally one, and a well-attested reading of Acts 13:33 quotes "Thou art my Son" as part of the first Psalm. The diversity of subject matter makes original unity improbable, but possibly our present first Psalm was prefixed unnumbered.*

***Psalm 1.*** *The theme of the first Psalm is the blessedness of keeping the Law and is enforced by the juxtaposition of two sharply contrasted pictures, one in bright light, another in deep shadow, and each heightening the other. Ebal and Gerizim face one another. The character and fate of the lover of the Law are sketched in vv. 1ff, and that of the "wicked" in vv. 4ff.*

**1:1–3.** The word "blessed" (HED #869) is usually taken as an exclamation, but may equally well be a simple affirmation. It declares a universal truth even more strongly, if so regarded. The characteristics which bring blessedness are first described negatively, and that order is significant. As long as there is so much evil in the world and society is what it is, godliness must be largely negative and its possessors a people whose laws are different from all people that be on earth. Live fish swim against the stream; dead ones go with it.

Increasing closeness and permanence of association are obvious in the progress from "walking" to "standing" and from "standing" to "sitting." Increasing boldness in evil is marked by the progress from "counsel" to "way," or course of life, and thence to "scoffing." Evil purposes come out in deeds, and deeds at last formulate bitter speech. Some men scoff because they have already sinned. The tongue is blackened and made sore by poison in the system. Therefore, goodness will avoid the smallest conformity with evil, as knowing that a sleeve caught in gears will draw in the whole body. But these negative characteristics are valuable mainly for their efficacy in contributing to the positive, as the wall around a young plantation is there for the sake of what grows behind it. On the other hand, these positive characteristics, the main one being a higher love, are the only basis for useful abstinence. Mere conventional, negative virtue is of little power or worth unless it flows from strong determination of the soul in another direction.

The good man's character being thus all condensed into one trait, the next Psalm gathers his blessedness up in one image. The tree is an eloquent figure, and water is the one factor that can turn a desert into a garden. Such a life will be rooted and steadfast. "Planted" is expressed by a word which suggests establishment (HED #8694). The good man's life is deeply anchored, and so rides out storms. It goes down through superficial fleeting things to that eternal will, and so stands unmoved and upright when winds howl.

Such a life is fed and refreshed. The Law of the LORD is both the soil and the stream. In the one aspect, fastening a life to it gives stability; in the other, it provides refreshment and a means of growth. Truly loved, that will becomes, in its manifold expressions, as the divided irrigation channels through which a great river is brought to the roots of each plant. If men do not find it as life-giving as rivers of water in a dry place, it is because they do not delight in it.

Such a life is vigorous and productive. It would be artificial straining to assign definite meanings to "fruit" and "leaf." All that belongs to vitality and beauty is included. These come naturally when the preceding condition is fulfilled. This stage of the Psalm is the appropriate place for deeds to come into view. By loving fellowship with God and delighting in his Law, the man is made capable of good. His virtues are growths, the outcome of life. The relation is more intimate still. "I am the vine, ye are the branches. He that abideth in me, and I in him, the same bringeth forth much fruit" (John 15:5).

Such a life will be prosperous. The figure is abandoned here. The meaning is not affected whether we translate "whatsoever he doeth shall prosper," or "whatsoever … he shall cause to succeed" (v. 3). That is not unconditionally true now, nor was it then, if it refers to what the world calls prospering, as many a sad and questioning line in the Psalter proves. They to whom the will of God is delight can never be hurt by evil, for all that meets them expresses and serves that will, and the fellow-servants of the King do not wound one another. If a life is rooted in God and a heart delights in his Law, that life will be prosperous, and that heart will be at rest.

| 866, 6449.121 | 7014.521 | | 3940, 3772 | 7857 | 3706 | 524, 3626, 4833 |
|---|---|---|---|---|---|---|
| rel part, v Qal impf 3ms | v Hiphil impf 3ms | 4. | neg part, adv | art, n mp | cj | cj, prep, art, n ms |
| אֲשֶׁר־יַעֲשֶׂה | יַצְלִיחַ | | לֹא־כֵן | הָרְשָׁעִים | כִּי | אִם־כַּמֹּץ |
| 'ăsher-ya'ăseh | yatslîach | | lō'-khēn | hāreshā'îm | kî | 'im-kammōts |
| that he does | it will succeed | | not so | the wicked | but | rather like the chaff |

| 866, 5264.122 | 7593 | | 6142, 3772 | 3940, 7251.126 | 7857 | 904, 5122 |
|---|---|---|---|---|---|---|
| rel part, v Qal impf 3fs, ps 3ms | n fs | 5. | prep, adv | neg part, v Qal impf 3mp | n mp | prep, art, n ms |
| אֲשֶׁר־תִּדְּפֶנּוּ | רוּחַ | | עַל־כֵּן | לֹא־יָקֻמוּ | רְשָׁעִים | בַּמִּשְׁפָּט |
| 'ăsher-tiddephennû | rûach | | 'al-kēn | lō'-yāqumû | reshā'îm | bammishpāṯ |
| which it blows it away | the wind | | therefore | he will not stand | the wicked | in the judgment |

| 2491 | 904, 5920 | 6926 | | 3706, 3156.151 | 3176 | 1932 |
|---|---|---|---|---|---|---|
| cj, n mp | prep, art, *n fs* | n mp | 6. | cj, v Qal act ptc ms | pn | *n ms* |
| וְחַטָּאִים | בַּעֲדַת | צַדִּיקִים | | כִּי־יוֹדֵעַ | יְהוָה | דֶּרֶךְ |
| wechaṯṯā'îm | ba'ădhath | tsaddîqîm | | kî-yôdhēa' | yehwāh | derekh |
| nor sinners | in the congregation of | the righteous | | because One Who knows | Yahweh | the way of |

| 6926 | 1932 | 7857 | 6.122 | | 4066 | 7570.116 | 1504 |
|---|---|---|---|---|---|---|---|
| n mp | cj, *n ms* | n mp | v Qal impf 3fs | 2:1 | intrg | v Qal pf 3cp | n mp |
| צַדִּיקִים | וְדֶרֶךְ | רְשָׁעִים | תֹּאבֵד | | לָמָּה | רָגְשׁוּ | גוֹיִם |
| tsaddîqîm | wedherekh | reshā'îm | tō'vēdh | | lāmmāh | rāgheshû | ghôyim |
| the righteous | but the way of | the wicked | it will perish | | why | are they restless | nations |

| 3947 | 1965.126, 7672 | | 3429.726 | 4567, 800 | 7619.152 |
|---|---|---|---|---|---|
| cj, n mp | v Qal impf 3mp, n ms | 2. | v Hithpael impf 3mp | *n mp*, n fs | cj, v Qal act ptc mp |
| וּלְאֻמִּים | יֶהְגּוּ־רִיק | | יִתְיַצְּבוּ | מַלְכֵי־אֶרֶץ | וְרוֹזְנִים |
| ûlă'ummîm | yehgû-rîq | | yithyatstsevû | malkhê-'erets | werôznîm |
| and the peoples | they plan vanity | | they take their stand | the kings of the earth | and rulers |

| 3354.216, 3266 | 6142, 3176 | 6142, 5081 | | 5607.320 |
|---|---|---|---|---|
| v Niphal pf 3cp, adv | prep, pn | cj, prep, n ms, ps 3ms | 3. | v Piel juss 1cp |
| נוֹסְדוּ־יָחַד | עַל־יְהוָה | וְעַל־מְשִׁיחוֹ | | נְנַתְּקָה |
| nôsdhû-yāchadh | 'al-yehwāh | we'al-meshîchô | | nenatteqāh |
| they conspire together | against Yahweh | and against his Anointed One | | let us cut off |

**and whatsoever he doeth shall prosper:** … Whatever it produces is good, *Anchor* … everything he does, *Berkeley* … and they succeed, *Fenton.*

**4. The ungodly are not so:** … bad, *Fenton* … evil men, *Good News* … How different, *JB* … what a different story, *LIVB* … the lawless, *Rotherham.*

**but are like the chaff:** … winnowed chaff, *Anchor* … straw, *Good News.*

**which the wind driveth away:** … drives along, *Anchor* … blows, *Berkeley* … blown around, *JB* … sweeps away, *Knox.*

**5. Therefore the ungodly shall not stand:** … wicked, *ASV* … lawless, *Rotherham* … there will be no mercy for sinners, *BB* … Sinners will be condemned, *Good News* … will not escape God's punishment, *NCV.*

**in the judgment:** … place of judgment, *Anchor* … when they are judged, *BB* … when judgment comes, *Knox.*

**nor sinners in the congregation of the righteous:** … the evil-doers will have no place among the upright, *BB* … kept apart from God's own people, *Good News* … community of the just, *Moffatt* … gathering of the upright, *JB* … reunion of the just, *Knox.*

**6. For the Lord knoweth:** … LORD cares about, *Beck* … regardeth, *MAST* … watches over, *NAB* … doth acknowledge, *Rotherham.*

**the way of the righteous:** … assembly of the just, *Anchor* … what happens to the righteous, *Beck* … good men's path the LORD prepares, *Fenton.*

**but the way of the ungodly shall perish:** … wicked will be destroyed, *NCV* … is doomed, *NEB* … is lost, *Young* … how soon is it lost to sight, *Knox.*

**2:1. Why do the heathen rage:** … so violently moved, *BB* … so angry, *NCV* … nations assembled in tumult, *Rotherham* … Why this uproar among the nations, *JB* … Why are the pagans seething, *Moffatt.*

**and the people imagine a vain thing?:** … plotting so uselessly, *Beck* … devise an empty scheme, *Berkeley* … Tribes contrive, *Fenton* … hatch their futile plots, *NEB* … impotent muttering, *JB.*

**1:4–6.** The second half of the Psalm gives the dark contrast of the fruitless, rootless life (vv. 4ff). The Hebrew flashes the whole dread antithesis on the view at once by its first word, "Not so," a universal negative, which reverses every part of the preceding picture. "Wicked" is preferable to "ungodly;" it is the opposite of "righteous" and therefore refers to one who lives not by the Law of God, but by his own will. The psalmist has no need to describe him further or enumerate his deeds. The fundamental trait of his character is enough. Two classes only, then, are recognized here. If a man does not have God's uttered will for his governor, he goes into the category of "wicked." That sounds like harsh doctrine, and not corresponding to the innumerable gradations of character actually seen. But it does correspond to facts, if they are grasped in their roots of motive and principle. If God is not the supreme delight, and his Law sovereign, some other object is men's delight and aim, and that departure from God taints a life, however fine it may be. It is a plain deduction from our relationship to God that lives lived irrespective of Him are sinful, whatever be their complexion otherwise.

The wicked's disappearance in the winnowing wind is the consequence and manifestation of its essential nullity. "Therefore" draws the conclusion of necessary transience. Just as the winnower throws up his shovel full of grain into the breeze and the chaff goes fluttering out of the floor because it is light, while the wheat falls on the heap because it is solid, so the wind of judgment will one day blow and deal with each man according to his nature. It will separate them, whirling away the one, and not the other. "One shall be taken, and the other left" (Matt. 24:40). When does this sifting take effect? The psalmist does not date it. There is a continually operative law of retribution, and there are crises of individual or national life, when the accumulated consequences of evil deeds fall on the doers. But the definite article prefixed to "judgment" seems to suggest some special "day" of separation. It is noteworthy that John the Baptist used the same figures of the tree and the chaff in his picture of the messianic judgments; that epoch may have been in the psalmist's mind.

The ground of these diverse fates is the different attitude of God to each life. The direction of the righteous man's life is watched, guarded, approved and blessed by God. Therefore, it will not fail to reach its goal. They who walk patiently in the paths which He has prepared will find them to be paths of peace, and they will not tread them unaccompanied.

The way or course of life which does not follow God perishes. A path perishes when, like some dim forest track, it dies out, leaving the traveler bewildered amid impenetrable forests, or when, like some treacherous Alpine track among rotten rocks, it crumbles beneath the tread. Every course of life but that of the man who delights in and keeps the Law of the LORD comes to a fatal end and leads to the brink of a precipice, over which the impetus of descent carries the reluctant foot. "The path of the just is as the shining light, which shineth more and more till the noontide of the day. The way of the wicked is as darkness; they know not at what they stumble" (Prov. 4:18f).

***Psalm 2.*** *The Psalm falls into four strophes of three verses each, in the first three of which the reader is made spectator and auditor of vividly painted scenes, while in the last the psalmist exhorts rebels to return to allegiance.*

**2:1–3.** In the first strophe, the conspiracy of banded rebels is set before us with extraordinary force. The singer does not delay to tell what he sees, but breaks into a question of astonished indignation as to what can be the cause of it all. Then, in a series of swift clauses, of which the vivid movement cannot be completely preserved in a translation, he lets us see what has so moved him. The masses of the "nations" are hurrying tumultuously to the mustering place; the "peoples" are meditating revolt, which is smitingly stigmatized in anticipation as "vanity." But it is no mere uprising of the common herd; "the kings of the earth" take their stand as in a battle line (v. 2), and the men of mark and influence lay their heads together and plot. All classes and orders are united in revolt, and haste and eagerness mark their action. The rule against which the revolt is directed is that of Yahweh and his Anointed. That is one rule, not two—the dominion of Yahweh exercised through the Messiah. The psalmist had grasped firmly the concept that God's visible rule is wielded by the Messiah, so that rebellion against one is rebellion against both. Their "bands" are the same.

All the self-will in the world does not alter the fact that the authority of Christ is sovereign over human wills. We cannot get away from it; but we can either lovingly embrace it, and then it is our life, or we can set ourselves against it, like an obstinate ox planting its feet and standing stock-still, and then the goad is driven deep and draws blood.

| 881, 4285 | 8390.520 | 4623 | 5895 | | 3553.151 | 904, 8452 |
|---|---|---|---|---|---|---|
| do, n fp, ps 3mp | cj, v Hiphil juss 1cp | prep, ps 1cp | n mp, ps 3mp | **4.** | v Qal act ptc ms | prep, art, n md |
| אֶת־מוֹסְרוֹתֵימוֹ | וְנַשְׁלִיכָה | מִמֶּנּוּ | עֲבֹתֵימוֹ | | יוֹשֵׁב | בַּשָּׁמַיִם |
| 'eth-môsrôthêmô | wenashlîkhāh | mimmennû | 'ăvōthêmô | | yôshēv | bashshāmayim |
| their fetters | and let us throw off | from us | their cords | | He Who sits | in the heavens |

| 7925.121 | 112 | 4074.121, 3937 | | 226 | 1744.321 | 420 |
|---|---|---|---|---|---|---|
| v Qal impf 3ms | n mp, ps 1cs | v Qal impf 3ms, prep, ps 3mp | **5.** | adv | v Piel impf 3ms | prep, ps 3mp |
| יִשְׂחָק | אֲדֹנָי | יִלְעַג־לָמוֹ | | אָז | יְדַבֵּר | אֵלֵימוֹ |
| yischāq | 'ădhōnāy | yil'agh-lāmô | | 'āz | yedhabbēr | 'ēlêmô |
| He laughs | the Lord | He scoffs at them | | then | He will speak | to them |

| 904, 653 | 904, 2841 | 963.321 | | 603 | 5445.115 |
|---|---|---|---|---|---|
| prep, n ms, ps 3ms | cj, prep, n ms, ps 3ms | v Piel impf 3ms, ps 3mp | **6.** | cj, pers pron | v Qal pf 1cs |
| בְאַפּוֹ | וּבַחֲרוֹנוֹ | יְבַהֲלֵמוֹ | | וַאֲנִי | נָסַכְתִּי |
| ve'appô | ûvachrônô | yevahlēmô | | wa'ănî | nāsakhtî |
| in his anger | and in his wrath | He will terrify them | | and I | I have consecrated |

| 4567 | 6142, 6995 | 2098, 7231 | | 5807.325 | 420 | 2805 |
|---|---|---|---|---|---|---|
| n ms, ps 1cs | prep, pn | *n ms*, n ms, ps 1cs | **7.** | v Piel juss 1cs | prep | *n ms* |
| מַלְכִּי | עַל־צִיּוֹן | הַר־קָדְשִׁי | | אֲסַפְּרָה | אֶל | חֹק |
| malkî | 'al-tsîyôn | har-qādheshî | | 'ăsapperāh | 'el | chōq |
| my King | on Zion | the mountain of my holy place | | let me recount | about | the decree of |

| 3176 | 569.111 | 420 | 1158 | 887 | 603 | 3219 | 3314.115 |
|---|---|---|---|---|---|---|---|
| pn | v Qal pf 3ms | prep, ps 1cs | n ms, ps 1cs | pers pron | pers pron | art, n ms | v Qal pf 1cs, ps 2ms |
| יְהוָה | אָמַר | אֵלַי | בְּנִי | אַתָּה | אֲנִי | הַיּוֹם | יְלִדְתִּיךָ |
| yehwāh | 'āmar | 'ēlay | benî | 'attāh | 'ănî | hayyôm | yelidhtîkhā |
| Yahweh | He said | to Me | my Son | You | I | today | I have brought you forth |

| | 8068.131 | 4623 | 5598.125 | 1504 | 5338 | 273 |
|---|---|---|---|---|---|---|
| **8.** | v Qal impv 2ms | prep, ps 1cs | cj, v Qal juss 1cs | n mp | n fs, ps 2ms | cj, n fs, ps 2ms |
| | שְׁאַל | מִמֶּנִּי | וְאֶתְּנָה | גוֹיִם | נַחֲלָתֶךָ | וַאֲחֻזָּתְךָ |
| | she'al | mimmenî | we'ettenāh | ghôyim | nachlāthekhā | wa'ăchuzzāthekhā |
| | ask | of Me | and let me give | nations | your inheritance | and your possession |

| 675, 800 | | 7778.123 | 904, 8101 | 1298 | 3626, 3747 |
|---|---|---|---|---|---|
| *n mp*, n fs | **9.** | v Qal impf 2ms, ps 3mp | prep, *n ms* | n ms | prep, *n ms* |
| אַפְסֵי־אָרֶץ | | תְּרֹעֵם | בְּשֵׁבֶט | בַּרְזֶל | כִּכְלִי |
| 'aphsê-'ārets | | terō'ēm | beshēvet | barzel | kikhlî |
| the ends of the earth | | You will shatter them | with a staff of | iron | like a vessel of |

**2. The kings of the earth set themselves:** … band themselues, *Geneva* … revolt, *Good News* … take up position, *JB* … stand in array, *Knox* … prepare to fight, *NCV.*

**and the rulers take counsel together:** … fixed in their purpose, *BB* … have met by appointment, *Rotherham* … a summit conference, *LIVB* … conspire, *NCB.*

**against the LORD:** … Yahweh, *Anchor* … LORD's Messiah, *Fenton* … Eternal, *Moffatt.*

**and against his anointed, saying:** … the king of his selection, *BB* … against His Christ, *Geneva* … his Messiah, *LIVB* … chosen one, *Moffatt* … his anointed king, *NEB.*

**3. Let us break their bands asunder:** … snap their bonds, *Anchor* … their chains be broken, *BB* … tear their ropes in pieces, *Beck* … break away from their bondage, *Knox* … that hold us back, *NCV.*

**and cast away their cords from us:** … throw off their yoke, *Anchor* … control, *Good News* … bonds, *JB* … rid ourselves of the toils, *Knox* … ropes that tie us down, *NCV.*

**4. He that sitteth in the heavens shall laugh:** … The Enthroned laughs down from heaven, *Anchor* … who dwells in heaven, *Berkeley* … is laughing at their threats, *Knox* … Heaven's dweller, *Fenton.*

**the Lord shall have them in derision:** … makes sport of them, *Anchor* … will mock at them, *Rotherham* … makes light of them, *Knox* … scoffs at them, *NASB* … my Prince will smile at them, *Fenton.*

**5. Then shall he speak unto them:** ... drives away their lieutenants, *Anchor* ... talks to them angrily, *Beck* ... warns them, *NCV* ... rebukes them, *JB* ... threatens them, *NEB.*

**in his wrath:** ... in his ire, *Anchor* ... his angry words come to their ears, *BB* ... in His indignation, *Berkeley.*

**and vex them:** ... distress them, *NKJV* ... terrify them, *NRSV* ... confound them, *Rotherham* ... fill with dread, *Fenton.*

**in his sore displeasure:** ... fierce fury, *LIVB* ... in his rage, *JB.*

**6. Yet have I set my king:** ... anointed, *Darby* ... installed, *Rotherham* ... I enthrone a king of my own choice, *Knox* ... established, *MAST.*

**upon my holy hill of Zion:** ... hill of my holiness, *Darby* ... on Zion's Holy Hill, *Fenton* ... his holy mountain, *Anchor* ... mount Sion, my sanctuary, *Knox* ... in Jerusalem, *NCV.*

**7. I will declare the decree:** ... shall announce, *REB* ... recite, *Anchor* ... reveal the everlasting purposes of God, *LIVB* ... Let me tell the Eternal's message, *Moffatt* ... concerning a statute, *Young.*

**the LORD hath said unto me:** ... the LIFE declared to me, *Fenton* ... His chosen one replies, *LIVB.*

**Thou art my Son; this day have I begotten thee:** ... given you being, *BB* ... become your Father, *NEB* ... fathered you, *JB* ... This is your Coronation Day, *LIVB* ... brought thee forth, *Young.*

**8. Ask of me, and I shall give thee the heathen:** ... Make your request to me, *BB* ... Ask of me what you will, *NEB* ... master of pagans, *Moffatt.*

**for thine inheritance:** ... the nations will be your patrimony, *Anchor* ... your Estate, *Fenton* ... as your birthright, *JB* ... your heritage, *NRSV* ... your domain, *REB.*

**and the uttermost parts of the earth:** ... the farthest limits, *BB* ... most distant, *Beck* ... Earth's bounds, *Fenton* ... the whole earth, *Good News* ... all the people on earth, *NCV.*

**for thy possession:** ... will be under your hand, *BB* ... you shall hold, *Fenton* ... will be yours, *NCV* ... for thy domain, *Knox* ... lord over all, *Moffatt.*

**9. Thou shalt break them:** ... herd them like sheep, *Knox* ... maul them, *Moffatt.*

**with a rod of iron:** ... sceptre of iron, *Darby* ... an iron staff, *Fenton* ... crook of iron, *Knox* ... an iron mace, *Moffatt.*

**thou shalt dash them in pieces:** ... shatter them, *Anchor* ... forms or breaks the pots, *Fenton* ... crush them, *Young.*

**like a potter's vessel:** ... pottery, *NCV* ... earthen dish, *NAB* ... earthenware, *Knox* ... clay pot, *NEB* ... jar, *Anchor.*

---

**2:4–6.** God's laughter passes into the utterance of his wrath at the time determined by Him. The silence is broken by his voice, and the motionless form flashes into action. One movement is enough to "vex" the enemies and fling them into panic, as a flock of birds put to flight by the lifting of an arm. There is a point, known to God alone, when He perceives that the fullness of time has come, and the opposition must be ended. By gentle patience, He has sought to draw people to obedience (although that side of his dealings is not presented in this Psalm), but the moment arrives when in worldwide catastrophes or crushing blows on individuals sleeping retribution wakes at the right moment, determined by considerations inappreciable by us: "Then shall He speak unto them in his wrath" (v. 5).

The last verse of this strophe is parallel with the last of the preceding, being also the dramatically introduced speech of the actor in the previous verses. The revolters' mutual encouragement is directly answered by the sovereign word of God, which discloses the reason for the futility of their attempts. The "I" of v. 6 is emphatic. On one side is that majestic "I have set my King"; on the other, a world of rebels. They may put their shoulders to the throne of the Anointed to overthrow it; but what of that? God's hand holds it firm, whatever forces press on it. All enmity of banded or single wills breaks against it and is dashed, becoming ineffectual.

**2:7–9.** Another speaker is heard next, the anointed King, Who, in the third strophe (vv. 7ff), bears witness to himself and claims universal dominion as his by a divine decree. "Thou art my son; today have I begotten thee"—so runs the first part of the decree. The allusion to Nathan's words to David is clear. In them, the prophet spoke of the succession of David's descendants, the king as a collective person, so to speak. The psalmist, knowing how incompletely any or all of these had fulfilled the words which were the patent of their kingship, repeats them in confident faith as certain to be accomplished in the Messiah-King, Who fills the future for him with a great light of hope. He did not know the historic Person in Whom the word has to be fulfilled, but it is difficult to resist the conclusion that he had before him the prospect of the King of Kings living as a man, the heir of the promises.

| 3443.151 | 5492.323 | | 6498 | 4567 | 7959.533 | 3364.233 |
|---|---|---|---|---|---|---|
| v Qal act ptc ms | v Piel impf 2ms, ps 3mp | **10.** | cj, adv | n mp | v Hiphil impv 2mp | v Niphal impv 2mp |
| יוֹצֵר | תְּנַפְּצֵם | | וְעַתָּה | מְלָכִים | הַשְׂכִּילוּ | הִוָּסְרוּ |
| yôtsēr | tenappetsēm | | we'attāh | melākhîm | haskîlû | hiwwāserû |
| the potter | You will shatter them | | and now | O kings | gain insight | be instructed |

| 8570.152 | 800 | | 5856.133 | 881, 3176 | 904, 3488 | 1559.133 |
|---|---|---|---|---|---|---|
| *v Qal act ptc mp* | n fs | **11.** | v Qal impv 2mp | do, pn | prep, n fs | cj, v Qal impv 2mp |
| שֹׁפְטֵי | אָרֶץ | | עִבְדוּ | אֶת־יְהוָה | בְּיִרְאָה | וְגִילוּ |
| shōphetê | 'ārets | | 'ivdhû | 'eth-yehwāh | beyir'āh | weghîlû |
| O judges of | the earth | | serve | Yahweh | with fear | and rejoice |

| 904, 7748 | | 5583.333, 1275 | 6678, 613.121 | 6.128 | 1932 |
|---|---|---|---|---|---|
| prep, n fs | **12.** | v Piel impv 2mp, n ms | adv, v Qal impf 3ms | cj, v Qal impf 2mp | *n ms* |
| בִּרְעָדָה | | נַשְּׁקוּ־בַר | פֶּן־יֶאֱנַף | וְתֹאבְדוּ | דֶרֶךְ |
| bir'ādhāh | | nashshequ-var | pen-ye'ĕnaph | wethō'vedhû | dherekh |
| with trembling | | kiss the Son | so that not He will be angry | and you will perish | the way |

| 3706, 1220.121 | 3626, 4746 | 653 | 869 | 3725, 2725.152 | 904 |
|---|---|---|---|---|---|
| cj, v Qal impf 3ms | prep, sub | n ms, ps 3ms | *n ms* | *adj, v Qal act ptc mp* | prep, ps 3ms |
| כִּי־יִבְעַר | כִּמְעַט | אַפּוֹ | אַשְׁרֵי | כָּל־חוֹסֵי | בוֹ |
| kî-yiv'ar | kim'aṭ | 'appô | 'ashrê | kol-chôsê | vô |
| because it will be kindled | like a moment | his nose | blessed | all those taking refuge | in Him |

| | 4344 | 3937, 1784 | 904, 1300.141 | 4623, 6686 | 84 | 1158 | | 3176 |
|---|---|---|---|---|---|---|---|---|
| **3:t** | n ms | prep, pn | prep, v Qal inf con, ps 3ms | prep, *n mp* | pn | n ms, ps 3ms | **1.** | pn |
| | מִזְמוֹר | לְדָוִד | בְּבָרְחוֹ | מִפְּנֵי | אַבְשָׁלוֹם | בְּנוֹ | | יְהוָה |
| | mizmôr | ledhāwidh | bevārechô | mippenê | 'avshālôm | benô | | yehwāh |
| | a Psalm | of David | during his fleeing | from before | Absalom | his son | | O Yahweh |

| 4242, 7525.116 | 7141 | 7521 | 7251.152 | 6142 | | 7521 |
|---|---|---|---|---|---|---|
| intrg, v Qal pf 3cp | n mp, ps 1cs | adj | v Qal act ptc mp | prep, ps 1cs | **2.** | adj |
| מָה־רַבּוּ | צָרָי | רַבִּים | קָמִים | עָלָי | | רַבִּים |
| māh-rabbû | tsārāy | rabbîm | qāmîm | 'ālāy | | rabbîm |
| why have they become numerous | my adversaries | many | those rising | against me | | many |

| 569.152 | 3937, 5497 | 375 | 3568 | 3937 | 904, 435 | 5734 | | 887 |
|---|---|---|---|---|---|---|---|---|
| v Qal act ptc mp | prep, n fs, ps 1cs | *sub* | n fs | prep, ps 3ms | prep, n mp | intrj | **3.** | cj, pers pron |
| אֹמְרִים | לְנַפְשִׁי | אֵין | יְשׁוּעָתָה | לוֹ | בֵאלֹהִים | סֶלָה | | וְאַתָּה |
| 'ōmerîm | lenaphshî | 'ên | yeshû'āthāh | lô | vē'lōhîm | selāh | | we'attāh |
| those saying | about myself | there is not | salvation | to him | by God | selah | | but You |

**10. Be wise now therefore, O ye kings:** ... Be mindful, *NEB* ... show discernment, *NASB* ... come to your senses, *JB* ... cautious, *Goodspeed* ... prudent, *Anchor.*

**be instructed, ye judges of the earth:** ... take warning, you rulers, *Anchor* ... take his teaching, *BB* ... be admonished, *Darby* ... learn your lesson, *JB.*

**11. Serve the LORD with fear:** ... Yahweh with reverence, *Anchor* ... Give worship to, *BB* ... be submissive, *JB* ... Obey the LORD, *NCV.*

**and rejoice with trembling:** ... live in trembling, O mortal men!, *Anchor* ... live in dread, *Beck* ... with awe, *Knox* ... shudder and submit to him, *Moffatt* ... exult, *Rotherham.*

**12. Kiss the Son:** ... bow down to him, *Good News* ... Do homage in purity, *MAST* ... the Chosen One, *Young.*

**lest he be angry:** ... or He'll get angry, *Beck* ... lest He grieve, *Fenton* ... do not brave his anger, *Knox.*

**and ye perish from the way:** ... your path be lost, *Fenton* ... go astray from the sure path, *Knox* ... end in ruin, *Moffatt* ... will be destroyed, *NCV* ... struck down in mid-course, *REB.*

**when his wrath is kindled:** ... ire flares up quickly, *Anchor* ... His anger can blaze, *Beck* ... If His face lights a spark, *Fenton* ... his fury flames up, *JB* ... fire of his vengeance, *Knox.*

**but a little:** ... suddenly, *Geneva* ... in a moment, *JB* ... in but a little time, *KJVII* ... soon, *ASV.*

**Blessed are all they:** ... Happy, *BB* ... But, oh, the joy, *Berkeley.*

**that put their trust in him:** ... take refuge, *ASV* ... put their faith in him, *BB* ... go to him for protection, *Good News* ... shelter beside him, *Moffatt.*

**3:t. A Psalm of David, when he fled from Absalom his son.**

**1. LORD, how are they increased:** ... have multiplied, *KJVII* ... See how they surround me, *Knox* ... how numerous, *REB.*

**that trouble me!:** ... who make attacks on me, *BB* ... my enemies, *Beck* ... distresses, *Young.*

**many are they:** ... in great numbers, *BB* ... are my foes, *Berkeley* ... Multitudes, *Rotherham.*

**that rise up against me:** ... are attacking me, *Beck* ... turn against me, *Good News* ... seek to harm me, *LIVB.*

**2. Many there be:** ... how countless, *JB* ... Unnumbered, *BB* ... Multitudes, *Rotherham* ... how many are my adversaries, *Anchor.*

**which say of my soul:** ... eye my life, *Anchor* ... say about my life, *Fenton* ... concerning me, *Goodspeed* ... saying about me, *NCV.*

**There is no help for him in God. Selah:** ... God will not save him, *Beck* ... no deliverance, *NASB* ... won't rescue him, *NCV* ... will not bring him victory, *NEB* ... He will not find safety in God, *REB.*

**3. But thou, O LORD, art a shield for me:** ... strength, O Lord, is round me, *BB* ... buckler, *Geneva* ... my champion, *Knox.*

---

Now, this idea of sonship, as belonging to the monarch, is much better illustrated by the fact that Israel, the nation, was so named, than by the boasts of Gentile dynasties to be sons of Baal or Amun-Ra. The relationship is moral and spiritual, involving divine care and love and appointment to office and demanding human obedience and use of dignity for God.

It is to be observed that our Psalm of the day of the King's self-attestation is the day of his being "begotten." The point of time referred to is not the beginning of personal existence, but of investiture with royalty. With accurate insight, then, into the meaning of the words, the NT takes them as fulfilled in the Resurrection (Acts 13:33; Rom. 1:4). In this day, as the first step in the process which was completed in the Ascension, Jesus, even though still in the flesh, was lifted above the limitations and weaknesses of earth and He was prepared to rise to the throne. The day of his resurrection was, as it were, the beginning of his reign over all.

The divine voice foretells victory over opposition and destruction to opposers. The scepter is of iron, although the hand that holds it once grasped the reed. The word rendered "break" (HED #7778) may also be translated, with a different set of vowels, "shepherd" and is so rendered by the LXX (which Rev. 2:27, etc., follows) and by some other versions. But in view of the parallelism of the next clause, "break " is to be preferred.

**2:10–12.** We have listened to three voices, and now, in vv. 10ff, the poet speaks in solemn exhortation: "Be wise now, ye kings." The "now" is argumentative, not temporal. It means "since things are so." The kings addressed are the rebel monarchs whose power seems so puny measured against that of "my King." Not only these are addressed, but all possessors of power and influence. Open-eyed consideration of the facts is true wisdom. The most senseless thing a person can do is to shut his eyes to them and steel his heart against their instruction. This pleading invitation to calm reflection is the purpose of all the preceding. To draw rebels to loyalty, which is life, is the meaning of all appeals to terror. God and his prophet desire that the conviction of the futility of rebellion with a poor ten thousand against the king of twenty thousands should lead to "sending an embassy" to sue for peace. The facts are before us, that we may be warned and wise.

The exhortation which follows in vv. 11f points to the conduct which will be dictated by wise reception of instruction. There is little difficulty with v. 11. The exhortation to "serve Yahweh with fear and rejoice with trembling" points to obedience founded on awe of God's majesty—the fear which love does not cast out, but perfects—and to the gladness which blends with reverence, but is not darkened by it. To love and cleave to God, to feel the silent awe of his greatness and holiness, giving dignity and solemnity to our gladness and from this inmost heaven of contemplation to come down to a life of practical obedience—this is God's command and man's blessedness.

***Psalm 3.*** *Another pair of Psalms follows the two of the Introduction. They are closely connected linguistically, structurally and in subject. The one is a morning, the other an evening hymn, and possibly they are placed at the beginning of the earliest Psalter for that reason.*

**3:1–2.** This Psalm falls into four strophes, three of which are marked by selah (HED #5734). In the first strophe (vv. 1f), the psalmist recounts his enemies. If we regard this as a morning Psalm, it is touchingly true to experience that the first waking

| 3176 | 4182 | 1185 | 3638 | 7597.551 | 7513 | | 7249 | 420, 3176 |
|---|---|---|---|---|---|---|---|---|
| pn | n ms | prep, ps 1cs | n ms, ps 1cs | cj, v Hiphil ptc ms | n ms, ps 1cs | **4.** | n ms, ps 1cs | prep, pn |
| יְהוָה | מָגֵן | בַּעֲדִי | כְּבוֹדִי | וּמֵרִים | רֹאשִׁי | | קוֹלִי | אֶל־יְהוָה |
| yehwāh | māghēn | ba'ădhî | kevôdhî | ûmērîm | rō'shî | | qôlî | 'el-yehwāh |
| Yahweh | a Shield | around me | my glory | and One Who lifts | my head | | my voice | to Yahweh |

| 7410.125 | 6257.121 | 4623, 2098 | 7231 | 5734 | | 603 |
|---|---|---|---|---|---|---|
| v Qal impf 1cs | cj, v Qal impf 3ms, ps 1cs | prep, *n ms* | n ms, ps 3ms | intrj | **5.** | pers pron |
| אֶקְרָא | וַיַּעֲנֵנִי | מֵהַר | קָדְשׁוֹ | סֶלָה | | אֲנִי |
| 'eqŏrā' | wayya'ănēnî | mēhar | qādheshô | selāh | | 'ănî |
| I will call aloud | and He will answer me | from the hill of | his holy place | selah | | I |

| 8311.115 | 3583.125 | 7301.515 | 3706 | 3176 | 5759.121 |
|---|---|---|---|---|---|
| v Qal pf 1cs | cj, v Qal impf 1cs | v Hiphil pf 1cs | cj | pn | v Qal impf 3ms, ps 1cs |
| שָׁכַבְתִּי | וָאִישָׁנָה | הֱקִיצוֹתִי | כִּי | יְהוָה | יִסְמְכֵנִי |
| shākhavtî | wā'îshānāh | hĕqîtsôthî | kî | yehwāh | yismekhēnî |
| I have lain down | and I have slept | I have awakened | because | Yahweh | He sustains me |

| | 3940, 3486.125 | 4623, 7526 | 6194 | 866 | 5623 | 8308.116 | 6142 |
|---|---|---|---|---|---|---|---|
| **6.** | neg part, v Qal impf 1cs | prep, *n fp* | n ms | rel pron | adv | v Qal pf 3cp | prep, ps 1cs |
| | לֹא־אִירָא | מֵרִבְבוֹת | עָם | אֲשֶׁר | סָבִיב | שָׁתוּ | עָלָי |
| | lō'-'îrā' | mērivevôth | 'ām | 'ăsher | sāvîv | shāthû | 'ālāy |
| | I am not afraid | of ten thousand | people | whom | all around | they have placed | against me |

| | 7251.131 | 3176 | 3588.531 | 435 | 3706, 5409.513 |
|---|---|---|---|---|---|
| **7.** | v Qal impv 2ms | pn | v Hiphil impv 2ms, ps 1cs | n mp, ps 1cs | cj, v Hiphil pf 2ms |
| | קוּמָה | יְהוָה | הוֹשִׁיעֵנִי | אֱלֹהַי | כִּי־הִכִּיתָ |
| | qûmāh | yehwāh | hôshî'ēnî | 'ĕlōhay | kî-hikkîthā |
| | rise | O Yahweh | save me | my God | because You have struck down |

| 881, 3725, 342.152 | 4029 | 8514 | 7857 | 8132.313 |
|---|---|---|---|---|
| do, *adj*, v Qal act ptc mp, ps 1cs | n ms | *n fd* | n mp | v Piel pf 2ms |
| אֶת־כָּל־אֹיְבַי | לֶחִי | שִׁנֵּי | רְשָׁעִים | שִׁבַּרְתָּ |
| 'eth-kol-'ōyevay | lechî | shinnê | reshā'îm | shibbartā |
| all my enemies | the jaw | the teeth of | the wicked | You have broken in pieces |

| | 3937, 3176 | 3568 | 6142, 6194 | 1318 | 5734 | | 3937, 5514.351 |
|---|---|---|---|---|---|---|---|
| **8.** | prep, pn | art, n fs | prep, n ms, ps 2ms | n fs, ps 2ms | intrj | **4:t** | prep, art, v Piel ptc ms |
| | לַיהוָה | הַיְשׁוּעָה | עַל־עַמְּךָ | בִרְכָתֶךָ | סֶלָה | | לַמְנַצֵּחַ |
| | layhwāh | hayshû'āh | 'al-'ammekhā | virkhāthekhā | selāh | | lamnatstsēach |
| | of Yahweh | the salvation | concerning your people | your blessing | selah | | to the director |

**my glory:** ... You give me glory, *Beck* ... you give me victory, *Good News* ... in triumph, *Moffatt* ... wonderful God, *NCV* ... My honour, *Young.*

**and the lifter up of mine head:** ... hold my head high, *JB* ... that keeps my head erect, *Knox* ... who gives me courage, *NCV.*

**4. I cried unto the LORD with my voice:** ... call to Yahweh, *Anchor* ... send up a cry, *BB* ... call aloud, *Beck* ... I will pray, *NCV.*

**and he heard me:** ... he answers me, *Anchor* ... and there finds hearing, *Knox.*

**out of his holy hill:** ... from his holy mountain, *Anchor* ... reaches his mountain sanctuary, *Knox* ... from his Temple in Jerusalem, *LIVB.*

**Selah:** ... Music, *Beck.*

**5. I laid me down and slept:** ... took my rest in sleep, *BB* ... can lie down and go to sleep, *NCV.*

**I awaked:** ... then again I was awake, *BB* ... rose vp againe, *Geneva.*

**for the LORD sustained me:** ... all night long the LORD protects me, *Good News* ... Safe in God's hand, *Knox* ... was watching over me, *LIVB* ... gives me strength, *NCV.*

**6. I will not be afraid of ten thousands of people:** ... the shafts of people, *Anchor* ... no human hosts, *Fenton* ... myriads, *Berkeley* ... the nations, *NEB* ... for God is guard, *Fenton.*

**that have set themselves against me round about:** ... deployed against me on every side, *Anchor* ... surround me, *LIVB* ... beset me, *Goodspeed.*

**7. Arise, O LORD:** ... Come to me, Lord, *BB* ... Bestir thyself, *Knox* ... rise up, *NCV.*

**save me, O my God:** ... keep me safe, *BB* ... rescue me, *JB* ... Deliver me, *NIV.*

**for thou hast smitten all mine enemies:** ... given all my haters blows, *BB* ... smashed, *KJVII* ... punish, *Good News* ... slap them, *LIVB* ... wilt all disable, *Moffatt.*

**upon the cheek bone:** ... on the jaw, *Anchor* ... face-bones, *BB* ... across the face, *JB.*

**thou hast broken the teeth:** ... thou wilt crush, *Moffatt* ... thine to break the fangs of malice, *Knox.*

**of the ungodly:** ... wicked, *Anchor* ... evil-doers, *BB* ... lawless, *Rotherham.*

**8. Salvation belongeth unto the LORD:** ... Only You can save, LORD, *Beck* ... The LORD can save his people, *NCV* ... From the LORD comes deliverance, *NIV.*

**thy blessing is upon thy people. Selah:** ... What joys he gives, *LIVB* ... bless your people, *NCV* ... thy blessing rest upon thy people, *NEB.*

---

thought should be the renewed rush of the trouble which sleep had for a time dammed back. His enemies are many, and they taunt him as forsaken of God. It is surely a strong thing to say that there is no correspondence here with David's situation during Absalom's revolt. It was no partial conspiracy.

Shimei's foul tongue spoke the general mind: "The LORD hath delivered the kingdom into the hand of Absalom" (2 Sam. 16:8). There had been enough sin in the king's recent past to give color to the interpretation of his present calamity as the sign of his being forsaken of God. The conviction that such was the fact would swell the rebel ranks.

The selah which parts the first from the second strophe is probably a direction for an instrumental interlude while the singer pauses.

**3:3–4.** The second strophe (vv. 3f) is the utterance of faith, based on experience, laying hold of Yahweh as defense. By an effort of will, the psalmist rises from the contemplation of surrounding enemies to that of the encircling Yahweh. In the thickest of danger and dread, there is a power of choice left a man as to what shall be the object of thought, whether trouble or the outstretched hand of the Christ. This harassed man flings himself out of the coil of troubles surrounding him and looks up to God. He sees in Him precisely what he needs most at the moment, for in that infinite nature is fulness corresponding to all emptiness of ours. He is "a shield around me" (v. 3), as He had promised to be to Abraham in his peril; "my glory," at a time when slander and shame were wrapping him about, and his kingdom seemed gone; "the lifter up of my head," sunk as it is both in sadness and calamity, since Yahweh can both cheer his spirit and restore his dignity.

**3:5–6.** The third strophe (vv. 5f) beautifully expresses the tranquil courage which comes from trust. Since sleeping and safe waking again in ordinary circumstances is no such striking proof of divine help that it would cause one in the psalmist's situation to give particular thought to it and to put his confidence in it, the view is to be taken that the psalmist in v. 5 is contemplating the experience which he has just made in his present situation. Surrounded by enemies, he was quite safe under God's protection and exposed to no peril even in the night. Correspondence with David's circumstances surely may be traced here. His little band had no fortress in Mahanaim, and Ahithophel's counsel to attack them by night was so natural that the possibility must have been present to the king. But another night had come and gone in safety, disturbed by no shout of an enemy. The nocturnal danger had passed, and day was again brightening.

**3:7–8.** The final strophe (vv. 7f) gives the culmination of faith in prayer. "Arise, Yahweh," is quoted from the ancient invocation (Num. 10:35) and expresses in strongly anthropomorphic form the desire for some interposition of divine power. Fearlessness is not so complete that the psalmist is beyond the need of praying. He is courageous because he knows that God will help, but he knows, too, that God's help depends on his prayer. The courage which does not pray is foolish and will break down into panic; that which fears enough to cry, "Arise, O LORD" (v. 7), will be vindicated by victory. This prayer is built on experience, as the preceding confidence was. The enemies are now, according to a very frequent figure in the Psalter, compared to wild beasts. Smiting on the cheek is usually a symbol of insult, but here it is better taken in close connection with the following "breaking the teeth" (v. 7). Deliverance from his enemies is the psalmist's main idea in the word here. It belongs to Yahweh, since its bestowal is his act.

**4:1.** The cry for an answer by deed is based on the name and on the past acts of God. Grammatically, it would be possible and regular to render

| 904, 5234 | 4344 | 3937, 1784 | | 904, 7410.141 | 6257.131 |
|---|---|---|---|---|---|
| prep, n fp | n ms | prep, pn | | prep, v Qal inf con, ps 1cs | v Qal impv 2ms, ps 1cs |
| בִּנְגִינוֹת | מִזְמוֹר | לְדָוִד | **1.** | בְּקָרְאִי | עֲנֵנִי |
| binghînôth | mizmôr | ledhāwidh | | beqāre'î | 'ănēnî |
| with the stringed instruments | a Psalm | of David | | during my calling | answer me |

| 435 | 6928 | 904, 7140 | 7622.513 | 3937 |
|---|---|---|---|---|
| *n mp* | n ms, ps 1cs | prep, art, n ms | v Hiphil pf 2ms | prep, ps 1cs |
| אֱלֹהֵי | צִדְקִי | בַּצָּר | הִרְחַבְתָּ | לִּי |
| 'ĕlōhê | tsidhqî | batstsār | hirchavtā | lî |
| O God of | my righteousness | in the narrow place | You have made wide | for me |

| 2706.131 | 8471.131 | 8940 | | 1158 | 382 | 5912, 4242 | 3638 |
|---|---|---|---|---|---|---|---|
| v Qal impv 2ms, ps 1cs | cj, v Qal impv 2ms | n fs, ps 1cs | | *n mp* | n ms | adv, intrg | n ms, ps 1cs |
| חָנֵּנִי | וּשְׁמַע | תְּפִלָּתִי | **2.** | בְּנֵי | אִישׁ | עַד־מֶה | כְבוֹדִי |
| chānnēnî | ûshema' | tephillāthî | | benê | 'îsh | 'adh-meh | khevôdhî |
| be gracious to me | and hear | my prayer | | O sons of | men | until what | my honor |

| 3937, 3759 | 154.128 | 7672 | 1272.328 | 3695 | 5734 | | 3156.133 |
|---|---|---|---|---|---|---|---|
| prep, n fs | v Qal impf 2mp | n ms | v Piel impf 2mp | n ms | intrj | | cj, v Qal impv 2mp |
| לִכְלִמָּה | תֶּאֱהָבוּן | רִיק | תְּבַקְשׁוּ | כָזָב | סֶלָה | **3.** | וּדְעוּ |
| likhlimmāh | te'ĕhāvûn | rîq | tevaqŏshû | khāzāv | selāh | | ûdhe'û |
| into an insult | will you love | worthlessness | will you seek | falsehood | selah | | and know |

| 3706, 6640.511 | 3176 | 2728 | 3937 | 3176 | 8471.121 |
|---|---|---|---|---|---|
| cj, v Hiphil pf 3ms | pn | n ms | prep, ps 3ms | pn | v Qal impf 3ms |
| כִּי־הִפְלָה | יְהוָה | חָסִיד | לוֹ | יְהוָה | יִשְׁמַע |
| kî-hiphlāh | yehwāh | chāsîdh | lô | yehwāh | yishma' |
| that He has made distinct | Yahweh | the godly | to Him | Yahweh | He hears |

| 904, 7410.141 | 420 | | 7553.133 | 414, 2490.128 | 569.133 |
|---|---|---|---|---|---|
| prep, v Qal inf con, ps 1cs | prep, ps 3ms | | v Qal impv 2mp | cj, adv, v Qal juss 2mp | v Qal impv 2mp |
| בְּקָרְאִי | אֵלָיו | **4.** | רִגְזוּ | וְאַל־תֶּחֱטָאוּ | אִמְרוּ |
| beqāre'î | 'ēlâv | | righzû | we'al-techĕtā'û | 'imrû |
| during my calling | to Him | | tremble | and do not sin | say |

| 904, 3949 | 6142, 5085 | 1887.133 | 5734 | | 2159.133 |
|---|---|---|---|---|---|
| prep, n ms, ps 2mp | prep, n ms, ps 2mp | cj, v Qal impv 2mp | intrj | | v Qal impv 2mp |
| בִלְבַבְכֶם | עַל־מִשְׁכַּבְכֶם | וְדֹמּוּ | סֶלָה | **5.** | זִבְחוּ |
| vilvavkhem | 'al-mishkavkhem | wedhōmmû | selāh | | zivchû |
| in your hearts | on your beds | and be silent | selah | | sacrifice |

| 2160, 6928 | 1019.133 | 420, 3176 | | 7521 | 569.152 |
|---|---|---|---|---|---|
| *n mp*, n ms | cj, v Qal impv 2mp | prep, pn | | adj | v Qal act ptc mp |
| זִבְחֵי־צֶדֶק | וּבִטְחוּ | אֶל־יְהוָה | **6.** | רַבִּים | אֹמְרִים |
| zivchê-tsedheq | ûvitchû | 'el-yehwāh | | rabbîm | 'ōmerîm |
| sacrifices of righteousness | and put trust your | with Yahweh | | many | those saying |

| 4449, 7495.520 | 3005 | 5558.131, 6142 | 214 | 6686 | 3176 |
|---|---|---|---|---|---|
| intrg, v Hiphil impf 1cp | adj | v Qal impv 2ms, prep, ps 1cp | *n ms* | n mp, ps 2ms | pn |
| מִי־יַרְאֵנוּ | טוֹב | נְסָה־עָלֵינוּ | אוֹר | פָּנֶיךָ | יְהוָה |
| mî-yar'ēnû | tôv | nesāh-'ālênû | 'ôr | pānêkhā | yehwāh |
| who shows us | good | lift up over us | the light of | your face | O Yahweh |

| | 5598.113 | 7977 | 904, 3949 | 4623, 6496 | 1765 | 8822 |
|---|---|---|---|---|---|---|
| | v Qal pf 2ms | n fs | prep, n ms, ps 1cs | prep, *n fs* | n ms, ps 3mp | cj, n ms, ps 3mp |
| **7.** | נָתַתָּה | שִׂמְחָה | בְלִבִּי | מֵעֵת | דְּגָנָם | וְתִירוֹשָׁם |
| | nāthattāh | simchāh | velibbî | mē'ēth | deghānām | wethîrôshām |
| | You have put | rejoicing | in my heart | from the time of | their grain | and their grape juice |

**4:t. To the chief Musician on Neginoth, A Psalm of David.**

**1. Hear me when I call:** ... Answer me when I pray, *NCV* ... listen to me, *Knox.*

**O God of my righteousness:** ... by whom I am made righteous, *Beck* ... my champion, *Moffatt* ... maintainer of my right, *NEB* ... O my just God, *NAB* ... vindication, *Anchor* ... my pitying GOD, *Fenton.*

**thou hast enlarged me:** ... Make things easier for me, *NCV* ... given relief, *Berkeley* ... set me at liberty, *Geneva* ... You have become greater to me, *KJVII* ... cared for me, *LIVB.*

**when I was in distress:** ... my troubles, *BB* ... hard-pressed, *Beck* ... hemmed in, *Moffatt* ... a strait place, *Rotherham* ... In adversity, *Young.*

**have mercy upon me:** ... pity, *Anchor* ... Be kind, *Beck* ... be gracious, *Berkeley* ... Shew me favour, *Rotherham* ... Be gentle, *Fenton.*

**and hear my prayer:** ... give ear, *BB* ... Hearken vnto, *Geneva.*

**2. O ye sons of men:** ... You mortals, *Beck* ... Great ones of the world, *Knox* ... Men of rank, *NAB* ... Ye sons of the great, *Rotherham.*

**how long will ye turn my glory into shame?:** ... libel my honour, *Fenton* ... will your hearts always be hardened, *Knox* ... how long will you be so misguided, *Moffatt* ... be dull of heart, *NAB* ... my honor become a reproach, *NASB.*

**how long will ye love vanity:** ... worthless idols, *Beck* ... futility, *Berkeley* ... set your heart on trifles, *NEB* ... love delusions, *NIV* ... vain words, *NRSV.*

**and seek after leasing? Selah:** ... chase after illusions, *JB* ... setting your heart on shadows, *Knox* ... aim at deception, *NASB* ... vain intrigues, *Moffatt* ... falsehood, *ASV.*

**3. But know that the LORD:** ... recognize that Yahweh, *Anchor* ... Remember, *Good News* ... be sure, *Knox* ... Mark this well, *LIVB.*

**hath set apart:** ... marks me out, *Moffatt* ... has singled out, *REB.*

**him that is godly for himself:** ... makes the one He loves someone special, *Beck* ... performs wonders for his faithful, *JB* ... who are loyal to him, *NCV* ... the redeemed, *Berkeley.*

**the LORD will hear when I call unto him:** ... give ear, *BB* ... whenever I call on his name, *Knox.*

**4. Stand in awe:** ... Be disquieted, *Anchor* ... Let there be fear in your hearts, *BB* ... Tremble, *Beck* ... When you are disturbed, *NRSV* ... Be deeply moved, *Rotherham.*

**and sin not:** ... practice not sin, *Fenton* ... sin no more, *Knox* ... do not do wrong, *NEB.*

**commune with your own heart:** ... examine your conscience, *Anchor* ... meditate, *Darby* ... reflect, *Fenton* ... search your hearts, *NIV* ... ponder it, *NRSV.*

**upon your bed:** ... as you lie awake, *Knox* ... at night, *Moffatt.*

**and be still. Selah:** ... make no sound, *BB* ... do not break silence, *NEB* ... hold your peace, *Moffatt* ... and weep, *Beck.*

**5. Offer the sacrifices of righteousness:** ... Offer legitimate sacrifices, *Anchor* ... Bring the proper sacrifices in the right spirit, *Beck* ... Give of pure offerings, *Fenton.*

**and put your trust in the LORD:** ... confide, *Darby* ... put your faith, *BB* ... trust the Eternal, *Moffatt.*

**6. There be many that say, Who will show us any good?:** ... If only someone could show us prosperity, *Beck* ... Who will put happiness

---

"my God of righteousness," i.e., "my righteous God"; but the pronoun is best attached to "righteousness" only, as the consideration that God is righteous is less relevant than that He is the source of the psalmist's righteousness. Since He is so, He may be expected to vindicate it by answering prayer by deliverance.

**4:2–5.** The strophe division keeps together the prayer and the beginning of the remonstrance to opponents, and does so in order to emphasize the eloquent, sharp juxtaposition of God and the "sons of men." The phrase is usually employed to mean "persons of position," but here the contrast between the varying height of men's molehills is not so much in view as the contrast between them all and the loftiness of God. By "the godly" is meant, of course, the psalmist. He is sure that he belongs to God and is set apart, so that no real evil can touch him; but does he build this confidence on his own character or on Yahweh's grace? The answer depends on the meaning of the pregnant word rendered "godly" (HED #2728), which here occurs for the first time in the Psalter. So far as its form is concerned, it may be either active, one who shows cheṣedh ("steadfast love," HED #2721) or passive, one to whom it is shown. The usage in the Psalter seems to decide in favor of the passive meaning, which is also more in accordance with the general biblical view, which traces all man's hopes and blessings, not to his attitude toward God, but to God's attitude toward him, and regards man's love as being derived from God.

**4:6.** The sudden appearance of the plural "us" suggests that the psalmist associates himself with

| 7525.116 | | 904, 8361 | 3267 | 8311.125 | 3583.125 | 3706, 887 |
|---|---|---|---|---|---|---|
| v Qal pf 3cp | 8. | prep, n ms | adv | v Qal juss 1cs | cj, v Qal juss 1cs | cj, pers pron |
| רַבּוּ | | בְּשָׁלוֹם | יַחְדָּו | אֶשְׁכְּבָה | וְאִישָׁן | כִּי־אַתָּה |
| rābû | | beshālôm | yachdāw | 'eshkevāh | we'îshān | kî-'attāh |
| they are numerous | | in peace | at the same time | let me lie down | and let me sleep | because You |

| 3176 | 3937, 945 | 3937, 1020 | 3553.523 | | 3937, 5514.351 | 5334 |
|---|---|---|---|---|---|---|
| pn | prep, n ms | prep, n ms | v Hiphil impf 2ms, ps 1cs | 5:t | prep, art, v Piel ptc ms | prep, art, n fp |
| יְהוָה | לְבָדָד | לָבֶטַח | תּוֹשִׁיבֵנִי | | לַמְנַצֵּחַ | אֶל־הַנְּחִילוֹת |
| yehwāh | levādhādh | lāvetach | tôshîvênî | | lamnatstsēach | 'el-hannechîlôth |
| O Yahweh | alone | with safety | You cause me to dwell | | to the director | with the flutes |

| 4344 | 3937, 1784 | | 571 | 237.531 | 3176 | 1032.131 | 1969 |
|---|---|---|---|---|---|---|---|
| n ms | prep, pn | 1. | n mp, ps 1cs | v Hiphil impv 2ms | pn | v Qal impv 2ms | n ms, ps 1cs |
| מִזְמוֹר | לְדָוִד | | אֲמָרַי | הַאֲזִינָה | יְהוָה | בִּינָה | הֲגִיגִי |
| mizmôr | ledhāwidh | | 'ămāray | ha'ăzînāh | yehwāh | bînāh | heghîghî |
| a Psalm | of David | | my words | listen to | O Yahweh | perceive | my groaning |

| | 7477.531 | 3937, 7249 | 8209.341 | 4567 | 435 | 3706, 420 |
|---|---|---|---|---|---|---|
| 2. | v Hiphil impv 2ms | prep, *n ms* | v Piel inf con, ps 1cs | n ms, ps 1cs | cj, n mp, ps 1cs | cj, prep, ps 2ms |
| | הַקְשִׁיבָה | לְקוֹל | שַׁוְעִי | מַלְכִּי | וֵאלֹהָי | כִּי־אֵלֶיךָ |
| | haqŏshîvāh | leqôl | shaw'î | malkî | wē'lōhāy | kî-'ēlêkhā |
| | be attentive | to the sound of | my crying for help | my King | and my God | because to You |

| 6663.725 | | 3176 | 1269 | 8471.123 | 7249 | 1269 |
|---|---|---|---|---|---|---|
| v Hithpael impf 1cs | 3. | pn | n ms | v Qal impf 2ms | n ms, ps 1cs | n ms |
| אֶתְפַּלָּל | | יְהוָה | בֹּקֶר | תִּשְׁמַע | קוֹלִי | בֹּקֶר |
| 'ethpallāl | | yehwāh | bōqer | tishma' | qôlî | bōqer |
| I pray | | O Yahweh | the morning | You will hear | my voice | the morning |

| 6424.125, 3937 | 7099.325 | | 3706 | 3940 | 418, 2760 |
|---|---|---|---|---|---|
| v Qal impf 1cs, prep, ps 2ms | cj, v Piel impf 1cs | 4. | cj | neg part | prep, adj |
| אֶעֱרָךְ־לְךָ | וַאֲצַפֶּה | | כִּי | לֹא | אֵל־חָפֵץ |
| 'e'ĕrākh-lekhā | wa'ătsappeh | | kî | lō' | 'ēl-chāphēts |
| I will prepare for You | and I will watch diligently | | because | not | a God pleased about |

| 7856 | 887 | 3940 | 1513.121 | 7737 | | 3940, 3429.726 |
|---|---|---|---|---|---|---|
| n ms | pers pron | neg part | v Qal impf 3ms, ps 2ms | n ms | 5. | neg part, v Hithpael impf 3mp |
| רֶשַׁע | אָתָּה | לֹא | יְגֻרְךָ | רָע | | לֹא־יִתְיַצְּבוּ |
| resha' | 'āttāh | lō' | yeghurkhā | rā' | | lō'-yithyatstsevû |
| offences | You | not | it will sojourn with You | evil | | they will not take a start |

before our eyes, *JB* … for a sight of better times, *Knox* … long for a sight of prosperous days, *Moffatt.*

**LORD, lift thou up:** … Look on us, *Good News* … look up, *Moffatt.*

**the light of thy countenance upon us:** … light of your face has fled from us, *Anchor* … light of Your face shine on us, *Beck* … the sunshine of thy favour, *Knox* … light of thy presence, *NEB.*

**7. Thou hast put gladness in my heart:** … happiness, *Anchor* … joy, *BB* … give to our hearts delight, *Fenton* … filled my heart, *NIV.*

**more than in the time that their corn and their wine increased:** … when their grain and their new wine are increased, *ASV* … season with plenty of new grain and wine, *Beck* … grain and wine abound, *Berkeley* … in abundance, *Darby* … corn and grapes, *Fenton.*

**8. I will both lay me down in peace, and sleep:** … In his peaceful presence, *Anchor* … take my rest, *BB* … I fall peacefully asleep, *NAB.*

**for thou, LORD, only makest me dwell in safety:** … keep me safe, *BB* … enable me to live without fear, *Beck* … make me rest secure, *JB* … bring security to my dwelling, *NAB.*

**5:t. To the chief Musician upon Nehiloth, A Psalm of David.**

**1. Give ear to my words, O LORD:** … Listen to what I'm saying, *Beck* … listen to my plea, *Knox* … Hear, *Berkeley.*

**consider my meditation:** … give thought to my heart-searchings, *BB* … give heed to my groaning, *RSV* …

attend to my thoughts, *Fenton* ... hear the murmur of my soul, *Moffatt* ... Understand my sadness, *NCV.*

**2. Hearken unto the voice of my cry, my King, and my God:** ... Be attentive, *Young* ... Give heed to the sound, *Anchor* ... Listen to me when I call for help, *Beck* ... my cry of petition, *Knox.*

**for unto thee will I pray:** ... because I'm pleading with you, *Beck* ... my prayer goes up, *Knox* ... I am calling out to thee, *Moffatt* ... when I say my prayers, *NEB* ... habitually, *Young.*

**3. My voice shalt thou hear:** ... My voice will come to you, *BB* ... wait thine answer, *Moffatt.*

**in the morning, O LORD:** ... At dawn, *Anchor* ... At daybreak, *JB* ... Each morning, *LIVB* ... early to win thy audience, *Knox.*

**in the morning:** ... at sunrise, *Good News.*

**will I direct my prayer unto thee:** ... I will draw up my case, *Anchor* ... lay my needs before you, *Beck* ... will I address myself, *Darby* ... set forth my plea, *Moffatt* ... prepare a sacrifice for thee, *RSV* ... I set in array for Thee, *Young.*

**and will look up:** ... fix my eyes on you, *JB* ... await thy pleasure, *Knox* ... wait thine answer, *Moffatt* ... And I look out, *Young* ... expectantly, *NAB.*

**4. For thou art not a God that hath pleasure in wickedness:** ... No evil thing claims thy divine assent, *Knox* ... delights in evil, *Anchor* ... in wrongdoing, *BB.*

**neither shall evil dwell with thee:** ... evil can be no guest of yours, *REB* ... Evil inhabiteth Thee not, *Young* ... cannot tolerate the slightest sin, *LIVB* ... live in Your presence, *KJVII* ... sojourn with thee, *ASV.*

**5. The foolish:** ... Those people who make fun of you, *NCV* ... boasters, *Anchor* ... arrogant, *ASV* ... sons of pride, *BB* ... Insolent fools, *Darby.*

**shall not stand:** ... have no place, *BB* ... Proud cannot endure, *Fenton* ... station not themselves, *Young* ... set themselves, *KJVII.*

**in thy sight:** ... before Your eyes, *Beck* ... in Thy presence, *Berkeley* ...

---

the persons whom he has been addressing. Furthermore, while he glances at the vain cries of the "many," he would make himself the mouthpiece of the nascent body of faith which he hopes may follow his beseechings.

**4:7–8.** Verses 7f are separated from v. 6 by their purely personal reference. The psalmist returns to the tone of his prayer in v. 1, only that petition has given place, as it should do, to possession and confident thankfulness. Yahweh's presence makes him safe, and being thus safe, he is secure and confident. So he shuts his eyes in peace, although he may be lying in the open, beneath the stars, without defenses or sentries. The face brings light in darkness, gladness in want, enlargement in straits, safety in peril, and every good that any person might need.

***Psalm 5.*** *Psalm 5 falls into two main parts: vv. 1–7 and 8–12. The first division deals with the inner side of the devout life and its access to God, to Whom sinful men cannot approach. The second deals with the outward side, the conduct, "the way" in which the psalmist seeks to be led, and in which sinful men come to ruin because they will not walk.*

**5:1–2.** In the first part of the Psalm, the central thought is that of access to God's presence, as the desire and purpose of the psalmist (vv. 1ff), as barred to evildoers (vv. 4ff), and as permitted to, and embraced as his chief blessing by, the singer (v. 7). The petition to be heard in vv. 1f passes into confidence that he is heard in v. 3. There is no shade of sadness or trace of struggle with doubt in this prayer, which is sunny and fresh, like the morning sky through which it ascends to God. "Consider [or understand] my meditation"—the brooding, silent thought is spread before God, Who knows unspoken desires and "understands thoughts afar off." The contrast between "understanding the meditation" and "hearkening to the voice of my cry" is scarcely unintentional and gives vividness to the picture of the musing psalmist, in whom, as he muses, the fire burns, and he speaks with his tongue in a "cry" as loud as the silence, from which it issued, had been deep.

**5:3–6.** He speaks his confidence and his resolve. "In the morning" is best taken literally, whether we suppose the Psalm to have been composed for a morning song or not. Apparently, the compilers of the first Psalter placed it next to Ps. 4, which they regarded as an evening hymn, for this reason. The clause "I will lay me down and sleep" (4:8) is beautifully followed by "My voice shalt thou hear in the morning" (5:3). The order of clauses in v. 3 is significant in its apparent breach of strict sequence, by which God's hearing is made to precede the psalmist's praying. It is the order dictated by confidence, and it is the order in which the thoughts rise in the trustful heart. He who is sure that

| 2054.152 | 3937, 5224 | 6084 | 7983.113 | 3725, 6713.152 | 201 | | 6.323 |
|---|---|---|---|---|---|---|---|
| v Qal act ptc mp | prep, prep | n fd, ps 2ms | v Qal pf 2ms | *adj, v Qal act ptc mp* | n ms | **6.** | v Piel impf 2ms |
| הוֹלְלִים | לְנֶגֶד | עֵינֶיךָ | שָׂנֵאתָ | כָּל־פֹּעֲלֵי | אָוֶן | | תְּאַבֵּד |
| hôlelîm | leneghedh | ‘ênêkhā | sānē’thā | kol-pō‘ălê | ’āwen | | te’abbēdh |
| boastful ones | facing | your eyes | You hate | all those who practice | iniquity | | You destroy |

| 1744.152 | 3695 | 382, 1879 | 4983 | 8911.321 | 3176 | | 603 |
|---|---|---|---|---|---|---|---|
| *v Qal act ptc mp* | n ms | *n ms*, n mp | cj, n fs | v Piel impf 3ms | pn | **7.** | cj, pers pron |
| דֹּבְרֵי | כָזָב | אִישׁ־דָּמִים | וּמִרְמָה | יְתָעֵב | יְהוָה | | וַאֲנִי |
| dōverê | khāzāv | ’îsh-dāmîm | ûmirmāh | yethā‘ēv | yehwāh | | wa’ănî |
| those who speak | falsehood | men of bloodshed | and fraud | He abhors | Yahweh | | and I |

| 904, 7524 | 2721 | 971.125 | 1041 | 8246.725 |
|---|---|---|---|---|
| prep, *n ms* | n ms, ps 2ms | v Qal juss 1cs | n ms, ps 2ms | v Hithpael juss 1cs |
| בְּרֹב | חַסְדְּךָ | אָבוֹא | בֵיתֶךָ | אֶשְׁתַּחֲוֶה |
| berōv | chasdekhā | ’āvô’ | vêthekhā | ’eshtachweh |
| in the abundance of | your steadfast love | let me enter | your house | let me worship |

| 420, 2033, 7231 | 904, 3488 | | 3176 | 5328.131 |
|---|---|---|---|---|
| prep, *n ms*, n ms, ps 2ms | prep, n fs, ps 2ms | **8.** | pn | v Qal impv 2ms, ps 1cs |
| אֶל־הֵיכַל־קָדְשְׁךָ | בְּיִרְאָתֶךָ | | יְהוָה | נְחֵנִי |
| ’el-hêkhal-qodhshekhā | beyir’āthekhā | | yehwāh | nechēnî |
| at the temple of your holy place | in fear of You | | O Yahweh | lead me |

| 904, 6930 | 3937, 4775 | 8234 | 3595.531 | 3937, 6686 | 1932 |
|---|---|---|---|---|---|
| prep, n fs, ps 2ms | prep, prep | n mp, ps 1cs | v Hiphil impv 2ms | prep, n mp, ps 1cs | n ms, ps 2ms |
| בְצִדְקָתֶךָ | לְמַעַן | שׁוֹרְרָי | הוֹשַׁר | לְפָנַי | דַּרְכֶּךָ |
| vetsidhqāthekhā | lema‘an | shôreray | hôshar | lephānay | darkekhā |
| by your righteousness | because of | my enemies | make straight | before me | your way |

| | 3706 | 375 | 904, 6552 | 3679.257 | 7419 | 2010 |
|---|---|---|---|---|---|---|
| **9.** | cj | *sub* | prep, n ms, ps 3ms | v Niphal ptc fs | n ms, ps 3mp | n fp |
| | כִּי | אֵין | בְּפִיהוּ | נְכוֹנָה | קִרְבָּם | הַוּוֹת |
| | kî | ’ên | bephîhû | nekhônāh | qirbām | hawwôth |
| | because | there is not | in their mouth | what is secured | their inmost being | destruction |

| 7197, 6858.155 | 1671 | 4098 | 2606.526 | | 843.531 | 435 |
|---|---|---|---|---|---|---|
| n ms, v Qal pass ptc ms | n ms, ps 3mp | n fs, ps 3mp | v Hiphil impf 3mp | **10.** | v Hiphil impv 2ms, ps 3mp | n mp |
| קֶבֶר־פָּתוּחַ | גְּרוֹנָם | לְשׁוֹנָם | יַחֲלִיקוּן | | הַאֲשִׁימֵם | אֱלֹהִים |
| qever-pāthûach | gerônām | leshônām | yachlîqûn | | ha’ăshîmēm | ’ĕlōhîm |
| an opened tomb | their throat | their tongues | they flatter | | pronounce them guilty | O God |

| 5489.126 | 4623, 4292 | 904, 7524 | 6840 |
|---|---|---|---|
| v Qal juss 3mp | prep, n fp, ps 3mp | prep, *n ms* | n mp, ps 3mp |
| יִפְּלוּ | מִמֹּעֲצוֹתֵיהֶם | בְּרֹב | פִּשְׁעֵיהֶם |
| yippelû | mimmō‘ătsôthêhem | berōv | pish‘êhem |
| may they fall | from their counsels | because of the abundance of | their offences |

| 5258.531 | 3706, 4947.116 | 904 | | 7975.126 |
|---|---|---|---|---|
| v Hiphil impv 2ms, ps 3mp | cj, v Qal pf 3cp | prep, ps 2ms | **11.** | cj, v Qal juss 3mp |
| הַדִּיחֵמוֹ | כִּי־מָרוּ | בָךְ | | וְיִשְׂמְחוּ |
| haddîchēmô | kî-mārû | vākh | | weyismechû |
| throw them out | because they have rebelled | in You | | let them be glad |

| 3725, 2725.152 | 904 | 3937, 5986 | 7728.326 | 5718.523 |
|---|---|---|---|---|
| *adj, v Qal act ptc mp* | prep, ps 2ms | prep, n ms | v Piel juss 3mp | cj, v Hiphil impf 2ms |
| כָּל־חוֹסֵי | בָךְ | לְעוֹלָם | יְרַנֵּנוּ | וְתָסֵךְ |
| khol-chôsê | vākh | le‘ôlām | yerannēnû | wethāsēkh |
| all those seeking refuge | in You | unto eternity | let them shout for joy | and You shelter |

under your gaze, *JB* ... can look thee in the face, *Moffatt.*

**thou hatest all workers of iniquity:** ... evildoers, *Anchor* ... who do wrong, *Beck* ... slaves of Vice, *Fenton* ... wicked people, *Good News.*

**6. Thou shalt destroy them:** ... send destruction, *BB* ... make an end, *REB.*

**that speak leasing:** ... who tell lies, *Anchor* ... whose words are false, *BB* ... speak falsehood, *MAST* ... all liars, *NEB.*

**the LORD will abhor:** ... despise, *Good News* ... detests, *Anchor.*

**the bloody and deceitful man:** ... those who kill and trick others, *NCV* ... craft and bloodshed, *Moffatt* ... murders and cheats, *Beck* ... bloodthirsty, *ASV* ... violent, *REB.*

**7. But as for me, I will come into thy house:** ... I have access to thy house, *Moffatt* ... Temple, *NCV.*

**in the multitude of thy mercy:** ... through your great love, *Anchor* ... in the full measure of your mercy, *BB* ... greatness of Thy unfailing love, *Berkeley* ... encompassed by thy mercy, *Knox* ... by thy great generosity, *Moffatt* ... abundant kindness, *NAB.*

**and in thy fear:** ... feeling of awe, *Beck* ... in reverence, *Berkeley* ... in Your fear, *KJVII* ... Because I fear and respect you, *NCV.*

**will I worship toward thy holy temple:** ... reverently bow, *Fenton* ... turning my eyes to, *BB* ... before thy sanctuary, *Knox.*

**8. Lead me, O LORD:** ... Be my guide, *BB* ... protect me, *REB* ... thou Eternal, *Moffatt.*

**in thy righteousness:** ... into your meadow, *Anchor* ... with faithful care, *Knox* ... as you promised me you would, *LIVB* ... as thou art just, *Moffatt* ... in your justice, *NAB.*

**because of mine enemies:** ... my rivals, *Anchor* ... those who hate me, *Beck* ... those who lie in wait, *JB* ... mine adversaries, *Rotherham* ... those who watch me, *Berkeley.*

**make thy way straight before my face:** ... show me the right thing to do, *NCV* ... Make even before me thy way, *Rotherham* ... Lead me to do your will, *Good News.*

**9. For there is no faithfulness in their mouth:** ... no truth in what they say, *Beck* ... nothing in their speech upon which one can rely, *Berkeley* ... nothing reliable, *NASB* ... from their lips, *JB.*

**their inward part is very wickedness:** ... his belly is an engulfing chasm, *Anchor* ... nothing but evil, *BB* ... perversion, *Darby* ... deep with mischief, *Moffatt* ... they want to destroy others, *NCV.*

**their throat is an open sepulchre:** ... an open place for the dead, *BB* ... open grave, *Beck* ... full of deadly deceit, *Good News* ... their mouths gaping tombs, *Knox.*

**they flatter with their tongue:** ... bring death, *Anchor* ... smooth are the words, *BB* ... their tongues seductive, *JB* ... smooth-tongued deceivers, *Moffatt* ... on their lips, *Knox.*

**10. Destroy thou them, O God:** ... Make them perish, *Anchor* ... Send them to destruction, *BB* ... make them suffer, *Beck* ... O'erthrow them, *Fenton* ... Punish them, *NAB.*

**let them fall by their own counsels:** ... evil designs, *BB* ... because of their schemes, *Anchor* ... by their own plans, *Beck* ... devices, *Goodspeed* ... their intrigues their own downfall, *JB* ... into their own traps, *NCV.*

**cast them out:** ... let them be forced out, *BB* ... drive them out, *Darby* ... thrust them from you, *JB* ... Banish them, *NIV.*

**in the multitude of their transgressions:** ... their numerous crimes, *Anchor* ... because they did so much wrong, *Beck* ... countless offences, *JB* ... iniquities, *Geneva* ... many sins, *NIV.*

**for they have rebelled against thee:** ... challenged you, *Anchor* ... have gone against your authority, *BB* ... turned against you, *NCV.*

**11. But let all those that put their trust in thee rejoice:** ... find their shelter, *Beck* ... seek refuge in you, *Anchor* ... shout for joy, *ASV* ... be happy, *NCV.*

**let them ever shout for joy:** ... forever singing with joy, *Anchor* ... with

---

God will hear will therefore address himself to speak. First comes the confidence, and then the resolve.

The "because" of v. 4 would naturally have heralded a statement of the psalmist's grounds for expecting that he would be welcomed in his approach, but the turn of thought, which postpones that and first regards God's holiness as shutting out the impure, is profoundly significant. The one idea of opposition between God and evil is put in a rich variety of shapes in vv. 4ff, which first deal with it negatively in three clauses ("not a God"; "not dwell"; "not stand in your sight") and then positively in the other three ("hate"; "will destroy"; "abhor").

**5:7.** In v. 7, the psalmist comes back to the personal reference, contrasting his own access to God with the separation of evildoers from his presence. But he does not assert that he has the right of entrance on the basis of purity. Very strikingly, he finds the ground of his right of entry to the palace in God's "multitude of mercy," not in his own innocence.

**5:8–12.** The whole of the devout man's desires for himself are summed up in that prayer

| | | | | |
|---|---|---|---|---|
| 6142<br>prep, ps 3mp<br>עָלֵימוֹ<br>'ālêmô<br>concerning them | 6192.126<br>cj, v Qal juss 3mp<br>וְיַעְלְצוּ<br>weya'ăltsû<br>that they may be glad | 904<br>prep, ps 2ms<br>בְךָ<br>vekhā<br>in You | 154.152<br>*v Qal act ptc mp*<br>אֹהֲבֵי<br>'ōhevê<br>those who love | 8428<br>n ms, ps 2ms<br>שְׁמֶךָ<br>shemekhā<br>your name |

| | | | | | | |
|---|---|---|---|---|---|---|
| **12.** | 3706, 887<br>cj, pers pron<br>כִּי־אַתָּה<br>kî-'attāh<br>because You | 1313.323<br>v Piel impf 2ms<br>תְּבָרֵךְ<br>tevārēkh<br>You bless | 6926<br>n ms<br>צַדִּיק<br>tsaddîq<br>the righteous | 3176<br>pn<br>יְהוָה<br>yehwāh<br>O Yahweh | 3626, 7065<br>prep, art, n fs<br>כַּצִּנָּה<br>katstsinnāh<br>like the large shield | 7814<br>n ms<br>רָצוֹן<br>rātsôn<br>favor |

| | | | | | |
|---|---|---|---|---|---|
| 6064.123<br>v Qal impf 2ms, ps 3ms<br>תַּעְטְרֶנּוּ<br>ta'ăṭrennû<br>You surround him | **6:t** | 3937, 5514.351<br>prep, art, v Piel ptc ms<br>לַמְנַצֵּחַ<br>lamnatstsēach<br>to the director | 904, 5234<br>prep, n fp<br>בִּנְגִינוֹת<br>binghînôth<br>with the stringed instruments | 6142, 8454<br>prep, art, adj<br>עַל־הַשְּׁמִינִית<br>'al-hashshemînîth<br>on the eighth | 4344<br>n ms<br>מִזְמוֹר<br>mizmôr<br>a Psalm |

| | | | | | |
|---|---|---|---|---|---|
| 3937, 1784<br>prep, pn<br>לְדָוִד<br>ledhāwidh<br>of David | **1.** | 3176<br>pn<br>יְהוָה<br>yehwāh<br>O Yahweh | 414, 904, 653<br>adv, prep, n ms, ps 3ms<br>אַל־בְּאַפְּךָ<br>'al-be'appekhā<br>not in your anger | 3306.523<br>v Hiphil juss 2ms, ps 1cs<br>תוֹכִיחֵנִי<br>thôkhîchēnî<br>may You chastise me | 414, 904, 2635<br>cj, adv, prep, n fs, ps 2ms<br>וְאַל־בַּחֲמָתְךָ<br>we'al-bachmāthekhā<br>and not in your wrath |

| | | | | | | |
|---|---|---|---|---|---|---|
| 3364.323<br>v Piel juss 2ms, ps 1cs<br>תְיַסְּרֵנִי<br>theyassērēnî<br>may You instruct me | **2.** | 2706.131<br>v Qal impv 2ms, ps 1cs<br>חָנֵּנִי<br>chonnēnî<br>be gracious to me | 3176<br>pn<br>יְהוָה<br>yehwāh<br>O Yahweh | 3706<br>cj<br>כִּי<br>kî<br>because | 545<br>adj<br>אֻמְלַל<br>'umlal<br>feeble | 603<br>pers pron<br>אָנִי<br>'ānî<br>I |

| | | | | | | |
|---|---|---|---|---|---|---|
| 7784.131<br>v Qal impv 2ms, ps 1cs<br>רְפָאֵנִי<br>rephā'ēnî<br>heal me | 3176<br>pn<br>יְהוָה<br>yehwāh<br>O Yahweh | 3706<br>cj<br>כִּי<br>kî<br>because | 963.216<br>v Niphal pf 3cp<br>נִבְהֲלוּ<br>nivhelû<br>they are dismayed | 6344<br>n fp, ps 1cs<br>עֲצָמָי<br>'ătsāmāy<br>my bones | **3.** | 5497<br>cj, n fs, ps 1cs<br>וְנַפְשִׁי<br>wenaphshî<br>and my soul |

| | | | | | | | |
|---|---|---|---|---|---|---|---|
| 963.212<br>v Niphal pf 3fs<br>נִבְהֲלָה<br>nivhelāh<br>it is dismayed | 4108<br>adv<br>מְאֹד<br>me'ōdh<br>very | 879<br>cj, pers pron<br>וְאַתְּ<br>we'atte<br>and You | 3176<br>pn<br>יְהוָה<br>yehwāh<br>O Yahweh | 5912, 5146<br>adv, intrg<br>עַד־מָתָי<br>'adh-māthāy<br>until when | **4.** | 8178.131<br>v Qal impv 2ms<br>שׁוּבָה<br>shûvāh<br>turn back | 3176<br>pn<br>יְהוָה<br>yehwāh<br>O Yahweh |

cries of joy, *BB* … shouting happily, *Beck* … endless songs of gladness, *JB* … everlasting triumph, *Knox.*

**because thou defendest them:** … will shelter them, *Anchor* … protect, *Beck* … make a covering over them, *Berkeley* … welcome protection, *Knox.*

**let them also that love thy name be joyful in thee:** … true lovers of thy name, *Knox* … shall exult, *Darby* … are truly happy, *Good News* … rejoice in you, *JB* … leap for joy, *Rotherham.*

**12. For thou, LORD:** … Eternal, *Moffatt* … Yahweh, *Rotherham.*

**wilt bless the righteous:** … givest the benediction to the just, *Knox* … those who obey you, *Good News* … who do what is right, *NCV* … the upright, *JB* … the godly man, *LIVB.*

**with favour wilt thou compass him:** … your grace will be round him, *BB* … And crown with a crown of delight, *Fenton* … throw thy loving-kindness about us, *Knox* … hedge him round, *NEB.*

**as with a shield:** … you will be his strength, *BB* … shielding them safe, *Moffatt* … like a soldier's shield, *NCV* … As a buckler, *Young* … an all-covering shield, *Rotherham.*

**6:t. To the chief Musician on Neginoth upon Sheminith, A Psalm of David.**

**1. O LORD, rebuke me not:** … do not be bitter with me, *BB* … don't be angry and punish me, *Beck* … when thou dost reprove me, *Knox* … don't correct me, *NCV* … do not condemn me, *NEB*

**in thine anger:** ... let it not be in anger, *Knox* ... when you are angry, *NCV* ... wrath, *BB*.

**neither chasten me:** ... discipline, *Berkeley* ... nor chastise me, *NAB* ... don't punish me, *NCV*.

**in thy hot displeasure:** ... wrath, *Anchor* ... in the heat of your passion, *BB* ... don't be furious, *Beck* ... in a rage, *Moffatt* ... when you are very angry, *NCV*.

**2. Have mercy upon me, O Lord:** ... Have pity, *Anchor* ... Be kind, *Beck* ... Be gracious, *Darby* ... Be merciful, *NIV* ... Show favour, *REB*.

**for I am weak:** ... I am languishing, *RSV* ... I am completely exhausted, *Good News* ... wasted away, *BB* ... withered away, *ASV* ... spent, *Anchor*.

**O Lord, heal me:** ... make me well, *BB*.

**for my bones are vexed:** ... I'm shaken to my bones, *Beck* ... my health is broken, *Moffatt* ... my body is racked with pain, *REB* ... my body is in terror, *NAB* ... in agony, *NIV*.

**3. My soul is also sore vexed:** ... is exceedingly disturbed, *Berkeley* ... my spirit is greatly shaken, *Goodspeed* ... I am upset and disturbed, *LIVB* ... utterly distraught, *REB* ... bitter trouble, *BB*.

**but thou, O Lord, how long?:** ... wilt thou delay, *Geneva* ... Lord, wilt thou never be content, *Knox* ... When will you act, *REB* ... will you wait to help me, *Good News*.

**4. Return, O Lord, deliver my soul:** ... save my life once more, *Moffatt* ... Come, O Lord, and make me well, *LIVB* ... grant a wretched soul relief, *Knox* ... make my soul free, *BB* ... rescue my life, *Anchor*.

**oh save me:** ... give me salvation, *BB* ... rescue me, *JB* ... succour me, *Moffatt* ... deliver me, *NEB*.

**for thy mercies' sake:** ... as befits your kindness, *Anchor* ... because You love me, *Beck* ... Thy covenant love, *Berkeley* ... as thou art ever merciful, *Knox* ... because of your unfailing love, *NIV*.

**5. For in death:** ... Once a person is dead, *Beck* ... In the world of the dead, *Good News* ... When death comes, *Knox* ... For if I die, *LIVB* ... Dead people, *NCV*.

**there is no remembrance of thee:** ... he can't remember You, *Beck* ... are no memorials made to Thee, *Berkeley* ... no mention of Thee, *NASB* ... None talk of thee, *NEB* ... no thought of thee, *Moffatt*.

**in the grave:** ... Sheol, *Anchor* ... underworld, *BB* ... in the tomb, *Knox* ... hades, *Rotherham*.

**who shall give thee thanks?:** ... who praises you, *Anchor* ... none can praise thee, *Knox*.

---

for guidance. All which the soul needs is included in these two: access to God in the depths of still prostration before his throne as the all-sufficient good for the inner life; guidance, as by a shepherd, on a plain path, chosen not by self-will but by God.

The picture of the evildoers is evidently the enemies. He complains that there is no faithfulness or steadfastness in "his mouth"—a distributive singular, which immediately passes into the plural—nothing there that a man can rely on, but all treacherous.

The psalmist is in the sanctuary, where he understands the end of the wicked and breaks into prayer which is also prophecy. The vindication of such prayers for the destruction of evildoers is that they are not the expressions of personal enmity ("They have rebelled against thee," v. 10) and that they correspond to one side of the divine character and acts, which was prominent in the OT epoch of revelation and is not superseded by the NT. The psalmist, on whom God looks with love, is safe from all evil; his heart dwells in God's house and his feet "travel on life's common way in cheerful godliness."

**6:1–3.** In vv. 1ff, we have a cluster of sharp, short cries to God for help, which all mean the same thing. In each, the great name of Yahweh is repeated, and the plea urged is simply the sore need of the suppliant. These are no vain repetitions, which are pressed out of a soul by the grip of the rack; and it is not taking the name of the Lord in vain (Deut. 5:11) when four times in three short verses the passionate cry for help is winged with it as the arrow with its feather. Thoughts of the Lord and the feeling of his pain fill the psalmist's consciousness. He does not at first appeal to God's revealed character, except insofar as the plaintive reiteration of the divine name carries such an appeal, but he spreads out his own wretchedness. He has faith in God's pity.

**6:4–5.** The next turn of thought is remarkable for the new pleas on which it rests—the triple prayer, "Return; deliver; save" (v. 4). God is his own motive, and his self-revelation in act must always be self-consistent in deed. Therefore, the plea is presented for the sake of his steadfast love. The psalmist beseeches Him to be what He is and to show himself as still being what He has always been.

| 2603.331 | 5497 | 3588.531 | 3937, 4775 | 2721 | | 3706 |
|---|---|---|---|---|---|---|
| v Piel impv 2ms | n fs, ps 1cs | v Hiphil impv 2ms, ps 1cs | prep, prep | n ms, ps 2ms | | cj |
| חַלְּצָה | נַפְשִׁי | הוֹשִׁיעֵנִי | לְמַעַן | חַסְדֶּךָ | **5.** | כִּי |
| challetsāh | naphshî | hôshî'ēnî | lema'an | chasdekhā | | kî |
| pull out | my soul | save me | because of | your steadfast love | | because |

| 375 | 904, 4323 | 2228 | 904, 8061 | 4449 | 3498.521, 3937 |
|---|---|---|---|---|---|
| *sub* | prep, art, n ms | n ms, ps 2ms | prep, pn | intrg | v Hiphil impf 3ms, prep, ps 2ms |
| אֵין | בַּמָּוֶת | זִכְרֶךָ | בִּשְׁאוֹל | מִי | יוֹדֶה־לָּךְ |
| 'ên | bammāweth | zikhrekhā | bish'ôl | mî | yôdheh-lākh |
| there is not | in death | a memory of You | in Sheol | who | he will praise You |

| | 3129.115 | 904, 599 | 7921.525 | 904, 3725, 4050 | 4433 |
|---|---|---|---|---|---|
| | v Qal pf 1cs | prep, n fs, ps 1cs | v Hiphil impf 1cs | prep, *adj*, n ms | n fs, ps 1cs |
| **6.** | יָגַעְתִּי | בְּאַנְחָתִי | אַשְׂחֶה | בְכָל־לַיְלָה | מִטָּתִי |
| | yāgha'ättî | be'anchāthî | 'ascheh | vekhol-laylāh | mittāthî |
| | I have become weary | in my groaning | I flood | during all the night | my bed |

| 904, 1893 | 6446 | 4678.525 | | 6485.112 | 4623, 3833 | 6084 |
|---|---|---|---|---|---|---|
| prep, n fs, ps 1cs | n fs, ps 1cs | v Hiphil impf 1cs | | v Qal pf 3fs | prep, n ms | n fs, ps 1cs |
| בְּדִמְעָתִי | עַרְשִׂי | אַמְסֶה | **7.** | עָשְׁשָׁה | מִכַּעַס | עֵינִי |
| bedhim'āthî | 'arsî | 'amseh | | 'āsheshāh | mikka'as | 'ênî |
| with my tears | my couch | I dissolve | | it is swollen | from vexation | my eye |

| 6514.112 | 904, 3725, 7173.152 | | 5681.133 | 4623 |
|---|---|---|---|---|
| v Qal pf 3fs | prep, *adj*, v Qal act ptc mp, ps 1cs | | v Qal impv 2mp | prep, ps 1cs |
| עָתְקָה | בְּכָל־צוֹרְרָי | **8.** | סוּרוּ | מִמֶּנִּי |
| 'ātheqāh | bekhol-tsôrerāy | | sûrû | mimmenî |
| it has become old | because of all my adversaries | | go away | from me |

| 3725, 6713.152 | 201 | 3706, 8471.111 | 3176 | 7249 | 1104 |
|---|---|---|---|---|---|
| *adj, v Qal act ptc mp* | n ms | cj, v Qal pf 3ms | pn | *n ms* | n ms, ps 1cs |
| כָּל־פֹּעֲלֵי | אָוֶן | כִּי־שָׁמַע | יְהוָה | קוֹל | בִּכְיִי |
| kol-pō'ălê | 'āwen | kî-shāma' | yehwāh | qôl | bikhyî |
| all those who practice | iniquity | because He has heard | Yahweh | the sound of | my weeping |

| | 8471.111 | 3176 | 8798 | 3176 | 8940 | 4089.121 |
|---|---|---|---|---|---|---|
| | v Qal pf 3ms | pn | n fs, ps 1cs | pn | n fs, ps 1cs | v Qal impf 3ms |
| **9.** | שָׁמַע | יְהוָה | תְּחִנָּתִי | יְהוָה | תְּפִלָּתִי | יִקָּח |
| | shāma' | yehwāh | techinnāthî | yehwāh | tephillāthî | yiqqāch |
| | He has heard | Yahweh | my supplication | Yahweh | my prayer | He accepts |

| | 991.126 | 963.226 | 4108 | 3725, 342.152 |
|---|---|---|---|---|
| | v Qal juss 3mp | cj, v Niphal juss 3mp | adv | *adj*, v Qal act ptc mp, ps 1cs |
| **10.** | יֵבֹשׁוּ | וְיִבָּהֲלוּ | מְאֹד | כָּל־אֹיְבָי |
| | yēvōshû | weyibbāhelû | me'ōdh | kol-'ōyevāy |
| | may they be ashamed | and may they be dismayed | very | all my enemies |

| 8178.126 | 991.126 | 7569 | | 8150 | 3937, 1784 | 866, 8301.111 |
|---|---|---|---|---|---|---|
| v Qal juss 3mp | v Qal juss 3mp | n ms | | n ms | prep, pn | rel part, v Qal pf 3ms |
| יָשֻׁבוּ | יֵבֹשׁוּ | רָגַע | **7:t** | שִׁגָּיוֹן | לְדָוִד | אֲשֶׁר־שָׁר |
| yāshuvû | yēvōshû | rāgha' | | shiggāyôn | ledhāwidh | 'äsher-shār |
| may they turn back | may they be ashamed | a moment | | a Shiggaion | of David | which he sang |

| 3937, 3176 | 6142, 1745, 3688 | 1176 | | 3176 | 435 | 904 |
|---|---|---|---|---|---|---|
| prep, pn | prep, *n mp*, pn | pn | | pn | n mp, ps 1cs | prep, ps 2ms |
| לַיהוָה | עַל־דִּבְרֵי־כוּשׁ | בֶּן־יְמִינִי | **1.** | יְהוָה | אֱלֹהַי | בְּךָ |
| layhwāh | 'al-divrê-khûsh | ben-yemînî | | yehwāh | 'ělōhay | bekhā |
| to Yahweh | concerning the matters of Cush | a Benjamite | | O Yahweh | my God | in You |

**6. I am weary:** ... wears me out, *Beck* ... I fainted, *Geneva* ... I am tired, *NCV* ... spent, *Knox.*

**with my groaning:** ... sobbing, *Anchor* ... voice of my sorrow, *BB* ... with sighs, *Fenton* ... moaning, *Goodspeed* ... of crying to you, *NCV.*

**all the night make I my bed to swim:** ... I soak my bed, *Anchor* ... wet with weeping, *BB* ... I flood my bed, *Goodspeed* ... I lie weeping on my bed, *Knox* ... my bed is drenched, *Moffatt.*

**I water my couch with my tears:** ... the drops flowing from my eyes, *BB* ... the tears drench my pillow, *Knox* ... my couch is wet, *Moffatt.*

**7. Mine eye is consumed:** ... My face is all sunken, *Rotherham* ... wasteth away, *ASV* ... are hollow, *Beck* ... I can hardly see, *Good News* ... Old, *Young.*

**because of grief:** ... with sorrow, *Anchor* ... with trouble, *BB* ... with vexation, *JB* ... from so much crying, *NCV* ... from provocation, *Young.*

**it waxeth old:** ... It is becoming old, *KJVII* ... faded their lustre, *Knox* ... oppress like age, *Fenton* ... they fail, *NIV.*

**because of all mine enemies:** ... under outrages from my foes, *Moffatt* ... so many are the adversaries, *Knox* ... oppressors, *Darby* ... My woes, *Fenton* ... my distress, *Beck.*

**8. Depart from me, all ye workers of iniquity:** ... Get away from me, *Beck* ... Leave me alone, *REB* ... all you that traffic in iniquity, *Knox* ... all you who do wrong, *Beck* ... all my passion, *Fenton.*

**for the LORD hath heard:** ... listens, *Moffatt.*

**the voice of my weeping:** ... my crying, *Beck* ... my tearful voice, *Fenton* ... my cry of distress, *Knox* ... to my wail, *Moffatt.*

**9. The LORD hath heard my supplication:** ... has heard me ask for money, *Beck* ... entreaty, *Goodspeed* ... my echoing groans, *Fenton* ... cry for help, *NCV* ... petition, *Geneva.*

**the LORD will receive my prayer:** ... has accepted, *Anchor* ... let my prayer come before him, *BB* ... will answer, *NCV* ... a boon divinely granted, *Knox.*

**10. Let all mine enemies be ashamed and sore vexed:** ... foes be humbled and greatly shaken, *Anchor* ... will feel miserable and terrified, *Beck* ... confounded, *Geneva* ... put to confusion, *JB* ... in utter terror, *NAB.*

**let them return:** ... turn back, *ASV* ... taken aback, *Knox* ... they shall fall back, *NAB* ... turn, *NCV.*

**and be ashamed suddenly:** ... in Perdition, *Anchor* ... in disgrace, *Beck* ... in a moment, *Berkeley* ... retreat in sudden confusion, *JB* ... dishonoured, *Fenton* ... discomfited, *Moffatt.*

**7:t. Shiggaion of David, which he sang unto the LORD, concerning the words of Cush the Benjamite.**

**1. O LORD my God:** ... Eternal One, my God, *Moffatt.*

---

**6:6–7.** The psalmist's sense of his own pains, which, in the two previous parts of the Psalm, had been contending with the thought of God, masters him in these dreary verses. The absence of the name of God is noteworthy as expressive of the psalmist's absorption in brooding over his misery. The vehemence of the manifestations of sorrow and the frankness of the record of these manifestations in the song may strike us as excessive, but the emotion which wails in these sad verses is only too familiar to people of all temperaments.

**6:8–10.** The triumphant dismissal of the wicked is a vivid way of expressing the certainty of their departure, with their murderous hate unslaked and balked. My enemies are workers of iniquity. That is a daring assumption, made still more remarkable by the previous confession that the psalmist's sorrow was God's rebuke and chastening. But a person has the right to believe that his cause is God's in the measure in which he makes God's cause his own. In the confidence that his prayer is heard, the psalmist can see things that are not as though they were. Although no change has passed on the beleaguering hosts, he triumphs in their certain rout and retreat. He significantly predicts in v. 10 the same fate for them which he had bewailed as his own.

***Psalm 7.*** *This is the only Psalm with the title "Shiggaion"(HED #8150). The word occurs in the OT only here and in Hab. 3:1, where it stands in the plural and with the preposition "upon" (HED #6142), as if to designate instruments. The meaning is unknown, and commentators, who do not like to say so, have trouble finding one. The root is a verb, "to wander," and the common explanation is that the word describes the disconnected character of the Psalm, which is full of swiftly succeeding emotions rather than sequential thoughts.*

**7:1–5.** The first section has two main thoughts: the cry for help and the protestation of innocence. It is in accordance with the bold triumphant tone of the Psalm that its first words are a profession of faith in Yahweh. It is important to look to God

| 2725.115 | 3588.531 | 4623, 3725, 7579.152 | 5522.531 |
|---|---|---|---|
| v Qal pf 1cs | v Hiphil impv 2ms, ps 1cs | prep, *adj*, v Qal act ptc mp | cj, v Hiphil impv 2ms, ps 1cs |
| חָסִיתִי | הוֹשִׁיעֵנִי | מִכָּל־רֹדְפַי | וְהַצִּילֵנִי |
| chās̱îthî | hôshî'ēnî | mikkol-rōdhephay | wehatstsîlênî |
| I have sought refuge | save me | from all my pursuers | and rescue me |

| 2. | 6678, 3072.121 | 3626, 765 | 5497 | 6811.151 | 375 | 5522.551 |
|---|---|---|---|---|---|---|
| | adv, v Qal impf 3ms | prep, n ms | n fs, ps 1cs | v Qal act ptc ms | cj, *sub* | v Hiphil ptc ms |
| | פֶּן־יִטְרֹף | כְּאַרְיֵה | נַפְשִׁי | פֹּרֵק | וְאֵין | מַצִּיל |
| | pen-yiṯrōph | ke'aryēh | naphshî | pōrēq | we'ên | matstsîl |
| | so that they will not tear | like a lion | me | dismembering | and there is not | a rescuer |

| 3. | 3176 | 435 | 524, 6449.115 | 2148 | 524, 3552, 5982 | 904, 3834 |
|---|---|---|---|---|---|---|
| | pn | n mp, ps 1cs | cj, v Qal pf 1cs | dem pron | cj, *sub*, n ms | prep, n fp, ps 1cs |
| | יְהוָה | אֱלֹהַי | אִם־עָשִׂיתִי | זֹאת | אִם־יֶשׁ־עָוֶל | בְּכַפָּי |
| | yehwāh | 'ĕlōhay | 'im-'āsîthî | zō'th | 'im-yesh-'āwel | bekhappāy |
| | O Yahweh | my God | if I have done | this | if there is wrongdoing | in my palms |

| 4. | 524, 1621.115 | 8396.151 | 7737 | 2603.325 | 7173.152 |
|---|---|---|---|---|---|
| | cj, v Qal pf 1cs | v Qal act ptc ms, ps 1cs | n ms | cj, v Piel impf 1cs | v Qal act ptc mp, ps 1cs |
| | אִם־גָּמַלְתִּי | שׁוֹלְמִי | רָע | וָאֲחַלְּצָה | צוֹרְרִי |
| | 'im-gāmaltî | shôlmî | rā' | wā'ăchalletsāh | tsôrerî |
| | if I have requited | the one who requites me | evil | or I am tearing out | my adversaries |

| 7674 | 5. | 7579.121 | 342.151 | 5497 | 5560.521 |
|---|---|---|---|---|---|
| adv | | v Qal juss 3ms | v Qal act ptc ms | n fs, ps 1cs | cj, v Hiphil juss 3ms |
| רֵיקָם | | יִרַדֹּף | אוֹיֵב | נַפְשִׁי | וְיַשֵּׂג |
| rêqām | | yiraddōph | 'ôyēv | naphshî | weyassēgh |
| without cause | | let him pursue | an enemy | me | and let him overtake |

| 7717.121 | 3937, 800 | 2522 | 3638 | 3937, 6312 | 8331.521 |
|---|---|---|---|---|---|
| cj, v Qal juss 3ms | prep, art, n fs | n mp, ps 1cs | cj, n ms, ps 1cs | prep, art, n ms | v Hiphil juss 3ms |
| וְיִרְמֹס | לָאָרֶץ | חַיָּי | וּכְבוֹדִי | לֶעָפָר | יַשְׁכֵּן |
| weyirmōs̱ | lā'ārets | chayyāy | ûkhevôdhî | le'āphār | yashkēn |
| and let him trample | to the ground | my life | and my honor | to the dust | let him make remain |

| 5734 | 6. | 7251.131 | 3176 | 904, 653 | 5558.231 | 904, 5887 |
|---|---|---|---|---|---|---|
| intrj | | v Qal impv 2ms | pn | prep, n ms, ps 2ms | v Niphal impv 2ms | prep, *n fp* |
| סֶלָה | | קוּמָה | יְהוָה | בְּאַפֶּךָ | הִנָּשֵׂא | בְּעַבְרוֹת |
| s̱elāh | | qûmāh | yehwāh | be'appekhā | hinnāsē' | be'avrôth |
| selah | | rise | O Yahweh | in your anger | lift yourself | because of the rage of |

| 7173.152 | 5996.131 | 420 | 5122 | 6943.313 |
|---|---|---|---|---|
| v Qal act ptc mp, ps 1cs | cj, v Qal impv 2ms | prep, ps 1cs | n ms | v Piel pf 2ms |
| צוֹרְרָי | וְעוּרָה | אֵלַי | מִשְׁפָּט | צִוִּיתָ |
| tsôrerāy | we'ûrāh | 'ēlay | mishpāṭ | tsiwwîthā |
| my adversaries | and arouse | for me | a judgment | You have commanded |

| 7. | 5920 | 3947 | 5621.322 | 6142 | 3937, 4953 |
|---|---|---|---|---|---|
| | cj, *n fs* | n mp | v Poel impf 3fs, ps 2ms | cj, prep, ps 3fs | prep, art, n ms |
| | וַעֲדַת | לְאֻמִּים | תְּסוֹבְבֶךָ | וְעָלֶיהָ | לַמָּרוֹם |
| | wa'ădhath | le'ummîm | tes̱ôvevekhā | we'ālêāh | lammārôm |
| | and the assembly of | peoples | may it gather around You | and over it | to the on high |

| 8178.131 | 8. | 3176 | 1833.121 | 6194 | 8570.131 |
|---|---|---|---|---|---|
| v Qal impv 2ms | | pn | v Qal juss 3ms | n mp | v Qal impv 2ms, ps 1cs |
| שׁוּבָה | | יְהוָה | יָדִין | עַמִּים | שָׁפְטֵנִי |
| shûvāh | | yehwāh | yādhîn | 'ammîm | shāpheṭēnî |
| return | | Yahweh | may He judge | peoples | judge me |

**in thee do I put my trust:** ... You are my Shelter, *Beck* ... my confidence is in thee, *Knox* ... I trust in you for protection, *NCV* ... take refuge, *ASV.*

**save me from all them that persecute me:** ... take me out of the hands, *BB* ... all my pursuers, *Anchor* ... of him who is cruel to me, *BB* ... from those who are chasing me, *NCV* ... rescue me, *REB.*

**and deliver me:** ... make me free, *BB* ... grant me deliverance, *Knox* ... keep me safe, *Moffatt* ... save me, *REB.*

**2. Lest he tear my soul:** ... deuour, *Geneva* ... else must I fall a helpless prey, *Knox* ... tear me apart, *NCV* ... before they tear at my throat, *NEB* ... pounce upon me, *LIVB.*

**like a lion:** ... like the lion's prey, *NAB* ... to the lion, *Knox.*

**rending it in pieces:** ... wounding it, *BB* ... crushing it, *Darby* ... break me, *Fenton* ... devour me, *Moffatt* ... ripping it, *KJVII.*

**while there is none to deliver:** ... no one to be my saviour, *BB* ... to rescue me, *Anchor* ... none to defend, *Fenton* ... beyond hope of rescue, *NEB* ... no deliverer, *Rotherham.*

**3. O LORD my God, if I have done this:** ... if I too have been at fault, *Knox* ... what have I done, *NCV* ... if I have done any of these things, *REB.*

**if there be iniquity in my hands:** ... have done any wrong, *BB* ... stained with guilt, *Knox* ... if I am guilty of injustice, *Moffatt* ... perversity, *Rotherham* ... wickednes, *Geneva.*

**4. If I have rewarded evil:** ... repaid my ally with treachery, *Anchor* ... if I have been a false friend, *Knox* ... ill-treated, *Moffatt* ... harm, *NRSV.*

**unto him that was at peace with me:** ... who did evil to me, *BB* ... my friend, *Beck* ... my wellwisher, *Young.*

**(yea, I have delivered him:** ... plundered anyone, *Beck* ... spared one, *JB* ... crushed, *Moffatt* ... wantonly despoiled, *REB* ... done violence, *Good News.*

**that without cause is mine enemy:):** ... without a reason, *Beck* ... vexed me, *Geneva* ... mine adversary, *MRB* ... unprovoked, *JB.*

**5. Let the enemy persecute my soul:** ... my hater go after my soul, *BB* ... chase me, *Beck* ... hunt me down, *JB* ... with his relentless pursuit, *Knox* ... come after me, *NEB* ... come in pursuit, *REB.*

**and take it:** ... overtake me, *Anchor* ... and catch me, *Beck* ... and capture me, *NCV.*

**yea, let him tread down my life:** ... trample my vitals, *Anchor* ... my life be crushed, *BB* ... bury me, *NCV* ... cut me down, *Good News.*

**upon the earth:** ... into the nether world, *Anchor* ... to the earth, *BB* ... into the ground, *Beck.*

**and lay mine honour in the dust. Selah:** ... glory, *ASV* ... fling down, *Fenton* ... crush my vital parts, *JB* ... level my pride, *Knox* ... lay me low, *Moffatt.*

**6. Arise, O LORD:** ... Come up, *BB* ... rise up, *Knox* ... Bestir thyself, *Moffatt.*

**in thine anger:** ... your wrath, *Anchor* ... be angry, *Beck.*

**lift up thyself:** ... countervail, *Knox* ... in outbursts of fury, *Moffatt* ... rouse thyself, *NEB* ... stand up, *NCV.*

**because of the rage of mine enemies:** ... against the arrogance of my adversaries, *Anchor* ... against the fury, *Beck* ... against my foes, *Goodspeed* ... the malice, *Knox* ... haughty outbursts, *Rotherham.*

**and awake for me:** ... Bestir yourself, *Anchor* ... be awake, *BB* ... arouse Thyself, *NASB* ... rise up, *Goodspeed* ... awake to aid us, *Moffatt.*

**to the judgment that thou hast commanded:** ... demand fairness, *NCV* ... Demand justice for me, *Fenton* ... give orders for the judging, *BB* ... a judgment appoint, *Anchor.*

**7. So shall the congregation of the people:** ... The meeting of the nations, *BB* ... have an assembly of peoples,

---

before looking at dangers and foes. He who begins with trust can go on to consider the fiercest antagonism without dismay.

Indignant repelling of slander follows the first burst of triumphant trust (vv. 3ff). Apparently, "the words of Cush" were calumnies poisoning Saul's suspicious nature, such as David refers to in 1 Sam. 24:9: "Wherefore hearkenest thou to men's words, saying, Behold, David seeketh thy hurt?" The special point of the falsehood is plain from the repudiation. David had been charged with attempting to injure one who was at peace with him. That is exactly what "men's words" charged on David, "saying, Behold, David seeketh thy hurt" (1 Samuel, as above). Thus, nobly throbbing with conscious innocence and fronting unmerited hate, the rush of words stops to let the musical accompaniment blare on for a while, as if defiant and confident.

**7:6–10.** The second section of the Psalm is a cry for the coming of the divine Judge. The previous prayer was content with deliverance, but this takes a bolder flight and asks for the manifestation of the punitive activity of God on the enemies, who,

| | | | |
|---|---|---|---|
| **3176**<br>pn<br>יְהוָה<br>yehwāh<br>O Yahweh | **3626, 6928**<br>prep, n ms, ps 1cs<br>כְּצִדְקִי<br>ketsidhqî<br>according to my righteousness | **3626, 8866**<br>cj, prep, n ms, ps 1cs<br>וּכְתֻמִּי<br>ûkhethummî<br>and according to my integrity | **6142**<br>prep, ps 1cs<br>עָלָי<br>'ālāy<br>concerning me |

| | | | | | |
|---|---|---|---|---|---|
| **9.** | **1625, 5167.121**<br>v Qal juss 3ms, part<br>יִגְמָר־נָא<br>yighmār-nā'<br>and let it be at an end please | **7737**<br>*n ms*<br>רַע<br>ra'<br>the evil of | **7857**<br>n mp<br>רְשָׁעִים<br>reshā'îm<br>the wicked | **3679.323**<br>cj, v Poel impf 2ms<br>וּתְכוֹנֵן<br>ûthekhônēn<br>but You establish | **6926**<br>n ms<br>צַדִּיק<br>tsaddîq<br>the righteous |

| | | | | | | | |
|---|---|---|---|---|---|---|---|
| **1010.151**<br>cj, v Qal act ptc ms<br>וּבֹחֵן<br>ûvōchēn<br>and examining | **3949**<br>n mp<br>לִבּוֹת<br>libbôth<br>intentions | **3749**<br>cj, n fp<br>וּכְלָיוֹת<br>ûkhelāyôth<br>and motives | **435**<br>n mp<br>אֱלֹהִים<br>'ĕlōhîm<br>God | **6926**<br>adj<br>צַדִּיק<br>tsaddîq<br>righteous | **10.** | **4182**<br>n ms, ps 1cs<br>מָגִנִּי<br>māghinî<br>my shield | **6142, 435**<br>prep, n mp<br>עַל־אֱלֹהִים<br>'al-'ĕlōhîm<br>beside God |

| | | | | | | |
|---|---|---|---|---|---|---|
| **3588.551**<br>v Hiphil ptc ms<br>מוֹשִׁיעַ<br>môshîa'<br>the One Who saves | **3596, 3949**<br>*adj*, n ms<br>יִשְׁרֵי־לֵב<br>yishrê-lēv<br>the upright of heart | **11.** | **435**<br>n mp<br>אֱלֹהִים<br>'ĕlōhîm<br>God | **8570.151**<br>v Qal act ptc ms<br>שׁוֹפֵט<br>shôphēṭ<br>a Judge | **6926**<br>adj<br>צַדִּיק<br>tsaddîq<br>righteous | **418**<br>cj, n ms<br>וְאֵל<br>we'ēl<br>and a God |

| | | | | | | |
|---|---|---|---|---|---|---|
| **2278.151**<br>v Qal act ptc ms<br>זֹעֵם<br>zō'ēm<br>One Who curses | **904, 3725, 3219**<br>prep, *adj*, n ms<br>בְּכָל־יוֹם<br>bekhol-yôm<br>in all the days | **12.** | **524, 3940**<br>cj, neg part<br>אִם־לֹא<br>'im-lō'<br>if not | **8178.121**<br>v Qal impf 3ms<br>יָשׁוּב<br>yāshûv<br>he turns back | **2820**<br>n fs, ps 3ms<br>חַרְבּוֹ<br>charbô<br>his sword | **4048.121**<br>v Qal impf 3ms<br>יִלְטוֹשׁ<br>yilṭôsh<br>He will sharpen |

| | | | | | |
|---|---|---|---|---|---|
| **7493**<br>n fs, ps 3ms<br>קַשְׁתּוֹ<br>qashtô<br>his bow | **1931.111**<br>v Qal pf 3ms<br>דָּרַךְ<br>dhārakh<br>He will bend | **3679.321**<br>cj, v Polel impf 3ms, ps 3fs<br>וַיְכוֹנְנֶהָ<br>waykhônenēāh<br>and He will secure it | **13.** | **3937**<br>cj, prep, ps 3ms<br>וְלוֹ<br>welô<br>and for him | **3679.511**<br>v Hiphil pf 3ms<br>הֵכִין<br>hēkhîn<br>He has prepared |

| | | | | | |
|---|---|---|---|---|---|
| **3747, 4323**<br>*n mp*, n ms<br>כְּלֵי־מָוֶת<br>kelê-māweth<br>weapons for death | **2784**<br>n mp, ps 3ms<br>חִצָּיו<br>chitstsâv<br>his arrows | **3937, 1875.152**<br>prep, v Qal act ptc mp<br>לְדֹלְקִים<br>ledhōleqîm<br>for burning ones | **6713.121**<br>v Qal impf 3ms<br>יִפְעָל<br>yiph'āl<br>he made | **14.** | **2079**<br>intrj<br>הִנֵּה<br>hinnēh<br>behold |

*Beck* … All the nations, *Knox* … a company of peoples, *Young* … Summon all nations, *Moffatt.*

**compass thee about:** … surround you, *Anchor* … gather around You, *Beck.*

**for their sakes therefore return thou on high:** … take your seat, then, over them, on high, *BB* … return thou thereon to the heights, *Goodspeed* … if thou wilt come back to thy throne, *Knox* … be seated on the lofty throne, *Moffatt* … rule them from above, *NCV.*

**8. The LORD shall judge the people:** … Let Yahweh judge the nations, *Anchor* … shall minister judgment to the peoples, *Darby* … O thou Eternal, judge of the world, *Moffatt* … thou who dost pass sentence on the nations, *NEB* … You are the judge of all mankind, *Good News.*

**judge me, O LORD:** … Vindicate me, *Berkeley* … justify me to the tribes, *Fenton* … do me justice, *Goodspeed* … Give me redress, *Knox* … defend me, *NCV* … Uphold my cause, *REB.*

**according to my righteousness:** … as my uprightness and my integrity deserve, *JB* … we are innocent, *Moffatt* … I am just, *NAB.*

**and according to mine integrity:** … let my virtue have its reward, *BB* … according to my innocence, *Beck* … establish my honour and truth, *Fenton* … because I have done no wrong, *NCV* … I am clearly innocent, *NEB.*

**that is in me:** … that is mine, *NAB* … upon me, *Berkeley.*

**9. Oh let the wickedness of the wicked:** ... evil of the evil-doer, *BB* ... Repay to the wicked their wrong, *Fenton* ... Avenge the treachery, *Anchor* ... malice of the ungodly, *Moffatt.*

**come to an end:** ... Stop those wicked actions, *NCV* ... Let wicked men do no more harm, *NEB* ... Surely thou wilt put an end to, *Knox.*

**but establish the just:** ... make the righteous secure, *Beck* ... Defending the honest true hearts, *Fenton* ... make the upright stand firm, *JB* ... prosper the innocent, *Knox* ... help those who do what is right, *NCV.*

**for the righteous God trieth the hearts and reins:** ... the searcher of mind and heart is God the Just, *Anchor* ... no thought or desire of ours can escape the scrutiny of thy divine justice, *Knox* ... The God of justice reads the inmost heart, *Moffatt* ... You know our thoughts and feelings, *NCV.*

**10. My defence is of God:** ... My Suzerain is the Most High God, *Anchor* ... my breast-plate, *BB* ... I rely on God to shield me, *REB* ... God Most High, is my King, *Beck* ... From the Lord, refuge of true hearts, my protection comes, *Knox.*

**which saveth the upright in heart:** ... the Savior of the upright of heart, *Anchor* ... My safety my trueness of heart, *Fenton* ... who preserueth the vpright in heart, *Geneva* ... saving the honest of heart, *JB* ... he saves those whose hearts are right, *NCV.*

**11. God judgeth the righteous:** ... El is a vindicator, *Anchor* ... God is a righteous judge, *ASV* ... judges ever true, *Knox* ... a judge who is perfectly fair, *LIVB.*

**and God is angry with the wicked:** ... a God that hath indignation, *ASV* ... GOD is provoked, *Fenton* ... a God at all times threatening, *JB* ... always ready to punish, *NCV* ... requites the raging enemy, *NEB* ... expresses his wrath, *NIV.*

**every day:** ... at all times, *Anchor* ... all the day, *Darby* ... always, *NCV* ... constant, *REB* ... day by day, *Knox.*

**12. If he turn not:** ... If anyone will not repent, *Beck* ... If they change not, *Fenton* ... Unless they be converted, *NAB* ... If he does not relent, *NIV.*

**he will whet his sword:** ... O that the Victor would again sharpen his sword, *Anchor* ... his sword will flash bright, *Knox* ... The enemy sharpens his sword again, *REB.*

**he hath bent his bow:** ... draw and aim his bow, *Anchor* ... strung His bow, *Berkeley* ... His bow he hath trodden, *Young.*

**and made it ready:** ... take aim, *Fenton* ... His bow is strung and stretched, *Moffatt* ... He prepareth it, *Young.*

**13. He hath also prepared for him the instruments of death:** ... lethal weapons, *Anchor* ... deadly weapons, *Geneva* ... darts, *Moffatt* ... shafts, *NEB* ... to kill him, *Beck.*

**he ordaineth his arrows against the persecutors:** ... he gives birth to treachery, *JB.*

**14. Behold, he travaileth with iniquity:** ... Look, he conceives malice, *Anchor* ... he travails with wickedness, *NASB* ... people who think up evil, *NCV* ... the enemy is in labour with iniquity, *NEB* ... Lo! he gendereth trouble, *Rotherham.*

---

as usual, are identified with "evildoers." The grand metaphors in "Arise," "Lift up thyself" and "Awake" mean the same thing in substance. The long periods during which evil works and flaunts with impunity are the times when God sits as if passive and, in a figure still more daring, as if asleep. When his destructive power flashed into act and some long-tolerated iniquity was smitten at a blow, the Hebrew singers saw therein God springing to his feet or awaking to judgment. Such long stretches of patient permission of evil and of swift punishment are repeated through the ages, and individual lives have them in miniature. The great judgments of nations and the small ones of single people embody the same principles, just as the tiniest crystal has the same angles and lines of cleavage as the greatest of its kind. Very beautifully does the order of the words in v. 9 suggest the kindred of the good man with God by closing each division of the verse with "righteous" (HED #6926). A righteous man has a claim on a righteous God. Most naturally then, the prayer ends with the calm confidence of v. 10: "My shield is upon God." God himself bears the defense of the psalmist. This confidence the psalmist has won by his prayer, and in it he ceases to be a suppliant and becomes a seer.

**7:11–17.** Retribution is set forth with solemn vigor under four figures. First, God is as an armed enemy sharpening his sword in preparation for action, which in the Hebrew is work of time represented as a process, and bending his bow, which is the work of a moment and in the Hebrew is represented as a completed act. Another second, and the arrow will whiz. Not only is the bow bent (v. 12), but the deadly arrows are aimed, and not only aimed, but continuously fed with flame.

The next figure in v. 14 insists on the automatic action of evil in bringing punishment. It is the OT version of "Sin when it is finished bringeth forth death." The evildoer is boldly represented as

| 2341.321, 201 | 2106.111 | 6219 | 3314.111 |
|---|---|---|---|
| v Piel impf 3ms, n ms | cj, v Qal pf 3ms | n ms | cj, v Qal pf 3ms |
| יְחַבֶּל־אָוֶן | וְהָרָה | עָמָל | וְיָלַד |
| yechabbel-'āwen | wehārāh | 'āmāl | weyāladh |
| he goes into labor with iniquity | yes he has become pregnant with | harm | and he has brought forth |

| 8632 | | 988 | 3868.111 | 2763.121 | 5489.121 | 904, 8273 | 6713.121 |
|---|---|---|---|---|---|---|---|
| n ms | 15. | n ms | v Qal pf 3ms | cj, v Qal impf 3ms, ps 3ms | cj, v Qal impf 3ms | prep, n fs | v Qal impf 3ms |
| שָׁקֶר | | בּוֹר | כָּרָה | וַיַּחְפְּרֵהוּ | וַיִּפֹּל | בְּשַׁחַת | יִפְעָל |
| shāqer | | bôr | kārāh | wayyachperēhû | wayyippōl | beshachath | yiph'āl |
| lies | | a pit | he has dug | when he dug it out | then he fell | in a pit | he made |

| | 8178.121 | 6219 | 904, 7513 | 6142 | 7221 | 2660 |
|---|---|---|---|---|---|---|
| 16. | v Qal impf 3ms | n ms, ps 3ms | prep, n ms, ps 3ms | cj, prep | n ms, ps 3ms | n ms, ps 3ms |
| | יָשׁוּב | עֲמָלוֹ | בְרֹאשׁוֹ | וְעַל | קָדְקֳדוֹ | חֲמָסוֹ |
| | yāshûv | 'ămālô | verō'shô | we'al | qādheqōdhô | chămāsô |
| | it returns | his harm | on his head | and on | the crown of his head | his violence |

| 3495.121 | | 3142.525 | 3176 | 3626, 6928 | 2252.325 |
|---|---|---|---|---|---|
| v Qal impf 3ms | 17. | v Hiphil juss 1cs | pn | prep, n ms, ps 3ms | cj, v Piel juss 1cs |
| יֵרֵד | | אוֹדֶה | יְהוָה | כְּצִדְקוֹ | וַאֲזַמְּרָה |
| yērēdh | | 'ôdheh | yehwāh | ketsidhqô | wa'ăzammerāh |
| it comes down | | let me praise | Yahweh | according to his righteousness | and let me sing praises to |

| 8428, 3176 | 6169 | | 3937, 5514.351 | 6142, 1713 | 4344 | 3937, 1784 |
|---|---|---|---|---|---|---|
| *n ms*, pn | n ms | 8:t | prep, art, v Piel ptc ms | prep, art, n fp | n ms | prep, pn |
| שֵׁם־יְהוָה | עֶלְיוֹן | | לַמְנַצֵּחַ | עַל־הַגִּתִּית | מִזְמוֹר | לְדָוִד |
| shēm-yehwāh | 'elyôn | | lamnatstsēach | 'al-haggittîth | mizmôr | ledhāwidh |
| the name of Yahweh | the Most High | | to the director | on the gittith | a Psalm | of David |

| | 3176 | 112 | 4242, 116 | 8428 | 904, 3725, 800 | 866 | 8896.112 |
|---|---|---|---|---|---|---|---|
| 1. | pn | n mp, ps 1cp | intrg, n ms | n ms, ps 2ms | prep, *adj*, art, n fs | rel part | v Qal pf 3fs |
| | יְהוָה | אֲדֹנֵינוּ | מָה־אַדִּיר | שִׁמְךָ | בְּכָל־הָאָרֶץ | אֲשֶׁר | תְּנָה |
| | yehwāh | 'ădhōnênû | māh-'addîr | shimkhā | bekhol-hā'ārets | 'ăsher | tenāh |
| | O Yahweh | our Lord | how majestic | your name | throughout all the earth | which | it recounts |

| 2003 | 6142, 8452 | | 4623, 6552 | 5985 | 3352.152 |
|---|---|---|---|---|---|
| n ms, ps 2ms | prep, art, n md | 2. | prep, *n ms* | n mp | cj, v Qal act ptc mp |
| הוֹדְךָ | עַל־הַשָּׁמָיִם | | מִפִּי | עוֹלְלִים | וְיֹנְקִים |
| hôdhkhā | 'al-hashshāmāyim | | mippî | 'ôlelîm | weyōneqîm |
| your splendor | above the heavens | | from the mouth of | children | and those who nurse |

**and hath conceived mischief:** ... the seed of wrongdoing has given birth to deceit, *BB* ... pregnant by Sin, *Fenton* ... labors with its dark details, *LIVB* ... conceiving spite, *JB* ... conceived perverseness, *Young*.

**and brought forth falsehood:** ... gives birth to treachery, *Anchor* ... gave birth only to empty promise, *Knox* ... hatching mischief and deception, *Moffatt* ... his brood is lies, *NEB* ... gives birth to disillusionment, *NIV*.

**15. He made a pit, and digged it:** ... has made a hole deep in the earth, *BB* ... digs a hole and keeps on digging, *Beck* ... digs and excavates a pit, *Goodspeed* ... They dug deep and sunk a wide ditch, *Fenton* ... He digs a trap, scoops it out, *JB*.

**and is fallen into the ditch:** ... fell into the hole he made, *Anchor* ... till he falls, *Beck* ... he falls into the snare he made himself, *JB* ... into his own pitfall he shall tumble, *Moffatt* ... they themselves get caught, *Good News*.

**which he made:** ... even while making it, *Berkeley* ... of his own setting, *Knox*.

**16. His mischief shall return upon his own head:** ... His mischief recoiled, *Anchor* ... The harm he plans comes back, *Beck* ... His own crime returns, *Fenton* ... The trouble he causes recoils on him, *NIV* ... they are punished by their own evil, *Good News*.

**and his violent dealing:** ... his violent behaviour, *BB* ... The crime he means to do, *Beck* ... his villainy

*Fenton* ... his brutality, *JB* ... May the violence he plans for others, *LIVB.*

**shall come down upon his own pate:** ... lights on his crown, *Fenton* ... upon his skull his malice redounded, *Anchor* ... on the top of his head, *Berkeley* ... will hurt only themselves, *NCV* ... boomerang upon himself, *LIVB.*

**17. I will praise the Lord:** ... will give thanks, *ASV* ... So I sing, *Fenton.*

**according to his righteousness:** ... as befits his justice, *Anchor* ... who is just, *Fenton* ... for his saving justice, *JB* ... for his just retribution, *Knox* ... because he does what is right, *NCV.*

**and will sing praise to the name:** ... I will make a song, *BB* ... sing a psalm, *NEB.*

**of the Lord most high:** ... Ever-living Most High, *Fenton.*

**8:t. To the chief Musician upon Gittith, A Psalm of David.**

**1. O Lord our Lord:** ... Yahweh, *JB* ... our Master, *Knox* ... our sovereign, *NEB.*

**how excellent is thy name:** ... how glorious, *Anchor* ... whose glory is higher than the heavens, *BB* ... majestic, *JB* ... honourable, *Young* ... your name is the most wonderful name, *NCV.*

**in all the earth!:** ... all over the earth, *Beck* ... O'er all Earth you made, *Fenton* ... throughout the world, *JB* ... fills all the earth, *Knox.*

**who hast set thy glory:** ... displayed Thy majesty, *Berkeley* ... Whose majesty is rehearsed, *MAST* ... set thy splendour, *Moffatt* ... whose glory is above the heavens chanted, *RSV.*

**above the heavens:** ... high above heaven itself, *Knox* ... in heaven above, *NCV.*

**2. Out of the mouth of babes and sucklings:** ... With the lips of striplings, *Anchor* ... even the unweaned, *Berkeley* ... babes in arms, *JB* ... like tiny children lisping out thy praise, *Moffatt* ... Thou hast made the lips of children, of infants at the breast, vocal with praise, *Knox.*

**hast thou ordained strength:** ... You built a fortress, *Anchor* ... fashioned praise, *NAB* ... rebuked the mighty, *NEB* ... founded a bulwark, *NRSV* ... laid a foundation of strength, *Rotherham.*

**because of thine enemies:** ... adversaries, *ASV* ... those who are against you, *BB* ... despite Your foes, *Beck* ... turn back the rebels, *Fenton* ... confound thy enemies, *Knox.*

**that thou mightest still:** ... conquer, *Fenton* ... put to shame, *BB* ... be silenced, *Berkeley* ... restrain the enemy, *REB.*

**the enemy and the avenger:** ... your adversaries, the foe, *Anchor* ... cruel and violent man, *BB* ... to silence malicious and revengeful tongues, *Knox* ... the hostile, *NAB* ... destroy those who try to get even, *NCV.*

---

"travailing with iniquity," and that metaphor is broken up into the two parts: He "hath conceived mischief" and "brought forth falsehood" (HED #6219). The "falsehood," which is the thing actually produced, is so called, not because it deceives others, but because it mocks its producer with false hopes and never fulfills his purposes. This is just the highly metaphorical way of saying that a sinner never does what he means to do, but that the end of all his plans is disappointment. The law of the universe condemns him to feed on ashes and to make and trust in lies.

A third figure brings out more fully the idea implied in "falsehood," namely, the failure of evil to accomplish its doer's purpose. Crafty attempts to trap others have an ugly habit of snaring their contriver. The irony of fortune tumbles the hunter into the pitfall dug by him for his prey.

The fourth figure (v. 16) represents the incidence of his evil on the evildoer as being as certain as the fall of a stone thrown straight up, which will infallibly come back in the line of its ascent. Retribution is as sure as gravitation, especially if there is an unseen hand above, adding impetus and direction to the falling weight.

So the end of all is thanksgiving. A stern but not selfish or unworthy thankfulness follows judgment, with praise which is not inconsistent with tears of pity, even as the act of judgment which calls it forth is not inconsistent with divine love.

**8:1–2.** The exclamation which begins and ends this Psalm determines its theme as being neither the nightly heaven, with all its stars, nor the dignity of man, but the name of the Lord as proclaimed by both. The biblical contemplation of nature and humanity starts from and ends in God. The main thought of the Psalm is the superiority of the revelation in man's nature and place to that in the vault of heaven.

Attesting to God's majesty are the apocalypse in the nightly heavens and the witness from the mouths of babes and sucklings. God's name is glorious in all the earth, first, because He has set his glory upon the heavens, which stretch their solemn magnificence above every land. It is his glory of which theirs is the shimmering reflection, visible to every eye upturned from this dim spot which men call earth.

| 3354.313 | 6010 | 3937, 4775 | 7173.152 | 3937, 8139.541 | 342.151 |
|---|---|---|---|---|---|
| v Piel pf 2ms | n ms | prep, prep | v Qal act ptc mp, ps 2ms | prep, v Hiphil inf con | v Qal act ptc ms |
| יִסַּדְתָּ | עֹז | לְמַעַן | צוֹרְרֶיךָ | לְהַשְׁבִּית | אוֹיֵב |
| yissadhtā | ʿōz | lᵉmaʿan | tsôrᵉrêkhā | lᵉhashbîth | ʾôyēv |
| You founded | strength | because of | your adversaries | to cause to stop | enemies |

| 5541.751 | | 3706, 7495.125 | 8452 | 4801 | 697 | 3507 |
|---|---|---|---|---|---|---|
| cj, v Hithpael ptc ms | 3. | cj, v Qal impf 1cs | n md, ps 2ms | *n mp* | n fp, ps 2ms | n ms |
| וּמִתְנַקֵּם | | כִּי־אֶרְאֶה | שָׁמֶיךָ | מַעֲשֵׂי | אֶצְבְּעֹתֶיךָ | יָרֵחַ |
| ûmithnaqqēm | | kî-ʾerʾeh | shāmêkhā | maʿăsê | ʾetsbᵉʿōthêkhā | yārēach |
| and avenging | | when I see | your heavens | the works of | your fingers | the moon |

| 3676 | 866 | 3679.313 | | 4242, 596 | 3706, 2226.123 |
|---|---|---|---|---|---|
| cj, n mp | rel part | v Polel pf 2ms | 4. | intrg, n ms | cj, v Qal impf 2ms, ps 3ms |
| וְכוֹכָבִים | אֲשֶׁר | כּוֹנָנְתָּה | | מָה־אֱנוֹשׁ | כִּי־תִזְכְּרֶנּוּ |
| wᵉkhôkhāvîm | ʾăsher | kônānᵉttāh | | māh-ʾĕnôsh | kî-thizkᵉrennû |
| and the stars | that | You established | | what a man | that You are mindful of him |

| 1158, 119 | 3706 | 6734.123 | | 2741.323 | 4746 | 4623, 435 |
|---|---|---|---|---|---|---|
| cj, *n ms*, n ms | cj | v Qal impf 2ms, ps 3ms | 5. | cj, v Piel impf 2ms, ps 3ms | sub | prep, n mp |
| וּבֶן־אָדָם | כִּי | תִפְקְדֶנּוּ | | וַתְּחַסְּרֵהוּ | מְעַט | מֵאֱלֹהִים |
| ûven-ʾādhām | kî | thiphqōdhennû | | wattᵉchassᵉrēhû | mᵉʿat | mēʾĕlōhîm |
| or the son of a man | that | You intervene for him | | and You have made him less | a little | than God |

| 3638 | 1994 | 6064.323 | | 5090.523 | 904, 4801 | 3135 |
|---|---|---|---|---|---|---|
| cj, n ms | cj, n ms | v Piel impf 2ms, ps 3ms | 6. | v Hiphil impf 2ms, ps 3ms | prep, *n mp* | n fd, ps 2ms |
| וְכָבוֹד | וְהָדָר | תְּעַטְּרֵהוּ | | תַּמְשִׁילֵהוּ | בְּמַעֲשֵׂי | יָדֶיךָ |
| wᵉkhāvôdh | wᵉhādhār | tᵉʿattᵉrēhû | | tamshîlēhû | bᵉmaʿăsê | yādhêkhā |
| and glory | and honor | You crowned him | | You caused him to rule | over the works of | your hands |

| 3725 | 8308.113 | 8809, 7559 | | 7063 | 511 | 3725 | 1612 |
|---|---|---|---|---|---|---|---|
| n ms | cj, v Qal pf 2ms | prep, n fp, ps 3ms | 7. | n ms | cj, n mp | adj, ps 3mp | cj, cj |
| כֹּל | שַׁתָּה | תַחַת־רַגְלָיו | | צֹנֶה | וַאֲלָפִים | כֻּלָּם | וְגַם |
| kōl | shattāh | thachath-raghlâv | | tsōneh | waʾălāphîm | kullām | wᵉgham |
| everything | You placed | under his feet | | small cattle | and large cattle | all of them | and also |

| 966 | 7899 | | 7109 | 8452 | 1759 | 3328 |
|---|---|---|---|---|---|---|
| *n fp* | n ms | 8. | *n fs* | n md | cj, *n mp* | art, n ms |
| בַּהֲמוֹת | שָׂדָי | | צִפּוֹר | שָׁמַיִם | וּדְגֵי | הַיָּם |
| bahmôth | sādhāy | | tsippôr | shāmayim | ûdhᵉghê | hayyām |
| the beasts of | the open country | | the birds of | the heavens | and the fish of | the sea |

| 5882.151 | 758 | 3328 | | 3176 | 112 | 4242, 116 | 8428 |
|---|---|---|---|---|---|---|---|
| v Qal act ptc ms | *n fp* | n mp | 9. | pn | n mp, ps 1cp | intrg, n ms | n ms, ps 2ms |
| עֹבֵר | אָרְחוֹת | יַמִּים | | יְהוָה | אֲדֹנֵינוּ | מָה־אַדִּיר | שִׁמְךָ |
| ʿōvēr | ʾārᵉchôth | yammîm | | yᵉhwāh | ʾădhōnênû | māh-ʾaddîr | shimkhā |
| passing through | the paths of | the seas | | O Yahweh | our Lord | how majestic | your name |

| 904, 3725, 800 | | 3937, 5514.351 | 6183 | 3937, 1158 | 4344 | 3937, 1784 |
|---|---|---|---|---|---|---|
| prep, *adj*, art, n fs | 9:t | prep, art, v Piel ptc ms | n fp | prep, art, n ms | n ms | prep, pn |
| בְּכָל־הָאָרֶץ | | לַמְנַצֵּחַ | עַלְמוּת | לַבֵּן | מִזְמוֹר | לְדָוִד |
| bᵉkhol-hāʾārets | | lamnatstsēach | ʿalmûth | labbēn | mizmôr | lᵉdhāwidh |
| throughout all the earth | | to the director | the young women | to the sons | a Psalm | of David |

| | 3142.525 | 3176 | 904, 3725, 3949 | 5807.325 | 3725, 6623.258 |
|---|---|---|---|---|---|
| 1. | v Hiphil juss 1cs | pn | prep, *adj*, n ms, ps 1cs | v Piel juss 1cs | *adj*, v Niphal ptc fp, ps 2ms |
| | אוֹדֶה | יְהוָה | בְּכָל־לִבִּי | אֲסַפְּרָה | כָּל־נִפְלְאוֹתֶיךָ |
| | ʾôdheh | yᵉhwāh | bᵉkhol-libbî | ʾăsappᵉrāh | kol-niphlᵉʾôthêkhā |
| | let me praise | Yahweh | with all my heart | let me recount | all your extraordinary deeds |

**3. When I consider thy heavens:** ... observe, *Berkeley* ... beholde, *Geneva* ... look up at, *JB* ... view, *Rotherham* ... When I look up into the night skies, *LIVB.*

**the work of thy fingers:** ... that Your fingers made, *Beck* ... shaped by your fingers, *JB.*

**the moon and the stars, which thou hast ordained:** ... which you have put in their places, *BB* ... which Thou hast made firm, *Berkeley* ... hast established, *Darby* ... formed, *Fenton* ... shaped, *Moffatt.*

**4. What is man:** ... what are human beings, *JB* ... But why are people important to you, *NCV* ... what is frail mortal, *REB* ... I cannot understand how you can bother with mere puny man, *LIVB.*

**that thou art mindful of him?:** ... that you spare a thought for them, *JB* ... that thou shouldest remember him, *Knox* ... that thou shouldst make mention of him, *Rotherham.*

**and the son of man:** ... What is Adam's Son, *Fenton* ... Adam's breed, *Knox* ... What is a mortal man, *Moffatt* ... Why do you take care of human beings, *NCV.*

**that thou visitest him?:** ... that you should care for him, *Anchor* ... that you take him into account, *BB* ... that You regard, *Fenton* ... that thou should'st heed him, *Moffatt* ... take notice of him, *REB* ... that Thou inspectest him, *Young.*

**5. For thou hast made him a little lower than the angels:** ... You depressed him below all Your Saints, *Fenton* ... little less than the gods, *Anchor* ... heavenly beings, *Berkeley* ... causest him to lack a little of Godhead, *Young* ... you have made him inferior only to yourself, *Good News.*

**and hast crowned him with glory and honour:** ... Honour and might, *Fenton* ... glory and splendour, *Darby* ... majesty and honour, *Moffatt* ... beauty, *JB* ... with honour and majesty compassest him, *Young.*

**6. Thou madest him to have dominion over the works of thy hands:** ... You have made him ruler over, *BB* ... Thou makest him master over all thy creatures, *NEB* ... giving him sway o'er all thy hands have made, *Moffatt.*

**thou hast put all things under his feet:** ... under his dominion, *Knox* ... under their control, *NCV* ... putting everything in subjection, *REB* ... you placed him over all creation, *Good News.*

**7. All sheep and oxen, yea, and the beasts of the field:** ... Small and large cattle—all of them, yes even the beasts of the steppe, *Anchor* ... sheep and cattle, and the wild animals too, *Beck* ... Flocks, Herds, *Fenton.*

**8. The fowl of the air, and the fish of the sea:** ... Birds of Heaven and Fish of the Stream, *Fenton.*

**and whatsoever passeth through the paths of the seas:** ... whatever goes through the deep waters, *BB* ... all that swims on the wet sea

---

The sudden drop from the glories of the heavens to the babble and prattle of infancy and childhood is most impressive. It gives extraordinary force to the paradox that the latter's witness is more powerful to silence gainsayers than that of the former.

**8:3–8.** The second part expands the theme of the first. The night sky is more overwhelming than the bare blue vault of day. Light conceals and darkness unveils the solemn glories. The silent depths, the inaccessible splendors, spoke to this psalmist, as they do to all sensitive souls, of the relative insignificance of humanity. But they spoke also of the God whose hand had fashioned them, and the thought of Him carried with it the assurance of his care for so small a creature, and therefore changed the aspect of his insignificance.

Verses 5–8 draw out the consequences of God's loving regard, which has made the insignificance of mankind the medium of a nobler manifestation of the divine name than streams from all the stars. The picture of humanity, as God made us is the only theme which concerns the psalmist; he paints it with colors drawn from the Genesis account, which tells of the Fall as well as the creation of humanity.

The rendering "than the angels" (v. 5) in the KJV comes from the LXX, but though defensible, it is less probable than the more lofty conception contained in the rendering "than God," which is vindicated, not only by lexical considerations, but as embodying an allusion to the original creation "in the image of God." The distance from the apex of creation to the Creator must ever be infinite; the perceived distance is shortened as a matter of hyperbole. That God is "mindful" of mankind at all may be termed "unfathomable." What we receive from God is certainly desperately undeserved.

**8:9.** The Psalm ends, as it began, with adoring wonder. This wonder is the result of the twofold witness which the Psalm has so nobly set forth: that God's name shines glorious through all the earth and that every eye may see its luster.

**9:1–2.** In the first pair of verses of Ps. 9, the song rushes out like some river breaking through a dam and flashing as it hurries on its course.

| | | | | | | |
|---|---|---|---|---|---|---|
| 2. | 7975.125 | 6192.125 | 904 | 2252.325 | 8428 | 6169 |
| | v Qal juss 1cs | cj, v Qal juss 1cs | prep, ps 2ms | v Piel juss 1cs | n ms, ps 2ms | n ms |
| | אֶשְׂמְחָה | וְאֶעֶלְצָה | בָךְ | אֲזַמְּרָה | שִׁמְךָ | עֶלְיוֹן |
| | 'esmechāh | we'e'eltsāh | vākh | 'ăzammerāh | shimkhā | 'elyôn |
| | let me rejoice | and let me be glad | in You | let me sing to | your name | the Most High |

| | | | | | |
|---|---|---|---|---|---|
| 3. | 904, 8178.141, 342.152 | 268 | 3911.226 | 6.126 | 4623, 6552 |
| | prep, v Qal inf con, v Qal act ptc mp, ps 1cs | adv | v Niphal impf 3mp | cj, v Qal impf 3mp | prep, n mp, ps 2ms |
| | בְּשׁוּב־אוֹיְבַי | אָחוֹר | יִכָּשְׁלוּ | וְיֹאבְדוּ | מִפָּנֶיךָ |
| | beshûv-'ôyvay | 'āchôr | yikkāshelû | weyō'vedhû | mippānêkhā |
| | when turning back my enemies | back | they stumble | and they perish | from before You |

| | | | | | |
|---|---|---|---|---|---|
| 4. | 3706, 6449.113 | 5122 | 1835 | 3553.113 | 3937, 3802 |
| | cj, v Qal pf 2ms | n ms, ps 1cs | cj, n ms, ps 1cs | v Qal pf 2ms | prep, n ms |
| | כִּי־עָשִׂיתָ | מִשְׁפָּטִי | וְדִינִי | יָשַׁבְתָּ | לְכִסֵּא |
| | kî-'āsîthā | mishpāṭî | wedhînî | yāshavtā | lekhissē' |
| | because You have executed | my justice | and my judgment | You have sat on | a throne |

| | | | | | |
|---|---|---|---|---|---|
| 8570.151 | 6928 | 5. | 1647.113 | 1504 | 6.313 |
| v Qal act ptc ms | n ms | | v Qal pf 2ms | n mp | v Piel pf 2ms |
| שׁוֹפֵט | צֶדֶק | | גָּעַרְתָּ | גוֹיִם | אִבַּדְתָּ |
| shôphēṭ | tsedheq | | gā'artā | ghôyim | 'ibbadhtā |
| administering justice | righteousness | | You have rebuked | the nations | You have destroyed |

| | | | | | | |
|---|---|---|---|---|---|---|
| 7857 | 8428 | 4364.113 | 3937, 5986 | 5911 | 6. | 342.151 |
| n ms | n ms, ps 3mp | v Qal pf 2ms | prep, n ms | cj, n ms | | art, v Qal act ptc ms |
| רָשָׁע | שְׁמָם | מָחִיתָ | לְעוֹלָם | וָעֶד | | הָאוֹיֵב |
| rāshā' | shemām | māchîthā | le'ôlām | wā'edh | | hā'ôyēv |
| the wicked | their name | You have wiped away | unto eternity | and everlasting | | the enemy |

| | | | | | |
|---|---|---|---|---|---|
| 8882.116 | 2823 | 3937, 5516 | 6111 | 5612.113 | 6.111 |
| v Qal pf 3cp | n fp | prep, art, n ms | cj, n fp | v Qal pf 2ms | v Qal pf 3ms |
| תַּמּוּ | חֳרָבוֹת | לָנֶצַח | וְעָרִים | נָתַשְׁתָּ | אָבַד |
| tammû | chărāvôth | lānetsach | we'ārîm | nāthashtā | 'āvadh |
| they are finished | desolate places | unto forever | and cities | You have driven out | it has perished |

| | | | | | | |
|---|---|---|---|---|---|---|
| 2228 | 2065 | 7. | 3176 | 3937, 5986 | 3553.121 | 3679.311 |
| n ms, ps 3mp | pers pron | | cj, pn | prep, n ms | v Qal impf 3ms | v Polel pf 3ms |
| זִכְרָם | הֵמָּה | | וַיהוָה | לְעוֹלָם | יֵשֵׁב | כּוֹנֵן |
| zikhrām | hēmmāh | | wayhwāh | le'ôlām | yēshēv | kônēn |
| their memory | they | | but Yahweh | unto eternity | He sits | He has established |

paths, *Moffatt* ... everything that lives under water, *NCV* ... all that moves along the paths of ocean, *NEB* ... the creatures in the seas, *Good News.*

**9. O Lord our Lord:** ... O Yahweh, *Anchor* ... O Lord our sovereign, *NEB.*

**how excellent is thy name in all the earth!:** ... glorious is your name, *Anchor* ... how wonderful, *Beck* ... How honourable, *Young* ... your name is the most wonderful name in all the earth, *NCV* ... the majesty and glory of your name fills the earth, *LIVB.*

**9:t. To the chief Musician upon Muth-labben, A Psalm of David.**

**1. I will praise thee, O Lord, with my whole heart:** ... give thanks, *ASV* ... with all my heart, *Anchor.*

**I will show forth all thy marvellous works:** ... declare your wonderful deeds, *Anchor* ... recount all your wonders, *JB* ... tell all the miracles you have done, *NCV* ... tell the story of thy marvellous acts, *NEB.*

**2. I will be glad and rejoice in thee:** ... I will rejoice and exult in you, *Anchor* ... and have delight in you, *BB* ... glad and triumphant in thee, *Knox* ... I thrill and triumph, *Moffatt.*

**I will sing praise to thy name, O thou most High:** ... sing hymns, *Anchor* ... sing to praise Your name, *Beck* ... sing psalms to thy name, *Knox.*

**3. When mine enemies are turned back:** ... haters, *BB* ... My enemies are in retreat, *JB* ... my foes are routed, *Moffatt.*

**they shall fall and perish:** ... They stumble, *ASV* ... they will be broken and overcome, *BB* ... how they faint and melt away, *Knox* ... stumbling to their ruin at thy frown, *Moffatt* ... overthrown and destroyed, *NCB* ... they are overwhelmed and die, *NCV.*

**at thy presence:** ... by your fury, *Anchor* ... at the sight of thee, *Knox* ... because of you, *NCV* ... at thy appearing, *NEB* ... from Thy face, *Young.*

**4. For thou hast maintained my right and my cause:** ... you gave approval to my right, *BB* ... You judged me with justice, *Beck* ... you have given fair judgment in my favour, *JB* ... You have heard my complaint, *NCV* ... you have vindicated me; you have endorsed my work, *LIVB.*

**thou satest in the throne:** ... you were seated in your high place, *BB* ... occupy the throne, *Berkeley.*

**judging right:** ... judged fairly, *Beck* ... seeing justice done, *Knox* ... passing just sentence, *Moffatt* ... judged by what was right, *NCV.*

**5. Thou hast rebuked the heathen:** ... You have said sharp words to the nations, *BB* ... You denounced nations, *Beck* ... thou hast curbed pagans, *Moffatt* ... You spoke strongly against the foreign nations, *NCV* ... You have condemned the heathen, *Good News.*

**thou hast destroyed the wicked:** ... you have sent destruction on the sinners, *BB* ... brought the wicked to nothing, *Knox* ... crushing the ungodly, *Moffatt* ... overwhelmed the ungodly, *NEB* ... Thou hast destroyed the lawless one, *Rotherham.*

**thou hast put out their name for ever and ever:** ... wiped out their name, *Beck* ... Erased their name from time, *Fenton* ... to times age-abiding and beyond, *Rotherham.*

**6. O thou enemy:** ... enemies of mine, *LIVB.*

**destructions are come to a perpetual end:** ... The enemy has been cut off, a neverending ruin, *Berkeley* ... complete are the desolations, *Rotherham* ... Spent is the enemy's power, doomed to everlasting ruin, *Knox* ... The enemies have vanished in everlasting ruins, *NRSV.*

**and thou hast destroyed cities:** ... the cities which thou hast overthrown, *ASV* ... You have given their towns to destruction, *BB* ... You uprooted their towns, *Beck* ... you have annihilated their cities, *JB* ... the towns thou hast torn up lie in lasting ruin, *Moffatt.*

**their memorial is perished with them:** ... they are forgotten, *Beck* ... the memory of them has died, *Knox* ... no more to be remembered, *Moffatt* ... and spoiled their fame, *Fenton.*

**7. But the LORD shall endure for ever:** ... Behold Yahweh who has reigned from eternity, *Anchor* ... The LORD for ever stays, *Fenton* ... Yahweh is enthroned for ever, *JB* ... The LORD thunders, *NEB.*

---

Each short clause begins with "aleph"; each makes the same fervid resolve. Wholehearted praise is sincere, and the singer's whole being is fused into it. The expression "all your extraordinary works" includes the great deliverances of the past, with which a living sense of God's working associates those of the present as one in character and source. Today is as full of God to this man as the sacred yesterdays of national history, and his deliverances as wonderful as those of old. But high above the joy in God's work is the joy in himself to which it leads, and "thy name, O thou most High" is the ground of all pure delight and the theme of all worthy praise.

**9:3–4.** The second stanza ("beth," vv. 3f) is best taken as giving the ground of praise. God's face blazes out on the foe, and they turn and flee from the field, but in their night they stumble, and like fugitives, once fallen they can rise no more. The underlying picture is of a battlefield and a disastrous rout. It is God's coming into action that scatters the enemy, as v. 4 tells by its "for." When He took his seat on the throne (of judgment rather than of royalty), they fled, and that act of assuming judicial activity maintained the psalmist's cause.

**9:5–6.** The third pair of verses ("gimel," vv. 5f) dwells on the grand picture of judgment and specifies for the first time the enemies as "the nations" or "heathen." This shows that the psalmist is not a private individual and probably implies that the whole Psalm is a hymn of victory in which the heat of battle still glows, but which writes no name on the trophy but that of God. The metaphor of a judgment seat is exchanged for a triumphant description of the destructions fallen on the land of the enemy, all in which God alone is recognized as the actor. "Thou hast rebuked"—just as his creative word was all-powerful, so his destructive word sweeps its objects into nothingness. There is a grand and solemn sequence in "Thou hast rebuked; ... Thou hast destroyed." His breath has made; his breath can unmake.

**9:7–8.** In the fourth pair of verses, a slight emendation of the text is approved of by most critics. The last word of v. 6 is the pronoun "they," which, though possible in such a position, is awk-

| 3937, 5122 | 3802 | | 2000 | 8570.121, 8725 | 904, 6928 | 1833.121 |
|---|---|---|---|---|---|---|
| prep, art, n ms | n ms, ps 3ms | 8. | cj, pers pron | v Qal impf 3ms, n fs | prep, n ms | v Qal impf 3ms |
| לַמִּשְׁפָּט | כִּסְאוֹ | | וְהוּא | יִשְׁפֹּט־תֵּבֵל | בְּצֶדֶק | יָדִין |
| lammishpāṭ | kis'ô | | wehû' | yishpōṭ-tēvēl | betsedheq | yādhîn |
| for the judgment | his throne | | and He | He judges the world | with righteousness | He judges |

| 3947 | 904, 4478 | | 2030.121 | 3176 | 5021 | 3937, 1847 | 5021 |
|---|---|---|---|---|---|---|---|
| n mp | prep, n mp | 9. | cj, v Qal juss 3ms | pn | n ms | prep, art, n ms | n ms |
| לְאֻמִּים | בְּמֵישָׁרִים | | וִיהִי | יְהוָה | מִשְׂגָּב | לַדָּךְ | מִשְׂגָּב |
| le'ummîm | bemêshārîm | | wîhî | yehwāh | misgāv | laddākh | misgāv |
| the peoples | with uprightness | | and may He be | Yahweh | a refuge | for the oppressed | a refuge |

| 3937, 6496 | 1250 | | 1019.126 | 904 | 3156.152 | 8428 |
|---|---|---|---|---|---|---|
| prep, *n fp* | n fs | 10. | cj, v Qal impf 3mp | prep, ps 2ms | *v Qal act ptc mp* | n ms, ps 2ms |
| לְעִתּוֹת | בַּצָּרָה | | וְיִבְטְחוּ | בְךָ | יוֹדְעֵי | שְׁמֶךָ |
| le'ittôth | batstsārāh | | weyivetchû | vekhā | yôdh'ê | shemekhā |
| for times of | drought | | and they put their trust | in You | those who know | your name |

| 3706 | 3940, 6013.113 | 1938.152 | 3176 | | 2252.333 | 3937, 3176 |
|---|---|---|---|---|---|---|
| cj | neg part, v Qal pf 2ms | v Qal act ptc mp, ps 2ms | pn | 11. | v Piel impv 2mp | prep, pn |
| כִּי | לֹא־עָזַבְתָּ | דֹרְשֶׁיךָ | יְהוָה | | זַמְּרוּ | לַיהוָה |
| kî | lō'-'āzavtā | dhōreshêkhā | yehwāh | | zammerû | layhwāh |
| because | You have not abandoned | those who seek You | O Yahweh | | sing praises | to Yahweh |

| 3553.151 | 6995 | 5222.533 | 904, 6194 | 6173 |
|---|---|---|---|---|
| v Qal act ptc ms | pn | v Hiphil impv 2 mp | prep, art, n mp | n fp, ps 3ms |
| יֹשֵׁב | צִיּוֹן | הַגִּידוּ | בָעַמִּים | עֲלִילוֹתָיו |
| yōshēv | tsîyôn | haggîdhû | vā'ammîm | 'ălîlôthâv |
| the One Who dwells in | Zion | tell | among the peoples | his deeds |

| | 3706, 1938.151 | 1879 | 881 | 2226.111 | 3940, 8319.111 |
|---|---|---|---|---|---|
| 12. | cj, v Qal act ptc ms | n mp | do, ps 3mp | v Qal pf 3ms | neg part, v Qal pf 3ms |
| | כִּי־דֹרֵשׁ | דָּמִים | אוֹתָם | זָכָר | לֹא־שָׁכַח |
| | kî-dhōrēsh | dāmîm | 'ôthām | zākhār | lō'-shākhach |
| | because One Who requires | bloodshed | them | He is mindful of | He does not forget |

| 7095 | 6270 | | 2706.131 | 3176 | 7495.131 | 6271 |
|---|---|---|---|---|---|---|
| *n fs* | n mp | 13. | v Qal impv 2ms ps 1cs | pn | v Qal impv 2ms | n ms, ps 1cs |
| צַעֲקַת | עֲנִיִּים | | חָנְנֵנִי | יְהוָה | רְאֵה | עָנְיִי |
| tsa'ăqath | 'ănîyîm | | chānenēnî | yehwāh | re'ēh | 'āneyî |
| the outcry of | the afflicted | | be gracious to me | O Yahweh | see | my affliction |

**he hath prepared his throne for judgment:** ... established his throne, *Anchor* ... ordained his throne, *Darby* ... keeping his throne firm, *JB* ... enthroned for government, *Moffatt* ... he has set up his throne, his judgment-seat, *NEB.*

**8. And he shall judge the world in righteousness:** ... It is he who governs the world with justice, *Anchor* ... By Right, He rules the world, *Fenton* ... he will judge the world in fairness, *NCV.*

**he shall minister judgment:** ... giving true decisions, *BB* ... By justice governs man, *Fenton* ... he will decide what is fair, *NCV* ... and try the cause of the peoples fairly, *NEB.*

**to the people in uprightness:** ... gives the people a fair trial, *Beck* ... upon the peoples with equity, *Darby* ... the world in uprightness, *JB.*

**9. The LORD also will be a refuge for the oppressed:** ... a high tower for those who are crushed down, *BB* ... The LORD defends those who suffer, *NCV* ... So the downtrodden are safe with the Eternal, *Moffatt.*

**a refuge in times of trouble:** ... in times of distress, *Darby* ... in time of peril, *Knox* ... in desperate hours, *Moffatt* ... a tower of strength in time of need, *NEB* ... for times of destitution, *Rotherham* ... times of adversity, *Young.*

**10. And they that know thy name:** ... those who cherish your name, *Anchor* ... Those who revere your name, *JB* ... Those who acknowledge thy name, *Knox* ... those who know what thou art, *Moffatt* ... those who know your mercy, *LIVB.*

**will put their trust in thee:** ... will confide in thee, *Darby* ... know Your power, *Fenton* ... can rely on you, *JB* ... put confidence in thee, *Rotherham* ... will count on you for help, *LIVB.*

**for thou, LORD, hast not forsaken them that seek thee:** ... for you do not abandon those who care for you, *Anchor* ... have ever given your help to those who were waiting for you, *BB* ... you never desert those who seek you, *JB* ... he will not leave those who come to him, *NCV.*

**11. Sing praises to the LORD:** ... Sings hymns to Yahweh, *Anchor* ... Sing psalms, *Darby* ... Sing praise to the Eternal, *Moffatt.*

**which dwelleth in Zion:** ... whose house is in Zion, *BB* ... enthroned in, *NAB* ... who is king on Mount Zion, *NCV* ... inhabiting, *Young* ... who rules in, *Good News.*

**declare among the people his doings:** ... publish his deeds, *Anchor* ... make his doings clear to the people, *BB* ... tell among the people the great things He does, *Beck* ... Proclaim to the Nations His fame, *Fenton* ... tell the Gentiles, *Knox.*

**12. When he maketh inquisition for blood:** ... makes search for blood, *BB* ... For He who avenges blood, *Berkeley.*

**he remembereth them:** ... does not forget them, *JB* ... cares for the afflicted, *Knox* ... how he bears you in mind, *Moffatt* ... is mindful of them, *NRSV* ... has an open ear, *LIVB.*

**he forgetteth not the cry of the humble:** ... the cry of the poor, *ASV* ... Nor abandons their cry, when oppressed, *Fenton* ... he does not ignore the cry of the afflicted, *JB* ... he never forgets the wail of the weak, *Moffatt* ... he will not forget the cries of those who suffer, *NCV.*

**13. Have mercy upon me, O LORD:** ... Have pity on me, *Anchor* ... be kind to me, *Beck* ... Be gracious to me, *Berkeley* ... Show me favour, *REB.*

**consider my trouble:** ... see my afflictions, *Anchor* ... pity my woes, *Fenton* ... Behold my humiliation, *Rotherham* ... See the sufferings, *Good News.*

---

ward. If it is transferred to the beginning of v. 7, and it is further supposed that "are perished" has dropped out, as might easily be the case, from the verb having just occurred in the singular, a striking antithesis is gained: "They perish, but Yahweh shall sit." Further, the pair of verses then begins with the fifth letter; and the only irregularity in the acrostic arrangement until v. 19 is the omission of the fourth letter, "daleth." A very significant change in tenses takes place at this point. Up to this point, the verbs have been perfects, implying a finished act; that is to say, until now, the Psalm has been dealing with facts of recent but completed experience. Now the verbs change to imperfects or futures.

**9:9–10.** The fifth pair turns to the glad contemplation of the purpose of all the pomp and terror of the judgment thus hoped for. The Judge is seated on high, and his elevation makes a "lofty stronghold" for the crushed or downtrodden.

The rare word rendered "trouble" (HED #1250) in v. 9 occurs only here and in 10:1. It means "a cutting off" (i.e., of hope of deliverance). The notion of distress intensified to despair is conveyed. God's judgments show that even in such extremity, He is an inexpugnable defense, like some hill fortress, inaccessible to any foe. A further result of judgment is the growing trust of devout souls (v. 10). To "know thy name" is here equivalent to learning God's character as made known by his acts, especially by the judgments anticipated. For such knowledge, some measure of devout trust is required, but further knowledge deepens trust.

**9:11–12.** All trusters and seekers are now called on to be a chorus to the solo of praise therein. The ground of the praise is the same past act which has already been set forth as that of the psalmist's thanksgiving, as is shown by the recurrence here of perfect tenses ("has remembered"; "has not forgotten"). The designation of God as "dwelling" in Zion (HED #3553) is perhaps better rendered, with allusion to the same word in v. 7, "sitteth." His seat had been there from the time the Ark was brought there. That earthly throne was the type of his heavenly seat, and from Zion He is conceived as executing judgment. The world wide destination of Israel's knowledge of God inspires the call to "declare among the people his doings." The "nations" are not merely the objects of destructive wrath, but are to be summoned to share in the blessing of knowing his mighty acts. The psalmist may not have been able to harmonize these two points of view as to Israel's relation to the Gentile world, but both thoughts vibrate in his song.

**9:13–14.** The second part of the Psalm begins with v. 13. The prayer in that verse is the only trace of trouble in the Psalm. The rest is tri-

| 4623, 7983.152 | 7597.351 | 4623, 8554 | 4323 | **14.** 3937, 4775 |
|---|---|---|---|---|
| prep, Qal act ptc mp, ps 1cs | v Polel ptc ms, ps 1cs | prep, *n mp* | n ms | prep, prep |
| מִשֹּׂנְאָי | מְרוֹמְמִי | מִשַּׁעֲרֵי | מָוֶת | לְמַעַן |
| missōn$^{e}$'āy | m$^{e}$rôm$^{e}$mî | mishsha'ărê | māweth | l$^{e}$ma'an |
| from those who hate me | O He Who lifts me up | from the gates of | death | so that |

| 5807.325 | 3725, 8747 | 904, 8554 | 1351, 6995 | 1559.125 |
|---|---|---|---|---|
| v Piel juss 1cs | *adj*, n fp ps 2ms | prep, *n mp* | *n fs*, pn | v Qal juss 1cs |
| אֲסַפְּרָה | כָּל־תְּהִלָּתֶיךָ | בְּשַׁעֲרֵי | בַּת־צִיּוֹן | אָגִילָה |
| 'ăsapp$^{e}$rāh | kol-t$^{e}$hillāthêkhā | b$^{e}$sha'ărê | vath-tsîyôn | 'āghîlāh |
| I may recount | all your praises | in the gates of | the daughter of Zion | let me rejoice |

| 904, 3568 | **15.** 2993.116 | 1504 | 904, 8273 | 6449.116 | 904, 7862, 2182 |
|---|---|---|---|---|---|
| prep, n fs, ps 2ms | v Qal pf 3cp | n mp | prep, n fs | v Qal pf 3cp | prep, n fs, rel part |
| בִּישׁוּעָתֶךָ | טָבְעוּ | גוֹיִם | בְּשַׁחַת | עָשׂוּ | בְּרֶשֶׁת־זוּ |
| bîshû'āthekhā | ṯāv$^{e}$'û | ghôyim | b$^{e}$shachath | 'āsû | b$^{e}$resheth-zû |
| in your salvation | they have sunk | the nations | in a pit | they made | in a net which |

| 3045.116 | 4058.212 | 7559 | **16.** 3156.211 | 3176 | 5122 |
|---|---|---|---|---|---|
| v Qal pf 3cp | v Niphal pf 3fs | n fs, ps 3mp | v Niphal pf 3ms | pn | n ms |
| טָמָנוּ | נִלְכְּדָה | רַגְלָם | נוֹדַע | יְהוָה | מִשְׁפָּט |
| ṯāmānû | nilk$^{e}$dhāh | raghlām | nôdha' | y$^{e}$hwāh | mishpāṯ |
| they hid | it has been caught | their foot | He makes himself known | Yahweh | a judgment |

| 6449.111 | 904, 6714 | 3834 | 5550.151 | 7857 | 1970 |
|---|---|---|---|---|---|
| v Qal pf 3ms | prep, *n ms* | n fp, ps 3ms | v Qal act ptc ms | n ms | n ms |
| עָשָׂה | בְּפֹעַל | כַּפָּיו | נוֹקֵשׁ | רָשָׁע | הִגָּיוֹן |
| 'āsāh | b$^{e}$phō'al | kappâv | nôqēsh | rāshā' | higgāyôn |
| He has executed | by the deeds of | their hands | One Who strikes down | the wicked | a meditation |

| 5734 | **17.** 8178.126 | 7857 | 3937, 8061 | 3725, 1504 | 8321 | 435 |
|---|---|---|---|---|---|---|
| intrj | v Qal impf 3mp | n mp | prep, n fs | *adj*, n mp | *adj* | n mp |
| סֶלָה | יָשׁוּבוּ | רְשָׁעִים | לִשְׁאוֹלָה | כָּל־גּוֹיִם | שְׁכֵחֵי | אֱלֹהִים |
| ṣelāh | yāshûvû | r$^{e}$shā'îm | lish'ôlāh | kol-gôyim | sh$^{e}$khēchê | 'ĕlōhîm |
| selah | they will return | the wicked | to Sheol | all the nations | forgetful of | God |

| **18.** 3706 | 3940 | 3937, 5516 | 8319.221 | 33 | 8951 | 6262 |
|---|---|---|---|---|---|---|
| cj | neg part | prep, art, n ms | v Niphal impf 3ms | n ms | *n fs* | n mp |
| כִּי | לֹא | לָנֶצַח | יִשָּׁכַח | אֶבְיוֹן | תִּקְוַת | עֲנָוִים |
| kî | lō' | lānetsach | yishshākhach | 'evyôn | tiqŏwath | 'ănāwîm |
| because | not | unto forever | they will be forgotten | the needy | the hope of | the lowly |

**which I suffer of them that hate me:** … brought on by my Enemy, *Anchor* … all that I suffer at my enemies' hands, *Knox* … see how I am afflicted by my foes, *NCB* … See how my enemies hurt me, *NCV.*

**thou that liftest me up from the gates of death:** … Snatch me from my foes, and the portals of Death, *Fenton* … O thou my deliverer from, *Goodspeed* … pull me back from, *JB* … thou who didst ever rescue me from, *Knox* … Lift me on high out of, *Rotherham* … Do not let me go through the gates of death, *NCV.*

**14. That I may show forth all thy praise:** … recount all your praises, *Anchor* … so I can proclaim your praise, *Beck* … declare, *Darby* … repeat, *NEB.*

**in the gates of the daughter of Zion:** … Zion's people, *Beck* … Bath-Zion, *Fenton* … Zion's city, *NEB* … before the people of Jerusalem, *Good News.*

**I will rejoice in thy salvation:** … rejoice in Thy deliverance, *Berkeley* … to exult in thy saving power, *Knox* … I will rejoice because you saved me, *NCV.*

**15. The heathen are sunk down:** … May the nations be mired, *Anchor* … The nations are plunged, *Goodspeed* … have fallen, *JB* … have been caught, *Knox* … The pagans have sunk, *Moffatt.*

**in the pit that they made:** … pits they construct, *Fenton* … into the trap they made, *JB* ... in their own deadly devices, *Knox*.

**in the net which they hid is their own foot taken:** ... may their feet get caught, *Anchor* ... their feet caught in the snare they laid, *JB* ... their feet have been trapped in the very toils they had laid, *Knox* ... their own feet are entangled, *NEB* ... caught in their own trap, *Good News*.

**16. The LORD is known by the judgment which he executeth:** ... shows who He is by His justice, *Beck* ... now it will be seen how the Lord defends the right, *Knox* ... The Eternal has shown what he is, by a sentence of doom, *Moffatt* ... In passing sentence, the LORD is manifest, *NAB* ... by his fair decisions, *NCV*.

**the wicked is snared in the work of his own hands. Higgaion. Selah:** ... were trapped by their own doings, *Beck* ... his own handiwork, *Goodspeed* ... contrive their own undoing, *Knox* ... as his hands have trapped the ungodly, *Moffatt* ... trapped in his own devices, *NEB*.

**17. The wicked shall be turned into hell:** ... will be turned into the underworld, *BB* ... To the place of death the wicked must return, *Knox* ... to the nether-world, *MAST* ... They rush blindly down to Sheol, *NEB*.

**and all the nations that forget God:** ... perish the nations that ignore God, *Anchor* ... heathens that have no thought of God, *Knox* ... who are heedless of God, *NEB* ... of all those who reject God, *Good News*.

**18. For the needy shall not always be forgotten:** ... the poor will not be without help, *BB* ... He never forgets the distressed, *Fenton* ... He does not forget the helpless, *Knox* ... one day the needy will be remembered, *Moffatt* ... those who have troubles, *NCV*.

**the expectation of the poor shall not perish for ever:** ... the hopes of those in need will not be crushed for ever, *BB* ... the hopes of the downtrodden will not always be disappointed, *Moffatt* ... The hope of the humble lost to the age, *Young* ... hope of the destitute be always vain, *NEB*.

**19. Arise, O LORD:** ... Up!, O Lord, *BB* ... Bestir thyself, *Knox* ... Take action, O Eternal, *Moffatt*.

**let not man prevail:** ... human strength shall not prevail, *JB* ... let not man have the upper hand, *Moffatt* ... Don't let people think they are strong, *NCV* ... Do not let man defy you, *Good News* ... restrain the power of mortals, *REB*.

**let the heathen be judged in thy sight:** ... nations be judged in thy presence, *Goodspeed* ... nations shall stand trial before you, *JB* ... pagans get their doom from thee, *Moffatt* ... summon the nations before thee for Judgment, *NEB* ... before Thy face, *Young*.

---

umph and exultation. This note, at first sight discordant, has sorely exercised commentators, and the violent solution is that the whole stanza should be regarded as "the cry of the meek." If the view of the structure of the Psalm given above is adopted, there is little difficulty in the connection. The victory has been completed over certain enemies, but there remain others. But God had lifted him thence, and the remembrance wings his prayer. A city's gates are the place of cheery life, stir, gossip and business. Anything proclaimed there flies far. God's end is the spread of his name, not for any good to Him, but because to know Him is life to us.

**9:15–16.** These verses repeat the thoughts of the "gimel" stanza (vv. 5f), recurring to the same significant perfects and dwelling on the new thought that the destruction of the enemy was self-caused. As in Ps. 7, the familiar figure of the pitfall catching the hunter expresses the truth that all evil, and especially malice, recoils on its contriver. A companion illustration is added of the fowler's (or hunter's) foot being caught in his own snare. Verse 16 presents the other view of retribution, which was the only one in vv. 5f, namely that it is a divine act. It is God Who executes judgment and Who "snareth the wicked," though it be "the work of his own hands" which weaves the snare. Both views are needed for the complete truth. This close of the retrospect of deliverance which is the main motive of the Psalm is appropriately marked by the musical direction "Higgaion, Selah," which calls for a strain of instrumental music to fill the pause of the song and to mark the rapture of triumph in accomplished deliverance.

**9:17–18.** The "yodh" stanza, like the "he" and "waw" stanzas (vv. 7–10), passes to confidence for the future. The correspondence is very close, but the two verses of this stanza represent the four of the earlier ones; thus, v. 17 answers to vv. 7f, while v. 18 corresponds to vv. 9f. To forget God is the sure way to be forgotten. The reason for the certain destruction of the nations who forget God and for the psalmist's assurance of it is the confidence he has that "the needy shall not always be forgotten" (v. 18). That confidence corresponds precisely to vv. 9f and also looks back to the "has remembered" and "not forgotten" of v. 12. They who remember God are remembered by Him.

| 6.122 | 3937, 5911 | | 7251.131 | 3176 | 414, 6022.121 | 596 |
|---|---|---|---|---|---|---|
| v Qal impf 3fs | prep, n ms | **19.** | v Qal impv 2ms | pn | adv, Qal juss 3ms | n ms |
| תֹּאבַד | לָעַד | | קוּמָה | יְהוָה | אַל־יָעֹז | אֱנוֹשׁ |
| tō'vadh | lā'adh | | qûmāh | yehwāh | 'al-yā'ōz | 'ĕnôsh |
| it will perish | unto eternity | | rise | O Yahweh | may he not prevail | a man |

| 8570.226 | 1504 | 6142, 6686 | | 8308.131 | 3176 | 4311 | 3937 |
|---|---|---|---|---|---|---|---|
| v Niphal juss 3mp | n mp | prep, n mp, ps 2ms | **20.** | v Qal impv 2ms | pn | n ms | prep, ps 3mp |
| יִשָּׁפְטוּ | גוֹיִם | עַל־פָּנֶיךָ | | שִׁיתָה | יְהוָה | מוֹרָה | לָהֶם |
| yishshāphetû | ghôyim | 'al-pānêkhā | | shîthāh | yehwāh | môrāh | lāhem |
| may they be judged | the nations | before You | | put | O Yahweh | fear | to them |

| 3156.126 | 1504 | 596 | 2065 | 5734 | | 4066 | 3176 | 6198.123 |
|---|---|---|---|---|---|---|---|---|
| v Qal juss 3mp | n mp | n ms | pers pron | intrj | **10:1** | intrg | pn | v Qal impf 2ms |
| יֵדְעוּ | גוֹיִם | אֱנוֹשׁ | הֵמָּה | סֶלָה | | לָמָה | יְהוָה | תַּעֲמֹד |
| yēdhe'û | ghôyim | 'ĕnôsh | hēmmāh | selāh | | lāmāh | yehwāh | ta'ămōdh |
| may they know | the nations | men | they | selah | | why | O Yahweh | do You stand |

| 904, 7632 | 6180.523 | 3937, 6496 | 1250 | | 904, 1375 | 7857 | 1875.121 |
|---|---|---|---|---|---|---|---|
| prep, adj | v Hiphil impf 2ms | prep, *n fp* | n fs | **2.** | prep, *n fs* | n ms | v Qal impf 3ms |
| בְּרָחוֹק | תַּעְלִים | לְעִתּוֹת | בַּצָּרָה | | בְּגַאֲוַת | רָשָׁע | יִדְלַק |
| berāchôq | ta'ălîm | le'ittôth | batstsārāh | | begha'ăwath | rāshā' | yidhlaq |
| far off | do You hide | for times of | drought | | in the pride of | the wicked | he burns |

| 6270 | 8945.226 | 904, 4343 | 2182 | 2913.116 | | 3706, 2054.311 |
|---|---|---|---|---|---|---|
| n ms | v Niphal impf 3mp | prep, n fp | rel part | v Qal pf 3cp | **3.** | cj, v Piel pf 3ms |
| עָנִי | יִתָּפְשׂוּ | בִּמְזִמּוֹת | זוּ | חָשָׁבוּ | | כִּי־הִלֵּל |
| 'ānî | yittāphesû | bimzimmôth | zû | chāshāvû | | kî-hillēl |
| the afflicted | they are grasped | in plots | which | they have devised | | because they boast |

| 7857 | 6142, 8707 | 5497 | 1239.151 | 1313.311 |
|---|---|---|---|---|
| n ms | prep, *n fs* | n fs, ps 3ms | cj, v Qal act ptc ms | v Piel pf 3ms |
| רָשָׁע | עַל־תַּאֲוַת | נַפְשׁוֹ | וּבֹצֵעַ | בֵּרֵךְ |
| rāshā' | 'al-ta'ăwath | naphshô | ûvōtsēa' | bērēkh |
| the wicked | about the longings of | his soul | and the one who unjustly profits | he has blessed |

| 5180.311 | 3176 | | 7857 | 3626, 1394 | 653 |
|---|---|---|---|---|---|
| v Piel pf 3ms | pn | **4.** | n ms | prep, *n ms* | n ms, ps 3ms |
| נִאֵץ | יְהוָה | | רָשָׁע | כְּגֹבַהּ | אַפּוֹ |
| ni'ēts | yehwāh | | rāshā' | keghōvahh | 'appô |
| He has rejected | Yahweh | | the wicked | according to the pride of | his nose |

| 1118, 1938.121 | 375 | 435 | 3725, 4343 | | 2523.126 | 1932 |
|---|---|---|---|---|---|---|
| neg part, v Qal impf 3ms | *sub* | n mp | *adj*, n fp, ps 3ms | **5.** | v Qal impf 3mp | n mp, ps 3ms |
| בַּל־יִדְרֹשׁ | אֵין | אֱלֹהִים | כָּל־מְזִמּוֹתָיו | | יָחִילוּ | דְרָכוֹ |
| bal-yidhrōsh | 'ên | 'ĕlōhîm | kol-mezimmôthâv | | yāchîlû | dhārekkw |
| he does not seek Him | there is not | God | all his thoughts | | they are firm | his ways |

| 904, 3725, 6496 | 4953 | 5122 | 4623, 5224 | 3725, 7173.152 | 6558.521 |
|---|---|---|---|---|---|
| prep, *adj*, n fs | adj | n mp, ps 2ms | prep, sub, ps 3ms | *adj*, v Qal act ptc mp, ps 3ms | v Hiphil impf 3ms |
| בְּכָל־עֵת | מָרוֹם | מִשְׁפָּטֶיךָ | מִנֶּגְדּוֹ | כָּל־צוֹרְרָיו | יָפִיחַ |
| bekhol-'ēth | mārôm | mishpāṭêkhā | minneghdô | kol-tsôrerâv | yāphîach |
| during all times | on high | your judgments | out of his sight | all his adversaries | he blows |

| 904 | | 569.111 | 904, 3949 | 1118, 4267.225 | 3937, 1810 |
|---|---|---|---|---|---|
| prep, ps 3mp | **6.** | v Qal pf 3ms | prep, n ms, ps 3ms | neg part, v Niphal impf 1cs | prep, n ms |
| בָּהֶם | | אָמַר | בְּלִבּוֹ | בַּל־אֶמּוֹט | לְדֹר |
| bāhem | | 'āmar | belibbô | bal-'emmôṭ | ledhōr |
| on them | | he has said | in his heart | I will not totter | unto generations |

**20. Put them in fear, O LORD:** ... Put, O Yahweh, a snaffle on them, *Anchor* ... frighten them, *Beck* ... Put them in terror, *Goodspeed* ... Teach them to fear you, *NCV* ... Make them afraid, *Good News.*

**that the nations may know themselves:** ... Let the Heathen know, *Fenton* ... let pagans know that they are only men, *Moffatt* ... make them know that they are only mortal beings, *Good News.*

**to be but men. Selah:** ... they're only human, *Beck* ... they are but puny men, *LIVB.*

**10:1. Why standest thou afar off, O LORD?:** ... Why do you keep far away, *BB* ... dost Thou stand at a distance, *Berkeley* ... Why, O LORD, do you stand aloof, *NAB.*

**why hidest thou thyself:** ... why dost thou make no sign, *Knox* ... stay hidden, *JB.*

**in times of trouble?:** ... distress, *Darby* ... need, *Goodspeed* ... destitution, *Rotherham* ... adversity, *Young* ... days of affliction, *Knox.*

**2. The wicked in his pride:** ... The evil-doer, *BB* ... In arrogance the wicked, *Berkeley* ... When the haughty bad, *Fenton* ... In the pride of the lawless one, *Rotherham.*

**doth persecute the poor:** ... harass the afflicted, *NAB* ... is cruel to the poor, *BB* ... hunts down the weak, *JB* ... The hearts of the oppressed burn within them, *Knox.*

**let them be taken in the devices that they have imagined:** ... may they be caught by their own schemes, *Beck* ... And catch in the traps they have set, *Fenton* ... caught in the devices the wicked have contrived, *NAB* ... may his crafty schemes be his own undoing, *NEB* ... Pour upon these men the evil they planned for others, *LIVB.*

**3. For the wicked boasteth of his heart's desire:** ... of his selfish lust, *Beck* ... wicked sings the praises of his own desires, *Goodspeed* ... so triumphant is the schemer, *Knox* ... the wicked man glories in his greed, *NAB* ... brag about the things they want, *NCV* ... is obsessed with his own desires, *NEB.*

**and blesseth the covetous:** ... he whose mind is fixed on wealth, *BB* ... the covetous vaunteth himself, *MAST* ... the covetous renounceth, yea, contemneth the LORD, *MRB* ... a dishonest gainer he hath blessed, *Young.*

**whom the LORD abhorreth:** ... but scorns the LORD, *Beck* ... curses and spurns the LORD, *Berkeley* ... spurns Yahweh, *JB* ... hath blasphemed Yahweh, *Rotherham* ... reviles the LORD, *NIV.*

**4. The wicked, through the pride of his countenance:** ... Because of his angry pride, *Beck* ... in his arrogance, *JB* ... sinner thinks in his pride, *Knox* ... in his insolence, *Moffatt* ... The lawless one in the loftiness of his countenance, *Rotherham.*

**will not seek after God:** ... won't ask Him for help, *Beck* ... will not inquire, *Berkeley* ... do not look for God, *NCV* ... he scorns the LORD, *NEB* ... he thinks that God doesn't matter, *Good News.*

**God is not in all his thoughts:** ... God is left out of all his plans, *Beck* ... his thoughts amount to this, There is no God at all, *Moffatt* ... there is no room for God in their thoughts, *NCV* ... leaves no place for God, *NEB* ... seem to think that God is dead, *LIVB.*

**5. His ways are always grievous:** ... In all circumstances his step is

---

**9:19–20.** The prayer of this concluding stanza circles round to the prayer in v. 13, as has been noticed, and so completes the whole Psalm symmetrically. The personal element in v. 13 has passed away; the prayer is general, just as the solo of praise in v. 1 broadened into the call for a chorus of voices in v. 12. The scope of the prayer is the very judgment which the previous stanza has contemplated as certain. So the two parts of the Psalm end with the thought that the "nations" may yet come to know the name of God, the one calling upon those who have experienced his deliverance to "declare among the peoples his doings" (v. 11), the other praying God to teach by chastisement what nations who forget Him have failed to learn from mercies.

**10:1–2.** The first stanza of Ps. 10 gives in its passionate cry a general picture of the situation, which is entirely different from that of Ps. 9. The two opposite characters, whose relations occupy much of these early Psalms, "the wicked" and "the poor," are, as usual, hunter and hunted, and God is passive, as if far away and hiding his eyes. Verse 2 spreads the facts of the situation before God. The first part of v. 2 may be translated, "Through the pride of the wicked the afflicted is burned," i.e., with anguish, pride being the fierce fire and burning being a vigorous expression for anguish or possibly for destruction.

**10:3–6.** The picture is drawn with extraordinary energy, and it describes first the character (vv. 3–6) and then the conduct of the wicked. The style reflects the vehemence of the psalmist's abhorrence, being full of gnarled phrases and harsh constructions. As with a scalpel, the inner heart of the man is laid open. Observe the recurrence of "saith," "thoughts" and "saith in his heart." But first comes a feature of character which is open and palpable.

| 1810 | 866 | 3940, 904, 7737 | | 427 | 6552 | 4529 | 4983 | 8826 |
|---|---|---|---|---|---|---|---|---|
| cj, n ms | rel part | neg part, prep, n ms | 7. | n fs | n ms, ps 3ms | adj | cj, n fp | cj, n ms |
| וָדֹר | אֲשֶׁר | לֹא־בְרָע | | אָלָה | פִּיהוּ | מָלֵא | וּמִרְמוֹת | וָתֹךְ |
| wādhōr | 'ăsher | lō'-v$^{e}$rā' | | 'ālāh | pîhû | mālē' | ûmirmôth | wāthōkh |
| and generations | which | not with evil | | cursing | his mouth | full | and deceit | and oppression |

| 8809 | 4098 | 6219 | 201 | | 3553.121 | 904, 4133 | 2793 | 904, 4718 |
|---|---|---|---|---|---|---|---|---|
| prep | n fs, ps 3ms | n ms | cj, n ms | 8. | v Qal impf 3ms | prep, *n ms* | n mp | prep, art, n mp |
| תַּחַת | לְשׁוֹנוֹ | עָמָל | וָאָוֶן | | יֵשֵׁב | בְּמַאְרַב | חֲצֵרִים | בַּמִּסְתָּרִים |
| tachath | l$^{e}$shônô | 'āmāl | wā'āwen | | yēshēv | b$^{e}$ma'ărav | chătsērîm | bammis̱tārîm |
| under | his tongue | harm | and iniquity | | he sits | in ambush of | villages | in hiding places |

| 2103.121 | 5538 | 6084 | 3937, 2590 | 7121.126 | | 717.121 |
|---|---|---|---|---|---|---|
| v Qal impf 3ms | n ms | n fd, ps 3ms | prep, n fs | v Qal impf 3mp | 9. | v Qal impf 3ms |
| יַהֲרֹג | נָקִי | עֵינָיו | לְחֶלְכָה | יִצְפֹּנוּ | | יֶאֱרֹב |
| yahrōgh | nāqî | 'ênâv | l$^{e}$chēl$^{e}$khāh | yitspōnû | | ye'ĕrōv |
| he kills | the innocent | his eyes | for the unfortunate | they hide | | he lies in wait |

| 904, 4718 | 3626, 765 | 904, 5712 | 717.121 | 3937, 2506.141 | 6270 |
|---|---|---|---|---|---|
| prep, art, n ms | prep, n ms | prep, n ms, ps 3ms | v Qal impf 3ms | prep, v Qal inf con | n ms |
| בַּמִּסְתָּר | כְּאַרְיֵה | בְסֻכֹּה | יֶאֱרֹב | לַחֲטוֹף | עָנִי |
| bammis̱tār | k$^{e}$'aryēh | v$^{e}$suk̲kōh | ye'ĕrōv | lachṯôph | 'ānî |
| in the hiding place | like a lion | in his hut | he lies in wait | to seize | the afflicted |

| 2506.121 | 6270 | 904, 5082.141 | 904, 7862 | | 1852.111 |
|---|---|---|---|---|---|
| v Qal impf 3ms | n ms | prep, v Qal inf con, ps 3ms | prep, n fs, ps 3ms | 10. | cj, v Qal pf 3ms |
| יַחְטֹף | עָנִי | בְּמָשְׁכוֹ | בְרִשְׁתּוֹ | | וַדָּכָה |
| yachṯōph | 'ānî | b$^{e}$māsh$^{e}$khô | v$^{e}$rishtô | | waddākhah |
| he seizes | the afflicted | when his drawing | into his net | | and he is crushed |

| 8249.121 | 5489.111 | 904, 6335 | 2590 | | 569.111 | 904, 3949 |
|---|---|---|---|---|---|---|
| v Qal impf 3ms | cj, v Qal pf 3ms | prep, adj, ps 3ms | n mp | 11. | v Qal pf 3ms | prep, n ms, ps 3ms |
| יָשֹׁחַ | וְנָפַל | בַּעֲצוּמָיו | חֶלְכָּאִים | | אָמַר | בְּלִבּוֹ |
| yāshōach | w$^{e}$nāphal | ba'ătsûmâv | chelkā'îm | | 'āmar | b$^{e}$libbô |
| he bows down | and he has fallen | by his might | the unfortunate | | he has said | in his heart |

| 8319.111 | 418 | 5846.511 | 6686 | 1118, 7495.111 | 3937, 5516 |
|---|---|---|---|---|---|
| v Qal pf 3ms | n ms | v Hiphil pf 3ms | n mp, ps 3ms | neg part, v Qal pf 3ms | prep, art, n ms |
| שָׁכַח | אֵל | הִסְתִּיר | פָּנָיו | בַּל־רָאָה | לָנֶצַח |
| shākhach | 'ēl | his̱tîr | pānâv | bal-rā'āh | lānetsach |
| he has forgotten | God | He has hidden | his face | He has not seen | unto forever |

| | 7251.131 | 3176 | 418 | 5558.131 | 3135 | 414, 8319.123 | 6270 |
|---|---|---|---|---|---|---|---|
| 12. | v Qal impv 2ms | pn | n ms | v Qal impv 2ms | n fs, ps 2ms | adv, v Qal juss 2ms | n mp |
| | קוּמָה | יְהוָה | אֵל | נְשָׂא | יָדֶךָ | אַל־תִּשְׁכַּח | עֲנִיִּים |
| | qûmāh | y$^{e}$hwāh | 'ēl | n$^{e}$sā' | yādhekhā | 'al-tishkach | 'ănîyîm |
| | rise | O Yahweh | O God | lift up | your hand | do not forget | the afflicted |

assured, *JB* … A wicked man succeeds in everything, *Good News* … At all times his path is perverse, *Fenton* … Life for him is always stable, *Moffatt.*

**thy judgments are far above out of his sight:** … your decisions are higher than he may see, *BB* … He flings Your Decrees from himself, *Fenton* … thy judgments are beyond his grasp, *NEB* … he banishes thy laws from his mind, *Knox.*

**as for all his enemies, he puffeth at them:** … he sneers at all his enemies, *NIV* … makes light of all his enemies, *Knox* … laughs at any who oppose him, *Moffatt* … all his foes he scorns, *NAB* … he scoffs at all restraint, *NEB.*

**6. He hath said in his heart, I shall not be moved:** … He says to himself, *Berkeley* … Nothing can shake me, *Beck* … Endless time, he thinks, cannot shake his untroubled existence, *Knox* … thinking he can never fail, *Moffatt* … Nothing bad will ever happen to me, *NCV.*

**for I shall never be in adversity:** …

through all generations I will never be in trouble, *BB* ... Nor ever experience distress, *Fenton* ... from age to age I shall be without misfortune, *NAB* ... never come to grief, *Moffatt* ... no misfortune can check my course, *NEB*.

**7. His mouth is full of cursing and deceit and fraud:** ... His speech is full of lies and browbeating, *JB* ... His mouth overflows with curses, calumny, and deceit, *Knox* ... His talk is all of perjury and craft, *Moffatt* ... Of oaths his mouth is full, *Young* ... curses, lies, and threats, *NCV*.

**under his tongue is mischief and vanity:** ... evil purposes and dark thoughts, *BB* ... falsehood hides under his tongue, *Fenton* ... his tongue is a storehouse of dissension and mischief, *Knox* ... they use their tongues for sin and evil, *NCV*.

**8. He sitteth in the lurking places of the villages:** ... waiting in the dark places of the towns, *BB* ... In ambush he sits in the streets, *Fenton* ... In the undergrowth he lies in ambush, *JB* ... He lurks round hamlets, *Moffatt*.

**in the secret places doth he murder the innocent:** ... In the covert places, *MRB* ... from ambush, *NIV* ... In hiding places, *Goodspeed* ... puts to death those who have done no wrong, *BB* ... to kill unawares the man who never wronged him, *Knox*.

**his eyes are privily set against the poor:** ... He watches intently for the downtrodden, *JB* ... his eyes are continually on his prey, *Knox* ... ever on the outlook for the hapless, *Moffatt* ... his eyes spy upon the unfortunate, *NAB* ... He is watching intently for some poor wretch, *NEB*.

**9. He lieth in wait secretly:** ... watches from his hiding-place, *Knox* ... lies in ambush, *Moffatt* ... lurketh in the covert, *MRB* ... crouches stealthily, *REB*.

**as a lion in his den:** ... in his hole, *BB* ... thicket, *Berkeley* ... lair, *Fenton* ... in cover, *NIV*.

**he lieth in wait to catch the poor:** ... waits there to catch the helpless, *Beck* ... Lies still to lay hold of the weak, *Fenton* ... lurking to pounce on the poor, *JB* ... to surprise his defenceless foe, *Knox* ... crouching to seize its victim, *NEB*.

**he doth catch the poor:** ... takes them away, *Beck* ... he may rob the weak, *Goodspeed* ... he pounces on him, *JB* ... So he catches him in the toils, *Knox*.

**when he draweth him into his net:** ... wrap them in folds of his net, *Fenton* ... dragging him in his net, *Beck* ... drags them off in his net, *NIV*.

**10. He croucheth, and humbleth himself:** ... who is crushed and sinks down, *Berkeley* ... He bends, and he thrusts, and he fells, *Fenton* ... stands there bowing and scraping, *Knox* ... He hunts the helpless till they drop, *Moffatt* ... He stoops and lies prone, *NAB*.

**that the poor may fall:** ... thus do the unfortunate fall, *Berkeley* ... O'erpowers the wretched, *Fenton* ... the helpless till they drop, *Moffatt* ... they are defeated, *NCV* ... he strikes and lays him low, *REB*.

**by his strong ones:** ... by his might, *Geneva* ... into his clutches, *JB* ... under his strength, *NIV* ... with his strong claws, *Rotherham* ... brute strength has defeated them, *Good News*.

**11. He hath said in his heart:** ... he thinks to himself, *Knox*.

**God hath forgotten:** ... forgets, *JB* ... God doesn't care, *Beck* ... God isn't watching, *LIVB* ... El forgets, *Anchor*.

**he hideth his face; he will never see it:** ... he has turned away his face to avoid seeing the end, *JB* ... He doesn't see what is happening, *NCV* ... he covers his face and never sees, *NIV* ... He hath veiled his face, *Rotherham* ... He has closed his eyes and will never see me, *Good News*.

---

He " boasts of his soul's desire." What is especially flagrant in that? The usual explanation is that he is not ashamed of his shameful lusts, but glories in them, or that he boasts of succeeding in all that he desires. But what will a good man do with his heart's desires? Verse 7 tells us, namely, breathe them to God; therefore, to boast of them instead is the outward expression of godless self-confidence and resolve to consult inclination and not God. The next trait of character is practical (indeed, there is no actual) atheism and denial of divine retribution.

**10:7–11.** Following the disclosure of the inner springs of life in the secret thoughts comes, in vv. 7–10, the outcome of these in word and deed. When the wicked's "mouth is full of cursing and deceit," the product is an affront to God and maledictions, lies and mischiefs for men. The vivid picture of a prowling lion seems to begin in v. 8, although it is sometimes taken as the unmetaphorical description of the wicked man's crime. The stealthy couching of the beast of prey, belong to the figure, which is abruptly changed in one clause (v. 9c) into that of a hunter with his net, and then is resumed and completed in v. 10. With great emphasis, the picture is rounded off (v. 11) with the repetition of the secret thought of no retribution from God.

**10:12–18.** The second part of the Psalm is the prayer, forced from the heart of the persecuted remnant, God's little flock in the midst of wolves.

| 13. | 6142, 4242 | 5180.311 | 7857 | 435 | 569.111 | 904, 3949 | 3940 |
|---|---|---|---|---|---|---|---|
| | prep, intrg | v Piel pf 3ms | n ms | n mp | v Qal pf 3ms | prep, n ms, ps 3ms | neg part |
| | עַל־מֶה | נִאֵץ | רָשָׁע | אֱלֹהִים | אָמַר | בְּלִבּוֹ | לֹא |
| | 'al-meh | ni'ēts | rāshā' | 'ĕlōhîm | 'āmar | belibbô | lō' |
| | why | has he rejected | the wicked | God | he has said | in his heart | not |

| 1938.123 | 14. | 7495.113 | 3706, 887 | 6219 | 3833 | 5202.523 |
|---|---|---|---|---|---|---|
| v Qal impf 2ms | | v Qal pf 2ms | cj, pers pron | n ms | cj, n ms | v Hiphil impf 2ms |
| תִּדְרֹשׁ | | רָאִתָה | כִּי־אַתָּה | עָמָל | וָכַעַס | תַּבִּיט |
| tidhrōsh | | rā'ithāh | kî-'attāh | 'āmāl | wākha'as | tabbîṭ |
| You will not require | | You have seen | because You | harm | and vexation | You regard |

| 3937, 5598.141 | 904, 3135 | 6142 | 6013.121 | 2590 | 3605 | 887 |
|---|---|---|---|---|---|---|
| prep, v Qal inf con | prep, n fd, ps 2ms | prep, ps 2ms | v Qal impf 3ms | n fs | n ms | pers pron |
| לָתֵת | בְּיָדֶךָ | עָלֶיךָ | יַעֲזֹב | חֵלֶכָה | יָתוֹם | אַתָּה |
| lāthēth | beyādhekhā | 'ālêkhā | ya'ăzōv | chēlekhāh | yāthôm | 'attāh |
| to allow | into your hands | beside You | he leaves | the unfortunate | orphans | You |

| 2030.113 | 6038.151 | 15. | 8132.131 | 2307 | 7857 | 7737 |
|---|---|---|---|---|---|---|
| v Qal pf 2ms | v Qal act ptc ms | | v Qal impv 2ms | *n fs* | n ms | cj, n ms |
| הָיִיתָ | עוֹזֵר | | שְׁבֹר | זְרוֹעַ | רָשָׁע | וָרָע |
| hāyîthā | 'ôzēr | | shevōr | zerôa' | rāshā' | wārā' |
| You have been | a Helper | | break | the arm of | the wicked | and evildoers |

| 1938.123, 7858 | 1118, 4834.123 | 16. | 3176 | 4567 | 5986 | 5911 |
|---|---|---|---|---|---|---|
| v Qal impf 2ms, n ms, ps 3ms | neg part, v Qal impf 2ms | | pn | n ms | n ms | cj, n ms |
| תִּדְרוֹשׁ־רִשְׁעוֹ | בַּל־תִּמְצָא | | יְהוָה | מֶלֶךְ | עוֹלָם | וָעֶד |
| tidhrôsh-rishe'ô | val-timtsā' | | yehwāh | melekh | 'ôlām | wā'edh |
| You will require his guilt | You will not find | | Yahweh | King | forever | and always |

| 6.116 | 1504 | 4623, 800 | 17. | 8707 | 6262 | 8471.113 |
|---|---|---|---|---|---|---|
| v Qal pf 3cp | n mp | prep, n fs, ps 3ms | | *n fs* | n mp | v Qal pf 2ms |
| אָבְדוּ | גוֹיִם | מֵאַרְצוֹ | | תַּאֲוַת | עֲנָוִים | שָׁמַעְתָּ |
| 'āvedhû | ghôyim | mē'artsô | | ta'ăwath | 'ănāwîm | shāma'āttā |
| they have perished | the nations | from his land | | the longing of | the lowly | You have heard |

| 3176 | 3679.523 | 3949 | 7477.523 | 238 | 18. | 3937, 8570.141 |
|---|---|---|---|---|---|---|
| pn | v Hiphil impf 2ms | n ms, ps 3mp | v Hiphil impf 2ms | n fs, ps 2ms | | prep, Qal inf con |
| יְהוָה | תָּכִין | לִבָּם | תַּקְשִׁיב | אָזְנֶךָ | | לִשְׁפֹּט |
| yehwāh | tākhîn | libbām | taqōshîv | 'āzenekhā | | lishpōṭ |
| O Yahweh | You will make strong | their heart | You will incline | your ear | | to execute justice |

**12. Arise, O LORD; O God, lift up thine hand:** ... bestir thyself, *Knox* ... Take action, O Eternal, *Moffatt* ... LORD, rise up and punish the wicked, *NCV* ... set thy hand to the task, *NEB* ... O God, crush them, *LIVB*.

**forget not the humble:** ... give thought to the poor, *BB* ... don't forget the oppressed, *Beck* ... Don't forget those who need help, *NCV* ... Do not forget the patient, *Rotherham* ... Remember those who are suffering, *Good News*.

**13. Wherefore doth the wicked contemn God?:** ... Why has the evil-doer a low opinion of God, *BB* ... why should the villain mock GOD, *Fenton* ... How dare ungodly men scorn God, *Moffatt* ... Why, O God, has the wicked man rejected thee, *NEB* ... Wherefore hath the lawless one blasphemed God, *Rotherham*.

**he hath said in his heart:** ... saying to himself, *Anchor* ... assuring himself, *JB*.

**Thou wilt not require it:** ... You will not make search for it, *BB* ... God won't punish us, *NCV* ... that Thou wilt not call to account, *Berkeley* ... to think that he will never exact punishment, *Knox* ... He will not avenge it, *NAB* ... you will never follow it up, *JB*.

**14. Thou hast seen it:** ... See for yourself, *Anchor* ... Lord, you see what they are doing, *LIVB*.

**for thou beholdest mischief and spite:** ... for your eyes are on sorrow and grief, *BB* ... for thou thyself beholdest trouble and vexation, *Darby* ... thou hast eyes for misery and distress, *Knox* ... See crime and wrong both advance, *Fenton* ... surely you see these cruel and evil things, *NCV.*

**to requite it with thy hand:** ... so You can take it in hand, *Beck* ... that Thou mayest repay it with Thine own hand, *Berkeley* ... To give them into thy power, *Goodspeed* ... thou takest the matter into thy own hands, *NEB* ... look at them and do something, *NCV* ... thou markest it, to punish it thyself, *Moffatt.*

**the poor committeth himself unto thee:** ... The victim commits himself to you, *NIV* ... The helpless can only trust You, *Fenton* ... The unfortunate leaves himself to thee, *Goodspeed* ... The destitute are cast on no care but thine, *Knox* ... The hapless can leave their plight to thee, *Moffatt.*

**thou art the helper of the fatherless:** ... you have been the helper of the child who has no father, *BB* ... To give the feeble Your strength, *Fenton* ... you are the only recourse of the orphan, *JB* ... thou Helper of the forlorn, *Moffatt.*

**15. Break thou the arm of the wicked and the evil man:** ... So shatter the criminal's arm, *Fenton* ... Break down the power of the wicked oppressor, *Knox* ... Shatter the ungodly's power, *Moffatt* ... Break the strength of the wicked, *NAB.*

**seek out his wickedness till thou find none:** ... go on searching for his sin till there is no more, *BB* ... Let his wickedness be sought and not found, *Goodspeed* ... punish his ill-doing, and let him be seen no more, *Knox* ... punish their wickedness; let them not survive, *NAB* ... Go after them until the last of them is destroyed, *LIVB.*

**16. The Lord is King for ever and ever:** ... Yahweh is the eternal and everlasting king, *Anchor* ... Lord, our Eternal King, *Fenton* ... Yahweh is king to times age-abiding and beyond, *Rotherham.*

**the heathen are perished out of his land:** ... nations are gone from his land, *BB* ... Drive pagans from the Land, *Fenton* ... heathen has vanished from his country, *JB* ... Destroy from your land those nations that do not worship you, *NCV.*

**17. Lord, thou hast heard the desire of the humble:** ... Hear, O Yahweh the lament of the poor, *Anchor* ... Thou hast heard the longing of the afflicted, *Berkeley* ... The sighing of the defenceless has found audience, *Knox* ... you have heard what the poor people want, *NCV* ... You will listen, O Lord, to the prayers of the lowly, *Good News.*

**thou wilt prepare their heart:** ... attentive to their heart's desire, *NEB* ... bring courage to their hearts, *Knox* ... Give quiet to, *Fenton* ... dost establish, *Berkeley* ... make strong, *BB.*

**thou wilt cause thine ear to hear:** ... give close heed, *Anchor* ... you will give them a hearing, *BB* ... Thou wilt incline Thine ear, *NASB* ... thou listenest to them, *Moffatt* ... Thou wilt make attentive thy ear, *Rotherham.*

**18. To judge the fatherless and the oppressed:** ... To give decision for the child without a father and for the broken-hearted, *BB* ... wilt give redress to the fatherless and the persecuted, *Knox* ... that the forlorn and the downtrodden may have justice, *Moffatt* ... To vindicate the orphan and the oppressed, *NASB* ... Protect the orphans and put an end to suffering, *NCV.*

**that the man of the earth may no more oppress:** ... no more shall the arrogant frighten men from the earth, *Anchor* ... And not permit again To

---

No trace of individual reference appeals in it, nor any breath of passion or vengeance, such as is found in some of the Psalms of persecution; but it glows with indignation at the blasphemies which are triumphant, for the moment, and cries aloud to God for a judicial act which shall shatter the dream that He does not see and will not requite. That impious boast, far more than the personal incidence of sufferings, moves the prayer.

At last comes the cry for the descent of God's uplifted hand (vv. 15f). It is not invoked to destroy, but simply to "break the arm" of the wicked, i.e., to make him powerless for mischief, as a swordsman with a shattered arm. One blow from God's hand lames, and the arm hangs useless. The impious denial of the divine retribution still affects the psalmist with horror, and he returns to it in the second clause of v. 15, in which he prays that God would "seek out"—i.e., require and requite, so as to abolish and make utterly non-existent—the wicked man's wickedness.

Desires can be translated into petitions. If the heart is humble, that divine breath will be breathed over and into it, which will prepare it to desire only what accords with God's will, and the prepared heart will always find God's ear open. The cry of the hapless, which has been put into their lips by God himself, is the appointed prerequisite of the manifestations of divine judgment which will relieve the earth of the incubus of "the man of the earth" (v. 18). "Shall not God avenge his own elect, though He bear long with them? I tell you that He will avenge them speedily" (Luke 18:7f). The prayer of the humble, like a whisper amid the avalanches, has power to start the swift, white destruction on its downward path; and when once that gliding mass has way on it, nothing which it smites can stand.

| 3605 | 1847 | 1118, 3362.521 | 5968 | 3937, 6442.141 | 596 |
|---|---|---|---|---|---|
| n ms | cj, n ms | neg part, v Hiphil impf 3ms | adv | prep, v Qal inf con | n ms |
| יָתוֹם | וָדָךְ | בַּל־יוֹסִיף | עוֹד | לַעֲרֹץ | אֱנוֹשׁ |
| yāthôm | wādhākh | bal-yôsîph | ‘ôdh | la‘ărōts | ’ĕnôsh |
| orphans | and the oppressed | it will not continue | continually | to frighten | a man |

| 4623, 800 | | 3937, 5514.351 | 3937, 1784 | | 904, 3176 | 2725.115 | 351 |
|---|---|---|---|---|---|---|---|
| prep, art, n fs | 11:t | prep, art, v Piel ptc ms | prep, pn | 1. | prep, pn | v Qal pf 1cs | intrg |
| מִן־הָאָרֶץ | | לַמְנַצֵּחַ | לְדָוִד | | בַּיהוָה | חָסִיתִי | אֵיךְ |
| min-hā’ārets | | lamnatstsēach | ledhāwidh | | bayhwāh | chās̱îthî | ’êkh |
| from the earth | | to the director | of David | | in Yahweh | I have sought refuge | how |

| 569.128 | 3937, 5497 | 5290.132 | 2098 | 7109 | | 3706 | 2079 | 7857 |
|---|---|---|---|---|---|---|---|---|
| v Qal impf 2mp | prep, n fs, ps 1cs | v Qal impv 2fs | n ms, ps 2mp | n fs | 2. | cj | intrj | art, n mp |
| תֹּאמְרוּ | לְנַפְשִׁי | נוּדוּ | הַרְכֶם | צִפּוֹר | | כִּי | הִנֵּה | הָרְשָׁעִים |
| tō’merû | lenaphshî | nûdhû | harkhem | tsippôr | | kî | hinnēh | hāreshā‘îm |
| do you say | to my soul | flee to | your mountain | a bird | | because | behold | the wicked |

| 1931.126 | 7493 | 3679.316 | 2777 | 6142, 3614 | 3937, 3498.141 | 1156, 669 |
|---|---|---|---|---|---|---|
| v Qal impf 3mp | n fs | v Polel pf 3cp | n ms, ps 3mp | prep, n ms | prep, v Qal inf con | prep, n ms |
| יִדְרְכוּן | קֶשֶׁת | כּוֹנְנוּ | חִצָּם | עַל־יֶתֶר | לִירוֹת | בְּמוֹ־אֹפֶל |
| yidhrekhûn | qesheth | kônenû | chitstsām | ‘al-yether | lîrôth | bemô-’ōphel |
| they bend | the bow | they have set | their arrow | on the string | to shoot | in the dark |

| 3937, 3596, 3949 | | 3706 | 8681 | 2117.226 | 6926 |
|---|---|---|---|---|---|
| prep, *n mp*, n ms | 3. | cj | art, n mp | v Niphal impf 3mp | n ms |
| לְיִשְׁרֵי־לֵב | | כִּי | הַשָּׁתוֹת | יֵהָרֵסוּן | צַדִּיק |
| leyishrê-lēv | | kî | hashshāthôth | yēhārēs̱ûn | tsaddîq |
| at the upright in heart | | because | the foundation | they are torn down | the righteous |

| 4242, 6713.111 | | 3176 | 904, 2033 | 7231 | 3176 | 904, 8452 | 3802 |
|---|---|---|---|---|---|---|---|
| intrg, v Qal pf 3ms | 4. | pn | prep, *n ms* | n ms, ps 3ms | pn | prep, art, n md | n ms, ps 3ms |
| מַה־פָּעָל | | יְהוָה | בְּהֵיכַל | קָדְשׁוֹ | יְהוָה | בַּשָּׁמַיִם | כִּסְאוֹ |
| mah-pā‘āl | | yehwāh | behêkhal | qādheshô | yehwāh | bashshāmayim | kis’ô |
| what can he do | | Yahweh | in the temple of | his holy place | Yahweh | in the heavens | his throne |

| 6084 | 2463.126 | 6310 | 1010.126 | 1158 | 119 | | 3176 |
|---|---|---|---|---|---|---|---|
| n fd, ps 3ms | v Qal impf 3mp | n md, ps 3ms | v Qal impf 3mp | *n mp* | n ms | 5. | pn |
| עֵינָיו | יֶחֱזוּ | עַפְעַפָּיו | יִבְחֲנוּ | בְּנֵי | אָדָם | | יְהוָה |
| ‘ênâv | yechězû | ‘aph‘appâv | yivchănû | benê | ’ādhām | | yehwāh |
| his eyes | they will behold | his eyelids | they examine | the children of | humankind | | Yahweh |

| 6926 | 1010.121 | 7857 | 154.151 | 2660 | 7983.112 | 5497 |
|---|---|---|---|---|---|---|
| n ms | v Qal impf 3ms | cj, n ms | cj, v Qal act ptc ms | n ms | v Qal pf 3fs | n fs, ps 3ms |
| צַדִּיק | יִבְחָן | וְרָשָׁע | וְאֹהֵב | חָמָס | שָׂנְאָה | נַפְשׁוֹ |
| tsaddîq | yivchān | werāshā‘ | we’ōhēv | chāmās̱ | sāne’āh | naphshô |
| the righteous | He examines | and the wicked | and the one that loves | violence | it hates | his soul |

| | 4442.521 | 6142, 7857 | 6595 | 813 | 1657 | 7593 | 2237 |
|---|---|---|---|---|---|---|---|
| 6. | v Hiphil impf 3ms | prep, n mp | *n mp* | n fs | cj, n fs | cj, *n fs* | n fp |
| | יַמְטֵר | עַל־רְשָׁעִים | פַּחִים | אֵשׁ | וְגָפְרִית | וְרוּחַ | זִלְעָפוֹת |
| | yamṯēr | ‘al-reshā‘îm | pachîm | ’ēsh | weghāpherîth | werûach | zil‘āphôth |
| | He will cause to rain | on the wicked | coals of | fire | and sulfur | and a wind of | intensity |

| 4669 | 3683 | | 3706, 6926 | 3176 | 6930 | 154.111 | 3596 |
|---|---|---|---|---|---|---|---|
| *n fs* | n fs, ps 3mp | 7. | cj, adj | pn | n fp | v Qal pf 3ms | n ms |
| מְנָת | כּוֹסָם | | כִּי־צַדִּיק | יְהוָה | צְדָקוֹת | אָהֵב | יָשָׁר |
| menāth | kôs̱ām | | kî-tsaddîq | yehwāh | tsedhāqôth | ’āhēv | yāshār |
| the portion of | their cup | | because righteous | Yahweh | righteous deeds | He loves | the upright |

drive men from the land, *Fenton* ... that fear may never drive men from their homes again, *NEB* ... so that no one on earth may ever again inspire terror, *REB*.

**11:t. To the chief Musician, A Psalm of David.**

**1. In the LORD put I my trust:** ... In Yahweh do I seek refuge, *Anchor* ... With the Eternal I take shelter, *Moffatt* ... I trust in the LORD for safety, *Good News*.

**how say ye to my soul:** ... How can you lie in wait for my life, *Anchor* ... how dare you tell me, then, *Moffatt* ... how can you say to me, *NAB* ... How foolish of you to say to me, *Good News*.

**Flee as a bird to your mountain?:** ... pursue me like a bird, *Anchor* ... Fly away to the hills, like a bird, *Fenton* ... Bird, flee to your mountain, *JB* ... Escape, like a frightened sparrow, to the hill-side, *Knox*.

**2. For, lo, the wicked bend their bow:** ... are bracing their bow, *Anchor* ... see how the wicked take aim with their bow, *Fenton* ... the rebels have strung their bows, *Knox* ... the wicked tread a bow, *Young*.

**they make ready their arrow upon the string:** ... have fitted their arrow, *Berkeley* ... set their arrows on the bowstrings, *NCV* ... aimed their arrows, *Good News*.

**that they may privily shoot at the upright in heart:** ... shoot from ambush, *Anchor* ... to shoot honest men from the shadows, *JB* ... They shoot from their dark places at those who are honest, *NCV* ... to shoot from the darkness at honest folk, *REB*.

**3. If the foundations be destroyed:** ... If the bases are broken down, *BB* ... When foundations are undermined, *NEB* ... they have thrown down all thou hadst built, *Knox* ... The pillars of the State are falling, *Moffatt* ... When all that is good falls apart, *NCV*.

**what can the righteous do?:** ... upright man, *BB* ... What has the righteous done, *Goodspeed* ... what hope, now, for the just man, *Knox* ... what can good people do, *NCV*.

**4. The LORD is in his holy temple:** ... Yahweh—in the temple is his holy seat, *Anchor* ... in the temple of his holiness, *Darby* ... in his holy palace, *Geneva* ... in his holy shrine, *Knox* ... Ah, but the Eternal is within his sacred place, *Moffatt*.

**the LORD's throne is in heaven:** ... the LORD is on his heavenly throne, *NIV* ... He still rules from heaven, *LIVB*.

**his eyes behold, his eyelids try, the children of men:** ... His eyes inspect, his pupils assay the sons of men, *Anchor* ... whose eye watches, whose glance can appraise, the deeds of men, *Knox* ... He sees what people do; he keeps his eye on them, *NCV* ... His gaze is upon mankind, his searching eye tests them, *REB* ... he takes their measure at a glance, *NEB*.

**5. The LORD trieth the righteous:** ... Yahweh is the Just One, *Anchor* ... The LORD puts the righteous to the proof, *Berkeley* ... The Lord searches the just, *NCB* ... Yahweh examines the upright, *JB* ... On good men the Eternal sets his stamp, *Moffatt* ... Innocent or sinful, he reads every heart, *Knox*.

**but the wicked and him that loveth violence his soul hateth:** ... for the lover of violent acts, *BB* ... the impious and violent, *Moffatt* ... and the friends of wrong-doing are his enemies, *Knox* ... but he hates the wicked and those who love to hurt others, *NCV* ... the lawless he hates with all his heart, *Good News*.

**6. Upon the wicked he shall rain snares, fire and brimstone:** ... Let him send upon the wicked bellows, fire, and sulphur, *Anchor* ... He will rain on the wicked distress, *Fenton* ... On the wicked he will rain coals of fire, *Goodspeed* ... Pitilessly his weapons rain down upon the offenders, *Knox*.

**and an horrible tempest; this shall be the portion of their cup:** ... burning wind, *ASV* ... scorching blasts fall to their lot, *Moffatt* ... The fiery and sulphurous breath Of the Simoon is destined for them, *Fenton* ... A whirlwind is what they will get, *NCV* ... such is the draught he brews for them, *Knox*.

---

***Psalm 11.*** *The structure of Ps. 11 is simple and striking. There are two vividly contrasted halves, the first giving the suggestions of timid counselors who see only along the low levels of earth, and the second the brave answer of faith which looks up into heaven.*

**11:1–3.** In the first part of the Psalm, the psalmist begins with an utterance of faith, which makes him recoil with wonder and aversion from the cowardly, well-meant counsels of his friends. "In Yahweh have I taken refuge"—a profession of faith in Ps. 7. It was laid as the basis of prayer for deliverance and is here the ground for steadfastly remaining where he stands. The metaphor of flight to a stronghold, which is in the word for "trust" (HED #2725), obviously colors the context, for what can be more absurd than that he who has sought and found shelter in God himself should listen to the whisperings of his own heart or to the advice of friends and hurry to some other hiding place?

**11:4–7.** So the Psalm turns, in its second part, from these creeping counsels, which see but half the field of vision, and that being the lower half, to soar and gaze on the upper half. God is in

| 2463.126 | 6686 | | 3937, 5514.351 | 6142, 8454 | 4344 | 3937, 1784 |
|---|---|---|---|---|---|---|
| v Qal impf 3mp | n mp, ps 3mp | **12:t** | prep, art, v Piel ptc ms | prep, art, adj | n ms | prep, pn |
| יֶחֱזוּ | פָנֵימוֹ | | לַמְנַצֵּחַ | עַל־הַשְּׁמִינִית | מִזְמוֹר | לְדָוִד |
| yechĕzû | phānêmô | | lamnatstsēach | 'al-hashshᵉmînîth | mizmôr | lᵉdhāwidh |
| they will behold | his face | | to the director | on the eighth | a Psalm | of David |

| | 3588.531 | 3176 | 3706, 1625.111 | 2728 | 3706, 6707.116 |
|---|---|---|---|---|---|
| **1.** | v Hiphil impv 2ms | pn | cj, v Qal pf 3ms | n ms | cj, v Qal pf 3cp |
| | הוֹשִׁיעָה | יְהוָה | כִּי־גָמַר | חָסִיד | כִּי־פַסּוּ |
| | hôshî'āh | yᵉhwāh | kî-ghāmar | chāsîdh | kî-phassû |
| | save | O Yahweh | because they are at an end | the godly | because they have disappeared |

| 548.156 | 4623, 1158 | 119 | | 8175 | 1744.326 | 382 | 882, 7739 |
|---|---|---|---|---|---|---|---|
| v Qal pass ptc mp | prep, *n mp* | n ms | **2.** | n ms | v Piel impf 3mp | n ms | prep, n ms, ps 3ms |
| אֱמוּנִים | מִבְּנֵי | אָדָם | | שָׁוְא | יְדַבְּרוּ | אִישׁ | אֶת־רֵעֵהוּ |
| 'ĕmûnîm | mibbᵉnê | 'ādhām | | shāwᵉ' | yᵉdhabbᵉrû | 'îsh | 'eth-rē'ēhû |
| the faithful | among the sons of | humankind | | vanity | they speak | each | with his fellow |

| 8004 | 2616 | 904, 3949 | 3949 | 1744.326 | | 3901.521 | 3176 | 3725, 8004 |
|---|---|---|---|---|---|---|---|---|
| *n fs* | n fp | prep, n ms | cj, n ms | v Piel impf 3mp | **3.** | v Hiphil juss 3ms | pn | *adj, n fd* |
| שְׂפַת | חֲלָקוֹת | בְּלֵב | וָלֵב | יְדַבֵּרוּ | | יַכְרֵת | יְהוָה | כָּל־שִׂפְתֵי |
| sᵉphath | chălāqôth | bᵉlēv | wālēv | yᵉdhabbērû | | yakhrēth | yᵉhwāh | kol-siphthê |
| lips of | flattery | with a heart | and a heart | they speak | | may He cut off | Yahweh | all lips of |

| 2616 | 4098 | 1744.353 | 1448 | | 866 | 569.116 | 3937, 4098 |
|---|---|---|---|---|---|---|---|
| n fp | n fs | v Piel, ptc fs | adj | **4.** | rel pron | v Qal pf 3cp | prep, n fs, ps 1cp |
| חֲלָקוֹת | לָשׁוֹן | מְדַבֶּרֶת | גְּדֹלוֹת | | אֲשֶׁר | אָמְרוּ | לִלְשֹׁנֵנוּ |
| chălāqôth | lāshôn | mᵉdhabbereth | gᵉdhōlôth | | 'ăsher | 'āmᵉrû | lilshōnēnû |
| flattery | the tongue | speaking | great | | who | they have said | with our tongue |

| 1428.520 | 8004 | 882 | 4449 | 112 | 3937 | | 4623, 8160 |
|---|---|---|---|---|---|---|---|
| v Hiphil impf 1cp | n fd, ps 1cp | prep, ps 1cp | intrg | n ms | prep, ps 1cp | **5.** | prep, *n ms* |
| נַגְבִּיר | שְׂפָתֵינוּ | אִתָּנוּ | מִי | אָדוֹן | לָנוּ | | מִשֹּׁד |
| naghbîr | sᵉphāthênû | 'ittānû | mî | 'ādhôn | lānû | | mishshōdh |
| we will prevail | our lips | with us | who | master | to us | | because devastation for |

**7. For the righteous LORD loveth righteousness:** … who loves just actions, *Anchor* … For the Lord is upright, *BB* … The Lord is just, and just are the deeds he loves, *Knox* … just is the Eternal, he loves justice, *Moffatt.*

**his countenance doth behold the upright:** … Our face shall gaze upon the Upright One, *Anchor* … The upright shall behold his face, *ASV* … his face is turned towards the upright man, *NEB* … none but upright souls shall enjoy his presence, *Knox* … the honest will ever see his face, *JB.*

**12:t. To the chief Musician upon Sheminith, A Psalm of David.**

**1. Help, LORD; for the godly man ceaseth:** … Send help, Lord, for mercy has come to an end, *BB* … for there is not a godly man left, *Geneva* … Lord, come to my rescue; piety is dead, *Knox* … the good people are all gone, *NCV.*

**for the faithful fail from among the children of men:** … faithful men have disappeared, *Anchor* … Where in all the world can dependable men be found, *LIVB* … in a base world, true hearts have grown rare, *Knox* … good faith between man and man is over, *NEB* … no true believers are left on earth, *NCV.*

**2. They speak vanity every one with his neighbour:** … Each one utters lies to his friend, *Fenton* … exchanges empty forms of speech with his neighbour, *Knox* … Empty and false are man's words to his fellow, *Moffatt* … they say one thing and mean another, *NCV* … They speak idly, *NKJV.*

**with flattering lips and with a double heart do they speak:** … pernicious lips and a double mind, *Anchor* … their tongues are smooth in their talk, and their hearts are full of deceit, *BB* … And with false lip, heart speaks to the heart, *Fenton* … and, smooth-tongued, speaks from an insincere heart, *JB* … everywhere false hearts and treacherous lips, *Knox.*

**3. The LORD shall cut off all flattering lips:** … Those treacherous lips, *Knox* … May the Lord destroy all smooth lips, *NCB* … Silence those flattering tongues, *Good News* … but the Lord will not deal gently with people who act like that, *LIVB.*

**and the tongue that speaketh proud things:** ... every tongue that speaks distortions, *Anchor* ... that makes great boasts, *Goodspeed* ... tongues that talk so loftily, *Moffatt* ... bragging tongues, *NCV.*

**4. Who have said, With our tongue will we prevail:** ... With our words we get what we want, *Good News* ... Our tongues will help us win, *NCV* ... We give rein to our tongues, *Moffatt* ... We will lie to our hearts' content, *LIVB.*

**our lips are our own:** ... our weapon is our lips, *Anchor* ... By the power of our lips we succeed, *Fenton* ... our lips are good friends to us, *Knox* ... We can say what we wish, *NCV* ... Words are our ally, *NEB.*

**who is lord over us?:** ... Who shall master us, *Anchor* ... we own no master, *Knox* ... who calls us to account, *Moffatt* ... and no one can stop us, *Good News.*

**5. For the oppression of the poor:** ... sobs of the poor, *Anchor* ... crushing of the poor, *BB* ... because the poor are being hurt, *NCV* ... on behalf of the helpless who are so ill used, *Knox* ... Because they rob the afflicted, *NAB.*

---

heaven; all is right with the world and with the good men who are trying to help to make it right. The poet opposes the vision of the opened heaven to the picture drawn by fear. In v. 4, the former part is not to be taken as a separate affirmation: "The LORD is," etc., but "Yahweh" is the subject, and the weight of the sentence falls on the last clause. The "holy palace" in which Yahweh is enthroned is not on earth, as the parallelism of the clauses shows. To the eyes that have seen that vision and before which it ever burns, all earthly sorrows and dangers seem small.

The double judgment of v. 5 has a gentler side, and the reason for the tempest of wrath is likewise that for the blessed hope of the upright, as the "for" of v. 7 teaches. "Yahweh is righteous." That is the rock foundation for the indomitable faith of the Psalter in the certain ultimate triumph of patient, afflicted righteousness. Because God in his own character is so, He loves righteous acts—his own and men's. God looks on the upright, as has been said, and the upright shall gaze on Him, here and now in the communion of that faith which is a better kind of sight and hereafter in the vision of heaven, which the psalmist was on the verge of anticipating. That mutual gaze is blessedness. They who, looking up, behold Yahweh are brave to front all foes and to keep calm hearts in the midst of alarms. Hope burns like a pillar of fire in them when it is gone out in others, and to all the suggestions of their own timidity or of others they have the answer, "In the LORD have I put my trust; how say ye to my soul, Flee?" "Here I stand; I can do no otherwise. God help me. Amen."

***Psalm 12.*** *One penalty of living near God is keen pain from low lives. The ears that hear God's Word cannot but be stunned and hurt by the babble of empty speech. This Psalm is profoundly melancholy, but without a trace of personal affliction. The psalmist is not sad for himself, but sick of the clatter of godless tongues, in which he discerns the outcome of godless lives. His complaint wakes echoes in hearts touched by the love of God and the visions of man's true life. It passes through four clearly marked stages, each consisting of two verses: despondent contemplation of the flood of corrupt talk which seems to submerge all (vv. 1f); a passionate prayer for divine intervention, wrung from the psalmist by the miserable spectacle (vv. 3f); the answer to that cry from the voice of God with the rapturous response of the psalmist to it (vv. 5f); and the confidence built on the divine Word, which rectifies the too despondent complaint at the beginning, but is still shaded by the facts which stare him in the face (vv. 7f).*

**12:1–2.** The cry for help abruptly beginning the Psalm tells of the sharp pain from which it comes. The psalmist has been brooding over the black outlook until his overcharged heart relieves itself in this single-worded prayer. As he looks around, he sees no exceptions to the prevailing evil. Like Elijah, he thinks that he is left alone, and love to God and men and reliableness and truth are vanished with their representatives.

As in Ps. 5, sins of speech are singled out, and of these "vanity" and "flattering lips and with a double heart" are taken as typical. As in Eph. 4:25, the guilt of falsehood is deduced from the bond of neighborliness, which it rends. The sin, to which a "high civilization" is especially prone, of saying pleasant things without meaning them, seems to this moralist as grave as to most men it seems slight.

**12:3–4.** The conscious adoption and cynical avowal of it are a mark of defiance of God: "With our tongue will we prevail"—an obscure expression which may be taken in various shades of meaning, e.g., as "We have power over," or "As to our tongues we are strong," or "We will give effect to

| 6270 | 4623, 617 | 33 | 6498 | 7251.125 | 569.121 | 3176 |
|---|---|---|---|---|---|---|
| n mp | prep, *n fs* | n mp | adv | v Qal impf 1cs | v Qal impf 3ms | pn |
| עֲנִיִּים | מֵאַנְקַת | אֶבְיוֹנִים | עַתָּה | אָקוּם | יֹאמַר | יְהוָה |
| ʿănîyîm | mēʾanqath | ʾevyônîm | ʿattāh | ʾāqûm | yōʾmar | yehwāh |
| the afflicted | because groaning for | the needy | now | I will arise | He says | Yahweh |

| 8308.125 | 904, 3589 | 6558.521 | 3937 | | 577 | 3176 | 577 | 2999 |
|---|---|---|---|---|---|---|---|---|
| v Qal impf 1cs | prep, n ms | v Hiphil impf 3ms | prep, ps 3ms | 6. | *n fp* | pn | n fp | adj |
| אָשִׁית | בְּיֵשַׁע | יָפִיחַ | לוֹ | | אִמְרוֹת | יְהוָה | אֲמָרוֹת | טְהֹרוֹת |
| ʾāshîth | beyēshaʿ | yāphîach | lô | | ʾimrôth | yehwāh | ʾămārôth | tehōrôth |
| I will place | by salvation | he blows | at him | | the words of | Yahweh | words | pure |

| 3826B | 7170.155 | 904, 6172 | 3937, 800 | 2298.455 | 8124 | | 887, 3176 |
|---|---|---|---|---|---|---|---|
| n ms | v Qal pass ptc ms | prep, n ms | prep, art, n fs | v Pual ptc ms | n fd | 7. | pers pron, pn |
| כֶּסֶף | צָרוּף | בַּעֲלִיל | לָאָרֶץ | מְזֻקָּק | שִׁבְעָתָיִם | | אַתָּה־יְהוָה |
| keseph | tsārûph | baʿălîl | lāʾārets | mezuqqāq | shivʿāthāyim | | ʾattāh-yehwāh |
| silver | refined | in a furnace | to the ground | refined | seven times | | You O Yahweh |

| 8490.123 | 5526.123 | 4623, 1810 | 2182 | 3937, 5986 | | 5623 |
|---|---|---|---|---|---|---|
| v Qal impf 2ms, ps 3mp | v Qal impf 2 ms, ps 1cp | prep, art, n ms | rel part | prep, n ms | 8. | adv |
| תִּשְׁמְרֵם | תִּצְּרֶנּוּ | מִן־הַדּוֹר | זוּ | לְעוֹלָם | | סָבִיב |
| tishmerēm | titstserennû | min-haddôr | zû | leʿôlām | | sāvîv |
| You protect them | You guard us | from the generation | this | unto eternity | | all around |

| 7857 | 2050.726 | 3626, 7597.141 | 2234 | 3937, 1158 |
|---|---|---|---|---|
| n mp | v Hithpael impf 3mp | prep, v Qal inf con | n fs | prep, *n mp* |
| רְשָׁעִים | יִתְהַלָּכוּן | כְּרֻם | זֻלּוּת | לִבְנֵי |
| reshāʿîm | yithhallākhûn | kerum | zullûth | livnê |
| the wicked | they walk back and forth | according to the exalting of | vileness | with the sons of |

| 119 | | 3937, 5514.351 | 4344 | 3937, 1784 | | 5912, 590 | 3176 | 8319.123 |
|---|---|---|---|---|---|---|---|---|
| n ms | 13:t | prep, art, v Piel ptc ms | n ms | prep, pn | 1. | prep, intrg | pn | v Qal impf 2ms, ps 1cs |
| אָדָם | | לַמְנַצֵּחַ | מִזְמוֹר | לְדָוִד | | עַד־אָנָה | יְהוָה | תִּשְׁכָּחֵנִי |
| ʾādhām | | lamnatstsēach | mizmôr | ledhāwidh | | ʿadh-ʾānāh | yehwāh | tishkāchēnî |
| humankind | | to the director | a Psalm | of David | | until when | O Yahweh | will You forget me |

| 5516 | 5912, 590 | 5846.523 | 881, 6686 | 4623 | | 5912, 590 | 8308.125 |
|---|---|---|---|---|---|---|---|
| n ms | prep, intrg | v Hiphil impf 2ms | do, n mp, ps 2ms | prep, ps 1cs | 2. | prep, intrg | v Qal impf 1cs |
| נֶצַח | עַד־אָנָה | תַּסְתִּיר | אֶת־פָּנֶיךָ | מִמֶּנִּי | | עַד־אָנָה | אָשִׁית |
| netsach | ʿadh-ʾānāh | tastîr | ʾeth-pānêkhā | mimmenî | | ʿadh-ʾānāh | ʾāshîth |
| forever | until when | will You hide | your face | from me | | until when | will I place |

**for the sighing of the needy:** ... groans of the needy, *Anchor* ... weeping of those in need, *BB* ... For the wretched who sigh, *Fenton* ... of the poor who cry out so bitterly, *Knox* ... moans of the helpless, *NCV.*

**now will I arise, saith the LORD:** ... come to his help, *BB* ... now will I act, *JB* ... I will bestir myself, *Knox* ... So I take action, says the Eternal One, *Moffatt.*

**I will set him in safety:** ... I will give my help to him who longs for it, *Anchor* ... I will give him the salvation which he is desiring, *BB* ... I will grant him the safekeeping, *Berkeley* ... I will win them the redress they long for, *Knox* ... I will set him in the safety for which he yearns, *NKJV.*

**from him that puffeth at him:** ... whom the wicked hath spared, *Geneva* ... to those who sigh for it, *JB* ... at whom they puff, *MAST* ... from those who malign them, *NIV* ... let him puff at him, *Rotherham.*

**6. The words of the LORD are pure words:** ... Yahweh's promises are promises unalloyed, *JB* ... The promises of the Lord are true metal, *Knox* ... The promises of the LORD can be trusted, *Good News* ... are flawless, *NIV* ... He speaks no careless word, *LIVB.*

**as silver tried in a furnace of earth:** ... silver purged in a crucible, of clay, *Anchor* ... tested by fire, *BB* ... refined with a flame, *Fenton* ... freed from dross, *NAB* ... they are as genuine as silver, *Good News.*

**purified seven times:** ... refined, *Anchor* ... burned clean, *BB* ...

cleansed from its earth, *Fenton* ... stains of earth gone, *Knox*.

**7. Thou shalt keep them, O LORD:** ... You, O Yahweh, have protected us, *Anchor* ... You, LORD, are the Guardian of men, *Fenton* ... will watch over them, *JB* ... So are we kept by thee, O thou Eternal, *Moffatt*.

**thou shalt preserve them:** ... you have guarded us, *Anchor* ... You will keep them, *BB* ... protect them, *JB* ... keep us ever safe, *Knox*.

**from this generation for ever:** ... from these evil days, *Knox* ... you will always protect us from such people, *NCV* ... from a profligate and evil generation, *NEB* ... from this generation unto times age-abiding, *Rotherham*.

**8. The wicked walk on every side:** ... When the wicked are left to go free, *Fenton* ... parade to and fro, *Goodspeed* ... where all around us the ungodly strut, *Moffatt* ... The wicked flaunt themselves on every side, *NEB* ... prowl on every side, *NKJV*.

**when the vilest men are exalted:** ... evil is honoured, *BB* ... and what is of little worth wins general esteem, *REB* ... where base creatures rise to power, *Moffatt* ... everyone loves what is wrong, *NCV* ... in the high place are the basest of men, *NAB*.

**13:t. To the chief Musician, A Psalm of David.**

**1. How long wilt thou forget me, O LORD? for ever?:** ... Will you eternally forget me, *Anchor* ... Will you for ever put me out of your memory,

---

our words." Possibly, it stands as the foundation of the daring defiance in the last clause of the verse and asserts that the speaker is the author of his power of speech and therefore responsible to none for its use. The literal phrase, "Our lips are with us," may be a further development of the same godless thought. "With us" is usually taken to mean "our allies," or confederates, but signifies rather "in our possession, to do as we will with them." "Who is lord over us?" There speaks godless insolence, shaking off dependence and asserting shamelessly license of speech and life, unhindered by obligations to God and his Law.

**12:5–6.** The twofold reason which rouses the divine activity is very strikingly put first in v. 5. Not merely the "oppression or spoiling of the meek," but that conjoined with the "sighing of the needy," bring God into the field. Not affliction alone, but affliction which impels to prayer, moves the LORD to "stir up his strength." "Now will I arise." That solemn "now" marks the crisis, or turning-point, when long forbearance ends and the crash of retribution begins. It is like the whir of the clock that precedes the striking. The swiftly following blow will ring out the old evil. The purpose of God's intervention is the safety of the afflicted who have sighed to Him; but while that is clear, the condensed language of v. 5 is rather obscure.

The listening psalmist responds in v. 6 to God's great word. That word stands, with strong force of contrast, side by side with the arrogant chatter of irresponsible frivolity and sounds majestic by the side of the shrill feebleness of the defiance. Now the psalmist lifts his voice in trustful acceptance of the oracle. The general sense of v. 6 is clear, and the metaphor which compares God's words to refined silver is familiar.

**12:7–8.** The last turn of the Psalm builds hope on the pure words just heard from heaven. When God speaks a promise, faith repeats it as a certitude and prophesies in the line of the revelation. "Thou shalt" is man's answer to God's "I will." In the strength of the divine word, the despondency of the opening strain is brightened. The godly and faithful shall not "fail from among the children of men," since God will keep them and his keeping shall preserve them. "This generation" (HED #1810) describes a class rather than an epoch. It refers to the vain talkers who have been sketched in such dark colors in the earlier part of the Psalm.

But even the pure words that promise safety and wake the response of faith do not wholly scatter the clouds. The Psalm recurs very pathetically at its close to the tone of its beginning. Notice the repetition of "the children of men" which links v. 8 with v. 1. If the fear that the faithful should fail is soothed by God's promise heard by the psalmist sounding in his soul, the hard fact of dominant evil is not altered thereby. That "vileness is set on high among the sons of men" is the description of the vile and unequitable world.

***Psalm 13.*** *This little Psalm begins in agitation and ends in calm. The waves run high at first, but swiftly sink to rest, and at last lie peacefully glinting in sunshine. The Psalm falls into three strophes, of which the first (vv. 1f) is the complaint of endurance strained almost to giving way; the second (vv. 3f) is prayer which feeds waning faith; and the third (vv. 5f, which are one in the Hebrew) is the voice of confidence, which, in the midst of trouble, makes future praise and deliverance a present experience.*

**13:1–2.** However true it is that sorrow is "but for a moment," it seems to last for an eternity. Sad hours are leaden footed, and joyful ones winged. If sorrows

| 6332 | 904, 5497 | 3123 | 904, 3949 | 3221 | 5912, 590 | 7597.121 |
|---|---|---|---|---|---|---|
| n fp | prep, n fs, ps 1cs | n ms | prep, n ms, ps 1cs | adv | prep, intrg | v Qal impf 3ms |
| עֵצוֹת | בְּנַפְשִׁי | יָגוֹן | בִּלְבָבִי | יוֹמָם | עַד־אָנָה | יָרוּם |
| ʽētsôth | b$^{e}$naphshî | yāghôn | bilvāvî | yômām | ʽadh-ʼānāh | yārûm |
| counsels | in my soul | agony | in my heart | daily | until when | will he be exalted |

| 342.151 | 6142 | | 5202.531 | 6257.131 | 3176 | 435 |
|---|---|---|---|---|---|---|
| v Qal act ptc ms, ps 1cs | prep, ps 1cs | 3. | v Hiphil impv 2ms | v Qal impv 2ms, ps 1cs | pn | n mp, ps 1cs |
| אֹיְבִי | עָלָי | | הַבִּיטָה | עֲנֵנִי | יְהוָה | אֱלֹהָי |
| ʼōy$^{e}$vî | ʽālāy | | habbîṭāh | ʽănēnî | y$^{e}$hwāh | ʼĕlōhāy |
| my enemy | over me | | regard | answer me | Yahweh | my God |

| 213.531 | 6084 | 6678, 3583.125 | 4323 | | 6678, 569.121 |
|---|---|---|---|---|---|
| v Hiphil impv 2ms | n fd, ps 1cs | adv, v Qal impf 1cs | art, n ms | 4. | adv, v Qal impf 3ms |
| הָאִירָה | עֵינַי | פֶּן־אִישַׁן | הַמָּוֶת | | פֶּן־יֹאמַר |
| hāʼîrāh | ʽênay | pen-ʼîshan | hammāweth | | pen-yōʼmar |
| luminate | my eyes | so that I will not sleep | the death | | so that he will not say |

| 342.151 | 3310.115 | 7141 | 1559.126 | 3706 | 4267.225 |
|---|---|---|---|---|---|
| v Qal act ptc ms, ps 1cs | v Qal pf 1cs, ps 3ms | n mp, ps 1cs | v Qal impf 3mp | cj | v Niphal impf 1cs |
| אֹיְבִי | יְכָלְתִּיו | צָרַי | יָגִילוּ | כִּי | אֶמּוֹט |
| ʼōy$^{e}$vî | y$^{e}$khāl$^{e}$ttîw | tsāray | yāghîlû | kî | ʼemmôṯ |
| my enemy | I have prevailed over him | my adversaries | they rejoice | when | I totter |

| | 603 | 904, 2721 | 1019.115 | 1559.121 | 3949 | 904, 3568 |
|---|---|---|---|---|---|---|
| 5. | cj, pers pron | prep, n ms, ps 2ms | v Qal pf 1cs | v Qal juss 3ms | n ms, ps 1cs | prep, n fs, ps 2ms |
| | וַאֲנִי | בְּחַסְדְּךָ | בָטַחְתִּי | יָגֵל | לִבִּי | בִּישׁוּעָתֶךָ |
| | waʼănî | b$^{e}$chasḏ$^{e}$khā | vāṭachtî | yāghēl | libbî | bîshûʽāthekhā |
| | but I | in your steadfast love | I have trusted | may it rejoice | my heart | in your salvation |

| | 8301.125 | 3937, 3176 | 3706 | 1621.111 | 6142 | | 3937, 5514.351 |
|---|---|---|---|---|---|---|---|
| 6. | v Qal juss 1cs | prep, pn | cj | v Qal pf 3ms | prep, ps 1cs | 14:t | prep, art, v Piel ptc ms |
| | אָשִׁירָה | לַיהוָה | כִּי | גָמַל | עָלָי | | לַמְנַצֵּחַ |
| | ʼāshîrāh | layhwāh | kî | ghāmal | ʽālāy | | lamnatstsēach |
| | let me sing | to Yahweh | because | He has rewarded | concerning me | | to the director |

| 3937, 1784 | | 569.111 | 5210 | 904, 3949 | 375 | 435 | 8271.516 |
|---|---|---|---|---|---|---|---|
| prep, pn | 1. | v Qal pf 3ms | n ms | prep, n ms, ps 3ms | *sub* | n mp | v Hiphil pf 3cp |
| לְדָוִד | | אָמַר | נָבָל | בְּלִבּוֹ | אֵין | אֱלֹהִים | הִשְׁחִיתוּ |
| l$^{e}$dhāwidh | | ʼāmar | nāvāl | b$^{e}$libbô | ʼên | ʼĕlōhîm | hishchîthû |
| of David | | He has said | the foolish | in his heart | there is not | God | they are depraved |

*BB* … Lord, must I still go all unremembered, *Knox* … Will you utterly forget me, *NAB* … will you leave me forgotten, *REB.*

**how long wilt thou hide thy face from me?:** … will your face for ever be turned away from me, *BB* … must thy look still be turned away from me, *Knox* … How long wilt thou withhold thy favour from me, *Moffatt* … How long will you look the other way when I am in need, *LIVB.*

**2. How long shall I take counsel in my soul:** … How long must I place doubts in my soul, *Anchor* … How long must I wrestle with my thoughts, *NIV* … How long must I nurse rebellion in my soul, *JB* … How long must I worry and feel sad in my heart all day, *NCV* … Each day brings a fresh load of care, *Knox.*

**having sorrow in my heart daily?:** … creating grief in my heart, *Anchor* … And torture my heart every day, *Fenton* … having weariness dayly, *Geneva* … fresh misery to my heart, *Knox* … grief in my heart day after day, *NAB.*

**how long shall mine enemy be exalted over me?:** … how long will he who is against me be given power over me, *BB* … While they lay their plots for my life, *Fenton* … shall my enemy lord it over me, *NEB* … is the enemy to domineer over me, *JB.*

**3. Consider and hear me, O LORD my God:** … Look at me, answer me, *Anchor* … Let my voice come before you, *BB* … EVER-LIVING! look down on my woes, *Fenton* … Have regard! answer me, O Yahweh my God, *Rotherham.*

**lighten mine eyes:** ... let your light be shining on me, *BB* ... Make my eyes gleam, *KJVII* ... revive me, *Moffatt* ... Restore my strength, *Good News* ... give me light in my darkness, *LIVB.*

**lest I sleep the sleep of death:** ... in the slumber of Death, *Fenton* ... before they close in death, *Knox* ... lest I sleep on into death, *Rotherham* ... don't let me die, *Good News.*

**4. Lest mine enemy say, I have prevailed against him:** ... lest my adversary say, I have overthrown him, *NEB* ... Or my foe will boast, I have overpowered him, *JB* ... do not let my enemies claim the mastery, *Knox* ... Otherwise my enemy will say, I have won, *NCV.*

**and those that trouble me rejoice:** ... mine adversaries be joyful, *Darby* ... my enemy have the joy, *JB* ... my persecutors triumph, *Knox* ... Don't let them gloat, *LIVB.*

**when I am moved:** ... when I slide, *Geneva* ... that I totter, *Rotherham* ... because I am shaken, *Goodspeed* ... over my downfall, *Moffatt* ... that I've been defeated, *NCV* ... of seeing me stumble, *JB* ... that I am down, *LIVB.*

**5. But I have trusted in thy mercy:** ... I cast myself on thy mercy, *Knox* ... But on thy kindness I indeed rely, *Moffatt* ... I trust in your love, *NCV* ... I rely on your constant love, *Good News* ... lovingkindness, *ASV.*

**my heart shall rejoice in thy salvation:** ... Let my heart delight in your saving help, *JB* ... soon may this heart boast of redress granted, *Knox* ... let me exult over thy saving aid, *Moffatt* ... My heart is happy because you saved me, *NCV* ... My heart shall rejoice, for thou hast set me free, *NEB.*

**6. I will sing unto the LORD:** ... let me sing to the name of Yahweh, *JB* ... sing in praise of the Lord, *Knox* ... let me be singing to the Eternal, *Moffatt.*

**because he hath dealt bountifully with me:** ... who has granted all my desire, *NEB* ... he has given me my reward, *BB* ... he has taken care of me, *NCV* ... He has been good to me, *NAB* ... my benefactor, *Knox.*

**14:t. To the chief Musician, A Psalm of David.**

**1. The fool hath said in his heart, There is no God:** ... There is no God above us, is the fond thought of reckless hearts, *Knox* ... Profane men think, *Moffatt* ... Fools say to themselves, *NCV* ... That man is a fool who says to himself, *LIVB* ... God will not do anything, *BB.*

**They are corrupt:** ... How vile men are, *NEB* ... Fools are evil, *NCV* ... They acted basely, *Goodspeed* ... warped natures everywhere, *Knox.*

---

passed to our consciousness as quickly as joys, or joys lingered as long as sorrows, life would be less weary.

That reiterated "How long?" betrays how weary sorrow was to the psalmist. Very significant is the progress of thought in the fourfold questioning complaint, which turns first to God, then to himself, then to the enemy. The root of his sorrow is that God seems to have forgotten him; therefore, his soul is full of plans for relief, and the enemy seems to be lifted above him. The "sorrow of the world" begins with the visible evil and stops with the inward pain.

**13:3–4.** The agitation of the first strophe is somewhat stilled in the second, in which the stream of prayer runs clear without such foam as the impatient questions of the first part. The second strophe falls into four clauses, which have an approximate correspondence to those of the first. "Consider and hear me, O LORD my God." The first petition corresponds to the hiding of God's face, and perhaps the second, by the law of inverted parallelism, may correspond to the forgetting. But in any case, the noticeable thing is the swift decisiveness of spring with which the psalmist's faith reaches firm ground here.

**13:5–6.** The storm has rolled away everything in the third strophe, in which faith has triumphed over doubt and anticipates the fulfillment of its prayer. The strophe begins with an emphatic opposition of the psalmist to the foe. Because he has thus trusted in God's mercy, the psalmist therefore is sure that that mercy will work for him salvation or deliverance from his peril. Anything is possible except that the appeal of faith to God's heart should not be answered. Whoever can say, "I have trusted," has the right to say, "I shall rejoice."

***Psalm 14.*** *This Psalm springs from the same situation as Pss. 10 and 12. It has several points of likeness to both. It resembles the former in its attribution to "the fool" of the heart speech, "There is no God," and the latter in its use of the phrases "sons of men" and "generation" as ethical terms and in its thought of a divine interference as the source of safety for the righteous. We have thus three Psalms closely connected, but separated from each other by Pss. 11 and 13. Now it is observable that these three have no personal references, unlike the two which part them. It would appear that the five are arranged on the principle of alternating a general complaint of the evil of the times with a more personal pleading of an individual sufferer.*

**14:1–3.** The heavy fact of widespread corruption presses on the psalmist and starts a train of

| 8911.516 | 6173 | 375 | 6449.151, 3005 | 2. | 3176 | 4623, 8452 |
|---|---|---|---|---|---|---|
| v Hiphil pf 3cp | n fs | *sub* | v Qal act ptc ms, adj | | pn | prep, n md |
| הִתְעִיבוּ | עֲלִילָה | אֵין | עֹשֵׂה־טוֹב | | יְהוָה | מִשָּׁמַיִם |
| hith'îvû | 'ălîlāh | 'ên | 'ōsēh-ṭôv | | yehwāh | mishshāmayim |
| they are abhorred | deeds | there is not | one who does good | | Yahweh | from the heavens |

| 8625.511 | 6142, 1158, 119 | 3937, 7495.141 | 1950B, 3552 |
|---|---|---|---|
| v Hiphil pf 3ms | prep, *n mp*, n ms | prep, v Qal inf con | intrg part, sub |
| הִשְׁקִיף | עַל־בְּנֵי־אָדָם | לִרְאוֹת | הֲיֵשׁ |
| hishqîph | 'al-benê-'ādhām | lir'ôth | hăyēsh |
| He looks down | on the children of humankind | to see | is there |

| 7959.551 | 1938.151 | 881, 435 | 3. | 3725 | 5681.111 |
|---|---|---|---|---|---|
| v Hiphil ptc ms | v Qal act ptc ms | do, n mp | | art, n ms | v Qal pf 3ms |
| מַשְׂכִּיל | דֹּרֵשׁ | אֶת־אֱלֹהִים | | הַכֹּל | סָר |
| maskîl | dōrēsh | 'eth-'ĕlōhîm | | hakkōl | sār |
| one who has understanding | one who seeks | God | | everyone | he has turned aside |

| 3267 | 447.216 | 375 | 6449.151, 3005 | 375 |
|---|---|---|---|---|
| adv | v Niphal pf 3cp | *sub* | v Qal act ptc ms, adj | *sub* |
| יַחְדָּו | נֶאֱלָחוּ | אֵין | עֹשֵׂה־טוֹב | אֵין |
| yachdāw | ne'ĕlāchû | 'ên | 'ōsēh-ṭôv | 'ên |
| at the same time | they have become corrupt | there is not | one who does good | there is not |

| 1612, 259 | 4. | 1950B, 3940 | 3156.116 | 3725, 6713.152 | 201 | 404.152 |
|---|---|---|---|---|---|---|
| cj, num | | intrg part, neg part | v Qal pf 3cp | *adj, v Qal act ptc mp* | n ms | *v Qal act ptc mp* |
| גַּם־אֶחָד | | הֲלֹא | יָדְעוּ | כָּל־פֹּעֲלֵי | אָוֶן | אֹכְלֵי |
| gam-'echādh | | hălō' | yādhe'û | kol-pō'ălê | 'āwen | 'ōkhelê |
| even one | | do not | they know | all those who practice | iniquity | those who devour |

| 6194 | 404.116 | 4035 | 3176 | 3940 | 7410.116 | 5. | 8427 |
|---|---|---|---|---|---|---|---|
| n ms, ps 1cs | v Qal pf 3cp | n ms | pn | neg part | v Qal pf 3cp | | adv |
| עַמִּי | אָכְלוּ | לֶחֶם | יְהוָה | לֹא | קָרָאוּ | | שָׁם |
| 'ammî | 'ākhelû | lechem | yehwāh | lō' | qārā'û | | shām |
| my people | they have eaten | bread | Yahweh | not | they have called on | | there |

| 6585.116 | 6586 | 3706, 435 | 904, 1810 | 6926 |
|---|---|---|---|---|
| v Qal pf 3cp | n ms | cj, n mp | prep, n ms | adj |
| פָּחֲדוּ | פַחַד | כִּי־אֱלֹהִים | בְּדוֹר | צַדִּיק |
| pāchădhû | phāchadh | kî-'ĕlōhîm | bedhôr | tsaddîq |
| they have trembled | terror | because God | with a generation | righteous |

| 6. | 6332, 6270 | 991.528 | 3706 | 3176 | 4406 | 7. | 4449 | 5598.121 |
|---|---|---|---|---|---|---|---|---|
| | *n fs*, n ms | v Hiphil impf 2mp | cj | pn | n ms, ps 3ms | | intrg | v Qal impf 3ms |
| | עֲצַת־עָנִי | תָבִישׁוּ | כִּי | יְהוָה | מַחְסֵהוּ | | מִי | יִתֵּן |
| | 'ătsath-'ānî | thāvîshû | kî | yehwāh | machsēhû | | mî | yittēn |
| | the counsel of the afflicted | you shame | except | Yahweh | his refuge | | who | he will allow |

**they have done abominable works:** … hateful things, *KJVII* … detestable, *Moffatt* … their deeds are vile, *NIV* … how depraved and loathsome, *NEB*.

**there is none that doeth good:** … not one of them does right, *JB* … There is not an innocent man among them, *Knox* … and cannot really be a good person at all, *LIVB*.

**2. The LORD looked down from heaven:** … from the heavens, *Darby* … looked forth from, *Goodspeed*.

**upon the children of men:** … on the children of Adam, *Fenton* … at the race of men, *Knox* … upon mankind, *Moffatt* … on all people, *NCV* … on all the human race, *REB*.

**to see if there were any that did understand:** … be one who ponders, *Anchor* … were any who had wisdom, *BB* … to see if any were acting wisely, *Berkeley* … to find one soul that reflects, *Knox* … to see if any have the sense, *Moffatt*.

**and seek God:** … would follow their GOD, *Fenton* … Enquiring after God,

*Rotherham* ... makes God its aim, *Knox* ... who want to please God, *LIVB* ... if anyone was looking to God for help, *NCV.*

**3. They are all gone aside:** ... Each one is stubborn, *Anchor* ... all have missed the mark, *Knox* ... But all are unfaithful, *REB* ... All have turned away, *JB* ... all are disloyal, *NEB.*

**they are all together become filthy:** ... together they are depraved, *Anchor* ... all alike turned sour, *JB* ... all are rotten to the core, *NEB* ... they have become perverse, *NAB* ... they are all equally bad, *Good News.*

**there is none that doeth good, no, not one:** ... none were practising good, *Fenton* ... an innocent man is nowhere to be found, *Knox.*

**4. Have all the workers of iniquity no knowledge?:** ... Do they know nothing, all the evildoers, *Goodspeed* ... What, can they learn nothing, all these traffickers in iniquity, *Knox* ... Are all these evildoers ignorant, *Good News* ... Don't the wicked understand, *NCV.*

**who eat up my people as they eat bread:** ... they take my people for food as they would take bread, *BB* ... this is the bread they eat, *JB* ... who feed themselves fat on this people of mine, *Knox* ... They live by robbing my people, *Good News* ... who devour my people with their extortion, *Moffatt.*

**and call not upon the LORD:** ... they make no prayer, *BB* ... never invoke the Lord's name, *Knox* ... They do not ask the LORD for help, *NCV.*

**5. There were they in great fear:** ... great terror, *Goodspeed* ... There they are, overwhelmed with dread, *NIV* ... Ha! there they are in a panic, *Moffatt* ... There they were in dire alarm, *NEB.*

**for God is in the generation of the righteous:** ... takes the side of the upright, *JB* ... when the Lord takes the part of the innocent, *Knox* ... is present in the company of the righteous, *NIV* ... was in the brotherhood of the godly, *NEB* ... is with those who love him, *LIVB.*

**6. Ye have shamed the counsel of the poor:** ... You evildoers frustrate the plans of the poor, *NIV* ... They scorn the poor's thoughts, *Fenton* ... You would baffle these weak folk, *Moffatt* ... Easily you thought to outwit the friendless, *Knox* ... You would confound the plans of the afflicted, *NAB.*

**because the LORD is his refuge:** ... is his support, *BB* ... will protect them, *NCV* ... whom the LORD Himself loves, *Fenton* ... because the Lord is his trust, *Geneva* ... But the Eternal is their resource, *Moffatt.*

**7. Oh that the salvation of Israel were come out of Zion!:** ... Who

---

thought which begins with a sad picture of the deluge of evil, rises to a vision of God's judgment of it, triumphs in the prospect of the sudden panic which shall shake the souls of the "workers of iniquity" when they see that God is with the righteous, and ends with a sigh for the coming of that time. The staple of the poem is the familiar contrast of a corrupt world and a righteous God Who judges, but it is cast into very dramatic and vivid form here.

We listen first to the psalmist's judgment of his generation (v. 1). Probably, it was very unlike the rosy hues with which a heart less in contact with God and the unseen would have painted the condition of things. Eras of great culture and material prosperity may have a very seamy side, which eyes accustomed to the light of God cannot fail to see. The root of the evil lay, as the psalmist believed, in a practical denial of God, and whoever thus denied Him was "a fool." It does not need formulated atheism in order to say in one's heart, "There is no God." Practical denial or neglect of his working in the world, rather than a creed of negation, is in the psalmist's mind. In effect, we say that there is no God when we shut Him up in a far-off heaven and never think of Him as concerned in our affairs. To attempt to strip Him of his justice and rob Him of his control is the part of a fool. The biblical conception of folly is moral perversity rather than intellectual feebleness, and whoever is morally and religiously wrong cannot be in reality intellectually right.

The next wave of thought (v. 2) brings into his consciousness the solemn contrast between the godless noise and activity of earth and the silent gaze of God that marks it all. God's heart yearns to find hearts that turn to Him, and He seeks those who seek Him; and only they are "wise." Other Scriptures present other reasons for that gaze of God from heaven, but this one in the midst of its solemnity is gracious with revelation of divine desires.

What is to be the issue of the strongly contrasted situation in these two verses—a world full of godless lawlessness beneath and a fixed eye piercing to the discernment of the inmost nature of actions and characters above? Verse 3 answers. We may almost venture to say that it shows a disappointed God, so sharply does it put the difference between what He desired to see and what He did see. The psalmist's sad estimate is repeated as the result of the divine search.

**14:4–7.** But a baffled quest cannot be the end. If Yahweh seeks in vain for goodness on earth, earth

| 4623, 6995 | 3568 | 3547 | 904, 8178.141 | 3176 | 8097 | 6194 |
|---|---|---|---|---|---|---|
| prep, pn | *n fs* | pn | prep, v Qal inf con | pn | *n fs* | n ms, ps 3ms |
| מִצִּיּוֹן | יְשׁוּעַת | יִשְׂרָאֵל | בְּשׁוּב | יְהוָה | שְׁבוּת | עַמּוֹ |
| mitstsîyôn | yeshû'ath | yisrā'ēl | beshûv | yehwāh | shevûth | 'ammô |
| from Zion | the salvation of | Israel | when returning | Yahweh | the captivity of | his people |

| 1559.121 | 3399 | 7975.121 | 3547 | | 4344 | 3937, 1784 | | 3176 |
|---|---|---|---|---|---|---|---|---|
| v Qal juss 3ms | pn | v Qal juss 3ms | pn | | n ms | prep, pn | | pn |
| יָגֵל | יַעֲקֹב | יִשְׂמַח | יִשְׂרָאֵל | **15:t** | מִזְמוֹר | לְדָוִד | **1.** | יְהוָה |
| yāghēl | ya'ăqōv | yismach | yisrā'ēl | | mizmôr | ledhāwidh | | yehōwāh |
| may they rejoice | Jacob | may they be glad | Israel | | a Psalm | of David | | Yahweh |

| 4449, 1513.121 | 904, 164 | 4449, 8331.121 | 904, 2098 | 7231 |
|---|---|---|---|---|
| intrg, v Qal impf 3ms | prep, n ms, ps 2ms | intrg, v Qal impf 3ms | prep, *n ms* | n ms, ps 2ms |
| מִי־יָגוּר | בְּאָהֳלֶךָ | מִי־יִשְׁכֹּן | בְּהַר | קָדְשֶׁךָ |
| mî-yāghûr | be'āhelekhā | mî-yishkōn | behar | qādheshekhā |
| who will stay | in your tabernacle | who will remain | on the mountain of | your holy place |

| | 2050.151 | 8879 | 6713.151 | 6928 | 1744.151 | 583 |
|---|---|---|---|---|---|---|
| | v Qal act ptc ms | adv | cj, v Qal act ptc ms | n ms | cj, v Qal act ptc ms | n fs |
| **2.** | הוֹלֵךְ | תָּמִים | וּפֹעֵל | צֶדֶק | וְדֹבֵר | אֱמֶת |
| | hôlēkh | tāmîm | ûphō'ēl | tsedheq | wedhōvēr | 'ĕmeth |
| | the one who walks | integrally | and one who practices | righteousness | and one who speaks | truth |

| 904, 3949 | | 3940, 7558.111 | 6142, 4098 | 3940, 6449.111 |
|---|---|---|---|---|
| prep, n ms, ps 3ms | | neg part, v Qal pf 3ms | prep, n ms, ps 3ms | neg part, v Qal pf 3ms |
| בִּלְבָבוֹ | **3.** | לֹא־רָגַל | עַל־לְשֹׁנוֹ | לֹא־עָשָׂה |
| bilvāvô | | lō'-rāghal | 'al-leshōnô | lō'-'āsāh |
| in his heart | | and he has not slandered | in front of his tongue | he has not done |

gives from Zion to Israel victory, *Fenton* ... Oh, that it might dawn over Sion, Israel's deliverance, *Knox* ... that God would come from Zion now to save his people, *LIVB.*

**when the LORD bringeth back the captivity of his people:** ... with Yahweh restoring the fortunes of his people, *Anchor* ... when the fate of his people is changed by the Lord, *BB* ... makes them prosperous again, *Good News* ... When Yahweh brings his people home, *JB* ... restores the well-being of his people, *NAB.*

**Jacob shall rejoice:** ... Then Jacob will laugh, *Fenton* ... Jacob shall exult, *Goodspeed* ... what joy for Jacob, *JB* ... Day of gladness for Jacob, *Knox.*

**and Israel shall be glad:** ... Israel shall rejoice, *Goodspeed* ... what happiness for Israel, *JB* ... day of Israel's triumph, *Knox* ... how glad will Israel be, *Moffatt.*

**15:t. A Psalm of David.**

**1. LORD, who shall abide in thy tabernacle?:** ... Yahweh, who will be a guest in your tent, *Anchor* ... who may have a resting-place in your Tent, *BB* ... who in Your Halls shall dwell, *Fenton* ... Who may sojourn in thy pavilion, *Goodspeed* ... who may dwell in your sanctuary, *NIV.*

**who shall dwell in thy holy hill?:** ... a living-place on your holy hill, *BB* ... who shall rest in thine Holy Mountaine, *Geneva* ... rest on the mountain where thy sanctuary is, *Knox* ... who may dwell on thy sacred hill, *Moffatt* ... Who may live on your holy mountain, *NCV.*

**2. He that walketh uprightly, and worketh righteousness:** ... who walks with integrity and practices justice, *Anchor* ... who does what is right, *Berkeley* ... One that guides his steps without fault, and gives to all their due, *Knox* ... Only those who are innocent, *NCV* ... Anyone who leads a blameless life and is truly sincere, *LIVB.*

**and speaketh the truth in his heart:** ... one whose heart is all honest purpose, *Knox* ... he whose words are from the heart, *Moffatt* ... who thinks the truth in his heart, *NAB* ... whose words are true and sincere, *Good News.*

**3. He that backbiteth not with his tongue:** ... He who does not trip over his tongue, *Anchor* ... who does not slander, *Berkeley* ... who keeps the tongue under control, *JB* ... who utters no treacherous word, *Knox* ... no scandal on his tongue to hurt his fellow, *Moffatt.*

**nor doeth evil to his neighbour:** ... doeth not evil to his companion, *Darby* ... who does not wrong a comrade, *JB* ... never defrauds a friend, *Knox* ... Who harms not his fellow man, *NAB.*

cannot go on forever in godless riot. Therefore, with eloquent abruptness, the voice from heaven crashes in upon the "fools" in the full career of their folly. The thunder rolls from a clear sky. God speaks in v. 4. The three clauses of the divine rebuke roughly correspond with those of v. 1 insofar as the first points to ignorance as the root of wrongdoing, the second charges positive sin, and the third refers to negative evil.

The psalmist sets before himself and us the two camps: the panic-stricken and confused mass of enemies ready to break into flight and the little flock of the "righteous generation," at peace in the midst of trouble and foes because God is in the midst of them. The permanent relations of God to the two sorts of men who are found in every generation and community are set forth in that strongly marked contrast.

In v. 6, the psalmist himself addresses the oppressors with triumphant confidence born of his previous contemplations. The first clause might be a question, but it is more probably a taunting affirmation: "You would frustrate the plans of the afflicted"—and you could not—"for Yahweh is his refuge." Here again, the briefer sentence brings out the eloquent contrast. The desire of malicious foe is unaccomplished, and there is but one explanation of the impotence of the mighty and the powerfulness of the weak, namely, that Yahweh is the stronghold of his saints.

So, finally, the whole course of thought gathers itself up in the prayer that the salvation of Israel—the true Israel, apparently—"were come out of Zion," God's dwelling, from which He comes forth in his delivering power. The salvation longed for is that just described. The voice of the oppressed handful of good men in an evil generation is heard in this closing prayer. It is encouraged by the visions which have passed before the psalmist. The assurance that God will intervene is the very essence of the cry to Him that He would. Because we know that He will deliver, therefore, we find it in our hearts to pray that He would deliver. The revelation of his gracious purposes animates the longings for their realization. Such a sigh of desire has no sadness in its longing and no doubt in its expectation.

***Psalm 15.*** *The ideal worshiper of Yahweh is painted in this Psalm in a few broad outlines. Zion is holy because God's "tent" is there. This is the only hint of date given by the Psalm. And all that can be said is that, if that consecration of thy hill was recent, the poet would naturally ponder all the more deeply the question of who were fit to dwell in the new solemnities of the abode of Yahweh. The tone of the Psalm, then, accords with the circumstances of the time when David brought the Ark to Jerusalem, but more than this cannot be affirmed. More important are its two main points: the conception of the guests of Yahweh and the statement of the ethical qualifications of these guests.*

*As to structure, the Psalm is simple. It has, first, the general question and answer in two verses of two clauses each (vv. 1f). Then the general description of the guest of God is expanded in three verses of three clauses each, the last of which closes with an assurance of stability, which varies and heightens the idea of dwelling in the tent of Yahweh.*

**15:1–2.** Technically, the two verbs in v. 1 differ in that the first implies transient and the second permanent abode. That difference, however, is not in the psalmist's mind, and the two phrases mean the same thing, with only the difference that the former brings out his conception of the rights of the guest. Clearly, then, the psalmist's question by no means refers only to an outward approach to an outward tabernacle, but the symbol in the very act of melting into the deep spiritual reality is signified here. The singer has been educated by the husks of ritual to pass beyond these and has learned that there is a better abode for Yahweh, and therefore for himself, than that pitched on Zion and frequented by impure and pure alike.

Verse 2 summarizes the qualifications of Yahweh's guest in one comprehensive demand that he should walk uprightly. That demand is then divided into the twin requirements of truthful speech and righteous deeds. The verbs are in the participial form, which emphasizes the notion of habitual action. The general answer is expanded in the three following verses.

**15:3–5.** Neither calumny (v. 3) nor the equally ignoble flattery of evildoers (v. 4) pollutes the lips of the ideal good man. If this reference to spoken estimates is allowed, the last clause of v. 4 completes the references to the right use of speech. The obligation of speaking "truth with his heart" is pursued into a third region: that of vows or promises. These must be conceived as not religious vows, but in accordance with the reference of the whole Psalm, to duties to neighbors, as oaths made to others. They must be kept, whatever consequences

| 3937, 7739 | 7750 | 2887 | 3940, 5558.111 | 6142, 7427 | | 995.255 |
|---|---|---|---|---|---|---|
| prep, n ms, ps 3ms | n fs | cj, n fs | neg part, v Qal pf 3ms | prep, n ms, ps 3ms | 4. | v Niphal ptc ms |
| לְרֵעֵהוּ | רָעָה | וְחֶרְפָּה | לֹא־נָשָׂא | עַל־קְרֹבוֹ | | נִבְזֶה |
| lerē'ēhû | rā'āh | wecherpāh | lō'-nāsā' | 'al-qōrōvô | | nivzeh |
| to his fellow | evil | and abuse | he has not raised | against his neighbor | | one who is despised |

| 904, 6084 | 4128.255 | 881, 3486.152 | 3176 | 3632.321 | 8123.211 |
|---|---|---|---|---|---|
| prep, n fd, ps 3ms | v Niphal ptc ms | cj, do, *v Qal act ptc mp* | pn | v Piel impf 3ms | v Niphal pf 3ms |
| בְּעֵינָיו | נִמְאָס | וְאֶת־יִרְאֵי | יְהוָה | יְכַבֵּד | נִשְׁבַּע |
| be'ênâv | nim'ās | we'eth-yir'ê | yehwāh | yekhabbēdh | nishba' |
| in his eyes | one who is rejected | but those who fear | Yahweh | he honors | he has sworn |

| 3937, 7778.541 | 3940 | 4306.521 | | 3826B | 3940, 5598.111 | 904, 5575 |
|---|---|---|---|---|---|---|
| prep, v Hiphil inf con | cj, neg part | v Hiphil impf 3ms | 5. | n ms, ps 3ms | neg part, v Qal pf 3ms | prep, n ms |
| לְהָרַע | וְלֹא | יָמִר | | כַּסְפּוֹ | לֹא־נָתַן | בְּנֶשֶׁךְ |
| lehāra' | welō' | yāmir | | kaspô | lō'-nāthan | beneshekh |
| to cause to be bad | and not | he will alter | | his silver | he has not given | with interest |

| 8245 | 6142, 5538 | 3940 | 4089.111 | 6449.151, 431 | 3940 |
|---|---|---|---|---|---|
| cj, n ms | prep, n ms | neg part | v Qal pf 3ms | *v Qal act ptc ms*, dem pron | neg part |
| וְשֹׁחַד | עַל־נָקִי | לֹא | לָקָח | עֹשֵׂה־אֵלֶּה | לֹא |
| weshōchadh | 'al-nāqî | lō' | lāqāch | 'ōsēh-'ēlleh | lō' |
| and a bribe | against the innocent | not | he has taken | the one who does these | not |

| 4267.221 | 3937, 5986 | | 4524 | 3937, 1784 | | 8490.131 | 418 |
|---|---|---|---|---|---|---|---|
| v Niphal impf 3ms | prep, n ms | 16:t | n ms | prep, pn | 1. | v Qal impv 2ms, ps 1cs | n ms |
| יִמּוֹט | לְעוֹלָם | | מִכְתָּם | לְדָוִד | | שָׁמְרֵנִי | אֵל |
| yimmôt | le'ôlām | | mikhtām | ledhāwidh | | shāmerēnî | 'ēl |
| he will totter | unto eternity | | a miktam | of David | | protect me | O God |

| 3706, 2725.115 | 904 | | 569.115 | 3937, 3176 | 112 | 887 | 3008 |
|---|---|---|---|---|---|---|---|
| cj, v Qal pf 1cs | prep, ps 2ms | 2. | v Qal pf 1cs | prep, pn | n mp, ps 1cs | pers pron | n fs, ps 1cs |
| כִּי־חָסִיתִי | בָךְ | | אָמַרְתְּ | לַיהוָה | אֲדֹנָי | אָתָּה | טוֹבָתִי |
| kî-chāsîthî | vākh | | 'āmart | layhwāh | 'ădhōnāy | 'āttāh | tôvāthî |
| because I have taken refuge | in You | | I have said | to Yahweh | my Lord | You | my good |

| 1118, 6142 | | 3937, 7202 | 866, 904, 800 | 2065 | 116 |
|---|---|---|---|---|---|
| neg part, prep, ps 2ms | 3. | prep, n mp | rel pron, prep, art, n fs | pers pron | cj, *n mp* |
| בַּל־עָלֶיךָ | | לִקְדוֹשִׁים | אֲשֶׁר־בָּאָרֶץ | הֵמָּה | וְאַדִּירֵי |
| bal-'ālêkhā | | liqōdhôshîm | 'ăsher-bā'ārets | hēmmāh | we'addîrê |
| not besides You | | about the holy ones | who in the land | they | and the nobles of |

| 3725, 2761, 904 | | 7528.126 | 6329 | 311 | 4257.116 |
|---|---|---|---|---|---|
| *adj*, n ms, ps 1cs, prep, ps 3mp | 4. | v Qal impf 3mp | n fp, ps 3mp | adj | v Qal pf 3cp |
| כָּל־חֶפְצִי־בָם | | יִרְבּוּ | עַצְּבוֹתָם | אַחֵר | מָהָרוּ |
| kol-chephtsî-vām | | yirbû | 'atstsevôthām | 'achēr | māhārû |
| all my delight in them | | they multiply | their agony | another | they have hastened |

| 1118, 5445.525 | 5447 | 4623, 1879 | 1118, 5558.125 | 881, 8428 |
|---|---|---|---|---|
| neg part, v Hiphil impf 1cs | n mp, ps 3mp | prep, n ms | cj, neg part, v Qal impf 1cs | do, n mp, ps 3mp |
| בַּל־אַסִּיךְ | נִסְכֵּיהֶם | מִדָּם | וּבַל־אֶשָּׂא | אֶת־שְׁמוֹתָם |
| bal-'assîkh | niskêhem | middām | ûval-'essā' | 'eth-shemôthām |
| I will not pour out | their drink offerings | of blood | and I will not carry | their names |

| 6142, 8004 | | 3176 | 4669, 2610 | 3683 | 887 | 8881.151 |
|---|---|---|---|---|---|---|
| prep, n fd, ps 1cs | 5. | pn | *n fs*, n ms, ps 1cs | cj, n fs, ps 1cs | pers pron | v Qal act ptc ms |
| עַל־שְׂפָתָי | | יְהוָה | מְנָת־חֶלְקִי | וְכוֹסִי | אַתָּה | תּוֹמִיךְ |
| 'al-sephāthāy | | yehwāh | menāth-chelqî | wekhôsî | 'attāh | tômîkh |
| upon my lips | | Yahweh | the share of my inheritance | and my cup | You | the One Who hold |

**nor taketh up a reproach against his neighbour:** ... nor spread rumors about his neighbors, *Good News* ... casts no slur on his fellow man, *NIV* ... does not take away the good name of his neighbour, *BB* ... do not gossip, *NCV* ... Who carries no hate in his breast, *Fenton.*

**4. In whose eyes a vile person is contemned:** ... The despicable man is rejected from his presence, *Anchor* ... speaks out against sin, *LIVB* ... They do not respect hateful people, *NCV* ... he who has contempt for rogues, *Moffatt* ... In his eyes a bad man is despised, *Goodspeed* ... He scorns the reprobate, *Knox.*

**but he honoureth them that fear the LORD:** ... but those who fear Yahweh he feasts, *Anchor* ... esteems those who revere the LORD, *Berkeley* ... respects those who reverence the LORD, *Fenton* ... keeping his reverence for such as fear God, *Knox* ... commends the faithful followers of the Lord, *LIVB.*

**He that sweareth to his own hurt:** ... They keep their promises to their neighbors, *NCV* ... changes not his pledged word, *NAB* ... He who takes an oath against himself, *BB* ... who stands by an oath at any cost, *JB.*

**and changeth not:** ... did not waver, *Anchor* ... come what may, *Knox* ... though he may lose by it, *Moffatt* ... even when it hurts, *NCV* ... even if it ruins him, *LIVB.*

**5. He that putteth not out his money to usury:** ... Who lends not his money to cheat, *Fenton* ... who asks no interest on loans, *JB* ... does not crush his debtors with high interest rates, *LIVB.*

**nor taketh reward against the innocent:** ... nor accept compensation from the hungry, *Anchor* ... or for payment give false decisions against men who have done no wrong, *BB* ... not take a bribe against the innocent, *Berkeley* ... do not take money to hurt innocent people, *NCV.*

**He that doeth these things shall never be moved:** ... shall never be brought low, *NEB* ... never be disturbed, *NAB* ... never be rejected, *Moffatt* ... such a man shall stand firm forever, *LIVB.*

---

may ensue. The Law prohibited the substitution of another animal sacrifice for that which had been vowed (Lev. 27:10); and the Psalm uses the same word for "changeth" (HED #4306), with evident allusion to the prohibition, which must therefore have been known to the psalmist. Usury and bribery were common sins, as they still are in communities on the same industrial and judicial level as that mirrored in the Psalm.

The psalmist's last word goes beyond his question, in the clear recognition that such a character as he has outlined not only dwells in Yahweh's tent, but will stand unmoved, though all the world should rock. He does not see how far onward that "forever" may stretch, but he is sure that righteousness is the one stable thing in the universe, and there may have shone before him the hope that it was possible to travel on beyond the horizon that bounds this life.

***Psalm 16.*** *The progress of thought in this Psalm is striking. The singer is first a bold confessor in the face of idolatry and apostasy (vv. 1–4). Then the inward sweetness of his faith fills his soul, as is the reward of brave avowal, and he buries himself in the pure delights of communion with Yahweh (vv. 5–8). Finally, on the ground of such experience, he rises to the assurance that "its very sweetness yieldeth proof" that he and it are born for undying life (vv. 9ff).*

**16:1–4.** The first turn of thought (vv. 1–4) is clear in its general purport. It is a profession of adherence to Yahweh and of attachment to his lovers in the face of idol worship which had drawn some away. The brief cry for preservation at the beginning does not necessarily imply actual danger, but refers to the possible antagonism of the idol worshipers provoked by the psalmist's bold testimony. The two meanings of martyr, a "witness" and a "sufferer," are closely intertwined. The psalmist needs to be preserved, and he has a claim to be so, for his profession of faith has brought the peril.

The remarkable expression in v. 2b is best understood as unfolding the depth of what lies in saying, "My God." It means the cleaving to Him of the whole nature as the all-comprehending supply of every desire and capacity. "Good for me is none besides thee." This is the same high strain as in the cognate Ps. 73:25, where, as here, the joy of communion is seen in the very act of creating the confidence of immortality.

With dramatic abruptness, he points to the unnamed recreants from Yahweh. "Their griefs are many—they exchange [Yahweh] for another." Apparently, there was some tendency in Israel to idolatry, which gives energy to the psalmist's vehement assertion that he will not offer their libations of blood or say the abhorred names of the gods they pronounced. This state of things would suit much of Israel's history, during which temptations to idol worship were continually present, and the bloody libations would point to such abominations of human sacrifice as we know characterized the worship of Molech and Chemosh.

| 1518 | | 2346 | 5489.116, 3937 | 904, 5461 | 652, 5338 |
|---|---|---|---|---|---|
| n ms, ps 1cs | | n mp | v Qal pf 3cp, prep, ps 1cs | prep, art, adj | cj, n fs |
| גּוֹרָלִי | 6. | חֲבָלִים | נָפְלוּ־לִי | בַּנְּעִמִים | אַף־נַחֲלָת |
| gôrālî | | chăvālîm | nāphelû-lî | banne'imîm | 'aph-nachlāth |
| my lot | | ropes | they have fallen for me | with pleasantness | also an inheritance |

| 8601.112 | 6142 | | 1313.325 | 881, 3176 | 866 | 3398.111 | 652, 4050 |
|---|---|---|---|---|---|---|---|
| v Qal pf 3fs | prep, ps 1cs | | v Piel impf 1cs | do, pn | rel pron | v Qal pf 3ms, ps 1cs | cj, n mp |
| שָׁפְרָה | עָלָי | 7. | אֲבָרֵךְ | אֶת־יְהוָה | אֲשֶׁר | יְעָצָנִי | אַף־לֵילוֹת |
| shāpherāh | 'ālāy | | 'ăvārēkh | 'eth-yehwāh | 'ăsher | ye'ātsānî | 'aph-lêlôth |
| it is beautiful | beside me | | I will bless | Yahweh | Who | He has counseled me | also by night |

| 3364.316 | 3749 | | 8187.315 | 3176 | 3937, 5224 | 8878 | 3706 |
|---|---|---|---|---|---|---|---|
| v Piel pf 3cp, ps 1cs | n fp, ps 1cs | | v Piel pf 1cs | pn | prep, prep, ps 1cs | adv | cj |
| יִסְּרוּנִי | כִלְיוֹתָי | 8. | שִׁוִּיתִי | יְהוָה | לְנֶגְדִּי | תָמִיד | כִּי |
| yisserûnî | khilyôthāy | | shiwwîthî | yehwāh | leneghdî | thāmîdh | kî |
| they instruct me | my kidneys | | I have set | Yahweh | before me | continually | because |

| 4623, 3332 | 1118, 4267.225 | | 3937, 3772 | 7975.111 | 3949 | 1559.121 |
|---|---|---|---|---|---|---|
| prep, n fs, ps 1cs | neg part, v Niphal impf 1cs | | prep, adv | v Qal pf 3ms | n ms, ps 1cs | cj, v Qal impf 3ms |
| מִימִינִי | בַּל־אֶמּוֹט | 9. | לָכֵן | שָׂמַח | לִבִּי | וַיָּגֶל |
| mîmînî | bal-'emmôṯ | | lākhēn | sāmach | libbî | wayyāghel |
| at my right hand | I will not totter | | therefore | it is glad | my heart | and it rejoices |

**16:t. Michtam of David.**

**1. Preserve me, O God:** ... Keep me safe, *BB* ... guard me, *Fenton* ... Protect me, *JB* ... Watch over me, *KJVII.*

**for in thee do I put my trust:** ... I have sought refuge in you, *Anchor* ... You are my shelter, *Beck* ... I trust in you for safety, *Good News.*

**2. O my soul, thou hast said unto the LORD:** ... I tell the LIFE, *Fenton* ... confess, *Knox.*

**Thou art my Lord:** ... You are my Prince, *Fenton* ... thou art my welfare, *Goodspeed* ... whom I own as my God, *Knox* ... Thou, LORD, art my felicity, *NEB.*

**my goodness extendeth not to thee:** ... there is none above you, *Anchor* ... Every good thing I have comes from you, *NCV* ... I have no pleasure but in You, *Fenton* ... my welfare rests on thee alone, *Moffatt* ... my happiness is in none of the sacred spirits of the earth, *JB.*

**3. But to the saints that are in the earth:** ... As for the holy ones who were in the land, *Anchor* ... As to the gods who are in the land, *Goodspeed* ... There are faithful souls in this land of his, *Knox* ... I want the company of the godly men and women, *LIVB.*

**and to the excellent:** ... the mighty ones, *Anchor* ... they are the glorious, *Berkeley* ... the lofty ones, *Goodspeed* ... the honourable, *Young* ... they are the true nobility, *LIVB.*

**in whom is all my delight:** ... My glory and joy is with them, *Fenton* ... wondrous delight he gives me in their companionship, *Knox* ... How wonderfully has he made me cherish, *NAB* ... they are the wonderful ones I enjoy, *NCV* ... My greatest pleasure is to be with them, *Good News* ... I have no pleasure in them, *Goodspeed.*

**4. Their sorrows shall be multiplied:** ... The furious bring griefs on themselves, *Fenton* ... Their images are many, *Goodspeed* ... lay up fresh store of sorrows, *Knox* ... Sorrow on sorrow is theirs, *Moffatt* ... find trouble without end, *NEB.*

**that hasten after another god:** ... who court other gods, *NAB* ... who have hastened backward, *Young* ... Those who rush to other gods, *Good News* ... that betake themselves to alien gods, *Knox* ... others praise them, *Goodspeed.*

**their drink offerings of blood will I not offer:** ... I surely will not pour libations to them from my hands, *Anchor* ... I will not take drink offerings from their hands, *BB* ... Not with these will I pour out the blood of sacrifice, *Knox* ... I will not offer blood to those idols, *NCV* ... I will not take part in their sacrifices, *Good News.*

**nor take up their names into my lips:** ... neither make mention of their names with my lips, *Geneva* ... I will not take forbidden names on my lips, *Knox* ... their names I will never mention, *Moffatt* ... I will not worship their gods, *Good News.*

**5. The LORD is the portion of mine inheritance:** ... you have assigned me my portion, *NIV* ... You, LORD, are all I have, *Good News* ... My birthrite, my cup is Yahweh, *JB* ... No, it is the Lord I claim for my prize, *Knox* ... Thou art what I get from life, *Moffatt.*

**and of my cup:** ... the wine of my cup, *BB* ... a cup of smooth wine, *Beck* ... the Lord who fills my cup, *Knox* ... thou thyself art my share, *Moffatt* ... and you give me all I need, *Good News.*

**thou maintainest my lot:** ... He guards all that is mine, *LIVB* ... my future is in your hands, *Good News* ... He takes care of me, *NCV* ... thou, and no other, wilt assure my inheritance to me, *Knox*

**6. The lines are fallen unto me in pleasant places:** ... Fair are the places marked out for me, *BB* ... How wonderful are your gifts to me, *Good News* ... The measuring-line marks out for me a delightful place, *JB* ... He sees that I am given pleasant brooks and meadows as my share, *LIVB* ... the measuring lines have fallen on pleasant sites, *NAB.*

**yea, I have a goodly heritage:** ... my heritage is something beautiful, *Beck* ... My estates are all smiling on me, *Fenton* ... My inheritance indeed pleases me, *Goodspeed* ... a blissful heritage is mine, *Moffatt* ... my birthright is indeed lovely, *JB.*

**7. I will bless the LORD:** ... give thanks to, *Fenton* ... I bless the Eternal, *Moffatt* ... I will praise the LORD, *NIV.*

**who hath given me counsel:** ... has been my guide, *BB* ... who directs, *Fenton* ... who has given me wisdom, *KJVII* ... who schools me, *Knox* ... he advises me, *NCV.*

**my reins also instruct me in the night seasons:** ... in the night-time wisdom comes to me in my inward parts, *NEB* ... at night my heart teaches me what is right, *Beck* ... even in the night my heart exhorts me, *NAB* ... in the night my conscience warns me, *Good News* ... Even at night, I feel his leading, *NCV.*

**8. I have set the LORD always before me:** ... I keep Yahweh continually before me, *Anchor* ... I wish the LORD always with me, *Fenton* ... Always I can keep the Lord within sight, *Knox* ... I am always aware of the LORD's presence, *Good News* ... I am always thinking of the Lord, *LIVB.*

**because he is at my right hand:** ... with him so close, *Moffatt* ... is close by my side, *NCV* ... he is near, *Good News.*

**I shall not be moved:** ... I will never swerve, *Anchor* ... I never need to stumble or to fall, *LIVB* ... never removed from my side, *Fenton* ... I will not be hurt, *NCV* ... nothing can shake me, *Good News.*

**9. Therefore my heart is glad:** ... rejoices, *Anchor* ... Then my heart's joy and vigour would laugh, *Fenton* ... Glad and merry am I, *Knox* ... Therefore my heart exults, *NEB.*

**and my glory rejoiceth:** ... my liver leaps with joy, *Anchor* ... My soul is delighted, *Beck* ... my tongue reioiceth, *Geneva* ... my spirit, *Goodspeed.*

**my flesh also shall rest in hope:** ... my body dwells at ease, *Anchor* ... lie down in content, *Fenton* ... shall rest in confidence, *Knox* ... unafraid, *NEB* ... Even my body has hope, *NCV.*

**10. For thou wilt not leave my soul in hell:** ... you will not let my soul be prisoned in the underworld, *BB* ... You will not leave Me in the grave, *Beck* ... wilt not leave My soul in the realm of the dead, *Berkeley* ... will not abandon me to Sheol, *JB* ...

---

**16:5–8.** In the second section, the devout soul warms itself in the light of God and tells itself how rich it is. "The portion of mine inheritance" might refer to an allotted share of either food or land, but v. 6 favors the latter interpretation. "Cup" (HED #3683) here is not so much an image for that which satisfies thirst, although that would be beautiful, as for that which is appointed for one to experience. Such a use of the figure is familiar and brings it into line with the other of inheritance, which is plainly the principal, as that of the cup is dropped in the following words. Every godly man has the same possession and the same prohibitions as the priests had. Like them he is landless, and instead of estates he has Yahweh. They presented in mere outward fashion what is the very law of the devout life. The consciousness of perfect rest in perfect satisfaction of need and desires ever follows possession of God. So the calm rapture of v. 6 is the true utterance of the heart acquainted with God, and of it alone. One possession only bears reflection. Whatever else a man has, if he does not have Yahweh for his portion, he will be dissatisfied and will not be able to say, "My inheritance is fair to me."

No wonder the psalmist breaks into blessing. "In the night seasons," he says, when things are more clearly seen in the dark than by day, many a whisper from Yahweh steals into his ears. The upshot is a firm resolve to make really his what is his. "I set Yahweh always before me," since He is "always my lot." That effort of faith is the very life of devotion, then dedication.

**16:9–11.** The psalmist feels the certainty in all his complex nature, heart, soul and flesh. All three have their portion in the joy which it brings. The foundation of the exultation of heart and soul and of the quiet rest of flesh is not so much the assurance that after death there will be life, and after the grave a resurrection, as the confidence that there will be no death at all.

| 3638 | 652, 1340 | 8331.121 | 3937, 1020 | | 3706 | 3940, 6013.123 | 5497 |
|---|---|---|---|---|---|---|---|
| n ms, ps 1cs | cj, n ms, ps 1cs | v Qal impf 3ms | prep, n ms | 10. | cj | neg part, v Qal impf 2ms | n fs, ps 1cs |
| כְּבוֹדִי | אַף־בְּשָׂרִי | יִשְׁכֹּן | לָבֶטַח | | כִּי | לֹא־תַעֲזֹב | נַפְשִׁי |
| kᵉvôdhî | 'aph-bᵉsārî | yishkōn | lāvetach | | kî | lō'-tha'ăzōv | naphshî |
| my glory | also my body | it remains | with safety | | because | You will not abandon | my soul |

| 3937, 8061 | 3940, 5598.123 | 2728 | 3937, 7495.141 | 8273 |
|---|---|---|---|---|
| prep, pn | neg part, v Qal impf 2ms | n ms, ps 2ms | prep, v Qal inf con | n fs |
| לִשְׁאוֹל | לֹא־תִתֵּן | חֲסִידְךָ | לִרְאוֹת | שָׁחַת |
| lish'ôl | lō'-thittēn | chăsîdhᵉkhā | lir'ôth | shachath |
| to Sheol | You will not allow | your godly ones | to see | a pit |

| | 3156.523 | 758 | 2522 | 7883 | 7977 | 881, 6686 | 5456 |
|---|---|---|---|---|---|---|---|
| 11. | v Hiphil impf 2ms, ps 1cs | *n ms* | n mp | *n ms* | n fp | do, n mp, ps 2ms | adj |
| | תּוֹדִיעֵנִי | אֹרַח | חַיִּים | שֹׂבַע | שְׂמָחוֹת | אֶת־פָּנֶיךָ | נְעִמוֹת |
| | thôdhî'ênî | 'ōrach | chayyîm | sōva' | sᵉmāchôth | 'eth-pānêkhā | nᵉ'imôth |
| | You cause me to know | the path of | life | fulness of | joy | your presence | pleasures |

| 904, 3332 | 5516 | | 8940 | 3937, 1784 | | 8471.131 | 3176 | 6928 |
|---|---|---|---|---|---|---|---|---|
| prep, n fs, ps 2ms | n ms | 17:t | n fs | prep, pn | 1. | v Qal impv 2ms | pn | n ms |
| בִּימִינְךָ | נֶצַח | | תְּפִלָּה | לְדָוִד | | שִׁמְעָה | יְהוָה | צֶדֶק |
| bîmînᵉkhā | netsach | | tᵉphillāh | lᵉdhāwidh | | shim'āh | yᵉhwāh | tsedheq |
| in your right hand | forever | | a Prayer | of David | | hear | O Yahweh | what is right |

| 7477.531 | 7726 | 237.531 | 8940 | 904, 3940 | 8004 | 4983 |
|---|---|---|---|---|---|---|
| v Hiphil impv 2ms | n fs, ps 1cs | v Hiphil impv 2ms | n fs, ps 1cs | prep, neg part | *n fd* | n fs |
| הַקְשִׁיבָה | רִנָּתִי | הַאֲזִינָה | תְּפִלָּתִי | בְּלֹא | שִׂפְתֵי | מִרְמָה |
| haqŏshîvāh | rinnāthî | ha'ăzînāh | thᵉphillāthî | bᵉlō' | siphthê | mirmāh |
| be attentive to | my lamentation | listen to | my prayer | not with | lips of | deceit |

| | 4623, 3937, 6686 | 5122 | 3428.121 | 6084 | 2463.127 | 4478 |
|---|---|---|---|---|---|---|
| 2. | prep, prep, n mp, ps 2ms | n ms, ps 1cs | v Qal juss 3ms | n fd, ps 2ms | v Qal juss 3fp | n mp |
| | מִלְּפָנֶיךָ | מִשְׁפָּטִי | יֵצֵא | עֵינֶיךָ | תֶּחֱזֶינָה | מֵישָׁרִים |
| | millᵉphānêkhā | mishpāṭî | yētsē' | 'ênêkhā | techĕzênāh | mêshārîm |
| | from your presence | my justice | may it go out | your eyes | may they behold | uprightness |

| | 1010.113 | 3949 | 6734.113 | 4050 | 7170.113 |
|---|---|---|---|---|---|
| 3. | v Qal pf 2ms | n ms, ps 1cs | v Qal pf 2ms | n ms | v Qal pf 2ms, ps 1cs |
| | בָּחַנְתָּ | לִבִּי | פָּקַדְתָּ | לַיְלָה | צְרַפְתַּנִי |
| | bāchantā | libbî | pāqadhtā | laylāh | tsᵉraphtanî |
| | You have examined | my heart | You have examined | at night | You have refined me |

| 1118, 4834.123 | 2246.115 | 1118, 5882.121, 6552 | | 3937, 6715 |
|---|---|---|---|---|
| neg part, v Qal impf 2ms | v Qal pf 1cs | neg part, v Qal impf 3ms, n ms, ps 1cs | 4. | prep, *n fp* |
| בַּל־תִּמְצָא | זַמֹּתִי | בַּל־יַעֲבָר־פִּי | | לִפְעֻלּוֹת |
| val-timtsā' | zammōthî | bal-ya'ăvār-pî | | liph'ullôth |
| You will not find | I have considered | it does not pass through my mouth | | about the works of |

never wilt thou let me sink to death, *Moffatt.*

**neither wilt thou suffer thine Holy One to see corruption:** ... you will not let your loved one see the place of death, *BB* ... or let Your loved One experience decay, *Beck* ... Thou wilt not let the godly one see the Pit, *Goodspeed* ... you cannot allow your faithful servant to see the abyss, *JB* ... You will not let your holy one rot, *NCV.*

**11. Thou wilt show me the path of life:** ... You will make me know the path of life eternal, *Anchor* ... You will make clear to me the way of life, *BB* ... You will teach me, *JB* ... thou wilt reveal the path to life, *Moffatt* ... You will teach me how to live a holy life, *NCV.*

**in thy presence is fulness of joy:** ... filling me with happiness before you, *Anchor* ... where you are joy is complete, *BB* ... plenty of joy in Your presence, *Beck* ... Being with you will fill me with joy, *NCV* ... unbounded joy in your presence, *JB.*

**at thy right hand there are pleasures for evermore:** ... delightful things at Your right hand forever, *Beck* ... are delights that will endure for ever, *Knox* ... bliss for evermore, *MAST* ... to the bliss of being close to thee forever, *Moffatt.*

**17:t. A Prayer of David.**

**1. Hear the right:** ... to my just complaint give ear, *Knox* ... my plea for vindication, *Anchor* ... Let my cause come to your ears, *BB* ... Listen to the innocent, *Moffatt* ... hear me begging for fairness, *NCV.*

**O LORD:** ... Yahweh, *Anchor* ... Eternal One, *Moffatt.*

**attend unto my cry:** ... Bend forward, *Fenton* ... pay attention, *JB* ... heed our wail, *Moffatt* ... do not spurn my cry for aid, *Knox.*

**give ear unto my prayer:** ... listen, *Fenton* ... lend an ear, *JB.*

**that goeth not out of feigned lips:** ... from false lips, *BB* ... innocent of all deceit, *NEB* ... no dishonesty on my lips, *Beck* ... lips that do not lie, *Fenton* ... no treacherous lips, *Knox.*

**2. Let my sentence come forth from thy presence:** ... my justice shine before you, *Anchor* ... Be my judge, *BB* ... Publicly acquit me, *LIVB* ... May my vindication come from you, *NIV* ... speed thy sentence in our favour, *Moffatt.*

**let thine eyes behold:** ... look upon, *ASV* ... may your eyes gaze, *Anchor.*

**the things that are equal:** ... my integrity, *Anchor.*

**3. Thou hast proved mine heart:** ... You have put my heart to the test, *BB* ... perceived my rights, *Fenton* ... Examine my heart, *Anchor.*

**thou hast visited me in the night:** ... searching me in the night, *BB* ... By nightly visits, *Fenton* ... examine me at night, *JB* ... probe me at night, *Anchor* ... Hast made inspection by night, *Rotherham.*

**thou hast tried me:** ... purified me by fire, *Goodspeed* ... Hast refined me, *Rotherham* ... test me with fire, *Anchor.*

**and shalt find nothing:** ... seen no evil purpose in me, *BB* ... hast found no evil intention, *Berkeley* ... found no crime in me, *Fenton* ... wilt find no treachery in me, *Knox.*

**I am purposed that my mouth shall not transgress:** ... My thoughts pass not over my mouth, *Young* ... no sin of speech, *Moffatt* ... my mouth does not go beyond my thoughts, *KJVII* ... I have not sinned with my mouth as most people do, *JB.*

**4. Concerning the works of men:** ... In respect to the acts of men, *Berkeley* ... As for what others do, *Beck* ... as for human acts, *Fenton.*

**by the word of thy lips I have kept me:** ... by Your word of warning, *Beck* ... I have kept the prescribed ways, *Goodspeed* ... I guarded myself against, *Berkeley.*

---

The correspondence between his effort of faith in v. 8 and his final position in v. 11 is striking. He who sets Yahweh continually before himself will, in due time, come where there are fullness of joys before God's face. He who here, amid distractions and sorrows, has kept Yahweh at his right hand as his Counselor, Defender and Companion, will one day stand at Yahweh's right hand and be satisfied forevermore with the uncloying and inexhaustible pleasures that abide there.

***Psalm 17.*** *The Psalm is called a "prayer," a title given to only four other Psalms, none of which are in Book 1. It has three movements, marked by the repetition of the name of God, which does not appear elsewhere, except in v. 14. These three are vv. 1–5, in which the cry for help is founded on a strong profession of innocence; vv. 6–12, in which it is based on a vivid description of the enemies; and vv. 13ff, in which it soars into the pure air of mystic devotion and thence looks downward on the transient prosperity of the foe and upward, in a rapture of hope, to the face of God.*

**17:1–2.** The petition proper and its ground are both strongly marked by conscious innocence and therefore sound strange to our ears, trained as we have been by the NT to deeper insight into sin. This sufferer asks God to "hear righteousness," i.e., his righteous cause. The fervor of his prayer is marked by its designation as "my cry," the high-pitched note which is usually the expression of joy, but here of sore need and strong desire. He boldly asks for his "sentence from thy face," and the ground of that petition is that "thine eyes behold rightly." Was there, then, no inner baseness that should have toned down such confidence? Was this prayer not much the same as the Pharisee's in Christ's parable? The answer is partly found in the considerations that the innocence professed is especially in regard to the occasions of the psalmist's present distress and that the acquittal by deliverance which he asks is God's testimony that as to these he was slandered and clear.

**17:3–5.** The general drift of vv. 3ff is clear, but the precise meaning and connection are extremely obscure. It has been twisted in all sorts of ways, the

| 119<br>n ms<br>אָדָם<br>'ādhām<br>humankind | 904, 1745<br>prep, *n ms*<br>בִּדְבַר<br>bidhvar<br>by the word of | 8004<br>n fd, ps 2ms<br>שְׂפָתֶיךָ<br>sephāthêkhā<br>your lips | 603<br>pers pron<br>אֲנִי<br>'ănî<br>I | 8490.115<br>v Qal pf 1cs<br>שָׁמַרְתִּי<br>shāmartî<br>I have kept watch | 758<br>*n fp*<br>אָרְחוֹת<br>'ārchôth<br>the paths of | 6782<br>n ms<br>פָּרִיץ<br>pārits<br>the violent |
|---|---|---|---|---|---|---|

| 5. | 8881.142<br>v Qal inf abs<br>תָּמֹךְ<br>tāmōkh<br>holding fast | 864<br>n fp, ps 1cs<br>אֲשֻׁרַי<br>'ăshuray<br>my steps | 904, 4724<br>prep, n mp, ps 2ms<br>בְּמַעְגְּלוֹתֶיךָ<br>bema'äggelôthêkhā<br>on your paths | 1118, 4267.216<br>neg part, v Niphal pf 3cp<br>בַּל־נָמוֹטּוּ<br>bal-nāmôṭû<br>they have not faltered | 6718<br>n fp, ps 1cs<br>פְעָמָי<br>phe'āmāy<br>my feet |
|---|---|---|---|---|---|

| 6. | 603, 7410.115<br>pers pron, v Qal pf 1cs, ps 2ms<br>אֲנִי־קְרָאתִיךָ<br>'ănî-qōrā'thîkhā<br>I have called You | 3706, 6257.123<br>cj, v Qal impf 2ms, ps 1cs<br>כִי־תַעֲנֵנִי<br>khî-tha'ănēnî<br>because You will answer me | 418<br>n ms<br>אֵל<br>'ēl<br>O God | 5371.531, 238<br>v Hiphil impv 2ms, n fs, ps 2ms<br>הַט־אָזְנְךָ<br>haṭ-'oznekhā<br>incline your ear |
|---|---|---|---|---|

| 3937<br>prep, ps 1cs<br>לִי<br>lî<br>to me | 8471.131<br>v Qal impv 2ms<br>שְׁמַע<br>shema'<br>hear | 577<br>n fs, ps 1cs<br>אִמְרָתִי<br>'imrāthî<br>my words | 7. | 6623.531<br>v Hiphil impv 2ms<br>הַפְלֵה<br>haphlēh<br>do something extraordinary | 2721<br>n mp, ps 2ms<br>חֲסָדֶיךָ<br>chăsādhêkhā<br>your steadfast love |
|---|---|---|---|---|---|

| 3588.551<br>v Hiphil ptc ms<br>מוֹשִׁיעַ<br>môshîa'<br>O Savior | 2725.152<br>v Qal act ptc mp<br>חוֹסִים<br>chôsîm<br>those who seek refuge | 4623, 7251.752<br>prep, v Hithpolel ptc mp<br>מִמִּתְקוֹמְמִים<br>mimmithqômemîm<br>from those who rise up | 904, 3332<br>prep, n fs, ps 2ms<br>בִּימִינֶךָ<br>bîmînekhā<br>by your right hand |
|---|---|---|---|

| 8. | 8490.131<br>v Qal impv 2ms, ps 1cs<br>שָׁמְרֵנִי<br>shāmerēnî<br>protect me | 3626, 385<br>prep, *n ms*<br>כְּאִישׁוֹן<br>ke'îshôn<br>like the pupil of | 1351, 6084<br>*n fs*, n fs<br>בַּת־עָיִן<br>bath-'āyin<br>the daughter of the eye | 904, 7009<br>prep, *n ms*<br>בְּצֵל<br>betsēl<br>in the shadow of | 3796<br>n fd, ps 2ms<br>כְּנָפֶיךָ<br>kenāphêkhā<br>your wings |
|---|---|---|---|---|---|

| 5846.523<br>v Hiphil impf 2ms, ps 1cs<br>תַּסְתִּירֵנִי<br>tastîrēnî<br>You hide me | 9. | 4623, 6686<br>prep, *n mp*<br>מִפְּנֵי<br>mippenê<br>from before | 7857<br>n mp<br>רְשָׁעִים<br>reshā'îm<br>the wicked | 2182<br>rel pron<br>זוּ<br>zû<br>who | 8161.116<br>v Qal pf 3cp, pf 1cs<br>שַׁדּוּנִי<br>shaddûnî<br>they ravage me | 342.152<br>v Qal act ptc mp, ps 1cs<br>אֹיְבַי<br>'ōyevay<br>my enemies |
|---|---|---|---|---|---|---|

| 904, 5497<br>prep, n fs<br>בְּנֶפֶשׁ<br>benephesh<br>on me | 5545.526<br>v Hiphil impf 3mp<br>יַקִּיפוּ<br>yaqqîphû<br>they encompass | 6142<br>prep, ps 1cs<br>עָלָי<br>'ālāy<br>beside me | 10. | 2561<br>n ms, ps 3mp<br>חֶלְבָּמוֹ<br>chelbāmô<br>their choicest parts | 5646.116<br>v Qal pf 3cp<br>סָגְרוּ<br>sāgherû<br>they have closed | 6552<br>n ms, ps 3mp<br>פִּימוֹ<br>pîmô<br>their mouth |
|---|---|---|---|---|---|---|

**from the paths of the destroyer:** ... from the ways of the violent, *BB* ... I shunned the broken paths, *Fenton* ... I have not done what evil people do, *NCV.*

**5. Hold up my goings in thy paths:** ... Maintain my steps in Your tracks, *KJVII* ... My steps have held fast to thy tracks, *Goodspeed* ... I kept close to Your ways, *Fenton* ... to the rugged paths, *Anchor* ... I have done what you told me, *NCV.*

**that my footsteps slip not:** ... My steps have not slidden, *Young* ... My legs held firmly, *Anchor* ... My footsteps never swerved, *Fenton* ... have not faltered, *Goodspeed* ... have not been shaken, *Rotherham.*

**6. I have called upon thee:** ... I call, for GOD replies, *Fenton* ... now I cry to thee, *Knox.*

**for thou wilt hear me, O God:** ... O that you would answer me, *Anchor* ... the God who ever hearest me, *Knox.*

**incline thine ear unto me, and hear my speech:** ... hear what I say, *JB.*

**7. Show thy marvellous lovingkindness:** ... Make clear the wonder of your mercy, *BB* ... Do Your wonderfully kind acts, *Beck* ... Show the evidence of your faithful love, *JB* ... Make passing great Thy mercies, *MAST.*

**O thou that savest by thy right hand them which put their trust in thee:** ... O Saviour of the confiding, *Young* ... thou that art the Sauiour, *Geneva* ... O savior of those who seek shelter, *Goodspeed* ... saviour of those who hope in your strength, *JB* ... none ever sought sanctuary at thy right hand in vain, *Knox* ... Strong Saviour, in thy kindness interpose, *Moffatt.*

**from those that rise up against them:** ... Fell those who revile you, *Anchor* ... From dominating foes, *Fenton* ... muzzle your assailants, *Anchor* ... From their adversaries, *Goodspeed* ... from withstanders, *Young.*

**8. Keep me as the apple of the eye:** ... Guard like my trembling eye, *Fenton* ... Protect me as you would your very eyes, *Good News* ... the pupil, the daughter of the eye, *Goodspeed* ... light of your eyes, *BB.*

**hide me under the shadow of thy wings:** ... covering me with the shade of your wings, *BB* ... as you hover over me, *LIVB.*

**9. From the wicked that oppress me, from my deadly enemies, who compass me about:** ... wicked who stripped me, *KJVII* ... from my mortal enemies, *Beck* ... wicked men who have maltreated me, *Berkeley* ... evil-doers who are violent to me, *BB* ... enemies encircle me with murder in their eyes, *LIVB.*

**10. They are inclosed in their own fat:** ... They close up their callous hearts, *NIV* ... They are clogged with their blubber, *Anchor* ... they have no pity, *Good News* ... They have closed their unfeeling heart, *NASB* ... Engrossed in themselves, *JB.*

**with their mouth they speak proudly:** ... speak arrogance itself, *Anchor* ... speaks haughty threats, *Fenton* ... they are mouthing arrogant words, *JB* ... their words are insolent, *Moffatt* ... and brag about themselves, *NCV.*

---

Masoretic accents have been disregarded, the division of verses set aside, and still no proposed rendering of parts of vv. 3ff, is wholly satisfactory. The psalmist deals with heart, lips and feet (i.e., thoughts, words and deeds) and declares the innocence of all. The knot has been untied in two ways: "My [evil] purpose shall not pass," or, taking the word as a verb and regarding the clause as hypothetical, "Should I think evil, it shall not pass."

Either of these renderings has the advantage of retaining the recognized meaning of the verb and of avoiding neglect of the accent. Such a rendering has been objected to as being inconsistent with the previous clause, but the psalmist may be looking back to it, feeling that his partial self-knowledge makes it a bold statement, and thus far limiting it, that if any evil thought is found in his heart, it is sternly repressed in silence.

Obscurity continues in v. 4. The usual rendering, "As for [or, during] the works of men, by the word of thy mouth I have kept me," is against the accents, which make the principal division of the verse fall after "lips." However, no satisfactory sense results if the accentuation is followed, unless we suppose a verb is implied, such as, "stand fast," getting the profession of steadfastness in the words of God's lips, in the face of men's self-willed doings. But this is precarious, and probably the ordinary way of cutting the knot by neglecting the accents is best. In any case, the avowal of innocence passes here from thoughts and words to acts.

**17:6–12.** The "I" in v. 6 is emphatic and may be taken as gathering up the psalmist's preceding declarations and humbly laying them before God as a plea. He says, "I, who thus cleave to thy ways, call upon thee, and my prayer is that of faith, which is sure of answer." That confidence does not make the petition superfluous, but rather encourages it.

The aspects of the divine character, which the psalmist employs to move God's heart and to encourage his own, are contained first in the name "God" and next in the reference to his habitual dealings with trusting souls, in v. 7. From of old it has been his way to be the Savior of those who take refuge in Him from their enemies, and his right hand has shielded them.

The eye which steadily looks on God can look calmly at dangers. It is with no lack of faith that the poet's thoughts turn to his enemies. Fears that have become prayers are already more than half conquered. By recounting his perils, the psalmist would move God to help, not bring himself to despair. In the expression of the enemy "spoiling" him or laying him waste, the word used is the same as that for the ravages of invaders. They are "enemies in soul," deadly, or perhaps "against [my] soul." They are pitiless and proud, closing their hearts, which prosperity has made "fat" or arrogant

| 1744.316<br>v Piel pf 3cp<br>דִּבְּרוּ<br>dibberû<br>they have spoken | 904, 1375<br>prep, n fs<br>בְגֵאוּת<br>veghē'ûth<br>with pride | **11.** | 864<br>n fp, ps 1cp<br>אַשֻּׁרֵינוּ<br>'ashshurênû<br>our steps | 6498<br>adv<br>עַתָּה<br>'attāh<br>now | 5621.116<br>v Qal pf 3cp, ps 1cs<br>סְבָבוּנִי<br>sevāvûnî<br>they surround me | 6084<br>n fd, ps 3mp<br>עֵינֵיהֶם<br>'ênêhem<br>their eyes | 8308.116<br>v Qal pf 3cp<br>יָשִׁיתוּ<br>yāshîthû<br>they have set |
|---|---|---|---|---|---|---|---|

| 3937, 5371.141<br>prep, v Qal inf con<br>לִנְטוֹת<br>lintôth<br>to bend | 904, 800<br>prep, art, n fs<br>בָּאָרֶץ<br>bā'ārets<br>on the ground | **12.** | 1886<br>n ms, ps 3ms<br>דִּמְיֹנוֹ<br>dimyōnô<br>his likeness | 3626, 765<br>prep, n ms<br>כְּאַרְיֵה<br>ke'aryēh<br>like a lion | 3826.121<br>v Qal impf 3ms<br>יִכְסוֹף<br>yikhsōph<br>he desires | 3937, 3072.141<br>prep, v Qal inf con<br>לִטְרוֹף<br>litrōph<br>to tear |
|---|---|---|---|---|---|---|

| 3626, 3841<br>cj, prep, n ms<br>וְכִכְפִיר<br>wekhikhphîr<br>and like a young lion | 3553.151<br>v Qal act ptc ms<br>יֹשֵׁב<br>yōshēv<br>sitting | 904, 4718<br>prep, n mp<br>בְּמִסְתָּרִים<br>bemistārîm<br>in ambush | **13.** | 7251.131<br>v Qal impv 2ms<br>קוּמָה<br>qûmāh<br>rise | 3176<br>pn<br>יְהוָה<br>yehwāh<br>O Yahweh | 7207.331<br>v Piel impv 2ms<br>קַדְּמָה<br>qaddemāh<br>confront |
|---|---|---|---|---|---|---|

| 6686<br>n mp, ps 3ms<br>פָנָיו<br>phānâv<br>their face | 3895.531<br>v Hiphil impv 2ms, ps 3ms<br>הַכְרִיעֵהוּ<br>hakhrî'ēhû<br>cause them to bow down | 6647.331<br>v Piel impv 2ms<br>פַּלְּטָה<br>palletāh<br>set free | 5497<br>n fs, ps 1cs<br>נַפְשִׁי<br>naphshî<br>my life | 4623, 7857<br>prep, n ms<br>מֵרָשָׁע<br>mērāshā'<br>from the wicked | 2820<br>n fs, ps 2ms<br>חַרְבֶּךָ<br>charbekhā<br>your sword |
|---|---|---|---|---|---|

| **14.** | 4623, 5139<br>prep, n mp<br>מִמְתִים<br>mimthîm<br>from men | 3135<br>n fs, ps 2ms<br>יָדְךָ<br>yādhekhā<br>your hand | 3176<br>pn<br>יְהוָה<br>yehwāh<br>O Yahweh | 4623, 5139<br>prep, n mp<br>מִמְתִים<br>mimthîm<br>from men | 4623, 2566<br>prep, n ms<br>מֵחֶלֶד<br>mēcheledh<br>of the world | 2610<br>n ms, ps 3mp<br>חֶלְקָם<br>chelqām<br>their portion | 904, 2522<br>prep, art, n mp<br>בַּחַיִּים<br>bachayyîm<br>in life |
|---|---|---|---|---|---|---|---|

| 7121.155<br>cj, v Qal pass ptc ms, ps 2ms<br>וּצְפִינְךָ<br>ûtsephînekhā<br>and what You have stored up | 4527.322<br>v Piel impf 3fs<br>תְּמַלֵּא<br>temallē'<br>it will be filled | 1027<br>n fs, ps 3mp<br>בִטְנָם<br>vitnām<br>their belly | 7881.126<br>v Qal impf 3mp<br>יִשְׂבְּעוּ<br>yisbe'û<br>they are satisfied | 1158<br>n mp<br>בָנִים<br>vānîm<br>children |
|---|---|---|---|---|

| 5299.516<br>cj, v Hiphil pf 3cp<br>וְהִנִּיחוּ<br>wehinîchû<br>and they have left behind | 3615<br>n ms, ps 3mp<br>יִתְרָם<br>yithrām<br>their remainder | 3937, 5985<br>prep, n mp, ps 3mp<br>לְעוֹלְלֵיהֶם<br>le'ôlelêhem<br>to their children | **15.** | 603<br>pers pron<br>אֲנִי<br>'ănî<br>I | 904, 6928<br>prep, n ms<br>בְּצֶדֶק<br>betsedheq<br>in righteousness |
|---|---|---|---|---|---|

| 2463.125<br>v Qal impf 1cs<br>אֶחֱזֶה<br>'echĕzeh<br>I will behold | 6686<br>n mp, ps 2ms<br>פָנֶיךָ<br>phānêkhā<br>your face | 7881.125<br>v Qal juss 1cs<br>אֶשְׂבְּעָה<br>'esbe'āh<br>let me be satisfied | 904, 7301.541<br>prep, v Hiphil inf con<br>בְהָקִיץ<br>vehāqîts<br>when awaking | 8874<br>n fs, ps 2ms<br>תְּמוּנָתֶךָ<br>temûnāthekhā<br>your form | **18:t** | 3937, 5514.351<br>prep, art, v Piel ptc ms<br>לַמְנַצֵּחַ<br>lamnatstsēach<br>to the director |
|---|---|---|---|---|---|---|

**11. They have now compassed us in our steps:** … at every step they dog us, *Moffatt* … Wherever we go, they have surrounded us, *Berkeley* … My legs tottered, they surrounded me, *Anchor* … Who are a wall round me, *Fenton* … their stealthy tread closes in on me, *Knox*.

**they have set their eyes bowing down to the earth:** … they fixed their eyes To pitch me into the very Land of Perdition, *Anchor* … looking determined to throw me to the ground, *Beck* … Who strive to strike to earth, *Fenton* … watching for a chance to hurl me to the ground, *JB*.

**12. Like as a lion that is greedy of his prey:** … that is avid for prey, *Anchor* … craving to tear, *Berkeley* … wanting to tear me to pieces, *Good News* … preparing to pounce, *JB*.

**and as it were a young lion lurking in secret places:** … crouching in ambush, *JB* … lying in his hiding-place, *Beck* ... lurks in ambush, *Anchor* ... Like Tigers in their Den, *Fenton* ... Lions whelpe lurking, *Geneva.*

**13. Arise, O LORD, disappoint him:** ... go before his face, *Young* ... O Yahweh, confront his fury, *Anchor* ... Eternal, *Moffatt* ... oppose him to his face, *Beck.*

**cast him down:** ... put him down on his knees, *Beck* ... throw him to the ground, *Knox* ... Cause him to bend, *Young.*

**deliver my soul from the wicked:** ... be my saviour from the evil-doer, *BB* ... Rescue my life from the wicked, *Anchor* ... Deliver my soul from the lawless one, *Rotherham.*

**which is thy sword:** ... Your sword defends my life, *Fenton* ... bare thy sword, *Knox.*

**14. From men which are thy hand, O LORD:** ... With your hand, *BB* ... Your hand from murderers, *Fenton* ... raise thy hand, *Knox* ... May thy hand slay them, *Moffatt.*

**from men of the world:** ... from men of this age, *Darby* ... From men who herd with beasts, *Fenton* ... mortal men, *Knox.*

**which have their portion in this life:** ... whose heritage is in this life, *BB* ... who have only this life and don't go on, *Beck* ... whose lot in life is fatness, *Goodspeed* ... whose only concern is earthly gain, *LIVB* ... whose reward is in this life, *NCV.*

**and whose belly thou fillest:** ... gorged as they are, *NEB* ... whom you make full, *BB* ... whose stomach Thou dost fill, *Berkeley* ... You still the hunger, *NIV* ... They have plenty of food, *NCV.*

**with thy hid treasure:** ... with what thou hast stored for them, *RSV* ... with your secret wealth, *BB* ... from your store, *JB* ... with thy good things, *NEB.*

**they are full of children:** ... They have many sons, *NCV* ... May their children enjoy abundance, *Anchor* ... may their sons be satisfied, *Beck* ... may there be enough for their children, *Good News* ... their children will have all they desire, *JB.*

**and leave the rest of their substance:** ... leave their wealth, *Anchor* ... leave their remainder, *Berkeley* ... leave what they have left, *Beck* ... leave their surplus, *JB* ... much money, *NCV.*

**to their babes:** ... young ones, *Berkeley* ... infants, *Beck* ... children's children, *Good News* ... new heirs, *Knox.*

**15. As for me, I will behold thy face in righteousness:** ... in my uprightness, *JB* ... with upright heart, *Knox* ... our innocent lives, *Moffatt.*

**I shall be satisfied:** ... I will be saturated, *Anchor* ... it will be joy enough, *BB* ... enjoy thy favour, *Moffatt.*

**when I awake, with thy likeness:** ... with your being, *Anchor* ... with beholding thy form, *ASV* ... with thine image, *Geneva* ... And wake content with You, *Fenton* ... I shall be filled with the vision of you, *JB.*

**18:t. To the chief Musician, A Psalm of David, the servant of the LORD, who spake unto the LORD the words of this song in the day that the LORD delivered him from the hand of all his enemies, and from the hand of Saul: And he said,**

---

against the entrance of compassion and boasting of their own power and contemptuous scoffs at his weakness. They ring him round, watching his steps.

**17:13–15.** The third part renews the cry for deliverance and unites the points of view of the preceding parts in inverted order, describing first the enemies and then the psalmist. But with these significant differences, he describes the fruits of his communion with God, that now the former are painted, not in their fierceness, but in their transitory attachments and low delights, and that the latter does not bemoan his own helplessness or build on his own integrity, but feeds his soul on his confidence of the vision of God and the satisfaction which it will bring. The smoke clouds that rolled in the former parts have caught fire, and one clear shoot of flame aspires heavenward. He who makes his needs known to God gains for immediate answer "the peace of God, which passeth understanding" (Phil. 4:7), and can await God's time for the rest. The crouching lion is still ready to spring, but the psalmist hides himself behind God, Whom he asks to face the brute and make him grovel at his feet.

***Psalm 18.*** *The description of the theophany (vv. 7–19) and that of the psalmist's God-won victories (vv. 32–46) appear to refer to the same facts, transfigured in the former case by devout imagination and presented in the latter in their actual form. These two portions make the two central masses around which the Psalm is built up. They are connected by a transitional section, of which the main theme is the power of character to determine God's aspect to a man as exemplified in the singer's experience; and they are preceded and followed by an introduction and a conclusion, throbbing with gratitude and love to Yahweh, the Deliverer.*

**18:1–3.** The preluding invocation in vv. 1ff at once touches the high-water mark of OT devotion and

| 3937, 5860 | 3176 | 3937, 1784 | 866 | 1744.311 | 3937, 3176 | 881, 1745 | 8303 |
|---|---|---|---|---|---|---|---|
| prep, *n ms* | pn | prep, pn | rel pron | v Piel pf 3ms | prep, pn | do, *n mp* | art, **n ts** |
| לְעֶבֶד | יְהוָה | לְדָוִד | אֲשֶׁר | דִּבֶּר | לַיהוָה | אֶת־דִּבְרֵי | הַשִּׁירָה |
| le'evedh | yehwāh | ledhāwidh | 'ăsher | dibber | layhwāh | 'eth-divrê | hashshîrāh |
| to the servant of | Yahweh | of David | who | he spoke | to Yahweh | the words of | the song |

| 2148 | 904, 3219 | 5526.511, 3176 | 881 | 4623, 3834 | 3725, 342.152 |
|---|---|---|---|---|---|
| art, dem pron | prep, n ms | v Hiphil pf 3ms, pn | do, ps 3ms | prep, *n fs* | *n ms*, v Qal act ptc mp, ps 3ms |
| הַזֹּאת | בְּיוֹם | הִצִּיל־יְהוָה | אוֹתוֹ | מִכַּף | כָּל־אֹיְבָיו |
| hazzō'th | beyôm | hitstsîl-yehwāh | 'ôthô | mikkaph | kol-'ōyevâv |
| the this | on the day | Yahweh preserved | him | from the hand of | all his enemies |

| 4623, 3135 | 8062 | 569.121 | | 7638.125 | 3176 | 2483 |
|---|---|---|---|---|---|---|
| cj, prep, *n fs* | pn | v Qal impf 3ms | **1.** | v Qal impf 1cs, ps 2ms | pn | n ms, ps 1cs |
| וּמִיַּד | שָׁאוּל | וַיֹּאמַר | | אֶרְחָמְךָ | יְהוָה | חִזְקִי |
| ûmîyadh | shā'ûl | wayyō'mar | | 'erchāmekhā | yehwāh | chizqî |
| and from the hand of | Saul | and he said | | I love You | O Yahweh | my Strength |

| | 3176 | 5748 | 4859 | 6647.351 | 418 | 6962 |
|---|---|---|---|---|---|---|
| **2.** | pn | n ms, ps 1cs | cj, n fs, ps 1cs | cj, v Piel ptc ms, ps 1cs | n ms, ps 1cs | n ms, ps 1cs |
| | יְהוָה | סַלְעִי | וּמְצוּדָתִי | וּמְפַלְטִי | אֵלִי | צוּרִי |
| | yehwāh | sal'î | ûmetsûdhāthî | ûmephaltî | 'ēlî | tsûrî |
| | Yahweh | my Rock | and my Fortress | and the One Who sets me free | my God | my Rock |

| 2725.125, 904 | 4182 | 7451, 3589 | 5021 |
|---|---|---|---|
| v Qal impf 1cs, prep, ps 3ms | n ms, ps 1cs | cj, *n fs*, n ms, ps 1cs | n ms, ps 1cs |
| אֶחֱסֶה־בּוֹ | מָגִנִּי | וְקֶרֶן־יִשְׁעִי | מִשְׂגַּבִּי |
| 'echĕseh-bô | māghinnî | weqeren-yish'î | misgabbî |
| I will take refuge in Him | my Shield | and the Horn of my salvation | my Stronghold |

| | 2054.455 | 7410.125 | 3176 | 4623, 342.152 | 3588.225 |
|---|---|---|---|---|---|
| **3.** | v Pual ptc ms | v Qal impf 1cs | pn | cj, prep, v Qal act ptc mp, ps 1cs | v Niphal impf 1cs |
| | מְהֻלָּל | אֶקְרָא | יְהוָה | וּמִן־אֹיְבַי | אִוָּשֵׁעַ |
| | mehullāl | 'eqōrā' | yehwāh | ûmin-'ōyevay | 'iwwāshēa' |
| | One Who is praised | I will call | Yahweh | and from my enemies | I am saved |

| | 680.116 | 2346, 4323 | 5337 | 1139 | 1227.326 |
|---|---|---|---|---|---|
| **4.** | v Qal pf 3cp, ps 1cs | *n mp*, n ms | cj, *n mp* | n ms | v Piel impf 3mp, ps 1cs |
| | אֲפָפוּנִי | חֶבְלֵי־מָוֶת | וְנַחֲלֵי | בְלִיַּעַל | יְבַעֲתוּנִי |
| | 'ăphāphûnî | chevlê-māweth | wenachlê | veliya'al | yeva'ăthûnî |
| | they have encompassed me | the cords of death | and the wadis of | destruction | they terrified me |

| | 2346 | 8061 | 5621.116 | 7207.316 | 4305 | 4323 |
|---|---|---|---|---|---|---|
| **5.** | *n mp* | pn | v Qal pf 3cp, ps 1cs | v Piel pf 3cp, ps 1cs | *n mp* | n ms |
| | חֶבְלֵי | שְׁאוֹל | סְבָבוּנִי | קִדְּמוּנִי | מוֹקְשֵׁי | מָוֶת |
| | chevlê | she'ôl | sevāvûnî | qiddemûnî | môqōshê | māweth |
| | the cords of | Sheol | they surround me | they confronted me | the snares of | death |

| | 904, 7140, 3937 | 7410.125 | 3176 | 420, 435 | 8209.325 | 8471.121 |
|---|---|---|---|---|---|---|
| **6.** | prep, art, n ms, prep, ps 1cs | v Qal impf 1cs | pn | cj, prep, n mp, ps 1cs | v Piel impf 1cs | v Qal impf 3ms |
| | בַּצַּר־לִי | אֶקְרָא | יְהוָה | וְאֶל־אֱלֹהַי | אֲשַׁוֵּעַ | יִשְׁמַע |
| | batstsar-lî | 'eqōrā' | yehwāh | we'el-'ĕlōhay | 'ăshawwē'a | yishma' |
| | in my adversity | I call to | Yahweh | and to my God | I cried for help | He heard |

| 4623, 2033 | 7249 | 8210 | 3937, 6686 | 971.122 | 904, 238 |
|---|---|---|---|---|---|
| prep, n ms, ps 3ms | n ms, ps 1cs | cj, n fs, ps 1cs | prep, n mp, ps 3ms | v Qal impf 3fs | prep, n fd, ps 3ms |
| מֵהֵיכָלוֹ | קוֹלִי | וְשַׁוְעָתִי | לְפָנָיו | תָּבוֹא | בְאָזְנָיו |
| mēhêkhālô | qôlî | weshaw'āthî | lephānâv | tāvô' | ve'āzenâv |
| from his temple | my voice | and my cry for help | to his presence | it entered | into his ears |

**1. I will love thee:** ... I will give you my love, *BB*.

**O LORD, my strength:** ... You are my defender, *Good News* ... my only defender, *Knox* ... O Eternal, *Moffatt*.

**2. The LORD is my rock:** ... my stronghold, *Berkeley* ... my rock-fastness, *Knox* ... my crag, *Moffatt*.

**and my fortress:** ... my walled town, *BB* ... my bulwark, *Young* ... I can run to him for safety, *NCV*.

**and my deliverer:** ... saviour, *BB* ... champion, *REB*.

**my God, my strength:** ... my safe Retreat, *Fenton* ... hiding-place, *Knox*.

**in whom I will trust:** ... I take refuge, *Berkeley* ... where I find shelter, *Beck* ... I flee for safety, *Knox*.

**my buckler:** ... shield, *Anchor* ... breastplate, *BB*.

**and the horn of my salvation:** ... my weapon of deliverance, *Knox*.

**and my high tower:** ... stronghold, *Anchor* ... mountain Refuge, *Beck* ... retreat, *Moffatt*.

**3. I will call upon the LORD:** ... Praised be the LORD, I exclaim, *NAB* ... I called Yahweh, *Anchor* ... I will send up my cry, *BB* ... When weak I cried to GOD, *Fenton* ... When I invoke his name, *Knox*.

**who is worthy to be praised:** ... who is to be praised, *BB* ... who deserves praise, *Beck*.

**so shall I be saved from mine enemies:** ... safe from those who are against me, *BB* ... Who saved me from my foes, *Fenton* ... I am secure from my enemies, *Knox* ... I am rescued from my foes, *Moffatt*.

**4. The sorrows of death compassed me:** ... pangs of death, *NKJV* ... cords of death, *BB* ... waves, *Knox*.

**and the floods of ungodly men:** ... floods of ungodliness, *ASV* ... deep flowed the perilous tide, *Knox* ... torrents of perdition, *NRSV* ... streams of the worthless, *Young*.

**made me afraid:** ... put me in fear, *BB* ... assailed me, *Berkeley* ... overwhelmed me, *Beck* ... to daunt me, *Knox* ... hemmed me in, *KJVII*.

**5. The sorrows of hell:** ... ropes of Death, *Fenton* ... grave, *Knox* ... cords of Sheol, *ASV* ... bands of Sheol, *Darby* ... meshes of hades, *Rotherham*.

**compassed me about:** ... tightened about me, *REB* ... entangled me, *Moffatt* ... wrapped around me, *NCV* ... a noose had twined, *Fenton*.

**the snares of death:** ... cords of the nether world, *NAB* ... nets of death, *BB* ... fatal snares, *Moffatt*.

**prevented me:** ... enmeshed me, *NAB* ... had trapped my feet, *Knox* ... were set to catch me, *NEB* ... lying ahead of me, *JB* ... surprised me, *Moffatt*.

**6. In my distress:** ... in my plight, *Moffatt* ... In mine adversity, *Young* ... trouble, *BB* ... anguish of heart, *NEB* ... affliction, *Knox*.

**I called upon the LORD:** ... my voice went up to the Lord, *BB*.

**and cried unto my God:** ... I called to Yahweh, *JB* ... One cry to the Lord, *Knox*.

**he heard my voice:** ... my voice came to his hearing, *BB* ... listened to my voice, *Knox*.

**out of his temple:** ... He heard my voice from his palace, *Goodspeed*.

**and my cry came before him, even into his ears:** ... my cry for help came to His ears, *Beck* ... my cry unto him reached his ears, *Goodspeed* ... the complaint I made before him found a hearing, *Knox* ... my call for help reached his ears, *NCV*.

**7. Then the earth shook and trembled:** ... earth swayed and quaked, *Beck* ... reeled and rocked, *RSV* ...

---

is conspicuous among its noblest utterances. Nowhere else in Scripture is the form of the word employed which is here used for "love" (HED #7638). It has depth and tenderness. How far into the center this man had penetrated, who could thus isolate and unite Yahweh and himself and could feel that they two were alone and knit together by love! The first word for "rock" (HED #5748) is more properly "crag" or "cliff," thus suggesting inaccessibility, and the second (HED #6962), a "rock mass," thus giving the notion of firmness or solidity. The shade of difference need not be pressed, but the general idea is that of safety, by elevation above the enemy and by reason of the unchangeable strength of Yahweh.

**18:4–6.** The superb idealization of past deliverances under the figure of a theophany is prepared for by a retrospect of dangers, which still palpitates with the memory of former fears. No better description of David's early life could have been given than that contained in the two vivid figures. "Destruction" is better than "ungodly men" as the rendering of the unusual word "belial" (HED #1139). Thus, the psalmist pictures himself as standing on a diminishing bit of solid ground, around which a rising flood runs strong, breaking on its crumbling narrowness. Islanded thus, he is all but lost. With swift transition, he casts the picture of his distress into another metaphor.

| | 1649.122 | 7782.122 | 800 | 4279 | 2098 | 7553.126 |
|---|---|---|---|---|---|---|
| **7.** | cj, v Qal impf 3fs | cj, v Qal impf 3fs | art, n fs | cj, *n mp* | n mp | v Qal impf 3mp |
| | וַתִּגְעַשׁ | וַתִּרְעַשׁ | הָאָרֶץ | וּמוֹסְדֵי | הָרִים | יִרְגָּזוּ |
| | wattigh'ash | wattir'ash | hā'ārets | ûmôsdhê | hārîm | yirgāzû |
| | and it shook | and it quaked | the earth | and the foundations of | the mountains | they trembled |

| 1649.726 | 3706, 2835.111 | 3937 | | 6148.111 | 6476 | 904, 653 |
|---|---|---|---|---|---|---|
| cj, v Hithpael impf 3mp | cj, v Qal pf 3ms | prep, ps 3ms | **8.** | v Qal pf 3ms | n ms | prep, n ms, ps 3ms |
| וַיִּתְגָּעֲשׁוּ | כִּי־חָרָה | לוֹ | | עָלָה | עָשָׁן | בְאַפּוֹ |
| wayyithgā'ăshû | kî-chārāh | lô | | 'ālāh | 'āshān | be'appô |
| and they shook | because He became angry | at them | | it went up | smoke | into his nose |

| 813, 4623, 6552 | 404.122 | 1544 | 1220.116 | 4623 | | 5371.121 |
|---|---|---|---|---|---|---|
| cj, n fs, prep, n ms, ps 3ms | v Qal impf 3fs | n fp | v Qal pf 3cp | prep, ps 3ms | **9.** | cj, v Qal impf 3ms |
| וְאֵשׁ־מִפִּיו | תֹּאכֵל | גֶּחָלִים | בָּעֲרוּ | מִמֶּנּוּ | | וַיֵּט |
| we'ēsh-mippîw | tō'khēl | gechālîm | bā'ărû | mimmennû | | wayyēṭ |
| and fire from his mouth | it devoured | coals | they burned | from it | | they bent down |

| 8452 | 3495.121 | 6441 | 8809 | 7559 | | 7680.121 |
|---|---|---|---|---|---|---|
| n md | cj, v Qal impf 3ms | cj, n ms | prep | n fd, ps 3ms | **10.** | cj, v Qal impf 3ms |
| שָׁמַיִם | וַיֵּרַד | וַעֲרָפֶל | תַּחַת | רַגְלָיו | | וַיִּרְכַּב |
| shāmayim | wayyēradh | wa'ărāphel | tachath | raghlâv | | wayyirkav |
| the heavens | and they came down | and thick darkness | under | his feet | | and He rode |

| 6142, 3872 | 5990.121 | 1723.121 | 6142, 3796, 7593 | | 8308.121 |
|---|---|---|---|---|---|
| prep, n ms | cj, v Qal impf 3ms | cj, v Qal impf 3ms | prep, *n fd*, n fs | **11.** | v Qal impf 3ms |
| עַל־כְּרוּב | וַיָּעֹף | וַיֵּדֶא | עַל־כַּנְפֵי־רוּחַ | | יָשֶׁת |
| 'al-kerûv | wayyā'ōph | wayyēdhe' | 'al-kanphê-rûach | | yāsheth |
| on a cherub | and He flew | and He flew | upon the wings of the wind | | he placed |

| 2932 | 5848 | 5623 | 5712 | 2932, 4448 | 5880 | 8263 |
|---|---|---|---|---|---|---|
| n ms | n ms, ps 3ms | sub, ps 3ms | n fs, ps 3ms | *n fs*, n md | *n mp* | n mp |
| חֹשֶׁךְ | סִתְרוֹ | סְבִיבוֹתָיו | סֻכָּתוֹ | חֶשְׁכַת־מַיִם | עָבֵי | שְׁחָקִים |
| chōshekh | sithrô | sevîvôthâv | sukkāthô | cheshkhath-mayim | 'āvê | shechāqîm |
| darkness | his cover | all around Him | his hut | the darkness of the waters | thickness of | clouds |

| | 4623, 5227 | 5224 | 5880 | 5882.116 | 1287 |
|---|---|---|---|---|---|
| **12.** | prep, n fs | sub, ps 3ms | n mp, ps 3ms | v Qal pf 3cp | n ms |
| | מִנֹּגַהּ | נֶגְדּוֹ | עָבָיו | עָבְרוּ | בָּרָד |
| | minnōghahh | neghdô | 'āvâv | 'āverû | bārādh |
| | out of the brightness | before Him | his thickness | they passed through | hailstones |

| 1544, 813 | | 7769.521 | 904, 8452 | 3176 | 6169 | 5598.121 |
|---|---|---|---|---|---|---|
| cj, *n fp*, n fs | **13.** | cj, v Hiphil impf 3ms | prep, art, n md | pn | cj, n ms | v Qal impf 3ms |
| וְגַחֲלֵי־אֵשׁ | | וַיַּרְעֵם | בַּשָּׁמַיִם | יְהוָה | וְעֶלְיוֹן | יִתֵּן |
| weghachlê-'ēsh | | wayyar'ēm | bashshāmayim | yehwāh | we'elyôn | yittēn |
| and coals of fire | | and it thundered | in the heavens | Yahweh | and the Most High | He gave |

| 7249 | 1287 | 1544, 813 | | 8365.121 | 2784 | 6571.521 |
|---|---|---|---|---|---|---|
| n ms, ps 3ms | n ms | cj, *n fp*, n fs | **14.** | cj, v Qal impf 3ms | n mp, ps 3ms | cj, v Hiphil impf 3ms, ps 3mp |
| קֹלוֹ | בָּרָד | וְגַחֲלֵי־אֵשׁ | | וַיִּשְׁלַח | חִצָּיו | וַיְפִיצֵם |
| qōlô | bārādh | weghachlê-'ēsh | | wayyishlach | chitstsâv | wayphîtsēm |
| his voice | hailstones | and coals of fire | | and He sent out | his arrows | and He scattered them |

| 1326 | 7525.111 | 2072.121 | | 7495.226 |
|---|---|---|---|---|
| cj, n mp | v Qal pf 3ms | cj, v Qal impf 3ms, ps 3mp | **15.** | cj, Niphal impf 3mp |
| וּבְרָקִים | רָב | וַיְהֻמֵּם | | וַיֵּרָאוּ |
| ûverāqîm | rāv | wayhummēm | | wayyērā'û |
| and lightnings | He multiplied | and He threw them into confusion | | and they appeared |

Earth thereupon shivered and shook, *Knox* ... trouble and shock came on the earth, *BB.*

**the foundations also of the hills:** ... bases of the mountains, *BB* ... foundations also of the mountains, *ASV* ... mountains' foundations shuddered, *JB* ... hills were quivering to their base, *Moffatt* ... foundations of hills are troubled, *Young.*

**moved and were shaken, because he was wroth:** ... angry, *BB* ... indignant, *Berkeley* ... quaked at his blazing anger, *JB* ... when his wrath flared up, *NCB.*

**8. There went up a smoke out of his nostrils:** ... from his nose, *BB* ... smoke fumed from his nostrils, *Moffatt.*

**and fire out of his mouth devoured:** ... a fire of destruction from his mouth, *BB* ... from His mouth came a devouring fire, *Beck* ... scorching fire from his lips, *Moffatt* ... consuming fire came from his mouth, *NIV.*

**coals were kindled by it:** ... made coals glow, *Beck* ... coals burned forth from it, *Darby* ... kindling coals to flame, *Knox* ... glowing coals and searing heat, *NEB* ... Live coals were kindled from it, *Rotherham.*

**9. He bowed the heavens also:** ... inclined the heavens, *NAB* ... spread apart the heavens, *Anchor* ... swept the skies aside, *NEB* ... heavens were bent, *BB* ... tore the sky open, *Good News.*

**and came down:** ... so that he might come down, *BB* ... came down to earth, *Knox* ... came to my defense, *LIVB* ... as he descended, *NEB.*

**and darkness was under his feet:** ... storm cloud, *Anchor* ... gloom, *Fenton* ... dark cloud, *Knox.*

**10. And he rode upon a cherub:** ... Mounted on a mighty angel, *LIVB* ... seated on a storm-cloud, *BB* ... On whirlwinds rode, *Fenton* ... on his winged creature, *Good News* ... cherubmounted, *Knox.*

**and did fly:** ... flew swiftly, *Good News.*

**yea, he did fly upon the wings of the wind:** ... soared on wings outstretched, *Anchor* ... darting along, *Beck.*

**11. He made darkness his secret place:** ... darkness around Him, *Beck* ... shrouded in darkness, *Knox* ... hidingplace, *ASV.*

**his pavilion round about him:** ... canopy, *NASB* ... the rain cloud his pavilion, *Anchor* ... tent, *Darby* ... tabernacle, *KJVII.*

**were dark waters:** ... dark with water, *Berkeley* ... black rain-storm, *Knox.*

**and thick clouds of the skies:** ... dense cloud, *JB* ... deep mist, *Knox* ... clouds of vapours, *Rotherham.*

**12. At the brightness that was before him:** ... brightness of his presence, *NIV* ... radiance, *REB* ... Light shone ahead of Him, *Beck.*

**his thick clouds passed:** ... light clouds, *Anchor* ... His clouds issued forth, *Berkeley* ... dark, misty rainclouds, *NAB* ... his clouds rolled along, *Rotherham.*

**hail stones and coals of fire:** ... hail and blazing fire, *Fenton* ... while coals were kindled, *Knox.*

**13. The LORD also thundered in the heavens:** ... Yahweh, *Rotherham.*

**and the Highest gave his voice:** ... Most High gave forth, *Anchor* ... resounded, *NIV* ... Highest uttered his voice, *Rotherham.*

**hail stones and coals of fire:** ... Hailstones and flashing fire, *Fenton.*

**14. Yea, he sent out his arrows, and scattered them:** ... He forged his arrows, *Anchor* ... when he rained down his arrows, *Knox.*

**and he shot out lightnings:** ... volleys of his lightning, *Knox* ... increased lightnings, *Geneva* ... frequent lightnings, *NAB* ... Lightnings in abundance, *NKJV* ... multiplied his shafts, *Anchor.*

**and discomfited them:** ... sent them echoing, *NEB* ... sent them running, *Good News* ... hurled and routed them, *Goodspeed* ... they fled in confusion, *Knox* ... threw them in a panic, *Beck.*

**15. Then the channels of waters:** ... fountainheads of the sea, *Anchor* ...

---

**18:7–8.** The phenomena of a thunderstorm are the substratum of the grand description of Yahweh's delivering self-manifestation. The garb is lofty poetry, but a definite fact lies beneath, namely, some deliverance in which the psalmist saw Yahweh's coming in storm and lightning flash to destroy and therefore to save. Faith sees more truly because it sees more deeply than sense. What would have appeared to an ordinary onlooker as merely a remarkable escape was to its subject the manifestation of a present God.

**18:9–16.** Thus kindled, God's wrath flashes into action, as is wonderfully painted in that great storm piece in vv. 9–15. The stages of a violent thunder tempest are painted with unsurpassable force and brevity.

Blacker grows the gloom, in which awed hearts are conscious of a present Deity shrouded behind the livid folds of the thunder-clouds, as in a tent. Down rushes the rain; the darkness is "a darkness of waters," and also "thick clouds of the skies," or "cloud masses," a mingled chaos of rain

| 665 | 4448 | 1580.226 | 4279 | 8725 |
|---|---|---|---|---|
| *n mp* | n md | cj, Niphal impf 3mp | *n mp* | n fs |
| אֲפִיקֵי | מַיִם | וַיִּגָּלוּ | מוֹסְדוֹת | תֵּבֵל |
| 'ăphîqê | mayim | wayyiggālû | môsdhôth | tēvēl |
| the channels of | the waters | and they were uncovered | the foundations of | the world |

| 4623, 1648 | 3176 | 4623, 5580 | 7593 | 653 | | 8365.121 |
|---|---|---|---|---|---|---|
| prep, n fs, ps 2ms | pn | prep, *n fs* | *n fs* | n ms, ps 2ms | 16. | v Qal impf 3ms |
| מִגַּעֲרָתְךָ | יְהוָה | מִנִּשְׁמַת | רוּחַ | אַפֶּךָ | | יִשְׁלַח |
| migga'ărāthekhā | yehwāh | minishmath | rûach | 'appekhā | | yishlach |
| from your rebuke | O Yahweh | from the blowing of | the breath of | your nose | | He reached out |

| 4623, 4953 | 4089.121 | 5056.521 | 4623, 4448 | 7521 |
|---|---|---|---|---|
| prep, n ms | v Qal impf 3ms, ps 1cs | v Hiphil impf 3ms, ps 1cs | prep, n md | adj |
| מִמָּרוֹם | יִקָּחֵנִי | יַמְשֵׁנִי | מִמַּיִם | רַבִּים |
| mimmārôm | yiqqāchēnî | yamshēnî | mimmayim | rabbîm |
| from on high | He took me | He drew me out | from the waters | many |

| | 5522.521 | 4623, 342.151 | 6006 | 4623, 7983.152 |
|---|---|---|---|---|
| 17. | v Hiphil impf 3ms, ps 1cs | prep, v Qal act ptc ms, ps 1cs | adj | cj, prep, v Qal act ptc mp, ps 1cs |
| | יַצִּילֵנִי | מֵאֹיְבִי | עָז | וּמִשֹּׂנְאַי |
| | yatstsîlēnî | mē'ōyevî | 'āz | ûmissōne'ay |
| | He rescued me | from my enemy | strong | and from those who hate me |

| 3706, 563.116 | 4623 | | 7207.326 | 904, 3219, 344 |
|---|---|---|---|---|
| cj, v Qal pf 3cp | prep, ps 1cs | 18. | v Piel impf 3mp, ps 1cs | prep, *n ms*, n ms, ps 1cs |
| כִּי־אָמְצוּ | מִמֶּנִּי | | יְקַדְּמוּנִי | בְיוֹם־אֵידִי |
| kî-'āmetsû | mimmenî | | yeqaddemûnî | veyôm-'êdhî |
| because they were stronger | than me | | they confronted me | in the day of my calamity |

| 2030.121, 3176 | 3937, 5117 | 3937 | | 3428.521 | 3937, 4962 |
|---|---|---|---|---|---|
| cj, v Qal impf 3ms, pn | prep, n ms | prep, ps 1cs | 19. | cj, v Hiphil impf 3ms, ps 1cs | prep, art, n ms |
| וַיְהִי־יְהוָה | לְמִשְׁעָן | לִי | | וַיּוֹצִיאֵנִי | לַמֶּרְחָב |
| wayhî-yehwāh | lemish'ān | lî | | wayyôtsî'ēnî | lammerchāv |
| but Yahweh was | for a support | to me | | and He led me | into a broad place |

| 2603.321 | 3706 | 2759.111 | 904 | | 1621.121 | 3176 |
|---|---|---|---|---|---|---|
| v Piel impf 3ms, ps 1cs | cj | v Qal pf 3ms | prep, ps 1cs | 20. | v Qal impf 3ms, ps 1cs | pn |
| יְחַלְּצֵנִי | כִּי | חָפֵץ | בִּי | | יִגְמְלֵנִי | יְהוָה |
| yechalletsēnî | kî | chāphēts | bî | | yighmelēnî | yehwāh |
| and He set me apart | because | He was pleased | with me | | He rewarded me | Yahweh |

| 3626, 6928 | 3623, 1281 | 3135 | 8178.521 |
|---|---|---|---|
| prep, n ms, ps 1cs | prep, *n ms* | n fd, ps 1cs | v Hiphil impf 3ms |
| כְּצִדְקִי | כְּבֹר | יָדַי | יָשִׁיב |
| ketsidhqî | kevōr | yādhay | yāshîv |
| according to my righteousness | according to the cleanness of | my hands | He recompensed |

| 3937 | | 3706, 8490.115 | 1932 | 3176 | 3940, 7855.115 |
|---|---|---|---|---|---|
| prep, ps 1cs | 21. | cj, v Qal pf 1cs | *n mp* | pn | cj, neg part, v Qal pf 1cs |
| לִי | | כִּי־שָׁמַרְתִּי | דַּרְכֵי | יְהוָה | וְלֹא־רָשַׁעְתִּי |
| lî | | kî-shāmartî | darkhê | yehwāh | welō'-rāsha'ättî |
| me | | because I have observed | the ways of | Yahweh | and I have not acted wickedly |

| 4623, 435 | | 3706 | 3725, 5122 | 3937, 5224 | 2807 |
|---|---|---|---|---|---|
| prep, n mp, ps 1cs | 22. | cj | *adj*, n mp, ps 3ms | prep, prep, ps 1cs | cj, n fp, ps 3ms |
| מֵאֱלֹהָי | | כִּי | כָל־מִשְׁפָּטָיו | לְנֶגְדִּי | וְחֻקֹּתָיו |
| mē'ĕlōhāy | | kî | khol-mishpāṭāv | leneghdî | wechuqqōthâv |
| from my God | | because | all his ordinances | before me | and his statutes |

deep beds, *BB* ... floor of the sea, *Beck* ... fearful mighty streams, *Fenton* ... springs of ocean, *JB.*

**were seen:** ... were exposed, *Anchor* ... became visible, *Berkeley* ... came to light, *Knox* ... receded from the shore, *LIVB* ... were revealed, *NEB.*

**and the foundations of the world were discovered:** ... bases, *BB* ... world's supports, *Fenton* ... were laid bare, *Anchor* ... uncovered, *BB.*

**at thy rebuke, O Lord:** ... at thy storming, *Moffatt* ... because of your words of wrath, *BB* ... when thou didst threaten them, *Knox* ... roared at them in anger, *Good News.*

**at the blast of the breath of thy nostrils:** ... because of the breath from your mouth, *BB* ... At your fierce breathing wrath, *Fenton* ... when thou didst blow upon them with the breath of thy anger, *Knox* ... at the snorting, *Moffatt* ... the breath of the spirit of Thine anger, *Young.*

**16. He sent from above:** ... reached from on high, *Berkeley* ... reached down from the height, *NEB.*

**he took me, he drew me:** ... snatched me, *Anchor* ... took hold of me, *Beck* ... draws me, *Moffatt.*

**out of many waters:** ... waters deep, *Anchor* ... great waters, *BB* ... watery depths, *JB* ... that flood, *Knox.*

**17. He delivered me from my strong enemy:** ... rescued me from my powerful Foe, *Anchor* ... made me free from my strong hater, *BB* ... saved me from triumphant malice, *Knox.*

**and from them which hated me:** ... those who were against me, *BB.*

**for they were too strong for me:** ... too mighty for me, *ASV* ... grew too powerful for me, *NEB* ... far too strong, *Moffatt.*

**18. They prevented me:** ... went before me, *Anchor* ... encountered me, *Darby* ... came on me, *BB* ... when they faced me at every turn, *Knox.*

**in the day of my calamity:** ... in the hour of my peril, *NEB* ... on the day of my death, *Anchor* ... in the day of my trouble, *BB* ... day of disaster, *JB* ... in my distress, *Moffatt.*

**but the Lord was my stay:** ... the Lord held me steady, *LIVB* ... was my support, *BB* ... my buttress, *NEB* ... my guardian power, *Fenton* ... stood by me, *Knox.*

**19. He brought me forth also into a large place:** ... brought me out, *Beck* ... the broad domain, *Anchor* ... roomy place, *Berkeley* ... set me at large, *JB* ... untrammelled liberty, *REB.*

**he delivered me:** ... liberated me, *Anchor* ... was my saviour, *BB* ... where I was free, *Beck* ... into freedom again, *Knox.*

**because he delighted in me:** ... he loved me, *Anchor* ... fauoured me, *Geneva* ... he was pleased with me, *Good News* ... his great love befriended me, *Knox.*

**20. The Lord rewarded me according to my righteousness:** ... spared me, *NCV* ... because I was just, *Anchor* ... as my righteousness deserved, *NEB.*

**according to the cleanness of my hands:** ... because my hands were innocent, *Anchor* ... what my clean hands deserve, *Beck* ... pureness of mine hand, *Geneva* ... my conduct was spotless, *REB.*

**hath he recompensed me:** ... repaid me, *Anchor* ... he would make return, *Knox.*

**21. For I have kept the ways of the Lord:** ... Have I not kept true to the Lord's paths, *Knox.*

**and have not wickedly departed from my God:** ... have not been guilty, *Anchor* ... was not disloyal, *NAB* ... have not been turned away in sin, *BB* ... haven't wickedly turned away, *Beck* ... never sinned by swerving, *Moffatt.*

---

and clouds. Then lightning tears a way through the blackness, and the language becomes abrupt, like the flash. In vv. 12f, the fury of the storm rages. Blinding light and deafening thunderclaps gleam and rattle through the broken words.

Then comes the purpose of all the dread magnificence, strangely small except to the psalmist. Heaven and earth have been shaken and lightnings set leaping through the sky for nothing greater than to drag one half-drowned man from the floods. But the result of the theophany is small only in the same way that its cause was small. This same poor man cried, and the cry set Yahweh's activity in motion. The deliverance of a single soul may seem a small thing, but if the soul has prayed it is no longer small, for God's good name is involved.

**18:17–19.** The psalmist lays aside the figure in vv. 17f and comes to the bare fact of his deliverance from enemies, and perhaps from one especially formidable ("my enemy," v. 17). The prose of the whole would have been that he was in great danger and without means of averting it, but had a hair-breadth escape. But the outside of a fact is not all of it, and in this mystical life of ours, poetry gets nearer the heart of things than does prose, and true communion with God nearer than either.

**18:20–29.** The note slightly touched at the close of the description of the deliverance domi-

| 3940, 5681.525 | 4623 | 23. | 2030.125 | 8879 | 6196 | 8490.725 |
|---|---|---|---|---|---|---|
| neg part, v Hiphil impf 1cs | prep, ps 1cs | | cj, v Qal impf 1cs | adj | prep, ps 3ms | cj, v Hithpael impf 1cs |
| לֹא־אָסִיר | מֶנִּי | | וָאֱהִי | תָמִים | עִמּוֹ | וָאֶשְׁתַּמֵּר |
| lō'-'āsîr | menî | | wā'ěhî | thāmîm | 'immô | wā'eshtammēr |
| I did not set aside | away from me | | but I was | blameless | with Him | and I kept myself |

| 4623, 5988 | 24. | 8178.521, 3176 | 3937 | 3626, 6928 |
|---|---|---|---|---|
| prep, n ms ps 1cs | | cj, v Hiphil impf 3ms, pn | prep, ps 1cs | prep, n ms, ps 1cs |
| מֵעֲוֺנִי | | וַיָּשֶׁב־יְהוָה | לִי | כְצִדְקִי |
| mē'āwōnî | | wayyāshev-yehwāh | lî | khetsidhqî |
| from my transgression | | and Yahweh recompensed | me | according to my righteousness |

| 3626, 1281 | 3135 | 3937, 5224 | 6084 | 25. | 6196, 2728 |
|---|---|---|---|---|---|
| prep, *n ms* | n fd, ps 1cs | prep, prep | n fd, ps 3ms | | prep, n ms |
| כְּבֹר | יָדַי | לְנֶגֶד | עֵינָיו | | עִם־חָסִיד |
| kevōr | yādhay | leneghedh | 'ênâv | | 'im-chāsîdh |
| according to the cleanness of | my hands | before | his eyes | | with the godly |

| 2720.723 | 6196, 1429 | 8879 | 8882.723 | 26. | 6196, 1331.255 |
|---|---|---|---|---|---|
| v Hithpael impf 2ms | prep, *n ms* | adj | v Hithpael impf 2ms | | prep, v Niphal ptc ms |
| תִּתְחַסָּד | עִם־גְּבַר | תָּמִים | תִּתַּמָּם | | עִם־נָבָר |
| tithchassādh | 'im-gevar | tāmîm | tittammām | | 'im-nāvār |
| You exhibit steadfast love | with a man | blameless | You exhibit blamelessness | | with the pure |

| 1331.723 | 6196, 6379 | 6871.723 | 27. | 3706, 887 |
|---|---|---|---|---|
| v Hithpael impf 2ms | cj, prep, n ms | v Hithpael impf 2ms | | cj, pers pron |
| תִּתְבָּרָר | וְעִם־עִקֵּשׁ | תִּתְפַּתָּל | | כִּי־אַתָּה |
| tithbārār | we'im-'iqqēsh | tithpattāl | | kî-'attāh |
| You exhibit purity | and with the perverse | You act with cunning | | because You |

| 6196, 6270 | 3588.523 | 6084 | 7597.154 | 8584.523 | 28. | 3706, 887 |
|---|---|---|---|---|---|---|
| n ms, adj | v Hiphil impf 2ms | cj, n fd | v Qal act ptc fp | v Hiphil impf 2ms | | cj, pers pron |
| עַם־עָנִי | תוֹשִׁיעַ | וְעֵינַיִם | רָמוֹת | תַּשְׁפִּיל | | כִּי־אַתָּה |
| 'am-'ānî | thôshîa' | we'ênayim | rāmôth | tashpîl | | kî-'attāh |
| an afflicted people | You save | but eyes | lifting | You bring low | | because You |

| 213.523 | 5552 | 3176 | 435 | 5226.521 | 2932 |
|---|---|---|---|---|---|
| v Hiphil impf 2ms | n ms, ps 1cs | pn | n mp, ps 1cs | v Hiphil impf 3ms | n ms, ps 1cs |
| תָּאִיר | נֵרִי | יְהוָה | אֱלֹהַי | יַגִּיהַּ | חָשְׁכִּי |
| tā'îr | nērî | yehwāh | 'ělōhay | yaggîahh | chāshekkî |
| You light | my lamp | O Yahweh | my God | it shines | my darkness |

| 29. | 3706, 904 | 7608.125 | 1447 | 904, 435 | 1860.325, 8229 | 30. | 418 |
|---|---|---|---|---|---|---|---|
| | cj, prep, ps 2ms | v Qal impf 1cs | n ms | cj, prep, n mp, ps 1cs | v Piel impf 1cs, n ms | | art, n ms |
| | כִּי־בְךָ | אָרֻץ | גְּדוּד | וּבֵאלֹהַי | אֲדַלֶּג־שׁוּר | | הָאֵל |
| | kî-vekhā | 'āruts | gedhûdh | ûvē'lōhay | 'ădhallegh-shûr | | hā'ēl |
| | because with You | I can run to | a troop | and with my God | I can leap over a wall | | God |

| 8879 | 1932 | 577, 3176 | 7170.157 | 4182 | 2000 | 3937, 3725 |
|---|---|---|---|---|---|---|
| adj | n ms, ps 3ms | *n fs*, pn | v Qal pass ptc fs | n ms | pers pron | prep, *n ms* |
| תָּמִים | דַּרְכּוֹ | אִמְרַת־יְהוָה | צְרוּפָה | מָגֵן | הוּא | לְכֹל |
| tāmîm | darkô | 'imrath-yehwāh | tserûphāh | māghēn | hû' | lekhōl |
| blameless | his ways | the words of Yahweh | refined | a shield | He | to all |

| 2725.152 | 904 | 31. | 3706 | 4449 | 438 | 4623, 1146 | 3176 | 4449 |
|---|---|---|---|---|---|---|---|---|
| art, v Qal act ptc mp | prep, ps 3ms | | cj | intrg | n ms | prep, prep | pn | cj, intrg |
| הַחֹסִים | בּוֹ | | כִּי | מִי | אֱלוֹהַּ | מִבַּלְעֲדֵי | יְהוָה | וּמִי |
| hachōsîm | bô | | kî | mî | 'ělôahh | mibbal'ădhê | yehwāh | ûmî |
| those who take refuge | in Him | | because | who | God | besides | Yahweh | and who |

**22. For all his judgments:** ... ordinances, *ASV* ... decisions, *BB* ... laws, *Beck* ... rules, *Moffatt.*

**were before me:** ... are all before my mind, *Moffatt* ... are before my eyes, *NEB.*

**and I did not put away his statutes from me:** ... I did not cast away his commaundements, *Geneva* ... I don't lay aside His rules, *Beck* ... I never set aside his orders, *Moffatt* ... I have not failed to follow his decrees, *NEB.*

**23. I was also upright before him:** ... perfect, *ASV* ... faultless, *Berkeley* ... blameless, *Beck* ... I have always been candid with him, *Anchor.*

**and I kept myself from mine iniquity:** ... having guarded myself against my sinfulness, *Berkeley* ... from vice, *Fenton* ... from my wickednesse, *Geneva* ... from doing wrong, *Beck* ... from wilful sin, *NEB.*

**24. Therefore hath the Lord recompensed me:** ... returned my due, *Fenton.*

**according to my righteousness:** ... because I was just, *Anchor* ... because he knows that I am innocent, *Good News* ... for acting uprightly, *JB.*

**according to the cleanness of my hands in his eyesight:** ... my hands were innocent, *Anchor* ... my life clean, *Moffatt* ... purity of my life, *NEB* ... Over-against his eyes, *Young.*

**25. With the merciful thou wilt show thyself merciful:** ... you are faithful, *Anchor* ... you are kind to him who is kind, *Beck* ... you are loyal to those who are loyal, *NCV* ... With the gracious thou dost shew, *Darby.*

**with an upright man thou wilt show thyself upright:** ... with the candid you are candid, *Anchor* ... perfect, *Berkeley* ... sincere with him who is sincere, *Beck* ... You are straight, *Fenton.*

**26. With the pure thou wilt show thyself pure:** ... With the sincere you are sincere, *Anchor* ... He who is holy will see that you are holy, *BB.*

**and with the froward thou wilt show thyself froward:** ... with the cunning you are crafty, *Anchor* ... whose way is not straight you will be a hard judge, *BB* ... treacherous, *Moffatt* ... perverse, *ASV* ... crooked, *Goodspeed* ... ready to contend, *Rotherham.*

**27. For thou wilt save:** ... you are the Strong One, *Anchor* ... you are the saviour, *BB* ... Thou deliverest, *Berkeley.*

**the afflicted people:** ... the poor, *Anchor* ... those who are in trouble, *BB* ... humble folk, *Knox* ... an oppressed people, *Rotherham.*

**but wilt bring down high looks:** ... you humble the eyes that are proud, *Anchor* ... haughty eyes thou wilt bring down, *ASV* ... eyes full of pride will be made low, *BB* ... you humiliate those with haughty looks, *JB.*

**28. For thou wilt light my candle:** ... You shine for me, *Anchor* ... Thou causest my lamp to shine, *Berkeley* ... that keepest the lamp of my hopes still burning, *Knox* ... dost make my lamp burn bright, *NEB.*

**the Lord my God will enlighten my darkness:** ... the dark will be made bright, *BB* ... who drives my gloom, *Fenton* ... wilt make my darkness shine, *Moffatt.*

**29. For by thee I have run through a troop:** ... With your help I storm a rampart, *REB* ... By your help I have made a way through the wall, *BB* ... By You I stormed the breach, *Fenton* ... through thee I can break down a rampart, *Goodspeed.*

**and by my God have I leaped over a wall:** ... And from God scaled the wall, *Fenton* ... in my God's strength I shall leap over all their defences, *Knox.*

**30. As for God, his way is perfect:** ... God is unerring in his ways,

---

nates the second part of the Psalm, of which the main theme is the correspondence of God's dealings with character, as illustrated in the singer's experience, and thence generalized into a law of the divine administration. It begins with startling protestations of innocence. These are rounded into a whole by the repetition, at the beginning and end, of the same statement that God dealt with the psalmist according to his righteousness and cleanhandedness. Unless a Christian can say, "I keep myself from mine iniquity," he has no right to look for the sunshine of God's face to gladden his eyes, nor for the strength of God's hand to pluck his feet from the net. In noble and daring words, the psalmist proclaims, as a law of God's dealings, his own experience generalized (vv. 25ff).

In vv. 27ff, the personal element comes again to the front. The individualizing name "my God" occurs in each verse, and the deliverance underlying the theophany is described in terms that prepare for the fuller celebration of victory in the last part of the Psalm. God lights the psalmist's lamp, by which is meant not the continuance of his family (as the expression elsewhere means), but the preservation of his own life, with the added idea, especially in v. 28b, of prosperity. Verse 29 tells how the lamp was kept alight, namely, by the singer's victory in actual battle, in which his swift rush had overtaken the enemy and his agile limbs had scaled their walls.

**18:30–31.** Once more, the song passes to the wider truths taught by the personal deliverance. "Our God" takes the place of "my God," and "all who take

| 6962 | 2190 | 435 | | 418 | 246.351 | 2524 | 5598.121 |
|---|---|---|---|---|---|---|---|
| n ms | prep | n mp, ps 1cp | **32.** | art, n ms | art, v Piel ptc ms, ps 1cs | n ms | cj, v Qal impf 3ms |
| צוּר | זוּלָתִי | אֱלֹהֵינוּ | | הָאֵל | הַמְאַזְּרֵנִי | חָיִל | וַיִּתֵּן |
| tsûr | zûlāthî | 'ĕlōhênû | | hā'ēl | ham'azz$^{e}$rēnî | chāyil | wayyittēn |
| a rock | except | our God | | God | the One Who girds me | strength | and He makes |

| 8879 | 1932 | | 8187.351 | 7559 | 3626, 359 | 6142 | 1154 |
|---|---|---|---|---|---|---|---|
| adj | n ms, ps 1cs | **33.** | v Piel ptc ms | n fd, ps 1cs | prep, art, n fp | cj, prep | n fp, ps 1cs |
| תָּמִים | דַּרְכִּי | | מְשַׁוֶּה | רַגְלַי | כָּאַיָּלוֹת | וְעַל | בָּמֹתַי |
| tāmîm | darkî | | m$^{e}$shawweh | raghlay | kā'ayyālôth | w$^{e}$'al | bāmōthay |
| blameless | my way | | setting | my feet | like female deer | and on | my high places |

| 6198.521 | | 4064.351 | 3135 | 3937, 4560 | 5365.312 |
|---|---|---|---|---|---|
| v Hiphil impf 3ms, ps 1cs | **34.** | v Piel ptc ms | n fd, ps 1cs | prep, art, n fs | cj, v Piel pf 3fs |
| יַעֲמִידֵנִי | | מְלַמֵּד | יָדַי | לַמִּלְחָמָה | וְנִחֲתָה |
| ya'ămîdhēnî | | m$^{e}$lammēdh | yādhay | lammilchāmāh | w$^{e}$nichăthāh |
| He causes me to stand | | He teaches | my hands | for the battle | and it is pulled back in |

| 7493, 5333 | 2307 | | 5598.123, 3937 | 4182 | 3589 |
|---|---|---|---|---|---|
| *n fs*, n fs | n fp, ps 1cs | **35.** | cj, v Qal impf 2ms, prep, ps 1cs | *n ms* | n ms, ps 2ms |
| קֶשֶׁת־נְחוּשָׁה | זְרוֹעֹתָי | | וַתִּתֶּן־לִי | מָגֵן | יִשְׁעֶךָ |
| qesheth-n$^{e}$chûshāh | z$^{e}$rô'ōthāy | | wattitten-lî | māghēn | yish'ekhā |
| a bow of bronze | my arms | | You have given me | the shield of | your salvation |

| 3332 | 5777.122 | 6265 | 7528.522 |
|---|---|---|---|
| cj, n fs, ps 2ms | v Qal impf 3fs, ps 1cs | cj, n fs, ps 2ms | v Hiphil impf 3fs, ps 1cs |
| וִימִינְךָ | תִּסְעָדֵנִי | וְעַנְוַתְךָ | תַּרְבֵּנִי |
| wîmîn$^{e}$khā | this'ādhēnî | w$^{e}$'anwathkhā | tharbēnî |
| and your right hand | it supported me | and your condescension | it makes me great |

| | 7620.523 | 7082 | 8809 | 3940 | 4726.116 | 7457 |
|---|---|---|---|---|---|---|
| **36.** | v Hiphil impf 2ms | n ms, ps 1cs | prep, ps 1cs | cj, neg part | v Qal pf 3cp | n fd, ps 1cs |
| | תַּרְחִיב | צַעֲדִי | תַּחְתָּי | וְלֹא | מָעֲדוּ | קַרְסֻלָּי |
| | tarchîv | tsa'ădhî | thachtāy | w$^{e}$lō' | mā'ădhû | qarsullāy |
| | You have made wide | my step | beneath me | and not | they faltered | my ankles |

| | 7579.125 | 342.152 | 5560.525 | 3940, 8178.125 |
|---|---|---|---|---|
| **37.** | v Qal impf 1cs | v Qal act ptc mp, ps 1cs | cj, v Hiphil impf 1cs, ps 3mp | cj, neg part, v Qal impf 1cs |
| | אֶרְדּוֹף | אוֹיְבַי | וְאַשִּׂיגֵם | וְלֹא־אָשׁוּב |
| | 'erdôph | 'ôyvay | w$^{e}$'assîghēm | w$^{e}$lō'-'āshûv |
| | I pursued | my enemies | and I overtook them | and I did not turn back |

| 5912, 3735.341 | | 4410.125 | 3940, 3310.126 | 7251.141 | 5489.126 |
|---|---|---|---|---|---|
| adv, v Piel inf con, ps 3mp | **38.** | v Qal impf 1cs, ps 3mp | cj, neg part, v Qal impf 3mp | v Qal inf con | v Qal impf 3mp |
| עַד־כַּלּוֹתָם | | אֶמְחָצֵם | וְלֹא־יֻכְלוּ | קוּם | יִפְּלוּ |
| 'adh-kallôthām | | 'emchātsēm | w$^{e}$lō'-yukhlû | qûm | yipp$^{e}$lû |
| until their finishing | | I wounded them | and they were not able | to rise | they fell |

| 8809 | 7559 | | 246.323 | 2524 | 3937, 4560 | 3895.523 |
|---|---|---|---|---|---|---|
| prep | n fd, ps 1cs | **39.** | cj, v Piel impf 2ms, ps 1cs | n ms | prep, art, n fs | v Hiphil impf 2ms |
| תַּחַת | רַגְלָי | | וַתְּאַזְּרֵנִי | חַיִל | לַמִּלְחָמָה | תַּכְרִיעַ |
| tachath | raghlāy | | watt$^{e}$'azz$^{e}$rēnî | chayil | lammilchāmāh | takhrî'a |
| beneath | my feet | | for You girded me | strength | for the battle | You caused to bow |

| 7251.152 | 8809 | | 342.152 | 5598.113 | 3937 | 6439 |
|---|---|---|---|---|---|---|
| v Qal act ptc mp, ps 1cs | prep, ps 1cs | **40.** | cj, v Qal act ptc mp, ps 1cs | v Qal pf 2ms | prep, ps 1cs | n ms |
| קָמַי | תַּחְתָּי | | וְאֹיְבַי | נָתַתָּה | לִי | עֹרֶף |
| qāmay | tachtāy | | w$^{e}$'ōy$^{e}$vay | nāthattāh | lî | 'ōreph |
| those who rise against me | under me | | and my enemies | You have given | to me | backs |

*Moffatt* ... his dominion is complete, *Anchor* ... The ways of God are without fault, *NCV* ... Such is my God, unsullied in dealings, *Knox*.

**the word of the LORD is tried:** ... word of Yahweh is refined in the furnace, *JB* ... command of Yahweh is well tested, *Anchor* ... the LORD's promise has been tested by fire, *Beck* ... The speech of the LORD is sincere, *Goodspeed*.

**he is a buckler:** ... The Suzerain is he, *Anchor* ... he is a breast-plate, *BB*.

**to all those that trust in him:** ... to all who go to Him for shelter, *Beck* ... of all who take refuge in him, *JB*.

**31. For who is God save the LORD? or who is a rock save our God?:** ... Who is the mountain but our God, *Anchor* ... What other refuge can there be, except our God, *Knox*.

**32. It is God that girdeth me with strength:** ... a strong band about me, *BB* ... God is my protection, *NCV*.

**and maketh my way perfect:** ... who makes my pathway safe, *Good News* ... bids me go on my way untroubled, *Knox* ... He makes my way free from fault, *NCV*.

**33. He maketh my feet like hinds' feet:** ... like roes' feet, *BB* ... like those of a doe, *Berkeley* ... like a deer that does not stumble, *NCV* ... Makes my legs like a stag's, *Fenton*.

**and setteth me upon my high places:** ... brought me to stand upon his heights, *Anchor* ... gives me a sure footing, *Beck* ... making me stand securely, *Goodspeed* ... helps me stand on the steep mountains, *NCV*.

**34. He teacheth my hands to war:** ... makes my hands expert in war, *BB* ... trained my hands for battle, *Anchor*.

**so that a bow of steel is broken by mine arms:** ... a bow of brass, *ASV* ... bronze bow, *Beck* ... iron bow, *LIVB* ... strongest bow, *Good News*.

**35. Thou hast also given me the shield of thy salvation:** ... shield of victory, *Anchor* ... saving shield, *NAB*.

**and thy right hand hath holden me up:** ... sustained me, *Anchor* ... has been my support, *BB*.

**and thy gentleness hath made me great:** ... thy louing kindness has caused mee to increase, *Geneva* ... Thy lowliness maketh me great, *Young* ... you have stooped to make me great, *NAB* ... Thy condescension, *MAST*.

**36. Thou hast enlarged my steps under me:** ... You have given me long-striding legs, *Anchor* ... Thou givest me room for my steps, *NEB* ... You have made my steps wide, *BB* ... you give me the strides of a giant, *JB*.

**that my feet did not slip:** ... my ankles did not give way, *Anchor* ... my ankles don't waver, *Beck* ... They never failed or shook, *Fenton* ... my tread never falters, *Knox*.

**37. I have pursued mine enemies:** ... go after my haters, *BB* ... I chase my enemies, *Beck*.

**and overtaken them:** ... and catch up with them, *Beck*.

**neither did I turn again:** ... and don't go back, *Beck*.

**till they were consumed:** ... till they're completely defeated, *Beck* ... till I have made an end of them, *Knox* ... overcome, *BB* ... annihilated, *Anchor*.

**38. I have wounded them that they were not able to rise:** ... I smash them so they can't get up, *Beck* ... I smote them so that they could not rise, *Anchor* ... I pinned them to the ground; all were helpless before me, *LIVB* ... I thrust them through, so that they were not able to rise, *RSV*.

**they are fallen under my feet:** ... they lie defeated before me, *Good News* ... hurl them down at my feet, *Knox* ... I placed my feet upon their necks, *LIVB*.

**39. For thou hast girded me with strength unto the battle:** ... I have

---

refuge in Him" are discerned as gathering around the solitary psalmist and as sharing in his blessings. The large truths of these verses are the precious fruit of distress and deliverance. Both have cleared the singer's eyes to see and tuned his lips to sing.

**18:32–36.** The remainder of the Psalm describes the victorious campaign of the psalmist and the establishment of his kingdom. There is difficulty in determining the tenses of the verbs in some verses, and interpreters vary between pasts and futures.

Many mythologies have told how the gods arm their champions, but the psalmist reaches a loftier height than these. He ventures to think of God as doing the humble office of bracing on his girdle, but the girdle is itself strength. God, whose own "way is perfect" (v. 30), makes his servant's "way" in some measure like his own. No doubt, the figure must be interpreted in a manner congruous with its context, as chiefly implying "perfection" in regard to the purpose in hand—namely, warfare. Light of foot as a deer and able to climb to the robber forts perched on crags, as a chamois would, his hands deft and his muscular arms strong to bend the bow which others could not use, he is the ideal of a warrior of old, and all these natural powers he again ascribes to God's gift.

**18:37–42.** Then follow six verses full of the stir and tumult of battle. There is no necessity for the change to futures in the verbs of vv. 37f. The

| 7983.356 | 7059.525 | | 8209.326 | 375, 3588.551 |
|---|---|---|---|---|
| cj, v Piel ptc mp, ps 1cs | v Hiphil impf 1cs, ps 3mp | **41.** | v Piel impf 3mp | cj, *sub*, v Hiphil ptc ms |
| וּמְשַׂנְאַי | אַצְמִיתֵם | | יְשַׁוְּעוּ | וְאֵין־מוֹשִׁיעַ |
| ûmᵉsan'ay | 'atsmîthēm | | yᵉshawwᵉ'û | wᵉ'ên-môshîa' |
| and those who hated me | I exterminated them | | they cried for help | but there was not a Savior |

| 6142, 3176 | 3940 | 6257.111 | | 8262.125 | 3626, 6312 |
|---|---|---|---|---|---|
| prep, pn | cj, neg part | v Qal pf 3ms, ps 3mp | **42.** | cj, v Qal impf 1cs, ps 3mp | prep, n ms |
| עַל־יְהוָה | וְלֹא | עָנָם | | וְאֶשְׁחָקֵם | כְּעָפָר |
| 'al-yᵉhwāh | wᵉlō' | 'ānām | | wᵉ'eshchāqēm | kᵉ'āphār |
| on Yahweh | but not | He answered them | | I pulverized them | like dust |

| 6142, 6686, 7593 | 3626, 3027 | 2445 | 7671.525 |
|---|---|---|---|
| prep, *n mp*, n fs | prep, *n ms* | n mp | v Hiphil impf 1cs, ps 3mp |
| עַל־פְּנֵי־רוּחַ | כְּטִיט | חוּצוֹת | אֲרִיקֵם |
| 'al-pᵉnê-rûach | kᵉṭîṭ | chûtsôth | 'ărîqēm |
| on the surface of the wind | like the mud of | the streets | I empty them |

| | 6647.323 | 4623, 7663 | 6194 | 7947.123 | 3937, 7513 | 1504 |
|---|---|---|---|---|---|---|
| **43.** | v Piel impf 2ms, ps 1cs | prep, *n mp* | n ms | v Qal impf 2ms, ps 1cs | prep, *n ms* | n mp |
| | תְּפַלְּטֵנִי | מֵרִיבֵי | עָם | תְּשִׂימֵנִי | לְרֹאשׁ | גּוֹיִם |
| | tᵉphallᵉṭēnî | mērîvê | 'ām | tᵉsîmēnî | lᵉrō'sh | gôyim |
| | You set me free | from the contentions of | people | You appointed me | for a leader of | nations |

| 6194 | 3940, 3156.115 | 5856.126 | | 3937, 8475 | 238 | 8471.226 |
|---|---|---|---|---|---|---|
| n ms | neg part, v Qal pf 1cs | v Qal impf 3mp, ps 1cs | **44.** | prep, *n ms* | n fs | v Niphal impf 3mp |
| עַם | לֹא־יָדַעְתִּי | יַעַבְדוּנִי | | לְשֵׁמַע | אֹזֶן | יִשָּׁמְעוּ |
| 'am | lō'-yādha'ättî | ya'avdhûnî | | lᵉshēma' | 'ōzen | yishshāmᵉ'û |
| a people | I had not known | they served me | | at the report of | the ear | they listened |

| 3937 | 1158, 5424 | 3703.326, 3937 | | 1158, 5424 | 5209.126 |
|---|---|---|---|---|---|
| prep, ps 1cs | *n mp*, n ms | v Piel impf 3mp, prep, ps 1cs | **45.** | *n mp*, n ms | v Qal impf 3mp |
| לִי | בְּנֵי־נֵכָר | יְכַחֲשׁוּ־לִי | | בְּנֵי־נֵכָר | יִבֹּלוּ |
| lî | bᵉnê-nēkhār | yᵉkhachshû-lî | | bᵉnê-nēkhār | yibbōlû |
| to me | sons of a foreign land | they disavowed to me | | sons of a foreign land | they withered |

| 2827.126 | 4623, 4675 | | 2508, 3176 | 1313.155 | 6962 |
|---|---|---|---|---|---|
| cj, v Qal impf 3mp | prep, n fp, ps 3mp | **46.** | adj, pn | cj, v Qal pass ptc ms | n ms, ps 1cs |
| וְיַחְרְגוּ | מִמִּסְגְּרוֹתֵיהֶם | | חַי־יְהוָה | וּבָרוּךְ | צוּרִי |
| wᵉyachrᵉghû | mimmisgᵉrôthêhem | | chay-yᵉhwāh | ûvārûkh | tsûrî |
| and they came out trembling | from their bulwarks | | Yahweh living | and blessed | my Rock |

| 7597.121 | 438 | 3589 | | 418 | 5598.151 | 5543 |
|---|---|---|---|---|---|---|
| cj, v Qal impf 3ms | *n mp* | n ms, ps 1cs | **47.** | art, n ms | art, v Qal act ptc ms | n fp |
| וְיָרוּם | אֱלוֹהֵי | יִשְׁעִי | | הָאֵל | הַנּוֹתֵן | נְקָמוֹת |
| wᵉyārûm | 'ĕlôhê | yish'î | | hā'ēl | hannôthēn | nᵉqāmôth |
| and He is exalted | the God of | my salvation | | God | the One Who gave | vengeances |

been armed by you, *BB* ... You girthed my waist for war, *Fenton.*

**thou hast subdued under me those that rose up against me:** ... Held up my knees beneath, *Fenton* ... you have made low under me, *BB* ... make those who attack me bow at my feet, *Beck* ... made my assailants sink under me, *NRSV.*

**40. Thou hast also given me the necks of mine enemies:** ... You enable me to put my feet on the back of my enemies, *Beck* ... you gave me the neck of my foes, *Anchor* ... Thou hast also made mine enemies turn their backs unto me, *ASV* ... As for my foes thou didst give me their neck, *Rotherham.*

**that I might destroy them that hate me:** ... my enemies I exterminated, *Anchor* ... That I might cut off them that hate me, *ASV* ... so I wipe out those who hate me, *Beck.*

**41. They cried, but there was none to save them:** ... They implored, but the Savior was not there, *Anchor* ... They shrieked, but no one saved,

*Fenton* ... Loudly they cry out to the Lord, bereft of aid, *Knox.*

**even unto the LORD, but he answered them not:** ... Most High Yahweh, *Anchor.*

**42. Then did I beat them:** ... I pulverized them, *Anchor* ... I beat them fine, *Beck* ... I pound them to pieces, *Moffatt* ... they were crushed, *BB.*

**small as the dust before the wind:** ... like the dust in the square, *Anchor.*

**I did cast them out:** ... I clear them away, *Beck* ... I poured them out, *NIV* ... tread them, *Geneva* ... trample them, *JB* ... they were drained out, *BB.*

**as the dirt in the streets:** ... like the mud in the streets, *Anchor* ... like the waste of the streets, *BB* ... flat as the clay, *Geneva* ... mire in the lanes, *Rotherham.*

**43. Thou hast delivered me:** ... made me free, *BB* ... You free me, *JB.*

**from the strivings of the people:** ... a people in revolt, *Beck* ... from the shafts of people, *Anchor* ... contentions, *Geneva* ... feuds, *Goodspeed* ... domestic broils to rid me, *Knox.*

**and thou hast made me the head of the heathen:** ... protected me from the venom of nations, *Anchor* ... made me the head of nations, *Berkeley* ... leader of nations, *Beck* ... chief of Tribes, *Fenton.*

**a people whom I have not known:** ... An alien people, *Anchor* ... people of whom I had no knowledge, *BB* ... And hands I knew not served, *Fenton* ... outsiders, *Moffatt.*

**shall serve me:** ... obey me, *Beck* ... now become my subjects, *Good News.*

**44. As soon as they hear of me:** ... when my name comes to their ears, *BB* ... Unhearing ears now hear, *Fenton* ... At the hearing of the ear, *Young.*

**they shall obey me:** ... they will be ruled by me, *BB* ... they render homage, *Moffatt.*

**the strangers:** ... men of other countries, *BB* ... outsiders, *Berkeley* ... Foreigners, *Beck* ... sons of the stranger, *MAST.*

**shall submit themselves unto me:** ... feign obedience to me, *Young* ... put themselves under my authority, *BB* ... come cringing to me, *Darby* ... fawn upon me, *Goodspeed* ... dwindle away before me, *MAST.*

**45. The strangers shall fade away:** ... Foreigners shrivel up, *Anchor* ... foreigners grow faint of heart, *JB* ... Foreigners wilt like leaves, *Beck* ... Strangers shall shrinke away, *Geneva.*

**and be afraid out of their close places:** ... they will come out of their secret places shaking with fear, *BB* ... come trembling out of their fortifications, *Beck* ... come slinking out of their strongholds, *Knox* ... come frightened from their hideouts, *NKJV* ... creep from hiding dens, *Fenton.*

**46. The LORD liveth:** ... May Yahweh live, *Anchor* ... Live LORD, *Fenton* ... God is alive, *LIVB* ... The Eternal is living, *Moffatt.*

**and blessed be my rock:** ... Praised be my Mountain, *Anchor* ... my strength, *Geneva* ... my defender, *Good News* ... who is the great rock of protection, *LIVB* ... blest be my Might, *Moffatt.*

**and let the God of my salvation be exalted:** ... And exalted the God of my triumph, *Anchor* ... Let high honor come to God, *Beck* ... The GOD who gave success, *Fenton* ... God of my deliverance be exalted, *Goodspeed.*

**47. It is God that avengeth me:** ... who sends punishment on my haters,

---

whole is a picture of past conflict, for which the psalmist had been equipped by God. It is a literal fight, the triumph of which still glows in the singer's heart and flames in his vivid words. We see him in swift pursuit, pressing hard on the enemy, crushing them with his fierce onset, trampling them under foot. They break and flee, shrieking out prayers, which the pursuer has a stern joy in knowing to be fruitless. His blows fall like those of a great pestle and crush the fleeing wretches who are scattered by his irresistible charge like dust whirled by the storm. The last clause of the picture of the routed foe is also given by the reading in 2 Sam. 22:43, "I did stamp them as the mire of the streets." Such delight in the enemy's despair and destruction, such gratification at hearing their vain cries to Yahweh, are far away from Christian sentiments. Nothing but confusion and mischief can come of slurring over the difference. The light of battle which blazes in them is not the fire which Jesus longed to kindle upon earth.

**18:43–45.** Thus far the enemies seem to have been native foes rebelling against God's anointed or, if the reference to the Sauline persecution is upheld, seeking to prevent his reaching his throne. But in the concluding verses of this part, a transition is made to victory over "strangers," i.e., foreign nations. The phrase "the strivings of the people" seems to point back to the war described already, while "Thou hast made me the head of the nations" refers to external conquests.

**18:46–50.** A noble close comes to a noble hymn, in which the singer's strong wing never flags, nor the rush of thought and feeling slackens. Even more absolutely than in the rest of the Psalm, every victory is ascribed to Yahweh. He alone acts;

| 3937 | 1744.521 | 6194 | 8809 | | 6647.351 |
|---|---|---|---|---|---|
| prep, ps 1cs | cj, v Hiphil impf 3ms | n mp | prep, ps 1cs | | v Piel ptc ms, ps 1cs |
| לִי | וַיַּדְבֵּר | עַמִּים | תַּחְתָּי | **48.** | מְפַלְּטִי |
| lî | wayyadhbēr | ‘ammîm | tachtāy | | mephalleṭî |
| to me | and He subdued | peoples | under me | | the One Who set me free |

| 4623, 342.152 | 652 | 4623, 7251.152 | 7597.323 | 4623, 382 |
|---|---|---|---|---|
| prep, v Qal act ptc mp, ps 1cs | cj | prep, v Qal act ptc mp, ps 1cs | v Polel impf 2ms, ps 1cs | prep, *n ms* |
| מֵאֹיְבָי | אַף | מִן־קָמַי | תְּרוֹמְמֵנִי | מֵאִישׁ |
| mē’ōyevāy | ’aph | min-qāmay | terômemēnî | mē’îsh |
| from my enemies | indeed | from those who rise against me | You exalted me | from men of |

| 2660 | 5522.523 | | 6142, 3772 | 3142.525 | 904, 1504 | 3176 |
|---|---|---|---|---|---|---|
| n ms | v Hiphil impf 2ms, ps 1cs | | prep, adv | v Hiphil juss 1cs, ps 2ms | prep, art, n mp | pn |
| חָמָס | תַּצִּילֵנִי | **49.** | עַל־כֵּן | אוֹדְךָ | בַגּוֹיִם | יְהוָה |
| chāmās | tatstsîlēnî | | ‘al-kēn | ’ôdhkhā | vaggôyim | yehwāh |
| violence | You rescued me | | therefore | let me praise You | among the nations | O Yahweh |

| 3937, 8428 | 2252.325 | | 1461.551 | 3568 | 4567 |
|---|---|---|---|---|---|
| cj, prep, n ms, ps 2ms | v Piel juss 1cs | | v Hiphil ptc ms | *n fp* | n ms, ps 3ms |
| וּלְשִׁמְךָ | אֲזַמֵּרָה | **50.** | מִגְדֹּל | יְשׁוּעוֹת | מַלְכּוֹ |
| ûlăshimkhā | ’ăzammērāh | | mighdōl | yeshû‘ôth | malkô |
| and to your name | let me sing | | making great | the deliverances of | his king |

| 6449.151 | 2721 | 3937, 5081 | 3937, 1784 | 3937, 2320 |
|---|---|---|---|---|
| cj, v Qal act ptc ms | n ms | prep, n ms, ps 3ms | prep, pn | cj, prep, n ms, ps 3ms |
| וְעֹשֶׂה | חֶסֶד | לִמְשִׁיחוֹ | לְדָוִד | וּלְזַרְעוֹ |
| we‘ōseh | chesedh | limshîchô | ledhāwidh | ûlăzar‘ô |
| and He demonstrates | steadfast love | to his anointed one | to David | and to his descendants |

| 5912, 5986 | | 3937, 5514.351 | 4344 | 3937, 1784 | | 8452 | 5807.352 | 3638, 418 |
|---|---|---|---|---|---|---|---|---|
| adv, n ms | | prep, art, v Piel ptc ms | n ms | prep, pn | | art, n md | v Piel ptc mp | *n ms*, n ms |
| עַד־עוֹלָם | **19:t** | לַמְנַצֵּחַ | מִזְמוֹר | לְדָוִד | **1.** | הַשָּׁמַיִם | מְסַפְּרִים | כְּבוֹד־אֵל |
| ‘adh-‘ôlām | | lamnatstsēach | mizmôr | ledhāwidh | | hashshāmayim | mesapperîm | kevôdh-’ēl |
| until forever | | to the director | a Psalm | of David | | the heavens | recounting | the glory of God |

| 4801 | 3135 | 5222.551 | 7842 | | 3219 | 3937, 3219 | 5218.521 |
|---|---|---|---|---|---|---|---|
| cj, *n ms* | n fd, ps 3ms | v Hiphil ptc ms | art, n ms | | n ms | prep, n ms | v Hiphil impf 3ms |
| וּמַעֲשֵׂה | יָדָיו | מַגִּיד | הָרָקִיעַ | **2.** | יוֹם | לְיוֹם | יַבִּיעַ |
| ûma‘ăsēh | yādhâv | maggîdh | hārāqîa‘ | | yôm | leyôm | yabbîa‘ |
| and the works of | his hands | telling | the firmament | | day | to day | it pours forth |

| 575 | 4050 | 3937, 4050 | 2425.321, 1907 | | 375, 575 | 375 | 1745 |
|---|---|---|---|---|---|---|---|
| n ms | cj, n ms | prep, n ms | v Piel impf 3ms, n fs | | *sub*, n ms | cj, *sub* | n mp |
| אֹמֶר | וְלַיְלָה | לְלַיְלָה | יְחַוֶּה־דָּעַת | **3.** | אֵין־אֹמֶר | וְאֵין | דְּבָרִים |
| ’ōmer | welaylāh | lelaylāh | yechawweh-dā‘ath | | ’ên-’ōmer | we’ên | devārîm |
| speech | and night | to night | it declares knowledge | | there is not speech | and there is not | words |

| 1136 | 8471.120 | 7249 | | 904, 3725, 800 | 3428.111 | 7241 |
|---|---|---|---|---|---|---|
| neg part | v Qal impf 1cp | n ms, ps 3mp | | prep, *adj*, art, n fs | v Qal pf 3ms | n ms, ps 3mp |
| בְּלִי | נִשְׁמָע | קוֹלָם | **4.** | בְּכָל־הָאָרֶץ | יָצָא | קַוָּם |
| belî | nishmā‘ | qôlām | | bekhol-hā’ārets | yātsā’ | qawwām |
| not | we listen | their voice | | throughout all the earth | it went out | their line |

| 904, 7381 | 8725 | 4543 | 3937, 8507 | 7947.111, 164 | 904 | | 2000 |
|---|---|---|---|---|---|---|---|
| cj, *n ms* | n fs | n fp, ps 3mp | prep, art, n fs | v Qal pf 3ms, n ms | prep, ps 3mp | | cj, pers pron |
| וּבִקְצֵה | תֵּבֵל | מִלֵּיהֶם | לַשֶּׁמֶשׁ | שָׂם־אֹהֶל | בָּהֶם | **5.** | וְהוּא |
| ûviqtsēh | thēvēl | millêhem | lashshemesh | sām-’ōhel | bāhem | | wehû’ |
| and to the end of | the world | their words | for the sun | He has set a tent | on them | | and it |

*BB* ... who gives me salvation, *Beck* ... who executes retribution for me, *Berkeley* ... who lets me enjoy my vengeance, *Moffatt* ... who grantest me vengeance, *NEB*.

**and subdueth the people under me:** ... puts peoples under my rule, *BB* ... subjected the peoples to me, *Darby* ... humbles the people under me, *KJVII* ... layest nations prostrate at my feet, *NEB*.

**48. He delivereth me from mine enemies:** ... He rescueth me from mine enemies, *ASV* ... who released from foes, *Fenton*.

**yea, thou liftest me up above those that rise up against me:** ... Thou dost exalt me higher than my assailants, *Berkeley* ... thou dost exalt me above my adversaries, *Goodspeed* ... so that I am high above the reach of their assaults, *Knox* ... Above my withstanders thou raisest me, *Young*.

**thou hast delivered me from the violent man:** ... rescued me from calumniators, *Anchor* ... Who freed from treacherous men, *Fenton* ... proof against their violence, *Knox*.

**49. Therefore will I give thanks unto thee, O LORD:** ... Because of this I will give you praise, *BB* ... I will extol Thee, *Berkeley*.

**among the heathen:** ... among the nations, *Anchor* ... before pagans, *Moffatt* ... among the Gentiles, *NKJV*.

**and sing praises unto thy name:** ... celebrate your name in song, *Anchor* ... will make a song of praise to your name, *BB* ... And chant Psalms to His name, *Fenton*.

**50. Great deliverance giveth he to his king:** ... Who made his king famous through victories, *Anchor* ... Great salvation does he give to his king, *BB* ... He saves his king time after time, *JB*.

**and showeth mercy to his anointed:** ... shows His sanctioned kindness, *Fenton* ... shows constant love, *Good News* ... displays his faithful love, *JB*.

**to David, and to his seed for evermore:** ... offspring, *Anchor* ... descendants, *Beck* ... his dynasty, *Moffatt*.

**19:t. To the chief Musician, A Psalm of David.**

**1. The heavens declare the glory of God:** ... heavens are recounting the honour of God, *Young* ... telling how wonderful God is, *Beck* ... the sky reveals God's glory, *Good News* ... heavens proclaim God's splendour, *Moffatt*.

**and the firmament showeth his handiwork:** ... the skies announce what his hands have made, *NCV* ... sky manifests the work of his hands, *Anchor* ... the arch of the sky makes clear the work of his hands, *BB* ... sky announces what His hands have made, *Beck*.

**2. Day unto day uttereth speech:** ... Each day echos its secret to the next, *Knox* ... day after day takes up the tale, *Moffatt* ... One day tells the next a lively story, *Beck* ... One day speaks to another, *NEB*.

**and night unto night showeth knowledge:** ... one night informs the next, *Beck* ... Night whispers news to night, *Fenton* ... each night passes on to the next its revelation of knowledge, *Knox*.

**3. There is no speech nor language:** ... Without speech and without words, *Anchor* ... No utterance at all, *JB* ... no word, no accent of theirs, *Knox*.

**where their voice is not heard:** ... their voice makes no sound, *BB* ... not a sound to be heard, *JB* ... sound of any voice not heard, *NEB*.

**4. Their line is gone out through all the earth:** ... Yet their sound goes out, *Beck* ... their message goes out, *Good News* ... their language, *Darby* ... Their music goes out, *NEB*.

---

the psalmist is simply the recipient. To have learned by life's struggles and deliverances that Yahweh is a living God and "my Rock" is to have gathered life's best fruit. A morning of tempest has cleared into sunny calm, as it always will, if the tempest drives him to God. He who cries to Yahweh when the floods of destruction make him afraid will in due time have to admit that Yahweh lives. If we begin with "The LORD is my Rock," we will end with "Blessed be my Rock."

The last verse of the Psalm is sometimes regarded as a liturgical addition, and the mention of David gratuitously supposed to be adverse to his authorship, but there is nothing unnatural in a king's mentioning himself in such a connection nor in the reference to his dynasty, which is evidently based upon the promise of perpetual dominion given through Nathan. The Christian reader knows that the mercy granted to the king in that great promise was much more wonderful than the singer knew, fulfilled in the Son of David, whose kingdom is an everlasting kingdom and who bears God's name to all the nations.

**19:1–6.** Verses 1–6 sing the silent declaration by the heavens. The details of exposition must first be dealt with. "Declare" (HED #5807) and "makes known" (HED #5222) are participles, and thus express the continuity of the acts. The substance of the witness is set forth with distinct reference to its limitations, for "glory" has here no moral element, but simply means what Paul calls "eternal power and Godhead." "His handiwork," in like manner,

| 3626, 2968 | 3428.151 | 4623, 2751 | 7919.121 | 3626, 1399 |
|---|---|---|---|---|
| prep, n ms | v Qal act ptc ms | prep, n fs, ps 3ms | v Qal impf 3ms | prep, n ms |
| כְּחָתָן | יֹצֵא | מֵחֻפָּתוֹ | יָשִׂישׂ | כְּגִבּוֹר |
| kechāthān | yōtsē' | mēchuppāthô | yāsîs | keghibbôr |
| like a bridegroom | going out | from his chamber | he rejoices | like a strong man |

| 3937, 7608.141 | 758 | | 4623, 7381 | 8452 | 4296 | 8958 |
|---|---|---|---|---|---|---|
| prep, v Qal inf con | n ms | 6. | prep, *n ms* | art, n md | n ms, ps 3ms | cj, n fs, ps 3ms |
| לָרוּץ | אֹרַח | | מִקְצֵה | הַשָּׁמַיִם | מוֹצָאוֹ | וּתְקוּפָתוֹ |
| lārûts | 'ōrach | | miqŏtsēh | hashshāmayim | môtsā'ô | ûthequphāthô |
| to run | a path | | from the end of | the heavens | its going out | and its turning point |

| 6142, 7381 | 375 | 5846.255 | 4623, 2635 | | 8784 | 3176 | 8879 |
|---|---|---|---|---|---|---|---|
| prep, n fp, ps 3mp | cj, *sub* | v Niphal ptc ms | prep, n fs, ps 3ms | 7. | *n fs* | pn | adj |
| עַל־קְצוֹתָם | וְאֵין | נִסְתָּר | מֵחַמָּתוֹ | | תּוֹרַת | יְהוָה | תְּמִימָה |
| 'al-qŏtsôthām | we'ên | nistār | mēchammāthô | | tôrath | yehwāh | temîmāh |
| on their ends | and there is not | hidden | from its heat | | the Law of | Yahweh | perfect |

| 8178.553 | 5497 | 5925 | 3176 | 548.257 | 2549.553 | 6864 |
|---|---|---|---|---|---|---|
| *v Hiphil ptc fs* | n fs | *n fs* | pn | v Niphal ptc fs | *v Hiphil ptc fs* | n ms |
| מְשִׁיבַת | נָפֶשׁ | עֵדוּת | יְהוָה | נֶאֱמָנָה | מַחְכִּימַת | פֶּתִי |
| meshîvath | nāphesh | 'ēdhûth | yehwāh | ne'ĕmānāh | machkîmath | pethî |
| causing to return | the soul | the testimony of | Yahweh | reliable | making wise | the simple |

| | 6740 | 3176 | 3596 | 7975.352, 3949 | 4851 | 3176 | 1276 |
|---|---|---|---|---|---|---|---|
| 8. | *n mp* | pn | adj | *v Piel ptc mp*, n ms | *n fs* | pn | adj |
| | פִּקּוּדֵי | יְהוָה | יְשָׁרִים | מְשַׂמְּחֵי־לֵב | מִצְוַת | יְהוָה | בָּרָה |
| | piqqûdhê | yehwāh | yeshārîm | mesammechê-lēv | mitswath | yehwāh | bārāh |
| | the precepts of | Yahweh | upright | rejoicing of the heart | the commandment of | Yahweh | pure |

| 213.553 | 6084 | | 3488 | 3176 | 2999 | 6198.153 | 3937, 5911 |
|---|---|---|---|---|---|---|---|
| *v Hiphil ptc fs* | n fd | 9. | *n fs* | pn | adj | v Qal act ptc fs | prep, n ms |
| מְאִירַת | עֵינָיִם | | יִרְאַת | יְהוָה | טְהוֹרָה | עוֹמֶדֶת | לָעַד |
| me'îrath | 'ênāyim | | yir'ath | yehwāh | tehôrāh | 'ômedheth | lā'adh |
| luminating | the eyes | | the fear of | Yahweh | clean | standing | unto eternity |

| 5122, 3176 | 583 | 6927.116 | 3267 | | 2629.256 | 4623, 2174 |
|---|---|---|---|---|---|---|
| *n mp*, pn | n fs | v Qal pf 3cp | adv | 10. | art, v Niphal ptc mp | prep, n ms |
| מִשְׁפְּטֵי־יְהוָה | אֱמֶת | צָדְקוּ | יַחְדָּו | | הַנֶּחֱמָדִים | מִזָּהָב |
| mishpetê-yehwāh | 'ĕmeth | tsādhequ | yachdāw | | hannechĕmādhîm | mizzāhāv |
| the ordinances of Yahweh | reliability | they are righteous | altogether | | more desirable | than gold |

**and their words to the end of the world:** ... the wide world over, *Moffatt* ... to the edge, *Anchor* ... all over the earth, *Beck* ... to the extremity, *Darby* ... the design stands out, *JB*.

**In them hath he set a tabernacle for the sun:** ... In the heavens an abode is fixed for the sun, *REB* ... God made a home in the sky for the sun, *Good News*.

**5. Which is as a bridegroom:** ... like a newly married man, *BB* ... And comes to seek his bride, *Fenton*.

**coming out of his chamber:** ... comes forth from his pavilion, *JB* ... comes from his bed, *Knox* ... from his bedroom, *NCV* ... coming from his bride-tent, *BB*.

**and rejoiceth as a strong man to run a race:** ... like a strong runner starting on his way, *BB* ... like an athlete eager to run, *Good News* ... delights like a champion in the course to be run, *JB* ... like some great runner who sees the track before him, *Knox* ... like a giant, joyfully runs its course, *NCB*.

**6. His going forth is from the end of the heaven:** ... starting from one end of the sky, *Beck* ... He starts from distant skies, *Fenton* ... From one end of the heavens is his starting-point, *Goodspeed* ... Riding on the one horizon, *JB*.

**and his circuit unto the ends of it:** ... and his circle, *BB* ... his compasse, *Geneva* ... whirls their full extent, *Fenton* ... and moving around, *Beck*.

**and there is nothing hid from the heat thereof:** ... which is not open to his heat, *BB* ... nothing can escape,

*JB* ... missing nothing with his heat, *Moffatt* ... Nothing can hide from its glowing heat, *Beck.*

**7. The law of the LORD is perfect:** ... How perfect are your laws, O LIFE, *Fenton* ... The Eternal's law is a sound law, *Moffatt.*

**converting the soul:** ... refreshing my soul, *Anchor* ... giving new life to the soul, *BB* ... They guide the mind aright, *Fenton.*

**the testimony of the LORD is sure:** ... decree of Yahweh is stable, *Anchor* ... decree of the LORD is trustworthy, *Goodspeed* ... the witness, *BB* ... plans of GOD, *Fenton* ... the Lord's unchallengeable decrees, *Knox.*

**making wise the simple:** ... giving my mind wisdom, *Anchor* ... giving wisdom to the foolish, *BB* ... how they make the simple learned, *Knox* ... that instructs the open-minded, *Moffatt.*

**8. The statutes of the LORD are right:** ... precepts, *ASV* ... orders, *BB* ... instructions, *Beck.*

**rejoicing the heart:** ... making glad the heart, *BB* ... delighting the mind, *Beck* ... a joy to the heart, *Moffatt* ... make people happy, *NCV.*

**the commandment of the LORD is pure:** ... rule of the Lord is holy, *BB* ... radiant, *Anchor* ... clear, *Moffatt* ... shines clear, *NEB.*

**enlightening the eyes:** ... More than the eyes can see, *Fenton* ... a light to the mind, *Moffatt* ... they light up the way, *NCV* ... gives light to the eyes, *NEB.*

**9. The fear of the LORD is clean:** ... The LORD's command to fear Him is clean, *Beck* ... reverence of the LORD, *Berkeley* ... fear of the LORD is unsullied, *REB.*

**enduring for ever:** ... has no end, *BB* ... forever the same, *Beck* ... which is binding for ever, *Knox* ... standing to the age, *Young.*

**the judgments of the LORD are true and righteous altogether:** ... ordinances, *ASV* ... decisions, *BB* ... rulings, *Moffatt.*

**10. More to be desired are they than gold:** ... more valuable than gold, *Goodspeed* ... more to be prized than gold, *Moffatt* ... more precious than gold, *NAB.*

**yea, than much fine gold:** ... even than much shining gold, *BB* ... than a hoard of pure gold, *Knox* ... than plenty of rare gold, *Moffatt* ... than a heap of purest gold, *NAB.*

**sweeter also than honey and the honeycomb:** ... and the droppings of the honeycomb, *ASV* ... even when it flows from the honeycomb, *Beck* ... drippings of the comb, *Berkeley* ... sweeter than syrup or honey, *NEB* ... Even liquid honey of the comb, *Young.*

---

limits the revelation. The heavens by day are so marvelously unlike the heavens by night that the psalmist's imagination conjures up two long processions, each member of which passes on the word entrusted to him to his successor—the blazing days with heaven naked but for one great light and the still nights with all their stars. Verse 3 has given commentators much trouble in attempting to smooth its paradox. In v. 4, the thought of the great voices returns. "Their line" is usually explained as meaning their sphere of influence, marked out, as it were, by a measuring cord. If that rendering is adopted, v. 4b would in effect say, "Their words go as far as their realm." Or the rendering "sound" may be deduced, although somewhat precariously, from that of line, since a line stretched is musical. In any case, the teaching of the verse is plain from the last clause, namely, the universality of the revelation. The psalmist is protesting against stellar worship, which some of his neighbors practiced. The sun was a creature, not a god; his "race" was marked out by the same hand which in depths beyond the visible heavens had pitched a "tent" for his nightly rest. We smile at the simple astronomy; the religious depth is as deep as ever.

**19:7–10.** In vv. 7–11, the clauses are constructed on a uniform plan, each containing a name for the Law, an attribute of it, and one of its effects. The abundance of synonyms indicates familiarity and clear views of the many sides of the subject. The psalmist had often brooded on the thought of what that Law was, because, loving its Giver, he must love the gift. So he calls it "Law," or teaching, since there he found the best lessons for character and life.

These synonyms have each an attribute attached, which, together, give a grand aggregate of qualities discerned by a devout heart to inhere in that Law which is to so many just a restraint and a foe. It is "perfect," as containing without flaw or defect the ideal of conduct; "sure" or reliable, as worthy of being absolutely followed and certain to be completely fulfilled; "right," as prescribing the straight road to humanity's true goal; "pure" or bright, as being light like the sun, but of a higher quality than that material brilliance; "clean," as contrasted with the foulness bedaubing false religious and making idol worship unutterably loathsome; and "true" and "wholly righteous," as corresponding accurately to the mind of Yahweh and the facts of humanity and as

| 4623, 6580 | 7521 | 5142 | 4623, 1756 | 5499 | 6951 |
|---|---|---|---|---|---|
| cj, prep, n ms | adj | cj, adj | prep, n ms | cj, *n ms* | n mp |
| וּמִפַּז | רָב | וּמְתוּקִים | מִדְּבַשׁ | וְנֹפֶת | צוּפִים |
| ûmippaz | rāv | ûmethûqîm | middevash | wenōpheth | tsûphîm |
| even than fine gold | abundant | and sweeter | than honey | even honey from | a honeycomb |

| | 1612, 5860 | 2178.255 | 904 | 904, 8490.141 | 6358 | 7521 |
|---|---|---|---|---|---|---|
| **11.** | adv, n ms, ps 2ms | v Niphal ptc ms | prep, ps 3mp | prep, v Qal inf con, ps 3mp | n ms | adj |
| | גַּם־עַבְדְּךָ | נִזְהָר | בָּהֶם | בְּשָׁמְרָם | עֵקֶב | רָב |
| | gam-'avdekhā | nizhār | bāhem | beshāmerām | 'ēqev | rāv |
| | also your servant | warned | by them | when observing them | wages | abundant |

| | 8149 | 4449, 1032.121 | 5846.258 | 5536.331 | | 1612 |
|---|---|---|---|---|---|---|
| **12.** | n fp | intrg, v Qal impf 3ms | prep, v Niphal ptc fp | v Piel impv 2ms, ps 1cs | **13.** | cj |
| | שְׁגִיאוֹת | מִי־יָבִין | מִנִּסְתָּרוֹת | נַקֵּנִי | | גַּם |
| | sheghî'ôth | mî-yāvîn | ministārôth | naqqēnî | | gam |
| | errors | who can discern | among what is hidden | acquit me | | also |

| 4623, 2170 | 2910.131 | 5860 | 414, 5090.126, 904 | 226 |
|---|---|---|---|---|
| prep, n mp | v Qal impv 2ms | n ms, ps 2ms | neg part, v Qal juss 3mp, prep, ps 1cs | adv |
| מִזֵּדִים | חֲשֹׂךְ | עַבְדֶּךָ | אַל־יִמְשְׁלוּ־בִי | אָז |
| mizzēdhîm | chāsōkh | 'avdekhā | 'al-yimshelû-vî | 'āz |
| from presumptuous sins | keep back | your servant | may they not rule over me | then |

| 8882.125 | 5536.315 | 4623, 6840 | 7521 | | 2030.126 | 3937, 7814 |
|---|---|---|---|---|---|---|
| v Qal impf 1cs | cj, v Piel pf 1cs | perp, n ms | adj | **14.** | v Qal juss 3mp | prep, n ms |
| אֵיתָם | וְנִקֵּיתִי | מִפֶּשַׁע | רָב | | יִהְיוּ | לְרָצוֹן |
| 'êthām | weniqqêthî | mippesha' | rāv | | yihyû | lerātsôn |
| I will be blameless | and I have been acquitted | from offence | many | | may they be | for favor |

| 571, 6552 | 1970 | 3949 | 3937, 6686 | 3176 | 6962 |
|---|---|---|---|---|---|
| *n mp*, n ms, ps 1cs | cj, *n ms* | n ms, ps 1cs | prep, n mp, ps 2ms | pn | n ms, ps 1cs |
| אִמְרֵי־פִי | וְהֶגְיוֹן | לִבִּי | לְפָנֶיךָ | יְהוָה | צוּרִי |
| 'imrê-phî | weheghyôn | libbî | lephānêkhā | yehwāh | tsûrî |
| the words of my mouth | and the meditation of | my heart | in your presence | O Yahweh | my Rock |

| 1381.151 | | 3937, 5514.351 | 4344 | 3937, 1784 | | 6257.121 | 3176 |
|---|---|---|---|---|---|---|---|
| cj, v Qal act ptc ms, ps 1cs | **20:t** | prep, art, v Piel ptc ms | n ms | prep, pn | **1.** | v Qal juss 3ms, ps 2ms | pn |
| וְגֹאֲלִי | | לַמְנַצֵּחַ | מִזְמוֹר | לְדָוִד | | יַעַנְךָ | יְהוָה |
| weghō'ălî | | lamnatstsēach | mizmôr | ledhāwidh | | ya'ankhā | yehwāh |
| and my Redeemer | | to the director | a Psalm | of David | | may He answer you | Yahweh |

| 904, 3219 | 7150 | 7891.321 | 8428 | 435 | 3399 |
|---|---|---|---|---|---|
| prep, *n ms* | n fs | v Piel juss 3ms, ps 2ms | *n ms* | *n mp* | pn |
| בְּיוֹם | צָרָה | יְשַׂגֶּבְךָ | שֵׁם | אֱלֹהֵי | יַעֲקֹב |
| beyôm | tsārāh | yesaggevkhā | shēm | 'ĕlōhê | ya'ăqōv |
| in the day of | adversity | may He shelter you | the name of | the God of | Jacob |

**11. Moreover by them is thy servant warned:** … is your servant made conscious of danger, *BB* … Your servant gets light from them, *Beck* … Your servant walks, *Fenton* … Thy servant also is instructed, *Goodspeed.*

**and in keeping of them:** … Delights to keep their tracks, *Fenton* … observing them how jealously, *Knox.*

**there is great reward:** … there is rich profit, *Moffatt.*

**12. Who can understand his errors?:** … Who can know his unintentional errors, *Beck* … how can I ever know what sins are lurking in my heart, *LIVB* … People cannot see their own mistakes, *NCV* … who can detect his lapses, *Moffatt.*

**cleanse thou me from secret faults:** … From my aberrations cleanse me, *Anchor* … from hidden faults, *Beck* … From those that are secret pardon me, *Berkeley* … Of unconscious ones, hold me guiltless, *Goodspeed.*

**13. Keep back thy servant also:** … restrain thy servant, *Goodspeed* … preserve, *JB.*

**from presumptuous sins:** ... sins of self-will, *NEB* ... deliberate wrongs, *LIVB* ... wanton sin, *NAB* ... sins of pride, *BB* ... from the insolent, *NRSV.*

**let them not have dominion over me:** ... don't let them get control over me, *Beck* ... lest they get the better of me, *NEB* ... never let it be my master, *JB* ... so long as this does not lord it over me, *Knox.*

**then shall I be upright:** ... blameless, *Anchor* ... without fault, *Knox.*

**and I shall be innocent:** ... acquitted, *Goodspeed.*

**from the great transgression:** ... of the great crime, *Anchor* ... from great sin, *BB* ... from gross transgression, *Berkeley* ... free from crimes, *Fenton* ... free from grave sin, *JB.*

**14. Let the words of my mouth:** ... May what I say please You, *Beck* ... Let my mouth's speech be sweet, *Fenton* ... Every word on my lips, *Knox.*

**and the meditation of my heart:** ... thoughts of my heart, *Anchor* ... what I think, *Beck* ... the soft utterance of my heart, *Rotherham.*

**be acceptable in thy sight, O LORD:** ... according to your will, *Anchor* ... be pleasing in your eyes, *BB* ... be what You like, *Beck.*

**my strength, and my redeemer:** ... my Mountain, and my Redeemer, *Anchor* ... my rock and my avenger, *Goodspeed.*

**20:t. To the chief Musician, A Psalm of David.**

**1. The LORD hear thee in the day of trouble:** ... May Yahweh grant you triumph in time of siege, *Anchor* ... The LORD answer you in time of distress, *NAB.*

**the name of the God of Jacob defend thee:** ... be your bulwark, *Anchor* ... may you be placed on high, *BB* ... lift you up on a safe height, *Beck* ... be your tower of strength, *NEB.*

---

being in full accordance with the justice which has its seat in the bosom of God.

The effects are summed up in the latter clauses of these verses, which stand, as it were, a little apart and by the slight pause are made more emphatic. The rhythm rises and falls like the upspringing and sinking of a fountain. The Law "restores the soul," or rather refreshes the life, as food does. It "makes the simple wise" by its sure testimony, giving practical guidance to narrow understandings and wills open to easy beguiling by sin. It "rejoices the heart," since there is no gladness equal to that of knowing and doing the will of God. It "enlightens the eyes" with brightness beyond that of the created light which rules the day. The relation of clauses changes slightly in v. 9, and a second attribute takes the place of the effect. It "endures for ever," and, as we have seen, is "wholly righteous."

**19:11–14.** The contemplation of the Law cannot but lead to self-examination, and that to petition. So the psalmist passes into prayer. His shortcomings are appalling, for "by the Law is the knowledge of sin," and he feels that beyond the sin which he knows, there is a dark region in him where foul things nestle and breed fast. "Secret faults" are those hidden, not from men, but from himself. He discovers that he has hitherto undiscovered sins. Lurking evils are most dangerous because, like aphides on the underside of a rose leaf, they multiply so quickly unobserved. Small deeds make up life, and small, unnoticed sins darken the soul. Mud in water, at the rate of a grain to a glassful, will make a lake opaque.

The closing aspiration is that Yahweh would accept the song and prayer. There is an allusion to the acceptance of a sacrifice, for the phrase "be acceptable" is frequent in connection with the sacrificial ritual. When the words of the mouth coincide with the meditation of the heart, we may hope that prayers for cleansing from and defense against sin, offered to Him whom our faith recognizes as our "strength" and our "Redeemer," will be as a sacrifice of a sweet smell, pleasing to God.

***Psalm 20.*** *This is a battle song, followed by a chant of victory. They are connected in subject and probably in occasion, but fight and triumph have fallen dim to us, although we can still feel how hotly the fire once glowed. The passion of loyalty and love for the king expressed in these Psalms fits no reign in Judah so well as the bright noonday of David's, when "whatever the king did pleased all the people."*

**20:1–5.** The prayer in vv. 1–5 breathes distrust of self and confidence in Yahweh, the temper which brings victory, not only to Israel, but to all fighters for God. Here is no boasting of former victories, or of man's bravery and strength, or of a captain's skill. One name is invoked. It alone rouses courage and pledges triumph. "The name of the God of Jacob set thee on high." That name is almost regarded as a person, as is often the case. Attributes and acts are ascribed to it which properly belong to the Unnameable Whom it names, as if with some dim inkling that the agent of revealing a person must be a person. The name is the

| 2. | 8365.121, 6039 | 4623, 7231 | 4623, 6995 | 5777.121 |
|---|---|---|---|---|
| | v Qal juss 3ms, n ms, ps 2ms | prep, n ms | cj, prep, pn | v Qal juss 3ms, ps 2ms |
| | יִשְׁלַח־עֶזְרְךָ | מִקֹּדֶשׁ | וּמִצִּיּוֹן | יִסְעָדֶךָּ |
| | yishlach-'ezrekhā | miqqōdhesh | ûmitstsîyôn | yis'ādhekhā |
| | may He send help to you | from the holy place | and from Zion | may He support you |

| 3. | 2226.121 | 3725, 4647 | 6150 | 1941.321 | 5734 |
|---|---|---|---|---|---|
| | v Qal juss 3ms | *adj*, n fp, ps 2ms | cj, n fp, ps 2ms | v Piel juss 3ms | intrj |
| | יִזְכֹּר | כָּל־מִנְחֹתֶךָ | וְעוֹלָתְךָ | יְדַשְּׁנֶה | סֶלָה |
| | yizkōr | kol-minchōthekhā | we'ôlāthekhā | yedhashshenneh | selāh |
| | may He be mindful of | all your offerings | and your burnt offerings | may He make fat | selah |

| 4. | 5598.121, 3937 | 3626, 3949 | 3725, 6332 | 4527.321 |
|---|---|---|---|---|
| | v Qal juss 3ms, prep, ps 2ms | prep, n ms, ps 2ms | cj, *adj*, n fs, ps 2ms | v Piel juss 3ms |
| | יִתֶּן־לְךָ | כִלְבָבֶךָ | וְכָל־עֲצָתְךָ | יְמַלֵּא |
| | yitten-lekhā | khilvāvekhā | wekhol-'ătsāthekhā | yemalle' |
| | may He give you | according to your heart | and all your counsel | may He cause to be full |

| 5. | 7728.320 | 904, 3568 | 904, 8428, 435 |
|---|---|---|---|
| | v Piel juss 1cp | prep, n fs, ps 2ms | cj, prep, *n ms*, n mp, ps 1cp |
| | נְרַנְּנָה | בִּישׁוּעָתֶךָ | וּבְשֵׁם־אֱלֹהֵינוּ |
| | nerannenāh | bîshû'āthekhā | ûveshēm-'ělōhênû |
| | may we shout for joy | because of your salvation | and in the name of our God |

| 1763.120 | 4527.321 | 3176 | 3725, 5048 | 6. | 6498 | 3156.115 |
|---|---|---|---|---|---|---|
| v Qal juss 1cp | v Piel juss 3ms | pn | *adj*, n fp, ps 2ms | | adv | v Qal pf 1cs |
| נִדְגֹּל | יְמַלֵּא | יְהוָה | כָּל־מִשְׁאֲלוֹתֶיךָ | | עַתָּה | יָדַעְתִּי |
| nidhgōl | yemallē' | yehwāh | kol-mish'ălôthêkhā | | 'attāh | yādha'ttî |
| may we lift the banner | may He cause to be full | Yahweh | all your requests | | now | I know |

| 3706 | 3588.511 | 3176 | 5081 | 6257.121 | 4623, 8452 |
|---|---|---|---|---|---|
| cj | v Hiphil pf 3ms | pn | n ms, ps 3ms | v Qal impf 3ms, ps 3ms | prep, *n md* |
| כִּי | הוֹשִׁיעַ | יְהוָה | מְשִׁיחוֹ | יַעֲנֵהוּ | מִשְּׁמֵי |
| kî | hôshîa' | yehwāh | limshîchô | ya'ănēhû | mishshemê |
| because | He will save | Yahweh | his anointed one | He will answer him | from the heavens of |

| 7231 | 904, 1400 | 3589 | 3332 | 7. | 431 | 904, 7681 | 431 |
|---|---|---|---|---|---|---|---|
| n ms, ps 3ms | prep, n fp | n ms | n fs, ps 3ms | | dem pron | prep, art, n ms | cj, dem pron |
| קָדְשׁוֹ | בִּגְבֻרוֹת | יֵשַׁע | יְמִינוֹ | | אֵלֶּה | בָרֶכֶב | וְאֵלֶּה |
| qādheshô | bighvurôth | yēsha' | yemînô | | 'ēlleh | vārekhev | we'ēlleh |
| his holy place | with might | salvation | his right hand | | these | with the chariots | and these |

| 904, 5670 | 601 | 904, 8428, 3176 | 435 | 2226.520 |
|---|---|---|---|---|
| prep, art, n mp | cj, pers pron | prep, *n ms*, pn | n mp, ps 1cp | v Hiphil impf 1cp |
| בַסּוּסִים | וַאֲנַחְנוּ | בְּשֵׁם־יְהוָה | אֱלֹהֵינוּ | נַזְכִּיר |
| vassûsîm | wa'ănachnû | beshēm-yehwāh | 'ělōhênû | nazkîr |
| with the horses | but we | with the name of Yahweh | our God | we will cause to remember |

| 8. | 2065 | 3895.116 | 5489.116 | 601 | 7251.119 | 5967.720 |
|---|---|---|---|---|---|---|
| | pers pron | v Qal pf 3cp | cj, v Qal pf 3cp | cj, pers pron | v Qal pf 1cp | cj, v Hithpolel impf 1cp |
| | הֵמָּה | כָּרְעוּ | וְנָפָלוּ | וַאֲנַחְנוּ | קַמְנוּ | וַנִּתְעוֹדָד |
| | hēmmāh | kāre'û | wenāphālû | wa'ănachnû | qamnû | wanith'ôdhādh |
| | they | they will kneel | and they will fall | but we | we will rise | and we will stand upright |

| 9. | 3176 | 3588.512 | 4567 | 6257.121 | 904, 3219, 7410.141 |
|---|---|---|---|---|---|
| | pn | v Hiphil pf 3fs | art, n ms | v Qal juss 3ms, ps 1cp | prep, *n ms*, v Qal inf con, ps 1cp |
| | יְהוָה | הוֹשִׁיעָה | הַמֶּלֶךְ | יַעֲנֵנוּ | בְיוֹם־קָרְאֵנוּ |
| | yehwāh | hôshî'āh | hammelekh | ya'ănēnû | veyôm-qāre'ēnû |
| | O Yahweh | He will save | the king | may He answer us | in the day of our calling |

**2. Send thee help from the sanctuary:** ... From His blest dwelling, *Fenton.*

**and strengthen thee out of Zion:** ... from Zion sustain you, *Anchor* ... and support you from Zion, *Beck.*

**3. Remember all thy offerings:** ... may he keep all your offerings in mind, *BB* ... remember with pleasure the gifts you have given him, *LIVB* ... all your meal offerings, *NASB* ... Remember every present of thine, *Rotherham.*

**and accept thy burnt sacrifice:** ... be pleased with the fat of your burnt offerings, *BB* ... turne thy burnt offerings into ashes, *Geneva* ... regard with favor your burnt sacrifices, *NRSV* ... And thy burnt-offering doth reduce to ashes, *Young.*

**Selah:** ... Music, *Beck.*

**4. Grant thee according to thine own heart:** ... May he give you what you strive for, *Anchor* ... your heart's desire, *BB* ... what you want, *NCV.*

**and fulfil all thy counsel:** ... every plan of yours accomplish, *Anchor* ... put all your purposes into effect, *BB* ... carry out all your plans, *Beck* ... Make all your plans succeed, *Fenton* ... graciously accept your holocaust, *NAB.*

**5. We will rejoice in thy salvation, and in the name of our God:** ... That we might exult in your victory, *Anchor* ... We will be glad in your salvation, *BB* ... we'll shout joyfully over the victory given you, *Beck* ... We then will cheer, at your success, *Fenton* ... Let us sing aloud in praise of your victory, *NEB.*

**we will set up our banners:** ... we will put up our flags, *BB* ... set up our standards, *Goodspeed* ... draw up our ranks, *JB* ... let us do homage, *NEB* ... flags flying with praise to God, *LIVB.*

**the LORD fulfil all thy petitions:** ... give you all your requests, *BB* ... give you everything you ask for, *Beck.*

**6. Now know I:** ... Now I am certain, *BB* ... Shall I doubt, *Knox* ... Now I am sure, *Moffatt.*

**that the LORD saveth his anointed:** ... that Yahweh has given his anointed victory, *Anchor* ... that the Lord gives salvation to his king, *BB* ... protects the king he has anointed, *Knox.*

**he will hear him from his holy heaven:** ... he will give him an answer, *BB* ... He will respond, *JB* ... as He answers, *Beck.*

**with the saving strength of his right hand:** ... with the strength of salvation, *BB* ... with mighty deeds, *Beck.*

**7. Some trust in chariots, and some in horses:** ... Some put their faith in carriages, *BB* ... Some boast in chariots, *NASB.*

**but we will remember:** ... But we will make mention, *ASV* ... but we will boast, *Beck.*

**the name of the LORD our God:** ... we trust on our LIVING GOD, *Fenton.*

**8. They are brought down and fallen:** ... overwhelmed and defeated, *NCV* ... bowed down and fallen, *ASV* ... bent down and made low, *BB* ... They slumped and fell, *Anchor* ... They will totter to their knees and fall, *Beck* ... They both will shake, and fall, *Fenton.*

**but we are risen, and stand upright:** ... while we stood erect and reassured, *Anchor* ... but we will rise and stand up, *Beck* ... we march forward and win, *NCV* ... But we in triumph rise, *Fenton* ... we have risen and station ourselves upright, *Young.*

**9. Save, LORD:** ... Come to our help, Lord, *BB.*

**let the king hear us:** ... answer us, *ASV* ... give our Leader success, *Fenton.*

---

revealed character, which is contemplated as having existence in some sense apart from Him whose character it is. In vv. 3f, they add the incense of their intercession to his sacrifices. The background of the Psalm is probably the altar on which the accustomed offerings before a battle were being presented (1 Sam. 13:9). The prayer for acceptance of the burnt offering is very graphic, since the word rendered "accept" (HED #4527) is literally "to esteem fat."

**20:6–9.** The sacrifice has been offered, and the choral prayer has gone up. Silence follows, the worshipers watching the curling smoke as it rises, and then a single voice breaks out into a burst of glad assurance that sacrifice and prayer are answered. Who speaks? The most natural answer is, "the king," and the fact that he speaks of himself as Yahweh's anointed in the third person does not present a difficulty. What is the reference in that "now" at the beginning of v. 6? May we venture to suppose that the king's heart swelled at the exhibition of his subjects' devotion and hailed it as a pledge of victory? The future is brought into the present by the outstretched hand of faith, for this single speaker knows that "Yahweh has saved," although no blow has yet been struck. Chariots and horses are very terrible, especially to raw soldiers unaccustomed to their whirling onset, but the name is mightier, as Pharaoh and his array proved by the Reed Sea.

The certain issue of the fight is given in v. 8 in a picturesque fashion, made more vigorous by the tenses which describe completed acts. When the

| 21:t | 3937, 5514.351 | 4344 | 3937, 1784 | 1. | 3176 | 904, 6007 | 7975.121, 4567 |
|---|---|---|---|---|---|---|---|
| | prep, art, v Piel ptc ms | n ms | prep, pn | | pn | prep, n ms, ps 2ms | v Qal impf 3ms, n ms |
| | לַמְנַצֵּחַ | מִזְמוֹר | לְדָוִד | | יְהוָה | בְּעָזְּךָ | יִשְׂמַח־מֶלֶךְ |
| | lamnatstsēach | mizmôr | ledhāwidh | | yehwāh | be'āzzekhā | yismach-melekh |
| | to the director | a Psalm | of David | | O Yahweh | in your strength | the king rejoices |

| 904, 3568 | 4242, 1559.121 | 4108 | 2. | 8707 | 3949 | 5598.113 |
|---|---|---|---|---|---|---|
| cj, prep, n fs, ps 2ms | intrg, v Qal impf 3ms | adv | | *n fs* | n ms, ps 3ms | v Qal pf 2ms |
| וּבִישׁוּעָתְךָ | מַה־יָּגֶיל | מְאֹד | | תַּאֲוַת | לִבּוֹ | נָתַתָּה |
| ûvîshû'āthekhā | mah-yāghêl | me'ōdh | | ta'awath | libbô | nāthattāh |
| and in your salvation | how does he rejoice | very | | the longing of | his heart | You have given |

| 3937 | 807 | 8004 | 1118, 4661.113 | 5734 | 3. | 3706, 7207.323 |
|---|---|---|---|---|---|---|
| prep, ps 3ms | cj, *n fs* | n fd, ps 3ms | neg part, v Qal pf 2ms | intrj | | cj, v Piel impf 2ms, ps 3ms |
| לּוֹ | וַאֲרֶשֶׁת | שְׂפָתָיו | בַּל־מָנַעְתָּ | סֶלָה | | כִּי־תְקַדְּמֶנּוּ |
| lô | wa'ăresheth | sephāthâv | bal-māna'ăttā | selāh | | kî-theqaddemennû |
| to him | and the desire of | his lips | You have not withheld | selah | | because You meet him |

| 1318 | 3005 | 8308.123 | 3937, 7513 | 6065 | 6580 | 4. | 2522 | 8068.111 |
|---|---|---|---|---|---|---|---|---|
| *n fp* | adj | v Qal impf 2ms | prep, n ms, ps 3ms | *n fs* | n ms | | n mp | v Qal pf 3ms |
| בִּרְכוֹת | טוֹב | תָּשִׁית | לְרֹאשׁוֹ | עֲטֶרֶת | פָּז | | חַיִּים | שָׁאַל |
| birkhôth | ṭôv | tāshîth | lerō'shô | 'ăṭereth | pāz | | chayyîm | shā'al |
| blessings | good | You set | on his head | a crown of | pure gold | | life | he asked |

| 4623 | 5598.113 | 3937 | 775 | 3219 | 5986 | 5911 | 5. | 1448 |
|---|---|---|---|---|---|---|---|---|
| prep, ps 2ms | v Qal pf 2ms | prep, ps 3ms | *n ms* | n mp | n ms | cj, n ms | | adj |
| מִמְּךָ | נָתַתָּה | לּוֹ | אֹרֶךְ | יָמִים | עוֹלָם | וָעֶד | | גָּדוֹל |
| mimmekhā | nāthattāh | lô | 'ōrekh | yāmîm | 'ôlām | wā'edh | | gādhôl |
| from You | You gave | to him | length of | days | forever | and everlasting | | great |

| 3638 | 904, 3568 | 2003 | 1994 | 8187.323 | 6142 |
|---|---|---|---|---|---|
| n ms, ps 3ms | prep, n fs, ps 2ms | n ms | cj, n ms | v Piel impf 2ms | prep, ps 3ms |
| כְּבוֹדוֹ | בִּישׁוּעָתֶךָ | הוֹד | וְהָדָר | תְּשַׁוֶּה | עָלָיו |
| kevôdhô | bîshû'āthekhā | hôdh | wehādhār | teshawweh | 'ālâv |
| his glory | in your salvation | majesty | and honor | You place | on him |

| 6. | 3706, 8308.123 | 1318 | 3937, 5911 | 2397.323 | 904, 7977 | 881, 6686 |
|---|---|---|---|---|---|---|
| | cj, v Qal impf 2ms, ps 3ms | n fp | prep, n ms | v Piel impf 2ms, ps 3ms | prep, n fs | do, n mp, ps 2ms |
| | כִּי־תְשִׁיתֵהוּ | בְרָכוֹת | לָעַד | תְּחַדֵּהוּ | בְשִׂמְחָה | אֶת־פָּנֶיךָ |
| | kî-theshîthēhû | verākhôth | lā'adh | techaddēhû | vesimchāh | 'eth-pānêkhā |
| | indeed You make him | blessings | unto eternity | You make him glad | with joy | your presence |

**when we call:** … and answer us in the hour of our calling, *NEB* … answer our appeal this day, *Moffatt.*

**21:t. To the chief Musician, A Psalm of David.**

**1. The king shall joy in thy strength, O LORD; and in thy salvation how greatly shall he rejoice!:** … Eternal One, the king rejoices in thy power, *Moffatt* … may the king rejoice, Lord, in thy protection, *Knox* … in Your victory how very delighted he is, *Beck.*

**2. Thou hast given him his heart's desire:** … Never a wish in his heart hast thou disappointed, *Knox.*

**and hast not withholden the request of his lips. Selah:** … and didn't keep from him what he asked for, *Beck* … not denied him the prayer of his lips, *JB* … and have not refused what he requested, *REB.*

**3. For thou preventest him:** … you set before him, *Anchor* … you go before him, *BB* … you come to meet him, *JB* … You welcomed him to the throne, *LIVB* … Thou puttest before him, *Young.*

**with the blessings of goodness:** … blessings of welfare, *Moffatt* … blessings of good things, *BB* … with liberall blessings, *Geneva* … With happy auguries, *Knox* … with success and prosperity, *LIVB.*

**thou settest a crown of pure gold on his head:** … a crown of fair gold, *BB* … a royal crown of solid gold, *LIVB.*

**4. He asked life of thee:** ... Long continuance of his reign, *Knox.*

**and thou gavest it him:** ... life thou gavest, *Moffatt.*

**even length of days for ever and ever:** ... Extended and lengthened his days, *Fenton* ... to last unfailing till the end of time, *Knox* ... to times age-abiding and beyond, *Rotherham* ... Age-during—and for ever, *Young* ... so his years go on and on, *NCV.*

**5. His glory is great in thy salvation:** ... By Your aid his power is great, *Fenton* ... Great is his glory through your saving help, *JB* ... Great is the renown thy protection, *Knox* ... Your victory has brought him great glory, *REB.*

**honour and majesty hast thou laid upon him:** ... honour and authority, *BB* ... honour and fame. With blessing You always endowed, *Fenton* ... you invest him with splendour and majesty, *JB* ... glory and high honour thou hast made his, *Knox.*

**6. For thou hast made him most blessed for ever:** ... You confer on him everlasting blessings, *JB* ... An everlasting monument of thy goodness, *Knox.*

**thou hast made him exceeding glad:** ... you have given him joy, *BB* ... Thou dost delight him with joy, *Berkeley.*

**with thy countenance:** ... in the light of your face, *BB* ... as he joyfully looks at You, *Beck* ... by Thy presence, *Berkeley* ... by the smile of thy favour, *Knox* ... with the joy of your presence, *NIV.*

---

brief struggle is over, this is what will be seen—the enemy defeated and Israel risen from subjection and standing firm. Then comes a closing cry for help, which, according to the traditional division of the verse, has one very short clause and one long drawn out, like the blast of the trumpet sounding the charge. The intensity of appeal is condensed in the former clause into the one word, "save," and the renewed utterance of the name, thrice referred to in this short Psalm, as the source at once of strength and confidence.

***Psalm 21.*** *This Psalm is a pendant to the preceding. There the people prayed for the king; here they give thanks for him. There they asked that his desires might be fulfilled; here they bless Yahweh, Who has fulfilled them. There the battle was impending; here it has been won, although foes are still in the field. There the victory was prayed for; here it is prophesied.*

**21:1–6.** The former Psalm had asked for strength to be given to the king; this begins with thanks for the strength in which the king rejoices. In the former, the people had anticipated triumph in the king's salvation or victory; here they celebrate his exceeding exultation in it.

It was his, since he was victor, but it was Yahweh's, since He was Giver of victory. Loyal subjects share in the king's triumph and connect it with him, but he himself traces it to God.

The extraordinarily lofty language in which Yahweh's gifts are described in the subsequent verses has, no doubt, analogies in the Assyrian hymns. However, the abject reverence and partial deification which these breathe were foreign to the relations of Israel to its kings, who were not separated from their subjects by such a gulf as divided the great sovereigns of the East from theirs. The figure of the king is then brought still nearer to the light of Yahweh, and words which are consecrated to express divine attributes are applied to him in v. 5. "Glory, honor and majesty" are predicated of him, as the royal recipient and the divine Giver are clearly separated, even while the luster raying from Yahweh is conceived of as falling in brightness upon the king.

**21:7–13.** The task of the ideal king was to crush and root out opposition to his monarchy, which was Yahweh's. Very terrible are the judgments of his hand, which sound like those of Yahweh rather than those inflicted by a man. In v. 8, the construction is slightly varied in the two clauses, the verb "reach" having a preposition attached in the former, and not in the latter; the difference may be reproduced by the distinction between "reach toward" and "reach." The seeking hand is stretched out after, and then it grasps, its victims. The comparison of the "fiery oven" is inexact in form, but the very negligence helps the impression of agitation and terribleness. The enemy is not likened to a furnace, but to the fuel cast into it. Then, in v. 12, the dread scene is completed by the picture of the flying foe and the overtaking pursuer, who first puts them to flight and then, getting in front of them, sends his arrows full in their faces. The ideal of the king has a side of terror, and while his chosen weapon is patient love, he has other arrows in his quiver.

As in Ps. 20, the close is a brief petition, which asks the fulfillment of the anticipations in vv. 8–13, and traces, as in v. 1, the king's triumph to Yahweh's strength. The loyal love of the nation will take its monarch's victory as its own joy and be glad in the manifestation of Yahweh's power. That is the true

| 7. 3706, 4567 | 1019.151 | 904, 3176 | 904, 2721 | 6169 |
|---|---|---|---|---|
| cj, art, n ms | v Qal act ptc ms | prep, pn | cj, prep, *n ms* | n ms |
| כִּי־הַמֶּלֶךְ | בֹּטֵחַ | בַּיהוָה | וּבְחֶסֶד | עֶלְיוֹן |
| kî-hammelekh | bōṭēach | bayhwāh | ûvechesedh | 'elyôn |
| because the king | trusting | in Yahweh | and in the steadfast love of | the Most High |

| 1118, 4267.221 | 8. 4834.122 | 3135 | 3937, 3725, 342.152 | 3332 |
|---|---|---|---|---|
| neg part, v Niphal impf 3ms | v Qal impf 3fs | n fs, ps 2ms | prep, *n ms*, v Qal act ptc mp, ps 2ms | n fs, ps 2ms |
| בַּל־יִמּוֹט | תִּמְצָא | יָדְךָ | לְכָל־אֹיְבֶיךָ | יְמִינְךָ |
| bal-yimmôṭ | timtsā' | yādhekhā | lekhol-'ōyevêkhā | yemînekhā |
| he will not totter | it will find | your hand | all your enemies | your right hand |

| 4834.122 | 7983.152 | 9. 8308.123 | 3626, 8902 | 813 | 3937, 6496 |
|---|---|---|---|---|---|
| v Qal impf 3fs | v Qal act ptc mp, ps 2ms | v Qal impf 2ms, ps 3mp | prep, *n ms* | n fs | prep, *n fs* |
| תִּמְצָא | שֹׂנְאֶיךָ | תְּשִׁיתֵמוֹ | כְּתַנּוּר | אֵשׁ | לְעֵת |
| timtsā' | sōne'êkhā | teshîthēmô | kethannûr | 'ēsh | le'ēth |
| it will find | those who hate you | You will make them | like an oven of | fire | at the time of |

| 6686 | 3176 | 904, 653 | 1142.321 | 404.122 | 813 |
|---|---|---|---|---|---|
| n mp, ps 2ms | pn | prep, n ms, ps 3ms | v Piel impf 3ms, ps 3mp | cj, v Qal impf 3fs, ps 3mp | n fs |
| פָּנֶיךָ | יְהוָה | בְּאַפּוֹ | יְבַלְּעֵם | וְתֹאכְלֵם | אֵשׁ |
| pānêkhā | yehwāh | be'appô | yevalle'ēm | wethō'khelēm | 'ēsh |
| your presence | Yahweh | in his anger | He will swallow them | and it will consume them | fire |

| 10. 6780 | 4623, 800 | 6.323 | 2320 | 4623, 1158 | 119 |
|---|---|---|---|---|---|
| n ms, ps 3mp | prep, n fs | v Piel impf 2ms | cj, n ms, ps 3mp | prep, *n mp* | n ms |
| פִּרְיָמוֹ | מֵאֶרֶץ | תְּאַבֵּד | וְזַרְעָם | מִבְּנֵי | אָדָם |
| piryāmô | mē'erets | te'abbēdh | wezar'ām | mibbenê | 'ādhām |
| their offspring | from the earth | You will destroy | and their seed | among the sons of | humankind |

| 11. 3706, 5371.116 | 6142 | 7750 | 2913.116 | 4343 |
|---|---|---|---|---|
| cj, v Qal pf 3cp | prep, ps 2ms | n fs | v Qal pf 3cp | n fs |
| כִּי־נָטוּ | עָלֶיךָ | רָעָה | חָשְׁבוּ | מְזִמָּה |
| kî-nāṭû | 'ālêkhā | rā'āh | chāshevû | mezimmāh |
| when they have turned aside | against you | evil | they have devised | a plot |

| 1118, 3310.126 | 12. 3706 | 8308.123 | 8327 | 904, 4479 | 3679.323 |
|---|---|---|---|---|---|
| neg part, v Qal impf 3mp | cj | v Qal impf 2ms, ps 3mp | n ms | prep, n mp, ps 2ms | v Polel impf 2ms |
| בַּל־יוּכָלוּ | כִּי | תְּשִׁיתֵמוֹ | שֶׁכֶם | בְּמֵיתָרֶיךָ | תְּכוֹנֵן |
| bal-yûkhālû | kî | teshîthēmô | shekhem | bemêthārêkhā | tekhônēn |
| they will not be able | because | You will put them | backs | with your bows | you will fix |

| 6142, 6686 | 13. 7597.123 | 3176 | 904, 6007 | 8301.120 | 2252.320 |
|---|---|---|---|---|---|
| prep, n mp, ps 3mp | v Qal juss 2ms | pn | prep, n ms, ps 2ms | v Qal juss 1cp | cj, v Piel juss 1cp |
| עַל־פְּנֵיהֶם | רוּמָה | יְהוָה | בְּעֻזֶּךָ | נָשִׁירָה | וּנְזַמְּרָה |
| 'al-penêhem | rûmāh | yehwāh | ve'uzzekhā | nāshîrāh | ûnezammerāh |
| on their faces | be exalted | O Yahweh | in your strength | let us sing | and let us praise |

| 1400 | 22:t 3937, 5514.351 | 6142, 370 | 8266 | 4344 |
|---|---|---|---|---|
| n fs, ps 2ms | prep, art, v Piel ptc ms | prep, *n fs* | art, n ms | n ms |
| גְּבוּרָתֶךָ | לַמְנַצֵּחַ | עַל־אַיֶּלֶת | הַשַּׁחַר | מִזְמוֹר |
| gevûrāthekhā | lamnatstsēach | 'al-'ayyeleth | hashshachar | mizemôr |
| your might | to the director | according to the female deer of | the early dawn | a Psalm |

| 3937, 1784 | 1. 418 | 418 | 4066 | 6013.113 | 7632 | 4623, 3568 |
|---|---|---|---|---|---|---|
| prep, pn | n ms, ps 1cs | n ms, ps 1cs | intrg | v Qal pf 2ms, ps 1cs | adj | prep, n fs, ps 1cs |
| לְדָוִד | אֵלִי | אֵלִי | לָמָה | עֲזַבְתָּנִי | רָחוֹק | מִישׁוּעָתִי |
| ledhāwidh | 'ēlî | 'ēlî | lāmāh | 'ăzavtānî | rāchôq | mîshû'āthî |
| of David | my God | my God | why | have You forsaken me | far | from my salvation |

**7. For the king trusteth in the LORD:** ... the king has faith, *BB* ... he depends upon the steadfast love of the God, *LIVB*.

**and through the mercy of the most High:** ... through the unfailing love of, *NIV*... the loving care of, *REB* ... because of the covenant-love of, *Berkeley* ... the love of God above, *Beck*.

**he shall not be moved:** ... will never swerve, *Anchor* ... he will always be secure, *Good News* ... he will not be shaken, *NASB* ... will keep him from falling, *JB* ... doesn't let him fail, *Beck*.

**8. Thine hand shall find out all thine enemies:** ... Your hand will make a search, *BB* ... Your hand will contact all your enemies, *Berkeley* ... your left hand overtook all your foes, *Anchor* ... shall seize those who oppose you, *Fenton*.

**thy right hand shall find out those that hate thee:** ... overtook those who hate you, *Anchor* ... will not leave their malice unpunished, *Knox*.

**9. Thou shalt make them as a fiery oven:** ... At the time of your appearing you will make them like a fiery furnace, *NIV* ... You put them as into a blazing furnace, *Anchor* ... And throw them like fuel to fire, *Fenton* ... they will wither away like grass in the oven, *Knox*.

**in the time of thine anger: the LORD shall swallow them up in his wrath, and the fire shall devour them:** ... in his wrath will put an end to them, *BB* ... when the LORD in his rage, Consumes and devours them, *Fenton* ... whirled away by the Lord's anger, burnt up in flames, *Knox* ... will engulf them in his anger, *JB*.

**10. Their fruit shalt thou destroy from the earth:** ... Thou wilt rid the land of their breed, *Knox* ... Their race you made perish, *Anchor* ... It will exterminate their offspring, *NEB* ... You will purge the earth of their descendants, *JB* ... Makes their produce to fail from the Land, *Fenton* ... None of their descendants will survive, *Good News*.

**and their seed from among the children of men:** ... and their children from the sons of men, *Anchor* ... And their race from the sons of Mankind, *Fenton* ... their race will vanish from the world of men, *Knox* ... and rid mankind of their posterity, *NEB* ... the king will kill them all, *Good News*.

**11. For they intended evil against thee:** ... they plotted a revolt, *Anchor*.

**they imagined a mischievous device:** ... Which they planned as a futile device, *Fenton* ... devised malice, *Anchor* ... devised a scheme, *Rotherham* ... an evil design in their minds, *BB* ... See how all their false designs against thee, *Knox*.

**which they are not able to perform:** ... which they were not able to put into effect, *BB* ... they cannot accomplish, *Rotherham* ... they will be unable to put it into practice, *Berkeley* ... but their traps won't work, *NCV* ... all their plots came to nothing, *Knox*.

**12. Therefore shalt thou make them turn their back, when thou shalt make ready:** ... Thou makest them a butt, *Young* ... Their backs will be turned, *BB* ... So break all their backs by Your might, *Fenton* ... you will make them turn tail, *JB* ... you will force them to retreat, *Moffatt*.

**thine arrows upon thy strings against the face of them:** ... with your bowstrings you aimed at their faces, *Anchor* ... by shooting your arrows at their faces, *Beck* ... bent is thy bow to meet their onslaught, *Knox* ... when you aim at them with drawn bow, *NIV*.

**13. Be thou exalted, LORD:** ... Be extolled, O LORD, *NAB* ... Be supreme, LORD, *NCV*.

**in thine own strength: so will we sing and praise thy power:** ... We will write songs to celebrate your mighty acts, *LIVB* ... We will sing, chant the praise of your might, *NAB* ... With song and with string we will sound forth thy power, *Rotherham* ... our song, our psalm, shall be of thy greatness, *Knox* ... That we may play and sing of thy power, *Goodspeed*.

**22:t. To the chief Musician upon Aijeleth Shahar, A Psalm of David.**

---

voice of devotion which recognizes God, not man, in all victories and answers the flashing of his delivering power by the thunder of praise.

*Psalm 22. To a reader who shares in this understanding of the Psalm, it must be holy ground, to be trodden reverently and with thoughts adoringly fixed on Jesus so as to prefigure the sacred sorrows of the Man of Sorrows. Cold analysis is out of place, yet there is a distinct order even in the groans and a manifest contrast in the two halves of the Psalm (vv. 1–21 and 22–31). "Thou answerest not" is the keynote of the former; "Thou hast answered me," of the latter. The one paints the sufferings, the other the glory that should follow. Both point to Jesus: the former by the desolation which it breathes, the latter by the worldwide consequences of these solitary sufferings which it foresees.*

**22:1–2.** Surely opposites were never more startlingly blended in one gush of feeling than in that complaint of mingled faith and despair, "My God! my God, why hast thou forsaken me?" (Mark 15:34). The evidence to the psalmist that he was for-

| 1745 | 8058 | | 435 | 7410.125 | 3221 | 3940 | 6257.123 |
|---|---|---|---|---|---|---|---|
| *n mp* | n fs, ps 1cs | | n mp, ps 1cs | v Qal impf 1cs | adv | cj, neg part | v Qal impf 2ms |
| דִּבְרֵי | שַׁאֲגָתִי | 2. | אֱלֹהַי | אֶקְרָא | יוֹמָם | וְלֹא | תַעֲנֶה |
| divrê | sha'ăghāthî | | 'ĕlōhay | 'eqŏrā' | yômām | wᵉlō' | tha'ăneh |
| the words of | my groaning | | my God | I call | by day | but not | You answer |

| 4050 | 3940, 1800 | 3937 | | 887 | 7202 | 3553.151 | 8747 |
|---|---|---|---|---|---|---|---|
| cj, n ms | cj, neg part, n fs | prep, ps 1cs | | cj, pers pron | adj | v Qal act ptc ms | *n fp* |
| וְלַיְלָה | וְלֹא־דוּמִיָּה | לִי | 3. | וְאַתָּה | קָדוֹשׁ | יוֹשֵׁב | תְּהִלּוֹת |
| wᵉlaylāh | wᵉlō'-dhûmîyāh | lî | | wᵉ'attāh | qādhôsh | yôshēv | tᵉhillôth |
| and by night | but no silence | for me | | and You | holy | sitting on | the praises of |

| 3547 | | 904 | 1019.116 | 1 | 1019.116 | 6647.323 |
|---|---|---|---|---|---|---|
| pn | | prep, ps 2ms | v Qal pf 3cp | n mp, ps 1cp | v Qal pf 3cp | cj, v Piel impf 2ms, ps 3mp |
| יִשְׂרָאֵל | 4. | בְּךָ | בָּטְחוּ | אֲבֹתֵינוּ | בָּטְחוּ | וַתְּפַלְּטֵמוֹ |
| yisrā'ēl | | bᵉkhā | bāṭᵉchû | 'ăvōthênû | bāṭᵉchû | wattᵉphallᵉṭēmô |
| Israel | | in You | they trusted | our ancestors | they trusted | and You set them free |

| | 420 | 2283.116 | 4561.216 | 904 | 1019.116 |
|---|---|---|---|---|---|
| | prep, ps 2ms | v Qal pf 3cp | cj, v Niphal pf 3cp | prep, ps 2ms | v Qal pf 3cp |
| 5. | אֵלֶיךָ | זָעֲקוּ | וְנִמְלָטוּ | בְּךָ | בָטְחוּ |
| | 'ēlêkhā | zā'ăqû | wᵉnimlāṭû | bᵉkhā | vāṭᵉchû |
| | to You | they cried out | and they fled to safety | in You | they trusted |

| 3940, 991.116 | | 609 | 8770 | 3940, 382 | 2887 | 119 |
|---|---|---|---|---|---|---|
| cj, neg part, v Qal pf 3cp | | cj, pers pron | n fs | cj, neg part, n ms | *n fs* | n ms |
| וְלֹא־בוֹשׁוּ | 6. | וְאָנֹכִי | תוֹלַעַת | וְלֹא־אִישׁ | חֶרְפַּת | אָדָם |
| wᵉlō'-vôshû | | wᵉ'ānōkhî | thôla'ath | wᵉlō'-'îsh | cherpath | 'ādhām |
| and they were not ashamed | | but I | a maggot | and not a man | disgrace from | men |

| 995.155 | 6194 | | 3725, 7495.152 | 4074.526 | 3937 |
|---|---|---|---|---|---|
| cj, *v Qal pass ptc ms* | n ms | | *adj*, v Qal act ptc mp, ps 1cs | v Hiphil impf 3mp | prep, ps 1cs |
| וּבְזוּי | עָם | 7. | כָּל־רֹאַי | יַלְעִגוּ | לִי |
| ûvᵉzûy | 'ām | | kol-rō'ay | yal'ighû | lî |
| and despised by | people | | all those who see me | they deride | me |

| 6604.526 | 904, 8004 | 5309.526 | 7513 | | 1597.131 | 420, 3176 |
|---|---|---|---|---|---|---|
| v Hiphil impf 3mp | prep, n fs | v Hiphil impf 3mp | n ms | | v Qal impv 2ms | prep, pn |
| יַפְטִירוּ | בְשָׂפָה | יָנִיעוּ | רֹאשׁ | 8. | גֹּל | אֶל־יְהוָה |
| yaphṭîrû | vᵉsāphāh | yānî'û | rō'sh | | gōl | 'el-yᵉhwāh |
| they open wide | with the lips | they shake | the head | | roll | to Yahweh |

**1. My God, my God, why hast thou forsaken me?:** … why are you turned away from me, *BB* … why have you rejected me, *NCV* … why desert me, *Moffatt.*

**why art thou so far from helping me:** … why have you abandoned me, *Good News* … You seem far from saving me, *NCV* … so far from helping me, *Berkeley* … so farre from mine health, *Geneva* … dismissing my plea, *Anchor.*

**and from the words of my roaring?:** … Loudly I call, but my prayer cannot reach thee, *Knox* … of my crying, *BB* … of my groaning, *Berkeley* … of my loud lamentation, *Rotherham* … as I roar out, *Beck.*

**2. O my God, I cry in the daytime:** … I make my cry in the day, *BB.*

**but thou hearest not:** … and you give no answer, *BB.*

**and in the night season, and am not silent:** … And by night—no respite for me, *Anchor* … night can bring no rest to me, *Fenton* … but I haue no audience, *Geneva.*

**3. But thou art holy:** … Thou art there none the less, dwelling in the holy place, *Knox* … But You are safe, *Fenton* … While you sit upon the holy throne, *Anchor* … are enthroned in the sanctuary, *REB.*

**O thou that inhabitest the praises of Israel:** … You are praised by Israel, *Beck* … enthroned upon the praises of Israel, *Berkeley* … Glory of Israel, *Anchor* … Israel's ancient boast, *Knox.*

**4. Our fathers trusted in thee:** … Our ancestors put their trust in you,

*Good News* ... On thee our fathers did rely, *Moffatt* ... had faith in you, *BB* ... confided in thee, *Darby.*

**they trusted, and thou didst deliver them:** ... they had faith and you were their saviour, *BB* ... relied, and thou didst rescue them, *Moffatt.*

**5. They cried unto thee, and were delivered:** ... They sent up their cry to you and were made free, *BB* ... They called to you and escaped from danger, *Good News* ... To you they cried, and they escaped, *NCB.*

**they trusted in thee, and were not confounded:** ... they were never disappointed when they sought your aid, *LIVB* ... no need to be ashamed of such trust as theirs, *Knox* ... were not put to shame, *BB* ... were not disgraced, *Goodspeed* ... had not turned pale, *Rotherham.*

**6. But I am a worm, and no man:** ... I am like a worm instead of a man, *NCV* ... and not human, *NRSV.*

**a reproach of men:** ... the scorn of men, *Anchor* ... cursed by men, *BB* ... a shame of men, *Geneva* ... I am a by-word to all, *Knox.*

**and despised of the people:** ... the most despicable of the people, *Anchor* ... looked down on by the people, *BB* ... the contempt of the people, *Geneva* ... the laughing-stock of all the rabble, *Knox.*

**7. All they that see me laugh me to scorn:** ... All those who catch sight of me fall to mocking, *Knox* ... make sport of me, *Anchor* ... make fun of me, *Good News.*

**they shoot out the lip:** ... they gape at me, *Anchor* ... with mouths wide open, *Beck* ... hurl insults, *NIV* ... stick out their tongues, *Good News* ... mock me with parted lips, *NAB.*

**they shake the head, saying:** ... they wag their heads, *Anchor* ... toss their heads, *Goodspeed.*

**8. He trusted on the LORD that he would deliver him:** ... Commit thyself, *ASV* ... He put his confidence in the LORD, *Beck* ... Is this the one who rolled his burden on the Lord, *LIVB* ... If he likes you, maybe he will rescue you, *NCV.*

**let him deliver him, seeing he delighted in him:** ... Let him rescue him, if he cares for him, *Anchor* ... let Him save him if He choose, *Fenton* ... Why doesn't he save you, *Good News* ... why does not the Lord come to his rescue and set his favourite free, *Knox.*

---

saken was the apparent rejection of his prayers for deliverance. We may suppose that the pathetic fate of David's predecessor hovered before his thoughts: "I am sore distressed ... God is departed from me and answereth me no more." But, while lower degrees of this conflict of trust and despair belong to all deep religious life and are experienced by saintly sufferers in all ages, the voice that rang through the darkness on Calvary was the cry of Him who experienced its force in supreme measure and in fulfillment of the matter. None but He can ask that question, "Why?" with conscience void of offense. No living person but He has known the mortal agony of utter separation from God. None but He has clung to God with absolute trust even in the horror of great darkness. In Christ's consciousness of being forsaken by God lie elements peculiar to it alone, for the separating agent was the gathered sins of the whole world, laid on Him and accepted by Him in the perfection of his sacrificial identification of himself with men. Unless in that dread hour He was bearing a world's sin, there is no worthy explanation of his cry, and many a silent martyr has faced death for Him with courage derived from Him.

***22:3–21.*** *After the introductory strophe of 2 verses, there come seven strophes, of which three contain 3 verses each (vv. 3–11), followed by two of 2 verses each (vv. 12–15), and these again by two with 3 verses each (vv. 16–21).*

**22:3–5.** A beautiful bold image is given of God enthroned "on the praises of Israel." These praises are evoked by former acts of grace answering prayers, and of them is built a yet nobler throne than the outstretched wings of the cherubim. The daring metaphor penetrates deeply into God's delight in men's praise and the power of Israel's voice to exalt Him in the world. How could a God thus enthroned cease to give mercies like those which were perpetually commemorated thereby? The same half-wistful, half-confident retrospect is continued in the remaining verses of this strophe (vv. 4f), which look back to the experience of the patriarchs.

**22:6–8.** Such remembrances make the contrast of present sufferings and of a far-off God more bitter, and a fresh wave of agony rolls over the psalmist's soul. He feels himself crushed and as incapable of resistance as a worm bruised in all its soft length by an armed heel. The very semblance of manhood has faded. One can scarcely fail to recall "his visage was so marred more than any man" (Isa. 52:14) and the designation of Yahweh's servant Israel as "thou worm" (Isa. 41:14). The taunts that wounded the psalmist so sorely have long since fallen dumb, and the wounds are all healed. But the immortal words in which he wails the pain of misapprehension and rejection are engraved forever on the heart of the world. No suffering is more acute than that of a sensitive soul,

| 6647.321 | 5522.521 | 3706 | 2759.111 | 904 | 9. 3706, 887 |
|---|---|---|---|---|---|
| v Piel juss 3ms, ps 3ms | v Hiphil juss 3ms, ps 3ms | cj | v Qal pf 3ms | prep, ps 3ms | cj, pers pron |
| יְפַלְּטֵהוּ | יַצִּילֵהוּ | כִּי | חָפֵץ | בּוֹ | כִּי־אַתָּה |
| yephalleṭēhû | yatstsîlēhû | kî | chāphēts | bô | kî-'attāh |
| and let Him set him free | may He rescue him | because | He delights | in him | because You |

| 1554.151 | 4623, 1027 | 1019.551 |
|---|---|---|
| v Qal act ptc ms, ps 1cs | prep, n fs | v Hiphil ptc ms, ps 1cs |
| גֹּחִי | מִבָּטֶן | מַבְטִיחִי |
| ghōchî | mibbāṭen | mavṭîchî |
| the One Who causes me to break forth | from the womb | the One Who causes me to trust |

| 6142, 8157 | 525 | 10. 6142 | 8390.615 | 4623, 7641 | 4623, 1027 |
|---|---|---|---|---|---|
| prep, *n md* | n fs, ps 1cs | prep, ps 2ms | v Hophal pf 1cs | prep, n ms | prep, *n fs* |
| עַל־שְׁדֵי | אִמִּי | עָלֶיךָ | הָשְׁלַכְתִּי | מֵרָחֶם | מִבֶּטֶן |
| 'al-shedhê | 'immî | 'ālêkhā | hāshelakhtî | mērāchem | mibbeṭen |
| on the breasts of | my mother | on You | I was thrown | from the womb | from the womb of |

| 525 | 418 | 887 | 11. 414, 7651.123 | 4623 | 3706, 7150 | 7427 |
|---|---|---|---|---|---|---|
| n fs, ps 1cs | n ms, ps 1cs | pers pron | adv, v Qal juss 2ms | prep, ps 1cs | cj, n fs | adj |
| אִמִּי | אֵלִי | אָתָּה | אַל־תִּרְחַק | מִמֶּנִּי | כִּי־צָרָה | קְרוֹבָה |
| 'immî | 'ēlî | 'āttāh | 'al-tirchaq | mimmenî | kî-tsārāh | qŏrôvāh |
| my mother | my God | You | do not be far away | from me | because adversity | near |

| 3706, 375 | 6038.151 | 12. 5621.116 | 6749 | 7521 | 48 |
|---|---|---|---|---|---|
| cj, *sub* | v Qal act ptc ms | v Qal pf 3cp, ps 1cs | n mp | adj | *adj* |
| כִּי־אֵין | עוֹזֵר | סְבָבוּנִי | פָּרִים | רַבִּים | אַבִּירֵי |
| kî-'ên | 'ôzēr | sevāvûnî | pārîm | rabbîm | 'abbîrê |
| because there is not | one who helps | they surround me | young bulls | many | the mighty of |

| 1347 | 3932.316 | 13. 6722.116 | 6142 | 6552 | 765 |
|---|---|---|---|---|---|
| pn | v Piel pf 3cp, ps 1cs | v Qal pf 3cp | prep, ps 1cs | n ms, ps 3mp | n ms |
| בָשָׁן | כִּתְּרוּנִי | פָּצוּ | עָלַי | פִּיהֶם | אַרְיֵה |
| vāshān | kitterûnî | pātsû | 'ālay | pîhem | 'aryēh |
| the Bashan | they have surrounded me | they have opened wide | against me | their mouth | a lion |

| 3072.151 | 8057.151 | 14. 3626, 4448 | 8581.215 | 6754.716 |
|---|---|---|---|---|
| v Qal act ptc ms | cj, v Qal act ptc ms | prep, art, n mp | v Niphal pf 1cs | cj, v Hithpael pf 3cp |
| טֹרֵף | וְשֹׁאֵג | כַּמַּיִם | נִשְׁפַּכְתִּי | וְהִתְפָּרְדוּ |
| ṭōrēph | weshō'ēgh | kammayim | nishpakhtî | wehithpāredhû |
| tearing | and roaring | like water | I have been poured out | they are separated |

| 3725, 6344 | 2030.111 | 3949 | 3626, 1804 | 4701.255 | 904, 8761 | 4753 |
|---|---|---|---|---|---|---|
| *adj*, n fp, ps 1cs | v Qal pf 3ms | n ms, ps 1cs | prep, art, n ms | v Niphal ptc ms | prep, *n ms* | n mp, ps 1cs |
| כָּל־עַצְמוֹתָי | הָיָה | לִבִּי | כַּדּוֹנַג | נָמֵס | בְּתוֹךְ | מֵעָי |
| kol-'atsmôthāy | hāyāh | libbî | kaddônāgh | nāmēs | bethôkh | mē'āy |
| all my bones | it is | my heart | like wax | melting | in the middle of | my inner being |

**9. But thou art he that took me out of the womb:** … it was you who took care of me from the day of my birth, *BB* … What hand but thine drew me out from my mother's womb, *Knox* … You have been my guide since I was first formed, *NAB* … You had my mother give birth to me, *NCV* … thou art he that severed me from the womb, *Rotherham.*

**thou didst make me hope:** … Thou didst give me security, *Goodspeed* … Who else was my refuge, *Knox* … you gave me faith, *BB* … made me tranquil, *Anchor* … made Me feel safe, *Beck.*

**when I was upon my mother's breasts:** … when I hung at the breast, *Knox.*

**10. I was cast upon thee from the womb:** … I was in your hands even before my birth, *BB* … From the hour of my birth, thou art my guardian, *Knox* … To you I was committed at birth, *NCB* … To your care I was entrusted, *REB.*

**thou art my God from my mother's belly:** … from My

**they look and stare upon me:** ... their looks are fixed on me, *BB* ... They watch; they gloat over Me, *Beck* ... they stand there watching me, *Knox* ... they look expectingly, *Young.*

**18. They part my garments among them:** ... Amongst them share my clothes, *Fenton* ... divide, *Anchor* ... apportion, *Young* ... distribute, *Goodspeed.*

**and cast lots upon my vesture:** ... they threw lots for my clothing, *NCV* ... over my robe they cast lots, *Anchor* ... by the decision of chance they take my clothing, *BB* ... for my robe cast dice, *Fenton* ... for my clothing they cause a lot to fall, *Young.*

**19. But be not thou far from me, O LORD:** ... do not stand at a distance, *Knox.*

**O my strength, haste thee to help me:** ... O thou my succor, *ASV* ... O, my army, hasten to my help, *Anchor* ... My GOD! Oh, haste to help, *Fenton* ... if thou wouldst aid me, come speedily to my side, *Knox* ... come quickly to my aid, *NRSV.*

**20. Deliver my soul from the sword:** ... Rescue my neck, *Anchor* ... My life guard from the sword, *Fenton.*

**my darling from the power of the dog:** ... my lonely self, *Berkeley* ... my precious life from the axe, *NEB* ... my loneliness from the grip of the dog, *NAB* ... save my life from these curs, *Moffatt* ... From the paw of a dog mine only one, *Young.*

**21. Save me from the lion's mouth: for thou hast heard me:** ... You have answered Me, *NKJV.*

**from the horns of the unicorns:** ... from the horns of the high places, *Young* ... Protect from tossing horns, *Fenton* ... horns of wild oxen, *Anchor* ... wild bull, *Beck* ... buffaloes, *Darby.*

**22. I will declare thy name unto my brethren:** ... Then I will tell my fel-

---

which killed by exhaustion. It stretched the body as on a rack and was attended with agonies of thirst. It requires considerable courage to slavishly brush aside such coincidences as accidental, in obedience to a theory of interpretation. But the picture is not completed when the bodily sufferings are set forth. A mysterious attribution of them all to God closes the strophe. "Thou hast brought me to the dust of death"—It is God's hand that has laid all these on him. No doubt this may be, and probably was in the psalmist's thought, only a devout recognition of Providence working through calamities; but the words receive full force only by being regarded as parallel with those of Isa. 53:10, "He hath put Him to grief." In like manner, the apostolic preaching regards Christ's murderers as God's instruments.

**22:16–18.** The next strophe returns to the three-verse arrangement and blends the contents of the two preceding, dealing both with the assailing enemies and the enfeebled sufferer. The former metaphor of wild animals encircling him is repeated with variations. A baser order of foes than bulls and lions, namely, a troop of cowardly curs, are snarling and snapping around him.

The picture of bodily sufferings has one more touch in "I can count all my bones." Crucifixion was a slow process, and we recall the long hours in which the crowds sated their hatred through their eyes.

It is extremely unlikely that the psalmist's garments were literally parted among his foes. Surely, this is a distinct instance of divine guidance molding a psalmist's words so as to fill them with a deeper meaning than the speaker knew. He who so shaped them saw the soldiers dividing the rest of the garments and gambling for the seamless cloak, and He was "the Spirit of Christ which was in" the singer.

**22:19–21.** The next strophe closes the first part with petition which, in the last words, becomes thanksgiving and realizes the answer so fervently besought. The initial complaint of God's distance is again turned into prayer, and the former metaphors of wild beasts are gathered into one long cry for deliverance from the dangerous weapons of each, the dog's paw, the lion's mouth, the wild oxen's horns. The psalmist speaks of his "soul" or life as "my only one," referring not to his isolation, but to his life as that which, once lost, could never be regained. He has but one life; therefore, he clings to it and cannot but believe that it is precious in God's eyes. Then, all at once, up shoots a clear light of joy, and he knows that he has not been speaking to a deaf or remote God, but that his cry is answered.

The consequences of the psalmist's deliverance are described in the last part (vv. 22–31) in language so wide that it is hard to suppose that any man could think his personal experiences so important and far-reaching. The whole congregation of Israel is to share in his thanksgiving and to learn more of God's name through him (vv. 22–26). This does not bound his anticipations, for they traverse the whole world and embrace all lands and ages and contemplate that the story of his sufferings and triumph will prove a true gospel, bringing every country and generation to remember and turn to Yahweh. The exuberant language becomes but one mouth. Such consequences, so widespread and agelong, can fol-

| 6257.113 | | 5807.325 | 8428 | 3937, 250 | 904, 8761 | 7235 |
|---|---|---|---|---|---|---|
| v Qal pf 2ms, ps 1cs | 22. | v Piel juss 1cs | n ms, ps 2ms | prep, n mp, ps 1cs | prep, *n ms* | n ms |
| עֲנִיתָנִי | | אֲסַפְּרָה | שִׁמְךָ | לְאֶחָי | בְּתוֹךְ | קָהָל |
| 'ănîthānî | | 'ăsapperāh | shimkhā | le'echāy | bethôkh | qāhāl |
| You will answer me | | let me recount | your name | to my brothers | in the midst of | the assembly |

| 2054.325 | | 3486.152 | 3176 | 2054.333 | 3725, 2320 | 3399 |
|---|---|---|---|---|---|---|
| v Piel juss 1cs, ps 2ms | 23. | *v Qal act ptc mp* | pn | v Piel impv 2mp, ps 3ms | *adj*, n ms | pn |
| אֲהַלְלֶךָּ | | יִרְאֵי | יְהוָה | הַלְלוּהוּ | כָּל־זֶרַע | יַעֲקֹב |
| 'ăhalelekhā | | yir'ê | yehwāh | halelûhû | kol-zera' | ya'ăqōv |
| let me praise You | | those who fear | Yahweh | praise Him | all the seed of | Jacob |

| 3632.333 | 1513.133 | 4623 | 3725, 2320 | 3547 | | 3706 |
|---|---|---|---|---|---|---|
| v Piel impv 2mp, ps 3ms | cj, v Qal impv 2mp | prep, ps 3ms | *adj*, n ms | pn | 24. | cj |
| כַּבְּדוּהוּ | וְגוּרוּ | מִמֶּנּוּ | כָּל־זֶרַע | יִשְׂרָאֵל | | כִּי |
| kabbedhûhû | weghûrû | mimmennû | kol-zera' | yisrā'ēl | | kî |
| glorify Him | and be afraid | of Him | all the seed of | Israel | | because |

| 3940, 995.111 | 3940 | 8628.311 | 6269 | 6270 | 3940, 5846.511 |
|---|---|---|---|---|---|
| neg part, v Qal pf 3ms | cj, neg part | v Piel pf 3ms | *n fs* | n ms | cj, neg part, v Hiphil pf 3ms |
| לֹא־בָזָה | וְלֹא | שִׁקַּץ | עֱנוּת | עָנִי | וְלֹא־הִסְתִּיר |
| lō'-vāzāh | welō' | shiqqats | 'ĕnûth | 'ānî | welō'-histîr |
| He has not despised | and not | He detested | the affliction of | the afflicted | and He has not hidden |

| 6686 | 4623 | 904, 8209.341 | 420 | 8471.111 | | 4623, 882 |
|---|---|---|---|---|---|---|
| n mp, ps 3ms | prep, ps 3ms | cj, prep, v Piel inf con, ps 3ms | prep, ps 3ms | v Qal pf 3ms | 25. | prep, prep, ps 2ms |
| פָּנָיו | מִמֶּנּוּ | וּבְשַׁוְּעוֹ | אֵלָיו | שָׁמֵעַ | | מֵאִתְּךָ |
| pānâv | mimmennû | ûveshawwe'ô | 'ēlâv | shāmēa' | | mē'ittekhā |
| his face | from him | and during his crying for help | to Him | He heard | | from with You |

| 8747 | 904, 7235 | 7521 | 5266 | 8396.325 | 5224 | 3487 |
|---|---|---|---|---|---|---|
| n fs, ps 1cs | prep, n ms | adj | n mp, ps 1cs | v Piel impf 1cs | prep | adj, ps 3ms |
| תְּהִלָּתִי | בְּקָהָל | רָב | נְדָרַי | אֲשַׁלֵּם | נֶגֶד | יְרֵאָיו |
| thehillāthî | beqāhāl | rāv | nedhāray | 'ăshallēm | neghedh | yerē'âv |
| my praise | in the assembly | great | my vows | I will pay | before | fearful of Him |

| | 404.126 | 6262 | 7881.126 | 2054.326 | 3176 | 1938.152 |
|---|---|---|---|---|---|---|
| 26. | v Qal impf 3mp | n mp | cj, v Qal impf 3mp | v Piel impf 3mp | pn | v Qal act ptc mp, ps 3ms |
| | יֹאכְלוּ | עֲנָוִים | וְיִשְׂבָּעוּ | יְהַלְלוּ | יְהוָה | דֹּרְשָׁיו |
| | yō'khelû | 'ănāwîm | weyisbā'û | yehalelû | yehwāh | dōreshâv |
| | they will eat | the lowly | and they are satisfied | they will praise | Yahweh | those who seek Him |

| 2513.121 | 3949 | 3937, 5911 | | 2226.126 | 8178.126 | 420, 3176 |
|---|---|---|---|---|---|---|
| v Qal juss 3ms | n ms, ps 2mp | prep, n ms | 27. | v Qal impf 3mp | cj, v Qal impf 3mp | prep, pn |
| יְחִי | לְבַבְכֶם | לָעַד | | יִזְכְּרוּ | וְיָשֻׁבוּ | אֶל־יְהוָה |
| yechî | levavkhem | lā'adh | | yizkerû | weyāshuvû | 'el-yehwāh |
| may it live | your heart | unto eternity | | they will remember | and they will turn | to Yahweh |

| 3725, 675, 800 | 8246.726 | 3937, 6686 | 3725, 5121 | 1504 |
|---|---|---|---|---|
| *adj, n mp*, n fs | cj, v Hithpael impf 3mp | prep, n mp, ps 2ms | *adj, n fp* | n mp |
| כָּל־אַפְסֵי־אָרֶץ | וְיִשְׁתַּחֲווּ | לְפָנֶיךָ | כָּל־מִשְׁפְּחוֹת | גּוֹיִם |
| kol-'aphsê-'ārets | weyishtachwû | lephānêkhā | kol-mishpechôth | gôyim |
| all the ends of the earth | and they will worship | in your presence | all the families of | nations |

| | 3706 | 3937, 3176 | 4548 | 5090.151 | 904, 1504 | | 404.116 |
|---|---|---|---|---|---|---|---|
| 28. | cj | prep, pn | art, n fs | cj, v Qal act ptc ms | prep, art, n mp | 29. | v Qal pf 3cp |
| | כִּי | לַיהוָה | הַמְּלוּכָה | וּמֹשֵׁל | בַּגּוֹיִם | | אָכְלוּ |
| | kî | layhwāh | hammelûkhāh | ûmōshēl | baggôyim | | 'ākhelû |
| | because | to Yahweh | the kingship | and a Ruler | among the nations | | they have eaten |

low Israelites about you, *NCV* ... I will tell your name to my brothers and sisters, *NRSV* ... I shall declare your fame to my associates, *REB* ... I'll tell my friends Your name, *Fenton.*

**in the midst of the congregation will I praise thee:** ... In the midst of the convocation, *Rotherham* ... praise you in the public meeting, *NCV* ... And thank among the crowd, *Fenton.*

**23. Ye that fear the LORD, praise him:** ... You who revere the LORD, *Berkeley* ... Praise the Eternal, ye his worshippers, *Moffatt.*

**all ye the seed of Jacob, glorify him:** ... descendants, *Beck* ... all you race of Jacob, honor him, *Anchor* ... All Jacob's race extol, *Fenton.*

**and fear him, all ye the seed of Israel:** ... Stand in awe of him, *Anchor* ... and revere him, *Darby* ... Israel's race adore, *Fenton.*

**24. For he hath not despised nor abhorred the affliction of the afflicted:** ... he has not despised the poor man's plight, *Moffatt* ... he has not spurned or disdained the wretched man in his misery, *NAB* ... He does not ignore those in trouble, *NCV* ... he has not scorned the downtrodden, *NEB.*

**neither hath he hid his face from him:** ... kept his face covered from him, *BB* ... he has not turned and walked away, *LIVB* ... He doesn't hide from them, *NCV* ... nor shrunk in loathing from his plight, *NEB.*

**but when he cried unto him, he heard:** ... but he has given an answer to his cry, *BB* ... my cry for help did not go unheeded, *Knox* ... he answered my appeal for help, *Moffatt.*

**25. My praise shall be of thee in the great congregation:** ... One hundred times will I repeat to you my song of praise, *Anchor* ... Of thee cometh my praise in the great assembly, *ASV* ... In crowds I thank for this, *Fenton* ... Thou dost inspire praise in the full assembly, *NEB.*

**I will pay my vows before them that fear him:** ... I will fulfill my vows, *Anchor* ... Take what I owe thee, *Knox* ... I will make my offerings before his worshippers, *BB.*

**26. The meek shall eat and be satisfied: they shall praise the LORD that seek him:** ... The afflicted, *Berkeley* ... Let the pious partake of the feast to their heart's desire, *Moffatt* ... The poor will have a feast of good things, *BB* ... the humble eat and be satisfied, *Beck* ... The patient wronged-ones shall eat and be satisfied, *Rotherham.*

**your heart shall live for ever:** ... Refreshed be your hearts eternally, *Knox* ... Their hearts shall rejoice with everlasting joy, *LIVB* ... May your hearts be ever merry, *NCB* ... wish me Long life and happiness, *Moffatt.*

**27. All the ends of the world:** ... In all parts, *Beck* ... The furthest dwellers on earth, *Knox* ... from earth's very verge, *Moffatt* ... The whole land bows to you, *Fenton.*

**shall remember and turn unto the LORD:** ... will keep it in mind and be turned to the Lord, *BB* ... will bethink themselves of the Lord, *Knox.*

**and all the kindreds of the nations:** ... all the families, *BB* ... all the Pagan Tribes, *Fenton.*

**shall worship before thee:** ... shall bow down before him, *NAB.*

**28. For the kingdom is the LORD's:** ... to the Lord royalty belongs, *Knox* ... dominion is the LORD's, *NAB* ... kingly power belongs to the LORD, *NEB* ... to Yahweh belongeth the kingdom, *Rotherham* ... truly is Yahweh the King, *Anchor.*

**and he is the governor among the nations:** ... He o'er the Heathen rules, *Fenton* ... the ruler over the nations, *Anchor* ... the whole world's homage is his due, *Knox.*

**29. All they that be fat upon earth shall eat and worship:** ... All the

---

low from the story of but one life. If the sorrows of the preceding part can only be a description of the passion, the glories of the second can only be a vision of the universal and eternal kingdom of Christ. It is a gospel before the Gospels and an apocalypse before Revelation.

**22:22–26.** The delivered singer vows to make God's name known to his brethren. The epistle to the Hebrews quotes the vow as not only expressive of our Lord's true manhood, but as specifying its purpose. Jesus became man that men might learn to know God, and the knowledge of his name streams most brightly from the cross. The death and resurrection, the sufferings and glory of Christ open deeper regions into the character of God than even his gracious life disclosed. Having arisen from the dead and been exalted to the throne, He has "a new song" in his immortal lips and more to teach concerning God than He had before.

**22:27–31.** The universal and perpetual diffusion of the kingdom and knowledge of God is the theme of the closing strain. That diffusion is not definitely stated as the issue of the sufferings or deliverance, but the very fact that such a universal knowledge comes into view here requires that it should be so regarded, else the unity of the Psalm is shattered. While, therefore, the ground alleged in v. 28 for this universal recognition of God is only his universal dominion, we must suppose that the history of the singer as told to the world is the great

| | | | |
|---|---|---|---|
| 8246.726 | 3725, 1943, 800 | 3937, 6686 | 3895.126 |
| cj, v Hithpael impf 3mp | *adj, adj,* n fs | prep, n mp, ps 3ms | v Qal impf 3mp |
| וַיִּשְׁתַּחֲווּ | כָּל־דִּשְׁנֵי־אֶרֶץ | לְפָנָיו | יִכְרְעוּ |
| wayyishtachᵉwwû | kol-dishnê-'erets | lᵉphānâv | yikhreʻû |
| and they will worship | all the fat of the earth | before Him | they will bow |

| | | | | | |
|---|---|---|---|---|---|
| 3725, 3495.152 | 6312 | 5497 | 3940 | 2513.311 | **30.** 2320 |
| *adj, v Qal act ptc mp* | n ms | cj, n fs, ps 3ms | neg part | v Piel pf 3ms | n ms |
| כָּל־יוֹרְדֵי | עָפָר | וְנַפְשׁוֹ | לֹא | חִיָּה | זֶרַע |
| kol-yôrdhê | ʻāphār | wᵉnaphshô | lō' | chîyāh | zera' |
| all those going down to | the dust | and their soul | not | they can keep alive | seed |

| | | | | |
|---|---|---|---|---|
| 5856.121 | 5807.421 | 3937, 112 | 3937, 1810 | **31.** 971.126 |
| v Qal impf 3ms, ps 3ms | v Pual impf 3ms | prep, n mp, ps 1cs | prep, art, n ms | v Qal impf 3mp |
| יַעַבְדֶנּוּ | יְסֻפַּר | לַאדֹנָי | לַדּוֹר | יָבֹאוּ |
| ya'avdhennû | yᵉsuppar | la'dhōnāy | laddôr | yāvō'û |
| they will serve Him | they will be told | about the Lord | to the generation | they will come |

| | | | | | | |
|---|---|---|---|---|---|---|
| 5222.526 | 6930 | 3937, 6194 | 3314.255 | 3706 | 6449.111 | **23:t** 4344 |
| cj, v Hiphil impf 3mp | n fs, ps 3ms | prep, n ms | v Niphal ptc ms | cj | v Qal pf 3ms | n ms |
| וְיַגִּידוּ | צִדְקָתוֹ | לְעַם | נוֹלָד | כִּי | עָשָׂה | מִזְמוֹר |
| wᵉyaggîdhû | tsidhqāthô | lᵉ'am | nôlādh | kî | 'āsāh | mizmôr |
| and they will tell | his righteousness | to a people | those born | that | He has done | a Psalm |

| | | | | | | |
|---|---|---|---|---|---|---|
| 3937, 1784 | **1.** 3176 | 7749.151 | 3940 | 2741.125 | **2.** 904, 5295 | 1940 |
| prep, pn | pn | v Qal act ptc ms, ps 1cs | neg part | v Qal impf 1cs | prep, *n fp* | n ms |
| לְדָוִד | יְהוָה | רֹעִי | לֹא | אֶחְסָר | בִּנְאוֹת | דֶּשֶׁא |
| lᵉdhāwidh | yᵉhwāh | rō'î | lō' | 'echsār | bin'ôth | deshe' |
| of David | Yahweh | my Shepherd | not | I will lack | in pastures of | fresh growth |

| | | | | |
|---|---|---|---|---|
| 7547.521 | 6142, 4448 | 4640 | 5273.321 | **3.** 5497 |
| v Hiphil impf 3ms, ps 1cs | prep, *n mp* | n fp | v Piel impf 3ms, ps 1cs | n fs, ps 1cs |
| יַרְבִּיצֵנִי | עַל־מֵי | מְנֻחוֹת | יְנַהֲלֵנִי | נַפְשִׁי |
| yarbîtsēnî | 'al-mê | mᵉnuchôth | yᵉnahlēnî | naphshî |
| He causes me to lie down | beside the waters of | resting places | He leads me | my soul |

| | | | | |
|---|---|---|---|---|
| 8178.321 | 5328.521 | 904, 4724, 6928 | 3937, 4775 | 8428 |
| v Polel impf 3ms | v Hiphil impf 3ms, ps 1cs | prep, *n mp*, n ms | prep, prep | n ms, ps 3ms |
| יְשׁוֹבֵב | יַנְחֵנִי | בְמַעְגְּלֵי־צֶדֶק | לְמַעַן | שְׁמוֹ |
| yᵉshôvēv | yanchēnî | vᵉma'ggᵉlê-tsedheq | lᵉma'an | shᵉmô |
| He restores | He leads me | in the worn paths of righteousness | because of | his name |

| | | | | | | |
|---|---|---|---|---|---|---|
| **4.** 1612 | 3706, 2050.125 | 904, 1548 | 7024 | 3940, 3486.125 | 7737 | 3706, 887 |
| cj | cj, v Qal impf 1cs | prep, *n ms* | n ms | neg part, v Qal impf 1cs | n ms | cj, pers pron |
| גַּם | כִּי־אֵלֵךְ | בְּגֵיא | צַלְמָוֶת | לֹא־אִירָא | רָע | כִּי־אַתָּה |
| gam | kî-'ēlēkh | bᵉghê' | tsalmāweth | lō'-'îrā' | rā' | kî-'attāh |
| even | when I walk | in the valley of | darkness | I will not fear | evil | because You |

great ones, *Rotherham* ... the powerful people, *NCV* ... all the rich people, *Beck* ... All the prosperous, *Berkeley.*

**all they that go down to the dust shall bow before him:** ... all who will one day die, *NCV* ... how can those who go down to the grave bow before him, *NEB* ... shall all who sleep in the earth bow down, *NRSV* ... Before him shall kneel, *Rotherham.*

**and none can keep alive his own soul:** ... folk who cannot keep themselves alive, *Moffatt* ... For the Victor himself restores to life, *Anchor* ... Even he that cannot keep his soul alive, *ASV* ... even he who has not enough for the life of his soul, *BB* ... But I shall live for his sake, *NEB.*

**30. A seed shall serve him:** ... The people in the future will serve him, *NCV* ... May my progeny serve him, *Anchor* ... There will be descendants that serve Him, *Beck.*

**it shall be accounted to the Lord for a generation:** ... the next generation has news of the Lord, *Moffatt* ... when those of a coming age are told about the Lord, *Beck.*

**31. They shall come, and shall declare his righteousness:** ... May they begin to recount his generosity, *Anchor* ... shall speak of the Lord's name, *Knox* ... his saving deeds shall be declared, *Moffatt* ... They will tell that he does what is right, *NCV* ... proclaim his deliverance, *NRSV.*

**unto a people that shall be born:** ... To men as yet unborn, *Fenton* ... to a race that must yet be born, *Knox.*

**that he hath done this:** ... for He has performed it, *Berkeley* ... That he has wrought it, *Goodspeed* ... the justice he has shown, *NAB* ... will hear what God has done, *NCV.*

**23:t. A Psalm of David.**

**1. The LORD is my shepherd:** ... Yahweh, *Anchor* ... The Lord takes care of me as his sheep, *BB* ... My LORD attends, *Fenton.*

**I shall not want:** ... I will not be without any good thing, *BB* ... I shall not lack, *Anchor* ... I have everything I need, *Beck.*

**2. He maketh me to lie down in green pastures:** ... He makes a resting-place for me in green fields, *BB* ... He lets me rest in verdant fields, *Fenton* ... green meadows he will make me lie down, *Anchor* ... In verdant pastures he gives me repose, *NAB* ... In pastures of tender grass, *Young.*

**he leadeth me beside the still waters:** ... he is my guide by the quiet waters, *BB* ... Near tranquil waters will he guide me, *Anchor* ... by the pleasant brooks, *Fenton* ... to quiet pools of fresh water, *Good News* ... to calm water, *NCV.*

**3. He restoreth my soul:** ... He brings me back, my life refreshed, *Fenton* ... renews life within me, *NEB* ... refreshes my soul, *NAB* ... revives my spirit, *REB.*

**he leadeth me in the paths of righteousness:** ... leads me on paths that are right, *NCV.*

**for his name's sake:** ... for the good of his name, *NCV.*

**4. Yea, though I walk through the valley of the shadow of death:** ... valley dark as death, *NEB* ... a valley death-shadowed, *Rotherham* ... deep shade, *BB* ... Death's dark Vale, *Fenton* ... glen of gloom, *Moffatt.*

**I will fear no evil:** ... fear no harm, *Beck* ... will not be afraid, *NCV.*

**for thou art with me:** ... You are there, *Fenton* ... you are at my side, *NAB.*

**thy rod and thy staff they comfort me:** ... rod and your support, *BB* ... crook, *Knox* ... club, *Moffatt.*

---

fact which brings home to men the truth of God's government over and care for them. True, men know God apart from revelation and from the Gospel, but He is to them a forgotten God, and the great influence which helps them to "remember and turn to Yahweh" is the message of the cross and the throne of Jesus.

The Psalm had just laid down the condition of partaking in the sacrificial meal as being lowliness, and (v. 29) it prophecies that the "fat" shall also share in it. That can only be if they become "humble."

As universality in extent, so perpetuity in duration is anticipated for the story of the psalmist's deliverance and for the praise to God thence accruing. "A seed shall serve Him"—that is one generation of obedient worshipers. "It shall be told of Yahweh unto the [next] generation"—that is, a second, who shall receive from their progenitors, the seed that serves, the blessed story. "They ... shall declare his righteousness unto a people that shall be born." "He has done it." "It is finished." No one word can express all that was accomplished in that sacrifice. Eternity will not fully supply the missing word, for the consequences of that finished work go on unfolding forever, and are forever unfinished, because forever increasing.

***Psalm 23.*** *Psalm 23 is the pure utterance of personal trust in Yahweh, darkened by no fears or complaints and so perfectly at rest that it has nothing more to ask. For the time desire is stilled in satisfaction. One tone, and that the most blessed which can sound in a life, is heard through the whole. It is the Psalm of quiet trust, undisturbed even by its joy, which is quiet too. The fire glows, but does not flame or crackle. The one thought is expanded in two kindred images: that of the shepherd and that of the host. The same ideas are substantially repeated under both forms.*

**23:1–4.** Verses 1–4 present the realities of the devout life under the image of the divine Shepherd and his lamb. The comparison of rulers to shepherds is familiar to many tongues and could scarcely fail to occur to a pastoral people like the Jews, nor is the application to Yahweh's relation to the people so concealed that we need to relegate the Psalms in which it occurs to a late era in the national history. The psalmist lovingly lingers on the image and draws out the various aspects of the shepherd's

| 6200 | 8101 | 5120 | 2065 | 5341.326 | 5. 6424.123 |
|---|---|---|---|---|---|
| prep, ps 1cs | n ms, ps 2ms | cj, n fs, ps 2ms | pers pron | v Piel impf 3mp, ps 1cs | v Qal impf 2ms |
| עִמָּדִי | שִׁבְטְךָ | וּמִשְׁעַנְתֶּךָ | הֵמָּה | יְנַחֲמֻנִי | תַּעֲרֹךְ |
| ‘immādhî | shivṭekhā | ûmish‘antekhā | hēmmāh | yenachmunî | ta‘ărōkh |
| with me | your rod | and your staff | they | they comfort me | You prepare |

| 3937, 6686 | 8374 | 5224 | 7173.152 | 1941.313 | 904, 8467 | 7513 |
|---|---|---|---|---|---|---|
| prep, n mp, ps 1cs | n ms | prep | v Qal act ptc mp, ps 1cs | v Piel pf 2ms | prep, art, n ms | n ms, ps 1cs |
| לְפָנַי | שֻׁלְחָן | נֶגֶד | צֹרְרָי | דִּשַּׁנְתָּ | בַשֶּׁמֶן | רֹאשִׁי |
| lephānay | shulchān | neghedh | tsōrerāy | dishshantā | vashshemen | rō'shî |
| before me | a table | before | my adversaries | You have made fat | with the oil | my head |

| 3683 | 7596 | 6. 395 | 3008 | 2721 | 7579.126 |
|---|---|---|---|---|---|
| n fs, ps 1cs | n ms | adv | n ms | cj, n ms | v Qal impf 3mp, ps 1cs |
| כּוֹסִי | רְוָיָה | אַךְ | טוֹב | וָחֶסֶד | יִרְדְּפוּנִי |
| kôsî | rewāyāh | 'akh | ṭôv | wāchesedh | yirdephûnî |
| my cup | something which overflows | surely | good | and steadfast love | they will pursue me |

| 3725, 3219 | 2522 | 8178.115 | 904, 1041, 3176 | 3937, 775 | 3219 |
|---|---|---|---|---|---|
| *adj, n mp* | n mp, ps 1cs | cj, v Qal pf 1cs | prep, *n ms*, pn | prep, *n ms* | n mp |
| כָּל־יְמֵי | חַיָּי | וְשַׁבְתִּי | בְּבֵית־יְהוָה | לְאֹרֶךְ | יָמִים |
| kol-yemê | chayyāy | weshavtî | bevêth-yehwāh | le'ōrekh | yāmîm |
| all the days of | my life | and I will return | into the Temple of Yahweh | for length of | days |

| 24:t 3937, 1784 | 4344 | 1. 3937, 3176 | 800 | 4530 | 8725 | 3553.152 |
|---|---|---|---|---|---|---|
| prep, pn | n ms | prep, pn | art, n fs | cj, n ms, ps 3fs | n fs | cj, *v Qal act ptc mp* |
| לְדָוִד | מִזְמוֹר | לַיהוָה | הָאָרֶץ | וּמְלוֹאָהּ | תֵּבֵל | וְיֹשְׁבֵי |
| ledhāwidh | mizmôr | layhwāh | hā'ārets | ûmelô'āhh | tēvēl | weyōshevê |
| of David | a Psalm | to Yahweh | the earth | and its fulness | the world | and those who dwell |

| 904 | 2. 3706, 2000 | 6142, 3328 | 3354.111 | 6142, 5282 | 3679.321 |
|---|---|---|---|---|---|
| prep, ps 3fs | cj, pers pron | prep, n mp | v Qal pf 3ms, ps 3fs | cj, prep, n fp | v Polel impf 3ms, ps 3fs |
| בָהּ | כִּי־הוּא | עַל־יַמִּים | יְסָדָהּ | וְעַל־נְהָרוֹת | יְכוֹנְנֶהָ |
| vāhh | kî-hû' | 'al-yammîm | yesādhāhh | we'al-nehārôth | yekhôneneāh |
| in it | because He | on the seas | He founded it | and on the rivers | He established it |

| 3. 4449, 6148.121 | 904, 2098, 3176 | 4449, 7251.121 | 904, 4887 |
|---|---|---|---|
| intrg, v Qal impf 3ms | prep, *n ms*, pn | cj, intrg, v Qal impf 3ms | prep, *n ms* |
| מִי־יַעֲלֶה | בְהַר־יְהוָה | וּמִי־יָקוּם | בִּמְקוֹם |
| mî-ya'ăleh | vehar-yehwāh | ûmî-yāqûm | bimqôm |
| who will go up | on the mountain of Yahweh | and who will rise | in the place of |

| 7231 | 4. 5538 | 3834 | 1276, 3949 | 866 | 3940, 5558.111 | 3937, 8175 |
|---|---|---|---|---|---|---|
| n ms, ps 3ms | *adj* | n fd | cj, *adj*, n ms | rel part | neg part, v Qal pf 3ms | prep, art, n ms |
| קָדְשׁוֹ | נְקִי | כַפַּיִם | וּבַר־לֵבָב | אֲשֶׁר | לֹא־נָשָׂא | לַשָּׁוְא |
| qādheshô | neqî | khappayim | ûvar-lēvāv | 'ăsher | lō'-nāsā' | lashshāwe' |
| his holy place | clean of | hands | and pure of heart | who | he has not lifted | to what is false |

**5. Thou preparest a table before me:** … make ready a table, *BB* … spread my board, *Fenton* … prepare a banquet, *Good News* … provide delicious food, *LIVB* … Thou art my host, spreading a feast, *Moffatt.*

**in the presence of mine enemies:** … in front of my adversaries, *Anchor* … in front of my haters, *BB* … where all my enemies can see me, *Good News* … Over-against my adversaries, *Young.*

**thou anointest my head with oil; my cup runneth over:** … You generously anoint my head, *Anchor* … thou hast richly bathed my head with oil, *NEB* … you welcome me as an honored guest and fill my cup to the brim, *Good News.*

**6. Surely goodness and mercy shall follow me:** … goodness and lovingkindness, *ASV* … unfailing love, *Berkeley.*

**all the days of my life:** ... On every day I live, *Fenton.*

**and I will dwell:** ... I will have a place, *BB* ... your house will be my home, *Good News* ... the Eternal's guest, within his household, *Moffatt.*

**in the house of the LORD for ever:** ... for days without end, *Anchor* ... all my days, *BB* ... for the length of the days, *Darby* ... to an old age, *Goodspeed* ... my whole life long, *NRSV.*

**24:t. A Psalm of David.**

**1. The earth is the LORD's:** ... To Yahweh belong the earth, *JB.*

**and the fulness thereof:** ... with all its wealth, *BB* ... and everything in it, *Beck* ... all it contains, *JB.*

**the world, and they that dwell therein:** ... all its people, *Beck* ... all who live there, *JB.*

**2. For he hath founded it upon the seas:** ... He laid its foundation over the seas, *Beck* ... He founded it upon periods, *Fenton* ... Who else has built it out from the sea, *Knox* ... He built it on the waters, *NCV.*

**and established it upon the floods:** ... planted it firm upon the waters beneath, *NEB* ... poised it on the hidden streams, *Knox* ... constructed to move in its spheres, *Fenton* ... upon the currents doth make it firm, *Rotherham.*

**3. Who shall ascend into the hill of the LORD?:** ... Who should mount, *Fenton* ... Who dares climb, *Knox* ... the mountain of Yahweh, *Anchor.*

---

care and of the flock's travels, with a ripeness and calmness which suggests that we listen to a much-experienced man. The sequence in which the successive pictures occur is noteworthy. Guidance to refreshment comes first and is described in v. 2 in words which fall as softly as the gentle streams of which they speak. The noontide is fierce, and the land lies baking in the sun; but deep down in some wadi runs a brook, and along its course the herbage is bright with perpetual moisture, and among the lush grass are cool lairs where the flock may rest.

But the midday or nightly rest is intended to fit for effort, and so a second little picture follows in v. 3, presenting another aspect of the shepherd's care and the sheep's course. Out again onto the road, in spite of heat and dust, the flock goes. "Paths of righteousness" is perhaps best taken as "straight paths," as that rendering keeps within the bounds of the metaphor; but since the sheep are men, straight paths for them must be paths of righteousness. That guidance is "for his name's sake." God has regard to his revealed character in shepherding his lamb and will give direction because He is what He is and in order that He may be known to be what He has declared himself.

**23:5–6.** The second image of the divine Host and his guest is expanded in vv. 5f. The ideas are substantially the same as in the first part. Repose and provision, danger and change, again fill the foreground; again there is forecast of a more remote future. But all is intensified, the need and the supply being painted in stronger colors and the hope being brighter. The devout man is God's guest while he marches through foes and travels toward perpetual repose in the house of Yahweh.

Yahweh supplies his servants' wants in the midst of conflict. The table spread in the sight of the enemy is a more signal token of care and power than the green pastures are. Life is not only journey and effort, but conflict, and it is possible not only to have seasons of refreshment interspersed in the weary march, but to find a sudden table spread by the same unseen hand which holds back the foes who look on with grim eyes, powerless to intercept the sustenance or disturb the guests. This is the condition of God's servant—always conflict, but always a spread table.

In the last verse, we seem to pass to pure anticipation. Memory melts into hope, and that brighter than the forecast which closed the first part. There the psalmist's trust simply refused to yield to fear, while keenly conscious of evil which might warrant it. But here he has risen higher, and the alchemy of his happy faith and experience has converted evil into something fairer. "Only good and mercy shall follow me."

The closing hope of dwelling in the house of Yahweh to length of days rises above even the former verse. The singer knew himself a guest of God's at the table spread before the foe, but that was, as it were, refreshment on the march, while this is continual abiding in the home. Such an unbroken continuity of abode in the house of Yahweh is a familiar aspiration in other Psalms and is always regarded as possible, even while hands are engaged in ordinary duties and cares. The Psalms which conceive of the religious life under this image are marked by a peculiar depth and inwardness.

**24:1–6.** Yahweh's dwelling on Zion did not mean his desertion of the rest of the world, nor did his choice of Israel imply his abdication of rule over, or withdrawal of blessings from, the nations. The light which glorified the bare hilltop where the

| 5497 | 3940 | 8123.211 | 3937, 4983 | | 5558.121 | 1318 | 4623, 881 | 3176 |
|---|---|---|---|---|---|---|---|---|
| n fs, ps 1cs | cj, neg part | v Niphal pf 3ms | prep, n fs | | v Qal impf 3ms | n fs | prep, do | pn |
| נַפְשִׁי | וְלֹא | נִשְׁבַּע | לְמִרְמָה | **5.** | יִשָּׂא | בְרָכָה | מֵאֵת | יְהוָה |
| naphshî | welō' | nishba' | lemirmāh | | yissā' | verākhāh | mē'ēth | yehwāh |
| my soul | and not | he has sworn | to deceit | | he will lift up | a blessing | from | Yahweh |

| 6930 | 4623, 435 | 3589 | | 2172 | 1810 |
|---|---|---|---|---|---|
| cj, n fs | prep, *n mp* | n ms, ps 3ms | | dem pron | *n ms* |
| וּצְדָקָה | מֵאֱלֹהֵי | יִשְׁעוֹ | **6.** | זֶה | דּוֹר |
| ûtsedhāqāh | mē'ĕlōhê | yish'ô | | zeh | dôr |
| and righteousness | from the God of | his salvation | | this | the generation of |

| 1938.152 | 1272.352 | 6686 | 3399 | 5734 | | 5558.133 | 8554 |
|---|---|---|---|---|---|---|---|
| v Qal act ptc mp, ps 3ms | *v Piel ptc mp* | n mp, ps 2ms | pn | intrj | | v Qal impv 2mp | n mp |
| דֹּרְשָׁו | מְבַקְשֵׁי | פָנֶיךָ | יַעֲקֹב | סֶלָה | **7.** | שְׂאוּ | שְׁעָרִים |
| dōreshāw | mevaqōshê | phānêkhā | ya'ăqōv | selāh | | se'û | she'ārîm |
| those who seek Him | those who seek | your face | O Jacob | selah | | lift up | O gates |

| 7513 | 5558.233 | 6860 | 5986 | 971.121 | 4567 | 3638 |
|---|---|---|---|---|---|---|
| n mp, ps 2mp | cj, v Niphal impv 2mp | *n mp* | n ms | cj, v Qal juss 3ms | *n ms* | art, n ms |
| רָאשֵׁיכֶם | וְהִנָּשְׂאוּ | פִּתְחֵי | עוֹלָם | וְיָבוֹא | מֶלֶךְ | הַכָּבוֹד |
| rā'shêkhem | wehinnāse'û | pithchê | 'ôlām | weyāvô' | melekh | hakkāvôdh |
| your heads | and be lifted up | O doors of | antiquity | that He may enter | the King of | the glory |

| | 4449 | 2172 | 4567 | 3638 | 3176 | 6021 | 1399 | 3176 | 1399 |
|---|---|---|---|---|---|---|---|---|---|
| | intrg | dem pron | *n ms* | art, n ms | pn | adj | cj, adj | pn | *adj* |
| **8.** | מִי | זֶה | מֶלֶךְ | הַכָּבוֹד | יְהוָה | עִזּוּז | וְגִבּוֹר | יְהוָה | גִּבּוֹר |
| | mî | zeh | melekh | hakkāvôdh | yehwāh | 'izzûz | weghibbôr | yehwāh | gibbôr |
| | who | this | the King of | the glory | Yahweh | strong | and mighty | Yahweh | mighty in |

| 4560 | | 5558.133 | 8554 | 7513 | 5558.133 | 6860 | 5986 |
|---|---|---|---|---|---|---|---|
| n fs | | v Qal impv 2mp | n mp | n mp, ps 2mp | cj, v Qal impv 2mp | *n mp* | n ms |
| מִלְחָמָה | **9.** | שְׂאוּ | שְׁעָרִים | רָאשֵׁיכֶם | וּשְׂאוּ | פִּתְחֵי | עוֹלָם |
| milchāmāh | | se'û | she'ārîm | rā'shêkhem | ûse'û | pithchê | 'ôlām |
| battle | | lift up | O gates | your heads | and lift up | O doors of | antiquity |

| 971.121 | 4567 | 3638 | | 4449 | 2000 | 2172 | 4567 | 3638 |
|---|---|---|---|---|---|---|---|---|
| cj, v Qal juss 3ms | *n ms* | art, n ms | | intrg | pers pron | dem pron | *n ms* | art, n ms |
| וְיָבֹא | מֶלֶךְ | הַכָּבוֹד | **10.** | מִי | הוּא | זֶה | מֶלֶךְ | הַכָּבוֹד |
| weyāvō' | melekh | hakkāvôdh | | mî | hû' | zeh | melekh | hakkāvôdh |
| that He may enter | the King of | the glory | | who | He | this | the King of | the glory |

**or who shall stand in his holy place?:** ... Who shall take a stand, *JB* ... Who may stand within his sacred shrine, *Moffatt* ... appear in his sanctuary, *Knox.*

**4. He that hath clean hands:** ... The clean handed, *Fenton* ... innocent handes, *Geneva* ... The guiltless in act, *Knox* ... whose hands are sinless, *NAB.*

**and a pure heart:** ... true heart, *BB* ... heart unstained, *Moffatt* ... whose heart is clean, *NAB.*

**who hath not lifted up his soul unto vanity:** ... who has not raised his mind to an idol, *Anchor* ... whose desire has not gone out to foolish things, *BB* ... Who incites not his mind to deceive, *Fenton* ... one who never set his heart on lying tales, *Knox* ... unto falsehood, *ASV.*

**nor sworn deceitfully:** ... who does not swear an oath in order to deceive, *JB* ... who has not taken a false oath, *BB* ... who have not made promises in the name of a false god, *NCV* ... or swore treacherously to his neighbour, *Knox* ... who does not feast upon vice, *Fenton* ... and has not committed perjury, *NEB.*

**5. He shall receive the blessing from the LORD:** ... He will receive bliss from the LORD, *Fenton* ... Shall bear away a blessing from Yahweh, *Rotherham.*

**and righteousness from the God of his salvation:** ... generous treatment from his saving God, *Anchor* ... vindicated by the God who saves him, *Beck* ... justification from the God of his deliverance, *Goodspeed* ... a boon from God his saviour, *Moffatt.*

**6. This is the generation:** ... Such is the company of those who seek him, *NRSV* ... his the true breed that still looks, *Knox* ... Such are the men who are in quest of him, *Moffatt.*

**of them that seek him, that seek thy face, O Jacob. Selah:** ... of those whose hearts are turned to you, *BB* ... who come for help to the God of Jacob, *Beck* ... still longs for the presence of the God of Jacob, *Knox* ... Who seek Thy face—even Jacob, *NASB.*

**7. Lift up your heads, O ye gates:** ... Raise your arches, *Moffatt* ... Gates, open all the way, *NCV* ... Swing back, doors, higher yet, *Knox* ... Lift up, O gates, your lintels, *NAB.*

**and be ye lift up:** ... be ye raised, *Berkeley* ... reach higher, *Knox.*

**ye everlasting doors:** ... O gates of the Eternal, *Anchor* ... Draw up your ancient doors, *Fenton* ... O doors age-during, *Young* ... age-abiding doors, *Rotherham.*

**and the King of glory shall come in:** ... let the Glorious King come in, *Fenton* ... let the King enter in triumph, *Knox* ... may enter, *Berkeley.*

**8. Who is this King of glory?:** ... Who is this great King, *Knox.*

**The LORD strong and mighty:** ... The LORD of Strength and Might, *Fenton* ... It is Yahweh, strong and valiant, *JB.*

**the LORD mighty in battle:** ... The LORD, a hero in battle, *Beck* ... The mighty LORD of War, *Fenton.*

**9. Lift up your heads, O ye gates; even lift them up, ye everlasting doors:** ... Swing back, doors, higher yet; reach higher, immemorial gates, *Knox.*

**and the King of glory shall come in:** ... Admit the Glorious King, *Fenton* ... shall enter, *JB.*

**10. Who is this King of glory? The LORD of hosts, he is the King of glory. Selah:** He is the LORD of Armies, *Fenton* ... Yahweh Saboath, *JB* ... The LORD All-Powerful, *NCV.*

**25:t. A Psalm of David.**

---

Ark rested was reflected thence over all the world. "The glory" was there concentrated, not confined. This Psalm guards against all superstitious misconceptions and protests against national narrowness in exactly the same way as Exo. 19:5 bases Israel's selection from among all peoples on the fact that "all the earth is mine."

"Who may ascend?" was a picturesquely appropriate question for singers toiling upward, and "who may stand?" for those who hoped presently to enter the sacred presence. The one requirement is purity. Here that requirement is deduced from the majesty of Yahweh, as set forth in vv. 1f and from the designation of his dwelling as "holy." This is the postulate of the whole Psalter. In v. 4, it may be noted that, of the four enumerated, the two central aspects of purity refer to the inward life ("pure heart"; "lifts not his desire unto vanity"), and these are embedded, as it were, in the outward life of deeds and words. Purity of act is expressed by "clean hands"—neither red with blood, nor foul with grubbing in dunghills for gold and other so-called good. Purity of speech is condensed into the one virtue of truthfulness ("swears not to a falsehood"). But the outward will only be right if the inward disposition is pure, and that inward purity will only be realized when desires are carefully curbed and directed. As is the desire, so is the man.

In v. 5, the possessor of such purity is represented as receiving "a blessing, even righteousness," from God. The expression is equivalent to "salvation" in the next clause.

Verse 6 seems to carry the adumbration of truth not yet disclosed a step further. A great planet is trembling into visibility and is divined before it is seen. The emphasis in this verse is on "seek," and the implication is that those who seek find. If we seek God's face, we shall receive purity. There the Psalm touches the foundation. The divine heart so earnestly desires to give righteousness that to seek is to find. The abrupt introduction of "Jacob" is made more emphatic by the musical interlude which closes the first part.

**24:7–10.** There is a pause, while the procession ascends the hill of the LORD, revolving the stringent qualifications for entrance. It stands before the barred gates, while possibly part of the choir is within. The advancing singers summon the doors to open and receive the incoming Yahweh. Their portals are too low for Him to enter, and therefore they are called upon to lift their lintels. They are gray with age, and around them cluster long memories; therefore, they are addressed as "gates of ancient time." The question from within expresses ignorance and hesitation and dramatically represents the ancient gates as sharing the relation of the former inhabitants to the God of Israel, whose name they did not know and whose authority they did not own. It heightens the force of the triumphant shout proclaiming his mighty name. He is

| 3176 | 6893 | 2000 | 4567 | 3638 | 5734 | | 3937, 1784 | | 420 | 3176 |
|---|---|---|---|---|---|---|---|---|---|---|
| pn | n fp | pers pron | *n ms* | art, n ms | intrj | | prep, pn | | prep, ps 2ms | pn |
| יְהוָה | צְבָאוֹת | הוּא | מֶלֶךְ | הַכָּבוֹד | סֶלָה | **25:t** | לְדָוִד | **1.** | אֵלֶיךָ | יְהוָה |
| yehwāh | tsevā'ōth | hû' | melekh | hakkāvôdh | selāh | | ledhāwidh | | 'ēlêkhā | yehwāh |
| Yahweh | Hosts | He | the King of | the glory | selah | | of David | | to You | O Yahweh |

| 5497 | 5558.125 | | 435 | 904 | 1019.115 | 414, 991.125 |
|---|---|---|---|---|---|---|
| n fs, ps 1cs | v Qal impf 1cs | | n mp, ps 1cs | prep, ps 2ms | v Qal pf 1cs | adv, v Qal juss 1cs |
| נַפְשִׁי | אֶשָּׂא | **2.** | אֱלֹהַי | בְּךָ | בָטַחְתִּי | אַל־אֵבוֹשָׁה |
| naphshî | 'essā' | | 'ĕlōhay | bekhā | vātachtî | 'al-'ēvôshāh |
| my soul | I will lift up | | my God | in You | I have trusted | let me not be ashamed |

| 414, 6192.126 | 342.152 | 3937 | | 1612 | 3725, 7245.152 | 3940 |
|---|---|---|---|---|---|---|
| adv, v Qal juss 3mp | v Qal act ptc mp, ps 1cs | prep, ps 1cs | | cj | *adj*, v Qal act ptc mp, ps 2ms | neg part |
| אַל־יַעַלְצוּ | אֹיְבַי | לִי | **3.** | גַּם | כָּל־קֹוֶיךָ | לֹא |
| 'al-ya'altsû | 'ōyevay | lî | | gam | kol-qōwêkhā | lō' |
| may they not exult | my enemies | at me | | also | all those who hope in You | not |

| 991.126 | 991.126 | 931.152 | 7674 |
|---|---|---|---|
| v Qal juss 3mp | v Qal juss 3mp | art, v Qal act ptc mp | adv |
| יֵבֹשׁוּ | יֵבֹשׁוּ | הַבּוֹגְדִים | רֵיקָם |
| yēvōshû | yēvōshû | habbôghdhîm | rêqām |
| may they be ashamed | may they be ashamed | those who act treacherously | without cause |

| | 1932 | 3176 | 3156.531 | 758 | 4064.331 |
|---|---|---|---|---|---|
| | n mp, ps 2ms | pn | v Hiphil impv 2ms, ps 1cs | n fp, ps 2ms | v Piel impv 2ms, ps 1cs |
| **4.** | דְּרָכֶיךָ | יְהוָה | הוֹדִיעֵנִי | אֹרְחוֹתֶיךָ | לַמְּדֵנִי |
| | derākhêkhā | yehwāh | hôdhî'ēnî | 'ōrechôthêkhā | lammedhēnî |
| | your ways | O Yahweh | cause me to know | your paths | teach me |

| | 1931.531 | 904, 583 | 4064.331 | 3706, 887 | 435 |
|---|---|---|---|---|---|
| | v Hiphil impv 2ms, ps 1cs | prep, n fs, ps 2ms | cj, v Piel impv 2ms, ps 1cs | cj, pers pron | *n mp* |
| **5.** | הַדְרִיכֵנִי | בַאֲמִתֶּךָ | וְלַמְּדֵנִי | כִּי־אַתָּה | אֱלֹהֵי |
| | hadhrîkhēnî | va'ămittekhā | welammedhēnî | kî-'attāh | 'ĕlōhê |
| | lead me | in your truth | and teach me | because You | the God of |

| 3589 | 881 | 7245.315 | 3725, 3219 | | 2226.131, 7638 | 3176 |
|---|---|---|---|---|---|---|
| n ms, ps 1cs | do, ps 2ms | v Piel pf 1cs | *adj*, art, n ms | | v Qal impv 2ms, n mp, ps 2ms | pn |
| יִשְׁעִי | אוֹתְךָ | קִוִּיתִי | כָּל־הַיּוֹם | **6.** | זְכֹר־רַחֲמֶיךָ | יְהוָה |
| yish'î | 'ôthkhā | qiwwîthî | kol-hayyôm | | zekhōr-rachmêkhā | yehwāh |
| my salvation | You | I have hoped in | all the day | | be mindful of your mercy | O Yahweh |

| 2721 | 3706 | 4623, 5986 | 2065 | | 2496 |
|---|---|---|---|---|---|
| cj, n mp, ps 2ms | cj | prep, n ms | pers pron | | *n fp* |
| וַחֲסָדֶיךָ | כִּי | מֵעוֹלָם | הֵמָּה | **7.** | חַטֹּאות |
| wachsādhêkhā | kî | mē'ôlām | hēmmāh | | chattō'wth |
| and your steadfast love | because | from ancient times | they | | the sins of |

**1. Unto thee, O LORD, do I lift up my soul:** ... To you, O Yahweh, I raise my mind, *Anchor* ... I long for You, LORD, *Beck* ... I lift up my desire, *Goodspeed* ... Adoration I offer, Yahweh, *JB*.

**2. O my God, I trust in thee:** ... I give myself to you, *NCV* ... I confide in thee, *Darby*.

**let me not be ashamed:** ... don't let me down, *Beck* ... Save me from the shame of defeat, *Good News* ... oh disappoint me not, *Moffatt* ... disgraced, *NCV* ... confounded, *Geneva*.

**let not mine enemies triumph over me:** ... Let not my foes gloat over me, *Anchor* ... Let not my foes exult, *Goodspeed* ... let not my enemies boast of my downfall, *Knox* ... not let my enemies laugh at me, *NCV*.

**3. Yea, let none that wait on thee be ashamed:** ... None who invoke you aloud will be humiliated, *Anchor* ... Let no servant of yours be put to shame, *BB* ... No one who looks to You for help will be disappointed,

*Beck* ... Do not let those who wait for you be put to shame, *NRSV.*

**let them be ashamed which transgress without cause:** ... humiliated will be the faithless through idle talk, *Anchor* ... those who sin without excuse will be disgraced, *NCV* ... those shall be ashamed who are vainly disloyal, *Berkeley* ... as they are disappointed who lightly break their troth, *Knox* ... that deal treacherously without cause, *MAST.*

**4. Show me thy ways, O LORD:** ... make me know, *Anchor* ... Make your steps clear to me, *BB* ... Direct my way, Lord, as thou wilt, *Knox.*

**teach me thy paths:** ... give me knowledge of your ways, *BB.*

**5. Lead me in thy truth, and teach me:** ... Cause me to tread in Thy truth, *Young* ... Be my guide and teacher in the true way, *BB.*

**for thou art the God of my salvation:** ... thou art my delivering God, *Rotherham.*

**on thee do I wait all the day:** ... I am waiting for your word all the day, *BB.*

**6. Remember, O LORD, thy tender mercies and thy lovingkindnesses:** ... Forget not, Lord, thy pity, *Knox* ... how ancient are your compassion and your kindness, *Anchor* ... keep in mind your pity and your mercies, *BB* ... Goodness and faithful love, *JB.*

**for they have been ever of old:** ... thy mercies of long ago, *Knox* ... they have been from the earliest times, *BB* ... they are from everlasting, *Berkeley* ... from age-past times, *Rotherham.*

**7. Remember not the sins of my youth:** ... Do not keep in mind my sins when I was young, *BB.*

**nor my transgressions:** ... wrongdoing, *BB* ... offenses, *Goodspeed* ... frailties, *Knox* ... rebellings, *KJVII* ... wrong things, *NCV.*

**according to thy mercy:** ... think mercifully of me, *Knox* ... in remembering my sins be kind to me, *Moffatt.*

---

Yahweh, the self-existent God, Who has made a Covenant with Israel and fights for his people as these gray walls bear witness. His warrior might have wrested them from their former possessors, and the gates must open for their Conqueror. The repeated question is animated: "Who then is He?" The King of glory!" The answer peals forth the great name, "Yahweh of Hosts."

**25:1–3.** The first prayer section embraces the three standing needs: protection, guidance and forgiveness. With these are intertwined their pleas according to the logic of faith—the suppliant's uplifted desires and God's eternal tenderness and manifested mercy. The order of mention of the needs proceeds inward from without, for protection from enemies is superficial as compared with illumination as to duty, and deeper than even that, as well as prior in order of time (and therefore last in order of enumeration), is pardon. Similarly, the pleas go deeper as they succeed each other, for the psalmist's trust and waiting is superficial as compared with the plea breathed in the name of "the God of my salvation." That general designation leads to the gaze upon the ancient and changeless mercies, which constitute the measure and pattern of God's working ("according to," v. 7), and upon the self-originated motive, which is the deepest and strongest of all arguments with Him ("for thy goodness' sake," v. 7).

**25:4–7.** The prayer for deliverance glides into that for guidance, since the latter is the deeper need and the former will scarcely be answered unless the suppliant's will docilely offers the latter. The soul lifted to Yahweh will long to know his will and submit itself to his manifold teachings. "Thy ways" and "thy paths" necessarily mean here the ways in which Yahweh desires that the psalmist should go. "In thy truth" is ambiguous, both as to the preposition and the noun. The clause may either present God's truth (i.e., faithfulness) as his motive for answering the prayer or his truth (i.e., the objective revelation) as the path for men. Predominant usage inclines to the former signification of the noun, but the possibility still remains of regarding God's faithfulness as the path in which the psalmist desires to be led, i.e., to experience it. The cry for forgiveness strikes a deeper note of pathos and, as asking a more wondrous blessing, grasps still more firmly the thought of what Yahweh is and always has been. The appeal is made to "thy compassions and loving kindnesses," as belonging to his nature and to their past exercise as having been "from of old."

Emboldened thus, the psalmist can look back on his own past, both on his outbursts of youthful passion and levity, which he calls "failures," as missing the mark, and on the darker evils of later manhood, which he calls "rebellions," and can trust that Yahweh will think upon him "according to his mercy," and "for the sake of his goodness" or love. The vivid realization of that eternal mercy as the very mainspring of God's actions, and as setting forth in many an ancient deed the eternal pattern of his dealings, enables a man to bear the thought of his own sins.

| 5454 | 6840 | 414, 2226.123 | 3626, 2721 |
|---|---|---|---|
| n mp, ps 1cs | cj, n mp, ps 1cs | adv, v Qal juss 2ms | prep, n ms, ps 2ms |
| נְעוּרַי | וּפְשָׁעַי | אַל־תִּזְכֹּר | כְּחַסְדְּךָ |
| ne‘ûray | ûphesha‘ay | 'al-tizkōr | kechas̱dekhā |
| my youth | and my transgressions | do not remember | according to your steadfast love |

| 2226.131, 3937, 887 | 3937, 4775 | 3008 | 3176 | | 3005, 3596 | 3176 |
|---|---|---|---|---|---|---|
| v Qal impv 2ms, prep, ps 1cs, pers pron | prep, prep | n ms, ps 2ms | pn | **8.** | adj, cj, adj | pn |
| זְכָר־לִי־אַתָּה | לְמַעַן | טוּבְךָ | יְהוָה | | טוֹב־וְיָשָׁר | יְהוָה |
| zekhār-lî-'attāh | lema‘an | ṯûvkhā | yehwāh | | tôv-weyāshār | yehwāh |
| remember me | because of | your good | O Yahweh | | good and upright | Yahweh |

| 6142, 3772 | 3498.521 | 2491 | 904, 1932 | | 1931.521 | 6262 | 904, 5122 |
|---|---|---|---|---|---|---|---|
| prep, adv | v Hiphil impf 3ms | n mp | prep, art, n ms | **9.** | v Hiphil juss 3ms | n mp | prep, art, n ms |
| עַל־כֵּן | יוֹרֶה | חַטָּאִים | בַּדָּרֶךְ | | יַדְרֵךְ | עֲנָוִים | בַּמִּשְׁפָּט |
| ‘al-kēn | yôreh | chaṯṯā'îm | baddārekh | | yadhrēkh | ‘ănāwîm | bammishpāṯ |
| therefore | He instructs | sinners | on the way | | may He lead | the lowly | with justice |

| 4064.321 | 6262 | 1932 | | 3725, 758 | 3176 | 2721 | 583 |
|---|---|---|---|---|---|---|---|
| cj, v Piel impf 3ms | n mp | n ms, ps 3ms | **10.** | *adj, n fp* | pn | n ms | cj, n fs |
| וִילַמֵּד | עֲנָוִים | דַּרְכּוֹ | | כָּל־אָרְחוֹת | יְהוָה | חֶסֶד | וֶאֱמֶת |
| wîlammēdh | ‘ănāwîm | darkô | | kol-'ārechôth | yehwāh | ches̱edh | we'ĕmeth |
| and He teaches | the lowly | his way | | all the paths of | Yahweh | steadfast love | and reliability |

| 3937, 5526.152 | 1311 | 5921 | | 3937, 4775, 8428 | 3176 |
|---|---|---|---|---|---|
| prep, *v Qal act ptc ms* | n fs, ps 3ms | cj, n fp, ps 3ms | **11.** | prep, prep, n ms, ps 2ms | pn |
| לְנֹצְרֵי | בְרִיתוֹ | וְעֵדֹתָיו | | לְמַעַן־שִׁמְךָ | יְהוָה |
| lenōtserê | verîthô | we‘ēdhōthâv | | lema‘an-shimkhā | yehwāh |
| to those who keep | his Covenant | and his testimonies | | because of your name | O Yahweh |

| 5739.113 | 3937, 5988 | 3706 | 7521, 2000 | | 4449, 2172 | 382 |
|---|---|---|---|---|---|---|
| cj, v Qal pf 2ms | prep, n ms, ps 1cs | cj | adj, pers pron | **12.** | intrg, dem pron | art, n ms |
| וְסָלַחְתָּ | לַעֲוֹנִי | כִּי | רַב־הוּא | | מִי־זֶה | הָאִישׁ |
| wes̱ālachtā | la‘ăwōnî | kî | rav-hû' | | mî-zeh | hā'îsh |
| and You have forgiven | my guilt | because | abundant it | | who this | the man |

| 3486.151 | 3176 | 3498.521 | 904, 1932 | 1013.121 | | 5497 |
|---|---|---|---|---|---|---|
| *v Qal act ptc ms* | pn | v Hiphil impf 3ms, ps 3ms | prep, n ms | v Qal impf 3ms | **13.** | n fs, ps 3ms |
| יְרֵא | יְהוָה | יוֹרֶנּוּ | בְּדֶרֶךְ | יִבְחָר | | נַפְשׁוֹ |
| yerē' | yehwāh | yôrennû | bedherekh | yivchār | | naphshô |
| the one who fears | Yahweh | He will teach him | in the way | He will choose | | his soul |

| 904, 3005 | 4053.122 | 2320 | 3542.121 | 800 | | 5660 |
|---|---|---|---|---|---|---|
| prep, adj | v Qal impf 3fs | cj, n ms, ps 3ms | v Qal impf 3ms | n fs | **14.** | *n ms* |
| בְּטוֹב | תָּלִין | וְזַרְעוֹ | יִירַשׁ | אָרֶץ | | סוֹד |
| beṯôv | tālîn | wezar‘ô | yîrash | 'ārets | | s̱ôdh |
| in good | it will lodge | and his descendants | they will possess | the land | | the consultation of |

| 3176 | 3937, 3486.152 | 1311 | 3937, 3156.541 | | 6084 |
|---|---|---|---|---|---|
| pn | prep, v Qal act ptc mp, ps 3ms | cj, n fs, ps 3ms | prep, v Hiphil inf con, ps 3mp | **15.** | n fd, ps 1cs |
| יְהוָה | לִירֵאָיו | וּבְרִיתוֹ | לְהוֹדִיעָם | | עֵינַי |
| yehwāh | lîrē'âv | ûverîthô | lehôdhî‘ām | | ‘ênay |
| Yahweh | to those who fear Him | and his Covenant | causing them to know | | my eyes |

| 8878 | 420, 3176 | 3706 | 2000, 3428.521 | 4623, 7862 | 7559 |
|---|---|---|---|---|---|
| adv | prep, pn | cj | pers pron, v Hiphil impf 3ms | prep, n fs | n fd, ps 1cs |
| תָּמִיד | אֶל־יְהוָה | כִּי | הוּא־יוֹצִיא | מֵרֶשֶׁת | רַגְלָי |
| tāmîdh | 'el-yehwāh | kî | hû'-yôtsî' | mēresheth | raghlāy |
| continually | to Yahweh | because | He He causes to go out | from a net | my feet |

**remember thou me for thy goodness' sake, O LORD:** ... as your faithful love dictates, *JB.*

**8. Good and upright is the LORD: therefore will he teach sinners in the way:** ... He will instruct sinners, *Berkeley* ... he brings sinners back to the path, *JB* ... he teaches any who go astray, *Moffatt* ... guiding out strayed feet back to the path, *Knox.*

**9. The meek will he guide in judgment:** ... He causeth the humble to tread in judgment, *Young* ... He enables the humble to live right, *Beck* ... Judiciously he guides the humble, *JB* ... In his own laws he will train the humble, *Knox* ... May he guide patient wronged-ones to be righted, *Rotherham.*

**and the meek will he teach his way:** ... and teaches the poor, *Anchor* ... instructing the poor in his way, *JB* ... teach such oppressed-ones his way, *Rotherham.*

**10. All the paths of the LORD:** ... All the ways, *NEB.*

**are mercy and truth:** ... kindness and constancy, *NAB* ... mercy and good faith, *BB* ... smooth and safe, *Fenton.*

**unto such as keep his covenant and his testimonies:** ... to men who keep his covenant and his charge, *NEB* ... for those who keep his covenant stipulations, *Anchor* ... who follow the demands of his agreement, *NCV* ... To those who guard His Law and Proofs, *Fenton* ... his decrees, *JB.*

**11. For thy name's sake, O LORD:** ... Because of your name, *BB* ... Glorify Your name, *Beck* ... for the honor of your name, *LIVB.*

**pardon mine iniquity; for it is great:** ... forgive my iniquity, *Anchor* ... let me have forgiveness for my sin, *BB* ... Pardon my guilt, *Goodspeed* ... forgive my wickedness, *NEB.*

**12. What man is he that feareth the LORD?:** ... who reveres the LORD, *Berkeley* ... who respect Yahweh, what of them, *JB* ... Whoever reverences the Eternal, learns, *Moffatt* ... respect, *NCV.*

**him shall he teach:** ... him will he show, *Anchor* ... the Lord will be his teacher, *BB* ... Him He shall instruct, *Berkeley* ... He will point them to the best way, *NCV.*

**in the way that he shall choose:** ... the path, *Anchor* ... in the way of his pleasure, *BB.*

**13. His soul shall dwell at ease:** ... He shall live within God's circle of blessing, *LIVB* ... His soul will be full of good things, *BB* ... shall dwell in prosperity, *Berkeley* ... They will always be prosperous, *Good News.*

**and his seed shall inherit the earth:** ... his offspring, *Berkeley* ... his progeny, *Anchor* ... his posterity shall hold their land, *Moffatt* ... his descendants will possess the land, *Goodspeed* ... his seed will have the earth for its heritage, *BB.*

**14. The secret of the LORD is with them that fear him:** ... Intimacy with Yahweh have they who revere him, *Rotherham* ... The LORD directs His friends, *Fenton* ... ONLY those who fear Yahweh possess his secret, *JB* ... The LORD tells his secrets to those who respect him, *NCV.*

**and he will show them his covenant:** ... he will make his agreement clear to them, *BB* ... show you what His covenant means, *Beck* ... his covenant, for their instruction, *NAB.*

**15. Mine eyes are ever toward the LORD:** ... Permanently my eyes are on Yahweh, *JB* ... I fix my eyes continually, *Knox.*

**for he shall pluck my feet out of the net:** ... He will keep me from any traps, *NCV* ... He can get my feet out of every trap, *Beck* ... he will free my

---

**25:8–15.** The contemplation of the divine character prepares the way for the transition to the second group of verses, which are mainly meditation on that character and on God's dealings and the blessedness of those who fear Him. The thought of God beautifully draws the singer from himself. How deeply and lovingly he had pondered on the name of the LORD before he attained to the grand truth that his goodness and very uprightness pledged Him to show sinners where they should walk! Since there is at the heart of things an infinitely pure and equally loving Being, nothing is more impossible than that He should wrap himself in thick darkness and leave men to grope after duty. Revelation of the path of life in some fashion is the only conduct consistent with his character.

The participants, then, in this blessed knowledge have a threefold character: sinners; humble; keepers of the Covenant and testimonies. Then passing from self, the singer again recurs to his theme, reiterating in vivid language and with some amplification the former thoughts. In vv. 8ff, the character of Yahweh is the main subject, and the men whom He blessed were in the background. In vv. 12ff, they stand forward. Their designation now is the wide one of "those who fear Yahweh," and the blessings they receive are, first, that of being taught the way, which has been prominent thus far, but here has a new phase, as being "the way that he should choose." God's teaching illuminates the path and tells a man what he ought to do, while his freedom of choice is uninfringed.

| 16. | 6680.131, 420 | 2706.131 | 3706, 3279 | 6270 | 603 |
|---|---|---|---|---|---|
| | v Qal impv 2ms, prep, ps 1cs | cj, v Qal impv 2ms, ps 1cs | cj, adj | cj, adj | pers pron |
| | פְּנֵה־אֵלַי | וְחָנֵּנִי | כִּי־יָחִיד | וְעָנִי | אָנִי |
| | penēh-'ēlay | wechānnēnî | kî-yāchîdh | we'ānî | 'ānî |
| | turn to me | and be gracious to me | because lonely | and afflicted | I |

| 17. | 7150 | 3949 | 7620.516 | 4623, 4855 | 3428.531 |
|---|---|---|---|---|---|
| | *n fp* | n ms, ps 1cs | v Hiphil pf 3cp | prep, n fp, ps 1cs | v Hiphil impv 2ms, ps 1cs |
| | צָרוֹת | לְבָבִי | הִרְחִיבוּ | מִמְּצוּקוֹתַי | הוֹצִיאֵנִי |
| | tsārôth | levāvî | hirchîvû | mimmetsûqôthay | hôtsî'ēnî |
| | the troubles of | my heart | they have made wide | from my distress | You bring me out |

| 18. | 7495.131 | 6271 | 6219 | 5558.131 | 3937, 3725, 2496 |
|---|---|---|---|---|---|
| | v Qal impv 2ms | n ms, ps 1cs | cj, n ms, ps 1cs | cj, v Qal impv 2ms | prep, *adj*, n fp, ps 1cs |
| | רְאֵה | עָנְיִי | וַעֲמָלִי | וְשָׂא | לְכָל־חַטֹּאותָי |
| | re'ēh | 'āneyî | wa'ămālî | wesā' | lekhol-chattō'wthāy |
| | see | my affliction | and my trouble | and forgive | all my sins |

| 19. | 7495.131, 342.152 | 3706, 7525.116 | 7985 | 2660 | 7983.116 |
|---|---|---|---|---|---|
| | v Qal impv 2ms, v Qal act ptc mp, ps 1cs | cj, v Qal pf 3cp | cj, *n fs* | n ms | v Qal pf 3cp, ps 1cs |
| | רְאֵה־אוֹיְבַי | כִּי־רָבּוּ | וְשִׂנְאַת | חָמָס | שְׂנֵאוּנִי |
| | re'ēh-'ôyvay | kî-rābbû | wesin'ath | chāmās | senē'ûnî |
| | see my enemies | that they are many | and hatred of | violence | they hated me |

| 20. | 8490.131 | 5497 | 5522.531 | 414, 991.125 |
|---|---|---|---|---|
| | v Qal impv 2ms | n fs, ps 1cs | cj, v Hiphil impv 2ms, ps 1cs | adv, v Qal juss 1cs |
| | שָׁמְרָה | נַפְשִׁי | וְהַצִּילֵנִי | אַל־אֵבוֹשׁ |
| | shāmerāh | naphshî | wehatstsîlēnî | 'al-'ēvôsh |
| | protect | my life | and rescue me | let me not be ashamed |

| 3706, 2725.115 | 904 | 21. | 8866, 3598 | 5526.126 |
|---|---|---|---|---|
| cj, v Qal pf 1cs | prep, ps 2ms | | n ms, cj, n ms | v Qal juss 3mp, ps 1cs |
| כִּי־חָסִיתִי | בָךְ | | תֹּם־וָיֹשֶׁר | יִצְּרוּנִי |
| kî-chāsîthî | vākh | | tōm-wāyōsher | yitstserûnî |
| because I have taken refuge | in You | | blamelessness and uprightness | may they guard me |

| 3706 | 7245.315 | 22. | 6540.131 | 435 | 881, 3547 | 4623, 3725 | 7150 |
|---|---|---|---|---|---|---|---|
| cj | v Piel pf 1cs, ps 2ms | | v Qal impv 2ms | n mp | do, pn | prep, adj | n fp, ps 3ms |
| כִּי | קִוִּיתִיךָ | | פְּדֵה | אֱלֹהִים | אֶת־יִשְׂרָאֵל | מִכֹּל | צָרוֹתָיו |
| kî | qiwwîthîkhā | | pedhēh | 'ĕlōhîm | 'eth-yisrā'ēl | mikkōl | tsārôthâv |
| because | I put my hope in You | | ransom | O God | Israel | from all | their troubles |

| 26:t | 3937, 1784 | 1. | 8570.131 | 3176 | 3706, 603 | 904, 8866 | 2050.115 |
|---|---|---|---|---|---|---|---|
| | prep, pn | | v Qal impv 2ms, ps 1cs | pn | cj, pers pron | prep, n ms, ps 1cs | v Qal pf 1cs |
| | לְדָוִד | | שָׁפְטֵנִי | יְהוָה | כִּי־אֲנִי | בְּתֻמִּי | הָלַכְתִּי |
| | ledhāwidh | | shāphetēnî | yehwāh | kî-'ănî | vethummî | hālakhtî |
| | of David | | judge me | Yahweh | because I | in my blamelessness | I have walked |

feet from the snare, *JB* … he will clear me from perplexities, *Moffatt.*

**16. Turn thee unto me:** … Quick, turn to me, *JB* … Look toward me, *NAB.*

**and have mercy upon me:** … be kind to me, *Beck* … be gracious, *Berkeley* … pity me, *JB.*

**for I am desolate and afflicted:** … friendless and forlorn, *Knox* … alone and oppressed, *Anchor* … troubled and have no helper, *BB* … lonely and miserable, *Beck* … alone and wretched as I am, *JB.*

**17. The troubles of my heart are enlarged:** … Enlarge the straits of my heart, *Goodspeed* … my problems go from bad to worse, *LIVB* … My troubles have grown larger, *NCV* … Anguish cramps my heart, *Anchor* … Relieve the distress of my heart, *Beck.*

**O bring thou me out of my distresses:** … take me out of my sorrows, *BB* … bring me out of my constraint, *JB* … brought me from my woes, *Fenton* ... out of my straits brought me forth, *Rotherham.*

**18. Look upon mine affliction and my pain:** ... Spare a glance for my misery and pain, *JB* ... Behold my humiliation, *Rotherham* ... my travail, *ASV* ... and my trouble, *Anchor.*

**and forgive all my sins:** ... freed me from my wrongs, *Fenton* ... to my sins be merciful, *Knox* ... pardon all my sins, *Moffatt.*

**19. Consider mine enemies; for they are many:** ... See how numerous are my foes, *Anchor* ... See how those who are against me are increased, *BB* ... See how many enemies I have, *Beck* ... Take note how countless are my enemies, *JB* ... how viciously they hate me, *LIVB.*

**and they hate me with cruel hatred:** ... my treacherous enemies who hate me, *Anchor* ... they hate me cruelly, *Moffatt* ... with the hatred of violence do they hate me, *Rotherham* ... how bitter is the grudge they bear me, *Knox* ... bitter is their hate of me, *BB.*

**20. O keep my soul, and deliver me:** ... Take my soul into thy keeping, *Knox* ... Guard my soul, *NASB* ... Defend me, *NEB* ... Preserve my life and rescue me, *Anchor* ... Protect and rescue me, *Beck.*

**let me not be ashamed:** ... humiliated, *Anchor* ... disappointed, *Beck* ... disgraced, *NCV.*

**for I put my trust in thee:** ... in you I find refuge, *REB* ... because I've come to You for shelter, *Beck* ... My trust on you held up, *Fenton* ... as I take shelter with thee, *Moffatt.*

**21. Let integrity and uprightness:** ... innocence and honesty, *Beck* ... Uprightness and purity, *Knox* ... devotion and my loyalty, *Moffatt* ... blamelessness and uprightness, *Rotherham.*

**preserve me:** ... safeguard me, *Anchor* ... protect, *Beck* ... bodyguards, *LIVB* ... watch over me, *Rotherham.*

**for I wait on thee:** ... when I invoke you, *Anchor* ... as I look to You for help, *Beck.*

**22. Redeem Israel, O God, out of all his troubles:** ... free Israel, *Beck* ... Ransom Israel, O God, from all its anguish, *Anchor* ... When wilt thou deliver Israel, *Knox* ... bring Israel safe out of all its troubles, *Moffatt.*

**26:t. A Psalm of David.**

**1. Judge me, O LORD; for I have walked in mine integrity: I have trusted also in the LORD; therefore I shall not slide:** ... Vindicate me, O LORD, *Berkeley* ... I have trusted in the LORD without wavering, *RSV* ... I move not from my trust in the LORD, *Fenton* ... and put unfaltering trust in you, *REB.*

---

**25:16–22.** When Yahweh turns to a man, the light streaming from his face makes darkness day. The pains on which He "looks" are soothed, and the enemies whom He beholds shrivel beneath his eye. The psalmist believes that God's presence, in the deeper sense of that phrase, as manifested partly through delivering acts and partly through inward consciousness, is his one need, in which all deliverances and gladnesses are enwrapped. He plaintively pleads, "For I am alone and afflicted." The soul that has awakened to the sense of the awful solitude of personal being, and stretched out yearning desires to the only God, and felt that with Him it would know no pain in loneliness, will not cry in vain. The "look" on the psalmist's affliction and pain will be tender and sympathetic, as a mother eagle's on her sick eaglet; that on his foes will be stern and destructive, many though they be. In v. 11, the prayer for pardon was sustained by the plea that the sin was "great." In v. 19, that for deliverance from foes rests on the fact that "they are many," for which the verb cognate with the adjective of v. 11 is used. Thus, both dangers without and evils within are regarded as crying out, by their multitude, for God's intervention. The wreath is twined so that its end is brought around to its beginning. "Let me not be ashamed, for I trust in thee," is the second petition of the first part repeated; and "I wait on thee," which is the last word of the Psalm, omitting the superfluous verse, echoes the clause which it is proposed to transfer to v. 1. Thus, the two final verses correspond to the two initial ones.

***Psalm 26.*** *The image of "the way" which is characteristic of Ps. 25 reappears in a modified form in this Psalm, which speaks of "walking in integrity" and truth and of "feet standing in an even place." Other resemblances to the preceding Psalm are the use of "redeem" and "be merciful" as well as the references to God's steadfast love and truth, in which the psalmist walks, and to his own integrity.*

**26:1–3.** The two keynotes are both struck in the first group of three verses, in which vv. 2f are substantially an expansion of v. 1. The prayer, "Judge me," asks for a divine act of deliverance based upon a divine recognition of the psalmist's sincerity and unwavering trust. Both the prayer and its ground are startling. It grates upon ears accustomed to the tone of the NT, that a suppliant should allege his single-eyed simplicity and steadfast faith

| 904, 3176 | 1019.115 | 3940 | 4726.125 | | 1010.131 | 3176 |
|---|---|---|---|---|---|---|
| cj, prep, pn | v Qal pf 1cs | neg part | v Qal impf 1cs | **2.** | v Qal impv 2ms, ps 1cs | pn |
| וּבַיהוָה | בָּטַחְתִּי | לֹא | אֶמְעָד | | בְּחָנֵנִי | יְהוָה |
| ûvayhwāh | bātachtî | lō' | 'em'ādh | | bechānēnî | yehwāh |
| and in Yahweh | I have trusted | not | I have faltered | | examine me | Yahweh |

| 5441.331 | 7170.131 | 3749 | 3949 | | 3706, 2721 |
|---|---|---|---|---|---|
| cj, v Piel impv 2ms, ps 1cs | v Qal impv 2ms | n fp, ps 1cs | cj, n ms, ps 2ms | **3.** | cj, n ms, ps 2ms |
| וְנַסֵּנִי | צְרוֹפָה | כִלְיוֹתַי | וְלִבִּי | | כִּי־חַסְדְּךָ |
| wenassēnî | tserôphāh | khilyôthay | welibbî | | kî-chasdekhā |
| and put me to the test | refine | my kidneys | and my heart | | because your steadfast love |

| 3937, 5224 | 6084 | 2050.715 | 904, 583 | | 3940, 3553.115 | 6194, 5139, 8175 |
|---|---|---|---|---|---|---|
| prep, prep | n fp, ps 1cs | cj, v Hithpael pf 1cs | prep, n fs, ps 2ms | **4.** | neg part, v Qal pf 1cs | prep, *n mp*, n ms |
| לְנֶגֶד | עֵינָי | וְהִתְהַלַּכְתִּי | בַּאֲמִתֶּךָ | | לֹא־יָשַׁבְתִּי | עִם־מְתֵי־שָׁוְא |
| leneghedh | 'ênāy | wehithhallakhtî | ba'ămittekhā | | lō'-yāshavtî | 'im-methê-shāwe' |
| before | my eyes | and I have walked | in your truth | | I have not sat | with men of falsehood |

| 6196 | 6180.256 | 3940 | 971.125 | | 7983.115 | 7235 | 7778.552 |
|---|---|---|---|---|---|---|---|
| cj, prep | v Niphal ptc mp | neg part | v Qal impf 1cs | **5.** | v Qal pf 1cs | *n ms* | v Hiphil ptc mp |
| וְעִם | נַעֲלָמִים | לֹא | אָבוֹא | | שָׂנֵאתִי | קְהַל | מְרֵעִים |
| we'im | na'ălāmîm | lō' | 'āvô' | | sānē'thî | qōhal | merē'îm |
| and with | those concealed | not | I will enter | | I hated | the assembly of | evildoers |

| 6194, 7857 | 3940 | 3553.125 | | 7647.125 | 904, 5539 | 3834 |
|---|---|---|---|---|---|---|
| cj, prep, n mp | neg part | v Qal impf 1cs | **6.** | v Qal impf 1cs | prep, n ms | n fp, ps 1cs |
| וְעִם־רְשָׁעִים | לֹא | אֵשֵׁב | | אֶרְחַץ | בְּנִקָּיוֹן | כַּפָּי |
| we'im-reshā'îm | lō' | 'ēshēv | | 'erchats | beniqqāyôn | kappāy |
| and with the wicked | not | I will sit | | I will wash | in innocence | my hands |

| 5621.325 | 881, 4326 | 3176 | | 3937, 8471.541 | 904, 7249 | 8756 |
|---|---|---|---|---|---|---|
| cj, v Poel juss 1cs | do, n ms, ps 2ms | pn | **7.** | prep, v Hiphil inf con | prep, *n ms* | n fs |
| וַאֲסֹבְבָה | אֶת־מִזְבַּחֲךָ | יְהוָה | | לַשְׁמִעַ | בְּקוֹל | תּוֹדָה |
| wa'ăsōvevāh | 'eth-mizbachkhā | yehwāh | | lashmia' | beqôl | tôdhāh |
| and let me go about | your altar | Yahweh | | to cause to hear | with a voice of | thanksgiving |

| 5807.341 | 3725, 6623.258 | | 3176 | 154.115 | 4737 |
|---|---|---|---|---|---|
| cj, v Piel inf con | *adj*, v Niphal ptc fp, ps 2ms | **8.** | pn | v Qal pf 1cs | *n ms* |
| וּלְסַפֵּר | כָּל־נִפְלְאוֹתֶיךָ | | יְהוָה | אָהַבְתִּי | מְעוֹן |
| ûlăsappēr | kol-niphle'ôthêkhā | | yehwāh | 'āhavtî | me'ôn |
| and to recount | all your extraordinary deeds | | Yahweh | I have loved | the habitation of |

| 1041 | 4887 | 5088 | 3638 | | 414, 636.123 | 6196, 2490 |
|---|---|---|---|---|---|---|
| n ms, ps 2ms | cj, *n ms* | *n ms* | n ms, ps 2ms | **9.** | adv, v Qal juss 2ms | prep, n mp |
| בֵּיתֶךָ | וּמְקוֹם | מִשְׁכַּן | כְּבוֹדֶךָ | | אַל־תֶּאֱסֹף | עִם־חַטָּאִים |
| bêthekhā | ûmeqôm | mishkan | kevôdhekhā | | 'al-te'ĕsōph | 'im-chattā'îm |
| your Temple | and the place of | the dwelling of | your glory | | do not add | with sinners |

**2. Examine me, O LORD, and prove me; try my reins and my heart:** … assay my inmost desires and thoughts, *Knox* … test my soul and my heart, *NCB* … try my heart and my mind, *KJVII* … let the fire make clean my thoughts and my heart, *BB*.

**3. For thy lovingkindness is before mine eyes: and I have walked in thy truth:** … For Thy mercy is before mine eyes, *MAST* … I see how kind you are; I live in Your truth, *Beck* … I have walked faithful to you, *Anchor* … and I live my life by your truth, *JB*.

**4. I have not sat with vain persons, neither will I go in with dissemblers:** … I have not associated with deceptive men, *Berkeley* … I have not sat with men of falsehood, *ASV* … Nor will I go with pretenders, *NASB* … among worthless men, nor do I mix with hypocrites, *NEB*.

**5. I have hated the congregation of evildoers; and will not sit with the wicked:** … I hate the wicked party, I never would join the ungodly,

*Moffatt* ... And with reprobates I will not sit down, *Goodspeed* ... And with lawless men would I not sit, *Rotherham* ... and avoid the wicked, *Good News.*

**6. I will wash mine hands in innocency: so will I compass thine altar, O LORD:** ... With the pure in heart I will wash my hands clean, *Knox* ... I will make my hands clean from sin, *BB* ... but blamelessly I wash my hands, *Moffatt* ... and march around Your altar, *Beck.*

**7. That I may publish with the voice of thanksgiving, and tell of all thy wondrous works:** ... Giving voice to my thanks, *NAB* ... To proclaim with a voice of praise, *Goodspeed* ... That I may make the voice of thanksgiving to be heard, *MRB* ... and tell of all the miracles you have done, *NCV.*

**8. LORD, I have loved the habitation of thy house:** ... I have loved the dwelling place of Your house, *KJVII* ... I love the beauty of thy house, *NEB* ... LORD I love the Court of Your House, *Fenton.*

**and the place where thine honour dwelleth:** ... the place where thy glory dwells, *RSV* ... Even the place of the habitation of thy glory, *Rotherham* ... the tenting-place of your glory, *NCB.*

**9. Gather not my soul with sinners:** ... Do not take my soul away along with sinners, *NASB* ... Do not sweep me away with sinners, *NRSV.*

**nor my life with bloody men:** ... nor my life with bloodthirsty men, *Berkeley* ... nor cast me out with those who thirst for blood, *REB* ... nor my life with men of idols, *Anchor* ... spare me from the fate of murderers, *Good News.*

---

as pleas with God, and the strange tone continues through the whole Psalm. The threefold prayer in v. 2 invites divine scrutiny and bares the inmost recesses of affection and impulse for testing, proving by circumstances and smelting by any fire. The psalmist is ready for the ordeal because he has kept God's "steadfast love" (HED #2721) steadily in sight through all the glamour of earthly brightnesses, and his outward life has been all, as it were, transacted in the sphere of God's truthfulness; i.e., the inward contemplation of his mercy and faithfulness has been the active principle of his life.

**26:4–5.** Such high and sweet communion cannot but breed profound distaste for the society of evildoers. The eyes which have God's steadfast love ever before them are endowed with penetrative clearness of vision into the true hollowness of most of the objects pursued by men, and with a terrible sagacity which detects hypocrisy and shams. Association with such men is necessary, but it is impossible for a man whose heart is truly in touch with God not to feel ill at ease when brought into contact with those who have no share in his deepest convictions and emotions. "Men of vanity" is a general designation for the ungodly. "Those who mask themselves" are another class, namely hypocrites who conceal their pursuit of vanity under the show of religion. The psalmist's revulsion is intensified in v. 5 into "hate," because the evildoers and sinners spoken of there are of a deeper tint of blackness and are banded together in a "congregation," the opposite and parody of the assemblies of the righteous.

**26:6–7.** The psalmist, then, in the next two verses, opposes access to the house of God and the solemn joy of thankful praises sounding there to the loathed consorting with evil. He will not sit with men of vanity because he will enter the sanctuary. Outward participation in its worship may be included in his vows and wishes, but the tone of the verses rather points to a symbolic use of the externalities of ritual. Cleansing the hands alludes to priestly lustration. Compassing the altar is not known to have been a Jewish practice, but it may be taken as simply a picturesque way of describing himself as one of the joyous circle of worshipers, and the sacrifice is praise. It may also indicate an unwillingness to leave the place of worship, given the transitory statement of v. 8.

**26:8–10.** Verse 8 shows the aspects which drew the psalmist's love. It was "the shelter of thy house," where he could hide himself from the strife of tongues and escape the pain of herding with evildoers; it was "the place of the dwelling of thy glory," the abode of that symbol of divine presence which flamed between the cherubim and lit the darkness of the innermost shrine. Because the singer felt his true home to be there, he prayed that his soul might not be gathered with sinners, i.e., that he might not be involved in their fate. He has had no fellowship with them in their evil, and therefore he asks that he may be separate from them in their punishment. To "gather the soul" is equivalent to taking away the life. The picture of the evildoers from whom the psalmist recoils is darker in these last verses than before. It is evidently a portrait and points to a state of society in which violence, outrage and corruption were rampant. The psalmist washed his hands in innocence, but these men had violence and bribes in theirs. They were therefore persons in authority, prostitut-

| 5497 | 6196, 596 | 1879 | 2522 | | 866, 904, 3135 | 2239 |
|---|---|---|---|---|---|---|
| n fs, ps 1cs | cj, prep, *n mp* | n mp | n mp, ps 1cs | **10.** | rel pron, prep, n fd, ps 3mp | n fs |
| נַפְשִׁי | וְעִם־אַנְשֵׁי | דָמִים | חַיָּי | | אֲשֶׁר־בִּידֵיהֶם | זִמָּה |
| naphshî | wᵉ'im-'anshê | dhāmîm | chayyāy | | 'ăsher-bîdhêhem | zimmāh |
| my soul | or with men of | bloodshed | my life | | who in their hands | shameful deeds |

| 3332 | 4527.112 | 8245 | | 603 | 904, 8866 | 2050.125 |
|---|---|---|---|---|---|---|
| cj, n fs, ps 3mp | v Qal pf 3fs | n ms | **11.** | cj, pers pron | prep, n ms, ps 1cs | v Qal impf 1cs |
| וִימִינָם | מָלְאָה | שֹּׁחַד | | וַאֲנִי | בְּתֻמִּי | אֵלֵךְ |
| wîmînām | mālᵉ'āh | shōchadh | | wa'ănî | bᵉthummî | 'ēlēkh |
| and their right hand | it is full of | bribes | | and I | in my blamelessness | I will walk |

| 6540.131 | 2706.131 | | 7559 | 6198.112 | 904, 4473 |
|---|---|---|---|---|---|
| v Qal impv 2ms, ps 1cs | cj, v Qal impv 2ms, ps 1cs | **12.** | n fs, ps 1cs | v Qal pf 3fs | prep, n ms |
| פְּדֵנִי | וְחָנֵּנִי | | רַגְלִי | עָמְדָה | בְמִישׁוֹר |
| pᵉdhēnî | wᵉchānnēnî | | raghlî | 'āmᵉdhāh | vᵉmîshôr |
| ransom me | and be gracious to me | | my foot | it stands | on level ground |

| 904, 4882 | 1313.325 | 3176 | | 3937, 1784 | | 3176 | 214 | 3589 |
|---|---|---|---|---|---|---|---|---|
| prep, n mp | v Piel impf 1cs | pn | **27:t** | prep, pn | **1.** | pn | n ms, ps 1cs | cj, n ms, ps 1cs |
| בְּמַקְהֵלִים | אֲבָרֵךְ | יְהוָה | | לְדָוִד | | יְהוָה | אוֹרִי | וְיִשְׁעִי |
| bᵉmaqŏhēlîm | 'ăvārēkh | yᵉhwāh | | lᵉdhāwidh | | yᵉhwāh | 'ôrî | wᵉyish'î |
| in the assembly | I will bless | Yahweh | | of David | | Yahweh | my light | and my salvation |

| 4623, 4449 | 3486.125 | 3176 | 4735, 2522 | 4623, 4449 | 6585.125 |
|---|---|---|---|---|---|
| prep, intrg | v Qal impf 1cs | pn | *n ms*, n mp, ps 1cs | prep, intrg | v Qal impf 1cs |
| מִמִּי | אִירָא | יְהוָה | מָעוֹז־חַיַּי | מִמִּי | אֶפְחָד |
| mimmî | 'îrā' | yᵉhwāh | mā'ôz-chayyay | mimmî | 'ephchādh |
| of whom | will I be afraid | Yahweh | the stronghold of my life | of whom | will I be terrified |

| | 904, 7414.141 | 6142 | 7778.552 | 3937, 404.141 | 881, 1340 | 7141 |
|---|---|---|---|---|---|---|
| **2.** | prep, v Qal inf con | prep, ps 1cs | v Hiphil ptc mp | prep, v Qal inf con | do, n ms, ps 1cs | n mp, ps 1cs |
| | בִּקְרֹב | עָלַי | מְרֵעִים | לֶאֱכֹל | אֶת־בְּשָׂרִי | צָרַי |
| | biqŏrōv | 'ālay | mᵉrē'îm | le'ĕkhōl | 'eth-bᵉsārî | tsāray |
| | when nearing | against me | evildoers | to devour | my flesh | my adversaries |

| 342.152 | 3937 | 2065 | 3911.116 | 5489.116 |
|---|---|---|---|---|
| cj, v Qal act ptc mp, ps 1cs | prep, ps 1cs | pers pron | v Qal pf 3cp | cj, v Qal pf 3cp |
| וְאֹיְבַי | לִי | הֵמָּה | כָּשְׁלוּ | וְנָפָלוּ |
| wᵉ'ōyᵉvay | lî | hēmmāh | khāshᵉlû | wᵉnāphālû |
| and my enemies | against me | they | they will stumble | and they will fall |

| | 524, 2684.122 | 6142 | 4402 | 3940, 3486.121 | 3949 | 524, 7251.122 |
|---|---|---|---|---|---|---|
| **3.** | cj, v Qal impf 3fs | prep, ps 1cs | n ms | neg part, v Qal impf 3ms | n ms, ps 1cs | cj, v Qal impf 3fs |
| | אִם־תַּחֲנֶה | עָלַי | מַחֲנֶה | לֹא־יִירָא | לִבִּי | אִם־תָּקוּם |
| | 'im-tachneh | 'ālay | machneh | lō'-yîrā' | libbî | 'im-tāqûm |
| | though it is encamped | against me | a regiment | it will not fear | my heart | though it rises |

| 6142 | 4560 | 904, 2148 | 603 | 1019.151 | | 259 | 8068.115 | 4623, 881, 3176 |
|---|---|---|---|---|---|---|---|---|
| prep, ps 1cs | n fs | prep, dem pron | pers pron | v Qal act ptc ms | **4.** | num | v Qal pf 1cs | prep, do, pn |
| עָלַי | מִלְחָמָה | בְּזֹאת | אֲנִי | בוֹטֵחַ | | אַחַת | שָׁאַלְתִּי | מֵאֵת־יְהוָה |
| 'ālay | milchāmāh | bᵉzō'th | 'ănî | vôṭēach | | 'achath | shā'altî | mē'ēth-yᵉhwāh |
| against me | a battle | in this | I | one who trusts | | one | I asked | from Yahweh |

| 881 | 1272.325 | 3553.141 | 904, 1041, 3176 | 3725, 3219 | 2522 |
|---|---|---|---|---|---|
| do, ps 3fs | v Piel impf 1cs | v Qal inf con, ps 1cs | prep, *n ms*, pn | *adj, n mp* | n mp, ps 1cs |
| אוֹתָהּ | אֲבַקֵּשׁ | שִׁבְתִּי | בְּבֵית־יְהוָה | כָּל־יְמֵי | חַיַּי |
| 'ôthāhh | 'ăvaqqēsh | shivtî | bᵉvêth-yᵉhwāh | kol-yᵉmê | chayyay |
| it | I will seek | my dwelling | in the Temple of Yahweh | all the days of | my life |

**10. In whose hands is mischief, and their right hand is full of bribes:** ... In whose hands is wickedness, *ASV* ... In whose hands is craftiness, *MAST* ... whose right hands take money for judging falsely, *BB* ... whose hands are stained with guilt, *JB.*

**11. But as for me, I will walk in mine integrity: redeem me, and be merciful unto me:** ... But I lead a blameless life, *NIV* ... But I live my life without reproach, *NEB* ... In innocence I will go on my way; ransom me, *JB.*

**12. My foot standeth in an even place: in the congregations will I bless the LORD:** ... My foot stands on a level place, *NASB* ... And when my foot rests on the temple floor, *Moffatt* ... I stand in a safe place. LORD, I praise you in the great meeting, *NCV* ... My feet are planted on firm ground; I shall bless the LORD in the full assembly, *REB.*

**27:t. A Psalm of David.**

**1. The LORD is my light and my salvation; whom shall I fear? the LORD is the strength of my life; of whom shall I be afraid?:** ... The LORD is the defense of my life, *NASB* ... The LORD is the refuge of my life, *NEB* ... The LORD, is my light and my Victor, *Fenton* ... The Lord watches over my life; whom shall I hold in dread?, *Knox.*

**2. When the wicked, even mine enemies and my foes, came upon me to eat up my flesh, they stumbled and fell:** ... When evildoers assail me, uttering slanders against me, *RSV* ... When evildoers pressed in upon me, *Goodspeed* ... When wicked men besiege me, *Anchor* ... to devour my flesh, *NRSV.*

**3. Though an host should encamp against me, my heart shall not fear: though war should rise against me, in this will I be confident:** ... Though there come up against me—a battle, *Rotherham* ... if war was made on me, my faith would not be moved, *BB* ... if armed men should fall upon me, even then I would be undismayed, *REB* ... even then will I trust, *NCB.*

**4. One thing have I desired of the LORD, that will I seek after; that I may dwell in the house of the LORD all the days of my life, to behold the beauty of the LORD, and to inquire in his temple:** ... That I may gaze on the loveliness of the LORD and contemplate his temple, *NAB* ... and to meditate in His temple, *Berkeley* ... To behold the graciousness of the LORD, *MAST* ... and to pray in His temple, *KJVII.*

---

ing justice. The description fits too many periods too well to give a clue to the date of the Psalm.

**26:11–12.** Once more the consciousness of difference and the resolve not to be like such men break forth in the closing couple of verses. The Psalm began with the profession that he had walked in his integrity; it ends with the vow that he will. It had begun with the prayer "Judge me"; it ends with the expansion of it into "Redeem me"—from existing dangers, from evildoers, or from their fate—and "Be gracious unto me," the positive side of the same petition. He who purposes to walk uprightly has the right to expect God's delivering and giving hand to be extended to him. The resolve to walk uprightly unaccompanied with the prayer for that hand to hold up is just as rash as the prayer without the resolve is vain. But if these two go together, quiet confidence will steal into the heart, and although there be no change in circumstances, the mood of mind will be so soothed and lightened that the suppliant will feel that he has suddenly emerged from the steep gorge where he has been struggling and shut up and stands on level ground.

**27:1–3.** The first half of the Psalm is the exultant song of soaring faith. But even in it there sounds an undertone. The refusal to be afraid glances sideways at outstanding causes for fear. The names of Yahweh as "Light," "Salvation" and "the Stronghold of my life," imply darkness, danger and besetting foes. The hopes of safety in Yahweh's tent, of a firm standing on a rock, and of the head being lifted above surrounding foes are not the hopes of a man at ease, but of one threatened on all sides and triumphant only because he clasps Yahweh's hand. The first words of the Psalm carry it all in germ.

**27:4–6.** Clearly, the terms forbid the limitation of meaning to mere external presence in a material sanctuary. "All the days of my life" points to a continuance inward and capable of accomplishment, wherever the body may be. Very beautifully does the Psalm describe the occupation of God's guest as "gazing upon the pleasantness of Yahweh." In that expression, the construction of the verb with a preposition implies a steadfast and penetrating contemplation, and the word rendered "beauty" or "pleasantness" (HED #5461) may mean "friendliness," but it is perhaps better taken in a more general meaning, as equivalent to the whole gathered delight of the divine character, the supremely fair and sweet. "To inquire" (HED #1266) may be rendered "to consider," but the rendering "meditate [or contemplate] in" is better, as the palace would scarcely be a worthy object of consideration. It is natural that the gaze on the goodness of Yahweh should be followed by loving meditation on what

| 3706 | | 904, 2033 | 3937, 1266.341 | 904, 5461, 3176 | 3937, 2463.141 |
|---|---|---|---|---|---|
| cj | | prep, n ms, ps 3ms | cj, prep, v Piel inf con | prep, *n ms*, pn | prep, v Qal inf con |
| כִּי | **5.** | בְּהֵיכָלוֹ | וּלְבַקֵּר | בְּנֹעַם־יְהוָה | לַחֲזוֹת |
| kî | | behêkhālô | ûlăvaqqēr | benō'am-yehwāh | lachzôth |
| because | | in his Temple | and to inquire | on the beauty of Yahweh | to behold |

| 904, 5848 | 5846.521 | 7750 | 904, 3219 | 904, 5712 | 7121.121 |
|---|---|---|---|---|---|
| prep, *n ms* | v Hiphil impf 3ms, ps 1cs | n fs | prep, *n ms* | prep, n ms, ps 3ms | v Qal impf 3ms, ps 1cs |
| בְּסֵתֶר | יַסְתִּרֵנִי | רָעָה | בְּיוֹם | בְּסֻכֹּה | יִצְפְּנֵנִי |
| besēther | yastirēnî | rā'āh | beyôm | besukkōh | yitspenēnî |
| in the cover of | He will hide me | evil | in the day of | in his shelter | He will conceal me |

| 6142 | 7513 | 7597.121 | 6498 | | 7597.321 | 904, 6962 | 164 |
|---|---|---|---|---|---|---|---|
| prep | n ms, ps 1cs | v Qal impf 3ms | cj, adv | | v Polel impf 3ms, ps 1cs | prep, n ms | n ms, ps 3ms |
| עַל | רֹאשִׁי | יָרוּם | וְעַתָּה | **6.** | יְרוֹמְמֵנִי | בְּצוּר | אָהֳלוֹ |
| 'al | rō'shî | yārûm | we'attāh | | yerômemēnî | betsûr | 'āhelô |
| over | my head | He will lift up | and now | | He will set me on high | on a rock | his tent |

| 8980 | 2160 | 904, 164 | 2159.125 | 5623 | 342.152 |
|---|---|---|---|---|---|
| n fs | *n mp* | prep, n ms, ps 3ms | cj, v Qal juss 1cs | adv, ps 1cs | v Qal act ptc mp, ps 1cs |
| תְרוּעָה | זִבְחֵי | בְּאָהֳלוֹ | וְאֶזְבְּחָה | סְבִיבוֹתַי | אֹיְבַי |
| therû'āh | zivchê | ve'āhelô | we'ezbechāh | sevîvôthay | 'ōyevay |
| a shout of joy | sacrifices of | in his tent | and let me sacrifice | all around me | my enemies |

| 7410.125 | 7249 | 8471.131, 3176 | | 3937, 3176 | 2252.325 | 8301.125 |
|---|---|---|---|---|---|---|
| v Qal impf 1cs | n ms, ps 1cs | v Qal impv 2ms, pn | | prep, pn | cj, v Piel juss 1cs | v Qal juss 1cs |
| אֶקְרָא | קוֹלִי | שְׁמַע־יְהוָה | **7.** | לַיהוָה | וַאֲזַמְּרָה | אָשִׁירָה |
| 'eqōrā' | qôlî | shema'-yehwāh | | layhwāh | wa'ăzammerāh | 'āshîrāh |
| I will call | my voice | hear Yahweh | | to Yahweh | and let me sing praises | let me sing |

| 1272.333 | 3949 | 569.111 | 3937 | | 6257.131 | 2706.131 |
|---|---|---|---|---|---|---|
| v Piel impv 2mp | n ms, ps 1cs | v Qal pf 3ms | prep, ps 2ms | | cj, v Qal impv 2ms, ps 1cs | cj, v Qal impv 2ms, ps 1cs |
| בַּקְּשׁוּ | לִבִּי | אָמַר | לְךָ | **8.** | וַעֲנֵנִי | וְחָנֵּנִי |
| baqqeshû | libbî | 'āmar | lekhā | | wa'ănēnî | wechonnēnî |
| seek | my heart | it has said | to You | | and answer me | and be gracious to me |

| 4623 | 6686 | 414, 5846.523 | | 1272.325 | 3176 | 881, 6686 | 6686 |
|---|---|---|---|---|---|---|---|
| prep, ps 1cs | n mp, ps 2ms | adv, v Hiphil juss 2ms | | v Piel impf 1cs | pn | do, n mp, ps 2ms | n mp, ps 1cs |
| מִמֶּנִּי | פָּנֶיךָ | אַל־תַּסְתֵּר | **9.** | אֲבַקֵּשׁ | יְהוָה | אֶת־פָּנֶיךָ | פָּנָי |
| mimmenî | pānêkhā | 'al-tastēr | | 'ăvaqqēsh | yehwāh | 'eth-pānêkhā | phānāy |
| from me | your face | do not hide | | I will seek | Yahweh | your face | my face |

| 414, 5389.123 | 2030.113 | 6046 | 5860 | 414, 5371.523, 904, 653 |
|---|---|---|---|---|
| adv, v Qal juss 2ms, ps 1cs | v Qal pf 2ms | n fs, ps 1cs | n ms, ps 2ms | adv, v Hiphil juss 2ms, prep, n ms |
| אַל־תִּטְּשֵׁנִי | הָיִיתָ | עֶזְרָתִי | עַבְדֶּךָ | אַל־תַּט־בְּאַף |
| 'al-titteshēnî | hāyîthā | 'ezrāthî | 'avdekhā | 'al-tat-be'aph |
| do not leave me behind | You have been | my Help | your servant | do not turn in anger |

| 525 | 3706, 1 | | 3589 | 435 | 414, 6013.123 |
|---|---|---|---|---|---|
| cj, n fs, ps 1cs | cj, n ms, ps 1cs | | n ms, ps 1cs | *n mp* | cj, adv, v Qal juss 2ms, ps 1cs |
| וְאִמִּי | כִּי־אָבִי | **10.** | יִשְׁעִי | אֱלֹהֵי | וְאַל־תַּעַזְבֵנִי |
| we'immî | kî-'āvî | | yish'î | 'ĕlōhê | we'al-ta'azvēnî |
| and my mother | because my father | | my salvation | the God of | and do not abandon me |

| 3176 | 3498.531 | | 636.121 | 3176 | 6013.116 |
|---|---|---|---|---|---|
| pn | v Hiphil impv 2ms, ps 1cs | | v Qal impf 3ms, ps 1cs | cj, pn | v Qal pf 3cp, ps 1cs |
| יְהוָה | הוֹרֵנִי | **11.** | יַאַסְפֵנִי | וַיהוָה | עֲזָבוּנִי |
| yehwāh | hôrēnî | | ya'asphēnî | wayhwāh | 'ăzāvûnî |
| O Yahweh | teach me | | He will gather me | and Yahweh | they have abandoned me |

| 1932 | 5328.131 | 904, 758 | 4473 | 3937, 4775 | 8234 |
|---|---|---|---|---|---|
| n ms, ps 2ms | cj, v Qal impv 2ms, ps 1cs | prep, *n ms* | n ms | prep, prep | n mp, ps 1cs |
| דַּרְכֶּךָ | וּנְחֵנִי | בְּאֹרַח | מִישׁוֹר | לְמַעַן | שׁוֹרְרָי |
| darkekhā | ûnechēnî | be'ōrach | mîshôr | lema'an | shôrerāy |
| your way | and lead me | in a path of | level ground | because of | my enemies |

12.

| 414, 5598.123 | 904, 5497 | 7141 | 3706 | 7251.116, 904 |
|---|---|---|---|---|
| adv, v Qal juss 2ms, ps 1cs | prep, *n fs* | n mp, ps 1cs | cj | v Qal pf 3cp, prep, ps 1cs |
| אַל־תִּתְּנֵנִי | בְּנֶפֶשׁ | צָרָי | כִּי | קָמוּ־בִי |
| 'al-tittenēnî | benephesh | tsārāy | kî | qāmû-vî |
| do not give me | by the desire of | my adversaries | because | they have risen against me |

**5. For in the time of trouble he shall hide me in his pavilion: in the secret of his tabernacle shall he hide me; he shall set me up upon a rock:** ... He hideth me in a secret place of His tent, *Young* ... For he hides me away under his roof on the day of evil, *JB* ... he will raise me beyond reach of distress, *NEB* ... and sets me high up on His mountain, *Beck*.

**6. And now shall mine head be lifted up above mine enemies round about me: therefore will I offer in his tabernacle sacrifices of joy; I will sing, yea, I will sing praises unto the Lord:** ... He will now lift me up to victory, *Moffatt* ... He shall lift me up upon a rock, *MRB* ... so I shall acclaim him in his tent with sacrifice, *REB* ... And now my head is high, *Goodspeed*.

**7. Hear, O Lord, when I cry with my voice: have mercy also upon me, and answer me:** ... Listen to my pleading, Lord, *LIVB* ... the sound of my call; have pity on me, *NAB* ... be gracious unto me, *Darby* ... show me favour, *NEB*.

**8. When thou saidst, Seek ye my face; my heart said unto thee, Thy face, Lord, will I seek:** ... True to my heart's promise, I have eyes only for thee, *Knox* ... Come, my heart says, Come to Him for help, *Beck* ... So I come to worship you, Lord, *NCV* ... you my glance seeks; your presence, *NCB*.

**9. Hide not thy face far from me; put not thy servant away in anger: thou hast been my help; leave me not, neither forsake me, O God of my salvation:** ... So hide not Your presence from me, *Fenton* ... Do not reject me nor abandon me, *Anchor* ... do not give me up or take your support from me, *BB* ... without you I am helpless, *JB*.

**10. When my father and my mother forsake me, then the Lord will take me up:** ... may abandon me, *Good News* ... will take care of me, *NKJV* ... will receive me, *NIV* ... yet the Lord will gather me vp, *Geneva*.

**11. Teach me thy way, O Lord, and lead me in a plain path, because of mine enemies:** ... and lead me by a level road, *Moffatt* ... lead me on the path of integrity, *JB* ... lead me in a straight path because of my oppressors, *NIV* ... Because of them that lie in wait for me, *MAST* ... do not give me up to the greed of my enemies, *REB*.

**12. Deliver me not over unto the will of mine enemies:** ... Do not deliver me over to the desire of my adversaries, *NASB* ... Don't give me up to the will of my enemies, *Beck* ... Do not put me into the throat of my adversaries, *Anchor*.

**for false witnesses are risen up against me, and such as breathe out cruelty:** ... because they tell lies about me, *NCV* ... liars stand up to

---

that earnest look had seen. The two acts complete the joyful employment of a soul communing with God: first perceiving and then reflecting upon his uncreated beauty of goodness.

Such intimacy of communion brings security from external dangers. The guest has a claim for protection. Therefore, the assurance of v. 5 follows the longing of v. 4. Borne up by such thoughts, the singer feels himself lifted clear above the reach of surrounding foes and, with the triumphant "now" of v. 6, stretches out his hand to bring future deliverance into the midst of present distress.

**27:7–14.** The general petitions of vv. 7–10 become more specific as the song nears its close. As in Ps. 25, guidance and protection are now the psalmist's needs. The analogy of other psalms suggests an ethical meaning for "the plain path" of v. 11, and that significance, rather than that of a safe road, is to be preferred for the sake of preserving a difference between this and the following prayer for deliverance. The figures of his enemies stand out more threateningly than before (v. 12). Is that all his gain from his prayer? Is it not a faint-hearted descent from v. 6, where, from the height of his divine security, he looked down on them who were far below and unable to reach him? Now they have "risen up," and He has dropped down among them. But such changes of mood are not inconsis-

| | | | | | | |
|---|---|---|---|---|---|---|
| 5915, 8632 | 3417 | 2660 | | 4020 | 548.515 | 3937, 7495.141 |
| *n mp*, n ms | cj, *n ms* | n ms | | cj | v Hiphil pf 1cs | prep, v Qal inf con |
| עֲדֵי־שֶׁקֶר | וִיפֵחַ | חָמָס | 13. | לוּלֵא | הֶאֱמַנְתִּי | לִרְאוֹת |
| ʿēdhê-sheqer | wîphēach | chāmās̱ | | lûlē' | he'ĕmantî | lir'ôth |
| witnesses of lies | and witnesses of | violence | | surely | I have believed | to see |

| | | | | | |
|---|---|---|---|---|---|
| 904, 3008, 3176 | 904, 800 | 2522 | | 7245.331 | 420, 3176 |
| prep, *n ms*, pn | prep, *n fs* | n mp | | v Piel impv 2ms | prep, pn |
| בְּטוּב־יְהוָה | בְּאֶרֶץ | חַיִּים | 14. | קַוֵּה | אֶל־יְהוָה |
| beṭûv-yehwāh | be'erets | chayyîm | | qawwēh | 'el-yehwāh |
| with the goodness of Yahweh | in the land of | the living | | hope | to Yahweh |

| | | | | | | |
|---|---|---|---|---|---|---|
| 2480.131 | 563.521 | 3949 | 7245.331 | 420, 3176 | | 3937, 1784 |
| v Qal impv 2ms | cj, v Hiphil juss 3ms | n ms, ps 2ms | cj, v Piel impv 2ms | prep, pn | | prep, pn |
| חֲזַק | וְיַאֲמֵץ | לִבֶּךָ | וְקַוֵּה | אֶל־יְהוָה | 28:t | לְדָוִד |
| chăzaq | weya'ămēts | libbekhā | weqawwēh | 'el-yehwāh | | ledhāwidh |
| be strong | and let it be firm | your heart | and hope | to Yahweh | | of David |

| | | | | | | |
|---|---|---|---|---|---|---|
| | 420 | 3176 | 7410.125 | 6962 | 414, 2896.123 | 4623 |
| | prep, ps 2ms | pn | v Qal impf 1cs | n ms, ps 1cs | adv, v Qal juss 2ms | prep, ps 1cs |
| 1. | אֵלֶיךָ | יְהוָה | אֶקְרָא | צוּרִי | אַל־תֶּחֱרַשׁ | מִמֶּנִּי |
| | 'ēlêkhā | yehwāh | 'eqŏrā' | tsûrî | 'al-techĕrash | mimmenî |
| | to You | Yahweh | I will call | my Rock | do not be deaf | from me |

| | | | |
|---|---|---|---|
| 6678, 2924.123 | 4623 | 5090.215 | 6196, 3495.152 |
| adv, v Qal impf 2ms | prep, ps 1cs | cj, v Niphal pf 1cs | prep, *v Qal act ptc mp* |
| פֶּן־תֶּחֱשֶׁה | מִמֶּנִּי | וְנִמְשַׁלְתִּי | עִם־יוֹרְדֵי |
| pen-techĕsheh | mimmenî | wenimshaltî | 'im-yôrdhê |
| so that You will not be silent | from me | then I would become similar | with those who go down to |

| | | | | | | |
|---|---|---|---|---|---|---|
| 988 | | 8471.131 | 7249 | 8800 | 904, 8209.341 | 420 |
| n ms | | v Qal impv 2ms | *n ms* | n mp, ps 1cs | prep, v Piel inf con, ps 1cs | prep, ps 2ms |
| בוֹר | 2. | שְׁמַע | קוֹל | תַּחֲנוּנַי | בְּשַׁוְּעִי | אֵלֶיךָ |
| vôr | | shema' | qôl | tachnûnay | beshawwe'î | 'ēlêkhā |
| the Pit | | hear | the sound of | my supplication | during my crying for help | to You |

| | | | |
|---|---|---|---|
| 904, 5558.141 | 3135 | 420, 1735 | 7231 |
| prep, v Qal inf con, ps 1cs | n fd, ps 1cs | prep, *n ms* | n ms, ps 2ms |
| בְּנָשְׂאִי | יָדַי | אֶל־דְּבִיר | קָדְשֶׁךָ |
| benāse'î | yādhay | 'el-devîr | qādheshekhā |
| during my lifting | my hands | toward the innermost room of | your holy place |

| | | | | | |
|---|---|---|---|---|---|
| | 414, 5082.123 | 6196, 7857 | 6196, 6713.152 | 201 | 1744.152 |
| | adv, v Qal juss 2ms, ps 1cs | prep, n mp | cj, prep, *v Qal act ptc mp* | n ms | *v Qal act ptc mp* |
| 3. | אַל־תִּמְשְׁכֵנִי | עִם־רְשָׁעִים | וְעִם־פֹּעֲלֵי | אָוֶן | דֹּבְרֵי |
| | 'al-timshekhēnî | 'im-reshā'îm | we'im-pō'ălê | 'āwen | dōverê |
| | do not drag me away | with the wicked | and with those who practice | iniquity | those who speak |

| | | | | | |
|---|---|---|---|---|---|
| 8361 | 6196, 7739 | 7750 | 904, 3949 | | 5598.131, 3937 |
| n ms | prep, n mp, ps 3mp | cj, n fs | prep, n ms, ps 3mp | | v Qal impv 2ms, prep, ps 3mp |
| שָׁלוֹם | עִם־רֵעֵיהֶם | וְרָעָה | בִּלְבָבָם | 4. | תֶּן־לָהֶם |
| shālôm | 'im-rē'êhem | werā'āh | bilvāvām | | ten-lāhem |
| peace | with their fellows | but evil | in their hearts | | give to them |

| | | | |
|---|---|---|---|
| 3626, 6714 | 3626, 7741 | 4770 | 3626, 4801 |
| prep, n ms, ps 3mp | cj, prep, *n ms* | n mp, ps 3mp | prep, *n ms* |
| כְּפָעֳלָם | וּכְרֹעַ | מַעַלְלֵיהֶם | כְּמַעֲשֵׂה |
| kephā'ālām | ûkheroa' | ma'alelêhem | kema'ăsēh |
| according to their deeds | and according to the evilness of | their deeds | according to the work of |

| 3135 | 5598.131 | 3937 | 8178.531 | 1618 | 3937 | 3706 |
|---|---|---|---|---|---|---|
| n fd, ps 3mp | v Qal impv 2ms | prep, ps 3mp | v Hiphil impv 2ms | n ms, ps 3mp | prep, ps 3mp | **5.** cj |
| יְדֵיהֶם | תֵּן | לָהֶם | הָשֵׁב | גְּמוּלָם | לָהֶם | כִּי |
| y$^{e}$dhêhem | tēn | lāhem | hāshēv | g$^{e}$mûlām | lāhem | kî |
| their hands | give | to them | cause to return | their recompense | to them | because |

| 3940 | 1032.126 | 420, 6715 | 3176 | 420, 4801 | 3135 |
|---|---|---|---|---|---|
| neg part | v Qal impf 3mp | prep, *n fp* | pn | cj, prep, *n ms* | n fd, ps 3ms |
| לֹא | יָבִינוּ | אֶל־פְּעֻלֹּת | יְהוָה | וְאֶל־מַעֲשֵׂה | יָדָיו |
| lō' | yāvînû | 'el-p$^{e}$'ullōth | y$^{e}$hwāh | w$^{e}$'el-ma'ăsēh | yādhâv |
| not | they perceive | about the deeds of | Yahweh | or about the work of | his hands |

give evidence against me, breathing malice, *NEB* ... and such as breathe forth violence, *Goodspeed.*

**13. I had fainted, unless I had believed to see the goodness of the LORD in the land of the living:** ... I would have lost heart, unless I had believed, *NKJV* ... I had almost given up my hope of seeing the blessing of the Lord, *BB* ... My faith is, I will yet live to see the Lord's mercies, *Knox* ... I believe that I shall see the bounty of the LORD, *NAB.*

**14. Wait on the LORD: be of good courage, and he shall strengthen thine heart: wait, I say, on the LORD:** ... Yet trust on the LORD, and be bold, *Fenton* ... Hope in the LORD; be strong, and He shall make your heart strong, *KJVII* ... be strong, and let your heart take courage, *NRSV* ... let your heart show itself mighty, *Berkeley.*

**28:t. A Psalm of David.**

**1. Unto thee will I cry, O LORD my rock; be not silent to me: lest, if thou be silent to me, I become like them that go down into the pit:** ... be not deaf to me, *RSV* ... if You say nothing to me, *KJVII* ... I call out to you for help, *NCV.*

**2. Hear the voice of my supplications, when I cry unto thee, when I lift up my hands toward thy holy oracle:** ... Hear my cry for mercy as I call to you for help, *NIV* ... Hear and pity my voice as I shout out to you, *Fenton* ... the sound of my pleading, *NAB* ... Your holy sanctuary, *NKJV.*

**3. Draw me not away with the wicked, and with the workers of iniquity, which speak peace to their neighbours, but mischief is in their hearts:** ... Do not drag me away with the ungodly, *REB* ... and with those who do wrong, *Goodspeed* ... with treachery in their hearts, *JB* ... With the lawless, *Rotherham* ... who speak smoothly to their fellows, *Moffatt.*

**4. Give them according to their deeds, and according to the wickedness of their endeavours: give them after the work of their hands; render to them their desert:** ... Reward them for their works, *NEB* ... Repay them their recompense, *NASB* ... and give them what they deserve, *Beck* ... as their actions merit, *Anchor.*

**5. Because they regard not the works of the LORD, nor the operation of his hands, he shall destroy them, and not build them up:** ... They don't understand what the LORD has done or what he has made, *NCV* ... they will be broken down and not lifted up by him, *BB* ... do not observe the LORD's doings, *Berkeley* ... may he tear them down, *NCB.*

---

tent with unchanged faith, if only the gaze which discerns the precipice at either side is not turned away from the goal ahead and above or from Him who holds up his servant. The effect of that clearer sight of the enemies is very beautifully given in the abrupt half-sentence of v. 13.

So the Psalm goes back to the major key at last, and in the closing verse, prayer passes into self-encouragement. The heart that spoke to God now speaks to itself. Faith exhorts sense and soul to "wait on Yahweh."

***Psalm 28.*** *This Psalm is built on the familiar plan of groups of two verses each, with the exception that the prayer, which is its center, runs over into three. The course of thought is as familiar as the structure. Invocation is followed by petition, then exultant anticipation of the answer as already given. Then all closes with wider petitions for the whole people.*

**28:1–2.** Verses 1f, are a prelude to the prayer proper, calling for the divine acceptance on the double ground of the psalmist's helplessness apart from God's help and of his outstretched hands appealing to God enthroned above the mercy seat. He is in such straits that, unless his prayer brings an answer in act, he must sink into the pit of Sheol and be made like those that lie huddled there in its darkness. On the edge of the slippery slope, he stretches out his hands toward the innermost sanctuary (for so means the word rendered "oracle" by a mistaken etymology, HED #1735).

**28:3–5.** The prayer itself (vv. 3ff) touches lightly on the petition that the psalmist may be delivered from the fate of the wicked and then

| 2117.121 | 3940 | 1161.121 | | 1313.155 | 3176 |
|---|---|---|---|---|---|
| v Qal impf 3ms, ps 3mp | cj, neg part | v Qal impf 3ms, ps 3mp | 6. | v Qal pass ptc ms | pn |
| יֶהֶרְסֵם | וְלֹא | יִבְנֵם | | בָּרוּךְ | יְהוָה |
| yehersēm | welō' | yivnēm | | bārûkh | yehwāh |
| He will tear them down | and not | He will build them | | blessed | Yahweh |

| 3706, 8471.111 | 7249 | 8800 | | 3176 | 6010 | 4182 |
|---|---|---|---|---|---|---|
| cj, v Qal pf 3ms | *n ms* | n mp, ps 1cs | 7. | pn | n ms, ps 1cs | cj, n ms, ps 1cs |
| כִּי־שָׁמַע | קוֹל | תַּחֲנוּנָי | | יְהוָה | עֻזִּי | וּמָגִנִּי |
| kî-shāma' | qôl | tachnûnāy | | yehwāh | 'uzzî | ûmāghinî |
| because He has heard | the sound of | my supplication | | Yahweh | my Strength | and my Shield |

| 904 | 1019.111 | 3949 | 6038.215 | 6159.121 | 3949 |
|---|---|---|---|---|---|
| prep, ps 3ms | v Qal pf 3ms | n ms, ps 1cs | cj, v Niphal pf 1cs | cj, v Qal impf 3ms | n ms, ps 1cs |
| בוֹ | בָטַח | לִבִּי | וְנֶעֱזָרְתִּי | וַיַּעֲלֹז | לִבִּי |
| bô | vātach | libbî | wene'ězārettî | wayya'ălōz | libbî |
| in Him | it has trusted | my heart | and I have been helped | and it exults | my heart |

| 4623, 8302 | 3142.525 | | 3176 | 6010, 3937 | 4735 |
|---|---|---|---|---|---|
| cj, prep, n ms, ps 1cs | v Hiphil impf 1cs, ps 3ms | 8. | pn | n ms, prep, ps 3mp | cj, n ms |
| וּמִשִּׁירִי | אֲהוֹדֶנּוּ | | יְהוָה | עֹז־לָמוֹ | וּמָעוֹז |
| ûmishshîrî | 'ăhôdhennû | | yehwāh | 'ōz-lāmô | ûmā'ôz |
| and from my song | I will praise Him | | Yahweh | a Strength to them | and a Refuge |

| 3568 | 5081 | 2000 | | 3588.531 | 881, 6194 | 1313.331 |
|---|---|---|---|---|---|---|
| *n fp* | n ms, ps 3ms | pers pron | 9. | v Hiphil impv 2ms | do, n ms, ps 2ms | cj, v Piel impv 2ms |
| יְשׁוּעוֹת | מְשִׁיחוֹ | הוּא | | הוֹשִׁיעָה | אֶת־עַמֶּךָ | וּבָרֵךְ |
| yeshû'ôth | limshîchô | hû' | | hôshî'āh | 'eth-'ammekhā | ûvārēkh |
| the deliverances of | his anointed one | He | | save | your people | and bless |

| 881, 5338 | 7749.131 | 5558.331 | 5912, 5986 | | 4344 |
|---|---|---|---|---|---|
| do, n fs, ps 2ms | cj, v Qal impv 2ms, ps 3mp | cj, v Piel impv 2ms, ps 3mp | prep, art, n ms | 29:t | n ms |
| אֶת־נַחֲלָתֶךָ | וּרְעֵם | וְנַשְּׂאֵם | עַד־הָעוֹלָם | | מִזְמוֹר |
| 'eth-nachlāthekhā | ûre'ēm | wenasse'ēm | 'adh-hā'ôlām | | mizmôr |
| your inheritance | and shepherd them | and carry them | until forever | | a Psalm |

| 3937, 1784 | | 1957.133 | 3937, 3176 | 1158 | 418 | 1957.133 | 3937, 3176 | 3638 |
|---|---|---|---|---|---|---|---|---|
| prep, pn | 1. | v Qal impv 2mp | prep, pn | *n mp* | n mp | v Qal impv 2mp | prep, pn | n ms |
| לְדָוִד | | הָבוּ | לַיהוָה | בְּנֵי | אֵלִים | הָבוּ | לַיהוָה | כָּבוֹד |
| ledhāwidh | | hāvû | layhwāh | benê | 'ēlîm | hāvû | layhwāh | kāvôdh |
| of David | | ascribe | to Yahweh | the sons of | God | ascribe | to Yahweh | glory |

| 6010 | | 1957.133 | 3937, 3176 | 3638 | 8428 | 8246.733 | 3937, 3176 |
|---|---|---|---|---|---|---|---|
| cj, n ms | 2. | v Qal impv 2mp | prep, pn | *n ms* | n ms, ps 3ms | v Hithpael impv 2mp | prep, pn |
| וָעֹז | | הָבוּ | לַיהוָה | כְּבוֹד | שְׁמוֹ | הִשְׁתַּחֲווּ | לַיהוָה |
| wā'ōz | | hāvû | layhwāh | kevôdh | shemô | hishtachwû | layhwāh |
| and strength | | ascribe | to Yahweh | the glory of | his name | worship | to Yahweh |

| 904, 1997, 7231 | | 7249 | 3176 | 6142, 4448 | 418, 3638 |
|---|---|---|---|---|---|
| prep, *n fs*, n ms | 3. | *n ms* | pn | prep, n md | prep, art, n ms |
| בְּהַדְרַת־קֹדֶשׁ | | קוֹל | יְהוָה | עַל־הַמָּיִם | אֵל־הַכָּבוֹד |
| behadhrath-qōdhesh | | qôl | yehwāh | 'al-hammāyim | 'ēl-hakkāvôdh |
| with an adornment of holiness | | the voice of | Yahweh | on waters | the God of glory |

| 7769.511 | 3176 | 6142, 4448 | 7521 | | 7249, 3176 | 904, 3699 | 7249 |
|---|---|---|---|---|---|---|---|
| v Hiphil pf 3ms | pn | prep, n mp | adj | 4. | *n ms*, pn | prep, art, n ms | *n ms* |
| הִרְעִים | יְהוָה | עַל־מַיִם | רַבִּים | | קוֹל־יְהוָה | בַּכֹּחַ | קוֹל |
| hir'îm | yehwāh | 'al-mayim | rabbîm | | qôl-yehwāh | bakkōach | qôl |
| He has thundered | Yahweh | on waters | many | | the voice of Yahweh | with power | the voice of |

**and in his temple doth every one speak of his glory:** ... while in his palace all are chanting, *Moffatt* ... While in his palace everything says, Glory, *Goodspeed* ... While in his temple—all of it, a vision of the Glorious One, *Anchor* ... all tell His might in His Home, *Fenton.*

**10. The LORD sitteth upon the flood; yea, the LORD sitteth King for ever:** ... The Lord had his seat as king when the waters came on the earth, *BB* ... Out of a raging flood, the Lord makes a dwelling-place, *Knox* ... the LORD sits enthroned as king for ever, *RSV* ... the LORD is a king on His throne forever, *Beck.*

**11. The LORD will give strength unto his people; the LORD will bless his people with peace:** ... Yahweh will give his people victory, *Anchor* ... will bless his people with prosperity, *Rotherham.*

**30:t. A Psalm and Song at the dedication of the house of David.**

**1. I will extol thee, O LORD; for thou hast lifted me up, and hast not made my foes to rejoice over me:** ... I praise you to the heights, *JB* ... thou

---

ture and grouped in verses of two clauses each, the second of which echoes the first, like the long-drawn roll that pauses, slackens and yet persists. Seven times "the voice of Yahweh" is heard, like the apocalyptic "seven thunders before the throne." The poet's eye travels with the swift tempest, and his picture is full of motion, sweeping from the waters above the firmament to earth and from the northern boundary of the land to the far south. First, we hear the mutterings in the sky (v. 3). If we understood "the waters" as meaning the Mediterranean, we should have the picture of the storm working up from the sea. But it is better to take the expression as referring to the super-terrestrial reservoirs or the rain flood stored in the thunderclouds. Up there the peals roll before their fury shakes the earth. It was not enough in the poet's mind to call the thunder the voice of Yahweh, but it must be brought into still closer connection with Him by the plain statement that it is He Who "thunders" and Who rides on the stormclouds as they hurry across the sky. To catch tones of a divine voice, full of power and majesty, in a noise so entirely explicable as a thunderclap, is, no doubt, unscientific; but the Hebrew contemplation of nature is occupied with another set of ideas than scientific and is entirely unaffected by these.

While the psalmist speaks, the swift tempest has come down with a roar and a crash on the northern mountains, and Lebanon and "Simon" (a Sidonian name for Hermon) reel, and the firm-boled, stately cedars are shivered. The structure of the verses already noticed, in which the second clause reduplicates with some specializing the thought of the first, makes it probable that in v. 6a the mountains, and not the cedars, are meant by "them." The trees are broken; the mountains shake.

The two-claused verses are interrupted by one of a single clause (v. 7), the brevity of which vividly suggests the suddenness and speed of the flash. The thunder is conceived of as the principal phenomenon and as creating the lightning, as if it hewed out the flash from the dark mass of cloud.

While tumult of storm and crash of thunder have been raging and rolling below, the singer hears "a deeper voice across the storm," the songs of the "sons of God" in the Temple palace above, chanting the praise to which he had summoned them. "In his temple every one is saying, Glory!" That is the issue of all storms. The clear eyes of the angels see, and their "loud uplifted trumpets" celebrate the lustrous self-manifestation of Yahweh Who rides upon the storm and makes the rush of the thunder minister to the fruitfulness of earth.

**29:10–11.** But what of the effects down here? The concluding strophe tells. Its general sense is clear, although the first clause of v. 10 is ambiguous. The source of the difficulty in rendering is twofold. The preposition (HED #3937) may mean "for"—in order to bring about—or, according to some, "on" or "above" or "at." The word rendered "flood" (HED #4138) is only used elsewhere in reference to the Noachian deluge, and with the definite article, which is most naturally explained as fixing the reference to that event; but it has been objected that the allusion would be far-fetched and out of place. Therefore, the rendering "rain-storm" has been suggested. In the absence of any instance of the word's being used for anything but the Deluge, it is safest to retain the meaning of "flood," an allusion to the torrents of thunder rain which closed the thunderstorm. And all ends with a sweet, calm word, assuring Yahweh's people of a share in the "strength" which spoke in the thunder, and, better still, of peace.

***Psalm 30.*** *The title of this Psalm is apparently a composite, the usual "Psalm of David" having been enlarged by "A Song at the Dedication of the House," which may indicate its later liturgical use, rather than its first destination.*

| 3937, 6194 | 5598.121 | 3176 | 1313.321 | 881, 6194 | 904, 8361 | | 4344 |
|---|---|---|---|---|---|---|---|
| prep, n ms, ps 3ms | v Qal impf 3ms | pn | v Piel impf 3ms | do, n ms, ps 3ms | prep, art, n ms | **30:t** | n ms |
| לְעַמּוֹ | יִתֵּן | יְהוָה | יְבָרֵךְ | אֶת־עַמּוֹ | בַשָּׁלוֹם | | מִזְמוֹר |
| l$^{e}$ammô | yittēn | y$^{e}$hwāh | y$^{e}$vārēkh | 'eth-'ammô | vashshālôm | | mizmôr |
| to his people | He will give | Yahweh | He will bless | his people | with peace | | a Psalm |

| 8302, 2700 | 1041 | 3937, 1784 | | 7597.325 | 3176 | 3706 |
|---|---|---|---|---|---|---|
| *n ms, n fs* | art, n ms | prep, pn | **1.** | v Polel impf 1cs, ps 2ms | pn | cj |
| שִׁיר־חֲנֻכַּת | הַבַּיִת | לְדָוִד | | אֲרוֹמִמְךָ | יְהוָה | כִּי |
| shîr-chănukkath | habbayith | l$^{e}$dhāwidh | | 'ărômimkhā | y$^{e}$hwāh | kî |
| a Song of dedication for | the Temple | of David | | I will exalt You | O Yahweh | because |

| 1861.313 | 3940, 7975.313 | 342.152 | 3937 |
|---|---|---|---|
| v Piel pf 2ms, ps 1cs | cj, neg part, v Piel pf 2ms | v Qal act ptc mp, ps 1cs | prep, ps 1cs |
| דִלִּיתָנִי | וְלֹא־שִׂמַּחְתָּ | אֹיְבַי | לִי |
| dhillîthānî | w$^{e}$lō'-simmachtā | 'ōy$^{e}$vay | lî |
| You have drawn me out | and You have not allowed to rejoice | my enemies | to me |

| | 3176 | 435 | 8209.315 | 420 | 7784.123 | | 3176 |
|---|---|---|---|---|---|---|---|
| **2.** | pn | n mp, ps 1cs | v Piel pf 1cs | prep, ps 2ms | cj, v Qal impf 2ms, ps 1cs | **3.** | pn |
| | יְהוָה | אֱלֹהָי | שִׁוַּעְתִּי | אֵלֶיךָ | וַתִּרְפָּאֵנִי | | יְהוָה |
| | y$^{e}$hwāh | 'ĕlōhāy | shiwwa'ăttî | 'ēlêkhā | wattirpā'ēnî | | y$^{e}$hwāh |
| | O Yahweh | my God | I have cried for help | to You | and You healed me | | O Yahweh |

| 6148.513 | 4623, 8061 | 5497 | 2513.313 | 4623, 3495.152, 988 |
|---|---|---|---|---|
| v Hiphil pf 2ms | prep, pn | n fs, ps 1cs | v Piel pf 2ms, ps 1cs | prep, *v Qal act ptc mp,* n ms |
| הֶעֱלִיתָ | מִן־שְׁאוֹל | נַפְשִׁי | חִיִּיתַנִי | מִיָּוֹרְדֵי־בוֹר |
| he'ĕlîthā | min-sh$^{e}$'ôl | naphshî | chîyîthanî | mîyāwrdhî-vôr |
| You have brought up | from Sheol | my soul | You have kept me alive | from those who go down to the Pit |

| | 2252.333 | 3937, 3176 | 2728 | 3142.533 | 3937, 2228 |
|---|---|---|---|---|---|
| **4.** | v Piel impv 2mp | prep, pn | n mp, ps 3ms | cj, v Hiphil impv 2mp | prep, *n ms* |
| | זַמְּרוּ | לַיהוָה | חֲסִידָיו | וְהוֹדוּ | לְזֵכֶר |
| | zamm$^{e}$rû | layhwāh | chăsîdhâv | w$^{e}$hôdhû | l$^{e}$zēkher |
| | sing praises | to Yahweh | his godly ones | and praise | at the memorial of |

| 7231 | | 3706 | 7569 | 904, 653 | 2522 | 904, 7814 | 904, 6394 |
|---|---|---|---|---|---|---|---|
| n ms, ps 3ms | **5.** | cj | n ms | prep, n ms, ps 3ms | n mp | prep, n ms, ps 3ms | prep, art, n ms |
| קָדְשׁוֹ | | כִּי | רֶגַע | בְּאַפּוֹ | חַיִּים | בִּרְצוֹנוֹ | בָּעֶרֶב |
| qādh$^{e}$shô | | kî | regha' | b$^{e}$'appô | chayyîm | birtsônô | bā'erev |
| his holy place | | because | a moment | with his anger | a lifetime | with his favor | in the evening |

| 4053.121 | 1104 | 3937, 1269 | 7726 | | 603 | 569.115 |
|---|---|---|---|---|---|---|
| v Qal impf 3ms | n ms | cj, prep, art, n ms | n fs | **6.** | cj, pers pron | v Qal pf 1cs |
| יָלִין | בֶכִי | וְלַבֹּקֶר | רִנָּה | | וַאֲנִי | אָמַרְתִּי |
| yālîn | bekhî | w$^{e}$labbōqer | rinnāh | | wa'ănî | 'āmartî |
| one will spend the night | weeping | but at the morning | joy | | and I | I said |

| 904, 8356 | 1118, 4267.225 | 3937, 5986 | | 3176 | 904, 7814 |
|---|---|---|---|---|---|
| prep, n ms, ps 1cs | neg part, v Niphal impf 1cs | prep, n ms | **7.** | pn | prep, n ms, ps 2ms |
| בְשַׁלְוִי | בַּל־אֶמּוֹט | לְעוֹלָם | | יְהוָה | בִּרְצוֹנְךָ |
| v$^{e}$shalwî | bal-'emmôt | l$^{e}$'ôlām | | y$^{e}$hwāh | birtsônkhā |
| in my contentment | I will not totter | unto eternity | | O Yahweh | with your favor |

| 6198.513 | 3937, 2121 | 6010 | 5846.513 | 6686 | 2030.115 |
|---|---|---|---|---|---|
| v Hiphil pf 2ms | prep, n ms, ps 1cs | n ms | v Hiphil pf 2ms | n mp, ps 2ms | v Qal pf 1cs |
| הֶעֱמַדְתָּה | לְהַרְרִי | עֹז | הִסְתַּרְתָּ | פָנֶיךָ | הָיִיתִי |
| he'ĕmadhtāh | l$^{e}$har$^{e}$rî | 'ōz | histartā | phānêkhā | hāyîthî |
| You caused me to stand | at my mountain | strength | You have hidden | your face | I was |

hast drawn me up, *Young* ... for thou hast delivered me, *Darby* ... You did not let my enemies laugh at me, *NCV.*

**2. O LORD my God, I cried unto thee, and thou hast healed me:** ... and thou hast restored me, *Geneva* ... and You made me well, *Beck* ... and thou didst grant me recovery, *Knox.*

**3. O LORD, thou hast brought up my soul from the grave: thou hast kept me alive, that I should not go down to the pit:** ... Thou hast revived me, *Berkeley* ... you spared me, *NIV* ... you restored me to life, *Anchor* ... you preserved me, *NCB.*

**4. Sing unto the LORD, O ye saints of his, and give thanks at the remembrance of his holiness:** ... all you his loyal servants, *REB* ... praise his unforgettable holiness, *JB* ... to his holy name, *RSV* ... as you recall his sacred name, *Moffatt.*

**5. For his anger endureth but a moment; in his favour is life: weeping may endure for a night, but joy cometh in the morning:** ... For his wrath is only for a minute, *BB* ... Tears may linger at nightfall, *NEB* ... But by the morning 'tis a Shout of Triumph, *Rotherham.*

**6. And in my prosperity I said, I shall never be moved:** ... When all was well with me, *Beck* ... But I said in my tranquillity, I shall not be shaken, *Rotherham* ... Once, in my security, I said, I shall never be disturbed, *NAB* ... I will never stumble, *Anchor.*

**7. LORD, by thy favour thou hast made my mountain to stand strong: thou didst hide thy face, and I was troubled:** ... thou hadst established me as a strong mountain, *RSV* ... you had endowed me with majesty and strength, *NCB* ... But You hid Your Presence, and I became weak, *Fenton* ... and I was at peace no more, *Knox.*

---

**30:1–3.** The very first word tells of David's exuberant thankfulness and stands in striking relation to God's act which evokes it. Yahweh has raised him from the very sides of the pit, and therefore what else should he do but exalt Yahweh by praising and commemorating his deeds? The song runs over in varying expressions for his deliverance. He gives praise to the LORD for lifting him up, keeping his enemies from rejoicing over his pain, healing, rescuing him from Sheol and the company who descend there, and restoring him to life. Possibly, the prose fact was recovery from sickness, but the metaphor of healing is so frequent that the literal use of the word here is questionable. As Calvin remarks, sackcloth (v. 11) is not a sick man's garb. Each verse has the name set on it as a seal. The best result of God's goodness is a firmer assurance of a personal relationship with Him. The stress of these three verses lies on the reiterated contemplation of God's fresh act of mercy and on the reiterated invocation of his name, which is not vain repetition, but represents distinct acts of consciousness, drawing near to delight the soul in thoughts of Him.

**30:4–5.** True thankfulness is expansive, and joy craves for sympathy. So the psalmist invites other voices to join his song, since he is sure that there are others who have shared his experience. The antitheses in v. 5 are obvious. In the first part of the verse, "anger" and "favor" are plainly contrasted, and it is natural to suppose that "a moment" and "life" are also contrasted. A suitable rendering, then, is, "A moment passes in his anger, a life [i.e., a lifetime] in his favor." Sorrow is brief; blessings are long.

A similar double antithesis molds the beautiful image of the last clause. Night and morning are contrasted, as are weeping and joy. The latter contrast is more striking, if it be observed that "joy" is literally a "joyful shout," raised by the voice that had been breaking into audible weeping. The thought may either be that of the substitution of joy for sorrow or of the transformation of sorrow into joy. No grief lasts in its first bitterness. Recuperative forces begin to appear slowly.

**30:6–7.** In v. 6, the psalmist's foolish confidence is emphatically contrasted with the truth won by experience and stated in v. 5. The word sometimes rendered "prosperity" (HED #8356) may be taken as also meaning "security." Even devout hearts are apt to count upon the continuance of present good. The bottom of the crater of Vesuvius once had great trees growing, the produce of centuries of quiescence. It would be difficult to think, when looking at them, that they would ever be torn up and whirled aloft in flame by a new outburst.

Lapse from dependence is recorded in v. 7. The sudden crash of false security is graphically reproduced by the abrupt clauses without connecting particles. It was the "favor" already celebrated which gave the stability which had been abused. Its effect is described in somewhat difficult terms. The word "dismayed" (HED #963) is that used for Saul's conflicting emotions and despair in the witch's house at Endor, and for the agitation of Joseph's brethren when they heard that the man who had their lives in his hand was their wronged brother. Thus, the psalmist was alarmed and filled with fear mixed with disconcerting thoughts.

| | | | | | | |
|---|---|---|---|---|---|---|
| 963.255 | | 420 | 3176 | 7410.125 | 420, 112 | 2706.725 |
| v Niphal ptc ms | 8. | prep, ps 2ms | pn | v Qal impf 1cs | cj, prep, n mp, ps 1cs | v Hithpael impf 1cs |
| נִבְהָל | | אֵלֶיךָ | יְהוָה | אֶקְרָא | וְאֶל־אֲדֹנָי | אֶתְחַנָּן |
| nivhāl | | 'ēlêkhā | yehwāh | 'eqŏrā' | we'el-'ădhōnāy | 'ethchannān |
| dismayed | | to You | O Yahweh | I will call | and to the Lord | I made supplication |

| | | | | | |
|---|---|---|---|---|---|
| | 4242, 1240 | 904, 1879 | 904, 3495.141 | 420, 8273 | 1950B, 3142.521 |
| 9. | intrg, n ms | prep, n ms, ps 1cs | prep, v Qal inf con, ps 1cs | prep, n fp | intrg part, v Hiphil impf 3ms, ps 2ms |
| | מַה־בֶּצַע | בְּדָמִי | בְּרִדְתִּי | אֶל־שָׁחַת | הֲיוֹדְךָ |
| | mah-betsa' | bedhāmî | beridhtî | 'el-shāchath | hăyôdhkhā |
| | what profit | in my blood | during my going down | to the Pit | will it praise You |

| | | | | | |
|---|---|---|---|---|---|
| 6312 | 1950B, 5222.521 | 583 | | 8471.131, 3176 | 2706.131 |
| n ms | intrg part, v Hiphil impf 3ms | n fs, ps 2ms | 10. | v Qal impv 2ms, pn | cj, v Qal impv 2ms, ps 1cs |
| עָפָר | הֲיַגִּיד | אֲמִתֶּךָ | | שְׁמַע־יְהוָה | וְחָנֵּנִי |
| 'āphār | hăyaggîdh | 'ămittekhā | | shema'-yehwāh | wechānnēnî |
| dust | will it tell about | your reliability | | hear O Yahweh | and be gracious to me |

| | | | | | |
|---|---|---|---|---|---|
| 3176 | 2030.131, 6038.151 | 3937 | | 2089.113 | 4705 |
| pn | v Qal impv 2ms, v Qal act ptc ms | prep, ps 1cs | 11. | v Qal pf 2ms | n ms, ps 1cs |
| יְהוָה | הֱיֵה־עֹזֵר | לִי | | הָפַכְתָּ | מִסְפְּדִי |
| yehwāh | hĕyēh-'ōzēr | lî | | hāphakhtā | mispedhî |
| O Yahweh | be a Helper | to me | | You have changed | my mourning rites |

| | | | | | |
|---|---|---|---|---|---|
| 3937, 4369 | 3937 | 6858.313 | 8012 | 246.323 | 7977 |
| prep, n ms | prep, ps 1cs | v Piel pf 2ms | n ms, ps 1cs | cj, v Piel impf 2ms, ps 1cs | n fs |
| לְמָחוֹל | לִי | פִּתַּחְתָּ | שַׂקִּי | וַתְּאַזְּרֵנִי | שִׂמְחָה |
| lemāchôl | lî | pittachtā | saqqî | watte'azzerēnî | simchāh |
| into dancing | to me | You have opened | my sackcloth | and You girded me with | rejoicing |

| | | | | | | | |
|---|---|---|---|---|---|---|---|
| | 3937, 4775 | 2252.321 | 3638 | 3940 | 1887.121 | 3176 | 435 |
| 12. | prep, prep | v Piel impf 3ms, ps 2ms | n ms | cj, neg part | v Qal impf 3ms | pn | n mp, ps 1cs |
| | לְמַעַן | יְזַמֶּרְךָ | כָבוֹד | וְלֹא | יִדֹּם | יְהוָה | אֱלֹהַי |
| | lema'an | yezammerkhā | khāvôdh | welō' | yiddōm | yehwāh | 'ĕlōhay |
| | so that | it will sing praises to You | glory | and not | it will be silent | O Yahweh | my God |

| | | | | | | | |
|---|---|---|---|---|---|---|---|
| 3937, 5986 | 3142.525 | | 3937, 5514.351 | 4344 | 3937, 1784 | | 904 |
| prep, n ms | v Hiphil impf 1cs, ps 2ms | 31:t | prep, art, v Piel ptc ms | n ms | prep, pn | 1. | prep, ps 2ms |
| לְעוֹלָם | אוֹדֶךָּ | | לַמְנַצֵּחַ | מִזְמוֹר | לְדָוִד | | בְּךָ |
| le'ôlām | 'ôdhekhā | | lamnatstsēach | mizmôr | ledhāwidh | | bekhā |
| unto eternity | I will praise You | | to the director | a Psalm | of David | | in You |

| | | | | |
|---|---|---|---|---|
| 3176 | 2725.115 | 414, 991.125 | 3937, 5986 | 904, 6930 |
| pn | v Qal pf 1cs | adv, v Qal juss 1cs | prep, n ms | prep, n fs, ps 2ms |
| יְהוָה | חָסִיתִי | אַל־אֵבוֹשָׁה | לְעוֹלָם | בְּצִדְקָתְךָ |
| yehwāh | chāsîthî | 'al-'ēvôshāh | le'ôlām | betsidhqāthekhā |
| Yahweh | I have sought refuge | let me not be ashamed | unto eternity | in your righteousness |

| | | | | | | |
|---|---|---|---|---|---|---|
| 6647.331 | | 5371.531 | 420 | 238 | 4259 | 5522.531 |
| v Piel impv 2ms, ps 1cs | 2. | v Hiphil impv 2ms | prep, ps 1cs | n fs, ps 2ms | adv | v Hiphil impv 2ms, ps 1cs |
| פַּלְּטֵנִי | | הַטֵּה | אֵלַי | אָזְנְךָ | מְהֵרָה | הַצִּילֵנִי |
| phalletēnî | | hattēh | 'ēlay | 'oznekhā | mehērāh | hatstsîlēnî |
| set me free | | incline | to me | your ear | quickly | rescue me |

| | | | | | |
|---|---|---|---|---|---|
| 2030.131 | 3937 | 3937, 6962, 4735 | 3937, 1041 | 4849 | 3937, 3588.541 |
| v Qal impv 2ms | prep, ps 1cs | prep, *n ms*, n ms | prep, *n ms* | n fp | prep, v Hiphil inf con, ps 1cs |
| הֱיֵה | לִי | לְצוּר־מָעוֹז | לְבֵית | מְצוּדוֹת | לְהוֹשִׁיעֵנִי |
| hĕyēh | lî | letsûr-mā'ôz | levêth | metsûdhôth | lehôshî'ēnî |
| be | to me | a Rock of refuge | a House of | a fortress | to save me |

**8. I cried to thee, O LORD; and unto the LORD I made supplication:** ... Unto Thee, O LORD did I call, *MAST* ... to my God I cry for mercy, *JB* ... and to the LORD I sought with prayer, *KJVII* ... appealing to my God, *Moffatt.*

**9. What profit is there in my blood, when I go down to the pit? Shall the dust praise thee? shall it declare thy truth?:** ... What gain is there in my destruction, *NIV* ... In my going down unto corruption, *Young* ... Will it tell of your faithfulness, *NRSV* ... Shall it declare Thy truth, *Berkeley.*

**10. Hear, O LORD, and have mercy upon me: LORD, be thou my helper:** ... and be gracious to me, *NEB* ... and have pity on me, *NAB.*

**11. Thou hast turned for me my mourning into dancing: thou hast put off my sackcloth, and girded me with gladness:** ... Change my weeping to dancing, *Beck* ... You took away my clothes of sadness, and clothed me in happiness, *NCV* ... you have taken away my clothing of grief, and given me robes of joy, *BB.*

**12. To the end that my glory may sing praise to thee, and not be silent. O LORD my God, I will give thanks unto thee for ever:** ... so that my soul may praise you, *NRSV* ... Therefore shall my tongue prayse thee and not cease, *Geneva* ... that my heart may sing to you and not be silent, *NIV* ... So may this heart never tire of singing praises, *Knox.*

**31:t. To the chief Musician, A Psalm of David.**

**1. In thee, O LORD, do I put my trust; let me never be ashamed: deliver me in thy righteousness:** ... O LORD, I take refuge, *NAB* ... keep me safe in your righteousness, *BB* ... in your saving justice deliver me, rescue me, *JB* ... don't let me be disappointed. Because of Your righteousness rescue me, *Beck.*

**2. Bow down thine ear to me; deliver me speedily:** ... Incline your ear to me, *NRSV* ... Grant me audience, and make haste to rescue me, *Knox* ... come quickly to my rescue, *REB.*

**be thou my strong rock, for an house of defence to save me:** ... Be my rock of refuge, A fortress of defense, *NKJV* ... a strong city to save me, *NCV* ... a fortress to save me, *KJVII* ... a Place of security, For saving me, *Rotherham.*

---

**30:8–10.** The approach to God is told in vv. 8ff, of which the two latter are a quotation of the prayer then projected by the psalmist. The ground of this appeal for deliverance from a life-threatening danger is as in Hezekiah's prayer (Isa. 38:18f), and it reflects the same conception of the state of the dead as Ps. 6:5. If the suppliant dies, his voice will be missed from the chorus which sings God's praise on earth. "The dust" (i.e., "the grave") is a region of silence. Here, where life yielded daily proofs of God's "truth" (i.e., "faithfulness"), it could be extolled, but there dumb tongues could bring Him no "profit" of praise. The boldness of the thought that God is in some sense advantaged by men's magnifying of his faithfulness, the cheerless gaze into the dark realm, and the implication that to live is desired not only for the sake of life's joys, but in order to show forth God's dealings, are all remarkable. The tone of the prayer indicates the imperfect view of the future life which shadows many Psalms and could only be completed by the historical facts of the Resurrection and Ascension.

**30:11–12.** With quick transition, corresponding to the swiftness of the answer to prayer, the closing pair of verses tells of the instantaneous change which that answer wrought. Just as in the earlier metaphor weeping was transformed into joy, here mourning is turned into dancing, and God's hand unties the cord which loosely binds the sackcloth robe and arrays the mourner in festival attire. The same conception of the sweetness of grateful praise to the ear of God which was presented in the prayer recurs here, where the purpose of God's gifts is regarded as being man's praise.

***Psalm 31.*** *The swift transitions of emotions in this Psalm may seem strange to colder natures whose lives run smoothly, but they reveal a soulmate to those who have known what it is to ride on the top of the wave and then to go down into its trough. What is peculiar to the Psalm is not only the inclusion of the whole gamut of feeling, but also the force with which each key is struck and the persistence through all of the one underlying tone of cleaving to Yahweh.*

*The stream of the psalmist's thoughts now runs in shadow of grim cliffs and vexed by opposing rocks, and now opens out in sunny stretches of smoothness; but its source is "In thee, Yahweh, do I take refuge" (v. 1), and its end is "Be strong, and let your heart take courage, all ye that wait for Yahweh" (v. 24).*

**31:1–4.** The first turn of the stream is in vv. 1–4, which consist of petitions and their grounds. The prayers reveal the suppliant's state. They are the familiar cries of an afflicted soul common to many Psalms and presenting no special features. The needs of the human heart are uniform, and the cry of distress is much alike on all lips. This sufferer asks, as his fel-

| 3. | 3706, 5748 | 4859 | 887 | 3937, 4775 | 8428 |
|---|---|---|---|---|---|
| | cj, n ms, ps 1cs | cj, n fs, ps 1cs | pers pron | cj, prep, prep | n ms, ps 2ms |
| | כִּי־סַלְעִי | וּמְצוּדָתִי | אָתָּה | וּלְמַעַן | שִׁמְךָ |
| | kî-s̱al'î | ûmetsûdhāthî | 'āttāh | ûlăma'an | shimkhā |
| | because my Rock | and my Fortress | You | and for the sake of | your name |

| 5328.523 | 5273.323 | 4. | 3428.523 | 4623, 7862 | 2182 |
|---|---|---|---|---|---|
| v Hiphil impf 2ms, ps 1cs | cj, v Piel impf 2ms, ps 1cs | | v Hiphil impf 2ms, ps 1cs | prep, n fs | rel part |
| תַּנְחֵנִי | וּתְנַהֲלֵנִי | | תּוֹצִיאֵנִי | מֵרֶשֶׁת | זוּ |
| tanchēnî | ûthenahlēnî | | tôtsî'ēnî | mēresheth | zû |
| You lead me | and You guide me | | and You cause me to go out | from a net | which |

| 3045.116 | 3937 | 3706, 887 | 4735 | 5. | 904, 3135 | 6734.525 | 7593 |
|---|---|---|---|---|---|---|---|
| v Qal pf 3cp | prep, ps 1cs | cj, pers pron | n ms, ps 1cs | | prep, n fs, ps 2ms | v Hiphil impf 1cs | n fs, ps 1cs |
| טָמְנוּ | לִי | כִּי־אַתָּה | מָעוּזִּי | | בְּיָדְךָ | אַפְקִיד | רוּחִי |
| ṭāmenû | lî | kî-'attāh | mā'ûzzî | | beyādhekhā | 'aphqîdh | rûchî |
| they have hidden | for me | because You | my Refuge | | into your hand | I commit | my spirit |

| 6540.113 | 881 | 3176 | 418 | 583 | 6. | 7983.115 | 8490.152 |
|---|---|---|---|---|---|---|---|
| v Qal pf 2ms | do, ps 1cs | pn | *n ms* | n fs | | v Qal pf 1cs | art, v Qal act ptc mp |
| פָּדִיתָה | אוֹתִי | יְהוָה | אֵל | אֱמֶת | | שָׂנֵאתִי | הַשֹּׁמְרִים |
| pādhîthāh | 'ôthî | yehwāh | 'ēl | 'ĕmeth | | sānē'thî | hashshōmerîm |
| You have ransomed | me | O Yahweh | a God of | faithfulness | | I hated | those who observe |

| 1961, 8175 | 603 | 420, 3176 | 1019.115 | 7. | 1559.125 |
|---|---|---|---|---|---|
| *n mp*, n ms | cj, pers pron | prep, pn | v Qal pf 1cs | | v Qal juss 1cs |
| הַבְלֵי־שָׁוְא | וַאֲנִי | אֶל־יְהוָה | בָּטָחְתִּי | | אָגִילָה |
| havlê-shāwe' | wa'ănî | 'el-yehwāh | bāṭachttî | | 'āghîlāh |
| vanities of worthlessness | but I | to Yahweh | I have trusted | | let me rejoice |

| 7975.125 | 904, 2721 | 866 | 7495.113 | 881, 6271 | 3156.113 |
|---|---|---|---|---|---|
| cj, v Qal juss 1cs | prep, n ms, ps 2ms | cj | v Qal pf 2ms | do, n ms, ps 1cs | v Qal pf 2ms |
| וְאֶשְׂמְחָה | בְּחַסְדֶּךָ | אֲשֶׁר | רָאִיתָ | אֶת־עָנְיִי | יָדַעְתָּ |
| we'esmechāh | bechas̱dekhā | 'ăsher | rā'îthā | 'eth-'āneyî | yādha'attā |
| and let me be glad | in your steadfast love | because | You have seen | my affliction | You have known |

| 904, 7141 | 5497 | 8. | 3940 | 5646.513 |
|---|---|---|---|---|
| prep, *n fp* | n fs, ps 1cs | | cj, neg part | v Hiphil pf 2ms, ps 1cs |
| בְּצָרוֹת | נַפְשִׁי | | וְלֹא | הִסְגַּרְתַּנִי |
| betsārôth | naphshî | | welō' | his̱gartanî |
| about the adversaries of | my soul | | and not | You have surrendered me |

| 904, 3135, 342.151 | 6198.513 | 904, 4962 | 7559 |
|---|---|---|---|
| prep, *n fs*, v Qal act ptc ms | v Hiphil pf 2ms | prep, art, n ms | n fd, ps 1cs |
| בְּיַד־אוֹיֵב | הֶעֱמַדְתָּ | בַמֶּרְחָב | רַגְלָי |
| beyadh-'ôyēv | he'ĕmadhtā | vammerchāv | raghlāy |
| into the hand of the enemy | You have made to stand | in the wide place | my feet |

| 9. | 2706.131 | 3176 | 3706 | 7140, 3937 | 6485.112 | 904, 3833 | 6084 |
|---|---|---|---|---|---|---|---|
| | v Qal impv 2ms, ps 1cs | pn | cj | n ms, prep, ps 1cs | v Qal pf 3fs | prep, n ms | n fs, ps 1cs |
| | חָנֵּנִי | יְהוָה | כִּי | צַר־לִי | עָשְׁשָׁה | בְכַעַס | עֵינִי |
| | chānnēnî | yehwāh | kî | tsar-lî | 'āsheshāh | vekha'as | 'ênî |
| | be gracious to me | O Yahweh | because | adversity to me | it is swollen | with grief | my eye |

| 5497 | 1027 | 10. | 3706 | 3735.116 | 904, 3123 | 2522 |
|---|---|---|---|---|---|---|
| n fs, ps 1cs | cj, n fs, ps 1cs | | cj | v Qal pf 3cp | prep, n ms | n mp, ps 1cs |
| נַפְשִׁי | וּבִטְנִי | | כִּי | כָלוּ | בְיָגוֹן | חַיַּי |
| naphshî | ûviṭnî | | kî | khālû | veyāghôn | chayyay |
| my soul | and my stomach | | because | they have come to an end | with agony | my life |

**3. For thou art my rock and my fortress; therefore for thy name's sake lead me, and guide me:** ... Thou art to me both rock and stronghold, *NEB* ... my strong tower; go in front of me and be my guide, because of your name, *BB* ... lead me and guide by Your power, *Fenton* ... guide me and lead me as you have promised, *Good News.*

**4. Pull me out of the net that they have laid privily for me: for thou art my strength:** ... You will free me from the snare they set for me, *NAB* ... For thou art my stronghold, *ASV* ... because you are my protection, *NCV.*

**5. Into thine hand I commit my spirit: thou hast redeemed me, O LORD God of truth:** ... I put my life into thy hands, *Moffatt* ... Into Your hands I entrust my spirit, *Beck* ... Into your hand I entrust my life, *Anchor* ... thou faithful God, *Goodspeed.*

**6. I have hated them that regard lying vanities: but I trust in the LORD:** ... I hate those who cling to worthless idols, *NIV* ... I have hated the teachers, of empty ideas, *Fenton* ... but my hope is in the Lord, *BB.*

**7. I will be glad and rejoice in thy mercy: for thou hast considered my trouble; thou hast known my soul in adversities:** ... I will delight and rejoice in your faithful love, *JB* ... and have cared for me in my distress, *REB* ... because thou hast seen my affliction, *RSV* ... you took care of me against the Adversary, *Anchor.*

**8. And hast not shut me up into the hand of the enemy: thou hast set my feet in a large room:** ... You haven't surrendered me to the enemy, *Beck* ... Thou hast not abandoned me to the power of the enemy, *NEB* ... but have set me in a safe place, *NCV.*

**9. Have mercy upon me, O LORD, for I am in trouble:** ... Be gracious unto me, *MAST* ... have compassion on my distress, *Knox* ... for I am in anguish, *Berkeley.*

**mine eye is consumed with grief, yea, my soul and my belly:** ... my eye wastes away from grief, *NRSV* ... my health is wasting under my woe, *Moffatt.*

**10. For my life is spent with grief, and my years with sighing: my strength faileth because of mine iniquity, and my bones are consumed:** ... For my life hath been consumed in sorrow, *Young* ... My

---

lows have done and will do, for deliverance, a swift answer, shelter and defense, guidance and leading, and escape from the net spread for him. These are the commonplaces of prayer which God is not wearied of hearing, and which fit us all. The last place to look for originality is in sighing. The pleas on which the petitions rest are also familiar. The man who trusts in Yahweh has a right to expect that his trust will not be put to shame, since God is faithful. Therefore, the first plea is the psalmist's faith, expressed in v. 1 by the word which literally means "to flee to a refuge" (HED #2725). The fact that he has done so makes his deliverance a work of God's righteousness. The metaphor latent in "flee for refuge" comes into full sight in that beautiful plea in v. 3, which unsympathetic critics would call illogical, "Be for me a refuge rock, for ... thou art my rock." Be what Thou art; manifest thyself in act to be what Thou art in nature: be what I, thy poor servant, have taken Thee to be. My heart has clasped Thy revelation of Thyself and fled to this strong tower. Let me not be deceived and find it incapable of sheltering me from my foes.

**31:5–8.** Verses 5–8 prolong the tone of the preceding, with some difference, inasmuch as God's past acts are more specifically dwelt on as the ground of confidence. In this turn of the stream, faith does not so much supplicate as meditate, plucking the flower of confidence from the nettle of past dangers and deliverances and renewing its acts of surrender. The sacred words which Jesus made his own on the Cross, and which have been the last utterance of so many saints, were meant by the psalmist to apply to life, not to death. "Lying vanities" are all other helpers feigning deity to one who has felt the clasp of that great, tender hand; unless the soul feels them to be such, it will never strongly clutch or firmly hold its true stay. Such trust has its crown in joyful experience of God's mercy even before the actual deliverance comes to pass, as wind-borne fragrance meets the traveler before he sees the spice gardens from which it comes. The cohortative verbs in v. 7 may be petition ("Let me rejoice"), or they may be anticipation of future gladness, but in either case some waft of joy has already reached the singer, as it inevitably would, when his faith was thus renewing itself and his eyes were gazing on God's deeds of old. The past tenses in vv. 7f refer to former experiences. God's sight of the psalmist's affliction was not idle contemplation, but implied active intervention. "Crown my soul in adversities" (or possibly, "of my soul in distresses") is the same as to care for it. It is enough to know that God sees the secret sorrows, the obscure trials which can be told to none.

**31:9–10.** Is it inconceivable that such sunny confidence should be suddenly clouded and followed, as in the third turn of thought (vv. 9–13), by plaintive absorption in the sad realities of present

| 8523 | 904, 599 | 3911.111 | 904, 5988 | 3699 | 6344 |
|---|---|---|---|---|---|
| cj, n fp, ps 1cs | prep, n fs | v Qal pf 3ms | prep, n ms, ps 1cs | n ms, ps 1cs | cj, n fp, ps 1cs |
| וּשְׁנוֹתַי | בַּאֲנָחָה | כָּשַׁל | בַּעֲוֺנִי | כֹחִי | וַעֲצָמַי |
| ûshᵉnôthay | ba'ănāchāh | kāshal | ba'ăwōnî | khōchî | wa'ătsāmay |
| and my years | with groaning | it has stumbled | because of my guilt | my strength | and my bones |

| 6485.116 | | 4623, 3725, 7173.152 | 2030.115 | 2887 |
|---|---|---|---|---|
| v Qal pf 3cp | **11.** | prep, *adj*, v Qal act ptc mp, ps 1cs | v Qal pf 1cs | n fs |
| עָשְׁשׁוּ | | מִכָּל־צֹרְרַי | הָיִיתִי | חֶרְפָּה |
| 'āshēshû | | mikkol-tsōrᵉray | hāyîthî | cherpāh |
| they have wasted away | | from all my adversaries | I have become | a disgrace |

| 3937, 8333 | 4108 | 6586 | 3937, 3156.452 | 7495.152 | 904, 2445 |
|---|---|---|---|---|---|
| cj, prep, n mp, ps 1cs | adv | cj, n ms | prep, Pual ptc mp, ps 1cs | v Qal act ptc mp, ps 1cs | prep, art, n ms |
| וְלִשְׁכֵנַי | מְאֹד | וּפַחַד | לִמְיֻדָּעָי | רֹאַי | בַּחוּץ |
| wᵉlishkhēnay | mᵉ'ōdh | ûphachadh | limyuddā'āy | rō'ay | bachûts |
| and to my neighbors | very | and a terror | to those known by me | those who see me | in the street |

| 5252.116 | 4623 | | 8319.215 | 3626, 4322.151 | 4623, 3949 |
|---|---|---|---|---|---|
| v Qal pf 3cp | prep, ps 1cs | **12.** | v Niphal pf 1cs | prep, v Qal act ptc ms | prep, n ms |
| נָדְדוּ | מִמֶּנִּי | | נִשְׁכַּחְתִּי | כְּמֵת | מִלֵּב |
| nādhᵉdhû | mimmenî | | nishkachtî | kᵉmēth | millēv |
| they have fled | from me | | I have been forgotten | like a dead man | from the heart |

| 2030.115 | 3626, 3747 | 6.151 | | 3706 | 8471.115 | 1730 | 7521 |
|---|---|---|---|---|---|---|---|
| v Qal pf 1cs | prep, n ms | v Qal act ptc ms | **13.** | cj | v Qal pf 1cs | *n fs* | adj |
| הָיִיתִי | כִּכְלִי | אֹבֵד | | כִּי | שָׁמַעְתִּי | דִּבַּת | רַבִּים |
| hāyîthî | kikhlî | 'ōvēdh | | kî | shāma'ättî | dibbath | rabbîm |
| I have become | like a vessel | breaking | | because | I have heard | the slander of | many |

| 4171 | 4623, 5623 | 904, 3354.241 | 3266 | 6142 | 4089.141 | 5497 |
|---|---|---|---|---|---|---|
| n ms | prep, adv | prep, v Niphal inf con, ps 3mp | adv | prep, ps 1cs | prep, v Qal inf con | n fs, ps 1cs |
| מָגוֹר | מִסָּבִיב | בְּהִוָּסְדָם | יַחַד | עָלַי | לָקַחַת | נַפְשִׁי |
| māghôr | missāvîv | bᵉhiwwāsᵉdhām | yachadh | 'ālay | lāqachath | naphshî |
| terror | all around | during their conspiring | together | against me | to take | my life |

| 2246.116 | | 603 | 6142 | 1019.115 | 3176 | 569.115 | 435 |
|---|---|---|---|---|---|---|---|
| v Qal pf 3cp | **14.** | cj, pers pron | prep, ps 2ms | v Qal pf 1cs | pn | v Qal pf 1cs | n mp, ps 1cs |
| זָמָמוּ | | וַאֲנִי | עָלֶיךָ | בָטַחְתִּי | יְהוָה | אָמַרְתִּי | אֱלֹהָי |
| zāmāmû | | wa'ănî | 'ālêkhā | vātachtî | yᵉhwāh | 'āmartî | 'ĕlōhay |
| they have plotted | | but I | with You | I have trusted | O Yahweh | I have said | my God |

| 887 | | 904, 3135 | 6496 | 5522.531 | 4623, 3135, 342.152 |
|---|---|---|---|---|---|
| pers pron | **15.** | prep, n fs, ps 2ms | n fp, ps 1cs | v Hiphil impv 2ms, ps 1cs | prep, *n fs*, v Qal act ptc mp, ps 1cs |
| אַתָּה | | בְּיָדְךָ | עִתֹּתָי | הַצִּילֵנִי | מִיַּד־אוֹיְבַי |
| 'attāh | | bᵉyādhᵉkhā | 'ittōthāy | hatstsîlēnî | mîyadh-'ôyvay |
| You | | into your hand | my time | rescue me | from the hand of my enemies |

| 4623, 7579.152 | | 213.531 | 6686 | 6142, 5860 | 3588.531 |
|---|---|---|---|---|---|
| cj, prep, v Qal act ptc mp, ps 1cs | **16.** | v Hiphil impv 2 ms | n mp, ps 2ms | prep, n ms, ps 2ms | v Hiphil impv 2ms, ps 1cs |
| וּמֵרֹדְפָי | | הָאִירָה | פָּנֶיךָ | עַל־עַבְדֶּךָ | הוֹשִׁיעֵנִי |
| ûmērōdhᵉphāy | | hā'îrāh | phānêkhā | 'al-'avdekhā | hôshî'ēnî |
| and from my pursuers | | cause to shine | your face | on your servant | save me |

| 904, 2721 | | 3176 | 414, 991.125 | 3706 | 7410.115 |
|---|---|---|---|---|---|
| prep, n ms, ps 2ms | **17.** | pn | adv, v Qal juss 1cs | cj | v Qal pf 1cs, ps 2ms |
| בְחַסְדֶּךָ | | יְהוָה | אַל־אֵבוֹשָׁה | כִּי | קְרָאתִיךָ |
| vᵉchasdekhā | | yᵉhwāh | 'al-'ēvôshāh | kî | qōrā'thîkhā |
| by your steadfast love | | O Yahweh | let me not be ashamed | because | I have called to You |

strength hath staggered with my humiliation, *Rotherham* ... And my body has wasted away, *NASB.*

**11. I was a reproach among all mine enemies, but especially among my neighbours, and a fear to mine acquaintance:** ... I have become an object of scorn even to my neighbhors, *Anchor* ... I'm a curse to my neighbors, *Beck* ... I am a dread to my friends, *NIV.*

**they that did see me without fled from me:** ... they are afraid and run, *NCV* ... men shun me in the street, *Moffatt.*

**12. I am forgotten as a dead man out of mind: I am like a broken vessel:** ... I have passed out of mind like one who is dead, *NRSV* ... I have become like some article thrown away, *REB* ... I am discarded like a worn-out utensil, *Berkeley* ... I am like a useless vessel, *MAST.*

**13. For I have heard the slander of many: fear was on every side:** ... On every side their busy whispering comes to my ears, *Knox* ... Terror on every side, *ASV.*

**while they took counsel together against me, they devised to take away my life:** ... as they scheme together against me, *RSV* ... in league against me as they are and plotting to take my life, *NEB.*

**14. But I trusted in thee, O Lord: I said, Thou art my God:** ... But I had faith in you, *BB* ... But I have relied upon You, *Fenton* ... I therefore in thee have put my trust, *Rotherham.*

**15. My times are in thy hand: deliver me from the hand of mine enemies, and from them that persecute me:** ... every moment of my life is in your hands, *JB* ... In your hands is my destiny, *NCB* ... Save me from my enemies and from those who are chasing me, *NCV* ... rescue me from the clutches of my enemies, *NAB.*

**16. Make thy face to shine upon thy servant: save me for thy mercies' sake:** ... And let Your face smile on Your slave, *Fenton* ... Save me in thy lovingkindness, *Rotherham* ... Deliver me through thy kindness, *Goodspeed* ... Save me because of your love, *NCV.*

**17. Let me not be ashamed, O Lord; for I have called upon thee: let the wicked be ashamed, and let them be silent in the grave:** ... so let disgrace fall not on me, *JB* ... let me not be humiliated, when I call you, *Anchor* ... don't let me be disappointed, but let the wicked end in shame, *Beck* ... they shall be silenced in the realm of the dead, *Berkeley.*

---

distress? The very remembrance of a brighter past may have sharpened the sense of present trouble. But it is to be noted that these complaints are prayer, not aimless, self-pitying wailing. In vv. 9f, the physical and mental effects of anxiety are graphically described. Sunken eyes, an enfeebled soul and a wasted body are gaunt witnesses of his distress. He is so weak that cares seem to him to have gnawed his very bones. All that he can do is to sigh. And worse than all, conscience tells him that his own sin underlies his trouble, and so he is without inward stay. The picture seems exaggerated to easygoing, prosperous people, but many a sufferer has since recognized himself in it as in a mirror and been thankful for words which gave voice to his pained heart, and cheering him with the sense of companionship in the gloom.

**31:11–18.** Verses 11f are mainly the description of the often repeated experience of friends forsaking the troubled. "Among all my enemies" somewhat anticipates v. 13 in assigning the reason for the cowardly desertion. The three phrases "neighbors," "acquaintances" and "they that did see me without" indicate concentric circles of increasing diameter. The psalmist is in the middle of those who are afraid to have anything to do with one who has such strong and numerous foes.

In v. 12, the desertion is bitterly summed up, like the oblivion that waits for the dead. The unsympathizing world goes on its way, and friends find new interests and forget the broken man who used to be so much to them as completely as if he were in his grave, or as they do the damaged cup, flung on the rubbish heap. Verse 13 discloses the nature of the calamity which has had these effects. Whispering slanders buzz around him; he is ringed about with causes for fear, since enemies are plotting his death. Jeremiah uses the phrase as if it were a proverb or familiar expression.

Again the key changes, modulated into confident petition. We see the recoil of the devout soul to God, because it recognizes its need and helplessness. This turn of the Psalm begins with a strong emphatic adversative: "But I—I trust in Yahweh." The word for "trust" (HED #1019) is the same as in v. 6 and means "to hang" or "to lean upon," or, as we say, "to depend on." He utters his trust in his prayer, which occupies the rest of this part of the Psalm. A prayer, which is the voice of trust, does not begin with petition, but with renewed adherence to God and happy consciousness of the soul's relation to Him, and then it melts into supplication for the blessings which are consequences of that relationship. To feel, because of dreary circumstances,

| 991.126 | 7857 | 1887.126 | 3937, 8061 | | 487.227 | 8004 |
|---|---|---|---|---|---|---|
| v Qal juss 3mp | n mp | v Qal juss 3mp | prep, pn | **18.** | v Niphal juss 3fp | *n fd* |
| יֵבֹשׁוּ | רְשָׁעִים | יִדְּמוּ | לִשְׁאוֹל | | תֵּאָלַמְנָה | שִׂפְתֵי |
| yēvōshû | reshā'îm | yiddemû | lish'ôl | | tē'ālamnāh | siphthê |
| may they be ashamed | the wicked | let them be silent | to Sheol | | let them be mute | lips of |

| 8632 | 1744.154 | 6142, 6926 | 6515 | 904, 1375 | 973 | | 4242 |
|---|---|---|---|---|---|---|---|
| n ms | art, v Qal act ptc fp | prep, n ms | adj | prep, n fs | cj, n ms | **19.** | intrg |
| שֶׁקֶר | הַדֹּבְרוֹת | עַל־צַדִּיק | עָתָק | בְּגַאֲוָה | וָבוּז | | מָה |
| shāqer | haddōverôth | 'al-tsaddîq | 'āthāq | begha'ăwāh | wāvûz | | māh |
| lies | those which speak | against the righteous | insolent | with pride | and contempt | | what |

| 7521, 3008 | 866, 7121.113 | 3937, 3486.152 | 6713.113 |
|---|---|---|---|
| adj, n ms, ps 2ms | rel part, v Qal pf 2ms | prep, v Qal act ptc mp, ps 2ms | v Qal pf 2ms |
| רַב־טוּבְךָ | אֲשֶׁר־צָפַנְתָּ | לִירֵאֶיךָ | פָּעַלְתָּ |
| rav-ṯûvkhā | 'ăsher-tsāphantā | lîrē'êkhā | pā'altā |
| your abundant goodness | which You have stored | to those who fear You | You have enacted |

| 3937, 2725.152 | 904 | 5224 | 1158 | 119 |
|---|---|---|---|---|
| prep, art, v Qal act ptc mp | prep, ps 2ms | prep | *n mp* | n ms |
| לַחֹסִים | בָּךְ | נֶגֶד | בְּנֵי | אָדָם |
| lachōsîm | bākh | neghedh | benê | 'ādhām |
| to those who seek refuge | in You | before | the children of | humankind |

| | 5846.523 | 904, 5848 | 6686 | 4623, 7696 | 382 |
|---|---|---|---|---|---|
| **20.** | v Hiphil impf 2ms, ps 3mp | prep, *n ms* | n mp, ps 2ms | prep, *n mp* | n ms |
| | תַּסְתִּירֵם | בְּסֵתֶר | פָּנֶיךָ | מֵרֻכְסֵי | אִישׁ |
| | tas̱tîrēm | bes̱ēther | pānêkhā | mērukhs̱ê | 'îsh |
| | You hide them | in the cover of | your presence | from the conspirators of | men |

| 7121.123 | 904, 5712 | 4623, 7663 | 4098 | | 1313.155 | 3176 |
|---|---|---|---|---|---|---|
| v Qal impf 2ms, ps 3mp | prep, n fs | prep, *n ms* | n fp | **21.** | v Qal pass ptc ms | pn |
| תִּצְפְּנֵם | בְּסֻכָּה | מֵרִיב | לְשֹׁנוֹת | | בָּרוּךְ | יְהוָה |
| titspenēm | bes̱ukkāh | mērîv | leshōnôth | | bārûkh | yehwāh |
| You have stored them | in a shelter | from the contention of | tongues | | blessed | Yahweh |

| 3706 | 6623.511 | 2721 | 3937 | 904, 6111 | 4857 |
|---|---|---|---|---|---|
| cj | v Hiphil pf 3ms | n ms, ps 3ms | prep, ps 1cs | prep, *n fs* | n ms |
| כִּי | הִפְלִיא | חַסְדּוֹ | לִי | בְּעִיר | מָצוֹר |
| kî | hiphlî' | chas̱dô | lî | be'îr | mātsôr |
| because | He has done extraordinary things | his steadfast love | to me | in a city of | siege works |

| | 603 | 569.115 | 904, 2753.141 | 1673.215 | 4623, 5224 | 6084 |
|---|---|---|---|---|---|---|
| **22.** | cj, pers pron | v Qal pf 1cs | prep, v Qal inf con, ps 1cs | v Niphal pf 1cs | prep, prep | n fd, ps 2ms |
| | וַאֲנִי | אָמַרְתִּי | בְחָפְזִי | נִגְרַזְתִּי | מִנֶּגֶד | עֵינֶיךָ |
| | wa'ănî | 'āmartî | vechāphezî | nighraztî | minneghedh | 'ênêkhā |
| | and I | I have said | in my hurrying | I have been cut off | from before | your eyes |

| 409 | 8471.113 | 7249 | 8800 | 904, 8209.341 | 420 |
|---|---|---|---|---|---|
| adv | v Qal pf 2ms | *n ms* | n mp, ps 1cs | prep, v Piel inf con, ps 1cs | prep, ps 2ms |
| אָכֵן | שָׁמַעְתָּ | קוֹל | תַּחֲנוּנַי | בְּשַׁוְּעִי | אֵלֶיךָ |
| 'ākhēn | shāma'ttā | qôl | tachnûnay | beshawwe'î | 'ēlêkhā |
| surely | You have heard | the voice of | my supplication | during my crying for help | to You |

| | 154.133 | 881, 3176 | 3725, 2728 | 548.156 | 5526.151 | 3176 |
|---|---|---|---|---|---|---|
| **23.** | v Qal impv 2mp | do, pn | *adj*, n mp, ps 3ms | v Qal pass ptc mp | v Qal act ptc ms | pn |
| | אֶהֱבוּ | אֶת־יְהוָה | כָּל־חֲסִידָיו | אֱמוּנִים | נֹצֵר | יְהוָה |
| | 'ehĕvû | 'eth-yehwāh | kol-chăs̱idhāv | 'ĕmûnîm | nōtsēr | yehwāh |
| | love | Yahweh | all his godly ones | the faithful | One Who guards | **Yahweh** |

**18. Let the lying lips be put to silence; which speak grievous things proudly and contemptuously against the righteous:** ... let silence fall on those treacherous lips, that spoke maliciously of the innocent, *Knox* ... Let the lying lips be dumb, *ASV* ... Which speak arrogantly against the righteous, *MAST* ... that speak insolence against the just in pride and scorn, *NAB.*

**19. Oh how great is thy goodness, which thou hast laid up for them that fear thee; which thou hast wrought for them that trust in thee before the sons of men!:** ... What wealth of kindness thou hast laid up for thy worshippers, *Moffatt* ... which you bestow in the sight of men on those who take refuge in you, *NIV* ... Which you have prepared for those who trust in You, *NKJV* ... made manifest before mortal eyes for all who turn to you for shelter, *REB.*

**20. Thou shalt hide them in the secret of thy presence from the pride of man:** ... You will keep them safe in your house from the designs of man, *BB* ... In the shelter of your presence you hide them from human plots, *NRSV* ... from the conspiracies of men, *Rotherham.*

**thou shalt keep them secretly in a pavilion from the strife of tongues:** ... thou holdest them safe under thy shelter, *RSV* ... thou keepest them beneath thy roof, safe from contentious men, *NEB.*

**21. Blessed be the LORD: for he hath shown me his marvellous kindness in a strong city:** ... A Strong-hold was His kindness to me, *Fenton* ... for wondrous favour shown me in a desperate plight, *Moffatt* ... so strong the wall of his protection, *Knox* ... who worked a miracle of unfailing love for me when I was in sore straits, *NEB.*

**22. For I said in my haste, I am cut off from before thine eyes: nevertheless thou heardest the voice of my supplications when I cried unto thee:** ... I had said in my alarm, I am driven far from your sight, *NRSV* ... Yet you heard my cry for mercy, *NIV* ... but You heard me plead and call to You for help, *Beck* ... When I cried to thee for aid, *Goodspeed.*

**23. O love the LORD, all ye his saints: for the LORD preserveth the faithful, and plentifully rewardeth the proud doer:** ... all ye his men of lovingkindness, *Rotherham* ... The LORD keeps

---

that God is one's own makes miraculous sunrise at midnight. Built on that act of trust claiming its portion in God is the recognition of God's all-regulating hand, shaping the psalmist's "time" and the changing periods, each of which has its definite character, responsibilities and opportunities. Every man's life is a series of crises, in each of which there is some special work to be done or lesson to be learned, some particular virtue to be cultivated or sacrifice made. The opportunity does not return.

He who stands by God and looks forward can, by the light of that face, see the end of much transient bluster, "with pride and contempt," against the righteous. Lying lips fall dumb; praying lips, like the psalmist's, are opened to show forth God's praise. His prayer is still audible across the centuries; the mutterings of his enemies only live in his mention of them.

**31:19–20.** That assurance prepares the way for the noble burst of thanksgiving, as for accomplished deliverance, which ends the Psalm, springing up in a joyous outpouring of melody, like a lark from a bare furrow. The ear catches a twitter hushed again and renewed more than once before the full song breaks out. The psalmist has been absorbed with his own troubles until now, but thankfulness expands his vision, and suddenly there is with him a multitude of fellow-dependents on God's goodness. He hungers alone, but he feasts in company. The abundance of God's "goodness" is conceived of as a treasure stored, and in part openly displayed, before the sons of men.

**31:21–22.** The "strong city" is worthily interpreted as being God himself, although the historical explanation is tempting. God's mercy makes a true man ashamed of his doubts, and therefore the thanksgiving of v. 21 leads to the confession of v. 22. Agitated into despair, the psalmist had thought that he was "cut off from before thine eyes"—hidden so as not to be helped—but the event has shown that God both heard and saw him. If alarm does not so make us think that God is blind to our need and deaf to our cry as to make us dumb, we shall be taught the folly of our fears by his answers to our prayers. These will have a voice of gentle rebuke and ask us, "O thou of little faith, wherefore didst thou doubt?" (Matt. 14:31). He delivers first and lets the deliverance stand in place of chiding.

**31:23–24.** The whole closes with a summons to all whom Yahweh loves to love Him for his mercy's sake. The joyful singer longs for a chorus to join his single voice, as all devout hearts do. He generalizes his own experience, as all who have experienced deliverance themselves are entitled and bound to do, and discerns that in his single case the broad law is attested that the faithful are guarded whatever dangers assail, and "the proud doer" abundantly is repaid for all his contempt and hatred of

| 8396.351 | 6142, 3613 | 6449.151 | 1375 | | 2480.133 |
|---|---|---|---|---|---|
| cj, v Piel ptc ms | prep, n ms | *v Qal act ptc ms* | n fs | **24.** | v Qal impv 2mp |
| וּמְשַׁלֵּם | עַל־יֶתֶר | עֹשֵׂה | גַאֲוָה | | חִזְקוּ |
| ûmeshallēm | 'al-yether | 'ōsēh | gha'ăwāh | | chizqû |
| and One Who repays | concerning what remains | one who acts with | pride | | be strong |

| 563.521 | 3949 | 3725, 3282.352 | 3937, 3176 | | 3937, 1784 | 5030 |
|---|---|---|---|---|---|---|
| cj, v Hiphil juss 3ms | n ms, ps 2mp | *adj*, art, v Piel ptc mp | prep, pn | **32:t** | prep, pn | n ms |
| וְיַאֲמֵץ | לְבַבְכֶם | כָּל־הַמְיַחֲלִים | לַיהוָה | | לְדָוִד | מַשְׂכִּיל |
| weya'ămēts | levavkhem | kol-hamyachlîm | layhwāh | | ledhāwidh | maskîl |
| and may it be courageous | your heart | all those who wait | for Yahweh | | of David | a Maskil |

| | 869 | 5558.155, 6840 | 3803.155 | 2494 | | 869 | 119 | 3940 |
|---|---|---|---|---|---|---|---|---|
| **1.** | *n mp* | *v Qal pass ptc ms*, n ms | *v Qal pass ptc ms* | n fs | **2.** | *n ms* | n ms | neg part |
| | אַשְׁרֵי | נְשׂוּי־פֶּשַׁע | כְּסוּי | חֲטָאָה | | אַשְׁרֵי | אָדָם | לֹא |
| | 'ashrê | nesûy-pesha' | kesûy | chătā'āh | | 'ashrê | 'ādhām | lō' |
| | blessed | offenses are forgiven | covered | sin | | blessed | a man | not |

| 2913.121 | 3176 | 3937 | 5988 | 375 | 904, 7593 | 7711 |
|---|---|---|---|---|---|---|
| v Qal impf 3ms | pn | prep, ps 3ms | n ms | cj, *sub* | prep, n fs, ps 3ms | n fs |
| יַחְשֹׁב | יְהוָה | לוֹ | עָוֺן | וְאֵין | בְּרוּחוֹ | רְמִיָּה |
| yachshōv | yehwāh | lô | 'āwōn | we'ên | berûchô | remîyāh |
| He reckons | Yahweh | to him | guilt | and there is not | in his spirit | deceit |

| | 3706, 2896.515 | 1126.116 | 6344 | 904, 8058 | 3725, 3219 | | 3706 |
|---|---|---|---|---|---|---|---|
| **3.** | cj, v Hiphil pf 1cs | v Qal pf 3cp | n fp, ps 1cs | prep, n fs, ps 1cs | *adj*, art, n ms | **4.** | cj |
| | כִּי־הֶחֱרַשְׁתִּי | בָּלוּ | עֲצָמָי | בְּשַׁאֲגָתִי | כָּל־הַיּוֹם | | כִּי |
| | kî-hechĕrashtî | bālû | 'ătsāmāy | besha'ăghāthî | kol-hayyôm | | kî |
| | when I was silent | they wore out | my bones | during my groaning | all the day | | because |

| 3221 | 4050 | 3632.122 | 6142 | 3135 | 2089.211 | 4097 |
|---|---|---|---|---|---|---|
| adv | cj, n ms | v Qal impf 3fs | prep, ps 1cs | n fs, ps 2ms | v Niphal pf 3ms | n ms, ps 1cs |
| יוֹמָם | וָלַיְלָה | תִּכְבַּד | עָלַי | יָדֶךָ | נֶהְפַּךְ | לְשַׁדִּי |
| yômām | wālaylāh | tikhbadh | 'ālay | yādhekhā | nehpakh | leshaddî |
| by day | and by night | it was heavy | on me | your hand | it was overthrown | my cakes |

| 904, 2821 | 7302 | 5734 | | 2496 | 3156.525 | 5988 |
|---|---|---|---|---|---|---|
| prep, *n mp* | n ms | intrj | **5.** | n fs, ps 1cs | v Hiphil impf 1cs, ps 2ms | cj, n ms, ps 1cs |
| בְּחַרְבֹנֵי | קָיִץ | סֶלָה | | חַטָּאתִי | אוֹדִיעֲךָ | וַעֲוֺנִי |
| becharvōnê | qayits | selāh | | chattā'thî | 'ôdhî'ăkhā | wa'ăwōnî |
| in the heat of | the summer | selah | | my sin | I admitted | and my transgression |

| 3940, 3803.315 | 569.115 | 3142.525 | 6142 | 6840 | 3937, 3176 | 887 |
|---|---|---|---|---|---|---|
| neg part, v Piel pf 1cs | v Qal pf 1cs | v Hiphil juss 1cs | prep | n ms, ps 1cs | prep, pn | cj, pers pron |
| לֹא־כִסִּיתִי | אָמַרְתִּי | אוֹדֶה | עֲלֵי | פְשָׁעַי | לַיהוָה | וְאַתָּה |
| lō'-khissîthî | 'āmartî | 'ôdheh | 'ălê | peshā'ay | layhwāh | we'attāh |
| I have not hidden | I said | let me confess | concerning | my offense | to Yahweh | and You |

| 5558.113 | 5988 | 2496 | 5734 | | 6142, 2148 | 6663.721 | 3725, 2728 |
|---|---|---|---|---|---|---|---|
| v Qal pf 2ms | *n ms* | n fs, ps 1cs | intrj | **6.** | prep, dem pron | v Hithpael juss 3ms | *adj*, n ms |
| נָשָׂאתָ | עֲוֺן | חַטָּאתִי | סֶלָה | | עַל־זֹאת | יִתְפַּלֵּל | כָּל־חָסִיד |
| nāsā'thā | 'ăwōn | chattā'thî | selāh | | 'al-zō'th | yithpallēl | kol-chāsîdh |
| You forgave | the guilt of | my sin | selah | | concerning this | let them pray | all the godly |

| 420 | 3937, 6496 | 4834.141 | 7828 | 3937, 8279 | 4448 | 7521 | 420 | 3940 |
|---|---|---|---|---|---|---|---|---|
| prep, ps 2ms | prep, *n fs* | v Qal inf con | adv | prep, *n ms* | n md | adj | prep, ps 3ms | neg part |
| אֵלֶיךָ | לְעֵת | מְצֹא | רַק | לְשֵׁטֶף | מַיִם | רַבִּים | אֵלָיו | לֹא |
| 'ēlêkhā | le'ēth | metsō' | raq | leshēteph | mayim | rabbîm | 'ēlāv | lō' |
| to You | at the time of | finding | only | a flood of | waters | many | to him | not |

those who are constant, *NAB* ... The LORD protects those who truly believe, *NCV* ... but more than requites those who act proudly, *NCB.*

**24. Be of good courage, and he shall strengthen your heart, all ye that hope in the LORD:** ... Be strong, and let your heart take courage, *MRB* ... All ye that wait for the LORD, *MAST* ... Put away fear and let your heart be strong, *BB* ... be strong, and he shall establish your heart, *Geneva.*

**32:t. A Psalm of David, Maschil.**

**1. Blessed is he whose transgression is forgiven, whose sin is covered:** ... Happy is he whose fault is taken away, *NAB* ... whose sin is blotted out, *REB* ... Whose sin is pardoned, *Rotherham* ... whose disobedience is forgiven, *NEB.*

**2. Blessed is the man unto whom the LORD imputeth not iniquity, and in whose spirit there is no guile:** ... to whom the LORD charges no guilt, *Goodspeed* ... Whose fault the LORD counts not to him, And there is in his mind no defect, *Fenton* ... and in whose spirit there is no deceit, *NRSV* ... the heart that hides no treason, *Knox.*

**3. When I kept silence, my bones waxed old through my roaring all the day long:** ... When I kept things to myself, I felt weak deep inside me, *NCV* ... my bones were wasted, because of my crying all through the day, *BB* ... I wore out my limbs, *Beck* ... become old have my bones, *Young.*

**4. For day and night thy hand was heavy upon me: my moisture is turned into the drought of summer. Selah:** ... my strength was sapped as in the heat of summer, *NIV* ... my heart grew parched as stubble in summer drought, *JB* ... my strength was dried up, *RSV.*

**5. I acknowledged my sin unto thee, and mine iniquity have I not hid. I said, I will confess my transgressions unto the LORD; and thou forgavest the iniquity of my sin. Selah:** ... my guilt I covered not, *NCB* ... My sin I made

---

the just. Therefore, the last result of contemplating God's ways with his servants is an incentive to courage, strength and patient waiting for the LORD.

***Psalm 32.*** *Across the dimness of many years, we hear this man speaking our sins, our penitence, our joy. The antique words are as fresh, and fit as close to our experiences, as if they had been welled up from a living heart today. The theme is the way of forgiveness and its blessedness. This is set forth in two parts: the first (vv. 1–5) is a leaf from the psalmist's autobiography, and the second (v. 6 to end) is the generalization of individual experience and its application to others.*

**32:1–2.** The psalmist begins abruptly with an exclamation ("Oh, the blessedness"). His new joy wells up irrepressibly. To think that he who had gone so far down in the mire, and has locked his lips in silence for so long, should find himself so blessed! Joy so exuberant cannot content itself with one statement of its grounds. It runs over in synonyms for sin and its forgiveness, which are not unnecessary repetition or accidental redundancy. The heart is too full to be emptied at one outpouring. The first designation, rendered "transgression" (HED #6840), conceives of it as rebellion against rightful authority; the second, "sin" (HED #2494), describes it as knowingly missing a mark. The last synonym, "iniquity" (HED #5988) means "crookedness" or "distortion."

The three expressions for pardon are also eloquent in their variety. The first word (HED #5558) means "taken away" or "lifted off," as a burden from aching shoulders. It implies more than holding back penal consequences. The second (HED #3803), "covered," paints pardon as God's shrouding the foul thing from his pure eyes so that his action is no longer determined by its existence. The third (HED #3940, 2913) describes forgiveness as God's not reckoning a man's sin to him, in which expression hovers some allusion to canceling a debt.

**32:3–4.** Retrospect of the dismal depth from which it has climbed is natural to a soul sunning itself on high. Therefore, on the overflowing description of present blessedness follows a shuddering glance downward to past unrest. Sullen silence caused the one; frank acknowledgment brought the other. He who will not speak his sin to God has to groan. A dumb conscience often makes a loud-voiced pain. This man's sin had indeed missed its aim, for it had brought about three things: rotting bones (which may be merely a strong metaphor or may be a physical fact), the consciousness of God's displeasure dimly felt as if a great hand were pressing him down, and the drying up of the sap of his life, as if the fierce heat of summer had burned the marrow in his bones. These were the fruits of pleasant sin, and by reason of them, many a moan broke from his locked lips. Stolid indifference may delay remorse, but its serpent fang strikes sooner or later, and then strength and joy die. The selah indicates a swell or prolongation of the accompaniment to emphasize this terrible picture of a soul gnawing itself.

**32:5.** The abrupt turn to the description of the opposite disposition in v. 5 suggests a sudden gush of penitence. As at a bound, the soul passes from

| | | | | | |
|---|---|---|---|---|---|
| 5236.526<br>v Hiphil impf 3mp<br>יַגִּיעוּ<br>yaggî'û<br>they will reach | 7. 887<br>pers pron<br>אַתָּה<br>'attāh<br>You | 5848<br>n ms<br>סֵתֶר<br>sēther<br>a hiding place | 3937<br>prep, ps 1cs<br>לִי<br>lî<br>to me | 4623, 7140<br>prep, n ms<br>מִצַּר<br>mitstsar<br>from adversity | 5526.123<br>v Qal impf 2ms, ps 1cs<br>תִּצְּרֵנִי<br>titsts$^{e}$rēnî<br>You guard me |
| 7724<br>*n mp*<br>רָנֵּי<br>rānnê<br>victory shouts of | 6647B<br>n ms<br>פַלֵּט<br>phallēt<br>deliverance | 5621.323<br>v Poel impf 2ms, ps 1cs<br>תְּסוֹבְבֵנִי<br>t$^{e}$sôv$^{e}$vēnî<br>You surround me with | 5734<br>intrj<br>סֶלָה<br>selāh<br>selah | 8. 7959.525<br>v Hiphil juss 1cs, ps 2ms<br>אַשְׂכִּילְךָ<br>'askîl$^{e}$khā<br>let me instruct you | |
| 3498.525<br>cj, v Hiphil juss 1cs, ps 2ms<br>וְאוֹרְךָ<br>w$^{e}$'ôrkhā<br>yes let me teach you | 904, 1932, 2182<br>prep, n ms, dem pron<br>בְּדֶרֶךְ־זוּ<br>b$^{e}$dherekh-zû<br>in this way | 2050.123<br>v Qal impf 2ms<br>תֵלֵךְ<br>thēlēkh<br>you will go | 3398.125<br>v Qal juss 1cs<br>אִיעֲצָה<br>'î'ătsāh<br>let me advise | 6142<br>prep, ps 2ms<br>עָלֶיךָ<br>'ālêkhā<br>concerning you | 6084<br>n fs, ps 1cs<br>עֵינִי<br>'ênî<br>my eye |
| 9. 414, 2030.128<br>adv, v Qal juss 2mp<br>אַל־תִּהְיוּ<br>'al-tihyû<br>do not be | 3626, 5670<br>prep, n ms<br>כְּסוּס<br>k$^{e}$sûs<br>like a horse | 3626, 6755<br>prep, n ms<br>כְּפֶרֶד<br>k$^{e}$pheredh<br>like a mule | 375<br>*sub*<br>אֵין<br>'ên<br>there is not | 1032.541<br>v Hiphil inf con<br>הָבִין<br>hāvîn<br>one who understands | 904, 5141, 7734<br>prep, n ms, cj, n ms<br>בְּמֶתֶג־וָרֶסֶן<br>b$^{e}$methegh-wāresen<br>with bit and bridle |
| 5927<br>n ms, ps 3ms<br>עֶדְיוֹ<br>'edhyô<br>his petulence | 3937, 1141.141<br>prep, v Qal inf con<br>לִבְלוֹם<br>livlôm<br>to restrain | 1118<br>neg part<br>בַּל<br>bal<br>not | 7414.141<br>v Qal inf con<br>קְרֹב<br>qŏrōv<br>coming near | 420<br>prep, ps 2ms<br>אֵלֶיךָ<br>'ēlêkhā<br>to you | 10. 7521<br>adj<br>רַבִּים<br>rabbîm<br>many |
| | | | | | 4480<br>n mp<br>מַכְאוֹבִים<br>makh'ôvîm<br>the sufferings |
| 3937, 7857<br>prep, art, n ms<br>לָרָשָׁע<br>lārāshā'<br>to the wicked | 1019.151<br>cj, art, v Qal act ptc ms<br>וְהַבּוֹטֵחַ<br>w$^{e}$habbôtēach<br>but the one who trusts | 904, 3176<br>prep, pn<br>בַּיהוָה<br>bayhwāh<br>in Yahweh | 2721<br>n ms<br>חֶסֶד<br>chesedh<br>steadfast love | 5621.321<br>v Poel impf 3ms, ps 3ms<br>יְסוֹבְבֶנּוּ<br>y$^{e}$sôv$^{e}$vennû<br>it surrounds him | |
| 11. 7975.133<br>v Qal impv 2mp<br>שִׂמְחוּ<br>simchû<br>rejoice | 904, 3176<br>prep, pn<br>בַּיהוָה<br>vayhwāh<br>in Yahweh | 1559.133<br>cj, v Qal impv 2mp<br>וְגִילוּ<br>w$^{e}$ghîlû<br>and rejoice | 6926<br>n mp<br>צַדִּיקִים<br>tsaddîqîm<br>O righteous ones | 7728.533<br>cj, v Hiphil impv 2mp<br>וְהַרְנִינוּ<br>w$^{e}$harnînû<br>and shout for joy | |

known to you, and did not hide my guilt from you, *Anchor* … With sorrow I will confess my disobedience to the LORD, *NEB* … then you for your part remitted the penalty of my sin, *REB*.

**6. For this shall every one that is godly pray unto thee in a time when thou mayest be found: surely in the floods of great waters they shall not come nigh unto him:** … For this cause let every saint make his prayer to you at a time when you are near, *BB* … every faithful man pray to you in time of stress, *NCB* … they will never reach your faithful, *JB* … the rush of mighty waters shall not reach them, *NRSV*.

**7. Thou art my hiding place; thou shalt preserve me from trouble; thou shalt compass me about with songs of deliverance. Selah:** … Thou art a refuge for me from distress, *NEB* … You surround me with people who are rescued, *Beck* … for thou wilt be his shelter, safeguarding him in peril, *Moffatt* … you guard me and enfold me in salvation, *REB*.

**8. I will instruct thee and teach thee in the way which thou shalt go: I will guide thee with mine eye:** … let my prudence watch over thee, *Knox* … and train you in the way you shall go, *Berkeley* … and show you the way you should walk, *NAB* … I cause mine eye to take counsel concerning thee, *Young*.

**9. Be ye not as the horse, or as the mule, which have no understanding: whose mouth must be held in with bit and bridle, lest they come near unto thee:** … like a mule without discernment, *Rotherham* …

Whose temper must be restrained, *Goodspeed* ... must his petulance be curbed; Then you can approach him, *Anchor* ... else it will not keep with you, *RSV.*

**10. Many sorrows shall be to the wicked: but he that trusteth in the LORD, mercy shall compass him about:** ... Countless troubles are in store for the wicked, *JB* ... but the LORD's love surrounds those who trust him, *NCV* ... but the LORD's unfailing love, *NIV* ... but mercy goes all around him who trusts in the LORD, *KJVII.*

**11. Be glad in the LORD, and rejoice, ye righteous: and shout for joy, all ye that are upright in heart:** ... and rejoice you righteous ones, *NASB* ... The Holy are glad and delight in the LIFE, *Fenton* ... sing aloud, all you of honest heart, *REB* ... give cries of joy, all you whose hearts are true, *BB.*

**33:1. Rejoice in the LORD, O ye righteous: for praise is comely for the upright:** ... SHOUT for joy in the

---

dreary remorse. The break with the former self is complete and effected in one wrench. Some things are best done by degrees, and some, of which forsaking sin is one, are best done quickly. As swift as the resolve to crave pardon, so swift is the answer giving it. We are reminded of that gospel compressed into a verse, "David said unto Nathan, I have sinned against the LORD. And Nathan said unto David, The LORD also hath put away thy sin" (2 Sam. 12:13). It parts the autobiographical section from the more general one which follows.

**32:6–7.** In the second part, the solitary soul translates its experience into exhortations for all and woos men to follow on the same path by setting forth in rich variety the joys of pardon. The exhortation first dwells on the positive blessings associated with penitence (vv. 6f) and next on the degradation and sorrow involved in obstinate hard-heartedness (vv. 8ff). The natural impulse of him who has known both is to beseech others to share his happy experience, and the psalmist's course of thought obeys that impulse.

The penitent, praying, pardoned man is set as on a rock islet in the midst of floods, whether these be conceived of as temptation to sin or as calamities. The hortatory tone is broken in v. 7 by the recurrence of the personal element, since the singer's heart was too full for silence. But there is no real interruption, for the joyous utterance of one's own faith is often the most winning persuasive, and a devout man can scarcely hold out to others the sweetness of finding God without at the same time tasting what He offers. The shout of joy is caught up by the selah.

**32:8.** The tone now changes into solemn warning against obstinate disregard of God's leading. It is usual to suppose that the psalmist still speaks, but surely "I will guide thee with mine eye" does not fit human lips. It is to be observed, also, that in v. 8 a single person, who is most naturally taken to be the same as he who spoke his individual faith in v. 7, is addressed. In other words, the psalmist's confidence evokes a divine response. With his eye upon his servant, God will show him the way and will keep him ever in sight as he travels on it.

**32:9–10.** Verses 9f are a warning against brutish obstinance. The former verse has difficulties in detail, but its drift is plain. The gracious guidance which avails for those made docile by forgiveness and trust is contrasted with the harsh constraint which must curb and coerce mulish natures. The only things which such understand are bits and bridles. They will not come near to God without such rough outward constraint any more than an unbroken horse will approach a man unless dragged by a halter. That untamableness except by force is the reason why many sorrows must strike the wicked. They who are at first driven are afterwards drawn and taught to know no delight so great as that of coming and keeping near God.

The antithesis of "wicked" and "he that trusteth in Yahweh" is as significant as teaching that faith is the true opposite of sinfulness. Not less full of meaning is the sequence of "trust," "righteousness" and "uprightness of heart" in vv. 10f. Faith leads to righteousness, and they are upright, not those who have never fallen, but those who have been raised from their fall by pardon.

**32:11.** The Psalm ends with a general summons to joy. All share in the solitary soul's exultation. The depth of penitence measures the height of gladness. The breath that was spent in "roaring all the day long" is used for shouts of deliverance. Every tear sparkles like a diamond in the sunshine of pardon, and he who begins with the lowly cry for forgiveness will end with lofty songs of joy and be made, by God's guidance and Spirit, righteous and upright in heart.

***Psalm 33.*** *This is the last of the four Psalms in Book One which have no title, the others being Pss. 1, 2, which are introductory, and Ps. 10, which is closely*

| **3725, 3596, 3949**<br>*adj, adj,* n ms<br>כָּל־יִשְׁרֵי־לֵב<br>kol-yishrê-lēv<br>all the upright of heart | **33:1** | **7728.333**<br>v Piel impv 2mp<br>רַנְּנוּ<br>rann$^{e}$nû<br>shout for joy | **6926**<br>n mp<br>צַדִּיקִים<br>tsaddîqîm<br>O righteous ones | **904, 3176**<br>prep, pn<br>בַּיהוָה<br>bayhwāh<br>in Yahweh | **3937, 3596**<br>prep, n mp<br>לַיְשָׁרִים<br>layshārîm<br>to the Upright One |
|---|---|---|---|---|---|

| **5172**<br>adj<br>נָאוָה<br>nā'wāh<br>proper | **8747**<br>n fs<br>תְהִלָּה<br>t$^{e}$hillāh<br>praise | **2.** | **3142.533**<br>v Hiphil impv 2mp<br>הוֹדוּ<br>hôdhû<br>praise | **3937, 3176**<br>prep, pn<br>לַיהוָה<br>layhwāh<br>Yahweh | **904, 3780**<br>prep, n ms<br>בְּכִנּוֹר<br>b$^{e}$khinnôr<br>with the zither | **904, 5213**<br>prep, *n ms*<br>בְּנֵבֶל<br>b$^{e}$nēvel<br>with the harp of | **6452**<br>num<br>עָשׂוֹר<br>ʻāsôr<br>ten |
|---|---|---|---|---|---|---|---|

| **2252.333, 3937**<br>v Piel impv 2mp, prep, ps 3ms<br>זַמְּרוּ־לוֹ<br>zamm$^{e}$rû-lô<br>sing praises to Him | **3.** | **8301.133, 3937**<br>v Qal impv 2mp, prep, ps 3ms<br>שִׁירוּ־לוֹ<br>shîrû-lô<br>sing to Him | **8302**<br>n ms<br>שִׁיר<br>shîr<br>a song | **2413**<br>adj<br>חָדָשׁ<br>chādhāsh<br>new | **3296.533**<br>v Hiphil impv 2mp<br>הֵיטִיבוּ<br>hêṭîvû<br>make good |
|---|---|---|---|---|---|

| **5235.341**<br>v Piel inf con<br>נַגֵּן<br>naggēn<br>play a stringed instrument | **904, 8980**<br>prep, n fs<br>בִּתְרוּעָה<br>bithrûʻāh<br>with a shout of joy | **4.** | **3706, 3596**<br>cj, adj<br>כִּי־יָשָׁר<br>kî-yāshār<br>because upright | **1745, 3176**<br>*n ms*, pn<br>דְּבַר־יְהוָה<br>d$^{e}$var-y$^{e}$hwāh<br>the word of Yahweh |
|---|---|---|---|---|

| **3725, 4801**<br>cj, *adj*, n ms, ps 3ms<br>וְכָל־מַעֲשֵׂהוּ<br>w$^{e}$khol-maʻăsēhû<br>and all his work | **904, 536**<br>prep, n fs<br>בֶּאֱמוּנָה<br>be'ĕmûnāh<br>with faithfulness | **5.** | **154.151**<br>v Qal act ptc ms<br>אֹהֵב<br>'ōhēv<br>One Who loves | **6930**<br>n fs<br>צְדָקָה<br>ts$^{e}$dhāqāh<br>righteousness | **5122**<br>cj, n ms<br>וּמִשְׁפָּט<br>ûmishpāṭ<br>and justice |
|---|---|---|---|---|---|

| **2721**<br>*n ms*<br>חֶסֶד<br>chesedh<br>the steadfast love of | **3176**<br>pn<br>יְהוָה<br>y$^{e}$hwāh<br>Yahweh | **4527.112**<br>v Qal pf 3fs<br>מָלְאָה<br>māl$^{e}$'āh<br>it is full of | **800**<br>art, n fs<br>הָאָרֶץ<br>hā'ārets<br>the earth | **6.** | **904, 1745**<br>prep, *n ms*<br>בִּדְבַר<br>bidhvar<br>by the word of | **3176**<br>pn<br>יְהוָה<br>y$^{e}$hwāh<br>Yahweh | **8452**<br>n md<br>שָׁמַיִם<br>shāmayim<br>the heavens |
|---|---|---|---|---|---|---|---|

| **6449.216**<br>v Niphal pf 3cp<br>נַעֲשׂוּ<br>naʻăsû<br>they were made | **904, 7593**<br>cj, prep, *n fs*<br>וּבְרוּחַ<br>ûv$^{e}$rûach<br>and with the breath of | **6552**<br>n ms, ps 3ms<br>פִּיו<br>pîw<br>his mouth | **3725, 6893**<br>*adj*, n ms, ps 3mp<br>כָּל־צְבָאָם<br>kol-ts$^{e}$vā'ām<br>all their host | **7.** | **3788.151**<br>v Qal act ptc ms<br>כֹּנֵס<br>kōnēs<br>gathering | **3626, 5243**<br>prep, art, n ms<br>כַּנֵּד<br>kannēdh<br>like a heap |
|---|---|---|---|---|---|---|

| **4448**<br>*n mp*<br>מֵי<br>mê<br>the waters of | **3328**<br>art, n ms<br>הַיָּם<br>hayyām<br>the sea | **5598.151**<br>v Qal act ptc ms<br>נֹתֵן<br>nōthēn<br>putting | **904, 212**<br>prep, n mp<br>בְּאֹצָרוֹת<br>b$^{e}$'ōtsārôth<br>into storehouses | **8745**<br>n fp<br>תְּהוֹמוֹת<br>t$^{e}$hômôth<br>the deeps | **8.** | **3486.126**<br>v Qal juss 3mp<br>יִירְאוּ<br>yîr$^{e}$'û<br>let them fear | **4623, 3176**<br>prep, pn<br>מֵיְהוָה<br>mêy$^{e}$hwāh<br>of Yahweh |
|---|---|---|---|---|---|---|---|

| **3725, 800**<br>*adj*, art, n fs<br>כָּל־הָאָרֶץ<br>kol-hā'ārets<br>all the earth | **4623**<br>prep, ps 3ms<br>מִמֶּנּוּ<br>mimmennû<br>of Him | **1513.126**<br>v Qal juss 3mp<br>יָגוּרוּ<br>yāghûrû<br>let them be afraid | **3725, 3553.152**<br>*adj, v Qal act ptc mp*<br>כָּל־יֹשְׁבֵי<br>kol-yōsh$^{e}$vê<br>all the dwellers of | **8725**<br>n fs<br>תֵבֵל<br>thēvēl<br>the world | **9.** | **3706**<br>cj<br>כִּי<br>kî<br>because | **2000**<br>pers pron<br>הוּא<br>hû'<br>He |
|---|---|---|---|---|---|---|---|

| **569.111**<br>v Qal pf 3ms<br>אָמַר<br>'āmar<br>He said | **2030.121**<br>cj, v Qal impf 3ms<br>וַיֶּהִי<br>wayyehî<br>and it was | **2000, 6943.311**<br>pers pron, v Piel pf 3ms<br>הוּא־צִוָּה<br>hû'-tsiwwāh<br>He He commanded | **6198.121**<br>cj, v Qal impf 3ms<br>וַיַּעֲמֹד<br>wayyaʻămōdh<br>and it stood | **10.** | **3176**<br>pn<br>יְהוָה<br>y$^{e}$hwāh<br>Yahweh | **6815.511**<br>v Hiphil pf 3ms<br>הֵפִיר<br>hēphîr<br>He has thwarted |
|---|---|---|---|---|---|---|

LORD, you that are righteous, *REB* ... praise comes well from the honest, *JB* ... songs of praise befit the upright soul, *Moffatt* ... for it is beautiful to praise, *Beck.*

**2. Praise the LORD with harp: sing unto him with the psaltery and an instrument of ten strings:** ... sing to him with stringed instruments, *Good News* ... Play to him on the ten-stringed lute, *Goodspeed* ... with the ten-stringed lyre chant his praises, *NAB* ... make music to him on the ten-stringed lyre, *NIV.*

**3. Sing unto him a new song; play skilfully with a loud noise:** ... Play skillfully with a shout of joy, *NKJV* ... play sweetly with sounds of gladness, *Anchor* ... play skilfully with a joyful sound, *Berkeley* ... make sweet music for your cry of victory, *JB.*

**4. For the word of the LORD is right; and all his works are done in truth:** ... His work is done in faithfulness, *NASB* ... he is faithful in all he does, *NIV* ... and all his work endures, *NEB* ... he is faithful in all his dealings, *Knox.*

**5. He loveth righteousness and judgment: the earth is full of the goodness of the LORD:** ... His delight is in righteousness and wisdom, *BB* ... And His mercies replenish the earth, *Fenton* ... the earth is filled with the LORD's unfailing love, *REB* ... full of the steadfast love of the LORD, *NRSV.*

**6. By the word of the LORD were the heavens made; and all the host of them by the breath of his mouth:** ... By the breath from his mouth, he made all the stars, *NCV* ... and all their host by his mere word, *Moffatt* ... by the spirit of his mouth all their host, *Rotherham* ... all the host of heaven was formed at his command, *REB.*

**7. He gathereth the waters of the sea together as an heap: he layeth up the depth in storehouses:** ... He gathered the sea like water in a goatskin, *NEB* ... stores up the waters of the sea as in a cistern, treasures up all its waves, *Knox* ... gathers the waters of the sea as in a flask, *NCB* ... gathered the waters of the sea as in a bottle, *NRSV.*

**8. Let all the earth fear the LORD: let all the inhabitants of the world stand in awe of him:** ... let all the people of the world be in holy fear of him, *BB* ... let all who dwell in the world revere him, *NCB* ... let all the people of the world revere him, *NIV* ... inhabitants of the world be reverent before Him, *Berkeley.*

**9. For he spake, and it was done; he commanded, and it stood fast:** ... For he spoke, and it was made, *NAB* ... He ordered and it came into being, *Beck* ... spoke and they came

---

*connected with Ps. 9. Some have endeavored to establish a similar connection between Pss. 32 and 33, but while the closing summons to the righteous in the former is substantially repeated in the opening words of the latter, there is little other trace of connection, except the references in both to "the eye" of Yahweh (32:8; 33:18); and no two Psalms could be more different in subject and tone than these.*

**33:1–3.** The opening summons to praise takes us far away from the solitary wrestlings and communings in former Psalms. Now the singers lift up their voices, singing, "Rejoice in the LORD, O ye righteous." But the clear recognition of purity as the condition of access to God speaks in this invocation as distinctly as in any of the preceding. "The righteous" whose lives conform to the divine will, and only they, can shout aloud their joy in Yahweh. Praise fits and adorns the lips of the "upright" (HED #3596) only, whose spirits are without twist of self-will and sin. The direction of character expressed in the word is horizontal rather than vertical and is better represented by "straight" than "upright." Praise gilds the gold of purity and adds grace even to the beauty of holiness. Experts tell us that the kinnôr ("zither"; HED #3780) and nevel ("harp"; HED #5218) were both stringed instruments, differing in the position of the sounding board, which was below in the former and above in the latter, and also in the covering of the strings.

**33:4–5.** This new song is saturated with reminiscences of old ones, and it deals with familiar thoughts which have come to the psalmist with fresh power. He magnifies the moral attributes manifested in God's self-revelation, his unfailing word and his providential government. "The word of Yahweh," in v. 4, is to be taken in the wide sense of every utterance of his thought or will (Calvin). It underlies his "works," as is more largely declared in the following verses. There is but one omnipotent will at work everywhere, and that is a will whose law for itself is the love of righteousness and truth. The majestic simplicity and universality of the cause are answered by the simplicity and universality of the result, the flooding of the whole world with blessing.

**33:6–9.** The work of creation is set forth in vv. 6–9, as the effect of the divine word alone. The psalmist is fascinated not by the glories created, but by the wonder of the process of creation. The divine will uttered itself, and the universe was. Of course, the thought is parallel with that of Genesis, "And God said, Let there be ...and there was." We are not to antedate the Christian teaching of a personal word of God, the Agent of creation. The image of "a

| 6332, 1504 | 5285.511 | 4422 | 6194 | | 6332 | 3176 |
|---|---|---|---|---|---|---|
| *n fs*, n mp | v Hiphil pf 3ms | *n fp* | n mp | | *n fs* | pn |
| עֲצַת־גּוֹיִם | הֵנִיא | מַחְשְׁבוֹת | עַמִּים | **11.** | עֲצַת | יְהוָה |
| 'ătsath-gôyim | hēnî' | machshevôth | 'ammîm | | 'ătsath | yehwāh |
| the counsel of the nations | He has frustrated | the plans of | the peoples | | the counsel of | Yahweh |

| 3937, 5986 | 6198.122 | 4422 | 3949 | 3937, 1810 | 1810 | | 869 |
|---|---|---|---|---|---|---|---|
| prep, n ms | v Qal impf 3fs | *n fp* | n ms, ps 3ms | prep, n ms | cj, n ms | | *n ms* |
| לְעוֹלָם | תַּעֲמֹד | מַחְשְׁבוֹת | לִבּוֹ | לְדֹר | וָדֹר | **12.** | אַשְׁרֵי |
| le'ôlām | ta'ămōdh | machshevôth | libbô | ledhōr | wādhōr | | 'ashrê |
| unto eternity | they stand | the plans of | his heart | unto generations | and generations | | blessed |

| 1504 | 866, 3176 | 435 | 6194 | 1013.111 | 3937, 5338 | 3937 |
|---|---|---|---|---|---|---|
| art, n ms | rel pron, pn | n mp, ps 3ms | art, n ms | v Qal pf 3ms | prep, n fs | prep, ps 3ms |
| הַגּוֹי | אֲשֶׁר־יְהוָה | אֱלֹהָיו | הָעָם | בָּחַר | לְנַחֲלָה | לוֹ |
| haggôy | 'ăsher-yehwāh | 'ĕlōhāv | hā'ām | bāchar | lenachlāh | lô |
| the nation | whom Yahweh | their God | the people | He has chosen | for an inheritance | to Him |

| | 4623, 8452 | 5202.511 | 3176 | 7495.111 | 881, 3725, 1158 | 119 |
|---|---|---|---|---|---|---|
| | prep, n md | v Hiphil pf 3ms | pn | v Qal pf 3ms | do, *adj*, *n mp* | art, n ms |
| **13.** | מִשָּׁמַיִם | הִבִּיט | יְהוָה | רָאָה | אֶת־כָּל־בְּנֵי | הָאָדָם |
| | mishshāmayim | hibbîṭ | yehwāh | rā'āh | 'eth-kol-benê | hā'ādhām |
| | from the heavens | He has looked down | Yahweh | He saw | all the children of | humankind |

| | 4623, 4487, 3553.141 | 8148.511 | 420 | 3725, 3553.152 | 800 |
|---|---|---|---|---|---|
| | prep, *n ms*, v Qal inf con, ps 3ms | v Hiphil pf 3ms | prep | *adj*, *v Qal act ptc mp* | art, n fs |
| **14.** | מִמְּכוֹן־שִׁבְתּוֹ | הִשְׁגִּיחַ | אֶל | כָּל־יֹשְׁבֵי | הָאָרֶץ |
| | mimmekhôn-shivtô | hishgîach | 'el | kol-yōshevê | hā'ārets |
| | from the place of his sitting | He has stared | at | all the dwellers of | the earth |

| | 3443.151 | 3266 | 3949 | 1032.551 | 420, 3725, 4801 |
|---|---|---|---|---|---|
| | art, v Qal act ptc ms | adv | n ms, ps 3mp | art, v Hiphil ptc ms | prep, *adj*, n mp, ps 3mp |
| **15.** | הַיֹּצֵר | יַחַד | לִבָּם | הַמֵּבִין | אֶל־כָּל־מַעֲשֵׂיהֶם |
| | hayyōtsēr | yachadh | libbām | hammēvîn | 'el-kol-ma'ăsêhem |
| | the One Who fashions | together | their hearts | the One Who understands | about all their deeds |

| | 375, 4567 | 3588.255 | 904, 7524, 2524 | 1399 |
|---|---|---|---|---|
| | *sub*, art, n ms | v Niphal ptc ms | prep, *n ms*, n ms | n ms |
| **16.** | אֵין־הַמֶּלֶךְ | נוֹשָׁע | בְּרָב־חָיִל | גִּבּוֹר |
| | 'ên-hammelekh | nôshā' | berāv-chāyil | gibbôr |
| | there is not the king | saved | by an abundance of strength | a warrior |

| 3940, 5522.221 | 904, 7524, 3699 | | 8632 | 5670 | 3937, 9009 |
|---|---|---|---|---|---|
| neg part, v Niphal impf 3ms | prep, *n ms*, n ms | | n ms | art, n ms | prep, n fs |
| לֹא־יִנָּצֵל | בְּרָב־כֹּחַ | **17.** | שֶׁקֶר | הַסּוּס | לִתְשׁוּעָה |
| lō'-yinnātsēl | berāv-kōach | | sheqer | hassûs | lithshû'āh |
| he will not be rescued | by an abundance of power | | vanity | the horse | for a victory |

| 904, 7524 | 2524 | 3940 | 4561.321 | | 2079 | 6084 |
|---|---|---|---|---|---|---|
| cj, prep, *n ms* | n ms, ps 3ms | neg part | v Piel impf 3ms | | intrj | *n fs* |
| וּבְרֹב | חֵילוֹ | לֹא | יְמַלֵּט | **18.** | הִנֵּה | עֵין |
| ûverōv | chêlô | lō' | yemallēṭ | | hinnēh | 'ên |
| even with the abundance of | his strength | not | it can provide safety | | behold | the eye of |

| 3176 | 420, 3486.152 | 3937, 3282.352 | 3937, 2721 |
|---|---|---|---|
| pn | prep, v Qal act ptc mp, ps 3ms | prep, art, v Piel ptc mp | prep, n ms, ps 3ms |
| יְהוָה | אֶל־יְרֵאָיו | לַמְיַחֲלִים | לְחַסְדּוֹ |
| yehwāh | 'el-yere'âv | lamyachlîm | lechasdô |
| Yahweh | toward those who fear Him | to those who wait | for his steadfast love |

into life, He commanded, and then they appeared, *Fenton* ... no sooner had he commanded, than there it stood!, *JB*.

**10. The LORD bringeth the counsel of the heathen to nought: he maketh the devices of the people of none effect:** ... upsets the plans of nations; he ruins all their plans, *NCV* ... made void the counsel of nations, *Young* ... he frustrates the plans of the peoples, *RSV* ... maketh the thoughts of the peoples to be of no effect, *ASV*.

**11. The counsel of the LORD standeth for ever, the thoughts of his heart to all generations:** ... But the plan of the LORD stands forever, *NAB* ... The plans of His heart from generation to generation, *NASB* ... what He proposes is for all time, *Beck* ... his ideas will last from now on, *NCV*.

**12. Blessed is the nation whose God is the LORD; and the people whom he hath chosen for his own inheritance:** ... How blest the nation Yahweh its God has blest, *Anchor* ... the people he has chosen for his own, *REB* ... the people whom he has chosen as his heritage, *RSV* ... And the people He takes for His own, *Fenton*.

**13. The LORD looketh from heaven; he beholdeth all the sons of men:** ... he sees all humankind, *NRSV* ... he sees all the children of Adam, *JB* ... he sees the whole race of men, *NEB* ... he watches all mankind, *Knox*.

**14. From the place of his habitation he looketh upon all the inhabitants of the earth:** ... From His dwelling place He looks on all the people of the earth, *KJVII* ... From the place of His habitation He looketh intently, *MAST* ... From his house he keeps watch on all who are living, *BB* ... place where He sits enthroned He looks down on all who live on earth, *Beck*.

**15. He fashioneth their hearts alike; he considereth all their works:** ... He who fashions their hearts to be human, *Berkeley* ... he alone moulds their hearts, *JB* ... He made their hearts and understands everything they do, *NCV* ... forms the hearts of all, who considers everything they do, *NIV*.

**16. There is no king saved by the multitude of an host: a mighty man is not delivered by much strength:** ... Armies do not bring victory to a king, *Moffatt* ... A king is not saved by his great army, *RSV* ... No warrior delivers himself through his massive strength, *Anchor* ... Nor a Hero prevail by his strength, *Fenton*.

**17. An horse is a vain thing for safety: neither shall he deliver any by his great strength:** ... The war horse is a vain hope for victory, *NRSV* ... No one can rely on his horse to save him, *REB* ... despite its great strength it can't help you escape, *Beck* ... it cannot provide escape, *NCB*.

**18. Behold, the eye of the LORD is upon them that fear him, upon them**

---

heap" is probably due to the same optical delusion which has coined the expression "the high seas," since, to an eye looking seaward from the beach, the level waters seem to rise as they recede; or it may merely express the gathering together in a mass. Possibly, the mention of storehouses suggests those of the Flood, when these were opened, and that thought, crossing the psalmist's mind, led to the exhortation in v. 8 to fear Yahweh. The power displayed in creation is, however, a sufficient ground for the summons to reverent obedience, and v. 9 may be but an emphatic repetition of the substance of the foregoing description.

**33:10–12.** From the original creation, the psalmist's mind runs over the ages between it and him and sees the same mystical might of the divine will working in what we call providential government. God's bare word has power without material means. His very thoughts, unspoken, are endowed with immortal vigor and are the only real powers in history. God's "thoughts stand," as creation does, lasting on through all men's fleeting years. With reverent boldness, the Psalm parallels the processes (if we may so speak) of the divine mind with those of the human, "counsel" and "thoughts" being attributed to both. But how different are the solemn thoughts of God and those of men, insofar as they are not in accordance with his!

If this historical allusion is not recognized, the connection of these verses is somewhat obscure, but still discernible. The people who stand in special relation to God are blessed, because that eye, which sees all men, rests on them in steadfast love and with gracious purpose of special protection.

**33:13–17.** There is a wide all-seeingness, characterized by three words in an ascending scale of closeness of observance in vv. 13f. It is possible to God, being Creator. "He fashions their hearts individually," or "one by one...." seems the best interpretation of v. 15a, and then He is determined to mean his intimate knowledge of all his creatures' doings. The sudden turn to the impotence of earthly might, as illustrated by the king, hero and battle-horse, may be taken as intended to contrast the weakness of such strength both with the preceding picture of divine omniscience and might, and with the succeeding assurance of safety in Yahweh.

**33:18–22.** The true reason for the blessedness of the chosen people is that God's eye is on them, not merely with cold omniscience or with critical

| 19. | 3937, 5522.541<br>prep, v Hiphil inf con<br>לְהַצִּיל<br>lᵉhatstsîl<br>for his rescuing | 4623, 4323<br>prep, n ms<br>מִמָּוֶת<br>mimmāweth<br>from death | 5497<br>n fs, ps 3mp<br>נַפְשָׁם<br>naphshām<br>their soul | 3937, 2513.341<br>cj, v Piel inf con, ps 3mp<br>וּלְחַיּוֹתָם<br>ûlăchayyôthām<br>and to keep them alive | 904, 7743<br>prep, art, n ms<br>בָּרָעָב<br>bārā'āv<br>during the famine |
|---|---|---|---|---|---|

| 20. | 5497<br>n fs, ps 1cp<br>נַפְשֵׁנוּ<br>naphshēnû<br>our soul | 2542.312<br>v Piel pf 3fs<br>חִכְּתָה<br>chikkᵉthāh<br>it waits | 3937, 3176<br>prep, pn<br>לַיהוָה<br>layhwāh<br>for Yahweh | 6039<br>n ms, ps 1cp<br>עֶזְרֵנוּ<br>'ezrēnû<br>our Help | 4182<br>cj, n ms, ps 1cp<br>וּמָגִנֵּנוּ<br>ûmāghinnēnû<br>and our Shield | 2000<br>pers pron<br>הוּא<br>hû'<br>He | 21. | 3706, 904<br>cj, prep, ps 3ms<br>כִּי־בוֹ<br>kî-vô<br>because in Him |
|---|---|---|---|---|---|---|---|---|

| 7975.121<br>v Qal impf 3ms<br>יִשְׂמַח<br>yismach<br>it will be glad | 3949<br>n ms, ps 1cp<br>לִבֵּנוּ<br>libbēnû<br>our heart | 3706<br>cj<br>כִּי<br>kî<br>because | 904, 8428<br>prep, *n ms*<br>בְשֵׁם<br>vᵉshēm<br>in the name of | 7231<br>n ms, ps 3ms<br>קָדְשׁוֹ<br>qādhᵉshô<br>his holiness | 1019.119<br>v Qal pf 1cp<br>בָטָחְנוּ<br>vāṯachănû<br>we have trusted |
|---|---|---|---|---|---|

| 22. | 2030.121, 2721<br>v Qal juss 3ms, n ms, ps 2ms<br>יְהִי־חַסְדְּךָ<br>yᵉhî-chasdᵉkhā<br>may your steadfast love be | 3176<br>pn<br>יְהוָה<br>yᵉhwāh<br>O Yahweh | 6142<br>prep, ps 1cp<br>עָלֵינוּ<br>'ālênû<br>on us | 3626, 866<br>prep, rel part<br>כַּאֲשֶׁר<br>ka'ăsher<br>just as | 3282.319<br>v Piel pf 1cp<br>יִחַלְנוּ<br>yichalnû<br>we have waited | 3937<br>prep, ps 2ms<br>לָךְ<br>lākh<br>for You |
|---|---|---|---|---|---|---|

| 34:t | 3937, 1784<br>prep, pn<br>לְדָוִד<br>lᵉdhāwidh<br>of David | 904, 8521.341<br>prep, v Piel inf con, ps 3ms<br>בְּשַׁנּוֹתוֹ<br>bᵉshannôthô<br>during his changing | 881, 3051<br>do, n ms, ps 3ms<br>אֶת־טַעְמוֹ<br>'eth-ṯa'āmô<br>his senses | 3937, 6686<br>prep, *n mp*<br>לִפְנֵי<br>liphnê<br>before | 40<br>pn<br>אֲבִימֶלֶךְ<br>'ăvîmelekh<br>Abimelech | 1691.321<br>cj, v Piel impf 3ms, ps 3ms<br>וַיְגָרְשֵׁהוּ<br>waygharᵉshēhû<br>then he drove him out |
|---|---|---|---|---|---|---|

| 2050.121<br>cj, v Qal impf 3ms<br>וַיֵּלַךְ<br>wayyēlakh<br>and he went | 1. | 1313.325<br>v Piel juss 1cs<br>אֲבָרְכָה<br>'ăvārᵉkhāh<br>let me bless | 881, 3176<br>do, pn<br>אֶת־יְהוָה<br>'eth-yᵉhwāh<br>Yahweh | 904, 3725, 6496<br>prep, *adj*, n fs<br>בְּכָל־עֵת<br>bᵉkhol-'ēth<br>during all times | 8878<br>adv<br>תָּמִיד<br>tāmîdh<br>continually | 8747<br>n fs, ps 3ms<br>תְּהִלָּתוֹ<br>tᵉhillāthô<br>his praise | 904, 6552<br>prep, n ms, ps 1cs<br>בְּפִי<br>bᵉphî<br>in my mouth |
|---|---|---|---|---|---|---|---|

| 2. | 904, 3176<br>prep, pn<br>בַּיהוָה<br>bayhwāh<br>in Yahweh | 2054.722<br>v Hithpael impf 3fs<br>תִּתְהַלֵּל<br>tithhallēl<br>it will praise | 5497<br>n fs, ps 1cs<br>נַפְשִׁי<br>naphshî<br>my soul | 8471.126<br>v Qal juss 3mp<br>יִשְׁמְעוּ<br>yishmᵉ'û<br>let them hear | 6262<br>n mp<br>עֲנָוִים<br>'ănāwîm<br>the lowly | 7975.126<br>cj, v Qal juss 3mp<br>וְיִשְׂמָחוּ<br>wᵉyismāchû<br>and let them be glad |
|---|---|---|---|---|---|---|

| 3. | 1461.333<br>v Piel impv 2mp<br>גַּדְּלוּ<br>gaddᵉlû<br>declare great | 3937, 3176<br>prep, pn<br>לַיהוָה<br>layhwāh<br>Yahweh | 882<br>prep, ps 1cs<br>אִתִּי<br>'ittî<br>with me | 7597.320<br>cj, v Polel juss 1cp<br>וּנְרוֹמְמָה<br>ûnᵉrômᵉmāh<br>and let us exalt | 8428<br>n ms, ps 3ms<br>שְׁמוֹ<br>shᵉmô<br>his name | 3267<br>adv<br>יַחְדָּו<br>yachdāw<br>together | 4. | 1938.115<br>v Qal pf 1cs<br>דָּרַשְׁתִּי<br>dārashtî<br>I sought |
|---|---|---|---|---|---|---|---|---|

| 881, 3176<br>do, pn<br>אֶת־יְהוָה<br>'eth-yᵉhwāh<br>Yahweh | 6257.111<br>cj, v Qal pf 3ms, ps 1cs<br>וְעָנָנִי<br>wᵉ'ānānî<br>and He answered me | 4623, 3725, 4173<br>cj, prep, *adj*, n fp, ps 1cs<br>וּמִכָּל־מְגוּרוֹתַי<br>ûmikkol-mᵉghûrôthay<br>and from all my fears | 5522.511<br>v Hiphil pf 3ms, ps 1cs<br>הִצִּילָנִי<br>hitstsîlānî<br>He rescued me | 5. | 5202.516<br>v Hiphil pf 3cp<br>הִבִּיטוּ<br>hibbîṯû<br>they looked |
|---|---|---|---|---|---|

| 420<br>prep, ps 3ms<br>אֵלָיו<br>'ēlâv<br>to Him | 5281.116<br>cj, v Qal pf 3cp<br>וְנָהָרוּ<br>wᵉnāhārû<br>and they were radiant | 6686<br>cj, n mp, ps 3mp<br>וּפְנֵיהֶם<br>ûphᵉnêhem<br>and their faces | 414, 2763.126<br>adv, v Qal juss 3mp<br>אַל־יֶחְפָּרוּ<br>'al-yechăppārû<br>may they not be downcast | 6. | 2172<br>dem pron<br>זֶה<br>zeh<br>this |
|---|---|---|---|---|---|

**that hope in his mercy:** ... Those who wait for his goodness, *Goodspeed* ... towards those who hope for his unfailing love, *NEB* ... those who rely on his faithful love, *JB* ... on those who revere Him, *Berkeley.*

**19. To deliver their soul from death, and to keep them alive in famine:** ... that he may rescue them from death, *Moffatt* ... and to keep them living in time of need, *BB* ... and spares their lives in times of hunger, *NCV* ... and preserve them in spite of famine, *NAB.*

**20. Our soul waiteth for the LORD: he is our help and our shield:** ... We wait in hope for the LORD, *NIV* ... Our souls therefore cling to the LORD, *Fenton* ... Patiently we wait for the Lord's help, *Knox* ... our warrior, our shield is he, *Anchor.*

**21. For our heart shall rejoice in him, because we have trusted in his holy name:** ... For in him our hearts are glad, *NEB* ... Yes, our hearts delight in Him, *Beck* ... Our heart is glad in him, *NRSV* ... in his holy name is our hope, *BB.*

**22. Let thy mercy, O LORD, be upon us, according as we hope in thee:** ... May your unfailing love rest upon us, *NIV* ... May your kindness, O LORD, be upon us, *NAB* ... LORD, show your love to us, *NCV* ... let your faithful love rest on us, as our hope has rested in you, *JB.*

**34:t. A Psalm of David, when he changed his behaviour before Abimelech; who drove him away, and he departed.**

**1. I will bless the LORD at all times: his praise shall continually be in my mouth:** ... His praise is constantly in my mouth, *Goodspeed* ... I will bless the LORD continually, *NEB* ... I will extol the LORD at all times; his praise will always be on my lips, *NIV.*

**2. My soul shall make her boast in the LORD: the humble shall hear thereof, and be glad:** ... In the LORD I shall glory, *REB* ... The patient oppressed-ones shall hear and be glad, *Rotherham* ... My whole being praises the LORD. The poor will hear, *NCV* ... the meek shall hear, and rejoice, *Darby.*

**3. O magnify the LORD with me, and let us exalt his name together:** ... Come, sing the Lord's praise with me, let us extol, *Knox* ... And in union proclaiming His NAME, *Fenton* ... Glorify the LORD with me, *NAB* ... let us be witnesses together of his great name, *BB.*

**4. I sought the LORD, and he heard me, and delivered me from all my fears:** ... He answered me, and freed me from all my fears, *Berkeley* ... and rescued me from everything I dreaded, *Beck* ... from all my terrors he rescued me, *Anchor.*

**5. They looked unto him, and were lightened: and their faces were not ashamed:** ... Look to him, and be

---

consideration of their works, but with the direct purpose of sheltering them from surrounding evil. The stress of the characterization of these guarded and nourished favorites of heaven is now laid not upon a divine act of choice, but upon their looking to Him. His eye meets with love the upturned patient eye of humble expectation and loving fear.

What should be the issue of such thoughts, but the glad profession of trust, with which the Psalm fittingly ends, corresponding to the invocation to praise which began it! Once, in each of these three closing verses, do the speakers profess their dependence on God. The attitude of waiting with fixed hope and patient submission is the characteristic of God's true servants in all ages. In it are blended consciousness of weakness and vulnerability, dread of assault, reliance on divine love, confidence of safety, patience, submission and strong aspiration.

***Psalm 34.*** *The occasion of this Psalm, according to the superscription, was that humiliating episode when David pretended insanity to save his life from the ruler of Goliath's city of Gath.*

*The course of thought is obvious. There is first a vow of praise in which others are summoned to unite (vv. 1ff); then follows a section in which personal experience and invocation to others are similarly blended (vv. 4-10); and finally a purely didactic section, analyzing the practical manifestations of "the fear of the LORD" and enforcing it by the familiar contrast of the blessedness of the righteous and the miserable fate of the ungodly. Throughout, we find familiar turns of thought and expression, such as are usual in acrostic Psalms.*

**34:1–3.** The solitary heart hungers for sympathy in its joy, as in its sorrow, but knows full well that such can only be given by those who have known like bitterness and have learned submission in the same way. We must be purged of self in order to be glad in another's deliverance, and we must be pupils in the same school in order to be entitled to take his experience as our encouragement and to make a chorus to his solo of thanksgiving. The invocation is so natural an expression of the instinctive desire for companionship in praise that one needs not to look for any particular group to whom it is addressed. The call is appropriate in the mouth of David, the leader of his band of devoted followers.

**34:4–6.** The second section of the Psalm (vv. 4–10) is at first biographical, and then it generalizes personal experience into broad universal truth.

| 6270 | 7410.111 | 3176 | 8471.111 | 4623, 3725, 7150 | 3588.511 |
|---|---|---|---|---|---|
| n ms | v Qal pf 3ms | cj, pn | v Qal pf 3ms | cj, prep, *adj*, n fp, ps 3ms | v Hiphil pf 3ms, ps 3ms |
| עָנִי | קָרָא | וַיהוָה | שָׁמֵעַ | וּמִכָּל־צָרוֹתָיו | הוֹשִׁיעוֹ |
| ‘ānî | qārā' | wayhwāh | shāmēa‘ | ûmikkol-tsārôthâv | hôshî‘ô |
| the afflicted | he called | and Yahweh | He heard | and from all his trouble | He saved him |

| 7. | 2684.151 | 4534, 3176 | 5623 | 3937, 3486.152 |
|---|---|---|---|---|
| | v Qal act ptc ms | *n ms*, pn | adv | prep, v Qal act ptc mp, ps 3ms |
| | חֹנֶה | מַלְאַךְ־יְהוָה | סָבִיב | לִירֵאָיו |
| | chōneh | mal'akh-yehwāh | sāvîv | lîrē'âv |
| | encamping | the angels of Yahweh | all around | to those who fear Him |

| 2603.321 | 8. | 3049.133 | 7495.133 | 3706, 3005 | 3176 | 869 | 1429 |
|---|---|---|---|---|---|---|---|
| cj, v Piel impf 3ms, ps 3mp | | v Qal impv 2mp | cj, v Qal impv 2mp | cj, adj | pn | *n ms* | art, n ms |
| וַיְחַלְּצֵם | | טַעֲמוּ | וּרְאוּ | כִּי־טוֹב | יְהוָה | אַשְׁרֵי | הַגֶּבֶר |
| waychallетsēm | | ta‘ămû | ûre'û | kî-tôv | yehwāh | 'ashrê | haggever |
| and He sets them apart | | perceive | and see | that good | Yahweh | blessed | the man |

| 2725.121, 904 | 9. | 3486.133 | 881, 3176 | 7202 | 3706, 375 | 4408 |
|---|---|---|---|---|---|---|
| v Qal impf 3ms, prep, ps 3ms | | v Qal impv 2mp | do, pn | n mp, ps 3ms | cj, *sub* | n ms |
| יֶחֱסֶה־בּוֹ | | יְראוּ | אֶת־יְהוָה | קְדֹשָׁיו | כִּי־אֵין | מַחְסוֹר |
| yechĕseh-bô | | yer'û | 'eth-yehwāh | qōdhōshâv | kî-'ên | machsôr |
| he takes refuge in Him | | fear | Yahweh | his holy ones | because there is not | lack |

| 3937, 3486.152 | 10. | 3841 | 7609.116 | 7742.116 |
|---|---|---|---|---|
| prep, v Qal act ptc mp, ps 3ms | | n mp | v Qal pf 3cp | cj, v Qal pf 3cp |
| לִירֵאָיו | | כְּפִירִים | רָשׁוּ | וְרָעֵבוּ |
| lîrē'âv | | kephîrîm | rāshû | werā‘ēvû |
| to those who fear Him | | young lions | they are in want | and they are hungry |

| 1938.152 | 3176 | 3940, 2742.126 | 3725, 3008 | 11. | 2050.133, 1158 |
|---|---|---|---|---|---|
| cj, *v Qal act ptc mp* | pn | neg part, v Qal impf 3mp | *adj*, n ms | | v Qal impv 2mp, n mp |
| וְדֹרְשֵׁי | יְהוָה | לֹא־יַחְסְרוּ | כָל־טוֹב | | לְכוּ־בָנִים |
| wedhōreshê | yehwāh | lō'-yachserû | khol-tôv | | lekhû-vānîm |
| but those who seek | Yahweh | they will not lack | any good thing | | come O children |

| 8471.133, 3937 | 3488 | 3176 | 4064.325 | 12. | 4449, 382 | 2760 |
|---|---|---|---|---|---|---|
| v Qal impv 2mp, prep, ps 1cs | *n fs* | pn | v Piel juss 1cs, ps 2mp | | intrg, art, n ms | art, adj |
| שִׁמְעוּ־לִי | יִרְאַת | יְהוָה | אֲלַמֶּדְכֶם | | מִי־הָאִישׁ | הֶחָפֵץ |
| shim‘û-lî | yir'ath | yehwāh | 'ălammedhkhem | | mî-hā'îsh | hechāphēts |
| listen to me | the fear of | Yahweh | let me teach you | | who the man | the desirous |

| 2522 | 154.151 | 3219 | 3937, 7495.141 | 3005 | 13. | 5526.131 | 4098 | 4623, 7737 |
|---|---|---|---|---|---|---|---|---|
| n mp | v Qal act ptc ms | n mp | prep, v Qal inf con | adj | | v Qal impv 2ms | n fs, ps 2ms | prep, n ms |
| חַיִּים | אֹהֵב | יָמִים | לִרְאוֹת | טוֹב | | נְצֹר | לְשׁוֹנְךָ | מֵרָע |
| chayyîm | 'ōhēv | yāmîm | lir'ôth | tôv | | netsōr | leshônkhā | mērā‘ |
| life | one who loves | days | to see | good | | guard | your tongue | from evil |

radiant, *RSV* … look to him, and you shall beam with joy, *Moffatt* … Ever look to him, and in him find happiness, *Knox* … Let your eyes be turned to him and you will have light, *BB*.

**6. This poor man cried, and the LORD heard him:** … When the afflicted man called out, *NAB* … Here was a poor wretch who cried to the LORD, *NEB* … This oppressed one cried, and Yahweh heard, *Rotherham* … A pauper calls out and Yahweh hears, *JB*.

**and saved him out of all his troubles:** … and was saved from every trouble, *NRSV* … And from all his distresses saved him, *Young* … and be rescued from all their afflictions, *Knox* … and from all his anguish he saved him, *Anchor*.

**7. The angel of the LORD encampeth round about them that fear him, and delivereth them:** … And rescues them, *NASB* … And He armeth them, *Young* … those who fear God, and he saves them, *NCV* … to keep them safe, *BB*.

**8. O taste and see that the Lord is good: blessed is the man that trusteth in him:** ... Taste and drink deeply, for Yahweh is sweet, *Anchor* ... blessed is the man who takes refuge in him, *NIV* ... happy the man who takes refuge, *NCB* ... happy is the man who has faith in him, *BB* ... who takes shelter with him!, *Moffatt.*

**9. O fear the Lord, ye his saints: for there is no want to them that fear him:** ... all you his holy people; for those who fear him lack nothing, *NEB* ... fear Him, and you will lack nothing, *Beck* ... there is no lack to those who revere Him, *Berkeley* ... For none who fear Him are in need, *Fenton.*

**10. The young lions do lack, and suffer hunger:** ... The great grow poor and hungry, *NAB* ... Young lions have come short, and suffered hunger, *Rotherham* ... may go needy and hungry, *JB* ... Justly do the proud fall into hunger and want, *Knox.*

**but they that seek the Lord shall not want any good thing:** ... but those who look to the Lord will have every good thing, *NCV* ... will lack no blessing, *Anchor* ... shall not lack any good thing, *NKJV.*

**11. Come, ye children, hearken unto me: I will teach you the fear of the Lord:** ... Come, children, listen to me, *Anchor* ... hear me, *NAB* ... Come, sons and daughters, *Berkeley* ... The reverence of Yahweh will I teach you, *Rotherham.*

**12. What man is he that desireth life, and loveth many days, that he may see good?:** ... and takes delight in prosperous days, *NCB* ... You must do these things to enjoy life and have many happy days, *NCV* ... and desires a long life to enjoy all good things, *NEB* ... And loves length of days, *NASB.*

**13. Keep thy tongue from evil, and thy lips from speaking guile:** ... Then stop talking evil and saying deceitful things, *Beck* ... keep your lips from deceit, *Moffatt* ... and thy lips free from every treacherous word, *Knox* ... from speaking falsely, *KJVII.*

**14. Depart from evil, and do good; seek peace, and pursue it:** ... Turn aside from evil, *Young* ... Turn from insult and do what is kind, *Fenton* ... make a search for peace, desiring it with all your heart, *BB* ... turn away from evil and practice good; seek peace and keep after it, *Berkeley.*

---

Verses 4f are a pair, as are vv. 6f, and in each the same fact is narrated first in reference to the single soul and then in regard to all the servants of Yahweh. "This poor man" is taken to be the psalmist, even though some have supposed it is an individualized way of saying "poor men." The former explanation seems the more natural, preserving the parallelism between the two groups of verses. To "look unto him" is the same thing as is expressed in the individualized verses by the two phrases "sought" and "cried unto," only the metaphor is changed into that of the silent, wistful directing of beseeching and sad eyes to God. Whoever turns his face to Yahweh will receive reflected brightness on his face, as when a mirror is directed sunwards, the dark surface will flash into sudden glory. Weary eyes will gleam. Faces turned to the sun are sure to be radiant.

**34:7.** Davidic authorship gives special force to the great assurance of v. 7. The fugitive, in his rude shelter in the cave of Adullam, perhaps thinks of Jacob, who, in his hour of defenseless need, was heartened by the vision of the angel encampment surrounding his own little band and named the place Mahanaim, "the two camps." That fleeting vision was a temporary manifestation of abiding reality. Wherever there is a camp of them that fear God, there is another, of which the helmed and sworded angel that appeared to Joshua is captain, and the name of every such place is Two Camps.

**38:8–10.** Faith, consecration and aspiration are their marks. These are the essentials of the religious life, regardless of the degree of revelation. These were its essentials in the psalmist's time, and they are so today. The consequent blessings are as abiding as these. These may all be summed up in one—the satisfaction of every need and desire. There are two ways of seeking for satisfaction: that of effort, violence and reliance on one's own teeth and claws to get one's meat; the other of patient, submissive trust. They that "seek Yahweh" shall assuredly find Him, and in Him everything. He is multiform, and his goodness takes many shapes, according to the curves of the vessels which it fills. "Seek ye first the kingdom of God ... and all these things shall be added unto you" (Matt. 6:33).

**34:11–14.** The mention of the "fear of the Lord" prepares the way for the transition to the third part of the Psalm. It is purely didactic, and, in its simple moral teaching and familiar contrast of the fates of the righteous and ungodly, it has affinities with the Book of Proverbs; but these are not so special as to require the supposition of contemporaneity. It is unfashionable now to lean toward the Davidic authorship, but would not the supposition that the "children" (who are to be taught the elements of religion) are the band of outlaws who have gathered around the fugitive give appropriateness to the transition from the thanksgiving of the first part

| 8004 | 4623, 1744.341 | 4983 | | 5681.131 | 4623, 7737 | 6449.131, 3008 |
|---|---|---|---|---|---|---|
| cj, n fd, ps 2ms | prep, v Piel inf con | n fs | | v Qal impv 2ms | prep, n ms | cj, v Qal impv 2ms, n ms |
| וּשְׂפָתֶיךָ | מִדַּבֵּר | מִרְמָה | **14.** | סוּר | מֵרָע | וַעֲשֵׂה־טוֹב |
| ûsᵉphāthêkhā | middabbēr | mirmāh | | s̱ûr | mērā' | wa'ăsēh-ṭôv |
| and your lips | from speaking | deceit | | turn aside | from evil | and do what is good |

| 1272.331 | 8361 | 7579.131 | | 6084 | 3176 | 420, 6926 |
|---|---|---|---|---|---|---|
| v Piel impv 2ms | n ms | cj, v Qal impv 2ms, ps 3ms | | *n fd* | pn | prep, n mp |
| בַּקֵּשׁ | שָׁלוֹם | וְרָדְפֵהוּ | **15.** | עֵינֵי | יְהוָה | אֶל־צַדִּיקִים |
| baqqēsh | shālôm | wᵉrādhᵉphēhû | | 'ênê | yᵉhwāh | 'el-tsaddîqîm |
| seek | peace | and pursue it | | the eyes of | Yahweh | toward the righteous |

| 238 | 420, 8216 | | 6686 | 3176 | 904, 6449.152 | 7737 |
|---|---|---|---|---|---|---|
| cj, n fd, ps 3ms | prep, n fs, ps 3mp | | *n mp* | pn | prep, *v Qal act ptc mp* | n ms |
| וְאָזְנָיו | אֶל־שַׁוְעָתָם | **16.** | פְּנֵי | יְהוָה | בְּעֹשֵׂי | רָע |
| wᵉ'āzᵉnâv | 'el-shaw'āthām | | pᵉnê | yᵉhwāh | bᵉ'ōsê | rā' |
| and his ears | toward their cry for help | | the face of | Yahweh | on those who do | evil |

| 3937, 3901.541 | 4623, 800 | 2228 | | 7094.116 | 3176 |
|---|---|---|---|---|---|
| prep, v Hiphil inf con | prep, n fs | n ms, ps 3mp | | v Qal pf 3cp | cj, pn |
| לְהַכְרִית | מֵאֶרֶץ | זִכְרָם | **17.** | צָעֲקוּ | וַיהוָה |
| lᵉhakhrîth | mē'erets | zikhrām | | tsā'ăqû | wayhwāh |
| to cut off | from the earth | their memory | | they have cried for help | and Yahweh |

| 8471.111 | 4623, 3725, 7150 | 5522.511 | | 7427 | 3176 |
|---|---|---|---|---|---|
| v Qal pf 3ms | cj, prep, *adj*, n fp, ps 3mp | v Hiphil pf 3ms, ps 3mp | | adj | pn |
| שָׁמֵעַ | וּמִכָּל־צָרוֹתָם | הִצִּילָם | **18.** | קָרוֹב | יְהוָה |
| shāmēa' | ûmikkol-tsārôthām | hitstsîlām | | qārôv | yᵉhwāh |
| He heard | and from all their troubles | and He rescues them | | near | Yahweh |

| 3937, 8132.256, 3949 | 881, 1851, 7593 | 3588.521 | | 7521 | 7750 |
|---|---|---|---|---|---|
| prep, *v Niphal ptc mp*, n ms | cj, do, *n mp*, n fs | v Hiphil impf 3ms | | adj | *n fp* |
| לְנִשְׁבְּרֵי־לֵב | וְאֶת־דַּכְּאֵי־רוּחַ | יוֹשִׁיעַ | **19.** | רַבּוֹת | רָעוֹת |
| lᵉnishbᵉrê-lēv | wᵉ'eth-dakkᵉ'ê-rûach | yôshîa' | | rabbôth | rā'ôth |
| to those broken of heart | and the crushed of spirit | He saves | | many | the troubles of |

| 6926 | 4623, 3725 | 5522.521 | 3176 | | 8490.151 |
|---|---|---|---|---|---|
| n ms | cj, prep, adj, ps 3mp | v Hiphil impf 3ms, ps 3ms | pn | | v Qal act ptc ms |
| צַדִּיק | וּמִכֻּלָּם | יַצִּילֶנּוּ | יְהוָה | **20.** | שֹׁמֵר |
| tsaddîq | ûmikkullām | yatstsîlennû | yᵉhwāh | | shōmēr |
| the righteous | but from all of them | He rescues him | Yahweh | | guarding |

| 3725, 6344 | 259 | 4623, 2078 | 3940 | 8132.212 | | 4322.322 | 7857 |
|---|---|---|---|---|---|---|---|
| *adj*, n fp, ps 3ms | num | prep, pers pron | neg part | v Niphal pf 3fs | | v Polel impf 3fs | n ms |
| כָּל־עַצְמוֹתָיו | אַחַת | מֵהֵנָּה | לֹא | נִשְׁבָּרָה | **21.** | תְּמוֹתֵת | רָשָׁע |
| kol-'atsmôthâv | 'achath | mēhēnnāh | lō' | nishbārāh | | tᵉmôthēth | rāshā' |
| all his bones | one | of them | not | it will be broken | | it slaughters | the wicked |

| 7750 | 7983.152 | 6926 | 843.126 | | 6540.151 | 3176 |
|---|---|---|---|---|---|---|
| n fs | cj, *v Qal act ptc mp* | n ms | v Qal impf 3mp | | v Qal act ptc ms | pn |
| רָעָה | וְשֹׂנְאֵי | צַדִּיק | יֶאְשָׁמוּ | **22.** | פּוֹדֶה | יְהוָה |
| rā'āh | wᵉsōnᵉ'ê | tsaddîq | ye'ăshāmû | | pôdheh | yᵉhwāh |
| evil | and those who hate | the righteous | they will be guilty | | One Who ransoms | Yahweh |

| 5497 | 5860 | 3940 | 843.126 | 3725, 2725.152 | 904 |
|---|---|---|---|---|---|
| *n fs* | n mp, ps 3ms | cj, neg part | v Qal impf 3mp | adj, art, v Qal act ptc mp | prep, ps 3ms |
| נֶפֶשׁ | עֲבָדָיו | וְלֹא | יֶאְשְׁמוּ | כָּל־הַחֹסִים | בּוֹ |
| nephesh | 'ăvādhâv | wᵉlō' | ye'ăshmû | kol-hachōs̱îm | bô |
| the soul of | his servants | and not | they will be guilty | all those taking refuge | in Him |

**15. The eyes of the LORD are upon the righteous, and his ears are open unto their cry:** ... The eyes of Yahweh are on the just, *Anchor* ... and his ears are toward their cry, *Darby* ... The LORD has eyes for the just, and ears for their cry, *NAB* ... and his ears are attentive to their cry, *NIV.*

**16. The face of the LORD is against them that do evil, to cut off the remembrance of them from the earth:** ... The Lord confronts the evildoers, *NCB* ... and he will wipe out all memory of them, *Beck* ... The LORD rejects doers of wrong, *Fenton* ... to root up their memory from off the earth, *Berkeley.*

**17. The righteous cry, and the LORD heareth, and delivereth them out of all their troubles:** ... The cry of the upright comes before the Lord, *BB* ... They cry in anguish and Yahweh hears, *JB* ... The LORD hears good people when they cry out to him, *NCV* ... and from all their distress he rescues them, *NAB.*

**18. The LORD is nigh unto them that are of a broken heart; and saveth such as be of a contrite spirit:** ... The LORD is close to those whose courage is broken, *REB* ... So near is he to patient hearts, *Knox* ... and saves those who are of a humble spirit, *KJVII* ... And saves those who are crushed in spirit, *NASB.*

**19. Many are the afflictions of the righteous: but the LORD delivereth him out of them all:** ... The good man's misfortunes may be many, *NEB* ... Great are the troubles of the righteous, *Geneva* ... Many are the ills of the righteous, *Goodspeed* ... but the LORD rescues them from them all, *NRSV.*

**20. He keepeth all his bones: not one of them is broken:** ... and protects every bone in you, *Beck* ... He guards all his bones, *NKJV* ... He watches over all his bones, *Anchor* ... And provides that not one of them break, *Fenton.*

**21. Evil shall slay the wicked: and they that hate the righteous shall be desolate:** ... Evil will put an end to the sinner, *BB* ... Calamity shall slay the wicked, *Berkeley* ... And they that hate the righteous shall be held guilty, *MAST* ... and the enemies of the just pay for their guilt, *NCB.*

**22. The LORD redeemeth the soul of his servants: and none of them that trust in him shall be desolate:** ... and none of them that trust in him shall bear guilt, *Darby* ... that trust in him shall be condemned, *MRB* ... and no punishment befalls those who

---

to the didactic tone of the second? The psalmist's belief that doing good was the sure way to enjoy good was a commonplace of OT teaching. Unquestionable goodness, in the sense of blessedness, is inseparable from good in the sense of righteousness, as evil which is suffering is from evil which is sin, but the conception of what constitutes blessedness and sorrow must be modified so as to throw most weight on inward experiences.

**34:15–16.** The remainder of the Psalm runs out into a detailed description of the joyful fate of the lovers of good, broken only by one tragic verse (v. 21), like a black rock in the midst of a sunny stream, telling how evil and evildoers end. In v. 17, as in v. 5, the verb has no subject expressed, but the supplement of "the righteous" is naturally drawn from the context and is found in the Septuagint. Whether this is part of the original text, or a supplement, is unknown. The construction may, as in v. 6, indicate that whoever cries to Yahweh is heard. Some propose to transpose vv. 15f to get a nearer subject for the verb in the "righteous" of v. 15, and defend the inversion by referring to the alphabetic order in Lam. 2ff, where similarly "pe" precedes "ayin"; but the present order of verses is better at putting the principal theme of this part of the Psalm—the blessedness of the righteous—in the foreground, and the opposite thought as its foil.

**34:17–20.** The main thought of vv. 17–20 is the experience of vv. 4–7 thrown into the form of general maxims. They are the commonplaces of religion but come with strange freshness to a man when they have been verified in his life. Happy are they who can cast their personal experience into such proverbial sayings and, having by faith individualized the general promises, can re-generalize the individual experience! The psalmist does not promise untroubled, outward good. His anticipation is of troubled lives, delivered because of crying to Yahweh. "Many are the afflictions," but more are the deliverances. Many are the blows, and painful is the pressure, but they break no bones, although they rack and wrench the frame. Significant, too, is the sequence of synonyms—righteous, brokenhearted, crushed in spirit, servants, them that take refuge in Yahweh. The first of these refers mainly to conduct, and the second to that submission of will and spirit which sorrow rightly borne brings about, substantially equivalent to "the humble" or "afflicted" of vv. 2 and 6. The third again deals mostly with practice, and the last touches the foundation of all service, submission and righteousness, as laid in the act of faith in Yahweh.

**34:21–22.** The last group of vv. 21f puts the teaching of the Psalm in one terrible contrast, "Evil shall slay the wicked." It would be a mere platitude

| 35:t | 3937, 1784 | | 7662.131 | 3176 | 881, 3516 | 4032.131 |
|---|---|---|---|---|---|---|
| | prep, pn | 1. | v Qal impv 2ms | pn | do, n mp, ps 1cs | v Qal impv 2ms |
| | לְדָוִד | | רִיבָה | יְהוָה | אֶת־יְרִיבַי | לְחַם |
| | ledhāwidh | | rîvāh | yehwāh | 'eth-yerîvay | lecham |
| | of David | | contend | O Yahweh | those who contend against me | fight against |

| 881, 4032.152 | | 2480.531 | 4182 | 7065 | 7251.131 |
|---|---|---|---|---|---|
| do, v Qal act ptc mp, ps 1cs | 2. | v Hiphil impv 2ms | n ms | cj, n fs | cj, v Qal impv 2ms |
| אֶת־לֹחֲמָי | | הַחֲזֵק | מָגֵן | וְצִנָּה | וְקוּמָה |
| 'eth-lōchāmāy | | hachzēq | māghēn | wetsinnāh | weqûmāh |
| those who fight against me | | take hold of | a shield | and a large shield | and rise |

| 904, 6046 | | 7671.531 | 2698 | 5646.141 | 3937, 7410.141 |
|---|---|---|---|---|---|
| prep, n fs, ps 1cs | 3. | cj, v Hiphil impv 2ms | n fs | cj, v Qal inf con | prep, v Qal inf con |
| בְּעֶזְרָתִי | | וְהָרֵק | חֲנִית | וּסְגֹר | לִקְרַאת |
| be'ezrāthî | | wehārēq | chănîth | ûseghōr | liqŏra'th |
| as my help | | and draw out | the spear | when closing off | to meet |

| 7579.152 | 569.131 | 3937, 5497 | 3568 | 603 | | 991.126 |
|---|---|---|---|---|---|---|
| v Qal act ptc mp, ps 1cs | v Qal impv 2ms | prep, n fs, ps 1cs | n fs, ps 2fs | pers pron | 4. | v Qal juss 3mp |
| רֹדְפָי | אֱמֹר | לְנַפְשִׁי | יְשֻׁעָתֵךְ | אָנִי | | יֵבֹשׁוּ |
| rōdhephāy | 'ĕmōr | lenaphshî | yeshu'āthēkh | 'ānî | | yēvōshû |
| my pursuers | say | to my soul | your salvation | I | | may they be ashamed |

| 3757.226 | 1272.352 | 5497 | 5657.226 | 268 |
|---|---|---|---|---|
| cj, v Niphal juss 3mp | *v Piel ptc mp* | n fs, ps 1cs | v Niphal juss 3mp | adv |
| וְיִכָּלְמוּ | מְבַקְשֵׁי | נַפְשִׁי | יִסֹּגוּ | אָחוֹר |
| weyikkālemû | mevaqŏshê | naphshî | yissōghû | 'āchôr |
| and let them be dishonored | those who seek | my soul | and let them retreat | back |

| 2763.126 | 2913.152 | 7750 | | 2030.126 | 3626, 4833 |
|---|---|---|---|---|---|
| cj, v Qal juss 3mp | *v Qal act ptc mp* | n fs, ps 1cs | 5. | v Qal juss 3mp | prep, n ms |
| וְיַחְפְּרוּ | חֹשְׁבֵי | רָעָתִי | | יִהְיוּ | כְּמֹץ |
| weyachperû | chōshevê | rā'āthî | | yihyû | kemōts |
| and let them be ashamed | those who devise | my disaster | | may they be | like chaff |

| 3937, 6686, 7593 | 4534 | 3176 | 1815.151 | | 2030.121, 1932 | 2932 |
|---|---|---|---|---|---|---|
| prep, *n mp*, n fs | cj, *n ms* | pn | v Qal act ptc ms | 6. | v Qal juss 3ms, n ms, ps 3mp | n ms |
| לִפְנֵי־רוּחַ | וּמַלְאַךְ | יְהוָה | דּוֹחֶה | | יְהִי־דַרְכָּם | חֹשֶׁךְ |
| liphnê-rûach | ûmal'akh | yehwāh | dôcheh | | yehî-dharkām | chōshekh |
| before the wind | and the Angel of | Yahweh | pushing | | may their way be | darkness |

| 2620 | 4534 | 3176 | 7579.151 | | 3706, 2703 |
|---|---|---|---|---|---|
| cj, n fp | cj, *n ms* | pn | v Qal act ptc ms, ps 3mp | 7. | cj, adv |
| וַחֲלַקְלַקּוֹת | וּמַלְאַךְ | יְהוָה | רֹדְפָם | | כִּי־חִנָּם |
| wachlaqŏlaqqôth | ûmal'akh | yehwāh | rōdhephām | | kî-chinnām |
| and slippery places | and the Angel of | Yahweh | and pursuing them | | because without cause |

seek refuge in him, *REB* … and there will be no penalty, *JB.*

**35:t. A Psalm of David.**

**1. Plead my cause, O LORD, with them that strive with me: fight against them that fight against me:** … Accuse my accusers, Yahweh, attack my attackers, *JB* … be at war with those who make war against me, *BB.*

**2. Take hold of shield and buckler, and stand up for mine help:** … Pick up the shield and armor, *NCV* … rise up to help me, *NRSV* … stand up as my champion, *Moffatt.*

**3. Draw out also the spear, and stop the way against them that persecute me:** … Couch the spear, and close in with my hunters, *Fenton* … Draw the spear and javelin against my pursuers, *RSV* … spear and step in to encounter my pursuers, *Berkeley* … spear and javelin to meet those hunting me down, *Beck.*

**say unto my soul, I am thy salvation:** ... whisper in my heart, I am here to save thee, *Knox* ... Let me hear you declare, *REB* ... I am thy deliverance, *Goodspeed* ... I am your victory, *Anchor.*

**4. Let them be confounded and put to shame that seek after my soul:** ... Shame and humiliation on those who are out to kill me!, *JB* ... put to shame and brought to dishonor Who seek after my life, *NKJV.*

**let them be turned back and brought to confusion that devise my hurt:** ... plan my downfall retreat, *REB* ... who devise evil against me, *NASB* ... and may those who plan to hurt me retreat in dismay, *NEB* ... may those who plot my ruin be turned back in dismay, *NIV.*

**5. Let them be as chaff before the wind: and let the angel of the LORD chase them:** ... Let them be like dust from the grain before the wind, *BB* ... And the angel of the LORD driving them on, *MRB* ... angel of the Lord to scatter them, *Knox* ... angel of the LORD forces them away, *NCV.*

**6. Let their way be dark and slippery: and let the angel of the LORD persecute them:** ... Let their path be pitch-dark and most slippery, *Berkeley* ... Let their destiny be Darkness and Destruction, *Anchor* ... With the angel of the LORD pursuing them, *NASB.*

---

if "evil" meant misfortune. The same thought of the inseparable connection of the two senses of that word, which runs through the context, is expressed here in the most terse fashion. To do evil is to suffer evil, and all sin is suicide. Its wages is death. Every sin is a strand in the hangman's rope, which the sinner nooses and puts round his own neck. That is so because every sin brings guilt, and guilt brings retribution. The meaning in vv. 21f is much more than "desolate" (HED #843). The word means "to be condemned or held guilty." Yahweh is the Judge; before his bar, all actions and characters are set. His unerring estimate of each brings with it, here and now, consequences of reward and punishment which prophesy a future, more perfect judgment. The redemption of the soul of God's servants is the antithesis to that awful experience, and they only, who take refuge in Him, escape it. The full Christian significance of this final contrast is in the Apostle's words, "There is therefore now no condemnation to them which are in Christ Jesus" (Rom. 8:1).

***Psalm 35.*** *The psalmist's life is in danger. He is the victim of ungrateful hatred. False accusations of crimes that he never dreamed of are brought against him. He professes innocence and appeals to Yahweh to be his Advocate and also his Judge. The prayer in v. 1a uses the same word and metaphor as David does in his remonstrance with Saul (1 Sam. 24:15).*

**35:1–3.** The most striking features of the first part are the boldness of the appeal to Yahweh to fight for the psalmist and the terrible imprecations and magnificent picture in vv. 5f. The relation between the two petitions of v. 1, "Plead with them that strive with me" and "fight against them that fight against me," may be variously determined. Both may be figurative, the former drawn from legal processes and the latter from the battlefield. But more likely, the psalmist was really the object of armed attack, and the "fighting" was a grim reality. The two defensive weapons are probably matched by two offensive ones in v. 3. The ordinary translation gives a satisfactory sense, but the other is more in accordance with the following preposition, with the accents and with the parallelism of target and shield. In either case, how beautifully the spiritual reality breaks through the warlike metaphor! This armed Yahweh, grasping shield and drawing spear, utters no battle shout, but whispers consolation to the trembling man crouching behind his shield. The outward side of the divine activity, turned to the foe, is martial and menacing; the inner side is full of tender, secret breathings of comfort and love.

**35:4–6.** When all considerations are taken into account, these prayers against enemies remain distinctly inferior to the code of Christian ethics. The more frankly the fact is recognized, the better. But, if we turn from the moral to the poetic side of these verses, what stern beauty there is in that awful picture of the fleeing foe, with the angel of Yahweh pressing hand on their broken ranks! The hope which has been embodied in the legends of many nations, that the gods were seen fighting for their worshipers, is the psalmist's faith and in its essence is ever true. That angel, whom we heard of in the previous Psalm as defending the defenseless encampment of them that fear Yahweh, fights with and scatters the enemies like chaff before the wind. One more touch of terror is added in that picture of flight in the dark, on a slippery path, with the celestial avenger close on the fugitives' heels, as when the Amorite kings fled down the pass of Beth-Horon, and "Yahweh cast down great stones from heaven upon them" (Josh. 10:11). Aeschylus or Dante has nothing more concentrated or suggestive of terror and beauty than this picture.

| 3045.116, 3937 | 8273 | 7862 | 2703 | 2763.116 | 3937, 5497 |
|---|---|---|---|---|---|
| v Qal pf 3cp, prep, ps 1cs | n fs | n fs, ps 3mp | adv | v Qal pf 3cp | prep, n fs, ps 1cs |
| טָמְנוּ־לִי | שַׁחַת | רִשְׁתָּם | חִנָּם | חָפְרוּ | לְנַפְשִׁי |
| ṭāmᵉnû-lî | shachath | rishtām | chinnām | chāphᵉrû | lᵉnaphshî |
| they hid for me | a pit | their net | without cause | they dug | for my life |

| 8. | 971.122 | 8177 | 3940, 3156.121 | 7862 | 866, 3045.111 |
|---|---|---|---|---|---|
| | v Qal juss 3fs, ps 3ms | n fs | neg part, v Qal impf 3ms | cj, n fs, ps 3ms | rel part, v Qal pf 3ms |
| | תְּבוֹאֵהוּ | שׁוֹאָה | לֹא־יֵדָע | וְרִשְׁתּוֹ | אֲשֶׁר־טָמַן |
| | tᵉvô'ēhû | shô'āh | lō'-yēdhā' | wᵉrishtô | 'ăsher-ṭāman |
| | let it come to him | ruin | he does not know | and his net | which he has hidden |

| 4058.122 | 904, 8177 | 5489.121, 904 | 9. | 5497 | 1559.122 | 904, 3176 |
|---|---|---|---|---|---|---|
| v Qal juss 3fs, ps 3ms | prep, n fs | v Qal juss 3ms, prep, ps 3fs | | cj, n fs, ps 1cs | v Qal impf 3fs | prep, pn |
| תִּלְכְּדוֹ | בְּשׁוֹאָה | יִפָּל־בָּהּ | | וְנַפְשִׁי | תָּגִיל | בַּיהוָה |
| tilkᵉdhô | bᵉshô'āh | yippāl-bāhh | | wᵉnaphshî | tāghîl | bayhwāh |
| may it capture him | in ruin | let him fall in it | | and my soul | it will rejoice | in Yahweh |

| 7919.122 | 904, 3568 | 10. | 3725 | 6344 | 569.127 | 3176 | 4449 | 3765 |
|---|---|---|---|---|---|---|---|---|
| v Qal impf 3fs | prep, n fs, ps 3ms | | *adj* | n fp, ps 1cs | v Qal impf 3fp | pn | intrg | prep, ps 2ms |
| תָּשִׂישׂ | בִּישׁוּעָתוֹ | | כָּל | עַצְמוֹתַי | תֹּאמַרְנָה | יְהוָה | מִי | כָמוֹךָ |
| tāsîs | bîshû'āthô | | kol | 'atsmôthay | tō'marnāh | yᵉhwāh | mî | khāmôkhā |
| it will rejoice | in his salvation | | all | my bones | they say | O Yahweh | who | like You |

| 5522.551 | 6270 | 4623, 2481 | 4623 | 6270 | 33 |
|---|---|---|---|---|---|
| v Hiphil ptc ms | n ms | prep, n ms | prep, ps 3ms | cj, n ms | cj, n ms |
| מַצִּיל | עָנִי | מֵחָזָק | מִמֶּנּוּ | וְעָנִי | וְאֶבְיוֹן |
| matstsîl | 'ānî | mēchāzāq | mimmennû | wᵉ'ānî | wᵉ'evyôn |
| One Who rescues | the afflicted | from those stronger | than him | and the afflicted | and the needy |

| 1528.151 | 11. | 7251.126 | 5915 | 2660 | 866 | 3940, 3156.115 |
|---|---|---|---|---|---|---|
| prep, v Qal act ptc ms, ps 3ms | | v Qal impf 3mp | *n mp* | n ms | rel pron | neg part, v Qal pf 1cs |
| מִגֹּזְלוֹ | | יְקוּמוּן | עֵדֵי | חָמָס | אֲשֶׁר | לֹא־יָדַעְתִּי |
| miggōzᵉlô | | yᵉqûmûn | 'ēdhê | chāmās̱ | 'ăsher | lō'-yādha'ättî |
| from those who rob him | | they rise up | witnesses of | violence | whom | I had not known |

| 8068.126 | 12. | 8396.326 | 7750 | 8809 | 3009B | 8315 | 3937, 5497 |
|---|---|---|---|---|---|---|---|
| v Qal impf 3mp, ps 1cs | | v Piel impf 3mp, ps 1cs | n fs | prep | adj | n ms | prep, n fs, ps 1cs |
| יִשְׁאָלוּנִי | | יְשַׁלְּמוּנִי | רָעָה | תַּחַת | טוֹבָה | שְׁכוֹל | לְנַפְשִׁי |
| yish'ālûnî | | yᵉshallᵉmûnî | rā'āh | tachath | ṭôvāh | shᵉkhôl | lᵉnaphshî |
| they ask me | | they repay me | evil | instead of | good | bereavement | to my soul |

| 13. | 603 | 904, 2571.141 | 3961 | 8012 | 6257.315 | 904, 6948 |
|---|---|---|---|---|---|---|
| | cj, pers pron | prep, v Qal inf con, ps 3mp | n ms, ps 1cs | n ms | v Piel pf 1cs | prep, art, n ms |
| | וַאֲנִי | בַּחֲלוֹתָם | לְבוּשִׁי | שָׂק | עִנֵּיתִי | בַצּוֹם |
| | wa'ănî | bachlôthām | lᵉvûshî | sāq | 'innêthî | vatstsôm |
| | but I | during their being sick | my clothes | sackcloth | I was afflicted | with fasting |

| 5497 | 8940 | 6142, 2536 | 8178.122 | 14. | 3626, 7739, 3626, 250 | 3937 |
|---|---|---|---|---|---|---|
| n fs, ps 1cs | cj, n fs, ps 1cs | prep, n ms, ps 1cs | v Qal impf 3fs | | prep, n ms, prep, n ms | prep, ps 1cs |
| נַפְשִׁי | וּתְפִלָּתִי | עַל־חֵיקִי | תָשׁוּב | | כְּרֵעַ־כְּאָח | לִי |
| naphshî | ûthᵉphillāthî | 'al-chêqî | thāshûv | | kᵉrēa'-kᵉ'āch | lî |
| my soul | and my prayer | on my lap | it turned back | | as a friend like a brother | to me |

| 2050.715 | 3626, 58, 525 | 7222.151 | 8246.115 |
|---|---|---|---|
| v Hithpael pf 1cs | prep, *adj*, n fs | v Qal act ptc ms | v Qal pf 1cs |
| הִתְהַלָּכְתִּי | כַּאֲבֶל־אֵם | קֹדֵר | שַׁחוֹתִי |
| hithhallākhtî | ka'ăvel-'ēm | qōdhēr | shachôthî |
| I walked about | like mourning for a mother | being unkempt | I bowed down |

**7. For without cause have they hid for me their net in a pit, which without cause they have digged for my soul:** ... For unprovoked they have hidden a net for me, *NEB* ... unprovoked they have dug a pit to trap me, *REB* ... without cause they dug a pit for my life, *RSV* ... in which to take my soul, *BB.*

**8. Let destruction come upon him at unawares; and let his net that he hath hid catch himself: into that very destruction let him fall:** ... May they be destroyed suddenly when they least expect it, *Beck* ... There shall reach him a ruin he could not know, *Rotherham* ... their own snare entrap them!, *Knox* ... let them fall in it—to their ruin, *NRSV.*

**9. And my soul shall be joyful in the LORD: it shall rejoice in his salvation:** ... and delight in his salvation, *NIV* ... exult in his victory, *Anchor* ... I will be happy when he saves me, *NCV* ... joyful at his deliverance, *Moffatt.*

**10. All my bones shall say, LORD, who is like unto thee, which deliverest the poor from him that is too strong for him, yea, the poor and the needy from him that spoileth him?:** ... All my being shall say, *NCB* ... The rescuer of the afflicted man, *NAB* ... the poor and wretched from those who prey on them, *NEB* ... from him that robbeth him, *ASV.*

**11. False witnesses did rise up; they laid to my charge things that I knew not:** ... Unrighteous witnesses rise up, *MRB* ... Malicious accusers come forward, *Moffatt* ... They ask me things that I do not know, *NKJV* ... they put questions to me about crimes of which I had no knowledge, *BB.*

**12. They rewarded me evil for good to the spoiling of my soul:** ... repay my kindness with cruelty, *JB* ... bringing bereavement to my soul, *NAB* ... loneliness has come to my soul, *KJVII* ... lying in wait to take my life, *NEB.*

**13. But as for me, when they were sick, my clothing was sackcloth:** ... Yet when they were ill, *REB* ... Tho' I had in their griefs worn a sack, *Fenton.*

**I humbled my soul with fasting; and my prayer returned into mine own bosom:** ... and showed my sorrow by going without food, *NCV* ... I afflicted myself with fasting, *NRSV* ... prayed from my heart's depths, *Knox* ... When my prayers returned to me unanswered, *NIV.*

**14. I behaved myself as though he had been my friend or brother: I bowed down heavily, as one that mourneth for his mother:** ... as though I grieved for my friend or my brother, *RSV* ... I was bent over in mourning, *Anchor* ... As in sorrow for a mother I bowed down mourning, *Goodspeed.*

**15. But in mine adversity they rejoiced, and gathered themselves together: yea, the abjects gathered themselves together against me, and I knew it not; they did tear me,**

---

**35:7–10.** The familiar figures of the hunter's snare and pitfall recur here, as expressing crafty plans for destruction, and pass, as in other places, into the wish that the *lex talionis* may fall on the would-be ensnarer. His own deliverance, not the other's destruction, makes the singer joyful in Yahweh, and what he vows to celebrate is not the retributive, but the delivering, aspect of the divine act. In such joy there is nothing unworthy of the purest forgiving love to foes. The relaxation of the tension of anxiety and fear brings the sweetest moments, in the sweetness which soul and body seem to share. The very bones, which were consumed and waxed old (Pss. 6:3; 32:3), are also at ease and, in their sense of well-being, have a tongue to ascribe it to Yahweh's delivering hand. No physical enjoyment surpasses the delight of simple freedom from long torture of pain, nor are there many experiences so poignantly blessed as that of passing out of tempest into calm.

**35:11–14.** The second division (vv. 11–16) runs parallel with the first, with some differences. The reference to "unjust witnesses" and their charges of crimes which he had never dreamed of may be but the reappearance of the image of a lawsuit, as in v. 1, but is more probably fact. We may venture to think of the slanders which poisoned Saul's jealous mind. Just as in "They requite me evil for good," we have at least a remarkable verbal coincidence with the latter's burst of tearful penitence (1 Sam. 24:17): "Thou art more righteous than I, for thou hast rendered unto me good, whereas I have rendered unto thee evil." What a wail breaks the continuity of the sentence in the pathetic words of v. 12b!: "Bereavement to my soul!" The word is used again in Isa. 48:7f, where it is translated "loss of children."

**35:15–16.** The reverse of this picture of true sympathy is given in the conduct of its objects when it was the psalmist's turn to sorrow. Gleefully, they flock together to mock and triumph. His calamity was as good as a feast to the ingrates. Verses 15f are in parts obscure, but the general sense is clear. The word rendered "abjects" (HED #5411) is unique and, consequently, its meaning is doubtful; various conjectural emendations have been proposed.

| | 904, 7028 | 7975.116 | 636.216 | 636.216 | 6142 |
|---|---|---|---|---|---|
| **15.** | cj, prep, n ms, ps 1cs | v Qal pf 3cp | cj, v Niphal pf 3cp | v Niphal pf 3cp | prep, ps 1cs |
| | וּבְצַלְעִי | שָׂמְחוּ | וְנֶאֱסָפוּ | נֶאֶסְפוּ | עָלַי |
| | ûvetsal'î | sāmechû | wene'ěsāphû | ne'esphû | 'ālay |
| | and when my stumbling | they were glad | and they gathered | they gathered | against me |

| 5411 | 3940 | 3156.115 | 7458.116 | 3940, 1887.116 | | 904, 2715 |
|---|---|---|---|---|---|---|
| n mp | cj, neg part | v Qal pf 1cs | v Qal pf 3cp | cj, neg part, v Qal pf 3cp | **16.** | prep, *adj* |
| נֵכִים | וְלֹא | יָדַעְתִּי | קָרְעוּ | וְלֹא־דָמּוּ | | בְּחַנְפֵי |
| nēkhîm | welō' | yādha'ättî | qāre'û | welō'-dhāmmû | | bechanphê |
| stricken ones | but not | I knew | they tore | and they were not silent | | as the godless of |

| 4074.152 | 4734 | 2892.142 | 6142 | 8514 | | 112 | 3626, 4242 |
|---|---|---|---|---|---|---|---|
| *v Qal act ptc mp* | n ms | v Qal inf abs | prep, ps 1cs | n fd, ps 3mp | **17.** | n mp, ps 1cs | prep, intrg |
| לַעֲגֵי | מָעוֹג | חָרֹק | עָלַי | שִׁנֵּימוֹ | | אֲדֹנָי | כַּמָּה |
| la'ăghê | mā'ôgh | chārōq | 'ālay | shinnêmô | | 'ădhōnāy | kammāh |
| those who deride | one bent over | gnashing | against me | their teeth | | O my Lord | like what |

| 7495.123 | 8178.531 | 5497 | 4623, 8055 | 4623, 3841 | 3279 |
|---|---|---|---|---|---|
| v Qal impf 2ms | v Hiphil impv 2ms | n fs, ps 1cs | prep, n mp, ps 3mp | prep, n mp | adv, ps 1cs |
| תִּרְאֶה | הָשִׁיבָה | נַפְשִׁי | מִשֹּׁאֵיהֶם | מִכְּפִירִים | יְחִידָתִי |
| tir'eh | hāshîvāh | naphshî | mishshō'êhem | mikkephîrîm | yechîdhāthî |
| will You look | restore | my soul | from their ravages | from the young lions | my only |

| | 3142.525 | 904, 7235 | 7521 | 904, 6194 | 6335 | 2054.325 |
|---|---|---|---|---|---|---|
| **18.** | v Hiphil juss 1cs, ps 2ms | prep, n ms | adj | prep, n ms | adj | v Piel juss 1cs, ps 2ms |
| | אוֹדְךָ | בְּקָהָל | רָב | בְּעַם | עָצוּם | אֲהַלְלֶךָּ |
| | 'ôdhkhā | beqāhāl | rāv | be'am | 'ātsûm | 'ăhalelekhā |
| | let me praise You | in the assembly | large | with a people | numerous | let me praise You |

| | 414, 7975.126, 3937 | 342.152 | 8632 | 7983.152 | 2703 |
|---|---|---|---|---|---|
| **19.** | adv, v Qal juss 3mp, prep, ps 1cs | v Qal act ptc mp, ps 1cs | n ms | v Qal act ptc mp, ps 1cs | adv |
| | אַל־יִשְׂמְחוּ־לִי | אֹיְבַי | שֶׁקֶר | שֹׂנְאַי | חִנָּם |
| | 'al-yismechû-lî | 'ōyevay | sheqer | sōne'ay | chinnām |
| | do not be glad about me | my enemies | vanity | those who hate me | without cause |

| 7460.126, 6084 | | 3706 | 3940 | 8361 | 1744.326 | 6142 |
|---|---|---|---|---|---|---|
| v Qal juss 3mp, n fs | **20.** | cj | neg part | n ms | v Piel impf 3mp | cj, prep |
| יִקְרְצוּ־עָיִן | | כִּי | לֹא | שָׁלוֹם | יְדַבֵּרוּ | וְעַל |
| yiqŏrtsû-'āyin | | kî | lō' | shālôm | yedhabbērû | we'al |
| let them squint the eye | | because | not | peace | they speak | and concerning |

| 7568, 800 | 1745 | 4983 | 2913.126 | | 7622.526 | 6142 |
|---|---|---|---|---|---|---|
| *adj*, n fs | *n mp* | n fp | v Qal impf 3mp | **21.** | cj, v Hiphil impf 3mp | prep, ps 1cs |
| רִגְעֵי־אֶרֶץ | דִּבְרֵי | מִרְמוֹת | יַחֲשֹׁבוּן | | וַיַּרְחִיבוּ | עָלַי |
| righ'ê-'erets | divrê | mirmôth | yachshōvûn | | wayyarchîvû | 'ālay |
| the quiet of the earth | words of | deceit | they devise | | and they make wide | against me |

| 6552 | 569.116 | 1955 | 1955 | 7495.112 | 6084 | | 7495.113 | 3176 |
|---|---|---|---|---|---|---|---|---|
| n ms, ps 3mp | v Qal pf 3cp | intrj | intrj | v Qal pf 3fs | n fd, ps 1cp | **22.** | v Qal pf 2ms | pn |
| פִּיהֶם | אָמְרוּ | הֶאָח | הֶאָח | רָאֲתָה | עֵינֵינוּ | | רָאִיתָה | יְהוָה |
| pîhem | 'āmerû | he'āch | he'āch | rā'āthāh | 'ênênû | | rā'îthāh | yehwāh |
| their mouth | they said | aha | aha | they have seen | our eyes | | You have seen | O Yahweh |

| 414, 2896.123 | 112 | 414, 7651.123 | 4623 | | 5996.531 | 7301.531 |
|---|---|---|---|---|---|---|
| adv, v Qal juss 2ms | n mp, ps 1cs | adv, v Qal juss 2ms | prep, ps 1cs | **23.** | v Hiphil impv 2ms | cj, v Hiphil impv 2ms |
| אַל־תֶּחֱרַשׁ | אֲדֹנָי | אַל־תִּרְחַק | מִמֶּנִּי | | הָעִירָה | וְהָקִיצָה |
| 'al-techěrash | 'ădhōnāy | 'ăl-tirchaq | mimmenî | | hā'îrāh | wehāqîtsāh |
| do not be deaf | O my Lord | do not be far away | from me | | arouse | and awake |

and ceased not: ... the slanderers gathered themselves together, *Darby*... When I stumble they gather in glee, *JB* ... But they joy and collect, as I grieve, *Fenton* ... they never came to an end of wounding me, *BB.*

**16. With hypocritical mockers in feasts, they gnashed upon me with their teeth:** ... they impiously mocked more and more, *NRSV* ... If I fall they surround me, *JB* ... When I slipped, they mocked and derided me, *REB* ... Like the ungodly they maliciously mocked, *NIV.*

**17. Lord, how long wilt thou look on? rescue my soul from their destructions, my darling from the lions:** ... Bring back my soul out of their raging, *Rotherham* ... Save me from the roaring beasts, *NCB* ... my life from the lions, *BB* ... save my unhappy life from human lions, *Moffatt.*

**18. I will give thee thanks in the great congregation: I will praise thee among much people:** ... Would extol to a powerful race, *Fenton* ... Let me live to praise and thank thee before the multitude, *Knox* ... in the mighty throng I will praise thee, *RSV* ... among a mighty people I will praise Thee, *Berkeley.*

**19. Let not them that are mine enemies wrongfully rejoice over me:** ... those who fight me without any reason!, *LIVB* ... Let not my unprovoked enemies rejoice over me, *NAB.*

**neither let them wink with the eye that hate me without a cause:** ... nor leer at me in triumph, *NEB* ... smirk with delight over my sorrow, *Good News* ... Do not let them make fun of me; they have no cause to hate me, *NCV.*

**20. For they speak not peace: but they devise deceitful matters against them that are quiet in the land:** ... they speake not as friendes, *Geneva* ... Their words are hostile and against the peaceful they hatch intrigues, *REB* ... but plot to betray people living quietly in the land, *Beck* ... but attack the oppressed in the land, *Anchor.*

**21. Yea, they opened their mouth wide against me, and said, Aha, aha, our eye hath seen it:** ... they shout in their joy, feasting their eyes on me, *NEB* ... We saw him with our own eyes, *NAB* ... We saw it ourselves, *Beck* ... What a sight for us to see, *REB.*

**22. This thou hast seen, O Lord: keep not silence: O Lord, be not far from me:** ... Lord, do not leave me alone, *NCV* ... Lord, keep not far away, *Moffatt* ... be not unmoved, *BB.*

**23. Stir up thyself, and awake to my judgment, even unto my cause, my God and my Lord:** ... and awake to my vindication, *NKJV* ... awake to my defense, *Anchor* ... rise up to do me justice, *Goodspeed.*

---

**35:17–21.** The picture of his danger is followed, as in the former part, by the psalmist's prayer. To him, God's beholding without interposing is strange, and the time seems protracted. The moments creep when he is sorrow-laden, and God's help seems slow to tortured hearts. But his impatience is soothed, and, although the man who cries "How long?" may feel that he lives among lions, he will quickly change his petition into thanksgiving. The designation of the life as "my only one," as in 22:20, enhances the earnestness of petition by the thought that, once lost, it can never be restored. A man has but one life; he therefore holds it dear. The mercy implored for the individual will be reason to praise God before many people. The thankfulness is no longer a private soliloquy, as in vv 9f. Individual blessings should be publicly acknowledged, and this fullness of praise may be used as a plea with God Who delivers men that they may show forth the excellencies of Him Who has called them out of trouble into his marvelous peace.

The third division goes over nearly the same ground as before with the difference that the prayer for deliverance is more extended and that the resulting praise comes from the great congregation, joining in as the chorus of the singer's solo. The former references to innocence and causeless hatred, lies and plots and open-mouthed rage are repeated. "Our eyes have seen," say the enemies, counting their plots as good as successful and snorting contempt of their victim's helplessness.

**35:22–26.** Usually Yahweh's "seeing," in the Psalter, is the same as his helping; but here, as in v. 17, the two things are separated, as they so often are, for the trial of faith. God's inaction does not disprove his knowledge, but the pleading soul presses on Him that He would not be deaf to its cry nor far from its help. The greedy eyes of the enemy around the psalmist gloat on their prey, but he cries aloud to his God and dares to speak to Him as if He were deaf and far off, inactive and asleep. The imagery of the lawsuit reappears in fuller form here. "My cause" (HED #7663) in v. 23 is a noun cognate with the verb rendered "plead" or "strive" in v. 1 (HED #7662); "Judge me" (HED #8570) in v. 24 does not mean "Pronounce sentence on my character and conduct," but, "Do me right in this case of mine versus my gratuitous foes."

The prayer for their confusion, which clearly has no wider scope than concerning the matter in

| | | | | | |
|---|---|---|---|---|---|
| **3937, 5122**<br>prep, n ms, ps 1cs<br>לְמִשְׁפָּטִי<br>lᵉmishpāṭî<br>for my justice | **435**<br>n mp, ps 1cs<br>אֱלֹהַי<br>'ĕlōhay<br>my God | **112**<br>cj, n mp, ps 1cs<br>וַאדֹנָי<br>wa'dhōnāy<br>and my Lord | **3937, 7663**<br>prep, n ms, ps 1cs<br>לְרִיבִי<br>lᵉrîvî<br>for my case | **24.** | **8570.131**<br>v Qal impv 2ms, ps 1cs<br>שָׁפְטֵנִי<br>shāphᵉṭēnî<br>judge me |

| | | | |
|---|---|---|---|
| **3626, 6928**<br>prep, n ms, ps 2ms<br>כְּצִדְקְךָ<br>khᵉtsidhqŏkhā<br>according to your righteousness | **3176**<br>pn<br>יְהוָה<br>yᵉhwāh<br>O Yahweh | **435**<br>n mp, ps 1cs<br>אֱלֹהָי<br>'ĕlōhāy<br>my God | **414, 7975.126, 3937**<br>cj, adv, v Qal juss 3mp, prep, ps 1cs<br>וְאַל־יִשְׂמְחוּ־לִי<br>wᵉ'al-yismᵉchû-lî<br>and let them not be glad about me |

| | | | | | |
|---|---|---|---|---|---|
| **25.** | **414, 569.126**<br>adv, v Qal juss 3mp<br>אַל־יֹאמְרוּ<br>'al-yō'mᵉrû<br>may thcy not say | **904, 3949**<br>prep, n ms, ps 3mp<br>בְלִבָּם<br>vᵉlibbām<br>in their heart | **1955**<br>intrj<br>הֶאָח<br>he'āch<br>aha | **5497**<br>n fs, ps 1cp<br>נַפְשֵׁנוּ<br>naphshēnû<br>our desire | **414, 569.126**<br>adv, v Qal juss 3mp<br>אַל־יֹאמְרוּ<br>'al-yō'mᵉrû<br>may they not say |

| | | | | |
|---|---|---|---|---|
| **1142.319**<br>v Piel pf 1cp, ps 3ms<br>בִּלַּעֲנוּהוּ<br>billa'ănûhû<br>we have swallowed him | **26.** | **991.126**<br>v Qal juss 3mp<br>יֵבֹשׁוּ<br>yēvōshû<br>may they be ashamed | **2763.126**<br>cj, v Qal juss 3mp<br>וְיַחְפְּרוּ<br>wᵉyachpᵉrû<br>and let them be ashamed | **3267**<br>adv<br>יַחְדָּו<br>yachdāw<br>at the same time |

| | | | |
|---|---|---|---|
| **7976**<br>*adj*<br>שְׂמֵחֵי<br>sᵉmēchê<br>those glad about | **7750**<br>n fs, ps 1cs<br>רָעָתִי<br>rā'āthî<br>my disaster | **3980.126, 1350**<br>v Qal juss 3mp, n fs<br>יִלְבְּשׁוּ־בֹשֶׁת<br>yilbᵉshû-vōsheth<br>may they be clothed with shame | **3759**<br>cj, n fs<br>וּכְלִמָּה<br>ûkhᵉlimmāh<br>and dishonor |

| | | | | |
|---|---|---|---|---|
| **1461.552**<br>art, v Hiphil ptc mp<br>הַמַּגְדִּילִים<br>hammaghdîlîm<br>those causing to be great | **6142**<br>prep, ps 1cs<br>עָלָי<br>'ālāy<br>against me | **27.** | **7728.126**<br>v Qal juss 3mp<br>יָרֹנּוּ<br>yārōnnû<br>let them shout for joy | **7975.126**<br>cj, v Qal juss 3mp<br>וְיִשְׂמְחוּ<br>wᵉyismᵉchû<br>and let them be glad |

| | | | | | | |
|---|---|---|---|---|---|---|
| **2760**<br>*adj*<br>חֲפֵצֵי<br>chăphētsê<br>the desirous of | **6928**<br>n ms, ps 1cs<br>צִדְקִי<br>tsidhqî<br>my vindication | **569.126**<br>cj, v Qal juss 3mp<br>וְיֹאמְרוּ<br>wᵉyō'mᵉrû<br>and let them say | **8878**<br>adv<br>תָמִיד<br>thāmîdh<br>continually | **1461.121**<br>v Qal impf 3ms<br>יִגְדַּל<br>yighdal<br>He is great | **3176**<br>pn<br>יְהוָה<br>yᵉhwāh<br>Yahweh | **2760**<br>art, adj<br>הֶחָפֵץ<br>hechāphēts<br>the desirous |

| | | | | | | |
|---|---|---|---|---|---|---|
| **8361**<br>*n ms*<br>שְׁלוֹם<br>shᵉlôm<br>the welfare of | **5860**<br>n ms, ps 3ms<br>עַבְדּוֹ<br>'avdô<br>his servant | **28.** | **4098**<br>cj, n ms, ps 1cs<br>וּלְשׁוֹנִי<br>ûlᵉshônî<br>and my tongue | **1965.122**<br>v Qal impf 3fs<br>תֶּהְגֶּה<br>tehgeh<br>it will utter | **6928**<br>n ms, ps 2ms<br>צִדְקֶךָ<br>tsidhqekhā<br>your righteousness | **3725, 3219**<br>*adj*, art, n ms<br>כָּל־הַיּוֹם<br>kol-hayyôm<br>all the day |

| | | | | | | |
|---|---|---|---|---|---|---|
| **8747**<br>n fs, ps 2ms<br>תְּהִלָּתֶךָ<br>tᵉhillāthekhā<br>your praise | **36:t** | **3937, 5514.351**<br>prep, art, v Piel ptc ms<br>לַמְנַצֵּחַ<br>lamnatstsēach<br>to the director | **3937, 5860, 3176**<br>prep, *n ms*, pn<br>לְעֶבֶד־יְהוָה<br>lᵉ'evedh-yᵉhwāh<br>of the servant of Yahweh | **3937, 1784**<br>prep, pn<br>לְדָוִד<br>lᵉdhāwidh<br>of David | **1.** | **5177, 6840**<br>*n ms*, n ms<br>נְאֻם־פֶּשַׁע<br>nᵉ'um-pesha'<br>a declaration of offense |

| | | | | | |
|---|---|---|---|---|---|
| **3937, 7857**<br>prep, art, n ms<br>לָרָשָׁע<br>lārāshā'<br>to the wicked | **904, 7419**<br>prep, *n ms*<br>בְּקֶרֶב<br>bᵉqerev<br>in the midst of | **3949**<br>n ms, ps 1cs<br>לִבִּי<br>libbî<br>my heart | **375, 6586**<br>*sub, n ms*<br>אֵין־פַּחַד<br>'ên-pachadh<br>there is not trembling about | **435**<br>n mp<br>אֱלֹהִים<br>'ĕlōhîm<br>God | **3937, 5224**<br>prep, prep<br>לְנֶגֶד<br>lᵉneghedh<br>before |

**24. Judge me, O LORD my God, according to thy righteousness; and let them not rejoice over me:** ... Do me justice, because you are just, *NAB* ... In your saving justice give judgement for me, *JB* ... let them not triumph long, *Fenton* ... do not let them gloat over me, *NIV.*

**25. Let them not say in their hearts, Ah, so would we have it: let them not say, We have swallowed him up:** ... We destroyed him, *NCV* ... We have engorged him, *Anchor* ... We have ruined him, *Beck* ... We haue devoured him, *Geneva.*

**26. Let them be ashamed and brought to confusion together that rejoice at mine hurt: let them be clothed with shame and dishonour that magnify themselves against me:** ... Let all who profit at my expense be covered with shame, *JB* ... be put to shame and confusion altogether who rejoice at my calamity, *RSV* ... humiliated altogether who rejoice at my distress, *NASB.*

**27. Let them shout for joy, and be glad, that favour my righteous cause:** ... Joy and gladness be theirs, who applaud my innocence, *Knox* ... shout in triumph and rejoice Who are desiring my justification, *Rotherham* ... those who are on my side, *BB* ... who are pleased at my vindication, *Goodspeed.*

**yea, let them say continually, Let the LORD be magnified, which hath pleasure in the prosperity of his servant:** ... All glory to the LORD who would see his servant thrive, *NEB* ... he wills the prosperity of his servant, *NCB* ... Who enraptures His servant with peace, *Fenton* ... Who delighteth in the peace of His servant, *MAST.*

**28. And my tongue shall speak of thy righteousness and of thy praise all the day long:** ... my tongue shall recount your saving justice, *JB* ... And I shall declare your saving power and your praise, *REB* ... of thy justice and thy praise, *Moffatt.*

**36:t. To the chief Musician, A Psalm of David the servant of the LORD.**

**1. The transgression of the wicked saith within my heart, that there is no fear of God before his eyes:** ... Sin is the oracle of the wicked in the depths of his heart, *JB* ... A wicked person's talk is prompted by sin in his heart, *REB* ... An oracle is within my heart concerning the sinfulness of the wicked, *NIV* ... Sin appeals to the wicked deep in his heart; no dread of God is present, *Berkeley.*

---

hand recurs. It is no breach of Christian charity to pray that hostile devices may fail. The vivid imagination of the poet hears the triumphant exclamations of gratified hatred, "Aha! our desire! We have swallowed him," and sums up the character of his enemies in the two traits of malicious joy in his hurt and self exaltation in their hostility toward him.

**35:27–28.** At last the prayer, which has run through so many moods of feeling, settles itself into restful contemplation of the sure results of Yahweh's sure deliverance. One receives the blessing; many rejoice in it. In significant antithesis to the enemies' joy is the joy of the rescued man's lovers and favorers. Their "saying" stands over against the silenced boastings of the losers of the suit. The latter "magnified themselves," but the end of Yahweh's deliverance will be that true hearts will magnify Him. That is the right end of mercies received. Whether there be many voices to join in praise or not, the voice of the one who received the blessings should not be silent, and even when he pauses in his song, his heart should keep singing daylong and lifelong praises.

***Psalm 36.*** *The supposition that the somber picture of "the wicked" in vv. 1–4 was originally unconnected with the glorious hymn in vv. 5–9 fails to emphasize the difference between the sober pace of pedestrian prose and the swift flight of winged poetry. It also fails to comprehend the instinctive turning of a devout meditative spectator from the darkness of earth and its sins to the light above. The one refuge from the sad vision of evil here is in the faith that God is above it all, and that his name is Mercy.*

**36:1–4.** The two clauses of v. 1 are simply set side by side, leaving the reader to identify their logical relation. Possibly the absence of the fear of God may be regarded as both the occasion and the result of the oracle of transgression, since, in fact, it is both. Still more obscure is v. 2. Who is the "flatterer"? The answers are conflicting. Some say he is the "wicked," but if so, "in his own eyes" is superfluous; others say "God," but that requires a doubtful meaning for "flatters," namely, "treats gently," and is open to the same objection as the preceding in regard to "in his own eyes." The most natural supposition is that "transgression," which was represented in v. 1 as "speaking," is meant here also. Clearly, the person in whose eyes the flattery is real is the wicked, and therefore, its speaker must be another. "Sin beguiled me," says Paul, and therein echoes this psalmist. Transgression in its oracle is one of those manipulating fiends that haggle us in a double sense, promising delights and impunity. But the closing words of v. 2 are a crux. Sin is cruel, and a traitor. This profound glimpse into the depths of a soul without the fear of God is followed by the picture of the consequences of such

| 6084<br>n fd, ps 3ms<br>עֵינָיו<br>'ênâv<br>his eyes | 2. | 3706, 2606.511<br>cj, v Hiphil pf 3ms<br>כִּי־הֶחֱלִיק<br>kî-hechĕlîq<br>because he has flattered | 420<br>prep, ps 3ms<br>אֵלָיו<br>'ēlâv<br>toward himself | 904, 6084<br>prep, n fd, ps 3ms<br>בְּעֵינָיו<br>be'ênâv<br>in his eyes | 3937, 4834.141<br>prep, v Qal inf con<br>לִמְצֹא<br>limtsō'<br>to find |
|---|---|---|---|---|---|

| 5988<br>n ms, ps 3ms<br>עֲוֺנוֹ<br>'ăwōnô<br>his transgression | 3937, 7983.141<br>prep, v Qal inf con<br>לִשְׂנֹא<br>lisnō'<br>to hate | 3. | 1745, 6552<br>*n mp*, n ms, ps 3ms<br>דִּבְרֵי־פִיו<br>divrê-phîw<br>the words of his mouth | 201<br>n ms<br>אָוֶן<br>'āwen<br>iniquity | 4983<br>cj, n fs<br>וּמִרְמָה<br>ûmirmāh<br>and deceit | 2403.111<br>v Qal pf 3ms<br>חָדַל<br>chādhal<br>he has refrained |
|---|---|---|---|---|---|---|

| 3937, 7959.541<br>prep, v Hiphil inf con<br>לְהַשְׂכִּיל<br>lehaskîl<br>to act wisely | 3937, 3296.541<br>prep, v Hiphil inf con<br>לְהֵיטִיב<br>lehêṯîv<br>to cause to be good | 4. | 201<br>n ms<br>אָוֶן<br>'āwen<br>iniquity | 2913.121<br>v Qal impf 3ms<br>יַחְשֹׁב<br>yachshōv<br>he devises | 6142, 5085<br>prep, n ms, ps 3ms<br>עַל־מִשְׁכָּבוֹ<br>'al-mishkāvô<br>on his bed | 3429.721<br>v Hithpael impf 3ms<br>יִתְיַצֵּב<br>yithyatstsēv<br>he takes his stand |
|---|---|---|---|---|---|---|

| 6142, 1932<br>prep, n ms<br>עַל־דֶּרֶךְ<br>'al-derekh<br>on a road | 3940, 3005<br>neg part, adj<br>לֹא־טוֹב<br>lō'-ṯôv<br>not good | 7737<br>n ms<br>רָע<br>rā'<br>evil | 3940<br>neg part<br>לֹא<br>lō'<br>not | 4128.121<br>v Qal impf 3ms<br>יִמְאָס<br>yim'ās̱<br>he despises | 5. | 3176<br>pn<br>יְהוָה<br>yehwāh<br>O Yahweh | 904, 8452<br>prep, art, n md<br>בְּהַשָּׁמַיִם<br>behashshāmayim<br>in the heavens |
|---|---|---|---|---|---|---|---|

| 2721<br>n ms, ps 2ms<br>חַסְדֶּךָ<br>chas̱dekhā<br>your steadfast love | 536<br>n fs, ps 2ms<br>אֱמוּנָתְךָ<br>'ĕmûnāthekhā<br>your faithfulness | 5912, 8263<br>prep, n mp<br>עַד־שְׁחָקִים<br>'adh-shechāqîm<br>up to the clouds | 6. | 6930<br>n fs, ps 2ms<br>צִדְקָתְךָ<br>tsidhqāthekhā<br>your righteousness |
|---|---|---|---|---|

| 3626, 2121, 418<br>prep, *n mp*, n ms<br>כְּהַרְרֵי־אֵל<br>keharerê-'ēl<br>like the mountains of God | 5122<br>n ms, ps 2ms<br>מִשְׁפָּטְךָ<br>mishpāṭekhā<br>your judgment | 8745<br>n fs<br>תְּהוֹם<br>tehôm<br>the deep | 7521<br>adj<br>רַבָּה<br>rabbāh<br>great | 119, 966<br>n ms, cj, n fs<br>אָדָם־וּבְהֵמָה<br>'ādhām-ûvehēmāh<br>man and beast | 3588.523<br>v Hiphil impf 2ms<br>תוֹשִׁיעַ<br>thôshîa'<br>You save |
|---|---|---|---|---|---|

| 3176<br>pn<br>יְהוָה<br>yehwāh<br>O Yahweh | 7. | 4242, 3479<br>intrg, adj<br>מַה־יָּקָר<br>mah-yāqār<br>how precious | 2721<br>n ms, ps 2ms<br>חַסְדְּךָ<br>chasdekhā<br>your steadfast love | 435<br>n mp<br>אֱלֹהִים<br>'ĕlōhîm<br>O God | 1158<br>cj, *n mp*<br>וּבְנֵי<br>ûvenê<br>and the sons of | 119<br>n ms<br>אָדָם<br>'ādhām<br>humankind |
|---|---|---|---|---|---|---|

| 904, 7009<br>prep, *n ms*<br>בְּצֵל<br>betsēl<br>in the shadow of | 3796<br>n fd, ps 2ms<br>כְּנָפֶיךָ<br>kenāphêkhā<br>your wings | 2725.126<br>v Qal impf 3mp<br>יֶחֱסָיוּן<br>yechĕs̱āyûn<br>they take refuge | 8. | 7588.126<br>v Qal impf 3mp<br>יִרְוְיֻן<br>yirweyun<br>they feast | 4623, 1942<br>prep, *n ms*<br>מִדֶּשֶׁן<br>middeshen<br>from the fatness of |
|---|---|---|---|---|---|

| 1041<br>n ms, ps 2ms<br>בֵּיתֶךָ<br>bêthekhā<br>your household | 5337<br>cj, *n ms*<br>וְנַחַל<br>wenachal<br>and the stream of | 5941<br>n mp, ps 2ms<br>עֲדָנֶיךָ<br>'ădhānêkhā<br>your bliss | 8615.523<br>v Hiphil impf 2ms, ps 3mp<br>תַשְׁקֵם<br>thashqēm<br>You give drink to them | 9. | 3706, 6196<br>cj, prep, ps 2ms<br>כִּי־עִמְּךָ<br>kî-'immekhā<br>because with You |
|---|---|---|---|---|---|

| 4888<br>*n ms*<br>מְקוֹר<br>meqôr<br>the fountain of | 2522<br>n mp<br>חַיִּים<br>chayyîm<br>life | 904, 214<br>prep, n ms, ps 2ms<br>בְּאוֹרְךָ<br>be'ôrkhā<br>in your light | 7495.120, 214<br>v Qal impf 1cp, n ms<br>נִרְאֶה־אוֹר<br>nir'eh-'ôr<br>we see light | 10. | 5082.131<br>v Qal impv 2ms<br>מְשֹׁךְ<br>meshōkh<br>stretch | 2721<br>n ms, ps 2ms<br>חַסְדְּךָ<br>chasdekhā<br>your steadfast love |
|---|---|---|---|---|---|---|

**2. For he flattereth himself in his own eyes, until his iniquity be found to be hateful:** ... They think too much of themselves so they don't see their sin and hate it, *NCV* ... But his God will destroy him with his glance having discovered his impious slander, *Anchor* ... For it deceives him in his own eyes, *Goodspeed* ... and is not aware of his sin to hate it, *Beck*.

**3. The words of his mouth are iniquity and deceit: he hath left off to be wise, and to do good:** ... The words of his mouth are wickedness and deceit, *NASB* ... His speech is wicked and full of lies, *Good News* ... he has turned his back on wisdom, *NEB* ... The words of his mouth are empty and false; he has ceased to understand how to do good, *NCB*.

**4. He deviseth mischief upon his bed; he setteth himself in a way that is not good; he abhorreth not evil:** ... hatches malicious plots even in his bed, *JB* ... plots evil on his bed, *KJVII* ... they do not reject evil, *NRSV*.

**5. Thy mercy, O Lord, is in the heavens; and thy faithfulness reacheth unto the clouds:** ... your kindness reaches to heaven, *NAB* ... Your mercy Lord reaches the hills, Your truthfulness goes to the clouds, *Fenton* ... and your strong purpose is as high as the clouds, *BB* ... thy loyalty soars to the very skies, *Moffatt*.

**6. Thy righteousness is like the great mountains; thy judgments are a great deep:** ... your saving justice is like towering mountains, *JB* ... justice stands firm as the everlasting hills, the wisdom of thy decrees is deep as the abyss, *Knox*.

**O Lord, thou preservest man and beast:** ... you protect both people and animals, *NCV* ... You make man and beast thrive, *Anchor* ... Thy providence is over man and beast, *Moffatt* ... you save humans and animals alike, *NRSV*.

**7. How excellent is thy lovingkindness, O God!:** ... How precious is your kindness, *NCB* ... How precious your bounty, *Fenton* ... How priceless is your unfailing love, *NIV* ... How good is your loving mercy, *BB*.

**therefore the children of men put their trust under the shadow of thy wings:** ... Men and angels come for shelter under the shadow of Your wings, *Beck* ... the shadow of thy wings seek refuge, *Rotherham*.

**8. They shall be abundantly satisfied with the fatness of thy house:** ... They have their fill of the prime gifts of your house, *NAB* ... feast on the abundance of thy house, *RSV*.

**and thou shalt make them drink of the river of thy pleasures:** ... thou givest them water from the flowing stream of thy delights, *NEB* ... let them drink from your delicious streams, *JB*.

**9. For with thee is the fountain of life: in thy light shall we see light:** ... thy brightness breaks on our eyes

---

practical atheism, as seen in conduct. It is deeply charged with blackness and unrelieved by any gleam of light. Falsehood, abandonment of all attempts to do right, insensibility to the hallowing influences of nightly solitude, when men are inclined to see their evil more clearly in the dark, like phosphorus streaks on the wall, obstinate planting the feet in ways not good, a silenced conscience which has no movement of aversion to evil—these are the fruits of that oracle of transgression when it has its perfect work.

**36:5–6.** The two strophes of the second division (vv. 5f, and 7ff) present the glorious realities of the divine name in contrast with the false oracle of vv. 1f, and the blessedness of God's guests in contrast with the gloomy picture of the "wicked" in vv. 3f. It is noteworthy that the first- and last-named "attributes" are the same. "Steadfast love" (HED #2721) begins and ends the glowing series. That stooping, active love encloses, like a golden circlet, all else that men can know or say of the perfection whose name is God.

The point of comparison with "the mountains of God" is, as in the previous clauses, their loftiness, which expresses greatness and elevation above our reach; but the subsidiary ideas of permanence and sublimity are not to be overlooked. "The mountains shall depart, and the hills be removed, but his righteousness endures forever" (Isa. 54:10). There is safe hiding in the fastness of that everlasting hill.

**36:7–9.** The secret of blessedness and test of true wisdom lie in a sober estimate of the worth of God's steadfast love as compared with all other treasures. Such an estimate leads to trust in Him, as the psalmist implies by his juxtaposition of the two clauses of v. 7.

The Psalm follows the refugees into their hiding place and shows how much more than bare shelter they find there. They are God's guests and royally entertained as such. The joyful priestly feasts in the Temple color the metaphor, but the idea of hospitable reception of guests is the more prominent. They partake of him and are saturated with his sufficiency, drink of his delights in some deep sense, bathe in the fountain of life, and have his light for their organ, medium and object of sight. These great sentences defy all exposition. They touch on the rim of infinite things, whereof only the nearer fringe comes within our perception in this life.

**36:10–12.** Prayer wins prophetic certitude. From his serene shelter under the wing, the suppliant

| 3937, 3156.152 | 6930 | 3937, 3596, 3949 | | 414, 971.122 |
|---|---|---|---|---|
| prep, v Qal act ptc mp, ps 2ms | cj, n fs, ps 2ms | prep, *n mp*, n ms | **11.** | adv, v Qal juss 3fs, ps 1cs |
| לְיֹדְעֶיךָ | וְצִדְקָתְךָ | לְיִשְׁרֵי־לֵב | | אַל־תְּבוֹאֵנִי |
| lᵉyōdhᵉ'êkhā | wᵉtsidhqāthᵉkhā | lᵉyishrê-lēv | | 'al-tᵉvô'ēnî |
| to those who know You | and your righteousness | to the upright in heart | | do not let it come |

| 7559 | 1375 | 3135, 7857 | 414, 5290.522 | | 8427 |
|---|---|---|---|---|---|
| *n fs* | n fs | cj, *n fs*, n mp | adv, v Hiphil juss 3fs, ps 1cs | **12.** | adv |
| רֶגֶל | גַּאֲוָה | וְיַד־רְשָׁעִים | אַל־תְּנִדֵנִי | | שָׁם |
| reghel | ga'ăwāh | wᵉyadh-rᵉshā'îm | 'al-tᵉnidhēnî | | shām |
| the foot of | the proud | and the hand of the wicked | may it not drive me away | | there |

| 5489.116 | 6713.152 | 201 | 1815.416 | 3940, 3310.116 |
|---|---|---|---|---|
| v Qal pf 3cp | *v Qal act ptc mp* | n ms | v Pual pf 3cp | cj, neg part, v Qal pf 3cp |
| נָפְלוּ | פֹּעֲלֵי | אָוֶן | דֹּחוּ | וְלֹא־יָכְלוּ |
| nāphᵉlû | pō'ălê | 'āwen | dōchû | wᵉlō'-yākhᵉlû |
| they will fall | those who practice | iniquity | they will be pushed | and they will not be able |

| 7251.141 | | 3937, 1784 | | 414, 2835.723 | 904, 7778.552 | 414, 7349.323 |
|---|---|---|---|---|---|---|
| v Qal inf con | **37:t** | prep, pn | **1.** | adv, v Hithpael juss 2ms | prep, art, v Hiphil ptc mp | adv, v Piel juss 2ms |
| קוּם | | לְדָוִד | | אַל־תִּתְחַר | בַּמְּרֵעִים | אַל־תְּקַנֵּא |
| qûm | | lᵉdhāwidh | | 'al-tithchar | bammᵉrē'îm | 'al-tᵉqannē' |
| to rise | | of David | | do not be annoyed | with evildoers | do not be envious |

| 904, 6449.152 | 5983 | | 3706 | 3626, 2785 | 4259 | 4589.126 |
|---|---|---|---|---|---|---|
| prep, *v Qal act ptc mp* | n fs | **2.** | cj | prep, art, n ms | adv | v Qal impf 3mp |
| בְּעֹשֵׂי | עַוְלָה | | כִּי | כֶחָצִיר | מְהֵרָה | יִמָּלוּ |
| bᵉ'ōsê | 'awlāh | | kî | khechātsîr | mᵉhērāh | yimmālû |
| with those who practice | wrongdoing | | because | like the grass | quickly | they will wither |

| 3626, 3537 | 1940 | 5209.126 | | 1019.131 | 904, 3176 |
|---|---|---|---|---|---|
| cj, prep, n ms | n ms | v Qal impf 3mp | **3.** | v Qal impv 2ms | prep, pn |
| וּכְיֶרֶק | דֶּשֶׁא | יִבּוֹלוּן | | בְּטַח | בַּיהוָה |
| ûkhᵉyereq | deshe' | yibbôlûn | | bᵉtach | bayhwāh |
| and like green plants | fresh growth | they will wither | | trust | in Yahweh |

| 6449.131, 3008 | 8331.131, 800 | 7749.131 | 536 | | 6253.731 |
|---|---|---|---|---|---|
| cj, v Qal impv 2ms, n ms | v Qal impv 2ms, n fs | cj, v Qal impv 2ms | n fs | **4.** | cj, v Hithpael impv 2ms |
| וַעֲשֵׂה־טוֹב | שְׁכָן־אֶרֶץ | וּרְעֵה | אֱמוּנָה | | וְהִתְעַנַּג |
| wa'ăsēh-ṭôv | shᵉkhān-'erets | ûrᵉ'ēh | 'ĕmûnāh | | wᵉhith'annagh |
| and do what is good | stay in the land | and shepherd | faithfulness | | and take pleasure |

| 6142, 3176 | 5598.121, 3937 | 5048 | 3949 | | 1597.131 |
|---|---|---|---|---|---|
| prep, pn | cj, v Qal juss 3ms, prep, ps 2ms | *n fp* | n ms, ps 2ms | **5.** | v Qal impv 2ms |
| עַל־יְהוָה | וְיִתֶּן־לְךָ | מִשְׁאֲלֹת | לִבֶּךָ | | גּוֹל |
| 'al-yᵉhwāh | wᵉyitten-lᵉkhā | mish'ălōth | libbekhā | | gôl |
| concerning Yahweh | and may He give to you | the requests of | your heart | | roll |

| 6142, 3176 | 1932 | 1019.131 | 6142 | 2000 | 6449.121 |
|---|---|---|---|---|---|
| prep, pn | n ms, ps 2ms | cj, v Qal impv 2ms | prep, ps 3ms | cj, pers pron | v Qal impf 3ms |
| עַל־יְהוָה | דַּרְכֶּךָ | וּבְטַח | עָלָיו | וְהוּא | יַעֲשֶׂה |
| 'al-yᵉhwāh | darkekhā | ûvᵉtach | 'ālâv | wᵉhû' | ya'ăseh |
| on Yahweh | your way | and put your trust | in Him | and He | He will do |

| | 3428.511 | 3626, 214 | 6928 | 5122 | 3626, 6937 |
|---|---|---|---|---|---|
| **6.** | cj, v Hiphil pf 3ms | prep, art, n ms | n ms, ps 2ms | cj, n ms, ps 2ms | prep, art, n mp |
| | וְהוֹצִיא | כָאוֹר | צִדְקֶךָ | וּמִשְׁפָּטֶךָ | כַּצָּהֳרָיִם |
| | wᵉhôtsî' | khā'ôr | tsidhqekhā | ûmishpāṭekhā | katstsāhᵒrāyim |
| | and He will bring out | like the light | your vindication | and your justice | like the noonday |

like dawn, *Knox* ... in your field we shall see the light, *Anchor* ... You are the giver of life. Your light lets us enjoy life, *NCV* ... and in thy smile we have the light of life, *Moffatt.*

**10. O continue thy lovingkindness unto them that know thee; and thy righteousness to the upright in heart:** ... Keep up your kindness toward your friends, *NCB* ... justice toward men of honest heart, *NEB* ... your just defense of the upright, *NAB* ... thy justification to the right-minded, *Goodspeed.*

**11. Let not the foot of pride come against me, and let not the hand of the wicked remove me:** ... feet of proud men step on me or hand of the wicked throw me down, *Beck* ... hand of the wicked drive me away, *NASB* ... the hand of the lawless scare me away, *Rotherham* ... Nor let mine be the hands to oppress, *Fenton.*

**12. There are the workers of iniquity fallen: they are cast down, and shall not be able to rise:** ... Those who do evil have been defeated, *NCV* ... See how the evildoers lie fallen, *NIV* ... They have been overthrown, *Young* ... flung down, never to rise again, *JB.*

**37:t. A Psalm of David.**

**1. Fret not thyself because of evildoers, neither be thou envious against the workers of iniquity:** ... Don't get upset about evil people, *Beck* ... nor indignant with those who do wrong, *Anchor* ... nor jealous of those who do wrong, *NCB* ... Be not incensed because of wrongdoers, *Goodspeed.*

**2. For they shall soon be cut down like the grass, and wither as the green herb:** ... Quick as the grass they wither, fading like the green of the fields, *JB* ... like green plants they will soon die away, *NIV* ... And they wither, as do the green leaves, *Fenton* ... like green herbs they wilt, *NAB.*

**3. Trust in the LORD, and do good; so shalt thou dwell in the land, and verily thou shalt be fed:** ... so you will live in the land, and enjoy security, *NRSV* ... Dwell in the land, and enjoy faithfulness, *Young* ... inhabit the land and practice faithfulness, *Berkeley* ... you shall be fed on truth, *KJVII.*

**4. Delight thyself also in the LORD:** ... rest thy delight on Yahweh, *Rotherham* ... Depend upon the LORD, *NEB* ... Seek your happiness in the LORD, *Good News.*

**and he shall give thee the desires of thine heart:** ... grant you your heart's requests, *NCB* ... and he will give you what you want, *NCV.*

**5. Commit thy way unto the LORD; trust also in him; and he shall bring it to pass:** ... Put your life in the hands of the Lord, *BB* ... Commit your destiny to Yahweh, be confident in him, *JB* ... Leave all to him, rely on him, and he will see to it, *Moffatt* ... And trust Him because He can save, *Fenton.*

**6. And he shall bring forth thy righteousness as the light, and thy judgment as the noonday:** ... he will bring your innocence to light, *Moffatt* ... He will make your righteousness shine clear as the day, *REB* ... and the justice of your cause like

---

looks out on the crowd of baffled foes and sees the end which gives the lie to the oracle of transgression and its flatteries. "They are struck down" (HED #1815) the same word as in the picture of the pursuing angel of the LORD in Ps. 35. Here the agent of their fall is unnamed, but one power only can inflict such irrevocable ruin. God, Who is the Shelter of the upright in heart, has at last found out the sinners' iniquity, and his hatred of sin stands ready to smite once and smite no more (1 Sam. 26:8).

***Psalm 37.*** *Verses 1–9 form a group, characterized by exhortations to trust and assurances of triumph. The second section will then be vv. 10–22, which, while reiterating the ground tone of the whole, does so with a difference, inasmuch as its main thought is the destruction of the wicked, in contrast with the triumph of the righteous in the preceding verses. A third division will be vv. 23–29, of which the chief feature is the adduction of the psalmist's own experience as authenticating his teaching in regard to the divine care of the righteous, and that extended to his descendants. The last section (vv. 30–40) gathers up all, reasserts the main thesis and confirms it by again adducing the psalmist's experience in confirmation of the other half of his assurances, namely, the destruction of the wicked.*

**37:1–2.** The tendency to murmur at flaunting wrong must be repressed if the disposition of trust is to be cultivated. On the other hand, full obedience to the negative precepts is only possible when the positive ones have been obeyed with some degree of completeness. The caretaking of the soul must involve removing weeds as well as sowing, but the true way to take away nourishment from the baser is to throw the strength of the soil into growing the nobler crop. Why should we blaze with indignation when so much hotter a glow will dry up the cut grass? Let it wave in brief glory, without interference. The scythe and the sunshine will soon make an end.

**37:3–9.** The blessed results of trust and active goodness are stable dwelling in the land, and nourishment there is from a faithful God. The thoughts move within the OT circle, but their substance is

| 7. | 1887.131<br>v Qal impv 2ms<br>דּוֹם<br>dôm<br>be still | 3937, 3176<br>prep, pn<br>לַיהוָה<br>layhwāh<br>to Yahweh | 2435.723<br>cj, v Hithpolel juss 2ms<br>וְהִתְחוֹלֵל<br>wehithchôlēl<br>and writhe within yourself | 3937<br>prep, ps 3ms<br>לוֹ<br>lô<br>for Him | 414, 2835.723<br>adv, v Hithpael juss 2ms<br>אַל־תִּתְחַר<br>'al-tithchar<br>do not be annoyed |
|---|---|---|---|---|---|

| 904, 7014.551<br>prep, v Hiphil ptc ms<br>בְּמַצְלִיחַ<br>bematslîach<br>with one who prospers | 1932<br>n ms, ps 3ms<br>דַּרְכּוֹ<br>darkô<br>his journey | 904, 382<br>prep, n ms<br>בְּאִישׁ<br>be'îsh<br>with a man | 6449.151<br>v Qal act ptc ms<br>עֹשֶׂה<br>'ōseh<br>one who makes | 4343<br>n fp<br>מְזִמּוֹת<br>mezimmôth<br>plots | 8. | 7791.531<br>v Hiphil impv 2ms<br>הֶרֶף<br>hereph<br>desert |
|---|---|---|---|---|---|---|

| 4623, 652<br>prep, n ms<br>מֵאַף<br>mē'aph<br>from anger | 6013.131<br>cj, v Qal impv 2ms<br>וַעֲזֹב<br>wa'ăzōv<br>and abandon | 2635<br>n fs<br>חֵמָה<br>chēmāh<br>wrath | 414, 2835.723<br>adv, v Hithpael juss 2ms<br>אַל־תִּתְחַר<br>'al-tithchar<br>do not be annoyed | 395, 7778.541<br>adv, prep, v Hiphil inf con<br>אַךְ־לְהָרֵעַ<br>'akh-lehārēa'<br>only to do evil |
|---|---|---|---|---|

| 9. | 3706, 7778.552<br>cj, v Hiphil ptc mp<br>כִּי־מְרֵעִים<br>kî-merē'îm<br>because the evildoers | 3901.226<br>v Niphal impf 3mp<br>יִכָּרֵתוּן<br>yikkārēthûn<br>they will be cut off | 7245.152<br>cj, *v Qal act ptc mp*<br>וְקֹוֵי<br>weqōwê<br>and those who hope for | 3176<br>pn<br>יְהוָה<br>yehwāh<br>Yahweh | 2065<br>pers pron<br>הֵמָּה<br>hēmmāh<br>they |
|---|---|---|---|---|---|

| 3542.126, 800<br>v Qal impf 3mp, n fs<br>יִירְשׁוּ־אָרֶץ<br>yîreshû-'ārets<br>they will possess the land | 10. | 5968<br>cj, adv<br>וְעוֹד<br>we'ôdh<br>and still | 4746<br>sub<br>מְעַט<br>me'aṭ<br>a little | 375<br>cj, *sub*<br>וְאֵין<br>we'ên<br>and there is not | 7857<br>n ms<br>רָשָׁע<br>rāshā'<br>the wicked |
|---|---|---|---|---|---|

| 1032.713<br>cj, v Hithpolel pf 2ms<br>וְהִתְבּוֹנַנְתָּ<br>wehithbônantā<br>and you will direct your attention | 6142, 4887<br>prep, n ms, ps 3ms<br>עַל־מְקוֹמוֹ<br>'al-meqômô<br>concerning his place | 375<br>cj, sub, ps 3ms<br>וְאֵינֶנּוּ<br>we'ênennû<br>but he is not | 11. | 6262<br>cj, n mp<br>וַעֲנָוִים<br>wa'ănāwîm<br>but the lowly |
|---|---|---|---|---|

| 3542.126, 800<br>v Qal impf 3mp, n fs<br>יִירְשׁוּ־אָרֶץ<br>yîreshû-'ārets<br>they will possess the land | 6253.716<br>cj, v Hithpael pf 3cp<br>וְהִתְעַנְּגוּ<br>wehith'anneghû<br>and they will take pleasure | 6142, 7524<br>prep, *n ms*<br>עַל־רֹב<br>'al-rōv<br>over the abundance of | 8361<br>n ms<br>שָׁלוֹם<br>shālôm<br>peace |
|---|---|---|---|

| 12. | 2246.151<br>v Qal act ptc ms<br>זֹמֵם<br>zōmēm<br>one who plans | 7857<br>n ms<br>רָשָׁע<br>rāshā'<br>the wicked | 3937, 6926<br>prep, art, n ms<br>לַצַּדִּיק<br>latstsaddîq<br>about the righteous | 2892.151<br>cj, v Qal act ptc ms<br>וְחֹרֵק<br>wechōrēq<br>and one who gnashes | 6142<br>prep, ps 3ms<br>עָלָיו<br>'ālâv<br>on him | 8514<br>n fp, ps 3ms<br>שִׁנָּיו<br>shinnâv<br>his teeth |
|---|---|---|---|---|---|---|

| 13. | 112<br>n mp, ps 1cs<br>אֲדֹנָי<br>'ădhōnāy<br>my Lord | 7925.121, 3937<br>v Qal impf 3ms, prep, ps 3ms<br>יִשְׂחַק־לוֹ<br>yischaq-lô<br>He laughs at him | 3706, 7495.111<br>cj, v Qal pf 3ms<br>כִּי־רָאָה<br>kî-rā'āh<br>because He has seen | 3706, 971.121<br>cj, v Qal impf 3ms<br>כִּי־יָבֹא<br>kî-yāvō'<br>that it is coming | 3219<br>n ms, ps 3ms<br>יוֹמוֹ<br>yômô<br>his day |
|---|---|---|---|---|---|

| 14. | 2820<br>n fs<br>חֶרֶב<br>cherev<br>a sword | 6858.116<br>v Qal pf 3cp<br>פָּתְחוּ<br>pāthechû<br>they have drawn | 7857<br>n mp<br>רְשָׁעִים<br>reshā'îm<br>the wicked | 1931.116<br>cj, v Qal pf 3cp<br>וְדָרְכוּ<br>wedhārekhû<br>and they have bent | 7493<br>n fs, ps 3mp<br>קַשְׁתָּם<br>qashtām<br>their bow | 3937, 5489.541<br>prep, v Hiphil inf con<br>לְהַפִּיל<br>lehappîl<br>to cause to fall |
|---|---|---|---|---|---|---|

the sun at noon, *NEB* ... bright as the noonday shall be your vindication, *NCB.*

**7. Rest in the LORD, and wait patiently for him:** ... Wait and trust the LORD, *NCV* ... Stand still and look to the LORD for help, *Beck* ... Resign all, and rely on the LORD, *Fenton* ... wait with longing for him, *Rotherham.*

**fret not thyself because of him who prospereth in his way, because of the man who bringeth wicked devices to pass:** ... Be not vexed at the successful path of the man who does malicious deeds, *NAB* ... do not strive to outdo the successful, *NEB* ... wicked schemes to pass, *NKJV.*

**8. Cease from anger, and forsake wrath: fret not thyself in any wise to do evil:** ... Quit being angry, and dismiss fury, *Berkeley* ... Fret not yourself; it does nothing but harm, *Goodspeed* ... Don't be upset; it only leads to trouble, *NCV* ... it only leads to doing wrong, *Beck.*

**9. For evildoers shall be cut off: but those that wait upon the LORD, they shall inherit the earth:** ... and patient souls, that wait for the Lord, succeed them, *Knox* ... who trust in the LORD hold the Land, *Fenton* ... and the land left to those who wait for the Eternal, *Moffatt* ... shall possess the land, *RSV.*

**10. For yet for a little while, and the wicked shall not be: yea, thou shalt diligently consider his place, and it shall not be:** ... though you mark his place he will not be there, *NAB* ... If you peer into his house, he will not be there, *Anchor* ... though you look for them, they will not be found, *NIV* ... And he shall have vanished, *Rotherham.*

**11. But the meek shall inherit the earth; and shall delight themselves in the abundance of peace:** ... People who are not proud, *NCV* ... the humble shall inherit the land, *MAST* ... shall possess the land, *Darby* ... and enjoy untold prosperity, *NEB.*

**12. The wicked plotteth against the just, and gnasheth upon him with his teeth:** ... The godless man makes plots against the good, *Moffatt* ... Tho' the wicked may rage at the good, *Fenton* ... grinding his teeth at him, *Beck* ... lifting up the voice of wrath against him, *BB.*

**13. The Lord shall laugh at him: for he seeth that his day is coming:** ... and laughs at his malice, *Knox* ... their day of judgement is coming, *REB* ... knowing that his end is in sight, *JB.*

**14. The wicked have drawn out the sword, and have bent their bow, to**

---

eternally true, for they who take God for their portion have a safe abode and feed their souls on his unalterable adherence to his promises and on the abundance flowing thence.

The subsequent precepts bear a certain relation to each other and, taken together, make a lovely picture of the inner secret of the devout life: Delight thyself in Yahweh; roll thy way on Him; trust in Him; be silent to Yahweh. No man will commit his way to God who does not delight in Him. Unless he has so committed his way, he cannot rest in the LORD. The heart that delights in God, finding its truest joy in Him and being well and at ease when consciously moving in Him as an all-encompassing atmosphere and reaching towards Him with the deepest of its desires, will live far above the region of disappointment. For desire and fruition go together. Longings fixed on Him fulfill themselves. We can have as much of God as we wish. If He is our delight, we shall wish nothing contrary to or apart from Him, and wishes which are directed to Him cannot be in vain. To delight in God is to possess our delight and to find fulfilled in Him wishes and abiding joys. "Commit thy way unto Him" (v. 5), or roll it upon Him in the exercise of trust, and, as the verse says with grand generality, omitting an object for the verb, "He will do" all that is wanted, or will finish the work. To roll one's way upon Yahweh implies subordination of will, judgment to Him and quiet confidence in his guidance. If the heart delights in Him and the will waits silent before Him and a happy consciousness of dependence fills the soul, the desert will not be trackless, nor will the travelers fail to hear the voice which says, "This is the way; walk ye in it" (Isa. 30:21). He who trusts is led, and God works for him, clearing away clouds and obstructions. His good may be evil spoken of, but the vindication by fact will make his righteousness shine spotless. His cause may be apparently hopeless, but God will deliver him. The section returns upon itself and once more ends with the unhesitating assurance, based upon the very essence of God's Covenant with the nation that righteousness is the condition of inheritance, and sin the cause of certain destruction. The narrower application of the principle, which was all that stage of revelation made clear to the psalmist, melts away for us into the Christian certainty that righteousness is the condition of dwelling in the true Land of Promise and that sin is always death, in germ or in full fruitage.

**37:10–15.** The refrain occurs next in v. 22, and the portion thus marked off (vv. 10–22) may be dealt with as a smaller whole. After a repetition (vv. 10f) of the main thesis slightly expanded, it sketches in vivid outline the fury of "the wicked" against "the just" and the grim retribution that turns

| 6270 | 33 | 3937, 2983.141 | 3596, 1932 | | 2820 | 971.122 |
|---|---|---|---|---|---|---|
| n ms | cj, n ms | prep, v Qal inf con | *adj*, n ms | | n fs, ps 3mp | v Qal impf 3fs |
| עָנִי | וְאֶבְיוֹן | לִטְבוֹחַ | יִשְׁרֵי־דָרֶךְ | **15.** | חַרְבָּם | תָּבוֹא |
| ʿānî | weʾevyôn | liṯvôach | yishrê-dhārekh | | charbām | tāvôʾ |
| the afflicted | and the needy | to slaughter | the upright of the way | | their sword | it will enter |

| 904, 3949 | 7493 | 8132.227 | | 3005, 4746 | 3937, 6926 |
|---|---|---|---|---|---|
| prep, n ms, ps 3mp | cj, n fp, ps 3mp | v Niphal impf 3fp | | adj, sub | prep, art, n ms |
| בְּלִבָּם | וְקַשְּׁתוֹתָם | תִּשָּׁבַרְנָה | **16.** | טוֹב־מְעַט | לַצַּדִּיק |
| velibbām | weqashshethôthām | tishshāvarnāh | | ṯôv-meʿaṯ | latstsaddîq |
| into their heart | and their bows | they will be broken | | better a little | for the righteous |

| 4623, 2066 | 7857 | 7521 | | 3706 | 2307 | 7857 | 8132.227 |
|---|---|---|---|---|---|---|---|
| prep, *n ms* | n mp | adj | | cj | *n fp* | n mp | v Niphal impf 3fp |
| מֵהֲמוֹן | רְשָׁעִים | רַבִּים | **17.** | כִּי | זְרוֹעוֹת | רְשָׁעִים | תִּשָּׁבַרְנָה |
| mēhemôn | reshāʿîm | rabbîm | | kî | zerôʿôth | reshāʿîm | tishshāvarnāh |
| than wealth of | the wicked | many | | because | the arms of | the wicked | they will be broken |

| 5759.151 | 6926 | 3176 | | 3156.151 | 3176 | 3219 |
|---|---|---|---|---|---|---|
| cj, v Qal act ptc ms | n mp | pn | | v Qal act ptc ms | pn | *n mp* |
| וְסוֹמֵךְ | צַדִּיקִים | יְהוָה | **18.** | יוֹדֵעַ | יְהוָה | יְמֵי |
| wesômēkh | tsaddîqîm | yehwāh | | yôdhēaʿ | yehwāh | yemê |
| but One Who sustains | the righteous | Yahweh | | One Who knows | Yahweh | the days of |

| 8879 | 5338 | 3937, 5986 | 2030.122 | | 3940, 991.126 |
|---|---|---|---|---|---|
| n mp | cj, n fs, ps 3mp | prep, n ms | v Qal impf 3fs | | neg part, v Qal impf 3mp |
| תְמִימִם | וְנַחֲלָתָם | לְעוֹלָם | תִּהְיֶה | **19.** | לֹא־יֵבֹשׁוּ |
| themîmim | wenachlāthām | leʿôlām | tihyeh | | lōʾ-yēvōshû |
| the blameless | and their inheritance | unto eternity | it will be | | they will not be ashamed |

| 904, 6496 | 7750 | 904, 3219 | 7743 | 7881.126 | | 3706 | 7857 |
|---|---|---|---|---|---|---|---|
| prep, *n fs* | n fs | cj, prep, *n mp* | n ms | v Qal impf 3mp | | cj | n mp |
| בְּעֵת | רָעָה | וּבִימֵי | רְעָבוֹן | יִשְׂבָּעוּ | **20.** | כִּי | רְשָׁעִים |
| beʿēth | rāʿāh | ûvîmê | reʿāvôn | yisbāʿû | | kî | reshāʿîm |
| in the time of | evil | and in the days of | famine | they are satiated | | yet | the wicked |

| 6.126 | 342.152 | 3176 | 3626, 3479 | 3862 | 3735.116 |
|---|---|---|---|---|---|
| v Qal impf 3mp | cj, *v Qal act ptc mp* | pn | prep, adj | n mp | v Qal pf 3cp |
| יֹאבֵדוּ | וְאֹיְבֵי | יְהוָה | כִּיקַר | כָּרִים | כָּלוּ |
| yōʾvēdhû | weʾōyevê | yehwāh | kîqar | kārîm | kālû |
| they perish | and the enemies of | Yahweh | like precious | pastures | they will come to an end |

| 904, 6476 | 3735.116 | | 4004.151 | 7857 | 3940 |
|---|---|---|---|---|---|
| prep, art, n ms | v Qal pf 3cp | | v Qal act ptc ms | n ms | cj, neg part |
| בֶעָשָׁן | כָּלוּ | **21.** | לֹוֶה | רָשָׁע | וְלֹא |
| veʿāshān | kālû | | lōweh | rāshāʿ | welōʾ |
| with the smoke | they will come to an end | | one who borrows | the wicked | but not |

| 8396.321 | 6926 | 2706.151 | 5598.151 | | 3706 |
|---|---|---|---|---|---|
| v Piel impf 3ms | cj, n ms | v Qal act ptc ms | cj, v Qal act ptc ms | | cj |
| יְשַׁלֵּם | וְצַדִּיק | חוֹנֵן | וְנוֹתֵן | **22.** | כִּי |
| yeshallēm | wetsaddîq | chônēn | wenôthēn | | kî |
| he repays | and the righteous | one who is gracious | and one who gives | | because |

| 4623, 1313.456 | 3542.126 | 800 | 7327.456 | 3901.226 |
|---|---|---|---|---|
| v Pual ptc mp, ps 3ms | v Qal impf 3mp | n fs | cj, v Pual ptc mp, ps 3ms | v Niphal impf 3mp |
| מְבֹרָכָיו | יִירְשׁוּ | אָרֶץ | וּמְקֻלָּלָיו | יִכָּרֵתוּ |
| mevōrākhâv | yîreshû | ʾārets | ûmequllālâv | yikkārēthû |
| those blessed by Him | they will possess | the land | but those cursed by Him | they will be cut off |

**cast down the poor and needy, and to slay such as be of upright conversation:** ... Evil-doers have drawn the sword, *Berkeley* ... To bring down the oppressed, *Rotherham* ... and to slaughter honest men, *NEB* ... to kill those who walk uprightly, *KJVII.*

**15. Their sword shall enter into their own heart, and their bows shall be broken:** ... will destroy their own selves, *Fenton* ... pierce their own hearts, *NIV* ... their bows shall be shivered, *Anchor.*

**16. A little that a righteous man hath is better than the riches of many wicked:** ... which the good man has is better than the wealth of evil-doers, *BB* ... Than the abundance of many wicked, *MRB* ... better than the godless man's great wealth, *Moffatt* ... Than the abundance of the lawless who are mighty, *Rotherham.*

**17. For the arms of the wicked shall be broken: but the LORD upholdeth the righteous:** ... The power of the wicked will be broken, *NCV* ... For the resources of the wicked, *Goodspeed* ... For the arms of the bad will be smashed, *Fenton* ... the weapons of the wicked shall be shattered, *JB.*

**18. The LORD knoweth the days of the upright: and their inheritance shall be for ever:** ... The lives of the just are in Yahweh's care, their birthright will endure, *JB* ... Yahweh looks after the possessions of the honest, *Anchor* ... knows the days of the blameless, and their heritage will abide, *RSV* ... watches over the lives of the wholehearted, *NAB.*

**19. They shall not be ashamed in the evil time: and in the days of famine they shall be satisfied:** ... in the days of famine they will have abundance, *NASB* ... not be miserable in bad times and in days of famine will eat all they want, *Beck* ... When times are bad, he shall not be distressed, *NEB* ... In times of disaster they will not wither, *NIV.*

**20. But the wicked shall perish, and the enemies of the LORD shall be as the fat of lambs: they shall consume; into smoke shall they consume away:** ... The LORD's enemies will be like the flowers of the fields, *NCV* ... like a brand in the furnace, Shall vanish in smoke, *Goodspeed* ... like the beauty of the meadows, vanish, *NCB* ... like a parched field Will vanish in smoke and dissolve, *Fenton* ... like fuel in a furnace, *REB.*

**21. The wicked borroweth, and payeth not again: but the righteous showeth mercy, and giveth:** ... The godless never pays back, *Moffatt* ... is generous and donates, *Berkeley* ... dealeth graciously, *ASV* ... the just man is kindly, *NCB.*

**22. For such as be blessed of him shall inherit the earth; and they that be cursed of him shall be cut off:** ... you will own the land, *Beck* ... shall be destroyed, *NEB* ... And those whom He curses decay, *Fenton.*

---

their weapons into agents of their destruction. How dramatically contrasted are the two pictures, of the quiet righteous in the former section and of this raging enemy, with his gnashing teeth and arsenal of murder! And with what crushing force the thought of the awful laughter of Yahweh in foresight of the swift flight toward the blind miscreant of the day of his fall, which has already, as it were, set out on its road, smites his elaborate preparations into dust! Silently, the good man sits wrapped in his faith. All around are raging, armed foes. Above, the laughter of God rolls thunderous, and from the throne the obedient "day" is winging its flight like an eagle with lightning bolts in its claws. What can the end be but another instance of the solemn *lex talionis*, by which a man's evil slays himself?

**37:16–22.** The longer antithesis is enclosed between two parallel shorter ones, and a certain variety breaks up the sameness of the swing from one side to the other and suggests a pause in the flow of the Psalm. The elongated verse (v. 20) reiterates the initial metaphor of withering herbage (cf. v. 2) with an addition, for the rendering "fat of lambs" must be given up as incongruous and only plausible on account of the emblem of smoke in the next clause. But the two metaphors are independent. Just as in v. 2, so here, the gay "beauty of the pastures," so soon to wilt and be changed into brown barrenness, mirrors the fate of the wicked. Verse 2 shows the grass fallen before the scythe; v. 20 lets us see it in its flush of loveliness, so tragically unlike what it will be when its "day" has come. The figure of smoke is a stereotype in all tongues for evanescence. The thick wreaths thin away and melt. Another peculiar form of the standing antithesis appears in the "lamedh" strophe (vv. 21, 27), which sets forth the gradual impoverishment of the wicked and prosperity as well as beneficence of the righteous and, by the "for" of v. 22, traces these up to the "curse and blessing of God, which become manifest in the final destiny of the two" (Delitzsch). Not dishonesty, but bankruptcy, is the cause of "not paying again"; while, on the other hand, the blessing of God not only enriches, but softens, making the heart which has received grace a wellspring of grace to needy ones, even if they are foes. The form of the contrast suggests its dependence on the promises in Deut. 12:44; 15:6, 28. Thus, the refrain is once more reached, and a new departure taken.

| 23. | 4623, 3176 | 4866, 1429 | 3679.416 | 1932 | 2759.121 |
|---|---|---|---|---|---|
| | prep, pn | *n mp*, n ms | v Polal pf 3cp | cj, n ms, ps 3ms | v Qal impf 3ms |
| | מֵיְהוָה | מִצְעֲדֵי־גֶבֶר | כּוֹנָנוּ | וְדַרְכּוֹ | יֶחְפָּץ |
| | mēyehwāh | mits'ădhê-ghever | kônānû | wedharkô | yechăppāts |
| | from Yahweh | the steps of a man | they are established | and his way | he delights in |

| 24. | 3706, 5489.121 | 3940, 3014.621 | 3706, 3176 | 5759.151 | 3135 |
|---|---|---|---|---|---|
| | cj, v Qal impf 3ms | neg part, v Hophal impf 3ms | cj, pn | v Qal act ptc ms | n fs, ps 3ms |
| | כִּי־יִפֹּל | לֹא־יוּטָל | כִּי־יְהוָה | סוֹמֵךְ | יָדוֹ |
| | kî-yippōl | lō'-yûṯāl | kî-yehwāh | ŝômēkh | yādhô |
| | though he falls | he will be cast headlong | because Yahweh | One Who supports | his hand |

| 25. | 5470 | 2030.115 | 1612, 2290.115 | 3940, 7495.115 | 6926 | 6013.255 |
|---|---|---|---|---|---|---|
| | n ms | v Qal pf 1cs | cj, v Qal pf 1cs | cj, neg part, v Qal pf 1cs | n ms | v Niphal ptc ms |
| | נַעַר | הָיִיתִי | גַּם־זָקַנְתִּי | וְלֹא־רָאִיתִי | צַדִּיק | נֶעֱזָב |
| | na'ar | hāyîthî | gam-zāqantî | welō'-rā'îthî | tsaddîq | ne'ĕzāv |
| | a youth | I was | also I have been old | but not I have seen | the righteous | abandoned |

| 2320 | 1272.351, 4035 | 26. | 3725, 3219 | 2706.151 | 4004.551 |
|---|---|---|---|---|---|
| cj, n ms, ps 3ms | v Piel ptc ms, n ms | | *adj*, art, n ms | v Qal act ptc ms | cj, v Hiphil ptc ms |
| וְזַרְעוֹ | מְבַקֶּשׁ־לָחֶם | | כָּל־הַיּוֹם | חוֹנֵן | וּמַלְוֶה |
| wezar'ô | mevaqqesh-lāchem | | kol-hayyôm | chônēn | ûmalweh |
| nor his descendants | seeking bread | | all the day | one who is gracious | and one who lends |

| 2320 | 3937, 1318 | 27. | 5681.131 | 4623, 7737 | 6449.131, 3005 |
|---|---|---|---|---|---|
| cj, n ms, ps 3ms | prep, n fs | | v Qal impv 2ms | prep, n ms | cj, v Qal impv 2ms, adj |
| וְזַרְעוֹ | לִבְרָכָה | | סוּר | מֵרָע | וַעֲשֵׂה־טוֹב |
| wezar'ô | livrākhāh | | ŝûr | mērā' | wa'ăsēh-ṭôv |
| and his descendants | for a blessing | | turn aside | from evil | and do good |

| 8331.131 | 3937, 5986 | 28. | 3706 | 3176 | 154.151 | 5122 |
|---|---|---|---|---|---|---|
| cj, v Qal impv 2ms | prep, n ms | | cj | pn | v Qal act ptc ms | n ms |
| וּשְׁכֹן | לְעוֹלָם | | כִּי | יְהוָה | אֹהֵב | מִשְׁפָּט |
| ûshekhōn | le'ôlām | | kî | yehwāh | 'ōhēv | mishpāṯ |
| and stay | unto eternity | | because | Yahweh | One Who loves | justice |

| 3940, 6013.121 | 881, 2728 | 3937, 5986 | 8490.216 |
|---|---|---|---|
| cj, neg part, v Qal impf 3ms | do, n mp, ps 3ms | prep, n ms | v Niphal pf 3cp |
| וְלֹא־יַעֲזֹב | אֶת־חֲסִידָיו | לְעוֹלָם | נִשְׁמָרוּ |
| welō'-ya'ăzōv | 'eth-chăŝîdhâv | le'ôlām | nishmārû |
| and He will not abandon | his godly ones | unto eternity | they will be protected |

| 2320 | 7857 | 3901.211 | 29. | 6926 |
|---|---|---|---|---|
| cj, *n ms* | n mp | v Niphal pf 3ms | | n mp |
| וְזֶרַע | רְשָׁעִים | נִכְרָת | | צַדִּיקִים |
| wezera' | reshā'îm | nikhrāth | | tsaddîqîm |
| but the descendants of | the wicked | they will be cut off | | the righteous |

| 3542.126, 800 | 8331.126 | 3937, 5911 | 6142 |
|---|---|---|---|
| v Qal impf 3mp, n fs | cj, v Qal impf 3mp | prep, n ms | prep, ps 3fs |
| יִירְשׁוּ־אָרֶץ | וְיִשְׁכְּנוּ | לָעַד | עָלֶיהָ |
| yîreshû-'ārets | weyishkenû | lā'adh | 'ālêāh |
| they will take possession of the land | and they will stay | unto eternity | on it |

| 30. | 6552, 6926 | 1965.121 | 2551 | 4098 | 1744.322 | 5122 |
|---|---|---|---|---|---|---|
| | *n ms*, n ms | v Qal impf 3ms | n fs | cj, n fs, ps 3ms | v Piel impf 3fs | n ms |
| | פִּי־צַדִּיק | יֶהְגֶּה | חָכְמָה | וּלְשׁוֹנוֹ | תְּדַבֵּר | מִשְׁפָּט |
| | pî-tsaddîq | yehgeh | chokhmāh | ûlāshônô | tedhabbēr | mishpāṯ |
| | the mouth of the righteous | he utters | wisdom | and his tongue | it speaks | justice |

**23. The steps of a good man are ordered by the LORD: and he delighteth in his way:** ... he makes his steps firm, *NIV* ... They have been prepared, *Young* ... who makes sure his stride, *Anchor* ... and approves of his conduct, *REB.*

**24. Though he fall, he shall not be utterly cast down: for the LORD upholdeth him with his hand:** ... though we stumble, *NRSV* ... When he trips he is not thrown sprawling, *JB* ... he will not be without help, *BB* ... for the hand of the LORD sustains him, *NAB.*

**25. I have been young, and now am old; yet have I not seen the righteous forsaken, nor his seed begging bread:** ... I have never seen good people left helpless, *NCV* ... or his offspring begging bread, *Berkeley* ... Nor his descendants, *NKJV* ... or his children, *RSV.*

**26. He is ever merciful, and lendeth; and his seed is blessed:** ... He is ever giving liberally and lending, *RSV* ... they always have something to give away, something wherewith to bless their families, *Moffatt* ... and their children become a blessing, *NRSV* ... so his descendants reap a blessing, *JB.*

**27. Depart from evil, and do good; and dwell for evermore:** ... do good, and be at rest continually, *Knox* ... and live at peace for ever, *NEB* ... then you will dwell in the land forever, *NIV* ... And so settle down unto times age-abiding, *Rotherham.*

**28. For the LORD loveth judgment, and forsaketh not his saints; they are preserved for ever:** ... For Yahweh loves the just man, and never deserts his devoted ones, *Anchor* ... LORD loves what is right, and forsakes not his faithful, *NAB* ... and will not leave those who worship him, *NCV* ... will not desert those devoted to Him, *Beck.*

**but the seed of the wicked shall be cut off:** ... and the children of the wicked destroyed, *NEB* ... the families of the godless shall be doomed, *Moffatt* ... But the descendants of the wicked are cut off, *Goodspeed.*

**29. The righteous shall inherit the land, and dwell therein for ever:** ... The upright will have the earth for their heritage, *BB* ... The just shall possess the land and dwell in it forever, *NCB* ... The godly shall be firmly planted in the land, *LIVB.*

**30. The mouth of the righteous speaketh wisdom, and his tongue talketh of judgment:** ... Wisdom comes from the lips of the upright, *JB* ... And his tongue speaks justice, *NASB* ... And his tongue speaks for justice alone, *Fenton* ... and he says what is fair, *NCV.*

**31. The law of his God is in his heart; none of his steps shall slide:** ... teachings of his God, *NCV* ... the law of God rules in his heart, *Knox* ... His steps shall not swerve, *Rotherham* ... He never will cease to advance, *Fenton.*

---

**37:23–29.** The third section is shorter than the preceding (vv. 23–29) and has as its center the psalmist's confirmation from his own experience of the former part of his antithesis, the fourth section similarly confirming the second. All this third part is positive, with the divine favor streaming upon the righteous, the only reference to the wicked being in the refrain at the close. The first strophe (vv. 23f) declares God's care for the former under the familiar image of guidance and support to a traveler. As in vv. 5, 7, the "way" is an emblem of active life and is designated as "his" who treads it. The intention of the Psalm, the context of the metaphor and the parallelism with the verses just referred to settle the reference of the ambiguous pronouns "he" and " his" in v. 23b. God delights in the good man's way (Ps. 1:6), and that is the reason for his establishing his goings. That promise is not to be limited to either the material or moral region. The ground tone of the Psalm is that the two regions coincide insofar as prosperity in the outer is the infallible index of rightness in the inner. The dial has two sets of hands, one within and one without, but both are, as it were, mounted on the same spindle, and they move accurately alike. Steadfast treading in the path of duty and successful undertakings are both included, since they are inseparable in fact. Even the fixed faith of the psalmist has to admit that the good man's path is not always smooth. If facts had not often contradicted his creed, he would never have sung his song; hence, he takes into account the case of such a man's falling and seeks to reduce its importance by the considerations of its recoverability and of God's keeping hold of the man's hand all the while.

**37:30–31.** The last section, like the preceding, has the psalmist's experience for its center and traces the entail of conduct to a second generation of evildoers as the former did to the seed of the righteous. Both sections begin with the promise of firmness for the "goings" or "steps" of the righteous, but the later verses expand the thought by a fuller description of the moral conditions of stability. "The law of his God is in his heart"—that is the foundation on which all permanence is built. From that as center, there issues forth wise and just words on the one hand and stable deeds on the other. That is true in the psalmist's view in reference to outward success and

| 31. | 8784 | 435 | 904, 3949 | 3940 | 4726.122 | 863 |
|---|---|---|---|---|---|---|
| | *n fs* | n mp, ps 3ms | prep, n ms, ps 3ms | neg part | v Qal impf 3fs | n fp, ps 3ms |
| | תּוֹרַת | אֱלֹהָיו | בְּלִבּוֹ | לֹא | תִמְעַד | אֲשֻׁרָיו |
| | tôrath | 'ĕlōhâv | b$^{e}$libbô | lō' | thim'adh | 'ăshurâv |
| | the Law of | his God | in his heart | not | they falter | steps |

| 32. | 7099.151 | 7857 | 3937, 6926 | 1272.351 |
|---|---|---|---|---|
| | v Qal act ptc ms | n ms | prep, art, n ms | cj, v Piel ptc ms |
| | צוֹפֶה | רָשָׁע | לַצַּדִּיק | וּמְבַקֵּשׁ |
| | tsôpheh | rāshā' | latstsaddîq | ûm$^{e}$vaqqēsh |
| | one who keeps looking | the wicked | for the righteous | and one who seeks |

| 3937, 4322.541 | 33. | 3176 | 940, 6013.121 | 904, 3135 | 3940 |
|---|---|---|---|---|---|
| prep, v Hiphil inf con, ps 3ms | | pn | neg part, v Qal impf 3ms, ps 3ms | prep, n fs, ps 3ms | cj, neg part |
| לַהֲמִיתוֹ | | יְהוָה | לֹא־יַעַזְבֶנּוּ | בְיָדוֹ | וְלֹא |
| lahmîthô | | y$^{e}$hwāh | lō'-ya'azvennû | v$^{e}$yādhô | w$^{e}$lō' |
| to kill him | | Yahweh | He will not abandon him | into his hand | and not |

| 7855.521 | 904, 8570.241 | 34. | 7245.331 | 420, 3176 | 8490.131 |
|---|---|---|---|---|---|
| v Hiphil impf 3ms, ps 3ms | prep, v Niphal inf con, ps 3ms | | v Piel impv 2ms | prep, pn | cj, v Qal impv 2ms |
| יַרְשִׁיעֶנּוּ | בְּהִשָּׁפְטוֹ | | קַוֵּה | אֶל־יְהוָה | וּשְׁמֹר |
| yarshî'ennû | b$^{e}$hishshāph$^{e}$ṭô | | qawwēh | 'el-y$^{e}$hwāh | ûsh$^{e}$mōr |
| He will declare him guilty | during his being judged | | hope | to Yahweh | and observe |

| 1932 | 7597.321 | 3937, 3542.141 | 800 | 904, 3901.241 | 7857 |
|---|---|---|---|---|---|
| n ms, ps 3ms | cj, v Polel impf 3ms, ps 2ms | prep, v Qal inf con | n fs | prep, v Niphal inf con | n mp |
| דַּרְכּוֹ | וִירוֹמִמְךָ | לָרֶשֶׁת | אָרֶץ | בְּהִכָּרֵת | רְשָׁעִים |
| darkô | wîrômimkhā | lāresheth | 'ārets | b$^{e}$hikkārēth | r$^{e}$shā'îm |
| his way | and He will lift you up | to possess | the land | when the cutting off of | the wicked |

| 7495.123 | 35. | 7495.115 | 7857 | 6422 | 6408.751 | 3626, 248 |
|---|---|---|---|---|---|---|
| v Qal impf 2ms | | v Qal pf 1cs | n ms | adj | cj, v Hithpael ptc ms | prep, n ms |
| תִּרְאֶה | | רָאִיתִי | רָשָׁע | עָרִיץ | וּמִתְעָרֶה | כְּאֶזְרָח |
| tir'eh | | rā'îthî | rāshā' | 'ārîts | ûmith'āreh | k$^{e}$'ezrāch |
| you will see | | I have seen | the wicked | terrible | and one who exposes himself | like a native |

| 7776 | 36. | 5882.121 | 2079 | 375 | 1272.325 | 3940 |
|---|---|---|---|---|---|---|
| adj | | cj, v Qal impf 3ms | cj, intrj | sub, ps 3ms | cj, v Piel impf 1cs, ps 3ms | cj, neg part |
| רַעֲנָן | | וַיַּעֲבֹר | וְהִנֵּה | אֵינֶנּוּ | וָאֲבַקְשֵׁהוּ | וְלֹא |
| ra'ănān | | wayya'ăvōr | w$^{e}$hinnēh | 'ênennû | wā'ăvaqōshēhû | w$^{e}$lō' |
| in luxury | | but he passed by | and behold | he was not | and I sought for him | but not |

| 4834.211 | 37. | 8490.131, 8865 | 7495.131 | 3596 | 3706, 321 |
|---|---|---|---|---|---|
| v Niphal pf 3ms | | v Qal impv 2ms, n ms | cj, v Qal impv 2ms | n ms | cj, n fs |
| נִמְצָא | | שְׁמָר־תָּם | וּרְאֵה | יָשָׁר | כִּי־אַחֲרִית |
| nimtsā' | | sh$^{e}$mār-tām | ûr$^{e}$'ēh | yāshār | kî-'achrîth |
| he was found | | watch the blameless | and look at | the upright | because an end |

| 3937, 382 | 8361 | 38. | 6839.152 | 8436.216 | 3267 | 321 |
|---|---|---|---|---|---|---|
| prep, *n ms* | n ms | | cj, v Qal act ptc mp | v Niphal pf 3cp | adv | *n fs* |
| לְאִישׁ | שָׁלוֹם | | וּפֹשְׁעִים | נִשְׁמְדוּ | יַחְדָּו | אַחֲרִית |
| l$^{e}$'îsh | shālôm | | ûphōsh$^{e}$'îm | nishm$^{e}$dhû | yachdāw | 'achrîth |
| for the man of | peace | | but transgressors | they will be destroyed | at the same time | the end of |

| 7857 | 3901.212 | 39. | 9009 | 6926 | 4623, 3176 | 4735 |
|---|---|---|---|---|---|---|
| n mp | v Niphal pf 3fs | | cj, *n fs* | n mp | prep, pn | n ms, ps 3mp |
| רְשָׁעִים | נִכְרָתָה | | וּתְשׁוּעַת | צַדִּיקִים | מֵיְהוָה | מָעוּזָּם |
| r$^{e}$shā'îm | nikhrāthāh | | ûth$^{e}$shû'ath | tsaddîqîm | mēy$^{e}$hwāh | mā'ûzzām |
| the wicked | they will be cut off | | but the salvation of | the righteous | of Yahweh | their fortress |

**32. The wicked watcheth the righteous, and seeketh to slay him:** ... The sinners are watching the upright man, *BB* ... spies on the just, *NCB* ... seek to put them to death, *REB* ... and tries to kill him, *Beck*.

**33. The LORD will not leave him in his hand, nor condemn him when he is judged:** ... Yahweh will never abandon him to the clutches of the wicked, *JB* ... Nor will he declare him guilty, *Goodspeed* ... in his power, *NAB* ... when brought to trial, *NIV*.

**34. Wait on the LORD, and keep his way, and he shall exalt thee to inherit the land: when the wicked are cut off, thou shalt see it:** ... you shall look upon the destruction of the wicked, *Berkeley* ... He will help you to conquer the land, *Fenton* ... wicked men shall perish, *Geneva* ... he will keep you safe, *NEB*.

**35. I have seen the wicked in great power, and spreading himself like a green bay tree:** ... a wicked man thriving, *Anchor* ... a green tree in its native soil, *Darby* ... covering the earth like a great tree, *BB* ... towering like any cedar of Lebanon, *Moffatt*.

**36. Yet he passed away, and, lo, he was not: yea, I sought him, but he could not be found:** ... there was no sign of him, *BB* ... I passed by one day, and he was gone, *NEB* ... and they were no more, *NRSV* ... he had vanished, *Rotherham*.

**37. Mark the perfect man, and behold the upright: for the end of that man is peace:** ... Watch the wholehearted man, *NAB* ... Watch integrity and look upon right, *Goodspeed* ... there is a future for the peaceable, *Moffatt* ... for the man of peace leaves descendants, *REB*.

**38. But the transgressors shall be destroyed together: the end of the wicked shall be cut off:** ... But perverse men shall wholly be destroyed, *Anchor* ... The future of the wicked, *NKJV* ... and their children annihilated, *JB* ... and their graceless names forgotten, *Knox*.

**39. But the salvation of the righteous is of the LORD: he is their strength in the time of trouble:** ... Their strong place in a time of adversity, *Young* ... and keeps them safe when trouble comes, *Beck* ... their fortress, *Berkeley* ... he is their refuge, *RSV*.

---

continuance, but still more profoundly in regard to steadfast progress in paths of righteousness. He who orders his footsteps by God's known will is saved from much hesitancy, vacillation and stumbling, and he plants a firm foot even on slippery places.

**37:32–34.** Once more, the picture of the enmity of the wicked recurs, as in vv. 12ff, with the difference that there the emphasis was laid on the destruction of the plotters, and here it is put on the vindication of the righteous by acts of deliverance (vv. 32f). In v. 34, another irregularity occurs, in its being the only verse in a strophe and being prolonged to three clauses. This may be intended to give emphasis to the exhortation contained in it, which, like that in v. 27, is the only one in its section. The two key words "inherit" and "cut off" are brought together. Not only are the two fates set in contrast, but the waiters on Yahweh are promised the sight of the destruction of the wicked. Satisfaction at the sight is implied. There is nothing unworthy in solemn thankfulness when God's judgments break the teeth of some devouring lion. Divine judgments minister occasion for praise even from pure spirits before the throne, and men relieved from the incubus of godless oppression may well draw a long breath of relief, which passes into celebration of his righteous acts. No doubt there is a higher tone, which remembers truth and pity even in that solemn joy; but Christian feeling does not destroy but modifies the psalmist's thankfulness for the sweeping away of godless antagonism to goodness.

**37:35–36.** His assurance to those who wait on Yahweh has his own experience as its guarantee (v. 35), just as the complimentary assurance in v. 24 had in v. 25. The earlier metaphors of the green herbage and the beauty of the pastures are heightened now. A venerable, wide-spreading giant of the forests, rooted in its native soil, is grander than those humble growths, but for lofty cedars or lowly grass the end is the same. Twice the psalmist stood at the same place; once the great tree laid its large limbs across the field and lifted a firm bole. Again he came, and a clear space revealed how great had been the bulk which shadowed it. Not even a stump was left to tell where the leafy glory had been.

**37:37–38.** Verses 37f make the "Shin" strophe, and simply reiterate the antithesis which has molded the whole Psalm, with the addition of that reference to a second generation which appeared in the third and fourth parts. The word rendered in the AV and RV "latter end" (HED #321) here means "posterity." The "perfect man" is further designated as a "man of peace."

**37:39–40.** The Psalm might have ended with this gathering together of its contents in one final emphatic statement, but the poet will not leave the stern words of destruction as his last. Therefore, he

| 904, 6496 | 7150 | | 6038.121 | 3176 | 6647.321 |
|---|---|---|---|---|---|
| prep, *n fs* | n fs | 40. | cj, v Qal impf 3ms, ps 3mp | pn | cj, v Piel impf 3ms, ps 3mp |
| בְּעֵת | צָרָה | | וַיַּעְזְרֵם | יְהוָה | וַיְפַלְּטֵם |
| be'ēth | tsārāh | | wayya'ăzrēm | yehwāh | wayphalleṭēm |
| in the time of | adversity | | and He helps them | Yahweh | and He sets them free |

| 6647.321 | 4623, 7857 | 3588.521 | 3706, 2725.116 |
|---|---|---|---|
| v Piel impf 3ms, ps 3mp | prep, n mp | cj, v Hiphil impf 3ms, ps 3mp | cj, v Qal pf 3cp |
| יְפַלְּטֵם | מֵרְשָׁעִים | וְיוֹשִׁיעֵם | כִּי־חָסוּ |
| yephalleṭēm | mēreshā'îm | weyôshî'ēm | kî-chāsû |
| He sets them free | from the wicked | and He saves them | because they have taken refuge |

| 904 | | 4344 | 3937, 1784 | 3937, 2226.541 | | 3176 | 414, 904, 7397 |
|---|---|---|---|---|---|---|---|
| prep, ps 3ms | 38:t | n ms | prep, pn | prep, v Hiphil inf con | 1. | pn | adv, prep, n ms, ps 2ms |
| בוֹ | | מִזְמוֹר | לְדָוִד | לְהַזְכִּיר | | יְהוָה | אַל־בְּקֶצְפְּךָ |
| vô | | mizmôr | ledhāwidh | lehazkîr | | yehwāh | 'al-beqetspekhā |
| in Him | | a Psalm | of David | to cause to remember | | O Yahweh | not in your anger |

| 3306.523 | 904, 2635 | 3364.323 | | 3706, 2777 |
|---|---|---|---|---|
| v Hiphil juss 2ms, ps 1cs | cj, prep, n fs, ps 2ms | v Piel impf 2ms, ps 1cs | 2. | cj, n mp, ps 2ms |
| תוֹכִיחֵנִי | וּבַחֲמָתְךָ | תְיַסְּרֵנִי | | כִּי־חִצֶּיךָ |
| thôkhîchēnî | ûvachmāthekhā | theyassérēnî | | kî-chitstsêkhā |
| chastise me | nor in your wrath | rebuke me | | because your arrows |

| 5365.216 | 904 | 5365.122 | 6142 | 3135 |
|---|---|---|---|---|
| v Niphal pf 3cp | prep, ps 1cs | cj, v Qal impf 3fs | prep, ps 1cs | n fs, ps 2ms |
| נִחֲתוּ | בִי | וַתִּנְחַת | עָלַי | יָדֶךָ |
| nichăthû | vî | wattinchath | 'ālay | yādhekhā |
| they have penetrated | into me | and it comes down | on me | your hand |

| | 375, 5149 | 904, 1340 | 4623, 6686 | 2279 | 375, 8361 |
|---|---|---|---|---|---|
| 3. | sub, n ms | prep, n ms, ps 1cs | prep, *n mp* | n ms, ps 2ms | sub, n ms |
| | אֵין־מְתֹם | בִּבְשָׂרִי | מִפְּנֵי | זַעְמֶךָ | אֵין־שָׁלוֹם |
| | 'ên-methōm | bivsārî | mippenê | za'ămekhā | 'ên-shālôm |
| | there is not an uninjured place | in my flesh | from before | your indignation | there is not health |

| 904, 6344 | 4623, 6686 | 2496 | | 3706 | 5988 | 5882.116 |
|---|---|---|---|---|---|---|
| prep, n fp, ps 1cs | prep, *n mp* | n fs, ps 1cs | 4. | cj | n mp, ps 1cs | v Qal pf 3cp |
| בַּעֲצָמַי | מִפְּנֵי | חַטָּאתִי | | כִּי | עֲוֹנֹתַי | עָבְרוּ |
| ba'ătsāmay | mippenê | chaṭṭā'thî | | kî | 'ăwōnōthay | 'āverû |
| in my bones | from before | my sin | | because | my transgressions | they have gone past |

| 7513 | 3626, 5014 | 3633 | 3632.126 | 4623 | | 919.516 |
|---|---|---|---|---|---|---|
| n ms, ps 1cs | prep, n ms | adj | v Qal impf 3mp | prep, ps 1cs | 5. | v Hiphil pf 3cp |
| רֹאשִׁי | כְּמַשָּׂא | כָבֵד | יִכְבְּדוּ | מִמֶּנִּי | | הִבְאִישׁוּ |
| rō'shî | kemassā' | khāvēdh | yikhbedhû | mimmenî | | hiv'îshû |
| my head | like a burden | heavy | they are heavier | than me | | they have begun to stink |

| 4905.216 | 2337 | 4623, 6686 | 198 | | 5971.215 |
|---|---|---|---|---|---|
| v Niphal pf 3cp | n fp, ps 1cs | prep, *n mp* | n fs, ps 1cs | 6. | v Niphal pf 1cs |
| נָמַקּוּ | חַבּוּרֹתָי | מִפְּנֵי | אִוַּלְתִּי | | נַעֲוֵיתִי |
| nāmaqqû | chabbûrōthāy | mippenê | 'iwwaltî | | na'ăwêthî |
| they have festered | my wounds | from before | my foolishness | | I have been bent down |

| 8246.115 | 5912, 4108 | 3725, 3219 | 7222.151 | 2050.315 | | 3706, 3814 |
|---|---|---|---|---|---|---|
| v Qal pf 1cs | adv, adv | *adj*, art, n ms | v Qal act ptc ms | v Piel pf 1cs | 7. | cj, n mp, ps 1cs |
| שַׁחֹתִי | עַד־מְאֹד | כָּל־הַיּוֹם | קֹדֵר | הִלָּכְתִּי | | כִּי־כְסָלַי |
| shachōthî | 'adh-me'ōdh | kol-hayyôm | qōdhēr | hillākhettî | | kî-khesālay |
| I have bowed down | until very | all the day | being unkempt | I walk about | | because my loins |

**40. And the LORD shall help them, and deliver them: he shall deliver them from the wicked, and save them, because they trust in him:** ... He rescues them from the wicked and makes them victorious, *Goodspeed* ... And saves from the hand of the bad, *Fenton* ... and keep them safe, *BB* ... because they take refuge in him, *NIV.*

**38:t. A Psalm of David, to bring to remembrance.**

**1. O LORD, rebuke me not in thy wrath: neither chasten me in thy hot displeasure:** ... let not your hand be on me in the heat of your passion, *BB* ... Nor in Your hot anger correct, *Fenton* ... Nor correct me in thy fury, *Goodspeed* ... do not discipline me in wrath, *JB.*

**2. For thine arrows stick fast in me, and thy hand presseth me sore:** ... For your arrows have rained down on me, *REB* ... arrows are gone deep into me, *MAST* ... arrows have wounded me, *NCV* ... For your arrows have pierced me, and your hand has come down upon me, *NIV.*

**3. There is no soundness in my flesh because of thine anger; neither is there any rest in my bones because of my sin:** ... Because You're angry, there's not a healthy spot in my body, *Beck* ... there is no health in my limbs, thanks to my sins, *Moffatt* ... there is no health in my whole frame because of my sin, *NEB* ... Peace is not in my bones because of my sin, *Young.*

**4. For mine iniquities are gone over mine head: as an heavy burden they are too heavy for me:** ... have overwhelmed me; they are like a heavy burden, beyond my strength, *NAB* ... as a heavy load they are too weighty for me, *Berkeley* ... hangs on me like a heavy burden, *Knox.*

**5. My wounds stink and are corrupt because of my foolishness:** ... My wounds fester and are loathsome, *NIV* ... My wounds grow foul and fester, *NRSV* ... My wounds are of bad odour, *Rotherham* ... My wounds are poisoned and evil-smelling, because of my foolish behaviour, *BB.*

**6. I am troubled; I am bowed down greatly; I go mourning all the day long:** ... I am bowed down and brought very low, *NIV* ... all the day long I go about in gloom, *Anchor* ... I am sad all day long, *NCV* ... All the day I am walking in gloom, *Fenton.*

**7. For my loins are filled with a loathsome disease: and there is no soundness in my flesh:** ... I am burning with fever, and my whole body is sore, *NCV* ... For my loins are filled with burning, *RSV* ... my loins are full of inflammation, *NKJV* ... and there's nothing healthy in my body, *Beck.*

---

adds a sweet, drawn-out close, like the calm, extended clouds that lie motionless in the western sky after a day of storm, in which he once more sings of the blessedness of those who wait on Yahweh. Trouble will come, notwithstanding his assurances that righteousness is blessedness; but in it Yahweh will be a fortress home, and out of it He will save them.

***Psalm 38.*** *This is a long-drawn wail, passionate at first, but gradually calming itself into submission and trust, although never passing from the minor key. The name of God is invoked three times (vv. 1, 9, 15), and each time the psalmist looks up, his burden is somewhat easier to carry, and some low beginnings of contentment steal into his heart and mingle with his lament. Sorrow finds relief in repeating its plaint. It is the mistake of cold-blooded readers to look for consecution of thought in the cries of a wounded soul, but it is also a mistake to be blind to the gradual sinking of the waves in this Psalm, which begins with deprecating God's wrath and ends with quietly nestling close to Him as "my salvation."*

**38:1–4.** The first part of the Psalm is entirely occupied with the subjective aspect of the psalmist's affliction. Three elements are conspicuous: God's judgments, the singer's consciousness of sin, and his mental and probably physical sufferings. Are the "arrows" and crushing weight of God's "hand," which he deprecates in the first verses, the same as the sickness and wounds, whether of mind or body, which he next describes so pathetically? They are generally taken to be so, but the language of this section and the contents of the remainder of the Psalm rather point to a distinction between them. It would seem that there are three stages, not two, as that interpretation would make them. Unspecified calamities, recognized by the sufferer as God's chastisements, have roused his conscience, and its gnawing has superinduced mental and bodily pain.

The second of these is the sense of sin, which the psalmist feels is taking all "peace" or well-being out of his "bones," as a flood rolling its black waters over his head, as a weight beneath which he cannot stand upright, and again as foolishness, since its only effect has been to bring to him not what he hoped to win by it, but this miserable plight.

**38:5–8.** Then, he pours himself out, with the monotonous repetition so natural to self-pity, in a graphic accumulation of pictures of disease, which may be taken as symbolic of mental distress, but are better understood literally. With the whole, Isa. 1:5f should be compared, and the partial resemblances of Isa. 53 should not be overlooked. No fastidiousness keeps the psalmist from describing offensive

| 4527.116 | 7319.255 | 375 | 5149 | 904, 1340 |
|---|---|---|---|---|
| v Qal pf 3cp | v Niphal ptc ms | cj, *sub* | n ms | prep, n ms, ps 1cs |
| מָלְאוּ | נִקְלֶה | וְאֵין | מְתֹם | בִּבְשָׂרִי |
| māl$^{e}$ʾû | niqŏleh | w$^{e}$ʾên | m$^{e}$thōm | bivsārî |
| they are filled with | burning | and there is not | an uninjured place | in my flesh |

| 8. | 6555.215 | 1852.215 | 5912, 4108 | 8057.115 | 4623, 5279 |
|---|---|---|---|---|---|
| | v Niphal pf 1cs | cj, v Niphal pf 1cs | adv, adv | v Qal pf 1cs | prep, *n fs* |
| | נְפוּגוֹתִי | וְנִדְכֵּיתִי | עַד־מְאֹד | שָׁאַגְתִּי | מִנַּהֲמַת |
| | n$^{e}$phûghôthî | w$^{e}$nidhkêthî | ʿadh-m$^{e}$ʾōdh | shāʾaghtî | minnahmath |
| | I have become weak | and I have been crushed | until very | I have groaned | from the tumult of |

| 3949 | 9. | 112 | 5224 | 3725, 8707 | 599 | 4623 |
|---|---|---|---|---|---|---|
| n ms, ps 1cs | | n mp, ps 1cs | prep, ps 2ms | *adj*, n fs, ps 1cs | cj, n fs, ps 1cs | prep, ps 2ms |
| לִבִּי | | אֲדֹנָי | נֶגְדְּךָ | כָל־תַּאֲוָתִי | וְאַנְחָתִי | מִמְּךָ |
| libbî | | ʾădhōnāy | neghd$^{e}$khā | khol-taʾăwāthî | w$^{e}$ʾanchāthî | mimm$^{e}$khā |
| my heart | | O my Lord | before You | all my longing | and my groaning | from You |

| 3940, 5846.212 | 10. | 3949 | 5692.311 | 6013.111 | 3699 |
|---|---|---|---|---|---|
| neg part, v Niphal pf 3fs | | n ms, ps 1cs | v Pealal pf 3ms | v Qal pf 3ms, ps 1cs | n ms, ps 1cs |
| לֹא־נִסְתָּרָה | | לִבִּי | סְחַרְחַר | עֲזָבַנִי | כֹחִי |
| lōʾ-nistārāh | | libbî | s$^{e}$charchar | ʿăzāvanî | khōchî |
| it was not hidden | | my heart | it beats convulsively | it has abandoned me | my strength |

| 214, 6084 | 1612, 2062 | 375 | 882 | 11. | 154.152 |
|---|---|---|---|---|---|
| cj, *n ms*, n fd, ps 1cs | cj, pers pron | *sub* | prep, ps 1cs | | v Qal act ptc mp, ps 1cs |
| וְאוֹר־עֵינַי | גַּם־הֵם | אֵין | אִתִּי | | אֹהֲבַי |
| w$^{e}$ʾôr-ʿênay | gam-hēm | ʾên | ʾittî | | ʾōh$^{e}$vay |
| and the light of my eyes | also they | there is not | with me | | those who love me |

| 7739 | 4623, 5224 | 5237 | 6198.126 | 7427 | 4623, 7632 |
|---|---|---|---|---|---|
| cj, n mp, ps 1cs | prep, prep | n ms, ps 1cs | v Qal impf 3mp | cj, n mp, ps 1cs | prep, adj |
| וְרֵעַי | מִנֶּגֶד | נִגְעִי | יַעֲמֹדוּ | וּקְרוֹבַי | מֵרָחֹק |
| w$^{e}$rēʿay | minneghedh | nighʿî | yaʿămōdhû | ûqŏrôvay | mērāchōq |
| and my companions | from before | my plague | they stand | and my relatives | from far away |

| 6198.116 | 12. | 5550.326 | 1272.352 | 5497 | 1938.152 | 7750 |
|---|---|---|---|---|---|---|
| v Qal pf 3cp | | cj, v Piel impf 3mp | *v Piel ptc mp* | n fs, ps 1cs | cj, *v Qal act ptc mp* | n fs, ps 1cs |
| עָמָדוּ | | וַיְנַקְשׁוּ | מְבַקְשֵׁי | נַפְשִׁי | וְדֹרְשֵׁי | רָעָתִי |
| ʿāmādhû | | waynaqŏshû | m$^{e}$vaqŏshê | naphshî | w$^{e}$dhōr$^{e}$shê | rāʿāthî |
| they stand | | and they lay a snare | those who seek | my soul | but those who seek | my disaster |

| 1744.316 | 2010 | 4983 | 3725, 3219 | 1965.126 | 13. | 603 | 3626, 2901 |
|---|---|---|---|---|---|---|---|
| v Piel pf 3cp | n fp | cj, n fp | *adj*, art, n ms | v Qal impf 3mp | | cj, pers pron | prep, adj |
| דִּבְּרוּ | הַוּוֹת | וּמִרְמוֹת | כָּל־הַיּוֹם | יֶהְגּוּ | | וַאֲנִי | כְחֵרֵשׁ |
| dibb$^{e}$rû | hawwôth | ûmirmôth | kol-hayyôm | yehgû | | waʾănî | kh$^{e}$chērēsh |
| they have spoken | destruction | and deceit | all the day | they utter | | and I | as deaf |

| 3940 | 8471.125 | 3626, 489 | 3940 | 6858.121, 6552 | 14. | 2030.125 | 3626, 382 |
|---|---|---|---|---|---|---|---|
| neg part | v Qal impf 1cs | cj, prep, adj | neg part | v Qal impf 3ms, n ms, ps 3ms | | cj, v Qal impf 1cs | prep, n ms |
| לֹא | אֶשְׁמָע | וּכְאִלֵּם | לֹא | יִפְתַּח־פִּיו | | וָאֱהִי | כְּאִישׁ |
| lōʾ | ʾeshmāʿ | ûkh$^{e}$ʾillēm | lōʾ | yiphtach-pîw | | wāʾěhî | k$^{e}$ʾîsh |
| not | I hear | and as mute | not | he opens his mouth | | and I was | like a man |

| 866 | 3940, 8471.151 | 375 | 904, 6552 | 8763 | 15. | 3706, 3937 |
|---|---|---|---|---|---|---|
| rel pron | neg part, v Qal act ptc ms | cj, *sub* | prep, n ms, ps 3ms | n fp | | cj, prep, ps 2ms |
| אֲשֶׁר | לֹא־שֹׁמֵעַ | וְאֵין | בְּפִיו | תּוֹכָחוֹת | | כִּי־לְךָ |
| ʾăsher | lōʾ-shōmēaʿ | w$^{e}$ʾên | b$^{e}$phîw | tôkhāchôth | | kî-l$^{e}$khā |
| who | not hearing | and there is not | in his mouth | reprimands | | because for You |

**8. I am feeble and sore broken: I have roared by reason of the disquietness of my heart:** ... I am spent and utterly crushed, I groan and moan in my heart, *Anchor* ... I groan because of the agitation of my heart, *NASB* ... I roar with anguish of heart, *NCB* ... I groan because of my heart murmurings, *Berkeley.*

**9. Lord, all my desire is before thee; and my groaning is not hid from thee:** ... You hear my every sigh, *LIVB* ... You know all my longing, and my sighing isn't hidden, *Beck* ... my sorrow is not kept secret from you, *BB* ... thou art no stranger to my sighs, *Moffatt.*

**10. My heart panteth, my strength faileth me: as for the light of mine eyes, it also is gone from me:** ... restless my heart, gone my strength; the very light that shone in my eyes is mine no longer, *Knox* ... my strength forsakes me; the very light of my eyes has failed me, *NAB* ... my strength has ebbed away, and the light has gone out of my eyes, *NEB* ... the light has faded from my eyes, *REB.*

**11. My lovers and my friends stand aloof from my sore; and my kinsmen stand afar off:** ... Friends and companions shun my disease, *JB* ... Those who love me and my friends stand back from my plague, *Goodspeed* ... keep away from my disease; my relations keep far away, *BB* ... avoid me because of my wounds; my neighbors stay far away, *NIV.*

**12. They also that seek after my life lay snares for me:** ... Those who wish me dead defame me, *NEB* ... who seek my life set their traps, *REB* ... those seeking my soul lay a snare, *Young.*

**and they that seek my hurt speak mischievous things, and imagine deceits all the day long:** ... they talk of ruining me, and all the day discuss intrigues, *Moffatt* ... they look to my misfortune, they speak of ruin, *NAB* ... and meditate treachery all the day long, *RSV.*

**13. But I, as a deaf man, heard not; and I was as a dumb man that openeth not his mouth:** ... a deaf man, who does not listen, *Berkeley* ... I kept my ears shut like a man without hearing; like a man without a voice, *BB* ... And I, all the while, am deaf to their threats, dumb before my accusers, *Knox* ... like a mute, who cannot open his mouth, *NIV.*

**14. Thus I was as a man that heareth not, and in whose mouth are no reproofs:** ... hearing nothing, has no sharp answer to make, *JB* ... and whose tongue offers no defence, *NEB* ... in whose mouth is no response, *NKJV* ... in whose mouth is no retort, *NRSV.*

**15. For in thee, O LORD, do I hope: thou wilt hear, O Lord my God:** ... do I wait; Thou wilt answer, *Goodspeed* ... I look to You, LORD, for help, *Beck* ... Yet my hope, LORD,

---

details. His body is scourged and livid with multicolored, swollen welts from the lash, and these discharge foul-smelling matter.

This vivid picture of the effects of the sense of personal sin will seem superficial to modern Christianity, exaggerated and alien from experience; but the deeper a man's godliness, the more he will listen with sympathy, with understanding and with appropriation of such piercing laments as his own. Contrast the utter deadness of the religious hymns of all other nations with the fresh vitality of the Psalms. As long as hearts are penetrated with the consciousness of evil done and loved, these strains will fit themselves to men's lips.

**38:9–14.** Because the psalmist's recounting of his pains was in the form of a prayer and not a soliloquy or mere cry of anguish, it calms him. We make the wound deeper by turning round the arrow in it, when we dwell upon suffering without thinking of God; but when, like the psalmist, we tell all to Him, healing begins. Thus, the second part (vv. 9–14) is perceptibly calmer, and though still agitated, its thought of God is more trustful. Silent submission at the close takes the place of the "roaring," the shrill cry of agony which ended the first part. A further variation of tone is that, instead of the entirely subjective description of the psalmist's sufferings in vv. 1–8, the desertion by friends and the hostility of foes are now the main elements of trial. The psalmist returns to speak of his sickness in v. 10, which is really a picture of syncope or fainting. The heart's action is described by a rare word (HED #5692), which in its root means "to go round and round" and is here in an intensive form expressive of violent motion, or possibly is to be regarded as a diminutive rather than an intensive, expressive of the thinner though quicker pulse. Then comes the collapse of strength and failure of sight. But this echo of the preceding part immediately gives place to the new element in the psalmist's sorrow, arising from the behavior of friends and foes repeated by most sufferers in this selfish world. They keep far away from his "stroke," says the Psalm, using the same word as is employed for leprosy, and as is used in the verb in Isa. 53:4 ("stricken"). There is a tone of wonder and disappointment in the untranslatable play of language in v. 11b. "My near relations stand far off"—kin are not always kind. Friends have deserted because foes have beset him. Probably we

| 3176 | 3282.515 | 887 | 6257.123 | 112 | 435 | | 3706, 569.115 |
|---|---|---|---|---|---|---|---|
| pn | v Hiphil pf 1cs | pers pron | v Qal impf 2ms | n mp, ps 1cs | n mp, ps 1cs | **16.** | cj, v Qal pf 1cs |
| יְהוָה | הוֹחָלְתִּי | אַתָּה | תַעֲנֶה | אֲדֹנָי | אֱלֹהָי | | כִּי־אָמַרְתִּי |
| yehwāh | hôchālettî | 'attāh | tha'äneh | 'ădhōnāy | 'ĕlōhāy | | kî-'āmartî |
| Yahweh | I have waited | You | You answer | O my Lord | my God | | because I have said |

| 6678, 7975.126, 3937 | 904, 4267.141 | 7559 | 6142 |
|---|---|---|---|
| adv, v Qal impf 3mp, prep, ps 1cs | prep, v Qal inf con | n fs, ps 1cs | prep, ps 1cs |
| פֶּן־יִשְׂמְחוּ־לִי | בְּמוֹט | רַגְלִי | עָלַי |
| pen-yismechû-lî | bemôṭ | raghlî | 'ālay |
| so that they will not be glad about me | when faltering | my foot | against me |

| 1461.516 | | 3706, 603 | 3937, 7028 | 3679.255 | 4480 |
|---|---|---|---|---|---|
| v Hiphil pf 3cp | **17.** | cj, pers pron | prep, n ms | v Niphal ptc ms | cj, n ms, ps 1cs |
| הִגְדִּילוּ | | כִּי־אֲנִי | לְצֶלַע | נָכוֹן | וּמַכְאוֹבִי |
| highdîlû | | kî-'ănî | letsela' | nākhôn | ûmakh'ôvî |
| they have declared great | | because I | for stumbling | ready | and my pain |

| 5224 | 8878 | | 3706, 5988 | 5222.525 | 1720.125 |
|---|---|---|---|---|---|
| prep, ps 1cs | adv | **18.** | cj, n ms, ps 1cs | v Hiphil impf 1cs | v Qal impf 1cs |
| נֶגְדִּי | תָמִיד | | כִּי־עֲוֹנִי | אַגִּיד | אֶדְאַג |
| neghdî | thāmîdh | | kî-'ăwōnî | 'aggîdh | 'edh'agh |
| before me | continually | | because my trangression | I will tell | I worry |

| 4623, 2496 | | 342.152 | 2522 | 6343.116 |
|---|---|---|---|---|
| prep, n fs, ps 1cs | **19.** | cj, v Qal act ptc mp, ps 1cs | adj | v Qal pf 3cp |
| מֵחַטָּאתִי | | וְאֹיְבַי | חַיִּים | עָצֵמוּ |
| mēchaṯṯā'thî | | we'ōyevay | chayyîm | 'ātsēmû |
| from my sin | | and my enemies | living | they have become innumerable |

| 7525.116 | 7983.152 | 8632 | | 8396.352 | 7750 |
|---|---|---|---|---|---|
| cj, v Qal pf 3cp | v Qal act ptc mp, ps 1cs | n ms | **20.** | cj, *v Piel ptc mp* | n fs |
| וְרַבּוּ | שֹׂנְאַי | שָׁקֶר | | וּמְשַׁלְּמֵי | רָעָה |
| werabbû | sōne'ay | shāqer | | ûmeshallemê | rā'āh |
| yes they have become numerous | those who hate me | treachery | | and those who repay | evil |

| 8809 | 3009B | 7930.126 | 8809 | 7579.141 | | 414, 6013.123 |
|---|---|---|---|---|---|---|
| prep | adj | v Qal impf 3mp, ps 1cs | prep | v Qal inf con, ps 1cs | **21.** | adv, v Qal juss 2ms, ps 1cs |
| תַּחַת | טוֹבָה | יִשְׂטְנוּנִי | תַּחַת | רְדוֹפִי | | אַל־תַּעַזְבֵנִי |
| tachath | ṯôvāh | yisṯenûnî | tachath | redhôphî | | 'al-ta'azvēnî |
| instead of | good | they are adverse to me | instead of | my pursuing | | do not abandon me |

| 3176 | 435 | 414, 7651.123 | 4623 | | 2456.131 | 3937, 6046 | 112 |
|---|---|---|---|---|---|---|---|
| pn | n mp, ps 1cs | adv, v Qal juss 2ms | prep, ps 1cs | **22.** | v Qal impv 2ms | prep, n fs, ps 1cs | n mp, ps 1cs |
| יְהוָה | אֱלֹהַי | אַל־תִּרְחַק | מִמֶּנִּי | | חוּשָׁה | לְעֶזְרָתִי | אֲדֹנָי |
| yehwāh | 'ĕlōhay | 'al-tirchaq | mimmenî | | chûshāh | le'ezrāthî | 'ădhōnāy |
| O Yahweh | my God | do not be far away | from me | | hurry | for my help | O my Lord |

| 9009 | | 3937, 5514.351 | 3937, 3154 | 4344 | 3937, 1784 | | 569.115 | 8490.125 |
|---|---|---|---|---|---|---|---|---|
| n fs, ps 1cs | **39:t** | prep, art, v Piel ptc ms | prep, pn | n ms | prep, pn | **1.** | v Qal pf 1cs | v Qal juss 1cs |
| תְּשׁוּעָתִי | | לַמְנַצֵּחַ | לִידִיתוּן | מִזְמוֹר | לְדָוִד | | אָמַרְתִּי | אֶשְׁמְרָה |
| teshû'āthî | | lamnatstsēach | lîdhîthûn | mizmôr | ledhāwidh | | 'āmartî | 'eshmerāh |
| my salvation | | to the director | to Jeduthun | a Psalm | of David | | I have said | let me guard |

| 1932 | 4623, 2490.141 | 4098 | 8490.125 | 3937, 6552 | 4407 |
|---|---|---|---|---|---|
| n mp, ps 1cs | prep, v Qal inf con | prep, n fs, ps 1cs | v Qal juss 1cs | prep, n ms, ps 1cs | n ms |
| דְרָכַי | מֵחֲטוֹא | בִלְשׁוֹנִי | אֶשְׁמְרָה | לְפִי | מַחְסוֹם |
| dherākhay | mēchăṯô' | vilshônî | 'eshmerāh | lephî | machsôm |
| my ways | from sinning | with my tongue | let me guard | my mouth | a muzzle |

relies upon You, *Fenton* ... I trust you, LORD. You will answer, *NCV.*

**16. For I said, Hear me, lest otherwise they should rejoice over me: when my foot slippeth, they magnify themselves against me:** ... Don't let them laugh at me or brag when I am defeated, *NCV* ... I thought they would triumph on me, *Fenton* ... my foot slips, don't let them ridicule me, *Beck* ... who, when my foot wavers, would puff themselves up against me, *Berkeley.*

**17. For I am ready to halt, and my sorrow is continually before me:** ... I am very near to falling, and my grief is with me always, *NCB* ... my pain is continually before me, *MAST* ... and my pain is ever with me, *RSV* ... misery clouds my view, *Knox.*

**18. For I will declare mine iniquity; I will be sorry for my sin:** ... I therefore confess to my faults, And deeply I grieve for my sins, *Fenton* ... I acknowledge my guilt; I grieve over my sin, *NAB* ... I am full of anxiety because of my sin, *NASB* ... I am troubled by my sin, *NCV* ... my grief is ever before me, *Anchor.*

**19. But mine enemies are lively, and they are strong: and they that hate me wrongfully are multiplied:** ... mine enemies are strong in health, *MAST* ... my undeserved enemies are strong; many are my foes without cause, *NCB* ... But many are my enemies, all without cause, *REB* ... Many are those who are my vigorous enemies, *NIV.*

**20. They also that render evil for good are mine adversaries; because I follow the thing that good is:** ... and bitterly accuse me for trying to do good, *Beck* ... they are hostile toward me because I aim at what is best, *Berkeley* ... accuse me because I pursue the good, *Rotherham* ... harass me for pursuing good, *NAB.*

**21. Forsake me not, O LORD: O my God, be not far from me:** ... Yahweh, do not desert me, *JB* ... be not distant from me, *Anchor* ... Do not give me up, O Lord, *BB* ... Do not abandon me, *Good News.*

**22. Make haste to help me, O Lord my salvation:** ... hasten to my defence, O Lord, my only refuge, *Knox* ... Quickly come and help me, my Lord and Savior, *NCV* ... Hasten to my help; O Lord, to my rescue!, *Goodspeed* ... My Lord my deliverance, *Rotherham.*

---

have here the facts which in the previous part are conceived of as the "arrows" of God.

Open and secret enemies, laying snares for him as for some hunted wild creature, eagerly seeking his life, speaking "destructions" as if they would kill him with their words and perpetually whispering lies about him, were recognized by him as instruments of God's judgment and evoked his consciousness of sin, which again led to actual disease. But the bitter schooling led to something else more blessed, namely, to silent resignation.

**38:15–18.** How does this confidence spring in so troubled a heart? The fourfold "for" (HED #3706) beginning each verse from vv. 15–18 weaves them all into a chain. The first gives the reason for the submissive silence as being quiet confidence. The succeeding three may be taken as either dependent on each other, or, as is perhaps better, as coordinate and all-assigning reasons for that confidence. Either construction yields worthy and natural meanings. If the former be adopted, trust in God's undertaking of the silent sufferer's cause is based upon the prayer which broke his silence. Dumb to men, he had breathed to God his petition for help and had supported it with the plea, "Lest they rejoice over me." He had feared that they would, because he knew that he was ready to fall and had ever before him his pain, since he felt himself forced to lament and confess his sin. But it seems to yield a richer meaning, if the "for's" be regarded as coordinate. They then become a striking and instructive example of faith's logic, the ingenuity of pleading which finds encouragements in discouragements. The suppliant is sure of an answer because he has told God his fear, and yet again because he is so near falling and therefore needs help so much, and again because he has made a complete confession of his sin. Trust in God's help, distrust of self, consciousness of weakness, and penitence make anything possible; it is a false supposition that the prayer which embodies them is flung up to an unanswering God. They are prevalent pleas which He will not ignore. They are grounds of assurance to him who prays.

**38:19–22.** The juxtaposition of consciousness of sin in v. 18 with the declaration that love of good was the cause of being persecuted brings out the twofold attitude, in regard to God and men, which a devout soul may permissibly and sometimes necessarily assume. There may be the truest sense of sinfulness, along with a clear-hearted affirmation of innocence in regard to men and a conviction that it is good and goodwill to them, not evil in the sufferer, which makes him the butt of hatred. Not less instructive is the double view of the same facts presented in the beginning and end of this Psalm. They were to the psalmist first regarded as God's chastisement in wrath, his "arrows" and heavy "hand," because of sin. Now they are men's enmity, because of his love

| 904, 5968 | 7857 | 3937, 5224 | | 487.215 | 1800 | 2924.515 | 4623, 3005 |
|---|---|---|---|---|---|---|---|
| prep, adv | n ms | prep, prep, ps 1cs | | v Niphal pf 1cs | n fs | v Hiphil pf 1cs | prep, adj |
| בְּעֹד | רָשָׁע | לְנֶגְדִּי | 2. | נֶאֱלַמְתִּי | דוּמִיָּה | הֶחֱשֵׁיתִי | מִטּוֹב |
| be'ōdh | rāshā' | leneghdî | | ne'ělamtî | dhûmîyāh | hechěshêthî | miṭṭôv |
| when continuing | the wicked | before me | | I was mute | silence | I was silent | from good |

| 3629 | 6138.211 | | 2657.111, 3937 | 904, 7419 |
|---|---|---|---|---|
| cj, n ms, ps 1cs | v Niphal pf 3ms | | v Qal pf 3ms, n ms, ps 1cs | prep, n ms, ps 1cs |
| וּכְאֵבִי | נֶעְכָּר | 3. | חַם־לִבִּי | בְּקִרְבִּי |
| ûkhe'ēvî | ne'ākkār | | cham-libbî | beqirbî |
| and my anguish | it has become disastrous | | my heart became hot | within me |

| 904, 1969 | 1220.122, 813 | 1744.315 | 904, 4098 | | 3156.531 |
|---|---|---|---|---|---|
| prep, n ms, ps 1cs | v Qal impf 3fs, n fs | v Piel pf 1cs | prep, n fs, ps 1cs | | v Hiphil impv 2ms, ps 1cs |
| בַהֲגִיגִי | תִבְעַר־אֵשׁ | דִּבַּרְתִּי | בִּלְשׁוֹנִי | 4. | הוֹדִיעֵנִי |
| bahghîghî | thiv'ar-'ēsh | dibbartî | bilshônî | | hôdhî'ēnî |
| during my sighing | fire burns | I spoke | with my tongue | | cause me to know |

| 3176 | 7377 | 4201 | 3219 | 4242, 2026 | 3156.125 | 4242, 2404 |
|---|---|---|---|---|---|---|
| pn | n ms, ps 1cs | cj, *n fs* | n mp, ps 1cs | intrg, pers pron | v Qal juss 1cs | intrg, adj |
| יְהוָה | קִצִּי | וּמִדַּת | יָמַי | מַה־הִיא | אֵדְעָה | מֶה־חָדֵל |
| yehwāh | qitstsî | ûmiddath | yāmay | mah-hî' | 'ēdhe'āh | meh-chādhēl |
| O Yahweh | my end | and the measure of | my days | what it | let me know | how fleeting |

| 603 | | 2079 | 3056 | 5598.113 | 3219 | 2566 | 3726, 375 |
|---|---|---|---|---|---|---|---|
| pers pron | | intrj | n mp | v Qal pf 2ms | n mp, ps 1cs | cj, n ms, ps 1cs | prep, sub |
| אָנִי | 5. | הִנֵּה | טְפָחוֹת | נָתַתָּה | יָמַי | וְחֶלְדִּי | כְאַיִן |
| 'ānî | | hinnēh | ṭephāchôth | nāthattāh | yāmay | wecheldî | khe'ayin |
| I | | behold | handbreadths | You have allowed | my days | and my lifespan | like there is not |

| 5224 | 395 | 3725, 1961 | 3725, 119 | 5507.255 | 5734 | | 395, 904, 7021 |
|---|---|---|---|---|---|---|---|
| prep, ps 2ms | adv | *adj*, n ms | *adj*, n ms | v Niphal ptc ms | intrj | | adv, prep, n ms |
| נֶגְדֶּךָ | אַךְ | כָּל־הֶבֶל | כָּל־אָדָם | נִצָּב | סֶלָה | 6. | אַךְ־בְּצֶלֶם |
| neghdekhā | 'akh | kol-hevel | kol-'ādhām | nitstsāv | ṣelāh | | 'akh-betselem |
| before You | only | all breath | all of humankind | taking a stand | selah | | only in a shadow |

| 2050.721, 382 | 395, 1961 | 2064.126 | 6914.121 | 3940, 3156.121 |
|---|---|---|---|---|
| v Hithpael impf 3ms, n ms | adv, n ms | v Qal impf 3mp | v Qal impf 3ms | cj, neg part, v Qal impf 3ms |
| יִתְהַלֶּךְ־אִישׁ | אַךְ־הֶבֶל | יֶהֱמָיוּן | יִצְבֹּר | וְלֹא־יֵדַע |
| yithhallekh-'îsh | 'akh-hevel | yehěmāyûn | yitsbōr | welō'-yēdha' |
| a man walks about | only a breath | they are in turmoil | he heaps up | and he does not know |

| 4449, 636.151 | | 6498 | 4242, 7245.315 | 112 | 8760 | 3937 |
|---|---|---|---|---|---|---|
| intrg, v Qal act ptc ms, ps 3mp | | cj, adv | intrg, v Piel pf 1cs | n mp, ps 1cs | n fs, ps 1cs | prep, ps 2ms |
| מִי־אֹסְפָם | 7. | וְעַתָּה | מַה־קִּוִּיתִי | אֲדֹנָי | תּוֹחַלְתִּי | לְךָ |
| mî-'ōsephām | | we'attāh | mah-qiwwîthî | 'ădhōnāy | tôchaltî | lekhā |
| who gathering them | | and now | what have I waited for | my Lord | my hope | to You |

**39:t. To the chief Musician, even to Jeduthun, A Psalm of David.**

**1. I said, I will take heed to my ways, that I sin not with my tongue: I will keep my mouth with a bridle, while the wicked is before me:** … I will guard my path, From sinning with my tongue, *Fenton* … I will guard my mouth as with a muzzle, while the wicked are in my presence, *NASB* … I will be careful how I act and will not sin by what I say, *NCV* … I will watch how I behave so that I do not sin by my tongue, *JB*.

**2. I was dumb with silence, I held my peace, even from good; and my sorrow was stirred:** … I refrained from speaking, I was deeply stirred by anguish, *Anchor* … I kept silence, dumb and ill at ease. Yet this only stirred my grief, *Moffatt* … I refrained from good, And my pain was aroused, *Goodspeed* … So my agony was quickened, *NEB*.

**3. My heart was hot within me, while I was musing the fire burned: then spake I with my**

**tongue:** ... hot grew my heart within me; in my thoughts, a fire blazed forth, *NCB* ... the fire kindled by my thoughts, so that at last I kept silence no longer, *Knox* ... My heart had been smouldering within me, but at the thought of this it flared up, *JB* ... As I pondered my mind was inflamed, and I began to speak, *REB.*

**4. LORD, make me to know mine end, and the measure of my days, what it is; that I may know how frail I am:** ... Let me know how short-lived I am, *MAST* ... how long I will live. Let me know how long I have, *NCV* ... Let me know how transient I am, *Berkeley* ... how many days I have left, so that I know how fleeting my life is, *Beck.*

**5. Behold, thou hast made my days as an handbreadth; and mine age is as nothing before thee:** ... only a breath is any human existence, *NCB* ... You have made my days no longer than a hand's measure, *BB* ... A short span you have made my days, *NAB* ... the span of my years is as nothing before you, *NIV.*

**verily every man at his best state is altogether vanity. Selah:** ... every man is but vapor, every man a false image, *Anchor* ... he moves like a phantom, *NEB* ... Certainly every man at his best state is but vapor, *NKJV.*

**6. Surely every man walketh in a vain show: surely they are disquieted in vain:** ... Only, in an image doth each walk habitually, *Young* ... Surely as a shadow doth every man wander, *Rotherham* ... Surely everyone goes about like a shadow. Surely for nothing they are in turmoil, *NRSV* ... Surely they are in an uproar for nothing, *KJVII.*

**he heapeth up riches, and knoweth not who shall gather them:** ... he heaps up stores, and knows not who will use them, *NAB* ... and there is no knowing who will enjoy them, *REB.*

**7. And now, Lord, what wait I for? my hope is in thee:** ... What then can I expect, O Lord?, *Moffatt* ... what am I to hope for?, *JB* ... And now, what shall I exclaim, *Anchor* ... In thee alone I trust, *Knox.*

---

of good. Is there not an entire contradiction between these two views of suffering, its cause and source? Certainly not, but rather the two views differ only in the angle of vision and may be combined, like stereoscopic pictures, into one rounded, harmonious whole. To be able so to combine them is one of the rewards of such pleading trust as that which breathes its plaintive music through this Psalm and wakes responsive notes in devout hearts still.

***Psalm 39.*** *Protracted suffering, recognized as chastisement for sin, had wasted the psalmist's strength. It had been borne for a while in silence, but the rush of emotion had burst the floodgates. The Psalm does not repeat the words which forced themselves from the hot heart, but preserves for us the calmer flow which followed. It falls into four parts, the first three of which contain three verses each, and the fourth is expanded into four, divided into two couples.*

**39:1–3.** In the first part, the frustrated resolve of silence is recorded. Its motive was fear of sinning in speech "while the wicked is before me." That phrase is often explained as meaning that the sight of the prosperity of the godless in contrast with his own sorrows tempted the singer to break out into arraigning God's providence and that he schooled himself to look at their insolent ease unmurmuringly. But the Psalm has no other references to other men's flourishing condition; it is more in accordance with its tone to suppose that his own pains, and not their pleasures, prompted him to withhold words. Repression of utterance only feeds the fire, and sooner or later the "muzzle" (HED #4407) is torn off, and pent-up reeling breaks into speech, often the wilder for the violence done to nature by the attempt to deny it its way. The psalmist's motive was right, and in a measure, his silence was so, but his resolve did not at first go deep enough. It is the heart, not the mouth, that has to be silenced. To build a dam across a torrent without diminishing the sources that supply its waters only increases weight and pressure and ensures a muddy flood when it bursts.

**39:4–6.** Does the Psalm proceed to recount what its author said when he broke silence? It may appear so at first sight. On the other hand, the calm prayer which follows, beginning with v. 4, is not of the character of the wild and whirling words which were suppressed for fear of sinning, nor does the fierce fire of which the Psalm has been speaking flame in it.

The thought of brevity naturally draws after it that of illusoriness. Just because life is so frail does it assume the appearance of being futile. Both ideas are blended in the metaphors of "a breath" and "a shadow." There is a solemn earnestness in the threefold "surely," confirming each clause of the seer's insight into earth's hollowness. How emphatically he puts it in the almost redundant language, "Surely nothing but a breath is every man, stand he ever so firm." The truth proclaimed is undeniably certain. It covers the whole ground of earthly life, and it includes the most prosperous and firmly established.

| 2026 | | 4623, 3725, 6840 | 5522.531 | 2887 | 5210 |
|---|---|---|---|---|---|
| pers pron | 8. | prep, *adj*, n mp, ps 1cs | v Hiphil impv 2ms, ps 1cs | *n fs* | n ms |
| הִיא | | מִכָּל־פְּשָׁעַי | הַצִּילֵנִי | חֶרְפַּת | נָבָל |
| hî' | | mikkol-peshā'ay | hatstsîlēnî | cherpath | nāvāl |
| it | | from all my offenses | rescue me | the disgrace of | a fool |

| 414, 7947.123 | | 487.215 | 3940 | 6858.125, 6552 | 3706 | 887 |
|---|---|---|---|---|---|---|
| adv, v Qal juss 2ms, ps 1cs | 9. | v Niphal pf 1cs | neg part | v Qal impf 1cs, n ms, ps 1cs | cj | pers pron |
| אַל־תְּשִׂימֵנִי | | נֶאֱלַמְתִּי | לֹא | אֶפְתַּח־פִּי | כִּי | אַתָּה |
| 'al-tesîmēnî | | ne'ĕlamtî | lō' | 'ephtach-pî | kî | 'attāh |
| do not put on me | | I have become mute | not | I have opened my mouth | because | You |

| 6449.113 | | 5681.531 | 4623, 6142 | 5236 | 4623, 8738 |
|---|---|---|---|---|---|
| v Qal pf 2ms | 10. | v Hiphil impv 2ms | prep, prep, ps 1cs | n ms, ps 2ms | prep, *n fs* |
| עָשִׂיתָ | | הָסֵר | מֵעָלַי | נִגְעֶךָ | מִתִּגְרַת |
| 'āsîthā | | hāsēr | mē'ālay | nigh'ekhā | mittighrath |
| You have done | | remove | from beside me | your striking | from the blow of |

| 3135 | 603 | 3735.115 | | 904, 8763 | 6142, 5988 |
|---|---|---|---|---|---|
| n fs, ps 2ms | pers pron | v Qal pf 1cs | 11. | prep, n fp | prep, n ms |
| יָדְךָ | אֲנִי | כָלִיתִי | | בְּתוֹכָחוֹת | עַל־עָוֹן |
| yādhekhā | 'ănî | kholîthî | | bethôkhāchôth | 'al-'āwōn |
| your hand | I | I have come to an end | | with chastisements | concerning transgression |

| 3364.313 | 382 | 4678.523 | 3626, 6468 | 2629.155 | 395 | 1961 |
|---|---|---|---|---|---|---|
| v Piel pf 2ms | n ms | cj, v Hiphil impf 2ms | prep, art, n ms | v Qal pass ptc ms, ps 3ms | adv | n ms |
| יִסַּרְתָּ | אִישׁ | וַתֶּמֶס | כָּעָשׁ | חֲמוּדוֹ | אַךְ | הֶבֶל |
| yissartā | 'îsh | wattemes | kā'āsh | chămûdhô | 'akh | hevel |
| You have rebuked | man | You cause to melt | like the moth | what is desired of him | only | a breath |

| 3725, 119 | 5734 | | 8471.131, 8940 | 3176 | 8210 | 237.531 |
|---|---|---|---|---|---|---|
| *adj*, n ms | intrj | 12. | v Qal impv 2ms, n fs, ps 1cs | pn | cj, n fs, ps 1cs | v Hiphil impv 2ms |
| כָּל־אָדָם | סֶלָה | | שִׁמְעָה־תְפִלָּתִי | יְהוָה | וְשַׁוְעָתִי | הַאֲזִינָה |
| kol-'ādhām | selāh | | shim'āh-thephillāthî | yehwāh | weshaw'āthî | ha'ăzînāh |
| all of humankind | selah | | hear my prayer | Yahweh | and my cry for help | listen to |

| 420, 1893 | 414, 2896.123 | 3706 | 1658 | 609 | 6196 | 8785 |
|---|---|---|---|---|---|---|
| prep, n fs, ps 1cs | adv, v Qal juss 2ms | cj | n ms | pers pron | prep, ps 2ms | n ms |
| אֶל־דִּמְעָתִי | אַל־תֶּחֱרַשׁ | כִּי | גֵר | אָנֹכִי | עִמָּךְ | תוֹשָׁב |
| 'el-dim'āthî | 'al-techĕrash | kî | ghēr | 'ānōkhî | 'immākh | tôshāv |
| to my tears | do not be deaf | because | a resident-alien | I | with You | a dweller |

| 3626, 3725, 1 | | 8541.531 | 4623 | 1122.525 | 904, 3071 | 2050.125 |
|---|---|---|---|---|---|---|
| prep, *adj*, n mp, ps 1cs | 13. | v Hiphil impv 2ms | prep, ps 1cs | cj, v Hiphil juss 1cs | prep, adv | v Qal impf 1cs |
| כְּכָל־אֲבוֹתָי | | הָשַׁע | מִמֶּנִּי | וְאַבְלִיגָה | בְּטֶרֶם | אֵלֵךְ |
| kekhol-'ăvôthāy | | hāsha' | mimmenî | we'avlîghāh | beterem | 'ēlēkh |
| like all my ancestors | | look away | from me | that I may smile | before | I will go |

**8. Deliver me from all my transgressions: make me not the reproach of the foolish:** ... Deliver me from all who do me wrong, *REB* ... Make me free from all my sins, *BB* ... do not make me the scorn of fools, *NIV* ... Make me not the scorn of the reprobate, *Goodspeed.*

**9. I was dumb, I opened not my mouth; because thou didst it:** ... I am speechless; I will not open my mouth, *Berkeley* ... I speak no more since you yourself have been at work, *JB* ... I am silent and don't open my mouth—if You would only act, *Beck* ... for it is thou who orderest life, *Moffatt.*

**10. Remove thy stroke away from me: I am consumed by the blow of thine hand:** ... No longer let your hand be hard on me, *BB* ... Take thy plague away from me, *Geneva* ... at the blow of your hand I wasted away, *NAB* ... I am exhausted by your hostility, *REB.*

**11. When thou with rebukes dost correct man for iniquity, thou makest his beauty to consume away like a moth: surely every man is vanity. Selah:** ... You chastise mortals in punishment for sin, *NRSV* ... thou consumed as a moth all that was delightful within him, Surely a breath are all men, *Rotherham* ... you dissolve like a cobweb all that is dear to him, *NAB* ... all his charm festers and drains away; indeed man is only a puff of wind, *NEB.*

**12. Hear my prayer, O LORD, and give ear unto my cry; hold not thy peace at my tears: for I am a stranger with thee, and a sojourner, as all my fathers were:** ... to my tears be not speechless; for I am a passing guest with Thee, *Berkeley* ... listen to my cry for help; be not deaf to my weeping. For I dwell with you as an alien, *NIV* ... A sojourner, like all my ancestors, *Goodspeed.*

**13. O spare me, that I may recover strength, before I go hence, and be no more:** ... Look away from me, and let me recover strength, *Darby* ... Let your wrath be turned away from me, so that I may be comforted, *BB* ... Turn your gaze away from me, that I may smile again, before I

---

The sheaves are piled up, but in whose barn are they to be housed? Surely, if the farmer is not the ultimate owner, his toil has been for a breath.

All this is no fantastic pessimism. Still less is it an account of what life must be. If any man's life is nothing but toiling for a breath and if he himself is nothing but a breath, it is his own fault. They who are joined to God have in their embers something that is alive. If they labor for Him, they do not labor for vanity, nor do they leave their possessions when they die.

**39:7–9.** The burden is still on the psalmist's shoulders. His sufferings are not ended, although his trust has taken the poison out of them. Therefore, his renewed grasp of God leads at once to prayer for deliverance from his "transgressions," in which cry may be included both sins and their chastisement. "The fool" (HED #5210) is the name of a class, not of an individual, and, as always in Scripture, it denotes moral and religious obliquity, not intellectual feebleness. The expression is substantially equivalent to "the wicked" (HED #7857) of v. 1, and a similar motive to that which there induced the psalmist to be silent is here urged as a plea with God for the sufferer's deliverance. Taunts launched at a good man suffering will glance off him and appear to reach his God.

Verse 9 pleads as a reason for God's deliverance; the psalmist's silence is under what he recognized as God's chastisement. The question arises whether this is the same silence as is referred to in vv. 1f, and many authorities take that view. But that silence was broken by a rush of words from a hot heart and, if the account of the connection in the Psalm given above is correct, by a subsequent more placid meditation and prayer.

**39:10–11.** The last part is somewhat abnormally long and falls into two parts separated by selah; the musical note does not here coincide with the greater divisions. The two pairs of verses are both petitions for removal of sickness, either real or figurative. Their pleading persistence presents substantially the same prayer and supports it by the same considerations of man's transience. The pattern of perfect resignation is repeated three times, praying, saying the same words; his suffering followers may do the same, and yet neither sin by impatience, nor weary the Judge by their continual coming. The psalmist sees in his pains God's "striking" and pleads the effects already produced on him as a reason for cessation. He is already wasted by the assault of God's hand. One more buffet, and he feels that he must die.

**39:12–13.** The second subdivision of this part (vv. 12f) reiterates the former with some difference of tone. There is a beautiful climax of earnestness in the psalmist's appeal to God. His prayer swells into crying and that again melts into tears, which go straight to the great Father's heart. Weeping eyes are never turned to heaven in vain; the gates of mercy open wide when the hot drops touch them. But his fervor of desire is not this suppliant's chief argument with God. His meditation has won for him deeper insight.

The closing prayer in v. 13 has a strange sound. "Look away from me" is surely a singular petition, and the effect of God's averting his face is not less singular. The devout psalmist had no notion of a neutral God, nor could he ever be content with simple cessation of the tokens of divine displeasure. The ever-outflowing, divine activity must reach every person. It may come in one or other of the two forms of favor or of displeasure, but come it will, and each can determine which side of that pillar of fire and cloud is turned to him.

***Psalm 40.*** *In the first part, the current of thought starts from thankfulness for individual deliverances (vv. 1ff); widens into contemplation of the blessedness of trust and the riches of divine*

| 375 | | 3937, 5514.351 | 3937, 1784 | 4344 | | 7245.342 | 7245.315 |
|---|---|---|---|---|---|---|---|
| cj, sub, ps 1cs | | prep, art, v Piel ptc ms | prep, pn | n ms | | v Piel inf abs | v Piel pf 1cs |
| וְאֵינֶנִּי | **40:t** | לַמְנַצֵּחַ | לְדָוִד | מִזְמוֹר | **1.** | קַוֹּה | קִוִּיתִי |
| we'ênenî | | lamnatstsēach | ledhāwidh | mizmôr | | qawwōh | qiwwîthî |
| and I am not | | to the director | of David | a Psalm | | hoping | I have completely hoped in |

| 3176 | 5371.121 | 420 | 8471.121 | 8210 | | 6148.521 |
|---|---|---|---|---|---|---|
| pn | cj, v Qal impf 3ms | prep, ps 1cs | cj, v Qal impf 3ms | n fs, ps 1cs | | cj, v Hiphil impf 3ms, ps 1cs |
| יְהוָה | וַיֵּט | אֵלַי | וַיִּשְׁמַע | שַׁוְעָתִי | **2.** | וַיַּעֲלֵנִי |
| yehwāh | wayyēṭ | 'ēlay | wayyishma' | shaw'āthî | | wayya'ălēnî |
| Yahweh | and He inclined | to me | and He heard | my cry for help | | and He brought me up |

| 4623, 988 | 8064 | 4623, 3027 | 3223 | 7251.521 | 6142, 5748 | 7559 |
|---|---|---|---|---|---|---|
| prep, *n ms* | n ms | prep, *n ms* | art, n ms | cj, v Hiphil impf 3ms | prep, n ms | n fd, ps 1cs |
| מִבּוֹר | שָׁאוֹן | מִטִּיט | הַיָּוֵן | וַיָּקֶם | עַל־סֶלַע | רַגְלַי |
| mibbôr | shā'ôn | miṭṭîṭ | hayyāwēn | wayyāqem | 'al-sela' | raghlay |
| from a pit of | tumult | from the soggy mire of | the mud | and He caused to rise | on a rock | my feet |

| 3679.311 | 863 | | 5598.121 | 904, 6552 | 8302 | 2413 | 8747 |
|---|---|---|---|---|---|---|---|
| v Polel pf 3ms | n fp, ps 1cs | | cj, v Qal impf 3ms | prep, n ms, ps 1cs | n ms | adj | n fs |
| כּוֹנֵן | אֲשֻׁרָי | **3.** | וַיִּתֵּן | בְּפִי | שִׁיר | חָדָשׁ | תְּהִלָּה |
| kônēn | 'ăshurāy | | wayyittēn | bephî | shîr | chādhāsh | tehillāh |
| He established | my steps | | and He gives | in my mouth | a song | new | praise |

| 3937, 435 | 7495.126 | 7521 | 3486.126 | 1019.126 | 904, 3176 |
|---|---|---|---|---|---|
| prep, n mp, ps 1cp | v Qal impf 3mp | adj | cj, v Qal impf 3mp | cj, v Qal impf 3mp | prep, pn |
| לֵאלֹהֵינוּ | יִרְאוּ | רַבִּים | וְיִירָאוּ | וְיִבְטְחוּ | בַּיהוָה |
| lē'lōhênû | yir'û | rabbîm | weyîrā'û | weyivṭechû | bayhwāh |
| to our God | they will see | many | and they will fear | and they will put their trust | in Yahweh |

| | 869 | 1429 | 866, 7947.111 | 3176 | 4623, 1020 | 3940, 6680.111 |
|---|---|---|---|---|---|---|
| | *n ms* | art, n ms | rel pron, v Qal pf 3ms | pn | prep, n ms, ps 3ms | cj, neg part, v Qal pf 3ms |
| **4.** | אַשְׁרֵי | הַגֶּבֶר | אֲשֶׁר־שָׂם | יְהוָה | מִבְטַחוֹ | וְלֹא־פָנָה |
| | 'ashrê | haggever | 'ăsher-sām | yehōwāh | mivṭachô | welō'-phānāh |
| | blessed | the man | who he has placed on | Yahweh | from his trust | and he has not turned |

| 420, 7581 | 7911.152 | 3695 | | 7521 | 6449.113 | 887 | 3176 |
|---|---|---|---|---|---|---|---|
| prep, n mp | cj, *v Qal act ptc mp* | n ms | | adj | v Qal pf 2ms | pers pron | pn |
| אֶל־רְהָבִים | וְשָׂטֵי | כָזָב | **5.** | רַבּוֹת | עָשִׂיתָ | אַתָּה | יְהוָה |
| 'el-rehāvîm | wesāṭê | khāzāv | | rabbôth | 'āsîthā | 'attāh | yehwāh |
| to the proud | or those who go off after | falsehood | | many | You have done | You | O Yahweh |

| 435 | 6623.258 | 4422 | 420 | 375 | 6424.141 |
|---|---|---|---|---|---|
| n mp, ps 1cs | v Niphal ptc fp, ps 2ms | cj, n fp, ps 2ms | prep, ps 1cp | *sub* | v Qal inf con |
| אֱלֹהַי | נִפְלְאֹתֶיךָ | וּמַחְשְׁבֹתֶיךָ | אֵלֵינוּ | אֵין | עֲרֹךְ |
| 'ělōhay | niphle'ōthêkhā | ûmachshevōthêkhā | 'ēlênû | 'ên | 'ărōkh |
| my God | your extraordinary deeds | and your thoughts | to us | there is not | confronting |

| 420 | 5222.525 | 1744.325 | 6343.116 | 4623, 5807.341 |
|---|---|---|---|---|
| prep, ps 2ms | v Hiphil juss 1cs | cj, v Piel juss 1cs | v Qal pf 3cp | prep, v Piel inf con |
| אֵלֶיךָ | אַגִּידָה | וַאֲדַבֵּרָה | עָצְמוּ | מִסַּפֵּר |
| 'ēlêkhā | 'aggîdhāh | wa'ădhabbērāh | 'ātsemû | missappēr |
| to You | let me declare | and let me speak | they have become innumerable | from counting |

| | 2160 | 4647 | 3940, 2759.113 | 238 | 3868.113 | 3937 |
|---|---|---|---|---|---|---|
| | n ms | cj, n fs | neg part, v Qal pf 2ms | n fd | v Qal pf 2ms | prep, ps 1cs |
| **6.** | זֶבַח | וּמִנְחָה | לֹא־חָפַצְתָּ | אָזְנַיִם | כָּרִיתָ | לִּי |
| | zevach | ûminchāh | lō'-chāphatstā | 'āzenayim | kārîthā | lî |
| | a sacrifice | or an offering | You do not desire | ears | You have dug | for me |

depart, *NRSV* ... Look from me, and I brighten up before I go, *Young*.

**40:t. To the chief Musician, A Psalm of David.**

**1. I waited patiently for the Lord; and he inclined unto me, and heard my cry:** ... he stooped toward me, *NCB* ... at last he turned his look towards me, *Knox* ... his heart was turned to me, *BB*.

**2. He brought me up also out of an horrible pit, out of the miry clay, and set my feet upon a rock, and established my goings:** ... raised from the Pit of Despair, *Fenton* ... steadied my steps, *Moffatt* ... drew me up from the pit of ruin, *Goodspeed* ... and gave me a firm place to stand, *NIV*.

**3. And he hath put a new song in my mouth, even praise unto our God: many shall see it, and fear, and shall trust in the Lord:** ... a song of praise, *NRSV* ... a hymn of praise, *Anchor* ... Many people will see this and worship him, *NCV* ... Many will be awestruck at the sight, *JB*.

**4. Blessed is that man that maketh the Lord his trust, and respecteth not the proud, nor such as turn aside to lies:** ... And hath not turned unto the arrogant, *MAST* ... and does not look to brutal and treacherous men, *NEB* ... who turns not to idolatry, *NAB* ... to those who lapse into falsehood, *NASB*.

**5. Many, O Lord my God, are thy wonderful works which thou hast done, and thy thoughts which are to us-ward:** ... how long is the story of thy marvellous deeds!, *Knox* ... your wonders and your purposes are for our good, *REB*.

**they cannot be reckoned up in order unto thee: if I would declare and speak of them, they are more than can be numbered:** ... no one can be compared with You, *Beck* ... you have no peer, *Anchor*.

**6. Sacrifice and offering thou didst not desire; mine ears hast thou opened: burnt offering and sin offering hast thou not required:** ... you have given me receptive ears, *REB* ... ears hast thou prepared me, *Darby* ... open to obedience you gave me, *NAB*.

---

*mercies (vv. 4f); moved by these and taught what is acceptable to God, it rises to self consecration as a living sacrifice (vv. 6ff); and, finally, pleads for experience of God's grace in all its forms on the ground of past faithful stewardship in celebrating these (vv. 9ff). The second part is one long-drawn cry for help, which admits no such analysis, although its notes are various.*

**40:1–3.** The first outpouring of the song is one long sentence in which the clauses follow one another like sunlit ripples and tell the whole process of the psalmist's deliverance. It began with patient waiting; it ended with a new song. The voice first raised in a cry, shrill and yet submissive enough to be heard, above, is at last tuned into new forms of uttering the old praise. The two clauses of v. 1 ("I" and "He") set over against each other, as separated by the distance between heaven and earth, the psalmist and his God. He does not begin with his troubles, but with his faith.

The suppliant and God have come closer together in v. 2, which should not be regarded as beginning a new sentence. As in Ps. 28, prayer brings God down to help. His hand reaches to the man prisoned in a pit or struggling in a swamp; he is dragged out, set on a rock and feels firm ground beneath his feet. Obviously, the whole representation is purely figurative, and it is hopelessly flat and prosaic to refer it to Jeremiah's experience.

God's deliverance gives occasion for fresh praise. The psalmist has to add his voice to the great chorus, and this sense of being but one of a multitude, who have been blessed alike and therefore should bless alike, occasions the significant interchange in v. 3 of "my" and "our," which needs no theory of the speaker being the nation to explain it. It is ever a joy to the heart swelling with the sense of God's mercies to be aware of the many who share the mercies and gratitude. The cry for deliverance is a solo; the song of praise is choral.

**40:4–5.** The transition from purely personal experience to more general thoughts is completed in vv. 4f. Just as the psalmist began with telling of his own patient expectation and then passed on to speak of God's help, so in these two verses, he sets forth the same sequence in terms studiously cast into the most comprehensive form. Happy indeed are they who can translate their own experience into these two truths for all men: that trust is blessedness and that God's mercies are one long sequence, made up of numberless constituent parts.

Verse 5 corresponds with v. 4 in that it sets forth in similar generality the great deeds with which God is going to answer man's trust. But the personality of the poet breaks very beautifully through the impersonal utterances when he names Yahweh as "my God," thus claiming his separate share in the general mercies.

**40:6–8.** In v. 6, the psalmist is entirely occupied with God's declarations of his requirements, and he presents these in a remarkable fashion, inserting the clause, "Ears hast Thou pierced for me," between the two parallel clauses in regard to

| 6150 | 2494 | 3940 | 8068.113 | | 226 | 569.115 |
|---|---|---|---|---|---|---|
| n fs | cj, n fs | neg part | v Qal pf 2ms | 7. | adv | v Qal pf 1cs |
| עוֹלָה | וַחֲטָאָה | לֹא | שָׁאָלְתָּ | | אָז | אָמַרְתִּי |
| 'ôlāh | wachtā'āh | lō' | shā'āl$^e$ttā | | 'āz | 'āmartî |
| a burnt offering | and a sin offering | not | You have requested | | then | I said |

| 2079, 971.115 | 904, 4178, 5809 | 3918.155 | 6142 |
|---|---|---|---|
| intrj, v Qal pf 1cs | prep, *n fs*, n ms | v Qal pass ptc ms | prep, ps 1cs |
| הִנֵּה־בָאתִי | בִּמְגִלַּת־סֵפֶר | כָּתוּב | עָלָי |
| hinnēh-vā'thî | bimghillath-sēpher | kāthûv | 'ālāy |
| behold I have come | on the roll of the scroll | written | about me |

| | 3937, 6449.141, 7814 | 435 | 2759.115 | 8784 | 904, 8761 |
|---|---|---|---|---|---|
| 8. | prep, v Qal inf con, n ms, ps 2ms | n mp, ps 1cs | v Qal pf 1cs | cj, n fs, ps 2ms | prep, *n ms* |
| | לַעֲשׂוֹת־רְצוֹנְךָ | אֱלֹהַי | חָפָצְתִּי | וְתוֹרָתְךָ | בְּתוֹךְ |
| | la'ăsôth-r$^e$tsônkhā | 'ělōhay | chāphāts$^e$ttî | w$^e$thôrāth$^e$khā | b$^e$thôkh |
| | to do your will | my God | I have delighted | and your Law | in the middle of |

| 4753 | | 1339.315 | 6928 | 904, 7235 | 7521 | 2079 | 8004 |
|---|---|---|---|---|---|---|---|
| n mp, ps 1cs | 9. | v Piel pf 1cs | n ms | prep, n ms | adj | intrj | n fd, ps 1cs |
| מֵעָי | | בִּשַּׂרְתִּי | צֶדֶק | בְּקָהָל | רָב | הִנֵּה | שְׂפָתַי |
| mē'āy | | bissartî | tsedheq | b$^e$qāhāl | rāv | hinnēh | s$^e$phāthay |
| my inner being | | I have told news | righteousness | in the assembly | abundant | behold | my lips |

| 3940 | 3727.125 | 3176 | 887 | 3156.113 | | 6930 |
|---|---|---|---|---|---|---|
| neg part | v Qal impf 1cs | pn | pers pron | v Qal pf 2ms | 10. | n fs, ps 2ms |
| לֹא | אֶכְלָא | יְהוָה | אַתָּה | יָדָעְתָּ | | צִדְקָתְךָ |
| lō' | 'ekhlā' | y$^e$hwāh | 'attāh | yādhā'āttā | | tsidhqāth$^e$khā |
| not | I have restrained | O Yahweh | You | You know | | your righteousness |

| 3940, 3803.315 | 904, 8761 | 3949 | 536 | 9009 | 569.115 |
|---|---|---|---|---|---|
| neg part, v Piel pf 1cs | prep, *n ms* | n ms, ps 1cs | n fs, ps 2ms | cj, n fs, ps 2ms | v Qal pf 1cs |
| לֹא־כִסִּיתִי | בְּתוֹךְ | לִבִּי | אֱמוּנָתְךָ | וּתְשׁוּעָתְךָ | אָמָרְתִּי |
| lō'-khissîthî | b$^e$thôkh | libbî | 'ěmûnāth$^e$khā | ûth$^e$shû'āth$^e$khā | 'āmār$^e$ttî |
| I did not hide | in the middle of | my heart | your faithfulness | and your salvation | I have said |

| 3940, 3701.315 | 2721 | 583 | 3937, 7235 | 7521 |
|---|---|---|---|---|
| neg part, v Piel pf 1cs | n ms, ps 2ms | cj, n fs, ps 2ms | prep, n ms | adj |
| לֹא־כִחַדְתִּי | חַסְדְּךָ | וַאֲמִתְּךָ | לְקָהָל | רָב |
| lō'-khichadhtî | chasd$^e$khā | wa'ămitt$^e$khā | l$^e$qāhāl | rāv |
| I have not concealed | your steadfast love | and your faithfulness | to the assembly | abundant |

| | 887 | 3176 | 3940, 3727.123 | 7641 | 4623 | 2721 |
|---|---|---|---|---|---|---|
| 11. | pers pron | pn | neg part, v Qal impf 2ms | n mp, ps 2ms | prep, ps 1cs | n ms, ps 2ms |
| | אַתָּה | יְהוָה | לֹא־תִכְלָא | רַחֲמֶיךָ | מִמֶּנִּי | חַסְדְּךָ |
| | 'attāh | y$^e$hwāh | lō'-thikhlā' | rachmêkhā | mimmenî | chasd$^e$khā |
| | You | O Yahweh | You do not restrain | your mercy | from me | your steadfast love |

| 583 | 8878 | 5526.126 | | 3706 |
|---|---|---|---|---|
| cj, n fs, ps 2ms | adv | v Qal juss 3mp, ps 1cs | 12. | cj |
| וַאֲמִתְּךָ | תָּמִיד | יִצְּרוּנִי | | כִּי |
| wa'ămitt$^e$khā | tāmîdh | yitsts$^e$rûnî | | kî |
| and your faithfulness | continually | may they guard me | | because |

| 680.116, 6142 | 7750 | 5912, 375 | 4709 | 5560.516 |
|---|---|---|---|---|
| v Qal pf 3cp, prep, ps 1cs | n fp | adv, sub | n ms | v Hiphil pf 3cp, ps 1cs |
| אָפְפוּ־עָלַי | רָעוֹת | עַד־אֵין | מִסְפָּר | הִשִּׂיגוּנִי |
| 'āph$^e$phû-'ālay | rā'ôth | 'adh-'ên | mispār | hissîghûnî |
| they have encompassed against me | troubles | until there is not | a number | they have overtaken me |

**7. Then said I, Lo, I come: in the volume of the book it is written of me:** ... In the scroll of the Book, *NKJV* ... to fulfil what is written of me, *Knox* ... which is prescribed for me, *MAST.*

**8. I delight to do thy will, O my God: yea, thy law is within my heart:** ... To do thy good-pleasure, *Rotherham* ... I desired to doe thy good will, *Geneva* ... to please and serve thee is my joy, *Moffatt* ... Your teachings, *NCV.*

**9. I have preached righteousness in the great congregation: lo, I have not refrained my lips, O LORD, thou knowest:** ... told the glad news of deliverance, *NRSV* ... proclaimed tidings of righteousness, *Young* ... I announced your justice in the vast assembly, *NAB* ... kept back my lips, *KJVII.*

**10. I have not hid thy righteousness within my heart; I have declared thy faithfulness and thy salvation: I have not concealed thy lovingkindness and thy truth from the great congregation:** ... thy saving help within my heart, *RSV* ... kept secret your mercy or your faith, *BB* ... Thy vindication, *Goodspeed* ... your saving justice locked in the depths of my heart, *JB.*

**11. Withhold not thou thy tender mercies from me, O LORD: let thy lovingkindness and thy truth continually preserve me:** ... don't hold back Your love from me, *Beck* ... let thy mercy and faithfulness, *Knox* ... have always safeguarded me, *Anchor* ... Thy compassion from me, *NASB.*

**12. For innumerable evils have compassed me about: mine iniquities have taken hold upon me, so that I am not able to look up; they are more than the hairs of mine head: therefore my heart faileth me:** ... My sins have caught me, *NCV* ... For troubles surround me, *JB* ... For misfortunes beyond counting, *NEB* ... So I have abandoned my heart, *Fenton.*

**13. Be pleased, O LORD, to deliver me: O LORD, make haste to help me:** ... to take me out of danger, *BB* ... to save me, *NIV* ... come quickly to my help, *REB* ... to rescue me, *NCB.*

---

sacrifice. Why should the connection be thus broken? The psalmist no doubt refers to the Mosaic practice of piercing the ear of the slave who has grown to love his master so much that he cannot abide serving any other (Deut. 15:16f).

Verses 7f are occupied with the response to God's requirements thus manifested by his gift of capacity to hear his voice. As soon as he had learned the meaning of his ears, he found the right use of his tongue. The thankful heart was moved to swift acceptance of the known will of God. The clearest recognition of his requirements may coexist with resistance to them, and it needs the impulse of loving contemplation of God's unnumbered wonders to vivify it into glad service. "Behold, I am come," is the language of a servant entering his master's presence in obedience to his call. In v. 7, the second clause interrupts just as in v. 6. There the interruption spoke of the organ of receiving divine messages as to duty; here it speaks of the messages themselves: "In the roll of the book is my duty prescribed for me." The promise implied in piercing the ear is fulfilled by giving a permanent written law.

**40:9–11.** "Righteousness," the good news that the Ruler of all is inflexibly just, with a justice which scrupulously meets all creatures' needs and becomes penal and awful only to the rejecters of its tender aspect; "faithfulness," the inviolable adherence to every promise; "salvation," the actual fullness of deliverance and well-being flowing from these attributes, often linked together as expressing at once the warmth and the unchangeableness of the divine heart—these have been the psalmist's themes. Therefore, they are his hope, and he is sure that, as he has been their singer, they will be his preservers. Verse 11 is not prayer, but bold confidence. It echoes the preceding verse, since "I did not restrain" (v. 9) corresponds with "Thou will not restrain," and "Thy steadfast love and thy troth" with the mention of the same attributes in v 10. The psalmist is not so much asserting his claims as giving voice to his faith. He does not so much think that his utterance is deserving of remuneration as that God's character makes impossible the supposition that he, who had so loved and sung his great name in its manifold glories, should find that name unavailing in his hour of need.

**40:12.** Are there any deliverances in this perilous and incomplete life so entire and permanent that they leave no room for future perils? Must not prevision of coming dangers accompany thankfulness for past escapes? Our Pharaohs are seldom drowned in the Red Sea, and we do not often see their corpses stretched on the sand. The change of tone, of which so much use is made as against the original unity of the Psalm, begins with v. 12; but that verse has a very strong and beautiful link of connection with the previous part, in the description of besetting evils as innumerable.

**40:13–17.** From v. 13 onward, Ps. 70 repeats this Psalm, with unimportant verbal differences.

| **5988**<br>n mp, ps 1cs<br>עֲוֹנֹתַי<br>'ăwōnōthay<br>my transgressions | **3940, 3310.115**<br>cj, neg part, v Qal pf 1cs<br>וְלֹא־יָכֹלְתִּי<br>w$^e$lō'-yākhōl$^e$ttî<br>and I have not been able | **3937, 7495.141**<br>prep, v Qal inf con<br>לִרְאוֹת<br>lir'ôth<br>to see | **6343.116**<br>v Qal pf 3cp<br>עָצְמוּ<br>'āts$^e$mû<br>they have become more innumerable |
|---|---|---|---|

| **4623, 8000**<br>prep, *n fp*<br>מִשַּׂעֲרוֹת<br>missa'ărôth<br>than the hairs of | **7513**<br>n ms, ps 1cs<br>רֹאשִׁי<br>rō'shî<br>my head | **3949**<br>cj, n ms, ps 2ms<br>וְלִבִּי<br>w$^e$libbî<br>and my heart | **6013.111**<br>v Qal pf 3ms, ps 1cs<br>עֲזָבָנִי<br>'ăzāvānî<br>it has abandoned me | **13.** | **7813.131**<br>v Qal impv 2ms<br>רְצֵה<br>r$^e$tsēh<br>be pleased | **3176**<br>pn<br>יְהוָה<br>y$^e$hwāh<br>O Yahweh |
|---|---|---|---|---|---|---|

| **3937, 5522.541**<br>prep, v Hiphil inf con, ps 1cs<br>לְהַצִּילֵנִי<br>l$^e$hatstsilēnî<br>to rescue me | **3176**<br>pn<br>יְהוָה<br>y$^e$hwāh<br>O Yahweh | **3937, 6046**<br>prep, n fs, ps 1cs<br>לְעֶזְרָתִי<br>l$^e$'ezrāthî<br>for my help | **2456.131**<br>v Qal impv 2ms<br>חוּשָׁה<br>chûshāh<br>hurry | **14.** | **991.126**<br>v Qal juss 3mp<br>יֵבֹשׁוּ<br>yēvōshû<br>may they be ashamed |
|---|---|---|---|---|---|

| **2763.126**<br>cj, v Qal juss 3mp<br>וְיַחְפְּרוּ<br>w$^e$yachp$^e$rû<br>yes let them be ashamed | **3266**<br>adv<br>יַחַד<br>yachadh<br>together | **1272.352**<br>*v Piel ptc mp*<br>מְבַקְשֵׁי<br>m$^e$vaqŏshê<br>those who seek | **5497**<br>n fs, ps 1cs<br>נַפְשִׁי<br>naphshî<br>my soul | **3937, 5793.141**<br>prep, v Qal inf con, ps 3fs<br>לִסְפּוֹתָהּ<br>lispôthāhh<br>to take it away |
|---|---|---|---|---|

| **5657.226**<br>v Niphal juss 3mp<br>יִסֹּגוּ<br>yissōghû<br>and let them retreat | **268**<br>adv<br>אָחוֹר<br>'āchôr<br>back | **3757.226**<br>cj, v Niphal juss 3mp<br>וְיִכָּלְמוּ<br>w$^e$yikkāl$^e$mû<br>and let them be dishonored | **2760**<br>*adj*<br>חֲפֵצֵי<br>chăphētsê<br>the desirous of | **7750**<br>n fs, ps 1cs<br>רָעָתִי<br>rā'āthî<br>my disaster |
|---|---|---|---|---|

| **15.** | **8460.126**<br>v Qal juss 3mp<br>יָשֹׁמּוּ<br>yāshōmmû<br>let them be appalled | **6142, 6358**<br>prep, *n ms*<br>עַל־עֵקֶב<br>'al-'ēqev<br>concerning the result of | **1350**<br>n fs, ps 3mp<br>בָּשְׁתָּם<br>bāsh$^e$ttām<br>their shame | **569.152**<br>art, v Qal act ptc mp<br>הָאֹמְרִים<br>hā'ōm$^e$rîm<br>those saying | **3937**<br>prep, ps 1cs<br>לִי<br>lî<br>to me | **1955**<br>intrj<br>הֶאָח<br>he'āch<br>aha |
|---|---|---|---|---|---|---|

| **1955**<br>intrj<br>הֶאָח<br>he'āch<br>aha | **16.** | **7919.126**<br>v Qal juss 3mp<br>יָשִׂישׂוּ<br>yāsîsû<br>let them rejoice | **7975.126**<br>cj, v Qal juss 3mp<br>וְיִשְׂמְחוּ<br>w$^e$yism$^e$chû<br>and let them be glad | **904**<br>prep, ps 2ms<br>בְּךָ<br>b$^e$khā<br>in You | **3725, 1272.352**<br>*adj*, v Piel ptc mp, ps 2ms<br>כָּל־מְבַקְשֶׁיךָ<br>kol-m$^e$vaqŏshêkhā<br>all those seeking You |
|---|---|---|---|---|---|

| **569.126**<br>v Qal juss 3mp<br>יֹאמְרוּ<br>yō'm$^e$rû<br>and may they say | **8878**<br>adv<br>תָּמִיד<br>thāmîdh<br>continually | **1461.121**<br>v Qal impf 3ms<br>יִגְדַּל<br>yighdal<br>He is great | **3176**<br>pn<br>יְהוָה<br>y$^e$hwāh<br>Yahweh | **154.152**<br>*v Qal act ptc mp*<br>אֹהֲבֵי<br>'ōh$^e$vê<br>those who love | **9009**<br>n fs, ps 2ms<br>תְּשׁוּעָתֶךָ<br>t$^e$shû'āthekhā<br>your salvation |
|---|---|---|---|---|---|

| **17.** | **603**<br>cj, pers pron<br>וַאֲנִי<br>wa'ănî<br>and I | **6270**<br>adj<br>עָנִי<br>'ānî<br>afflicted | **33**<br>cj, adj<br>וְאֶבְיוֹן<br>w$^e$'evyôn<br>and needy | **112**<br>n mp, ps 1cs<br>אֲדֹנָי<br>'ădhōnāy<br>my Lord | **2913.121**<br>v Qal juss 3ms<br>יַחֲשָׁב<br>yachshāv<br>may He reckon | **3937**<br>prep, ps 1cs<br>לִי<br>lî<br>to me | **6046**<br>n fs, ps 1cs<br>עֶזְרָתִי<br>'ezrāthî<br>my help |
|---|---|---|---|---|---|---|---|

| **6647.351**<br>cj, v Piel ptc ms, ps 1cs<br>וּמְפַלְטִי<br>ûm$^e$phaltî<br>and the One Who sets me free | **887**<br>pers pron<br>אַתָּה<br>'attāh<br>You | **435**<br>n mp, ps 1cs<br>אֱלֹהַי<br>'ĕlōhay<br>O my God | **414, 310.323**<br>adv, v Piel juss 2ms<br>אַל־תְּאַחַר<br>'al-t$^e$'achar<br>do not delay | **41:t** | **3937, 5514.351**<br>prep, art, v Piel ptc ms<br>לַמְנַצֵּחַ<br>lamnatstsēach<br>to the director |
|---|---|---|---|---|---|

| | | | | | | | |
|---|---|---|---|---|---|---|---|
| 4344 | 3937, 1784 | 1. | 869 | 7959.551 | 420, 1859 | 904, 3219 | 7750 |
| n ms | prep, pn | | *n ms* | v Hiphil ptc ms | prep, n ms | prep, *n ms* | n fs |
| מִזְמוֹר | לְדָוִד | | אַשְׁרֵי | מַשְׂכִּיל | אֶל־דָּל | בְּיוֹם | רָעָה |
| mizmôr | ledhāwidh | | 'ashrê | maskîl | 'el-dāl | beyôm | rā'āh |
| a Psalm | of David | | blessed | the one who considers | about the poor | on the day of | trouble |

| | | | | | |
|---|---|---|---|---|---|
| 6647.321 | 3176 | 2. | 3176 | 8490.121 | 2513.321 |
| v Piel impf 3ms, ps 3ms | pn | | pn | v Qal impf 3ms, ps 3ms | cj, v Piel impf 3ms, ps 3ms |
| יְמַלְּטֵהוּ | יְהוָה | | יְהוָה | יִשְׁמְרֵהוּ | וִיחַיֵּהוּ |
| yemalletēhû | yehwāh | | yehwāh | yishmerēhû | wîchayyēhû |
| He delivers him | Yahweh | | Yahweh | He protects him | and He keeps him alive |

**14. Let them be ashamed and confounded together that seek after my soul to destroy it; let them be driven backward and put to shame that wish me evil:** ... to mutual confusion, *NKJV* ... and brought to dishonour, *MRB* ... to take away my life!, *Goodspeed* ... That delight in my hurt, *MAST.*

**15. Let them be desolate for a reward of their shame that say unto me, Aha, aha:** ... shamed into silence, *NCV* ... Let those be appalled because of their shame, *NASB* ... Let them be destroyed, *Geneva* ... Joy, joy! is their cry, *Knox.*

**16. Let all those that seek thee rejoice and be glad in thee: let such as love thy salvation say continually, The Lord be magnified:** ... may all who look to You for help, *Beck* ... joy and happiness in you, *JB* ... The Lord be glorified, *NAB* ... Great is the Lord, *RSV.*

**17. But I am poor and needy; yet the Lord thinketh upon me: thou art my help and my deliverer; make no tarrying, O my God:** ... I am weak and wretched, *Moffatt* ... Though I am afflicted, *NCB* ... the Lord has me in mind, *BB* ... make no delay, *NEB.*

**41:t. To the chief Musician, A Psalm of David.**

**1. Blessed is he that considereth the poor: the Lord will deliver him in time of trouble:** ... How happy is he that is attentive to the poor, *Rotherham* ... Who is acting wisely unto the poor, *Young* ... Happy is he who has regard for the lowly and the poor, *NAB* ... concern for the helpless, *REB* ... Blessings are his, who considers the weak; in the day of misfortune the Lord will deliver, *Berkeley.*

**2. The Lord will preserve him, and keep him alive; and he shall be**

The first of these is the omission of "Be pleased" in v. 13, which binds this second part to the first and points back to "thy pleasure" (v. 8). The prayer for the confusion of enemies closely resembles that in Ps. 35, v. 14 being almost identical with vv. 4 and 26 there, and v. 15 recalling v. 21 of that Psalm. The prayer that enemies may fail in their designs is consistent with the most Christ-like spirit, and nothing more is asked by the psalmist, but the tinge of satisfaction with which he dwells on their discomfiture, however natural, belongs to the less lofty moral standard of his stage of revelation. He uses extraordinarily forcible words to paint their bewilderment and mortification.

Very plaintively and touchingly does the low sigh of personal need follow this triumphant intercession for the company of the saints. "My God, delay not"—there he embraces both in one act of faithful longing. His need calls for, and God's loving counsels ensure, a swift response. He who delights when an afflicted and poor man calls Him "my God" will not be slack to vindicate his servant's confidence and magnify his own name. That appeal goes straight to the heart of God.

***Psalm 41.*** *The Psalm may be divided into four strophes, of which the two middle strophes cohere very closely. Verses 1ff give the mercy requited to the merciful; vv. 4ff, after a brief prayer and confession, begin the picture of the psalmist's sufferings, which is carried through the next strophe (vv. 7ff), with the difference that in the former the scene is mainly the sick man's chamber and in the latter the meeting place of the secret conspirators. Verses 10ff build on this picture of distress a prayer for deliverance and rise to serene confidence in its certain answer. The closing doxology is not part of the Psalm, but is appended as the conclusion of the first book of the Psalter.*

**41:1–3.** The "happy" of v. 1 is caught up in the abruptly introduced "He shall be counted happy" of v. 2, which may carry tacit reference to the malicious slanders that aggravated the psalmist's sufferings, and anticipates deliverance so perfect that all who see him shall think him fortunate. The next clause rises into direct address of Yahweh and is shown by the form of the negative in the Hebrew to be petition, not assertion, thus strongly confirming the view that "me" lurks below "him" in this context. A similar

| 861.421 | 904, 800 | 414, 5598.123 | 904, 5497 | 342.152 | | 3176 |
|---|---|---|---|---|---|---|
| v Pual impf 3ms | prep, art, n fs | cj, v Qal juss 2mp, ps 3ms | prep, *n fs* | v Qal act ptc mp, ps 3ms | **3.** | pn |
| יְאֻשַּׁר | בָּאָרֶץ | וְאַל־תִּתְּנֵהוּ | בְּנֶפֶשׁ | אֹיְבָיו | | יְהוָה |
| ye'ushshar | bā'ārets | we'al-tittenēhû | benephesh | 'ōyevâv | | yehwāh |
| he is blessed | in the land | so do not give him | into the desire of | his enemies | | Yahweh |

| 5777.121 | 6142, 6446 | 1793 | 3725, 5085 | 2089.113 | 904, 2582 |
|---|---|---|---|---|---|
| v Qal impf 3ms, ps 3ms | prep, *n fs* | n ms | *adj*, n ms, ps 3ms | v Qal pf 2ms | prep, n ms, ps 3ms |
| יִסְעָדֶנּוּ | עַל־עֶרֶשׂ | דְּוָי | כָּל־מִשְׁכָּבוֹ | הָפַכְתָּ | בְחָלְיוֹ |
| yis'ādhennû | 'al-'eres | dewāy | kol-mishkāvô | hāphakhtā | vechāleyô |
| He sustains him | on the bed of | illness | all his bed | You have changed | during his sickness |

| | 603, 569.115 | 3176 | 2706.131 | 7784.131 | 5497 |
|---|---|---|---|---|---|
| **4.** | pers pron, v Qal pf 1cs | pn | v Qal impv 2ms, ps 1cs | v Qal impv 2ms | n fs, ps 1cs |
| | אֲנִי־אָמַרְתִּי | יְהוָה | חָנֵּנִי | רְפָאָה | נַפְשִׁי |
| | 'ănî-'āmartî | yehwāh | chonnēnî | rephā'āh | naphshî |
| | I I have said | O Yahweh | be gracious to me | heal | my soul |

| 3706, 2490.115 | 3937 | | 342.152 | 569.126 | 7737 | 3937 | 5146 |
|---|---|---|---|---|---|---|---|
| cj, v Qal pf 1cs | prep, ps 2ms | **5.** | v Qal act ptc mp, ps 1cs | v Qal impf 3mp | n ms | prep, ps 1cs | intrg |
| כִּי־חָטָאתִי | לָךְ | | אוֹיְבַי | יֹאמְרוּ | רַע | לִי | מָתַי |
| kî-chāṭā'thî | lākh | | 'ôyvay | yō'merû | ra' | lî | māthay |
| because I have sinned | against You | | my enemies | they say | evil | about me | when |

| 4322.121 | 6.111 | 8428 | | 524, 971.111 | 3937, 7495.141 | 8175 |
|---|---|---|---|---|---|---|
| v Qal impf 3ms | cj, v Qal pf 3ms | n ms, ps 3ms | **6.** | cj, cj, v Qal pf 3ms | prep, v Qal inf con | n ms |
| יָמוּת | וְאָבַד | שְׁמוֹ | | וְאִם־בָּא | לִרְאוֹת | שָׁוְא |
| yāmûth | we'āvadh | shemô | | we'im-bā' | lir'ôth | shāwe' |
| will he die | so it will have perished | his name | | and when he comes | to see | vanity |

| 1744.321 | 3949 | 7192.121, 201 | 3937 | 3428.121 | 3937, 2445 |
|---|---|---|---|---|---|
| v Piel impf 3ms | n ms, ps 3ms | v Qal impf 3ms, n ms | prep, ps 3ms | v Qal impf 3ms | prep, art, n ms |
| יְדַבֵּר | לִבּוֹ | יִקְבָּץ־אָוֶן | לוֹ | יֵצֵא | לַחוּץ |
| yedhabbēr | libbô | yiqōbbāts-'āwen | lô | yētsē' | lachûts |
| it speaks | his heart | he harvests iniquity | for himself | he goes out | to the streets |

| 1744.321 | | 3266 | 6142 | 4042.726 | 3725, 7983.152 | 6142 |
|---|---|---|---|---|---|---|
| v Piel impf 3ms | **7.** | adv | prep, ps 1cs | v Hithpael impf 3mp | *adj*, v Qal act ptc mp, ps 1cs | prep, ps 1cs |
| יְדַבֵּר | | יַחַד | עָלַי | יִתְלַחֲשׁוּ | כָּל־שֹׂנְאָי | עָלַי |
| yedhabbēr | | yachadh | 'ālay | yithlachshû | kol-sōne'āy | 'ālay |
| he speaks | | together | against me | they whisper | all those who hate me | against me |

| 2913.126 | 7750 | 3937 | | 1745, 1139 | 3441.155 | 904 | 866 |
|---|---|---|---|---|---|---|---|
| v Qal impf 3mp | n fs | prep, ps 1cs | **8.** | *n ms*, n ms | v Qal pass ptc ms | prep, ps 3ms | cj, rel part |
| יַחְשְׁבוּ | רָעָה | לִי | | דְּבַר־בְּלִיַּעַל | יָצוּק | בּוֹ | וַאֲשֶׁר |
| yachshevû | rā'āh | lî | | devar-beliya'al | yātsûq | bô | wa'āsher |
| they devise | evil | for me | | a thing of worthlessness | poured out | on him | and where |

| 8311.111 | 3940, 3362.521 | 3937, 7251.141 | | 1612, 382 | 8361 |
|---|---|---|---|---|---|
| v Qal pf 3ms | neg part, v Hiphil impf 3ms | prep, v Qal inf con | **9.** | cj, *n ms* | n ms, ps 1cs |
| שָׁכַב | לֹא־יוֹסִיף | לָקוּם | | גַּם־אִישׁ | שְׁלוֹמִי |
| shākhav | lō'-yôsîph | lāqûm | | gam-'îsh | shelômî |
| he lay down | he will not continue | to stand | | also the man of | my peace |

| 866, 1019.115 | 904 | 404.151 | 4035 | 1461.511 | 6142 | 6357 |
|---|---|---|---|---|---|---|
| rel part, v Qal pf 1cs | prep, ps 3ms | v Qal act ptc ms | n ms, ps 1cs | v Hiphil pf 3ms | prep, ps 1cs | n ms |
| אֲשֶׁר־בָּטַחְתִּי | בוֹ | אוֹכֵל | לַחְמִי | הִגְדִּיל | עָלַי | עָקֵב |
| 'ăsher-bāṭachtî | vô | 'ôkhēl | lachmî | highdîl | 'ālay | 'āqēv |
| whom I trusted | in him | the one who ate | my bread | he made great | onto me | a heel |

**blessed upon the earth: and thou wilt not deliver him unto the will of his enemies:** ... The LORD will protect him, *NASB* ... he shall be made happy in the land, *Darby* ... unto the greed of his enemies, *MAST* ... and not surrender him to the desire of his foes, *NIV.*

**3. The LORD will strengthen him upon the bed of languishing: thou wilt make all his bed in his sickness:** ... him on his sickbed, he will take away all his ailment when he is ill, *NCB* ... transforming his every illness to health, *REB* ... in their illness you heal all their infirmities, *NRSV* ... Thou dost restore him to health, *NASB.*

**4. I said, LORD, be merciful unto me: heal my soul; for I have sinned against thee:** ... I entreat, LORD, have pity on me, *Fenton* ... make my soul well, because my faith is in you, *BB* ... Cure me for I have sinned, *JB* ... bring healing to a soul that has sinned against thee, *Knox.*

**5. Mine enemies speak evil of me, When shall he die, and his name perish?:** ... enemies wonder in malice when I will die, *NRSV* ... When will he die and his name disappear, *Beck* ... When will he die and be forgotten, *NCV.*

**6. And if he come to see me, he speaketh vanity: his heart gathereth iniquity to itself; when he goeth abroad, he telleth it:** ... When people come to see me their talk is hollow, *JB* ... They just come to get bad news. Then they go and gossip, *NCV* ... When any of them visits me, his heart is false, *Moffatt* ... stores up malice for himself, goes outside and gossips, *Anchor.*

**7. All that hate me whisper together against me: against me do they devise my hurt:** ... and love to make the worst of everything, *NEB* ... they are designing my downfall, *BB* ... against me they imagine the worst, *NAB* ... they plot against me to hurt me, *KJVII.*

**8. An evil disease, say they, cleaveth fast unto him: and now that he lieth he shall rise up no more:** ... A fatal sickness has a grip on him, *JB* ... A vile disease has beset him, *NIV* ... He is loaded with crimes, *Fenton* ... May a deadly disease be poured out on him, *Beck.*

**9. Yea, mine own familiar friend, in whom I trusted, which did eat of my bread, hath lifted up his heel against me:** ... intimate friend, who shared my bread, has lifted his heel to trip me, *Knox* ... ate at my table, exults over my misfortune, *NEB* ... has acted deceitfully against me, *Goodspeed* ... trips me up heavily, *Moffatt.*

**10. But thou, O LORD, be merciful unto me, and raise me up, that I may requite them:** ... have pity on me, *NCB* ... restore me that I may repay them in full, *REB* ... And I give recompence to them, *Young* ... That I may repay them, *Anchor.*

---

transition from the third to the second person occurs in v. 3, as if the psalmist drew closer to his God. There is also a change of tense in the verbs there: "Yahweh will sustain"; "Thou hast turned," the latter tense converting the general truth expressed in the former clause into a fact of experience.

**41:4–6.** The second and third strophes (vv. 4–9) are closely connected. In them, the psalmist recounts his sorrows and pains, but first breathes a prayer for mercy and bases it no longer on his mercifulness, but on his sin. Only a shallow experience will find contradiction here to either the former words or to the later profession of "integrity" (v. 12). The petition for soul-healing does not prove that sickness in the following verses is figurative. While he speaks thus to Yahweh, his enemies speak in a different tone. The "evil" which they utter is not calumny, but malediction. Their hatred is impatient for his death. The time seems long until they can hear of it. One of them comes on a hypocritical visit of solicitude ("see" is used for visiting the sick in 2 Ki. 8:29) and speaks lying condolence, while he greedily collects encouraging symptoms that the disease is hopeless. Then he hurries back to tell how much worse he had found the patient, and that ignoble crew delights in the good news. The second strophe ends with the exit of the false friend.

**41:7–9.** The third section carries him to the meeting place of the plotters, who eagerly receive and retail the good news that the sick man is worse. They feed their ignoble hate by picturing further ill as laying hold of him. Their wish is parent to their thought, which is confirmed by the report of their emissary. "A thing of Belial is poured out on him," or "is fastened upon him," they say. That unusual expression may refer either to moral or physical evil. In the former sense, it would here mean the sufferer's sin, in the latter, a fatal disease. The connection makes the physical reference the more likely. Our LORD's quotation of part of v. 9, with the significant omission of "in whom I trusted," does not imply the messianic character of the entire Psalm, but is an instance of an event and a saying which were not meant as prophetic, finding fuller realization in the life of the perfect type of suffering godliness than in the original sufferer.

**41:10–13.** The last strophe recurs to prayer and soars to confidence born of communion. A hand stretched out in need and trust soon comes back filled with blessings. Therefore, here the moment

| | 887 | 3176 | 2706.131 | 7251.531 | 8396.325 | 3937 |
|---|---|---|---|---|---|---|
| | cj, pers pron | pn | v Qal impv 2ms, ps 1cs | cj, v Hiphil impv 2ms | cj, v Piel juss 1cs | prep, ps 3mp |
| **10.** | וְאַתָּה | יְהוָה | חָנֵּנִי | וַהֲקִימֵנִי | וַאֲשַׁלְּמָה | לָהֶם |
| | we'attāh | yehwāh | channēnî | wahqîmēnî | wa'ăshallemāh | lāhem |
| | but You | O Yahweh | be gracious to me | and raise me up | that I may requite | to them |

| | 904, 2148 | 3156.115 | 3706, 2759.113 | 904 | 3706 |
|---|---|---|---|---|---|
| | prep, dem pron | v Qal pf 1cs | cj, v Qal pf 2ms | prep, ps 1cs | cj |
| **11.** | בְּזֹאת | יָדַעְתִּי | כִּי־חָפַצְתָּ | בִּי | כִּי |
| | bezō'th | yādha'ttî | kî-chāphatstā | bî | kî |
| | by this | I know | that You take delight | in me | because |

| 3940, 7607.521 | 342.151 | 6142 | | 603 | 904, 8866 |
|---|---|---|---|---|---|
| neg part, v Hiphil impf 3ms | v Qal act ptc ms, ps 1cs | prep, ps 1cs | | cj, pers pron | prep, n ms, ps 1cs |
| לֹא־יָרִיעַ | אֹיְבִי | עָלָי | **12.** | וַאֲנִי | בְּתֻמִּי |
| lō'-yārîa' | 'ōyevî | 'ālāy | | wa'ănî | bethummî |
| he does not shout victoriously | my enemy | over me | | and I | in my blamelessness |

| 8881.113 | 904 | 5507.523 | 3937, 6686 | 3937, 5986 |
|---|---|---|---|---|
| v Qal pf 2ms | prep, ps 1cs | cj, v Hiphil impf 2ms, ps 1cs | prep, n mp, ps 2ms | prep, n ms |
| תָּמַכְתָּ | בִּי | וַתַּצִּיבֵנִי | לְפָנֶיךָ | לְעוֹלָם |
| tāmakhtā | bî | wattatstsîvēnî | lephānêkhā | le'ôlām |
| You have held fast | on me | and You have stationed me | in your presence | unto eternity |

| | 1313.155 | 3176 | 435 | 3547 | 4623, 5986 | 5912 | 5986 | 549 |
|---|---|---|---|---|---|---|---|---|
| | v Qal pass ptc ms | pn | *n mp* | pn | prep, art, n ms | cj, adv | art, n ms | intrj |
| **13.** | בָּרוּךְ | יְהוָה | אֱלֹהֵי | יִשְׂרָאֵל | מֵהָעוֹלָם | וְעַד | הָעוֹלָם | אָמֵן |
| | bārûkh | yehwāh | 'ĕlōhê | yisrā'ēl | mēhā'ôlām | we'adh | hā'ôlām | 'āmēn |
| | blessed | Yahweh | the God of | Israel | from eternity | even until | eternity | amen |

| 549 | | 3937, 5514.351 | 5030 | 3937, 1158, 7432 | | 3626, 358 | 6045.122 |
|---|---|---|---|---|---|---|---|
| cj, intrj | | prep, art, v Piel ptc ms | n ms | prep, *n mp*, pn | | prep, n fs | v Qal impf 3fs |
| וְאָמֵן | **42:t** | לַמְנַצֵּחַ | מַשְׂכִּיל | לִבְנֵי־קֹרַח | **1.** | כְּאַיָּל | תַּעֲרֹג |
| we'āmēn | | lamnatstsēach | maskîl | livnê-qōrach | | ke'ayyāl | ta'ărōgh |
| and amen | | to the director | a Maskil | of the sons of Korah | | like a male deer | it longs |

| 6142, 665, 4448 | 3772 | 5497 | 6045.122 | 420 | 435 | | 7039.122 | 5497 |
|---|---|---|---|---|---|---|---|---|
| prep, *n mp*, n mp | adv | n fs, ps 1cs | v Qal impf 3fs | prep, ps 2ms | n mp | | v Qal pf 3fs | n fs, ps 1cs |
| עַל־אֲפִיקֵי־מָיִם | כֵּן | נַפְשִׁי | תַעֲרֹג | אֵלֶיךָ | אֱלֹהִים | **2.** | צָמְאָה | נַפְשִׁי |
| 'al-'ăphîqê-māyim | kēn | naphshî | tha'ărōgh | 'ēlêkhā | 'ĕlōhîm | | tsāme'āh | naphshî |
| over streams of water | so | my soul | it longs | toward You | O God | | it is thirsty | my soul |

| 3937, 435 | 3937, 418 | 2508 | 5146 | 971.125 | 7495.225 | 6686 | 435 |
|---|---|---|---|---|---|---|---|
| prep, n mp | prep, n ms | adj | intrg | v Qal impf 1cs | cj, v Niphal impf 1cs | *n mp* | n mp |
| לֵאלֹהִים | לְאֵל | חָי | מָתַי | אָבוֹא | וְאֵרָאֶה | פְּנֵי | אֱלֹהִים |
| lē'lōhîm | le'ēl | chāy | māthay | 'āvô' | we'ērā'eh | penê | 'ĕlōhîm |
| for God | for God | alive | when | will I go | and will I appear in | the presence of | God |

| | 2030.122, 3937 | 1893 | 4035 | 3221 | 4050 | 904, 569.141 | 420 |
|---|---|---|---|---|---|---|---|
| | v Qal pf 3fs, prep, ps 1cs | n fs, ps 1cs | n ms | adv | cj, n ms | prep, v Qal inf con | prep, ps 1cs |
| **3.** | הָיְתָה־לִּי | דִמְעָתִי | לֶחֶם | יוֹמָם | וָלָיְלָה | בֶּאֱמֹר | אֵלַי |
| | hāyethāh-lî | dhim'āthî | lechem | yômām | wālāyelāh | be'ĕmōr | 'ēlay |
| | they have been to me | my tears | food | by day | and by night | while saying | to me |

| 3725, 3219 | 347 | 435 | | 431 | 2226.125 | 8581.125 | 6142 |
|---|---|---|---|---|---|---|---|
| *adj*, art, n ms | intrg | n mp, ps 2ms | | dem pron | v Qal juss 1cs | cj, v Qal juss 1cs | prep, ps 1cs |
| כָּל־הַיּוֹם | אַיֵּה | אֱלֹהֶיךָ | **4.** | אֵלֶּה | אֶזְכְּרָה | וְאֶשְׁפְּכָה | עָלַי |
| kol-hayyôm | 'ayyēh | 'ĕlōhêkhā | | 'ēlleh | 'ezkerāh | we'eshpekhāh | 'ālay |
| all the day | where | your God | | these | let me remember | and let me pour out | beside me |

**11. By this I know that thou favourest me, because mine enemy doth not triumph over me:** ... because my hater does not overcome me, *BB* ... mine enemy shall not raise a shout over me, *Rotherham.*

**12. And as for me, thou upholdest me in mine integrity, and settest me before thy face for ever:** ... Because I am innocent, you support me, *NCV* ... You will help me, because I do what is right, *Good News* ... will keep me unscathed, and set me in your presence for ever, *JB.*

**13. Blessed be the LORD God of Israel from everlasting, and to everlasting. Amen, and Amen:** ... from the beginning to the end of time, *Knox* ... from eternity and to eternity, *Anchor* ... through eternal days and for ever. So be it, *BB* ... From the age that is past even unto the age yet to come, *Rotherham.*

**42:t. To the chief Musician, Maschil, for the sons of Korah.**

**1. As the hart panteth after the water brooks, so panteth my soul after thee, O God:** ... As a deer pants, *Berkeley* ... My whole being, *Goodspeed* ... so my soul longs for you, *NCB* ... I yearn for you, *JB.*

**2. My soul thirsteth for God, for the living God: when shall I come and appear before God?:** ... My soul is dry for need of God, *BB* ... Oh Source of Life, *Fenton* ... to drink in deeply the presence of God, *Anchor* ... see the face of God, *Rotherham.*

**3. My tears have been my meat day and night, while they continually say unto me, Where is thy God?:** ... I have lived on my tears, *Moffatt* ... my bread, *Darby* ... my food, *NKJV* ... say to me day after day, *NAB.*

**4. When I remember these things, I pour out my soul in me:** ... my very heart, *Geneva* ... my soul in distress, *REB.*

**for I had gone with the multitude, I went with them to the house of God, with the voice of joy and praise, with a multitude that kept holyday:** ... and led them in procession, *NRSV* ... singing and confession, *Young* ... glad shouts and songs of thanksgiving, *RSV.*

---

of true petition is the moment of realized answer. The prayer traverses the malicious hopes of enemies. They had said, "He will rise no more"; it prays, "Raise me up." It touches a note which at first sounds discordant in the desire "that I may requite them."

But the last words of the Psalm shine with the assurance of present favor and with boundless hope. The man is still lying on his sickbed, ringed by whispering foes. There is no change without, but he has tightened his hold of God and therefore can feel that his enemies' whispers will never rise or swell into a shout of victory over him.

***Psalms 42–43.*** *The second book of the Psalter is characterized by the use of the divine name "Elohim" instead of "Yahweh." It begins with a cluster of seven Psalms (reckoning Pss. 42 and 43 as one) of which the superscription is most probably regarded as ascribing their authorship to "the sons of Korah." These were Levites, and (according to 1 Chr. 9:19) the office of keepers of the door of the sanctuary had been hereditary in their family from the time of Moses. Some of them were among the faithful adherents of David at Ziklag (1 Chr. 12:6), and in the new model of worship inaugurated by him the Korahites were doorkeepers and musicians. They retained the former office in the second Temple (Neh. 9:19). The ascription of authorship to a group is remarkable and has led to the suggestion that the superscription does not specify the authors but the persons for whose use the Psalms in question were composed. The Hebrew would bear either meaning; but if the latter is adopted, all these Psalms are anonymous.*

*The two Psalms (42, 43) are plainly one. The absence of a title for the second, the identity of tone throughout, the recurrence of several phrases, and especially of the refrain, put this beyond doubt. The separation, however, is old, since it is found in the Septuagint. It is useless to speculate on its origin.*

*The Psalm of 42 and 43 falls into three parts, each closing with the same refrain.*

**42:1–5.** The "soul" (HED #5497) is feminine in Hebrew and is here compared to the female deer, for "pants" is the feminine form of the verb, although its noun is masculine. It is better therefore to translate "hind" than "hart." The soul is the seat of emotions and desires. It pants and thirsts, is cast down and disquieted. It is poured out; it can be bidden to hope. Thus, tremulous, timid and mobile, it is beautifully compared to a hind. The true object of its longings is always God, however little it knows for what it is thirsting. But they are happy in their very yearnings who are conscious of the true direction of these and can say that it is God for Whom they thirst.

This man's longing was intensified by his unwilling exile from the sanctuary, a special privation to a door keeper of the Temple. His situation and mood closely resemble those in another Korahite Psalm (Ps. 84), in which, as here, the soul

| 5497 | 3706 | 5882.125 | 904, 5710 | 1768.725 | 5912, 1041 | 435 |
|---|---|---|---|---|---|---|
| n fs, ps 1cs | cj | v Qal impf 1cs | prep, art, n ms | v Hithpael impf 1cs, ps 3mp | prep, *n ms* | n mp |
| נַפְשִׁי | כִּי | אֶעֱבֹר | בַּסָּךְ | אֶדַּדֵּם | עַד־בֵּית | אֱלֹהִים |
| naphshî | kî | 'e'ĕvōr | bassākh | 'eddaddēm | 'adh-bêth | 'ĕlōhîm |
| my soul | that | I passed on | with the booth | I went with them | unto the Temple of | God |

| 904, 7249, 7726 | 8756 | 2066 | 2379.151 |
|---|---|---|---|
| prep, *n ms*, n fs | cj, n fs | n ms | v Qal act ptc ms |
| בְּקוֹל־רִנָּה | וְתוֹדָה | הָמוֹן | חוֹגֵג |
| b$^{e}$qôl-rinnāh | w$^{e}$thôdhāh | hāmôn | chôghēgh |
| with the voice of a shout of joy | and thanksgiving | a multitude | observing a festival |

| 5. | 4242, 8246.724 | 5497 | 2064.124 | 6142 | 3282.532 |
|---|---|---|---|---|---|
| | intrg, v Hithpoel impf 2fs | n fs, ps 1cs | cj, v Qal impf 2fs | prep, ps 1cs | v Hiphil impv 2fs |
| | מַה־תִּשְׁתּוֹחֲחִי | נַפְשִׁי | וַתֶּהֱמִי | עָלָי | הוֹחִילִי |
| | mah-tishtôchăchî | naphshî | wattehĕmî | 'ālāy | hôchîlî |
| | why are you bent down | my soul | and are you tumultuous | against me | wait |

| 3937, 435 | 3706, 5968 | 3142.525 | 3568 | 6686 | 6. | 435 |
|---|---|---|---|---|---|---|
| prep, n mp | cj, adv | v Hiphil impf 1cs, ps 3ms | *n fp* | n mp, ps 3ms | | n mp, ps 1cs |
| לֵאלֹהִים | כִּי־עוֹד | אוֹדֶנּוּ | יְשׁוּעוֹת | פָּנָיו | | אֱלֹהַי |
| lē'lōhîm | kî-'ôdh | 'ôdhennû | y$^{e}$shû'ôth | pānâv | | 'ĕlōhay |
| for God | because still | I will praise Him | the deliverances of | his presence | | my God |

| 6142 | 5497 | 8249.722 | 6142, 3772 | 2226.125 | 4623, 800 | 3497 |
|---|---|---|---|---|---|---|
| prep, ps 1cs | n fs, ps 1cs | v Hithpoel impf 3fs | prep, adv | v Qal impf 1cs, ps 2ms | prep, *n fs* | pn |
| עָלַי | נַפְשִׁי | תִשְׁתּוֹחָח | עַל־כֵּן | אֶזְכָּרְךָ | מֵאֶרֶץ | יַרְדֵּן |
| 'ālay | naphshî | thishtôchāch | 'al-kēn | 'ezkār$^{e}$khā | mē'erets | yardēn |
| against me | my soul | it makes itself low | therefore | I will remember You | from the land of | Jordan |

| 2874 | 4623, 2098 | 4867B | 7. | 8745, 420, 8745 | 7410.151 | 3937, 7249 |
|---|---|---|---|---|---|---|
| cj, pn | prep, *n ms* | pn | | n fs, prep, n fs | v Qal act ptc ms | prep, *n ms* |
| וְחֶרְמוֹנִים | מֵהַר | מִצְעָר | | תְּהוֹם־אֶל־תְּהוֹם | קוֹרֵא | לְקוֹל |
| w$^{e}$chermônîm | mēhar | mits'ār | | t$^{e}$hôm-'el-t$^{e}$hôm | qôrē' | l$^{e}$qôl |
| and Hermon | from Mount | Mizar | | deep to deep | calling | to the sound of |

| 7069 | 3725, 5053 | 1570 | 6142 | 5882.116 | 8. | 3221 |
|---|---|---|---|---|---|---|
| n mp, ps 2ms | *adj*, n mp, ps 2ms | cj, n mp, ps 2ms | prep, ps 1cs | v Qal pf 3cp | | adv |
| צִנּוֹרֶיךָ | כָּל־מִשְׁבָּרֶיךָ | וְגַלֶּיךָ | עָלָי | עָבָרוּ | | יוֹמָם |
| tsinnôrêkhā | kol-mishbārêkhā | w$^{e}$ghallêkhā | 'ālay | 'āvārû | | yômām |
| your waterfalls | all your waves | and your billows | over me | they have passed over | | by day |

| 6943.321 | 3176 | 2721 | 904, 4050 | 8301 | 6196 | 8940 |
|---|---|---|---|---|---|---|
| v Piel impf 3ms | pn | n ms, ps 3ms | cj, prep, art, n ms | n ms, ps 3ms | prep, ps 1cs | n fs |
| יְצַוֶּה | יְהוָה | חַסְדּוֹ | וּבַלַּיְלָה | שִׁירֹה | עִמִּי | תְּפִלָּה |
| y$^{e}$tsawweh | y$^{e}$hwāh | chasdô | ûvallaylāh | shîrōh | 'immî | t$^{e}$phillāh |
| He commands | Yahweh | his steadfast love | and in the night | his song | with me | a prayer |

| 3937, 418 | 2522 | 9. | 569.125 | 3937, 418 | 5748 | 4066 | 8319.113 |
|---|---|---|---|---|---|---|---|
| prep, *n ms* | n mp, ps 1cs | | v Qal juss 1cs | prep, n ms | n ms, ps 1cs | intrg | v Qal pf 2ms, ps 1cs |
| לְאֵל | חַיָּי | | אוֹמְרָה | לְאֵל | סַלְעִי | לָמָה | שְׁכַחְתָּנִי |
| l$^{e}$'ēl | chayyāy | | 'ômrāh | l$^{e}$'ēl | sal'î | lāmāh | sh$^{e}$khachtānî |
| to the God of | my life | | let me say | to God | my Rock | why | have You forgotten me |

| 4066, 7222.151 | 2050.125 | 904, 4040 | 342.151 |
|---|---|---|---|
| intrg, v Qal act ptc ms | v Qal impf 1cs | prep, *n ms* | v Qal act ptc ms |
| לָמָּה־קֹדֵר | אֵלֵךְ | בְּלַחַץ | אוֹיֵב |
| lāmmāh-qōdhēr | 'ēlēkh | b$^{e}$lachats | 'ôyēv |
| why being unkempt | do I walk about | under the oppression of | the enemy |

**5. Why art thou cast down, O my soul? and why art thou disquieted in me?:** ... Why are you in despair, *NASB* ... why am I in such turmoil, *Beck* ... How deep I am sunk in misery, *NEB.*

**hope thou in God: for I shall yet praise him for the help of his countenance:** ... help of His face, *KJVII* ... For the salvation, *MAST* ... Wait for God's help, *Knox.*

**6. O my God, my soul is cast down within me: therefore will I remember thee from the land of Jordan, and of the Hermonites, from the hill Mizar:** ... In my sad mood, *Knox* ... from Depression's Land I think, *Fenton* ... my soul is in despair, *NASB.*

**7. Deep calleth unto deep at the noise of thy waterspouts: all thy waves and thy billows are gone over me:** ... Flood follows flood, *Moffatt* ... Troubles have come again and again, *NCV* ... at the voice of thy cataracts, *Rotherham* ... have swept over me, *NIV.*

**8. Yet the LORD will command his lovingkindness in the daytime, and in the night his song shall be with me, and my prayer unto the God of my life:** ... makes his unfailing love shine forth, *NEB* ... will send his mercy, *BB* ... bestows his grace, *NAB* ... the song it inspires in me, *JB.*

**9. I will say unto God my rock, Why hast thou forgotten me? why go I mourning because of the oppression of the enemy?:** ... my refuge, *Berkeley* ... I walk about mournfully, *NRSV* ... harassment by the Foe, *Anchor* ... the cruelty of the enemy, *KJVII.*

**10. As with a sword in my bones, mine enemies reproach me; while**

---

"faints for the courts of the LORD," and as here the panting hind, so there the glancing swallows flitting about the eaves are woven into the song. Unnamed foes taunt the psalmist with the question, "Where is thy God?" There is no necessity to conclude that these were heathens, although the taunt is usually put into heathen lips (Pss. 79:10; 52:2), but it would be quite as natural from co-religionists, flouting their fervor and personal grasp of God and taking their sorrows as tokens of God's abandonment of them. That is the world's way with the calamities of a devout man, whose humble cry, "my God," it resents as presumption or hypocrisy.

Verse 5 has the refrain in a form slightly different from that of the other two instances of its occurrence (v. 11 and 43:5). But the text is probably faulty. The shifting of the initial word of v. 6 to the end of v. 5 and the substitution of "my" for "his" bring the three refrains into line and avoid the harsh expression "help of his countenance." Since no reason for the variation is discernible and the proposed slight change of text improves construction and restores uniformity, it is probably to be adopted. If it is, the second part of the Psalm is also conformed to the other two in regard to its not beginning with the divine name.

**42:6–8.** With wise resolve, he finds in dejection a reason for nestling closer to God. In reference to the description of the psalmist's locality, the preposition "from" (HED #4623) is chosen (rather than "in") with a subtle purpose. It suggests that the psalmist's faith will bridge over the interval between himself and the sanctuary: "I can send my thoughts to Thee from the distant frontier." The region intended seems to be the northeastern corner of Palestine, near the lower slopes of Hermon. The plural Hermons is probably used in reference to the group of crests. Mizar is probably the name of a hill otherwise unknown and specifies the singer's locality more minutely, although not helpfully to us. Many ingenious attempts have been made to explain the name either as symbolic or as a common noun and not a proper name.

The twofold emotions of v. 6 recur in vv. 7f, where there is first renewed despondency and then reaction into hope. The imagery of floods lifting up their voices, cataracts sounding as they fall and breaking waves rolling over the half-drowned psalmist has been supposed to be suggested by the scenery in which he was. But the rushing noise of Jordan in its rocky bed seems scarcely enough to deserve being described as "flood calling to flood," and "breakers and rollers" is an exaggeration if applied to any commotion possible on such a stream. The imagery is so usual that it needs no assumption of having been occasioned by the poet's locality. The dry and thirsty land there and the rush of waters here mean the same thing, so flexible is nature in a poet's hands.

**42:9–11.** Then follows a gleam of hope, like a rainbow spanning the waterfall. With the alternation of mood already noticed as characteristic, the singer looks forward, even from the midst of overwhelming seas of trouble, to a future day when God will give his angel, mercy or steadfast love, charge concerning him and draw him out of many waters. That day of extrication will surely be followed by a night of music and of thankful prayer (for supplication is not the only element in prayer) to Him Who by his deliverance has shown himself to be the God

| | 904, 7816 | 904, 6344 | 2884.316 | 7173.152 |
|---|---|---|---|---|
| **10.** | prep, n ms | prep, n fp, ps 1cs | v Piel pf 3cp, ps 1cs | v Qal act ptc mp, ps 1cs |
| | בְּרֶצַח | בְּעַצְמוֹתַי | חֵרְפוּנִי | צוֹרְרָי |
| | beretsach | beʿatsmôthay | chērephûnî | tsôrerāy |
| | with a deadly stroke | in my bones | they have taunted me | my adversaries |

| 904, 569.141 | 420 | 3725, 3219 | 347 | 435 | | 4242, 8246.724 |
|---|---|---|---|---|---|---|
| prep, v Qal inf con, ps 3mp | prep, ps 1cs | *adj*, art, n ms | intrg | n mp, ps 2ms | **11.** | intrg, v Hithpoel impf 2fs |
| בְּאָמְרָם | אֵלַי | כָּל־הַיּוֹם | אַיֵּה | אֱלֹהֶיךָ | | מַה־תִּשְׁתּוֹחֲחִי |
| beʾāmerām | ʾēlay | kol-hayyôm | ʾayyēh | ʾělōhêkhā | | mah-tishtôchăchî |
| while their saying | to me | all the day | where | your God | | why are you bent down |

| 5497 | 4242, 2064.124 | 6142 | 3282.532 | 3937, 435 | 3706, 5968 |
|---|---|---|---|---|---|
| n fs, ps 1cs | cj, intrg, v Qal impf 2fs | prep, ps 1cs | v Hiphil impv 2fs | prep, n mp | cj, adv |
| נַפְשִׁי | וּמַה־תֶּהֱמִי | עָלָי | הוֹחִילִי | לֵאלֹהִים | כִּי־עוֹד |
| naphshî | ûmah-tehĕmî | ʿālāy | hôchîlî | lēʾlōhîm | kî-ʿôdh |
| my soul | and why are you tumultuous | against me | wait | for God | because still |

| 3142.525 | 3568 | 6686 | 435 | | 8570.131 |
|---|---|---|---|---|---|
| v Hiphil impf 1cs, ps 3ms | *n fs* | n mp, ps 1cs | cj, n mp, ps 1cs | **43:1** | v Qal impv 2ms, ps 1cs |
| אוֹדֶנּוּ | יְשׁוּעֹת | פָּנַי | וֵאלֹהָי | | שָׁפְטֵנִי |
| ʾôdhennû | yeshûʿōth | pānay | wēʾlōhāy | | shāpheṯēnî |
| I will praise Him | the salvations of | my countenance | and my God | | vindicate me |

| 435 | 7662.131 | 7663 | 4623, 1504 | 3940, 2728 | 4623, 382, 4983 |
|---|---|---|---|---|---|
| n mp | cj, v Qal impv 2ms | n ms, ps 1cs | prep, n ms | neg part, adj | prep, *n ms*, n fs |
| אֱלֹהִים | וְרִיבָה | רִיבִי | מִגּוֹי | לֹא־חָסִיד | מֵאִישׁ־מִרְמָה |
| ʾělōhîm | werîvāh | rîvî | miggôy | lōʾ-chās̱îdh | mēʾîsh-mirmāh |
| O God | and contend for | my case | from a nation | not godly | from a man of deceit |

| 5983 | 6647.323 | | 3706, 887 | 435 | 4735 | 4066 |
|---|---|---|---|---|---|---|
| cj, n fs | v Piel impf 2ms, ps 1cs | **2.** | cj, pers pron | *n mp* | n ms, ps 1cs | intrg |
| וְעַוְלָה | תְּפַלְּטֵנִי | | כִּי־אַתָּה | אֱלֹהֵי | מָעוּזִּי | לָמָה |
| weʿawlāh | thephalleṯēnî | | kî-ʾattāh | ʾělōhê | māʿûzzî | lāmāh |
| and wrongdoing | You set me free | | because You | the God of | my Refuge | why |

| 2269.113 | 4066, 7222.151 | 2050.725 | 904, 4040 | 342.151 |
|---|---|---|---|---|
| v Qal pf 2ms, ps 1cs | intrg, v Qal act ptc ms | v Hithpael impf 1cs | prep, *n ms* | v Qal act ptc ms |
| זְנַחְתָּנִי | לָמָּה־קֹדֵר | אֶתְהַלֵּךְ | בְּלַחַץ | אוֹיֵב |
| zenachtānî | lāmmāh-qōdhēr | ʾethhallēkh | belachats | ʾôyēv |
| have You rejected me | why being unkempt | do I walk about | under the oppression of | the enemy |

| | 8365.131, 214 | 583 | 2065 | 5328.526 | 971.526 |
|---|---|---|---|---|---|
| **3.** | v Qal impv 2ms, n ms, ps 2ms | cj, n fs, ps 2ms | pers pron | v Hiphil juss 3mp, ps 1cs | v Hiphil juss 3mp, ps 1cs |
| | שְׁלַח־אוֹרְךָ | וַאֲמִתְּךָ | הֵמָּה | יַנְחוּנִי | יְבִיאוּנִי |
| | shelach-ʾôrkhā | waʾămittekhā | hēmmāh | yanchûnî | yevîʾûnî |
| | send out your light | and your truth | they | and let them lead me | and let them bring me |

| 420, 2098, 7231 | 420, 5088 | | 971.125 | 420, 4326 |
|---|---|---|---|---|
| prep, *n ms*, n ms, ps 2ms | cj, prep, n mp, ps 2ms | **4.** | cj, v Qal juss 1cs | prep, *n ms* |
| אֶל־הַר־קָדְשְׁךָ | וְאֶל־מִשְׁכְּנוֹתֶיךָ | | וְאָבוֹאָה | אֶל־מִזְבַּח |
| ʾel-har-qodhshekhā | weʾel-mishkenôthêkhā | | weʾāvôʾāh | ʾel-mizbach |
| to the mountain of your holy place | even to your Tabernacle | | and let me go | to the altar of |

| 435 | 420, 418 | 7977 | 1561 | 3142.525 | 904, 3780 | 435 |
|---|---|---|---|---|---|---|
| n mp | prep, n ms | *n fs* | n ms, ps 1cs | cj, v Hiphil juss 1cs, ps 2ms | prep, n ms | n mp |
| אֱלֹהִים | אֶל־אֵל | שִׂמְחַת | גִּילִי | וְאוֹדְךָ | בְכִנּוֹר | אֱלֹהִים |
| ʾělōhîm | ʾel-ʾēl | simchath | gîlî | weʾôdhkhā | vekhinnôr | ʾělōhîm |
| God | to God | the gladness of | my rejoicing | and let me praise You | with the zither | O God |

**they say daily unto me, Where is thy God?:** ... With piercing pain, *Goodspeed* ... racked by the ceaseless taunts of my persecutors, *Knox* ... it's a crushing of my bones, *Beck* ... deadly wound in my body, *RSV.*

**11. Why art thou cast down, O my soul? and why art thou disquieted within me? hope thou in God:** ... I am sunk in misery, *NEB* ... why moanest thou within me?, *MAST* ... Put your hope in God, *NIV* ... In GOD I still possess my trust, *Fenton.*

**for I shall yet praise him, who is the health of my countenance, and my God:** ... my Saviour, *JB* ... my deliverer, *REB.*

**43:1. Judge me, O God, and plead my cause against an ungodly nation:** ... fight my fight against a faithless people, *NCB* ... plead my cause against a merciless people, *Berkeley* ... Against an unmerciful race, *Fenton* ... Argue my case against those who don't follow you, *NCV.*

**O deliver me from the deceitful and unjust man:** ... rescue me from liars and evil men, *REB* ... from deceitful and evil people rescue me, *Beck* ... those who are treacherous and unjust, *JB.*

**2. For thou art the God of my strength: why dost thou cast me off? why go I mourning because of the oppression of the enemy?:** ... For you are the God in whom I take refuge, *NRSV* ... Why have you rejected me, *NIV* ... I go in sorrow because of the attacks of my haters, *BB* ... I go like a mourner because my foes oppress me, *NEB.*

**3. O send out thy light and thy truth: let them lead me; let them bring me unto thy holy hill, and to thy tabernacles:** ... light and faithfulness; may they guide me, *Goodspeed* ... bring me home to thine own sacred hill, *Moffatt* ... holy hill and to thy dwelling, *RSV.*

**4. Then will I go unto the altar of God, unto God my exceeding joy: yea, upon the harp will I praise**

---

of the rescued man's life. The epithet answers to that of the former part, "the living God," from which it differs by but one additional letter. He Who has life in himself is the Giver and Rescuer of our lives, and to Him they are to be rendered in thankful sacrifice. Once more the contending currents meet in vv. 9f, in the former of which confidence and hope utter themselves in the resolve to appeal to God and in the name given to Him as "my Rock"; while another surge of despondency breaks, in the question in which the soul interrogates God, as the better self had interrogated her, and contrasts almost reproachfully God's apparent forgetfulness, manifested by his delay in deliverance, with her remembrance of Him. It is not a question asked for enlightenment's sake, but is an exclamation of impatience, if not of rebuke. Verse 10 repeats the enemies' taunt, which is there represented as being like crushing blows which broke the bones. And then once more, above this conflict of emotion soars the clear note of the refrain, summoning to self-command, calmness and unfaltering hope.

**43:1–2.** But the victory is not quite won, and therefore Ps. 43 follows. It is sufficiently distinct in tone to explain its separation from the preceding, inasmuch as it is prayer throughout, and the note of joy is dominant, even while an undertone of sadness links it with the previous parts. The unity is vouched by the considerations already noticed, by the incompleteness of Ps. 42 without such triumphant close and of Ps. 43 without such despondent beginning. The prayer of vv. 1f blends the two elements, which were at war in the second part, and for the moment, the darker is the more prominent. The situation is described as in the preceding parts. Perhaps there was one "man" of special mischief prominent among them, but it is not safe to treat that expression as anything but a collective. Verse 2 looks back to 42:9, the former clause in each verse being practically equivalent, and the second in Ps. 43 being a quotation of the second in v. 9, with a variation in the form of the verb to suggest more vividly the picture of weary, slow, dragging gait, fit for a man clad in mourning garb.

**43:3–5.** But the gloomier mood has shot its last bolt. Grief which finds no fresh words is beginning to dry up. The stage of mechanical repetition of complaints is not far from that of cessation of them. So the higher mood conquers at last and breaks into a burst of joyous petition, which passes swiftly into realization of the future joys whose coming shines thus far off. Hope and trust hold the field. The certainty of return to the Temple overbears the pain of absence from it, and the vivid realization of the gladness of worshiping again at the altar takes the place of the vivid remembrance of former festival.

The actual return to the Temple is desired because thereby new praise will be occasioned. Not mere bodily presence there, but joyful outpouring of triumph and gladness is the object of the psalmist's longing. He began with yearning after the living God. In his sorrow, he could still think of Him at intervals as the help of his counte-

| 435 | | 4242, 8246.724 | 5497 | 4242, 2064.124 | 6142 |
|---|---|---|---|---|---|
| n mp, ps 1cs | | intrg, v Hithpoel impf 2fs | n fs, ps 1cs | cj, intrg, v Qal impf 2fs | prep, ps 1cs |
| אֱלֹהָי | **5.** | מַה־תִּשְׁתּוֹחֲחִי | נַפְשִׁי | וּמַה־תֶּהֱמִי | עָלָי |
| 'ĕlōhāy | | mah-tishtôchăchî | naphshî | ûmah-tehĕmî | 'ālāy |
| my God | | why are you bent down | my soul | and why are you tumultuous | against me |

| 3282.532 | 3937, 435 | 3706, 5968 | 3142.525 | 3568 | 6686 |
|---|---|---|---|---|---|
| v Hiphil impv 2fs | prep, n mp | cj, adv | v Hiphil impf 1cs, ps 3ms | *n fs* | n mp, ps 1cs |
| הוֹחִילִי | לֵאלֹהִים | כִּי־עוֹד | אוֹדֶנּוּ | יְשׁוּעֹת | פָּנַי |
| hôchîlî | lē'lōhîm | kî-'ôdh | 'ôdhennû | yeshû'ōth | pānay |
| wait | for God | because still | I will praise Him | the salvation of | my countenance |

| 435 | | 3937, 5514.351 | 3937, 1158, 7432 | 5030 | | 435 | 904, 238 |
|---|---|---|---|---|---|---|---|
| cj, n mp, ps 1cs | | prep, art, v Piel ptc ms | prep, *n mp*, pn | n ms | | n mp | prep, n fd, ps 1cp |
| וֵאלֹהָי | **44:t** | לַמְנַצֵּחַ | לִבְנֵי־קֹרַח | מַשְׂכִּיל | **1.** | אֱלֹהִים | בְּאָזְנֵינוּ |
| wē'lōhāy | | lamnatstsēach | livnê-qōrach | maskîl | | 'ĕlōhîm | be'āzenênû |
| and my God | | to the director | of the sons of Korah | a Maskil | | O God | with our ears |

| 8471.119 | 1 | 5807.316, 3937 | 6714 | 6713.113 | 904, 3219 |
|---|---|---|---|---|---|
| v Qal pf 1cp | n mp, ps 1cp | v Piel pf 3cp, prep, ps 1cp | n ms | v Qal pf 2ms | prep, n mp, ps 3mp |
| שָׁמַעְנוּ | אֲבוֹתֵינוּ | סִפְּרוּ־לָנוּ | פֹּעַל | פָּעַלְתָּ | בִימֵיהֶם |
| shāma'ănû | 'ăvôthênû | sipperû-lānû | pō'al | pā'altā | vîmêhem |
| we have heard | our ancestors | they have recounted to us | the deeds | You performed | in their days |

| 904, 3219 | 7208 | | 887 | 3135 | 1504 | 3542.513 | 5378.123 |
|---|---|---|---|---|---|---|---|
| prep, *n mp* | n ms | | pers pron | n fs, ps 2ms | n mp | v Hiphil pf 2ms | cj, v Qal impf 2ms, ps 3mp |
| בִּימֵי | קֶדֶם | **2.** | אַתָּה | יָדְךָ | גּוֹיִם | הוֹרַשְׁתָּ | וַתִּטָּעֵם |
| bîmê | qedhem | | 'attāh | yādhekhā | gôyim | hôrashtā | wattittā'ēm |
| in the days of | antiquity | | You | your hand | nations | You subdued | and You planted them |

| 7778.523 | 3947 | 8365.323 | | 3706 | 3940 | 904, 2820 |
|---|---|---|---|---|---|---|
| v Hiphil impf 2ms | n mp | cj, v Piel impf 2ms, ps 3mp | | cj | neg part | prep, n fs, ps 3mp |
| תָּרַע | לְאֻמִּים | וַתְּשַׁלְּחֵם | **3.** | כִּי | לֹא | בְחַרְבָּם |
| tāra' | le'ummîm | watteshallechēm | | kî | lō' | vecharbām |
| You brought evil on | peoples | and You sent them out | | because | not | with their sword |

| 3542.116 | 800 | 2307 | 3940, 3588.512 | 3937 |
|---|---|---|---|---|
| v Qal pf 3cp | n fs | cj, n fs, ps 3mp | neg part, v Hiphil pf 3fs | prep, ps 3mp |
| יָרְשׁוּ | אָרֶץ | וּזְרוֹעָם | לֹא־הוֹשִׁיעָה | לָמוֹ |
| yāreshû | 'ārets | ûzărô'ām | lō'-hôshî'āh | lāmô |
| they took possession of | the land | and their arm | it was not victorious | to them |

| 3706, 3332 | 2307 | 214 | 6686 | 3706 |
|---|---|---|---|---|
| cj, n fs, ps 2ms | cj, n fs, ps 2ms | cj, *n ms* | n mp, ps 2ms | cj |
| כִּי־יְמִינְךָ | וּזְרוֹעֲךָ | וְאוֹר | פָּנֶיךָ | כִּי |
| kî-yemînekhā | ûzărō'ăkhā | we'ôr | pānêkhā | kî |
| because your right hand | and your arm | and the light of | your countenance | because |

| 7813.113 | | 887, 2000 | 4567 | 435 | 6943.331 | 3568 |
|---|---|---|---|---|---|---|
| v Qal pf 2ms, ps 3mp | | pers pron, pers pron | n ms, ps 1cs | n mp | v Piel impv 2ms | *n fp* |
| רְצִיתָם | **4.** | אַתָּה־הוּא | מַלְכִּי | אֱלֹהִים | צַוֵּה | יְשׁוּעוֹת |
| retsîthām | | 'attāh-hû' | malkî | 'ĕlōhîm | tsawwēh | yeshû'ôth |
| You delighted in them | | You He | my King | God | command | the victories of |

| 3399 | | 904 | 7141 | 5231.320 | 904, 8428 | 983.120 |
|---|---|---|---|---|---|---|
| pn | | prep, ps 2ms | n mp, ps 1cp | v Piel impf 1cp | prep, n ms, ps 2ms | v Qal impf 1cp |
| יַעֲקֹב | **5.** | בְּךָ | צָרֵינוּ | נְנַגֵּחַ | בְּשִׁמְךָ | נָבוּס |
| ya'ăqōv | | bekhā | tsārênû | nenaggēach | beshimkhā | nāvûs |
| Jacob | | in You | our adversaries | we gore | in your name | we trample |

**thee, O God my God:** ... the joy of my life, *Beck* ... To the God of my pleasure and joy, *Fenton* ... the God of my joy and delight, *REB* ... the giver of triumphant happiness, *Knox.*

**5. Why art thou cast down, O my soul? and why art thou disquieted within me?:** ... why do you groan within me, *Berkeley* ... Why do you sigh within me, *NAB* ... why have you become disturbed within me, *NASB.*

**hope in God: for I shall yet praise him, who is the health of my countenance, and my God:** ... For I shall again be thanking him in the presence of my savior, *NCB* ... As the triumph of my presence, and my God, *Rotherham* ... he is my present helpe and my God, *Geneva* ... The salvation of my countenance, *Young.*

**44:t. To the chief Musician for the sons of Korah, Maschil.**

**1. We have heard with our ears, O God, our fathers have told us, what work thou didst in their days, in the times of old:** ... in the days of old your hand worked wonders, *Anchor* ... about the great things you did in their time, *Good News* ... of thy doings in ancient years, *Moffatt* ... what deeds you performed in their days, *NRSV.*

**2. How thou didst drive out the heathen with thy hand, and plantedst them; how thou didst afflict the people, and cast them out:** ... Thou didst dispossess the nations, *Goodspeed* ... With your power you forced the nations out of the land, *NCV* ... you crushed the peoples and made our fathers flourish, *NIV* ... to settle them, you laid waste the inhabitants, *REB.*

**3. For they got not the land in possession by their own sword, neither did their own arm save them:** ... not with their own sword did they conquer the land, *NCB* ... nor their own arms which made them victorious, *JB* ... own arm gain deliverance for them, *Berkeley.*

**but thy right hand, and thine arm, and the light of thy countenance, because thou hadst a favour unto them:** ... it was your great power and strength, *NCV* ... in your love for them, *NAB* ... thou didst delight in them, *RSV.*

**4. Thou art my King, O God: command deliverances for Jacob:** ... my Commander, the Savior of Jacob, *Anchor* ... at thy bidding Jacob is victorious, *NEB* ... Who orders for Jacob success, *Fenton.*

**5. Through thee will we push down our enemies: through thy name will we tread them under that rise up against us:** ... under thy protection we crushed their onslaught, *Knox* ... your name we trample our foes, *NIV* ... by your name will they be crushed under our feet, *BB* ... we trampled on those who attacked us, *Beck.*

---

nance and call Him "my God." He ends with naming Him "the gladness of my joy." Whoever begins as he did will finish where he climbed. The refrain is repeated for a third time and is followed by no relapse into sadness. The effort of faith should be persistent, even if old bitternesses begin again and "break the low beginnings of content"; for, even if the wild waters burst through the dam once and again, they do not utterly wash it away, and there remains a foundation on which it may be built up anew. Each swing of the gymnast lifts him higher until he is on a level with a firm platform on which he can spring and stand secure. Faith may have a long struggle with fear, but it will have the last word, and that word will be "the help of my countenance and my God."

***Psalm 44.*** *The Psalm falls into four parts: a wistful look backwards to days already "old," when God fought for them (vv. 1–8); a sad contrast in present oppression (vv. 9–16); a profession of unfaltering national adherence to the Covenant notwithstanding all these ills (vv. 17–22); and a fervent cry to a God Who seems asleep to awake and rescue his martyred people (vv. 23–26).*

**44:1–8.** The first part (vv. 1–8) recalls the fact that shone so brightly in all the past, the continual exercise of divine power giving victory to their weakness, and builds thereon a prayer that the same law of his providence might be fulfilled now. The bitter side of the retrospect forces itself into consciousness in the next part, but here memory is the handmaid of faith. The whole process of the Exodus and the conquest of Canaan is gathered up as one great "work" of God's hand. The former inhabitants of the land were uprooted like old trees to give room for planting the "vine out of Egypt." Two stages in the settlement are distinguished in v. 2: first came the "planting" and next the growth; for the phrase "didst spread them forth" carries on the metaphor of the tree and expresses the extension of its roots and branches. The ascription of victory to God is made more emphatic by the negatives in v. 3, which take away all credit of it from the people's own weapons or strength. The consciousness of our own impotence must accompany adequate recognition of God's agency in our deliverances.

On this grand generalization of the meaning of past centuries, a prayer is built for their repetition in the prosaic present. The psalmist did not think that

| 7251.152 | 6. | 3706 | 3940 | 904, 7493 | 1019.125 | 2820 | 3940 |
|---|---|---|---|---|---|---|---|
| v Qal act ptc mp, ps 1cp | | cj | neg part | prep, n fs, ps 1cs | v Qal impf 1cs | cj, n fs, ps 1cs | neg part |
| קָמֵינוּ | | כִּי | לֹא | בְקַשְׁתִּי | אֶבְטָח | וְחַרְבִּי | לֹא |
| qāmênû | | kî | lō' | veqashtî | 'evṭāch | wecharbî | lō' |
| those who rise against us | | because | not | in my bow | I will trust | and my sword | not |

| 3588.522 | 7. | 3706 | 3588.513 | 4623, 7141 | 7983.352 |
|---|---|---|---|---|---|
| v Hiphil impf 3fs, ps 1cs | | cj | v Hiphil pf 2ms, ps 1cp | prep, n mp, ps 1cp | cj, v Piel ptc mp, ps 1cp |
| תּוֹשִׁיעֵנִי | | כִּי | הוֹשַׁעְתָּנוּ | מִצָּרֵינוּ | וּמְשַׂנְאֵינוּ |
| thôshî'ēnî | | kî | hôsha'ttānû | mitstsārênû | ûmesan'ênû |
| it will save me | | because | You have saved us | from our adversaries | and those who hate us |

| 991.513 | 8. | 904, 435 | 2054.319 | 3725, 3219 | 8428 | 3937, 5986 |
|---|---|---|---|---|---|---|
| v Hiphil pf 2ms | | prep, n mp | v Piel pf 1cp | *adj*, art, n ms | cj, n ms, ps 2ms | prep, n ms |
| הֱבִישׁוֹתָ | | בֵּאלֹהִים | הִלַּלְנוּ | כָּל־הַיּוֹם | וְשִׁמְךָ | לְעוֹלָם |
| hĕvîshôthā | | bē'lōhîm | hillalnû | khol-hayyôm | weshimkhā | le'ôlām |
| You have put to shame | | in God | we have boasted | all the day | and your name | unto eternity |

| 3142.520 | 5734 | 9. | 652, 2269.113 | 3757.523 |
|---|---|---|---|---|
| v Hiphil juss 1cp | intrj | | cj, v Qal pf 2ms | cj, v Hiphil impf 2ms, ps 1cp |
| נוֹדֶה | סֶלָה | | אַף־זָנַחְתָּ | וַתַּכְלִימֵנוּ |
| nôdheh | selāh | | 'aph-zānachtā | wattakhlîmēnû |
| let us praise | selah | | also You have rejected | and You have dishonored us |

| 3940, 3428.123 | 904, 6893 | 10. | 8178.523 | 268 | 4623, 7141 |
|---|---|---|---|---|---|
| cj, neg part, v Qal impf 2ms | prep, n mp, ps 1cp | | v Hiphil impf 2ms, ps 1cp | adv | prep, n ms |
| וְלֹא־תֵצֵא | בְּצִבְאוֹתֵינוּ | | תְּשִׁיבֵנוּ | אָחוֹר | מִנִּי־צָר |
| welō'-thētsē' | betsiv'ôthênû | | teshîvênû | 'āchôr | minî-tsār |
| and You have not gone out | with our armies | | You caused us to turn | back | from the adversary |

| 7983.352 | 8536.116 | 3937 | 11. | 5598.123 | 3626, 6887 |
|---|---|---|---|---|---|
| cj, v Piel ptc mp, ps 1cp | v Qal pf 3cp | prep, ps 3mp | | v Qal impf 2ms, ps 1cp | prep, n fs |
| וּמְשַׂנְאֵינוּ | שָׁסוּ | לָמוֹ | | תִּתְּנֵנוּ | כְּצֹאן |
| ûmesan'ênû | shāsû | lāmô | | tittenēnû | ketsō'n |
| and those who hate us | they have despoiled | to them | | You have given us | like sheep |

| 4120 | 904, 1504 | 2306.313 | 12. | 4513.123, 6194 |
|---|---|---|---|---|
| n ms | cj, prep, art, n mp | v Piel pf 2ms, ps 1cp | | v Qal impf 2ms, n ms, ps 2ms |
| מַאֲכָל | וּבַגּוֹיִם | זֵרִיתָנוּ | | תִּמְכֹּר־עַמְּךָ |
| ma'ăkhāl | ûvaggôyim | zērîthānû | | timkōr-'ammekhā |
| food | and among the nations | You have scattered us | | You have sold your people |

| 904, 3940, 2019 | 3940, 7528.313 | 904, 4378B | 13. | 7947.123 | 2887 |
|---|---|---|---|---|---|
| prep, neg part, n ms | cj, neg part, v Piel pf 2ms | prep, n mp, ps 3mp | | v Qal impf 2ms, ps 1cp | n fs |
| בְלֹא־הוֹן | וְלֹא־רִבִּיתָ | בִּמְחִירֵיהֶם | | תְּשִׂימֵנוּ | חֶרְפָּה |
| velō'-hôn | welō'-ribbîthā | bimchîrêhem | | tesîmēnû | cherpāh |
| with not wealth | and You have not made great | with their price | | You have made us | a disgrace |

| 3937, 8333 | 4075 | 7331 | 3937, 5623 | 14. | 7947.123 | 5091 |
|---|---|---|---|---|---|---|
| prep, n mp, ps 1cp | n ms | cj, n ms | prep, sub, ps 1cp | | v Qal impf 2ms, ps 1cp | n ms |
| לִשְׁכֵנֵינוּ | לַעַג | וָקֶלֶס | לִסְבִיבוֹתֵינוּ | | תְּשִׂימֵנוּ | מָשָׁל |
| lishkhēnênû | la'agh | wāqeles | lisvîvôthênû | | tesîmēnû | māshāl |
| of our neighbors | derision | and mockery | to those all around us | | You have made us | a byword |

| 904, 1504 | 4637, 7513 | 904, 3947 | 15. | 3725, 3219 | 3759 |
|---|---|---|---|---|---|
| prep, art, n mp | *n ms*, n ms | prep, n mp | | *adj*, art, n ms | n fs, ps 1cs |
| בַּגּוֹיִם | מְנוֹד־רֹאשׁ | בַּלְאֻמִּים | | כָּל־הַיּוֹם | כְּלִמָּתִי |
| baggôyim | menôdh-rō'sh | bal'ummîm | | kol-hayyôm | kelimmāthî |
| among the nations | shaking of the head | among the peoples | | all the day | my dishonor |

**6. For I will not trust in my bow, neither shall my sword save me:** ... put confidence, *Darby* ... nor will my victory be won, *REB* ... will not be my salvation, *BB* ... wins the battle, *Moffatt.*

**7. But thou hast saved us from our enemies, and hast put them to shame that hated us:** ... give us victory, *NIV* ... Thou hast freed us, *Berkeley* ... make those who hate us to fail, *Fenton* ... put them to confusion, *Geneva.*

**8. In God we boast all the day long, and praise thy name for ever. Selah:** ... we gloried day by day, *NCB* ... we will give thanks, *NRSV* ... Thy name to the age we thank, *Young* ... we praise unceasingly, *Knox.*

**9. But thou hast cast off, and put us to shame; and goest not forth with our armies:** ... rejected and confounded us, *Rotherham* ... put us in disgrace, *NAB* ... and brought us to dishonor, *NASB* ... with our hosts, *ASV.*

**10. Thou makest us to turn back from the enemy: and they which hate us spoil for themselves:** ... take our goods for themselves, *KJVII* ... from the adversary, *MRB* ... forced us to retreat before the foe, *REB* ... plunder us as they please, *Beck.*

**11. Thou hast given us like sheep appointed for meat; and hast scattered us among the heathen:** ... You made us a flock to be devoured, *Anchor* ... Will You let us be eaten like sheep, *Fenton* ... thou hast dispersed us, *Goodspeed* ... have scattered us among the nations, *NIV* ... among the nations, *JB.*

**12. Thou sellest thy people for nought, and dost not increase thy wealth by their price:** ... thou hast bartered away thy people, *Knox* ... gaining nothing from their sale, *NIV* ... made no profit on the sale, *NCV* ... demanding no high price for them, *RSV.*

**13. Thou makest us a reproach to our neighbours, a scorn and a derision to them that are round about us:** ... mockery and contempt, *NEB* ... and make fun of us, *Beck* ... scoffing, *ASV* ... You make us a curse, *KJVII.*

**14. Thou makest us a byword among the heathen, a shaking of the head among the people:** ... Our name is a word of shame among the nations, *BB* ... a laughingstock among the peoples, *NAB* ... among the Gentiles, *Berkeley* ... shake their heads over us, *JB.*

**15. My confusion is continually before me, and the shame of my face hath covered me:** ... all day long the disgrace is before me, *Moffatt* ... dishonour before me, *Fenton* ... I am covered with shame, *REB* ... my humiliation has overwhelmed me, *NASB.*

---

God was nearer in some majestic past than now. Therefore, v. 4 begins with an emphatic recognition of the constancy of the divine nature in that strong expression "thou thyself," and with an individualizing transition for a moment to the singular in "my King," in order to give most forcible utterance to the thought that He was the same to each man of that generation as He had been to the fathers. On that unchanging relation rests the prayer, "Command deliverance for Jacob," as if a multitude of several acts of deliverance stood before God, as servants waiting to be sent on his errands. Just as "God" ("Elohim") takes the place of "Yahweh" in this second book of the Psalter, so in it "Jacob" frequently stands for "Israel." The prayer is no sooner spoken than the confidence in its fulfillment lifts the suppliant's heart buoyantly above present defeat, which will in the next turn of thought insist on being felt. Such is the magic of every act of true appeal to God. However dark the horizon, there is light if a man looks straight up. Thus, this psalmist breaks into anticipatory tributes of victory. The vivid image of v. 5 is taken from the manner of fighting common to wild horned animals, buffaloes and the like, who first prostrate their foe by their fierce charge and then trample him. The individualizing "my" reappears in v. 6, where the negation that had been true of the ancestors is made his own by the descendant. Each man must, as his own act, appropriate the universal relation of God to men and make God his God, and must also disown for himself reliance on himself. So he will enter into participation in God's victories. Remembrance of the victorious past and confidence in a like victorious future blend in the closing burst of praise and vow for its continuance, which vow takes for granted the future continued manifestation of deliverances as occasions for uninterrupted thanksgivings. Well might some long-drawn, triumphant notes from the instruments prolong the impression of the jubilant words.

**44:9–16.** The song drops in the second part (vv. 9–16) from these clear heights with lyric suddenness. The grim facts of defeat and consequent exposure to mocking laughter from enemies force themselves into sight and seem utterly to contradict the preceding verses. But the first part speaks with the voice of faith and the second with that of sense, both in very close sequence or even simultaneously. In v. 9, the two verbs are united by the absence of "us" with the first, and the difference of tense in the Hebrew brings out

| 5224<br>prep, ps 1cs<br>נֶגְדִּי<br>neghdî<br>before me | 1350<br>cj, *n fs*<br>וּבֹשֶׁת<br>ûvōsheth<br>and the shame of | 6686<br>n mp, ps 1cs<br>פָּנַי<br>pānay<br>my countenance | 3803.312<br>v Piel pf 3fs, ps 1cs<br>כִּסָּתְנִי<br>kissāthenî<br>it has covered me | **16.** | 4623, 7249<br>prep, *n ms*<br>מִקּוֹל<br>miqqôl<br>about the sound of |
|---|---|---|---|---|---|

| 2884.351<br>v Piel ptc ms<br>מְחָרֵף<br>mechārēph<br>taunters | 1472.351<br>cj, v Piel ptc ms<br>וּמְגַדֵּף<br>ûmeghaddēph<br>and blasphemers | 4623, 6686<br>prep, *n mp*<br>מִפְּנֵי<br>mippenê<br>from before | 342.151<br>v Qal act ptc ms<br>אוֹיֵב<br>'ôyēv<br>the enemy | 5541.751<br>cj, v Hithpael ptc ms<br>וּמִתְנַקֵּם<br>ûmithnaqqēm<br>and the avenger | **17.** | 3725, 2148<br>*adj*, dem pron<br>כָּל־זֹאת<br>kol-zō'th<br>all this |
|---|---|---|---|---|---|---|

| 971.112<br>v Qal pf 3fs, ps 1cp<br>בָּאַתְנוּ<br>bā'athnû<br>it has come to us | 3940<br>cj, neg part<br>וְלֹא<br>welō'<br>but not | 8319.119<br>v Qal pf 1cp, ps 2ms<br>שְׁכַחֲנוּךָ<br>shekhachnûkhā<br>we have forgotten You | 3940, 8631.319<br>cj, neg part, v Piel pf 1cp<br>וְלֹא־שִׁקַּרְנוּ<br>welō'-shiqqarnû<br>and we have not lied | 904, 1311<br>prep, n fs, ps 2ms<br>בִּבְרִיתֶךָ<br>bivrîthekhā<br>by your Covenant |
|---|---|---|---|---|

| **18.** | 3940, 5657.211<br>neg part, v Niphal pf 3ms<br>לֹא־נָסוֹג<br>lō'-nāsōgh<br>it has not withdrawn | 268<br>adv<br>אָחוֹר<br>'āchôr<br>back | 3949<br>n ms, ps 1cp<br>לִבֵּנוּ<br>libbēnû<br>our heart | 5371.122<br>cj, v Qal impf 3fs<br>וַתֵּט<br>wattēt<br>nor it has turned aside | 863<br>n fp, ps 1cp<br>אֲשֻׁרֵינוּ<br>'ăshurênû<br>our steps | 4623<br>prep<br>מִנִּי<br>minî<br>from | 758<br>n ms, ps 2ms<br>אָרְחֶךָ<br>'ārechekhā<br>your path |
|---|---|---|---|---|---|---|---|

| **19.** | 3706<br>cj<br>כִּי<br>kî<br>because | 1852.313<br>v Piel pf 2ms, ps 1cp<br>דִכִּיתָנוּ<br>dhikkîthānû<br>You have crushed us | 904, 4887<br>prep, *n ms*<br>בִּמְקוֹם<br>bimqôm<br>in the place of | 8895<br>n mp<br>תַּנִּים<br>tanîm<br>jackals | 3803.323<br>cj, v Piel impf 2ms<br>וַתְּכַס<br>wattekhas<br>and You have covered | 6142<br>prep, ps 1cp<br>עָלֵינוּ<br>'ālênû<br>over us |
|---|---|---|---|---|---|---|

| 904, 7024<br>prep, n ms<br>בְצַלְמָוֶת<br>vetsalmāweth<br>with deep darkness | **20.** | 524, 8319.119<br>cj, v Qal pf 1cp<br>אִם־שָׁכַחְנוּ<br>'im-shākhachnû<br>if we had forgotten | 8428<br>*n ms*<br>שֵׁם<br>shēm<br>the name of | 435<br>n mp, ps 1cp<br>אֱלֹהֵינוּ<br>'ĕlōhênû<br>our God | 6816.120<br>cj, v Qal impf 1cp<br>וַנִּפְרֹשׂ<br>waniphrōs<br>and we spread out | 3834<br>n fp, ps 1cp<br>כַּפֵּינוּ<br>kappênû<br>our palms |
|---|---|---|---|---|---|---|

| 3937, 418<br>prep, n ms<br>לְאֵל<br>le'ēl<br>to a god | 2299<br>adj<br>זָר<br>zār<br>foreign | **21.** | 1950B, 3940<br>intrg part, neg part<br>הֲלֹא<br>hălō'<br>would not | 435<br>n mp<br>אֱלֹהִים<br>'ĕlōhîm<br>God | 2811.121, 2148<br>v Qal impf 3ms, pers pron<br>יַחֲקָר־זֹאת<br>yachqār-zō'th<br>He examine this | 3706, 2000<br>cj, pers pron<br>כִּי־הוּא<br>kî-hû'<br>because He |
|---|---|---|---|---|---|---|

| 3156.151<br>v Qal act ptc ms<br>יֹדֵעַ<br>yōdhēa'<br>One Who knows | 8920<br>*n fp*<br>תַּעֲלֻמוֹת<br>ta'ălumôth<br>the secrets of | 3949<br>n ms<br>לֵב<br>lēv<br>the heart | **22.** | 3706, 6142<br>cj, prep, ps 2ms<br>כִּי־עָלֶיךָ<br>kî-'ālêkhā<br>because of You | 2103.419<br>v Pual pf 1cp<br>הֹרַגְנוּ<br>hōraghnû<br>we have been killed | 3725, 3219<br>*adj*, art, n ms<br>כָל־הַיּוֹם<br>khol-hayyôm<br>all the day |
|---|---|---|---|---|---|---|

| 2913.219<br>v Niphal pf 1cp<br>נֶחְשַׁבְנוּ<br>nechshavnû<br>we have been reckoned | 3626, 6887<br>prep, *n fs*<br>כְּצֹאן<br>ketsō'n<br>as sheep for | 2989<br>n fs<br>טִבְחָה<br>tivchāh<br>slaughter | **23.** | 5996.131<br>v Qal impv 2ms<br>עוּרָה<br>'ûrāh<br>arouse | 4066<br>intrg<br>לָמָּה<br>lāmmāh<br>why | 3583.123<br>v Qal impf 2ms<br>תִישַׁן<br>thîshan<br>do You sleep |
|---|---|---|---|---|---|---|

| 112<br>n mp, ps 1cs<br>אֲדֹנָי<br>'ădhōnāy<br>O my Lord | 7301.531<br>v Hiphil impv 2ms<br>הָקִיצָה<br>hāqîtsāh<br>awake | 414, 2269.123<br>adv, v Qal juss 2ms<br>אַל־תִּזְנַח<br>'al-tiznach<br>do not reject | 3937, 5516<br>prep, art, n ms<br>לָנֶצַח<br>lānetsach<br>unto forever | **24.** | 4066, 6686<br>intrg, n mp, ps 2ms<br>לָמָּה־פָנֶיךָ<br>lāmmāh-phānêkhā<br>why your face | 5846.523<br>v Hiphil impf 2ms<br>תַסְתִּיר<br>thastîr<br>do You hide |
|---|---|---|---|---|---|---|

**16. For the voice of him that reproacheth and blasphemeth; by reason of the enemy and avenger:** ... the voice of the scoffer and the scorner, *Berkeley* ... at the words of the taunters and revilers, *NRSV* ... the voice of Derision and Libel, *Fenton* ... reproach and revile me, because of the enemy, who is bent on revenge, *NIV.*

**17. All this is come upon us; yet have we not forgotten thee, neither have we dealt falsely in thy covenant:** ... nor have we been disloyal to your covenant, *NCB* ... have not violated your covenant, *LIVB* ... nor were we untrue, *Beck* ... we have not been false to your word, *BB.*

**18. Our heart is not turned back, neither have our steps declined from thy way:** ... steps departed from thy way, *RSV* ... we haven't stopped following you, *NCV* ... Nor our step swerved from thy path, *Goodspeed* ... never swerved from thine own road, *Moffatt.*

**19. Though thou hast sore broken us in the place of dragons, and covered us with the shadow of death:** ... thrust us down into a place of misery and covered us over with darkness, *NCB* ... crushed us in the place of jackals, *Darby* ... down in the place of wild dogs, *Rotherham* ... you have crushed us as the sea serpent was crushed, *REB.*

**20. If we have forgotten the name of our God, or stretched out our hands to a strange god:** ... spread out our hands in prayer to the gods of the alien, *Knox* ... our hands in prayer to any other, *NEB* ... stretched out our palms to an alien god, *Anchor* ... prayed to a foreign god, *Good News.*

**21. Shall not God search this out? for he knoweth the secrets of the heart:** ... Would not God have discovered this, *NAB* ... Would not God have searched into this, *Rotherham* ... he knows what is in our hearts, *NCV* ... because you know our secret thoughts, *Good News.*

**22. Yea, for thy sake are we killed all the day long; we are counted as sheep for the slaughter:** ... because of thee we are slain the whole day long, *Goodspeed* ... we are facing death threats constantly because of serving you!, *LIVB* ... we are being massacred all day long, *JB.*

**23. Awake, why sleepest thou, O Lord? arise, cast us not off for ever:** ... Be not angry forever, *Anchor* ... do not banish us from thy presence for ever, *Knox.*

---

the dependence of the second on the first, as effect and cause. God's rejection is the reason for the nation's disgrace by defeat. In the subsequent verses, the thoughts of rejection and disgrace are expanded, the former in v. 9b to v. 12 and the latter in vv. 13–16. The poet paints with few strokes the whole disastrous rout. We see the fated band going out to battle, with no pillar of cloud or Ark of the Covenant at their head. They have but their own weapons and sinews to depend on—not, as of old, a divine Captain. No description of a fight under such conditions is needed, for it can have only one issue, so the next clause shows panic-struck flight. Whoever goes into battle without God comes out of it without victory.

Defeat brings dishonor. The nearer nations, such as Edomites, Ammonites and other ancestral foes, are ready with their gibes. The more distant peoples make a proverb out of the tragedy and nod their heads in triumph and scorn. The cowering creature, in the middle of this ring of mockers, is covered with shame as he hears the babel of heartless jests at his expense and steals a glance at the fierce faces round him.

**44:17–22.** The third part brings closely together professions of righteousness, which sound strange in Christian ears, and complaints of suffering and closes with the assertion that these two are cause and effect. The sufferers are a nation of martyrs and know themselves to be so. This tone is remarkable when the nation is the speaker; for although we find individuals asserting innocence and complaining of undeserved afflictions in many Psalms, a declaration of national conformity with the Law is in sharp contradiction both to history and to the uniform tone of prophets. This psalmist asserts not only national freedom from idolatry, but adherence in heart and act to the Covenant. No period before the exile was clear of the taint of idol worship and free from calamity. "The place of jackals" is apparently the field of defeat referred to in the second part, where obscene creatures would gather to feast on the plundered corpses. The Christian consciousness cannot appropriate the psalmist's asseverations of innocence; neither should the difference between them be slurred over. On the other hand, his words should not be exaggerated into charges of injustice against God, nor claims of absolute sinlessness. He does not feel that present national distresses have the same origin as had past ones. There has been no such falling away to account for them. But he does not arraign God's government. He knows why the miseries have come and that he and his fellows are martyrs. He does not fling that fact down as an accusation of Providence, but as the foundation of a prayer and as a plea for God's help. The words may sound daring; still they are not blasphemy, but supplication.

**44:23–26.** The fourth part is importunate prayer. Its frank anthropomorphisms of a sleeping

| 8319.123 | 6270 | 4041 | | 3706 | 8190.112 | 3937, 6312 |
|---|---|---|---|---|---|---|
| v Qal impf 2ms | n ms, ps 1cp | cj, n ms, ps 1cp | 25. | cj | v Qal pf 3fs | prep, art, n ms |
| תִּשְׁכַּח | עָנְיֵנוּ | וְלַחֲצֵנוּ | | כִּי | שָׁחָה | לֶעָפָר |
| tishkach | 'āneyēnû | welachtsēnû | | kî | shāchāh | le'āphār |
| You forget | our affliction | and our oppression | | because | it has sunk down | to the dust |

| 5497 | 1740.112 | 3937, 800 | 1027 | | 7251.131 | 6046 | 3937 |
|---|---|---|---|---|---|---|---|
| n fs, ps 1cp | v Qal pf 3fs | prep, art, n fs | n fs, ps 1cp | 26. | v Qal impv 2ms | n fs | prep, ps 1cp |
| נַפְשֵׁנוּ | דָּבְקָה | לָאָרֶץ | בִּטְנֵנוּ | | קוּמָה | עֶזְרָתָה | לָנוּ |
| naphshēnû | dāveqāh | lā'ārets | biṭnēnû | | qûmāh | 'ezrāthāh | lānû |
| our soul | it has stuck | to the ground | our belly | | rise | a Help | to us |

| 6540.131 | 3937, 4775 | 2721 | | 3937, 5514.351 | 6142, 8236 |
|---|---|---|---|---|---|
| cj, v Qal impv 2ms, ps 1cp | prep, prep | n ms, ps 2ms | 45:t | prep, art, v Piel ptc ms | prep, n mp |
| וּפְדֵנוּ | לְמַעַן | חַסְדֶּךָ | | לַמְנַצֵּחַ | עַל־שֹׁשַׁנִּים |
| ûphedhēnû | lema'an | chasdekhā | | lamnatstsēach | 'al-shōshanîm |
| and ransom us | because of | your steadfast love | | to the director | according to the lilies |

| 3937, 1158, 7432 | 5030 | 8302 | 3151 | | 7653.111 | 3949 | 1745 | 3005 |
|---|---|---|---|---|---|---|---|---|
| prep, *n mp*, pn | n ms | *n ms* | adj | 1. | v Qal pf 3ms | n ms, ps 1cs | n ms | adj |
| לִבְנֵי־קֹרַח | מַשְׂכִּיל | שִׁיר | יְדִידֹת | | רָחַשׁ | לִבִּי | דָּבָר | טוֹב |
| livnê-qōrach | maskîl | shîr | yedhîdhōth | | rāchash | libbî | dāvār | ṭôv |
| of the sons of Korah | a Maskil | a song for | a beloved | | it is stirred | my heart | a word | good |

| 569.151 | 603 | 4801 | 3937, 4567 | 4098 | 6056 | 5810 | 4248 |
|---|---|---|---|---|---|---|---|
| v Qal act ptc ms | pers pron | n mp, ps 1cs | prep, n ms | n fs, ps 1cs | *n ms* | n ms | adj |
| אֹמֵר | אֲנִי | מַעֲשַׂי | לְמֶלֶךְ | לְשׁוֹנִי | עֵט | סוֹפֵר | מָהִיר |
| 'ōmēr | 'ānî | ma'ăsay | lemelekh | leshônî | 'ēṭ | sôphēr | māhîr |
| saying | I | my works | to the king | my tongue | a stylus of | a scribe | quick |

| | 3412.313 | 4623, 1158 | 119 | 3441.611 | 2682 | 904, 8004 |
|---|---|---|---|---|---|---|
| 2. | v Pealal pf 2ms | prep, *n mp* | n ms | v Hophal pf 3ms | n ms | prep, n fd, ps 2ms |
| | יָפְיָפִיתָ | מִבְּנֵי | אָדָם | הוּצַק | חֵן | בְּשְׂפְתוֹתֶיךָ |
| | yāpheyāphîthā | mibbenê | 'ādhām | hûtsaq | chēn | besphethôthêkhā |
| | You are beautiful | from the sons of | humankind | it has been poured out | favor | on your lips |

| 6142, 3772 | 1313.311 | 435 | 3937, 5986 | | 2391.131, 2820 | 6142, 3525 |
|---|---|---|---|---|---|---|
| prep, adv | v Piel pf 3ms, ps 2ms | n mp | prep, n ms | 3. | v Qal impv 2ms, n fs, ps 2ms | prep, n fs |
| עַל־כֵּן | בֵּרַכְךָ | אֱלֹהִים | לְעוֹלָם | | חֲגוֹר־חַרְבְּךָ | עַל־יָרֵךְ |
| 'al-kēn | bērakhekhā | 'ĕlōhîm | le'ôlām | | cheghôr-charbekhā | 'al-yārēkh |
| therefore | He has blessed you | God | unto eternity | | gird on your sword | on the thigh |

| 1399 | 2003 | 1996 | | 1996 | 7014.131 | 7680.131 |
|---|---|---|---|---|---|---|
| *adj* | n ms, ps 2ms | cj, n ms, ps 2ms | 4. | cj, n ms, ps 2ms | v Qal impv 2ms | v Qal impv 2ms |
| גִּבּוֹר | הוֹדְךָ | וַהֲדָרֶךָ | | וַהֲדָרְךָ | צְלַח | רְכַב |
| gibbôr | hôdhkhā | wahdhārekhā | | wahdhārekhā | tselach | rekhav |
| O mighty One | your splendor | and your majesty | | and your majesty | succeed | ride |

| 6142, 1745, 583 | 6266, 6928 | 3498.522 | 3486.258 |
|---|---|---|---|
| prep, *n ms*, n fs | cj, n fs, n ms | cj, v Hiphil juss 3fs, ps 2ms | v Niphal ptc fp |
| עַל־דְּבַר־אֱמֶת | וְעַנְוָה־צֶדֶק | וְתוֹרְךָ | נוֹרָאוֹת |
| 'al-devar-'ĕmeth | we'anwāh-tsedheq | wethôrkhā | nôrā'ôth |
| concerning the matter of truth | and meekness righteousness | may it teach you | fearful things |

| 3332 | | 2784 | 8532.156 | 6194 | 8809 | 5489.126 | 904, 3949 |
|---|---|---|---|---|---|---|---|
| n fs, ps 2ms | 5. | n mp, ps 2ms | v Qal pass ptc mp | n mp | prep, ps 2ms | v Qal juss 3mp | prep, *n ms* |
| יְמִינֶךָ | | חִצֶּיךָ | שְׁנוּנִים | עַמִּים | תַּחְתֶּיךָ | יִפְּלוּ | בְּלֵב |
| yemînekhā | | chitstsêkhā | shenûnîm | 'ammîm | tachtêkhā | yippelû | belēv |
| your right hand | | your arrows | sharpened | peoples | under you | may they fall | in the heart of |

**24. Wherefore hidest thou thy face, and forgettest our affliction and our oppression?:** ... forgetting that we are poor and harrassed, *JB* ... Don't forget our suffering and trouble, *Good News* ... heedless of our misery and our sufferings, *NEB* ... why do you give no thought to our trouble and our cruel fate, *BB*.

**25. For our soul is bowed down to the dust: our belly cleaveth unto the earth:** ... our body lies low on the ground, *Moffatt* ... We have been pushed down into the dirt, *NCV* ... Our necks are bowed down in the dust, *Beck* ... we sink down to the dust, *REB*.

**26. Arise for our help, and redeem us for thy mercies' sake:** ... for thy love's sake set us free, *NEB* ... Ransom us as befits your kindness, *Anchor* ... release us because of thy kindness, *Goodspeed* ... in thy mercy, claim us for thy own, *Knox*.

**45:t. To the chief Musician upon Shoshannim, for the sons of Korah, Maschil, A Song of loves.**

**1. My heart is inditing a good matter: I speak of the things which I have made touching the king: my tongue is the pen of a ready writer:** ... I will recite my poem concerning the king, *Rotherham* ... I am telling my works to a king, *Young* ... my tongue runs swiftly like the pen of an expert scribe, *REB* ... my tongue is nimble as the pen of a skillful scribe, *NCB*.

**2. Thou art fairer than the children of men: grace is poured into thy lips: therefore God hath blessed thee for ever:** ... You are the most handsome of men, *NRSV* ... fairer than a child of Adam, *Fenton* ... Thine is more than mortal beauty, *Knox* ... the most beautiful of men, Your lips pour out an undeserved love, *Beck*.

**3. Gird thy sword upon thy thigh, O most mighty, with thy glory and thy majesty:** ... clothe yourself with splendor and majesty, *NIV* ... Put on your sword, make it ready at your side, *BB* ... Put on your sword, powerful warrior, *NCV* ... Warrior, strap your sword at your side, *JB*.

**4. And in thy majesty ride prosperously because of truth and meekness and righteousness:** ... ride on triumphant, *NCB* ... majesty ride on victoriously for the cause of truth, *NRSV* ... ride on to execute true sentence and just judgement, *NEB* ... On behalf of faithfulness and humility, *Rotherham*.

**and thy right hand shall teach thee terrible things:** ... shall teach You fearful things, *KJVII* ... shall teach You awesome things, *NKJV* ... hand will perform awesome deeds, *REB*.

**5. Thine arrows are sharp in the heart of the king's enemies; whereby the people fall under thee:** ... let the nations fall beneath your

---

God, forgetting his people, surely need little defense. Sleep withdraws from knowledge of and action on the external world, and hence is attributed to God, when He allows evils to run unchecked. He is said to "awake," or, with another figure, to "arise," as if starting from his throned calm, when by some great act of judgment He smites flourishing evil into nothingness. Injustice is surely done to these cries, when they are supposed to be in opposition to the other psalmist's word: "He that keepeth Israel slumbers not, nor sleeps" (Ps. 121:4). Some commentators call these closing petitions commonplace, and so they are. Extreme need and agony of supplication have other things to think of than originality, and so long as sorrows are so commonplace and like each other, the cries of the sorrowful will be very much alike. God is pleased with well-worn prayers, which have fitted many lips, and is not so fastidious as some critics.

***Psalm 45.*** *The Psalm has two main divisions, prefaced by a prelude (v. 1) and followed by a prediction of the happy issue of the marriage and enduring and wide dominion. The main parts are respectively addressed to the royal bridegroom (vv. 2–9), to the bride (vv. 10–15) and to the king (vv. 16f).*

**45:1.** The picture of the king begins with two features on which the old-world ideal of a monarch laid stress: personal beauty and gracious speech. This monarch is fairer than the sons of men. The note of superhuman excellence is struck at the outset, and although the surface reference is only to physical beauty, that is conceived of as the indication of a fair nature which molds the fair form. The body takes the form of the soul.

**45:2.** From such characteristics, the psalmist draws an inference: "Therefore God hath blessed thee for ever"; for that "therefore" does not introduce the result of the preceding excellences, but the cause of them. The psalmist knows that God has blessed the king because he sees these beauties. They are the visible signs and tokens of the divine benediction. In its reference to Christ, the thought expressed is that his superhuman beauty is to all men the proof of a unique operation of God. Abiding divinity is witnessed by perfect humanity.

**45:3–5.** The scene changes with startling suddenness to the fury of battle. In a burst of lyric enthusiasm, forgetting for a moment nuptials and wedding marches, the singer calls on the king to array himself for war and to rush on the foe. Very striking is this combination of gentleness and warrior strength—a

| 342.152 | 4567 | | 3802 | 435 | 5986 | 5911 | 8101 |
|---|---|---|---|---|---|---|---|
| *v Qal act ptc mp* | art, n ms | 6. | n ms, ps 2ms | n mp | n ms | cj, n ms | *n ms* |
| אֹויְבֵי | הַמֶּלֶךְ | | כִּסְאֲךָ | אֱלֹהִים | עוֹלָם | וָעֶד | שֵׁבֶט |
| 'ôyvê | hammelekh | | kis̱'ăkhā | 'ĕlōhîm | 'ôlām | wā'edh | shēveṯ |
| the enemies of | the king | | your throne | God | forever | and everlasting | a scepter of |

| 4473 | 8101 | 4577 | | 154.113 | 6928 | 7983.123 |
|---|---|---|---|---|---|---|
| n ms | *n ms* | n fs, ps 2ms | 7. | v Qal pf 2ms | n ms | cj, v Qal impf 2ms |
| מִישֹׁר | שֵׁבֶט | מַלְכוּתֶךָ | | אָהַבְתָּ | צֶּדֶק | וַתִּשְׂנָא |
| mîshōr | shēveṯ | malkhûthekhā | | 'āhavtā | tsedheq | wattisnā' |
| uprightness | the scepter of | your kingdom | | You love | righteousness | and You hate |

| 7856 | 6142, 3772 | 5066.111 | 435 | 435 | 8467 | 8050 |
|---|---|---|---|---|---|---|
| n ms | prep, adv | v Qal pf 3ms, ps 2ms | n mp | n mp, ps 2ms | *n ms* | n ms |
| רֶשַׁע | עַל־כֵּן | מְשָׁחֲךָ | אֱלֹהִים | אֱלֹהֶיךָ | שֶׁמֶן | שָׂשׂוֹן |
| resha' | 'al-kēn | meshāchăkhā | 'ĕlōhîm | 'ĕlōhêkhā | shemen | sāsôn |
| wickedness | therefore | He has anointed you | God | your God | oil of | gladness |

| 4623, 2358 | | 4915, 167 | 7390 | 3725, 933 | 4623, 2033 |
|---|---|---|---|---|---|
| prep, n mp, ps 2ms | 8. | n ms, cj, n mp | n fp | *adj*, n mp, ps 2ms | prep, *n mp* |
| מֵחֲבֵרֶיךָ | | מֹר־וַאֲהָלוֹת | קְצִיעוֹת | כָּל־בִּגְדֹתֶיךָ | מִן־הֵיכְלֵי |
| mēchăvērêkhā | | mōr-wa'ăhālôth | qōtsî'ôth | kol-bighdhōthêkhā | min-hêkhelê |
| from your associates | | myrrh and aloe | cassia | all your garments | from palaces of |

| 8514 | 4625 | 7975.316 | | 1351 | 4567 |
|---|---|---|---|---|---|
| n fs | n mp | v Piel pf 3cp, ps 2ms | 9. | *n fp* | n mp |
| שֵׁן | מִנִּי | שִׂמְּחוּךָ | | בְּנוֹת | מְלָכִים |
| shēn | minî | simmechûkhā | | benôth | melākhîm |
| ivory | stringed instruments | they have made you glad | | daughters of | kings |

| 904, 3479 | 5507.212 | 8152 | 3937, 3332 | 904, 3929 |
|---|---|---|---|---|
| prep, adj, ps 2ms | v Niphal pf 3fs | n fs | prep, n fs, ps 2ms | prep, *n ms* |
| בְּיִקְּרוֹתֶיךָ | נִצְּבָה | שֵׁגַל | לִימִינְךָ | בְּכֶתֶם |
| beyiqqerôthêkhā | nitstsevāh | shēghal | lîmînekhā | bekhethem |
| among your prized women | she is stationed | the queen | at your right side | in the pure gold of |

| 209 | | 8471.132, 1351 | 7495.132 | 5371.532 | 238 | 8319.132 |
|---|---|---|---|---|---|---|
| pn | 10. | v Qal impv 2fs, n fs | cj, v Qal impv 2fs | cj, v Hiphil impv 2fs | n fs, ps 2fs | cj, v Qal impv 2fs |
| אוֹפִיר | | שִׁמְעִי־בַת | וּרְאִי | וְהַטִּי | אָזְנֵךְ | וְשִׁכְחִי |
| 'ôphîr | | shim'î-vath | ûre'î | wehattî | 'āzenēkh | weshikhchî |
| Ophir | | hear O daughter | and see | and incline | your ear | and forget |

| 6194 | 1041 | 1 | | 181.721 | 4567 | 3418 |
|---|---|---|---|---|---|---|
| n ms, ps 2fs | cj, *n ms* | n ms, ps 2fs | 11. | cj, v Hithpael juss 3ms | art, n ms | n ms, ps 2fs |
| עַמֵּךְ | וּבֵית | אָבִיךְ | | וְיִתְאָו | הַמֶּלֶךְ | יָפְיֵךְ |
| 'ammēkh | ûvêth | 'āvîkh | | weyith'āw | hammelekh | yāpheyēkh |
| your people | and the household of | your father | | and he will crave for | the king | your beauty |

feet, *NIV* … Nations will be defeated before you, *NCV* … Beneath you they will fall, *Fenton* … peoples are subject to you, *NAB.*

**6. Thy throne, O God, is for ever and ever: the sceptre of thy kingdom is a right sceptre:** … must be a scepter of equity, *Anchor* … a sceptre of justice, *JB* … your royal sceptre a sceptre of righteousness, *NEB* … You will rule your kingdom with fairness, *NCV.*

**7. Thou lovest righteousness, and hatest wickedness: therefore God, thy God, hath anointed thee with the oil of gladness above thy fellows:** … oil of joy on your head, lifting you high over all other kings, *BB* … oil of joy above Your companions, *Beck* … oil of gladness beyond thy partners, *Rotherham.*

**8. All thy garments smell of myrrh, and aloes, and cassia, out of the ivory palaces, whereby they have made thee glad:** … music of ivory harps is ravishing your heart, *Moffatt* … ivory palaces stringed instruments delight you, *Goodspeed* ... stringed instruments have made thee glad, *MAST* ... from ivory palaces string music brings you joy, *NCB*.

**9. Kings' daughters were among thy honourable women: upon thy right hand did stand the queen in gold of Ophir:** ... A princess takes her place among the noblest of your women, *NEB* ... Your bride stands at your right side wearing gold, *NCV* ... Standing beside you is the queen, wearing jewelry of finest gold, *LIVB* ... at your right hand is the royal bride, *NIV*.

**10. Hearken, O daughter, and consider, and incline thine ear; forget also thine own people, and thy father's house:** ... forget your own nation and your ancestral home, *JB* ... Forget your Tribe, and Home, *Fenton* ... forget your people and your relatives, *Good News*.

**11. So shall the king greatly desire thy beauty: for he is thy Lord; and worship thou him:** ... The king is enthralled by your beauty, *NIV* ... King longs for your beauty, *Beck* ... A King desires your love, *Fenton* ... you should obey him, *NCV* ... then bow down to him, *Rotherham*.

**12. And the daughter of Tyre shall be there with a gift; even the rich among the people shall entreat thy**

---

union which has been often realized in heroic figures, which is needful for the highest type of either, and which is fulfilled in the Lamb of God, Who is the Lion of the tribe of Judah. The king is to gird on his sword and to array himself, as in glittering armor, in his splendor and majesty and, thus arrayed, to mount his chariot or, less probably, to bestride his warhorse and hurl himself on the yielding ranks of the enemy. He presses forward, crushing obstacles and forcing a path. But Israel's king could be no vulgar conqueror, impelled by lust of dominion or glory. His sword is to be girt "on behalf of truth, meekness, and righteousness." These abstracts may be used for concretes—namely, the possessors of the qualities named. But the limitation is not necessary. The monarch's warfare is for the spread of these. The Hebrew binds the two latter closely together by an anomalous construction, which may be represented by connecting the two words with a hyphen. They are regarded as a double star. Then follows a verse of hurry: "Thy right hand shall teach thee terrible things." He has no allies. The canvas has no room for soldiers. The picture is like the Assyrian sculptures in which the king stands erect and alone in his chariot, a giant in comparison with the tiny figures beneath him.

**45:6–7.** The perpetuity of the king's throne is guaranteed, not only by his theocratic appointment by God, but by the righteousness of his rule. His scepter is not a rod of iron (that is only needed for breaking), but "a sceptre of uprightness." He is righteous in character as well as in official acts. He loves righteousness and therefore cannot but "hate iniquity." His broad shield shelters all who love and seek after righteousness, and he wars against evil wherever it shows itself. Therefore, his throne stands firm and is the world's hope.

The king's love of righteousness leads to his being "anointed with the oil of gladness above his fellows." This anointing is not that of a coronation, but that of a feast. His "fellows" may either be other kings or his attendant companions at his marriage. The psalmist looks as deep into individual life as he has just looked into politics and ascribes to righteousness lofty powers in that region too. The heart which loves it will be joyful, whatever befalls. Since Christ is the fulfillment of the psalmist's picture, and the perfectly realized perfection of manhood, the psalmist's words here are most fully applicable to Him.

**45:8.** In v. 8, the Psalm reaches its main theme: the marriage of the king. The previous verses have painted his grace of person, his heroic deeds in battle and his righteous rule. Now he stands ready to pass into the palace to meet his bride. His festival robes are so redolent of perfumes that they seem to be composed of nothing but woven fragrance. There are difficulties in the rendering of v. 8a, but that adopted above is generally accepted as the most probable. The clause then describes the burst of jubilant music which welcomed and rejoiced the king as he approached the "palaces of ivory" where his bride awaited his coming.

**45:9.** Verse 9 carries the king into his harem. The inferior wives are of royal blood, but nearest him and superior to these is the queen consort glittering with golden ornaments. This feature of the psalmist's description can only have reference to the actual historical occasion of the Psalm and warns against overlooking that in seeking a prophetic reference to the Christ in every particular.

**45:10–12.** The second main part of the Psalm is an address to the bride and a description of her beauty and state. The singer assumes a fatherly tone, speaking to her as "daughter." She is a foreigner by birth and is called upon to give up all her former associations with wholehearted consecration to her new duties. It is difficult to imagine Jezebel or Athaliah as the recipient of these counsels, and it

| 3706, 2000 | 112 | 8246.732, 3937 | | 1351, 7145 | 904, 4647 |
|---|---|---|---|---|---|
| cj, pers pron | n mp, ps 2fs | cj, v Hithpael impv 2fs, prep, ps 3ms | 12. | cj, *n fs*, pn | prep, n fs |
| כִּי־הוּא | אֲדֹנַיִךְ | וְהִשְׁתַּחֲוִי־לוֹ | | וּבַת־צֹר | בְּמִנְחָה |
| kî-hû' | 'ădhōnayikh | wehishtachwî-lô | | ûvath-tsōr | beminchāh |
| because He | your lord | and bow down to him | | and the daughter of Tyre | with a gift |

| 6686 | 2571.326 | 6474 | 6194 | | 3725, 3639 | 1351, 4567 | 6687 |
|---|---|---|---|---|---|---|---|
| n mp, ps 2fs | v Piel impf 3mp | *adj* | n ms | 13. | *adj*, adj | *n fs*, n ms | adv |
| פָּנַיִךְ | יְחַלּוּ | עֲשִׁירֵי | עָם | | כָּל־כְּבוּדָּה | בַּת־מֶלֶךְ | פְּנִימָה |
| pānayikh | yechallû | 'ăshîrê | 'ām | | kol-kevûddāh | vath-melekh | penîmāh |
| your face | they will flatter | rich | people | | all glorious | the daughter of the king | inside |

| 4623, 5051 | 2174 | 3961 | | 3937, 7846 | 3095.622 | 3937, 4567 |
|---|---|---|---|---|---|---|
| prep, *n fp* | n ms | n ms, ps 3fs | 14. | prep, n fp | v Hophal impf 3fs | prep, art, n ms |
| מִמִּשְׁבְּצוֹת | זָהָב | לְבוּשָׁהּ | | לִרְקָמוֹת | תּוּבַל | לַמֶּלֶךְ |
| mimmishbetsôth | zāhāv | levûshāhh | | lirqamōth | tûval | lammelekh |
| from settings of | gold | her clothes | | with embroidered garments | she is brought | to the king |

| 1359 | 313 | 7752 | 971.658 | 3937 | | 3095.627 |
|---|---|---|---|---|---|---|
| n fp | prep, ps 3fs | n fp, ps 3fs | v Hophal ptc fp | prep, ps 2ms | 15. | v Hophal impf 3fp |
| בְּתוּלוֹת | אַחֲרֶיהָ | רֵעוֹתֶיהָ | מוּבָאוֹת | לָךְ | | תּוּבַלְנָה |
| bethûlôth | 'achrêāh | rē'ôthêāh | mûvā'ôth | lākh | | tûvalnāh |
| virgins | after her | her companions | brought | to You | | they have been brought |

| 904, 7977 | 1561 | 971.127 | 904, 2033 | 4567 | | 8809 | 1 |
|---|---|---|---|---|---|---|---|
| prep, n fp | cj, n ms | v Qal impf 3fp | prep, *n ms* | n ms | 16. | prep | n mp, ps 2ms |
| בִּשְׂמָחֹת | וָגִיל | תְּבֹאֶינָה | בְּהֵיכַל | מֶלֶךְ | | תַּחַת | אֲבֹתֶיךָ |
| bismāchōth | wāghîl | tevō'ênāh | behêkhal | melekh | | tachath | 'ăvōthêkhā |
| with gladness | and rejoicing | they enter | in the temple of | the king | | instead of | your fathers |

| 2030.126 | 1158 | 8308.123 | 3937, 8015 | 904, 3725, 800 |
|---|---|---|---|---|
| v Qal impf 3mp | n mp, ps 2ms | v Qal impf 2ms, ps 3mp | prep, n mp | prep, *adj*, art, n fs |
| יִהְיוּ | בָנֶיךָ | תְּשִׁיתֵמוֹ | לְשָׂרִים | בְּכָל־הָאָרֶץ |
| yihyû | vānêkhā | teshîthēmô | lesārîm | bekhol-hā'ārets |
| they will be | your sons | You will make them | into princes | throughout all the earth |

| | 2226.525 | 8428 | 904, 3725, 1810 | 1810 | 6142, 3772 | 6194 |
|---|---|---|---|---|---|---|
| 17. | v Hiphil juss 1cs | n ms, ps 2ms | prep, *adj*, n ms | cj, n ms | prep, adv | n mp |
| | אַזְכִּירָה | שִׁמְךָ | בְּכָל־דֹּר | וָדֹר | עַל־כֵּן | עַמִּים |
| | 'azkîrāh | shimkhā | bekhol-dōr | wādhōr | 'al-kēn | 'ammîm |
| | let me commemorate | your name | in all generations | and generations | therefore | peoples |

| 3142.526 | 3937, 5986 | 5911 | | 3937, 5514.351 | 3937, 1158, 7432 |
|---|---|---|---|---|---|
| v Hiphil impf 3mp, ps 2ms | prep, n ms | cj, n ms | 46:t | prep, art, v Piel ptc ms | prep, *n mp*, pn |
| יְהוֹדֻךָ | לְעֹלָם | וָעֶד | | לַמְנַצֵּחַ | לִבְנֵי־קֹרַח |
| yehôdhukhā | le'ōlām | wā'edh | | lamnatstsēach | livnê-qōrach |
| they will praise You | for eternity | and everlasting | | to the director | of the sons of Korah |

**favour:** … shall seek your favor with gifts, *Berkeley* … the richest of the people with all kinds of wealth, *NRSV* … those who have wealth among the people will be looking for your approval, *BB* … the noblest of its citizens will be courting thy favour, *Knox*.

**13. The king's daughter is all glorious within: her clothing is of wrought gold:** … daughter is altogether wonderful, *Beck* … The princess is very beautiful, *NCV*.

**14. She shall be brought unto the king in raiment of needlework:** … In embroidered apparel she is borne in to the king, *NCB* … in many-colored robes she is led to the king, *NRSV* … In divers colours she is brought to the king, *Young* … robes of many colors, *NKJV*.

**the virgins her companions that follow her shall be brought unto thee:** … virgins, her companions, accompanying her, *Berkeley* … her escort, in her train, *RSV* … Come, follow, shepherd girls, *Fenton* … followed by her bridesmaids, *Good News*.

**15. With gladness and rejoicing shall they be brought: they shall enter into the king's palace:** ... With joy and rapture will they come, *BB* ... What a joyful, glad procession as they enter, *LIVB* ... escorted with the noise of revels and rejoicing, *NEB* ... let her be led with joy and gladness, *Anchor.*

**16. Instead of thy fathers shall be thy children, whom thou mayest make princes in all the earth:** ... Your sons will take the place Your ancestors had, *Beck* ... Instead of your ancestors you will have sons, *JB* ... and divide a world between them for their domains, *Knox* ... Thou shalt make them rulers in all the earth, *Rotherham.*

**17. I will make thy name to be remembered in all generations: therefore shall the people praise thee for ever and ever:** ... cause your name to be celebrated, *NRSV* ... I will perpetuate your memory, *NIV* ... make your name memorable, *NAB* ... I shall declare your fame, *REB.*

**46:t. To the chief Musician for the sons of Korah, A Song upon Alamoth.**

**1. God is our refuge and strength, a very present help in trouble:** ... God is our shelter and stronghold, *Anchor* ... we shall find him very near, *Moffatt* ... sovereign aid he has brought us in the hour of peril, *Knox* ... A help in adversities found most surely, *Young.*

---

does not seem to the writer that identifying the recipient would add anything to the enjoyment of the Psalm. The exhortation to give up all for love's sake goes to the heart of the sacred relation of husband and wife and witnesses to the lofty ideal of that relation which prevailed in Israel, even though polygamy was not forbidden. The sweet necessity of wedded love subordinates all other love, as a deeper well, when sunk, draws the surface waters and shallower springs into itself.

A picture of the reflected honor and influence of the bride follows in v. 12. When she stands by the king's side, those around recognize her dignity and seek to secure her favor. It is a personification of the Tyrians according to a familiar idiom.

**45:13–15.** In vv. 13ff the bride's apparel and nuptial procession are described. She is "all glorious within," which does not mean, as is ordinarily supposed, that she possesses an inner beauty of soul, but that the poet conceives of her as standing in the inner chamber where she has been arrayed in her splendor. In v. 14, the marriage procession is described. The words rendered "embroidered robes" are by some taken to mean "tapestry of diverse colors" or richly woven carpets spread for the bride to walk on and by others colored cushions, to which she is led in order to sit beside the bridegroom. But the word (HED #7846) means "apparel" elsewhere, and either of the other meanings introduces an irrelevant detail of another kind into the picture. The analogy of other Scripture metaphors leads at once to interpreting the bride's attire as symbolic of the purity of character belonging to the Church. The Apocalypse dresses "the Lamb's wife" in "fine linen, clean and white" (Rev. 19:7f). The Psalm arrays her in garments gleaming with gold, which symbolize splendor and glory, and in embroidered robes, which suggest the patient use of the slow needle and the variegated harmony of color attained at last. There is no marriage between Christ and the soul unless it is robed in the beauty of righteousness and manifold graces of character.

**45:16–17.** The closing verses are addressed, not to the bride, but to the king, and can only in a very modified way and partially be supposed to pass beyond the Jewish monarch and refer to the true King. The Psalm had a historical basis, and it has also a prophetic meaning, because the king of Israel was himself a type, and Jesus Christ is the fulfillment of the ideal never realized by its successive occupants. Both views of its nature must be kept in view in its interpretation, and it need cause no surprise if, at some points, the rind of prose fact is, so to speak, thicker than at others or if certain features absolutely refuse to lend themselves to the spiritual interpretation.

***Psalm 46.*** *The structure is simple. The three strophes into which the Psalm falls set forth substantially the same thought, that God's presence is safety and peace, whatever storms may roar. This general theme is exhibited in the first strophe (vv. 1ff) in reference to natural convulsions; in the second (vv. 4–7) in reference to the rage of hostile kingdoms; and in the third (vv. 8–11) men are summoned to behold a recent example of God's delivering might, which establishes the truth of the preceding utterances and has occasioned the Psalm. The grand refrain which closes the second and third strophes should probably be restored at the end of v. 3.*

**46:1–3.** In the first strophe, the psalmist paints chaos once again by the familiar figures of a changed earth, tottering mountains sinking in the raging sea from which they rose at creation, and a wild ocean with thunderous dash appalling

| 6142, 6183 | 8302 | | 435 | 3937 | 4406 | 6010 | 6046 |
|---|---|---|---|---|---|---|---|
| prep, n fp | n ms | | n mp | prep, ps 1cp | n ms | cj, n ms | n fs |
| עַל־עֲלָמוֹת | שִׁיר | 1. | אֱלֹהִים | לָנוּ | מַחֲסֶה | וָעֹז | עֶזְרָה |
| 'al-'ălāmôth | shîr | | 'ĕlōhîm | lānû | machseh | wā'ōz | 'ezrāh |
| according to the young women | a song | | God | for us | a Refuge | and Strength | a Help |

| 904, 7150 | 4834.255 | 4108 | | 6142, 3772 | 3940, 3486.120 | 904, 4306.541 |
|---|---|---|---|---|---|---|
| prep, n fp | v Niphal ptc ms | adv | | prep, adv | neg part, v Qal impf 1cp | prep, v Hiphil inf con |
| בְצָרוֹת | נִמְצָא | מְאֹד | 2. | עַל־כֵּן | לֹא־נִירָא | בְּהָמִיר |
| vetsārôth | nimtsā' | me'ōdh | | 'al-kēn | lō'-nîrā' | behāmîr |
| when trouble | One Who is found | very | | therefore | we will not fear | when changing |

| 800 | 4267.141 | 2098 | 904, 3949 | 3328 | | 2064.126 |
|---|---|---|---|---|---|---|
| n fs | cj, prep, v Qal inf con | n mp | prep, *n ms* | n mp | | v Qal impf 3mp |
| אָרֶץ | וּבְמוֹט | הָרִים | בְּלֵב | יַמִּים | 3. | יֶהֱמוּ |
| 'ārets | ûvemôt | hārîm | belev | yammîm | | yehĕmû |
| the earth | and when tottering | mountains | in the heart of | the seas | | they are tumultuous |

| 2666.126 | 4448 | 7782.126, 2098 | 904, 1375 | 5734 | | 5282 | 6631 |
|---|---|---|---|---|---|---|---|
| v Qal impf 3mp | n mp, ps 3ms | v Qal impf 3mp, n mp | prep, n fs, ps 3ms | intrj | | n ms | n mp, ps 3ms |
| יֶחְמְרוּ | מֵימָיו | יִרְעֲשׁוּ־הָרִים | בְּגַאֲוָתוֹ | סֶלָה | 4. | נָהָר | פְּלָגָיו |
| yechămrû | mêmâv | yir'ăshû-hārîm | begha'ăwāthô | selāh | | nāhār | pelāghâv |
| they foam | its waters | mountains quake | during its swelling | selah | | a river | its streams |

| 7975.326 | 6111, 435 | 7202 | 5088 | 6169 | | 435 |
|---|---|---|---|---|---|---|
| v Piel impf 3mp | *n fs*, n mp | adj | *n mp* | n ms | | n mp |
| יְשַׂמְּחוּ | עִיר־אֱלֹהִים | קְדֹשׁ | מִשְׁכְּנֵי | עֶלְיוֹן | 5. | אֱלֹהִים |
| yesammechû | 'îr-'ĕlōhîm | qōdhōsh | mishkenê | 'elyôn | | 'ĕlōhîm |
| they make glad | the city of God | holy | the Tabernacle of | the Most High | | God |

| 904, 7419 | 1118, 4267.222 | 6038.121 | 435 | 3937, 6680.141 | 1269 |
|---|---|---|---|---|---|
| prep, n ms, ps 3fs | neg part, v Niphal impf 3fs | v Qal impf 3ms, ps 3fs | n mp | prep, v Qal inf con | n ms |
| בְּקִרְבָּהּ | בַּל־תִּמּוֹט | יַעְזְרֶהָ | אֱלֹהִים | לִפְנוֹת | בֹּקֶר |
| beqirbāhh | bal-timmôt | ya'ăzreāh | 'ĕlōhîm | liphnôth | bōqer |
| in its midst | it will not totter | He will help it | God | when turning into | the morning |

| | 2064.116 | 1504 | 4267.116 | 4608 | 5598.111 | 904, 7249 |
|---|---|---|---|---|---|---|
| | v Qal pf 3cp | n mp | v Qal pf 3cp | n fp | v Qal pf 3ms | prep, n ms, ps 3ms |
| 6. | הָמוּ | גוֹיִם | מָטוּ | מַמְלָכוֹת | נָתַן | בְּקוֹלוֹ |
| | hāmû | ghôyim | mātû | mamlākhôth | nāthan | beqôlô |
| | they have raged | nations | they have tottered | kingdoms | he gives | with his voice |

| 4265.122 | 800 | | 3176 | 6893 | 6196 | 5021, 3937 | 435 | 3399 | 5734 |
|---|---|---|---|---|---|---|---|---|---|
| v Qal impf 3fs | n fs | | pn | n fp | prep, ps 1cp | n ms, prep, ps 1cp | *n mp* | pn | intrj |
| תָּמוּג | אָרֶץ | 7. | יְהוָה | צְבָאוֹת | עִמָּנוּ | מִשְׂגָּב־לָנוּ | אֱלֹהֵי | יַעֲקֹב | סֶלָה |
| tāmûgh | 'ārets | | yehwāh | tsevā'ôth | 'immānû | misgāv-lānû | 'ĕlōhê | ya'ăqōv | selāh |
| it melts | the earth | | Yahweh | Hosts | with us | a Refuge to us | the God of | Jacob | selah |

| | 2050.133, | 4821 | 3176 | 866, 7947.111 | 8439 |
|---|---|---|---|---|---|
| | v Qal impv 2mp, v Qal impv 2mp | *n fp* | pn | rel part, v Qal pf 3ms | n fp |
| 8. | לְכוּ־חֲזוּ | מִפְעֲלוֹת | יְהוָה | אֲשֶׁר־שָׂם | שַׁמּוֹת |
| | lekhû-chăzû | miph'ălôth | yehwāh | 'ăsher-sām | shammôth |
| | come behold | the works of | Yahweh | which He has effected | desolations |

| 904, 800 | | 8139.551 | 4560 | 5912, 7381 | 800 | 7493 | 8132.321 |
|---|---|---|---|---|---|---|---|
| prep, art, n fs | | v Hiphil ptc ms | n fp | prep, *n ms* | art, n fs | n fs | v Piel impf 3ms |
| בָּאָרֶץ | 9. | מַשְׁבִּית | מִלְחָמוֹת | עַד־קְצֵה | הָאָרֶץ | קֶשֶׁת | יְשַׁבֵּר |
| bā'ārets | | mashbîth | milchāmôth | 'adh-qōtsēh | hā'ārets | qesheth | yeshabbēr |
| in the land | | causing to cease | wars | unto the ends of | the land | the bow | He breaks |

**2. Therefore will not we fear, though the earth be removed, and though the mountains be carried into the midst of the sea:** ... though the earth be shaken, *NAB* ... though the earth give way, *NIV* ... though mountains tumble into the depths of the sea, *JB* ... the mountains be moved in the heart of the seas, *MRB.*

**3. Though the waters thereof roar and be troubled, though the mountains shake with the swelling thereof. Selah:** ... though its waters rage and foam, *NCB* ... and the mountains quake before his majesty, *NEB* ... the mountains quake at its swelling pride, *NASB* ... though the mountains tremble with its tumult, *NRSV.*

**4. There is a river, the streams whereof shall make glad the city of God, the holy place of the tabernacles of the most High:** ... that brings joy to the city of God, *NCV* ... whose streams make glad the resting-place of God, *BB* ... The holiest dwelling-place of the Most High, *MAST* ... the holy habitation of the Most High, *RSV.*

**5. God is in the midst of her; she shall not be moved: God shall help her, and that right early:** ... God is in the city—she can't fall, *Beck* ... She shrinks not with GOD in her midst, *Fenton* ... when morning comes, God is her aid, *Moffatt* ... God will help her at break of dawn, *Goodspeed.*

**6. The heathen raged, the kingdoms were moved: he uttered his voice, the earth melted:** ... Though nations are in turmoil, *NAB* ... Nations are in uproar, kingdoms fall, *NIV* ... at the sound of his voice the earth became like wax, *BB* ... God thundered, and the earth melted, *Geneva.*

**7. The LORD of hosts is with us; the God of Jacob is our refuge. Selah:** ... The LORD All-Powerful is with us, *NCV* ... A tower for us is the God of Jacob, *Young* ... The God of Jacob is our stronghold, *NASB* ... the God of Jacob is our fortress, *REB.*

**8. Come, behold the works of the LORD, what desolations he hath made in the earth:** ... Come near, and see God's acts, *Knox* ... the astounding things he has wrought on earth, *NCB* ... what ruins He has made in the earth, *KJVII* ... What power they show to the earth, *Fenton.*

**9. He maketh wars to cease unto the end of the earth; he breaketh the bow, and cutteth the spear in sunder; he burneth the chariot in the fire:** ... he puts an end to wars over the whole wide world, *JB* ... from end to end of the earth he stamps out war, *NEB* ... He breaks the bow into pieces and snaps the spear in two, *Berkeley* ... and shatters the spear, *RSV.*

---

the ear and yeasty foam terrifying the eye, sweeping in triumphant insolence over all the fair earth. It is prosaic to insist on an allegorical meaning for the picture. It is rather a vivid sketch of utter confusion, dashed in with three or four bold strokes, an impossible case supposed in order to bring out the unshaken calm of those who have God for an ark in such a deluge. He is not only a sure Refuge and Stronghold, but one easily accessible when troubles come.

**46:4–7.** The second strophe brings a new picture to view with impressive suddenness, which is even more vividly dramatic if the refrain is not supplied. Right against the vision of confusion comes one of peace. The abrupt introduction of "a river" as an isolated noun, which dislocates grammatical structure, is almost an exclamation. "There is a river" enfeebles the swing of the original. We might almost translate, "Lo! a river!" Jerusalem was unique among historical cities in that it had no great river. It had one tiny thread of water, of which perhaps the psalmist was thinking.

With what vigor the short, crashing clauses of v. 6 describe the wrath and turbulence of the nations and the instantaneous dissolving of their strength into weakness at a word from those awful lips! The verse may be taken as hypothetical or as historical. In either case, we see the sequence of events as by a succession of lightning flashes. The hurry of the style, marked by the omission of connecting particles, reflects the swiftness of incident.

Again the triumph of the refrain peals forth, with its musical accompaniment prolonging the impression. In it the psalmist gives voice, for himself and his fellows, to their making of their own general truths which the Psalm has been declaring. The two names of God set forth a twofold ground for confidence. "Yahweh of Hosts" is all the more emphatic here, since the second book of the Psalter usually uses "Elohim." It proclaims God's eternal, self-existent Being and his covenant relation, as well as his absolute authority over the ranked forces of the universe, personal or impersonal, spiritual or material. The LORD of all these legions is with us. When we say "The God of Jacob," we reach back into the past and lay hold of the Helper of the men of old as ours. What He has been, He is; what He did, He is doing still.

**46:8–11.** The third strophe summons to contemplate with fixed attention the "desolations" made by some great manifestation of God's delivering power. It is presupposed that these are still visible. Broken bows, splintered spears and half-charred chariots strew the ground, and Israel

| 7401.311 | 2698 | 5906 | 8041.121 | 904, 813 | | 7791.533 |
|---|---|---|---|---|---|---|
| cj, v Piel pf 3ms | n fs | n fp | v Qal impf 3ms | prep, art, n fs | 10. | v Hiphil impv 2mp |
| וְקִצֵּץ | חֲנִית | עֲגָלוֹת | יִשְׂרֹף | בָּאֵשׁ | | הַרְפּוּ |
| wᵉqitstsēts | chănîth | ʿăghālôth | yisrōph | bāʾēsh | | harpû |
| and He has shattered | the spear | wagons | He burns | with the fire | | leave off |

| 3156.133 | 3706, 609 | 435 | 7597.125 | 904, 1504 | 7597.125 | 904, 800 |
|---|---|---|---|---|---|---|
| cj, v Qal impv 2mp | cj, pers pron | n mp | v Qal impf 1cs | prep, art, n mp | v Qal impf 1cs | prep, art, n fs |
| וּדְעוּ | כִּי־אָנֹכִי | אֱלֹהִים | אָרוּם | בַּגּוֹיִם | אָרוּם | בָּאָרֶץ |
| ûdhᵉʿû | kî-ʾānōkhî | ʾělōhîm | ʾārûm | baggôyim | ʾārûm | bāʾārets |
| and be aware | that I | God | I am exalted | among the nations | I am exalted | in the earth |

| | 3176 | 6893 | 6196 | 5021, 3937 | 435 | 3399 | 5734 | | 3937, 5514.351 |
|---|---|---|---|---|---|---|---|---|---|
| 11. | pn | n fp | prep, ps 1cp | n ms, prep, ps 1cp | *n mp* | pn | intrj | 47:t | prep, art, v Piel ptc ms |
| | יְהוָה | צְבָאוֹת | עִמָּנוּ | מִשְׂגָּב־לָנוּ | אֱלֹהֵי | יַעֲקֹב | סֶלָה | | לַמְנַצֵּחַ |
| | yᵉhwāh | tsᵉvāʾôth | ʿimmānû | misgāv-lānû | ʾělōhê | yaʿăqōv | selāh | | lamnatstsēach |
| | Yahweh | Hosts | with us | a Refuge to us | the God of | Jacob | selah | | to the director |

| 3937, 1158, 7432 | 4344 | | 3725, 6194 | 8965.133, 3834 | 7607.533 | 3937, 435 |
|---|---|---|---|---|---|---|
| prep, *n mp*, pn | n ms | 1. | *adj*, art, n mp | v Qal impv 2mp, n fs | v Hiphil impv 2mp | prep, n mp |
| לִבְנֵי־קֹרַח | מִזְמוֹר | | כָּל־הָעַמִּים | תִּקְעוּ־כָף | הָרִיעוּ | לֵאלֹהִים |
| livnê-qōrach | mizmôr | | kol-hāʿammîm | tiqʿû-khāph | hārîʿû | lēʾlōhîm |
| of the sons of Korah | a Psalm | | all the peoples | clap your hands | shout | to God |

| 904, 7249 | 7726 | | 3706, 3176 | 6169 | 3486.255 | 4567 | 1448 |
|---|---|---|---|---|---|---|---|
| prep, *n ms* | n fs | 2. | cj, pn | n ms | v Niphal ptc ms | n ms | adj |
| בְּקוֹל | רִנָּה | | כִּי־יְהוָה | עֶלְיוֹן | נוֹרָא | מֶלֶךְ | גָּדוֹל |
| bᵉqôl | rinnāh | | kî-yᵉhwāh | ʿelyôn | nôrāʾ | melekh | gādhôl |
| with a voice of | shouts of joy | | because Yahweh | the Most High | fearful | a King | great |

| 6142, 3725, 800 | | 1744.521 | 6194 | 8809 | 3947 | 8809 | 7559 |
|---|---|---|---|---|---|---|---|
| prep, *adj*, art, n fs | 3. | v Hiphil impf 3ms | n mp | prep, ps 1cs | cj, n mp | prep | n fd, ps 1cp |
| עַל־כָּל־הָאָרֶץ | | יַדְבֵּר | עַמִּים | תַּחְתֵּינוּ | וּלְאֻמִּים | תַּחַת | רַגְלֵינוּ |
| ʿal-kol-hāʾārets | | yadhbēr | ʿammîm | tachtênû | ûlāʾummîm | tachath | raghlênû |
| on all the earth | | He subdues | peoples | under us | and peoples | beneath | our feet |

| | 1013.121, 3937 | 881, 5338 | 881 | 1377 | 3399 | 866, 154.111 | 5734 |
|---|---|---|---|---|---|---|---|
| 4. | v Qal impf 3ms, prep, ps 1cp | do, n fs, ps 1cp | do | *n ms* | pn | rel pron, v Qal pf 3ms | intrj |
| | יִבְחַר־לָנוּ | אֶת־נַחֲלָתֵנוּ | אֶת | גְּאוֹן | יַעֲקֹב | אֲשֶׁר־אָהֵב | סֶלָה |
| | yivchar-lānû | ʾeth-nachlāthēnû | ʾeth | gᵉʾôn | yaʿăqōv | ʾăsher-ʾāhēv | selāh |
| | He chooses for us | our inheritance | | the pride of | Jacob | whom He loves | selah |

| | 6148.111 | 435 | 904, 8980 | 3176 | 904, 7249 | 8223 |
|---|---|---|---|---|---|---|
| 5. | v Qal pf 3ms | n mp | prep, n fs | pn | prep, *n ms* | n ms |
| | עָלָה | אֱלֹהִים | בִּתְרוּעָה | יְהוָה | בְּקוֹל | שׁוֹפָר |
| | ʿālāh | ʾělōhîm | bithrûʿāh | yᵉhōwāh | bᵉqôl | shôphār |
| | He went up | God | with a shout of joy | Yahweh | with the sound of | a ram's horn |

**10. Be still, and know that I am God: I will be exalted among the heathen, I will be exalted in the earth:** … Stop and realize that I am God, *Beck* … Cease striving and know that I am God, *NASB* … I am exalted among the nations, *NRSV* … high over nations, high over the world, *Moffatt.*

**11. The LORD of hosts is with us; the God of Jacob is our refuge. Selah:** … The Lord of armies is with us, *BB* … our stronghold is the God of Jacob, *NCB* … A high tower for us is the God of Jacob, *Rotherham* … Jacob's GOD is a Fortress to us, *Fenton.*

**47:t. To the chief Musician, A Psalm for the sons of Korah.**

**1. O clap your hands, all ye people; shout unto God with the voice of triumph:** … letting your voices go up to God with joy, *BB* … Let all the Tribes clap with their hands, *Fenton* … shout to God with cries of gladness, *NAB* … with a voice of singing, *Young.*

**2. For the LORD most high is terrible; he is a great King over all the**

**earth:** ... the Most High, is to be feared, *Moffatt* ... How awesome is the LORD Most High, *REB* ... For the LORD Most High is awe-inspiring, *Berkeley* ... he is the sovereign Ruler of all the earth, *Knox.*

**3. He shall subdue the people under us, and the nations under our feet:** ... He lays the nations prostrate beneath us, *NEB* ... He defeated nations for us, *NCV* ... He will subjugate Peoples under us, *Rotherham* ... He shall humble the people under us, *KJVII.*

**4. He shall choose our inheritance for us, the excellency of Jacob whom he loved. Selah:** ... He chose our possession for us, *Goodspeed* ... He chose our land for us, *Beck* ... the pride of Jacob whom he loves, *RSV* ... The glory Jacob whom he loved, *ASV.*

**5. God is gone up with a shout, the LORD with the sound of a trumpet:** ... God is gone vp with triumph, *Geneva* ... God is gone up amidst shouting, *MAST* ... God mounts his throne amid shouts of joy, *NAB* ... God has ascended with a shout, *NASB.*

---

could go forth without fear and feast their eyes on these tokens of what God had done for them. The language is naturally applied to the relics of Sennacherib's annihilated force. In any case, it points to a recent act of God, the glad surprise of which palpitates all through the Psalm. The field of history is littered with broken, abandoned weapons, once flourished in hands long since turned to dust; yet the city and throne of God against which they were lifted remain unharmed. The voice which melted the earth speaks at the close of the Psalm, not now with destructive energy, but in warning, through which tones of tenderness can be caught. God desires that foes would cease their vain strife before it proves fatal. "Desist" (HED #7791) is here an elliptical expression, of which the full form is "Let your hands drop"; or, as we say, "Ground your weapons," and learn how vain is a contest with Him Who is God and whose fixed purpose is that all nations shall know and exalt Him. The prospect hinted at in the last words, of a world submissive to its King, softens the terrors of his destructive manifestations, reveals their inmost purpose and opens to foes the possibility of passing, not as conquerors, but as subjects, and therefore fellow citizens, through the gate into the city.

***Psalm 47.*** *Psalm 47 has little complexity in structure or thought. It is a gush of pure rapture. It rises to prophetic foresight and, by reason of a comparatively small historical occasion, has a vision of the worldwide expansion of the kingdom of God. It falls into two strophes of four verses each, with one longer verse appended to the latter.*

**47:1–2.** In the first strophe (vv. 1–4), the nations are invited to welcome God as their King, not only because of his divine exaltation and worldwide dominion, but also because of his deeds for "Jacob." The same divine act which in Ps. 46 is represented as quelling wars and melting the earth and in Ps. 48 as bringing dismay, pain and flight, is here contemplated as attracting the nations to worship. The psalmist knows that destructive providences have their gracious aspect and that God's true victory over men is not won when opposition is crushed and hearts are made to quake, but when recognition of his sway and joy in it swell the heart. The quick clatter of clapping hands is the sign of homage to the King.

**47:3–4.** Verses 3f seem to state the grounds for the summons in v. 1. The tenses in these verses present a difficulty in the way of taking them for a historical retrospect of the conquest and partition of Canaan, which but for that objection would be the natural interpretation. It is possible to take them as "a truth of experience inferred from what had just been witnessed, the historical fact being expressed not in historical form, but generalized and idealized" (Delitzsch). The just accomplished deliverance repeated in essence the wonders of the first entrance on possession of the land and revealed the continuous working of the same divine hand, ever renewing the choice of Jacob's inheritance and ever scattering its enemies. "The pride of Jacob" is a phrase in apposition with "our inheritance." The Holy Land was the object of pride to Jacob, not in an evil sense, but in that he boasted of it as a precious treasure entrusted to him by God. The root fact of all God's ancient and continued blessings is that He "loved." His own heart, not Jacob's deserts, prompted his mercies.

**47:5–8.** The second strophe is distinguished from the first by the increased fervor of its calls to praise, by its still more exultant rush, and by its omission of reference to Jacob. It is wholly concerned with the peoples whom it invites to take up the song. As in the former strophe the singer showed to the peoples God working in the world, here he bids them look up and see Him ascending on high. Now that He ascended, what is it but that He also descended first? The mighty deliverance

| 6. | 2252.333 | 435 | 2252.333 | 2252.333 | 3937, 4567 | 2252.333 | 7. | 3706 |
|---|---|---|---|---|---|---|---|---|
| | v Piel impv 2mp | n mp | v Piel impv 2mp | v Piel impv 2mp | prep, n ms, ps 1cp | v Piel impv 2mp | | cj |
| | זַמְּרוּ | אֱלֹהִים | זַמֵּרוּ | זַמְּרוּ | לְמַלְכֵּנוּ | זַמֵּרוּ | | כִּי |
| | zammerû | 'ĕlōhîm | zammērû | zammerû | lemalkēnû | zammērû | | kî |
| | sing praises to | God | sing praises | sing praises | to our King | sing praises | | because |

| 4567 | 3725, 800 | 435 | 2252.333 | 5030 | 8. | 4566.111 | 435 |
|---|---|---|---|---|---|---|---|
| *n ms* | *adj*, art, n fs | n mp | v Piel impv 2mp | n ms | | v Qal pf 3ms | n mp |
| מֶלֶךְ | כָּל־הָאָרֶץ | אֱלֹהִים | זַמְּרוּ | מַשְׂכִּיל | | מָלַךְ | אֱלֹהִים |
| melekh | kol-hā'ārets | 'ĕlōhîm | zammerû | maskîl | | mālakh | 'ĕlōhîm |
| the King of | all the earth | God | sing praises | a Maskil | | He reigns | God |

| 6142, 1504 | 435 | 3553.111 | 6142, 3802 | 7231 | 9. | 5259 | 6194 |
|---|---|---|---|---|---|---|---|
| prep, n mp | n mp | v Qal pf 3ms | prep, *n ms* | n ms, ps 3ms | | *n mp* | n mp |
| עַל־גּוֹיִם | אֱלֹהִים | יָשַׁב | עַל־כִּסֵּא | קָדְשׁוֹ | | נְדִיבֵי | עַמִּים |
| 'al-gôyim | 'ĕlōhîm | yāshav | 'al-kissē' | qādheshô | | nedhîvê | 'ammîm |
| over the nations | God | He sits | on the throne of | his holy place | | the nobles of | peoples |

| 636.216 | 6194 | 435 | 80 | 3706 | 3937, 435 | 4182, 800 |
|---|---|---|---|---|---|---|
| v Niphal pf 3cp | *n ms* | *n mp* | pn | cj | prep, n mp | *n mp*, n fs |
| נֶאֱסָפוּ | עַם | אֱלֹהֵי | אַבְרָהָם | כִּי | לֵאלֹהִים | מָגִנֵּי־אֶרֶץ |
| ne'ĕsāphû | 'am | 'ĕlōhê | 'avrāhām | kî | lē'lōhîm | māghinnê-'erets |
| they gather | the people of | the God of | Abraham | because | to God | the shields of the earth |

| 4108 | 6148.211 | 48:t | 8302 | 4344 | 3937, 1158, 7432 | 1. | 1448 | 3176 | 2054.455 |
|---|---|---|---|---|---|---|---|---|---|
| adv | v Niphal pf 3ms | | n ms | n ms | prep, *n mp*, pn | | adj | pn | cj, v Pual ptc ms |
| מְאֹד | נַעֲלָה | | שִׁיר | מִזְמוֹר | לִבְנֵי־קֹרַח | | גָּדוֹל | יְהוָה | וּמְהֻלָּל |
| me'ōdh | na'ălāh | | shîr | mizmôr | livnê-qōrach | | gādhôl | yehwāh | ûmehullāl |
| very | He is uplifted | | a Song | a Psalm | of the sons of Korah | | great | Yahweh | and praised |

| 4108 | 904, 6111 | 435 | 2098, 7231 | 2. | 3413 | 5312 | 5026 |
|---|---|---|---|---|---|---|---|
| adv | prep, *n fs* | n mp, ps 1cp | *n ms*, n ms, ps 3ms | | *adj* | n ms | *n ms* |
| מְאֹד | בְּעִיר | אֱלֹהֵינוּ | הַר־קָדְשׁוֹ | | יְפֵה | נוֹף | מְשׂוֹשׂ |
| me'ōdh | be'îr | 'ĕlōhênû | har-qādheshô | | yephēh | nôph | mesôs |
| very | in a city of | our God | the mountain of his holiness | | beautiful | elevation | the joy of |

| 3725, 800 | 2098, 6995 | 3526 | 7103 | 7439 | 4567 | 7521 | 3. | 435 |
|---|---|---|---|---|---|---|---|---|
| *adj*, art, n fs | *n ms*, pn | *n fd* | n ms | *n fs* | n ms | adj | | n mp |
| כָּל־הָאָרֶץ | הַר־צִיּוֹן | יַרְכְּתֵי | צָפוֹן | קִרְיַת | מֶלֶךְ | רָב | | אֱלֹהִים |
| kol-hā'ārets | har-tsîyôn | yarkethê | tsāphôn | qiryath | melekh | rāv | | 'ĕlōhîm |
| all the earth | Mount Zion | the remote part of | the north | the city of | the king | great | | God |

| 904, 783 | 3156.211 | 3937, 5021 | 4. | 3706, 2079 | 4567 |
|---|---|---|---|---|---|
| prep, n mp, ps 3fs | v Niphal pf 3ms | prep, n ms | | cj, intrj | art, n mp |
| בְּאַרְמְנוֹתֶיהָ | נוֹדַע | לְמִשְׂגָּב | | כִּי־הִנֵּה | הַמְּלָכִים |
| be'armenôthêāh | nôdha' | lemisgāv | | kî-hinnēh | hammelākhîm |
| in its citadels | He makes himself known | for a Refuge | | because behold | the kings |

**6. Sing praises to God, sing praises: sing praises unto our King, sing praises:** ... Sing psalms of God, *Darby* ... let the music sound for our king, *JB* ... Music of praise for God, *Moffatt* ... sing your highest praises to our King, *LIVB*.

**7. For God is the King of all the earth: sing ye praises with understanding:** ... sing hymns of praise, *NCB* ... sing psalms with all your skill, *REB* ... Give praise, O understanding one, *Young* ... so sing a song of praise to him, *NCV*.

**8. God reigneth over the heathen: God sitteth upon the throne of his holiness:** ... God rules over all the nations, *Berkeley* ... God hath become king over the nations, *Rotherham* ... God sits enthroned in holiness, *Knox* ... God is on the high seat of his holy rule, *BB*.

**9. The princes of the people are gathered together, even the people of the God of Abraham: for the shields of the earth belong unto God: he is greatly exalted:** ... May those who are willing among the nations rally round, *Beck* ... for the kings of the earth belong to God, *NIV* ... For God's are the guardians of the earth, *NAB* ... He is lifted up on high, *KJVII.*

**48:t. A Song and Psalm for the sons of Korah.**

**1. Great is the LORD, and greatly to be praised in the city of our God, in the mountain of his holiness:** ... great honour is his due, *Knox* ... worthy to be mightily praised, *Rotherham* ... loudly to be praised, *Moffatt.*

**2. Beautiful for situation, the joy of the whole earth, is mount Zion, on the sides of the north, the city of the great King:** ... fairest of heights, is the joy of all the earth, *NAB* ... It is beautiful in its loftiness, *NIV* ... Beautiful in its high position, *BB* ... rising beautifully, *Beck.*

**3. God is known in her palaces for a refuge:** ... as a high fortress, *Darby* ... known for a stronghold, *MAST* ... revealed as a tower of strength, *REB* ... God has shown himself a sure defense, *RSV.*

**4. For, lo, the kings were assembled, they passed by together:** ... joined forces, when they advanced together, *NIV* ... they marched up together, *Berkeley* ... and came to attack the city, *NCV.*

---

of which the triumph throbs through this trilogy of tributes of victory was God's coming down. Now He has gone back to his throne and seated himself there, not as having ceased to work in the world—for He is still King over it all—but as having completed a delivering work. He does not withdraw when He goes up. He does not cease to work here below when He sits enthroned in his palace-temple above. The "shout" and "voice of a trumpet," which accompany that ascent, are borrowed from the ordinary attendants on a triumphal procession. He soars as in a chariot of praises, from whose lips the Psalm does not say, but probably it intends Israel to be understood as the singer. To that choir the nations are called to join their voices and harps, since God is their King too, and not Jacob's only. The word often rendered "with understanding" (HED #5030) is a noun, the name of a description of the Psalm, which occurs in several Psalm titles, and is best understood as "a skillful song." Verse 8 gathers up the reasons for the peoples' homage to God. He has become King over them by his recent act, having manifested and established his dominion. He has now "sat down on his throne," as having accomplished his purpose and as thence administering the world's affairs.

**47:9.** A final verse, of double the length of the others, stands somewhat apart from the preceding strophe both in rhythm and in thought. It crowns the whole. The invitations to the nations are conceived of as having been welcomed and obeyed. And there rises before the poet's eye a fair picture of a great convocation, such as might wait before a world-ruling monarch's throne on the day of his coronation. The princes of the nations, like tributary kings, come flocking to do homage as if they surely knew their sovereign LORD was by.

***Psalm 48.*** *The Psalm falls into three parts, of which the first (vv. 1f) is introductory, celebrating the glory of Zion as the city of God; the second (vv. 3–8) recounts in glowing words the deliverance of Zion; and the third tells of the consequent praise and trust of the inhabitants of Zion (vv. 9–14).*

**48:1–2.** The general sense of the first part is plain, but v. 2 is difficult. "Mount Zion" is obviously the subject, and "lovely in loftiness" and "joy of all the earth" predicates, but the grammatical connection of the two last clauses is obscure. Further, the meaning of "the sides of the north" has not been satisfactorily ascertained. The supposition that there is an allusion in the phrase to the mythological mountain of the gods, with which Zion is compared, is surely most unnatural. We are not forcing NT ideas into OT words when we see in the Psalm an eternal truth. An idea is one thing; the fact which more or less perfectly embodies it is another. The idea of God's dwelling with men had a previous "embodiment" in the presence in the Temple. It is more perfect in the dwelling of Jesus among us and then the Holy Spirit in the Church, and will have its complete fulfillment when the city "having the glory of God" shall appear, and He will dwell with men and be their God. God in her, not anything of her own, makes Zion lovely and pleasant. "For it was perfect through my comeliness which I had put upon thee, saith the LORD" (Ezek. 16:14).

**48:3–8.** The second part pictures Zion's deliverance with picturesque vigor (vv. 3–8). Verse 3 sums up the whole as the act of God by which He has made himself known as that which the refrain of Ps. 46 declared Him to be—a refuge, or, literally, a high tower. Then follows the muster of the hosts.

As in Ps. 46:6, the clauses, piled up without cement or connecting particles, convey an impression of hurry, culminating in the rush of panic-struck

| 3366.216 | 5882.116 | 3267 | | 2065 | 7495.116 | 3772 | 8867.116 |
|---|---|---|---|---|---|---|---|
| v Niphal pf 3cp | v Qal pf 3cp | adv | | pers pron | v Qal pf 3cp | adv | v Qal pf 3cp |
| נוֹעֲדוּ | עָבְרוּ | יַחְדָּו | **5.** | הֵמָּה | רָאוּ | כֵּן | תָּמָהוּ |
| nô'ădhû | 'āverû | yachdāw | | hēmmāh | rā'û | kēn | tāmāhû |
| they assembled | they passed on | together | | they | they saw | so | they were stunned |

| 963.216 | 2753.216 | | 7748 | 270.112 | 8427 | 2527 |
|---|---|---|---|---|---|---|
| v Niphal pf 3cp | v Niphal pf 3cp | | n fs | v Qal pf 3fs, ps 3mp | adv | n ms |
| נִבְהֲלוּ | נֶחְפָּזוּ | **6.** | רְעָדָה | אֲחָזָתַם | שָׁם | חִיל |
| nivhelû | nechpāzû | | re'ādhāh | 'ăchāzātham | shām | chîl |
| they were dismayed | they quickly retreated | | trembling | it takes hold of them | there | anguish |

| 3626, 3314.153 | | 904, 7593 | 7205 | 8132.323 | 605 | 8998 |
|---|---|---|---|---|---|---|
| prep, art, v Qal act ptc fs | | prep, *n fs* | n ms | v Piel impf 2ms | n fp | pn |
| כַּיּוֹלֵדָה | **7.** | בְּרוּחַ | קָדִים | תְּשַׁבֵּר | אֳנִיּוֹת | תַּרְשִׁישׁ |
| kayyôlēdhāh | | berûach | qādhîm | teshabbēr | 'ănîyôth | tarshîsh |
| like a woman in childbirth | | with a wind from | the east | You shattered | ships | Tarshish |

| | 3626, 866 | 8471.119 | 3772 | 7495.119 | 904, 6111, 3176 | 6893 | 904, 6111 |
|---|---|---|---|---|---|---|---|
| | prep, rel part | v Qal pf 1cp | adv | v Qal pf 1cp | prep, *n fs*, pn | n fp | prep, *n fs* |
| **8.** | כַּאֲשֶׁר | שָׁמַעְנוּ | כֵּן | רָאִינוּ | בְּעִיר־יְהוָה | צְבָאוֹת | בְּעִיר |
| | ka'ăsher | shāma'ănû | kēn | rā'înû | be'îr-yehwāh | tsevā'ôth | be'îr |
| | just as | we have heard | so | we have seen | in the city of Yahweh | Hosts | in the city of |

| 435 | 435 | 3679.321 | 5912, 5986 | 5734 | | 1880.319 | 435 |
|---|---|---|---|---|---|---|---|
| n mp, ps 1cp | n mp | v Polel impf 3ms, ps 3fs | adv, n ms | intrj | | v Piel pf 1cp | n mp |
| אֱלֹהֵינוּ | אֱלֹהִים | יְכוֹנְנֶהָ | עַד־עוֹלָם | סֶלָה | **9.** | דִּמִּינוּ | אֱלֹהִים |
| 'ĕlōhênû | 'ĕlōhîm | yekhôneneāh | 'adh-'ôlām | s̱elāh | | dimmînû | 'ĕlōhîm |
| our God | God | He established it | until forever | selah | | we have compared | O God |

| 2721 | 904, 7419 | 2033 | | 3626, 8428 | 435 | 3772 | 8747 |
|---|---|---|---|---|---|---|---|
| n ms, ps 2ms | prep, *n ms* | n ms, ps 2ms | | prep, n ms, ps 2ms | n mp | adv | n fs, ps 2ms |
| חַסְדֶּךָ | בְּקֶרֶב | הֵיכָלֶךָ | **10.** | כְּשִׁמְךָ | אֱלֹהִים | כֵּן | תְּהִלָּתְךָ |
| chas̱dekhā | beqerev | hêkhālekhā | | keshimkhā | 'ĕlōhîm | kēn | tehillāthekhā |
| your steadfast love | in the middle of | your Temple | | like your name | O God | so | your praise |

| 6142, 7384, 800 | 6928 | 4527.112 | 3332 | | 7975.121 | 2098, 6995 |
|---|---|---|---|---|---|---|
| prep, *n mp*, n fs | n ms | v Qal pf 3fs | n fs, ps 2ms | | v Qal juss 3ms | *n ms*, pn |
| עַל־קַצְוֵי־אֶרֶץ | צֶדֶק | מָלְאָה | יְמִינֶךָ | **11.** | יִשְׂמַח | הַר־צִיּוֹן |
| 'al-qatswê-'erets | tsedheq | māle'āh | yemînekhā | | yismach | har-tsîyôn |
| on the ends of the earth | righteousness | it is full | your right hand | | let it be glad | Mount Zion |

| 1559.127 | 1351 | 3171 | 3937, 4775 | 5122 | | 5621.133 | 6995 |
|---|---|---|---|---|---|---|---|
| v Qal juss 3fp | *n fp* | pn | prep, prep | n mp, ps 2ms | | v Qal impv 2mp | pn |
| תָּגֵלְנָה | בְּנוֹת | יְהוּדָה | לְמַעַן | מִשְׁפָּטֶיךָ | **12.** | סֹבּוּ | צִיּוֹן |
| tāghēlenāh | benôth | yehûdhāh | lema'an | mishpāṭêkhā | | s̱ōbû | tsîyôn |
| let them rejoice | the daughters of | Judah | because of | your judgments | | walk around | Zion |

| 5545.533 | 5807.133 | 4166 | | 8308.133 | 3949 | 3937, 2526 |
|---|---|---|---|---|---|---|
| cj, v Hiphil impv 2mp, ps 3fs | v Qal impv 2mp | n mp, ps 3fs | | v Qal impv 2mp | n ms, ps 2mp | prep, n ms, ps 3fs |
| וְהַקִּיפוּהָ | סִפְרוּ | מִגְדָּלֶיהָ | **13.** | שִׁיתוּ | לִבְּכֶם | לְחֵילָה |
| wehaqqîphûāh | s̱iphrû | mighdālêāh | | shîthû | libbekhem | lechêlāh |
| and encircle it | count | her towers | | set | your heart | its ramparts |

| 6694.333 | 783 | 3937, 4775 | 5807.328 | 3937, 1810 | 315 | | 3706 |
|---|---|---|---|---|---|---|---|
| v Piel impv 2mp | n mp, ps 3fs | prep, prep | v Piel impf 2mp | prep, n ms | adv | | cj |
| פַּסְּגוּ | אַרְמְנוֹתֶיהָ | לְמַעַן | תְּסַפְּרוּ | לְדוֹר | אַחֲרוֹן | **14.** | כִּי |
| pas̱seghû | 'armenôthêāh | lema'an | tes̱apperû | ledhôr | 'achrôn | | kî |
| reflect on | her citadels | so that | you will recount | to the generations | behind | | because |

**5. They saw it, and so they marvelled; they were troubled, and hasted away:** ... they feared, and shook in dread, *Fenton* ... they were in panic, they took to flight, *RSV* ... when they saw, they panicked and fled away, *JB* ... filled with alarm they panic, *REB.*

**6. Fear took hold upon them there, and pain, as of a woman in travail:** ... Trembling seized them on the spot, *JB* ... pains as of a woman in labor, *NRSV* ... they hurt like a woman having a baby, *NCV* ... throes like those of childbirth, *Berkeley.*

**7. Thou breakest the ships of Tarshish with an east wind:** ... when an east wind wrecks them, *NEB* ... an east wind wrecks ocean going ships, *Beck* ... like ships tossing in a furious storm, *Good News* ... You destroyed them like ships of Tarshish, *NIV.*

**8. As we have heard, so have we seen in the city of the LORD of hosts, in the city of our God: God will establish it for ever. Selah:** ... God will always keep his city safe. It is the city of the LORD All-Powerful, *NCV* ... God will make her secure forever, *Anchor* ... What we had heard we saw now with our own eyes, *REB* ... in the city of Yahweh Sabaoth, *JB.*

**9. We have thought of thy lovingkindness, O God, in the midst of thy temple:** ... We have pondered upon thy goodness, *Goodspeed* ... we re-enact the story of thy true love, *NEB* ... We ponder your steadfast love, *NRSV* ... we give thanks for our deliverance, *Knox.*

**10. According to thy name, O God, so is thy praise unto the ends of the earth: thy right hand is full of righteousness:** ... right hand is full of justice, *Beck* ... right hand is filled with victory, *RSV* ... You rule with justice, *Good News.*

**11. Let mount Zion rejoice, let the daughters of Judah be glad, because of thy judgments:** ... The daughters of Judah are joyful, *Young* ... of Judah delight because of your saving justice, *JB* ... Your hand fills the earth with all good, *Fenton* ... because of your wise decisions, *BB.*

**12. Walk about Zion, and go round about her: tell the towers thereof:** ... Go round Zion in procession, count the number of her towers, *REB.*

**13. Mark ye well her bulwarks, consider her palaces; that ye may tell it to the generation following:** ... Set your mind upon her wall, *Goodspeed* ... Notice well her defence-walls, *Berkeley* ... Consider her high places, *Young* ... so you can tell your descendants in the future, *Beck.*

**14. For this God is our God for ever and ever: he will be our guide even**

---

fugitives. No cause for the rout is named. No weapons were drawn in the city. An unseen hand "smites once, and smites no more"; for once is enough. The process of deliverance is not told, for a hymn of victory is not a chronicle. One image explains it all and signals the divine breath as the sole agent. "Thou breakest the ships of Tarshish with an east wind" is not history, but metaphor. The unwieldy, huge vessel, however strong for fight, is unfit for storms and, caught in a gale, rolls heavily in the trough of the sea and is driven on a lee shore and ground to pieces on its rocks. "God blew upon them, and they were scattered," as the medal struck on the defeat of the Armada had. In the companion Psalm, God's uttered voice did all. Here the breath of the tempest, which is the breath of his lips, is the sole agent.

The past, of which the nation had heard from its fathers, lives again in their own history, and that verification of traditional belief by experience is to a devout soul the chief blessing of its deliverances. There is rapture in the thought that "As we have heard, so have we seen." The present ever seems commonplace. The sky is farthest from earth right overhead, but touches the ground on the horizon behind and before. Miracles were in the past; God will be manifestly in the far-off future, but the present is apt to seem empty of Him. But if we rightly mark his dealings with us, we shall learn that nothing in his past has so passed that it is not present. As the companion Psalm says, "The God of Jacob is our refuge," this exclaims, "As we have heard, so have we seen."

**48:9–11.** The third part (vv. 9–14) deals with the praise and trust of the inhabitants of Zion. Deliverance leads to thankful meditation on the steadfast love which it so signally displayed, and the ransomed people first gather in the Temple, which was the scene of God's manifestation of his grace and therefore is the fitting place for them to ponder it. The worldwide consequences of the great act of steadfast love almost shut out of sight for the moment its bearing on the worshipers. It is a lofty height to which the song climbs, when it regards national deliverance chiefly as an occasion for wider diffusion of God's praise. His "name" is the manifestation of his character in act. The psalmist is sure that wherever that character is declared, praise will follow, because he is sure that that character is perfectly and purely good and that God cannot act except in such a way as to magnify himself.

**48:12–14.** The close may be slightly separated from vv. 9ff. The citizens who have been cooped up by the siege are bidden to come forth and, free

| 2172 | 435 | 435 | 5986 | 5911 | 2000 | 5268.321 |
|---|---|---|---|---|---|---|
| dem pron | n mp | n mp, ps 1cp | n ms | cj, n ms | pers pron | v Piel impf 3ms, ps 1cp |
| זֶה | אֱלֹהִים | אֱלֹהֵינוּ | עוֹלָם | וָעֶד | הוּא | יְנַהֲגֵנוּ |
| zeh | 'ĕlōhîm | 'ĕlōhênû | 'ôlām | wā'edh | hû' | yenahghēnû |
| this | God | our God | forever | and everlasting | He | He will guide us |

| 6142, 4322.141 | | 3937, 5514.351 | 3937, 1158, 7432 | 4344 | | 8471.133, 2148 |
|---|---|---|---|---|---|---|
| prep, v Qal inf con | **49:t** | prep, art, v Piel ptc ms | prep, *n mp*, pn | n ms | **1.** | v Qal impv 2mp, dem pron |
| עַל־מוּת | | לַמְנַצֵּחַ | לִבְנֵי־קֹרַח | מִזְמוֹר | | שִׁמְעוּ־זֹאת |
| 'al-mûth | | lamnatstsēach | livnê-qōrach | mizmôr | | shim'û-zō'th |
| unto dying | | to the director | of the sons of Korah | a Psalm | | hear this |

| 3725, 6194 | 237.533 | 3725, 3553.152 | 2566 | | 1612, 1158 | 119 |
|---|---|---|---|---|---|---|
| *adj*, art, n mp | v Hiphil impv 2mp | *adj, v Qal act ptc mp* | n ms | **2.** | cj, *n mp* | n ms |
| כָּל־הָעַמִּים | הַאֲזִינוּ | כָּל־יֹשְׁבֵי | חָלֶד | | גַּם־בְּנֵי | אָדָם |
| kol-hā'ammîm | ha'ăzînû | kol-yōshevê | chāledh | | gam-benê | 'ādhām |
| all the peoples | listen | all the dwellers of | the world | | both the sons of | humankind |

| 1612, 1158, 382 | 3266 | 6474 | 33 | | 6552 | 1744.321 | 2554 |
|---|---|---|---|---|---|---|---|
| cj, *n mp*, n ms | adv | n ms | cj, n ms | **3.** | n ms, ps 1cs | v Piel impf 3ms | n fp |
| גַּם־בְּנֵי־אִישׁ | יַחַד | עָשִׁיר | וְאֶבְיוֹן | | פִּי | יְדַבֵּר | חָכְמוֹת |
| gam-benê-'îsh | yachadh | 'āshîr | we'evyôn | | pî | yedhabbēr | chokhmôth |
| and the sons of one man | together | the rich | and the needy | | my mouth | it will speak | wisdom |

| 1967 | 3949 | 8722 | | 5371.525 | 3937, 5091 | 238 |
|---|---|---|---|---|---|---|
| cj, *n fs* | n ms, ps 1cs | n fp | **4.** | v Hiphil impf 1cs | prep, n ms | n fs, ps 1cs |
| וְהָגוּת | לִבִּי | תְבוּנוֹת | | אַטֶּה | לְמָשָׁל | אָזְנִי |
| wehāghûth | libbî | thevûnôth | | 'atteh | lemāshāl | 'āzenî |
| and the meditation of | my heart | understanding | | I will incline | to a proverb | my ear |

| 6858.125 | 904, 3780 | 2512 | | 4066 | 3486.125 | 904, 3219 | 7737 |
|---|---|---|---|---|---|---|---|
| v Qal impf 1cs | prep, n ms | n fs, ps 1cs | **5.** | intrg | v Qal impf 1cs | prep, *n mp* | n ms |
| אֶפְתַּח | בְּכִנּוֹר | חִידָתִי | | לָמָּה | אִירָא | בִּימֵי | רָע |
| 'ephtach | bekhinnôr | chîdhāthî | | lāmmāh | 'îrā' | bîmê | rā' |
| I will uncover | with the zither | my riddle | | why | will I be afraid | in the days of | evil |

| 5988 | 6357 | 5621.121 | | 1019.152 | 6142, 2524 |
|---|---|---|---|---|---|
| *n ms* | n mp, ps 1cs | v Qal impf 3ms, ps 1cs | **6.** | art, v Qal act ptc mp | prep, n ms, ps 3mp |
| עֲוֹן | עֲקֵבַי | יְסוּבֵּנִי | | הַבֹּטְחִים | עַל־חֵילָם |
| 'ăwōn | 'ăqēvay | yesûbbēnî | | habbōṯechîm | 'al-chêlām |
| the transgression of | my heels | it surrounds me | | those who trust | on their wealth |

| 904, 7524 | 6484 | 2054.726 | | 250 | 3940, 6540.142 |
|---|---|---|---|---|---|
| cj, prep, *n ms* | n ms, ps 3mp | v Hithpoel impf 3mp | **7.** | n ms | neg part, v Qal inf abs |
| וּבְרֹב | עָשְׁרָם | יִתְהַלָּלוּ | | אָח | לֹא־פָדֹה |
| ûverōv | 'āsherām | yithhallālû | | 'āch | lō'-phādhōh |
| and in the abundance of | their riches | they boast | | a brother | not ransoming |

**unto death:** … He will be our guide forever, *NRSV* … our Shepherd eternally, *Knox* … He will guide us from now on, *NCV.*

**49:1. To the chief Musician, A Psalm for the sons of Korah.**

**1. Hear this, all ye people; give ear, all ye inhabitants of the world:** … all who live in this world, *NIV* … LISTEN, you nations far and wide, *Knox* … inhabitants of this passing world, *Rotherham* … all you nations, *NEB.*

**2. Both low and high, rich and poor, together:** … together rich and needy, *Young* … Of lowly birth or high degree, *NAB* … the poor, and those who have wealth, *BB* … Sons of men, and all mankind, *Goodspeed.*

**3. My mouth shall speak of wisdom; and the meditation of my heart shall be of understanding:** … my heart good sense to whisper, *JB* … thoughts of my heart shall be of insight, *Berkeley* … prudence shall be the utterance of my **heart**,

*NCB* ... heart speaks with understanding, *NCV.*

**4. I will incline mine ear to a parable: I will open my dark saying upon the harp:** ... I will open my riddle, *Darby* ... and interpret a mystery to the music of the lyre, *REB* ... with a lyre clarify my puzzling thoughts, *Beck.*

**5. Wherefore should I fear in the days of evil, when the iniquity of my heels shall compass me about?:** ... And the wicked surrounding my feet, *Fenton* ... iniquity of my foes surrounds me, *NASB* ... wicked deceivers surround me, *NIV* ... my persecutors surrounds me, *RSV.*

**6. They that trust in their wealth, and boast themselves in the multitude of their riches:** ... trust in their money and brag about their riches, *NCV* ... brag of how very rich they are, *Beck* ... boast of their great possessions, *Knox* ... Those who trust on their power, *Fenton.*

**7. None of them can by any means redeem his brother, nor give to God a ransom for him:** ... no man can ever ransom himself nor pay God the price of that release, *NEB* ... Or give a price for himself to God, *Goodspeed* ... not give to God his atonement, *Young* ... none can buy himself off, *Moffatt.*

---

from fear, to compass the city without and pass between its palaces within and so see how untouched they are. The towers and bulwark or rampart remain unharmed with not a stone smitten from its place. Within, the palaces stand without a trace of damage to their beauty. Whatever perishes in any assault, that which is of God will abide. After all musterings of the enemy, the uncaptured walls will rise in undiminished strength, and the fair palaces which they guard glitter in untarnished splendor. And this complete exemption from harm is to be told to the generation following that they may learn what a God this God is, and how safely and well He will guide all generations.

***Psalm 49.*** *After a solemn summons to all the world to hear the psalmist's utterance of what he has learned by divine teaching (vv. 1–4), the Psalm is divided into two parts, each closed with a refrain. The former of these (vv. 5–12) contrasts the arrogant security of the prosperous godless with the end that awaits them, while the second (vv. 13–20) contrasts the dreary lot of these victims of vain self-confidence with the blessed reception after death into God's own presence, which the psalmist grasped as a certainty for himself and thereon bases an exhortation to possess souls in patience while the godless prosper and to be sure that their lofty structures will topple into hideous ruin.*

**49:1–3.** The psalmist calls for universal attention, not only because his lessons fit all classes, but because they are in themselves "wisdom" and because he himself had first bent his ear to receive them before he strung his lyre to utter them. The fellow-psalmist, in Ps. 73, presents himself as struggling with doubt and painfully groping his way to his conclusion. This psalmist presents himself as a divinely inspired teacher who has received into purged and attentive ears, in many a whisper from God, and as the result of many an hour of silent waiting, the word which he would now proclaim on the housetops. The discipline of the teacher of religious truth is the same at all times. There must be the bent ear before there is the message which men will recognize as important and true.

**49:4–6.** There is no parable in the ordinary sense in the Psalm. The word seems to have acquired the wider meaning of a weighty didactic utterance, as in Ps. 78:2. The expression "Open my riddle" is ambiguous and is by some understood to mean the proposal and by others, the solution of the puzzle; but the phrase is more naturally understood of solving than of setting a riddle, and if so, the disproportion between the characters and fortunes of good and bad is the mystery or riddle, and the Psalm is its solution.

How vain the boasting in wealth when all its heaps cannot buy a day of life! This familiar thought is not all the psalmist's contribution to the solution of the mystery of life's unequal partition of worldly good, but it prepares the way for it, and it lays a foundation for his refusal to be afraid, however pressed by insolent enemies. Very significantly, he sets the conclusion, to which observation of the transience of human prosperity has led him, at the beginning of his "parable."

**49:7–9.** It is necessary to observe that there is no reference here to any other "redemption" than that of the body from physical death. There is a distinct intention to contrast the man's limited power with God's, for v. 15 points back to this verse and declares that God can do what man cannot. Verse 8 must be taken as a parenthesis, and the construction carried on from vv. 7 to 9, which specifies the purpose of the ransom, if it were possible. No man can secure for another continuous life or an escape from the necessity of seeing the pit—going down to the

| 6540.121 | 382 | 3940, 5598.121 | 3937, 435 | 3853 | | 3478.121 |
|---|---|---|---|---|---|---|
| v Qal impf 3ms | n ms | neg part, v Qal impf 3ms | prep, n mp | n ms, ps 3ms | 8. | cj, v Qal impf 3ms |
| יִפְדֶּה | אִישׁ | לֹא־יִתֵּן | לֵאלֹהִים | כָּפְרוֹ | | וְיֵקַר |
| yiphdeh | 'îsh | lō'-yittēn | lē'lōhîm | kāpherô | | weyēqar |
| he completely ransoms | a man | he does not give | to God | his ransom | | for it is costly |

| 6548 | 5497 | 2403.111 | 3937, 5986 | | 2513.121, 5968 |
|---|---|---|---|---|---|
| *n ms* | n fs, ps 3mp | cj, v Qal pf 3ms | prep, n ms | 9. | cj, v Qal juss 3ms, adv |
| פִּדְיוֹן | נַפְשָׁם | וְחָדַל | לְעוֹלָם | | וִיחִי־עוֹד |
| pidhyôn | naphshām | wechādhal | le'ôlām | | wîchî-'ôdh |
| the redemption of | their life | so it has ceased | unto everlasting | | and may he live continually |

| 3937, 5516 | 3940 | 7495.121 | 8273 | | 3706 | 7495.121 | 2550 | 4322.126 |
|---|---|---|---|---|---|---|---|---|
| prep, art, n ms | neg part | v Qal impf 3ms | art, n fs | 10. | cj | v Qal impf 3ms | n mp | v Qal impf 3mp |
| לָנֶצַח | לֹא | יִרְאֶה | הַשָּׁחַת | | כִּי | יִרְאֶה | חֲכָמִים | יָמוּתוּ |
| lanetsach | lō' | yir'eh | hashshāchath | | kî | yir'eh | chăkhāmîm | yāmûthû |
| unto forever | not | he will see | the Pit | | indeed | he will see | the wise | they die |

| 3266 | 3809 | 1221 | 6.126 | 6013.116 | 3937, 311 | 2524 |
|---|---|---|---|---|---|---|
| adv | n ms | cj, n ms | v Qal impf 3mp | cj, v Qal pf 3cp | prep, adj | n ms, ps 3mp |
| יַחַד | כְּסִיל | וָבַעַר | יֹאבֵדוּ | וְעָזְבוּ | לַאֲחֵרִים | חֵילָם |
| yachadh | kesîl | wāva'ar | yō'vēdhû | we'āzevû | la'ăchērîm | chêlām |
| together | the foolish | and the stupid | they perish | and they are abandoned | to others | their wealth |

| | 7419 | 1041 | 3937, 5986 | 5088 | 3937, 1810 |
|---|---|---|---|---|---|
| 11. | n ms, ps 3mp | n mp, ps 3mp | prep, n ms | n mp, ps 3mp | prep, n ms |
| | קִרְבָּם | בָּתֵּימוֹ | לְעוֹלָם | מִשְׁכְּנֹתָם | לְדֹר |
| | qirbām | bātêmô | le'ôlām | mishkenōthām | ledhōr |
| | their inmost being | their households | unto eternity | their dwelling places | unto generations |

| 1810 | 7410.116 | 904, 8428 | 6142 | 124 | | 119 |
|---|---|---|---|---|---|---|
| cj, n ms | v Qal pf 3cp | prep, n mp, ps 3mp | prep | n fp | 12. | cj, n ms |
| וָדֹר | קָרְאוּ | בִשְׁמוֹתָם | עֲלֵי | אֲדָמוֹת | | וְאָדָם |
| wādhōr | qāre'û | vishmôthām | 'ălê | 'ădhāmôth | | we'ādhām |
| and generations | they called | by their names | on | their lands | | and humankind |

| 904, 3480 | 1118, 4053.121 | 5090.211 | 3626, 966 | 1880.216 |
|---|---|---|---|---|
| prep, n ms | neg part, v Qal impf 3ms | v Niphal pf 3ms | prep, art, n fp | v Niphal pf 3cp |
| בִּיקָר | בַּל־יָלִין | נִמְשַׁל | כַּבְּהֵמוֹת | נִדְמוּ |
| bîqār | bal-yālîn | nimshal | kabbehēmôth | nidhmû |
| with costly goods | he will not stay | he is like | like the beasts | they have become silent |

| | 2172 | 1932 | 3815 | 3937 | 313 | 904, 6552 |
|---|---|---|---|---|---|---|
| 13. | dem pron | n ms, ps 3mp | n ms | prep, ps 3mp | cj, prep, ps 3mp | prep, n ms, ps 3mp |
| | זֶה | דַרְכָּם | כֵּסֶל | לָמוֹ | וְאַחֲרֵיהֶם | בְּפִיהֶם |
| | zeh | dharkām | kesel | lāmô | we'achrêhem | bephîhem |
| | this | they way | foolishness | to them | and after them | with their mouth |

| 7813.126 | 5734 | | 3626, 6887 | 3937, 8061 | 8308.116 | 4323 |
|---|---|---|---|---|---|---|
| v Qal impf 3mp | intrj | 14. | prep, art, n fs | prep, pn | v Qal pf 3cp | n ms |
| יִרְצוּ | סֶלָה | | כַּצֹּאן | לִשְׁאוֹל | שַׁתּוּ | מָוֶת |
| yirtsû | selāh | | katstsō'n | lish'ôl | shattû | māweth |
| they take pleasure | selah | | like the sheep | to Sheol | they have been appointed | death |

| 7749.121 | 7575.126 | 904 | 3596 | 3937, 1269 | 7007 |
|---|---|---|---|---|---|
| v Qal impf 3ms, ps 3mp | cj, v Qal impf 3mp | prep, ps 3mp | n mp | prep, art, n ms | cj, n ms, ps 3mp |
| יִרְעֵם | וַיִּרְדּוּ | בָם | יְשָׁרִים | לַבֹּקֶר | וְצִירָם |
| yir'ēm | wayyirdû | vām | yeshārîm | labbōqer | wetsîrām |
| it will shepherd them | and they will rule | over them | the upright | at the morning | and their form |

| 3937, 1126.341 | 8061 | 4623, 2166 | 3937 | | 395, 435 | 6540.121 | 5497 |
|---|---|---|---|---|---|---|---|
| prep, v Piel inf con | pn | prep, n ms | prep, ps 3ms | | adv, n mp | v Qal impf 3ms | n fs, ps 1cs |
| לְבַלּוֹת | שְׁאוֹל | מִזְּבֻל | לוֹ | 15. | אַךְ־אֱלֹהִים | יִפְדֶּה | נַפְשִׁי |
| levallôth | she'ôl | mizzevul | lô | | 'akh-'ĕlōhîm | yiphdeh | naphshî |
| for the decaying of | Sheol | of dwelling | to them | | surely God | He will ransom | my soul |

**8. (For the redemption of their soul is precious, and it ceaseth for ever:):** ... because the price of a life is high, *NCV* ... he shall cease forever, *Anchor* ... redemption of their life is costly and can never suffice, *Berkeley* ... And must be let alone for ever, *MRB*.

**9. That he should still live for ever, and not see corruption:** ... should live on forever and never see the grave, *NRSV* ... or avoid the grave, *Beck* ... he might have eternal life, and never see the underworld, *BB* ... live on forever and not see decay, *NIV*.

**10. For he seeth that wise men die, likewise the fool and the brutish person perish, and leave their wealth to others:** ... the senseless and the stupid pass away, *NCB* ... And to others abandon their power, *Fenton* ... their riches will go to others, *Knox* ... and leave their wealth behind, *JB*

**11. Their inward thought is, that their houses shall continue for ever, and their dwelling places to all generations; they call their lands after their own names:** ... Their heart is: Their houses are to the age, *Young* ... those who come after them give their names to their lands, *BB* ... Though they give their names to estates, the grave is their eternal home, *REB*.

**12. Nevertheless man being in honour abideth not: he is like the beasts that perish:** ... But man, though high in honor, does not remain, *KJVII* ... But a son of earth though wealthy cannot tarry, *Rotherham* ... But man is an ox without understanding, *Goodspeed* ... Short is man's enjoyment of earthly goods, *Knox*.

**13. This their way is their folly: yet their posterity approve their sayings. Selah:** ... Such is the fate of the self-satisfied, *Moffatt* ... This is what will happen to those who trust in themselves, *NCV* ... and of all who seek to please them, *NEB* ... and those coming after them who like what they said, *Beck*.

**14. Like sheep they are laid in the grave; death shall feed on them:** ... Death shall be their shepherd, *NRSV* ... Like sheep they are appointed for the nether-world, *MAST*.

**and the upright shall have dominion over them in the morning; and their beauty shall consume in the grave from their dwelling:** ... and those who are honest will rule over them, *JB* ... And their form shall be for Sheol to consume, *NASB*.

**15. But God will redeem my soul from the power of the grave: for he shall receive me. Selah:** ... But God will ransom me, from the hand of Sheol, *Anchor* ... for he will take me

depths of death. It would cost more than all the rich man's store; wherefore he, the would-be ransomer, must abandon the attempt forever.

**49:10–13.** Like the godless man in Ps. 10, this rich man has reached a height of false security, which cannot be put into words without exposing its absurdity, but which still haunts his inmost thoughts. The fond imagination of perpetuity is not driven out by the plain facts of life and death. He acts on the presumption of permanence.

Then comes with a crash the stern refrain which pulverizes all this insanity of arrogance. The highest distinction among men gives no exemption from the grim law which holds all corporeal life in its gripe. The psalmist does not look, and probably did not see, beyond the external fact of death. He knows nothing of a future for the men whose portion is in this life. As we shall see in the second part of the Psalm, the confidence in immortality is for him a deduction from the fact of communion with God here, and, apparently, his bent ear had received no whisper as to any distinction between the godless man and the beast in regard to their deaths. They are alike "brought to silence." The awful dumbness of the dead strikes on his heart and imagination as most pathetic. That skull had a tongue in it and could sing once, but now the pale lips are locked in eternal silence, and some ears hunger in vain for the sound of a voice that is still.

**49:14–15.** To this condition of dismal inactivity, as of sheep penned in a fold, of loss of beauty, of wasting and homelessness, the psalmist opposes the fate which he has risen to anticipate for himself. Verse 15 is plainly antithetical, not only to v. 14, but to v. 7. The "redemption" which was impossible with men is possible with God. The emphatic particle of asseveration and restriction at the beginning (HED #395) is, as we have remarked, characteristic of the parallel Ps. 63. It here strengthens the expression of confidence, and points to God as alone able to deliver his servant from the "hand of Sheol." That deliverance is clearly not escape from the universal lot, as the second clause of the verse makes emphatic.

| 4623, 3135, 8061 | 3706 | 4089.121 | 5734 | 16. | 414, 3486.123 |
|---|---|---|---|---|---|
| prep, *n fs*, pn | cj | v Qal impf 3ms, ps 1cs | intrj | | adv, Qal juss 2ms |
| מִיַּד־שְׁאוֹל | כִּי | יִקָּחֵנִי | סֶלָה | | אַל־תִּירָא |
| mîyadh-sheʾôl | kî | yiqqāchēnî | selāh | | 'al-tîrā' |
| from the hand of Sheol | because | He will receive me | selah | | do not be afraid |

| 3706, 6483.521 | 382 | 3706, 7528.121 | 3638 | 1041 | 17. | 3706 |
|---|---|---|---|---|---|---|
| cj, v Hiphil impf 3ms | n ms | cj, v Qal impf 3ms | *n ms* | n ms, ps 3ms | | cj |
| כִּי־יַעֲשִׁר | אִישׁ | כִּי־יִרְבֶּה | כְּבוֹד | בֵּיתוֹ | | כִּי |
| kî-ya'ăshir | 'îsh | kî-yirbeh | kevôdh | bêthô | | kî |
| when he becomes rich | a man | when it is abundant | the glory of | his household | | because |

| 3940 | 904, 4323 | 4089.121 | 3725 | 3940, 3495.121 | 313 | 3638 |
|---|---|---|---|---|---|---|
| neg part | prep, n ms, ps 3ms | v Qal impf 3ms | art, n ms | neg part, v Qal impf 3ms | prep, ps 3ms | n ms, ps 3ms |
| לֹא | בְמוֹתוֹ | יִקַּח | הַכֹּל | לֹא־יֵרֵד | אַחֲרָיו | כְּבוֹדוֹ |
| lō' | vemôthô | yiqqach | hakkōl | lō'-yērēdh | 'achrâv | kevôdhô |
| not | when his death | he will take | everything | it will not go down | after him | his glory |

| 18. | 3706, 5497 | 904, 2522 | 1313.321 | 3142.526 |
|---|---|---|---|---|
| | cj, n fs, ps 3ms | prep, n mp, ps 3ms | v Piel impf 3ms | cj, v Hiphil impf 3mp, ps 2ms |
| | כִּי־נַפְשׁוֹ | בְּחַיָּיו | יְבָרֵךְ | וְיוֹדֻךָ |
| | kî-naphshô | bechayyâv | yevārēkh | weyôdhukhā |
| | because his life | during his lifetime | he declares blessed | and they praise you |

| 3706, 3296.523 | 3937 | 19. | 971.123 | 5912, 1810 | 1 |
|---|---|---|---|---|---|
| cj, v Hiphil impf 2ms | prep, ps 2ms | | v Qal impf 2ms | prep, *n ms* | n mp, ps 3ms |
| כִּי־תֵיטִיב | לָךְ | | תָּבוֹא | עַד־דּוֹר | אֲבוֹתָיו |
| kî-thêṭîv | lākh | | tāvô' | 'adh-dôr | 'ăvôthâv |
| because you seem good | to yourself | | you will go | to the generation of | his ancestors |

| 5912, 5516 | 3940, 7495.121 | 214 | 20. | 119 | 904, 3480 | 3940 |
|---|---|---|---|---|---|---|
| adv, n ms | neg part, v Qal impf 3ms | n ms | | n ms | prep, n ms | cj, neg part |
| עַד־נֵצַח | לֹא־יִרְאוּ | אוֹר | | אָדָם | בִּיקָר | וְלֹא |
| 'adh-nētsach | lō'-yir'û | 'ôr | | 'ādhām | bîqār | welō' |
| until forever | he will not see | light | | humankind | with costly goods | and not |

| 1032.121 | 5090.211 | 3626, 966 | 1880.216 | 50:t | 4344 | 3937, 637 |
|---|---|---|---|---|---|---|
| v Qal impf 3ms | v Niphal pf 3ms | prep, art, n fp | v Niphal pf 3cp | | n ms | prep, pn |
| יָבִין | נִמְשַׁל | כַּבְּהֵמוֹת | נִדְמוּ | | מִזְמוֹר | לְאָסָף |
| yāvîn | nimshal | kabbehēmôth | nidhmû | | mizmôr | le'āsāph |
| he discerns | he is like | like the beasts | they have become silent | | a Psalm | of Asaph |

| 1. | 418 | 435 | 3176 | 1744.311 | 7410.121, 800 | 4623, 4350, 8507 |
|---|---|---|---|---|---|---|
| | n ms | n mp | pn | v Piel pf 3ms | cj, v Qal impf 3ms, n fs | prep, *n ms*, n fs |
| | אֵל | אֱלֹהִים | יְהוָה | דִּבֶּר | וַיִּקְרָא־אָרֶץ | מִמִּזְרַח־שֶׁמֶשׁ |
| | 'ēl | 'ĕlōhîm | yehwāh | dibber | wayyiqŏrā'-'ārets | mimmizrach-shemesh |
| | God | God | Yahweh | He speaks | and He summons the earth | from the rising of the sun |

| 5912, 4136 | 2. | 4623, 6995 | 4497, 3418 | 435 | 3423.511 | 3. | 971.121 |
|---|---|---|---|---|---|---|---|
| adv, n ms, ps 3ms | | prep, pn | *n ms*, n ms | n mp | v Hiphil pf 3ms | | v Qal juss 3ms |
| עַד־מְבֹאוֹ | | מִצִּיּוֹן | מִכְלַל־יֹפִי | אֱלֹהִים | הוֹפִיעַ | | יָבֹא |
| 'adh-mevō'ô | | mitstsîyôn | mikhlal-yōphî | 'ĕlōhîm | hôphîa' | | yāvō' |
| until its setting | | from Zion | perfection of beauty | God | He has shone forth | | may He come |

| 435 | 414, 2896.121 | 813, 3937, 6686 | 404.122 | 5623 |
|---|---|---|---|---|
| n mp, ps 1cp | cj, adv, v Qal juss 3ms | n fs, prep, n mp, ps 3ms | v Qal impf 3fs | cj, prep, ps 3ms |
| אֱלֹהֵינוּ | וְאַל־יֶחֱרַשׁ | אֵשׁ־לְפָנָיו | תֹּאכֵל | וּסְבִיבָיו |
| 'ĕlōhênû | we'al-yechĕrash | 'ēsh-lephānâv | tō'khēl | ûsevîvâv |
| our God | and may He not keep silent | fire before Him | it devours | and all around Him |

from the power of death, *BB* ... But GOD will deliver my life, *Fenton* ... he will surely take me to himself, *NIV.*

**16. Be not thou afraid when one is made rich, when the glory of his house is increased:** ... Do not be overawed when a man grows rich, *NIV* ... Be not envious when a man grows rich, *Anchor* ... and lives in ever greater splendour, *JB* ... when the wealth of his house becomes great, *NCB.*

**17. For when he dieth he shall carry nothing away: his glory shall not descend after him:** ... For when he dies, he shall take none of it, *NAB* ... For at his death he receiveth nothing, *Young* ... magnificence will not follow him to the grave, *Knox* ... and his wealth will not go with him, *NEB.*

**18. Though while he lived he blessed his soul: and men will praise thee, when thou doest well to thyself:** ... Though while he lives he congratulates himself, *NASB* ... Though in his lifetime he counts himself happy, *REB* ... Even though they were praised when they were alive, *NCV* ... and people praise you, when you do well for yourself, *Berkeley.*

**19. He shall go to the generation of his fathers; they shall never see light:** ... but he will join his fathers who lived before him, *Beck* ... he shall join the circle of his forebears, *NCB* ... they will go to the company of their ancestors, *NRSV* ... and they shall not liue for euer, *Geneva.*

**20. Man that is in honour, and understandeth not, is like the beasts that perish:** ... A son of earth though wealthy who discerneth not, *Rotherham* ... Men in honour, and yet without sense, *Fenton* ... Man, like the animals, does not go on for ever, *BB* ... Man cannot abide in his pomp, *RSV.*

**50:t. A Psalm of Asaph.**

**The mighty God, even the LORD, hath spoken, and called the earth from the rising of the sun unto the going down thereof:** ... and summoned the world from the rising to the setting sun, *NEB* ... has sent out his voice, and the earth is full of fear, *BB* ... his message goes out to all the earth, *Knox* ... from east to west he summons the earth, *JB.*

**2. Out of Zion, the perfection of beauty, God hath shined:** ... God shines from Jerusalem, whose beauty is perfect, *NCV* ... God appears in glory-light, *Berkeley* ... GOD's perfect beauty shines from Zion, *Fenton* ... the city perfect in its beauty, *Good News.*

**3. Our God shall come, and shall not keep silence: a fire shall devour before him, and it shall be very tempestuous round about him:** ... around him a raging tempest, *Anchor* ... and it shall be very stormy all around Him, *KJVII* ... a great storm rages round about him, *LIVB.*

---

**49:16–20.** As the first part began with the psalmist encouraging himself to put away fear, so the whole ends with the practical application of the truths declared, in the exhortation to others not to be terrified or bewildered out of their faith by the insolent inflated prosperity of the godless. The lofty height of wholesome mysticism reached in the anticipation of personal immortality is not maintained in this closing part. The ground of the exhortation is simply the truth proclaimed in the first part with additional emphasis on the thought of the necessary parting from all wealth and pomp. Shrouds have no pockets. All the external is left behind, and much of the inward too—such as habits, desires, ways of thinking and acquirements which have been directed to and bounded by the seen and temporal. What is not left behind is character and desert. The man of this world is wrenched from his possessions by death, but he who has made God his portion here carries his portion with him and does not enter into that other state in utter nakedness. But it is hard for them that trust in riches to enter into the kingdom! (Matt. 19:23).

***Psalm 50.*** *This is the first of the Asaph Psalms. The structure is clear and simple. There is, first, a magnificent description of God's coming to judgment and summoning heaven and earth to witness while He judges his people (vv. 1–6). The second part (vv. 7–15) proclaims the worthlessness of sacrifice; and the third (vv. 16–21) brands hypocrites who pollute God's statutes by taking them into their lips while their lives are foul. A closing strophe of two verses (22f) gathers up the double lesson of the whole.*

**50:1–3.** The earth from east to west is summoned, not to be judged, but to witness God judging his people. The peculiarity of this theophany is that God is not represented as coming from afar or from above, but as letting his light blaze out from Zion, where He sits enthroned. As his presence made the city "the joy of the whole earth" (Ps. 48:2), so it makes Zion the sum of all beauty. The idea underlying the representation of his shining out of Zion is that his presence among his people makes certain his judgment of their worship. It is the poetic clothing of the prophetic announcement, "You only have I known of all the families of the earth; therefore will I punish you for all your iniquities" (Amos 3:2). The seer beholds the dread pomp of the advent of the judge and describes it with accessories familiar in such pictures: devour-

| 7994.212 | 4108 | | 7410.121 | 420, 8452 | 4623, 6142 | 420, 800 |
|---|---|---|---|---|---|---|
| v Niphal pf 3fs | adv | | v Qal impf 3ms | prep, art, n md | prep, prep | cj, prep, art, n fs |
| נִשְׂעֲרָה | מְאֹד | 4. | יִקְרָא | אֶל־הַשָּׁמַיִם | מֵעָל | וְאֶל־הָאָרֶץ |
| nis‘ārāh | me’ōdh | | yiqrā’ | ’el-hashshāmayim | mē‘āl | we’el-hā’ārets |
| it is tempestuous | very | | He calls | to the heavens | from above | and to the earth |

| 3937, 1833.141 | 6194 | | 636.133, 3937 | 2728 | 3901.152 |
|---|---|---|---|---|---|
| prep, v Qal inf con | n ms, ps 3ms | | v Qal impv 2mp, prep, ps 1cs | n mp, ps 1cs | *v Qal act ptc mp* |
| לָדִין | עַמּוֹ | 5. | אִסְפוּ־לִי | חֲסִידָי | כֹּרְתֵי |
| lādhîn | ‘ammô | | ’isphû-lî | chăsîdhāy | kōrethê |
| to judge | his people | | gather to Me | my godly ones | the ones who cut |

| 1311 | 6142, 2160 | | 5222.526 | 8452 | 6928 | 3706, 435 |
|---|---|---|---|---|---|---|
| n fs, ps 1cs | prep, n ms | | cj, v Hiphil impf 3mp | n md | n ms, ps 3ms | cj, n mp |
| בְרִיתִי | עֲלֵי־זָבַח | 6. | וַיַּגִּידוּ | שָׁמַיִם | צִדְקוֹ | כִּי־אֱלֹהִים |
| verîthî | ‘ălê-zāvach | | wayyaggîdhû | shāmayim | tsidhqô | kî-’ĕlōhîm |
| my Covenant | on a sacrifice | | and they tell | the heavens | his righteousness | because God |

| 8570.151 | 2000 | 5734 | | 8471.131 | 6194 | 1744.325 | 3547 |
|---|---|---|---|---|---|---|---|
| v Qal act ptc ms | pers pron | intrj | | v Qal impv 2ms | n ms, ps 1cs | cj, v Piel juss 1cs | pn |
| שֹׁפֵט | הוּא | סֶלָה | 7. | שִׁמְעָה | עַמִּי | וַאֲדַבֵּרָה | יִשְׂרָאֵל |
| shōphēt | hû’ | selāh | | shim‘āh | ‘ammî | wa’ădhabbērāh | yisrā’ēl |
| a Judge | He | selah | | hear | O my people | and let Me speak | O Israel |

| 5967.525 | 904 | 435 | 435 | 609 | | 3940 |
|---|---|---|---|---|---|---|
| cj, v Hiphil juss 1cs | prep, ps 2ms | n mp | n mp, ps 2ms | pers pron | | neg part |
| וְאָעִידָה | בָּךְ | אֱלֹהִים | אֱלֹהֶיךָ | אָנֹכִי | 8. | לֹא |
| we’ā‘îdhāh | bākh | ’ĕlōhîm | ’ĕlōhêkhā | ’ānōkhî | | lō’ |
| and let Me testify | against you | God | your God | I | | not |

| 6142, 2160 | 3306.525 | 6150 | 3937, 5224 |
|---|---|---|---|
| prep, n mp, ps 2ms | v Hiphil impf 1cs, ps 2ms | cj, n fp, ps 2ms | prep, prep, ps 1cs |
| עַל־זְבָחֶיךָ | אוֹכִיחֶךָ | וְעוֹלֹתֶיךָ | לְנֶגְדִּי |
| ‘al-zevāchêkhā | ’ôkhîchekhā | we‘ôlōthêkhā | leneghdî |
| concerning your sacrifices | I will rebuke you | nor your burnt offerings | before me |

| 8878 | | 3940, 4089.125 | 4623, 1041 | 6749 | 4623, 4494 | 6500 |
|---|---|---|---|---|---|---|
| adv | | neg part, v Qal impf 1cs | prep, n ms, ps 2ms | n ms | prep, n mp, ps 2ms | n mp |
| תָמִיד | 9. | לֹא־אֶקַּח | מִבֵּיתְךָ | פָר | מִמִּכְלְאֹתֶיךָ | עַתּוּדִים |
| thāmîdh | | lō’-’eqqach | mibbêthekhā | phār | mimmikhle’ōthêkhā | ‘attûdhîm |
| continually | | I will not receive | from your household | a young bull | from your folds | he-goats |

| | 3706, 3937 | 3725, 2516, 3402 | 966 | 904, 2121, 512 | | 3156.115 |
|---|---|---|---|---|---|---|
| | cj, prep, ps 1cs | *adj, n fs*, n ms | n fp | prep, *n mp*, num | | v Qal pf 1cs |
| 10. | כִּי־לִי | כָל־חַיְתוֹ־יָעַר | בְּהֵמוֹת | בְּהַרְרֵי־אָלֶף | 11. | יָדַעְתִּי |
| | kî-lî | khol-chaythô-yā‘ar | behēmôth | behar erê-’āleph | | yādha‘ttî |
| | because to Me | all the animals of the forest | the cattle | on one thousand hills | | I know |

| 3725, 5991 | 2098 | 2205 | 7899 | 6200 | | 524, 7742.125 |
|---|---|---|---|---|---|---|
| *adj, n ms* | n mp | cj, *n ms* | n ms | prep, ps 1cs | | cj, v Qal impf 1cs |
| כָּל־עוֹף | הָרִים | וְזִיז | שָׂדָי | עִמָּדִי | 12. | אִם־אֶרְעַב |
| kol-‘ôph | hārîm | wezîz | sādhay | ‘immādhî | | ’im-’er‘av |
| all the birds of | the mountains | and the swarms of | the field | with Me | | if I were hungry |

| 3940, 569.125 | 3937 | 3706, 3937 | 8725 | 4530 | | 404.125 |
|---|---|---|---|---|---|---|
| neg part, v Qal impf 1cs | prep, ps 2ms | cj, prep, ps 1cs | n fs | cj, n ms, ps 3fs | | intrg part, v Qal impf 1cs |
| לֹא־אֹמַר | לָךְ | כִּי־לִי | תֵּבֵל | וּמְלֹאָהּ | 13. | הַאוֹכַל |
| lō’-’ōmar | lākh | kî-lî | thēvēl | ûmelō’āh | | ha’ôkhal |
| I would not say | to you | because to Me | the world | and its fulness | | do I eat |

**4. He shall call to the heavens from above, and to the earth, that he may judge his people:** ... to the trial of his people, *Moffatt* ... he summons heaven and earth to witness the judgement pronounced on his people, *Knox.*

**5. Gather my saints together unto me; those that have made a covenant with me by sacrifice:** ... Gather to me my consecrated ones, *NIV* ... Gather to me my faithful ones, *NRSV* ... who sealed my covenant by sacrifice, *JB* ... Who have solemnised my covenant, *Rotherham.*

**6. And the heavens shall declare his righteousness: for God is judge himself. Selah:** ... The heavens proclaim his saving justice, *JB* ... For God executeth judgment himself, *Darby* ... Which GOD Himself decrees, *Fenton* ... The heavens themselves pronounce him just, *Knox.*

**7. Hear, O my people, and I will speak; O Israel, and I will testify against thee: I am God, even thy God:** ... I will be a witness against you, *BB* ... Here are my charges against you, *LIVB.*

**8. I will not reprove thee for thy sacrifices or thy burnt offerings, to have been continually before me:** ... I do not rebuke you for your sacrifices, *NIV* ... I do not criticize you for your sacrifices, *Beck* ... shall I not find fault with your sacrifices, *NEB* ... for your holocausts are before me always, *NCB.*

**9. I will take no bullock out of thy house, nor he goats out of thy folds:** ... I shall take no young bull out of your house, *NASB* ... But the gifts I accept are not cattle from thy stock, *Knox* ... Nor ram from your folds, *Goodspeed* ... But I do not need bulls from your stalls, *NCV.*

**10. For every beast of the forest is mine, and the cattle upon a thousand hills:** ... beasts by the thousand on my mountains, *NAB* ... For every wild animal of the forest is mine, *NRSV* ... for all the wild things of the wood are mine, *Moffatt* ... the beasts in the towering mountains, *Anchor.*

**11. I know all the fowls of the mountains: and the wild beasts of the field are mine:** ... I own all roaming creatures on the plains, *Moffatt* ... and every living thing in the fields is mine, *NCV* ... the teeming life of the fields is my care, *NEB* ... whatever stirs in the plains, belongs to me, *NAB.*

**12. If I were hungry, I would not tell thee: for the world is mine, and the fulness thereof:** ... for the earth is mine and all its wealth, *BB* ... world is mine and everything in it, *Beck* ... Mine are the whole World's fruits, *Fenton* ... the world and all it holds is mine, *JB.*

---

ing fire is his forerunner, as clearing a path for Him among tangles of evil, and wild tempests whirl around his stable throne. "He cannot be silent"—the form of the negation in the original is emotional or emphatic, conveying the idea of the impossibility of his silence in the face of such corruptions.

**50:4–6.** The opening of the court or preparation for the judgment follows. That divine voice speaks, summoning heaven and earth to attend as spectators of the solemn process. The universal significance of God's relation to and dealings with Israel and the vindication of his righteousness by his inflexible justice dealt out to their faults are grandly taught in this making heaven and earth assessors of that tribunal. The court having been thus constituted, the Judge on his seat and the spectators standing around, the accused are next brought in. There is no need to be prosaically definite as to the attendants who are bidden to escort them. His officers are everywhere, and to ask who they are in the present case is to apply to poetry the measuring lines meant for prose. It is more important to note the name by which the persons to be judged are designated. They are "my favored ones, who have made a covenant with me by sacrifice." These terms carry an indictment, recalling the lavish mercies so unworthily requited and the solemn obligations so unthankfully broken.

**50:7–11.** The second part (vv. 7–15) deals with one of the two permanent tendencies which work for the corruption of religion—namely, the reliance on external worship and neglect of the emotions of thankfulness and trust. God appeals first to the relation into which He has entered with the people, as giving Him the right to judge. There may be a reference to the Mosaic formula, "I am Yahweh, your God," which is here converted, in accordance with the usage of this book of the Psalter, into "God, your God." The formula, which was the seal of laws when enacted, is also the warrant for the action of the Judge. He has no fault to find with the external acts of worship. They are abundant and continually before Him. But the gross stupidity of supposing that man's gift makes the offering to be God's more truly than before is laid bare in the fine, sympathetic glance at the free, wild life of forest, mountain and plain, which is all God's possession, and present to his upholding thought, and by the side of which man's folds are very small affairs. The cattle in v. 10 are not the usual domesticated animals, but the larger wild animals. They graze or roam on the mountains of a thousand.

**50:12–15.** Verses 12f turn the stream of irony on another absurdity involved in the superstition attacked—the grossly material thought of God

| 1340 | 48 | 1879 | 6500 | 8685.125 | | 2159.131 | 3937, 435 |
|---|---|---|---|---|---|---|---|
| *n ms* | adj | cj, *n ms* | n mp | v Qal impf 1cs | **14.** | v Qal impv 2ms | prep, n mp |
| בְּשַׂר | אַבִּירִים | וְדַם | עַתּוּדִים | אֶשְׁתֶּה | | זְבַח | לֵאלֹהִים |
| besar | 'abbîrîm | wedham | 'attûdhîm | 'eshteh | | zevach | lē'lōhîm |
| the meat of | mighty ones | or the blood of | he-goats | do I drink | | sacrifice | to God |

| 8756 | 8396.331 | 3937, 6169 | 5266 | | 7410.131 |
|---|---|---|---|---|---|
| n fs | cj, v Piel impv 2ms | prep, n ms | n mp, ps 2ms | **15.** | cj, v Qal impv 2ms, ps 1cs |
| תּוֹדָה | וְשַׁלֵּם | לְעֶלְיוֹן | נְדָרֶיךָ | | וּקְרָאֵנִי |
| tôdhāh | weshallēm | le'elyôn | nedhārêkhā | | ûqŏrā'ēnî |
| a thank offering | and pay | to the Most High | your vows | | then call Me |

| 904, 3219 | 7150 | 2603.325 | 3632.323 | | 3937, 7857 |
|---|---|---|---|---|---|
| prep, *n ms* | n fs | v Piel impf 1cs, ps 2ms | cj, v Piel impf 2ms, ps 1cs | **16.** | cj, prep, art, n ms |
| בְּיוֹם | צָרָה | אֲחַלֶּצְךָ | וּתְכַבְּדֵנִי | | וְלָרָשָׁע |
| beyôm | tsārāh | 'ăchalletskhā | ûthekhabbedhēnî | | welārāshā' |
| on the day of | trouble | and I will set you apart | and you will glorify Me | | but to the wicked |

| 569.111 | 435 | 4242, 3937 | 5807.341 | 2807 | 5558.123 | 1311 |
|---|---|---|---|---|---|---|
| v Qal pf 3ms | n mp | intrg, prep, ps 2ms | prep, v Piel inf con | n mp, ps 1cs | cj, v Qal impf 2ms | n fs, ps 1cs |
| אָמַר | אֱלֹהִים | מַה־לְּךָ | לְסַפֵּר | חֻקָּי | וַתִּשָּׂא | בְרִיתִי |
| 'āmar | 'ĕlōhîm | mah-lekhā | lesappēr | chuqqāy | wattissā' | verîthî |
| He has said | God | what to you | to recount | my statutes | or to bear | my Covenant |

| 6142, 6552 | | 887 | 7983.113 | 4284 | 8390.523 | 1745 |
|---|---|---|---|---|---|---|
| prep, n ms, ps 2ms | **17.** | cj, pers pron | v Qal pf 2ms | n ms | cj, v Hiphil impf 2ms | n mp, ps 1cs |
| עֲלֵי־פִיךָ | | וְאַתָּה | שָׂנֵאתָ | מוּסָר | וַתַּשְׁלֵךְ | דְּבָרַי |
| 'ălê-phîkhā | | we'attāh | sānē'thā | mûsār | wattashlēkh | devāray |
| on your mouth | | for you | you hate | chastisement | and you throw away | my words |

| 313 | | 524, 7495.113 | 1631 | 7813.123 | 6196 | 6196 |
|---|---|---|---|---|---|---|
| prep, ps 2ms | **18.** | cj, v Qal pf 2ms | n ms | cj, v Qal impf 2ms | prep, ps 3ms | cj, prep |
| אַחֲרֶיךָ | | אִם־רָאִיתָ | גַנָּב | וַתִּרֶץ | עִמּוֹ | וְעִם |
| 'achrêkhā | | 'im-rā'îthā | ghannāv | wattirets | 'immô | we'im |
| behind you | | if you have seen | a thief | then you are favorably disposed | with him | and with |

| 5178.352 | 2610 | | 6552 | 8365.113 | 904, 7750 | 4098 |
|---|---|---|---|---|---|---|
| v Piel ptc mp | n ms, ps 2ms | **19.** | n ms, ps 2ms | v Qal pf 2ms | prep, n fs | cj, n fs, ps 2ms |
| מְנָאֲפִים | חֶלְקֶךָ | | פִּיךָ | שָׁלַחְתָּ | בְרָעָה | וּלְשׁוֹנְךָ |
| menā'ăphîm | chelqekhā | | pîkhā | shālachtā | verā'āh | ûlăshônkhā |
| adulterers | your portion | | your mouth | you have put forth | with evil | so your tongue |

| 7044.522 | 4983 | | 3553.123 | 904, 250 | 1744.323 |
|---|---|---|---|---|---|
| v Hiphil impf 3fs | n fs | **20.** | v Qal impf 2ms | prep, n ms, ps 2ms | v Piel impf 2ms |
| תַּצְמִיד | מִרְמָה | | תֵּשֵׁב | בְּאָחִיךָ | תְדַבֵּר |
| tatsmîdh | mirmāh | | tēshēv | be'āchîkhā | thedhabbēr |
| it harnesses | deceit | | you sit | against your brother | you speak |

| 904, 1158, 525 | 5598.123, 1908 | | 431 | 6449.113 | 2896.515 |
|---|---|---|---|---|---|
| prep, *n ms*, n fs, ps 2ms | v Qal impf 2ms, n ms | **21.** | dem pron | v Qal pf 2ms | cj, v Hiphil pf 1cs |
| בְּבֶן־אִמְּךָ | תִּתֶּן־דֹּפִי | | אֵלֶּה | עָשִׂיתָ | וְהֶחֱרַשְׁתִּי |
| beven-'immekhā | titten-dōphî | | 'ēlleh | 'āsîthā | wehecherashtî |
| against the son of your mother | you give damage | | these | you have done | yet I was silent |

| 1880.313 | 2030.141, 2030.125 | 3765 | 3306.525 |
|---|---|---|---|
| v Piel pf 2ms | v Qal inf con, v Qal impf 1cs | prep, ps 2ms | v Hiphil juss 1cs, ps 2ms |
| דִּמִּיתָ | הֱיוֹת־אֶהְיֶה | כָמוֹךָ | אוֹכִיחֲךָ |
| dimmîthā | hĕyôth-'ehyeh | khāmôkhā | 'ôkhîchăkhā |
| you thought | I was being | like you | let me argue a case against you |

**13. Will I eat the flesh of bulls, or drink the blood of goats?:** ... eat the flesh of oxen, *Goodspeed* ... eat the flesh of mighty oxen, *Rotherham* ... blood of male goats, *NASB* ... I don't need your sacrifices of flesh and blood, *LIVB*.

**14. Offer unto God thanksgiving; and pay thy vows unto the most High:** ... Offer to God praise as your sacrifice, *Anchor* ... The sacrifice thou must offer to God is a sacrifice of praise, *Knox* ... Sacrifice thank offerings to God, *NIV*.

**15. And call upon me in the day of trouble: I will deliver thee, and thou shalt glorify me:** ... Call Me in Sorrow's day, *Fenton* ... I will come to your rescue, *NEB* ... and you will honor me, *NCV* ... I will save you, *Good News*.

**16. But unto the wicked God saith, What hast thou to do to declare my statutes, or that thou shouldest take my covenant in thy mouth?** ... What right have you to recite my laws, *NIV* ... What are you doing, talking of my laws, *BB* ... and make so free with the words of my covenant, *NEB* ... how can you recite my commandments, *Anchor*.

**17. Seeing thou hatest instruction, and castest my words behind thee:** ... For you hate discipline, *NASB* ... you hate correction, *REB* ... casting every warning of mine to the winds, *Knox* ... and turn your back on what I say, *NCV* ... when you hate me to control you, *Moffatt*.

**18. When thou sawest a thief, then thou consentedst with him, and hast been partaker with adulterers:** ... You make friends with a thief as soon as you see one, *JB* ... see a thief, you delight to associate with him, *Berkeley* ... you were joined with those who took other men's wives, *BB* ... and share the life of adulterers, *Beck*.

**19. Thou givest thy mouth to evil, and thy tongue frameth deceit:** ... kept weaving deceit, *Rotherham* ... harness your tongue to deceit, *NIV* ... And mislead by your tongue, *Fenton* ... and harness your tongue to slander, *NEB*.

**20. Thou sittest and speakest against thy brother; thou slanderest thine own mother's son:** ... against your mother's son you spread rumors, *NAB* ... stabbing your own mother's son in the back, *NEB* ... imputing faults to your own mother's son, *REB* ... on the son of your mother you bring ruin, *Berkeley*.

**21. These things hast thou done, and I kept silence; thou thoughtest that I was altogether such an one as thyself:** ... Do you think that I am really like you?, *JB* ... You plan to destroy; should I be like you, *Beck* ... you thought that I was one like yourself, *RSV*.

---

involved in it. What good do bulls' flesh and goats' blood do to Him? But if these are expressions of thankful love, they are delightful to Him. Therefore, the section ends with the declaration that the true sacrifice is thanksgiving and the discharge of vows. Men honor God by asking and taking, not by giving. They glorify Him when, by calling on Him in trouble, they are delivered; and then, by thankfulness and service, as well as by the evidence which their experience gives—that prayer is not in vain—they again glorify Him. All sacrifices are God's before they are offered and do not become any more his by being offered. He neither needs nor can partake of material sustenance. But men's hearts are not his without their glad surrender in the same way as after it; and thankful love, trust and obedience are as the food of God, sacrifices acceptable and well pleasing to Him.

**50:16–21.** The third part of the Psalm is still sterner in tone. It strikes at the other great corruption of worship by hypocrites. As has been often remarked, it condemns breaches of the second table of the Law, just as the former part may be regarded as dealing with transgressions of the first. The eighth, seventh and ninth commandments are referred to in vv. 18f as examples of the hypocrites' sins. The irreconcilable contradiction of their professions and conduct is vividly brought out in the juxtaposition of "declare my statutes" and "castest my words behind thee." They do two opposite things with the same words—at the same time proclaiming them with all lip service and scornfully flinging them behind their backs in their conduct.

Hypocrisy finds encouragement in impunity. God's silence is an emphatic way of expressing his patient tolerance of evil unpunished. Such "longsuffering" is meant to lead to repentance and indicates God's unwillingness to smite. But as experience shows, it is often abused, and "because sentence against an evil work is not executed speedily, the heart of the sons of men is thoroughly set in them to do evil." The gross mind has gross conceptions of God. One nemesis of hypocrisy is the dimming of the idea of the righteous Judge. All sin darkens the image of God. When men turn away from God's self-revelation, as they do by transgression and most fatally by hypocrisy, they cannot but make a God after their own image. Such men sink deeper in evil until He speaks. Then comes an apocalypse to the dreamer, when there is flashed before him what God is and what he himself is. How terror-stricken the gaze of these eyes before which God

| 6424.125 | 3937, 6084 | | 1032.133, 5167 | 2148 | 8319.152 | 438 |
|---|---|---|---|---|---|---|
| cj, v Qal juss 1cs | prep, n fd, ps 2ms | **22.** | v Qal impv 2mp, part | dem pron | *v Qal act ptc mp* | n ms |
| וְאֶעֶרְכָה | לְעֵינֶיךָ | | בִּינוּ־נָא | זֹאת | שֹׁכְחֵי | אֱלוֹהַּ |
| we'e'erkhāh | le'ênêkhā | | bînû-nā' | zō'th | shōkhechê | 'ĕlôahh |
| and let me set in order | to your eyes | | understand please | this | those who forget | God |

| 6678, 3072.125 | 375 | 5522.551 | | 2159.151 | 8756 |
|---|---|---|---|---|---|
| adv, v Qal impf 1cs | cj, *sub* | v Hiphil ptc ms | **23.** | v Qal act ptc ms | n fs |
| פֶּן־אֶטְרֹף | וְאֵין | מַצִּיל | | זֹבֵחַ | תּוֹדָה |
| pen-'eṭrōph | we'ên | matstsîl | | zōvēach | tôdhāh |
| so that I will not tear | and there is not | a rescuer | | one who sacrifices | a thank offering |

| 3632.321 | 7947.151 | 1932 | 7495.525 | 904, 3589 |
|---|---|---|---|---|
| v Piel impf 3ms, ps 1cs | cj, v Qal act ptc ms | n ms | v Hiphil impf 1cs, ps 3ms | prep, *n ms* |
| יְכַבְּדָנְנִי | וְשָׂם | דֶּרֶךְ | אַרְאֶנּוּ | בְּיֵשַׁע |
| yekhabbedhānenî | wesām | derekh | 'ar'ennû | beyēsha' |
| he honors Me | and the one who sets | a way | I will cause him to look | on the salvation of |

| 435 | | 3937, 5514.351 | 4344 | 3937, 1784 | 904, 971.141, 420 | 5600 |
|---|---|---|---|---|---|---|
| n mp | **51:t** | prep, art, v Piel ptc ms | n ms | prep, pn | prep, v Qal inf con, prep, ps 3ms | pn |
| אֱלֹהִים | | לַמְנַצֵּחַ | מִזְמוֹר | לְדָוִד | בְּבוֹא־אֵלָיו | נָתָן |
| 'ĕlōhîm | | lamnatstsēach | mizmôr | ledhāwidh | bevô'-'ēlâv | nāthān |
| God | | to the director | a Psalm | of David | when coming to him | Nathan |

| 5204 | 3626, 866, 971.111 | 420, 1368 | | 2706.131 | 435 |
|---|---|---|---|---|---|
| art, n ms | prep, rel part, v Qal pf 3ms | prep, pn | **1.** | v Qal impv 2ms, ps 1cs | n mp |
| הַנָּבִיא | כַּאֲשֶׁר־בָּא | אֶל־בַּת־שָׁבַע | | חָנֵּנִי | אֱלֹהִים |
| hannāvî' | ka'ăsher-bā' | 'el-bath-shāva' | | chonnēnî | 'ĕlōhîm |
| the prophet | when he went in | to Bathsheba | | be gracious to me | O God |

| 3626, 2721 | 3626, 7524 | 7641 | 4364.131 |
|---|---|---|---|
| prep, n ms, ps 2ms | prep, *n ms* | n mp, ps 2ms | v Qal impv 2ms |
| כְּחַסְדֶּךָ | כְּרֹב | רַחֲמֶיךָ | מְחֵה |
| kechasdekhā | kerōv | rachmêkhā | mechēh |
| according to your steadfast love | according to the abundance of | your mercy | wipe clean |

| 6840 | | 7528.542 | 3645.331 | 4623, 5988 | 4623, 2496 |
|---|---|---|---|---|---|
| n mp, ps 1cs | **2.** | v Hiphil inf abs | v Piel impv 2ms, ps 1cs | prep, n ms ps 1cs | cj, prep, n fs, ps 1cs |
| פְּשָׁעָי | | הַרְבֵּה | כַּבְּסֵנִי | מֵעֲוֺנִי | וּמֵחַטָּאתִי |
| phesha'āy | | harbēh | kabbesēnî | mē'ăwōnî | ûmēchattā'thî |
| my offenses | | making abundant | wash me | from my guilt | and from my sin |

| 3000.331 | | 3706, 6840 | 603 | 3156.125 | 2496 | 5224 |
|---|---|---|---|---|---|---|
| v Piel impv 2ms, ps 1cs | **3.** | cj, n mp, ps 1cs | pers pron | v Qal impf 1cs | cj, n fs, ps 1cs | prep, ps 1cs |
| טַהֲרֵנִי | | כִּי־פְשָׁעַי | אֲנִי | אֵדָע | וְחַטָּאתִי | נֶגְדִּי |
| ṭahrēnî | | kî-phesha'ay | 'ănî | 'ēdhā' | wechattā'thî | neghdî |
| cleanse me | | because my offenses | I | I am aware of | and my sin | before me |

**but I will reprove thee, and set them in order before thine eyes:** ... set the cause before, *MAST* ... I will correct you by drawing them up before your eyes, *NCB* ... I will censure you and put the case in order, *Berkeley.*

**22. Now consider this, ye that forget God, lest I tear you in pieces, and there be none to deliver:** ... lest I rend you and there be no one to rescue you, *NAB* ... without hope of a rescuer, *JB* ... or his hand will fall suddenly, and there will be no delivering you, *Knox* ... for fear that you may be crushed under my hand, with no one to give you help, *BB.*

**23. Whoso offereth praise glorifieth me: and to him that ordereth his conversation aright will I show the salvation of God:** ... And walk GOD's saving path, *Fenton* ... He that sacrificeth a thankoffering, *Rotherham* ... I cause him to look on the salvation of God, *Young* ... If you set your life in order, I will have you drink your fill of God's salvation, *Beck.*

**51:t. To the chief Musician, A Psalm of David, when Nathan the prophet came unto him, after he had gone in to Bath-sheba.**

**1. Have mercy upon me, O God, according to thy lovingkindness: according unto the multitude of thy tender mercies blot out my transgressions:** ... Have pity on me ... take away my sin, *BB* ... wipe out my wrong, *Beck* ... blot out my crime, *Fenton* ... tenderness wipe away my offences, *JB* ... your unfailing love, *NIV*.

**2. Wash me throughly from mine iniquity, and cleanse me from my sin:** ... Let all my wrongdoing be washed away, and make me clean from evil, *BB* ... wash me from every stain of guilt, and purge me, *Moffatt* ... from mine iniquity, *Rotherham*.

**3. For I acknowledge my transgressions: and my sin is ever before me:** ... I am conscious of my error, *BB* ... I realize the wrong I've done, *Beck* ... I am conscious, *Berkeley* ... I certainly sinned against You, *Fenton* ... I know about my wrongs, and I can't forget my sin, *NCV*.

**4. Against thee, thee only, have I sinned, and done this evil in thy sight:** ... You are the only one I have sinned against, *NCV* ... before your eyes committed the crime, *Anchor* ... I have done what you see to be wrong, *JB* ... done what displeases thee, *NEB*.

**that thou mightest be justified when thou speakest, and be clear when thou judgest:** ... That you may be

---

arrays the deeds of a life, seen for the first time in their true character! It will be the hypocrite's turn to keep silence then, and his thought of a complacent God like himself will perish before the stern reality.

**50:22–23.** The whole teaching of the Psalm is gathered up in the two closing verses. "Ye that forget God" includes both the superstitious formalists and the hypocrites. Reflection upon such truths as those of the Psalm will save them from otherwise inevitable destruction. "This" points to v. 23, which is a compendium of both parts of the Psalm. The true worship, which consists in thankfulness and praise, is opposed in v. 23a to mere externalisms of sacrifice, as being the right way of glorifying God. The promise to him who thus acts is that he shall see God's salvation, both in the narrower sense of daily interpositions for deliverance and in the wider of a full and final rescue from all evil and endowment with all good. The Psalm has as keen an edge for modern as for ancient sins. Superstitious reliance on externals of worship survives, although sacrifices have ceased; and hypocrites, with their mouths full of the Gospel, still cast God's words behind them, as did those ancient hollow-hearted proclaimers and breakers of the Law.

***Psalm 51.*** *In vv. 1–9, the psalmist's cry is chiefly for pardon; in vv. 10ff, he prays chiefly for purity; in vv. 13–17, he vows grateful service. Verses 18f are probably a later addition.*

*The Psalm begins with at once grasping the character of God as the sole ground of hope. That character has been revealed in an infinite number of acts of love. The very number of the psalmist's sins drove him to contemplate the yet greater number of God's mercies. For where but in an infinite placableness and steadfast love could he find pardon? This Psalm followed Nathan's assurance of forgiveness, and its petitions are David's efforts to lay hold of that assurance. The revelation of God's love precedes and causes true penitence. Our prayer for forgiveness is the appropriation of God's promise of forgiveness. The assurance of pardon does not lead to a light estimate of sin, but drives it home to the conscience.*

**51:1–2.** The petitions of vv. 1f teach us how the psalmist thought of sin. They are all substantially the same, and their repetition discloses the depth of longing in the suppliant. The language fluctuates between plural and singular nouns, designating the evil as "transgressions" and as "iniquity" and "sin." The psalmist regards it, first, as a multitude of separate acts, then as all gathered together into a grim unity. The single deeds of wrongdoing pass before him. But these have a common root; and we must not only recognize acts, but that alienation of heart from which they come—not only sin as it comes out in the life, but as it is coiled around our hearts. Sins are the manifestations of sin. The psalmist is ready to submit to any painful discipline, if only he may be cleansed.

**51:3.** The petitions for cleansing are, in v. 3, urged on the ground of the psalmist's consciousness of sin. Penitent confession is a condition of forgiveness. There is no need to take this verse as giving the reason why the psalmist offered his prayer, rather than as presenting a plea why it should be answered. Some commentators have adopted the former explanation from a fear lest the other should give countenance to the notion that repentance is a meritorious cause of forgiveness, but that is unnecessary scrupulousness. "Sin is always sin, and deserving of punishment, whether it is confessed or not. Still, confession of sin is of importance on this account—that God will be gracious to none but to those who confess their sin" (Luther).

| 8878 | 4. | 3937 | 3937, 940 | 2490.115 | 7737 | 904, 6084 |
|---|---|---|---|---|---|---|
| adv | | prep, ps 2ms | prep, n ms, ps 2ms | v Qal pf 1cs | cj, art, n ms | prep, n fd, ps 2ms |
| תָּמִיד | | לְךָ | לְבַדְּךָ | חָטָאתִי | וְהָרַע | בְּעֵינֶיךָ |
| thāmîdh | | lekhā | levaddekhā | chāṭā'thî | wehāra' | be'ênêkhā |
| continually | | against You | only You | I have sinned | and what is evil | in your eyes |

| 6449.115 | 3937, 4775 | 6927.123 | 904, 1744.141 | 2218.123 |
|---|---|---|---|---|
| v Qal pf 1cs | prep, prep | v Qal impf 2ms | prep, v Qal inf con, ps 2ms | v Qal impf 2ms |
| עָשִׂיתִי | לְמַעַן | תִּצְדַּק | בְּדָבְרֶךָ | תִּזְכֶּה |
| 'āsîthî | lema'an | titsdaq | bedhāverekhā | tizkeh |
| I have done | so that | You are righteous | in your speaking | You are blameless |

| 904, 8570.141 | 5. | 2075, 904, 5988 | 2523.315 | 904, 2491 |
|---|---|---|---|---|
| prep, v Qal inf con, ps 2ms | | intrj, prep, n ms | v Polal pf 1cs | cj, prep, n ms |
| בְשָׁפְטֶךָ | | הֵן־בְּעָווֹן | חוֹלָלְתִּי | וּבְחֵטְא |
| veshāphetekhā | | hēn-be'āwôn | chôlālettî | ûvechēṭe' |
| in your judging | | behold in transgression | I caused labor pains | and by a sinner |

| 3285.312 | 525 | 6. | 2075, 583 | 2760.113 | 904, 3021 |
|---|---|---|---|---|---|
| v Piel pf 3fs, ps 1cs | n fs, ps 1cs | | intrj, n fs | v Qal pf 2ms | prep, art, n fp |
| יֶחֱמַתְנִי | אִמִּי | | הֵן־אֱמֶת | חָפַצְתָּ | בַטֻּחוֹת |
| yechĕmathnî | 'immî | | hēn-'ĕmeth | chāphatstā | vattuchôth |
| she was in heat to conceive me | my mother | | behold faithfulness | You desire | in the secret places |

| 904, 5845.155 | 2551 | 3156.523 | 7. | 2490.323 | 904, 230 |
|---|---|---|---|---|---|
| cj, prep, v Qal pass ptc ms | n fs | v Hiphil impf 2ms, ps 1cs | | v Piel impf 2ms, ps 1cs | prep, n ms |
| וּבְסָתֻם | חָכְמָה | תוֹדִיעֵנִי | | תְּחַטְּאֵנִי | בְאֵזוֹב |
| ûvesāthum | chokhmāh | thôdhî'ēnî | | techatte'ēnî | ve'ēzôv |
| yes in the secret place | wisdom | You cause me to know | | You purify me | with hyssop |

| 3000.125 | 3645.323 | 4623, 8345 | 3967.525 | 8. | 8471.523 |
|---|---|---|---|---|---|
| cj, v Qal impf 1cs | v Piel impf 2ms, ps 1cs | cj, prep, n ms | v Hiphil impf 1cs | | v Hiphil impf 2ms, ps 1cs |
| וְאֶטְהָר | תְּכַבְּסֵנִי | וּמִשֶּׁלֶג | אַלְבִּין | | תַּשְׁמִיעֵנִי |
| we'eṭhār | tekhabbesēnî | ûmishshelegh | 'albîn | | tashmî'ēnî |
| and I am clean | You wash me | and more than snow | I am white | | You cause me to hear |

| 8050 | 7977 | 1559.127 | 6344 | 1852.313 | 9. | 5846.531 | 6686 |
|---|---|---|---|---|---|---|---|
| n ms | cj, n fs | v Qal impf 3fp | n fp | v Piel pf 2ms | | v Hiphil impv 2ms | n mp, ps 2ms |
| שָׂשׂוֹן | וְשִׂמְחָה | תָּגֵלְנָה | עֲצָמוֹת | דִּכִּיתָ | | הַסְתֵּר | פָּנֶיךָ |
| sāsôn | wesimchāh | tāghēlenāh | 'ătsāmôth | dikkîthā | | hastēr | pānêkhā |
| joy | and gladness | they rejoice | the bones | You have crushed | | hide | your face |

| 4623, 2491 | 3725, 5988 | 4364.131 | 10. | 3949 | 2999 |
|---|---|---|---|---|---|
| prep, n mp, ps 1cs | cj, *adj*, n mp, ps 1cs | v Qal impv 2ms | | n ms | adj |
| מֵחֲטָאָי | וְכָל־עֲוֹנֹתַי | מְחֵה | | לֵב | טָהוֹר |
| mēchăṭā'āy | wekhol-'ăwōnōthay | mechēh | | lēv | ṭāhôr |
| from my sins | and all my transgressions | wipe clean | | a heart | clean |

| 1282.131, 3937 | 435 | 7593 | 3679.255 | 2412.331 | 904, 7419 |
|---|---|---|---|---|---|
| v Qal impv 2ms, prep, ps 1cs | n mp | cj, *n fs* | v Niphal ptc ms | v Piel impv 2ms | prep, n ms, ps 1cs |
| בְּרָא־לִי | אֱלֹהִים | וְרוּחַ | נָכוֹן | חַדֵּשׁ | בְּקִרְבִּי |
| berā'-lî | 'ĕlōhîm | werûach | nākhôn | chaddēsh | beqirbî |
| create for me | God | and a spirit | established | make new | in my inmost being |

| 11. | 414, 8390.523 | 4623, 3937, 6686 | 7593 | 7231 |
|---|---|---|---|---|
| | adv, v Hiphil juss 2ms, ps 1cs | prep, prep, n mp, ps 2ms | cj, *n fs* | n ms, ps 2ms |
| | אַל־תַּשְׁלִיכֵנִי | מִלְּפָנֶיךָ | וְרוּחַ | קָדְשְׁךָ |
| | 'al-tashlîkhēnî | millephānêkhā | werûach | qodhshekhā |
| | do not throw me aside | from your presence | and the Spirit of | your holiness |

justified in your sentence, vindicated when you condemn, *NAB* ... And so you are just when you sentence, *Anchor* ... so that your words may be seen to be right ... when you are judging, *BB* ... and your victory may appear when you give judgement, *JB*.

**5. Behold, I was shapen in iniquity; and in sin did my mother conceive me:** ... I was sinful at birth, *NIV* ... I was born guilty, *NRSV* ... in sinful state I was born, *Berkeley* ... a sinner from the moment of conception, *JB*.

**6. Behold, thou desirest truth in the inward parts: and in the hidden part thou shalt make me to know wisdom:** ... Your desire is for what is true, *BB* ... You want to teach me to be wise, *Beck* ... you delight in sincerity of heart, and in secret you teach me wisdom, *JB* ... teach me wisdom in my secret heart, *RSV*.

**7. Purge me with hyssop, and I shall be clean: wash me, and I shall be whiter than snow:** ... Sprinkle me with hyssop, *REB* ... Unsin me, I'll indeed be purer than gushing water, *Anchor* ... Purify me, *ASV* ... Make me free from sin with hyssop, *BB*.

**8. Make me to hear joy and gladness; that the bones which thou hast broken may rejoice:** ... Make me full of joy and rapture, *BB* ... Let me hear the sounds, *Good News* ... let the bones you crushed be happy again, *NCV* ... let the bones dance, *NEB*.

**9. Hide thy face from my sins, and blot out all mine iniquities:** ... Turn your face from my sins, *Anchor* ... from my wrongdoing, and take away all my sins, *BB* ... wipe out all my wrongs, *Beck*.

**10. Create in me a clean heart, O God; and renew a right spirit within me:** give me a right spirit, *BB* ... Create a pure heart ... loyal spirit, *Good News* ... clean heart, O God, filled with clean thoughts and right desires, *LIVB* ... a resolute spirit, *Anchor* ... renew a steadfast spirit within me, *Darby*.

**11. Cast me not away from thy presence; and take not thy holy spirit from me:** ... do not drive me from thy presence, *NEB* ... Do not put me away from before you, *BB* ... deprive me not, *Moffatt*.

---

**51:4.** Verse 4 sounds the depths in both of its clauses. In the first, the psalmist shuts out all other aspects of his guilt and is absorbed in its solemnity as viewed in relation to God. It is questioned how David could have thought of his sin, which had in so many ways been "against" others, as having been "against thee, thee only." David's deed had been a crime against Bathsheba, against Uriah, against his family and his realm; but these were not its blackest characteristics. Every crime against man is sin against God.

The second clause of v. 4 opens the question whether "in order that" (HED #4775), which is always used in the OT in its full meaning as expressing intention, or sometimes in the looser signification of "so that," expressing result.

**51:5–6.** Verses 5f are marked as closely related by the "behold" (HED #2075) at the beginning of each. The psalmist passes from penitent contemplation and confession of his acts of sin to acknowledging his sinful nature, derived from sinful parents. "Original sin" is theological terminology corresponding to the physical scientific realm of "heredity." The psalmist is not responsible for later dogmatic developments of the idea, but he feels that he has to confess not only his acts but his nature.

**51:7–9.** Meditation on the sin which was ever before the psalmist passes into renewed prayers for pardon, which partly reiterate those already offered in vv. 1f. The petition in v. 7 for purging with hyssop alludes to sprinkling of lepers and unclean persons and indicates both a consciousness of great impurity and a clear perception of the symbolic meaning of ritual cleansings. "Wash me" repeats a former petition, but now the psalmist can venture to dwell more on the thought of future purity than he could do then. The approaching answer begins to make its brightness visible through the gloom, and it seems possible to the suppliant that even his stained nature will glisten like sunlit snow. Nor does that expectation exhaust his confidence. He hopes for "joy and gladness." His bones have been crushed—i.e., his whole self has been, as it were, ground to powder by the weight of God's hand, but restoration is possible. A penitent heart is not too bold when it asks for joy. There is no real well-founded gladness without the consciousness of divine forgiveness. The psalmist closes his petitions for pardon (v. 9) with asking God to "hide thy face from my sins," so that they be, as it were, no more existent for Him, and, by a repetition of the initial petition in v. 1, for the blotting out of "all mine iniquities."

**51:10–12.** The second principal division begins with v. 10 and is a prayer for purity, followed by vows of glad service. The prayer is contained in three verses (vv. 10ff), of which the first implores complete renewal of nature, the second beseeches that there may be no break between the suppliant and God, and the third asks for the joy and willingness to

| 414, 4089.123 | 4623 | | 8178.531 | 3937 | 8050 | 3589 | 7593 |
|---|---|---|---|---|---|---|---|
| adv, v Qal juss 2ms | prep, ps 1cs | **12.** | v Hiphil impv 2ms | prep, ps 1cs | *n ms* | n ms, ps 2ms | cj, *n fs* |
| אַל־תִּקַּח | מִמֶּנִּי | | הָשִׁיבָה | לִּי | שְׂשׂוֹן | יִשְׁעֶךָ | וְרוּחַ |
| 'al-tiqqach | mimmenî | | hāshîvāh | lî | sesôn | yish'ekhā | werûach |
| do not take | from me | | cause to return | to me | the joy of | your salvation | and a spirit |

| 5259 | 5759.123 | | 4064.325 | 6839.152 | 1932 | 2491 | 420 |
|---|---|---|---|---|---|---|---|
| adj | v Qal impf 2ms, ps 1cs | **13.** | v Piel juss 1cs | v Qal act ptc mp | n mp, ps 2ms | cj, n mp | prep, ps 2ms |
| נְדִיבָה | תִסְמְכֵנִי | | אֲלַמְּדָה | פֹשְׁעִים | דְּרָכֶיךָ | וְחַטָּאִים | אֵלֶיךָ |
| nedhîvāh | thismekhēnî | | 'ălammedhāh | phōshe'îm | derākhêkhā | wechattā'îm | 'ēlêkhā |
| willing | You sustain me | | let me teach | transgressors | your ways | and sinners | to You |

| 8178.126 | | 5522.531 | 4623, 1879 | 435 | 435 | 9009 |
|---|---|---|---|---|---|---|
| v Qal impf 3mp | **14.** | v Hiphil impv 2ms, ps 1cs | prep, n mp | n mp | *n mp* | n fs, ps 1cs |
| יָשׁוּבוּ | | הַצִּילֵנִי | מִדָּמִים | אֱלֹהִים | אֱלֹהֵי | תְּשׁוּעָתִי |
| yāshûvû | | hatstsîlēnî | middāmîm | 'ĕlōhîm | 'ĕlōhê | teshû'āthî |
| they will return | | rescue me | from bloodshed | O God | the God of | my salvation |

| 7728.322 | 4098 | 6930 | | 112 | 8004 | 6858.123 |
|---|---|---|---|---|---|---|
| v Piel impf 3fs | n fs, ps 1cs | n fs, ps 2ms | **15.** | n mp, ps 1cs | n fd, ps 1cs | v Qal impf 2ms |
| תְּרַנֵּן | לְשׁוֹנִי | צִדְקָתֶךָ | | אֲדֹנָי | שְׂפָתַי | תִּפְתָּח |
| terannēn | leshônî | tsidhqāthekhā | | 'ădhōnāy | sephāthay | tiphtāch |
| it will shout for joy | my tongue | your righteousness | | O my Lord | my lips | You open |

| 6552 | 5222.521 | 8747 | | 3706 | 3940, 2759.123 | 2160 |
|---|---|---|---|---|---|---|
| cj, n ms, ps 1cs | v Hiphil impf 3ms | n fs, ps 2ms | **16.** | cj | neg part, v Qal impf 2ms | n ms |
| וּפִי | יַגִּיד | תְּהִלָּתֶךָ | | כִּי | לֹא־תַחְפֹּץ | זֶבַח |
| ûphî | yaggîdh | tehillāthekhā | | kî | lō'-thachpōts | zevach |
| and my mouth | it will tell | your praise | | because | You do not delight in | a sacrifice |

| 5598.125 | 6150 | 3940 | 7813.123 | | 2160 |
|---|---|---|---|---|---|
| cj, v Qal juss 1cs | n fs | neg part | v Qal impf 2ms | **17.** | *n mp* |
| וְאֶתֵּנָה | עוֹלָה | לֹא | תִרְצֶה | | זִבְחֵי |
| we'ettēnāh | 'ôlāh | lō' | thirtseh | | zivchê |
| and if I were to give | a burnt offering | not | You would be pleased | | the sacrifices for |

| 435 | 7593 | 8132.257 | 3949, 8132.256 | 1852.257 | 435 | 3940 |
|---|---|---|---|---|---|---|
| n mp | *n fs* | v Niphal ptc fs | *n ms*, v Niphal ptc ms | cj, v Niphal ptc fs | n mp | neg part |
| אֱלֹהִים | רוּחַ | נִשְׁבָּרָה | לֵב־נִשְׁבָּר | וְנִדְכֶּה | אֱלֹהִים | לֹא |
| 'ĕlōhîm | rûach | nishbārāh | lēv-nishbār | wenidhkeh | 'ĕlōhîm | lō' |
| God | a spirit | broken | a broken heart | and crushed | God | not |

| 995.123 | | 3296.531 | 904, 7814 | 881, 6995 | 1161.123 | 2440 |
|---|---|---|---|---|---|---|
| v Qal impf 2ms | **18.** | v Hiphil impv 2ms | prep, n ms, ps 2ms | do, pn | v Qal impf 2ms | *n fp* |
| תִבְזֶה | | הֵיטִיבָה | בִרְצוֹנְךָ | אֶת־צִיּוֹן | תִּבְנֶה | חוֹמוֹת |
| thivzeh | | hêtîvāh | virtsônkhā | 'eth-tsîyôn | tivneh | chômôth |
| You will despise | | cause to be good | in your pleasure | Zion | You build | the wall of |

**12. Restore unto me the joy of thy salvation; and uphold me with thy free spirit:** ... Give me back the joy of your salvation, and a willing spirit sustain in me, *NAB* ... Keep me strong, *NCV* ... revive in me the joy of thy deliverance, *NEB*.

**13. Then will I teach transgressors thy ways; and sinners shall be converted unto thee:** ... I will teach the rebellious, *Beck* ... I teach the wicked to follow thy paths, *Knox* ... will teach transgressors the ways that lead to thee, *NEB* ... will I make your ways clear to wrongdoers; and sinners will be turned to you, *BB*.

**14. Deliver me from bloodguiltiness, O God, thou God of my salvation: and my tongue shall sing aloud of thy righteousness:** ... Save me from bloodguilt, *NIV* ... Deliver me from the tears of death, *Anchor* ... I will sing the praises of thy justice, *NEB* ... I shall sing the praises of your saving power, *REB*.

**15. O Lord, open thou my lips: and my mouth shall show forth thy**

**praise:** ... open my lips, and my mouth shall proclaim your praise, *NAB* ... let me speak so I may praise you, *NCV* ... so that my mouth may make clear your praise, *BB*.

**16. For thou desirest not sacrifice; else would I give it: thou delightest not in burnt offering:** ... Sacrifice gives you no pleasure, burnt offering you do not desire, *JB* ... Thou hast no mind for sacrifice, *Knox* ... a mere burnt offering doesn't please You, *Beck*.

**17. The sacrifices of God are a broken spirit: a broken and a contrite heart, O God, thou wilt not despise:** ... you will not reject a humble and repentant heart, *Good News* ... a heart contrite and crushed, *Anchor* ... a broken and sorrowing heart, *BB*.

**18. Do good in thy good pleasure unto Zion: build thou the walls of Jerusalem:** ... Grant happiness to Sion, *Moffatt* ... Be bountiful, *NAB* ... Do whatever good you wish for Jerusalem, *NCV* ... make Zion prosper, *NIV* ... in thy great love send prosperity to Sion, so that the walls of Jerusalem may rise again, *Knox*.

**19. Then shalt thou be pleased with the sacrifices of righteousness, with burnt offering and whole burnt offering: then shall they offer bullocks upon thine altar:** ... the right kind of sacrifices, *Beck* ... proper sacrifices, *Good News* ... bulls will be offered, *NIV* ... you will have delight in the offerings of righteousness, *BB*.

---

serve that which would flow from the granting of the desires preceding. In each verse, the second clause has "spirit" for its leading word, and the middle one of the three asks concerning the Holy Spirit.

"A steadfast spirit" is needful in order to keep a cleansed heart clean; and, on the other hand, when, by cleanness of heart, a man is freed from the perturbations of rebellious desires and the weakening influences of sin, his spirit will be steadfast. The two characteristics sustain each other. If we remember how it had fared with his predecessor, from whom, because of impenitence, "the spirit of the LORD departed, and an evil spirit from the LORD troubled him" (1 Sam. 16:14), we understand how Saul's successor, trembling as he remembers his fate, prays with peculiar emphasis, "Take not thy Holy Spirit from me."

The last member of the triad looks back to former petitions, and asks for restoration of the "joy of thy salvation" (v. 12). To serve God because we must is not service. To serve Him because we had rather do his will than anything else is the service which delights Him and blesses us. Such obedience is freedom. "I will walk at liberty; for I keep thy precepts" (Ps. 119:45).

**51:13–15.** The last part of the Psalm runs over with joyful vows—first, of magnifying God's name (vv. 13ff) and then of offering true sacrifices. A man who has passed through such experiences as the psalmist's and has received the blessings for which he prayed cannot be silent. The instinct of hearts touched by God's mercies is to speak of them to others. And no man who can say "I will tell what He has done for my soul" is without the most persuasive argument to bring to bear on others. A piece of autobiography will touch men who are unaffected by elaborate reasonings and deaf to polished eloquence. The impulse and the capacity to "teach transgressors thy ways" are given in the experience of sin and forgiveness, and if anyone has not the former, it is questionable whether he has, in any real sense or large measure, received the latter. The prayer for deliverance from blood guiltiness in v. 14 breaks for a moment the flow of vows, but only for a moment. It indicates how amid them the psalmist preserved his sense of guilt and how little he was disposed to think lightly of the sins of whose forgiveness he had prayed himself into the assurance. Its emergence here, like a black rock pushing its grimness up through a sparkling, sunny sea, is no sign of doubt whether his prayers had been answered; but it marks the abiding sense of sinfulness, which must ever accompany abiding gratitude for pardon and abiding holiness of heart. It seems hard to believe, as the advocates of a national reference in the Psalm are obliged to do, that "blood guiltiness" has no special reference to the psalmist's crime, but is employed simply as typical of sin in general.

**51:16–19.** Verse 16 introduces the reason for the preceding vow of grateful praise, as is shown by the initial "for" (HED #3706). The psalmist will bring the sacrifices of a grateful heart, making his lips musical, because he has learned that these, and not ritual offerings, are acceptable.

The psalmist's last words are immortal: "A broken and contrite heart, O God, thou wilt not despise." But they derive still deeper beauty and pathos when it is observed that they are spoken after confession has been answered to his consciousness by pardon. The "joy of thy salvation," (v. 12) for which he had prayed, has begun to flow into his heart. The "bones" which had been "crushed" are beginning to reknit and thrills of gladness, to steal through his frame; but still he feels that with all

| 3503 | | 226 | 2759.123 | 2160, 6928 | 6150 |
|---|---|---|---|---|---|
| pn | 19. | adv | v Qal impf 2ms | n mp, n ms | n fs |
| יְרוּשָׁלָם | | אָז | תַּחְפֹּץ | זִבְחֵי־צֶדֶק | עוֹלָה |
| yerûshālām | | 'āz | tachpōts | zivchê-tsedheq | 'ôlāh |
| Jerusalem | | then | You will delight in | sacrifices of righteousness | a burnt offering |

| 3752 | 226 | 6148.526 | 6142, 4326 | 6749 |
|---|---|---|---|---|
| cj, sub | adv | v Hiphil impf 3mp | prep, n ms, ps 2ms | n mp |
| וְכָלִיל | אָז | יַעֲלוּ | עַל־מִזְבַּחֲךָ | פָרִים |
| wekhālîl | 'āz | ya'ălû | 'al-mizbachkhā | phārîm |
| even a whole offering | then | they will cause to go up | on your altar | young bulls |

| | 3937, 5514.351 | 5030 | 3937, 1784 | 904, 971.141 | 1721 | 128 | 5222.521 |
|---|---|---|---|---|---|---|---|
| 52:t | prep, art, v Piel ptc ms | n ms | prep, pn | prep, v Qal inf con | pn | art, pn | cj, v Hiphil impf 3ms |
| | לַמְנַצֵּחַ | מַשְׂכִּיל | לְדָוִד | בְּבוֹא | דּוֹאֵג | הָאֲדֹמִי | וַיַּגֵּד |
| | lamnatstsēach | maskîl | ledhāwidh | bevô' | dô'ēgh | hā'ădhōmî | wayyaggēdh |
| | to the director | a Maskil | of David | when coming | Doeg | the Edomite | and he reported |

| 3937, 8062 | 569.121 | 3937 | 971.111 | 1784 | 420, 1041 | 289 |
|---|---|---|---|---|---|---|
| prep, pn | cj, v Qal impf 3ms | prep, ps 3ms | v Qal pf 3ms | pn | prep, n ms | pn |
| לְשָׁאוּל | וַיֹּאמֶר | לוֹ | בָּא | דָוִד | אֶל־בֵּית | אֲחִימֶלֶךְ |
| leshā'ûl | wayyō'mer | lô | bā' | dhāwidh | 'el-bêth | 'ăchîmelekh |
| to Saul | and he said | to him | he has come | David | to the house of | Ahimelech |

| | 4242, 2054.723 | 904, 7750 | 1399 | 2721 | 418 | 3725, 3219 |
|---|---|---|---|---|---|---|
| 1. | intrg, v Hithpael impf 2ms | prep, n fs | art, n ms | n ms | n ms | adj, art, n ms |
| | מַה־תִּתְהַלֵּל | בְּרָעָה | הַגִּבּוֹר | חֶסֶד | אֵל | כָּל־הַיּוֹם |
| | mah-tithhallēl | berā'āh | haggibbôr | chesedh | 'ēl | kol-hayyôm |
| | why do you boast | in evil | O mighty man | the steadfast love of | God | all the day |

| | 2010 | 2913.122 | 4098 | 3626, 8926 | 4048.455 | 6449.151 | 7711 |
|---|---|---|---|---|---|---|---|
| 2. | n fp | v Qal impf 3fs | n fs, ps 2ms | prep, n ms | v Pual ptc ms | v Qal act ptc ms | n fs |
| | הַוּוֹת | תַּחְשֹׁב | לְשׁוֹנֶךָ | כְּתַעַר | מְלֻטָּשׁ | עֹשֵׂה | רְמִיָּה |
| | hawwôth | tachshōv | leshônekhā | ketha'ar | meluttāsh | 'ōsēh | remîyāh |
| | destruction | it devises | your tongue | like a razor | sharpened | one who acts with | deceit |

| | 154.113 | 7737 | 4623, 3005 | 8632 | 4623, 1744.341 | 6928 | 5734 | | 154.113 |
|---|---|---|---|---|---|---|---|---|---|
| 3. | v Qal pf 2ms | n ms | prep, adj | n ms | prep, v Piel inf con | n ms | intrj | 4. | v Qal pf 2ms |
| | אָהַבְתָּ | רָע | מִטּוֹב | שֶׁקֶר | מִדַּבֵּר | צֶדֶק | סֶלָה | | אָהַבְתָּ |
| | 'āhavtā | rā' | mittôv | sheqer | middabbēr | tsedheq | selāh | | 'āhavtā |
| | you love more | evil | than good | lies | than speaking | what is correct | selah | | you love |

| 3725, 1745, 1144 | 4098 | 4983 | | 1612, 418 | 5606.121 | 3937, 5516 |
|---|---|---|---|---|---|---|
| adj, n mp, n ms | n fs | n fs | 5. | cj, n ms | v Qal impf 3ms, ps 2ms | prep, art, n ms |
| כָּל־דִּבְרֵי־בָלַע | לְשׁוֹן | מִרְמָה | | גַּם־אֵל | יִתָּצְךָ | לָנֶצַח |
| khol-divrê-vāla' | leshôn | mirmāh | | gam-'ēl | yittātsekhā | lānetsach |
| all the words of confusion | a tongue of | deceit | | indeed God | He will tear you down | unto forever |

| 2954.121 | 5442.121 | 4623, 164 | 8657.311 |
|---|---|---|---|
| v Qal impf 3ms, ps 2ms | cj, v Qal impf 3ms, ps 2ms | prep, n ms | cj, v Piel pf 3ms, ps 2ms |
| יַחְתְּךָ | וְיִסָּחֲךָ | מֵאֹהֶל | וְשֵׁרֶשְׁךָ |
| yachtekhā | weyissāchăkhā | mē'ōhel | weshēreshkhā |
| He will take you away | and He will tear you away | from a tent | and He will uproot you |

| 4623, 800 | 2522 | 5734 | | 7495.126 | 6926 | 3486.126 |
|---|---|---|---|---|---|---|
| prep, n fs | n mp | intrj | 6. | cj, v Qal impf 3mp | n mp | cj, v Qal impf 3mp |
| מֵאֶרֶץ | חַיִּים | סֶלָה | | וְיִרְאוּ | צַדִּיקִים | וְיִירָאוּ |
| mē'erets | chayyîm | selāh | | weyir'û | tsaddîqîm | weyîrā'û |
| from the land of | the living | selah | | and they will see | the righteous | and they will fear |

**52:t. To the chief Musician, Maschil, A Psalm of David, when Doeg the Edomite came and told Saul, and said unto him, David is come to the house of Ahimelech.**

**1. Why boastest thou thyself in mischief, O mighty man? the goodness of God endureth continually:** ... Why do you boast of wickedness, O champion?, *Anchor* ... in evil ... The mercy of God endures forever, *KJVII* ... Why do you take pride in wrongdoing, lifting yourself up against the upright man, *BB* ... The lovingkindness of God is exercised continually, *Berkeley*.

**2. Thy tongue deviseth mischiefs; like a sharp razor, working deceitfully:** ... deviseth destruction, *MAST* ... making up lies, *NCV* ... plots destruction, *NIV*.

**3. Thou lovest evil more than good; and lying rather than to speak righteousness. Selah:** ... rather than truthful speech, *REB* ... lying instead of telling the truth, *Anchor* ... for deceit than for works of righteousness, *BB* ... saying what is right, *Beck*.

**4. Thou lovest all devouring words, O thou deceitful tongue:** ... destroying words, *Berkeley* ... destructive words, *Goodspeed* ... the word that brings men to ruin, *Knox* ... anything that will do harm, O man with the lying tongue, *LIVB*.

**5. God shall likewise destroy thee for ever, he shall take thee away, and pluck thee out of thy dwelling-place, and root thee out of the land of the living. Selah:** ... God will pull you down for that, he will snatch you right away, *Moffatt* ... God himself shall demolish you; forever he shall break you, *NAB* ... God will put an end to you for ever, *BB* ... He will grab you and throw you out of your tent, *NCV* ... leave you ruined and homeless, *NEB*.

**6. The righteous also shall see, and fear, and shall laugh at him:** ... will laugh at the evildoer, *NRSV* ... righteous will look on, awestruck, then laugh, *REB* ... The just will look on in dread, but then will laugh, *Anchor*.

---

these happy experiences contrite consciousness of his sin must mingle. It does not rob his joy of one rapture, but it keeps it from becoming careless. He goes safely who goes humbly. The more sure a man is that God has put away the iniquity of his sin, the more should he remember it, for the remembrance will vivify gratitude and bind close to Him without Whom there can be no steadfastness of spirit nor purity of life. The clean heart must continue contrite if it is not to cease to be clean.

The liturgical addition implies that Jerusalem is in ruins. It cannot be supposed without violence to come from David. It is not needed in order to form a completion to the Psalm, which ends more impressively and has an inner unity and coherence if the deep words of v. 17 are taken as its close.

***Psalm 52.*** *The prominence given to sins of speech is peculiar. We should have expected high-handed violence rather than these. But the psalmist is tracking the deeds to their source; and it is not so much the tyrant's words as his love of a certain kind of words which is adduced as proof of his wickedness. These words have two characteristics in addition to boastfulness: they are false and destructive.*

**52:1–4.** Such words lead to acts which make a tyrant. They flow from perverted preference of evil to good. Thus, the deeds of oppression are followed up to their den and birthplace. Part of the description of the "words" corresponds to the fatal effect of Doeg's report, but nothing in it answers to the other part—falsehood (1 Sam. 22:9f). The psalmist's hot indignation speaks in the triple, direct address to the tyrant, which comes in each case like a lightning flash at the end of a clause (vv. 1f, 4). In the second of these, the epithet "framing deceit" does not refer to the "sharpened razor," but to the tyrant. If referred to the former, it weakens rather than strengthens the metaphor by bringing in the idea that the sharp blade misses its proper aim and wounds cheeks instead of shearing off hair. The selah of v. 3 interrupts the description in order to fix attention, by a pause filled up by music, on the hideous picture thus drawn.

**52:5.** That description is resumed and summarized in v. 4, which, by the selahs, is closely bound to v. 5 in order to enforce the necessary connection of sin and punishment, which is strongly underlined by the "also" or "so" (HED #1612) at the beginning of the latter verse. The stern prophecy of destruction is based upon no outward signs of failure in the oppressor's might, but wholly on confidence in God's continual steadfast love, which must assume attributes of justice when its objects are oppressed.

**52:6–7.** The third movement of thought (vv. 6f) deals with the effects of this retribution. It is a conspicuous demonstration of God's justice and of the folly of reliance on anything but himself. The fear which it produces in the "righteous" is reverential awe, no dread that the same should happen to them. Whether history and experience teach evil men that "verily he is a God that judgeth" (Ps. 58:11), their lessons are not wasted on devout and righteous souls. There is one safe stronghold, and only one. He who conceits him-

| 6142 | 7925.126 | | 2079 | 1429 | 3940 | 7947.121 | 435 |
|---|---|---|---|---|---|---|---|
| cj, prep, ps 3ms | v Qal impf 3mp | 7. | intrj | art, n ms | neg part | v Qal impf 3ms | n mp |
| וְעָלָיו | יִשְׂחָקוּ | | הִנֵּה | הַגֶּבֶר | לֹא | יָשִׂים | אֱלֹהִים |
| weʿālâv | yischāqû | | hinnēh | haggever | lō' | yāsîm | 'ĕlōhîm |
| and concerning him | they will laugh | | behold | the man | not | he makes | God |

| 4735 | 1019.121 | 904, 7524 | 6484 | 6022.121 |
|---|---|---|---|---|
| n ms, ps 3ms | cj, v Qal impf 3ms | prep, *n ms* | n ms, ps 3ms | v Qal impf 3ms |
| מָעוּזּוֹ | וַיִּבְטַח | בְּרֹב | עָשְׁרוֹ | יָעֹז |
| māʿûzzô | wayyivṭach | bᵉrōv | ʿāshᵉrô | yāʿōz |
| his refuge | but he trusts | in the abundance of | his riches | he demonstrates strength |

| 904, 2010 | | 603 | 3626, 2215 | 7776 | 904, 1041 | 435 |
|---|---|---|---|---|---|---|
| prep, n fs, ps 3ms | 8. | cj, pers pron | prep, n ms | adj | prep, *n ms* | n mp |
| בְּהַוָּתוֹ | | וַאֲנִי | כְּזַיִת | רַעֲנָן | בְּבֵית | אֱלֹהִים |
| bᵉhawwāthô | | waʾănî | kᵉzayith | raʿănān | bᵉvêth | 'ĕlōhîm |
| by his destruction | | but I | like an olive tree | luxurious | into the Temple of | God |

| 1019.115 | 904, 2721, 435 | 5986 | 5911 | | 3142.525 |
|---|---|---|---|---|---|
| v Qal pf 1cs | prep, *n ms*, n mp | n ms | cj, n ms | 9. | v Hiphil juss 1cs, ps 2ms |
| בָּטַחְתִּי | בְּחֶסֶד־אֱלֹהִים | עוֹלָם | וָעֶד | | אוֹדְךָ |
| bāṭachtî | vᵉchesedh-'ĕlōhîm | ʿôlām | wāʿedh | | 'ôdhkhā |
| I have trusted | in the steadfast love of God | forever | and everlasting | | let me praise You |

| 3937, 5986 | 3706 | 6449.113 | 7245.325 | 8428 | 3706, 3005 | 5224 |
|---|---|---|---|---|---|---|
| prep, n ms | cj | v Qal pf 2ms | cj, v Piel juss 1cs | n ms, ps 2ms | cj, adj | prep |
| לְעוֹלָם | כִּי | עָשִׂיתָ | וַאֲקַוֶּה | שִׁמְךָ | כִּי־טוֹב | נֶגֶד |
| lᵉʿôlām | kî | ʿāsîthā | waʾăqawweh | shimkhā | khî-ṭôv | neghedh |
| unto eternity | because | You have done | and let me hope in | your name | because good | before |

| 2728 | | 3937, 5514.351 | 6142, 4395 | 5030 | 3937, 1784 | | 569.111 |
|---|---|---|---|---|---|---|---|
| n mp, ps 2ms | 53:t | prep, art, v Piel ptc ms | prep, n fs | n ms | prep, pn | 1. | v Qal pf 3ms |
| חֲסִידֶיךָ | | לַמְנַצֵּחַ | עַל־מָחֲלַת | מַשְׂכִּיל | לְדָוִד | | אָמַר |
| chăsîdhêkhā | | lamnatstsēach | ʿal-māchălath | maskîl | lᵉdhāwidh | | 'āmar |
| your godly ones | | to the director | on the mahalath | a Maskil | of David | | he has said |

| 5210 | 904, 3949 | 375 | 435 | 8271.516 |
|---|---|---|---|---|
| n ms | prep, n ms, ps 3ms | *sub* | n mp | v Hiphil pf 3cp |
| נָבָל | בְּלִבּוֹ | אֵין | אֱלֹהִים | הִשְׁחִיתוּ |
| nāvāl | bᵉlibbô | 'ên | 'ĕlōhîm | hishchîthû |
| the foolish | in his heart | there is not | God | they are depraved |

| 8911.516 | 5982 | 375 | 6449.151, 3005 | | 435 |
|---|---|---|---|---|---|
| cj, v Hiphil pf 3cp | n ms | *sub* | v Qal act ptc ms, adj | 2. | n mp |
| וְהִתְעִיבוּ | עָוֶל | אֵין | עֹשֵׂה־טוֹב | | אֱלֹהִים |
| wᵉhithʿîvû | ʿāwel | 'ên | ʿōsēh-ṭôv | | 'ĕlōhîm |
| and they have acted abominably | perverseness | there is not | one who does good | | God |

| 4623, 8452 | 8625.511 | 6142, 1158 | 119 | 3937, 7495.141 | 1950B, 3552 |
|---|---|---|---|---|---|
| prep, n md | v Hiphil pf 3ms | prep, *n mp* | n ms | prep, v Qal inf con | intrg part, sub |
| מִשָּׁמַיִם | הִשְׁקִיף | עַל־בְּנֵי | אָדָם | לִרְאוֹת | הֲיֵשׁ |
| mishshāmayim | hishqîph | ʿal-bᵉnê | 'ādhām | lir'ôth | hăyēsh |
| from the heavens | He looks down | on the children of | humankind | to see | is there |

| 7959.551 | 1938.151 | 881, 435 | | 3725 | 5657.111 | 3267 |
|---|---|---|---|---|---|---|
| v Hiphil ptc ms | v Qal act ptc ms | do, n mp | 3. | adj, ps 3ms | v Qal pf 3ms | adv |
| מַשְׂכִּיל | דֹּרֵשׁ | אֶת־אֱלֹהִים | | כֻּלּוֹ | סָג | יַחְדָּו |
| maskîl | dōrēsh | 'eth-'ĕlōhîm | | kullô | sāgh | yachdāw |
| one who acts wisely | one who seeks | God | | all of them | they have deviated | together |

| 447.216 | 375 | 6449.151, 3005 | 375 | 1612, 259 |
|---|---|---|---|---|
| v Niphal pf 3cp | *sub* | v Qal act ptc ms, adj | *sub* | cj, num |
| נֶאֱלָחוּ | אֵין | עֹשֵׂה־טוֹב | אֵין | גַּם־אֶחָד |
| ne'ĕlāchû | 'ên | 'ōsēh-ṭôv | 'ên | gam-'echādh |
| they have become corrupt | there is not | one who does good | there is not | even one |

| | 1950B, 3940 | 3156.116 | 6713.152 | 201 | 404.152 | 6194 |
|---|---|---|---|---|---|---|
| 4. | intrg part, neg part | v Qal pf 3cp | *v Qal act ptc mp* | n ms | *v Qal act ptc mp* | n ms, ps 1cs |
| | הֲלֹא | יָדְעוּ | פֹּעֲלֵי | אָוֶן | אֹכְלֵי | עַמִּי |
| | hălō' | yādh$^e$'û | pō'ălê | 'āwen | 'ōkh$^e$lê | 'ammî |
| | do not | they know | those who practice | iniquity | those who devour | my people |

**7. Lo, this is the man that made not God his strength; but trusted in the abundance of his riches, and strengthened himself in his wickedness:** ... So much for someone who would not place his reliance in God, *JB* ... who would have none of God's help, *Knox* ... So this was the great man who would not upon God rely, but ... on his power of money!, *Moffatt* ... his strength in harmful plots, *NAB* ... And was strong in his evil desire, *NASB*.

**8. But I am like a green olive tree in the house of God: I trust in the mercy of God for ever and ever:** ... like a spreading olive-tree, *NEB* ... like an olive tree flourishing in the house of God; I trust in God's unfailing love for ever, *NIV* ... trust in the steadfast love of God forever, *NRSV*.

**9. I will praise thee for ever, because thou hast done it: and I will wait on thy name; for it is good before thy saints:** I will give honour to your name, *BB* ... thank You forever for what You did, *Beck* ... in the presence of thy saints I will proclaim that thy name is good, *Goodspeed*.

**53:t. To the chief Musician upon Mahalath, Maschil, A Psalm of David.**

**1. The fool hath said in his heart, There is no God. Corrupt are they, and have done abominable iniquity: there is none that doeth good:** ... Profane men think, "There is no God!," *Moffatt* ... They are corrupt, vile and unjust, not one of them does right, *JB* ... They acted basely; they did abominable things, *Goodspeed* ... there is not an innocent man among them, *Knox*.

**2. God looked down from heaven upon the children of men, to see if there were any that did understand, that did seek God:** ... To see if there be one who ponders, one who searches for God, *Anchor* ... to see if there were any who had wisdom, *BB* ... who comes to God for help, *Beck* ... to find one soul that reflects, *Knox*.

**3. Every one of them is gone back: they are altogether become filthy; there is none that doeth good, no, not one:** ... all have missed the mark and rebelled against him, *Knox* ... they have become perverse, *NAB* ... They have together become corrupt, *NKJV* ... all have turned their backs on him, *LIVB*.

**4. Have the workers of iniquity no knowledge? who eat up my people as they eat bread: they have not called upon God:** ... Will all these evildoers never learn?, *NAB* ... evildoers who devour my people as if eating bread, and never call to God, *REB* ... they take my people for food, as they would take bread; they make no prayer to God, *BB*.

self to be strong in his own evil and, instead of relying on God, trusts in material resources, will sooner or later be leveled with the ground, dragged, resisting vainly the tremendous grasp from his tent and laid prostrate, as melancholy a spectacle as a great tree blown down by a tempest with its roots turned up to the sky and its arms with drooping leaves trailing on the ground.

**52:8–9.** A swift turn of feeling carries the singer to rejoice in the contrast of his own lot. No uprooting does he fear. It may be questioned whether the words "in the house of God" refer to the psalmist or to the olive tree. Apparently, there were trees in the Temple area (Ps. 92:13), but the parallel in the next clause, "in the mercy of God," points to the reference of the words to the speaker. Dwelling in enjoyment of God's fellowship, as symbolized by and realized through presence in the sanctuary, whether it were at Nob or in Jerusalem, he dreads no such forcible removal as had befallen the tyrant. Communion with God is the source of flourishing and fruitfulness, and the guarantee of its own continuance.

***Psalm 53.*** *In this Psalm, we have a recast of Ps. 14, differing from its original in substituting Elohim for Yahweh (four times) and in the language of v. 5. There are also other slight deviations not affecting the sense. For the exposition, the reader is referred to that of Ps. 14. It is only necessary here to take note of the divergences.*

**53:1–4.** The first of these occurs in v. 1. The forcible rough construction "they corrupt, they

| 404.116 | 4035 | 435 | 3940 | 7410.116 | | 8427 |
|---|---|---|---|---|---|---|
| v Qal pf 3cp | n ms | n mp | neg part | v Qal pf 3cp | | adv |
| אָכְלוּ | לֶחֶם | אֱלֹהִים | לֹא | קָרָאוּ | **5.** | שָׁם |
| 'ākhelû | lechem | 'ĕlōhîm | lō' | qārā'û | | shām |
| they have eaten | bread | God | not | they have called on | | there |

| 6585.116, 6586 | 3940, 2030.111 | 6586 | 3706, 435 | 6582.311 |
|---|---|---|---|---|
| v Qal pf 3cp, n ms | neg part, v Qal pf 3ms | n ms | cj, n mp | v Piel pf 3ms |
| פָּחֲדוּ־פַחַד | לֹא־הָיָה | פָּחַד | כִּי־אֱלֹהִים | פִּזַּר |
| pāchădhû-phachadh | lō'-hāyāh | phāchadh | kî-'ĕlōhîm | pizzar |
| they are terrified with terror | it is not | terror | because God | He will scatter |

| 6344 | 2699.151 | 991.513 | 3706, 435 |
|---|---|---|---|
| *n fp* | v Qal act ptc ms, ps 2ms | v Hiphil pf 2ms | cj, n mp |
| עַצְמוֹת | חֹנָךְ | הֱבִשֹׁתָה | כִּי־אֱלֹהִים |
| 'atsmôth | chōnākh | hĕvishōthāh | kî-'ĕlōhîm |
| the bones of | the one who encamps against you | you will cause to be ashamed | because God |

| 4128.111 | | 4449 | 5598.121 | 4623, 6995 | 3568 | 3547 | 904, 8178.141 |
|---|---|---|---|---|---|---|---|
| v Qal pf 3ms, ps 3mp | | intrg | v Qal impf 3ms | prep, pn | *n fp* | pn | prep, v Qal inf con |
| מְאָסָם | **6.** | מִי | יִתֵּן | מִצִּיּוֹן | יְשֻׁעוֹת | יִשְׂרָאֵל | בְּשׁוּב |
| me'āsām | | mî | yittēn | mitstsîyôn | yeshu'ôth | yisrā'ēl | beshûv |
| He has rejected them | | who | he will allow | from Zion | deliverances for | Israel | when returning |

| 435 | 8097 | 6194 | 1559.121 | 3399 | 7975.121 | 3547 |
|---|---|---|---|---|---|---|
| n mp | *n fs* | n ms, ps 3ms | v Qal juss 3ms | pn | v Qal juss 3ms | pn |
| אֱלֹהִים | שְׁבוּת | עַמּוֹ | יָגֵל | יַעֲקֹב | יִשְׂמַח | יִשְׂרָאֵל |
| 'ĕlōhîm | shevûth | 'ammô | yāghēl | ya'ăqōv | yismach | yisrā'ēl |
| God | the captivity of | his people | may he rejoice | Jacob | may he be glad | Israel |

| | 3937, 5514.351 | 904, 5234 | 5030 | 3937, 1784 | 904, 971.141 |
|---|---|---|---|---|---|
| | prep, art, v Piel ptc ms | prep, n fp | n ms | prep, pn | prep, v Qal inf con |
| **54:t** | לַמְנַצֵּחַ | בִּנְגִינֹת | מַשְׂכִּיל | לְדָוִד | בְּבוֹא |
| | lamnatstsēach | binghînōth | maskîl | ledhāwidh | vevō' |
| | to the director | with the stringed instruments | a Maskil | of David | when going |

| 2213 | 569.126 | 3937, 8062 | 1950B, 3940 | 1784 | 5846.751 | 6196 |
|---|---|---|---|---|---|---|
| art, pn | cj, v Qal impf 3mp | prep, pn | intrg part, neg part | pn | v Hithpael ptc ms | prep, ps 1cp |
| הַזִּיפִים | וַיֹּאמְרוּ | לְשָׁאוּל | הֲלֹא | דָוִד | מִסְתַּתֵּר | עִמָּנוּ |
| hazzîphîm | wayyō'merû | leshā'ûl | hălō' | dhāwidh | mistattēr | 'immānû |
| the Ziphites | and they said | to Saul | is not | David | hiding | among us |

| | 435 | 904, 8428 | 3588.531 | 904, 1400 | 1833.123 |
|---|---|---|---|---|---|
| | n mp | prep, n ms, ps 2ms | v Hiphil impv 2ms, ps 1cs | cj, prep, n fs, ps 2ms | v Qal impf 2ms, ps 1cs |
| **1.** | אֱלֹהִים | בְּשִׁמְךָ | הוֹשִׁיעֵנִי | וּבִגְבוּרָתְךָ | תְדִינֵנִי |
| | 'ĕlōhîm | beshimkhā | hôshî'ēnî | ûvighvûrāthekhā | thedhînēnî |
| | O God | in your name | save me | and by your strength | judge me |

| | 435 | 8471.131 | 8940 | 237.531 | 3937, 571, 6552 | | 3706 |
|---|---|---|---|---|---|---|---|
| | n mp | v Qal impv 2ms | n fs, ps 1cs | v Hiphil impv 2ms | prep, *n mp*, n ms, ps 1cs | | cj |
| **2.** | אֱלֹהִים | שְׁמַע | תְּפִלָּתִי | הַאֲזִינָה | לְאִמְרֵי־פִי | **3.** | כִּי |
| | 'ĕlōhîm | shema' | tephillāthî | ha'ăzînāh | le'imrê-phî | | kî |
| | O God | hear | my prayer | listen | to the words of my mouth | | because |

| 2299 | 7251.116 | 6142 | 6422 | 1272.316 | 5497 | 3940 | 7947.116 |
|---|---|---|---|---|---|---|---|
| n mp | v Qal pf 3cp | prep, ps 1cs | cj, n mp | v Piel pf 3cp | n fs, ps 1cs | neg part | v Qal pf 3cp |
| זָרִים | קָמוּ | עָלַי | וְעָרִיצִים | בִּקְשׁוּ | נַפְשִׁי | לֹא | שָׂמוּ |
| zārîm | qāmû | 'ālay | we'ārîtsîm | biqōshû | naphshî | lō' | sāmû |
| strangers | they have risen | against me | and tyrants | they seek | my life | not | they have placed |

**5. There were they in great fear, where no fear was: for God hath scattered the bones of him that encampeth against thee: thou hast put them to shame, because God hath despised them:** ... overwhelmed with dread, where there was nothing to dread, *NIV* ... for God scatters the bones of your besiegers ... because God has rejected them, *Berkeley* ... they are mocked because God rejects them, *JB*.

**6. Oh that the salvation of Israel were come out of Zion! When God bringeth back the captivity of his people, Jacob shall rejoice, and Israel shall be glad:** ... deliverance might come!, *Berkeley* ... When the fate of his people is changed by God, *BB* ... When God restores His people, *Beck* ... How I pray that victory will come, *Good News*.

**54:t. To the chief Musician on Neginoth, Mashil, A Psalm of David, when the Ziphims came and said to Saul, Doth not David hide himself with us?**

**1. Save me, O God, by thy name, and judge me by thy strength:** ... by the virtue of thy name deliver me, *Knox* ... by your might defend my cause, *NAB* ... vindicate me, *NASB* ... show that I am innocent, *NCV*.

**2. Hear my prayer, O God; give ear to the words of my mouth:** ... listen to my supplication, *NEB* ... Let my prayer come before you, *BB* ... hear my pleading, *Berkeley*.

**3. For strangers are risen up against me, and oppressors seek after my soul: they have not set God before them. Selah:** ... haughty men have risen up against me, and fierce men seek my life, *NAB* ... violent men seek my life, *Berkeley* ... no room in their thoughts for God, *JB*.

---

make abominable," is smoothed down by the insertion of "and." The author apparently thought that the loosely piled words needed a piece of mortar to hold them together, but his emendation weakens as well as smoothes. On the other hand, he has aimed at increased energy of expression by substituting "iniquity" for "doings" in the same clause, which results in tautology and is no improvement. In v. 3, the word for "turned aside" (HED #7251) is varied, without substantial difference of meaning. The alteration is very slight, affecting only one letter, and may be due to error in transcription or to mere desire to emend. In v. 4, "all," which in Ps. 14 precedes "workers of iniquity," is omitted, probably as unnecessary.

**53:5–6.** The most important changes are in v. 5, which stands for vv. 5f of Ps. 14. The first is the insertion of "where no fear was." These words may be taken as describing causeless panic or, less probably, as having a subjective reference and being equal to "while in the midst of careless security." They evidently point to some fact, possibly the destruction of Sennacherib's army. Their insertion shows that the object of the alterations was to adapt an ancient Psalm as a hymn of triumph for recent deliverance, thus altering its application from evildoers within Israel to enemies without. The same purpose is obvious in the transformations effected in the remainder of this verse. The tremulous hope of the original, "God is his refuge" swells into commemoration of an accomplished fact in "God has rejected them." The natural supposition is that some great deliverance of Israel had just taken place and inspired this singular attempt to fit old words to new needs. Whatever the historical occasion may have been, the two singers unite in one final aspiration, a sigh of longing for the coming of Israel's full salvation, which is intensified in the recast by being put in the plural ("salvation of Israel were come") instead of the singular, as in Ps. 14, to express the completeness and deliverance thus yearned for of old, and not yet come in its perfection.

***Psalm 54.*** *The structure is simple, like the thought and expression. The Psalm falls into two parts, divided by selah, of which the former is prayer, spreading before God the suppliant's straits; and the latter is confident assurance, blended with petition and vows of thanksgiving.*

**54:1–3.** The order in which the psalmist's thoughts run in the first part (vv. 1ff) is noteworthy. He begins with appeal to God and summons before his vision the characteristics in the divine nature on which he builds his hope. Then he pleads for the acceptance of his prayer, and only when thus heartened does he recount his perils. That is a deeper faith which begins with what God is and from that place proceeds to look calmly at foes than that which is driven to God in the second place as a consequence of an alarmed gaze on dangers. In the latter case, fear strikes out a spark of faith in the darkness; in the former, faith controls fear.

"Strangers," in v. 3, would most naturally mean foreigners, but not necessarily so. The meaning would naturally pass into that of enemies —men who, even though of the psalmist's own blood, behave to him in a hostile manner. The word, then, does not negate the tradition in the superscription; although the men of Ziph belonged to the tribe of Judah, they might still be called "strangers." The verse recurs in Ps. 84:14, with a

| 435 | 3937, 5224 | 5734 | | 2079 | 435 | 6038.151 | 3937 | 112 |
|---|---|---|---|---|---|---|---|---|
| n mp | prep, prep, ps 3mp | intrj | | intrj | n mp | v Qal act ptc ms | prep, ps 1cs | n mp, ps 1cs |
| אֱלֹהִים | לְנֶגְדָּם | סֶלָה | 4. | הִנֵּה | אֱלֹהִים | עֹזֵר | לִי | אֲדֹנָי |
| 'ĕlōhîm | leneghdām | selāh | | hinnēh | 'ĕlōhîm | 'ōzēr | lî | 'ădhōnāy |
| God | before them | selah | | behold | God | a Helper | to me | my Lord |

| 904, 5759.152 | 5497 | | 8178.121 | 7737 | 3937, 8234 |
|---|---|---|---|---|---|
| prep, *v Qal act ptc mp* | n fs, ps 1cs | | v Qal juss 3ms | art, adj | prep, n mp, ps 1cs |
| בְּסֹמְכֵי | נַפְשִׁי | 5. | יָשׁוּב | הָרַע | לְשֹׁרְרָי |
| besōmekhê | naphshî | | yāshôv | hāra' | leshōrerāy |
| with those who sustain | my life | | it will turn back | the evil | to my enemies |

| 904, 583 | 7059.531 | | 904, 5249 | 2159.125, 3937 |
|---|---|---|---|---|
| prep, n fs, ps 2ms | v Hiphil impv 2ms, ps 3mp | | prep, n fs | v Qal juss 1cs, prep, ps 2ms |
| בַּאֲמִתֶּךָ | הַצְמִיתֵם | 6. | בִּנְדָבָה | אֶזְבְּחָה־לָּךְ |
| ba'ămittekhā | hatsmîthēm | | bindhāvāh | 'ezbechāh-lākh |
| by your steadfast love | annihilate them | | with a freewill offering | let me sacrifice to You |

| 3142.525 | 8428 | 3176 | 3706, 3005 | | 3706 | 4623, 3725, 7150 |
|---|---|---|---|---|---|---|
| v Hiphil juss 1cs | n ms, ps 2ms | pn | cj, adj | | cj | prep, *adj*, n fs |
| אוֹדֶה | שִׁמְךָ | יְהוָה | כִּי־טוֹב | 7. | כִּי | מִכָּל־צָרָה |
| 'ôdheh | shimkhā | yehwāh | kî-ṭôv | | kî | mikkol-tsārāh |
| let me praise | your name | O Yahweh | because good | | because | from all adversity |

| 5522.511 | 904, 342.152 | 7495.112 | 6084 | | 3937, 5514.351 |
|---|---|---|---|---|---|
| v Hiphil pf 3ms, ps 1cs | cj, prep, v Qal act ptc mp, ps 1cs | v Qal pf 3fs | n fs, ps 1cs | | prep, art, v Piel ptc ms |
| הִצִּילָנִי | וּבְאֹיְבַי | רָאֲתָה | עֵינִי | 55:t | לַמְנַצֵּחַ |
| hitstsîlānî | ûve'ōyevay | rā'ăthāh | 'ênî | | lamnatstsēach |
| He has rescued me | and over my enemies | it has seen | my eye | | to the director |

| 904, 5234 | 5030 | 3937, 1784 | | 237.531 | 435 | 8940 |
|---|---|---|---|---|---|---|
| prep, n fp | n ms | prep, pn | | v Hiphil impv 2ms | n mp | n fs, ps 1cs |
| בִּנְגִינֹת | מַשְׂכִּיל | לְדָוִד | 1. | הַאֲזִינָה | אֱלֹהִים | תְּפִלָּתִי |
| binghînōth | maskîl | ledhāwidh | | ha'ăzînāh | 'ĕlōhîm | tephillāthî |
| with the stringed instruments | a Maskil | of David | | listen to | O God | my prayer |

| 414, 6180.723 | 4623, 8798 | | 7477.531 | 3937 |
|---|---|---|---|---|
| cj, adv, v Hithpael juss 2ms | prep, n fs, ps 1cs | | v Hiphil impv 2ms | prep, ps 1cs |
| וְאַל־תִּתְעַלַּם | מִתְּחִנָּתִי | 2. | הַקְשִׁיבָה | לִי |
| we'al-tith'allam | mittechinnāthî | | haqŏshîvāh | lî |
| and do not conceal yourself | from my supplication | | be attentive | to me |

| 6257.131 | 7586.525 | 904, 7945 | 2016.525 |
|---|---|---|---|
| cj, v Qal impv 2ms, ps 1cs | v Hiphil impf 1cs | prep, n ms, ps 1cs | cj, v Hiphil impf 1cs |
| וַעֲנֵנִי | אָרִיד | בְּשִׂיחִי | וְאָהִימָה |
| wa'ănēnî | 'ārîdh | besîchî | we'āhîmāh |
| and answer me | I am restless | because of my complaint | and I am thrown into confusion |

**4. Behold, God is mine helper: the Lord is with them that uphold my soul:** ... God is my ally, *Berkeley* ... the Lord has my safety in his keeping, *Knox* ... sustains me, *NIV* ... great supporter of my soul, *BB*.

**5. He shall reward evil unto mine enemies: cut them off in thy truth:** ... Turn back the evil upon my foes; in your faithfulness destroy them, *NAB* ... Let evil recoil on those who slander me, *NIV* ... Let the evil works of my haters come back on them again; let them be cut off by your good faith, *BB*.

**6. I will freely sacrifice unto thee: I will praise thy name, O LORD; for it is good:** ... I make my offerings to you, *BB* ... Liberally I will sacrifice to thee, *Goodspeed*.

**7. For he hath delivered me out of all trouble: and mine eye hath seen his desire upon mine enemies:** ... from all distress you have rescued me, *NAB* ... And my eye has looked with satisfaction upon my enemies,

*NASB* ... and I look on my enemies' downfall with delight, *NEB*.

**55:t. To the chief Musician on Neginoth, Maschil, A Psalm of David.**

**1. Give ear to my prayer, O God; and hide not thyself from my supplication:** ... let not your ear be shut, *BB* ... hide not Yourself from my cry, *KJVII* ... hide not Thyself from my petition, *Berkeley*.

**2. Attend unto me, and hear me: I mourn in my complaint, and make a noise:** ... Hear me and answer, for my cares give me no peace, *NEB* ... trouble me and I am distraught, *NIV* ... I have been made low in sorrow, *BB* ... I am restless and troubled, *Beck* ... In restlessness I groan and am distracted, *Berkeley*.

**3. Because of the voice of the enemy, because of the oppression of the wicked: for they cast iniq-**

---

variation of reading, namely, "proud" instead of "strangers." The same variation is found here in some manuscripts and in the Targum. But probably it has crept in here in order to bring our Psalm into correspondence with the other, and it is better to retain the existing reading, which is that of the Septuagint and other ancient authorities.

**54:4–5.** Prayer is, as so often in the Psalter, followed by immediately deepened assurance of victory. The suppliant rises from his knees and points the enemies around him to his one Helper. In v. 4b, a literal rendering would mislead. "The LORD is among the upholders of my soul" seems to bring God down to a level on which others stand. The psalmist does not mean this, but that God gathers up in himself supremely the qualities belonging to the conception of an upholder. It is, in form, an inclusion of God in a certain class. It is, in meaning, the assertion that He is the only true representative of the class.

That petition is, like others in similar Psalms, proper to the spiritual level of the OT, and not to that of the NT; and it is far more reverent, as well as accurate, to recognize fully the distinction than to try to slur it over. At the same time, it is not to be forgotten that the same lofty consciousness of the identity of his cause with God's, which we have already had to notice, operating here in these wishes for the enemies' destruction, gives another aspect to them than that of mere outbursts of private vengeance.

**54:6–7.** The faith which has prayed has grown so sure of answer that it already begins to think of the thank offerings. This is not like a superstitious vow. This praying man knows that he is heard, and he is not so much vowing as joyfully anticipating his glad sacrifice. The same incipient personification of the name as in v. 1 is very prominent in the closing strains. Thank offerings—not merely statutory and obligatory, but brought by free, uncommanded impulse—are to be offered to "thy name," because that name is good. Verse 7 probably should be taken as going even further in the same direction of personification, for "thy name" is probably to be taken as the subject of "hath delivered." The tenses of the verbs in v. 7 are perfects. They contemplate the deliverance as already accomplished.

The closing words express confidence in the enemies' defeat and destruction, with a tinge of feeling that is not permissible to Christians. But the supplement, "his desire," is perhaps rather too strongly expressive. Possibly, there needs no supplement at all, and the expression simply paints the calm security of the man protected by God, who can look upon impotent hostility without the tremor of an eyelid, because he knows Who is his Helper.

***Psalm 55.*** *The Psalm may be regarded as divided into three parts, in each of which a different phase of agitated feeling predominates, but not exclusively. Strong excitement does not marshal emotions or their expression according to artistic proprieties of sequence, and this Psalm is all ablaze with it. That vehemence of emotion sufficiently accounts for both the occasional obscurities and the manifest lack of strict accuracy in the flow of thought, without the assumption of dislocation of parts or piecing it with a fragment of another Psalm. When the heart is writhing within, and tumultuous feelings are knocking at the door of the lips, the words will be troubled and heaped together, and dominant thoughts will repeat themselves in defiance of logical continuity. Still, complaint and longing sound through the wailing, yearning notes of vv. 1–8; hot indignation and terrible imprecations in the stormy central portion (vv. 9–15); and a calmer note of confidence and hope, through which, however, the former indignation surges up again, is audible in the closing verses (vv. 16–23).*

**55:1–4.** The psalmist pictures his emotions in the first part, with but one reference to their cause and but one verse of petition. He begins, indeed, with asking that his prayer may be heard; and it is well when a troubled heart can raise itself above the sea of troubles to stretch a hand toward God. Such an effort of faith already prophesies firm footing on the safe shore. But very pathetic and

| 3. | 4623, 7249 | 342.151 | 4623, 6686 | 6363 | 7857 |
|---|---|---|---|---|---|
| | prep, *n ms* | v Qal act ptc ms | prep, *n mp* | *n fs* | n ms |
| | מִקּוֹל | אוֹיֵב | מִפְּנֵי | עָקַת | רָשָׁע |
| | miqqôl | 'ôyēv | mippᵉnê | 'āqath | rāshā' |
| | from the sound of | an enemy | from before | the oppression of | the wicked |

| 3706, 4267.526 | 6142 | 201 | 904, 653 | 7929.126 |
|---|---|---|---|---|
| cj, v Hiphil impf 3mp | prep, ps 1cs | n ms | cj, prep, n ms | v Qal impf 3mp, ps 1cs |
| כִּי־יָמִיטוּ | עָלַי | אָוֶן | וּבְאַף | יִשְׂטְמוּנִי |
| kî-yāmîṭû | 'ālay | 'āwen | ûve'aph | yisṯᵉmûnî |
| because they cause to totter | over me | iniquity | and in anger | they are at enmity with me |

| 4. | 3949 | 2523.121 | 904, 7419 | 372 | 4323 | 5489.116 | 6142 |
|---|---|---|---|---|---|---|---|
| | n ms, ps 1cs | v Qal impf 3ms | prep, n ms, ps 1cs | cj, *n fp* | n ms | v Qal pf 3cp | prep, ps 1cs |
| | לִבִּי | יָחִיל | בְּקִרְבִּי | וְאֵימוֹת | מָוֶת | נָפְלוּ | עָלָי |
| | libbî | yāchîl | bᵉqirbî | wᵉ'êmôth | māweth | nāphᵉlû | 'ālāy |
| | my heart | it writhes | within me | and the horrors of | death | they have fallen | upon me |

| 5. | 3488 | 7747 | 971.121 | 904 | 3803.322 | 6671 |
|---|---|---|---|---|---|---|
| | n fs | cj, n ms | v Qal impf 3ms | prep, ps 1cs | cj, v Piel impf 3fs, ps 1cs | n fs |
| | יִרְאָה | וָרַעַד | יָבֹא | בִי | וַתְּכַסֵּנִי | פַּלָּצוּת |
| | yir'āh | wāra'adh | yāvō' | vî | wattᵉkhassēnî | pallātsûth |
| | fear | and trembling | it has come | on me | and it covers me | shuddering |

| 6. | 569.125 | 4449, 5598.121, 3937 | 78 | 3626, 3225 | 5990.125 |
|---|---|---|---|---|---|
| | cj, v Qal impf 1cs | intrg, v Qal impf 3ms, prep, ps 1cs | n ms | prep, art, n fs | v Qal juss 1cs |
| | וָאֹמַר | מִי־יִתֶּן־לִּי | אֵבֶר | כַּיּוֹנָה | אָעוּפָה |
| | wā'ōmar | mî-yitten-lî | 'ēver | kayyônāh | 'ā'ûphāh |
| | and I say | who will allow to me | wings | like the dove | that I might fly |

| 8331.125 | 7. | 2079 | 7651.525 | 5252.141 | 4053.125 |
|---|---|---|---|---|---|
| cj, v Qal juss 1cs | | intrj | v Hiphil juss 1cs | v Qal inf con | v Qal juss 1cs |
| וְאֶשְׁכֹּנָה | | הִנֵּה | אַרְחִיק | נְדֹד | אָלִין |
| wᵉ'eshkōnāh | | hinnēh | 'archîq | nᵉdhōdh | 'ālîn |
| and that I might settle | | behold | let me go far away | to escape | that I might lodge |

| 904, 4198 | 5734 | 8. | 2456.525 | 4817 | 3937 | 4623, 7593 | 5779.153 |
|---|---|---|---|---|---|---|---|
| prep, art, n ms | intrj | | v Hiphil juss 1cs | n ms | prep, ps 1cs | prep, n fs | v Qal act ptc fs |
| בַּמִּדְבָּר | סֶלָה | | אָחִישָׁה | מִפְלָט | לִי | מֵרוּחַ | סֹעָה |
| bammidhbār | selāh | | 'āchîshāh | miphlāṯ | lî | mērûach | sō'āh |
| in the wilderness | selah | | let me hurry | a retreat | to me | from the wind | driving |

| 4623, 5787 | 9. | 1142.331 | 112 | 6629.331 | 4098 | 3706, 7495.115 |
|---|---|---|---|---|---|---|
| prep, n ms | | v Piel impv 2ms | n mp, ps 1cs | v Piel impv 2ms | n fs, ps 3mp | cj, v Qal pf 1cs |
| מִסַּעַר | | בַּלַּע | אֲדֹנָי | פַּלַּג | לְשׁוֹנָם | כִּי־רָאִיתִי |
| missā'ar | | balla' | 'ădhōnāy | pallagh | lᵉshônām | kî-rā'îthî |
| from the gale | | swallow | O my Lord | split | their tongues | because I have seen |

| 2660 | 7663 | 904, 6111 | 10. | 3221 | 4050 | 5621.326 | 6142, 2440 |
|---|---|---|---|---|---|---|---|
| n ms | cj, n ms | prep, art, n fs | | adv | cj, n ms | v Poel impf 3mp, ps 3fs | prep, n fp, ps 3fs |
| חָמָס | וְרִיב | בָּעִיר | | יוֹמָם | וָלַיְלָה | יְסוֹבְבֻהָ | עַל־חוֹמֹתֶיהָ |
| chāmās | wᵉrîv | bā'îr | | yômām | wālaylāh | yᵉsôvᵉvuāh | 'al-chômōthêāh |
| violence | and contention | in the city | | by day | and by night | they surround it | on its walls |

| 201 | 6219 | 904, 7419 | 11. | 2010 | 904, 7419 |
|---|---|---|---|---|---|
| cj, n ms | cj, n ms | prep, n ms, ps 3fs | | n fp | prep, n ms, ps 3fs |
| וְאָוֶן | וְעָמָל | בְּקִרְבָּהּ | | הַוּוֹת | בְּקִרְבָּהּ |
| wᵉ'āwen | wᵉ'āmāl | bᵉqirbāhh | | hawwôth | bᵉqirbāhh |
| and iniquity | and trouble | in the middle of it | | destruction | in the middle of it |

**uity upon me, and in wrath they hate me:** ... For they engulf me with their mischief and in anger they assault me, *Berkeley* ... for they bring down suffering upon me and revile me in their anger, *NIV* ... they attack me with fury, *Goodspeed* ... with fury they persecute me, *NAB*.

**4. My heart is sore pained within me: and the terrors of death are fallen upon me:** ... My heart is full of whirling thoughts; the fear of death stands over me, *Knox* ... My heart is in anguish, *NASB* ... heart is severely pained within me, *NKJV*.

**5. Fearfulness and trembling are come upon me, and horror hath overwhelmed me:** ... assail me and my whole frame shudders, *REB* ... horror has covered me, *KJVII* ... horror overpowers me, *Berkeley*.

**6. And I said, Oh that I had wings like a dove! for then would I fly away, and be at rest:** ... That I might fly away and dwell in peace, *Goodspeed* ... To fly off, and seek myself rest?, *Fenton*.

**7. Lo, then would I wander far off, and remain in the wilderness. Selah:** ... in the wilderness would I settle!, *Anchor* ... would lodge, *ASV* ... living in the waste land, *BB*.

**8. I would hasten my escape from the windy storm and tempest:** ... would hurry and find myself a shelter, *Good News* ... find a refuge, *JB* ... might find speedy refuge, *Knox* ... escape from the furious blast, *Moffatt*.

**9. Destroy, O Lord, and divide their tongues: for I have seen violence and strife in the city:** ... Send destruction on them, *BB* ... confuse their words, *NCV* ... confound their speech, *NIV* ... Frustrate and divide their counsels, *REB* ... I see violence and conflict, *Beck*.

**10. Day and night they go about it upon the walls thereof: mischief also and sorrow are in the midst of it:** ... Day and night they encircle the walls, *Fenton* ... trouble and misery are in the city, *Beck* ... all the while there is wrong and oppression at the heart of it, *Knox*.

**11. Wickedness is in the midst thereof: deceit and guile depart not from her streets:** ... Destruction is in her midst; Oppression and deceit do not depart, *NASB* ... Destructive forces are at work in the city; threats and lies never leave its streets, *NIV* ... oppression and fraud do not depart, *NRSV*.

---

true to the experience of many a sorrowing heart is the psalmist's immediately subsequent dilating on his griefs. There is a dumb sorrow, and there is one which unpacks its heart in many words and knows not when to stop. The psalmist is distracted in his bitter brooding on his troubles. The word means "to move restlessly," (HED #2523) and may either apply to body or mind, perhaps to both; for Eastern demonstrativeness is not paralyzed by sorrow, but stimulated to bodily tokens. He can do nothing but groan or moan. His heart is "sore pained" within him. Like an avalanche, deadly terrors have fallen on him and crushed him. Fear and trembling have pierced into his inner being, and "horror" (HED #372, a rare word, which the Septuagint here renders "darkness") wraps him round or covers him, as a cloak does. It is not so much the pressure of present evil, as the shuddering anticipation of a heavier storm about to burst, which is indicated by these pathetic expressions.

**55:5–8.** Then, from out of all this plaintive description of the psalmist's agitation and its causes, starts up that immortal strain which answers to the deepest longings of the soul and has touched responsive chords in all whose lives are not hopelessly outward and superficial—the yearning for repose. It may be ignoble, or lofty and pure; it may mean only cowardice or indolence; but it is deepest in those who stand most unflinchingly at their posts and crush it down at the command of duty. Unless a soul knows that yearning for a home in stillness, afar from the sphere of our sorrow, it will remain a stranger to many high and noble things. The psalmist was moved to utter this longing by his painful consciousness of encompassing evils; but the longing is more than a desire for exemption from these. It is the cry of the homeless soul, which, like the dove from the ark, finds no resting-place in a world full of carrion and would fain return whence it came. No obligation of duty keeps migratory birds in a land where winter is near. The selah at the close of v. 7 deepens the sense of still repose by a prolonged instrumental interlude.

**55:9–11.** The second part turns from subjective feelings to objective facts. A cry for help and a yearning for a safe solitude were natural results of the former; but when the psalmist's eye turns to his enemies, a flash of anger lights it, and, instead of the meek longings of the earlier verses, prayers for their destruction are vehemently poured out. The state of things in the city corresponds to what must have been the condition of Jerusalem during the incubation of Absalom's conspiracy, but it is sufficiently general to fit any time of strained party feeling. The caldron simmers, ready to boil over. The familiar evils, of which so many Psalms complain, are in full vigor. The psalmist enumerates them with a wealth of words which indicates their abun-

| 3940, 4318.521 | 4623, 7624 | 8826 | 4983 | | 3706 | 3940, 342.151 |
|---|---|---|---|---|---|---|
| cj, neg part, v Hiphil impf 3ms | prep, n ms, ps 3fs | n ms | cj, n fs | **12.** | cj | neg part, v Qal act ptc ms |
| וְלֹא־יָמִישׁ | מֵרְחֹבָהּ | תֹּךְ | וּמִרְמָה | | כִּי | לֹא־אוֹיֵב |
| welō'-yāmîsh | mērechōvāhh | tōkh | ûmirmāh | | kî | lō'-'ôyēv |
| and it does not withdraw | from its plaza | extortion | and fraud | | because | not an enemy |

| 2884.321 | 5558.125 | 3940, 7983.351 | 6142 | 1461.511 |
|---|---|---|---|---|
| cj, v Piel impf 3ms, ps 1cs | cj, v Qal impf 1cs | neg part, v Piel ptc ms, ps 1cs | prep, ps 1cs | v Hiphil pf 3ms |
| יְחָרְפֵנִי | וְאֶשָּׂא | לֹא־מְשַׂנְאִי | עָלַי | הִגְדִּיל |
| yechārephēnî | we'essā' | lō'-mesan'î | 'ālay | highdîl |
| he taunts me | then I could carry | not one who hates me | against me | He caused to be great |

| 5846.225 | 4623 | | 887 | 596 | 3626, 6425 | 443 |
|---|---|---|---|---|---|---|
| cj, v Niphal impf 1cs | prep, ps 3ms | **13.** | cj, pers pron | n ms | prep, n ms, ps 1cs | n ms, ps 1cs |
| וְאֶסָּתֵר | מִמֶּנּוּ | | וְאַתָּה | אֱנוֹשׁ | כְּעֶרְכִּי | אַלּוּפִי |
| we'essāthēr | mimmennû | | we'attāh | 'ĕnôsh | ke'erkî | 'allûphî |
| then I could hide myself | from him | | but you | a man | like my value | my close friend |

| 3156.455 | | 866 | 3267 | 5159.520 | 5660 | 904, 1041 |
|---|---|---|---|---|---|---|
| cj, v Pual ptc ms, ps 1cs | **14.** | rel pron | adv | v Hiphil impf 1cp | n ms | prep, *n ms* |
| וּמְיֻדָּעִי | | אֲשֶׁר | יַחְדָּו | נַמְתִּיק | סוֹד | בְּבֵית |
| ûmeyuddā'î | | 'ăsher | yachdāw | namtîq | sôdh | bevêth |
| and one known to me | | who | together | we caused to be sweet | consultation | in the Temple of |

| 435 | 2050.320 | 904, 7572 | | 5565.521 | 4323 | 6142 |
|---|---|---|---|---|---|---|
| n mp | v Piel impf 1cp | prep, n ms | **15.** | v Hiphil juss 3ms | n ms | prep, ps 3mp |
| אֱלֹהִים | נְהַלֵּךְ | בְּרָגֶשׁ | | יַשִּׁיא | מָוֶת | עָלֵימוֹ |
| 'ĕlōhîm | nehallēkh | berāghesh | | yashshî' | māweth | 'ālêmô |
| God | we walked | among the crowd | | may it deceive | death | concerning them |

| 3495.126 | 8061 | 2522 | 3706, 7750 | 904, 4172 | 904, 7419 |
|---|---|---|---|---|---|
| v Qal juss 3mp | pn | adj | cj, n fp | prep, n ms, ps 3mp | prep, n ms, ps 3mp |
| יֵרְדוּ | שְׁאוֹל | חַיִּים | כִּי־רָעוֹת | בִּמְגוּרָם | בְּקִרְבָּם |
| yēredhû | she'ôl | chayyîm | kî-rā'ôth | bimghûrām | beqirbām |
| may they go down to | Sheol | alive | because of the evils | in their sojourning | in their midst |

| | 603 | 420, 435 | 7410.125 | 3176 | 3588.521 | | 6394 |
|---|---|---|---|---|---|---|---|
| **16.** | pers pron | prep, n mp | v Qal impf 1cs | cj, pn | v Hiphil impf 3ms, ps 1cs | **17.** | n ms |
| | אֲנִי | אֶל־אֱלֹהִים | אֶקְרָא | וַיהוָה | יוֹשִׁיעֵנִי | | עֶרֶב |
| | 'ănî | 'el-'ĕlōhîm | 'eqōrā' | wayhwāh | yôshî'ēnî | | 'erev |
| | I | to God | I will call | and Yahweh | He will save me | | evening |

| 1269 | 6937 | 7943.125 | 2064.125 | 8471.121 | 7249 |
|---|---|---|---|---|---|
| cj, n ms | cj, n md | v Qal juss 1cs | cj, v Qal juss 1cs | cj, v Qal impf 3ms | n ms, ps 1cs |
| וָבֹקֶר | וְצָהֳרַיִם | אָשִׂיחָה | וְאֶהֱמֶה | וַיִּשְׁמַע | קוֹלִי |
| wāvōqer | wetsāherayim | 'āsîchāh | we'ehĕmeh | wayyishma' | qôlî |
| and morning | and noon | let me complain | and let me groan | and He will hear | my voice |

| | 6540.111 | 904, 8361 | 5497 | 4623, 7414.141 | 3706, 904, 7521 |
|---|---|---|---|---|---|
| **18.** | v Qal pf 3ms | prep, n ms | n fs, ps 1cs | prep, v Qal inf con, prep, ps 1cs | cj, prep, adj |
| | פָּדָה | בְשָׁלוֹם | נַפְשִׁי | מִקְּרָב־לִי | כִּי־בְרַבִּים |
| | pādhāh | veshālôm | naphshî | miqqerāv-lî | kî-verabbîm |
| | He has ransomed | in safety | my life | from drawing near to me | though with many |

| 2030.116 | 6200 | | 8471.121 | 418 | 6257.521 |
|---|---|---|---|---|---|
| v Qal pf 3cp | prep, ps 1cs | **19.** | v Qal impf 3ms | n ms | cj, v Hiphil impf 3ms, ps 3mp |
| הָיוּ | עִמָּדִי | | יִשְׁמַע | אֵל | וְיַעֲנֵם |
| hāyû | 'immādhî | | yishma' | 'ēl | weya'ănēm |
| they are | against me | | He hears | God | and He will afflict them |

**12. For it was not an enemy that reproached me; then I could have borne it: neither was it he that hated me that did magnify himself against me; then I would have hid myself from him:** ... it was not my hater who said evil of me; that would have been no grief to me, *BB* ... if it were one that hated me who attacked me—I could hide from him, *Beck.*

**13. But it was thou, a man mine equal, my guide, and mine acquaintance:** ... you, a man like myself, my companion and my friend, *LIVB* ... a person of my own rank, a comrade and dear friend, *JB* ... my companion and confidant, *Anchor* ... my familiar friend, *NRSV.*

**14. We took sweet counsel together, and walked unto the house of God in company:** ... Sweet was our fellowship, *Moffatt* ... worshiped together in the Temple, *Good News.*

**15. Let death seize upon them, and let them go down quick into hell: for wickedness is in their dwellings, and among them:** ... take my enemies by surprise; let them go down alive to the grave, *NIV* ... for evil is in their homes and in their hearts, *NRSV* ... let them go down living into the underworld, *BB.*

**16. As for me, I will call upon God; and the LORD shall save me:** ... I will call to God for help, *NCV* ... I appeal to God, *REB* ... I will make my prayer to God, *BB.*

**17. Evening, and morning, and at noon, will I pray, and cry aloud: and he shall hear my voice:** ... I will sigh and moan; and he will hear, *Goodspeed* ... I complain and I groan, *JB* ... I will cry aloud and make my plea known, *Knox.*

**18. He hath delivered my soul in peace from the battle that was against me: for there were many with me:** ... He ransoms me unharmed, *NIV* ... gave me back my peace, *NEB* ... given it peace, *BB.*

**19. God shall hear, and afflict them, even he that abideth of old. Selah. Because they have no changes, therefore they fear not God:** ... May God who sits on His ancient throne hear and put them down, *Beck* ... humble them, *MAST* ... they will not change; they do not fear God, *NCV.*

---

dance. Violence, strife, iniquity, mischief, oppression and deceit—a goodly company to patrol the streets and fill the open places of the city! Verse 10a is sometimes taken as carrying on the personification of violence and strife in v. 9 by painting these as going their rounds on the walls like sentries, but it is better to suppose that the actual foes are meant and that they are keeping up a strict watch to prevent the psalmist's escape.

**55:12–14.** The abruptness with which the thought of the traitor is interjected here and in the subsequent reference to him indicates how the singer's heart was oppressed by the treason, and the return to the subject in v. 20 is equally significant of his absorbed and pained brooding on the bitter fact. That is a slight pain which is removed by one cry. Rooted griefs and overwhelming sorrows demand many repetitions.

The psalmist feels that the defection of his false friend is the worst blow of all. He could have braced himself to bear an enemy's reviling, and he could have found weapons to repel, or a shelter in which to escape from, open foes, but the baseness which forgets all former sweet companionship in secret and all association in public and in worship is more than he can bear up against. The voice of wounded love is too plain in the words for the hypothesis that the singer is the personified nation. Traitors are too common to allow for a very confident affirmation that the Psalm must point to Ahithophel, and the description of the disloyal friend as the equal of the psalmist does not quite fit that case.

**55:15.** As he thinks of all the sweetness of past intimacy, turned to gall by such dastardly treachery, his anger rises. The description of the city and of the one enemy in whom all its wickedness is, as it were, concentrated, is framed in a terrible circlet of prayers for the destruction of the foes. The translation "desolations" (HED #7750) follows the Hebrew text, while the alternative and in some respects preferable reading "May death come suddenly" follows the Hebrew marginal correction. There are difficulties in both, and the correction does not so much smooth the language as to be obviously an improvement. The general sense is clear, whichever reading is preferred.

**55:16–18.** The third part of the Psalm returns to gentler tones of devotion and trust. The great name of Yahweh appears here significantly. To that Ever-Living One, the Covenant God, will the psalmist cry, in assurance of an answer. "Evening, and morning, and at noon" designate the whole day by its three principal divisions and mean, in effect, "continually." Happy are they who are impelled to unintermitting prayer by the sight of unslumbering enmity! Enemies may go their rounds "day and night," but they will do little harm, if the poor, hunted man, whom they watch so closely, lifts his cries to heaven "evening and morning and at noon." The psalmist goes back to his first words. He had begun by say-

| 3553.151 | 7208 | 5734 | 866 | 375 | 2588 | 3937 | 3940 |
|---|---|---|---|---|---|---|---|
| cj, v Qal act ptc ms | n ms | intrj | rel pron | *sub* | n fp | prep, ps 3ms | cj, neg part |
| וְיֹשֵׁב | קֶדֶם | סֶלָה | אֲשֶׁר | אֵין | חֲלִיפוֹת | לָמוֹ | וְלֹא |
| weyōshēv | qedhem | selāh | 'ăsher | 'ên | chălîphôth | lāmô | welō' |
| and One Who sits | antiquity | selah | Who | there is not | changes | to Him | and not |

| 3486.116 | 435 | | 8365.111 | 3135 | 904, 8361 |
|---|---|---|---|---|---|
| v Qal pf 3cp | n mp | **20.** | v Qal pf 3ms | n fd, ps 3ms | prep, n mp, ps 3ms |
| יָרְאוּ | אֱלֹהִים | | שָׁלַח | יָדָיו | בִּשְׁלֹמָיו |
| yāre'û | 'ĕlōhîm | | shālach | yādhâv | bishlōmâv |
| they have feared | God | | he stretched out | his hands | against his peaceful ones |

| 2591.311 | 1311 | | 2606.116 | 4397 | 6552 |
|---|---|---|---|---|---|
| v Piel pf 3ms | n fs, ps 3ms | **21.** | v Qal pf 3cp | *n fp* | n ms, ps 3ms |
| חִלֵּל | בְּרִיתוֹ | | חָלְקוּ | מַחְמָאֹת | פִּיו |
| chillēl | berîthô | | chāleqû | machmā'ōth | pîw |
| He has profaned | his covenant | | they were smooth | the butters of | his mouth |

| 7417, 3949 | 7690.116 | 1745 | 4623, 8467 | 2065 |
|---|---|---|---|---|
| cj, *n ms*, n ms, ps 3ms | v Qal pf 3cp | n mp, ps 3ms | prep, n ms | cj, pers pron |
| וּקֲרָב־לִבּוֹ | רַכּוּ | דְבָרָיו | מִשֶּׁמֶן | וְהֵמָּה |
| ûqŏrāv-libbô | rakkû | dhevārâv | mishshemen | wehēmmāh |
| and the encroachment of his heart | they were softer | his words | than olive oil | but they |

| 6869 | | 8390.531 | 6142, 3176 | 3163 | 2000 | 3677.321 |
|---|---|---|---|---|---|---|
| n fp | **22.** | v Hiphil impv 2ms | prep, pn | n ms, ps 2ms | cj, pers pron | v Pilpel impf 3ms, ps 2ms |
| פְתִחוֹת | | הַשְׁלֵךְ | עַל־יְהוָה | יְהָבְךָ | וְהוּא | יְכַלְכְּלֶךָ |
| phethichôth | | hashlēkh | 'al-yehwāh | yehāvekhā | wehû' | yekhalkelekhā |
| divulgences | | throw | on Yahweh | your burden | and He | He will sustain you |

| 3940, 5598.121 | 3937, 5986 | 4268 | 3937, 6926 | | 887 | 435 |
|---|---|---|---|---|---|---|
| neg part, v Qal impf 3ms | prep, n ms | n ms | prep, art, n ms | **23.** | cj, pers pron | n mp |
| לֹא־יִתֵּן | לְעוֹלָם | מוֹט | לַצַּדִּיק | | וְאַתָּה | אֱלֹהִים |
| lō'-yittēn | le'ôlām | môṭ | latstsaddîq | | we'attāh | 'ĕlōhîm |
| He will not allow | unto eternity | tottering | for the righteous | | but You | O God |

| 3495.523 | 3937, 908 | 8273 | 596 | 1879 | 4983 |
|---|---|---|---|---|---|
| v Hiphil impf 2ms, ps 3mp | prep, n ms | n fs | *n mp* | n mp | cj, n fs |
| תּוֹרִדֵם | לִבְאֵר | שַׁחַת | אַנְשֵׁי | דָמִים | וּמִרְמָה |
| tôridhēm | liv'ēr | shachath | 'anshê | dhāmîm | ûmirmāh |
| You will cause to go down | into a cistern | a pit | men of | bloodshed | and deceit |

| 3940, 2779.126 | 3219 | 603 | 1019.125, 904 | | 3937, 5514.351 |
|---|---|---|---|---|---|
| neg part, v Qal impf 3mp | n mp, ps 3mp | cj, pers pron | v Qal impf 1cs, prep, ps 2ms | **56:t** | prep, art, v Piel ptc ms |
| לֹא־יֶחֱצוּ | יְמֵיהֶם | וַאֲנִי | אֶבְטַח־בָּךְ | | לַמְנַצֵּחַ |
| lō'-yechĕtsû | yemêhem | wa'ănî | 'evṭach-bākh | | lamnatstsēach |
| they will not be divided | their days | but I | I will trust in You | | to the director |

**20. He hath put forth his hands against such as be at peace with him: he hath broken his covenant:** … Each lays hands on his friends and violates his covenant, *Beck* … going back on their oaths, *JB* … Such men do violence to those at peace with them and break their promised word, *NEB*.

**21. The words of his mouth were smoother than butter, but war was in his heart: his words were softer than oil, yet were they drawn swords:** … His talk is smoother than butter, but he means to fight, *Beck* … Smoother than cream was his speech, but his intention was war, *Anchor*.

**22. Cast thy burden upon the LORD, and he shall sustain thee: he shall never suffer the righteous to be moved:** … and he will be your support; he will not let the upright man be moved, *BB* … never allow the righteous to be shaken, *NASB* … will never let the righteous fall, *NIV* … and He will keep you, *KJVII*.

**23. But thou, O God, shalt bring them down into the pit of destruction: bloody and deceitful men shall not live out half their days; but I will trust in thee:** ... you, O God, will bring down the wicked into the pit of corruption, *NIV* ... Men of bloodshed and deceit will not live out half their days, *NASB.*

**56:t. To the chief Musician upon Johath-elem-rechokim, Michtam of David, when the Philistines took him in Gath.**

**1. Be merciful unto me, O God: for man would swallow me up; he fighting daily oppresseth me:** ... Have pity on me, God!, *Anchor* ... for man is attempting my destruction; every day he makes cruel attacks against me, *BB* ... men tram-

---

ing that he was distracted as he mused, unable to do anything but groan, and in v. 17 he repeats that he will still do so. Has he, then, won nothing by his prayer but the prolongation of his first dreary tone of feeling? He has won this—that his musing is not accompanied by distraction and that his groaning is not involuntary expression of pain, but articulate prayer, and therefore accompanied by the confidence of being heard. Communion with God and prayerful trust in his help do not at once end sadness and sobbing, but they do change their character and lighten the blackness of grief. A soul hidden in God has an invisible defense which repels assaults.

**55:19–21.** The principal difficulty in the latter part of v. 19 is the meaning of the word rendered "changes" (HED #2588). The persons spoken of are those whom God will hear and answer in his judicial character, in which He has been throned from of old. Their not having "changes" is closely connected with their not fearing God. The word is elsewhere used for changes of raiment or for the relief of military guards. Calvin and others take the changes intended to be vicissitudes of fortune and hence draw the true thought that unbroken prosperity tends to forgetfulness of God. Others take the changes to be those of mind or conduct from evil to good, while others fall back upon the metaphor of relieving guard, which they connect with the picture in v. 10 of the patrols on the walls, illustrating that they have no cessation in their wicked watchfulness. It must be acknowledged that none of these meanings is quite satisfactory; but probably the first, which expresses the familiar thought of the godlessness attendant on uninterrupted prosperity, is best.

Then follows another reference to the traitorous friend, which by its very abruptness declares how deep the wound is that he has inflicted. The psalmist does not stand alone. He classes with himself those who remained faithful to him. The traitor has not yet thrown off his mask, although the psalmist has penetrated his still-retained disguise. He comes with smooth words, but, in the vigorous language of v. 21, "war was in his heart." The fawning softness of words served only to gather information so as to pass it on to the enemy, disclosing confidences.

**55:22.** Verse 22 has been singularly taken as the smooth words which cut so deep, but surely that is a very strained interpretation. Much rather does the psalmist exhort himself and all who have the same bitterness to taste, to commit themselves to Yahweh. What is it which he exhorts us to cast on Him? The word employed is used here only (HED #3163), and its meaning is therefore questionable. The Septuagint and others translate "care." Others, relying on Talmudical usage, prefer "burden," which is appropriate to the following promise of being held erect. However crushing our loads of duty or of sorrow, we receive strength to carry them with straight backs, if we cast them on Yahweh. The promise is not that He will take away the pressure, but that He will hold us up under it. Similarly, the last clause declares that the righteous will not be allowed to stumble. Faith is mentioned before righteousness. The two must go together.

**55:23.** The last verse sums up the diverse fates of the "bloody and deceitful men" versus that of the psalmist. The terrible prayers of the middle portion of the Psalm have wrought the assurance of their fulfillment, just as the cries of faith have brought the certainty of theirs. So the two closing verses of the Psalm turn both parts of the earlier petitions into prophecies; and over against the trustful, righteous psalmist, standing erect and unmoved, there is set the picture of the "bloody and deceitful men," chased down the black slopes to the depths of destruction by the same God whose hand holds up the man that trusts in Him.

***Psalm 56.*** *The Psalm is simple in structure. Like others ascribed to David during the Sauline period, it has a refrain, which divides it into two parts; but these are of substantially the same purport, with the difference that the second part enlarges the description of the enemies' assaults and rises to confident anticipation of their defeat. In that confidence, the singer adds a closing expression of thankfulness for the deliverance already realized in faith.*

| 6142, 3225 | 488 | 7632 | 3937, 1784 | 4524 | 904, 270.141 | 881 |
|---|---|---|---|---|---|---|
| prep, *n fs* | n ms | adj | prep, pn | n ms | prep, v Qal inf con | do, ps 3ms |
| עַל־יוֹנַת | אֵלֶם | רְחֹקִים | לְדָוִד | מִכְתָּם | בֶּאֱחֹז | אֹתוֹ |
| 'al-yônath | 'ēlem | rechōqîm | ledhāwidh | mikhtām | be'ĕchōz | 'ōthô |
| according to the dove of | silence | far away | of David | a Miktam | when seizing | him |

| 6674 | 904, 1709 | | 2706.131 | 435 | 3706, 8079.111 | 596 |
|---|---|---|---|---|---|---|
| pn | prep, pn | | v Qal impv 2ms, ps 1cs | n mp | cj, v Qal pf 3ms, ps 1cs | n ms |
| פְּלִשְׁתִּים | בְּגַת | **1.** | חָנֵּנִי | אֱלֹהִים | כִּי־שְׁאָפַנִי | אֱנוֹשׁ |
| phelishtîm | beghath | | channēnî | 'ĕlōhîm | kî-she'āphanî | 'ĕnôsh |
| the Philistines | in Gath | | be gracious to me | O God | because they are anxious to get me | men |

| 3725, 3219 | 4032.151 | 4040.121 | | 8079.116 | 8234 |
|---|---|---|---|---|---|
| *adj*, art, n ms | v Qal act ptc ms | v Qal impf 3ms, ps 1cs | | v Qal pf 3cp | n mp, ps 1cs |
| כָּל־הַיּוֹם | לֹחֵם | יִלְחָצֵנִי | **2.** | שָׁאֲפוּ | שׁוֹרְרַי |
| kol-hayyôm | lōchēm | yilchātsēnî | | shā'ăphû | shôreray |
| all the day | fighters | they torment me | | they are anxious to get me | my enemies |

| 3725, 3219 | 3706, 7521 | 4032.152 | 3937 | 4953 | | 3219 | 3486.125 |
|---|---|---|---|---|---|---|---|
| *adj*, art, n ms | cj, adj | v Qal act ptc mp | prep, ps 1cs | adv | | n ms | v Qal impf 1cs |
| כָּל־הַיּוֹם | כִּי־רַבִּים | לֹחֲמִים | לִי | מָרוֹם | **3.** | יוֹם | אִירָא |
| kol-hayyôm | kî-rabbîm | lōchămîm | lî | mārôm | | yôm | 'îrā' |
| all the day | because many | those who fight | against me | arrogantly | | a day | I will be afraid |

| 603 | 420 | 1019.125 | | 904, 435 | 2054.325 | 1745 | 904, 435 | 1019.115 |
|---|---|---|---|---|---|---|---|---|
| pers pron | prep, ps 2ms | v Qal impf 1cs | | prep, n mp | v Piel impf 1cs | n ms, ps 3ms | prep, n mp | v Qal pf 1cs |
| אֲנִי | אֵלֶיךָ | אֶבְטָח | **4.** | בֵּאלֹהִים | אֲהַלֵּל | דְּבָרוֹ | בֵּאלֹהִים | בָּטַחְתִּי |
| 'ănî | 'ēlêkhā | 'evṭāch | | bē'lōhîm | 'ăhallēl | devārô | bē'lōhîm | bāṭachtî |
| I | to You | I will trust | | in God | I will praise | his word | in God | I have trusted |

| 3940 | 3486.125 | 4242, 6449.121 | 1340 | 3937 | | 3725, 3219 | 1745 |
|---|---|---|---|---|---|---|---|
| neg part | v Qal impf 1cs | intrg, v Qal impf 3ms | n ms | prep, ps 1cs | | *adj*, art, n ms | n mp, ps 1cs |
| לֹא | אִירָא | מַה־יַּעֲשֶׂה | בָשָׂר | לִי | **5.** | כָּל־הַיּוֹם | דְּבָרַי |
| lō' | 'îrā' | mah-ya'ăseh | vāsār | lî | | kol-hayyôm | devāray |
| not | I will be afraid | what can it do | flesh | to me | | all the day | my words |

| 6321.326 | 6142 | 3725, 4422 | 3937, 7737 | | 1513.126 | 7121.526 |
|---|---|---|---|---|---|---|
| v Piel impf 3mp | prep, ps 1cs | *adj*, n fp, ps 3mp | prep, art, n ms | | v Qal impf 3mp | v Hiphil impf 3mp |
| יְעַצֵּבוּ | עָלַי | כָּל־מַחְשְׁבֹתָם | לָרָע | **6.** | יָגוּרוּ | יַצְפִּינוּ |
| ye'atstsēvû | 'ālay | kol-machshevōthām | lārā' | | yāghûrû | yatspînû |
| they hurt | against me | all their thoughts | for evil | | they are foreigners | they hide |

| 2065 | 6357 | 8490.126 | 3626, 866 | 7245.316 | 5497 | | 6142, 201 |
|---|---|---|---|---|---|---|---|
| pers pron | n mp, ps 1cs | v Qal impf 3mp | prep, rel part | v Piel pf 3cp | n fs, ps 1cs | | prep, n ms |
| הֵמָּה | עֲקֵבַי | יִשְׁמֹרוּ | כַּאֲשֶׁר | קִוּוּ | נַפְשִׁי | **7.** | עַל־אָוֶן |
| hēmmāh | 'ăqēvay | yishmōrû | ka'ăsher | qiwwû | naphshî | | 'al-'āwen |
| they | my heels | they watch for | just as | they wait for | my life | | concerning iniquity |

| 6647B, 3937 | 904, 653 | 6194 | 3495.531 | 435 | | 5244 |
|---|---|---|---|---|---|---|
| n ms, prep, ps 3mp | prep, n ms | n mp | v Hiphil impv 2ms | n mp | | n ms, ps 1cs |
| פַּלֶּט־לָמוֹ | בְּאַף | עַמִּים | הוֹרֵד | אֱלֹהִים | **8.** | נֹדִי |
| palleṭ-lāmô | be'aph | 'ammîm | hôrēdh | 'ĕlōhîm | | nōdhî |
| deliverance to them | in anger | peoples | make to go down | O God | | my flowing tears |

| 5807.113 | 887 | 7947.131 | 1893 | 904, 5170 | 1950B, 3940 |
|---|---|---|---|---|---|
| v Qal pf 2ms | pers pron | v Qal impv 2ms | n fs, ps 1cs | prep, n ms, ps 2ms | intrg part, neg part |
| סָפַרְתָּה | אָתָּה | שִׂימָה | דִמְעָתִי | בְנֹאדֶךָ | הֲלֹא |
| sāphartāh | 'āttāh | sîmāh | dhim'āthî | venō'dhekhā | hălō' |
| You have counted | You | place | my tears | in your bottle | is not |

ple on me, *Beck* ... the adversary oppresses me, *Goodspeed*.

**2. Mine enemies would daily swallow me up: for they be many that fight against me, O thou most High:** ... My slanderers pursue me all day long; many are attacking me in their pride, *NIV* ... Daily would my enemies devour me; for many are they who proudly fight against me, *Berkeley*.

**3. What time I am afraid, I will trust in thee:** ... When I am afraid, I will trust in You, *KJVII* ... when I have fears, I put my trust in you, *Anchor* ... I will have faith in you, *BB* ... I will have confidence in Thee, *Berkeley*.

**4. In God I will praise his word, in God I have put my trust; I will not fear what flesh can do unto me:** ... In God I trust—I'm not afraid; what can flesh do to me?, *Beck* ... in God have I put my hope, *BB* ... what can mortal man do to me, *JB*.

**5. Every day they wrest my words: all their thoughts are against me for evil:** ... their only thought is to harm me, *JB* ... They are always twisting what I say, *LIVB* ... All day long they distort my words, *NASB* ... all their thoughts are hostile, *NEB* ... they are always plotting to harm me, *NIV*.

**6. They gather themselves together, they hide themselves, they mark my steps, when they wait for my soul:** ... They conspire, they lurk, they watch my steps, eager to take my life, *NIV* ... They come together, they are waiting in secret places, they take note of my steps, *BB* ... They watch where I go because they're eager to kill me, *Beck*.

**7. Shall they escape by iniquity? in thine anger cast down the people, O God:** ... By evil-doing they will not get free from punishment. In wrath, O God, let the peoples be made low, *BB* ... With the wrong they do, can they escape?, *Beck* ... Because of this crime reject them, in your anger, God, strike down the nations, *JB*.

**8. Thou tellest my wanderings: put thou my tears into thy bottle: are they not in thy book?:** ... You have recorded my troubles. You have kept a list of my tears. Aren't they in your records?, *NCV* ... You yourself have counted up my sorrows, *JB* ... Record my lament; list my tears on your scroll, *NIV* ... Thou takest note of my roaming, *Berkeley*.

---

**56:1–4.** The first part begins with that significant contrast which is the basis of all peaceful fronting of a hostile world or any evil. On one side stands man, whose very name here suggests feebleness, and on the other is God. "Man" (HED #596) in v. 1 is plainly a collective. The psalmist masses the foes, whom he afterwards individualizes and knows only too well to be a multitude, under that generic appellation, which brings out their inherent frailty. Be they ever so many, still they all belong to the same class, and an infinite number of nothings only sums up into nothing. The divine unit is more than all these. The enemy is said to "be anxious to get" the psalmist (HED #8079), as a wild beast open-mouthed and ready to devour; or, according to others, the word means "to crush." The thing meant by the strong metaphor is given in vv. 1bf, namely, the continual hostile activity of the foe. The word rendered "arrogantly" (HED #4953) is literally "on high," and it has been suggested that the literal meaning should be retained. He supposes that the antagonists "held an influential position in a princely court." Even more literally, the word may describe the enemies as occupying a post of vantage from which they shower down missiles.

The antagonists are continually at work, and the psalmist on his part strives to meet their schemings and to subdue his own fears with as continuous a faith. Therefore, the situation has three elements: the busy malice of the foes; the effort of the psalmist, his only weapon against them, to hold fast his confidence; and the power and majesty of God, who will be gracious when besought. The refrain gathers up these three in a significantly different order. The preceding verses arranged them as God, man and the trusting singer; the refrain puts them as God, the trusting singer and man.

**56:5–7.** The second part covers the same ground. Trust, like love, never finds it grievous to write the same things. There is delight, and there is strengthening for the temper of faith, in repeating the contemplation of the earthly facts which make it necessary and the super-sensuous facts which make it blessed. A certain expansion of the various parts of the theme, as compared with the first portion of the Psalm, is obvious. Again the phrase "every day" occurs in reference to the unwearying hostility which dogs the singer.

Verse 7 brings in a new element not found in the first part, namely, the prayer for the destruction of these unwearied watchers. The introduction of a prayer for a worldwide judgment in the midst of so intensely individual a Psalm is remarkable and favors the theory that the afflicted man of the Psalm is really the nation, but it may be explained on the ground that, as in Ps. 7:8, the judgment on behalf of one man is contemplated as only one smaller manifestation of the same judicial activity which brings about the universal judgment. This single reference to the theme

| 904, 5815 | | 226 | 8178.126 | 342.152 | 268 | 904, 3219 | 7410.125 |
|---|---|---|---|---|---|---|---|
| prep, n fs, ps 2ms | **9.** | adv | v Qal impf 3mp | v Qal act ptc mp, ps 1cs | adv | prep, n ms | v Qal impf 1cs |
| בְּסִפְרָתֶךָ | | אָז | יָשׁוּבוּ | אוֹיְבַי | אָחוֹר | בְּיוֹם | אֶקְרָא |
| bᵉsiphrāthekhā | | 'āz | yāshûvû | 'ôyvay | 'āchôr | bᵉyôm | 'eqōrā' |
| in your book | | then | they will turn back | my enemies | back | on the day | I call |

| 2172, 3156.115 | 3706, 435 | 3937 | | 904, 435 | 2054.325 | 1745 | 904, 3176 |
|---|---|---|---|---|---|---|---|
| dem pron, v Qal pf 1cs | cj, n mp | prep, ps 1cs | **10.** | prep, n mp | v Piel impf 1cs | n ms | prep, pn |
| זֶה־יָדַעְתִּי | כִּי־אֱלֹהִים | לִי | | בֵּאלֹהִים | אֲהַלֵּל | דָּבָר | בַּיהוָה |
| zeh-yādha'ăttî | kî-'ĕlōhîm | lî | | bē'lōhîm | 'ăhallēl | dāvār | bayhwāh |
| this I know | because God | for me | | in God | I will praise | a word | in Yahweh |

| 2054.325 | 1745 | | 904, 435 | 1019.115 | 3940 | 3486.125 | 4242, 6449.121 |
|---|---|---|---|---|---|---|---|
| v Piel impf 1cs | n ms | **11.** | prep, n mp | v Qal pf 1cs | neg part | v Qal impf 1cs | intrg, v Qal impf 3ms |
| אֲהַלֵּל | דָּבָר | | בֵּאלֹהִים | בָּטַחְתִּי | לֹא | אִירָא | מַה־יַּעֲשֶׂה |
| 'ăhallēl | dāvār | | bē'lōhîm | bāṭachtî | lō' | 'îrā' | mah-ya'ăseh |
| I will praise | a word | | in God | I have trusted | not | I will be afraid | what can he do |

| 119 | 3937 | | 6142 | 435 | 5266 | 8396.325 | 8756 |
|---|---|---|---|---|---|---|---|
| n ms | prep, ps 1cs | **12.** | prep, ps 1cs | n mp | n mp, ps 2ms | v Piel impf 1cs | n fp |
| אָדָם | לִי | | עָלַי | אֱלֹהִים | נְדָרֶיךָ | אֲשַׁלֵּם | תּוֹדֹת |
| 'ādhām | lî | | 'ālay | 'ĕlōhîm | nᵉdhārêkhā | 'ăshallēm | tôdhōth |
| humankind | to me | | on me | O God | your vows | I will pay | thank offerings |

| 3937 | | 3706 | 5522.513 | 5497 | 4623, 4323 | 1950B, 3940 | 7559 |
|---|---|---|---|---|---|---|---|
| prep, ps 2ms | **13.** | cj | v Hiphil pf 2ms | n fs, ps 1cs | prep, n ms | intrg part, neg part | n fd, ps 1cs |
| לָךְ | | כִּי | הִצַּלְתָּ | נַפְשִׁי | מִמָּוֶת | הֲלֹא | רַגְלַי |
| lākh | | kî | hitstsaltā | naphshî | mimmāweth | hălō' | raghlay |
| to You | | because | You have rescued | my life | from death | are not | my feet |

| 4623, 1818 | 3937, 2050.741 | 3937, 6686 | 435 | 904, 214 | 2522 |
|---|---|---|---|---|---|
| prep, n ms | prep, v Hithpael inf con | prep, *n mp* | n mp | prep, *n ms* | art, n mp |
| מִדֶּחִי | לְהִתְהַלֵּךְ | לִפְנֵי | אֱלֹהִים | בְּאוֹר | הַחַיִּים |
| middechî | lᵉhithhallēkh | liphnê | 'ĕlōhîm | bᵉ'ôr | hachayyîm |
| from falling | to walk | before | God | in the light of | the living |

| | 3937, 5514.351 | 414, 8271.528 | 3937, 1784 | 4524 | 904, 1300.141 |
|---|---|---|---|---|---|
| **57:t** | prep, art, v Piel ptc ms | adv, v Hiphil juss 2mp | prep, pn | n ms | prep, v Qal inf con, ps 3ms |
| | לַמְנַצֵּחַ | אַל־תַּשְׁחֵת | לְדָוִד | מִכְתָּם | בְּבָרְחוֹ |
| | lamnatstsēach | 'al-tashchēth | lᵉdhāwidh | mikhtām | bᵉvārᵉchô |
| | to the director | do not destroy | of David | a Miktam | during his fleeing |

| 4623, 6686, 8062 | 904, 4792 | | 2706.131 | 435 | 2706.131 | 3706 |
|---|---|---|---|---|---|---|
| prep, *n mp*, pn | prep, art, n fs | **1.** | v Qal impv 2ms, ps 1cs | n mp | v Qal impv 2ms, ps 1cs | cj |
| מִפְּנֵי־שָׁאוּל | בַּמְּעָרָה | | חָנֵּנִי | אֱלֹהִים | חָנֵּנִי | כִּי |
| mippᵉnê-shā'ûl | bammᵉ'ārāh | | chānnēnî | 'ĕlōhîm | chānnēnî | kî |
| from before Saul | in the cave | | be gracious to me | O God | be gracious to me | because |

| 904 | 2725.112 | 5497 | 904, 7009, 3796 | 2725.125 | 5912 |
|---|---|---|---|---|---|
| prep, ps 2ms | v Qal pf 3fs | n fs, ps 1cs | cj, prep, *n ms*, n fd, ps 2ms | v Qal impf 1cs | adv |
| בְךָ | חָסָיָה | נַפְשִׁי | וּבְצֵל־כְּנָפֶיךָ | אֶחְסֶה | עַד |
| vᵉkhā | chāṣāyāh | naphshî | ûvᵉtsēl-kᵉnāphêkhā | 'echṣeh | 'adh |
| in You | it takes refuge | my soul | and in the shadow of your wings | I will take refuge | until |

| 5882.121 | 2010 | | 7410.125 | 3937, 435 | 6169 | 3937, 418 |
|---|---|---|---|---|---|---|
| v Qal impf 3ms | n fp | **2.** | v Qal impf 1cs | prep, n mp | n ms | prep, art, n ms |
| יַעֲבֹר | הַוּוֹת | | אֶקְרָא | לֵאלֹהִים | עֶלְיוֹן | לָאֵל |
| ya'ăvōr | hawwôth | | 'eqōrā' | lē'lōhîm | 'elyôn | lā'ēl |
| it passes by | destruction | | I will call | to God | the Most High | to the God |

**9. When I cry unto thee, then shall mine enemies turn back: this I know; for God is for me:** ... One cry raised to thee, and my enemies are driven back, *Knox* ... On the day I call for help, my enemies will be defeated. I know that God is on my side, *NCV* ... for God is with me, *KJVII.*

**10. In God will I praise his word: in the LORD will I praise his word:** ... I praise God for his word to me, *NCV* ... Of God do I boast, *Anchor.*

**11. In God have I put my trust: I will not be afraid what man can do unto me:** ... I put my hope; I will have no fear of what man may do, *BB* ... In God have I put my confidence, *Darby* ... In God I put my trust, *JB* ... What can people do to me, *NCV.*

**12. Thy vows are upon me, O God: I will render praises unto thee:** ... I must keep my promises to you. I will give you my offerings to thank you, *NCV* ... I keep the memory of my debt to you, O God; I will give you the offerings of praise, *BB* ... I'm under vows to You, O God, I will carry them out by praising You, *Beck.*

**13. For thou hast delivered my soul from death: wilt not thou deliver my feet from falling, that I may walk before God in the light of the living?:** ... thou hast rescued me from death, *Goodspeed* ... You have kept me from being defeated, *NCV* ... You have rescued me from death, and kept my foot from stumbling, that I might walk before God in the land of the living, *Beck.*

**57:t. To the chief Musician, Al-taschith, Michtam of David, when he fled from Saul in the cave.**

**1. Be merciful unto me, O God, be merciful unto me: for my soul trusteth in thee: yea, in the shadow of thy wings will I make my refuge, until these calamities be overpast:** ... Be gracious unto me, O God, *Darby* ... in You my life finds protection, *Beck* ... in the shadow of Thy wings I will shelter, *Berkeley* ... till these troubles are past, *BB* ... my soul has reliance on You; I will trust in Your canopy's shade, Until my distressers have passed, *Fenton.*

**2. I will cry unto God most high; unto God that performeth all things for me:** ... I call to God the Most

---

which fills so considerable a part of the other Psalms of this class is in harmony with the whole tone of this gem of quiet faith, which is too much occupied with the blessedness of its own trust to have many thoughts of the end of others. It passes, therefore, quickly to dwell on yet another phase of that blessedness.

**56:8.** The tender words of v. 8 need little clarifying. They have brought comfort to many and have helped to dry many tears. How the psalmist presses close to God, and how sure he is of his gentle care and love! God's book, or reckoning, contains the count of all the tears as well as wanderings of his servant. The certainty that it is so is expressed by the interrogative form of the clause.

**56:9–11.** The "then" (HED #226) of v. 9 may be either temporal or logical. It may mean "things being so," or "in consequence of this," or it may mean "at the time when" and may refer to the further specification of period in the next clause. That same day which has already been designated as that of the enemies' panting after the psalmist's life and wresting of his words and, on the other hand, as that of his fear is now the time of his prayer and consequently of their defeat and flight. The confidence which struggled with fear in the closing words of the first part is now consolidated into certain knowledge that God is on the singer's side and that in a very deep sense He belongs to him. This is the foundation of his hope of deliverance, and in this clear knowledge he chants once more his refrain. As is often the case, slight differences, mainly due to artistic love of variety in uniformity, occur in the repeated refrain. "Word" stands instead of "his word," "man" instead of "flesh."

**56:12–13.** The psalmist's exuberant confidence overflows the limits of his song in a closing couple of verses which are outside its scheme. So sure is he of deliverance that, as often in similar Psalms, his thoughts are busied in preparing his sacrifice of thanks before the actual advent of the mercy for which it is to be offered. Such swift-footed gratitude is the daughter of very vivid faith. The ground of the thank offering is deliverance of "the soul," for which foes have "waited." The Psalm crowns its celebration of God's miracles of deliverance by declaring the aim of them all to be that their recipient may walk before God— i.e., in continual consciousness of cognizance of his deeds, and "in the light of the living" or "of life." The expression seems here to mean simply the present life, as contrasted with the darkness and inactivity of Sheol, but we can scarcely help remembering the deeper meaning given to it by Him who said that to follow Him was to have the light of life.

***Psalm 57.*** *There is no very sharp division of parts in the Psalm. A grand refrain separates it into two portions, in the former of which prayer for deliverance and contemplation of dangers prevail, while in the latter, the foe is beheld as already baffled, and exuberant praise is poured forth and vowed.*

**57:1.** As in Ps. 54 and often, the first part begins with an act of faith reaching out to God and strengthening itself by the contemplation of his

| 1625.151 | 6142 | | 8365.121 | 4623, 8452 | 3588.521 |
|---|---|---|---|---|---|
| v Qal act ptc ms | prep, ps 1cs | 3. | v Qal impf 3ms | prep, n md | cj, v Hiphil impf 3ms, ps 1cs |
| גֹּמֵר | עָלָי | | יִשְׁלַח | מִשָּׁמַיִם | וְיוֹשִׁיעֵנִי |
| gōmēr | ʻālāy | | yishlach | mishshāmayim | weyôshîʻēnî |
| One Who avenges | concerning me | | He stretches forth | from the heavens | and He saves me |

| 2884.311 | 8079.151 | 5734 | 8365.121 | 435 | 2721 |
|---|---|---|---|---|---|
| v Piel pf 3ms | v Qal act ptc ms, ps 1cs | intrj | v Qal impf 3ms | n mp | n ms, ps 3ms |
| חֵרֵף | שֹׁאֲפִי | סֶלָה | יִשְׁלַח | אֱלֹהִים | חַסְדּוֹ |
| chērēph | shō'ăphî | selāh | yishlach | 'ĕlōhîm | chasdô |
| He has scorned | those who are anxious to get me | selah | He sends forth | God | his steadfast love |

| 583 | | 5497 | 904, 8761 | 3952 | 8311.125 | 3993.152 |
|---|---|---|---|---|---|---|
| cj, n fs, ps 3ms | 4. | n fs, ps 1cs | prep, *n ms* | n mp | v Qal juss 1cs | v Qal act ptc mp |
| וַאֲמִתּוֹ | | נַפְשִׁי | בְּתוֹךְ | לְבָאִם | אֶשְׁכְּבָה | לֹהֲטִים |
| wa'ămittô | | naphshî | bethôkh | levā'im | 'eshkevāh | lōhetîm |
| and his faithfulness | | my soul | in the middle of | lions | let me lie down | those ablaze |

| 1158, 119 | 8514 | 2698 | 2777 | 4098 | 2820 | 2392 |
|---|---|---|---|---|---|---|
| *n mp*, n ms | n fd, ps 3mp | n fs | cj, n mp | cj, n fs, ps 3mp | n fs | adj |
| בְּנֵי־אָדָם | שִׁנֵּיהֶם | חֲנִית | וְחִצִּים | וּלְשׁוֹנָם | חֶרֶב | חַדָּה |
| benê-'ādhām | shinnêhem | chănîth | wechitstsîm | ûlăshônām | cherev | chaddāh |
| the sons of humankind | their teeth | the spear | and arrows | and their tongue | a sword | sharp |

| | 7597.131 | 6142, 8452 | 435 | 6142 | 3725, 800 | 3638 | | 7862 |
|---|---|---|---|---|---|---|---|---|
| 5. | v Qal impv 2ms | prep, art, n md | n mp | prep | *adj*, art, n fs | n ms, ps 2ms | 6. | n fs |
| | רוּמָה | עַל־הַשָּׁמַיִם | אֱלֹהִים | עַל | כָּל־הָאָרֶץ | כְּבוֹדֶךָ | | רֶשֶׁת |
| | rûmāh | 'al-hashshāmayim | 'ĕlōhîm | 'al | kol-hā'ārets | kevôdhekhā | | resheth |
| | be exalted | above the heavens | O God | above | all the earth | your glory | | a net |

| 3679.516 | 3937, 6718 | 3847.111 | 5497 | 3868.116 | 3937, 6686 | 8290 |
|---|---|---|---|---|---|---|
| v Hiphil pf 3cp | prep, n fp, ps 1cs | v Qal pf 3ms | n ms, ps 1cs | v Qal pf 3cp | prep, n mp, ps 1cs | n fs |
| הֵכִינוּ | לִפְעָמַי | כָּפַף | נַפְשִׁי | כָּרוּ | לְפָנַי | שִׁיחָה |
| hēkhînû | liph'āmay | kāphaph | naphshî | kārû | lephānay | shîchāh |
| they have set | for my steps | it has bowed down | my soul | they dug | before me | a pit |

| 5489.116 | 904, 8761 | 5734 | | 3679.255 | 3949 | 435 | 3679.255 |
|---|---|---|---|---|---|---|---|
| v Qal pf 3cp | prep, n ms, ps 3fs | intrj | 7. | v Niphal ptc ms | n ms, ps 1cs | n mp | v Niphal ptc ms |
| נָפְלוּ | בְתוֹכָהּ | סֶלָה | | נָכוֹן | לִבִּי | אֱלֹהִים | נָכוֹן |
| nāphelû | vethôkhāhh | selāh | | nākhôn | libbî | 'ĕlōhîm | nākhôn |
| they have fallen | into the middle of it | selah | | established | my heart | O God | established |

| 3949 | 8301.125 | 2252.325 | | 5996.131 | 3638 | 5996.131 | 5213 |
|---|---|---|---|---|---|---|---|
| n ms, ps 1cs | v Qal juss 1cs | cj, v Piel juss 1cs | 8. | v Qal impv 2ms | n ms, ps 1cs | v Qal impv 2ms | art, n ms |
| לִבִּי | אָשִׁירָה | וַאֲזַמֵּרָה | | עוּרָה | כְבוֹדִי | עוּרָה | הַנֵּבֶל |
| libbî | 'āshîrāh | wa'ăzammērāh | | 'ûrāh | khevôdhî | 'ûrāh | hannēvel |
| my heart | let me sing | and let me sing praises | | awaken | my glory | awaken | the harp |

High, to God, my benefactor, *NAB* ... to God who has done everything for me, *JB* ... the God who has ever befriended me, *Knox* ... To God who accomplishes all things for me, *NASB*.

**3. He shall send from heaven, and save me from the reproach of him that would swallow me up. Selah. God shall send forth his mercy and his truth:** ... God will send forth His lovingkindness and His truth, *NASB* ... He will send his truth and his love that never fails, he will send from heaven and save me, *NEB* ... take me from the power of him whose desire is for my destruction. God will send out his mercy and his good faith, *BB* ... saves me from the slander of him who hounds me, *Beck*.

**4. My soul is among lions: and I lie even among them that are set on fire, even the sons of men, whose teeth are spears and arrows, and their tongue a sharp sword:** ... I myself must lie down among lions—men who devour, *Beck* ... I lie surrounded by lions, greedy for human prey, *JB*.

**5. Be thou exalted, O God, above the heavens; let thy glory be above all the earth:** ... O God, mount high above the heavens, till thy glory overshadows the whole earth, *Knox* ... God is supreme over the skies; his majesty covers the earth, *NCV* ... Be praised above the heavens, *KJVII.*

**6. They have prepared a net for my steps; my soul is bowed down: they have digged a pit before me, into the midst whereof they are fallen themselves. Selah:** ... They dug a pit in front of me and then fell into it, *Beck* ... They spread out a net for my feet. Dug pitfalls to capture my life;—But they have sunk into their pit!, *Fenton.*

**7. My heart is fixed, O God, my heart is fixed: I will sing and give praise:** ... my heart is ready; I will sing, and make music for you, *JB* ... My heart is steadfast, *NAB* ... I will sing and raise a psalm, *NEB* ... My heart is confident, *Berkeley.*

**8. Awake up, my glory; awake, psaltery and harp: I myself will awake early:** ... Wake up, my soul. Wake up, harp and lyre! I will wake up the dawn, *NCV* ... You are my glory; let the instruments of music be awake; I myself will be awake with the dawn, *BB.*

---

character and acts. That energy of confidence wins assurance of help, and only after that calming certitude has filled the soul does the psalmist turn his eye directly on his enemies. His faith does not make him oblivious of his danger, but it minimizes his dread. An eye that has seen God sees little terror in the most terrible things.

**57:2.** Hidden in his shelter, the psalmist, in v. 2, tells himself the grounds on which he may be sure that his cry to God will not be in vain. His name is "Most High," and his elevation is the pledge of his irresistible might. He is the "God" (the strong) who accomplishes all that the psalmist needs, and his past manifestations in that character make his future interventions certain.

**57:3.** The wish to destroy the psalmist is itself blasphemy or is accompanied with blasphemy; therefore, God will surely send down what will bring it to nought. The same identification of his own cause with God's, which marks many of the Psalms ascribed to the persecuted David, underlies this sudden reference to the enemy and warrants the conclusion drawn that help will come. The selah at the end of the clause is unusual in the middle of a verse; but it may be intended to underscore, as it were, the impiety of the enemy and so corresponds with the other selah in v. 6, which is also in an unusual place and points attention to the enemy's ruin, as this does to his wickedness.

**57:4.** The psalmist's contemplation of his forlorn lair among men worse than beasts of prey drives him back to realize again his refuge in God. He, as it were, wrenches his mind round to look at God rather than at the enemies. Clear perception of peril and weakness works best when it results in a clear recognition of God's help and causes faithful prayer.

**57:5–6.** The reference to the enemies in v. 6 is of a triumphant sort, which naturally prepares for the burst of praise following. The familiar figures of the net and pit, by both of which wild animals are caught, and the familiar picture of the hunter trapped in his own pitfall, need no elucidation. There is a grim irony of events. A pit is dug for others, but somehow and somewhere the digger finds himself at the bottom of it with his net wrapped round his own limbs. The selah at the end of v. 6 calls spectators to gather around the sight of the ensnared plotter, who lies helplessly in the pit.

**57:7–11.** The psalmist is done with the enemies; they are at the bottom of the pit. In full confidence of triumph and deliverance, he breaks out into a grand burst of praise. "My heart is fixed," or "steadfast." Twice the psalmist repeats this, as he does other emphatic thoughts, in this Psalm (cf. vv. 2, 4, 8f). Knit to God, a heart is firm. The psalmist's was steadfast because it had taken refuge in God; and so, even before his rescue from his enemies came to pass, he was emancipated from the fear of them and could lift this song of praise. He had said that he must lie down among lions. But wherever his bed may be, he is sure that he will rise from it; and however dark the fight, he is sure that a morning will come. In a bold and beautiful figure, he says that he will "wake the dawn" with his song.

He ends his song with the conviction, which has become to him matter of experience, that these divine attributes tower to heaven and, in their height, symbolize their own infinitude. Nor is the other truth suggested by v. 10 to be passed over, that the manifestation of these attributes on earth leads to their being more gloriously visible in heaven. These two angels, who come forth from on high to do God's errands for his poor, trusting servant, go back, their work done, and are hailed as victors by the celestial inhabitants. By God's manifestation of these attributes to a man, his glory is exalted above the heavens and all the earth. The same thought is more definitely expressed in Paul's declaration that "the prin-

| 3780 | 5996.525 | 8266 | | 3142.525 | 904, 6194 | 112 |
|---|---|---|---|---|---|---|
| cj, n ms | v Hiphil juss 1cs | n ms | | v Hiphil juss 1cs, ps 2ms | prep, art, n mp | n mp, ps 1cs |
| וְכִנּוֹר | אָעִירָה | שָׁחַר | 9. | אוֹדְךָ | בָעַמִּים | אֲדֹנָי |
| wekhinnôr | 'ā'îrāh | shāchar | | 'ôdhkhā | vā'ammîm | 'ădhōnāy |
| and the zither | let me awaken | the dawn | | let me praise You | among the peoples | O my Lord |

| 2252.325 | 904, 3947 | | 3706, 1448 | 5912, 8452 |
|---|---|---|---|---|
| v Piel juss 1cs, ps 2ms | prep, art, n mp | | cj, adj | prep, n md |
| אֲזַמֶּרְךָ | בַּלְאֻמִּים | 10. | כִּי־גָדֹל | עַד־שָׁמַיִם |
| 'ăzammerkhā | bal'ummîm | | kî-ghādhōl | 'adh-shāmayim |
| let me sing praises to You | among the peoples | | because great | unto the heavens |

| 2721 | 5912, 8263 | 583 | | 7597.131 | 6142, 8452 |
|---|---|---|---|---|---|
| n ms, ps 2ms | cj, prep, n mp | n fs, ps 2ms | | v Qal impv 2ms | prep, n md |
| חַסְדֶּךָ | וְעַד־שְׁחָקִים | אֲמִתֶּךָ | 11. | רוּמָה | עַל־שָׁמַיִם |
| chasdekhā | we'adh-shechāqîm | 'ămittekhā | | rûmāh | 'al-shāmayim |
| your steadfast love | even unto the clouds | your faithfulness | | be exalted | above the heavens |

| 435 | 6142 | 3725, 800 | 3638 | | 3937, 5514.351 | 414, 8271.528 | 3937, 1784 |
|---|---|---|---|---|---|---|---|
| n mp | prep | *adj*, art, n fs | n ms, ps 2ms | | prep, art, v Piel ptc ms | adv, v Hiphil juss 2mp | prep, pn |
| אֱלֹהִים | עַל | כָּל־הָאָרֶץ | כְּבוֹדֶךָ | 58:t | לַמְנַצֵּחַ | אַל־תַּשְׁחֵת | לְדָוִד |
| 'ĕlōhîm | 'al | kol-hā'ārets | kevôdhekhā | | lamnatstsēach | 'al-tashchēth | ledhāwidh |
| O God | above | all the earth | your glory | | to the director | do not destroy | of David |

| 4524 | | 1950B, 562 | 488 | 6928 | 1744.328 | 4478 | 8570.128 |
|---|---|---|---|---|---|---|---|
| n ms | | intrg part, adv | n ms | n ms | v Piel impf 2mp | n mp | v Qal impf 2mp |
| מִכְתָּם | 1. | הַאֻמְנָם | אֵלֶם | צֶדֶק | תְּדַבֵּרוּן | מֵישָׁרִים | תִּשְׁפְּטוּ |
| mikhtām | | ha'umnām | 'ēlem | tsedheq | tedhabbērûn | mêshārîm | tishpetû |
| a Miktam | | is indeed | silence | righteousness | do you speak | uprightness | do you judge |

| 1158 | 119 | | 652, 904, 3949 | 5984 | 6713.128 | 904, 800 |
|---|---|---|---|---|---|---|
| *n mp* | n ms | | cj, prep, n ms | n fp | v Qal impf 2mp | prep, art, n fs |
| בְּנֵי | אָדָם | 2. | אַף־בְּלֵב | עוֹלֹת | תִּפְעָלוּן | בָּאָרֶץ |
| benê | 'ādhām | | 'aph-belēv | 'ôlōth | tiph'ālûn | bā'ārets |
| the children of | humankind | | surely in the heart | wrongdoings | you commit | in the land |

| 2660 | 3135 | 6668.328 | | 2197.116 | 7857 | 4623, 7641 |
|---|---|---|---|---|---|---|
| *n ms* | n fd, ps 2mp | v Piel impf 2mp | | v Qal pf 3cp | n mp | prep, n ms |
| חֲמַס | יְדֵיכֶם | תְּפַלֵּסוּן | 3. | זֹרוּ | רְשָׁעִים | מֵרָחֶם |
| chămas | yedhêkhem | tephallēsûn | | zōrû | reshā'îm | mērāchem |
| the violence of | your hands | you weigh | | they turned aside | the wicked | from the womb |

| 8912.116 | 4623, 1027 | 1744.152 | 3695 | | 2635, 3937 |
|---|---|---|---|---|---|
| v Qal pf 3cp | prep, n fs | *v Qal act ptc mp* | n ms | | n fs, prep, ps 3mp |
| תָּעוּ | מִבֶּטֶן | דֹּבְרֵי | כָזָב | 4. | חֲמַת־לָמוֹ |
| tā'û | mibbeten | dōverê | khāzāv | | chămath-lāmô |
| they wandered off | from the womb | those who speak | falsehood | | venom to them |

| 3626, 1883 | 2635, 5357 | 3765, 6874 | 2901 | 334.521 | 238 |
|---|---|---|---|---|---|
| prep, *n fs* | *n fs*, n ms | prep, n ms | adj | v Hiphil juss 3ms | n fs, ps 3ms |
| כִּדְמוּת | חֲמַת־נָחָשׁ | כְּמוֹ־פֶתֶן | חֵרֵשׁ | יַאְטֵם | אָזְנוֹ |
| kidhmûth | chămath-nāchāsh | kemô-phethen | chērēsh | ya'ṭēm | 'āzenô |
| like the likeness of | the venom of a snake | like a cobra | deaf | it stops up | its ear |

| | 866 | 3940, 8471.121 | 3937, 7249 | 4042.352 | 2357.151 | 2358 | 2549.455 |
|---|---|---|---|---|---|---|---|
| | rel part | neg part, v Qal impf 3ms | prep, *n ms* | v Piel ptc mp | v Qal act ptc ms | n mp | v Pual ptc ms |
| 5. | אֲשֶׁר | לֹא־יִשְׁמַע | לְקוֹל | מְלַחֲשִׁים | חוֹבֵר | חֲבָרִים | מְחֻכָּם |
| | 'āsher | lō'-yishma' | leqôl | melachshîm | chôvēr | chăvārîm | mechukkām |
| | which | it does not hear | the sound of | enchanters | charmers | charms | those made wise |

**9. I will praise thee, O Lord, among the people: I will sing unto thee among the nations:** ... I will chant your praise among the nations, *NAB* ... sing psalms while the Gentiles listen, *Knox* ... will sing songs about you to all the nations, *NCV*.

**10. For thy mercy is great unto the heavens, and thy truth unto the clouds:** ... reaches to the skies, *NCV* ... and your righteousness goes up to the clouds, *BB* ... towers to heaven, your constancy to the clouds, *JB* ... wide as the heavens and thy truth reaches to the skies, *NEB*.

**11. Be thou exalted, O God, above the heavens: let thy glory be above all the earth:** ... O God, mount high above the heavens, till thy glory overshadows the whole earth, *Knox* ... God you are supreme above the skies. Let your glory be over all the earth, *NCV* ... Be lifted up, O God, higher than the heavens, *BB*.

**58:t. To the chief Musician, Al-taschith, Michtam of David.**

**1. Do ye indeed speak righteousness, O congregation? do ye judge uprightly, O ye sons of men?:** ... Will you, O judges, really say what is right? Will you judge the people fairly?, *Beck* ... Do ye judge with equity, *Darby* ... Do you decide impartially, *NEB*.

**2. Yea, in heart ye work wickedness; ye weigh the violence of your hands in the earth:** ... No, in your hearts you devise wrongs; your hands deal out violence on earth, *NRSV* ... The purposes of your hearts are evil; your hands are full of cruel doings on the earth, *BB* ... No, you act with perverse minds, and your hands commit violence in the land, *Beck* ... No, in secret you devise injustice, *Moffatt* ... you willingly commit crimes; on earth you look to the fruits of extortion, *NAB*.

**3. The wicked are estranged from the womb: they go astray as soon as they be born, speaking lies:** ... Wicked men, from birth they have taken to devious ways, *NEB* ... The wicked are strangers to God from the womb, *KJVII* ... From the womb the wicked are perverted, *NCB*.

**4. Their poison is like the poison of a serpent: they are like the deaf adder that stoppeth her ear:** ... They are like a deaf cobra shutting its ears, *Beck* ... like that of a stubborn snake that stops its ears, *NAB*.

**5. Which will not hearken to the voice of charmers, charming never so wisely:** ... will not listen to the sound of the charmer, however skillfully he may play, *REB* ... cannot hear the music of the snake charmer, no matter how well he plays, *NCV*.

---

cipalities and powers in heavenly places might be known by the church the manifold wisdom of God."

***Psalm 58.*** *The Psalm is a wealth of somber imagination, which produces the most solemn effects with the homeliest metaphors and in its awed and yet satisfied contemplation of the fate of evildoers. It parts itself into three portions: a dark picture of abounding evil (vv. 1–5); its punishment prayed for (vv. 6–9); and the consequent joy of the righteous and widespread recognition of the rule of a just God (vv. 10f).*

**58:1–5.** It is to be noted that the Psalm says no more about the sins of unjust authorities, but passes on to describe the "wicked" generally. The transition may suggest that under unjust rulers, all wrongdoers find impunity and so multiply and worsen, or it may simply be that these former are now merged in the class to which they belong. The type of "wickedness" gibbeted is the familiar one of maligners and persecutors. From birth onward, they have continuously been doers of evil. The psalmist is not laying down theological propositions about heredity, but describing the inveterate habit of sin which has become a second nature and makes amendment hopeless. The reference to "lies" naturally suggests the image of the serpent's poison. An envenomed tongue is worse than any snake's bite. And the mention of the serpent stimulates the poet's imagination to yet another figure, which puts most graphically that disregard of warnings, entreaties and every voice, human or divine, that marks long practiced, customary sinfulness. There can be no more striking symbol of determined disregard to the calls of patient love and the threats of outraged justice than that of the snake lying coiled, with its head in the center of its motionless folds, as if its ears were stopped by its own bulk, while the enchanter plays his softest notes and speaks his strongest spells in vain. This psalmist thinks such men exist. There are none whom the mightiest spell, that of God's love in Christ, could not conquer and free from their poison, but there are those who will close their ears to its plaintive sweetness. This is the condemnation that light has come and men love darkness, and they would rather lie coiled in their holes than have their fangs extracted.

**58:6–9.** The general drift of the second part is to call down divine retribution on these obstinate, irreclaimable evildoers. Figure is heaped on figure in a fashion suggestive of intense emotion. The transience of insolent evil and the completeness of its destruction are the thoughts common to them all. There are difficulties in translation, but these should not hide the tremendous force of the gloomy words.

| | 435 | 2117.131, 8514 | 904, 6552 | 4600 | 3841 | 5606.131 |
|---|---|---|---|---|---|---|
| **6.** | n mp | v Qal impv 2ms, n fd, ps 3mp | prep, n ms, ps 3mp | *n fp* | n mp | v Qal impv 2ms |
| | אֱלֹהִים | הֲרָס־שִׁנֵּימוֹ | בְּפִימוֹ | מַלְתְּעוֹת | כְּפִירִים | נְתֹץ |
| | 'ĕlōhîm | herāṣ-shinnêmô | bephîmô | malteʻôth | kephîrîm | nethōts |
| | O God | tear out their teeth | in their mouth | the jawbones of | young lions | tear down |

| 3176 | | 4128.226 | 3765, 4448 | 2050.726, 3937 | 1931.121 |
|---|---|---|---|---|---|
| pn | **7.** | v Niphal juss 3mp | prep, n md | v Hithpael impf 3mp, prep, ps 3mp | v Qal impf 3ms |
| יְהוָה | | יִמָּאֲסוּ | כְמוֹ־מַיִם | יִתְהַלְּכוּ־לָמוֹ | יִדְרֹךְ |
| yehwāh | | yimmā'ăsû | khemô-mayim | yithhallekhû-lāmô | yidhrōkh |
| O Yahweh | | let them be rejected | like waters | they go away from them | they trample |

| 2777 | 3626 | 4589.726 | | 3765 | 8117 | 8886 | 2050.121 |
|---|---|---|---|---|---|---|---|
| n mp, ps 3ms | prep, ps 3mp | v Hithpoel juss 3mp | **8.** | prep | n ms | n ms | v Qal impf 3ms |
| חִצּוֹ | כְּמוֹ | יִתְמֹלָלוּ | | כְּמוֹ | שַׁבְּלוּל | תֶּמֶס | יַהֲלֹךְ |
| chitstsô | kemô | yithmōlālû | | kemô | shabbelûl | temes | yahlōkh |
| their arrows | like them | let them dry up | | like | a snail | melting | they will go |

| 5491 | 828 | 1118, 2463.116 | 8507 | | 904, 3071 | 1032.526 | 5709 |
|---|---|---|---|---|---|---|---|
| *n ms* | n fs | neg part, v Qal pf 3cp | n fs | **9.** | prep, adv | v Hiphil impf 3mp | n fp, ps 2mp |
| נֵפֶל | אֵשֶׁת | בַּל־חָזוּ | שָׁמֶשׁ | | בְּטֶרֶם | יָבִינוּ | סִּירֹתֵיכֶם |
| nēphel | 'ēsheth | bal-chāzû | shāmesh | | beṭerem | yāvînû | ṣîrōthêkhem |
| a miscarriage of | a woman | not they have beheld | the sun | | before | they perceive | your pots |

| 331 | 3765, 2508 | 3765, 2841 | 7994.121 | | 7975.121 |
|---|---|---|---|---|---|
| n ms | cj, adj | cj, n ms | v Qal impf 3ms, ps 3ms | **10.** | v Qal impf 3ms |
| אָטָד | כְּמוֹ־חַי | כְּמוֹ־חָרוֹן | יִשְׂעָרֶנּוּ | | יִשְׂמַח |
| 'āṭādh | kemô-chay | kemô-chārôn | yisʻārennû | | yismach |
| the brambles | like the living | so the burning | He will whisk them away | | he will be glad |

| 6926 | 3706, 2463.111 | 5542 | 6718 | 7647.121 | 904, 1879 | 7857 |
|---|---|---|---|---|---|---|
| n ms | cj, v Qal pf 3ms | n ms | n fp, ps 3ms | v Qal impf 3ms | prep, *n ms* | art, n ms |
| צַדִּיק | כִּי־חָזָה | נָקָם | פְּעָמָיו | יִרְחַץ | בְּדַם | הָרָשָׁע |
| tsaddîq | kî-chāzāh | nāqām | peʻāmāv | yirchats | bedham | hārāshā' |
| the righteous | when he has beheld | vengeance | his feet | he will rinse | in the blood of | the wicked |

| | 569.121 | 119 | 395, 6780 | 3937, 6926 | 395 | 3552, 435 | 8570.152 |
|---|---|---|---|---|---|---|---|
| **11.** | cj, v Qal impf 3ms | n ms | adv, n ms | prep, art, n ms | adv | *sub*, n mp | v Qal act ptc mp |
| | וְיֹאמַר | אָדָם | אַךְ־פְּרִי | לַצַּדִּיק | אַךְ | יֵשׁ־אֱלֹהִים | שֹׁפְטִים |
| | weyō'mar | 'ādhām | 'akh-perî | latstsaddîq | 'akh | yēsh-'ĕlōhîm | shōpheṭîm |
| | and they will say | humankind | surely fruit | for the righteous | surely | there is God | judging |

| 904, 800 | | 3937, 5514.351 | 414, 8271.528 | 3937, 1784 | 4524 | 904, 8365.141 |
|---|---|---|---|---|---|---|
| prep, art, n fs | **59:t** | prep, art, v Piel ptc ms | adv, v Hiphil juss 2mp | prep, pn | n ms | prep, v Qal inf con |
| בָּאָרֶץ | | לַמְנַצֵּחַ | אַל־תַּשְׁחֵת | לְדָוִד | מִכְתָּם | בִּשְׁלֹחַ |
| bā'ārets | | lamnatstsēach | 'al-tashchēth | ledhāwidh | mikhtām | bishlōach |
| on the earth | | to the director | do not destroy | of David | a Miktam | when sending out |

| 8062 | 8490.126 | 881, 1041 | 3937, 4322.541 | | 5522.531 |
|---|---|---|---|---|---|
| pn | cj, v Qal impf 3mp | do, art, n ms | prep, v Hiphil inf con, ps 3ms | **1.** | v Hiphil impv 2ms, ps 1cs |
| שָׁאוּל | וַיִּשְׁמְרוּ | אֶת־הַבַּיִת | לַהֲמִיתוֹ | | הַצִּילֵנִי |
| shā'ûl | wayyishmerû | 'eth-habbayith | lahmîthô | | hatstsîlēnî |
| Saul | and they watched | the house | to kill him | | rescue me |

| 4623, 342.152 | 435 | 4623, 7251.752 | 7891.323 |
|---|---|---|---|
| prep, v Qal act ptc mp, ps 1cs | n mp, ps 1cs | prep, v Hithpolel ptc mp, ps 1cs | v Piel impf 2ms, ps 1cs |
| מֵאֹיְבַי | אֱלֹהָי | מִמִּתְקוֹמְמַי | תְּשַׂגְּבֵנִי |
| mē'ōyevay | 'ĕlōhāy | mimithqômemay | tesaggevēnî |
| from my enemies | O my God | from those who rise up against me | You make me inaccessible |

**6. Break their teeth, O God, in their mouth: break out the great teeth of the young lions, O LORD:** ... the jaws of the unbelievers, *NEB* ... break their cruel fangs; Lord, shatter their jaws, strong as the jaws of lions, *Knox*.

**7. Let them melt away as waters which run continually: when he bendeth his bow to shoot his arrows, let them be as cut in pieces:** ... Let them vanish like water flowing off, *NAB* ... Let them disappear like water that flows away. Let them be cut short like a broken arrow, *NCV* ... When he aims his arrows, let them be as headless shafts, *NASB*.

**8. As a snail which melteth, let every one of them pass away: like the untimely birth of a woman, that they may not see the sun:** ... Like one ravaged by consumption, may he pass away, *Anchor* ... like the slug that melts as it moves, *JB* ... Like the miscarriages of a woman which never see the sun, *NASB*.

**9. Before your pots can feel the thorns, he shall take them away as with a whirlwind, both living, and in his wrath:** ... Before they are conscious of it, let them be cut down like thorns; let a strong wind take them away like waste growth, *BB* ... whether still alive or burnt may God sweep them away, *Beck* ... whether green or ablaze, *NRSV*.

**10. The righteous shall rejoice when he seeth the vengeance: he shall wash his feet in the blood of the wicked:** ... rejoice when he sees the fair punishment, *Berkeley* ... he beholds his victory, *Anchor* ... innocent man will triumph, *Knox*.

**11. So that a man shall say, Verily there is a reward for the righteous: verily he is a God that judgeth in the earth:** ... the good do get their due; yes, a God rules on earth indeed, *Moffatt* ... innocence has its reward, *Knox* ... there is after all a God who dispenses justice on earth, *REB*.

**59:t. To the chief Musician, Al-taschith, Michtam of David; when Saul sent, and they watched the house to kill him.**

**1. Deliver me from mine enemies, O my God: defend me from them**

---

In v. 7a their destruction is sought, while in the second clause of the same verse the defeat of their attempts is desired. Verse 8 then expands the former wish, and v. 9 the latter. This plain symmetrical arrangement makes the proposals to resort to transposition unnecessary. Mountain torrents quickly run themselves dry, and the more furious their rush, the swifter their exhaustion. They leave a chaos of whitened stones that lie bleaching in the fierce sun when the wild spate is past. So stormy and so short will be the career of evildoers.

The prayer for destruction is caught up again in v. 8, in two daring figures which tremble on the verge of lowering the key of the whole, but, by escaping that peril, produce the contrary effect and heighten it. A slug leaves a shining track of slime as it creeps, which exudes from its soft body, and thus it seems to disintegrate itself by its own motion. It is the same thought of the suicidal character of bad men's efforts which was expressed by the stream foaming itself away.

The scope of the figure seems discoverable through the obscurity. It is a vigorous picture of half-accomplished plans suddenly reduced to utter failure and leaving their concocters hungry for the satisfaction which seemed so near. The cookery may go on merrily and the thorns crackle cheerily, but the simoom comes, topples over the tripod on which the pot swung and blows the fire away in a hundred directions. Peter's gibbet was ready, and the morning of his execution was near; but when day dawned, "there was no small stir among the soldiers, what was become of [him]." The wind had blown him away from the expectation of the people of the Jews into safe quarters, and the fire was dispersed.

**58:10–11.** The closing part (vv. 10f) breathes a stern spirit of joy over the destruction of the wicked. It is a terrible picture of the righteous bathing his feet in the blood of the wicked (Ps. 68:23). It expresses not only the dreadful abundance of blood, but also the satisfaction of the "righteous" at its being shed. There is an ignoble and there is a noble and Christian satisfaction in even the destructive providences of God. God's righteousness can do no less than take his full vengeance at the proper time. It is not right for men to execute vengeance, but we must remember that the reason it is not right is that it is completely righteous for God to do so.

***Psalm 59.*** *The Psalm falls into two principal divisions (vv. 1–9 and 1–17), each closing with a refrain, and each subdivided into two minor sections, the former of which in each case ends with selah, and the latter begins with another refrain. The two parts travel over much the same ground of petition, description of the enemies, confidence in deliverance and in the defeat of the foes. But in the first half the psalmist prays for himself, and in the second he prays against his persecutors! Assured confidence in his own deliverance takes the place of alarmed gaze on their might and cruelty.*

**59:1–5.** The former half of the first part begins and ends with petitions. Imbedded in these is a plaintive recounting of the plottings of the adver-

| 2. | 5522.531 | 4623, 6713.152 | 201 | 4623, 596 | 1879 |
|---|---|---|---|---|---|
| | v Hiphil impv 2ms, ps 1cs | prep, *v Qal act ptc mp* | n ms | cj, prep, *n mp* | n mp |
| | הַצִּילֵנִי | מִפֹּעֲלֵי | אָוֶן | וּמֵאַנְשֵׁי | דָמִים |
| | hatstsîlēnî | mippō'ălê | 'āwen | ûmē'anshê | dhāmîm |
| | rescue me | from those who practice | iniquity | and from men of | bloodshed |

| 3588.531 | 3. | 3706 | 2079 | 717.116 | 3937, 5497 | 1513.126 |
|---|---|---|---|---|---|---|
| v Hiphil impv 2ms, ps 1cs | | cj | intrj | v Qal pf 3cp | prep, n fs, ps 1cs | v Qal juss 3mp |
| הוֹשִׁיעֵנִי | | כִּי | הִנֵּה | אָרְבוּ | לְנַפְשִׁי | יָגוּרוּ |
| hôshî'ēnî | | kî | hinnēh | 'ār$^{e}$vû | l$^{e}$naphshî | yāghûrû |
| save me | | because | behold | they lie in wait | for my life | let them be afraid |

| 6142 | 6006 | 3940, 6840 | 3940, 2496 | 3176 | 4. | 1136, 5988 |
|---|---|---|---|---|---|---|
| prep, ps 1cs | adj | neg pat, n ms, ps 1cs | cj, neg part, n fs, ps 1cs | pn | | neg part, n ms |
| עָלַי | עַזִּים | לֹא־פִשְׁעִי | וְלֹא־חַטָּאתִי | יְהוָה | | בְּלִי־עָוֹן |
| 'ālay | 'azîm | lō'-phish'î | w$^{e}$lō'-chattā'thî | y$^{e}$hwāh | | b$^{e}$lî-'āwōn |
| concerning me | defiant ones | not my offense | and not my sin | O Yahweh | | no guilt |

| 7608.126 | 3679.726 | 5996.131 | 3937, 7410.141 | 7495.131 |
|---|---|---|---|---|
| v Qal impf 3mp | cj, v Hithpolel impf 3mp | v Qal impv 2ms | prep, v Qal inf con, ps 1cs | cj, v Qal impv 2ms |
| יְרוּצוּן | וְיִכּוֹנָנוּ | עוּרָה | לִקְרָאתִי | וּרְאֵה |
| y$^{e}$rûtsûn | w$^{e}$yikkônānû | 'ûrāh | liqrā'thî | ûr$^{e}$'ēh |
| they run | and they prepare | arouse | to meet me | and see |

| 5. | 887 | 3176, 435 | 6893 | 435 | 3547 | 7301.531 | 3937, 6734.141 |
|---|---|---|---|---|---|---|---|
| | cj, pers pron | pn, n mp | n fp | *n mp* | pn | v Hiphil impv 2ms | prep, v Qal inf con |
| | וְאַתָּה | יְהוָה־אֱלֹהִים | צְבָאוֹת | אֱלֹהֵי | יִשְׂרָאֵל | הָקִיצָה | לִפְקֹד |
| | w$^{e}$'attāh | y$^{e}$hwāh-'ĕlōhîm | ts$^{e}$vā'ôth | 'ĕlōhê | yisrā'ēl | hāqîtsāh | liphqōdh |
| | and You | Yahweh God | Hosts | the God of | Israel | awake | to punish |

| 3725, 1504 | 414, 2706.123 | 3725, 931.152 | 201 | 5734 | 6. | 8178.126 |
|---|---|---|---|---|---|---|
| *adj*, art, n mp | adv, v Qal juss 2ms | *adj, v Qal act ptc mp* | n ms | intrj | | v Qal impf 3mp |
| כָּל־הַגּוֹיִם | אַל־תָּחֹן | כָּל־בֹּגְדֵי | אָוֶן | סֶלָה | | יָשׁוּבוּ |
| kol-haggôyim | 'al-tāchōn | kol-bōgh$^{e}$dhê | 'āwen | selāh | | yāshûvû |
| all the nations | do not be gracious | all those who act treacherously | iniquity | selah | | they return |

| 3937, 6394 | 2064.126 | 3626, 3732 | 5621.326 | 6111 | 7. | 2079 |
|---|---|---|---|---|---|---|
| prep, art, n ms | v Qal impf 3mp | prep, art, n ms | cj, v Poel impf 3mp | n fs | | intrj |
| לָעֶרֶב | יֶהֱמוּ | כַכָּלֶב | וִיסוֹבְבוּ | עִיר | | הִנֵּה |
| lā'erev | yehĕmû | khakkālev | wîsôv$^{e}$vû | 'îr | | hinnēh |
| at the evening | they howl | like the dogs | and they surround | a city | | behold |

| 5218.526 | 904, 6552 | 2820 | 904, 8004 | 3706, 4449 | 8471.151 |
|---|---|---|---|---|---|
| v Hiphil impf 3mp | prep, n ms, ps 3mp | n fp | prep, n fd, ps 3mp | cj, intrg | v Qal act ptc ms |
| יַבִּיעוּן | בְּפִיהֶם | חֲרָבוֹת | בְּשִׂפְתוֹתֵיהֶם | כִּי־מִי | שֹׁמֵעַ |
| yabbî'ûn | b$^{e}$phîhem | chărāvôth | b$^{e}$siphthôthêhem | kî-mî | shōmēa' |
| they allow to gush forth | with their mouth | swords | with their lips | because who | hearing |

| 8. | 887 | 3176 | 7925.123, 3937 | 4074.123 | 3937, 3725, 1504 | 9. | 6010 |
|---|---|---|---|---|---|---|---|
| | cj, pers pron | pn | v Qal impf 2ms, prep, ps 3mp | v Qal impf 2ms | prep, adj, n mp | | n ms, ps 3ms |
| | וְאַתָּה | יְהוָה | תִּשְׂחַק־לָמוֹ | תִּלְעַג | לְכָל־גּוֹיִם | | עֻזּוֹ |
| | w$^{e}$'attāh | y$^{e}$hwāh | tischaq-lāmô | til'agh | l$^{e}$khol-gôyim | | 'uzzô |
| | but You | O Yahweh | You laugh at them | You deride | all nations | | his strength |

| 420 | 8490.125 | 3706, 435 | 5021 | 10. | 435 | 2721 |
|---|---|---|---|---|---|---|
| prep, ps 2ms | v Qal juss 1cs | cj, n mp | n ms, ps 1cs | | *n mp* | n ms, ps 3ms |
| אֵלֶיךָ | אֶשְׁמֹרָה | כִּי־אֱלֹהִים | מִשְׂגַּבִּי | | אֱלֹהֵי | חַסְדּוֹ |
| 'ēlêkhā | 'eshmōrāh | kî-'ĕlōhîm | misgabbî | | 'ĕlōhê | chasdô |
| to You | let me watch | because God | my Stronghold | | the God of | his steadfast love |

**that rise up against me:** ... Set me on high from them that rise up against me, *ASV* ... be my stronghold from my assailants, *JB* ... Set me securely on high away from those who rise up, *NASB*.

**2. Deliver me from the workers of iniquity, and save me from bloody men:** ... from men of violence save me, *JB* ... Rescue me from evildoers, *NAB* ... Save me from those who do evil and from murderers, *NCV*.

**3. For, lo, they lie in wait for my soul: the mighty are gathered against me; not for my transgression, nor for my sin, O LORD:** ... Here they are, lurking to take my life, a fierce gang to attack me! And for no sin or crime of mine, *Moffatt* ... Fierce men launch an attack against me, *NASB* ... for no offense or sin of mine, *NIV* ... my evildoing, *BB*.

**4. They run and prepare themselves without my fault: awake to help me, and behold:** ... they rush to the attack, *Knox* ... come forward and see!, *Fenton* ... Rouse yourself to see it, and aid me, *NAB*.

**5. Thou therefore, O LORD God of hosts, the God of Israel, awake to visit all the heathen: be not merciful to any wicked transgressors. Selah:** ... Do not be gracious to any who are treacherous in iniquity, *NASB* ... have no pity on any worthless traitors, *NCB* ... spare none of those who treacherously plot evil, *Berkeley*.

**6. They return at evening: they make a noise like a dog, and go round about the city:** ... come back at nightfall, like yelping dogs, to prowl about the city, *Knox* ... come back at night. Like dogs they growl and roam around the city, *NCV*.

**7. Behold, they belch out with their mouth: swords are in their lips: for who, say they, doth hear?:** ... From their mouths comes a stream of nonsense, *NEB* ... they bellow out with their mouth, *KJVII* ... Insults come from their lips, because they say, "Who's listening?", *NCV* ... hate is dropping from their lips; curses are on their tongues: they say, Who gives attention to it, *BB* ... they foam at their mouth, *Berkeley* ... blasphemies are on their lips, *NAB*.

**8. But thou, O LORD, shalt laugh at them; thou shalt have all the heathen in derision:** ... all the while thou, Lord, makest light of them, *Knox* ... Thou dost scoff at all the nations, *NASB* ... you make fun of all of them, *NCV* ... Thou shalt mock at all the nations, *Be*rkeley.

**9. Because of his strength will I wait upon thee: for God is my**

---

saries, which were spread before God's eyes, accompanied with protestations of innocence. The prayers, which enclose, as in a circlet, this description of unprovoked hatred, are varied so that the former petitions are directed to the singer's deliverance while the latter invoke judgment on his antagonists.

The strong assertion of innocence is, of course, to be limited to the psalmist's conduct to his enemies. They attack him without provocation. The psalmist calls God to look upon the doings of his enemies. Privy plots and open assaults are both directed against him. The enemy lie in wait for his life, but also, with fell eagerness like that of soldiers making haste to rank themselves in battle-array, they "run and prepare themselves." This is probably simply metaphor, for the rest of the Psalm does not seem to contemplate actual warfare.

The imminence of peril forces an urgent prayer from the threatened man. So urgent is it that it breaks in on the parallelism of v. 4, substituting its piercing cry "Awake, behold!" for the proper second clause carrying on the description in the first. The singer makes haste to grasp God's hand because he feels the pressure of the wind blowing in his face. It is wise to break off the contemplation of enemies and dangers by crying to God.

**59:6–8.** The comparison of the psalmist's enemies to dogs occurs in another Psalm ascribed to David (Ps. 22:16, 20). They are like the masterless, gaunt, savage curs which infest the streets of Eastern cities, hungrily hunting for scraps and ready to growl or snarl at every passerby. Although the dog is not a nocturnal animal, evening would naturally be a time when these would specially prowl round the city in search of food, if disappointed during the day. The picture suggests the enemies' eagerness, lawlessness, foulness and persistence. The word rendered "belch" (HED #5218) means "to gush out," and it is found in a good sense in Ps. 19:1. Here it may perhaps be taken as meaning "foam," with some advantage to the truth of the picture. "Swords are in their lips"—i.e., their talk is of slaying the psalmist, or their slanders cut like swords; and the crown of their evil is their scoff at the apparently deaf and passive God.

With startling suddenness, as if one quick touch drew aside a curtain, the vision of God as He really regards the enemies is flashed on them in v. 8. The strong antithesis expressed by the "thou therefore," as in v. 5, comes with overwhelming force. Below is the crowd of greedy foes, obscene, cruel and blasphemous; above, throned in dread repose, which is not carelessness or ignorance as they dream, is Yahweh, mocking their fancied security.

**59:9.** Verse 9 is the refrain closing the first part. The reading of the Hebrew text, "his strength," must be given up, as unintelligible, and the slight alter-

| 7207.321 | 435 | 7495.521 | 904, 8234 | | 414, 2103.123 |
|---|---|---|---|---|---|
| v Piel impf 3ms, ps 1cs | n mp | v Hiphil impf 3ms, ps 1cs | prep, n mp, ps 1cs | **11.** | adv, v Qal juss 2ms, ps 3mp |
| יְקַדְּמֵנִי | אֱלֹהִים | יַרְאֵנִי | בְשֹׁרְרָי | | אַל־תַּהַרְגֵם |
| yeqaddemênî | 'ĕlōhîm | yar'ēnî | veshōrerāy | | 'al-taharghēm |
| He meets me | God | He causes me to see | over my enemies | | do not kill them |

| 6678, 8319.126 | 6194 | 5309.531 | 904, 2524 |
|---|---|---|---|
| adv, v Qal impf 3mp | n ms, ps 1cs | v Hiphil impv 2ms, ps 3mp | prep, n ms, ps 2ms |
| פֶּן־יִשְׁכְּחוּ | עַמִּי | הֲנִיעֵמוֹ | בְחֵילְךָ |
| pen-yishkechû | 'ammî | henî'ēmô | vechêlekhā |
| so that they will not forget | my people | You cause them to tremble | by your power |

| 3495.531 | 4182 | 112 | | 2496, 6552 | 1745, 8004 |
|---|---|---|---|---|---|
| cj, v Hiphil impv 2ms, ps 3mp | n ms, ps 1cs | n mp, ps 1cs | **12.** | *n fs*, n ms, ps 3mp | *n ms*, n fs, ps 3mp |
| וְהוֹרִידֵמוֹ | מָגִנֵּנוּ | אֲדֹנָי | | חַטַּאת־פִּימוֹ | דְּבַר־שְׂפָתֵימוֹ |
| wehôrîdhēmô | māghinnēnû | 'ădhōnāy | | chatta'th-pîmô | devar-sephāthêmô |
| cause them to go down | our Shield | O my Lord | | the sin of their mouth | the words of their lips |

| 4058.226 | 904, 1377 | 4623, 427 | 4623, 3704 | 5807.326 |
|---|---|---|---|---|
| cj, v Niphal juss 3mp | prep, n ms, ps 3mp | cj, prep, n fs | cj, prep, n ms | v Piel impf 3mp |
| וְיִלָּכְדוּ | בִגְאוֹנָם | וּמֵאָלָה | וּמִכַּחַשׁ | יְסַפֵּרוּ |
| weyillākhedhû | vigh'ônām | ûmē'ālāh | ûmikkachash | yesapperû |
| and let them be trapped | in their pride | and from cursing | and from lying | they announce |

| | 3735.331 | 904, 2735 | 3735.331 | 375 | 3156.126 | 3706, 435 |
|---|---|---|---|---|---|---|
| **13.** | v Piel impv 2ms | prep, n fs | v Piel impv 2ms | cj, sub, ps 3mp | cj, v Qal juss 3mp | cj, n mp |
| | כַּלֵּה | בְחֵמָה | כַּלֵּה | וְאֵינֵמוֹ | וְיֵדְעוּ | כִּי־אֱלֹהִים |
| | kallēh | vechēmāh | kallēh | we'ênēmô | weyēdhe'û | kî-'ĕlōhîm |
| | bring to an end | in wrath | bring to an end | so they are not | that they may know | that God |

| 5090.151 | 904, 3399 | 3937, 675 | 800 | 5734 | | 8178.126 | 3937, 6394 |
|---|---|---|---|---|---|---|---|
| v Qal act ptc ms | prep, pn | prep, *n mp* | art, n fs | intrj | **14.** | v Qal impf 3mp | prep, art, n ms |
| מֹשֵׁל | בְּיַעֲקֹב | לְאַפְסֵי | הָאָרֶץ | סֶלָה | | וְיָשׁוּבוּ | לָעֶרֶב |
| mōshēl | beya'ăqōv | le'aphsê | hā'ārets | selāh | | weyāshûvû | lā'erev |
| the Ruler | over Jacob | to the ends of | the earth | selah | | and they return | at the evening |

| 2064.126 | 3626, 3732 | 5621.326 | 6111 | | 2065 | 5309.126 |
|---|---|---|---|---|---|---|
| v Qal impf 3mp | prep, art, n ms | cj, v Poel impf 3mp | n fs | **15.** | pers pron | v Qal impf 3mp |
| יֶהֱמוּ | כַכָּלֶב | וִיסוֹבְבוּ | עִיר | | הֵמָּה | יְנוּעוּן |
| yehĕmû | khakkālev | wîsôvevû | 'îr | | hēmmāh | yenû'ûn |
| they howl | like the dogs | and they surround | a city | | they | they tremble |

| 3937, 404.141 | 524, 3940 | 7881.126 | 4053.126 | | 603 |
|---|---|---|---|---|---|
| prep, v Qal inf con | cj, neg part | v Qal impf 3mp | cj, v Qal impf 3mp | **16.** | cj, pers pron |
| לֶאֱכֹל | אִם־לֹא | יִשְׂבְּעוּ | וַיָּלִינוּ | | וַאֲנִי |
| le'ĕkhōl | 'im-lō' | yisbe'û | wayyālînû | | wa'ănî |
| to devour | if not | they are satisfied | then they spend the night | | but I |

| 8301.125 | 6010 | 7728.325 | 3937, 1269 | 2721 |
|---|---|---|---|---|
| v Qal impf 1cs | n ms, ps 2ms | cj, v Piel impf 1cs | prep, art, n ms | n ms, ps 2ms |
| אָשִׁיר | עֻזֶּךָ | וַאֲרַנֵּן | לַבֹּקֶר | חַסְדֶּךָ |
| 'āshîr | 'uzzekhā | wa'ărannēn | labbōqer | chasdekhā |
| I will sing | your strength | and I will shout for joy | at the morning | your steadfast love |

| 3706, 2030.113 | 5021 | 3937 | 4642 | 904, 3219 | 7140, 3937 |
|---|---|---|---|---|---|
| cj, v Qal pf 2ms | n ms | prep, ps 1cs | cj, n ms | prep, *n ms* | n ms, prep, ps 1cs |
| כִּי־הָיִיתָ | מִשְׂגָּב | לִי | וּמָנוֹס | בְּיוֹם | צַר־לִי |
| kî-hāyîthā | misgāv | lî | ûmānôs | beyôm | tsar-lî |
| because You are | a Refuge | to me | and a Stronghold | in the day of | adversity to me |

**defence:** ... My strength, I keep my eyes fixed on you. For my stronghold is God, *JB* ... God, my strength, I am looking to you, because God is my defender, *NCV* ... God is my stronghold, *Berkeley* ... God is my fortress, *Goodspeed* ... for thou, O God, art my strong tower, *NEB*.

**10. The God of my mercy shall prevent me: God shall let me see my desire upon mine enemies:** ... God who loves me faithfully is coming to meet me, God will let me feast my eyes on those who lie in wait for me, *JB* ... God of my mercy shall go before me, *KJVII* ... God with his lovingkindness will meet me, *ASV* ... God will let me see my desire effected on my haters, *BB*.

**11. Slay them not, lest my people forget: scatter them by thy power; and bring them down, O Lord our shield:** ... Pity them not, *Moffatt* ... Lord, our protector, do not kill them, or my people will forget, *NCV* ... Put them not to death, for so my people will keep the memory of them: let them be sent in all directions by your power, *BB* ... Shake them by thy power, *Goodspeed* ... bring them low, *JB*.

**12. For the sin of their mouth and the words of their lips let them even be taken in their pride: and for cursing and lying which they speak:** ... Down with the guilty tongues, the boastful lips; let their own pride ensnare them, *Knox* ... Each word they utter is a sin; so let their own pride trap them, for all their perjury and false talk, *Moffatt* ... By the sin of their mouths and the word of their lips let them be caught in their arrogance, *NAB* ... for their curses and their deceit, *BB*.

**13. Consume them in wrath, consume them, that they may not be: and let them know that God ruleth in Jacob unto the ends of the earth. Selah:** ... put an end to them, so that they may not be seen again, *BB* ... in anger destroy them, destroy them till they're gone. Then they'll know God rules over Jacob and to the most distant parts of the world, *Beck* ... Destroy in indignation, destroy, that they may be no more, *Berkeley*.

**14. And at evening let them return; and let them make a noise like a dog, and go round about the city:** ... prowling through the town, *JB* ... Back come they at nightfall, like yelping dogs, and prowl, *Knox*.

**15. Let them wander up and down for meat, and grudge if they be not satisfied:** ... They wander around to devour, and if they don't get all they want, they go on all night, *Beck* ... they stay out all night, if they are not filled, *Berkeley* ... If they are not satisfied, they grumble, *Goodspeed*.

**16. But I will sing of thy power; yea, I will sing aloud of thy mercy in the morning: for thou hast been my defence and refuge in the day of my trouble:** ... I will sing of thy strength; I will extol thy kindness in the morning, *Goodspeed* ... in the morning acclaim your faithful love, *JB*.

---

ation required for reading "my" instead of "his" adopted, as in the second instance of the refrain in v. 17. The variation of the two refrains is not only in accordance with usage, but brings out a delicate phase of progress in confidence. He who begins with waiting for God ends with singing praise to God. The silence of patient expectance is changed for the melody of received deliverance.

**59:10–13.** The first part of the second division, like the corresponding portion of the first division, is mainly prayer, but with the significant difference that the petitions now are directed, not to the psalmist's deliverance, but to his enemies' punishment. For himself, he is sure that his God will come to meet him with his steadfast love and that, thus met and helped, he will look on, secure, at their ruin. The Hebrew margin proposes to read "The God of my loving kindness will meet me"—an incomplete sentence, which does not tell with what God will meet him. But the text needs only the change of one vowel point in order to yield the perfectly appropriate reading, "My God shall meet me with his steadfast love," which is distinctly to be preferred. Every word which the adversaries speak is sin. Their own self-sufficient pride, which is revolt against dependence on God, is like a trap to catch them. They speak curses and lies, for which retribution is due. This recounting of their crimes, not so much against the psalmist, although involving him, as against God, fires his indignation anew, and he flames out with petitions which seem to forget the former ones for lingering destruction: "Consume them in wrath, consume them." The contradiction may be apparent only, and this passionate cry may presuppose the fulfillment of the former. The psalmist will then desire two dreadful things—first, protracted suffering, and then a crushing blow to end it. His ultimate desire in both is the same. He would have the evildoers spared long enough to be monuments of God's punitive justice; he would have them ended, that the crash of their fall may reverberate afar and proclaim that God rules in Jacob.

**59:14–15.** The second part of this division begins (v. 14) with the same words as the corresponding part of the first division (v. 6) so that there is a kind of refrain here. The futures in vv. 14f may be either simple futures or jussives. In the latter case, the petitions of the preceding verses would be con-

| 17. | 6010 | 420 | 2252.325 | 3706, 435 | 5021 | 435 |
|---|---|---|---|---|---|---|
| | n ms, ps 1cs | prep, ps 2ms | v Piel juss 1cs | cj, n mp | n ms, ps 1cs | *n mp* |
| | עֻזִּי | אֵלֶיךָ | אֲזַמֵּרָה | כִּי־אֱלֹהִים | מִשְׂגַּבִּי | אֱלֹהֵי |
| | 'uzzî | 'ēlêkhā | 'ăzammērāh | kî-'ĕlōhîm | misgabbî | 'ĕlōhê |
| | my strength | to You | let me sing praises | because God | my Stronghold | the God of |

| 2721 | 60:t | 3937, 5514.351 | 6142, 8236 | 5925 | 4524 | 3937, 1784 |
|---|---|---|---|---|---|---|
| n ms, ps 1cs | | prep, art, v Piel ptc ms | prep, n ms | n fs | n ms | prep, pn |
| חַסְדִּי | | לַמְנַצֵּחַ | עַל־שׁוּשַׁן | עֵדוּת | מִכְתָּם | לְדָוִד |
| chasdî | | lamnatstsēach | 'al-shûshan | 'ēdhûth | mikhtām | ledhāwidh |
| my steadfast love | | to the director | on the shushan | a Testimony | a Miktam | of David |

| 3937, 4064.341 | 904, 5510.541 | 881 | 786 | 786 | 881, 782 | 6941 |
|---|---|---|---|---|---|---|
| prep, v Piel inf con | prep, v Hiphil inf con, ps 3ms | do | pn | pn | cj, do, pn | pn |
| לְלַמֵּד | בְּהַצּוֹתוֹ | אֵת | אֲרַם | נַהֲרַיִם | וְאֶת־אֲרַם | צוֹבָה |
| lelammēdh | behatstsôthô | 'eth | 'ăram | nahrayim | we'eth-'ăram | tsôvāh |
| for teaching | during his struggling with | | Aram | Naharaim | and Aram | Zobah |

| 8178.121 | 3200 | 5409.521 | 881, 110 | 904, 1550 | 8530 | 6461 |
|---|---|---|---|---|---|---|
| cj, v Qal impf 3ms | pn | cj, v Hiphil impf 3ms | do, pn | prep, pn | num | num |
| וַיָּשָׁב | יוֹאָב | וַיַּךְ | אֶת־אֱדוֹם | בְּגֵיא־מֶלַח | שְׁנֵים | עָשָׂר |
| wayyāshāv | yô'āv | wayyakh | 'eth-'ĕdhôm | beghê'-melach | shenêm | 'āsār |
| then he returned | Joab | and he struck down | Edom | in the Valley of Salt | two | ten |

| 512 | 1. | 435 | 2269.113 | 6805.113 | 613.113 |
|---|---|---|---|---|---|
| num | | n mp | v Qal pf 2ms, ps 1cp | v Qal pf 2ms, ps 1cp | v Qal pf 2ms |
| אָלֶף | | אֱלֹהִים | זְנַחְתָּנוּ | פְּרַצְתָּנוּ | אָנַפְתָּ |
| 'āleph | | 'ĕlōhîm | zenachtānû | pheratstānû | 'ānaphtā |
| thousands | | O God | You have rejected us | You have broken through us | You have been angry |

| 8178.323 | 3937 | 2. | 7782.513 | 800 | 6727.113 |
|---|---|---|---|---|---|
| v Polel impf 2ms | prep, ps 1cp | | v Hiphil pf 2ms | n fs | v Qal pf 2ms, ps 3fs |
| תְּשׁוֹבֵב | לָנוּ | | הִרְעַשְׁתָּה | אֶרֶץ | פְּצַמְתָּהּ |
| teshôvēv | lānû | | hir'ashtāh | 'erets | petsamtāhh |
| O restore | us | | You have caused to quake | the land | You have split it open |

| 7792.131 | 8133 | 3706, 4267.112 | 3. | 7495.513 | 6194 | 7482 |
|---|---|---|---|---|---|---|
| v Qal impv 2ms | n mp, ps 3fs | cj, v Qal pf 3fs | | v Hiphil pf 2ms | n ms, ps 2ms | adj |
| רְפָה | שְׁבָרֶיהָ | כִּי־מָטָה | | הִרְאִיתָה | עַמְּךָ | קָשָׁה |
| rephāh | shevārêāh | khî-māṭāh | | hir'îthāh | 'ammekhā | qāshāh |
| repair | its breaches | because it has tottered | | You have seen | your people | hard |

| 8615.513 | 3302 | 8992 | 4. | 5598.113 | 3937, 3486.152 |
|---|---|---|---|---|---|
| v Hiphil pf 2ms, ps 1cp | *n ms* | n fs | | v Qal pf 2ms | prep, v Qal act ptc mp, ps 2ms |
| הִשְׁקִיתָנוּ | יַיִן | תַּרְעֵלָה | | נָתַתָּה | לִּירֵאֶיךָ |
| hishqîthānû | yayin | tar'ēlāh | | nāthattāh | lîrē'êkhā |
| You have made us drink | wine of | staggering | | You have given | to those who fear You |

| 5438 | 3937, 5449.741 | 4623, 6686 | 7486 | 5734 | 5. | 3937, 4775 | 2603.226 |
|---|---|---|---|---|---|---|---|
| n ms | prep, v Hithpoel inf con | prep, *n mp* | n ms | intrj | | prep, prep | v Niphal impf 3mp |
| נֵּס | לְהִתְנוֹסֵס | מִפְּנֵי | קֹשֶׁט | סֶלָה | | לְמַעַן | יֵחָלְצוּן |
| nēs | lehithnôsēs | mippenê | qōsheṭ | selāh | | lema'an | yēchāletsûn |
| a banner | to raise a banner | from before | truth | selah | | so that | they will be girded |

| 3148 | 3588.531 | 3332 | 6257.131 | 6. | 435 | 1744.311 |
|---|---|---|---|---|---|---|
| adj, ps 2ms | v Hiphil impv 2ms | n fs, ps 2ms | cj, v Qal impv 2ms, ps 1cp | | n mp | v Piel pf 3ms |
| יְדִידֶיךָ | הוֹשִׁיעָה | יְמִינְךָ | וַעֲנֵנוּ | | אֱלֹהִים | דִּבֶּר |
| yedhîdhêkhā | hôshî'āh | yemînekhā | wa'ănēnû | | 'ĕlōhîm | dibber |
| your beloved | save | your right hand | and answer us | | God | He has spoken |

**17. Unto thee, O my strength, will I sing: for God is my defence, and the God of my mercy:** ... I will sing praises to you, *NCV* ... my fortress, *NIV* ... God is my high tower, even the God of my mercy, *BB* ... the God who shows me steadfast love, *NRSV*.

**60:t. To the chief Musician upon Shushan-eduth, Michtam of David, to teach; when he strove with Aram-naharaim and with Aram-zobah, when Joab returned, and smote of Edom in the valley of salt twelve thousand.**

**1. O God, thou hast cast us off, thou hast scattered us, thou hast been displeased; O turn thyself to us again:** ... thou hast been angry and rebuked us, *NEB* ... you have sent us in all directions, *BB* ... You have been angry—restore us, *Beck* ... you have rejected us, broken us, you were angry, come back to us, *JB*.

**2. Thou hast made the earth to tremble; thou hast broken it: heal the breaches thereof; for it shaketh:** ... You have made the land quake and split open—heal its fractures, *Beck* ... earth is shaking and broken, *BB* ... Heal the wounds of the land, *Knox*.

**3. Thou hast shown thy people hard things: thou hast made us to drink the wine of astonishment:** ... You have shown your people desperate times, *NIV* ... Heavy the burden thou didst lay on us, *Knox* ... You have made your people feel hardships, *NAB* ... wine to drink that makes us stagger, *NASB*.

**4. Thou hast given a banner to them that fear thee, that it may be displayed because of the truth. Selah:** ... Give a safe place, *BB* ... hast given a banner to those who revere Thee, *Berkeley* ... You gave a signal to those who fear you to let them escape out of range of the bow, *JB* ... thou hast set up a standard to rally thy faithful servants, *Knox*.

**5. That thy beloved may be delivered; save with thy right hand, and hear me:** ... That your loved ones may escape; *NAB* ... Save us by Your right hand and give us victory in order to free Your dear people, *Beck*.

**6. God hath spoken in his holiness; I will rejoice, I will divide Shechem, and mete out the valley of Succoth:** ... God promised in his

---

tinued here, and the pregnant truth would show that continuance in sin is the punishment of sin. But probably the imprecations are better confined to the former part, as the selah draws a broad line of demarcation. If the verses are taken as simply predictive, the point of the reintroduction of the figure of the pack of dogs hunting for their prey lies in v. 15.

**59:16–17.** A clear strain of trust springs up, like a lark's morning song. The singer contrasts himself with his baffled foes. "They" is repeated in the Hebrew text at the beginning of v. 15 for emphasis and is matched with the emphatic "but I" which begins v. 16. His "morning" is similarly set over against their "night." So petition, complaint, imprecation all merge into a song of joy and trust, and the whole ends with the refrain significantly varied and enlarged. In its first form, the psalmist said, "For thee will I watch!"; in its second he rises to "To thee will I sing."

***Psalm 60.*** *It falls into three parts of four verses each, of which the first (vv. 1–4) is complaint of defeat and prayer for help; the second (vv. 5–8), a divine oracle assuring victory; and the third (vv. 9–12), the flash of fresh hope kindled by God's word.*

**60:1–4.** The first part blends complaint and prayer in the first pair of verses, in each of which there is first a description of the desperate state of Israel and then a cry for help. The nation is broken, as a wall is broken down, or as an army whose ordered ranks are shattered and scattered. Some crushing defeat is meant, which in v. 2 is further described as an earthquake. The land trembles and then gapes in hideous clefts, and houses become gaunt ruins. The state is disorganized as in consequence of defeat. It is an unpoetic mixture of fact and figure to see in the "rending" of the land allusion to the separation of the kingdoms, especially as that was not the result of defeat.

There is almost a tone of wonder in the designation of Israel as "thy people," so sadly does the fate meted out to them contrast with their name. Stranger still and more anomalous is it that, as v. 3b laments, God's own hand has commended such a chalice to their lips as should fill them with infatuation. The construction "wine of staggering" is unusual. The best explanation of the phrase is that God not only sent the disaster which had shaken the nation like an earthquake, but had sent, too, the presumptuous self confidence which had led to it.

Verse 4 has received two opposite interpretations, being taken by some as a prolongation of the tone of lament over disaster and by others as commemoration of God's help. The latter meaning violently interrupts the continuity of thought. The natural view is that which sees v. 4 as a continuation of the description of calamity of v. 3.

**60:5–8.** The second part begins with a verse which Delitzsch and others regard as really connected, notwithstanding the selah at the end of v. 4, with the preceding. But it is quite intelligible as

| 904, 7231 | 6159.125 | 2606.325 | 8328 | 6231 | 5713 | 4200.325 |
|---|---|---|---|---|---|---|
| prep, n ms, ps 3ms | v Qal juss 1cs | v Piel juss 1cs | pn | cj, *n ms* | pn | v Piel juss 1cs |
| בְּקָדְשׁוֹ | אֶעְלֹזָה | אֲחַלְּקָה | שְׁכֶם | וְעֵמֶק | סֻכּוֹת | אֲמַדֵּד |
| beqādheshô | 'e'ālōzāh | 'ăchalleqāh | shekhem | we'ēmeq | sukkôth | 'ămaddēdh |
| in his holy place | let me exult | let me divide | Shechem | and the Valley of | Succoth | let me measure |

| | 3937 | 3113B | 3937 | 4667 | 688 | 4735 | 7513 |
|---|---|---|---|---|---|---|---|
| **7.** | prep, ps 1cs | pn | cj, prep, ps 1cs | pn | cj, pn | *n ms* | n ms, ps 1cs |
| | לִי | גִלְעָד | וְלִי | מְנַשֶּׁה | וְאֶפְרַיִם | מָעוֹז | רֹאשִׁי |
| | lî | ghil'ādh | welî | menashsheh | we'ephrayim | mā'ôz | rō'shî |
| | to me | Gilead | and to me | Manasseh | and Ephraim | the stronghold of | my head |

| 3171 | 2809.351 | | 4262 | 5707 | 7649 | 6142, 110 | 8390.125 |
|---|---|---|---|---|---|---|---|
| pn | v Poel ptc ms, ps 1cs | **8.** | pn | *n ms* | n ms, ps 1cs | prep, pn | v Hiphil impf 1cs |
| יְהוּדָה | מְחֹקְקִי | | מוֹאָב | סִיר | רַחְצִי | עַל־אֱדוֹם | אַשְׁלִיךְ |
| yehûdhāh | mechōqeqî | | mô'āv | sîr | rachtsî | 'al-'ědhôm | 'ashlîkh |
| Judah | my scepter | | Moab | the basin of | my washing | on Edom | I will throw |

| 5458 | 6142 | 6673 | 7607.732 | | 4449 | 3095.521 | 6111 | 4857 |
|---|---|---|---|---|---|---|---|---|
| n fs, ps 1cs | prep | pn | v Hithpolel impv 2fs | **9.** | intrg | v Hiphil impf 3ms, ps 1cs | *n fs* | n ms |
| נַעֲלִי | עָלַי | פְּלֶשֶׁת | הִתְרֹעָעִי | | מִי | יֹבִלֵנִי | עִיר | מָצוֹר |
| na'ălî | 'ālay | pelesheth | hithrō'ā'î | | mî | yōvilēnî | 'îr | mātsôr |
| my sandal | over | Philistia | I will shout | | who | he will bring me | a city of | a fortress |

| 4449 | 5328.111 | 5912, 110 | | 1950B, 3940, 887 | 435 | 2269.113 |
|---|---|---|---|---|---|---|
| intrg | v Qal pf 3ms, ps 1cs | prep, pn | **10.** | intrg part, neg part, pers pron | n mp | v Qal pf 2ms, ps 1cp |
| מִי | נָחַנִי | עַד־אֱדוֹם | | הֲלֹא־אַתָּה | אֱלֹהִים | זְנַחְתָּנוּ |
| mî | nāchanî | 'adh-'ědhôm | | hălō'-'attāh | 'ělōhîm | zenachtānû |
| who | he will lead me | unto Edom | | will You not | O God | You have rejected us |

| 3940, 3428.123 | 435 | 904, 6893 | | 1957, 3937 | 6054 |
|---|---|---|---|---|---|
| cj, neg part, v Qal impf 2ms | n mp | prep, n mp, ps 1cp | **11.** | v Qal impv 2ms, prep, ps 1cp | n fs |
| וְלֹא־תֵצֵא | אֱלֹהִים | בְּצִבְאוֹתֵינוּ | | הָבָה־לָּנוּ | עֶזְרָת |
| welō'-thētsē' | 'ělōhîm | betsiv'ôthênû | | hāvāh-lānû | 'ezrāth |
| and You have not gone out | O God | with our armies | | give to us | help |

| 4623, 7141 | 8175 | 9009 | 119 | | 904, 435 | 6449.120, 2524 |
|---|---|---|---|---|---|---|
| prep, n ms | cj, n ms | *n fs* | n ms | **12.** | prep, n mp | v Qal impf 1cp, n ms |
| מִצָּר | וְשָׁוְא | תְּשׁוּעַת | אָדָם | | בֵּאלֹהִים | נַעֲשֶׂה־חָיִל |
| mitstsār | weshāwe' | teshû'ath | 'ādhām | | bē'lōhîm | na'ăseh-chāyil |
| from the adversary | for vanity | the salvation of | humankind | | with God | we will act with valor |

| 2000 | 983.121 | 7141 | | 3937, 5514.351 | 6142, 5234 |
|---|---|---|---|---|---|
| cj, pers pron | v Qal impf 3ms | n mp, ps 1cp | **61:t** | prep, art, v Piel ptc ms | prep, n fs |
| וְהוּא | יָבוּס | צָרֵינוּ | | לַמְנַצֵּחַ | עַל־נְגִינַת |
| wehû' | yāvûs | tsārênû | | lamnatstsēach | 'al-neghînath |
| and He | He will trample | our adversaries | | to the director | on the stringed instruments |

sanctuary: Exultantly I will apportion Shechem, *NAB* … God has said in his holy place, I will be glad: I will make a division of Shechem, and the valley of Succoth will be measured out, *BB* … God spoke from his sanctuary, *Anchor* … I will be exultant and divide up Shechem, *Beck* … In triumph I will divide up Shechem, *JB*.

**7. Gilead is mine, and Manasseh is mine; Ephraim also is the strength of mine head; Judah is my lawgiver:** … Ephraim is the defense of My head, *Berkeley* … Ephraim also is the helmet of My head, *NASB*.

**8. Moab is my washpot; over Edom will I cast out my shoe: Philistia, triumph thou because of me:** … Moab is like my washbowl. I throw my sandals at Edom. I shout at Philistia, *NCV* … Philistia is the target of my anger, *NEB* … Philistia, shout and acclaim me, *REB*.

**9. Who will bring me into the strong city? who will lead me into Edom?:** … Who will bring me to the Rock City?, *Anchor* … fortified city?, *Beck* ...Who will take me into the strong town? who will be my guide into Edom, *BB*.

**10. Wilt not thou, O God, which hadst cast us off? and thou, O God, which didst not go out with our armies?:** ... O God, hast abandoned us, *NEB* ... the God who has rejected us, *JB* ... you do not go out with our armies, *NCV* ... do you no longer lead our armies to battle, *REB*.

**11. Give us help from trouble: for vain is the help of man:** ... Give us help against the enemy, for human deliverance is useless!, *Beck* ... Bring us help in our time of crisis, any human help is worthless, *JB* ... for there is no help in man, *BB*.

**12. Through God we shall do valiantly: for he it is that shall tread down our enemies:** ... we can win with God's help. He will defeat our enemies, *NCV* ... it is He who will tread down our adversaries, *NASB* ... He will trample down our enemies, *Beck* ... through him our haters will be crushed under our feet, *BB*.

**61:t. To the chief Musician upon Neginah, A Psalm of David.**

**1. Hear my cry, O God; attend unto my prayer:** ... Let my cry come to you, O God; let your ears be open to my prayer, *BB* ... listen to my prayer!, *Anchor* ... hear my prayer!, *Beck* ... Hear, O God, my pleading, *Berkeley* ... heed my prayer, *Moffatt*.

---

independent and is in its place as the introduction to the divine oracle which follows and makes the kernel of the Psalm. There is a beautiful strength of confidence in the psalmist's words regarding the beaten, scattered people as "thy beloved." He appeals to Him to answer, in order that a result so accordant with God's heart as the deliverance of his beloved ones may be secured. And the prayer has no sooner passed his lips than he hears the thunderous response, "God hath spoken in his holiness." That infinite elevation of his nature above creatures is the pledge of the fulfillment of his word.

The following verses contain the substance of the oracle; but it is too daring to suppose that they reproduce its words; for "I will rejoice" can scarcely be reverently put into the mouth of God. The substance of the whole is a twofold promise—of a united Israel and a submissive heathendom. Shechem on the west and Succoth on the east of Jordan, Gilead and Manasseh on the east and Ephraim and Judah on the west are the possession of the speaker, whether he is king or representative of the nation. No trace of a separation of the kingdoms is here. Ephraim, the strongest tribe of the Northern Kingdom, is the "strength of my head," the helmet, or perhaps with allusion to the horns of an animal as symbols of offensive weapons. Judah is the ruling tribe, the commander's baton, or possibly "lawgiver," as in Gen. 49. Israel thus compact together may count on conquests over hereditary foes.

Their defeat is foretold in contemptuous images. The basin for washing the feet was "a vessel unto dishonor," and in Israel's great house no higher function for his ancestral enemy, when conquered, would be found. The meaning of casting the shoe upon or over Edom is difficult. It may be a symbol for taking possession of property.

**60:9–12.** The third part is taken by some commentators to breathe the same spirit as the first part. Some speak of it as a "relapse into despondency," while others more truly hear in it the tones of rekindled trust. In v. 9, there is a remarkable change of tense from "Who will bring?" in the first clause to "Who will lead?" in the second. This is best explained by the supposition that some victory over Edom had preceded the Psalm, which is regarded by the singer as a guarantee of success in his assault of "the fenced city," probably Petra. There is no need to supplement v. 10 so as to read, "Wilt not Thou, O God, which," etc. The psalmist recurs to his earlier lament, not as if he thought that it still held true, but just because it does not. It explained the reason of past disasters, and being now reversed by the divine oracle becomes the basis of the prayer which follows. It is as if he had said, "We were defeated because Thou didst cast us off. Now help as Thou hast promised, and we shall do deeds of valor." It is impossible to suppose that the result of the divine answer, which makes the very heart of the Psalm, should be a hopeless repetition of the initial despondency. Rather glad faith acknowledges past weakness and traces past failures to self caused abandonment by a loving God, Who let his people be worsted that they might learn Who was their strength, and ever goes forth with those who go forth to war with the consciousness that all help but his is vain, and with the hope that in Him even their weakness shall do deeds of prowess. "Had cast us off?" may be the utterance of despair, but it may also be that of assured confidence and the basis of a prayer that will be answered by God's present help.

***Psalm 61.*** *The scheme of this Psalm is an introductory verse, followed by two parallel pairs of verses, each consisting of petition and its grounding*

| 3937, 1784 | | 8471.131 | 435 | 7726 | 7477.531 | 8940 | | 4623, 7381 |
|---|---|---|---|---|---|---|---|---|
| prep, pn | 1. | v Qal impv 2ms | n mp | n fs, ps 1cs | v Hiphil impv 2ms | n fs, ps 1cs | 2. | prep, *n ms* |
| לְדָוִד | | שִׁמְעָה | אֱלֹהִים | רִנָּתִי | הַקְשִׁיבָה | תְּפִלָּתִי | | מִקְצֵה |
| ledhāwidh | | shim'āh | 'ĕlōhîm | rinnāthî | haqŏshîvāh | tephillāthî | | miqŏtsēh |
| of David | | hear | O God | my lamentation | be attentive to | my prayer | | from the end of |

| 800 | 420 | 7410.125 | 6063.141 | 3949 | 904, 6962, 7597.121 | 4623 |
|---|---|---|---|---|---|---|
| art, n fs | prep, ps 2ms | v Qal impf 1cs | prep, v Qal inf con | n ms, ps 1cs | prep, n ms, v Qal impf 3ms | prep, ps 1cs |
| הָאָרֶץ | אֵלֶיךָ | אֶקְרָא | בַּעֲטֹף | לִבִּי | בְּצוּר־יָרוּם | מִמֶּנִּי |
| hā'ārets | 'ēlêkhā | 'eqŏrā' | ba'ătōph | libbî | betsûr-yārûm | mimmenî |
| the earth | to You | I will call | when being weak | my heart | on a rock it is higher | than I |

| 5328.523 | | 3706, 2030.113 | 4406 | 3937 | 4166, 6010 | 4623, 6686 |
|---|---|---|---|---|---|---|
| v Hiphil impf 2ms, ps 1cs | 3. | cj, v Qal pf 2ms | n ms | prep, ps 1cs | *n ms*, n ms | prep, *n mp* |
| תַנְחֵנִי | | כִּי־הָיִיתָ | מַחְסֶה | לִי | מִגְדַּל־עֹז | מִפְּנֵי |
| thanchēnî | | kî-hāyîthā | machseh | lî | mighdal-'ōz | mippenê |
| lead me | | because You are | a Refuge | to me | a Tower of strength | from before |

| 342.151 | | 1513.125 | 904, 164 | 5986 | 2725.125 | 904, 5848 |
|---|---|---|---|---|---|---|
| v Qal act ptc ms | 4. | v Qal juss 1cs | prep, n ms, ps 2ms | n mp | v Qal juss 1cs | prep, *n ms* |
| אוֹיֵב | | אָגוּרָה | בְאָהָלְךָ | עוֹלָמִים | אֶחֱסֶה | בְסֵתֶר |
| 'ôyēv | | 'āghûrāh | ve'āhālekhā | 'ôlāmîm | 'echĕseh | vesēther |
| the enemy | | let me stay | in your tent | forever | let me seek refuge | under the shelter of |

| 3796 | 5734 | | 3706, 887 | 435 | 8471.113 | 3937, 5266 | 5598.113 |
|---|---|---|---|---|---|---|---|
| n fd, ps 2ms | intrj | 5. | cj, pers pron | n mp | v Qal pf 2ms | prep, n mp, ps 1cs | v Qal pf 2ms |
| כְּנָפֶיךָ | סֶלָה | | כִּי־אַתָּה | אֱלֹהִים | שָׁמַעְתָּ | לִנְדָרָי | נָתַתָּ |
| kenāphêkhā | selāh | | kî-'attāh | 'ĕlōhîm | shāma'ttā | lindhāray | nāthattā |
| your wings | selah | | because You | O God | You have heard | my vows | You have given |

| 3544 | 3486.152 | 8428 | | 3219 | 6142, 3219, 4567 |
|---|---|---|---|---|---|
| *n fs* | *v Qal act ptc mp* | n ms, ps 2ms | 6. | n mp | prep, *n mp*, n ms |
| יְרֻשַּׁת | יִרְאֵי | שְׁמֶךָ | | יָמִים | עַל־יְמֵי־מֶלֶךְ |
| yerushshath | yir'ê | shemekhā | | yāmîm | 'al-yemê-melekh |
| a possession for | those who fear | your name | | days | upon the days of the king |

| 3362.523 | 8523 | 3765, 1810 | 1810 | | 3553.121 | 5986 | 3937, 6686 |
|---|---|---|---|---|---|---|---|
| v Hiphil impf 2ms | n fp, ps 3ms | prep, n ms | cj, n ms | 7. | v Qal impf 3ms | n ms | prep, *n mp* |
| תּוֹסִיף | שְׁנוֹתָיו | כְּמוֹ־דֹר | וָדֹר | | יֵשֵׁב | עוֹלָם | לִפְנֵי |
| tôsîph | shenôthâv | kemô-dhōr | wādhōr | | yēshēv | 'ôlām | liphnê |
| You add | his years | like generations | and generations | | He sits | forever | before |

| 435 | 2721 | 583 | 4630.331 | 5526.126 | | 3772 |
|---|---|---|---|---|---|---|
| n mp | n ms | cj, n fs | v Piel impv 2ms | v Qal impf 3mp, ps 3ms | 8. | adv |
| אֱלֹהִים | חֶסֶד | וֶאֱמֶת | מַן | יִנְצְרֻהוּ | | כֵּן |
| 'ĕlōhîm | chesedh | we'ĕmeth | man | yintseruhû | | kēn |
| God | steadfast love | and faithfulness | allot | they will watch over him | | so |

**2. From the end of the earth will I cry unto thee, when my heart is overwhelmed: lead me to the rock that is higher than I:** ... when my heart is overcome, *BB* ... as my heart grows faint, *NAB* ... Carry me away to a high mountain, *NCV* ... Lead me to a Rock that towers above me, *Beck*.

**3. For thou hast been a shelter for me, and a strong tower from the enemy:** ... my high tower, *BB* ... Thou art a refuge to me, *Berkeley* ... You ever were my defence, *Fenton*.

**4. I will abide in thy tabernacle for ever: I will trust in the covert of thy wings. Selah:** ... Let me stay in your tent for ever, taking refuge in the shelter of your wings, *JB* ... take refuge in the shelter, *NIV* ... I will make your tent my resting-place, *BB*.

**5. For thou, O God, hast heard my vows: thou hast given me the heritage of those that fear thy name:** ... You heard my promises, God—Gave possessions for honouring Your Name, *Fenton* ... Thou hast granted the wish of those who fear, *Goodspeed* ... revere Thy name, *Berkeley*.

**6. Thou wilt prolong the king's life: and his years as many generations:** ... To the king's life add length of days, *NEB* ... while generations come and go, may his life still last, *Knox* ... turning his years into endless generations, *Anchor*.

**7. He shall abide before God for ever: O prepare mercy and truth, which may preserve him:** ... sit enthroned before God forever, *Anchor* ... may mercy and righteousness keep him safe, *BB* ... ordain lovingkindness and truth to keep him, *Berkeley* ... your faithful love and constancy watch over him, *JB*.

**8. So will I sing praise unto thy name for ever, that I may daily perform my vows:** ... every day I will keep my promises, *NCV* ... sing psalms in honour of thy name, *NEB* ... giving to God that which is right day by day, *BB*.

**62:t. To the chief Musician, to Jeduthun, A Psalm of David.**

---

*in past mercies (vv. 2f, and 4f), and these again succeeded by another pair containing petitions for "the king," while a final single verse, corresponding to the introductory one, joyfully foresees lifelong praise evoked by the certain answers to the singer's prayer.*

**61:1.** The fervor of the psalmist's supplication is strikingly expressed by his use in the first clause of the word which is ordinarily employed for the shrill notes of rejoicing. It describes the quality of the sound as penetrating and emotional, not the nature of the emotion expressed by it. Joy is usually louder-tongued than sorrow, but this suppliant's need has risen so high that his cry is resonant. To himself he seems to be at "the end of the earth," for he measures distance not as a map maker, but as a worshiper.

**61:2–3.** The one desire of such a suppliant is for restoration of access to God. The psalmist embodies that yearning in its more outward form, but not without penetrating to the inner reality in both the parallel petitions which follow. In the first of these (v. 2b), the thought is more full than the condensed expression of it. "Lead me to" or "in," says he, meaning, "Lead me to and set me on." His imagination sees a great cliff towering above him on which, if he could be planted, he might defy pursuit or assault. But he is distant from it, and the inaccessibility which, were he in its clefts, would be his safety, is now his despair. Therefore, he turns to God and asks Him to bear him up in his hands that he may set his foot on that rock. The figure has been, strangely enough, interpreted to mean a rock of difficulty, but not in the Psalter.

**61:4–5.** The second pair of verses, containing petition and its ground in past experience (vv. 4f), brings out still more clearly the psalmist's longing for the sanctuary. The futures in v. 4 may be taken either as simple expressions of certainty or, more probably, as precative, as is suggested by the parallelism with the preceding pair. The "tent" of God is the sanctuary, possibly so called because, at the date of the Psalm, "the ark of God dwelleth within curtains" (2 Sam. 7:2). The "shelter of your wings" may then be an allusion to the Shekinah and outspread pinions of the cherubim. Those in God's dwelling have provision and protection.

**61:6–7.** Very naturally, then, follows the closing prayer in vv. 6f. The purely individual character of the rest of the Psalm, which is resumed in the last verse, where the singer, speaking in the first person, represents his continual praise as the result of the answer to his petitions for the king, makes these petitions hopelessly irrelevant, unless the psalmist is the king and these prayers are for himself. The transition to the third person does not necessarily negate this interpretation, which seems to be required by the context. The prayer sounds hyperbolical, but has a parallel in Ps. 21:4 and need not be vindicated by taking the dynasty rather than the individual to be meant or by diverting it to a messianic reference. It is a prayer for length of days, in order that the deliverance already begun may be perfected, and that the psalmist may dwell in the house of the LORD forever (cf. Pss. 23:6; 27:4). He asks that he may sit enthroned before God forever—that is, that his dominion may by God's favor be established and his throne upheld in peace.

The final petition has, as has been noticed above, parallels in Pss. 42, 43, to which may be added the personifications of goodness and steadfast love in Ps. 43:6. These bright harnessed angels stand sentries over the devout suppliant, set on their guard by the great Commander, and no harm can come to him over whom God's steadfast love and faithfulness keep daily and nightly watch.

**61:8.** Thus guarded, the psalmist's prolonged life will be one long anthem of praise, and the days added to his days will be occupied with the fulfillment of his vows made in trouble and redeemed in his prosperity. What congruity is there between this closing verse, which is knit closely to the preceding by that "so," and the previous pair of verses, unless the king is himself the petitioner? "He sits forever before

| 2252.325 | 8428 | 3937, 5911 | 3937, 8396.341 | 5266 | 3219 | 3219 |
|---|---|---|---|---|---|---|
| v Piel juss 1cs | n ms, ps 2ms | prep, n ms | prep, v Piel inf con, ps 1cs | n mp, ps 1cs | n ms | n ms |
| אֲזַמְּרָה | שִׁמְךָ | לָעַד | לְשַׁלְּמִי | נְדָרַי | יוֹם | יוֹם |
| 'ăzammerāh | shimkhā | lā'adh | leshallemî | nedhāray | yôm | yôm |
| let me sing praises to | your name | unto eternity | for my making complete | my vows | a day | a day |

| 62:t | 3937, 5514.351 | 6142, 3147 | 4344 | 3937, 1784 | 1. | 395 | 420, 435 | 1800 |
|---|---|---|---|---|---|---|---|---|
| | prep, art, v Piel ptc ms | prep, pn | n ms | prep, pn | | adv | prep, n mp | n fs |
| | לַמְנַצֵּחַ | עַל־יְדוּתוּן | מִזְמוֹר | לְדָוִד | | אַךְ | אֶל־אֱלֹהִים | דּוּמִיָּה |
| | lamnatstsēach | 'al-yedhûthûn | mizmôr | ledhāwidh | | 'akh | 'el-'ĕlōhîm | dûmîyāh |
| | to the director | according to Jeduthun | a Psalm | of David | | only | to God | silence |

| 5497 | 4623 | 3568 | 2. | 395, 2000 | 6962 | 3568 | 5021 |
|---|---|---|---|---|---|---|---|
| n fs, ps 1cs | prep, ps 3ms | n fs, ps 1cs | | adv, pers pron | n ms, ps 1cs | cj, n fs, ps 1cs | n ms, ps 1cs |
| נַפְשִׁי | מִמֶּנּוּ | יְשׁוּעָתִי | | אַךְ־הוּא | צוּרִי | וִישׁוּעָתִי | מִשְׂגַּבִּי |
| naphshî | mimmennû | yeshû'āthî | | 'akh-hû' | tsûrî | wîshû'āthî | misgabbî |
| my soul | from Him | my salvation | | only He | my Rock | and my Salvation | my Stronghold |

| 3940, 4267.225 | 7521 | 3. | 5912, 590 | 2133.328 | 6142, 382 |
|---|---|---|---|---|---|
| neg part, v Niphal impf 1cs | adv | | prep, intrg | v Poel impf 2mp | prep, n ms |
| לֹא־אֶמּוֹט | רַבָּה | | עַד־אָנָה | תְּהוֹתְתוּ | עַל־אִישׁ |
| lō'-'emmôṯ | rabbāh | | 'adh-'ānāh | tehôthethû | 'al-'îsh |
| I will not falter | greatly | | until when | will you overwhelm with reproofs | against a man |

| 7815.328 | 3725 | 3626, 7306 | 5371.155 | 1474 | 1815.157 |
|---|---|---|---|---|---|
| v Piel impf 2mp | adj, ps 2mp | prep, n ms | v Qal pass ptc ms | n ms | art, v Qal pass ptc fs |
| תְּרָצְּחוּ | כֻּלְּכֶם | כְּקִיר | נָטוּי | גָּדֵר | הַדְּחוּיָה |
| terātstsechû | khullekhem | keqîr | nāṯûy | gādhēr | haddechûyāh |
| will you continually murder | all of you | like a wall | bent down | a fence | which is pushed |

| 4. | 395 | 4623, 7874 | 3398.116 | 3937, 5258.541 | 7813.126 | 3695 |
|---|---|---|---|---|---|---|
| | adv | prep, n fs, ps 3ms | v Qal pf 3cp | prep, v Hiphil inf con | v Qal impf 3mp | n ms |
| | אַךְ | מִשְּׂאֵתוֹ | יָעֲצוּ | לְהַדִּיחַ | יִרְצוּ | כָזָב |
| | 'akh | misse'ēthô | yā'ătsû | lehaddîach | yirtsû | khāzāv |
| | only | from his exaltation | they plan | to oust | they take pleasure | falsehood |

| 904, 6552 | 1313.326 | 904, 7419 | 7327.326, 5734 | 5. | 395 | 3937, 435 |
|---|---|---|---|---|---|---|
| prep, n ms, ps 3ms | v Piel impf 3mp | cj, prep, n ms, ps 3mp | v Piel impf 3mp, intrj | | adv | prep, n mp |
| בְּפִיו | יְבָרֵכוּ | וּבְקִרְבָּם | יְקַלְלוּ־סֶלָה | | אַךְ | לֵאלֹהִים |
| bephîw | yevārēkhû | ûveqirbām | yeqalelû-s̱elāh | | 'akh | lē'lōhîm |
| in his mouth | they bless | and within them | they curse selah | | only | to God |

| 1887.141 | 5497 | 3706, 4623 | 8951 | 6. | 395, 2000 | 6962 |
|---|---|---|---|---|---|---|
| v Qal inf con, ps 1cs | n fs, ps 1cs | cj, prep, ps 3ms | n fs, ps 1cs | | adv, pers pron | n ms, ps 1cs |
| דּוֹמִּי | נַפְשִׁי | כִּי־מִמֶּנּוּ | תִּקְוָתִי | | אַךְ־הוּא | צוּרִי |
| dômmî | naphshî | kî-mimmennû | tiqôwāthî | | 'akh-hû' | tsûrî |
| my being silent | my soul | because from Him | my hope | | only He | my Rock |

| 3568 | 5021 | 3940 | 4267.225 | 7. | 6142, 435 | 3589 |
|---|---|---|---|---|---|---|
| cj, n fs, ps 1cs | n ms, ps 1cs | neg part | v Niphal impf 1cs | | prep, n mp | n ms, ps 1cs |
| וִישׁוּעָתִי | מִשְׂגַּבִּי | לֹא | אֶמּוֹט | | עַל־אֱלֹהִים | יִשְׁעִי |
| wîshû'āthî | misgabbî | lō' | 'emmôṯ | | 'al-'ĕlōhîm | yish'î |
| and my Salvation | my Stronghold | not | I will falter | | upon God | my Salvation |

| 3638 | 6962, 6010 | 4406 | 904, 435 | 8. | 1019.133 | 904 |
|---|---|---|---|---|---|---|
| cj, n ms, ps 1cs | *n ms*, n ms, ps 1cs | n ms, ps 1cs | prep, n mp | | v Qal impv 2mp | prep, ps 3ms |
| וּכְבוֹדִי | צוּר־עֻזִּי | מַחְסִי | בֵּאלֹהִים | | בִּטְחוּ | בוֹ |
| ûkhevôdhî | tsûr-'uzzî | machs̱î | bē'lōhîm | | biṯchû | vô |
| and my Honor | my Rock of strength | my Refuge | in God | | trust | in Him |

**1. Truly my soul waiteth upon God: from him cometh my salvation:** ... My soul, put all your faith in God, *BB* ... my heart is calm before God, for He saves me, *Beck* ... To God alone is my spirit resigned, *Goodspeed.*

**2. He only is my rock and my salvation; he is my defence; I shall not be greatly moved:** ... He is my defender; I will not be defeated, *NCV* ... he is my high tower, *BB* ... I'll not be shaken, *Beck* ... never shall I be overthrown, *Moffatt.*

**3. How long will ye imagine mischief against a man? ye shall be slain all of you: as a bowing wall shall ye be, and as a tottering fence:** ... will you set on a victim, all together, intent on murder, *JB* ... All of you are like a leaning wall, a sagging fence, *Anchor* ... will you go on designing evil against a man, *BB.*

**4. They only consult to cast him down from his excellency: they delight in lies: they bless with their mouth, but they curse inwardly. Selah:** ... put him down from his place of honour; their delight is in deceit, *BB* ... Trickery is their only plan, *JB* ... they plan to dislodge me, *NAB* ... they bless him, the hypocrites, but revile him in their hearts, *NEB.*

**5. My soul, wait thou only upon God; for my expectation is from him:** ... Leave it all quietly to God, *Moffatt* ... I find rest in God, *NCV* ... from him comes my hope, *BB* ... all my trust is in him, *Knox.*

**6. He only is my rock and my salvation: he is my defence; I shall not be moved:** ... my tower of strength, *NEB* ... my mountain Refuge, *Beck* ... will not be defeated, *NCV.*

**7. In God is my salvation and my glory: the rock of my strength, and my refuge, is in God:** ... my mighty rock and my protection, *NCV.*

---

God"—how does that lead up to "So will I sing praises unto thy name for ever"? Surely the natural answer is that "he" and "I" are the same person.

***Psalm 62.*** *The Psalm is in three strophes of four verses each, the divisions being marked by selah. The two former have a long refrain at the beginning, instead of, as usually, at the end. In the first, the psalmist sets his quiet trust in contrast with the furious assaults of his foes; while, in the second, he stirs himself to renewed exercise of it and exhorts others to share with him in the security of God as a place of refuge. In the third strophe, the nothingness of man is set in strong contrast to the power and steadfast love of God, and the exhortation from trust in material wealth urged as the negative side of the previous exhortation to trust in God.*

**62:1–2.** The noble saying of v. 1a is hard to translate without weakening. The initial word (HED #395) may have the meanings of "only" or "surely." The former seems more appropriate in this Psalm, where it occurs six times, in one only of which (v. 4) does the latter seem the more natural rendering, although even there the other is possible. It is, however, to be noticed that its restrictive power is not always directed to the adjacent word; and here it may either present God as the exclusive object of the psalmist's waiting trust or his whole soul as being nothing else but silent resignation. The reference to God is favored by v. 2, but the other is possible.

**62:3–4.** The assurance of personal safety is inseparable from such a thought of God. Nothing which does not shake the rock can shake the frail tent pitched on it. As long as the tower stands, its inhabitant can look down from his inaccessible fastness with equanimity, although assailed by crowds. Thus, the psalmist turns swiftly in the latter pair of verses making up the first strophe to address remonstrances to his enemies, as engaged in a useless effort, and then drops direct address and speaks of their hostility and treachery. The bulging wall outlasts its would-be destroyers. But appeal to them is vain for they have one settled purpose absorbing them, namely, to cast him down from his height. He is, then, probably in some position of distinction, threatened by false friends who are plotting his deposition while their words are fair. All these circumstances agree well with the Davidic authorship.

**62:5–6.** The second strophe reiterates the refrain, with slight but significant variations, and substitutes for the address to and contemplation of the plotters a meditation on the psalmist's own security and an invitation to others to share it. In v. 5, the refrain is changed from a declaration of the psalmist's silent waiting to self exhortation. The "expectation" in v. 5b is substantially equivalent to the "salvation" in v. 1b. It means not the emotion, but the thing expected. The change in expression from "salvation" to "expectation" makes prominent the psalmist's attitude. In his silence, his wistful eyes look up, watching for the first far-off brightening which tells him that help is on its road from the throne. Salvation will not come unexpected, and expectation will not look in vain.

**62:7–8.** The second pair of verses in this strophe substitutes for the description of their fierce rush the triumphant reiteration of what God is to the psalmist and an invitation to others to come with him into that strong refuge. The transition to

| 904, 3725, 6496 | 6194 | 8581.133, 3937, 6686 | 3949 | 435 | 4406, 3937 | 5734 |
|---|---|---|---|---|---|---|
| prep, *adj*, n fs | n ms | v Qal impv 2mp, prep, n mp, ps 3ms | n ms, ps 2mp | n mp | n ms, prep, ps 1cp | intrj |
| בְּכָל־עֵת | עָם | שִׁפְכוּ־לְפָנָיו | לְבַבְכֶם | אֱלֹהִים | מַחֲסֶה־לָּנוּ | סֶלָה |
| vekhol-ʿēth | ʿām | shiphkhû-lephānâv | levavkhem | 'ĕlōhîm | machseh-lānû | selāh |
| in all times | O people | pour out before Him | your heart | God | a Refuge to us | selah |

9.

| 395 | 1961 | 1158, 119 | 3695 | 1158 | 382 | 904, 4118 |
|---|---|---|---|---|---|---|
| adv | n ms | *n mp*, n ms | n ms | *n mp* | n ms | prep, n md |
| אַךְ | הֶבֶל | בְּנֵי־אָדָם | כָּזָב | בְּנֵי | אִישׁ | בְּמֹאזְנַיִם |
| 'akh | hevel | benê-'ādhām | kāzāv | benê | 'îsh | bemō'zenayim |
| only | a breath | the children of humankind | falsehood | the children of | men | in the balances |

| 3937, 6148.141 | 2065 | 4623, 1961 | 3266 | 10. 414, 1019.128 | 904, 6480 |
|---|---|---|---|---|---|
| prep, v Qal inf con | pers pron | prep, n ms | adv | adv, v Qal juss 2mp | prep, n ms |
| לַעֲלוֹת | הֵמָּה | מֵהֶבֶל | יָחַד | אַל־תִּבְטְחוּ | בְעֹשֶׁק |
| laʿălôth | hēmmāh | mēhevel | yāchadh | 'al-tivtechû | veʿōsheq |
| to go up | they | from a breath | altogether | do not trust | in extortion |

| 904, 1529 | 414, 1960.128 | 2524 | 3706, 5286.121 | 414, 8308.128 | 3949 |
|---|---|---|---|---|---|
| cj, prep, n ms | adv, v Qal juss 2mp | n ms | cj, v Qal impf 3ms | adv, v Qal juss 2mp | n ms |
| וּבְגָזֵל | אַל־תֶּהְבָּלוּ | חַיִל | כִּי־יָנוּב | אַל־תָּשִׁיתוּ | לֵב |
| ûveghāzēl | 'al-tehbālû | chayil | kî-yānûv | 'al-tāshîthû | lēv |
| and in robberry | do not be vain | riches | whether they will prosper | do not set | the heart |

11.

| 259 | 1744.311 | 435 | 8692, 2182 | 8471.115 | 3706 | 6010 | 3937, 435 |
|---|---|---|---|---|---|---|---|
| num | v Piel pf 3ms | n mp | num, dem pron | v Qal pf 1cs | cj | n ms | prep, n mp |
| אַחַת | דִּבֶּר | אֱלֹהִים | שְׁתַּיִם־זוּ | שָׁמָעְתִּי | כִּי | עֹז | לֵאלֹהִים |
| 'achath | dibber | 'ĕlōhîm | shettayim-zû | shāmāʿttî | kî | ʿōz | lē'lōhîm |
| one | He spoke | God | twice this | I heard | that | strength | to God |

12.

| 3937, 112 | 2721 | 3706, 887 | 8396.323 | 3937, 382 |
|---|---|---|---|---|
| cj, prep, ps 2ms, n mp, ps 1cs | n ms | cj, pers pron | v Piel impf 2ms | prep, n ms |
| וּלְךָ־אֲדֹנָי | חָסֶד | כִּי־אַתָּה | תְשַׁלֵּם | לְאִישׁ |
| ûlăkhā-'ădhōnāy | chāsedh | kî-'attāh | theshallēm | le'îsh |
| and to You O Lord | steadfast love | because You | You requite | to a man |

| 3626, 4801 | 63:t 4344 | 3937, 1784 | 904, 2030.141 | 904, 4198 |
|---|---|---|---|---|
| prep, n ms, ps 3ms | n ms | prep, pn | prep, v Qal inf con, ps 3ms | prep, *n ms* |
| כְמַעֲשֵׂהוּ | מִזְמוֹר | לְדָוִד | בִּהְיוֹתוֹ | בְּמִדְבַּר |
| kemaʿăsēhû | mizmôr | ledhāwidh | bihyôthô | bemidhbar |
| according to his works | a Psalm | of David | when his being | in the wilderness of |

| 3171 | 1. 435 | 418 | 887 | 8264.325 | 7039.122 | 3937 | 5497 |
|---|---|---|---|---|---|---|---|
| pn | n mp | n ms, ps 1cs | pers pron | v Piel impf 1cs, ps 2ms | v Qal pf 3fs | prep, ps 2ms | n fs, ps 1cs |
| יְהוּדָה | אֱלֹהִים | אֵלִי | אַתָּה | אֲשַׁחֲרֶךָּ | צָמְאָה | לְךָ | נַפְשִׁי |
| yehûdhāh | 'ĕlōhîm | 'ēlî | 'attāh | 'ăshachrekhā | tsāme'āh | lekhā | naphshî |
| Judah | O God | my God | You | I search for You | it is thirsty | for You | my soul |

**8. Trust in him at all times; ye people, pour out your heart before him: God is a refuge for us. Selah:** ... Always rely on him, *Moffatt* ... Have faith in him at all times, *BB*.

**9. Surely men of low degree are vanity, and men of high degree are a lie: to be laid in the balance, they are altogether lighter than vanity:** ... men of low birth are nothing, and men of high position are not what they seem, *BB* ... Mortal men are only a breath, even important men a delusion. They are altogether less than a vapor, *Beck*.

**10. Trust not in oppression, and become not vain in robbery: if riches increase, set not your heart upon them:** ... Rely not on extortion, pride not yourselves on robbery, *Moffatt* ... do not be proud of stolen goods, *NEB*.

**11. God hath spoken once; twice have I heard this; that power belongeth unto God:** ... strength belongs to God, *Berkeley* ... power is only from God, *Fenton*.

**12. Also unto thee, O Lord, belongeth mercy: for thou renderest to every man according to his work:** ... you repay everyone as their deeds deserve, *JB* ... according to what he does, *Beck* ... You reward, *NCV*.

**63:t. A Psalm of David, when he was in the wilderness of Judah.**

**1. O God, thou art my God; early will I seek thee: my soul thirsteth for thee, my flesh longeth for thee in a dry and thirsty land, where no water is:** ... I'm eagerly looking for You, I'm thirsting for You. My body faints with longing for You, more than a dry and parched land, *Beck* ... for you my flesh pines and my soul thirsts like the earth, parched, lifeless and without water, *NAB* ... I long for you. My whole being desires you; like a dry, worn-out, and waterless land, *Good News*.

---

addressing the "people" is natural. The phrase would then apply to his immediate followers, who were one with him in peril and whom he would have one with him in trust. But the Septuagint has another reading, which involves only the insertion of a letter that may easily have dropped out in the word rendered "time" and which makes the verse run more smoothly. It reads "all the congregation of the people." Every man who has learned that God is a refuge for him is thereby assured that He is the same for all men and thereby moved to beseech them to make the like blessed discovery. The way into that hiding place is trust. "Pour out your heart before him," says the psalmist. "In every thing by prayer and supplication with thanksgiving let your requests be made known unto God," says Paul (Phil. 4:6). They both mean the same thing.

**62:9–10.** The third strophe sets the emptiness of men in strong contrast to the sufficiency of God. "Vanity" is literally "a breath" (HED #1911) and would better be so rendered in v. 9, but for the recurrence of the verb from the same root in v. 10, which requires the rendering "be not vain." It is desirable to preserve identity of translation so as to retain the play of words. But by doing so, v. 9 is somewhat weakened. The eyes that have been looking on God are cleared to see the shadowy nothingness of men of all degrees. The differences of high and low dwindle when seen from that "high tower," (Pss. 1:2; 144:2) as lower lands appear flat when viewed from a mountaintop. They are but "breath," so fleeting, unsubstantial are they. They are a "lie," insofar as hopes directed to them are deceived and trust misplaced. The singer is not cynically proclaiming man's worthlessness, but asserting his insufficiency as the object of man's trust.

The folly and misery of false trust are vigorously set forth by that word "become vain." The curse of misplaced confidence is that it brings down a man to the level of what he trusts in, as the blessing of wisely placed trust is that it lifts him to that level. Trust in vanity is vain and makes the truster "vanity." Wind is not a nourishing diet. It may inflate, or, as Paul says about knowledge, may "puff up," but not "build up" (1 Cor. 4:6).

**62:11–12.** So far the psalmist has spoken. But his silent waiting has been rewarded with a clear voice from heaven, confirming that of his faith. The synthesis of power and steadfast love is in the God whom men are invited to trust; and such trust can never be disappointed; for his power and his steadfast love will cooperate to "render to a man according to his work." The last word of the Psalm adds the conception of righteousness to those of power and steadfast love. But the psalmist seems to have in view mainly one direction in which that rendering "to every man according to his work" is active, namely, in answering the trust which turns away from human power which is weakness, and from human love which may change and must die, to anchor itself on the might and tenderness of God. Such work of faith will not be in vain, for these twin attributes of power and love are pledged to requite it with security and peace.

***Psalm 63.*** *The recurrence of the expression "My soul" in vv. 1, 5, 8 suggests the divisions into which the Psalm falls. Following that clue, we recognize three parts, in each of which a separate phase of the experience of the soul in its communion with God is presented as realized in sequence by the psalmist. The soul longs and thirsts for God (vv. 1–4). The longing soul is satisfied in God (vv. 5ff). The satisfied soul cleaves to and presses after God (vv. 8–11). These stages melt into each other in the Psalm as in experience, but are still discernible.*

**63:1.** In the first strophe, the psalmist gives expression in immortal words to his longing after God. Like many a sad singer before and after him, he finds in the dreary scene around an image of yet drearier experiences within. He sees his own mood reflected in the gray monotony of the sterile desert, stretching waterless on every side, and seamed with cracks, like mouths gaping for the rain that does not come. He is weary and thirsty physically, but there is a more agonizing craving is in his spirit.

| 3762.111 | 3937 | 1340 | 904, 800, 6993 | 6106 | 1136, 4448 | | 3772 |
|---|---|---|---|---|---|---|---|
| v Qal pf 3ms | prep, ps 2ms | n ms, ps 1cs | prep, *n fs*, n fs | cj, adj | neg part, n mp | | adv |
| כָּמַהּ | לְךָ | בְשָׂרִי | בְּאֶרֶץ־צִיָּה | וְעָיֵף | בְּלִי־מָיִם | 2. | כֵּן |
| kāmahh | lekhā | vesārî | be'erets-tsîyāh | we'āyēph | belî-māyim | | kēn |
| it yearns | for You | my flesh | in a waterless land | and weary | no water | | so |

| 904, 7231 | 2463.115 | 3937, 7495.141 | 6010 | 3638 |
|---|---|---|---|---|
| prep, art, n ms | v Qal pf 1cs, ps 2ms | prep, v Qal inf con | n ms, ps 2ms | cj, n ms, ps 2ms |
| בַּקֹּדֶשׁ | חֲזִיתִיךָ | לִרְאוֹת | עֻזְּךָ | וּכְבוֹדֶךָ |
| baqqōdhesh | chăzîthîkhā | lir'ôth | 'uzzekhā | ûkhevôdhekhā |
| in the holy place | I have beheld You | to see | your strength | and your glory |

| | 3706, 3005 | 2721 | 4623, 2522 | 8004 | 8099.326 | | 3772 |
|---|---|---|---|---|---|---|---|
| | cj, adj | n ms, ps 2ms | prep, n mp | n fd, ps 1cs | v Piel impf 3mp, ps 2ms | | adv |
| 3. | כִּי־טוֹב | חַסְדְּךָ | מֵחַיִּים | שְׂפָתַי | יְשַׁבְּחוּנְךָ | 4. | כֵּן |
| | kî-ṭôv | chasdekhā | mēchayyîm | sephāthay | yeshabbechûnkhā | | kēn |
| | because better | your steadfast love | than life | my lips | they will exult in You | | so |

| 1313.325 | 904, 2522 | 904, 8428 | 5558.125 | 3834 | | 3765 | 2562 |
|---|---|---|---|---|---|---|---|
| v Piel impf 1cs, ps 2ms | prep, n mp, ps 1cs | prep, n ms, ps 2ms | v Qal impf 1cs | n fd, ps 1cs | | prep | n ms |
| אֲבָרֶכְךָ | בְחַיָּי | בְּשִׁמְךָ | אֶשָּׂא | כַפָּי | 5. | כְּמוֹ | חֵלֶב |
| 'ăvārekhekhā | vechayyāy | beshimkhā | 'essā' | khappāy | | kemô | chēlev |
| I will bless You | during my lifetime | in your name | I will lift up | my hands | | like | choice parts |

| 1942 | 7881.122 | 5497 | 8004 | 7729 | 2054.321, 6552 |
|---|---|---|---|---|---|
| cj, n ms | v Qal impf 3fs | n fs, ps 1cs | cj, *n fd* | n fp | v Piel impf 3ms, n ms, ps 1cs |
| וָדֶשֶׁן | תִּשְׂבַּע | נַפְשִׁי | וְשִׂפְתֵי | רְנָנוֹת | יְהַלֶּל־פִּי |
| wādheshen | tisba' | naphshî | wesiphthê | renānôth | yehallel-pî |
| and fatness | it is satisfied | my soul | and lips with | shouts of joy | my mouth will praise |

| | 524, 2226.115 | 6142, 3435 | 904, 847 | 1965.125, 904 |
|---|---|---|---|---|
| | cj, v Qal pf 1cs, ps 2ms | prep, n mp, ps 1cs | prep, n fp | v Qal impf 1cs, prep, ps 2ms |
| 6. | אִם־זְכַרְתִּיךָ | עַל־יְצוּעָי | בְּאַשְׁמֻרוֹת | אֶהְגֶּה־בָּךְ |
| | 'im-zekhartîkhā | 'al-yetsû'āy | be'ashmurôth | 'ehgeh-bākh |
| | when I remember You | on my beddings | in the night watches | I will meditate on You |

| | 3706, 2030.113 | 6046 | 3937 | 904, 7009 | 3796 |
|---|---|---|---|---|---|
| | cj, v Qal pf 2ms | n fs | prep, ps 1cs | cj, prep, *n ms* | n fd, ps 2ms |
| 7. | כִּי־הָיִיתָ | עֶזְרָתָה | לִּי | וּבְצֵל | כְּנָפֶיךָ |
| | kî-hāyîthā | 'ezrāthāh | lî | ûvetsēl | kenāphêkhā |
| | because You have been | a Help | to me | and in the shadow of | your wings |

| 7728.325 | | 1740.112 | 5497 | 313 | 904 | 8881.112 |
|---|---|---|---|---|---|---|
| v Piel impf 1cs | | v Qal pf 3fs | n fs, ps 1cs | prep, ps 2ms | prep, ps 1cs | v Qal pf 3fs |
| אֲרַנֵּן | 8. | דָּבְקָה | נַפְשִׁי | אַחֲרֶיךָ | בִּי | תָּמְכָה |
| 'ărannēn | | dāveqāh | naphshî | 'achrêkhā | bî | tāmekhāh |
| I will shout for joy | | it has stuck | my soul | after You | on me | it has taken hold of |

**2. To see thy power and thy glory, so as I have seen thee in the sanctuary:** … to look upon thy power and, *NEB* … I have seen you in the Temple and have seen your strength, *NCV* … I have seen you in the holy place, *BB*.

**3. Because thy lovingkindness is better than life, my lips shall praise thee:** … your mercy is better than, *BB* … Your love is better than, *Beck* … Better your faithful love than life itself, *JB* … my lips shall glorify you, *NCB* … my songs of praise can no more be withheld, *Knox*.

**4. Thus will I bless thee while I live: I will lift up my hands in thy name:** … bless thee all my life, *NEB* … may I bless you throughout my life eternal, in your heaven raise my hands, *Anchor* … lifting my hands in prayer to thee, *Moffatt*.

**5. My soul shall be satisfied as with marrow and fatness; and my mouth shall praise thee with joyful lips:** … soul will be comforted, as with good food, *BB* … You satisfy my hunger as with rich food; I praise You with jubilant lips, *Beck* ... All my longings fulfilled as with fat and rich foods, *JB*.

**6. When I remember thee upon my bed, and meditate on thee in the night watches:** ... My thoughts shall go out to thee at dawn, as I lie awake remembering thee, *Knox* ... I think about you through the night, *NCV* ... I muse on you in the watches of the night, *JB*.

**7. Because thou hast been my help, therefore in the shadow of thy wings will I rejoice:** ... Because of your protection, I sing, *NCV* ... I will have joy in the shade of your wings, *BB* ... shadow of Your wings I shout happily, *Beck* ... I will sing joyfully, *Berkeley*.

**8. My soul followeth hard after thee: thy right hand upholdeth me:** ... I humbly follow thee with all my heart, and thy right hand is my support, *NEB* ... soul follows close behind You, *NKJV* ... soul clings to you, *NRSV* ... your hand keeps me safe, *Good News*.

**9. But those that seek my soul, to destroy it, shall go into the lower**

---

**63:2.** These attributes were peculiarly manifested amid the imposing sanctities where the light of the shekinah, which was especially designated as "the glory," shone above the Ark. The first clause of v. 3 is closely connected with the preceding and gives the reason for some of the emotion expressed there, as the introductory "because" (HED #3706) shows. But there is a question as to which part of the preceding verses it refers. It is probably best taken as assigning the reason for their main subject, namely, the psalmist's thirst after God.

**63:3–4.** The deep desires of this psalmist were occasioned by his seclusion from outward forms of worship, which were to him so intimately related to the inward reality that he felt farther away from God in the wilderness than when he caught glimpses of his face through the power and glory which he saw visibly manifested in the sanctuary. But in his isolation, he learns to equate his desert yearnings with his sanctuary contemplations and thus glides from longing to fruition. His devotion, nourished by forms, is seen in the Psalm in the very act of passing on to independence of form, and so springs break out for him in the desert. His passion of yearning after God rebukes and shames our faint desires.

The remaining clauses of vv. 3 and 4 form a transition to the full consciousness of satisfaction which animates the psalmist in the second part. The resolve to praise and the assurance that he will have occasion to praise succeed his longing with startling swiftness.

**63:5.** Thus, the psalmist passes imperceptibly to the second strophe, in which the longing soul becomes the satisfied soul. The emblem of a feast is naturally suggested by the previous metaphor of thirst. The same conviction, which urged the psalmist forward in his search after God, now assures him of absolute satisfaction in finding Him. When the rain comes in the desert, what was baked earth is soon rich pasture, and the dry torrent beds, where the white stones glittered ghastly in the sunshine, are musical with rushing streams and fringed with budding oleanders.

**63:6–7.** That feast leaves no bitter taste. The remembrance of it is all but as sweet as its enjoyment was. Thus, in v. 6 the psalmist recounts how, in the silent hours of night, when many joys are seen to be hollow and conscience wakes to condemn coarse delights, he recalled his blessednesses in God and, like a ruminant animal, tasted their sweetness a second time. The verse is best regarded as an independent sentence. So blessed was the thought of God that, if once it rose in his wakeful mind as he lay on his bed, he "meditated" on it all the night. Past deliverances minister to present trust and assure future joy. The prerogative of the soul, blessed in the sense of possessing God, is to discern in all that has been the manifestations of his help and to anticipate in all that is to come the continuance of the same. Thus, the second strophe gathers up the experiences of the satisfied soul as being fruition, praise, sweet lingering memories that fill the night of darkness and fear, and settled trust in the coming of a future which will follow as a part of such a present and past.

**63:8–11.** The third strophe presents a stage in the devout soul's experience which naturally follows the two preceding. Verse 8 has a beautifully pregnant expression for the attitude of the satisfied soul. Literally rendered, the words run, "has stuck my soul after You," thus uniting the ideas of close contact and eager pursuit. Such union, however impossible in the region of lower aims, is the very characteristic of communion with God, in which fruition subsists along with longing, since God is infinite, and the closest approach to and fullest possession of Him are capable of increase. Satisfaction tends to become satiety when that which produces it is a creature whose limits are soon reached, but the cup which God gives to a

| 3332 | 9. | 2065 | 3937, 8177 | 1272.326 | 5497 | 971.126 |
|---|---|---|---|---|---|---|
| n fs, ps 2ms | | cj, pers pron | prep, n fs | v Piel impf 3mp | n fs, ps 1cs | v Qal impf 3mp |
| יְמִינֶךָ | | וְהֵמָּה | לְשׁוֹאָה | יְבַקְשׁוּ | נַפְשִׁי | יָבֹאוּ |
| yemînekhā | | wehēmmāh | leshô'āh | yevaqōshû | naphshî | yāvō'û |
| your right hand | | but they | for destruction | they seek | my soul | they will go |

| 904, 8812 | 800 | 10. | 5240.526 | 6142, 3135, 2820 |
|---|---|---|---|---|
| prep, *n fp* | art, n fs | | v Hiphil impf 3mp, ps 3ms | prep, *n fd*, n fs |
| בְּתַחְתִּיּוֹת | הָאָרֶץ | | יַגִּירֻהוּ | עַל־יְדֵי־חֶרֶב |
| bethachtîyôth | hā'ārets | | yaggîruhû | 'al-yedhê-chārev |
| into the lowest parts of | the earth | | they will deliver it over | on the power of the sword |

| 4669 | 8217 | 2030.126 | 11. | 4567 | 7975.121 | 904, 435 | 2054.721 |
|---|---|---|---|---|---|---|---|
| *n fs* | n mp | v Qal impf 3mp | | cj, art, n ms | v Qal impf 3ms | prep, n mp | v Hithpael impf 3ms |
| מְנָת | שֻׁעָלִים | יִהְיוּ | | וְהַמֶּלֶךְ | יִשְׂמַח | בֵּאלֹהִים | יִתְהַלֵּל |
| menāth | shu'ālîm | yihyû | | wehammelekh | yismach | bē'lōhîm | yithhallēl |
| a portion for | foxes | they will be | | but the king | he will be glad | in God | he will boast |

| 3725, 8123.255 | 904 | 3706 | 5727.221 | 6552 |
|---|---|---|---|---|
| *adj*, art, v Niphal ptc ms | prep, ps 3ms | cj | v Niphal impf 3ms | *n ms* |
| כָּל־הַנִּשְׁבָּע | בּוֹ | כִּי | יִסָּכֵר | פִּי |
| kol-hanishbā' | bô | kî | yissākhēr | pî |
| all those who swear | by Him | because | they will be stopped up | the mouths of |

| 1744.152, 8632 | 64:t | 3937, 5514.351 | 4344 | 3937, 1784 | 1. | 8471.131, 435 | 7249 |
|---|---|---|---|---|---|---|---|
| *v Qal act ptc mp*, n ms | | prep, art, v Piel ptc ms | n ms | prep, pn | | v Qal impv 2ms, n mp | n ms, ps 1cs |
| דּוֹבְרֵי־שָׁקֶר | | לַמְנַצֵּחַ | מִזְמוֹר | לְדָוִד | | שְׁמַע־אֱלֹהִים | קוֹלִי |
| dhôvrê-shāqer | | lamnatstsēach | mizmôr | ledhāwidh | | shema'-'ĕlōhîm | qôlî |
| those who speak lies | | to the director | a Psalm | of David | | hear O God | my voice |

| 904, 7945 | 4623, 6586 | 342.151 | 5526.123 | 2522 |
|---|---|---|---|---|
| prep, n ms, ps 1cs | prep, *n ms* | v Qal act ptc ms | v Qal impf 2ms | n mp, ps 1cs |
| בְשִׂיחִי | מִפַּחַד | אוֹיֵב | תִּצֹּר | חַיָּי |
| vesîchî | mippachadh | 'ôyēv | titstsōr | chayyāy |
| in my complaint | from the terror of | the enemy | You guard | my life |

| 2. | 5846.523 | 4623, 5660 | 7778.552 | 4623, 7573 |
|---|---|---|---|---|
| | v Hiphil impf 2ms, ps 1cs | prep, *n ms* | v Hiphil ptc mp | prep, *n fs* |
| | תַּסְתִּירֵנִי | מִסּוֹד | מְרֵעִים | מֵרִגְשַׁת |
| | tastîrēnî | missōdh | merē'îm | mērighshath |
| | You hide me | from the schemes of | evildoers | from the restlessness of |

| 6713.152 | 201 | 3. | 866 | 8532.116 | 3626, 2820 | 4098 |
|---|---|---|---|---|---|---|
| *v Qal act ptc mp* | n ms | | rel pron | v Qal pf 3cp | prep, art, n fs | n fs, ps 3mp |
| פֹּעֲלֵי | אָוֶן | | אֲשֶׁר | שָׁנְנוּ | כַחֶרֶב | לְשׁוֹנָם |
| pō'ălê | 'āwen | | 'ăsher | shānenû | khacherev | leshônām |
| those who practice | iniquity | | who | they are sharpened | like the sword | their tongue |

| 1931.116 | 2777 | 1745 | 4914 | 4. | 3937, 3498.141 | 904, 4718 | 8865 |
|---|---|---|---|---|---|---|---|
| v Qal pf 3cp | n ms, ps 3mp | n ms | adj | | prep, v Qal inf con | prep, art, n mp | n ms |
| דָּרְכוּ | חִצָּם | דָּבָר | מָר | | לִירוֹת | בַּמִּסְתָּרִים | תָּם |
| dārekhû | chitstsām | dāvār | mār | | lîrôth | bammistārîm | tām |
| they journey | their arrows | a word | bitter | | to shoot | in hiding places | blamelessness |

| 6849 | 3498.526 | 3940 | 3486.126 | 5. | 2480.326, 3937 | 1745 |
|---|---|---|---|---|---|---|
| adv | v Hiphil impf 3mp, ps 3ms | cj, neg part | v Qal impf 3mp | | v Piel impf 3mp, prep, ps 3mp | n ms |
| פִּתְאֹם | יֹרֻהוּ | וְלֹא | יִירָאוּ | | יְחַזְּקוּ־לָמוֹ | דָּבָר |
| pith'ōm | yōruhû | welō' | yîrā'û | | yechazzequ-lāmô | dāvār |
| suddenly | they shoot at him | and not | they are afraid | | they hold fast to them | a matter |

**parts of the earth:** ... those whose desire is my soul's destruction, *BB* ... those who seek to ruin my soul, *Berkeley* ... go down to the depths of the earth, *JB* ... go down to the grave, *NCV*.

**10. They shall fall by the sword: they shall be a portion for foxes:** ... killed with swords and eaten by wild dogs, *NCV* ... shall be given over to the power of the sword, *Goodspeed* ... They will be a prey for foxes, *NASB*.

**11. But the king shall rejoice in God; every one that sweareth by him shall glory: but the mouth of them that speak lies shall be stopped:** ... Everyone who swears by Him will feel happy, *Beck* ... All who make promises in his name will praise him, but the mouths of liars will be shut, *NCV* ... the voice of falsehood shall be silenced, *NEB* ... but the false mouth will be stopped, *BB*.

**64:t. To the chief Musician, A Psalm of David.**

**1. Hear my voice, O God, in my prayer: preserve my life from fear of the enemy:** ... let the voice of my grief come to your ear, *BB* ... Hear my voice, O God, in my complaint; guard my life against the terror of the enemy, *Berkeley* ... Listen, God, to my voice as I plead, *JB* ... keep me safe from the threats of the enemy, *NEB*.

**2. Hide me from the secret counsel of the wicked; from the insurrection of the workers of iniquity:** ... Shelter me from the council of the wicked, from the gathering of evildoers, *Anchor* ... Hide me from men secretly talking about doing evil, from the mob of wicked men, *Beck* ... from the conspiracy of wicked men, from the noisy gangs of the evil-doers, *Berkeley*.

**3. Who whet their tongue like a sword, and bend their bows to shoot their arrows, even bitter words:** ... They aimed bitter speech as their arrow, *NASB* ... sharpen their tongues like swords and shoot bitter words like arrows, *NCV* ... aim poisoned words like arrows, *Berkeley*.

**4. That they may shoot in secret at the perfect: suddenly do they shoot at him, and fear not:** ... in secret they may let loose their arrows at the upright, *BB* ... shoot suddenly, without warning, *Beck* ... shoot unexpectedly and without self-reproach, *Berkeley* ... shoot in secret at the blameless one, *KJVII* ... at the innocent, *Anchor*.

**5. They encourage themselves in an evil matter: they commune of laying snares privily; they say, Who shall see them?:** ... They strengthen for themselves a wicked scheme; They talk of laying snares, *Goodspeed* ... They support each other in their evil designs, *JB* ...

---

thirsty soul has no cloying in its sweetness. On the other hand, to seek after Him has no pain or unrest along with it, since the desire for fuller possession comes from the felt joy of present attainment. Thus, in constant interchange satisfaction and desire beget each other, and each carries with it some trace of the other's blessedness.

We descend from the heights of mystic communion in the remainder of the Psalm. But in the singer's mind, his enemies were God's enemies and, as v. 11 shows, were regarded as apostates from God in being traitors to "the king." They did not "swear by him"—i.e., they did not acknowledge God as God. Therefore, such being their character, the psalmist's confidence that God's right hand upheld him necessarily passes into assurance of their defeat. The meaning is plain—a battle is impending, and the psalmist is sure that his enemies will be slain and their corpses torn by beasts of prey.

***Psalm 64.*** *Familiar notes are struck in this Psalm, which has no very distinctive features. Complaint of secret slanderers, the comparison of their words to arrows and swords, their concealed snares, their blasphemous defiance of detection, the sudden flashing out of God's retribution, the lesson thereby read to and learned by men, the vindication of God's justice, and praise from all true hearts are frequent themes. They are woven here into a whole which much resembles many other Psalms.*

**64:1–2.** In the first pair of verses, complaint is sublimed into prayer and so becomes strengthening instead of weakening. He who can cry "Hear, O God, guard, hide" has already been able to hide in a safe refuge. "The terror of the enemy" is already dissipated when the trembling heart grasps at God, and an escape from facts that warrant terror will come in good time. This man knows his life is in danger. There are secret gatherings of his enemies, and he can almost hear their loud voices as they plan his ruin. What can he do in such circumstances but fling himself on God? He has thought of resistance. He can only pray, and no man is helpless who can look up. However high and closely engirding may be the walls that men or sorrows build around us, there is always an opening in the dungeon roof through which heaven is visible and prayers can mount.

**64:3–4.** The next two pairs of verses (vv. 3–6) describe the machinations of the enemies in language for the most part familiar, but presenting some difficulties. The metaphors of a slanderous tongue as a sword and mischief-meaning words as arrows have occurred in several other Psalms (e.g., 55:21; 57:4; 59:7). The reference may either be to calumnies or to murderous threats and plans. The

| | | | | | | |
|---|---|---|---|---|---|---|
| 7737 | 5807.326 | 3937, 3045.141 | 4305 | 569.116 | 4449 | 7495.121, 3937 |
| n ms | v Piel impf 3mp | prep, v Qal inf con | n mp | v Qal pf 3cp | intrg | v Qal impf 3ms, prep, ps 3mp |
| רָע | יְסַפְּרוּ | לִטְמוֹן | מוֹקְשִׁים | אָמְרוּ | מִי | יִרְאֶה־לָּמוֹ |
| rā' | yesapperû | litmôn | môqōshîm | 'āmerû | mî | yir'eh-lāmô |
| evil | they announce | to hide | snares | they said | who | he can see them |

| | | | | | | |
|---|---|---|---|---|---|---|
| 6. | 2769.126, 5984 | 8882.116 | 2770 | 2769.455 | 7419 | 382 |
| | v Qal impf 3mp, n fp | v Qal pf 1cp | n ms | v Pual ptc ms | cj, *n ms* | n ms |
| | יַחְפְּשׂוּ־עוֹלֹת | תַּמְנוּ | חֵפֶשׂ | מְחֻפָּשׂ | וְקֶרֶב | אִישׁ |
| | yachpesû-'ôlōth | tamnû | chēphes | mechuppās | weqerev | 'îsh |
| | they search out perversity | they complete | a plot | searched out | and the inward part of | man |

| | | | | | | | |
|---|---|---|---|---|---|---|---|
| 3949 | 6233 | 7. | 3498.521 | 435 | 2777 | 6849 | 2030.116 |
| cj, n ms | adj | | cj, v Hiphil impf 3ms, ps 3mp | n mp | n ms | adv | v Qal pf 3cp |
| וְלֵב | עָמֹק | | וַיֹּרֵם | אֱלֹהִים | חֵץ | פִּתְאוֹם | הָיוּ |
| welēv | 'āmōq | | wayyōrēm | 'ĕlōhîm | chēts | pith'ôm | hāyû |
| and the heart | deep | | and He will shoot at them | God | arrows | suddenly | they will be |

| | | | | |
|---|---|---|---|---|
| 4485 | 8. | 3911.526 | 6142 | 4098 |
| n fp, ps 3mp | | cj, v Hiphil impf 3mp, ps 3ms | prep, ps 3mp | n fs, ps 3mp |
| מַכּוֹתָם | | וַיַּכְשִׁילוּהוּ | עָלֵימוֹ | לְשׁוֹנָם |
| makkôthām | | wayyakhshîlûhû | 'ālêmô | leshônām |
| their wounds | | and He will cause them to stumble | against them | their tongue |

| | | | | | |
|---|---|---|---|---|---|
| 5252.726 | 3725, 7495.151 | 904 | 9. | 3486.126 | 3725, 119 |
| v Hithpoel impf 3mp | *adj*, v Qal act ptc ms | prep, ps 3mp | | cj, v Qal impf 3mp | *adj*, n ms |
| יִתְנֹדְדוּ | כָּל־רֹאֵה | בָם | | וַיִּירְאוּ | כָּל־אָדָם |
| yithnōdhedhû | kol-rō'ēh | vām | | wayyîre'û | kol-'ādhām |
| they will shake their heads | all those seeing | over them | | and they will fear | all humankind |

| | | | | | | |
|---|---|---|---|---|---|---|
| 5222.526 | 6714 | 435 | 4801 | 7959.516 | 10. | 7975.121 |
| cj, v Hiphil impf 3mp | *n ms* | n mp | cj, n ms, ps 3ms | v Hiphil pf 3cp | | v Qal juss 3ms |
| וַיַּגִּידוּ | פֹּעַל | אֱלֹהִים | וּמַעֲשֵׂהוּ | הִשְׂכִּילוּ | | יִשְׂמַח |
| wayyaggîdhû | pō'al | 'ĕlōhîm | ûma'ăsēhû | hiskîlû | | yismach |
| and they will report | the deeds of | God | and his works | they will ponder | | may he be glad |

| | | | | |
|---|---|---|---|---|
| 6926 | 904, 3176 | 2725.111 | 904 | 2054.726 |
| n ms | prep, pn | cj, v Qal pf 3ms | prep, ps 3ms | cj, v Hithpael juss 3mp |
| צַדִּיק | בַּיהוָה | וְחָסָה | בוֹ | וְיִתְהַלְלוּ |
| tsaddîq | bayhwāh | wechāsāh | vô | weyithhalelû |
| the righteous | in Yahweh | for he has taken refuge | in Him | and let him boast |

| | | | | | | | | |
|---|---|---|---|---|---|---|---|---|
| 3725, 3596, 3949 | 65:t | 3937, 5514.351 | 4344 | 3937, 1784 | 8302 | 1. | 3937 | 1800 |
| *adj, adj*, n ms | | prep, art, v Piel ptc ms | n ms | prep, pn | n ms | | prep, ps 2ms | n fs |
| כָּל־יִשְׁרֵי־לֵב | | לַמְנַצֵּחַ | מִזְמוֹר | לְדָוִד | שִׁיר | | לְךָ | דֻמִיָּה |
| kol-yishrê-lēv | | lamnatstsēach | mizmôr | ledhāwidh | shîr | | lekhā | dhumîyāh |
| all the upright of heart | | to the director | a Psalm | of David | a Song | | to You | silence |

they conspire to set snares, *NAB* ... They encourage each other to do wrong, *NCV*.

**6. They search out iniquities; they accomplish a diligent search: both the inward thought of every one of them, and the heart, is deep:** ... They seek mischief with diligent search, *Fenton* ... they make a careful search, *KJVII* ... they hatch their secret plans with skill and cunning, *NEB* ... They work out wicked schemes; they are ready with a well-conceived plan, *Berkeley* ... They conceal a well-laid plot, *Goodspeed*.

**7. But God shall shoot at them with an arrow; suddenly shall they be wounded:** ... suddenly they are struck, *NAB* ... struck down, *NCV* ... Suddenly their wounds are there, *Goodspeed* ... Suddenly his arrow will pierce them, *LIVB*.

**8. So they shall make their own tongue to fall upon themselves: all that see them shall flee away:** ... make their tongue a stumbling-block, *Goodspeed* ... He brings them down because of their tongue, *JB* ... their mischievous tongues are their undoing, *NEB* ... Their own words will be used against them, *NCV*.

**9. And all men shall fear, and shall declare the work of God; for they shall wisely consider of his doing:** ... they will proclaim the works of God and ponder what he has done, *NIV* ... tell what God has brought about, *NRSV* ... man will stand in awe, *Anchor* ... understand his work, *Goodspeed*.

**10. The righteous shall be glad in the LORD, and shall trust in him; and all the upright in heart shall glory:** ... have hope in him; and all the lovers of righteousness will give him glory, *BB* ... righteous are delighted in the LORD and find shelter in Him, and ... feel happy, *Beck* ... shall offer praise, *Berkeley* ... rejoices in the LORD and takes refuge in Him, *Goodspeed*.

**65:t. To the chief Musician, A Psalm and Song of David.**

---

latter is more probable. Secret plots are laid, which are suddenly unmasked. From out of some covert of seeming friendship an unlooked-for arrow whizzes. The archers "shoot at him, and fear not." They are sure of remaining concealed and fear neither man's detection of them nor God's.

**64:5–6.** The same ideas are enlarged on in the third verse pair under a new metaphor. Instead of arrows flying in secret, we have now snares laid to catch unsuspecting prey. "They encourage themselves in an evil plan" pictures mutual encouragement and fixed determination. They discuss the best way of entrapping the psalmist and, as in the preceding verse, flatter themselves that their subtle schemes are too well buried to be observed, whether by their victim or by God. Verse 6 tells without a figure the fact meant in both figures. "They search out iniquities" and plume themselves upon the cleverness of their unsuspected plots. The second clause of the verse is obscure. But the suppositions the plotters are speaking as they did in the last clause of the preceding verse and that "they say" or the like expression is omitted for the sake of dramatic effect remove much of the difficulty. "We have schemed a well-schemed plan" is their complacent estimate.

**64:7–8.** God's retribution scatters their dreams of impunity, as the next pair of verses tells. The verbs are in the past tense, although the events described are still in the future, for the psalmist's faith reckons them to be as good as done. They were shooting at him. God will shoot at them. The archer becomes a target. Punishment is molded after the guise of sin. Verse 8b is with difficulty made intelligible with the existing reading. Probably, the best that can be done with it is to render it as above, although it must be acknowledged that "their tongue comes upon them" needs a good deal of explanation to be made to mean that the consequences of their sins of speech fall on them. The drift of the clause must be that retribution falls on the offending tongue.

**64:9–10.** The Psalm closes with the familiar thought that these judgments will move to wholesome awe and be told from lip to lip, while they become to the righteous occasion of joy, incitements to find refuge in God and material for triumph. These are large consequences to flow from one man's deliverance. The anticipation would be easily explained if we took the speaker to be the personified nation. But it would be equally intelligible if he were in any way a conspicuous or representative person. The humblest may feel that his experience of divine deliverance witnesses, to as many as know it, of a delivering God. That is a high type of godliness which, like this psalmist, counts the future as so certain that it can be spoken of as present even in peril. It augurs a still higher godliness to welcome deliverance, not only for the ease it brings to the suppliant, but for the glory it brings to God.

***Psalm 65.*** *This Psalm with the two Psalms that follow form a group, with one great thought dominant in each, namely, that God's manifestations of grace and providence to Israel are witnesses to the world. Psalm 65 falls into three parts, which set forth a threefold revelation of God in his acts. The first (vv. 1–4) deals with the most intimate privileges of the men who dwell in his house. The second (vv. 5–8) points to his rule in nature, the tokens of God's power in the mighty things of creation: mountains, ocean, day and night, the radiant east and the solemn sunset west. The third (vv. 9–13) gives a lovely picture of the annual miracle which brings harvest joys.*

**65:1–3.** The experience of accepted prayers has taught the psalmist that it is God's nature and property to be "the hearer of prayer" (HED #8471; the word is a participle, expressive of a permanent characteristic), and therefore, he is sure that "all flesh," in its weariness and need of an ear into which to pour necessities and sorrows, will come to Him. His eye travels far beyond Israel and contemplates mankind as coming to worship. But one black barrier rises between men

| 8747 | 435 | 904, 6995 | 3937 | 8396.321, 5266 | | 8471.151 | 8940 |
|---|---|---|---|---|---|---|---|
| n fs | n mp | prep, pn | cj, prep, ps 2ms | v Pual impf 3ms, n ms | | v Qal act ptc ms | n fs |
| תְּהִלָּה | אֱלֹהִים | בְּצִיּוֹן | וּלְךָ | יְשֻׁלַּם־נֶדֶר | 2. | שֹׁמֵעַ | תְּפִלָּה |
| thehillāh | 'ělōhîm | betsîyôn | ûlākhā | yeshullam-nedher | | shōmēa' | tephillāh |
| praise | God | in Zion | and to You | vows will be paid | | the One Who hears | prayers |

| 5912 | 3725, 1340 | 971.126 | | 1745 | 5988 | 1428.116 | 4623 |
|---|---|---|---|---|---|---|---|
| prep, ps 2ms | *adj*, n ms | v Qal impf 3mp | | *n mp* | n fp | v Qal pf 3cp | prep, ps 1cs |
| עָדֶיךָ | כָּל־בָּשָׂר | יָבֹאוּ | 3. | דִּבְרֵי | עֲוֺנֹת | גָּבְרוּ | מֶנִּי |
| 'ādhêkhā | kol-bāsār | yāvō'û | | divrê | 'āwōnōth | gāverû | menî |
| unto You | all flesh | they will come | | matters of | guiltiness | they have prevailed | of me |

| 6840 | 887 | 3848.323 | | 869 | 1013.123 | 7414.323 |
|---|---|---|---|---|---|---|
| n mp, ps 1cp | pers pron | v Piel impf 2ms, ps 3mp | | *n ms* | v Qal impf 2ms | cj, v Piel impf 2ms |
| פְּשָׁעֵינוּ | אַתָּה | תְכַפְּרֵם | 4. | אַשְׁרֵי | תִּבְחַר | וּתְקָרֵב |
| peshā'ênû | 'attāh | thekhapperēm | | 'ashrê | tivchar | ûtheqārēv |
| our offenses | You | You cover them | | blessed | You choose | and You bring near |

| 8331.121 | 2793 | 7881.120 | 904, 3008 | 1041 | 7202 |
|---|---|---|---|---|---|
| v Qal impf 3ms | n mp, ps 2ms | v Qal juss 1cp | prep, *n ms* | n ms, ps 2ms | adj |
| יִשְׁכֹּן | חֲצֵרֶיךָ | נִשְׂבְּעָה | בְּטוּב | בֵּיתֶךָ | קְדֹשׁ |
| yishkōn | chātsērêkhā | nisbe'āh | betûv | bêthekhā | qōdhōsh |
| he remains in | your courts | let us be satisfied | with the goodness of | your Temple | holy |

| 2033 | | 3486.258 | 904, 6928 | 6257.123 | 435 | 3589 |
|---|---|---|---|---|---|---|
| n ms, ps 2ms | | v Niphal ptc fp | prep, n ms | v Qal impf 2ms, ps 1cp | *n mp* | n ms, ps 1cp |
| הֵיכָלֶךָ | 5. | נוֹרָאוֹת | בְּצֶדֶק | תַּעֲנֵנוּ | אֱלֹהֵי | יִשְׁעֵנוּ |
| hêkhlekhā | | nôrā'ôth | betsedheq | ta'ănēnû | 'ělōhê | yish'ēnû |
| your Temple | | fearful things | with righteousness | You answer us | O God of | our salvation |

| 4148 | 3725, 7381, 800 | 3328 | 7632 | | 3679.551 |
|---|---|---|---|---|---|
| *n ms* | *adj*, *n mp*, n fs | cj, n ms | adj | | v Hiphil ptc ms |
| מִבְטָח | כָּל־קַצְוֵי־אֶרֶץ | וְיָם | רְחֹקִים | 6. | מֵכִין |
| mivtāch | kol-qatswê-'erets | weyām | rechōqîm | | mēkhîn |
| the Trust of | all the ends of the earth | and the seas | far away | | One Who establishes |

| 2098 | 904, 3699 | 246.255 | 904, 1400 | | 8099.551 | 8064 |
|---|---|---|---|---|---|---|
| n mp | prep, n ms, ps 3ms | v Niphal ptc ms | prep, n fs | | v Hiphil ptc ms | *n ms* |
| הָרִים | בְּכֹחוֹ | נֶאְזָר | בִּגְבוּרָה | 7. | מַשְׁבִּיחַ | שְׁאוֹן |
| hārîm | bekhōchô | ne'āzār | bighvûrāh | | mashbîach | she'ôn |
| the mountains | by his strength | girded | with might | | One Who quiets | the raging of |

| 3328 | 8064 | 1570 | 2066 | 3947 | | 3486.126 |
|---|---|---|---|---|---|---|
| n mp | *n ms* | n ms, ps 3mp | cj, *n ms* | n mp | | cj, v Qal impf 3mp |
| יַמִּים | שְׁאוֹן | גַּלֵּיהֶם | וַהֲמוֹן | לְאֻמִּים | 8. | וַיִּירְאוּ |
| yammîm | she'ôn | gallêhem | wahmôn | le'ummîm | | wayyîre'û |
| the seas | the roaring of | their waves | and the uproar of | peoples | | and they are afraid |

| 3553.152 | 7381 | 4623, 225 | 4296, 1269 | 6394 |
|---|---|---|---|---|
| *v Qal act ptc mp* | n fp | prep, n fp, ps 2ms | *n mp*, n ms | cj, n ms |
| יֹשְׁבֵי | קְצָוֺת | מֵאוֹתֹתֶיךָ | מוֹצָאֵי־בֹקֶר | וָעֶרֶב |
| yōshevê | qōtsāwōth | mē'ōthōthêkhā | môtsā'ê-vōqer | wā'erev |
| those who dwell at | the ends | from your signs | the coming out of the morning | and the evening |

| 7728.523 | | 6734.113 | 800 | 8224.323 |
|---|---|---|---|---|
| v Hiphil impf 2ms | | v Qal pf 2ms | art, n fs | cj, v Polel impf 2ms, ps 3fs |
| תַּרְנִין | 9. | פָּקַדְתָּ | הָאָרֶץ | וַתְּשֹׁקְקֶהָ |
| tarnîn | | pāqadhtā | hā'ārets | watteshōqeqeāh |
| You cause to shout for joy | | You have intervened on | the earth | and You cause it to be abundant |

**1. Praise waiteth for thee, O God, in Sion: and unto thee shall the vow be performed:** ... It is right for, O God, you to have praise in Zion: to you let the offering be made, *BB* ... vow be paid, *KJVII* ... It is fitting to praise You, *Beck* ... vow shall be fulfilled, *Berkeley*.

**2. O thou that hearest prayer, unto thee shall all flesh come:** ... All men shall lay their guilt before thee, *NEB* ... To thee all mankind must look for pardon, *Knox*.

**3. Iniquities prevail against me: as for our transgressions, thou shalt purge them away:** ... Iniquities got the better of me, *Berkeley* ... Evils have overcome us: but as for our sins, you will take them away, *BB* ... only thou canst blot them out, *NEB* ... you forgave, *NIV*.

**4. Blessed is the man whom thou choosest, and causest to approach unto thee, that he may dwell in thy courts: we shall be satisfied with the goodness of thy house, even of thy holy temple:** ... choose and invite to dwell, *JB* ... choose and bring near to dwell, *Goodspeed* ... sacred temple, *Berkeley*.

**5. By terrible things in righteousness wilt thou answer us, O God of our salvation; who art the confidence of all the ends of the earth, and of them that are afar off upon the sea:** ... You will give us an answer in righteousness by great acts of power, *BB* ... Through terrible deeds thou dost answer us, *Goodspeed* ... hope of the whole wide world, even the distant islands, *JB*.

**6. Which by his strength setteth fast the mountains; being girded with power:** ... By your strength you hold the mountains steady, being clothed in power, *JB* ... thou by whose might the mountains are made firm, *Moffatt* ... You made the mountains by your strength; you are dressed in power, *NCV* ... You set the mountains in place by your strength, showing your mighty power, *Good News* ... who is robed with power, *BB*.

**7. Which stilleth the noise of the seas, the noise of their waves, and the tumult of the people:** ... Who pacifies loud roaring Oceans, Loud billows, and murmurs of nations!, *Fenton* ... Who silenced the roaring ... the turmoil, *Anchor* ... Who makes the loud voice of the sea quiet, *BB* ... quiet the raging seas, *Beck* ... moaning of their waves, and the clamor of the nations, *Berkeley*.

**8. They also that dwell in the uttermost parts are afraid at thy tokens: thou makest the outgoings of the morning and evening to rejoice:** ... Thy portents strike terror at the world's end, fill the lands of sunrise and sunset with rejoicing, *Knox* ... who dwell in the far regions are afraid, *Goodspeed* ... The nations are in uproar, in panic, *JB*.

**9. Thou visitest the earth, and waterest it: thou greatly enrichest**

---

and God, the separating power of which the singer has painfully felt. Sin chokes the stream that would flow from seeking hearts into the ocean of God. The very act of gathering himself up to pray and praise quickens the sense of sinfulness in the psalmist. Therefore, his look turns swiftly inward for the only time in the Psalm. The consciousness of transgression wakes the sense of personality and isolation as nothing else will, and for one bitter moment the singer is, as it were, prisoned in the solitude of individual responsibility. God covers sins, for none but God can cope with the evil things that are too strong for man. I can neither keep them out, nor drive them out when they have come in, nor cleanse the stains that their hooves have made; but God can and does cover them.

**65:4.** The strophe ends with an exclamation celebrating the blessedness of dwelling with God. That refers, no doubt, to Israel's prerogative of access to the Temple; but the inward and outward are blended, as in many places in the Psalter where dwelling in the house of the LORD is yearned for or rejoiced in. The universalism of the Psalm does not forget the special place held by the nation whom God "has chosen and brought near." But the reality beneath the symbol is too familiar and sweet to this singer for him to suppose that mere outward access exhausts the possibilities of blessed communion.

**65:5.** The second strophe (vv. 5–8) celebrates another aspect of God's manifestation by deeds, which has, in like manner, a message for the ends of the earth. Israel is again the immediate recipient of God's acts, but they reverberate through the world. Therefore, in v. 5, the two clauses are not merely adjacent, but connected. It is because God is ever revealing himself to the nation (for the tense of the verb "answer" expresses continuous action) that He is revealed as the trust of the whole earth.

**65:6–8.** From the self-revelation of God in history, the Psalm passes to his mighty deeds in nature (vv. 6f), and from these it returns to his providential guidance of human affairs (v. 7b). The two specimens of divine power celebrated in vv. 6f, are suggested by the closing words of v. 5. "The ends of the earth" were, according to ancient cosmography, girdled by mountains, and God has set these fast. The dash of "the remotest seas" is hushed by Him. Two mighty things are selected to witness to the Mightier, Who made and manages them. The firm bulk of the mountains is firm because He is strong. The tossing waves are still because He bids them be silent. The mention

| | | | | | | |
|---|---|---|---|---|---|---|
| 7521 | 6483.523 | 6631 | 435 | 4527.111 | 4448 | 3679.523 |
| adv | v Hiphil impf 2ms, ps 3fs | *n ms* | n mp | v Qal pf 3ms | n mp | v Hiphil impf 2ms |
| רַבַּת | תַּעְשְׁרֶנָּה | פֶּלֶג | אֱלֹהִים | מָלֵא | מָיִם | תָּכִין |
| rabbath | ta'ăshrennāh | pelegh | 'ĕlōhîm | male' | māyim | tākhîn |
| greatly | You enrich it | the channel of | God | it is full of | water | You prepare |

| | | | | | | |
|---|---|---|---|---|---|---|
| 1765 | 3706, 3772 | 3679.523 | | 8854 | 7588.342 | 5367.342 |
| n ms, ps 3mp | cj, adv | v Hiphil impf 2ms, ps 3fs | **10.** | n mp, ps 3fs | v Piel inf abs | v Piel inf abs |
| דְּגָנָם | כִּי־כֵן | תְּכִינֶהָ | | תְּלָמֶיהָ | רַוֵּה | נַחֵת |
| deghānām | kî-khēn | tekhîneāh | | telāmêāh | rawwēh | nachēth |
| their grain | even so | You prepare it | | its furrows | thoroughly watering | settling |

| | | | | | | |
|---|---|---|---|---|---|---|
| 1446 | 904, 7534 | 4265.323 | 7049 | 1313.323 | | 6064.313 |
| n mp, ps 3fs | prep, n mp | v Polel impf 2ms, ps 3fs | n ms, ps 3fs | v Piel impf 2ms | **11.** | v Piel pf 2ms |
| גְּדוּדֶיהָ | בִּרְבִיבִים | תְּמֹגְגֶנָּה | צִמְחָהּ | תְּבָרֵךְ | | עִטַּרְתָּ |
| gedhûdhêāh | birvîvîm | temōghehennāh | tsimchāhh | tevārēkh | | 'iṭṭartā |
| it furrows | with showers | You level it | its plants | You bless | | You have crowned |

| | | | | | | |
|---|---|---|---|---|---|---|
| 8523 | 3008 | 4724 | 7780.126 | 1942 | | 7780.126 |
| *n fs* | n fs, ps 2ms | cj, n mp, ps 2ms | v Qal impf 3mp | n ms | **12.** | v Qal impf 3mp |
| שְׁנַת | טוֹבָתֶךָ | וּמַעְגָּלֶיךָ | יִרְעֲפוּן | דָּשֶׁן | | יִרְעֲפוּ |
| shenath | ṭôvāthekhā | ûma'ăggālêkhā | yir'ăphûn | dāshen | | yir'ăphû |
| a year of | your good things | and your worn paths | they run | fatness | | they drip |

| | | | | |
|---|---|---|---|---|
| 5295 | 4198 | 1561 | 1421 | 2391.127 |
| *n fp* | n ms | cj, n ms | n fp | v Qal impf 3fp |
| נְאוֹת | מִדְבָּר | וְגִיל | גְּבָעוֹת | תַּחְגֹּרְנָה |
| ne'ôth | midhbār | weghîl | gevā'ôth | tachgōrenāh |
| the grasslands of | the wilderness | and rejoicing | the hills | they gird themselves |

| | | | | | |
|---|---|---|---|---|---|
| | 3980.116 | 3862 | 6887 | 6231 | 6063.126, 1277 |
| **13.** | v Qal pf 3cp | n mp | art, n fs | cj, n mp | v Qal impf 3mp, n ms |
| | לָבְשׁוּ | כָרִים | הַצֹּאן | וַעֲמָקִים | יַעַטְפוּ־בָר |
| | lāveshû | khārîm | hatstsō'n | wa'ămāqîm | ya'aṭphû-vār |
| | they clothe themselves | the meadows | the flocks | and valleys | they are gorged with grain |

| | | | | | | | |
|---|---|---|---|---|---|---|---|
| 7607.726 | 652, 8301.126 | | 3937, 5514.351 | 8302 | 4344 | | 7607.533 |
| v Hithpolel impf 3mp | cj, v Qal impf 3mp | **66:t** | prep, art, v Piel ptc ms | n ms | n ms | **1.** | v Hiphil impv 2mp |
| יִתְרוֹעֲעוּ | אַף־יָשִׁירוּ | | לַמְנַצֵּחַ | שִׁיר | מִזְמוֹר | | הָרִיעוּ |
| yithrô'ă'û | 'aph-yāshîrû | | lamnatstsēach | shîr | mizmôr | | hārî'û |
| they cry out | indeed they sing | | to the director | a Song | a Psalm | | shout |

| | | | | | | | |
|---|---|---|---|---|---|---|---|
| 3937, 435 | 3725, 800 | | 2252.333 | 3638, 8428 | 7947.133 | 3638 | 8747 |
| prep, n mp | *adj*, art, n fs | **2.** | v Piel impv 2mp | *n ms*, n ms, ps 3ms | v Qal impv 2mp | n ms | n fs, ps 3ms |
| לֵאלֹהִים | כָּל־הָאָרֶץ | | זַמְּרוּ | כְבוֹד־שְׁמוֹ | שִׂימוּ | כָבוֹד | תְּהִלָּתוֹ |
| lē'lōhîm | kol-hā'ārets | | zammerû | khevôdh-shemô | sîmû | khāvôdh | tehillāthô |
| to God | all the earth | | sing praises to | the glory of his name | place | glory | his praise |

**it with the river of God, which is full of water: thou preparest them corn, when thou hast so provided for it:** … make her fruitful with your rain. With water fill the heavenly channel, provide her grain; For this you brought her into being, *Anchor* … and having made it ready, you give men grain, *BB*.

**10. Thou waterest the ridges thereof abundantly: thou settlest the furrows thereof: thou makest it soft with showers: thou blessest the springing thereof:** … loosening the clods, multiplying, with soft showers, the grain, *Knox* … you water its furrows abundantly, level its ridges, soften it with showers and bless its shoots, *JB*.

**11. Thou crownest the year with thy goodness; and thy paths drop fatness:** … hast crowned the year with Thy bounty, *NASB* … your paths overflow with a rich harvest, *NCB* … You give the year a good harvest, and you load the wagons with many crops, *NCV* … dost crown the year with thy good gifts and the palm-trees drip with sweet juice,

*NEB* ... your carts overflow with abundance, *NIV*.

**12. They drop upon the pastures of the wilderness: and the little hills rejoice on every side:** ... pastures of the wilderness overflow, the hills gird themselves with joy, *NRSV* ... open pastures are lush and the hills wreathed in happiness, *REB* ... Falling on the grass of the waste land: and the little hills are glad, *BB* ... hills are encircled with glee, *Fenton*.

**13. The pastures are clothed with flocks; the valleys also are covered over with corn; they shout for joy, they also sing:** ... grass-land is thick with flocks; the valleys are full of grain; they give glad cries and songs of joy, *BB* ... meadows are covered with flocks, the valleys clothed with wheat, *JB* ... everywhere the hymn of praise, *Knox*.

**66:t. To the chief Musician, A Song or Psalm.**

**1. Make a joyful noise unto God, all ye lands:** ... Everything on earth, shout with joy to God, *NCV* ... Acclaim our God, all men on earth, *NEB* ... Send up a glad cry to God, all the earth, *BB*.

**2. Sing forth the honour of his name: make his praise glorious:** ... Sing about his glory, *NCV* ... sing psalms to the glory of his name, glorify him with your praises, *JB* ... give praise and glory to him, *BB* ... render Him glorious praise, *Berkeley*.

---

of the sea, the standing emblem of unrest and rebellious power, suggests the "tumult of the peoples" on which similar repressive power is exercised. The great deeds of God, putting down tyranny and opposition to Israel, which is rebellion against himself, strike terror, which is wholesome and is purified into reverence, into the distant lands. Therefore, from the place where the sun rises to where it sinks in the west through all the earth—there rings out a shout of joy.

**65:9–10.** God reveals himself not only in the sanctities of his house or in his dread "signs" in nature and history, but in the yearly recurring harvest, which was waving, as yet unreaped, while the poet sang. The local coloring, which regards rain as the chief factor in fertility and the special gift of God, is noticeable. In such a land as Palestine, irrigation seems the one thing needful to turn desert into fruitful field. To "water" the soil is there emphatically to "enrich" it. The psalmist uses for "river" the technical word for an irrigation cutting (HED #6631), as if he would represent God in the guise of the Cultivator, Who digs his ditches that the sparkling blessing may reach all his field.

**65:11–13.** The poet stands in the joyous time when all the beauty of summer flushes the earth, and the harvest is yet a hope, not a possibly disappointing reality. It is near enough to fill his song with exultation. It is far enough off to let him look on the whitened fields, and not on the bristly stubble. So he regards the "crown" as already set on a year of goodness. He sees God's chariot passing in triumph and blessing over the land and leaving abundance wherever its wheel tracks go. Out in the uncultivated prairie, where sweet grass unsown by man grows, is the flush of greenery where, before the rain, was baked and gaping earth. The hills that wear a girdle of forest trees halfway up toward their barren summits wave their foliage, as if glad. The white fleeces of flocks are dotted over the vivid verdure of every meadow, and one cannot see the ground for the tall corn that stands waiting for the sickle, in each fertile plain. The psalmist hears a hymn of glad praise rising from all these happy and sunny things, and for its melody he hushes his own, that he and we may listen to the fair music that all creatures make to their great Lord.

***Psalm 66.*** *Five strophes, three of which are marked by selah, make up Ps. 66. That musical indication is missing at the close of the third strophe (v. 12), which is also the close of the first or choral part, and its absence may be connected with the transition to a single voice. A certain progress in thought is noticeable, as will appear as we proceed.*

**66:1–4.** The first strophe calls upon all the earth to praise God for his works. The special deeds which fire the psalmist are not yet mentioned, although they are present to his mind. The summons of the world to praise passes over into prophecy that it shall praise. The manifestation of God's character by act will win homage. The great thought that God has but to be truly known in order to be reverenced is an axiom with this psalmist, and no less certain is he that such knowledge and such praise will one day fill the world. True, he discerns that submission will not always be genuine, for he uses the same word to express it as occurs in Ps. 18:44, which represents "feigned homage." Every great religious awakening has a fringe of adherents, imperfectly affected by it, whose professions outrun reality, although they themselves are but half conscious that they feign. Although this sobering estimate of the shallowness of a widely diffused recognition of God tones down the psalmist's expectations and has been abundantly confirmed by later experience, his great hope

| **3.** 569.133 | 3937, 435 | 4242, 3486.255 | 4801 | 904, 7524 | 6010 |
|---|---|---|---|---|---|
| v Qal impv 2mp | prep, n mp | intrg, v Niphal ptc ms | n mp, ps 2ms | prep, *n ms* | n ms, ps 2ms |
| אִמְרוּ | לֵאלֹהִים | מַה־נּוֹרָא | מַעֲשֶׂיךָ | בְּרֹב | עֻזְּךָ |
| 'imrû | lē'lōhîm | mah-nôrā' | ma'ăsêkhā | berōv | 'uzzekhā |
| say | to God | how fearful | your works | in the abundance of | your strength |

| 3703.326 | 3937 | 342.152 | **4.** 3725, 800 | 8246.726 | 3937 |
|---|---|---|---|---|---|
| v Piel impf 3mp | prep, ps 2ms | v Qal act ptc mp, ps 2ms | *adj*, art, n fs | v Hithpael impf 3mp | prep, ps 2ms |
| יְכַחֲשׁוּ | לְךָ | אֹיְבֶיךָ | כָּל־הָאָרֶץ | יִשְׁתַּחֲווּ | לְךָ |
| yekhachshû | lekhā | 'ōyevêkhā | kol-hā'ārets | yishtachwû | lekhā |
| they disavow | to You | your enemies | all the earth | they worship | You |

| 2252.326, 3937 | 2252.326 | 8428 | 5734 | **5.** 2050.133 |
|---|---|---|---|---|
| cj, v Piel impf 3mp, prep, ps 2ms | v Piel impf 3mp | n ms, ps 2ms | intrj | v Qal impv 2mp |
| וִיזַמְּרוּ־לָךְ | יְזַמְּרוּ | שִׁמְךָ | סֶלָה | לְכוּ |
| wîzammerû-lākh | yezammerû | shimkhā | selāh | lekhû |
| and they sing praises to You | they sing praises to | your name | selah | come |

| 7495.133 | 4821 | 435 | 3486.255 | 6173 | 6142, 1158 | 119 |
|---|---|---|---|---|---|---|
| cj, v Qal impv 2mp | *n fp* | n mp | v Niphal ptc ms | n fs | prep, *n mp* | n ms |
| וּרְאוּ | מִפְעֲלוֹת | אֱלֹהִים | נוֹרָא | עֲלִילָה | עַל־בְּנֵי | אָדָם |
| ûre'û | miph'ălôth | 'ĕlōhîm | nôrā' | 'ălîlāh | 'al-benê | 'ādhām |
| and see | the works of | God | fearful | deeds | on the children of | humankind |

| **6.** 2089.111 | 3328 | 3937, 3114 | 904, 5282 | 5882.126 | 904, 7559 | 8427 |
|---|---|---|---|---|---|---|
| v Qal pf 3ms | n ms | prep, n fs | prep, art, n ms | v Qal impf 3mp | prep, n fs | adv |
| הָפַךְ | יָם | לְיַבָּשָׁה | בַּנָּהָר | יַעַבְרוּ | בְרָגֶל | שָׁם |
| hāphakh | yām | leyabbāshāh | bannāhār | ya'avrû | verāghel | shām |
| He turned | the sea | into dry ground | in the river | they passed | on foot | there |

| 7975.120, 904 | **7.** 5090.151 | 904, 1400 | 5986 | 6084 | 904, 1504 |
|---|---|---|---|---|---|
| v Qal juss 1cp, prep, ps 3ms | v Qal act ptc ms | prep, n fs, ps 3ms | n ms | n fd, ps 3ms | prep, art, n mp |
| נִשְׂמְחָה־בּוֹ | מֹשֵׁל | בִּגְבוּרָתוֹ | עוֹלָם | עֵינָיו | בַּגּוֹיִם |
| nismechāh-bô | mōshēl | bighvûrāthô | 'ôlām | 'ênāv | baggôyim |
| let us be glad in Him | the Ruler | with his might | forever | his eyes | among the nations |

| 7099.127 | 5842.152 | 414, 7597.526 | 3937 | 5734 | **8.** 1313.333 |
|---|---|---|---|---|---|
| v Qal impf 3fp | art, v Qal act ptc mp | adv, v Hiphil juss 3mp | prep, ps 3mp | intrj | v Piel impv 2mp |
| תִּצְפֶּינָה | הַסּוֹרְרִים | אַל־יָרִימוּ | לָמוֹ | סֶלָה | בָּרְכוּ |
| titspênāh | hassôrerîm | 'al-yārîmû | lāmô | selāh | bārekhû |
| they keep watch | the stubborn ones | do not let them exalt | themselves | selah | bless |

| 6194 | 435 | 8471.533 | 7249 | 8747 | **9.** 7947.151 | 5497 |
|---|---|---|---|---|---|---|
| n mp | n mp, ps 1cp | cj, v Hiphil impv 2mp | *n ms* | n fs, ps 3ms | art, v Qal act ptc ms | n fs, ps 1cp |
| עַמִּים | אֱלֹהֵינוּ | וְהַשְׁמִיעוּ | קוֹל | תְּהִלָּתוֹ | הַשָּׂם | נַפְשֵׁנוּ |
| 'ammîm | 'ĕlōhênû | wehashmî'û | qôl | tehillāthô | hassām | naphshēnû |
| O peoples | our God | and cause to hear | the sound of | his praise | the One Who sets | our life |

**3. Say unto God, How terrible art thou in thy works! through the greatness of thy power shall thine enemies submit themselves unto thee:** … What dread, Lord, thy acts inspire!, *Knox* … How tremendous are your deeds! for your great strength your enemies fawn upon you, *NAB* … How awesome are Thy works! Because of the greatness of Thy power Thine enemies will give feigned obedience to Thee, *NASB*.

**4. All the earth shall worship thee, and shall sing unto thee; they shall sing to thy name. Selah:** … All the earth bows down to you, *NIV* … The whole world bows low in your presence, *REB* … All the earth worships you and sings praises to you, *NCV* … All men on earth fall prostrate in thy presence, *NEB*.

**5. Come and see the works of God: he is terrible in his doing toward the children of men:** … He is fearful in His deeds toward the children, *KJVII* … terrifying in action before men, *Anchor* … he is to be feared in all he does to the children of, *BB* …

what He does for human beings inspires awe, *Beck*.

**6. He turned the sea into dry land: they went through the flood on foot: there did we rejoice in him:** ... let us delight in Him, *Beck* ... then we all gave thanks to Him, *Fenton* ... rejoiced because of what he did, *Good News*.

**7. He ruleth by his power for ever; his eyes behold the nations: let not the rebellious exalt themselves. Selah:** ... He watches every movement of the nations. O rebel lands, he will deflate your pride, *LIVB* ... eyes keep watch on the nations to forestall rebellion against him, *JB* ... let rebellious souls tame their pride, *Knox* ... eyes survey the nations, till not a rebel dares to raise his head, *Moffatt*.

**8. O bless our God, ye people, and make the voice of his praise to be heard:** ... Bless our God, all nations; let his praise be heard far and near, *NEB* ... praise our God; loudly sing his praise, *NCV* ... Let all hear how you praise Him, *Beck* ... with full voice proclaim his praise!, *Anchor*.

**9. Which holdeth our soul in life, and suffereth not our feet to be moved:** ... he brings us to life and keeps our feet from stumbling, *JB* ... He kept us alive and didn't let our feet slip, *Beck* ... Who has kept us among the living, And has not suffered our feet to stumble, *Goodspeed*.

---

remains as an early utterance of the conviction, which has gathered assurance and definiteness by subsequent Revelation and is now familiar to all. The world is God's. His self-revelation will win hearts. There shall be true submission and joyous praise, girdling the earth as it rolls. The psalmist dwells mainly on the majestic and awe-inspiring aspect of God's acts. His greatness of power bears down opposition. But the later strophes introduce other elements of the divine nature and syllables of the name, although the inmost secret of the "power of God" in the weakness of manhood and the all-conquering might of love is not yet ripe for utterance.

**66:5–7.** The second strophe advances to a closer contemplation of the deeds of God, which the nations are summoned to behold. He is not only "dread" in his doings toward mankind at large, but Israel's history is radiant with the manifestation of his name, and that past lives on, so that ancient experiences give the measure and manner of today's working.

The retrospect embraces the two standing instances of God's delivering help—the passage of the Red Sea and of Jordan—and these are not dead deeds in a far-off century. For the singer calls on his own generation to rejoice "there" in Him. Verse 6c is by some translated as "There did we rejoice," and more accurately by others, "Let us rejoice." In the former case, the essential solidarity of all generations of the nation is most vividly set forth. But the same idea is involved in the correct rendering, according to which the men of the psalmist's period are entitled and invoked to associate themselves in thought with that long-past generation, and to share in their joy, since they do possess the same power which was present then.

God's work is never antiquated. It is all a revelation of eternal activities. What He has been, He is. What He did, He does. Therefore, faith may feed on all the records of old time and expect the repetition of all that they contain. Such an application of history to the present makes the nerve of this strophe. For v. 7, following on the retrospect, declares the perpetuity of God's rule and that his eyes still keep an outlook as a watchman on a tower might do to mark the enemies' designs in order that He may intervene, as of old, for his people's deliverance. He "looked forth upon the Egyptians through the pillar of fire and of cloud" (Exo. 14:24). Thus, He still marks the actions and plans of Israel's foes. Therefore, it were wise for the "rebellious" not to rear their heads so high in opposition.

**66:8–12.** The familiar figures for affliction reappear, namely, proving and refining in a furnace. A less common metaphor is that of being imprisoned in a dungeon, as the word rendered "net" (HED #4848) probably means. Another peculiar image is that of v. 12: "Thou hast caused men to ride over our head." The word for "men" (HED #596) here connotes feebleness and frailty, characteristics which make tyranny more intolerable. The somewhat harsh metaphor is best explained as setting forth insolent and crushing domination, whether the picture intended is that of ruthless conquerors driving their chariots over their prone victims or that of their sitting as an incubus on their shoulders and making them like beasts of burden. Fire and water are standing figures for affliction. With great force, these accumulated symbols of oppression are confronted by one abrupt clause ending the strophe and describing in a breath the perfect deliverance which sweeps them all away: "Thou broughtest us out into a wealthy place." There is no need for the textual alteration of the last word into "a wide place." The word (HED #7598)

| 904, 2522 | 3940, 5598.111 | 3937, 4267.141 | 7559 | | 3706, 1010.113 |
|---|---|---|---|---|---|
| prep, art, n mp | cj, neg part, v Qal pf 3ms | prep, v Qal inf con | n fs, ps 1cp | 10. | cj, v Qal pf 2ms, ps 1cp |
| בַּחַיִּים | וְלֹא־נָתַן | לַמּוֹט | רַגְלֵנוּ | | כִּי־בְחַנְתָּנוּ |
| bachayyîm | welō'-nāthan | lammôṭ | raghlēnû | | kî-vechantānû |
| among the living | and He does not allow | to falter | our foot | | You have tested us |

| 435 | 7170.113 | 3626, 7170.141, 3826B | | 971.513 | 904, 4848 |
|---|---|---|---|---|---|
| n mp | v Qal pf 2ms, ps 1cp | prep, v Qal inf con, n ms | 11. | v Hiphil pf 2ms, ps 1cp | prep, art, n fs |
| אֱלֹהִים | צְרַפְתָּנוּ | כִּצְרָף־כָּסֶף | | הֲבֵאתָנוּ | בַמְּצוּדָה |
| 'ĕlōhîm | tseraphtānû | kitsrāph-kāseph | | hevē'thānû | vammetsûdhāh |
| O God | You have refined us | like the refining of silver | | You have brought us | into the net |

| 7947.113 | 4293 | 904, 5158 | | 7680.513 | 596 | 3937, 7513 |
|---|---|---|---|---|---|---|
| v Qal pf 2ms | n fs | prep, n md, ps 1cp | 12. | v Hiphil pf 2ms | n ms | prep, n ms, ps 1cp |
| שַׂמְתָּ | מוּעָקָה | בְמָתְנֵינוּ | | הִרְכַּבְתָּ | אֱנוֹשׁ | לְרֹאשֵׁנוּ |
| samtā | mû'āqāh | vemāthenênû | | hirkavtā | 'ĕnôsh | lerō'shēnû |
| You laid | affliction | on our loins | | You caused to ride | men | our heads |

| 971.119, 904, 813 | 904, 4448 | 3428.523 | 3937, 7596 |
|---|---|---|---|
| v Qal pf 1cp, prep, art, n fs | cj, prep, art, n md | cj, v Hiphil impf 2ms, ps 1cp | prep, art, n fs |
| בָּאנוּ־בָאֵשׁ | וּבַמַּיִם | וַתּוֹצִיאֵנוּ | לָרְוָיָה |
| bā'nû-vā'ēsh | ûvammayim | wattôtsî'ēnû | lārewāyāh |
| we went through fire | and through water | but You led us out | to a thoroughly watered place |

| | 971.125 | 1041 | 904, 6150 | 8396.325 | 3937 | 5266 |
|---|---|---|---|---|---|---|
| 13. | v Qal impf 1cs | n ms, ps 2ms | prep, n fp | v Piel impf 1cs | prep, ps 2ms | n mp, ps 1cs |
| | אָבוֹא | בֵיתְךָ | בְעוֹלוֹת | אֲשַׁלֵּם | לְךָ | נְדָרָי |
| | 'āvô' | vêthekhā | ve'ôlôth | 'ăshallēm | lekhā | nedhārāy |
| | I will enter | your Temple | with burnt offerings | I will complete | to You | my vows |

| | 866, 6722.116 | 8004 | 1744.311, 6552 | 904, 7140, 3937 |
|---|---|---|---|---|
| 14. | rel part, v Qal pf 3cp | n fd, ps 1cs | cj, v Piel pf 3ms, n ms, ps 1cs | prep, art, n ms, prep, ps 1cs |
| | אֲשֶׁר־פָּצוּ | שְׂפָתָי | וְדִבֶּר־פִּי | בַּצַּר־לִי |
| | 'ăsher-pātsû | sephāthāy | wedhibber-pî | batstsar-lî |
| | which they have opened wide | my lips | and my mouth spoke | in my adversity |

| | 6150 | 4354 | 6148.525, 3937 | 6196, 7285 | 356 | 6449.125 |
|---|---|---|---|---|---|---|
| 15. | n fp | n mp | v Hiphil impf 1cs, prep, ps 2ms | prep, *n fs* | n mp | v Qal impf 1cs |
| | עֹלוֹת | מֵחִים | אַעֲלֶה־לָּךְ | עִם־קְטֹרֶת | אֵילִים | אֶעֱשֶׂה |
| | 'ōlôth | mēchîm | 'a'ăleh-lākh | 'im-qŏṭōreth | 'êlîm | 'e'ĕseh |
| | burnt offerings | provisions | I will cause to go up to You | with incense of | rams | I will make |

| 1267 | 6196, 6500 | 5734 | | 2050.133, 8471.133 | 5807.325 |
|---|---|---|---|---|---|
| n ms | prep, n mp | intrj | 16. | v Qal impv 2mp, v Qal impv 2mp | cj, v Piel juss 1cs |
| בָקָר | עִם־עַתּוּדִים | סֶלָה | | לְכוּ־שִׁמְעוּ | וַאֲסַפְּרָה |
| vāqār | 'im-'attûdhîm | selāh | | lekhû-shim'û | wa'ăsapperāh |
| cows | with goats | selah | | come hear | and let me recount |

| 3725, 3486.152 | 435 | 866 | 6449.111 | 3937, 5497 | | 420 |
|---|---|---|---|---|---|---|
| *adj, v Qal act ptc mp* | n mp | rel part | v Qal pf 3ms | prep, n fs, ps 1cs | 17. | prep, ps 3ms |
| כָּל־יִרְאֵי | אֱלֹהִים | אֲשֶׁר | עָשָׂה | לְנַפְשִׁי | | אֵלָיו |
| kol-yir'ê | 'ĕlōhîm | 'ăsher | 'āsāh | lenaphshî | | 'ēlâv |
| all those who fear | God | what | He has done | for my soul | | to Him |

| 6552, 7410.115 | 7597.411 | 8809 | 4098 | | 201 | 524, 7495.115 |
|---|---|---|---|---|---|---|
| n ms, ps 1cs, v Qal pf 1cs | cj, Polal pf 3ms | prep | n fs, ps 1cs | 18. | n ms | cj, v Qal pf 1cs |
| פִּי־קָרָאתִי | וְרוֹמַם | תַּחַת | לְשׁוֹנִי | | אָוֶן | אִם־רָאִיתִי |
| pî-qārā'thî | werômam | tachath | leshônî | | 'āwen | 'im-rā'îthî |
| my mouth proclaimed | He was exalted | beneath | my tongue | | iniquity | if I had seen |

**10. For thou, O God, hast proved us: thou hast tried us, as silver is tried:** ... thou hast put us to the proof, tested us as men test silver in the fire, *Knox* ... you have put us to the test, refined us like silver, *JB* ... Thou hast tried us, *NASB* ... you have purified us like silver, *NCV*.

**11. Thou broughtest us into the net; thou laidst affliction upon our loins:** ... You let us be trapped and put a heavy load on us, *NCV* ... You brought us into prison and laid burdens on our backs, *NIV* ... caught us in a net, and put misery on our bodies, *Beck* ... put a heavy strain on our backs, *JB* ... laid a heavy burden on our hips, *Berkeley*.

**12. Thou hast caused men to ride over our heads; we went through fire and through water: but thou broughtest us out into a wealthy place:** ... brought us to an overflowing abundance, *Berkeley* ... brought us forth to a spacious place, *Goodspeed* ... led us out to breathe again, *JB*.

**13. I will go into thy house with burnt offerings: I will pay thee my vows:** ... I enter thy house with sacrifices, *Moffatt* ... I will bring holocausts to your house, *NAB* ... shall bring whole-offerings into your house, *REB* ... come to your Temple with burnt offerings, *NCV*.

**14. Which my lips have uttered, and my mouth hath spoken, when I was in trouble:** ... my lips have made and my mouth promised on oath during my distress, *REB* ... vows poured out by my lips, vows uttered in my agony, *Moffatt*.

**15. I will offer unto thee burnt sacrifices of fatlings, with the incense of rams; I will offer bullocks with goats. Selah:** ... fat beasts I will offer thee, the odour of burning rams, bullocks and goats in sacrifice, *Moffatt* ... With the smoke of rams; I shall make an offering of bulls with male goats, *NASB* ... will bring you offerings of fat animals, *NCV*.

**16. Come and hear, all ye that fear God, and I will declare what he hath done for my soul:** ... I tell what he has done for me, *Anchor* ... I may make clear to you what he has done, *BB* ... I tell of the great mercies he has shewn me, *Knox*.

**17. I cried unto him with my mouth, and he was extolled with my tongue:** ... no sooner had I called to him than I was praising him for answering me, *Moffatt* ... praise was on the tip of my tongue, *NAB* ... his high praise was on my lips, *NEB*.

**18. If I regard iniquity in my heart, the Lord will not hear me:** ... If I had meant to do wrong, The Lord would not have listened to me, *Beck* ... If He had seen Sin in my heart, Th' ALMIGHTY would not have heard me, *Fenton* ... Had I cherished deceit in my heart, The Lord would not have heard, *Goodspeed* ... Had I been aware of guilt in my heart, the Lord would not have listened, *JB*.

---

is that employed in Ps. 23:5. "My cup is overfulness" and "abundance" yields a satisfactory meaning here, although not closely corresponding to any of the preceding metaphors for affliction.

**66:13–15.** The fourth strophe begins the solo part. It clothes in a garb appropriate to a sacrificial system the thought expressed in more spiritual dress in the next strophe, that God's deliverance should evoke men's praise. The abundance and variety of sacrifices named, and the fact that "rams" were not used for the offerings of individuals, seem to suggest that the speaker is representing the nation in some sense and it has been supposed that he may be the high priest. But this is merely conjecture, and the explanation may be that there is a certain ideal and poetic tone over the representation that does not confine itself to scrupulous accuracy.

**66:16–20.** The last strophe passes beyond sacrificial symbols and gives the purest utterance to the emotions and resolves which ought to well up in a devout soul on occasion of God's goodness. Not only does the psalmist teach us how each individual must take the general blessing for his very own—of which act the faith which takes the world's Christ for my Christ is the supreme example—but he teaches us that the obligation laid on all recipients of God's mercy is to tell it forth and that the impulse is as certain to fol low real reception as the command is imperative. Just as Israel received deliverances that the whole earth might learn how strong and gracious was Israel's God, we receive his blessings, and chiefly his highest gift of life in Christ, not only that we may live, but that, living, we may "declare the works of the LORD." He has little possession of God's grace who has not felt the necessity of speech and the impossibility of the lips being locked when the heart is full.

***Psalm 67.*** *The structure of the Psalm has been variously conceived. Clearly, the selahs do not glide as to divisions in the flow of thought. But it may be noted that the seven verses in the Psalm each have two clauses, with the exception of the middle one (v. 4), which has three. Its place and its abnormal length mark it as the core around which, as it were, the whole is built up. Further, it is as if encased in two verses (vv. 3, 5), which in their four clauses are a fourfold repetition of a single aspiration. These three verses are the heart of the Psalm enclosed in two strophes of two verses each.*

| 904, 3949 | 3940 | 8471.121 | 112 | | 409 | 8471.111 | 435 |
|---|---|---|---|---|---|---|---|
| prep, n ms, ps 1cs | neg part | v Qal impf 3ms | n mp, ps 1cs | **19.** | adv | v Qal pf 3ms | n mp |
| בְלִבִּי | לֹא | יִשְׁמַע | אֲדֹנָי | | אָכֵן | שָׁמַע | אֱלֹהִים |
| velibbî | lō' | yishma' | 'ădhōnāy | | 'ākhēn | shāma' | 'ĕlōhîm |
| in my heart | not | He hears | my Lord | | surely | He has heard | God |

| 7477.511 | 904, 7249 | 8940 | | 1313.155 | 435 | 866 |
|---|---|---|---|---|---|---|
| v Hiphil pf 3ms | prep, *n ms* | n fs, ps 1cs | **20.** | v Qal pass ptc ms | n mp | cj |
| הִקְשִׁיב | בְּקוֹל | תְּפִלָּתִי | | בָּרוּךְ | אֱלֹהִים | אֲשֶׁר |
| hiqŏshîv | beqôl | tephillāthî | | bārûkh | 'ĕlōhîm | 'ăsher |
| He was attentive | by the voice of | my prayer | | blessed | God | because |

| 3940, 5681.511 | 8940 | 2721 | 4623, 882 | | 3937, 5514.351 |
|---|---|---|---|---|---|
| neg part, v Hiphil pf 3ms | n fs, ps 1cs | cj, n ms, ps 3ms | prep, prep, ps 1cs | **67:t** | prep, art, v Piel ptc ms |
| לֹא־הֵסִיר | תְּפִלָּתִי | וְחַסְדּוֹ | מֵאִתִּי | | לַמְנַצֵּחַ |
| lō'-hēsîr | tephillāthî | wechasdô | mē'ittî | | lamnatstsēach |
| He has not removed | my prayer | or his steadfast love | from with me | | to the director |

| 904, 5234 | 4344 | 8302 | | 435 | 2706.321 |
|---|---|---|---|---|---|
| prep, n fp | n ms | n ms | **1.** | n mp | v Piel juss 3ms, ps 1cp |
| בִּנְגִינֹת | מִזְמוֹר | שִׁיר | | אֱלֹהִים | יְחָנֵּנוּ |
| binghînōth | mizmôr | shîr | | 'ĕlōhîm | yechonnēnû |
| with the stringed instruments | a Psalm | a Song | | God | may He be gracious to us |

| 1313.321 | 213.521 | 6686 | 882 | 5734 | | 3937, 3156.141 |
|---|---|---|---|---|---|---|
| cj, v Piel juss 3ms, ps 1cp | v Hiphil juss 3ms | n mp, ps 3ms | prep, ps 1cp | intrj | **2.** | prep, v Qal inf con |
| וִיבָרְכֵנוּ | יָאֵר | פָּנָיו | אִתָּנוּ | סֶלָה | | לָדַעַת |
| wîvārekhēnû | yā'ēr | pānāv | 'ittānû | selāh | | lādha'ath |
| and may He bless us | may He cause to shine | his face | with us | selah | | to know |

| 904, 800 | 1932 | 904, 3725, 1504 | 3568 | | 3142.526 |
|---|---|---|---|---|---|
| prep, art, n fs | n ms, ps 2ms | prep, *adj*, n mp | n fs, ps 2ms | **3.** | v Hiphil juss 3mp, ps 2ms |
| בָּאָרֶץ | דַּרְכֶּךָ | בְּכָל־גּוֹיִם | יְשׁוּעָתֶךָ | | יוֹדוּךָ |
| bā'ārets | darkekhā | bekhol-gôyim | yeshû'āthekhā | | yôdhûkhā |
| throughout the earth | your way | throughout all the nations | your salvation | | let them praise You |

| 6194 | 435 | 3142.526 | 6194 | 3725 | | 7975.126 |
|---|---|---|---|---|---|---|
| n mp | n mp | v Hiphil juss 3mp, ps 2ms | n mp | adj, ps 3mp | **4.** | v Qal juss 3mp |
| עַמִּים | אֱלֹהִים | יוֹדוּךָ | עַמִּים | כֻּלָּם | | יִשְׂמְחוּ |
| 'ammîm | 'ĕlōhîm | yôdhûkhā | 'ammîm | kullām | | yismechû |
| peoples | O God | let them praise You | peoples | all of them | | let them be glad |

| 7728.326 | 3947 | 3706, 8570.123 | 6194 | 4473 | 3947 |
|---|---|---|---|---|---|
| cj, Piel juss 3mp | n mp | cj, v Qal impf 2ms | n mp | n ms | cj, n mp |
| וִירַנְּנוּ | לְאֻמִּים | כִּי־תִשְׁפֹּט | עַמִּים | מִישׁוֹר | וּלְאֻמִּים |
| wîrannenû | le'ummîm | kî-thishpōt | 'ammîm | mîshôr | ûlā'ummîm |
| and let them shout for joy | peoples | because You judge | peoples | equity | and the peoples |

| 904, 800 | 5341.523 | 5734 | | 3142.526 | 6194 | 435 | 3142.526 |
|---|---|---|---|---|---|---|---|
| prep, art, n fs | v Hiphil impf 2ms | intrj | **5.** | v Hiphil juss 3mp, ps 2ms | n mp | n mp | v Hiphil juss 3mp, ps 2ms |
| בָּאָרֶץ | תַּנְחֵם | סֶלָה | | יוֹדוּךָ | עַמִּים | אֱלֹהִים | יוֹדוּךָ |
| bā'ārets | tanchēm | selāh | | yôdhûkhā | 'ammîm | 'ĕlōhîm | yôdhûkhā |
| in the land | You comfort | selah | | let them praise You | peoples | O God | let them praise You |

| 6194 | 3725 | | 800 | 5598.112 | 3090 | 1313.321 | 435 |
|---|---|---|---|---|---|---|---|
| n mp | adj, ps 3mp | **6.** | n fs | v Qal pf 3fs | n fs, ps 3fs | v Piel impf 3ms, ps 1cp | n mp |
| עַמִּים | כֻּלָּם | | אֶרֶץ | נָתְנָה | יְבוּלָהּ | יְבָרְכֵנוּ | אֱלֹהִים |
| 'ammîm | kullām | | 'erets | nāthenāh | yevûlāhh | yevārekhēnû | 'ĕlōhîm |
| peoples | all of them | | the earth | it has yielded | its produce | He has blessed us | God |

**19. But verily God hath heard me; he hath attended to the voice of my prayer:** ... but in fact God did listen, attentive to the sound of my prayer, *JB* ... to my prayer he has paid heed, *Moffatt* ... he has hearkened to the sound of my prayer, *NAB*.

**20. Blessed be God, which hath not turned away my prayer, nor his mercy from me:** ... Praise God, who did not ignore my prayer or hold back his love from me, *NCV* ... has not withdrawn his love and care from me, *NEB* ... has not rejected my prayer or withheld his love from me, *NIV* ... or removed his steadfast love from me, *NRSV*.

**67:t. To the chief Musician on Neginoth, A Psalm or Song.**

**1. God be merciful unto us, and bless us; and cause his face to shine upon us; Selah:** ... God favour and bless us, And shine with His presence on us, *Fenton* ... God have pity on us, *Anchor* ... let the light of his face be shining on us, *BB*.

**2. That thy way may be known upon earth, thy saving health among all nations:** ... the earth will acknowledge your ways, and all nations your power to save, *JB* ... make known among all nations thy saving power, *Knox* ... so thy purpose may be plain to men, *Moffatt* ... among all nations, your salvation, *NAB*.

**3. Let the people praise thee, O God; let all the people praise thee:** ... the people should praise you, *NCV* ... the peoples will praise you all together, *Anchor* ... Let Nations call You their GOD, *Fenton*.

**4. O let the nations be glad and sing for joy: for thou shalt judge the people righteously, and govern the nations upon earth. Selah:** ... nations will be glad and shout happily, *Beck* ... for you judge the world with justice, you judge the peoples with fairness, *JB* ... for thou wilt judge the peoples equitably; and the nations upon earth, thou wilt guide them, *Darby*.

**5. Let the people praise thee, O God; let all the people praise thee:** ... Let Nations call You their GOD, You, let all the Nations proclaim, *Fenton* ... nations praise you, *JB* ... may all races praise thee, *Moffatt* ... Honour to thee, O God, from the nations, *Knox*.

**6. Then shall the earth yield her increase; and God, even our own God, shall bless us:** ... The land has yielded her harvest by the blessing of God, *Moffatt* ... earth has yielded its fruits, *NAB* ... land has given its crops, *NCV* ... land has produced its harvest, *Good News*.

---

**67:1–2.** The priestly blessing (Num. 6:24ff) molds v. 1, but with the substitution of God for Yahweh and of "among us" for "upon us." Israel is the world's high priest, lifting up intercessions and holy hands of benediction for mankind. What self-effacement, and what profound insight into and sympathy with the mind of God breathe in that arrangement of desires in which the gracious luster of God's face shining on us is longed for chiefly that thence it may be reflected into the dark places of earth to gladden sad and seeking eyes! This psalmist did not know in how true a sense the Light would come to dwell among men of Israel's race and thence to flood the world, but his yearning is a foreshadowing of the spirit of Christianity.

**67:3–5.** The central core of the Psalm may either be taken as a summons to the nations or as an expression of desire for them. The depth of the longing or the stringency of the summons is wonderfully given by that fourfold repetition of the same words in vv. 3 and 5, with the emphatic "all of them" in the second clause of each. Not less significant is the use of three names for the aggregations of men—"nations" (v. 2), "peoples" and "tribes." All are included, whatever bond knits them in communities, whatever their societies call themselves, however many they are. The very vagueness gives sublimity and universality. We can fill the vast outline drawn by these sweeping strokes, and wider knowledge should not be attended with narrowed desires nor feebler confidence that the Light shall lighten every land.

It is noticeable that in this central portion the deeds of God among the nations are set forth as the ground of their praise and joy in Him. Israel had the light of his face, and that would draw men to Him. But all peoples have the strength of his arm to be their defender and the guidance of his hand by providences and in other ways unrecognized by them. The "judgments" here contemplated are, of course, not retribution for evil, but the aggregate of dealings by which God shows his sovereignty in all the earth. The psalmist does not believe that God's goodness has been confined to Israel, nor that the rest of the world has been left orphaned. He agrees with Paul: "That which may be known of God is manifest in them, for God hath shown it unto them" (Rom. 1:19).

**67:6–7.** The final strophe is substantially a repetition of vv. 1f, with the addition that a past fact is laid as the foundation of the desires or hopes of future blessings. "The earth has yielded her increase." This may show that the Psalm is a harvest hymn, but it does not necessarily imply this. The thought may have been born at any time. The singer takes the plain fact that, year by year, by mysterious quickening which he recognizes as

| 435 | | 1313.321 | 435 | 3486.126 | 881 | 3725, 675, 800 |
|---|---|---|---|---|---|---|
| n mp, ps 1cp | | v Piel impf 3ms, ps 1cp | n mp | cj, v Qal impf 3mp | do, ps 3ms | *adj, n mp*, n fs |
| אֱלֹהֵינוּ | 7. | יְבָרְכֵנוּ | אֱלֹהִים | וְיִירְאוּ | אֹתוֹ | כָּל־אַפְסֵי־אָרֶץ |
| 'ělōhênû | | yevārekhēnû | 'ělōhîm | weyîre'û | 'ōthô | kol-'aphsê-'ārets |
| our God | | He has blessed us | God | and they will fear | Him | all the ends of the earth |

| | 3937, 5514.351 | 3937, 1784 | 4344 | 8302 | | 7251.121 | 435 | 6571.126 |
|---|---|---|---|---|---|---|---|---|
| | prep, art, v Piel ptc ms | prep, pn | n ms | n ms | | v Qal impf 3ms | n mp | v Qal impf 3mp |
| 68:t | לַמְנַצֵּחַ | לְדָוִד | מִזְמוֹר | שִׁיר | 1. | יָקוּם | אֱלֹהִים | יָפוּצוּ |
| | lamnatstsēach | ledhāwidh | mizmôr | shîr | | yāqûm | 'ělōhîm | yāphûtsû |
| | to the director | of David | a Psalm | a Song | | He will arise | God | and they will be scattered |

| 342.152 | 5308.126 | 4623, 7983.352 | 4623, 6686 |
|---|---|---|---|
| v Qal act ptc mp, ps 3ms | cj, v Qal impf 3mp | v Piel ptc mp, ps 3ms | prep, n mp, ps 3ms |
| אוֹיְבָיו | וְיָנוּסוּ | מְשַׂנְאָיו | מִפָּנָיו |
| 'ôyvâv | weyānûsû | mesan'âv | mippānâv |
| his enemies | and they will flee | those who hate Him | from before Him |

| | 3626, 5264.241 | 6476 | 5264.123 | 3626, 4701.241 | 1804 | 4623, 6686, 813 |
|---|---|---|---|---|---|---|
| | prep, v Niphal inf con | n ms | v Qal impf 2ms | prep, v Niphal inf con | n ms | prep, *n mp*, n fs |
| 2. | כְּהִנְדֹּף | עָשָׁן | תִּנְדֹּף | כְּהִמֵּס | דּוֹנַג | מִפְּנֵי־אֵשׁ |
| | kehindōph | 'āshān | tindōph | kehimmēs | dônagh | mippenê-'ēsh |
| | like the driving away of | smoke | You drive away | like the melting of | wax | from before fire |

| 6.126 | 7857 | 4623, 6686 | 435 | | 6926 | 7975.126 |
|---|---|---|---|---|---|---|
| v Qal impf 3mp | n mp | prep, *n mp* | n mp | | cj, n mp | v Qal impf 3mp |
| יֹאבְדוּ | רְשָׁעִים | מִפְּנֵי | אֱלֹהִים | 3. | וְצַדִּיקִים | יִשְׂמְחוּ |
| yō'vedhû | reshā'îm | mippenê | 'ělōhîm | | wetsaddîqîm | yismechû |
| they will perish | the wicked | from before | God | | but the righteous | they will be glad |

| 6192.126 | 3937, 6686 | 435 | 7919.126 | 904, 7977 | | 8301.133 | 3937, 435 |
|---|---|---|---|---|---|---|---|
| v Qal impf 3mp | prep, *n mp* | n mp | cj, v Qal impf 3mp | prep, n fs | | v Qal impv 2mp | prep, n mp |
| יַעַלְצוּ | לִפְנֵי | אֱלֹהִים | וְיָשִׂישׂוּ | בְשִׂמְחָה | 4. | שִׁירוּ | לֵאלֹהִים |
| ya'altsû | liphnê | 'ělōhîm | weyāsîsû | vesimchāh | | shîrû | lē'lōhîm |
| they will exult | before | God | they will be jubilant | with joy | | sing | to God |

| 2252.333 | 8428 | 5744.133 | 3937, 7680.151 | 904, 6400 | 904, 3161 | 8428 |
|---|---|---|---|---|---|---|
| v Piel impv 2mp | n ms, ps 3ms | v Qal impv 2mp | prep, art, v Qal act ptc ms | prep, art, n fp | prep, pn | n ms, ps 3ms |
| זַמְּרוּ | שְׁמוֹ | סֹלּוּ | לָרֹכֵב | בָּעֲרָבוֹת | בְּיָהּ | שְׁמוֹ |
| zammerû | shemô | sōllû | lārōkhēv | bā'ărāvôth | beyāhh | shemô |
| sing praises to | his name | build up | to the One Who rides | in the deserts | in Yah | his name |

| 6159.133 | 3937, 6686 | | 1 | 3605 | 1837 | 496 |
|---|---|---|---|---|---|---|
| cj, v Qal impv 2mp | prep, n mp, ps 3ms | | *n ms* | n mp | cj, *n ms* | n fp |
| וְעִלְזוּ | לְפָנָיו | 5. | אֲבִי | יְתוֹמִים | וְדַיַּן | אַלְמָנוֹת |
| we'ilzû | lephānâv | | 'ăvî | yethômîm | wedhayyan | 'almānôth |
| yes exult | before Him | | the Father of | the orphans | and the Vindicator of | the widows |

| 435 | 904, 4737 | 7231 | | 435 | 3553.551 | 3279 |
|---|---|---|---|---|---|---|
| n mp | prep, *n ms* | n ms, ps 3ms | | n mp | v Hiphil ptc ms | n mp |
| אֱלֹהִים | בִּמְעוֹן | קָדְשׁוֹ | 6. | אֱלֹהִים | מוֹשִׁיב | יְחִידִים |
| 'ělōhîm | bim'ôn | qādheshô | | 'ělōhîm | môshîv | yechîdhîm |
| God | in the Tabernacle of | his holy place | | God | One Who causes to dwell | the lonely |

| 1041 | 3428.551 | 629 | 904, 3692 | 395 | 5842.152 | 8331.116 |
|---|---|---|---|---|---|---|
| n ms | v Hiphil ptc ms | n mp | prep, art, n fp | adv | v Qal act ptc mp | v Qal pf 3cp |
| בַּיְתָה | מוֹצִיא | אֲסִירִים | בַּכּוֹשָׁרוֹת | אַךְ | סוֹרְרִים | שָׁכְנוּ |
| baythāh | môtsî' | 'ăsîrîm | bakkôshārôth | 'akh | sōrerîm | shākhenû |
| to a house | One Who leads out | prisoners | into prosperity | only | stubborn ones | they will dwell in |

**7. God shall bless us; and all the ends of the earth shall fear him:** ... God grant us ever his blessing, and may earth, far and wide, do him reverence, *Knox* ... May God go on blessing us and all the most distant parts of the world worship Him, *Beck* ... and be revered by the whole wide world, *JB*.

**68:t. To the chief Musician, A Psalm or Song of David.**

**1. Let God arise, let his enemies be scattered: let them also that hate him flee before him:** ... let those who hate him run away from him, *NCV* ... Let God be seen, and let his haters be put to flight; let those who are against him be turned back before Him, *BB* ... his foes be scattered, *Goodspeed*.

**2. As smoke is driven away, so drive them away: as wax melteth before the fire, so let the wicked perish at the presence of God:** ... You disperse them like smoke, *JB* ... Vanish the wicked at God's presence as the smoke vanishes, *Knox* ... so perish the ungodly before God, *Moffatt*.

**3. But let the righteous be glad; let them rejoice before God: yea, let them exceedingly rejoice:** ... the just rejoice and exult before God, *NAB* ... those who do right should be glad and should rejoice before God, *NCV* ... righteous are joyful, they exult before God, *NEB* ... let the upright be glad; let them have delight before God, *BB*.

**4. Sing unto God, sing praises to his name: extol him that rideth upon the heavens by his name JAH, and rejoice before him:** ... Sing to God, ... rejoice in Yahweh, dance before him, *JB* ... Extol him who rides upon the stormclouds, *Goodspeed*.

**5. A father of the fatherless, and a judge of the widows, is God in his holy habitation:** ... a father to the orphan, and gives the widow redress, this God who dwells apart in holiness, *Knox* ... defender of widows is God in his holy dwelling, *NAB* ... father to those who have no father, *BB*.

**6. God setteth the solitary in families: he bringeth out those which are bound with chains: but the rebellious dwell in a dry land:** ... Those who are without friends, God puts in families, *BB* ... God gives the lonely a home to live in; He releases prisoners, making them happy. But the rebellious must live in a parched land, *Beck* ... God brings home the desolate; He leads prisoners forth into prosperity, *Goodspeed* ... leaves none but the rebels to find their abode in the wilderness, *Knox*.

---

being of God, the fertile earth "causes the things sown in it to bring forth and bud" (Isa. 61:11), as an evidence of divine care and kindliness, which warrants the desire and the confidence that all blessings will be given. It seems a large inference from such a premise, but it is legitimate for those who recognize God as working in nature and have eyes to read the parables amid which we live. The psalmist reminds God of his own acts and, further, of his own name and builds on these his petitions and his faith. Because He is our God, He will bless us, and since the earth has, by his gift, "yielded her increase," He will give the better food which souls need. This the singer desires, not only because he and his brethren need it, but because a happy people are the best witnesses for a good King, and worshipers "satisfied with favor and full of the blessing of the LORD" (Deut. 33:23) proclaim most persuasively, "Taste, and see that God is good" (Ps. 34:8).

***Psalm 68.*** *The main division at v. 18 parts the Psalm into two equal halves, which are again easily subdivided into strophes. The first strophe (vv. 1–6) may be regarded as introductory to the chief theme of the first half, namely, the triumphant march of the conquering God to his sanctuary.*

*With the second strophe (vv. 7–10) begins the historical retrospect, which is continued until, at the end of the fourth (v. 18), God is enthroned in the sanctuary, there to dwell forever. In the second strophe, the wilderness life is described. The third (vv. 11–14) tells of the victories which won the land. The fourth triumphantly contrasts the glory of the mountain where God at last has come to dwell, with the loftier peaks across the Jordan on which no such luster gleams.*

**68:1–6.** God "arises" when He displays by some signal act his care for his people. That strong anthropomorphism sets forth the plain truth that there come crises in history when causes, long silently working, suddenly produce their world-shaking effects. God has seemed to sit passively, but the heavens open, and all but blind eyes can see Him, standing ready to smite that He may deliver. When He rises to his feet, the enemy scatters in panic. His presence revealed is enough. The emphatic repetition of "before" in these verses is striking, especially when fully rendered—from his face (v. 1); from the face of the fire (v. 2); from the face of God (v. 2); before his face (vv. 3f). To his foes, that face is dreadful, and they would fain cower away from its light; his friends sun themselves in its brightness. The same fire consumes and vivifies. All depends on the character of the recipients. In the Psalm, "the righteous" are Israel, the ideal nation.

| 6975 | | 435 | 904, 3428.141 | 3937, 6686 | 6194 | 904, 7081.141 |
|---|---|---|---|---|---|---|
| n fs | 7. | n mp | prep, v Qal inf con, ps 2ms | prep, *n mp* | n ms, ps 2ms | prep, v Qal inf con, ps 2ms |
| צְחִיחָה | | אֱלֹהִים | בְּצֵאתְךָ | לִפְנֵי | עַמֶּךָ | בְּצַעְדְּךָ |
| tsᵉchîchāh | | 'ĕlōhîm | bᵉtsē'thᵉkhā | liphnê | 'ammekhā | bᵉtsa'addᵉkhā |
| a parched land | | O God | during your going out | before | your people | during your marching |

| 904, 3574 | 5734 | | 800 | 7782.112 | 652, 8452 | 5382.116 | 4623, 6686 |
|---|---|---|---|---|---|---|---|
| prep, n ms | intrj | 8. | n fs | v Qal pf 3fs | cj, n md | v Qal pf 3cp | prep, *n mp* |
| בִּישִׁימוֹן | סֶלָה | | אֶרֶץ | רָעָשָׁה | אַף־שָׁמַיִם | נָטְפוּ | מִפְּנֵי |
| vishîmôn | s̱elāh | | 'erets | rā'āshāh | 'aph-shāmayim | nāṭᵉphû | mippᵉnê |
| through the desert | selah | | the earth | it quaked | also the heavens | they dripped | from before |

| 435 | 2172 | 5703 | 4623, 6686 | 435 | 435 | 3547 | | 1700 | 5249 |
|---|---|---|---|---|---|---|---|---|---|
| n mp | dem pron | pn | prep, *n mp* | n mp | *n mp* | pn | 9. | n ms | n fp |
| אֱלֹהִים | זֶה | סִינַי | מִפְּנֵי | אֱלֹהִים | אֱלֹהֵי | יִשְׂרָאֵל | | גֶּשֶׁם | נְדָבוֹת |
| 'ĕlōhîm | zeh | s̱înay | mippᵉnê | 'ĕlōhîm | 'ĕlōhê | yisrā'ēl | | geshem | nᵉdhāvôth |
| God | this | Sinai | from before | God | the God of | Israel | | rain | freewill offerings |

| 5311.523 | 435 | 5338 | 3942.211 | 887 | 3679.313 |
|---|---|---|---|---|---|
| v Hiphil impf 2ms | n mp | n fs, ps 2ms | cj, v Niphal pf 3ms | pers pron | v Polel pf 2ms, ps 3fs |
| תָּנִיף | אֱלֹהִים | נַחֲלָתְךָ | וְנִלְאָה | אַתָּה | כוֹנַנְתָּהּ |
| tānîph | 'ĕlōhîm | nachlāthᵉkhā | wᵉnil'āh | 'attāh | khônantāhh |
| You spread around | O God | your inheritance | when it languished | You | You made it firm |

| | 2516 | 3553.116, 904 | 3679.523 | 904, 3008 | 3937, 6270 | 435 |
|---|---|---|---|---|---|---|
| 10. | n fs, ps 2ms | v Qal pf 3cp, prep, ps 3fs | v Hiphil impf 2ms | prep, n fs, ps 2ms | prep, art, n ms | n mp |
| | חַיָּתְךָ | יָשְׁבוּ־בָהּ | תָּכִין | בְּטוֹבָתְךָ | לֶעָנִי | אֱלֹהִים |
| | chayyāthᵉkhā | yāshᵉvû-vāhh | tākhîn | bᵉṭôvāthᵉkhā | le'ānî | 'ĕlōhîm |
| | your livestock | they dwelled in it | You prepared | in your goodness | for the needy | O God |

| | 112 | 5598.121, 575 | 1339.354 | 6893 | 7521 | | 4567 |
|---|---|---|---|---|---|---|---|
| 11. | n mp, ps 1cs | v Qal impf 3ms, n ms | art, v Piel ptc fp | n ms | adj | 12. | *n mp* |
| | אֲדֹנָי | יִתֶּן־אֹמֶר | הַמְבַשְּׂרוֹת | צָבָא | רָב | | מַלְכֵי |
| | 'ădhōnāy | yitten-'ōmer | hamvassᵉrôth | tsāvā' | rāv | | malkhê |
| | my Lord | He gave a word | the ones bearing good news | a host | large | | the kings of |

| 6893 | 5252.126 | 5252.126 | 5295 | 1041 | 2606.323 | 8395 |
|---|---|---|---|---|---|---|
| n fp | v Qal impf 3mp | v Qal impf 3mp | cj, *n fs* | n ms | v Piel impf 2ms | n ms |
| צְבָאוֹת | יִדֹּדוּן | יִדֹּדוּן | וּנְוַת | בַּיִת | תְּחַלֵּק | שָׁלָל |
| tsᵉvā'ôth | yiddōdhûn | yiddōdhûn | ûnᵉwath | bayith | tᵉchallēq | shālāl |
| armies | they will flee | they will flee | and the grasslands of | the household | You will divide | booty |

| | 524, 8311.128 | 1033 | 8610 | 3796 | 3225 | 2750.211 | 904, 3826B |
|---|---|---|---|---|---|---|---|
| 13. | cj, v Qal impf 2mp | prep | n fd | *n fd* | n fs | v Niphal pf 3ms | prep, art, n ms |
| | אִם־תִּשְׁכְּבוּן | בֵּין | שְׁפַתָּיִם | כַּנְפֵי | יוֹנָה | נֶחְפָּה | בַּכֶּסֶף |
| | 'im-tishkᵉvûn | bên | shᵉphattāyim | kanphê | yônāh | nechpāh | vakkes̱eph |
| | if You remain | between | the sheepfolds | the wings of | a dove | they are overlaid | with silver |

**7. O God, when thou wentest forth before thy people, when thou didst march through the wilderness; Selah:** ... led your people out when you marched through the desert, *NCV* ... went out in front of Your people and marched through the desert, *Beck* ... set out at the head of your people, when you strode over the desert, *JB*.

**8. The earth shook, the heavens also dropped at the presence of God: even Sinai itself was moved at the presence of God, the God of Israel:** ... the earth rocked, the heavens pelted down rain at the presence of God, *JB* ... how the earth trembled, how the sky broke at God's coming, how even Sinai shook, *Knox*.

**9. Thou, O God, didst send a plentiful rain, whereby thou didst confirm thine inheritance, when it was weary:** ... when Your land was exhausted, You refreshed it, *Beck* ... you sent much rain; you refreshed your tired land, *NCV* ... You gave abundant showers, O God; you refreshed your weary inheritance, *NIV* ... did freely send the rain, giving strength to the weariness of your heritage, *BB*.

**10. Thy congregation hath dwelt therein: thou, O God, hast prepared of thy goodness for the poor:** ... Your living family settled there, *Beck* ... Your family found a home, which you in your generosity provided for the humble, *JB* ... and in thy goodness thou didst meet their needs, *Moffatt* ... Your flock settled in it; in your goodness, O God, you provided it for the needy, *NAB*.

**11. The Lord gave the word: great was the company of those that published it:** ... a great army told the news, *NCV* ... great was the company of those who proclaimed it, *NIV* ... Lord uttered the word that made a mighty army rejoice, *Beck*.

**12. Kings of armies did flee apace: and she that tarried at home divided the spoil:** ... they fled and the woman staying home got her share of the spoil, *Beck* ... household shall divide the spoils, *NAB* ... the women in the houses make a division of their goods, *BB*.

**13. Though ye have lain among the pots, yet shall ye be as the wings of a dove covered with silver, and her feathers with yellow gold:** ... Some of you lingered among the sheepfolds, *Beck* ... When you lie among the sheepfolds, *KJVII* ... Will you take your rest among the flocks? like the wings of a dove, *BB* ... feathers with glistening gold, *Berkeley* ... glittering gold, *Goodspeed*.

---

The "wicked" are its heathen foes, but the principle underlying the impassioned words demands a real assimilation of moral character to the divine as a condition of being at ease in the Light.

The "deserts" are, in consonance with the immediately following reminiscences, those of the Exodus. Those who discover in the Psalm the hopes of the captives in Babylon take them to be the waste wilderness stretching between Babylon and Palestine. But it is better to see in them simply a type drawn from the past, of guidance through any needs or miseries. Verses 5f draw out at length the blessed significance of the name Yah (HED #3161), in order to hearten to earnest desire and expectance of Him. They are best taken as in apposition with "him" in v. 4. Well may we exult before Him who is the orphans' father, the widows' advocate. There may be significance in the contrast between what He is when "in his holy habitation" and when He arises to ride through the deserts. Even in the times when he seems to be far above, dwelling in the separation of his unapproachable holiness, He is still caring and acting for the sad and helpless. But when He comes forth, it is to make the solitary to dwell in a home, to bring out prisoners into prosperity. Are these simply expressions for God's general care of the afflicted, like the former clauses, or do they point back to the Exodus? A very slight change in the text gives the reading, "Makes the solitary to return home"; but even without that alteration, the last clause of the verse is so obviously an allusion to the disobedient, "whose carcasses fell in the wilderness" (Heb. 3:17), that the whole verse is best regarded as pointing back to that time. The "home" to which the people were led is the same as the "prosperity" into which the prisoners are brought, namely, the rest and well-being of Canaan, while the fate of the "rebellious" is, as it ever is, to live and die amidst the drought-stricken barrenness which they have chosen.

**68:7–10.** Verses 7f are from Deborah's song, with slight omissions and alterations, notably of "Yahweh" into "God." The phrase "before" still rings in the psalmist's ears, and he changes Deborah's words, in the first clause of v. 7, so as to give the picture of God marching in front of his people, instead of, as the older song represented Him, coming from the east to meet them marching from the west. The majestic theophany at the giving of the Law is taken as the culmination of his manifestations in the wilderness. Verses 9f are capable of two applications. According to one, they anticipate the chronological order and refer to the fertility of the land and the abundance enjoyed by Israel when established there. According to the other, they refer to the sustenance of the people in the wilderness. The former view has in its favor the ordinary use of "inheritance" for the land, the likelihood that "rain" should be represented as falling on soil rather than on people and the apparent reference in "dwelt therein" to the settlement in Canaan. The objection to it is that the reference to peaceful dwelling in the land is out of place, since the next strophe pictures the conquest. If, then, the verses belong to the age of wandering, to what do they refer?

**68:11–12.** The next strophe is abrupt and disconnected, as if echoing the hurry of battle and the tumult of many voices on the field. The general drift is unmistakable, but the meaning of part is the despair of commentators. The whole scene of the conflict, flight and division of the spoil is flashed before us in brief clauses, panting with excitement and blazing with the glow of victory. "The LORD giveth the word," which sees God as

| 79 | 904, 3541 | 2843 | | 904, 6816.341 | 8163 | 4567 | 904 |
|---|---|---|---|---|---|---|---|
| cj, n fp, ps 3fs | prep, adj | n ms | **14.** | prep, v Piel inf con | n ms | n mp | prep, ps 3fs |
| וְאֶבְרוֹתֶיהָ | בִּירַקְרַק | חָרוּץ | | בְּפָרֵשׂ | שַׁדַּי | מְלָכִים | בָּהּ |
| we'evrôthêāh | bîraqōraq | chārûts | | bephārēs | shadday | melākhîm | bāhh |
| and its pinions | with alloyed | gold | | when scattering | the Almighty | kings | in it |

| 8344.523 | 904, 7023 | | 2098, 435 | 2098, 1347 | 2098 |
|---|---|---|---|---|---|
| v Hiphil impf 2ms | prep, pn | **15.** | *n ms*, n mp | *n ms*, pn | n ms |
| תַּשְׁלֵג | בְּצַלְמוֹן | | הַר־אֱלֹהִים | הַר־בָּשָׁן | הַר |
| tashlēgh | betsalmôn | | har-'ĕlōhîm | har-bāshān | har |
| You caused to snow | on Zalmon | | the mountain of God | the mountains of the Bashan | mountains |

| 1418 | 2098, 1347 | | 4066 | 7812.328 | 2098 | 1418 |
|---|---|---|---|---|---|---|
| adj | *n ms*, pn | **16.** | intrg | v Piel impf 2mp | n mp | adj |
| גַּבְנֻנִּים | הַר־בָּשָׁן | | לָמָּה | תְּרַצְּדוּן | הָרִים | גַּבְנֻנִּים |
| gavnunîm | har-bāshān | | lāmmāh | teratstsedhûn | hārîm | gavnunîm |
| humped | the mountains of the Bashan | | why | do you look with envy | mountains | humped |

| 2098 | 2629.111 | 435 | 3937, 3553.141 | 652, 3176 | 8331.121 | 3937, 5516 |
|---|---|---|---|---|---|---|
| art, n ms | v Qal pf 3ms | n mp | prep, v Qal inf con, ps 3ms | cj, pn | v Qal impf 3ms | prep, art, n ms |
| הָהָר | חָמַד | אֱלֹהִים | לְשִׁבְתּוֹ | אַף־יְהוָה | יִשְׁכֹּן | לָנֶצַח |
| hāhār | chāmadh | 'ĕlōhîm | leshivtô | 'aph-yehwāh | yishkōn | lānetsach |
| the hills | He desired | God | for his dwelling | indeed Yahweh | He remains | unto forever |

| | 7681 | 435 | 7531 | 512 | 8519 | 112 | 904 | 5703 |
|---|---|---|---|---|---|---|---|---|
| **17.** | *n ms* | n mp | num | num | n ms | n mp, ps 1cs | prep, ps 3mp | pn |
| | רֶכֶב | אֱלֹהִים | רִבֹּתַיִם | אַלְפֵי | שִׁנְאָן | אֲדֹנָי | בָּם | סִינַי |
| | rekhev | 'ĕlōhîm | ribbōthayim | 'alphê | shin'ān | 'ădhōnāy | vām | sînay |
| | the chariot of | God | myriads | thousands | repeated | my Lord | among them | Sinai |

| 904, 7231 | | 6148.113 | 3937, 4953 | 8091.113 | 8104 | 4089.113 |
|---|---|---|---|---|---|---|
| prep, art, n ms | **18.** | v Qal pf 2ms | prep, art, n ms | v Qal pf 2ms | n ms | v Qal pf 2ms |
| בַּקֹּדֶשׁ | | עָלִיתָ | לַמָּרוֹם | שָׁבִיתָ | שֶּׁבִי | לָקַחְתָּ |
| baqqōdhesh | | 'ālîthā | lammārôm | shāvîthā | shevî | lāqachtā |
| in the holy place | | You went up | to the on high | You took captive | captives | You received |

| 5152 | 904, 119 | 652 | 5842.152 | 3937, 8331.141 | 3161 | 435 |
|---|---|---|---|---|---|---|
| n fp | prep, art, n ms | cj, cj | v Qal act ptc mp | prep, v Qal inf con | pn | n mp |
| מַתָּנוֹת | בָּאָדָם | וְאַף | סוֹרְרִים | לִשְׁכֹּן | יָהּ | אֱלֹהִים |
| mattānôth | bā'ādhām | we'aph | sôrerîm | lishkōn | yāhh | 'ĕlōhîm |
| tributes | among humankind | and even | stubborn ones | to dwell | Yah | God |

| | 1313.155 | 112 | 3219 | 3219 | 6227.121, 3937 | 418 | 3568 | 5734 |
|---|---|---|---|---|---|---|---|---|
| **19.** | v Qal pass ptc ms | n mp, ps 1cs | n ms | n ms | v Qal impf 3ms, prep, ps 1cp | art, n ms | n fs, ps 1cp | intrj |
| | בָּרוּךְ | אֲדֹנָי | יוֹם | יוֹם | יַעֲמָס־לָנוּ | הָאֵל | יְשׁוּעָתֵנוּ | סֶלָה |
| | bārûkh | 'ădhōnāy | yôm | yôm | ya'ămās-lānû | hā'ēl | yeshû'āthēnû | selāh |
| | blessed | my Lord | a day | a day | He carries us | God | our salvation | selah |

**14. When the Almighty scattered kings in it, it was white as snow in Salmon:** … Almighty made kings fly therein, *Goodspeed* … scattered kings like snow on Mount Zalmon, *NCV* … scatters kings far and wide like snowflakes falling, *NEB*.

**15. The hill of God is as the hill of Bashan; an high hill as the hill of Bashan:** … a mountain studded with peaks is the Bashan range, *Berkeley* … a hill with high tops is the hill of Bashan, *BB* … Basan's hills are high, Basan's hills are rugged, *Knox* … a haughty mountain, *JB*.

**16. Why leap ye, ye high hills? this is the hill which God desireth to dwell in; yea, the LORD will dwell in it for ever:** … Why do you gaze with envious hostility, *Berkeley* … Why look you jealously, you rugged mountains, at the mountain God has chosen for his throne, *NAB* … Why do you mountains with many peaks look with envy on the mountain that God chose for his home, *NCV* … the mountain God has chosen for His resting place, *KJVII*.

**17. The chariots of God are twenty thousand, even thousands of angels: the Lord is among them, as in Sinai, in the holy place:** ... See where God comes, with chariots innumerable for his escort; thousands upon thousands, *Knox* ... chariots of God are myriads, thousands upon thousands, *NASB* ... God comes with millions of chariots, *NCV* ... Lord came from Sinai into the sanctuary, *Goodspeed.*

**18. Thou hast ascended on high, thou hast led captivity captive: thou hast received gifts for men; yea, for the rebellious also, that the LORD God might dwell among them:** ... When you went up to the heights, you led a parade of captives, *NCV* ... You have gone up on high, taking your prisoners with you, *BB* ... you have taken men as tribute, even rebels that Yahweh God might have a dwelling-place, *JB*.

**19. Blessed be the Lord, who daily loadeth us with benefits, even the God of our salvation. Selah:** ... Praise be to the Lord, who is our support day by day, *BB* ... He carries our load for us, *Beck* ... who daily bears our burden, *Goodspeed* ... day after day, he carries us along, *JB*.

---

the only actor in Israel's history. This battle is the LORD's. There is no description of conflict. But one mighty word is hurled from heaven.

**68:13–14.** Verses 13f are among the most difficult to translate in the Psalter. The separate clauses offer no great difficulties, but the connection is enigmatic indeed. "Will ye lie among the sheepfolds?" comes from Deborah's song (Judg. 5:16) and is, in that verse, a reproach flung at Reuben for preferring pastoral ease to warlike effort. Is it meant as a reproach here? The question will then retain the taunting force which it has in Deborah's song, while it pictures a very different kind of couching among the sheepfolds, namely, the hiding there from pursuit. The kings are first seen in full flight. Then the triumphant psalmist flings after them the taunt, "Will ye hide among the cattle?" The second and third clauses are then parallel with the second of v. 12 and carry on the description of the home-keeping matron, "the dove," adorned with rich spoils and glorious in her apparel. We thus have a complete parallelism between the two verses, which both lay side by side the contrasted pictures of the defeated kings and the women. We further establish continuity between the three verses (13ff) insofar as the "kings" are dealt within them all.

Verse 14 is even harder than the preceding. What does "in it" refer to? Is the second clause a metaphor, requiring to be eked out with "It is like as when"? If it is figurative, what does it mean? Salmon was an inconsiderable hill in central Palestine, deriving its name as is probable, from forests on its sides. Many commentators look to that characteristic for explanation of the riddle. Snow on the dark hill would show very white. So after the defeat, the bleached bones of the slain, or, as others, their glittering armor, would cover the land. Others take the point of comparison to be the change from trouble to joy which follows the foe's defeat and is likened to the change of the dark hillside to a gleaming snow field.

**68:15–17.** The battle is over, and now the Conqueror enters his palace-temple. The third strophe soars with its theme, describing his triumphal entry thither and permanent abiding there. The long years between the conquest of Canaan and the establishment of the Ark on Zion dwindle to a span, for God's enthronement there was in one view the purpose of the conquest, which was incomplete until that was effected. There is no need to suppose any reference in the mention of Bashan to the victories over Og, its ancient king. The noble figure needs no historic allusion to explain it. His triumphal procession is not composed of earthly warriors, for none such had appeared in the battle. Angels surround Him in numbers innumerable, which language strains its power in endeavoring to reckon. "Myriads" (HED #7531) says the psalmist—an indefinite expression for a countless host. But all their wide-flowing ranks are clustered around the Conqueror, whose presence makes their multitude a unity even as it gives their immortal frames their life and strength and their faces all their lustrous beauty. "God is in the midst of them"; therefore, they conquer and exult. Sinai is in the sanctuary.

**68:18.** Paul's quotation of this verse in Eph. 4:8 reveals that the ascent of the Ark to Zion was a type. Conflict, conquest, triumphant ascent to a lofty home, tribute, widespread submission and access for rebels to the royal presence—all these, which the psalmist saw as facts or hopes in their earthly form, are repeated in loftier fashion in Christ and are only attainable through his universal reign. The apostle significantly alters "received among" into "gave to," sufficiently showing that he is not arguing from a verbal prophecy, but from a typical fact.

**68:19–21.** The Psalm reaches its climax in God's enthronement on Zion. Its subsequent strophes set forth the results thereof. The first of these,

| 20. | 418 | 3937 | 418 | 3937, 4321 | 3937, 3176 | 112 | 3937, 4323 | 8777 |
|---|---|---|---|---|---|---|---|---|
| | art, n ms | prep, ps 1cp | n ms | prep, n fp | cj, prep, pn | n mp, ps 1cs | prep, art, n ms | n fp |
| | הָאֵל | לָנוּ | אֵל | לְמוֹשָׁעוֹת | וְלֵיהוִה | אֲדֹנָי | לַמָּוֶת | תּוֹצָאוֹת |
| | hā'ēl | lānû | 'ēl | lemôshā'ôth | welêhwih | 'ădhōnāy | lammāweth | tôtsā'ôth |
| | God | to us | a God | of salvation | and to Yahweh | my Lord | death | goings out |

| 21. | 395, 435 | 4410.121 | 7513 | 342.152 | 7221 | 7998 |
|---|---|---|---|---|---|---|
| | adv, n mp | v Qal impf 3ms | *n ms* | v Qal act ptc mp, ps 3ms | *n ms* | n ms |
| | אַךְ־אֱלֹהִים | יִמְחַץ | רֹאשׁ | אֹיְבָיו | קָדְקֹד | שֵׂעָר |
| | 'akh-'ĕlōhîm | yimchats | rō'sh | 'ōyevâv | qādheqōdh | sē'ār |
| | surely God | He shatters | the head of | his enemies | a crown of the head of | hair |

| 2050.751 | 904, 844 | 22. | 569.111 | 112 | 4623, 1347 |
|---|---|---|---|---|---|
| v Hithpael ptc ms | prep, n mp, ps 3ms | | v Qal pf 3ms | n mp, ps 1cs | prep, pn |
| מִתְהַלֵּךְ | בַּאֲשָׁמָיו | | אָמַר | אֲדֹנָי | מִבָּשָׁן |
| mithhallēkh | ba'ăshāmâv | | 'āmar | 'ădhōnāy | mibbāshān |
| the one who walks about | in his guilt | | He has said | my Lord | from the Bashan |

| 8178.525 | 8178.525 | 4623, 4852 | 3328 | 23. | 3937, 4775 | 4410.122 |
|---|---|---|---|---|---|---|
| v Hiphil impf 1cs | v Hiphil impf 1cs | prep, *n fp* | n ms | | prep, prep | v Qal impf 3fs |
| אָשִׁיב | אָשִׁיב | מִמְּצֻלוֹת | יָם | | לְמַעַן | תִּמְחַץ |
| 'āshîv | 'āshîv | mimmetsulôth | yām | | lema'an | timchats |
| I will bring back | I will bring back | from the depths of | the sea | | so that | it will smash |

| 7559 | 904, 1879 | 4098 | 3732 | 4623, 342.152 | 4633 |
|---|---|---|---|---|---|
| n fs, ps 2ms | prep, n ms | *n fs* | n mp, ps 2ms | prep, v Qal act ptc mp | n ms, ps 3ms |
| רַגְלְךָ | בְּדָם | לְשׁוֹן | כְּלָבֶיךָ | מֵאֹיְבִים | מִנֵּהוּ |
| raghlekhā | bedhām | leshôn | kelāvêkhā | mē'ōyevîm | minnēhû |
| your foot | in the blood | the tongue of | your dogs | from the enemies | their portion |

| 24. | 7495.116 | 2049 | 435 | 2049 | 418 | 4567 |
|---|---|---|---|---|---|---|
| | v Qal pf 3cp | n fp, ps 2ms | n mp | *n fp* | n ms, ps 1cs | n ms, ps 1cs |
| | רָאוּ | הֲלִיכוֹתֶיךָ | אֱלֹהִים | הֲלִיכוֹת | אֵלִי | מַלְכִּי |
| | rā'û | helîkhôthêkhā | 'ĕlōhîm | helîkhôth | 'ēlî | malkî |
| | they have seen | your processions | O God | the processions of | my God | my King |

| 904, 7231 | 25. | 7208.316 | 8301.152 | 313 | 5235.152 |
|---|---|---|---|---|---|
| prep, art, n ms | | v Piel pf 3cp | v Qal act ptc mp | prep | v Qal act ptc mp |
| בַּקֹּדֶשׁ | | קִדְּמוּ | שָׁרִים | אַחַר | נֹגְנִים |
| vaqqōdhesh | | qiddemû | shārîm | 'achar | nōghenîm |
| into the holy place | | they are in front | the singers | behind | the stringed musicians |

| 904, 8761 | 6183 | 8943.154 | 26. | 4882 | 1313.333 | 435 |
|---|---|---|---|---|---|---|
| prep, *n ms* | n fp | v Qal act ptc fp | | prep, n mp | v Piel impv 2mp | n mp |
| בְּתוֹךְ | עֲלָמוֹת | תּוֹפֵפוֹת | | בְּמַקְהֵלוֹת | בָּרְכוּ | אֱלֹהִים |
| bethôkh | 'ălāmôth | tôphēphôth | | bemaqhēlôth | bārekhû | 'ĕlōhîm |
| in the midst of | the young women | timbrel players | | in the assemblies | bless | God |

**20. He that is our God is the God of salvation; and unto GOD the Lord belong the issues from death:** … God is a saving God for us; the LORD, my Lord, controls the passageways of death, *NAB* … This God of ours is a God who saves; from Lord Yahweh comes escape from death, *JB* … the Lord is our Master, that saves men from peril of death, *Knox*.

**21. But God shall wound the head of his enemies, and the hairy scalp of such an one as goeth on still in his trespasses:** … Surely God crushes the heads of his enemies, the hairy crowns of those who stalk about in their guilt, *NAB* … God himself will smite the head of his enemies, *NEB* … The heads of the haters of God will be crushed, *BB*.

**22. The Lord said, I will bring again from Bashan, I will bring my people again from the depths of the sea:** … I will restore my people, the Lord says; I will restore them to their land, from Basan, from the shore of the high seas, *Knox* … deep parts of the sea, *BB*.

**23. That thy foot may be dipped in the blood of thine enemies, and the**

**tongue of thy dogs in the same:** ... foot may be red with blood, *BB* ... you can bathe your feet in blood and your dogs' tongues can get a share of the enemy, *Beck* ... your dogs may have a portion of your enemies, *Berkeley* ... the tongue of your dogs have its share of your foes, *Goodspeed.*

**24. They have seen thy goings, O God; even the goings of my God, my King, in the sanctuary:** ... Thy processions are seen, *Goodspeed* ... They view your progress, O God, *NAB* ... people have seen your victory march; God my King marched into the holy place, *NCV.*

**25. The singers went before, the players on instruments followed after; among them were the damsels playing with timbrels:** ... singers are in front and the instruments are behind, *NCV* ... at its head the singers, next come minstrels, girls among them playing on tambourines, *NEB* ... Singers lead; at the rear, the stringed instruments, *Goodspeed* ... singers go first, and the harpers behind, *Fenton.*

**26. Bless ye God in the congregations, even the Lord, from the fountain of Israel:** ... In choirs, they bless God, *Goodspeed* ... since the foundation of Israel, *JB* ... Israel's offspring!, *Moffatt.*

---

the fifth of the Psalm (vv. 19–23), suddenly drops from strains of exultation to a plaintive note and then again, just as suddenly, breaks out into stern rejoicing over the ruin of the foe. There is wonderful depth of insight and tenderness in laying side by side the two thoughts of God, that He sits on high as Conqueror and that He daily bears our burdens, or perhaps bears us as a shepherd might his lambs.

It is but for a moment, and what follows is startlingly different. Israel's escape from death is secured by the destruction of the enemy, and in it the psalmist has joy. He pictures the hand that sustained him and his fellows so tenderly, shattering the heads of the rebellious. These are described as long-haired, an emblem of strength and insolence which one is almost tempted to connect with Absalom. The same idea of determined and flaunting sin is conveyed by the expression "goes on in his guiltinesses." There will be such rebels, even though the house of God is open for them to dwell in, and there can be but one end for such. If they do not submit, they will be crushed. The psalmist is as sure of that as of God's gentleness, and his two clauses do state the alternative that every man has to face—either to let God bear his burden or to be smitten by Him.

**68:22–23.** Verses 22f give a terrible picture of the end of the rebels. The psalmist hears the voice of the LORD promising to bring some unnamed fugitives from Bashan and the depths of the sea in order that they may be slain and that he (or Israel) may bathe his foot in their blood and his dogs may lick it as they did Ahab's. Who are to be brought back? Some have thought that the promise referred to Israel, but it is more natural to apply it to the flying foe. There is no reference to Bashan either as the kingdom of an ancient enemy or as envying Zion (v. 15). But the high land of Bashan in the east and the depths of the sea to the west are taken (cf. Amos 9:1ff) as representing the farthest and most inaccessible hiding places. Wherever the enemies lurk, thence they will be dragged and slain.

The existing text is probably to be emended by the change of one letter in the verb, so as to read "shall wash" or bathe, as in Ps. 58:10, and the last clause to be read, "that the tongue of thy dogs may have its portion from the enemy." The blood runs ankle-deep, and the dogs feast on the carcasses or lick it—a dreadful picture of slaughter and fierce triumph. It is not to be softened, spiritualized or explained away.

There is, no doubt, a legitimate Christian joy in the fall of opposition to Christ's kingdom, and the purest benevolence has sometimes a right to be glad when hoary oppressions are swept away and their victims set free, but such rejoicing is not after the Christian law unless it is mingled with pity, of which the Psalm has no trace.

**68:24–27.** A festal procession is the second result of his enthronement, of which the deliverance and triumph described in the preceding strophe were the first. The people escaped from death flock to thank their Deliverer. Such seems to be the connection of the whole, especially of vv. 24f. Instead of myriads of angels surrounding the conquering God, here are singers and flute players and damsels beating their timbrels, like Miriam and her choir. Their shrill call in v. 26 summons all who "spring from the fountain of Israel" to bless God. After these musicians and singers, the psalmist sees tribe after tribe go up to the sanctuary and points to each as it passes. His enumeration is not free from difficulties, both in regard to the epithets employed and the specification of the tribes.

A more important question is the reason for the selection of the four tribes named. The mention of

| 3176 | 4623, 4888 | 3547 | | 8427 | 1175 | 7087 | 7575.151 |
|---|---|---|---|---|---|---|---|
| pn | prep, *n ms* | pn | 27. | adv | pn | adj | v Qal act ptc ms, ps 3mp |
| יְהוָה | מִמְּקוֹר | יִשְׂרָאֵל | | שָׁם | בִּנְיָמִן | צָעִיר | רֹדֵם |
| yehwāh | mimmeqôr | yisrā'ēl | | shām | binyāmin | tsā'îr | rōdhēm |
| Yahweh | from the fountain of | Israel | | there | Benjamin | least | their ruler |

| 8015 | 3171 | 7565 | 8015 | 2157 | 8015 | 5503 |
|---|---|---|---|---|---|---|
| *n mp* | pn | n fs, ps 3mp | *n mp* | pn | *n mp* | pn |
| שָׂרֵי | יְהוּדָה | רִגְמָתָם | שָׂרֵי | זְבֻלוּן | שָׂרֵי | נַפְתָּלִי |
| sārê | yehûdhāh | righmāthām | sārê | zevulûn | sārê | naphtālî |
| the officials of | Judah | their heap of stones | the officials of | Zebulun | the officials of | Naphtali |

| | 6943.311 | 435 | 6010 | 6022.131 | 435 | 2182 |
|---|---|---|---|---|---|---|
| 28. | v Piel pf 3ms | n mp, ps 2ms | n ms, ps 2ms | v Qal impv 2ms | n mp | dem pron |
| | צִוָּה | אֱלֹהֶיךָ | עֻזֶּךָ | עוּזָּה | אֱלֹהִים | זוּ |
| | tsiwwāh | 'ĕlōhêkhā | 'uzzekhā | 'ûzzāh | 'ĕlōhîm | zû |
| | He has commanded | your God | your Strength | exhibit strength | O God | this |

| 6713.113 | 3937 | | 4623, 2033 | 6142, 3503 | 3937 | 3095.526 |
|---|---|---|---|---|---|---|
| v Qal pf 2ms | prep, ps 1cp | 29. | prep, n ms, ps 2ms | prep, pn | prep, ps 2ms | v Hiphil impf 3mp |
| פָּעַלְתָּ | לָנוּ | | מֵהֵיכָלֶךָ | עַל־יְרוּשָׁלָם | לְךָ | יוֹבִילוּ |
| pā'altā | lānû | | mēhêkhālekhā | 'al-yerûshālām | lekhā | yôvîlû |
| You have enacted | for us | | from your Temple | upon Jerusalem | to You | they bring |

| 4567 | 8282 | | 1647.131 | 2516 | 7354 | 5920 | 48 |
|---|---|---|---|---|---|---|---|
| n mp | n ms | 30. | v Qal impv 2ms | *n fs* | n ms | *n fs* | n mp |
| מְלָכִים | שָׁי | | גְּעַר | חַיַּת | קָנֶה | עֲדַת | אַבִּירִים |
| melākhîm | shāy | | ge'ar | chayyath | qāneh | 'ădhath | 'abbîrîm |
| kings | presents | | rebuke | the animals of | the reeds | the herds of | bulls |

| 904, 5903 | 6194 | 7806.751 | 904, 7809, 3826B | 1002.311 | 6194 |
|---|---|---|---|---|---|
| prep, *n mp* | n mp | v Hithpael ptc ms | prep, *n mp*, n ms | v Piel pf 3ms | n mp |
| בְּעֶגְלֵי | עַמִּים | מִתְרַפֵּס | בְרַצֵּי־כָסֶף | בִּזַּר | עַמִּים |
| be'eghlê | 'ammîm | mithrappēs | beratstsê-khāseph | bizzar | 'ammîm |
| among the calves of | peoples | trampling | on the pieces of silver | He has scattered | peoples |

| 7420 | 2759.126 | | 885.126 | 2943 | 4623 | 4875 | 3688 |
|---|---|---|---|---|---|---|---|
| n fp | v Qal impf 3mp | 31. | v Qal impf 3mp | n mp | prep | pn | pn |
| קְרָבוֹת | יֶחְפָּצוּ | | יֶאֱתָיוּ | חַשְׁמַנִּים | מִנִּי | מִצְרָיִם | כּוּשׁ |
| qōrāvôth | yechăppātsû | | ye'ĕthāyû | chashmanîm | minî | mitsrāyim | kûsh |
| near ones | they delight in | | they come | bronze items | from | Egypt | Cush |

| 7608.522 | 3135 | 3937, 435 | | 4608 | 800 | 8301.133 | 3937, 435 |
|---|---|---|---|---|---|---|---|
| v Hiphil impf 3fs | n fd, ps 3ms | prep, n mp | 32. | *n fp* | art, n fs | v Qal impv 2mp | prep, n mp |
| תָּרִיץ | יָדָיו | לֵאלֹהִים | | מַמְלְכוֹת | הָאָרֶץ | שִׁירוּ | לֵאלֹהִים |
| tārîts | yādhâv | lē'lōhîm | | maml'khôth | hā'ārets | shîrû | lē'lōhîm |
| they cause to hurry | their hands | to God | | O kingdoms of | the earth | sing | to God |

**27. There is little Benjamin with their ruler, the princes of Judah and their council, the princes of Zebulun, and the princes of Naphtali:** … Benjamin, the youngest, leading them; the princes of Judah in a body, *NAB* … princes of Judah in their throng, *NASB*.

**28. Thy God hath commanded thy strength: strengthen, O God, that which thou hast wrought for us:** … God, order up your power; show the mighty power you have used for us before, *NCV* … Summon your power, O God; show us your strength, O God, as you have done before, *NIV* … Exert Your strength, *Beck* … that godlike power which has acted for us, *NEB*.

**29. Because of thy temple at Jerusalem shall kings bring presents unto thee:** … from your temple high above Jerusalem. Kings will come to you bearing tribute, *JB* … Kings freely bring You gifts, *Fenton*

... Kings will bring their wealth to you, to your Temple in Jerusalem, *NCV*.

**30. Rebuke the company of spearmen, the multitude of the bulls, with the calves of the people, till every one submit himself with pieces of silver: scatter thou the people that delight in war:** ... Say sharp words to the beast among the water-plants, *BB* ... prostrating themselves with pieces of silver, *Berkeley* ... Trample upon those who rejoice in spoil, *Goodspeed*.

**31. Princes shall come out of Egypt; Ethiopia shall soon stretch out her hands unto God:** ... Egypt sends ambassadors, and Ethiopia hurries to submit to God, *Moffatt* ... From Egypt nobles will come, *JB* ... Ethiopia makes her peace with God, *Knox*.

**32. Sing unto God, ye kingdoms of the earth; O sing praises unto the Lord; Selah:** ... raise your voices in God's honour, *Knox* ... oh celebrate the Lord, *Moffatt* ... chant praise to the LORD, *NAB* ... sing psalms to the LORD, *NEB*.

---

Benjamin and Judah is natural, but why are Zebulun and Naphtali the only representatives of the other tribes? The defenders of a late date answer (as has been already noticed) that it was because in the late period when the Psalm was written, Galilee and Judea "formed the two orthodox provinces." The objection to this is that in the post-exilic period, there were no distinct tribes of Zebulun and Naphtali and no princes to rule.

The mention of these tribes as sharing in the procession to the sanctuary on Zion would have been impossible during the period of the Northern Kingdom. If, then, these two periods are excluded, what is left but the Davidic? The fact seems to be that we have here another glance at Deborah's song, in which the daring valor of these two tribes is set in contrast with the sluggish cowardice of Reuben and the other northern ones. Those who had done their part in the wars of the LORD now go up in triumph to his house. That is the reward of God's faithful soldiers.

**68:28–31.** The next strophe is the prayer of the procession. It falls into two parts of two verses each, of which the former verse is petition and the latter confident anticipation of the results of answered prayer. The symmetry of the whole requires the substitution in v. 28 of "command" for "hath commanded." God's strength is poetically regarded as distinct from himself and almost personified, as "steadfast love" is in Ps. 42:8. The prayer is substantially equivalent to the following petition in v. 28b. Note how "strength" occurs four times in vv. 33ff. The prayer for its present manifestation is, in accordance with the historical retrospect of the first part, based upon God's past acts. It has been proposed to detach "from thy Temple" from v. 29, and to attach it to v. 28. This gets over a difficulty, but unduly abbreviates v. 29 and is not in harmony with the representation in the former part, which magnifies what God has wrought, not "from the Temple," but in his progress thither. No doubt the retention of the words in v. 29 introduces a singular expression there. How can presents be brought to God "from thy Temple"? The only explanation is that "Temple" is used in a restricted sense for the "holy place," as distinguished from the "holy of holies," in which the Ark was contained. The tribute bearers stand in that outer sanctuary and thence present their tokens.

Verse 30c is extremely obscure. The first word (HED #7806) is a participle, which is variously taken as meaning "casting oneself to the ground" (i.e, in submission) and "trampling to the ground." It is also variously referred to the nations and their leaders spoken of in the previous verse and to God. In the former case, it would describe their attitude of submission in consequence of "rebuke," in the latter, God's subjugation of them. The slightest change would make the word an imperative, thus bringing it into line with "rebuke"; but, even without this, the reference to God is apparently to be preferred.

One verse then tells what the result of that will be. "Great ones" shall come from the land of the beast of the reeds, and Ethiopia shall make haste to stretch out tribute-bearing hands to God. The vision of a world subjugated and loving its subjugation is rising before the poet. That is the end of the ways of God with Israel. So deeply had this psalmist been led into comprehension of the divine purpose; so clearly was he given to see the future, "and all the wonder that should be."

**68:32–35.** Therefore, he breaks forth at the last into invocation to all the kingdoms of the earth to sing to God. He had sung of his majesty as, of old, Yahweh "rode through the deserts," and that phrase described his intervention in the field of history on behalf of Israel. Now the singer calls for praise from all the earth to Him who rides in the "most ancient heavens," and that expression sets forth his

| 2252.333 | 112 | 5734 | | 3937, 7680.151 | 904, 8452 |
|---|---|---|---|---|---|
| v Piel impv 2mp | n mp, ps 1cs | intrj | | prep, art, v Qal act ptc ms | prep, *n md* |
| זַמְּרוּ | אֲדֹנָי | סֶלָה | 33. | לָרֹכֵב | בִּשְׁמֵי |
| zammᵉrû | ʼădhōnāy | selāh | | lārōkhēv | bishmê |
| sing praises to | my Lord | selah | | to the One Who rides | in the heavens of |

| 8452, 7208 | 2075 | 5598.121 | 904, 7249 | 7249 | 6010 |
|---|---|---|---|---|---|
| *n md*, n ms | intrj | v Qal impf 3ms | prep, n ms, ps 3ms | *n ms* | n ms |
| שְׁמֵי־קֶדֶם | הֵן | יִתֵּן | בְקוֹלוֹ | קוֹל | עֹז |
| shᵉmê-qedhem | hēn | yittēn | bᵉqôlô | qôl | ʻōz |
| the heavens of antiquity | behold | He gives | with his strength | a voice of | strength |

| | 5598.133 | 6010 | 3937, 435 | 6142, 3547 | 1375 | 6010 | 904, 8263 |
|---|---|---|---|---|---|---|---|
| | v Qal impv 2mp | n ms | prep, n mp | prep, pn | n fs, ps 3ms | cj, n ms, ps 3ms | prep, art, n mp |
| 34. | תְּנוּ | עֹז | לֵאלֹהִים | עַל־יִשְׂרָאֵל | גַּאֲוָתוֹ | וְעֻזּוֹ | בַּשְּׁחָקִים |
| | tᵉnû | ʻōz | lēʼlōhîm | ʻal-yisrāʼēl | gaʼăwāthô | weʻuzzô | bashshᵉchāqîm |
| | ascribe | strength | to God | over Israel | his majesty | and his strength | in the clouds |

| | 3486.255 | 435 | 4623, 4881 | 418 | 3547 | 2000 | 5598.151 |
|---|---|---|---|---|---|---|---|
| | v Niphal ptc ms | n mp | prep, n mp, ps 2ms | *n ms* | pn | pers pron | v Qal act ptc ms |
| 35. | נוֹרָא | אֱלֹהִים | מִמִּקְדָּשֶׁיךָ | אֵל | יִשְׂרָאֵל | הוּא | נֹתֵן |
| | nôrāʼ | ʼĕlōhîm | mimmiqŏddāshêkhā | ʼēl | yisrāʼēl | hûʼ | nōthēn |
| | fearful | O God | from your sanctuary | the God of | Israel | He | One Who gives |

| 6010 | 8925 | 3937, 6194 | 1313.155 | 435 | | 3937, 5514.351 |
|---|---|---|---|---|---|---|
| n ms | cj, n fp | prep, art, n ms | v Qal pass ptc ms | n mp | | prep, art, v Piel ptc ms |
| עֹז | וְתַעֲצֻמוֹת | לָעָם | בָּרוּךְ | אֱלֹהִים | 69:t | לַמְנַצֵּחַ |
| ʻōz | wethaʻătsumôth | lāʻām | bārûkh | ʼĕlōhîm | | lamnatstsēach |
| strength | and vitality | to the people | blessed | God | | to the director |

| 6142, 8236 | 3937, 1784 | | 3588.531 | 435 | 3706 | 971.116 | 4448 |
|---|---|---|---|---|---|---|---|
| prep, n mp | prep, pn | | v Hiphil impv 2ms, ps 1cs | n mp | cj | v Qal pf 3cp | n md |
| עַל־שֹׁשַׁנִּים | לְדָוִד | 1. | הוֹשִׁיעֵנִי | אֱלֹהִים | כִּי | בָאוּ | מַיִם |
| ʻal-shôshanîm | lᵉdhāwidh | | hôshîʻēnî | ʼĕlōhîm | kî | vāʼû | mayim |
| according to the lilies | of David | | save me | O God | because | they have come | waters |

| 5912, 5497 | | 2993.115 | 3223 | 4852 | 375 | 4772 | 971.115 |
|---|---|---|---|---|---|---|---|
| prep, n fs | | v Qal pf 1cs | prep, *n ms* | n fs | cj, *sub* | n ms | v Qal pf 1cs |
| עַד־נָפֶשׁ | 2. | טָבַעְתִּי | בִּיוֵן | מְצוּלָה | וְאֵין | מָעֳמָד | בָּאתִי |
| ʻadh-nāphesh | | ṭāvaʻttî | bîwēn | mᵉtsûlāh | weʼên | māʻămādh | bāʼthî |
| unto the throat | | I have sunk down | in mud | the deep | and there is not | a foothold | I have entered |

| 904, 4774, 4448 | 8119 | 8278.112 | | 3129.115 |
|---|---|---|---|---|
| prep, *n mp*, n md | cj, n fs | v Qal pf 3fs, ps 1cs | | v Qal pf 1cs |
| בְמַעֲמַקֵּי־מַיִם | וְשִׁבֹּלֶת | שְׁטָפָתְנִי | 3. | יָגַעְתִּי |
| vᵉmaʻămaqqê-mayim | wᵉshibbōleth | shᵉṭāphāthᵉnî | | yāghaʻttî |
| into the deep part of the waters | and the flood | it has flowed over me | | I have become weary |

| 904, 7410.141 | 2893.211 | 1671 | 3735.116 | 6084 | 3282.351 |
|---|---|---|---|---|---|
| prep, v Qal inf con, ps 1cs | v Niphal pf 3ms | n ms, ps 1cs | v Qal pf 3cp | n fd, ps 1cs | v Piel ptc ms |
| בְקָרְאִי | נִחַר | גְרוֹנִי | כָּלוּ | עֵינַי | מְיַחֵל |
| vᵉqārᵉʼî | nichar | gᵉrônî | kālû | ʻênay | mᵉyachēl |
| in my calling out | it is burning | my throat | they are failing | my eyes | from waiting |

| 3937, 435 | | 7525.116 | 4623, 8000 | 7513 | 7983.152 |
|---|---|---|---|---|---|
| prep, n mp, ps 1cs | | v Qal pf 3cp | prep, *n fp* | n ms, ps 1cs | v Qal act ptc mp, ps 1cs |
| לֵאלֹהָי | 4. | רַבּוּ | מִשַּׂעֲרוֹת | רֹאשִׁי | שֹׂנְאַי |
| lēʼlōhāy | | rabbû | missaʻărôth | rōʼshî | sōnᵉʼay |
| for my God | | they are more numerous | than the hairs of | my head | those who hate me |

**33. To him that rideth upon the heavens of heavens, which were of old; lo, he doth send out his voice, and that a mighty voice:** ... There he speaks, with a voice of power, *JB* ... utters his word in a voice of thunder, *Knox* ... Behold, his voice resounds, the voice of power, *NAB* ... Listen, His voice thunders mightily, *Beck*.

**34. Ascribe ye strength unto God: his excellency is over Israel, and his strength is in the clouds:** ... acknowledge the power of God; His majesty is over Israel and His power in the skies, *Beck* ... Pay honour to God, the God whose splendour rests over Israel, who holds dominion high among the clouds, *Knox* ... Confess the power of God!, *NAB* ... Announce that God is powerful, *NCV*.

**35. O God, thou art terrible out of thy holy places: the God of Israel is he that giveth strength and power unto his people. Blessed be God:** ... Awesome is God in his sanctuary, *JB* ... God, you are wonderful in your Temple, *NCV* ... you are to be feared in your holy place, *BB* ... Awe-inspiring art Thou, O God, *Berkeley*.

**69:t. To the chief Musician upon Shoshannim, A Psalm of David.**

**1. Save me, O God; for the waters are come in unto my soul:** ... waters come up to my lips, *Berkeley* ... waters come up to My neck, *Beck* ... water mounts to my chin, *Goodspeed* ... see how the waters close about me, shoulder-high, *Knox* ... waters have closed in on my very being, *JB*.

**2. I sink in deep mire, where there is no standing: I am come into deep waters, where the floods overflow me:** ... I am sinking in the deepest swamp and there is no firm ground, *JB* ... I am sinking deep in the mud, where foothold there is none, *Moffatt* ... there is nothing to stand on. I am in deep water, and the flood covers me, *NCV* ... flood overwhelms me, *NAB*.

**3. I am weary of my crying: my throat is dried: mine eyes fail while I wait for my God:** ... I am tired from calling for help; my throat is sore. My eyes are tired from waiting for God to help me, *NCV* ... I am worn out calling for help; my throat is parched. My eyes fail, looking for my God, *NIV* ... my throat is burning: my eyes are wasted with waiting, *BB* ... My throat is hoarse. My eyes are bleary looking for My God, *Beck* ... my eyes grow dim as I wait for God to help me, *NEB*.

---

transcendent majesty and eternal, universal sway. The psalmist had hymned the victory won when "God gave the word." Now he bids earth listen as "He gives his voice, a voice of strength," which moves and controls all creatures and events. Therefore, all nations are summoned to give strength to God, who gives all fulnesses of strength to his people. The Psalm closes with the utterance of the thought which has animated it throughout—that God's deeds for and in Israel are the manifestation for the world of his power and that these will one day lead all men to bless the God of Israel, Who shines out in dread majesty from the sanctuary, which is henceforth his abode forever.

***Psalm 69.*** *The Psalm falls into two equal parts (vv. 1–18 and 19–36). In the former part, three turns of thought or feeling may be traced: vv. 1–6 being mainly a cry for divine help, with plaintive spreading out of the psalmist's extremity of need; vv. 7–12 basing the prayer on the fact that his sufferings flow from his religion; and vv. 13–18 being a stream of petitions for deliverance, with continuous allusion to the description of his trials in vv. 1–6. The second part (vv. 19–36) begins with renewed description of the psalmist's affliction (vv. 19ff) and thence passes to invocation of God's justice on his foes (vv. 22–28), which takes the place of the direct petitions for deliverance in the first part. The whole closes with trustful anticipation of answers to prayer, which will call forth praise from ever-widening circles, first from the psalmist himself, then from the oppressed righteous, and finally from heaven, earth and sea.*

*The numerous citations of this Psalm in the NT have led many commentators to maintain its directly messianic character. But its confessions of sin and imprecations of vengeance are equally incompatible with that view. It is messianic as typical rather than as prophetic, exhibiting a history, whether of king, prophet, righteous man or personified nation, in which the same principles are at work as are manifest in their supreme energy and highest form in the Prince of righteous sufferers. But the correspondence of such a detail as giving gall and vinegar with the history of Jesus carries us beyond the region of types and is a witness that God's Spirit shaped the utterances of the psalmist for a purpose unknown to himself and worked in like manner on the rude soldiers, whose clumsy mockery and clumsy kindness fulfilled ancient words. There is surely something more here than coincidence or similarity between the experience of one righteous sufferer and another.*

**69:1–6.** The psalmist begins with metaphors in vv. 1f and translates these into grim prose in vv. 3f and then, with acknowledgment of sinfulness, cries for God's intervention in vv. 5f.

| 2703 | 6343.116 | 7059.552 | 342.152 | 8632 |
|---|---|---|---|---|
| adv | v Qal pf 3cp | v Hiphil ptc mp, ps 1cs | v Qal act ptc mp, ps 1cs | n ms |
| חִנָּם | עָצְמוּ | מַצְמִיתַי | אֹיְבַי | שֶׁקֶר |
| chinnām | 'ātsemû | matsmîthay | 'ōyevay | sheqer |
| without cause | they have become innumerable | those who destroy me | my enemies | lies |

| 866 | 3940, 1528.115 | 226 | 8178.525 | | 435 | 887 | 3156.113 |
|---|---|---|---|---|---|---|---|
| rel part | neg part, v Qal pf 1cs | adv | v Hiphil impf 1cs | **5.** | n mp | pers pron | v Qal pf 2ms |
| אֲשֶׁר | לֹא־גָזַלְתִּי | אָז | אָשִׁיב | | אֱלֹהִים | אַתָּה | יָדַעְתָּ |
| 'āsher | lō'-ghāzaltî | 'āz | 'āshîv | | 'ĕlōhîm | 'attāh | yādha'ttā |
| what | I did not steal | then | I will return | | O God | You | You have known |

| 3937, 198 | 846 | 4623 | 3940, 3701.216 | | 414, 991.126 |
|---|---|---|---|---|---|
| prep, n fs, ps 1cs | cj, n fp, ps 1cs | prep, ps 2ms | neg part, v Niphal pf 3cp | **6.** | adv, v Qal juss 3mp |
| לְאִוַּלְתִּי | וְאַשְׁמוֹתַי | מִמְּךָ | לֹא־נִכְחָדוּ | | אַל־יֵבֹשׁוּ |
| le'iwwaltî | we'ashmôthay | mimmekhā | lō'-nikhchādhû | | 'al-yēvōshû |
| my foolishness | and my guiltiness | from You | they are not hidden | | let them not be put to shame |

| 904 | 7245.152 | 112 | 3176 | 6893 | 414, 3757.226 |
|---|---|---|---|---|---|
| prep, ps 1cs | v Qal act ptc mp, ps 2ms | n mp, ps 1cs | pn | n fp | adv, v Niphal juss 3mp |
| בִי | קֹוֶיךָ | אֲדֹנָי | יְהוִה | צְבָאוֹת | אַל־יִכָּלְמוּ |
| vî | qōwêkhā | 'ădhōnāy | yehwih | tsevā'ôth | 'al-yikkālemû |
| by me | those who wait for You | my Lord | Yahweh | Hosts | do not let them be dishonored |

| 904 | 1272.352 | 435 | 3547 | | 3706, 6142 | 5558.115 | 2887 |
|---|---|---|---|---|---|---|---|
| prep, ps 1cs | v Piel ptc mp, ps 2ms | *n mp* | pn | **7.** | cj, prep, ps 2ms | v Qal pf 1cs | n fs |
| בִי | מְבַקְשֶׁיךָ | אֱלֹהֵי | יִשְׂרָאֵל | | כִּי־עָלֶיךָ | נָשָׂאתִי | חֶרְפָּה |
| vî | mevaqōshêkhā | 'ĕlōhê | yisrā'ēl | | kî-'ālêkhā | nāsā'thî | cherpāh |
| by me | those who seek You | the God of | Israel | | because of You | I have carried | disgrace |

| 3803.312 | 3759 | 6686 | | 2197.655 | 2030.115 | 3937, 250 | 5425 |
|---|---|---|---|---|---|---|---|
| v Piel pf 3fs | n fs | n mp, ps 1cs | **8.** | v Hophal ptc ms | v Qal pf 1cs | prep, n mp, ps 1cs | cj, n ms |
| כִּסְּתָה | כְלִמָּה | פָּנָי | | מוּזָר | הָיִיתִי | לְאֶחָי | וְנָכְרִי |
| kissethāh | khelimmāh | phānāy | | mûzār | hāyîthî | le'echāy | wenākherî |
| it has covered | dishonor | my face | | turned away | I have been | of my brothers | and a foreigner |

| 3937, 1158 | 525 | | 3706, 7352 | 1041 | 404.112 |
|---|---|---|---|---|---|
| prep, *n mp* | n fs, ps 1cs | **9.** | cj, *n fs* | n ms, ps 2ms | v Qal pf 3fs, ps 1cs |
| לִבְנֵי | אִמִּי | | כִּי־קִנְאַת | בֵּיתְךָ | אֲכָלָתְנִי |
| livnê | 'immî | | kî-qin'ath | bêthekhā | 'ăkhālāthenî |
| to the sons of | my mother | | because zeal for | your household | it has devoured me |

| 2887 | 2884.152 | 5489.116 | 6142 | | 1098.125 |
|---|---|---|---|---|---|
| cj, *n fp* | v Qal act ptc mp, ps 2ms | v Qal pf 3cp | prep, ps 1cs | **10.** | cj, v Qal impf 1cs |
| וְחֶרְפּוֹת | חוֹרְפֶיךָ | נָפְלוּ | עָלָי | | וָאֶבְכֶּה |
| wecherpôth | chôrphêkhā | nāphelû | 'ālāy | | wā'evkeh |
| and the disgrace of | those who taunt me | they have fallen | on me | | when I am weeping |

| 904, 6948 | 5497 | 2030.122 | 3937, 2887 | 3937 | | 5598.125 |
|---|---|---|---|---|---|---|
| prep, art, n ms | n fs, ps 1cs | cj, v Qal impf 3fs | prep, art, n fp | prep, ps 1cs | **11.** | cj, v Qal impf 1cs |
| בַצּוֹם | נַפְשִׁי | וַתְּהִי | לַחֲרָפוֹת | לִי | | וָאֶתְּנָה |
| vatstsôm | naphshî | wattehî | lachrāphôth | lî | | wā'ettenāh |
| with fasting | O my soul | then it will be | for the taunting | to me | | and I made |

| 3961 | 8012 | 2030.125 | 3937 | 3937, 5091 | | 7943.126 | 904 |
|---|---|---|---|---|---|---|---|
| n ms, ps 1cs | n ms | cj, v Qal impf 1cs | prep, ps 3mp | prep, n ms | **12.** | v Qal impf 3mp | prep, ps 1cs |
| לְבוּשִׁי | שָׂק | וָאֱהִי | לָהֶם | לְמָשָׁל | | יָשִׂיחוּ | בִי |
| levûshî | sāq | wā'ĕhî | lāhem | lemāshāl | | yāsîchû | vî |
| my clothes | sackcloth | and I became | to them | a proverb | | they ridicule | about me |

**4. They that hate me without a cause are more than the hairs of mine head: they that would destroy me, being mine enemies wrongfully, are mighty: then I restored that which I took not away:** ... They that hate me without a reason are more numerous than the hairs on my head. Those who wish to destroy me are powerful; *Berkeley* ... those who are against me, falsely desiring my destruction, are very strong, *BB* ... Those who seek to get rid of me are powerful, my treacherous enemies, *JB* ... I am no match for the oppressors that wrong me. Should I make amends to them, I, that never robbed them, *Knox* ... Must I restore what I did not steal, *NAB*.

**5. O God, thou knowest my foolishness; and my sins are not hid from thee:** ... thou knowest my rash doing, no fault of mine is hidden from thy sight, *Knox* ... you know what I have done wrong; I cannot hide my guilt from you, *NCV* ... my guilty deeds are not hidden from thee, *NEB* ... my wrongdoing is clear to you, *BB*.

**6. Let not them that wait on thee, O Lord GOD of hosts, be ashamed for my sake: let not those that seek thee be confounded for my sake, O God of Israel:** ... May they who seek you not be disgraced through me, *Anchor* ... let not those who are waiting for you be made low because of me, O God, *BB* ... May it never happen that those who seek Thee be brought to dishonor on my account, *Berkeley* ... Those who hope in you must not be made fools of because of me, *JB*.

**7. Because for thy sake I have borne reproach; shame hath covered my face:** ... For you, I carry this shame, and my face is covered with disgrace, *NCV* ... I endure scorn for your sake, *NIV* ... Because of you I have suffered abuse, and disgrace has covered, *Anchor* ... for your sake I bear insult, *NAB* ... Dishonor has covered my face, *NASB*.

**8. I am become a stranger unto my brethren, and an alien unto my mother's children:** ... strange to my brothers, and like a man from a far country, *BB* ... a foreigner to My mother's sons, *Beck* ... unknown to my own mother's son, *Fenton* ... an outcast among my own brethren, *Knox* ... estranged from my brothers, alienated from my own mother's sons, *JB*.

**9. For the zeal of thine house hath eaten me up; and the reproaches of them that reproached thee are fallen upon me:** ... My strong love for your Temple completely controls me. When people insult you, it hurts me, *NCV* ... Was it not jealousy for the honour of thy house that consumed me, *Knox* ... and insults directed against you fall on me, *JB* ... the insults of those who blaspheme you fall upon me, *NAB*.

**10. When I wept, and chastened my soul with fasting, that was to my reproach:** ... they make fun of me, *NCV* ... lay myself open to many reproaches, *NEB* ... endure scorn, *NIV* ... they insulted me, *NRSV*.

**11. I made sackcloth also my garment; and I became a proverb to them:** ... became the butt of their jokes, *Beck* ... became a laughingstock to them, *Berkeley* ... people make sport of me, *NIV* ... they said evil of me, *BB*.

---

The psalmist had to bear unjust charges and to make restitution of what he had never taken. Causeless hatred justified itself by false accusations, and innocence had but to bear silently and to save life at the expense of being robbed in the name of justice.

He turns from enemies to God, but his profession of innocence assumes a touching and unusual form. He does not, as might be expected, say, "Thou knowest my guiltlessness," but, "Thou knowest my foolishness." A true heart, while conscious of innocence in regard to men and of having done nothing to evoke their enmity, is, even in the act of searching itself, arrested by the consciousness of its many sins in God's sight and will confess these the more penitently because it stands upright before men and asserts its freedom from all crime against them. Insofar as men's hatred is God's instrument, it inflicts merited chastisement. That does not excuse men, but it needs to be acknowledged by the sufferer, if things are to be right between him and God. Then, after such confession, he can pray, as this psalmist does, that God's mercy may deliver him, so that others who, like him, wait on God may not be disheartened or swept from their confidence by the spectacle of his vain hopes and unanswered cries. The psalmist has a strong consciousness of his representative character and, as in so many other Psalms, thinks that his experience is of wide significance as a witness for God. This consciousness points to something special in his position, whether we find the speciality in his office or in the supposed personification of the nation or in poetic consciousness heightened by the sense of being an organ of God's Spirit.

**69:7–12.** In vv. 7–12, the prayer for deliverance is urged on the ground that the singer's sufferings are the result of his devotion. Psalm 44:13–22 may be compared, and Jer. 15:15 is an even closer parallel. Fasting and sackcloth are mentioned again together in Ps. 35:13, and Lam. 3:14 and Job 30:9 resemble v. 12b. Surrounded by a godless generation, the psalmist's earnestness of faith and concern

| 3553.152 | 8554 | 5234 | 8685.152 | 8336 |
|---|---|---|---|---|
| *v Qal act ptc mp* | n ms | cj, n fp | *v Qal act ptc mp* | n ms |
| יֹשְׁבֵי | שָׁעַר | וּנְגִינוֹת | שׁוֹתֵי | שֵׁכָר |
| yōshᵉvê | shā'ar | ûnᵉghînôth | shôthê | shēkhār |
| those who sit in | the gate | and stringed instruments | those who drink | strong drink |

| 13. | 603 | 8940, 3937 | 3176 | 6496 | 7814 | 435 |
|---|---|---|---|---|---|---|
| | cj, pers pron | n fs, ps 1cs, prep, ps 2ms | pn | *n fs* | n ms | n mp |
| | וַאֲנִי | תְפִלָּתִי־לְךָ | יְהוָה | עֵת | רָצוֹן | אֱלֹהִים |
| | wa'ănî | thᵉphillāthî-lᵉkhā | yᵉhwāh | 'ēth | rātsôn | 'ĕlōhîm |
| | and I | my prayer to You | O Yahweh | the time of | favor | O God |

| 904, 7524, 2721 | 6257.131 | 904, 583 | 3589 |
|---|---|---|---|
| prep, *n ms*, n ms, ps 2ms | v Qal impv 2ms, ps 1cs | prep, n fs | n ms, ps 2ms |
| בְּרָב־חַסְדֶּךָ | עֲנֵנִי | בֶּאֱמֶת | יִשְׁעֶךָ |
| bᵉrāv-chasdekhā | 'ănēnî | be'ĕmeth | yish'ekhā |
| in the abundance of your steadfast love | answer me | in truth | your salvation |

| 14. | 5522.531 | 4623, 3027 | 414, 2993.125 | 5522.225 |
|---|---|---|---|---|
| | v Hiphil impv 2ms, ps 1cs | prep, n ms | cj, adv, v Qal juss 1cs | v Niphal juss 1cs |
| | הַצִּילֵנִי | מִטִּיט | וְאַל־אֶטְבָּעָה | אִנָּצְלָה |
| | hatstsîlēnî | miṭṭîṭ | wᵉ'al-'eṭbā'āh | 'innātsᵉlāh |
| | rescue me | from the soggy mire | that I may not sink down | may I be rescued |

| 4623, 7983.152 | 4623, 4774, 4448 | 15. | 414, 8278.122 |
|---|---|---|---|
| prep, v Qal act ptc mp, ps 1cs | cj, prep, *n mp*, n mp | | adv, v Qal juss 3fs, ps 1cs |
| מִשֹּׂנְאַי | וּמִמַּעֲמַקֵּי־מָיִם | | אַל־תִּשְׁטְפֵנִי |
| missōnᵉ'ay | ûmimma'ămaqqê-māyim | | 'al-tishṭᵉphēnî |
| from those who hate me | and from the deep part of the waters | | do not let it flow over me |

| 8119 | 4448 | 414, 1142.122 | 4852 | 414, 335.122, 6142 | 908 |
|---|---|---|---|---|---|
| *n fs* | n md | cj, adv, v Qal juss 3fs, ps 1cs | n fs | cj, adv, v Qal juss 3fs, prep, ps 1cs | n fs |
| שִׁבֹּלֶת | מַיִם | וְאַל־תִּבְלָעֵנִי | מְצוּלָה | וְאַל־תֶּאְטַר־עָלַי | בְּאֵר |
| shibbōleth | mayim | wᵉ'al-tivlā'ēnî | mᵉtsûlāh | wᵉ'al-te'ṭar-'ālay | bᵉ'ēr |
| the flood of | waters | and may it not swallow me | the deep | and may it not close over me | the pit |

| 6552 | 16. | 6257.131 | 3176 | 3706, 3005 | 2721 |
|---|---|---|---|---|---|
| n ms, ps 3fs | | v Qal impv 2ms, ps 1cs | pn | cj, adj | n ms, ps 2ms |
| פִּיהָ | | עֲנֵנִי | יְהוָה | כִּי־טוֹב | חַסְדֶּךָ |
| pîāh | | 'ănēnî | yᵉhwāh | kî-ṭôv | chasdekhā |
| its mouth | | answer me | O Yahweh | because good | your steadfast love |

| 3626, 7524 | 7641 | 6680.131 | 420 | 17. | 414, 5846.523 |
|---|---|---|---|---|---|
| prep, *n ms* | n mp, ps 2ms | v Qal impv 2ms | prep, ps 1cs | | cj, adv, v Hiphil juss 2ms |
| כְּרֹב | רַחֲמֶיךָ | פְּנֵה | אֵלָי | | וְאַל־תַּסְתֵּר |
| kᵉrōv | rachmêkhā | pᵉnēh | 'ēlāy | | wᵉ'al-tastēr |
| according to the abundance of | your mercy | turn | to me | | and do not hide |

| 6686 | 4623, 5860 | 3706, 7140, 3937 | 4257.331 | 6257.131 |
|---|---|---|---|---|
| n mp, ps 2ms | prep, n ms, ps 2ms | cj, n ms, prep, ps 1cs | v Piel impv 2ms | v Qal impv 2ms, ps 1cs |
| פָּנֶיךָ | מֵעַבְדֶּךָ | כִּי־צַר־לִי | מַהֵר | עֲנֵנִי |
| pānêkhā | mē'avdekhā | kî-tsar-lî | mahēr | 'ănēnî |
| your face | from your servant | because adversity to me | hurry | answer me |

| 18. | 7414.131 | 420, 5497 | 1381.131 | 3937, 4775 | 342.152 |
|---|---|---|---|---|---|
| | v Qal impv 2ms | prep, n fs, ps 1cs | v Qal impv 2ms, ps 3fs | prep, prep | v Qal act ptc mp, ps 1cs |
| | קָרְבָה | אֶל־נַפְשִׁי | גְאָלָהּ | לְמַעַן | אֹיְבַי |
| | qārᵉvāh | 'el-naphshî | ghᵉ'ālāhh | lᵉma'an | 'ōyᵉvay |
| | be near | to my soul | redeem it | because of | my enemies |

**12. They that sit in the gate speak against me; and I was the song of the drunkards:** ... They make fun of me in public places, *NCV* ... song to those who are given to strong drink, *BB* ... Those who sit at the gate gossip about Me, and drunkards make up songs about Me, *Beck*.

**13. But as for me, my prayer is unto thee, O Lord, in an acceptable time: O God, in the multitude of thy mercy hear me, in the truth of thy salvation:** ... at an opportune moment, O God, in Thy plenteous grace, answer me with the truth of Thy salvation, *Berkeley* ... in your great kindness answer me, *Anchor* ... O God, give me an answer in your great mercy, for your salvation is certain, *BB*.

**14. Deliver me out of the mire, and let me not sink: let me be delivered from them that hate me, and out of the deep waters:** ... Rescue me from the mire before I sink in, *JB* ... let me be rescued from the muddy depths, so that no flood may carry me away, *NEB* ... With your faithful help rescue me, lest I be submerged by the mire. me be rescued from my Enemy, and from the bottomless waters, *Anchor*.

**15. Let not the waterflood overflow me, neither let the deep swallow me up, and let not the pit shut her mouth upon me:** ... Let not the floods sweep me away, And let not the Gulfs swallow down, *Fenton* ... Let me not be covered by the flowing waters; let not the deep waters go over my head, and let me not be shut up in the underworld, *BB* ... Keep the flood waters from overwhelming me, *Berkeley*.

**16. Hear me, O Lord; for thy lovingkindness is good: turn unto me according to the multitude of thy tender mercies:** ... Answer me, Yahweh, for your faithful love is generous, *JB* ... Listen to me, Lord, of thy gracious mercy, look down upon me in the abundance of thy pity, *Knox* ... Answer me, O Lord, for bounteous is your kindness; in your great mercy turn toward me, *NAB*.

**17. And hide not thy face from thy servant; for I am in trouble: hear me speedily:** ... Do not hide from me, your servant, I am in trouble. Hurry to help me!, *NCV* ... I am in distress; answer me quickly, *NASB* ... Haste to answer for I am in grief, *Fenton*.

**18. Draw nigh unto my soul, and redeem it: deliver me because of mine enemies:** ... Come to my side, redeem me, ransom me because of my enemies, *JB* ... Draw near in my distress, and grant deliverance; relieve me, so hard pressed by my enemies, *Knox* ... come to me, rescue my life, set me in safety from my foes, *Moffatt*.

---

for God's honor made him an object of dislike, a target for drunken ridicule. These broke the strong ties of kindred and acted as separating forces more strongly than brotherhood did, as a uniting one. "Zeal of thine house" presupposes the existence of the Temple and also either its neglect or its desecration. That sunken condition of the sanctuary distressed the psalmist more than personal calamity, and it was the departure of Israel from God that made him clothe himself in sackcloth and fast and weep. But so far had deterioration gone that his mourning and its cause supplied materials for tipsy mirth, and his name became a byword and a butt for malicious gossip. The whole picture is that of the standing experience of the godly among the godless. The perfect example of devotion and communion had to pass through these waters where they ran deepest and chilliest, but all who have his Spirit have their share of the same fate.

**69:13–18.** The last division of this first part (vv. 13–18) begins by setting in strong contrast the psalmist's prayer and the drunkard's song. He is sure that his cry will be heard, so he calls the present time "an acceptable time" and appeals, as often in the Psalter, to the multitude of God's steadfast love and the faithfulness of his promise of salvation. Such a pleading with God on the ground of his manifested character is heard in vv. 13, 16, thus enclosing the prayer for deliverance in a wrapping of reminders to God of his own name. The petitions here echo the description of peril in the former part—mire and watery depths—and add another kindred image in that of the "pit shutting her mouth" over the suppliant. He is plunged in a deep dungeon, well-shaped; and if a stone is rolled on to its opening, his last gleam of daylight will be gone, and he will be buried alive. Beautifully do the pleas from God's character and those from the petitioner's sore need alternate, the latter predominating in vv. 17f. His thoughts pass from his own desperate condition to God's mercy and from God's mercy to his own condition, and he has the reward of faith in that he finds in his straits reasons for his assurance that this is a time of favor, as well as pleas to urge with God. They make the black backing which turns his soul into a mirror, reflecting God's promises in its trust.

**69:19–21.** The second part of the Psalm (vv. 19–36) has, like the former, three main divisions. The first of these, like vv. 1–6, is mainly a renewed spreading before God of the psalmist's trouble (vv. 19–21). He speaks no more of mire

| 6540.131 | | 887 | 3156.113 | 2887 | 1350 | 3759 |
|---|---|---|---|---|---|---|
| v Qal impv 2ms, ps 1cs | **19.** | pers pron | v Qal pf 2ms | n fs, ps 1cs | cj, n fs, ps 1cs | cj, n fs, ps 1cs |
| פְּדֵנִי | | אַתָּה | יָדַעְתָּ | חֶרְפָּתִי | וּבָשְׁתִּי | וּכְלִמָּתִי |
| pedhênî | | 'attāh | yādha'āttā | cherpāthî | ûvāshettî | ûkhelimmāthî |
| ransom me | | You | You have known | my disgrace | and my shame | and my dishonor |

| 5224 | 3725, 7173.152 | | 2887 | 8132.112 | 3949 | 5316.125 |
|---|---|---|---|---|---|---|
| prep, ps 2ms | *adj*, v Qal act ptc mp, ps 1cs | **20.** | n fs | v Qal pf 3fs | n ms, ps 1cs | cj, v Qal impf 1cs |
| נֶגְדְּךָ | כָּל־צוֹרְרָי | | חֶרְפָּה | שָׁבְרָה | לִבִּי | וָאָנוּשָׁה |
| neghdekhā | kol-tsôrerāy | | cherpāh | shāverāh | libbî | wā'ānûshāh |
| before You | all my adversaries | | disgrace | it has broken | my heart | yes I was deceived |

| 7245.325 | 3937, 5290.141 | 375 | 3937, 5341.352 | 3940 |
|---|---|---|---|---|
| cj, v Piel impf 1cs | prep, v Qal inf con | cj, sub | cj, prep, art, v Piel ptc mp | cj, neg part |
| וָאֲקַוֶּה | לָנוּד | וָאַיִן | וְלַמְנַחֲמִים | וְלֹא |
| wā'ăqawweh | lānûdh | wā'ayin | welamnachmîm | welō' |
| and I hoped | for shaking of the head | but there was not | indeed for comforters | but not |

| 4834.115 | | 5598.126 | 904, 1295 | 7514 | 3937, 7040 | 8615.526 |
|---|---|---|---|---|---|---|
| v Qal pf 1cs | **21.** | cj, v Qal impf 3mp | prep, n fs, ps 1cs | n ms | cj, prep, n ms, ps 1cs | v Hiphil impf 3mp, ps 1cs |
| מָצָאתִי | | וַיִּתְּנוּ | בְּבָרוּתִי | רֹאשׁ | וְלִצְמָאִי | יַשְׁקוּנִי |
| mātsā'thî | | wayyittenû | bevārûthî | rō'sh | welitsmā'î | yashqûnî |
| I found | | and they gave | with my food | poison | and for my thirst | they gave me to drink |

| 2663 | | 2030.121, 8374 | 3937, 6686 | 3937, 6583 | 3937, 8361 | 3937, 6583 |
|---|---|---|---|---|---|---|
| n ms | **22.** | v Qal juss 3ms, n ms, ps 3mp | prep, n mp, ps 3mp | prep, n ms | cj, prep, n mp | prep, n ms |
| חֹמֶץ | | יְהִי־שֻׁלְחָנָם | לִפְנֵיהֶם | לְפָח | וְלִשְׁלוֹמִים | לְמוֹקֵשׁ |
| chōmets | | yehî-shulchānām | liphnêhem | lephāch | welishlômîm | lemôqēsh |
| vinegar | | let their table become | before them | for a net | and for safety | for a snare |

| | 2931.127 | 6084 | 4623, 7495.141 | 5158 | 8878 |
|---|---|---|---|---|---|
| **23.** | v Qal juss 3fp | n fd, ps 3mp | prep, v Qal inf con | cj, n md, ps 3mp | adv |
| | תֶּחְשַׁכְנָה | עֵינֵיהֶם | מֵרְאוֹת | וּמָתְנֵיהֶם | תָּמִיד |
| | techăshakhnāh | 'ênêhem | mēre'ôth | ûmāthenêhem | tāmîdh |
| | may they become dark | their eyes | from seeing | and their loins | continually |

| 4726.531 | | 8581.131, 6142 | 2279 | 2841 | 653 |
|---|---|---|---|---|---|
| v Hiphil impv 2ms | **24.** | v Qal impv 2ms, prep, ps 3mp | n ms, ps 2ms | cj, *n ms* | n ms, ps 2ms |
| הַמְעַד | | שְׁפָךְ־עֲלֵיהֶם | זַעְמֶךָ | וַחֲרוֹן | אַפְּךָ |
| ham'adh | | shephākh-'ălêhem | za'ămekhā | wachrôn | 'appekhā |
| cause to shake | | pour out on them | your indignation | and the wrath of | your anger |

| 5560.521 | | 2030.122, 3029 | 8460.257 | 904, 164 | 414, 2030.121 |
|---|---|---|---|---|---|
| v Hiphil juss 3ms, ps 3mp | **25.** | v Qal juss 3fs, n fs, ps 3mp | v Niphal ptc fs | prep, n mp, ps 3mp | adv, v Qal juss 3ms |
| יַשִּׂיגֵם | | תְּהִי־טִירָתָם | נְשַׁמָּה | בְּאָהֳלֵיהֶם | אַל־יְהִי |
| yassîghēm | | tehî-ṭîrāthām | neshammāh | be'āhelêhem | 'al-yehî |
| let it overtake them | | let their encampment be | desolate | in their tents | may he not be |

| 3553.151 | | 3706, 887 | 866, 5409.513 | 7579.116 |
|---|---|---|---|---|
| v Qal act ptc ms | **26.** | cj, pers pron | rel part, v Hiphil pf 2ms | v Qal pf 3cp |
| יֹשֵׁב | | כִּי־אַתָּה | אֲשֶׁר־הִכִּיתָ | רָדָפוּ |
| yōshēv | | kî-'attāh | 'ăsher-hikkîthā | rādhāphû |
| a dweller | | because You | whom You have struck down | they have pursued |

| 420, 4480 | 2592 | 5807.326 | | 5598.131, 5988 |
|---|---|---|---|---|
| cj, prep, *n ms* | n mp, ps 2ms | v Piel impf 3mp | **27.** | v Qal impv 2ms, n ms |
| וְאֶל־מַכְאוֹב | חֲלָלֶיךָ | יְסַפֵּרוּ | | תְּנָה־עָוֹן |
| we'el-makh'ôv | chălālêkhā | yesappērû | | tenāh-'āwōn |
| and about the pain of | your slain ones | they will recount | | ascribe guilt |

**19. Thou hast known my reproach, and my shame, and my dishonour: mine adversaries are all before thee:** ... Thou knowest what reproaches I bear, all my anguish is seen by thee, *NEB* ... You know how I'm insulted, put to shame, and disgraced—My enemies are all before You, *Beck* ... Every one of my oppressors is known to you, *JB*.

**20. Reproach hath broken my heart; and I am full of heaviness: and I looked for some to take pity, but there was none; and for comforters, but I found none:** ... Reproach has broken my heart, and I feel depressed, *Berkeley* ... Insult has broken my heart past cure, *JB* ... Insult has broken my heart, and I am weak, I looked for sympathy, but there was none, *NAB* ... I made a search for some to have pity on me, but there was no one, *BB*.

**21. They gave me also gall for my meat; and in my thirst they gave me vinegar to drink:** ... They gave me poison for my food; and bitter wine for my drink, *BB* ... When I hungered,—they opium gave,—When I thirsted,—sharp acid to drink, *Fenton* ... For food men hand me poisonous drugs, and vinegar, *Moffatt*.

**22. Let their table become a snare before them: and that which should have been for their welfare, let it become a trap:** ... Let their table before them be for their destruction, *BB* ... Make their table before them a trap, A punishment to them, and snare, *Fenton* ... May the table they spread be their own ruin, *Moffatt* ... Let their own feasts cause their ruin, *NCV*.

**23. Let their eyes be darkened, that they see not; and make their loins continually to shake:** ... May their eyes grow too dim to see, and make their thighs continually shake, *Anchor* ... Let their eyes be blind so that they may not see; let their bodies for ever be shaking, *BB* ... Let their eyes be obscured from the light, *Fenton*.

**24. Pour out thine indignation upon them, and let thy wrathful anger take hold of them:** ... Let your curse come on them; let the heat of your wrath overtake them, *BB* ... Vent your fury on them, let your burning anger overtake them, *JB* ... Pour out your wrath upon them, *NAB* ... let your raging fury overtake them, *Anchor*.

**25. Let their habitation be desolate; and let none dwell in their tents:** ... Let their Castles be wrecks, *Fenton* ... Give their houses to destruction, and let there be no one in their tents, *BB* ... May their camp turn to ruins, *Beck* ... In their tents may there be no inhabitant, *Goodspeed*.

**26. For they persecute him whom thou hast smitten; and they talk to the grief of those whom thou hast wounded:** ... for hounding someone you had already stricken, for redoubling the pain of one you had wounded, *JB* ... they kept after him whom you smote, and added to the pain of him you wounded, *NAB* ... They chase after those you have hurt, *NCV*.

**27. Add iniquity unto their iniquity: and let them not come into thy righteousness:** ... Add guilt to their guilt, *Goodspeed* ... Let their punishment be increased, *BB* ... Give them the punishment their sin deserves. Exclude them from Your

---

and flood, but we hear the moan of a broken heart and that wail which sounds sad across the centuries and wakes echoes in many solitary hearts. The psalmist's eyes had failed, while he looked upward for a God whose coming seemed slow, but they had looked yet more wearily and vainly for human pity and comforters and found none. Instead of pity, He had received only aggravation of misery. Such seems to be the force of giving gall for food and vinegar to his thirst. The precise meaning of the word rendered "gall" (HED #7514) is uncertain, but the general idea of something bitter is sufficient. That was all that his foes would give Him when hungry. Vinegar, which would make Him more thirsty still, was all that they offered for his thirst. According to Matthew, the potion of wine (or vinegar) "mingled with gall" was offered to and rejected by Jesus before being fastened to the cross. He does not expressly quote the Psalm, but probably refers to it. John, on the other hand, does tell us that Jesus, "that the scripture might be fulfilled, said, I thirst" and sees its fulfillment in the kindly act of moistening the parched lips.

**69:22–28.** But the immediately succeeding section warns us against pushing the messianic character of the Psalm too far, for these fearful imprecations cannot have any analogies in Christ's words (vv. 22–28). The form of the wish in "Let their table become a snare" is explained by remembering that the Eastern table was often a leather flap laid on the ground, which the psalmist desires may start up as a snare and close upon the feasters as they sit securely around it. Disease, continual terror, dimmed eyes, paralyzed or quaking loins, ruin falling on their homes, and desolation round their encampment so that they have no descendants are the least of the evils invoked. The psalmist's desires go further than this material disaster. He prays that iniquity may be added to their iniquity, i.e., that they may be held guilty of sin after sin, and that they may have no portion in God's righteousness, i.e., in the gifts which flow from his adherence to his Covenant.

| 6142, 5988 | 414, 971.126 | 904, 6930 |
|---|---|---|
| prep, n ms, ps 3mp | cj, adv, v Qal juss 3mp | prep, n fs, ps 2ms |
| עַל־עֲוֺנָם | וְאַל־יָבֹאוּ | בְּצִדְקָתֶךָ |
| 'al-'ăwōnām | we'al-yāvō'û | betsidhqāthekhā |
| concerning their transgression | that they might not enter | into your righteousness |

| | 4364.226 | 4623, 5809 | 2522 | 6196 | 6926 |
|---|---|---|---|---|---|
| **28.** | v Niphal juss 3mp | prep, *n ms* | n mp | cj, prep | n mp |
| | יִמָּחוּ | מִסֵּפֶר | חַיִּים | וְעִם | צַדִּיקִים |
| | yimmāchû | missēpher | chayyîm | we'im | tsaddîqîm |
| | let them be wiped off | from the book of | life | and with | the righteous |

| 414, 3918.226 | | 603 | 6270 | 3628.151 | 3568 | 435 |
|---|---|---|---|---|---|---|
| adv, v Niphal juss 3mp | **29.** | cj, pers pron | adj | cj, v Qal act ptc ms | n fs, ps 2ms | n mp |
| אַל־יִכָּתֵבוּ | | וַאֲנִי | עָנִי | וְכוֹאֵב | יְשׁוּעָתְךָ | אֱלֹהִים |
| 'al-yikkāthēvû | | wa'ănî | 'ānî | wekhô'ēv | yeshû'āthekhā | 'ĕlōhîm |
| let them not be written | | and I | afflicted | and one in pain | your salvation | O God |

| 7891.323 | | 2054.325 | 8428, 435 | 904, 8302 | 1461.325 |
|---|---|---|---|---|---|
| v Piel juss 2ms, ps 1cs | **30.** | v Piel juss 1cs | *n ms*, n mp | prep, n ms | cj, v Piel juss 1cs, ps 3ms |
| תְּשַׂגְּבֵנִי | | אֲהַלְלָה | שֵׁם־אֱלֹהִים | בְּשִׁיר | וַאֲגַדְּלֶנּוּ |
| tesaggevēnî | | 'ăhalelāh | shēm-'ĕlōhîm | beshîr | wa'ăghaddelennû |
| make me inaccessible | | let me praise | the name of God | with a song | and let me magnify Him |

| 904, 8756 | | 3296.122 | 3937, 3176 | 4623, 8228 | 6749 | 7450.551 |
|---|---|---|---|---|---|---|
| prep, n fs | **31.** | cj, v Qal impf 3fs | prep, pn | prep, n ms | n ms | v Hiphil ptc ms |
| בְתוֹדָה | | וְתִיטַב | לַיהוָה | מִשּׁוֹר | פָּר | מַקְרִן |
| vethôdhāh | | wethîṭav | layhwāh | mishshôr | pār | maqrin |
| with thanksgiving | | and it will seem better | to Yahweh | than an ox | a bull | having horns |

| 6788.551 | | 7495.116 | 6262 | 7975.126 | 1938.152 | 435 |
|---|---|---|---|---|---|---|
| v Hiphil ptc ms | **32.** | v Qal pf 3cp | n mp | v Qal juss 3mp | *v Qal act ptc mp* | n mp |
| מַפְרִיס | | רָאוּ | עֲנָוִים | יִשְׂמָחוּ | דֹּרְשֵׁי | אֱלֹהִים |
| maphrîs | | rā'û | 'ănāwîm | yismāchû | dōreshê | 'ĕlōhîm |
| having hooves | | they have seen | the lowly | may they be glad | those who search for | God |

| 2513.121 | 3949 | | 3706, 8471.151 | 420, 33 | 3176 |
|---|---|---|---|---|---|
| cj, v Qal juss 3ms | n ms, ps 2mp | **33.** | cj, v Qal act ptc ms | prep, n mp | pn |
| וִיחִי | לְבַבְכֶם | | כִּי־שֹׁמֵעַ | אֶל־אֶבְיוֹנִים | יְהוָה |
| wîchî | levavkhem | | kî-shōmēa' | 'el-'evyônîm | yehwāh |
| and may it revive | your heart | | because One Who listens | to the needy | Yahweh |

| 881, 629 | 3940 | 995.111 | | 2054.326 | 8452 | 800 |
|---|---|---|---|---|---|---|
| cj, do, n mp, ps 3ms | neg part | v Qal pf 3ms | **34.** | v Piel juss 3mp, ps 3ms | n md | cj, n fs |
| וְאֶת־אֲסִירָיו | לֹא | בָזָה | | יְהַלְלוּהוּ | שָׁמַיִם | וָאָרֶץ |
| we'eth-'ăsîrāv | lō' | vāzāh | | yehalelûhû | shāmayim | wā'ārets |
| and his prisoners | not | He despises | | may they praise Him | the heavens | and the earth |

| 3328 | 3725, 7718.151 | 904 | | 3706 | 435 | 3588.521 | 6995 |
|---|---|---|---|---|---|---|---|
| n mp | cj, *adj*, v Qal act ptc ms | prep, ps 3mp | **35.** | cj | n mp | v Hiphil impf 3ms | pn |
| יַמִּים | וְכָל־רֹמֵשׂ | בָּם | | כִּי | אֱלֹהִים | יוֹשִׁיעַ | צִיּוֹן |
| yammîm | wekhol-rōmēs | bām | | kî | 'ĕlōhîm | yôshîa' | tsîyôn |
| the seas | and everything moving | in them | | because | God | He will save | Zion |

| 1161.121 | 6111 | 3171 | 3553.116 | 8427 | 3542.126 |
|---|---|---|---|---|---|
| cj, v Qal impf 3ms | *n fp* | pn | cj, v Qal pf 3cp | adv | cj, v Qal impf 3mp, ps 3fs |
| וְיִבְנֶה | עָרֵי | יְהוּדָה | וְיָשְׁבוּ | שָׁם | וִירֵשׁוּהָ |
| weyivneh | 'ārê | yehûdhāh | weyāshevû | shām | wîrēshûāh |
| and He will build | the cities of | Judah | and they will dwell | there | and they will possess it |

righteousness, *Beck* ... let them not enter into Thy justification, *Berkeley*.

**28. Let them be blotted out of the book of the living, and not be written with the righteous:** ... Wipe their names from the book of life, and do not list them with those who do what is right, *NCV* ... erase them from the book of life, do not enrol them among the upright, *JB* ... and never be written among the just, *Knox*.

**29. But I am poor and sorrowful: let thy salvation, O God, set me up on high:** ... I am afflicted and in pain, *Anchor* ... let me be lifted up by your salvation, O Lord, *BB* ... I am suffering and in pain. By Your saving power lift Me to a safe height, O God, *Beck*.

**30. I will praise the name of God with a song, and will magnify him with thanksgiving:** ... I will extol him by thanksgiving, *JB* ... and I will glorify him with thanksgiving, *NAB* ... and will honor him by giving thanks, *NCV*.

**31. This also shall please the LORD better than an ox or bullock that hath horns and hoofs:** ... That will please the LORD more than offering him cattle, more than sacrificing a bull with horns and hoofs, *NCV* ... will please the LORD more than the offering of a bull, a young bull with horn and cloven hoof, *NEB* ... This will be more pleasing to the Lord than an ox, or a young ox of full growth, *BB*.

**32. The humble shall see this, and be glad: and your heart shall live that seek God:** ... The poor will see it and be glad: you who are lovers of God, let your hearts have life, *BB* ... Look, you who are oppressed and rejoice; you who go to God for help, may your spirits be refreshed, *Beck* ... you who seek God, let your heart revive!, *Berkeley* ... Let your courage revive, you who seek God, *JB*.

**33. For the LORD heareth the poor, and despiseth not his prisoners:** ... God listens to the poor, he has never scorned his captive people, *JB* ... Lord listens to the prayer of the destitute, *Knox* ... Eternal listens to a life in need, *Moffatt* ... LORD hears the poor, and his own who are in bonds he spurns not, *NAB*.

**34. Let the heaven and earth praise him, the seas, and every thing that moveth therein:** ... Heavens, and the Earth give Him thanks, *Fenton* ... sky and earth praise him, *NEB* ... the seas and all that stirs in them, *Anchor*.

**35. For God will save Zion, and will build the cities of Judah: that they may dwell there, and have it in possession:** ... God delivers Zion, *Goodspeed* ... people will live there on their own land, *JB* ... the cities of Juda will rise from their ruins, *Knox*.

---

The climax of all these maledictions is the awful wish that the persecutors may be blotted out of the book of life or of the living. To blot out these names is not only to kill, but to exclude from the national community and so from all the privileges of the people of God. The psalmist desires for his foes the accumulation of all the ills that flesh is heir to, the extirpation of their families and their absolute exclusion from the company of the living and the righteous. It is impossible to bring such utterances into harmony with the teachings of Jesus, and the attempt to vindicate them ignores plain facts and does violence to plain words.

**69:29–36.** The Psalm ends with glad anticipations of deliverance and vows of thanksgiving. The psalmist is sure that God's salvation will lift him high above his enemies and as sure that then he will be as grateful as he is now earnest in prayer and surest of all that his thankful voice will sound sweeter in God's ear than any sacrifice would smell in his nostrils. There is no contempt of sacrifices expressed in "horned and hoofed," but simply the idea of maturity which fits the animal to be offered.

The single voice of praise will be caught up, the singer thinks, by a great chorus of those who would have been struck dumb with confusion if his prayer had not been answered (v. 6) and who, in like manner, are gladdened by seeing his deliverance. The grace bestowed on one brings thanksgivings from many, which overflow to the glory of God. The sudden transition in v. 32b to direct address to the seekers after God, as if they stood beside the solitary singer, gives vividness to the anticipation. The insertion of "behold" is warranted, and tells what revives the beholders' hearts. The seekers after God feel the pulse of a quicker life throbbing, when they see the wonders wrought through prayer. The singer's thoughts go beyond his own deliverance to that of Israel. "His servants" is most naturally understood as referring to the exiled nation. And this wider manifestation of God's restoring power will evoke praise from a wider circle, even from heaven, earth and sea. The circumstances contemplated in vv. 33–36 are evidently those of a captivity. God's people are in bondage, the cities of Judah are in ruins, the inhabitants scattered far from their homes. The only reason for taking the closing verses as being a liturgical addition is unwillingness to admit exilic or post-exilic Psalms. But these verses cannot be fairly interpreted without recognizing that they presuppose that Israel is in bondage, or at least on the verge of it. The circum-

| 36. | 2320 | 5860 | 5336.126 | 154.152 | 8428 |
|---|---|---|---|---|---|
| | cj, *n ms* | n mp, ps 3ms | v Qal impf 3mp, ps 3fs | cj, *v Qal act ptc mp* | n ms, ps 3ms |
| | וְזֶרַע | עֲבָדָיו | יִנְחָלוּהָ | וְאֹהֲבֵי | שְׁמוֹ |
| | wᵉzeraʻ | ʻăvādhâv | yinchālûāh | wᵉ'ōhᵉvê | shᵉmô |
| | and the descendants of | his servants | they will inherit it | and those who love | his name |

| 8331.126, 904 | 70:t | 3937, 5514.351 | 3937, 1784 | 3937, 2226.541 | 1. | 435 |
|---|---|---|---|---|---|---|
| v Qal impf 3mp, prep, ps 3fs | | prep, art, v Piel ptc ms | prep, pn | prep, v Hiphil inf con | | n mp |
| יִשְׁכְּנוּ־בָהּ | | לַמְנַצֵּחַ | לְדָוִד | לְהַזְכִּיר | | אֱלֹהִים |
| yishkᵉnû-vāhh | | lamnatstsēach | lᵉdhāwidh | lᵉhazkîr | | 'ĕlōhîm |
| they will remain in it | | to the director | of David | to cause to remember | | O God |

| 3937, 5522.541 | 3176 | 3937, 6046 | 2456.131 | 2. | 991.126 |
|---|---|---|---|---|---|
| prep, v Hiphil inf con, ps 1cs | pn | prep, n fs, ps 1cs | v Qal impv 2ms | | v Qal juss 3mp |
| לְהַצִּילֵנִי | יְהוָה | לְעֶזְרָתִי | חוּשָׁה | | יֵבֹשׁוּ |
| lᵉhatstsîlēnî | yᵉhwāh | lᵉʻezrāthî | chûshāh | | yēvōshû |
| to rescue me | O Yahweh | for my help | hurry | | may they be ashamed |

| 2763.126 | 1272.352 | 5497 | 5657.226 | 268 |
|---|---|---|---|---|
| cj, v Qal juss 3mp | *v Piel ptc mp* | n fs, ps 1cs | v Niphal juss 3mp | adv |
| וְיַחְפְּרוּ | מְבַקְשֵׁי | נַפְשִׁי | יִסֹּגוּ | אָחוֹר |
| wᵉyachpᵉrû | mᵉvaqŏshê | naphshî | yissōghû | 'āchôr |
| indeed may they be ashamed | those who seek | my life | and may they retreat | back |

| 3757.226 | 2760 | 7750 | 3. | 8178.126 |
|---|---|---|---|---|
| cj, v Niphal juss 3mp | *adj* | n fs, ps 1cs | | v Qal juss 3mp |
| וְיִכָּלְמוּ | חֲפֵצֵי | רָעָתִי | | יָשׁוּבוּ |
| wᵉyikkālᵉmû | chăphētsê | rāʻāthî | | yāshûvû |
| and let them be dishonored | the desirous of | my disaster | | may they return |

| 6142, 6358 | 1350 | 569.152 | 1955 | 1955 | 4. | 7919.126 |
|---|---|---|---|---|---|---|
| prep, *n ms* | n fp, ps 3mp | art, v Qal act ptc mp | intrj | intrj | | v Qal juss 3mp |
| עַל־עֵקֶב | בָּשְׁתָּם | הָאֹמְרִים | הֶאָח | הֶאָח | | יָשִׂישׂוּ |
| ʻal-ʻēqev | bāshᵉttām | hā'ōmᵉrîm | he'āch | he'āch | | yāsîsû |
| because of the result of | their shame | those saying | aha | aha | | may they rejoice |

| 7975.126 | 904 | 3725, 1272.352 | 569.126 | 8878 |
|---|---|---|---|---|
| cj, v Qal juss 3mp | prep, ps 2ms | *adj*, v Piel ptc mp, ps 2ms | cj, v Qal juss 3mp | n ms |
| וְיִשְׂמְחוּ | בְּךָ | כָּל־מְבַקְשֶׁיךָ | וְיֹאמְרוּ | תָמִיד |
| wᵉyismᵉchû | bᵉkhā | kol-mᵉvaqŏshêkhā | wᵉyō'mᵉrû | thāmîdh |
| and may they be glad | in You | all those seeking You | and may they say | continually |

| 1461.121 | 435 | 154.152 | 3568 | 5. | 603 | 6270 | 33 |
|---|---|---|---|---|---|---|---|
| v Qal impf 3ms | n mp | *v Qal act ptc mp* | n fs, ps 2ms | | cj, pers pron | adj | cj, adj |
| יִגְדַּל | אֱלֹהִים | אֹהֲבֵי | יְשׁוּעָתֶךָ | | וַאֲנִי | עָנִי | וְאֶבְיוֹן |
| yighdal | 'ĕlōhîm | 'ōhĕvê | yᵉshûʻāthekhā | | wa'ănî | ʻānî | wᵉ'evyôn |
| He is great | God | those who love | your salvation | | but I | afflicted | and needy |

| 435 | 2456.131, 3937 | 6039 | 6647.351 | 887 | 3176 |
|---|---|---|---|---|---|
| n mp | v Qal impv 2ms, prep, ps 1cs | n ms, ps 1cs | cj, v Piel ptc ms, ps 1cs | pers pron | pn |
| אֱלֹהִים | חוּשָׁה־לִּי | עֶזְרִי | וּמְפַלְטִי | אַתָּה | יְהוָה |
| 'ĕlōhîm | chûshāh-lî | ʻezrî | ûmᵉphaltî | 'attāh | yᵉhwāh |
| O God | hurry to me | my Help | and the One Who sets me free | You | Yahweh |

| 414, 310.323 | 71:1 | 904, 3176 | 2725.115 | 414, 991.125 |
|---|---|---|---|---|
| adv, v Piel juss 2ms | | prep, ps 2ms, pn | v Qal pf 1cs | adv, v Qal juss 1cs |
| אַל־תְּאַחַר | | בְּךָ־יְהוָה | חָסִיתִי | אַל־אֵבוֹשָׁה |
| 'al-tᵉ'achar | | bᵉkhā-yᵉhwāh | chāsîthî | 'al-'ēvôshāh |
| do not delay | | in You O Yahweh | I have sought refuge | let me not be ashamed |

**36. The seed also of his servants shall inherit it: and they that love his name shall dwell therein:** ... The offspring of His servants shall inherit it, and they who love His name shall abide in it, *Berkeley* ... the descendants of his servants shall inherit it, and those who love his name shall inhabit it, *NAB* ... those who love him will live there, *NCV*.

**70:t. To the chief Musician, A Psalm of David, to bring to remembrance.**

**1. Make haste, O God, to deliver me; make haste to help me, O Lord:** ... O God, rescue me, *Anchor* ... come quickly and help me, *JB* ... come quickly and save me. Lord, hurry to help me, *NCV*.

**2. Let them be ashamed and confounded that seek after my soul: let them be turned backward, and put to confusion, that desire my hurt:** ... Let those who are trying to kill me be ashamed and disgraced, *NCV* ... be humiliated and put to confusion, *Anchor* ... be disappointed and ashamed, and those who delight in harming me turn back in disgrace, *Beck*.

**3. Let them be turned back for a reward of their shame that say, Aha, aha:** ... Let them shrink away covered with shame, those who say, *JB* ... Let those who make fun of me stop because of their shame, *NCV* ... let those who cry 'Hurrah!' at my downfall turn back at the shame they incur, *NEB*.

**4. Let all those that seek thee rejoice and be glad in thee: and let such as love thy salvation say continually, Let God be magnified:** ... Let God be exalted, *NIV* ... Let all those who are looking for you be glad and have joy in you, *BB* ... may all who look to You for help find joy and delight in You. May those who love You for saving them always say, "God is great!", *Beck* ... may they continually say, "Great is God," who love thy deliverance, *Goodspeed*.

**5. But I am poor and needy: make haste unto me, O God: thou art my help and my deliverer; O Lord, make no tarrying:** ... I am afflicted and poor; *NAB* ... I am poor and helpless; God, hurry to me, *NCV* ... God haste to my aid, and relief, *Fenton*.

**71:1. In thee, O Lord, do I put my trust: let me never be put to confusion:** ... let me never be put to shame, *KJVII* ... let me not be humiliated, *Anchor* ... have I put my hope, *BB* ... don't ever let me be disgraced, *Beck*.

---

stances of Jeremiah's life and times coincide closely with those of the psalmist.

**70:1–5.** This Psalm is all but identical with the last verses of Ps. 50:13–17. Some unimportant alterations have been made, principally in the divine names, but the principle on which they have been made is not obvious. It is scarcely correct to say, with Delitzsch, that the Psalm "has been transformed, so as to become Elohistic"; for although it twice replaces the name of Yahweh with that of Elohim (vv. 1, 4), it makes the converse change in v. 5, last clause, by reading Yahweh instead of "Elohim," as in Ps. 50.

Other changes are of little moment. The principal are in vv. 3 and 5. In the former, the vehement wish that the psalmist's mockers may be paralyzed with shame is softened down into a desire that they may be turned back. The two verbs are similar in sound, and the substitution may have been accidental, a slip of memory or a defect in hearing, or it may have been an artistic variation of the original. In v. 5, a prayer that God will hasten to the psalmist's help takes the place of an expression of confidence that "Yahweh purposes [good]" to him, and again there is similarity of sound in the two words. This change is like the subtle alteration which a painter might make on his picture by taking out one spot of highlight. The gleam of confidence is changed to a call of need, and the tone of the whole Psalm is thereby made more plaintive.

Some have proposed that this Psalm is the original and Ps. 50 a composite, but most commentators agree in regarding this as a fragment of that Psalm. The cut has not been very cleanly made, for the necessary verb "be pleased" has been left behind, and the symmetry of v. 1 is destroyed as a result. The awkward incompleteness of this beginning witnesses that the Psalm is a fragment.

***Psalm 71.*** *Echoes of former Psalms make the staple of this one and even those parts of it which are not quotations have little individuality. The themes are familiar, and the expression of them is scarcely less so. There is no well-defined structure and little continuity of thought or feeling. Verses 13 and 24b serve as a kind of partial refrain and may be taken as dividing the Psalm into two parts, but there is little difference between the contents of the two. Verses 1ff are slightly varied from Ps. 31:1ff. The character of the differences would be best appreciated by setting the two passages side by side.*

**71:1–4.** The two verbs, which in Ps. 31 are in separate clauses ("deliver" and "rescue"), are here brought together. "Speedily" is omitted, and "save" is substituted for "deliver," which has been drawn into the preceding clause. Obviously, no difference of meaning is intended to be conveyed.

| 3937, 5986 | | 904, 6930 | 5522.523 | 6647.528 |
|---|---|---|---|---|
| prep, n ms | **2.** | prep, n fs, ps 2ms | v Hiphil impf 2ms, ps 1cs | cj, v Hiphil impf 2mp, ps 1cs |
| לְעוֹלָם | | בְּצִדְקָתְךָ | תַּצִּילֵנִי | וּתְפַלְּטֵנִי |
| le'ôlām | | betsidhqāthekhā | tatstsîlēnî | ûthephalleṯēnî |
| unto eternity | | in your righteousness | You rescue me | and You set me free |

| 5371.531, 420 | 238 | 3588.531 | | 2030.131 | 3937 |
|---|---|---|---|---|---|
| v Hiphil impv 2ms, prep, ps 1cs | n fs, ps 2ms | cj, v Hiphil impv 2ms, ps 1cs | **3.** | v Qal impv 2ms | prep, ps 1cs |
| הַטֵּה־אֵלַי | אָזְנְךָ | וְהוֹשִׁיעֵנִי | | הֱיֵה | לִי |
| haṯṯēh-'ēlay | 'oznekhā | wehôshî'ēnî | | hĕyēh | lî |
| incline to me | your ear | and save me | | be | to me |

| 3937, 6962 | 4735 | 3937, 971.141 | 8878 | 6943.313 | 3937, 3588.541 |
|---|---|---|---|---|---|
| prep, *n ms* | n ms | prep, v Qal inf con | adv | v Piel pf 2ms | prep, v Hiphil inf con, ps 1cs |
| לְצוּר | מָעוֹן | לָבוֹא | תָּמִיד | צִוִּיתָ | לְהוֹשִׁיעֵנִי |
| letsûr | mā'ôn | lāvô' | tāmîdh | tsiwwîthā | lehôshî'ēnî |
| for a rock of | refuge | for going to | continually | You have commanded | to save me |

| 3706, 5748 | 4859 | 887 | | 435 | 6647.331 | 4623, 3135 |
|---|---|---|---|---|---|---|
| cj, n ms, ps 1cs | cj, n fs, ps 1cs | pers pron | **4.** | n mp, ps 1cs | v Piel impv 2ms, ps 1cs | prep, *n fs* |
| כִּי־סַלְעִי | וּמְצוּדָתִי | אָתָּה | | אֱלֹהַי | פַּלְּטֵנִי | מִיַּד |
| kî-sal'î | ûmetsûdhāthî | 'āttāh | | 'ĕlōhay | palleṯēnî | mîyadh |
| because my Rock | and my Fortress | You | | my God | set me free | from the hand of |

| 7857 | 4623, 3834 | 5979.351 | 2661.151 |
|---|---|---|---|
| n ms | prep, *n fs* | v Piel ptc ms | cj, v Qal act ptc ms |
| רָשָׁע | מִכַּף | מְעַוֵּל | וְחוֹמֵץ |
| rāshā' | mikkaph | me'awwēl | wechômēts |
| the wicked | from the palm of | those who commit wrongdoing | and from those who oppress |

| | 3706, 887 | 8951 | 112 | 3176 | 4148 | 4623, 5454 | | 6142 |
|---|---|---|---|---|---|---|---|---|
| **5.** | cj, pers pron | n fs, ps 1cs | n mp, ps 1cs | pn | n ms, ps 1cs | prep, n mp, ps 1cs | **6.** | prep, ps 2ms |
| | כִּי־אַתָּה | תִקְוָתִי | אֲדֹנָי | יְהוִה | מִבְטַחִי | מִנְּעוּרָי | | עָלֶיךָ |
| | kî-'attāh | thiqōwāthî | 'ădhōnāy | yehwih | mivṯachî | minne'ûrāy | | 'ālêkhā |
| | because You | my Hope | my Lord | Yahweh | my trust | from my youth | | on You |

| 5759.215 | 4623, 1027 | 4623, 4732 | 525 | 887 | 1522.151 |
|---|---|---|---|---|---|
| v Niphal pf 1cs | prep, n fs | prep, *n mp* | n fs, ps 1cs | pers pron | v Qal act ptc ms, ps 1cs |
| נִסְמַכְתִּי | מִבֶּטֶן | מִמְּעֵי | אִמִּי | אַתָּה | גוֹזִי |
| nismakhtî | mibbeṯen | mimme'ê | 'immî | 'attāh | ghôzî |
| I have leaned | from the womb | from the womb of | my mother | You | the One Who takes me |

| 904 | 8747 | 8878 | | 3626, 4295 | 2030.115 | 3937, 7521 | 887 |
|---|---|---|---|---|---|---|---|
| prep, ps 2ms | n fs, ps 1cs | adv | **7.** | prep, n ms | v Qal pf 1cs | prep, adj | cj, pers pron |
| בְּךָ | תְהִלָּתִי | תָמִיד | | כְּמוֹפֵת | הָיִיתִי | לְרַבִּים | וְאַתָּה |
| bekhā | thehillāthî | thāmîdh | | kemôphēth | hāyîthî | lerabbîm | we'attāh |
| in You | my praise | continually | | like a bad sign | I have been | to many | but You |

| 4406, 6010 | | 4527.221 | 6552 | 8747 | 3725, 3219 | 8930 |
|---|---|---|---|---|---|---|
| n ms, ps 1cs, n ms | **8.** | v Niphal impf 3ms | n ms, ps 1cs | n fs, ps 2ms | *adj*, art, n ms | n fs, ps 2ms |
| מַחֲסִי־עֹז | | יִמָּלֵא | פִי | תְּהִלָּתֶךָ | כָּל־הַיּוֹם | תִּפְאַרְתֶּךָ |
| machsi-'ōz | | yimmālē' | phî | tehillāthekhā | kol-hayyôm | tiph'artekhā |
| my Refuge of strength | | it is filled with | my mouth | your praise | all the day | your splendor |

| | 414, 8390.523 | 3937, 6496 | 2294 | 3626, 3735.141 | 3699 |
|---|---|---|---|---|---|
| **9.** | adv, v Hiphil juss 2ms, ps 1cs | prep, *n fs* | n fs | prep, v Qal inf con | n ms, ps 1cs |
| | אַל־תַּשְׁלִיכֵנִי | לְעֵת | זִקְנָה | כִּכְלוֹת | כֹּחִי |
| | 'al-tashlîkhēnî | le'ēth | ziqōnāh | kikhlôth | kōchî |
| | do not throw me away | at the time of | old age | when the ending of | my strength |

**2. Deliver me in thy righteousness, and cause me to escape: incline thine ear unto me, and save me:** ... rescue me and help me escape, *Beck* ... In Your goodness relieve me and guard, *Fenton* ... listen to me and save me, *JB* ... listen to my cry, *Knox.*

**3. Be thou my strong habitation, whereunto I may continually resort: thou hast given commandment to save me; for thou art my rock and my fortress:** ... Be a stronghold, a fortress, *Moffatt* ... Be my rock of refuge, *NAB* ... you are my rock and my strong, walled city, *NCV* ... For you have issued the order to save me, *LIVB.*

**4. Deliver me, O my God, out of the hand of the wicked, out of the hand of the unrighteous and cruel man:** ... from the clutches of unjust and cruel men, *NEB* ... from the hands of those who are unjust and cruel, *Beck.*

**5. For thou art my hope, O Lord GOD: thou art my trust from my youth:** ... My confidence from my youth, *Goodspeed* ... my trust, Yahweh, since boyhood, *JB* ... the hope and confidence of my youth, *Knox* ... I have trusted in you since I was young, *Good News.*

**6. By thee have I been holden up from the womb: thou art he that took me out of my mother's bowels: my praise shall be continually of thee:** ... On you I depend from birth, *NAB* ... you helped me even on the day of my birth. I will always praise you, *NCV* ... From birth I have leaned upon thee, my protector since I left my mother's womb, *NEB.*

**7. I am as a wonder unto many; but thou art my strong refuge:** ... I am a wonder to all, *BB* ... but You are my strong shelter, *Beck* ... Thou art my strong refuge, *Berkeley* ... you have been my strong defender, *Good News.*

**8. Let my mouth be filled with thy praise and with thy honour all the day:** ... mouth has been filled with your praise, and with your glorious deeds throughout the day, *Anchor* ... filled with your splendour all day long, *JB* ... all day long I honor you, *NCV* ... All day long I'll praise and honor you, *LIVB.*

**9. Cast me not off in the time of old age; forsake me not when my strength faileth:** ... Do not give me up when I am old; be my help even when my strength is gone, *BB* ... Don't discard me when I'm old or leave me when I lose my strength, *Beck* ... When my strength fails, do not forsake me, *Goodspeed.*

---

The difference between "a strong rock" and "rock of habitation" is but one letter. That between "for a house of defense" and "to go to continually: thou hast commanded" is extremely slight. Some have proposed these variations between Ps. 31 and Ps. 71 as a textual corruption, but more probably this psalmist intentionally altered the words of the older Psalm. Most of the old versions have the existing text, but the Septuagint seems to have read the Hebrew here as in Ps. 31. That thought of God as a habitation to which the soul may continually find access goes very deep into the secrets of the devout life. The variation in v. 3 is recommended by observing the frequent recurrence of "continually" in this Psalm, of which that word may almost be said to be the motto. Nor is the thought of God's command given to his multitude of unnamed servants to save this poor man, one which we can afford to lose.

**71:5–6.** Verses 5f, are a similar variation of Ps. 22:9f. "By thee have I been holden up from the womb," says this psalmist; "I was cast upon thee from the womb," says the original passage. The variation beautifully brings out, not only reliance on God, but the divine response to that reliance by lifelong upholding. That strong arm answers leaning weakness with firm support, and whosoever relies on it is upheld by it. The word rendered above "protector" (HED #1522) is doubtful. It is substituted for that in Ps. 22:9, which means "One that takes out," and some commentators would attach the same meaning to the word used here, referring it to God's goodness before and at birth. But it could be taken as equivalent to "benefactor," "provider," or some such designation, and as referring to God's lifelong care.

**71:7–8.** The psalmist has been "a wonder" to many spectators, either in the sense that they have gazed astonished at God's goodness, or, as accords better with the adversative character of the next clause ("but thou art my strong refuge") that his sufferings have been unexampled. Both ideas may well be combined, for the life of every man, if rightly studied, is full of miracles both of mercy and judgment. If the Psalm is the voice of an individual, the natural conclusion from such words is that his life was conspicuous, but it is obvious that the national reference is appropriate here.

On this thankful retrospect of lifelong help and lifelong trust, the Psalm builds a prayer for future protection from eager enemies, who think that the charmed life is vulnerable at last.

**71:9–13.** Verses 9–13 rise to a height of emotion above the level of the rest of the Psalm. On one hypothesis, we have in them the cry of an old man, whose strength diminishes as his dangers increase. Something undisclosed in his circumstances gave color to the greedy hopes of his enemies. Often pros-

| 414, 6013.123 | | 3706, 569.116 | 342.152 | 3937 |
|---|---|---|---|---|
| adv, v Qal juss 2ms, ps 1cs | | cj, v Qal pf 3cp | v Qal act ptc mp, ps 1cs | prep, ps 1cs |
| אַל־תַּעַזְבֵנִי | 10. | כִּי־אָמְרוּ | אוֹיְבַי | לִי |
| ʾal-taʿazvēnî | | kî-ʾāmᵉrû | ʾôyvay | lî |
| do not abandon me | | because they have said | my enemies | to me |

| 8490.152 | 5497 | 3398.216 | 3267 | | 3937, 569.141 |
|---|---|---|---|---|---|
| cj, *v Qal act ptc mp* | n fs, ps 1cs | v Niphal pf 3cp | adv | | prep, v Qal inf con |
| וְשֹׁמְרֵי | נַפְשִׁי | נוֹעֲצוּ | יַחְדָּו | 11. | לֵאמֹר |
| wᵉshōmᵉrê | naphshî | nôʿātsû | yachdāw | | lēʾmōr |
| and those who keep watch for | my life | they have consulted | together | | saying |

| 435 | 6013.111 | 7579.133 | 8945.133 | 3706, 375 |
|---|---|---|---|---|
| n mp | v Qal pf 3ms, ps 3ms | v Qal impv 2mp | cj, v Qal impv 2mp, ps 3ms | cj, *sub* |
| אֱלֹהִים | עֲזָבוֹ | רִדְפוּ | וְתִפְשׂוּהוּ | כִּי־אֵין |
| ʾĕlōhîm | ʿăzāvô | ridhphû | wᵉthiphsûhû | kî-ʾēn |
| God | He has abandoned him | pursue | so grasp him | because there is not |

| 5522.551 | | 435 | 414, 7651.123 | 4623 | 435 | 3937, 6046 | 2924.131 |
|---|---|---|---|---|---|---|---|
| v Hiphil ptc ms | | n mp | adv, v Qal juss 2ms | prep, ps 1cs | n mp, ps 1cs | prep, n fs, ps 1cs | v Qal impv 2ms |
| מַצִּיל | 12. | אֱלֹהִים | אַל־תִּרְחַק | מִמֶּנִּי | אֱלֹהַי | לְעֶזְרָתִי | חִישָׁה |
| matstsîl | | ʾĕlōhîm | ʾăl-tirchaq | mimmenî | ʾĕlōhay | lᵉʿezrāthî | chîshāh |
| a rescuer | | O God | do not be far away | from me | O my God | for my help | hurry |

| | 991.126 | 3735.126 | 7930.152 | 5497 |
|---|---|---|---|---|
| | v Qal juss 3mp | v Qal juss 3mp | *v Qal act ptc mp* | n fs, ps 1cs |
| 13. | יֵבֹשׁוּ | יִכְלוּ | שֹׂטְנֵי | נַפְשִׁי |
| | yēvōshû | yikhlû | sōṭᵉnê | naphshî |
| | may they be ashamed | and may they come to an end | the accusers of | my life |

| 6057.126 | 2887 | 3759 | 1272.352 | 7750 | | 603 |
|---|---|---|---|---|---|---|
| v Qal juss 3mp | n fs | cj, n fs | *v Piel ptc mp* | n fs, ps 1cs | | cj, pers pron |
| יַעֲטוּ | חֶרְפָּה | וּכְלִמָּה | מְבַקְשֵׁי | רָעָתִי | 14. | וַאֲנִי |
| yaʿăṭû | cherpāh | ûkhᵉlimmāh | mᵉvaqŏshê | rāʿāthî | | waʾănî |
| may they be covered with | disgrace | and dishonor | those who seek | my disaster | | but I |

| 8878 | 3282.325 | 3362.515 | 6142, 3725, 8747 | | 6552 | 5807.321 |
|---|---|---|---|---|---|---|
| adv | v Piel impf 1cs | cj, v Hiphil pf 1cs | prep, *adj*, n fs, ps 2ms | | n ms, ps 1cs | v Piel impf 3ms |
| תָּמִיד | אֲיַחֵל | וְהוֹסַפְתִּי | עַל־כָּל־תְּהִלָּתֶךָ | 15. | פִּי | יְסַפֵּר |
| tāmîdh | ʾăyachēl | wᵉhôsaphtî | ʿal-kol-tᵉhillāthekhā | | pî | yᵉsappēr |
| continually | I will wait | and I will add | onto all your praise | | my mouth | it will recount |

| 6930 | 3725, 3219 | 9009 | 3706 | 3940 | 3156.115 | 5818 |
|---|---|---|---|---|---|---|
| n fs, ps 2ms | *adj*, art, n ms | n fs, ps 2ms | cj | neg part | v Qal pf 1cs | n fp |
| צִדְקָתֶךָ | כָּל־הַיּוֹם | תְּשׁוּעָתֶךָ | כִּי | לֹא | יָדַעְתִּי | סְפֹרוֹת |
| tsidhqāthekhā | kol-hayyôm | tᵉshûʿāthekhā | kî | lōʾ | yādhaʿttî | sᵉphōrôth |
| your righteousness | all the day | your salvation | because | not | I know | the numbers |

| | 971.125 | 904, 1400 | 112 | 3176 | 2226.525 |
|---|---|---|---|---|---|
| | v Qal impf 1cs | prep, *n fp* | n mp, ps 1cs | pn | v Hiphil impf 1cs |
| 16. | אָבוֹא | בִּגְבֻרוֹת | אֲדֹנָי | יְהוִה | אַזְכִּיר |
| | ʾāvôʾ | bighvurôth | ʾădhōnāy | yᵉhwih | ʾazkîr |
| | I will enter | with the might of | my Lord | Yahweh | I will cause to remember |

| 6930 | 3937, 945 | | 435 | 4064.313 | 4623, 5454 |
|---|---|---|---|---|---|
| n fs, ps 2ms | prep, n ms, ps 2ms | | n mp | v Piel pf 2ms, ps 1cs | prep, n mp, ps 1cs |
| צִדְקָתְךָ | לְבַדֶּךָ | 17. | אֱלֹהִים | לִמַּדְתַּנִי | מִנְּעוּרָי |
| tsidhqāthᵉkhā | lᵉvaddekhā | | ʾĕlōhîm | limmadhtanî | minnᵉʿûrāy |
| your righteousness | You alone | | O God | You have taught me | from my youth |

**10. For mine enemies speak against me; and they that lay wait for my soul take counsel together:** ... My enemies make plans against me, *NCV* ... my haters are waiting secretly for me, *BB* ... because my enemies talk about me, and those who watch to take my life plan together, *Beck* ... those with designs on my life are plotting together, *JB*.

**11. Saying, God hath forsaken him: persecute and take him; for there is none to deliver him:** ... pursue and seize him for there is none to rescue, *Anchor* ... God has given him up, *BB* ... Pursue and grab him—there's nobody to rescue him, *Beck* ... Hound him down, for God has deserted him, *JB*.

**12. O God, be not far from me: O my God, make haste for my help:** ... do not keep thy distance from me, *Knox* ... My God, hurry to help me, *NCV* ... come quickly, O my God, to help me, *NIV* ... my God, hurry to my aid, *Good News*.

**13. Let them be confounded and consumed that are adversaries to my soul; let them be covered with reproach and dishonour that seek my hurt:** ... be overcome and put to shame, *BB* ... May those who accuse me come to a shameful end, *Beck* ... May they be covered with abuse and shame who seek to injure me, *Goodspeed* ... may those intent on harming me be covered with insult and infamy, *JB*.

**14. But I will hope continually, and will yet praise thee more and more:** ... my hope will never fade, *JB* ... will always hope, *NAB* ... will wait in continual hope, *NEB* ... and increasing in all your praise, *BB*.

**15. My mouth shall show forth thy righteousness and thy salvation all the day; for I know not the numbers thereof:** ... mouth would count your faithful deeds, *Anchor* ... mouth will make clear your righteousness and your salvation, *BB* ... although they're more than I can number, *Beck* ... your saving power, *JB*.

**16. I will go in the strength of the Lord God: I will make mention of thy righteousness, even of thine only:** ... I will come and tell about your powerful works, *NCV* ... I will give news of the great acts of the Lord God, *BB* ... the triumphs You alone perform, *Beck* ... I will praise your power, Sovereign LORD, *Good News*.

**17. O God, thou hast taught me from my youth: and hitherto have I declared thy wondrous works:** ... you have taught me from boyhood, *JB* ... To this day I tell about the miracles you do, *NCV* ... all my life I have proclaimed thy marvellous works, *NEB* ... you have been my teacher from the time when I was young, *BB*.

---

perous careers are overclouded at the end, and the piteous spectacle is seen of age overtaken by tempests which its feebleness cannot resist and which are all the worse to face because of the calms preceding them. On the national hypothesis, the Psalm is the prayer of Israel at a late stage of its history from which it looks back to the miracles of old, and then to the ring of enemies rejoicing over its apparent weakness, and then upwards to the eternal helper.

Verses 12f are woven out of other Psalms. Verse 12a, "Be not far from me," is found in 22:11, 19; 35:22; 38:21, etc. "Haste for my help" is found in 38:22; 40:13; 70:1. For v. 13, compare 35:4, 26; 40:14; 70:2. With this as a sort of refrain, the first part of the Psalm ends.

**71:14–16.** The second part goes over substantially the same ground, but with lighter heart. The confidence of deliverance is more vivid, and it, as well as the vow of following praise, bulk larger. The singer has thinned away his anxieties by speaking them to God and has by the same process solidified his faith. Aged eyes should see God, the Helper, more clearly when earth begins to look gray and dim. The forward look of such finds little to stay it on this side of heaven. As there seems less and less to hope for here, there should be more and more there. Youth is the time for buoyant anticipation, according to the world's notions, but age may have far brighter lights ahead than youth had leisure to see. "I will hope always" becomes sublime from aged lips, which are so often shaped to say, "I have nothing left to hope for now."

This psalmist's words may well be a pattern for old men, who need fear no failure of buoyancy, nor any collapse of gladness, if they will fix their thoughts where this singer did his. Other subjects of thought and speech will pall and run dry, but he whose theme is God's righteousness and the salvation that flows from it will never lack materials for animating meditation and grateful praise, "I know not the numbers thereof." It is something to have fast hold of an inexhaustible subject. It will keep an old man young.

**71:17–19.** The psalmist recognizes his task, which is also his joy, to declare God's wondrous works and prays for God's help until he has discharged it. The consciousness of a vocation to speak to later generations inspires him and assures him that he is immortal until his work is done. His anticipations have been fulfilled beyond his knowledge. His words will last as long as the world. But men with narrower spheres may be animated by the

| 5912, 2077 | 5222.525 | 6623.258 | | 1612 | 5912, 2294 | 7939 |
|---|---|---|---|---|---|---|
| cj, prep, adv | v Hiphil impf 1cs | v Niphal ptc fp, ps 2ms | **18.** | cj, cj | adv, n fs | cj, n fs |
| וְעַד־הֵנָּה | אַגִּיד | נִפְלְאוֹתֶיךָ | | וְגַם | עַד־זִקְנָה | וְשֵׂיבָה |
| wᵉʿadh-hēnnāh | ʾaggîdh | niphlᵉʾôthêkhā | | wᵉgham | ʿadh-ziqnāh | wᵉsêvāh |
| and until here | I will tell | your extraordinary deeds | | and also | until old age | and gray hair |

| 435 | 414, 6013.123 | 5912, 5222.525 | 2307 | 3937, 1810 |
|---|---|---|---|---|
| n mp | adv, v Qal juss 2ms, ps 1cs | adv, v Hiphil impf 1cs | n fs, ps 2ms | prep, n ms |
| אֱלֹהִים | אַל־תַּעַזְבֵנִי | עַד־אַגִּיד | זְרוֹעֲךָ | לְדוֹר |
| ʾĕlōhîm | ʾal-taʿazvēnî | ʿadh-ʾaggîdh | zᵉrôʿăkhā | lᵉdhôr |
| O God | do not abandon me | until I tell about | your arm | to a generation |

| 3937, 3725, 971.121 | 1400 | | 6930 | 435 | 5912, 4953 |
|---|---|---|---|---|---|
| prep, *adj*, v Qal impf 3ms | n fs, ps 2ms | **19.** | cj, n fs, ps 2ms | n mp | prep, n ms |
| לְכָל־יָבוֹא | גְּבוּרָתֶךָ | | וְצִדְקָתְךָ | אֱלֹהִים | עַד־מָרוֹם |
| lᵉkhol-yāvôʾ | gᵉvûrāthekhā | | wᵉtsidhqāthᵉkhā | ʾĕlōhîm | ʿadh-mārôm |
| to all who come to | your might | | and your righteousness | O God | to the heights |

| 866, 6449.113 | 1448 | 435 | 4449 | 3765 | | 866 | 7495.513 |
|---|---|---|---|---|---|---|---|
| rel pron, v Qal pf 2ms | adj | n mp | intrg | prep, ps 2ms | **20.** | rel pron | v Hiphil pf 2ms, ps 1cp |
| אֲשֶׁר־עָשִׂיתָ | גְדֹלוֹת | אֱלֹהִים | מִי | כָמוֹךָ | | אֲשֶׁר | הִרְאִיתַנוּ |
| ʾăsher-ʿāsîthā | ghᵉdhōlôth | ʾĕlōhîm | mî | khāmôkhā | | ʾăsher | hirʾîthanû |
| You Who have done | great things | O God | who | like You | | Who | You have caused us to see |

| 7150 | 7521 | 7737 | 8178.123 | 2513.323 | 4623, 8745 | 800 |
|---|---|---|---|---|---|---|
| n fp | adj | cj, adj | v Qal impf 2ms | v Piel impf 2ms, ps 1cp | cj, prep, *n fp* | art, n fs |
| צָרוֹת | רַבּוֹת | וְרָעוֹת | תָּשׁוּב | תְּחַיֵּינוּ | וּמִתְּהֹמוֹת | הָאָרֶץ |
| tsārôth | rabbôth | wᵉrāʿôth | tāshûv | tᵉchayyênû | ûmittᵉhōmôth | hāʾārets |
| troubles | many | and evil | You will return | You preserve us | and from the depths of | the earth |

| 8178.123 | 6148.523 | | 7528.523 | 1449 |
|---|---|---|---|---|
| v Qal impf 2ms | v Hiphil impf 2ms, ps 1cs | **21.** | v Hiphil juss 2ms | n fs, ps 1cs |
| תָּשׁוּב | תַּעֲלֵנִי | | תֶּרֶב | גְּדֻלָּתִי |
| tāshûv | taʿălēnî | | terev | gᵉdhullāthî |
| You will return | You will bring me up | | may You make great | my greatness |

| 5621.123 | 5341.323 | | 1612, 603 | 3142.525 |
|---|---|---|---|---|
| cj, v Qal juss 2ms | v Piel impf 2ms, ps 1cs | **22.** | cj, pers pron | v Hiphil juss 1cs, ps 2ms |
| וְתִסֹּב | תְּנַחֲמֵנִי | | גַּם־אֲנִי | אוֹדְךָ |
| wᵉthissōv | tᵉnachmēnî | | gam-ʾănî | ʾôdhkhā |
| and may You surround | You will comfort me | | also I | let me praise You |

| 904, 3747, 5213 | 583 | 435 | 2252.325 | 3937 |
|---|---|---|---|---|
| prep, *n ms*, n ms | n fs, ps 2ms | n mp, ps 1cs | v Piel juss 1cs | prep, ps 2ms |
| בִכְלִי־נֶבֶל | אֲמִתְּךָ | אֱלֹהָי | אֲזַמְּרָה | לְךָ |
| vikhlî-nevel | ʾămittᵉkhā | ʾĕlōhāy | ʾăzammᵉrāh | lᵉkhā |
| with the instrument of the harp | your reliability | O my God | let me sing praises | to You |

| 904, 3780 | 7202 | 3547 | | 7728.327 | 8004 | 3706 |
|---|---|---|---|---|---|---|
| prep, n ms | *n ms* | pn | **23.** | v Piel impf 3fp | n fd, ps 1cs | cj |
| בְכִנּוֹר | קְדוֹשׁ | יִשְׂרָאֵל | | תְּרַנֵּנָּה | שְׂפָתַי | כִּי |
| vᵉkhinnôr | qōdhôsh | yisrāʾēl | | tᵉrannēnnāh | sᵉphāthay | kî |
| with the zither | O Holy One of | Israel | | they will shout for joy | my lips | so |

| 2226.325, 3937 | 5497 | 866 | 6540.113 | | 1612, 4098 |
|---|---|---|---|---|---|
| v Piel juss 1cs, prep, ps 2ms | cj, n fs, ps 1cs | rel part | v Qal pf 2ms | **24.** | cj, n fs, ps 1cs |
| אֲזַמְּרָה־לָּךְ | וְנַפְשִׁי | אֲשֶׁר | פָּדִיתָ | | גַּם־לְשׁוֹנִי |
| ʾăzammᵉrāh-lākh | wᵉnaphshî | ʾăsher | pādhîthā | | gam-lᵉshônî |
| let me sing praises to You | and my soul | which | You have ransomed | | also my tongue |

**18. Now also when I am old and grayheaded, O God, forsake me not; until I have shown thy strength unto this generation, and thy power to every one that is to come:** ... till I tell this age what Your arm has done, *Beck* ... to this generation and Thy power to all descendants, *Berkeley* ... I will tell those who live after me about your might, *NCV*.

**19. Thy righteousness also, O God, is very high, who hast done great things: O God, who is like unto thee:** ... righteousness reaches to heaven, *Beck* ... You have done great things, *NCV* ... O God; Who is Thy equal?, *Berkeley*.

**20. Thou, which hast shown me great and sore troubles, shalt quicken me again, and shalt bring me up again from the depths of the earth:** ... hast made me experience troubles great and sore, *Berkeley* ... hast made us see many dangers and disasters, *Goodspeed* ... will give me life again, *BB* ... You will restore me to life again, *Beck*.

**21. Thou shalt increase my greatness, and comfort me on every side:** ... wilt add to my stature, *Berkeley* ... add to our honour, and comfort us, *Moffatt* ... and comfort me over and over, *NAB* ... will make me greater than ever, *NCV*.

**22. I will also praise thee with the psaltery, even thy truth, O my God: unto thee will I sing with the harp, O thou Holy One of Israel:** ... With full voice I will praise you on the harp, *Anchor* ... with instruments of music, *BB* ... will praise You with a lute for being faithful, *Beck* ... will praise you with music, telling of your faithfulness to all your promises, *LIVB*.

**23. My lips shall greatly rejoice when I sing unto thee; and my soul, which thou hast redeemed:** ... lips shall ring with joy and praise, *Moffatt* ... lips will resound with joy, *Anchor* ... to which you have given salvation, *BB*.

**24. My tongue also shall talk of thy righteousness all the day long: for they are confounded, for they are brought unto shame, that seek my hurt:** ... and those who are out to harm me, *Beck* ... my tongue muses on your saving justice, *JB* ... will be ashamed and disgraced, *NCV* ... defeated and disgraced, *Good News*.

---

same consciousness, and they who have rightly understood the purpose of God's mercies to themselves will, like the psalmist, recognize in their own participation in his salvation an imperative command to make it known and an assurance that nothing shall by any means harm them until they have fulfilled their witnessing. A many-wintered saint should be a convincing witness for God.

**71:20–21.** Verse 20, with its sudden transition to the plural, may simply show that the singer passes out from individual contemplation to the consciousness of the multitude of fellow sufferers and fellow participants in God's mercy. Such transition is natural, for the most private passages of a good man's communion with God are swift to bring up the thought of others like-minded and similarly blessed. "Suddenly there was with the angel a multitude of the heavenly host praising" (Luke 2:13). Every solo swells into a chorus. Again the song returns to "my" and "me," the confidence of the single soul being reinvigorated by the thought of sharers in blessing.

**71:22–24.** So all ends with the certainty of, and the vow of praise for, deliverances already realized in faith, although not in fact. But the imitative character of the Psalm is maintained even in this last triumphant vow, for v. 24a is almost identical with 35:28, and v. 24b, as has been already pointed out, is copied from several other Psalms. But imitative words are nonetheless sincere, and new thankfulness may be run into old molds without detriment to its acceptableness to God and preciousness to men.

***Psalm 72.*** *The superscription ascribes this Psalm to Solomon. Its contents have led several commentators to take the superscription in a meaning for which there is no warrant, as designating the subject, not the author. Clearly, the whole is a prayer for the king, but why should he not be both suppliant and object of supplication? Modern critics reject this as incompatible with the "phraseological evidence" and adduce the difference between the historical Solomon and the ideal of the Psalm as negating reference to him. The impossibility of Solomon praying thus for himself does not seem so completely established that the hypothesis must be abandoned, however.*

*The psalmist's prayers are broadly massed. In vv. 1–4, he prays for the foundation of the king's reign in righteousness, which will bring peace; in vv. 5ff, for its perpetuity, and in vv. 8–11, for its universality; while in vv. 12–15 the ground of both these characteristics is laid in the king's becoming the champion of the oppressed. A final prayer for the increase of his people and the perpetuity and worldwide glory of his name concludes the Psalm, to which are appended in vv. 18ff a doxology, closing the second book of the Psalter.*

| 3725, 3219 | 1965.122 | 6930 | 3706, 991.116 |
|---|---|---|---|
| *adj*, art, n ms | v Qal impf 3fs | n fs, ps 2ms | cj, v Qal pf 3cp |
| כָּל־הַיּוֹם | תֶּהְגֶּה | צִדְקָתֶךָ | כִּי־בֹשׁוּ |
| kol-hayyôm | tehgeh | tsidhqāthekhā | kî-vōshû |
| all the day | it will utter | your righteousness | because they have been ashamed |

| 3706, 2763.116 | 1272.352 | 7750 | | 3937, 8406 | | 435 |
|---|---|---|---|---|---|---|
| cj, v Qal pf 3cp | *v Piel ptc mp* | n fs, ps 1cs | 72:t | prep, pn | 1. | n mp |
| כִּי־חָפְרוּ | מְבַקְשֵׁי | רָעָתִי | | לִשְׁלֹמֹה | | אֱלֹהִים |
| khî-chāpherû | mevaqōshê | rā'āthî | | lishlōmōh | | 'ĕlōhîm |
| indeed they have been put to shame | those who seek | my disaster | | of Solomon | | O God |

| 5122 | 3937, 4567 | 5598.131 | 6930 | 3937, 1158, 4567 |
|---|---|---|---|---|
| n mp, ps 2ms | prep, n ms | v Qal impv 2ms | cj, n fs, ps 2ms | prep, *n ms*, n ms |
| מִשְׁפָּטֶיךָ | לְמֶלֶךְ | תֵּן | וְצִדְקָתְךָ | לְבֶן־מֶלֶךְ |
| mishpāṭêkhā | lemelekh | tēn | wetsidhqāthekhā | leven-melekh |
| your judgments | to the king | give | and your righteousness | to the son of the king |

| | 1833.121 | 6194 | 904, 6928 | 6270 | 904, 5122 | | 5558.126 |
|---|---|---|---|---|---|---|---|
| 2. | v Qal juss 3ms | n ms, ps 2ms | prep, n ms | cj, n mp, ps 2ms | prep, n ms | 3. | v Qal impf 3mp |
| | יָדִין | עַמְּךָ | בְצֶדֶק | וַעֲנִיֶּיךָ | בְמִשְׁפָּט | | יִשְׂאוּ |
| | yādhîn | 'ammekhā | vetsedheq | wa'ănîyêkhā | vemishpāṭ | | yis'û |
| | may he judge | your people | with righteousness | and your afflicted | with justice | | they will bear |

| 2098 | 8361 | 3937, 6194 | 1421 | 904, 6930 |
|---|---|---|---|---|
| n mp | n ms | prep, art, n ms | cj, n fp | prep, n fs |
| הָרִים | שָׁלוֹם | לָעָם | וּגְבָעוֹת | בִּצְדָקָה |
| hārîm | shālôm | lā'ām | ûghevā'ôth | bitsdhāqāh |
| the mountains | peace | for the people | and the hills | in righteousness |

| | 8570.121 | 6270, 6194 | 3588.521 | 3937, 1158 | 33 |
|---|---|---|---|---|---|
| 4. | v Qal juss 3ms | *n mp*, n ms | v Hiphil impf 3ms | prep, *n mp* | n ms |
| | יִשְׁפֹּט | עֲנִיֵּי־עָם | יוֹשִׁיעַ | לִבְנֵי | אֶבְיוֹן |
| | yishpōṭ | 'ănîyê-'ām | yôshîa' | livnê | 'evyôn |
| | he will administer justice for | the afflicted of the people | he will save | the sons of | the needy |

| 1850.321 | 6479.151 | | 3486.126 | 6196, 8507 | 3937, 6686 | 3507 |
|---|---|---|---|---|---|---|
| cj, v Piel impf 3ms | v Qal act ptc ms | 5. | v Qal impf 3mp, ps 2ms | prep, n fs | cj, prep, *n mp* | n ms |
| וִידַכֵּא | עוֹשֵׁק | | יִירָאוּךָ | עִם־שָׁמֶשׁ | וְלִפְנֵי | יָרֵחַ |
| wîdhakkē' | 'ôshēq | | yîrā'ûkhā | 'im-shāmesh | weliphnê | yārēach |
| and he will crush | the oppressor | | they will fear you | with the sun | and before | the moon |

| 1810 | 1810 | | 3495.121 | 3626, 4443 | 6142, 1519 | 3626, 7534 |
|---|---|---|---|---|---|---|
| *n ms* | n mp | 6. | v Qal impf 3ms | prep, n ms | prep, n ms | prep, n mp |
| דּוֹר | דּוֹרִים | | יֵרֵד | כְּמָטָר | עַל־גֵּז | כִּרְבִיבִים |
| dôr | dôrîm | | yērēdh | kemāṭār | 'al-gēz | kirvîvîm |
| generation of | generations | | he will come down | like rain | on the mown grass | like showers |

| 2309 | 800 | | 6775.121, 904, 3219 | 6926 | 7524 |
|---|---|---|---|---|---|
| *n ms* | n fs | 7. | v Qal impf 3ms, prep, n mp, ps 3ms | n ms | cj, *n ms* |
| זַרְזִיף | אָרֶץ | | יִפְרַח־בְּיָמָיו | צַדִּיק | וְרֹב |
| zarzîph | 'ārets | | yiphrach-beyāmâv | tsaddîq | werōv |
| the raindrops of | the earth | | he will blossom in his days | the righteous | and the abundance of |

| 8361 | 5912, 1136 | 3507 | | 7575.121 | 4623, 3328 | 5912, 3328 | 4623, 5282 |
|---|---|---|---|---|---|---|---|
| n ms | adv, neg part | n ms | 8. | cj, v Qal juss 3ms | prep, n ms | prep, n ms | cj, prep, n ms |
| שָׁלוֹם | עַד־בְּלִי | יָרֵחַ | | וְיֵרְדְּ | מִיָּם | עַד־יָם | וּמִנָּהָר |
| shālôm | 'adh-belî | yārēach | | weyērd | mîyām | 'adh-yām | ûminnāhār |
| peace | until not | the moon | | and may he rule | from sea | unto sea | and from the Euphrates |

**72:t. A Psalm for Solomon.**

**1. Give the king thy judgements, O God, and thy righteousness unto the king's son:** ... Give the king your authority, *BB* ... grant the king Thy justice, *Berkeley* ... with your own fair judgement, *JB* ... your good judgment and the king's son your goodness, *NCV*.

**2. He shall judge thy people with righteousness, and thy poor with judgment:** ... may judge thy people rightly and deal out justice to the poor and suffering, *NEB* ... your afflicted ones with justice, *NIV* ... and your oppressed with judgment, *Anchor* ... and make true decisions for the poor, *BB*.

**3. The mountains shall bring peace to the people, and the little hills, by righteousness:** ... provide your people with prosperity in righteousness, *REB* ... mountains bring well-being to the people, *Beck* ... Let there be peace on the mountains, *NCV* ... the hills the fruit of righteousness, *NIV*.

**4. He shall judge the poor of the people, he shall save the children of the needy, and shall break in pieces the oppressor:** ... May he defend the oppressed of the people, *Anchor* ... And give deliverance to the poor, *Goodspeed* ... save the children of the poor, *Beck* ... and shall crush the cruel one, *KJVII*.

**5. They shall fear thee as long as the sun and moon endure, throughout all generations:** ... In the sight of the sun and the moon, *JB* ... throughout the ages, *Goodspeed*.

**6. He shall come down like rain upon the mown grass: as showers that water the earth:** ... as the rain that drops on the meadow grass, *Knox* ... May his rule be like rainfall upon meadows, *Moffatt*.

**7. In his days shall the righteous flourish; and abundance of peace so long as the moon endureth:** ... may the upright do well, *BB* ... let righteousness bloom, *Fenton* ... Let goodness be plentiful while he lives, *NCV* ... prosperity abound until the moon is no more, *NEB*.

**8. He shall have dominion also from sea to sea, and from the river unto the ends of the earth:** ... His empire shall stretch, *JB* ... He will rule, *Beck* ... from the Euphrates to the ends, *Good News*.

---

**72:1–3.** The first petitions of the Psalm all ask for one thing for the king, namely, that he should give righteous judgment. They reflect the antique conception of a king as the fountain of justice, himself making and administering law and giving decisions. Thrice in the first four verses does "righteousness" occur as the foundation attribute of an ideal king. Caprice, self-interest and tyrannous injustice were rank in the world's monarchies round the psalmist. Bitter experience and sad observation had taught him that the first condition of national prosperity was a righteous ruler. This king sits on an ancestral throne. His people are God's people. Since, then, he is God's viceroy, the desire cannot be vain that in his heart there may be some reflection of God's righteousness and that his decisions may accord with God's. One cannot but remember Solomon's prayer for "an understanding heart" that he might judge this people nor forget how darkly his later reign showed against its bright beginning.

**72:4.** A special manifestation of judicial righteousness is the vindication of the oppressed and the punishment of the oppressor (v. 4). The word rendered "judge" in v. 4 (HED #8570) differs from that in v. 2 (HED #1833) and is the same from which the name of the judges in Israel is derived. Like them, this king is not only to pronounce decisions, as the word in v. 2 means, but is to execute justice by acts of deliverance, which smite in order to rescue. Functions which policy and dignity require to be kept apart in the case of earthly rulers are united in the ideal monarch. He executes his own sentences. His acts are decisions.

**72:5–7.** The perpetuity of the king's reign and of his subjects' peace is the psalmist's second aspiration (vv. 5ff). The "thee" of v. 5 presents a difficulty, as it is doubtful to whom it refers. Throughout the Psalm, the king is spoken of and never to, and if it is further noticed that in the preceding verses God has been directly addressed and "thy" used thrice in regard to Him, then it will appear more natural to take the reference in v. 5 to be to Him. The fear of God would be diffused among the king's subjects, as a consequence of his rule in righteousness. The king is, as it were, the shadow on earth of God's righteousness and consequently becomes an organ for the manifestation thereof in such manner as to draw men to true devotion. The psalmist's desires are for something higher than external prosperity, and his conceptions of the kingly office are very sacred. Not only peace and material well-being, but also the fear of Yahweh, are longed for by him to be diffused in Israel. And he prays that these blessings may be perpetual.

The psalmist turns for a moment from his prayer for the perpetuity of the king's rule to linger upon the thought of its blessedness as set forth in the lovely image of v. 6. Rain upon mown grass is no blessing, as every farmer knows, but what is meant

| 5912, 675, 800 | | 3937, 6686 | 3895.126 | 6993 | 342.152 |
|---|---|---|---|---|---|
| prep, *n mp*, n fs | 9. | prep, n mp, ps 3ms | v Qal impf 3mp | n mp | cj, v Qal act ptc mp, ps 3ms |
| עַד־אַפְסֵי־אָרֶץ | | לְפָנָיו | יִכְרְעוּ | צִיִּים | וְאֹיְבָיו |
| 'adh-'aphsê-'ārets | | lephānâv | yikhre'û | tsîyîm | we'ōyevâv |
| unto the ends of the earth | | before him | they will bow | the dry places | and his enemies |

| 6312 | 4031.326 | | 4567 | 8998 | 339 | 4647 |
|---|---|---|---|---|---|---|
| n ms | v Piel impf 3mp | 10. | *n mp* | pn | cj, n mp | n fs |
| עָפָר | יְלַחֵכוּ | | מַלְכֵי | תַּרְשִׁישׁ | וְאִיִּים | מִנְחָה |
| 'āphār | yelachēkhû | | malkhê | tharshîsh | we'îyîm | minchāh |
| dust | they will lick | | the kings of | Tarshish | and the islands | a tribute |

| 8178.526 | 4567 | 8088 | 5619 | 841 | 7414.526 |
|---|---|---|---|---|---|
| v Hiphil impf 3mp | *n mp* | pn | cj, pn | n ms | v Hiphil impf 3mp |
| יָשִׁיבוּ | מַלְכֵי | שְׁבָא | וּסְבָא | אֶשְׁכָּר | יַקְרִיבוּ |
| yāshîvû | malkhê | shevā' | ûsevā' | 'eshkār | yaqōrîvû |
| they will cause to return | the kings of | Sheba | and Seba | gifts | they will bring near |

| | 8246.726, 3937 | 3725, 4567 | 3725, 1504 | 5856.126 |
|---|---|---|---|---|
| 11. | cj, v Hithpael impf 3mp, prep, ps 3ms | *adj*, n mp | *adj*, n mp | v Qal impf 3mp, ps 3ms |
| | וְיִשְׁתַּחֲווּ־לוֹ | כָל־מְלָכִים | כָּל־גּוֹיִם | יַעַבְדוּהוּ |
| | weyishtachwû-lô | khol-melākhîm | kol-gôyim | ya'avdhûhû |
| | and they will bow down to him | all the kings | all the nations | they will serve him |

| | 3706, 5522.521 | 33 | 8209.351 | 6270 | 375, 6038.151 |
|---|---|---|---|---|---|
| 12. | cj, v Hiphil impf 3ms | n ms | v Piel ptc ms | cj, n ms | cj, *sub*, v Qal act ptc ms |
| | כִּי־יַצִּיל | אֶבְיוֹן | מְשַׁוֵּעַ | וְעָנִי | וְאֵין־עֹזֵר |
| | kî-yatstsîl | 'evyôn | meshawwēa' | we'ānî | we'ên-'ōzēr |
| | because he rescues | the needy | crying out | and the afflicted | when there is not a helper |

| 3937 | | 2441.121 | 6142, 1859 | 33 | 5497 | 33 |
|---|---|---|---|---|---|---|
| prep, ps 3ms | 13. | v Qal impf 3ms | prep, n ms | cj, n ms | cj, *n fp* | n mp |
| לוֹ | | יָחֹס | עַל־דָּל | וְאֶבְיוֹן | וְנַפְשׁוֹת | אֶבְיוֹנִים |
| lô | | yāchōs | 'al-dal | we'evyôn | wenaphshôth | 'evyônîm |
| to him | | he has pity | on the poor | and the needy | indeed the lives of | the needy |

| 3588.521 | | 4623, 8826 | 4623, 2660 | 1381.121 | 5497 |
|---|---|---|---|---|---|
| v Hiphil impf 3ms | 14. | prep, n ms | cj, prep, n ms | v Qal impf 3ms | n fs, ps 3mp |
| יוֹשִׁיעַ | | מִתּוֹךְ | וּמֵחָמָס | יִגְאַל | נַפְשָׁם |
| yôshîa' | | mittôkh | ûmēchāmās | yigh'al | naphshām |
| he saves | | from oppression | and from violence | he redeems | their life |

| 3478.121 | 1879 | 904, 6084 | | 2513.121 | 5598.121, 3937 |
|---|---|---|---|---|---|
| cj, v Qal impf 3ms | n ms, ps 3mp | prep, n fd, ps 3ms | 15. | cj, v Qal juss 3ms | cj, v Qal juss 3ms, prep, ps 3ms |
| וְיֵיקַר | דָּמָם | בְּעֵינָיו | | וִיחִי | וְיִתֶּן־לוֹ |
| weyêqar | dāmām | be'ênâv | | wîchî | weyitten-lô |
| and it is precious | their blood | in his eyes | | and may he live | and may they give to him |

**9. They that dwell in the wilderness shall bow before him; and his enemies shall lick the dust:** ... Let the people of the desert bow down to him, *NCV* ... desert tribes will bow before him, *NIV* ... His foes, *NAB* ... humbled in the dust, *Knox*.

**10. The kings of Tarshish and of the isles shall bring presents: the kings of Sheba and Seba shall offer gifts:** ... kings of Tarshish and of the lands by the sea will pay tribute, *Beck* ... kings of Tarshish and the coast-lands, *Goodspeed* ... render tribute, *Anchor* ... come back with offerings, *BB*.

**11. Yea, all kings shall fall down before him: all nations shall serve him:** ... may all kings prostrate themselves before him, *Anchor* ... all kings will do him homage, all nations become his servants, *JB* ... all nations yield to him, *Moffatt*.

**12. For he shall deliver the needy when he crieth; the poor also, and him that hath no helper:** ... he will deliver the wretched who cry,

And the poor who have none to console, *Fenton* ... be a saviour to the poor, *BB* ... and the oppressed who have nobody to help them, *Beck.*

**13. He shall spare the poor and needy, and shall save the souls of the needy:** ... takes pity upon, *Goodspeed* ... saves the needy from death, *JB* ... He shall have pity for the lowly and the poor, *NAB* ... in their need and helplessness, they shall have his compassion, *Knox.*

**14. He shall redeem their soul from deceit and violence: and precious shall their blood be in his sight:** ... will rescue their life from oppression and violence, *NASB* ... will save them from cruel people, *NCV* ... he redeems their lives from lawless oppression, *Anchor* ... and their blood will be of value in his eyes, *BB.*

**15. And he shall live, and to him shall be given of the gold of Sheba: prayer also shall be made for him continually; and daily shall he be praised:** ... and blessings be his all day long, *Beck* ... they shall bless Him all the day, *Berkeley* ... blessings invoked on him all day, *JB* ... may ceaseless prayer be made, *Moffatt.*

**16. There shall be an handful of corn in the earth upon the top of the mountains; the fruit thereof shall shake like Lebanon: and they of the city shall flourish like grass of the earth:** ... May there be an abundance of grain upon the earth,

---

is, not the grass which has already been mown, but the naked meadow from which it has been taken. It needs drenching showers in order to sprout again and produce an aftermath. The psalmist heightens the metaphor by the introduction of the mown meadow as stimulated to new growth. A righteous king will insure prosperity to the righteous, and the number of such will increase. Both these ideas seem to be contained in the figure of their flourishing, which is literally bud or shoot. As the people become more and more prevailingly righteous, they receive more abundant and unbroken peace. The psalmist had seen deeply into the conditions of national prosperity, as well as those of individual tranquility, when he based these on rectitude.

**72:8–11.** With v. 8, the singer takes a still loftier flight and prays for the universality of the king's dominion. In that verse, the form of the verb is that which expresses desire, but in v. 9 and following verses, the verbs may be rendered as simple futures. Confident prayers insensibly melt into assurances of their own fulfillment. As the psalmist pours out his petitions, they glide into prophecies, for they are desires fashioned upon promises and bear, in their very earnestness, the pledge of their realization. As to the details of the form which the expectation of universal dominion here takes, it need only be noted that we have to do with a poet, not with a geographer. We are not to treat the expressions as if they were instructions to a boundary commission and to be laid down upon a map. "The sea" is probably the Mediterranean, but what the other sea which makes the opposite boundary may be is hard to say. The poet's eyes have looked east and west, and in v. 9 he turns to the south and sees the desert tribes, unconquered as they have hitherto been, groveling before the king and his enemies in abject submission at his feet. The word rendered "desert peoples" (HED #6993) is that used in Ps. 74:14 for wild beasts inhabiting the desert, but here it can only mean "wilderness tribes." There seems no need to alter the text, as has been proposed, to read "adversaries." In v. 10, the psalmist again looks westward, across the mysterious ocean of which he, like all his nation, knew so little. The great city of Tarshish lay for him at the farthest bounds of the world, and between him and it, or perhaps still farther out in the waste unknown, were islands from which rich and strange things sometimes reached Judaea. These shall bring their wealth in token of fealty. Again, he looks southward to Sheba in Arabia and Seba far south below Egypt and foresees their submission. Wide beyond his dreams and needy beyond his imagination, should own the sway of a king, endowed with God's righteousness and communicative of God's peace in a manner and measure beyond his desires.

**72:12–13.** The world is so full of sorrow and men are so miserable and needy that he who can stanch their wounds, solace their griefs and shelter their lives will win their hearts and be crowned their king. Thrones based on force are as if set on an iceberg which melts away. There is no solid foundation for rule except helpfulness. In the world and for a little while they that exercise authority are called benefactors, but in the long run the terms of the sentence are inverted, and they that are rightly called benefactors exercise authority.

**72:14–15.** The king is represented in v. 14 as taking on himself the office of goel, or kinsman-redeemer, and ransoming his subjects' lives from "deceit and violence." That "precious shall their blood be in his sight" is another way of saying that they are too dear to him to be suffered to perish.

| 4623, 2174 | 8088 | 6663.721 | 1185 | 8878 | 3725, 3219 |
|---|---|---|---|---|---|
| prep, *n ms* | pn | cj, v Hithpael juss 3ms | prep, ps 3ms | adv | *adj*, art, n ms |
| מִזְּהַב | שְׁבָא | וְיִתְפַּלֵּל | בַּעֲדוֹ | תָּמִיד | כָּל־הַיּוֹם |
| mizzehav | shevā' | weyithpallēl | ba'ădhô | thāmîdh | kol-hayyôm |
| from the gold of | Sheba | and may they pray | for him | continually | all the day |

| 1313.321 | | 2030.121 | 6697, 1277 | 904, 800 | 904, 7513 |
|---|---|---|---|---|---|
| v Piel juss 3ms, ps 3ms | **16.** | v Qal juss 3ms | *n fs*, n ms | prep, art, n fs | prep, *n ms* |
| יְבָרְכֶנְהוּ | | יְהִי | פִּסַּת־בַּר | בָּאָרֶץ | בְּרֹאשׁ |
| yevārekhenhû | | yehî | phissath-bar | bā'ārets | berō'sh |
| may they bless him | | may it be | the abundance of grain | in the land | on the top of |

| 2098 | 7783.121 | 3626, 3976 | 6780 | 6957.126 | 4623, 6111 |
|---|---|---|---|---|---|
| n mp | v Qal juss 3ms | prep, art, pn | n ms, ps 3ms | cj, v Qal juss 3mp | prep, n fs |
| הָרִים | יִרְעַשׁ | כַּלְּבָנוֹן | פִּרְיוֹ | וְיָצִיצוּ | מֵעִיר |
| hārîm | yir'ash | kallevānôn | piryô | weyātsîtsû | mē'îr |
| the mountains | and may it rustle | like Lebanon | its fruit | may they blossom | from the city |

| 3626, 6448 | 800 | | 2030.121 | 8428 | 3937, 5986 | 3937, 6686, 8507 |
|---|---|---|---|---|---|---|
| prep, *n ms* | art, n fs | **17.** | v Qal juss 3ms | n ms, ps 3ms | prep, n ms | prep, *n mp*, n fs |
| כְּעֵשֶׂב | הָאָרֶץ | | יְהִי | שְׁמוֹ | לְעוֹלָם | לִפְנֵי־שֶׁמֶשׁ |
| ke'ēsev | hā'ārets | | yehî | shemô | le'ôlām | liphnê-shemesh |
| like the grass of | the land | | may it be | his name | unto eternity | before the sun |

| 5396.521 | 8428 | 1313.726 | 904 | 3725, 1504 |
|---|---|---|---|---|
| v Hiphil juss 3ms | n ms, ps 3ms | cj, v Hithpael juss 3mp | prep, ps 3ms | *adj*, n mp |
| יָנִין | שְׁמוֹ | וְיִתְבָּרְכוּ | בוֹ | כָּל־גּוֹיִם |
| yānîn | shemô | weyithbārekhû | vô | kol-gôyim |
| may it shoot up | his name | and may they bless | by him | all the nations |

| 861.326 | | 1313.155 | 3176 | 435 | 435 | 3547 |
|---|---|---|---|---|---|---|
| v Piel juss 3mp, ps 3ms | **18.** | v Qal pass ptc ms | pn | n mp | *n mp* | pn |
| יְאַשְּׁרוּהוּ | | בָּרוּךְ | יְהוָה | אֱלֹהִים | אֱלֹהֵי | יִשְׂרָאֵל |
| ye'ashsherûhû | | bārûkh | yehwāh | 'ĕlōhîm | 'ĕlōhê | yisrā'ēl |
| they will declare him blessed | | blessed | Yahweh | God | the God of | Israel |

| 6449.151 | 6623.258 | 3937, 945 | | 1313.155 | 8428 |
|---|---|---|---|---|---|
| *v Qal act ptc ms* | v Niphal ptc fp | prep, n ms, ps 3ms | **19.** | cj, v Qal pass ptc ms | *n ms* |
| עֹשֵׂה | נִפְלָאוֹת | לְבַדּוֹ | | וּבָרוּךְ | שֵׁם |
| 'ōsēh | niphlā'ōth | levaddô | | ûvārûkh | shēm |
| One Who does | extraordinary deeds | by himself | | and blessed | the name of |

| 3638 | 3937, 5986 | 4527.221 | 3638 | 881, 3725 | 800 | 549 |
|---|---|---|---|---|---|---|
| n ms, ps 3ms | prep, n ms | cj, v Niphal juss 3ms | n ms, ps 3ms | do, *n ms* | art, n fs | intrj |
| כְּבוֹדוֹ | לְעוֹלָם | וְיִמָּלֵא | כְבוֹדוֹ | אֶת־כֹּל | הָאָרֶץ | אָמֵן |
| kevôdhô | le'ôlām | weyimmālē' | khevôdhô | 'eth-kōl | hā'ārets | 'āmēn |
| his glory | unto eternity | and may it be full | his glory | the entirety of | the earth | amen |

| 549 | | 3735.116 | 8940 | 1784 | 1158, 3571 | | 4344 | 3937, 637 |
|---|---|---|---|---|---|---|---|---|
| cj, intrj | **20.** | v Pual pf 3cp | *n fp* | pn | *n ms*, pn | **73:t** | n ms | prep, pn |
| וְאָמֵן | | כָּלּוּ | תְפִלּוֹת | דָּוִד | בֶּן־יִשָׁי | | מִזְמוֹר | לְאָסָף |
| we'āmēn | | kollû | thephillôth | dāwidh | ben-yishāy | | mizmôr | le'āsāph |
| and amen | | they have ended | the prayers of | David | the son of Jesse | | a Psalm | of Asaph |

| | 395 | 3005 | 3937, 3547 | 435 | 3937, 1276 | 3949 | | 603 | 3626, 4746 |
|---|---|---|---|---|---|---|---|---|---|
| **1.** | adv | adj | prep, pn | n mp | prep, adj | n ms | **2.** | cj, pers pron | prep, sub |
| | אַךְ | טוֹב | לְיִשְׂרָאֵל | אֱלֹהִים | לְבָרֵי | לֵבָב | | וַאֲנִי | כִּמְעַט |
| | 'akh | tôv | leyisrā'ēl | 'ĕlōhîm | levārê | lēvāv | | wa'ănî | kim'at |
| | surely | good | Israel | God | to the pure of | heart | | but I | like a moment |

*NAB* ... Let the fields grow plenty of grain and the hills be covered with crops, *NCV* ... may its stems be unnumbered like the grass of the earth, *BB*.

**17. His name shall endure for ever: his name shall be continued as long as the sun: and men shall be blessed in him: all nations shall call him blessed:** ... and His name increase as long as the sun shines, *Beck* ... may His reputation flourish, *Berkeley* ... Let his name for ever remain, *Fenton*.

**18. Blessed be the Lord God, the God of Israel, who only doeth wondrous things:** ... who alone works wonders, *JB* ... who does wonderful deeds as none else, *Knox* ... who alone does marvellous things, *NEB*.

**19. And blessed be his glorious name for ever: and let the whole earth be filled with his glory; Amen, and Amen:** ... fill all the Earth with His Might, *Fenton* ... Let his glory fill the whole world, *NCV*.

**20. The prayers of David the son of Jesse are ended:** ... This concludes the prayers of, *NIV*.

**73:t. A Psalm of Asaph.**

**1. Truly God is good to Israel, even to such as are of a clean heart:** ... What bounty God shews, *Knox* ... to the upright God is good, to hearts unstained, *Moffatt* ... to those whose hearts are pure, *Beck*.

**2. But as for me, my feet were almost gone; my steps had well nigh**

---

This king's treasure is the life of his subjects. Therefore, he will put forth his power to preserve them and deliver them. The result of such tender care and delivering love is set forth in v. 15, but in obscure language. The plain way of understanding the verse is to suppose that the person spoken of in all the clauses is the same, and then the question comes whether he is the king or the ransomed man. On the whole, it is best to suppose that the ransomed man is the subject throughout and that the verse describes his glad tribute and continual thankfulness. Ransomed from death, he brings offerings to his deliverer.

**72:16–20.** The last part of the Psalm (vv. 16f) returns to petitions for the growth of the nation and the perpetual flourishing of the king's name. The fertility of the land and the increase of its people are the psalmist's desires, which are also certainties, as expressed in v. 16. He sees in imagination the whole land waving with abundant harvests, which reach even to the tops of the mountains and rustle in the summer air with a sound like the cedars of Lebanon when they move their layers of greenness to the breeze. Such hopes had only partial fulfillment in Israel, and have had inadequate fulfillment up until now. But they lie on the horizon of the future, and they shall one day be reached. Much that is dim is treasured in them. There may be a renovated world from which the curse of barrenness has been banished. There shall be a swift increase of the subjects of the King, until the earlier hope of the Psalm is fulfilled, and all nations shall serve Him.

But bright as are the poet's visions concerning the kingdom, his last gaze is fastened on its king, and he prays that his name may last forever and may send forth shoots as long as the sun shines in the sky. He probably meant no more than a prayer for the continual duration of the dynasty, and his conception of the name as sending forth shoots was probably that of its being perpetuated in descendants. But as has been already noticed, the perpetuity, which he conceived of as belonging to a family and an office, really belongs to the one King, Jesus Christ, whose name is above every name. The psalmist's last desire is that the ancient promise to the fathers may be fulfilled in the King, their descendant, in whom men shall bless themselves. It still is true that in Christ all blessings for humanity are stored and that therefore, if men are to be truly blessed, they must plunge themselves into Him and in Him find all that they need for blessedness and nobility of life and character. Since He is our supreme type of whatsoever things are fair and of good report, and if we have bowed ourselves to Him because He has delivered us from death, then we share in his life, and all his blessings are parted among us.

***Psalm 73.*** *The perennial problem of reconciling God's moral government with observed facts is grappled with in this Psalm, as in Pss. 37 and 49. It tells how the prosperity of the godless, in apparent flat contradiction of divine promises, had all but swept the psalmist from his faith, and how he was led through the doubt and struggle to closer communion with God.*

*The Psalm falls into two divisions: in the first (vv. 1–14), the psalmist tells of his doubts and in the second (vv. 15–28), of his victory over them. The body of the Psalm is divided into groups of four verses, and it has an introduction and conclusion of two verses each.*

**73:1–2.** The introduction (vv. 1f) asserts, with an accent of assurance, the conviction which the psalmist had all but lost and therefore had the more

| 5371.155 | 7559 | 3626, 375 | 8581.412 | 863 | | 3706, 7349.315 |
|---|---|---|---|---|---|---|
| v Qal pass ptc ms | n fd, ps 1cs | prep, sub | v Pual pf 3fs | n fp, ps 1cs | | cj, v Piel pf 1cs |
| נָטוּי | רַגְלָי | כְּאַיִן | שֻׁפְּכָה | אֲשֻׁרָי | **3.** | כִּי־קִנֵּאתִי |
| nāṭûy | raghlāy | k$^{e}$'ayin | shupp$^{e}$khāh | 'ăshurāy | | kî-qinnē'thî |
| stumbled ones | my feet | like there is not | they gushed out | my steps | | because I was jealous |

| 904, 2054.152 | 8361 | 7857 | 7495.125 | | 3706 | 375 |
|---|---|---|---|---|---|---|
| prep, art, v Qal act ptc mp | *n ms* | n mp | v Qal impf 1cs | | cj | *sub* |
| בַּהוֹלְלִים | שְׁלוֹם | רְשָׁעִים | אֶרְאֶה | **4.** | כִּי | אֵין |
| bahôl$^{e}$lîm | sh$^{e}$lôm | r$^{e}$shā'îm | 'er'eh | | kî | 'ên |
| with those who boast | the prosperity of | the wicked | I saw | | because | there were not |

| 2890 | 3937, 4323 | 1304 | 190 | | 904, 6219 | 596 |
|---|---|---|---|---|---|---|
| n fp | prep, n ms, ps 3mp | cj, adj | n ms, ps 3mp | | prep, *n ms* | n ms |
| חַרְצֻבּוֹת | לְמוֹתָם | וּבָרִיא | אוּלָם | **5.** | בַּעֲמַל | אֱנוֹשׁ |
| chartsubbôth | l$^{e}$môthām | ûvārî' | 'ûlām | | ba'ămal | 'ĕnôsh |
| pangs | leading to their death | and fattened | their body | | with the trouble of | a man |

| 375 | 6196, 119 | 3940 | 5236.426 | | 3937, 3772 |
|---|---|---|---|---|---|
| sub, ps 3mp | cj, prep, n ms | neg part | v Pual impf 3mp | | prep, adv |
| אֵינֵמוֹ | וְעִם־אָדָם | לֹא | יְנֻגָּעוּ | **6.** | לָכֵן |
| 'ênēmô | w$^{e}$'im-'ādhām | lō' | y$^{e}$nuggā'û | | lākhēn |
| there is not to them | and among humankind | not | they have been harmed | | therefore |

| 6290.112 | 1375 | 6063.121, 8309 | 2660 | 3937 | | 3428.111 |
|---|---|---|---|---|---|---|
| v Qal pf 3fs, ps 3mp | n fs | v Qal impf 3ms, n ms | n ms | prep, ps 3mp | | v Qal pf 3ms |
| עֲנָקַתְמוֹ | גַאֲוָה | יַעֲטָף־שִׁית | חָמָס | לָמוֹ | **7.** | יָצָא |
| 'ănāqathmô | gha'ăwāh | ya'ăṭāph-shîth | chāmās̱ | lāmô | | yātsā' |
| it is placed around their neck | pride | a garment covers | violence | to them | | it goes out |

| 4623, 2561 | 6084 | 5882.116 | 5031 | 3949 | | 4302.126 |
|---|---|---|---|---|---|---|
| prep, n ms | n fs, ps 3mp | v Qal pf 3cp | *n fp* | n ms | | v Qal impf 3mp |
| מֵחֵלֶב | עֵינֵמוֹ | עָבְרוּ | מַשְׂכִּיּוֹת | לֵבָב | **8.** | יָמִיקוּ |
| mēchēlev | 'ênēmô | 'āverû | maskîyôth | lēvāv | | yāmîqû |
| from fatness | their eye | they have passed by | the imaginations of | heart | | they scoff |

| 1744.326 | 904, 7737 | 6480 | 4623, 4953 | 1744.326 | | 8308.116 |
|---|---|---|---|---|---|---|
| cj, v Piel impf 3mp | prep, n ms | n ms | prep, n ms | v Piel impf 3mp | | v Qal pf 3cp |
| וִידַבְּרוּ | בְרָע | עֹשֶׁק | מִמָּרוֹם | יְדַבֵּרוּ | **9.** | שַׁתּוּ |
| wîdhabb$^{e}$rû | v$^{e}$rā' | 'ōsheq | mimmārôm | y$^{e}$dhabbērû | | shattû |
| and they speak | with evil | oppression | from the heights | they speak | | they have set |

| 904, 8452 | 6552 | 4098 | 2050.122 | 904, 800 | | 3937, 3772 |
|---|---|---|---|---|---|---|
| prep, art, n md | n ms, ps 3mp | cj, n fs, ps 3mp | v Qal impf 3fs | prep, art, n fs | | prep, adv |
| בַשָּׁמַיִם | פִּיהֶם | וּלְשׁוֹנָם | תִּהֲלַךְ | בָּאָרֶץ | **10.** | לָכֵן |
| vashshāmayim | pîhem | ûlāshônām | tihlakh | bā'ārets | | lākhēn |
| in the heavens | their mouth | and their tongue | it walks about | throughout the earth | | therefore |

**slipped:** … I almost lost my balance; my feet all but slipped, *NAB* … my feet came close to stumbling, *NASB* … I had almost stopped believing; I had almost lost my faith, *NCV* … my foothold had all but given way, *NEB*.

**3. For I was envious at the foolish, when I saw the prosperity of the wicked:** … I envied the arrogant when I saw, *NIV* … I saw the peace of the wicked, *KJVII* … when I saw the well-being of the wrong-doers, *BB*.

**4. For there are no bands in their death: but their strength is firm:** … Their bodies are healthy and sleek, *Beck* … their body is well nourished, *Berkeley* … Sound and healthy is their bodies, *Goodspeed*.

**5. They are not in trouble as other men; neither are they plagued like other men:** … are free from the burdens of mortals, *NAB* … they don't have problems like other people, *NCV* … they have no part in Adam's afflictions, *JB* … are free from the burdens common to man, *NIV*.

**6. Therefore pride compasseth them about as a chain; violence covereth them as a garment:** ... Pride therefore encircles their neck, *Berkeley* ... They deck themselves with pride, adorn their crown with crime, *Fenton* ... they wear pride like a necklace, *REB* ... and crime the garment that covers them, *Beck*.

**7. Their eyes stand out with fatness: they have more than heart could wish:** ... they have more than their heart's desire, *BB* ... They transcend the imaginations of the heart, *Goodspeed* ... do not control their selfish desires, *NCV* ... Their eyes bulge with abundance, *NKJV*.

**8. They are corrupt, and speak wickedly concerning oppression: they speak loftily:** ... They scoff and speak with malice; loftily they threaten oppression, *NRSV* ... high-handedly they threaten oppression, *REB* ... They are rotten and speak with wicked cruelty, *KJVII* ... they talk disdainfully, *Berkeley*.

**9. They set their mouth against the heavens, and their tongue walketh through the earth:** ... They speak evil of God in heaven and give arrogant orders to men on earth, *Good News* ... Their mouth claims heaven for themselves, *JB* ... their words strut through the earth, *LIVB* ... tongue ranges the earth, *Goodspeed*.

**10. Therefore his people return hither: and waters of a full cup are wrung out to them:** ... His people turn to them, swallow their words, *Beck* ... So people turn to follow them, and see no wrong in them, *Moffatt* ... So their people turn to them and give them whatever they want, *NCV* ... my people follow their lead, *NEB*.

---

truly won. The initial word "surely" (HED #395) is an indication of his past struggle when the truth that God was good to Israel had seemed so questionable.

The disavowal of conquered doubts follows on this clear note of certitude. There is a tinge of shame in the emphatic "I" of v. 2 and in the broken construction and the change of subject to "my feet" and "my steps." The psalmist looks back to that dreary time and sees more clearly than he had, while he was caught in the toils of perplexity and doubt, how narrow had been his escape from casting away his confidence. He shudders as he remembers it, but he can do so now from the vantage point of tried and regained faith.

**73:3–4.** In the first quatrain of verses, the prosperity of the godless, which had been the psalmist's stumbling block, is described. Two things are specified—physical health and exemption from calamity. The former is the theme of v. 4. Its first clause is doubtful. The word rendered "bands" (HED #2890) only occurs here and in Isa. 58:6. It literally means "bands" but may pass into the figurative signification of pains and is sometimes by some taken in that meaning here and the whole clause as asserting that the wicked have painless and peaceful deaths. But such a declaration is impossible in the face of vv. 18f, which assert the very opposite and would be out of place at this point of the Psalm, which is here occupied with the lives, not the deaths, of the ungodly. The text describes the prosperous worldling as free from troubles or diseases, which would be like chains on a captive by which he is dragged to execution. It thus gives a parallel to the next clause, which describes their bodies as stalwart.

**73:5–6.** Verse 5 carries on the description and paints the wicked's exemption from trouble. The first clause is literally, "In the trouble of man, they are not." Thus the prosperous worldlings appeared to the psalmist, in his times of skepticism, as possessing charmed lives, which were free from all the ills that came from frailty and mortality and, as like superior beings, lifted above the universal lot. Very graphically does v. 6 paint them as having pride for their necklace and violence for their robe. A proud man carries a stiff neck and a high head. As the clothing wraps the body and is visible to the world, so insolent violence, masterfulness enforced by material weapons and contemptuous of others' rights, characterized these men who had never learned gentleness in the school of suffering.

**73:7–9.** The next group of verses further describes the unfeeling insolence begotten of unbroken prosperity and the crowd of admirers and imitators attendant on the successful wicked. Verse 8 deals with the manifestation of these in speech. Well-to-do wickedness delights in making suffering goodness the butt of its coarse jeers. It does not need much wit to do that. Clumsy jests are easy, and poverty is often the helpless object of vulgar wealth's ridicule. But there is a dash of ferocity in such laughter, and such jests pass quickly into earnest and wicked oppression. From the heights, they speak, fancying themselves set on a pedestal above the common masses. The Septuagint, followed by many moderns, attaches "oppression" to the second clause, which makes the verse more symmetrical, but the existing division of clauses yields an appropriate sense.

| 8178.521 | 6194 | 2057 | 4448 | 4529 | 4842.226 | 3937 |
|---|---|---|---|---|---|---|
| v Hiphil impf 3ms | n ms, ps 3ms | adv | cj, n mp | adj | v Niphal impf 3mp | prep, ps 3mp |
| יָשִׁיב | עַמּוֹ | הֲלֹם | וּמֵי | מָלֵא | יִמָּצוּ | לָמוֹ |
| yāshîv | 'ammô | helōm | ûmê | mālē' | yimmātsû | lāmô |
| they return | his people | here | and waters | full | they are drained | for them |

| 11. | 569.116 | 353 | 3156.111, 418 | 3552 | 1907 | 904, 6169 |
|---|---|---|---|---|---|---|
| | cj, v Qal pf 3cp | intrg | v Qal pf 3ms, n ms | cj, sub | n fs | prep, n ms |
| | וְאָמְרוּ | אֵיכָה | יָדַע־אֵל | וְיֵשׁ | דֵּעָה | בְעֶלְיוֹן |
| | we'āmerû | 'êkhāh | yādha'-'ēl | weyēsh | dē'āh | ve'elyôn |
| | and they have said | how | does God know | and is there | knowledge | in the Most High |

| 12. | 2079, 431 | 7857 | 8358 | 5986 | 7892.516, 2524 |
|---|---|---|---|---|---|
| | intrj, dem pron | n mp | cj, *adj* | n ms | v Hiphil pf 3cp, n ms |
| | הִנֵּה־אֵלֶּה | רְשָׁעִים | וְשַׁלְוֵי | עוֹלָם | הִשְׂגּוּ־חָיִל |
| | hinnēh-'ēlleh | reshā'îm | weshalwê | 'ôlām | hisgû-chāyil |
| | behold these | the wicked | and at ease | forever | they have increased riches |

| 13. | 395, 7672 | 2218.315 | 3949 | 7647.125 | 904, 5539 | 3834 |
|---|---|---|---|---|---|---|
| | adv, n ms | v Piel pf 1cs | n ms, ps 1cs | cj, v Qal impf 1cs | prep, n ms | n fp, ps 1cs |
| | אַךְ־רִיק | זִכִּיתִי | לְבָבִי | וָאֶרְחַץ | בְּנִקָּיוֹן | כַּפָּי |
| | 'akh-rîq | zikkîthî | levāvî | wā'erchats | beniqqāyôn | kappāy |
| | surely worthlessness | I have cleansed | my heart | and I have washed | in innocence | my hands |

| 14. | 2030.125 | 5236.155 | 3725, 3219 | 8763 | 3937, 1269 |
|---|---|---|---|---|---|
| | cj, v Qal impf 1cs | v Qal pass ptc ms | *adj*, art, n ms | cj, n fs, ps 1cs | prep, art, n mp |
| | וָאֱהִי | נָגוּעַ | כָּל־הַיּוֹם | וְתוֹכַחְתִּי | לַבְּקָרִים |
| | wā'ěhî | nāghûa' | kol-hayyôm | wethôkhachtî | labbeqārîm |
| | and I was | stricken | all the day | and my chastenings | at the mornings |

| 15. | 524, 569.115 | 5807.325 | 3765 | 2079 | 1810 | 1158 |
|---|---|---|---|---|---|---|
| | cj, v Qal pf 1cs | v Piel juss 1cs | prep | intrj | *n ms* | n mp, ps 2ms |
| | אִם־אָמַרְתִּי | אֲסַפְּרָה | כְמוֹ | הִנֵּה | דוֹר | בָנֶיךָ |
| | 'im-'āmartî | 'ăsapperāh | khemô | hinnēh | dhôr | bānêkhā |
| | if I had said | let me recount | so | behold | the generation of | your children |

| 931.115 | 16. | 2913.325 | 3937, 3156.141 | 2148 | 6219 | 2026 |
|---|---|---|---|---|---|---|
| v Qal pf 1cs | | cj, v Piel impf 1cs | prep, v Qal inf con | dem pron | n ms | pers pron |
| בָגָדְתִּי | | וָאֲחַשְּׁבָה | לָדַעַת | זֹאת | עָמָל | הִיא |
| vāghādhettî | | wā'ăchashshevāh | lādha'ath | zō'th | 'āmāl | hî' |
| I would have acted deceitfully | | but I thought | to know | this | harm | it |

| 904, 6084 | 17. | 5912, 971.125 | 420, 4881, 418 | 1032.125 | 3937, 313 |
|---|---|---|---|---|---|
| prep, n fd, ps 1cs | | adv, v Qal impf 1cs | prep, *n mp*, n ms | v Hiphil juss 1cs | prep, n fs, ps 3mp |
| בְעֵינָי | | עַד־אָבוֹא | אֶל־מִקְדְּשֵׁי־אֵל | אָבִינָה | לְאַחֲרִיתָם |
| ve'ênāy | | 'adh-'āvô' | 'el-miqōddeshê-'ēl | 'āvînāh | le'achrîthām |
| in my eyes | | until I went | to the sanctuaries of God | let me understand | about their future |

**11. And they say, How doth God know? and is there knowledge in the most High?:** … How will the Lord see this, *BB* … and the Most High understand?, *Beck* … They say, "God will not know; the Most High will not find out," *Good News*.

**12. Behold, these are the ungodly, who prosper in the world; they increase in riches:** … That is what the wicked are like, *JB* … always carefree, while they increase in wealth, *NAB* … they are secure and their riches increase, *Berkeley* … always at ease, and getting richer, *NCV*.

**13. Verily I have cleansed my heart in vain, and washed my hands in innocency:** … kept my heart from stain, *Moffatt* … have I kept my heart pure, *Goodspeed* … washed my hands clean in pureness of living, *Knox*.

**14. For all the day long have I been plagued, and chastened every morning:** … I suffer affliction day after day, *NAB* … have suffered all day long, *NCV* … I suffer torment, *NEB* … have been troubled all the day, *BB*.

**15. If I say, I will speak thus; behold, I should offend against the generation of thy children:** ... had I said, 'I shall talk like them,' *JB* ... I would have betrayed Your people, *Beck* ... I would have let your people down, *NCV* ... I would have been a traitor to your people, *LIVB*.

**16. When I thought to know this, it was too painful for me:** ... when I pondered to understand this, it was too overwhelming for me, *Berkeley* ... I set myself to think this out, *NEB* ... When I tried to understand all this, *NIV* ... it was too difficult for my mind, *Anchor*.

**17. Until I went into the sanctuary of God; then understood I their end:** ... and perceived their ending, *Berkeley* ... saw the end of the evil-doers, *BB* ... saw the end in store for them, *Beck* ... understood what was destined to become of them, *JB*.

---

The description of arrogant speech is carried on in v. 9, which has been variously understood as referring in v. 9a to blasphemy against God ("they set their mouth against the heavens") and in v. 9b to slander against men; or, as in v. 9a, continuing the thought of v. 8b and designating their words as spoken as if from heaven itself and in v. 9b ascribing to their words sovereign power among men. But it is better to regard "heaven" and "earth" as the ordinary designation of the whole visible frame of things and to take the verse as describing the self-sufficiency which gives its opinions and lays down the law about everything and, on the other hand, the currency and influence which are accorded by the popular voice to the dicta of prosperous worldlings.

The next group begins with an utterance of unbelief or doubt, but it is difficult to reach certainty as to the speakers.

**73:10–14.** Verse 10 is enigmatic. There are several obscure points in it. First, the verb in the Hebrew text (HED #8178) means "turns" (transitive), which the Hebrew margin corrects into "returns" (intransitive). With the former reading, "his people" is the object of the verb, and the implied subject is the prosperous wicked man, the change to the singular "he" from the plural "they" of the preceding clauses being not unusual in Hebrew. With the latter reading, "his people" is the subject. "Waters of abundance" is probably a figure for fulness of material good, which rewards the humiliation of servile adherents to the prosperous worldling.

It is very natural to refer the "they" to the last-mentioned persons, namely, the people who have been led to attach themselves to the prosperous sinners and who by the example of these are led to question the reality of God's acquaintance with and moral government of human affairs. The question is, as often, in reality a denial. But "they" may have a more general sense, equivalent to our own colloquial use of it for an indefinite multitude.

Verse 11 would then be a question anxiously raised by faith that was beginning to reel; v. 12 would be a statement of the anomalous fact which staggered it; and vv. 13f would be the complaint of the afflicted godly. The psalmist's repudiation of a share in such incipient skepticism would begin with v. 15. There is much in favor of this view of the speakers, but against it is the psalmist's acknowledgment, in v. 2, that his own confidence in God's moral government had been shaken, of which there is no further trace in the Psalm, unless vv. 13f express the conclusion which he had been tempted to draw, and which, as he proceeds to say, he had fought down. If these two verses are ascribed to him, v. 12 is best regarded as a summary of the whole preceding part. Only v. 11 is the utterance either of the prosperous sinner and his adherents (in which case it is a question which means denial) or is that of troubled faith (in which case it is a question that would fain be an affirmation, but has been forced unwillingly to regard the very pillars of the universe as trembling).

**73:15–16.** Verses 15–18 tell how the psalmist strove with and finally conquered his doubts and saw enough of the great arc of the divine dealings to be sure that the anomaly, which had exercised his faith, was capable of complete reconciliation with the righteousness of providence. It is instructive to note that he silenced his doubts, out of regard to "the generation of thy children" that is, to the true Israel, the pure in heart.

Silent brooding over his problem did not bring light, as v. 16 tells us. The more he thought over it, the more insoluble it seemed to him. There are chambers which the key of thinking will not open. Unwelcome as the lesson is, we have to learn that every lock will not yield to even prolonged and strenuous investigation. The lamp of the understanding throws its beams far, but there are depths of darkness too deep and dark for them, and they are wisest who know its limits and do not try to use it in regions where it is useless.

**73:17–18.** But faith finds a path where speculation discerns none. The psalmist "went into the sanctuary of God," and there light streamed in on him, in which he saw light. It was not mere entrance into the

| 18. 395 | 904, 2616 | 8308.123 | 3937 | 5489.513 | 3937, 5060 |
|---|---|---|---|---|---|
| adv | prep, art, n fp | v Qal impf 2ms | prep, ps 3mp | v Hiphil pf 2ms, ps 3mp | prep, n fp |
| אַךְ | בַּחֲלָקוֹת | תָּשִׁית | לָמוֹ | הִפַּלְתָּם | לְמַשּׁוּאוֹת |
| 'akh | bachlāqōth | tāshîth | lāmô | hippaltām | lemashshû'ôth |
| only | in the slippery places | You set | them | You cause them to fall | to destruction |

| 19. 351 | 2030.116 | 3937, 8439 | 3626, 7569 | 5673.116 | 8882.116 |
|---|---|---|---|---|---|
| intrg | v Qal pf 3cp | prep, art, n fs | prep, n ms | v Qal pf 3cp | v Qal pf 3cp |
| אֵיךְ | הָיוּ | לְשַׁמָּה | כְרָגַע | סָפוּ | תַּמּוּ |
| 'êkh | hāyû | leshammāh | kherāgha' | sāphû | thammû |
| how | they are | unto destruction | like a moment | they come to an end | they are complete |

| 4623, 1130 | 20. 3626, 2573 | 4623, 7301.541 | 112 | 904, 5996.541 | 7021 |
|---|---|---|---|---|---|
| prep, n fp | prep, art, n ms | prep, v Hiphil inf con | n mp, ps 1cs | prep, v Hiphil inf con | n ms, ps 3mp |
| מִן־בַּלָּהוֹת | כַּחֲלוֹם | מֵהָקִיץ | אֲדֹנָי | בָּעִיר | צַלְמָם |
| min-ballāhôth | kachlôm | mēhāqîts | 'ădhōnāy | bā'îr | tsalmām |
| from terrors | like the dream | from awaking | my Lord | when awaking | their images |

| 995.123 | 21. 3706 | 2661.721 | 3949 | 3749 | 8532.725 |
|---|---|---|---|---|---|
| v Qal impf 2ms | cj | v Hithpael impf 3ms | n ms, ps 1cs | cj, n fp, ps 1cs | v Hithpoel impf 1cs |
| תִּבְזֶה | כִּי | יִתְחַמֵּץ | לְבָבִי | וְכִלְיוֹתַי | אֶשְׁתּוֹנָן |
| tivzeh | kî | yithchammēts | levāvî | wekhilyôthay | 'eshtônān |
| You will despise | because | it was embittered | my heart | and my kidneys | I was pierced |

| 22. 603, 1221 | 3940 | 3156.125 | 966 | 2030.115 | 6196 | 23. 603 |
|---|---|---|---|---|---|---|
| cj, pers pron, adj | cj, neg part | v Qal impf 1cs | n fp | v Qal pf 1cs | prep, ps 2ms | cj, pers pron |
| וַאֲנִי־בַעַר | וְלֹא | אֵדָע | בְּהֵמוֹת | הָיִיתִי | עִמָּךְ | וַאֲנִי |
| wa'ănî-va'ar | welō' | 'ēdhā' | behēmôth | hāyîthî | 'immākh | wa'ănî |
| and I stupid | but not | I know | beasts | I was | with You | yet I |

| 8878 | 6196 | 270.113 | 904, 3135, 3332 | 24. 904, 6332 |
|---|---|---|---|---|
| adv | prep, ps 2ms | v Qal pf 2ms | prep, *n fs*, n fs, ps 1cs | prep, n fs, ps 2ms |
| תָּמִיד | עִמָּךְ | אָחַזְתָּ | בְּיַד־יְמִינִי | בַּעֲצָתְךָ |
| thāmîdh | 'immākh | 'āchaztā | beyadh-yemînî | ba'ătsāthekhā |
| continually | with You | You hold fast | on the hand of my right side | with your counsel |

| 5328.523 | 313 | 3638 | 4089.123 | 25. 4449, 3937 |
|---|---|---|---|---|
| v Hiphil impf 2ms, ps 1cs | cj, adv | n ms | v Qal impf 2ms, ps 1cs | intrg, prep, ps 1cs |
| תַנְחֵנִי | וְאַחַר | כָּבוֹד | תִּקָּחֵנִי | מִי־לִי |
| thanchēnî | we'achar | kāvôdh | tiqqāchēnî | mî-lî |
| You lead me | and afterward | honor | You will receive me | who to me |

| 904, 8452 | 6196 | 3940, 2759.115 | 904, 800 | 26. 3735.111 | 8083 |
|---|---|---|---|---|---|
| prep, art, n md | cj, prep, ps 2ms | neg part, v Qal pf 1cs | prep, art, n fs | v Qal pf 3ms | n ms, 1cs |
| בַשָּׁמָיִם | וְעִמְּךָ | לֹא־חָפַצְתִּי | בָאָרֶץ | כָּלָה | שְׁאֵרִי |
| vashshāmāyim | we'immekhā | lō'-chāphatstî | vā'ārets | kālāh | she'ērî |
| in the heavens | even with You | I do not desire | on the earth | it has come to an end | my body |

**18. Surely thou didst set them in slippery places: thou castedst them down into destruction:** … You have put them in danger, *NCV* … where there was danger of slipping, *BB* … ready to plunge them in ruin, *Knox* … making them fall into Desolation, *Anchor*.

**19. How are they brought into desolation, as in a moment! they are utterly consumed with terrors:** … they perish in their fears, *Fenton* … are instantly destroyed, *Good News* … completely wiped out in terrifying ways!, *Beck*.

**20. As a dream when one awaketh; so, O Lord, when thou awakest, thou shalt despise their image:** … when aroused, Thou wilt despise their form, *NASB* … Lord, when you rise up, they will disappear, *NCV* … like images in sleep which are dismissed on waking, *NEB*.

**21. Thus my heart was grieved, and I was pricked in my reins:** … and my spirit embittered, *NIV* … my emotions had dried up, *Anchor* …

feel bitter and stirred up inside, *Beck* ... I was pierced deep within, *Berkeley*.

**22. So foolish was I, and ignorant: I was as a beast before thee:** ... I became a stupid fool, *Anchor* ... without knowledge, *BB* ... like an animal in Your presence, *Beck* ... a reasonless creature in Thy sight, *Berkeley*.

**23. Nevertheless I am continually with thee: thou hast holden me by my right hand:** ... am always with thee, *Goodspeed* ... I stayed in your presence, *JB* ... you hold me by the hand, *Good News*.

**24. Thou shalt guide me with thy counsel, and afterward receive me to glory:** ... You guide me with your advice, and later you will receive me in honor, *NCV* ... welcome me into glory, *Knox*.

**25. Whom have I in heaven but thee? and there is none upon earth that I desire beside thee:** ... having thee, I desire nothing else on earth, *NEB*.

**26. My flesh and my heart faileth: but God is the strength of my heart, and my portion for ever:** ... My body and my mind may become weak, *NCV* ... But my heart's rock, *Goodspeed* ... and my part forever, *KJVII* ... my eternal heritage, *BB* ... eternally my inheritance, *Knox*.

**27. For, lo, they that are far from thee shall perish: thou hast**

---

place of worship, but closer approach to the God Who dwelt there and cleared away the mists. Communion with God solves many problems which thinking leaves unresolved. The eye which has gazed on God is purged for much vision besides. Such communion, in its seclusion from worldly agitations, enables a man to take calmer, saner views of life. The lesson which the psalmist learned in the solemn stillness of the sanctuary was the end of ungodly prosperity. That changes the aspect of the envied position of the prosperous sinner, for his very prosperity is seen to contribute to his downfall, as well as to make that downfall more tragic by contrast. His sure footing, exempt as he seemed from the troubles, was really on a treacherous slope, like smooth sheets of rock on a mountainside. To stand on them is to slide down to hideous ruin.

**73:19–20.** The theme of the end of the prosperous sinners is continued in the next group (vv. 19–22). In v. 19, the psalmist seems to stand as an amazed spectator of the crash, which tumbles into chaos the seemingly solid fabric of their insolent prosperity. An exclamation breaks from his lips as he looks. And then destruction is foretold for all of them under the solemn and magnificent image of v. 20. God has seemed to sleep, letting evil run its course, but He "rouses" himself and comes forth in judicial acts. Life is full of such awakings of God, both in regard to individuals and nations, which if a man duly regards he will find the problem of the Psalm less insoluble than at first it appears. But if there are lives which being without goodness are also without chastisement, death comes at last to such as God's awaking and a very awful dissipating of earthly prosperity into a shadowy nothing.

**73:21–22.** Verses 21f are generally taken as one sentence and translated, "When my heart became bitter ... then I was like an animal." They are better regarded as the psalmist's penitent explanation of his struggle. His recognition that his doubts had their source, not in defect in God's providence, but in his own ignorance and hasty irritation, which took offense without cause, prepares him for the sweet, clear note of purely spiritual aspiration and fruition which follows in the next strophe.

**73:23–24.** He had all but lost his hold of God, but although his feet had almost gone astray, his hand had been grasped by God, and that strong hold had kept him from utterly falling. The pledge of continual communion with God is not our own vacillating, wayward hearts, but God's gentle, strong clasp, which will not let us go. Conscious of constant fellowship and feeling thrillingly God's touch in his inmost spirit, the psalmist rises to a height of joyous assurance far above doubts and perplexities caused by the unequal distribution of earth's trivial good. For him, all life will be illumined by God's counsel, which will guide him as a shepherd leads his sheep and which he will obey as a sheep follows his shepherd. How small the delights of the prosperous men seem now! Whether we translate "with glory" or "to glory," there can be no question that the psalmist is looking beyond life on earth to dwelling with God in glory. We have, in this utterance, the expression of the conviction, inseparable from any true, deep communion with God, that such communion can never be at the mercy of death. The real proof of a life beyond the grave is the resurrection of Jesus, and the pledge of it is present enjoyment of fellowship with God.

**73:25–26.** Such thoughts lift the psalmist to a height from which earth's troubles show small, and as they diminish, the perplexity arising from their distribution diminishes in proportion. They fade

| 3949 | 6962, 3949 | 2610 | 435 | 3937, 5986 | | 3706, 2079 |
|---|---|---|---|---|---|---|
| cj, n ms, ps 1cs | *n ms*, n ms, ps 1cs | cj, n ms, ps 1cs | n mp | prep, n ms | **27.** | cj, intrj |
| וּלְבָבִי | צוּר־לְבָבִי | וְחֶלְקִי | אֱלֹהִים | לְעוֹלָם | | כִּי־הִנֵּה |
| ûlāvāvî | tsûr-levāvî | wechelqî | 'ělōhîm | le'ôlām | | kî-hinnēh |
| and my heart | the Rock of my heart | and my portion | God | unto eternity | | because behold |

| 7652 | 6.126 | 7059.513 | 3725, 2265.151 | 4623 |
|---|---|---|---|---|
| adj, ps 2ms | v Qal impf 3mp | v Hiphil pf 2ms | *adj*, v Qal act ptc ms | prep, ps 2ms |
| רְחֵקֶיךָ | יֹאבֵדוּ | הִצְמַתָּה | כָּל־זוֹנֶה | מִמֶּךָ |
| rechēqêkhā | yō'vēdhû | hitsmattāh | kol-zôneh | mimmekhā |
| those far from You | they perish | You will annihilate | all the unfaithful | from You |

| | 603 | 7420 | 435 | 3937, 3005 | 8308.115 | 904, 112 | 3176 | 4406 |
|---|---|---|---|---|---|---|---|---|
| **28.** | cj, pers pron | *n fs* | n mp | prep, ps 1cs, adj | v Qal pf 1cs | prep, n mp, ps 1cs | pn | n ms, ps 1cs |
| | וַאֲנִי | קִרֲבַת | אֱלֹהִים | לִי־טוֹב | שַׁתִּי | בַּאדֹנָי | יְהוִה | מַחְסִי |
| | wa'ănî | qirvath | 'ělōhîm | lî-ţôv | shattî | ba'dhōnāy | yehōwih | machsî |
| | but I | being near | God | to me good | I have put | on my Lord | Yahweh | my Refuge |

| 3937, 5807.341 | 3725, 4536 | | 5030 | 3937, 637 | | 4066 | 435 | 2269.113 |
|---|---|---|---|---|---|---|---|---|
| prep, v Piel inf con | *adj*, n fp, ps 2ms | **74:t** | n ms | prep, pn | **1.** | intrg | n mp | v Qal pf 2ms |
| לְסַפֵּר | כָּל־מַלְאֲכוֹתֶיךָ | | מַשְׂכִּיל | לְאָסָף | | לָמָה | אֱלֹהִים | זָנַחְתָּ |
| lesappēr | kol-mal'ăkhôthêkhā | | maskîl | le'āsāph | | lāmāh | 'ělōhîm | zānachtā |
| to recount | all your handiworks | | a Maskil | of Asaph | | why | O God | have You rejected |

| 3937, 5516 | 6475.121 | 653 | 904, 6887 | 4993 | | 2226.131 |
|---|---|---|---|---|---|---|
| prep, art, n ms | v Qal impf 3ms | n ms, ps 2ms | prep, *n fs* | n fs, ps 2ms | **2.** | v Qal impv 2ms |
| לָנֶצַח | יֶעְשַׁן | אַפְּךָ | בְּצֹאן | מַרְעִיתֶךָ | | זְכֹר |
| lānetsach | ye'ăshan | 'appekhā | betsō'n | mar'îthekhā | | zekhōr |
| unto forever | it smokes | your nose | against the sheep of | your pasture | | remember |

| 5920 | 7353.113 | 7208 | 1381.113 | 8101 |
|---|---|---|---|---|
| n fs, ps 2ms | v Qal pf 2ms | adv | v Qal pf 2ms | *n ms* |
| עֲדָתְךָ | קָנִיתָ | קֶּדֶם | גָּאַלְתָּ | שֵׁבֶט |
| 'ădhāthekhā | qānîthā | qedhem | gā'altā | shēveţ |
| your congregation | You have bought | in former times | You have redeemed | the tribe of |

| 5338 | 2098, 6995 | 2172 | 8331.113 | 904 | | 7597.531 |
|---|---|---|---|---|---|---|
| n fs, ps 2ms | *n ms*, pn | dem pron | v Qal pf 2ms | prep, ps 3ms | **3.** | v Hiphil impv 2ms |
| נַחֲלָתֶךָ | הַר־צִיּוֹן | זֶה | שָׁכַנְתָּ | בּוֹ | | הָרִימָה |
| nachlāthekhā | har-tsîyôn | zeh | shākhantā | bô | | hārîmāh |
| your inheritance | Mount Zion | this | You have stayed | on it | | raise |

| 6718 | 3937, 5061 | 5516 | 3725, 7778.511 | 342.151 | 904, 7231 |
|---|---|---|---|---|---|
| n fp, ps 2ms | prep, *n fp* | n ms | *adj*, v Hiphil pf 3ms | v Qal act ptc ms | prep, art, n ms |
| פְּעָמֶיךָ | לְמַשֻּׁאוֹת | נֶצַח | כָּל־הֵרַע | אוֹיֵב | בַּקֹּדֶשׁ |
| phe'āmêkhā | lemashshu'ôth | netsach | kol-hēra' | 'ôyēv | baqqōdhesh |
| your steps | for ruins of | forever | all he has done evil | an enemy | in the holy place |

| | 8057.116 | 7173.152 | 904, 7419 | 4287 | 7947.116 |
|---|---|---|---|---|---|
| **4.** | v Qal pf 3cp | v Qal act ptc mp, ps 2ms | prep, *n ms* | n ms, ps 2ms | v Qal pf 3cp |
| | שָׁאֲגוּ | צֹרְרֶיךָ | בְּקֶרֶב | מוֹעֲדֶךָ | שָׂמוּ |
| | shā'ăghû | tsōrerêkhā | beqerev | mô'ădhekhā | sāmû |
| | they have roared | your adversaries | in the midst of | your meeting place | they have put |

| 225 | 225 | | 3156.221 | 3626, 971.551 | 3937, 4762 |
|---|---|---|---|---|---|
| n mp, ps 3mp | n mp | **5.** | v Niphal impf 3ms | prep, v Hiphil ptc ms | prep, n fs |
| אוֹתֹתָם | אֹתוֹת | | יִוָּדַע | כְּמֵבִיא | לְמַעְלָה |
| 'ôthōthām | 'ōthôth | | yiwwādha' | kemēvî' | lema'ālāh |
| their signs | signs | | it is known | like one who causes to go | to the ascent |

**destroyed all them that go a whoring from thee:** ... will come to destruction, *BB* ... you destroy everyone who is unfaithful to you, *NAB* ... You have destroyed all who go lusting away from You, *KJVII*.

**28. But it is good for me to draw near to God: I have put my trust in the Lord GOD, that I may declare all thy works:** ... I know no other content but clinging to God, *Knox* ... it is best for me to come close to God, *Beck* ... I have made the LORD my refuge, *Berkeley* ... That I may recount all thy wonders, *Goodspeed*.

**74:t. Maschil of Asaph.**

**1. O God, why hast thou cast us off for ever? why doth thine anger smoke against the sheep of thy pasture?:** ... why have you put us away from you for ever?, *BB* ... Why do your nostrils smoke, *Anchor* ... why does Your anger blaze against the sheep, *Beck*.

**2. Remember thy congregation, which thou hast purchased of old; the rod of thine inheritance, which thou hast redeemed; this mount Zion, wherein thou hast dwelt:** ... Remember your flock, *NAB* ... You saved us, and we are your very own, *NCV* ... your own tribe which you redeemed, *JB*.

**3. Lift up thy feet unto the perpetual desolations; even all that the enemy hath done wickedly in the sanctuary:** ... restore what was ruined beyond repair, *NEB* ... all the evil which your haters have done in the holy place, *BB* ... see what havoc thy enemies have wrought in the holy place, *Knox* ... Walk through the awful ruins, *LIVB*.

**4. Thine enemies roar in the midst of thy congregations; they set up**

---

away altogether when he feels how rich he is in possessing God. Surely the very summit of devotional rapture is reached in the immortal words which follow! Heaven without God would be a waste to this man. With God, he neither needs nor desires anything on earth. If the impossible should be actual and heart as well as flesh should fail, his naked self would be clothed and rich, steadfast and secure, as long as he had God. He is so closely knit to God that he knows he will not lose Him when he dies, but have Him for his very own forever. Why should he care how earth's vain goods come and go? Whatever outward calamities or poverty may be his lot, there is no riddle in that divine government which thus enriches the devout heart, and the richest ungodly man is poor because he shuts himself out from the one all-sufficient and enduring wealth.

**73:27–28.** A final pair of verses, answering to the introductory pair, gathers up the double truth which the psalmist has learned to grasp more firmly by occasion of his doubts. To be absent from God is to perish. Distance from Him is separation from life. Drawing near to Him is the only good, and the psalmist has deliberately chosen it as his good, let worldly prosperity come or go as it list, or, rather, as God shall choose. By the effort of his own volition he has made God his Refuge, and safe in Him he can bear the sorrows of the godly and look unenvying on the fleeting prosperity of sinners. With insight drawn from communion, he can recount with faith and praise all God's works and find in none of them a stumbling block, nor fail to find in any of them material for a song of thankfulness.

***Psalm 74.*** *The Psalm begins with a complaining cry to God (vv. 1ff), which passes into a piteous detail of the nation's misery (vv. 4–9), whence it rises into petition (vv. 10f), stays trembling faith by gazing upon his past deeds of help and the wonders of his creative power (vv. 12–17), and closes with beseeching God to vindicate the honor of his own name by the deliverance of his people (vv. 18–23).*

**74:1–3.** The main emphasis of the prayer in vv. 1–3 lies on the pleas which it presents, drawn from Israel's relation to God. The characteristic Asaphic designation "thy flock" stands in v. 1 and appeals to the Shepherd, both on the ground of his tenderness and of his honor as involved in the security of the sheep. A similar appeal lies in the two words "acquire" (HED #7353) and "redeem" (HED #1381), in both of which the deliverance from Egypt is referred to, the former expression suggesting the price at which the acquisition was made, as well as the obligations of ownership, and the latter, the office of the goel, the kinsman-redeemer, on whom devolved the duty of obtaining satisfaction for blood. The double designations of Israel as "thy congregation" and as "the tribe of thine inheritance" probably point to the religious and civil aspects of the national life. The strongest plea is put last, namely, God's dwelling on Zion. For all these reasons, the psalmist asks and expects Him to come with swift footsteps to the desolations, which have endured so long that the impatience of despair blends with the cry for help and calls them "everlasting," even while it prays that they may be built up again. The fact that the enemy of God and of his flock has marred everything in the sanctuary is enough, the psalmist thinks, to move God to action.

**74:4–9.** The same thought, that the nation's calamities are really dishonoring to God and there-

| 904, 5625, 6320 | 7423 | | 6496 | 6855 | 3266 | 904, 3910 |
|---|---|---|---|---|---|---|
| prep, *n ms*, n ms | n fp | 6. | cj, adv | n mp, ps 3fs | adv | prep, n ms |
| בְּסֲבָךְ־עֵץ | קַרְדֻּמּוֹת | | וְעַת | פִּתּוּחֶיהָ | יָּחַד | בְּכַשִּׁיל |
| bisvākh-'ēts | qardummôth | | we'ēth | pittûchêâh | yāchadh | bekhashshîl |
| in a thicket of wood | axes | | and a time | its engravings | together | with the hatchet |

| 3717 | 2056.126 | | 8365.316 | 904, 813 | 4881 | 3937, 800 |
|---|---|---|---|---|---|---|
| cj, n fp | v Qal impf 3mp | 7. | v Piel pf 3cp | prep, art, n fs | n ms, ps 2ms | prep, art, n fs |
| וְכֵילַפֹּת | יַהֲלֹמוּן | | שִׁלְחוּ | בָאֵשׁ | מִקְדָּשֶׁךָ | לָאָרֶץ |
| wekhêlappōth | yahlōmûn | | shilchû | vā'ēsh | miqŏddāshekhā | lā'ārets |
| and hammers | they have struck | | they sent out | with the fire | your Sanctuary | to the ground |

| 2591.316 | 5088, 8428 | | 569.116 | 904, 3949 | 3347.120 |
|---|---|---|---|---|---|
| v Piel pf 3cp | *n ms*, n ms, ps 2ms | 8. | v Qal pf 3cp | prep, n ms, ps 3mp | v Qal juss 1cp, ps 3mp |
| חִלְּלוּ | מִשְׁכַּן־שְׁמֶךָ | | אָמְרוּ | בְלִבָּם | נִינָם |
| chillelû | mishkan-shemekhā | | 'āmerû | velibbām | nînām |
| they profaned | the Tabernacle of your name | | they said | in their heart | let us subdue them |

| 3266 | 8041.116 | 3725, 4287, 418 | 904, 800 | | 225 | 3940 |
|---|---|---|---|---|---|---|
| adv | v Qal pf 3cp | *adj, n mp*, n ms | prep, art, n fs | 9. | n mp, ps 1cp | neg part |
| יַחַד | שָׂרְפוּ | כָל־מוֹעֲדֵי־אֵל | בָּאָרֶץ | | אוֹתֹתֵינוּ | לֹא |
| yāchadh | sārephû | khol-mô'ădhê-ēl | bā'ārets | | 'ôthōthênû | lō' |
| together | they burned | all the meeting places of God | throughout the land | | our signs | not |

| 7495.119 | 375, 5968 | 5204 | 3940, 882 | 3156.151 | 5912, 4242 |
|---|---|---|---|---|---|
| v Qal pf 1cp | *sub*, adv | n ms | cj, neg part, prep, ps 1cp | v Qal act ptc ms | adv, intrg |
| רָאִינוּ | אֵין־עוֹד | נָבִיא | וְלֹא־אִתָּנוּ | יֹדֵעַ | עַד־מָה |
| rā'înû | 'ên-'ôdh | nāvî' | welō'-'ittānû | yōdhēa' | 'adh-māh |
| we have seen | there is not anymore | a prophet | and not with us | one who knows | until what |

| | 5912, 5146 | 435 | 2884.321 | 7141 | 5180.321 | 342.151 | 8428 |
|---|---|---|---|---|---|---|---|
| 10. | adv, intrg | n mp | v Piel impf 3ms | n ms | v Piel impf 3ms | v Qal act ptc ms | n ms, ps 2ms |
| | עַד־מָתַי | אֱלֹהִים | יְחָרֶף | צָר | יְנָאֵץ | אוֹיֵב | שִׁמְךָ |
| | 'adh-māthay | 'ĕlōhîm | yechāreph | tsār | yenā'ēts | 'ôyēv | shimkhā |
| | until when | O God | will they taunt | the adversary | will they spurn | the enemy | your name |

| 3937, 5516 | | 4066 | 8178.523 | 3135 | 3332 | 4623, 7414 |
|---|---|---|---|---|---|---|
| prep, art, n ms | 11. | intrg | v Hiphil impf 2ms | n fs, ps 2ms | cj, n fs, ps 2ms | prep, *n ms* |
| לָנֶצַח | | לָמָּה | תָשִׁיב | יָדְךָ | וִימִינֶךָ | מִקֶּרֶב |
| lānetsach | | lāmmāh | thāshîv | yādhekhā | wîmînekhā | miqqerev |
| unto forever | | why | do You cause to return | your hand | even your right hand | from the middle of |

| 2536 | 3735.331 | | 435 | 4567 | 4623, 7208 | 6713.151 |
|---|---|---|---|---|---|---|
| n ms, ps 2ms | v Piel impv 2ms | 12. | cj, n mp | n ms, ps 1cs | prep, n ms | v Qal act ptc ms |
| חוֹקְךָ | כַלֵּה | | וֵאלֹהִים | מַלְכִּי | מִקֶּדֶם | פֹּעֵל |
| chôqŏkhā | khallēh | | wē'lōhîm | malkî | miqqedhem | pō'ēl |
| your bosom | bring to an end | | for God | my King | from antiquity | One Who works |

**their ensigns for signs:** ... enemies bawled inside thy house, *Moffatt* ... they have set up their tokens of victory, *NAB* ... raised their flags there, *NCV* ... They set up their banners for signs, *NKJV*.

**5. A man was famous according as he had lifted up axes upon the thick trees:** ... It was like a man using axes on, *KJVII* ... They are cutting down, *BB* ... It looks as if one had brought down the axe on brushwood, *Berkeley* ... like woodmen felling trees, *Moffatt*.

**6. But now they break down the carved work thereof at once with axes and hammers:** ... with chisel and hammer they hack at all its paneling, *NAB* ... doors are broken down with hammers and iron blades, *BB*.

**7. They have cast fire into thy sanctuary, they have defiled by casting down the dwellingplace of thy name to the ground:** ... burned your Temple to the ground, *NCV* ... tore down and polluted the shrine sacred to thy name, *NEB* ... polluted and tore down the sanctuary bearing Your name, *Beck.*

**8. They said in their hearts, Let us destroy them together: they have burned up all the synagogues of God in the land:** ... We will oppress them also, *Goodspeed* ... Let us put an end to them all together, *BB* ... "Let us subdue them completely," *Berkeley* ... 'Let us crush them at one stroke!' They burned down every sacred shrine, *JB.*

**9. We see not our signs: there is no more any prophet: neither is there among us any that knoweth how long:** ... Our emblems are nowhere to be seen, *Knox* ... We are given no miraculous signs, *NIV* ... We do not see our symbols, *Berkeley* ... The prophets are gone, and who can say when it all will end, *LIVB.*

**10. O God, how long shall the adversary reproach? shall the enemy blaspheme thy name for ever?:** ... how long shall the enemy speak evil, *KJVII* ... how long will those who are against us say cruel things?, *BB* ... Will the enemy scorn Your name forever?, *Beck* ... Shall the enemy revile thy name forever, *Goodspeed.*

**11. Why withdrawest thou thy hand, even thy right hand? pluck it out of thy bosom:** ... Why do you hold back your power?, *NCV* ... keep your right hand hidden in the folds of your robe, *JB* ... must it always lie idle in thy bosom, *Knox* ... Take it from the folds of your garment and destroy them!, *NIV.*

**12. For God is my King of old, working salvation in the midst of the earth:** ... You have been our king from the beginning, *Good News* ... from the past God is my King, *BB* ... performing victories throughout the country, *Beck* ... author of saving acts throughout the earth, *JB.*

---

fore worthy of his intervention, colors the whole of the description of these in vv. 4–9. The invaders are "your adversaries." It is in the place where God met Israel that their bestial noises, like those of lions over their prey, echoed. It is "your Sanctuary" which they have set on fire, "the Tabernacle of your name" which they have profaned. It is "the meeting places of God" which they have burned throughout the land. Only at the end of the sad catalog is the misery of the people touched on, and that, not so much as inflicted by human foes, as by the withdrawal of God's Spirit. This is, in fact, the dominant thought of the whole Psalm. It says very little about the sufferings resulting from the success of the enemy, but constantly returns to the insult to God and the reproach adhering to his name therefrom. The essence of it all is in the concluding prayer, "plead thine own cause" (v. 22).

In vv. 5f, a change of tense represents the action described in them, as if in progress at the moment before the singer's eyes. "They seem" (HED #3156) is literally "he is known" (or "makes himself known"), which may refer to the invaders, the change from plural to singular being frequent in Hebrew, or it may be taken impersonally, meaning "it seems." In either case, it introduces a comparison between the hacking and hewing by the spoilers in the Temple and the work of a woodman swinging on high his axe in the forest. "And now" (HED #6496) seems to indicate the next step in the scene, which the psalmist picturesquely conceives as passing before his horror-stricken sight. All is hewn down as if it were no more than so much growing timber. With v. 7, the tenses change to the calmer tone of historical narration. The plundered Temple is set on fire. In v. 8, the word "let us crush them" (HED #3347) has been erroneously taken as a noun and rendered "their brood," a verb like "we will root out" being supplied. The "meeting places of God in the land" cannot be old sanctuaries, nor the high places, which were Israel's sin, for no psalmist could have adduced the destruction of these as a reason for God's intervention. They can only be the synagogues. The expression is a strong argument for the later date of the Psalm. Equally strong is the lament in v. 9 over the removal of the "signs"—i.e., as in v. 4, the emblems of religion, or the sacrifices and festivals suppressed by Antiochus which were the tokens of the Covenant between God and Israel. The silence of prophecy cannot be alleged of the Chaldean period without some straining of facts and of the words here, nor is it true that then there was universal ignorance of the duration of the calamity, for Jeremiah had foretold it.

**74:10–11.** Verses 10f are the kernel of the Psalm, the rest of which is folded round them symmetrically. Starting from this center and working outward, we note that it is preceded by six verses dilating on the profanations of the name of God and followed by six setting forth the glories of that name in the past. The connection of these two portions of the Psalm is obvious. The outer shell is the prayer in three verses which begins the Psalm, and that in six verses which closes it. Verse 10 takes up the despairing "how long" from the end of the preceding portion and turns it into a question to God. The psalmist cannot endure that this condition should drag on indefinitely, as if "for ever," and his

| 3568 | 904, 7419 | 800 | | 887 | 6815.313 | 904, 6010 | 3328 |
|---|---|---|---|---|---|---|---|
| n fp | prep, *n ms* | art, n fs | **13.** | pers pron | v Poel pf 2ms | prep, n ms, ps 2ms | n ms |
| יְשׁוּעוֹת | בְּקֶרֶב | הָאָרֶץ | | אַתָּה | פוֹרַרְתָּ | בְעָזְּךָ | יָם |
| yeshû'ôth | beqerev | hā'ārets | | 'attāh | phôrartā | ve'āzzekhā | yām |
| deliverances | in the midst of | the earth | | You | You divided | by your strength | the Sea |

| 8132.313 | 7513 | 8906 | 6142, 4448 | | 887 | 7827.313 |
|---|---|---|---|---|---|---|
| v Piel pf 2ms | *n mp* | n mp | prep, art, n mp | **14.** | pers pron | v Piel pf 2ms |
| שִׁבַּרְתָּ | רָאשֵׁי | תַנִּינִים | עַל־הַמָּיִם | | אַתָּה | רִצַּצְתָּ |
| shibbartā | rā'shê | thanînîm | 'al-hammāyim | | 'attāh | ritstsatstā |
| You have broken in pieces | the heads of | the sea monsters | on the waters | | You | You crushed |

| 7513 | 4018 | 5598.123 | 4120 | 3937, 6194 | 3937, 6993 | | 887 |
|---|---|---|---|---|---|---|---|
| *n mp* | n ms | v Qal impf 2ms, ps 3ms | n ms | prep, n ms | prep, n mp | **15.** | pers pron |
| רָאשֵׁי | לִוְיָתָן | תִּתְּנֶנּוּ | מַאֲכָל | לְעָם | לְצִיִּים | | אַתָּה |
| rā'shê | liwyāthān | tittenennû | ma'ăkhol | le'ām | letsîyîm | | 'attāh |
| the heads of | the leviathan | You gave it | food | for people | to the dry places | | You |

| 1260.113 | 4754 | 5337 | 887 | 3111.513 | 5282 | 393 |
|---|---|---|---|---|---|---|
| v Qal pf 2ms | n ms | cj, n ms | pers pron | v Hiphil pf 2ms | *n fp* | adj |
| בָקַעְתָּ | מַעְיָן | וָנָחַל | אַתָּה | הוֹבַשְׁתָּ | נַהֲרוֹת | אֵיתָן |
| vāqa'ttā | ma'ăyān | wānāchal | 'attāh | hôvashtā | nahrôth | 'êthān |
| You split open | springs | and streams | You | You caused to dry up | the rivers of | ever flowing |

| | 3937 | 3219 | 652, 3937 | 4050 | 887 | 3679.513 | 4115 |
|---|---|---|---|---|---|---|---|
| **16.** | prep, ps 2ms | n ms | cj, prep, ps 2ms | n ms | pers pron | v Hiphil pf 2ms | n ms |
| | לְךָ | יוֹם | אַף־לְךָ | לָיְלָה | אַתָּה | הֲכִינוֹתָ | מָאוֹר |
| | lekhā | yôm | 'aph-lekhā | lāyelāh | 'attāh | hekhînôthā | mā'ôr |
| | to You | the day | also to You | the night | You | You established | the luminaries |

| 8507 | | 887 | 5507.513 | 3725, 1398 | 800 | 7302 |
|---|---|---|---|---|---|---|
| cj, n fs | **17.** | pers pron | v Hiphil pf 2ms | *adj, n fp* | n fs | n ms |
| וָשָׁמֶשׁ | | אַתָּה | הִצַּבְתָּ | כָּל־גְּבוּלוֹת | אָרֶץ | קַיִץ |
| wāshāmesh | | 'attāh | hitstsavtā | kol-gevûlôth | 'ārets | qayits |
| and the sun | | You | You stationed | all the boundaries of | the earth | the summer |

| 2886 | 887 | 3443.113 | | 2226.131, 2148 | 342.151 |
|---|---|---|---|---|---|
| cj, n ms | pers pron | v Qal pf 2ms, ps 3mp | **18.** | v Qal impv 2ms, dem pron | v Qal act ptc ms |
| וָחֹרֶף | אַתָּה | יְצַרְתָּם | | זְכָר־זֹאת | אוֹיֵב |
| wāchōreph | 'attāh | yetsartām | | zekhār-zō'th | 'ôyēv |
| and the winter | You | You fashioned them | | remember this | the enemy |

| 2884.311 | 3176 | 6194 | 5210 | 5180.316 | 8428 |
|---|---|---|---|---|---|
| v Piel pf 3ms | pn | cj, n ms | adj | v Piel pf 3cp | n ms, ps 2ms |
| חֵרֵף | יְהוָה | וְעָם | נָבָל | נִאֲצוּ | שְׁמֶךָ |
| chērēph | yehwāh | we'am | nāvāl | ni'ătsû | shemekhā |
| they have taunted | Yahweh | and a people | foolish | they have spurned | your name |

| | 414, 5598.123 | 3937, 2508 | 5497 | 8782 | 2508 | 6270 |
|---|---|---|---|---|---|---|
| **19.** | adv, v Qal juss 2ms | prep, *n fs* | *n fs* | n fs, ps 2ms | *n fs* | n mp, ps 2ms |
| | אַל־תִּתֵּן | לְחַיַּת | נֶפֶשׁ | תּוֹרֶךָ | חַיַּת | עֲנִיֶּיךָ |
| | 'al-tittēn | lechayyath | nephesh | tôrekhā | chayyath | 'ănîyêkhā |
| | do not give | for the life of | the soul of | your turtledove | the life of | your afflicted |

| 414, 8319.123 | 3937, 5516 | | 5202.531 | 3937, 1311 | 3706 | 4527.116 |
|---|---|---|---|---|---|---|
| adv, v Qal juss 2ms | prep, art, n ms | **20.** | v Hiphil impv 2ms | prep, art, n fs | cj | v Qal pf 3cp |
| אַל־תִּשְׁכַּח | לָנֶצַח | | הַבֵּט | לַבְּרִית | כִּי | מָלְאוּ |
| 'al-tishkach | lānetsach | | habbēṭ | labberîth | kî | māle'û |
| do not forget | unto forever | | look | at the Covenant | because | they are filled with |

**13. Thou didst divide the sea by thy strength: thou brakest the heads of the dragons in the waters:** ... You stirred up the sea by your might, *NAB* ... by your power you split the sea in two, *JB* ... crush the power of the monster beneath its waters, *Knox* ... shattering the Dragon's heads upon the waves, *Moffatt.*

**14. Thou brakest the heads of leviathan in pieces, and gavest him to be meat to the people inhabiting the wilderness:** ... and gave him to the desert creatures as food, *NCV* ... throw him to the sharks for food, *NEB* ... giving him as food, *Berkeley* ... heads of the leviathan and give them as food to the sharks in the sea, *Beck.*

**15. Thou didst cleave the fountain and the flood: thou driedst up mighty rivers:** ... You made valleys for fountains and springs, *BB* ... You opened fountains and brooks, *Fenton* ... Thou didst dry up unfailing rivers, *Goodspeed* ... turned primordial rivers into dry land, *JB.*

**16. The day is thine, the night also is thine: thou hast prepared the light and the sun:** ... Day and night alike belong to you, *LIVB* ... you caused sun and light to exist, *JB* ... you fashioned the moon and the sun, *NAB.*

**17. Thou hast set all the borders of the earth: thou hast made summer and winter:** ... It was you who set all the boundaries of the earth, *NIV* ... you who fixed the zones of the earth, *Anchor* ... summer and winter, thou didst create them both, *NEB.*

**18. Remember this, that the enemy hath reproached, O Lord, and that the foolish people have blasphemed thy name:** ... Keep this in mind, O Lord, *BB* ... how the enemy has defied You, *Beck* ... reviles Thy name, *Berkeley* ... And a reprobate people reviled thy name, *Goodspeed.*

**19. O deliver not the soul of thy turtledove unto the multitude of the wicked: forget not the congregation of thy poor for ever:** ... Do not surrender your turtledove to the beast, *JB* ... forget not thy poor peo-

---

prayer question "how long?" is next exchanged for another similar blending of petition and inquiry, "Why withdrawest thou thy hand?" Both are immediately translated into that petition which they both really mean. "From the middle of your bosom" is a pregnant phrase, like that in v. 7b, and has to be completed as above, although, possibly, the verb stands absolutely as equivalent to "bring to an end"—i.e., of such a state of things.

**74:12–17.** The psalmist's petition is next grounded on the revelation of God's name in Israel's past and in creative acts of power. These at once encourage him to expect that God will pluck his hand out from the folds of his robe where it lies inactive and appeal to God to be what He has been of old and to rescue the name which He has thus magnified from insult. There is singular solemnity in the emphatic reiteration of "thou" in these verses. The Hebrew does not usually express the pronominal nominative to a verb, unless special attention is to be called to it, but in these verses, it does so uniformly with one exception, and the sevenfold repetition of the word brings forcibly into view the divine personality and former deeds which pledge God to act now. Remembrance of past wonders made present misery more bitter, but it also fanned into a flame the spark of confidence that the future would be like the past. One characteristic of the Asaph Psalms is wistful retrospect, which is sometimes the basis of rebuke, and sometimes of hope and sometimes of deepened sorrow, but is here, in part an appeal to God and in part consolation. The familiar instances of his working drawn from the Exodus history appear in the Psalm. First comes the dividing of the Red Sea, which is regarded chiefly as occasioning the destruction of the Egyptians who are symbolized by the "sea-monsters" and by "leviathan" (the crocodile). Their fate is an omen of what the psalmist hopes may befall the oppressors of his own day.

In v. 15, another pregnant expression occurs, which is best filled out as above, the reference being to cleaving the rock for the flow of water, with which is contrasted in v. 15b the drying up of the Jordan. Thus, the whole of the Exodus period is covered. It is noteworthy that the psalmist adduces only wonders wrought on waters, being possibly guided in his selection by the familiar poetic use of floods and seas as emblems of hostile power and unbridled insolence. From the wonders of history, he passes to those of creation and chiefly of that might by which times alternate, and each constituent of the kosmos has its appointed limits. Day and night, summer and winter, recur by God's continual operation. Is there to be no dawning for Israel's night of weeping and no summer making glad the winter of its discontent? "Thou hast set all the borders of the earth." Would God not bid back this surging ocean which has transgressed its limits and filled the breadth of his land? All the lights in the sky, and chiefly the greatest of them, He established. Surely, He will end this eclipse in which his people groped.

**74:18–23.** Thus, the psalmist lifts himself to the height of confident although humble prayer with which the Psalm closes, recurring to the opening

| 4423, 800 | 5295 | 2660 | | 414, 8178.121 | 1847 |
|---|---|---|---|---|---|
| *n mp*, n fs | *n fp* | n ms | 21. | adv, v Qal juss 3ms | n ms |
| מַחְשַׁכֵּי־אֶרֶץ | נְאוֹת | חָמָס | | אַל־יָשֹׁב | דַּךְ |
| machshakkê-'erets | ne'ôth | chāmās̱ | | 'al-yāshōv | dakh |
| the hiding places of the land | the abodes of | violence | | may they not return | the oppressed |

| 3757.255 | 6270 | 33 | 2054.326 | 8428 | | 7251.131 |
|---|---|---|---|---|---|---|
| v Niphal ptc ms | n ms | cj, n ms | v Piel juss 3mp | n ms, ps 2ms | 22. | v Qal impv 2ms |
| נִכְלָם | עָנִי | וְאֶבְיוֹן | יְהַלְלוּ | שְׁמֶךָ | | קוּמָה |
| nikhlām | 'ānî | we'evyôn | yehalelû | shemekhā | | qûmāh |
| the dishonored | the afflicted | and the needy | may they praise | your name | | rise |

| 435 | 7662.131 | 7663 | 2226.131 | 2887 | 4655, 5210 | 3725, 3219 |
|---|---|---|---|---|---|---|
| n mp | v Qal impv 2ms | n ms, ps 2ms | v Qal impv 2ms | n fs, ps 2ms | prep, n ms | *adj*, art, n ms |
| אֱלֹהִים | רִיבָה | רִיבֶךָ | זְכֹר | חֶרְפָּתְךָ | מִנִּי־נָבָל | כָּל־הַיּוֹם |
| 'ĕlōhîm | rîvāh | rîvekhā | zekhōr | cherpāthekhā | minî-nāvāl | kol-hayyôm |
| O God | contend | your case | remember | your abuse | from the foolish | all the day |

| | 414, 8319.123 | 7249 | 7173.152 | 8064 | 7251.152 |
|---|---|---|---|---|---|
| 23. | adv, v Qal juss 2ms | *n ms* | v Qal act ptc mp, ps 2ms | *n ms* | v Qal act ptc mp, ps 2ms |
| | אַל־תִּשְׁכַּח | קוֹל | צֹרְרֶיךָ | שְׁאוֹן | קָמֶיךָ |
| | 'al-tishkach | qôl | tsōrerêkhā | she'ôn | qāmêkhā |
| | do not forget | the voice of | your adversaries | the uproar of | those who rise up against You |

| 6148.151 | 8878 | | 3937, 5514.351 | 414, 8271.528 | 4344 | 3937, 637 | 8302 |
|---|---|---|---|---|---|---|---|
| v Qal act ptc ms | adv | 75:t | prep, art, v Piel ptc ms | adv, v Hiphil juss 2mp | n ms | prep, pn | n ms |
| עֹלֶה | תָּמִיד | | לַמְנַצֵּחַ | אַל־תַּשְׁחֵת | מִזְמוֹר | לְאָסָף | שִׁיר |
| 'ōleh | thāmîdh | | lamnatstsēach | 'al-tashchēth | mizmôr | le'ās̱āph | shîr |
| going up | continually | | to the director | do not destroy | a Psalm | of Asaph | a Song |

| | 3142.519 | 3937 | 435 | 3142.519 | 7427 | 8428 | 5807.316 |
|---|---|---|---|---|---|---|---|
| 1. | v Hiphil pf 1cp | prep, ps 2ms | n mp | v Hiphil pf 1cp | cj, adj | n ms, ps 2ms | v Piel pf 3cp |
| | הוֹדִינוּ | לְךָ | אֱלֹהִים | הוֹדִינוּ | וְקָרוֹב | שְׁמֶךָ | סִפְּרוּ |
| | hôdhînû | lekhā | 'ĕlōhîm | hôdhînû | weqārôv | shemekhā | s̱ipperû |
| | we give thanks | to You | O God | we give thanks | for near | your name | they have recounted |

| 6623.258 | | 3706 | 4089.125 | 4287 | 603 | 4478 |
|---|---|---|---|---|---|---|
| v Niphal ptc fp, ps 2ms | 2. | cj | v Qal impf 1cs | n ms | pers pron | n mp |
| נִפְלְאוֹתֶיךָ | | כִּי | אֶקַּח | מוֹעֵד | אֲנִי | מֵישָׁרִים |
| niphle'ôthêkhā | | kî | 'eqqach | mô'ēdh | 'ănî | mêshārîm |
| your extraordinary deeds | | when | I take | the appointed time | I | uprightness |

| 8570.125 | | 4265.256 | 800 | 3725, 3553.152 | 609 | 8834.315 |
|---|---|---|---|---|---|---|
| v Qal impf 1cs | 3. | v Niphal ptc mp | n fs | cj, *n ms*, v Qal act ptc mp, ps 3fs | pers pron | v Piel pf 1cs |
| אֶשְׁפֹּט | | נְמֹגִים | אֶרֶץ | וְכָל־יֹשְׁבֶיהָ | אָנֹכִי | תִכַּנְתִּי |
| 'eshpōṯ | | nemōghîm | 'erets | wekhol-yōshevêāh | 'ānōkhî | thikkantî |
| I will judge with | | melting | the earth | and all its dwellers | I | I have examined |

ple for all time, *Moffatt* ... the lives of your afflicted ones, *NAB*.

**20. Have respect unto the covenant: for the dark places of the earth are full of the habitations of cruelty:** ... Have regard for your covenant, *NIV* ... violence fills every dark corner of this land, *NCV* ... the dark places of the earth are full of pride and cruel acts, *BB*.

**21. O let not the oppressed return ashamed: let the poor and needy praise thy name:** ... Do not let the humble go away disappointed, *Knox* ... Let not the downtrodden return in shame, *Berkeley* ... the wretched will sing to Your NAME, *Fenton* ... give the poor and needy cause to praise your name, *JB*.

**22. Arise, O God, plead thine own cause: remember how the foolish man reproacheth thee daily:** ... Rise up, O God, maintain thy own cause, *NEB* ... remember how fools mock you, *NIV* ... defend your cause, *NAB* ... all day long, *NCV.*

**23. Forget not the voice of thine enemies: the tumult of those that rise up against thee increaseth continually:** ... The uproar, *NASB* ... those who rise up against You, *KJVII* ... Do not ignore the clamor of your adversaries, *Anchor* ... the outcry of those who come against you goes up, *BB.*

**75:t. To the chief Musician, Al-taschith, A Psalm or Song of Asaph.**

**1. Unto thee, O God, do we give thanks, unto thee do we give thanks: for that thy name is near thy wondrous works declare:** ... those who give honour to your name, *BB* ... we tell of the wonderful things You have done, *Beck* ... they who call upon thy name, *Goodspeed* ... We proclaim, *Good News.*

**2. When I shall receive the congregation I will judge uprightly:** ... I set the time for trial, *NCV* ... At the appointed time, *JB* ... I will judge strictly, *Knox* ... I will judge with equity, *NAB.*

**3. The earth and all the inhabitants thereof are dissolved: I bear up the pillars of it. Selah:** ... Though every living creature tremble and the earth itself be shaken, *Good News* ...

---

tones. Its center is, as we have seen, a double remonstrance—"how long?" and "why?" The encircling circumference is earnest supplication, of which the keynote is "Remember" (HED #2226; vv. 2 and 18).

The gist of this closing prayer is the same appeal to God to defend his own honor, which we have found in the former verses. It is put in various forms here. Twice (vv. 18 and 22) God is besought to remember the reproach insolently heaped on his name and apparently warranted by his inaction. The claim of Israel for deliverance is based, in v. 19, upon its being "thy turtledove," which, therefore, cannot be abandoned without sullying his fame. The psalmist spreads the "Covenant" before God, as reminding Him of his obligations under it. He asks that such deeds may be done as will give occasion to the afflicted and needy to "praise thy name," which is being besmirched by their calamities. Finally, in wonderfully bold words, he calls on God to take up what is, after all, "his own" quarrel, and, if the cry of the afflicted does not move Him, to listen to the loud voices of those who blaspheme Him all the day. Reverent earnestness of supplication sometimes sounds like irreverence; but when the heart's depths boil in earnest, God understands the meaning of what sounds strange and recognizes the profound trust in his faithfulness and love which underlies bold words.

***Psalm 75.*** *This Psalm deals with the general thought of God's judgment in history, especially on heathen nations. It has no clear marks of connection with any particular instance of that judgment.*

*The kernel of the Psalm is a majestic divine utterance, proclaiming that God's judgment is at hand. The limits of that divine word are doubtful, but it is best taken as occupying two pairs of verses (vv. 2–5). It is preceded by one verse of praise, followed by three (vv. 6ff) of warning, spoken by the psalmist and by two (vv. 9f) in which he again praises God the Judge and stands forth as an instrument of his judicial acts.*

**75:1.** In v. 1, which is as a prelude to the great voice from heaven, we hear the nation giving thanks beforehand for the judgment which is about to fall. The second part of the verse is doubtful. It may be taken thus: "And your name is near; they have recounted your extraordinary deeds." Delitzsch comments that the Church "welcomes the future acts of God with fervent thanks, and all they that belong to it declare beforehand God's wondrous works."

**75:2.** Two great principles are declared—one in regard to the time and the other in regard to the animating spirit of God's judgment. Literally, the first words of the verse read, "When I take the appointed time." The thought is that He has his own appointed time at which his power will flash forth into action. His servants may be tempted to think that He delays too long; his enemies, that He will never break his silence. But the slow hand traverses the dial in time, and at last the hour strikes and the crash comes punctually and completely at the moment. The purposes of delay are presented in Scripture as twofold: on the one hand, "that the goodness of God leadeth thee to repentance" (Rom. 2:4), and on the other, that evil may work itself out and show its true character.

**75:3.** Such a "set time" has arrived, as v. 3 proceeds to declare. Oppression and corruption have gone so far that "the earth and all the inhabitants" are as if "dissolved." All things are rushing to ruin. The psalmist does not distinguish between the physical and the moral here. His figure is employed in reference to both orders, which he regards as indissolubly connected. Possibly, he is echoing Ps. 46:6, "The earth melted," although there the "melting" is an expression for dread occasioned by God's voice, and here rather refers to the results of "the proud man's wrong." At such a supreme moment, when the solid framework of society and of the world itself seems to

| 6204 | 5734 | | 569.115 | 3937, 2054.152 | 414, 2054.528 | 3937, 7857 |
|---|---|---|---|---|---|---|
| n mp, ps 3fs | intrj | 4. | v Qal pf 1cs | prep, art, v Qal act ptc mp | adv, v Hiphil juss 2mp | cj, prep, art, adj |
| עַמּוּדֶיהָ | סֶלָה | | אָמַרְתִּי | לַהוֹלְלִים | אַל־תָּהֹלּוּ | וְלָרְשָׁעִים |
| 'ammûdhêāh | selāh | | 'āmartî | lahôlelîm | 'al-tāhōllû | welāreshā'îm |
| its pillars | selah | | I have said | to those who boast | do not boast | and to the wicked |

| 414, 7597.528 | 7451 | | 414, 7597.528 | 3937, 4953 | 7451 | 1744.328 |
|---|---|---|---|---|---|---|
| adv, v Hiphil juss 2mp | n fs | 5. | adv, v Hiphil juss 2mp | prep, art, n ms | n fs, ps 2mp | v Piel juss 2mp |
| אַל־תָּרִימוּ | קָרֶן | | אַל־תָּרִימוּ | לַמָּרוֹם | קַרְנְכֶם | תְּדַבְּרוּ |
| 'al-tārîmû | qāren | | 'al-tārîmû | lammārôm | qarnkhem | tedhabberû |
| do not raise | the horn | | do not raise | to the on high | your horn | may you speak |

| 904, 6939 | 6515 | | 3706 | 3940 | 4623, 4296 | 4623, 4790 | 3940 |
|---|---|---|---|---|---|---|---|
| prep, n ms | adj | 6. | cj | neg part | prep, n ms | cj, prep, n ms | cj, neg part |
| בְצַוָּאר | עָתָק | | כִּי | לֹא | מִמּוֹצָא | וּמִמַּעֲרָב | וְלֹא |
| vetsawwā'r | 'āthāq | | kî | lō' | mimmôtsā' | ûmimma'ărāv | welō' |
| with a neck | insolent | | because | not | from the east | or from the west | and not |

| 4623, 4198 | 7597.541 | | 3706, 435 | 8570.151 | 2172 | 8584.521 |
|---|---|---|---|---|---|---|
| prep, n ms | v Hiphil inf con | 7. | cj, n mp | v Qal act ptc ms | dem pron | v Hiphil impf 3ms |
| מִמִּדְבַּר | הָרִים | | כִּי־אֱלֹהִים | שֹׁפֵט | זֶה | יַשְׁפִּיל |
| mimmidhbar | hārîm | | kî-'ĕlōhîm | shōphēt | zeh | yashpîl |
| from the wilderness | raising | | because God | a Judge | this one | He abases |

| 2172 | 7597.521 | | 3706 | 3683 | 904, 3135, 3176 | 3302 | 2666.111 |
|---|---|---|---|---|---|---|---|
| cj, dem pron | v Hiphil impf 3ms | 8. | cj | n fs | prep, *n fs*, pn | cj, n ms | v Qal pf 3ms |
| וְזֶה | יָרִים | | כִּי | כוֹס | בְּיַד־יְהוָה | וְיַיִן | חָמַר |
| wezeh | yārîm | | kî | khôs | beyadh-yehwāh | weyayin | chāmar |
| and this one | He exalts | | because | a cup | in the hand of Yahweh | and wine | it has foamed |

| 4529 | 4688 | 5240.521 | 4623, 2172 | 395, 8491 | 4842.126 |
|---|---|---|---|---|---|
| adj | n ms | cj, v Hiphil impf 3ms | prep, dem pron | adv, n mp, ps 3fs | v Qal impf 3mp |
| מָלֵא | מֶסֶךְ | וַיַּגֵּר | מִזֶּה | אַךְ־שְׁמָרֶיהָ | יִמְצוּ |
| mālē' | mesekh | wayyaggēr | mizzeh | 'akh-shemārêāh | yimtsû |
| full | the mixture | and He will pour out | from this | surely its dregs | they will drain |

| 8685.126 | 3725 | 7857, 800 | | 603 | 5222.525 | 3937, 5986 |
|---|---|---|---|---|---|---|
| v Qal impf 3mp | *n ms* | *n mp*, n fs | 9. | cj, pers pron | v Hiphil impf 1cs | prep, n ms |
| יִשְׁתּוּ | כֹּל | רִשְׁעֵי־אָרֶץ | | וַאֲנִי | אַגִּיד | לְעֹלָם |
| yishtû | kōl | rish'ê-'ārets | | wa'ănî | 'aggîdh | le'ōlām |
| they will drink | the entirety of | the wicked of the earth | | but I | I will tell | for eternity |

| 2252.325 | 3937, 435 | 3399 | | 3725, 7451 | 7857 | 1468.325 |
|---|---|---|---|---|---|---|
| v Piel juss 1cs | prep, *n mp* | pn | 10. | cj, *adj*, *n fd* | n mp | v Piel impf 1cs |
| אֲזַמְּרָה | לֵאלֹהֵי | יַעֲקֹב | | וְכָל־קַרְנֵי | רְשָׁעִים | אֲגַדֵּעַ |
| 'ăzammerāh | lē'lōhê | ya'ăqōv | | wekhol-qarnê | reshā'îm | 'ăghaddēa' |
| let me sing praises | to the God of | Jacob | | and all the horns of | the wicked | I will cut off |

When the earth and all its people quake, *NIV* ... I am the support of its pillars, *BB*.

**4. I said unto the fools, Deal not foolishly: and to the wicked, Lift not up the horn:** ... I tell the impious, 'Never flaunt your power,' *Moffatt* ... I warned the proud to cease their arrogance! I told the wicked to lower their insolent gaze, *LIVB* ... I said to the boastful, "Do not boast!," *JB* ... Rebel no more, I cry to the rebels, *Knox*.

**5. Lift not up your horn on high: speak not with a stiff neck:** ... Do not lift your horns against heaven, *NIV* ... speak not haughtily against the Rock, *NAB* ... Do not speak with insolent pride, *NASB* ... nor speak arrogantly against your Creator, *NEB*.

**6. For promotion cometh neither from the east, nor from the west, nor from the south:** ... exaltation comes neither from the east, *NKJV* ... For honour does not come from the east, or from the west, or uplifting from the south, *BB* … and not from the wilderness comes lifting up, *NRSV.*

**7. But God is the judge: he putteth down one, and setteth up another:** … humbling one man and exalting another, *Knox* … this one he lowers, this one he lifts, *Moffatt* … he judges one person as guilty and another as innocent, *NCV* … He promotes one and deposes another, *LIVB.*

**8. For in the hand of the LORD there is a cup, and the wine is red; it is full of mixture; and he poureth out of the same: but the dregs thereof, all the wicked of the earth shall wring them out, and drink them:** … it is full of wine mixed with spices, *NCV* … he will make all the sinners of the earth take of it, even to the last drop, *BB* … yes, the wicked of the earth must swallow it and drink its dregs, *Berkeley.*

**9. But I will declare for ever; I will sing praises to the God of Jacob:** … I will forever rejoice, *Goodspeed* … I shall speak out for ever, *JB* … Evermore will I triumph, singing praises, *Knox* … I will glorify the Eternal One, *Beck.*

**10. All the horns of the wicked also will I cut off; but the horns of the righteous shall be exalted:** … I will break off, *NAB* … He will take all power away from the wicked, *NCV* … horns of the ungodly I will strike down, *Berkeley.*

---

be on the point of dissolution, the mighty divine personality intervenes. That strong hand is thrust forth to grasp the tottering pillars and stay their fall; or, in plain words, God himself then intervenes to reestablish the moral order of society and thus to save the sufferers (cf. Hannah's song in 1 Sam. 2:8). That intervention has necessarily two aspects, being on the one hand restorative and on the other punitive.

**75:4–5.** Therefore, in vv. 4f, follow divine warnings to the "fools" and "wicked," whose insolent boasting and tyranny have provoked it. The word rendered "fools" (HED #2054) seems to include the idea of boastfulness as well as folly in the biblical sense of that word, which points to moral rather than to merely intellectual aberration. "Lifting up the horn" is a symbol of arrogance. According to the accents, the word rendered "stiff" is not to be taken as attached to "neck," but as the object of the verb "to speak." But it is more natural to take the word in its usual construction as an epithet of "neck," expressive of superciliously holding a high head.

**75:6–8.** The exact point where the divine oracle passes into the psalmist's own words is doubtful. Verse 7 is evidently his, and that verse is so closely connected with v. 6 that it is best to make the break at the end of v. 5 and to suppose that what follows is the singer's application of the truths which he has heard. Two renderings of v. 6b are possible, which, although very different in English, turn on the minute difference in the Hebrew of one vowel sign. The same letters spell the Hebrew word meaning "mountains" and that meaning "lifting up." With one punctuation of the preceding word, "wilderness," we must translate "from the wilderness of mountains." "Lifting up" occurs so often in this Psalm, that it is more natural to take the word in that meaning here, especially as the next verse ends with it, in a different tense, and thus makes a sort of rhyme with this verse. The metaphor of v. 8 in which judgment is represented as a cup of foaming wine, which God puts to the lips of the nations, receives great expansion in the prophets, especially in Jeremiah, and recurs in Revelation. There is a grim contrast between the images of festivity and hospitality called up by the picture of a host presenting the wine cup to his guests and the stern compulsion which makes the "wicked" gulp down the nauseous draught held by God to their reluctant lips. The utmost extremity of punitive inflictions, unflinchingly inflicted, is suggested by the terrible imagery. And the judgment is to be worldwide, for "all the wicked of the earth" are to drink, and that to the dregs.

**75:9.** And how does the prospect affect the psalmist? It moves him, first, to solemn praise—not only because God has proved himself by these terrible things in righteousness to be the God of his people, but also because He has thereby manifested his own character as righteous and hating evil. It is no selfish or cruel joy which stirs in devout hearts when God comes forth in history and smites oppressing insolence. It is but a spurious benevolence which affects to recoil from the conception of a God who judges and smites when needful. This psalmist not only praised, but in his degree, vowed to imitate.

**75:10.** The last verse is best understood as his declaration of his own purpose, although some commentators have proposed to transfer it to the earlier part of the Psalm, regarding it as part of the divine oracle. But it is in its right place where it stands. God's servants are his instruments in carrying out his judgments, and there is a very real sense in which all of them should seek to fight against dominant evil and to cripple the power of tyrannous godlessness.

***Psalm 76.*** *The Psalm is divided into four strophes of three verses each. The first two describe the*

| 7597.327 | 7451 | 6926 | | 3937, 5514.351 | 904, 5234 |
|---|---|---|---|---|---|
| v Polal impf 3fp | *n fp* | n ms | | prep, art, v Piel ptc ms | prep, n fp |
| תְּרוֹמַמְנָה | קַרְנוֹת | צַדִּיק | 76:t | לַמְנַצֵּחַ | בִּנְגִינֹת |
| teromamnāh | qarnōth | tsaddîq | | lamnatstsēach | binghînōth |
| they will be exalted | the horns of | the righteous | | to the director | with the stringed instruments |

| 4344 | 3937, 637 | 8302 | | 3156.255 | 904, 3171 | 435 | 904,3547 | 1448 | 8428 |
|---|---|---|---|---|---|---|---|---|---|
| n ms | prep, pn | n ms | | v Niphal ptc ms | prep, pn | n mp | prep, pn | adj | n ms, ps 3ms |
| מִזְמוֹר | לְאָסָף | שִׁיר | 1. | נוֹדָע | בִּיהוּדָה | אֱלֹהִים | בְּיִשְׂרָאֵל | גָּדוֹל | שְׁמוֹ |
| mizmôr | le'āsāph | shîr | | nôdhā' | bîhûdhāh | 'ĕlōhîm | beyisrā'ēl | gādhôl | shemô |
| a Psalm | of Asaph | a Song | | known | in Judah | God | in Israel | great | his name |

| | 2030.121 | 904, 8401 | 5712 | 4737 | 904, 6995 | | 8427 | 8132.311 |
|---|---|---|---|---|---|---|---|---|
| | cj, v Qal impf 3ms | prep, pn | n ms, ps 3ms | cj, n fs, ps 3ms | prep, pn | | adv | v Piel pf 3ms |
| 2. | וַיְהִי | בְשָׁלֵם | סֻכּוֹ | וּמְעוֹנָתוֹ | בְצִיּוֹן | 3. | שָׁמָּה | שִׁבַּר |
| | wayhî | veshālēm | sukkô | ûme'ônāthô | vetsîyôn | | shāmmāh | shibbar |
| | and it is | in Salem | his booth | and his residence | in Zion | | to there | He shattered |

| 7859, 7493 | 4182 | 2820 | 4560 | 5734 | | 213.255 | 887 |
|---|---|---|---|---|---|---|---|
| *n mp*, n fs | n ms | cj, n fs | cj, n fs | intrj | | v Niphal ptc ms | pers pron |
| רִשְׁפֵי־קָשֶׁת | מָגֵן | וְחֶרֶב | וּמִלְחָמָה | סֶלָה | 4. | נָאוֹר | אַתָּה |
| rishphê-qāsheth | māghēn | wecherev | ûmilchāmāh | selāh | | nā'ôr | 'attāh |
| the flames of the arrow | a shield | and a sword | and weapons | selah | | luminous | You |

| 116 | 4623, 2121, 3073 | | 8394.716 | 48 | 3949 |
|---|---|---|---|---|---|
| adj | prep, *n mp*, n ms | | v Hithpoel pf 3cp | *adj* | n ms |
| אַדִּיר | מֵהַרְרֵי־טָרֶף | 5. | אֶשְׁתּוֹלְלוּ | אַבִּירֵי | לֵב |
| 'addîr | mēharerê-tāreph | | 'eshtôlelû | 'abbîrê | lēv |
| more majestic | than the mountains of prey | | they have been plundered | the mighty of | heart |

| 5305.116 | 8535 | 3940, 4834.116 | 3725, 596, 2524 | 3135 |
|---|---|---|---|---|
| v Qal pf 3cp | n fs, ps 3mp | cj, neg part, v Qal pf 3cp | *adj, n mp*, n ms | n fd, ps 3mp |
| נָמוּ | שְׁנָתָם | וְלֹא־מָצְאוּ | כָל־אַנְשֵׁי־חַיִל | יְדֵיהֶם |
| nāmû | shenāthām | welō'-mātse'û | khol-'anshê-chayil | yedhêhem |
| they went to sleep | their sleep | and they did not find | all the men of the army | their hands |

| | 4623, 1648 | 435 | 3399 | 7578.255 | 7681 | 5670 | | 887 |
|---|---|---|---|---|---|---|---|---|
| | prep, n fs, ps 2ms | *n mp* | pn | v Niphal ptc ms | cj, n ms | cj, n ms | | pers pron |
| 6. | מִגַּעֲרָתְךָ | אֱלֹהֵי | יַעֲקֹב | נִרְדָּם | וְרֶכֶב | וָסוּס | 7. | אַתָּה |
| | migga'ărāthekhā | 'ĕlōhê | ya'ăqōv | nirdām | werekhev | wāsûs | | 'attāh |
| | from your rebuke | O God of | Jacob | sleeping deeply | both chariot | and horse | | You |

| 3486.255 | 887 | 4449, 6198.121 | 3937, 6686 | 4623, 226 | 653 |
|---|---|---|---|---|---|
| v Niphal ptc ms | pers pron | cj, intrg, v Qal impf 3ms | prep, n mp, ps 2ms | prep, adv | n ms, ps 2ms |
| נוֹרָא | אַתָּה | וּמִי־יַעֲמֹד | לְפָנֶיךָ | מֵאָז | אַפֶּךָ |
| nôrā' | 'attāh | ûmî-ya'ămōdh | lephānêkhā | mē'āz | 'appekhā |
| fearful | You | and who can stand | in your presence | from then | your anger |

**76:t. To the chief Musician on Neginoth, A Psalm or Song of Asaph.**

**1. In Judah is God known:** … In Judah God has shown himself, *Anchor* … In Judah God has renown, *Berkeley* … God is acknowledged in Judah, *JB*.

**his name is great in Israel:** … his name is honored in Israel, *Good News* … in Israel that his name is extolled, *Knox* … his fame is high in Israel, *Moffatt*.

**2. In Salem also is his tabernacle, and his dwellingplace in Zion:** … His covert was in Salem, and his lair in Zion, *Anchor* … his tent, his resting-place in Zion, *BB* … In Shalem is His Throne, And His Home is in Zion!, *Fenton* … in Zion his battle-quarters are set up, *NEB*.

**3. There brake he the arrows of the bow, the shield, and the sword, and the battle:** … There with his thunderbolts he shattered the bow, shield, and sword, and weapons of war, *Anchor* ... put an end to body-cover, sword, and fight, *BB* ... the flaming arrows, the shield, the sword, and war itself, *Beck* ... It was there he broke the archers' volleys, broke shield, and sword, and battle array, *Knox*.

**Selah:** ... Music, *Beck* ... Pause, *JB*.

**4. Thou art more glorious and excellent:** ... O Luminous One, you are majestic!, *Anchor* ... You are shining and full of glory, *BB* ... Terrible art thou, *Goodspeed* ... Radiant you are, and renowned, *JB* ... How princely was thy dawning, *Knox*.

**than the mountains of prey:** ... more than the eternal mountains, *BB* ... Beyond the heaps of spoil, *Fenton* ... mightier than a devouring lion, *Goodspeed* ... than the hills full of animals, *NCV*.

**5. The stouthearted are spoiled:** ... Soldiers with their prowess perished, *Anchor* ... Gone is the wealth of the strong, *BB* ... Valiant men were plundered, *Beck* ... Devastated are the stout-hearted, *Goodspeed* ... The stout-hearted are bereft of sense, *MAST* ... The brave soldiers were stripped, *NCV* ... men that lust for plunder stand aghast, *NEB*.

**they have slept their sleep:** ... their last sleep has overcome them, *BB* ... They sank into sleep, *NASB* ... as they lay asleep in death, *NCV* ... the boldest swoon away, *NEB*.

**and none of the men of might have found their hands:** ... and were found no more, *Anchor* ... the men of war have become feeble, *BB* ... not a fighting man could lift a hand, *Beck* ... Those warriors lost their hands!, *Fenton* ... all their strength and skill was useless, *Good News* ... Not one warrior had the strength to stop it, *NCV*.

**6. At thy rebuke:** ... At your roar, *Anchor* ... At the voice of your wrath, *BB* ... When you threatened them, *Good News* ... at your reproof, *JB* ... at thy stroke, *Moffatt* ... when you spoke strongly, *NCV*.

**O God of Jacob, both the chariot and horse are cast into a dead sleep:** ... both chariot and horse lay

---

*act; the latter two deal with its results, in an awed world and thankful praise.*

**76:1–3.** The emphatic words in the first strophe are those which designate the scene of the divine act. The glow of humble pride, of wonder and thankfulness, is perceptible in the fourfold reiteration: "in Judah, in Israel, in Salem, in Zion." All of these names are gathered up in the eloquent "there" of v. 3. The true point of view from which to regard God's acts is that they are his self-revelation. The reason why Israel is the object of the acts which manifest his name is that there He has chosen to dwell. And since He dwells there, the special act of judgment which the Psalm celebrates was there performed. "The lightnings of the bow" picturesquely designate arrows, from their swift flight and deadly impact (cf. Ps. 46:9).

**76:4–6.** The second strophe comes closer to the fact celebrated and describes with magnificent sweep, brevity and vividness the death sleep of the enemy. But before it shows the silent corpses, it lifts one exclamation of reverence to the God who has thus manifested his power. The word rendered "excellent" (HED #116) is doubtful, and by a slight transposition of letters, it becomes, as in v. 7 which begins the next strophe, "dread." In v. 4b, the rendering "more excellent than" yields a comparison which can scarcely be called worthy. It is little to say of God that He is more glorious than the enemies' "mountains of prey," although Delitzsch tries to recommend this rendering by supposing that God is represented as towering above "the Lebanon of the hostile army of peoples." The Hebrew idiom expresses comparison (adding the -er ending to the noun in English) by the preposition "from" following the adjective, some take the construction as indicating point of departure rather than comparison. God comes forth as "glorious," from the lofty heights where He sits supreme. But "mountains of prey" is a singular phrase, which can only be explained by the supposition that God is conceived of as a Conqueror Who has laid up his spoils in his inaccessible storehouse on high. Yet the Septuagint translates "everlasting mountains," fitting the context well and implying a text, which might easily be misinterpreted as meaning "prey" and may afterwards have crept into the body of the text. If this alteration is not adopted, the meaning will be as just stated.

Verse 5 gives some support to the existing text by its representation of the stout-hearted foe as "spoiled." They are robbed of their might, their weapons and their life. How graphically the psalmist sets before the eyes of his readers the process of destruction from its beginning! He shows us the warriors falling asleep in the drowsiness of death. How feeble their "might" is now! One vain struggle, as in the throes of death, and the hands which shot the "lightnings of the bow" against Zion are stiff forevermore. One word from the sovereign lips of the God of Jacob and all the noise of the camp is hushed; we look out upon a field of the dead, lying in awful stillness, dreamlessly sleeping their long slumber.

| 8. | | | | | | |
|---|---|---|---|---|---|---|
| | **4623, 8452** | **8471.513** | **1835** | **800** | **3486.112** | **8618.112** |
| | prep, n md | v Hiphil pf 2ms | n ms | n fs | v Qal pf 3fs | cj, v Qal pf 3fs |
| | מִשָּׁמַיִם | הִשְׁמַעְתָּ | דִּין | אֶרֶץ | יָרְאָה | וְשָׁקָטָה |
| | mishshāmayim | hishma'āttā | dîn | 'erets | yāre'āh | weshāqātāh |
| | from the heavens | You caused to hear | judgment | the earth | it was afraid | and it kept quiet |

| 9. | | | | | |
|---|---|---|---|---|---|
| | **904, 7251.141, 3937, 5122** | **435** | **3937, 3588.541** | **3725, 6262, 800** | **5734** |
| | prep, v Qal inf con, prep, art, n ms | n mp | prep, v Hiphil inf con | *adj, n mp*, n fs | intrj |
| | בְּקוּם־לַמִּשְׁפָּט | אֱלֹהִים | לְהוֹשִׁיעַ | כָּל־עַנְוֵי־אָרֶץ | סֶלָה |
| | beqûm-lammishpāt | 'ělōhîm | lehôshîa' | kol-'anwê-'erets | selāh |
| | when rising for the judgment | God | to save | all the lowly of the earth | selah |

| 10. | | | | | |
|---|---|---|---|---|---|
| | **3706, 2635** | **119** | **3142.522** | **8086** | **2635** |
| | cj, *n fs* | n ms | v Hiphil impf 3fs, ps 2ms | *n fs* | n fp |
| | כִּי־חֲמַת | אָדָם | תּוֹדֶךָּ | שְׁאֵרִית | חֵמֹת |
| | kî-chămath | 'ādhām | tôdhekhā | she'ērîth | chēmōth |
| | surely the wrath of | humankind | it will praise You | the remaining of | the wrath |

| | | 11. | | | | |
|---|---|---|---|---|---|---|
| **2391.123** | | **5265.133** | **8396.333** | **3937, 3176** | **435** | **3725, 5623** |
| v Qal impf 2ms | | v Qal impv 2mp | cj, v Piel impv 2mp | prep, pn | n mp, ps 2mp | *adj*, n mp, ps 3ms |
| תַּחְגֹּר | | נִדְרוּ | וְשַׁלְּמוּ | לַיהוָה | אֱלֹהֵיכֶם | כָּל־סְבִיבָיו |
| tachgōr | | nidhrû | weshallemû | layhwāh | 'ělōhêkhem | kol-sevîvâv |
| You will gird on | | make a vow | and complete | to Yahweh | your God | all those around Him |

| | | | 12. | | | |
|---|---|---|---|---|---|---|
| **3095.526** | **8282** | **3937, 4307** | | **1245.121** | **7593** | **5233** |
| v Hiphil juss 3mp | n ms | prep, art, n ms | | v Qal impf 3ms | *n fs* | n mp |
| יוֹבִילוּ | שַׁי | לַמּוֹרָא | | יִבְצֹר | רוּחַ | נְגִידִים |
| yôvîlû | shay | lammôrā' | | yivtsōr | rûach | neghîdhîm |
| let them bring | tribute | to the fearsome One | | He removes | the spirit of | the leaders |

| | | 77:t | | | |
|---|---|---|---|---|---|
| **3486.255** | **3937, 4567, 800** | | **3937, 5514.351** | **6142, 3147** | **3937, 637** |
| v Niphal ptc ms | prep, *n mp*, n fs | | prep, art, v Piel ptc ms | prep, pn | prep, pn |
| נוֹרָא | לְמַלְכֵי־אָרֶץ | | לַמְנַצֵּחַ | עַל־יְדוּתוּן | לְאָסָף |
| nôrā' | lemalkhê-'ārets | | lamnatstsēach | 'al-yedhûthûn | le'āsāph |
| the fearsome One | to the kings of the earth | | to the director | according to Jeduthun | of Asaph |

| | 1. | | | | | | |
|---|---|---|---|---|---|---|---|
| **4344** | | **7249** | **420, 435** | **7094.125** | **7249** | **420, 435** | **237.511** |
| n ms | | n ms, ps 1cs | prep, n mp | cj, v Qal juss 1cs | n ms, ps 1cs | prep, n mp | cj, v Hiphil pf 3ms |
| מִזְמוֹר | | קוֹלִי | אֶל־אֱלֹהִים | וְאֶצְעָקָה | קוֹלִי | אֶל־אֱלֹהִים | וְהַאֲזִין |
| mizmôr | | qôlî | 'el-'ělōhîm | we'ets'āqāh | qôlî | 'el-'ělōhîm | weha'ăzîn |
| a Psalm | | my voice | to God | and let me cry out | my voice | to God | that He will listen |

stunned, *Anchor* ... chariots and horses were paralyzed, *Beck* ... horses and riders fell dead, *NCV.*

**7. Thou, even thou, art to be feared:** ... As for You, You terrify, *Beck* ... Thou thyself art terrible, *Goodspeed* ... You, you alone strike terror!, *JB* ... But you indeed are awesome!, *NRSV.*

**and who may stand in thy sight when once thou art angry?:** ... and who will be able to face your fury, your wrath of old?, *Anchor* ... who may keep his place before you in the time of your wrath?, *BB* ... who can stand before thee, because of the intensity of thine anger?, *Goodspeed.*

**8. Thou didst cause judgment to be heard from heaven:** ... From heaven you gave your decision, *BB* ... when God rouses himself to execute his sentence, *Knox.*

**the earth feared, and was still:** ... the earth hushed in fear, *Beck* ... the land feared and was quiet, *NIV.*

**9. When God arose to judgment:** ... when God takes his stand to give judgement, *JB* ... to act on earth, *Moffatt.*

**to save all the meek of the earth:** ... for the salvation of the poor on the earth, *BB* ... to save all who suffer on earth, *Beck* ... To save the weak on Earth, *Fenton* ... to save all the humble of the earth, *JB.*

**Selah:** ... Music, *Beck* ... Pause, *JB.*

**10. Surely the wrath of man shall praise thee:** ... the most violent of men will give thanks to thee,

*Goodspeed* ... Human anger serves only to praise you, *JB*.

**the remainder of wrath shalt thou restrain:** ... The survivors of your rage will encircle you, *Anchor* ... their surplus of anger will honor You, *Beck* ... the remainder of fury wilt thou gird on thyself, *Darby* ... The most persistently violent will put on sackcloth, *Goodspeed*.

**11. Vow, and pay unto the LORD your God:** ... Give to the Lord your God what is his by right, *BB* ... Make and fulfil your vows to Yahweh your God, *JB*.

**let all that be round about him bring presents unto him that ought to be feared:** ... let those who surround him make offerings to the Awesome One, *JB* ... Bring gifts to honour Him, *Fenton*.

**12. He shall cut off the spirit of princes:** ... Who fathoms the mind of princes, *Anchor* ... puts an end to the wrath of rulers, *BB* ... he it is that cows the hearts of princes, *Knox* ... strips chiefs of their courage, *Moffatt*.

**he is terrible to the kings of the earth:** ... who should be feared by the kings of the earth, *Anchor* ... He is awesome to the kings of the earth, *NKJV*.

**77:t. To the chief Musician, to Jeduthun, A Psalm of Asaph.**

**1. I cried unto God with my voice, even unto God with my voice:** ... My voice is to God; I call; my voice is to God, *Berkeley* ... I will shout with my voice to my GOD, *Fenton* ... A cry to my God in loud appeal, a cry to my God, *Knox*.

**and he gave ear unto me:** ... to win his hearing, *Knox* ... and He

---

**76:7–9.** The third strophe passes from the description of the destruction of the enemy to paint its widespread results in the manifestation to a hushed world of God's judgment. In it, anger and love are wondrously blended. While no creature can bear the terrible blaze of his face, or endure the weight of his onset "in the time of his anger," the most awful manifestations thereof have a side of tenderness and an inner purpose of blessing. With judgment is the promise of mercy. It is worthy of God to smite the oppressor and to save the "afflicted," who not only suffer, but trust. When He makes his judgments reverberate from on high, earth should keep an awed stillness, as nature does when thunder peals. When some gigantic and hoary iniquity crashes to its fall, there is a moment of awed silence after the hideous tumult.

**76:10–12.** The last strophe is mainly a summons to praise God for his manifestation of delivering judgment. Verse 10 is obscure. The first clause is intelligible enough. Since God magnifies his name by his treatment of opposing men, who set themselves against Him, their very foaming fury subserves his praise. That is a familiar thought with all the Scripture writers who meditate on God's dealings. But the second clause is hard. Whose "wraths" are spoken of in it? God's or man's? The change from the singular ("wrath of man") to plural ("wraths") makes it all but certain that God's fullness of "wrath" is meant here. It is set over against the finite and puny "wrath" of men, as an ocean might be contrasted with a shallow pond. If so, God's girding himself with the residue of his own wrath will mean that, after every such forth-putting of it as the Psalm has been hymning, there still remains an unexhausted store ready to flame out if need arise. It is a stern and terrible thought of God, but it is solemnly true. His steadfast love out-measures man's, and so does his judicial judgment. All divine attributes partake of infinitude, and the stores of his punitive anger are not less deep than those of his gentle goodness.

Therefore, men are summoned to vow and pay their vows. While Israel is called to worship, the nations around, who have seen that field of the dead, are called to do homage and bring tribute to Him, Who, as it so solemnly shows, can cut off the breath of the highest or can cut down their pride as a grape-gatherer does the ripe cluster (for such is the allusion in the word "cuts down"). The last clause of the Psalm, which stands somewhat disconnected from the preceding, gathers up the lessons of the tremendous event which inspired it when it sets Him forth as to be feared by the kings of the earth.

***Psalm 77.*** *The Psalm falls into two parts: in the first part (vv. 1–9), deepest gloom wraps the singer's spirit, while in the latter (vv. 10–20), the clouds break. Each of these parts falls into three strophes of three verses, except for the last, which has five. Selah stands at the end of the first and third. In like manner, the first strophe of the second part (vv. 10ff) has no selah, but the second has (vv. 13ff), the closing strophe (vv. 16–20) being thus parted off.*

**77:1–3.** The psalmist's agitation colors his language, which fluctuates in the first six verses between expressions of resolve or desire (vv. 1, 3, 6) and simple statement of fact (vv. 2, 4f). He has prayed long and earnestly, and nothing has been laid in answer on his outstretched palm. Therefore, his cry has died down into a sigh. He fain would lift his voice to God, but dark thoughts make him dumb for

| 420 | | 904, 3219 | 7150 | 112 | 1938.115 | 3135 | 4050 |
|---|---|---|---|---|---|---|---|
| prep, ps 1cs | 2. | prep, *n ms* | n fs, ps 1cs | n mp, ps 1cs | v Qal pf 1cs | n fs, ps 1cs | n ms |
| אֵלָי | | בְּיוֹם | צָרָתִי | אֲדֹנָי | דָּרָשְׁתִּי | יָדִי | לַיְלָה |
| 'ēlāy | | bᵉyôm | tsārāthî | 'ădhōnāy | dārāshᵉttî | yādhî | laylāh |
| to me | | in the day of | my adversity | my Lord | I have sought | my hand | at night |

| 5240.212 | 3940 | 6555.122 | 4126.312 | 5341.241 | 5497 |
|---|---|---|---|---|---|
| v Niphal pf 3fs | cj, neg part | v Qal impf 3fs | v Piel pf 3fs | v Niphal inf con | n fs, ps 1cs |
| נִגְּרָה | וְלֹא | תָפוּג | מֵאֲנָה | הִנָּחֵם | נַפְשִׁי |
| niggᵉrāh | wᵉlō' | thāphûgh | mē'ănāh | hinnāchēm | naphshî |
| it was poured out | and not | it became weary | it refused | comforting | my soul |

| | 2226.125 | 435 | 2064.125 | 7943.125 | 6063.722 | 7593 |
|---|---|---|---|---|---|---|
| 3. | v Qal juss 1cs | n mp | cj, v Qal juss 1cs | v Qal juss 1cs | cj, v Hithpael impf 3fs | n fs, ps 1cs |
| | אֶזְכְּרָה | אֱלֹהִים | וְאֶהֱמָיָה | אָשִׂיחָה | וְתִתְעַטֵּף | רוּחִי |
| | 'ezkᵉrāh | 'ĕlōhîm | wᵉ'ehĕmāyāh | 'āsîchāh | wᵉthith'aṯṯēph | rûchî |
| | may I remember | God | and let me be in tumult | let me ponder | for it faints | my spirit |

| 5734 | | 270.113 | 8495 | 6084 | 6717.215 | 3940 | 1744.325 |
|---|---|---|---|---|---|---|---|
| intrj | 4. | v Qal pf 2ms | *n fp* | n fd, ps 1cs | v Niphal pf 1cs | cj, neg part | v Piel impf 1cs |
| סֶלָה | | אָחַזְתָּ | שְׁמֻרוֹת | עֵינָי | נִפְעַמְתִּי | וְלֹא | אֲדַבֵּר |
| s̱elāh | | 'āchaztā | shᵉmurōth | 'ênāy | niph'amtî | wᵉlō' | 'ădhabbēr |
| selah | | You have seized | the eyelids of | my eyes | I have been troubled | and not | I can speak |

| | 2913.315 | 3219 | 4623, 7208 | 8523 | 5986 | | 2226.125 |
|---|---|---|---|---|---|---|---|
| 5. | v Piel pf 1cs | n mp | prep, n ms | *n fp* | n mp | 6. | v Qal juss 1cs |
| | חִשַּׁבְתִּי | יָמִים | מִקֶּדֶם | שְׁנוֹת | עוֹלָמִים | | אֶזְכְּרָה |
| | chishshavtî | yāmîm | miqqedhem | shᵉnôth | 'ôlāmîm | | 'ezkᵉrāh |
| | I have considered | days | from antiquity | the years of | eternities | | may I remember |

| 5234 | 904, 4050 | 6196, 3949 | 7943.125 | 2769.321 |
|---|---|---|---|---|
| n fs, ps 1cs | prep, art, n ms | prep, n ms, ps 1cs | v Qal juss 1cs | cj, v Piel impf 3ms |
| נְגִינָתִי | בַּלָּיְלָה | עִם־לְבָבִי | אָשִׂיחָה | וַיְחַפֵּשׂ |
| nᵉghînāthî | ballāyᵉlāh | 'im-lᵉvāvî | 'āsîchāh | waychappēs |
| my stringed instrument | in the night | with my heart | let me meditate | that it will examine |

| 7593 | | 1950B, 3937, 5986 | 2269.121 | 112 | 3940, 3362.521 |
|---|---|---|---|---|---|
| n fs, ps 1cs | 7. | intrg part, prep, n mp | v Qal impf 3ms | n mp, ps 1cs | cj, neg part, v Hiphil impf 3ms |
| רוּחִי | | הַלְעוֹלָמִים | יִזְנַח | אֲדֹנָי | וְלֹא־יֹסִיף |
| rûchî | | hal'ôlāmîm | yiznach | 'ădhōnāy | wᵉlō'-yōs̱iph |
| my spirit | | forever | will He reject | my Lord | and will He not do again |

hears me, *Beck* … Oh, that he would listen, *LIVB.*

**2. In the day of my trouble I sought the Lord:** … When I'm in trouble, I go to my Lord for help, *Beck* … I turn to the Lord in my hour of need, *Moffatt.*

**my sore ran in the night, and ceased not:** … His hand attacks at night and does not slacken, *Anchor* … My hand was stretched out in the night, and slacked not, *ASV* … all night long I lift my hands in prayer, *Good News* … My tears ran unceasingly, *REB.*

**my soul refused to be comforted:** … His mind refuses to relent, *Anchor* … I refuse to calm down, *Beck* … but I cannot find comfort, *Good News* … I refused all comfort, *REB.*

**3. I remembered God, and was troubled:** … I will keep God in memory, with sounds of grief, *BB* … When I remember God, I moan, *NCB* … I sigh, and my mind is depressed, *Fenton.*

**I complained, and my spirit was overwhelmed:** … I think of Him, and my spirit faints, *Beck* … when my spirit was faint, I pondered, *Berkeley* … as I lay thinking, darkness came over my spirit, *NEB* … I meditate, and feeble is my spirit, *Young.*

**Selah:** … Music, *Beck* … Pause, *JB.*

**4. Thou holdest mine eyes waking:** … You keep my eyes from sleep, *BB* … You keep my eyelids open, *Beck* … Thou holdest fast the lids of mine eyes, *MAST* … My eyelids were tightly closed, *REB.*

**I am so troubled that I cannot speak:**… I pace the floor and do not recline, *Anchor* ... I am too upset to say anything, *NCV* ... I was dazed and I could not speak, *NEB* ... I was driven to and fro and could not speak, *Rotherham.*

**5. I have considered the days of old:** ... I think of the times that are past, *Fenton* ... I think of the early days, *Beck.*

**the years of ancient times:** ... Of the years to Eternity gone!, *Fenton* ... the years of long ago, *Beck* ... I remembered distant years, *REB.*

**6. I call to remembrance my song in the night:** ... At night I play the lyre, *Beck* ... deep musings occupy my thoughts at midnight, *Knox* ... all night long I meditated, *REB.*

**I commune with mine own heart:** ... my mind thinking, *Beck* ... with my heart I meditated, *Berkeley* ... I speak with my own heart, *KJVII.*

**and my spirit made diligent search:** ... That my spirit might be healed, *Anchor* ... and my spirit searching, *Beck* ... I meditate and search my spirit, *NRSV.*

**7. Will the Lord cast off for ever?:** ... Will the Lord put me away for ever?, *BB* ... Has th' ALMIGHTY forgotten for ever?, *Fenton* ... Is the Lord's rejection final, *JB.*

**and will he be favourable no more?:** ... Will He always cease to be kind?, *Fenton* ... Will he never again be pleased with us?, *Good News* ... And never again be gracious?, *Goodspeed.*

---

supplication and eloquent only in self-pitying monologue. A man must have waded through similar depths to understand this pathetic bewilderment of spirit. They who glide smoothly over a sunlit surface of sea little know the terrors of sinking, with choked lungs, into the abyss. A little experience will go further than much learning in penetrating the meaning of these moanings of lamed faith. They begin with an elliptical phrase, which, in its fragmentary character, reveals the psalmist's discomposure. "My voice to God" evidently needs some such completion as is supplied above, and the form of the following verb ("cry") suggests that the supplied one should express wish or effort.

The repetition of the phrase in v. 1b strengthens the impression of agitation. The last words of that clause may be a petition, "give ear," but are probably better taken as above. The psalmist would cry to God, that he may be heard. He has cried, as he goes on to tell in a calmer mood in v. 2, and has apparently not been heard. He describes his unintermitted supplications by a strong metaphor. The word rendered "stretched out" (HED #5240) is literally "poured out as water" and is applied to weeping eyes (Lam. 3:49). The Targum substitutes "eye" for "hand" here, but that is commentary, not translation.

The clause which we render "without ceasing" (HED #5555) is literally "and grew not stiff." That word, too, is used of tears, and derivatives from it are found in the passage just referred to in Lam. 3:49 ("intermission") and in Lam. 2:18 ("rest"). It carries on the metaphor of a stream, the flow of which is unchecked. The application of this metaphor to the hand is harsh, but the meaning is plain—that all night long the psalmist extended his hand in the attitude of prayer, as if open to receive God's gift. His voice "rose like a fountain night and day," but brought no comfort to his soul. He bewails himself in the words which tell of Jacob's despair when he heard that Joseph was dead, so rooted and inconsolable does he think his sorrows. The thought of God has changed its nature, as if the sun were to become a source of darkness. When he looks up, he can only sigh; when he looks within, his spirit is clothed or veiled, i.e., wrapped in melancholy.

**77:4–6.** In the next strophe of three verses (vv. 4ff), the psalmist plunges yet deeper into gloom and unfolds more clearly its occasion. Sorrow, like a beast of prey, devours at night; every sad heart knows how eyelids, however wearied, refuse to close upon as wearied eyes, which gaze wide opened into the blackness and see dreadful things there. This man felt as if God's finger was pushing up his lids and forcing him to stare out into the night. Buffeted, as if laid on an anvil and battered with the shocks of doom, he cannot speak; he can only moan, as he is doing. Prayer seems to be impossible. But to say, "I cannot pray; would that I could!" is surely prayer which will reach its destination, although the sender knows it not. The psalmist had found no ease in remembering God. He finds as little in remembering a brighter past. That he should have turned to history in seeking for consolation implies that his affliction was national in its sweep, however intensely personal in its pressure. This retrospective meditation on the great deeds of old is characteristic of the Asaph Psalms. It ministers in them to many moods, as memory always does. In this Psalm, we have it feeding two directly opposite emotions. It may be the nurse of bitter despair, or of bright-eyed hope. When the thought of God occasions only sighs, the remembrance of his acts can only make the present more doleful. The heavy spirit finds

| 3937, 7813.141 | 5968 | | 1950B, 674.111 | 3937, 5516 | 2721 |
|---|---|---|---|---|---|
| prep, v Qal inf con | adv | | intrg part, v Qal pf 3ms | prep, art, n ms | n ms, ps 3ms |
| לִרְצוֹת | עוֹד | **8.** | הֶאָפֵס | לָנֶצַח | חַסְדּוֹ |
| lirtsôth | 'ôdh | | he'āphēs̱ | lānetsach | chas̱dô |
| to be pleased | anymore | | has it ceased | unto forever | his steadfast love |

| 1625.111 | 575 | 3937, 1810 | 1810 | | 1950B, 8319.111 |
|---|---|---|---|---|---|
| v Qal pf 3ms | n ms | prep, n ms | cj, n ms | | intrg part, v Qal pf 3ms |
| גָּמַר | אֹמֶר | לְדֹר | וָדֹר | **9.** | הֲשָׁכַח |
| gāmar | 'ōmer | ledhōr | wādhōr | | heshākhach |
| it has come to an end | words | unto generations | and generations | | has He forgotten |

| 2706.141 | 418 | 524, 7376.111 | 904, 653 | 7641 | 5734 | | 569.125 |
|---|---|---|---|---|---|---|---|
| v Qal inf con | n ms | intrg, v Qal pf 3ms | prep, n ms | n mp, ps 3ms | intrj | | cj, v Qal impf 1cs |
| חַנּוֹת | אֵל | אִם־קָפַץ | בְּאַף | רַחֲמָיו | סֶלָה | **10.** | וָאֹמַר |
| channôth | 'ēl | 'im-qāphats | be'aph | rachmâv | s̱elāh | | wā'ōmar |
| to be gracious | God | or has He shut | in anger | his compassions | selah | | and I say |

| 2571.341 | 2026 | 8521.141 | 3332 | 6169 | | 2226.125 |
|---|---|---|---|---|---|---|
| v Piel inf con, ps 1cs | pers pron | v Qal inf con | *n fs* | n ms | | v Qal impf 1cs |
| חַלּוֹתִי | הִיא | שְׁנוֹת | יְמִין | עֶלְיוֹן | **11.** | אַזְכִּיר |
| challôthî | hî' | shenôth | yemîn | 'elyôn | | 'azkîr |
| my being sick | it | the changing of | the right hand of | the Most High | | I will remember |

| 4770, 3161 | 3706, 2226.125 | 4623, 7208 | 6624 | | 1965.115 |
|---|---|---|---|---|---|
| *n mp*, pn | cj, v Qal juss 1cs | prep, n ms | n ms, ps 2ms | | cj, v Qal pf 1cs |
| מַעַלְלֵי־יָהּ | כִּי־אֶזְכְּרָה | מִקֶּדֶם | פִּלְאֶךָ | **12.** | וְהָגִיתִי |
| ma'alelê-yāhh | kî-'ezkerāh | miqqedhem | pil'ekhā | | wehāghîthî |
| the deeds of Yah | indeed let me remember | from times past | your miracles | | and I will meditate |

| 904, 3725, 6714 | 904, 6173 | 7943.125 | | 435 | 904, 7231 | 1932 |
|---|---|---|---|---|---|---|
| prep, *n ms*, n ms, ps 2ms | cj, prep, n fp, ps 2ms | v Qal juss 1cs | | n mp | prep, art, n ms | n ms, ps 2ms |
| בְּכָל־פָּעֳלֶךָ | וּבַעֲלִילוֹתֶיךָ | אָשִׂיחָה | **13.** | אֱלֹהִים | בַּקֹּדֶשׁ | דַּרְכֶּךָ |
| vekhol-pā'ālekhā | ûva'ălîlôthêkhā | 'āsîchāh | | 'ĕlōhîm | baqqōdhesh | darkekhā |
| on all your works | and on your deeds | let me ponder | | God | in the holy place | your way |

| 4449, 418 | 1448 | 3626, 435 | | 887 | 418 | 6449.151 | 6624 |
|---|---|---|---|---|---|---|---|
| intrg, n ms | adj | prep, n mp | | pers pron | art, n ms | *v Qal act ptc ms* | n ms |
| מִי־אֵל | גָּדוֹל | כֵּאלֹהִים | **14.** | אַתָּה | הָאֵל | עֹשֵׂה | פֶלֶא |
| mî-'ēl | gādhôl | kē'lōhîm | | 'attāh | hā'ēl | 'ōsēh | phele' |
| who a god | great | like God | | You | the God | One Who does | miracles |

**8. Is his mercy clean gone for ever?:** ... Is his lovingkindness clean gone for ever?, *ASV* ... Has he stopped loving us?, *Good News* ... Has his unfailing love now failed us utterly, *NEB*.

**doth his promise fail for evermore?:** ... have visions from him come to an end?, *Anchor* ... has his word come to nothing?, *BB* ... must his promise time and again be unfulfilled?, *NEB*.

**9. Hath God forgotten to be gracious?:** ... Have the inmost parts of God dried up, *Anchor* ... Has God put away the memory of his pity?, *BB*.

**hath he in anger shut up his tender mercies?:** ... are his mercies shut up by his wrath?, *BB* ... Has he slammed the door in anger on his love, *LIVB* ... Is he too angry to pity us?, *NCV*.

**Selah:** ... Music, *Beck* ... Pause, *JB*.

**10. And I said, This is my infirmity:** ... And I said, It is a weight on my spirit, *BB* ... Then I said, It makes me feel sick, *Beck* ... Then said I, This is my weakness, *Darby* ... And I said, This is my death, *Geneva* ... Yes, this is my grief, *Moffatt* ... Perhaps his sickness is this, *Anchor*.

**but I will remember the years of the right hand of the most High:** ... the right hand of the Most High has withered, *Anchor* ... might change, *Beck* ... The years are in the Highest's right hand, *Fenton* ... altered the fashion of his dealings with men, *Knox* ... no longer has the strength he had, *Moffatt*.

**11. I will remember the works of the LORD:** ... I will keep in mind the works of Jah, *BB* ... I remember the deeds of the Lord, *NCB* ... I will meditate on all your works, *NIV* ... I will remember the doings of Yah, *Rotherham.*

**surely I will remember thy wonders of old:** ... for I remembered Thy miracles of old, *Berkeley* ... and consider all your mighty deeds, *NIV.*

**12. I will meditate also of all thy work:** ... To ponder over all thy doings, *Knox.*

**and talk of thy doings:** ... And muse on thy doings, *ASV* ... while my mind goes over your acts of power, *BB* ... pass thy wonders in review, *Knox* ... And talk of your deeds, *NKJV.*

**13. Thy way, O God, is in the sanctuary:** ... O God, your dominion is over the holy ones, *Anchor* ... Your way, O God, is holy, *BB.*

**who is so great a God as our God?:** ... Who is a great God like Elohim?, *Rotherham.*

**14. Thou art the God that doest wonders:** ... Thy own wonderful acts acclaim thy Deity, *Knox* ... Thou art the God who workest miracles, *NEB.*

---

reasons for heaviness in God's past and in its own. The psalmist in his sleepless vigils remembers other wakeful times, when his song filled the night with music and "awoke the dawn."

Verse 6 is parallel with v. 3. The three keywords, "remember," "muse" and "spirit," recur. There musing ended in wrapping the spirit in deeper gloom. Here it stings that spirit to activity in questionings, which the next strophe flings out in vehement number and startling plainness. It is better to be pricked to even such interrogations by affliction than to be made torpid by it. All depends on the temper in which they are asked. If that is right, answers which will scatter gloom are not far off.

**77:7–9.** The comparison of present national evils with former happiness naturally suggests such questions. Obviously, the casting off spoken of in v. 7 is that of the nation, and hence its mention confirms the view that the psalmist is suffering under public calamities. All the questions mean substantially one thing—has God changed? They are not, as some questions are, the strongest mode of asserting their negative, nor are they, like others, a more than half assertion of their affirmative; but they are what they purport to be—the anxious interrogations of an afflicted man, who would fain be sure that God is the same as ever, but is staggered by the dismal contrast of "now" and "then." He faces with trembling the terrible possibilities, and, however his language may seem to regard failure of resources or fickleness of purpose or limitations in long-suffering as conceivable in God, his doubts are better put into plain speech than lying diffused and darkening, like poisonous mists, in his heart. A thought, be it good or bad, can be dealt with when it is made articulate. Formulating vague conceptions is like cutting a channel in a bog for the water to run. One gets it together in manageable shape, and the soil is drained. So the end of the despondent half of the Psalm is marked by the bringing to distinct speech of the suspicions which floated in the singer's mind and made him miserable. The selah bids us dwell on the questions so as to realize their gravity and prepare ourselves for their answer.

**77:10–12.** The second part begins in v. 10 with an obscure and much-commented-on verse, of which two explanations are possible, depending mainly on the meanings of the two words "sickness" and "years." The former word (HED #2571) may mean "my wounding" or "my sickness." The latter is by many commentators taken to be an infinitive verb, with the signification "to be changed" (HED #8521), and by others to be a plural noun meaning "years" (HED #8523) as in v. 5. Neglecting some minor differences, we may say that those who understand the word to mean "being changed" explain the whole thus: "This is my wound ["misery," "sorrow"], that the right hand of the Most High has changed." But the use of the word in v. 5 for "years" creates a strong presumption that its sense is the same here. As to the other word, its force is best seen by reference to a closely parallel passage in Jer. 10:19—"I said, Truly this is my grief, and I must bear it"; where the word for "grief," although not the same as in the Psalm, is cognate. The most probable meaning, then, for the expression here is, "This my affliction is sent from God, and I must bear it with resignation." A change comes with the recognition of two great truths: first, that the calamity is laid on Israel and on the psalmist as a member of the nation by God and has not come because of that impossible change in Him which the bitter questions had suggested; and, second, the unchangeable eternity of God's delivering power. That second truth comes to him as with a flash, and the broken words of v. 10b hail the sudden rising of the new star.

**77:13–15.** The strophe in vv. 13ff fixes on the one great redeeming act of the Exodus as the pledge

| 3156.513 | 904, 6194 | 6010 | | 1381.113 | 904, 2307 |
|---|---|---|---|---|---|
| v Hiphil pf 2ms | prep, art, n mp | n ms, ps 2ms | | v Qal pf 2ms | prep, n fs |
| הוֹדַעְתָּ | בָעַמִּים | עֻזֶּךָ | **15.** | גָּאַלְתָּ | בִּזְרוֹעַ |
| hôdha'ättā | vā'ammîm | 'uzzekhā | | gā'altā | bizrôa' |
| You have caused to know | among the peoples | your strength | | You redeemed | with an arm |

| 6194 | 1158, 3399 | 3231 | 5734 | | 7495.116 | 4448 | 435 |
|---|---|---|---|---|---|---|---|
| n ms, ps 2ms | *n mp*, pn | cj, pn | intrj | | v Qal pf 3cp, ps 2ms | n md | n mp |
| עַמֶּךָ | בְּנֵי־יַעֲקֹב | וְיוֹסֵף | סֶלָה | **16.** | רָאוּךָ | מַּיִם | אֱלֹהִים |
| 'ammekhā | benê-ya'ăqōv | weyôsēph | selāh | | rā'ûkhā | mayim | 'ĕlōhîm |
| your people | the children of Jacob | and Joseph | selah | | they saw You | the waters | God |

| 7495.116 | 4448 | 2523.126 | 652 | 7553.126 | 8745 |
|---|---|---|---|---|---|
| v Qal pf 3cp, ps 2ms | n md | v Qal impf 3mp | cj | v Qal impf 3mp | n fp |
| רָאוּךָ | מַּיִם | יָחִילוּ | אַף | יִרְגְּזוּ | תְהֹמוֹת |
| rā'ûkhā | mayim | yāchîlû | 'aph | yirgezû | thehōmôth |
| they saw You | the waters | they were in anguish | indeed | they trembled | the depths |

| | 2316.416 | 4448 | 5854 | 7249 | 5598.116 | 8263 | 652, 2777 |
|---|---|---|---|---|---|---|---|
| | v Pual pf 3cp | n md | n mp | n ms | v Qal pf 3cp | n mp | cj, n mp, ps 2ms |
| **17.** | זֹרְמוּ | מַּיִם | עָבוֹת | קוֹל | נָתְנוּ | שְׁחָקִים | אַף־חֲצָצֶיךָ |
| | zōremû | mayim | 'āvôth | qôl | nāthenû | shechāqîm | 'aph-chătsātsêkhā |
| | they were poured out | the waters | the clouds | sounds | they gave | clouds | indeed your arrows |

| 2050.726 | | 7249 | 7770 | 904, 1574 | 213.516 | 1326 |
|---|---|---|---|---|---|---|
| v Hithpael impf 3mp | | *n ms* | n ms, ps 2ms | prep, art, n ms | v Hiphil pf 3cp | n mp |
| יִתְהַלָּכוּ | **18.** | קוֹל | רַעַמְךָ | בַּגַּלְגַּל | הֵאִירוּ | בְרָקִים |
| yithhallākhû | | qôl | ra'amkhā | baggalgal | hē'îrû | verāqîm |
| they went forth | | the sound of | your thunder | in the wheel | they illuminated | lightning |

| 8725 | 7553.112 | 7782.122 | 800 | | 904, 3328 | 1932 | 8111 |
|---|---|---|---|---|---|---|---|
| n fs | v Qal pf 3fs | cj, v Qal impf 3fs | art, n fs | | prep, art, n ms | n ms, ps 2ms | cj, n mp, ps 2ms |
| תֵּבֵל | רָגְזָה | וַתִּרְעַשׁ | הָאָרֶץ | **19.** | בַּיָּם | דַּרְכֶּךָ | וּשְׁבִילֶיךָ |
| tēvēl | rāghezāh | wattir'ash | hā'ārets | | bayyām | darkekhā | ûshevîlêkhā |
| the world | it trembled | and it quaked | the earth | | in the sea | your way | and your paths |

| 904, 4448 | 7521 | 6357 | 3940 | 3156.216 | | 5328.113 | 3626, 6887 |
|---|---|---|---|---|---|---|---|
| prep, n md | adj | cj, n mp, ps 2ms | neg part | v Niphal pf 3cp | | v Qal pf 2ms | prep, art, n fs |
| בְּמַיִם | רַבִּים | וְעִקְּבוֹתֶיךָ | לֹא | נֹדָעוּ | **20.** | נָחִיתָ | כַּצֹּאן |
| bemayim | rabbîm | we'iqqevôthêkhā | lō' | nōdhā'û | | nāchîthā | khatstsō'n |
| in the waters | many | but your heels | not | they have been known | | You led | like the sheep |

**thou hast declared thy strength among the people:** ... even to the Gentiles thou wouldst make thy power known, *Knox* ... thou hast shown the nations thy power, *NEB.*

**15. Thou hast with thine arm redeemed thy people, the sons of Jacob and Joseph:** ... With your arm you have made your people free, the sons of Jacob and Joseph, *BB* ... By Your Arm you rescued Your people, The children of Jacob and Joseph!, *Fenton* ... You have redeemed Your people with Your power, the sons of Jacob and Joseph, *KJVII.*

**Selah:** ... Music, *Beck* ... Pause, *JB.*

**16. The waters saw thee, O God, the waters saw thee:** ... When the Red Sea saw you, *LIVB.*

**they were afraid:** ... and shook, *Beck* ... they suffered pangs, *Goodspeed* ... They were in birth-throes, *Rotherham.*

**the depths also were troubled:** ... The very deeps were convulsed, *Goodspeed* ... the ocean was troubled to its depths, *NEB.*

**17. The clouds poured out water:** ... rain rushed from the clouds, *Moffatt.*

**the skies sent out a sound:** ... the skies in thunder crashed, *Moffatt* ... the skies resounded with thunder, *NIV.*

**thine arrows also went abroad:** ... Thy lightning arrows zigzagged, *Berkeley* ... Your lightning flashed back and forth like arrows, *NCV.*

**18. The voice of thy thunder was in the heaven:** ... The voice of thy thunder was in the whirlwind, *ASV* ... The voice of your thunder went rolling on, *BB* ... The crash of your thunder was the whirlwind, *NRSV* ... The voice of Thy thunder is in the spheres, *Young.*

**the lightnings lightened the world:** ... Lightning lit up the world, *NCV.*

**the earth trembled and shook:** ... the nether world quaked and shook, *Anchor.*

**19. Thy way is in the sea:** ... You walked through the waves, *Good News* ... Thy way led through the sea, *Knox.*

**and thy path in the great waters:** ... you crossed the deep sea, *Good News* ... the deep tide made a road for thee, *Knox.*

**and thy footsteps are not known:** ... but your footprints could not be seen, *Good News* ... and none may read the traces of thy passage, *Knox.*

**20. Thou leddest thy people like a flock by the hand of Moses and Aaron:** ... You guided your people like a flock shepherded by Moses and Aaron, *REB* ... where thou, with Moses and Aaron for thy shepherds, didst bring thy people out on their journey, *Knox.*

---

of future deeds of a like kind, as need requires. The language is deeply tinged with reminiscences of Exo. 15. "In holiness" (not "in the sanctuary"), the question "Who is so great a God?" and the epithet "Who doest wonders" all come from Exo. 15:11. "[Thine] arm" in the Psalm recalls "by the greatness of thine arm" in Exodus (v. 16), and the psalmist's "redeemed thy people" reproduces "the people which thou hast redeemed" (Exo. 15:13). The separate mention of "sons of Joseph" can scarcely be accounted for if the Psalm is prior to the division of the kingdoms. But the purpose of the designation is doubtful. It may express the psalmist's protest against the division as a breach of ancient national unity or his longings for reunion.

**77:16–20.** The final strophe differs from the others in structure. It contains five verses instead of three, and the verses are (with the exception of the last) composed of three clauses each instead of two. Some commentators have supposed that vv. 16–19 are an addition to the original Psalm and that they do not cohere well with the preceding. This view denies that there is any allusion in the closing verses to the passage of the Red Sea and takes the whole as simply a description of a theophany, like that in Ps. 18. But surely the writhing of the waters as if in pangs at the sight of God is such an allusion. Verse 19, too, is best understood as referring to the path through the sea, whose waters returned and covered God's footprints from human eyes. Unless there is such a reference in vv. 16–19, the connection with the preceding and with v. 20 is no doubt loose. But that is not so much a reason for denying the right of these verses to a place in the Psalm as for recognizing the reference. Why should a mere description of a theophany, which had nothing to do with the psalmist's theme, have been tacked on to it? No doubt, the thunders, lightnings and storm so grandly described here are unmentioned in Exodus and, quite possibly, may be simply poetic heightening of the scene, intended to suggest how majestic was the intervention which freed Israel. Some commentators, indeed, have claimed the picture as giving additional facts concerning the passage of the Red Sea.

The picture in the Psalm is most striking. The continuous short clauses crash and flash like the thunders and lightnings. That energetic metaphor of the waters writhing as if panic-struck is more violent than Western taste approves, but its emotional vigor as a rendering of the fact is unmistakable. "Thine arrows went to and fro" is a very imperfect transcript of the Hebrew, which suggests the swift zigzag of the fierce flashes. In v. 18, one word (HED #1574) offers some difficulty. It literally means "a wheel" and is apparently best rendered as above, the thunder being poetically conceived of as the sound of the rolling wheels of God's chariot. There are several coincidences between vv. 16–19 of the Psalm and Hab. 3:10–15, namely, the expression "writhed in pain," applied in Habakkuk to the mountains; the word rendered "overflowing" (KJV) or "tempest" (RV) in Hab. 3:10, cognate with the verb in v. 17 of the Psalm, and there rendered "poured out"; and the designation of lightnings as God's arrows. Delitzsch strongly maintains the priority of the Psalm; others as strongly that of the prophet.

The last verse returns to the two-claused structure of the earlier part. It comes in lovely contrast with the majestic and terrible picture preceding, like the wonderful setting forth of the purpose of the other theophany in Ps. 18, which was for no higher end than to draw one poor man from the mighty waters. All this pomp of divine appearance, with lightnings, thunders, a heaving earth and a shrinking sea, had for its end the leading of the people of God to their land, as a shepherd does his flock. The image is again an echo of Exo. 15:13. The thing intended is not merely

| 6194 | 904, 3135, 5057 | 172 | | 5030 | 3937, 637 | | 237.531 |
|---|---|---|---|---|---|---|---|
| n ms, ps 2ms | prep, *n fs*, pn | cj, pn | **78:t** | n ms | prep, pn | **1.** | v Hiphil impv 2ms |
| עַמֶּךָ | בְּיַד־מֹשֶׁה | וְאַהֲרֹן | | מַשְׂכִּיל | לְאָסָף | | הַאֲזִינָה |
| 'ammekhā | beyadh-mōsheh | we'ahrōn | | maskîl | le'āsāph | | ha'ăzînāh |
| your people | by the hand of Moses | and Aaron | | a Maskil | of Asaph | | listen |

| 6194 | 8784 | 5371.533 | 238 | 3937, 571, 6552 | | 6858.125 |
|---|---|---|---|---|---|---|
| n ms, ps 1cs | n fs, ps 1cs | v Hiphil impv 2mp | n fs, ps 2mp | prep, *n mp*, n ms, ps 1cs | **2.** | v Qal juss 1cs |
| עַמִּי | תּוֹרָתִי | הַטּוּ | אָזְנְכֶם | לְאִמְרֵי־פִי | | אֶפְתְּחָה |
| 'ammî | tôrāthî | hattû | 'oznekhem | le'imrê-phî | | 'ephtechāh |
| O my people | my teaching | incline | your ear | to the words of my mouth | | let me open |

| 904, 5091 | 6552 | 5218.525 | 2512 | 4623, 7208 | | 866 | 8471.119 |
|---|---|---|---|---|---|---|---|
| prep, n ms | n ms, ps 1cs | v Hiphil juss 1cs | n fp | prep, n ms | **3.** | rel part | v Qal pf 1cp |
| בְמָשָׁל | פִי | אַבִּיעָה | חִידוֹת | מִנִּי־קֶדֶם | | אֲשֶׁר | שָׁמַעְנוּ |
| vemāshāl | pî | 'abbî'āh | chîdhôth | minî-qedhem | | 'āsher | shāma'ănû |
| in a proverb | my mouth | and let me gush forth | riddles | from antiquity | | which | we have heard |

| 3156.120 | 1 | 5807.316, 3937 | | 3940 | 3701.320 |
|---|---|---|---|---|---|
| cj, v Qal impf 1cp, ps 3mp | cj, n mp, ps 1cp | v Piel pf 3cp, prep, ps 1cp | **4.** | neg part | v Piel impf 1cp |
| וַנֵּדָעֵם | וַאֲבוֹתֵינוּ | סִפְּרוּ־לָנוּ | | לֹא | נְכַחֵד |
| wannēdhā'ēm | wa'ăvôthênû | sipperû-lānû | | lō' | nekhachēdh |
| and we have known them | and our fathers | they have recounted to us | | not | we will hide |

| 4623, 1158 | 3937, 1810 | 315 | 5807.352 | 8747 | 3176 | 6020 |
|---|---|---|---|---|---|---|
| prep, n mp, ps 3mp | prep, n ms | adj | v Piel ptc mp | *n fp* | pn | cj, n ms, ps 3ms |
| מִבְּנֵיהֶם | לְדוֹר | אַחֲרוֹן | מְסַפְּרִים | תְּהִלּוֹת | יְהוָה | וֶעֱזוּזוֹ |
| mibbenêhem | ledhôr | 'achrôn | mesapperîm | tehillôth | yehwāh | we'ĕzûzô |
| from their children | to the generation | next | recounting | the praises of | Yahweh | and his strength |

| 6623.257 | 866 | 6449.111 | | 7251.521 | 5925 | 904, 3399 |
|---|---|---|---|---|---|---|
| cj, v Niphal ptc fs, ps 3ms | rel part | v Qal pf 3ms | **5.** | cj, v Hiphil impf 3ms | n fs | prep, pn |
| וְנִפְלְאוֹתָיו | אֲשֶׁר | עָשָׂה | | וַיָּקֶם | עֵדוּת | בְּיַעֲקֹב |
| weniphle'ôthâv | 'ăsher | 'āsāh | | wayyāqem | 'ēdhûth | beya'ăqōv |
| and his extraordinary deeds | which | He has done | | and He established | a testimony | in Jacob |

| 8784 | 7949.111 | 904, 3547 | 866 | 6943.311 | 881, 1 | 3937, 3156.541 |
|---|---|---|---|---|---|---|
| cj, n fs | v Qal pf 3ms | prep, pn | rel part | v Piel pf 3ms | do, n mp, ps 1cp | prep, v Hiphil inf con, ps 3mp |
| וְתוֹרָה | שָׂם | בְּיִשְׂרָאֵל | אֲשֶׁר | צִוָּה | אֶת־אֲבוֹתֵינוּ | לְהוֹדִיעָם |
| wethôrāh | sām | beyisrā'ēl | 'ăsher | tsiwwāh | 'eth-'ăvôthênû | lehôdhî'ām |
| and a Law | He placed | in Israel | which | He commanded | our ancestors | causing them to know |

| 3937, 1158 | | 3937, 4775 | 3156.126 | 1810 | 315 | 1158 | 3314.226 |
|---|---|---|---|---|---|---|---|
| prep, n mp, ps 3mp | **6.** | prep, prep | v Qal impf 3mp | n ms | adj | n mp | v Niphal impf 3mp |
| לִבְנֵיהֶם | | לְמַעַן | יֵדְעוּ | דּוֹר | אַחֲרוֹן | בָּנִים | יִוָּלֵדוּ |
| livnêhem | | lema'an | yēdhe'û | dôr | 'achrôn | bānîm | yiwwālēdhû |
| to their children | | so that | they will know | the generation | next | children | they will be born |

| 7251.126 | 5807.326 | 3937, 1158 | | 7947.126 | 904, 435 | 3815 |
|---|---|---|---|---|---|---|
| v Qal impf 3mp | cj, v Piel impf 3mp | prep, n mp, ps 3mp | **7.** | cj, v Qal impf 3mp | prep, n mp | n ms, ps 3mp |
| יָקֻמוּ | וִיסַפְּרוּ | לִבְנֵיהֶם | | וְיָשִׂימוּ | בֵּאלֹהִים | כִּסְלָם |
| yāqumû | wîsapperû | livnêhem | | weyāsîmû | vē'lōhîm | kislām |
| they will rise | and they will recount | to their children | | and they will set | in God | their hope |

| 3940 | 8319.126 | 4770, 418 | 4851 | 5526.126 | | 3940 |
|---|---|---|---|---|---|---|
| cj, neg part | v Qal impf 3mp | *n mp*, n ms | cj, n fp, ps 3ms | v Qal impf 3mp | **8.** | cj, neg part |
| וְלֹא | יִשְׁכְּחוּ | מַעַלְלֵי־אֵל | וּמִצְוֹתָיו | יִנְצֹרוּ | | וְלֹא |
| welō' | yishkechû | ma'alelê-'ēl | ûmitswōthâv | yintsōrû | | welō' |
| and not | they will forget | the works of God | and his commandments | they will keep | | and not |

**78:t. Maschil of Asaph.**

**1. Give ear, O my people, to my law:** ... Give ear, my people, to my teaching, *Anchor* ... My people, listen to my instruction, *Beck* ... Listen, my people, to this testament of mine, *Knox.*

**incline your ears to the words of my mouth:** ... let your ears be bent down to the words of my mouth, *BB* ... pay attention to what I say, *Beck* ... do not turn a deaf ear to the words I utter, *Knox.*

**2. I will open my mouth in a parable:** ... On Maxims I open My lips, *Fenton* ... I will speak to you in poetry, *JB* ... I will speak using stories, *NCV.*

**I will utter dark sayings of old:** ... I will reveal riddles of old, *Anchor* ... and speak of the ancient mysteries, *Beck* ... as I utter lessons from ancient times, *Berkeley* ... on the deep lessons of the past, *Moffatt.*

**3. Which we have heard and known, and our fathers have told us:** ... which we have heard and known, for our fathers related them to us, *Berkeley* ... Which we formerly heard of and learnt, And our fathers recorded for us, *Fenton.*

**4. We will not hide them from their children, showing to the generation to come:** ... We will not keep them secret from our children; we will make clear to the coming generation, *BB* ... which were not hidden from their children but told to the next generation, *Beck.*

**the praises of the LORD, and his strength, and his wonderful works that he hath done:** ... The glorious deeds of Yahweh and his triumph, and his miracles that he has wrought, *Anchor* ... the Eternal's praise and power, the wonders he has done, *Moffatt* ... the praiseworthy deeds of the LORD, his power, and the wonders he has done, *NIV.*

**5. For he established a testimony in Jacob, and appointed a law in Israel, which he commanded our fathers, that they should make them known to their children:** ... How he established the truth in Jacob and set up the law in Israel. How He ordered our fathers to teach their children, *Beck* ... When in Jacob He set up the Witness, And in Israel settled the law, Which He had commanded our fathers, To teach to the people, their sons, *Fenton* ... He laid on Jacob a solemn charge and established a law in Israel, which he commanded our fathers to teach their sons, *NEB.*

**6. That the generation to come might know them, even the children which should be born; who should arise and declare them to their children:** ... so that a new generation might learn it; sons would be born to take their place, and teach it to their own sons after them, *Knox.*

**7. That they might set their hope in God, and not forget the works of God, but keep his commandments:** ... So that they might put their hope in God, and not let God's works go out of their minds, but keep his laws, *BB* ... so as to put their confidence in God and not to forget God's works,

---

the passage of the Red Sea, but the whole process of guidance begun there amid the darkness.

***Psalm 78.*** *This Psalm is closely related to Pss. 105–107. Like them, it treats the history of Israel, especially the Exodus and wilderness wanderings, for purposes of edification, rebuke and encouragement. The past is held up as a mirror to the present generation. It has been one long succession of miracles of mercy met by equally continuous ingratitude, which has ever been punished by national calamities. The Psalm departs singularly from chronological order. It arranges its contents in two principal masses, each introduced by the same formula (vv. 12, 43) referring to "wonders in Egypt and the field of Zoan." There are no regular strophes, but a tendency to run into paragraphs of four verses, with occasional irregularities.*

**78:1–4.** Verses 1–4 declare the singer's didactic purpose. He deeply feels the solidarity of the nation through all generations—how fathers and children are knit by mystic ties and by possession of an eternal treasure, the mighty deeds of God, of which they are bound to pass on the record from age to age. The history of ancient days is "a parable" and a "riddle" or "dark saying," as containing examples of great principles and lessons which need reflection to discern and draw out. From that point of view, the psalmist will sum up the past. He is not a chronicler, but a religious teacher. His purpose is edification, rebuke, encouragement, the deepening of godly fear and obedience. In a word, he means to give the spirit of the nation's history.

**78:5–8.** Verses 5–8 base this purpose on God's declared will that the knowledge of his deeds for Israel might be handed down from fathers to sons: the obligations of parents for the religious training of their children, the true bond of family unity, the ancient order of things when oral tradition was the principal means of preserving national history, the peculiarity of this nation's annals, as celebrating no heroes and recording only the deeds of God by men, the contrast between the changing bearers of the story and the undying deeds which they had to tell. These are all expressed in these verses, so pathetic in their gaze upon the linked series of short-lived men, so stern in their final declaration that divine com-

| 2030.126 | 3626, 1 | 1810 | 5842.151 | 4947.151 | 1810 |
|---|---|---|---|---|---|
| v Qal impf 3mp | prep, n mp, ps 3mp | n ms | v Qal act ptc ms | cj, v Qal act ptc ms | n ms |
| יִהְיוּ | כַּאֲבוֹתָם | דּוֹר | סוֹרֵר | וּמֹרֶה | דּוֹר |
| yihyû | ka'ăvôthām | dôr | sôrēr | ûmōreh | dôr |
| they will be | like their ancestors | a generation | stubborn ones | and rebels | a generation |

| 3940, 3679.511 | 3949 | 3940, 548.212 | 882, 418 | 7593 |
|---|---|---|---|---|
| neg part, v Hiphil pf 3ms | n ms, ps 3ms | cj, neg part, v Niphal pf 3fs | prep, n ms | n fs, ps 3ms |
| לֹא־הֵכִין | לִבּוֹ | וְלֹא־נֶאֶמְנָה | אֶת־אֵל | רוּחוֹ |
| lō'-hēkhîn | libbô | w$^{e}$lō'-ne'emnāh | 'eth-'ēl | rûchô |
| it was not steadfast | their heart | and it was not faithful | God | his spirit |

| 9. | 1158, 688 | 5583.152 | 7700.152, 7493 | 2089.116 | 904, 3219 | 7417 |
|---|---|---|---|---|---|---|
| | *n mp*, pn | *v Qal act ptc mp* | *v Qal act ptc mp*, n fs | v Qal pf 3cp | prep, *n ms* | n ms |
| | בְּנֵי־אֶפְרַיִם | נוֹשְׁקֵי | רוֹמֵי־קָשֶׁת | הָפְכוּ | בְּיוֹם | קְרָב |
| | b$^{e}$nê-'ephrayim | nôshqê | rômê-qāsheth | hāph$^{e}$khû | b$^{e}$yôm | qŏrāv |
| | the sons of Ephraim | the kissing of | the shooting of arrows | they turned | on the day of | battle |

| 10. | 3940 | 8490.116 | 1311 | 435 | 904, 8784 | 4126.316 |
|---|---|---|---|---|---|---|
| | neg part | v Qal pf 3cp | *n fs* | n mp | cj, prep, n fs, ps 3ms | v Piel pf 3cp |
| | לֹא | שָׁמְרוּ | בְּרִית | אֱלֹהִים | וּבְתוֹרָתוֹ | מֵאֲנוּ |
| | lō' | shām$^{e}$rû | b$^{e}$rîth | 'ĕlōhîm | ûv$^{e}$thôrāthô | mē'ănû |
| | not | they observed | the Covenant of | God | and in his Law | they refused |

| 3937, 2050.141 | 11. | 8319.126 | 6173 | 6623.258 | 866 |
|---|---|---|---|---|---|
| prep, v Qal inf con | | cj, v Qal impf 3mp | n fp, ps 3ms | cj, v Niphal ptc fp, ps 3ms | rel part |
| לָלֶכֶת | | וַיִּשְׁכְּחוּ | עֲלִילוֹתָיו | וְנִפְלְאוֹתָיו | אֲשֶׁר |
| lālekheth | | wayyishk$^{e}$chû | 'ălîlôthâv | w$^{e}$niphl$^{e}$'ôthâv | 'ăsher |
| to walk | | and they forgot | his deeds | even his extraordinary deeds | which |

| 7495.511 | 12. | 5224 | 1 | 6449.111 | 6624 | 904, 800 | 4875 |
|---|---|---|---|---|---|---|---|
| v Hiphil pf 3ms, ps 3mp | | prep | n mp, ps 3mp | v Qal pf 3ms | n ms | prep, *n fs* | pn |
| הֶרְאָם | | נֶגֶד | אֲבוֹתָם | עָשָׂה | פֶּלֶא | בְּאֶרֶץ | מִצְרַיִם |
| her'ām | | neghedh | 'ăvôthām | 'āsāh | phele' | b$^{e}$'erets | mitsrayim |
| He had caused them to see | | before | their fathers | He did | miracles | in the land of | Egypt |

| 7898, 7091 | 13. | 1260.111 | 3328 | 5882.521 |
|---|---|---|---|---|
| *n ms*, pn | | v Qal pf 3ms | n ms | cj, v Hiphil impf 3ms, ps 3mp |
| שְׂדֵה־צֹעַן | | בָּקַע | יָם | וַיַּעֲבִירֵם |
| s$^{e}$dhēh-tsō'an | | bāqa' | yām | wayya'ăvîrēm |
| the field of Zoan | | He divided | the sea | and He caused them to pass over |

| 5507.521, 4448 | 3765, 5243 | 14. | 5328.521 | 904, 6281 | 3221 |
|---|---|---|---|---|---|
| cj, v Hiphil impf 3ms, n md | cj, n ms | | cj, v Hiphil impf 3ms, ps 3mp | prep, art, n ms | adv |
| וַיַּצֶּב־מַיִם | כְּמוֹ־נֵד | | וַיַּנְחֵם | בֶּעָנָן | יוֹמָם |
| wayyatstsev-mayim | k$^{e}$mô-nēdh | | wayyanchēm | be'ānān | yômām |
| and He caused the waters to stand | like a dam | | and He led them | with a cloud | by day |

but to keep His commandments, *Berkeley* ... He charged them to put their trust in God, *NEB* ... That they might set in Elohim their confidence, And not forget the doings of El, *Rotherham*.

**8. And might not be as their fathers, a stubborn and rebellious generation:** ... a stiff-necked and uncontrolled generation, *BB* ... a stubborn and defiant breed, *Knox*.

**a generation that set not their heart aright, and whose spirit was not stedfast with God:** ... a generation whose heart was not firm, whose spirit was unfaithful to God, *Anchor* ... heart was hard, whose spirit was not true to God, *BB* ... did not prepare its heart; and its spirit was not faithful to God, *Berkeley* ... A race that would not fix its heart, Whose spirit was not true to GOD, *Fenton* ... weak of purpose, their spirit fickle towards God, *JB*.

**9. The children of Ephraim, being armed, and carrying bows, turned back in the day of battle:** ...

Ephraim's men, armed with bows, turned and ran on the day of battle, *Beck* ... The archer sons of Ephraim turned tail when the time came for fighting, *JB* ... as archers handling the bow, That turned back in the day of battle, *MAST* ... a disappointing bow, that fails upon the day of battle, *Moffatt.*

**10. They kept not the covenant of God, and refused to walk in his law:** ... They were not ruled by God's word, and they would not go in the way of his law, *BB* ... Nor regarded their bond with their GOD, And in His laws who would not walk, *Fenton* ... they would not keep their compact with God, they would not follow his directions, *Moffatt.*

**11. And forgat his works, and his wonders that he had shown them:** ... And remembered not His mighty acts, And wonders they had themselves seen!, *Fenton* ... And they forgot His deeds, And His miracles that He had shown them, *NASB.*

**12. Marvellous things did he in the sight of their fathers, in the land of Egypt, in the field of Zoan:** ... The wonders for their fathers done, In Mitzer's land,—on Tzoan's plains!, *Fenton.*

**13. He divided the sea, and caused them to pass through:** ... He cleft the sea and led them through, *Goodspeed* ... He split the sea and brought them through, *JB* ... He divided the Red Sea and led them through, *NCV.*

**and he made the waters to stand as an heap:** ... he made the waters stand like a dike, *Anchor* ... making the water stand up like a wall, *Beck* ... made the waters stand up like a dam, *JB.*

**14. In the daytime also he led them with a cloud, and all the night with a light of fire:** ... when he led them

---

mandment and mercy had been in vain and that instead of a tradition of goodness, there had been a transmission of stubbornness and departure from God, repeating itself with tragic uniformity. The devout poet, who knows what God meant family life to be and to do, sadly recognizes the grim contrast presented by its reality. Yet he will make one more attempt to break the flow of evil from father to son. Perhaps his contemporaries will listen and shake themselves clear of this entail of disobedience.

**78:9–11.** The reference to Ephraim in vv. 9ff is not to be taken as alluding to any cowardly retreat from actual battle. Verse 9 seems to be a purely figurative way of expressing what is put without a metaphor in the two following verses. Ephraim's revolt from God's Covenant was like the conduct of soldiers, well armed and refusing to charge the foe. The better their weapons, the greater the cowardice and ignominy of the recreants. So the faithlessness of Ephraim was made darker in criminality by its knowledge of God and experience of his mercy. These should have knit the tribe to Him. A general truth of wide application is implied—that the measure of capacity is the measure of obligation. Guilt increases with endowment, if the latter is misused. A poor soldier, with no weapon but a sling or a stick, might sooner be excused for flight than a fully armed archer. The mention of Ephraim as prominent in faithlessness may be an allusion to the separation of the kingdoms. That allusion has been denied on the ground that it is the wilderness history which is here before the psalmist's mind. But the historical retrospect does not begin until v. 12, and this introduction may well deal with an event later than those detailed in the following verses. Whether the break by the ten tribes is here in view or not, the psalmist sees that the wayward and powerful tribe of Ephraim had been a center of religious disaffection, and there is no reason why his view should not be believed, or should be supposed to be due to mere prejudiced hostility.

**78:12.** The historical details begin with v. 12, but, as has been noticed above, the psalmist seems to change his intention of first narrating the wonders in Egypt and passes on to dilate on the wilderness history. Zoan is the famous Egyptian city of Tanis, built by the Hyksos about 1700 B.C. The wonders enumerated are the familiar ones of the passage of the Red Sea, the guidance by the pillar of cloud and fire and the miraculous supply of water from the rock. In vv. 15f, the poet brings together the two instances of such supply which were separated from each other by the forty years of wandering, the first having occurred at Horeb in the first year, and the second at Kadesh in the last year. The two words "rocks" (HED #7162) in v. 15 and "cliff" (HED #5748) in v. 16 are taken from the two narratives of these miracles in Exo. 17 and Num. 20.

**78:13–20.** The group of four verses (13–16) sets forth God's mighty deeds; the next quartet of verses (17–20) tells of Israel's requital. It is significant of the thoughts which filled the singer's heart that he begins the latter group with declaring that, notwithstanding such tokens of God's care, the people "went on to sin yet more," although he had specified no previous acts of sin. He combines widely separated instances of their murmurings as he had combined distant instances of God's miraculous

| 3725, 4050 | 904, 214 | 813 | | 1260.321 | 7162 | 904, 4198 |
|---|---|---|---|---|---|---|
| cj, *adj*, art, n ms | prep, *n ms* | n fs | | v Piel impf 3ms | n mp | prep, art, n ms |
| וְכָל־הַלַּיְלָה | בְּאוֹר | אֵשׁ | **15.** | יְבַקַּע | צֻרִים | בַּמִּדְבָּר |
| wekhol-hallaylāh | be'ôr | 'ēsh | | yevaqqa‘ | tsurîm | bammidhbār |
| and all the night | with a light of | fire | | and He split | rocks | in the wilderness |

| 8615.521 | 3626, 8745 | 7521 | | 3428.521 | 5320.152 |
|---|---|---|---|---|---|
| cj, v Hiphil impf 3ms | prep, n fp | adj | | cj, v Hiphil impf 3ms | v Qal act ptc mp |
| וַיַּשְׁק | כִּתְהֹמוֹת | רַבָּה | **16.** | וַיּוֹצִא | נוֹזְלִים |
| wayyashqō | kithhōmôth | rabbāh | | wayyôtsi' | nôzlîm |
| and He gave drink | like the deeps | great | | and He caused to come out | streaming |

| 4623, 5748 | 3495.521 | 3626, 5282 | 4448 | | 3362.526 | 5968 |
|---|---|---|---|---|---|---|
| prep, n ms | cj, v Hiphil impf 3ms | prep, art, n mp | n mp | | cj, v Hiphil impf 3mp | adv |
| מִסָּלַע | וַיּוֹרֶד | כַּנְּהָרוֹת | מָיִם | **17.** | וַיּוֹסִיפוּ | עוֹד |
| missāla‘ | wayyôredh | kannehārôth | māyim | | wayyôsîphû | ‘ôdh |
| from a rock | and He caused to go down | like rivers | water | | but they continued | anymore |

| 3937, 2490.141, 3937 | 3937, 4947.541 | 6169 | 904, 6993 |
|---|---|---|---|
| prep, v Qal inf con, prep, ps 3ms | prep, v Hiphil inf con | n ms | prep, art, n fs |
| לַחֲטֹא־לוֹ | לַמְרוֹת | עֶלְיוֹן | בַּצִּיָּה |
| lachtō'-lô | lamrôth | ‘elyôn | batstsîyāh |
| to sin against Him | to rebel against | the Most High | in the waterless region |

| | 5441.326, 418 | 904, 3949 | 3937, 8068.141, 406 | 3937, 5497 |
|---|---|---|---|---|
| | cj, v Piel impf 3mp, n ms | prep, n ms, ps 3mp | prep, v Qal inf con, n ms | prep, n fs, ps 3mp |
| **18.** | וַיְנַסּוּ־אֵל | בִּלְבָבָם | לִשְׁאָל־אֹכֶל | לְנַפְשָׁם |
| | waynassû-'ēl | bilvāvām | lish'āl-'ōkhel | lenaphshām |
| | they put God to the test | in their hearts | to ask for food | for their desire |

| | 1744.326 | 904, 435 | 569.116 | 1950B, 3310.121 | 418 | 3937, 6424.141 | 8374 |
|---|---|---|---|---|---|---|---|
| | cj, v Piel impf 3mp | prep, n mp | v Qal pf 3cp | intrg part, v Qal impf 3ms | n ms | prep, v Qal inf con | n ms |
| **19.** | וַיְדַבְּרוּ | בֵּאלֹהִים | אָמְרוּ | הֲיוּכַל | אֵל | לַעֲרֹךְ | שֻׁלְחָן |
| | waydhabberû | bē'lōhîm | 'āmerû | hăyûkhal | 'ēl | la‘ărōkh | shulchān |
| | and they spoke | against God | they said | is He able | God | to set in order | a table |

| 904, 4198 | | 2075 | 5409.511, 6962 | 2183.126 | 4448 | 5337 |
|---|---|---|---|---|---|---|
| prep, art, n ms | | intrj | v Hiphil pf 3ms, n ms | cj, v Qal impf 3mp | n md | cj, n mp |
| בַּמִּדְבָּר | **20.** | הֵן | הִכָּה־צוּר | וַיָּזוּבוּ | מַיִם | וּנְחָלִים |
| bammidhbār | | hēn | hikkāh-tsûr | wayyāzûvû | mayim | ûnechālîm |
| in the wilderness | | behold | He struck a rock | and it gushed out | water | and streams |

| 8278.126 | 1950B, 1612, 4035 | 3310.121 | 5598.141 | 524, 3679.521 | 8083 |
|---|---|---|---|---|---|
| v Qal impf 3mp | intrg part, cj, n ms | v Qal impf 3ms | v Qal inf con | cj, v Hiphil impf 3ms | n ms |
| יִשְׁטֹפוּ | הֲגַם־לֶחֶם | יוּכַל | תֵּת | אִם־יָכִין | שְׁאֵר |
| yishṭōphû | hăgham-lechem | yûkhal | tēth | 'im-yākhîn | she'ēr |
| they overflowed | also bread | is He able | to give | or can He allow | flesh |

| 3937, 6194 | | 3937, 3772 | 8471.111 | 3176 | 5882.721 | 813 |
|---|---|---|---|---|---|---|
| prep, n ms, ps 3ms | | prep, adv | v Qal pf 3ms | pn | cj, v Hithpael impf 3ms | cj, n fs |
| לְעַמּוֹ | **21.** | לָכֵן | שָׁמַע | יְהוָה | וַיִּתְעַבָּר | וְאֵשׁ |
| le‘ammô | | lākhēn | shāma‘ | yehwāh | wayyith‘abbār | we'ēsh |
| to his people | | therefore | He heard | Yahweh | then He was infuriated | and a fire |

| 5564.212 | 904, 3399 | 1612, 653 | 6148.111 | 904, 3547 | | 3706 | 3940 |
|---|---|---|---|---|---|---|---|
| v Niphal pf 3fs | prep, pn | cj, cj, n ms | v Qal pf 3ms | prep, pn | | cj | neg part |
| נִשְּׂקָה | בְיַעֲקֹב | וְגַם־אַף | עָלָה | בְיִשְׂרָאֵל | **22.** | כִּי | לֹא |
| nisseqāh | veya‘ăqōv | wegham-'aph | ‘ālāh | veyisrā'ēl | | kî | lō' |
| it was kindled | against Jacob | and also anger | it went up | against Israel | | because | not |

with a cloud by day, with glowing fire all through the night?, *Knox.*

**15. He clave the rocks in the wilderness:** ... The rocks of the waste land were broken by his power, *BB* ... He split rocks in the wilderness, *Beck* ... He pierced the rock, too, in the desert, *Knox.*

**and gave them drink as out of the great depths:** ... and watered the vast wasteland itself, *Anchor* ... and let them drink as from deep water, *Beck* ... let them drink as though from the limitless depths, *JB* ... and gave them water in copious floods, *NCB.*

**16. He brought streams also out of the rock, and caused waters to run down like rivers:** ... bidding the very stones yield water, till fountains gushed from them, abundant as rivers, *Knox.*

**17. And they sinned yet more against him by provoking the most High in the wilderness:** ... But they kept on sinning against Him, rebelling against the Most High in the desert, *Beck* ... But they only sinned against him more than ever, defying the Most High in barren country, *JB.*

**18. And they tempted God in their heart by asking meat for their lust:** ... They tested God in their heart by asking food for their gullet, *Anchor* ... they deliberately challenged God by demanding food to their hearts' content, *JB* ... with a doubt of God in their mind they demanded the food they craved, *Moffatt* ... according to their desire, *ASV.*

**19. Yea, they spake against God; they said, Can God furnish a table in the wilderness?:** ... They said bitter words against God, saying, Is God able to make ready a table in the waste land?, *BB* ... They sneered at their GOD, and they said:—Can GOD in the Desert spread feasts?, *Fenton* ... They insulted God by saying, Can God make a banquet in the desert, *JB.*

**20. Behold, he smote the rock, that the waters gushed out, and the streams overflowed; can he give bread also? can he provide flesh for his people?:** ... He did, indeed, smite the rock, so that the water flowed, *Goodspeed* ... can he give us food as well, and furnish flesh to his people?, *Moffatt.*

**21. Therefore the LORD heard this, and was wroth: so a fire was kindled against Jacob, and anger also came up against Israel:** ... So, when the LORD heard it, He got angry, His fire burned against Jacob and His anger blazed at Israel, *Beck.*

**22. Because they believed not in God, and trusted not in his salvation:** ... Because they had no faith in God, and no hope in his salvation, *BB.*

---

supply of water. The complaints which preceded the fall of the manna and the first supply of quails (Exo. 16) and those which led to the second giving of these (Num. 11) are thrown together, as one in kind. The speech put into the mouths of the murmurers in vv. 19f is a poetic casting into bitter, blasphemous words of the half-conscious thoughts of the faithless, sensuous crowd. They are represented as almost upbraiding God with his miracle, as quite unmoved to trust by it, and as thinking that it has exhausted his power. When they were half dead with thirst, they thought much of the water, but now they depreciate that past wonder as a comparatively small thing. So to the churlish heart, which cherishes eager desires after some unattained earthly good, past blessings diminish as they recede and leave neither thankfulness nor trust. There is a dash of intense bitterness and ironic levity concerning their relation to God in their question, "Can He provide flesh for his people?" Much good that name has done us, starving here! The root of all this blasphemous talk was sensuous desire. Because the people yielded to it, they "tempted God"—that is, they "unbelievingly and defiantly demanded, instead of trustfully waiting and praying" (Delitzsch). To ask food for their desires was sin; to ask it for their need would have been faith.

**78:21–29.** In v. 21, the allusion is to the "fire of the LORD," which, according to Num. 11:3, burned in the camp just before the second giving of quails. It comes in here out of chronological order, for the sending of manna follows it, but the psalmist's didactic purpose renders him indifferent to chronology. The manna is called "grain of heaven" and "bread of the mighty ones"—i.e., angels, as the Septuagint renders the word. Both designations point to its heavenly origin without its being necessary to suppose that the poet thought of angels as really eating it. The description of the fall of the quails (vv. 26–29) is touched with imaginative beauty. The word rendered "He caused to gust" (HED #5450) is originally applied to the breaking up of an encampment and that rendered "He led out" (HED #5268) to a shepherd leading his flock. Both words are found in the Pentateuch, the first in reference to the wind that brought the quails (Num. 11:31), the latter in reference to that which brought the plague of locusts (Exo. 10:13). So the winds are conceived of as God's servants, issuing from their tents at his command and guided by Him as a shepherd leads his sheep. "He let it fall in the midst of their camp" graphically describes the dropping down of the wearied, storm-beaten birds.

| 548.516 | 904, 435 | 3940 | 1019.116 | 904, 3568 | | 6943.321 |
|---|---|---|---|---|---|---|
| v Hiphil pf 3cp | prep, n mp | cj, neg part | v Qal pf 3cp | prep, n fs, ps 3ms | 23. | cj, v Piel impf 3ms |
| הֶאֱמִינוּ | בֵּאלֹהִים | וְלֹא | בָטְחוּ | בִּישׁוּעָתוֹ | | וַיְצַו |
| he'ĕmînû | bē'lōhîm | welō' | vāṭechû | bîshû'āthô | | waytsaw |
| they believed | in God | and not | they trusted | in his salvation | | and He commanded |

| 8263 | 4623, 4762 | 1878 | 8452 | 6858.111 | | 4442.521 |
|---|---|---|---|---|---|---|
| n mp | prep, sub | cj, *n fp* | n md | v Qal pf 3ms | 24. | cj, v Hiphil impf 3ms |
| שְׁחָקִים | מִמָּעַל | וְדַלְתֵי | שָׁמַיִם | פָּתָח | | וַיַּמְטֵר |
| shechāqîm | mimmā'al | wedhalthê | shāmayim | pāthāch | | wayyamṭēr |
| clouds | from the above | and the doors of | the heavens | they opened | | and He caused to rain |

| 6142 | 4620 | 3937, 404.141 | 1765, 8452 | 5598.111 | 3937 |
|---|---|---|---|---|---|
| prep, ps 3mp | n ms | prep, v Qal inf con | cj, *n ms*, n md | v Qal pf 3ms | prep, ps 3mp |
| עֲלֵיהֶם | מָן | לֶאֱכֹל | וּדְגַן־שָׁמַיִם | נָתַן | לָמוֹ |
| 'ălêhem | mān | le'ĕkhōl | ûdheghan-shāmayim | nāthan | lāmô |
| on them | manna | to eat | yes the grain of the heavens | He gave | to them |

| | 4035 | 48 | 404.111 | 382 | 6990 | 8365.111 | 3937 | 3937, 7883 |
|---|---|---|---|---|---|---|---|---|
| 25. | *n ms* | n mp | v Qal pf 3ms | n ms | n fs | v Qal pf 3ms | prep, ps 3mp | prep, n ms |
| | לֶחֶם | אַבִּירִים | אָכַל | אִישׁ | צֵידָה | שָׁלַח | לָהֶם | לָשֹׂבַע |
| | lechem | 'abbîrîm | 'ākhal | 'îsh | tsêdhāh | shālach | lāhem | lāsōva' |
| | bread of | mighty ones | they ate | men | provisions | He sent | to them | satiation |

| | 5450.521 | 7205 | 904, 8452 | 5268.321 | 904, 6010 | 8816 |
|---|---|---|---|---|---|---|
| 26. | v Hiphil juss 3ms | n ms | prep, art, n md | cj, v Piel impf 3ms | prep, n ms, ps 3ms | n fs |
| | יַסַּע | קָדִים | בַּשָּׁמָיִם | וַיְנַהֵג | בְּעֻזּוֹ | תֵימָן |
| | yassa' | qādhîm | bashshāmāyim | waynahēgh | be'uzzô | thêmān |
| | He caused to gust | an east wind | in the heavens | and He led out | by his strength | a south wind |

| | 4442.521 | 6142 | 3626, 6312 | 8083 | 3626, 2437 | 3328 |
|---|---|---|---|---|---|---|
| 27. | cj, v Hiphil impf 3ms | prep, ps 3mp | prep, art, n ms | n ms | cj, prep, *n ms* | n mp |
| | וַיַּמְטֵר | עֲלֵיהֶם | כֶּעָפָר | שְׁאֵר | וּכְחוֹל | יַמִּים |
| | wayyamṭēr | 'ălêhem | ke'āphār | she'ēr | ûkhechôl | yammîm |
| | and He caused to rain | on them | like the dust | flesh | and like the sand of | the seas |

| 5991 | 3796 | | 5489.521 | 904, 7419 | 4402 | 5623 |
|---|---|---|---|---|---|---|
| *n ms* | n fs | 28. | cj, v Hiphil impf 3ms | prep, *n ms* | n ms, ps 3ms | adv |
| עוֹף | כָּנָף | | וַיַּפֵּל | בְּקֶרֶב | מַחֲנֵהוּ | סָבִיב |
| 'ôph | kānāph | | wayyappēl | beqerev | machnēhû | sāvîv |
| birds with | wings | | and He caused to fall | in the midst of | their camp | all around |

| 3937, 5088 | | 404.126 | 7881.126 | 4108 | 8707 |
|---|---|---|---|---|---|
| prep, n fp, ps 3ms | 29. | cj, v Qal impf 3mp | cj, v Qal impf 3mp | adv | cj, n fs, ps 3mp |
| לְמִשְׁכְּנֹתָיו | | וַיֹּאכְלוּ | וַיִּשְׂבְּעוּ | מְאֹד | וְתַאֲוָתָם |
| lemishkenōthâv | | wayyō'khelû | wayyisbe'û | me'ōdh | wetha'ăwāthām |
| to their homes | | and they ate | and they were satisfied | very | and their craving |

| 971.521 | 3937 | | 3940, 2197.116 | 4623, 8707 | 5968 | 406 |
|---|---|---|---|---|---|---|
| v Hiphil impf 3ms | prep, ps 3mp | 30. | neg part, v Qal pf 3cp | prep, n fs, ps 3mp | adv | n ms, ps 3mp |
| יָבִא | לָהֶם | | לֹא־זָרוּ | מִתַּאֲוָתָם | עוֹד | אָכְלָם |
| yāvi' | lāhem | | lō'-zārû | mitta'ăwāthām | 'ôdh | 'ākhelām |
| He caused to come | to them | | they did not turn aside | from their craving | still | their food |

| 904, 6552 | | 653 | 435 | 6148.111 | 904 | 2103.121 |
|---|---|---|---|---|---|---|
| prep, n ms, ps 3mp | 31. | cj, *n ms* | n mp | v Qal pf 3ms | prep, ps 3mp | cj, v Qal impf 3ms |
| בְּפִיהֶם | | וְאַף | אֱלֹהִים | עָלָה | בָּהֶם | וַיַּהֲרֹג |
| bephîhem | | we'aph | 'ĕlōhîm | 'ālāh | vāhem | wayyahrōgh |
| in their mouth | | so the anger of | God | it went up | against them | and He killed |

| | | | |
|---|---|---|---|
| 904, 5104<br>prep, n mp, ps 3mp<br>בְּמִשְׁמַנֵּיהֶם<br>b$^e$mishmannêhem<br>among their choice ones | 1005<br>cj, *n mp*<br>וּבַחוּרֵי<br>ûvachûrê<br>indeed the chosen ones of | 3547<br>pn<br>יִשְׂרָאֵל<br>yisrā'ēl<br>Israel | 3895.511<br>v Hiphil pf 3ms<br>הִכְרִיעַ<br>hikhrîa'<br>He caused to collapse |

**32.**

| | | | |
|---|---|---|---|
| 904, 3725, 2148<br>prep, *n ms*, dem pron<br>בְּכָל־זֹאת<br>b$^e$khol-zō'th<br>in all this | 2490.116, 5968<br>v Qal pf 3cp, adv<br>חָטְאוּ־עוֹד<br>chāṯ$^e$'û-'ôdh<br>they sinned still | 3940, 548.516<br>cj, neg part, v Hiphil pf 3cp<br>וְלֹא־הֶאֱמִינוּ<br>w$^e$lō'-he'ĕmînû<br>and they did not believe | 904, 6623.258<br>prep, v Niphal ptc fp, ps 3ms<br>בְּנִפְלְאוֹתָיו<br>b$^e$niphl$^e$'ôthâv<br>in his extraordinary deeds |

**33.**

| | | | |
|---|---|---|---|
| 3735.321, 904, 1961<br>cj, v Piel impf 3ms, prep, art, n ms<br>וַיְכַל־בַּהֶבֶל<br>waykhal-bahevel<br>so He brought to an end with the breath | 3219<br>n mp, ps 3mp<br>יְמֵיהֶם<br>y$^e$mêhem<br>their days | 8523<br>cj, n fp, ps 3mp<br>וּשְׁנוֹתָם<br>ûsh$^e$nôthām<br>and their years | 904, 965<br>prep, art, n fs<br>בַּבֶּהָלָה<br>babbehālāh<br>in sudden terror |

**23. Though he had commanded the clouds from above, and opened the doors of heaven:** ... Yet he commanded the clouds above, and opened the doors of heaven, *ASV* ... Even so he gave orders to the skies above, he opened the sluice-gates of heaven, *JB*.

**24. And had rained down manna upon them to eat:** ... And He caused manna to rain upon them for food, *MAST*.

**and had given them of the corn of heaven:** ... and gave them the grain of heaven, *Anchor* ... Providing their corn from the skies!, *Fenton* ... he gave them the wheat of heaven, *JB* ... and gave them heavenly bread, *NCB*.

**25. Man did eat angels' food: he sent them meat to the full:** ... the bread of the mighty: He sent them food to the full, *ASV* ... Man took part in the food of strong ones; he sent them meat in full measure, *BB* ... the bread of angels, and He sent them plenty of food, *Beck*.

**26. He caused an east wind to blow in the heaven: and by his power he brought in the south wind:** ... He let loose the east wind in the heavens, And in his might he guided the south wind, *Goodspeed*.

**27. He rained flesh also upon them as dust, and feathered fowls like as the sand of the sea:** ... he rained down meat on them like dust, *JB* ... meat down on them like a dust storm, birds flying thick as the sand of the seashore, *REB*.

**28. And he let it fall in the midst of their camp, round about their habitations:** ... And he let it come down into their resting-place, round about their tents, *BB* ... tumbling into the middle of his camp, all around his dwelling-place, *JB* ... letting them fall inside the camp, close to their very tents, *Moffatt*.

**29. So they did eat, and were well filled:** ... So they ate and were fully satisfied, *Berkeley* ... Then they ate, and they gorged to excess, *Fenton* ... were wholly surfeited, *NCB*.

**for he gave them their own desire:** ... He brought them what they craved, *Anchor* ... for that they lusted after, he brought to them, *Darby*.

**30. They were not estranged from their lust:** ... They did not desist from their complaining, *Anchor* ... But they were not turned from their desires, *BB* ... but they didn't get over their craving, *Beck* ... And they did not hold back from their greed, *Fenton*.

**But while their meat was yet in their mouths:** ... still eating up their food, *Moffatt*.

**31. The wrath of God came upon them, and slew the fattest of them:** ... God's anger rose against them; he slew their sturdiest, *Anchor* ... when God got angry with them and killed some of their husky men, *Beck* ... rose against them and slew their best men, *NCB*.

**and smote down the chosen men of Israel:** ... And smote down the young men of Israel, *ASV* ... and felled the choicest of Israel, *Berkeley* ... laying the pick of Israel low, *Moffatt*.

**32. For all this they sinned still, and believed not for his wondrous**

**78:30–33.** Verses 30–33 paint the swift punishment of the people's unbelief in language almost identical with Num. 11:33. The psalmist twice stigmatizes their sin as "lust" and uses the word which enters into the tragic name given to the scene of the sin and the punishment (the "graves of lust"). In vv. 32f, the fainthearted despondency after the return of the spies and the punishment of it by the sentence of death on all that generation seem to be alluded to.

**78:34–37.** The next group of four verses describes the people's superficial and transient repentance, "When he slew them, then they sought him"—

| 34. | | | | |
|---|---|---|---|---|
| | 524, 2103.111 | 1938.116 | 8178.116 | 8264.316, 418 |
| | cj, v Qal pf 3ms, ps 3mp | cj, v Qal pf 3cp, ps 3ms | cj, v Qal pf 3cp | cj, v Piel pf 3cp, n ms |
| | אִם־הֲרָגָם | וּדְרָשׁוּהוּ | וְשָׁבוּ | וְשִׁחֲרוּ־אֵל |
| | 'im-heraghām | ûdherāshûhû | weshāvû | weshichărû-'ēl |
| | when He killed them | then they sought Him | and they turned | and they sought God earnestly |

| 35. | | | | | | |
|---|---|---|---|---|---|---|
| | 2226.126 | 3706, 435 | 6962 | 418 | 6169 | 1381.151 |
| | cj, v Qal impf 3mp | cj, n mp | n ms, ps 3mp | cj, n ms | n ms | v Qal act ptc ms, ps 3mp |
| | וַיִּזְכְּרוּ | כִּי־אֱלֹהִים | צוּרָם | וְאֵל | עֶלְיוֹן | גֹּאֲלָם |
| | wayyizkerû | kî-'ĕlōhîm | tsûrām | we'ēl | 'elyôn | gō'ălām |
| | and they remembered | that God | their Rock | and God | the Most High | their Redeemer |

| 36. | | | | |
|---|---|---|---|---|
| | 6858.326 | 904, 6552 | 904, 4098 | 3694.326, 3937 |
| | cj, v Piel impf 3mp, ps 3ms | prep, n ms, ps 3mp | cj, prep, n fs, ps 3mp | v Piel impf 3mp, prep, ps 3ms |
| | וַיְפַתּוּהוּ | בְּפִיהֶם | וּבִלְשׁוֹנָם | יְכַזְּבוּ־לוֹ |
| | wayphattûhû | bephîhem | ûvilshônām | yekhazzevû-lô |
| | and they tried to persuade | with their mouth | and with their tongue | they lied to Him |

| 37. | | | | | |
|---|---|---|---|---|---|
| | 3949 | 3940, 3679.255 | 6196 | 3940 | 548.216 |
| | cj, n ms, ps 3mp | neg part, v Niphal ptc ms | prep, ps 3ms | cj, neg part | v Niphal pf 3cp |
| | וְלִבָּם | לֹא־נָכוֹן | עִמּוֹ | וְלֹא | נֶאֶמְנוּ |
| | welibbām | lō'-nākhôn | 'immô | welō' | ne'emnû |
| | and their heart | it was not steadfast | with Him | and not | they were reliable |

| | | | | | | |
|---|---|---|---|---|---|---|
| 904, 1311 | | 2000 | 7631 | 3848.321 | 5988 | 3940, 8271.521 |
| prep, n fs, ps 3ms | 38. | cj, pers pron | adj | v Piel impf 3ms | n ms | cj, neg part, v Hiphil impf 3ms |
| בִּבְרִיתוֹ | | וְהוּא | רַחוּם | יְכַפֵּר | עָוֹן | וְלֹא־יַשְׁחִית |
| bivrîthô | | wehû' | rachûm | yekhappēr | 'āwōn | welō'-yashchîth |
| with the Covenant | | but He | compassionate | He forgave | guilt | and He did not destroy |

| | | | | |
|---|---|---|---|---|
| 7528.511 | 3937, 8178.541 | 653 | 3940, 5996.521 | 3725, 2635 |
| cj, v Hiphil pf 3ms | prep, v Hiphil inf con | n ms, ps 3ms | cj, neg part, v Hiphil impf 3ms | *adj*, n fs, ps 3ms |
| וְהִרְבָּה | לְהָשִׁיב | אַפּוֹ | וְלֹא־יָעִיר | כָּל־חֲמָתוֹ |
| wehirbāh | lehāshîv | 'appô | welō'-yā'îr | kol-chămāthô |
| and He made abundant | to turn back | his anger | and He did not arouse | all his wrath |

| 39. | | | | | | | |
|---|---|---|---|---|---|---|---|
| | 2226.121 | 3706, 1340 | 2065 | 7593 | 2050.151 | 3940 | 8178.121 |
| | cj, v Qal impf 3ms | cj, n ms | pers pron | n fs | v Qal act ptc ms | cj, neg part | v Qal impf 3ms |
| | וַיִּזְכֹּר | כִּי־בָשָׂר | הֵמָּה | רוּחַ | הוֹלֵךְ | וְלֹא | יָשׁוּב |
| | wayyizkōr | kî-vāsār | hēmmāh | rûach | hôlēkh | welō' | yāshûv |
| | and He remembered | that flesh | they | a wind | proceeding | and not | it returns |

| 40. | | | | | |
|---|---|---|---|---|---|
| | 3626, 4242 | 4947.526 | 904, 4198 | 6321.526 | 904, 3574 |
| | prep, intrg | v Hiphil impf 3mp, ps 3ms | prep, art, n ms | v Hiphil impf 3mp, ps 3ms | prep, n ms |
| | כַּמָּה | יַמְרוּהוּ | בַמִּדְבָּר | יַעֲצִיבוּהוּ | בִּישִׁימוֹן |
| | kammāh | yamrûhû | vammidhbār | ya'ătsîvûhû | bîshîmôn |
| | like what | they rebelled against Him | in the wilderness | they caused Him grief | in the desert |

| 41. | | | | | |
|---|---|---|---|---|---|
| | 8178.126 | 5441.326 | 418 | 7202 | 3547 |
| | cj, v Qal impf 3mp | cj, v Piel impf 3mp | n ms | cj, *n ms* | pn |
| | וַיָּשׁוּבוּ | וַיְנַסּוּ | אֵל | וּקְדוֹשׁ | יִשְׂרָאֵל |
| | wayyāshûvû | waynassû | 'ēl | ûqŏdhôsh | yisrā'ēl |
| | and they turned | and they put to the test | God | even the Holy One of | Israel |

| | | | | | |
|---|---|---|---|---|---|
| 8757.516 | | 3940, 2226.116 | 881, 3135 | 3219 | 866, 6540.111 |
| v Hiphil pf 3cp | 42. | neg part, v Qal pf 3cp | do, n fs, ps 3ms | n ms | rel part, v Qal pf 3ms, ps 3mp |
| הִתְווּ | | לֹא־זָכְרוּ | אֶת־יָדוֹ | יוֹם | אֲשֶׁר־פָּדָם |
| hithwû | | lō'-zākherû | 'eth-yādhô | yôm | 'ăsher-pādhām |
| they caused to mark | | they did not remember | his hand | the day | which He ransomed them |

**works:** ... For all this they went on sinning even more, and had no faith in his great wonders, *BB* ... In spite of all this, they sinned still more and had no confidence in His wondrous works, *Berkeley.*

**33. Therefore their days did he consume in vanity, and their years in trouble:** ... Their days he made vanish more quickly than vapor, and their years more quickly than a fleeting phantom, *Anchor* ... So their days were wasted like a breath, and their years in trouble, *BB* ... So He made their days disappear like a fog, made their years end in sudden disaster, *Berkeley* ... So he brought their days to an end in a breath, And their years in sudden ruin, *Goodspeed.*

**34. When he slew them, then they sought him: and they returned and inquired early after God:** ...When he sent death on them, then they made search for him; turning to him and looking for him with care, *BB* ... When He struck them down, they searched for Him, repented, and eagerly looked for God, *Beck* ... Anytime he killed them, they would look to him for help, *NCV.*

**35. And they remembered that God was their rock, and the high God their redeemer:** ... They remembered that God was their protector, that the Almighty came to their aid, *Good News* ... remembering God was their strength, and God Most High their preserver, *Moffatt.*

**36. Nevertheless they did flatter him with their mouth, and they lied unto him with their tongues:** ... So they beguiled him with their mouth, And lied to him with their tongue, *Goodspeed* ... They tried to hoodwink him with their mouths, their tongues were deceitful towards him, *JB* ... But their words were all lies; nothing they said was sincere, *Good News.*

**37. For their heart was not right with him, neither were they stedfast in his covenant:** ... In their hearts they didn't stand true to Him but were unfaithful to His covenant, *Beck* ... they had a wavering mind, they were not loyal to his compact, *Moffatt.*

**38. But he, being full of compassion, forgave their iniquity, and destroyed them not:** ... But he the Merciful forgave their sin, and did not destroy them, *Anchor* ... But he, being full of pity, has forgiveness for sin, and does not put an end to man, *BB* ... kindly pardoned their sin, Destroyed not, *Fenton* ... wiped out their guilt and did not smother his own natural affection, *NEB.*

**yea, many a time turned he his anger away, and did not stir up all his wrath:** ... frequently turning back his wrath, and not being violently angry, *BB* ... And frequently he restrains his anger, And does not arouse all his rage, *Goodspeed* ... often he will avert his wrath, without one angry breath, *Moffatt.*

**39. For he remembered that they were but flesh; a wind that passeth away, and cometh not again:** ... He remembered that they were only human, *NCV* ... He remembered they were only flesh, a breeze that blows and doesn't come back, *Beck* ... So he remembered they were mortal men, their life no better than a passing breeze, *Moffatt.*

**40. How oft did they provoke him in the wilderness, and grieve him in the desert!:** ... How often did they oppose him in the wilderness, And grieve him in the desert, *Goodspeed* ... They turned against God so often in the desert and grieved him there, *NCV.*

**41. Yea, they turned back and tempted God, and limited the Holy One of Israel:** ... Again they put God to the test, and gave pain to the Holy One of Israel, *BB* ... Over and over they tempted God and made Israel's holy One feel sad, *Beck* ... They tried God again and again, And vexed the holy one of Israel, *Goodspeed* ... set bounds to the Holy One of Israel, *MAST.*

**42. They remembered not his hand, nor the day when he deliv-**

---

i.e., when the fiery serpents were sent among them. But such seeking after God, which is properly not seeking Him at all but only seeking to escape from evil, neither goes deep nor lasts long. Thus, the end of it was only lip reverence, proved to be false by life, and soon ended. "Their heart was not steadfast." The pressure being removed, they returned to their habitual position, as all such penitents do.

**78:38–39.** From the midst of this sad narrative of faithlessness springs up, like a fountain in a weary land or a flower among half-cooled lava blocks, the lovely description of God's forbearance in vv. 38f. It must not be read as if it merely carried on the narrative and was in continuation of the preceding clauses. The psalmist does not say "He was full of compassion," although that would be much in the circumstances, but he is declaring God's eternal character. His compassions are unfailing. It is always his desire to cover sin and to spare. Therefore, He exercised these gracious forbearances toward those obstinate transgressors. He was true to his own compassion in remembering their mortality and feebleness. What a melancholy sound, as of wind blowing among forgotten graves, has that summing up of human life as "a breath that goes and comes not again!"

**78:40–51.** The second portion of the Psalm begins with v. 40. The first group of historical details dealt first with God's mercies and passed on to man's requital. The second starts with man's

| 4623, 7141 | | 866, 7947.111 | 904, 4875 | 225 | 4295 |
|---|---|---|---|---|---|
| prep, n ms | 43. | rel part, v Qal pf 3ms | prep, pn | n mp, ps 3ms | cj, n mp, ps 3ms |
| מִנִי־צָר | | אֲשֶׁר־שָׂם | בְּמִצְרַיִם | אֹתוֹתָיו | וּמוֹפְתָיו |
| minî-tsār | | 'ăsher-sām | b$^{e}$mitsrayim | 'ōthôthâv | ûmôphthâv |
| from the adversary | | that He had set | against Egypt | his signs | and his wonders |

| 904, 7898, 7091 | | 2089.121 | 3937, 1879 | 3083 | 5320.152 |
|---|---|---|---|---|---|
| prep, *n ms*, pn | 44. | cj, v Qal impf 3ms | prep, n ms | n mp, ps 3mp | cj, v Qal act ptc mp, ps 3mp |
| בִּשְׂדֵה־צֹעַן | | וַיַּהֲפֹךְ | לְדָם | יְאֹרֵיהֶם | וְנֹזְלֵיהֶם |
| bisdhēh-tsō'an | | wayyahphōkh | l$^{e}$dhām | y$^{e}$'ōrêhem | w$^{e}$nōz$^{e}$lêhem |
| in the field of Zoan | | and He changed | into blood | their rivers | and their streaming ones |

| 1118, 8685.126 | | 8365.321 | 904 | 6389 | 404.121 | 7131 |
|---|---|---|---|---|---|---|
| neg part, v Qal impf 3mp | 45. | v Piel impf 3ms | prep, ps 3mp | n ms | cj, v Qal impf 3ms, ps 3mp | cj, n fs |
| בַּל־יִשְׁתָּיוּן | | יְשַׁלַּח | בָּהֶם | עָרֹב | וַיֹּאכְלֵם | וּצְפַרְדֵּעַ |
| bal-yishtāyûn | | y$^{e}$shallach | bāhem | 'ārōv | wayyō'kh$^{e}$lēm | ûts$^{e}$phardēa' |
| they could not drink | | He sent | among them | the fly | and it devoured them | and the frog |

| 8271.522 | | 5598.121 | 3937, 2730 | 3090 |
|---|---|---|---|---|
| cj, v Hiphil impf 3fs, ps 3mp | 46. | cj, v Qal impf 3ms | prep, art, n ms | n ms, ps 3mp |
| וַתַּשְׁחִיתֵם | | וַיִּתֵּן | לֶחָסִיל | יְבוּלָם |
| wattashchîthēm | | wayyittēn | lechāsîl | y$^{e}$vûlām |
| and it destroyed them | | and He gave | to the young locust | their produce |

| 3127 | 3937, 722 | | 2103.121 | 904, 1287 | 1655 |
|---|---|---|---|---|---|
| cj, n ms, ps 3mp | prep, art, n ms | 47. | v Qal impf 3ms | prep, art, n ms | n fs, ps 3mp |
| וִיגִיעָם | לָאַרְבֶּה | | יַהֲרֹג | בַּבָּרָד | גַּפְנָם |
| wîghî'ām | lā'arbeh | | yahrōgh | babbārādh | gaphnām |
| and the product of their labor | to the locust | | He killed | with the hail | their vines |

| 8622 | 904, 2705 | | 5646.521 | 3937, 1287 | 1194 |
|---|---|---|---|---|---|
| cj, n fp, ps 3mp | prep, art, n ms | 48. | cj, v Hiphil impf 3ms | prep, art, n ms | n ms, ps 3mp |
| וְשִׁקְמוֹתָם | בַּחֲנָמַל | | וַיַּסְגֵּר | לַבָּרָד | בְּעִירָם |
| w$^{e}$shiqōmôthām | bachnāmal | | wayyasgēr | labbārādh | b$^{e}$'îrām |
| and their sycamore fig trees | with the frost | | and He handed over | to the hail | their cattle |

| 4898 | 3937, 7859 | | 8365.321, 904 | 2841 | 653 | 5887 |
|---|---|---|---|---|---|---|
| cj, n mp, ps 3mp | prep, art, n mp | 49. | v Piel impf 3ms, prep, ps 3mp | *n ms* | n ms, ps 3ms | n fs |
| וּמִקְנֵיהֶם | לָרְשָׁפִים | | יְשַׁלַּח־בָּם | חֲרוֹן | אַפּוֹ | עֶבְרָה |
| ûmiqōnêhem | lār$^{e}$shāphîm | | y$^{e}$shallach-bām | chărôn | 'appô | 'evrāh |
| and their livestock | to the lightning | | He sent out against them | the anger of | his nose | wrath |

| 2279 | 7150 | 5097 | 4534 | 7737 | | 6668.321 | 5593 |
|---|---|---|---|---|---|---|---|
| cj, n ms | cj, n fs | *n fs* | *n mp* | adj | 50. | v Piel impf 3ms | n ms |
| וָזַעַם | וְצָרָה | מִשְׁלַחַת | מַלְאֲכֵי | רָעִים | | יְפַלֵּס | נָתִיב |
| wāza'am | w$^{e}$tsārāh | mishlachath | mal'ăkhê | rā'îm | | y$^{e}$phallēs | nāthîv |
| and indignation | and adversity | a regiment of | angels of | disastrous | | He made level | a path |

| 3937, 653 | 3940, 2931.111 | 4623, 4323 | 5497 | 2517 | 3937, 1746 |
|---|---|---|---|---|---|
| prep, n ms, ps 3ms | neg part, v Qal pf 3ms | prep, n ms | n fs, ps 3mp | cj, n fs, ps 3mp | prep, art, n ms |
| לְאַפּוֹ | לֹא־חָשַׂךְ | מִמָּוֶת | נַפְשָׁם | וְחַיָּתָם | לַדֶּבֶר |
| l$^{e}$'appô | lō'-chāsakh | mimmāweth | naphshām | w$^{e}$chayyāthām | laddever |
| because of his anger | He did not restrain | from death | their life | but their life | to the plague |

| 5646.511 | | 5409.521 | 3725, 1111 | 904, 4875 | 7519 |
|---|---|---|---|---|---|
| v Hiphil pf 3ms | 51. | cj, v Hiphil impf 3ms | *adj*, n ms | prep, pn | *n fs* |
| הִסְגִּיר | | וַיַּךְ | כָּל־בְּכוֹר | בְּמִצְרָיִם | רֵאשִׁית |
| hisgîr | | wayyakh | kol-b$^{e}$khôr | b$^{e}$mitsrāyim | rē'shîth |
| He handed over | | and He struck down | all the firstborn | in Egypt | the beginning of |

**ered them from the enemy:** ... They did not remember his power, the day when he ransomed them from the adversary, *Anchor* ... They did not keep in mind the work of his hand, or the day when he took them from the power of their haters, *BB* ... his prowess on the day when he saved them from the enemy, *NEB.*

**43. How he had wrought his signs in Egypt, and his wonders in the field of Zoan:** ... How he set his signs in Egypt, and his miracles in the field of Zoan, *Darby* ... the portents that he wrought in Egypt, his marvels in the land of Zoan, *Moffatt.*

**44. And had turned their rivers into blood:** ... He turned their Nile into blood, *Beck* ... He turned their streams into blood, *NEB.*

**and their floods, that they could not drink:** ... and they were not able to get drink from their streams, *BB* ... and they could not drink the running water, *NEB.*

**45. He sent divers sorts of flies among them, which devoured them; and frogs, which destroyed them:** ... He sent among them swarms of flies that ate them; frogs too that devastated them, *Berkeley* ... dog-flies among them, which devoured them, and frogs, which destroyed them, *Darby* ... locusts on them, to devour, and defiled them by means of the frogs, *Fenton* ... horse-flies to eat them up, and frogs to devastate them, *JB.*

**46. He gave also their increase unto the caterpillar, and their labour unto the locust:** ... He gave their crops to grasshoppers and what they worked for to locusts, *Beck* ... to locusts and their produce to grasshoppers, *Berkeley* ... vermin their produce, And their gardens to grasshoppers gave, *Fenton* ... harvest over to locusts, their produce to the grubs, *REB.*

**47. He destroyed their vines with hail, and their sycamore trees with frost:** ... He sent ice for the destruction of their vines; their trees were damaged by the bitter cold, *BB* ... he devastated their vines with hailstones, their fig trees with torrents of rain, *REB.*

**48. He gave up their cattle also to the hail, and their flocks to hot thunderbolts:** ... Ice was rained down on their cattle; thunder-storms sent destruction among the flocks, *BB* ... And He shut up their towns by the hail, And their ware-rooms, by lightning's bright flash, *Fenton* ... And how he gave their cattle over to the plague, And their flocks to the pestilence, *Goodspeed.*

**49. He cast upon them the fierceness of his anger, wrath, and indignation, and trouble, by sending evil angels among them:** ... He sent them His blazing anger, wrath, fury, and distress - an escort of troublesome messengers, *Beck* ... Sending forth evil spirits, He cast upon them bursting anger, His overflowing wrath, indignation, and distress, *Berkeley* ... He caused them great distress by pouring out his anger and fierce rage, which came as messengers of death, *Good News* ... He sent his strong anger against them, his destroying angels, *NCV.*

**50. He made a way to his anger; he spared not their soul from death, but gave their life over to the pestilence:** ... He let his wrath have its way; he did not keep back their soul from death, but gave their life to disease, *BB* ... straight and swift his anger sped, unsparing, letting the deadly pestilence prey on life, *Moffatt* ... He did not keep them from dying but let them die by a terrible disease, *NCV* ... and delivered their beasts to the plague, *NCB.*

**51. And smote all the firstborn in Egypt; the chief of their strength in the tabernacles of Ham:** ... He struck all the first-born in Egypt, the flower of the youth in the tents of Ham, *JB* ... The first issue of their virility in the tents of Ham, *NASB* ... the oldest son of each family of Ham, *NCV.*

---

ingratitude, which it paints in the darkest colors as provoking Him, grieving Him, tempting Him and vexing Him. The psalmist is not afraid to represent God as affected with such emotions by reason of men's indifference and unbelief. His language is not to be waved aside as anthropomorphic and antiquated. No doubt, we come nearer to the unattainable truth when we conceive of God as grieved by men's sins and delighting in their trust than when we think of Him as an impassive infinitude, serenely indifferent to tortured or sinful hearts. For does He not continually reach out in love?

The psalmist traces Israel's sin to forgetfulness of God's mercy, and thus glides into a swift summing up of the plagues of Egypt, regarded as conducive to Israel's deliverance. They are not arranged chronologically, although the list begins with the first. Then follows three of those in which animals were the destroyers: namely, the fourth, that of flies; the second, that of frogs; and the eighth, that of locusts. Then comes the seventh, that of hail; and, according to some commentators, the fifth, that of the murrain, in v. 49, followed by the tenth in v. 51. But the grand, somber imagery of v. 49 is too majestic for such application. It rather sums up the whole series of plagues, likening them to an embassy (literally, "a sending") of angels of evil. They are a grim company to come forth from his presence—wrath, indignation and trouble. The same power which sent them out on their errand

| 202 | 904, 164, 2626 | 52. | 5450.521 | 3626, 6887 |
|---|---|---|---|---|
| n mp | prep, *n mp*, pn | | cj, v Hiphil impf 3ms | prep, art, n fs |
| אוֹנִים | בְּאָהֳלֵי־חָם | | וַיַּסַּע | כַּצֹּאן |
| 'ônîm | bᵉ'āhᵉlê-chām | | wayyassa' | katstsō'n |
| their procreative power | in the tents of Ham | | then He caused to pull out | like the sheep |

| 6194 | 5268.321 | 3626, 5953 | 904, 4198 | 53. | 5328.521 |
|---|---|---|---|---|---|
| n ms, ps 3ms | cj, v Piel impf 3ms, ps 3mp | prep, art, n ms | prep, art, n ms | | cj, v Hiphil impf 3ms, ps 3mp |
| עַמּוֹ | וַיְנַהֲגֵם | כַּעֵדֶר | בַּמִּדְבָּר | | וַיַּנְחֵם |
| 'ammô | waynahghēm | ka'ēdher | bammidhbār | | wayyanchēm |
| his people | and He guided them | like the flock | in the wilderness | | and He led them |

| 3937, 1020 | 3940 | 6585.116 | 881, 342.152 | 3803.311 | 3328 |
|---|---|---|---|---|---|
| prep, n ms | cj, neg part | v Qal pf 3cp | cj, do, v Qal act ptc mp, ps 3mp | v Piel pf 3ms | art, n ms |
| לָבֶטַח | וְלֹא | פָּחָדוּ | וְאֶת־אוֹיְבֵיהֶם | כִּסָּה | הַיָּם |
| lāveṭach | wᵉlō' | phāchādhû | wᵉ'eth-'ôyvêhem | kissāh | hayyām |
| with safety | and not | they trembled | but their enemies | it brought to an end | the sea |

| 54. | 971.521 | 420, 1397 | 7231 | 2098, 2172 | 7353.112 |
|---|---|---|---|---|---|
| | cj, v Hiphil impf 3ms, ps 3mp | prep, *n ms* | n ms, ps 3ms | n ms, dem pron | v Qal pf 3fs |
| | וַיְבִיאֵם | אֶל־גְּבוּל | קָדְשׁוֹ | הַר־זֶה | קָנְתָה |
| | wayvî'ēm | 'el-gᵉvûl | qādhᵉshô | har-zeh | qānᵉthāh |
| | and He brought them | to the boundary of | his holy place | the mountain which | it acquired |

| 3332 | 55. | 1691.321 | 4623, 6686 | 1504 | 5489.521 |
|---|---|---|---|---|---|
| n fs, ps 3ms | | cj, v Piel impf 3ms | prep, n mp, ps 3mp | n mp | cj, v Hiphil impf 3ms, ps 3mp |
| יְמִינוֹ | | וַיְגָרֶשׁ | מִפְּנֵיהֶם | גּוֹיִם | וַיַּפִּילֵם |
| yᵉmînô | | wayghāresh | mippᵉnêhem | gôyim | wayyappîlēm |
| his right hand | | and He drove out | from before them | nations | and He caused to fall |

| 904, 2346 | 5338 | 8331.521 | 904, 164 | 8101 | 3547 |
|---|---|---|---|---|---|
| prep, n ms | n fs | cj, v Hiphil impf 3ms | prep, n mp, ps 3mp | *n mp* | pn |
| בְּחֶבֶל | נַחֲלָה | וַיַּשְׁכֵּן | בְּאָהֳלֵיהֶם | שִׁבְטֵי | יִשְׂרָאֵל |
| bᵉchevel | nachlāh | wayyashkēn | bᵉ'āhᵉlêhem | shivṭê | yisrā'ēl |
| with ropes | an inheritance | and He caused to settle | in their tents | the tribes of | Israel |

| 56. | 5441.326 | 4947.526 | 881, 435 | 6169 |
|---|---|---|---|---|
| | cj, v Piel impf 3mp | cj, v Hiphil impf 3mp | do, n mp | n ms |
| | וַיְנַסּוּ | וַיַּמְרוּ | אֶת־אֱלֹהִים | עֶלְיוֹן |
| | waynassû | wayyamrû | 'eth-'ĕlōhîm | 'elyôn |
| | but they put to the test | and they rebelled against | God | the Most High |

| 5921 | 3940 | 8490.116 | 57. | 5657.226 | 931.126 |
|---|---|---|---|---|---|
| cj, n fp, ps 3ms | neg part | v Qal pf 3cp | | cj, v Niphal impf 3mp | cj, v Qal impf 3mp |
| וְעֵדוֹתָיו | לֹא | שָׁמָרוּ | | וַיִּסֹּגוּ | וַיִּבְגְּדוּ |
| wᵉ'ēdhôthâv | lō' | shāmārû | | wayyissōghû | wayyivgᵉdhû |
| and his Testimonies | not | they observed | | and they turned aside | and they acted treacherously |

| 3626, 1 | 2089.216 | 3626, 7493 | 7711 | 58. | 3832.526 |
|---|---|---|---|---|---|
| prep, n mp, ps 3mp | v Niphal pf 3cp | prep, *n fs* | n fs | | cj, v Hiphil impf 3mp, ps 3ms |
| כַּאֲבוֹתָם | נֶהְפְּכוּ | כְּקֶשֶׁת | רְמִיָּה | | וַיַּכְעִיסוּהוּ |
| ka'ăvôthām | nehpᵉkhû | kᵉqesheth | rᵉmîyāh | | wayyakh'îsûhû |
| like their fathers | they turned against | like a bow of | deceit | | and they provoked Him |

| 904, 1154 | 904, 6702 | 7349.526 | 59. | 8471.111 |
|---|---|---|---|---|
| prep, n fp, ps 3mp | cj, prep, n mp, ps 3mp | v Hiphil impf 3mp, ps 3ms | | v Qal pf 3ms |
| בְּבָמוֹתָם | וּבִפְסִילֵיהֶם | יַקְנִיאוּהוּ | | שָׁמַע |
| bᵉvāmôthām | ûviphsîlêhem | yaqnî'ûhû | | shāma' |
| with their high places | and with their idols | and they caused Him to be zealous | | He heard |

**52. But made his own people to go forth like sheep, and guided them in the wilderness like a flock:** ... but his people he led forth like sheep and guided them like a herd in the desert, *NCB* ... But he brought his people out like a flock; he led them like sheep through the desert, *NIV.*

**53. And he led them on safely, so that they feared not: but the sea overwhelmed their enemies:** ... he led them safely on, without a fear, when the sea drowned their foes, *Moffatt* ... He guided them safely, so they were unafraid; but the sea engulfed their enemies, *NIV.*

**54. And he brought them to the border of his sanctuary, even to this mountain, which his right hand had purchased:** ... And he was their guide to his holy land, even to the mountain, which his right hand had made his, *BB* ... He brought them to His holy domain, to the mountain which His right hand had gained, *Berkeley* ... He brought them to his holy land, the hill-country won by his right hand, *JB.*

**55. He cast out the heathen also before them, and divided them an inheritance by line, and made the tribes of Israel to dwell in their tents:** ... He drove out the nations before them, and by lot made their patrimony fall to them; He settled the tribes of Israel in their tents, *Anchor* ... He drove out peoples before them and allotted them a measured inheritance; He settled the tribes of Israel in their tents, *Berkeley.*

**56. Yet they tempted and provoked the most high God, and kept not his testimonies:** ... But they were bitter against the Most High God, testing him, and not keeping his laws, *BB* ... Still they tempted God and rebelled against the Most High and didn't live by His truth, *Beck* ... But they tried and vexed God, the Most High, And did not keep his injunctions, *Goodspeed.*

**57. But turned back, and dealt unfaithfully like their fathers: they were turned aside like a deceitful bow:** ... Their hearts were turned back and untrue like their fathers; they were turned to one side like a twisted bow, *BB* ... as perverse and treacherous as their ancestors, they gave way like a faulty bow, *JB* ... renegades, traitors like their fathers, they changed, they went slack like a bow, *NEB* ... like a crooked bow that does not shoot straight, *NCV.*

**58. For they provoked him to anger with their high places, and moved him to jealousy with their graven images:** ... They made Him angry by worshiping on their high places, and made Him jealous with their idols, *Beck* ... by building places to worship gods; they made him jealous with their idols, *NCV.*

**59. When God heard this, he was wroth, and greatly abhorred Israel:** ... When this came to God's ears he was very angry, and gave up Israel completely, *BB* ... God heard them and got furious. He vehemently rejected Israel, *Beck* ... he put them out of mind and utterly rejected Israel, *NEB.*

**60. So that he forsook the tabernacle of Shiloh, the tent which he placed among men:** ... and abandoned His home in Shiloh, the tabernacle where He lived among people, *Beck.*

---

prepared a way before them, and the crowning judgment, which in the psalmist's view was also the crowning mercy, was the death of the firstborn.

**78:52–59.** The next quartet of verses passes lightly over the wilderness history and the settlement in the land and hastens on to a renewed narration of repeated rebellion, which occupies the next group (vv. 56–59). These verses cover the period from the entrance into Canaan to the fall of the sanctuary of Shiloh during which there was a continual tendency to relapse into idolatry. That is the special sin here charged against the Israelites during the time of the judges. The figure of a "deceitful bow" in v. 57 well describes the people as failing to fulfill the purpose of their choice by God. As such a weapon does not shoot true and makes the arrow fly wide, so Israel foiled all divine attempts and failed to carry God's message to the world or to fulfill his will in themselves. Hence, the next verses tell with intense energy and pathos the sad story of Israel's humiliation under the Philistines. The language is extraordinarily strong in its description of God's loathing and rejection of the nation and sanctuary and is instinct with sorrow, blended with stern recognition of his righteousness in judgment. What a tragic picture the psalmist draws: Shiloh, the dwelling place of God, empty forevermore; the "Glory"—that is, the Ark—in the enemy's hands; everywhere stiffening corpses; a pall of silence over the land; no brides and no joyous bridal chants; the very priests massacred, unlamented by their widows who had wept so many tears already that the fountain of them was dried up, and even sorrowing love was dumb with horror and despair!

**78:60–72.** The two last groups of verses paint God's great mercy in delivering the nation from such misery. The daring figure of his awaking as from sleep and dashing upon Israel's foes—who are also his—with a shout like that of a hero stimulated by wine is more accordant with

| 435 | 5882.721 | 4128.121 | 4108 | 904, 3547 | | 5389.121 |
|---|---|---|---|---|---|---|
| n mp | cj, v Hithpael impf 3ms | cj, v Qal impf 3ms | adv | prep, pn | 60. | cj, v Qal impf 3ms |
| אֱלֹהִים | וַיִּתְעַבָּר | וַיִּמְאַס | מְאֹד | בְּיִשְׂרָאֵל | | וַיִּטֹּשׁ |
| 'ĕlōhîm | wayyith'abbār | wayyim'as | me'ōdh | beyisrā'ēl | | wayyittōsh |
| God | then He was infuriated | and He rejected | very | in Israel | | and He left behind |

| 5088 | 8350 | 164 | 8331.311 | 904, 119 | | 5598.121 |
|---|---|---|---|---|---|---|
| *n ms* | pn | n ms | v Piel pf 3ms | prep, art, n ms | 61. | cj, v Qal impf 3ms |
| מִשְׁכַּן | שִׁלוֹ | אֹהֶל | שִׁכֵּן | בָּאָדָם | | וַיִּתֵּן |
| mishkan | shilô | 'ōhel | shikkēn | bā'ādhām | | wayyittēn |
| the Tabernacle of | Shiloh | the Tent | He remained in | among humankind | | and He gave |

| 3937, 8104 | 6010 | 8930 | 904, 3135, 7141 | | 5646.521 |
|---|---|---|---|---|---|
| prep, art, n ms | n ms, ps 3ms | cj, n fs, ps 3ms | prep, *n fs*, n ms | 62. | cj, v Hiphil impf 3ms |
| לַשְּׁבִי | עֻזּוֹ | וְתִפְאַרְתּוֹ | בְּיַד־צָר | | וַיַּסְגֵּר |
| lashshevî | 'uzzô | wethiph'artô | veyadh-tsār | | wayyasgēr |
| to captivity | his strength | and his splendor | into the hand of the adversary | | and He handed over |

| 3937, 2820 | 6194 | 904, 5338 | 5882.711 | | 1005 |
|---|---|---|---|---|---|
| prep, art, n fs | n ms, ps 3ms | cj, prep, n fs, ps 3ms | v Hithpael pf 3ms | 63. | n mp, ps 3ms |
| לַחֶרֶב | עַמּוֹ | וּבְנַחֲלָתוֹ | הִתְעַבָּר | | בַּחוּרָיו |
| lacherev | 'ammô | ûvenachlāthô | hith'abbār | | bachûrâv |
| to the sword | his people | and against his inheritance | He became infuriated | | his young men |

| 404.112, 813 | 1359 | 3940 | 2054.416 | | 3669 | 904, 2820 |
|---|---|---|---|---|---|---|
| v Qal pf 3fs, n fs | cj, n fp, ps 3ms | neg part | v Pual pf 3cp | 64. | n mp, ps 3ms | prep, art, n fs |
| אָכְלָה־אֵשׁ | וּבְתוּלֹתָיו | לֹא | הוּלָּלוּ | | כֹּהֲנָיו | בַּחֶרֶב |
| 'ākhelāh-'ēsh | ûvethûlōthâv | lō' | hûllālû | | kōhenâv | bacherev |
| the fire devoured | and his young women | not | they were adorned | | his priests | by the sword |

| 5489.116 | 496 | 3940 | 1098.127 | | 3477.121 | 3626, 3585 | 112 |
|---|---|---|---|---|---|---|---|
| v Qal pf 3cp | cj, n fp, ps 3ms | neg part | v Qal impf 3fp | 65. | cj, v Qal impf 3ms | prep, adj | n mp, ps 1cs |
| נָפָלוּ | וְאַלְמְנֹתָיו | לֹא | תִבְכֶּינָה | | וַיִּקַץ | כְּיָשֵׁן | אֲדֹנָי |
| nāphālû | we'almenōthâv | lō' | thivkênāh | | wayyiqats | keyāshēn | 'ădhōnāy |
| they fell | and his widows | not | they wept | | then He awoke | as sleeping | my Lord |

| 3626, 1399 | 7728.751 | 4623, 3302 | | 5409.521, 7141 | 268 |
|---|---|---|---|---|---|
| prep, n ms | v Hithpoel ptc ms | prep, n ms | 66. | cj, v Hiphil impf 3ms, n mp, ps 3ms | adv |
| כְּגִבּוֹר | מִתְרוֹנֵן | מִיָּיִן | | וַיַּךְ־צָרָיו | אָחוֹר |
| keghibbôr | mithrônēn | mîyāyin | | wayyakh-tsārâv | 'āchôr |
| like a strong man | shouting | from wine | | and He struck down his adversaries | back |

| 2887 | 5986 | 5598.111 | 3937 | | 4128.121 | 904, 164 | 3231 |
|---|---|---|---|---|---|---|---|
| *n fs* | n ms | v Qal pf 3ms | prep, ps 3mp | 67. | cj, v Qal impf 3ms | prep, *n ms* | pn |
| חֶרְפַּת | עוֹלָם | נָתַן | לָמוֹ | | וַיִּמְאַס | בְּאֹהֶל | יוֹסֵף |
| cherpath | 'ôlām | nāthan | lāmô | | wayyim'as | be'ōhel | yôsēph |
| a disgrace of | forever | He gave | to them | | and He rejected | against the tent of | Joseph |

| 904, 8101 | 688 | 3940 | 1013.111 | | 1013.121 | 881, 8101 | 3171 |
|---|---|---|---|---|---|---|---|
| cj, prep, *n ms* | pn | neg part | v Qal pf 3ms | 68. | cj, v Qal impf 3ms | do, *n ms* | pn |
| וּבְשֵׁבֶט | אֶפְרַיִם | לֹא | בָחָר | | וַיִּבְחַר | אֶת־שֵׁבֶט | יְהוּדָה |
| ûveshēvet | 'ephrayim | lō' | vāchār | | wayyivchar | 'eth-shēvet | yehûdhāh |
| and against the tribe of | Ephraim | not | He chose | | but He chose | the tribe of | Judah |

| 881, 2098 | 6995 | 866 | 154.111 | | 1161.121 | 3765, 7597.152 | 4881 |
|---|---|---|---|---|---|---|---|
| do, *n ms* | pn | rel part | v Qal pf 3ms | 69. | cj, v Qal impf 3ms | prep, v Qal act ptc mp | n ms, ps 3ms |
| אֶת־הַר | צִיּוֹן | אֲשֶׁר | אָהֵב | | וַיִּבֶן | כְּמוֹ־רָמִים | מִקְדָּשׁוֹ |
| 'eth-har | tsîyôn | 'ăsher | 'āhēv | | wayyiven | kemô-rāmîm | miqdāshô |
| Mount | Zion | which | He loves | | and He built | like high places | his Sanctuary |

| 3626, 800<br>prep, n fs<br>כְּאֶרֶץ<br>k$^{e}$'erets<br>like the earth | 3354.111<br>v Qal pf 3ms, ps 3fs<br>יְסָדָהּ<br>y$^{e}$sādhāhh<br>He founded it | 3937, 5986<br>prep, n ms<br>לְעוֹלָם<br>l$^{e}$'ôlām<br>unto eternity | **70.** | 1013.121<br>cj, v Qal impf 3ms<br>וַיִּבְחַר<br>wayyivchar<br>and He chose | 904, 1784<br>prep, pn<br>בְּדָוִד<br>b$^{e}$dhāwidh<br>with David | 5860<br>n ms, ps 3ms<br>עַבְדּוֹ<br>'avdô<br>his servant |
|---|---|---|---|---|---|---|

| 4089.121<br>cj, v Qal impf 3ms, ps 3ms<br>וַיִּקָּחֵהוּ<br>wayyiqqāchēhû<br>and He took him | 4623, 4494<br>prep, *n mp*<br>מִמִּכְלְאֹת<br>mimmikhl$^{e}$'ōth<br>from the folds of | 6887<br>n fs<br>צֹאן<br>tsō'n<br>the sheep | **71.** | 4623, 313<br>prep, prep<br>מֵאַחַר<br>mē'achar<br>from after | 5979.154<br>v Qal act ptc fp<br>עָלוֹת<br>'ālôth<br>the sucklings |
|---|---|---|---|---|---|

**61. And delivered his strength into captivity, and his glory into the enemy's hand:** ... He gave his fortress to the captors, his glorious ark into the hand of the adversary, *Anchor* ... And he let his strength be taken prisoner, and gave his glory into the hands of his hater, *BB* ... he let his great ark be captured, let his splendid ark fall to the foe, *Moffatt* ... he surrendered the symbol of his strength into captivity and his pride into enemy hands, *NEB.*

**62. He gave his people over also unto the sword; and was wroth with his inheritance:** ... He let the sword kill His people and was furious with His own, *Beck.*

**63. The fire consumed their young men:** ... Fire devoured their young men, *JB* ... The young men died by fire, *NCV.*

**and their maidens were not given to marriage:** ... And their virgins had no marriage-song, *ASV* ... and their maidens were not serenaded, *Berkeley* ... and the young women had no one to marry, *NCV* ... and his maidens could raise no lament for them, *NEB.*

**64. Their priests fell by the sword; and their widows made no lamentation:** ... The sword struck down their priests, and their widows couldn't even weep, *Beck.*

**65. Then the Lord awaked as one out of sleep, and like a mighty man that shouteth by reason of wine:** ... Then the Lord awoke like one who had slept, like a warrior resting after wine, *Anchor* ... Then the LORD was aroused as one from sleep, like a strong man heated from wine, *Berkeley* ... The Lord arose as though he had been asleep, like a strong man fighting-mad with wine, *JB* ... Like a mighty man recovering from wine, *MAST.*

**66. And he smote his enemies in the hinder parts:** ... He smote his adversaries on the rear, *Anchor* ... His haters were turned back by his blows, *BB* ... he struck his enemies on the rump, *JB.*

**he put them to a perpetual reproach:** ... he covered them with everlasting shame, *Anchor* ... and shamed for ever, *BB* ... He caused them unending disgrace, *Berkeley.*

**67. Moreover he refused the tabernacle of Joseph, and chose not the tribe of Ephraim:** ... But abandoned His dwelling with Joseph, And chose not the Tribe of Ephraim, *Fenton* ... He rejected the house of Joseph, And chose not the tribe of Ephraim, *Goodspeed* ... Moreover He abhorred the tent of Joseph, And chose not the tribe of Ephraim, *MAST.*

**68. But chose the tribe of Judah, the mount Zion which he loved:** ... But it was Judah's Tribe He selected, Zion's Hill as the spot which He loved, *Fenton.*

**69. And he built his sanctuary like high palaces, like the earth which he hath established for ever:** ... He built His sanctuary like the high heavens and founded it forever like the earth, *Beck* ... And he built his shrine like heaven, like the earth which he founded forever, *NCB* ... Like the earth, he built it to last forever, *NCV.*

**70. He chose David also his servant, and took him from the sheepfolds:** ... He chose David to be his servant, took him from the sheepfold, *JB.*

**71. From following the ewes great with young he brought him to feed Jacob his people, and Israel his inheritance:** ... From looking after the sheep which were giving milk, he took him to give food to Jacob his people, and to Israel his heritage, *BB.*

---

Eastern fervor than with our colder imagination. But it wonderfully expresses the sudden transition from a period, during which God seemed passive and careless of his people's wretchedness, to one in which his power flashed forth triumphant for their defense. The prose fact is the long series of victories over the Philistines and other oppressors, which culminated in the restoration of the Ark, the selection of Zion as its abode, which involved the rejection of Shiloh and consequently of Ephraim (in whose territory Shiloh was), and the accession of David. The Davidic kingdom is, in the psalmist's view, the final form of Israel's national existence; and the sanctuary, like the kingdom, is perpetual as the lofty heavens or the firm earth. Nor were his visions vain, for that

| 971.511 | 3937, 7749.141 | 904, 3399 | 6194 | 904, 3547 | 5338 |
|---|---|---|---|---|---|
| v Hiphil pf 3ms, ps 3ms | prep, v Qal inf con | prep, pn | n ms, ps 3ms | cj, prep, pn | n fs, ps 3ms |
| הֱבִיאוֹ | לִרְעוֹת | בְּיַעֲקֹב | עַמּוֹ | וּבְיִשְׂרָאֵל | נַחֲלָתוֹ |
| hĕvî'ô | lir'ôth | beya'ăqōv | 'ammô | ûveyisrā'ēl | nachlāthô |
| He brought him | to shepherd | over Jacob | his people | and over Israel | his inheritance |

| | 7749.121 | 3626, 8866 | 3949 | 904, 8722 | 3834 |
|---|---|---|---|---|---|
| **72.** | cj, v Qal impf 3ms, ps 3mp | prep, *n ms* | n ms, ps 3ms | cj, prep, *n fp* | n fp, ps 3ms |
| | וַיִּרְעֵם | כְּתֹם | לְבָבוֹ | וּבִתְבוּנוֹת | כַּפָּיו |
| | wayyir'ēm | kethōm | levāvô | ûvithvûnôth | kappâv |
| | and he tended them | with the blamelessness of | his heart | and with the skills of | his hands |

| 5341.521 | | 4344 | 3937, 637 | | 435 | 971.116 | 1504 |
|---|---|---|---|---|---|---|---|
| v Hiphil impf 3ms, ps 3mp | **79:t** | n ms | prep, pn | **1.** | n mp | v Qal pf 3cp | n mp |
| יַנְחֵם | | מִזְמוֹר | לְאָסָף | | אֱלֹהִים | בָּאוּ | גוֹיִם |
| yanchēm | | mizmôr | le'āsāph | | 'ĕlōhîm | bā'û | ghôyim |
| He led them | | a Psalm | of Asaph | | O God | they have come | nations |

| 904, 5338 | 3041.316 | 881, 2033 | 7231 | 7947.116 |
|---|---|---|---|---|
| prep, n fs, ps 2ms | v Piel pf 3cp | do, *n ms* | n ms, ps 2ms | v Qal pf 3cp |
| בְּנַחֲלָתֶךָ | טִמְּאוּ | אֶת־הֵיכַל | קָדְשֶׁךָ | שָׂמוּ |
| benachlāthekhā | ṭimme'û | 'eth-hêkhal | qādheshekhā | sāmû |
| into your inheritance | they have profaned | the Temple of | your holy place | they have put |

| 881, 3503 | 3937, 6070 | | 5598.116 | 881, 5215 | 5860 | 4120 |
|---|---|---|---|---|---|---|
| do, pn | prep, n mp | **2.** | v Qal pf 3cp | do, *n fs* | n mp, ps 2ms | n ms |
| אֶת־יְרוּשָׁלַם | לְעִיִּים | | נָתְנוּ | אֶת־נִבְלַת | עֲבָדֶיךָ | מַאֲכָל |
| 'eth-yerûshālam | le'iyîm | | nāthenû | 'eth-nivlath | 'ăvādhêkhā | ma'ăkhāl |
| Jerusalem | into ruins | | they have given | the corpses of | your servants | food |

| 3937, 5991 | 8452 | 1340 | 2728 | 3937, 2516, 800 |
|---|---|---|---|---|
| prep, *n ms* | art, n md | *n ms* | n mp, ps 2ms | prep, *n fs*, n fs |
| לְעוֹף | הַשָּׁמָיִם | בְּשַׂר | חֲסִידֶיךָ | לְחַיְתוֹ־אָרֶץ |
| le'ôph | hashshāmāyim | besar | chăṣîdhêkhā | lechaythô-'ārets |
| for the birds of | the heavens | the flesh of | your godly ones | to the beasts of the earth |

| | 8581.116 | 1879 | 3626, 4448 | 5623 | 3503 | 375 |
|---|---|---|---|---|---|---|
| **3.** | v Qal pf 3cp | n ms, ps 3mp | prep, art, n mp | adv | pn | cj, *sub* |
| | שָׁפְכוּ | דָּמָם | כַּמַּיִם | סְבִיבוֹת | יְרוּשָׁלָם | וְאֵין |
| | shāphekhû | dhāmām | kammayim | ṣevîvôth | yerûshālām | we'ên |
| | they have poured out | their blood | like water | all around | Jerusalem | and there is not |

| 7196.151 | | 2030.119 | 2887 | 3937, 8333 | 4075 | 7331 |
|---|---|---|---|---|---|---|
| v Qal act ptc ms | **4.** | v Qal pf 1cp | n fs | prep, n mp, ps 1cp | n ms | cj, n ms |
| קוֹבֵר | | הָיִינוּ | חֶרְפָּה | לִשְׁכֵנֵינוּ | לַעַג | וָקֶלֶס |
| qôvēr | | hāyînû | cherpāh | lishkhēnênû | la'agh | wāqeles |
| one burying | | we have become | a disgrace | to our neighbors | derision | and mockery |

| 3937, 5623 | | 5912, 4242 | 3176 | 613.123 | 3937, 5516 | 1220.122 |
|---|---|---|---|---|---|---|
| prep, sub, ps 1cp | **5.** | adv, intrg | pn | v Qal impf 2ms | prep, art, n ms | v Qal impf 3fs |
| לִסְבִיבוֹתֵינוּ | | עַד־מָה | יְהוָה | תֶּאֱנַף | לָנֶצַח | תִּבְעַר |
| liṣvîvôthênû | | 'adh-māh | yehwāh | te'ĕnaph | lānetsach | tiv'ar |
| to those all around us | | until when | Yahweh | will You be angry | unto forever | will it burn |

| 3765, 813 | 7352 | | 8581.131 | 2635 | 420, 1504 | 866 |
|---|---|---|---|---|---|---|
| prep, n fs | n fs, ps 2ms | **6.** | v Qal impv 2ms | n fs, ps 2ms | prep, art, n mp | rel part |
| כְּמוֹ־אֵשׁ | קִנְאָתֶךָ | | שְׁפֹךְ | חֲמָתְךָ | אֶל־הַגּוֹיִם | אֲשֶׁר |
| kemô-'ēsh | qin'āthekhā | | shephōkh | chămāthekhā | 'el-haggôyim | 'ăsher |
| like fire | your zeal | | pour out | your wrath | against the nations | who |

**72. So he fed them according to the integrity of his heart:** ... So he was their shepherd according to the integrity of his heart, *ASV* ... So He shepherds them with a pure heart, *Beck* ... He pastured them with unblemished heart, *JB* ... And he tended them with a sincere heart, *NCB*.

**and guided them by the skilfulness of his hands:** ... guiding them by the wisdom of his hands, *BB* ... with a sensitive hand he led them, *JB*.

**79:t. A Psalm of Asaph.**

**1. O God, the heathen are come into thine inheritance; thy holy temple have they defiled; they have laid Jerusalem on heaps:** ... O God, the heathen have invaded your patrimony, they have defiled your holy temple, they have made Jerusalem a heap of ruins, *Anchor* ... they have made your holy Temple unclean; they have made Jerusalem a mass of broken walls, *BB* ... GOD! the Heathen have entered Your land! Defiling Your Holy Abode, They make round Jerusalem ruins, *Fenton* ... they have laid Jerusalem in ruins, *Moffatt*.

**2. The dead bodies of thy servants have they given to be meat unto the fowls of the heaven:** ... They have given the bodies of your servants as food to the wild birds, *NCV* ... They have thrown out the dead bodies of thy servants to feed the birds of the air, *NEB*.

**the flesh of thy saints unto the beasts of the earth:** ... the flesh of your devoted ones, to the beasts of the earth, *Anchor* ... the flesh of Thy worshipers to the beasts of the earth, *Berkeley* ... They have given the bodies of those who worship you to the wild animals, *NCV* ... everyone loyal to you they have made carrion for wild beasts, *REB*.

**3. Their blood have they shed like water round about Jerusalem; and there was none to bury them:** ... Their blood has been flowing like water round about Jerusalem; there was no one to put them in their last resting-place, *BB* ... No one was left to bury the dead, *NCV*.

**4. We are become a reproach to our neighbours, a scorn and derision to them that are round about us:** ... We have become the taunt of our neighbors, the mockery and scorn of those around us, *Anchor* ... A scoffing and derision to them that are round about us, *ASV* ... We are looked down on by our neighbours, we are laughed at and made sport of by those who are round us, *BB* ... We are a joke to the other nations; they laugh and make fun of us, *NCV*.

**5. How long, LORD? wilt thou be angry for ever?:** ... How long will you be angry, Yahweh? For ever?,

---

kingdom subsists and will subsist forever, and the true sanctuary, the dwelling place of God among men, is still more closely intertwined with the kingdom and its King than the psalmist knew. The perpetual duration of both is, in truth, the greatest of God's mercies, outshining all earlier deliverances. They who truly have become the subjects of the Christ, the King of Israel and of the world, and who dwell with God in his house by dwelling with Jesus, will not rebel against Him anymore or ever forget his wonders, but faithfully tell them to the generations to come.

***Psalm 79.*** *The division is not perfectly clear, but it is probably best to recognize three strophes of four verses each, with an appended verse of conclusion. The first spreads before God his people's miseries. The second and third are prayer for deliverance and confession of sin; but they differ, in that the former strophe dwells mainly upon the desired destruction of the enemy and the latter upon the rescue of Israel, while a subordinate diversity is that ancestral sins are confessed in the one and those of the present generation in the other. Verse 13 stands out of the strophe scheme as a kind of epilogue.*

**79:1–4.** The first strophe vividly describes the ghastly sights that wrung the psalmist's heart and will move God to pity and help. The same thought as was expressed in Ps. 74 underlies the emphatic repetition of "Thy" in this strophe—namely, the implication of God's fair name in his people's disasters. "Thine inheritance" is invaded, and "thy holy temple" defiled by the "heathen." The corpses of "thy servants" lie unburied, torn by vultures' beaks and jackals' claws. The blood of "thy saints" saturates the ground. It was not easy to hold fast by the reality of God's special relation to a nation thus apparently deserted, but the psalmist's faith stood even such a strain and is not dashed by a trace of doubt. Such times are the test and triumph of trust. If genuine, it will show brightest against the blackest background. The word in v. 1 rendered "heathen" (HED #1504) is usually translated "nations," but here it also connotes idolatry (v. 6). Their worship of strange gods, rather than their alien nationality, makes their invasion of God's inheritance a tragic anomaly. The psalmist remembers the prophecy of Micah (Mic. 3:12) that Jerusalem should become heaps and sadly repeats it as fulfilled at last. Verse 3 is quoted in 1 Macc. 7:16f, and v. 4 is found in Ps. 44:13, which is by many commentators referred to as the Maccabean period.

**79:5–8.** The second strophe passes to direct petition which, as it were, gives voice to the stiffened corpses strewing the streets and the righteous blood

| 3940, 3156.116 | 6142 | 4608 | 866 | 904, 8428 | 3940 | 7410.116 |
|---|---|---|---|---|---|---|
| neg part, v Qal pf 3cp, ps 2ms | cj, prep | n fp | rel part | prep, n ms, ps 2ms | neg part | v Qal pf 3cp |
| לֹא־יְדָעוּךָ | וְעַל | מַמְלָכוֹת | אֲשֶׁר | בְּשִׁמְךָ | לֹא | קָרָאוּ |
| lō'-yedhā'ûkhā | we'al | mamlākhôth | 'ăsher | beshimkhā | lō' | qārā'û |
| they have not known You | and on | kingdoms | which | on your name | not | they have called |

| 7. | 3706 | 404.111 | 881, 3399 | 881, 5295 | 8460.516 |
|---|---|---|---|---|---|
| | cj | v Qal pf 3ms | do, pn | cj, do, n ms, ps 3ms | v Hiphil pf 3cp |
| | כִּי | אָכַל | אֶת־יַעֲקֹב | וְאֶת־נָוֵהוּ | הֵשַׁמּוּ |
| | kî | 'ākhal | 'eth-ya'ăqōv | we'eth-nāwēhû | hēshammû |
| | because | they have devoured | Jacob | and his abode | they have laid waste |

| 8. | 414, 2226.131, 3937 | 5988 | 7518 | 4257.341 |
|---|---|---|---|---|
| | adv, v Qal juss 2ms, prep, ps 1cp | *n mp* | adj | v Piel inf con |
| | אַל־תִּזְכָּר־לָנוּ | עֲוֹנֹת | רִאשֹׁנִים | מַהֵר |
| | 'al-tizkār-lānû | 'ăwōnōth | ri'shōnîm | mahēr |
| | do not call to mind against us | the transgressions of | those before | acting quickly |

| 7207.326 | 7641 | 3706 | 1870.119 | 4108 | 9. | 6038.131 |
|---|---|---|---|---|---|---|
| v Piel juss 3mp, ps 1cp | n mp, ps 2ms | cj | v Qal pf 1cp | adv | | v Qal impv 2ms, ps 1cp |
| יְקַדְּמוּנוּ | רַחֲמֶיךָ | כִּי | דַלּוֹנוּ | מְאֹד | | עָזְרֵנוּ |
| yeqaddemûnû | rachmêkhā | kî | dhallônû | me'ōdh | | 'āzerēnû |
| let them meet us | your mercies | because | we have become lowly | very | | help us |

| 435 | 3589 | 6142, 1745 | 3638, 8428 |
|---|---|---|---|
| *n mp* | n ms, ps 1cp | prep, *n ms* | *n ms*, n ms, ps 2ms |
| אֱלֹהֵי | יִשְׁעֵנוּ | עַל־דְּבַר | כְּבוֹד־שְׁמֶךָ |
| 'ělōhê | yish'ēnû | 'al-devar | kevôdh-shemekhā |
| O God of | our salvation | on account of the word of | the glory of your name |

| 5522.531 | 3848.331 | 6142, 2496 | 3937, 4775 | 8428 | 10. | 4066 |
|---|---|---|---|---|---|---|
| cj, v Hiphil impv 2ms, ps 1cp | cj, v Piel impv 2ms | prep, n fp, ps 1cp | prep, prep | n ms, ps 2ms | | intrg |
| וְהַצִּילֵנוּ | וְכַפֵּר | עַל־חַטֹּאתֵינוּ | לְמַעַן | שְׁמֶךָ | | לָמָּה |
| wehatstsîlēnû | wekhappēr | 'al-chaṯṯō'thênû | lema'an | shemekhā | | lāmmāh |
| and rescue us | and forgive | concerning our sins | because of | your name | | why |

| 569.126 | 1504 | 347 | 435 | 3156.221 | 904, 1504 | 3937, 6084 |
|---|---|---|---|---|---|---|
| v Qal impf 3mp | art, n mp | intrg | n mp, ps 3mp | v Niphal juss 3ms | prep, art, n mp | prep, n fd, ps 1cp |
| יֹאמְרוּ | הַגּוֹיִם | אַיֵּה | אֱלֹהֵיהֶם | יִוָּדַע | בַּגּיִּם | לְעֵינֵינוּ |
| yō'merû | haggôyim | 'ayyēh | 'ělōhêhem | yiwwādha' | baggiyîm | le'ênênû |
| will they say | the nations | where | their God | let it be known | among the nations | before our eyes |

| 5543 | 1879, 5860 | 8581.155 | 11. | 971.123 |
|---|---|---|---|---|
| *n fs* | *n ms*, n mp, ps 2ms | art, v Qal pass ptc ms | | v Qal juss 2ms |
| נִקְמַת | דַּם־עֲבָדֶיךָ | הַשָּׁפוּךְ | | תָּבוֹא |
| niqōmath | dam-'ăvādhêkhā | hashshāphûkh | | tāvô' |
| the avenging of | the blood of your servants | that which has been poured out | | may it come |

*JB* ... How long, O LORD, wilt thou be roused to such fury?, *NEB*.

**shall thy jealousy burn like fire?:** ... Will Your zeal go on burning like fire?, *Beck* ... Is your jealousy to go on smouldering like a fire, *JB* ... Must thy jealousy rage like a fire?, *NEB*.

**6. Pour out thy wrath upon the heathen that have not known thee, and upon the kingdoms that have not called upon thy name:** ... Let your wrath be on the nations who have no knowledge of you, and on the kingdoms who have not made prayer to your name, *BB* ... Pour out Thy fury on the Gentiles who do not acknowledge Thee, and on the kingdoms that do not call upon Thy name, *Berkeley* ... Vent thy rage on pagans who disown thee, on realms that never call to thee, *Moffatt*.

**7. For they have devoured Jacob, and laid waste his dwelling place:** ... They have gobbled up the people of Jacob and destroyed their land, *NCV*.

**8. O remember not against us former iniquities:** ... Do not record to our debit, O Scribe, the iniquities of our forefathers, *Anchor* ... Don't hold our fathers' sins against us, *Beck* ... Do not remember against us our early sins, *Goodspeed.*

**let thy tender mercies speedily prevent us: for we are brought very low:** ... Let your acts of mercy come to meet us, because we are down and out, *Anchor* ... Hurry to come to us with Your mercy—we are helpless, *Beck* ... may your compassion quickly come to us, for we are brought very low, *NAB.*

**9. Help us, O God of our salvation, for the glory of thy name:** ... Strengthen and save us, O GOD! Because of Your GLORIOUS NAME, *Fenton* ... Help us, O God our saviour, for the sake of thine own honour, *Moffatt* ... God our Savior, help us so people will praise you, *NCV.*

**and deliver us, and purge away our sins, for thy name's sake:** ... take us out of danger and give us forgiveness for our sins, because of your name, *BB* ... and cancel thou our sins; rescue us, as thou art God, *Moffatt* ... And deliver us, and provide atonement for our sins, *NKJV* ... Rescue us then and put a propitiatory-covering over our sins, *Rotherham.*

**10. Wherefore should the heathen say, Where is their God?:** ... for why should pagans sneer, "Where is their God?," *Moffatt* ... Why should the nations ask, 'Where is their God?,' *NEB.*

**let him be known among the heathen in our sight by the revenging of the blood of thy servants which is shed:** ... May there be known among the nations, in our sight, *Goodspeed* ... Let payment for the blood of your servants be made openly among the nations before our eyes, *BB* ... Tell the other nations in our presence that you punish those who kill your servants, *NCV.*

**11. Let the sighing of the prisoner come before thee; according to the greatness of thy power preserve**

---

crying from the ground. The psalmist goes straight to the cause of calamity—the anger of God—and in the close of the strophe confesses the sins which had kindled it. Beneath the play of politics and the madness of Antiochus, he discerned God's hand at work. He reiterates the fundamental lesson, which prophets were never weary of teaching, that national disasters are caused by the anger of God, which is excited by national sins. That conviction is the first element in his petitions. A second is the twin conviction that the "heathen" are used by God as his instrument of chastisement, but that, when they have done their work, they are called to account for the human passion—cruelty, lust of conquest and the like—which impelled them to it. Even as they poured out the blood of God's people, they have God's wrath poured out on them, because "they have devoured Jacob."

The same double point of view is frequently taken by the prophets. For example, in Isaiah's magnificent prophecy against the Assyrian (Isa. 10) where the conqueror is first addressed as "the rod of mine anger," and then his punishment is foretold, because, while executing God's purpose, he had been unconscious of his mission and had been gratifying his ambition. These two convictions go very deep into the philosophy of history. Though modified in their application to modern states and politics, they are true in substance still. The Goths who swept down on Rome, the Arabs who crushed a corrupt Christianity, and the French who stormed across Europe were God's scavengers, gathered vulture-like around carrion, but they were each responsible for their cruelty and were punished for the fruit of their stout hearts.

The closing verse of the strophe (v. 8) is intimately connected with the next, which we take as beginning the third strophe, but this connection does not set aside the strophical division, although it somewhat obscures it. The distinction between the similar petitions of vv. 8f is sufficient to warrant our recognition of that division, even while acknowledging that the two parts coalesce more closely than usual. The psalmist knows that the heathen have been hurled against Israel because God is angry, and he knows that God's anger is no arbitrarily kindled flame, but one lit and fed by Israel's sins. He knows, too, that there is a fatal entail by which the iniquities of the fathers are visited on the children. Therefore, he asks first that these ancestral sins may not be "remembered," nor their consequences discharged on the children's heads. The evil that men do lives after them (Deut. 5:9), and history affords abundant instances of the accumulated consequences of ancestors' crimes lighting on descendants that had abandoned the ancient evil and were possibly doing their best to redress it. Guilt is not transmitted, but results of wrong are, and it is one of the tragedies of history that "one soweth and another reapeth" the bitter fruit. Upon one generation may, and often does, come the blood of all the righteous men that many generations have slain (Matt. 23:35).

**79:9–12.** The last strophe continues the strain begun in v. 8, but with significant deepening into confession of the sins of the existing generation. The

| 3937, 6686 | 617 | 629 | 3626, 1465 | 2307 |
|---|---|---|---|---|
| prep, n mp, ps 2ms | *n fs* | n ms | prep, *n ms* | n fs, ps 2ms |
| לְפָנֶיךָ | אֶנְקַת | אָסִיר | כְּגֹדֶל | זְרוֹעֲךָ |
| lephānêkhā | 'enqath | 'āsîr | keghōdhel | zerô'ăkhā |
| to your presence | the groaning of | prisoners | according to the greatness of | your arm |

| 3613.531 | 1158 | 8876 | | 8178.531 | 3937, 8333 | 8124 |
|---|---|---|---|---|---|---|
| v Hiphil impv 2ms | *n mp* | n fs | **12.** | cj, v Hiphil impv 2ms | prep, n mp, ps 1cp | n fd |
| הוֹתֵר | בְּנֵי | תְמוּתָה | | וְהָשֵׁב | לִשְׁכֵנֵינוּ | שִׁבְעָתַיִם |
| hôthēr | benê | themûthāh | | wehāshēv | lishkhēnênû | shiv'āthayim |
| cause to remain | the children of | death | | and return | to our neighbors | seven times |

| 420, 2536 | 2887 | 866 | 2884.316 | 112 | | 601 |
|---|---|---|---|---|---|---|
| prep, n ms, ps 3mp | n fs, ps 3mp | rel part | v Piel pf 3cp, ps 2ms | n mp, ps 1cs | **13.** | cj, pers pron |
| אֶל־חֵיקָם | חֶרְפָּתָם | אֲשֶׁר | חֵרְפוּךָ | אֲדֹנָי | | וַאֲנַחְנוּ |
| 'el-chêqām | cherpāthām | 'ăsher | chērephûkhā | 'ădhōnāy | | wa'ănachnû |
| to their bosom | their abuse | which | they have abused You | my Lord | | then we |

| 6194 | 6887 | 4993 | 3142.520 | 3937 | 3937, 5986 |
|---|---|---|---|---|---|
| n ms, ps 2ms | cj, *n fs* | n fs, ps 2ms | v Hiphil impf 1cp | prep, ps 2ms | prep, n ms |
| עַמְּךָ | וְצֹאן | מַרְעִיתֶךָ | נוֹדֶה | לְךָ | לְעוֹלָם |
| 'ammekhā | wetsō'n | mar'îthekhā | nôdheh | lekhā | le'ôlām |
| your people | and the sheep of | your pasturage | we will praise | You | unto eternity |

| 3937, 1810 | 1810 | 5807.320 | 8747 | | 3937, 5514.351 | 420, 8236 |
|---|---|---|---|---|---|---|
| prep, n ms | cj, n ms | v Piel impf 1cp | n fs, ps 2ms | **80:t** | prep, art, v Piel ptc ms | prep, n mp |
| לְדֹר | וָדֹר | נְסַפֵּר | תְּהִלָּתֶךָ | | לַמְנַצֵּחַ | אֶל־שֹׁשַׁנִּים |
| ledhōr | wādhōr | nesappēr | tehillāthekhā | | lamnatstsēach | 'el-shōshanîm |
| unto generations | and generations | we will recount | your praise | | to the director | to the lilies |

| 5925 | 3937, 637 | 4344 | | 7749.151 | 3547 | 237.531 | 5268.151 |
|---|---|---|---|---|---|---|---|
| n fs | prep, pn | n ms | **1.** | *v Qal act ptc ms* | pn | v Hiphil impv 2ms | v Qal act ptc ms |
| עֵדוּת | לְאָסָף | מִזְמוֹר | | רֹעֵה | יִשְׂרָאֵל | הַאֲזִינָה | נֹהֵג |
| 'ēdhûth | le'āsāph | mizmôr | | rō'ēh | yisrā'ēl | ha'ăzînāh | nōhēgh |
| a Testimony | of Asaph | a Psalm | | O Shepherd of | Israel | listen | the One Who leads |

| 3626, 6887 | 3231 | 3553.151 | 3872 | 3423.531 | | 3937, 6686 | 688 |
|---|---|---|---|---|---|---|---|
| prep, art, n fs | pn | v Qal act ptc ms | art, n mp | v Hiphil impv 2ms | **2.** | prep, *n mp* | pn |
| כַּצֹּאן | יוֹסֵף | יֹשֵׁב | הַכְּרוּבִים | הוֹפִיעָה | | לִפְנֵי | אֶפְרַיִם |
| katstsō'n | yôsēph | yōshēv | hakkerûvîm | hôphî'āh | | liphnê | 'ephrayim |
| like the sheep | Joseph | the One Who sits on | the cherubim | shine | | before | Ephraim |

| 1175 | 4667 | 5996.331 | 881, 1400 | 2050.131 | 3937, 3568 |
|---|---|---|---|---|---|
| cj, pn | cj, pn | v Polel impv 2ms | do, n fs, ps 2ms | cj, v Qal impv 2ms | prep, n fs |
| וּבִנְיָמִן | וּמְנַשֶּׁה | עוֹרְרָה | אֶת־גְּבוּרָתֶךָ | וּלְכָה | לִישֻׁעָתָה |
| ûvinyāmin | ûmenashsheh | 'ōrerāh | 'eth-gevûrāthekhā | ûlākhāh | lîshu'āthāh |
| and Benjamin | and Manasseh | arouse | your might | and come | for salvation |

**thou those that are appointed to die:** ... May the groan of the prisoner come before thee!, *Goodspeed* ... Let the prisoners' sighing come before you; with your great power free those doomed to death, *NCB.*

**12. And render unto our neighbours sevenfold into their bosom their reproach, wherewith they have reproached thee, O Lord:** ... Pay back our neighbors, seven times into their laps, for the insults with which they defied You, Lord, *Beck* ... And repay our neighbors sevenfold into their bosoms the disgrace they have inflicted on you, O Lord, *NCB* ... the curse with which they have cursed You, O Lord, *KJVII.*

**13. So we thy people and sheep of thy pasture will give thee thanks for ever: we will shew forth thy praise to all generations:** ... Then we, Your people, the sheep that You shepherd, will thank You forever and tell from age to age the wonderful things You have done, *Beck* ... the sheep of your pasture, will praise you forever; from generation to generation we will recount your praise, *NIV.*

**80:t. To the chief Musician upon Shoshannim-Eduth, A Psalm of Asaph.**

**1. Give ear, O Shepherd of Israel, thou that leadest Joseph like a flock:** ... Give ear, O Keeper of Israel, guiding Joseph like a flock, *BB* ... Shepherd of Israel; listen, you who lead Joseph like a flock, *JB.*

**thou that dwellest between the cherubims, shine forth:** ... O Enthroned upon the Cherubim, shine forth, *Anchor* ... you who have your seat on the winged ones, let your glory be seen, *BB* ... You sit on your throne between the gold creatures with wings, *NCV* ... Inhabiting the cherubs—shine forth, *Young.*

**2. Before Ephraim and Benjamin and Manasseh stir up thy strength, and come and save us:** ... As you lead Ephraim, Benjamin, and Manasseh, stir up Your power and come to save us, *Beck* ... over Ephraim, Benjamin and Manasseh; rouse your valour and come to our help, *JB* ... Rouse thy victorious might from slumber, come to our rescue, *NEB.*

---

psalmist knows that the present disaster is no case of the fathers having eaten sour grapes and the children's teeth being set on edge, but that he and his contemporaries had repeated the fathers' transgressions. The ground of his plea for cleansing and deliverance is the glory of God's name, which he emphatically puts at the end of both clauses of v. 9. He repeats the same thought in another form in the question of v. 10, "Wherefore should the heathen say, Where is their God?" If Israel, sinful though it is and therefore meriting chastisement, is destroyed, there will be a blot on God's name, and the "heathen" will take it as proof, not that Israel's God was just, but that He was too feeble or too far off to hear prayers or to send succors. It is bold faith which blends acknowledgment of sins with such a conviction of the inextricable intertwining of God's glory and the sinners' deliverance. Lowly confession is wonderfully wedded to confidence that seems almost too lofty. But the confidence is in its inmost core as lowly as the confession, for it disclaims all right to God's help and clasps his name as its only but sufficient plea.

The final strophe dwells more on the sufferings of the survivors than the earlier parts of the Psalm do, and in this respect contrasts with Ps. 74, which is all but entirely silent as to these. Not only does the spilt blood of dead confessors cry for vengeance, since they died for their faith as "thy servants," but the groans and sighs of the living who are captives and "sons of death"—i.e., doomed to die if unrescued by God—appeal to Him. The expressions "the groaning of prisoners" and "the chidlren of death" occur in Ps. 102:20, from which, if this is a composition of Maccabean date, they are here quoted. The strophe ends with recurring to the central thought of both this and the companion Psalm—the reproach on God from his servants' calamities—and prays that the enemies' taunts may be paid back into their bosoms sevenfold, i.e., in fullest measure.

**79:13.** The epilogue in v. 13 has the image of a flock, so frequent in the Asaph Psalms, suggesting tender thoughts of the shepherd's care and of his obligations. Deliverance will evoke praise, and instead of the sad succession of sin and suffering from generation to generation, the solidarity of the nation will be more happily expressed by ringing songs, transmitted from father to son and gathering volume as they flow from age to age.

***Psalm 80.*** *The triple refrain in vv. 3, 7, 19 divides the Psalm into three unequal parts. The last of these is disproportionately long and may be further broken up into three parts, of which the first (vv. 8–11) describes the luxuriant growth of Israel under the parable of a vine, the second (vv. 12–14) brings to view the bitter contrast of present ruin and with an imperfect echo of the refrain melts into the petitioning tone of the third (vv. 15–19), which is all prayer.*

**80:1–3.** In the first strophe, "Shepherd of Israel" reminds us of Jacob's blessing of Ephraim and Manasseh, in which he invoked "the God who shepherded me all my life long" to "bless the lads," and of the title in Gen. 49:24, "the shepherd, the stone of Israel." The comparison of the nation to a flock is characteristic of the Asaph Psalms and here refers to the guidance of the people at the Exodus. Delitzsch regards the notions of the earthly and heavenly sanctuary as being blended in the designation of God as sitting throned on the cherubim, but it is better to take the reference as being to his dwelling in the Temple. The word rendered "shine forth" (HED #3423) occurs in Ps. 50:2, where it expresses his coming from "Zion," and so it does here. The same metaphor underlies the subsequent petition in v. 3. In both, God is thought of as light, and the manifestation of his delivering help is likened to the blazing out of the sun from behind a cloud.

In reference to the mention of the tribes in v. 2, we need only add to what has been already said, that

| 3937<br>prep, ps 1cp<br>לָנוּ<br>lānû<br>for us | 3. | 435<br>n mp<br>אֱלֹהִים<br>'ĕlōhîm<br>O God | 8178.531<br>v Hiphil impv 2ms, ps 1cp<br>הֲשִׁיבֵנוּ<br>heshîvēnû<br>restore us | 213.531<br>cj, v Hiphil impv 2ms<br>וְהָאֵר<br>wehā'ēr<br>and illuminate | 6686<br>n mp, ps 2ms<br>פָּנֶיךָ<br>pānêkhā<br>your face | 3588.220<br>cj, v Niphal juss 1cp<br>וְנִוָּשֵׁעָה<br>weniwwāshē'āh<br>that we may be saved |
|---|---|---|---|---|---|---|

| 4. | 3176<br>pn<br>יְהוָה<br>yehwāh<br>O Yahweh | 435<br>n mp<br>אֱלֹהִים<br>'ĕlōhîm<br>God | 6893<br>n fp<br>צְבָאוֹת<br>tsevā'ôth<br>Hosts | 5912, 5146<br>adv, intrg<br>עַד־מָתַי<br>'adh-māthay<br>until when | 6475.113<br>v Qal pf 2ms<br>עָשַׁנְתָּ<br>'āshantā<br>will You smoke | 904, 8940<br>prep, *n fs*<br>בִּתְפִלַּת<br>bithphillath<br>against the prayers of | 6194<br>n ms, ps 2ms<br>עַמֶּךָ<br>'ammekhā<br>your people |
|---|---|---|---|---|---|---|---|

| 5. | 404.513<br>v Hiphil pf 2ms, ps 3mp<br>הֶאֱכַלְתָּם<br>he'ĕkhaltām<br>You have fed them | 4035<br>*n ms*<br>לֶחֶם<br>lechem<br>the bread of | 1893<br>n fs<br>דִּמְעָה<br>dim'āh<br>tears | 8615.523<br>cj, v Hiphil impf 2ms, ps 3mp<br>וַתַּשְׁקֵמוֹ<br>wattashqēmô<br>and You have given them drink | 904, 1893<br>prep, n fp<br>בִּדְמָעוֹת<br>bidhmā'ôth<br>with tears |
|---|---|---|---|---|---|

| 8386<br>n ms<br>שָׁלִישׁ<br>shālîsh<br>a third of a measure | 6. | 7947.123<br>v Qal impf 2ms, ps 1cp<br>תְּשִׂימֵנוּ<br>tesîmēnû<br>You have appointed to us | 4209<br>n ms<br>מָדוֹן<br>mādhôn<br>strife | 3937, 8333<br>prep, n mp, ps 1cp<br>לִשְׁכֵנֵינוּ<br>lishkhēnênû<br>of our neighbors | 342.152<br>cj, v Qal act ptc mp, ps 1cp<br>וְאֹיְבֵינוּ<br>we'ōyevênû<br>and our enemies |
|---|---|---|---|---|---|

| 4074.126, 3937<br>v Qal impf 3mp, prep, ps 3mp<br>יִלְעֲגוּ־לָמוֹ<br>yil'ăghû-lāmô<br>they scoff to themselves | 7. | 435<br>n mp<br>אֱלֹהִים<br>'ĕlōhîm<br>O God | 6893<br>n fp<br>צְבָאוֹת<br>tsevā'ôth<br>Hosts | 8178.531<br>v Hiphil impv 2ms, ps 1cp<br>הֲשִׁיבֵנוּ<br>heshîvēnû<br>restore us | 213.531<br>cj, v Hiphil impv 2ms<br>וְהָאֵר<br>wehā'ēr<br>and cause to shine | 6686<br>n mp, ps 2ms<br>פָּנֶיךָ<br>pānêkhā<br>your face |
|---|---|---|---|---|---|---|

| 3588.220<br>cj, v Niphal juss 1cp<br>וְנִוָּשֵׁעָה<br>weniwwāshē'āh<br>that we may be saved | 8. | 1655<br>n fs<br>גֶּפֶן<br>gephen<br>a vine | 4623, 4875<br>prep, pn<br>מִמִּצְרַיִם<br>mimmitsrayim<br>from Egypt | 5450.523<br>v Hiphil impf 2ms<br>תַּסִּיעַ<br>tassîa'<br>You pulled out | 1691.323<br>v Piel impf 2ms<br>תְּגָרֵשׁ<br>teghārēsh<br>and You drove out | 1504<br>n mp<br>גּוֹיִם<br>gôyim<br>nations |
|---|---|---|---|---|---|---|

| 5378.123<br>cj, v Qal impf 2ms, ps 3fs<br>וַתִּטָּעֶהָ<br>wattittā'eāh<br>and You planted it | 9. | 6680.313<br>v Piel pf 2ms<br>פִּנִּיתָ<br>pinîthā<br>You cultivated | 3937, 6686<br>prep, n mp, ps 3fs<br>לְפָנֶיהָ<br>lephānêāh<br>before it | 8657.523<br>cj, v Hiphil impf 2ms<br>וַתַּשְׁרֵשׁ<br>wattashrēsh<br>and You caused to take root | 8659<br>n mp, ps 3fs<br>שָׁרָשֶׁיהָ<br>shārāshêāh<br>its roots |
|---|---|---|---|---|---|

**3. Turn us again, O God, and cause thy face to shine; and we shall be saved:** … O God, return to us! and let your face shine that we may be saved, *Anchor* … Take us back again, O God; let us see the shining of your face, and let us be safe, *BB* … restore us to power; a smile of thy favour, and we are saved!, *Moffatt* … Show us your kindness so we can be saved, *NCV.*

**4. O Lord God of hosts, how long wilt thou be angry against the prayer of thy people?:** … O Lord God of armies, how long will your wrath be burning against the rest of your people?, *BB* … Yahweh, God Sabaoth, how long will you flare up at your people's prayer?, *JB* … will thine anger fume, though thy people are praying?, *Moffatt.*

**5. Thou feedest them with the bread of tears:** … You feed them with bread made with tears, *Fenton* … You have made sorrow their daily bread, *REB.*

**and givest them tears to drink in great measure:** … and have given them tears to drink three times, *Beck* … and tears of threefold grief their drink, *NEB* … you have made them drink tears by the bowlful, *NIV* … and copious tears their drink, *REB.*

**6. Thou makest us a strife unto our neighbours:** … You make us a By-word to friends, *Fenton* … Thou dost make us a butt for our neighbors, *Goodspeed* … You make us a target for our neighbors, *KJVII* … You have left us to be fought over by our neighbors, *NCB.*

**and our enemies laugh among themselves:** … And our foes make mock of us, *Goodspeed.*

**7. Turn us again, O God of hosts, and cause thy face to shine; and we shall be saved:** ... O God of Hosts, return to us! and let your face shine that we may be saved, *Anchor* ... Take us back again, O God of armies; let us see the shining of your face, and let us be safe, *BB* ... restore us to power; a smile of thy favour, and we are saved!, *Moffatt.*

**8. Thou hast brought a vine out of Egypt: thou hast cast out the heathen, and planted it:** ... A vine from Egypt you transplanted; you drove away the nations and planted it, *NAB* ... You forced out other nations and planted us in the land, *NCV.*

**9. Thou preparedst room before it, and didst cause it to take deep root, and it filled the land:** ... Thou didst clear the land before it, so it took root and filled the land, *Berkeley.*

---

the petitions of v. 1, which look back to the wilderness marches when the Ark led the caravan, naturally suggested the mention of the three tribes who were together reckoned as "the camp of Ephraim" and who in the removal of the encampment "set forth third"—that is, immediately in the rear of the Tabernacle. The order of march explains not only the collocation here, but the use of the word "before." Joseph and Benjamin were children of the same mother, and the schism which parted their descendants is, to the psalmist's faith, as transient as unnatural. Once again shall the old unity be seen, when the brothers' sons shall again dwell and fight side by side, and God shall again go forth before them for victory.

The prayer of the refrain, "turn us" (HED #8178) is not to be taken as for restoration from exile, which is negatived by the whole tone of the Psalm, or as for spiritual quickening, but simply asks for the return of the glories of ancient days. The petition that God would let his face shine upon the nation alludes to the priestly benediction (Num. 6:25), thus again carrying us back to the wilderness. Such a flashing forth is all that is needed to change blackest night into day. To be "saved" (HED #3588) means here to be rescued from the assaults of hostile nations. The poet was sure that Israel's sole defense was God and that one gleam of his face would shrivel up the strongest foes like unclean, slimy creatures which writhe and die in sunshine. The same conviction is valid in a higher sphere. Whatever elevation of meaning is given to "saved," the condition of it is always this—the manifestation of God's face. That brings light into all dark hearts. To behold that light and to walk in it and to be transformed by beholding as they are who lovingly and steadfastly gaze is salvation.

**80:4–7.** A piteous tale of suffering is wailed forth in the second strophe. The peculiar accumulation of the divine names in vv. 4, 19 is found also in Pss. 59:5 and 84:8. It is grammatically anomalous, as the word for "God" (Elohim) does not undergo the modification which would show that the next word is to be connected with it by "of." Hence, some have regarded "Sabbaoth" (hosts) as being almost equivalent to a proper name of God, which it afterwards undoubtedly became, while others have explained the construction by supposing the phrase to be elliptical, requiring after "God" the supplement "God of." This accumulation of divine names is by some taken as a sign of late date. Is it not a mark of the psalmist's intensity rather than of his period? In accordance with the Elohistic character of the Asaph Psalms, the common expression "Yahweh of Hosts" is expanded, but the hypothesis that the expansion was the work of a redactor is unnecessary. It may quite as well have been that of the author.

The urgent question "How long?" is not petulant impatience, but hope deferred, and though sick at heart still cleaving to God and remonstrating for long protracted calamities. The bold imagery of v. 4b cannot well be reproduced in translation. The rendering "wilt thou be angry?" is but a feeble reproduction of the vigorous original, which runs "wilt thou smoke?" Other Psalms (e.g., 74:1) speak of God's anger as smoking, but here the figure is applied to God himself. What a contrast it presents to the petition in the refrain! That "light" of Israel has become "as a flaming fire." A terrible possibility of darkening and consuming wrath lies in the divine nature and the very emblem of light suggests it. Verse 6 adds one more touch to the picture—gleeful neighbors cynically rejoicing to their hearts' content (literally, "for themselves") over Israel's calamities. Thus, in three verses, the psalmist points to an angry God, a weeping nation and mocking foes, a trilogy of woe. On all he bases an urgent repetition of the refrain, which is made more imploring by the expanded name under which God is invoked to help. Instead of the simple "God," as in v. 3, he now says "God of Hosts." As sense of need increases, a true suppliant goes deeper into God's revealed character.

**80:8–11.** From v. 8 onward, the parable of the vine as representing Israel fills the singer's mind. As has been already noticed, this part of the Psalm may be regarded as one long strophe, the parts of which

| 4527.323, 800 | | 3803.416 | 2098 | 7009 | 6287 |
|---|---|---|---|---|---|
| cj, v Piel impf 2ms, n fs | 10. | v Pual pf 3cp | n mp | n ms, ps 3fs | cj, n mp, ps 3fs |
| וַתְּמַלֵּא־אָרֶץ | | כָּסּוּ | הָרִים | צִלָּהּ | וַעֲנָפֶיהָ |
| wattemallē'-'ārets | | kāssû | hārîm | tsillāhh | wa'ănāphêāh |
| and it filled the land | | they were covered with | the mountains | its shadow | and its branches |

| 753, 417 | | 8365.322 | 7393 | 5912, 3328 | 420, 5282 | 3229 |
|---|---|---|---|---|---|---|
| *n mp*, n ms | 11. | v Piel impf 3fs | n mp, ps 3fs | prep, n ms | cj, prep, n ms | n fp, ps 3fs |
| אַרְזֵי־אֵל | | תְּשַׁלַּח | קְצִירֶהָ | עַד־יָם | וְאֶל־נָהָר | יוֹנְקוֹתֶיהָ |
| 'arzê-'ēl | | teshallach | qōtsîreāh | 'adh-yām | we'el-nāhār | yônqôthêāh |
| cedars of strength | | it put forth | its branches | unto the Sea | and to the River | its shoots |

| | 4066 | 6805.113 | 1474 | 741.116 |
|---|---|---|---|---|
| 12. | intrg | v Qal pf 2ms | n mp, ps 3fs | cj, v Qal pf 3cp, ps 3fs |
| | לָמָּה | פָּרַצְתָּ | גְדֵרֶיהָ | וְאָרוּהָ |
| | lāmmāh | pāratstā | ghedhērêāh | we'ārûāh |
| | why | have You broken through | its stone walls | that they have gathered it |

| 3725, 5882.152 | 1932 | | 3894.321 | 2478 | 4623, 3402 |
|---|---|---|---|---|---|
| *adj, v Qal act ptc mp* | n ms | 13. | v Piel impf 3ms, ps 3fs | n ms | prep, n ms |
| כָּל־עֹבְרֵי | דָרֶךְ | | יְכַרְסְמֶנָּה | חֲזִיר | מִיָּעַר |
| kol-'ōverê | dhārekh | | yekharsemennāh | chăzîr | mîyā'ar |
| all those passing by | the way | | it has bitten it off | a wild boar | from the forest |

| 2205 | 7899 | 7749.121 | | 435 | 6893 | 8178.131, 5167 |
|---|---|---|---|---|---|---|
| cj, *n ms* | n ms | v Qal impf 3ms, ps 3fs | 14. | n mp | n fp | v Qal impv 2ms, part |
| וְזִיז | שָׂדָי | יִרְעֶנָּה | | אֱלֹהִים | צְבָאוֹת | שׁוּב־נָא |
| wezîz | sādhay | yir'ennāh | | 'ĕlōhîm | tsevā'ôth | shûv-nā' |
| and the swarms of | the field | they feed on it | | O God | Hosts | turn please |

| 5202.531 | 4623, 8452 | 7495.131 | 6734.131 | 1655 | 2148 |
|---|---|---|---|---|---|
| v Hiphil impv 2ms | prep, n md | cj, v Qal impv 2ms | cj, v Qal impv 2ms | n fs | dem pron |
| הַבֵּט | מִשָּׁמַיִם | וּרְאֵה | וּפְקֹד | גֶּפֶן | זֹאת |
| habbēṭ | mishshāmayim | ûre'ēh | ûpheqōdh | gephen | zō'th |
| look down | from the heavens | and see | and intervene | a vine | this |

| | 3774 | 866, 5378.112 | 3332 | 6142, 1158 |
|---|---|---|---|---|
| 15. | cj, n fs | rel part, v Qal pf 3fs | n fs, ps 2ms | cj, prep, n ms |
| | וְכַנָּה | אֲשֶׁר־נָטְעָה | יְמִינֶךָ | וְעַל־בֵּן |
| | wekhannāh | 'ăsher-nāṭe'āh | yemînekhā | we'al-bēn |
| | and the stalk | which it planted | your right hand | and concerning the son |

**10. The hills were covered with the shadow of it, and the boughs thereof were like the goodly cedars:** … The mountains were covered with its shade, and the great trees with its branches, *BB.*

**11. She sent out her boughs unto the sea, and her branches unto the river:** … It spread its branches to the sea and its shoots to the River, *Berkeley* … It extended its branches to the Mediterranean Sea and as far as the Euphrates River, *Good News.*

**12. Why hast thou then broken down her hedges, so that all they which pass by the way do pluck her?:** … Why are its walls broken down by your hands, so that all who go by may take its fruit?, *BB* … Why did You break down its stone fences? All who pass by are picking its fruit, *Beck* … Now everyone who passes by steals from us, *NCV.*

**13. The boar out of the wood doth waste it, and the wild beast of the field doth devour it:** … The swine from the forest devour, And the beasts of the field eat its leaves, *Fenton* … Like wild pigs they walk over us; like wild animals they feed on us, *NCV* … The wild boar from the thickets gnaws it, and swarming insects from the fields feed on it, *NEB.*

**14. Return, we beseech thee, O God of hosts: look down from heaven, and behold, and visit this vine:** … God All-Powerful, come back, *NCV* … God of armies, come back, look from heaven and see. Come to help this vine, *Beck* … O God of hosts return, we pray thee,—Look down out of the heavens and see, And inspect this vine, *Rotherham.*

**15. And the vineyard which thy right hand hath planted, and the branch that thou madest strong for thyself:** ... Protect what Thy right hand has planted, the son whom Thou hast raised for Thyself, *Berkeley* ... And the root that Your right hand has planted, And the Child You had reared for Yourself, *Fenton* ... Even upon the son thou didst secure for thyself, *Rotherham.*

**16. It is burned with fire, it is cut down: they perish at the rebuke of thy countenance:** ... They have thrown it on the fire like dung, *JB* ... Let those who would burn it with fire or cut it down perish before you at your rebuke, *NAB* ... Now it is cut down and burned with fire; you destroyed us by your angry looks, *NCV.*

---

follow in orderly sequence and are held closely together, as shown by the recurrence of the refrain at the close only. Three stages are discernible in it—a picture of what has been, the contrast of what is now and a prayer for speedy help. The emblem of the vine, which has received so great development in the prophets and has been hallowed forever by our LORD's use of it, seems to have been suggested to the psalmist by the history of Joseph, to which he has already alluded. For in Jacob's blessing (Gen. 49:22), Joseph is likened to a fruitful bough. Other OT writers have drawn out the manifold felicities of the emblem as applied to Israel. But these need not concern us here, where the point is rather God's husbandry and the vine's growth, both of which are in startling contrast with a doleful present. The figure is carried out with much beauty in detail. The Exodus was the vine's transplanting; the destruction of the Canaanites was the grubbing up of weeds to clear the ground for it; the numerical increase of the people was its making roots and spreading far. In v. 10b, the rendering may be either that adopted above, or "And the cedars of God [were covered with] its branches." The latter preserves the parallelism of clauses and the unity of representation in vv. 10f, which will then deal throughout with the spreading growth of the vine. But the cedars would not have been called "of God"—which implies their great size—unless their dimensions had been in point, which would not be the case if they were only thought of as espaliers for the vine. And the image of its running over the great trees of Lebanon is unnatural. The rendering as above is to be preferred, even though it somewhat mars the unity of the picture. The extent of ground covered by the vine is described in v. 11 as stretching from the Mediterranean to the Euphrates (Deut. 11:24; 1 Ki. 4:24). Such had been the glories of the past, and they had all been the work of God's hand.

**80:12–13.** In v. 12, the miserable contrast of present desolation is spread before God with the bold and yet submissive question "Why?" The vineyard wall is thrown down, and the vine lies exposed to every vagrant passenger and to every destructive creature. Swine from the woods burrow at its roots, and "whatever moves on the plain" (cf. Ps. 50:11, the only other place where the expression occurs) feeds on it. The parallelism forbids the supposition that any particular enemy is meant by the wild boar. Some would transpose v. 16 so as to stand after v. 13, which they think improves the connection and brings the last part of the Psalm into symmetrical form, in three equal parts, containing four verses each.

**80:14.** Verse 14 sounds like an imperfect echo of the refrain significantly modified, so as to beseech that God would "turn" himself, even as He had been implored to "turn" his people. The purpose of his turning is that He may "look and see" the condition of the desolated vineyard and thence be moved to interfere for its restoration. The verse may be regarded as closing one of the imperfectly developed strophes of this last part, but it belongs in substance to the following petitions, although in form it is more closely connected with the preceding verses. The picture of Israel's misery passes insensibly into prayer, and the burden of that prayer is, first, that God would behold the sad facts, prior to his actions in view of them.

**80:15–19.** The last part is prayer for God's help. The meaning of the word in v. 15 rendered "stalk" (HED #3774) is difficult. Many commentators translate it as a noun and regard it as referring to something related to a "plant." The verse then depends on the preceding verb in v. 14, "to intervene." This construction is opposed by the auxiliary verb, but to render it "to protect," would require a change in the vocalization. There may be an allusion to Jacob's blessing in v. 15b, for in it (Gen. 49:22) Joseph is called a "fruitful bough," literally meaning "son." If so, the figure of the vine is retained in v. 15b as well as in the first part.

The apparent interruption of the petitions by v. 16 is accounted for by the sharp pang that shot into the psalmist's heart, when he recalled the past divine acts, which seemed so contradicted now. But the bit-

| 563.313 | 3937 | | 8041.157 | 904, 813 | 3807.157 |
|---|---|---|---|---|---|
| v Piel pf 2ms | prep, ps 2ms | 16. | v Qal pass ptc fs | prep, art, n fs | v Qal pass ptc fs |
| אִמַּצְתָּה | לָּךְ | | שְׂרֻפָה | בָאֵשׁ | כְּסוּחָה |
| 'immatstāh | lākh | | s$^{e}$ruphāh | vā'ēsh | k$^{e}$sûchāh |
| You have made strong | for yourself | | burned | with the fire | cut off |

| 4623, 1648 | 6686 | 6.126 | | 2030.122, 3135 | 6142, 382 |
|---|---|---|---|---|---|
| prep, *n fs* | n mp, ps 2ms | v Qal impf 3mp | 17. | v Qal juss 3fs, n fs, ps 2ms | prep, *n ms* |
| מִגַּעֲרַת | פָּנֶיךָ | יֹאבֵדוּ | | תְּהִי־יָדְךָ | עַל־אִישׁ |
| migga'ărath | pānêkhā | yō'vēdhû | | t$^{e}$hî-yādh$^{e}$khā | 'al-'îsh |
| from the rebuke of | your presence | they perish | | may your hand be | on the man of |

| 3332 | 6142, 1158, 119 | 563.313 | 3937 |
|---|---|---|---|
| n fs, ps 2ms | prep, *n ms*, n ms | v Piel pf 2ms | prep, ps 2ms |
| יְמִינֶךָ | עַל־בֶּן־אָדָם | אִמַּצְתָּ | לָּךְ |
| y$^{e}$mînekhā | 'al-ben-'ādhām | 'immatstā | lākh |
| your right hand | on the son of humankind | You have made strong | for yourself |

| | 3940, 5657.120 | 4623 | 2513.323 | 904, 8428 | 7410.120 |
|---|---|---|---|---|---|
| 18. | cj, neg part, v Qal impf 1cp | prep, ps 2ms | v Piel impf 2ms, ps 1cp | cj, prep, n ms, ps 2ms | v Qal impf 1cp |
| | וְלֹא־נָסוֹג | מִמֶּךָּ | תְּחַיֵּנוּ | וּבְשִׁמְךָ | נִקְרָא |
| | w$^{e}$lō'-nāsôgh | mimmekhā | t$^{e}$chayyēnû | ûv$^{e}$shimkhā | niqōrā' |
| | that we will not deviate | from You | revive us | and on your name | we will call |

| | 3176 | 435 | 6893 | 8178.531 | 213.531 | 6686 |
|---|---|---|---|---|---|---|
| 19. | pn | n mp | n fp | v Hiphil impv 2ms | v Hiphil impv 2ms | n mp, ps 2ms |
| | יְהוָה | אֱלֹהִים | צְבָאוֹת | הֲשִׁיבֵנוּ | הָאֵר | פָּנֶיךָ |
| | y$^{e}$hwāh | 'ĕlōhîm | ts$^{e}$vā'ôth | h$^{e}$shîvēnû | hā'ēr | pānêkhā |
| | O Yahweh | God | Hosts | return | cause to shine | your face |

| 3588.220 | | 3937, 5514.351 | 6142, 1713 | 3937, 637 | | 7728.533 | 3937, 435 |
|---|---|---|---|---|---|---|---|
| cj, v Niphal juss 1cp | 81:t | prep, art, v Piel ptc ms | prep, art, n fp | prep, pn | 1. | v Hiphil impv 2mp | prep, n mp |
| וְנִוָּשֵׁעָה | | לַמְנַצֵּחַ | עַל־הַגִּתִּית | לְאָסָף | | הַרְנִינוּ | לֵאלֹהִים |
| w$^{e}$niwwāshē'āh | | lamnatstsēach | 'al-haggittîth | l$^{e}$'āsāph | | harnînû | lē'lōhîm |
| that we may be saved | | to the director | on the gittith | of Asaph | | shout for joy | to God |

| 6010 | 7607.533 | 3937, 435 | 3399 | | 5558.133, 2256 | 5598.133, 8929 |
|---|---|---|---|---|---|---|
| n ms, ps 1cp | v Hiphil impv 2mp | prep, *n mp* | pn | 2. | v Qal impv 2mp, n fs | cj, v Qal impv 2mp, n ms |
| עוּזֵּנוּ | הָרִיעוּ | לֵאלֹהֵי | יַעֲקֹב | | שְׂאוּ־זִמְרָה | וּתְנוּ־תֹף |
| 'ûzzēnû | hārî'û | lē'lōhê | ya'ăqōv | | s$^{e}$'û-zimrāh | ûth$^{e}$nû-thōph |
| our Strength | shout | to the God of | Jacob | | lift up a song | and give the timbrel |

| 3780 | 5456 | 6196, 5213 | | 8965.133 | 904, 2414 | 8223 |
|---|---|---|---|---|---|---|
| n ms | adj | prep, n ms | 3. | v Qal impv 2mp | prep, art, n ms | n ms |
| כִּנּוֹר | נָעִים | עִם־נָבֶל | | תִּקְעוּ | בַחֹדֶשׁ | שׁוֹפָר |
| kinnôr | nā'îm | 'im-nāvel | | tiqō'û | vachōdhesh | shôphār |
| the zither | lovely | with the harp | | blow | during the new moon | a ram's horn |

**17. Let thy hand be upon the man of thy right hand, upon the son of man whom thou madest strong for thyself:** … Let Your hand guard the man of Your choice, Adam's Son whom You raised for Yourself, *Fenton.*

**18. So will not we go back from thee: quicken us, and we will call upon thy name:** … Then we shall not depart from Thee; revive us and we shall call upon Thy name!, *Berkeley* … Never again will we turn away from you, give us life and we will call upon your name, *JB* … We have not turned back from thee, so grant us new life, and we will invoke thee by name, *NEB.*

**19. Turn us again, O LORD God of hosts, cause thy face to shine; and we shall be saved:** … O Yahweh, God of Hosts, return to us! let your face shine that we may be saved, *Anchor* … Take us back, O Lord God of armies; let us see the shining of your face, and let us be safe, *BB* … O God of hosts, restore us to power; a smile of thy favour, and we are saved!, *Moffatt* ... Show us your kindness so we can be saved, *NCV.*

**81:t. To the chief Musician upon Gittith, A Psalm of Asaph.**

**1. Sing aloud unto God our strength: make a joyful noise unto the God of Jacob:** ... Sing out in praise of God our refuge, *NEB* ... Let us cheer to GOD, our Helper; Let us cheer for Jacob's GOD!, *Fenton* ... Cry aloud to God our strength, Shout to the God of Jacob, *Young.*

**2. Take a psalm, and bring hither the timbrel:** ... Raise a melody; beat the drum, *REB* ... Raise a melody and strike the timbrel, *Rotherham* ... Lift up a song, and give out a timbrel, *Young* ... Take pipe and tabor, *NEB.* **the pleasant harp with the psaltery:** ... take tuneful harp and lute, *NEB* ... the sweet lyre with the harp, *RSV.*

**3. Blow up the trumpet in the new moon, in the time appointed, on our solemn feast day:** ... At the new moon blow the ram's horn, and blow it at the full moon on the day of our pilgrim-feast, *REB.*

---

terness, although it surges up, is overcome, and his petitions return to their former strain in v. 17, which pathetically takes up, as it were, the broken thread by repeating "right hand" from v. 15a and "that thou madest strong for thyself" from v. 15b. Israel, not an individual, is the "man of thy right hand," in which designation, coupled with "son," there may be an allusion to the name of Benjamin (v. 2), the "son of the right hand." Human weakness clothed in divine strength is indicated in that designation for Israel, "the son of man whom thou madest strong for thyself." The inmost purpose of God's gifts is that their recipients may be the proclaimers of his praise. Israel's sacred calling, its own weakness and the strength of the God who endows it are all set forth, not now as lessons to it, but as pleas with Him whose gifts are without repentance and whose purposes cannot be foiled by man's unworthiness or opposition.

The Psalm closes with a vow of grateful adhesion to God as the result of his renewed mercy. They who have learned how bitter a thing it is to turn away from God and how blessed when He turns again to them and turns back their miseries and their sins have good reason for not again departing from Him. But if they are wise to remember their own weakness, they will not only humbly vow future faithfulness, but earnestly implore continual help, since only the constant communication of a divine quickening will open their lips to call upon God's name.

The refrain in its most expanded form closes the Psalm. Growing intensity of desire and realization of the pleas and pledges hived in the name are expressed by its successive forms: God, God of Hosts and Yahweh, the God of Hosts. The faith that grasps all that is contained in that full-toned name already feels the light of God's face shining upon it and is sure that its prayer for salvation is not in vain.

***Psalm 81.*** *The presupposed existence of the full Temple ceremonially shows that the Psalm was not written in exile, nor at a time of religious persecution. Its warning against idolatry would be needless in a post-exilic Psalm, as no such tendency existed after the return from captivity. But we cannot go beyond such general indications. The theory that the Psalm is composed of two fragments exaggerates the difference between the two parts into which it falls. These are the summons to the feast (vv. 1–5) and the lessons of the feast (vv. 6–16).*

**81:1–3.** Some suggest that the summons in v. 1 is addressed to the whole congregation, in v. 2 to the Levites, the appointed singers and musicians, and in v. 3 to the priests who are entrusted with blowing the Shophar, or horn (Josh. 6:4; 2 Chr. 20:28). One can almost hear the tumult of joyful sounds in which the roar of the multitude, the high-pitched notes of singers, the deeper clash of timbrels, the twanging of stringed instruments and the hoarse blare of rams' horns mingle in concordant discord, grateful to Eastern ears, however unmusical to ours. The religion of Israel allowed and required exuberant joy. It sternly rejected painting and sculpture, but abundantly employed music, the most ethereal of the arts, which stirs emotions and longings too delicate and deep for speech. Whatever differences in form have necessarily attended the progress from the worship of the Temple to that of the Church, the free play of joyful emotion should mark the latter even more than the former. Decorum is good, but not if purchased by the loss of ringing gladness. The psalmist's summons has a meaning still.

**81:4–5.** The reason for it is given in vv. 4, 5a. The feast (not the musical accompaniments) is appointed by God. The psalmist employs designations for it, which are usually applied to "the word of the LORD"; statute, ordinance and testimony are all found in Pss. 19, 119 with that meaning. A triple designation of the people corresponds with these triple names for the feast. Israel, Jacob and Joseph

| | | | | | | | |
|---|---|---|---|---|---|---|---|
| 904, 3801 | 3937, 3219 | 2374 | | 3706 | 2805 | 3937, 3547 | 2000 |
| prep, art, n ms | prep, *n ms* | n ms, ps 1cp | | cj | n ms | prep, pn | pers pron |
| בַּכֶּסֶה | לְיוֹם | חַגֵּנוּ | **4.** | כִּי | חֹק | לְיִשְׂרָאֵל | הוּא |
| bakkēs̱eh | leyôm | chaggēnû | | kî | chōq | leyisrā'ēl | hû' |
| during the full moon | at the day of | our feast | | because | a statute | for Israel | it |

| | | | | | | |
|---|---|---|---|---|---|---|
| 5122 | 3937, 435 | 3399 | | 5925 | 904, 3186 | 7947.111 |
| n ms | prep, *n mp* | pn | | n fs | prep, pn | v Qal pf 3ms, ps 3ms |
| מִשְׁפָּט | לֵאלֹהֵי | יַעֲקֹב | **5.** | עֵדוּת | בִּיהוֹסֵף | שָׂמוֹ |
| mishpāṯ | lē'lōhê | ya'ăqōv | | 'ēdhûth | bîhôs̱ēph | sāmô |
| an ordinance | of the God of | Jacob | | a testimony | in Joseph | He established it |

| | | | | | |
|---|---|---|---|---|---|
| 904, 3428.141 | 6142, 800 | 4875 | 8004 | 3940, 3156.115 | 8471.125 |
| prep, v Qal inf con, ps 3ms | prep, *n fs* | pn | n fs | neg part, v Qal pf 1cs | v Qal impf 1cs |
| בְּצֵאתוֹ | עַל־אֶרֶץ | מִצְרָיִם | שְׂפַת | לֹא־יָדַעְתִּי | אֶשְׁמָע |
| betsē'thô | 'al-'erets | mitsrāyim | sephath | lō'-yādha'ăttî | 'eshmā' |
| when his going out | against the land of | Egypt | a language | I had not known | I hear |

| | | | | | | |
|---|---|---|---|---|---|---|
| | 5681.515 | 4623, 5630 | 8327 | 3834 | 4623, 1783 | 5882.127 |
| | v Hiphil pf 1cs | prep, n ms | n ms, ps 3ms | n fp, ps 3ms | prep, n ms | v Qal impf 3fp |
| **6.** | הֲסִירוֹתִי | מִסֵּבֶל | שִׁכְמוֹ | כַּפָּיו | מִדּוּד | תַּעֲבֹרְנָה |
| | hes̱îrôthî | mis̱s̱ēvel | shikhmô | kappâv | middûdh | ta'ăvōrenāh |
| | I removed | of the burden | his shoulder | his hands | from the basket | they passed on |

| | | | | |
|---|---|---|---|---|
| | 904, 7150 | 7410.113 | 2603.325 | 6257.125 |
| | prep, art, n fs | v Qal pf 2ms | cj, v Piel impf 1cs, ps 2ms | v Qal impf 1cs, ps 2ms |
| **7.** | בַּצָּרָה | קָרָאתָ | וָאֲחַלֶּצְךָ | אֶעֶנְךָ |
| | batstsārāh | qārā'thā | wā'ăchalletsekhā | 'e'enkhā |
| | during the adversity | you called | and I separated you away | I answered you |

| | | | | | |
|---|---|---|---|---|---|
| 904, 5848 | 7770 | 1010.125 | 6142, 4448 | 4971 | 5734 |
| prep, *n ms* | n ms | v Qal impf 1cs, ps 2ms | prep, *n mp* | pn | intrj |
| בְּסֵתֶר | רַעַם | אֶבְחָנְךָ | עַל־מֵי | מְרִיבָה | סֶלָה |
| bes̱ēther | ra'am | 'evchānekhā | 'al-mê | merîvāh | s̱elāh |
| in the secret place of | thunder | I tested you | beside the waters of | Meribah | selah |

| | | | | | | |
|---|---|---|---|---|---|---|
| | 8471.131 | 6194 | 5967.525 | 904 | 3547 | 524, 8471.123, 3937 |
| | v Qal impv 2ms | n ms, ps 1cs | cj, v Hiphil juss 1cs | prep, ps 2ms | pn | cj, v Qal impf 2ms, prep, ps 1cs |
| **8.** | שְׁמַע | עַמִּי | וְאָעִידָה | בָּךְ | יִשְׂרָאֵל | אִם־תִּשְׁמַע־לִי |
| | shema' | 'ammî | we'ā'îdhāh | bākh | yisrā'ēl | 'im-tishma'-lî |
| | hear | O my people | so let Me admonish | with you | O Israel | if you will listen to Me |

| | | | | | | | |
|---|---|---|---|---|---|---|---|
| | 3940, 2030.121 | 904 | 418 | 2299 | 3940 | 8246.723 | 3937, 418 |
| | neg part, v Qal impf 3ms | prep, ps 2ms | n ms | adj | cj, neg part | v Hithpael impf 2ms | prep, *n ms* |
| **9.** | לֹא־יִהְיֶה | בְךָ | אֵל | זָר | וְלֹא | תִשְׁתַּחֲוֶה | לְאֵל |
| | lō'-yihyeh | vekhā | 'ēl | zār | welō' | thishtachweh | le'ēl |
| | it will not be | among you | a god | foreign | and not | you will bow down | to a god of |

**4. For this was a statute for Israel, and a law of the God of Jacob:** ... This is a law for Israel, an ordiance of the God of Jacob, *REB.*

**5. This he ordained in Joseph for a testimony, when he went out through the land of Egypt:** ... This is the testimony God gave in behalf of Joseph when He went to war against Egypt, *Beck* ... He gave this rule to the people of Joseph when they went out of the land of Egypt, *NCV* ... He established it as a statute for Joseph when he went out against Egypt, *NIV* ... laid as a solemn charge on Joseph at the exodus from Egypt, *REB.*

**where I heard a language that I understood not:** ... I heard a language I did not know, saying, *NCV* ... where we heard a language we did not understand, *NIV* ... I hear a voice I had not known, *NRSV.*

**6. I removed his shoulder from the burden: his hands were delivered from the pots:** ... When I lifted the load from his shoulders, his hands let go the builder's basket, *NEB* ... I relieved your shoulder of the burden; your hands were freed from the basket, *RSV.*

**7. Thou calledst in trouble, and I delivered thee:** ... You cried to me in trouble and I saved you, *LIVB* ... In distress you called, and I rescued you, *NRSV.*

**I answered thee in the secret place of thunder:** ... unseen, I answered you in thunder, *NCB* ... I answered you out of a thundercloud, *NIV.*

**I proved thee at the waters of Meribah:** ... I tested your loyalty at the Water of Meribah, *Beck* ... and tested thee at the Waters of Rebellion, *Knox.*

**Selah:** ... Music, *Beck* ... Pause, *JB.*

**8. Hear, O my people, and I will testify unto thee: O Israel, if thou wilt hearken unto me:** ... My people, listen. I am warning you, *NCV.*

**9. There shall no strange god be in thee; neither shalt thou worship any strange god:** ... you must allow no foreign god, no worship of an outside god, *Moffatt* ... You must not have foreign gods; you must not worship any false god, *NCV.*

---

are synonyms, the use of the last of these having probably the same force here as in the preceding Psalm, namely, to express the singer's longing for the restoration of the shattered unity of the nation. The summons to the feast is based not only on divine appointment, but also on divine purpose in that appointment. It was "a testimony," a rite commemorative of a historical fact, and therefore an evidence of it to future times. There is no better proof of such a fact than a celebration of it, which originates contemporaneously and continues through generations. The feast in question was thus simultaneous with the event commemorated, as v. 5b tells. It was God, not Israel, as is often erroneously supposed, who "went forth." For the following preposition (HED #6142) is not "from," which might refer to the national departure, but "over" or "against," which cannot have such a reference, since Israel did not, in any sense, go "over" or "against" the land. God's triumphant forthputting of power over the whole land, especially in the death of the firstborn, on the night of the Passover, is meant to be remembered forever and is at once the fact commemorated by the feast and a reason for obeying his appointment of it.

So far the thoughts and language are limpid, but v. 5c interrupts their clear flow. Who is the speaker thus suddenly introduced? What is the "language" (literally, "lip") which he "knew not"? The usual explanation is that the speaker is the psalmist and that the language which he hears is the voice of God, the substance of which follows in the remainder of the Psalm. The inner coherence of the two parts of the Psalm is, on this explanation, so obvious, that there is no need nor room for the hypothesis of two fragments having been fused into one.

**81:6–7.** The divine voice begins by recapitulating the facts which the feast was intended to commemorate—namely, the act of emancipation from Egyptian bondage (v. 6), and the miracles of the wilderness sojourn (v. 7). The compulsory labor from which God delivered the people is described by two terms, of which the former ("burden") is borrowed from Exodus where it frequently occurs (Exo. 1:11; 5:4; 6:6), and the latter ("basket") is by some supposed to mean the wickerwork implemented for carrying, which the monuments show was in use in Egypt (so Septuagint, etc.), and by others to mean an earthen vessel. The years of desert wandering are summed up (v. 7) as one long continuance of benefits from God. Whenever they cried to Him in their trouble, He delivered them. He spoke to them "from the secret place of thunder." That expression is generally taken to refer to the pillar of cloud, but seems more naturally to be regarded as alluding to the thick darkness, in which God was shrouded on Sinai when He spoke his Law amid thunderings and lightnings. "The proving at the waters of Meribah" is, according to the connection and in harmony with Exo. 17:6, to be regarded as a benefit, binding Israel more closely to God.

**81:8–10.** That retrospect next becomes the foundation of a divine exhortation to the people, which is to be regarded as spoken originally to Israel in the wilderness, as v. 11 shows. These verses put into words the meaning of the wilderness experience and sum up the laws spoken on Sinai, which they in part repeat. The purpose of God's lavish benefits was to bind Israel to himself. "Hear, O my people," reminds us of Deut. 5:1 and 6:4. "I will testify unto thee" (HED #5967) here means "solemn warning to" rather than "testifying against" the person addressed. With infinite pathos, the tone of the divine speaker changes from that of authority to pleading and the utterance of a yearning wish, like a sigh. "O Israel, if thou wilt hearken unto me." God desires nothing so earnestly as that, but his divine desire is tragically

| 5424 | | 609 | 3176 | 435 | 6148.551 |
|---|---|---|---|---|---|
| n ms | 10. | pers pron | pn | n mp, ps 2ms | v Hiphil ptc ms |
| נֵכָר | | אָנֹכִי | יְהוָה | אֱלֹהֶיךָ | הַמַּעַלְךָ |
| nēkhār | | 'ānōkhî | yehwāh | 'ĕlōhêkhā | hamma'alkhā |
| a foreign land | | I | Yahweh | your God | the One Who caused you to go up |

| 4623, 800 | 4875 | 7620.531, 6552 | 4527.325 |
|---|---|---|---|
| prep, *n fs* | pn | v Hiphil impv 2ms, n ms, ps 2ms | cj, v Piel impf 1cs, ps 3ms |
| מֵאֶרֶץ | מִצְרָיִם | הַרְחֶב־פִּיךָ | וַאֲמַלְאֵהוּ |
| mē'erets | mitsrāyim | harchev-pîkhā | wa'ămal'ēhû |
| from the land of | Egypt | open wide your mouth | that I may fill it |

| | 3940, 8471.111 | 6194 | 3937, 7249 | 3547 | 3940, 13.111 | 3937 |
|---|---|---|---|---|---|---|
| 11. | cj, neg part, v Qal pf 3ms | n ms, ps 1cs | prep, n ms, ps 1cs | cj, pn | neg part, v Qal pf 3ms | prep, ps 1cs |
| | וְלֹא־שָׁמַע | עַמִּי | לְקוֹלִי | וְיִשְׂרָאֵל | לֹא־אָבָה | לִי |
| | welō'-shāma' | 'ammî | leqôlî | weyisrā'ēl | lō'-'āvāh | lî |
| | but they did not listen | my people | to my voice | and Israel | they were not willing | for Me |

| | 8365.325 | 904, 8656 | 3949 | 2050.126 |
|---|---|---|---|---|
| 12. | cj, v Piel impf 1cs, ps 3ms | prep, *n fs* | n ms, ps 3mp | v Qal impf 3mp |
| | וָאֲשַׁלְּחֵהוּ | בִּשְׁרִירוּת | לִבָּם | יֵלְכוּ |
| | wā'ăshallechēhû | bishrîrûth | libbām | yēlekhû |
| | so I sent them out | because of the stubbornness of | their heart | they walked |

| 904, 4292 | | 4001 | 6194 | 8471.151 | 3937 | 3547 | 904, 1932 |
|---|---|---|---|---|---|---|---|
| prep, n fp, ps 3mp | 13. | intrj | n ms, ps 1cs | v Qal act ptc ms | prep, ps 1cs | pn | prep, n mp, ps 1cs |
| בְּמוֹעֲצוֹתֵיהֶם | | לוּ | עַמִּי | שֹׁמֵעַ | לִי | יִשְׂרָאֵל | בִּדְרָכַי |
| bemô'ătsôthêhem | | lû | 'ammî | shōmēa' | lî | yisrā'ēl | bidhrākhay |
| in their counsels | | O that | my people | ones who listen | to Me | Israel | in my ways |

| 2050.326 | | 3626, 4746 | 342.152 | 3789.525 | 6142 |
|---|---|---|---|---|---|
| v Piel impf 3mp | 14. | prep, sub | v Qal act ptc mp, ps 3mp | v Hiphil impf 1cs | cj, prep |
| יְהַלֵּכוּ | | כִּמְעַט | אוֹיְבֵיהֶם | אַכְנִיעַ | וְעַל |
| yehallēkhû | | kim'aṭ | 'ôyvêhem | 'akhnîa' | we'al |
| they would walk | | like a moment | their enemies | I would subdue | and against |

| 7141 | 8178.525 | 3135 | | 7983.352 | 3176 |
|---|---|---|---|---|---|
| n mp, ps 3mp | v Hiphil impf 1cs | n fs, ps 1cs | 15. | *v Piel ptc mp* | pn |
| צָרֵיהֶם | אָשִׁיב | יָדִי | | מְשַׂנְאֵי | יְהוָה |
| tsārêhem | 'āshîv | yādhî | | mesan'ê | yehwāh |
| their adversaries | I would turn | my hand | | those who hate | Yahweh |

| 3703.326, 3937 | 2030.121 | 6496 | 3937, 5986 | | 404.521 |
|---|---|---|---|---|---|
| v Piel impf 3mp, prep, ps 3ms | cj, v Qal juss 3ms | n fs, ps 3mp | prep, n ms | 16. | cj, v Hiphil impf 3ms, ps 3ms |
| יְכַחֲשׁוּ־לוֹ | וִיהִי | עִתָּם | לְעוֹלָם | | וַיַּאֲכִילֵהוּ |
| yekhachshû-lô | wîhî | 'ittām | le'ôlām | | wayya'ăkhîlēhû |
| they would disavow to Me | that it would be | their time | unto eternity | | and He would feed them |

| 4623, 2561 | 2498 | 4623, 6962 | 1756 | 7881.525 | | 4344 |
|---|---|---|---|---|---|---|
| prep, *n ms* | n fs | cj, prep, n ms | n ms | v Hiphil impf 1cs, ps 2ms | 82:t | n ms |
| מֵחֵלֶב | חִטָּה | וּמִצּוּר | דְּבַשׁ | אַשְׂבִּיעֶךָ | | מִזְמוֹר |
| mēchēlev | chiṭṭāh | ûmitstsûr | devash | 'asbî'ekhā | | mizmôr |
| from the fat of | the wheat | and from the rock | honey | I would satisfy you | | a Psalm |

| 3937, 637 | | 435 | 5507.255 | 904, 5920, 418 | 904, 7419 | 435 |
|---|---|---|---|---|---|---|
| prep, pn | 1. | n mp | v Niphal ptc ms | prep, *n fs*, n ms | prep, *n ms* | n mp |
| לְאָסָף | | אֱלֹהִים | נִצָּב | בַּעֲדַת־אֵל | בְּקֶרֶב | אֱלֹהִים |
| le'āsāph | | 'ĕlōhîm | nitstsāv | ba'ădhath-'ēl | beqerev | 'ĕlōhîm |
| of Asaph | | God | taking a stand | in the congregation of God | in the midst of | gods |

**10. I am the LORD thy God, which brought thee out of the land of Egypt:** ... I, Yahweh, am your God, who brought you here from Egypt, *JB* ... I am your God, I the Eternal, who brought you out of Egypt's land, *Moffatt.*

**open thy mouth wide, and I will fill it:** ... you have only to open your mouth for me to fill it, *JB* ... Open your mouth and I will feed you, *NCV.*

**11. But my people would not hearken to my voice:** ... My people would not listen to me, *JB.*

**and Israel would none of me:** ... Israel would not submit to me, *NRSV* ... And Israel hath not consented to Me, *Young.*

**12. So I gave them up unto their own hearts' lust:** ... so I left them to their own self-will, *Moffatt* ... so I gave them up to the hardness of their hearts, *NCB* ... so I sent them off, stubborn as they were, *NEB* ... So I gave them over to their stubborn hearts, *RSV.*

**and they walked in their own counsels:** ... to follow their own devices, *Moffatt.*

**13. Oh that my people had hearkened unto me, and Israel had walked in my ways!:** ... If my people would but listen to me, if Israel would follow my ways, *NIV.*

**14. I should soon have subdued their enemies, and turned my hand against their adversaries:** ... I should soon bring their enemies to their knees and turn my hand against their foes, *REB.*

**15. The haters of the LORD should have submitted themselves unto him: but their time should have endured for ever:** ... Those who hate the LORD would pretend obedience to Him; And their time of punishement would be forever, *NASB* ... Those who hate the LORD would cringe toward him, and their fate would last for ever, *RSV* ... but their fate would endure forever, *NCB.*

**16. He should have fed them also with the finest of the wheat:** ... But he would feed you with the choicest foods, *LIVB* ... While Israel I would

---

and mysteriously foiled. The awful human power of resisting his voice and of making his efforts vain, and the still more awful fact of the exercise of that power, were clear before the psalmist, whose daring anthropopathy teaches a deep lesson and warns us against supposing that men have to do with an impassive Deity. That wonderful utterance of divine wish is almost a parenthesis. It gives a moment's glimpse into the heart of God, and then the tone of command is resumed. The reason for exclusive devotion to God is based in v. 10, as in Exo. 20:2, on his omnipotence and exclusity. He is all-powerful. Further, He is the only real God. The others are all false. Yahweh is all Israel needed for their physical needs as well.

**81:11–12.** In vv. 11f, the divine voice laments the failure of benefits and commandments and promises to win Israel to God. There is a world of baffled tenderness and almost wondering rebuke in the designation of the rebels as "my people." It would have been no cause of astonishment if other nations had not listened, but that the tribes bound by so many kindnesses should have been deaf is a sad marvel. Who should listen to "my voice" if "my people" do not? The penalty of not yielding to God is to be left unyielding. The worst punishment of sin is the prolongation and consequent intensifying of the sin. A heart that willfully closes itself against God's pleadings brings on itself the nemesis, that it becomes incapable of opening, as a self-torturing Hindu fakir may clench his fist so long, that at last his muscles lose their power, and it remains shut for his lifetime. The issue of such stubbornness is walking in their own counsels, the practical life being regulated entirely by self-originated and God-forgetting dictates of prudence or inclination. He who will not have the divine guide has to grope his way as well as he can. There is no worse fate for a man than to be allowed to do as he chooses. The ditch, sooner or later, receives the man who lets his active powers, which are in themselves blind, be led by his understanding, which he has himself blinded by forbidding it to look to the One Light of life.

**81:13–16.** In v. 13, the divine voice turns to address the joyous crowd of festal worshipers, exhorting them to that obedience which is the true keeping of the feast and holding forth bright promises of the temporal blessings which, in accordance with the fundamental conditions of Israel's prosperity, should follow thereon. The sad picture of ancient rebellion just drawn influences the language in this verse, in which "my people," "hearken" and "walk" recur. The antithesis to walking in one's own counsels is walking in God's ways, suppressing native stubbornness and becoming docile to his guidance. The highest blessedness of man is to have a will submissive to God's will and to carry out that submission in all details of life. Self-engineered paths are always hard and, if pursued to the end, lead into the dark. The listening heart will not lack guidance, and obedient feet will find God's way the way of peace, which steadily climbs to unfading light.

| 8570.121<br>v Qal impf 3ms<br>יִשְׁפֹּט<br>yishpōṭ<br>He judges | 2. | 5912, 5146<br>adv, intrg<br>עַד־מָתַי<br>'adh-māthay<br>until when | 8570.128, 5982<br>v Qal impf 2mp, n ms<br>תִּשְׁפְּטוּ־עָוֶל<br>tishpeṭû-'āwel<br>will you make judgments of wrongdoing | 6686<br>cj, *n mp*<br>וּפְנֵי<br>ûphenê<br>and the face of | 7857<br>n mp<br>רְשָׁעִים<br>reshā'îm<br>the wicked |
|---|---|---|---|---|---|

| 5558.128, 5734<br>v Qal impf 2mp, intrj<br>תִּשְׂאוּ־סֶלָה<br>tis'û-selāh<br>will you lift up selah | 3. | 8570.133, 1859<br>v Qal impv 2mp, n ms<br>שִׁפְטוּ־דָל<br>shiphṭû-dhal<br>give a judgment to the poor | 3605<br>cj, n ms<br>וְיָתוֹם<br>weyāthôm<br>and the orphan | 6270<br>n ms<br>עָנִי<br>'ānî<br>the afflicted |
|---|---|---|---|---|

| 7609.151<br>cj, v Qal act ptc ms<br>וָרָשׁ<br>wārāsh<br>and those destitute | 6927.533<br>v Hiphil impv 2mp<br>הַצְדִּיקוּ<br>hatsdîqû<br>vindicate | 4. | 6647.333, 1859<br>v Piel impv 2mp, n ms<br>פַּלְּטוּ־דַל<br>palleṭû-dhal<br>set free the poor | 33<br>cj, n ms<br>וְאֶבְיוֹן<br>we'evyôn<br>and the needy | 4623, 3135<br>prep, *n fs*<br>מִיַּד<br>mîyadh<br>from the hand of |
|---|---|---|---|---|---|

| 7857<br>n mp<br>רְשָׁעִים<br>reshā'îm<br>the wicked | 5522.533<br>v Hiphil impv 2mp<br>הַצִּילוּ<br>hatstsîlû<br>rescue | 5. | 3940<br>neg part<br>לֹא<br>lō'<br>not | 3156.116<br>v Qal pf 3cp<br>יָדְעוּ<br>yādhe'û<br>they know | 3940<br>cj, neg part<br>וְלֹא<br>welō'<br>and not | 1032.126<br>v Qal impf 3mp<br>יָבִינוּ<br>yāvînû<br>they have understanding |
|---|---|---|---|---|---|---|

| 904, 2934<br>prep, art, n fs<br>בַּחֲשֵׁכָה<br>bachshēkhāh<br>in darkness | 2050.726<br>v Hithpael impf 3mp<br>יִתְהַלָּכוּ<br>yithhallākhû<br>they walk around | 4267.226<br>v Niphal impf 3mp<br>יִמּוֹטוּ<br>yimmôṭû<br>they totter | 3725, 4279<br>*adj, n mp*<br>כָּל־מוֹסְדֵי<br>kol-môsdhê<br>all the foundations of | 800<br>n fs<br>אָרֶץ<br>'ārets<br>the earth |
|---|---|---|---|---|

| 6. | 603, 569.115<br>pers pron, v Qal pf 1cs<br>אֲנִי־אָמַרְתִּי<br>'ănî-'āmartî<br>I I have said | 435<br>n mp<br>אֱלֹהִים<br>'ĕlōhîm<br>gods | 894<br>pers pron<br>אַתֶּם<br>'attem<br>you | 1158<br>cj, *n mp*<br>וּבְנֵי<br>ûvenê<br>and the sons of | 6169<br>n ms<br>עֶלְיוֹן<br>'elyôn<br>the Most High | 3725<br>adj, ps 2mp<br>כֻּלְּכֶם<br>kullekhem<br>all of you | 7. | 409<br>adv<br>אָכֵן<br>'ākhēn<br>surely |
|---|---|---|---|---|---|---|---|---|

| 3626, 119<br>prep, n ms<br>כְּאָדָם<br>ke'ādhām<br>like humankind | 4322.128<br>v Qal impf 2mp<br>תְּמוּתוּן<br>temûthûn<br>you will die | 3626, 259<br>cj, prep, num<br>וּכְאַחַד<br>ûkhe'achadh<br>and like one of | 8015<br>art, n mp<br>הַשָּׂרִים<br>hassārîm<br>the officials | 5489.128<br>v Qal impf 2mp<br>תִּפֹּלוּ<br>tippōlû<br>you will fall | 8. | 7251.131<br>v Qal impv 2ms<br>קוּמָה<br>qûmāh<br>rise |
|---|---|---|---|---|---|---|

feed with the best of wheat, *NAB* … He causeth him to eat of the fat of wheat, *Young*.

**and with honey out of the rock should I have satisfied thee:** … with honey from the rock to their hearts' content, *Moffatt*.

**82:t. A Psalm of Asaph.**

**1. God standeth in the congregation of the mighty:** … God is in the meeting-place of God, *BB* … God standeth in the assembly of God, *Darby* … God stands out in the council of the gods, *Moffatt* … God takes his place in the court of heaven, *REB*.

**he judgeth among the gods:** … in the midst of the judges He gives judgment, *Berkeley* … surrounded by the gods he gives judgement, *JB* … among the gods he rules supreme, *Moffatt*.

**2. How long will ye judge unjustly, and accept the persons of the wicked?:** … How long will you defend the unjust, and show partiality to the wicked?, *Anchor* … How long will you show greater kindness to the wicked?, *NCV*.

**Selah:** … Music, *Beck* … Pause, *JB*.

**3. Defend the poor and fatherless:** … Give ear to the cause of the poor and the children without fathers, *BB* … Dispense justice to the weak and the orphan, *Berkeley* … Uphold the cause of the weak and the fatherless, *REB*.

**do justice to the afflicted and needy:** … let those who are troubled and in need have their rights, *BB* … and see right done to the afflicted and destitute, *REB*.

**4. Deliver the poor and needy:** ... Be the saviour of the poor and those who have nothing, *BB* ... Deliver the lowly and the oppressed, *Berkeley.*

**rid them out of the hand of the wicked:** ... save them from the clutches of the wicked, *JB.*

**5. They know not, neither will they understand; they walk on in darkness:** ... They don't know or understand anything as they walk around in the dark, *Beck* ... Who unknown, unseen in the darkness, proceed, *Fenton* ... You don't understand. You walk in the dark, *NCV* ... But these gods know nothing and understand nothing, they walk about in darkness, *REB.*

**all the foundations of the earth are out of course:** ... All the foundations of the earth are shaken, *ASV* ... all the foundations of the earth are moved, *Darby* ... To remove all the landmarks away, *Fenton* ... while the world is falling apart, *NCV.*

**6. I have said, Ye are gods; and all of you are children of the most High:** ... It was I who said, You are gods, all of you are sons of the Most High, *Beck* ... I had thought, "Are you gods, are all of you sons of the Most High?," *JB* ... This is my sentence: Gods you may be, sons all of you of a high god, *NEB.*

**7. But ye shall die like men, and fall like one of the princes:** ... but as human beings you die and fall like any of the princes, *Beck* ... yet, like mere men, you shall die, you shall perish like a demon, *Moffatt.*

**8. Arise, O God, judge the earth: for thou shalt inherit all nations:** ... Bestir thyself, Lord, bring the world to judgement; all the nations are thy own domain, *Knox* ... God,

---

The blessings attached in the Psalm to such conformity with God's will are of an external kind, as was to be expected at the OT stage of revelation. They are mainly two—victory and abundance. The momentary emergence of the psalmist's personality would lead him to say "He," and the renewed sense of being, but the echo of the divine voice, would lead of the recurrence to the "I," in which God speaks directly. The words are best taken as in line with the other hypothetical promises in the preceding verses. The whole verse looks back to Deut. 32:13f. "Honey out of the rock" is not a natural product, but the parallel "oil out of the flinty rock," which follows in Deuteronomy, shows that we are here, not on the ground of the concrete, but of the ideal and that the expression is a hyperbole for incomparable abundance. Those who hearken to God's voice will have all desires satisfied and needs supplied. They will find furtherance in hindrances and fertility in barrenness; rocks will drop honey, and stones will become bread.

***Psalm 82.*** *In Ps. 1, God is represented as gathering his people together to be judged; in this Psalm, He has gathered them together for his judgment on judges. The former Psalm begins at an earlier point of the great cause than this one does. In it, unnamed messengers go forth to summon the nation. In this Psalm, the first verse shows us the assembled congregation, the accused and the divine Judge standing in "the midst."*

**82:1.** The scene pictured in v. 1 has been variously interpreted. "The congregation of God" is most naturally understood according to the parallel in Ps. 1, and the familiar phrase "the congregation of Israel" as being the assembled nation. Its interpretation and that of the "gods" who are judged hang together. If the assembly is the nation, the persons at the bar can scarcely be other than those who have exercised injustice on the nation. If, on the other hand, the "gods" are ideal or angelic beings, the assembly will necessarily be a heavenly one. The use of the expressions "the congregation of Yahweh" (Num. 27:17; 31:16; Josh. 22:16f) and "thy congregation" (Ps. 74:2) makes the former interpretation the more natural and therefore exercises some influence in determining the meaning of the other difficult word.

**82:2–4.** In vv. 2ff, God speaks in stern upbraiding and command. The abrupt pealing forth of the divine voice, without any statement of who speaks, is extremely dramatic and impressive. The judgment hall is filled with a hushed crowd. No herald is needed to proclaim silence. Strained expectance sits on every ear. Then the silence is broken. These authoritative accents can come but from one speaker. The crimes rebuked are those to which rulers, in such a state of society as was in Israel, are especially prone, and such as must have been universal at the time of the psalmist. These sharp arrows were not launched against imaginary evils. These princes were like those gibbeted forever in Isa. 1—lovers of gifts and followers after rewards, murderers rather than judges, and more fit to be "rulers of Sodom" than of God's city. They had prostituted their office by injustice, had favored the rich and neglected the poor, had been deaf to the cry of the helpless, had steeled their hearts against the miseries of the afflicted and left them to perish in the gripe of the wicked. Such is the indictment. Does it sound applicable to angels?

**82:5–8.** For a moment, the divine voice pauses. Will its tones reach any consciences? No.

| 435 | 8570.131 | 800 | 3706, 887 | 5336.123 | 904, 3725, 1504 |
|---|---|---|---|---|---|
| n mp | v Qal impv 2ms | art, n fs | cj, pers pron | v Qal impf 2ms | prep, *n ms*, art, n mp |
| אֱלֹהִים | שָׁפְטָה | הָאָרֶץ | כִּי־אַתָּה | תִנְחַל | בְּכָל־הַגּוֹיִם |
| 'ĕlōhîm | shāphᵉṭāh | hā'ārets | kî-'attāh | thinchal | bᵉkhol-haggôyim |
| O God | judge | the earth | because You | You have taken possession | among all the nations |

| 83:t | 8302 | 4344 | 3937, 637 | 1. | 435 | 414, 1885, 3937 | 414, 2896.123 |
|---|---|---|---|---|---|---|---|
| | n ms | n ms | prep, pn | | n mp | adv, n ms, prep, ps 2ms | adv, v Qal juss 2ms |
| | שִׁיר | מִזְמוֹר | לְאָסָף | | אֱלֹהִים | אַל־דֳּמִי־לָךְ | אַל־תֶּחֱרַשׁ |
| | shîr | mizmôr | lᵉ'āsāph | | 'ĕlōhîm | 'al-dᵉmî-lākh | 'al-techĕrash |
| | a Song | a Psalm | of Asaph | | O God | not silence to You | do not be deaf |

| 414, 8618.123 | 418 | 2. | 3706, 2079 | 342.152 | 2064.126 |
|---|---|---|---|---|---|
| cj, adv, v Qal juss 2ms | n ms | | cj, intrj | v Qal act ptc mp, ps 2ms | v Qal impf 3mp |
| וְאַל־תִּשְׁקֹט | אֵל | | כִּי־הִנֵּה | אוֹיְבֶיךָ | יֶהֱמָיוּן |
| wᵉ'al-tishqōṭ | 'ēl | | kî-hinnēh | 'ôyvêkhā | yehĕmāyûn |
| and do not keep quiet | O God | | because behold | your enemies | they are in an uproar |

| 7983.352 | 5558.116 | 7513 | 3. | 6142, 6194 |
|---|---|---|---|---|
| cj, v Piel ptc mp, ps 2ms | v Qal pf 3cp | *n ms* | | prep, n ms, ps 2ms |
| וּמְשַׂנְאֶיךָ | נָשְׂאוּ | רֹאשׁ | | עַל־עַמְּךָ |
| ûmᵉsan'êkhā | nāsᵉ'û | rō'sh | | 'al-'ammᵉkhā |
| and those who hate You | they have lifted up | the head | | over your people |

| 6429.526 | 5660 | 3398.726 | 6142, 7121.156 |
|---|---|---|---|
| v Hiphil impf 3mp | n ms | cj, v Hithpael impf 3mp | prep, v Qal pass ptc mp, ps 2ms |
| יַעֲרִימוּ | סוֹד | וְיִתְיָעֲצוּ | עַל־צְפוּנֶיךָ |
| ya'ărîmû | sôdh | wᵉyithyā'ătsû | 'al-tsᵉphûnêkhā |
| they have caused to be subtle | consultation | and they counsel | against those hidden by You |

| 4. | 569.116 | 2050.133 | 3701.520 | 4623, 1504 |
|---|---|---|---|---|
| | v Qal pf 3cp | v Qal impv 2mp | cj, v Hiphil juss 1cp, ps 3mp | prep, n ms |
| | אָמְרוּ | לְכוּ | וְנַכְחִידֵם | מִגּוֹי |
| | 'āmᵉrû | lᵉkhû | wᵉnakhchîdhēm | miggôy |
| | they said | come | and let us annihilate them | from a nation |

| 3940, 2226.221 | 8428, 3547 | 5968 | 5. | 3706 | 3398.216 | 3949 |
|---|---|---|---|---|---|---|
| cj, neg part, v Niphal impf 3ms | *n ms*, pn | adv | | cj | v Niphal pf 3cp | n ms |
| וְלֹא־יִזָּכֵר | שֵׁם־יִשְׂרָאֵל | עוֹד | | כִּי | נוֹעֲצוּ | לֵב |
| wᵉlō'-yizzākhēr | shēm-yisrā'ēl | 'ôdh | | kî | nô'ătsû | lēv |
| that it will not be remembered | the name of Israel | anymore | | indeed | they have consulted | a heart |

| 3267 | 6142 | 1311 | 3901.126 | 6. | 164 | 110 | 3579 | 4262 |
|---|---|---|---|---|---|---|---|---|
| adv | prep, ps 2ms | n fs | v Qal impf 3mp | | *n mp* | pn | cj, pn | pn |
| יַחְדָּו | עָלֶיךָ | בְּרִית | יִכְרֹתוּ | | אָהֳלֵי | אֱדוֹם | וְיִשְׁמְעֵאלִים | מוֹאָב |
| yachdāw | 'ālêkhā | bᵉrîth | yikhrōthû | | 'āhᵉlê | 'ĕdhôm | wᵉyishmᵉ'ē'lîm | mô'āv |
| together | against You | a covenant | they have cut | | the tents of | Edom | and Ishmaelites | Moab |

come and judge the earth, because you own all the nations, *NCV* ... Arise, O God, and judge the earth; for thou dost pass all nations through thy sieve, *NEB*.

**83:t. A Song or Psalm of Asaph.**

**1. Keep not thou silence, O God: hold not thy peace, and be not still, O God:** ... O God, do not stand idly by, mute and inactive, O God!, *Berkeley* ... Be silent, Lord, no longer. O God, do not keep still now, do not hold back now!, *Knox* ... O God, do not remain unmoved; be not silent, O God, and be not still!, *NAB*.

**2. For, lo, thine enemies make a tumult: and they that hate thee have lifted up the head:** ... For now hear Your Enemies growl, And Your haters lift up their head, *Fenton* ... for your enemies raise an uproar, and those who are hostile to you carry their heads high, *REB*.

**3. They have taken crafty counsel against thy people, and consulted against thy hidden ones:** ... They are laying plans against your people, conspiring against those you cherish, *JB* ... Against thy people they craftily devise a secret plot, And conspire against thy treasured ones, *Rotherham* ... They lay crafty plans against thy people; they consult together against thy protected ones, *RSV.*

**4. They have said, Come, and let us cut them off from being a nation; that the name of Israel may be no more in remembrance:** ... 'Let us wipe them out as a nation,' they say; 'let the name of Israel be remembered no more,' *REB.*

**5. For they have consulted together with one consent: they are confederate against thee:** ... With one mind they have conspired to form a league against you, *REB.*

**6. The tabernacles of Edom, and the Ishmaelites; of Moab, and the Hagarenes:** ... the tents of Edom and the Ismaelites, Moab and the Agarenes, *NCB* ... the families of Edom, the Ishmaelites, Moabites and Hagarenes, *NEB.*

**7. Gebal, and Ammon, and Amalek; the Philistines with the inhabitants of Tyre:** ... Gebal, Ammon and

---

There is no sign of contrition among the judges, who are thus solemnly being judged. Therefore, God speaks again, as if wondering, grieved and indignant "at the blindness of their hearts," as his Son was when his words met the same reception from the same class. Verse 5 might almost be called a divine lament over human impenitence, ere the voice swells into the fatal sentence. One remembers Christ's tears as He looked across the valley to the city glittering in the morning sun. His tears did not hinder his pronouncing its doom, nor did his pronouncing its doom hinder his tears. These judges were without knowledge. They walked in darkness because they walked in selfishness and never thought of God's judgment. Their gait was insolent, as the form of the word "walk to and fro" (HED #2050) implies. And since they who were set to be God's representatives on earth and to show some gleam of his justice and compassion were ministers of injustice and vice regents of evil, fostering what they should have crushed and crushing whom they should have fostered, the foundations of society were shaken, and unless these were swept away, it would be dissolved into chaos. Therefore, the sentence must fall, as it does in vv. 6f. The grant of dignity is withdrawn. They are stripped of their honors, as a soldier is stripped of his uniform before he is driven from his corps. The judge's robe, which they have smirched, is plucked off their shoulders, and they stand as common men.

***Psalm 83.*** *The Psalm naturally falls into two parts, separated by selah, of which the first (vv. 1–8) describes Israel's extremity, and the second (vv. 9–18) is its supplication.*

**83:1–5.** The psalmist begins with earnest invocation of God's help, beseeching Him to break his apparent inactivity and silence. "Keep not thou silence" is like Isa. 62:7. God seems passive. It needs only his voice to break the dreary silence, and the foes will be scattered. There is strong reason for his intervention, for they are his enemies who riot and roar like the hoarse chafing of an angry sea, for so the word rendered "they are in an uproar" (HED #2064) implies (Ps. 46:3). It is "thy people" who are the object of their crafty conspiracy, and it is implied that these are thus hated because they are God's people. Israel's prerogative, which evokes the heathen's rage, is the ground of Israel's confidence and the plea urged to God by it. Are we not your "hidden ones"? And shall a hostile world be able to pluck us from our safe hiding place in the hollow of your hand? The idea of preciousness, as well as that of protection, is included in the word. Men store their treasures in secret places; God hides his treasures in the secret of his face, the glorious privacy of light inaccessible. How vain are the plotters' whisperings against such a people!

The conspiracy has for its aim nothing short of blotting out the national existence and the very name of Israel. It is therefore high-handed opposition to God's counsel, and the confederacy is against Him. The true antagonists are not Israel and the world, but God and the world. Calmness, courage and confidence spring in the heart with such thoughts. They who can feel that they are hid in God may look out, as from a safe islet on the wildest seas, and fear nothing. And all who will may hide in Him.

**83:6–8.** The enumeration of the confederates in vv. 6ff groups together peoples who probably were never really united for any common end. Hatred is a very potent cement, and the most discordant elements may be fused together in the fire of a common animosity. What a motley assemblage is here! What could bring together in one company Ishmaelites and Tyrians, Moab and Asshur? The first seven names in the list of allies had their seats to the east and southeast of Palestine. Edom, Moab, Ammon and Amalek were ancestral foes, the last of which had been destroyed in the time of Hezekiah

| 1973<br>cj, pn<br>וְהַגְרִים<br>wehaghrîm<br>and Hagrites | 7. | 1413<br>pn<br>גְּבָל<br>gevāl<br>Gebal | 6205<br>cj, pn<br>וְעַמּוֹן<br>we'ammôn<br>and Ammon | 6222<br>cj, pn<br>וַעֲמָלֵק<br>wa'ămālēq<br>and Amalek | 6673<br>pn<br>פְּלֶשֶׁת<br>pelesheth<br>Philistia | 6196, 3553.152<br>prep, *v Qal act ptc mp*<br>עִם־יֹשְׁבֵי<br>'im-yōshevê<br>with the dwellers of | 7145<br>pn<br>צוֹר<br>tsôr<br>Tyre |
|---|---|---|---|---|---|---|---|

| 8. | 1612, 831<br>cj, pn<br>גַּם־אַשּׁוּר<br>gam-'ashshûr<br>also Assyria | 4004.211<br>v Niphal pf 3ms<br>נִלְוָה<br>nilwāh<br>they have allied | 6196<br>prep, ps 3mp<br>עִמָּם<br>'immām<br>with them | 2030.116<br>v Qal pf 3cp<br>הָיוּ<br>hāyû<br>they are | 2307<br>n fs<br>זְרוֹעַ<br>zerôa'<br>the arm | 3937, 1158, 4013<br>prep, *n mp*, pn<br>לִבְנֵי־לוֹט<br>livnê-lôt<br>of the children of Lot | 5734<br>intrj<br>סֶלָה<br>selāh<br>selah |
|---|---|---|---|---|---|---|---|

| 9. | 6449.131, 3937<br>v Qal impv 2ms, prep, ps 3mp<br>עֲשֵׂה־לָהֶם<br>'ăsēh-lāhem<br>do to them | 3626, 4220<br>prep, pn<br>כְּמִדְיָן<br>kemidhyān<br>like Midian | 3626, 5705<br>prep, pn<br>כְּסִיסְרָא<br>kesiserā'<br>like Sisera | 3626, 3094<br>prep, pn<br>כְיָבִין<br>kheyāvîn<br>like Jabin | 904, 5336<br>prep, *n ms*<br>בְּנַחַל<br>benachal<br>at the wadi of | 7312<br>pn<br>קִישׁוֹן<br>qîshôn<br>Kishon |
|---|---|---|---|---|---|---|

| 10. | 8436.216<br>v Niphal pf 3cp<br>נִשְׁמְדוּ<br>nishmedhû<br>they were destroyed | 904, 6088<br>prep, pn<br>בְעֵין־דֹּאר<br>ve'ên-dō'r<br>at En-Dor | 2030.116<br>v Qal pf 3cp<br>הָיוּ<br>hāyû<br>they were | 1889<br>n ms<br>דֹּמֶן<br>dōmen<br>dung | 3937, 124<br>prep, art, n fs<br>לָאֲדָמָה<br>lā'ădhāmāh<br>for the ground | 11. | 8308.131<br>v Qal impv 2ms, ps 3mp<br>שִׁיתֵמוֹ<br>shîthēmô<br>make them |
|---|---|---|---|---|---|---|---|

| 5259<br>n ms, ps 3mp<br>נְדִיבֵמוֹ<br>nedhîvēmô<br>their nobles | 3626, 6398<br>prep, pn<br>כְּעֹרֵב<br>ke'ōrēv<br>like Oreb | 3626, 2147<br>cj, prep, pn<br>וְכִזְאֵב<br>wekhiz'ēv<br>and like Zeeb | 3626, 2161<br>cj, prep, pn<br>וּכְזֶבַח<br>ûkhezevach<br>and like Zebah | 3626, 7026<br>cj, prep, pn<br>וּכְצַלְמֻנָּע<br>ûkhetsalmunnā'<br>and like Zalmunna | 3725, 5444<br>*adj*, n mp, ps 3mp<br>כָּל־נְסִיכֵמוֹ<br>kol-nesîkhēmô<br>all their officials |
|---|---|---|---|---|---|

| 12. | 866<br>rel pron<br>אֲשֶׁר<br>'ăsher<br>who | 569.116<br>v Qal pf 3cp<br>אָמְרוּ<br>'āmerû<br>they said | 3542.120<br>v Qal juss 1cp<br>נִירְשָׁה<br>nîreshāh<br>let us take possession | 3937<br>prep, ps 1cp<br>לָנוּ<br>lānû<br>for ourselves | 881<br>do<br>וֹד<br>'ēth | 5295<br>*n fp*<br>נְאוֹת<br>ne'ôth<br>the pasturage of |
|---|---|---|---|---|---|---|

| 435<br>n mp<br>אֱלֹהִים<br>'ĕlōhîm<br>God | 13. | 435<br>n mp, ps 1cs<br>אֱלֹהַי<br>'ĕlōhay<br>O my God | 8308.131<br>v Qal impv 2ms, ps 3mp<br>שִׁיתֵמוֹ<br>shîthēmô<br>make them | 3626, 1574<br>prep, art, n ms<br>כַּגַּלְגַּל<br>kaggalgal<br>like a wheel | 3626, 7475<br>prep, n ms<br>כְּקַשׁ<br>keqash<br>like chaff | 3937, 6686, 7593<br>prep, *n mp*, n fs<br>לִפְנֵי־רוּחַ<br>liphnê-rûach<br>before the wind |
|---|---|---|---|---|---|---|

| 14. | 3626, 813<br>prep, n fs<br>כְּאֵשׁ<br>ke'ēsh<br>like a fire | 1220.122, 3402<br>v Qal impf 3fs, n ms<br>תִּבְעַר־יָעַר<br>tiv'ar-yā'ar<br>it consumes the forest | 3626, 3988<br>cj, prep, n fs<br>וּכְלֶהָבָה<br>ûkhelehāvāh<br>and like a flame | 3993.322<br>v Piel impf 3fs<br>תְּלַהֵט<br>telahēt<br>it enflames | 2098<br>n mp<br>הָרִים<br>hārîm<br>the mountains |
|---|---|---|---|---|---|

Amalek, Philistia, with the people of Tyre, *NIV.*

**8. Assur also is joined with them: they have helped the children of Lot:** … Assyria also has joined them; they are the strong arm of the children of Lot, *RSV.*

**Selah:** … Music, *Beck* … Pause, *JB.*

**9. Do unto them as unto the Midianites; as to Sisera, as to Jabin, at the brook of Kison:** … Deal with them as with Sisera, as with Jabin by the torrent of Kishon, *NEB.*

**10. Which perished at En-dor:** … who fell vanquished as Midian fell at En-harod, *NEB.*

**they became as dung for the earth:** … whose decaying corpses fertilized the soil, *LIVB* … and were spread on the battlefield like dung, *NEB* … They became manure for the soil!, *Rotherham.*

**11. Make their nobles like Oreb, and like Zeeb: yea, all their princes as Zebah, and as Zalmunna:** …

... Treat their leaders like Oreb and Zeeb, all their commanders like Zebah and Zalmunna, *JB*.

**12. Who said, Let us take to ourselves the houses of God in possession:** ... Who said, We will seize for ourselves The very finest meadows, *Goodspeed* ... who said, Let us take for oursevles the dwelling place of God, *NCB* ... who said, 'Let us take possession for ourselves of the pastures of God,' *RSV*.

**13. O my God, make them like a wheel:** ... Make them like tumbleweed, *NIV* ... Scatter them, my God, like thistledown, *REB* ... make them like whirling dust, *RSV* ... make them as a rolling thing, *Young*.

**as the stubble before the wind:** ... like straw before the wind, *Moffatt* ... like chaff before the wind, *RSV*.

**14. As the fire burneth a wood, and as the flame setteth the mountains on fire:** ... Like fire raging through the forest or flames which blaze across the hills, *NEB*.

---

(1 Chr. 4:43). The mention of descendants of Ishmael and Hagar, nomad Arab tribes to the south and east, recalls their ancestors' expulsion from the patriarchal family. Gebal is probably the mountainous region to the south of the Dead Sea. Then the psalmist turns to the west, to the ancient foe Philistia and Tyre, "the two peoples of the Mediterranean coast, which also appear in Amos (ch. 1; cf. Joel 3) as making common cause with the Edomites against Israel" (Delitzsch). Asshur brings up the rear—a strange post for it to occupy, to be reduced to be an auxiliary to "the children of Lot," i.e. Moab and Ammon. The ideal character of this roll is supported by this singular inferiority of position, as well as by the composition of the allied force and by the allusion to the shameful origin of the two leading peoples, which is the only reference to Lot besides the narrative in Genesis.

**83:9–12.** The confederacy is formidable, but the psalmist does not enumerate its members merely in order to emphasize Israel's danger. He is contrasting this miscellaneous conglomeration of many peoples with the Almighty One, against Whom they are vainly banded. Faith can look without a tremor on battalions of enemies, knowing that one poor man with God at his back outnumbers them all. Let them come from east and west, south and north, and close around Israel; God alone is mightier than they. So, after a pause marked by selah, in which there is time to let the thought of the multitudinous enemies sink into the soul, the Psalm passes into prayer, which throbs with confident assurance and anticipatory triumph. The singer recalls ancient victories and prays for their repetition. To him, as to every devout man, today's exigencies are as sure of divine help as any of yesterday's were, and what God has done is pledge and specimen of what He is doing and will do. The battle is left to be waged by Him alone. The psalmist does not seem to think of Israel's drawing sword, but rather that it should stand still and see God fighting for it. The victory of Gideon over Midian, to which Isaiah also refers as the very type of complete conquest (Isa. 9:3), is named first, but thronging memories drive it out of the singer's mind for a moment, while he goes back to the other crushing defeat of Jabin and Sisera at the hands of Barak and Deborah (Judg. 4–5). He adds a detail to the narrative in Judges, when he localizes the defeat at Endor, which lies on the eastern edge of the great plain of Esdraelon. In v. 11, he returns to his first example of defeat—the slaughter of Midian by Gideon. Oreb ("raven") and Zeeb ("wolf") were in command of the Midianites and were killed by the Ephraimites in the retreat. Zebah and Zalmunnah were kings of Midian and fell by Gideon's own hand (Judg. 8:21). The psalmist bases his prayer for such a dread fate for the foes on their insolent purpose and sacrilegious purpose of making the dwellings (or possibly, the pastures) of God their own property. Not because the land and its peaceful homes belonged to the suppliant and his nation, but because they were God's, does he thus pray. The enemies had drawn the sword; it was permissible to pray that they might fall by the sword or by some divine intervention, since such was the only way of defeating their God-insulting plans.

**83:13–16.** The Psalm rises to high poetic fervor and imaginative beauty in the terrible petitions of vv. 13–16. The word rendered "whirling dust" (HED #1574) in v. 13 is somewhat doubtful. It literally means "a wheel," but what particular thing of the sort is difficult to determine. The reference is perhaps to spherical masses of dry weeds which course over the plains. Thomson (*Land and Book*, 1870, p. 563) suggests it is the wild artichoke, which, when ripe, forms a globe of about a foot in diameter. "In autumn the branches become dry and as light as a feather, the parent stem breaks off at the ground, and the wind carries these vegetable globes whithersoever it pleaseth. At the proper season thousands of them come scudding over the

| 15. | 3772 | 7579.123 | 904, 5787 | 904, 5679 |
|---|---|---|---|---|
| | adv | v Qal impf 2ms, ps 3mp | prep, n ms, ps 2ms | cj, prep, n fs, ps 2ms |
| | כֵּן | תִּרְדְּפֵם | בְּסַעֲרֶךָ | וּבְסוּפָתְךָ |
| | kēn | tirdephēm | besa'ărekhā | ûvesûphāthekhā |
| | so | You will pursue them | with your windstorm | and with your gale |

| 963.323 | 16. | 4527.331 | 6686 | 7320 | 1272.326 |
|---|---|---|---|---|---|
| v Piel impf 2ms, ps 3mp | | v Piel impv 2ms | n mp, ps 3mp | n ms | cj, v Piel juss 3mp |
| תְּבַהֲלֵם | | מַלֵּא | פְּנֵיהֶם | קָלוֹן | וִיבַקְשׁוּ |
| thevahlēm | | mallē' | phenêhem | qālôn | wîvaqōshû |
| You will cause them to be dismayed | | fill with | their faces | shame | and may they seek |

| 8428 | 3176 | 17. | 991.126 | 963.226 | 5912, 5911 |
|---|---|---|---|---|---|
| n ms, ps 2ms | pn | | v Qal juss 3mp | cj, v Niphal impf 3mp | adv, adv |
| שְׁמֶךָ | יְהוָה | | יֵבֹשׁוּ | וְיִבָּהֲלוּ | עֲדֵי־עַד |
| shimkhā | yehwāh | | yēvōshû | weyibbāhelû | 'ădhê-'adh |
| your name | O Yahweh | | may they be ashamed | and may they be dismayed | unto everlasting |

| 2763.126 | 6.126 | 18. | 3156.126 | 3706, 887 | 8428 |
|---|---|---|---|---|---|
| cj, v Qal juss 3mp | cj, v Qal juss 3mp | | cj, v Qal juss 3mp | cj, pers pron | n ms, ps 2ms |
| וְיַחְפְּרוּ | וְיֹאבֵדוּ | | וְיֵדְעוּ | כִּי־אַתָּה | שִׁמְךָ |
| weyachperû | weyō'vēdhû | | weyēdhe'û | kî-'attāh | shimkhā |
| and may they be ashamed | and may they perish | | and may they know | that You | your name |

| 3176 | 3937, 940 | 6169 | 6142, 3725, 800 | 84:t | 3937, 5514.351 | 6142, 1713 |
|---|---|---|---|---|---|---|
| pn | prep, n ms, ps 2ms | n ms | prep, *adj*, art, n fs | | prep, art, v Piel ptc ms | prep, art, n fp |
| יְהוָה | לְבַדֶּךָ | עֶלְיוֹן | עַל־כָּל־הָאָרֶץ | | לַמְנַצֵּחַ | עַל־הַגִּתִּית |
| yehwāh | levaddekhā | 'elyôn | 'al-kol-hā'ārets | | lamnatstsēach | 'al-haggittîth |
| Yahweh | only You | the Most High | over all the earth | | to the director | on the gittith |

| 3937, 1158, 7432 | 4344 | 1. | 4242, 3151 | 5088 | 3176 | 6893 | 2. | 3826.212 |
|---|---|---|---|---|---|---|---|---|
| prep, *n mp*, pn | n ms | | intrg, adj | n mp, ps 2ms | pn | n fp | | v Niphal pf 3fs |
| לִבְנֵי־קֹרַח | מִזְמוֹר | | מַה־יְּדִידוֹת | מִשְׁכְּנוֹתֶיךָ | יְהוָה | צְבָאוֹת | | נִכְסְפָה |
| livnê-qōrach | mizmôr | | mah-yedhîdhôth | mishkenôthêkhā | yehwāh | tsevā'ôth | | nikhsephāh |
| of the sons of Korah | a Psalm | | how beloved | your Tabernacle | O Yahweh | Hosts | | it longs for |

| 1612, 3735.112 | 5497 | 3937, 2793 | 3176 | 3949 | 1340 |
|---|---|---|---|---|---|
| cj, cj, v Qal pf 3fs | n fs, ps 1cs | prep, *n fp* | pn | n ms, ps 1cs | cj, n ms, ps 1cs |
| וְגַם־כָּלְתָה | נַפְשִׁי | לְחַצְרוֹת | יְהוָה | לִבִּי | וּבְשָׂרִי |
| wegham-kālethāh | naphshî | lechatsrôth | yehwāh | libbî | ûvesārî |
| and also it languishes | my soul | for the courts of | Yahweh | my heart | and my flesh |

| 7728.326 | 420 | 418, 2508 | 3. | 1612, 7109 | 4834.112 | 1041 | 1925 |
|---|---|---|---|---|---|---|---|
| v Piel impf 3mp | prep | n ms, adj | | cj, n fs | v Qal pf 3fs | n ms | cj, n fs |
| יְרַנְּנוּ | אֶל | אֵל־חָי | | גַּם־צִפּוֹר | מָצְאָה | בַיִת | וּדְרוֹר |
| yerannenû | 'el | 'ēl-chāy | | gam-tsippôr | māts'āh | vayith | ûdherôr |
| they shout for joy | to | the living God | | also the birds | they find | a house | and the swallow |

**15. So persecute them with thy tempest, and make them afraid with thy storm:** … so do Thou pursue them with Thy wind, and terrify them with Thy tornado, *Berkeley.*

**16. Fill their faces with shame; that they may seek thy name, O LORD:** … Fill their faces with confusion, That they may seek thy name, *ASV* … Heap shame on their heads until, LORD, they seek your name, *REB* … Fill thou their faces with dishonour, That men may seek thy Name O Yahweh, *Rotherham.*

**17. Let them be confounded and troubled for ever; yea, let them be put to shame, and perish:** … Let them turn pale and be terrified to futurity, Yea let them blush and perish, *Rotherham* … Let them be put to shame and dismayed for ever; let them perish in disgrace, *RSV.*

**18. That men may know that thou, whose name alone is JEHOVAH, art the most high over all the earth:** … Let them learn what Your power is, LORD,—Only YOU, are

Supreme over Earth, *Fenton* ... till they, too, know the meaning of the divine name, acknowledge thee as the most high God, the Overlord of earth, *Knox.*

**84:t. To the chief Musician upon Gittith, A Psalm for the sons of Korah.**

**1. How amiable are thy tabernacles, O LORD of hosts!:** ... How lovely is your dwelling, O Yahweh of Hosts!, *Anchor* ... How dear are your tents, O Lord of armies!, *BB.*

**2. My soul longeth, yea, even fainteth for the courts of the LORD:** ... The passion of my soul's desire is for the house of the Lord, *BB* ... My soul longs, yes, is homesick for the courts of the LORD, *Berkeley* ... My spirit longs and pines for the courts of the LORD, *Goodspeed* ... I want more than anything to be in the courtyards of the LORD's Temple, *NCV.*

**my heart and my flesh crieth out for the living God:** ... My heart and my body shout happily to the living God, *Beck* ... The living God! at his name my heart, my whole being thrills with joy, *Knox* ... now soul and body thrill with joy over the living God, *Moffatt* ... My whole being wants to be with the living God, *NCV.*

**3. Yea, the sparrow hath found an house, and the swallow a nest for herself, where she may lay her young, even thine altars, O LORD of hosts, my King, and my God:** ... For the bird finds a home, and the swallow a nest, Where they lodge their young On Your altar, O LORD of Rest, My King and my GOD!, *Fenton*

---

plain, rolling, leaping, bounding." So understood, the clause would form a complete parallel with the next, which compares the fleeing foe to stubble, not rooted, but loose and whirled before the wind. The metaphor of v. 14 is highly poetic, likening the flight of the foe to the swift rush of a forest fire, which licks up (for so the word rendered "burneth," HED #1220, means) the woods on the hillsides and leaves a bare, blackened space. Still more terrible is the petition in v. 15, which asks that God himself should chase the flying remnants and beat them down, helpless and panic-stricken, with storm and hurricane, as He did the other confederacy of Canaanite kings when they fled down the pass of Beth-Horon, and "Yahweh cast down great stones on them from heaven" (Josh. 10:10f).

**83:17–18.** But there is a deeper desire in the psalmist's heart than the enemies' destruction. He wishes that they should be turned into God's friends, and he wishes for their chastisement as the means to that end. That they may seek the face of Yahweh is the sum of his aspirations, as it is the inmost meaning of God's punitive acts. The end of the judgment of the world, which is continually going on by means of the history of the world, is none other than what this psalmist contemplated as the end of the defeat of that confederacy of God's enemies—that rebels should seek his face, not in enforced submission, but with true desire to sun themselves in its light and with heart-felt acknowledgment of his name as supreme through all the earth. The thought of God as standing alone in his majestic omnipotence, while a world is vainly arrayed against Him, which we have traced in vv. 5ff, is prominent in the close of the Psalm.

God alone is the Most High. He is revealed to men by his name. It stands alone, as He in his nature does. The highest good of men is to know that the sovereign name is unique and high above all creatures, hostile or obedient. Such knowledge is God's aim in punishment and blessing. Its universal extension must be the deepest wish of all who have for themselves learned how strong a fortress against a world in arms that name is. Their desires for the foes of God and themselves are not in harmony with God's heart, nor with this psalmist's song, unless they are that his enemies may be led by salutary defeat of their enterprises and experience of the weight of God's hand to bow, in loving obedience, low before the name which, whether they recognize the fact or not, is high above all the earth.

***Psalm 84.*** *It is divided into three parts by the selahs. The last verse of the first part prepares the way for the first of the second by sounding the note of "Blessed are they," which is prolonged in v. 5. The last verse of the second part (v. 8) similarly prepares for the first of the third (v. 9) by beginning the prayer which is prolonged there. In each part, there is a verse pronouncing blessing on Yahweh's worshipers, and the variation in the designations of these gives the key to the progress of thought in the Psalm.*

**84:1–2.** The abrupt exclamation beginning the Psalm is the breaking into speech the thought which had long increased itself in silence. The intensity of his desires is expressed very strikingly by two words, of which the former, (HED #3826), "longs," literally means "grows pale," and the latter, "fails" or "languishes" (HED #3735). His whole being, body and spirit, is one cry for the living God. The word rendered "cry out" (HED #7728) is usually employed for the shrill cry of joy, and that meaning

| 7348 | 3937 | 866, 8308.112 | 686 | 881, 4326 | 3176 | 6893 |
|---|---|---|---|---|---|---|
| n ms | prep, ps 3fs | rel part, v Qal pf 3fs | n mp, ps 3fs | do, n fp, ps 2ms | pn | n fp |
| קֵן | לָהּ | אֲשֶׁר־שָׁתָה | אֶפְרֹחֶיהָ | אֶת־מִזְבְּחוֹתֶיךָ | יְהוָה | צְבָאוֹת |
| qēn | lāhh | 'ăsher-shāthāh | 'ephrōchêāh | 'eth-mizb$^{e}$chôthêkhā | y$^{e}$hwāh | ts$^{e}$vā'ôth |
| a nest | for herself | where she puts | her young birds | your altars | O Yahweh | Hosts |

| 4567 | 435 | | 869 | 3553.152 | 1041 | 5968 |
|---|---|---|---|---|---|---|
| n ms, ps 1cs | cj, n mp, ps 1cs | 4. | *n mp* | *v Qal act ptc mp* | n ms, ps 2ms | adv |
| מַלְכִּי | וֵאלֹהָי | | אַשְׁרֵי | יוֹשְׁבֵי | בֵיתֶךָ | עוֹד |
| malkî | wē'lōhāy | | 'ashrê | yôshvê | vêthekhā | 'ôdh |
| my King | and my God | | blessed | the dwellers of | your Temple | continually |

| 2054.326 | 5734 | | 869 | 119 | 6010, 3937 | 904 | 4697 |
|---|---|---|---|---|---|---|---|
| v Piel impf 3mp, ps 2ms | intrj | 5. | *n mp* | n ms | n ms, prep, ps 3ms | prep, ps 2ms | n fp |
| יְהַלְלוּךָ | סֶלָה | | אַשְׁרֵי | אָדָם | עוֹז־לוֹ | בָךְ | מְסִלּוֹת |
| y$^{e}$hal$^{e}$lûkhā | selāh | | 'ashrê | 'ādhām | 'ôz-lô | vākh | m$^{e}$sillôth |
| they will praise You | selah | | blessed | the man | strength to him | with You | the highways |

| 904, 3949 | | 5882.152 | 904, 6231 | 1097 | 4754 |
|---|---|---|---|---|---|
| prep, n ms, ps 3mp | 6. | *v Qal act ptc mp* | prep, *n ms* | art, n ms | n ms |
| בִּלְבָבָם | | עֹבְרֵי | בְּעֵמֶק | הַבָּכָא | מַעְיָן |
| bilvāvām | | 'ōv$^{e}$rê | b$^{e}$'ēmeq | habbākhā' | ma'ăyān |
| in their hearts | | those passing through | in the Valley of | the Baca | a place of springs |

| 8308.126 | 1612, 1318 | 6057.521 | 4310 | | 2050.126 | 4623, 2524 |
|---|---|---|---|---|---|---|
| v Qal impf 3mp, ps 3ms | cj, n fp | v Hiphil impf 3ms | n ms | 7. | v Qal impf 3mp | prep, n ms |
| יְשִׁיתוּהוּ | גַּם־בְּרָכוֹת | יַעְטֶה | מוֹרֶה | | יֵלְכוּ | מֵחַיִל |
| y$^{e}$shîthûhû | gam-b$^{e}$rākhôth | ya'ăṭeh | môreh | | yēl$^{e}$khû | mēchayil |
| they make it | also blessings | it enwraps | the early rain | | they proceed | from strength |

| 420, 2524 | 7495.221 | 420, 435 | 904, 6995 | | 3176 | 435 | 6893 | 8471.131 |
|---|---|---|---|---|---|---|---|---|
| prep, n ms | v Niphal impf 3ms | prep, n mp | prep, pn | 8. | pn | n mp | n fp | v Qal impv 2ms |
| אֶל־חָיִל | יֵרָאֶה | אֶל־אֱלֹהִים | בְּצִיּוֹן | | יְהוָה | אֱלֹהִים | צְבָאוֹת | שִׁמְעָה |
| 'el-chāyil | yērā'eh | 'el-'ĕlōhîm | b$^{e}$tsîyôn | | y$^{e}$hwāh | 'ĕlōhîm | ts$^{e}$vā'ôth | shim'āh |
| to strength | it appears | to God | in Zion | | Yahweh | God | Hosts | hear |

... at thy altar, Lord of hosts, my king and my God, *Knox.*

**4. Blessed are they that dwell in thy house: they will be still praising thee:** ... Happy are they whose resting-place is in your house, *BB* ... Happy are those who live at Your house, always praising You, *Beck.*

**Selah:** ... Music, *Beck* ... Pause, *JB.*

**5. Blessed is the man whose strength is in thee:** ... How happy are the men whose strength is in thee!, *Goodspeed.*

**in whose heart are the ways of them:** ... in whose heart are the highways to Zion, *ASV* ... Their minds are on the pilgrim roads, *Beck.*

**6. Who passing through the valley of Baca make it a well:** ... Passing through the valley of Weeping they make it a place of springs, *ASV* ... Going through the valley of balsam-trees, they make it a place of springs, *BB* ... They pass thro' the Valley of Tears, And find it a Valley of Springs, *Fenton.*

**the rain also filleth the pools:** ... it is clothed with blessings by the early rain, *BB* ... Which the showers have covered with pools, *Fenton* ... and the LORD provides even men who lose their way with pools to quench their thirst, *NEB.*

**7. They go from strength to strength, every one of them in Zion appeareth before God:** ... They go from city to city till each appears before God in Zion, *Beck* ... So they pass on from outer wall to inner, and the God of gods shows himself in Zion, *NEB.*

**8. O LORD God of hosts, hear my prayer: give ear, O God of Jacob:** ... Lord of hosts, listen to my prayer; God of Israel, grant me audience!, *Knox.*

**Selah:** ... Music, *Beck.*

**9. Behold, O God our shield, and look upon the face of thine anointed:** ... O God, our Suzerain, behold, look upon the face of your anointed, *Anchor* ... O God, look upon our lord the king and accept thy anointed prince with favour, *NEB.*

is by many retained here. But the cognate noun is not infrequently employed for any loud or high-pitched call, especially for fervent prayer (Ps. 88:2), and it is better to suppose that this clause expresses emotion substantially parallel to that of the former one than that it makes a contrast to it. "The living God" is an expression only found in Ps. 42 and is one of the points of resemblance between it and this Psalm. That name is more than a contrast with the gods of the heathen. It lays bare the reason for the psalmist's longings. By communion with Him, Who possesses life in its fulness and is its Fountain for all that live, he will draw supplies of that life which can only be gained in the spiritual world. Nothing short of the Almighty can quench the immortal thirst of the soul, made after God's own life and restless until it rests in Him. The surface current of this singer's desires ran toward the sanctuary; the depth of them set toward God; and, for the stage of revelation at which he stood, the deeper was best satisfied through the satisfaction of the more superficial. The one is modified by the progress of Christian enlightenment, but the other remains eternally the same.

**84:3–4.** All creatures find environment suited to their need and are at rest in it; man walks like a stranger on earth and restlessly seeks for rest. Where but in God is it to be found? Who that seeks it in Him shall fail to find it? What their nests are to the swallows, God is to man. The solemnity of the direct address to God at the close of v. 3 would be out of place if the altar were the dwelling of the birds, but is entirely natural if the psalmist is thinking of the Temple as the home of his spirit. By the accumulation of sacred and dear names and by the lovingly reiterated "my" which claims personal relation to God, he deepens his conviction of the blessedness which would be his, were he in that abode of his heart, and lingeringly tells his riches, as a miser might delight to count his gold, piece by piece.

The first part closes with an exclamation which gathers into one all-expressive word the joy of communion with God. They who have it are "blessed" with something more sacred and lasting than happiness, with something deeper and more tranquil than joy, even with a calm delight, not altogether unlike the still, yet not stagnant, rest of supreme felicity which fills the life of the living and ever-blessed God. That thought is prolonged by the music.

**84:5–8.** The second strophe (vv. 5–8) is knit to the first, chain-wise, by taking up again the closing strain, "Blessed the man!" But it turns the blessedness in another direction. Not only are they blessed who have found their rest in God, but so also are they who are seeking it. The goal is sweet, but scarcely less sweet are the steps toward it. The fruition of God has delights beyond all that earth can give, but the desire after Him, too, has delights of its own. The experiences of the soul seeking God in his sanctuary are here cast into the image of pilgrim bands going up to the Temple. There may be local allusions in the details. The "ways" in v. 5 are the pilgrims' paths to the sanctuary.

Verse 6 is highly imaginative and profoundly true. If a man has "the ways" in his heart, he will pass through "the valley of weeping" and turn it into a "place of fountains." His very tears will fill the wells. Sorrow borne as a help to pilgrimage changes into joy and refreshment. The remembrance of past grief nourishes the soul which is aspiring to God. God puts our tears into his bottle; we lose the benefit of them and fail to discern their true intent, unless we gather them into a well, which may refresh us in many a weary hour thereafter. If we do, there will be another source of fertility, plentifully poured out upon our life's path. The early rain covers it with blessings. Heaven-descended gifts will not be wanting, nor the smiling harvests which they quicken and mature. God meets the pilgrims' love and faith with gently falling influences, which bring forth rich fruit. Trials borne aright bring down fresh bestowments of power for fruitful service. Thus possessed of a charm which transforms grief and recipients of strength from on high, the pilgrims are not tired by travel as others are, but grow stronger day by day, and their progressive increase in vigor is a pledge that they will joyously reach their journey's end and stand in the courts of the LORD's house. The seekers after God are superior to the law of decay. It may affect their physical powers, but they are borne up by an unfulfilled and certain hope and reinvigorated by continual supplies from above; therefore, although in their bodily frame they faint and grow weary like other men, they shall not utterly fail, but waiting on Yahweh, they "will renew their strength." The fabled fountain of perpetual youth rises at the foot of God's throne, and its waters meet those who journey there.

Such are the elements of the blessedness of those who seek God's presence. With that great promise of certain finding of the good and the God Whom they seek, the description and the strophe properly end. But just as the first part prepared the way for the second, so the second does for the third

| 8940 | 237.531 | 435 | 3399 | 5734 | | 4182 | 7495.131 | 435 |
|---|---|---|---|---|---|---|---|---|
| n fs, ps 1cs | v Hiphil impv 2ms | *n mp* | pn | intrj | 9. | n ms, ps 1cp | v Qal impv 2ms | n mp |
| תְּפִלָּתִי | הַאֲזִינָה | אֱלֹהֵי | יַעֲקֹב | סֶלָה | | מָגִנֵּנוּ | רְאֵה | אֱלֹהִים |
| thephillāthî | ha'ăzînāh | 'ĕlōhê | ya'ăqōv | selāh | | māghinnēnû | re'ēh | 'ĕlōhîm |
| my prayer | listen | O God of | Jacob | selah | | our Shield | see | O God |

| 5202.531 | 6686 | 5081 | | 3706 | 3005, 3219 | 904, 2793 |
|---|---|---|---|---|---|---|
| cj, v Hiphil impv 2ms | *n mp* | n ms, ps 2ms | 10. | cj | adj, n ms | prep, n mp, ps 2ms |
| וְהַבֵּט | פְּנֵי | מְשִׁיחֶךָ | | כִּי | טוֹב־יוֹם | בַּחֲצֵרֶיךָ |
| wehabbēṭ | penê | meshîchekhā | | kî | ṭôv-yôm | bachtsērêkhā |
| and look at | the face of | your anointed one | | because | better a day | in your courtyards |

| 4623, 512 | 1013.115 | 5804.741 | 904, 1041 | 435 |
|---|---|---|---|---|
| prep, num | v Qal pf 1cs | v Hithpoel inf con | prep, *n ms* | n mp, ps 1cs |
| מֵאָלֶף | בָּחַרְתִּי | הִסְתּוֹפֵף | בְּבֵית | אֱלֹהַי |
| mē'āleph | bāchartî | histôphēph | bevêth | 'ĕlōhay |
| than one thousand | I have chosen | to stand at the doorway | in the Temple of | my God |

| 4623, 1806.141 | 904, 164, 7856 | | 3706 | 8507 | 4182 | 3176 | 435 |
|---|---|---|---|---|---|---|---|
| prep, v Qal inf con | prep, *n mp*, n ms | 11. | cj | n ms | cj, n ms | pn | n mp |
| מִדּוּר | בְּאָהֳלֵי־רֶשַׁע | | כִּי | שֶׁמֶשׁ | וּמָגֵן | יְהוָה | אֱלֹהִים |
| middûr | be'āhelê-resha' | | kî | shemesh | ûmāghēn | yehwāh | 'ĕlōhîm |
| than to dwell | in tents of wickedness | | because | a Sun | and a Shield | Yahweh | God |

| 2682 | 3638 | 5598.121 | 3176 | 3940 | 4661.121, 3008 | 3937, 2050.152 |
|---|---|---|---|---|---|---|
| n ms | cj, n ms | v Qal impf 3ms | pn | neg part | v Qal impf 3ms, n ms | prep, art, v Qal act ptc mp |
| חֵן | וְכָבוֹד | יִתֵּן | יְהוָה | לֹא | יִמְנַע־טוֹב | לַהֹלְכִים |
| chēn | wekhāvôdh | yittēn | yehwāh | lō' | yimna'-ṭôv | lahōlekhîm |
| favor | and glory | He gives | Yahweh | not | He withholds good things | to those who walk |

| 904, 8879 | | 3176 | 6893 | 869 | 119 | 1019.151 | 904 |
|---|---|---|---|---|---|---|---|
| prep, adj | 12. | pn | n fp | *n mp* | n ms | v Qal act ptc ms | prep, ps 2ms |
| בְּתָמִים | | יְהוָה | צְבָאוֹת | אַשְׁרֵי | אָדָם | בֹּטֵחַ | בָּךְ |
| bethāmîm | | yehwāh | tsevā'ôth | 'ashrê | 'ādhām | bōṭēach | bākh |
| with blamelessness | | O Yahweh | Hosts | blessed | the man | the one who trusts | in You |

| | 3937, 5514.351 | 3937, 1158, 7432 | 4344 | | 7813.113 | 3176 | 800 |
|---|---|---|---|---|---|---|---|
| 85:t | prep, art, v Piel ptc ms | prep, *n mp*, pn | n ms | 1. | v Qal pf 2ms | pn | n fs, ps 2ms |
| | לַמְנַצֵּחַ | לִבְנֵי־קֹרַח | מִזְמוֹר | | רָצִיתָ | יְהוָה | אַרְצֶךָ |
| | lamnatstsēach | livnê-qōrach | mizmôr | | rātsîthā | yehwāh | 'artsekhā |
| | to the director | of the sons of Korah | a Psalm | | You showed favor to | Yahweh | your land |

| 8178.113 | 8097 | 3399 | | 5558.113 | 5988 | 6194 | 3803.313 |
|---|---|---|---|---|---|---|---|
| v Qal pf 2ms | *n fs* | pn | 2. | v Qal pf 2ms | *n ms* | n ms, ps 2ms | v Piel pf 2ms |
| שַׁבְתָּ | שְׁבוּת | יַעֲקֹב | | נָשָׂאתָ | עֲוֹן | עַמֶּךָ | כִּסִּיתָ |
| shavtā | shevûth | ya'ăqōv | | nāsā'thā | 'āwōn | 'ammekhā | kissîthā |
| You turned | the captivity of | Jacob | | You forgave | the guilt of | your people | You pardoned |

**10. For a day in thy courts is better than a thousand:** ... How much better is one day in your court than a thousand in the Cemetery!, *Anchor* ... A day in Your courts is better than a thousand elsewhere, *Beck* ... Better one day in your courts than a thousand at my own devices, *JB* ... For a day in Thy courts is better than a thousand outside, *NASB.*

**I had rather be a doorkeeper in the house of my God, than to dwell in the tents of wickedness:** ... It is better to be a door-keeper in the house of my God, than to be living in the tents of sin, *BB.*

**11. For the LORD God is a sun and shield:** ... Truly Sun and Suzerain is Yahweh God, *Anchor* ... is our sun and our strength, *BB* ... is a rampart and shield, *JB.*

**the LORD will give grace and glory:** ... grace and glory he bestows, *NAB* ... the LORD gives us kindness and honor, *NCV.*

**no good thing will he withhold from them that walk uprightly:** ...

The LORD doesn't keep back anything good from those who live innocently, *Beck* ... He does not withhold prosperity from them that walk in integrity, *Goodspeed* ... no good thing does he withhold from those whose walk is blameless, *NIV.*

**12. O LORD of hosts, blessed is the man that trusteth in thee:** ... O Lord of armies, happy is the man whose hope is in you, *BB* ... happy the name who trusts in thee!, *NEB* ... blessed is the man that confideth in thee!, *Darby.*

**85:t. To the chief Musician, A Psalm for the sons of Korah.**

**1. LORD, thou hast been favourable unto thy land:** ... Thou hast accepted, *Young* ... You have refreshed, LORD, your land, *Fenton* ... LORD, you have been kind to your land, *NCV.*

**thou hast brought back the captivity of Jacob:** ... changing the fate of Jacob, *BB* ... you have restored the well-being of Jacob, *NCB* ... thou didst restore the fortunes of Jacob, *RSV.*

**2. Thou hast forgiven the iniquity of thy people:** ... Thou hast borne away the iniquity of Thy people, *Young.*

**thou hast covered all their sin:** ... burying away the record of their

---

by breaking forth into prayer. No wonder that the thoughts which he has been dwelling on should move the singer to supplication so that these blessednesses may be his. According to some, v. 8 is the prayer of the pilgrim on arriving in the Temple, but it is best taken as the psalmist's own.

**84:9–12.** Nothing fills life so full or stretches the hours to hold so much of real living as communion with God, which works, on those who have plunged into its depths, some assimilation to the timeless life of Him with Whom "one day is as a thousand years." There may be a reference to the Korahites' function of door keepers, in that touchingly beautiful choice of the psalmist's, rather to lie on the threshold of the Temple than to dwell in the tents of wickedness. Whether there is or not, the sentiment breathes sweet humility and deliberate choice. Just as the poet has declared that the briefest moment of communion is in his sight to be preferred to years of earthly delight, so he counts the humblest office in the sanctuary as better than ought besides. The least degree of fellowship with God has delights superior to the greatest measure of worldly joys. And this man, knowing that, chose accordingly. How many of us know it, and yet cannot say with him, "Rather would I lie on the door-sill of the Temple than sit in the chief places of the world's feasts!"

Such a choice is the only rational one. It is the choice of supreme good, correspondent to man's deepest needs and lasting as his being. Therefore, the psalmist vindicates his preference and encourages himself in it by the thoughts in v. 11, which he introduces with "for" (HED #3706). Because God is who He is and gives what He does, it is the highest wisdom to take Him for our true good and never to let Him go. He is "Sun and Shield." This is the only place in which He is directly called "a Sun," although the idea conveyed is common. He is "the master light of all our seeing," the fountain of warmth, illumination and life.

But high as is the psalmist's flight of mystic devotion, he does not soar so far as to lose sight of plain morality, as mystics have often been apt to do. It is the man who walks in his integrity who may hope to receive these blessings. Without holiness, no man shall see the Lord; neither access to his house nor the blessings flowing from his presence can belong to him who is faithless to his own convictions of duty. The pilgrim paths are paths of righteousness. The psalmist's last word translates his metaphors of dwelling in and traveling toward the house of Yahweh into their simple meaning, "Blessed is the man that trusteth in thee." That trust both seeks and finds God. There has never been but one way to his presence, and that is the way of trust. "I am the way.... No man cometh to the Father but by me" (John 14:6). So coming, we shall find and then shall seek more eagerly and find more fully, and thus shall possess at once the joys of fruition and of desires always satisfied, never satiated, but continually renewed.

***Psalm 85.*** *Three parts of increasing length comprise Ps. 85. The first is three verses (vv. 1ff), recounting God's acts of mercy already received; the second, of four verses (vv. 4–7), is a plaintive prayer in view of still remaining national afflictions; and the third (vv. 8–13) is a glad report by the psalmist of the divine promises which his waiting ear had heard and which might well quicken the most fainthearted into triumphant hope.*

**85:1–3.** In the first strophe, one great fact is presented in a threefold aspect and traced wholly to Yahweh. "You caused to return the captivity of Jacob." That expression is sometimes used in a figurative sense for any restoration of prosperity, but is here to be taken literally.

The psalmist uses two significant words for "pardon," both of which occur in Ps. 32. In v. 2, a sin is regarded as a weight pressing down the

| 3725, 2496 | 5734 | | 636.113 | 3725, 5887 | 8178.513 | 4623, 2841 |
|---|---|---|---|---|---|---|
| *adj*, n fs, ps 3mp | intrj | 3. | v Qal pf 2ms | *adj*, n fs, ps 2ms | v Hiphil pf 2ms | prep, *n ms* |
| כָּל־חַטָּאתָם | סֶלָה | | אָסַפְתָּ | כָּל־עֶבְרָתֶךָ | הֱשִׁיבוֹתָ | מֵחֲרוֹן |
| khol-chattā'thām | selāh | | 'āsaphtā | khol-'evrāthekhā | hĕshîvôthā | mēchărôn |
| all their sin | selah | | You gathered in | all your rage | You turned | from the heat of |

| 653 | | 8178.131 | 435 | 3589 | 6815.531 | 3833 |
|---|---|---|---|---|---|---|
| n ms, ps 2ms | 4. | v Qal impv 2ms, ps 1cp | *n mp* | n ms, ps 1cp | cj, v Hiphil impv 2ms | n ms, ps 2ms |
| אַפֶּךָ | | שׁוּבֵנוּ | אֱלֹהֵי | יִשְׁעֵנוּ | וְהָפֵר | כַּעַסְךָ |
| 'appekhā | | shûvēnû | 'ĕlōhê | yish'ēnû | wehāphēr | ka'askhā |
| your nose | | return to us | O God of | our salvation | and suspend | your anger |

| 6196 | | 1950B, 3937, 5986 | 613.123, 904 | 5082.123 | 653 |
|---|---|---|---|---|---|
| prep, ps 1cp | 5. | intrg part, prep, n ms | v Qal impf 2ms, prep, ps 1cp | v Qal impf 2ms | n ms, ps 2ms |
| עִמָּנוּ | | הַלְעוֹלָם | תֶּאֱנַף־בָּנוּ | תִּמְשֹׁךְ | אַפְּךָ |
| 'immānû | | hal'ôlām | te'ĕnaph-bānû | timshōkh | 'appekhā |
| with us | | to eternity | will You be angry with us | will You prolong | your anger |

| 3937, 1810 | 1810 | | 1950B, 3940, 887 | 8178.123 | 2513.323 |
|---|---|---|---|---|---|
| prep, n ms | cj, n ms | 6. | intrg part, neg part, pers pron | v Qal impf 2ms | v Piel impf 2ms, ps 1cp |
| לְדֹר | וָדֹר | | הֲלֹא־אַתָּה | תָּשׁוּב | תְּחַיֵּנוּ |
| ledhōr | wādhōr | | hălō'-'attāh | tāshûv | techayyēnû |
| unto generations | and generations | | will You not | will You return | will You revive us |

| 6194 | 7975.126, 904 | | 7495.531 | 3176 | 2721 |
|---|---|---|---|---|---|
| cj, n ms, ps 2ms | v Qal impf 3mp, prep, ps 2ms | 7. | v Hiphil impv 2ms, ps 1cp | pn | n ms, ps 2ms |
| וְעַמְּךָ | יִשְׂמְחוּ־בָךְ | | הַרְאֵנוּ | יְהוָה | חַסְדֶּךָ |
| we'ammekhā | yismechû-vākh | | har'ēnû | yehwāh | chasdekhā |
| and your people | they will be glad in You | | show us | O Yahweh | your steadfast love |

| 3589 | 5598.123, 3937 | | 8471.125 | 4242, 1744.321 | 418 | 3176 |
|---|---|---|---|---|---|---|
| cj, n ms, ps 2ms | v Qal impf 2ms, prep, ps 1cp | 8. | v Qal juss 1cs | intrg, v Piel impf 3ms | art, n ms | pn |
| וְיֶשְׁעֲךָ | תִּתֶּן־לָנוּ | | אֶשְׁמְעָה | מַה־יְדַבֵּר | הָאֵל | יְהוָה |
| weyesh'ăkhā | titten-lānû | | 'eshme'āh | mah-yedhabbēr | hā'ēl | yehwāh |
| and your salvation | You will give to us | | let me hear | what He speaks | God | Yahweh |

| 3706 | 1744.321 | 8361 | 420, 6194 | 420, 2728 | 414, 8178.126 |
|---|---|---|---|---|---|
| cj | v Piel impf 3ms | n ms | prep, n ms, ps 3ms | cj, prep, n mp, ps 3ms | cj, adv, v Qal juss 3mp |
| כִּי | יְדַבֵּר | שָׁלוֹם | אֶל־עַמּוֹ | וְאֶל־חֲסִידָיו | וְאַל־יָשׁוּבוּ |
| kî | yedhabbēr | shālôm | 'el-'ammô | we'el-chăsîdhâv | we'al-yāshûvû |
| because | He will speak | peace | to his people | and to his godly ones | and may they not turn |

| 3937, 3816 | | 395 | 7427 | 3937, 3486.152 | 3589 | 3937, 8331.141 | 3638 |
|---|---|---|---|---|---|---|---|
| prep, n fs | 9. | adv | adj | prep, v Qal act ptc mp, ps 3ms | n ms, ps 3ms | prep, v Qal inf con | n ms |
| לְכִסְלָה | | אַךְ | קָרוֹב | לִירֵאָיו | יִשְׁעוֹ | לִשְׁכֹּן | כָּבוֹד |
| lekhislāh | | 'akh | qārôv | lîrē'âv | yish'ô | lishkōn | kāvôdh |
| to folly | | surely | near | to those who fear Him | his salvation | for dwelling of | glory |

sins, *Knox* … you pardoned all their sin, *NRSV.*

**Selah:** … Music, *Beck* … Pause, *JB.*

**3. Thou hast taken away all thy wrath:** … Thou hast taken back all thy anger, *NEB* … Thou hast withdrawn all thine indignation, *Rotherham.*

**thou hast turned thyself from the fierceness of thine anger:** … and turned from thy bitter wrath, *NEB* … thou didst turn from thy hot anger, *RSV.*

**4. Turn us, O God of our salvation, and cause thine anger toward us to cease:** … Restore us again, O God of our salvation, and put away thy indignation toward us, *RSV* … Turn back to us, O God of our salvation, And make void Thine anger with us, *Young.*

**5. Wilt thou be angry with us for ever? wilt thou draw out thine anger to all generations?:** … Will you be angry with us forever? Will you stay angry from now on, *NCV.*

**6. Wilt thou not revive us again:** ... Won't you give us life again?, *NCV.*

**that thy people may rejoice in thee?:** ... so Your people can delight in You, *Beck.*

**7. Show us thy mercy, O LORD, and grant us thy salvation:** ... LORD, show us your love and grant us your deliverance, *REB.*

**8. I will hear what God the LORD will speak:** ... Let me hear the words of the LORD, *NEB.*

**for he will speak peace unto his people, and to his saints:** ... Yahweh's message is peace, for his people, for his faithful, *JB* ... For he will bespeak prosperity to his people And to his men of lovingkindness, *Rotherham.*

**but let them not turn again to folly:** ... but they mustn't go back to foolishness, *Beck* ... if only they renounce their folly, *JB* ... to those who turn to him in their hearts, *RSV.*

**9. Surely his salvation is nigh them that fear him:** ... God will soon save those who respect him, *NCV* ... Deliverance is near to those who worship him, *REB.*

---

nation, which God's mercy lifts off and takes away; in v. 2b, it is conceived of as a hideous stain or foulness, which his mercy hides, so that it is no longer an offense to heaven. Verse 3 ventures still deeper into the sacred recesses of the divine nature and traces the forgiveness, which in act had produced so happy a change in Israel's position, to its source in a change in God's disposition. "You gathered in all your rage," as a man does his breath, or, if the comparison may be ventured, as some creature armed with a sting retracts it into its sheath. "Thou hast turned thyself from the fierceness of thine anger" gives the same idea under another metaphor. The word "turn" (HED #8178) has a singular fascination for this psalmist. He uses it five times (vv. 1, 3f, 6 and 8). God's turning from his anger is the reason for Israel's returning from captivity.

**85:4–7.** The abruptness of the transition from joyous thanksgiving to the sad minor of lamentation and supplication is striking, but most natural, if the psalmist was one of the band of returning exiles, surrounded by the ruins of a happier past and appalled by the magnitude of the work before them, the slenderness of their resources and the fierce hostility of their neighbors. The prayer of v. 4, "Turn us," is best taken as using the word in the same sense as in v. 1, where God is said to have "turned" the captivity of Jacob, meaning "to prosper." In like manner, the petitions of v. 5 look back to v. 3 and pray that the anger which there had been spoken of as passed may indeed utterly cease. The partial restoration of the people implied, in the psalmist's view, a diminution rather than a cessation of God's punitive wrath, and he beseeches Him to complete that which He had begun.

The relation of the first to the second strophe is not only that of contrast, but the prayers of the latter are founded upon the facts of the former, which constitute both grounds for the suppliant's hope of answer and pleas with God. He cannot mean to deliver by halves. The mercies received are incomplete, and his work must be perfect. So the contrast between the bright dawning of the return and its clouded day is not wholly depressing; for the remembrance of what has been heartens for the assurance that what is shall not always be, but will be followed by a future more correspondent to God's purpose as shown in that past. When we are tempted to gloomy thoughts by the palpable incongruities between God's ideals and man's realization of them, we may take a hint from this psalmist and, instead of concluding that the ideal was a phantasm, argue with ourselves that the incomplete actually will one day give way to the perfect embodiment. God leaves no work unfinished. He never leaves off until He has finished. His beginnings guarantee congruous endings. He does not half withdraw his anger, and if He seems to do so, it is only because men have but half turned from their sins. This Psalm is rich in teaching as to the right way of regarding the incompleteness of great movements which, in their incipient stages, were evidently of God. It instructs us to keep the divine intervention which started them clearly in view; to make the shortcomings, which mar them, a subject of lowly prayer; and to be sure that all which He begins He will finish and that the end will fully correspond to the promise of the beginning. A "day of the LORD" which rose in brightness may cloud over as its hours roll, but "at eventide it shall be light," and none of the morning promise will be unfulfilled.

**85:8–9.** The third strophe (vv. 8–13) brings solid hopes, based upon divine promises, to bear on present discouragements. In v. 8, the psalmist, like Habakkuk (Hab. 2:1), encourages himself to listen to what God will speak. The word "I will hear" (HED #8471) expresses resolve or desire, and might be rendered "Let me hear" or "I would hear." Faithful prayer will always be followed by patient and faithful waiting for response from God. God

| 904, 800<br>prep, n fs, ps 1cp<br>בְּאַרְצֵנוּ<br>be'artsēnû<br>in our land | 10. | 2721, 583<br>n ms, cj, n fs<br>חֶסֶד־וֶאֱמֶת<br>chesedh-we'ěmeth<br>steadfast love and reliability | 6539.216<br>v Niphal pf 3cp<br>נִפְגָּשׁוּ<br>niphgāshû<br>they will meet | 6928<br>n ms<br>צֶדֶק<br>tsedheq<br>righteousness | 8361<br>cj, n ms<br>וְשָׁלוֹם<br>weshālôm<br>and peace |
|---|---|---|---|---|---|

| 5583.116<br>v Qal pf 3cp<br>נָשָׁקוּ<br>nāshāqû<br>they will kiss | 11. | 583<br>n fs<br>אֱמֶת<br>'ěmeth<br>reliability | 4623, 800<br>prep, n fs<br>מֵאֶרֶץ<br>mē'erets<br>from the earth | 7048.122<br>v Qal impf 3fs<br>תִּצְמָח<br>titsmāch<br>it will sprout | 6928<br>cj, n ms<br>וְצֶדֶק<br>wetsedheq<br>and righteousness | 4623, 8452<br>prep, n md<br>מִשָּׁמַיִם<br>mishshāmayim<br>from the heavens |
|---|---|---|---|---|---|---|

| 8625.255<br>v Niphal ptc ms<br>נִשְׁקָף<br>nishqāph<br>looking down | 12. | 1612, 3176<br>cj, pn<br>גַּם־יְהוָה<br>gam-yehwāh<br>also Yahweh | 5598.121<br>v Qal impf 3ms<br>יִתֵּן<br>yittēn<br>He will give | 3008<br>art, n ms<br>הַטּוֹב<br>hattôv<br>what is good | 800<br>cj, n fs, ps 1cp<br>וְאַרְצֵנוּ<br>we'artsēnû<br>and our land | 5598.122<br>v Qal impf 3fs<br>תִּתֵּן<br>tittēn<br>it will give | 3090<br>n ms, ps 3fs<br>יְבוּלָהּ<br>yevûlāhh<br>it produce |
|---|---|---|---|---|---|---|---|

| 13. | 6928<br>n ms<br>צֶדֶק<br>tsedheq<br>righteousness | 3937, 6686<br>prep, n mp, ps 3ms<br>לְפָנָיו<br>lephānâv<br>before Him | 2050.321<br>v Piel impf 3ms<br>יְהַלֵּךְ<br>yehallēkh<br>it will go | 7947.121<br>cj, v Qal juss 3ms<br>וְיָשֵׂם<br>weyāsēm<br>and it establishes | 3937, 1932<br>prep, n ms<br>לְדֶרֶךְ<br>ledherekh<br>for the way | 6718<br>n fs, ps 3ms<br>פְּעָמָיו<br>pe'āmâv<br>his footsteps |
|---|---|---|---|---|---|---|

| 86:t | 8940<br>n fs<br>תְּפִלָּה<br>tephillāh<br>a Prayer | 3937, 1784<br>prep, pn<br>לְדָוִד<br>ledhāwidh<br>of David | 1. | 5371.531, 3176<br>v Hiphil impv 2ms, pn<br>הַטֵּה־יְהוָה<br>hattēh-yehwāh<br>incline O Yahweh | 238<br>n fs, ps 2ms<br>אָזְנְךָ<br>'oznekhā<br>your ear | 6257.131<br>v Qal impv 2ms, ps 1cs<br>עֲנֵנִי<br>'ănēnî<br>answer me | 3706, 6270<br>cj, n ms<br>כִּי־עָנִי<br>kî-'ānî<br>because the afflicted |
|---|---|---|---|---|---|---|---|

| 33<br>cj, n ms<br>וְאֶבְיוֹן<br>we'evyôn<br>and the needy | 603<br>pers pron<br>אָנִי<br>'ānî<br>I | 2. | 8490.131<br>v Qal impv 2ms<br>שָׁמְרָה<br>shāmerāh<br>protect | 5497<br>n fs, ps 1cs<br>נַפְשִׁי<br>naphshî<br>my life | 3706, 2728<br>cj, adj<br>כִּי־חָסִיד<br>kî-chāsîdh<br>because godly | 603<br>pers pron<br>אָנִי<br>'ānî<br>I | 3588.531<br>v Hiphil impv 2ms<br>הוֹשַׁע<br>hôsha'<br>save |
|---|---|---|---|---|---|---|---|

**that glory may dwell in our land:** ... That honor may dwell in our land, *Goodspeed* ... till his great Presence dwells within our land, *Moffatt.*

**10. Mercy and truth are met together; righteousness and peace have kissed each other:** ... Love and truth belong to God's people; goodness and peace will be theirs, *NCV* ... Love and faithfulness have come together; justice and peace have embraced, *REB.*

**11. Truth shall spring out of the earth:** ... Truth sprouts forth from the earth, *Berkeley* ... Faithfulness will spring up from the ground, *RSV.*

**and righteousness shall look down from heaven:** ... and Justice will lean down from heaven, *JB* ... and justice shall look down from heaven, *NAB.*

**12. Yea, the LORD shall give that which is good; and our land shall yield her increase:** ... The LORD will grant prosperity, and our land will yield its harvest, *REB.*

**13. Righteousness shall go before him; and shall set us in the way of his steps:** ... make His footsteps into a way, *NASB* ... Justice shall go in front of him and the path before his feet shall be peace, *NEB* ... prepares the way for his steps, *NIV.*

**86:t. A Prayer of David.**

**1. Bow down thine ear, O LORD, hear me: for I am poor and needy:** ... Listen, LORD, and answer me for I am miserable and poor, *Beck* ... Turn thy ear, Lord, and listen to me in my helplessness and my need, *Knox.*

**2. Preserve my soul; for I am holy:** ... Protect my life for I am devoted to you, *Anchor* ... Keep my soul, for I am true to you, *BB* ... Oh, keep my life, for I am dedicated, *Berkeley* ... Protect me, because I worship you, *NCV* ... Guard me, for I am faithful, *REB.*

**O thou my God, save thy servant that trusteth in thee:** ... O my God, give salvation to your servant, whose hope is in you, *BB.*

**3. Be merciful unto me, O Lord:** ... You are my God, take pity on me, Lord, *JB.*

will not be silent, when his servant appeals to Him with recognition of his past mercies joined with longing that these may be perfected. No voice will break the silence of the heavens; but, in the depths of the waiting soul, there will spring a sweet assurance which comes from God and is really his answer to prayer telling the suppliant that "He will speak peace unto his people" and warning them not to turn away from Him to other helps, which is folly. "His saints" seems here to be meant as coextensive with "his people." Israel is regarded as having entered into covenant relations with God; and the designation is the pledge that what God speaks will be "peace" (HED #8361). That word is to be taken in its widest sense as meaning, first and chiefly, peace with Him who has "turned himself from his anger," and then, generally, well being of all kinds, outward and inward, as a consequence of that rectified relation with God.

**85:10–11.** The lovely personifications in vv. 10–13 have passed into Christian poetry and art, but are not clearly apprehended when they are taken to describe the harmonious meeting and cooperation in Christ's great work of apparently opposing attributes of the divine nature. No such thoughts are in the psalmist's mind. Steadfast love and faithfulness are constantly associated in Scripture as divine attributes. Righteousness and peace are as constantly united, as belonging to the perfection of human character. Verse 10 seems to refer to the manifestation of God's steadfast love and faithfulness in its first clause and to the exhibition of his people's virtues and consequent happiness in its second. In all God's dealings for his people, his steadfast love blends with faithfulness. In all his people's experience, righteousness and peace are inseparable. The point of the assurance in v. 10 is that heaven and earth are blended in permanent amity. These four radiant angels "dwell in the land." Then in v. 11, there comes a beautiful inversion of the two pairs of personifications; in each, only one member reappears. Faithfulness, which in v. 10 came into view principally as a divine attribute, is in v. 11 conceived of as a human virtue. It "springs out of the earth"—that is, it is produced among men. But all human virtue is an echo of the divine.

**85:12.** The same idea is further presented in v. 12 in its most general form. God gives that which is good, both outward and inward blessings, and thus fructified by bestowments from above, earth yields her increase. His gifts precede men's returns. Without sunshine and rain, there are no harvests. More widely still, God gives first before He asks. He does not gather where He has not strawed, nor reap what He has not sown. Nor does He only sow, but He "blesses the springing thereof," and to Him should the harvest be rendered. He gives before we can give. Isaiah 45:8 is closely parallel, representing in like manner the cooperation of heaven and earth in the new world of messianic times.

**85:13.** In v. 13, the thought of the blending of heaven and earth or of divine attributes as being the foundation and parents of their human analogues is still more vividly expressed. Righteousness, which in v. 10 was regarded as exercised by men and in v. 11 as looking down from heaven, is now represented both as a herald preceding God's royal progress and as following in his footsteps. But the same righteousness which precedes also follows Him and points his footsteps as the way for us. The incongruity of this double position of God's herald makes the force of the thought greater. In Him, the righteousness of God is brought near, and trusting in Him each of us may tread in his footsteps and have his righteousness fulfilled in us "who walk, not after the flesh, but after the spirit" (Rom. 8:4).

***Psalm 86.*** *This Psalm is a mosaic of quotations and familiar phrases of petition. But it is nonetheless individual, and the psalmist is heavily burdened, or less truly beseeching and trustful, because he casts his prayer into well-worn words. There is no fully developed strophical arrangement, but there is a discernible flow of thought, and the Psalm may be regarded as falling into three parts.*

*Verses 6–13 may be taken together, as the prayer proper, to which vv. 1–5 are introductory. In them, there is, first, a repetition of the cry for help and of the declaration of need (vv. 6f); then a joyful contemplation of God's unapproachable majesty and works, which insure the ultimate recognition of his name by all nations (vv. 8ff); then a profoundly and tenderly spiritual prayer for guidance and consecration—more pressing still than outward deliverance (v. 11); and, finally, as in so many Psalms, anticipatory thanksgivings for future deliverance, but conceived of as present by vivid faith.*

**86:1–5.** The first part of Ps. 86 (vv. 1–5) is a series of petitions, each supported by a plea. The petitions are the well-worn ones which spring from universal need, and there is a certain sequence in them. They begin with "Bow down thine ear," the first of a suppliant's desires, which, as it were, clears

| 5860 | 887 | 435 | 1019.151 | 420 | | 2706.131 | 112 |
|---|---|---|---|---|---|---|---|
| n ms, ps 2ms | pers pron | n mp, ps 1cs | art, v Qal act ptc ms | prep, ps 2ms | **3.** | v Qal impv 2ms, ps 1cs | n mp, ps 1cs |
| עַבְדֶּךָ | אַתָּה | אֱלֹהַי | הַבּוֹטֵחַ | אֵלֶיךָ | | חָנֵּנִי | אֲדֹנָי |
| 'avdᵉkhā | 'attāh | 'ĕlōhay | habbôṭēach | 'ēlêkhā | | chānnēnî | 'ădhōnāy |
| your servant | You | my God | the one who trusts | to You | | be gracious to me | O my Lord |

| 3706 | 420 | 7410.125 | 3725, 3219 | | 7975.331 | 5497 | 5860 | 3706 |
|---|---|---|---|---|---|---|---|---|
| cj | prep, ps 2ms | v Qal impf 1cs | *adj*, art, n ms | **4.** | v Piel impv 2ms | *n fs* | n ms, ps 2ms | cj |
| כִּי | אֵלֶיךָ | אֶקְרָא | כָּל־הַיּוֹם | | שַׂמֵּחַ | נֶפֶשׁ | עַבְדֶּךָ | כִּי |
| kî | 'ēlêkhā | 'eqōrā' | kol-hayyôm | | sammēach | nephesh | 'avdekhā | kî |
| because | to You | I will call | all the day | | make glad | the soul of | your servant | because |

| 420 | 112 | 5497 | 5558.125 | | 3706, 887 | 112 |
|---|---|---|---|---|---|---|
| prep, ps 2ms | n mp, ps 1cs | n fs, ps 1cs | v Qal impf 1cs | **5.** | cj, pers pron | n mp, ps 1cs |
| אֵלֶיךָ | אֲדֹנָי | נַפְשִׁי | אֶשָּׂא | | כִּי־אַתָּה | אֲדֹנָי |
| 'ēlêkhā | 'ădhōnāy | naphshî | 'essā' | | kî-'attāh | 'ădhōnāy |
| to You | O my Lord | my soul | I will lift up | | because You | O my Lord |

| 3005 | 5740 | 7521, 2721 | 3937, 3725, 7410.152 |
|---|---|---|---|
| adj | cj, adj | cj, *adj*, n ms | prep, *adj*, v Qal act ptc mp, ps 2ms |
| טוֹב | וְסַלָּח | וְרַב־חֶסֶד | לְכָל־קֹרְאֶיךָ |
| ṭôv | wᵉsallāch | wᵉrav-chesedh | lᵉkhol-qōrᵉ'êkhā |
| good | and ready to forgive | and abundant in steadfast love | to all those who call You |

| | 237.531 | 3176 | 8940 | 7477.531 | 904, 7249 | 8798 |
|---|---|---|---|---|---|---|
| **6.** | v Hiphil impv 2ms | pn | n fs, ps 1cs | cj, v Hiphil impv 2ms | prep, *n ms* | n mp, ps 1cs |
| | הַאֲזִינָה | יְהוָה | תְּפִלָּתִי | וְהַקְשִׁיבָה | בְּקוֹל | תַּחֲנוּנוֹתָי |
| | ha'ăzînāh | yᵉhwāh | tᵉphillāthî | wᵉhaqōshîvāh | bᵉqôl | tachnûnôthāy |
| | listen to | O Yahweh | my prayer | and be attentive | by the voice of | my supplications |

| | 904, 3219 | 7150 | 7410.125 | 3706 | 6257.123 |
|---|---|---|---|---|---|
| **7.** | prep, *n ms* | n fs, ps 1cs | v Qal impf 1cs, ps 2ms | cj | v Qal impf 2ms, ps 1cs |
| | בְּיוֹם | צָרָתִי | אֶקְרָאֶךָּ | כִּי | תַעֲנֵנִי |
| | bᵉyôm | tsārāthî | 'eqōrā'ekhā | kî | tha'ănēnî |
| | in the day of | my adversity | I will call You | because | You will answer me |

| | 3725, 3765 | 904, 435 | 112 | 375 | 3626, 4801 |
|---|---|---|---|---|---|
| **8.** | *sub*, prep, ps 2ms | prep, art, n mp | n mp, ps 1cs | cj, *sub* | prep, n mp, ps 2ms |
| | אֵין־כָּמוֹךָ | בָאֱלֹהִים | אֲדֹנָי | וְאֵין | כְּמַעֲשֶׂיךָ |
| | 'ên-kāmôkhā | vā'ĕlōhîm | 'ădhōnāy | wᵉ'ên | kᵉma'ăsêkhā |
| | there is no one like You | among the gods | O my Lord | and there is not | like your works |

| | 3725, 1504 | 866 | 6449.113 | 971.126 | 8246.726 | 3937, 6686 |
|---|---|---|---|---|---|---|
| **9.** | *adj*, n mp | rel part | v Qal pf 2ms | v Qal impf 3mp | cj, v Hithpael impf 3mp | prep, n mp, ps 2ms |
| | כָּל־גּוֹיִם | אֲשֶׁר | עָשִׂיתָ | יָבוֹאוּ | וְיִשְׁתַּחֲווּ | לְפָנֶיךָ |
| | kol-gôyim | 'ăsher | 'āsîthā | yāvô'û | wᵉyishtachwû | lᵉphānêkhā |
| | all the nations | that | You have made | they will come | and they will worship | in your presence |

| 112 | 3632.326 | 3937, 8428 | | 3706, 1448 | 887 | 6449.151 |
|---|---|---|---|---|---|---|
| n mp, ps 1cs | cj, v Piel impf 3mp | prep, n ms, ps 2ms | **10.** | cj, adj | pers pron | cj, *v Qal act ptc ms* |
| אֲדֹנָי | וִיכַבְּדוּ | לִשְׁמֶךָ | | כִּי־גָדוֹל | אַתָּה | וְעֹשֵׂה |
| 'ădhōnāy | wîkhabbᵉdhû | lishmekhā | | kî-ghādhôl | 'attāh | wᵉ'ōsēh |
| O my Lord | and they will glorify | your name | | because great | You | and One Who does |

| 6623.258 | 887 | 435 | 3937, 940 | | 3498.531 | 3176 |
|---|---|---|---|---|---|---|
| v Niphal ptc fp | pers pron | n mp | prep, n ms, ps 2ms | **11.** | v Hiphil impv 2ms, ps 1cs | pn |
| נִפְלָאוֹת | אַתָּה | אֱלֹהִים | לְבַדֶּךָ | | הוֹרֵנִי | יְהוָה |
| niphlā'ōth | 'attāh | 'ĕlōhîm | lᵉvaddekhā | | hôrênî | yᵉhwāh |
| what is extraordinary | You | God | only You | | teach me | O Yahweh |

**for I cry unto thee daily:** ... For unto thee do I cry all the day long, *ASV.*

**4. Rejoice the soul of thy servant: for unto thee, O Lord, do I lift up my soul:** ... Make glad the soul of your servant; for it is lifted up to you, O Lord, *BB* ... Give your servant joy because I lift up my heart to You, *Beck.*

**5. For thou, Lord, art good, and ready to forgive; and plenteous in mercy unto all them that call upon thee:** ... You, Lord, are kind and forgiving, full of love for all who call to You, *Beck.*

**6. Give ear, O LORD, unto my prayer; and attend to the voice of my supplications:** ... Yahweh, hear my prayer, listen to the sound of my pleading, *JB* ... LORD, hear my prayer, and listen when I ask for mercy, *NCV.*

**7. In the day of my trouble I will call upon thee: for thou wilt answer me:** ... When I'm in trouble, I call You because You answer me, *Beck.*

**8. Among the gods there is none like unto thee, O Lord; neither are there any works like unto thy works:** ... There is no god like you, O Lord; there are no works like your works, *BB.*

**9. All nations whom thou hast made shall come and worship before thee, O Lord; and shall glorify thy name:** ... All the nations you have made will come and worship before you, O Lord; they will bring glory to your name, *NIV.*

**10. For thou art great, and doest wondrous things: thou art God alone:** ... For you are great and do marvelous deeds; you alone are God, *NIV.*

---

the way for those which follow. Trusting that he will not ask in vain, the psalmist then prays that God would "keep" his soul as a watchful guardian or sentry does and that, as the result of such care, he may be saved from impending perils. Nor do his desires limit themselves to deliverance. They rise to more inward and select manifestations of God's heart of tenderness, for the prayer "Be merciful" asks for such and so goes deeper into the blessedness of the devout life than the preceding. And the crown of all these requests is "Rejoice the soul of thy servant," with the joy which flows from experience of outward deliverance and of inward whispers of God's grace, heard in the silent depths of communion with Him. It matters not that every petition has parallels in other Psalms, which this singer is quoting. His desires are nonetheless his, because they have been shared by a company of devout souls before him. His expression of them is nonetheless his, because his very words have been uttered by others. There is rest in thus associating oneself with an innumerable multitude who have cried to God. The petition in v. 1 is like that in Ps. 55:2. Verse 2 sounds like a reminiscence of Ps. 25:20; v. 3 closely resembles Ps. 57:1.

The pleas on which the petitions are grounded are also beautifully wreathed together. First, the psalmist asks to be heard because he is afflicted and poor (cf. Ps. 40:17). Our need is a valid plea with a faithful God. The sense of it drives us to Him, and our recognition of poverty and need must underlie all faithful appeal to Him. The second plea is capable of two interpretations. Here, the psalmist is urging God's gracious relation to him, which, once entered on, pledges God to unchanging continuance in manifesting his steadfast love. But, although the psalmist does not plead his character, he does, in the subsequent pleas, present his faith, his daily and day-long prayers and his lifting of his desires, aspirations and whole self above the trivialities of earth to set them on God. These are valid pleas with Him. It cannot be that trust fixed on Him should be disappointed, or that cries perpetually rising to his ears should be unanswered, or that a soul stretching its tendrils heavenward should fail to find the strong stay, around which it can cling and climb. God owns the force of such appeals and delights to be moved to answer by the spreading before Him of his servant's faith and longings.

But all of the psalmist's other pleas are merged at last in that one contained in v. 5, where he gazes on the revealed name of God and thinks of Him as He had been described of old, and as this suppliant delights to set to his seal that he has found Him to be—good and placable, and rich in steadfast love. God is his own motive, and faith can find nothing mightier to urge with God, or any surer answer to its own doubts to urge with itself, than the unfolding of all that lies in the name of the LORD. These pleas, like the petitions which they support, are largely echoes of older words. "Afflicted and poor" comes, as just noticed, from Ps. 40:17. The designation of "one whom God favors" is from Ps. 4:3. "Unto thee, O LORD, do I lift up my soul" is taken verbatim from Ps. 25:1. The explication of the contents of the name of the LORD, like the fuller one in v. 15, is based upon Exo. 34:6.

**86:6–10.** Echoes of earlier Psalms sound through the whole, but the general impression is not that of imitation, but of genuine personal need and devotion. Verse 7 is like Ps. 17:6 and other passages; v. 8a is from Exo. 15:11; v. 8b is modeled on Deut. 3:24; v. 9, on Ps. 22:27; v. 11a, on Ps. 27:11;

| 1932 | 2050.325 | 904, 583 | 3265.331 | 3949 | 3937, 3486.141 | 8428 |
|---|---|---|---|---|---|---|
| n ms, ps 2ms | v Piel impf 1cs | prep, n fs, ps 2ms | v Piel impv 2ms | n ms, ps 1cs | prep, v Qal inf con | n ms, ps 2ms |
| דַּרְכֶּךָ | אֲהַלֵּךְ | בַּאֲמִתֶּךָ | יַחֵד | לְבָבִי | לְיִרְאָה | שְׁמֶךָ |
| darkekhā | 'ăhallēkh | ba'ămittekhā | yachēdh | levāvî | leyir'āh | shemekhā |
| your way | I will walk | in your truth | unite | my heart | to fear | your name |

| 12. | 3142.525 | 112 | 435 | 904, 3725, 3949 | 3632.325 |
|---|---|---|---|---|---|
| | v Hiphil juss 1cs, ps 2ms | n mp, ps 1cs | n mp, ps 1cs | prep, *adj*, n ms, ps 1cs | cj, v Piel juss 1cs |
| | אוֹדְךָ | אֲדֹנָי | אֱלֹהַי | בְּכָל־לְבָבִי | וַאֲכַבְּדָה |
| | 'ôdhkhā | 'ădhōnāy | 'ĕlōhay | bekhol-levāvî | wa'ăkhabbedhāh |
| | let me praise You | O my Lord | my God | with all my heart | and let me glorify |

| 8428 | 3937, 5986 | 13. | 3706, 2721 | 1448 | 6142 |
|---|---|---|---|---|---|
| n ms, ps 2ms | prep, n ms | | cj, n ms, ps 2ms | adj | prep, ps 1cs |
| שִׁמְךָ | לְעוֹלָם | | כִּי־חַסְדְּךָ | גָּדוֹל | עָלָי |
| shimkhā | le'ôlām | | kî-chasdekhā | gādhôl | 'ālāy |
| your name | unto eternity | | because your steadfast love | great | concerning me |

| 5522.513 | 5497 | 4623, 8061 | 8812 | 14. | 435 | 2170 |
|---|---|---|---|---|---|---|
| cj, v Hiphil pf 2ms | n fs, ps 1cs | prep, n ms | adj | | n mp | adj |
| וְהִצַּלְתָּ | נַפְשִׁי | מִשְּׁאוֹל | תַּחְתִּיָּה | | אֱלֹהִים | זֵדִים |
| wehitstsaltā | naphshî | mishshe'ôl | tachtîyāh | | 'ĕlōhîm | zēdhîm |
| and You have rescued | my soul | from Sheol | the lowest | | O God | presumptuous |

| 7251.116, 6142 | 5920 | 6422 | 1272.316 | 5497 |
|---|---|---|---|---|
| v Qal pf 3cp, prep, ps 1cs | cj, *n fs* | adj | v Piel pf 3cp | n fs, ps 1cs |
| קָמוּ־עָלַי | וַעֲדַת | עָרִיצִים | בִּקְשׁוּ | נַפְשִׁי |
| qāmû-'ālay | wa'ădhath | 'ārîtsîm | biqōshû | naphshî |
| they have risen up against You | and an assembly of | violent | they have sought | my life |

| 3940 | 7947.116 | 3937, 5224 | 15. | 887 | 112 | 420, 7631 |
|---|---|---|---|---|---|---|
| cj, neg part | v Qal pf 3cp, ps 2ms | prep, prep, ps 3mp | | cj, pers pron | n mp, ps 1cs | n ms, adj |
| וְלֹא | שָׂמוּךָ | לְנֶגְדָּם | | וְאַתָּה | אֲדֹנָי | אֵל־רַחוּם |
| welō' | sāmûkhā | leneghdām | | we'attāh | 'ădhōnāy | 'ēl-rachûm |
| and not | they have set | before them | | but You | O my Lord | a compassionate God |

| 2688 | 774 | 653 | 7521, 2721 | 583 | 16. | 6680.131 |
|---|---|---|---|---|---|---|
| cj, adj | *adj* | n md | cj, *adj*, n ms | cj, n fs | | v Qal impv 2ms |
| וְחַנּוּן | אֶרֶךְ | אַפַּיִם | וְרַב־חֶסֶד | וֶאֱמֶת | | פְּנֵה |
| wechannûn | 'erekh | 'appayim | werav-chesedh | we'ĕmeth | | penēh |
| and gracious | long of | nostrils | and abundant in steadfast love | and reliability | | turn |

| 420 | 2706.131 | 5598.131, 6010 | 3937, 5860 | 3588.531 |
|---|---|---|---|---|
| prep, ps 1cs | cj, v Qal impv 2ms, ps 1cs | v Qal impv 2ms, n ms, ps 2ms | prep, n ms, ps 2ms | cj, v Hiphil impv 2ms |
| אֵלַי | וְחָנֵּנִי | תְּנָה־עֻזְּךָ | לְעַבְדֶּךָ | וְהוֹשִׁיעָה |
| 'ēlay | wechonnēnî | tenāh-'uzzekhā | le'avdekhā | wehôshî'āh |
| to me | and be gracious to me | give your strength | to your servant | and save |

**11. Teach me thy way, O LORD; I will walk in thy truth: unite my heart to fear thy name:** … Make your way clear to me, O Lord; I will go on my way in your faith: let my heart be glad in the fear of your name, *BB* … LORD, teach me what you want me to do, and I will live by your truth. Teach me to respect you completely, *NCV* … let my heart's one aim be to fear your name, *JB*.

**12. I will praise thee, O Lord my God, with all my heart: and I will glorify thy name for evermore:** … with my whole heart, *ASV*.

**13. For great is thy mercy toward me: and thou hast delivered my soul from the lowest hell:** … Since your love is great, O Most High, you will rescue me from deepest Sheol, *Anchor* … you have taken my soul up from the deep places of the underworld, *BB* … You have shown great love to me, and You have saved me from the deepest grave, *Beck* … thou hast delivered my soul from the lowest pit, *MRB*.

**14. O God, the proud are risen against me, and the assemblies of violent men have sought after my soul; and have not set thee before them:** ... The cruel, GOD, rose against me, False witnesses sought for my life, And before them they placed not YOUR NAME,—No fear of You was before them, *Fenton* ... O God! arrogant men have risen up against me; a gang of brutal men seek my life, *Berkeley*.

**15. But thou, O Lord, art a God full of compassion, and gracious, long-suffering, and plenteous in mercy and truth:** ... But you, my Lord, are El the Compassionate and Merciful, slow to anger, rich in kindness and fidelity, *Anchor* ... But thou, Lord, art a Lord of mercy and pity, patient, full of compassion, true to thy promise, *Knox* ... But Lord, you are a God who shows mercy and is kind. You don't become angry quickly, *NCV*.

**16. O turn unto me, and have mercy upon me; give thy strength unto thy servant, and save the son of thine handmaid:** ... Look upon

---

v. 11b, on Ps. 26:3; "Sheol beneath" is from Deut. 32:22. But, withal, there are unity and progress in this cento of citations. The psalmist begins with reiterating his cry that God would hear and in v. 7 advances to the assurance that He will. Then in vv. 8ff, he turns from all his other pleas to dwell on his final plea (v. 5) of the divine character. As in the former verse he had rested his calm hope on God's willingness to help, so now he strengthens himself in assurance of an answer by the thought of God's unmatched power, the unique majesty of his works and his sole divinity. Verse 8 might seem to assert only Yahweh's supremacy above other gods of the heathen, but v. 10 shows that the psalmist speaks the language of pure Monotheism. Most naturally, the prophetic assurance that all nations shall come and worship Him is deduced from his sovereign power and incomparableness. It cannot be that "all nations whom thou hast made" shall forever remain ignorant of the hand that made them. Sooner or later that great character will be seen by all men in its solitary elevation, and universal praise shall correspond to his sole divinity.

**86:11–13.** The thought of God's sovereign power carries the psalmist beyond remembrance of his immediate outward needs and stirs higher desires in him. Hence spring the beautiful and spiritual petitions of v. 11, which seek for clearer insight into God's will concerning the psalmist's conduct, breathe aspirations after a "walk" in that God-appointed way and culminate in one of the sweetest and deepest prayers of the Psalter: "Unite my heart to fear thy name." There, at least, the psalmist speaks words borrowed from no other, but springing fresh from his heart's depths. Jeremiah 32:39 is the nearest parallel, and the commandment in Deut. 6:5 to love God "with all thine heart" may have been in the psalmist's mind, but the prayer is all his own. He has known the misery of a divided heart, the affections and purposes of which are drawn in manifold directions and are arrayed in conflict against each other. There is no peace or blessedness, neither is any nobility of life possible, without wholehearted devotion to one great object; and there is no object capable of evoking such devotion or worthy to receive it, except Him who is "God alone." Divided love is no love. It must be all in all or not at all. With deep truth, the command to love God with all the heart is based upon his unity—"Hear, O Israel: The LORD our God is one LORD. And thou shalt love the LORD thy God with all thine heart" (Deut. 6:4f). The very conception of religion requires that it should be exclusive and should dominate the whole nature. It is only God Who is great enough to fill and engage all our capacities. As in many other Psalms, there is anticipation of an answer to the prayers, and v. 13 speaks of God's steadfast love as freshly manifested to him and of deliverance from the dismal depths of the unseen world, which threatened to swallow him up. It seems more in accordance with the usage in similar Psalms to regard v. 13 as thus recounting with prophetic certainty the coming deliverance as if it were accomplished than to suppose that in it the psalmist is falling back on former instances of God's rescuing grace.

**86:14–17.** In the closing part (vv. 14–17), the psalmist describes more precisely his danger. He is surrounded by a rabble rout of proud and violent men, whose enmity to him is, as in so many of the Psalms of persecuted singers, a proof of their forgetfulness of God. Right against this rapid outline of his perils he sets the grand unfolding of the character of God in v. 15. It is still fuller than that in v. 5 and, like it, rests on Exo. 34. Such juxtaposition is all that is needed to show how little he has to fear from the hostile crew. On the one hand, they are, in their insolence and masterfulness, eagerly hunting after his life; on the other is God, with his infinite pity and steadfast love. Happy are they who can discern high above dangers and foes the calm presence of the only God and with hearts undis-

| **3937, 1158, 526** | | **6449.131, 6196** | **225** | **3937, 3009B** | **7495.126** |
|---|---|---|---|---|---|
| prep, *n ms*, n fs, ps 2ms | **17.** | v Qal impv 2ms, prep, ps 1cs | n ms | prep, n fs | cj, v Qal juss 3mp |
| לְבֶן־אֲמָתֶךָ | | עֲשֵׂה־עִמִּי | אוֹת | לְטוֹבָה | וְיִרְאוּ |
| leven-'ămāthekhā | | 'ăsēh-'immî | 'ôth | letôvāh | weyir'û |
| the son of your female servant | | make with me | a sign | for good | that they may see |

| **7983.152** | **991.126** | **3706, 887** | **3176** | **6038.113** |
|---|---|---|---|---|
| v Qal act ptc mp, ps 1cs | cj, v Qal juss 3mp | cj, pers pron | pn | v Qal pf 2ms, ps 1cs |
| שֹׂנְאַי | וְיֵבֹשׁוּ | כִּי־אַתָּה | יְהוָה | עֲזַרְתַּנִי |
| sōne'ay | weyēvōshû | kî-'attāh | yehwāh | 'ăzartanî |
| those who hate me | that they may be ashamed | because You | O Yahweh | You have helped me |

| **5341.313** | | **3937, 1158, 7432** | **4344** | **8302** | | **3357** |
|---|---|---|---|---|---|---|
| cj, v Piel pf 2ms, ps 1cs | **87:t** | prep, *n mp*, pn | n ms | n ms | **1.** | n fs, ps 3ms |
| וְנִחַמְתָּנִי | | לִבְנֵי־קֹרַח | מִזְמוֹר | שִׁיר | | יְסוּדָתוֹ |
| wenichamtānî | | livnê-qōrach | mizmôr | shîr | | yesûdhāthô |
| and You have comforted me | | of the sons of Korah | a Psalm | a Song | | his foundations |

| **904, 2121, 7231** | | **154.151** | **3176** | **8554** | **6995** | **4623, 3725** |
|---|---|---|---|---|---|---|
| prep, *n mp*, n ms | **2.** | v Qal act ptc ms | pn | *n mp* | pn | prep, adj |
| בְּהַרְרֵי־קֹדֶשׁ | | אֹהֵב | יְהוָה | שַׁעֲרֵי | צִיּוֹן | מִכֹּל |
| behareré-qōdhesh | | 'ōhēv | yehwāh | sha'ărê | tsîyôn | mikkōl |
| on the mountains of the holy place | | One Who loves more | Yahweh | the gates of | Zion | than all |

| **5088** | **3399** | | **3632.258** | **1744.451** | **904** | **6111** | **435** |
|---|---|---|---|---|---|---|---|
| *n mp* | pn | **3.** | v Niphal ptc fp | v Pual ptc ms | prep, ps 2ms | *n fs* | art, n mp |
| מִשְׁכְּנוֹת | יַעֲקֹב | | נִכְבָּדוֹת | מְדֻבָּר | בָּךְ | עִיר | הָאֱלֹהִים |
| mishkenôth | ya'ăqōv | | nikhbādhôth | medhubbār | bākh | 'îr | hā'ĕlōhîm |
| the dwelling places of | Jacob | | glorious things | being spoken | in You | O city of | God |

| **5734** | | **2226.525** | **7581** | **928** | **3937, 3156.152** | **2079** | **6673** |
|---|---|---|---|---|---|---|---|
| intrj | **4.** | v Hiphil impf 1cs | pn | cj, pn | prep, v Qal act ptc mp, ps 1cs | intrj | pn |
| סֶלָה | | אַזְכִּיר | רַהַב | וּבָבֶל | לְיֹדְעָי | הִנֵּה | פְלֶשֶׁת |
| selāh | | 'azkîr | rahav | ûvāvel | leyōdhe'āy | hinnēh | phelesheth |
| selah | | I will cause to remember | Rahab | and Babylon | to those who know me | behold | Philistia |

| **7145** | **6196, 3688** | **2172** | **3314.411, 8427** | | **3937, 6995** | **569.221** | **382** | **382** |
|---|---|---|---|---|---|---|---|---|
| cj, pn | prep, pn | dem pron | v Pual pf 3ms, adv | **5.** | cj, prep, pn | v Niphal impf 3ms | n ms | cj, n ms |
| וְצוֹר | עִם־כּוּשׁ | זֶה | יֻלַּד־שָׁם | | וּלְצִיּוֹן | יֵאָמַר | אִישׁ | וְאִישׁ |
| wetsôr | 'im-kûsh | zeh | yulladh-shām | | ûlătsîyôn | yē'āmar | 'îsh | we'îsh |
| and Tyre | with Cush | this one | he was born there | | and of Zion | it will be said | a man | and a man |

me and be merciful to me; rescue, with thy sovereign aid, one whose mother bore him to thy service, *Knox*.

**17. Show me a token for good; that they which hate me may see it, and be ashamed:** … Work a miracle for me, O Good One, that my enemies might see and be humiliated, *Anchor* … To prove to me it is well, do a miracle, that those who hate me may see it and feel ashamed, *Beck* … Make me a wonder of Mercy, That my haters may see it and fail, *Fenton*.

**because thou, LORD, hast helped me, and comforted me:** … because You, O LORD, are my help and my comfort, *Beck*.

**87:t. A Psalm or Song for the sons of Korah.**

**1. His foundation is in the holy mountains:** … O city founded by him on the holy mountains, *Anchor* … His house is resting on the holy mountain, *BB* … It stands on the Holy Hills!, *Fenton* … God layd his foundations among the holy mountaines, *Geneva*.

**2. The LORD loveth the gates of Zion more than all the dwellings of Jacob:** … He loves its gates more than any other place in Israel, *NCV*.

**3. Glorious things are spoken of thee, O city of God:** … Noble things are said of you, O town of God, *BB* … City of God, wonderful things are said about you, *NCV*.

**Selah:** … Music, *Beck* … Pause, *JB*.

**4. I will make mention of Rahab and Babylon to them that know me:** … I shall inscribe Rahab and

Babylon among those who acknowledge me, *Anchor* ... I will count Egypt and Babylon among those who acknowledge Me, *Beck* ... I will count Egypt and Babylon among my friends, *NEB.*

**behold Philistia, and Tyre, with Ethiopia; this man was born there:** ... There is Philistia, Tyre, and Ethiopia—each one claims that he was born there, *Beck* ... People from Philistia, Tyre, and Cush will be born there, *NCV.*

**5. And of Zion it shall be said, This and that man was born in her:** ... But it will be said of Zion, Every race is born in her, *Beck* ... but Sion!—her name shall be Mother, for every follower of mine belongs to her by birth, *Moffatt* ... and Zion shall be called a mother in whom men of every race are born, *NEB.*

**and the highest himself shall establish her:** ... and the Most

---

tracted and undismayed can oppose to all that assails them the impenetrable shield of the name of the LORD! It concerns our peaceful fronting of the darker facts of life, that we cultivate the habit of never looking at dangers or sorrows without seeing the helping God beside and above them.

The Psalm ends with prayer for present help. If God is, as the psalmist has seen Him to be, "full of compassion, and gracious," it is no presumptuous petition that the streams of these perfections should be made to flow toward a needy suppliant. "Be gracious to me" asks that the light, which pours through the universe, may fall on one heart, which is surrounded by earth-born darkness. As in the introductory verses, so in the closing petitions, the psalmist grounds his prayer principally on God's manifested character and secondarily on his own relationship to God. Thus, in v. 16, he pleads that he is God's servant and "the son of thine handmaid" (cf. Ps. 116:16). That expression does not imply any special piety in the psalmist's mother, but pleads his hereditary relation as servant to God. To the devout heart, all common things are from God and bear witness for Him. Even blind eyes and hard hearts may be led to see and feel that God is the helper and comforter of humble souls who trust in Him. A heart that is made at peace with itself by the ear of God and has but one dominant purpose and desire will long for God's mercies, not only because they have a bearing on its own outward well-being, but because they will demonstrate that it is no vain thing to wait on the LORD. They may lead some, who cherished enmity to God's servant and alienation from himself, to learn the sweetness of his name and the security of trust in Him.

***Psalm 87.*** *The structure of this Psalm is simple. The Psalm is divided by selah into two strophes, to which a closing verse is appended. The first strophe bursts abruptly into rapturous praise of Zion, the beloved of God. The second predicts the gathering of all nations into her citizenship, and the closing verse apparently paints the exuberant joy of the festal crowds, who shall then throng her streets.*

**87:1–3.** The abrupt beginning of the first strophe offends some commentators, who have tried to smooth v. 1 into propriety and tameness by suggesting possible preliminary clauses, which they suppose to have dropped out. But there is no canon which forbids a singer, with the rush of inspiration on him, either poetic or other, to plunge into the heart of his theme.

The psalmist's fervent love for Jerusalem is something more than national pride. It is the apotheosis of that emotion, clarified and hallowed into religion. Zion is founded by God himself. The mountains on which it stands are made holy by the divine dwelling. On their heads shines a glory before which the light that lies on the rock crowned by the Parthenon or on the seven hills of Rome pales. Not only is the Temple mountain meant, but the city is the psalmist's theme. The hills on which it stands are emblems of the firmness of its foundation in the divine purpose on which it reposes. It is beloved of God, and that, as the form of the word "loves" (HED #154) shows, with an abiding affection. The "glorious things" which are spoken of Zion may be either the immediately following divine oracle or, more probably, prophetic utterances, such as many of those in Isaiah, which predict its future glory. The divine utterance which follows expresses the substance of these. So far, the Psalm is not unlike other outpourings in praise of Zion, such as Ps. 48. But in the second strophe, to which the first is introductory, the singer strikes a note all his own.

**87:4–6.** There can be no doubt as to who the speaker is in v. 4. The abrupt introduction of a divine oracle accords with a normal usage in the Psalter, which adds much to the solemnity of the words. If we regard the "glorious things" mentioned in v. 3 as being the utterances of earlier prophets, the psalmist has had his ears purged to hear God's voice, by meditation on and sympathy with these. The faithful use of what God has said prepares for hearing further disclosures of his lips. The enumeration of nations in v. 4 carries a great

| 3314.411, 904 | 2000 | 3679.321 | 6169 | | 3176 | 5807.121 |
|---|---|---|---|---|---|---|
| v Pual pf 3ms, prep, ps 3fs | cj, pers pron | v Polel impf 3ms, ps 3fs | n ms | | pn | v Qal impf 3ms |
| יֻלַּד־בָּהּ | וְהוּא | יְכוֹנְנֶהָ | עֶלְיוֹן | 6. | יְהוָה | יִסְפֹּר |
| yulladh-bāhh | wehû' | yekhôneneāh | ‘elyôn | | yehwāh | yispōr |
| he will be born in her | and He | He will establish her | the Most High | | Yahweh | He will record |

| 904, 3918.141 | 6194 | 2172 | 3314.411, 8427 | 5734 | | 8301.152 | 3626, 2591.152 |
|---|---|---|---|---|---|---|---|
| prep, v Qal inf con | n mp | dem pron | v Pual pf 3ms, adv | intrj | | v Qal act ptc mp | prep, v Qal act ptc mp |
| בִּכְתוֹב | עַמִּים | זֶה | יֻלַּד־שָׁם | סֶלָה | 7. | וְשָׁרִים | כְּחֹלְלִים |
| bikhthôv | ‘ammîm | zeh | yulladh-shām | selāh | | weshārîm | kechōlelîm |
| when writing | peoples | this one | he was born there | selah | | and singers | like flute players |

| 3725, 4754 | 904 | | 8302 | 4344 | 3937, 1158 | 7432 | 3937, 5514.351 |
|---|---|---|---|---|---|---|---|
| *adj*, n mp, ps 1cs | prep, ps 2ms | | n ms | n ms | prep, *n mp* | pn | prep, art, v Piel ptc ms |
| כָּל־מַעְיָנַי | בָּךְ | 88:t | שִׁיר | מִזְמוֹר | לִבְנֵי | קֹרַח | לַמְנַצֵּחַ |
| kol-ma‘äyānay | bākh | | shîr | mizmôr | livnê | qōrach | lamnatstseāch |
| all my springs | in You | | a Song | a Psalm | of the sons of | Korah | to the director |

| 6142, 4395 | 3937, 6257.341 | 5030 | 3937, 2037 | 249 | | 3176 | 435 |
|---|---|---|---|---|---|---|---|
| prep, n fs | prep, v Piel inf con | n ms | prep, pn | art, pn | | pn | *n mp* |
| עַל־מַחֲלַת | לְעַנּוֹת | מַשְׂכִּיל | לְהֵימָן | הָאֶזְרָחִי | 1. | יְהוָה | אֱלֹהֵי |
| ‘al-māchălath | le‘annôth | maskîl | lehêmān | hā'ezrāchî | | yehwāh | 'ĕlōhê |
| on the mahalath | leannoth | a Maskil | of Heman | the Ezrahite | | Yahweh | the God of |

| 3568 | 3219, 7094.115 | 904, 4050 | 5224 | | 971.122 | 3937, 6686 |
|---|---|---|---|---|---|---|
| n fs, ps 1cs | n ms, v Qal pf 1cs | prep, art, n ms | prep, ps 2ms | | v Qal juss 3fs | prep, n mp, ps 2ms |
| יְשׁוּעָתִי | יוֹם־צָעַקְתִּי | בַלַּיְלָה | נֶגְדֶּךָ | 2. | תָּבוֹא | לְפָנֶיךָ |
| yeshû‘āthî | yôm-tsā‘aqŏttî | vallaylāh | neghdekhā | | tāvô' | lephānêkhā |
| my salvation | by day I have cried out | in the night | before You | | may it come | in your presence |

| 8940 | 5371.531, 238 | 3937, 7726 | | 3706, 7881.112 |
|---|---|---|---|---|
| n fs, ps 1cs | v Hiphil impv 2ms, n fs, ps 2ms | prep, n fs, ps 1cs | | cj, v Qal pf 3fs |
| תְּפִלָּתִי | הַטֵּה־אָזְנְךָ | לְרִנָּתִי | 3. | כִּי־שָׂבְעָה |
| tephillāthî | hattēh-'oznekhā | lerinnāthî | | kî-sāve‘āh |
| my prayer | incline your ear | to my lamentation | | because it has become satiated |

| 904, 7750 | 5497 | 2522 | 3937, 8061 | 5236.511 | | 2913.215 |
|---|---|---|---|---|---|---|
| prep, n fp | n fs, ps 1cs | cj, n mp, ps 1cs | prep, pn | v Hiphil pf 3ms | | v Niphal pf 1cs |
| בְרָעוֹת | נַפְשִׁי | וְחַיַּי | לִשְׁאוֹל | הִגִּיעוּ | 4. | נֶחְשַׁבְתִּי |
| verā‘ôth | naphshî | wechayyay | lish'ôl | higgî‘û | | nechshavtî |
| with troubles | my soul | and my life | to Sheol | it has approached | | I have been reckoned |

High will make her secure, *Anchor* … God Most High will strengthen her, *NCV.*

**6. The LORD shall count, when he writeth up the people, that this man was born there:** … The Lord will keep in mind, when he is writing the records of the people, that this man had his birth there, *BB* … The LORD writes in the Book of the Peoples, That 'There the MESSIAH was born,' *Fenton.*

**Selah:** … Music, *Beck* … Pause, *JB.*

**7. As well the singers as the players on instruments shall be there: all my springs are in thee:** … And all who have suffered in you will sing as well as dance, *Anchor* … They that sing as well as they that dance shall say, All my fountains are in thee, *ASV* … There will be singing and dancing, for all will find their home in you, *Beck* … Singers and dancers alike say, 'The source of all good is in you', *REB.*

**88:t. A Song or Psalm for the sons of Korah, to the chief Musician upon Mahalath Leannoth, Maschil of Heman the Ezrahite.**

**1. O LORD God of my salvation, I have cried day and night before thee:** … I call for help by day, O LORD, my God; I cry before thee at night, *Goodspeed* … LORD God, day and night I cry bitterly to thee, *Knox* … O LORD, my God, by day I cry out; at night I clamor in your presence, *NAB.*

**2. Let my prayer come before thee: incline thine ear unto my cry:** … may my prayer reach your presence, hear my cry for help, *JB.*

**3. For my soul is full of troubles:** … For my soul is full of evils, *BB* …

I've had enough troubles, *Beck* ... My body is filled full of pains, *Fenton* ... For I am filled with misery, *JB.*

**and my life draweth nigh unto the grave:** ... and my life has reached Sheol, *Anchor* ... and my life has come near to the underworld, *BB.*

**4. I am counted with them that go down into the pit:** ... I count as one of those who go down into the abyss, *Knox.*

**I am as a man that hath no strength:** ... I have become like a man for whom there is no help, *BB* ... I am as a man without manly strength, *Berkeley.*

**5. Free among the dead, like the slain that lie in the grave, whom thou rememberest no more: and they are cut off from thy hand:** ... In Death is my cot like the slaughtered, My couch is in the Grave, Where you remember them no longer, cut off as they are from your love, *Anchor* ... My soul is among the dead, like those in the underworld, to

---

lesson. First comes the ancient enemy, Egypt, designated by the old name of contempt (Rahab, i.e. pride), but from which the contempt has faded; then follows Babylon, the more recent inflicter of many miseries, once so detested, but toward whom animosity has died down. Philistia was the old neighbor and foe, which from the beginning had hung on the skirts of Israel and been ever ready to utilize her disasters and add to them. Tyre is the type of godless luxury and inflated material prosperity and, although often in friendly alliance with Israel, as being exposed to the same foes which harassed her, she was as far from knowing God as the other nations were. Cush, or Ethiopia, seems mentioned as a type of distant peoples rather than because of its hostility to Israel. "That man was born in her." God's voice ceases, and in v. 5 the psalmist takes up the wonderful promise which he has just heard. He slightly shifts his point of view, for while the nations that were to be gathered into Zion were named in the divine utterance, the Zion into which they are gathered is foremost in the Psalm.

Verse 6 represents Yahweh as writing the names of individuals in the book and of saying in regard to each as He writes, "This man was born there." In like manner, in v. 5 the form of expression is "this and that man," which brings out the same thought, with the addition that there is an unbroken series of new citizens. It is by accession of single souls that the population of Zion is increased. God's register resolves the community into its component units. Men are born one by one, and one by one they enter the true kingdom. In the ancient world, the community was more than the individual.

**87:7.** Verse 7 is extremely obscure because it is so abrupt and condensed. But probably the translation adopted above, although by no means free from difficulty or doubt, brings out the meaning which is most in accordance with the preceding. It may be supposed to flash vividly before the reader's imagination the picture of a triumphal procession of rejoicing citizens, singers as well as dancers, who chant as they advance a joyous chorus in praise of the city in which they have found all fountains of joy and satisfaction welling up for their refreshment and delight.

***Psalm 88.*** *The resulting division into three parts gives, first, the psalmist's description of his hopeless condition as, in effect, already dead (vv. 1–8); second, an expostulation with God on the ground that, if the psalmist is actually numbered with the dead, he can no more be the object of divine help, nor bring God praise (vv. 9–12); and, third, a repetition of the thoughts of the first part, with slight variation and addition.*

**88:1–2.** The central portion of the first division is occupied with an expansion of the thought that the psalmist is already as good as dead (vv. 3b–6). The condition of the dead is drawn with a powerful hand, and the picture is full of solemn grandeur and hopelessness. It is preceded in vv. 1f by an invocation which has many parallels in the Psalms, but which here is peculiarly striking. This saddest of them all has for its first words the name which ought to banish sadness. He who can call on Yahweh as the God of his salvation has power to still agitation and to flush despair with some light of hope as from an unrisen sun. But this poet feels no warmth from the beams, and the mists surge up, if not to hide the light, yet to obscure it. All the more admirable, then, is the persistence of his cry; and all the more precious the lesson that faith is not to let present experience limit its conceptions. God is nonetheless the God of salvation and nonetheless to be believed to be so, although no consciousness of his saving power blesses the heart at the moment.

**88:3–5.** With "for" in v. 3, the psalmist begins the dreary description of his affliction, the desperate and all-but-deadly character which he spreads before God as a reason for hearing his prayer. Despair sometimes strikes men dumb, and sometimes makes them eloquent. The sorrow which has

| 6196, 3495.152 | 988 | 2030.115 | 3626, 1429 | 375, 357 |
|---|---|---|---|---|
| prep, *v Qal act ptc mp* | n ms | v Qal pf 1cs | prep, n ms | *sub*, n ms |
| עִם־יוֹרְדֵי | בוֹר | הָיִיתִי | כְּגֶבֶר | אֵין־אֱיָל |
| 'im-yôrdhê | vôr | hāyîthî | keghever | 'ên-'ĕyāl |
| with those who go down to | the Pit | I am | like a mighty man | there is not strength |

5.

| 904, 4322.152 | 2775 | 3765 | 2592 | 8311.152 | 7197 | 866 | 3940 |
|---|---|---|---|---|---|---|---|
| prep, art, v Qal act ptc mp | adj | prep | adj | *v Qal act ptc mp* | n ms | rel pron | neg part |
| בַּמֵּתִים | חָפְשִׁי | כְּמוֹ | חֲלָלִים | שֹׁכְבֵי | קֶבֶר | אֲשֶׁר | לֹא |
| bammēthîm | chāpheshî | kemô | chălālîm | shōkhevê | qever | 'ăsher | lō' |
| among the dead | free | like | the slain | those who lie in | a tomb | who | not |

| 2226.113 | 5968 | 2065 | 4623, 3135 | 1535.216 |
|---|---|---|---|---|
| v Qal pf 2ms, ps 3mp | adv | cj, pers pron | prep, n fs, ps 2ms | v Niphal pf 3cp |
| זְכַרְתָּם | עוֹד | וְהֵמָּה | מִיָּדְךָ | נִגְזָרוּ |
| zekhartām | 'ôdh | wehēmmāh | mîyādhekhā | nighzārû |
| You remember them | anymore | and they | from your hand | they have been cut down |

6.

| 8308.113 | 904, 988 | 8812 | 904, 4423 | 904, 4852 | 7. | 6142 |
|---|---|---|---|---|---|---|
| v Qal pf 2ms, ps 1cs | prep, *n ms* | adj | prep, n mp | prep, n fp | | prep, ps 1cs |
| שַׁתַּנִי | בְּבוֹר | תַּחְתִּיּוֹת | בְּמַחֲשַׁכִּים | בִּמְצֹלוֹת | | עָלַי |
| shattanî | bevôr | tachtîyôth | bemachshakkîm | bimtsōlôth | | 'ālay |
| You have put me | in the Pit | lower | in the dark places | in the depths | | upon me |

| 5759.112 | 2635 | 3725, 5053 | 6257.313 | 5734 |
|---|---|---|---|---|
| v Qal pf 3fs | n fs, ps 2ms | cj, *adj*, n mp, ps 2ms | v Piel pf 2ms | intrj |
| סָמְכָה | חֲמָתֶךָ | וְכָל־מִשְׁבָּרֶיךָ | עִנִּיתָ | סֶלָה |
| sāmekhāh | chămāthekhā | wekhol-mishbārêkhā | 'innîthā | selāh |
| it has leaned | your wrath | and all your waves | You have afflicted with | selah |

8.

| 7651.513 | 3156.456 | 4623 | 8308.113 |
|---|---|---|---|
| v Hiphil pf 2ms | v Pual ptc mp, ps 1cs | prep, ps 1cs | v Qal pf 2ms, ps 1cs |
| הִרְחַקְתָּ | מְיֻדָּעַי | מִמֶּנִּי | שַׁתַּנִי |
| hirchaqtā | meyuddā'ay | mimmenî | shattanî |
| You have caused to be far away | those whom I know | from me | You have made me into |

| 8774 | 3937 | 3727.155 | 3940 | 3428.125 | 9. | 6084 | 1717.112 |
|---|---|---|---|---|---|---|---|
| n fp | prep, ps 3mp | v Qal pass ptc ms | cj, neg part | v Qal impf 1cs | | n fs, ps 1cs | v Qal pf 3fs |
| תוֹעֵבוֹת | לָמוֹ | כָּלֻא | וְלֹא | אֵצֵא | | עֵינִי | דָּאֲבָה |
| thô'ēvôth | lāmô | kālu' | welō' | 'ētsē' | | 'ênî | dhā'ăvāh |
| abominable things | to them | restrained | and not | I can go out | | my eye | it has pined |

| 4655 | 6271 | 7410.115 | 3176 | 904, 3725, 3219 | 8275.315 |
|---|---|---|---|---|---|
| prep | n ms | v Qal pf 1cs, ps 2ms | pn | prep, *adj*, n ms | v Piel pf 1cs |
| מִנִּי | עֹנִי | קְרָאתִיךָ | יְהוָה | בְּכָל־יוֹם | שִׁטַּחְתִּי |
| minî | 'ōnî | qōrā'thîkhā | yehwāh | bekhol-yôm | shittachtî |
| from | affliction | I have called to You | O Yahweh | during every day | I have spread out |

whom you give no more thought; for they are cut off from your care, *BB* … I am stiff, like the wounded to death, Who forgotten, are laid in the tomb, And who are cut off from Your side, *Fenton* … I have been left as dead, like a body lying in a grave whom you don't remember anymore, cut off from your care, *NCV.*

**6. Thou hast laid me in the lowest pit, in darkness, in the deeps:** … I am sunk in the depth of the Pit; In the gloom and the Shadow of Death, *Fenton* … Such is the place where thou hast laid me, in a deep pit where the dark waters swirl, *Knox* … You have plunged me into the bottom of the pit, into the dark abyss, *NAB.*

**7. Thy wrath lieth hard upon me, and thou hast afflicted me with all thy waves:** … Your anger lies heavy on me; with all Your waves You overwhelm me, *Beck* … heavily thy anger weighs down on me, and thou dost overwhelm me with its full flood, *Knox.*

**Selah:** … Music, *Beck* … Pause, *JB*

**8. Thou hast put away mine acquaintance far from me; thou hast made me an abomination unto them:** ... You have taken my friends far away from me and made them loathe me, *Beck* ... You have taken from me my closest friends and have made me repulsive to them, *NIV.*

**I am shut up, and I cannot come forth:** ... I am shut in and can't get out, *Beck* ... I lie in a prison whence there is no escape, *Knox.*

**9. Mine eye mourneth by reason of affliction:** ... My eyes are wasting away because of my trouble, *BB* ... and my health pines away under my trouble, *Moffatt* ... My eyes are weak from crying, *NCV* ... my eyes are dim with grief, *NIV.*

**LORD, I have called daily upon thee, I have stretched out my hands unto thee:** ... I have called upon thee, O LORD, all day long; I have spread out my hands toward thee, *Goodspeed* ... LORD, I have prayed to you every day; I have lifted my hands in prayer to you, *NCV.*

**10. Wilt thou shew wonders to the dead?:** ... Do You do wonderful things for the dead, *Beck* ... Do you show your miracles for the dead?, *NCV.*

**shall the dead arise and praise thee?:** ... will the shades come back to give you praise?, *BB* ... Do their ghosts get up and praise You, *Beck.*

---

a voice is less crushing than that which is tongueless. This overcharged heart finds relief in self-pitying depiction of its burdens and in the exercise of a gloomy imagination, which draws out in detail the picture of the feebleness, the recumbent stillness, the seclusion and darkness of the dead. They have "no strength." Their vital force has ebbed away, and they are but as weak shadows, having an impotent existence which does not deserve to be called life. The remarkable expression of v. 5, "free among the dead," is to be interpreted in the light of Job 3:19, which counts it as one blessing of the grave that there "the servant is free from his master." But the psalmist thinks that "freedom" is loathsome, not desirable, for it means removal from the stir of a life the heaviest duties and cares of which are better than the torpid immunity from these, which makes the state of the dead a dreary monotony. They lie stretched out and motionless. No ripple of cheerful activity stirs that stagnant sea. One unvarying attitude is theirs. It is not the stillness of rest which prepares for work, but of incapacity of action or of change. They are forgotten by Him Who remembers all that are. They are parted from the guiding and blessing influence of the hand that upholds all being. In some strange fashion, they are and yet are not.

**88:6.** Their death has a representation of life. Their shadowy life is death. Being and non-being may both be predicated of them. The psalmist speaks in riddles and looks into its gloomy depths, and he sees little but gloom. It needed the resurrection of Jesus to flood these depths with light and to completely show that the life beyond may be fuller of bright activity than life here—a state in which vital strength is increased beyond all earthly experience and wherein God's all-quickening hand grasps more closely and communicates richer gifts than are attainable in that death which sense calls life.

**88:7.** Verse 7 traces the psalmist's sorrows to God. It breathes not complaints but submission, or at least recognition of his hand, and they who in the very outburst of their pains still exalt God to his rightful position are not far from saying, "Let Him do what seemeth Him good" (Judg. 10:15) or from the peace that comes from a compliant will. The recognition implies, too, consciousness of sin which has deserved the wrath of God, and in such consciousness lies the germ of blessing. Sensitive nerves may quiver, as they feel the dreadful weight with which that wrath presses down on them as if to crush them, but if the man lies still and lets the pressure do its work, it will not force out his life, but only his evil, as foul water is squeezed from cloth.

**88:8.** Verse 8 approaches nearer to a specification of the psalmist's affliction. If taken literally, it points to some loathsome disease which had long clung to him and made even his friends shrink from companionship, and thus had condemned him to isolation. The desertion by friends is a common feature in the psalmists' complaints. The seclusion, as in a prison house, is, no doubt, appropriate to a quarantined condition, but may also simply refer to the loneliness and compulsory inaction arising from heavy trials.

**88:9–12.** If the recurring cry to Yahweh in v. 9 is taken, as we have suggested it should be, as marking a new turn in the thoughts, the second part of the Psalm will include vv. 9–12. Verses 1–12 are apparently the daily prayer referred to in v. 9. They appeal to God to preserve the psalmist from the state of death, which he has just depicted himself as having in effect already entered, by the consideration which is urged in other Psalms as a reason for divine intervention (6:5; 30:9; etc.), namely, that his power had no field for its manifestation in the grave and that He could draw no revenue of praise from

| 420 | 3834 | | 1950B, 3937, 4322.152 | 6449.123, 6624 |
|---|---|---|---|---|
| prep, ps 2ms | n fd, ps 1cs | 10. | intrg part, prep, art, v Qal act ptc mp | v Qal impf 2ms, n ms |
| אֵלֶיךָ | כַּפָּי | | הֲלַמֵּתִים | תַּעֲשֶׂה־פֶּלֶא |
| 'ēlêkhā | khappāy | | helammēthîm | ta'āseh-pele' |
| to You | my hands | | for the dead | will You do extraordinary deeds |

| 524, 7787 | 7251.126 | 3142.526 | 5734 | | 1950B, 5807.421 |
|---|---|---|---|---|---|
| cj, n mp | v Qal impf 3mp | v Hiphil juss 3mp, ps 2ms | intrj | 11. | intrg part, v Pual impf 3ms |
| אִם־רְפָאִים | יָקוּמוּ | יוֹדוּךָ | סֶלָה | | הַיְסֻפַּר |
| 'im-rephā'îm | yāqûmû | yôdhûkhā | selāh | | haysuppar |
| or the shadows of the dead | will they rise | let them praise You | selah | | will it be recounted |

| 904, 7197 | 2721 | 536 | 904, 11 | | 1950B, 3156.221 |
|---|---|---|---|---|---|
| prep, art, n ms | n ms, ps 2ms | n fs, ps 2ms | prep, art, n ms | 12. | intrg part, v Niphal impf 3ms |
| בַּקֶּבֶר | חַסְדֶּךָ | אֱמוּנָתְךָ | בָּאֲבַדּוֹן | | הֲיִוָּדַע |
| baqqever | chasdekhā | 'ĕmûnāthekhā | bā'ăvaddôn | | hăyiwwādha' |
| in the tomb | your steadfast love | your faithfulness | in Abaddon | | will it be known |

| 904, 2932 | 6624 | 6930 | 904, 800 | 5570 |
|---|---|---|---|---|
| prep, art, n ms | n ms, ps 2ms | cj, n fs, ps 2ms | prep, *n fs* | n fs |
| בַּחֹשֶׁךְ | פִּלְאֶךָ | וְצִדְקָתְךָ | בְּאֶרֶץ | נְשִׁיָּה |
| bachōshekh | pil'ekhā | wetsidhqāthekhā | be'erets | neshîyāh |
| in the darkness | your extraordinary deeds | and your righteousness | in the land of | forgetfulness |

| | 603 | 420 | 3176 | 8209.315 | 904, 1269 | 8940 |
|---|---|---|---|---|---|---|
| 13. | cj, pers pron | prep, ps 2ms | pn | v Piel pf 1cs | cj, prep, art, n ms | n fs, ps 1cs |
| | וַאֲנִי | אֵלֶיךָ | יְהוָה | שִׁוַּעְתִּי | וּבַבֹּקֶר | תְּפִלָּתִי |
| | wa'ănî | 'ēlêkhā | yehwāh | shiwwa'ättî | ûvabbōqer | tephillāthî |
| | but I | to You | O Yahweh | I have cried for help | and in the morning | my prayer |

| 7207.322 | | 4066 | 3176 | 2269.123 | 5497 | 5846.523 | 6686 |
|---|---|---|---|---|---|---|---|
| v Piel impf 3fs, ps 2ms | 14. | intrg | pn | v Qal impf 2ms | n fs, ps 1cs | v Hiphil impf 2ms | n mp, ps 2ms |
| תְּקַדְּמֶךָּ | | לָמָה | יְהוָה | תִּזְנַח | נַפְשִׁי | תַּסְתִּיר | פָּנֶיךָ |
| theqaddemekhā | | lāmāh | yehwāh | tiznach | naphshî | tastîr | pānêkhā |
| it has been before You | | why | O Yahweh | do You reject | me | do You hide | your face |

| 4623 | | 6270 | 603 | 1510.151 | 4623, 5471 | 5558.115 | 372 |
|---|---|---|---|---|---|---|---|
| prep, ps 1cs | 15. | adj | pers pron | cj, v Qal act ptc ms | prep, n ms | v Qal pf 1cs | n fp, ps 2ms |
| מִמֶּנִּי | | עָנִי | אֲנִי | וְגֹוֵעַ | מִנֹּעַר | נָשָׂאתִי | אֵמֶיךָ |
| mimmenî | | 'ānî | 'ănî | weghōwēa' | minnō'ar | nāsā'thî | 'ēmêkhā |
| from me | | afflicted | I | and dying | from a youth | I have borne | your terrors |

| 6566.125 | | 6142 | 5882.116 | 2841 | 1190 |
|---|---|---|---|---|---|
| v Qal juss 1cs | 16. | prep, ps 1cs | v Qal pf 3cp | n mp, ps 2ms | n mp, ps 2ms |
| אָפוּנָה | | עָלַי | עָבְרוּ | חֲרוֹנֶיךָ | בִּעוּתֶיךָ |
| 'āphûnāh | | 'ālay | 'āverû | chărônêkhā | bi'ûthêkhā |
| let me become weary | | over me | they have passed | your wrath | your terrors |

| 7059.316 | | 5621.116 | 3626, 4448 | 3725, 3219 |
|---|---|---|---|---|
| v Pilel pf 3cp, ps 1cs | 17. | v Qal pf 3cp, ps 1cs | prep, art, n md | *adj*, art, n ms |
| צִמְּתוּתֻנִי | | סַבּוּנִי | כַּמַּיִם | כָּל־הַיּוֹם |
| tsimmethûthunî | | sabbûnî | khammayim | kol-hayyôm |
| they have silenced me | | they have surrounded me | like the waters | all the day |

| 5545.516 | 6142 | 3266 | | 7651.513 | 4623 |
|---|---|---|---|---|---|
| v Hiphil pf 3cp | prep, ps 1cs | adv | 18. | v Hiphil pf 2ms | prep, ps 1cs |
| הִקִּיפוּ | עָלַי | יָחַד | | הִרְחַקְתָּ | מִמֶּנִּי |
| hiqqîphû | 'ālay | yāchadh | | hirchaqōttā | mimmenî |
| they have encircled | upon me | together | | You have caused to be far away | from me |

**Selah:** ... Music, *Beck* ... Pause, *JB.*

**11. Shall thy lovingkindness be declared in the grave? or thy faithfulness in destruction?:** ... Will the story of your mercy be given in the house of the dead? will news of your faith come to the place of destruction?, *BB* ... Does anybody in the grave tell about Your love, do they talk about Your faithfulness in that place of decay, *Beck* ... Will your loyalty be told in the place of death?, *NCV.*

**12. Shall thy wonders be known in the dark? and thy righteousness in the land of forgetfulness?:** ... Are your wonders made known in the darkness, or your justice in the land of oblivion?, *NAB.*

**13. But unto thee have I cried, O LORD; and in the morning shall my prayer prevent thee:** ... But to You I have cried, O LORD; and in the morning my prayer shall go before You, *KJVII.*

**14. LORD, why castest thou off my soul? why hidest thou thy face from me?:** ... Then why do You, LORD, leave my soul, And hide up Your Presence from me?, *Fenton.*

**15. I am afflicted and ready to die from my youth up: while I suffer thy terrors I am distracted:** ... I have been troubled and in fear of death from the time when I was young; your wrath is hard on me, and I have no strength, *BB* ... I am afflicted and dying from early life; while I suffer Your terrors, I pine away, *KJVII.*

**16. Thy fierce wrath goeth over me; thy terrors have cut me off:** ... Thy blazing anger passes over me; Thy terrors destroy me, *Berkeley.*

**17. They came round about me daily like water; they compassed me about together:** ... they surround me like water all day long; together they encircle me, *Berkeley.*

**18. Lover and friend hast thou put far from me, and mine acquaintance into darkness:** ... You have sent my friends and lovers far from me; I am gone from the memory of those who are dear to me, *BB* ... You have removed from me anyone who might love me or be a friend. The friend I know is—darkness, *Beck* ... Companion and neighbor you have taken away from me; my only friend is darkness, *NCB.*

---

the pale lips that lay silent there. The conception of the state of the dead is even more dreary than that in vv. 4f. They are "shades," which conveys the idea of relaxed feebleness. Their dwelling is Abaddon—"destruction," "darkness," "the land of forgetfulness," whose inhabitants neither remember nor are remembered, either by God or man. In that cheerless region, God had no opportunity to show his wonders of delivering mercy, for monotonous immobility was stamped upon it, and out of that realm of silence no glad songs of praise could sound. Such thoughts are in startling contrast with the hopes that sparkle in some Psalms (such as 16:10; etc.), and they show that clear, permanent assurance of future blessedness was not granted to the ancient Church. Nor could there be sober certainty of it until after Christ's resurrection. But it is also to be noticed that this Psalm neither affirms nor denies a future resurrection. It does affirm continuous personal existence after death, however thin and shadowy. It is not concerned with what may lie far ahead, but is speaking of the present state of the dead, as it was conceived of at that stage of revelation by a devout soul in its hours of despondency.

**88:13–14.** The last part (vv. 13–18) is marked, like the two preceding, by the repetition of the name of Yahweh and of the allusion to the psalmist's continual prayer. It is remarkable and perhaps significant that the time of prayer should here be "the morning." The psalmist had asked in v. 2 that his prayer might enter into God's presence; he now vows that it will come to meet Him. Possibly some lightening of his burden may be hinted at by the reference to the time of his petition. Morning is the hour of hope, of new vigor, of a fresh beginning, which may not be merely a prolongation of dreary yesterdays. But if there is any such alleviation, it is only for a moment, and then the cloud settles down still more heavily. But one thing the psalmist has won by his cry: He now longs to know the reason for his affliction. He is confident that God is righteous when He afflicts, and heavy as his sorrow is, he has passed beyond mere complaint concerning it to the wish to understand it.

**88:15–18.** Such a cry is never offered in vain, even though it should be followed, as it is here, by plaintive reiterations of the sufferer's pains. These are now little more than a summary of the first part. The same idea of being in effect dead even while alive is repeated in v. 15, in which the psalmist wails that from youth he has been but a dying man, so close to him had death seemed, or so death-like had been his life. He has borne God's terrors until he is distracted. The word rendered "I am distracted" (HED #6566) is only used here in the OT and consequently is obscure. In v. 16, the word for "wrath" (HED #2841) is in the plural, to express the manifold outbursts of that deadly indignation. The word means

| 154.151 | 7739 | 3156.456 | 4423 | | 5030 | 3937, 394 |
|---|---|---|---|---|---|---|
| v Qal act ptc ms | cj, n ms | v Pual ptc mp, ps 1cs | n ms | **89:t** | n ms | prep, pn |
| אֹהֵב | וָרֵעַ | מְיֻדָּעַי | מַחְשָׁךְ | | מַשְׂכִּיל | לְאֵיתָן |
| 'ōhēv | wārēa' | meyuddā'ay | machshākh | | maskîl | le'êthān |
| those who love | and friends | those known by me | a dark place | | a Maskil | of Ethan |

| 249 | | 2721 | 3176 | 5986 | 8301.125 | 3937, 1810 | 1810 |
|---|---|---|---|---|---|---|---|
| art, pn | **1.** | *n mp* | pn | n ms | v Qal juss 1cs | prep, n ms | cj, n ms |
| הָאֶזְרָחִי | | חַסְדֵי | יְהוָה | עוֹלָם | אָשִׁירָה | לְדֹר | וָדֹר |
| hā'ezrāchî | | chasdhê | yehwāh | 'ôlām | 'āshîrāh | ledhōr | wādhōr |
| the Ezrahite | | the steadfast love of | Yahweh | forever | let me sing | unto generations | and generations |

| 3156.525 | 536 | 904, 6552 | | 3706, 569.115 | 5986 |
|---|---|---|---|---|---|
| v Hiphil impf 1cs | n fs, ps 2ms | prep, n ms, ps 1cs | **2.** | cj, v Qal pf 1cs | n ms |
| אוֹדִיעַ | אֱמוּנָתְךָ | בְּפִי | | כִּי־אָמַרְתִּי | עוֹלָם |
| 'ôdhîa' | 'ĕmûnāthekhā | bephî | | kî-'āmartî | 'ôlām |
| I will cause to know | your faithfulness | with my mouth | | because I have said | forever |

| 2721 | 1161.221 | 8452 | 3679.523 | 536 | 904 |
|---|---|---|---|---|---|
| n ms | v Niphal impf 3ms | n md | v Hiphil impf 2ms | n fs, ps 2ms | prep, ps 3mp |
| חֶסֶד | יִבָּנֶה | שָׁמַיִם | תָּכִן | אֱמוּנָתְךָ | בָהֶם |
| chesedh | yibbāneh | shāmayim | tākhin | 'ĕmûnāthekhā | vāhem |
| steadfast love | it was built | the heavens | You established | your faithfulness | in them |

| | 3901.115 | 1311 | 3937, 1008 | 8123.215 | 3937, 1784 | 5860 | | 5912, 5986 |
|---|---|---|---|---|---|---|---|---|
| **3.** | v Qal pf 1cs | n fs | prep, n ms, ps 1cs | v Niphal pf 1cs | prep, pn | n ms, ps 1cs | **4.** | adv, n ms |
| | כָּרַתִּי | בְרִית | לִבְחִירִי | נִשְׁבַּעְתִּי | לְדָוִד | עַבְדִּי | | עַד־עוֹלָם |
| | kārattî | verîth | livchîrî | nishba'ttî | ledhāwidh | 'avdî | | 'adh-'ôlām |
| | I have cut | a covenant | for my chosen one | I swore | to David | my servant | | until forever |

| 3679.525 | 2320 | 1161.115 | 3937, 1810, 1810 | 3802 | 5734 |
|---|---|---|---|---|---|
| v Hiphil impf 1cs | n ms, ps 2ms | cj, v Qal pf 1cs | prep, n ms, cj, n ms | n ms, ps 2ms | intrj |
| אָכִין | זַרְעֲךָ | וּבָנִיתִי | לְדֹר־וָדוֹר | כִּסְאֲךָ | סֶלָה |
| 'ākhîn | zar'ekhā | ûvānîthî | ledhōr-wādhôr | kis'ăkhā | selāh |
| I will establish | your seed | and I will build | for generations and generations | your throne | selah |

**89:t. Maschil of Ethan the Ezrahite.**

**1. I will sing of the mercies of the LORD for ever:** ... Your love, Yahweh, for ever shall I sing, *Anchor* ... I will sing of Your love forever, *Beck* ... The favors of the LORD I will sing for ever, *NAB.*

**with my mouth will I make known thy faithfulness to all generations:** ... I will make known to all coming ages how faithful You are, *Beck* ... age after age I shall proclaim your fidelity, *Anchor* ... Throughout the ages I will proclaim thy faithfulness with my mouth, *Goodspeed* ... Young and old shall hear of your blessings, *LIVB.*

**2. For I have said, Mercy shall be built up for ever:** ... Kindness will be renewed forever, *Goodspeed* ... Your grace is forever built, *Beck* ... for thy love hast promised to be lasting, *Moffatt* ... Thy true love is as firm as the ancient earth, *NEB.*

**thy faithfulness shalt thou establish in the very heavens:** ... The heavens! Thou dost establish Thy faithfulness in them, *Young* ... you have fixed your constancy firm in the heavens, *JB* ... how You firmly set up Your faithfulness there, *Beck* ... thy faithfulness fixed as the heavens, *NEB.*

**3. I have made a covenant with my chosen:** ... covenant with mine elect, *Darby* ... With my chosen a Treaty I made, *Fenton* ... I have made an agreement with the man of my selection, *BB* ... solemn agreement with my chosen servant David, *LIVB.*

**I have sworn unto David my servant:** ... David My Slave, *Fenton* ... I have made an oath to David my servant, *BB* ... I have made a promise to my servant David, *NCV* ... sworn an oath to my servant David, *JB.*

**4. Thy seed will I establish for ever:** ... Forever will I confirm your posterity, *NCB* ... Establish your line for ever, *REB* ... made your dynasty firm for ever, *JB* ... A descendant of yours will always be king, *Good News.*

**and build up thy throne to all generations:** ... built your throne stable age after age, *JB* ... age after age I will bid thy throne endure, *Knox* ... Your kingdom will go on and on, *NCV* ... I will preserve your dynasty forever, *Good News.*

literally "heat," and we may represent the psalmist's thought as being that the wrath shoots forth many fierce tongues of licking flame or, like a lava stream, pours out in many branches. The word rendered "cut me off" (HED #7059) is anomalous and is variously translated "annihilate," "extinguish" or as above. The wrath which was a fiery flame in v. 16 is an overwhelming flood in v. 17. The complaint of v. 8 recurs in v. 18 in still more tragic form. All human sympathy and help are far away, and the psalmist's only familiar friend is darkness. There is an infinitude of despair in that sad irony. But there is a gleam of hope, although faint and far, like faint daylight seen from the innermost recesses of a dark tunnel, in his recognition that his dismal solitude is the work of God's hand; for, if God has made a heart or a life empty of human love, it is that He may himself fill it with his own sweet and all-compensating presence.

***Psalm 89.*** *The foundation of this Psalm is the promise in 2 Sam. 7, which guaranteed the perpetuity of the Davidic kingdom. Many of the characteristic phrases of the prophecy recur here—the promises that the children of wickedness shall not afflict them and that the transgressions of David's descendants should be followed by chastisement only, not by rejection. The contents of Nathan's oracle are first given in brief in vv. 3f and again in detail and with poetic embellishments in vv. 19–37.*

*The complaint and petitions of the latter part are the true burden of the Psalm, to which the celebration of divine attributes in vv. 1–18 and the expansion of the fundamental promise in vv. 19–37 are meant to lead up. The attributes specified are those of faithfulness (vv. 1f, 5, 8, 14) and of power, which render the fulfillment of God's promises certain. By such contemplations, the psalmist would fortify himself against the whispers of doubt, which were beginning to make themselves heard in his mind and would find in the character of God both assurance that his promise shall not fail and a powerful plea for his prayer that it may not fail.*

*The structure of the Psalm can scarcely be called strophical. There are three well-marked turns in the flow of thought: first, the hymn to the divine attributes (vv. 1–18); second, the expansion of the promise, which is the basis of the monarchy (vv. 19–37); and, finally, the lament and prayer that God would be true to his attributes and promises in view of present afflictions (vv. 38–51). For the most part, the verses are grouped in pairs which are occasionally lengthened into triplets.*

**89:1–2.** The psalmist begins with announcing the theme of his song—the steadfast love and faithfulness of God. Surrounded by disasters, which seem in violent contradiction to God's promise to David, he falls back on thoughts of the mercy which gave it and the faithfulness which will surely accomplish it. The resolve to celebrate these in such circumstances argues a faith victorious over doubt and a faith putting forth energetic efforts to maintain itself. This bird can sing in mid-winter. True, the song has other notes than joyous ones, but they, too, extol God's steadfast love and faithfulness even while they seem to question them. Self-command, which insists on a man's averting his thoughts from a gloomy outward presence to gaze on God's loving purpose and unalterable veracity, is no small part of practical religion. The psalmist will sing because he said that these two attributes were ever in operation and lasting as the heavens. "Mercy shall be built up for ever," its various manifestations being conceived as each being a stone in the stately building which is in continual course of progress through all ages and can never be completed, since fresh stones will continually be laid as long as God lives and pours forth his blessings. Much less can it ever fall into ruin, as impatient sense would persuade the psalmist that it is doing in his day. The parallel declaration as to God's faithfulness takes the heavens as the type of duration and immobility and conceives that attribute to be eternal and fixed, as they are. These convictions could not burn in the psalmist's heart without forcing him to speak. Lover, poet and devout man, in their several ways, feel the same necessity of utterance. Not every Christian can sing, but all can and should speak. They will, if their faith is strong.

**89:3–5.** The divine promise on which the Davidic throne rests is summed up in the abruptly introduced pair of verses (vv. 3f). That promise is the second theme of the Psalm; and just as the overture in some great musical composition sounds for the first time phrases which are to be recurrent and elaborated in the sequel, so its ruling thoughts are briefly put in the first four verses of the Psalm. Verses 1f stand first, but are second in time to vv. 3f. God's oracle preceded the singer's praise. The language of these two verses echoes the original passage in 2 Sam. 7, as in "David my servant," "establish, for ever" and "build," expressions which were used in v. 2, with a view to their recurrence in v. 4. The music keeps before the mind the perpetual duration of David's throne.

| 5. | 3142.526 | 8452 | 6624 | 3176 | 652, 536 |
|---|---|---|---|---|---|
| | cj, v Hiphil impf 3mp | n md | n ms, ps 2ms | pn | cj, n fs, ps 2ms |
| | וְיוֹדוּ | שָׁמַיִם | פִּלְאֲךָ | יְהוָה | אַף־אֱמוּנָתְךָ |
| | weyôdhû | shāmayim | pil'ăkhā | yehwāh | 'aph-'ĕmûnāthekhā |
| | and they praise | the heavens | your extraordinary deeds | O Yahweh | also your reliability |

| 904, 7235 | 7202 | 6. | 3706 | 4449 | 904, 8262 | 6424.121 |
|---|---|---|---|---|---|---|
| prep, *n ms* | n mp | | cj | intrg | prep, art, n ms | v Qal impf 3ms |
| בִּקְהַל | קְדֹשִׁים | | כִּי | מִי | בַשַּׁחַק | יַעֲרֹךְ |
| biqŏhal | qŏdhōshîm | | kî | mî | vashshachaq | ya'ărōkh |
| in the assembly of | the holy ones | | because | who | in the clouds | will he be set in order |

| 3937, 3176 | 1880.121 | 3937, 3176 | 904, 1158 | 418 | 7. | 418 | 6442.255 |
|---|---|---|---|---|---|---|---|
| prep, pn | v Qal impf 3ms | prep, pn | prep, *n mp* | n mp | | n ms | v Niphal ptc ms |
| לַיהוָה | יִדְמֶה | לַיהוָה | בִּבְנֵי | אֵלִים | | אֵל | נַעֲרָץ |
| layhwāh | yidhmeh | layhwāh | bivnê | 'ēlîm | | 'ēl | na'ărāts |
| opposite Yahweh | will he be like | Yahweh | among the sons of | the gods | | God | terrifying |

| 904, 5660, 7231 | 7521 | 3486.255 | 6142, 3725, 5623 |
|---|---|---|---|
| prep, *n ms*, n mp | adj | cj, v Niphal ptc ms | prep, *adj*, sub, ps 3ms |
| בְּסוֹד־קְדֹשִׁים | רַבָּה | וְנוֹרָא | עַל־כָּל־סְבִיבָיו |
| besôdh-qŏdhōshîm | rabbāh | wenôrā' | 'al-kol-sevîvâv |
| in the consultation of the holy ones | great | and fearful | above all that is around Him |

| 8. | 3176 | 435 | 6893 | 4449, 3765 | 2731 | 3161 | 536 | 5623 |
|---|---|---|---|---|---|---|---|---|
| | pn | *n mp* | n fp | intrg, prep, ps 2ms | adj | pn | cj, n fs, ps 2ms | sub, ps 2ms |
| | יְהוָה | אֱלֹהֵי | צְבָאוֹת | מִי־כָמוֹךָ | חֲסִין | יָהּ | וֶאֱמוּנָתְךָ | סְבִיבוֹתֶיךָ |
| | yehwāh | 'ĕlōhê | tsevā'ôth | mî-khāmôkhā | chăsîn | yāhh | we'ĕmûnāthekhā | sevîvôthêkhā |
| | O Yahweh | God of | Hosts | who like You | strong | O Yah | and your truth | all around You |

| 9. | 887 | 5090.151 | 904, 1375 | 3328 | 904, 5558.141 | 1570 | 887 |
|---|---|---|---|---|---|---|---|
| | pers pron | v Qal act ptc ms | prep, *n fs* | art, n ms | prep, v Qal inf con | n mp, ps 3ms | pers pron |
| | אַתָּה | מוֹשֵׁל | בְּגֵאוּת | הַיָּם | בְּשׂוֹא | גַלָּיו | אַתָּה |
| | 'attāh | môshēl | beghē'ûth | hayyām | besô' | ghallâv | 'attāh |
| | You | the Ruler | over the raging of | the sea | when lifting up | its waves | You |

| 8099.323 | 10. | 887 | 1850.313 | 3626, 2592 | 7581 | 904, 2307 |
|---|---|---|---|---|---|---|
| v Piel impf 2ms, ps 3mp | | pers pron | v Piel pf 2ms | prep, art, n ms | pn | prep, *n fs* |
| תְשַׁבְּחֵם | | אַתָּה | דִכִּאתָ | כֶחָלָל | רָהַב | בִּזְרוֹעַ |
| theshabbechēm | | 'attāh | dhikki'thā | khechālāl | rāhav | bizrôa' |
| You quiet them | | You | You have crushed | like the slain | Rahab | with the arm of |

| 6010 | 6582.313 | 342.152 | 11. | 3937 | 8452 | 652, 3937 |
|---|---|---|---|---|---|---|
| n ms, ps 2ms | v Piel pf 2ms | v Qal act ptc mp, ps 2ms | | prep, ps 2ms | n md | cj, prep, ps 2ms |
| עֻזְּךָ | פִּזַּרְתָּ | אוֹיְבֶיךָ | | לְךָ | שָׁמַיִם | אַף־לְךָ |
| 'uzzekhā | pizzartā | 'ôyvêkhā | | lekhā | shāmayim | 'aph-lekhā |
| your strength | You scattered | your enemies | | to You | the heavens | also to You |

| 800 | 8725 | 4530 | 887 | 3354.113 | 12. | 7103 | 3332 |
|---|---|---|---|---|---|---|---|
| n fs | n fs | cj, n ms, ps 3fs | pers pron | v Qal pf 2ms, ps 3mp | | n ms | cj, n fs |
| אָרֶץ | תֵּבֵל | וּמְלֹאָהּ | אַתָּה | יְסַדְתָּם | | צָפוֹן | וְיָמִין |
| 'ārets | tēvēl | ûmelō'āhh | 'attāh | yesadhtām | | tsāphôn | weyāmîn |
| the earth | the world | and its fulness | You | You have founded them | | the north | and the south |

| 887 | 1282.113 | 8724 | 2874 | 904, 8428 | 7728.326 |
|---|---|---|---|---|---|
| pers pron | v Qal pf 2ms, ps 3mp | pn | cj, pn | prep, n ms, ps 2ms | v Piel impf 3mp |
| אַתָּה | בְרָאתָם | תָּבוֹר | וְחֶרְמוֹן | בְּשִׁמְךָ | יְרַנֵּנוּ |
| 'attāh | verā'thām | tāvôr | wechermôn | beshimkhā | yerannēnû |
| You | You created them | Tabor | and Hermon | in your name | they shout for joy |

**Selah:** ... Music, *Beck* ... Pause, *JB.*

**5. And the heavens shall praise thy wonders, O LORD:** ... euen the heauens shall prayse thy wonderous worke, *Geneva* ... the heavens confess Thy wonders, *Young* ... The heavens sing of the wonderful things you do, *Good News.*

**thy faithfulness also in the congregation of the saints:** ... Yea thy faithfulness in the convocation of holy ones, *Rotherham* ... in the divine assembly, *Goodspeed* ... in the assembly of holy ones, *Berkeley.*

**6. For who in the heaven can be compared unto the LORD?:** ... For who in the skies can rank with the Lord?, *NCB* ... In the skies who is there like the LORD, *NEB* ... who above can rank with the Eternal, *Moffatt* ... are not those heavens, Lord, witnesses of thy wonderful power, *Knox.*

**who among the sons of the mighty can be likened unto the LORD?:** ... Who among the heavenly beings is like the LORD, *RSV* ... who like the LORD in the court of heaven, *REB* ... what angel can compare with the Eternal?, *Moffatt.*

**7. God is greatly to be feared in the assembly of the saints:** ... When the holy ones meet, it is God they fear, *NCV* ... A God dreaded in the great council of the holy ones, *MAST* ... God is terrible in the council of the holy ones, *NAB* ... in the council of the holy ones, *NASB.*

**and to be had in reverence of all them that are about him:** ... And awesome above all those who are around Him?, *NASB* ... He is more frightening than all who surround him, *NCV* ... and to be honoured over all those who are about him, *BB* ... too great and awesome for all around him, *Anchor.*

**8. O LORD God of hosts, who is a strong LORD like unto thee?:** ... LORD God of armies, who is like You, *Beck* ... who can compare with thee, *Moffatt* ... who is mighty as thou art, *RSV* ... who is equal to You, *Fenton.*

**or to thy faithfulness round about thee?:** ... in all thy love and faithfulness?, *Moffatt* ... Your Strength, LIFE, and Truth are around, *Fenton* ... your faithful ones surround you, *Anchor* ... you are powerful and completely trustworthy, *NCV.*

**9. Thou rulest the raging of the sea: when the waves thereof arise, thou stillest them:** ... Thy sway is over the proud sea, *Moffatt* ... proud swelling of the sea, *MAST* ... rule over the sea in storm, *BB* ... calming the turmoil of its wave, *REB.*

**10. Thou hast broken Rahab in pieces, as one that is slain; thou hast scattered thine enemies with thy strong arm:** ... crushed Rahab with a mortal blow, *NCB* ... wounded lies Rahab at thy feet, by the strong arm that has routed thy enemies, *Knox* ... When Rahab You trod down to death, And Your foes with a strong arm dispersed, *Fenton* ... You crushed the sea monster Rahab; by your power you scattered your enemies, *NCV.*

**11. The heavens are thine, the earth also is thine: as for the world and the fulness thereof, thou hast founded them:** ... The skies and earth belong to you, *NCV* ... the world and everything in it—You made them, *Beck* ... author, thou, of the world and all it holds, *Knox* ... You formed the World's sphere and its times, *Fenton.*

**12. The north and the south thou hast created them: Tabor and Hermon shall rejoice in thy name:**

---

**89:6–8.** In vv. 6–18, the psalmist sets forth the power and faithfulness of God, which ensure the fulfillment of his promises. He is the incomparably great and terrible God Who subdues the mightiest forces of nature and tames the proudest nations (vv. 9f), Who is Maker and Lord of the world (vv. 11f), Who rules with power, but also with righteousness, faithfulness and grace (vv. 13f), and Who, therefore, makes his people blessed and safe (vv. 15–18). Since God is such a God, his promise cannot remain unfulfilled. Power and willingness to execute it to the last tittle are witnessed by heaven and earth, by history and experience. Dark as the present may be, it would, therefore, be folly to doubt for a moment.

The psalmist begins his contemplations of the glory of the divine nature with figuring the very heavens as vocal with his praise. Not only the object, but the givers of that praise are noteworthy. The heavens are personified, as in Ps. 19, and from their silent depths comes music. There is One higher, mightier, older, more unperturbed, pure and enduring than they, Whom they extol by their luster which they owe to Him. They praise God's "wonder" (which here means not so much his marvelous acts, as the wonderfulness of his being, his incomparable greatness and power) and his faithfulness, the two guarantees of the fulfillment of his promises. Nor are the visible heavens his only praisers. The holy ones, sons of the mighty—the angels—bow before Him Who is high above their holiness and might and own Him for God alone.

**89:9–18.** With v. 9, the hymn descends to earth and magnifies God's power and faithfulness as manifested there. The sea is, as always, the emblem of rebellious tumult. Its insolence is calmed by Him. And the proudest of the nations, such as Rahab ("Pride," a current name for Egypt), had cause to own his power when He brought the waves of the sea over

| 13. | 3937 | 2307 | 6196, 1400 | 6022.122 | 3135 | 7597.122 | 3332 |
|---|---|---|---|---|---|---|---|
| | prep, ps 2ms | n fs | prep, n fs | v Qal impf 3fs | n fs, ps 2ms | v Qal impf 3fs | n fs, ps 2ms |
| | לְךָ | זְרוֹעַ | עִם־גְּבוּרָה | תָּעֹז | יָדְךָ | תָּרוּם | יְמִינֶךָ |
| | lekhā | zerôa' | 'im-gevûrāh | tā'ōz | yādhekhā | tārûm | yemînekhā |
| | to You | an arm | with might | it is strong | your hand | it is high | your right hand |

| 14. | 6928 | 5122 | 4487 | 3802 | 2721 | 583 |
|---|---|---|---|---|---|---|
| | n ms | cj, n ms | *n ms* | n ms, ps 2ms | n ms | cj, n fs |
| | צֶדֶק | וּמִשְׁפָּט | מְכוֹן | כִּסְאֶךָ | חֶסֶד | וֶאֱמֶת |
| | tsedheq | ûmishpāṯ | mekhôn | kis'ekhā | chesedh | we'ĕmeth |
| | righteousness | and justice | the foundation of | your throne | steadfast love | and reliability |

| 7207.326 | 6686 | 15. | 869 | 6194 | 3156.152 | 8980 | 3176 |
|---|---|---|---|---|---|---|---|
| v Piel impf 3mp | n mp, ps 2ms | | *n mp* | art, n ms | *v Qal act ptc mp* | n fs | pn |
| יְקַדְּמוּ | פָנֶיךָ | | אַשְׁרֵי | הָעָם | יוֹדְעֵי | תְרוּעָה | יְהוָה |
| yeqaddemû | phānêkhā | | 'ashrê | hā'ām | yôdh'ê | therû'āh | yehwāh |
| they meet | your face | | blessed | the people | those who know | a shout | O Yahweh |

| 904, 214, 6686 | 2050.326 | 16. | 904, 8428 | 1559.126 | 3725, 3219 |
|---|---|---|---|---|---|
| prep, *n ms*, n mp, ps 2ms | v Piel impf 3mp | | prep, n ms, ps 2ms | v Qal impf 3mp | *adj*, art, n ms |
| בְּאוֹר־פָּנֶיךָ | יְהַלֵּכוּן | | בְּשִׁמְךָ | יְגִילוּן | כָּל־הַיּוֹם |
| be'ôr-pānêkhā | yehallēkhûn | | beshimkhā | yeghîlûn | kol-hayyôm |
| by the light of your face | they walk | | in your name | they rejoice | all the day |

| 904, 6930 | 7597.126 | 17. | 3706, 8930 | 6010 | 887 |
|---|---|---|---|---|---|
| cj, prep, n fs, ps 2ms | v Qal impf 3mp | | cj, *n fs* | n ms, ps 3mp | pers pron |
| וּבְצִדְקָתְךָ | יָרוּמוּ | | כִּי־תִפְאֶרֶת | עֻזָּמוֹ | אָתָּה |
| ûvetsidhqāthekhā | yārûmû | | kî-thiph'ereth | 'uzzāmô | 'āttāh |
| and in your righteousness | they exult | | because the splendor of | their strength | You |

| 904, 7814 | 7597.122 | 7451 | 18. | 3706 | 3937, 3176 | 4182 |
|---|---|---|---|---|---|---|
| cj, prep, n ms, ps 2ms | v Qal impf 3fs | n fs, ps 1cp | | cj | prep, pn | n ms, ps 1cp |
| וּבִרְצֹנְךָ | תָּרִים | קַרְנֵנוּ | | כִּי | לַיהוָה | מָגִנֵּנוּ |
| ûvirtsōnekhā | tārîm | qarnēnû | | kî | layhwāh | māghinnēnû |
| and by your favor | it is exalted | our horn | | because | to Yahweh | our Shield |

| 3937, 7202 | 3547 | 4567 | 19. | 226 | 1744.313, 904, 2469 |
|---|---|---|---|---|---|
| cj, prep, *n ms* | pn | n ms, ps 1cp | | adv | v Piel pf 2ms, prep, n ms |
| וְלִקְדוֹשׁ | יִשְׂרָאֵל | מַלְכֵּנוּ | | אָז | דִּבַּרְתָּ־בְחָזוֹן |
| weliqōdhôsh | yisrā'ēl | malkēnû | | 'āz | dibbartā-vechāzôn |
| and to the Holy One of | Israel | our King | | then | You spoke with a vision |

… The north wind and the south are of thy fashioning; thy name wakes the glad echoes of Thabor and Hermon, *Knox* … You created Zaphon and Amanus, Tabor and Hermon ring out with Your name, *Beck* … Tabor and Hermon, applaud to Your Name, *Fenton* … Tabor and Hermon hills acclaim thee, *Moffatt.*

**13. Thou hast a mighty arm: strong is thy hand, and high is thy right hand:** … God of the strong arm, the sure, the uplifted hand, *Knox* … Strength of arm and valour are thine; thy hand is mighty, thy right hand lifted high, *NEB* … Your arm is endued with power; your hand is strong, your right hand exalted, *NIV* … Yours is a powerful arm, O Warrior! your left hand is triumphant, your right hand raised in victory!, *Anchor.*

**14. Justice and judgment are the habitation of thy throne: mercy and truth shall go before thy face:** … Faithful love and Constancy march before you, *JB* … The seat of thy kingdom is resting on righteousness and right judging: mercy and good faith come before your face, *BB* … Your Throne stands on Goodness and Right, Before You, march Mercy and Truth, *Fenton.*

**15. Blessed is the people that know the joyful sound: they shall walk, O LORD, in the light of thy countenance:** … Blessed are those who have learned to acclaim you, who walk in the light of your presence, *NIV* … Happy is the people that knows well the shout of praise, that lives, Lord, in the smile of thy protection!, *Knox* … happy are the people who know the festal trumpet-call,

*Goodspeed* ... they walk in the light of Your face, *Beck.*

**16. In thy name shall they rejoice all the day: and in thy righteousness shall they be exalted:** ... In Your Name they can laugh all the day; And can in Your Goodness exult, *Fenton* ... Evermore they take pride in thy name, rejoice over thy just dealings, *Knox* ... They rejoice in your presence all day, and are jubilant over your generosity, *Anchor* ... All day long they exult, O thou Eternal, and extol they equity, *Moffatt.*

**17. For thou art the glory of their strength: and in thy favour our horn shall be exalted:** ... For thou art our pride, thou are strength, and, thanks to thy favour, our honour is high, *Moffatt* ... You are the flower of their strength, by your favour our strength is triumphant, *JB* ... You are yourself the strength in which they glory; through your favour we hold our heads high, *REB* ... in your pleasure will our horn be lifted up, *BB.*

**18. For the LORD is our defence; and the Holy One of Israel is our king:** ... For our shield appertaineth to the Lord, *Geneva* ... because the LORD is our ruler, *Beck* ... we are defended by the Eternal, by our King, the Majestic One of Israel,

---

her hosts, thus in one act exemplifying his sovereign sway over both nature and nations. He is Maker and therefore Lord of heaven and earth. In all quarters of the world, his creative hand is manifest, and his praise sounds. Tabor and Hermon may stand, as the parallelism requires, for west and east, although some suppose that they are simply named as conspicuous summits. They "shall rejoice in thy name" is an expression like that used in v. 16 in reference to Israel. The poet thinks of the softly swelling Tabor with its verdure and of the lofty Hermon with its snows, as sharing in that gladness and praising Him to Whom they owe their beauty and majesty. Creation vibrates with the same emotions which thrill the poet. The sum of all the preceding is gathered up in v. 13, which magnifies the might of God's arm.

But more blessed still for the psalmist in the midst of national gloom is the other thought of the moral character of God's rule. His throne is broad-based upon the sure foundation of righteousness and justice. The pair of attributes always closely connected—namely, steadfast love and faithfulness—are here, as frequently, personified. They "go before thy face," that is, in order to present themselves before Him. "The two genii of the his tory of redemption (Ps. 43:3) stand before his countenance, like attendant maidens, waiting the slightest indication of his will" (Delitzsch).

Since God is such a God, his Israel is blessed, whatever its present plight. So the psalmist closes the first part of his song with rapturous celebration of the favored nation's prerogatives. "The festal shout" or "the trumpet-blast" is probably the music at the festivals (Num. 23:21; 31:6), and "those who know it" means "those who are familiar with the worship of this great God." The elements of their blessedness are then unfolded. "They walk in the light of thy countenance." Their outward life is passed in continual happy consciousness of the divine presence, which becomes to them a source of gladness and guidance. "In thy name shall they rejoice all the day." God's self-manifestation, and the knowledge of Him which arises therefrom, become the occasion of a calm, perpetual joy, which is secure from change, because its roots go deeper than the region where change works. "In thy righteousness shall they be exalted." Through God's strict adherence to his Covenant, not by any power of their own, shall they be lifted above foes and fears. "Thou art the glory of their strength." In themselves they are weak, but God, not any arm of flesh, is their strength, and by possession of Him they are not only clothed with might, but resplendent with beauty. Human power is often unlovely; God-given strength is, like armor inlaid with gold, ornament as well as defense. "In thy favour our horn shall be exalted." The psalmist identifies himself at last with the people whose blessedness he has so glowingly celebrated. He could keep up the appearance of distinction no longer. "They" gives place to "we" unconsciously, as his heart swells with the joy which he paints. Depressed as he and his people are for the moment, he is sure that there is lifting up. The emblem of the lifted horn is common, as expressive of victory. The psalmist is confident of Israel's triumph, because he is certain that the nation, as represented by and, as it were, concentrated in its king, belongs to God, Who will not lose what is his. The rendering of v. 18 in the KJV cannot be sustained. "Defence" in the first clause is parallel with "our king" in the second, and the meaning of both clauses is that the king of Israel is God's, and therefore, secure. That ownership rests on the promise to David, and on it, in turn, is rested the psalmist's confidence that Israel and its king are possessed of a charmed life and shall be exalted, however now abject and despondent.

**89:19–25.** The second part (vv. 19–37) draws out in detail, and at some points with heightened col-

| 3937, 2728 | 569.123 | 8187.315 | 6039 | 6142, 1399 | 7597.515 |
|---|---|---|---|---|---|
| prep, n mp, ps 2ms | cj, v Qal impf 2ms | v Piel pf 1cs | n ms | prep, adj | v Hiphil pf 1cs |
| לַחֲסִידֶיךָ | וַתֹּאמֶר | שִׁוִּיתִי | עֵזֶר | עַל־גִּבּוֹר | הֲרִימוֹתִי |
| lachsîdhêkhā | wattō'mer | shiwwîthî | 'ēzer | 'al-gibbôr | h$^{e}$rîmôthî |
| to your godly ones | and You said | I have set | help | upon the mighty | and I have exalted |

| 1013.155 | 4623, 6194 | | 4834.115 | 1784 | 5860 | 904, 8467 | 7231 |
|---|---|---|---|---|---|---|---|
| v Qal pass ptc ms | prep, n ms | **20.** | v Qal pf 1cs | pn | n ms, ps 1cs | prep, *n ms* | n ms, ps 1cs |
| בָּחוּר | מֵעָם | | מָצָאתִי | דָּוִד | עַבְדִּי | בְּשֶׁמֶן | קָדְשִׁי |
| vāchûr | mē'ām | | mātsā'thî | dāwidh | 'avdî | b$^{e}$shemen | qādh$^{e}$shî |
| a chosen one | from the people | | I have found | David | my servant | with the oil of | my holiness |

| 5066.115 | | 866 | 3135 | 3679.222 | 6196 | 652, 2307 |
|---|---|---|---|---|---|---|
| v Qal pf 1cs, ps 3ms | **21.** | cj | n fs, ps 1cs | v Niphal impf 3fs | prep, ps 3ms | cj, n fs, ps 1cs |
| מְשַׁחְתִּיו | | אֲשֶׁר | יָדִי | תִּכּוֹן | עִמּוֹ | אַף־זְרוֹעִי |
| m$^{e}$shachtîw | | 'ăsher | yādhî | tikkôn | 'immô | 'aph-z$^{e}$rô'î |
| I have anointed him | | because | my hand | it is permanently | with him | also my arm |

| 563.322 | | 3940, 5565.521 | 342.151 | 904 |
|---|---|---|---|---|
| v Piel impf 3fs, ps 3ms | **22.** | neg part, v Hiphil impf 3ms | v Qal act ptc ms | prep, ps 3ms |
| תְּאַמְּצֶנּוּ | | לֹא־יַשִּׁא | אוֹיֵב | בּוֹ |
| th$^{e}$'amm$^{e}$tsennû | | lō'-yashshi' | 'ôyēv | bô |
| it will strengthen him | | not he will lend | an enemy | with him |

| 1158, 5983 | 3940 | 6257.321 | | 3936.115 | 4623, 6686 |
|---|---|---|---|---|---|
| cj, *n ms*, n fs | neg part | v Piel impf 3ms, ps 3ms | **23.** | cj, v Qal pf 1cs | prep, n mp, ps 3ms |
| וּבֶן־עַוְלָה | לֹא | יְעַנֶּנּוּ | | וְכַתּוֹתִי | מִפָּנָיו |
| ûven-'awlāh | lō' | y$^{e}$'annennû | | w$^{e}$khattôthî | mippānâv |
| and the son of wickedness | not | he will afflict him | | I will hammer | before him |

| 7141 | 7983.356 | 5238.125 | | 536 | 2721 |
|---|---|---|---|---|---|
| n mp, ps 3ms | cj, v Piel ptc mp, ps 3ms | v Qal impf 1cs | **24.** | cj, n fs, ps 1cs | cj, n ms, ps 1cs |
| צָרָיו | וּמְשַׂנְאָיו | אֶגּוֹף | | וֶאֱמוּנָתִי | וְחַסְדִּי |
| tsārâv | ûm$^{e}$san'âv | 'eggōph | | we'ĕmûnāthî | w$^{e}$chasdî |
| his adversaries | and those who hate him | I will strike | | and my reliability | and my steadfast love |

| 6196 | 904, 8428 | 7597.122 | 7451 | | 7947.115 | 904, 3328 |
|---|---|---|---|---|---|---|
| prep, ps 3ms | cj, prep, n ms, ps 1cs | v Qal impf 3fs | n fs, ps 3ms | **25.** | cj, v Qal pf 1cs | prep, art, n ms |
| עִמּוֹ | וּבִשְׁמִי | תָּרוּם | קַרְנוֹ | | וְשַׂמְתִּי | בַיָּם |
| 'immô | ûvishmî | tārûm | qarnô | | w$^{e}$samtî | vayyām |
| with him | and in my name | it will be exalted | his horn | | and I will put | on the sea |

| 3135 | 904, 5282 | 3332 | | 2000 | 7410.121 | 1 | 887 |
|---|---|---|---|---|---|---|---|
| n fs, ps 3ms | cj, prep, art, n mp | n fs, ps 3ms | **26.** | pers pron | v Qal impf 3ms, ps 1cs | n ms, ps 1cs | pers pron |
| יָדוֹ | וּבַנְּהָרוֹת | יְמִינוֹ | | הוּא | יִקְרָאֵנִי | אָבִי | אַתָּה |
| yādhô | ûvann$^{e}$hārôth | y$^{e}$mînô | | hû' | yiqŏrā'ēnî | 'āvî | 'attāh |
| his hand | and on the rivers | his right hand | | he | he will call Me | my Father | You |

| 418 | 6962 | 3568 | | 652, 603 | 1111 | 5598.125 |
|---|---|---|---|---|---|---|
| n ms, ps 1cs | cj, *n ms* | n fs, ps 1cs | **27.** | cj, pers pron | n ms | v Qal impf 1cs, prep, ps 3ms |
| אֵלִי | וְצוּר | יְשׁוּעָתִי | | אַף־אָנִי | בְּכוֹר | אֶתְּנֵהוּ |
| 'ēlî | w$^{e}$tsûr | y$^{e}$shû'āthî | | 'aph-'ānî | b$^{e}$khôr | 'ett$^{e}$nēhû |
| my God | and the Rock of | my salvation | | also I | the firstborn | I will allow to him |

| 6169 | 3937, 4567, 800 | | 3937, 5986 | 8490.125, 3937 |
|---|---|---|---|---|
| n ms | prep, *n mp*, n fs | **28.** | prep, n ms | v Qal impf 1cs, prep, ps 3ms |
| עֶלְיוֹן | לְמַלְכֵי־אָרֶץ | | לְעוֹלָם | אֶשְׁמָור־לוֹ |
| 'elyôn | l$^{e}$malkhê-'ārets | | l$^{e}$'ôlām | 'eshmāwr-lô |
| the most high | of the kings of the earth | | unto eternity | I will keep for him |

*Moffatt* ... Truly Yahweh is our Suzerain, *Anchor.*

**19. Then thou spakest in vision to thy holy one, and saidst, I have laid help upon one that is mighty; I have exalted one chosen out of the people:** ... I set a boy above a warrior, *Beck* ... I have granted help to a warrior, *REB* ... I have placed help upon a mighty one, *Young* ... I have set the crown on one who is mighty, *NRSV.*

**20. I have found David my servant; with my holy oil have I anointed him:** ... Here was my servant David; on him my consecrating oil has been poured, *Knox* ... I have made discovery of David my servant; I have put my holy oil on his head, *BB* ... And consecrated him as king, *Moffatt* ... I appointed by My Sacred Oil, *Fenton.*

**21. With whom my hand shall be established: mine arm also shall strengthen him:** ... I will steady him with my hand, *NCV* ... My hand will always be with him, *JB* ... With a firm hand I will help him, *Beck* ... with whom My hand shall be steadfast, *Berkeley.*

**22. The enemy shall not exact upon him; nor the son of wickedness afflict him:** ... No enemy shall deceive him, *NCB* ... The enemy shall not outwit him, the wicked shall not humble him, *RSV* ... No enemy will subject him to tribute; no wicked man will oppress him, *NIV* ... Nor shall a son of perversity humiliate him, *Rotherham.*

**23. And I will beat down his foes before his face, and plague them that hate him:** ... I will beat to pieces his adversaries before him, *MAST* ... beaten down, every foe, at his onset, baffled, at their ill will, *Knox* ... strike his opponents dead, *JB* ... And those hating him I plague, *Young.*

**24. But my faithfulness and my mercy shall be with him: and in my name shall his horn be exalted:** ... My faithfulness and steadfast love shall be with him, *RSV* ... Through me he will be strong, *NCV* ... by my favour he shall rise to preeminence, *Knox* ... My fidelity and love shall be with him, and through my Name he shall be victorious, *Anchor.*

**25. I will set his hand also in the sea, and his right hand in the rivers:** ... I shall establish his power over the sea, his dominion over the rivers, *JB* ... I will extend his power to the sea, and his authority far as the Euphrates, *Moffatt* ... I will make his power rest on the sea; to the streams of the great river, *Knox* ... I will extend his rule over the Sea and his dominion as far as the River, *NEB.*

**26. He shall cry unto me, Thou art my father, my God, and the rock of my salvation:** ... He will call to Me, 'You are my Father, my God and Rock who saves me', *Beck* ... He shall say to me, 'You are my father; My GOD, and my Tower of retreat!,' *Fenton* ... He will say to me, 'Thou art my father, my God, my rock and safe refuge,' *NEB.*

**27. Also I will make him my firstborn, higher than the kings of the earth:** ... I also first-born do appoint

---

oring, the fundamental prophecy by Nathan. It falls into two parts, of which the former (vv. 19–27) refers more especially to the promises given to David and the latter (vv. 28–37) to those relating to his descendants. In v. 19, "vision" is quoted from 2 Sam. 7:17; "then" points back to the period of giving the promise; and "one chosen" is possibly Nathan, but more probably David. The Masoretic reading, however, which is followed by many ancient versions, has the plural "favored ones," which Delitzsch takes to mean Samuel and Nathan. "Help" means the help which, through the king, comes to his people, and especially, as appears from the use of the word "hero," aid in battle. But since the selection of David for the throne is the subject in hand, the emendation which reads for "help" recommends itself as probable. David's prowess, his humble origin and his devotion to God's service are brought into view in vv. 19f, as explaining and magnifying the divine choice. His dignity is all from God. Consequently, as the next pair of verses goes on to say, God's protecting hand will ever be with him, since He cannot set a man in any position and fail to supply the gifts needed for it. Whom He chooses, He will protect. Sheltered behind that strong hand, the king will be safe from all assaults. The word rendered "steal upon" (HED #5565) in v. 22 is doubtful and by some is taken to mean "to exact," as a creditor does, but that gives a flat and incongruous turn to the promise. For v. 22b, compare 2 Sam. 7:10. Victory over all enemies is next promised in vv. 23ff and is traced to the perpetual presence with the king of God's faithfulness and steadfast love, the two attributes of which so much has been sung in the former part. The manifestation of God's character (his name) will secure the exaltation of David's horn—the victorious exercise of his God-given strength. Therefore, a wide extension of his kingdom is promised in v. 25, from the Mediterranean to the Euphrates and its canals, on which God will lay the king's hand—will put them in his possession.

**89:26–27.** The next pair of verses deals with the inward side of the relations of God and the king. On David's part, there will be child-like love, with all the lowliness of trust and obedience which lies in the recognition of God's fatherhood, and on God's

| 2721 | 1311 | 548.257 | 3937 | | 7947.115 | 3937, 5911 |
|---|---|---|---|---|---|---|
| n ms, ps 1cs | cj, n fs, ps 1cs | v Niphal ptc fs | prep, ps 3ms | | cj, v Qal pf 1cs | prep, n ms |
| חַסְדִּי | וּבְרִיתִי | נֶאֱמֶנֶת | לוֹ | **29.** | וְשַׂמְתִּי | לָעַד |
| chas̱dî | ûverîthî | ne'ĕmeneth | lô | | wesamtî | lā'adh |
| my steadfast love | and my covenant | firm | for him | | I will establish | unto eternity |

| 2320 | 3802 | 3626, 3219 | 8452 | | 524, 6013.126 | 1158 |
|---|---|---|---|---|---|---|
| n ms, ps 3ms | cj, n ms, ps 3ms | prep, *n mp* | n md | | cj, v Qal impf 3mp | n mp, ps 3ms |
| זַרְעוֹ | וְכִסְאוֹ | כִּימֵי | שָׁמָיִם | **30.** | אִם־יַעַזְבוּ | בָנָיו |
| zar'ô | wekhis̱'ô | kîmê | shāmāyim | | 'im-ya'azvû | vānâv |
| his seed | and his throne | like the days of | the heavens | | if they abandon | his sons |

| 8784 | 904, 5122 | 3940 | 2050.126 | | 524, 2807 | 2591.326 |
|---|---|---|---|---|---|---|
| n fs, ps 1cs | cj, prep, n mp, ps 1cs | neg part | v Qal impf 3mp | | cj, n fp, ps 1cs | v Piel impf 3mp |
| תּוֹרָתִי | וּבְמִשְׁפָּטַי | לֹא | יֵלֵכוּן | **31.** | אִם־חֻקֹּתַי | יְחַלֵּלוּ |
| tôrāthî | ûvemishpāṭay | lō' | yēlēkhûn | | 'im-chuqqōthay | yechallēlû |
| my Law | and by my ordinances | not | they walk | | if my statutes | they violate |

| 4834 | 3940 | 8490.126 | | 6734.115 | 904, 8101 |
|---|---|---|---|---|---|
| cj, n fp, ps 1cs | neg part | v Qal impf 3mp | | cj, v Qal pf 1cs | prep, *n ms* |
| וּמִצְוֹתַי | לֹא | יִשְׁמֹרוּ | **32.** | וּפָקַדְתִּי | בְשֵׁבֶט |
| ûmitswōthay | lō' | yishmōrû | | ûphāqadhtî | veshēveṯ |
| and my commandments | not | they observe | | then I will intervene | with the staff of |

| 6840 | 904, 5237 | 5988 | | 2721 |
|---|---|---|---|---|
| n ms, ps 3mp | cj, prep, n mp | n ms, ps 3mp | | cj, n ms, ps 1cs |
| פִּשְׁעָם | וּבִנְגָעִים | עֲוֹנָם | **33.** | וְחַסְדִּי |
| pish'ām | ûvinghā'îm | 'ăwōnām | | wechas̱dî |
| their offenses | and with blows | their transgressions | | but my steadfast love |

| 3940, 6815.525 | 4623, 6196 | 3940, 8631.325 | 904, 536 |
|---|---|---|---|
| neg part, v Hiphil impf 1cs | prep, prep, ps 3ms | cj, neg part, v Piel impf 1cs | prep, n fs, ps 1cs |
| לֹא־אָפִיר | מֵעִמּוֹ | וְלֹא־אֲשַׁקֵּר | בֶּאֱמוּנָתִי |
| lō'-'āphîr | mē'immô | welō'-'ăshaqqēr | be'ĕmûnāthî |
| I will not suspend | from with him | and I will not act deceitfully | with my faithfulness |

| | 3940, 2591.325 | 1311 | 4296 | 8004 | 3940 | 7983.325 |
|---|---|---|---|---|---|---|
| | neg part, v Piel impf 1cs | n fs, ps 1cs | cj, *n ms* | n fd, ps 1cs | neg part | v Piel impf 1cs |
| **34.** | לֹא־אֲחַלֵּל | בְּרִיתִי | וּמוֹצָא | שְׂפָתַי | לֹא | אֲשַׁנֶּה |
| | lō'-'ăchallēl | berîthî | ûmôtsā' | sephāthay | lō' | 'ăshanneh |
| | I will not violate | my Covenant | and what goes out of | my lips | not | I will change |

| | 259 | 8123.215 | 904, 7231 | 524, 3937, 1784 | 3694.325 | | 2320 |
|---|---|---|---|---|---|---|---|
| | num | v Niphal pf 1cs | prep, n ms, ps 1cs | cj, prep, pn | v Piel impf 1cs | | n ms, ps 3ms |
| **35.** | אַחַת | נִשְׁבַּעְתִּי | בְקָדְשִׁי | אִם־לְדָוִד | אֲכַזֵּב | **36.** | זַרְעוֹ |
| | 'achath | nishba'ttî | veqādheshî | 'im-ledhāwidh | 'ăkhazzēv | | zar'ô |
| | one time | I swore | by my holiness | if to David | I lie | | his seed |

him, Highest of the kings of the earth, *Young* ... Yes! I will make him Imperial, The First of the Kings of the Earth, *Fenton* ... I will acknowledge him as my first-born, overlord to all the kings of the earth, *Knox* ... I shall give him the rank of firstborn, *REB*.

**28. My mercy will I keep for him for evermore, and my covenant shall stand fast with him:** ... I will always keep my word to him, my compact with him is secure, *Moffatt* ... Age-abidingly will I keep for him my lovingkindness, *Rotherham* ... I will continue my favour towards him for ever, my covenant with him shall remain unbroken, *Knox* ... I will guard him for ever by Mercy, And secure My Treaty to him, *Fenton*.

**29. His seed also will I make to endure for ever, and his throne as the days of heaven:** ... I will give him posterity that never fails, *Knox* ... I will make his family continue, and his kingdom will last as long as the skies, *NCV* ... I will put his offspring on his seat, and his throne will be like heaven's days, *Anchor* ... I have established his dynasty for ever, *JB*.

**30. If his children forsake my law, and walk not in my judgments:** ... If his descendants reject my teachings and do not follow my laws, *NCV* ... and are not ruled by my decisions, *BB* ... and walk not according to my ordinances, *NCB* ... And by My Decrees cease to walk, *Fenton.*

**31. If they break my statutes, and keep not my commandments:** ... If My statutes they pollute, *Young* ... If my rules are not broken, and my orders are not kept, *BB* ... if they violate My laws and don't do what I order, *Beck* ... if they ignore my demands, *NCV.*

**32. Then will I visit their transgression with the rod, and their iniquity with stripes:** ... I will scourge them for their sin, *Knox* ... And their guilt with blows, *Goodspeed* ... and their malice with whiplashes, *Anchor* ... and lash them for their lawlessness, *Moffatt.*

**33. Nevertheless my lovingkindness will I not utterly take from him, nor suffer my faithfulness to fail:** ... but I shall never withdraw from him my faithful love, I shall not belie my constancy, *JB* ... Yet I will not deprive him of my true love nor let my faithfulness prove false, *NEB* ... never will I be guilty of unfaithfulness, never will I violate my covenant, or alter the decree once spoken, *Knox* ... But My mercy not take from his People, Nor will I be false to My Truth, *Fenton.*

**34. My covenant will I not break, nor alter the thing that is gone out of my lips:** ... I will not renounce my covenant nor change my promised purpose, *NEB* ... I profane not My covenant, *Young* ... My Treaty will never be broken, *Fenton* ... I will not desecrate My covenant, *Berkeley.*

**35. Once have I sworn by my holiness that I will not lie unto David:** ... Once and for all I have took a solemn oath, and I will keep my word to David, *Moffatt* ... I will not be false unto David, *MAST* ... I will never forget about David, *Fenton* ... never will I break faith with David, *JB.*

**36. His seed shall endure for ever, and his throne as the sun before me:** ... his posterity shall continue for ever, his royalty, too, shall last on in my presence like the sun, *Knox* ... his throne as long as the sun before me, *RSV.*

---

part there will be the acknowledgment of the relation and the adoption of the king as his "first-born" and therefore in a special sense beloved and exalted. Israel is called by the same name in other places, in reference to its special prerogative among the nations. The national dignity is concentrated in the king, who stands to other monarchs as Israel to other nations and is to them "Most High," the august divine title, which here may possibly mean that David is to the rulers of the earth an image of God. The reciprocal relation of Father and Son is not here conceived in its full inwardness and depth as Christianity knows it, for it has reference to office rather than to the person sustaining the office, but it is approximating thereto. There is an echo of the fundamental passage in v. 26 (cf. 2 Sam. 7:14).

**89:28–37.** From v. 28 onward, the psalmist turns to expand the promises to David's line. His words are mainly a poetic paraphrase of 2 Sam. 7:14. Transgression shall indeed be visited with chastisement, which the fatherly relation requires, as the original passage indicates by the juxtaposition of the promise "I will be his Father" and the declaration "I will chasten him." But it will be chastisement only, and not rejection. The unchangeableness of God's loving purpose is very strongly and beautifully put in v. 33, in which the twin attributes of steadfast love and faithfulness are again blended as the ground of sinful men's hope. The word rendered above "break off" (HED #6815) occasions a difficulty, both in regard to its form and its appropriateness in this connection. The clause is a quotation from 2 Sam. 7:15, and the emendation which substitutes for "break off" the more natural word used there—withdraw—is to be preferred. In v. 33b, the paradoxical expression of being false to my faithfulness suggests the contradiction inherent in the very thought that He can break his plighted word. The same idea is again put in striking form in v. 34: "My covenant will I not break," even though degenerate sons of David "profane" God's statute. His word, once spoken, is inviolable. He is bound by his oath. He has given his holiness as the pledge of his word, and until that holiness wanes, those utterances which He has sealed with it cannot be recalled. The certainty that sin does not alter God's promise is not traced here to his placableness, but to his immutable nature and to the obligations under which He is laid by his own word and acts. That unchangeableness is a rock foundation on which sinful men may build their certitude. It is much to know that they cannot chase away God's mercy nor exhaust his gentle long-suffering. It is even more to know that his holiness guarantees that they cannot sin away his promises, or by any breach of his commandments provoke Him to break his Covenant.

The allusions to the ancient promise are completed in vv. 36f, with the thought of the perpetual continuance of the Davidic line and kingdom, expressed by the familiar comparison of its duration

| 3937, 5986 | 2030.121 | 3802 | 3626, 8507 | 5224 | | 3626, 3507 |
|---|---|---|---|---|---|---|
| prep, n ms | v Qal impf 3ms | cj, n ms, ps 3ms | prep, art, n fs | prep, ps 1cs | **37.** | prep, n ms |
| לְעוֹלָם | יִהְיֶה | וְכִסְאוֹ | כַּשֶּׁמֶשׁ | נֶגְדִּי | | כְּיָרֵחַ |
| leʿôlām | yihyeh | wekhisʾô | khashshemesh | neghdî | | keyārēach |
| unto eternity | it will be | and his throne | like the sun | before Me | | like the moon |

| 3679.221 | 5986 | 5915 | 904, 8262 | 548.255 | 5734 | | 887 |
|---|---|---|---|---|---|---|---|
| v Niphal impf 3ms | n ms | cj, n ms | prep, art, n ms | v Niphal ptc ms | intrj | **38.** | cj, pers pron |
| יִכּוֹן | עוֹלָם | וְעֵד | בַּשַּׁחַק | נֶאֱמָן | סֶלָה | | וְאַתָּה |
| yikkôn | ʿôlām | weʿēdh | bashshachaq | neʾĕmān | selāh | | weʾattāh |
| it is established | forever | and a testimony | in the clouds | reliable | selah | | but You |

| 2269.113 | 4128.123 | 5882.713 | 6196, 5081 |
|---|---|---|---|
| v Qal pf 2ms | cj, v Qal impf 2ms | v Hithpael pf 2ms | prep, n ms, ps 2ms |
| זָנַחְתָּ | וַתִּמְאָס | הִתְעַבַּרְתָּ | עִם־מְשִׁיחֶךָ |
| zānachtā | wattimʾās | hithʿabbartā | ʿim-meshîchekhā |
| You have rejected | and You have despised | You have become enraged | with your anointed one |

| | 5185.313 | 1311 | 5860 | 2591.313 | 3937, 800 | 5325 |
|---|---|---|---|---|---|---|
| **39.** | v Piel pf 2ms | *n fs* | n ms, ps 2ms | v Piel pf 2ms | prep, art, n fs | n ms, ps 3ms |
| | נֵאַרְתָּה | בְּרִית | עַבְדֶּךָ | חִלַּלְתָּ | לָאָרֶץ | נִזְרוֹ |
| | nēʾartāh | berîth | ʿavdekhā | chillaltā | lāʾārets | nizrô |
| | You have anulled | the covenant of | your servant | You have violated | to the ground | his diadem |

| | 6805.113 | 3725, 1481 | 7947.113 | 4152 | 4425 |
|---|---|---|---|---|---|
| **40.** | v Qal pf 2ms | *adj*, n fp, ps 3ms | v Qal pf 2ms | n mp, ps 3ms | n fs |
| | פָּרַצְתָּ | כָּל־גְּדֵרֹתָיו | שַׂמְתָּ | מִבְצָרָיו | מְחִתָּה |
| | pāratstā | khol-gedhērōthâv | samtā | mivtsārâv | mechittāh |
| | You have broken through | all his walls | You have laid | his fortressess | a ruins |

| | 8537.116 | 3725, 5882.152 | 1932 | 2030.111 | 2887 |
|---|---|---|---|---|---|
| **41.** | v Qal pf 3cp, ps 3ms | *adj, v Qal act ptc mp* | n ms | v Qal pf 3ms | n fs |
| | שַׁסֻּהוּ | כָּל־עֹבְרֵי | דָרֶךְ | הָיָה | חֶרְפָּה |
| | shassuhû | kol-ʿōverê | dhārekh | hāyāh | cherpāh |
| | they have despoiled him | all those passing by | the way | he has become | a disgrace |

| 3937, 8333 | | 7597.513 | 3332 | 7141 | 7975.513 |
|---|---|---|---|---|---|
| prep, adj, ps 3ms | **42.** | v Hiphil pf 2ms | *n fs* | n mp, ps 3ms | v Hiphil pf 2ms |
| לִשְׁכֵנָיו | | הֲרִימוֹתָ | יְמִין | צָרָיו | הִשְׂמַחְתָּ |
| lishkhēnâv | | herîmôthā | yemîn | tsārâv | hismachtā |
| to his neighbors | | You have exalted | the right hand of | his adversaries | You have made glad |

| 3725, 342.152 | | 652, 8178.523 | 6962 | 2820 | 3940 |
|---|---|---|---|---|---|
| *adj*, v Qal act ptc mp, ps 3ms | **43.** | cj, v Hiphil impf 2ms | *n ms* | n fs, ps 3ms | cj, neg part |
| כָּל־אוֹיְבָיו | | אַף־תָּשִׁיב | צוּר | חַרְבּוֹ | וְלֹא |
| kol-ʾôyvâv | | ʾaph-tāshîv | tsûr | charbô | welōʾ |
| all his enemies | | also You have turned back | the flint of | his knife | and not |

| 7251.513 | 904, 4560 | | 8178.513 | 4623, 3002 |
|---|---|---|---|---|
| v Hiphil pf 2ms, ps 3ms | prep, art, n fs | **44.** | v Hiphil pf 2ms | prep, n ms, ps 3ms |
| הֲקֵימֹתוֹ | בַּמִּלְחָמָה | | הִשְׁבַּתָּ | מִטְּהָרוֹ |
| heqêmōthô | bammilchāmāh | | hishbattā | mittehārô |
| You have caused him to rise up | in the battle | | You have caused to cease | from his purity |

| 3802 | 3937, 800 | 4188.313 | | 7403.513 | 3219 |
|---|---|---|---|---|---|
| cj, n ms, ps 3ms | prep, art, n fs | v Piel pf 2ms | **45.** | v Hiphil pf 2ms | *n mp* |
| וְכִסְאוֹ | לָאָרֶץ | מִגַּרְתָּה | | הִקְצַרְתָּ | יְמֵי |
| wekhisʾô | lāʾārets | miggartāh | | hiqōtsartā | yemê |
| and his throne | to the ground | You have thrown down | | You have made short | the days of |

**37. It shall be established for ever as the moon, and as a faithful witness in heaven:** ... As the moon it shall always remain reliable, *Berkeley* ... like the moon's eternal orb, that bears witness in heaven unalterable, *Knox* ... Like the moon will his descendants live on, and his seat will be stabler than the sky, *Anchor* ... And as the faithful witness in the sky, *MRB.*

**Selah:** ... Music, *Beck* ... Pause, *JB.*

**38. But thou hast cast off and abhorred, thou hast been wroth with thine anointed:** ... But you have rejected, you have spurned, you have been very angry with your anointed one, *NIV* ... But you have put him away in disgust; you have been angry with the king of your selection, *BB* ... And yet thou hast scorned, discarded, stormed against thy chosen!, *Moffatt* ... Thou hast raged against thine anointed, *Goodspeed.*

**39. Thou hast made void the covenant of thy servant: thou hast profaned his crown by casting it to the ground:** ... You have renounced the covenant, *NIV* ... You have repudiated the covenant with Your servant and made his crown unholy in the dust, *Beck* ... you have had no respect for his crown, it has come down even to the earth, *BB* ... defiled his crown and flung it to the ground, *NEB.*

**40. Thou hast broken down all his hedges; thou hast brought his strong holds to ruin:** ... Thou hast breached all his walls, *RSV* ... Thou hast broken down all his fences, *MAST* ... You have torn down all his city walls; you have turned his strong cities into ruins, *NCV* ... reduced his fortifications to rubble, *Anchor.*

**41. All that pass by the way spoil him: he is a reproach to his neighbours:** ... scorn of his neighbors, *RSV* ... he has become the taunt of his neighbors, *Anchor* ... a laughing-stock to his neighbours, *Knox* ... He has become a jest to his neighbors, *Goodspeed.*

**42. Thou hast set up the right hand of his adversaries; thou hast made all his enemies to rejoice:** ... You have increased the power of his adversaries, *REB* ... exalted the right hand of his antagonists, *Berkeley* ... granted aid to the attacking armies, *Knox* ... allowed his enemies to triumph, *Moffatt.*

**43. Thou hast also turned the edge of his sword, and hast not made him to stand in the battle:** ... foiling the thrust of his sword, *Knox* ... you have snapped off his sword on a rock, and failed to support him in battle, *JB* ... though hast let his sharp sword be driven back and left him without help in battle, *NEB* ... and didn't let him attack in battle, *Beck.*

**44. Thou hast made his glory to cease, and cast his throne down to the ground:** ... You have deprived him of his luster, *NCB* ... Thou hast robbed him of the bright glory that once was, *Knox* ... You have removed the scepter from his hand, *NRSV* ... Thou hast brought an end to his splendour, *Rotherham.*

**45. The days of his youth hast thou shortened: thou hast covered him with shame:** ... cut short the days of his youth and vigour, *NEB* ... You have made him old before

---

to that of the sun and moon. Verse 37b is best understood as mentioned above. Some take the faithful witness to be the moon; others the rainbow, and render the phrase, "and as a faithful witness." But the designation of the moon as a witness is unexampled and almost unintelligible. It is better to take the clause as independent and to suppose that Yahweh is his own witness and that the psalmist here speaks in his own person, the quotation of the promises being ended. Some have enclosed the clause in a parenthesis and compared it to Rev. 3:14.

**89:38–45.** The third part begins with v. 38 and consists of two portions in the first of which the psalmist complains with extraordinary boldness of remonstrance and describes the contrast between these lofty promises and the sad reality (vv. 38–45). In the second, he prays for the removal of the contradiction of God's promise by Israel's affliction and bases this petition on the double ground of the shortness of life and the dishonor done to his own name thereby.

The expostulation very nearly crosses the boundary of reverent remonstrance when it charges God with having himself "abhorred" or, according to another rendering, "made void" his covenant, and cast the king's crown to the ground. The devastation of the kingdom is described in vv. 40f in language borrowed from Ps. 80:12. The pronouns grammatically refer to the king, but the ideas of the land and the monarch are blended. The next pair of verses (vv. 42f) venture still further in remonstrance by charging God with taking the side of Israel's enemies and actively intervening to procure its defeat. The last pair of verses of this part (vv. 44f) speak more exclusively of the king, or perhaps of the monarchy. The language, especially in v. 45a, seems most naturally understood of an individual. Delitzsch takes such to be its application and supposes it to describe the king as having been prematurely aged by calamity; while others prefer to regard the expression as lamenting that the early days of the monarchy's vigor had so soon

| 6156 | 6057.513 | 6142 | 992 | 5734 | | 5912, 4242 | 3176 |
|---|---|---|---|---|---|---|---|
| n mp, ps 3ms | v Hiphil pf 2ms | prep, ps 3ms | n fs | intrj | | adv, intrg | pn |
| עֲלוּמָיו | הֶעֱטִיתָ | עָלָיו | בּוּשָׁה | סֶלָה | 46. | עַד־מָה | יְהוָה |
| 'ălûmâv | he'ĕṭîthā | 'ālâv | bûshāh | selāh | | 'adh-māh | yehwāh |
| his youth | You have wrapped | upon him | shame | selah | | until what | O Yahweh |

| 5846.223 | 3937, 5516 | 1220.122 | 3765, 813 | 2635 | | 2226.131, 603 |
|---|---|---|---|---|---|---|
| v Niphal impf 2ms | prep, art, n ms | v Qal impf 3fs | prep, n fs | n fs, ps 2ms | | v Qal impv 2ms, pers pron |
| תִּסָּתֵר | לָנֶצַח | תִּבְעַר | כְּמוֹ־אֵשׁ | חֲמָתֶךָ | 47. | זְכָר־אֲנִי |
| tissāthēr | lānetsach | tiv'ar | kemô-'ēsh | chămāthekhā | | zekhār-'ănî |
| will You hide | unto forever | it will burn | like fire | your wrath | | remember I |

| 4242, 2566 | 6142, 4242, 8175 | 1282.113 | 3725, 1158, 119 |
|---|---|---|---|
| intrg, n ms | prep, intrg, n ms | v Qal pf 2ms | *adj, n mp*, n ms |
| מֶה־חָלֶד | עַל־מַה־שָּׁוְא | בָּרָאתָ | כָּל־בְּנֵי־אָדָם |
| meh-chāledh | 'al-mah-shāwe' | bārā'thā | khol-benê-'ādhām |
| what length of life | concerning what vanity | have You created | all the children of humankind |

| | 4449 | 1429 | 2513.121 | 3940 | 7495.121, 4323 | 4561.321 | 5497 |
|---|---|---|---|---|---|---|---|
| | intrg | n ms | v Qal impf 3ms | cj, neg part | v Qal impf 3ms, n ms | v Piel impf 3ms | n fs, ps 3ms |
| 48. | מִי | גֶבֶר | יִחְיֶה | וְלֹא | יִרְאֶה־מָּוֶת | יְמַלֵּט | נַפְשׁוֹ |
| | mî | ghever | yichăyeh | welō' | yir'eh-māweth | yemallēṭ | naphshô |
| | who | a man | can he live | and not | he will see death | can he set free | his soul |

| 4623, 3135, 8061 | 5734 | | 347 | 2721 | 7518 | 112 |
|---|---|---|---|---|---|---|
| prep, *n fs*, n fs | intrj | | intrg | n mp, ps 2ms | art, adj | n mp, ps 1cs |
| מִיַּד־שְׁאוֹל | סֶלָה | 49. | אַיֵּה | חֲסָדֶיךָ | הָרִאשֹׁנִים | אֲדֹנָי |
| mîyadh-she'ôl | selāh | | 'ayyēh | chăsādhêkhā | hāri'shōnîm | 'ădhōnāy |
| from the power of Sheol | selah | | where | your steadfast love | the former times | O my Lord |

| 8123.213 | 3937, 1784 | 904, 536 | | 2226.131 | 112 | 2887 |
|---|---|---|---|---|---|---|
| v Niphal pf 2ms | prep, pn | prep, n fs, ps 2ms | | v Qal impv 2ms | n mp, ps 1cs | *n fs* |
| נִשְׁבַּעְתָּ | לְדָוִד | בֶּאֱמוּנָתֶךָ | 50. | זְכֹר | אֲדֹנָי | חֶרְפַּת |
| nishba'āttā | ledhāwidh | be'ĕmûnāthekhā | | zekhōr | 'ădhōnāy | cherpath |
| You swore | to David | by your faithfulness | | remember | O my Lord | disgrace from |

| 5860 | 5558.141 | 904, 2536 | 3725, 7521 | 6194 | | 866 |
|---|---|---|---|---|---|---|
| n mp, ps 2ms | v Qal inf con, ps 1cs | prep, n ms, ps 1cs | *adj*, adj | n mp | | rel pron |
| עֲבָדֶיךָ | שְׂאֵתִי | בְחֵיקִי | כָּל־רַבִּים | עַמִּים | 51. | אֲשֶׁר |
| 'ăvādhêkhā | se'ēthî | vechêqî | kol-rabbîm | 'ammîm | | 'ăsher |
| your servants | my bearing | in my bosom | all the many | peoples | | who |

| 2884.316 | 342.152 | 3176 | 866 | 2884.316 | 6357 |
|---|---|---|---|---|---|
| v Piel pf 3cp | v Qal act ptc mp, ps 2ms | pn | rel pron | v Piel pf 3cp | *n mp* |
| חֵרְפוּ | אוֹיְבֶיךָ | יְהוָה | אֲשֶׁר | חֵרְפוּ | עִקְּבוֹת |
| chērephû | 'ôyevêkhā | yehwāh | 'ăsher | chērephû | 'iqqevôth |
| they have taunted | your enemies | O Yahweh | who | they have taunted | the heels of |

his time, *BB* … cut his manhood short before its time; confusion overwhelms him, *Knox* … robed his young manhood with sterility, *Anchor.*

**Selah:** … Music, *Beck* … Pause, *JB.*

**46. How long, LORD? wilt thou hide thyself for ever? shall thy wrath burn like fire?:** … Lord, wilt thou always turn thy face away so obdurately, will the flame of thy anger never be quenched?, *Knox* … Is your anger to go on smouldering like a fire, *JB.*

**47. Remember how short my time is: wherefore hast thou made all men in vain?:** … how frail you created all the children of men!, *NCB* … Remember how fleeting is my life. For what futility you have created all men!, *NIV* … Why did you create us? For nothing?, *NCV* … Why create in vain all Adam's Sons, *Fenton.*

**48. What man is he that liveth, and shall not see death? shall he deliver his soul from the hand of the**

**grave?:** ... Who can save himself from the power of Sheol?, *REB* ... Does any man live without experiencing death; can any rescue his life from the grave, *Beck* ... What man is there so strong that he shall live and not see death, *Berkeley* ... but deliver himself from the nether world, *NCB*.

**Selah:** ... Music, *Beck* ... Pause, *JB*.

**49. Lord, where are thy former lovingkindnesses, which thou swarest unto David in thy truth?:** ... Lord, where is your steadfast love of old, *NRSV* ... Where are your ancient favors, O Lord, *NCB* ... Where are those earlier acts of love, O Lord, Which you promised on your fidelity to David?, *Anchor* ... which thou didst pledge to David faithfully?, *Moffatt*.

**50. Remember, Lord, the reproach of thy servants; how I do bear in my bosom the reproach of all the mighty people:** ... Remember how a world's taunts assail thy people, and this one heart must bear them all, *Knox* ... Keep in mind O Lord, the shame of your servants, and how the bitter words of all the people have come into my heart, *BB* ... the taunts hurled at they servant, how I have borne in my heart the calumnies of the nations, *NEB*.

**51. Wherewith thine enemies have reproached, O LORD; wherewith they have reproached the footsteps of thine anointed:** ... How thy foes insult, O LORD, *Goodspeed* ... so have thy enemies taunted us, O LORD, taunted the successors of

---

been succeeded by decrepitude like that of age. That family, which had been promised perpetual duration and dominion, had lost its luster and was like a dying lamp. That throne, which God had promised should stand forever, had fallen to the ground. Senile weakness had stricken the monarchy, and disaster, which made it an object of contempt, wrapped it like a garment instead of the royal robe. A long, sad wail of the music fixes the picture on the mind of the hearer.

**89:46–48.** Then follows prayer, which shows how consistent with true reverence and humble dependence the outspoken vigor of the preceding remonstrance is. The boldest thoughts about the apparent contradiction of God's words and deeds are not too bold, if spoken straight to Him, rather than against Him, and if they lead the speaker to prayer for the removal of the anomaly. In v. 46, there is a quotation from Ps. 79:5. The question "How long" is the more imploring because life is so short. There is but a little while during which it is possible for God to manifest himself as full of steadfast love and faithfulness. The psalmist lets his feelings of longing to see for himself the manifestation of these attributes peep forth for a moment in that pathetic sudden emergence of "I" instead of "we" or "men" in v. 47a. His language is somewhat obscure, but the sense is clear. The meaning is plain enough, when it is observed that, "I" is placed first for the sake of emphasis. It is a tender thought that God may be moved to show forth his steadfast love by remembrance of the brief period within which a man's opportunity of beholding it is restricted and by the consideration that so soon he will have to look on a grimmer sight and "see death." The music again comes in with a melancholy cadence, emphasizing the sadness which enwraps man's short life, if no gleams of God's steadfast love fall on its fleeting days.

**89:49–51.** The last three verses urge yet another plea—that of the dishonor accruing to God from the continuance of Israel's disasters. A second "remember" presents that plea, which is preceded by the wistful question "where are thy former steadfast love?" The psalmist looks back on the glories of early days, and the retrospect is bitter and bewildering. That these were sworn to David in God's faithfulness staggers him, but he makes the fact a plea with God. Then in vv. 50f, he urges the insults and reproaches which enemies hurled against him and against "thy servants," and therefore against God.

Verse 50b is obscure. To "bear in my bosom" usually implies tender care, but here can only mean sympathetic participation. The psalmist again lets his own personality appear for a moment, while he identifies himself as a member of the nation with "thy servants" and "thine anointed." The reproaches cut deep into the singer's heart, but they glance off from the earthly objects and strike the majesty of Heaven. God's people cannot be flouted without his honor being touched. Therefore, the prayer goes up that the LORD would remember these jeers which mocked Him as well as his afflicted people and would arise to action on behalf of his own name. His steadfast love and faithfulness, which the psalmist has magnified and on which he rests his hopes, are darkened in the eyes of men and even of his own nation by the calamities, which give point to the rude gibes of the enemy. Therefore, the closing petitions beseech God to think on these reproaches and to bring into act once more his steadfast love and to vindicate his faithfulness, which He had sealed to David by his oath.

| 5081 | | 1313.155 | 3176 | 3937, 5986 | 549 | 549 | | 8940 |
|---|---|---|---|---|---|---|---|---|
| n ms, ps 2ms | 52. | v Qal pass ptc ms | pn | prep, n ms | intrj | cj, intrj | 90:t | n fs |
| מְשִׁיחֶךָ | | בָּרוּךְ | יְהוָה | לְעוֹלָם | אָמֵן | וְאָמֵן | | תְּפִלָּה |
| meshîchekhā | | bārûkh | yehwāh | le'ôlām | 'āmēn | we'āmēn | | tephillāh |
| your anointed one | | blessed | Yahweh | unto eternity | amen | and amen | | a Prayer |

| 3937, 5057 | 382, 435 | | 112 | 4737 | 887 | 2030.113 | 3937 |
|---|---|---|---|---|---|---|---|
| prep, pn | *n ms*, art, n mp | 1. | n mp, ps 1cs | n ms | pers pron | v Qal pf 2ms | prep, ps 1cp |
| לְמֹשֶׁה | אִישׁ־הָאֱלֹהִים | | אֲדֹנָי | מָעוֹן | אַתָּה | הָיִיתָ | לָנוּ |
| lemōsheh | 'îsh-hā'ĕlōhîm | | 'ădhōnāy | mā'ôn | 'attāh | hāyîthā | lānû |
| of Moses | the man of God | | O my Lord | a dwelling place | You | You have been | to us |

| 904, 1810 | 1810 | | 904, 3071 | 2098 | 3314.416 |
|---|---|---|---|---|---|
| prep, n ms | cj, n ms | 2. | prep, adv | n mp | v Pual pf 3cp |
| בְּדֹר | וָדֹר | | בְּטֶרֶם | הָרִים | יֻלָּדוּ |
| bedhōr | wādhōr | | beterem | hārîm | yullādhû |
| in generations | and generations | | before | the mountains | they have brought forth |

| 2523.323 | 800 | 8725 | 4623, 5986 | 5912, 5986 | 887 | 418 |
|---|---|---|---|---|---|---|
| cj, Polel impf 2ms | n fs | cj, n fs | cj, prep, n ms | adv, n ms | pers pron | n ms |
| וַתְּחוֹלֵל | אֶרֶץ | וְתֵבֵל | וּמֵעוֹלָם | עַד־עוֹלָם | אַתָּה | אֵל |
| wattechôlēl | 'erets | wethēvēl | ûmē'ôlām | 'adh-'ôlām | 'attāh | 'ēl |
| and You caused to writhe | the earth | and the world | and from eternity | unto eternity | You | God |

| | 8178.523 | 596 | 5912, 1851 | 569.123 | 8178.133 | 1158, 119 |
|---|---|---|---|---|---|---|
| 3. | v Hiphil impf 2ms | n ms | adv, adj | cj, v Qal impf 2ms | v Qal impv 2mp | *n mp*, n ms |
| | תָּשֵׁב | אֱנוֹשׁ | עַד־דַּכָּא | וַתֹּאמֶר | שׁוּבוּ | בְנֵי־אָדָם |
| | tāshēv | 'ĕnôsh | 'adh-dakkā' | wattō'mer | shûvû | venê-'ādhām |
| | You turn back | a man | until crushed | and You say | turn back | children of humankind |

| | 3706 | 512 | 8523 | 904, 6084 | 3626, 3219 | 896 | 3706 | 5882.121 |
|---|---|---|---|---|---|---|---|---|
| 4. | cj | num | n fp | prep, n fd, ps 2ms | prep, n ms | sub | cj | v Qal impf 3ms |
| | כִּי | אֶלֶף | שָׁנִים | בְּעֵינֶיךָ | כְּיוֹם | אֶתְמוֹל | כִּי | יַעֲבֹר |
| | kî | 'eleph | shānîm | be'ênêkhā | keyôm | 'əthmôl | kî | ya'ăvōr |
| | because | one thousand | years | in your eyes | about a day | yesterday | when | it passes by |

| 847 | 904, 4050 | | 2316.113 | 8517 | 2030.126 | 904, 1269 |
|---|---|---|---|---|---|---|
| cj, n fs | prep, art, n ms | 5. | v Qal pf 2ms, ps 3mp | n fs | v Qal impf 3mp | prep, art, n ms |
| וְאַשְׁמוּרָה | בַלָּיְלָה | | זְרַמְתָּם | שֵׁנָה | יִהְיוּ | בַּבֹּקֶר |
| we'ashmûrāh | vallāyelāh | | zeramtām | shēnāh | yihyû | babbōqer |
| or a watch | in the night | | You have flooded them | sleep | they are | in the morning |

| 3626, 2785 | 2599.121 | | 904, 1269 | 6957.121 | 2599.111 | 3937, 6394 |
|---|---|---|---|---|---|---|
| prep, art, n ms | v Qal impf 3ms | 6. | prep, art, n ms | v Qal impf 3ms | cj, v Qal pf 3ms | prep, art, n ms |
| כֶּחָצִיר | יַחֲלֹף | | בַּבֹּקֶר | יָצִיץ | וְחָלָף | לָעֶרֶב |
| kechātsîr | yachlōph | | babbōqer | yātsîts | wechālāph | lā'erev |
| like the grass | it is replaced | | in the morning | it flourishes | and it is replaced | at the evening |

thy anointed king, *NEB* ... shall they hurl taunts, Lord, these, thy enemies, after the man thou thyself hast anointed?, *Knox* ... they have mocked every step of your anointed one, *NIV.*

**52. Blessed be the LORD for evermore. Amen, and Amen:** ... Let the Lord be praised for ever. So be it, So be it, *BB* ... Blessed be Yahweh for ever. Amen, Amen, *JB.*

**90:t. A Prayer of Moses the man of God.**

**1. LORD, thou hast been our dwellingplace in all generations:** ... You are our home through all the ages, *Beck* ... O Lord, our mainstay, come! Be ours from age to age!, *Anchor* ... A dwelling-place has thou become to us, *Rotherham* ... you have been our home since the beginning, *NCV.*

**2. Before the mountains were brought forth, or ever thou hadst formed the earth and the world, even from everlasting to everlast-**

**ing, thou art God:** ... Before the mountains were born, or the earth and the world came to birth—From eternity to eternity you are!, *Anchor* ... Or the Earth and the World rolled in their spheres, You, GOD, were from Ever to Ever, *Fenton* ... You have always been, and you will always be, *NCV.*

**3. Thou turnest man to destruction; and sayest, Return, ye children of men:** ... Thou turnest man to contrition, *MAST* ... Thou crumblest man away, summoning men back to the dust, *Moffatt* ... You send man back to dust, *BB* ... And wilt thou bring man to dust again, that thou sayest, Return, children of Adam, to what you were?, *Knox.*

**4. For a thousand years in thy sight are but as yesterday when it is past, and as a watch in the night:** ... a thousand years is like the passing of the day, or like a few hours in the night, *NCV* ... are like the flight of yesterday, like an hour passing in the night, *Moffatt* ... or as one of the night-watches, *Knox.*

**5. Thou carriest them away as with a flood; they are as a sleep: in the morning they are like grass which groweth up:** ... Thou cuttest them off; they are as a dream, *Goodspeed* ... Swiftly thou bearest our lives away, as a waking dream, or the green grass, *Knox* ... If you pluck them while they're sleeping, in the morning they will be like cut grass, *Beck* ... Year after year thou sowest men like grass that grows anew, *Moffatt.*

**6. In the morning it flourisheth, and groweth up; in the evening it is cut down, and withereth:** ... that blooms fresh with the morning; night finds it faded and dead, *Knox* ... in the morning it sprouts and shoots up;

---

**89:52.** Verse 52 is no part of the original Psalm, but is the closing doxology of Book Three.

***Psalm 90.*** *This Psalm falls into three parts, of which the two former contain six verses each, while the last has only five. In the first section (vv. 1–6), the transitoriness of men is set over against the eternity of God; in the second (vv. 7–12), that transitoriness is traced to its reason, namely sin; and in the third, prayer that God would visit his servants is built upon both his eternity and their fleeting days.*

**90:1.** The short v. 1 blends both of the thoughts which are expanded in the following verses, while in it the singer breathes awed contemplation of the eternal God as the dwelling place or asylum of generations that follow each other, swift and unremembered, as the waves that break on some lonely shore. God is invoked as "LORD," the sovereign Ruler, the name which connotes his elevation and authority. But, although lofty, He is not inaccessible.

**90:2.** What God has been to successive generations results from his character. Verse 2 soars to the contemplation of his absolute eternity, stretching boundless on either side of this bank and shoal of time—"from everlasting to everlasting, thou art God"; and in that name is proclaimed his self-derived strength, which, being eternal, is neither derived from nor diminished by time that first gives to and then withdraws from all creatures their feeble power. The remarkable expressions for the coming forth of the material world from the abyss of deity regard creation as a birth. The Hebrew text reads in v. 2b as above, "Thou gavest birth to," but a very small change in a single vowel gives the possibly preferable reading which preserves the parallelism of a passive verb in both clauses, "Or the earth and the world were brought forth."

**90:3.** The poet turns now to the other member of his antithesis. Over against God's eternality is set the succession of man's generations, which has been already referred to in v. 1. This thought of successiveness is lost unless v. 3b is understood as the creative fiat which replaces by a new generation those who have been turned back to dust. Death and life, decay and ever-springing growth, are in continual alternation. The leaves, which are men, drop; the buds swell and open. The ever-knitted web is being ever run down and woven together again.

**90:4.** The psalmist rises still higher in v. 4. It is much to say that God is eternal, but it is more to say that He is raised above time, and that none of the terms in which men describe duration have any meaning for Him. A thousand years, which to a man seem so long, are to Him dwindled to nothing, since He is eternal without beginning or end. He can crowd a fullness of action into narrow limits. Moments can do the work of centuries.

**90:5–6.** The passing of mortal life has hitherto been contemplated in immediate connection with God's permanence, and the psalmist's tone has been a wonderful blending of melancholy and trust. But in v. 5, the sadder side of his contemplations becomes predominant. Frail man, frail because sinful, is his theme. The figures which set forth man's mortality are grand in their unelaborated brevity. They are like some of Michaelangelo's solemn statues. "Thou carriest them away"—a bold metaphor, suggesting the rush of a mighty stream, bearing on its tawny bosom crops, household goods and corpses and hurrying with its spoils to the sea.

| 4589.321 | 3111.111 | | 3706, 3735.119 | 904, 653 |
|---|---|---|---|---|
| v Poel impf 3ms | cj, v Qal pf 3ms | **7.** | cj, v Qal pf 1cp | prep, n ms, ps 2ms |
| יְמוֹלֵל | וְיָבֵשׁ | | כִּי־כָלִינוּ | בְאַפֶּךָ |
| yemôlēl | weyāvēsh | | kî-kholînû | ve'appekhā |
| it withers | and it dries up | | because we have come to an end | by your anger |

| 904, 2635 | 963.219 | | 8308.113 | 5988 | 3937, 5224 |
|---|---|---|---|---|---|
| cj, prep, n fs, ps 2ms | v Niphal pf 1cp | **8.** | v Qal pf 2ms | n mp, ps 1cp | prep, n ms, ps 2ms |
| וּבַחֲמָתְךָ | נִבְהָלְנוּ | | שַׁתָּ | עֲוֹנֹתֵינוּ | לְנֶגְדֶּךָ |
| ûvachmāthekhā | nivhālenû | | shattā | ‘ăwōnōthênû | leneghdekhā |
| and by your wrath | we have been dismayed | | You have placed | our trangressions | before You |

| 6180.155 | 3937, 4115 | 6686 | | 3706 | 3725, 3219 |
|---|---|---|---|---|---|
| v Qal pass ptc ms, ps 1cp | prep, *n ms* | n mp, ps 2ms | **9.** | cj | *adj*, n mp, ps 1cp |
| עֲלֻמֵנוּ | לִמְאוֹר | פָּנֶיךָ | | כִּי | כָל־יָמֵינוּ |
| ‘ălumēnû | lim'ôr | pānêkhā | | kî | khol-yāmênû |
| our concealed things | to the light of | your face | | because | all our days |

| 6680.116 | 904, 5887 | 3735.319 | 8523 | 3765, 1966 |
|---|---|---|---|---|
| v Qal pf 3cp | prep, n fs, ps 2ms | v Piel pf 1cp | n fp, ps 1cp | prep, n ms |
| פָּנוּ | בְעֶבְרָתֶךָ | כִּלִּינוּ | שָׁנֵינוּ | כְמוֹ־הֶגֶה |
| pānû | ve‘evrāthekhā | killînû | shānênû | khemô-hegheh |
| they have turned away | because of your rage | we make an end of | our years | like an utterance |

| | 3219, 8523 | 904 | 8124 | 8523 | 524 | 904, 1400 | 8470 | 8523 |
|---|---|---|---|---|---|---|---|---|
| **10.** | *n mp*, n fp, ps 1cp | prep, ps 3mp | num | n fs | cj, cj | prep, n fp | num | n fs |
| | יְמֵי־שְׁנוֹתֵינוּ | בָהֶם | שִׁבְעִים | שָׁנָה | וְאִם | בִּגְבוּרֹת | שְׁמוֹנִים | שָׁנָה |
| | yemê-shenôthênû | vāhem | shiv‘îm | shānāh | we'im | bighvûrōth | shemônîm | shānāh |
| | the days of our years | among them | seventy | years | or if | with might | eighty | years |

| 7582 | 6219 | 201 | 3706, 1500.111 | 2540 | 5990.120 |
|---|---|---|---|---|---|
| cj, n ms, ps 3mp | n ms | cj, n ms | cj, v Qal pf 3ms | adv | cj, v Qal impf 1cp |
| וְרָהְבָּם | עָמָל | וָאָוֶן | כִּי־גָז | חִישׁ | וַנָּעֻפָה |
| werāhebbām | ‘āmāl | wā'āwen | kî-ghāz | chîsh | wannā‘uphāh |
| then their pestilence | harm | and disaster | when they have passed by | quickly | then we fly away |

| | 4449, 3156.151 | 6010 | 653 | 3626, 3488 | 5887 |
|---|---|---|---|---|---|
| **11.** | intrg, v Qal act ptc ms | *n ms* | n ms, ps 2ms | cj, prep, n fs, ps 2ms | n fs, ps 2ms |
| | מִי־יוֹדֵעַ | עֹז | אַפֶּךָ | וּכְיִרְאָתְךָ | עֶבְרָתֶךָ |
| | mî-yôdhēa‘ | ‘ōz | 'appekhā | ûkheyir'āthekhā | ‘evrāthekhā |
| | who one who knows | the strength of | your anger | and like the fear of You | your rage |

| | 3937, 4630.141 | 3219 | 3772 | 3156.531 | 971.520 | 3949 |
|---|---|---|---|---|---|---|
| **12.** | prep, v Qal inf con | n mp, ps 1cp | adv | v Hiphil impv 2ms | cj, v Hiphil juss 1cp | *n ms* |
| | לִמְנוֹת | יָמֵינוּ | כֵּן | הוֹדַע | וְנָבִא | לְבַב |
| | limnôth | yāmênû | kēn | hôdha‘ | wenāvi' | levav |
| | to count | our days | so | make known | that we may cause to come | the heart of |

in the evening it is cut down and dries up, *KJVII* … if they blossom and are cut in the morning in the evening they will wither and dry up, *Beck* … that in the dawn is fresh and flourishing, and by the twilight fades and withers, *Moffatt.*

**7. For we are consumed by thine anger, and by thy wrath are we troubled:** … For we have been destroyed by your wrath, dismayed by your anger, *JB* … We are destroyed by your anger; we are terrified by your hot anger, *NCV* … For we faint at Your anger, And die at Your Wrath, *Fenton* … For under thine anger we perish, we sink in terror at thy wrath, *Moffatt.*

**8. Thou hast set our iniquities before thee, our secret sins in the light of thy countenance:** … You have taken note of our guilty deeds, our secrets in the full light of your presence, *JB* … You have put the evil we have done right in front of you; you clearly see our secret sins, *NCV* … Near you, our passions are set, Our faults in the light of Your face.

*Fenton* ... and our lusts in the full light of thy presence, *NEB.*

**9. For all our days are passed away in thy wrath: we spend our years as a tale that is told:** ... our years are like a cobweb wiped away, *Goodspeed* ... our years come to an end like a breath, *BB* ... we have spent our years like a sigh, *NAB* ... we spend our years as a passing thought, *Darby.*

**10. The days of our years are threescore years and ten; and if by reason of strength they be fourscore years, yet is their strength labour and sorrow; for it is soon cut off, and we fly away:** ... our life is seventy years, Perchance through strength eighty years, *Goodspeed* ... its pride is only trouble and sorrow, for it comes to an end and we are quickly gone, *BB* ... And most of them are fruitless toil, for they pass quickly and we drift away, *NAB* ... if there is great strength, eighty years—yet their best involves toil and grief, for it is soon gone, and we vanish, *Berkeley.*

**11. Who knoweth the power of thine anger? even according to thy fear, so is thy wrath:** ... Yet who weighs the full weight of thy displeasure? Which of us dreads thine anger, *Moffatt* ... Who can understand the violence of your wrath, or that those who fear you can be the object of your fury?, *Anchor* ... Who knows the force of Thy anger, and Thy awesomeness according to Thy indignation?, *Berkeley* ... For your wrath is as great as the fear that is due you, *NIV.*

**12. So teach us to number our days, that we may apply our hearts unto wisdom:** ... Teach us to count every passing day, till our hearts find wisdom, *Knox* ... that our minds may learn wisdom, *REB* ... That we may present to Thee a heart of wisdom, *NASB* ... that we may acquire discerning minds, *Berkeley.*

---

"They are as asleep." Some would take this to mean falling into the sleep of death; others would regard life as compared to a sleep. Luther noted, "Before we are rightly conscious of being alive, we cease to live." It is tempting to attach "in the morning" to "a sleep," but the recurrence of the expression in v. 7 points to the retention of the present division of clauses, according to which the springing grass greets the eye at dawn, as if created by a night's rain. The word rendered "springs afresh" (HED #6957) is taken in two opposite meanings, being by some rendered "passes away," and by others as above. Both meanings come from the same radical notion of change, but the latter is evidently the more natural and picturesque here as preserving, untroubled by any intrusion of an opposite thought.

**90:7–12.** The central portion of the Psalm narrows the circle of the poet's vision to Israel and brings out the connection between death and sin. The transition from truths of universal application is marked by the use of "we" and "us," while the past tenses indicate that the Psalm is recounting history. That transitoriness assumes a still more tragic aspect when regarded as the result of the collision of God's "wrath" with frail man. How can such stubble be wasted into ashes by such fire? And yet this is the same psalmist who has just discerned that the unchanging LORD is the dwelling-place of all generations. The change from the previous thought of the eternal God as the dwelling place of frail men is very marked in this section, in which the destructive anger of God is in view. But the singer felt no contradiction between the two thoughts, and there is none. We do not understand the full blessedness of believing that God is our asylum until we understand that He is our asylum from all that is destructive in himself; nor do we know the significance of the universal experience of decay and death until we learn that it is not the result of our finite being, but of sin.

That one note sounds on in solemn persistence through these verses, therein echoing the characteristic Mosaic lesson, and corresponding with the history of the people in the desert. In v. 7, the cause of their wasting away is declared to be God's wrath, which has scattered them as in panic (Ps. 58:5). The occasion of that lightning flash of anger is confessed in v. 8 to be the sins which, however hidden, stand revealed before God. The expression for "the light of thy face" is slightly different from the usual one, a word being employed which means a luminary and is used in Gen. 1 for the heavenly bodies. The ordinary phrase is always used as expressing favor and blessing, but there is an illumination, as from an all-revealing light, which flashes into all dark corners of human experience, and "there is nothing hid from the heat thereof" (Ps. 19:6). Sin smitten by that light must die. Therefore, in v. 9 the consequence of its falling on Israel's transgressions is set forth. Their days vanish as mists before the sun or as darkness glides out of the sky in the morning. Their noisy years are but as a murmur, scarcely breaking the deep silence and forgotten as soon as faintly heard. The psalmist sums up his sad contemplations in v. 10, in which life is regarded as not only rigidly circumscribed within a poor seventy or, at most, eighty years, but as being unsatisfying and burdensome by reason of its transitoriness. The "pride" which is but trouble and vanity is that which

| 2551 | | 8178.131 | 3176 | 5912, 5146 | 5341.231 |
|---|---|---|---|---|---|
| n fs | 13. | v Qal impv 2ms | pn | adv, intrg | cj, v Niphal impv 2ms |
| חָכְמָה | | שׁוּבָה | יְהוָה | עַד־מָתָי | וְהִנָּחֵם |
| chokhmāh | | shûvāh | yehwāh | ʻadh-māthāy | wehinnāchēm |
| wisdom | | return | O Yahweh | until when | and be compassionate |

| 6142, 5860 | | 7881.331 | 904, 1269 | 2721 |
|---|---|---|---|---|
| prep, n mp, ps 2ms | 14. | v Piel impv 2ms, ps 1cp | prep, art, n ms | n ms, ps 2ms |
| עַל־עֲבָדֶיךָ | | שַׂבְּעֵנוּ | בַבֹּקֶר | חַסְדֶּךָ |
| ʻal-ʻăvādhêkhā | | sabbeʻēnû | vabbōqer | chasdekhā |
| concerning your servants | | satisfy us | in the morning | your steadfast love |

| 7728.320 | 7975.120 | 904, 3725, 3219 | | 7975.331 |
|---|---|---|---|---|
| cj, v Piel juss 1cp | cj, v Qal juss 1cp | prep, *adj*, n mp, ps 1cp | 15. | v Piel impv 2ms, ps 1cp |
| וּנְרַנְּנָה | וְנִשְׂמְחָה | בְּכָל־יָמֵינוּ | | שַׂמְּחֵנוּ |
| ûnerannenāh | wenismechāh | bekhol-yāmênû | | sammechēnû |
| that we may shout for joy | that we may be glad | during all our days | | make us glad |

| 3626, 3219 | 6257.313 | 8523 | 7495.119 | 7750 | | 7495.221 |
|---|---|---|---|---|---|---|
| prep, n mp | v Piel pf 2ms, ps 1cp | n fp | v Qal pf 1cp | n fs | 16. | v Niphal juss 3ms |
| כִּימוֹת | עִנִּיתָנוּ | שְׁנוֹת | רָאִינוּ | רָעָה | | יֵרָאֶה |
| kîmôth | ʻinnîthānû | shenôth | rāʼînû | rāʻāh | | yērāʼeh |
| like the days | You answered us | years | we have seen | evil | | may it be manifested |

| 420, 5860 | 6714 | 1994 | 6142, 1158 | | 2030.121 |
|---|---|---|---|---|---|
| prep, n mp, ps 2ms | n ms, ps 2ms | cj, n ms, ps 2ms | prep, n mp, ps 3mp | 17. | cj, v Qal juss 3ms |
| אֶל־עֲבָדֶיךָ | פָעֳלֶךָ | וַהֲדָרְךָ | עַל־בְּנֵיהֶם | | וִיהִי |
| ʼel-ʻăvādhêkhā | phāʻălekhā | wahdhārekhā | ʻal-benêhem | | wîhî |
| to your servants | your deeds | and your majesty | on your children | | and may it be |

| 5461 | 112 | 435 | 6142 | 4801 | 3135 | 3679.331 |
|---|---|---|---|---|---|---|
| *n ms* | n mp, ps 1cs | n mp, ps 1cp | prep, ps 1cp | cj, *n ms* | n fd, ps 1cp | v Polel impv 2ms |
| נֹעַם | אֲדֹנָי | אֱלֹהֵינוּ | עָלֵינוּ | וּמַעֲשֵׂה | יָדֵינוּ | כּוֹנְנָה |
| nōʻam | ʼădhōnāy | ʼĕlōhênû | ʻālênû | ûmaʻăsēh | yādhênû | kônenāh |
| the pleasure of | my Lord | our God | on us | and the work of | our hands | establish |

| 6142 | 4801 | 3135 | 3679.331 | | 3553.151 |
|---|---|---|---|---|---|
| prep, ps 1cp | cj, *n ms* | n fd, ps 1cp | v Polel impv 2ms, ps 3ms | 91:1 | v Qal act ptc ms |
| עָלֵינוּ | וּמַעֲשֵׂה | יָדֵינוּ | כּוֹנְנֵהוּ | | יֹשֵׁב |
| ʻālênû | ûmaʻăsēh | yādhênû | kônenēhû | | yōshēv |
| concerning us | yes the work of | our hands | establish it | | the one who dwells |

**13. Return, O Lord, how long? and let it repent thee concerning thy servants:** ... how long? let your purpose for your servants be changed, *BB* ... how long? And have compassion upon thy servants, *Rotherham.*

**14. O satisfy us early with thy mercy; that we may rejoice and be glad all our days:** ... With Your mercy refresh us at dawn, *Fenton* ... Each morning fill us with your faithful love, we shall sing and be happy all our days, *JB* ... that we may shout for joy and happiness all our days, *Anchor* ... then we'll shout happily and be glad as long as we live, *Beck.*

**15. Make us glad according to the days wherein thou hast afflicted us, and the years wherein we have seen evil:** ... Now give us as much joy as you gave us sorrow, *NCV* ... Grant us days of gladness for the days you have humbled us, for the years when we have known misfortune, *REB* ... happiness that shall atone for the time when thou didst afflict us, for the long years of ill fortune, *Knox* ... the years when we experienced disaster, *JB.*

**16. Let thy work appear unto thy servants, and thy glory unto their children:** ... Let these eyes see thy purpose accomplished, to our own sons reveal thy glory, *Knox* ... Show your servants the deeds you do, let their children enjoy your splendour!, *JB* ... And thy splendor be upon their children, *Goodspeed.*

**17. And let the beauty of the Lord our God be upon us: and establish thou the work of our hands upon us; yea, the work of our hands establish thou it:** ... May the sweetness of the Lord be upon us, to confirm the work we have done!, *JB* ... May all delightful things be ours, O Lord our God; establish firmly all we do, *NEB* ... Give us success in what we do; yes, give us success in what we do, *NCV* ... and prosper for us the work of our hands, *NRSV.*

**91:1. He that dwelleth in the secret place of the most High shall abide under the shadow of the Almighty:** ... Those who go to God Most High for safety will be protected by the Almighty, *NCV* ... Let him who sits enthroned in the shelter of the Most High, passes the night in the shadow of Shaddai, *Anchor* ... Who rests in the Highest's Retreat, Reclined in the Almighty's shade, *Fenton* ... You who live in the secret place of Elyon, spend your nights in the shelter of Shaddai, *JB.*

**2. I will say of the LORD, He is my refuge and my fortress: my God; in him will I trust:** ... Say: 'O Yahweh, my refuge amd my mountain fastness, My God, in whom I trust!,' *Anchor* ... Can say this, The LORD is my hope, And I trust in my GOD as

---

John calls "the pride of life" (1 John 2:16), the objects which, apart from God, men desire to win, and glory in possessing. The self-gratulation would be less ridiculous or tragic if the things which evoke it lasted longer, or if we lasted longer to possess them. But seeing that they swiftly pass as we do, surely it is but "trouble" to fight for what is "vanity" when that which is won melts away so soon.

Plainly, then, man's wisdom is to seek to know two things—the power of God's anger and the measure of his own days. But alas for human levity and bondage to sense, how few look beyond the external, or lay to heart the solemn truth that God's wrath is inevitably operative against sin, and how few have any such just conception of it as to lead to reverential awe, proportioned to the divine character which should evoke it! Ignorance and inoperative knowledge divide mankind between them, and only a small remnant have let the truth plow deep into their inmost being and plant there holy fear of God. Therefore, the psalmist prays for himself and his people, as knowing the temptations to inconsiderate disregard and to inadequate feeling of God's opposition to sin, that his power would take untaught hearts in hand and teach them this—to count their days. Then we shall bring home, as from a ripened harvest field, the best fruit which life can yield, "a heart of wisdom," which having learned the power of God's anger and the number of our days turns itself to the eternal dwelling place, and no more is sad when it sees life ebbing away, or the generations moving in unbroken succession into the darkness.

**90:13–17.** The psalmist believes that God's justice has in store for his servants joys and blessings proportioned to the duration of their trials. He is not thinking of any future beyond the grave, but his prayer is a prophecy, which is often fulfilled even in this life and always hereafter. Sorrows rightly borne here are factors determining the glory that shall follow. There is a proportion between the years of affliction and the millennia of glory. But the final prayer, based upon all these thoughts of God's eternity and man's transitoriness, is not for blessedness, but for vision and divine favor on work done for Him. The deepest longing of the devout heart should be for the manifestation to itself and others of God's work. The psalmist is not only asking that God would put forth his acts in interposition for himself and his fellow servants, but also that the full glory of these far-reaching deeds may be disclosed to their understandings as well as experienced in their lives. And since he knows that through the ages an increasing purpose runs, he prays that coming generations may see even more glorious displays of divine power than his contemporaries have done. The psalmist's closing prayer reaches further than he knew. Lives on which the favor of God has come down like a dove and in which his will has been done are not flooded away, nor do they die into silence like a whisper, but carry in themselves the seeds of immortality and are akin to the eternity of God.

***Psalm 91.*** *We have this distribution of parts: v. 1, the broad statement of the blessedness of dwelling with God; v. 2, a solo, the voice of a heart encouraged thereby to exercise personal trust; vv. 3–8, answers, setting forth the security of such a refuge; v. 9a, solo, reiterating with sweet monotony the word of trust; vv. 9b–13, the first voice or chorus repeating with some variation the assurances of vv. 3–8; and vv. 14ff, God's acceptance of the trust and confirmation of the assurances.*

**91:1–2.** There is, no doubt, difficulty in v. 1; for, if it is taken as an independent sentence, it sounds tautological, since there is no well-marked difference between "sitting" and "lodging," nor much between "secret place" and "shadow." But possibly the idea of safety is more strongly conveyed by "shadow" than by "secret place," and the meaning of the apparently identical assertion may be that he who quietly enters into communion with God thereby passes into his protection. The psalmist speaks to Yahweh with the exclamation of

| 904, 5848 | 6169 | 904, 7009 | 8163 | 4053.721 | | 569.125 |
|---|---|---|---|---|---|---|
| prep, *n ms* | n ms | prep, *n ms* | n ms | v Hithpolel impf 3ms | **2.** | v Qal impf 1cs |
| בְּסֵתֶר | עֶלְיוֹן | בְּצֵל | שַׁדַּי | יִתְלוֹנָן | | אֹמַר |
| besēther | 'elyôn | betsēl | shadday | yithlônān | | 'ōmar |
| under the cover of | the Most High | in the shadow of | the Almighty | he will lodge | | I will say |

| 3937, 3176 | 4406 | 4859 | 435 | 1019.125, 904 | | 3706 | 2000 |
|---|---|---|---|---|---|---|---|
| prep, pn | n ms, ps 1cs | cj, n fs, ps 1cs | n mp, ps 1cs | v Qal impf 1cs, prep, ps 3ms | **3.** | cj | pers pron |
| לַיהוָה | מַחְסִי | וּמְצוּדָתִי | אֱלֹהַי | אֶבְטַח־בּוֹ | | כִּי | הוּא |
| layhwāh | machsî | ûmetsûdhāthî | 'ĕlōhay | 'evṭach-bô | | kî | hû' |
| to Yahweh | my Refuge | and my Fortress | my God | I will trust in Him | | because | He |

| 5522.521 | 4623, 6583 | 3463 | 4623, 1746 | 2010 |
|---|---|---|---|---|
| v Hiphil impf 3ms, ps 2ms | prep, *n ms* | n ms | prep, *n ms* | n fp |
| יַצִּילְךָ | מִפַּח | יָקוּשׁ | מִדֶּבֶר | הַוּוֹת |
| yatstsîlekhā | mippach | yāqûsh | middever | hawwôth |
| He will rescue you | from the snare of | the fowler | from the pestilence of | destruction |

| | 904, 79 | 5718.521 | 3937 | 8809, 3796 | 2725.123 |
|---|---|---|---|---|---|
| **4.** | prep, n fs, ps 3ms | v Hiphil juss 3ms | prep, ps 2ms | cj, prep, n fd, ps 3ms | v Qal impf 2ms |
| | בְּאֶבְרָתוֹ | יָסֶךְ | לָךְ | וְתַחַת־כְּנָפָיו | תֶּחְסֶה |
| | be'evrāthô | yāsekh | lākh | wethachath-kenāphâv | techăseh |
| | under his feathers | He will cover | you | and beneath his wings | you can take refuge |

| 7065 | 5695 | 583 | | 3940, 3486.123 | 4623, 6586 | 4050 |
|---|---|---|---|---|---|---|
| n fs | cj, n fs | n fs, ps 3ms | **5.** | neg part, v Qal impf 2ms | prep, *n ms* | n ms |
| צִנָּה | וְסֹחֵרָה | אֲמִתּוֹ | | לֹא־תִירָא | מִפַּחַד | לָיְלָה |
| tsinnāh | wesōcherāh | 'ămittô | | lō'-thîrā' | mippachadh | lāyelāh |
| a large shield | and a buckler | his faithfulness | | you will not be afraid | of the terror of | the night |

| 4623, 2777 | 5990.121 | 3221 | | 4623, 1746 | 904, 669 | 2050.121 |
|---|---|---|---|---|---|---|
| prep, n ms | v Qal impf 3ms | adv | **6.** | prep, n ms | prep, art, n ms | v Qal impf 3ms |
| מֵחֵץ | יָעוּף | יוֹמָם | | מִדֶּבֶר | בָּאֹפֶל | יַהֲלֹךְ |
| mēchēts | yā'ûph | yômām | | middever | bā'ōphel | yahlōkh |
| of the arrow | it flies | by day | | of the pestilence | in the darkness | it goes about |

| 4623, 7269 | 8161.121 | 6937 | | 5489.121 | 4623, 6917 | 512 |
|---|---|---|---|---|---|---|
| prep, n ms | v Qal impf 3ms | n mp | **7.** | v Qal impf 3ms | prep, n ms, ps 2ms | num |
| מִקֶּטֶב | יָשׁוּד | צָהֳרָיִם | | יִפֹּל | מִצִּדְּךָ | אֶלֶף |
| miqqeṭev | yāshûdh | tsāherāyim | | yippōl | mitstsiddekhā | 'eleph |
| of destruction | it lays waste | noon | | they will fall | from your side | one thousand |

| 7526 | 4623, 3332 | 420 | 3940 | 5242.121 | | 7828 |
|---|---|---|---|---|---|---|
| cj, num | prep, n fs, ps 2ms | prep, ps 2ms | neg part | v Qal impf 3ms | **8.** | adv |
| וּרְבָבָה | מִימִינֶךָ | אֵלֶיךָ | לֹא | יִגָּשׁ | | רַק |
| ûrevāvāh | mîmînekhā | 'ēlêkhā | lō' | yiggāsh | | raq |
| even ten thousand | from your right side | to you | not | it will approach | | only |

my Fort, *Fenton* ... Who says of the Lord, He is my safe place and my tower of strength: he is my God, in whom is my hope, *BB* ... The LORD is my safe retreat, my God the fastness in which I trust, *NEB.*

**3. Surely he shall deliver thee from the snare of the fowler, and from the noisome pestilence:** ... For He will release from the web, From the bird catcher's note of deceit, *Fenton* ... He it is will rescue thee from every treacherous lure, every destroying plague, *Knox* ... Certainly it is He who rescues you from the hunter's trap and from the fatal pestilence, *Berkeley* ... and from the deadly pit, *Moffatt.*

**4. He shall cover thee with his feathers, and under his wings shalt thou trust: his truth shall be thy shield and buckler:** ... under his wings you will be safe: his good faith will be your salvation, *BB* ... His arm is a shield and an armor, *Beck* ... A shield and buckler is his faithfulness, *Rotherham.*

**5. Thou shalt not be afraid for the terror by night; nor for the arrow that flieth by day:** ... Thou shalt not be afraid Of the dread of the night, *Rotherham* ... You need not fear the pack of the night, *Anchor* ... You will not fear the terrors abroad at night, *REB* ... you will not fear the hunters' trap by night or the arrow that flies by day, *NEB.*

**6. Nor for the pestilence that walketh in darkness; nor for the destruction that wasteth at noonday:** ... The plague that prowls in the dark, the scourge that stalks at noon, *Anchor* ... the plague that stalks in the darkness, the scourge that wreaks havoc at high noon, *JB* ... pestilence, walking in gloom, Nor contagion that wastes in the noon, *Fenton* ... nor sudden death at noon, *Moffatt.*

**7. A thousand shall fall at thy side, and ten thousand at thy right hand; but it shall not come nigh thee:** ... And a myriad at thy right hand, *Young* ... you yourself will remain unscathed, *JB* ... but the plague will never reach you, *Moffatt* ... But upon you they will not alight, *Fenton.*

**8. Only with thine eyes shalt thou behold and see the reward of the wicked:** ... You will only watch and see the wicked punished, *NCV* ... You have only to keep your eyes open to see how the wicked are repaid, *JB* ... With your own eyes you will observe this; you will see the retribution on the wicked, *REB* ... and see the requital of the wicked, *NCB.*

---

yearning trust. He can only call Him by precious names, the use which, in however broken a fashion, is an appeal that goes straight to his heart, as it comes straight from the suppliant's. The singer lovingly accumulates the divine names in the first verses. He calls God "Most High," "Almighty," when he utters the general truth of the safety of souls that enter his secret place; but, when he speaks his own trust, he addresses Yahweh and adds to the wide designation "God" the little word "my," which claims personal possession of his fulness of deity. The solo voice does not say much, but it says enough. There has been much underground work before that clear jet of personal "appropriating faith" could spring into light.

**91:3–4.** We might have looked for a selah here, if this Psalm had stood in the earlier books, but we can feel the brief pause before the choral answer comes in vv. 3–8. It sets forth in lofty poetry the blessings that such a trust secures. Its central idea is that of safety. That safety is guaranteed in regard to two classes of dangers—those from enemies, and those from diseases. Both are conceived of as divided into secret and open perils. Verse 3 proclaims the trustful soul's immunity, and v. 4 beautifully describes the divine protection which secures it. Verses 5f expand the general notion of safety, into defense against secret and open foes and secret and open pestilences; while vv. 7f sum up the whole, in a vivid contrast between the multitude of victims and the man sheltered in God, and looking out from his refuge on the wide-rolling flood of destruction. As in Ps. 18:5, death is represented as a "fowler" into whose snares men heedlessly flutter, unless held back by God's delivering hand. The mention of pestilence in v. 3 somewhat anticipates the proper order, as the same idea recurs in its appropriate place in v. 6. The beautiful description of God sheltering the trustful man beneath his pinions recalls Deut. 32:11 and Ps. 17:8; 63:7. The mother eagle, spreading her dread wing over her eaglets, is a wonderful symbol of the union of power and gentleness. It would be a bold hand which would drag the fledglings from that warm hiding place and dare the terrors of that beak and claws. But this pregnant verse (v. 4) not only tells of the strong defense which God is, but also sets in clear light man's way of reaching that asylum. "Under his wings shalt thou trust." It is the word which is often vaguely rendered "trust" (HED #2725), but which, if we retain its original signification, becomes illuminative as to what that trust is. The flight of the soul, conscious of nakedness and peril, to the safe shelter of God's breast is a description of faith which, in practical value, surpasses much learned dissertation. His faithfulness is our sure defense, and faith is our shield only in a secondary sense, its office being but to grasp our true defense and to keep us well behind that.

**91:5–8.** The assaults of enemies and the devastations of pestilence are taken in vv. 5f as types of all perils. These evils speak of a less artificial stage of society than that in which our experience moves, but they serve us as symbols of more complex dangers besetting outward and inward life. "The terror by night" seems best understood as parallel with the "arrow that flieth by day," insofar as both refer to actual attacks by enemies. Nocturnal surprises were favorite methods of assault in early warfare. Such an explanation is worthier than the supposition that the psalmist means demons that haunt the night. In v. 6, pestilence is personified as stalking, shrouded in darkness, the more terrible because it strikes unseen. Verse 6b has been understood, as by the

| 904, 6084 | 5202.523 | 8405 | 7857 | 7495.123 | | 3706, 887 |
|---|---|---|---|---|---|---|
| prep, n fd, ps 2ms | v Hiphil impf 2ms | cj, *n fs* | n mp | v Qal impf 2ms | **9.** | cj, pers pron |
| בְּעֵינֶיךָ | תַבִּיט | וְשִׁלֻּמַת | רְשָׁעִים | תִּרְאֶה | | כִּי־אַתָּה |
| be'ênêkhā | thabbîṯ | weshillumath | reshā'îm | tir'eh | | kî-'attāh |
| with your eyes | you will look upon | and the requital of | the wicked | you will see | | indeed You |

| 3176 | 4406 | 6169 | 7947.113 | 4737 | | 3940, 589.422 |
|---|---|---|---|---|---|---|
| pn | n ms, ps 1cs | n ms | v Qal pf 2ms | n ms, ps 2ms | **10.** | neg part, v Pual impf 3fs |
| יְהוָה | מַחְסִי | עֶלְיוֹן | שַׂמְתָּ | מְעוֹנֶךָ | | לֹא־תְאֻנֶּה |
| yehwāh | machsî | 'elyôn | samtā | me'ônekhā | | lō'-the'unneh |
| O Yahweh | my Refuge | the Most High | You have put | your dwelling place | | it will not happen |

| 420 | 7750 | 5237 | 3940, 7414.121 | 904, 164 | | 3706 | 4534 |
|---|---|---|---|---|---|---|---|
| prep, ps 2ms | n fs | cj, n ms | neg part, v Qal impf 3ms | prep, n ms, ps 2ms | **11.** | cj | n mp, ps 3ms |
| אֵלֶיךָ | רָעָה | וְנֶגַע | לֹא־יִקְרַב | בְּאָהֳלֶךָ | | כִּי | מַלְאָכָיו |
| 'ēlêkhā | rā'āh | wenegha' | lō'-yiqŏrav | be'āhelekhā | | kî | mal'ākhâv |
| to you | evil | and a wound | it will not come near | into your tent | | because | his angels |

| 6943.321, 3937 | 3937, 8490.141 | 904, 3725, 1932 | | 6142, 3834 |
|---|---|---|---|---|
| v Piel impf 3ms, prep, ps 2ms | prep, v Qal inf con, ps 2ms | prep, *n ms*, n mp, ps 2ms | **12.** | prep, n fd |
| יְצַוֶּה־לָּךְ | לִשְׁמָרְךָ | בְּכָל־דְּרָכֶיךָ | | עַל־כַּפַּיִם |
| yetsawweh-lākh | lishmārekhā | bekhol-derākhêkhā | | 'al-kappayim |
| He commands for you | to guard you | in all your ways | | on the hands |

| 5558.126 | 6678, 5238.123 | 904, 63 | 7559 | | 6142, 8256 |
|---|---|---|---|---|---|
| v Qal impf 3mp, ps 2ms | cj, v Qal impf 2ms | prep, art, n fs | n fs, ps 2ms | **13.** | prep, n ms |
| יִשָּׂאוּנְךָ | פֶּן־תִּגֹּף | בָּאֶבֶן | רַגְלֶךָ | | עַל־שַׁחַל |
| yissā'ûnkhā | pen-tiggōph | bā'even | raghlekhā | | 'al-shachal |
| they will lift you up | so that you will not strike | on the stone | your foot | | on the lion cub |

| 6874 | 1931.123 | 7717.123 | 3841 | 8906 | | 3706 |
|---|---|---|---|---|---|---|
| cj, n ms | v Qal impf 2ms | v Qal impf 2ms | n ms | cj, n ms | **14.** | cj |
| וָפֶתֶן | תִּדְרֹךְ | תִּרְמֹס | כְּפִיר | וְתַנִּין | | כִּי |
| wāphethen | tidhrōkh | tirmōs | kephîr | wethanîn | | kî |
| and the cobra | you will tread on | you will trample on | the young lion | and the serpent | | because |

| 904 | 2945.111 | 6647.325 | 7891.325 | 3706, 3156.111 |
|---|---|---|---|---|
| prep, ps 1cs | v Qal pf 3ms | cj, v Piel impf 1cs, ps 3ms | v Piel impf 1cs, ps 3ms | cj, v Qal pf 3ms |
| בִי | חָשַׁק | וַאֲפַלְּטֵהוּ | אֲשַׂגְּבֵהוּ | כִּי־יָדַע |
| vî | chāshaq | wa'ăphallețēhû | 'ăsaggevēhû | kî-yādha' |
| with Me | he is devoted | then I will set him free | I will make him inaccessible | because he knows |

| 8428 | | 7410.121 | 6257.125 | 6196, 609 | 904, 7150 |
|---|---|---|---|---|---|
| n ms, ps 1cs | **15.** | v Qal impf 3ms, ps 1cs | cj, v Qal impf 1cs, ps 3ms | prep, ps 3ms, pers pron | prep, n fs |
| שְׁמִי | | יִקְרָאֵנִי | וְאֶעֱנֵהוּ | עִמּוֹ־אָנֹכִי | בְצָרָה |
| shemî | | yiqŏrā'ēnî | we'e'ĕnēhû | 'immô-'ānōkhî | vetsārāh |
| my name | | he calls on Me | and I answer him | with him I | in adversity |

**9. Because thou hast made the LORD, which is my refuge, even the most High, thy habitation:** … Because you have said, I am in the hands of the Lord, The Most High is my resting-place, *BB* … For you, the LORD is a safe retreat; you have made the Most High your refuge, *NEB* … Whilst you have the LORD your guard, You placed on the Highest your hope, *Fenton* … If you consider Yahweh himself your refuge, the Most High your mainstay, *Anchor.*

**10. There shall no evil befall thee, neither shall any plague come nigh thy dwelling:** … No disaster shall befall you, no calamity shall come upon your home, *NEB* … So sickness will not approach you, Contagion not enter your Rest, *Fenton* … There shall not be sent unto thee misfortune, Nor shall plague come near into thy tent, *Rotherham* … no scourge come near your tent, *RSV.*

**11. For he shall give his angels charge over thee, to keep thee in all thy ways:** … For you He will order His angels to keep guard upon your paths, *Fenton* ... For he will give you into the care of his angels to keep you wherever you go, *BB* ... For to his angels he has given command about you, that they guard you in all your ways, *NAB* ... For He gives His angels orders regarding you, *Berkeley*.

**12. They shall bear thee up in their hands, lest thou dash thy foot against a stone:** ... They will support you with their hands, *Berkeley* ... In their hands they will keep you up, so that your foot may not be crushed against a stone, *BB* ... lest thou shouldst chance to trip on a stone, *Knox* ... for fear you strike your foot against a stone, *REB*.

**13. Thou shalt tread upon the lion and adder: the young lion and the dragon shalt thou trample under feet:** ... step on asp and cobra, you shall tread safely on snake and serpent, *NEB* ... trample the great lion and the serpent, *NIV* ... the young lion and the great snake will be crushed under your feet, *BB* ... trample on young lion and crocodile, *Rotherham*.

**14. Because he hath set his love upon me, therefore will I deliver him: I will set him on high, because he hath known my name:** ... Because he has anchored his love in Me, I will deliver him. I will place him securely on high, for he has faith in My name, *Berkeley* ... If he clings to me, I will rescue him; I will be his bulwark, if he acknowledges my Name, *Anchor* ... I will protect those who know me, *NCV*.

**15. He shall call upon me, and I will answer him: I will be with him in trouble; I will deliver him, and honour him:** ... When his cry comes up to me, I will give him an answer:

---

Targum and Septuagint, to refer to demons who exercise their power in noonday. But this explanation rests upon a misreading of the word rendered "wasteth" (HED #8161). The other, translated "sickness" (HED #1746), is only found, besides this place, in Deut. 32:24 ("destruction") and Isa. 28:2 ("a destroying storm," literally, a "storm of destruction") and in somewhat different form in Hos. 13:14. It comes from a root meaning "to cut," and seems here to be a synonym for pestilence. The trustful man, sheltered in God, looks on while thousands fall round him—as Israel looked from their homes on the Passover night—and sees that there is a God that judges and recompenses evildoers by evil suffered.

**91:9–13.** This second utterance of trust is almost identical with the first. Faith has no need to vary its expression. "The LORD, which is my refuge" is enough for it. God's mighty name and its personal possession of all which that name means, as its own hiding place, are its treasures, which it does not weary of recounting. Love loves to repeat itself. The deepest emotions, like songbirds, have but two or three notes, which they sing over and over again all the long day through. He that can use this singer's words of trust has a vocabulary rich enough.

The responsive assurances are, in like manner, substantially identical with the preceding ones, but differences may be discerned by which these are heightened in comparison with the former. The promise of immunity is more general. Instead of two typical forms of danger, the widest possible exemption from all forms of it is declared in v. 10. No evil shall come near, no scourge approach, the "tent" of the man whose real and permanent "dwelling place" is Yahweh. There is great beauty and significance in that contrast of the two homes in which a godly man lives. His housing, as far as his outward life is concerned, is in a transitory abode, which tomorrow may be rolled up and moved to another camping place in the desert, but he abides, insofar as his true being is concerned, in God, the permanent dwelling place through all generations. The transitory outward life has reflected on it some light of peaceful security from that true home. It is further noteworthy that the second group of assurances is concerned with active life, while the first only represented a passive condition of safety beneath God's wing. In vv. 11f, his angels take the place of protectors, and the sphere in which they protect is "in all thy ways"— in the activities of ordinary life. The dangers there are of stumbling, whether that be construed as referring to outward difficulties or to temptations to sin.

The perils, further specified in v. 13, correspond to those of the previous part in being open and secret: the lion with its roar and leap, the adder with its stealthy glide among the herbage and its unlooked-for bite. So, the two sets of assurances, taken together, cover the whole ground of life, both in its moments of hidden communion in the secret place of the Most High and in its times of diligent discharge of duty on life's common way. Perils of communion and perils of work are equally real, and equally may we be sheltered from them. God himself spreads his wing over the trustful man and sends his messengers to keep him in all the paths appointed for him by God. The angels have no charge to take stones out of the way. Hinderances are good for us. Smooth paths weary and make presumptuous. Rough ones bring out our best and drive us to look to God.

**91:14–16.** Finally, God himself speaks, and confirms and deepens the previous assurances. That He is represented as speaking of, not to, his servant

| | | | | | |
|---|---|---|---|---|---|
| 2603.325 | 3632.325 | 16. | 775 | 3219 | 7881.525 |
| v Piel impf 1cs, ps 3ms | cj, v Piel impf 1cs, ps 3ms | | *n ms* | n mp | v Hiphil impf 1cs, ps 3ms |
| אֲחַלְּצֵהוּ | וַאֲכַבְּדֵהוּ | | אֹרֶךְ | יָמִים | אַשְׂבִּיעֵהוּ |
| 'ăchalletsēhû | wa'ăkhabbedhēhû | | 'ōrekh | yāmîm | 'asbî'ēhû |
| I will set him apart | and I will honor him | | length of | days | I will satiate him with |

| | | | | | | |
|---|---|---|---|---|---|---|
| 7495.525 | 904, 3568 | 92:t | 4344 | 8302 | 3937, 3219 | 8141 |
| cj, v Hiphil impf 1cs, ps 3ms | prep, n fs, ps 1cs | | n ms | n ms | prep, *n ms* | art, n fs |
| וְאַרְאֵהוּ | בִּישׁוּעָתִי | | מִזְמוֹר | שִׁיר | לְיוֹם | הַשַּׁבָּת |
| we'ar'ēhû | bîshû'āthî | | mizmôr | shîr | leyôm | hashshabbāth |
| and I will cause him to look | on my salvation | | a Psalm | a Song | for the day of | the Sabbath |

| | | | | | | |
|---|---|---|---|---|---|---|
| 1. | 3005 | 3937, 3142.541 | 3937, 3176 | 3937, 2252.341 | 3937, 8428 | 6169 |
| | adj | prep, v Hiphil inf con | prep, pn | cj, prep, v Piel inf con | prep, n ms, ps 2ms | n ms |
| | טוֹב | לְהֹדוֹת | לַיהוָה | וּלְזַמֵּר | לְשִׁמְךָ | עֶלְיוֹן |
| | ṯôv | lehōdhôth | layhwāh | ûlăzammēr | leshimkhā | 'elyôn |
| | good | to praise | Yahweh | and to sing praises | to your name | the Most High |

| | | | | | |
|---|---|---|---|---|---|
| 2. | 3937, 5222.541 | 904, 1269 | 2721 | 536 | 904, 4050 |
| | prep, v Hiphil inf con | prep, art, n ms | n ms, ps 2ms | cj, n fs, ps 2ms | prep, art, n mp |
| | לְהַגִּיד | בַּבֹּקֶר | חַסְדֶּךָ | וֶאֱמוּנָתְךָ | בַּלֵּילוֹת |
| | lehaggîdh | babbōqer | chasdekhā | we'ĕmûnāthekhā | ballêlôth |
| | to expound | in the morning | your steadfast love | and your faithfulness | during the nights |

| | | | | | | | |
|---|---|---|---|---|---|---|---|
| 3. | 6142, 6452 | 6142, 5213 | 6142 | 1970 | 904, 3780 | 4. | 3706 |
| | prep, n ms | cj, prep, n ms | prep | n ms | prep, n ms | | cj |
| | עֲלֵי־עָשׂוֹר | וַעֲלֵי־נָבֶל | עֲלֵי | הִגָּיוֹן | בְּכִנּוֹר | | כִּי |
| | 'ălê-'āsôr | wa'ălê-nāvel | 'ălê | higgāyôn | bekhinnôr | | kî |
| | on the tenths | and on the harp | according to | a meditation | with the zither | | because |

| | | | | |
|---|---|---|---|---|
| 7975.313 | 3176 | 904, 6714 | 904, 4801 | 3135 |
| v Piel pf 2ms, ps 1cs | pn | prep, n ms, ps 2ms | prep, *n mp* | n fd, ps 2ms |
| שִׂמַּחְתַּנִי | יְהוָה | בְּפָעֳלֶךָ | בְּמַעֲשֵׂי | יָדֶיךָ |
| simmachtanî | yehwāh | bephā'ālekhā | bema'ăsê | yādhêkhā |
| You make me glad | O Yahweh | because of your deeds | because of the works of | your hands |

| | | | | | | |
|---|---|---|---|---|---|---|
| 7728.325 | 5. | 4242, 1461.116 | 4801 | 3176 | 4108 | 6230.116 |
| v Piel impf 1cs | | intrg, v Qal pf 3cp | n mp, ps 2ms | pn | adv | v Qal pf 3cp |
| אֲרַנֵּן | | מַה־גָּדְלוּ | מַעֲשֶׂיךָ | יְהוָה | מְאֹד | עָמְקוּ |
| 'ărannēn | | mah-gādhelû | ma'ăsêkhā | yehwāh | me'ōdh | 'āmeqû |
| I will shout for joy | | how great are they | your works | O Yahweh | very | they are deep |

I will be with him in trouble; I will make him free from danger and give him honour, *BB* … I will listen, in affliction I am at his side, to bring him safety and honour, *Knox* … He calls,—I reply I am with You; I deliver and help in distress, *Fenton* … From his anguish will I rescue him, and I will feast him, *Anchor.*

**16. With long life will I satisfy him, and show him my salvation:** … Length of days he shall have to content him, and find in me deliverance, *Knox* … With length of days will I content him, and make him drink deeply of my salvation, *Anchor* … And let him behold My salvation, *NASB* … And make him to behold My salvation, *MAST.*

**92:t. A Psalm or Song for the sabbath day.**

**1. It is a good thing to give thanks unto the LORD, and to sing praises unto thy name, O most High:** … LORD, to praise You is sweet, And HIGHEST, to sing Your Name, *Fenton* … Sweet it is to praise the Lord, to sing, most high God, in honour of thy name, *Knox* … and to make melody to your name, O Most High, *BB.*

**2. To show forth thy lovingkindness in the morning, and thy faithfulness every night:** … It is good to tell of your love in the morning and of your loyalty at night, *NCV* … to proclaim your love at daybreak, and your fidelity through the watches of the night, *Anchor* … your kindness at dawn and your faithfulness throughout the night, *NCB* … To make clear your mercy in the morning, and your unchanging faith every night, *BB.*

**3. Upon an instrument of ten strings, and upon the psaltery; upon the harp with a solemn sound:** ... With the ten-stringed lute, and with the harp; With resounding music upon the lyre, *NASB* ... On ten strings and on psaltery, On higgaion, with harp, *Young* ... to the music of the lute and the harp, to the melody of the lyre, *RSV* ... on the harp with deep thought, *KJVII.*

**4. For thou, LORD, hast made me glad through thy work: I will triumph in the works of thy hands:** ... Your acts, LORD, fill me with exultation; I shout in triumph at your mighty deeds, *REB* ... For your works, LORD, delight, I am cheered by the work of your hands, *Fenton* ... hast made me glad by thy work; at the works of thy hands I sing for joy, *RSV* ... thy doings have made me glad, O thou Eternal, I sing for joy at all thou hast done, *Moffatt.*

**5. O LORD, how great are thy works! and thy thoughts are very deep:** ... How great are thy deeds, O Eternal, how deep are thy designs!, *Moffatt* ... How great have grown thy works Yahweh, how very deep are laid thy plans!, *Rotherham* ... How great are thy deeds, O LORD! How fathomless thy thoughts!, *NEB* ... How magnificent is thy creation, Lord, how unfathomable are thy purposes!, *Knox.*

---

increases the majesty of the utterance by seeming to call the universe to hear and converts promises to an individual into promises to everyone who will fulfill the requisite conditions. These are threefold.

God desires that men should cling to Him, know his name and call on Him. The word rendered "devoted" (HED #2945) includes more than "setting love upon" one. It means "to bind" or "to knit oneself" to anything, and so embraces the cleaving of a fixed heart, of a "recollected" mind and of an obedient will. Such clinging demands effort, for every hand relaxes its grasp, unless ever and again tightened. He who thus clings will come to know God's name, with the knowledge which is born of experience and is loving familiarity, not mere intellectual apprehension. Such clinging and knowledge will find utterance in continual communion with God, not only when needing deliverance, but in perpetual aspiration after Him.

The promises to such a one go very deep and stretch very far. "I will deliver him." So the previous assurance that no evil shall come nigh to him is explained and brought into correspondence with the facts of life. Evil may be experienced. Sorrows will come, but they will not touch the central core of the true life, and from them God will deliver, not only by causing them to cease, but by fitting us to bear.

"With long life will I satisfy him" is, no doubt, a promise belonging more especially to OT times, but if we put emphasis on "satisfy," rather than on the extended duration, it may fairly suggest that life is long enough to the trustful soul whatever its duration, and that the guest, who has sat at God's table here, is not unwilling to rise from it when his time comes, being "satisfied with favour, and full with the blessing of the LORD" (Deut. 33:23). The vision of God's salvation, which is set last, seems from its position in the series to point to a vision which comes after earth's troubles and length of days. The psalmist's language implies not a mere casual beholding, but a fixed gaze. Such seeing is possession. The crown of God's promises to the man who makes God his dwelling place is a full, rapturous experience of a full salvation, which follows on the troubles and deliverances of earth and brings a more dazzling honor and a more perfect satisfaction.

***Psalm 92.*** *Here are five strophes of three verses each, of which the first is introductory; the second and third, a pair setting forth the aspect of providence toward the wicked; and the fourth and fifth, another pair, magnifying its dealings with the righteous.*

**92:1–3.** Verses 1ff are in any case introductory. In form, they are addressed to Yahweh, in thankful acknowledgment of the privilege and joy of praise. In reality, they are a summons to men to taste its gladness and to fill each day and brighten every night by music of thanksgiving. The devout heart feels that worship is "good," not only as being acceptable to God and conformable to man's highest duty, but as being the source of delight to the worshiper. Nothing is more characteristic of the Psalter than the joy which often dances and sings through its strains. Nothing affords a surer test of the reality of worship than the worshiper's joy in it. With much significance and beauty, "thy steadfast love" is to be the theme of each morning, as we rise to a new day and find his mercy, radiant as the fresh sunshine, waiting to bless our eyes, and "thy faithfulness" is to be sung in the night seasons, as we part from another day which has witnessed to his fulfillment of all his promises.

**92:4–6.** The second strophe contains the reason for praise—the greatness and depth of the divine works and purposes. The works meant are, as is obvious from the whole strain of the Psalm, those of God's government of the world. The theme which exercised earlier psalmists reappears here, but the struggles of

| 4422 | | 382, 1221 | 3940 | 3156.121 | 3811 | 3940, 1032.121 |
|---|---|---|---|---|---|---|
| n fp, ps 2ms | 6. | *n ms*, adj | neg part | v Qal impf 3ms | cj, n ms | neg part, v Qal impf 3ms |
| מַחְשְׁבֹתֶיךָ | | אִישׁ־בַּעַר | לֹא | יֵדָע | וּכְסִיל | לֹא־יָבִין |
| machsh$^{e}$vōthêkhā | | 'îsh-ba'ar | lō' | yēdhā' | ûkh$^{e}$sîl | lō'-yāvîn |
| your thoughts | | a stupid man | not | he knows | and the fool | he does not understand |

| 881, 2148 | | 904, 6775.141 | 7857 | 3765 | 6448 | 6957.126 |
|---|---|---|---|---|---|---|
| do, dem pron | 7. | prep, v Qal inf con | n mp | prep | n ms | cj, v Qal impf 3mp |
| אֶת־זֹאת | | בִּפְרֹחַ | רְשָׁעִים | כְּמוֹ | עֵשֶׂב | וַיָּצִיצוּ |
| 'eth-zō'th | | biphrōach | r$^{e}$shā'îm | k$^{e}$mô | 'ēsev | wayyātsîtsû |
| this | | because sprouting | the wicked | like | grass | and they flourish |

| 3725, 6713.152 | 201 | 3937, 8436.241 | 5912, 5911 | | 887 | 4953 |
|---|---|---|---|---|---|---|
| *adj, v Qal act ptc mp* | n ms | prep, v Niphal inf con, ps 3mp | prep, n ms | 8. | cj, pers pron | adj |
| כָּל־פֹּעֲלֵי | אָוֶן | לְהִשָּׁמְדָם | עֲדֵי־עַד | | וְאַתָּה | מָרוֹם |
| kol-pō'ălê | 'āwen | l$^{e}$hishshām$^{e}$dhām | 'ădhê-'adh | | w$^{e}$'attāh | mārôm |
| all those who practice | iniquity | to their being destroyed | until everlasting | | but You | on high |

| 3937, 5986 | 3176 | | 3706 | 2079 | 342.152 | 3176 | 3706, 2079 |
|---|---|---|---|---|---|---|---|
| prep, n ms | pn | 9. | cj | intrj | v Qal act ptc mp, ps 2ms | pn | cj, intrj |
| לְעֹלָם | יְהוָה | | כִּי | הִנֵּה | אֹיְבֶיךָ | יְהוָה | כִּי־הִנֵּה |
| l$^{e}$'ōlām | y$^{e}$hwāh | | kî | hinnēh | 'ōy$^{e}$vêkhā | y$^{e}$hwāh | kî-hinnēh |
| to eternity | O Yahweh | | because | behold | your enemies | O Yahweh | because behold |

| 342.152 | 6.126 | 6815.726 | 3725, 6713.152 | 201 |
|---|---|---|---|---|
| v Qal act ptc mp, ps 2ms | v Qal impf 3mp | v Hithpael impf 3mp | *adj, v Qal act ptc mp* | n ms |
| אֹיְבֶיךָ | יֹאבֵדוּ | יִתְפָּרְדוּ | כָּל־פֹּעֲלֵי | אָוֶן |
| 'ōy$^{e}$vêkhā | yō'vēdhû | yithpār$^{e}$dhû | kol-pō'ălê | 'āwen |
| your enemies | they perish | they will be scattered | all those who practice | iniquity |

| | 7597.523 | 3626, 7508 | 7451 | 1140.115 | 904, 8467 | 7776 |
|---|---|---|---|---|---|---|
| 10. | cj, v Hiphil impf 2ms | prep, n ms | n fs, ps 1cs | v Qal pf 1cs | prep, n ms | adj |
| | וַתָּרֶם | כִּרְאֵים | קַרְנִי | בַּלֹּתִי | בְּשֶׁמֶן | רַעֲנָן |
| | wattārem | kir'êm | qarnî | ballōthî | b$^{e}$shemen | ra'ănān |
| | but You have exalted | like a wild ox | my horn | I have mixed | with olive oil | fresh |

| | 5202.522 | 6084 | 904, 8230 | 904, 7251.152 | 6142 |
|---|---|---|---|---|---|
| 11. | cj, v Hiphil impf 3fs | n fs, ps 1cs | prep, n mp, ps 1cs | prep, art, v Qal act ptc mp | prep, ps 1cs |
| | וַתַּבֵּט | עֵינִי | בְּשׁוּרָי | בַּקָּמִים | עָלַי |
| | wattabbēṯ | 'ênî | b$^{e}$shûrāy | baqqāmîm | 'ālay |
| | and it has looked down | my eye | over my wall | on those who rise up | against me |

| 7778.552 | 8471.127 | 238 | | 6926 | 3626, 8887 | 6775.121 |
|---|---|---|---|---|---|---|
| v Hiphil ptc mp | v Qal impf 3fp | n fd, ps 1cs | 12. | n ms | prep, art, n ms | v Qal impf 3ms |
| מְרֵעִים | תִּשְׁמַעְנָה | אָזְנָי | | צַדִּיק | כַּתָּמָר | יִפְרָח |
| m$^{e}$rē'îm | tishma'ănāh | 'āz$^{e}$nāy | | tsaddîq | kattāmār | yiphrāch |
| evildoers | they have heard | my ears | | the righteous | like the palm tree | they sprout up |

**6. A brutish man knoweth not; neither doth a fool understand this:** … the dull man does not see, the senseless does not understand, *Moffatt* … Stupid people cannot realise this, fools do not grasp it, *JB* … Anyone who does not grasp this is a stupid person, and a fool does not understand it, *REB* … And still, too dull to learn, too slow to grasp his lesson, the wrong-doer, *Knox*.

**7. When the wicked spring as the grass, and when all the workers of iniquity do flourish; it is that they shall be destroyed for ever:** … Wicked people grow like grass. Evil people seem to do well, but they will be destroyed forever, *NCV* … When the wicked sprouted like weeds, and all the evildoers thrived, He completely destroyed them for all time!, *Anchor* … all who do wrong blossom like flowers only to be killed off forever, *Beck* … when bad men thrive like grass, and evildoers flourish, 'tis only to be rooted up forever, *Moffatt*.

**8. But thou, LORD, art most high for evermore:** … But you, Yahweh, are the Exalted from eternity, *Anchor* … while you, LORD, reign for ever,

*REB* ... whereas you are supreme for ever, Yahweh, *JB* ... honored forever, *NCV.*

**9. For, lo, thine enemies, O LORD, for, lo, thine enemies shall perish; all the workers of iniquity shall be scattered:** ... For, look, how Your foeman, O LORD Yes! see, how Your enemies perish, And the products of Wickedness fail, *Fenton* ... Vanished away the enemies, Lord, vanished away, and all their busy wickedness scattered to the winds!, *Knox* ... For see! your haters, O Lord, will be put to death; all workers of evil will be put to flight, *BB* ... all those who habitually sin shall bring about their own separation, *Berkeley.*

**10. But my horn shalt thou exalt like the horn of an unicorn: I shall be anointed with fresh oil:** ... But thou wilt exalt as those of the buffalo, my horn, I have been anointed, with fresh oil, *Rotherham* ... But Thou hast magnified my horn like that of the wild ox; I am anointed with invigorating oil, *Berkeley* ... But thou dost raise me high to honour, thou doest revive my failing strength, *Moffatt* ... But You set up my horn like a bull's That bellows in richness of food, *Fenton.*

**11. Mine eye also shall see my desire on mine enemies, and mine ears shall hear my desire of the wicked that rise up against me:** ... I gloat over all who speak ill of me, I listen for the downfall of my cruel foes, *NEB* ... My eyes see those who watch for me, my ears hear the evildoers attacking me, *Beck* ... I caught sight of the ambush against me, overheard the plans of the wicked, *JB.*

**12. The righteous shall flourish like the palm tree: he shall grow like a cedar in Lebanon:** ... The good man will be like a tall tree in his strength; his growth will be as the wide-stretching trees of Lebanon, *BB* ... shoot forth like a palm-tree; he shall grow like a cedar on Lebanon, *Darby* ... The innocent man will flourish as the palm-tree flourishes; he will grow to greatness as the cedars grow on Lebanon, *Knox.*

---

faith with unbelief, which are so profoundly and pathetically recorded in Ps. 73. are ended for this singer. He bows in trustful adoration before the greatness of the works and the unsearchable depth of the purpose of God which directs the works. The sequence of vv. 4ff is noteworthy. The central place is occupied by v. 5—a wondering and reverent exclamation, evoked by the very mysteries of providence. On either side of it stand verses describing the contrasted impression made by these on devout and on gross minds. The psalmist and his fellows are "gladdened," although he cannot see to the utmost verge or deepest abyss of works or plans. What he does see is good, and if sight does not go down to the depths, it is because eyes are weak, not because these are less pellucid than the sunlit shallows. What gladdens the trustful soul, which is in sympathy with God, only bewilders the "brutish man"—the man who by immersing his faculties in sense has descended to the animal level. It is too grave and weighty for the "fool," the man of incurable levity and self conceit, to trouble himself to ponder. The eye sees what it is capable of seeing. A man's judgment of God's dealings depends on his relationship to God and on the dispositions of his soul.

**92:7–9.** The sterner aspect of providence is dealt with in the next strophe. Some recent signal destruction of evildoers seems to be referred to. It exemplifies once more the old truth, which another psalmist had sung (Ps. 37:2), that the prosperity of evildoers is short-lived, like the blossoming herbage, and not only short-lived, but itself the occasion of their destruction. The apparent success of the wicked is as a pleasant slope that leads downward. The quicker the blossoming, the sooner the petals fall. The prosperity of fools shall destroy them. As the middle verse in the previous strophe was central in idea as well as in place, so in this one. Verse 8 states the great fact from which the overthrow of the wicked results, which is declared in the verses before and after. God's eternal elevation above the transitory and the evil is not merely contrasted with these, but is assigned as the reason why what is evil is transitory. We might render "thou, LORD, art most high for evermore," as, in effect, the Septuagint and other old versions do; but the application of such an epithet to God is unexampled, and the rendering above is preferable.

All God's enemies shall perish, as the psalmist reiterates, with triumphant reduplication of the designation of the foes, as if he would make plain that the very name "God's enemies" contained a prophecy of their destruction. However closely banded, they "shall be scattered." Evil may make conspiracies for a time, for common hatred of good brings discordant elements into strange fellowship, but in its real nature it is divisive, and sooner or later allies in wickedness become foes, leaving no two of them together. The only lasting human association is that which binds men to one another, because all are bound to God.

**92:10–12.** From the scattered fugitives, the psalmist turns first to joyful contemplation of his own blessedness and then to wider thoughts of the general well-being of all God's friends. The more personal references are comprised in the fourth strophe (vv. 10ff). The metaphor of the exalted horn

| | | | | | | |
|---|---|---|---|---|---|---|
| 3626, 753<br>prep, n ms<br>כְּאֶרֶז<br>ke'erez<br>like a cedar | 904, 3976<br>prep, art, pn<br>בַּלְּבָנוֹן<br>ballevānôn<br>in the Lebanon | 7889.121<br>v Qal impf 3ms<br>יִשְׂגֶּה<br>yisgeh<br>they become large | **13.** | 8694.156<br>v Qal pass ptc mp<br>שְׁתוּלִים<br>shethûlîm<br>transplanted | 904, 1041<br>prep, *n ms*<br>בְּבֵית<br>bevêth<br>in the Temple of | 3176<br>pn<br>יְהוָה<br>yehwāh<br>Yahweh |

| | | | | | | | |
|---|---|---|---|---|---|---|---|
| 904, 2793<br>prep, *n fp*<br>בְּחַצְרוֹת<br>bechatsrôth<br>in the courts of | 435<br>n mp, ps 1cp<br>אֱלֹהֵינוּ<br>'ĕlōhênû<br>our God | 6775.526<br>v Hiphil impf 3mp<br>יַפְרִיחוּ<br>yaphrîchû<br>they sprout up | **14.** | 5968<br>adv<br>עוֹד<br>'ôdh<br>continually | 5286.126<br>v Qal impf 3mp<br>יְנוּבוּן<br>yenûvûn<br>they thrive | 904, 7939<br>prep, n fs<br>בְּשֵׂיבָה<br>besêvāh<br>in old age | 1943<br>adj<br>דְּשֵׁנִים<br>deshēnîm<br>fat |

| | | | | | | |
|---|---|---|---|---|---|---|
| 7776<br>cj, adj<br>וְרַעֲנַנִּים<br>wera'ănanîm<br>and fresh | 2030.126<br>v Qal impf 3ms<br>יִהְיוּ<br>yihyû<br>they are | **15.** | 3937, 5222.541<br>prep, v Hiphil inf con<br>לְהַגִּיד<br>lehaggîdh<br>to expound | 3706, 3596<br>cj, adj<br>כִּי־יָשָׁר<br>kî-yāshār<br>because upright | 3176<br>pn<br>יְהוָה<br>yehwāh<br>Yahweh | 6962<br>n ms, ps 1cs<br>צוּרִי<br>tsûrî<br>my Rock |

| | | | | | | |
|---|---|---|---|---|---|---|
| 3940, 5984<br>cj, neg part, n fs<br>וְלֹא־עַלָתָה<br>welō'-'ōlāthāh<br>and no perversity | 904<br>prep, ps 3ms<br>בּוֹ<br>bô<br>in Him | **93:1** | 3176<br>pn<br>יְהוָה<br>yehwāh<br>Yahweh | 4566.111<br>v Qal pf 3ms<br>מָלָךְ<br>mālākh<br>He reigns | 1378<br>n fs<br>גֵּאוּת<br>gē'ûth<br>majesty | 3980.111<br>v Qal pf 3ms<br>לָבֵשׁ<br>lāvēsh<br>He is clothed with |

| | | | | | |
|---|---|---|---|---|---|
| 3980.111<br>v Qal pf 3ms<br>לָבֵשׁ<br>lāvēsh<br>He is clothed with | 3176<br>pn<br>יְהוָה<br>yehwāh<br>Yahweh | 6010<br>n ms<br>עֹז<br>'ōz<br>strength | 246.711<br>v Hithpael pf 3ms<br>הִתְאַזָּר<br>hith'azzār<br>He is girded with | 652, 3679.222<br>cj, v Niphal impf 3fs<br>אַף־תִּכּוֹן<br>'aph-tikkôn<br>indeed it is established | 8725<br>n fs<br>תֵּבֵל<br>tēvēl<br>the world |

| | | | | | | |
|---|---|---|---|---|---|---|
| 1118, 4267.222<br>neg part, v Niphal impf 3fs<br>בַּל־תִּמּוֹט<br>bal-timmôṯ<br>it will not totter | **2.** | 3679.255<br>v Niphal ptc ms<br>נָכוֹן<br>nākhôn<br>established | 3802<br>n ms, ps 2ms<br>כִּסְאֲךָ<br>kis̱'ākhā<br>your throne | 4623, 226<br>prep, adv<br>מֵאָז<br>mē'āz<br>from then | 4623, 5986<br>prep, n ms<br>מֵעוֹלָם<br>mē'ôlām<br>from eternity | 887<br>pers pron<br>אַתָּה<br>'āttāh<br>You |

**13. Those that be planted in the house of the LORD shall flourish in the courts of our God:** … Transplanted to the house of Yahweh, they will richly flourish in the court of our God, *Anchor* … They are planted in the LORD's house, they blossom like flowers in the courts of our God, *Beck* … will come up tall and strong in his gardens, *BB* … they flourish in the courts of our God, *Moffatt.*

**14. They shall still bring forth fruit in old age; they shall be fat and flourishing:** … When they are old they will still produce fruit; they will be healthy and fresh, *NCV* … Still full of sap in old age, they will remain fresh and green, *Anchor* … They shall bear fruit even in old age; vigorous and sturdy shall they be, *NAB* … they still bear fruit in old age; they are luxuriant, wide-spreading trees, *REB.*

**15. To show that the LORD is upright: he is my rock, and there is no unrighteousness in him:** … the LORD means what He says. He's my Rock, and there's no iniquity in Him!, *Beck* … proclaiming, 'The LORD is upright; he is my Rock, and there is no wickedness in him,' *NIV* … the LORD is right, My rock, in whom there is no wrong, *Goodspeed* … there is no perverseness in Him!, *Young.*

**93:1. The LORD reigneth, he is clothed with majesty; the LORD is clothed with strength, wherewith he hath girded himself:** … The LORD is King! He dresses in majesty, *Beck* … Yahweh reigns, in majesty robed, Robed is Yahweh, belted with victory, *Anchor.*

**the world also is stablished, that it cannot be moved:** … The world also was made to stand firm and can't be moved, *Beck* … Indeed, the world is established immovable, *Goodspeed* … Surely he hath fixed the world, It shall not be shaken, *Rotherham* … Yes! fixed like Earth's orbit secure, *Fenton.*

**2. Thy throne is established of old: thou art from everlasting:** … Thy throne has been established from of old, *Goodspeed* … The seat of your power has been from the past; you are eternal, *BB* … You settled Your Throne—For, from ever, YOU WERE!, *Fenton* … LORD, your kingdom was set up long ago; you are everlasting, *NCV.*

expresses, as in Pss. 75:10 and 39:17, triumph or the vindication of the psalmist by his deliverance. Verse 10b is very doubtful. The word usually rendered "I am anointed" (HED #1140) is peculiar. Another view of the word takes it for an infinitive used as a noun, with the meaning "growing old" or "wasting strength." This translation ("my wasting strength with rich oil") is that of the Septuagint and other ancient versions. If adopted, the verb must be understood as repeated from the preceding clause, and the slight incongruity thence arising can be lessened by giving a somewhat wider meaning to "exalted," such as "strengthen" or the like. The psalmist would then represent his deliverance as being like refreshing a failing old age, by anointing with fresh oil.

Thus triumphant and quickened, he expects to gaze on the downfall of his foes. He uses the same expression as is found in Ps. 91:8, with a similar connotation of calm security and possibly of satisfaction. There is no need for heightening his feelings into "desire." A less personal verse (v. 12) forms the transition to the last strophe, which is concerned with the community of the righteous. Here the singular number is retained. By "the righteous" the psalmist does not exactly mean himself, but he blends his own individuality with that of the ideal character so that he is both speaking of his own future and declaring a general truth. The wicked "spring as the grass" (v. 7), but the righteous "spring like the palm." The point of comparison is apparently the gracefulness of the tree, which lifts its slender but upright stem and is ever verdant and fruitful. The cedar in its massive strength, its undecaying vigor, and the broad shelves of its foliage, green among the snows of Lebanon, stands in strong contrast to the palm. Gracefulness is wedded to strength, and both are perennial in lives devoted to God and right. Evil blooms quickly, and quickly dies. What is good lasts. One cedar outlives a hundred generations of the grass and flowers that encircle its steadfast feet.

**92:13–15.** The last part extends the thoughts of v. 12 to all the righteous. It does not name them, for it is needless to do so. Imagery and reality are fused together in this strophe. It is questionable whether there were trees planted in the courts of the Temple, but the psalmist's thought is that the righteous will surely be found there and that it is their native soil, in which rooted, they are permanent. The facts underlying the somewhat violent metaphor are that true righteousness is found only in the dwellers with God, that they who anchor themselves in Him, as a tree in the earth, are both established in and fed from Him. The law of physical decay does not enfeeble all the powers of devout men, even while they are subject to it. As aged palm trees bear the heaviest clusters, so lives that are planted in and nourished from God know no term of their fruitfulness and are full of sap and verdant when lives that have shut themselves off from Him are like an old stump, gaunt and dry, fit only for firewood. Such lives are prolonged and made fruitful, as standing proofs that Yahweh is upright, rewarding all who cleave to Him and do his will, with conservation of strength, and ever-growing power to do his will.

Verse 15 is a reminiscence of Deut. 32:4. The last clause is probably to be taken in connection with the preceding, but it may also be regarded as a final avowal of the psalmist's faith, the last result of his contemplations of the mysteries of providence. These but drive him to cling close to Yahweh as his sole refuge and his sure shelter and to ring out this as the end which shall one day be manifest as the net result of providence—that there is no least trace of unrighteousness in Him.

***Psalm 93.*** *This short Psalm strikes the keynote for the group (Pss. 93–100). It is overture to the oratorio, prelude of the symphony. Yahweh's reign, the stability of his throne, the consequent fixity of the natural order, his supremacy over all noisy rage of opposition and lawlessness, either in nature or among men, are set forth with magnificent energy and brevity. But the King of the world is not a mere nature-compelling love. He has spoken to humanity, and the stability of the natural order but faintly shadows the firmness of his "testimonies," which are worthy of absolute reliance and which make the souls that do rely on them stable as the firm earth and steadfast with a steadfastness derived from Yahweh's throne. He not only reigns over, but dwells among men, and his power keeps his dwelling place inviolate and lasting as his reign.*

**93:1–3.** Verse 1 describes a state. "Yahweh reigns" by some specific manifestation of his sovereignty. Not as though He had not been King before, as v. 2 immediately goes on to point out, but that He has shown the world by a recent deed the eternal truth that He reigns. His coronation has been by his own hands. No others have arrayed Him in his royal robes. The psalmist dwells with emphatic reiteration on the thought that Yahweh has clothed himself with majesty and girded himself with

| | 5558.116 | 5282 | 3176 | 5558.116 | 5282 | 7249 | 5558.126 |
|---|---|---|---|---|---|---|---|
| | v Qal pf 3cp | n mp | pn | v Qal pf 3cp | n mp | n ms, ps 3mp | v Qal impf 3mp |
| 3. | נָשְׂאוּ | נְהָרוֹת | יְהוָה | נָשְׂאוּ | נְהָרוֹת | קוֹלָם | יִשְׂאוּ |
| | nāse'û | nehārôth | yehwāh | nāse'û | nehārôth | qôlām | yis'û |
| | they have lifted | the floods | O Yahweh | they have lifted | the floods | their voice | they will lift |

| 5282 | 1853 | | 4623, 7249 | 4448 | 7521 | 116 |
|---|---|---|---|---|---|---|
| n mp | n ms, ps 3mp | | prep, *n mp* | n md | adj | adj |
| נְהָרוֹת | דָּכְיָם | 4. | מִקֹּלוֹת | מַיִם | רַבִּים | אַדִּירִים |
| nehārôth | dākheyām | | miqqōlôth | mayim | rabbîm | 'addîrîm |
| the floods | their pounding | | than the sounds of | the waters | more abundant | mightier |

| 5053, 3328 | 116 | 904, 4953 | 3176 | | 5926 | 548.216 | 4108 |
|---|---|---|---|---|---|---|---|
| *n mp*, n ms | adj | prep, art, n ms | pn | | n fp, ps 2ms | v Niphal pf 3cp | adv |
| מִשְׁבְּרֵי־יָם | אַדִּיר | בַּמָּרוֹם | יְהוָה | 5. | עֵדֹתֶיךָ | נֶאֶמְנוּ | מְאֹד |
| mishberê-yām | 'addîr | bammārôm | yehwāh | | 'ēdhōthêkhā | ne'emnû | me'ōdh |
| the waves of the sea | mightier | on high | Yahweh | | your testimonies | reliable | very |

| 3937, 1041 | 5172, 7231 | 3176 | 3937, 775 | 3219 | | 418, 5543 |
|---|---|---|---|---|---|---|
| prep, n ms, ps 2ms | adj, n ms | pn | prep, *n ms* | n mp | | *n ms*, n fp |
| לְבֵיתְךָ | נַאֲוָה־קֹדֶשׁ | יְהוָה | לְאֹרֶךְ | יָמִים | 94:1 | אֵל־נְקָמוֹת |
| levêthekhā | na'ăwāh-qōdhesh | yehwāh | le'ōrekh | yāmîm | | 'ēl-neqāmôth |
| to your Temple | proper holiness | O Yahweh | for length of | days | | a God of vengeances |

| 3176 | 418 | 5543 | 3423.531 | | 5558.231 | 8570.151 | 800 |
|---|---|---|---|---|---|---|---|
| pn | *n ms* | n fp | v Hiphil impv 2ms | | v Niphal impv 2ms | *v Qal act ptc ms* | art, n fs |
| יְהוָה | אֵל | נְקָמוֹת | הוֹפִיַע | 2. | הִנָּשֵׂא | שֹׁפֵט | הָאָרֶץ |
| yehwāh | 'ēl | neqāmôth | hôphiya' | | hinnāsē' | shōphēṭ | hā'ārets |
| Yahweh | a God of | vengeances | shine | | rise up | O Judge of | the earth |

| 8178.531 | 1618 | 6142, 1373 | | 5912, 5146 | 7857 | 3176 | 5912, 5146 |
|---|---|---|---|---|---|---|---|
| v Hiphil impv 2ms | n ms | prep, adj | | adv, intrg | n mp | pn | adv, intrg |
| הָשֵׁב | גְּמוּל | עַל־גֵּאִים | 3. | עַד־מָתַי | רְשָׁעִים | יְהוָה | עַד־מָתַי |
| hāshēv | gemûl | 'al-gē'îm | | 'adh-māthay | reshā'îm | yehwāh | 'adh-māthay |
| cause to return | deserts | on the proud | | until when | the wicked | O Yahweh | until when |

**3. The floods have lifted up, O LORD, the floods have lifted up their voice; the floods lift up their waves:** … Loud the rivers echo, Lord, loud the rivers echo, crashing down in flood, *Knox* … The rivers send up, O Lord, the rivers send up their voices; they send them up with a loud cry, *BB* … The rivers have risen, O LORD; the streams have swirled up with their roar; the floods are surging high, *Berkeley*.

**4. The LORD on high is mightier than the noise of many waters, yea, than the mighty waves of the sea:** … The sound of the water is loud; the ocean waves are powerful, but the Lord above is much greater, *NVC* … Above the sound of expansive waters, of mighty ocean breakers, the LORD on high stands supreme, *Berkeley* … Magnificent the roar of eddying waters; magnificent the sea's rage; magnificent above these, the Lord reigns in heaven, *Knox* … Stronger than thundering waters, Mightier than the breakers of the sea, Mightier than high heaven was Yahweh, *Anchor*.

**5. Thy testimonies are very sure: holiness becometh thine house, O LORD, for ever:** … LORD, your laws will stand forever, *NCV* … The truths you wrote can be trusted absolutely. In Your temple, LORD, holiness is beautiful forever, *Beck* … Thy testimonies are so trustworthy; holiness is the mark of Thy house, O LORD, forevermore, *Berkeley*.

**94:1. O LORD God, to whom vengeance belongeth; O God, to whom vengeance belongeth, show thyself:** … The LORD is a God who punishes, *NCV* … O God, in whose hands is punishment, O God of punishment, let your shining face be seen, *BB* … O GOD of Justice, O LORD! O GOD of glorious Right!, *Fenton* … O LORD, Thou God of retribution, Thou God of retribution, shine forth!, *Berkeley*.

**2. Lift up thyself, thou judge of the earth: render a reward to the proud:** … give the presumptuous their deserts!, *Anchor* … let the haughty have what they deserve!, *Moffatt* … let their reward come to the men of pride, *BB* … repay the arrogant as they deserve, *REB*.

**3. LORD, how long shall the wicked, how long shall the wicked triumph?:** … O LORD, how long shall

strength. All the stability of nature is a consequence of his self-created and self-manifested power. That strength holds a reeling world steady. The psalmist knew nothing about the fixity of natural law, but his thought goes down below that fixity and finds its reason in the constant forth-putting of divine power. Verse 2 goes far back as well as deep down or high up when it travels into the dim, unbounded past and sees there amidst its mists one shining, solid substance, Yahweh's throne, which stood firm before every "then." The word rendered "of old" (HED #5986) is literally "from then," as if to express the priority of that throne to every period of defined time. And even that grand thought can be capped by a grander climax: "Thou art from everlasting." Therefore, the world stands firm.

But there are things in the firm world that are not firm. There are "streams" or perhaps "floods," which seem to own no control, in their hoarse dash and devastating rush. The sea is ever the symbol of rebellious opposition and of ungoverned force. Here both the natural and symbolic meanings are present. And the picture is superbly painted. The sound of the blows of the breakers against the rocks, or as they clash with each other, is vividly repeated in the word rendered "waves" (HED #5282), which means rather, "roaring," and here seems to express the thud of the waves against an obstacle.

**93:4.** Verse 4 is difficult to construe. The word rendered "mighty" is, according to the accentuation, attached to "waves," but stands in an unusual position if it is to be so taken. It seems better to disregard the accents and to take "mighty" as a second adjective belonging to "waters." These will then be described as both multitudinous and proud in their strength, while "waves" will stand in apposition to waters. Yahweh's might is compared with these. It would be but a poor measure of it to say that it was more than they; but the comparison means that He subdues the floods and proves his power by taming and calming them. Evidently, we are to see shining through the nature picture Yahweh's triumphant subjugation of rebellious men, which is one manifestation of his kingly power.

**93:5.** "Holiness" (HED #7231) in v. 5 expresses an attribute of Yahweh's house, not a quality of the worshipers therein. It cannot but be preserved from assault, since He dwells there. A king who cannot keep his own palace safe from invaders can have little power. If this Psalm is (as it evidently is) postexilic, how could the singer, remembering the destruction of the Temple, speak thus? Because he had learned the lesson of that destruction, that the earthly house in which Yahweh dwelt among men had ceased to be his by reason of the sins of its frequenters. The kingship of Yahweh is proclaimed eloquently and tragically by the desolated shrine.

***Psalm 94.*** *The structure and course of thought are transparent. First comes an invocation to God as the Judge of the earth (vv. 1f); then follow groups of four verses each, subdivided into pairs. The first of these (vv. 3–6) pictures the doings of the oppressors, the second (vv. 7–11) quotes their delusion that their crimes are unseen by Yahweh and refutes their dream of impunity, and it is closed by a verse in excess of the normal number, emphatically asserting the truth which the mockers denied. The third group declares the blessedness of the men whom God teaches and the certainty of his retribution to vindicate the cause of the righteous (vv. 12–15). Then follow the singer's own cry for help in his own need, as one of the oppressed community, and a sweet reminiscence of former aid, which calms his present anxieties. The concluding group goes back to description of the lawless lawmakers and their doings and ends with trust that the retribution prayed for in the first verses will truly be dealt out to them and that thereby both the singer, as a member of the nation, and the community will find Yahweh, Who is both "my God" and "our God," a high tower.*

**94:1–2.** The reiterations in the first two verses are not oratorical embellishments, but they reveal intense feeling and pressing need. It is a cold prayer which contents itself with one utterance. A man in straits continues to cry for help until it comes, or until he sees it coming. To this singer, the one aspect of Yahweh's reign which was forced on him by Israel's dismal circumstances was the judicial. There are times when no thought of God is so full of strength as that He is "the LORD God of recompenses," as Jeremiah calls Him (Jer. 51:56), and when the longing of good men is that He would flash forth and slay evil by the brightness of his coming. They who have no profound loathing of sin, or who have never felt the crushing weight of legalized wickedness, may shrink from such aspirations as the psalmist's and brand them as ferocious, but hearts longing for the triumph of righteousness will not take offense at them.

**94:3–6.** The first group lifts the cry of suffering faith, which has almost become impatience, but turns to God and so checks complaints of his delay and converts them into prayer. "LORD, how long" is the bur-

| 7857 | 6159.126 | | 5218.526 | 1744.326 | 6515 | 569.726 |
|---|---|---|---|---|---|---|
| n mp | v Qal impf 3mp | 4. | v Hiphil impf 3mp | v Piel impf 3mp | adv | v Hithpael impf 3mp |
| רְשָׁעִים | יַעֲלֹזוּ | | יַבִּיעוּ | יְדַבְּרוּ | עָתָק | יִתְאַמְּרוּ |
| reshā'îm | ya'ălōzû | | yabbî'û | yedhabberû | 'āthāq | yith'ammerû |
| the wicked | will they exult | | they bubble up | they speak | insolently | they say about themselves |

| 3725, 6713.152 | 201 | | 6194 | 3176 | 1850.326 | 5338 |
|---|---|---|---|---|---|---|
| *adj, v Qal act ptc mp* | n ms | 5. | n ms, ps 2ms | pn | v Piel impf 3mp | cj, n fs, ps 2ms |
| כָּל־פֹּעֲלֵי | אָוֶן | | עַמְּךָ | יְהוָה | יְדַכְּאוּ | וְנַחֲלָתְךָ |
| kol-pō'ălê | 'āwen | | 'ammekhā | yehwāh | yedhakke'û | wenachlāthekhā |
| all those who practice | iniquity | | your people | O Yahweh | they crush | and your inheritance |

| 6257.326 | | 496 | 1658 | 2103.126 | 3605 | 7815.326 |
|---|---|---|---|---|---|---|
| v Piel impf 3mp | 6. | n fs | cj, n ms | v Qal impf 3mp | cj, n mp | v Piel impf 3mp |
| יְעַנּוּ | | אַלְמָנָה | וְגֵר | יַהֲרֹגוּ | וִיתוֹמִים | יְרַצֵּחוּ |
| ye'annû | | 'almānāh | wegher | yahrōghû | wîthômîm | yeratstsechû |
| they afflict | | the widow | and the resident-alien | they kill | and the orphans | they murder |

| | 569.126 | 3940 | 7495.121, 3161 | 3940, 1032.121 | 435 | 3399 |
|---|---|---|---|---|---|---|
| 7. | cj, v Qal impf 3mp | neg part | v Qal impf 3ms, pn | cj, neg part, v Qal impf 3ms | *n mp* | pn |
| | וַיֹּאמְרוּ | לֹא | יִרְאֶה־יָּהּ | וְלֹא־יָבִין | אֱלֹהֵי | יַעֲקֹב |
| | wayyō'merû | lō' | yir'eh-yāhh | welō'-yāvîn | 'ĕlōhê | ya'ăqōv |
| | and they say | not | Yah sees | neither does He perceive | the God of | Jacob |

| | 1032.133 | 1220.152 | 904, 6194 | 3809 | 5146 | 7959.528 |
|---|---|---|---|---|---|---|
| 8. | v Qal impv 2mp | v Qal act ptc mp | prep, art, n ms | cj, n mp | intrg | v Hiphil impf 2mp |
| | בִּינוּ | בֹּעֲרִים | בָּעָם | וּכְסִילִים | מָתַי | תַּשְׂכִּילוּ |
| | bînû | bō'ărîm | bā'ām | ûkhesîlîm | māthay | taskîlû |
| | understand | stupid ones | among the people | and fools | when | will you become wise |

| | 1950B, 5378.151 | 238 | 1950B, 3940 | 8471.121 | 524, 3443.151 | 6084 |
|---|---|---|---|---|---|---|
| 9. | intrg, v Qal act ptc ms | n fs | intrg part, neg part | v Qal impf 3ms | cj, v Qal act ptc ms | n fs |
| | הֲנֹטַע | אֹזֶן | הֲלֹא | יִשְׁמָע | אִם־יֹצֵר | עַיִן |
| | hănōṯa' | 'ōzen | hălō' | yishmā' | 'im-yōtsēr | 'ayin |
| | the One Who plants | the ear | does not | He hear | or the One Who forms | the eye |

| 1950B, 3940 | 5202.521 | | 1950B, 3364.151 | 1504 | 1950B, 3940 | 3306.521 |
|---|---|---|---|---|---|---|
| intrg part, neg part | v Hiphil impf 3ms | 10. | intrg, v Qal act ptc ms | n mp | intrg part, neg part | v Hiphil impf 3ms |
| הֲלֹא | יַבִּיט | | הֲיֹסֵר | גּוֹיִם | הֲלֹא | יוֹכִיחַ |
| hălō' | yabbîṯ | | hăyōsēr | gôyim | hălō' | yôkhîach |
| does not | He look | | the One Who rebukes | nations | does not | He reprove |

| 4064.351 | 119 | 1907 | | 3176 | 3156.151 | 4422 |
|---|---|---|---|---|---|---|
| art, v Piel ptc ms | n ms | n fs | 11. | pn | v Qal act ptc ms | *n fp* |
| הַמְלַמֵּד | אָדָם | דָּעַת | | יְהוָה | יֹדֵעַ | מַחְשְׁבוֹת |
| hamlammēdh | 'ādhām | dā'ath | | yehwāh | yōdhea' | machshevôth |
| the One Who teaches | humankind | knowledge | | Yahweh | One Who knows | the plans of |

sinners, how long shall the wicked be jubilant!, *Berkeley* ... How long will sinners, O Lord, how long will sinners have joy over us?, *BB* ... How long will the wicked be happy? How long, LORD?, *NCV.*

**4. How long shall they utter and speak hard things? and all the workers of iniquity boast themselves?:** ... They boast freely; they speak arrogantly; all the wrongdoers brag about themselves, *Berkeley* ... They pour forth words they speak arrogantly, All the workers of iniquity do boast, *Rotherham* ... Mouthing insolent speeches, boasting, all the evildoers?, *NAB* ... They bluster and boast, they flaunt themselves, all the evil-doers, *JB.*

**5. They break in pieces thy people, O LORD, and afflict thine heritage:** ... LORD, they crush your people and make your children suffer, *NCV* ... Your people, Yahweh, they crushed, and your patrimony they afflicted, *Anchor* ... See, Lord, how they crush down thy people, afflict the land of thy choice, *Knox* ... and oppress your chosen nation, *REB.*

**6. They slay the widow and the stranger, and murder the fatherless:** ... They kill widows and foreigners and murder orphans, *NCV* ... Widow, and Stranger murder, And Orphans they oppress, *Fenton* ... They kill the widow and the immigrant; they murder orphans, *Berkeley* ... bring the orphan to a violent death, *JB*.

**7. Yet they say, The LORD shall not see, neither shall the God of Jacob regard it:** ... and they say 'The LORD does not see; the God of Jacob does not perceive,' *RSV* ... The LORD is not looking; the God of Jacob pays no attention, *Berkeley* ... nor does the God of Jacob understand, *NJKV* ... Nor does the God of Jacob pay heed, *NASB*.

**8. Understand, ye brutish among the people: and ye fools, when will ye be wise?:** ... You mindless ones among the people, understand; you fools, when will you get wise, *Beck* ... Fools, when will you learn some sense?, *JB* ... Take heed yourselves, most stupid of people, *REB* ... Pay heed, rather, yourselves, dull hearts that count among my people; fools, learn your lesson ere it is too late, *Knox*.

**9. He that planted the ear, shall he not hear? he that formed the eye, shall he not see?:** ... Can't the creator of ears hear? Can't the maker of eyes see?, *NCV* ... Or that fashioneth the eye shall he not have power to see?, *Rotherham* ... He who makes the ear, is He deaf? He who forms the eye, is He blind?, *Berkeley* ... Is God deaf and blind—he who makes ears and eyes, *LIVB*.

**10. He that chastiseth the heathen, shall not he correct? he that teacheth man knowledge, shall not he know?:** ... Does he who disciplines nations not punish? Does he who teaches man not lack knowledge?, *NIV* ... Is the instructor of nations unable to punish? Is the teacher of mankind without knowledge?, *Anchor* ... He who gives nations their schooling, who taught man all that man knows, will he not call you to account?, *Knox*.

**11. The LORD knoweth the thoughts of man, that they are vanity:** ... The LORD knows human thoughts, That as themselves, are weak, *Fenton* ... he knows that they

---

den of many a tried heart, and the seer heard it from the souls beneath the altar. This Psalm passes quickly to dilate on the crimes of the rulers which forced out that prayer. The portrait has many points of likeness to that drawn in Ps. 73. Here, as there, boastful speech and haughty carriage are made prominent, being put before even cruelty and oppression. "They pour out; they speak arrogance." Both verbs have the same object. Insolent self-exaltation pours from the fountain of their pride in copious jets. They give themselves airs like princes. The verb in this clause (HED #6159) may mean "to say among themselves" or "to boast," but is now usually regarded as meaning "to behave like a prince," meaning "to carry oneself insolently." These oppressors were grinding the nation to powder, and what made their crime darker was that it was Yahweh's people and inheritance which they thus harassed. Helplessness should be a passport to a ruler's care, but it had become a mark for murderous attack. Widow, stranger and orphan are named as types of defenselessness.

**94:7–11.** Nothing in this strophe indicates that these oppressors are foreigners. Nor does the delusion that Yahweh neither saw nor cared for their doings, which the next strophe (vv. 7–11) states and confutes, imply that they were so. The language derives its darkest shade from being used by Hebrews who are thereby declaring themselves apostates from God as well as oppressors of his people. Their mad, practical atheism makes the psalmist blaze up in indignant rebuke and impetuous argumentation. He turns to them and addresses them in rough, plain words, strangely contrasted with their arrogant utterances regarding themselves. They are "brutish" (cf. Ps. 73:22) and "fools." The psalmist, in his height of moral indignation, towers above these petty tyrants, and tells them home truths very profitable for such people, however dangerous to their utterer. There is no obligation to speak smooth words to rulers whose rule is injustice and their religion impiety. Ahab had his Elijah, and Herod his John the Baptist. The succession has been continued through the ages.

Delitzsch and others, who take the oppressors to be foreigners, are obliged to suppose that the psalmist turns in v. 8 to those Israelites who had been led to doubt God by the prosperity of the wicked; but there is nothing, except the exigencies of that mistaken supposition, to show that any others than the deniers of God's providence who have just been quoted are addressed as "among the people." Their denial was the more inexcusable because they belonged to the people whose history was one long proof that Yahweh did see and recompense evil.

Two considerations are urged by the psalmist. First, he argues that nothing can be in the effect which is not in the cause, that the Maker of men's eyes cannot be blind, nor the Planter of their ears deaf. The thought has wide applications. It hits the center in regard to many modern denials as well as

| 119 | 3706, 2065 | 1961 | | 869 | 1429 | 866, 3364.323 | 3161 |
|---|---|---|---|---|---|---|---|
| n ms | cj, pers pron | n ms | 12. | *n mp* | art, n ms | rel part, v Piel impf 2ms, ps 3ms | pn |
| אָדָם | כִּי־הֵמָּה | הָבֶל | | אַשְׁרֵי | הַגֶּבֶר | אֲשֶׁר־תְּיַסְּרֶנּוּ | יָהּ |
| 'ādhām | kî-hēmmāh | hāvel | | 'ashrê | haggever | 'äsher-teyasserennû | yāhh |
| humankind | because they | a breath | | blessed | the man | whom You rebuke him | O Yah |

| 4623, 8784 | 4064.323 | | 3937, 8618.541 | 3937 | 4623, 3219 | 7737 |
|---|---|---|---|---|---|---|
| cj, prep, n fs, ps 2ms | v Piel impf 2ms, ps 3ms | 13. | prep, v Hiphil inf con | prep, ps 3ms | prep, *n mp* | n ms |
| וּמִתּוֹרָתְךָ | תְלַמְּדֶנּוּ | | לְהַשְׁקִיט | לוֹ | מִימֵי | רָע |
| ûmittôrāthekhā | thelammedhennû | | lehashqîṭ | lô | mîmê | rā' |
| and from your Law | You teach him | | to make calm | for him | from the days of | evil |

| 5912 | 3868.221 | 3937, 7857 | 8273 | | 3706 | 3940, 5389.121 | 3176 |
|---|---|---|---|---|---|---|---|
| adv | v Niphal impf 3ms | prep, art, n ms | n fs | 14. | cj | neg part, v Qal impf 3ms | pn |
| עַד | יִכָּרֶה | לָרָשָׁע | שָׁחַת | | כִּי | לֹא־יִטֹּשׁ | יְהוָה |
| 'adh | yikkāreh | lārāshā' | shāchath | | kî | lō'-yittōsh | yehwāh |
| until | it has been dug | for the wicked | a pit | | because | He will not leave | Yahweh |

| 6194 | 5338 | 3940 | 6013.121 | | 3706, 5912, 6928 |
|---|---|---|---|---|---|
| n ms, ps 3ms | cj, n fs, ps 3ms | neg part | v Qal impf 3ms | 15. | cj, prep, n ms |
| עַמּוֹ | וְנַחֲלָתוֹ | לֹא | יַעֲזֹב | | כִּי־עַד־צֶדֶק |
| 'ammô | wenachlāthô | lō' | ya'ăzōv | | kî-'adh-tsedheq |
| his people | and his inheritance | not | He will abandon | | because unto the righteous |

| 8178.121 | 5122 | 313 | 3725, 3596, 3949 | | 4449, 7251.121 | 3937 |
|---|---|---|---|---|---|---|
| v Qal impf 3ms | n ms | cj, prep, ps 3ms | *adj, adj,* n ms | 16. | intrg, v Qal impf 3ms | prep, ps 1cs |
| יָשׁוּב | מִשְׁפָּט | וְאַחֲרָיו | כָּל־יִשְׁרֵי־לֵב | | מִי־יָקוּם | לִי |
| yāshûv | mishpāṭ | we'achrâv | kol-yishrê-lēv | | mî-yāqûm | lî |
| He turns back | justice | and after Him | all the upright of heart | | who rises up | for me |

| 6196, 7778.152 | 4449, 3429.721 | 3937 | 6196, 6713.152 | 201 |
|---|---|---|---|---|
| prep, *v Qal act ptc mp* | intrg, v Hithpael impf 3ms | prep, ps 1cs | prep, *v Qal act ptc mp* | n ms |
| עִם־מְרֵעִים | מִי־יִתְיַצֵּב | לִי | עִם־פֹּעֲלֵי | אָוֶן |
| 'im-merē'îm | mî-yithyatstsēv | lî | 'im-pō'ălê | 'āwen |
| against evildoers | who takes a stand | for me | against the workers of | iniquity |

| | 4020 | 3176 | 6046 | 3937 | 3626, 4746 | 8331.112 | 1798 |
|---|---|---|---|---|---|---|---|
| 17. | cj | pn | n fs | prep, ps 1cs | prep, sub | v Qal pf 3fs | n fs |
| | לוּלֵי | יְהוָה | עֶזְרָתָה | לִי | כִּמְעַט | שָׁכְנָה | דוּמָה |
| | lûlê | yehwāh | 'ezrāthāh | lî | kim'aṭ | shākhenāh | dhûmāh |
| | if not | Yahweh | a Help | to me | like a moment | it would have dwelled in | silence |

are futile, *NIV* ... The LORD knows the devices of men, That they are but a breath, *Goodspeed* ... The LORD knows that the thoughts of everyone are but a puff of wind, *REB*.

**12. Blessed is the man whom thou chastenest, O LORD, and teachest him out of thy law:** ... Happy, Lord, is the man whom thou dost chasten, reading him the lesson of thy law!, *Knox* ... Blessed is the man whom You, LORD, correct and teach from Your Word, *Beck* ... those you instruct, Yahweh, whom you teach by the means of your law, *JB* ... Happy is the man who is guided by you, *BB*.

**13. That thou mayest give him rest from the days of adversity, until the pit be digged for the wicked:** ... For him, thou wilt lighten the time of adversity, digging a pit all the while to entrap the sinner, *Knox* ... that he may enjoy security during the days of distress, till a pit be dug for the wicked, *Berkeley* ... to give them respite in evil times, till a pit is dug for the wicked, *JB*.

**14. For the LORD will not cast off his people, neither will he forsake his inheritance:** ... Yahweh will not abandon his people, he will not desert his heritage, *JB* ... The LORD leaves not His Race, Nor casts off His Estate, *Fenton* ... The LORD will not abandon his people nor forsake his chosen, *NEB* ... The LORD doesn't reject His people of forsake His own, *Beck*.

**15. But judgment shall return unto righteousness: and all the upright in heart shall follow it:** ... But the tribunal of justice will restore **equity**

and with it all upright hearts, *Anchor* ... Judgement will again be fair, and all who are honest will follow it, *NCV* ... no, goodness shall have justice done to it—the future is with men of upright mind, *Moffatt* ... But brings the Good their Right, The just of heart, their pay, *Fenton.*

**16. Who will rise up for me against the evildoers? or who will stand up for me against the workers of iniquity:** ... Will anyone rise against the wicked in my behalf?, *Beck* ... Who takes my part against the oppressor? Who rallies to my side against the wrong-doers?, *Knox* ... Against the vile, who joined?, *Fenton* ... Who is my champion against the ungodly, who sides with me against the evildoers, *Moffatt.*

**17. Unless the LORD had been my help, my soul had almost dwelt in silence:** ... If the LORD had not helped me, I would have died in a minute, *NCV* ... If the Lord had not been my

---

in regard to these blunt, ancient ones. Can a universe plainly full of purpose have come from a purposeless source? Can finite persons have emerged from an impersonal infinity? Have we not a right to argue upwards from man to God his Maker and to find in Him the archetype of all human capacity?

In v. 10, a second argument is employed, which turns on the thought that God is the educator of mankind. That office of instructor cannot be carried out unless He is also their chastiser, when correction is needed. The psalmist looks beyond the bounds of Israel, the recipient of special revelation (cf. v. 12), and recognizes what seldom appears in the OT, but is unquestionably there—the great thought that He is teaching all mankind by manifold ways, and especially by the Law written in their hearts. Jewish particularism, the exaggeration into a lie of the truth of God's special revelation to Israel, came to forget or deny God's education of mankind. The teaching of the strophe is gathered up in v. 11, which exceeds the normal number of four verses in each group and asserts strongly the conclusion for which the psalmist has been arguing.

**94:12–15.** In this strophe, the psalmist turns from the oppressors to their victims and changes his tone from fiery remonstrance to gracious consolation. The true point of view from which to regard the oppressors' wrong is to see in it part of God's educational processes. Yahweh, Who "teachest" all men by conscience, "teachest" Israel and by the Law "teachest" the right interpretation of such afflictive providences. Happy is he who accepts that higher education! A further consolation lies in considering the purpose of the special revelation to Israel, which will be realized in patient hearts that are made wise thereby; this is a calm repose of submission and trust, which are not disturbed by any stormy weather. There is possible for the harassed man peace subsisting at the heart of endless agitation.

If we recognize that life is mainly educational, we shall neither be astonished nor disturbed by sorrows. It is not to be wondered why the schoolmaster has a rod and uses it sometimes. There is rest from evil even while in evil, if we understand the purpose of evil. Yet another consolation lies in the steadfast anticipation of its transience and of the retribution measured to its doers. That is no unworthy source of comfort. And the ground on which it rests is the impossibility of God's forsaking his people, his inheritance. These designations of Israel look back to v. 5, where the crushed and afflicted are designated by the same words. Israel's relationship to Yahweh made the calamities more startling, but it also makes their cessation, and retribution for them on their inflicters, more certain. It is the trial and triumph of faith to be sure that Yahweh has not deserted the victims of the oppressors. He cannot change his purpose; therefore, sorrows and prosperity are but divergent methods, concurring in carrying out his unalterable design. The individual sufferer may take comfort from his belonging to the community to which the presence of Yahweh is guaranteed forever. The singer puts his convictions thus: "judgment shall return unto righteousness," by which he seems to mean that the administration of justice, which at present was being trampled under foot, "shall return unto righteousness." In other words, there shall be no schism between the judgments of earthly tribunals and justice. The psalmist's hope is that of all good men and sufferers from unjust rulers. All the upright in heart long for such a state of things and follow after it, either in the sense of delight in it or of seeking to bring it about. *Dem Recht mussen alle frommen Herzen zufallen*—Luther ("All the upright of heart must follow the righteousness"). The psalmist's hope is realized in the sovereign God, whose own judgments are truth and Who infuses righteousness and the love of it into all who trust in Him.

**94:16–19.** The singer comes closer to his own experience in the next strophe, in which he claims his share in these general sources of rest and patience and thankfully thinks of past times when he found that they yielded him streams in the desert.

| 5497<br>n fs, ps 1cs<br>נַפְשִׁי<br>naphshî<br>my life | **18.** | 524, 569.115<br>cj, v Qal pf 1cs<br>אִם־אָמַרְתִּי<br>'im-'āmartî<br>when I said | 4267.112<br>v Qal pf 3fs<br>מָטָה<br>māṭāh<br>it has faltered | 7559<br>n fs, ps 1cs<br>רַגְלִי<br>raghlî<br>my foot | 2721<br>n ms, ps 2ms<br>חַסְדְּךָ<br>chas̱dᵉkhā<br>your steadfast love | 3176<br>pn<br>יְהוָה<br>yᵉhwāh<br>O Yahweh |
|---|---|---|---|---|---|---|

| 5777.121<br>v Qal impf 3ms, ps 1cs<br>יִסְעָדֵנִי<br>yis̱'ādhēnî<br>it supported me | **19.** | 904, 7524<br>prep, *n ms*<br>בְּרֹב<br>bᵉrōv<br>in the abundance of | 8040<br>n mp, ps 1cs<br>שַׂרְעַפַּי<br>sar'appay<br>my disturbing thoughts | 904, 7419<br>prep, n ms, ps 1cs<br>בְּקִרְבִּי<br>bᵉqirbî<br>within me |
|---|---|---|---|---|

| 8904<br>n mp, ps 2ms<br>תַּנְחוּמֶיךָ<br>tanchûmêkhā<br>your consolations | 8551.326<br>v Pilpel impf 3mp<br>יְשַׁעַשְׁעוּ<br>yᵉsha'ash'û<br>they cause to be free of care | 5497<br>n fs, ps 1cs<br>נַפְשִׁי<br>naphshî<br>my soul | **20.** | 1950B, 2357.421<br>intrg, v Pual impf 3ms, ps 2ms<br>הַיְחָבְרְךָ<br>haychovrᵉkhā<br>will it be allied with You | 3802<br>*n ms*<br>כִּסֵּא<br>kissē'<br>the seat of |
|---|---|---|---|---|---|

| 2010<br>n fp<br>הַוּוֹת<br>hawwôth<br>destruction | 3443.151<br>v Qal act ptc ms<br>יֹצֵר<br>yōtsēr<br>one who fashions | 6219<br>n ms<br>עָמָל<br>'āmāl<br>harm | 6142, 2805<br>prep, n ms<br>עֲלֵי־חֹק<br>'ălê-chōq<br>on a statute | **21.** | 1443.126<br>v Qal impf 3mp<br>יָגוֹדּוּ<br>yāghôddû<br>they band together | 6142, 5497<br>prep, *n fs*<br>עַל־נֶפֶשׁ<br>'al-nephesh<br>against the life of |
|---|---|---|---|---|---|---|

| 6926<br>n ms<br>צַדִּיק<br>tsaddîq<br>the righteous | 1879<br>cj, n ms<br>וְדָם<br>wᵉdhām<br>and blood | 5538<br>adj<br>נָקִי<br>nāqî<br>innocent | 7855.526<br>v Hiphil impf 3mp<br>יַרְשִׁיעוּ<br>yarshî'û<br>they declare guilty | **22.** | 2030.121<br>cj, v Qal impf 3ms<br>וַיְהִי<br>wayhî<br>but He becomes | 3176<br>pn<br>יְהוָה<br>yᵉhwāh<br>Yahweh | 3937<br>prep, ps 1cs<br>לִי<br>lî<br>to me |
|---|---|---|---|---|---|---|---|

| 3937, 5021<br>prep, n ms<br>לְמִשְׂגָּב<br>lᵉmisgāv<br>for a Refuge | 435<br>cj, n mp, ps 1cs<br>וֵאלֹהַי<br>wē'lōhay<br>and my God | 3937, 6962<br>prep, *n ms*<br>לְצוּר<br>lᵉtsûr<br>for a Rock of | 4406<br>n ms, ps 1cs<br>מַחְסִי<br>machs̱î<br>my Hiding Place | **23.** | 8178.521<br>cj, v Hiphil impf 3ms<br>וַיָּשֶׁב<br>wayyāshev<br>and He will cause to return |
|---|---|---|---|---|---|

| 6142<br>prep, ps 3mp<br>עֲלֵיהֶם<br>'ălêhem<br>on them | 881, 201<br>do, n ms, ps 3mp<br>אֶת־אוֹנָם<br>'eth-'ônām<br>their iniquity | 904, 7750<br>cj, prep, n fs, ps 3mp<br>וּבְרָעָתָם<br>ûvᵉrā'āthām<br>and because of their evil | 7059.521<br>v Hiphil impf 3ms, ps 3mp<br>יַצְמִיתֵם<br>yatsmîthēm<br>He will annihilate them |
|---|---|---|---|

helper, my soul would quickly have gone down into death, *BB* … It is the Lord that helps me; but for that, the grave would soon be my resting-place, *Knox* … The LORD was my ally, When life fell, nearly dumb, *Fenton.*

**18. When I said, My foot slippeth; thy mercy, O LORD, held me up:** … When I say, 'My foot is slipping,' your kindness, O LORD, sustains me, *NAB* … I need only say, 'I am slipping,' for your faithful love, Yahweh, to support me, *JB* … When I said, 'My foot is sinking,' your love, Yahweh, supported me, *Anchor.*

**19. In the multitude of my thoughts within me thy comforts delight my soul:** … Anxious thoughts may fill my heart, but thy presence is my joy and consolation, *NEB* … When cares abound within me, your comfort gladdens my soul, *NAB* … Whenever perplexing cares crowd my inmost self, Thy consolations cheer my soul, *Berkeley* … amid all the thronging cares that fill my heart, my soul finds comfort in thy consolation, *Knox.*

**20. Shall the throne of iniquity have fellowship with thee, which frameth mischief by a law?:** … Can evil rulers have thee for an ally, who work us injury by law, *Moffatt* … Can the seat of iniquity associate with you, the architect of disorder receive your protection?, *Anchor* … Can a corrupt throne be allied with you—one that brings on misery by its decrees?, *NIV* … They use the law to cause suffering, *NCV.*

**21. They gather themselves together against the soul of the righteous, and condemn the innocent blood:** … They are banded together against the soul of the upright, to give decisions against those who have done no wrong, *BB* ... who attack honest men, and doom the innocent to death, *Moffatt* ... Who hunt the good man's life, And shed the saintly blood, *Fenton* ... Let them harry the just as they will, pass sentence of death upon the innocent, *Knox.*

**22. But the LORD is my defence; and my God is the rock of my refuge:** ... But the LORD has been my high retreat, my God, my impregnable rock of safety, *Berkeley* ... But the LORD is my defender; my God is the rock of my protection, *NCV* ... Be, LORD, to me a Peak, My GOD, a Rock of Hope, *Fenton.*

**23. And he shall bring upon them their own iniquity, and shall cut them off in their own wickedness; yea, the LORD our God shall cut them off:** ... He has made them pay for their crime, and He will destroy them in their sin; the LORD our God will make an end of them, *Berkeley* ... And will cut them off in their own evil; The LORD our God will cut them off, *MAST* ... He made their malice recoil upon them, and for their wickedness annihilated them; Yahweh our God annihilated them, *Anchor.*

**95:1. O come, let us sing unto the LORD: let us make a joyful noise to the rock of our salvation:** ... let us sing joyfully to Yahweh, let us hail the Rock who saved us, *Anchor* ... to the Eternal, let us sing loudly to our saving Strength, *Moffatt* ... let us cheer to the LORD, Hurray for the Rock that we trust, *Fenton* ... rejoice we in the Lord's honour; cry we out merrily to God, our strength and deliverer, *Knox.*

---

He looks out upon the multitude of "evildoers," and asks for a moment the question which faithless sense is ever suggesting and pronouncing unanswerable: "Who will rise up for me?" As long as our eyes range along the level of earth, they see none such. But the empty earth should turn our gaze to the occupied throne. There sits the answer to our almost despairing question. Rather, there He stands, as the first Christian martyr saw Him, risen to his feet in swift readiness to help his servant (Acts 7:55f). Experience confirms the hope of Yahweh's aid, for unless in the past He had been the singer's help, he could not have lived until this hour, but must have gone down into the silent land. No man who still draws breath is without tokens of God's sufficient care and ever present help. The mystery of continued life is a witness for God. And not only does the past thus proclaim where a man's help is, but devout reflection on it will bring to light many times when doubts and tremors were disappointed. Conscious weakness appeals to confirming strength. If we feel our foot giving and fling up our hands toward Him, He will grasp them and steady us in the most slippery places. Therefore, when divided thoughts hesitate between hope and fear, God's consolations steal into agitated minds, and there is a great calm.

**94:20–23.** The last strophe weaves together in the finale, as a musician does in the last bars of his composition, the main themes of the Psalm—the evil deeds of unjust rulers, the trust of the psalmist, his confidence in the final annihilation of the oppressors and the consequent manifestation of God as the God of Israel. The height of crime is reached when rulers use the forms of justice as masks for injustice and give legal sanction to "mischief." The ancient world groaned under such travesties of the sanctity of Law, and the modern world is not free from them. The question often tortures faithful hearts, "Can such doings be sanctioned by God, or in any way be allied to Him?" To the psalmist, the worst part of these rulers' wickedness was that, in his doubting moments, it raised the terrible suspicion that God was perhaps on the side of the oppressors. But when such thoughts came surging on him, he fell back—as we all have to do—on personal experience and on an act of renewed trust. He remembered what God had been to him in past moments of peril, and he claimed Him for the same now. Strong in that individual experience and conviction, he won the confidence that all which Yahweh had to do with the throne of destruction was, not to connive at its evil, but to overthrow it and root out the evildoers whose own sin will be their ruin. Then Yahweh will be known, not only for the God Who belongs to and works for the single soul, but Who is "our God," the refuge of the community, Who will not forsake his inheritance.

***Psalm 95.*** *This Psalm is divided into two parts. Each derives force from the other. After the congregation had spoken its joyful summons to itself to worship, Yahweh spoke warning words as to the requisite heart preparation, without which worship is vain.*

*There could be no more impressive way of teaching the conditions of acceptable worship than to set side by side a glad call to praise and a solemn warning against repeating the rebellions of the wilderness. These would be still more appropriate if this were a post-exilic hymn; for the second return from captivity would be felt to be the analog of the first, and the dark story of former hard-heartedness would fit very close to present circumstances.*

| 7059.521 | 3176 | 435 | | 2050.133 | 7228.320 | 3937, 3176 |
|---|---|---|---|---|---|---|
| v Hiphil impf 3ms, ps 3mp | pn | n mp, ps 1cp | **95:1** | v Qal impv 2mp | v Piel juss 1cp | prep, pn |
| יַצְמִיתֵם | יְהוָה | אֱלֹהֵינוּ | | לְכוּ | נְרַנְּנָה | לַיהוָה |
| yatsmîthēm | yehwāh | 'ĕlōhênû | | lekhû | nerannenāh | layhwāh |
| He will annihilate them | Yahweh | our God | | come | let us shout for joy | to Yahweh |

| 7607.520 | 3937, 6962 | 3589 | | 7207.320 | 6686 |
|---|---|---|---|---|---|
| v Hiphil juss 1cp | prep, *n ms* | n ms, ps 1cp | **2.** | v Piel juss 1cp | n mp, ps 3ms |
| נָרִיעָה | לְצוּר | יִשְׁעֵנוּ | | נְקַדְּמָה | פָנָיו |
| nārî'āh | letsûr | yish'ēnû | | neqaddemāh | phānâv |
| let us shout | to the Rock of | our salvation | | let us meet together with | his presence |

| 904, 8756 | 904, 2256 | 7607.520 | 3937 | | 3706 | 418 | 1448 |
|---|---|---|---|---|---|---|---|
| prep, n fs | prep, n mp | v Hiphil juss 1cp | prep, ps 3ms | **3.** | cj | n ms | adj |
| בְתוֹדָה | בִּזְמִרוֹת | נָרִיעַ | לוֹ | | כִּי | אֵל | גָּדוֹל |
| bethôdhāh | bizmirôth | nāria' | lô | | kî | 'ēl | gādhôl |
| with thanksgiving | with songs of praise | let us shout | to Him | | because | God | great |

| 3176 | 4567 | 1448 | 6142, 3725, 435 | | 866 | 904, 3135 | 4416, 800 |
|---|---|---|---|---|---|---|---|
| pn | cj, n ms | adj | prep, *n ms*, n mp | **4.** | rel part | prep, n fs, ps 3ms | *n mp*, n fs |
| יְהוָה | וּמֶלֶךְ | גָּדוֹל | עַל־כָּל־אֱלֹהִים | | אֲשֶׁר | בְּיָדוֹ | מֶחְקְרֵי־אָרֶץ |
| yehwāh | ûmelekh | gādhôl | 'al-kol-'ĕlōhîm | | 'ăsher | beyādhô | mechăqōrê-'ārets |
| Yahweh | and a King | great | above all gods | | Who | in his hand | the depths of the earth |

| 8776 | 2098 | 3937 | | 866, 3937 | 3328 | 2000 |
|---|---|---|---|---|---|---|
| cj, *n fp* | n mp | prep, ps 3ms | **5.** | rel part, prep, ps 3ms | art, n ms | cj, pers pron |
| וְתוֹעֲפוֹת | הָרִים | לוֹ | | אֲשֶׁר־לוֹ | הַיָּם | וְהוּא |
| wethô'ăphôth | hārîm | lô | | 'ăsher-lô | hayyām | wehû' |
| and the heights of | the mountains | to Him | | Who to Him | the sea | for He |

| 6449.111 | 3116 | 3135 | 3443.116 | | 971.133 | 8246.720 |
|---|---|---|---|---|---|---|
| v Qal pf 3ms, ps 3ms | cj, n fs | n fd, ps 3ms | v Qal pf 3cp | **6.** | v Qal impv 2mp | v Hithpael juss 1cp |
| עָשָׂהוּ | וְיַבֶּשֶׁת | יָדָיו | יָצָרוּ | | בֹּאוּ | נִשְׁתַּחֲוֶה |
| 'āsāhû | weyabbesheth | yādhâv | yātsārû | | bō'û | nishtachweh |
| He made | and the dry ground | his hands | they formed | | come | let us worship |

| 3895.120 | 1313.120 | 3937, 6686, 3176 | 6449.151 | | 3706 | 2000 |
|---|---|---|---|---|---|---|
| cj, v Qal juss 1cp | v Qal juss 1cp | prep, *n mp*, pn | v Qal act ptc ms, ps 1cp | **7.** | cj | pers pron |
| וְנִכְרָעָה | נִבְרְכָה | לִפְנֵי־יְהוָה | עֹשֵׂנוּ | | כִּי | הוּא |
| wenikhrā'āh | nivrekhāh | liphnê-yehwāh | 'ōsēnû | | kî | hû' |
| and let us bow down | let us kneel | before Yahweh | our Maker | | because | He |

| 435 | 601 | 6194 | 4993 | 6887 | 3135 | 3219 |
|---|---|---|---|---|---|---|
| n mp, ps 1cp | cj, pers pron | *n ms* | n fs, ps 3ms | cj, *n fs* | n fs, ps 3ms | art, n ms |
| אֱלֹהֵינוּ | וַאֲנַחְנוּ | עַם | מַרְעִיתוֹ | וְצֹאן | יָדוֹ | הַיּוֹם |
| 'ĕlōhênû | wa'ănachnû | 'am | mar'îthô | wetsō'n | yādhô | hayyôm |
| our God | but we | the people of | his pasture | and the sheep of | his hand | today |

**2. Let us come before his presence with thanksgiving, and make a joyful noise unto him with psalms:** … Let us come before his face with praises; and make melody with holy songs, *BB* … Be early before Him with praise, And to Him hurrah in our Psalms, *Fenton* … with praises court his presence, singing a joyful psalm!, *Knox* … and extol him with music and song, *NIV.*

**3. For the LORD is a great God, and a great King above all gods:** … For a great God is the Eternal, the King of all the gods, *Moffatt* … For Yahweh is the great El, the Great King over all the gods, *Anchor* … For a Great GOD is the LORD, A Great King above every God!, *Fenton* … A high God is the Lord, a king high above all the gods, *Knox.*

**4. In his hand are the deep places of the earth: the strength of the hills is his also:** … The depths of the earth are at His finger tips; the tallest summits belong to Him, *Berkeley* … the farthest places of the earth are in his hands, and the folds of the hills are his, *NEB* ... In His hands are the bounds of the Earth, And His are the wings of the Hills, *Fenton* ... beneath his hand lie the depths of the earth, his are the mountain peaks, *Knox*.

**5. The sea is his, and he made it: and his hands formed the dry land:** ... His own hands have moulded its Tribes, *Fenton* ... his the ocean, for who but he created it? What other power fashioned the dry land?, *Knox* ... the dry land his hands molded, *Anchor* ... and the dry land which his hands fashioned, *REB*.

**6. O come, let us worship and bow down: let us kneel before the LORD our maker:** ... Enter! let us bow down and bend low, Let us kneel before Yahweh our maker, *Rotherham* ... Come! Let us throw ourselves at his feet in homage, let us kneel before the LORD who made us, *NEB*.

**7. For he is our God; and we are the people of his pasture, and the sheep of his hand. Today if ye will hear his voice:** ... the flock in his care, *REB* ... And what are we, but folk of his pasturing, sheep that follow his beckoning hand?, *Knox* ... to whom he gives food, and the sheep of his flock. Today, if you would only give ear to his voice!, *BB* ... the flock of his grazing plot. Today, hear the awesome One when he proclaims, *Anchor*.

---

**95:1–2.** The invocation to praise in vv. 1f gives a striking picture of the joyful tumult of the Temple worship. Shrill cries of gladness, loud shouts of praise and songs with musical accompaniments rang simultaneously through the courts and to Western ears would have sounded as din rather than as music and as more exuberant than reverent. The spirit expressed is almost as strange to many moderns as the manner of its expression. That swelling joy which throbs in the summons, that consciousness that jubilation is a conspicuous element in worship, that effort to rise to a height of joyful emotion, are very foreign to much of our worship. And their absence, or presence only in minute amount, flattens much devotion and robs the Church of one of its chief treasures. No doubt, there must often be sad strains blended with praise. But it is a part of Christian duty, and certainly of Christian wisdom, to try to catch that tone of joy in worship which rings in this Psalm.

**95:3–5.** The three following verses give Yahweh's creative and sustaining power and his consequent ownership of this fair world as the reasons for worship. He is King by right of creation. Surely, it is forcing unnatural meanings on words to maintain that the psalmist believed in the real existence of the "gods" whom he disparagingly contrasts with Yahweh. The fact that these were worshiped sufficiently warrants the comparison. To treat it as in any degree inconsistent with monotheism is unnecessary and would scarcely have occurred to a reader but for the exigencies of a theory. The repeated reference to the "hand" of Yahweh is striking. In it are held the deeps; it is a hand forming the land as a potter fashions his clay; it is a shepherd's hand, protecting and feeding his flock (v. 7). The same Power created and sustains the physical universe and guides and guards Israel. The psalmist has no time for details; he can only single out extremes and leave us to infer that what is true of these is true of all that is enclosed between them. The depths and the heights are Yahweh's. The word rendered "heights" (HED #8776) is doubtful. Etymologically, it should mean "fatigue," but it is not found in that sense in any of the places where it occurs. The parallelism requires the meaning of "heights" to contrast with "depths," and this rendering is found in the Septuagint and is adopted by most moderns. The word is then taken to come from a root meaning "to be high." Some of those who adopt the translation "summits" attempt to get that meaning out of the root meaning "fatigue" by supposing that the labor of getting to the top of the mountain is alluded to in the name. But it is simpler to trace the word to the other root, "to be high." The ownerless sea is owned by Him; He made both its watery waste and the solid earth.

**95:6–7b.** But that all-creating Hand has put forth more wondrous energies than those of which heights and depths, sea and land, witness. Therefore, the summons is again addressed to Israel to bow before "Yahweh our Maker." The creation of a people to serve Him is the work of his grace and is a nobler effect of his power than material things. It is remarkable that the call to glad praise should be associated with thoughts of his greatness as shown in creation, while lowly reverence is enforced by remembrance of his special relation to Israel. We should have expected the converse. The revelation of the shepherd's love in his work of creating a people for himself is most fittingly adored by his sheep prostrate before Him. "The sheep of his hand" suggests not merely the creative, but the sustaining and protecting power of God.

**95:7c–8.** The sudden turn from jubilant praise and recognition of Israel's prerogative as its occasion to grave warning is made more impressive by its occurring in the middle of a verse. God's voice

| | | | | | |
|---|---|---|---|---|---|
| **524, 904, 7249** | **8471.128** | | **414, 7481.528** | **3949** | **3626, 4971** |
| cj, prep, n ms, ps 3ms | v Qal impf 2mp | **8.** | adv, v Hiphil juss 2mp | n ms, ps 2mp | prep, pn |
| אִם־בְּקֹלוֹ | תִשְׁמָעוּ | | אַל־תַּקְשׁוּ | לְבַבְכֶם | כִּמְרִיבָה |
| 'im-beqōlô | thishmā'û | | 'al-taqōshû | levavkhem | kimrîvāh |
| if by his voice | you listen | | do not cause to be hard | your heart | like Meribah |

| | | | | | | |
|---|---|---|---|---|---|---|
| **3626, 3219** | **4681** | **904, 4198** | | **866** | **5441.316** | **1** |
| prep, *n ms* | pn | prep, art, n ms | **9.** | rel part | v Piel pf 3cp, ps 1cs | n mp, ps 2mp |
| כְּיוֹם | מַסָּה | בַּמִּדְבָּר | | אֲשֶׁר | נִסּוּנִי | אֲבוֹתֵיכֶם |
| keyôm | massāh | bammidhbār | | 'ăsher | nissûnî | 'ăvôthêkhem |
| like the day of | Massah | in the wilderness | | when | they put Me to the test | your ancestors |

| | | | | | | |
|---|---|---|---|---|---|---|
| **1010.116** | **1612, 7495.116** | **6714** | | **727** | **8523** | **7248.125** |
| v Qal pf 3cp, ps 1cs | cj, v Qal pf 3cp | n ms, ps 1cs | **10.** | num | n fs | v Qal impf 1cs |
| בְּחָנוּנִי | גַּם־רָאוּ | פָּעֳלִי | | אַרְבָּעִים | שָׁנָה | אָקוּט |
| bechānûnî | gam-rā'û | phā'ălî | | 'arbā'îm | shānāh | 'āqûṯ |
| they tested Me | yet they had seen | my deeds | | forty | years | I was disgusted |

| | | | | | | |
|---|---|---|---|---|---|---|
| **904, 1810** | **569.125** | **6194** | **8912.152** | **3949** | **2062** | **2062** |
| prep, n ms | cj, v Qal impf 1cs | n ms | *v Qal act ptc mp* | n ms | pers pron | cj, pers pron |
| בְּדוֹר | וָאֹמַר | עַם | תֹּעֵי | לֵבָב | הֵם | וְהֵם |
| bedhôr | wā'ōmar | 'am | tō'ê | lēvāv | hēm | wehēm |
| with a generation | and I said | a people | going astray in | the heart | they | and they |

| | | | | | |
|---|---|---|---|---|---|
| **3940, 3156.116** | **1932** | | **866, 8123.215** | **904, 653** | **524, 971.126** |
| neg part, v Qal pf 3cp | n mp, ps 1cs | **11.** | rel part, v Niphal pf 1cs | prep, n ms, ps 1cs | cj, v Qal impf 3mp |
| לֹא־יָדְעוּ | דְרָכָי | | אֲשֶׁר־נִשְׁבַּעְתִּי | בְאַפִּי | אִם־יְבֹאוּן |
| lō'-yādhe'û | dherākhāy | | 'ăsher-nishba'ttî | ve'appî | 'im-yevō'ûn |
| they do not know | my ways | | whom I swore to | in my anger | that they would not enter |

| | | | | | | | |
|---|---|---|---|---|---|---|---|
| **420, 4638** | | **8301.133** | **3937, 3176** | **8302** | **2413** | **8301.133** | **3937, 3176** |
| prep, n fs, ps 1cs | **96:1** | v Qal impv 2mp | prep, pn | n ms | adj | v Qal impv 2mp | prep, pn |
| אֶל־מְנוּחָתִי | | שִׁירוּ | לַיהוָה | שִׁיר | חָדָשׁ | שִׁירוּ | לַיהוָה |
| 'el-menûchāthî | | shîrû | layhwāh | shîr | chādhāsh | shîrû | layhwāh |
| to my rest | | sing | to Yahweh | a song | new | sing | to Yahweh |

**8. Harden not your heart, as in the provocation, and as in the day of temptation in the wilderness:** … if you would only listen to my voice today, and be not stubborn as at Meribah, as once at Massa in the wilderness, *Moffatt* … Do not be stubborn, as your ancestors were at Meribah, as they were that day at Massah, *NCV.*

**9. When your fathers tempted me, proved me, and saw my work:** … When your forefathers made trial of me, tested me, though they had seen what I did, *REB* … Your fathers put me to the test, challenged me, as if they lacked proof of my power, *Knox* … When your fathers perverted themselves, To try Me, tho' seeing My works, *Fenton.*

**10. Forty years long was I grieved with this generation, and said, It is a people that do err in their heart, and they have not known my ways:** … For forty years I was disgusted with that generation and said, They are a people whose heart strays, *Berkeley* … For forty years I abhorred that generation and said: They are a people whose hearts are astray, *REB* … Forty years I loathed that generation, and I said: They are a people of erring heart, *NAB* … They are a senseless people, who care not for my ways, *Moffatt.*

**11. Unto whom I sware in my wrath that they should not enter into my rest:** … I was angry and made a promise, They will never enter my rest, *NCV* … Therefore I vowed in My indignation, They shall never enter My rest, *Berkeley* … They shall never attain my rest, *Knox.*

**96:1. O sing unto the LORD a new song: sing unto the LORD, all the earth:** … in the Lord's honour, let the whole earth make melody!, *Knox* … O make a new song to the Lord; let all the earth make melody to the Lord, *BB* … Sing to Yahweh a song that is new, Sing to Yahweh all the earth, *Rotherham.*

**2. Sing unto the LORD, bless his name; show forth his salvation from day to day:** … sing to the LORD, all men on earth, *NEB* … Proclaim from sea to sea his victory, *Anchor* … Publish his deliverance abroad from day to day, *Goodspeed* … Sing to the Eternal, praise him, breaks in upon the joyful acclamations with solemn effect. The shouts of the adoring multitude fade on the poet's trembling ear, as that deeper voice is heard. We cannot persuade ourselves that this magnificent transition is due to the afterthought of a compiler. Such an one would surely have stitched his fragments more neatly together than to make the seam run through the center of a verse—an irregularity which would seem small to a singer in the heat of his inspiration. Verse 7c may be either a wish or the protasis to the apodosis in v. 8. "If ye would but listen to his voice!" is an exclamation, made more forcible by the omission of what would happen then. But it is not necessary to regard the clause as optative. The conditional meaning, which connects it with what follows, is probably preferable and is not set aside by the expression "his voice" instead of "My voice." "Today" stands first with strong emphasis, to enforce the critical character of the present moment. It may be the last opportunity. At all events, it is an opportunity and therefore to be grasped and used. A doleful history of unthankfulness lay behind; but still the divine voice sounds, and still the fleeting moments offer space for softening of heart and docile hearkening. The madness of delay when time is hurrying on and the longsuffering patience of God are wonderfully proclaimed in that one word, which the Epistle to the Hebrews lays hold of with so deep insight as all-important.

**95:9–11.** The warning points Israel back to ancestral sins, the tempting of God in the second year of the Exodus by the demand for water (Exo. 17:1–7). The scene of that murmuring received both names, Massah ("temptation") and Meribah ("strife").

It is difficult to decide the exact force of v. 9b. "Saw My work" is most naturally taken as referring to the divine acts of deliverance and protection seen by Israel in the desert, which aggravated the guilt of their faithlessness. But the word rendered "and" (HED #1612) will, in that case, have to be taken as meaning "although"—a sense which cannot be established. It seems better, therefore, to take "work" (HED #6714) in the unusual meaning of acts of judgment—his "strange work." Israel's tempting of God was the more indicative of hardheartedness that it was persisted in, in spite of chastisements. Possibly, both thoughts are to be combined, and the whole varied stream of blessings and punishments is referred to in the wide expression. Both forms of God's work should have touched these hard hearts. It mattered not whether He blessed or punished. They were impervious to both. The awful issue of this obstinate rebellion is set forth in terrible words. The sensation of physical loathing followed by sickness is daringly ascribed to God. We cannot but remember what John heard in Patmos from the lips into which grace was poured: "I will spew thee out of my mouth" (Rev. 3:16).

But before He cast Israel out, He pled with them, as v. 10b goes on to tell: "He said, 'A people that do err in their heart are they.'" He said so, by many a prophet and many a judgment, in order that they might come back to the true path. The desert-wanderings were but a symbol, as they were a consequence, of their wanderings in heart. They did not know his ways; therefore, they chose their own. They strayed in heart; therefore, they had an ever-increasing ignorance of the right road. For the averted heart and the blind understanding produce each other.

The issue of the long-protracted departure from the path which God had marked was, as it ever is, condemnation to continue in the pathless wilderness and exclusion from the land of rest which God had promised them and in which He himself had said that He would make his resting-place in their midst. But what befell Israel in outward fact was symbolic of universal spiritual truth. The hearts that love devious ways can never be restful. The path which leads to calm is traced by God, and only those who tread it with softened hearts, earnestly listening to his voice, will find repose even on the road and come at last to the land of peace. For others, they have chosen the desert, and in it they will wander wearily, forever roaming with a hungry heart.

The author of the Epistle to the Hebrews is laying hold of the very kernel of the Psalm when he adduces the fact that so many centuries after Moses the warning was still addressed to Israel, and the possibility of entering the rest of God and the danger of missing it still urged, as showing that the rest of God remained to be won by later generations, and proclaiming the eternal truth that "we which have believed do enter into rest."

***Psalm 96.*** *The praise of Yahweh as King has, in the preceding Psalms, chiefly celebrated his reign over Israel. But this grand coronation anthem takes a wider sweep, and hymns that kingdom as extending to all nations and as reaching beyond men for the joy and blessing of a renovated earth. It falls into four strophes, of which the first three contain three verses each, while the last extends to four. These strophes are like concentric circles,*

| 3725, 800 | | 8301.133 | 3937, 3176 | 1313.333 | 8428 | 1339.333 |
|---|---|---|---|---|---|---|
| *adj*, art, n fs | | v Qal impv 2mp | prep, pn | v Piel impv 2mp | n ms, ps 3ms | v Piel impv 2mp |
| כָּל־הָאָרֶץ | **2.** | שִׁירוּ | לַיהוָה | בָּרְכוּ | שְׁמוֹ | בַּשְּׂרוּ |
| kol-hā'ārets | | shîrû | layhwāh | bārekhû | shemô | basserû |
| all the earth | | sing | to Yahweh | bless | his name | tell the news |

| 4623, 3219, 3937, 3219 | 3568 | | 5807.333 | 904, 1504 | 3638 |
|---|---|---|---|---|---|
| prep, n ms, prep, n ms | n fs, ps 3ms | | v Piel impv 2mp | prep, art, n mp | n ms, ps 3ms |
| מִיּוֹם־לְיוֹם | יְשׁוּעָתוֹ | **3.** | סַפְּרוּ | בַגּוֹיִם | כְּבוֹדוֹ |
| mîyôm-leyôm | yeshû'āthô | | sapperû | vaggôyim | kevôdhô |
| from day to day | his salvation | | recount | among the nations | his glory |

| 904, 3725, 6194 | 6623.258 | | 3706 | 1448 | 3176 |
|---|---|---|---|---|---|
| prep, *adj*, art, n mp | v Niphal ptc fp, ps 3ms | | cj | adj | pn |
| בְּכָל־הָעַמִּים | נִפְלְאוֹתָיו | **4.** | כִּי | גָּדוֹל | יְהוָה |
| bekhol-hā'ammîm | niphle'ôthâv | | kî | ghādhôl | yehwāh |
| among all the peoples | his extraordinary deeds | | because | great | Yahweh |

| 2054.455 | 4108 | 3486.255 | 2000 | 6142, 3725, 435 | | 3706 |
|---|---|---|---|---|---|---|
| cj, v Pual ptc ms | adv | v Niphal ptc ms | pers pron | prep, *adj*, n mp | | cj |
| וּמְהֻלָּל | מְאֹד | נוֹרָא | הוּא | עַל־כָּל־אֱלֹהִים | **5.** | כִּי |
| ûmehullāl | me'ōdh | nôrā' | hû' | 'al-kol-'ĕlōhîm | | kî |
| and One Who is praised | very | fearful | He | over all gods | | because |

| 3725, 435 | 6194 | 462 | 3176 | 8452 | 6449.111 | | 2003, 1994 |
|---|---|---|---|---|---|---|---|
| *adj, n mp* | art, n mp | adj | cj, pn | n md | v Qal pf 3ms | | n ms, cj, n ms |
| כָּל־אֱלֹהֵי | הָעַמִּים | אֱלִילִים | וַיהוָה | שָׁמַיִם | עָשָׂה | **6.** | הוֹד־וְהָדָר |
| kol-'ĕlōhê | hā'ammîm | 'ĕlîlîm | wayhwāh | shāmayim | 'āsāh | | hôdh-wehādhār |
| all the gods of | the peoples | idols | but Yahweh | the heavens | He made | | majesty and honor |

| 3937, 6686 | 6010 | 8930 | 904, 4881 | | 1957.133 | 3937, 3176 | 5121 |
|---|---|---|---|---|---|---|---|
| prep, n mp, ps 3ms | n ms | cj, n fs | prep, n ms, ps 3ms | | v Qal impv 2mp | prep, pn | *n fp* |
| לְפָנָיו | עֹז | וְתִפְאֶרֶת | בְּמִקְדָּשׁוֹ | **7.** | הָבוּ | לַיהוָה | מִשְׁפְּחוֹת |
| lephānâv | 'ōz | wethiph'ereth | bemiqŏddāshô | | hāvû | layhwāh | mishpechôth |
| before Him | strength | and beauty | in his Sanctuary | | ascribe | to Yahweh | O families of |

| 6194 | 1957.133 | 3937, 3176 | 3638 | 6010 | | 1957.133 | 3937, 3176 | 3638 |
|---|---|---|---|---|---|---|---|---|
| n mp | v Qal impv 2mp | prep, pn | n ms | cj, n ms | | v Qal impv 2mp | prep, pn | *n ms* |
| עַמִּים | הָבוּ | לַיהוָה | כָּבוֹד | וָעֹז | **8.** | הָבוּ | לַיהוָה | כְּבוֹד |
| 'ammîm | hāvû | layhwāh | kāvôdh | wā'ōz | | hāvû | layhwāh | kevôdh |
| peoples | ascribe | to Yahweh | glory | and strength | | ascribe | to Yahweh | the glory of |

| 8428 | 5558.133, 4647 | 971.133 | 3937, 2793 | | 8246.733 | 3937, 3176 |
|---|---|---|---|---|---|---|
| n ms, ps 3ms | v Qal impv 2mp, n fs | cj, v Qal impv 2mp | prep, n fp, ps 3ms | | v Hithpael impv 2mp | prep, pn |
| שְׁמוֹ | שְׂאוּ־מִנְחָה | וּבֹאוּ | לְחַצְרוֹתָיו | **9.** | הִשְׁתַּחֲווּ | לַיהוָה |
| shemô | se'û-minchāh | ûvō'û | lechatsrôthâv | | hishtachwû | layhwāh |
| his name | carry an offering | and come | to his courts | | worship | Yahweh |

day after day tell of his saving aid, *Moffatt* ... publish his salvation from day to day, *Darby.*

**3. Declare his glory among the heathen, his wonders among all people:** ... Recount Among the nations his glory, Among all the peoples his wonders, *Rotherham* ... Publish his glory among the heathen; his wonderful acts for all the world to hear, *Knox* ... let pagans hear about his glory, let every nation know his wondrous deeds, *Moffatt.*

**4. For the LORD is great, and greatly to be praised: he is to be feared above all gods:** ... His splendour above all the Powers, *Fenton* ... because the LORD is great; he should be praised at all times, *NCV* ... awesome is he, beyond all gods, *NCB.*

**5. For all the gods of the nations are idols: but the LORD made the heavens:** ... For all the gods of peoples are things of nought, *Rotherham* ... They are but fancied gods the heathen call divine; the Lord, not they, made the heavens, *Knox* ... For all the gods of the peoples are nonentities, While the LORD made the heavens, *Goodspeed* ... are false gods, *BB.*

**6. Honour and majesty are before him: strength and beauty are in his sanctuary:** ... Honour and beauty are his escort; worship and magnificence the attendants of his shrine, *Knox* ... splendour and majesty are before him, strength and beauty at his side, *Anchor* ... Honour and glory are before him: strong and fair is his holy place, *BB* ... he has power and beauty in his Temple, *NCV.*

**7. Give unto the LORD, O ye kindreds of the people, give unto the LORD glory and strength:** ... Tribes of the heathen, make your offering to the Lord, an offering to the Lord of glory and homage, *Knox* ... Ascribe to the LORD, O families of the peoples, ascribe to the LORD glory and strength, *NRSV.*

**8. Give unto the LORD the glory due unto his name: bring an offering, and come into his courts:** ... Bring gifts, and enter into his courts, *NCB* ... bring an oblation and come into his courts, *Darby* ... Lift up a present and come in to His courts, *Young* ... bring sacrifice, come into his courts, *Knox.*

**9. O worship the LORD in the beauty of holiness: fear before him, all the earth:** ... Worship the LORD in holy splendor; tremble before him, all the earth, *NRSV* ... O give worship to the Lord in holy robes; be in fear before him, all the earth, *BB* ... Stand in His presence with awe, all the earth, *Berkeley* ... kneel before God in sacred vestments, tremble before him all the earth, *Moffatt* ... in holy attire worship the LORD; tremble before him, all the earth, *REB.*

---

*drawn round that eternal throne. The first summons Israel to its high vocation of Yahweh's evangelist, the herald who proclaims the enthronement of the King. The second sets Him above all the "Nothings" which usurp the name of gods, and thus prepares the way for his sole monarchy. The third summons outlying nations to bring their homage and flings open the Temple gates to all men, inviting them to put on priestly robes and do priestly acts there. The fourth calls on Nature in its heights and depths, heaven and earth, sea, plain and forest, to add their acclaim to the shouts which hail the establishment of Yahweh's visible dominion.*

**96:1–3.** The Psalm is probably a lyric echo, in which the prophet-singer sees the beginning of Yahweh's worldwide display of his dominion. He knew not how many weary years were to pass in a weary and God-defying world, before his raptures became facts. But though his vision tarries, his song is no overheated imagining, which has been chilled down for succeeding generations into a baseless hope. The perspective of the world's chronology hid from him the deep valley between his standpoint and the fulfillment of his glowing words. Mankind still marches burdened, down among the mists, but it marches toward the sunlit heights. The call to sing a new song is quoted from Isa. 42:10. The word in v. 2b rendered "tell the news" (HED #1339) is also a favorite word with Isaiah (40:9; 52:7, etc.). Verse 3a closely resembles Isa. 66:19.

**96:4–6.** The second strophe is full of allusions to earlier Psalms and prophets. The new manifestation of Yahweh's power has vindicated his supremacy above the vanities which the peoples call gods and has thereby given new force to old triumphant words which magnified his exalted name. Long ago a psalmist had sung, after a signal defeat of assailants of Jerusalem, that God was "great and greatly to be praised" (Ps. 48:1), and this psalmist makes the old words new. "Feared" (HED #3486) reminds us of Ps. 47:2. The contemptuous name of the nations' gods as "nothings" is frequent in Isaiah. The heavens, which roof over all the earth, declare to every land Yahweh's creative power, and his supremacy above all gods. But the singer's eye pierces their abysses and sees some gleams of that higher sanctuary of which they are but the floor. There stand honor and majesty, strength and beauty. The psalmist does not speak of "attributes." His vivid imagination conceives of these as servants, attending on Yahweh's royal state. Whatsoever things are lovely, and whatsoever are august, are at home in that sanctuary. Strength and beauty are often separated in a disordered world, and each is maimed thereby, but in their perfection they are indissolubly blended. Men call many things strong and fair which have no affinity with holiness; but the archetypes of both are in the Holy Place, and any strength which has not its roots there is weakness, and any beauty which is not a reflection from "the beauty" of the LORD our God is but a mask concealing ugliness.

**96:7–9.** The third strophe builds on this supremacy of Yahweh, whose dwelling-place is the seat of all things worthy to be admired, the summons to all nations to render praise to Him. It is mainly a variation of Ps. 29:1f, where the summons is addressed to angels. Here "the families of the peoples" are called on to ascribe to Yahweh "glory and strength," or "the glory of his name" (i.e., of his character as revealed). The call presupposes a new manifestation of his kingship, as conspicuous and earth-shaking as the thunderstorm of the original

| 904, 1997, 7231 | 2523.133 | 4623, 6686 | 3725, 800 | | 569.133 |
|---|---|---|---|---|---|
| prep, *n fs*, n ms | v Qal impv 2mp | prep, n mp, ps 3ms | *adj*, art, n fs | **10.** | v Qal impv 2mp |
| בְּהַדְרַת־קֹדֶשׁ | חִילוּ | מִפָּנָיו | כָּל־הָאָרֶץ | | אִמְרוּ |
| behadhrath-qōdhesh | chîlû | mippānâv | kol-hā'ārets | | 'imrû |
| with an adornment of holiness | tremble | before Him | all the earth | | say |

| 904, 1504 | 3176 | 4566.111 | 652, 3679.222 | 8725 | 1118, 4267.222 |
|---|---|---|---|---|---|
| prep, art, n mp | pn | v Qal pf 3ms | cj, v Niphal impf 3fs | n fs | neg part, v Niphal impf 3fs |
| בַּגּוֹיִם | יְהוָה | מָלָךְ | אַף־תִּכּוֹן | תֵּבֵל | בַּל־תִּמּוֹט |
| vaggôyim | yehwāh | mālākh | 'aph-tikkôn | tēvēl | bal-timmôṯ |
| among the nations | Yahweh | He reigns | indeed it is established | the world | it will not totter |

| 1833.121 | 6194 | 904, 4478 | | 7975.126 | 8452 | 1559.122 |
|---|---|---|---|---|---|---|
| v Qal impf 3ms | n mp | prep, n mp | **11.** | v Qal juss 3mp | art, n md | cj, v Qal juss 3fs |
| יָדִין | עַמִּים | בְּמֵישָׁרִים | | יִשְׂמְחוּ | הַשָּׁמַיִם | וְתָגֵל |
| yādhîn | 'ammîm | bemêshārîm | | yismechû | hashshāmayim | wethāghēl |
| He will judge | peoples | with uprightness | | may they be glad | the heavens | and may it rejoice |

| 800 | 7769.121 | 3328 | 4530 | | 6159.121 | 7899 |
|---|---|---|---|---|---|---|
| art, n fs | v Qal juss 3ms | art, n ms | cj, n ms, ps 3ms | **12.** | v Qal juss 3ms | n ms |
| הָאָרֶץ | יִרְעַם | הַיָּם | וּמְלֹאוֹ | | יַעֲלֹז | שָׂדַי |
| hā'ārets | yir'am | hayyām | ûmelō'ô | | ya'ălōz | sādhay |
| the earth | and may it rage | the sea | and it fulness | | may it exult | the field |

| 3725, 866, 904 | 226 | 7728.326 | 3725, 6320, 3402 | | 3937, 6686 |
|---|---|---|---|---|---|
| cj, *adj*, rel part, prep, ps 3ms | adv | v Piel impf 3mp | *adj*, *n mp*, n ms | **13.** | prep, *n mp* |
| וְכָל־אֲשֶׁר־בּוֹ | אָז | יְרַנְּנוּ | כָּל־עֲצֵי־יָעַר | | לִפְנֵי |
| wekhol-'ăsher-bô | 'āz | yerannenû | kol-'ătsê-yā'ar | | liphnê |
| and all that in it | then | they will shout for joy | all the trees of the forest | | before |

| 3176 | 3706 | 971.111 | 3706 | 971.111 | 3937, 8570.141 | 800 | 8570.121, 8725 |
|---|---|---|---|---|---|---|---|
| pn | cj | v Qal pf 3ms | cj | v Qal pf 3ms | prep, Qal inf con | art, n fs | v Qal impf 3ms, n fs |
| יְהוָה | כִּי | בָא | כִּי | בָא | לִשְׁפֹּט | הָאָרֶץ | יִשְׁפֹּט־תֵּבֵל |
| yehwāh | kî | vā' | kî | vā' | lishpōṯ | hā'ārets | yishpōṯ-tēvēl |
| Yahweh | because | He comes | because | He comes | to judge | the earth | He judges the world |

| 904, 6928 | 6194 | 904, 536 | | 3176 | 4566.111 | 1559.122 |
|---|---|---|---|---|---|---|
| prep, n ms | cj, n mp | prep, n fs, ps 3ms | **97:1** | pn | v Qal pf 3ms | v Qal impf 3fs |
| בְּצֶדֶק | וְעַמִּים | בֶּאֱמוּנָתוֹ | | יְהוָה | מָלָךְ | תָּגֵל |
| betsedheq | we'ammîm | be'ĕmûnāthô | | yehwāh | mālākh | tāghēl |
| with righteousness | and peoples | with truth | | Yahweh | He reigns | may it rejoice |

| 800 | 7975.126 | 339 | 7521 | | 6281 | 6441 | 5623 |
|---|---|---|---|---|---|---|---|
| art, n fs | v Qal juss 3mp | n mp | adj | **2.** | n ms | cj, n ms | adv, ps 3ms |
| הָאָרֶץ | יִשְׂמְחוּ | אִיִּים | רַבִּים | | עָנָן | וַעֲרָפֶל | סְבִיבָיו |
| hā'ārets | yismechû | 'iyîm | rabbîm | | 'ānān | wa'ărāphel | sevîvâv |
| the earth | may they be glad | the islands | many | | clouds | and thick darkness | around Him |

**10. Say among the heathen that the LORD reigneth: the world also shall be established that it shall not be moved: he shall judge the people righteously:** ... The Lord is king now, he has put the world in order, never to be thrown into confusion more; he gives the nations a just award, *Knox* ... To the Nations, proclaim the LORD King;—Who fixed its unchangeable sphere, And its Peoples, He governs by Laws, *Fenton* ... He will judge the peoples with equity, *NRSV.*

**11. Let the heavens rejoice, and let the earth be glad; let the sea roar, and the fulness thereof:** ... Let the Skies smile, and the Earth laugh; Let the Sea roar, and all it contains, *Fenton* ... let the sea and what fills it resound, *NCB* ... and all the sea contains, give thunderous applause, *Knox* ... let the sea in its vastness continually roar, *Berkeley.*

**12. Let the field be joyful, and all that is therein: then shall all the trees of the wood rejoice:** ... The fields, and all the burden they bear, full of expectancy; no tree in the forest but will rejoice, *Knox* ... let all the trees of the wood be sounding with joy, *BB* ... all the trees of the forest rustle with praise, *Berkeley* ... the trees of the forest sing for joy, *NRSV.*

**13. Before the LORD: for he cometh, for he cometh to judge the earth: he shall judge the world with righteousness, and the people with his truth:** ... to rule the world with justice and the nations faithfully, *Moffatt* ... brings the world justice, to every race of men its promised award, *Knox* ... To the LORD, for He comes, For He comes to give justice on Earth, To govern its circuit by right, And its Peoples by Truth, *Fenton* ... judge the world with fairness, *NCV.*

**97:1. The LORD reigneth; let the earth rejoice; let the multitude of isles be glad thereof:** ... The Lord is King, let the earth have joy; let all the sea-lands be glad, *BB* ... The Eternal reigns! Let earth rejoice, let many a shore be glad, *Moffatt* ... faraway lands should be glad, *NCV* ... let the many coastlands be glad!, *RSV.*

**2. Clouds and darkness are round about him: righteousness and judgment are the habitation of his throne:** ... Dark clouds are round him; his kingdom is based on righteousness and right judging, *BB* ... See where he sits, clouds and darkness about him, justice and right the pillars of his throne, *Knox* ... His kingdom is built on what is right and fair, *NCV.*

---

Psalm. As in it the "sons of God" were called to worship in priestly garb, so here, still more emphatically, Gentile nations are invited to assume the priestly office, to "take an offering and come into his courts." The issue of Yahweh's manifestation of kingly sway will be that Israel's prerogative of priestly access to Him will be extended to all men and that the lowly worship of earth will have characteristics which assimilate it to that of the elder brethren who ever stand before Him and also characteristics which distinguish it from that and are necessary while the worshipers are housed in flesh. Material offerings and places consecrated to worship belong to earth. The "sons of God" above have them not, for they need them not.

**96:10–12.** The last strophe has four verses, instead of the normal three. The psalmist's chief purpose in it is to extend his summons for praise to the whole creation; but he cannot refrain from once more ringing out the glad tidings for which praise is to be rendered. He falls back in v. 10 on Ps. 93:1 and Ps. 9:8. In his quotation from the former Psalm, he brings more closely together the thoughts of Yahweh's reign and the fixity of the world, whether that is taken with a material reference, or as predicting the calm perpetuity of the moral order established by his merciful rule and equitable judgment. The thought that inanimate nature will share in the joy of renovated humanity inspires many glowing prophetic utterances, eminently those of Isaiah—as, e.g., Isa. 35. The converse thought, that it shared in the consequences of man's sin, is deeply stamped on the Genesis narrative. The same note is struck with unhesitating force in Rom. 8 and elsewhere in the NT. A poet invests nature with the hues of his own emotions, but this summons of the psalmist is more than poetry. How the transformation is to be effected is not revealed, but the consuming fires will refine, and at last man will have a dwelling place where environment will correspond to character, where the external will image the inward state, where a new form of the material will be the perpetual ally of the spiritual and perfected manhood will walk in a new heaven and new earth, where there is righteousness and no evil.

**96:13.** In the last verse of the Psalm, the singer appears to extend his prophetic gaze from the immediate redeeming act by which Yahweh assumes royal majesty to a still future "coming," during which He will judge the earth. "The accession is a single act; the judging is a continual process. Note that 'judging' has no terrible sound to a Hebrew." Verse 13c is a verbatim quotation from Ps. 9:8.

***Psalm 97.*** *In this Psalm, the first group of verses celebrates the royal state of the King (vv. 1–3); the second describes his coming as a past fact (vv. 4ff); the third portrays the twofold effects of Yahweh's appearance on the heathen and on Zion (vv. ff); and the last applies the lessons of the whole to the righteous, in exhortation and encouragement (vv. 1ff). The same dependence on earlier Psalms and prophets which marks others of this group is obvious here. The psalmist's mind is saturated with old sayings, which he finds flashed up into new meaning by recent experiences.*

**97:1–3.** The first strophe is mosaic-work. Verse 1 may be compared with Isa. 42:10; 51:5. Verse 2a is from Exo. 19:9, 16, etc.; and Ps. 18:9. Verse 2b is quoted from Ps. 89:14. Verse 3a recalls Pss. 50:3 and 18:8. The appearance of God on Sinai is the type of all later theophanies, and the reproduction of its principal features witnesses to the conviction that that transient manifestation was the unveiling of permanent reality. The veil had

| 6928 | 5122 | 4487 | 3802 | | 813 | 3937, 6686 | 2050.123 |
|---|---|---|---|---|---|---|---|
| n ms | cj, n ms | *n ms* | n ms, ps 3ms | **3.** | n fs | prep, n mp, ps 3ms | v Qal impf 2ms |
| צֶדֶק | וּמִשְׁפָּט | מְכוֹן | כִּסְאוֹ | | אֵשׁ | לְפָנָיו | תֵּלֵךְ |
| tsedheq | ûmishpāṭ | mekhôn | kis̱'ô | | 'ēsh | lephānâv | tēlēkh |
| righteousness | and justice | the foundation of | his throne | | fire | before Him | it proceeds |

| 3993.322 | 5623 | 7141 | | 213.516 | 1325 | 8725 | 7495.112 |
|---|---|---|---|---|---|---|---|
| cj, v Piel impf 3fs | adv | n mp, ps 3ms | **4.** | v Hiphil pf 3cp | n mp, ps 3ms | n fs | v Qal pf 3fs |
| וּתְלַהֵט | סָבִיב | צָרָיו | | הֵאִירוּ | בְרָקָיו | תֵּבֵל | רָאֲתָה |
| ûthelahēṭ | s̱āvîv | tsārâv | | hē'îrû | verāqâv | tēvēl | rā'ăthāh |
| and it ignites | all around | his adversaries | | they illuminate | his lightnings | the world | it sees |

| 2523.522 | 800 | | 2098 | 3626, 1804 | 4701.216 | 4623, 3937, 6686 | 3176 |
|---|---|---|---|---|---|---|---|
| cj, v Hiphil impf 3fs | art, n fs | **5.** | n mp | prep, art, n ms | v Niphal pf 3cp | prep, prep, *n mp* | pn |
| וַתָּחֵל | הָאָרֶץ | | הָרִים | כַּדּוֹנַג | נָמַסּוּ | מִלִּפְנֵי | יְהוָה |
| wattāchēl | hā'ārets | | hārîm | kaddônagh | nāmas̱s̱û | milliphnê | yehwāh |
| and it writhes | the earth | | the mountains | like the wax | they melt | from before | Yahweh |

| 4623, 3937, 6686 | 112 | 3725, 800 | | 5222.516 | 8452 | 6928 |
|---|---|---|---|---|---|---|
| prep, prep, *n mp* | *n ms* | *adj*, art, n fs | **6.** | v Hiphil pf 3cp | art, n md | n ms, ps 3ms |
| מִלִּפְנֵי | אֲדוֹן | כָּל־הָאָרֶץ | | הִגִּידוּ | הַשָּׁמַיִם | צִדְקוֹ |
| milliphnê | 'ădhôn | kol-hā'ārets | | higgîdhû | hashshāmayim | tsidhqô |
| from before | the Lord of | all the earth | | they declare | the heavens | his righteousness |

| 7495.116 | 3725, 6194 | 3638 | | 991.126 | 3725, 5856.152 | 6705 |
|---|---|---|---|---|---|---|
| cj, v Qal pf 3cp | *adj*, art, n mp | n ms, ps 3ms | **7.** | v Qal juss 3mp | *adj, v Qal act ptc mp* | n ms |
| וְרָאוּ | כָל־הָעַמִּים | כְּבוֹדוֹ | | יֵבֹשׁוּ | כָּל־עֹבְדֵי | פֶסֶל |
| werā'û | khol-hā'ammîm | kevôdhô | | yēvōshû | kol-'ōvedhê | phes̱el |
| and they see | all the peoples | his glory | | may they be ashamed | all the servants of | an idol |

| 2054.752 | 904, 462 | 8246.716, 3937 | 3725, 435 | | 8471.112 |
|---|---|---|---|---|---|
| art, v Hithpael ptc mp | prep, art, n mp | v Hithpael pf 3cp, prep, ps 3ms | *adj*, n mp | **8.** | v Qal pf 3fs |
| הַמִּתְהַלְלִים | בָּאֱלִילִים | הִשְׁתַּחֲווּ־לוֹ | כָּל־אֱלֹהִים | | שָׁמְעָה |
| hammithhalelîm | bā'ĕlîlîm | hishtachwû-lô | kol-'ĕlōhîm | | shāme'āh |
| those who boast | in idols | they will bow down to Him | all gods | | it hears |

| 7975.122 | 6995 | 1559.127 | 1351 | 3171 | 3937, 4775 | 5122 |
|---|---|---|---|---|---|---|
| cj, v Qal impf 3fs | pn | cj, v Qal impf 3fp | *n fp* | pn | prep, prep | n mp, ps 2ms |
| וַתִּשְׂמַח | צִיּוֹן | וַתָּגֵלְנָה | בְּנוֹת | יְהוּדָה | לְמַעַן | מִשְׁפָּטֶיךָ |
| wattismach | tsîyôn | wattāghēlenāh | benôth | yehûdhāh | lema'an | mishpāṭêkhā |
| and it is glad | Zion | and they rejoice | the daughters of | Judah | because of | your judgments |

**3. A fire goeth before him, and burneth up his enemies round about:** … Fire goes before him, sets ablaze his enemies all around, *JB* … A fire issues from His presence and consumes His enemies on every side, *Berkeley* … fire burns in front of him and blazes round his steps, *Moffatt* … consumes his adversaries on every side, *NRSV*.

**4. His lightnings enlightened the world: the earth saw, and trembled:** … In the flash of his lightning, how shines the world revealed, how earth trembled at the sight!, *Knox* … The world is lit up beneath his lightening-flash; the earth sees it and writhes in pain, *NEB* … his lightnings illumine the world, till earth shivers at the sight, *Moffatt* … His bright flames give light to the world; the earth saw it with fear, *BB*.

**5. The hills melted like wax at the presence of the LORD, at the presence of the Lord of the whole earth:** … The Hills like wax dissolve, Before the LORD,—Before the King of Earth!, *Fenton* … Mountains melt like wax at the LORD's approach, the Lord of all the earth, *REB* … The hills melt like wax at the presence of the Lord; his presence whom all the earth obeys, *Knox*.

**6. The heavens declare his righteousness, and all the people see his glory:** … The heavens announce his just claim, all the people see his glory, *Anchor* … The skies proclaim His Power, All Tribes His glory see, *Fenton* … proclaim his high authority, all nations see his majesty, *Moffatt* … his faithfulness; no nation but the sight of his glory, *Knox*.

**7. Confounded be all they that serve graven images, that boast themselves of idols: worship him, all ye gods:** ... All who worship images, and brag about vain idols, will come to a shameful end, *Beck* ... Shame on all who serve images, who pride themselves on their idols; bow down to him, all you gods, *JB* ... the men that worship carved images, and make their boast of false gods! him only all the powers of heaven, prostrate, adore, *Knox*.

**8. Zion heard, and was glad; and the daughters of Judah rejoiced because of thy judgments, O LORD:** ... Zion gave ear and was glad; and the daughters of Judah were full of joy, because of your decisions, O Lord, *BB* ... Zion is happy to hear it; Judah's towns are delighted with Your judgments LORD, *Beck* ... When Jerusalem hears this, she is

---

dropped again, but what had been once seen continued always, although unseen; and the veil could and would be drawn aside, and the long-hidden splendor blaze forth again. The combination of the pieces of mosaic in a new pattern here is striking. Three thoughts fill the singer's mind. God is King, and his reign gladdens the world, even away out to the dimly seen lands that are washed by the western ocean. "The islands" drew Isaiah's gaze. Prophecy began in him to look seaward or westward, little knowing how the course of empire was to take its way there, but feeling that whatever lands might lie toward the setting sun were ruled, and would be gladdened, by Yahweh.

Gladness passes into awe in v. 2a, as the seer beholds the cloud and gloom which encircle the throne. The transcending infinitude of the divine nature, the mystery of much of the divine acts, are symbolized by these; but the curtain is the picture. To know that God cannot be known is a large part of the knowledge of Him. Faith, built on experience, enters into the cloud and is not afraid, but confidently tells what it knows to be within the darkness. "Righteousness and judgment"—the eternal principle and the activity thereof in the several acts of the King—are the bases of his throne, more solid than the covering cloud. Earth can rejoice in his reign, even though darkness may make parts of it painful riddles, if the assurance is held fast that absolute righteousness is at the center and that the solid core of all is judgment. Destructive power, symbolized in v. 3 by fire which devours his adversaries, the fire which flashed first on Sinai, is part of the reason for the gladness of earth in his reign. For his foes are the world's foes too; and a God who could not smite into nothingness that which lifted itself against his dominion would be no God for whom the isles could wait. These three characteristics, mystery, righteousness, power to consume, attach to Yahweh's royalty and should make every heart rejoice.

**97:4–6.** In the second strophe, the tenses suddenly change into pure narrative. Verse 4a is quoted from Ps. 77:18. With v. 4b, may be compared Ps. 77:16. Verse 5a is like Mic. 1:4, and in a less degree Ps. 68:2. "The LORD of the whole earth" is an unusual designation, first found in a significant connection in Josh. 3:11, 13 as emphasizing his triumph over heathen gods in leading the people into Canaan and afterwards found in Zech. 4:14; 6:5; and Mic. 4:13. Verse 6a comes from the theophany in Ps. 50:6; and v. 6b has parallels in both parts of Isaiah—e.g., Isa. 35:2; 40:5; 52:10—passages which refer to the restoration from Babylon. The picture is grand as a piece of word-painting. The world lies wrapped in thunder gloom, and is suddenly illumined by the fierce blaze of lightning. The awestruck silence of nature is wonderfully given by v. 4b: " The earth saw, and trembled." But the picture is symbol, and the lightning-flash is meant to set forth the sudden, swift forth-darting of God's delivering power, which awes a gazing world, while the hills melting like wax from before his face solemnly proclaim how terrible its radiance is and how easily the mere showing of himself annihilates all high things that oppose themselves. Terrible powers, which tower above his people's ability to overcome them, vanish when He looks out from the deep darkness. The end of his appearance and of the consequent removal of obstacles is the manifestation of his righteousness and glory. The heavens are the scene of the divine appearance, although earth is the theater of its working. They "declare his righteousness," not because, as in Ps. 19 they are said to tell forth his glory by their myriad lights, but because in them He has shone forth in his great act of deliverance of his oppressed people. Israel receives the primary blessing, but is blessed, not for itself alone, but that all peoples may see in it Yahweh's glory. Thus, once more the Psalm recognizes the worldwide destination of national mercies and Israel's place in the divine economy as being of universal significance.

**97:7–9.** The third strophe (vv. 7ff) sets forth the results of the theophany on foes and friends. The worshipers of "the idols" (literally, "the nothings"; cf.

| 3176 | | 3706, 887 | 3176 | 6169 | 6142, 3725, 800 | 4108 | 6148.213 |
|---|---|---|---|---|---|---|---|
| pn | 9. | cj, pers pron | pn | n ms | prep, *adj*, art, n fs | adv | v Niphal pf 2ms |
| יְהוָה | | כִּי־אַתָּה | יְהוָה | עֶלְיוֹן | עַל־כָּל־הָאָרֶץ | מְאֹד | נַעֲלֵיתָ |
| yehwāh | | kî-'attāh | yehwāh | 'elyôn | 'al-kol-hā'ārets | me'ōdh | na'ălêthā |
| O Yahweh | | because You | O Yahweh | the Most High | over all the earth | very | You are up |

| 6142, 3725, 435 | | 154.152 | 3176 | 7983.131 | 7737 | 8490.151 | 5497 |
|---|---|---|---|---|---|---|---|
| prep, *adj*, n mp | 10. | *v Qal act ptc mp* | pn | v Qal impv 2mp | n ms | v Qal act ptc ms | *n fp* |
| עַל־כָּל־אֱלֹהִים | | אֹהֲבֵי | יְהוָה | שִׂנְאוּ | רָע | שֹׁמֵר | נַפְשׁוֹת |
| 'al-kol-'ĕlōhîm | | 'ōhevê | yehwāh | sin'û | rā' | shōmēr | naphshôth |
| above all gods | | those who love | Yahweh | hate | evil | guarding | the lives of |

| 2728 | 4623, 3135 | 7857 | 5522.521 | | 214 | 2319.155 |
|---|---|---|---|---|---|---|
| n mp, ps 3ms | prep, *n fs* | n mp | v Hiphil impf 3ms, ps 3mp | 11. | n ms | v Qal pass ptc ms |
| חֲסִידָיו | מִיַּד | רְשָׁעִים | יַצִּילֵם | | אוֹר | זָרֻעַ |
| chăsîdhâv | mîyadh | reshā'îm | yatstsîlēm | | 'ōr | zārua' |
| his godly ones | from the hand of | the wicked | He rescues them | | a light | sown |

| 3937, 6926 | 3937, 3596, 3949 | 7977 | | 7975.133 | 6926 |
|---|---|---|---|---|---|
| prep, art, n ms | cj, prep, *adj*, n ms | n fs | 12. | v Qal impv 2mp | n mp |
| לַצַּדִּיק | וּלְיִשְׁרֵי־לֵב | שִׂמְחָה | | שִׂמְחוּ | צַדִּיקִים |
| latstsaddîq | ûlăyishrê-lēv | simchāh | | simchû | tsaddîqîm |
| for the righteous | and for the upright of heart | rejoicing | | rejoice | O righteous ones |

| 904, 3176 | 3142.533 | 3937, 2228 | 7231 | | 4344 | | 8301.133 |
|---|---|---|---|---|---|---|---|
| prep, pn | cj, v Hiphil impv 2mp | prep, *n ms* | n ms, ps 3ms | 98:t | n ms | 1. | v Qal impv 2mp |
| בַּיהוָה | וְהוֹדוּ | לְזֵכֶר | קָדְשׁוֹ | | מִזְמוֹר | | שִׁירוּ |
| bayhwāh | wehôdhû | lezēkher | qādheshô | | mizmôr | | shîrû |
| in Yahweh | and give thanks | at the remembrance of | his holiness | | a Psalm | | sing |

| 3937, 3176 | 8302 | 2413 | 3706, 6623.258 | 6449.111 | 3588.512, 3937 |
|---|---|---|---|---|---|
| prep, pn | n ms | adj | cj, v Niphal ptc fp | v Qal pf 3ms | v Hiphil pf 3fs, prep, ps 3ms |
| לַיהוָה | שִׁיר | חָדָשׁ | כִּי־נִפְלָאוֹת | עָשָׂה | הוֹשִׁיעָה־לּוֹ |
| layhwāh | shîr | chādhāsh | kî-niphlā'ôth | 'āsāh | hôshî'āh-lô |
| to Yahweh | a song | new | because extraordinary deeds | He has done | it has saved for Him |

| 3332 | 2307 | 7231 | | 3156.511 | 3176 | 3568 |
|---|---|---|---|---|---|---|
| n fs, ps 3ms | cj, *n fs* | n ms, ps 3ms | 2. | v Hiphil pf 3ms | pn | n fs, ps 3ms |
| יְמִינוֹ | וּזְרוֹעַ | קָדְשׁוֹ | | הוֹדִיעַ | יְהוָה | יְשׁוּעָתוֹ |
| yemînô | ûzărôa' | qādheshô | | hôdhîa' | yehwāh | yeshû'āthô |
| his right hand | and the arm of | his holiness | | He has made known | Yahweh | his salvation |

glad, and the towns of Judah rejoice, *NCV* … because of your acts of providence, Yahweh, *Anchor.*

**9. For thou, LORD, art high above all the earth: thou art exalted far above all gods:** … for thou art the Most High o'er all the earth, thou hast proved greater than all gods, *Moffatt* … art thou not sovereign Lord of earth, beyond measure exalted above all gods?, *Knox* … Thou transcendest far above all gods, *Berkeley* … And over all the Powers, *Fenton* … thou art exalted exceedingly above all gods, *Darby.*

**10. Ye that love the LORD, hate evil: he preserveth the souls of his saints; he delivereth them out of the hand of the wicked:** … Yahweh, who loves those who hate evil, who protects the lives of his devoted, Will rescue them from the hand of the wicked, *Anchor.*

**11. Light is sown for the righteous, and gladness for the upright in heart:** … A harvest of light is sown for the righteous, and joy for all good men, *NEB* … Light is shed upon the righteous and joy on the upright in heart, *NIV* … Light dawns for the just, and happiness for men of upright mind, *Moffatt* … Light is sown like a seed for the righteous, And gladness for the upright in heart, *NASB.*

**12. Rejoice in the LORD, ye righteous; and give thanks at the remembrance of his holiness:** … You that are righteous, rejoice in the LORD and praise his holy name, *NEB* … Be happy in the LORD, you righteous, and praise Him as you remember how holy He is, *Beck* … rejoice, ye just, in the Eternal, give thanks as you recall his sacred name, *Moffatt*

... Let the Righteous rejoice in the LORD, And thank for remembering His Saints, *Fenton.*

**98:t. A Psalm.**

**1. O sing unto the LORD a new song; for he hath done marvellous things: his right hand, and his holy arm, hath gotten him the victory:** ... Sing to the LORD, Sing a new song for His wonderful act, *Fenton* ... a song of wonder at his doings; how his own right hand, his own holy arm, brought him victory, *Knox* ... His right hand, and his holy arm, hath wrought salvation for him, *MRB.*

**2. The LORD hath made known his salvation: his righteousness hath he openly shown in the sight of the heathen:** ... The Lord has given proof of his saving power, has vindicated his just dealings, *Knox* ... Yahweh has made known his saving power, revealed his saving justice for the nations to see, *JB* ... The LORD has made known his victory, he has revealed his vindication in the sight of the nations, *RSV* ... the Eternal has let the nations see his triumph and his victory, *Moffatt.*

---

96:5) are put to confusion by the demonstration by fact of Yahweh's sovereignty over their helpless deities. Verse 7a, b, recall Isa. 52:17; 44:9. As the worshipers are ashamed, so the gods themselves are summoned to fall down before this triumphant Yahweh, as Dagon did before the Ark. Surely it is a piece of most prosaic pedantry to argue, from this flash of scorn, that the psalmist believed that the gods whom he had just called "nothings" had a real existence and that therefore he was not a pure monotheist.

The shame of the idolaters and the prostration of their gods heighten the gladness of Zion, which the Psalm describes in old words that had once celebrated another flashing forth of Yahweh's power (Ps. 48:11). But there is no need for a transposition of v. 7 and v. 8, since there is no ambiguity as to what Zion heard, if the existing order is retained, and her gladness is quite as worthy a consequence of the exaltation of Yahweh in v. 9 as the subjugation of the false gods would be. (Cf. v. 9 with Ps. 83:18; and Ps. 47:2.)

**97:10–12.** The last strophe draws exhortation and promises from the preceding. There is a marked diminution of dependence on earlier passages in this strophe, in which the psalmist points for his own generation the lessons of the great deliverance which he has been celebrating. Verse 12a is like Ps. 32:11; v. 12b is from Ps. 30:4; but the remainder is the psalmist's own earnest exhortation and firm faith, cast into words which come warm from his own heart's depths. Love toward Yahweh necessarily implies hatred of evil, which is enmity with the Holy Spirit. That higher love will not be kept in energy, unless it is guarded by wholesome antipathy to everything foul. The capacity for love of the noble is maimed unless there is hearty hatred of the ignoble. Love to God is no idle affection, but withdraws a man from rival loves. The stronger the attraction, the stronger the recoil. The closer we cleave to God, the more decided our shrinking from all that would weaken our hold of Him.

A specific reference in the exhortation to temptations to idolatry is possible, though not necessary. All times have their "evil" (HED #7737) with which God's people are ever tempted to comply. The exhortation is never out of place, nor the encouragement which accompanies it ever illusory. In such firm adherence to Yahweh, many difficulties will rise, and foes be made; but those who obey it will not lack protection. Mark the alternation of names for such. They are first called lovers of God; they are then designated as "his saints." That which is first in time is last in mention. The effect is in view before it is traced to its cause. "We love Him because He first loved us" (1 John 4:19). Then follow names drawn from the moral perfecting which will ensue on recognition and reception of God's favor and on the cherishing of the love which fulfills the Law. They who love because they are loved become righteous and upright-hearted because they love. For such the psalmist has promise as well as exhortation. Not only are they preserved in and from dangers, but "light is sown" for them. Darkness often wraps the righteous, and it is not true to experience to say that his way is always in the sunlight.

***Psalm 98.*** *The two preceding Psalms correspond in number and division of verses. The first begins with a summons to sing to Yahweh; the second, with a proclamation that He is King. A precisely similar connection exists between this and the following Psalm. Psalm 98 is an echo of Ps. 96, and Ps. 99 of Ps. 97. The number of verses in each of the second pair is nine, and in each there is a threefold division. The general theme of both pairs is the same, but with considerable modifications. The abundant allusions to older passages continue here, and the second part of Isaiah is especially familiar to the singer.*

**98:1–3.** The first strophe, although modeled on the first of Ps. 96, presents the theme in a different fashion. Instead of reiterating through three verses

| 3937, 6084 | 1504 | 1580.311 | 6930 | | 2226.111 |
|---|---|---|---|---|---|
| prep, *n fd* | art, n mp | v Piel pf 3ms | n fs, ps 3ms | | v Qal pf 3ms |
| לְעֵינֵי | הַגּוֹיִם | גִּלָּה | צִדְקָתוֹ | **3.** | זָכַר |
| le'ênê | haggôyim | gillāh | tsidhqāthô | | zākhar |
| before the eyes of | the nations | He has revealed | his righteousness | | He has called to mind |

| 2721 | 536 | 3937, 1041 | 3547 | 7495.116 |
|---|---|---|---|---|
| n ms, ps 3ms | cj, n fs, ps 3ms | prep, *n ms* | pn | v Qal pf 3cp |
| חַסְדּוֹ | וֶאֱמוּנָתוֹ | לְבֵית | יִשְׂרָאֵל | רָאוּ |
| chasdô | we'ĕmûnāthô | levêth | yisrā'ēl | rā'û |
| his steadfast love | and his reliability | to the household of | Israel | they saw |

| 3725, 675, 800 | 881 | 3568 | 435 | | 7607.533 | 3937, 3176 |
|---|---|---|---|---|---|---|
| *adj*, *n mp*, n fs | do | *n fs* | n mp, ps 1cp | | v Hiphil impv 2mp | prep, pn |
| כָל־אַפְסֵי־אָרֶץ | אֵת | יְשׁוּעַת | אֱלֹהֵינוּ | **4.** | הָרִיעוּ | לַיהוָה |
| khol-'aphsê-'ārets | 'ēth | yeshû'ath | 'ĕlōhênû | | hārî'û | layhwāh |
| all the ends of the earth | | the salvation of | our God | | shout | to Yahweh |

| 3725, 800 | 6723.133 | 7728.333 | 2252.333 | | 2252.333 | 3937, 3176 |
|---|---|---|---|---|---|---|
| *adj*, art, n fs | v Qal impv 2mp | cj, v Piel impv 2mp | cj, v Piel impv 2mp | | v Piel impv 2mp | prep, pn |
| כָּל־הָאָרֶץ | פִּצְחוּ | וְרַנְּנוּ | וְזַמֵּרוּ | **5.** | זַמְּרוּ | לַיהוָה |
| kol-hā'ārets | pitschû | werannenû | wezammērû | | zammerû | layhwāh |
| all the earth | break forth | and shout for joy | and sing praises | | sing praises | to Yahweh |

| 904, 3780 | 904, 3780 | 7249 | 2256 | | 904, 2792 |
|---|---|---|---|---|---|
| prep, n ms | prep, n ms | cj, *n ms* | n fs | | prep, art, n fp |
| בְּכִנּוֹר | בְּכִנּוֹר | וְקוֹל | זִמְרָה | **6.** | בַּחֲצֹצְרוֹת |
| bekhinnôr | bekhinnôr | weqôl | zimrāh | | bachtsōtserôth |
| with the zither | with the zither | and the sound of | a song of praise | | with the trumpets |

| 7249 | 8223 | 7607.533 | 3937, 6686 | 4567 | 3176 | | 7769.121 |
|---|---|---|---|---|---|---|---|
| cj, *n ms* | n ms | v Hiphil impv 2mp | prep, *n mp* | art, n ms | pn | | v Qal juss 3ms |
| וְקוֹל | שׁוֹפָר | הָרִיעוּ | לִפְנֵי | הַמֶּלֶךְ | יְהוָה | **7.** | יִרְעַם |
| weqôl | shôphār | hārî'û | liphnê | hammelekh | yehwāh | | yir'am |
| and the sound of | the ram's horn | shout | before | the King | Yahweh | | may it rage |

| 3328 | 4530 | 8725 | 3553.152 | 904 | | 5282 |
|---|---|---|---|---|---|---|
| art, n ms | cj, n ms, ps 3ms | n fs | cj, *v Qal act ptc mp* | prep, ps 3fs | | n mp |
| הַיָּם | וּמְלֹאוֹ | תֵּבֵל | וְיֹשְׁבֵי | בָהּ | **8.** | נְהָרוֹת |
| hayyām | ûmelō'ô | tēvēl | weyōshevê | vāhh | | nehārôth |
| the sea | and its fulness | the world | and those who dwell | in it | | the floods |

| 4356.126, 3834 | 3266 | 2098 | 7728.326 | | 3937, 6686, 3176 |
|---|---|---|---|---|---|
| v Qal juss 3mp, n fs | adv | n mp | v Piel juss 3mp | | prep, *n mp*, pn |
| יִמְחֲאוּ־כָף | יַחַד | הָרִים | יְרַנֵּנוּ | **9.** | לִפְנֵי־יְהוָה |
| yimchă'û-khāph | yachadh | hārîm | yerannēnû | | liphnê-yehwāh |
| may they clap their hands | together | the mountains | let them shout for joy | | before Yahweh |

**3. He hath remembered his mercy and his truth toward the house of Israel: all the ends of the earth have seen the salvation of our God:** … He has remembered his love for Jacob, his faithfulness toward the house of Israel. All the ends of the earth have seen the victory of our God, *REB* … his constancy, his love for the house of Israel. All the ends of the earth have seen the victory of our God, *NEB* … Remember his love and fidelity, O house of Israel! all you ends of the earth, See the victory of our God!, *Anchor* … All the distant parts of the world have seen how our God can save, *Beck.*

**4. Make a joyful noise unto the LORD, all the earth: make a loud noise, and rejoice, and sing praise:** … our God. Break forth, and cry aloud, and sing, *Young* … Acclaim the LORD, all the earth; break into songs of joy, sing psalms, *REB* … Shout to the LORD, all the world; break into happy shouting, and sing to praise Him, *Beck* … Shout aloud to the LORD, all the earth; Rejoice, be jubilant, and sing praises, *Goodspeed.*

**5. Sing unto the LORD with the harp; with the harp, and the voice of a psalm:** ... Sing praise to the LORD with the harp, with the harp and melodious song, *NAB* ... Sing praises to the LORD with the lyre, with the lyre and the sound of melody!, *RSV* ... Play to Yahweh on the harp, to the sound of instruments, *JB* ... Praise the Lord with the harp, with the harp and psaltery's music, *Knox.*

**6. With trumpets and sound of cornet make a joyful noise before the LORD, the King:** ... the sound of the horn sing joyfully before the King, the LORD, *NAB* ... to the sound of trumpet and horn, acclaim the presence of the King, *JB* ... with trumpets of metal, and the music of the braying horn! Keep holiday in the presence of the Lord, our King, *Knox.*

**7. Let the sea roar, and the fulness thereof; the world, and they that dwell therein:** ... resound and everything in it, the world, and all who live in it, *NIV* ... be thundering, with all its waters; the world, *BB* ... and all within it thunder praise, *Moffatt* ... Let the sea in its vastness roar in praise, *Berkeley.*

**8. Let the floods clap their hands: let the hills be joyful together:** ... Let the streams make sounds of joy with their hands; let the mountains be glad together, *BB* ... let the rivers clap their hands, let mountains sing in chorus, *Moffatt* ... Floods clap hand, together hills cry aloud, *Young.*

**9. Before the LORD; for he cometh to judge the earth: with righteousness shall he judge the world, and the people with equity:** ... He comes to judge the earth; brings the world justice, to very race of men its due award, *Knox* ... at Yahweh's approach, for he is coming to judge the earth, *JB* ... the peoples with unfaltering fairness, *Berkeley* ... and giving true decisions for the peoples, *BB.*

---

the summons to Israel to praise Yahweh and declare his glory to the nations, this Psalm passes at once from the summons to praise, in order to set forth the divine deed which evokes the praise, and which, the psalmist thinks, will shine by its own luster to "the ends of the earth," whether it has human voices to celebrate it or not. This psalmist speaks more definitely of Yahweh's wonders of deliverance. Israel appears rather as the recipient than as the celebrator of God's steadfast love. The sun shines to all nations, whether any voices say "Look," or no. Verse 1a is from Ps. 96:1; vv. 1c–3 weave together snatches of various passages in the second part of Isaiah, especially Isa. 52:10; 59:16; 63:5. The remarkable expression "brought salvation to Him" (from the second passage in Isaiah) is rendered by many "helped Him," and that rendering gives the sense but obliterates the connection with "salvation," emphatically repeated in the two following verses. "The salvation of our God," Who seemed to have forgotten his people, as Isa. 49:2 represents Israel as complaining, but now before "the eyes of all nations" has shown how well He remembers and faithfully keeps his covenant obligations Israel is, indeed, Yahweh's witness and should ring out her grateful joy; but Yahweh's deed speaks more loudly than Israel's proclamation of it can ever do.

**98:4–6.** The second strophe corresponds to the third of Ps. 96; but whereas there the Gentiles were summoned to bring offerings into the courts of Yahweh, here it is rather the glad tumult of vocal praise, mingled with the twang of harps and the blare of trumpets and horns, which is present to the singer's imagination. He hears the swelling chorus echoing through the courts, which are conceived as wide enough to hold "all the earth." He has some inkling of the great thought that the upshot of God's redeeming self manifestation will be glad music from a redeemed world. His call to mankind throbs with emotion and sounds like a prelude to the melodious commingling of voice and instrument which he at once enjoins and foretells. His words are largely echoes of Isaiah. (Compare Isa. 44:23; 49:13; 52:9 for "break forth into," and 51:3 for "voice of melody.")

**98:7–9.** The final strophe is almost identical with that of Ps. 96 but, in accordance with the variation found in vv. 1ff, omits the summons to Israel to proclaim God's Kinghood among the nations. It also inverts the order of clauses in v. 7, and in v. 7b quotes from Ps. 24:1, where also "the fulness of it" precedes, with the result of having no verb expressed which suits the nouns, since "the world and the dwellers therein" cannot well be called on to "thunder." Instead of the "plain" and "trees of the forest" in the original, v. 8 substitutes "streams" and "mountains." The bold figure of the streams clapping hands, in token of homage to the King (2 Ki. 11:12; Ps. 47:1) occurs in Isa. 55:12. The meeting waves are conceived of as striking against each other, with a sound resembling that of applauding palms. Verse 9 is quoted from Ps. 96, with the omission of the second "He cometh" (which many versions of the Septuagint retain) and the substitution of "equity" for "his faithfulness."

***Psalm 99.*** *Delitzsch has well called this Psalm "an earthly echo of the seraphic" threefold proclamation of the divine holiness, which Isaiah heard*

| 3706 | 971.111 | 3937, 8570.141 | 800 | 8570.121, 8725 | 904, 6928 | 6194 |
|---|---|---|---|---|---|---|
| cj | v Qal pf 3ms | prep, Qal inf con | art, n fs | v Qal impf 3ms, n fs | prep, n ms | cj, n mp |
| כִּי | בָא | לִשְׁפֹּט | הָאָרֶץ | יִשְׁפֹּט־תֵּבֵל | בְּצֶדֶק | וְעַמִּים |
| kî | vā' | lishpōṭ | hā'ārets | yishpōṭ-tēvēl | betsedheq | we'ammîm |
| because | He comes | to judge | the earth | He judges the world | with righteousness | and peoples |

| 904, 4478 | | 3176 | 4566.111 | 7553.126 | 6194 | 3553.151 |
|---|---|---|---|---|---|---|
| prep, n mp | | pn | v Qal pf 3ms | v Qal juss 3mp | n mp | v Qal act ptc ms |
| בְּמֵישָׁרִים | 99:1 | יְהוָה | מָלָךְ | יִרְגְּזוּ | עַמִּים | יֹשֵׁב |
| bemêshārîm | | yehwāh | mālākh | yirgezû | 'ammîm | yōshēv |
| with uprightness | | Yahweh | He reigns | may they tremble | peoples | the One Who sits on |

| 3872 | 5302.122 | 800 | | 3176 | 904, 6995 | 1448 | 7597.151 | 2000 |
|---|---|---|---|---|---|---|---|---|
| n mp | v Qal juss 3fs | art, n fs | | pn | prep, pn | adj | cj, v Qal act ptc ms | pers pron |
| כְּרוּבִים | תָּנוּט | הָאָרֶץ | 2. | יְהוָה | בְּצִיּוֹן | גָּדוֹל | וְרָם | הוּא |
| kerûvîm | tānûṭ | hā'ārets | | yehwāh | betsîyôn | gādhôl | werām | hû' |
| the cherubim | may it quake | the earth | | Yahweh | in Zion | great | and the exalted One | He |

| 6142, 3725, 6194 | | 3142.526 | 8428 | 1448 | 3486.255 | 7202 | 2000 |
|---|---|---|---|---|---|---|---|
| prep, *adj*, art, n mp | | v Hiphil juss 3mp | n ms, ps 2ms | adj | cj, v Niphal ptc ms | adj | pers pron |
| עַל־כָּל־הָעַמִּים | 3. | יוֹדוּ | שִׁמְךָ | גָּדוֹל | וְנוֹרָא | קָדוֹשׁ | הוּא |
| 'al-kol-hā'ammîm | | yôdhû | shimkhā | gādhôl | wenôrā' | qādhôsh | hû' |
| over all the peoples | | let them praise | your name | great | and fearful | holy | He |

| | 6010 | 4567 | 5122 | 154.111 | 887 | 3679.313 | 4478 |
|---|---|---|---|---|---|---|---|
| | cj, *n ms* | n ms | n ms | v Qal pf 3ms | pers pron | v Polel pf 2ms | n mp |
| 4. | וְעֹז | מֶלֶךְ | מִשְׁפָּט | אָהֵב | אַתָּה | כּוֹנַנְתָּ | מֵישָׁרִים |
| | we'ōz | melekh | mishpāṭ | 'āhēv | 'attāh | kônantā | mêshārîm |
| | and the strength of | the King | justice | He loves | You | You established | uprightness |

| 5122 | 6930 | 904, 3399 | 887 | 6449.113 | | 7597.133 | 3176 |
|---|---|---|---|---|---|---|---|
| n ms | cj, n fs | prep, pn | pers pron | v Qal pf 2ms | | v Polel impv 2mp | pn |
| מִשְׁפָּט | וּצְדָקָה | בְּיַעֲקֹב | אַתָּה | עָשִׂיתָ | 5. | רוֹמְמוּ | יְהוָה |
| mishpāṭ | ûtsedhāqāh | beya'ăqōv | 'attāh | 'āsîthā | | rômemû | yehwāh |
| justice | and righteousness | in Jacob | You | You have executed | | exalt | Yahweh |

| 435 | 8246.733 | 3937, 1986 | 7559 | 7202 | 2000 | | 5057 |
|---|---|---|---|---|---|---|---|
| n mp, ps 1cp | cj, Hithpael impv 2mp | prep, *n ms* | n fd, ps 3ms | adj | pers pron | | pn |
| אֱלֹהֵינוּ | וְהִשְׁתַּחֲווּ | לַהֲדֹם | רַגְלָיו | קָדוֹשׁ | הוּא | 6. | מֹשֶׁה |
| 'ĕlōhênû | wehishtachwû | lahdhōm | raghlâv | qādhôsh | hû' | | mōsheh |
| our God | and worship | at the footstool of | his feet | holy | He | | Moses |

**99:1. The Lord reigneth; let the people tremble: he sitteth between the cherubims; let the earth be moved:** … The Lord is king, the nations are adread; he is throned above the Cherubim, and earth trembles before him, *Knox* … The Lord is King; let the peoples be in fear: his seat is on the winged ones; let the earth be moved, *BB* … Let the nations shake! He is enthroned! Let the world quake!, *Moffatt* … He's on a throne among the angels—the earth shakes, *Beck.*

**2. The Lord is great in Zion; and he is high above all the people:** … Yahweh is too great for Zion, exalted is he beyond all the Strong Ones, *Anchor* … Great is the Lord who dwells in Sion, sovereign ruler of all the peoples!, *Knox* … The Lord is majestic in Zion; He is supreme above all the nations, *Berkeley* … The Lord in Jerusalem is great; he is supreme over all the peoples, *NCV.*

**3. Let them praise thy great and terrible name; for it is holy:** … Let them praise your name, O Great and Awesome One! Holy is he, *Anchor* … Let them all praise that great name of thine, a name terrible and holy, *Knox* … They praise Your Mighty Name, The dreadful, and the Holy!, *Fenton* … Praise to him, so great and dread! A mighty Majesty is he, *Moffatt.*

**4. The king's strength also loveth judgment; thou dost establish equity, thou executest judgment and righteousness in Jacob:** … You are a king who loves justice, you established honesty, justice and uprightness; in Jacob it is you who are active, *JB* … The King's energy is keenly set on justice; Thou dost establish equity; Thou dost guarantee justice and truth in Jacob, *Berkeley* ... justice and judgment in Jacob you have wrought, *NAB*.

**5. Exalt ye the LORD our God, and worship at his footstool; for he is holy:** ... worship at the Temple, his footstool, *NCV* ... And prostrate yourselves at His footstool, *MAST* ... and bow down at his footstool, *REB* ... bow in worship at His footstool, *Berkeley*.

**6. Moses and Aaron among his priests, and Samuel among them that call upon his name; they called upon the LORD, and he answered them:** ... who gave honour to his name; they made prayers to the Lord, *BB* ... those priests of his, ... how the Lord listened when they called upon him, *Knox* ... who invoked his name; They called to Yahweh, and he himself answered them, *Anchor* ... his worshippers have still a Samuel; and the Eternal answers, when they call to him, *Moffatt*.

---

*(Isa. 6:3). It is, as already noted, a pendant to Ps. 98, but is distinguished from the other Psalms of this group by its greater originality, the absence of distinct allusion to the great act of deliverance celebrated in them and its absorption in the one thought of the divine holiness. Their theme is the event by which Yahweh manifested to the world his sovereign rule; this Psalm passes beyond the event and grasps the eternal central principle of that rule—namely, holiness. The same thought has been touched on in the other members of the group, but here it is the single subject of praise. Its exhibition in God's dealings with Israel is here traced in ancient examples, rather than in recent instances; but the viewpoint of the other Psalms is retained, insofar as the divine dealings with Israel are regarded as the occasion for the world's praise.*

**99:1–3.** The first strophe dwells in general terms on Yahweh's holiness, by which august conception is meant, not only moral purity, but separation from, by elevation above, the finite and imperfect. Verse 1 vividly paints in each clause the glory reigning in heaven and its effect on an awestruck world. We might render the verbs in the second part of each clause as futures or as optatives ("shall tremble," "shall totter," or "let peoples tremble," etc.), but the thought is more animated if they are taken as describing the result of the theophany. The participial clause "throned on the cherubim" adds detail to the picture of Yahweh as King. It should not, strictly speaking, be rendered with a finite verb. When that vision of Him sitting in royal state is unveiled, all people are touched with reverence, and the solid earth staggers. But the glory which is made visible to all men has its earthly seat in Zion and shines from thence into all lands. It is by his deeds in Israel that God's exaltation is made known. The psalmist does not call on men to bow before a veiled majesty, of which they only know that it is free from all creatural limitations, lowliness and imperfections; but before a God, Who has revealed himself in acts and has thereby made himself a name. "Great and terrible" is that name, but it is a sign of his steadfast love that it is known by men, and thanksgiving, not dumb trembling, befits men who know it. The refrain might be rendered "It is holy," referring to the name, but vv. 5 and 9 make the rendering "Holy is He" more probable. The meaning is unaffected whichever translation is adopted.

**99:4–5.** Yahweh is holy, not only because lifted above and separated from creatural limitations, but because of his righteousness. The second strophe therefore proclaims that all his dominion is based on uprightness and is a continual passing of that into acts of "judgment and righteousness. The "and" at the beginning of v. 4 following the refrain is singular and has led many commentators to link the words with v. 3a and, taking the refrain as parenthetical, to render, "Let them give thanks to thy great and dread name, [for it is holy], and [to] the strength of the King [who] loveth," etc. But the presence of the refrain is an insuperable bar to this rendering. One King only is spoken of in this Psalm, and it is the inmost principle and outward acts of his rule which are stated as the psalmist's reason for summoning men to prostrate themselves at his footstool. The "and" at the beginning of the strophe links its whole thought with that of the preceding and declares eloquently how closely knit together are Yahweh's exaltation and his righteousness. The singer is in haste to assert the essentially moral character of infinite power.

God is no arbitrary ruler. His reign is for the furtherance of justice. Its basis is "equity," and its separate acts are "judgment and righteousness." These have been done in and for Jacob. Therefore, the call to worship rings out again. It is addressed to an undefined multitude, which, as the tone of all this group of Psalms leads us to suppose, includes all of humanity. They are summoned to lift high the praise of Him Who, in himself, is so high and to cast themselves low in prostrate adoration at his footstool—i.e., at his sanctuary on Zion (v. 9). Thus again, in the center strophe of this Psalm, as in Pss. 96 and 98, all

| 172 | 904, 3669 | 8442 | 904, 7410.152 | 8428 | 7410.152 |
|---|---|---|---|---|---|
| cj, pn | prep, n mp, ps 3ms | cj, pn | prep, v *Qal act ptc mp* | n ms, ps 3ms | v Qal act ptc mp |
| וְאַהֲרֹן | בְּכֹהֲנָיו | וּשְׁמוּאֵל | בְּקֹרְאֵי | שְׁמוֹ | קֹרְאִים |
| we'ahrōn | bekhōhenâv | ûshmû'ēl | beqōre'ê | shemô | qōri'ym |
| and Aaron | with his priests | and Samuel | with those who called on | his name | calling |

| 420, 3176 | 2000 | 6257.121 | | 904, 6204 | 6281 | 1744.321 | 420 |
|---|---|---|---|---|---|---|---|
| prep, pn | cj, pers pron | v Qal impf 3ms, ps 3mp | **7.** | prep, *n ms* | n ms | v Piel impf 3ms | prep, ps 3mp |
| אֶל־יְהוָה | וְהוּא | יַעֲנֵם | | בְּעַמּוּד | עָנָן | יְדַבֵּר | אֲלֵיהֶם |
| 'el-yehwāh | wehû' | ya'ănēm | | be'ammûdh | 'ānān | yedhabbēr | 'ălêhem |
| to Yahweh | and He | He answered them | | in the pillar of | the cloud | He spoke | to them |

| 8490.116 | 5926 | 2805 | 5598.111, 3937 | | 3176 | 435 |
|---|---|---|---|---|---|---|
| v Qal pf 3cp | n fp, ps 3ms | cj, n ms | v Qal pf 3ms, prep, ps 3mp | **8.** | pn | n mp, ps 1cp |
| שָׁמְרוּ | עֵדֹתָיו | וְחֹק | נָתַן־לָמוֹ | | יְהוָה | אֱלֹהֵינוּ |
| shāmerû | 'ēdhōthâv | wechōq | nāthan-lāmō | | yehwāh | 'ĕlōhênû |
| they observed | his testimonies | and statutes | He gave to them | | O Yahweh | our God |

| 887 | 6257.113 | 418 | 5558.151 | 2030.113 | 3937 |
|---|---|---|---|---|---|
| pers pron | v Qal pf 2ms, ps 3mp | n ms | v Qal act ptc ms | v Qal pf 2ms | prep, ps 3mp |
| אַתָּה | עֲנִיתָם | אֵל | נֹשֵׂא | הָיִיתָ | לָהֶם |
| 'attāh | 'ănîthām | 'ēl | nōsē' | hāyîthā | lāhem |
| You | You answered them | a God | forgiving | You were | to them |

| 5541.151 | 6142, 6173 | | 7597.133 | 3176 |
|---|---|---|---|---|
| cj, v Qal act ptc ms | prep, n fp, ps 3mp | **9.** | v Polel impv 2mp | pn |
| וְנֹקֵם | עַל־עֲלִילוֹתָם | | רוֹמְמוּ | יְהוָה |
| wenōqēm | 'al-'ălîlôthām | | rômemû | yehwāh |
| but One Who takes vengeance | concerning their wrongdoing | | exalt | Yahweh |

| 435 | 8246.733 | 3937, 2098 | 7231 | 3706, 7202 | 3176 |
|---|---|---|---|---|---|
| n mp, ps 1cp | cj, v Hithpael impv 2mp | prep, *n ms* | n ms, ps 3ms | cj, adj | pn |
| אֱלֹהֵינוּ | וְהִשְׁתַּחֲווּ | לְהַר | קָדְשׁוֹ | כִּי־קָדוֹשׁ | יְהוָה |
| 'ĕlōhênû | wehishtachwû | lehar | qādheshô | kî-qādhôsh | yehwāh |
| our God | and worship | at the mountain of | his holy place | because holy | Yahweh |

| 435 | | 4344 | 3937, 8756 | | 7607.533 | 3937, 3176 | 3725, 800 |
|---|---|---|---|---|---|---|---|
| n mp, ps 1cp | **100:t** | n ms | prep, n fs | **1.** | v Hiphil impv 2mp | prep, pn | *adj*, art, n fs |
| אֱלֹהֵינוּ | | מִזְמוֹר | לְתוֹדָה | | הָרִיעוּ | לַיהוָה | כָּל־הָאָרֶץ |
| 'ĕlōhênû | | mizmôr | lethôdhāh | | hārî'û | layhwāh | kol-hā'ārets |
| our God | | a Psalm | of thanksgiving | | shout | to Yahweh | all the earth |

**7. He spake unto them in the cloudy pillar: they kept his testimonies, and the ordinance that he gave them:** … GOD from the Clouding Pillar spoke!—They kept the proofs and Laws He gave, *Fenton* … They kept his decrees and the law which he gave them, *Goodspeed* … kept his statutes and decrees he gave, *NIV* … they keep the commands he has laid down, *Moffatt.*

**8. Thou answeredst them, O LORD our God: thou wast a God that forgavest them, though thou tookest vengeance of their inventions:** … you were a forgiving God to them, but an avenger of their wrongdoings, *NRSV* … Yahweh our God, you yourself answered them. For them you became El the Forgiver; Most High Vindicator, you dealt severely with them, *Anchor* … didst listen to them, and they found thee a God of pardon; yet every fault of theirs thou wert quick to punish, *Knox* … You were their help, And punished all their foes, *Fenton.*

**9. Exalt the LORD our God, and worship at his holy hill; for the LORD our God is holy:** … and prostrate yourselves at his holy mountains, *Anchor* … and do worship the holy mountain where he dwells, *Knox* … worshipping with your faces turned to his holy hill, *BB* … and worship at his sacred hill: for the Eternal is a mighty Majesty, *Moffatt.*

**100:t. A Psalm of praise.**

**1. Make a joyful noise unto the LORD, all ye lands:** … Sing joyfully to the LORD, all you lands, *NAB* … Shout praise, all earth, to the Eternal, *Moffatt* … Hurrah to the LORD all the Earth, *Fenton.*

of humanity is called to praise the God Who has revealed himself in Israel; but while in the former of these two Psalms worship was represented as sacrificial, and in the second as loud music of voice and instrument, here silent prostration is the fitting praise of the holiness of the infinitely exalted Yahweh.

**99:6–7.** The third strophe turns to examples drawn from the great ones of old, which at once encourage to worship and teach the true nature of worship, while they also set in clear light Yahweh's holiness in dealing with his worshipers. Priestly functions were exercised by Moses, as in sprinkling the blood of the Covenant (Exo. 24) and in the ceremonial connected with the consecration of Aaron and his sons (Lev. 8), as well as at the first celebration of worship in the Tabernacle (Exo. 40:18). In the wider sense of the word "priest" (HED #3669), he acted as mediator and intercessor, as in Exo. 17:12, in the fight against Amalek, and 32:30ff, after the worship of the golden calf. Samuel, too, interceded for Israel after their seeking a king (1 Sam. 12:19ff), and offered sacrifices (1 Sam. 7:9). Jeremiah couples them together as intercessors with God (Jer. 15:1).

From these venerable examples, the psalmist draws instruction as to the nature of the worship befitting the holiness of Yahweh. He goes deeper than all sacrifices, or than silent awe. To call on God is the best adoration. The cry of a soul, conscious of emptiness and need and convinced of his fulness and of the love which is the soul of his power, is never in vain. "They called, and He"—even He in all the unreachable separation of his loftiness from their lowliness—"answered them." There is a commerce of desire and bestowal between the holy Yahweh and us. But these answers come on certain conditions, which are plain consequences of his holiness, namely, that his worshipers should keep his testimonies, by which He has witnessed both to his own character and to their duty. The psalmist seems to lose sight of his special examples and to extend his view to the whole people when he speaks of answers from the pillar of cloud, which cannot apply to Samuel's experience.

**99:8–9.** The persons spoken of in v. 8 as receiving answers may indeed be Moses, Aaron and Samuel, all of whom were punished for evil deeds, as well as answered when they cried; but more probably they are the whole community. The great principle, firmly grasped and clearly proclaimed by the singer, is that a holy God is a forgiving God, willing to hearken to men's cry and rich to answer with needed gifts, and that indissolubly interwoven with the pardon, which He in his holiness gives, is retribution for evil. God loves too well to grant impunity. Forgiveness is something far better than escape from penalties. It cannot be worthy of God to bestow or salutary for men to receive, unless it is accompanied with such retribution as may show the pardoned man how deadly his sin was. "Whatsoever a man soweth that shall he also reap" (Gal. 6:7) is a law not abrogated by forgiveness. The worst penalty of sin, indeed—namely, separation from God—is wholly turned aside by repentance and forgiveness; but for the most part the penalties which are inflicted on earth and which are the natural results of sin whether in character, memory, habit, or circumstances are not removed by pardon. Their character is changed; they become loving chastisement for our profit.

Such, then, is the worship which all men are invited to render to the holy Yahweh. Prostrate awe should pass into the cry of need, desire and aspiration. It will be heard, if it is verified as real by obedience to God's known will. The answers will be fresh witnesses of God's holiness, which declares itself equally in forgiveness and in retribution. Therefore, once more the clear summons to all mankind rings out, and once more the proclamation of his holiness is made.

There is joyful confidence of access to the inaccessible in the reiteration in v. 9 of "Yahweh our God." "Holy is He," sang the psalmist at first, but all the gulf between Yahweh and us is bridged over when to the name which emphasizes the eternal, self existent being of the holy One we can add "our God." Then humble prostration is reconcilable with confident approach; and his worshipers have not only to lie lowly at his footstool, but to draw near, with childlike frankness, to his heart.

***Psalm 100.*** *The Psalms of the King end with this full-toned call to all the earth to pay Him homage. It differs from the others of the group, by making no distinct mention either of Yahweh's royal title or of the great act of deliverance which was his visible exercise of sovereignty. But it resembles them in its jubilant tone, its urgent invitation to all men to walk in the light which shone on Israel and its conviction that the mercies shown to the nation had blessing in them for all the world. The structure is simple. A call to praise Yahweh is twice given, and each is followed by reasons for his praise, which is grounded in the first instance (v. 3) on his dealings with Israel and in the second on his character as revealed by all his works.*

**100:1–2.** Verse 1 consists of but a single clause and, as Delitzsch says, is like the signal-

| | | | | | | |
|---|---|---|---|---|---|---|
| **2.** | **5856.133**<br>v Qal impv 2mp<br>עִבְדוּ<br>'ivdhû<br>serve | **881, 3176**<br>do, pn<br>אֶת־יְהוָה<br>'eth-yehwāh<br>Yahweh | **904, 7977**<br>prep, n fs<br>בְּשִׂמְחָה<br>besimchāh<br>with gladness | **971.133**<br>v Qal impv 2mp<br>בֹּאוּ<br>bō'û<br>come | **3937, 6686**<br>prep, n mp, ps 3ms<br>לְפָנָיו<br>lephānâv<br>before Him | **904, 7729**<br>prep, n fs<br>בִּרְנָנָה<br>birnānāh<br>with shouts of joy |

| | | | | | | | |
|---|---|---|---|---|---|---|---|
| **3.** | **3156.133**<br>v Qal impv 2mp<br>דְּעוּ<br>de'û<br>know | **3706, 3176**<br>cj, pn<br>כִּי־יְהוָה<br>kî-yehwāh<br>that Yahweh | **2000**<br>pers pron<br>הוּא<br>hû'<br>He | **435**<br>n mp<br>אֱלֹהִים<br>'ĕlōhîm<br>God | **2000, 6449.111**<br>pers pron, v Qal pf 3ms, ps 1cp<br>הוּא־עָשָׂנוּ<br>hû'-'āsānû<br>He He made us | **3940**<br>cj, neg part<br>וְלֹא<br>welō'<br>and not | **601**<br>pers pron<br>אֲנַחְנוּ<br>'ănachnû<br>we |

| | | | | | | |
|---|---|---|---|---|---|---|
| **6194**<br>n ms, ps 3ms<br>עַמּוֹ<br>'ammô<br>his people | **6887**<br>cj, *n fs*<br>וְצֹאן<br>wetsō'n<br>but the sheep of | **4993**<br>n fs, ps 3ms<br>מַרְעִיתוֹ<br>mar'îthô<br>his pasture | **4.** | **971.133**<br>v Qal impv 2mp<br>בֹּאוּ<br>bō'û<br>enter | **8554**<br>n mp, ps 3ms<br>שְׁעָרָיו<br>she'ārâv<br>his gates | **904, 8756**<br>prep, n fs<br>בְּתוֹדָה<br>bethôdhāh<br>with thanksgiving |

| | | | | | | |
|---|---|---|---|---|---|---|
| **2793**<br>n fp, ps 3ms<br>חֲצֵרֹתָיו<br>chătsērōthâv<br>his courts | **904, 8747**<br>prep, n fs<br>בִּתְהִלָּה<br>bithhillāh<br>with praise | **3142.533, 3937**<br>v Hiphil impv 2mp, prep, ps 3ms<br>הוֹדוּ־לוֹ<br>hôdhû-lô<br>ascribe majesty to Him | **1313.333**<br>v Piel impv 2mp<br>בָּרְכוּ<br>bārekhû<br>bless | **8428**<br>n ms, ps 3ms<br>שְׁמוֹ<br>shemô<br>his name | **5.** | **3706, 3005**<br>cj, adj<br>כִּי־טוֹב<br>kî-ṯôv<br>because good |

| | | | | | |
|---|---|---|---|---|---|
| **3176**<br>pn<br>יְהוָה<br>yehōwāh<br>Yahweh | **3937, 5986**<br>prep, n ms<br>לְעוֹלָם<br>le'ôlām<br>unto eternity | **2721**<br>n ms, ps 3ms<br>חַסְדּוֹ<br>chasdô<br>his steadfast love | **5912, 1810**<br>cj, prep, n ms<br>וְעַד־דֹּר<br>we'adh-dōr<br>even unto generations | **1810**<br>cj, n ms<br>וָדֹר<br>wādhōr<br>and generations | **536**<br>n fs, ps 3ms<br>אֱמוּנָתוֹ<br>'ĕmûnāthô<br>his faithfulness |

| | | | | | | | |
|---|---|---|---|---|---|---|---|
| **101:t** | **3937, 1784**<br>prep, pn<br>לְדָוִד<br>ledhāwidh<br>of David | **4344**<br>n ms<br>מִזְמוֹר<br>mizmôr<br>a Psalm | **1.** | **2721, 5122**<br>n ms, cj, n ms<br>חֶסֶד־וּמִשְׁפָּט<br>chesedh-ûmishpāṯ<br>steadfast love and justice | **8301.125**<br>v Qal juss 1cs<br>אָשִׁירָה<br>'āshîrāh<br>let me sing | **3937**<br>prep, ps 2ms<br>לְךָ<br>lekhā<br>to You | **3176**<br>pn<br>יְהוָה<br>yehwāh<br>O Yahweh |

| | | | | | | |
|---|---|---|---|---|---|---|
| **2252.325**<br>v Piel juss 1cs<br>אֲזַמֵּרָה<br>'ăzammērāh<br>let me sing praises | **2.** | **7959.525**<br>v Hiphil juss 1cs<br>אַשְׂכִּילָה<br>'askîlāh<br>may I cause to succeed | **904, 1932**<br>prep, n ms<br>בְּדֶרֶךְ<br>bedherekh<br>on a way | **8879**<br>adj<br>תָּמִים<br>tāmîm<br>blameless | **5146**<br>intrg<br>מָתַי<br>māthay<br>when | **971.123**<br>v Qal impf 2ms<br>תָּבוֹא<br>tāvô'<br>will You come |

**2. Serve the LORD with gladness: come before his presence with singing:** ... Serve Yahweh with rejoicing, Enter before him, with shouts of triumph, *Rotherham* ... sacrifice gladly to the Eternal, enter his presence with songs of praise, *Moffatt* ... Serve the LORD with delight; Come into His Presence with cheering, *Fenton.*

**3. Know ye that the LORD he is God: it is he that hath made us, and not we ourselves; we are his people, and the sheep of his pasture:** ... Be sure that Yahweh is God, he made us, we belong to him, his people, the flock of his sheepfold, *JB* ... he himself made us when we, his people and the flock of his pasture, were nothing, *Anchor* ... confess that the Eternal is God, 'tis he who made us, we are his, the people whom he shepards, *Moffatt* ... we are his people, and the sheep to whom he gives food, *BB.*

**4. Enter into his gates with thanksgiving, and into his courts with praise: be thankful unto him, and bless his name:** ... Come into his doors with joy, and into his house with praise; give him honour, blessing his name, *BB* ... Enter into His gates with thanksgiving and into His courts with praise. Give thanks to Him; bless His name!, *Berkeley* ... Come into His gates to give thanks, into His courts to praise. Thank Him, bless His name, *Beck.*

**5. For the LORD is good; his mercy is everlasting; and his truth endureth to all generations:** ... For THE LIFE is eternally kind,—His mercy will last for all time, And for ages His Truth, *Fenton* ... Gracious is the Lord, everlasting his mercy; age after age, he is faithful to his promise still, *Knox* ... His love is forever, and his loyalty goes on and on, *NCV* ... his kindness is everlasting; And his faithfulness endures throughout the ages, *Goodspeed*.

**101:t. A Psalm of David.**

**1. I will sing of mercy and judgment:** ... I will be kind and just, *Moffatt* ... of loving-kindness and judgment, *Darby* ... of your love and justice, *NIV* ... Of Mercy and Justice I sing, *Fenton*.

**unto thee, O LORD, will I sing:** ... to you, Yahweh, will I chant, *Anchor* ... to you, Yahweh, will I make music, *JB* ... to you, O Lord, will I make melody, *BB*.

**2. I will behave myself wisely in a perfect way:** ... I will carefully observe the path of the perfect, *Berkeley* ... persevere in the way of integrity, *NCB* ... give heed to the blameless way, *NASB*.

**O when wilt thou come unto me?:** ... grant me thy presence?, *Knox* ...

---

blast of a trumpet. It rings out a summons to "all the earth," as in Ps. 98:4, which is expanded in v. 2. The service there enjoined is that of worship in the Temple, as in v. 4. Thus, the characteristic tone of this group of Psalms echoes here, in its close, and all men are called and welcomed to the Sanctuary. There is no more a court of the Gentiles. Not less striking than the universality of the Psalm is its pulsating gladness. The depths of sorrow, both of that which springs from outward calamities and of that more heart-breaking sort which wells up from dark fountains in the soul, have been sounded in many a Psalm. But the Psalter would not reflect all the moods of the devout soul, unless it had some strains of unmingled joy. There is no music without passages in minor keys; but joy has its rights and place too, and they know but little of the highest kind of worship who do not sometimes feel their hearts swell with gladness more poignant and exuberant than earth can minister.

**100:3.** The reason for the world's gladness is given in v. 3. It is Yahweh's special relation to Israel. So far as the language of the verse is concerned, it depends on Ps. 95:7. "He hath made us" does not refer to creation, but to the constituting of Israel the people of God. "We are his" is the reading of the Hebrew margin and is evidently to be preferred to that of the text, "Not we ourselves." The difference in Hebrew is only in one letter, and the pronunciation of both readings would be the same. Jewish text-critics count fifteen passages, in which a similar mistake has been made in the text. Here, the comparison of Ps. 95 and the connection with the next clause of v. 3 are decidedly in favor of the amended reading. It is to be observed that this is the only place in the Psalm in which "we" and "us" are used; and it is natural to lay stress on the opposition between "ye" in v. 3a, and "we" and "us" in b. The collective Israel speaks and calls all men to rejoice in Yahweh, because of his grace to it. The Psalm is, not a national song of thanksgiving, a song which starts from national blessings and discerns in them a message of hope and joy for all men. Israel was meant to be a sacred hearth on which a fire was kindled, that was to warm all the house. God revealed himself in Israel, but to the world.

**100:4–5.** The call to praise is repeated in v. 4 with more distinct reference to the open Temple gates into which all the nations may now enter. The psalmist sees, in prophetic hope, crowds pouring in with glad alacrity through the portals, and then hears the joyful tumult of their many voices rising in a melodious surge of praise. His eager desire and large-hearted confidence that so it will one day be are vividly expressed by the fourfold call in v. 4. And the reason which should draw all men to bless God's revealed character is that his self-revelation, whether to Israel or to others, shows the basis of that character. As older singers sang, "his steadfast love endures for ever" (Ps. 106), and as a thousand generations in Israel and throughout the earth have proved his faithful adherence to his word and discharge of all obligations under which He has come to his creatures give a basis for trust and a perpetual theme for joyful thanksgiving. Therefore, all the world has an interest in Yahweh's royalty and should, and one day shall, compass his throne with joyful homage and obey his commands with willing service.

***Psalm 101.*** *The Psalm falls into two main parts. In the first, the king lays down the rule of his own conduct; in the second, he declares war against the slanderers, arrogant upstarts and traffickers in lies. His ambition is to have Yahweh's city worthy of its true King, when He shall deign to come and dwell in it. Therefore his face will be gracious to all good men and his hand heavy on all evildoers.*

**101:1.** It is as a king that the psalmist vows to praise these twin characteristics of the divine rule; and his song is to be accompanied by melodious deeds, which shape themselves after that pattern for rulers and all men. Earthly power is then strongest when, like God's, it is informed by steadfast love and based on righteousness. In this connection, it is significant that this Psalm, describing

| 420 | 2050.725 | 904, 8866, 3949 | 904, 7419 | 1041 |
|---|---|---|---|---|
| prep, ps 1cs | v Hithpael impf 1cs | prep, *n ms*, n ms, ps 1cs | prep, *n ms* | n ms, ps 1cs |
| אֵלָי | אֶתְהַלֵּךְ | בְּתָם־לְבָבִי | בְּקֶרֶב | בֵּיתִי |
| 'ēlāy | 'ethhallēkh | bethām-levāvî | beqerev | bêthî |
| to me | I will walk | with the integrity of my heart | in the middle of | my house |

| 3. 3940, 8308.125 | 3937, 5224 | 6084 | 1745, 1139 | 6449.141, 5697 | 7983.115 |
|---|---|---|---|---|---|
| neg part, v Qal impf 1cs | prep, prep | n fd, ps 1cs | *n ms*, n ms | v Qal inf con, n mp | v Qal pf 1cs |
| לֹא־אָשִׁית | לְנֶגֶד | עֵינַי | דְּבַר־בְּלִיָּעַל | עֲשֹׂה־סֵטִים | שָׂנֵאתִי |
| lō'-'āshîth | leneghedh | 'ênay | devar-belîyā'al | 'ăsōh-sēṭîm | sānē'thî |
| I will not set | before | my eyes | worthless things | doing transgressions | I hate |

| 3940 | 1740.121 | 904 | 4. 3949 | 6379 | 5681.121 | 4623 | 7737 | 3940 |
|---|---|---|---|---|---|---|---|---|
| neg part | v Qal impf 3ms | prep, ps 1cs | n ms | adj | v Qal impf 3ms | prep, ps 1cs | n ms | neg part |
| לֹא | יִדְבַּק | בִּי | לֵבָב | עִקֵּשׁ | יָסוּר | מִמֶּנִּי | רָע | לֹא |
| lō' | yidhbaq | bî | lēvāv | 'iqqēsh | yāsûr | mimmenî | rā' | lō' |
| not | it will cling | on me | a heart | distorted | it will turn aside | from me | evil | not |

| 3156.125 | 5. 4102.351 | 904, 5848 | 7739 | 881 | 7059.525 |
|---|---|---|---|---|---|
| v Qal impf 1cs | *v Poel ptc ms* | prep, art, *n ms* | n ms, ps 3ms | do, ps 3ms | v Hiphil impf 1cs |
| אֵדָע | מְלוֹשְׁנִי | בַסֵּתֶר | רֵעֵהוּ | אוֹתוֹ | אַצְמִית |
| 'ēdhā' | melôshnî | vassēther | rē'ēhû | 'ôthô | 'atsmîth |
| I will know | the slanderer of | in the secret place | his fellow | him | I will annihilate |

| 1392, 6084 | 7622 | 3949 | 881 | 3940 | 404.125 | 6. 6084 |
|---|---|---|---|---|---|---|
| *adj*, n fd | cj, *adj* | n ms | do, ps 3ms | neg part | v Qal impf 1cs | n fd, ps 1cs |
| גְּבַהּ־עֵינַיִם | וּרְחַב | לֵבָב | אֹתוֹ | לֹא | אוּכָל | עֵינַי |
| gevahh-'ênayim | ûrechav | lēvāv | 'ōthô | lō' | 'ûkhol | 'ênay |
| haughty eyes | and broad of | heart | him | not | I will allow | my eyes |

| 904, 548.256, 800 | 3937, 3553.141 | 6200 | 2050.151 | 904, 1932 | 8879 |
|---|---|---|---|---|---|
| prep, *v Niphal ptc mp*, n fs | prep, v Qal inf con | prep, ps 1cs | v Qal act ptc ms | prep, *n ms* | adj |
| בְּנֶאֶמְנֵי־אֶרֶץ | לָשֶׁבֶת | עִמָּדִי | הֹלֵךְ | בְּדֶרֶךְ | תָּמִים |
| bene'emnê-'erets | lāsheveth | 'immādhî | hōlēkh | bedherekh | tāmîm |
| on the faithful ones of the land | for dwelling | with me | one who walks | on a way | blameless |

| 2000 | 8664.321 | 7. 3940, 3353.121 | 904, 7419 | 1041 |
|---|---|---|---|---|
| pers pron | v Piel impf 3ms, ps 1cs | neg part, v Qal impf 3ms | prep, *n ms* | n ms, ps 1cs |
| הוּא | יְשָׁרְתֵנִי | לֹא־יֵשֵׁב | בְּקֶרֶב | בֵּיתִי |
| hû' | yeshārethēnî | lō'-yēshēv | beqerev | bêthî |
| he | he will minister to me | he will not dwell | in the middle of | my house |

| 6449.151 | 7711 | 1744.151 | 8632 | 3940, 3679.221 |
|---|---|---|---|---|
| *v Qal act ptc ms* | n fs | *v Qal act ptc ms* | n mp | neg part, v Niphal impf 3ms |
| עֹשֵׂה | רְמִיָּה | דֹּבֵר | שְׁקָרִים | לֹא־יִכּוֹן |
| 'ōsēh | remîyāh | dōvēr | sheqārîm | lō'-yikkôn |
| one who acts with | deceit | one speaking | lies | he will not be established |

till thou commest to me, *Geneva* … whatever may befall me, *NEB.*

**I will walk within my house with a perfect heart:** … My conduct among my house will be blameless, *REB* … with integrity of heart within my house, *RSV* … live an innocent life in my house, *NCV* … in the integrity of my heart, within my house, *NAB* … to and fro in the blamelessness of my heart,—in the midst of my house, *Rotherham.*

**3. I will set no wicked thing before mine eyes:** … anything that is base, *NRSV* … no worthless thing, *NASB* … not set before my eyes anything sordid, *JB* … no vile thing, *NIV.*

**I hate the work of them that turn aside; it shall not cleave to me:** … None such will I have at my side, *Knox* … hold on to me, *KJVII* … cling to me, *NKJV.*

**4. A froward heart shall depart from me:** … A perverse heart, *ASV* … A crooked heart, *NCB* … false heart I will send away, *BB* …

Perverseness of heart shall be far from me, *RSV.*

**I will not know a wicked person:** ... I disown evil men, *Moffatt* ... I will not know evil, *Darby* ... know nothing of evil, *NRSV* ... know no evil thing, *MAST.*

**5. Whoso privily slandereth his neighbour, him will I cut off:** ... I'll silence anyone who secretly slanders, *Beck* ... will I destroy, *MRB* ... will I root out, *Rotherham.*

**him that hath an high look and a proud heart will not I suffer:** ... The supercilious and high-minded I cannot endure, *Goodspeed* ... I will not tolerate one who is conceited and arrogant, *Berkeley* ... I will not allow people to be proud and look down on others, *NCV* ... I will not endure, *NKJV.*

**6. Mine eyes shall be upon the faithful of the land, that they may dwell with me:** ... I shall choose for my companions the faithful in the land, *REB* ... I will choose the most loyal for my companions, *NEB* ... were upon my faithful countrymen, *Anchor.*

**he that walketh in a perfect way, he shall serve me:** ... Those who follow straight paths, *Fenton* ... walks in the way that is blameless, *NRSV* ... in the way of integrity shall be in my service, *NAB* ... shall minister unto me, *MRB.*

**7. He that worketh deceit shall not dwell within my house:** ... The liar shall not dwell in my house, *Fenton* ... There is no room in my house, *JB* ... No welcome here for schemers, *Knox.*

**he that telleth lies shall not tarry in my sight:** ... no liar shall set himself up where I can see him, *NEB* ... no liar will establish himself in my presence, *REB* ... shall not be established before mine eyes, *ASV* ... Never lingered before my eyes, *Anchor.*

---

what a king should be, has been placed immediately after the series which tells who the true King of Israel and the world is, in Whom these same attributes are ever linked together.

**101:2–4.** Verses 2ff outline the king's resolves for himself. With noble self-control, this ruler of men sets before himself the narrow, thorny way of perfectness, not the broad, flowery road of indulgence. He owns a law above himself and a far-off goal of moral completeness, which, he humbly feels, is yet unattained, but which he vows will never be hidden from his undazzled eyes by the glitter of lower earthly good or the rank mists of sensual pleasures.

After this most significant interruption, the stream of resolutions runs on again. In the comparative privacy of his house, he will "walk with a perfect heart," ever seeking to translate his convictions of right into practice and regulating his activities by conscience. The recesses of an Eastern palace were often foul with lust and hid extravagances of caprice and self-indulgence, but this ruler will behave there as one who has Yahweh for a guest. The language of v. 3 is very energetic. The phrase "worthless things" is literally "a thing of Belial"; "doing transgressions" is literally "doing deeds that turn aside," i.e., from the course prescribed. He will not take the former as models for imitation or objects of desire. The latter kindle wholesome hatred, and if ever he is tempted to dally with sin, he will shake it off, as a venomous reptile that has fastened on him. A perfect heart will expel "a distorted heart," but neither will the one be gained nor the other banished without vehement and persistent effort. This man does not trust the improvement of his character to chance or expect it to come of itself. He means to bend his strength to effect it. He cannot but "know evil," in the sense of being aware of it and conscious of its seductions, but he will not "know" (HED #3156) it, in the sense of letting it into his inner nature, or with the knowledge which is experience and love.

**101:5–6.** From v. 5 onwards the king lays down the principles of his public action, and that mainly in reference to bad men. One verse suffices to tell of his fostering care of good men. The rest describes how he means to be a terror to evildoers. The vices against which he will implacably war are not gross crimes that ordinarily bring down the sword of public justice. This monarch has regard to more subtle evils—slander, superciliousness, inflated vanity ("proud heart" in v. 5, HED #7622, is literally "broad in heart," i.e., dilated with self-sufficiency or ambition). His eyes are quick to mark "the faithful of the land." He looks for those whose faithfulness to God guarantees their fidelity to men and general reliableness. His servants will be like himself, followers who walk "in a perfect way." In that court, dignity and office will go, not to talent, or to crafty arts of servility, or to birth, but to moral and religious qualities.

**101:7–8.** In the last two verses, the attention of the Psalm returns to evildoers. The actors and speakers of lies will be cleared out of the palace. The psalmist longs to get rid of the stifling atmosphere of deceit and to have honest men round him, as many a

| 3937, 5224 | 6084 | | 3937, 1269 | 7059.525 | 3725, 7857, 800 |
|---|---|---|---|---|---|
| prep, prep | n fd, ps 1cs | **8.** | prep, art, n mp | v Hiphil impf 1cs | *adj, adj,* n fs |
| לְנֶגֶד | עֵינָי | | לַבְּקָרִים | אַצְמִית | כָּל־רִשְׁעֵי־אָרֶץ |
| leneghedh | ‘ênāy | | labbeqārîm | ’atsmîth | kol-rish‘ê-’ārets |
| before | my eyes | | at the mornings | I will annihilate | all the wicked of the land |

| 3937, 3901.541 | 4623, 6111, 3176 | 3725, 6713.152 | 201 | | 8940 |
|---|---|---|---|---|---|
| prep, v Hiphil inf con | prep, *n fs*, pn | *adj, v Qal act ptc mp* | n ms | **102:t** | n fs |
| לְהַכְרִית | מֵעִיר־יְהוָה | כָּל־פֹּעֲלֵי | אָוֶן | | תְּפִלָּה |
| lehakhrîth | mē‘îr-yehwāh | kol-pō‘ălê | ’āwen | | tephillāh |
| to cut off | from the city of Yahweh | all those who practice | iniquity | | a Prayer |

| 3937, 6270 | 3706, 6063.121 | 3937, 6686 | 3176 | 8581.121 | 7945 | | 3176 |
|---|---|---|---|---|---|---|---|
| prep, n ms | cj, v Qal impf 3ms | cj, prep, *n mp* | pn | v Qal impf 3ms | n ms, ps 3ms | **1.** | pn |
| לְעָנִי | כִּי־יַעֲטֹף | וְלִפְנֵי | יְהוָה | יִשְׁפֹּךְ | שִׂיחוֹ | | יְהוָה |
| le‘ānî | khî-ya‘ăṭōph | weliphnê | yehwāh | yishpōkh | sîchô | | yehwāh |
| for the afflicted | when he is faint | and before | Yahweh | he pours out | his complaint | | O Yahweh |

| 8471.131 | 8940 | 8210 | 420 | 971.122 | | 414, 5846.523 |
|---|---|---|---|---|---|---|
| v Qal impv 2ms | n fs, ps 1cs | cj, n fs, ps 1cs | prep, ps 2ms | v Qal juss 3fs | **2.** | adv, v Hiphil juss 2ms |
| שִׁמְעָה | תְפִלָּתִי | וְשַׁוְעָתִי | אֵלֶיךָ | תָבוֹא | | אַל־תַּסְתֵּר |
| shim‘āh | thephillāthî | weshaw‘āthî | ’ēlêkhā | thāvô’ | | ’al-tastēr |
| hear | my prayer | and my cry for help | to You | may it come | | do not hide |

| 6686 | 4623 | 904, 3219 | 7140 | 3937 | 5371.531, 420 | 238 |
|---|---|---|---|---|---|---|
| n mp, ps 2ms | prep, ps 1cs | prep, *n ms* | n ms | prep, ps 1cs | v Hiphil impv 2ms, prep, ps 1cs | n fs, ps 2ms |
| פָּנֶיךָ | מִמֶּנִּי | בְּיוֹם | צַר | לִי | הַטֵּה־אֵלַי | אָזְנְךָ |
| pānêkhā | mimmenî | beyôm | tsar | lî | haṭṭēh-’ēlay | ’āzenekhā |
| your face | from me | on the day of | adversity | to me | incline to me | your ear |

| 904, 3219 | 7410.125 | 4257.341 | 6257.131 | | 3706, 3735.116 |
|---|---|---|---|---|---|
| prep, n ms | v Qal impf 1cs | v Piel inf con | v Qal impv 2ms, ps 1cs | **3.** | cj, v Qal pf 3cp |
| בְּיוֹם | אֶקְרָא | מַהֵר | עֲנֵנִי | | כִּי־כָלוּ |
| beyôm | ’eqōrā’ | mahēr | ‘ănēnî | | kî-khālû |
| on the day | I call | acting quickly | answer me | | because they have come to an end |

| 904, 6476 | 3219 | 6344 | 3626, 4303 | 2893.216 |
|---|---|---|---|---|
| prep, n ms | n mp, ps 1cs | cj, n fp, ps 1cs | prep, n ms | v Niphal pf 3cp |
| בְעָשָׁן | יָמָי | וְעַצְמוֹתַי | כְּמוֹקֵד | נִחָרוּ |
| ve‘āshān | yāmāy | we‘atsmôthay | kemô-qēdh | nichārû |
| with smoke | my days | and my bones | like a hearth | they are burned |

| | 5409.611, 3626, 6448 | 3111.121 | 3949 | 3706, 8319.115 |
|---|---|---|---|---|
| **4.** | v Hophal pf 3ms, prep, art, n ms | cj, v Qal impf 3ms | n ms, ps 1cs | cj, v Qal pf 1cs |
| | הוּכָּה־כָעֵשֶׂב | וַיִּבַשׁ | לִבִּי | כִּי־שָׁכַחְתִּי |
| | hûkkāh-khā‘ēsev | wayyivash | libbî | kî-shākhachtî |
| | it has been struck down like the grass | and it has withered | my heart | because I have forgotten |

| 4623, 404.141 | 4035 | | 4623, 7249 | 599 | 1740.112 | 6344 |
|---|---|---|---|---|---|---|
| prep, v Qal inf con | n ms, ps 1cs | **5.** | prep, *n ms* | n fs, ps 1cs | v Qal pf 3fs | n fs, ps 1cs |
| מֵאֲכֹל | לַחְמִי | | מִקּוֹל | אַנְחָתִי | דָּבְקָה | עַצְמִי |
| mē’ăkhōl | lachmî | | miqqôl | ’anchāthî | dāveqāh | ‘atsmî |
| from eating | my bread | | from the sound of | my groaning | they have stuck | my bones |

| 3937, 1340 | | 1880.115 | 3937, 7179 | 4198 | 2030.115 |
|---|---|---|---|---|---|
| prep, n ms, ps 1cs | **6.** | v Qal pf 1cs | prep, *n fs* | n ms | v Qal pf 1cs |
| לִבְשָׂרִי | | דָּמִיתִי | לִקְאַת | מִדְבָּר | הָיִיתִי |
| livsārî | | dāmîthî | liqō’ath | midhbār | hāyîthî |
| to my flesh | | I have become like | the desert owl of | the wilderness | I have become |

**8. I will early destroy all the wicked of the land:** ... Morning after morning I will do away with all criminals within the country, *Berkeley* ... Every morning I will put to silence all the wicked, *NIV* ... will I put to death all the sinners, *BB* ... will I uproot All the lawless ones, *Rotherham.*

**that I may cut off all wicked doers from the city of the LORD:** ... And uproot from the city of the LORD all evildoers, *NAB* ... cutting off all the evildoers, *RSV* ... the workers of iniquity, *KJVII* ... I will rid the LORD's city of people who do evil, *NCV.*

**102:t. A Prayer of the afflicted, when he is overwhelmed, and poureth out his complaint before the LORD.**

**1. Hear my prayer, O LORD, and let my cry come unto thee:** ... let my cry for help reach thee, *NEB.*

**2. Hide not thy face from me in the day when I am in trouble:** ... of my distress, *NRSV.*

**incline thine ear unto me: in the day when I call answer me speedily:** ... make haste to heare me, *Geneva* ... Bow down Your ear to me, *KJVII* ... turn Your ear to me, *Beck* ... Listen to my prayer, *NEB* ... Pay attention to me, *NCV.*

**3. For my days are consumed like smoke:** ... See how this life of mine passes away like smoke, *Knox* ... vanish like smoke, *Goodspeed* ... pass away like smoke, *RSV.*

**and my bones are burned as an hearth:** ... my bones as a fire-brand have burned, *Young* ... my limbs are fevered like a fire, *Moffatt* ... burn like fire, *NCB* ... burning like an oven, *JB* ... burn like coals, *Fenton.*

**4. My heart is smitten, and withered like grass:** ... My heart is stricken, *NKJV* ... My heart is broken, *BB* ... Scorched like grass, my heart has withered, *Anchor.*

**so that I forget to eat my bread:** ... I have forgotten to eat my food, *Rotherham* ... I have neglected my regular food, *Berkeley* ... I neglect to eat my food, *REB.*

**5. By reason of the voice of my groaning my bones cleave to my skin:** ... As I groan my bones cling to my flesh, *Beck* ... bones hold fast to my skin, *KJVII* ... I am reduced to skin and bones, *NIV* ... My bones cling to my flesh, *NASB.*

**6. I am like a pelican of the wilderness:** ... a desert-owl in the wilderness, *REB* ... a vulture in the wilderness, *Anchor* ... a Stork in the Desert, *Fenton.*

---

ruler before and since has longed. But not only palace, but city, has to be swept clean, and one cleansing at the beginning of a reign will not be enough. So "at the mornings" the work has to be done again.

The Psalm is a God-given vision of what a king and a kingdom might and should be. David writes, "I will set no wicked thing before my eyes," yet from his "house," where he vowed to "walk with a perfect heart," he looked on Bathsheba. "He that worketh deceit shall not dwell within my house," David declares, yet Absalom, Ahithophel and the sons of Zeruiah stood round his throne. The shortcomings of the earthly shadows of God's rule force us to turn to the only perfect King and Kingdom, Jesus Christ and his realm, and to the city which "there shall in no wise enter into it any thing that defileth" (Rev. 21:27).

***Psalm 102.*** *The turns of thought are simple. While there is no clear strophical arrangement, there are four broadly distinguished parts: a prelude, invoking God to hearken (vv. 1f); a plaintive bemoaning of the psalmist's condition (vv. 3–11); a triumphant rising above his sorrows and rejoicing in the fair vision of a restored Jerusalem, whose temple courts the nations tread (vv. 12–22); and a momentary glance at his sorrows and brief life, which but spurs him to lay hold the more joyously on God's eternity, wherein he finds the pledge of the fulfillment of his hopes and of God's promises (vv. 23–28).*

**102:1–2.** The opening invocations in vv. 1f are mostly found in other psalms. "Let my cry come unto thee" recalls Ps. 18:6. "Hide not thy face" is like Ps. 27:9. "In the day when I am in trouble" recurs in Ps. 59:16. "Incline thine ear unto me" is in Ps. 31:2. "In the day when I call" is as in Ps. 56:9. "Answer me speedily" is found in Ps. 69:17. But the psalmist is not a mere compiler, weaving a web from old threads, but a suffering man, longing to give his desires voice in words which sufferers before him had hallowed and securing a certain solace by reiterating familiar petitions. They are nonetheless his own, because they have been the cry of others. Some aroma of the answers that they drew down in the past clings to them still and makes them fragrant to him.

**102:3–7.** Sorrow and pain are sometimes dumb, but in Eastern natures more often eloquent, finding ease in recounting their pangs. The psalmist's first words of self-lamentation echo familiar strains, as he bases his cry for speedy answer on the swiftness with which his days are being whirled away and melting like smoke as it escapes from a chimney. The image suggests another. The fire that makes the smoke is that in which his very bones are smoldering like a brand. The word for bones is in the singular, the bony

| 3626, 3684 | 2823 | | 8613.115 | 2030.125 | 3626, 7109 | 944.151 |
|---|---|---|---|---|---|---|
| prep, *n ms* | n fp | | v Qal pf 1cs | cj, v Qal impf 1cs | prep, n fs | v Qal act ptc ms |
| כְּכוֹס | חֳרָבוֹת | 7. | שָׁקַדְתִּי | וָאֶהְיֶה | כְּצִפּוֹר | בּוֹדֵד |
| kᵉkhôs | chărāvôth | | shāqadhtî | wā'ehyeh | kᵉtsippôr | bôdhēdh |
| like the small owl of | desolate places | | I keep watch | and I am | like a bird | being alone |

| 6142, 1437 | | 3725, 3219 | 2884.316 | 342.152 | 2054.456 |
|---|---|---|---|---|---|
| prep, n ms | | *adj*, art, n ms | v Piel pf 3cp, ps 1cs | v Qal act ptc mp, ps 1cs | v Poal ptc mp, ps 1cs |
| עַל־גָּג | 8. | כָּל־הַיּוֹם | חֵרְפוּנִי | אוֹיְבָי | מְהוֹלָלַי |
| 'al-gāgh | | kol-hayyôm | chērᵉphûnî | 'ôyvāy | mᵉhôlālay |
| on a roof | | all the day | they have taunted me | my enemies | those who denounce me |

| 904 | 8123.216 | | 3706, 684 | 3626, 4035 | 404.115 | 8616 |
|---|---|---|---|---|---|---|
| prep, ps 1cs | v Niphal pf 3cp | | cj, n ms | prep, art, n ms | v Qal pf 1cs | cj, n mp, ps 1cs |
| בִּי | נִשְׁבָּעוּ | 9. | כִּי־אֵפֶר | כַּלֶּחֶם | אָכָלְתִּי | וְשִׁקֻּוַי |
| bî | nishbā'û | | kî-'ēpher | kallechem | 'ākhālᵉttî | wᵉshiqquway |
| against me | they have sworn | | because ashes | like the bread | I have eaten | and my drink |

| 904, 1104 | 4687.115 | | 4623, 6686, 2279 | 7397 | 3706 |
|---|---|---|---|---|---|
| prep, n ms | v Qal pf 1cs | | prep, *n mp*, n ms, ps 2ms | cj, n ms, ps 2ms | cj |
| בִּבְכִי | מָסָכְתִּי | 10. | מִפְּנֵי־זַעַמְךָ | וְקִצְפֶּךָ | כִּי |
| bivkhî | māsākhᵉttî | | mippᵉnê-za'amkhā | wᵉqitspekhā | kî |
| with weeping | I have mixed | | from before your indignation | and your anger | because |

| 5558.113 | 8390.523 | | 3219 | 3626, 7009 |
|---|---|---|---|---|
| v Qal pf 2ms, ps 1cs | cj, v Hiphil impf 2ms, ps 1cs | | n mp, ps 1cs | prep, n ms |
| נְשָׂאתַנִי | וַתַּשְׁלִיכֵנִי | 11. | יָמַי | כְּצֵל |
| nᵉsā'thanî | wattashlîkhēnî | | yāmay | kᵉtsēl |
| You have picked me up | and You have thrown me down | | my days | like a shadow |

| 5371.155 | 603 | 3626, 6448 | 3111.125 | | 887 | 3176 | 3937, 5986 |
|---|---|---|---|---|---|---|---|
| v Qal pass ptc ms | cj, pers pron | prep, art, n ms | v Qal impf 1cs | | cj, pers pron | pn | prep, n ms |
| נָטוּי | וַאֲנִי | כָּעֵשֶׂב | אִיבָשׁ | 12. | וְאַתָּה | יְהוָה | לְעוֹלָם |
| nāṭûy | wa'ănî | kā'ēsev | 'îvāsh | | wᵉ'attāh | yᵉhwāh | lᵉ'ôlām |
| stretched out | and I | like the grass | I wither | | but You | O Yahweh | unto eternity |

| 3553.123 | 2228 | 3937, 1810 | 1810 | | 887 | 7251.123 |
|---|---|---|---|---|---|---|
| v Qal impf 2ms | cj, n ms, ps 2ms | prep, n ms | cj, n ms | | pers pron | v Qal impf 2ms |
| תֵּשֵׁב | וְזִכְרְךָ | לְדֹר | וָדֹר | 13. | אַתָּה | תָקוּם |
| tēshēv | wᵉzikhrᵉkhā | lᵉdhōr | wādhōr | | 'attāh | thāqûm |
| You dwell | and your remembrance | unto generations | and generations | | You | You will rise |

**I am like an owl of the desert:** … like the night-bird in a waste of sand, *BB* … of the waste places, *MRB* … in desolate places, *Darby.*

**7. I watch, and am as a sparrow alone upon the house top:** … I lie awake, *Berkeley* … I am sleepless, and I moan, *NAB* … I have become like a lonely bird on a housetop, *NASB* … I mourn like a lonely bird on the roof, *Moffatt.*

**8. Mine enemies reproach me all the day:** … All day long my foes insult me, *Goodspeed* … taunt me, *MAST* … reuile me dayly, *Geneva.*

**and they that are mad against me are sworn against me:** … in their rage against me they make a curse of me, *NCB* … those who rail against me use my name as a curse, *NIV* … those who deride me use my name for a curse, *NRSV* … do curse by me, *ASV.*

**9. For I have eaten ashes like bread, and mingled my drink with weeping:** … I eat ashes as my food, *NIV* … Ashes are the food that I eat, *JB* … Ashes are all my food, I drink nothing but what comes to me mingled with my tears, *Knox.*

**10. Because of thine indignation and thy wrath:** … because of your fury, *NCB* … In furious anger, *REB* … At the face of Your anger and wrath, *Fenton* … so angry and so furious art thou, *Moffatt.*

**for thou hast lifted me up, and cast me down:** … taken me up, and cast me away, *MAST* … You picked me up and threw me away, *Good News* … thou hast taken me up and flung me aside, *NEB* … thrown me down, *Berkeley.*

**11. My days are like a shadow that declineth:** … decline as the shadows lengthen, *NEB* ... a shadow stretched out, *KJVII* ... a shadow getting longer, *Beck* ... a shade which is stretched out, *BB*.

**and I am withered like grass:** ... wasting away, like grass in the sun, *Knox* ... I am like dried grass, *NCV*.

**12. But thou, O LORD, shalt endure for ever:** ... sittest enthroned for ever, *MAST* ... abide forever, *NCB*.

**and thy remembrance unto all generations:** ... thy memorial, *MRB* ... Thy name, *NASB* ... each generation in turn remembers you, *JB*.

**13. Thou shalt arise, and have mercy upon Zion:** ... You will rise up and have compassion, *NRSV* ... Arouse up Your pity for Zion, *Fenton* ... thou wilt have pity, *Goodspeed*.

**for the time to favour her, yea, the set time, is come:** ... the time to be gracious to her, *Darby* ... Surely the time appointed, *Rotherham* ... the appointed time, *RSV* ... for it is time to show favor to her, *NIV* ... it is time to have pity upon her, *ASV*.

---

framework being thought of as articulated into a whole. "Brand" (HED #2893) is a doubtful rendering of a word which ancient Jewish authorities render "hearth." The item is also used in Isa. 33:14. The same theme of physical decay is continued in v. 4, with a new image struck out by the ingenuity of pain. His heart is "smitten" as by sunstroke (cf. Ps. 121:6; Isa. 49:10; and for still closer parallels Hos. 9:16 and Jon. 4:7, in both of which the same effect of fierce sunshine is described as the sufferer here bewails). His heart withers like Jonah's gourd. The "so" in v. 4b can scarcely be taken as giving the reason for this withering. It must rather be taken as giving the proof that it was so withered, as might be concluded by beholders from the fact that he refused his food. The psalmist apparently intends in v. 5 to describe himself as worn to a skeleton by long and passionate lamentations. But his phrase is singular. One can understand that emaciation should be described by saying that the bones adhered to the skin, the flesh having wasted away, but that they stick to the flesh can only describe it, by giving a wide meaning to "flesh" (HED #1340), as including the whole outward part of the frame in contrast with the internal framework. Lamentations 4:8 gives the more natural expression. The psalmist has groaned himself into emaciation. Sadness and solitude go well together. We plunge into lonely places when we would give voice to our grief. The poet's imagination sees his own likeness in solitude-loving creatures. The "owl of the desert" is often seen in the rocky hills of Syria. The sparrow may be here a generic term for any small song-bird, but there is no need for departing from the narrower meaning. When one of them has lost his mate, he will sit on the housetop alone and lament by the hour.

**102:8–11.** Yet another drop of bitterness in the psalmist's cup is the frantic hatred which pours itself out in voluble mockery all day long, making a running accompaniment to his wail. Solitary as he is, he cannot get beyond his hearing of shrill insults. So miserable does he seem, that enemies take him and his distresses for a formula of imprecation and can find no blacker curse to launch at other foes than to wish that they may be like him. So ashes, the token of mourning, are his food instead of the bread which he had forgotten to eat, and there are more tears than wine in the cup he drinks.

But all this only tells how sad he is. A deeper depth opens when he remembers why he is sad. The bitterest thought to a sufferer is that his sufferings indicate God's displeasure. But it may be wholesome bitterness, which, leading to the recognition of the sin that evokes the wrath, may change into a solemn thankfulness for sorrows which are discerned to be chastisements, inflicted by that love of which indignation is one form. The psalmist confesses sin in the act of bewailing sorrow and sees behind all his pains the working of that hand whose interposition for him he ventures to implore. The tremendous metaphor of v. 10b pictures it as thrust forth from heaven to grasp the feeble sufferer, as an eagle stoops to plunge its talons into a lamb. It lifts him high, only to give more destructive impetus to the force with which it flings him down, to the place where he lies, a huddled heap of broken bones and wounds. His plaint returns to its beginning, lamenting the brief life which is being wasted away by sore distress. Lengthening shadows tell of approaching night. His day is nearing sunset. It will be dark soon, and, as he has said (v. 4), his very self is withering and becoming like dried-up herbage.

**102:12–14.** One can scarcely miss the tone of individual sorrow in the preceding verses, but national restoration, rather than personal deliverance, is the theme of the triumphant central part of the Psalm. That is no reason for flattening the previous verses into the voice of the personified Israel, but rather for hearing in them the sighing of one exile on whom the general burden weighed sorely. He lifts his tear-laden eyes to heaven and catches a

| 7638.323 | 6995 | 3706, 6496 | 3937, 2706.141 |
|---|---|---|---|
| v Piel impf 2ms | pn | cj, n fs | prep, v Qal inf con, ps 3fs |
| תְּרַחֵם | צִיּוֹן | כִּי־עֵת | לְחֶנְנָהּ |
| terachēm | tsîyôn | kî-ʿēth | lechenenāhh |
| and You will have compassion for | Zion | because a time | to favor her |

| 3706, 971.111 | 4287 | | 3706, 7813.116 | 5860 |
|---|---|---|---|---|
| cj, v Qal pf 3ms | n ms | **14.** | cj, v Qal pf 3cp | n mp, ps 2ms |
| כִּי־בָא | מוֹעֵד | | כִּי־רָצוּ | עֲבָדֶיךָ |
| kî-vā' | môʿēdh | | kî-rātsû | ʿăvādhêkhā |
| because it has come | the time of meeting | | because they are pleased with | your servants |

| 881, 63 | 881, 6312 | 2706.326 | | 3486.126 | 1504 | 881, 8428 | 3176 |
|---|---|---|---|---|---|---|---|
| do, n fp, ps 3fs | cj, do, n ms, ps 3fs | v Poel impf 3mp | **15.** | cj, v Qal impf 3mp | n mp | do, *n ms* | pn |
| אֶת־אֲבָנֶיהָ | וְאֶת־עֲפָרָהּ | יְחֹנֵנוּ | | וְיִירְאוּ | גוֹיִם | אֶת־שֵׁם | יְהוָה |
| 'eth-'ăvānêāh | we'eth-ʿăphārāhh | yechōnēnû | | weyîre'û | ghôyim | 'eth-shēm | yehwāh |
| her stones | and her dust | they favor | | and they will fear | nations | the name of | Yahweh |

| 3725, 4567 | 800 | 881, 3638 | | 3706, 1161.111 | 3176 | 6995 |
|---|---|---|---|---|---|---|
| cj, *adj*, *n mp* | art, n fs | do, n ms, ps 2ms | **16.** | cj, v Qal pf 3ms | pn | pn |
| וְכָל־מַלְכֵי | הָאָרֶץ | אֶת־כְּבוֹדֶךָ | | כִּי־בָנָה | יְהוָה | צִיּוֹן |
| wekhol-malkhê | hā'ārets | 'eth-kevôdhekhā | | kî-vānāh | yehwāh | tsîyôn |
| and all the kings of | the earth | your glory | | because He will build | Yahweh | Zion |

| 7495.211 | 904, 3638 | | 6680.111 | 420, 8940 | 6436 |
|---|---|---|---|---|---|
| v Niphal pf 3ms | prep, n ms, ps 3ms | **17.** | v Qal pf 3ms | prep, *n fs* | art, n ms |
| נִרְאָה | בִּכְבוֹדוֹ | | פָּנָה | אֶל־תְּפִלַּת | הָעַרְעָר |
| nir'āh | bikhvôdhô | | pānāh | 'el-tephillath | hā'ar'ār |
| He will appear | in his glory | | He will turn | toward the prayer of | the destitute |

| 3940, 995.111 | 881, 8940 | | 3918.222 | 2148 | 3937, 1810 | 315 |
|---|---|---|---|---|---|---|
| cj, neg part, v Qal pf 3ms | do, n fs, ps 3mp | **18.** | v Niphal juss 3fs | dem pron | prep, n ms | adv |
| וְלֹא־בָזָה | אֶת־תְּפִלָּתָם | | תִּכָּתֶב | זֹאת | לְדוֹר | אַחֲרוֹן |
| welō'-vāzāh | 'eth-tephillāthām | | tikkāthev | zō'th | ledhôr | 'achrôn |
| and He will not despise | their prayer | | let it be written | this | for a generation | afterward |

| 6194 | 1282.255 | 2054.321, 3161 | | 3706, 8625.511 | 4623, 4953 |
|---|---|---|---|---|---|
| cj, n ms | v Niphal ptc ms | v Piel impf 3ms, pn | **19.** | cj, v Hiphil pf 3ms | prep, *n ms* |
| וְעַם | נִבְרָא | יְהַלֶּל־יָהּ | | כִּי־הִשְׁקִיף | מִמְּרוֹם |
| weʿam | nivrā' | yehallel-yāhh | | kî-hishqîph | mimmerôm |
| and a people | being created | they will praise Yah | | because He looked down | from the height of |

**14. For thy servants take pleasure in her stones, and favour the dust thereof:** … For her stones are dear to your servants, *NCB* … And show favor to her dust, *NKJV* … and haue pitie on the dust, *Geneva* … even her dust moves them to pity, *REB*.

**15. So the heathen shall fear the name of the LORD:** … Then will the nations revere your name, *Anchor* … the nations will give honour, *BB* … Will not the heathen learn reverence, Lord, for thy glorious name, *Knox* … The nations too shall revere the name, *Berkeley*.

**and all the kings of the earth thy glory:** … all kings on earth will own thy majesty, *Moffatt* … kings on earth will honor you, *NCV* … will revere your glory, *NIV*.

**16. When the LORD shall build up Zion, he shall appear in his glory:** … builds Zion anew, he will be seen in his glory, *JB* … hath built up Zion, He hath appeared in his glory, *MRB* … In His Splendour He then will appear, *Fenton* … When he is seen in his glory, *Goodspeed*.

**17. He will regard the prayer of the destitute, and not despise their prayer:** … listen to the prayer of those stripped of everything, *Beck* … turn to the prayer of the forsaken, *KJVII* … turne vnto the prayer of the desolate, *Geneva* … does not scorn them when they pray, *NEB*.

**18. This shall be written for the generation to come: and the people which shall be created shall praise the LORD:** … Such legend inscribe we for a later age to read it; a new people will arise, to praise the Lord, *Knox* … that people yet unborn may

vision there which changes, as by magic, the key of his song—Yahweh sitting in royal state forever (cf. Pss. 9:7; 29:10). That silences complaints, breathes courage into the feeble and hope into the despairing. In another mood, the thought of the eternal rule of God might make man's mortality more bitter, but faith grasps it, as enfolding assurances which turn groaning into ringing praise. For the vision is not only of an everlasting One Who works a sovereign will, but of the age-long dominion of Him whose name is Yahweh, and since that name is the revelation of his nature, it, too, endures forever. It is the name of Israel's covenant-making and keeping God. Therefore, ancient promises have not gone to water, although Israel is an exile, and all the old comfort and confidence are still welling up from the name. Zion cannot die while Zion's God lives. God's servants are proven to be his true servants, because they favor what He favors. Their regards, turned to existing evils, are the precursors of divine intervention for the remedy of these. When good men begin to lay the Church's or the world's miseries to heart, it is a sign that God is beginning to heal them. The cry of God's servants can hasten the day of the LORD.

**102:15–17.** The psalmist anticipates that a rebuilt Zion will ensure a worshiping world. He expresses that confidence, which he shares with Isa. 40–66, in vv. 15–18. The name and glory of Yahweh will become objects of reverence to all the earth, because of the manifestation of them by the rebuilding of Zion, which is a witness to all men of his power and tender regard to his people's cry. The past tenses of vv. 16f do not indicate that the Psalm is later than the restoration of the Temple. It is contemplated as already accomplished, because it is the occasion of the "fear" prophesied in v. 15, and consequently prior in time to it. "Destitute" (HED #6436) in v. 17 is literally "naked" or "stripped." It is used in Jer. 17:6 as the name of a desert plant, probably a dwarf juniper, stunted and dry, but it seems to be employed here as simply designating utter destitution. Israel had been stripped of every beauty and made naked before her enemies. Despised, she has cried to God, and she is now clothed again with the garments of salvation, "as a bride adorneth herself with her jewels" (Isa. 61:10).

A wondering world will adore her delivering God. The glowing hopes of the psalmist and prophet seem to be dreams, since the restored Israel attracted no such observance and wrought no such convictions. But the singer was not wrong in believing that the coming of Yahweh in his glory for the rebuilding of Zion would sway the world to homage. His facts were right, but he did not know their perspective, nor could he understand how many weary years lay, like a deep gorge hidden from the eye of one who looks over a wide prospect, between the rebuilding of which he was thinking and that truer establishment of the city of God, which is again parted from the period of universal recognition of Yahweh's glory by so many sad and stormy generations. But the vision is true. The coming of Yahweh in his glory will be followed by a world's recognition of its light.

**102:18.** That praise accruing to Yahweh shall be not only universal, but shall go on sounding, with increasing volume in its tone, through coming generations. This expectation is set forth in vv. 18–22, which substantially reiterate the thought of the preceding with the addition that there is to be a new Israel, a people yet to be created (Ps. 22:31). The psalmist did not know the deep things of which he spoke. He did know that Israel was immortal and that the seed of life was in the tree that had cast its leaves and stood bare and apparently dead. But he did not know the process by which that new Israel was to be created, nor the new elements of which it was to consist. His confidence teaches us never to despair of the future of God's Church, however low its present state, but to look down the ages in calm certainty that, however externals may change, the succession of God's children will never fail nor the voice of their praise ever fall silent.

**102:19–22.** The course of God's intervention for Israel is described in vv. 19f. His looking down from heaven is equivalent to his observance, as the all-seeing Witness and Judge (cf. Pss. 14:2; 33:13f; etc.) and is preparatory to his hearing the sighing of the captive Israel, doomed to death. The language of v. 20 is apparently drawn from Ps. 79:11. The thought corresponds to that of v. 17. The purpose of his intervention is set forth in vv. 21f as being the declaration of Yahweh's name and praise in Jerusalem before a gathered world. The aim of Yahweh's dealings is that all men, through all generations, may know and praise Him. That is but another way of saying that He infinitely desires, and perpetually works for, men's highest good. For our sakes, He desires so much that we should know Him, since the knowledge is life eternal. He is not greedy of adulation nor dependent on recognition,

| 7231<br>n ms, ps 3ms<br>קָדְשׁוֹ<br>qādheshô<br>his holy place | 3176<br>pn<br>יְהוָה<br>yehwāh<br>Yahweh | 4623, 8452<br>prep, n md<br>מִשָּׁמַיִם<br>mishshāmayim<br>from the heavens | 420, 800<br>prep, n fs<br>אֶל־אֶרֶץ<br>'el-'erets<br>to the earth | 5202.511<br>v Hiphil pf 3ms<br>הִבִּיט<br>hibbîṯ<br>He looked down | **20.** | 3937, 8471.141<br>prep, v Qal inf con<br>לִשְׁמֹעַ<br>lishmōa'<br>to hear |
|---|---|---|---|---|---|---|

| 617<br>*n fs*<br>אֶנְקַת<br>'enqath<br>the groans of | 629<br>n ms<br>אָסִיר<br>'āsîr<br>prisoners | 3937, 6858.341<br>prep, v Piel inf con<br>לְפַתֵּחַ<br>lephattēach<br>to loose | 1158<br>*n mp*<br>בְּנֵי<br>benê<br>the children of | 8876<br>n fs<br>תְמוּתָה<br>themûthāh<br>death | **21.** | 3937, 5807.341<br>prep, v Piel inf con<br>לְסַפֵּר<br>lesappēr<br>to recount | 904, 6995<br>prep, pn<br>בְּצִיּוֹן<br>betsîyôn<br>in Zion |
|---|---|---|---|---|---|---|---|

| 8428<br>*n ms*<br>שֵׁם<br>shēm<br>the name of | 3176<br>pn<br>יְהוָה<br>yehwāh<br>Yahweh | 8747<br>cj, n fs, ps 3ms<br>וּתְהִלָּתוֹ<br>ûthehillāthô<br>and his praise | 904, 3503<br>prep, pn<br>בִּירוּשָׁלָם<br>bîrûshālām<br>in Jerusalem | **22.** | 904, 7192.241<br>prep, v Niphal inf con<br>בְּהִקָּבֵץ<br>behiqqāvēts<br>when gathering together | 6194<br>n mp<br>עַמִּים<br>'ammîm<br>peoples | 3267<br>adv<br>יַחְדָּו<br>yachdāw<br>together |
|---|---|---|---|---|---|---|---|

| 4608<br>cj, n fp<br>וּמַמְלָכוֹת<br>ûmamlākhôth<br>and kingdoms | 3937, 5856.141<br>prep, v Qal inf con<br>לַעֲבֹד<br>la'ăvōdh<br>to serve | 881, 3176<br>do, pn<br>אֶת־יְהוָה<br>'eth-yehwāh<br>Yahweh | **23.** | 6257.311<br>v Piel pf 3ms<br>עִנָּה<br>'innāh<br>He has afflicted | 904, 1932<br>prep, art, n ms<br>בַדֶּרֶךְ<br>vadderekh<br>on the way | 3699<br>n ms, ps 3ms<br>כֹּחוֹ<br>kōchô<br>his strength |
|---|---|---|---|---|---|---|

| 7403.311<br>v Piel pf 3ms<br>קִצַּר<br>qitstsar<br>He has made short | **24.** | 569.125<br>v Qal impf 1cs<br>אֹמַר<br>'ōmar<br>I say | 418<br>n ms, ps 1cs<br>אֵלִי<br>'ēlî<br>O my God | 414, 6148.523<br>adv, v Hiphil juss 2ms, ps 1cs<br>אַל־תַּעֲלֵנִי<br>'al-ta'ălēnî<br>do not cause me to go up | 904, 2783<br>prep, art, *n ms*<br>בַּחֲצִי<br>bachtsî<br>during the half of |
|---|---|---|---|---|---|

| 3219<br>n mp, ps 1cs<br>יָמָי<br>yāmāy<br>my days | 904, 1810<br>prep, n ms<br>בְּדוֹר<br>bedhôr<br>with a generation | 1810<br>n mp<br>דּוֹרִים<br>dôrîm<br>generations | 8523<br>n fp, ps 2ms<br>שְׁנוֹתֶיךָ<br>shenôthêkhā<br>your years | **25.** | 3937, 6686<br>prep, n mp<br>לְפָנִים<br>lephānîm<br>before | 800<br>art, n fs<br>הָאָרֶץ<br>hā'ārets<br>the earth |
|---|---|---|---|---|---|---|

| 3354.113<br>v Qal pf 2ms<br>יָסַדְתָּ<br>yāsadhtā<br>You laid a foundation | 4801<br>cj, *n ms*<br>וּמַעֲשֵׂה<br>ûma'ăsēh<br>and the works of | 3135<br>n fd, ps 2ms<br>יָדֶיךָ<br>yādhêkhā<br>your hands | 8452<br>n md<br>שָׁמָיִם<br>shāmāyim<br>the heavens | **26.** | 2065<br>pers pron<br>הֵמָּה<br>hēmmāh<br>they | 6.126<br>v Qal impf 3mp<br>יֹאבֵדוּ<br>yō'vēdhû<br>they will perish |
|---|---|---|---|---|---|---|

| 887<br>cj, pers pron<br>וְאַתָּה<br>we'attāh<br>but You | 6198.123<br>v Qal impf 2ms<br>תַעֲמֹד<br>tha'ămōdh<br>You will stand | 3725<br>cj, adj, ps 3mp<br>וְכֻלָּם<br>wekhullām<br>and all of them | 3626, 933<br>prep, art, n ms<br>כַּבֶּגֶד<br>kabbeghedh<br>like the garment | 1126.126<br>v Qal impf 3mp<br>יִבְלוּ<br>yivlû<br>they will wear out | 3626, 3961<br>prep, art, n ms<br>כַּלְּבוּשׁ<br>kallevûsh<br>like the garment |
|---|---|---|---|---|---|

praise the LORD, *REB* … let his future creatures praise the Lord, *NCB.*

**19. For he hath looked down from the height of his sanctuary; from heaven did the LORD behold the earth:** … the LORD from His high Dwelling looked, He bent from the Heavens, to Earth, *Fenton* … From heaven the LORD gazed upon the earth, *NASB* … looked at the earth, *NRSV.*

**20. To hear the groaning of the prisoner:** … to listen to the sighing of the captive, *JB* … He heard the moans, *NCV* … Hearing the cry, *BB.*

**to loose those that are appointed to death:** … to set free men under sentence of death, *NEB* … To loose sons of death, *Young* … condemned to death, *JB* … those doomed to death, *Goodspeed.*

**21. To declare the name of the LORD in Zion, and his praise in Jerusalem:** … To the end the Name of Yahweh might be celebrated, *Rotherham* … that the name of the

LORD may be proclaimed, *Berkeley* ... rehearsing his fame in Sion, *Moffatt* ... In Jerusalem, give to Him thanks, *Fenton.*

**22. When the people are gathered together, and the kingdoms, to serve the LORD:** ... the peoples and the kingdoms assemble to worship, *NIV* ... when peoples and kings meet there to pay him their homage, *Knox* ... with kings to serve him, *Anchor.*

**23. He weakened my strength in the way; he shortened my days:** ... He has broken my strength in mid-course, *RSV* ... He has broken down my strength, *NAB* ...He has broken my strength before my course is run, *REB.*

**24. I said, O my God, take me not away in the midst of my days:** ... don't take me away in the middle of my life, *Beck* ... Snatch me not away before half my days are done, *NEB* ... in middle age, *Berkeley.*

**thy years are throughout all generations:** ... for your years run on from age to age, *JB* ... For Your years are from ever to ever, *Fenton* ... from generation to generation, *Geneva.*

**25. Of old hast thou laid the foundation of the earth: and the heavens are the work of thy hands:** ... You have laid the foundation of the earth beforehand, *KJVII* ... you established the earth, *NCB* ... In the beginning you made the earth, *NCV* ... the foundations of earth when time began, *Knox.*

**26. They shall perish, but thou shalt endure: yea, all of them shall wax old like a garment:** ... they vanish, but thou shalt endure, *Moffatt* ... They will come to an end, but you will still go on, *BB* ... will wear out like a garment, *NASB* ... wear out like clothes, *Anchor.*

**as a vesture shalt thou change them, and they shall be changed:** ... they shall pass away, *MAST* ... they shall vanish, *Rotherham* ... and they pass away, *RSV.*

---

but He loves men too well not to rejoice in being understood and loved by them, since love ever hungers for return. The psalmist saw what shall one day be, when, far down the ages, he beheld the world gathered in the temple courts and heard the shout of their praise borne to him up the stream of time. He penetrated to the inmost meaning of the divine acts when he proclaimed that they were all done for the manifestation of the name, which cannot but be praised when it is known.

**102:23–24.** The psalmist has felt the exhaustion of long sorrow and the shortness of his term. Will God do all these glorious things of which he has been singing, and he, the singer, not be there to see? That would mingle bitterness in his triumphant anticipations, for it would be little to him, lying in his grave, that Zion should be built again. The hopes with which some would console us for the loss of the Christian assurance of immortality, that the race shall march on to new power and nobleness, are poor substitutes for continuance of our own lives and for our own participation in the glories of the future. The psalmist's prayer, which takes God's eternity as its reason for deprecating his own premature death, echoes the inextinguishable confidence of the devout heart that somehow even its fleeting being has a claim to be assimilated in duration to its eternal object of trust and aspiration. The contrast between God's years and man's days may be brooded on in bitterness or in hope. They who are driven by thinking of their own mortality to clutch God's eternity, use the one aright and will not be deprived of the other.

**102:25–26.** The solemn grandeur of vv. 25f needs little commentary, but it may be noted that a reminiscence of Isa. 11 runs through them, both in the description of the act of creation of heaven and earth (Isa. 48:13; 44:24) and in that of their decaying like a garment (Isa. 51:6; 54:10). That which has been created can be removed. The creatural is necessarily the transient. Possibly, too, the remarkable expression "changed" (HED #2599) as applied to the visible creation may imply the thought which had already been expressed in Isaiah and was destined to receive such deepening by the Christian truth of the new heavens and new earth—a truth the contents of which are unclear to us until it is fulfilled. But whatever may be the fate of creatures, He who receives no accession to his stable being by originating suffers no diminution by extinguishing them. Man's days, the earth"s ages, and the eons of the heavens pass, and still "thou shalt endure," the same unchanging Author of change. Measures of time fail when applied to his being, whose years have not that which all divisions of time have—an end. An unending year is a paradox, which in relation to God is a truth.

**102:27–28.** It is remarkable that the psalmist does not draw the conclusion that he himself shall receive an answer to his prayer, but that "the children of thy servants shall continue," i.e., in the land, and that there will always be an Israel "established before thee." He contemplates successive generations as in turn dwelling in the Promised Land (and perhaps in the ancient "dwelling place to all generations," even in God), but of his own

| Number | Grammar | Hebrew | Transliteration | English |
|---|---|---|---|---|
| 3940 | neg part | לֹא | lō' | not |
| 8523 | cj, n fp, ps 2ms | וּשְׁנוֹתֶיךָ | ûshenôthêkhā | and your years |
| 887, 2000 | cj, pers pron, pers pron | וְאַתָּה־הוּא | we'attāh-hû' | but You He |
| **27.** | | | | |
| 2599.126 | cj, v Qal impf 3mp | וְיַחֲלֹפוּ | weyachlōphû | and they will pass away |
| 2599.523 | v Hiphil impf 2ms, ps 3mp | תַּחֲלִיפֵם | tachlîphēm | You will change them |
| 2320 | cj, n ms, ps 3mp | וְזַרְעָם | wezar'ām | and their seed |
| 8331.126 | v Qal impf 3mp | יִשְׁכּוֹנוּ | yishkônû | they will stay |
| 1158, 5860 | *n mp*, n mp, ps 2ms | בְּנֵי־עֲבָדֶיךָ | benê-'ăvādhêkhā | the children of your servants |
| **28.** | | | | |
| 8882.126 | v Qal impf 3mp | יִתָּמּוּ | yittommû | they will be completed |
| 881, 3176 | do, pn | אֶת־יְהוָה | 'eth-yehwāh | Yahweh |
| 5497 | n fs, ps 1cs | נַפְשִׁי | naphshî | O my soul |
| 1313.332 | v Piel impv 2fs | בָּרְכִי | bārekhî | bless |
| **1.** | | | | |
| 3937, 1784 | prep, pn | לְדָוִד | ledhāwidh | of David |
| **103:t** | | | | |
| 3679.221 | v Niphal impf 3ms | יִכּוֹן | yikkôn | they will be established |
| 3937, 6686 | prep, n mp, ps 2ms | לְפָנֶיךָ | lephānêkhā | in your presence |
| 881, 3176 | do, pn | אֶת־יְהוָה | 'eth-yehwāh | Yahweh |
| 5497 | n fs, ps 1cs | נַפְשִׁי | naphshî | O my soul |
| 1313.332 | v Piel impv 2fs | בָּרְכִי | bārekhî | bless |
| **2.** | | | | |
| 7231 | n ms, ps 3ms | קָדְשׁוֹ | qādheshô | his holiness |
| 881, 8428 | do, *n ms* | אֶת־שֵׁם | 'eth-shēm | the name of |
| 3725, 7419 | cj, *adj*, n mp, ps 1cs | וְכָל־קְרָבָי | wekhol-qŏrāvay | and all my inmost parts |
| 3937, 3725, 5988 | prep, *adj*, n ms, ps 2fs | לְכָל־עֲוֺנֵכִי | lekhol-'ăwōnēkhî | all your transgressions |
| 5739.151 | art, v Qal act ptc ms | הַסֹּלֵחַ | hassōlēach | the One Who forgives |
| **3.** | | | | |
| 3725, 1618 | *adj*, n mp, ps 3ms | כָּל־גְּמוּלָיו | kol-gemûlâv | all his benefits |
| 414, 8319.124 | cj, adv, v Qal juss 2fs | וְאַל־תִּשְׁכְּחִי | we'al-tishkechî | and do not forget |
| 2522 | n mp, ps 2fs | חַיָּיְכִי | chayyāyekhî | your life |
| 4623, 8273 | prep, n fs | מִשַּׁחַת | mishshachath | from the Pit |
| 1381.151 | art, v Qal act ptc ms | הַגּוֹאֵל | haggô'ēl | the Redeemer |
| **4.** | | | | |
| 3937, 3725, 8794 | prep, *adj*, n mp, ps 2fs | לְכָל־תַּחֲלֻאָיְכִי | lekhol-tachlu'āyekhî | of all your diseases |
| 7784.151 | art, v Qal act ptc ms | הָרֹפֵא | hārōphē' | the Healer |
| 7881.551 | art, v Hiphil ptc ms | הַמַּשְׂבִּיעַ | hammasbiya' | the One Who satisfies |
| **5.** | | | | |
| 7641 | cj, n mp | וְרַחֲמִים | werachmîm | mercies |
| 2721 | n ms | חֶסֶד | chesedh | steadfast love |
| 6064.351 | art, v Piel ptc ms, ps 2fs | הַמְעַטְּרֵכִי | ham'atterēkhî | the One who crowns you with |
| 5454 | n fp, ps 2fs | נְעוּרָיְכִי | ne'ûrāyekhî | your youth |
| 3626, 5585 | prep, art, n ms | כַּנֶּשֶׁר | kannesher | like the eagle |
| 2412.723 | v Hithpael impf 2ms | תִּתְחַדֵּשׁ | tithchaddēsh | you renew |
| 5927 | n ms, ps 2fs | עֶדְיֵךְ | 'edhyēkh | your ornaments |
| 904, 3008 | prep, art, n ms | בַּטּוֹב | battôv | with good things |

**27. But thou art the same, and thy years shall have no end:** … but you never alter, and your years never end, *JB* … thy yeeres shall not faile, *Geneva* … your life will never end, *NCV.*

**28. The children of thy servants shall continue, and their seed shall be established before thee:** … of your servants shall live secure, *NRSV* … of your servants will live in your presence, *NIV* … Thy servants shall dwell securely, *MAST* … their descendants will stand firm before You, *Beck.*

**103:t. A Psalm of David.**

**1. Bless the LORD, O my soul: and all that is within me, bless his holy name:** … unite, all my powers, to bless that holy name, *Knox* … my innermost heart, *NEB* … with all my being I bless, *REB* … let all my being bless his sacred name, *Moffatt.*

**2. Bless the LORD, O my soul, and forget not all his benefits:** … And never forget all His gifts, *Fenton* . . let not all his blessings go from your memory, *BB* ... never forget all his acts of kindness, *JB.*

**3. Who forgiveth all thine iniquities:** ... pardons all your iniquities, *NAB* ... forgives all your offences, *JB* ... forgives all my wrongs, *Beck* ... forgives all my sins, *NCV.*

**who healeth all thy diseases:** ... heals all my sicknesses, *Goodspeed* ... heals all thy mortal ills, *Knox* ... all thine infirmities, *Geneva.*

**4. Who redeemeth thy life from destruction:** ... redeems your life from the Pit, *RSV* ... redeems your life from the grave, *Berkeley* ... redeems your life from ruin, *KJVII.*

**who crowneth thee with lovingkindness and tender mercies:** ... crowns you with steadfast love, *NRSV* ... crowns you with love and compassion, *NIV* ... and compassion, *NCB.*

**5. Who satisfieth thy mouth with good things:** ... Who is satisfying with good thy desire, *Young* ... will imbue your eternity with his beauty, *Anchor* ... he contents you with good things all your life, *JB* ... thine old age, *Darby.*

**so that thy youth is renewed like the eagle's:** ... restores thy youth, as the eagle's plumage is restored, *Knox* ... makes me young again, like the eagle, *NCV.*

**6. The LORD executeth righteousness and judgment for all that are oppressed:** ... does what is right and just, *Beck* ... works vindication and justice, *NRSV* ... secures justice and the rights of all the oppressed, *NCB.*

---

continuance he is silent. Was he not assured of that? Or was he so certain of the answer to his prayer that he had forgotten himself in the vision of the eternal God and the abiding Israel? The psalmist's oblivion of self results from rapt gazing on God's eternal being. The pledge of his servants' perpetuity may teach us that we reach the summit of faith when we lose ourselves in God.

The Book of Hebrews quotes vv. 25ff as spoken of "the Son" (Heb. 1:8). Such an application of the words rests on the fact that the Psalm speaks of the coming of Yahweh for redemption, Who is none other than Yahweh manifested fully in the Messiah. But Yahweh, whose coming brings redemption and his recognition by the world, is also Creator. Since the Incarnation is the coming of Yahweh, which the psalmist—like all the prophets—looked for as the consummation, He in Whom the redeeming Yahweh was manifested is He in Whom Yahweh the Creator "made the worlds." The writer of the epistle is declaring that the words point to Jesus as the crowning manifestation of the redeeming, and therefore necessarily of the creating, God.

***Psalm 103.*** *The psalmist's praise flows in one unbroken stream. There are no clear marks of division, but the river broadens as it runs, and personal benefits and individual praise open out into gifts which are seen to fill the universe and thanksgiving which is heard from every extremity of his wide dominion of steadfast love.*

**103:1–5.** In v. 1–5, the psalmist sings of his own experience. His spirit, or ruling self, calls on his "soul," the weaker and more feminine part, which may be cast down (Pss. 42; 43) by sorrow and needs stimulus and control, to contemplate God's gifts and to praise Him. A good man will rouse himself to such exercise and coerce his more sensuous and sluggish faculties to their noblest use. Memory must especially be directed, for it keeps woefully short-lived records of mercies, especially of continuous ones. God's gifts are all "benefits," whether they are bright or dark. The catalog of blessings lavished on the singer's soul begins with forgiveness and ends with immortal youth. The profound consciousness of sin, which was one aim of the Law to evoke, underlies the psalmist's praise, and he who does not feel that any blessings could come from heaven unless forgiveness cleared the way for them has yet to learn the deepest music of thankfulness. It is followed by healing of "all thy diseases," which is no cure of merely bodily ailments any more than redeeming of life "from destruction" is simply preservation of physical existence. In both, there is at least included—even if we do not say that it only is in view—the operation of the pardoning God in delivering from the sicknesses and death of the spirit.

How should a man thus dealt with grow old? The body may, but not the soul. There is no need to make the psalmist responsible for the fables of the eagle's renewal of its youth. The comparison with the monarch of the air does not refer to the process by which the soul's wings are made strong, but to the result in wings that never tire, but bear their possessor far up in the blue and toward the throne.

**103:6–10.** In vv. 6–18, the psalmist sweeps a greater circle and deals with God's blessings to mankind. He has Israel specifically in view in the earlier verses, but passes beyond Israel to "them that fear him." It is very instructive that he begins with the definite fact of God's revelation through Moses. He is not spinning an idea of a God out of his own

| 6. | 6449.151 | 6930 | 3176 | 5122 | 3937, 3725, 6456.156 |
|---|---|---|---|---|---|
| | *v Qal act ptc ms* | n fp | pn | cj, n mp | prep, *adj*, v Qal pass ptc mp |
| | עֹשֵׂה | צְדָקוֹת | יְהוָה | וּמִשְׁפָּטִים | לְכָל־עֲשׁוּקִים |
| | ʿōsēh | tsedhāqôth | yehwāh | ûmishpāṭîm | lekhol-ʿăshûqîm |
| | the One Who acts with | righteous deeds | Yahweh | and justice | for all those oppressed |

| 7. | 3156.521 | 1932 | 3937, 5057 | 3937, 1158 | 3547 | 6173 |
|---|---|---|---|---|---|---|
| | v Hiphil impf 3ms | n mp, ps 3ms | prep, pn | prep, *n mp* | pn | n fp, ps 3ms |
| | יוֹדִיעַ | דְּרָכָיו | לְמֹשֶׁה | לִבְנֵי | יִשְׂרָאֵל | עֲלִילוֹתָיו |
| | yôdhîaʿ | derākhâv | lemōsheh | livnê | yisrāʾēl | ʿălîlôthâv |
| | He caused to be known | his ways | to Moses | to the children of | Israel | his deeds |

| 8. | 7631 | 2688 | 3176 | 774 | 653 | 7521, 2721 |
|---|---|---|---|---|---|---|
| | adj | cj, adj | pn | *adj* | n md | cj, *adj*, n ms |
| | רַחוּם | וְחַנּוּן | יְהוָה | אֶרֶךְ | אַפַּיִם | וְרַב־חָסֶד |
| | rachûm | wechannûn | yehwāh | ʾerekh | ʾappayim | werav-chāsedh |
| | merciful | and gracious | Yahweh | long of | nostrils | and abundant in steadfast love |

| 9. | 3940, 3937, 5516 | 7662.121 | 3940 | 3937, 5986 | 5386.121 | 10. | 3940 |
|---|---|---|---|---|---|---|---|
| | neg part, prep, art n ms | v Qal impf 3ms | cj, neg part | prep, n ms | v Qal impf 3ms | | neg part |
| | לֹא־לָנֶצַח | יָרִיב | וְלֹא | לְעוֹלָם | יִטּוֹר | | לֹא |
| | lōʾ-lānetsach | yārîv | welōʾ | leʿôlām | yiṭṭôr | | lōʾ |
| | not unto forever | He will contend | and not | unto eternity | he will keep back | | not |

| 3626, 2492 | 6449.111 | 3937 | 3940 | 3626, 5988 |
|---|---|---|---|---|
| prep, n mp, ps 1cp | v Qal pf 3ms | prep, ps 1cp | cj, neg part | prep, n mp, ps 1cp |
| כַחֲטָאֵינוּ | עָשָׂה | לָנוּ | וְלֹא | כַעֲוֹנֹתֵינוּ |
| khachetāʾênû | ʿāsāh | lānû | welōʾ | khaʿăwōnōthênû |
| according to our sins | He has acted | against us | and not | according to our transgressions |

| 1621.111 | 6142 | 11. | 3706 | 3626, 1393 | 8452 | 6142, 800 | 1428.111 |
|---|---|---|---|---|---|---|---|
| v Qal pf 3ms | prep, ps 1cp | | cj | prep, *adj* | n md | prep, art, n fs | v Qal pf 3ms |
| גָּמַל | עָלֵינוּ | | כִּי | כִגְבֹהַּ | שָׁמַיִם | עַל־הָאָרֶץ | גָּבַר |
| gāmal | ʿālênû | | kî | khighvōahh | shāmayim | ʿal-hāʾārets | gāvar |
| He has rewarded | on us | | because | like the high | the heavens | on the earth | it is excellent |

| 2721 | 6142, 3486.152 | 12. | 3626, 7651.141 | 4350 | 4623, 4790 |
|---|---|---|---|---|---|
| n ms, ps 3ms | prep, v Qal act ptc mp, ps 3ms | | prep, v Qal inf con | n ms | prep, n ms |
| חַסְדּוֹ | עַל־יְרֵאָיו | | כִּרְחֹק | מִזְרָח | מִמַּעֲרָב |
| chasdô | ʿal-yerēʾâv | | kirchōq | mizrāch | mimmaʿărāv |
| his steadfast love | concerning those who fear Him | | as being far | the rising | from the setting |

| 7651.511 | 4623 | 881, 6840 | 13. | 3626, 7638.341 | 1 |
|---|---|---|---|---|---|
| v Hiphil pf 3ms | prep, ps 1cp | do, n mp, ps 1cp | | prep, v Piel inf con | n ms |
| הִרְחִיק | מִמֶּנּוּ | אֶת־פְּשָׁעֵינוּ | | כְּרַחֵם | אָב |
| hirchîq | mimmennû | ʾeth-peshāʿênû | | kerachēm | ʾāv |
| He has caused to be far | from us | our offenses | | like having compassion | a father |

| 6142, 1158 | 7638.311 | 3176 | 6142, 3486.152 |
|---|---|---|---|
| prep, n mp | v Piel pf 3ms | pn | prep, v Qal act ptc mp, ps 3ms |
| עַל־בָּנִים | רִחַם | יְהוָה | עַל־יְרֵאָיו |
| ʿal-bānîm | richam | yehwāh | ʿal-yerēʾâv |
| concerning his children | He has compassion | Yahweh | concerning those who fear Him |

| 14. | 3706, 2000 | 3156.111 | 3444 | 2226.155 | 3706, 6312 | 601 | 15. | 596 |
|---|---|---|---|---|---|---|---|---|
| | cj, pers pron | v Qal pf 3ms | n ms, ps 1cp | v Qal pass ptc ms | cj, n ms | pers pron | | n ms |
| | כִּי־הוּא | יָדַע | יִצְרֵנוּ | זָכוּר | כִּי־עָפָר | אֲנָחְנוּ | | אֱנוֹשׁ |
| | kî-hûʾ | yādhaʿ | yitsrēnû | zākhûr | kî-ʿāphār | ʾănāchnû | | ʾěnôsh |
| | because He | He knows | our form | being called to mind | that dust | we | | a man |

**7. He made known his ways unto Moses, his acts unto the children of Israel:** ... he let Moses see this purpose, and Israel his methods, *Moffatt* ... He gave knowledge of his way to Moses, *BB* ... And His power to Israel's Sons, *Fenton.*

**8. The LORD is merciful and gracious, slow to anger, and plenteous in mercy:** ... abounding in steadfast love, *RSV* ... and abounding in kindness, *NAB* ... abundant in lovingkindness, *ASV* ... Compassionate and gracious is Yahweh, *Rotherham.*

**9. He will not always chide: neither will he keep his anger for ever:** ... He will not always show contention nor maintain it forever, *Berkeley* ... He will not always strive with us, *NASB* ... He will not always accuse, *NIV* ... nor will He watch forever, *KJVII.*

**10. He hath not dealt with us after our sins; nor rewarded us according to our iniquities:** ... He has not treated us as our sins deserve, *REB* ... Nor punished us, *NKJV* ... Nor requited us, *MAST.*

**11. For as the heaven is high above the earth, so great is his mercy toward them that fear him:** ... so his strong love stands high over all who fear him, *NEB* ... His kindness hath been mighty, *Young* ... so great is his steadfast love, *NRSV* ... so surpassing is his kindness toward those who fear him, *NCB.*

**12. As far as the east is from the west, so far hath he removed our transgressions from us:** ... As far as the rising of the sun is from its setting, *Beck* ... he put far from us our trangressions, *Rotherham* ... he clears away our guilt from us, *Knox.*

**13. Like as a father pitieth his children, so the LORD pitieth them that fear him:** ... as a father has mercy on his children, *NCV* ... As tenderly as a father treats his children, *JB* ... tenderly sympathizes with those who revere Him, *Berkeley.*

**14. For he knoweth our frame; he remembereth that we are dust:** ... For he knows our form, mindful that we are clay, *Anchor* ... For He knows

---

consciousness, but he has learned all that he knows of Him from his historical self-revelation. A hymn of praise which does not have revelation for its basis will have many a quaver of doubt. The God of men's imaginations, consciences or yearnings is a dim shadow. The God to whom love turns undoubting and praise rises without one note of discord is the God who has spoken his own name by deeds which have entered into the history of the world. And what has He revealed himself to be? The psalmist answers almost in the words of the proclamation made to Moses (vv. 8f). The lawgiver had prayed, "I pray thee ... show me now thy way, that I may know thee" (Exo. 33:13); and the prayer had been granted, when "the LORD passed by before him," and proclaimed his name as "merciful and gracious, longsuffering, and abundant in goodness and truth" (Exo. 34:6). That proclamation fills the singer's heart, and his whole soul leaps up in him, as he meditates on its depth and sweetness. Now, after so many centuries of experience, Israel can repeat with full assurance the ancient self-revelation, which has been proved true by many "extraordinary" (HED #6623).

The psalmist's thoughts are still circling around the idea of forgiveness, with which he began his contemplations. He and his people equally need it, and the revelation of God's character bears directly on his relation to sin. Yahweh is "slow to anger"—i.e., slow to allow it to flash out in punishment—and as lavish of steadfast love as sparing of wrath. That character is disclosed by deeds. Yahweh's graciousness forces Him to "chide" (HED #7662) against a man's sins for the man's sake. But it forbids Him to be perpetually chastising and condemning, like a harsh taskmaster. Nor does He keep his anger ever burning, although He does keep his steadfast love aflame for a thousand generations. Lightning is transitory; sunshine, constant. Whatever his chastisements, they have been less than our sins. The heaviest is light and brief when compared with the tremendous weight of our guilt (v. 10; cf. 2 Cor. 4:16f).

**103:11–13.** The glorious metaphors in vv. 11f traverse heaven to the zenith and from sunrise to sunset to find distances wide enough to express the towering height of God's mercy and the completeness of his removal from us of our sins. That pure arch, the top stone of which no wings nor thoughts can reach, sheds down all light and heat that make growth and cherish life. It is high above us, but it pours blessings on us, and it bends down all around the horizon to kiss the low, dark earth. The steadfast love of Yahweh is similarly lofty, boundless, all-fructifying. In v. 11b, the parallelism would be more complete if a small textual alteration were adopted, which would give "high" instead of "great," but the slight departure which the existing text makes from precise correspondence with v. 11a is of little significance, and the thought is sufficiently intelligible as the words stand. Between east and west all distances lie. To the eye, they bound the world. So far does God's mercy bear away our sins. Forgiveness and cleansing are inseparably united.

**103:14–16.** But the song drops—or possibly, rises from these magnificent measures of the

| 3626, 2785 | 3219 | 3626, 7001 | 7898 | 3772 | 6957.121 | | 3706 | 7593 |
|---|---|---|---|---|---|---|---|---|
| prep, art, n ms | n mp, ps 3ms | prep, *n ms* | art, n ms | adv | v Qal impf 3ms | **16.** | cj | n fs |
| כֶּחָצִיר | יָמָיו | כְּצִיץ | הַשָּׂדֶה | כֵּן | יָצִיץ | | כִּי | רוּחַ |
| kechātsîr | yāmâv | ketsîts | hassādheh | kēn | yātsîts | | kî | rûach |
| like the grass | his days | like the flower of | the field | so | he blossoms | | because | the wind |

| 5882.112, 904 | 375 | 3940, 5422.521 | 5968 | 4887 |
|---|---|---|---|---|
| v Qal pf 3fs, prep, ps 3ms | cj, sub, ps 3ms | cj, neg part, v Hiphil impf 3ms, ps 3ms | adv | n ms, ps 3ms |
| עָבְרָה־בּוֹ | וְאֵינֶנּוּ | וְלֹא־יַכִּירֶנּוּ | עוֹד | מְקוֹמוֹ |
| ‘āverāh-bô | we’ênennû | welō’-yakkîrennû | ‘ôdh | meqômô |
| it passes over it | then it is not | and he does not recognize it | anymore | its place |

| | 2721 | 3176 | 4623, 5986 | 5912, 5986 |
|---|---|---|---|---|
| **17.** | cj, *n ms* | pn | prep, n ms | cj, adv, n ms |
| | וְחֶסֶד | יְהוָה | מֵעוֹלָם | וְעַד־עוֹלָם |
| | wechesedh | yehwāh | mē‘ôlām | we‘adh-‘ôlām |
| | but the steadfast love of | Yahweh | from eternity | even unto eternity |

| 6142, 3486.152 | 6930 | 3937, 1158 | 1158 |
|---|---|---|---|
| prep, v Qal act ptc mp, ps 3ms | cj, n fs, ps 3ms | prep, *n mp* | n mp |
| עַל־יְרֵאָיו | וְצִדְקָתוֹ | לִבְנֵי | בָנִים |
| ‘al-yerē’âv | wetsidhqāthô | livnê | vānîm |
| concerning those who fear Him | and his righteousness | to the children of | children |

| | 3937, 8490.152 | 1311 | 3937, 2226.152 | 6740 |
|---|---|---|---|---|
| **18.** | prep, *v Qal act ptc mp* | n fs, ps 3ms | cj, prep, *v Qal act ptc mp* | n mp, ps 3ms |
| | לְשֹׁמְרֵי | בְרִיתוֹ | וּלְזֹכְרֵי | פִקֻּדָיו |
| | leshōmerê | verîthô | ûlăzōkherê | phiqqudhâv |
| | to those who observe | his covenant | and to those who remember | his precepts |

| 3937, 6449.141 | | 3176 | 904, 8452 | 3679.511 | 3802 |
|---|---|---|---|---|---|
| prep, v Qal inf con, ps 3mp | **19.** | pn | prep, art, n md | v Hiphil pf 3ms | n ms, ps 3ms |
| לַעֲשׂוֹתָם | | יְהוָה | בַּשָּׁמַיִם | הֵכִין | כִּסְאוֹ |
| la‘ăsôthām | | yehwāh | bashshāmayim | hēkhîn | kis’ô |
| to do them | | Yahweh | in the heavens | He has established | his throne |

| 4577 | 904, 3725 | 5090.112 | | 1313.333 | 3176 | 4534 |
|---|---|---|---|---|---|---|
| cj, n fs, ps 3ms | prep, art, n ms | v Qal pf 3fs | **20.** | v Piel impv 2mp | pn | n mp, ps 3ms |
| וּמַלְכוּתוֹ | בַּכֹּל | מָשָׁלָה | | בָּרְכוּ | יְהוָה | מַלְאָכָיו |
| ûmalkhûthô | bakkōl | māshālāh | | bārekhû | yehwāh | mal’ākhâv |
| and his kingdom | over everything | it rules | | bless | Yahweh | his angels |

| 1399 | 3699 | 6449.152 | 1745 | 3937, 8471.141 | 904, 7249 |
|---|---|---|---|---|---|
| *n mp* | n ms | *v Qal act ptc mp* | n ms, ps 3ms | prep, v Qal inf con | prep, *n ms* |
| גִּבֹּרֵי | כֹּחַ | עֹשֵׂי | דְּבָרוֹ | לִשְׁמֹעַ | בְּקוֹל |
| gibbōrê | khōach | ‘ōsê | dhevārô | lishmōa‘ | beqôl |
| the mighty ones of | power | those who do | his word | to listen | by the voice of |

how we are made, *KJVII* ... he knows what we are made of, *Moffatt.*

**15. As for man, his days are as grass: as a flower of the field, so he flourisheth:** ... his beautiful growth is like the flower, *BB* ... Like a flower of the field, so he blooms, *Fenton* ... he flourishes like a flower, *RSV.*

**16. For the wind passeth over it, and it is gone; and the place thereof shall know it no more:** ... The wind sweeps over him and he is gone, *NAB* ... a wind passes over them, and they cease to be, *NEB* ... its place doth not discern it any more, *Young* ... and his home knows him no longer, *Anchor.*

**17. But the mercy of the LORD is from everlasting to everlasting upon them that fear him, and his righteousness unto children's children:** ... the LORD's love is with those who fear him, *NIV* ... But the louing kindness of the Lord endureth for euer and euer, *Geneva* ... But the kindness of the LORD is from age to age, *Goodspeed* ... But the Lord's worshippers know no beginning or end of his mercy, *Knox.*

**18. To such as keep his covenant, and to those that remember his commandments to do them:** ... to those who keep his agreement and who remember to obey his orders, *NCV* ... as long as they keep his covenant, and carefully obey his precepts, *JB* ... And to those that remember His precepts, *MAST* ... who keep his commandments in mind, *REB.*

**19. The LORD hath prepared his throne in the heavens; and his kingdom ruleth over all:** ... And His sovereignty rules over all, *NASB* ... and as King rules everything, *Beck* ... and his dominion covers all the world, *Moffatt.*

**20. Bless the LORD, ye his angels, that excel in strength, that do his commandments, hearkening unto the voice of his word:** ... That are

---

immeasurable to the homely image of a father's pity. We may lose ourselves amid the amplitudes of the lofty, wide-stretching sky, but this emblem of paternal love goes straight to our hearts. A pitying God! What can be added to that? But that fatherly pity is decisively limited to "them that fear him" (v. 11). It is possible, then, to put oneself outside the range of that abundant dew, and the universality of God's blessings does not hinder self-exclusion from them.

In vv. 14ff man's brief life is brought in, not as a sorrow or as a cloud darkening the sunny joy of the song, but as one reason for the divine compassion. "He, he knoweth our frame." The word rendered "frame" (HED #3444) is literally "formation" or "fashioning" and comes from the same root as the verb employed in Gen. 2:7 to describe man's creation, "the LORD God formed man of the dust of the ground." It is also used for the potter's action in molding earthen vessels (Isa. 29:16; etc.). So, in the next clause, "dust" (HED #6312) carries on the allusion to Genesis, and the general idea conveyed is that of frailty. Made from dust and fragile as an earthen vessel, man by his weakness appeals to Yahweh's compassion. A blow, delivered with the full force of that almighty hand, would "dash them in pieces like a potter's vessel" (Ps. 2:9). Therefore, God handles us tenderly, as mindful of the brittle material with which He has to deal. The familiar figure of fading vegetation so dear to the psalmists recurs here, but it is touched with peculiar delicacy, and there is something very sweet and uncomplaining in the singer's tone. The image of the fading flower, burned up by the dust storm and leaving one little spot in the desert robbed of its beauty, veils much of the terror of death and expresses no shrinking, though great pathos. Verse 16 may either describe the withering of the flower or the passing away of frail man. In the former case, the pronouns would be rendered by "it" and "its"; in the latter, by "he," "him" and "his." The latter seems the preferable explanation, in which v. 16b is verbally the same as Job 7:10. The contemplation of mortality tinges the song with a momentary sadness, which melts into the pensive, yet cheerful, assurance that mortality has an accompanying blessing, in that it makes a plea for pity from a father's heart.

**103:17–18.** But another, more triumphant thought springs up. A devout soul, filled with thankfulness based on faith in God's name and ways, cannot but be led by remembering man's brief life to think of God's eternal years. So the key changes at v. 17 from plaintive minors to jubilant notes. The psalmist pulls out all the stops of his organ, and rolls along his music in a great crescendo to the close. The contrast of God's eternity with man's transitoriness is like the similar trend of thought in Pss. 90; 102. The extension of his steadfast love to children's children and its limitation to those who fear Him and keep his Covenant in obedience rest upon Exo. 20:6; 34:7; Deut. 7:9. That limitation has been laid down twice already (vv. 11ff). All men share in that loving-kindness and receive the best gifts from it of which they are capable, but those who cling to God in loving reverence and who are moved by that blissful "fear" which has no torment to yield their wills to Him in inward submission and outward obedience do enter into the inner recesses of that steadfast love and are replenished with good, of which others are incapable.

**103:19–22.** From v. 19 to the end, the Psalm takes a still wider sweep. It now embraces the universe. But it is noticeable that there is no more about "steadfast love" in these verses. Man's sin and frailty make him a fit recipient of it, but we do not know that in all creation another being, capable of and needing it, is found. Amid starry distances, amid heights and depths, far beyond sunrise and sunset, God's all-including kingdom stretches and blesses all. Therefore, all creatures are called on to bless Him, since all are blessed by Him, each according to its nature and need. If they have consciousness, they owe Him praise. If they have not, they praise Him by being. The angels, "mighty ones of power," as the words literally read, are

| 1745<br>n ms, ps 3ms<br>דְּבָרוֹ<br>devārô<br>his word | 21. | 1313.333<br>v Piel impv 2mp<br>בָּרְכוּ<br>bārekhû<br>bless | 3176<br>pn<br>יְהוָה<br>yehwāh<br>Yahweh | 3725, 6893<br>*adj*, n mp, ps 3ms<br>כָּל־צְבָאָיו<br>kol-tsevā'âv<br>all his hosts | 8664.352<br>v Piel ptc mp, ps 3ms<br>מְשָׁרְתָיו<br>meshārethâv<br>his ministers | 6449.152<br>*v Qal act ptc mp*<br>עֹשֵׂי<br>'ōsê<br>those who do |
|---|---|---|---|---|---|---|

| 7814<br>n ms, ps 3ms<br>רְצוֹנוֹ<br>retsônô<br>his will | 22. | 1313.333<br>v Piel impv 2mp<br>בָּרְכוּ<br>bārekhû<br>bless | 3176<br>pn<br>יְהוָה<br>yehwāh<br>Yahweh | 3725, 4801<br>*adj*, n mp, ps 3ms<br>כָּל־מַעֲשָׂיו<br>kol-ma'ăsâv<br>all his works | 904, 3725, 4887<br>prep, *adj*, *n mp*<br>בְּכָל־מְקֹמוֹת<br>bekhol-meqōmôth<br>in all the places of | 4617<br>n fs, ps 3ms<br>מֶמְשַׁלְתּוֹ<br>memshaltô<br>his dominion |
|---|---|---|---|---|---|---|

| 1313.332<br>v Piel impv 2fs<br>בָּרְכִי<br>bārekhî<br>bless | 5497<br>n fs, ps 1cs<br>נַפְשִׁי<br>naphshî<br>O my soul | 881, 3176<br>do, pn<br>אֶת־יְהוָה<br>'eth-yehwāh<br>Yahweh | 104:1 | 1313.332<br>v Piel impv 2fs<br>בָּרְכִי<br>bārekhî<br>bless | 5497<br>n fs, ps 1cs<br>נַפְשִׁי<br>naphshî<br>O my soul | 881, 3176<br>do, pn<br>אֶת־יְהוָה<br>'eth-yehwāh<br>Yahweh | 3176<br>pn<br>יְהוָה<br>yehwāh<br>O Yahweh |
|---|---|---|---|---|---|---|---|

| 435<br>n mp, ps 1cs<br>אֱלֹהַי<br>'ĕlōhay<br>my God | 1461.113<br>v Qal pf 2ms<br>גָּדַלְתָּ<br>gādhaltā<br>You are great | 4108<br>adv<br>מְאֹד<br>me'ōdh<br>very | 2003<br>n ms<br>הוֹד<br>hôdh<br>majesty | 1994<br>cj, n ms<br>וְהָדָר<br>wehādhār<br>and honor | 3980.113<br>v Qal pf 2ms<br>לָבָשְׁתָּ<br>lāvāshettā<br>You are clothed with |
|---|---|---|---|---|---|

| 2. | 6057.151, 214<br>v Qal act ptc ms, n ms<br>עֹטֶה־אוֹר<br>'ōṭeh-'ôr<br>One Who enwraps himself with light | 3626, 7968<br>prep, art, n fs<br>כַּשַּׂלְמָה<br>kassalmāh<br>like the cloak | 5371.151<br>v Qal act ptc ms<br>נוֹטֶה<br>nôṭeh<br>One Who stretches out | 8452<br>n md<br>שָׁמַיִם<br>shāmayim<br>the heavens |
|---|---|---|---|---|

| 3626, 3523<br>prep, art, n fs<br>כַּיְרִיעָה<br>kayrî'āh<br>like the tent curtain | 3. | 7424.351<br>art, v Piel ptc ms<br>הַמְקָרֶה<br>hamqāreh<br>the One Who causes to meet | 904, 4448<br>prep, art, n md<br>בַמַּיִם<br>vammayim<br>with the waters | 6168<br>n fp, ps 3ms<br>עֲלִיּוֹתָיו<br>'ălîyôthâv<br>his upper rooms |
|---|---|---|---|---|

| 7947.151, 5854<br>art, v Qal act ptc ms, n mp<br>הַשָּׂם־עָבִים<br>hassām-'āvîm<br>the One Who makes clouds | 7687<br>n ms, ps 3ms<br>רְכוּבוֹ<br>rekhûvô<br>his chariot | 2050.351<br>art, v Piel ptc ms<br>הַמְהַלֵּךְ<br>hamhallēkh<br>the One Who walks | 6142, 3796, 7593<br>prep, *n fp*, n fs<br>עַל־כַּנְפֵי־רוּחַ<br>'al-kanphê-rûach<br>upon the wings of the wind |
|---|---|---|---|

| 4. | 6449.151<br>v Qal act ptc ms<br>עֹשֶׂה<br>'ōseh<br>the One Who makes | 4534<br>n mp, ps 3ms<br>מַלְאָכָיו<br>mal'ākhâv<br>his messengers | 7593<br>n fp<br>רוּחוֹת<br>rûchôth<br>the winds | 8664.352<br>v Piel ptc mp, ps 3ms<br>מְשָׁרְתָיו<br>meshārethâv<br>his ministers | 813<br>n fs<br>אֵשׁ<br>'ēsh<br>fire | 3993.151<br>v Qal act ptc ms<br>לֹהֵט<br>lōhēṭ<br>flaming |
|---|---|---|---|---|---|---|

| 5. | 3354.111, 800<br>v Qal pf 3ms, n fs<br>יָסַד־אֶרֶץ<br>yāsadh-'erets<br>He laid the foundation of the earth | 6142, 4487<br>prep, n mp, ps 3fs<br>עַל־מְכוֹנֶיהָ<br>'al-mekhônêāh<br>upon its foundations | 1118, 4267.222<br>neg part, v Niphal impf 3fs<br>בַּל־תִּמּוֹט<br>bal-timmôṭ<br>it will not totter | 5986<br>n ms<br>עוֹלָם<br>'ôlām<br>forever |
|---|---|---|---|---|

| 5911<br>cj, n ms<br>וָעֶד<br>wā'edh<br>even everlasting | 6. | 8745<br>n fs<br>תְּהוֹם<br>tehôm<br>the deep | 3626, 3961<br>prep, art, n ms<br>כַּלְּבוּשׁ<br>kallevûsh<br>like the garment | 3803.313<br>v Piel pf 2ms, ps 3ms<br>כִּסִּיתוֹ<br>kissîthô<br>You covered it | 6142, 2098<br>prep, n mp<br>עַל־הָרִים<br>'al-hārîm<br>on the mountains |
|---|---|---|---|---|---|

mighty in strength, *ASV* ... that execute his word, *Darby* ... That fulfil his word, *MRB* ... who do his bidding, obeying his spoken word, *NCB.*

**21. Bless ye the LORD, all ye his hosts; ye ministers of his, that do his pleasure:** ... Bless the LORD, all you His armies, *Berkeley* ... All you, His warriors, bless Him, *Fenton* ... You who serve Him, doing His will, *NASB* ... ministers who carry out his will!, *Goodspeed.*

**22. Bless the LORD, all his works in all places of his dominion: bless the LORD, O my soul:** ... Bless the Lord, all his works, everywhere in his domain, *NCB* ... Bless the LORD, all created things, *REB* ... in all places under his rule, *BB.*

**104:1. Bless the LORD, O my soul. O LORD my God, thou art very great; thou art clothed with honour and majesty:** ... My whole being, praise the LORD, *NCV* ... Honour and majesty Thou hast put on, *Young* ... Glory and beauty are thy clothing, *Knox* ... You dress in majesty and splendor, *Beck.*

**2. Who coverest thyself with light as with a garment: who stretchest out the heavens like a curtain:** ... Who is robed with the sun, *Anchor* ... wearing the light as a robe!, *JB* ... out the heavens like a tent, *NRSV.*

**3. Who layeth the beams of his chambers in the waters: who maketh the clouds his chariot: who walketh upon the wings of the wind:** ... He lays the beams of His upper rooms in the waters, *KJVII* ... you have constructed your palace upon the waters, *NAB* ... Building in the waters his upper chambers, *Rotherham.*

**4. Who maketh his angels spirits; his ministers a flaming fire:** ... Who makest winds Thy messengers, *MAST* ... fire and flame thy ministers, *RSV* ... His Couriers are the storms! His Agents flames of fire!, *Fenton* ... and flames of fire thy servants, *NEB.*

**5. Who laid the foundations of the earth, that it should not be removed for ever:** ... He hath fixed the earth on its foundations, *Rotherham* ... The earth thou hast planted on its own firm base, undisturbed for all time, *Knox* ...

---

"his," and they not only execute his behests, but stand attent before Him, listening to catch the first whispered indication of his will. "His hosts" are taken by some to mean the stars, but surely it is more congruous to suppose that beings who are his "ministers" and perform his "pleasure" are intelligent beings. Their praise consists in hearkening to and doing his word. But obedience is not all their praise, for they, too, bring Him tribute of conscious adoration in more melodious music than ever sounded on earth. That invisible choir praises the King of heaven, but later revelation has taught us that men shall teach a new song to "principalities and powers in heavenly places," because men only can praise Him whose steadfast love to them, sinful and dying, redeemed them by his blood.

**104:1–4.** Verse 1 would be normal in structure if the initial invocation were omitted, and as v. 35 would also be complete without it, the suggestion that it is, in both verses, a liturgical addition is plausible. The verse sums up the whole of the creative act in one grand thought. In that act, the invisible God has arrayed himself in splendor and glory, making visible these inherent attributes. That is the deepest meaning of creation. The universe is the garment of God.

This general idea lays the foundation for the following picture of the process of creation which is colored by reminiscences of Genesis. Here, as there, light is the first-born of heaven, but the influence of the preceding thought shapes the language, and light is regarded as God's vesture. The uncreated light, who is darkness to our eyes, arrays himself in created light, which reveals while it veils Him. Everywhere diffused, all-penetrating, all-gladdening, it tells of the presence in which all creatures live. This clause is the poetic rendering of the work of the first creative day. The next clause in like manner deals with that of the second. The mighty arch of heaven is lifted and expanded over earth, as easily as a man draws the cloth or skin sides and canopy of his circular tent over its framework. But our roof is his floor, and according to Genesis the firmament (literally, "expanse") separates the waters above from those beneath. So the Psalm pictures the divine Architect as laying the beams of his upper chambers (for so the word means) in these waters, above the tent roof. The fluid is solid at his will, and the most mobile becomes fixed enough to be the foundation of his royal abode. The custom of having chambers on the roof, for privacy and freshness, suggests the image.

**104:5.** In these introductory verses, the poet is dealing with the grander instances of creative power, especially as realized in the heavens. Not until v. 5 does he drop to earth. His first theme is God's dominion over the elemental forces, and so he goes on to represent the clouds as his chariot, the wind as bearing Him on its swift pinions, and, as the parallelism requires, the winds as his messengers, and devouring fire as his servants. The rendering of v. 4

6198.126, 4448 | v Qal impf 3mp, n mp | יַעַמְדוּ־מָיִם | ya'amdhû-māyim | the waters stood

7.

4623, 1648 | prep, n fs, ps 2ms | מִן־גַּעֲרָתְךָ | min-ga'ărāthᵉkhā | from your rebuke

5308.126 | v Qal impf 3mp | יְנוּסוּן | yᵉnûsûn | they fled

4623, 7249 | prep, *n ms* | מִן־קוֹל | min-qôl | from the sound of

7770 | n ms, ps 2ms | רַעַמְךָ | ra'amkhā | your thundering

---

2753.226 | v Niphal impf 3mp | יֵחָפֵזוּן | yēchāphēzûn | they hurried away

8.

6148.126 | v Qal impf 3mp | יַעֲלוּ | ya'ălû | they went up

2098 | n mp | הָרִים | hārîm | the mountains

3495.126 | v Qal impf 3mp | יֵרְדוּ | yērᵉdhû | they went down

1262 | n fp | בְקָעוֹת | vᵉqā'ôth | the valleys

420, 4887 | prep, *n ms* | אֶל־מְקוֹם | 'el-mᵉqôm | to the place

---

2172 | dem pron | זֶה | zeh | this

3354.113 | v Qal pf 2ms | יָסַדְתָּ | yāsadhtā | You allocated

3937 | prep, ps 3mp | לָהֶם | lāhem | for them

9.

1397, 7947.113 | n ms, v Qal pf 2ms | גְּבוּל־שַׂמְתָּ | gᵉvûl-samtā | You set a boundary

1118, 5882.126 | neg part, v Qal impf 3mp | בַּל־יַעֲבֹרוּן | bal-ya'ăvōrûn | they will not pass by

---

1118, 8178.126 | neg part, v Qal impf 3mp | בַּל־יְשׁוּבוּן | bal-yᵉshûvûn | they will not return

3937, 3803.341 | prep, v Piel inf con | לְכַסּוֹת | lᵉkhassôth | to cover

800 | art, n fs | הָאָרֶץ | hā'ārets | the earth

10.

8365.351 | art, v Piel ptc ms | הַמְשַׁלֵּחַ | hamshallēach | the One Who sends out

4754 | n mp | מַעְיָנִים | ma'yānîm | springs

---

904, 5337 | prep, art, n mp | בַּנְּחָלִים | bannᵉchālîm | in the valleys

1033 | prep | בֵּין | bên | between

2098 | n mp | הָרִים | hārîm | the mountains

2050.326 | v Piel impf 3mp | יְהַלֵּכוּן | yᵉhallēkhûn | they proceed

11.

8615.526 | v Hiphil impf 3mp | יַשְׁקוּ | yashqû | they give drink to

3725, 2516 | *adj*, n fs, ps 3ms | כָּל־חַיְתוֹ | kol-chaythô | all his animals

---

7899 | n ms | שָׂדָי | sādhāy | the field

8132.126 | v Qal impf 3mp | יִשְׁבְּרוּ | yishbᵉrû | they break

6751 | n mp | פְרָאִים | phᵉrā'îm | wild donkeys

7040 | n ms, ps 3mp | צְמָאָם | tsᵉmā'ām | their thirst

12.

6142 | prep, ps 3mp | עֲלֵיהֶם | 'ălêhem | beside them

5991, 8452 | *n ms*, art, n md | עוֹף־הַשָּׁמַיִם | 'ôph-hashshāmayim | the birds of the air

---

8331.121 | v Qal impf 3ms | יִשְׁכּוֹן | yishkôn | they stay

4623, 1033 | prep, prep | מִבֵּין | mibbên | from between

6304 | n mp | עֳפָאיִם | 'ăpho'yim | thick foliage

5598.126, 7249 | v Qal impf 3mp, n ms | יִתְּנוּ־קוֹל | yittᵉnû-qôl | they give a sound

13.

8615.551 | v Hiphil ptc ms | מַשְׁקֶה | mashqeh | the One Who causes to drink

---

2098 | n mp | הָרִים | hārîm | the mountains

4623, 6168 | prep, n fp, ps 3ms | מֵעֲלִיּוֹתָיו | mē'ălîyôthâv | from his upper room

4623, 6780 | prep, *n ms* | מִפְּרִי | mippᵉrî | from the fruit of

4801 | n mp, ps 2ms | מַעֲשֶׂיךָ | ma'ăsêkhā | your works

7881.122 | v Qal impf 3fs | תִּשְׂבַּע | tisba' | it is satiated

800 | art, n fs | הָאָרֶץ | hā'ārets | the earth

---

14.

7048.551 | v Hiphil ptc ms | מַצְמִיחַ | matsmîach | the One Who causes to sprout

2785 | n ms | חָצִיר | chātsîr | grass

3937, 966 | prep, art, n fs | לַבְּהֵמָה | labbᵉhēmāh | for the livestock

6448 | cj, n ms | וְעֵשֶׂב | wᵉ'ēsev | and herbs

3937, 5865 | prep, *n fs* | לַעֲבֹדַת | la'ăvōdhath | for the labor of

---

119 | art, n ms | הָאָדָם | hā'ādhām | the humankind

3937, 3428.541 | prep, v Hiphil inf con | לְהוֹצִיא | lᵉhôtsî' | to bring out

4035 | n ms | לֶחֶם | lechem | food

4623, 800 | prep, art, n fs | מִן־הָאָרֶץ | min-hā'ārets | from the earth

15.

3302 | cj, n ms | וְיַיִן | wᵉyayin | and wine

7975.321 | v Piel impf 3ms | יְשַׂמַּח | yᵉsammach | it makes glad

So that it will not totter forever and ever, *NASB*.

**6. Thou coveredst it with the deep as with a garment: the waters stood above the mountains:** ... Covering it with the sea as with a robe, *BB* ... with the ocean, as with a garment, you covered it, *NCB* ... The abyss! as with clothing Thou hast covered it, *Young* ... drawing the deep over it, till the waters stood above the mountains, *Moffatt*.

**7. At thy rebuke they fled; at the voice of thy thunder they hasted away:** ... At your roar they fled, *Anchor* ... which surged in retreat at Thy rebuke, at Thy thunderous command swirled away, *Berkeley* ... at the sound of your thunder they took to flight, *NAB* ... At the sound of thy thunder they fled in terror, *Goodspeed*.

**8. They go up by the mountains; they go down by the valleys unto the place which thou hast founded for them:** ... And the mountaines ascend, and the valleys descend to the place, *Geneva* ... The mountains rose, the valleys sank, *Darby* ... they flowed over the mountains, they went down into the valleys, to the place you assigned for them, *NIV*.

**9. Thou hast set a bound that they may not pass over; that they turn not again to cover the earth:** ... You set a boundary they cannot cross, *NIV* ... You set borders for the seas that they cannot cross, *NCV* ... That they might not return to cover the earth, *MAST* ... Or turn again to hide the land, *Fenton*.

**10. He sendeth the springs into the valleys, which run among the hills** ... He pours the streams into the valleys, *Moffatt* ... In the ravines you opened up springs, running down between the mountains, *JB* ... Yet there shall be torrents flooding the glens, watercourses among the hills, *Knox*.

**11. They give drink to every beast of the field: the wild asses quench their thirst:** ... They furnish drink for all the beasts of the field, *Goodspeed* ... The wild beasts all drink from them, *NEB*.

**12. By them shall the fowls of the heaven have their habitation, which sing among the branches:** ... The birds of the air nest beside them, *Berkeley* ... Beside them the birds of the heavens dwell, *NASB* ... The birds of heaven dwell by them; they give forth their voice from among the branches, *Darby* ... From amidst the foliage they utter a voice, *Rotherham*.

**13. He watereth the hills from his chambers: the earth is satisfied with the fruit of thy works:** ... He sends down rain from his storehouses on the hills, *BB* ... You water the mountains from your palace, *NCB* ... the earth is replete with the fruit of your works, *NAB*.

**14. He causeth the grass to grow for the cattle, and herb for the service of man: that he may bring forth food out of the earth:** ... and plants for people to use, *NRSV* ... And vegetation for the service of man, *NKJV* ... fruits and vegetables for man to cultivate, *Berkeley* ... bringing bread out of the earth, *NEB*.

**15. And wine that maketh glad the heart of man, and oil to make his face to shine, and bread which strengtheneth man's heart:** ... Making radiant his well-nourished face, *Rotherham* ... Making the face brighter than oil, *MAST* ... and bread which makes a man's heart strong, *KJVII*.

---

adopted in Hebrews from the Septuagint is less relevant to the psalmist's purpose of gathering all the forces which sweep through the wide heavens into one company of obedient servants of God than that adopted above and now generally recognized. It is to be observed that the verbs in vv. 2ff are participles, which express continuous action. These creative acts were not done once for all, but are going on still and always. Preservation is continued in creation.

**104:6–9.** With v. 6, we pass to the work of the third of the Genesis days, and the verb is in the form which describes a historical fact. The earth is conceived of as formed, and already molded into mountains and valleys, but all covered with "the deep" (HED #8745) like a vesture—a sadly different one from the robe of light which He wears. That weltering deep is bidden back to its future appointed bounds, and the process is grandly described, as if the waters were sentient and, panic-stricken at God's voice, took to flight. Verse 8a throws in a vivid touch, to the disturbance of grammatical smoothness. The poet has the scene before his eye, and as the waters flee he sees the earth emerging, the mountains soaring, and the vales sinking, and he breaks his sentence, as if in wonder at the lovely apparition, but returns, in v. 8b, to tell to what place the fugitive waters fled—namely, to the ocean depths. There they are hemmed in by God's will and, as was promised to Noah, shall not again run wasting over a drowned world.

**104:10–18.** The picture of the emerging earth, with its variations of valleys and mountains, remains before the psalmist's eye throughout vv. 10–18, which describe how it is clothed and peopled. These effects are due to the beneficent ministry of the same element, when guided and restrained by God, which swathed the world with desolation. Water runs through the vales, and rain

| 3949, 596 | 3937, 6934.541 | 6686 | 4623, 8467 | 4035 | 3949, 596 |
|---|---|---|---|---|---|
| *n ms*, n ms | prep, v Hiphil inf con | n mp | prep, n ms | cj, n ms | *n ms*, n ms |
| לְבַב־אֱנוֹשׁ | לְהַצְהִיל | פָּנִים | מִשָּׁמֶן | וְלֶחֶם | לְבַב־אֱנוֹשׁ |
| levav-'ĕnôsh | lehatshîl | pānîm | mishshāmen | welechem | levav-'ĕnôsh |
| the heart of men | to cause to shine | the face | from olive oil | and food | the heart of men |

| 5777.121 | | 7881.126 | 6320 | 3176 | 753 | 3976 | 866 |
|---|---|---|---|---|---|---|---|
| v Qal impf 3ms | **16.** | v Qal impf 3mp | *n mp* | pn | *n mp* | pn | rel part |
| יִסְעָד | | יִשְׂבְּעוּ | עֲצֵי | יְהוָה | אַרְזֵי | לְבָנוֹן | אֲשֶׁר |
| yis'ādh | | yisbe'û | 'ătsê | yehwāh | 'arzê | levānôn | 'ăsher |
| it sustains | | they are satisfied | the trees of | Yahweh | the cedars of | Lebanon | which |

| 5378.111 | | 866, 8427 | 7109 | 7361.326 | 2729 | 1293 |
|---|---|---|---|---|---|---|
| v Qal pf 3ms | **17.** | rel part, adv | n mp | v Piel impf 3mp | n fs | n mp |
| נָטָע | | אֲשֶׁר־שָׁם | צִפֳּרִים | יְקַנֵּנוּ | חֲסִידָה | בְּרוֹשִׁים |
| nāṭā' | | 'ăsher-shām | tsipperîm | yeqannēnû | chăsîdhāh | berôshîm |
| He has planted | | which there | the birds | they make a nest | the stork | in the juniper trees |

| 1041 | | 2098 | 1393 | 3937, 3386 | 5748 | 4406 |
|---|---|---|---|---|---|---|
| n ms, ps 3fs | **18.** | n mp | art, adj | prep, art, n mp | n mp | n ms |
| בֵּיתָהּ | | הָרִים | הַגְּבֹהִים | לַיְּעֵלִים | סְלָעִים | מַחְסֶה |
| bêthāhh | | hārîm | haggevōhîm | layye'ēlîm | selā'îm | machseh |
| her house | | the mountains | the high | for the wild goats | the rocks | a hiding place |

| 3937, 8596 | | 6449.111 | 3507 | 3937, 4287 | 8507 | 3156.111 |
|---|---|---|---|---|---|---|
| prep, art, n mp | **19.** | v Qal pf 3ms | n ms | prep, n mp | n ms | v Qal pf 3ms |
| לַשְׁפַנִּים | | עָשָׂה | יָרֵחַ | לְמוֹעֲדִים | שֶׁמֶשׁ | יָדַע |
| lashphanîm | | 'āsāh | yārēach | lemô'ădhîm | shemesh | yādha' |
| for the coneys | | He made | the moon | for appointed times | the sun | He knows |

| 4136 | | 8308.123, 2932 | 2030.121 | 4050 | 904, 7718.122 |
|---|---|---|---|---|---|
| n ms, ps 3ms | **20.** | v Qal impf 2ms, n ms | cj, v Qal impf 3ms | n ms | prep, ps 3ms, v Qal impf 3fs |
| מְבוֹאוֹ | | תָּשֶׁת־חֹשֶׁךְ | וַיְהִי | לַיְלָה | בּוֹ־תִרְמֹשׂ |
| mevô'ô | | tāsheth-chōshekh | wîhî | lāyelāh | bô-thirmōs |
| its going | | You make into darkness | and it is | night | during it they creep |

| 3725, 2516, 3402 | | 3841 | 8057.152 | 3937, 3073 | 3937, 1272.341 |
|---|---|---|---|---|---|
| *adj*, n fs, n ms | **21.** | art, n mp | v Qal act ptc mp | prep, art, n ms | cj, prep, v Piel inf con |
| כָּל־חַיְתוֹ־יָעַר | | הַכְּפִירִים | שֹׁאֲגִים | לַטָּרֶף | וּלְבַקֵּשׁ |
| kol-chaythô-yā'ar | | hakkephîrîm | shō'ăghîm | laṭṭāreph | ûlăvaqqēsh |
| all his animals the forest | | the young lions | roaring | about the prey | and seeking |

| 4623, 418 | 406 | | 2311.122 | 8507 | 636.226 | 420, 4881 |
|---|---|---|---|---|---|---|
| prep, n ms | n ms, ps 3mp | **22.** | v Qal impf 3fs | art, n ms | v Niphal impf 3mp | cj, prep, n fp, ps 3mp |
| מֵאֵל | אָכְלָם | | תִּזְרַח | הַשֶּׁמֶשׁ | יֵאָסֵפוּן | וְאֶל־מְעוֹנֹתָם |
| mē'ēl | 'ākhelām | | tizrach | hashshemesh | yē'āsēphûn | we'el-me'ônōthām |
| from God | their food | | it rises | the sun | they are gathered | and to their dens |

| 7547.126 | | 3428.121 | 119 | 3937, 6714 | 3937, 5865 | 5912, 6394 |
|---|---|---|---|---|---|---|
| v Qal impf 3mp | **23.** | v Qal impf 3ms | n ms | prep, n ms, ps 3ms | cj, prep, n fs, ps 3ms | adv, n ms |
| יִרְבָּצוּן | | יֵצֵא | אָדָם | לְפָעֳלוֹ | וְלַעֲבֹדָתוֹ | עֲדֵי־עָרֶב |
| yirbātsûn | | yētsē' | 'ādhām | lephā'ălô | wela'ăvōdhāthô | 'ădhê-'ārev |
| they lie down | | he goes out | a man | to his work | and to his labor | until evening |

| | 4242, 7525.116 | 4801 | 3176 | 3725 | 904, 2551 | 6449.113 |
|---|---|---|---|---|---|---|
| **24.** | intrg, v Qal pf 3cp | n mp, ps 2ms | pn | adj, ps 3mp | prep, n fs | v Qal pf 2ms |
| | מָה־רַבּוּ | מַעֲשֶׂיךָ | יְהוָה | כֻּלָּם | בְּחָכְמָה | עָשִׂיתָ |
| | māh-rabbû | ma'ăsêkhā | yehwāh | kullām | bechokhmāh | 'āsîthā |
| | how numerous are they | your works | O Yahweh | all of them | in wisdom | You have **done** |

**16. The trees of the LORD are full of sap; the cedars of Lebanon, which he hath planted:** ... The trees of the LORD have their fill, *Goodspeed* ... The high trees are satisfied, *Geneva* ... The trees of the LORD flourish, *REB* ... are filled with moisture, *ASV.*

**17. Where the birds make their nests: as for the stork, the fir trees are her house:** ... Where the birds have their resting-places; as for the stork, the tall trees are her house, *BB* ... on the highest branches the stork makes its home, *JB* ... the stork with her home in the cypress, *Moffatt* ... the stork makes her home in their tops, *NEB.*

**18. The high hills are a refuge for the wild goats; and the rocks for the conies:** ... The high mountains are for the wild goats, *Beck* ... the rocks are a refuge for the badgers, *RSV* ... The rocks are hiding places for the badgers, *NCV* ... the sheltering crags to the badgers, *Anchor.*

**19. He appointed the moon for seasons: the sun knoweth his going down:** ... He made the moon for the seasons, *NASB* ... The moon marks off the seasons, *NIV* ... He fixed the Moon her times, The Sun taught when to set, *Fenton.*

**20. Thou makest darkness, and it is night: wherein all the beasts of the forest do creep forth:** ... Thou settest darkness, *Young* ... Thou makest darkness settle down, so that during the night all forest animals may roam about, *Berkeley* ... all the beasts of the forest roam about, *NAB* ... when all the animals of the forest come creeping out, *NRSV.*

**21. The young lions roar after their prey, and seek their meat from God:** ... The young lions go thundering after their food, *BB* ... asking for their food, *Knox* ... seeking their food from God, *REB.*

**22. The sun ariseth, they gather themselves together, and lay them down in their dens:** ... The sun rises, and they steal away, *NIV* ... The sun ariseth, they get them away, *MRB* ... When the sun rises, they withdraw and couch in their dens, *NCB* ... they are gathered and lie down together in their dens, *KJVII.*

**23. Man goeth forth unto his work and to his labour until the evening:**

---

falls on the mountains. Therefore, the former bear herbs and corn, vines and olives, and the latter are clothed with trees not planted by human hand, the mighty cedars which spread their broad shelves of steadfast green high up among the clouds. Around the drinking places in the vales, thirsty creatures gather and birds flit and sing. Among the cedars, there are peaceful nests, and inaccessible cliffs have their sure-footed inhabitants. All depend on water, and water is God's gift. The psalmist's view of nature is characteristic in the direct ascription of all its processes to God. He makes the springs flow and sends rain on the peaks. Equally characteristic is the absence of any expression of a sense of beauty in the sparkling streams tinkling down the gloomy wadies, or in the rainstorms darkening the hills or in the green mantle of earth or in the bright creatures. The psalmist is thinking of use, not of beauty. The stork is on her nest, the goats on the mountains and the coney hurrying to their holes in the cliffs. Man appears as depending, like the lower creatures, on the fruit of the ground, but he has more varied supplies: bread and wine and oil. These not only satisfy material wants, but "gladden" and "strengthen" the heart. According to some, the word rendered "labor" (HED #5865) in v. 14 means "tillage," a meaning which is supported by v. 23, where the word is also rendered "labor," and which fits in well with the next clause of v. 14, "bring forth food out of the earth," which would describe the purpose of the tillage. His prerogative of labor is man's special characteristic in creation. It is a token of his superiority to the happy, careless creatures who toil not nor spin. Earth does not yield him its best products without his cooperation. There would thus be an allusion to him as the only worker in creation, similar to that in v. 23, and to the reference to the "ships" in v. 26. But the meaning of "tillage," is not suggested by the parallelism and does not introduce the new thought of cooperation with nature or God. Therefore, "labor" is to be preferred. The construction is somewhat difficult, but the rendering of "labor" seems best. The two clauses with infinitive verbs ("to bring forth" and "to cause to shine") are each followed by a clause in which the construction is varied into that with a finite verb, the meaning remaining the same, and all four clauses express the divine purpose in causing vegetation to spring. Then the psalmist looks up once more to the hills. "The trees of the LORD" are so called, not so much because they are great, but because, unlike vines and olives, they have not been planted or tended by man, nor do they belong to him. Far above the valleys, where men and the cattle dependent on him live on earth's cultivated bounties, the unowned woods stand and drink God's gift of rain, while wild creatures lead free lives amid mountains and rocks.

**104:19–23.** With v. 19, the psalmist passes to the fourth day, but thinks of moon and sun only in relation to the alternation of day and night as affect-

| 4527.112 | 800 | 7359 | 25. | 2172 | 3328 | 1448 | 7622 | 3135 |
|---|---|---|---|---|---|---|---|---|
| v Qal pf 3fs | art, n fs | n ms, ps 2ms | | dem pron | art, n ms | adj | cj, *adj* | n fd |
| מָלְאָה | הָאָרֶץ | קִנְיָנֶךָ | | זֶה | הַיָּם | גָּדוֹל | וּרְחַב | יָדָיִם |
| māle'āh | hā'ārets | qinyānekhā | | zeh | hayyām | gādhôl | ûrechav | yādhayim |
| it is full of | the earth | your acquisitions | | this | the sea | great | and wide of | hands |

| 8427, 7719 | 375 | 4709 | 2516 | 7278 | 6196, 1448 |
|---|---|---|---|---|---|
| adv, n ms | cj, *sub* | n ms | n fp | adj | prep, adj |
| שָׁם־רֶמֶשׂ | וְאֵין | מִסְפָּר | חַיּוֹת | קְטַנּוֹת | עִם־גְּדֹלוֹת |
| shām-remes | we'ên | mispār | chayyôth | qōṯannôth | 'im-gedhōlôth |
| there teeming creatures | and there is not | a number | living creatures | small | with large |

| 26. | 8427 | 605 | 2050.326 | 4018 | 2172, 3443.113 | 3937, 7925.341, 904 |
|---|---|---|---|---|---|---|
| | adv | n fp | v Piel impf 3mp | n ms | dem pron, v Qal pf 2ms | prep, v Piel inf con, prep, ps 3ms |
| | שָׁם | אֳנִיּוֹת | יְהַלֵּכוּן | לִוְיָתָן | זֶה־יָצַרְתָּ | לְשַׂחֶק־בּוֹ |
| | shām | 'ănîyôth | yehallēkhûn | liwyāthān | zeh-yātsartā | lesacheq-bô |
| | there | ships | they proceed | leviathan | this You formed | to laugh about it |

| 27. | 3725 | 420 | 7887.326 | 3937, 5598.141 | 406 | 904, 6496 |
|---|---|---|---|---|---|---|
| | adj, ps 3mp | prep, ps 2ms | v Piel impf 3mp | prep, v Qal inf con | n ms, ps 3mp | prep, n fs, ps 3ms |
| | כֻּלָּם | אֵלֶיךָ | יְשַׂבֵּרוּן | לָתֵת | אָכְלָם | בְּעִתּוֹ |
| | kullām | 'ēlêkhā | yesabbērûn | lāthēth | 'ākhelām | be'ittô |
| | all of them | to You | they wait | to give | their food | in its season |

| 28. | 5598.123 | 3937 | 4092.126 | 6858.123 | 3135 | 7881.126 |
|---|---|---|---|---|---|---|
| | v Qal impf 2ms | prep, ps 3mp | v Qal impf 3mp | v Qal impf 2ms | n fs, ps 2ms | v Qal impf 3mp |
| | תִּתֵּן | לָהֶם | יִלְקֹטוּן | תִּפְתַּח | יָדְךָ | יִשְׂבְּעוּן |
| | tittēn | lāhem | yilqōṯûn | tiphtach | yādhekhā | yisbe'ûn |
| | You give | to them | they gather | You open | your hand | they are satiated with |

| 3008 | 29. | 5846.523 | 6686 | 1009.226 | 636.123 | 7593 |
|---|---|---|---|---|---|---|
| n ms | | v Hiphil impf 2ms | n mp, ps 2ms | v Niphal impf 3mp | v Qal impf 2ms | n fs, ps 3mp |
| טוֹב | | תַּסְתִּיר | פָּנֶיךָ | יִבָּהֵלוּן | תֹּסֵף | רוּחָם |
| ṯôv | | tasṯîr | pānêkhā | yibbāhēlûn | tōsēph | rûchām |
| good things | | You hide | your face | they are dismayed | You gather | their life |

| 1510.126 | 420, 6312 | 8178.126 | 30. | 8365.323 | 7593 | 1282.226 |
|---|---|---|---|---|---|---|
| v Qal impf 3mp | cj, prep, n ms, ps 3mp | v Qal impf 3mp | | v Piel impf 2ms | n fs, ps 2ms | v Niphal impf 3mp |
| יִגְוָעוּן | וְאֶל־עֲפָרָם | יְשׁוּבוּן | | תְּשַׁלַּח | רוּחֲךָ | יִבָּרֵאוּן |
| yighwā'ûn | we'el-'ăphārām | yeshûvûn | | teshallach | rûchăkhā | yibbārē'ûn |
| they die | and to their dust | they return | | You send out | your Spirit | they are created |

... but man comes out to his work, *NEB* ... while man goes abroad to toil and drudge till the evening, *Knox* ... Then people go to work and work until evening, *NCV.*

**24. O LORD, how manifold are thy works! in wisdom hast thou made them all: the earth is full of thy riches:** ... how many are the things You made, You made them all by wisdom, *Beck* ... The earth is full of Thy possessions, *NASB* ... Full is the earth of thy possessions, *Young* ... There is nothing on earth but gives proof of thy creative power, *Knox.*

**25. So is this great and wide sea, wherein are things creeping innumerable, both small and great beasts:** ... in which are schools without number of living things, *NCB* ... Here is the vast immeasurable sea, in which move crawling things beyond number, *REB* ... In which are innumerable teeming things, Living things both small and great, *NKJV* ... in it are swarms too many to number, creatures tiny and large, *Berkeley.*

**26. There go the ships: there is that leviathan, whom thou hast made to play therein:** ... And where ships move about with Leviathan, which you formed to make sport of it, *NAB* ... leviathan, whom thou hast formed to take his pastime therein, *MRB* ... This sea-monster thou hast formed to sport therein, *Rotherham* ... The crocodile whom thou didst form to frolic therein, *Goodspeed.*

**27. These wait all upon thee; that thou mayest give them their meat in due season:** ... They all depend upon you, to feed them when they need it, *JB* ... All these rely on You, To give them daily food!, *Fenton* ... These all look to thee, to give them their food, *RSV* ... to give them their food at the proper time, *NEB*.

**28. That thou givest them they gather: thou openest thine hand, they are filled with good:** ... They take what you give them; they are full of the good things which come from your open hand, *BB* ... feasting from thine open hand, *Moffatt* ... when you open your hand, they are satisfied with good things, *NIV*.

**29. Thou hidest thy face, they are troubled: thou takest away their breath, they die, and return to their dust:** ... hide your face, they are dismayed, *NRSV* ... When you turn away from them, they become frightened, *NCV* ... Thou hidest Thy face, they vanish; Thou withdrawest their breath, they perish, *MAST* ... Take back your spirit, they die, and return to their clay, *Anchor*.

**30. Thou sendest forth thy spirit, they are created: and thou renewest the face of the earth:** ... sendest forth thy spirit, and there is fresh creation, *Knox* ... Send out your breath and life begins, *JB* ... renewest the face of the ground, *ASV*.

**31. The glory of the LORD shall endure for ever: the LORD shall rejoice in his works:** ... For ever may the glorious might of the Eternal

---

ing creatural life on earth. The moon is named first, because the Hebrew day began with the evening. It is the measurer by whose phases seasons (or, according to some, "festivals") are reckoned. The sun is a punctual servant, knowing the hour to set and duly keeping it. "Thou makest darkness, and it is night." God wills, and his will effects material changes. He says to his servant, night, "Come," and she comes. The psalmist had peopled the vales and mountains of his picture. Everywhere he had seen life fitted to its environment, and night is populous too. He had outlined swift sketches of tame and wild creatures, and now he half shows us beasts of prey stealing through the gloom. He puts his finger on two characteristics—their stealthy motions and their cries that made night hideous. Even their roar was a kind of prayer, although they did not know it was God from Whom they sought their food. The poet desired to show how there were creatures that found possibilities of happy life in all the variety of conditions fashioned by the creative Hand, which was thus shown to be moved by wisdom and love. The sunrise sends these nocturnal animals back to their dens, and the world is ready for man. "The sun ariseth," and the beasts of prey slunk to their lairs, and man's day of toil began—the mark of his pre-eminence, God's gift for his good, by which he uses creation for its highest end and fulfills God's purpose. Grateful is the evening rest when the day has been filled with strenuous toil.

**104:24.** The picture of earth and its inhabitants is now complete, and the dominant thought which it leaves on the psalmist's heart is cast into the exultant and wondering exclamation of v. 24. The variety as well as multitude of the forms in which God's creative idea is embodied, the wisdom which shapes all, his ownership of all, are the impressions made by the devout contemplation of nature. The scientist and the artist are left free to pursue their respective lines of investigation and impression, but scientist and artist must rise to the psalmist's point of view, if they are to learn the deepest lesson from the ordered kingdoms of nature and from the beauty which floods the world.

**104:25–26.** With the exclamation in v. 24, the psalmist has finished his picture of the earth, which he had seen as if emerging from the abyss and watched as it was gradually clothed with fertility and peopled with happy life. He turns, in vv. 25f, to the other half of his vision of creation and portrays the gathered and curbed waters which he now calls the "sea." As always in Scripture, it is described as it looks to a landsman, gazing out on it from the safe shore. The characteristics specified betray unfamiliarity with maritime pursuits. The psalmist is struck by the far-stretching roll of the waters out to the horizon, the mystery veiling the strange lives swarming in its depths and the extreme contrasts in the magnitude of its inhabitants. He sees the stately ships sail. The introduction of these into the picture is unexpected. We should have looked for an instance of the "small" creatures, to pair off with the great one, leviathan, in the next words.

**104:27–30.** Verses 27–30 mass all creatures of earth and sea, including man, as being dependent on God for sustenance and for life. Dumbly, these look expectant to Him, although man only knows to whom all living eyes are directed. The swift clauses in vv. 28ff, without connecting particles, vividly represent the divine acts as immediately followed by the creatural consequences. To this psalmist, the links in the chain were of little consequence. His thoughts were fixed on its two ends—the hand that sent its power thrilling through the links and the result realized in the creature's life. All natural phenomena are issues of God's present will. Preservation is as much his act, as inexplicable without Him, as creation. There would be nothing to "gather" unless He "gave." All sorts of supplies,

| 2412.323 | 6686 | 124 | | 2030.121 | 3638 | 3176 | 3937, 5986 |
|---|---|---|---|---|---|---|---|
| cj, v Piel impf 2ms | *n mp* | n fs | **31.** | v Qal juss 3ms | *n ms* | pn | prep, n ms |
| וּתְחַדֵּשׁ | פְּנֵי | אֲדָמָה | | יְהִי | כְבוֹד | יְהוָה | לְעוֹלָם |
| ûthechaddēsh | penê | 'ădhāmāh | | yehî | khevôdh | yehwāh | le'ôlām |
| You renew | the surface of | the ground | | may it be | the glory of | Yahweh | unto eternity |

| 7975.121 | 3176 | 904, 4801 | | 5202.551 | 3937, 800 |
|---|---|---|---|---|---|
| v Qal juss 3ms | pn | prep, n mp, ps 3ms | **32.** | art, v Hiphil ptc ms | prep, art, n fs |
| יִשְׂמַח | יְהוָה | בְּמַעֲשָׂיו | | הַמַּבִּיט | לָאָרֶץ |
| yismach | yehwāh | bema'ăsâv | | hammabbîṯ | lā'ārets |
| may he be glad | Yahweh | because of his works | | the One Who looks down | to the earth |

| 7746.122 | 5236.121 | 904, 2098 | 6475.126 | | 8301.125 | 3937, 3176 |
|---|---|---|---|---|---|---|
| cj, v Qal impf 3fs | v Qal impf 3ms | prep, art, n mp | cj, v Qal impf 3mp | **33.** | v Qal juss 1cs | prep, pn |
| וַתִּרְעָד | יִגַּע | בֶּהָרִים | וְיֶעֱשָׁנוּ | | אָשִׁירָה | לַיהוָה |
| wattir'ādh | yigga' | behārîm | weye'ĕshānû | | 'āshîrāh | layhwāh |
| and it trembles | He touches | on the mountains | and they smoke | | let me sing | to Yahweh |

| 904, 2522 | 2252.325 | 3937, 435 | 904, 5968 |
|---|---|---|---|
| prep, n mp, ps 1cs | v Piel juss 1cs | prep, n mp, ps 1cs | prep, adv, ps, 1cs |
| בְּחַיָּי | אֲזַמְּרָה | לֵאלֹהַי | בְּעוֹדִי |
| bechayyāy | 'ăzammerāh | lē'lōhay | be'ôdhî |
| during my lifetime | let me sing praises | to my God | during my continuing |

| | 6386.121 | 6142 | 7945 | 609 | 7975.125 | 904, 3176 |
|---|---|---|---|---|---|---|
| **34.** | v Qal juss 3ms | prep, ps 3ms | n ms, ps 1cs | pers pron | v Qal impf 1cs | prep, pn |
| | יֶעֱרַב | עָלָיו | שִׂיחִי | אָנֹכִי | אֶשְׂמַח | בַּיהוָה |
| | ye'ĕrav | 'ālâv | sîchî | 'ānōkhî | 'esmach | bayhwāh |
| | may it be pleasing | beside Him | my pondering | I | I will be glad | in Yahweh |

| | 8882.126 | 2491 | 4623, 800 | 7857 | 5968 | 375 |
|---|---|---|---|---|---|---|
| **35.** | v Qal juss 3mp | n mp | prep, art, n fs | cj, n mp | adv | sub, ps 3mp |
| | יִתַּמּוּ | חַטָּאִים | מִן־הָאָרֶץ | וּרְשָׁעִים | עוֹד | אֵינָם |
| | yittammû | chaṯṯā'îm | min-hā'ārets | ûreshā'îm | 'ôdh | 'ênām |
| | may they be finished | sinners | from the earth | that the wicked | anymore | they are not |

| 1313.332 | 5497 | 881, 3176 | 2054.333, 3161 | | 3142.533 | 3937, 3176 |
|---|---|---|---|---|---|---|
| v Piel impv 2fs | n fs, ps 1cs | do, pn | v Piel impv 2mp, pn | **105:1** | v Hiphil impv 2mp | prep, pn |
| בָּרְכִי | נַפְשִׁי | אֶת־יְהוָה | הַלְלוּ־יָהּ | | הוֹדוּ | לַיהוָה |
| bārekhî | naphshî | 'eth-yehwāh | halelû-yāhh | | hôdhû | layhwāh |
| bless | O my soul | Yahweh | praise Yah | | praise | to Yahweh |

last!, *Moffatt* ... Be thy glory O Yahweh to times age-abiding, *Rotherham* ... may Yahweh find joy in his works, *Anchor* ... may the LORD be glad in his works!, *NAB*.

**32. He looketh on the earth, and it trembleth: he toucheth the hills, and they smoke:** ... Who is looking to earth, and it trembleth, *Young* ... He just looks at the earth, and it shakes, *NCV* ... he touches the mountains, *NIV*... he touches the mountains, *NIV*.

**33. I will sing unto the LORD as long as I live: I will sing praise to my God while I have my being:** ... I will prayse my God, while I liue, *Geneva* ... and make music to my God as long as I exist, *Beck* ... I will sing praises to my God as long as I breathe, *Goodspeed* ... I shall sing psalms to my God all my life long, *REB*.

**34. My meditation of him shall be sweet: I will be glad in the LORD:** ... My thoughts of Him, *KJVII* ... My meditation shall be pleasant unto him, *Darby* ... Pleasing to him be my theme, *NCB* ... May my meditation please Him, *Beck*.

**35. Let the sinners be consumed out of the earth, and let the wicked be no more. Bless thou the LORD, O my soul. Praise ye the LORD:** ... Let Sinners die from Earth, And Villains cease to be; But my soul bless the LORD, Give honour to the LIFE!, *Fenton* ... But may sinners vanish from the earth and the wicked be no more, *NIV* ... Let sinners be destroyed from the earth, and let the wicked live no longer, *NCV* ... And the lawless no more shall exist, *Rotherham*.

**105:1. O give thanks unto the LORD; call upon his name: make**

which make the "good" of physical life, are in his hand, whether they be the food of the wild goats by the streams or of the conies among the cliffs or of the young lions in the night or of leviathan tumbling amidst the waves or of toiling man. Nor is it only the nourishment of life which comes straight from God to all, but life itself depends on his continual in-breathing. His face is creation's light; breath from Him is its life. The withdrawal of it is death. Every change in creatural condition is wrought by Him. He is the only fountain of life, and the reservoir of all the forces that minister to life or to inanimate being. But the psalmist will not end his contemplations with the thought of the fair creation returning to nothingness. He adds another verse (v. 30), which reads "thou renewest the face of the earth." Individuals pass, and the type remains. New generations spring up. The yearly miracle of spring brings greenness over the snow-covered or brown pastures and green begins to shoot from stiffened boughs. Many of last year's birds are dead, but there are nests in the cypresses and twitterings among the branches in the wadies. Life, not death, prevails in God's world.

**104:31–35.** So the psalmist gathers all up into a burst of praise. He desires that the glory of God, which accrues to Him from his works, may ever be rendered through devout recognition of Him as working them all by man, the only creature who can be the spokesman of creation. He further desires that, as God at first saw that all was "very good," He may ever continue thus to rejoice in his works, or in other words, that these may fulfill his purpose. Possibly, his rejoicing in his works is regarded as following upon man's giving glory to Him for them. That rejoicing, which is the manifestation both of his love and of his satisfaction, is all the more desired, because if his works do not please Him, there lies in Him a dread abyss of destructive power, which could sweep them into nothingness. Superficial readers may feel that the tone of v. 32 strikes a discord, but it is a discord which can be resolved into deeper harmony. One frown from God, and the solid earth trembles, as conscious to its depths of his displeasure. One touch of the hand that is filled with good, and the mountains smoke. Creation perishes if He is displeased. Well then may the psalmist pray that He may forever rejoice in his works and make them live by his smile.

Very beautifully and profoundly does the psalmist ask, in vv. 33f, that some echo of the divine joy may gladden his own heart and that his praise may be coeval with God's glory and his own life. This is the divine purpose in creation—that God may rejoice in it and chiefly in man its crown and that man may rejoice in Him. Such sweet commerce is possible between heaven and earth, and they have learned the lesson of creative power and love aright who by it have been led to share in the joy of God. The Psalm has been shaped in part by reminiscences of the creative days of creation. It ends with the divine Sabbath and with the prayer, which is also a hope, that man may enter into God's rest.

But there is one discordant note in creation's full-toned hymn, the fair music that all creatures made. There are sinners on earth. The last prayer of the psalmist is that that blot may be removed, so nothing may mar the realization of God's ideal nor be left to lessen the completeness of his delight in his work. And so the Psalm ends, as it began, with the singer's call to his own soul to bless Yahweh.

This is the first Psalm which closes with "Praise ye the LORD." It is appended to the two following Psalms, which close book four, and is again found in book five, in Pss. 111–13; 115–17, and in the final group, Pss. 146–150. It is probably a liturgical addition.

***Psalm 105.*** *Psalm 105 deals entirely with God's unfailing faithfulness to Israel, while Psalm 106 sets forth the sad contrast presented by Israel's continual faithlessness to God. Each theme is made more impressive by being pursued separately, then set over against the other. The long series of God's mercies massed together here confronts the dark uniformity of Israel's unworthy requital of them there. Half of the sky is pure blue and radiant sunshine; half is piled with unbroken clouds. Nothing drives home the consciousness of sin so surely as contemplation of God's loving acts.*

**105:1–4.** Verses 1–6 are a ringing summons to extol and contemplate God's great deeds for Israel. They are full of exultation, and in their reiterated short clauses, are like the joyful cries of a herald bringing good tidings to Zion. There is a beautiful progress of thought in these verses. They begin with the call to thank and praise Yahweh and to proclaim his doings among the people. That recognition of Israel's office as the world's evangelist does not require the supposition that the nation was dispersed in captivity, but simply shows that the singer understood the reason for the long series of mercies heaped on it. It is signifi-

| 7410.133 | 904, 8428 | 3156.533 | 904, 6194 | 6173 |
|---|---|---|---|---|
| v Qal impv 2mp | prep, n ms, ps 3ms | v Hiphil impv 2mp | prep, art, n mp | n fp, ps 3ms |
| קִרְאוּ | בִשְׁמוֹ | הוֹדִיעוּ | בָעַמִּים | עֲלִילוֹתָיו |
| qir'û | bishmô | hôdhî'û | vā'ammîm | 'ălîlôthâv |
| call | on his name | cause to be known | among the peoples | his deeds |

| | 8301.133, 3937 | 2252.333, 3937 | 7943.133 | 904, 3725, 6623.258 |
|---|---|---|---|---|
| 2. | v Qal impv 2mp, prep, ps 3ms | v Piel impv 2mp, prep, ps 3ms | v Qal impv 2mp | prep, *adj*, v Niphal ptc fp, ps 3ms |
| | שִׁירוּ־לוֹ | זַמְּרוּ־לוֹ | שִׂיחוּ | בְּכָל־נִפְלְאוֹתָיו |
| | shîrû-lô | zamm$^{e}$rû-lô | sîchû | b$^{e}$khol-niphl$^{e}$'ôthâv |
| | sing to Him | sing praises to Him | ponder | on all his extraordinary deeds |

| | 2054.733 | 904, 8428 | 7231 | 7975.121 | 3949 |
|---|---|---|---|---|---|
| 3. | v Hithpael impv 2mp | prep, *n ms* | n ms, ps 3ms | v Qal juss 3ms | *n ms* |
| | הִתְהַלְלוּ | בְּשֵׁם | קָדְשׁוֹ | יִשְׂמַח | לֵב |
| | hithhal$^{e}$lû | b$^{e}$shēm | qādh$^{e}$shô | yismach | lēv |
| | boast | about the name of | his holy place | may it be glad | the hearts of |

| 1272.352 | 3176 | | 1938.133 | 3176 | 6010 | 1272.333 | 6686 |
|---|---|---|---|---|---|---|---|
| *v Piel ptc mp* | pn | 4. | v Qal impv 2mp | pn | cj, n ms, ps 3ms | v Piel impv 2mp | n mp, ps 3ms |
| מְבַקְשֵׁי | יְהוָה | | דִּרְשׁוּ | יְהוָה | וְעֻזּוֹ | בַּקְּשׁוּ | פָנָיו |
| m$^{e}$vaqŏshê | y$^{e}$hwāh | | dirshû | y$^{e}$hwāh | w$^{e}$'uzzô | baqq$^{e}$shû | phānâv |
| those who seek | Yahweh | | seek | Yahweh | and his strength | seek | his face |

| 8878 | | 2226.133 | 6623.258 | 866, 6449.111 | 4295 |
|---|---|---|---|---|---|
| adv | 5. | v Qal impv 2mp | v Niphal ptc fp, ps 3ms | rel part, v Qal pf 3ms | n mp, ps 3ms |
| תָּמִיד | | זִכְרוּ | נִפְלְאוֹתָיו | אֲשֶׁר־עָשָׂה | מֹפְתָיו |
| tāmîdh | | zikhrû | niphl$^{e}$'ôthâv | 'ăsher-'āsāh | mōph$^{e}$thâv |
| continually | | remember | his extraordinary deeds | which He has done | his wonders |

| 5122, 6552 | | 2320 | 80 | 5860 | 1158 | 3399 |
|---|---|---|---|---|---|---|
| cj, *n mp*, n ms, ps 3ms | 6. | *n ms* | pn | n ms, ps 3ms | *n mp* | pn |
| וּמִשְׁפְּטֵי־פִיו | | זֶרַע | אַבְרָהָם | עַבְדּוֹ | בְּנֵי | יַעֲקֹב |
| ûmishp$^{e}$ṭê-phîw | | zera' | 'avrāhām | 'avdô | b$^{e}$nê | ya'ăqōv |
| and the judgments of his mouth | | O seed of | Abraham | his servant | the children of | Jacob |

| 1008 | | 2000 | 3176 | 435 | 904, 3725, 800 | 5122 |
|---|---|---|---|---|---|---|
| n mp, ps 3ms | 7. | pers pron | pn | n mp, ps 1cp | prep, *adj*, art, n fs | n mp, ps 3ms |
| בְּחִירָיו | | הוּא | יְהוָה | אֱלֹהֵינוּ | בְּכָל־הָאָרֶץ | מִשְׁפָּטָיו |
| b$^{e}$chîrâv | | hû' | y$^{e}$hwāh | 'ĕlōhênû | b$^{e}$khol-hā'ārets | mishpāṭâv |
| his chosen ones | | He | Yahweh | our God | throughout all the earth | his judgments |

| | 2226.111 | 3937, 5986 | 1311 | 1745 | 6943.311 | 3937, 512 |
|---|---|---|---|---|---|---|
| 8. | v Qal pf 3ms | prep, n ms | n fs, ps 3ms | n ms | v Piel pf 3ms | prep, *n ms* |
| | זָכַר | לְעוֹלָם | בְּרִיתוֹ | דָּבָר | צִוָּה | לְאֶלֶף |
| | zākhar | l$^{e}$'ôlām | b$^{e}$rîthô | dāvār | tsiwwāh | l$^{e}$'eleph |
| | He is mindful of | unto eternity | his covenant | the word | He has commanded | to one thousand |

| 1810 | | 866 | 3901.111 | 882, 80 | 8095 | 3937, 3545 |
|---|---|---|---|---|---|---|
| n ms | 9. | rel part | v Qal pf 3ms | prep, pn | cj, n fs, ps 3ms | prep, pn |
| דּוֹר | | אֲשֶׁר | כָּרַת | אֶת־אַבְרָהָם | וּשְׁבוּעָתוֹ | לְיִשְׂחָק |
| dôr | | 'ăsher | kārath | 'eth-'avrāhām | ûsh$^{e}$vû'āthô | l$^{e}$yischāq |
| generations | | which | He cut | with Abraham | and his oath | to Isaac |

| | 6198.521 | 3937, 3399 | 3937, 2805 | 3937, 3547 | 1311 | 5986 |
|---|---|---|---|---|---|---|
| 10. | cj, v Hiphil impf 3ms, ps 3fs | prep, pn | prep, n ms | prep, pn | *n fs* | n ms |
| | וַיַּעֲמִידֶהָ | לְיַעֲקֹב | לְחֹק | לְיִשְׂרָאֵל | בְּרִית | עוֹלָם |
| | wayya'ămîdheāh | l$^{e}$ya'ăqōv | l$^{e}$chōq | l$^{e}$yisrā'ēl | b$^{e}$rîth | 'ôlām |
| | and He caused it to stand | to Jacob | for a statute | to Israel | a Covenant of | everlasting |

**known his deeds among the people:** ... proclaim His doings among the nations, *Berkeley* ... invoke his name; make known among the nations his deeds, *NCB* ... make known among the nations what he has done, *NIV* ... Make known among the peoples his doings, *ASV.*

**2. Sing unto him, sing psalms unto him: talk ye of all his wondrous works:** ... Pay him honour with song and psalm, *NEB* ...Sing to him, make music for him, recount all his wonders!, *JB* ... meditate upon all his wondrous works, *Darby.*

**3. Glory ye in his holy name: let the heart of them rejoice that seek the LORD:** ... Triumph in that holy name; let every heart that longs for the Lord rejoice, *Knox* ... Praise His HOLY NAME; And seek the LORD gladly, *Fenton* ... You who look for the LORD, be glad at heart, *Beck* ... Be glad that you are his; let those who seek the LORD be happy, *NCV.*

**4. Seek the LORD, and his strength: seek his face evermore:** ... Look to the LORD and be strong; at all times seek his presence, *REB* ... let your hearts ever be turned to him, *BB* ... seek his presence continually, *NRSV.*

**5. Remember his marvellous works that he hath done; his wonders, and the judgments of his mouth:** ... Recall his wonders that he wrought, his prodigies, and the judgments, *Anchor* ... never forget the wonders he has done, his marvels and his sentences of doom, *Moffatt* ... the judgments he has uttered, *NAB* ... His portents and the just decisions of his mouth, *Rotherham.*

**6. O ye seed of Abraham his servant, ye children of Jacob his chosen:** ...O race of Abraham, *Moffatt* ... which are his elect, *Geneva* ... O sons of Jacob, His chosen ones!, *NASB.*

**7. He is the LORD our God: his judgments are in all the earth:** ... His judgments reach over the whole world, *Berkeley* ... he is judge of all the earth, *BB* ... over all the earth is his authority, *Anchor.*

**8. He hath remembered his covenant for ever, the word which he commanded to a thousand generations:** ... He hath remembered to the age His covenant, *Young* ... He is ever mindful of his covenant, *Darby* ... He is ever mindful of his covenant, the promise he ordained, *REB* ... the promise he laid down for a thousand generations, *JB.*

**9. Which covenant he made with Abraham, and his oath unto Isaac:** ... He will keep the agreement he made with Abraham, *NCV* ... He gave Abraham a promise, bound himself to Isaac by an oath, *Knox* ... his sworn promise to Isaac, *RSV* ... the oath he swore to Isaac, *NIV.*

**10. And confirmed the same unto Jacob for a law, and to Israel for an everlasting covenant:** ... And He established it unto Jacob for a statute,

---

cant that God's "deeds" are Israel's message to the world. By such deeds his "name" is spoken. What God has done is the best revelation of what God is. His messengers are not to speak their own thoughts about Him, but to tell the story of his acts and let these speak for Him. To seek Yahweh is to find his strength investing our feebleness. To turn our faces toward his in devout desire is to have our faces made bright by reflected light. And one chief way of seeking Yahweh is the remembrance of his merciful wonders of old, "He hath made his wonderful works to be remembered" (Ps. 111:4), and his design in them is that men should have solid basis for their hopes and be thereby encouraged to seek Him, as well as be taught what He is.

**105:5–7.** Thus, the psalmist reaches his main theme, which is to build a memorial of these deeds for an everlasting possession. The "wonders" (HED #4295) referred to in v. 5 are chiefly those wrought in Egypt, as the subsequent verses show.

Verse 6 contains, in the names given to Israel, the reason for their obeying the preceding summons. Their hereditary relation to God gives them the material and imposes on them the obligation and the honor of being "secretaries of God's praise." In v. 6a, "his servant" may be intended to designate the nation, as it often does in Isa. 40–46. "His chosen ones" in v. 6b would then be an exact parallel; but the recurrence of the expression in v. 42, with the individual reference, makes that reference more probable here.

**105:8–11.** The fundamental fact underlying all Israel's experience of God's care is his own loving will, which entered into covenant obligations, so that thereafter his mercies are ensured by his veracity no less than by his kindness. Hence, the Psalm begins its proper theme by hymning the faithfulness of God to his oath and painting the insignificance of the beginnings of the nation as showing that the ground of God's covenant relation was laid in himself, not in them. Israel's consciousness of holding a special relation to God never obscured, in the minds of psalmists and prophets, the twin truth that all the earth waited on Him and was the theater of his manifestations.

The obligations under which God has come to Israel are represented as a covenant, a word and an oath. In all, the general idea of explicit declaration of divine purpose, which henceforth becomes binding on God by reason of his faithfulness, is con-

| 11. | 3937, 569.141 | 3937 | 5598.125 | 881, 800, 3791 | 2346 | 5338 |
|---|---|---|---|---|---|---|
| | prep, v Qal inf con | prep, ps 2ms | v Qal impf 1cs | do, *n fs*, pn | *n ms* | n fs, ps 2mp |
| | לֵאמֹר | לְךָ | אֶתֵּן | אֶת־אֶרֶץ־כְּנָעַן | חֶבֶל | נַחֲלַתְכֶם |
| | lē'mōr | lekhā | 'ettēn | 'eth-'erets-kenā'an | chevel | nachlathkhem |
| | saying | to you | I will give | the land of Canaan | the portion of | your inheritance |

| 12. | 904, 2030.141 | 5139 | 4709 | 3626, 4746 | 1513.152 | 904 |
|---|---|---|---|---|---|---|
| | prep, v Qal inf con, ps 3mp | *n mp* | n ms | prep, sub | cj, v Qal act ptc mp | prep, ps 3fs |
| | בִּהְיוֹתָם | מְתֵי | מִסְפָּר | כִּמְעַט | וְגָרִים | בָּהּ |
| | bihyôthām | methê | mispār | kim'at | weghārîm | bāhh |
| | when their being | men of | a number | like a moment | then sojourning | in it |

| 13. | 2050.726 | 4623, 1504 | 420, 1504 | 4623, 4608 | 420, 6194 | 311 |
|---|---|---|---|---|---|---|
| | cj, v Hithpael impf 3mp | prep, n ms | prep, n ms | prep, n fs | prep, n ms | adj |
| | וַיִּתְהַלְּכוּ | מִגּוֹי | אֶל־גּוֹי | מִמַּמְלָכָה | אֶל־עַם | אַחֵר |
| | wayyithhallekhû | miggôy | 'el-gôy | mimmamlākhāh | 'el-'am | 'achēr |
| | and they were walking about | from a nation | to a nation | from a kingdom | to a people | another |

| 14. | 3940, 5299.511 | 119 | 3937, 6479.141 | 3306.521 | 6142 |
|---|---|---|---|---|---|
| | neg part, v Hiphil pf 3ms | n ms | prep, v Qal inf con, ps 3mp | cj, v Hiphil impf 3ms | prep, ps 3mp |
| | לֹא־הִנִּיחַ | אָדָם | לְעָשְׁקָם | וַיּוֹכַח | עֲלֵיהֶם |
| | lō'-hinîach | 'ādhām | le'āsheqām | wayyôkhach | 'ălêhem |
| | He did not allow | a man | to oppress them | but He reproved | concerning them |

| 4567 | 15. | 414, 5236.128 | 904, 5081 | 3937, 5204 | 414, 7778.528 |
|---|---|---|---|---|---|
| n mp | | adv, v Qal juss 2mp | prep, n mp, ps 1cs | cj, prep, n mp, ps 1cs | adv, v Hiphil juss 2mp |
| מְלָכִים | | אַל־תִּגְּעוּ | בִמְשִׁיחָי | וְלִנְבִיאַי | אַל־תָּרֵעוּ |
| melākhîm | | 'al-tigge'û | vimshîchāy | welinvî'ay | 'al-tārē'û |
| kings | | do not touch | on my anointed ones | and to my prophets | do not do evil |

| 16. | 7410.121 | 7743 | 6142, 800 | 3725, 4431, 4035 | 8132.111 |
|---|---|---|---|---|---|
| | cj, v Qal impf 3ms | n ms | prep, art, n fs | *adj, n ms*, n ms | v Qal pf 3ms |
| | וַיִּקְרָא | רָעָב | עַל־הָאָרֶץ | כָּל־מַטֵּה־לֶחֶם | שָׁבָר |
| | wayyiqŏrā' | rā'āv | 'al-hā'ārets | kol-mattēh-lechem | shāvār |
| | when He summoned | a famine | onto the land | all the staffs of bread | He broke |

| 17. | 8365.111 | 3937, 6686 | 382 | 3937, 5860 | 4513.211 | 3231 | 18. | 6257.316 |
|---|---|---|---|---|---|---|---|---|
| | v Qal pf 3ms | prep, n mp, ps 3mp | n ms | prep, n ms | v Niphal pf 3ms | pn | | v Piel pf 3cp |
| | שָׁלַח | לִפְנֵיהֶם | אִישׁ | לְעֶבֶד | נִמְכַּר | יוֹסֵף | | עִנּוּ |
| | shālach | liphnêhem | 'îsh | le'evedh | nimkar | yôsēph | | 'innû |
| | He sent | before them | a man | for a slave | he was sold | Joseph | | they afflicted |

| 904, 3644 | 7559 | 1298 | 971.112 | 5497 | 19. | 5912, 6496 |
|---|---|---|---|---|---|---|
| prep, art, n ms | n fd, ps 3ms | n ms | v Qal pf 3fs | n fs, ps 3ms | | prep, *n fs* |
| בַכֶּבֶל | רַגְלָיו | בַּרְזֶל | בָּאָה | נַפְשׁוֹ | | עַד־עֵת |
| vakkevel | raghlâv | barzel | bā'āh | naphshô | | 'adh-'ēth |
| with fetters | his feet | iron | it came to | his soul | | until the time of |

*MAST* … the decree by which he bound himself for Jacob, *NEB* … And settled with Jacob—The Bond made with Israel, *Fenton* … Ṭo Israel as a covenant age-abiding, *Rotherham.*

**11. Saying, Unto thee will I give the land of Canaan, the lot of your inheritance:** … As the portion of your inheritance, *NASB* … as your property measured out to you, *Beck* … As the allotment of your inheritance, *NKJV* … 'as your allotted holding,' *REB* … the measured line of your heritage, *BB.*

**12. When they were but a few men in number; yea, very few, and strangers in it:** … A small company it was, *NEB* … When they were few in number, a handful, and strangers, *NAB* … they were few in number, of little account, *NRSV* … Few in number were our fathers, few and foreigners, *Moffatt.*

**13. When they went from one nation to another, from one kingdom to another people:** … roaming from nation to nation, *REB* ... Wandering from nation to nation, *Anchor* ... And ever they passed on from country to country, *Knox* ... Among Tribes they wandered, Alone in the kingdoms, *Fenton.*

**14. He suffered no man to do them wrong: yea, he reproved kings for their sakes:** ... he allowed no one to oppress them, *RSV* ... but he let no one ill-treat them, *NEB* ... for their sake he rebuked kings, *NCB* ... And warned kings concerning them, *Goodspeed* ... for their sake he instructed kings, *JB.*

**15. Saying, Touch not mine anointed, and do my prophets no harm:** ... Put not your hand on those who have been marked with my holy oil, *BB* ... Never touch my chosen, *Moffatt* ... Don't touch my chosen people, *NCV* ... 'Strike not against Mine anointed, And to My prophets do not evil,' *Young* ... see that no harm comes to My prophets, *Berkeley.*

**16. Moreover he called for a famine upon the land: he brake the whole staff of bread:** ... and destroyed all their supplies of food, *NIV* ... and ruined the crop that sustained them, *NAB* ...He destroyed all the provision of bread, *NKJV* ... cut off their daily bread, *REB.*

**17. He sent a man before them, even Joseph, who was sold for a servant:** ... Therefore He sent a man to precede them, *Berkeley* ... He sent a man in front of them, *Moffatt* ... Joseph, who was given as a servant for a price, *BB* ... For a servant hath Joseph been sold, *Young.*

**18. Whose feet they hurt with fetters: he was laid in iron:** ... Into the

---

tained. But the conception of a covenant implies mutual obligations, and failure to discharge on one side relieves the other contracting party from his promise. A word simply includes the notion of articulate utterance, and an oath adds the thought of a solemn sanction and a pledge given. God swears by himself; that is, his own character is the guarantee of his promise. These various designations are thus heaped together, in order to heighten the thought of the firmness of his promise. It stands "for ever, ... to a thousand generations"; it is an "everlasting covenant." The psalmist triumphs, as it were, in the manifold repetition of it. Each of the fathers of the nation had it confirmed to himself: Abraham; Isaac when, ready to flee from the land in famine, he had renewed to him (Gen. 26:3) the oath which he had first heard as he stood, trembling but unharmed, by the rude altar where the ram lay in his stead (Gen. 22:16); and Jacob as he lay beneath the stars at Bethel. With Jacob (Israel), the singer passes from the individuals to the nation, as is shown by the alternation of "thee" and "your" in v. 11.

**105:12–15.** The lowly condition of the recipients of the promise not only exalts the love which chose them, but the power which preserved them and fulfilled it. And if, as may be the case, the Psalm is exilic or post-exilic, its picture of ancient days is like a mirror, reflecting present depression and bidding the downcast be of good cheer. He who made a strong nation out of that little horde of wanderers must have been moved by his own heart, not by anything in them, and what He did long ago, He can do today. God's past is the prophecy of God's future. Literally rendered, v. 12a, "When they were but a few men in number," i.e., "easily numbered" (cf. Gen. 34:30, where Jacob uses the same phrase). "Very few" in 12b is literally "like a little" and may either apply to number or to worth. It is used in the latter sense, in reference to "the heart of the wicked," in Prov. 10:20, and may have the same meaning here. That little band of wanderers who went about as sojourners among the kinglets of Canaan and Philistia with occasional visits to Egypt seemed very vulnerable, but God was, as He had promised to the first of them at a moment of extreme peril, their "shield," and in their lives there were instances of strange protection afforded them, which curbed kings, as in the case of Abram in Egypt (Gen. 12) and Gerar (Gen. 20) and of Isaac in the latter place (Gen. 26). The patriarchs were not, technically speaking, "anointed," but they had that of which anointing was but a symbol. They were divinely set apart and endowed for their tasks, and as consecrated to God's service their persons were inviolable. In a very profound sense, all God's servants are thus anointed and are immortal until their work is done. The patriarchs were not "prophets" in the narrower sense of the word, but Abraham is called so by God in Gen. 20:7. Prior to prophetic utterance is prophetic inspiration, and these men received divine communications and were possessed of the counsels of heaven. The designation is equivalent to Abraham's name the "friend of God." Thus both titles, which guaranteed a charmed, invulnerable life to their bearers, go deep into the permanent privileges of God-trusting souls. All such have an anointing from the Holy One and receive whispers from his lips. They are all under his protection, and for their sakes, kings of many a dynasty and age have been rebuked.

**105:16–18.** In vv. 16–22, the history of Joseph is poetically and summarily treated as a

| 971.141, 1745 | 577 | 3176 | 7170.112 | | 8365.111 | 4567 |
|---|---|---|---|---|---|---|
| v Qal inf con, n ms, ps 3ms | *n fs* | pn | v Qal pf 3fs, ps 3ms | **20.** | v Qal pf 3ms | n ms |
| בֹּא־דְבָרוֹ | אִמְרַת | יְהוָה | צְרָפָתְהוּ | | שָׁלַח | מֶלֶךְ |
| bō'-dhevārô | 'imrath | yehwāh | tserāphāthehû | | shālach | melekh |
| the coming of his word | the word of | Yahweh | it refined him | | he sent | the king |

| 5609.521 | 5090.151 | 6194 | 6858.321 | | 7947.111 |
|---|---|---|---|---|---|
| cj, v Hiphil impf 3ms, ps 3ms | *v Qal act ptc ms* | n mp | cj, v Piel impf 3ms, ps 3ms | **21.** | v Qal pf 3ms, ps 3ms |
| וַיַּתִּירֵהוּ | מֹשֵׁל | עַמִּים | וַיְפַתְּחֵהוּ | | שָׂמוֹ |
| wayattîrēhû | mōshēl | 'ammîm | wayphattechēhû | | sāmô |
| and he broke his fetters | the ruler of | peoples | and he released him | | he appointed him |

| 112 | 3937, 1041 | 5090.151 | 904, 3725, 7359 | | 3937, 646.141 |
|---|---|---|---|---|---|
| n ms | prep, n ms, ps 3ms | cj, v Qal act ptc ms | prep, *adj*, n ms, ps 3ms | **22.** | prep, v Qal inf con |
| אָדוֹן | לְבֵיתוֹ | וּמֹשֵׁל | בְּכָל־קִנְיָנוֹ | | לֶאְסֹר |
| 'ādhôn | levêthô | ûmōshēl | bekhol-qinyānô | | le'ăsōr |
| master | to his household | and a ruler | over all his acquisitions | | to bind |

| 8015 | 904, 5497 | 2292 | 2549.321 | | 971.121 | 3547 |
|---|---|---|---|---|---|---|
| n mp, ps 3ms | prep, n fs, ps 3ms | cj, n mp, ps 3ms | v Piel impf 3ms | **23.** | cj, v Qal impf 3ms | pn |
| שָׂרָיו | בְּנַפְשׁוֹ | וּזְקֵנָיו | יְחַכֵּם | | וַיָּבֹא | יִשְׂרָאֵל |
| sārâv | benaphshô | ûzāqēnâv | yechakkēm | | wayyāvō' | yiserā'ēl |
| his officials | with his soul | and his elders | he caused to be wise | | then he entered | Israel |

| 4875 | 3399 | 1513.111 | 904, 800, 2626 | | 6759.521 |
|---|---|---|---|---|---|
| pn | cj, pn | v Qal pf 3ms | prep, *n fs*, pn | **24.** | cj, Hiphil impf 3ms |
| מִצְרָיִם | וְיַעֲקֹב | גָּר | בְּאֶרֶץ־חָם | | וַיֶּפֶר |
| mitsrāyim | weya'ăqōv | gār | be'erets-chām | | wayyepher |
| Egypt | then Jacob | he sojourned | in the land of Ham | | and He caused to be fruitful |

| 881, 6194 | 4108 | 6343.521 | 4623, 7141 | | 2089.111 |
|---|---|---|---|---|---|
| do, n ms, ps 3ms | adv | cj, v Hiphil impf 3ms, ps 3ms | prep, n mp, ps 3ms | **25.** | v Qal pf 3ms |
| אֶת־עַמּוֹ | מְאֹד | וַיַּעֲצִמֵהוּ | מִצָּרָיו | | הָפַךְ |
| 'eth-'ammô | me'ōdh | wayya'ătsimēhû | mitstsārâv | | hāphakh |
| his people | very | and He made them stronger | than their adversaries | | he turned |

| 3949 | 3937, 7983.141 | 6194 | 3937, 5417.741 | 904, 5860 | | 8365.111 |
|---|---|---|---|---|---|---|
| n ms, ps 3mp | prep, v Qal inf con | n ms, ps 3ms | prep, v Hithpael inf con | prep, n mp, ps 3ms | **26.** | v Qal pf 3ms |
| לִבָּם | לִשְׂנֹא | עַמּוֹ | לְהִתְנַכֵּל | בַּעֲבָדָיו | | שָׁלַח |
| libbām | lisnō' | 'ammô | lehithnakkēl | ba'ăvādhâv | | shālach |
| their hearts | to hate | his people | to act deceitfully | with his servants | | He sent |

| 5057 | 5860 | 172 | 866 | 1013.111, 904 | | 7947.116, 904 |
|---|---|---|---|---|---|---|
| pn | n ms, ps 3ms | pn | rel pron | v Qal pf 3ms, prep, ps 3ms | **27.** | v Qal pf 3cp, prep, ps 3mp |
| מֹשֶׁה | עַבְדּוֹ | אַהֲרֹן | אֲשֶׁר | בָּחַר־בּוֹ | | שָׂמוּ־בָם |
| mōsheh | 'avdô | 'ahrōn | 'ăsher | bāchar-bô | | sāmû-vām |
| Moses | his servant | Aaron | whom | He had chosen with him | | they set among them |

iron entered his soul, *Rotherham* … his soul came into irons, *Darby* … Iron pierced to his soul, *Fenton.*

**19. Until the time that his word came:** … Vntill his appoynted time came, *Geneva* … that his word came to pass, *NASB* … Till his prediction came to pass, *NAB* … until what he had said came to pass, *NRSV* … In due time his prophecy was fulfilled, *JB.*

**the word of the LORD tried him:** … the word of the LORD proved him true, *NIV* … and the LORD's Word proved he was right, *Beck* … He was tested by the LORD's command, *REB* … Yahweh's promise was proved true by him, *Anchor.*

**20. The king sent and loosed him; even the ruler of the people, and let him go free:** … The king sent men to take off his chains, *BB* … The king of Egypt sent for Joseph and freed him, *NCV* … the ruler of nations released him, *NEB.*

**21. He made him lord of his house, and ruler of all his substance:** …

lord of all the possessions that were his, *Knox* ...ruler of all he owned, *KJVII* ... He appointed him manager of his estate, *Berkeley* ... made him master of his palace, *Anchor.*

**22. To bind his princes at his pleasure:** ... That he might give orders to his officers as he pleased, *Goodspeed* ... To imprison his princes at will, *NASB* ... to control his nobles as he pleased, *Moffatt.*

**and teach his senators wisdom:** ... his elders he maketh wise, *Young* ... teach his counsellors wisdom, *REB* ... so that his law-givers might get wisdom from him, *BB.*

**23. Israel also came into Egypt; and Jacob sojourned in the land of Ham:** ... was a stranger in the land of Ham, *Geneva* ... Jacob lived as an alien in the land, *NRSV* ... Jacob came to live in the land, *NEB.*

**24. And he increased his people greatly:** ... he made his people exceeding fruitful, *Rotherham* ... He made his people increase in numbers, *JB* ... he gave his people great increase of numbers, *Knox.*

**and made them stronger than their enemies:** ... he made them too numerous for their foes, *NIV* ... made them mightier than their oppressors, *Darby* ... till they outnumbered the Egyptians, *Moffatt.*

**25. He turned their heart to hate his people, to deal subtly with his servants:** ... they grew weary of his people's presence, devised ruin for his worshippers, *Knox* ... and dealt deceitfully with his servants, *NCB.*

**26. He sent Moses his servant; and Aaron whom he had chosen:** ... Aaron whom He had fixed on, *Young* ... Aaron, the man of his choice, *JB.*

**27. They showed his signs among them, and wonders in the land of Ham:** ... They were appointed to

---

link in the chain of providences which brought about the fulfillment of the Covenant. Possibly, the singer is thinking about a captive Israel in the present, while speaking about a captive Joseph in the past. In God's dealings, humiliation and affliction are often, he thinks, the precursors of glory and triumph. Calamities prepare the way for prosperity. So it was in that old time, and so it is still. In this resume of the history of Joseph, the points signalized are God's direct agency in the whole—the errand on which Joseph was sent ("before them") as a forerunner to "prepare a place for them" (Gen. 45:5), the severity of his sufferings, the trial of his faith by the contrast which his condition presented to what God had promised, and his final exaltation. The description of Joseph's imprisonment adds some dark touches to the account in Genesis, whether these are due to poetic idealizing or to tradition. In v. 18b, some would translate "iron came over his soul." This rendering follows the Vulgate (Jerome's Latin Bible, A.D. 400) and the picturesque Prayer-Book Version, "The iron entered into his soul." But the original is against this, as the word for iron is masculine and the verb is feminine, agreeing with the feminine noun "soul." The clause is simply a parallel to the preceding. "His soul" is best taken as a mere periphrasis for "he," although it may be used emphatically to suggest that his soul entered entirely in its resolve to obey God. The meaning is conveyed by the free rendering above.

**105:19–22.** Verse 19 is also ambiguous, from the uncertainty as to whose word is intended in v. 19a. It may be either God's or Joseph's. The latter is the more probable, as there appears to be an intentional contrast between "his word" in 19a and "the promise of Yahweh" in 19b. If this explanation is adopted, a choice is still possible between Joseph's interpretation of his fellow-prisoners' dreams, the fulfillment of which led to his liberation, and his earlier word recounting his own dreams, which led to his being sold by his brethren. In any case, the thought of the verse is a great and ever true one, that God's promise, while it remains unfulfilled and seems contradicted by present facts, serves as a test of the genuineness and firmness of a man's reliance on Him and his promise. That promise is by the psalmist almost personified, as putting Joseph to the test. Such testing is the deepest meaning of all afflictions. Fire will burn off a thin plating of silver from a copper coin and reveal the base metal beneath, but it will only brighten into a glow the one which is all silver.

There is a ring of triumph in the singer's voice as he tells of the honor and power heaped on the captive and of how the king of many nations "sent" (HED #8365), as the mightier King in heaven had done (vv. 20 and 17), and not only liberated but exalted him, giving him whose soul had been bound in fetters power to "bind princes according to his soul" and to instruct and command the elders of Egypt.

**105:23–27.** Verses 23–27 carry on the story to the next step in the evolution of God's purposes. The long years of the sojourn in Egypt are summarily dealt with, as they are in the narrative in Genesis and Exodus, and the salient points of

| 1745 | 225 | 4295 | 904, 800 | 2626 | | 8365.111 | 2932 |
|---|---|---|---|---|---|---|---|
| *n mp* | n mp, ps 3ms | cj, n mp | prep, *n fs* | pn | **28.** | v Qal pf 3ms | n ms |
| דִּבְרֵי | אֹתוֹתָיו | וּמֹפְתִים | בְּאֶרֶץ | חָם | | שָׁלַח | חֹשֶׁךְ |
| divrê | 'ōthôthâv | ûmōphethîm | be'erets | chām | | shālach | chōshekh |
| the words of | his signs | and wonders | in the land of | Ham | | He sent | darkness |

| 2931.521 | 3940, 4947.116 | 881, 1745 | | 2089.111 |
|---|---|---|---|---|
| cj, Hiphil impf 3ms | cj, neg part, v Qal pf 3cp | do, n mp, ps 3ms | **29.** | v Qal pf 3ms |
| וַיַּחְשִׁךְ | וְלֹא־מָרוּ | אֶת־דְּבָרָיו | | הָפַךְ |
| wayyachshikh | welō'-mārû | 'eth-devāryô | | hāphakh |
| and He caused to be dark | and they did not rebel against | his words | | He turned |

| 881, 4448 | 3937, 1879 | 4322.521 | 881, 1759 | | 8650.111 | 800 |
|---|---|---|---|---|---|---|
| do, n mp, ps 3mp | prep, n ms | cj, v Hiphil impf 3ms | do, n fs, ps 3mp | **30.** | v Qal pf 3ms | n fs, ps 3mp |
| אֶת־מֵימֵיהֶם | לְדָם | וַיָּמֶת | אֶת־דְּגָתָם | | שָׁרַץ | אַרְצָם |
| 'eth-mêmêhem | ledhām | wayyāmeth | 'eth-deghāthām | | shārats | 'artsām |
| their waters | into blood | He caused to die | their fish | | it swarmed with | their land |

| 7131 | 904, 2410 | 4567 | | 569.111 | 971.121 | 6389 | 3775 |
|---|---|---|---|---|---|---|---|
| n fp | prep, *n mp* | n mp, ps 3mp | **31.** | v Qal pf 3ms | cj, v Qal impf 3ms | n ms | n mp |
| צְפַרְדְּעִים | בְּחַדְרֵי | מַלְכֵיהֶם | | אָמַר | וַיָּבֹא | עָרֹב | כִּנִּים |
| tsephardeîm | bechadhrê | malkhêhem | | 'āmar | wayyāvō' | 'ārōv | kinîm |
| frogs | into the chambers of | their kings | | He said | and they entered | flies | gnats |

| 904, 3725, 1397 | | 5598.111 | 1700 | 1287 | 813 | 3988 |
|---|---|---|---|---|---|---|
| prep, *adj*, n ms, ps 3mp | **32.** | v Qal pf 3ms | n mp, ps 3mp | n ms | n fs | n fp |
| בְּכָל־גְּבוּלָם | | נָתַן | גִּשְׁמֵיהֶם | בָּרָד | אֵשׁ | לֶהָבוֹת |
| bekhol-gevûlām | | nāthan | gishmêhem | bārādh | 'ēsh | lehāvôth |
| over all their boundaries | | He gave | their rain | hailstones | fire | flames |

| 904, 800 | | 5409.521 | 1655 | 8711 | 8132.321 |
|---|---|---|---|---|---|
| prep, n fs, ps 3mp | **33.** | cj, v Hiphil impf 3ms | n fs, ps 3mp | cj, n fs, ps 3mp | cj, v Piel impf 3ms |
| בְּאַרְצָם | | וַיַּךְ | גַּפְנָם | וּתְאֵנָתָם | וַיְשַׁבֵּר |
| be'artsām | | wayyakh | gaphnām | ûthe'ēnāthām | wayshabbēr |
| throughout their land | | and He struck down | their vines | and their fig trees | and He shattered |

| 6320 | 1397 | | 569.111 | 971.121 | 722 | 3326 |
|---|---|---|---|---|---|---|
| *n ms* | n ms, ps 3mp | **34.** | v Qal pf 3ms | cj, v Qal impf 3ms | n ms | cj, n ms |
| עֵץ | גְּבוּלָם | | אָמַר | וַיָּבֹא | אַרְבֶּה | וְיֶלֶק |
| 'ēts | gevûlām | | 'āmar | wayyāvō' | 'arbeh | weyeleq |
| the trees of | their territory | | He said | and they entered | locusts | and young locusts |

| 375 | 4709 | | 404.121 | 3725, 6448 | 904, 800 |
|---|---|---|---|---|---|
| cj, *sub* | n ms | **35.** | cj, v Qal impf 3ms | *adj*, n ms | prep, n fs, ps 3mp |
| וְאֵין | מִסְפָּר | | וַיֹּאכַל | כָּל־עֵשֶׂב | בְּאַרְצָם |
| we'ên | mispār | | wayyō'khal | kol-'ēsev | be'artsām |
| and there was not | a number | | and they devoured | all the herbage | throughout their land |

| 404.121 | 6780 | 124 | | 5409.521 | 3725, 1111 |
|---|---|---|---|---|---|
| cj, v Qal impf 3ms | *n ms* | n fs, ps 3mp | **36.** | cj, v Hiphil impf 3ms | *adj*, n ms |
| וַיֹּאכַל | פְּרִי | אַדְמָתָם | | וַיַּךְ | כָּל־בְּכוֹר |
| wayyō'khal | perî | 'adhmāthām | | wayyakh | kol-bekhôr |
| and they devoured | the fruit of | their ground | | and He struck down | all the firstborn |

| 904, 800 | 7519 | 3937, 3725, 202 | | 3428.521 |
|---|---|---|---|---|
| prep, n fs, ps 3mp | n fs | prep, *adj*, n ms, ps 3mp | **37.** | cj, v Hiphil impf 3ms, ps 3mp |
| בְּאַרְצָם | רֵאשִׁית | לְכָל־אוֹנָם | | וַיּוֹצִיאֵם |
| be'artsām | rē'shîth | lekhol-'ônām | | wayyôtsî'ēm |
| throughout their land | the beginning | of all their procreative power | | He led them out |

announce his signs, *REB* ... They were his mouthpiece to announce his signs, *NEB* ... He set among them his threatening signs, And his wonders, *Rotherham* ... His miracles against the land of Egypt, *Berkeley.*

**28. He sent darkness, and made it dark:** ... Sent gloom and it darkened, *Fenton* ... He sent black night and made it dark, *BB* ... Darkness he sent, and darkness fell, *JB.*

**and they rebelled not against his word:** ... But they rebelled against his words, *Goodspeed* ... they did not rebel against His word, *NKJV* ... for had they not rebelled against his words?, *NIV* ... they were not disobedient vnto his commission, *Geneva* ... but still the Egyptians resisted his commands, *REB* ... so that they could not see his actions, *Anchor.*

**29. He turned their waters into blood, and slew their fish:** ... He turned their supply of water into blood, *Knox* ... caused their fish to die, *NASB.*

**30. Their land brought forth frogs in abundance, in the chambers of their kings:** ... land swarmed with frogs, *NCB* ... which went up into the bedrooms of their rulers, *NIV* ... even their princes' inner chambers, *NEB.*

**31. He spake, and there came divers sorts of flies:** ... At his command there came swarms of flies, *REB* ... He spoke and brought flies, *Anchor* ... at his word came flies, *JB* ... at his word, flies attacked them, *Knox.*

**and lice in all their coasts:** ... and gnats were everywhere in the country, *NCV* ... Mosquitoes throughout their country, *Goodspeed* ... in all their borders, *KJVII.*

**32. He gave them hail for rain:** ... He turned their rain into hail, *NIV* ... He gave them hail as their rain, *JB* ... ice for rain, *BB.*

**and flaming fire in their land:** ... and lightning that flashed through their land, *NRSV* ... and flashed fire over their country, *NEB* ... he produced lightning in their land, *Anchor* ... it brought fire that burned up their countryside, *Knox.*

**33. He smote their vines also and their fig trees:** ... He ruined their vines and their fig trees, *Berkeley* ... he shattered their vines and fig-trees, *Knox* ... and shattered the trees throughout their territory, *REB.*

**and brake the trees of their coasts:** ... and shattered the trees throughout their borders, *NAB* ... And splintered the trees of their territory, *NKJV* ... He destroyed their outlying forests, *Berkeley.*

**34. He spake, and the locusts came:** ... He gave the word, *Knox* ... He spoke—vermin came, *Fenton* ... then came the swarming locust, *Rotherham.*

**and caterpillars, and that without number:** ... And the cankerworm, *MRB* ... and young locusts, *RSV* ... and grasshoppers past counting, *Moffatt* ... And insects innumerable, *Goodspeed* ... wingless ones that couldn't be counted, *Beck.*

**35. And did eat up all the herbs in their land, and devoured the fruit of their ground:** ... And ate up all vegetation in their land, *NASB* ... everything that grew on their ground, *Beck* ... consumed all the produce of the soil, *NEB* ... taking all the fruit of the earth for food, *BB.*

**36. He smote also all the firstborn in their land:** ... He also destroyed all the firstborn, *NKJV* ... he struck down all the first-born in Egypt, *NEB* ... He put to death the first child of every family, *BB* ... He struck their country's heirs, *Fenton.*

**the chief of all their strength:** ... The first-fruit of all their strength, *Young* ... the oldest son of each family, *NCV* ... the first fruit of all their vigor, *Anchor.*

**37. He brought them forth also with silver and gold:** ... he led forth

---

its close alone are touched—the numerical growth of the people, the consequent hostility of the Egyptians and the mission of Moses and Aaron. The direct ascription to God of all the incidents mentioned is to be noted. The psalmist sees only one hand moving and has no hesitation in tracing to God the turning of the Egyptians' hearts to hatred. Many commentators, both old and new, try to weaken the expression by the explanation that the hatred was "indirectly the work of God, inasmuch as He lent increasing might to the people" (Delitzsch). But the psalmist means much more than this, just as Exodus does in attributing the hardening of Pharaoh's heart to God.

Verse 27, according to the existing text, breaks the series of verses beginning with a singular verb of which God is the subject, which stretch with only one other interruption from v. 24 to v. 37. It seems most probable, therefore, that the Septuagint is right in reading "He" instead of "they." The change is but the omission of one letter, and the error supposed is a frequent one. The word (HED #7947) literally means "set" or "planted," and "did" is an explanation rather than a rendering. The whole expression is remarkable. Literally, we should translate "he" (or "they") "set among them words" (or "matters") "of his signs"; but this would be unintelligible, and we must have recourse to produce the smoother of the words for English.

**105:28–41.** The following enumeration of the "signs" does not follow the order in Exodus, but begins with the ninth plague, perhaps because

| 904, 3826B | 2174 | 375 | 904, 8101 | 3911.151 | | 7975.111 |
|---|---|---|---|---|---|---|
| prep, n ms | cj, n ms | cj, *sub* | prep, n mp, ps 3ms | v Qal act ptc ms | **38.** | v Qal pf 3ms |
| בְּכֶסֶף | וְזָהָב | וְאֵין | בִּשְׁבָטָיו | כּוֹשֵׁל | | שָׂמַח |
| bekhes̱eph | wezāhāv | we'ên | bishvāṯāv | kôshēl | | sāmach |
| with silver | and gold | and there was not | among their tribes | one who stumbled | | they were glad |

| 4875 | 904, 3428.141 | 3706, 5489.111 | 6586 | 6142 |
|---|---|---|---|---|
| pn | prep, v Qal inf con, ps 3mp | cj, v Qal pf 3ms | n ms, ps 3mp | prep, ps 3mp |
| מִצְרַיִם | בְּצֵאתָם | כִּי־נָפַל | פַּחְדָּם | עֲלֵיהֶם |
| mitsrayim | betsē'thām | kî-nāphal | pachdām | 'ălêhem |
| Egypt | when their going out | because it had fallen | the terror of them | on them |

| | 6816.111 | 6281 | 3937, 4689 | 813 | 3937, 213.541 | 4050 | | 8068.111 |
|---|---|---|---|---|---|---|---|---|
| **39.** | v Qal pf 3ms | n ms | prep, n ms | cj, n fs | prep, v Hiphil inf con | n ms | **40.** | v Qal pf 3ms |
| | פָּרַשׂ | עָנָן | לְמָסָךְ | וְאֵשׁ | לְהָאִיר | לָיְלָה | | שָׁאַל |
| | pāras | 'ānān | lemās̱ākh | we'ēsh | lehā'îr | lāyelāh | | shā'al |
| | He spread out | a cloud | for a covering | and fire | to illuminate | at night | | they asked |

| 971.521 | 7967 | 4035 | 8452 | 3588.521 | | 6858.111 | 6962 |
|---|---|---|---|---|---|---|---|
| cj, Hiphil impf 3ms | n fs | cj, *n ms* | n md | v Hiphil impf 3ms, ps 3mp | **41.** | v Qal pf 3ms | n ms |
| וַיָּבֵא | שְׂלָו | וְלֶחֶם | שָׁמַיִם | יַשְׂבִּיעֵם | | פָּתַח | צוּר |
| wayyāvē' | selāw | welechem | shāmayim | yasbî'ēm | | pāthach | tsûr |
| and He brought | quail | and the bread of | the heavens | it satisfied them | | He opened | a rock |

| 2183.126 | 4448 | 2050.116 | 904, 6993 | 5282 |
|---|---|---|---|---|
| cj, v Qal impf 3mp | n mp | v Qal pf 3cp | prep, art, n fp | n ms |
| וַיָּזוּבוּ | מָיִם | הָלְכוּ | בַּצִּיּוֹת | נָהָר |
| wayyāzûvû | māyim | hālekhû | batstsîyôth | nāhār |
| and they gushed out | waters | they proceeded | in the waterless regions | a river |

| | 3706, 2226.111 | 881, 1745 | 7231 | 882, 80 | 5860 |
|---|---|---|---|---|---|
| **42.** | cj, v Qal pf 3ms | do, *n ms* | n ms, ps 3ms | prep, pn | n ms, ps 3ms |
| | כִּי־זָכַר | אֶת־דְּבַר | קָדְשׁוֹ | אֶת־אַבְרָהָם | עַבְדּוֹ |
| | kî-zākhar | 'eth-devar | qādheshô | 'eth-'avrāhām | 'avdô |
| | because He was mindful of | the word of | his holiness | with Abraham | his servant |

| | 3428.521 | 6194 | 904, 8050 | 904, 7726 | 881, 1008 |
|---|---|---|---|---|---|
| **43.** | cj, v Hiphil impf 3ms | n ms, ps 3ms | prep, n ms | prep, n fs | do, n mp, ps 3ms |
| | וַיּוֹצִא | עַמּוֹ | בְּשָׂשׂוֹן | בְּרִנָּה | אֶת־בְּחִירָיו |
| | wayyôtsi' | 'ammô | vesāsôn | berinnāh | 'eth-bechîrâv |
| | and He led out | his people | with joy | with a shout of joy | his chosen ones |

| | 5598.121 | 3937 | 800 | 1504 | 6221 | 3947 |
|---|---|---|---|---|---|---|
| **44.** | cj, v Qal impf 3ms | prep, ps 3mp | *n fp* | n mp | cj, *n ms* | n mp |
| | וַיִּתֵּן | לָהֶם | אַרְצוֹת | גּוֹיִם | וַעֲמַל | לְאֻמִּים |
| | wayyittēn | lāhem | 'artsôth | gôyim | wa'āmal | le'ummîm |
| | and He gave | to them | the lands of | nations | and the labor of | peoples |

Israel with silver and gold, *RSV* … He brought out Israel, laden with silver and gold, *NIV* … carrying spoil of gold and silver, *Moffatt.*

**and there was not one feeble person among their tribes:** … And there was none that stumbled among His tribes, *MAST* … with not a weakning among their tribes, *NAB* … And there was no straggler in their ranks, *Goodspeed* … among all their tribes no man fell, *NEB.*

**38. Egypt was glad when they departed: for the fear of them fell upon them:** … Egypt rejoiced at their going, *NCB* … For terror had fallen upon them, *Goodspeed* … because they were afraid of them, *Beck* … for dread of them had seized them, *Berkeley.*

**39. He spread a cloud for a covering; and fire to give light in the night:** … and lit up the night with fire, *NCV* … And fire to illumine by night, *NASB* … that turned to fire in the darkness, lighting their journey, *Knox* … fire to light up the night, *JB.*

**40. The people asked, and he brought quails, and satisfied them with the bread of heaven:** ... and bread of heaven in plenty, *Moffatt* ... and gave them food from heaven in abundance, *NRSV* ... The skies filled with bread!, *Fenton* ... and refreshed them with bread from heaven, *Berkeley.*

**41. He opened the rock, and the waters gushed out; they ran in the dry places like a river:** ... it ran like a river through the desert, *NCV* ... it flowed through the dry lands like a stream, *NAB* ... There ran a river in the sands, *Goodspeed* ... flowed like a river through the arid land, *Anchor.*

**42. For he remembered his holy promise, and Abraham his servant:** ... he remembered his own sacred pledge, *Moffatt* ... His Word he kept true, *Fenton* ... remembered his solemn promise, *NEB* ... Faithful to his sacred promise, *JB.*

**43. And he brought forth his people with joy, and his chosen with gladness:** ... his chosen ones in triumph, *REB* ... His chosen ones with singing, *MAST* ... chosen ones with shouts of joy, *NIV* ... With shouts of triumph, *Rotherham.*

**44. And gave them the lands of the heathen:** ... the lands of the nations, *NRSV* ... the lands of the Gentiles, *NKJV.*

**and they inherited the labour of the people:** ... they took the labor of the peoples in possession, *ASV* ... they took what the peoples had toiled for, *NCB* ... the wealth of nations they seized, *Anchor.*

---

of its severity, and then in the main adheres to the original sequence, although it inverts the order of the third and forth plagues (flies and gnats or mosquitoes, not "lice") and omits the fifth and sixth. The reason for this divergence is far from clear, but it may be noted that the first two in the psalmist's order attack the elements; the next three (frogs, flies, gnats) have to do with animal life; and the next two (hail and locusts), which embrace both of these categories, are considered chiefly as affecting vegetable products. The emphasis is laid in all on God's direct act. He sends darkness, He turns the waters into blood, and so on. The only other point needing notice in these verses is the statement in v. 28b. "They rebelled not against his word," which obviously is true only in reference to Moses and Aaron, who shrank not from their perilous embassage.

The tenth plague is briefly told, for the Psalm is hurrying on to the triumphant climax of the Exodus when, enriched with silver and gold, the tribes went forth, strong for their desert march, and Egypt rejoiced to see the last of them, for they said, "We be all dead men" (Exo. 12:33). There may be a veiled hope in this exultant picture of the Exodus, that present oppression will end in like manner. The wilderness sojourn is so treated in v. 39 as to bring into sight only the leading instances, sung in many Psalms, of God's protection, without one disturbing reference to the sins and failures which darkened the forty years. These are spread out at length, without flattery or minimizing, in the next Psalm, but here the theme is God's wonders. Therefore, the pillar of cloud which guided, covered and illumined the camp and the miracles which provided food and water are touched on in vv. 39ff, and then the psalmist gathers up the lessons which he would teach in three great thoughts.

**105:42–45.** The reason for God's merciful dealings with his people is his remembrance of his Covenant and of his servant Abraham, whose faith made a claim on God, for the fulfillment which would vindicate it. That Covenant has been amply fulfilled, for Israel came forth with ringing songs and took possession of lands which they had not tilled and houses which they had not built. The purpose of covenant and fulfillment is that the nation, thus admitted into a special relationship with God, should by his mercies be drawn to keep his commandments and, in obedience, find rest and closer fellowship with its God. The psalmist had learned that God gives before He demands or commands and that "love," springing from grateful reception of his benefits, "is the fulfilling of the Law" (Rom. 13:10). He anticipates the full Christian exhortation, "I beseech you, brethren, by the mercies of God, that ye present your bodies a living sacrifice" (Rom. 12:1).

***Psalm 106.*** *No trace of strophical arrangement is discernible. But after an introduction in some measure like that in Ps. 105, the psalmist plunges into his theme and draws out the long, sad story of Israel's faithlessness. He recounts seven instances during the wilderness sojourn (vv. 7–33) and then passes to those occurring in the Land (vv. 34–39), with which he connects the alternations of punishment and relenting on God's part and the obstinacy of transgression on Israel's, even down to the moment in which he speaks (vv. 40–46). The whole closes with a prayer for restoration to the land (v. 47), to which is appended the doxology (v. 48), the mark of the end of book four, and not a part of the Psalm.*

| 3542.126 | | 904, 5877 | 8490.126 | 2805 | 8784 |
|---|---|---|---|---|---|
| v Qal impf 3mp | 45. | prep, prep | v Qal impf 3mp | n mp, ps 3ms | cj, n fp, ps 3ms |
| יִירְשׁוּ | | בַּעֲבוּר | יִשְׁמְרוּ | חֻקָּיו | וְתוֹרֹתָיו |
| yîrāshû | | ba'ăvûr | yishmerû | chuqqâv | wethôrōthâv |
| they took possession of | | on account of | they observed | his statutes | and his instructions |

| 5526.126 | 2054.333, 3161 | | 2054.333, 3161 | 3142.533 | 3937, 3176 | 3706, 3005 |
|---|---|---|---|---|---|---|
| v Qal impf 3mp | v Piel impv 2mp, pn | 106:1 | v Piel impv 2mp, pn | v Hiphil impv 2mp | prep, pn | cj, adj |
| יִנְצֹרוּ | הַלְלוּ־יָהּ | | הַלְלוּיָהּ | הוֹדוּ | לַיהוָה | כִּי־טוֹב |
| yintsōrû | halelû-yāhh | | halelûyāhh | hôdhû | layhwāh | kî-ṭôv |
| they kept | praise Yah | | praise Yah | praise | Yahweh | because good |

| 3706 | 3937, 5986 | 2721 | | 4449 | 4589.321 | 1400 |
|---|---|---|---|---|---|---|
| cj | prep, n ms | n ms, ps 3ms | 2. | intrg | v Piel impf 3ms | *n fp* |
| כִּי | לְעוֹלָם | חַסְדּוֹ | | מִי | יְמַלֵּל | גְּבוּרוֹת |
| kî | le'ôlām | chasdô | | mî | yemallēl | gevûrôth |
| because | unto eternity | his steadfast love | | who | he can narrow down | the mighty deeds of |

| 3176 | 8471.521 | 3725, 8747 | | 869 | 8490.152 | 5122 |
|---|---|---|---|---|---|---|
| pn | v Hiphil impf 3ms | *adj*, n fs, ps 3ms | 3. | *n mp* | *v Qal act ptc mp* | n ms |
| יְהוָה | יַשְׁמִיעַ | כָּל־תְּהִלָּתוֹ | | אַשְׁרֵי | שֹׁמְרֵי | מִשְׁפָּט |
| yehwāh | yashmîa' | kol-tehillāthô | | 'ashrê | shōmerê | mishpāṭ |
| Yahweh | he can cause to hear | all his praises | | blessed | those who observe | justice |

| 6449.151 | 6930 | 904, 3725, 6496 | | 2226.131 | 3176 |
|---|---|---|---|---|---|
| *v Qal act ptc ms* | n fs | prep, *adj*, n fs | 4. | v Qal impv 2ms, ps 1cs | pn |
| עֹשֵׂה | צְדָקָה | בְכָל־עֵת | | זָכְרֵנִי | יְהוָה |
| 'ōsēh | tsedhāqāh | vekhol-'ēth | | zākherēnî | yehwāh |
| those who act with | righteousness | during all times | | remember me | O Yahweh |

| 904, 7814 | 6194 | 6734.131 | 904, 3568 | | 3937, 7495.141 |
|---|---|---|---|---|---|
| prep, *n ms* | n ms, ps 2ms | v Qal impv 2ms, ps 1cs | prep, n fs, ps 2ms | 5. | prep, v Qal inf con |
| בִּרְצוֹן | עַמֶּךָ | פָּקְדֵנִי | בִּישׁוּעָתֶךָ | | לִרְאוֹת |
| birtsôn | 'ammekhā | pāqōdhēnî | bîshû'āthekhā | | lir'ôth |
| during the favor of | your people | intervene for me | during your salvation | | to look |

| 904, 3009B | 1008 | 3937, 7975.141 | 904, 7977 | 1504 |
|---|---|---|---|---|
| prep, *n fs* | n mp, ps 2ms | prep, v Qal inf con | prep, *n fs* | n ms, ps 2ms |
| בְּטוֹבַת | בְּחִירֶיךָ | לִשְׂמֹחַ | בְּשִׂמְחַת | גּוֹיֶךָ |
| beṭôvath | bechîrêkhā | lismōach | besimchath | gôyekhā |
| on the good things of | your chosen ones | to be glad | with gladness | your nation |

| 3937, 2054.741 | 6196, 5338 | | 2490.119 | 6196, 1 |
|---|---|---|---|---|
| prep, v Hithpael inf con | prep, n fs, ps 2ms | 6. | v Qal pf 1cp | prep, n mp, ps 1cp |
| לְהִתְהַלֵּל | עִם־נַחֲלָתֶךָ | | חָטָאנוּ | עִם־אֲבוֹתֵינוּ |
| lehithhallēl | 'im-nachlāthekhā | | chāṭā'nû | 'im-'ăvôthênû |
| to boast | with your inheritance | | we have sinned | with our ancestors |

| 5971.519 | 7855.519 | | 1 | 904, 4875 | 3940, 7959.516 |
|---|---|---|---|---|---|
| v Hiphil pf 1cp | v Hiphil pf 1cp | 7. | n mp, ps 1cp | prep, pn | neg part, v Hiphil pf 3cp |
| הֶעֱוִינוּ | הִרְשָׁעְנוּ | | אֲבוֹתֵינוּ | בְמִצְרַיִם | לֹא־הִשְׂכִּילוּ |
| he'ĕwînû | hirshā'ănû | | 'ăvôthênû | vemitsrayim | lō'-hiskîlû |
| we have trangressed | we have acted wickedly | | our ancestors | in Egypt | they did not consider |

| 6623.258 | 3940 | 2226.116 | 881, 7524 | 2721 |
|---|---|---|---|---|
| v Niphal ptc fp, ps 2ms | neg part | v Qal pf 3cp | do, *n ms* | n mp, ps 2ms |
| נִפְלְאוֹתֶיךָ | לֹא | זָכְרוּ | אֶת־רֹב | חֲסָדֶיךָ |
| niphle'ôthêkhā | lō' | zākherû | 'eth-rōv | chăsādhêkhā |
| your extraordinary deeds | neither | did they remember | the abundance of | your steadfast love |

**45. That they might observe his statutes, and keep his laws. Praise ye the LORD:** ... This was so they would keep his orders and obey his teachings, *NCV* ... If they keep His decrees, And always His laws, *Fenton* ... so that they might do what He ordered, *Beck* ... they might be faithful to His statutes, *Berkeley*.

**106:1. Praise ye the LORD. O give thanks unto the LORD; for he is good: for his mercy endureth for ever:** ... his faithful love is everlasting!, *JB* ... His lovingkindness is everlasting, *NASB* ... His love continues forever, *NCV* ... his kindness never fails, *Moffatt*.

**2. Who can utter the mighty acts of the LORD? who can show forth all his praise?:** ... His Glories who can tell?, *Fenton* ... Who can put into words the mighty deeds of the LORD?, *Berkeley* ... express Yahweh's might, *Anchor*.

**3. Blessed are they that keep judgment:** ... Happy are they whose decisions are upright, *BB* ... How blessed are those who keep justice, *NASB* ... they who abide ever by his decrees, *Knox*.

**and he that doeth righteousness at all times:** ... who do always what is just, *NAB* ... who constantly do what is right, *NIV* ... whose conduct is always upright!, *JB*.

**4. Remember me, O LORD, with the favour that thou bearest unto thy people:** ... Keep me in mind, O Lord, when you are good to your people, *BB* ... remember me when you are kind to your people, *NCV*.

**O visit me with thy salvation:** ... help me when you deliver them, *NRSV* ... visit me with your saving help, *NAB* ... Come near to me with your saving power, *JB* ... look on me when you save them, *REB*.

**5. That I may see the good of thy chosen, that I may rejoice in the gladness of thy nation:** ... That I may behold the prosperity of Thy chosen, *MAST* ... that I may see the prosperity of your chosen ones, *NRSV* ... That I may see the benefit of Your chosen ones, *NKJV* ... enjoy the prosperity of your chosen, *Anchor*.

**that I may glory with thine inheritance:** ... the triumph of thy land, *Moffatt* ... join your inheritance in giving praise, *NIV* ... and boast with those who are Your own, *Beck* ... and exult with thy own people, *NEB*.

**6. We have sinned with our fathers, we have committed iniquity, we have done wickedly:** ... we have committed crimes; we have done wrong, *NCB* ... We have acted perversely, we have committed lawlessness, *Rotherham* ... we have gone astray and done wrong, *REB* ... We have done wrong; we have done evil, *NCV*.

**7. Our fathers understood not thy wonders in Egypt:** ... Our forefathers in Egypt disregarded your marvels, *REB* ... Our ancestors in Egypt did not learn from your miracles, *NCV* ... they gave no thought to your miracles, *NIV* ... Our fathers did not appreciate Thy miracles in Egypt, *Berkeley*.

---

**106:1–3.** The psalmist preludes his confession and contemplation of his people's sins by a glad remembrance of God's goodness and enduring steadfast love and by a prayer for himself. Some commentators regard these introductory verses as incongruous with the tone of the Psalm and as mere liturgical commonplace, which has been tacked on without much heed to fitness. But surely the thought of God's unspeakable goodness most appropriately precedes the psalmist's confession, for nothing so melts a heart in penitence as the remembrance of God's love, and nothing so heightens the evil of sin as the consideration of the patient goodness which it has long flouted. The blessing pronounced in v. 3 on those who "do righteousness" and keep the Law is not less natural before a Psalm which sets forth in melancholy detail the converse truth of the misery of those breaking the Law.

**106:4–5.** In vv. 4f, the psalmist interjects a prayer for himself, the abruptness of which strongly reminds us of similar jets of personal supplication in Nehemiah. The determination to make the "I" of the Psalter refer to the nation perversely insists on that personification here, in spite of the clear distinction thrice drawn in v. 5 between the psalmist and his people. The "salvation" in which he desires to share is the deliverance from exile for which he prays in the closing verse of the Psalm. There is something very pathetic in this momentary thought of self. It breathes wistful yearning, absolute confidence in the unrealized deliverance and lowly humility which bases its claim with God on that of the nation. Such a prayer stands in the closest relation to the theme of the Psalm, which draws out the dark record of national sin, in order to lead to that national repentance which, as all the history shows, is the necessary condition of "the good of thy chosen." Precisely because the hope of restoration is strong, the delineation of sin is unsparing.

**106:6–12.** With v. 6, the theme of the Psalm is given forth in language which recalls Solomon's and Daniel's similar confessions (1 Ki. 8:47; Dan. 9:5). The accumulation of synonyms for sin witnesses at once to the gravity and manifold offences and to the earnestness and comprehensiveness of the acknowledgment. The remarkable expression

| | | | | | |
|---|---|---|---|---|---|
| 4947.526<br>cj, v Hiphil impf 3mp<br>וַיַּמְרוּ<br>wayyamrû<br>but they rebelled | 6142, 3328<br>prep, n ms<br>עַל־יָם<br>ʿal-yām<br>beside the sea | 904, 3328, 5675<br>prep, *n ms*, n ms<br>בְּיַם־סוּף<br>beyam-sûph<br>by the Sea of Reeds | **8.** | 3588.521<br>cj, v Hiphil impf 3ms, ps 3mp<br>וַיּוֹשִׁיעֵם<br>wayyôshîʿēm<br>but He saved them | 3937, 4775<br>prep, prep<br>לְמַעַן<br>lemaʿan<br>because of |

| | | | | | |
|---|---|---|---|---|---|
| 8428<br>n ms, ps 3ms<br>שְׁמוֹ<br>shemô<br>his name | 3937, 3156.541<br>prep, v Hiphil inf con<br>לְהוֹדִיעַ<br>lehôdhîaʿ<br>to cause to know | 881, 1400<br>do, n fs, ps 3ms<br>אֶת־גְּבוּרָתוֹ<br>'eth-gevûrāthô<br>his might | **9.** | 1647.121<br>cj, v Qal impf 3ms<br>וַיִּגְעַר<br>wayyighʿar<br>He rebuked | 904, 3328, 5675<br>prep, *n ms*, n ms<br>בְּיַם־סוּף<br>beyam-sûph<br>by the Sea of Reeds |

| | | | |
|---|---|---|---|
| 2817.121<br>cj, v Qal impf 3ms<br>וַיֶּחֱרָב<br>wayyechĕrāv<br>and it dried up | 2050.521<br>cj, v Hiphil impf 3ms, ps 3mp<br>וַיּוֹלִיכֵם<br>wayyôlîkhēm<br>and He caused them to walk | 904, 8745<br>prep, art, n fp<br>בַּתְּהֹמוֹת<br>battehōmôth<br>on the deeps | 3626, 4198<br>prep, art, n ms<br>כַּמִּדְבָּר<br>kammidhbār<br>like the desert |

| | | | | |
|---|---|---|---|---|
| **10.** | 3588.521<br>cj, v Hiphil impf 3ms, ps 3ms<br>וַיּוֹשִׁיעֵם<br>wayyôshîʿēm<br>and He saved them | 4623, 3135<br>prep, *n fs*<br>מִיַּד<br>mîyadh<br>from the hand of | 7983.151<br>v Qal act ptc ms<br>שׂוֹנֵא<br>sônē'<br>the hater | 1381.121<br>cj, v Qal impf 3ms, ps 3mp<br>וַיִּגְאָלֵם<br>wayyigh'ālēm<br>and He redeemed them |

| | | | | | | |
|---|---|---|---|---|---|---|
| 4623, 3135<br>prep, *n fs*<br>מִיַּד<br>mîyadh<br>from the hand of | 342.151<br>v Qal act ptc ms<br>אוֹיֵב<br>'ôyēv<br>the enemy | **11.** | 3803.326, 4448<br>cj, v Piel impf 3mp, n md<br>וַיְכַסּוּ־מַיִם<br>waykhassû-mayim<br>and the waters covered | 7141<br>n mp, ps 3mp<br>צָרֵיהֶם<br>tsārêhem<br>their adversaries | 259<br>num<br>אֶחָד<br>'echādh<br>one | 4623<br>prep, ps 3mp<br>מֵהֶם<br>mēhem<br>from them |

| | | | | | | |
|---|---|---|---|---|---|---|
| 3940<br>neg part<br>לֹא<br>lō'<br>not | 3613.211<br>v Niphal pf 3ms<br>נוֹתָר<br>nôthār<br>they were left | **12.** | 548.526<br>cj, v Hiphil impf 3mp<br>וַיַּאֲמִינוּ<br>wayya'ămînû<br>then they believed | 904, 1745<br>prep, n mp, ps 3ms<br>בִדְבָרָיו<br>vidhvārâv<br>on his words | 8301.126<br>v Qal impf 3mp<br>יָשִׁירוּ<br>yāshîrû<br>they sang | 8747<br>n fs, ps 3ms<br>תְּהִלָּתוֹ<br>tehillāthô<br>his praise |

| | | | | | |
|---|---|---|---|---|---|
| **13.** | 4257.316<br>v Piel pf 3cp<br>מִהֲרוּ<br>mihrû<br>they hurried | 8319.116<br>v Qal pf 3cp<br>שָׁכְחוּ<br>shākhechû<br>they forgot | 4801<br>n mp, ps 3ms<br>מַעֲשָׂיו<br>maʿăsâv<br>his works | 3940, 2542.316<br>neg part, v Piel pf 3cp<br>לֹא־חִכּוּ<br>lō'-chikkû<br>they were not patient | 3937, 6332<br>prep, n fs, ps 3ms<br>לַעֲצָתוֹ<br>laʿătsāthô<br>for his counsel |

| | | | | | |
|---|---|---|---|---|---|
| **14.** | 181.726<br>cj, v Hithpael impf 3mp<br>וַיִּתְאַוּוּ<br>wayyith'awwû<br>but they desired | 8707<br>n fs<br>תַאֲוָה<br>tha'ăwāh<br>a desire | 904, 4198<br>prep, art, n ms<br>בַּמִּדְבָּר<br>bammidhbār<br>in the wilderness | 5441.326, 418<br>cj, v Piel impf 3mp, n ms<br>וַיְנַסּוּ־אֵל<br>waynassû-'ēl<br>and they put God to the test | 904, 3574<br>prep, n ms<br>בִּישִׁימוֹן<br>bîshîmôn<br>in the desert |

**they remembered not the multitude of thy mercies:** ... They have not remembered The abundance of Thy kind acts, *Young* ... or remember how much You loved them, *Beck* ... many acts of faithful love, *NEB* ... the abundance of thy steadfast love, *RSV.*

**but provoked him at the sea, even at the Red sea:** ... But rebelled against the Most High at the Red Sea, *Goodspeed* ... But were rebellious at the sea, *ASV* ... on their journey they rebelled by the Red Sea, *REB* ... At the Reed Sea our fathers defied the Most High, *Moffatt.*

**8. Nevertheless he saved them for his name's sake, that he might make his mighty power to be known:** ... to display his power, *Moffatt* ... to let them know His power, *Beck* ... to make known his power, he delivered them, *Knox.*

**9. He rebuked the Red sea also, and it was dried up: so he led them through the depths, as through the wilderness:** ... them through the deep as through a desert, *RSV* ... And they marched in the depth, as a field, *Fenton.*

**10. And he saved them from the hand of him that hated them, and redeemed them from the hand of the enemy:** ... saving them from hostile hands, rescuing them from the foe, *Moffatt* ... saved them from the hand of the foe, *NRSV* ... claimed them back from the enemy's hand, *NEB* ... He redeemed them from the enemies' grasp, *Berkeley.*

**11. And the waters covered their enemies: there was not one of them left:** ... And the waters covered their oppressors, *Darby* ... the water overwhelmed their pursuers, *Knox* ... waters closed over their adversaries, *NEB.*

**12. Then believed they his words; they sang his praise:** ... Then they had faith in his words, *BB* ... they believed His promises, *NIV* ... Then they put their trust in His word, *Fenton.*

**13. They soon forgat his works:** ... They hurried to forget His works, *KJVII* ... But soon they forgot what he had done, *Moffatt* ... soon forgot his deeds, *Goodspeed.*

**they waited not for his counsel:** ... they did not even wait for his plans, *JB* ... did not wait for his advice, *Anchor.*

**14. But lusted exceedingly in the wilderness:** ... They gave way to craving in the desert, *NAB* ... But craved intensely, *NASB* ... They complained bitterly in the desert, *Anchor* ... They became greedy for food in the desert, *NCV.*

**and tempted God in the desert:** ... And tested God, *NKJV* ... in the solitary wastes they challenged God, *JB* ... there in the desert they tried God's patience, *REB.*

---

"We have sinned with our fathers" is not to be weakened to mean merely that the present generation had sinned like their ancestors, but gives expression to the profound sense of national solidarity, which speaks in many other places of Scripture and rests on very deep facts in the life of nations and their individual members. The enumeration of ancestral sin begins with the murmurings of the faint-hearted fugitives by the Red Sea. In Ps. 105, the wonders in Egypt were dilated on and the events at the Red Sea unmentioned. Here the signs in Egypt are barely referred to and treated as past at the point where the Psalm begins, while the incidents by the Red Sea fill a large space in the song. Clearly, the two Psalms supplement each other. The reason given for Israel's rebellion in Ps. 106 is its forgetfulness of God's mighty deeds (v. 7a, b), while in Ps. 105 the remembrance of these is urgently enjoined. Thus, again, the connection of thought in the pair of Psalms is evident. Every man has experiences enough of God's goodness stored away in the chambers of his memory to cure him of distrust, if he would only look at them. But they lie unnoticed, and so fear has sway over him. No small part of the discipline needed for vigorous hope lies in vigorous exercise of remembrance. The drying up of the Red Sea is poetically represented here, with the omission of Moses' outstretched rod and the strong east wind, as the immediate consequence of God's omnipotent rebuke. Verse 9b is from Isa. 63:13 and picturesquely describes the march through that terrible gorge of heaped-up waters as being easy and safe as if it had been across some wide-stretching plain, with springy turf to tread on. The triumphant description of the completeness of the enemies' destruction in v. 11b is from Exo. 14:28, and "then believed they on his words" is in part quoted from Exo. 14:31, while Miriam's song is referred to in v. 12b.

**106:13–15.** The next instance of departure is the lusting for food (vv. 13ff). Again the evil is traced to forgetfulness of God's doings, to which in v. 13b is added impatient disinclination to await the unfolding of his counsel or plan. These evils cropped up with strange celerity. The memory of benefits was transient, as if they had been written on the blown sands of the desert. "They soon forgat his works" has to be said of many of us! We remember pain and sorrow longer than joy and pleasure. It is always difficult to bridle desires and be still until God discloses his purposes. We are all apt to try to force his hand open and to impose our wishes on Him, rather than to let his will mold us. So, on forgeting his works and lacking patience there followed then, as there follow still, eager longings after material good and a tempting of God. They "fell a-lusting" is from Num. 11:4. "Tempted God" is found in reference to the same incident in the other Psalm of historical retrospect (Ps. 78:18). He is "tempted" when unbelief demands proofs of his power, instead of waiting patiently for Him. In Num. 11:33, Yahweh is said to have smitten the people "with a very great plague." The Psalm specifies more particularly the nature of the stroke by saying he "sent leanness into their soul." The words are true in a deeper sense, though not so meant. For whoever sets his hot desires in self-willed fashion on material good and succeeds in securing their

| 15. | 5598.121 | 3937 | 8072 | 8365.321 | 7614 | 904, 5497 |
|---|---|---|---|---|---|---|
| | cj, v Qal impf 3ms | prep, ps 3mp | n fs, ps 3mp | cj, v Piel impf 3ms | n ms | prep, n fs, ps 3mp |
| | וַיִּתֵּן | לָהֶם | שֶׁאֱלָתָם | וַיְשַׁלַּח | רָזוֹן | בְּנַפְשָׁם |
| | wayyittēn | lāhem | she'ĕlāthām | wayshallach | rāzôn | b$^{e}$naphshām |
| | but He gave | to them | their request | but He sent | a wasting disease | on their life |

| 16. | 7349.326 | 3937, 5057 | 904, 4402 | 3937, 172 | 7202 | 3176 |
|---|---|---|---|---|---|---|
| | cj, v Piel impf 3mp | prep, pn | prep, art, n ms | prep, pn | *n ms* | pn |
| | וַיְקַנְאוּ | לְמֹשֶׁה | בַּמַּחֲנֶה | לְאַהֲרֹן | קְדוֹשׁ | יְהוָה |
| | wayqan'û | l$^{e}$mōsheh | bammachneh | le'ahrōn | qōdhôsh | y$^{e}$hwāh |
| | when they were jealous | of Moses | in the camp | of Aaron | the holy one of | Yahweh |

| 17. | 6858.122, 800 | 1142.122 | 1950 | 3803.322 | 6142, 5920 | 49 |
|---|---|---|---|---|---|---|
| | v Qal impf 3fs, n fs | cj, v Qal impf 3fs | pn | cj, v Piel impf 3fs | prep, *n fs* | pn |
| | תִּפְתַּח־אֶרֶץ | וַתִּבְלַע | דָּתָן | וַתְּכַס | עַל־עֲדַת | אֲבִירָם |
| | tiphtach-'erets | wattivla' | dāthān | watt$^{e}$khas | 'al-'ădhath | 'ăvîrām |
| | the earth opened | and it swallowed | Dathan | and it covered | upon the assembly of | Abiram |

| 18. | 1220.122, 813 | 904, 5920 | 3988 | 3993.322 | 7857 |
|---|---|---|---|---|---|
| | cj, v Qal impf 3fs, n fs | prep, n fs, ps 3mp | n fs | v Piel impf 3fs | n mp |
| | וַתִּבְעַר־אֵשׁ | בַּעֲדָתָם | לֶהָבָה | תְּלַהֵט | רְשָׁעִים |
| | wattiv'ar-'ēsh | ba'ădhāthām | lehāvāh | t$^{e}$lahēt | r$^{e}$shā'îm |
| | and a fire burned | among their assembly | a flame | it ignited | the wicked |

| 19. | 6449.126, 5903 | 904, 2822 | 8246.726 | 3937, 4691 | 20. | 4306.526 |
|---|---|---|---|---|---|---|
| | v Qal impf 3mp, n ms | prep, pn | cj, v Hithpael impf 3mp | prep, n fs | | cj, v Hiphil impf 3mp |
| | יַעֲשׂוּ־עֵגֶל | בְּחֹרֵב | וַיִּשְׁתַּחֲווּ | לְמַסֵּכָה | | וַיָּמִירוּ |
| | ya'ăsû-'ēghel | b$^{e}$chōrēv | wayyishtachwû | l$^{e}$massēkhāh | | wayyāmîrû |
| | they made a calf | in Horeb | and they worshiped | a cast image | | and they exchanged |

| 881, 3638 | 904, 8732 | 8228 | 404.151 | 6448 | 21. | 8319.116 | 418 |
|---|---|---|---|---|---|---|---|
| do, n ms, ps 3mp | prep, *n fs* | n ms | v Qal act ptc ms | n ms | | v Qal pf 3cp | n ms |
| אֶת־כְּבוֹדָם | בְּתַבְנִית | שׁוֹר | אֹכֵל | עֵשֶׂב | | שָׁכְחוּ | אֵל |
| 'eth-k$^{e}$vôdhām | b$^{e}$thavnîth | shôr | 'ōkhēl | 'ēsev | | shākh$^{e}$chû | 'ēl |
| their glory | with the image of | an ox | eating | grass | | they forgot | God |

| 3588.551 | 6449.151 | 1448 | 904, 4875 | 22. | 6623.258 |
|---|---|---|---|---|---|
| v Hiphil ptc ms, ps 3mp | v Qal act ptc ms | adj | prep, pn | | v Niphal ptc fp |
| מוֹשִׁיעָם | עֹשֶׂה | גְדֹלוֹת | בְּמִצְרָיִם | | נִפְלָאוֹת |
| môshî'ām | 'ōseh | gh$^{e}$dhōlôth | b$^{e}$mitsrāyim | | niphlā'ôth |
| their Savior | the One Who did | great deeds | in Egypt | | being extraordinary |

| 904, 800 | 2626 | 3486.258 | 6142, 3328. 5675 | 23. | 569.121 |
|---|---|---|---|---|---|
| prep, *n fs* | pn | v Niphal ptc fp | prep, *n ms*, n ms | | cj, v Qal impf 3ms |
| בְּאֶרֶץ | חָם | נוֹרָאוֹת | עַל־יַם־סוּף | | וַיֹּאמֶר |
| b$^{e}$'erets | chām | nôrā'ôth | 'al-yam-sûph | | wayyō'mer |
| in the land of | Ham | fearful | beside the Sea of Reeds | | so He said |

**15. And he gave them their request:** ... He let them have what they wanted, *Berkeley* ... he gave them what they asked, *NRSV.*

**but sent leanness into their soul:** ... sent a wasting disease into their souls, *BB* ... then sent a wasting sickness to plague them, *Knox* ... But sent to their bodies disease, *Fenton.*

**16. They envied Moses also in the camp, and Aaron the saint of the LORD:** ... When men in the camp were jealous of Moses, *RSV* ... They were full of envy against Moses among the tents, *BB* ... In the camp they grew envious of Moses, *NIV.*

**17. The earth opened and swallowed up Dathan, and covered the company of Abiram:** ... and buried Abiram's group, *Beck* ... And engulfed the company of Abiram, *NASB* ... and closed over Abiram's group, *NCV.*

**18. And a fire was kindled in their company:** ... fire flamed out against their faction, *JB* ... A fire broke out among their assemblage, *Berkeley* ...

fire raged through their company, *NEB* ... Fire blazed among their followers, *NIV.*

**the flame burned up the wicked:** ... a flame consumed the wicked, *NCB* ... the sinners were burned up by the flames, *BB* ... and the rebels perished by its flames, *Knox* ... the wicked perished in flames, *REB.*

**19. They made a calf in Horeb, and worshipped the molten image:** ... bowed low before cast metal, *JB* ... To a statue they bowed themselves down, *Fenton* ... and worshipped a metal image, *Moffatt.*

**20. Thus they changed their glory into the similitude of an ox that eateth grass:** ... Thus changed they my glory, *Rotherham* ... And change their Honour Into the form of an ox, *Young* ... So they traded their glorious God for a statue, *Beck* ... Thus they exchanged their glory, *MAST.*

**21. They forgat God their saviour, which had done great things in Egypt:** ... They forgot God who had delivered them, *Goodspeed* ... They forgot God their Deliverer, *KJVII* ... They forgot the God who saved them, *NIV* ... They forgot the God who was saving them, *JB.*

**22. Wondrous works in the land of Ham, and terrible things by the Red sea:** ... awesome happenings near the Reed Sea, *Anchor* ... At the Sea of Weeds terrors!, *Fenton* ... Of fearful things by the sea of Suph, *Young* ... and amazing things by the Red Sea, *NCV.*

**23. Therefore he said that he would destroy them, had not Moses his chosen stood before him in the breach:** ... What wonder if he threatened to make an end of them?, *Knox* ... So his purpose was to destroy them, *NEB* ... Then he spoke of exterminating them, *NCB.*

**to turn away his wrath, lest he should destroy them:** ... to keep his fury from ravaging them, *Anchor* ... to prevent his wrath from destroying them, *REB* ... to turn Him from wiping them out in His anger, *Berkeley* ... to avert his deadly wrath, *Moffatt.*

---

gratification gains with the satiety of his lower sense the loss of a shriveled spiritual nature. Full-fed flesh makes starved souls.

**106:16–18.** The third instance is the revolt headed by Korah, Dathan and Abiram against the exclusive Aaronic priesthood. It was rebellion against God, for He had set apart Aaron as his own, and therefore the unusual title of the "holy one of Yahweh" is here given to the high priest. The expression recalls the fierce protest of the mutineers, addressed to Moses and Aaron, "Ye take too much upon you, seeing all the congregation are holy" (Num. 16:3), and also Moses' answer, "The LORD will show ... who is holy" (v. 5). Envy often masquerades as the champion of the rights of the community, when it only wishes to grasp these for itself. These aristocratic democrats cared nothing for the prerogatives of the nation, although they talked about them. They wanted to pull down Aaron, not lift up Israel. Their end is described with stern brevity, in language colored by the narrative in Numbers from which the phrases "opened" (i.e., her mouth) and "covered" are drawn. Korah is not mentioned here, in which the Psalm follows Num. 16 and Deut. 11:6; whereas Num. 26:10 includes Korah in the destruction. The difficulty does not seem to have received any satisfactory solution. But it is too peremptory to undertake to divine the reason for the omission of Korah here and in Deut. 11:6, because he was a Levite and well known to temple poets." Such speculation as to motives is beyond necessity. In v. 18, the fate of the two hundred and fifty "princes of Israel" who took part in the revolt is recorded as in Num. 16:35.

**106:19–23.** The worship of the calf is the fourth instance in the narrative of which the psalmist follows Exo. 32, but seems also to have Deut. 9:8–12 floating in his mind, as appears from the use of the name "Horeb" (HED #2822), which is rare in Exodus and frequent in Deuteronomy. Verse 20 is apparently modeled on Jer. 2:11: "My people have changed their glory for that which doth not profit." Compare also Paul's "changed the glory of the incorruptible God into an image ... " (Rom. 1:23). "His glory" is read instead of "their glory" by old Jewish authority. It yields a worthy meaning, but the existing text is quite appropriate. It scarcely means that God was the source of Israel's glory or their boast, for the word is not found in that sense. It is much rather the name for the collective attributes of the revealed Godhead, and is here substantially equivalent to "their God," that lustrous Light which, in a special manner, belonged to the people of revelation, on Whom its first and brightest beams shone. The strange perverseness which turned them away from such a radiance of glory to bow down before an idol is strikingly set forth by the figure of bartering it for an image and that of an ox that ate grass. The one true substance was given away for a shadow. The lofty being whose light filled space surrendered: and for what? a brute that had to feed, and that on

| **3937, 8436.541** | **4020** | **5057** | **1008** | **6198.111** | **904, 6806** | **3937, 6686** |
|---|---|---|---|---|---|---|
| prep, v Hiphil inf con, ps 3mp | cj | pn | n ms, ps 3ms | v Qal pf 3ms | prep, art, n ms | prep, n mp, ps 3ms |
| לְהַשְׁמִידָם | לוּלֵי | מֹשֶׁה | בְּחִירוֹ | עָמַד | בַּפֶּרֶץ | לְפָנָיו |
| lehashmîdhām | lûlê | mōsheh | vechîrô | ʿāmadh | bapperets | lephānâv |
| to destroy them | if not | Moses | his chosen one | he had stood | in the space | before Him |

| **3937, 8178.541** | **2635** | **4623, 8271.541** | **24.** | **4128.126** | **904, 800** |
|---|---|---|---|---|---|
| prep, v Hiphil inf con | n fs, ps 3ms | prep, v Hiphil inf con | | cj, v Qal impf 3mp | prep, *n fs* |
| לְהָשִׁיב | חֲמָתוֹ | מֵהַשְׁחִית | | וַיִּמְאֲסוּ | בְּאֶרֶץ |
| lehāshîv | chămāthô | mēhashchîth | | wayyim'ăsû | be'erets |
| to cause to turn back | his wrath | from annihilating | | but they despised | by the land of |

| **2631** | **3940, 548.516** | **3937, 1745** | **25.** | **7566.226** | **904, 164** |
|---|---|---|---|---|---|
| n fs | neg part, v Hiphil pf 3cp | prep, n ms, ps 3ms | | cj, v Niphal impf 3mp | prep, n mp, ps 3mp |
| חֶמְדָּה | לֹא־הֶאֱמִינוּ | לִדְבָרוֹ | | וַיֵּרָגְנוּ | בְּאָהֳלֵיהֶם |
| chemdāh | lō'-he'ĕmînû | lidhvārô | | wayyērāghenû | ve'āhelêhem |
| desirable things | they did not believe | his word | | and they grumbled | in their tents |

| **3940** | **8471.116** | **904, 7249** | **3176** | **26.** | **5558.121** | **3135** | **3937** |
|---|---|---|---|---|---|---|---|
| neg part | v Qal pf 3cp | prep, *n ms* | pn | | cj, v Qal impf 3ms | n fs, ps 3ms | prep, ps 3mp |
| לֹא | שָׁמְעוּ | בְּקוֹל | יְהוָה | | וַיִּשָּׂא | יָדוֹ | לָהֶם |
| lō' | shāme'û | beqôl | yehwāh | | wayyissā' | yādhô | lāhem |
| not | they listened | by the voice of | Yahweh | | so He lifted | his hand | to them |

| **3937, 5489.541** | **881** | **904, 4198** | **27.** | **3937, 5489.541** | **2320** |
|---|---|---|---|---|---|
| prep, v Hiphil inf con | do, ps 3mp | prep, art, n ms | | cj, prep, v Hiphil inf con | n ms, ps 3mp |
| לְהַפִּיל | אוֹתָם | בַּמִּדְבָּר | | וּלְהַפִּיל | זַרְעָם |
| lehappîl | 'ôthām | bammidhbār | | ûlăhappîl | zar'ām |
| to cause to fall | them | in the wilderness | | and to cause to fall | their descendants |

| **904, 1504** | **3937, 2306.341** | **904, 800** | **28.** | **7044.226** | **3937, 1211B** |
|---|---|---|---|---|---|
| prep, art, n mp | cj, prep, v Piel inf con | prep, art, n fp | | cj, v Niphal impf 3mp | prep, pn |
| בַּגּוֹיִם | וּלְזָרוֹתָם | בָּאֲרָצוֹת | | וַיִּצָּמְדוּ | לְבַעַל |
| baggôyim | ûlăzārôthām | bā'ărātsôth | | wayyitstsāmedhû | leva'al |
| among the nations | and to scatter | among the lands | | then they joined themselves | to Baal |

| **1211B** | **404.126** | **2160** | **4322.152** | **29.** | **3832.526** |
|---|---|---|---|---|---|
| pn | cj, v Qal impf 3mp | *n mp* | v Qal act ptc mp | | cj, v Hiphil impf 3mp |
| פְּעוֹר | וַיֹּאכְלוּ | זִבְחֵי | מֵתִים | | וַיַּכְעִיסוּ |
| pe'ôr | wayyō'khelû | zivchê | mēthîm | | wayyakh'îsû |
| Peor | and they ate | the sacrifices of | the dead | | and they provoked to anger |

| **904, 4770** | **6805.122, 904** | **4186** | **30.** | **6198.121** | **6615** |
|---|---|---|---|---|---|
| prep, n mp, ps 3mp | cj, v Qal impf 3fs, prep, ps 3mp | n fs | | cj, v Qal impf 3ms | pn |
| בְּמַעַלְלֵיהֶם | וַתִּפְרָץ־בָּם | מַגֵּפָה | | וַיַּעֲמֹד | פִּינְחָס |
| bema'alelêhem | wattiphrāts-bām | maggēphāh | | wayya'ămōdh | pînechās |
| with their practices | then it broke out among them | a plague | | but he stood | Phinehas |

| **6663.321** | **6352.222** | **4186** | **31.** | **2913.222** | **3937** |
|---|---|---|---|---|---|
| cj, v Piel impf 3ms | cj, v Niphal impf 3fs | art, n fs | | cj, v Niphal impf 3fs | prep, ps 3ms |
| וַיְפַלֵּל | וַתֵּעָצַר | הַמַּגֵּפָה | | וַתֵּחָשֶׁב | לוֹ |
| wayphallēl | wattē'ātsar | hammaggēphāh | | wattēchāshev | lô |
| and he interceded | and it was stayed | the plague | | and it was reckoned | to him |

| **3937, 6930** | **3937, 1810** | **1810** | **5912, 5986** | **32.** | **7395.526** |
|---|---|---|---|---|---|
| prep, n fs | prep, n ms | cj, n ms | adv, n ms | | cj, v Hiphil impf 3mp |
| לִצְדָקָה | לְדֹר | וָדֹר | עַד־עוֹלָם | | וַיַּקְצִיפוּ |
| litsdhāqāh | ledhōr | wādhōr | 'adh-'ôlām | | wayyaqtsîphû |
| for righteousness | unto generations | and generations | until forever | | but they angered |

**24. Yea, they despised the pleasant land:** ... they despised the desirable land, *NAB* ... they scorned the desirable land, *MAST* ... They were disgusted with the good land, *BB* ... And they refused the delightful land, *Rotherham.*

**they believed not his word:** ... they did not believe his promise, *NIV* ... They did not believe in His path, *Fenton* ... having no faith in his promise, *NRSV.*

**25. But murmured in their tents, and hearkened not unto the voice of the LORD:** ... They muttered treason in their tents, *REB* ... they stayed in their tents and grumbled, *JB.*

**26. Therefore he lifted up his hand against them:** ... So with hand uplifted against them he made an oath, *REB* ... Raising His hand, He swore to them, *Beck* ... So he swore to them with uplifted hand, *NIV.*

**to overthrow them in the wilderness:** ... That He would cast them down in the wilderness, *NASB* ... to destroy them, *Geneva* ... he would let them perish in the desert, *Goodspeed* ... He would let them fall in the wilderness, *Berkeley.*

**27. To overthrow their seed also among the nations, and to scatter them in the lands:** ... To overthrow their descendants among the nations, *NKJV* ... nations, and disperse them throughout the lands, *Anchor* ... they should be lost among the peoples, *Knox* ... and disperse them throughout the world, *NEB.*

**28. They joined themselves also unto Baal-peor:** ... But they went to serve Baal at Peor, *Beck* ... And they submitted to the rites of Baal of Peor, *NAB.*

**and ate the sacrifices of the dead:** ... ate sacrifices offered to the dead, *Goodspeed* ... and at meat sacrificed to lifeless gods, *REB* ... and ate food offered to the dead, *Moffatt.*

**29. Thus they provoked him to anger with their inventions:** ... till their wicked ways roused God's anger, *Knox* ... with their deeds, *NASB* ... by their wicked deeds, *NIV* ... made the LORD angry by their practices, *Berkeley.*

**and the plague brake in upon them:** ... a plague broke out among them, *Darby* ... so many people became sick with a terrible disease, *NCV* ... and he sent disease on them, *BB.*

**30. Then stood up Phinehas, and executed judgment: and so the plague was stayed:** ... Phin-e-has stood up and carried out judgment, *KJVII* ... And so the plague was stopped, *NKJV* ... interceded, and the plague was checked, *Anchor* ... And the plague is restrained, *Young.*

**31. And that was counted unto him for righteousness unto all generations for evermore:** ... And that has been reckoned to him as righteousness, *NRSV* ... This was credited to his

---

herbage! Men usually make a profit, or think they do, on their barter, but what do they gain by exchanging God for anything? Yet we keep making the same mistake of parting with substance for shadows. And the reason which moved Israel is still operative. As before, the psalmist traces their mad apostasy to forgetfulness of God's deeds. The list of these is now increased by the addition of those at the Red Sea. With every step new links were added to the chain that should have bound the recipients of so many mercies to God. Therefore, each new act of departure was of a darker hue of guilt and drew on the apostates severer punishment, which also, rightly understood, was greater mercy.

"He said that He would destroy them" is quoted from Deut. 9:25. Moses' intercession for the people is here most vividly represented under the figure of a champion who rushes into the breach by which the enemy is about to pour into some beleaguered town and with his own body closes the gap and arrests the assault (cf. Ezek. 22:30).

**106:24–27.** The fifth instance is the refusal to go up to the land, which followed on the report of the spies. These verses are full of reminiscences of the Pentateuch and other parts of Scripture. "The delightsome land" (literally, "land of desire") is found in Jer. 3:19 and Zech. 7:14. "They despised" is from Num. 14:31. "They murmured in their tents" is from Deut. 1:27 (the only other place in which the word for murmuring occurs in this form). Lifting up the hand is used, as here, not in the usual sense of threatening to strike, but in that of swearing, in Exo. 6:8, and the oath itself is given in Num. 14:28, while the expression "lifted up My hand" occurs in that context in reference to God's original oath to the patriarch. The threat of exile (v. 27) does not occur in Numbers, but is found as the punishment of apostasy in Lev. 26:33 and Deut. 28:64. The verse, however, is found almost exactly in Ezek. 20:23, with the exception that there "scatter" stands instead of "make to fall." The difference in the Hebrew is only in the final letter of the words, and the reading in Ezekiel should probably be adopted here.

**106:28–31.** The sixth instance is the participation in the abominable Moabitish worship of "Baal-Peor," recorded in Num. 25. The peculiar phrase "joined themselves also unto" is taken from that chapter and seems to refer to the mystic, union supposed to exist between a god and its followers par-

| 6142, 4448 | 4971 | 7778.121 | 3937, 5057 | 904, 5877 |
|---|---|---|---|---|
| prep, *n mp* | pn | cj, v Qal impf 3ms | prep, pn | prep, prep, ps 3mp |
| עַל־מֵי | מְרִיבָה | וַיֵּרַע | לְמֹשֶׁה | בַּעֲבוּרָם |
| 'al-mê | merîvāh | wayyēra' | lemōsheh | ba'ăvûrām |
| beside the waters of | Meribah | and it was evil | to Moses | on account of them |

| 33. | 3706, 4947.516 | 881, 7593 | 1017.321 | 904, 8004 |
|---|---|---|---|---|
| | cj, v Hiphil pf 3cp | do n fs, ps 3ms | cj, v Piel impf 3ms | prep, n fd, ps 3ms |
| | כִּי־הִמְרוּ | אֶת־רוּחוֹ | וַיְבַטֵּא | בִּשְׂפָתָיו |
| | kî-himrû | 'eth-rûchô | wayvattē' | bisphāthâv |
| | because they caused to be bitter | his spirit | and he spoke rashly | with his lips |

| 34. | 3940, 8436.516 | 881, 6194 | 866 | 569.111 | 3176 | 3937 |
|---|---|---|---|---|---|---|
| | neg part, v Hiphil pf 3cp | do, art, n mp | rel part | v Qal pf 3ms | pn | prep, ps 3mp |
| | לֹא־הִשְׁמִידוּ | אֶת־הָעַמִּים | אֲשֶׁר | אָמַר | יְהוָה | לָהֶם |
| | lō'-hishmîdhû | 'eth-hā'ammîm | 'ăsher | 'āmar | yehwāh | lāhem |
| | they did not destroy | the peoples | which | He had said | Yahweh | to them |

| 35. | 6386.726 | 904, 1504 | 4064.126 | 4801 | 36. | 5856.126 |
|---|---|---|---|---|---|---|
| | cj, v Hithpael impf 3mp | prep, art, n mp | cj, v Qal impf 3mp | n mp, ps 3mp | | cj, v Qal impf 3mp |
| | וַיִּתְעָרְבוּ | בַגּוֹיִם | וַיִּלְמְדוּ | מַעֲשֵׂיהֶם | | וַיַּעַבְדוּ |
| | wayyith'ārevû | vaggôyim | wayyilmedhû | ma'ăsêhem | | wayya'avdhû |
| | but they intermixed | among the nations | and they learned | their works | | and they served |

| 881, 6322 | 2030.126 | 3937 | 3937, 4305 | 37. | 2159.126 | 881, 1158 |
|---|---|---|---|---|---|---|
| do, n mp, ps 3mp | cj, v Qal impf 3mp | prep, ps 3mp | prep, n ms | | cj, v Qal impf 3mp | do, n mp, ps 3mp |
| אֶת־עֲצַבֵּיהֶם | וַיִּהְיוּ | לָהֶם | לְמוֹקֵשׁ | | וַיִּזְבְּחוּ | אֶת־בְּנֵיהֶם |
| 'eth-'ătsabbêhem | wayyihyû | lāhem | lemôqēsh | | wayyizbechû | 'eth-benêhem |
| their cast images | and they became | to them | a snare | | and they sacrificed | their sons |

| 881, 1351 | 3937, 8158 | 38. | 8581.126 | 1879 | 5538 |
|---|---|---|---|---|---|
| cj, do, n fp, ps 3mp | prep, art, n mp | | cj, v Qal impf 3mp | n ms | adj |
| וְאֶת־בְּנוֹתֵיהֶם | לַשֵּׁדִים | | וַיִּשְׁפְּכוּ | דָם | נָקִי |
| we'eth-benôthêhem | lashshēdhîm | | wayyishpekhû | dhām | nāqî |
| and their daughters | to the demons | | and they poured out | blood | innocent |

| 1879, 1158 | 1351 | 866 | 2159.316 | 3937, 6322 | 3791 |
|---|---|---|---|---|---|
| *n ms*, n mp, ps 3mp | cj, n fp, ps 3mp | rel pron | v Piel pf 3cp | prep, *n mp* | pn |
| דַּם־בְּנֵיהֶם | וּבְנוֹתֵיהֶם | אֲשֶׁר | זִבְּחוּ | לַעֲצַבֵּי | כְּנָעַן |
| dam-benêhem | ûvenôthêhem | 'ăsher | zibbechû | la'ătsabbê | khenā'an |
| the blood of their sons | and their daughters | whom | they sacrificed | to the cast images of | Canaan |

| 2714.122 | 800 | 904, 1879 | 39. | 3041.126 | 904, 4801 |
|---|---|---|---|---|---|
| cj, v Qal impf 3fs | art, n fs | prep, art, n mp | | cj, v Qal impf 3mp | prep, n mp, ps 3mp |
| וַתֶּחֱנַף | הָאָרֶץ | בַּדָּמִים | | וַיִּטְמְאוּ | בְמַעֲשֵׂיהֶם |
| wattechĕnaph | hā'ārets | baddāmîm | | wayyiṭme'û | vema'ăsêhem |
| and it was defiled | the land | with bloodshed | | and they became unclean | by their acts |

virtue, *Anchor* … it was imputed to him for merit, *NAB* … And all generations coming after him kept the memory of his righteousness for ever, *BB*.

**32. They angered him also at the waters of strife:** … At the waters of Meribah they so angered Yahweh, *JB* … They roused the LORD's anger at the waters of Meribah, *REB* … At the waters of Meribah they enraged God, *Moffatt*.

**so that it went ill with Moses for their sakes:** … So that it went hard with Moses on their account, *NASB* … and got Moses into trouble, *Beck* … Moses was punished for their sake, *Knox* … which made it hard for Moses on their account, *Berkeley*.

**33. Because they provoked his spirit:** … they were rebellious against his spirit, *MRB* … for they made his spirit bitter, *NRSV* … Because they rebelled against His Spirit, *NKJV* … they embittered his spirit, *Goodspeed*.

**so that he spake unadvisedly with his lips:** … And he spoke **rashly with**

his lips, *MAST* ... he spoke in his haste, *Fenton* ... and utter words in haste, *Moffatt* ... he spoke unwisely with his lips, *KJVII.*

**34. They did not destroy the nations, concerning whom the LORD commanded them:** ... They did not exterminate the peoples, *NCB* ... They did not put an end to the peoples,.

**35. But were mingled among the heathen, and learned their works:** ... but intermarried with them, and adopted their ways, *JB* ... mingled with the nations and learned to do as they did, *RSV* ... and learned their customs, *Anchor* ... and adopted their customs, *NIV.*

**36. And they served their idols: which were a snare unto them:** ... which were a trap for them, *Beck* ... gave worship to images; which were a danger, *BB* ... and were ensnared by them, *REB.*

**37. Yea, they sacrificed their sons and their daughters unto devils:** ... daughters to destroyers, *Young* ... they sacrificed to foreign deities, *REB* ... daughters to demons, *NIV.*

**38. And shed innocent blood, even the blood of their sons and of their daughters, whom they sacrificed unto the idols of Canaan: and the land was polluted with blood:** ... they desecrated the land with torrents of blood, *Anchor* ... the land was made unclean with blood, *BB.*

**39. Thus were they defiled with their own works:** ... Thus they became unclean in their practices, *NASB* ... They became unclean through their acts, *Goodspeed* ... The people became unholy by their sins, *NCV* ... And corrupted themselves by their acts, *Fenton.*

---

ticipated in during sacrificial meals. These are called sacrifices of the dead, inasmuch as idols are dead in contrast with the living God. The judicial retribution inflicted according to divine command by the judges of Israel slaying "every one his man" is here called a "plague" (HED #4186), as in the foundation passage, Num. 25:9. The word (literally, "a stroke," i.e., from God) is usually applied to punitive sickness; but God smites when He bids men smite. Both the narrative in Numbers and the Psalm bring out vividly the picture of the indignant Phinehas springing to his feet from the midst of the passive crowd. He "rose up," says the former; he "stood up," says the latter. And his deed is described in the Psalm in relation to its solemn judicial character, without particularizing its details. The psalmist would partially veil both the sin and the horror of its punishment. Phinehas' javelin was a minister of God's justice, and the death of the two culprits satisfied that justice and stayed the plague. The word rendered "executed judgment" (HED #6663) has that meaning only, and such renderings as mediated or appeased give the effect of the deed and not the description of it contained in the word. "It was reckoned to him for righteousness," as Abraham's faith was (Gen. 15:6). It was indeed an act which had its origin "in the faithfulness that had its root in faith and which, for the sake of this its ultimate ground, gained him the acceptation of a righteous man, inasmuch as it proved him to be such" (Delitzsch). He showed himself a true son of Abraham in the midst of these degenerate descendants, and it was the same impulse of faith which drove his spear and which filled the patriarch's heart when he gazed into the silent sky and saw in its numberless lights the promise of his seed. Phinehas' reward was the permanence of the priesthood in his family.

**106:32–39.** The seventh instance is the rebellion at the waters of Meribah "Strife" in the fortieth year (Num. 20:2–13). The chronological order is here set aside, for the events recorded in vv. 28–31 followed those dealt with in vv. 32f. The reason is probably that here Moses himself is hurried into sin on account of the people's faithlessness, and so a climax is reached. The leader, long-tried, fell at last and was shut out from entering the land. That was in some aspects the masterpiece and triumph of the nation's sin. "It went ill with Moses for their sakes," as in Deut. 1:37; 3:26, "Yahweh was angry with me for your sakes." "His Spirit," in v. 33, is best taken as referring to the Spirit of God. The people's sin is repeatedly specified in the Psalm as being rebellion against God, and the absence of a more distinct definition of the person referred to is like the expression in v. 32 where "anger" is that of God, although his name is not mentioned. Isaiah 63:10 is a parallel to this clause, as other parts of the same chapter are to other parts of the Psalm. The question that has been often raised, as to what was Moses' sin, is solved in v. 33b, which makes his passionate words, wherein he lost his temper and arrogated to himself the power of fetching water from the rock, the focus of his offense. The psalmist has finished his melancholy catalog of sins in the wilderness with this picture of the great leader dragged down by the prevailing tone, and he next turns to the sins done in the land.

Two flagrant instances are given—disobedience to the command to exterminate the inhabitants

| 2265.126 | 904, 4770 | 40. | 2835.121 | 653, 3176 |
|---|---|---|---|---|
| cj, v Qal impf 3mp | prep, n mp, ps 3mp | | cj, v Qal impf 3ms | *n ms*, pn |
| וַיִּזְנוּ | בְּמַעַלְלֵיהֶם | | וַיִּחַר | אַף־יְהוָה |
| wayyiznû | bema'alelêhem | | wayyichar | yehwāh-'aph |
| and they acted like a prostitute | by their practices | | so it was kindled | the nose of Yahweh |

| 904, 6194 | 8911.321 | 881, 5338 | 41. | 5598.121 |
|---|---|---|---|---|
| prep, n ms, ps 3ms | cj, v Piel impf 3ms | do, n fs, ps 3ms | | cj, v Qal impf 3ms, ps 3mp |
| בְּעַמּוֹ | וַיְתָעֵב | אֶת־נַחֲלָתוֹ | | וַיִּתְּנֵם |
| be'ammô | waythā'ēv | 'eth-nachlāthô | | wayyittenēm |
| against his people | and it was abominable | his inheritance | | and He gave them |

| 904, 3135, 1504 | 5090.126 | 904 | 7983.152 |
|---|---|---|---|
| prep, *n fs*, n mp | cj, v Qal impf 3mp | prep, ps 3mp | v Qal act ptc mp, ps 3mp |
| בְּיַד־גּוֹיִם | וַיִּמְשְׁלוּ | בָהֶם | שֹׂנְאֵיהֶם |
| beyadh-gôyim | wayyimshelû | vāhem | sōne'êhem |
| into the hand of nations | and they ruled | over them | those who hated them |

| 42. | 4040.126 | 342.152 | 3789.226 | 8809 | 3135 |
|---|---|---|---|---|---|
| | cj, v Qal impf 3mp, ps 3mp | v Qal act ptc mp, ps 3mp | cj, v Niphal impf 3mp | prep | n fs, ps 3mp |
| | וַיִּלְחָצוּם | אוֹיְבֵיהֶם | וַיִּכָּנְעוּ | תַּחַת | יָדָם |
| | wayyilchātsûm | 'ôyvêhem | wayyikkāne'û | tachath | yādhām |
| | and they oppressed them | their enemies | and they were subdued | beneath | their hand |

| 43. | 6718 | 7521 | 5522.521 | 2065 | 4947.526 | 904, 6332 |
|---|---|---|---|---|---|---|
| | n fp | adj | v Hiphil impf 3ms, ps 3mp | cj, pers pron | v Hiphil impf 3mp | prep, n fs, ps 3mp |
| | פְּעָמִים | רַבּוֹת | יַצִּילֵם | וְהֵמָּה | יַמְרוּ | בַּעֲצָתָם |
| | pe'āmîm | rabbôth | yatstsîlēm | wehēmmāh | yamrû | va'ătsāthām |
| | times | many | He delivered them | but they | they rebelled | with their counsels |

| 4493.126 | 904, 5988 | 44. | 7495.121 | 904, 7140 |
|---|---|---|---|---|
| cj, v Qal impf 3mp | prep, n ms, ps 3mp | | cj, v Qal impf 3ms | prep, art, n ms |
| וַיָּמֹכּוּ | בַּעֲוֹנָם | | וַיַּרְא | בַּצַּר |
| wayyāmōkû | ba'ăwōnām | | wayyare' | batstsar |
| and they became low | because of their trangressions | | but He looked | on the adversity |

| 3937 | 904, 8471.141 | 881, 7726 | 45. | 2226.121 | 3937 |
|---|---|---|---|---|---|
| prep, ps 3mp | prep, v Qal inf con, ps 3ms | do, n fs, ps 3mp | | cj, v Qal impf 3ms | prep, ps 3mp |
| לָהֶם | בְּשָׁמְעוֹ | אֶת־רִנָּתָם | | וַיִּזְכֹּר | לָהֶם |
| lāhem | beshāme'ô | 'eth-rinnāthām | | wayyizkōr | lāhem |
| to them | when his hearing | their lamentation | | and He was mindful | to them |

| 1311 | 5341.221 | 3626, 7524 | 2721 |
|---|---|---|---|
| n fs, ps 3ms | cj, v Niphal impf 3ms | prep, *n ms* | n ms, ps 3ms |
| בְּרִיתוֹ | וַיִּנָּחֵם | כְּרֹב | חַסְדּוֹ |
| berîthô | wayyinnāchēm | kerōv | chasdô |
| his covenant | so He relented | according to the abundance of | his steadfast love |

| 46. | 5598.121 | 881 | 3937, 7641 | 3937, 6686 | 3725, 8091.152 |
|---|---|---|---|---|---|
| | cj, v Qal impf 3ms | do, ps 3mp | prep, n mp | prep, *n mp* | *adj*, v Qal act ptc mp, ps 3mp |
| | וַיִּתֵּן | אוֹתָם | לְרַחֲמִים | לִפְנֵי | כָּל־שׁוֹבֵיהֶם |
| | wayyittēn | 'ôthām | lerachmîm | liphnê | kol-shôvêhem |
| | and He gave | them | mercies | before | all those taking them captive |

| 47. | 3588.531 | 3176 | 435 | 7192.331 | 4623, 1504 |
|---|---|---|---|---|---|
| | v Hiphil impv 2ms, ps 1cp | pn | n mp, ps 1cp | cj, v Piel impv 2ms, ps 1cp | prep, art, n mp |
| | הוֹשִׁיעֵנוּ | יְהוָה | אֱלֹהֵינוּ | וְקַבְּצֵנוּ | מִן־הַגּוֹיִם |
| | hôshî'ēnû | yehwāh | 'ĕlōhênû | weqabbetsēnû | min-haggôyim |
| | save us | O Yahweh | our God | and gather us in | from the nations |

**and went a-whoring with their own inventions:** ... they followed their lusts and broke faith with God, *NEB* ... and went lusting in their own doings, *KJVII* ... and wanton in their crimes, *NAB* ... and were faithless in their conduct, *REB* ... by their deeds they prostituted themselves, *NIV.*

**40. Therefore was the wrath of the LORD kindled against his people, insomuch that he abhorred his own inheritance:** ... God's anger blazed against his people, his chosen race became abominable to him, *Knox* ... he loathed his heritage, *Goodspeed* ... He regarded His heritage with disgust, *Berkeley.*

**41. And he gave them into the hand of the heathen; and they that hated them ruled over them:** ... the hand of the nations, *RSV* ... and their opponents became their masters, *JB* ... they were ruled by their foes, *NEB* ... and let their enemies rule over them, *NCV.*

**42. Their enemies also oppressed them, and they were brought into subjection under their hand:** ... they were humbled under their power, *NCB* ... And they were bowed down under their hand, *Rotherham* ... forced them to submission, *Moffatt* ... they were humbled under their hand, *Anchor.*

**43. Many times did he deliver them; but they provoked him with their counsel:** ... but they were rebellious in their purposes, *NRSV* ... were rebellious in their counsel, *MRB* ... But they followed their own stubborn counsel, *Goodspeed.*

**and were brought low for their iniquity:** ... and sank ever deeper in their guilt, *JB* ... evildoing wasted them away, *Moffatt* ... and sank lower in their sin, *Beck* ... were brought low by their guilt, *NAB.*

**44. Nevertheless he regarded their affliction, when he heard their cry:** ... he looked with pity on their distress, *NEB* ... He looked upon their distress, *MAST* ... he took note of their distress, *NIV* ... when he heard their appeals to him, *Knox.*

**45. And he remembered for them his covenant:** ... for their sake he was mindful of his covenant, *NAB* ... And he recalled for them his covenant, *Goodspeed* ... he called to mind his covenant with them, *REB.*

**and repented according to the multitude of his mercies:** ... relented according to the greatness of His lovingkindness, *NASB* ... and in accordance with His great love changed His mind, *Beck* ... and showed compassion according to the abundance of his steadfast love, *NRSV* ... According to the abundance of His kindness, *Young.*

**46. He made them also to be pitied of all those that carried them captives:** ... He made all their captors feel sorry for them, *Beck* ... He put pity into the hearts of those who made

---

and the adoption of their bloody worship. The conquest of Canaan was partial, and, as often is the case, the conquerors were conquered, the invaders catching the manners of the invaded. Intermarriage poured a large infusion of alien blood into Israel, and the Canaanitish strain is perceptible today in the fellahin of the Holy Land. The proclivity to idolatry, which was natural in that stage of the world's history and was intensified by universal example, became more irresistible when reinforced by kinship and neighborhood, and the result foretold was realized—the idols "became a snare" (Judg. 2:1ff). The poet dwells with special abhorrence on the hideous practice of human sacrifices, which exercised so strong and horrible a fascination over the inhabitants of Canaan. The word "demons" (HED #8158) in v. 37 is found only here and in Deut. 32:17. The above rendering is that of the Septuagint. Its literal meaning seems to be "lords." It is thus a synonym for "Baalim." The epithet "Shaddai," exclusively applied to Yahweh, may be compared.

**106:40–43.** In vv. 40–46, the whole history of Israel is summed up as alternating periods of sin, punishment and deliverance, recurring in constantly repeated cycles, in which the mystery of human obstinance is set over against that of divine long-suffering, and one knows not whether to wonder most at the incurable levity which learned nothing from experience or the inexhaustible long-suffering which wearied not in giving wasted gifts. Chastisement and mercies were equally in vain. The outcome of God's many deliverances was that the Israelites rebelled in their counsel—they went on their own stiff-necked way, instead of waiting for and following God's merciful plan, which would have made them secure and blessed. The end of such obstinance of disobedience can only be that "they were brought low for their iniquity." The psalmist appears to be quoting Lev. 26:39, "They that are left of you shall pine away in their iniquity"; but he intentionally slightly alters the word, substituting one of nearly the same sound, but with the meaning of being brought low instead of fading away. To follow one's own will is to secure humiliation and degradation. Sin weakens the true strength and darkens the true glory of men.

**106:44–46.** In vv. 44ff, the singer rises from these sad and stern thoughts to recreate his spirit with the contemplation of the patient steadfast love of God. It persists through all man's sin and God's anger. The

| 3937, 3142.541 | 3937, 8428 | 7231 | 3937, 8099.741 | 904, 8747 |
|---|---|---|---|---|
| prep, v Hiphil inf con | prep, *n ms* | n ms, ps 2ms | prep, v Hithpael inf con | prep, n fs, ps 2ms |
| לְהֹדוֹת | לְשֵׁם | קָדְשֶׁךָ | לְהִשְׁתַּבֵּחַ | בִּתְהִלָּתֶךָ |
| lehōdhôth | leshēm | qādheshekhā | lehishtabbēach | bithhillāthekhā |
| to praise | the name of | your holiness | to revel | in your praise |

| | 1313.155, 3176 | 435 | 3547 | 4623, 5986 | 5912 | 5986 | 569.111 |
|---|---|---|---|---|---|---|---|
| 48. | v Qal pass ptc ms, pn | *n mp* | pn | prep, art, n ms | cj, prep | art, n ms | cj, v Qal pf 3ms |
| | בָּרוּךְ־יְהוָה | אֱלֹהֵי | יִשְׂרָאֵל | מִן־הָעוֹלָם | וְעַד | הָעוֹלָם | וְאָמַר |
| | bārûkh-yehwāh | 'ĕlōhê | yisrā'ēl | min-hā'ôlām | we'adh | hā'ôlām | we'āmar |
| | blessed Yahweh | the God of | Israel | from eternity | and unto | eternity | and they said |

| 3725, 6194 | 549 | 2054.333, 3161 | | 3142.533 | 3937, 3176 | 3706, 3005 | 3706 |
|---|---|---|---|---|---|---|---|
| *adj*, art, n ms | intrj | v Piel impv 2mp, pn | 107:1 | v Hiphil impv 2mp | prep, pn | cj, adj | cj |
| כָּל־הָעָם | אָמֵן | הַלְלוּ־יָהּ | | הֹדוּ | לַיהוָה | כִּי־טוֹב | כִּי |
| kol-hā'ām | 'āmēn | halelû-yāhh | | hōdhû | layhwāh | kî-ṭôv | kî |
| all the people | amen | praise Yah | | praise | Yahweh | because good | because |

| 3937, 5986 | 2721 | | 569.126 | 1381.156 | 3176 | 866 |
|---|---|---|---|---|---|---|
| prep, n ms | n ms, ps 3ms | 2. | v Qal juss 3mp | *v Qal pass ptc mp* | pn | rel pron |
| לְעוֹלָם | חַסְדּוֹ | | יֹאמְרוּ | גְּאוּלֵי | יְהוָה | אֲשֶׁר |
| le'ôlām | chasdô | | yō'merû | ge'ûlê | yehwāh | 'ăsher |
| unto eternity | his steadfast love | | let them say | the redeemed of | Yahweh | whom |

| 1381.111 | 4623, 3135, 7141 | | 4623, 800 | 7192.311 |
|---|---|---|---|---|
| v Qal pf 3ms, ps 3mp | prep, *n fs*, n ms | 3. | cj, prep, n fp | v Piel pf 3ms, ps 3mp |
| גְּאָלָם | מִיַּד־צָר | | וּמֵאֲרָצוֹת | קִבְּצָם |
| ge'ālām | mîyadh-tsār | | ûmē'ărātsôth | qibbetsām |
| He has redeemed them | from the hand of the adversary | | and from the lands | He gathered them in |

| 4623, 4350 | 4623, 4790 | 4623, 7103 | 4623, 3328 | | 8912.116 | 904, 4198 |
|---|---|---|---|---|---|---|
| prep, n ms | cj, prep, n ms | prep, n fs | cj, prep, n ms | 4. | v Qal pf 3cp | prep, art, n ms |
| מִמִּזְרָח | וּמִמַּעֲרָב | מִצָּפוֹן | וּמִיָּם | | תָּעוּ | בַּמִּדְבָּר |
| mimmizrāch | ûmimma'ărāv | mitstsāphôn | ûmîyām | | tā'û | vammidhbār |
| eastward | and westward | northward | and seaward | | they went astray | in the wilderness |

| 904, 3574 | 1932 | 6111 | 4319 | 3940 | 4834.116 | | 7744 | 1612, 7041 |
|---|---|---|---|---|---|---|---|---|
| prep, *n ms* | n ms | *n fs* | n ms | neg part | v Qal pf 3cp | 5. | adj | cj, adj |
| בִּישִׁימוֹן | דָּרֶךְ | עִיר | מוֹשָׁב | לֹא | מָצָאוּ | | רְעֵבִים | גַּם־צְמֵאִים |
| bîshîmôn | dārekh | 'îr | môshāv | lō' | mātsā'û | | re'ēvîm | gam-tsemē'îm |
| in a desert of | a way | a city for | dwelling | not | they found | | hungry | as well as thirsty |

them prisoners, *BB* ... he caused them to find compassion, *Darby* ... he won for them compassion from all who held them captive, *NCB*.

**47. Save us, O LORD our God, and gather us from among the heathen:** ... Deliver us, O LORD our God; bring us together from among the nations, *Berkeley* ... Deliver us, O Lord our God, and gather us again, scattered as we are among the heathen, *Knox*.

**to give thanks unto thy holy name, and to triumph in thy praise:** ... that we may give thanks to thy sacred name, *Moffatt* ... To praise your HOLY NAME, To rejoice in thanksgiving to You, *Fenton* ... holy name and glory in your praise, *NIV*.

**48. Blessed be the LORD God of Israel from everlasting to everlasting: and let all the people say, Amen. Praise ye the LORD:** ... Praise the LORD, the God of Israel. He always was and always will be, *NCV* ... Blessed be Yahweh, the God of Israel, from all eternity and for ever!, *JB* ... From age unto age, *Goodspeed*.

**107:1. O give thanks unto the LORD, for he is good: for his mercy endureth for ever:** ... It is good to give thanks to the LORD, *NEB* ... his love endures forever, *NIV* ... his kindness endures forever!, *NCB* ... his steadfast love, *RSV*.

**2. Let the redeemed of the LORD say so, whom he hath redeemed from the hand of the enemy:** ... redeemed from the hand of the adversary, *NASB* ... whom he has redeemed from trouble, *RSV* ... redeemed by the Eternal from their foes, *Moffatt* ... from the hand of the oppressor, *Darby*.

**3. And gathered them out of the lands, from the east, and from the west, from the north, and from the south:** ... bringing them back from foreign lands, *JB* ... gathered from other countries, *Beck* ... From north, and from the sea, *Young* ... gathered them in from sunrising and sunset, from the north country and the south, *Knox*.

**4. They wandered in the wilderness in a solitary way; they found no city to dwell in:** ... wandered in desert lands. They found no city in which to live, *NCV* ... wilderness in a desolate way, *NKJV* ... they saw no way to a resting-place, *BB* ... They found no city of habitation, *MAST*.

**5. Hungry and thirsty, their soul fainted in them:** ... their life was wasting away within them, *NAB* ... their life ebbed from them, *Anchor*

---

multitude of its manifestations far outnumbers that of our sins. His eye looks on Israel's distress with pity, and every sorrow on which He looks He desires to remove. Calamities melt away beneath his gaze, like damp stains in sunlight. His merciful "look" swiftly follows the afflicted man's cry. No voice acknowledges sin and calls for help in vain. The Covenant forgotten by men is nonetheless remembered by Him. The numberless number of his steadfast loves, greater than that of all men's sins, secures forgiveness after the most repeated transgressions. The law and measure of his "repenting" lie in the endless depths of his own heart. As the psalmist had sung at the beginning, that steadfast love endures forever; therefore, none of Israel's many sins went unchastised, and no chastisement outlasted their repentance. Solomon had prayed that God would "give them compassion before them who carried them captive" (1 Ki. 8:50), and thus has it been, as the psalmist joyfully sees. He may have written when the Babylonian captivity was near an end, and such instances as those of Daniel or Nehemiah may have been in his mind. In any case, it is beautifully significant that a Psalm that tells the doleful story of centuries of faithlessness should end with God's faithfulness to his promises, his inexhaustible forgiveness and the multitude of his steadfast loves. Such will be the last result of the world's history no less than of Israel's.

**106:47–48.** The Psalm closes with the prayer in v. 47, which shows that it was written in exile. It corresponds in part with the closing words of Ps. 105. Just as there, the purpose of God's mercies to Israel was said to be that they might be thereby moved to keep his statutes, so here the psalmist hopes and vows that the issue of his people's restoration will be thankfulness to God's holy name, and triumphant pealing forth from ransomed lips of his high praises. Verse 48 is the concluding doxology of the fourth book.

***Psalm 107.*** *Psalm 106 confessed the hereditary faithlessness of Israel and its chastisement by calamity and exile. Psalm 107 begins with summoning Israel as "the redeemed of the LORD" to praise Him for his enduring steadfast love in bringing them back from bondage and then takes a wider flight and celebrates the loving providence which delivers, in all varieties of peril and calamity, those who cry to God.*

**107:1–3.** The Psalm begins with venerable words, which it bids the recipients of God's last great mercy ring out once more. They who have yesterday been "redeemed from the hand of the enemy" have proof that his steadfast love endures forever, since it has come down to them through centuries. The characteristic fondness for quotations, which marks the Psalm, is in full force in the three introductory verses. Verse 1, of course, occurs in several Psalms. On the phrase, "the redeemed of the LORD," see Isa. 62:12. "Gathered them out of the lands" looks back to Ps. 106:47 and to many prophetic passages. The word rendered above "distress" (HED #7141) may mean oppressor and is frequently rendered so here, which rendering fits better the preceding word "hand." But the recurrence of the same word in the subsequent refrains (vv. 6, 13, 19, 28) makes the rendering "distress" preferable here. To ascribe to distress a "hand" is poetical personification, or the latter word may be taken in a somewhat wider sense as equivalent to a grasp or grip, as above. The return from Babylon is evidently in the poet's thoughts, but he widens it out into a restoration from every quarter. His enumeration of the points from which the exiles flock is irregular in that he says "from the west [literally, 'sea,' referring to the Mediterranean] from north." That quarter has, however, already been mentioned, and, therefore, it has been proposed that "sea" here means, abnormally, the Red Sea, or the southern portion of the Mediterranean. But possibly, the psalmist is quoting Isa. 49:12, where the same phrase occurs, and the north is set over against the sea—i.e., the west. The slight irregularity does not interfere with the picture of the streams of returning exiles from every quarter.

**107:4–9.** The first scene, that of a caravan lost in a desert, is probably suggested by the previous reference to the return of the "redeemed of the LORD," but is not to be taken as referring only to that. It is a

| 5497<br>n fs, ps 3mp<br>נַפְשָׁם<br>naphshām<br>their soul | 904<br>prep, ps 3mp<br>בָּהֶם<br>bāhem<br>in them | 6063.722<br>v Hithpael impf 3fs<br>תִּתְעַטָּף<br>tith'attāph<br>it fainted | **6.** | 7094.126<br>cj, v Qal impf 3mp<br>וַיִּצְעֲקוּ<br>wayyits'ăqû<br>then they cried out | 420, 3176<br>prep, pn<br>אֶל־יְהוָה<br>'el-yehwāh<br>to Yahweh | 904, 7140<br>prep, art, n ms<br>בַּצַּר<br>batstsar<br>during the adversity |
|---|---|---|---|---|---|---|

| 3937<br>prep, ps 3mp<br>לָהֶם<br>lāhem<br>to them | 4623, 4855<br>prep, n fp, ps 3mp<br>מִמְּצוּקוֹתֵיהֶם<br>mimmetsûqôthêhem<br>from their distress | 5522.521<br>v Hiphil impf 3ms, ps 3mp<br>יַצִּילֵם<br>yatstsîlēm<br>He rescued them | **7.** | 1931.521<br>cj, v Hiphil impf 3ms, ps 3mp<br>וַיַּדְרִיכֵם<br>wayyadhrîkhēm<br>and He caused them to tread | 904, 1932<br>prep, n ms<br>בְּדֶרֶךְ<br>bedherekh<br>on a way |
|---|---|---|---|---|---|

| 3596<br>adj<br>יְשָׁרָה<br>yeshārāh<br>upright | 3937, 2050.141<br>prep, v Qal inf con<br>לָלֶכֶת<br>lālekheth<br>to walk | 420, 6111<br>prep, *n fs*<br>אֶל־עִיר<br>'el-'îr<br>to a city of | 4319<br>n ms<br>מוֹשָׁב<br>môshāv<br>dwelling | **8.** | 3142.526<br>v Hiphil juss 3mp<br>יוֹדוּ<br>yôdhû<br>let them praise | 3937, 3176<br>prep, pn<br>לַיהוָה<br>layhwāh<br>Yahweh | 2721<br>n ms, ps 3ms<br>חַסְדּוֹ<br>chasdô<br>his steadfast love |
|---|---|---|---|---|---|---|---|

| 6623.258<br>cj, v Niphal ptc fp, ps 3ms<br>וְנִפְלְאוֹתָיו<br>weniphle'ôthâv<br>and his extraordinary deeds | 3937, 1158<br>prep, *n mp*<br>לִבְנֵי<br>livnê<br>to the sons of | 119<br>n ms<br>אָדָם<br>'ādhām<br>humankind | **9.** | 3706, 7881.511<br>cj, v Hiphil pf 3ms<br>כִּי־הִשְׂבִּיעַ<br>kî-hisbîa'<br>because He satisfies | 5497<br>n fs<br>נֶפֶשׁ<br>nephesh<br>the soul |
|---|---|---|---|---|---|

| 8630.153<br>v Qal act ptc fs<br>שֹׁקֵקָה<br>shōqēqāh<br>the dried out | 5497<br>cj, n fs<br>וְנֶפֶשׁ<br>wenephesh<br>and the soul | 7744<br>adj<br>רְעֵבָה<br>re'ēvāh<br>hungry | 4527.311, 3008<br>v Piel pf 3ms, n ms<br>מִלֵּא־טוֹב<br>millē'-tôv<br>He fills with good things | **10.** | 3553.152<br>*v Qal act ptc mp*<br>יֹשְׁבֵי<br>yōshevê<br>those sitting in | 2932<br>n ms<br>חֹשֶׁךְ<br>chōshekh<br>darkness |
|---|---|---|---|---|---|---|

| 7024<br>cj, n ms<br>וְצַלְמָוֶת<br>wetsalmāweth<br>and gloom | 629<br>*n mp*<br>אֲסִירֵי<br>'ăsîrê<br>prisoners in | 6270<br>n ms<br>עֳנִי<br>'ŏnî<br>affliction | 1298<br>cj, n ms<br>וּבַרְזֶל<br>ûvarzel<br>and iron | **11.** | 3706, 4947.516<br>cj, v Hiphil pf 3cp<br>כִּי־הִמְרוּ<br>kî-himrû<br>because they rebelled against | 577, 418<br>*n mp*, n ms<br>אִמְרֵי־אֵל<br>'imrê-'ēl<br>the words of God |
|---|---|---|---|---|---|---|

| 6332<br>cj, *n fs*<br>וַעֲצַת<br>wa'ătsath<br>and the counsel of | 6169<br>n ms<br>עֶלְיוֹן<br>'elyôn<br>the Most High | 5180.116<br>v Qal pf 3cp<br>נָאָצוּ<br>nā'ātsû<br>they disdained | **12.** | 3789.521<br>cj, v Hiphil impf 3ms<br>וַיַּכְנַע<br>wayyakhna'<br>and He humbled | 904, 6219<br>prep, art, n ms<br>בֶּעָמָל<br>be'āmāl<br>with forced labor |
|---|---|---|---|---|---|

| 3949<br>n ms, ps 3mp<br>לִבָּם<br>libbām<br>their heart | 3911.116<br>v Qal pf 3cp<br>כָּשְׁלוּ<br>kāshelû<br>they stumbled | 375<br>cj, *sub*<br>וְאֵין<br>we'ên<br>and there was not | 6038.151<br>v Qal act ptc ms<br>עֹזֵר<br>'ōzēr<br>a helper | **13.** | 2283.126<br>cj, v Qal impf 3mp<br>וַיִּזְעֲקוּ<br>wayyiz'ăqû<br>but they cried out |
|---|---|---|---|---|---|

… their spirit sank within them, *NEB.*

**6. Then they cried unto the LORD in their trouble, and he delivered them out of their distresses:** … in their peril, Out of their distresses he rescued them, *Rotherham* … he gave them salvation out of all their troubles, *BB.*

**7. And he led them forth by the right way:** … And guided them in a straight way, *Goodspeed* … till they came to a town to dwell in, *Anchor* … he led them by a direct way, *NCB* … he set them on the road, *JB.*

**that they might go to a city of habitation:** … To march to the City of Rest!, *Fenton* … to the residence city they sought, *Berkeley* … to the place where they should find a home, *Knox* … to a city where they could settle, *NIV.*

**8. Oh that men would praise the LORD for his goodness, and for his wonderful works to the children of men!:** … Let them give thanks unto the LORD for His mercy, *MAST* …

Let them thank the LORD for his steadfast love, *RSV* ... for his enduring love and for the marvellous things he has done for men, *NEB*.

**9. For he satisfieth the longing soul, and filleth the hungry soul with goodness:** ... He gives its desire to the unresting soul, *BB* ... He satisfies the thirsty and fills up the hungry, *NCV* ... filled the starving with good things, *JB* ... and fills them in their hunger, *Moffatt*.

**10. Such as sit in darkness and in the shadow of death:** ... They dwelt in darkness and gloom, *NAB* ... Such as inhabit darkness, *Darby* ... Some lay where darkness overshadowed them, *Knox*.

**being bound in affliction and iron:** ... prisoners in misery and in irons, *NRSV* ... bound fast in iron, *REB* ... fettered by torturing irons, *Anchor* ... in misery and chains, *NASB*.

**11. Because they rebelled against the words of God:** ... for defying the orders of Yahweh, *JB* ... they defied the commands of El, *Anchor*.

**and contemned the counsel of the most High:** ... And the counsel of the Most High despised, *Young* ... and despised the counsel, *NIV* ... and scorn what the Most High had planned, *Beck*.

**12. Therefore he brought down their heart with labour:** ... They were weak thro' the sin of their hearts, *Fenton* ... brought them low in trouble and sorrow, *Berkeley* ... he humbled their hearts with trouble, *NAB* ... So he broke their pride by hard work, *NCV*.

**they fell down, and there was none to help:** ... none else to aid their faltering steps, *Knox* ... if they fell there was no one to help, *JB*.

**13. Then they cried unto the LORD in their trouble, and he saved them out of their distresses:** ... their cry to the Lord in their sorrow, and he gives them salvation out of all their troubles, *BB* ... In their misery they cried out to the LORD, *NCV* ... from their straits he rescued them, *NCB* ... to save them from their evil plight, *Moffatt*.

---

perfectly general sketch of a frequent incident of travel. It is a remarkable trace of a state of society very unlike modern life, that two of the four instances of "distress" are due to the perils of journeying. By land and by sea men took their lives in their hands when they left their homes. Two points are signalized in this description: the first, the loss of the track; the second, the wanderers' hunger and thirst. "A waste of a way" is a singular expression, which has suggested various unnecessary textual emendations.

The travelers are driven to God by their "distress." He does not reject the cry which is forced out by the pressure of calamity; but as the structure of vv. 6f shows, his answer is simultaneous with the appeal to Him, and it is complete, as well as immediate. The track appears as suddenly as it had faded. God himself goes at the head of the march. The path is as straight as an arrow's flight, and soon they are in the city.

Verse 6 is the first instance of the refrain, which in each of the four pictures is followed by a verse (or, in the last of the four, by two verses) descriptive of the act of deliverance, which again is followed by the second refrain, calling on those who have experienced such a mercy to thank Yahweh. This is followed in the first two groups by a verse reiterating the reason for praise, the deliverance just granted, and in the last two, by a verse expanding the summons. Various may be the forms of need, but the supply of them all is one, and the way to get it is one, and one is the experience of the suppliants, and one should be their praise. Life's diversities have underlying them identity of soul's wants. Waiters on God have very different outward fortunes, but the broad outlines of their inward history are identical. This is the law of his providence: they cry, He delivers. This should be the harvest from his sowing of benefits—"Oh that men would praise the LORD." Some would translate v. 8, "Let them thankfully confess to Yahweh his steadfast love, and to the children of men [confess] his wonders"; but the usual rendering as above is better, as not introducing a thought which, however important, is scarcely in the psalmist's view here and as preserving the great thought of the Psalm—God's providence to all mankind.

**107:10–16.** The second scene, that of captives, probably retains some allusion to Babylon, although an even fainter one than in the preceding strophe. It has several quotations and references to Isaiah, especially to the latter half (Isa. 40–46). The deliverance is described in v. 16 in words borrowed from the prophecy as to Cyrus, the instrument of Israel's restoration (Isa. 14:2). The gloom of the prison house is described in language closely resembling Isa. 42:7; 49:9. The combination of "darkness and in the shadow of death" is found in Isa. 9:2. The cause of the captivity described is rebellion against God's counsel and word. These things point to Israel's Babylonian bondage, but the picture in the Psalm draws its color rather than its subject from that event and is quite general. The psalmist thinks that such bondage, and deliverance

| 420, 3176 | 904, 7140 | 3937 | 4623, 4855 | 3588.521 |
|---|---|---|---|---|
| prep, pn | prep, art, n ms | prep, ps 3mp | prep, n fp, ps 3mp | v Hiphil impf 3ms, ps 3mp |
| אֶל־יְהוָה | בַּצַּר | לָהֶם | מִמְּצֻקוֹתֵיהֶם | יוֹשִׁיעֵם |
| 'el-yehwāh | batstsar | lāhem | mimmetsuqôthêhem | yôshî'ēm |
| to Yahweh | during the adversity | to them | from their distress | He saved them |

| 14. | 3428.521 | 4623, 2932 | 7024 | 4283 | 5607.321 |
|---|---|---|---|---|---|
| | v Hiphil impf 3ms, ps 3mp | prep, n ms | cj, n ms | cj, n mp, ps 3mp | v Piel impf 3ms |
| | יוֹצִיאֵם | מֵחֹשֶׁךְ | וְצַלְמָוֶת | וּמוֹסְרוֹתֵיהֶם | יְנַתֵּק |
| | yôtsî'ēm | mēchōshekh | wetsalmāweth | ûmôsrôthêhem | yenattēq |
| | He brought them out | from darkness | and gloom | and their fetters | He cut off |

| 15. | 3142.526 | 3937, 3176 | 2721 | 6623.258 | 3937, 1158 |
|---|---|---|---|---|---|
| | v Hiphil juss 3mp | prep, pn | n ms, ps 3ms | cj, v Niphal ptc fp, ps 3ms | prep, *n mp* |
| | יוֹדוּ | לַיהוָה | חַסְדּוֹ | וְנִפְלְאוֹתָיו | לִבְנֵי |
| | yôdhû | layhwāh | chasdô | weniphle'ôthâv | livnê |
| | let them praise | Yahweh | his steadfast love | and his extraordinary deeds | to the sons of |

| 119 | 16. | 3706, 8132.311 | 1878 | 5361 | 1308 | 1298 |
|---|---|---|---|---|---|---|
| n ms | | cj, v Piel pf 3ms | *n fp* | n ms | cj, *n mp* | n ms |
| אָדָם | | כִּי־שִׁבַּר | דַּלְתוֹת | נְחֹשֶׁת | וּבְרִיחֵי | בַרְזֶל |
| 'ādhām | | kî-shibbar | dalthôth | nechōsheth | ûverîchê | varzel |
| humankind | | because He has shattered | the doors of | bronze | and the bars of | iron |

| 1468.311 | 17. | 192 | 4623, 1932 | 6840 | 4623, 5988 |
|---|---|---|---|---|---|
| v Piel pf 3ms | | n mp | prep, *n ms* | n ms, ps 3mp | cj, prep, n mp, ps 3mp |
| גִּדֵּעַ | | אֱוִלִים | מִדֶּרֶךְ | פִּשְׁעָם | וּמֵעֲוֺנֹתֵיהֶם |
| giddēa' | | 'ĕwilîm | midderekh | pish'ām | ûmē'ăwōnōthêhem |
| He has cut in two | | fools | from the way of | their offenses | and because of their transgression |

| 6257.726 | 18. | 3725, 406 | 8911.322 | 5497 | 5236.526 | 5912, 7881 |
|---|---|---|---|---|---|---|
| v Hithpael impf 3mp | | *adj*, n ms | v Piel impf 3fs | n fs, ps 3mp | cj, v Hiphil impf 3mp | prep, *n mp* |
| יִתְעַנּוּ | | כָּל־אֹכֶל | תְּתַעֵב | נַפְשָׁם | וַיַּגִּיעוּ | עַד־שַׁעֲרֵי |
| yith'annû | | kol-'ōkhel | tetha'ēv | naphshām | wayyaggî'û | 'adh-sha'ărê |
| they were afflicted | | all food | it abhorred | their soul | and they abhorred | unto the gates of |

| 4323 | 19. | 2283.126 | 420, 3176 | 904, 7140 | 3937 | 4623, 4855 |
|---|---|---|---|---|---|---|
| n ms | | cj, v Qal impf 3mp | prep, pn | prep, art, n ms | prep, ps 3mp | prep, n fp, ps 3mp |
| מָוֶת | | וַיִּזְעֲקוּ | אֶל־יְהוָה | בַּצַּר | לָהֶם | מִמְּצֻקוֹתֵיהֶם |
| māweth | | wayyiz'ăqû | 'el-yehwāh | batstsar | lāhem | mimmetsuqôthêhem |
| death | | but they cried out | to Yahweh | during the adversity | to them | from their distress |

| 3588.521 | 20. | 8365.121 | 1745 | 7784.121 | 4561.321 |
|---|---|---|---|---|---|
| v Hiphil impf 3ms, ps 3mp | | v Qal impf 3ms | n ms, ps 3ms | cj, v Qal impf 3ms, ps 3mp | cj, Piel impf 3ms |
| יוֹשִׁיעֵם | | יִשְׁלַח | דְּבָרוֹ | וְיִרְפָּאֵם | וִימַלֵּט |
| yôshî'ēm | | yishlach | devārô | weyirpā'ēm | wîmallēt |
| He saved them | | He sent | his word | and He healed them | and He set them free |

| 4623, 8255 | 21. | 3142.526 | 3937, 3176 | 2721 | 6623.258 |
|---|---|---|---|---|---|
| prep, n fp, ps 3mp | | v Hiphil juss 3mp | prep, pn | n ms, ps 3ms | cj, v Niphal ptc fp, ps 3ms |
| מִשְּׁחִיתוֹתָם | | יוֹדוּ | לַיהוָה | חַסְדּוֹ | וְנִפְלְאוֹתָיו |
| mishshechîthôthām | | yôdhû | layhwāh | chasdô | weniphle'ôthâv |
| from destruction | | let them praise | Yahweh | his steadfast love | and his extraordinary deeds |

| 3937, 1158 | 119 | 22. | 2159.126 | 2160 | 8756 |
|---|---|---|---|---|---|
| prep, *n mp* | n ms | | cj, v Qal juss 3mp | *n mp* | n fs |
| לִבְנֵי | אָדָם | | וְיִזְבְּחוּ | זִבְחֵי | תּוֹדָה |
| livnê | 'ādhām | | weyizbechû | zivchê | thôdhāh |
| to the sons of | humankind | | and let them sacrifice | sacrifices of | thanksgiving |

**14. He brought them out of darkness and the shadow of death, and brake their bands in sunder:** ... He brought them out of darkness and deepest gloom, *Goodspeed* ... deepest darkness, and burst their chains, *REB* ... And broke their chains in pieces, *NKJV.*

**15. Oh that men would praise the Lord for his goodness, and for his wonderful works to the children of men!:** ... Give thanks to the Lord for His mercy, *Fenton* ... for his lovingkindness, *ASV* ... Let them thank the Lord for his steadfast love, *NRSV* ... Let them thank the Lord for his enduring love, *NEB.*

**16. For he hath broken the gates of brass, and cut the bars of iron in sunder:** ... For he shatters the doors of bronze, *RSV* ... And bars of iron He hath cut, *Young* ... and burst the bars of iron, *NAB.*

**17. Fools because of their transgression, and because of their iniquities, are afflicted:** ... Fools are afflicted because of their rebellion, and because of their sins, *KJVII* ... Crazed because of the way of their transgression, *MAST* ... for their transgression suffered punishment, *REB* ... Some were sick through their sinful ways, *RSV.*

**18. Their soul abhorreth all manner of meat:** ... abhorred all kinds of food, *NASB* ... They loathed every kind of food, *Goodspeed* ... They sickened at the sight of food, *NEB.*

**and they draw near unto the gates of death:** ... And they shook at the gateway of Death, *Fenton* ... they almost died, *NCV* ... close to death's door, *Knox* ... were on the verge of death, *Moffatt.*

**19. Then they cry unto the Lord in their trouble, and he saveth them out of their distresses:** ... He delivered them from their troubles, *Berkeley* ... in their sorrow, and he gives them salvation out of all their troubles, *BB* ... from their straits he rescued them, *NCB* ... he rescued them from their plight, *JB.*

**20. He sent his word, and healed them, and delivered them from their destructions:** ... his word to heal them and snatch them out of the pit of death, *REB* ... And from their corruptions it freed, *Fenton* ... to save their lives from the grave, *Berkeley* ... to relieve them of their boils, *Anchor.*

**21. Oh that men would praise the Lord for his goodness, and for his wonderful works to the children of men!:** ... thank Yahweh for his faithful love, for his wonders for the children of Adam!, *JB* ... praise to the Lord for his mercy, and for the wonders which he does, *BB* ... Let them thank the Lord for his steadfast love, *RSV* ... and for the miracles he does for people, *NCV.*

**22. And let them sacrifice the sacrifices of thanksgiving, and declare his works with rejoicing:** ... Let them bring their thank offerings and gladly tell of His doings, *Berkeley* ... and recite his deeds with shouts of joy, *NEB* ... declare His works with singing, *MAST* ... tell of His works with joyful singing, *NASB.*

---

on repentance and prayer, are standing facts in providence, both in regard to nations and individuals. One may see, too, a certain parabolic aspect hinted at, as if the poet would have us catch a half-revealed intention to present calamity of any kind under this image of captivity. We note the slipping in of words that are not required for the picture, as when the fetters are said to be "affliction" as well as "iron." Verse 12, too, is not especially appropriate to the condition of prisoners; persons in fetters and gloom do not stumble, for they do not move. There may, therefore, be a partial glance at the parabolic aspect of captivity, such as poetic imagination, and especially biblical poetry, loves. At most, it is a delicate suggestion, shyly hiding while it shows itself and made too much of if drawn out in prosaic exposition.

We may perceive also the allegorical pertinence of his second picture, although we do not suppose that the singer intended such a use. For is not godless life ever bondage? And is not rebellion against God the sure cause of falling under a harsher dominion? And does He not listen to the cry of a soul that feels the slavery of subjection to self and sin? And is not true enlargement found in his free service? And does He not give power to break the strongest chains of habit? The synagogue at Nazareth, where the carpenter's Son stood up to read and found the place where it was written, "The Spirit of the Lord is upon me ... He hath sent me ... to preach deliverance to the captives" (Luke 4:18), warrants the symbolic use of the psalmist's imagery, which is, as we have seen, largely influenced by the prophet whose words Jesus quoted. The first scene taught that devout hearts never lack guidance from God. The second adds to their blessings freedom, the true liberty which comes with submission and acceptance of his Law.

**107:17–22.** Sickness, which yields the third type of suffering, is a more common experience than the two preceding. The picture is lightly sketched, emphasis being laid on the cause of the sickness, which is sin, in accordance with the prevailing view in the OT. The psalmist introduces the persons of whom he is to speak by the strongly condemnatory term "fools" (HED #192) which refers not to intellectual feebleness, but to moral perver-

| 5807.326 | 4801 | 904, 7726 | | 3495.152 | 3328 |
|---|---|---|---|---|---|
| cj, v Piel juss 3mp | n mp, ps 3ms | prep, n fs | 23. | *v Qal act ptc mp* | art, n ms |
| וִיסַפְּרוּ | מַעֲשָׂיו | בְּרִנָּה | | יוֹרְדֵי | הַיָּם |
| wîsapperû | ma'ăsāv | berinnāh | | yôrdhê | hayyām |
| and let them recount | his works | with a shout of joy | | those who went down to | the sea |

| 904, 604 | 6449.152 | 4536 | 904, 4448 | 7521 | | 2065 | 7495.116 | 4801 |
|---|---|---|---|---|---|---|---|---|
| prep, n fp | *v Qal act ptc mp* | n fs | prep, n md | adj | 24. | pers pron | v Qal pf 3cp | *n mp* |
| בָּאֳנִיּוֹת | עֹשֵׂי | מְלָאכָה | בְּמַיִם | רַבִּים | | הֵמָּה | רָאוּ | מַעֲשֵׂי |
| bā'ănîyôth | 'ōsê | melā'khāh | bemayim | rabbîm | | hēmmāh | rā'û | ma'ăsê |
| in ships | the ones doing | work | in waters | many | | they | they saw | the works of |

| 3176 | 6623.258 | 904, 4852 | | 569.121 | 6198.521 |
|---|---|---|---|---|---|
| pn | cj, v Niphal ptc fp, ps 3ms | prep, n fs | 25. | cj, v Qal impf 3ms | cj, v Hiphil impf 3ms |
| יְהוָה | וְנִפְלְאוֹתָיו | בִּמְצוּלָה | | וַיֹּאמֶר | וַיַּעֲמֵד |
| yehwāh | weniphle'ôthāv | bimtsûlāh | | wayyō'mer | wayya'ămēdh |
| Yahweh | and his extraordinary deeds | in the deep | | when He said | and He caused to stand |

| 7593 | 5788 | 7597.322 | 1570 | | 6148.126 | 8452 |
|---|---|---|---|---|---|---|
| *n fs* | n fs | cj, v Polel impf 3fs | n mp, ps 3ms | 26. | v Qal impf 3mp | n md |
| רוּחַ | סְעָרָה | וַתְּרוֹמֵם | גַּלָּיו | | יַעֲלוּ | שָׁמַיִם |
| rûach | se'ārāh | watterômēm | gallāv | | ya'ălû | shāmayim |
| the wind of | a storm | and it raised | its waves | | they went up to | the heavens |

| 3495.126 | 8745 | 5497 | 904, 7750 | 4265.722 | | 2379.126 |
|---|---|---|---|---|---|---|
| v Qal impf 3mp | n fp | n fs, ps 3mp | prep, n fs | v Hithpolel impf 3fs | 27. | v Qal impf 3mp |
| יֵרְדוּ | תְהוֹמוֹת | נַפְשָׁם | בְּרָעָה | תִתְמוֹגָג | | יָחוֹגּוּ |
| yēredhû | thehômôth | naphshām | berā'āh | thithmôghāgh | | yāchôggû |
| they went down to | the depths | their soul | into evil | it melted | | they reeled |

| 5309.126 | 3626, 8318 | 3725, 2551 | 1142.722 | | 7094.126 |
|---|---|---|---|---|---|
| cj, v Qal impf 3mp | prep, art, n ms | cj, *adj*, n fs, ps 3mp | v Hithpael impf 3fs | 28. | cj, v Qal impf 3mp |
| וְיָנוּעוּ | כַּשִּׁכּוֹר | וְכָל־חָכְמָתָם | תִּתְבַּלָּע | | וַיִּצְעֲקוּ |
| weyānû'û | kashshikkôr | wekhol-chokhmāthām | tithballā' | | wayyits'ăqû |
| and they staggered | like a drunk | and all their wisdom | it swallowed | | but they cried out |

| 420, 3176 | 904, 7140 | 3937 | 4623, 4855 | 3428.521 |
|---|---|---|---|---|
| prep, pn | prep, art, n ms | prep, ps 3mp | cj, prep, n fp, ps 3mp | v Hiphil impf 3ms, ps 3mp |
| אֶל־יְהוָה | בַּצָּר | לָהֶם | וּמִמְּצוּקֹתֵיהֶם | יוֹצִיאֵם |
| 'el-yehwāh | batstsar | lāhem | ûmimmetsûqōthêhem | yôtsî'ēm |
| to Yahweh | during the adversity | to them | and from their distress | and He brought them out |

| | 7251.521 | 5788 | 3937, 1888 | 2924.126 | 1570 |
|---|---|---|---|---|---|
| 29. | v Hiphil impf 3ms | n fs | prep, n fs | cj, v Qal impf 3mp | n mp, ps 3mp |
| | יָקֵם | סְעָרָה | לִדְמָמָה | וַיֶּחֱשׁוּ | גַּלֵּיהֶם |
| | yāqēm | se'ārāh | lidhmāmāh | wayyechĕshû | gallêhem |
| | He changed | a storm | into silence | and they were quieted | their waves |

| | 7975.126 | 3706, 8698.126 | 5341.521 | 420, 4366 |
|---|---|---|---|---|
| 30. | cj, v Qal impf 3mp | cj, v Qal impf 3mp | cj, v Hiphil impf 3ms, ps 3mp | prep, *n ms* |
| | וַיִּשְׂמְחוּ | כִּי־יִשְׁתֹּקוּ | וַיַּנְחֵם | אֶל־מְחוֹז |
| | wayyismechû | khî-yishtōqû | wayyanchēm | 'el-mechôz |
| | then they were glad | because they became calm | and He brought them | to the harbor of |

| 2761 | | 3142.526 | 3937, 3176 | 2721 | 6623.258 |
|---|---|---|---|---|---|
| n ms, ps 3mp | 31. | v Hiphil juss 3mp | prep, pn | n ms, ps 3ms | cj, v Niphal ptc fp, ps 3ms |
| חֶפְצָם | | יוֹדוּ | לַיהוָה | חַסְדּוֹ | וְנִפְלְאוֹתָיו |
| chephtsām | | yôdhû | layhwāh | chasdô | weniphle'ôthāv |
| their delight | | let them praise | Yahweh | his steadfast love | and his extraordinary deeds |

**23. They that go down to the sea in ships, that do business in great waters:** ... You Sailors who traverse the Sea On Oceans who work at Your Trade, *Fenton* ... Some crossed the sea in ships, trading in great waters, *Moffatt* ... plying their trade on the wide ocean, *REB*.

**24. These see the works of the LORD, and his wonders in the deep:** ... and his wonders in the abyss, *NCB* ... his wonders with the abyss, *Anchor* ... his wonderful doings amid the deep, *Knox*.

**25. For he commandeth, and raiseth the stormy wind, which lifteth up the waves thereof:** ... He spoke and raised a storm and made its waves dash high, *Beck* ... For he spoke and raised up the storm-wind, Which lifted its billows on high, *Goodspeed* ... For he spoke and stirred up a tempest that lifted high the waves, *NIV*.

**26. They mount up to the heaven, they go down again to the depths:** ... Up to the sky then down to the depths!, *JB* ... They descend the roaring deeps, *Rotherham*.

**their soul is melted because of trouble:** ... their hearts melted away in their plight, *NCB* ... their courage melting, *Moffatt* ... the disaster melts their courage, *Beck*.

**27. They reel to and fro, and stagger like a drunken man, and are at their wit's end:** ... tossed to and fro in peril, *NEB* ... and all their wisdom comes to nothing, *BB* ... They did not know what to do, *NCV* ... And all their wisdom was swallowed up, *MAST* ... and all their skill was of no avail, *REB*.

**28. Then they cry unto the LORD in their trouble, and he bringeth them out of their distresses:** ... He saved them from their sorry plight, *Berkeley* ... from their straits he rescued them, *NAB* ... and he relieved their distress, *Knox*.

**29. He maketh the storm a calm, so that the waves thereof are still:** ... he stilled the storm to a whisper, *Moffatt* ... He hushed the storm to a gentle breeze, *NCB* ... He caused the storm to be still, *NASB* ... the waves of the sea were hushed, *NIV*.

**30. Then are they glad because they be quiet; so he bringeth them unto their desired haven:** ... they smile as they see them abate, And rejoice at the comfort received, *Fenton* ... he bringeth them unto the haven where they would be, *MRB* ... when he guided them to their port of trade, *Anchor*.

**31. Oh that men would praise the LORD for his goodness, and for his wonderful works to the children of men!:** ... Let them give thanks to the Lord for his kindness and his won-

---

sity. All sin is folly. Nothing is so insane as to do wrong. The entirety of v. 17 lays more stress on the sin than on the sickness, and the initial designation of the sufferers as "fools" is quite in harmony with its tone. They are habitual evildoers, as is expressed by the weighty expression "fools because of their transgression." Not by one or two breaches of moral law, but by inveterate, customary sins, men ruin their physical health. So the psalmist uses a form of the verb in v. 17b which expresses that the sinner drags down his punishment with his own hands. That is, of course, eminently true in such gross forms of sin as sow to the flesh, and of the flesh reap corruption. But it is no less really true of all transgression, since all brings sickness to the soul. Verse 18 is apparently taken from Job 33:20ff. It paints with impressive simplicity the failing appetite and consequent ebbing strength. The grim portals, of which death keeps the keys, have all but received the sick men; but before they pass into their shadow they cry to Yahweh, and like the other men in distress they too are heard, feeble as their sick voice may be. The manner of their deliverance is strikingly portrayed by the phrase, "He sent his word, and healed them." As in Ps. 105:19, God's word is almost personified. It is the channel of the divine power. God's uttered will has power on material things. It is the same great thought as is expressed in "he spake and it was done" (Ps. 33:9). The psalmist did not know the Christian teaching that the personal Word of God is the agent of all the divine energy in the realm of nature and of history and that a far deeper sense than that which he attached to them would one day be found in his words, when the Incarnate Word was manifested, as himself bearing and bearing away the sicknesses of humanity and rescuing not only the dying from going down to the grave, but bringing up the dead who had long lain there. God, Who is Guide and Emancipator, is also Healer and Life-giver, and He is all these in the Word, which has become flesh and dwelt and dwells among men.

**107:23–32.** Another travel scene follows. The storm at sea is painted as a landsman would do it, but, specifically a landsman who had seen, from a safe shore, what he so vividly describes. He is impressed with the strange things that the bold men who venture to sea must meet, away out there beyond the point where sea and sky touch. With sure poetic instinct, he spends no time on trivial details, but dashes on his canvas the salient features of the tempest—the sudden springing up of the gale; the swift response of the

| 3937, 1158 | 119 | | 7597.326 | 904, 7235, 6194 |
|---|---|---|---|---|
| prep, *n mp* | n ms | | cj, v Polel juss 3mp, ps 3ms | prep, *n ms*, n ms |
| לִבְנֵי | אָדָם | **32.** | וִירֹמְמוּהוּ | בִּקְהַל־עָם |
| livnê | 'ādhām | | wîrōmemûhû | biqōhal-'ām |
| to the sons of | humankind | | and let them extol Him | in the assembly of the people |

| 904, 4319 | 2292 | 2054.326 | | 7947.121 | 5282 | 3937, 4198 |
|---|---|---|---|---|---|---|
| cj, prep, *n ms* | n mp | v Piel juss 3mp, ps 3ms | | v Qal juss 3ms | n mp | prep, n ms |
| וּבְמוֹשַׁב | זְקֵנִים | יְהַלְלוּהוּ | **33.** | יָשֵׂם | נְהָרוֹת | לְמִדְבָּר |
| ûvemôshav | zeqēnîm | yehalelûhû | | yāsēm | nehārôth | lemidhbār |
| and in the seat of | elders | may they praise Him | | may He change | the floods | into a wilderness |

| 4296 | 4448 | 3937, 7043 | | 800 | 6780 | 3937, 4559 |
|---|---|---|---|---|---|---|
| cj, *n mp* | n md | prep, n ms | | *n fs* | n ms | prep, n fs |
| וּמֹצָאֵי | מַיִם | לְצִמָּאוֹן | **34.** | אֶרֶץ | פְּרִי | לִמְלֵחָה |
| ûmōtsā'ê | mayim | letsimmā'ôn | | 'erets | perî | limlēchāh |
| and springs of | water | into dry places | | a land of | fruit | into a salty place |

| 4623, 7750 | 3553.152 | 904 | | 7947.121 | 4198 |
|---|---|---|---|---|---|
| prep, *n fs* | *v Qal act ptc mp* | prep, ps 3fs | | v Qal juss 3ms | n ms |
| מֵרָעַת | יֹשְׁבֵי | בָהּ | **35.** | יָשֵׂם | מִדְבָּר |
| mērā'ath | yōshevê | vāhh | | yāsēm | midhbār |
| because of the wickedness of | those who dwell | in it | | may He change | the wilderness |

| 3937, 95, 4448 | 800 | 6993 | 3937, 4296 | 4448 | | 3553.521 | 8427 |
|---|---|---|---|---|---|---|---|
| prep, *n ms*, n md | cj, *n fs* | adj | prep, *n mp* | n mp | | cj, v Hiphil impf 3ms | adv |
| לַאֲגַם־מַיִם | וְאֶרֶץ | צִיָּה | לְמֹצָאֵי | מָיִם | **36.** | וַיּוֹשֶׁב | שָׁם |
| la'ăgham-mayim | we'erets | tsîyāh | lemōtsā'ê | māyim | | wayyôshev | shām |
| into pools of water | and a land of | no water | into springs of | water | | and they dwelled | there |

| 7744 | 3679.326 | 6111 | 4319 | | 2319.126 | 7898 | 5378.126 |
|---|---|---|---|---|---|---|---|
| n mp | cj, v Polel impf 3mp | *n fs* | n ms | | cj, v Qal impf 3mp | n mp | cj, v Qal impf 3mp |
| רְעֵבִים | וַיְכוֹנְנוּ | עִיר | מוֹשָׁב | **37.** | וַיִּזְרְעוּ | שָׂדוֹת | וַיִּטְּעוּ |
| re'ēvîm | waykhônenû | 'îr | môshāv | | wayyizre'û | sādhôth | wayyitte'û |
| the hungry | and they founded | a city for | dwelling | | and they sowed | fields | and they planted |

| 3884 | 6449.126 | 6780 | 8721 | | 1313.321 | 7528.126 |
|---|---|---|---|---|---|---|
| n mp | cj, v Qal impf 3mp | *n ms* | n fs | | cj, v Piel impf 3ms, ps 3mp | cj, v Qal impf 3mp |
| כְרָמִים | וַיַּעֲשׂוּ | פְּרִי | תְבוּאָה | **38.** | וַיְבָרְכֵם | וַיִּרְבּוּ |
| kherāmîm | wayya'ăsû | perî | thevû'āh | | wayvārekhēm | wayyirbû |
| vineyards | and they made | fruit of | produce | | and He blessed them | and they multiplied |

| 4108 | 966 | 3940 | 4745.521 | | 4745.126 | 8249.126 |
|---|---|---|---|---|---|---|
| adv | cj, n fs, ps 3mp | neg part | v Hiphil impf 3ms | | cj, v Qal impf 3mp | cj, v Qal impf 3mp |
| מְאֹד | וּבְהֶמְתָּם | לֹא | יַמְעִיט | **39.** | וַיִּמְעֲטוּ | וַיָּשֹׁחוּ |
| me'ōdh | ûvehemtām | lō' | yam'it | | wayyim'ăṭû | wayyāshōchû |
| very | and they cattle | not | He diminished | | but they became few | and they became low |

| 4623, 6354 | 7750 | 3123 | | 8581.151 | 973 | 6142, 5259 |
|---|---|---|---|---|---|---|
| prep, n ms | n fs | cj, n ms | | v Qal act ptc ms | n ms | prep, n mp |
| מֵעֹצֶר | רָעָה | וְיָגוֹן | **40.** | שֹׁפֵךְ | בּוּז | עַל־נְדִיבִים |
| mē'ōtser | rā'āh | weyāghôn | | shōphēkh | bûz | 'al-nedhîvîm |
| from oppression | evil | and agony | | pouring out | contempt | on the leaders |

| 8912.521 | 904, 8744 | 3940, 1932 | | 7891.321 |
|---|---|---|---|---|
| cj, v Hiphil impf 3ms, ps 3mp | prep, n ms | neg part, n ms | | cj, v Piel impf 3ms |
| וַיַּתְעֵם | בְּתֹהוּ | לֹא־דָרֶךְ | **41.** | וַיְשַׂגֵּב |
| wayyath'ēm | bethōhû | lō'-dhārekh | | waysaggēv |
| and He led them astray | into a wasteland | not a way | | and He will make inaccessible |

drous deeds, *NCB* ... thank Yahweh for his faithful love, for his wonders for the children of Adam!, *JB* ... Let men give praise to the Lord for his mercy, *BB* ... Let them thank the LORD for his steadfast love, *NRSV.*

**32. Let them exalt him also in the congregation of the people, and praise him in the assembly of the elders:** ... let them praise him in the meeting of the older leaders, *NCV.*

**33. He turneth rivers into a wilderness, and the watersprings into dry ground:** ... He turned rivers into a desert, *Goodspeed* ... He changed rivers into desert, *Anchor* ... he changes rivers into desert sand, wells into dry ground, *Knox* ... And watersprings into a thirsty ground, *ASV.*

**34. A fruitful land into barrenness, for the wickedness of them that dwell therein:** ... he turns an oasis into a salt waste, to punish people for their sins, *Moffatt* ... fertile ground into a salt flat because the people living there are wicked, *Beck* ... because of the sins of those who are living there, *BB* ... because the people who live there are so wicked, *REB.*

**35. He turneth the wilderness into a standing water, and dry ground into watersprings:** ... He turns a desert into pools of water, a parched land into springs, *RSV* ... And a dry land become fountains of waters, *Young.*

**36. And there he maketh the hungry to dwell, that they may prepare a city for habitation:** ... there he brought the hungry to live, and they founded a city where they could settle, *NIV* ... There the hungry settle and build towns to live in, *Beck* ... has given the hungry a home, where they have built themselves a city, *JB* ... so that they may prepare a city to live in, *KJVII.*

**37. And sow the fields, and plant vineyards, which may yield fruits of increase:** ... plant farms, And make them to yield up their fruits, *Fenton* ... And they obtained a fruitful yield, *NAB* ... And gather a fruitful harvest, *NASB* ... reap a fruitful harvest, *NEB.*

**38. He blesseth them also, so that they are multiplied greatly; and suffereth not their cattle to decrease:** ... they increase, and their herds never diminish, *Moffatt* ... he keeps their cattle at full strength, *JB* ... and their cattle he never let diminish, *Anchor.*

**39. Again, they are minished and brought low through oppression, affliction, and sorrow:** ... Once, they were but few, worn down by stress of need and ill fortune, *Knox* ... Through oppression of evil and sorrow, *MAST* ... they were humbled by oppression, calamity and sorrow, *NIV* ... Tyrants lose their strength and are brought low, *REB.*

**40. He poureth contempt upon princes:** ... He puts an end to the pride of kings, *BB* ... He showed he was displeased with their leaders, *NCV.*

---

waves rolling high with new force in their mass and a new voice in their breaking; the pitching craft, now on the crest, now in the trough; the terror of the helpless crew; the loss of steering power; the heavy rolling of the unmanageable, clumsy ship; and the desperation of the sailors, whose wisdom or skill was "swallowed up," or came to nothing.

Their cry to Yahweh was heard above the shriek of the storm, and the tempest fell as suddenly as it rose. The description of the deliverance is extended beyond the normal single verse, just as that of the peril had been prolonged. It comes like a benediction after the onslaught of the storm. How gently the words echo the softness of the light air into which it has died down and the music which the wavelets make as they lap against the ship's sides! With what sympathy the poet thinks of the glad hearts on board and of their reaching the safe harbor for which they had longed when they thought they would never see it more! Surely it is a permissible application of these lovely words to read into them the Christian hope of preservation amid life's tempests, "Safe into the haven guide, O receive my soul at last." God the Guide, the Emancipator, the Healer, is also the Stiller of the storm, and they who cry to Him from the unquiet sea will reach the stable shore. And so it came to pass, they all came safe to land.

**107:33–38.** With v. 33, the Psalm changes its structure. The refrains, which came in so strikingly in the preceding strophes, are dropped. The complete pictures give place to mere outline sketches. In vv. 33–38, he describes a double change wrought on a land. The barrenness which blasts fertile soil is painted in language largely borrowed from Isaiah. "Verse 33a recalls Isa. 50:2b; v. 33b is like Isa. 35:7a" (Delitzsch). The opposite change of desert into fertile ground is pictured as in Isa. 41:18. The references in v. 36 to "the hungry" and to "a city for habitation" connect with the previous part of the Psalm and are against the supposition that the latter half is not originally part of it. The incidents described refer to no particular instance, but are as general as those of the former part. Many a land, which has been blasted by the vices of its inhabitants, has been transformed into a garden by new settlers.

**107:39–42.** Verse 39 introduces the reverse, which often befalls prosperous communities, especially in times when it is dangerous to seem rich for fear of rapacious rulers. If so, v. 40, which is quoted

| 33 | 4623, 5988 | 7947.121 | 3626, 6887 | 5121 | | 7495.126 |
|---|---|---|---|---|---|---|
| n ms | prep, n ms | cj, v Qal impf 3ms | prep, art, n fs | n fp | **42.** | v Qal impf 3mp |
| אֶבְיוֹן | מֵעוֹנִי | וַיָּשֶׂם | כַּצֹּאן | מִשְׁפָּחוֹת | | יִרְאוּ |
| 'evyôn | mē'ônî | wayyāsem | katstsō'n | mishpāchôth | | yir'û |
| the needy | from transgressions | and He made | like sheep | families | | they will see |

| 3596 | 7975.126 | 3725, 5983 | 7376.112 | 6552 | | 4449, 2550 |
|---|---|---|---|---|---|---|
| n mp | cj, v Qal impf 3mp | cj, *adj*, n fs | v Qal pf 3fs | n ms, ps 3fs | **43.** | intrg, adj |
| יְשָׁרִים | וְיִשְׂמָחוּ | וְכָל־עַוְלָה | קָפְצָה | פִּיהָ | | מִי־חָכָם |
| yeshārîm | weyismāchû | wekhol-'awlāh | qāphetsāh | pîāh | | mî-chākhām |
| the upright | and they will be glad | and all perversity | it will draw shut | its mouth | | who is wise |

| 8490.121, 431 | 1032.726 | 2721 | 3176 |
|---|---|---|---|
| cj, v Qal juss 3ms, dem pron | cj, v Hithpolel juss 3mp | *n mp* | pn |
| וְיִשְׁמָר־אֵלֶּה | וְיִתְבּוֹנְנוּ | חַסְדֵי | יְהוָה |
| weyishmār-'ēlleh | weyithbônenû | chasdhê | yehwāh |
| then let them observe these things | and let them understand | the steadfast love of | Yahweh |

| | 8302 | 4344 | 3937, 1784 | | 3679.255 | 3949 | 435 | 8301.125 |
|---|---|---|---|---|---|---|---|---|
| **108:t** | n ms | n ms | prep, pn | **1.** | v Niphal ptc ms | n ms, ps 1cs | n mp | v Qal juss 1cs |
| | שִׁיר | מִזְמוֹר | לְדָוִד | | נָכוֹן | לִבִּי | אֱלֹהִים | אָשִׁירָה |
| | shîr | mizmôr | ledhāwidh | | nākhôn | libbî | 'ĕlōhîm | 'āshîrāh |
| | a Song | a Psalm | of David | | steady | my heart | O God | let me sing |

| 2252.325 | 652, 3638 | | 5996.131 | 5213 | 3780 | 5996.525 |
|---|---|---|---|---|---|---|
| cj, v Piel juss 1cs | cj, n ms, ps 1cs | **2.** | v Qal impv 2ms | art, n ms | cj, n ms | v Hiphil juss 1cs |
| וַאֲזַמְּרָה | אַף־כְּבוֹדִי | | עוּרָה | הַנֵּבֶל | וְכִנּוֹר | אָעִירָה |
| wa'ăzammerāh | 'aph-kevôdhî | | 'ûrāh | hannēvel | wekhinnôr | 'ā'îrāh |
| yes let me sing praises | also my glory | | arouse | the harp | and the zither | let me awaken |

| 8266 | | 3142.525 | 904, 6194 | 3176 | 2252.325 |
|---|---|---|---|---|---|
| n ms | **3.** | v Hiphil juss 1cs, ps 2ms | prep, art, n mp | pn | cj, v Piel juss 1cs, ps 2ms |
| שָׁחַר | | אוֹדְךָ | בָעַמִּים | יְהוָה | וַאֲזַמֶּרְךָ |
| shāchar | | 'ôdhkhā | vā'ammîm | yehwāh | wa'ăzammerkhā |
| the dawn | | let me praise You | among the peoples | O Yahweh | and let me sing praises to You |

| 904, 3947 | | 3706, 1448 | 4762, 8452 | 2721 | 5912, 8263 |
|---|---|---|---|---|---|
| prep, n mp | **4.** | cj, adj | prep, n md | n ms, ps 2ms | cj, prep, n mp |
| בַּלְאֻמִּים | | כִּי־גָדוֹל | מֵעַל־שָׁמַיִם | חַסְדֶּךָ | וְעַד־שְׁחָקִים |
| bal'ummîm | | kî-ghādhôl | mē'al-shāmayim | chasdekhā | we'adh-shechāqîm |
| among the peoples | | because great | above the heavens | your steadfast love | and unto the clouds |

| 583 | | 7597.123 | 6142, 8452 | 435 | 6142 | 3725, 800 | 3638 |
|---|---|---|---|---|---|---|---|
| n fs, ps 2ms | **5.** | v Qal juss 2ms | prep, n md | n mp | cj, prep | *adj*, art, n fs | n ms, ps 2ms |
| אֲמִתֶּךָ | | רוּמָה | עַל־שָׁמַיִם | אֱלֹהִים | וְעַל | כָּל־הָאָרֶץ | כְּבוֹדְךָ |
| 'ămittekhā | | rûmāh | 'al-shāmayim | 'ĕlōhîm | we'al | kol-hā'ārets | kevôdhekhā |
| your faithfulness | | be exalted | above the heavens | O God | and above | all the earth | your glory |

**and causeth them to wander in the wilderness, where there is no way:** … and causeth them to wander in a pathless waste, *Darby* … and sends them astray through a trackless waste, *NCB.*

**41. Yet setteth he the poor on high from affliction:** … But He sets the needy securely on high away from affliction, *NASB* … The poor, however, He lifts out of their afflictions and miseries, *Berkeley.*

**and maketh him families like a flock:** … and made the families numerous like flocks, *NAB* … And guards them like sheep in His fold, *Fenton* … and made his clans like lambs, *Anchor.*

**42. The righteous shall see it, and rejoice: and all iniquity shall stop her mouth:** … The upright shall see it, and be glad, *MRB* … while all wrongdoers will be silent, *Berkeley* … malice will stand dumb with confusion, *Knox* … and all wickedness closes its mouth, *NCB.*

**43. Whoso is wise, and will observe these things:** ... Let any wise man ponder this, *Moffatt* ... Let the wise man lay these things to heart, *NEB* ... Let the wise give thought to these things, *BB* ... wise will give heed to these things, *ASV.*

**even they shall understand the lovingkindness of the LORD:** ... And diligently consider the lovingkindness of Yahweh, *Rotherham* ... shall consider the mercies of the LORD, *MRB* ... see for yourself the love of the LORD, *Beck* ... steadfast love, *RSV.*

**108:t. A Song or Psalm of David.**

**1. O God, my heart is fixed; I will sing and give praise, even with my glory:** ... a heart true to thy service, *Knox* ... My heart is steadfast; I will sing and chant praise, *NAB* ... I will sing praises, even with my soul, *NASB* ... I will sing and make music with all my soul, *NIV.*

**2. Awake, psaltery and harp: I myself will awake early:** ... Awake, harp; awake, lyre; for I will arouse the dawn!, *Berkeley* ... I will awaken the dawn!, *Rotherham* ... dawn shall find me watching, *Knox.*

**3. I will praise thee, O LORD, among the people: and I will sing praises unto thee among the nations:** ... and play music to praise You among the people, *Beck* ... I will confess thee, O LORD, among the peoples, *NEB* ... I will chant to the Nations of You, *Fenton.*

**4. For thy mercy is great above the heavens: and thy truth reacheth unto the clouds:** ... for your kindness towers to the heavens, *NCB* ... and your faithfulness to the skies, *NAB* ... For great is your love, higher than the heavens, *NIV* ... For thy loving-kindness is great above the heavens, *Darby.*

**5. Be thou exalted, O God, above the heavens: and thy glory above all the earth:** ... God, you are supreme above the skies, *NCV* ... Be lifted up, O God, *KJVII* ... may Thy glory tower over all the earth, *Berkeley* ... till thy glory overshadows the whole earth, *Knox* ... Up with thy glory over all the earth!, *Moffatt.*

---

from Job 12:21, 24, although introduced abruptly, does not disturb the sequence of thought. It grandly paints the judgment of God on such robber-princes, who are hunted from their seats by popular execration and have to hide themselves in the pathless waste from which those who cry to God were delivered (v. 4a, b). On the other hand, the oppressed are lifted, as by his strong arm, out of the depths and set on high, like a man perched safely on some crag above high water mark. Prosperity returning is followed by large increase and happy, peaceful family life, the chief good of man on earth. The outcome of the various methods of God's unvarying purpose is that all which is good is glad, and all which is evil is struck dumb. The two clauses of v. 42, which describe this double effect, are quoted from two passages in Job—v. 42a from 22:19, and 42b from v. 16.

**107:43.** The Psalm began with hymning the enduring steadfast love of Yahweh. It ends with a call to all who would be wise to give heed to the various dealings of God, as exemplified in the specimens chosen in it, that they may comprehend how, in all these, one purpose rules, and all are examples of the manifold steadfast love of Yahweh. This closing note is an echo of the last words of Hosea's prophecy. It is the broad truth which all thoughtful observance of providence brings home to a man, notwithstanding many mysteries and apparent contradictions. "All things work together for good to them that love God" (Rom. 8:28); and the more they love Him, the more clearly will they see, and the more happily will they feel, that so it is. How can a man contemplate the painful riddle of the world and keep his sanity without that faith? He who has it for his faith will have it for his experience.

***Psalm 108.*** *Two fragments of Davidic psalms are here put together here with slight variations. Verses 1–5 are from Ps. 57:7–11, and vv. 6–13 from Ps. 60:5–12. The return from Babylon would be an appropriate occasion for combining these ancient words. We have seen in preceding Psalms that Israel's past drew the thoughts of the singers of that period, and the conjecture may be hazarded that the recent deliverance suggested to some devout man, whose mind was steeped in the songs of former days, the closeness with which old strains suited new joys. If so, there is pathetic meaning in the summons to the "psaltery and harp," which had hung silent on the willows of Babylon so long, to wake their ancient minstrelsy once more, as well as exultant confidence that the God who had led David to victory still leads his people. The hopes of conquest are in the second part, the consciousness that while much has been achieved by God's help, much still remains to be won before Israel can sit secure. Verse 11 heightens the exultation of the rest of the song, and the cry for help against adversaries too strong for Israel's unassisted might are all appropriate to the early stages of the return.*

**108:1–5.** The variations from the original Psalms are of slight moment. In v. 1, the reduplication of the clause "Steadfast is my heart" is omitted,

| 6. | 3937, 4775 | 2603.226 | 3148 | 3588.531 | 3332 |
|---|---|---|---|---|---|
| | prep, prep | v Niphal impf 3mp | adj, ps 2ms | v Hiphil impv 2ms | n fs, ps 2ms |
| | לְמַעַן | יֵחָלְצוּן | יְדִידֶיךָ | הוֹשִׁיעָה | יְמִינְךָ |
| | l$^{e}$ma'an | yēchāl$^{e}$tsûn | y$^{e}$dhîdhêkhā | hôshî'āh | y$^{e}$mîn$^{e}$khā |
| | so that | they may be set apart | your beloved | save with | your right hand |

| 6257.131 | 7. | 435 | 1744.311 | 904, 7231 | 6159.125 | 2606.325 |
|---|---|---|---|---|---|---|
| cj, v Qal impv 2ms, ps 1cs | | n mp | v Piel pf 3ms | prep, n ms, ps 3ms | v Qal juss 1cs | v Piel juss 1cs |
| וַעֲנֵנִי | | אֱלֹהִים | דִּבֶּר | בְּקָדְשׁוֹ | אֶעְלֹזָה | אֲחַלְּקָה |
| wa'ănēnî | | 'ĕlōhîm | dibber | b$^{e}$qādh$^{e}$shô | 'e'ălōzāh | 'ăchall$^{e}$qāh |
| and answer me | | God | He spoke | in his holy place | let me exult | let me divide |

| 8328 | 6231 | 5713 | 4200.325 | 8. | 3937 | 3113B | 3937 |
|---|---|---|---|---|---|---|---|
| pn | cj, *n ms* | pn | v Piel juss 1cs | | prep, ps 1cs | pn | prep, ps 1cs |
| שְׁכֶם | וְעֵמֶק | סֻכּוֹת | אֲמַדֵּד | | לִי | גִלְעָד | לִי |
| sh$^{e}$khem | w$^{e}$'ēmeq | sukkôth | 'ămaddēdh | | lî | ghil'ādh | lî |
| Shechem | and the Valley of | Succoth | let me measure out | | to me | Gilead | to me |

| 4667 | 688 | 4735 | 7513 | 3171 | 2809.351 | 9. | 4262 | 5707 |
|---|---|---|---|---|---|---|---|---|
| pn | cj, pn | *n ms* | n ms, ps 1cs | pn | v Poel ptc ms, ps 1cs | | pn | *n ms* |
| מְנַשֶּׁה | וְאֶפְרַיִם | מָעוֹז | רֹאשִׁי | יְהוּדָה | מְחֹקְקִי | | מוֹאָב | סִיר |
| m$^{e}$nashsheh | w$^{e}$'ephrayim | mā'ôz | rō'shî | y$^{e}$hûdhāh | m$^{e}$chōq$^{e}$qî | | mô'āv | sîr |
| Manasseh | and Ephraim | the helmet of | my head | Judah | my ruler | | Moab | the tub of |

| 7649 | 6142, 110 | 8390.125 | 5458 | 6142, 6673 | 7607.725 |
|---|---|---|---|---|---|
| n ms, ps 1cs | prep, pn | v Hiphil impf 1cs | n fs, ps 1cs | prep, pn | v Hithpolel impf 1cs |
| רַחְצִי | עַל־אֱדוֹם | אַשְׁלִיךְ | נַעֲלִי | עֲלֵי־פְלֶשֶׁת | אֶתְרוֹעָע |
| rachtsî | 'al-'ĕdhôm | 'ashlîkh | na'ălî | 'ălê-ph$^{e}$lesheth | 'ethrô'ā' |
| my washing | on Edom | I will throw down | my sandal | against Philistia | I will make a battle cry |

| 10. | 4449 | 3095.521 | 6111 | 4152 | 4449 | 5328.111 | 5912, 110 |
|---|---|---|---|---|---|---|---|
| | intrg | v Hiphil impf 3ms, ps 1cs | *n fs* | n ms | intrg | v Qal pf 3ms, ps 1cs | prep, pn |
| | מִי | יֹבִלֵנִי | עִיר | מִבְצָר | מִי | נָחַנִי | עַד־אֱדוֹם |
| | mî | yōvilēnî | 'îr | mivtsār | mî | nāchanî | 'adh-'ĕdhôm |
| | who | will he bring Me | a city of | fortification | who | will he lead Me | unto Edom |

| 11. | 1950B, 3940, 435 | 2269.113 | 3940, 3428.123 | 435 | 904, 6893 |
|---|---|---|---|---|---|
| | intrg part, neg part, n mp | v Qal pf 2ms, ps 1cp | cj, neg part, v Qal impf 2ms | n mp | prep, n mp, ps 1cp |
| | הֲלֹא־אֱלֹהִים | זְנַחְתָּנוּ | וְלֹא־תֵצֵא | אֱלֹהִים | בְּצִבְאֹתֵינוּ |
| | hălō'-'ĕlōhîm | z$^{e}$nachtānû | w$^{e}$lō'-thētsē' | 'ĕlōhîm | b$^{e}$tsiv'ōthênû |
| | have not O God | You rejected us | indeed You have not gone out | O God | with our armies |

| 12. | 1957.131, 3937 | 6054 | 4623, 7140 | 8175 | 9009 |
|---|---|---|---|---|---|
| | v Qal impv 2ms, prep, ps 1cp | n fs | prep, n ms | cj, n ms | *n fp* |
| | הָבָה־לָּנוּ | עֶזְרָת | מִצָּר | וְשָׁוְא | תְּשׁוּעַת |
| | hāvāh-lānû | 'ezrāth | mitstsār | w$^{e}$shāw$^{e}$' | t$^{e}$shû'ath |
| | give to us | help | from the adversary | and vanity | the deliverances of |

| 119 | 13. | 904, 435 | 6449.120, 2524 | 2000 | 983.121 | 7141 |
|---|---|---|---|---|---|---|
| n ms | | prep, n mp | v Qal impf 1cp, n ms | cj, pers pron | v Qal impf 3ms | n mp, ps 1cp |
| אָדָם | | בֵּאלֹהִים | נַעֲשֶׂה־חָיִל | וְהוּא | יָבוּס | צָרֵינוּ |
| 'ādhām | | bē'lōhîm | na'ăseh-chāyil | w$^{e}$hû' | yāvûs | tsārênû |
| humankind | | with God | we will act with strength | for He | He will trample | our adversaries |

| 109:t | 3937, 5514.351 | 3937, 1784 | 4344 | 1. | 435 | 8747 | 414, 2896.123 | 2. | 3706 |
|---|---|---|---|---|---|---|---|---|---|
| | prep, art, v Piel ptc ms | prep, pn | n ms | | *n mp* | n fs, ps 1cs | adv, v Qal juss 2ms | | cj |
| | לַמְנַצֵּחַ | לְדָוִד | מִזְמוֹר | | אֱלֹהֵי | תְּהִלָּתִי | אַל־תֶּחֱרַשׁ | | כִּי |
| | lamnatstsēach | l$^{e}$dhāwidh | mizmôr | | 'ĕlōhê | th$^{e}$hillāthî | 'al-techĕrash | | kî |
| | to the director | of David | a Psalm | | O God of | my praise | do not be deaf | | because |

**6. That thy beloved may be delivered: save with thy right hand, and answer me:** ... That your loved ones may escape, *NCB* ... Your right hand, and hear me, *NKJV* ... To rescue those you love, *JB* ... so that those whom you love may be rescued, *NRSV* ... so Your dear people may be free, *Beck.*

**7. God hath spoken in his holiness; I will rejoice:** ... God has spoken from his sanctuary, *NIV* ... God's word came to us from his sanctuary, *Knox* ... God gave his sacred promise, *Moffatt* ... This is the word of the holy God, *BB.*

**I will divide Shechem, and mete out the valley of Succoth:** ... And measure out the valley of Succoth, *NASB* ... the Valley of Succoth measure off, *Anchor.*

**8. Gilead is mine; Manasseh is mine; Ephraim also is the strength of mine head; Judah is my lawgiver:** ... Ephraim is the defence of my head, Judah is my commander's staff, *Rotherham* ... Ephraim is the helmet for my head; Judah, my scepter, *NAB* ... Judah holds my royal scepter, *NCV* ... is the defence of my head; Judah is my sceptre, *ASV.*

**9. Moab is my washpot; over Edom will I cast out my shoe; over Philistia will I triumph:** ... over Edom I will claim my right, *Knox* ... Over Edom I shall throw My shoe; Over Philistia I will shout aloud, *NASB* ... Over Philistia do I cry aloud, *MAST* ... over Philistia I will shout in victory, *Berkeley.*

**10. Who will bring me into the strong city? who will lead me into Edom?:** ... Who will bring me to the fortified city?, *RSV* ... who will lead us inside the hill-fort?, *Moffatt* ... Who will bring me into the fenced city?, *MRB* ... Who can bring me to the impregnable city, *NEB.*

**11. Wilt not thou, O God, who hast cast us off?:** ... But you, O God—will you be angry with us, *Anchor* ... Have not you, O God, rejected us, *NCB* ... Have you not sent us away from you, O God?, *BB* ... We are not forsaken by God, *Fenton.*

**and wilt not thou, O God, go forth with our hosts?:** ... didst not go forth, O God, with our armies?, *Darby* ... O God, haven't You refused to go out with our armies?, *Beck* ... You do not go out, O God, with our armies, *NRSV* ... and do no longer lead our armies to battle?, *REB.*

**12. Give us help from trouble: for vain is the help of man:** ... Give us aid against the enemy, *NIV* ... for deliverance by man is a vain hope, *NEB* ... And vain is the salvation of man, *Young* ... Bring us help in our time of crisis, *JB* ... for worthless is the help of men, *NAB.*

**13. Through God we shall do valiantly: for he it is that shall tread down our enemies:** ... we shall do mighty things, for He shall trample our enemies, *KJVII* ... Only through God can we fight victoriously; only he can trample our oppressors, *Knox* ... but we can win with God's help, *NCV.*

**109:t. To the chief Musician, A Psalm of David.**

**1. Hold not thy peace, O God of my praise:** ... be not deaf to my song of praise, *Anchor* ... O God of my praise, be silent no longer, *NEB* ... do not leave me unbefriended, *Knox* ... Do not keep silent, O God of my praise!, *NKJV.*

**2. For the mouth of the wicked and the mouth of the deceitful are opened against me: they have spoken against me with a lying tongue:** ... Wicked people and liars have spoken against me, *NCV* ... For the mouth of the lawless one and the mouth of the deceiver against me are open, *Rotherham* ... for they have opened wicked and treacherous mouths against me, *NAB.*

---

and "my glory" is detached from v. 2, where it stands in Ps. 57 and is made a second subject, equivalent to "I." In v. 3a, "I will praise thee, O LORD" is repeated, but the auxilary verb "and" is prefixed to 3b. Verse 4 is not improved by the change of "unto the heavens" to "above the heavens," for an anti-climax is produced by following "above the heavens" with "unto the clouds."

**108:6–13.** In the second part, the only change affecting the sense is in v. 9, where the summons by Philistia to "shout aloud because of me," which is probably meant in sarcasm, is transformed into the plain expression of triumph, "Over Philistia will I triumph." The other changes are "me" for "us" in v. 6, the omission of "and" before "mine; Manasseh" in v. 8, and the substitution of a more usual synonym for "fenced" (HED #4152) in v. 10.

***Psalm 109.*** *This is the last and the most terrible of the imprecatory Psalms. Its central portion (vv. 6–20) consists of a series of wishes, addressed to God, of the heaping of all miseries on the heads of one "adversary" and of all his kith and kin. These maledictions are enclosed in prayers, which make the most striking contrast to them: vv. 1–5 are the plaint of a loving soul, shrinkingly conscious of an atmosphere of hatred and appealing gently to God; while vv. 21–31 expatiate in the presentation to Him of the suppliant's feebleness and cries for deliverance, but barely touch on the wished for requital of enemies.*

**109:1–5.** Divine retribution for evil was the truth of the OT, as forgiveness is that of the NT. The conflict between God's kingdom and its enemies was being keenly and perpetually waged, in most literal fashion. Devout men could not but long

6552 / *n ms* / פִּי / phî / the mouth of
7857 / n ms / רָשָׁע / rāshā' / the wicked
6552, 4983 / cj, *n ms*, n fs / וּפִי־מִרְמָה / ûphî-mirmāh / and mouths of deceit
6142 / prep, ps 1cs / עָלַי / 'ālay / against me
6858.116 / v Qal pf 3cp / פָּתָחוּ / pāthāchû / they have opened
1744.316 / v Piel pf 3cp / דִּבְּרוּ / dibbᵉrû / they have spoken

---

882 / prep, ps 1cs / אִתִּי / 'ittî / against me
4098 / *n fs* / לְשׁוֹן / lᵉshôn / tongues of
8632 / n ms / שָׁקֶר / shāqer / lies
**3.**
1745 / cj, *n mp* / וְדִבְרֵי / wᵉdhivrê / and words of
7985 / n fs / שִׂנְאָה / sin'āh / hate
5621.116 / v Qal pf 3cp, ps 1cs / סְבָבוּנִי / sᵉvāvûnî / they have surrounded me

---

4032.226 / cj, v Niphal impf 3mp, ps 1cs / וַיִּלָּחֲמוּנִי / wayyillāchămûnî / and they have fought against me
2703 / adv / חִנָּם / chinnām / without cause
**4.**
8809, 157 / prep, n fs, ps 1cs / תַּחַת־אַהֲבָתִי / tachath-'ahvāthî / instead of my love
7930.126 / v Qal impf 3mp, ps 1cs / יִשְׂטְנוּנִי / yisṯᵉnûnî / they have accused me

---

603 / cj, pers pron / וַאֲנִי / wa'ănî / and I
8940 / n fs / תְפִלָּה / thᵉphillāh / a prayer
**5.**
7947.126 / cj, v Qal impf 3mp / וַיָּשִׂימוּ / wayyāsîmû / and they have put
6142 / prep, ps 1cs / עָלַי / 'ālay / on me
7750 / n fs / רָעָה / rā'āh / evil
8809 / prep / תַּחַת / tachath / instead of
3009B / adj / טוֹבָה / ṭôvāh / good
7985 / cj, n fs / וְשִׂנְאָה / wᵉsin'āh / and hate
8809 / prep / תַּחַת / tachath / instead of

---

157 / n fs, ps 1cs / אַהֲבָתִי / 'ahvāthî / my love
**6.**
6734.531 / v Hiphil impv 2ms / הַפְקֵד / haphqēdh / intervene
6142 / prep, ps 3ms / עָלָיו / 'ālâv / against them
7857 / n ms / רָשָׁע / rāshā' / the wicked
7931 / cj, n ms / וְשָׂטָן / wᵉsāṭān / and the accuser
6198.121 / v Qal juss 3ms / יַעֲמֹד / ya'ămōdh / may he stand

---

6142, 3332 / prep, n fs, ps 3ms / עַל־יְמִינוֹ / 'al-yᵉmînô / on his right side
**7.**
904, 8570.241 / prep, v Niphal inf con, ps 3ms / בְּהִשָּׁפְטוֹ / bᵉhishshāphᵉṭô / during his being judged
3428.121 / v Qal juss 3ms / יֵצֵא / yētsē' / may he go out
7857 / n ms / רָשָׁע / rāshā' / the wicked
8940 / cj, n fs, ps 3ms / וּתְפִלָּתוֹ / ûthᵉphillāthô / and his prayer

---

2030.122 / v Qal impf 3fs / תִּהְיֶה / tihyeh / may it be
3937, 2494 / prep, art, n fs / לַחֲטָאָה / lachṭā'āh / for the sin
**8.**
2030.126, 3219 / v Qal juss 3mp, n mp, ps 3ms / יִהְיוּ־יָמָיו / yihyû-yāmâv / may his days be
4746 / sub / מְעַטִּים / mᵉ'aṭṭîm / few
6735 / n fs, ps 3ms / פְּקֻדָּתוֹ / pᵉquddāthô / his office
4089.121 / v Qal juss 3ms / יִקַּח / yiqqach / may he take
311 / adj / אַחֵר / 'achēr / another

---

**9.**
2030.126, 1158 / v Qal juss 3mp, n mp, ps 3ms / יִהְיוּ־בָנָיו / yihyû-vānâv / may his children be
3605 / n mp / יְתוֹמִים / yᵉthômîm / orphans
828 / cj, n fs, ps 3ms / וְאִשְׁתּוֹ / wᵉ'ishtô / and his wife
496 / n fs / אַלְמָנָה / 'almānāh / a widow
**10.**
5309.142 / cj, v Qal inf abs / וְנוֹעַ / wᵉnôa' / that wandering

---

5309.126 / v Qal impf 3mp / יָנוּעוּ / yānû'û / they will wander aimlessly
1158 / n mp, ps 3ms / בָנָיו / vānâv / his children
8068.316 / cj, v Piel pf 3cp / וְשִׁאֵלוּ / wᵉshi'ēlû / and they will beg
1938.116 / cj, v Qal pf 3cp / וְדָרְשׁוּ / wᵉdhārᵉshû / and they will search
4623, 2823 / prep, n fp, ps 3mp / מֵחָרְבוֹתֵיהֶם / mēchārᵉvôthêhem / among their ruins

---

**11.**
5550.321 / v Piel juss 3ms / יְנַקֵּשׁ / yᵉnaqqēsh / may he place a snare
5565.151 / v Qal act ptc ms / נוֹשֶׁה / nôsheh / a creditor
3937, 3725, 866, 3937 / prep, *adj*, rel part, prep, ps 3ms / לְכָל־אֲשֶׁר־לוֹ / lᵉkhol-'ăsher-lô / for all which to him
997.126 / cj, v Qal juss 3mp / וְיָבֹזּוּ / wᵉyāvōzzû / and may they plunder

**3. They compassed me about also with words of hatred; and fought against me without a cause:** ... with venomous words they surround, And assail me without any cause!, *Fenton* ... They also hemmed me in with words of hatred, *KJVII* ... They have also surrounded me with words of hatred, *NASB.*

**4. For my love they are my adversaries: but I give myself unto prayer:** ... in return for my love they denounced me, *REB* ... In return for my love they accuse me, even while I make prayer for them, *NRSV* ... In return for my friendship they denounce me, and all I can do is pray!, *JB* ... In return for my love they slandered me, but I prayed, *NCB.*

**5. And they have rewarded me evil for good, and hatred for my love:** ... hate in exchange for my love, *BB* ... rewarding me with cruelty for my kindness, *Moffatt* ... and hatred for my friendship, *NIV.*

**6. Set thou a wicked man over him: and let Satan stand at his right hand:** ... And let an adversary stand, *ASV* ... let an accuser bring him to trial, *RSV* ... let one be placed at his right hand to say evil of him, *BB.*

**7. When he shall be judged, let him be condemned:** ... when his case is tried, let him come off guilty, *Berkeley* ... At his trial may he emerge as guilty, *JB* ... let him be tried and sentenced, *Moffatt* ... When he is judged, let him come forth guilty, *NASB.*

**and let his prayer become sin:** ... may his prayer become a sin!, *Goodspeed* ... And their plea be considered a crime, *Fenton* ... pleading with heaven in vain, *Knox.*

**8. Let his days be few; and let another take his office:** ... Let another take his charge, *MAST* ... let another man replace him as leader, *NCV* ... may another seize his position, *NRSV* ... may his hoarded wealth fall to another!, *NEB.*

**9. Let his children be fatherless, and his wife a widow:** ... be orphans, And wives, widows in want!, *Fenton.*

**10. Let his children be continually vagabonds, and beg: let them seek their bread also out of their desolate places:** ... may their houses be investigated by the appraiser, *Anchor* ... beggars, driven from

---

for the triumph of that with which all good was associated and therefore for the defeat and destruction of its opposite. For no private injuries, or for these only insofar as the suffering singer is a member of the community which represents God's cause, does he ask the descent of God's vengeance, but for the insults and hurts inflicted on righteousness. The form of these maledictions belongs to a lower stage of revelation; the substance of them, considered as passionate desires for the destruction of evil, burning zeal for the triumph of Truth, which is God's cause, and unquenchable faith that He is just, is a part of Christian perfection.

***109:6–20.*** *In vv. 6–15, we have imprecations pure and simple, and it is noteworthy that so large a part of these verses refers to the family of the evildoer. In vv. 16–20, the grounds of the wished for destruction are laid in the sinner's perverted choice, and the automatic action of sin working its own punishment is vividly set forth.*

**109:6–8.** Verses 6ff are best taken in close connection, as representing the trial and condemnation of the object of the psalmist's imprecations before a tribunal. He prays that the man may be haled before a wicked judge. The word rendered "set" (HED #6734) is the root from which that rendered "office" (HED #6735) in v. 8 comes and here means to set in a position of authority—in a judicial position. His judge is to be "a wicked man" like himself, for such have no mercy on each other. An accuser is to stand at his right hand. The word rendered "adversary" (HED #7931) can mean "Satan," but the general meaning "hostile accuser" is to be preferred here. With such a judge and prosecutor the issue of the cause is certain—"May he go out [from the judgment hall] guilty." A more terrible petition follows, which is best taken in its most terrible sense. The condemned man cries for mercy, not to his earthly judge, but to God, and the psalmist can ask that the last despairing cry to heaven may be unanswered and even counted sin. It could only be so if the heart that framed it was still an evil heart, despairing, indeed, but obdurate. Then comes the end; when the sentence is executed. The criminal dies, and his office falls to another; his wife is a widow, and his children fatherless. This view of the connection gives unity to what is otherwise a mere heap of unconnected maledictions. It also brings out more clearly that the psalmist is seeking not merely the gratification of private animosity, but the vindication of public justice, even if ministered by an unjust judge. Peter's quotation of v. 8b in reference to Judas (Acts 1:20) does not involve the messianic character of the Psalm.

**109:9–15.** Verses 9–15 extend the maledictions to the enemy's children and parents, in accordance with the ancient strong sense of family solidarity, which was often expressed in practice by

| 2197.152 | 3127 | 12. | 414, 2030.121, 3937 | 5082.151 | 2721 |
|---|---|---|---|---|---|
| v Qal act ptc mp | n ms, ps 3ms | | adv, v Qal juss 3ms, prep, ps 3ms | v Qal act ptc ms | n ms |
| זָרִים | יְגִיעוֹ | | אַל־יְהִי־לוֹ | מֹשֵׁךְ | חָסֶד |
| zārîm | yeghî'ô | | 'al-yehî-lô | mōshēkh | chāsedh |
| strangers | his gain | | may it not be to him | extending | steadfast love |

| 414, 2030.121 | 2706.151 | 3937, 3605 | 13. | 2030.121, 321 | 3937, 3901.541 |
|---|---|---|---|---|---|
| cj, adv, v Qal juss 3ms | v Qal act ptc ms | prep, n mp, ps 3ms | | v Qal juss 3ms, n fs, ps 3ms | prep, v Hiphil inf con |
| וְאַל־יְהִי | חוֹנֵן | לִיתוֹמָיו | | יְהִי־אַחֲרִיתוֹ | לְהַכְרִית |
| we'al-yehî | chônēn | lîthômâv | | yehî-'achrîthô | lehakhrîth |
| and may it not be | being gracious | to his orphans | | and may his posterity be | to cut off |

| 904, 1810 | 311 | 4364.221 | 8428 | 14. | 2226.221 |
|---|---|---|---|---|---|
| prep, n ms | adj | v Niphal juss 3ms | n ms, ps 3mp | | v Niphal juss 3ms |
| בְּדוֹר | אַחֵר | יִמַּח | שְׁמָם | | יִזָּכֵר |
| bedhôr | 'achēr | yimmach | shemām | | yizzākhēr |
| in the generation | another | may it be wiped away | their name | | may it be remembered |

| 5988 | 1 | 420, 3176 | 2496 | 525 | 414, 4364.222 |
|---|---|---|---|---|---|
| *n ms* | n mp, ps 3ms | prep, pn | cj, *n fs* | n fs, ps 3ms | adv, v Niphal juss 3fs |
| עֲוֹן | אֲבֹתָיו | אֶל־יְהוָה | וְחַטַּאת | אִמּוֹ | אַל־תִּמָּח |
| 'ăwōn | 'ăvōthâv | 'el-yehwāh | wechatta'th | 'immô | 'al-timmāch |
| the guilt of | his fathers | to Yahweh | and the sin of | his mother | may it not be wiped away |

| 15. | 2030.126 | 5224, 3176 | 8878 | 3901.521 | 4623, 800 | 2228 |
|---|---|---|---|---|---|---|
| | v Qal juss 3mp | prep, pn | adv | cj, v Hiphil juss 3ms | prep, n fs | n ms, ps 3mp |
| | יִהְיוּ | נֶגֶד־יְהוָה | תָּמִיד | וְיַכְרֵת | מֵאֶרֶץ | זִכְרָם |
| | yihyû | neghedh-yehwāh | tāmîdh | weyakhrēth | mē'erets | zikhrām |
| | may they be | before Yahweh | continually | may He cut off | from the earth | their memory |

| 16. | 3391 | 866 | 3940 | 2226.111 | 6449.141 | 2721 | 7579.121 |
|---|---|---|---|---|---|---|---|
| | cj | rel part | neg part | v Qal pf 3ms | v Qal inf con | n ms | cj, v Qal impf 3ms |
| | יַעַן | אֲשֶׁר | לֹא | זָכַר | עֲשׂוֹת | חָסֶד | וַיִּרְדֹּף |
| | ya'an | 'ăsher | lō' | zākhar | 'ăsôth | chāsedh | wayyirdōph |
| | on account of | that | not | he remembered | to act with | kindness | but he pursued |

| 382, 6270 | 33 | 3630.255 | 3949 | 3937, 4322.341 | 17. | 154.121 |
|---|---|---|---|---|---|---|
| n ms, adj | cj, adj | cj, *v Niphal ptc ms* | n ms | prep, v Polel inf con | | cj, v Qal impf 3ms |
| אִישׁ־עָנִי | וְאֶבְיוֹן | וְנִכְאֵה | לֵבָב | לְמוֹתֵת | | וַיֶּאֱהַב |
| 'îsh-'ānî | we'evyôn | wenikh'ēh | lēvāv | lemôthēth | | wayye'ĕhav |
| an afflicted man | and needy | and broken of | heart | to kill | | and he loved |

| 7329 | 971.122 | 3940, 2759.111 | 904, 1318 | 7651.122 | 4623 |
|---|---|---|---|---|---|
| n fs | cj, v Qal impf 3fs, ps 3ms | cj, neg part, v Qal pf 3ms | prep, n fs | cj, v Qal impf 3fs | prep, ps 3ms |
| קְלָלָה | וַתְּבוֹאֵהוּ | וְלֹא־חָפֵץ | בִּבְרָכָה | וַתִּרְחַק | מִמֶּנּוּ |
| qōlālāh | wattevô'ēhû | welō'-chāphēts | bivrākhāh | wattirchaq | mimmennû |
| a curse | so it will come to him | and he did not delight | in a blessing | so it will be far | from him |

| 18. | 3980.121 | 7329 | 3626, 4196 | 971.122 | 3626, 4448 |
|---|---|---|---|---|---|
| | cj, v Qal impf 3ms | n fs | prep, n ms, ps 3ms | cj, v Qal impf 3fs | prep, art, n mp |
| | וַיִּלְבַּשׁ | קְלָלָה | כְּמַדּוֹ | וַתָּבֹא | כַמַּיִם |
| | wayyilbash | qōlālāh | kemaddô | wattāvō' | khammayim |
| | and he clothed himself with | a curse | like his clothes | and it will come | like the water |

| 904, 7419 | 3626, 8467 | 904, 6344 | 19. | 2030.122, 3937 | 3626, 933 |
|---|---|---|---|---|---|
| prep, n ms, ps 3ms | cj, prep, art, n ms | prep, n fp, ps 3ms | | v Qal juss 3fs, prep, ps 3ms | prep, n ms |
| בְּקִרְבּוֹ | וְכַשֶּׁמֶן | בְּעַצְמוֹתָיו | | תְּהִי־לוֹ | כְּבֶגֶד |
| beqirbô | wekhashshemen | be'atsmôthâv | | tehî-lô | keveghedh |
| in his inmost parts | and like olive oil | in his bones | | may it be to him | like a garment |

their ruined homes!, *REB* ... let them be sent away from the company of their friends, *BB* ... may they be driven out of the ruins they inhabit!, *RSV.*

**11. Let the extortioner catch all that he hath:** ... May a creditor seize all he has, *NIV* ... Let the people to whom he owes money take everything he owns, *NCV* ... Let his creditor take all his goods, *BB.*

**and let the strangers spoil his labour:** ... let the strangers take the fruit of his labor, *KJVII* ... may strangers plunder his earnings!, *Goodspeed* ... and strangers run off with his earnings!, *REB* ... And their earnings by strangers be robbed, *Fenton.*

**12. Let there be none to extend mercy unto him: neither let there be any to favour his fatherless children:** ... Let no one show him love, *NCV* ... no one to do him a kindness, nor anyone to pity his orphans, *NAB* ... no one pitying his fatherless children, *Anchor* ... or give help to his children when he is dead, *BB.*

**13. Let his posterity be cut off; and in the generation following let their name be blotted out:** ... Let all his descendants die, *NCV* ... from the age to come his name erased, *Anchor* ... May his line be doomed to extinction, *NEB* ... may his name be blotted out in the second generation!, *RSV.*

**14. Let the iniquity of his fathers be remembered with the LORD; and let not the sin of his mother be blotted out:** ... May the evil deeds of his father be remembered before the LORD, *Berkeley* ... and his own mother's wickedness never be wiped out!, *REB* ... may the sin of his mother have no forgiveness, *BB.*

**15. Let them be before the LORD continually, that he may cut off the memory of them from the earth:** ... till he banish the memory of these parents from the earth, *NAB* ... may Yahweh keep these constantly in mind, *JB* ... may the Lord keep it in mind, and wipe out their memory from the earth, *Knox.*

**16. Because that he remembered not to show mercy, but persecuted the poor and needy man:** ... For he never thought of doing a kindness, but hounded to death the poor, *NIV* ... never set himself to be loyal to his friend, *NEB* ... but hunted down the poor, *Beck.*

**that he might even slay the broken in heart:** ... And the broken-hearted to kill him, *Goodspeed* ... And murdered the broken in heart!, *Fenton* ... he persecuted to the death, *Moffatt.*

**17. As he loved cursing, so let it come unto him: as he delighted not in blessing, so let it be far from him:** ... No taste for blessing; let it never come his way!, *JB* ... He loved cursing; so may cursing overtake him!, *Berkeley.*

**18. As he clothed himself with cursing like as with his garment, so let it come into his bowels like water, and like oil into his bones:** ... Cursing others filled his body and his life, *NCV* ... And it came into his inward parts like water, *ASV* ... as his coat, may it soak into his body like water, *NRSV* ... And took it like drink to his breast, *Fenton.*

---

visiting the kindred of a convicted criminal with ruin and leveling his house to the ground. The psalmist wishes these consequences to fall in all their cruel severity and pictures the children as vagabonds, driven from the desolation which had in happier days been their home and seeking a scanty subsistence among strangers.

The imprecations of v. 11 at first sight seem to hark back to an earlier stage in the wicked man's career, contemplating him as still in life. But the wish that his wealth may be ensnared (HED #5550) by creditors and stolen by strangers is quite appropriate as a consequence of his sentence and execution; and the prayer in v. 12, that there may be no one to "extend mercy to him," is probably best explained by the parallel clause. A dead man lives a quasi-life in his children, and what is done to them is a prolongation of what was done to him. Helpless beggars, homeless and plundered, "the seed of evildoers," would naturally be short-lived, and the psalmist desires that they may be cut off, and the world freed from an evil race.

His wishes go backwards too, and reach to the previous as well as the subsequent generation. The foe had come of a bad stock—parents, son, and son's sons are to be involved in a common doom, because they were partakers of a common sin. The special reason for the terrible desire that the iniquity of his father and mother may never be blotted out seems to be the desire that the accumulated consequences of hereditary sin may fall on the heads of the third generation—a dread wish, which experience shows is often tragically fulfilled, even when the sufferers are far less guilty than their ancestors. "Father, forgive them" (Luke 23:34) is the strongest conceivable contrast to these awful prayers. But the psalmist's petition implies that the sins in question were unrepented sins, and is, in fact, a cry that, as such, they should be requited in the "cutting off the memory" of such a brood of evildoers "from the earth."

**109:16–20.** In v. 16, a new turn of thought begins, which is pursued until v. 20—the self-retributive action of a perverted choice of evil. "He remembered not" to be gracious to him who

| 6057.121 | 3937, 4337 | 8878 | 2391.121 | | 2148 | 6715 |
|---|---|---|---|---|---|---|
| v Qal impf 3ms | cj, prep, n ms | adv | v Qal impf 3ms, ps 3fs | **20.** | dem pron | *n fs* |
| יַעֲטֶה | וּלְמֵזַח | תָּמִיד | יַחְגְּרֶהָ | | זֹאת | פְּעֻלַּת |
| ya'ăṯeh | ûlămēzach | tāmîdh | yachg$^{e}$reāh | | zō'th | p$^{e}$'ullath |
| it is wrapped | and for a belt | continually | he girds it on | | this | the requital of |

| 7930.152 | 4623, 882 | 3176 | 1744.152 | 7737 | 6142, 5497 | | 887 |
|---|---|---|---|---|---|---|---|
| v Qal act ptc mp, ps 1cs | prep, prep | pn | cj, art, v Qal act ptc mp | n ms | prep, n fs, ps 1cs | **21.** | cj, pers pron |
| שֹׂטְנַי | מֵאֵת | יְהוָה | וְהַדֹּבְרִים | רָע | עַל־נַפְשִׁי | | וְאַתָּה |
| sōṭ$^{e}$nay | mē'ēth | y$^{e}$hwāh | w$^{e}$haddōv$^{e}$rîm | rā' | 'al-naphshî | | w$^{e}$'attāh |
| my accusers | from with | Yahweh | and those who speak | evil | against my life | | but You |

| 3176 | 112 | 6449.131, 882 | 3937, 4775 | 8428 | 3706, 3005 |
|---|---|---|---|---|---|
| pn | n mp, ps 1cs | v Qal impv 2ms, prep, ps 1cs | prep, prep | n ms, ps 2ms | cj, adj |
| יְהוִה | אֲדֹנָי | עֲשֵׂה־אִתִּי | לְמַעַן | שְׁמֶךָ | כִּי־טוֹב |
| y$^{e}$hwih | 'ădhōnāy | 'ăsēh-'ittî | l$^{e}$ma'an | sh$^{e}$mekhā | kî-ṭôv |
| O Yahweh | my Lord | act on behalf of me | because of | your name | because good |

| 2721 | 5522.531 | | 3706, 6270 | 33 | 609 | 3949 |
|---|---|---|---|---|---|---|
| n ms, ps 2ms | v Hiphil impv 2ms, ps 1cs | **22.** | cj, adj | cj, adj | pers pron | cj, n ms, ps 2ms |
| חַסְדְּךָ | הַצִּילֵנִי | | כִּי־עָנִי | וְאֶבְיוֹן | אָנֹכִי | וְלִבִּי |
| chasd$^{e}$khā | hatstsîlēnî | | kî-'ānî | w$^{e}$'evyôn | 'ānōkhî | w$^{e}$libbî |
| your steadfast love | rescue me | | because afflicted | and needy | I | and my heart |

| 2591.111 | 904, 7419 | | 3626, 7009, 3626, 5371.141 | 2050.215 |
|---|---|---|---|---|
| v Qal pf 3ms | prep, n ms, ps 1cs | **23.** | prep, n ms, prep, v Qal inf con, ps 3ms | v Niphal pf 1cs |
| חָלַל | בְּקִרְבִּי | | כְּצֵל־כִּנְטוֹתוֹ | נֶהֱלָכְתִּי |
| chālal | b$^{e}$qirbî | | k$^{e}$tsēl-kinṭôthô | nehĕlākh$^{e}$ttî |
| it has been pierced | within me | | like a shadow when its stretching out | I have proceeded |

| 5469.215 | 3626, 722 | | 1314 | 3911.116 | 4623, 6948 |
|---|---|---|---|---|---|
| v Niphal pf 1cs | prep, art, n ms | **24.** | n fp, ps 1cs | v Qal pf 3cp | prep, n ms |
| נִנְעַרְתִּי | כָּאַרְבֶּה | | בִּרְכַּי | כָּשְׁלוּ | מִצּוֹם |
| nin'artî | kā'arbeh | | birkay | kāsh$^{e}$lû | mitstsôm |
| I have been shaken off | like the locust | | my knees | they have staggered | from fasting |

| 1340 | 3703.111 | 4623, 8469 | | 603 | 2030.115 | 2887 | 3937 |
|---|---|---|---|---|---|---|---|
| cj, n ms, ps 1cs | v Qal pf 3ms | prep, n ms | **25.** | cj, pers pron | v Qal pf 1cs | n fs | prep, ps 3mp |
| וּבְשָׂרִי | כָּחַשׁ | מִשָּׁמֶן | | וַאֲנִי | הָיִיתִי | חֶרְפָּה | לָהֶם |
| ûv$^{e}$sārî | kāchash | mishshāmen | | wa'ănî | hāyîthî | cherpāh | lāhem |
| and my flesh | it has denied | of fatness | | and I | I am | a disgrace | to them |

| 7495.126 | 5309.526 | 7513 | | 6038.131 | 3176 | 435 |
|---|---|---|---|---|---|---|
| v Qal impf 3mp, ps 1cs | v Hiphil impf 3mp | n ms, ps 3mp | **26.** | v Qal impv 2ms, ps 1cs | pn | n mp, ps 1cs |
| יִרְאוּנִי | יְנִיעוּן | רֹאשָׁם | | עָזְרֵנִי | יְהוָה | אֱלֹהָי |
| yir'ûnî | y$^{e}$nî'ûn | rō'shām | | 'āz$^{e}$rēnî | y$^{e}$hwāh | 'ĕlōhāy |
| they see me | they shake | their heads | | help me | O Yahweh | my God |

| 3588.531 | 3626, 2721 | | 3156.126 | 3706, 3135 |
|---|---|---|---|---|
| v Hiphil impv 2ms, ps 1cs | prep, n ms, ps 2ms | **27.** | cj, v Qal juss 3mp | cj, n fs, ps 2ms |
| הוֹשִׁיעֵנִי | כְחַסְדֶּךָ | | וְיֵדְעוּ | כִּי־יָדְךָ |
| hôshî'ēnî | kh$^{e}$chasdekhā | | w$^{e}$yēdh$^{e}$'û | kî-yādh$^{e}$khā |
| save me | according to your steadfast love | | so may they know | that your hand |

| 2148 | 887 | 3176 | 6449.113 | | 7327.326, 2065 | 887 | 1313.323 |
|---|---|---|---|---|---|---|---|
| dem pron | pers pron | pn | v Qal pf 2ms, ps 3fs | **28.** | v Piel impf 3mp, pers pron | cj, pers pron | v Piel impf 2ms |
| זֹּאת | אַתָּה | יְהוָה | עֲשִׂיתָהּ | | יְקַלְלוּ־הֵמָּה | וְאַתָּה | תְבָרֵךְ |
| zō'th | 'attāh | y$^{e}$hwāh | 'ăsîthāhh | | y$^{e}$qal$^{e}$lû-hēmmāh | we'attāh | th$^{e}$vārēkh |
| this | You | Yahweh | You have done it | | they they curse | but You | You bless |

**19. Let it be unto him as the garment which covereth him, and for a girdle wherewith he is girded continually:** ... as a garment he shall wrap round him, *Rotherham* ... May it wrap him round like the clothes he puts on, *REB* ... for a belt with which he girds himself continually, *NKJV* ... and as a sash, daily let him gird it on, *Anchor.*

**20. Let this be the reward of mine adversaries from the LORD, and of them that speak evil against my soul:** ... Let this be the reward given to my haters from the Lord, *BB* ... This is the wage of mine accusers, *Young* ... the recompense from the LORD to my accusers and to those who threaten my life with evil, *Berkeley* ... speak evil against my life, *NRSV.*

**21. But do thou for me, O GOD the Lord, for thy name's sake: because thy mercy is good, deliver thou me:** ... work for me, LIVING LORD, For your NAME, for your mercy relieves, *Fenton* ... Since good is thy lovingkindness O rescue me, *Rotherham* ... out of the goodness of your love, deliver me, *NIV* ... Because your love is good, save me, *NCV.*

**22. For I am poor and needy, and my heart is wounded within me:** ... downtrodden and poor, and my heart within me is distraught, *REB* ... my heart is pierced through with anguish, *Knox* ... Poor and needy as I am, my wounds go right to the heart, *JB.*

**23. I am gone like the shadow when it declineth:** ... As a shadow when it is stretched out, I am gone, *KJVII* ... I am gone like a shadow at evening, *NRSV* ... I am gone like the shadow when it declineth, *MRB.*

**I am tossed up and down as the locust:** ... I am shaken off like a locust, *NKJV* ... I have lost my youth, truly I have aged, *Anchor* ... I am forced out of my place like a locust, *BB* ... I have been driven away as a locust, *Young.*

**24. My knees are weak through fasting; and my flesh faileth of fatness:** ... my body is thin and gaunt, *NIV* ... feeble for need of food; there is no fat on my bones, *BB* ... And my flesh has grown lean, without fatness, *NASB.*

**25. I became also a reproach unto them: when they looked upon me they shaked their heads:** ... They make a laughing-stock of me, *Knox* ... My enemies insult me, *NCV* ... To them I became a contempt, *Fenton* ... I have become the victim of their taunts; when they see me they toss their heads, *NEB.*

**26. Help me, O LORD my God: O save me according to thy mercy:** ... Deliver me in accordance with thy kindness!, *Goodspeed* ... oh help me, save me in thy love, *Moffatt* ... Save me according to your steadfast love, *NRSV* ... save me, by thy unfailing love, *NEB.*

**27. That they may know that this is thy hand; that thou, LORD, hast done it:** ... know this is your doing and you alone, LORD, have done it, *REB* ... And teach me that this was Your hand, *Fenton* ... Then they will know that your power has done this, *NCV.*

**28. Let them curse, but bless thou:** ... So let them curse, as long as you bless, *Anchor* ... They may give curses but you give blessing, *BB* ... They revile, and Thou dost bless, *Young.*

---

needed compassion; therefore, it is just that he should not be remembered on earth and that his sin should be remembered in heaven. He deliberately chose cursing rather than blessing as his attitude and act towards others; therefore, cursing comes to him and blessing remains far from him as others' attitudes and acts toward him. The world is a mirror which, on the whole, gives back the smile or the frown which we present to it.

Although the psalmist has complained that he had loved and been hated in return, he does not doubt that, in general, the curser is cursed back again and the blesser blessed. Outwardly and inwardly, the man is wrapped in and saturated with "cursing." Like a robe or a girdle, it encompasses him; like a draught of water, it passes into his inmost nature; like anointing oil oozing into the bones, it steals into every corner of his soul. His own doings come back to poison him. The kick of the gun which he fires is sure to hurt his own shoulder, and it is better to be in front of the muzzle than behind the trigger.

The last word of these maledictions is not only a wish, but a declaration of the law of divine retribution. The psalmist could not have found it in his heart to pray such a prayer unless he had been sure that Yahweh paid men's wages punctually in full, and that conviction is the kernel of his awful words. He is equally sure that his cause is God's, because he is sure that God's cause is his and that he suffers for righteousness and for the righteous Yahweh.

**109:21–31.** The final part returns to lowly, sad petitions for deliverance of the kind common to many Psalms. Very pathetically and as with a tightening of his grasp does the singer call on his helper by the double name "O GOD the Lord," and plead all the pleas with God which are hived in these names. The prayer in v. 21b resembles that in Ps. 69:16, another of the Psalms of imprecation. The image of the long drawn out shadow recurs in Ps.

| 7251.116 | 991.126 | 5860 | 7975.121 |
|---|---|---|---|
| v Qal pf 3cp | cj, v Qal impf 3mp | cj, n ms, ps 2ms | v Qal impf 3ms |
| קָמוּ | וַיֵּבֹשׁוּ | וְעַבְדְּךָ | יִשְׂמָח |
| qāmû | wayyēvōshû | we'avdekhā | yismāch |
| they have risen | but they will be put to shame | and your servant | he will be glad |

| 29. | 3980.126 | 7930.152 | 3759 | 6057.126 | 3626, 4752 |
|---|---|---|---|---|---|
| | v Qal impf 3mp | v Qal act ptc mp, ps 1cs | n fs | cj, v Qal impf 3mp | prep, art, n ms |
| | יִלְבְּשׁוּ | שׂוֹטְנַי | כְלִמָּה | וְיַעֲטוּ | כַמְעִיל |
| | yilbeshû | sôṭnay | kelimmāh | weya'ățû | kham'îl |
| | they will be clothed | my accusers | dishonor | and they will be wrapped | like a robe |

| 1350 | 30. | 3142.525 | 3176 | 4108 | 904, 6552 | 904, 8761 | 7521 |
|---|---|---|---|---|---|---|---|
| n fp, ps 3mp | | v Hiphil juss 1cs | pn | adv | prep, n ms, ps 1cs | cj, prep, *n ms* | adj |
| בָּשְׁתָּם | | אוֹדֶה | יְהוָה | מְאֹד | בְּפִי | וּבְתוֹךְ | רַבִּים |
| bāshettām | | 'ôdheh | yehwāh | me'ōdh | bephî | ûvethôkh | rabbîm |
| their shame | | let me praise | Yahweh | very | with my mouth | and in the midst of | many |

| 2054.325 | 31. | 3706, 6198.121 | 3937, 3332 | 33 | 3937, 3588.541 |
|---|---|---|---|---|---|
| v Piel juss 1cs, ps 3ms | | cj, v Qal impf 3ms | prep, *n fs* | n ms | prep, v Hiphil inf con |
| אֲהַלְלֶנּוּ | | כִּי־יַעֲמֹד | לִימִין | אֶבְיוֹן | לְהוֹשִׁיעַ |
| 'ăhalelennû | | kî-ya'ămōdh | lîmîn | 'evyôn | lehôshîa' |
| let me praise Him | | because He stands | at the right hand of | the needy | to save |

| 8570.152 | 5497 | 110:t | 3937, 1784 | 4344 | 1. | 5177 | 3176 |
|---|---|---|---|---|---|---|---|
| prep, *v Qal act ptc mp* | n fs, ps 3ms | | prep, pn | n ms | | *n ms* | pn |
| מִשֹּׁפְטֵי | נַפְשׁוֹ | | לְדָוִד | מִזְמוֹר | | נְאֻם | יְהוָה |
| mishshōphetê | naphshô | | ledhāwidh | mizmôr | | ne'um | yehwāh |
| from the judgments against | his life | | of David | a Psalm | | a declaration of | Yahweh |

| 3937, 112 | 3553.131 | 3937, 3332 | 5912, 8308.125 | 342.152 | 1986 |
|---|---|---|---|---|---|
| prep, n ms, ps 1cs | v Qal impv 2ms | prep, n fs, ps 1cs | adv, v Qal impf 1cs | v Qal act ptc mp, ps 2ms | n ms |
| לַאדֹנִי | שֵׁב | לִימִינִי | עַד־אָשִׁית | אֹיְבֶיךָ | הֲדֹם |
| la'dhōnî | shēv | lîmînî | 'adh-'āshîth | 'ōyevêkhā | hedhōm |
| to my Lord | sit | at my right hand | until I make | your enemies | a stool |

| 3937, 7559 | 2. | 4431, 6010 | 8365.121 | 3176 | 4623, 6995 |
|---|---|---|---|---|---|
| prep, n fp, ps 2ms | | *n ms*, n ms, ps 2ms | v Qal impf 3ms | pn | prep, pn |
| לְרַגְלֶיךָ | | מַטֵּה־עֻזְּךָ | יִשְׁלַח | יְהוָה | מִצִּיּוֹן |
| leraghlêkhā | | maṭṭēh-'uzzekhā | yishlach | yehwāh | mitstsîyôn |
| for your feet | | the staff of your strength | He has stretched out | Yahweh | from Zion |

**when they arise, let them be ashamed; but let thy servant rejoice:** ... May those who attack me come to a shameful end, *Beck* ... when they attack they will be put to shame, *NIV* ... let their attacks bring shame to them and joy to your servant!, *JB.*

**29. Let mine adversaries be clothed with shame, and let them cover themselves with their own confusion, as with a mantle:** ... Mine accusers shall be clothed with confusion, *Rotherham* ... Let my accusers be clothed with disgrace and let them wear their shame, *NAB* ... be clothed with dishonor, And let them cover themselves with their own shame as with a robe, *ASV* ... robed in their own dishonour!, *Moffatt.*

**30. I will greatly praise the Lord with my mouth; yea, I will praise him among the multitude:** ... I will give thanks to the Lord in a loud voice, *Berkeley* ... I will speak my thanks earnestly to the Lord, and in the midst of the throng I will praise him, *NCB* ... With my mouth I will give thanks abundantly to the Lord, *NASB.*

**31. For he shall stand at the right hand of the poor, to save him from those that condemn his soul:** ... stands at the right hand of the needy, to save him from those who condemn him to death, *RSV* ... To save from them who would pass sentence on his life, *Rotherham.*

**110:t. A Psalm of David.**

**1. The Lord said unto my Lord, Sit thou at my right hand, until I make thine enemies thy footstool:** ... till I put all those who are against you under your feet, *BB* ... until I put your enemies under your control, *NCV.*

102:11. The word rendered " I am gone" (HED # 8469) occurs here only and implies compulsory departure. The same idea of external force hurrying one out of life is picturesquely presented in the parallel clause. The psalmist complains, "I am tossed up and down," as a thing which a man wishes to get rid of is shaken out of the folds of a garment. He thinks of himself as being whirled away, helpless, as a swarm of locusts blown into the sea. The physical feebleness in v. 24 is probably to be taken literally, as descriptive of the havoc wrought on him by his persecutions and trouble of soul, but may be a metaphor for that trouble itself.

The expression in v. 24b rendered above "faileth of fatness" is literally "has become a liar," or faithless, which is probably a picturesque way of saying that the psalmist's flesh had, as it were, become a renegade from its former well nourished condition and was emaciated by his sorrow. Others would keep the literal meaning of the word rendered "fatness" (HED #8469), oil, and translate "My flesh has shrunk up for lack of oil."

One more glance at the enemies, now again regarded as many, and one more flash of confidence that his prayer is heard, close the Psalm. Once again, God is invoked by his name LORD, and the suppliant presses close to Him as "my God." Once again, he casts himself on that steadfast love, whose measure is wider than his thoughts and will ensure him larger answers than his desires. Once again, he builds all his hope on it and pleads no claims of his own. He longs for personal deliverance, not only for personal ends, but rather that it may be an undeniable manifestation of Yahweh's power. That is a high range of feeling which subordinates self to God even while longing for deliverance and wishes more that He should be glorified than that self should be blessed. There is almost a smile on the psalmist's face as he contrasts his enemies' curses with God's blessing and thinks how ineffectual these are and how omnipotent that is. He takes the issue of the strife between cursing men and a blessing God to be as good as already decided. So he can look with new equanimity on the energetic preparations of his foes; for he sees in faith their confusion and defeat and already feels some springing in his heart of the joy of victory and is sure of already clothing themselves with shame. It is the prerogative of faith to behold things that are not as though they were and to live as in the hour of triumph, even while in the thick of the fight.

The Psalm began with addressing "O God of my praise"; it ends with the confidence and the vow that the singer will yet praise Him. It painted an adversary standing at the right hand of the wicked to condemn him; it ends with the assurance that Yahweh stands at the right hand of his afflicted servant, as his advocate to protect him. The wicked man was to "go out guilty"; he whom God defends shall come forth from all that would judge his soul. "If God be for us, who can be against us?" (Rom 8:31) It is God that justifieth. Who is he that condemneth?" (Rom. 8:33f).

**110:1.** "The LORD said" introduces a fresh utterance heard by the psalmist, who thus claims to be the mouthpiece of the divine will. It is a familiar prophetic phrase, but usually found at the close—not, as here, at the beginning—of the utterance to which it refers (cf., however, Isa. 56:8; Zech. 12:1). The unusual position makes the divine origin of the following words more emphatic. "My LORD" is a customary title of respect in addressing a superior, but not in speaking of him. Its use here evidently implies that the psalmist regards Messiah as his King, and the best comment on it is Matt. 22:43: "How then doth David in spirit call him LORD"? The substance of the oracle follows. He who is exalted to sit at the right hand of a king is installed thereby as his associate in rule.

**110:2.** The divine oracle is silent, and the strain is taken up by the psalmist himself, who speaks in the spirit, in the remainder of the Psalm, no less than he did when uttering Yahweh's word. Messiah's dominion has a definite earthly center. From Zion is this King to rule. His mighty scepter, the symbol and instrument of his God-given power, is to stretch thence. How far? No limit is named to the sweep of his influence.

Verse 2b may be taken as the words of Yahweh, but more probably they are the loyal exclamation of the psalmist, moved to his heart's depths by the vision which makes the bliss of his solitude. The word rendered "rule" (HED #7575) is found also in Balaam's prophecy of Messiah (Num. 24:19) and in the messianic Ps. 72:8. The kingdom is to subsist in the midst of enemies. The normal state of the Church on earth is militant. Yet the enemies are not only a ring of antagonists around a center of submission, but into their midst his power penetrates, and Messiah dominates them too, for all their embattled hostility. A throne around which storms of rebellion rage is an insecure seat. But this throne is established through enmity, because it is upheld by Yahweh.

| 7575.131 | 904, 7419 | 342.152 | | 6194 | 5249 | 904, 3219 |
|---|---|---|---|---|---|---|
| v Qal impv 2ms | prep, *n ms* | v Qal act ptc mp, ps 2ms | | n ms, ps 2ms | n fp | prep, *n ms* |
| רְדֵה | בְּקֶרֶב | אֹיְבֶיךָ | **3.** | עַמְּךָ | נְדָבֹת | בְּיוֹם |
| redhēh | beqerev | 'ōyevêkhā | | 'ammekhā | nedhāvōth | beyôm |
| rule | in the midst of | your enemies | | your people | freewill offerings | on the day of |

| 2524 | 904, 1994, 7231 | 4623, 7641 | 5073 | 3937 | 3030 | 3317 |
|---|---|---|---|---|---|---|
| n ms, ps 2ms | prep, *n mp*, n ms | prep, *n ms* | n ms | prep, ps 2ms | n ms | n fp, ps 2ms |
| חֵילֶךָ | בְּהַדְרֵי־קֹדֶשׁ | מֵרֶחֶם | מִשְׁחָר | לְךָ | טַל | יַלְדֻתֶיךָ |
| chêlekhā | behadhrê-qōdhesh | mērechem | mishchār | lekhā | ṭal | yaldhuthêkhā |
| your army | with the honor of holiness | from the womb of | the dawn | to You | dew | your youth |

| | 8123.211 | 3176 | 3940 | 5341.221 | 887, 3669 | 3937, 5986 |
|---|---|---|---|---|---|---|
| | v Niphal pf 3ms | pn | cj, neg part | v Niphal impf 3ms | pers pron, n ms | prep, n ms |
| **4.** | נִשְׁבַּע | יְהוָה | וְלֹא | יִנָּחֵם | אַתָּה־כֹהֵן | לְעוֹלָם |
| | nishba' | yehwāh | welō' | yinnāchēm | 'attāh-khōhēn | le'ôlām |
| | He has sworn | Yahweh | and not | He will relent | You a priest | unto eternity |

| 6142, 1750 | 4581 | | 112 | 6142, 3332 | 4410.111 |
|---|---|---|---|---|---|
| prep, *n fs* | pn | | n mp, ps 1cs | prep, n fs, ps 2ms | v Qal pf 3ms |
| עַל־דִּבְרָתִי | מַלְכִּי־צֶדֶק | **5.** | אֲדֹנָי | עַל־יְמִינְךָ | מָחַץ |
| 'al-divrāthî | malkî-tsedheq | | 'ădhōnāy | 'al-yemînekhā | māchats |
| according to the manner of | Melchizedek | | my Lord | on your right hand | He will smash |

| 904, 3219, 653 | 4567 | | 1833.121 | 904, 1504 | 4527.151 | 1505 |
|---|---|---|---|---|---|---|
| prep, *n ms*, n ms, ps 3ms | n mp | | v Qal impf 3ms | prep, art, n mp | v Qal act ptc ms | n fp |
| בְּיוֹם־אַפּוֹ | מְלָכִים | **6.** | יָדִין | בַּגּוֹיִם | מָלֵא | גְוִיּוֹת |
| beyôm-'appô | melākhîm | | yādhîn | baggôyim | mālē' | ghewîyôth |
| in the day of his anger | kings | | He will judge | among the nations | being full of | corpses |

| 4410.111 | 7513 | 6142, 800 | 7521 | | 4623, 5337 | 904, 1932 | 8685.121 |
|---|---|---|---|---|---|---|---|
| v Qal pf 3ms | n ms | prep, n fs | adj | | prep, n ms | prep, art, n ms | v Qal impf 3ms |
| מָחַץ | רֹאשׁ | עַל־אֶרֶץ | רַבָּה | **7.** | מִנַּחַל | בַּדֶּרֶךְ | יִשְׁתֶּה |
| māchats | rō'sh | 'al-'erets | rabbāh | | minnachal | badderekh | yishteh |
| He will smash | the heads | upon the earth | wide | | from the stream | on the way | He will drink |

**2. The LORD shall send the rod of thy strength out of Zion: rule thou in the midst of thine enemies:** … When the LORD from Zion hands you the sceptre, *NEB* … The LORD sends your brave army from Zion, *Fenton* … The Lord will make thy empire spring up like a branch out of Sion, *Knox.*

**3. Thy people shall be willing in the day of thy power, in the beauties of holiness from the womb of the morning:** … Thy people are free-will gifts in the day of thy strength, in the honours of holiness, *Young* … Royal dignity has been yours from the day of your birth, sacred honour from the womb, *JB* … Your people shall be volunteers, *NKJV* … Arrayed in holy majesty, from the womb of the dawn, *NIV.*

**thou hast the dew of thy youth:** … you have the freshness of a child, *NCV* … vital and fresh like dewdrops of the dawn, *Moffatt* … like the dew, I have begotten you, *NCB* … Thine is the flower of Thy young men, *Berkeley.*

**4. The LORD hath sworn, and will not repent, Thou art a priest for ever after the order of Melchizedek:** … in the succession of Melchizedek, *NEB* … a priest for ever, a Melchizedek in my service, *REB* … You are a priest of the Eternal according to his pact, *Anchor* … in the line of Melchisedech, *Knox.*

**5. The Lord at thy right hand shall strike through kings in the day of his wrath:** … At your right the Lord will smash kings when He's angry, *Beck* … He has shattered kings on the day of his wrath, *Goodspeed* … he will crush kings on the day of his wrath, *NAB* … through kings in the day of his anger, *Darby.*

**6. He shall judge among the heathen, he shall fill the places with the dead bodies:** … He will execute judgment among the nations, filling them with corpses, *NRSV* … He will judge among the nations, *MAST.*

**he shall wound the heads over many countries:** … He shall strike through the head over a wide land, *MRB* … He will shatter the chief men over a broad country, *NASB* … He hath shattered the head over a land far extended, *Rotherham* … he will shatter chiefs over the wide earth, *RSV.*

**110:3.** The kingdom in relation to its subjects is the theme of v. 3, which accords with the warlike tone of the whole Psalm, by describing them as an army. The period spoken of is "the day of thy power," meaning the time when the forces are mustered and set in order for battle. The word rendered "freewill offerings" (HED #5249) may possibly mean simply "willingnesses," but it is better to retain the fuller and more picturesque meaning of glad, spontaneous sacrifices, which corresponds with the priestly character ascribed afterwards to the people.

The last two parts of v. 3 give another picture of the host. The usual explanation of the clause takes "youth" (HED #3317) as meaning, not the young vigor of the King, but, in a collective sense, the assembled warriors, just now twenty years old. The principal point of comparison of the army with the dew is probably its multitude (2 Sam. 17:12).

**110:4.** Verse 4 again enshrines a divine utterance, which is presented in an even more solemn manner than that of v. 1. The oath of Yahweh by himself represents the thing sworn as guaranteed by the divine character. God, as it were, pledges his own name, with its fullness of unchanging power, to the fulfillment of the Word, and this irrevocable and omnipotent decree is made still more impressive by the added assurance that He "will not repent." Thus inextricably intertwined with the augustness of God's nature, the union of the royal and priestly offices in the person of Messiah shall endure forever. Their opposition has resulted in many tragedies. Their union would probably be still more fatal, except in the case of One whose priestly sacrifice of himself as a willing offering is the basis of his royal sway.

The "order of Melchizedek" has received unexpected elucidation from the El-Amarna tablets, which bring to light, as a correspondent of the Pharaoh, one Ebed-Tob, king of Uru-Salim (the city of Salim, the god of peace). In one of his letters he says, "Behold, neither my father nor my mother have exalted me in this place; the prophecy [or perhaps, arm] of the mighty King has caused me to enter the house of my father." By the mighty King is meant the god whose sanctuary stood on the summit of Mount Moriah. The Psalm lays stress on the eternal duration of the royalty and priesthood of Messiah; and although in another messianic Psalm, the promised perpetuity may be taken to refer to the dynasty rather than the individual monarch. That explanation is impossible here, where a person is the theme.

**110:5–6.** The second part of the Psalm carries the King into the battlefield. He comes forth from the throne, where He sat at Yahweh's right hand, and now Yahweh stands at his right hand. The word rendered "Lord" in v. 5 (HED #112) is never used of any but God, and it is best to take it so here, even though to do so involves the necessity of supposing a change in the subject either in v. 6 or v. 7, which latter verse can only refer to the Messiah.

The destructive conflict described is said to take place "in the day of his wrath"—of Yahweh's wrath. If this is strictly interpreted, the period intended is not that of "the day of thine army," when by his priestly warriors the Priest-King wages a warfare among his enemies, which wins them to be his lovers, but that dread hour when He comes forth from his ascended glory to pronounce doom among the nations and to crush all opposition. Such a final apocalypse of the wrath of the Lamb is declared to us in clearer words, which may well be permitted to cast a light back on this Psalm (Rev. 19:11).

"He will smash kings" is the perfect of prophetic certainty or intuition, the scene being so vividly bodied before the singer that he regards it as accomplished. "He shall judge" or give doom "among the heathen"— the future of pure prediction.

Verse 6b is capable of various renderings. It may be rendered as above, or the verb may be intransitive and the whole clause translated, "shall fill the places with the dead bodies."

**110:7.** Verse 7 is usually taken as depicting the King as pausing in his victorious pursuit of the flying foe, to drink, like Gideon's men, from the brook, and then with renewed vigor pressing on. But is not the idea of the Messiah needing refreshment in that final conflict somewhat harsh? And may there not be here a certain desertion of the order of sequence, so that we are carried back to the time prior to the enthronement of the King? One is tempted to suggest the possibility of this closing verse being a full parallel with Phil. 2:7ff. On the way to his throne, Christ drank of "waters of affliction," and He is precisely therefore "highly exalted."

The choice for every man is either being crushed beneath his foot or being exalted to sit with Him on his throne. "To him that overcometh will I grant to sit down with me in my throne, even as I also overcame, and am set down with my Father in his throne" (Rev. 3:21). It is better to sit on his throne than to be his footstool.

| 6142, 3772 | 7597.521 | 7513 | | 2054.333 | 3161 | 3142.525 | 3176 |
|---|---|---|---|---|---|---|---|
| prep, adv | v Hiphil impf 3ms | n ms | **111:1** | v Piel impv 2mp | pn | v Hiphil juss 1cs | pn |
| עַל־כֵּן | יָרִים | רֹאשׁ | | הַלְלוּ | יָהּ | אוֹדֶה | יְהוָה |
| 'al-kēn | yārîm | rō'sh | | halelû | yāhh | 'ōdheh | yehwāh |
| therefore | He will raise | the head | | praise | Yah | let me praise | Yahweh |

| 904, 3725, 3949 | 904, 5660 | 3596 | 5920 | | 1448 | 4801 |
|---|---|---|---|---|---|---|
| prep, *adj*, n ms | prep, *n ms* | n mp | cj, n fs | **2.** | adj | *n mp* |
| בְּכָל־לְבָב | בְּסוֹד | יְשָׁרִים | וְעֵדָה | | גְּדֹלִים | מַעֲשֵׂי |
| bekhol-lēvāv | besôdh | yeshārîm | we'ēdhāh | | gedhōlîm | ma'ăsê |
| with all the heart | in the consultation of | the upright | and the congregation | | great | the works of |

| 3176 | 1938.156 | 3937, 3725, 2761 | | 2003, 1994 | 6714 |
|---|---|---|---|---|---|
| pn | v Qal pass ptc mp | prep, *adj*, n mp, ps 3mp | **3.** | n ms, cj, n ms | n ms, ps 3ms |
| יְהוָה | דְּרוּשִׁים | לְכָל־חֶפְצֵיהֶם | | הוֹד־וְהָדָר | פָּעֳלוֹ |
| yehwāh | derûshîm | lekhol-chephtsêhem | | hôdh-wehādhār | pā'ālô |
| Yahweh | inquired about | all those delighting in them | | majesty and honor | his deeds |

| 6930 | 6198.153 | 3937, 5911 | | 2228 | 6449.111 |
|---|---|---|---|---|---|
| cj, n fs, ps 3ms | v Qal act ptc fs | prep, n ms | **4.** | n ms | v Qal pf 3ms |
| וְצִדְקָתוֹ | עֹמֶדֶת | לָעַד | | זֵכֶר | עָשָׂה |
| wetsidhqāthô | 'ōmedheth | lā'adh | | zēkher | 'āsāh |
| and his righteousness | standing | unto eternity | | a memorial | He has made |

| 3937, 6623.258 | 2688 | 7631 | 3176 | | 3073 | 5598.111 |
|---|---|---|---|---|---|---|
| prep, v Niphal ptc fp, ps 3ms | adj | cj, adj | pn | **5.** | n ms | v Qal pf 3ms |
| לְנִפְלְאֹתָיו | חַנּוּן | וְרַחוּם | יְהוָה | | טֶרֶף | נָתַן |
| leniphle'ōthâv | channûn | werachûm | yehwāh | | ṭereph | nāthan |
| to his extraordinary deeds | gracious | and merciful | Yahweh | | food | He gives |

| 3937, 3486.152 | 2226.121 | 3937, 5986 | 1311 | | 3699 | 4801 |
|---|---|---|---|---|---|---|
| prep, v Qal act ptc mp, ps 3ms | v Qal impf 3ms | prep, n ms | n fs, ps 3ms | **6.** | *n ms* | n mp, ps 3ms |
| לִירֵאָיו | יִזְכֹּר | לְעוֹלָם | בְּרִיתוֹ | | כֹּחַ | מַעֲשָׂיו |
| lîrē'âv | yizkōr | le'ôlām | berîthô | | kōach | ma'ăsâv |
| to those who fear Him | He is mindful | unto eternity | his Covenant | | the power of | his works |

| 5222.511 | 3937, 6194 | 3937, 5598.141 | 3937 | 5338 | 1504 |
|---|---|---|---|---|---|
| v Hiphil pf 3ms | prep, n ms, ps 3ms | prep, v Qal inf con | prep, ps 3mp | *n fs* | n mp |
| הִגִּיד | לְעַמּוֹ | לָתֵת | לָהֶם | נַחֲלַת | גּוֹיִם |
| higgîdh | le'ammô | lāthēth | lāhem | nachlath | gôyim |
| He told | to his people | to give | to them | the inheritance of | nations |

**7. He shall drink of the brook in the way: therefore shall he lift up the head:** … then charges forward, triumphing, *Moffatt.*

**111:1. Praise ye the LORD. I will praise the LORD with my whole heart, in the assembly of the upright, and in the congregation:** … give thanks to the Lord with all my heart in the company and assembly of the just, *NCB* … in gatherings of good men for fellowship, *Moffatt* … in the secret meeting of the upright, *KJVII* … in the meeting of his good people, *NCV.*

**2. The works of the LORD are great, sought out of all them that have pleasure therein:** … studied by all who delight in them, *NRSV* … they are pondered by all who delight in them, *NIV.*

**3. His work is honourable and glorious: and his righteousness endureth for ever:** … faithful he abides to all eternity, *Knox* … Full of honor and majesty is his work, *RSV* … Majesty and glory are his work, and his justice endures forever, *NAB* … He will be righteous forever, *Beck.*

**4. He hath made his wonderful works to be remembered: the LORD is gracious and full of compassion:** … He hath made a memorial for His wonderful works, *MAST* … A memorial hath he made by his wonders, *Rotherham* … A memorial he made by his wonders, the Compassionate and Merciful Yahweh, *Anchor* … the Lord is full of pity and mercy, *BB.*

**5. He hath given meat unto them that fear him: he will ever be mindful of his covenant:** … He provides for those who revere Him, *Berkeley*

... he keeps his covenant always in mind, *REB* ... And always keeps His Bond, *Fenton* ... He remembers his agreement forever, *NCV.*

**6. He hath shown his people the power of his works, that he may give them the heritage of the heathen:** ... He showed his people what his strength could do, *NEB* ... To give them the inheritance of nations, *Young* ... To give them pagan lands, *Fenton.*

**7. The works of his hands are verity and judgment; all his commandments are sure:** ... truth and justice; All His precepts are sure, *NASB* ... faith and righteousness; all his laws are unchanging, *BB* ... faithful and right, and all His decrees are trustworthy, *Berkeley* ... all his precepts are faithful, *Darby.*

---

***Psalm 111.*** *Another series of Psalms headed with "hallelujah" begins here, and includes the two following Psalms. The prefix apparently indicates liturgical use. The present Psalm is closely allied to the next. Both are acrostic and correspond verse-to-verse. Together they represent God and the godly. This Psalm magnifies the divine character and acts; the other paints the ideal godly man as, in some real fashion, an imitator of God as a beloved child. Both have allusions to other Psalms and the Book of Proverbs, and they share with many of the Psalms of Book Five the character of being mainly rewarding from earlier works.*

**111:1–3.** The Psalmist begins by a vow to thank Yahweh with his whole heart and immediately proceeds to carry it out. "The upright" (HED #3596) is understood by some as a national designation. But it is more in accordance with usage to regard the psalmist as referring first to a narrower circle of like-minded lovers of good, to whose congenial ears he rejoices to sing. There was an Israel within Israel, who would sympathize with his song. The "congregation" (HED #5920) is then either the wider audience of the gathered people, or, as Delitzsch takes it, equivalent to "their congregation"— i.e., of the upright.

The theme of thanksgiving is, as ever, God's works for Israel; the first characteristic of these which the psalmist sings is their greatness. He will come closer presently and discern more delicate features, but now the magnitude of these colossal manifestations chiefly animates his song. Far-stretching in their mass and in their consequences, they are deep-rooted in God's own character. His great deeds draw the eager search of "them that have pleasure therein." These are the same sympathetic auditors to whom the song is primarily addressed. There were indolent beholders in Israel, before whom the works of God were passed without exciting the faintest desire to know more of their depth. Such careless onlookers, who see and see not, are rife in all ages. God shines out in his deeds, and they will not give one glance of sharpened interest. But the test of caring for his doings is the effort to comprehend their greatness and plunge oneself into their depths. The more one gazes, the more one sees. What was at first but dimly apprehended as great resolves itself, as we look. First, "honourable and glorious," the splendor of his reflected character, shine out from his deeds, and then, when still more deeply they are pondered, the central fact of their righteousness, their conformity to the highest standard of rectitude, becomes patent. Greatness and majesty, divorced from righteousness, would be no theme for praise. Such greatness is littleness, such splendor is phosphorescent corruption.

**111:4–6.** These general contemplations are followed in vv. 4ff by references to Israel's history as the greatest example of God's working. Some find in the clause "He hath made his wonderful works to be remembered" a reference to the Passover and other feasts commemorative of the deliverance from Egypt. But it is better to think of Israel itself as the "memorial" (HED #2228), or of the deeds themselves, in their remembrance by men, as being a monument of his power. The men whom God has blessed are standing evidences of his wonders. "Ye are my witnesses, saith the LORD" (Isa. 43:10). And the great attribute, which is commemorated by that "memorial," is Yahweh's gracious compassion. The psalmist presses steadily toward the center of the divine nature. God's works become eloquent of more and more precious truth as he listens to their voice. They spoke of greatness, honor, majesty and righteousness, but tenderer qualities are revealed to the loving and patient gazer. The two standing proofs of divine kindness are the miraculous provision of food in the desert and the possession of the Promised Land. But to the psalmist, these are not past deeds to be remembered only, but continually repeated operations. "He will ever be mindful of his covenant," and so the experiences of the fathers are lived over again by the children, and today is as full of God as yesterday was. Still He feeds us; still He gives us our heritage.

| 7. | 4801 | 3135 | 583 | 5122 | 548.256 | 3725, 6740 | 8. | 5759.156 |
|---|---|---|---|---|---|---|---|---|
| | *n mp* | n fd, ps 3ms | n fs | cj, n ms | v Niphal ptc mp | *adj*, n mp, ps 3ms | | v Qal pass ptc mp |
| | מַעֲשֵׂי | יָדָיו | אֱמֶת | וּמִשְׁפָּט | נֶאֱמָנִים | כָּל־פִּקּוּדָיו | | סְמוּכִים |
| | ma'ăsê | yādhâv | 'ĕmeth | ûmishpāṭ | ne'ĕmānîm | kol-piqqûdhâv | | semûkhîm |
| | the works of | his hands | truth | and justice | reliable | all his precepts | | sustaining |

| 3937, 5911 | 3937, 5986 | 6449.156 | 904, 583 | 3596 | 9. | 6545 |
|---|---|---|---|---|---|---|
| prep, n ms | prep, n ms | v Qal pass ptc mp | prep, n fs | cj, adj | | n fs |
| לָעַד | לְעוֹלָם | עֲשׂוּיִם | בֶּאֱמֶת | וְיָשָׁר | | פְּדוּת |
| lā'adh | le'ôlām | 'ăsûyim | be'ĕmeth | weyāshār | | pedhûth |
| unto eternity | unto eternity | being done | with faithfulness | and upright | | ransoming |

| 8365.111 | 3937, 6194 | 6943.311, 3937, 5986 | 1311 | 7202 |
|---|---|---|---|---|
| v Qal pf 3ms | prep, n ms, ps 3ms | v Piel pf 3ms, prep, n ms | n fs, ps 3ms | adj |
| שָׁלַח | לְעַמּוֹ | צִוָּה־לְעוֹלָם | בְּרִיתוֹ | קָדוֹשׁ |
| shālach | le'ammô | tsiwwāh-le'ôlām | berîthô | qādhôsh |
| He sent out | to his people | He commanded unto everlasting | his Covenant | holy |

| 3486.255 | 8428 | 10. | 7519 | 2551 | 3488 | 3176 | 7961 | 3005 |
|---|---|---|---|---|---|---|---|---|
| cj, v Niphal ptc ms | n ms, ps 3ms | | *n fs* | n fs | *n fs* | pn | n ms | adj |
| וְנוֹרָא | שְׁמוֹ | | רֵאשִׁית | חָכְמָה | יִרְאַת | יְהוָה | שֵׂכֶל | טוֹב |
| wenôrā' | shemô | | rē'shîth | chokhmāh | yir'ath | yehwāh | sēkhel | ṭôv |
| and terrible | his name | | the beginning | wisdom | the fear of | Yahweh | insight | good |

| 3937, 3725, 6449.152 | 8747 | 6198.153 | 3937, 5911 | 112:1 | 2054.333 | 3161 |
|---|---|---|---|---|---|---|
| prep, *adj*, v Qal act ptc mp, ps 3mp | n fs, ps 3ms | v Qal act ptc fs | prep, n ms | | v Piel impv 2mp | pn |
| לְכָל־עֹשֵׂיהֶם | תְּהִלָּתוֹ | עֹמֶדֶת | לָעַד | | הַלְלוּ | יָהּ |
| lekhol-'ōsêhem | tehillāthô | 'ōmedheth | lā'adh | | halelû | yāhh |
| to all those practicing | his praise | standing | unto eternity | | praise | Yah |

| 869, 382 | 3486.151 | 881, 3176 | 904, 4851 | 2759.111 | 4108 |
|---|---|---|---|---|---|
| *n mp*, n ms | v Qal act ptc ms | do, pn | prep, n fp, ps 3ms | v Qal pf 3ms | adv |
| אַשְׁרֵי־אִישׁ | יָרֵא | אֶת־יְהוָה | בְּמִצְוֹתָיו | חָפֵץ | מְאֹד |
| 'ashrê-'îsh | yārē' | 'eth-yehwāh | bemitswōthâv | chāphēts | me'ōdh |
| blessed the man | the one who fears | Yahweh | in his commandments | one who delights | very |

| 2. | 1399 | 904, 800 | 2030.121 | 2320 | 1810 | 3596 |
|---|---|---|---|---|---|---|
| | n ms | prep, art, n fs | v Qal impf 3ms | n ms, ps 3ms | n ms | adj |
| | גִּבּוֹר | בָּאָרֶץ | יִהְיֶה | זַרְעוֹ | דּוֹר | יְשָׁרִים |
| | gibbôr | bā'ārets | yihyeh | zar'ô | dôr | yeshārîm |
| | a mighty man | in the land | they will be | his descendants | a generation | upright |

| 1313.421 | 3. | 2019, 6484 | 904, 1041 | 6930 | 6198.153 |
|---|---|---|---|---|---|
| v Pual impf 3ms | | n ms, cj, n ms | prep, n ms, ps 3ms | cj, n fs, ps 3ms | v Qal act ptc fs |
| יְבֹרָךְ | | הוֹן־וָעֹשֶׁר | בְּבֵיתוֹ | וְצִדְקָתוֹ | עֹמֶדֶת |
| yevōrākh | | hôn-wā'ōsher | bevêthô | wetsidhqāthô | 'ōmedheth |
| they will be blessed | | wealth and riches | in his house | and his righteousness | standing |

**8. They stand fast for ever and ever, and are done in truth and uprightness:** … They are unshakably firm forever; they are faithfully and correctly put into action, *Beck* … reliable forever and ever, *NCB* … to be performed with faithfulness and uprightness, *NRSV* … to be performed with faithfulness and uprightness, *RSV*.

**9. He sent redemption unto his people: he hath commanded his covenant for ever: holy and reverend is his name:** … He has sent deliverance to his people; he has ratified his covenant forever, *NAB* … He has sent his people freedom, fixing his compact with them for all time, *Moffatt* … He has sent forth release for his people, *Goodspeed*.

**10. The fear of the LORD is the beginning of wisdom:** … Wisdom begins with respect for the LORD, *NCV* … The beginning of wisdom is the reverence of Yahweh, *Rotherham* … vain without his fear is learning, *Knox*.

**a good understanding have all they that do his commandments: his**

**praise endureth for ever:** ... and they who live by it grow in understanding, *REB* ... understanding of the Good One belongs to all those who acquire it, *Anchor* ... all those who obey Him have understanding, *KJVII* ... There is insight in all who observe it, *Berkeley.*

**112:1. Praise ye the LORD. Blessed is the man that feareth the LORD, that delighteth greatly in his commandments:** ... Happy are those who respect the LORD, who want what he commands, *NCV* ... Oh, the bliss of the man who reveres the LORD, *Berkeley* ... He who fears the LORD will succeed And whoever delights in His Laws, *Fenton* ... and finds great joy in his commandments, *NEB.*

**2. His seed shall be mighty upon earth: the generation of the upright shall be blessed:** ... Children of his shall win renown in their country, *Knox* ... His descendants will be mighty in the land, *Goodspeed* ... His children shall rise to power within the land, *Moffatt* ... the race of the honest shall receive blessings, *JB.*

**3. Wealth and riches shall be in his house: and his righteousness endureth for ever:** ... and his generosity endures for ever, *Anchor* ... A store of wealth will be in his house, *BB* ... his righteousness will stand sure for ever, *REB.*

---

**111:7–8.** From v. 7 onward, a new thought comes in. God has spoken as well as wrought. His very works carry messages of truth and judgment, and they are interpreted further by articulate precepts, which are at once a revelation of what He is and a law for what we should be. His Law stands as fast as his righteousness (vv. 3, 8). A man may utterly trust his commandments. They abide eternally, for duty is ever duty, and his Law, while it has a surface of temporary ceremony, has a core of immutable requirement. His commandments are done—appointed by Him—"in truth and uprightness." They are tokens of his grace and revelations of his character.

**111:9–10.** The two closing verses have three clauses each, partly from the exigencies of the acrostic structure and partly to secure a more impressive ending. Verse 9 sums up all of God's works in the two chief manifestations of his goodness which should ever live in Israel's thanks: his sending redemption and his establishing his everlasting Covenant—the two facts which are as fresh today, under new and better forms, as when long ago this unknown psalmist sang. And he gathers up the total impression which God's dealings should leave, in the great saying "holy and reverend is his name."

In v. 10, he somewhat passes the limits of his theme and trenches on the territory of the next Psalm, which is already beginning to shape itself in his mind. The designation of the fear of the Yahweh as "the beginning of wisdom" is from Prov. 1:7; 9:10. "Beginning" (HED #7519) may rather mean "principal part" (cf. Prov. 4:7, "principal thing"). The "they" of v. 10b is best referred, although the expression is awkward, to "commandments" in v. 7. Less probably, it is taken to allude to the "fear" and "wisdom" of the previous clause. The two clauses of this verse descriptive of the godly correspond in structure to v. 9a and b, and the last clause corresponds to the last of that verse, expressing the continual praise which should rise to that holy and dread name. Note that the perpetual duration, which has been predicated of God's attributes, precepts and Covenant (vv. 3, 5, 8f), is here ascribed to his praise. Man's songs cannot fall dumb, so long as God pours out himself in such deeds. As long as that sun streams across the desert, stony lips will part in music to hail its beams.

***Psalm 112.*** *The basis of righteousness and beneficence to men must be laid in reverence and conformity of will toward God. Therefore, the Psalm begins with proclaiming that, apart from all external consequences, these dispositions carry blessedness themselves. The close of the preceding Psalm had somewhat overpassed its limits, when it declared that "the fear of the LORD" was the beginning of wisdom and that to do his commandments was sound discretion.*

**112:1–3.** This Psalm echoes these sayings and so links itself to the former one. It deepens them by pointing out that the fear of Yahweh is a fountain of joy as well as of wisdom and that inward delight in the Law must precede outward doing of it. The familiar blessing attached in the OT to godliness, namely, prosperous posterity, is the first of the consequences of righteousness which the Psalm holds out. That promise belongs to another order of things from that of the NT; but the essence of it is true still, namely, that the only secure foundation for permanent prosperity is in the fear of Yahweh.

"The generation of the upright" (v. 2) does not merely mean the natural descendants of a good man as is usually the case with the word "generation" (HED #1810). Another result of righteousness is declared to be "wealth and riches" (v. 3), which, again, must be taken as applying more fully to the OT system of providence than to that of the NT.

| 3937, 5911 | | 2311.111 | 904, 2932 | 214 | 3937, 3596 | 2688 | 7631 |
|---|---|---|---|---|---|---|---|
| prep, n ms | | v Qal pf 3ms | prep, art, n ms | n ms | prep, n mp | adj | cj, adj |
| לָעַד | 4. | זָרַח | בַּחֹשֶׁךְ | אוֹר | לַיְשָׁרִים | חַנּוּן | וְרַחוּם |
| lā'adh | | zārach | bachōshekh | 'ôr | layshārîm | channûn | werachûm |
| unto eternity | | it rises | in the darkness | the light | for the upright | gracious | and merciful |

| 6926 | | 3005, 382 | 2706.151 | 4004.551 | 3677.321 | 1745 |
|---|---|---|---|---|---|---|
| cj, adj | | adj, n ms | v Qal act ptc ms | cj, v Hiphil ptc ms | v Pilpel impf 3ms | n mp, ps 3ms |
| וְצַדִּיק | 5. | טוֹב־אִישׁ | חוֹנֵן | וּמַלְוֶה | יְכַלְכֵּל | דְּבָרָיו |
| wetsaddîq | | ṭôv-'îsh | chônēn | ûmalweh | yekhalkēl | devārâv |
| and righteous | | a good man | one who is gracious | and one who lends | he upholds | his matters |

| 904, 5122 | | 3706, 3937, 5986 | 3940, 4267.221 | 3937, 2228 | 5986 | 2030.121 |
|---|---|---|---|---|---|---|
| prep, n ms | | cj, prep, n ms | neg part, v Niphal impf 3ms | prep, n ms | n ms | v Qal impf 3ms |
| בְּמִשְׁפָּט | 6. | כִּי־לְעוֹלָם | לֹא־יִמּוֹט | לְזֵכֶר | עוֹלָם | יִהְיֶה |
| bemishpāṭ | | kî-le'ôlām | lō'-yimmôṭ | lezēkher | 'ôlām | yihyeh |
| with justice | | because to eternity | he will not falter | for a memorial | forever | he will be |

| 6926 | | 4623, 8444 | 7750 | 3940 | 3486.121 | 3679.255 | 3949 |
|---|---|---|---|---|---|---|---|
| n ms | | prep, n fs | n ms | neg part | v Qal impf 3ms | v Niphal ptc ms | n ms, ps 3ms |
| צַדִּיק | 7. | מִשְּׁמוּעָה | רָעָה | לֹא | יִירָא | נָכוֹן | לִבּוֹ |
| tsaddîq | | mishshemû'āh | rā'āh | lō' | yîrā' | nākhôn | libbô |
| the righteous | | of a report | something evil | not | he will be afraid | steady | his heart |

| 1019.155 | 904, 3176 | | 5759.155 | 3949 | 3940 | 3486.121 | 5912 |
|---|---|---|---|---|---|---|---|
| v Qal pass ptc ms | prep, pn | | v Qal pass ptc ms | n ms, ps 3ms | neg part | v Qal impf 3ms | adv |
| בָּטֻחַ | בַּיהוָה | 8. | סָמוּךְ | לִבּוֹ | לֹא | יִירָא | עַד |
| bāṭuach | bayhwāh | | sāmûkh | libbô | lō' | yîrā' | 'adh |
| trusting | in Yahweh | | sustained | his heart | not | he will be afraid | until |

| 866, 3486.121 | 904, 7141 | | 6582.311 | 5598.111 | 3937, 33 |
|---|---|---|---|---|---|
| rel part, v Qal impf 3ms | prep, n mp, ps 3ms | | v Piel pf 3ms | v Qal pf 3ms | prep, art, n mp |
| אֲשֶׁר־יִרְאֶה | בְּצָרָיו | 9. | פִּזַּר | נָתַן | לָאֶבְיוֹנִים |
| 'ăsher-yir'eh | vetsārâv | | pizzar | nāthan | lā'evyônîm |
| that he sees | over his adversaries | | he has scattered | he has given | to the needy |

| 6930 | 6198.153 | 3937, 5911 | 7451 | 7597.122 | 904, 3638 |
|---|---|---|---|---|---|
| n fs, ps 3ms | v Qal act ptc fs | prep, n ms | n fs, ps 3ms | v Qal impf 3fs | prep, n ms |
| צִדְקָתוֹ | עֹמֶדֶת | לָעַד | קַרְנוֹ | תָּרוּם | בְּכָבוֹד |
| tsidhqāthô | 'ōmedheth | lā'adh | qarnô | tārûm | bekhāvôdh |
| his righteousness | standing | unto eternity | his horn | it will be exalted | in honor |

**4. Unto the upright there ariseth light in the darkness: he is gracious, and full of compassion, and righteous:** ... upright He shineth as a light, *MAST* ... the LORD is gracious, merciful, and righteous, *RSV* ... He dawns through the darkness, a light for the upright, *NAB* ... that is the Kind, Merciful, and Righteous One, *Beck.*

**5. A good man showeth favour, and lendeth: he will guide his affairs with discretion:** ... A good man deals graciously and lends, *NKJV* ... He shall maintain his cause in judgment, *ASV* ... who conducts his affairs with justice, *NIV* ... just and merciful in his dealings, *Knox.*

**6. Surely he shall not be moved for ever: the righteous shall be in everlasting remembrance:** ... Such a man will never fail, *Beck* ... never shall that man come to grief, *Moffatt* ... his goodness shall be remembered for all time, *NEB* ... the memory of the upright will be living for ever, *BB.*

**7. He shall not be afraid of evil tidings: his heart is fixed, trusting in the LORD:** ... Of an evil report he is not afraid, *Young* ... He shall not be afraid of bad news, *KJVII* ... They won't be afraid of bad news, *NCV* ... He need never fear any evil report; his heart will remain firm, *Berkeley.*

**8. His heart is established, he shall not be afraid, until he see his desire upon his enemies:** ... Until he looks with satisfaction on his adversaries, *NASB* ... in the end they will look in triumph on their foes, *NRSV* ... till he can gloat over his enemies, *JB* ... in the end he will see the downfall of his enemies, *REB.*

A parallelism of the most striking character between God and the godly emerges in v. 3b, where the same words are applied to the latter as were used of the former in the corresponding verse of Ps. 111. It would be giving too great evangelical definiteness to the psalmist's words to read into them the Christian teaching that man's righteousness is God's gift through Christ, but it is unwarranted to go to the other extreme and suppose that the psalmist put in the clause purely for poetic reasons. The psalmist has a very definite and noble thought. Man's righteousness is the reflection of God's and has in it some kindred with its original, which guarantees stability not all unlike the eternity of that source. Since v. 3b thus brings into prominence the ruling thought of the two Psalms, possibly we may venture to see a fainter utterance of that thought in the first clause of the verse, in which the "wealth and riches" in the righteous man's house may correspond to the "honor and glory" attendant on God's works (Ps. 111:3a).

**112:4.** Verse 4 blends consequences of righteousness and characterization of it in a remarkable way. The construction is doubtful. In v. 4a, "upright" (HED #3596) is in the plural, and the adjectives in v. 4b are in the singular number. They are appended abruptly to the preceding clause, and the loose structure has occasioned difficulty to expositors, which has been increased by the scruples of some who have not given due weight to the leading thought of correspondence between the human and divine and have hesitated to regard v. 4b as referring to the righteous man, seeing that in Ps. 111:4b it refers to God.

Hence, efforts have been made to find other renderings. Delitzsch would refer the clause to God, whom he takes to be meant by "light" in the previous clause, while others would translate, "As a light, he [the righteous] rises in darkness for the upright" and would then consider "gracious," etc., as in apposition with "light" and descriptive of the righteous man's character as such. But the very fact that the words are applied to God in the corresponding verse of the previous Psalm suggests their application here to the godly man, and the sudden change of number is not so harsh as to require the ordinary translation to be abandoned. However dark may be a good man's road, the very midnight blackness is a prophecy of sunrise; or, to use another figure, "If winter comes, can spring be far behind?" (cf. Ps. 97:11). The fountain of pity in human hearts must be fed from the great source of compassion in God's, if it is to gush out unremittingly and bless the deserts of sorrow and misery. He who has received "grace" will surely exercise grace. "Be ye therefore merciful, as your Father also is merciful" (Luke 6:36).

**112:5.** Verse 5 blends characteristics and consequences of goodness in reverse order from that in v. 4. The compassionate man of v. 4b does not let pity evaporate, but he is primarily moved by it to act and to lend money, and secondarily to lend any needful help or solace. Benevolence that is not translated into beneficence is a poor affair. There is no blessing in it or for it, but it is well with the man who turns emotions into deeds. Lazy compassion hurts him who indulges in it, but that which "lends" gets joy in the act of bestowing aid. The result of such active compassion is stated in v. 5b as being that such a one will "guide his affairs with discretion," by which seems to be meant the judgment of earthly tribunals. If compassion and charity guide a life, it will have few disputes and will contain nothing for which a judge can condemn. He who obeys the higher law will not break the lower.

**112:6–8.** Verses 6ff dwell mainly on one consequence of righteousness, namely, the stability which it imparts. While such a man lives, he shall be unmoved by shocks, and after he dies, his memory will live, like a summer evening's glow which lingers in the west until a new morning dawns.

In v. 7, the resemblance of the godly to God comes very beautifully to the surface. Psalm 111:7 deals with God's commandments as "trustworthy." The human parallel is an established heart. He who has learned to lean upon Yahweh (for such is the literal force of "trusting" here) and has proved the commandments utterly reliable as basis for his life will have his heart steadfast. The same idea is repeated in v. 8 with direct quotation of the corresponding verse of Ps. 111. In both, the word for "established" (HED #5759) is the same. The heart that delights in God's established commandments is established by them, and sooner or later will look in calm security on the fading away of all evil things and men, while it rests indeed because it rests in God. He who builds his transient life on the Rock of Ages wins rocklike steadfastness and some share in the perpetuity of his Refuge. Lives rooted in God are never uprooted.

**112:9–10.** The two final verses are elongated, like the corresponding verses in Ps. 111. Again,

| 10. | 7857 | 7495.121 | 3832.111 | 8514 | 2892.121 | 4701.211 |
|---|---|---|---|---|---|---|
| | n ms | v Qal impf 3ms | cj, v Qal pf 3ms | n fp, ps 3ms | v Qal impf 3ms | cj, v Niphal pf 3ms |
| | רָשָׁע | יִרְאֶה | וְכָעָס | שִׁנָּיו | יַחֲרֹק | וְנָמָס |
| | rāshā' | yir'eh | wekhā'ās | shinnâv | yachrōq | wenāmās |
| | the wicked | he will see | and he is furious | his teeth | he gnashes | and it melts |

| 8707 | 7857 | 6.122 | 113:1 | 2054.333 | 3161 | 2054.333 | 5860 |
|---|---|---|---|---|---|---|---|
| *n fs* | n mp | v Qal impf 3fs | | v Piel impv 2mp | pn | v Piel impv 2mp | *n mp* |
| תַּאֲוַת | רְשָׁעִים | תֹּאבֵד | | הַלְלוּ | יָהּ | הַלְלוּ | עַבְדֵי |
| ta'ăwath | reshā'îm | tō'vēdh | | halelû | yāhh | halelû | 'avdhê |
| the longing of | the wicked | it will perish | | praise | Yah | praise | O servants of |

| 3176 | 2054.333 | 881, 8428 | 3176 | 2. | 2030.121 | 8428 | 3176 | 1313.455 |
|---|---|---|---|---|---|---|---|---|
| pn | v Piel impv 2mp | do, *n ms* | pn | | v Qal juss 3ms | *n ms* | pn | v Pual ptc ms |
| יְהוָה | הַלְלוּ | אֶת־שֵׁם | יְהוָה | | יְהִי | שֵׁם | יְהוָה | מְבֹרָךְ |
| yehwāh | halelû | 'eth-shēm | yehwāh | | yehî | shēm | yehwāh | mevōrākh |
| Yahweh | praise | the name of | Yahweh | | may it be | the name of | Yahweh | blessed |

| 4623, 6498 | 5912, 5986 | 3. | 4623, 4350, 8507 | 5912, 4136 | 2054.455 |
|---|---|---|---|---|---|
| prep, adv | cj, adv, n ms | | prep, *n ms*, n fs | adv, n ms, ps 3ms | v Pual ptc ms |
| מֵעַתָּה | וְעַד־עוֹלָם | | מִמִּזְרַח־שֶׁמֶשׁ | עַד־מְבוֹאוֹ | מְהֻלָּל |
| mē'attāh | we'adh-'ôlām | | mimmizrach-shemesh | 'adh-mevô'ô | mehullāl |
| from now | even unto eternity | | from the rising of the sun | until its setting | praised |

| 8428 | 3176 | 4. | 7597.111 | 6142, 3725, 1504 | 3176 | 6142 | 8452 | 3638 |
|---|---|---|---|---|---|---|---|---|
| *n ms* | pn | | v Qal pf 3ms | prep, *adj*, n mp | pn | prep | art, n md | n ms, ps 3ms |
| שֵׁם | יְהוָה | | רָם | עַל־כָּל־גּוֹיִם | יְהוָה | עַל | הַשָּׁמַיִם | כְּבוֹדוֹ |
| shēm | yehwāh | | rām | 'al-kol-gôyim | yehwāh | 'al | hashshāmayim | kevôdhô |
| the name of | Yahweh | | it is high | above all nations | Yahweh | above | the heavens | his glory |

| 5. | 4449 | 3626, 3176 | 435 | 1391.551 | 3937, 3553.141 | 6. | 8584.551 |
|---|---|---|---|---|---|---|---|
| | intrg | prep, pn | n mp, ps 1cp | art, v Hiphil ptc ms | prep, v Qal inf con | | art, v Hiphil ptc ms |
| | מִי | כַּיהוָה | אֱלֹהֵינוּ | הַמַּגְבִּיהִי | לָשָׁבֶת | | הַמַּשְׁפִּילִי |
| | mî | kayhwāh | 'ĕlōhênû | hammaghbîhî | lāshāveth | | hammashpîlî |
| | who | like Yahweh | our God | the One Who is high | sitting | | the One Who goes low |

**9. He hath dispersed, he hath given to the poor:** ... He scattereth abroad, he giveth to the needy, *Darby* ... He has distributed freely, *RSV* ... He has scattered abroad his gifts to the poor, *NIV.*

**his righteousness endureth for ever; his horn shall be exalted with honour:** ... in honour he carries his head high, *NEB* ... his head will be raised in glory, *Anchor* ... The Lord will lift up his head in triumph, *Knox.*

**10. The wicked shall see it, and be grieved; he shall gnash with his teeth, and melt away:** ... The wicked will see this and become angry, *NCV* ... he will be wasted away with envy, *BB.*

**the desire of the wicked shall perish:** ... The craving of the lawless shall vanish, *Rotherham* ... The desires of the wicked will be frustrated, *JB* ... worldly hopes must fade and perish, *Knox* ... For the pride of the wicked will fail, *Fenton.*

**113:1. Praise ye the LORD. Praise, O ye servants of the LORD, praise the name of the LORD:** ... praise the name of the Lord together, *Knox.*

**2. Blessed be the name of the LORD from this time forth and for evermore:** ... Let blessing be on the name of the Lord, *BB* ... The LORD's name should be praised now and forever, *NCV.*

**3. From the rising of the sun unto the going down of the same the LORD's name is to be praised:** ... From where the sun rises to where it sets, *Berkeley* ... The Name of the LORD should be cheered!, *Fenton* ... let the Lord's name be praised continually, *Knox.*

**4. The LORD is high above all nations, and his glory above the heavens:** ... The LORD is supreme over all the nations, *NCV* ... The LORD is exalted over all the nations, *NIV* ... Above the heavens is His honour, *Young.*

**5. Who is like unto the LORD our God, who dwelleth on high:** ... That is enthroned on high, *MAST* ... That hath his seat on high, *ASV* ... That goeth on high to dwell, *Rotherham.*

**6. Who humbleth himself to behold the things that are in heaven, and in the earth!:** ... The One who

beneficence is put in the forefront as a kind of shorthand summing up of all virtues. And again in v. 9, the analogy is drawn out between God and the godly. Paul quotes the two former clauses of v. 9 as involving the truth that Christian giving does not impoverish (2 Cor. 9:9). The exercise of a disposition strengthens it; God takes care that the means of beneficence shall not be wanting to him who has the spirit of it. The later Jewish use of "righteousness" as a synonym for almsgiving has probably been influenced by this Psalm, in which beneficence is the principal trait in the righteous man's character. But there is no reason for supposing that the psalmist uses the word in that restricted sense.

Verse 10 is not parallel with the last verse of Ps. 111, which stands, as we have seen, somewhat beyond the scope of the rest of that Psalm. It gives one brief glimpse of the fate of the evildoer in opposition to the loving picture of the blessedness of the righteous. Thus, it too is rather beyond the immediate object of the Psalm of which it forms part. The wicked sees, in contrast with the righteous man's seeing in v. 8. The one looks with peace on the short duration of antagonistic power, and rejoices that there is a God of recompenses; the other grinds his teeth in envious rage, as he beholds the perpetuity of the righteous.

He shall "melt away," i.e., in jealousy or despair. Opposition to goodness, since it is enmity toward God, is self-condemned to impotence and final failure. Desires turned for satisfaction elsewhere than to God are sure to perish. The sharp contrast between the righteousness of the good man, which endures forever, in his steadfast, trustful heart, and the crumbling schemes and disappointed hopes which gnaw the life of the man whose aims go athwart God's will, solemnly proclaims an eternal truth. This Psalm, like Ps. 1, touches the two poles of possible human experience, in its first and last words, beginning with "blessed is the man" and ending with "shall perish."

***Psalm 113.*** *Three strophes of three verses each may be recognized, the first of which summons Israel to praise Yahweh and reaches out through all time and over all space in longing that God's name may be known and praised. The second strophe (vv. 4ff) magnifies God's exalted greatness; while the third (vv. 7ff) adores his condescension, manifested in his stooping to lift the lowly. The second and third of these strophes, however, overlap in the song, as do the facts which they celebrate. God's loftiness can never be adequately measured, unless his condescension is taken into account, and his condescension never sufficiently wondered at, unless his loftiness is felt.*

**113:1–3.** The call to praise is addressed to Israel, whose designation "servants of Yahweh" recalls Isaiah's characteristic use of that name in the singular number for the nation. With strong emphasis, the name of Yahweh is declared as the theme of praise. God's revelation of his character by deed and word must precede man's thanksgiving. They to whom that name has been entrusted by their reception of his mercies are bound to ring it out to all the world. And in the name itself, there lies enshrined the certainty that through all ages, it shall be blessed, and in every spot lit by the sun, shall shine as a brighter light and be hailed with praises. The psalmist has learned the worldwide significance of Israel's position as the depository of the name, and the fair vision of a universal adoration of it fills his heart. Verse 3b may be rendered "worthy to be praised is the name," but the context seems to suggest the rendering above.

**113:4–6.** The infinite exaltation of Yahweh above all dwellers on this low earth and above the very heavens does not lift Him too high for man's praise, for it is wedded to condescension as infinite. Incomparable is He; but still adoration can reach Him, and men do not clasp mist, but solid substance, when they grasp his name. That incomparable uniqueness of Yahweh is celebrated in v. 5a in strains borrowed from Exo. 15:11, while the striking description of loftiness combined with condescension in vv. 5b and 6 resembles Isa. 57:15. The literal rendering of vv. 5b and 6a is, "Who makes high to sit, who makes low to behold," which is best understood as above. It may be questioned whether "on the heavens and on the earth" designates the objects on which his gaze is said to be turned; or whether, as some understand the construction, it is to be taken with "Who is like Yahweh our God?" the intervening clauses being parenthetical; or whether, as others prefer, "in heaven" points back to "enthroned on high," and "on earth" to "looks far below." But the construction which regards the totality of created things, represented by the familiar phrase "the heavens and the earth," as being the objects on which Yahweh looks down from his inconceivable loftiness, accords best with the context and yields an altogether worthy meaning. Transcendent elevation,

| 3937, 7495.141 | 904, 8452 | 904, 800 | | 7251.551 | 4623, 6312 | 1859 |
|---|---|---|---|---|---|---|
| prep, v Qal inf con | prep, art, n md | cj, prep, n fs | | v Hiphil ptc ms | prep, n ms | n ms |
| לִרְאוֹת | בַּשָּׁמָיִם | וּבָאָרֶץ | **7.** | מְקִימִי | מֵעָפָר | דָּל |
| lir'ôth | bashshāmayim | ûvā'ārets | | meqîmî | mē'āphār | dāl |
| to see | in the heavens | and on the earth | | the One Who raises | from the dust | the poor |

| 4623, 858 | 7597.521 | 33 | | 3937, 3553.541 | 6196, 5259 | 6196 |
|---|---|---|---|---|---|---|
| prep, n fp | v Hiphil impf 3ms | n ms | | prep, v Hiphil inf con | prep, n mp | prep |
| מֵאַשְׁפֹּת | יָרִים | אֶבְיוֹן | **8.** | לְהוֹשִׁיבִי | עִם־נְדִיבִים | עִם |
| mē'ashpōth | yārîm | 'evyôn | | lehôshîvî | 'im-nedhîvîm | 'im |
| from the dunghill | He causes to rise | the needy | | to cause them to sit | with the nobles | with |

| 5259 | 6194 | | 3553.551 | 6371 | 1041 |
|---|---|---|---|---|---|
| *n mp* | n ms, ps 3ms | | v Hiphil ptc ms | *adj* | art, n ms |
| נְדִיבֵי | עַמּוֹ | **9.** | מוֹשִׁיבִי | עֲקֶרֶת | הַבַּיִת |
| nedhîvê | 'ammô | | môshîvî | 'ăqereth | habbayith |
| the nobles | his people | | He causes to dwell in | the barren women of | the household |

| 525, 1158 | 7977 | 2054.333, 3161 | | 904, 3428.141 | 3547 |
|---|---|---|---|---|---|
| *n fs*, art, n mp | n fs | v Piel impv 2mp, pn | | prep, v Qal inf con | pn |
| אֵם־הַבָּנִים | שְׂמֵחָה | הַלְלוּ־יָהּ | **114:1** | בְּצֵאת | יִשְׂרָאֵל |
| 'ēm-habbānîm | semēchāh | halelû-yāhh | | betsē'th | yisrā'ēl |
| the mother of the children | joy | praise Yah | | when coming out | Israel |

| 4623, 4875 | 1041 | 3399 | 4623, 6194 | 4079.151 | | 2030.112 | 3171 |
|---|---|---|---|---|---|---|---|
| prep, pn | *n ms* | pn | prep, n ms | v Qal act ptc ms | | v Qal pf 3fs | pn |
| מִמִּצְרָיִם | בֵּית | יַעֲקֹב | מֵעַם | לֹעֵז | **2.** | הָיְתָה | יְהוּדָה |
| mimmitsrāyim | bêth | ya'ăqōv | mē'am | lō'ēz | | hāyethāh | yehûdhāh |
| from Egypt | the house of | Jacob | from a people | speaking unintelligibly | | it became | Judah |

| 3937, 7231 | 3547 | 4617 | | 3328 | 7495.111 | 5308.121 | 3497 |
|---|---|---|---|---|---|---|---|
| prep, n ms, ps 3ms | pn | n fp, ps 3ms | | art, n ms | v Qal pf 3ms | cj, v Qal impf 3ms | art, pn |
| לְקָדְשׁוֹ | יִשְׂרָאֵל | מַמְשְׁלוֹתָיו | **3.** | הַיָּם | רָאָה | וַיָּנֹס | הַיַּרְדֵּן |
| leqādheshô | yisrā'ēl | mamshelôthâv | | hayyām | rā'āh | wayyānōs | hayyardēn |
| for his holy place | Israel | his dominion | | the sea | it saw | and it fled | the Jordan |

| 5621.121 | 3937, 268 | | 2098 | 7833.116 | 3626, 356 | 1421 |
|---|---|---|---|---|---|---|
| v Qal impf 3ms | prep, sub | | art, n mp | v Qal pf 3cp | prep, n mp | n fp |
| יִסֹּב | לְאָחוֹר | **4.** | הֶהָרִים | רָקְדוּ | כְּאֵילִים | גְּבָעוֹת |
| yissōv | le'āchôr | | hehārîm | rāqōdhû | khe'êlîm | gevā'ôth |
| it turned | backward | | the mountains | they skipped | like rams | hills |

stoops to look from heaven to earth?, *Anchor* ... and looks upon the heavens and the earth below?, *NAB* ... who looks far down on the heavens and the earth?, *NRSV.*

**7. He raiseth up the poor out of the dust, and lifteth the needy out of the dunghill:** ... And lifts the needy from the ash heap, *NASB* ... who lifts the weak out of the dust, *NEB* ... lifting him up from his low position, *BB.*

**8. That he may set him with princes, even with the princes of his people:** ... among the nobles of his people, *Darby* ... With the Chiefs of His Race!, *Fenton* ... with the noblest of His people, *Berkeley* ... enables him to sit with noblemen, *Beck.*

**9. He maketh the barren woman to keep house, and to be a joyful mother of children. Praise ye the LORD:** ... He grants the barren woman a home, Like a joyful mother of children, *NKJV* ... the childless woman abide in the household As the happy mother of its children, *Goodspeed* ... establishes in her home the barren wife as the joyful mother of children, *NCB* ... barren wife a happy mother in her home, *Moffatt.*

**114:1. When Israel went out of Egypt, the house of Jacob from a people of strange language:** ... the people of Jacob left that foreign country, *NCV* ... and the sons of Jacob heard no more a strange language, *Knox* ... the house of Jacob from a people of alien speech, *Berkeley* ... from a barbaric people, *Anchor.*

**2. Judah was his sanctuary, and Israel his dominion:** ... Judah he took to be his own, and Israel for his domain, *Moffatt* ... Israel was His kingdom, *KJVII* ... Israel his realm, *Rotherham.*

**3. The sea saw it, and fled: Jordan was driven back:** ... The sea looked and fled, Jordan turned back, *RSV* ... The sea fled at the sight, the Jordan turned back, *JB.*

**4. The mountains skipped like rams, and the little hills like lambs:** ... the hills like lambs of the flock, *REB* ... The little hills like young sheep, *MRB* ... mountains were jumping like goats, *BB* ... like young sheep, *MAST.*

**5. What ailed thee, O thou sea, that thou fleddest?:** ... Why have you fled, O sea, *Beck.*

---

condescension and omniscience are blended in the poet's thought. So high is Yahweh that the highest heavens are far beneath Him, and unless his gaze were all-discerning, would be but a dim speck. That He should enter into relations with creatures and that there should be creatures for Him to enter into relations with are due to his stooping graciousness. These far-darting looks are looks of tenderness and signify care as well as knowledge. Since all things lie in his sight, all receive from his hand.

**113:7–9.** The third strophe pursues the thought of the divine condescension as especially shown in stooping to the dejected and helpless and lifting them. The effect of the descent of One so high must be to raise the lowliness to which He bends. The words in vv. 7f are quoted from Hannah's song (1 Sam. 2:8). Probably, the singer has in his mind Israel's restoration from exile, that great act in which Yahweh had shown his condescending loftiness and had lifted his helpless people as from the ash-heap where they lay as outcasts. The same event seems to be referred to in v. 9 under a metaphor suggested by the story of Hannah, whose words have just been quoted. The barren women (HED #6371) is Israel (cf. Isa. 54:1). The expression in the original is somewhat obscure. It stands literally "the barren women of the household" and is susceptible to different explanations, but probably the simplest is to regard it as a contracted expression for the unfruitful wife in a house.

The singer did not know how far it would be transcended by a more wonderful, more heart-touching manifestation of stooping love when "the Word became flesh." How much more exultant and full should be the praises from the lips of those who do know how low that Word has stooped, how high He has risen, and how surely all who hold his hand will be lifted from any ash-heap and set on his throne, sharers in the royalty of Him who has been partaker of their weakness!

***Psalm 114.*** *The limpid clearness, the eloquent brevity of the Psalm is as obvious as its masterly structure. Its four pairs of verses, each laden with one thought, the dramatic vividness of the sudden questions in the third pair, the skillful suppression of the divine name until the close, where it is pealed out in full tones of triumph, make this little Psalm a gem.*

**114:1–2.** In vv. 1f, the slighting glance at the land left by the ransomed people is striking. The Egyptians are to this singer "a people of strange language," speaking a language which sounded to him barely articulate. The word carries a contempt similiar to that in the Greek "barbarian," which imitates the unmeaning babble of a foreign tongue. To such insignificance in the psalmist's mind had the once dreaded oppressors sunk! The great fact about the Exodus was that it was the birthday of the nation, the beginning of its entrance on its high prerogatives. If the consecration of Judah as "his sanctuary" took place when Israel went forth from Egypt, there can be no reference to the later erection of the material sanctuary in Jerusalem, and the names of Judah and Israel must both apply to the people, not to the land, which would be an anachronism to introduce here.

That deliverance from Egypt was the precursor to God's dwelling in Israel, thereby sanctifying or setting it apart to himself, "a kingdom of priests and an holy nation." Dwelling in the midst of them, He wrought wonders for them, as the Psalm goes on to hymn, but this is the grand foundation fact: Israel was brought out of bondage to be God's temple and kingdom. The higher deliverance of which that Exodus is a foreshadowing is, in like manner, intended to effect a still more wonderful and intimate indwelling of God in his Church. Redeemed humanity is meant to be God's temple and realm.

**114:3–6.** The historical substratum for vv. 3f is the twin miracles of drying up the Red Sea and the Jordan, which began and closed the Exodus, and the "quaking" of Sinai at the theophany accompanying the giving of the Law. These physical facts are imaginatively conceived as the effects of panic produced by some dread vision, and the psalmist heightens his representation by leaving unnamed the sight which dried the sea and shook the steadfast granite cliffs. In the third pair of verses, he changes his point of view from that of narrator to that of a wondering spectator and asks what terrible thing,

| 3626, 1158, 6887 | | 4242, 3937 | 3328 | 3706 | 5308.123 | 3497 | 5621.123 |
|---|---|---|---|---|---|---|---|
| prep, *n mp*, n fs | 5. | intrg, prep, ps 2ms | art, n ms | cj | v Qal impf 2ms | art, pn | v Qal impf 2ms |
| כִּבְנֵי־צֹאן | | מַה־לְּךָ | הַיָּם | כִּי | תָנוּס | הַיַּרְדֵּן | תִּסֹּב |
| kivnê-tsō'n | | mah-lekhā | hayyām | kî | thānûs | hayyardēn | tissōv |
| like the young of the flock | | what to you | O sea | that | you flee | the Jordan | you turn |

| 3937, 268 | | 2098 | 7833.128 | 3626, 356 | 1421 | 3626, 1158, 6887 |
|---|---|---|---|---|---|---|
| prep, sub | 6. | art, n mp | v Qal impf 2mp | prep, n mp | n fp | prep, *n mp*, n fs |
| לְאָחוֹר | | הֶהָרִים | תִּרְקְדוּ | כְאֵילִים | גְּבָעוֹת | כִּבְנֵי־צֹאן |
| le'āchôr | | hehārîm | tirqŏdhû | khe'êlîm | gevā'ôth | kivnê-tsō'n |
| backward | | the mountains | you skip | like rams | hills | like the young of the flock |

| | 4623, 3937, 6686 | 112 | 2253.132 | 800 | 4623, 3937, 6686 | 438 | 3399 |
|---|---|---|---|---|---|---|---|
| 7. | prep, prep, *n mp* | n ms | v Qal impv 2fs | n fs | prep, prep, *n mp* | *n ms* | pn |
| | מִלִּפְנֵי | אָדוֹן | חוּלִי | אָרֶץ | מִלִּפְנֵי | אֱלוֹהַּ | יַעֲקֹב |
| | milliphnê | 'ādhôn | chûlî | 'ārets | milliphnê | 'ĕlôahh | ya'ăqōv |
| | from before | the Lord | writhe | O earth | from before | the God of | Jacob |

| | 2089.151 | 6962 | 95, 4448 | 2597 | 3937, 4754, 4448 |
|---|---|---|---|---|---|
| 8. | art, v Qal act ptc ms, ps 1cs | art, n ms | *n ms*, n mp | n ms | prep, n ms, ps 3ms, n mp |
| | הַהֹפְכִי | הַצּוּר | אֲגַם־מָיִם | חַלָּמִישׁ | לְמַעְיְנוֹ־מָיִם |
| | hahōphekhî | hatstsûr | 'ăgham-māyim | challāmîsh | lema'ăynô-māyim |
| | the One Who changes for me | the rock | a pool of water | the flint | into his springs water |

| | 3940 | 3937 | 3176 | 3940 | 3937 | 3706, 3937, 8428 | 5598.131 |
|---|---|---|---|---|---|---|---|
| 115:1 | neg part | prep, ps 1cp | pn | neg part | prep, ps 1cp | cj, prep, n ms, ps 2ms | v Qal impv 2ms |
| | לֹא | לָנוּ | יְהוָה | לֹא | לָנוּ | כִּי־לְשִׁמְךָ | תֵּן |
| | lō' | lānû | yehwāh | lō' | lānû | kî-leshimkhā | tēn |
| | not | to us | O Yahweh | not | to us | rather to your name | give |

| 3638 | 6142, 2721 | 6142, 583 | | 4066 | 569.126 |
|---|---|---|---|---|---|
| n ms | prep, n ms, ps 2ms | prep, n fs, ps 2ms | 2. | intrg | v Qal impf 3mp |
| כָּבוֹד | עַל־חַסְדְּךָ | עַל־אֲמִתֶּךָ | | לָמָּה | יֹאמְרוּ |
| kāvôdh | 'al-chasdekhā | 'al-'ămittekhā | | lāmmāh | yō'merû |
| glory | because of your steadfast love | because of your reliability | | why | do they say |

| 1504 | 347, 5167 | 435 | | 435 | 904, 8452 | 3725 |
|---|---|---|---|---|---|---|
| art, n mp | intrg, part | n mp, ps 3mp | 3. | cj, n mp, ps 1cp | prep, art, n md | n ms |
| הַגּוֹיִם | אַיֵּה־נָא | אֱלֹהֵיהֶם | | וֵאלֹהֵינוּ | בַשָּׁמָיִם | כֹּל |
| haggôyim | 'ayyēh-nā' | 'ĕlōhêhem | | wē'lōhênû | vashshāmāyim | kōl |
| the nations | where please | their God | | yet our God | in the heavens | everything |

| 866, 2759.111 | 6449.111 | | 6322 | 3826B | 2174 | 4801 | 3135 |
|---|---|---|---|---|---|---|---|
| rel part, v Qal pf 3ms | v Qal pf 3ms | 4. | n mp, ps 3mp | n ms | cj, n ms | *n ms* | *n fd* |
| אֲשֶׁר־חָפֵץ | עָשָׂה | | עֲצַבֵּיהֶם | כֶּסֶף | וְזָהָב | מַעֲשֵׂה | יְדֵי |
| 'ăsher-chāphēts | 'āsāh | | 'ătsabbêhem | keseph | wezāhāv | ma'ăsēh | yedhê |
| all He desires | He does | | their cast images | silver | and gold | the work of | the hands of |

**thou Jordan, that thou wast driven back?:** … O Jordan, that you turned back, *NIV* … that you turn back?, *NRSV.*

**6. Ye mountains, that ye skipped like rams; and ye little hills, like lambs?:** … You hills, like the lambs of the flock?, *NCB* … like young sheep?, *MAST.*

**7. Tremble, thou earth, at the presence of the Lord, at the presence of the God of Jacob:** … Dance, O earth, at the presence of the Lord, *NEB* … From before the Lord be afraid, *Young* … Before the face of the Lord, tremble, O earth, *NAB.*

**8. Which turned the rock into a standing water, the flint into a fountain of waters:** … a hard rock into a spring of water, *NCV* … the rock into a pool of water, *ASV.*

**115:1. Not unto us, O LORD, not unto us, but unto thy name give glory, for thy mercy, and for thy truth's sake:** … to thy name, give honor; Because of thy kindness, because of thy faithfulness!,

*Goodspeed* ... for thy true love and for thy constancy, *NEB* ... not because of us, But because of your name display your glory, *Anchor* ... because of your love and faithfulness, *NIV.*

**2. Wherefore should the heathen say, Where is now their God?:** ... Why should the nations say?, *NASB* ... Why should the pagans say, *NCB* ... Why should the nations ask, 'Where, then, is their God?,' *REB.*

**3. But our God is in the heavens: he hath done whatsoever he hath pleased:** ... And all He wills, He does?, *Fenton* ... Whatsoever pleased Him He hath done, *MAST* ... and does anything He wants to do, *Beck* ... he creates whatever he chooses, *JB.*

**4. Their idols are silver and gold, the work of men's hands:** ... the handiwork of men, *NAB* ... the work of human hands, *NRSV.*

---

unseen by him, strikes such awe. All is silent now, and the wonders have long since passed. The sea rolls its waters again over the place where Pharaoh's host lie. The Jordan rushes down its steep valley as of old, and the savage peaks of Sinai know no tremors, but these momentary wonders proclaimed an eternal truth.

**114:7–8.** So the psalmist answers his own question and goes beyond it in summoning the whole earth to tremble, as sea, river and mountain had done, for the same vision before, which they had shrunk, is present to all nature. Now the psalmist can peal forth the name of Him, the sight of Whom wrought these wonders. It is "the LORD," the Sovereign Ruler, whose omnipotence and power over all creatures were shown when his touch made rock and flint forget their solidity and become fluid, even as his will made the waves solid as a wall, and his presence shook Sinai. He is still LORD of nature, and more blessed still, the God of Jacob. Both of these names were magnified in the two miracles (which, like those named in v. 3, are a pair) of giving drink to the thirsty pilgrims. With that thought of omnipotence blended with gracious care, the singer ceases. He has said enough to breed faith and hearten courage, and he drops his harp without a formal close. The effect is all the greater, although some critics prosaically insist the text is defective and put a row or two of asterisks at the end of v. 8, since it is not discernible what purpose the Psalm is to serve.

***Psalm 115.*** *Obviously, the Psalm is intended for temple worship and was meant to be sung by various voices. The distribution of its parts may be doubtful. Ewald would regard vv. 1–11 as the voice of the congregation while the sacrifice was being offered; vv. 12–15 as that of the priest announcing its acceptance; and vv. 16–18 as again the song of the congregation. But there is plainly a change of singer at v. 9; and the threefold summons to trust in Yahweh in the first clauses of vv. 9ff may with some probability be allotted to a ministering official, while the refrain, in the second clause of each of these verses, may be regarded as pealed out with choral force. The solo voice next pronounces the benediction on the same three classes to whom it had addressed the call to trust. And the congregation, thus receiving Yahweh's blessing, sends back its praise, as sunshine from a mirror, in v. 16ff.*

**115:1–2.** The prayer in vv. 1f beautifully blends profound consciousness of demerit and confidence that, unworthy as Israel is, its welfare is inextricably interwoven with Yahweh's honor. It goes very deep into the logic of supplication, even though the thing desired is but deliverance from human foes. Men win their pleas with God when they ask as a needy pauper. There must be thorough relinquishing of all claims based on self before there can be faithful urging of the one prevalent motive—God's care for his own fair fame. The underside of faith is self-distrust; the upper side is affiance on Yahweh. God has given pledges for his future by his past acts of self-revelation and cannot but be true to his name. His steadfast love is no transient mood, but rests on the solid basis of his faithfulness, like flowers rooted in the clefts of a rock. The taunts that had tortured another psalmist long before (Ps. 42:3) have been flung now from heathen lips with still more bitterness and call for Yahweh's thunderous answer. If Israel goes down before its foes, the heathen will have warrant to scoff.

**115:3–7.** But from their bitter tongues and his own fears, the singer turns, in the name of the sorely harassed congregation, to ring out the proclamation which answers the heathen taunt, before God answers it by deeds. "Our God is in heaven"—that is where He is; and He is not too far away to make his hand felt on earth. He is no impotent image; He does what He wills, executing fully his purposes; and conversely, He wills what He does, being constrained by no outward force, but drawing the determinations of his actions from the depths of his being. Therefore, whatever evil has befallen Israel is not a sign that it has lost Him, but a proof that He is near.

| 119 | | 6552, 3937 | 3940 | 1744.326 | 6084 | 3937 | 3940 |
|---|---|---|---|---|---|---|---|
| n ms | | n ms, prep, ps 3mp | cj, neg part | v Piel impf 3mp | n fd | prep, ps 3mp | cj, neg part |
| אָדָם | 5. | פֶּה־לָהֶם | וְלֹא | יְדַבֵּרוּ | עֵינַיִם | לָהֶם | וְלֹא |
| 'ādhām | | peh-lāhem | w$^{e}$lō' | y$^{e}$dhabbērû | 'ênayim | lāhem | w$^{e}$lō' |
| men | | a mouth to them | but not | they speak | eyes | to them | but not |

| 7495.126 | | 238 | 3937 | 3940 | 8471.126 | 653 | 3937 | 3940 |
|---|---|---|---|---|---|---|---|---|
| v Qal impf 3mp | | n fd | prep, ps 3mp | cj, neg part | v Qal impf 3mp | n ms | prep, ps 3mp | cj, neg part |
| יִרְאוּ | 6. | אָזְנַיִם | לָהֶם | וְלֹא | יִשְׁמָעוּ | אַף | לָהֶם | וְלֹא |
| yir'û | | 'āz$^{e}$nayim | lāhem | w$^{e}$lō' | yishmā'û | 'aph | lāhem | w$^{e}$lō' |
| they see | | ears | to them | but not | they hear | a nose | to them | but not |

| 7665B.526 | | 3135 | 3940 | 4318.526 | 7559 | 3940 | 2050.326 |
|---|---|---|---|---|---|---|---|
| v Hiphil impf 3mp | | n fd, ps 3mp | cj, neg part | v Hiphil impf 3mp | n fd, ps 3mp | cj, neg part | v Piel impf 3mp |
| יְרִיחוּן | 7. | יְדֵיהֶם | וְלֹא | יְמִישׁוּן | רַגְלֵיהֶם | וְלֹא | יְהַלֵּכוּ |
| y$^{e}$rîchûn | | y$^{e}$dhêhem | w$^{e}$lō' | y$^{e}$mîshûn | raghlêhem | w$^{e}$lō' | y$^{e}$hallēkhû |
| they smell | | their hands | but not | they feel | their feet | but not | they walk |

| 3940, 1965.126 | 904, 1671 | | 3765 | 2030.126 | 6449.152 | 3725 |
|---|---|---|---|---|---|---|
| neg part, v Qal impf 3mp | prep, n ms, ps 3mp | | prep, ps 3mp | v Qal impf 3mp | v Qal act ptc mp, ps 3mp | n ms |
| לֹא־יֶהְגּוּ | בִּגְרוֹנָם | 8. | כְּמוֹהֶם | יִהְיוּ | עֹשֵׂיהֶם | כֹּל |
| lō'-yehgû | bighrônām | | k$^{e}$môhem | yihyû | 'ōsêhem | kōl |
| they do not meditate | in their throat | | like them | they are | those who make them | everyone |

| 866, 1019.151 | 904 | | 3547 | 1019.131 | 904, 3176 | 6039 | 4182 |
|---|---|---|---|---|---|---|---|
| rel part, v Qal act ptc ms | prep, ps 3mp | | pn | v Qal impv 2ms | prep, pn | n ms, ps 3mp | cj, n ms, ps 3mp |
| אֲשֶׁר־בֹּטֵחַ | בָּהֶם | 9. | יִשְׂרָאֵל | בְּטַח | בַּיהוָה | עֶזְרָם | וּמָגִנָּם |
| 'ăsher-bōṭēach | bāhem | | yisrā'ēl | b$^{e}$ṭach | bayhwāh | 'ezrām | ûmāghinnām |
| who trusting | in them | | O Israel | trust | in Yahweh | their Help | and their Shield |

| 2000 | | 1041 | 172 | 1019.133 | 904, 3176 | 6039 | 4182 |
|---|---|---|---|---|---|---|---|
| pers pron | | *n ms* | pn | v Qal impv 2mp | prep, pn | n ms, ps 3mp | cj, n ms, ps 3mp |
| הוּא | 10. | בֵּית | אַהֲרֹן | בִּטְחוּ | בַיהוָה | עֶזְרָם | וּמָגִנָּם |
| hû' | | bêth | 'ahrōn | biṭchû | vayhwāh | 'ezrām | ûmāghinnām |
| He | | O household of | Aaron | trust | in Yahweh | their Help | and their Shield |

| 2000 | | 3486.152 | 3176 | 1019.133 | 904, 3176 | 6039 | 4182 |
|---|---|---|---|---|---|---|---|
| pers pron | | *v Qal act ptc mp* | pn | v Qal impv 2mp | prep, pn | n ms, ps 3mp | cj, n ms, ps 3mp |
| הוּא | 11. | יִרְאֵי | יְהוָה | בִּטְחוּ | בַיהוָה | עֶזְרָם | וּמָגִנָּם |
| hû' | | yir'ê | y$^{e}$hwāh | biṭchû | vayhwāh | 'ezrām | ûmāghinnām |
| He | | those who fear | Yahweh | trust | in Yahweh | their Help | and their Shield |

| 2000 | | 3176 | 2226.121 | 1313.321 | 1313.321 | 881, 1041 | 3547 |
|---|---|---|---|---|---|---|---|
| pers pron | | pn | v Qal pf 3ms, ps 1cp | v Piel impf 3ms | v Piel impf 3ms | do, *n ms* | pn |
| הוּא | 12. | יְהוָה | זְכָרָנוּ | יְבָרֵךְ | יְבָרֵךְ | אֶת־בֵּית | יִשְׂרָאֵל |
| hû' | | y$^{e}$hwāh | z$^{e}$khārānû | y$^{e}$vārēkh | y$^{e}$vārēkh | 'eth-bêth | yisrā'ēl |
| He | | Yahweh | He is mindful of us | He will bless | He will bless | the household of | Israel |

| 1313.321 | 881, 1041 | 172 | | 1313.321 | 3486.152 | 3176 |
|---|---|---|---|---|---|---|
| v Piel impf 3ms | do, *n ms* | pn | | v Piel impf 3ms | *v Qal act ptc mp* | pn |
| יְבָרֵךְ | אֶת־בֵּית | אַהֲרֹן | 13. | יְבָרֵךְ | יִרְאֵי | יְהוָה |
| y$^{e}$vārēkh | 'eth-bêth | 'ahrōn | | y$^{e}$vārēkh | yir'ê | y$^{e}$hwāh |
| He will bless | the household of | Aaron | | He will bless | those who fear | Yahweh |

| 7278 | 6196, 1448 | | 3362.521 | 3176 | 6142 | 6142 |
|---|---|---|---|---|---|---|
| art, adj | prep, art, adj | | v Hiphil juss 3ms | pn | prep, ps 2mp | prep, ps 2mp |
| הַקְּטַנִּים | עִם־הַגְּדֹלִים | 14. | יֹסֵף | יְהוָה | עֲלֵיכֶם | עֲלֵיכֶם |
| haqq$^{e}$ṭanîm | 'im-hagg$^{e}$dhōlîm | | yōsēph | y$^{e}$hwāh | 'ălêkhem | 'ălêkhem |
| the insignificant | with the great | | may He increase | Yahweh | on you | on you |

**5. They have mouths, but they speak not: eyes have they, but they see not:** ... Mouths have they, but they cannot speak, *Berkeley* ... They have mouths, but no voice, *BB* ... They have mouths, but do not speak; eyes, but do not see, *RSV.*

**6. They have ears, but they hear not: noses have they, but they smell not:** ... nostrils, and cannot smell, *NEB* ... ears, but do not hear; noses, but do not smell, *NRSV.*

**7. They have hands, but they handle not: feet have they, but they walk not: neither speak they through their throat:** ... Their hands! but they feel not, *Rotherham* ... Nor do they mutter through their throat, *Young* ... they give no sound through their throat, *Darby* ... hands, as well, but they cannot feel, *Berkeley.*

**8. They that make them are like unto them; so is every one that trusteth in them:** ... Their makers will end up like them, *JB* ... People who make idols will be like them, *NCV* ... No breath of life is in them!, *Moffatt.*

**9. O Israel, trust thou in the LORD: he is their help and their shield:** ... he is their help and their breast-plate, *BB* ... Helper and Suzerain is he!, *Anchor.*

**10. O house of Aaron, trust in the LORD: he is their help and their shield:** ... he is your helper and your protection, *NCV* ... He helps and shields them, *Beck.*

**11. Ye that fear the LORD, trust in the LORD: he is their help and their shield:** ... Helper and Suzerain is he!, *Anchor* ... All you who revere the LORD, *Berkeley* ... You worshippers of the Lord, have faith in the Lord, *BB.*

**12. The LORD hath been mindful of us: he will bless us; he will bless the house of Israel; he will bless the house of Aaron:** ... The LORD remembers us and will bless us, *NAB* ... He will bless the family of Israel; he will bless the family of Aaron, *NCV* ... He will bless Israel's family; He will bless Aaron's family, *Beck.*

**13. He will bless them that fear the LORD, both small and great:** ... He will bless those who reverence the LORD, *Goodspeed* ... both high and low, *REB* ... all who fear him, high and low alike, *NEB* ... from the smallest to the greatest, *NCV.*

**14. The LORD shall increase you more and more, you and your children:** ... May the LORD give you increase more and more, *NKJV*

---

The brief, pregnant assertion of God's omnipotence and sovereign freedom, which should tame the heathens' arrogance and teach the meaning of Israel's disasters, is set in eloquent opposition to the fiery indignation which dashes off the sarcastic picture of an idol. The tone of the description is like that of the manufacture of an image in Isa. 44:9–20. Psalm 135:15–18 repeats it verbatim. The vehemence of scorn in these verses suggests a previous, compelled familiarity with idolatry such as the exiles had. It corresponds with the revolution which that familiarity produced, by extirpating forever the former following after the gods of the nations.

**115:8.** But a deeper note is struck in v. 8, in the assertion that, as is the god, so becomes the worshiper. The psalmist probably means chiefly, if not exclusively, in respect to the impotence just spoken of. So the worshiper and his idol are called by the same name (Isa. 44:9, "vanity"), and in the tragic summary of Israel's sins and punishment in 2 Ki. 17:15, it is said that "they followed vanity, and became vain." But the statement is true in a wider sense. Worship is sure to breed likeness. A lustful, cruel god will make his devotees so. Men make gods after their own image, and when made, the gods make men after theirs. The same principle which degrades the idolater lifts the Christian to the likeness of Christ. The aim and effect of adoration is assimilation.

**115:9–11.** Probably, the congregation is now silent, and a single voice takes up the song, with the call, which the hollowness of idolatry makes so urgent and reasonable, to trust in Yahweh, not in vanities. It is thrice repeated, being first addressed to the congregation, then to the house of Aaron, and finally to a wider circle, those who "fear Yahweh." These are most naturally understood as proselytes, and in the prominence given to them, we see the increasing consciousness in Israel of its divine destination to be God's witness to the world. Exile had widened the horizon, and fair hopes that men who were not of Israel's blood would share Israel's faith and shelter under the wings of Israel's God stirred in many hearts. The crash of the triple choral answer to the summons comes with magnificent effect, in the second clauses of vv. 9f, triumphantly telling how safe are they who take refuge behind that strong buckler. The same threefold division into Israel, the house of Aaron and they who fear Yahweh occurs in Ps. 118:2ff, and, with the addition of "house of Levi," in Ps. 135.

**115:12–15.** Promises of blessing occupy vv. 12–15, which probably were sung by priests, or rather by Levites, the musicians of the temple service. In any case, these benedictions are authoritative assurances from commissioned lips, not utterances of hopeful faith. They are Yahweh's

| | | 15. | | | | | |
|---|---|---|---|---|---|---|---|
| 5912, 1158 | | | 1313.156 | 894 | 3937, 3176 | 6449.151 | 8452 |
| cj, prep, n mp, ps 2mp | | | v Qal pass ptc mp | pers pron | prep, pn | *v Qal act ptc ms* | n md |
| וְעַל־בְּנֵיכֶם | | | בְּרוּכִים | אַתֶּם | לַיהוָה | עֹשֵׂה | שָׁמַיִם |
| weʻal-benêkhem | | | berûkhîm | 'attem | layhwāh | ʻōsēh | shāmayim |
| and on your children | | | blessed | you | of Yahweh | the Maker of | the heavens |

| | 16. | | | | | |
|---|---|---|---|---|---|---|
| 800 | | 8452 | 8452 | 3937, 3176 | 800 | 5598.111 |
| cj, n fs | | art, n md | n md | prep, pn | cj, art, n fs | v Qal pf 3ms |
| וָאָרֶץ | | הַשָּׁמַיִם | שָׁמַיִם | לַיהוָה | וְהָאָרֶץ | נָתַן |
| wā'ārets | | hashshāmayim | shāmayim | layhwāh | wehā'ārets | nāthan |
| and the earth | | the heavens | the heavens | to Yahweh | and the earth | He has given |

| | 17. | | | | |
|---|---|---|---|---|---|
| 3937, 1158, 119 | | 3940 | 4322.152 | 2054.326, 3161 | 3940 |
| prep, *n mp*, n ms | | neg part | art, v Qal act ptc mp | v Piel impf 3mp, pn | cj, neg part |
| לִבְנֵי־אָדָם | | לֹא | הַמֵּתִים | יְהַלְלוּ־יָהּ | וְלֹא |
| livnê-'ādhām | | lō' | hammēthîm | yehalelû-yāhh | welō' |
| to the sons of humankind | | not | the dead | they will praise Yah | indeed not |

| | | 18. | | | | | |
|---|---|---|---|---|---|---|---|
| 3725, 3495.152 | 1798 | | 601 | 1313.320 | 3161 | 4623, 6498 | 5912, 5986 |
| *adj, v Qal act ptc mp* | n fs | | cj, pers pron | v Piel impf 1cp | pn | prep, adv | cj, adv, n ms |
| כָּל־יֹרְדֵי | דוּמָה | | וַאֲנַחְנוּ | נְבָרֵךְ | יָהּ | מֵעַתָּה | וְעַד־עוֹלָם |
| kol-yōredhê | dhûmāh | | wa'ănachnû | nevārēkh | yāhh | mē'attāh | we'adh-'ôlām |
| all those going down to | silence | | but we | we will bless | Yah | from now | even until eternity |

| | 116:1 | | | | | |
|---|---|---|---|---|---|---|
| 2054.333, 3161 | | 154.115 | 3706, 5471.121 | 3176 | 881, 7249 | 8800 |
| v Piel impv 2mp, pn | | v Qal pf 1cs | cj, v Qal impf 3ms | pn | do, n ms, ps 1cs | n mp, ps 1cs |
| הַלְלוּ־יָהּ | | אָהַבְתִּי | כִּי־יִשְׁמַע | יְהוָה | אֶת־קוֹלִי | תַּחֲנוּנָי |
| halelû-yāhh | | 'āhavtî | kî-yishma' | yehwāh | 'eth-qôlî | tachnûnāy |
| praise Yah | | I love | because He hears | Yahweh | my voice | my supplication |

| 2. | | | | | |
|---|---|---|---|---|---|
| | 3706, 5371.511 | 238 | 3937 | 904, 3219 | 7410.125 |
| | cj, v Hiphil pf 3ms | n fs, ps 3ms | prep, ps 1cs | cj, prep, n mp, ps 1cs | v Qal impf 1cs |
| | כִּי־הִטָּה | אָזְנוֹ | לִי | וּבְיָמַי | אֶקְרָא |
| | kî-hiṭṭāh | 'āzenô | lî | ûveyāmay | 'eqŏrā' |
| | because He inclines | his ear | to me | and during my days | I will call |

| 3. | | | | | |
|---|---|---|---|---|---|
| | 680.116 | 2346, 4323 | 4873 | 8061 | 4834.116 |
| | v Qal pf 3cp, ps 1cs | *n mp*, n ms | cj, *n mp* | pn | v Qal pf 3cp, ps 1cs |
| | אֲפָפוּנִי | חֶבְלֵי־מָוֶת | וּמְצָרֵי | שְׁאוֹל | מְצָאוּנִי |
| | 'ăphāphûnî | chevlê-māweth | ûmetsārê | she'ôl | metsā'ûnî |
| | they encompassed me | the cords of death | and the bondage of | Sheol | they found me |

| | | | 4. | | | | |
|---|---|---|---|---|---|---|---|
| 7150 | 3123 | 4834.125 | | 904, 8428, 3176 | 7410.125 | 588 | 3176 |
| n fs | cj, n ms | v Qal impf 1cs | | cj, prep, *n ms*, pn | v Qal impf 1cs | part | pn |
| צָרָה | וְיָגוֹן | אֶמְצָא | | וּבְשֵׁם־יְהוָה | אֶקְרָא | אָנָּה | יְהוָה |
| tsārāh | weyāghôn | 'emtsā' | | ûveshēm-yehwāh | 'eqŏrā' | 'ānnāh | yehwāh |
| adversity | and agony | I found | | then on the name of Yahweh | I called | please | Yahweh |

… May Yahweh add to your numbers, *JB* … will add unto you more, *Darby* … Yahweh multiply you, *Rotherham.*

**15. Ye are blessed of the LORD which made heaven and earth:** … Give Blessings to the LORD, Who made the Skies and Earth, *Fenton* … May you have the blessing of the Lord, *BB* … the Maker of heaven and earth, *NIV* … maker of heaven and earth, *Young.*

**16. The heaven, even the heavens, are the LORD's: but the earth hath he given to the children of men:** … heavens are the LORD's heavens, but the earth he has given to human beings, *NRSV* … Heaven belongs to the LORD, but he gave the earth to people, *NCV* … the earth He gave to mortal man, *Beck* … he has entrusted to the children of men, *Anchor.*

**17. The dead praise not the LORD, neither any that go down into silence:** … The dead cannot praise Yah, *Rotherham* … those who sink into silence, *JB* … or those who go down to the underworld, *BB* ... nor any who sink to the silent land, *Moffatt.*

**18. But we will bless the LORD from this time forth and for evermore. Praise the LORD:** ... both now and forevermore, *KJVII* ... But as for us, we will bless the LORD, *NASB* ... From henceforth, and unto the age, *Young.*

**116:1. I love the LORD, because he hath heard my voice and my supplications:** ... Out of love for me Yahweh did hear my plea for his mercy, *Anchor* ... I am filled with love when Yahweh listens to the sound of my prayer, *JB* ... because He has heard my voice and my prayers, *KJVII* ... and listens to my prayer, *NEB.*

**2. Because he hath inclined his ear unto me, therefore will I call upon him as long as I live:** ... He has let my request come before him, *BB* ... He paid attention to me, *NCV.*

**3. The sorrows of death compassed me, and the pains of hell gat hold upon me: I found trouble and sorrow:** ... The cords of death encircled me; And the tortures of Sheol found me, *Goodspeed* ... Anguish and torment held me fast, *NEB* ... And the pangs of Sheol laid hold of me, *NKJV* ... the anguish of the grave came upon me, *NIV.*

**4. Then called I upon the name of the LORD; O LORD, I beseech thee, deliver my soul:** ... 'O LORD, save my life!,' *NAB* ... O Lord, take my soul out of trouble, *BB* ... 'Please, LORD, rescue me!,' *Beck.*

---

response to Israel's obedience to the preceding summons, swiftly sent, as his answers ever are. Calm certainty that He will bless comes at once into the heart that deeply feels that He is its Shield; however, his manifestation of outward help may be lovingly delayed. The blessing is parted among those who had severally been called to trust and had obeyed the call. Universal blessings have special destinations. The fiery mass breaks up into cloven tongues and sits on each. Distinctions of position make no difference in its reception. Small vessels are filled, and great ones can be no more than full. Cedars and hyssop rejoice in impartial sunshine. When blessed, Israel increases in number, and there is an inheritance of good from generation to generation. The seal of such hopes is the name of Him who blesses, He "which made heaven and earth," to whose omnipotent, universal sway these impotent gods in human form are as a foil.

**115:16–18.** Finally, we may hear the united voices of the congregation thus blessed breaking into full-throated praise in vv. 16ff. As in v. 3, God's dwelling in heaven symbolized his loftiness and power, so here the thought that "the heavens are the LORD's" implies both the worshipers' trust in his mighty help and their lowliness even in trust. The earth is man's, but by Yahweh's gift. Therefore its inhabitants should remember the terms of their tenure and thankfully recognize his giving love. But heaven and earth do not include all the universe. There is another region, the land of silence, whither the dead descend. No voice of praise wakes its dumb sleep (cf. Isa. 38:18f). That pensive contemplation, on which the light of the NT assurance of immortality has not shone, gives keener edge to the bliss of present ability to praise Yahweh. We who know that to die is to have a new song put into immortal lips may still be stimulated to fill our brief lives here with the music of thanksgiving by the thought that—so far as our witness for God to men is concerned—most of us will "go down into silence" when we pass into the grave. Therefore, we should shun silence and bless Him while we live here.

***Psalm 116.*** *Four parts may be discerned in this Psalm, of which the first (vv. 1–4) mainly describes the psalmist's peril; the second (vv. 5–9), his deliverance; the third glances back to his alarm and thence draws reasons for his vow of praise (vv. 10–14); and the fourth bases the same vow on the remembrance of Yahweh's having loosed his bonds.*

**116:1–3.** The early verses of Ps. 18 obviously color the psalmist's description of his distress. That Psalm begins with an expression of love to Yahweh, which is echoed here, although a different word is employed. "I love" stands in v. 1 without an object, just as "I call" does in v. 2, and "I believed" and "have I spoken" in v. 10. Probably, "thee" has fallen out, which would be the more easy, as the next word begins with the letter which stands for it in Hebrew. Some propose the conjectural adoption of the same beginning as in v. 10, "I am confident." This change necessitates translating the following "for" as "that," whereas it is plainly to be taken, like the "for" at the beginning of v. 2, as causal.

Verse 3 is molded on Ps. 18:5, with a modification of the metaphors by the unusual expression "the cords of Sheol." The word rendered "cords" (HED #4323) may be employed simply as "distress" or "straits," but it is allowable to take it as picturing that gloomy realm as a confined gorge, like the throat of a pass, from which the psalmist could find no escape. He is like a creature caught in the toils of the hunter death. The stern rocks of a dark defile have all but closed upon him, but like a

| | | | | | | | |
|---|---|---|---|---|---|---|---|
| 4561.331<br>v Piel impv 2ms<br>מַלְּטָה<br>malleṭāh<br>set free | 5497<br>n fs, ps 1cs<br>נַפְשִׁי<br>naphshî<br>my soul | **5.** | 2688<br>adj<br>חַנּוּן<br>channûn<br>gracious | 3176<br>pn<br>יְהוָה<br>yehōwāh<br>Yahweh | 6926<br>cj, adj<br>וְצַדִּיק<br>wetsaddîq<br>and righteous | 435<br>cj, n mp, ps 1cp<br>וֵאלֹהֵינוּ<br>wē'lōhênû<br>and our God | 7638.351<br>v Piel ptc ms<br>מְרַחֵם<br>merachēm<br>One Who shows mercy |

| | | | | | | | |
|---|---|---|---|---|---|---|---|
| **6.** | 8490.151<br>v Qal act ptc ms<br>שֹׁמֵר<br>shōmēr<br>guarding | 6848<br>adj<br>פְּתָאִים<br>pethā'yim<br>the simple | 3176<br>pn<br>יְהוָה<br>yehōwāh<br>Yahweh | 1870.115<br>v Qal pf 1cs<br>דַּלּוֹתִי<br>dallôthî<br>I became low | 3937<br>cj, prep, ps 1cs<br>וְלִי<br>welî<br>then me | 3588.521<br>v Hiphil impf 3ms<br>יְהוֹשִׁיעַ<br>yehôshîa'<br>He saved | **7.** 8178.132<br>v Qal impv 2fs<br>שׁוּבִי<br>shûvî<br>return |

| | | | | | |
|---|---|---|---|---|---|
| 5497<br>n fs, ps 1cs<br>נַפְשִׁי<br>naphshî<br>my soul | 3937, 4640<br>prep, n mp, ps 2fs<br>לִמְנוּחָיְכִי<br>limnûchāyekhî<br>to your rest | 3706, 3176<br>cj, pn<br>כִּי־יְהוָה<br>kî-yehwāh<br>because Yahweh | 1621.111<br>v Qal pf 3ms<br>גָּמַל<br>gāmal<br>He has rewarded | 6142<br>prep, ps 2fs<br>עָלָיְכִי<br>'ālāyekhî<br>concerning you | **8.** 3706<br>cj<br>כִּי<br>kî<br>because |

| | | | | | | |
|---|---|---|---|---|---|---|
| 2603.313<br>v Piel pf 2ms<br>חִלַּצְתָּ<br>chillatstā<br>You have separated | 5497<br>n fs, ps 1cs<br>נַפְשִׁי<br>naphshî<br>my soul | 4623, 4323<br>prep, n ms<br>מִמָּוֶת<br>mimmāweth<br>from death | 881, 6084<br>do, n fs, ps 1cs<br>אֶת־עֵינִי<br>'eth-'ênî<br>my eye | 4623, 1893<br>prep, n fs<br>מִן־דִּמְעָה<br>min-dim'āh<br>from tears | 881, 7559<br>do, n fs, ps 1cs<br>אֶת־רַגְלִי<br>'eth-raghlî<br>my foot | 4623, 1818<br>prep, n ms<br>מִדֶּחִי<br>middechî<br>from stumbling |

| | | | | | | | |
|---|---|---|---|---|---|---|---|
| **9.** 2050.725<br>v Hithpael impf 1cs<br>אֶתְהַלֵּךְ<br>'ethhallēkh<br>I will walk | 3937, 6686<br>prep, *n mp*<br>לִפְנֵי<br>liphnê<br>before | 3176<br>pn<br>יְהוָה<br>yehwāh<br>Yahweh | 904, 800<br>prep, *n fp*<br>בְּאַרְצוֹת<br>be'artsôth<br>in the lands of | 2522<br>art, n mp<br>הַחַיִּים<br>hachayyîm<br>the living | **10.** | 548.515<br>v Hiphil pf 1cs<br>הֶאֱמַנְתִּי<br>he'ĕmantî<br>I have believed | 3706<br>cj<br>כִּי<br>kî<br>when |

| | | | | | | | |
|---|---|---|---|---|---|---|---|
| 1744.325<br>v Piel impf 1cs<br>אֲדַבֵּר<br>'ădhabbēr<br>I spoke | 603<br>pers pron<br>אֲנִי<br>'ănî<br>I | 6257.115<br>v Qal pf 1cs<br>עָנִיתִי<br>'ānîthî<br>I am afflicted | 4108<br>adv<br>מְאֹד<br>me'ōdh<br>very | **11.** | 603<br>pers pron<br>אֲנִי<br>'ănî<br>I | 569.115<br>v Qal pf 1cs<br>אָמַרְתִּי<br>'āmartî<br>I said | 904, 2753.141<br>prep, v Qal inf con, ps 1cs<br>בְחָפְזִי<br>vechāphezî<br>in my hurrying |

| | | | | | | |
|---|---|---|---|---|---|---|
| 3725, 119<br>*adj*, art, n ms<br>כָּל־הָאָדָם<br>kol-hā'ādhām<br>all men | 3694.151<br>v Qal act ptc ms<br>כֹּזֵב<br>kōzēv<br>liars | **12.** | 4242, 8178.525<br>intrg, v Hiphil impf 1cs<br>מָה־אָשִׁיב<br>māh-'āshîv<br>what will I return | 3937, 3176<br>prep, pn<br>לַיהוָה<br>layhwāh<br>to Yahweh | 3725, 8737<br>*adj*, n mp, ps 3ms<br>כָּל־תַּגְמוּלוֹהִי<br>kol-taghmûlôhî<br>all his benefits | 6142<br>prep, ps 1cs<br>עָלָי<br>'ālāy<br>on me |

**5. Gracious is the LORD, and righteous; yea, our God is merciful:** … our God is full of compassion, *REB* … The Lord was good and kind, And our GOD was benign, *Fenton* … Tender and true is the Eternal, our God indeed is pitiful, *Moffatt.*

**6. The LORD preserveth the simple: I was brought low, and he helped me:** … brought low, and He saved me, *NASB* … brought low, when to me he granted salvation, *Rotherham* … The LORD takes care of the helpless, *Berkeley* … when I was helpless, he saved me, *NCV.*

**7. Return unto thy rest, O my soul; for the LORD hath dealt bountifully with thee:** … to your tranquillity, for the Lord has been good to you, *NCB* … go back to your rest, the LORD has been kind to you, *Beck* … My heart, be at peace once again, for Yahweh has treated you generously, *JB.*

**8. For thou hast delivered my soul from death, mine eyes from tears, and my feet from falling:** … You stopped my eyes from crying; you kept me from being defeated, *NCV* … My life relieved from Death, Mine eyes relieved from tears, *Fenton* … For he has freed my soul from death, *NAB* … my feet from overthrowing, *Young.*

**9. I will walk before the LORD in the land of the living:** … I will live mindful of thee now, *Moffatt* … I shall walk before Yahweh in the Fields of Life, *Anchor* … I will walk in the presence of the LORD, *NEB.*

**10. I believed, therefore have I spoken: I was greatly afflicted:** … I still had faith, though I said, I am in great trouble, *BB* … I believed even when I had to speak of suffering so much, *Beck* ... I believe what I say; I am fully responsible for it, *Goodspeed* ... I was sure I should be swept away; my distress was bitter, *REB.*

**11. I said in my haste, All men are liars:** ... And in my dismay I said, *NIV* ... I said in my consternation, 'Men are all a vain hope,' *RSV* ... In panic I cried, 'How faithless all men are!,' *NEB* ... I had said in my panic, 'Everyone is lying,' *Beck.*

**12. What shall I render unto the LORD for all his benefits toward me?:** ... How shall I make a return to the LORD for all the good he has done, *NAB* ... All His benefits are upon me, *Young* ... How shall I give back to Yahweh, All his benefits unto me?, *Rotherham* ... All His bountiful dealings toward me?, *MAST.*

---

man from the bottom of a pit, he can send out one cry before the earth falls in and buries him. He cried to Yahweh, and the rocks flung his voice heavenwards. Sorrow is meant to drive to God. When cries become prayers, they are not in vain. The revealed character of Yahweh is the ground of a desperate man's hope. His own name is a plea which Yahweh will certainly honor. Many words are needless when peril is sore and the suppliant is sure of God. To name Him and to cry for deliverance are enough. "I beseech thee" represents a particle which is used frequently in this Psalm, and by some peculiarities in its use, here indicates a late date.

**116:4–6.** The psalmist does not pause to say definitely that he was delivered, but breaks into the celebration of the name on which he had called and from which the certainty of an answer followed. Since Yahweh is gracious, righteous (as strictly adhering to the conditions He has laid down) and merciful (as condescending in love to lowly and imperfect men), there can be no doubt how He will deal with trustful suppliants. The psalmist turns for a moment from his own experience to sun himself in the great thought of the name and thereby to come into touch with all who share his faith. The cry for help is wrung out by personal need, but the answer received brings into fellowship with a great multitude.

Yahweh's character leads up in v. 6 to a broad truth as to his acts, for it ensures that He cannot but care for the "simple," whose simplicity lays them open to assailants and whose single-hearted adhesion to God appeals unfailingly to his heart. Happy the man who, like the psalmist, can give confirmation, from his own experience, of the broad truths of God's protection to ingenuous and guileless souls! Each individual may, if he will, thus narrow to his own use the widest promises and put "I" and "me" wherever God has put "whosoever." If he does, he will be able to turn his own experience into universal maxims and encourage others to put "whosoever" where his grateful heart has put "I" and "me."

**116:7.** The deliverance, which is thus the direct result of the divine character and which extends to all the simple and therefore included the psalmist, leads to calm repose. The singer does not say so in cold words, but beautifully wooes his "soul" (HED #5497), his sensitive nature, which had trembled with fear in death's net, to come back to its rest. The word is in the plural, which may be only another indication of late date, but is more worthily understood as expressing the completeness of the repose, which in its fullness is only found in God and is made the more deep by contrast with previous "agitation."

**116:8–9.** Verses 8f, are quoted from Ps. 56:13 with slight variations, the most significant of which is the change of "light" into "lands." It is noticeable that the divine deliverance is thus described as surpassing the psalmist's petition. He requested, "Deliver my soul." Bare escape was all that he craved, but he received not only the deliverance of his soul from death, but over and above, his tears were wiped away by a loving hand, and his feet were stayed by a strong arm. God answers trustful cries and does not give the minimum consistent with safety, but the maximum of which we are capable. What shall a grateful heart do with such benefits? It responds, "I will walk before the LORD in the land of the living," joyously and unconstrainedly (for so the form of the word "walk," HED #2050, implies), as ever conscious of that presence which brings blessedness and requires holiness. The paths appointed may carry the traveler far, but into whatever lands he goes, he will have the same glad heart within to urge his feet and the same loving eye above to beam guidance on him.

**116:10–11.** The third part (vv. 10–14) recurs to the psalmist's mood in his trouble and bases on the retrospect of that and of God's mercy the vow of praise. Verse 10 may be variously understood. The "speaking" may be taken as referring to the preceding expressions of trust or thanksgivings for deliverance. The sentiment would then be that the psalmist was confident that he should one day thus speak, or the rendering may be "I believed in that I spake thus"—i.e., that he spake those trustful words of v. 9 was the result of sheer faith. The

| 13. | 3683, 3568 | 5558.125 | 904, 8428 | 3176 | 7410.125 | 14. | 5266 |
|---|---|---|---|---|---|---|---|
| | *n fs*, n fp | v Qal impf 1cs | cj, prep, *n ms* | pn | v Qal impf 1cs | | n mp, ps 1cs |
| | כּוֹס־יְשׁוּעוֹת | אֶשָּׂא | וּבְשֵׁם | יְהוָה | אֶקְרָא | | נְדָרַי |
| | kôs̱-yeshû'ôth | 'essā' | ûveshēm | yehwāh | 'eqōrā' | | nedhāray |
| | the cup of salvation | I will lift up | and on the name of | Yahweh | I will call | | my vows |

| 3937, 3176 | 8396.325 | 5222, 5167 | 3937, 3725, 6194 | 15. | 3479 | 904, 6084 |
|---|---|---|---|---|---|---|
| prep, pn | v Piel impf 1cs | prep, part | prep, *adj*, n ms, ps 3ms | | adj | prep, *n fd* |
| לַיהוָה | אֲשַׁלֵּם | נֶגְדָה־נָּא | לְכָל־עַמּוֹ | | יָקָר | בְּעֵינֵי |
| layhwāh | 'ăshallēm | neghdhāh-nā' | lekhol-'ammô | | yāqār | be'ênê |
| to Yahweh | I will complete | before please | to all his people | | precious | in the eyes of |

| 3176 | 4323 | 3937, 2728 | 16. | 588 | 3176 | 3706, 603 | 5860 |
|---|---|---|---|---|---|---|---|
| pn | art, n ms | prep, n mp, ps 3ms | | part | pn | cj, pers pron | n ms, ps 2ms |
| יְהוָה | הַמָּוְתָה | לַחֲסִידָיו | | אָנָּה | יְהוָה | כִּי־אֲנִי | עַבְדֶּךָ |
| yehwāh | hammāwethāh | lachs̱îdhâv | | 'ānnāh | yehwāh | kî-'ănî | 'avdekhā |
| Yahweh | the death | of his godly ones | | please | O Yahweh | because I | your servant |

| 603, 5860 | 1158, 526 | 6858.313 | 3937, 4283 |
|---|---|---|---|
| pers pron, n ms, ps 2ms | *n ms*, n fs, ps 2ms | v Piel pf 2ms | prep, n mp, ps 1cs |
| אֲנִי־עַבְדְּךָ | בֶּן־אֲמָתֶךָ | פִּתַּחְתָּ | לְמוֹסֵרָי |
| 'ănî-'avdekhā | ben-'ămāthekhā | pittachtā | lemôs̱ērāy |
| I your servant | the son of your female servant | You have opened | my fetters |

| 17. | 3937, 2159.125 | 2160 | 8756 | 904, 8428 | 3176 | 7410.125 |
|---|---|---|---|---|---|---|
| | prep, ps 2ms, v Qal impf 1cs | *n ms* | n fs | cj, prep, *n ms* | pn | v Qal impf 1cs |
| | לְךָ־אֶזְבַּח | זֶבַח | תּוֹדָה | וּבְשֵׁם | יְהוָה | אֶקְרָא |
| | lekhā-'ezbach | zevach | tôdhāh | ûveshēm | yehwāh | 'eqōrā' |
| | to You I will sacrifice | a sacrifice of | thanksgiving | and on the name of | Yahweh | I will call |

| 18. | 5266 | 3937, 3176 | 8396.325 | 5222, 5167 | 3937, 3725, 6194 | 19. | 904, 2793 |
|---|---|---|---|---|---|---|---|
| | n mp, ps 1cs | prep, pn | v Piel impf 1cs | prep, part | prep, *adj*, n ms, ps 3ms | | prep, *n fp* |
| | נְדָרַי | לַיהוָה | אֲשַׁלֵּם | נֶגְדָה־נָּא | לְכָל־עַמּוֹ | | בְּחַצְרוֹת |
| | nedhāray | layhwāh | 'ăshallēm | neghdhāh-nā' | lekhol-'ammô | | bechatsrôth |
| | my vows | to Yahweh | I will complete | before please | to all his people | | in the courts of |

| 1041 | 3176 | 904, 8761 | 3503 | 2054.333, 3161 | 117:1 | 2054.333 |
|---|---|---|---|---|---|---|
| *n ms* | pn | prep, n ms, ps 2fs | pn | v Piel impv 2mp, pn | | v Piel impv 2mp |
| בֵּית | יְהוָה | בְּתוֹכֵכִי | יְרוּשָׁלָם | הַלְלוּ־יָהּ | | הַלְלוּ |
| bêth | yehwāh | bethôkhēkhî | yerûshālām | halelû-yāhh | | halelû |
| the Temple of | Yahweh | in your midst | Jerusalem | praise Yah | | praise |

**13. I will take the cup of salvation, and call upon the name of the LORD:** … I'll raise Salvation's Cup, *Fenton* … I will take the cup of deliverance, *Goodspeed* … I will take the chalice of salvation, *Anchor.*

**14. I will pay my vows unto the LORD now in the presence of all his people:** … I shall fulfil my vows to Yahweh, witnessed by all his people, *JB* … I will give the LORD what I promised in front of all his people, *NCV.*

**15. Precious in the sight of the LORD is the death of his saints:** … is the death of his faithful ones, *NRSV* … is the death of those who die faithful to him, *NEB* … is the death of those who are loyal to him, *REB* … is the death of his devoted, *Moffatt.*

**16. O LORD, truly I am thy servant; I am thy servant, and the son of thine handmaid: thou hast loosed my bonds:** … You have freed me from my chains, *NCV* … I am your servant and my mother was your servant, *JB.*

**17. I will offer to thee the sacrifice of thanksgiving, and will call upon the name of the LORD:** … Then I will offer thanks, *Fenton* … and invoke the LORD by name, *NEB.*

**18. I will pay my vows unto the LORD now in the presence of all his people:** … I will make the offerings of my oath, even before all his people, *BB* … I will fulfill my vows, *NIV.*

**19. In the courts of the LORD's house, in the midst of thee, O Jerusalem. Praise ye the LORD:** … in the Temple courtyards in Jerusalem, *NCV* … courts of the LORD's temple, *Beck.*

thing spoken may also be the expressions which follow, and this seems to yield the most satisfactory meaning.

In the expression "Even when I said, I am afflicted and men fail me, I had not lost my faith," the psalmist is recalling the agitation which shook him, but feels that through it all, there was an unshaken center of rest in God. The presence of doubt and fear does not prove the absence of trust. There may live a spark of it, though almost buried below masses of cold unbelief. What he said was the complaint that he was greatly afflicted and the bitter wail that all men deceive or disappoint. He said so in his agitation (Ps. 31:22). But even in recognizing the folly of trusting in men, he was in some measure trusting God, and the trust, though tremulous, was rewarded.

**116:12–13.** Again, he hurries on to sing the issues of deliverance without waiting to describe it. That little dialogue of the devout soul with itself goes very deep. It is an illuminative word as to God's character, an emancipating word as to the true notion of service to Him, a guiding word as to common life. For it declares that men honor God most by taking his gifts with recognition of the Giver and that the return which He in his love seeks is only our thankful reception of his mercy. A giver who desires but these results is surely love. A religion which consists first in accepting God's gift, and then in praising by lip and life Him who gives, banishes the religion of fear, of barter, of unwelcome restrictions and commands. It is the exact opposite of the slavery which says, "Thou art an austere man, reaping where thou didst not sow." It is the religion of which the initial act is faith, and the continual activity is the appropriation of God's spiritual gifts. In daily life, there would be less despondency and weakening regrets over vanished blessings if men were more careful to take and enjoy thankfully all that God gives. But many of us have no eyes for other blessings, because one blessing is withdrawn or denied. If we treasured all that is given, we should be richer than most of us are.

**116:14.** In v. 14, the particle of beseeching (HED #5167) is added to "before," a singular form of expression which seems to imply desire that the psalmist may come into the Temple with his vows. He may have been thinking of the "sacrificial meal in connection with the peace offerings." In any case, blessings received in solitude should impel to public gratitude. God delivers his suppliants that they may magnify Him before men.

**116:15–19.** The last part repeats the refrain of v. 14, but with a different setting. Here the singer generalizes his own experience and finds increase of joy in the thought of the multitude who dwell safe under the same protection. The more usual form of expression for the idea in v. 15 is "their blood is precious" (Ps. 72:14). The meaning is that the death of God's saints is no trivial thing in God's eyes, to be lightly permitted (cf. the contrasted thought, 44:12).

Then, on the basis of that general truth, is built v. 16, which begins singularly with the same beseeching word which has already occurred in vv. 4 and 14. Here it is not followed by an expressed petition, but is a yearning of desire for continued or fuller manifestation of God's favor. The largest gifts, most fully accepted and most thankfully recognized, still leave room for longing, which is not pain, because it is conscious of tender relations with God that guarantee its fulfillment. The psalmist humbly says, "I am Thy servant." Therefore the longing which has no words needs none. "Thou hast loosed my bonds." His thoughts go back to "the cords of death" (v. 3), which had held him so tightly. God's hand has slackened them, and, by freeing him from that bondage, has bound him more closely than before to himself. "Being made free from sin, ye became the slaves of righteousness" shows that, in the full blessedness of received deliverance, the grateful heart offers itself to God, as moved by his mercies to become a living sacrifice, and calls on the name of Yahweh, in its hour of thankful surrender, as it had called on that name in its time of deep distress. Once more, the lonely suppliant, who had waded such deep waters without companion but Yahweh, seeks to feel himself one of the glad multitude in the courts of the house of Yahweh and to blend his single voice in the shout of a nation's praise. We suffer and struggle for the most part alone. Grief is a hermit, but joy is sociable; and thankfulness desires listeners to its praise. The perfect song is the chorus of a great "multitude which no man can number."

**117:1–2.** This shortest of the Psalms is not a fragment, although some manuscripts attach it to the preceding and some to the following Psalm. It contains large "riches in a narrow room," and its very brevity gives force to it. Paul laid his finger on its special significance, when he quoted it in proof that God meant his salvation to be for the whole race. Jewish narrowness was an after-growth and a

| 881, 3176<br>do, pn<br>אֶת־יְהוָה<br>'eth-yehwāh<br>Yahweh | 3725, 1504<br>*adj*, n mp<br>כָּל־גּוֹיִם<br>kol-gôyim<br>all the nations | 8099.333<br>v Piel impv 2mp, ps 3ms<br>שַׁבְּחוּהוּ<br>shabbechûhû<br>exalt Him | 3725, 531<br>*adj*, art, n fp<br>כָּל־הָאֻמִּים<br>kol-hā'ummîm<br>all the peoples | **2.** | 3706<br>cj<br>כִּי<br>kî<br>because | 1428.111<br>v Qal pf 3ms<br>גָּבַר<br>ghāvar<br>it prevails |
|---|---|---|---|---|---|---|

| 6142<br>prep, ps 1cp<br>עָלֵינוּ<br>'ālênû<br>concerning us | 2721<br>n ms, ps 3ms<br>חַסְדּוֹ<br>chasdô<br>his steadfast love | 583, 3176<br>cj, *n fs*, pn<br>וֶאֱמֶת־יְהוָה<br>we'ěmeth-yehwāh<br>and the reliability of Yahweh | 3937, 5986<br>prep, n ms<br>לְעוֹלָם<br>le'ôlām<br>unto eternity | 2054.333, 3161<br>v Piel impv 2mp, pn<br>הַלְלוּ־יָהּ<br>halelû-yāhh<br>praise Yah |
|---|---|---|---|---|

| **118:1** | 3142.533<br>v Hiphil impv 2mp<br>הוֹדוּ<br>hôdhû<br>praise | 3937, 3176<br>prep, pn<br>לַיהוָה<br>layhwāh<br>to Yahweh | 3706, 3005<br>cj, adj<br>כִּי־טוֹב<br>kî-ṯôv<br>because good | 3706<br>cj<br>כִּי<br>kî<br>because | 3937, 5986<br>prep, n ms<br>לְעוֹלָם<br>le'ôlām<br>unto eternity | 2721<br>n ms, ps 3ms<br>חַסְדּוֹ<br>chasdô<br>his steadfast love |
|---|---|---|---|---|---|---|

| **2.** | 569.121, 5167<br>v Qal juss 3ms, part<br>יֹאמַר־נָא<br>yō'mar-nā'<br>may they please say | 3547<br>pn<br>יִשְׂרָאֵל<br>yisrā'ēl<br>Israel | 3706<br>cj<br>כִּי<br>kî<br>that | 3937, 5986<br>prep, n ms<br>לְעוֹלָם<br>le'ôlām<br>unto eternity | 2721<br>n ms, ps 3ms<br>חַסְדּוֹ<br>chasdô<br>his steadfast love | **3.** | 569.126, 5167<br>v Qal juss 3mp, part<br>יֹאמְרוּ־נָא<br>yō'merû-nā'<br>may they please say |
|---|---|---|---|---|---|---|---|

| 1041, 172<br>*n ms*, pn<br>בֵית־אַהֲרֹן<br>vêth-'ahrōn<br>the household of Aaron | 3706<br>cj<br>כִּי<br>kî<br>that | 3937, 5986<br>prep, n ms<br>לְעוֹלָם<br>le'ôlām<br>unto eternity | 2721<br>n ms, ps 3ms<br>חַסְדּוֹ<br>chasdô<br>his steadfast love | **4.** | 569.126, 5167<br>v Qal juss 3mp, part<br>יֹאמְרוּ־נָא<br>yō'merû-nā'<br>may they please say |
|---|---|---|---|---|---|

| 3486.152<br>*v Qal act ptc mp*<br>יִרְאֵי<br>yir'ê<br>those who fear | 3176<br>pn<br>יְהוָה<br>yehwāh<br>Yahweh | 3706<br>cj<br>כִּי<br>kî<br>that | 3937, 5986<br>prep, n ms<br>לְעוֹלָם<br>le'ôlām<br>unto eternity | 2721<br>n ms, ps 3ms<br>חַסְדּוֹ<br>chasdô<br>his steadfast love | **5.** | 4623, 4873<br>prep, art, n ms<br>מִן־הַמֵּצַר<br>min-hammētsar<br>from the bondage | 7410.115<br>v Qal pf 1cs<br>קָרָאתִי<br>qārā'thî<br>I called to |
|---|---|---|---|---|---|---|---|

| 3161<br>pn<br>יָּהּ<br>yāhh<br>Yah | 6257.111<br>v Qal pf 3ms, ps 1cs<br>עָנָנִי<br>'ānānî<br>He answered me | 904, 4962<br>prep, art, n ms<br>בַמֶּרְחָב<br>vammerchāv<br>in the wide place | 3161<br>pn<br>יָהּ<br>yāhh<br>Yah | **6.** | 3176<br>pn<br>יְהוָה<br>yehwāh<br>Yahweh | 3937<br>prep, ps 1cs<br>לִי<br>lî<br>to me | 3940<br>neg part<br>לֹא<br>lō'<br>not | 3486.125<br>v Qal impf 1cs<br>אִירָא<br>'îrā'<br>I will be afraid |
|---|---|---|---|---|---|---|---|---|

| 4242, 6449.121<br>intrg, v Qal impf 3ms<br>מַה־יַּעֲשֶׂה<br>mah-ya'ăseh<br>what can he do | 3937<br>prep, ps 1cs<br>לִי<br>lî<br>to me | 119<br>n ms<br>אָדָם<br>'ādhām<br>a man | **7.** | 3176<br>pn<br>יְהוָה<br>yehwāh<br>Yahweh | 3937<br>prep, ps 1cs<br>לִי<br>lî<br>to me | 904, 6038.151<br>prep, v Qal act ptc ms, ps 1cs<br>בְּעֹזְרָי<br>be'ōzerāy<br>with the One Who helps me |
|---|---|---|---|---|---|---|

**117:1. O Praise the LORD, all ye nations: praise him, all ye people:** ... all you Gentiles! Laud Him, all you peoples!, *NKJV* ... laud him, all ye races, *Moffatt* ... let all the nations of the world do him honour, *Knox* ... extol him, all you peoples, *NIV.*

**2. For his merciful kindness is great toward us: and the truth of the LORD endureth for ever. Praise ye the LORD:** ... For mighty to us hath been His kindness, *Young* ... for his faithful love is strong and his constancy never-ending, *JB* ... For steadfast is his kindness toward us, *NAB.*

**118:1. O give thanks unto the LORD; for he is good: because his mercy endureth for ever:** ... his steadfast love endures forever!, *NRSV* ... for his kindness is eternal, *Anchor* ... his kindness never fails, *Moffatt* ... for his mercy is unchanging for ever, *BB.*

**2. Let Israel now say, that his mercy endureth for ever:** ... Declare it, house of Israel: his love endures for ever, *NEB* ... Let the House of Israel say, "His faithful love endures for ever,' *JB* ... That his kindness is everlasting, *Goodspeed*.

**3. Let the house of Aaron now say, that his mercy endureth for ever:** ... Aaron's family should say, 'He loves us forever,' *Beck* ... his lovingkindness endureth, *ASV* ... That His Mercy endures, *Fenton*.

**4. Let them now that fear the LORD say, that his mercy endureth for ever:** ... I pray you! let them who revere Yahweh say, *Rotherham* ... Let those who worship the LORD say, *Berkeley* ... Let those who respect the LORD say, *NCV*.

**5. I called upon the LORD in distress: the LORD answered me, and set me in a large place:** ... Out of my straits I called upon the LORD, *MAST* ... the LORD answered me and set me free, *RSV* ... In my anguish I cried to the LORD, and he answered by setting me free, *NIV* ... he answered me and gave me relief, *REB*.

**6. The LORD is on my side; I will not fear: what can man do unto me?:** ... What can mortals do to me?, *NRSV* ... People can't do anything to me, *NCV* ... what can human beings do to me?, *JB*.

**7. The LORD taketh my part with them that help me: therefore shall I see my desire upon them that hate me:** ... Yahweh is for me, my Great Warrior, *Anchor* ... I shall gaze in triumph on those who hate me, *Goodspeed* ... I shall see the downfall of my enemies, *REB* ... In victory I view those who hate me, *Beck*.

---

corruption. The historical limitations of God's manifestation to a special nation were means to its universal diffusion. The fire was gathered in a grate that it might warm the whole house. All men have a share in what God does for Israel. His grace was intended to fructify through it to all. The consciousness of being the special recipients of Yahweh's mercy was saved from abuse by being united with the consciousness of being endowed with blessing that they might diffuse blessing.

The psalmist's thought of what Israel's experience proclaimed concerning God's character is no less noteworthy. As often, steadfast love is united with faithfulness, which shines out in all God's dealings with his people. That steadfast love is "mighty over us"—the word used for being mighty (HED #1428) has the sense of prevailing, and so "where sin abounded, grace did much more abound." The permanence of the divine steadfast love is guaranteed by God's reliability, by which the fulfillment of every promise and the prolongation of every mercy are sealed to men. These two fair messengers have appeared in yet fairer form than the psalmist knew, and the world has to praise Yahweh for a worldwide gift, first bestowed on and rejected by a degenerate Israel, which thought that it owned the inheritance, and so lost it.

***Psalm 118.*** *Apparently, the Psalm falls into two halves, of which the former (vv. 1–16) seems to have been sung as a processional hymn while approaching the sanctuary, and the latter (vv. 17–29), partly at the Temple gates, partly by a chorus of priests within, and partly by the procession when it had entered. Every reader recognizes traces of antiphonal singing, but it is difficult to separate the parts with certainty. A clue may possibly be found by noting that verses marked by the occurrence of "I," "me" and "my" are mingled with others more impersonal. In the first part of the Psalm, we may suppose that a part of the procession sang the one and another portion the other series; while in the second part (vv. 17–29) the more personal verses were sung by the whole cortege arrived at the Temple, and the more generalized other part was taken by a chorus of priests or Levites within the sanctuary.*

**118:1–4.** First rings out from the full choir the summons to praise, which peculiarly belonged to the period of the restoration (Ezra 3:11; Pss. 106:1; 107:1). As in Ps. 115, three classes are called on: the whole house of Israel, the priests, and "those who fear Yahweh"—i.e., aliens who have taken refuge beneath the wings of Israel's God. The threefold designation expresses the thrill of joy in the recovery of national life; the high estimate of the priesthood as the only remaining God-appointed order, now that the monarchy was swept away; and the growing desire to draw the nations into the community of God's people.

**118:5–7.** Then, with v. 5, the single voice begins. His experience, now to be told, is the reason for the praise called for in the previous verses. It is the familiar sequence reiterated in many a Psalm and many a life—distress, or "a strait place" (Ps. 116:3), a cry to Yahweh, his answer by enlargement, and a consequent triumphant confidence, which has warrant in the past for believing that no hand can hurt him whom Yahweh's hand helps. Many a man passes through the psalmist's experience without thereby achieving the psalmist's settled faith and power to despise threatening calamities. We fail both in recounting clearly to

| 603 | 7495.125 | 904, 7983.152 | | 3005 | 3937, 2725.141 | 904, 3176 |
|---|---|---|---|---|---|---|
| cj, pers pron | v Qal impf 1cs | prep, v Qal act ptc mp, ps 1cs | **8.** | adj | prep, v Qal inf con | prep, pn |
| וַאֲנִי | אֶרְאֶה | בְשֹׂנְאָי | | טוֹב | לַחֲסוֹת | בַּיהוָה |
| wa'ănî | 'er'eh | v$^{e}$sōn$^{e}$'āy | | ṯôv | lachs̱ôth | bayhwāh |
| then I | I will see | over those who hate me | | better | to take refuge | in Yahweh |

| 4623, 1019.141 | 904, 119 | | 3005 | 3937, 2725.141 | 904, 3176 | 4623, 1019.141 | 904, 5259 |
|---|---|---|---|---|---|---|---|
| prep, v Qal inf con | prep, art, n ms | **9.** | adj | prep, v Qal inf con | prep, pn | prep, v Qal inf con | prep, n mp |
| מִבְּטֹחַ | בָּאָדָם | | טוֹב | לַחֲסוֹת | בַּיהוָה | מִבְּטֹחַ | בִּנְדִיבִים |
| mibb$^{e}$ṯōach | bā'ādhām | | ṯôv | lachs̱ôth | bayhwāh | mibb$^{e}$ṯōach | bindhîvîm |
| than to trust | in humankind | | better | to take refuge | in Yahweh | than to trust | in nobles |

| | 3725, 1504 | 5621.116 | 904, 8428 | 3176 | 3706 | 4271.525 |
|---|---|---|---|---|---|---|
| **10.** | *adj*, n mp | v Qal pf 3cp, ps 1cs | prep, *n ms* | pn | cj | v Hiphil impf 1cs, ps 3mp |
| | כָּל־גּוֹיִם | סְבָבוּנִי | בְּשֵׁם | יְהוָה | כִּי | אֲמִילַם |
| | kol-gôyim | s̱$^{e}$vāvûnî | b$^{e}$shēm | y$^{e}$hwāh | kî | 'ămîlam |
| | all the nations | they have surrounded me | in the name of | Yahweh | rather | I will cut them off |

| | 5621.116 | 1612, 5621.116 | 904, 8428 | 3176 | 3706 |
|---|---|---|---|---|---|
| **11.** | v Qal pf 3cp, ps 1cs | cj, v Qal pf 3cp, ps 1cs | prep, *n ms* | pn | cj |
| | סַבּוּנִי | גַם־סְבָבוּנִי | בְּשֵׁם | יְהוָה | כִּי |
| | s̱abbûnî | gham-s̱$^{e}$vāvûnî | b$^{e}$shēm | y$^{e}$hwāh | kî |
| | they have surrounded me | indeed they have surrounded me | in the name of | Yahweh | rather |

| 4271.525 | | 5621.116 | 3626, 1731 | 1906.416 |
|---|---|---|---|---|
| v Hiphil impf 1cs, ps 3mp | **12.** | v Qal pf 3cp, ps 1cs | prep, n fp | v Pual pf 3cp |
| אֲמִילַם | | סַבּוּנִי | כִדְבוֹרִים | דֹּעֲכוּ |
| 'ămîlam | | s̱abbûnî | khidhvôrîm | dō'ăkhû |
| I will cut them off | | they have surrounded me | like bees | they have been extinguished |

| 3626, 813 | 7259 | 904, 8428 | 3176 | 3706 | 4271.525 | | 1815.142 |
|---|---|---|---|---|---|---|---|
| prep, n fs | n mp | prep, *n ms* | pn | cj | v Hiphil impf 1cs, ps 3mp | **13.** | v Qal inf abs |
| כְּאֵשׁ | קוֹצִים | בְּשֵׁם | יְהוָה | כִּי | אֲמִילַם | | דַּחֹה |
| k$^{e}$'ēsh | qôtsîm | b$^{e}$shēm | y$^{e}$hwāh | kî | 'ămîlam | | dachōh |
| like a fire of | thornbushes | in the name of | Yahweh | because | I will cut them off | | pushing |

| 1815.113 | 3937, 5489.141 | 3176 | 6038.111 | | 6007 | 2257 |
|---|---|---|---|---|---|---|
| v Qal pf 2ms, ps 1cs | prep, v Qal inf con | cj, pn | v Qal pf 3ms, ps 1cs | **14.** | n ms, ps 1cs | cj, n fs |
| דְחִיתַנִי | לִנְפֹּל | וַיהוָה | עֲזָרָנִי | | עָזִּי | וְזִמְרָת |
| dh$^{e}$chîthanî | linpōl | wayhwāh | 'ăzārānî | | 'āzzî | w$^{e}$zimrāth |
| you shoved me | to falling | but Yahweh | He helped me | | my Strength | indeed Strength |

| 3161 | 2030.121, 3937 | 3937, 3568 | | 7249 | 7726 | 3568 | 904, 164 |
|---|---|---|---|---|---|---|---|
| pn | cj, v Qal impf 3ms, prep, ps 1cs | prep, n fs | **15.** | *n ms* | n fs | cj, n fs | prep, *n mp* |
| יָהּ | וַיְהִי־לִי | לִישׁוּעָה | | קוֹל | רִנָּה | וִישׁוּעָה | בְּאָהֳלֵי |
| yāhh | wayhî-lî | lîshû'āh | | qôl | rinnāh | wîshû'āh | b$^{e}$'āh$^{e}$lê |
| Yah | and He has become to me | for salvation | | the sound of | joy | and victory | in the tents of |

**8. It is better to trust in the LORD than to put confidence in man:** … It is better to rely on the LORD, *Berkeley* … It is better to take refuge in, *ASV* … than to trust in man, *NIV.*

**9. It is better to trust in the LORD than to put confidence in princes:** … have faith in the Lord than to put one's hope in rulers, *BB* … put confidence in nobles, *Darby* … Than to trust in princes, *NASB.*

**10. All nations compassed me about: but in the name of the LORD will I destroy them:** … The pagans all swarmed round me; I routed them, *Moffatt* … All nations hemmed me in, *KJVII* … in the name of the LORD I cut them off!, *RSV.*

**11. They compassed me about; yea, they compassed me about: but in the name of the LORD I will destroy them:** … I surely cut them off, *Young* … but with the LORD's power I defeated them, *NCV* … I cut off their foreskins, *Anchor.*

**12. They compassed me about like bees; they are quenched as the fire**

of thorns: for in the name of the LORD I will destroy them: ... but they died out as quickly as burning thorns, *NIV* ... they attack me, as fire attacks brushwood, *NEB* ... name of the LORD I will cut them off, *MRB*.

**13. Thou hast thrust sore at me that I might fall: but the LORD helped me:** ... You pushed me violently, that I might fall, *NKJV* ... Hard pressed, about to fall was I, *Berkeley* ... You pushed me violently so that I was falling, *NASB*.

**14. The LORD is my strength and song, and is become my salvation:** ... My strength and my courage is the Lord, and he has been my savior, *NCB* ... for he hath bene my deliuerance, *Geneva* ... he has been my Savior, *JB* ... He has saved me, *NCV*.

**15. The voice of rejoicing and salvation is in the tabernacles of the righteous: the right hand of the LORD doeth valiantly:** ... Shouts of deliverance in the camp of the victors!, *NEB* ... The right hand of the LORD has struck with power, *NAB* ... The LORD's right hand has done mighty things, *NIV* ... The LORD strengthens the hand of the Good, *Fenton*.

---

ourselves our deliverances and in drawing assurance from them for the future. Verse 5b is a pregnant construction. He "answered me in [or, into] an open place"—i.e., by bringing me into it. The contrast of a narrow gorge and a wide plain picturesquely expresses past restraints and present freedom of movement. Verse 6 is taken from Ps. 56:9, 11, and v. 7 is influenced by Ps. 54:4, reproducing the peculiar expression occurring there, "Yahweh is among my helpers," on which compare remarks on that passage.

**118:8–9.** Verses 8f are impersonal and generalize the experience of the preceding verses. They ring out loud, like a trumpet, and are the more intense for reiteration. Israel was but a feeble handful. The nation's very existence seemed to depend on the caprice of the protecting kings who had permitted the exiles' return. It had had bitter experience of the unreliableness of a monarch's whim. Now, with superb reliance, which was felt by the psalmist to be the true lesson of the immediate past, it peals out its choral confidence in Yahweh with a "heroism of faith which may well put us to the blush." These verses surpass the preceding in that they avow that faith in Yahweh makes men independent of human helpers, while the former verses declared that it makes superior to mortal foes. Fear of and confidence in man are both removed by trust in God. But it is perhaps harder to be weaned from the confidence than to rise above the fear.

**118:10–14.** The individual experience is resumed in vv. 10–14. The energetic reduplications strengthen the impression of multiplied attacks, corresponding with the facts of the restoration period. The same impression is accentuated by the use in v. 11a of two forms of the same verb, and in v. 12a by the metaphor of a swarm of angry bees (Deut. 1:44). Numerous, venomous, swift and hard to strike at as the enemies were, buzzing and stinging around, they were but insects after all, and a strong hand could crush them.

The psalmist does not merely look to God to interpose for him, as in vv. 6f, but expects that God will give him power to conquer by the use of his own strengthened arm. We are not only objects of divine protection, but organs of divine power. Trusting in the revealed character of Yahweh, we shall find conquering energy flowing into us from Him, and the most fierce assaults will die out as quickly as a fire of dry thorn twigs, which sinks into ashes the sooner the more it crackles and blazes.

Then the psalmist individualizes the multitude of foes, just as the collective Israel is individualized, and brings assailants and assailed down to two antagonists, engaged in desperate duel.

But a third Person intervenes. "The LORD helped me" (v. 13); as in old legends, the gods on their immortal steeds charged at the head of the hosts of their worshipers. Thus delivered, the singer breaks into the ancient strain, which had gone up on the shores of the sullen sea that rolled over Pharaoh's army and is still true after centuries have intervened: "The LORD is my strength and song, and is become my salvation." Miriam sang it, the restored exiles sang it, tried and trustful men in every age have sung and will sing it, until there are no more foes; and then, by the shores of the sea of glass mingled with fire, the calm victors will lift again the undying "song of Moses and of the Lamb."

**118:15–16.** Verses 15f are probably best taken as sung by the chorus, generalizing and giving voice to the emotions excited by the preceding verses. The same reiteration which characterized vv. 8f reappears here. Two broad truths are built on the individual voice's autobiography, namely, that trust in Yahweh and consequent conformity to his Law are never in vain, but always issue in joy; and that God's power, when put forth, always conquers.

| 6926 | 3332 | 3176 | 6449.153 | 2524 | | 3332 | 3176 |
|---|---|---|---|---|---|---|---|
| n mp | *n fs* | pn | v Qal act ptc fs | n ms | **16.** | *n fs* | pn |
| צַדִּיקִים | יְמִין | יְהוָה | עֹשָׂה | חָיִל | | יְמִין | יְהוָה |
| tsaddîqîm | yemîn | yehwāh | ‘ōsāh | chāyil | | yemîn | yehwāh |
| the righteous | the right hand of | Yahweh | executing | power | | the right hand of | Yahweh |

| 7597.312 | 3332 | 3176 | 6449.153 | 2524 | | 3940 | 4322.125 |
|---|---|---|---|---|---|---|---|
| v Polel pf 3fs | *n fs* | pn | v Qal act ptc fs | n ms | **17.** | neg part | v Qal impf 1cs |
| רוֹמֵמָה | יְמִין | יְהוָה | עֹשָׂה | חָיִל | | לֹא | אָמוּת |
| rômēmāh | yemîn | yehwāh | ‘ōsāh | chāyil | | lō’ | ’āmûth |
| it is raised high | the right hand of | Yahweh | executing | power | | not | I will die |

| 3706, 2513.125 | 5807.325 | 4801 | 3161 | | 3364.342 | 3364.311 |
|---|---|---|---|---|---|---|
| cj, v Qal impf 1cs | cj, v Piel impf 1cs | *n mp* | pn | **18.** | v Piel inf abs | v Piel pf 3ms, ps 1cs |
| כִּי־אֶחְיֶה | וַאֲסַפֵּר | מַעֲשֵׂי | יָהּ | | יַסֹּר | יִסְּרַנִּי |
| kî-’echăyeh | wa’ăsappēr | ma‘ăsê | yāhh | | yassōr | yisseranî |
| rather I will live | and I will recount | the works of | Yah | | rebuking | He thoroughly rebuked me |

| 3161 | 3937, 4323 | 3940 | 5598.111 | | 6858.133, 3937 |
|---|---|---|---|---|---|
| pn | cj, prep, art, n ms | neg part | v Qal pf 3ms, ps 1cs | **19.** | v Qal impv 2mp, prep, ps 1cs |
| יָהּ | וְלַמָּוֶת | לֹא | נְתָנָנִי | | פִּתְחוּ־לִי |
| yāhh | welammāweth | lō’ | nethānānî | | pithchû-lî |
| Yah | but to death | not | He has given me over | | open to me |

| 7881, 6926 | 971.125, 904 | 3142.525 | 3161 | | 2172, 7881 |
|---|---|---|---|---|---|
| *n mp*, n ms | v Qal impf 1cs, prep, ps 3mp | v Hiphil impf 1cs | pn | **20.** | dem pron, art, n ms |
| שַׁעֲרֵי־צֶדֶק | אָבֹא־בָם | אוֹדֶה | יָהּ | | זֶה־הַשַּׁעַר |
| sha‘ărê-tsedheq | ’āvō’-vām | ’ôdheh | yāhh | | zeh-hashsha‘ar |
| the gates of righteousness | I will enter into them | I will praise | Yah | | this the gate |

| 3937, 3176 | 6926 | 971.126 | 904 | | 3142.525 | 3706 |
|---|---|---|---|---|---|---|
| prep, pn | n mp | v Qal impf 3mp | prep, ps 3ms | **21.** | v Hiphil impf 1cs, ps 2ms | cj |
| לַיהוָה | צַדִּיקִים | יָבֹאוּ | בוֹ | | אוֹדְךָ | כִּי |
| layhwāh | tsaddîqîm | yāvō’û | vô | | ’ôdhkhā | kî |
| to Yahweh | the righteous | they will enter | into it | | I will praise You | because |

| 6257.113 | 2030.123, 3937 | 3937, 3568 | | 63 | 4128.116 |
|---|---|---|---|---|---|
| v Qal pf 2ms, ps 1cs | cj, v Qal impf 2ms, prep, ps 1cs | prep, n fs | **22.** | n fs | v Qal pf 3cp |
| עֲנִיתָנִי | וַתְּהִי־לִי | לִישׁוּעָה | | אֶבֶן | מָאֲסוּ |
| ‘ănîthānî | wattehî-lî | lîshû‘āh | | ’even | mā’ăsû |
| You have answered me | and You have become to me | for salvation | | a stone | they rejected |

| 1161.152 | 2030.112 | 3937, 7513 | 6682 | | 4623, 881 | 3176 | 2030.112 |
|---|---|---|---|---|---|---|---|
| art, v Qal act ptc mp | v Qal pf 3fs | prep, *n ms* | n fs | **23.** | prep, do | pn | v Qal pf 3fs |
| הַבּוֹנִים | הָיְתָה | לְרֹאשׁ | פִּנָּה | | מֵאֵת | יְהוָה | הָיְתָה |
| habbônîm | hāyethāh | lerō’sh | pinnāh | | mē’ēth | yehwāh | hāyethāh |
| the builders | it has become | for the top of | the corner | | from | Yahweh | it is |

**16. The right hand of the LORD is exalted: the right hand of the LORD doeth valiantly:** … right hand of the LORD works victoriously, *Goodspeed* … hand of the LORD is lifted up; the right hand of the LORD does mighty things, *KJVII* … The LORD's right-hand makes strong, *Fenton.*

**17. I shall not die, but live, and declare the works of the LORD:** … and recount the deeds of the LORD, *NRSV* … and I will tell what the LORD has done, *NCV* … I will give out the story of the works of the Lord, *BB* … and tell of the LORD's deeds, *Berkeley.*

**18. The LORD hath chastened me sore: but he hath not given me over unto death:** … but he did not surrender me to Death, *NEB* … yet he has not delivered me to death, *NCB.*

**19. Open to me the gates of righteousness: I will go into them, and I will praise the LORD:** … and give thanks to the LORD, *RSV* … Open to me the gates of justice, *NAB* … Open for me the gates of saving justice, *JB.*

**20. This gate of the LORD, into which the righteous shall enter:** ... 'Here is the Eternal's gate; the just alone can enter,' *Moffatt* ... the victors will enter through it, *REB* ... let the triumphant enter it!, *Anchor.*

**21. I will praise thee: for thou hast heard me, and art become my salvation:** ... will give you thanks, for you answered me, *NIV* ... and hast become my deliverer, *Berkeley* ... become my deliverance, *Goodspeed.*

**22. The stone which the builders refused is become the head stone of the corner:** ... the builders rejected Is become the head of the corner, *ASV* ... A Stone by the builders despised, Has gone to the head of the Spire!, *Fenton* ... builders rejected became the cornerstone, *Anchor* ... Has become the chief cornerstone, *NKJV.*

**23. This is the LORD's doing; it is marvellous in our eyes:** ... Yahweh's doing, and we marvel at it, *JB* ... we can but watch and wonder, *Moffatt* ... what a wonderful sight it is!, *Good News* ... and it is wonderful to us, *NCV.*

---

"The tents of the righteous" may possibly allude to the "tabernacles" constructed for the feast, at which the song was probably sung.

**118:17–19.** Verses 17ff belong to the individual voice. The procession has reached the Temple. Deeper thoughts than before now mark the retrospect of past trial and deliverance. Both are recognized to be from Yahweh. It is He Who has corrected, severely indeed, but still "in measure, not to bring to nothing, but to make capable and recipient of fuller life." The enemy thrust sore, with intent to make Israel fall; but God's strokes are meant to make us stand the firmer. It is beautiful that all thought of human foes has faded away, and God only is seen in all the sorrow. But his chastisement has wider purposes than individual blessedness. It is intended to make its objects the heralds of his name to the world. Israel is beginning to lay to heart more earnestly its worldwide vocation to "declare the works of Yahweh." The imperative obligation of all who have received delivering help from Him is to become missionaries of his name. The reed is cut and pared thin and bored with hot irons, and the very pith of it extracted, that it may be fit to be put to the owner's lips and give out music from his breath. Thus, conscious of its vocation and eager to render its due of sacrifice and praise, Israel asks that "the gates of righteousness" may be opened for the entrance of the long procession. The temple doors are so called, because righteousness is the condition of entrance (Isa. 26:2; cf. Ps. 24).

**118:20.** Verse 20 may belong to the individual voice, but is perhaps better taken as the answer, from within the Temple, of the priests or Levites who guarded the closed doors and who now proclaim what must be the character of those who would tread the sacred courts. The gate (not, as in v. 19, "gates") belongs to Yahweh, and therefore access by it is permitted to none but the righteous. That is an everlasting truth. It is possible to translate, "This is the gate of the Lord"—i.e., by which one comes to his presence; and that rendering would bring out still more emphatically the necessity of the condition laid down: "Without holiness no man shall see the LORD."

**118:21.** The condition is supposed to be met; for in v. 21, the individual voice again breaks into thanksgiving, for being allowed once more to stand in the house of Yahweh. The psalmist now says, "Thou hast heard me," although he had already sung that the LORD had answered him (v. 5). And he sings, "And art become my salvation," although he had already hailed Yahweh as having become such (v. 14). God's deliverance is not complete until full communion with Him is enjoyed. Dwelling in his house is the crown of all his blessings. We are set free from enemies, from sins and fears and struggles, that we may abide forever with Him, and only then do we realize the full sweetness of his redeeming hand, when we stand in his presence and commune evermore with Him.

**118:22–23.** Verses 22ff probably belong to the priestly chorus. They set forth the great truth made manifest by restored Israel's presence in the rebuilt Temple. The metaphor is suggested by the incidents connected with the rebuilding. The "stone" is obviously Israel—weak, contemptible, but now once more laid as the very foundation stone of God's house in the world. The broad truth taught by its history is that God lays as the basis of his building—i.e., uses for the execution of his purposes—that which the wisdom of man despises and tosses aside. The general truth contained here is that of Paul's great saying, "God hath chosen the weak things of the world that He might put to shame the things that are strong." It is the constant law, not because God chooses unfit instruments, but because the world's estimates of fitness are false, and the qualities which it admires are irrelevant with regard to his designs, while the requisite qualities are of another sort altogether. Therefore, it is a law which

| 2148 | 2026 | 6623.257 | 904, 6084 | | 2172, 3219 | 6449.111 | 3176 |
|---|---|---|---|---|---|---|---|
| dem pron | pers pron | v Niphal ptc fs | prep, n fd, ps 1cp | 24. | dem pron, art, n ms | v Qal pf 3ms | pn |
| זֹאת | הִיא | נִפְלָאת | בְּעֵינֵינוּ | | זֶה־הַיּוֹם | עָשָׂה | יְהוָה |
| zō'th | hî' | niphlā'th | be'ênênû | | zeh-hayyôm | 'āsāh | yehwāh |
| this | it | an extraordinary deed | in our eyes | | this the day | He made | Yahweh |

| 1559.120 | 7975.120 | 904 | | 588 | 3176 | 3588.531 | 5167 |
|---|---|---|---|---|---|---|---|
| v Qal juss 1cp | cj, v Qal juss 1cp | prep, ps 3ms | 25. | part | pn | v Hiphil impv 2ms | part |
| נָגִילָה | וְנִשְׂמְחָה | בוֹ | | אָנָּא | יְהוָה | הוֹשִׁיעָה | נָּא |
| nāghîlāh | wenismechāh | vô | | 'ānnā' | yehwāh | hôshî'āh | nā' |
| let us rejoice | and let us be glad | in it | | please | O Yahweh | save | please |

| 588 | 3176 | 7014.531 | 5167 | | 1313.155 | 971.151 | 904, 8428 |
|---|---|---|---|---|---|---|---|
| part | pn | v Hiphil impv 2ms | part | 26. | v Qal pass ptc ms | art, v Qal act ptc ms | prep, *n ms* |
| אָנָּא | יְהוָה | הַצְלִיחָה | נָּא | | בָּרוּךְ | הַבָּא | בְּשֵׁם |
| 'ānnā' | yehwāh | hatslîchāh | nā' | | bārûkh | habbā' | beshēm |
| please | O Yahweh | cause to succeed | please | | blessed | the one entering | in the name of |

| 3176 | 1313.319 | 4623, 1041 | 3176 | | 418 | 3176 |
|---|---|---|---|---|---|---|
| pn | v Piel pf 1cp, ps 2mp | prep, *n ms* | pn | 27. | n ms | pn |
| יְהוָה | בֵּרַכְנוּכֶם | מִבֵּית | יְהוָה | | אֵל | יְהוָה |
| yehwāh | bērakhnûkhem | mibbêth | yehwāh | | 'ēl | yehwāh |
| Yahweh | we bless you | from the Temple of | Yahweh | | God | Yahweh |

| 213.521 | 3937 | 646.133, 2374 | 904, 5895 | 5912, 7451 |
|---|---|---|---|---|
| cj, v Hiphil impf 3ms | prep, ps 1cp | v Qal impv 2mp, n ms | prep, n mp | prep, *n fp* |
| וַיָּאֶר | לָנוּ | אִסְרוּ־חַג | בַּעֲבֹתִים | עַד־קַרְנוֹת |
| wayyā'er | lānû | 'isrû-chagh | ba'ăvōthîm | 'adh-qarnôth |
| and He has illuminated | us | bind the festive procession | with ropes | onto the horns of |

| 4326 | | 418 | 887 | 3142.525 | 435 | 7597.325 |
|---|---|---|---|---|---|---|
| art, n ms | 28. | n ms, ps 1cs | pers pron | cj, v Hiphil impf 1cs, ps 2ms | n mp, ps 1cs | v Polel juss 1cs, ps 2ms |
| הַמִּזְבֵּחַ | | אֵלִי | אַתָּה | וְאוֹדֶךָּ | אֱלֹהַי | אֲרוֹמְמֶךָּ |
| hammizbēach | | 'ēlî | 'attāh | we'ôdhekhā | 'ĕlōhay | 'ărômemekhā |
| the altar | | my God | You | so I will praise You | my God | let me exalt You |

| | 3142.533 | 3937, 3176 | 3706, 3005 | 3706 | 3937, 5986 | 2721 |
|---|---|---|---|---|---|---|
| 29. | v Hiphil impv 2mp | prep, pn | cj, adj | cj | prep, n ms | n ms, ps 3ms |
| | הוֹדוּ | לַיהוָה | כִּי־טוֹב | כִּי | לְעוֹלָם | חַסְדּוֹ |
| | hôdhû | layhwāh | kî-ṭôv | kî | le'ôlām | chasdô |
| | praise | to Yahweh | because good | because | unto eternity | his steadfast love |

**24. This is the day which the LORD hath made; we will rejoice and be glad in it:** ... the day one which the LORD has acted, a day for us to exult and rejoice, *REB* ... let us rejoice and be glad in Him, *Beck* ... We will be full of joy and delight in it, *BB*.

**25. Save now, I beseech thee, O LORD: O LORD, I beseech thee, send now prosperity:** ... O LORD, grant us success, *NIV* ... Ah now Yahweh do send success, *Rotherham* ... make us now to prosper!, *MAST* ... send blessings now, *KJVII*.

**26. Blessed be he that cometh in the name of the LORD: we have blessed you out of the house of the LORD:** ... Blessed be he that entereth in the name, *MRB* ... We bless all of you from the Temple of the LORD, *NCV* ... A blessing from the Lord's house upon your company!, *Knox*.

**27. God is the LORD, which hath shown us light: bind the sacrifice with cords, even unto the horns of the altar:** ... Who is LIFE, Who gives to us life, *Fenton* ... adorn the horns of the altar, *Anchor* ... Join in procession with leafy boughs up to the horns of the altar, *NAB* ... Bind the festal procession with branches, *NRSV*.

**28. Thou art my God, and I will praise thee: thou art my God, I will exalt thee:** ... you are my God, and I will praise your greatness, *NCV* ... all praise to you, my God, *JB* ... my God, I honor You highly, *Beck* ...You are my God and I will give you thanks, *NIV*.

**29. O give thanks unto the LORD; for he is good: for his mercy endureth for ever:** ... for his love endures for ever, *NEB* ... for his

finds its highest exemplification in the foundation for God's true Temple, other than that which can no man lay. Israel is not only a figure of Christ—there is an organic unity between Him and them. Whatever, therefore, is true of Israel in a lower sense is true in its highest sense of Christ. Israel praised God in the gates of righteousness; the rejected Stone made the capstone is He Who was indeed rejected of men, but chosen of God and precious, the capstone of the living temple of the redeemed" (1 Pet. 2:4–8).

**118:24.** Verse 24 is best regarded as the continuation of the choral praise in vv. 22f. "The day" is that of the festival now in process, the joyful culmination of God's manifold deliverances. It is a day in which joy is duty, and no heart has a right to be too heavy to leap for gladness. Many of the jubilant worshipers no doubt had plenty of private sorrows, but the sight of the stone laid as the head of the corner should bring joy even to such. If sadness was ingratitude and almost treason, then what sorrow should now be so dense that it cannot be pierced by the light which lighteth every man? The joy of the LORD should float, like oil on stormy waves, above our troublesome sorrows and smooth their tossing.

**118:25.** Again, the single voice rises, not now in thanksgiving, as might have been expected, but in plaintive tones of earnest imploring (v. 25). Standing in the sanctuary, Israel is conscious of its perils, its need, its weakness, and so with pathetic reiteration of the particle of entreaty, which occurs twice in each clause of the verse, cries for continued deliverance from continuing evils and for prosperity in the course opening before it. The "day" in which unmingled gladness inspires our songs has not yet dawned, fair as are the many days which Yahweh has made. In the earthly house of the LORD, thanksgiving must ever pass into petition. An unending day comes when there will be nothing to dread and no need for the sadder notes occasioned by felt weakness and feared foes.

**118:26.** Verses 26f come from the chorus of priests, who welcome the entering procession and solemnly pronounce on them the benediction of Yahweh. They answer, in his name, the prayer of v. 25, and bless the single leader of the procession and the multitudes following. The use of "blessed" in v. 26a and of the "hosanna" (HED #3588, an attempted transliteration of the Hebrew "Save I beseech") from v. 25 at Christ's entrance into Jerusalem probably shows that the Psalm was regarded as messianic. It is so, in virtue of the relation already referred to between Israel and Christ. He "cometh in the name of Yahweh" in a deeper sense than did Israel, the servant of the LORD.

**118:27.** Verse 27a recalls the priestly benediction (Num. 6:25) and thankfully recognizes its ample fulfillment in Israel's history and especially in the dawning of new prosperity now. Verse 27b is difficult. Obviously, it should be a summons to worship, as thanksgiving for the benefits acknowledged in the first part of the verse. But the act of worship intended is hard to say. The rendering "Bind the sacrifice with cords, unto the horns of the altar" has against it the usual meaning of the word rendered sacrifice, which is rather festival, and the fact that the last words of the verse cannot possibly be translated "to the horns," etc., but must mean "as far as" or "even up to the horns," etc. There must, therefore, be a good deal supplied in the sentence, and commentators differ as to how to fill the gap. The verb rendered "bind" (HED #646) is used in 1 Ki. 20:14; 2 Chr. 13:3, in a sense which fits well with "procession" here—i.e., that of marshaling an army for battle. If this meaning is adopted, the middle part of the verse will be the summons to order the bough-bearing procession and the last part a call to march onward so as to encircle the altar. This meaning of the obscure verse may be provisionally accepted, while owning that our ignorance of the ceremonial referred to prevents complete under standing of the words.

**118:28–29.** Once more, Miriam's song supplies ancient language of praise for recent mercies, and the personified Israel compasses the altar with thanksgiving (v. 28). Then the whole multitude, both of those who had come up to the Temple and of those who had welcomed them there, join in the chorus of praise with which the Psalm begins and ends, and which was so often pealed forth in those days of early joy for the new manifestations of that steadfast love which endures through all days, both those of past evil and those of future, hoped-for good.

***Psalm 119.*** *The one thought pervading this Psalm is the surpassing excellence of the Law. The beauty and power of the Psalm lie in the unwearied reiteration of that single idea. There is music in its refrains, which is subtly varied. One or another of the usual synonyms for God's instructions to his people, including "law," "saying," "statutes," "commandments," "testimonies" and "judgments" occurs in every verse, except vv. 122 and 132. The prayers "Teach me," "Revive me," "Preserve me according*

| 119:1 | 869<br>n mp<br>אַשְׁרֵי<br>'ashrê<br>blessed | 8879, 1932<br>n mp, n ms<br>תְמִימֵי־דָרֶךְ<br>themîmê-dhārekh<br>those blameless of ways | 2050.152<br>art, v Qal act ptc mp<br>הַהֹלְכִים<br>hahōlekhîm<br>those walking | 904, 8784<br>prep, n fs<br>בְּתוֹרַת<br>bethôrath<br>in the Law of | 3176<br>pn<br>יְהוָה<br>yehwāh<br>Yahweh | 2. | 869<br>n mp<br>אַשְׁרֵי<br>'ashrê<br>blessed |
|---|---|---|---|---|---|---|---|

| 5526.152<br>v Qal act ptc mp<br>נֹצְרֵי<br>nōtserê<br>those who keep | 5959<br>n fp, ps 3ms<br>עֵדֹתָיו<br>'ēdhōthâv<br>his testimonies | 904, 3725, 3949<br>prep, adj, n ms<br>בְּכָל־לֵב<br>bekhol-lēv<br>with all the heart | 1938.126<br>v Qal impf 3mp, ps 3ms<br>יִדְרְשׁוּהוּ<br>yidhreshûhû<br>they search for Him | 3. | 652<br>cj<br>אַף<br>'aph<br>also |
|---|---|---|---|---|---|

| 3940, 6713.116<br>neg part, v Qal pf 3cp<br>לֹא־פָעֲלוּ<br>lō'-phā'ălû<br>they do not practice | 5983<br>n fs<br>עַוְלָה<br>'awlāh<br>wrongdoing | 904, 1932<br>prep, n mp, ps 3ms<br>בִּדְרָכָיו<br>bidhrākhâv<br>in his ways | 2050.116<br>v Qal pf 3cp<br>הָלָכוּ<br>hālākhû<br>they walk | 4. | 887<br>pers pron<br>אַתָּה<br>'attāh<br>You | 6943.313<br>v Piel pf 2ms<br>צִוִּיתָה<br>tsiwwîthāh<br>You have commanded |
|---|---|---|---|---|---|---|

| 6740<br>n mp, ps 2ms<br>פִקֻּדֶיךָ<br>phiqqudhêkhā<br>your precepts | 3937, 8490.141<br>prep, v Qal inf con<br>לִשְׁמֹר<br>lishmōr<br>to observe | 4108<br>adv<br>מְאֹד<br>me'ōdh<br>very | 5. | 305<br>intrj<br>אַחֲלַי<br>'achlay<br>oh that | 3679.226<br>v Niphal impf 3mp<br>יִכֹּנוּ<br>yikkōnû<br>they would be established | 1932<br>n mp, ps 1cs<br>דְרָכָי<br>dherākhāy<br>my ways |
|---|---|---|---|---|---|---|

| 3937, 8490.141<br>prep, v Qal inf con<br>לִשְׁמֹר<br>lishmōr<br>to observe | 2805<br>n mp, ps 2ms<br>חֻקֶּיךָ<br>chuqqêkhā<br>your statutes | 6. | 226<br>adv<br>אָז<br>'āz<br>then | 3940, 991.125<br>neg part, v Qal impf 1cs<br>לֹא־אֵבוֹשׁ<br>lō'-'ēvôsh<br>I will not be ashamed | 904, 5202.541<br>prep, v Hiphil inf con, ps 1cs<br>בְּהַבִּיטִי<br>behabbîṭî<br>when my looking |
|---|---|---|---|---|---|

| 420, 3725, 4851<br>prep, adj, n fp, ps 2ms<br>אֶל־כָּל־מִצְוֹתֶיךָ<br>'el-kol-mitsôthêkhā<br>to all your commandments | 7. | 3142.525<br>v Hiphil juss 1cs, ps 2ms<br>אוֹדְךָ<br>'ôdhkhā<br>let me praise You | 904, 3596<br>prep, adj<br>בְּיֹשֶׁר<br>beyōsher<br>with the upright of | 3949<br>n ms<br>לֵבָב<br>lēvāv<br>heart | 904, 4064.141<br>prep, v Qal inf con, ps 1cs<br>בְּלָמְדִי<br>belāmedhî<br>when my learning |
|---|---|---|---|---|---|

| 5122<br>n mp<br>מִשְׁפְּטֵי<br>mishpeṭê<br>the ordinances of | 6928<br>n ms, ps 2ms<br>צִדְקֶךָ<br>tsidhqekhā<br>your righteousness | 8. | 881, 2805<br>do, n mp, ps 2ms<br>אֶת־חֻקֶּיךָ<br>'eth-chuqqêkhā<br>your statutes | 8490.125<br>v Qal impf 1cs<br>אֶשְׁמֹר<br>'eshmōr<br>I will observe | 414, 6013.123<br>adv, v Qal juss 2ms, ps 1cs<br>אַל־תַּעַזְבֵנִי<br>'al-ta'azvēnî<br>do not abandon me |
|---|---|---|---|---|---|

| 5912, 4108<br>adv, adv<br>עַד־מְאֹד<br>'adh-me'ōdh<br>until very | 9. | 904, 4242<br>prep, art, intrg<br>בַּמֶּה<br>bammeh<br>by what | 2218.321, 5470<br>v Piel impf 3ms, n ms<br>יְזַכֶּה־נַּעַר<br>yezakkeh-na'ar<br>can a young man make pure | 881, 758<br>do, n ms, ps 3ms<br>אֶת־אָרְחוֹ<br>'eth-'ārechô<br>his path | 3937, 8490.141<br>prep, v Qal inf con<br>לִשְׁמֹר<br>lishmōr<br>to observe |
|---|---|---|---|---|---|

kindness endures forever, *NCB* ... For His lovingkindness is everlasting, *NASB* ... for his mercy is unchanging for ever, *BB*.

**119:1. ALEPH. Blessed are the undefiled in the way, who walk in the law of the LORD:** ... How happy the men of blameless life, *Rotherham* ... O the happiness of those perfect in the way, *Young* ... blessed they, who pass through life's journey unstained, *Knox* ... Happy are those whose lives are innocent, *Beck*.

**2. Blessed are they that keep his testimonies, and that seek him with the whole heart:** ... How happy are they who keep his decrees, *Goodspeed* ... Happy are they who obey his instruction, *REB* ... giving him undivided hearts, *Moffatt* ... who try to obey him with their whole heart, *NCV*.

**3. They also do no iniquity: they walk in his ways:** ... they do no unrighteousness, *MAST* ... who also do no wrong, *RSV* ... They do no evil; they go in his ways, *BB* ... For they practice no vices, *Fenton.*

**4. Thou hast commanded us to keep thy precepts diligently:** ... That we should observe them diligently, *ASV* ... You lay down your precepts to be carefully kept, *JB* ... hast laid down thy precepts for men to keep them faithfully, *NEB.*

**5. O that my ways were directed to keep thy statutes!:** ... that my ways may be established, *Berkeley* ... my ways were steadfast in obeying your decrees!, *NIV* ... how shall my steps be surely guided to keep faith with thy covenant?, *Knox* ... how I want my life to conform to Your laws, *Beck.*

**6. Then shall I not be ashamed, when I have respect unto all thy commandments:** ... having my eyes fixed on all your commandments, *NRSV* ... Then I should not be humiliated, if I gazed upon all your commandments, *Anchor* ... if I set my eyes on all Your commandments, *Beck* ... Attentive to all thy commandments, I go my way undismayed, *Knox.*

**7. I will praise thee with uprightness of heart, when I shall have learned thy righteous judgments:** ... learned your just ordinances, *NAB* ... praise thee in sincerity of heart as I learn thy just decrees, *NEB* ... I will give thanks to Thee with integrity of heart, *Berkeley* ... learned thy righteous regulations, *Rotherham.*

**8. I will keep thy statutes: O forsake me not utterly:** ... Your Decrees I will keep, so forsake me not ever, *Fenton* ... I will obey your demands, so please don't ever leave me, *NCV* ... I shall do your will; do not ever abandon me wholly, *JB.*

---

*to thy word," and the vows "I will keep," "observe," "meditate on" and "delight in thy Law" are frequently repeated. There are but few pieces in the psalmist's kaleidoscope, but they fall into many shapes of beauty; and although all his sentences are molded after the same general plan, the variety within such narrow limits is equally a witness of poetic power which turns the fetters of the acrostic structure into helps, and of devout heartfelt love for the Law of Yahweh. The Psalm is probably of later date; but its allusions to the singer's circumstances, whether they are taken as autobiographical or as having reference to the nation, are too vague to be used as clues to the period of its composition. The elaborate acrostic plan and the praises of the Law naturally suggest a time when it was familiar in an approximately complete form. It may be that the rulers referred to in vv. 23, 46 were foreigners, but the expression is too general to draw a conclusion from. It may be that the double-minded (v. 113) who err from God's statutes (v. 118) and forsake his Law (v. 53) are Israelites who have yielded to the temptations to apostatize. But these expressions, too, are of so general a nature that they do not give clear testimony of date.*

**119:1–8.** The first three verses are closely connected. They set forth in general terms the elements of the blessedness of the doers of the Law. To walk in it—to order the active life in conformity with its requirements—ensures perfectness. To keep God's testimonies is at once the consequence and the proof of seeking Him with wholehearted devotion and determination. To walk in his ways is the preservative from evildoing. And such men cannot but be blessed with a deep sacred blessedness, which puts to shame coarse and turbulent delights and feeds its pure fires from God himself.

Whether these verses are taken as exclamation or declaration, they lead up naturally to v. 4, which reverently gazes upon the loving act of God in the revelation of his will in the Law and bethinks itself of the obligations bound on us by that act. It is of God's mercy that He has commanded, and his words are meant to sway our wills, since He has broken the awful silence, not merely to instruct us, but to command; and nothing short of practical obedience will discharge our duties to his revelation. So the psalmist betakes himself to prayer, that he may be helped to realize the purpose of God in giving the Law.

His contemplation of the blessedness of obedience and of the divine act of declaring his will moves him to longing, and his consciousness of weakness and wavering makes the longing into prayer that his wavering may be consolidated into fixity of purpose and continuity of obedience. When a man's ways are established to observe, they will be established by observing God's statutes. For nothing can put to the blush one whose eye is directed to these. "Whatever record leap to light, He never shall be shamed." Nor will he cherish hopes that fail, nor desires that, when accomplished, are bitter of taste. To give heed to the commandments is the condition of learning them and recognizing how righteous they are; and such learning makes the learner's heart righteous like them and causes it to run over in thankfulness for the boon of knowledge of God's will.

By all these thoughts, the psalmist is brought to his fixed resolve in v. 8 to do what God meant him to do when He gave the Law and what the

| 3626, 1745 | | 904, 3725, 3949 | 1938.115 | 414, 8146.523 |
|---|---|---|---|---|
| prep, n ms, ps 2ms | **10.** | prep, *adj*, n ms, ps 1cs | v Qal pf 1cs, ps 2ms | adv, v Hiphil juss 2ms, ps 1cs |
| כִּדְבָרֶךָ | | בְּכָל־לִבִּי | דְרַשְׁתִּיךָ | אַל־תַּשְׁגֵּנִי |
| kidhvārekhā | | bekhol-libbî | dherashtîkhā | 'al-tashgēnî |
| according to your word | | with all my heart | I have inquired about You | do not let me go astray |

| 4623, 4851 | | 904, 3949 | 7121.115 | 577 | 3937, 4775 | 3940 |
|---|---|---|---|---|---|---|
| prep, n fp, ps 2ms | **11.** | prep, n ms, ps 1cs | v Qal pf 1cs | n fs, ps 2ms | prep, prep | neg part |
| מִמִּצְוֺתֶיךָ | | בְּלִבִּי | צָפַנְתִּי | אִמְרָתֶךָ | לְמַעַן | לֹא |
| mimmitswōthêkhā | | belibbî | tsāphantî | 'imrāthekhā | lema'an | lō' |
| from your commandments | | in my heart | I have stored | your word | so that | not |

| 2490.125, 3937 | | 1313.155 | 887 | 3176 | 4064.331 | 2805 |
|---|---|---|---|---|---|---|
| v Qal impf 1cs, prep, ps 2ms | **12.** | v Qal pass ptc ms | pers pron | pn | v Piel impv 2ms, ps 1cs | n mp, ps 2ms |
| אֶחֱטָא־לָךְ | | בָּרוּךְ | אַתָּה | יְהוָה | לַמְּדֵנִי | חֻקֶּיךָ |
| 'echĕṭā'-lākh | | bārûkh | 'attāh | yehwāh | lammedhēnî | chuqqêkhā |
| I will sin against You | | blessed | You | O Yahweh | teach me | your statutes |

| | 904, 8004 | 5807.315 | 3725 | 5122, 6552 | | 904, 1932 |
|---|---|---|---|---|---|---|
| **13.** | prep, n fd, ps 1cs | v Piel pf 1cs | adj | *n mp*, n ms, ps 2ms | **14.** | prep, *n ms* |
| | בִּשְׂפָתַי | סִפַּרְתִּי | כֹּל | מִשְׁפְּטֵי־פִיךָ | | בְּדֶרֶךְ |
| | bisphāthay | sippartî | kōl | mishpetê-phîkhā | | bedherekh |
| | with my lips | I have recounted | all | the ordinances of your mouth | | in the way of |

| 5959 | 7919.115 | 3626, 6142 | 3725, 2019 | | 904, 6740 | 7943.125 |
|---|---|---|---|---|---|---|
| n fp, ps 2ms | v Qal pf 1cs | prep, prep | *adj*, n ms | **15.** | prep, n mp, ps 2ms | v Qal juss 1cs |
| עֵדְוֺתֶיךָ | שַׂשְׂתִּי | כְּעַל | כָּל־הוֹן | | בְּפִקֻּדֶיךָ | אָשִׂיחָה |
| 'ēdhewōthêkhā | sastî | ke'al | kol-hôn | | bephiqqudhêkhā | 'āsîchāh |
| your testimonies | I have rejoiced | according to | all riches | | on your precepts | may I ponder |

| 5202.525 | 758 | | 904, 2807 | 8551.725 | 3940 | 8319.125 |
|---|---|---|---|---|---|---|
| cj, v Hiphil juss 1cs | n mp, ps 2ms | **16.** | prep, n fp, ps 2ms | v Hithpalpel impf 1cs | neg part | v Qal impf 1cs |
| וְאַבִּיטָה | אֹרְחֹתֶיךָ | | בְּחֻקֹּתֶיךָ | אֶשְׁתַּעֲשָׁע | לֹא | אֶשְׁכַּח |
| we'abbîṭāh | 'ōrechōthêkhā | | bechuqqōthêkhā | 'eshta'ăshā' | lō' | 'eshkach |
| and may I look on | your paths | | in your statutes | I delight | not | I can forget |

| 1745 | | 1621.131 | 6142, 5860 | 2513.125 | 8490.125 | 1745 |
|---|---|---|---|---|---|---|
| n ms, ps 2ms | **17.** | v Qal impv 2ms | prep, n ms, ps 2ms | v Qal juss 1cs | cj, v Qal juss 1cs | n ms, ps 2ms |
| דְּבָרֶךָ | | גְּמֹל | עַל־עַבְדְּךָ | אֶחְיֶה | וְאֶשְׁמְרָה | דְבָרֶךָ |
| devārekhā | | gemōl | 'al-'avdekhā | 'echăyeh | we'eshmerāh | dhevārekhā |
| your word | | requite | concerning your servant | let me live | that I may observe | your word |

**9. BETH. Wherewithal shall a young man cleanse his way? by taking heed thereto according to thy word:** ... How shall a young man be faultless in his way?, *NCB* ... How can young people keep their way pure?, *NRSV* ... keep his way pure? By living according to your word, *NIV* ... By guarding it according to thy word, *RSV*.

**10. With my whole heart have I sought thee: O let me not wander from thy commandments:** ... With all my heart I strive to find thee; let me not stray, *NEB* ... I have made search for you with all my heart, *BB* ... never may I stray from thy control!, *Moffatt*.

**11. Thy word have I hid in mine heart, that I might not sin against thee:** ... I treasure your promise in my heart, *REB* ... Buried deep in my heart, thy warnings shall keep me clear of sin, *Knox* ... Thy word have I stored up in my heart, *Berkeley* ... I have kept your sayings secretly in my heart, *BB*.

**12. Blessed art thou, O LORD: teach me thy statutes:** ... teach me Your laws, *Beck* ... teach me thy will, *Moffatt* ... LORD, you should be praised. Teach me your demands, *NCV* ... LORD You should be thanked, for You taught me Your Statutes, *Fenton*.

**13. With my lips have I declared all the judgments of thy mouth:** ... lips have I told All the ordinances of Thy mouth, *MAST* ... lips I recount all the laws that come from your mouth, *NIV* ... lips have I recounted All the regulations of thy mouth, *Rotherham*.

**14. I have rejoiced in the way of thy testimonies, as much as in all riches:** ... In the way of thy decrees I delight, As much as in all wealth, *Goodspeed* ... Thy testimonies I have joyed, As over all wealth, *Young* ... In the way of your instructions lies my joy, a joy beyond all wealth, *JB*.

**15. I will meditate in thy precepts, and have respect unto thy ways:** ... And contemplate Your ways, *NKJV* ... and fix my eyes on your ways, *NRSV* ... I will meditate on Your commandments, *KJVII* ... and keep your paths before my eyes, *REB* ... and gaze upon your paths, *Anchor.*

**16. I will delight myself in thy statutes: I will not forget thy word:** ... Be thy covenant ever my delight, thy words kept in memory, *Knox* ... I delight in your decrees; I will not neglect your word, *NIV* ... I enjoy obeying your demands, *NCV* ... I will not let your word go out of my mind, *BB*.

**17. GIMEL. Deal bountifully with thy servant, that I may live, and keep thy word:** ... Be generous to your servant and I shall live, *JB* ... Kindly help Your servant, that I may live and do what You say, *Beck* ... So will I observe thy word, *ASV.*

---

singer had just longed that he might be able to do, namely, to observe the statutes. But in his resolve, he remembers his weakness, and therefore, he glides into prayer for that presence without which resolves are transient and abortive.

**119:9–16.** The inference drawn from v. 9, that the psalmist was a young man, is precarious. The language would be quite as appropriate to an aged teacher desirous of guiding impetuous youth to sober self-control. While some verses favor the hypothesis of the author's youth (v. 141, and perhaps vv. 99ff), the tone of the whole, its rich experience and comprehensive grasp of the manifold relations of the Law to life, imply maturity of years and length of meditation. The Psalm is the ripe fruit of a life which is surely past its spring. But it is extremely questionable whether these apparently personal traits are really so. Much rather is the poet "thinking ... of the individuals of different ages and spiritual attainments who may use his works" (Cheyne, in loc.).

The word rendered "by taking heed" (HED #8490) has already occurred in vv. 4f ("observe"). The careful study of the word must be accompanied with as careful a study of self. The object observed there was the Law; here, it is the man himself. Study God's Law, says the psalmist, and study thyself in its light; so shall youthful impulses be bridled and the life's path be kept pure. That does not sound so like a young man's thought as an old man's maxim in which are crystallized many experiences.

The rest of the section intermingles petitions, professions and vows and is purely personal. The psalmist claims that he is one of those whom he has pronounced blessed, inasmuch as he has "sought" God with his "whole heart." Such longing is no mere idle aspiration, but must be manifested in obedience, as v. 2 has declared. If a man longs for God, he will best find Him by doing his will. But no heart-desire is so rooted as to guarantee that it shall not die, nor is past obedience a certain pledge of a like future.

Wherefore, the psalmist prays, not in reliance on his past, but in dread that he may falsify it, "Let me not wander." He had not only sought God in his heart, but had there hid God's Law, as its best treasure, and as an inward power controlling and stimulating. Evil cannot flow from a heart in which God's Law is lodged. That is the tree which sweetens the waters of the fountain. But the cry "teach me thy statutes" would be but faltering, if the singer could not rise above himself and take heart by gazing upon God, whose own great character is the guarantee that He will not leave a seeking soul in ignorance.

Professions and vows now take the place of petitions. "From the abundance of the heart the mouth speaketh," and the word hid in it will certainly not be concealed. It is buried deep, that it may grow high. It is hidden, that it may come abroad. Therefore, v. 13 tells of bold utterance, which is as incumbent on men as obedient deeds.

A sane estimate of earthly good will put it decisively below the knowledge of God and of his will. Lives which despise what the world calls riches, because they are smitten with the desire of any sort of wisdom, are ever nobler than those which keep the low levels. And highest of all is the life which gives effect to its conviction that man's true treasure is to know God's mind and will. To rejoice in his testimonies is to have wealth that cannot be lost and pleasures that cannot wither. That glad estimate will surely lead to happy meditation on them, by which their worth shall be disclosed and their sweep made plain. The miser loves to tell his gold; the saint, to ponder his wealth in God. The same double direction of the mind, already noted, reappears in v. 15, where quiet meditation on God's statutes is associated with attention to the ways which are called his, as being pointed out by and pleasing to

| 18. | 1580.131, 6084 | 5202.525 | 6623.258 | 4623, 8784 |
|---|---|---|---|---|
| | v Piel impv 2ms, n fd, ps 1cs | cj, v Hiphil juss 1cs | v Niphal ptc fp | prep, n fs, ps 2ms |
| | גַּל־עֵינַי | וְאַבִּיטָה | נִפְלָאוֹת | מִתּוֹרָתֶךָ |
| | gal-'ênay | we'abbîṭāh | niphlā'ôth | mittôrāthekhā |
| | uncover my eyes | that I may look on | extraordinary things | from your Law |

| 19. | 1658 | 609 | 904, 800 | 414, 5846.523 | 4623 | 4851 |
|---|---|---|---|---|---|---|
| | n ms | pers pron | prep, art, n fs | adv, v Hiphil juss 2ms | prep, ps 1cs | n fp, ps 2ms |
| | גֵּר | אָנֹכִי | בָאָרֶץ | אַל־תַּסְתֵּר | מִמֶּנִּי | מִצְוֺתֶיךָ |
| | gēr | 'ānōkhî | vā'ārets | 'al-tastēr | mimmenî | mitswōthêkhā |
| | a resident-alien | I | in the land | do not hide | from me | your commandments |

| 20. | 1685.112 | 5497 | 3937, 8704 | 420, 5122 | 904, 3725, 6496 | 21. | 1647.113 |
|---|---|---|---|---|---|---|---|
| | v Qal pf 3fs | n fs, ps 1cs | prep, n fs | prep, n mp, ps 2ms | prep, *adj*, n fs | | v Qal pf 2ms |
| | גָּרְסָה | נַפְשִׁי | לְתַאֲבָה | אֶל־מִשְׁפָּטֶיךָ | בְכָל־עֵת | | גָּעַרְתָּ |
| | gār$^e$sāh | naphshî | l$^e$tha'ăvāh | 'el-mishpāṭêkhā | v$^e$khol-'ēth | | gā'artā |
| | it despairs | my soul | of longing | toward your ordinances | during all times | | You rebuke |

| 2170 | 803.156 | 8146.152 | 4623, 4851 | 22. | 1580.131 |
|---|---|---|---|---|---|
| n mp | v Qal pass ptc mp | art, v Qal act ptc mp | prep, n fp, ps 2ms | | v Qal impv 2ms |
| זֵדִים | אֲרוּרִים | הַשֹּׁגִים | מִמִּצְוֺתֶיךָ | | גַּל |
| zēdhîm | 'ărûrîm | hashshōghîm | mimmitswōthêkhā | | gal |
| the insolent | cursed ones | those who go astray | from your commandments | | remove |

| 4623, 6142 | 2887 | 973 | 3706 | 5959 | 5526.115 | 23. | 1612 |
|---|---|---|---|---|---|---|---|
| prep, prep, ps 1cs | n fs | cj, n ms | cj | n fp, ps 2ms | v Qal pf 1cs | | cj |
| מֵעָלַי | חֶרְפָּה | וָבוּז | כִּי | עֵדֹתֶיךָ | נָצָרְתִּי | | גַּם |
| mē'ālay | cherpāh | wāvûz | kî | 'ēdhōthêkhā | nātsār$^e$ttî | | gam |
| from on me | disgrace | and contempt | because | your testimonies | I have kept | | also |

| 3553.116 | 8015 | 904 | 1744.216 | 5860 | 7943.121 |
|---|---|---|---|---|---|
| v Qal pf 3cp | n mp | prep, ps 1cs | v Niphal pf 3cp | n ms, ps 2ms | v Qal impf 3ms |
| יָשְׁבוּ | שָׂרִים | בִּי | נִדְבָּרוּ | עַבְדְּךָ | יָשִׂיחַ |
| yāsh$^e$vû | sārîm | bî | nidhbārû | 'avd$^e$khā | yāsîach |
| they have sat | officials | against me | they have been spoken | your servant | he ponders |

| 904, 2805 | 24. | 1612, 5959 | 8562 | 596 | 6332 | 25. | 1740.112 |
|---|---|---|---|---|---|---|---|
| prep, n mp, ps 2ms | | cj, n fp, ps 2ms | n mp, ps 1cs | *n mp* | n fs, ps 1cs | | v Qal pf 3fs |
| בְּחֻקֶּיךָ | | גַּם־עֵדֹתֶיךָ | שַׁעֲשֻׁעָי | אַנְשֵׁי | עֲצָתִי | | דָּבְקָה |
| b$^e$chuqqêkhā | | gam-'ēdhōthêkhā | sha'ăshu'āy | 'anshê | 'ătsāthî | | dāv$^e$qāh |
| on your statutes | | also your testimonies | my delight | the men of | my counsel | | it has stuck |

| 3937, 6312 | 5497 | 2513.331 | 3626, 1745 | 26. | 1932 |
|---|---|---|---|---|---|
| prep, art, n ms | n fs, ps 1cs | v Piel impv 2ms, ps 1cs | prep, n ms, ps 2ms | | n mp, ps 1cs |
| לֶעָפָר | נַפְשִׁי | חַיֵּנִי | כִּדְבָרֶךָ | | דְּרָכַי |
| le'āphār | naphshî | chayyēnî | kidhvārekhā | | d$^e$rākhay |
| to the dust | my soul | revive me | according to your word | | my ways |

**18. Open thou mine eyes, that I may behold wondrous things out of thy law:** ... Take the veil from my eyes, that I may see the marvels that spring from thy law, *NEB* ... contemplate the wonders of Thy law, *Berkeley* ... consider the wonders of your law, *NCB.*

**19. I am a stranger in the earth: hide not thy commandments from me:** ... A sojourner I am on earth, *Young* ... Though I am but a passing stranger here on earth, *REB* ... do not let your teachings be kept secret from me, *BB.*

**20. My soul breaketh for the longing that it hath unto thy judgments at all times:** ... My soul is consumed with longing for your ordinances, *NAB* ... is crushed with longing, *NASB* ... aches, desiring at all times Your Judgments, *Fenton* ... craves, truly longs for your ordinances, *Anchor.*

**21. Thou hast rebuked the proud that are cursed, which do err from thy commandments:** ... Thou hast destroyed the proud, *Geneva* ... You rebuke the insolent, accursed ones, who wander from your commandments,

*NRSV* ... Strip me of reproach and scorn, for I observe your stipulations, *Anchor* ... Reprove haughty villains, who slip from Your Orders, *Fenton.*

**22. Remove from me reproach and contempt; for I have kept thy testimonies:** ... cursing and scorn from me, *KJVII* ... relieve me from their insults and contempt, for I follow thine injunctions, *Moffatt* ... For I have kept thy decrees, *Goodspeed.*

**23. Princes also did sit and speak against me: but thy servant did meditate in thy statutes:** ... Even rulers have taken their seat against me, *Rotherham* ... Rulers sit scheming together against me; but I, your servant, shall study your statutes, *REB* ... slandered me, *Berkeley.*

**24. Thy testimonies also are my delight and my counsellors:** ... I delight in the truths You wrote—they are my advisers, *Beck* ... Your unchanging word is my delight, and the guide of my footsteps, *BB* ... Your rules give me pleasure; they give me good advice, *NCV.*

**25. DALETH. My soul cleaveth unto the dust: quicken thou me according to thy word:** ... My neck cleaves to the dust, restore me to life, *Anchor* ... I am laid low in the dust; preserve my life according to your word, *NIV.*

**26. I have declared my ways, and thou heardest me: teach me thy statutes:** ... I told You my ways, and You heard and You taught me Your Laws, *Fenton* ... I told you about my life, and you answered me. Teach me your demands, *NCV*

---

Him, but are ours, as being walked in by us. Inward delight in, and practical remembrance of the Law are vowed in v. 16, which covers the whole field of contemplative and active life.

**119:17–24.** In v. 17, the psalmist desires continued life, mainly because it affords the opportunity of continued obedience. He will "observe thy word," not only in token of gratitude, but because to him, life is precious chiefly because in its activities, he can serve God. Such a reason for wishing to live may easily change to a willingness to die, as it did with Paul, who had learned that a better obedience was possible when he had passed through the dark gates, and therefore could say, "To die is gain."

Verses 18f are connected, insofar as the former desires subjective illumination and the latter objective revelation. Opened eyes are useless, if commandments are hidden; and the disclosure of the latter is in vain unless there are eyes to see them. Two great truths lie in the former petition—namely, that scales cover our spiritual vision which only God can take away and that his revelation has in its depths truths and treasures which can only be discerned by his help.

The cognate petition in v. 19 is based upon the pathetic thought that man is a stranger on earth and therefore needs what will take away his sense of homelessness and unrest. All other creatures are adapted to their environments, but he has a consciousness that he is an exile here, a haunting, stinging sense, which vaguely feels after repose in his native land. "Thy commandments" can still it. To know God's will, with knowledge which is acceptance and love, gives rest and makes every place a mansion in the Father's house.

There may possibly be a connection between vv. 20 and 21—the terrible fate of those who wander from the commandments, as described in the latter verse, being the motive for the psalmist's longing expressed in the former. The "judgments" (HED #5122) for which he longed with a yearning which seemed to bruise his soul are not, as might be supposed, God's judicial acts, but the word is a synonym for "commandments" (HED #4851) as throughout the Psalm.

The last three verses of the section appear to be linked together. They relate to the persecutions of the psalmist for his faithfulness to God's Law. In v. 22, he prays that reproach and shame, which wrapped him like a covering, may be lifted from him; and his plea in v. 22b declares that he lay under these because he was true to God's statutes. In v. 23, we see the source of the reproach and shame, in the conclave of men in authority, whether foreign princes or Jewish rulers, who were busy slandering him and plotting his ruin; while, with wonderful beauty, the contrasted picture in 23b shows the object of that busy talk, sitting silently absorbed in meditation on the higher things of God's statutes. As long as a man can do that, he has a magic circle drawn round him, across which fears and cares cannot step.

Verse 24 heightens the impression of the psalmist's rest. "Also thy testimonies are my delight"—not only the subjects of his meditation, but bringing inward sweetness, although earth is in arms against him; and not only are they his delights, but "the men of his counsel," in whom he, solitary as he is, finds companionship that arms him with resources against that knot of whispering enemies.

**119:25–32.** The exigencies of the acrostic plan are very obvious in this section, five of the verses of which begin with "way" or "ways" (HED #1932), and two of the remaining three with "cleaves" (HED

| 5807.315 | 6257.123 | 4064.331 | 2805 |
|---|---|---|---|
| v Piel pf 1cs | cj, v Qal impf 2ms, ps 1cs | v Piel impv 2ms, ps 1cs | n mp, ps 2ms |
| סִפַּרְתִּי | וַתַּעֲנֵנִי | לַמְּדֵנִי | חֻקֶּיךָ |
| sippartî | watta'ănēnî | lammedhēnî | chuqqêkhā |
| I have recounted | and You answered me | teach me | your statutes |

| 27. 1932, 6740 | 1032.531 | 7943.125 |
|---|---|---|
| *n ms*, n mp, ps 2ms | v Hiphil impv 2ms, ps 1cs | cj, v Qal juss 1cs |
| דֶּרֶךְ־פִּקּוּדֶיךָ | הֲבִינֵנִי | וְאָשִׂיחָה |
| derekh-piqqûdhêkhā | hevînēnî | we'āsîchāh |
| the way of your precepts | cause me to understand | that I may ponder |

| 904, 6623.258 | 28. 1872.112 | 5497 | 4623, 8755 | 7251.331 |
|---|---|---|---|---|
| prep, v Niphal ptc fp, ps 2ms | v Qal pf 3fs | n fs, ps 1cs | prep, n fs | v Piel impv 2ms, ps 1cs |
| בְּנִפְלְאוֹתֶיךָ | דָּלְפָה | נַפְשִׁי | מִתּוּגָה | קַיְּמֵנִי |
| beniphle'ôthêkhā | dālephāh | naphshî | mittûghāh | qayyemēnî |
| on your extraordinary deeds | it drips | my soul | from sorrow | raise me up |

| 3626, 1745 | 29. 1932, 8632 | 5681.531 | 4623 | 8784 |
|---|---|---|---|---|
| prep, n ms, ps 2ms | *n ms*, n ms | v Hiphil impv 2ms | prep, ps 1cs | cj, n fs, ps 2ms |
| כִּדְבָרֶךָ | דֶּרֶךְ־שֶׁקֶר | הָסֵר | מִמֶּנִּי | וְתוֹרָתְךָ |
| kidhvārekhā | derekh-sheqer | hāsēr | mimmenî | wethôrāthekhā |
| according to your word | the way of deception | remove | from me | and your Law |

| 2706.131 | 30. 1932, 536 | 1013.115 | 5122 | 8187.315 |
|---|---|---|---|---|
| v Qal impv 2ms, ps 1cs | *n ms*, n fs | v Qal pf 1cs | n mp, ps 2ms | v Piel pf 1cs |
| חָנֵּנִי | דֶּרֶךְ־אֱמוּנָה | בָחָרְתִּי | מִשְׁפָּטֶיךָ | שִׁוִּיתִי |
| channēnî | derekh-'ĕmûnāh | vāchārettî | mishpāṭêkhā | shiwwîthî |
| be gracious to me | the way of faithfulness | I have chosen | your ordinances | I have set |

| 31. 1740.115 | 904, 5959 | 3176 | 414, 991.523 |
|---|---|---|---|
| v Qal pf 1cs | prep, n fp, ps 2ms | pn | adv, v Hiphil juss 2ms, ps 1cs |
| דָּבַקְתִּי | בְעֵדְוֹתֶיךָ | יְהוָה | אַל־תְּבִישֵׁנִי |
| dāvaqettî | ve'ēdhwōthêkhā | yehwāh | 'al-tevîshēnî |
| I cling | on your testimonies | O Yahweh | do not cause me to be ashamed |

| 32. 1932, 4851 | 7608.125 | 3706 | 7620.523 | 3949 |
|---|---|---|---|---|
| *n ms*, n fp, ps 2ms | v Qal impf 1cs | cj | v Hiphil impf 2ms | n ms, ps 1cs |
| דֶּרֶךְ־מִצְוֹתֶיךָ | אָרוּץ | כִּי | תַרְחִיב | לִבִּי |
| derekh-mitswōthêkhā | 'ārûts | kî | tharchîv | libbî |
| the way of your commandments | I will run to | because | You widen | my heart |

| 33. 3498.531 | 3176 | 1932 | 2805 | 5526.125 | 6358 |
|---|---|---|---|---|---|
| v Hiphil impv 2ms, ps 1cs | pn | *n ms* | n mp, ps 2ms | cj, v Qal juss 1cs, ps 3fs | adv |
| הוֹרֵנִי | יְהוָה | דֶּרֶךְ | חֻקֶּיךָ | וְאֶצְּרֶנָּה | עֵקֶב |
| hôrēnî | yehwāh | derekh | chuqqêkhā | we'etstserennāh | 'ēqev |
| teach me | O Yahweh | the way of | your statutes | that I may keep it | to the end |

| 34. 1032.531 | 5526.125 | 8784 | 8490.125 | 904, 3725, 3949 |
|---|---|---|---|---|
| v Hiphil impv 2ms, ps 1cs | cj, v Qal juss 1cs | n fs, ps 2ms | cj, v Qal juss 1cs, ps 3fs | prep, *adj*, n ms |
| הֲבִינֵנִי | וְאֶצְּרָה | תוֹרָתֶךָ | וְאֶשְׁמְרֶנָּה | בְכָל־לֵב |
| hevînēnî | we'etstserāh | thôrāthekhā | we'eshmerennāh | vekhol-lēv |
| cause me to discern | that I may keep | your Law | that I may observe it | with all the heart |

| 35. 1931.531 | 904, 5593 | 4851 | 3706, 904 | 2759.115 |
|---|---|---|---|---|
| v Hiphil impv 2ms, ps 1cs | prep, *n ms* | n fp, ps 2ms | cj, prep, ps 3ms | v Qal pf 1cs |
| הַדְרִיכֵנִי | בִּנְתִיב | מִצְוֹתֶיךָ | כִּי־בוֹ | חָפָצְתִּי |
| hadhrîkhēnî | binthîv | mitswōthêkhā | kî-vô | chāphātsettî |
| lead me | in the pathway of | your commandments | because in it | I delight |

... I tell you of my plight and you answer me, *REB*.

**27. Make me to understand the way of thy precepts: so shall I talk of thy wondrous works:** ... So shall I meditate on thy wondrous works, *ASV* ... Help me understand how You want me to live, *Beck* ... Make me to understand the way of Your commandments, *KJVII* ... that I may reflect on your wonders, *JB*.

**28. My soul melteth for heaviness: strengthen thou me according unto thy word:** ... My soul melteth for sadness, *Darby* ... My soul weeps because of grief, *NASB* ... I cannot rest for misery, *NEB* ... My soul is weary with sorrow, *NIV*.

**29. Remove from me the way of lying: and grant me thy law graciously:** ... Keep me far from the way of deceit, grant me the grace of your Law, *JB* ... and favor me with your law, *NAB* ... Don't let me be dishonest; have mercy on me by helping me obey your teachings, *NCV*.

**30. I have chosen the way of truth: thy judgments have I laid before me:** ... I have chosen the way of faithfulness, *MRB* ... I have taken the way of faith: I have kept your decisions before me, *BB*.

**31. I have stuck unto thy testimonies: O Lord, put me not to shame:** ... I cling to Your testimonies, *NKJV* ... I cling to your decrees, *NRSV* ... I hold fast to your instruction, *REB* ... the truths You wrote, *Beck*.

**32. I will run the way of thy commandments, when thou shalt enlarge my heart:** ... I will go quickly in the way of your teaching, because you have given me a free heart, *BB* ... open up my heart, *Berkeley*.

**33. HE. Teach me, O Lord, the way of thy statutes; and I shall keep it unto the end:** ... Show, Lord, the path to Your Plans, and I'll keep it for ever, *Fenton* ... And I will keep it at every step, *MAST* ... and in keeping them I shall find my reward, *NEB*.

**34. Give me understanding, and I shall keep thy law; yea, I shall observe it with my whole heart:** ... Give me discernment, *NAB* ... Cause me to understand, *Young* ... and I will keep what You teach and do it with all my heart, *Beck*.

**35. Make me to go in the path of thy commandments; for therein do I delight:** ... Guide me in the path of

---

#1740). The variety secured under such conditions is remarkable. The psalmist's soul cleaves to the dust—i.e., is bowed in mourning (cf. Ps. 44:25); but still, though thus darkened by sorrow and weeping itself away for grief (v. 28), it cleaves to "thy testimonies" (v. 31). Happy in their sorrow are they who, by reason of the force which bows their sensitive nature to the dust, cling the more closely in their true selves to the declared will of God! Their sorrow appeals to God's heart and is blessed if it dictates the prayer for his quickening (v. 25). Their cleaving to his Law warrants their hope that He will not put them to shame.

The first pair of verses in which "way" is the acrostic word (vv. 26f) sets "my ways" over against "the way of thy precepts." The psalmist has made God his confidant, telling Him all his life's story, and has found continual answers in gifts of mercy and inward whispers. He asks, therefore, for further illumination, which will be in accordance with these past mutual communications. Tell God thy ways, and He will teach thee his statutes. The franker our confession, the more fervent our longing for fuller knowledge of his will.

"The way of thy precepts" is the practical life according to these, the ideal which shall rebuke and transform "my ways." The singer's crooked course is spread before God, and he longs to see clearly the straight path of duty, on which he vows that he will meditate and find wonders in the revelation of God's will. Many a sunbeam is wasted for want of intent eyes. The prayer for understanding is vain without the vow of pondering.

The next pair of "way" verses (vv. 29f) contrasts ways of "lying" and of "faithfulness"—i.e., sinful life which is false toward God and erroneous in its foundation maxims and life which is true in practice to Him and to man's obligations. The psalmist prays that the former may be put far from him, for he feels that it is only too near and his unhelped feet too ready to enter on it. He recognizes the inmost meaning of the Law as an outcome of God's favor. It is not harsh, but glowing with love, God's best gift.

The prayer in v. 29 has the psalmist's deliberate choice in v. 30 as its plea. That choice does not lift him above the need of God's help, and it gives him a claim thereon. Our wills may seem fixed, but the gap between choice and practice is wide, and our feebleness will not bridge it, unless He strengthens us. So the last verse of this section humbly vows to transform meditation and choice into action and to "run the way of God's commandments" in thanksgiving for the joy with which, while the psalmist prays, he feels that his heart swells.

**119:33–40.** Verses 33f are substantially identical in their prayer for enlightenment and their vow of obedience. Both are based on the conviction that outward revelation is incomplete without inward illumination. Both recognize the necessary priority

| 36. | 5371.531, 3949 v Hiphil impv 2ms, n ms, ps 1cs הַט־לִבִּי haṭ-libbî incline my heart | 420, 5959 prep, n fp, ps 2ms אֶל־עֵדְוֹתֶיךָ 'el-'ēdhwōthêkhā toward your testimonies | 414 cj, adv וְאַל w^e'al and not | 420, 1240 prep, n ms אֶל־בָּצַע 'el-bātsa' toward gain | 37. | 5882.531 v Hiphil impv 2ms הַעֲבֵר ha'ăvēr cause to pass by |
|---|---|---|---|---|---|---|

| 6084 n fd, ps 1cs עֵינַי 'ênay my eyes | 4623, 7495.141 prep, v Qal inf con מֵרְאוֹת mēr^e'ôth from looking at | 8175 n ms שָׁוְא shāw^e' vanity | 904, 1932 prep, n ms, ps 2ms בִּדְרָכֶךָ bidhrākhekhā in your way | 2513.331 v Piel impv 2ms, ps 1cs חַיֵּנִי chayyēnî revive me | 38. | 7251.531 v Hiphil impv 2ms הָקֵם hāqēm establish |
|---|---|---|---|---|---|---|

| 3937, 5860 prep, n ms, ps 2ms לְעַבְדְּךָ l^e'avd^ekhā to your servant | 577 n fs, ps 2ms אִמְרָתֶךָ 'imrāthekhā your word | 866 rel part אֲשֶׁר 'ăsher which | 3937, 3488 prep, n fs, ps 2ms לְיִרְאָתֶךָ l^eyir'āthekhā for the fear of You | 39. | 5882.531 v Hiphil impv 2ms הַעֲבֵר ha'ăvēr cause to pass away | 2887 n fs, ps 1cs חֶרְפָּתִי cherpāthî my disgrace |
|---|---|---|---|---|---|---|

| 866 rel part אֲשֶׁר 'ăsher which | 3133.115 v Qal pf 1cs יָגֹרְתִּי yāghōr^ettî I dread | 3706 cj כִּי kî because | 5122 n mp, ps 2ms מִשְׁפָּטֶיךָ mishpāṭêkhā your ordinances | 3005 adj טוֹבִים ṭôvîm good | 40. | 2079 intrj הִנֵּה hinnēh behold | 8703.115 v Qal pf 1cs תָּאַבְתִּי tā'avtî I long for | 3937, 6740 prep, n mp, ps 2ms לְפִקֻּדֶיךָ l^ephiqqudhêkhā for your precepts |
|---|---|---|---|---|---|---|---|---|

| 904, 6930 prep, n fs, ps 2ms בְּצִדְקָתְךָ b^etsidhqāth^ekhā in your righteousness | 2513.331 v Piel impv 2ms, ps 1cs חַיֵּנִי chayyēnî revive me | 41. | 971.126 cj, v Qal juss 3mp, ps 1cs וִיבֹאֻנִי wîvō'unî and let them come to me | 2721 n ms, ps 2ms חֲסָדֶךָ chăsādhekhā your steadfast love |
|---|---|---|---|---|

| 3176 pn יְהוָה y^ehwāh O Yahweh | 9009 n fs, ps 2ms תְּשׁוּעָתְךָ t^eshû'āth^ekhā your salvation | 3626, 577 prep, n fs, ps 2ms כְּאִמְרָתֶךָ k^e'imrāthekhā according to your word | 42. | 6257.125 cj, v Qal juss 1cs וְאֶעֱנֶה w^e'e'ĕneh that I may answer | 2884.151 v Qal act ptc ms, ps 1cs חֹרְפִי chōr^ephî those who taunt me |
|---|---|---|---|---|---|

| 1745 n ms דָבָר dhāvār a word | 3706, 1019.115 cj, v Qal pf 1cs כִּי־בָטַחְתִּי kî-vāṭachtî because I have trusted | 904, 1745 prep, n ms, ps 2ms בִּדְבָרֶךָ bidhvārekhā in your word | 43. | 414, 5522.523 cj, adv, v Hiphil juss 2ms וְאַל־תַּצֵּל w^e'al-tatstsēl and do not pull out | 4623, 6552 prep, n ms, ps 1cs מִפִּי mippî from my mouth |
|---|---|---|---|---|---|

thy commandments, For therein do I find pleasure, *Rotherham* … lead me in thine obedience, for it is my joy, *Moffatt* … Lead me in the path of your commands, because that makes me happy, *NCV* … Eagerly I long to be guided in the way of thy obedience, *Knox*.

**36. Incline my heart unto thy testimonies, and not to covetousness:** … Bend my heart to your instructions, not to selfish gain, *JB* … Let my heart be turned to your unchanging word, and not to evil desire, *BB* … Dispose my heart towards your instruction, not towards love of gain, *REB* … And not unto dishonest gain, *Young*.

**37. Turn away mine eyes from beholding vanity; and quicken thou me in thy way:** … my eyes from all that is vile, grant me life by thy word, *NEB* … and give me life in thy ways, *RSV* … revive me in Thy ways, *NASB* … By Your power give me a new life, *Beck*.

**38. Stablish thy word unto thy servant, who is devoted to thy fear:** … Confirm thy word, *MRB* … Make Your word sure to Your servant, *KJVII* … Establish thy promise for thy servant, Which is for those who revere thee, *Goodspeed* … Fulfill for your servant your promise to those who fear you, *NAB*.

**39. Turn away my reproach which I fear: for thy judgments are good:** … Take away the shame I fear, because your laws are good, *NCV* … Take away the disgrace I dread, *NIV* … Remove my reproach because I revere you, *Anchor*.

**40. Behold, I have longed after thy precepts: quicken me in thy right-**

**eousness:** ... in your saving justice give me life, *JB* ... In Your Goodness revive me, *Fenton* ... Revive me in Your righteousness, *NKJV.*

**41. WAW. Let thy mercies come also unto me, O LORD, even thy salvation, according to thy word:** ... Let your steadfast love come to me, *NRSV* ... And let thy louing kindnesse come vnto mee, *Geneva* ... Let thy love come to my rescue, as thou hast promised, *Moffatt* ... May your unfailing love come to me, *NIV.*

**42. So shall I have wherewith to answer him that reproacheth me: for I trust in thy word:** ... then I shall have a word to answer the one reproaching me, *Berkeley* ... That I may have an answer for him that taunteth me, *MAST* ... So that I may have an answer for the man who would put me to shame, *BB* ... So I shall have something to answer him who mocks me, *KJVII.*

**43. And take not the word of truth utterly out of my mouth; for I have hoped in thy judgments:** ... Do not rob me of my power to speak the truth, for I put my hope in your decrees, *REB* ... for in your ordinances is my hope, *NCB.*

---

of enlightened reason as condition of obedient action and such action as the test and issue of enlightenment. Both vow that knowledge shall not remain barren. They differ in that the former verse pledges the psalmist to obedience unlimited in time, and the latter to obedience without reservation.

But even in uttering his vow, the singer remembers his need of God's help to keep it, and turns it, in v. 35, into petition, which he very significantly grounds on his heart's delight in the Law. Warm as that delight may be, circumstances and flesh will cool it, and it is ever a struggle to translate desires into deeds. Therefore, we need the sweet constraint of our divine helper to make us walk in the right way.

Again, in v. 36, the preceding profession is caught up and modulated into petition. "Incline my heart" stands to "In it I delight," just as "Make me walk" does to "I will observe it." Our purest joys in God and in his will depend on Him for their permanence and increase. Our hearts are apt to spill their affection on the earth, even while we would bear the cup filled to God. And one chief rival of "thy testimonies" is worldly gain from which there must be forcible detachment in order to experience, and see as accompaniment of, attachment to God. All possessions which come between us and Him are "plunder," unjust gain.

The heart is often led astray by the eyes. The senses bring fuel to its unholy flames. Therefore, the next petition (v. 37) asks that they may be made, as it were, to pass on one side of tempting things, which are branded as being "vanity" (HED #8175), without real substance or worth, however they may glitter and solicit the gaze. To look longingly on earth's good makes us torpid in God's ways; and to be earnest in the latter makes us dead to the former. There is but one real life for men, the life of union with God and of obedience to his commandments. Therefore, the singer prays to be revived in God's ways.

Experience of God's faithfulness to his plighted word will do much to deliver from earth's glamour, as v. 38 implies. The second clause is elliptical in Hebrew and is now usually taken as above, meaning that God's promise fulfilled leads men to reverence Him. But the rendering "who is devoted to thy fear" is tenable and perhaps better.

The "reproach" in v. 39 is probably that which would fall on the psalmist if he were unfaithful to God's Law. This interpretation gives the best meaning to v. 39b, which would then contain the reason for his desire to keep the "judgments"—i.e., the commandments, not the judicial acts—which he feels to be good. The section ends with a constantly recurring strain. God's righteousness, his strict discharge of all obligations, guarantees that no longing, turned to Him, can be left unsatisfied. The languishing desire will be changed into fuller joy of more vigorous life. The necessary precursor of deeper draughts from the fountain of life is thirst for it, which faithfully turns aside from earth's sparkling but drugged potions.

**119:41–48.** There are practically no Hebrew words beginning with the letter required as the initial in this section, except the conjunction "and" (HED #2134). Each verse begins with it, and it is best to retain it in translation, so as to reproduce in some measure the original impression of uniformity. The verses are aggregated rather than linked. "And" sometimes introduces a consequence, as probably in v. 42, and sometimes is superfluous in regard to the sense. A predominant reference to the duty of bearing witness to the truth runs through the section.

The prayer in v. 41 for the visits of God's steadfast love which, in sum, makes salvation, and is guaranteed by his word of promise, is urged on the ground that by experience of this, the psalmist will have his answer ready for all carpers who scoff at him and his patient faith. Such a

| | | | | | | |
|---|---|---|---|---|---|---|
| 1745, 583 | 5912, 4108 | 3706 | 3937, 5122 | 3282.315 | | 8490.125 |
| n ms, n fs | adv, adv | cj | prep, n ms, ps 2ms | v Piel pf 1cs | 44. | cj, v Qal juss 1cs |
| דְּבַר־אֱמֶת | עַד־מְאֹד | כִּי | לְמִשְׁפָּטֶךָ | יִחָלְתִּי | | וְאֶשְׁמְרָה |
| dhevar-'ĕmeth | 'adh-me'ōdh | kî | lemishpāṭekhā | yichālettî | | we'eshmerāh |
| a word of truth | until very | because | for your ordinances | I wait | | that I may observe |

| | | | | | | | |
|---|---|---|---|---|---|---|---|
| 8784 | 8878 | 3937, 5986 | 5911 | | 2050.725 | 904, 7622 | 3706 |
| n fs, ps 2ms | adv | prep, n ms | cj, n ms | 45. | cj, v Hithpael juss 1cs | prep, art, adj | cj |
| תּוֹרָתְךָ | תָמִיד | לְעוֹלָם | וָעֶד | | וְאֶתְהַלְּכָה | בָרְחָבָה | כִּי |
| thôrāthekhā | thāmîdh | le'ôlām | wā'edh | | we'ethhallekhāh | vārechāvāh | kî |
| your Law | continually | unto eternity | and everlasting | | that I may walk | in the wide | because |

| | | | | | |
|---|---|---|---|---|---|
| 6740 | 1938.115 | | 1744.325 | 904, 5959 | 5224 |
| n mp, ps 2ms | v Qal pf 1cs | 46. | cj, v Piel juss 1cs | prep, n fp, ps 2ms | prep |
| פִקֻּדֶיךָ | דָרָשְׁתִּי | | וַאֲדַבְּרָה | בְעֵדֹתֶיךָ | נֶגֶד |
| phiqqudhêkhā | dhārāshettî | | wa'ădhabberāh | ve'ēdhōthêkhā | neghedh |
| your precepts | I have inquired about | | that I may speak | about your testimonies | before |

| | | | | | | |
|---|---|---|---|---|---|---|
| 4567 | 3940 | 991.125 | | 8551.725 | 904, 4851 | 866 |
| n mp | cj, neg part | v Qal impf 1cs | 47. | cj, v Hithpalpel impf 1cs | prep, n fp, ps 2ms | rel part |
| מְלָכִים | וְלֹא | אֵבוֹשׁ | | וְאֶשְׁתַּעֲשַׁע | בְּמִצְוֹתֶיךָ | אֲשֶׁר |
| melākhîm | welō' | 'ēvôsh | | we'eshta'ăsha' | bemitswōthêkhā | 'ăsher |
| kings | and not | I will be ashamed | | for I delight | in your commandments | which |

| | | | | | |
|---|---|---|---|---|---|
| 154.115 | | 5558.125, 3834 | 420, 4851 | 866 | 154.115 |
| v Qal pf 1cs | 48. | cj, v Qal juss 1cs, n fd, ps 1cs | prep, n fp, ps 2ms | rel part | v Qal pf 1cs |
| אָהָבְתִּי | | וְאֶשָּׂא־כַפַּי | אֶל־מִצְוֹתֶיךָ | אֲשֶׁר | אָהָבְתִּי |
| 'āhāvettî | | we'essā'-khappay | 'el-mitswōthêkhā | 'ăsher | 'āhāvettî |
| I love | | that I may lift up my hands | to your commandments | which | I love |

| | | | | | | |
|---|---|---|---|---|---|---|
| 7943.125 | 904, 2805 | | 2226.131, 1745 | 3937, 5860 | 6142 | 866 |
| cj, v Qal juss 1cs | prep, n mp, ps 2ms | 49. | v Qal impv 2ms, n ms | prep, n ms, ps 2ms | prep | rel part |
| וְאָשִׂיחָה | בְחֻקֶּיךָ | | זְכֹר־דָּבָר | לְעַבְדֶּךָ | עַל | אֲשֶׁר |
| we'āsîchāh | vechuqqêkhā | | zekhōr-dāvār | le'avdekhā | 'al | 'ăsher |
| that I may ponder | about your statutes | | remember a word | to your servant | on | which |

| | | | | | | |
|---|---|---|---|---|---|---|
| 3282.313 | | 2148 | 5344 | 904, 6270 | 3706 | 577 |
| v Piel pf 2ms, ps 1cs | 50. | dem pron | n fs, ps 1cs | prep, n ms, ps 1cs | cj | n fs, ps 2ms |
| יִחַלְתָּנִי | | זֹאת | נֶחָמָתִי | בְעָנְיִי | כִּי | אִמְרָתְךָ |
| yichaltānî | | zō'th | nechāmāthî | ve'āneyî | kî | 'imrāthekhā |
| You have made me wait | | this | my comfort | in my affliction | that | your word |

| | | | | | | |
|---|---|---|---|---|---|---|
| 2513.312 | | 2170 | 4054.516 | 5912, 4108 | 4623, 8784 | 3940 |
| v Piel pf 3fs, ps 1cs | 51. | n mp | v Hiphil pf 3cp, ps 1cs | adv, adv | prep, n fs, ps 2ms | neg part |
| חִיָּתְנִי | | זֵדִים | הֱלִיצֻנִי | עַד־מְאֹד | מִתּוֹרָתְךָ | לֹא |
| chîyāthenî | | zēdhîm | hĕlîtsunî | 'adh-me'ōdh | mittôrāthekhā | lō' |
| it revives me | | the insolent | they scorn me | until very | away from your Law | not |

| | | | | | | |
|---|---|---|---|---|---|---|
| 5371.115 | | 2226.115 | 5122 | 4623, 5986 | 3176 | 5341.725 |
| v Qal pf 1cs | 52. | v Qal pf 1cs | n mp, ps 2ms | prep, n ms | pn | cj, v Hithpael impf 1cs |
| נָטִיתִי | | זָכַרְתִּי | מִשְׁפָּטֶיךָ | מֵעוֹלָם | יְהוָה | וָאֶתְנֶחָם |
| nāṭîthî | | zākhartî | mishpāṭêkhā | mē'ôlām | yehwāh | wā'ethnechām |
| I will incline | | I remember | your ordinances | from eternity | O Yahweh | and I am comforted |

| | | | | | | | |
|---|---|---|---|---|---|---|---|
| | 2237 | 270.112 | 4623, 7857 | 6013.152 | 8784 | | 2244 |
| 53. | n fs | v Qal pf 3fs, ps 1cs | prep, n mp | *v Qal act ptc mp* | n fs, ps 2ms | 54. | n mp |
| | זַלְעָפָה | אֲחָזַתְנִי | מֵרְשָׁעִים | עֹזְבֵי | תּוֹרָתֶךָ | | זְמִרוֹת |
| | zal'āphāh | 'ăchāzathnî | mēreshā'îm | 'ōzevê | tôrāthekhā | | zemirôth |
| | intensity | it seizes me | because the wicked | abandoning | your Law | | songs |

**44. So shall I keep thy law continually for ever and ever:** ... So shall I observe thy law, *ASV* ... That I may keep your law, Perpetual One, for ever, *Anchor* ... I will continually and forever be careful to do what You teach, *Beck* ... I will obey your teachings forever and ever, *NCV.*

**45. And I will walk at liberty: for I seek thy precepts:** ... Freely shall my feet tread, if thy will is all my quest, *Knox* ... That I may walk to and fro in a large place, *Rotherham* ... I shall live in all freedom, *JB* ... And I walk habitually in a broad place, *Young.*

**46. I will speak of thy testimonies also before kings, and will not be ashamed:** ... So that I may give knowledge of your unchanging word before kings, *BB* ... I bear testimony to thy law before kings, *Moffatt* ... I will also speak of your decrees before kings, *NRSV.*

**47. And I will delight myself in thy commandments, which I have loved:** ... I have all my comfort in the law I love, *Knox.*

**48. My hands also will I lift up unto thy commandments, which I have loved; and I will meditate in thy statutes:** ... I will welcome thy commandments, *NEB* ... I praise your commands, which I love, *NCV* ... I am devoted to your commandments, *REB* ... I shall raise my hands according to your commandments, *Anchor.*

**49. ZAYIN. Remember the word unto thy servant, upon which thou hast caused me to hope:** ... since you have given me hope, *NAB* ... on which I have trusted, *Fenton* ... on which I have built my hope, *JB* ... caused me to trust, *Geneva.*

**50. This is my comfort in my affliction: for thy word hath quickened me:** ... that thy promise gives me life, *RSV* ... Thy word has revived me, *NASB* ... comfort in my trouble, That thy promise revives me, *Goodspeed* ... Your promise preserves my life, *NIV.*

**51. The proud have had me greatly in derision: yet have I not declined from thy law:** ... Proud men bitterly scorn me, but I don't turn away from Your teaching, *Beck* ... The arrogant have had me in complete derision, yet I have not deviated, *Berkeley* ... Though the proud scoff bitterly at me, *NCB* ... Yet have I not swerved from thy law, *ASV.*

**52. I remembered thy judgments of old, O LORD; and have comforted myself:** ... I remember your ancient laws, *NIV* ... I have kept the memory of your decisions from times past, *BB* ... I have cherished thy decrees all my life long, *NEB* ... I console myself, *Moffatt.*

**53. Horror hath taken hold upon me because of the wicked that forsake thy law:** ... Burning indignation hath taken hold, *Darby* ... Fury seizes me as I think of the wicked, *REB* ... I tremble because of the wicked rejecting Your Laws, *Fenton.*

**54. Thy statutes have been my songs in the house of my pilgrimage:** ... Your laws have been my songs here where I'm a stranger, *Beck* ... are the theme of my song in

---

prayer is entirely accordant with the hypothesis that the speaker is the collective Israel, but not less so with the supposition that he is an individual. "Whereas I was blind, now I see" is an argument that silences sarcasm.

Verse 43 carries on the thought of witnessing and asks that "the word of truth"—i.e., the Law considered as disclosure of truth rather than of duty—may not be snatched from the witness' mouth, as it would be if God's promised steadfast love failed him. The condition of free utterance is rich experience. If prayers had gone up in vain from the psalmist's lips, no glad proclamation could come from them.

The verbs at the beginnings of vv. 44ff are best taken as optatives, expressing what the psalmist would do, and has done to some extent. There is no true religion without that longing for unbroken conformity with the manifest will of God. Whoever makes that his deepest desire, and seeks after God's precepts, will "walk at liberty," or at large, for restraints that are loved are not bonds, and freedom consists not in doing as I would, but in willing to do as I ought. Strong in such emancipation from the hindrances of one's own passions, and triumphant over external circumstances which may mold, but not dominate, a God-obeying life, the psalmist would fain open his mouth unabashed before rulers. The "kings" spoken of in v. 46 may be foreign rulers, possibly the representatives of the Persian monarch or later alien sovereigns or the expression may be quite general and the speaker be a private person who feels his courage rising as he enters into the liberty of perfect submission.

Verses 47f are general expressions of delight in the Law. Lifting the hands toward the commandments seems to be a figure for reverent regard, or longing, as one wistfully stretches them out toward some dear person or thing that one would draw closer. The phrase "which I have loved" in v. 48 overweights the clause and is probably a scribe's erroneous repetition of 47b.

**119:49–56.** This section has only one verse of petition, the others being mainly avowals of adherence to the Law in the face of various trials. The single petition (v. 49) pleads the relation of servant,

| 2030.116, 3937 | 2805 | 904, 1041 | 4171B | | 2226.115 | 904, 4050 |
|---|---|---|---|---|---|---|
| v Qal pf 3cp, prep, ps 1cs | n mp, ps 2mp | prep, *n ms* | n mp, ps 1cs | | v Qal pf 1cs | prep, art, n ms |
| הָיוּ־לִי | חֻקֶּיךָ | בְּבֵית | מְגוּרָי | **55.** | זָכַרְתִּי | בַלַּיְלָה |
| hāyû-lî | chuqqêkhā | b$^{e}$vêth | m$^{e}$ghûrāy | | zākhartî | vallaylāh |
| they have been to me | your statutes | in the house of | my sojourning | | I remember | in the night |

| 8428 | 3176 | 8490.125 | 8784 | | 2148 | 2030.122, 3937 | 3706 |
|---|---|---|---|---|---|---|---|
| n ms, ps 2ms | pn | cj, v Qal juss 1cs | n fs, ps 2ms | | dem pron | v Qal pf 3fs, prep, ps 1cs | cj |
| שִׁמְךָ | יְהוָה | וָאֶשְׁמְרָה | תּוֹרָתֶךָ | **56.** | זֹאת | הָיְתָה־לִּי | כִּי |
| shimkhā | y$^{e}$hwāh | wā'eshm$^{e}$rāh | tôrāthekhā | | zō'th | hāy$^{e}$thāh-lî | kî |
| your name | O Yahweh | that I may observe | your Law | | this | it is to me | that |

| 6740 | 5526.115 | | 2610 | 3176 | 569.115 | 3937, 8490.141 | 1745 |
|---|---|---|---|---|---|---|---|
| n mp, ps 2ms | v Qal pf 1cs | | n ms, ps 1cs | pn | v Qal pf 1cs | prep, v Qal inf con | n mp, ps 2ms |
| פִּקֻּדֶיךָ | נָצָרְתִּי | **57.** | חֶלְקִי | יְהוָה | אָמַרְתִּי | לִשְׁמֹר | דְּבָרֶיךָ |
| phiqqudhêkhā | nātsār$^{e}$ttî | | chelqî | y$^{e}$hwāh | 'āmartî | lishmōr | d$^{e}$vārêkhā |
| your precepts | I have kept | | my Portion | O Yahweh | I have said | to observe | your words |

| | 2571.315 | 6686 | 904, 3725, 3949 | 2706.131 | 3626, 577 |
|---|---|---|---|---|---|
| | v Piel pf 1cs | n mp, ps 2ms | prep, *adj*, n ms | v Qal impv 2ms, ps 1cs | prep, n fs, ps 2ms |
| **58.** | חִלִּיתִי | פָנֶיךָ | בְּכָל־לֵב | חָנֵּנִי | כְּאִמְרָתֶךָ |
| | chillîthî | phānêkhā | v$^{e}$khol-lēv | chānnēnî | k$^{e}$'imrāthekhā |
| | I have entreated | your face | with all the heart | be gracious to me | according to your word |

| | 2913.315 | 1932 | 8178.525 | 7559 | 420, 5959 | | 2456.115 |
|---|---|---|---|---|---|---|---|
| | v Piel pf 1cs | n mp, ps 1cs | cj, v Hiphil impf 1cs | n fd, ps 1cs | prep, n fp, ps 2ms | | v Qal pf 1cs |
| **59.** | חִשַּׁבְתִּי | דְרָכָי | וָאָשִׁיבָה | רַגְלַי | אֶל־עֵדֹתֶיךָ | **60.** | חַשְׁתִּי |
| | chishshavtî | dh$^{e}$rākhāy | wā'āshîvāh | raghlay | 'el-'ēdhōthêkhā | | chashtî |
| | I consider | my ways | and I turn back | my feet | to your testimonies | | I hurry |

| 3940 | 4244.725 | 3937, 8490.141 | 4851 | | 2346 | 7857 |
|---|---|---|---|---|---|---|
| cj, neg part | v Hithpalpel impf 1cs | prep, v Qal inf con | n fp, ps 2ms | | *n mp* | n mp |
| וְלֹא | הִתְמַהְמָהְתִּי | לִשְׁמֹר | מִצְוֹתֶיךָ | **61.** | חֶבְלֵי | רְשָׁעִים |
| w$^{e}$lō' | hithmahmāh$^{e}$ttî | lishmōr | mitswōthêkhā | | chevlê | r$^{e}$shā'îm |
| yes not | I delay | to observe | your commandments | | the cords of | the wicked |

| 5967.316 | 8784 | 3940 | 8319.115 | | 2783, 4050 | 7251.125 |
|---|---|---|---|---|---|---|
| v Piel pf 3cp, ps 1cs | n fs, ps 2ms | neg part | v Qal pf 1cs | | *n fp*, n ms | v Qal impf 1cs |
| עִוְּדֻנִי | תּוֹרָתְךָ | לֹא | שָׁכָחְתִּי | **62.** | חֲצוֹת־לַיְלָה | אָקוּם |
| 'iww$^{e}$dhunî | tôrāth$^{e}$khā | lō' | shākhāchättî | | chătsôth-laylāh | 'āqûm |
| they surrounded me | your Law | not | I forget | | the middle of the night | I will arise |

the place of my exile, *NCB* ... In my house of sojourn, *Rotherham* ... as I wander through the world, *Moffatt.*

**55. I have remembered thy name, O LORD, in the night, and have kept thy law:** ... All night, Yahweh, I hold your name in mind, *JB* ... Gloom of night finds me still thinking of thy name, *Knox* ... dwell upon your instruction, *REB* ... and I will obey your teachings, *NCV.*

**56. This I had, because I kept thy precepts:** ... This blessing has fallen to me, for I have kept your precepts, *NRSV* ... They have come to me, because I have studied Your Orders, *Fenton* ... This has been my practice: I obey your precepts, *NIV.*

**57. HETH. Thou art my portion, O LORD: I have said that I would keep thy words:** ... My Creator, Yahweh, I promise to observe your commandments, *Anchor* ... Thou, LORD, art all I have, *NEB* ... LORD, you are my share in life, *NCV* ... I promise to do what You say, *Beck.*

**58. I entreated thy favour with my whole heart: be merciful unto me according to thy word:** ... have pity on me according to your promise, *NAB* ... I looked for Your favor with my whole heart, *KJVII* ... With all my heart I have tried to please you, *REB.*

**59. I thought on my ways, and turned my feet unto thy testimonies:** ... I pondered my ways, *Berkeley* ... I have thought much about the course of my life and always turned back to thy instruction, *NEB* ... Thinking on how to live, I turn to thy directions, *Moffatt* ... Have I not planned out my path, turned aside to follow thy decrees?, *Knox.*

**60. I made haste, and delayed not to keep thy commandments:** ... I hurried and did not wait to obey, *NCV* ... I was quick to do your orders, and let no time be wasted, *BB* ... I was prompt and did not hesitate in keeping your commands, *NCB.*

**61. The bands of the wicked have robbed me: but I have not forgotten thy law:** ... The snares of the wicked have coiled around me, *Berkeley* ... The wicked put the ropes of their traps around me, but I don't forget Your teaching, *Beck* ... The cords of the wicked have wrapped me round, *ASV* ... Though the cords of the wicked ensnare me, *RSV.*

**62. At midnight I will rise to give thanks unto thee because of thy righteous judgments:** ... for the justice of your decrees, *REB* ... I will get up to give you praise, because of all your right decisions, *BB* ... righteous ordinances, *NASB.*

**63. I am a companion of all them that fear thee, and of them that**

---

as giving a claim on the great LORD of the household, and adduces God's having encouraged hope as imposing on Him an obligation to fulfill it. Expectations fairly deduced from his word are prophets of their own realization.

In v. 50, "this" points to the fact stated in v. 50b—namely, that the Word had already proved its power in the past by quickening the psalmist to new courage and hope—and declares that that remembered experience solaces his present sorrow. A heart that has been revived by life-giving contact with the Word has a hidden warmth beneath the deepest snows, and cleaves the more to that Word.

Verses 51ff describe the attitude of the lover of the Law in presence of the ungodly. He is as unmoved by shafts of ridicule as by the heavier artillery of slander and plots (v. 23). To be laughed out of one's faith is even worse than to be terrified out of it. The lesson is not needless in a day when adherence and obedience to the Word are smiled at in so many quarters as indicating inferior intelligence. The psalmist held fast by it, and while laughter, with more than a trace of bitterness, rung about him, threw himself back on God's ancient and enduring words, which made the scoffs sound very hollow and transient (v. 52). Righteous indignation, too, rises in a devout soul at sight of men's departure from God's law (v. 53). The word rendered "intensity" (HED #2237) is found in 11:6 ("a wind of burning") and is best taken as above, although some would render "horror." The wrath was not unmingled with compassion (v. 136), and while it is clearly an emotion belonging to the OT rather than to the Christian type of devotion, it should be present in softened form in our feelings toward evil.

In v. 54, the psalmist turns from gainsayers. He strikes again the note of v. 19, calling earth his place of transitory abode, or, as we might say, his inn. The brevity of life would be crushing, if God had not spoken to us. Since He has, the pilgrims can march "with songs and everlasting joy upon their heads," and all about their moving camp the sound of song may echo. To its lovers, God's Law is not "harsh and crabbed ... but musical as is Apollo's lute." This Psalm is one of the poet's songs. Even those of us who are not singers can and should meditate on God's Law, until its melodious beauty is disclosed and its commandments, that sometimes sound stern, set themselves to rhythm and harmony. As God's words took bitterness out of the thought of mortality, so his name remembered in the night brought light into darkness, whether physical or other. We often lose our memory of God and our hold of his hand when in sorrow, and grief sometimes thinks that it has a dispensation from obedience. So we will be the better for remembering the psalmist's experience and should, like him, cling to the name in the dark, and then we shall have light enough to "have kept thy law."

Verse 56 looks back on the mingled life of good and evil, of which some of the sorrows have just been touched, and speaks deep contentment with its portion. Whatever else is withheld or withdrawn, that lot is blessed which has been helped by God to keep his precepts, and they are happy and wise who deliberately prefer that good to all beside.

**119:57–64.** Verse 57 goes to the root of the matter in setting forth the resolve of obedience as the result of the consciousness of possessing God. He who feels, in his own happy heart, that Yahweh is his portion will be moved thereby to vow to keep his words. This psalmist had learned the evangelical lesson that he did not win God by keeping the Law, but that he was moved to keep the Law because he had won God; and he had also learned the companion truth, that the way to retain that possession is obedience.

Verse 58 corresponds in some measure to v. 57, but the order of clauses is inverted, v. 58a stating the psalmist's prayer, as v. 57b did his resolve, and v. 58b building on his cry the hope that God would be truly his portion and bestow his favor on him. But

| | | | | | | |
|---|---|---|---|---|---|---|
| 3937, 3142.541 | 3937 | 6142 | 5122 | 6928 | | 2358 |
| prep, v Hiphil inf con | prep, ps 2ms | prep | *n mp* | n ms, ps 2ms | | n ms |
| לְהוֹדוֹת | לָךְ | עַל | מִשְׁפְּטֵי | צִדְקֶךָ | **63.** | חָבֵר |
| lehôdhôth | lākh | 'al | mishpetê | tsidhqekhā | | chāvēr |
| to praise | You | concerning | the ordinances of | your righteousness | | a companion |

| | | | | |
|---|---|---|---|---|
| 603 | 3937, 3725, 866 | 3486.116 | 8490.152 | 6740 |
| pers pron | prep, *adj*, rel pron | v Qal pf 3cp, ps 2ms | cj, prep, *v Qal act ptc mp* | n mp, ps 2ms |
| אָנִי | לְכָל־אֲשֶׁר | יְרֵאוּךָ | וּלְשֹׁמְרֵי | פִּקּוּדֶיךָ |
| 'ānî | lekhol-'ăsher | yerē'ûkhā | ûlăshōmerê | piqqûdhêkhā |
| I | of all who | they fear You | and of those who observe | your precepts |

| | | | | | | |
|---|---|---|---|---|---|---|
| | 2721 | 3176 | 4527.112 | 800 | 2805 | 4064.331 |
| | n ms, ps 2ms | pn | v Qal pf 3fs | art, n fs | n mp, ps 2ms | v Piel impv 2ms, ps 1cs |
| **64.** | חַסְדְּךָ | יְהוָה | מָלְאָה | הָאָרֶץ | חֻקֶּיךָ | לַמְּדֵנִי |
| | chasdekhā | yehwāh | māle'āh | hā'ārets | chuqqêkhā | lammedhēnî |
| | your steadfast love | O Yahweh | it is full of | the earth | your statutes | teach me |

| | | | | | | | | |
|---|---|---|---|---|---|---|---|---|
| | 3005 | 6449.113 | 6196, 5860 | 3176 | 3626, 1745 | | 3005 | 3049 |
| | adj | v Qal pf 2ms | prep, n ms, ps 2ms | pn | prep, n ms, ps 2ms | | adj | n ms |
| **65.** | טוֹב | עָשִׂיתָ | עִם־עַבְדְּךָ | יְהוָה | כִּדְבָרֶךָ | **66.** | טוּב | טַעַם |
| | ṭôv | 'āsîthā | 'im-'avdekhā | yehwāh | kidhvārekhā | | ṭûv | ṭa'am |
| | good | You have acted | with your servant | O Yahweh | according to your word | | good | sense |

| | | | | | | |
|---|---|---|---|---|---|---|
| 1907 | 4064.331 | 3706 | 904, 4851 | 548.515 | | 3071 |
| cj, n fs | v Piel impv 2ms, ps 1cs | cj | prep, n fp, ps 2ms | v Hiphil pf 1cs | | adv |
| וָדַעַת | לַמְּדֵנִי | כִּי | בְמִצְוֺתֶיךָ | הֶאֱמָנְתִּי | **67.** | טֶרֶם |
| wādha'ath | lammedhēnî | kî | vemitswōthêkhā | he'ĕmānettî | | ṭerem |
| and knowledge | teach me | because | in your commandments | I believe | | before |

| | | | | | |
|---|---|---|---|---|---|
| 6257.125 | 603 | 8144.151 | 6498 | 577 | 8490.115 |
| v Qal impf 1cs | pers pron | v Qal act ptc ms | cj, adv | n fs, ps 2ms | v Qal pf 1cs |
| אֶעֱנֶה | אֲנִי | שֹׁגֵג | וְעַתָּה | אִמְרָתְךָ | שָׁמָרְתִּי |
| 'e'ĕneh | 'ănî | shōghēgh | we'attāh | 'imrāthekhā | shāmārettî |
| I was afflicted | I | sinning inadvertently | but now | your word | I have observed |

| | | | | |
|---|---|---|---|---|
| | 3005, 887 | 3296.551 | 4064.331 | 2805 |
| | adj, pers pron | cj, v Hiphil ptc ms | v Piel impv 2ms, ps 1cs | n mp, ps 2ms |
| **68.** | טוֹב־אַתָּה | וּמֵטִיב | לַמְּדֵנִי | חֻקֶּיךָ |
| | ṭôv-'attāh | ûmēṭîv | lammedhēnî | chuqqêkhā |
| | good You | and One Who causes to be good | teach me | your statutes |

| | | | | | | | |
|---|---|---|---|---|---|---|---|
| | 3059.116 | 6142 | 8632 | 2170 | 603 | 904, 3725, 3949 | 5526.125 |
| | v Qal pf 3cp | prep, ps 1cs | n ms | n mp | pers pron | prep, *adj*, n ms | v Qal impf 1cs |
| **69.** | טָפְלוּ | עָלַי | שֶׁקֶר | זֵדִים | אֲנִי | בְּכָל־לֵב | אֱצֹּר |
| | ṭāphelû | 'ālay | sheqer | zēdhîm | 'ănî | bekhol-lēv | 'ĕtstsōr |
| | they have smeared | on me | lies | the insolent | I | with all the heart | I keep |

| | | | | | | |
|---|---|---|---|---|---|---|
| 6740 | | 3063.111 | 3626, 2561 | 3949 | 603 | 8784 |
| n mp, ps 2ms | | v Qal pf 3ms | prep, art, n ms | n ms, ps 3mp | pers pron | n fs, ps 2ms |
| פִּקּוּדֶיךָ | **70.** | טָפַשׁ | כַּחֵלֶב | לִבָּם | אֲנִי | תּוֹרָתְךָ |
| piqqûdhêkhā | | ṭāphash | kachēlev | libbām | 'ănî | tôrāthekhā |
| your precepts | | it has become coated | like the fat | their hearts | I | your Law |

| | | | | | | |
|---|---|---|---|---|---|---|
| 8551.315 | | 3005, 3937 | 3706, 6257.415 | 3937, 4775 | 4064.125 | 2805 |
| v Pilpel pf 1cs | | adj, prep, ps 1cs | cj, v Pual pf 1cs | prep, prep | v Qal impf 1cs | n mp, ps 2ms |
| שִׁעֲשָׁעְתִּי | **71.** | טוֹב־לִי | כִּי־עֻנֵּיתִי | לְמַעַן | אֶלְמַד | חֻקֶּיךָ |
| shi'ăshā'ăttî | | ṭôv-lî | khî-'unnêthî | lema'an | 'elmadh | chuqqêkhā |
| I am delighted with | | good to me | that I was afflicted | so that | I would learn | your statutes |

**keep thy precepts:** ... I keep company with all thy worshippers who carry out thy will, *Moffatt* ... I am a friend to all who fear you, *NIV* ... I join all who fear, and regard Your Commands, *Fenton.*

**64. The earth, O LORD, is full of thy mercy: teach me thy statutes:** ... is full of thy loving-kindness, *Darby* ... How thy mercy fills the earth, *Knox* ... Teach me your demands, *NCV* ... Your faithful love fills the earth, Yahweh, teach me your judgements, *JB.*

**65. TETH. Thou hast dealt well with thy servant, O LORD, according unto thy word:** ... shown thy servant much kindness, fulfilling thy word, *NEB* ... You have done good to your servant, *NAB* ... Do good to your servant, Yahweh, according to your good word, *Anchor.*

**66. Teach me good judgment and knowledge: for I have believed thy commandments:** ... The goodness of reason and knowledge teach me, *Young* ... Teach me good discernment and knowledge, *MAST* ... I have put my faith in your teachings, *BB.*

**67. Before I was afflicted I went astray: but now have I kept thy word:** ... Before I suffered, I did wrong, but now I obey, *NCV* ... Before I was humbled, *NRSV* ... but now I hold to your promise, *NCB* ... I went astray before I was punished, *NEB.*

**68. Thou art good, and doest good; teach me thy statutes:** ... You are kind, and with Kindness, O! teach Your Plans, *Fenton* ... You are good and bountiful, *NAB* ... You are generous and act generously, *JB* ... You are good, and what you do is good; teach me your decrees, *NIV.*

**69. The proud have forged a lie against me: but I will keep thy precepts with my whole heart:** ... The arrogant smear me with lies, *NRSV* ... The arrogant have told lies about me, *Goodspeed* ... In vain my oppressors plot against me; thy will is all my quest, *Knox* ... but with all my heart I follow the way You want me to live, *Beck.*

**70. Their heart is as fat as grease; but I delight in thy law:** ... Their heart is without feeling, like fat, *KJVII* ... Their heart has become gross and fat, *NCB* ... Gross as lard is their heart, *Anchor* ... Their heart is covered with fat, *NASB.*

**71. It is good for me that I have been afflicted; that I might learn thy statutes:** ... It is good for me to have been in trouble—to learn thy will, *Moffatt* ... It is good for me to

---

the true ground of our hope is not our most wholehearted prayers, but God's promise.

The following five verses change from the key of petition into that of profession of obedience to, and delight in, the Law. The fruit of wise consideration of one's conduct is willing acceptance of God's Law as his witness of what is right for us. The only "ways" which sober consideration will approve are those marked out in mercy by Him, and meditation on conduct is worthless if it does not issue in turning our feet into these. Without such meditation we shall wander on byways and lose ourselves. Want of thought ruins men (v. 59). But such turning of our feet to the right road has many foes, and chief among them is lingering delay. Therefore, resolve must never be let cool, but be swiftly carried into action (v. 60). The world is full of snares, and they lie thick around our feet whenever these are turned toward God's ways. The only means of keeping clear of them is to fix heart and mind on God's Law. Then we shall be able to pick our steps among traps and pits (v. 61). Physical weariness limits obedience, and needful sleep relaxes nervous tension, so that many a strenuous worker and noble aspirant falls beneath his daylight self in wakeful night seasons. Blessed they who in the night see visions of God and meditate on his Law, not on earthly vanities or aims (v. 62). Society has its temptations as solitude has. The man whose heart has fed in secret on God and his Law will naturally gravitate toward likeminded people. Our relation to God and his uttered will should determine our affinities with men, and it is a bad sign when natural impulses do not draw us to those who fear God. Two men who have that fear in common are like each other in their deepest selves, however different they may be in other respects, than either of them is to those to whom he is likest in surface characteristics and unlike in this supreme trait (v. 63).

One pathetic petition closes the section. In v. 19, the psalmist had based his prayer for illumination on his being a stranger on earth; here he grounds it on the plenitude of God's steadfast love, which floods the world. It is the same plea in another form. All creatures bask in the light of God's love, which falls on each in a manner appropriate to its needs. Man's supreme need is the knowledge of God's statutes; therefore, the same all-embracing mercy, which cares for these happy, careless creatures, will not be implored in vain, to satisfy his nobler and more pressing want. All beings get their respective boons unasked; but the pre-eminence of ours is partly seen in this, that it cannot be given without the cooperation of our desire. It will be given wherever that condition is fulfilled (v. 64).

**119:65–72.** The restrictions of the acrostic structure are very obvious in this section, five of the

| | | | | | | | |
|---|---|---|---|---|---|---|---|
| 72. | 3005, 3937 | 8784, 6552 | 4623, 512 | 2174 | 3826B | 73. | 3135 |
| | adj, prep, ps 1cs | *n fs*, n ms, ps 2ms | prep, *n mp* | n ms | cj, n ms | | n fp, ps 2ms |
| | טוֹב־לִי | תּוֹרַת־פִּיךָ | מֵאַלְפֵי | זָהָב | וָכָסֶף | | יָדֶיךָ |
| | ṭôv-lî | thôrath-pîkhā | mē'alphê | zāhāv | wākhāseph | | yādhêkhā |
| | better to me | the Law of your mouth | than thousands of | gold | and silver | | your hands |

| | | | |
|---|---|---|---|
| 6449.116 | 3679.326 | 1032.531 | 4064.125 |
| v Qal pf 3cp, ps 1cs | cj, v Polel impf 3mp, ps 1cs | v Hiphil impv 2ms, ps 1cs | cj, v Qal juss 1cs |
| עָשׂוּנִי | וַיְכוֹנְנוּנִי | הֲבִינֵנִי | וְאֶלְמְדָה |
| 'āsûnî | waykhônenûnî | hevînēnî | we'elmedhāh |
| they have made me | and they establish me | cause me to discern | that I may learn |

| | | | | | |
|---|---|---|---|---|---|
| 4851 | 74. | 3486.152 | 7495.126 | 7975.126 | 3706 |
| n fp, ps 2ms | | v Qal act ptc mp, ps 2ms | v Qal juss 3mp, ps 1cs | cj, v Qal juss 3mp | cj |
| מִצְוֹתֶיךָ | | יְרֵאֶיךָ | יִרְאוּנִי | וְיִשְׂמָחוּ | כִּי |
| mitswōthêkhā | | yerē'êkhā | yir'ûnî | weyismāchû | kî |
| your commandments | | those who fear You | may they see me | and may they be glad | because |

| | | | | | | | |
|---|---|---|---|---|---|---|---|
| 3937, 1745 | 3282.315 | 75. | 3156.115 | 3176 | 3706, 6928 | 5122 | 536 |
| prep, n ms, ps 2ms | v Piel pf 1cs | | v Qal pf 1cs | pn | cj, adj | n mp, ps 2ms | cj, n fs |
| לִדְבָרְךָ | יִחָלְתִּי | | יָדַעְתִּי | יְהוָה | כִּי־צֶדֶק | מִשְׁפָּטֶיךָ | וֶאֱמוּנָה |
| lidhvārekhā | yichāletti | | yādha'ättî | yehwāh | kî-tsedheq | mishpāṭêkhā | we'ĕmûnāh |
| for your word | I wait | | I know | O Yahweh | that righteous | your ordinances | and truth |

| | | | | |
|---|---|---|---|---|
| 6257.313 | 76. | 2030.121, 5167 | 2721 | 3937, 5341.341 |
| v Piel pf 2ms, ps 1cs | | v Qal juss 3ms, part | n ms, ps 2ms | prep, v Piel inf con, ps 1cs |
| עִנִּיתָנִי | | יְהִי־נָא | חַסְדְּךָ | לְנַחֲמֵנִי |
| 'innîthānî | | yehî-nā' | chasdekhā | lenachmēnî |
| You have answered me with | | may it be please | your steadfast love | for my comforting |

| | | | | | |
|---|---|---|---|---|---|
| 3626, 577 | 3937, 5860 | 77. | 971.126 | 7641 | 2513.125 |
| prep, n fs, ps 2ms | prep, n ms, ps 2ms | | v Qal juss 3mp, ps 1cs | n mp, ps 2ms | cj, v Qal juss 1cs |
| כְּאִמְרָתְךָ | לְעַבְדֶּךָ | | יְבֹאוּנִי | רַחֲמֶיךָ | וְאֶחְיֶה |
| ke'imrāthekhā | le'avdekhā | | yevō'ûnî | rachmêkhā | we'echăyeh |
| according to your word | to your servant | | may they come | your mercies | that I may live |

| | | | | | |
|---|---|---|---|---|---|
| 3706, 8784 | 8562 | 78. | 991.126 | 2170 | 3706, 8632 |
| cj, n fs, ps 2ms | n mp, ps 1cs | | v Qal juss 3mp | n mp | cj, n ms |
| כִּי־תוֹרָתְךָ | שַׁעֲשֻׁעָי | | יֵבֹשׁוּ | זֵדִים | כִּי־שֶׁקֶר |
| kî-thôrāthekhā | sha'ăshu'āy | | yēvōshû | zēdhîm | kî-sheqer |
| because your Law | my delights | | may they be ashamed | the insolent | because lies |

| | | | | | | |
|---|---|---|---|---|---|---|
| 6003.316 | 603 | 7943.125 | 904, 6740 | 79. | 8178.126 | 3937 |
| v Piel pf 3cp, ps 1cs | pers pron | v Qal impf 1cs | prep, n mp, ps 2ms | | v Qal juss 3mp | prep, ps 1cs |
| עִוְּתוּנִי | אֲנִי | אָשִׂיחַ | בְּפִקּוּדֶיךָ | | יָשׁוּבוּ | לִי |
| 'iwwethûnî | 'ănî | 'āsîach | bephiqqûdhêkhā | | yāshûvû | lî |
| they have falsified to me | I | I will ponder | on your precepts | | may they return | to me |

have suffered in order to learn Your laws, *Beck* ... so I would learn your demands, *NCV* ... It is good for me that I was humbled, *NRSV.*

**72. The law of thy mouth is better unto me than thousands of gold and silver:** ... Is not the law thou hast given dearer to me than rich store of gold and silver?, *Knox* ... is more precious to me than thousands of pieces of silver and gold, *NIV* ... more precious to me than all the wealth in the world, *JB*.

**73. YODH. Thy hands have made me and fashioned me: give me understanding, that I may learn thy commandments:** ... Your hands have made me, and given me form: give me wisdom, *BB* ... Thy hands moulded me and made me what I am, *NEB* ... give me discernment, *NAB* ... give me insight that I may learn your commandments, *REB*.

**74. They that fear thee will be glad when they see me; because I have hoped in thy word:** ... may thy worshippers rejoice to see me waiting on thy word!, *Moffatt* ... because I trust Your promise, *Beck* ... because I wait for your word, *Anchor* ... Those fearing Thee see me and rejoice, *Young.*

**75. I know, O LORD, that thy judgments are right, and that thou in faithfulness hast afflicted me:** ... in punishing me you show your constancy, *JB* ... that it was right for you to punish me, *NCV* ... Your Decree, LORD, was just, and justly I suffered, *Fenton.*

**76. Let, I pray thee, thy merciful kindness be for my comfort, according to thy word unto thy servant:** ... Let thy steadfast love be ready to comfort me according to thy promise, *RSV* ... Let thy never-failing love console me, *NEB* ... Your faithful love must be my consolation, *JB* ... but now console me with thy love, *Moffatt.*

**77. Let thy tender mercies come unto me, that I may live: for thy law is my delight:** ... Let thy compassions reach me, *Rotherham* ... Let Your pity come and revive, *Fenton* ... because I delight in Your teaching, *Beck.*

**78. Let the proud be ashamed; for they dealt perversely with me without a cause: but I will meditate in thy precepts:** ... for they have distorted my cause with falsehood, *MAST* ... I will think upon Your commandments, *KJVII* ... be put to shame for oppressing me unjustly, *NCB* ... for they subvert me with a lie, *NASB.*

---

eight verses of which begin with "good" (HED #3005). The epithet is first applied in v. 65 to the whole of God's dealings with the psalmist. To the devout soul all life is of one piece, and its submission and faith exercise transmuting power on pains and sorrows, so that the psalmist can say "Let one more attest, I have lived, seen God's hand through a lifetime, And all was for best."

The epithet is next applied (v. 66) to the perception (literally, "taste") or faculty of discernment of good and evil, for which the psalmist prays, basing his petition on his belief of God's word. Swift, sure and delicate apprehension of right and wrong comes from such belief. The heart in which it reigns is sensitive as a goldsmith's scales or a thermometer which visibly sinks when a cloud passes before the sun. The instincts of faith work surely and rapidly.

The settled judgment that life had been good includes apparent evil (v. 67), which is real evil in so far as it pains, but is good, inasmuch as it scourges a wandering heart back to true obedience and therefore to well-being. The words of v. 67 are especially appropriate as the utterance of the Israel purified from idolatrous tendencies by captivity, but may also be the expression of individual experience.

The epithet is next applied to God himself (v. 68). How steadfast a gaze into the depths of the divine nature and over the broad field of the divine activity is in that short, all-including clause, containing but three words in the Hebrew, "Good art thou and doing good"! The prayer built on it is the one which continually recurs in this Psalm and is reached by many paths. Every view of man's condition, whether it is bright or dark, and every thought of God bring the psalmist to the same desire. Here God's character and beneficence, widespread and continual, prompt to the prayer, both because the knowledge of his will is our highest good and because a good God cannot but wish his servants to be like himself, in loving righteousness and hating iniquity.

Verses 69f are a pair, setting forth the antithesis, frequent in the Psalm, between evil men's conduct to the psalmist and his tranquil contemplation of, and delight in, God's precepts. False slanders buzz about him, but he cleaves to God's Law and is conscious of innocence. Men are dull and insensible, as if their hearts were waterproofed with a layer of grease, through which no gentle rain from heaven could steal; but the psalmist is all the more led to open his heart to the gracious influences of that Law, because others close theirs. If a bad man is not made worse by surrounding evil, he is made better by it.

Just as in vv. 65 and 68 the same thought of God's goodness is expressed, v. 71 repeats the thought of v. 67, with a slight deepening. There the beneficent influence of sorrow was simply declared as a fact; here it is thankfully accepted, with full submission and consent of the will.

"Good for me" means not only good in fact, but in my estimate. The repetition of the phrase at the beginning of the next verse throws light on its meaning in v. 71. The singer thinks that he has two real goods, pre-eminent among the uniform sequence of such, and these are, first, his sorrows, which he reckons to be blessings, because they have helped him to a firmer grasp of the other, the real good for every man, the Law which is sacred and venerable, because it has come from the very lips of deity. That is our true wealth. Happy are they whose estimate of it corresponds to its real worth and who have learned that material riches are dross compared with its solid preciousness!

**119:73–80.** Prayer for illumination is confined to the first and last verses of this section, the rest of which is mainly occupied with petitions for gracious providences, based upon the grounds of the

| 3486.152 | 3156.116 | 5959 | | 2030.121, 3949 | 8879 |
|---|---|---|---|---|---|
| v Qal act ptc mp, ps 2ms | cj, v Qal pf 3mp | n fp, ps 2ms | **80.** | v Qal juss 3ms, n ms, ps 1cs | adj |
| יְרֵאֶיךָ | וְיָדְעוּ | עֵדֹתֶיךָ | | יְהִי־לִבִּי | תָמִים |
| yerē'êkhā | weyādheû | 'ēdhōthêkhā | | yehî-libbî | thāmîm |
| those who fear You | so they will know | your testimonies | | may my heart be | blameless |

| 904, 2805 | 3937, 4775 | 3940 | 991.125 | | 3735.112 | 3937, 9009 | 5497 |
|---|---|---|---|---|---|---|---|
| prep, n mp, ps 2ms | prep, prep | neg part | v Qal impf 1cs | **81.** | v Qal pf 3fs | prep, n fs, ps 2ms | n fs, ps 1cs |
| בְּחֻקֶּיךָ | לְמַעַן | לֹא | אֵבוֹשׁ | | כָּלְתָה | לִתְשׁוּעָתְךָ | נַפְשִׁי |
| bechuqqêkhā | lema'an | lō' | 'ēvôsh | | kālethāh | lithshû'āthekhā | naphshî |
| on your statutes | so that | not | I will be ashamed | | it is failing | for your salvation | my soul |

| 3937, 1745 | 3282.315 | | 3735.116 | 6084 | 3937, 577 | 3937, 569.141 | 5146 |
|---|---|---|---|---|---|---|---|
| prep, n ms, ps 2ms | v Piel pf 1cs | **82.** | v Qal pf 3cp | n fd, ps 1cs | prep, n fs, ps 2ms | prep, v Qal inf con | intrg |
| לִדְבָרְךָ | יִחָלְתִּי | | כָּלוּ | עֵינַי | לְאִמְרָתֶךָ | לֵאמֹר | מָתַי |
| lidhvārekhā | yichālettî | | kālû | 'ênay | le'imrāthekhā | lē'mōr | māthay |
| for your word | I wait | | they are failing | my eyes | for your word | saying | when |

| 5341.323 | | 3706, 2030.115 | 3626, 5170 | 904, 7290 | 2805 | 3940 |
|---|---|---|---|---|---|---|
| v Piel impf 2ms, ps 1cs | **83.** | cj, v Qal pf 1cs | prep, n ms | prep, n ms | n mp, ps 2ms | neg part |
| תְּנַחֲמֵנִי | | כִּי־הָיִיתִי | כְּנֹאד | בְּקִיטוֹר | חֻקֶּיךָ | לֹא |
| tenachmēnî | | kî-hāyîthî | kenō'dh | beqîṭôr | chuqqêkhā | lō' |
| will you comfort me | | because I have become | like a bottle | in smoke | your statutes | not |

| 8319.115 | | 3626, 4242 | 3219, 5860 | 5146 | 6449.123 |
|---|---|---|---|---|---|
| v Qal pf 1cs | **84.** | prep, intrg | *n mp*, n ms, ps 2ms | intrg | v Qal impf 2ms |
| שָׁכָחְתִּי | | כַּמָּה | יְמֵי־עַבְדֶּךָ | מָתַי | תַּעֲשֶׂה |
| shākhāchttî | | kammāh | yemê-'avdekhā | māthay | ta'āseh |
| I forget | | like what | the days of your servant | when | will You execute |

| 904, 7579.152 | 5122 | | 3868.116 | 2170 | 8290 | 866 |
|---|---|---|---|---|---|---|
| prep, v Qal act ptc mp, ps 1cs | n ms | **85.** | v Qal pf 3cp, prep, ps 1cs | n mp | n fp | rel part |
| בְרֹדְפָי | מִשְׁפָּט | | כָּרוּ־לִי | זֵדִים | שִׁיחוֹת | אֲשֶׁר |
| verōdhephay | mishpāṭ | | kārû-lî | zēdhîm | shîchôth | 'ăsher |
| on my persecutors | a judgment | | they have dug for me | the insolent | pits | which |

| 3940 | 3626, 8784 | | 3725, 4851 | 536 | 8632 |
|---|---|---|---|---|---|
| neg part | prep, n fs, ps 2ms | **86.** | *adj*, n fp, ps 2ms | n fs | n ms |
| לֹא | כְּתוֹרָתֶךָ | | כָּל־מִצְוֺתֶיךָ | אֱמוּנָה | שֶׁקֶר |
| lō' | khethôrāthekhā | | kol-mitswōthêkhā | 'ĕmûnāh | sheqer |
| not | according to your Law | | all your commandments | truth | lies |

| 7579.116 | 6038.131 | | 3626, 4746 | 3735.316 |
|---|---|---|---|---|
| v Qal pf 3cp, ps 1cs | v Qal impv 2ms, ps 1cs | **87.** | prep, sub | v Piel pf 3cp, ps 1cs |
| רְדָפוּנִי | עָזְרֵנִי | | כִּמְעַט | כִּלּוּנִי |
| redhāphûnî | 'āzerēnî | | kim'aṭ | killûnî |
| they have persecuted me with | help me | | like a moment | they will make an end of me |

**79. Let those that fear thee turn unto me, and those that have known thy testimonies:** … Let those who respect you return to me, *NCV* … who revere thee turn to me, And those who know thy decrees!, *Goodspeed* … they may know your stipulations, *Anchor* … and acknowledge your decrees, *NAB*.

**80. Let my heart be sound in thy statutes; that I be not ashamed:** … Let my heart be perfect, *MRB* … My heart shall be faultless towards your will, *JB* … Let my heart be blameless regarding Your statutes, *NKJV*.

**81. KAPH. My soul fainteth for thy salvation: but I hope in thy word:** … I am worn out as I long for You to save me, *Beck* … Keeping watch for thy aid, my soul languishes, *Knox* … I long with all my heart for thy deliverance, *NEB*.

**82. Mine eyes fail for thy word, saying, When wilt thou comfort me?:** … My eyes are full of weariness with searching for your word,

*BB* ... My eyes are tired from looking for your promise, *NCV* ... My eyes strain after your promise, *NAB* ... My eyes peer longingly for Thy promise, *Berkeley.*

**83. For I am become like a bottle in the smoke; yet do I not forget thy statutes:** ... Though I am like a wineskin in the smoke, *NIV* ... become like one weeping from smoke, *Anchor.*

**84. How many are the days of thy servant? when wilt thou execute judgment on them that persecute me?:** ... What is left of Your servant's life?, *Beck* ... When wilt thou doom my persecutors?, *Moffatt* ... When will you punish my hunters?, *Fenton* ... How long must your servant endure?, *NRSV.*

**85. The proud have digged pits for me, which are not after thy law:** ... The proud who flout your law spread tales about me, *REB* ... They have nothing to do with your teachings, *NCV* ... in defiance of your Law, *JB.*

**86. All thy commandments are faithful: they persecute me wrongfully; help thou me:** *KJVII* ... commandments are enduring, *NRSV* ... your commands are steadfast, *NAB* ... they persecute me with lying, ... Help me, for they hound me with their lies, *NEB.*

**87. They had almost consumed me upon earth; but I forsook not thy precepts:** ... They have nearly destroyed me in the land, *Goodspeed* ... They have all but put an end to me on the earth, *NCB* ... They almost finished me in the land, *Berkeley* ... They almost wiped me from the earth, *NIV.*

---

psalmist's love of the Law and of the encouragement to others to trust, derivable from his experience. Verse 73 puts forcibly the thought that man is evidently an incomplete fragment, unless the gift of understanding is infused into his material frame. God has begun by shaping it and, therefore, is pledged to go on to bestow spiritual discernment, when his creature asks it. But that prayer will only be answered if the suppliant intends to use the gift for its right purpose of learning God's statutes.

Verse 74 prays that the psalmist may be a witness that hope in his Word is never vain, and so that his deliverances may be occasions of widespread gladness. God's honor is involved in answering his servant's trust.

Verses 75f are linked together. The word "judgments" (HED #5122) in v. 75 seems to refer here to providential acts, not as generally in this Psalm, the Law. The acknowledgment of the justice and faithfulness which send sorrows precedes the two verses of petition for "steadfast love" and "compassions." Sorrows still sting and burn, although recognized as sent in love, and the tried heart yearns for these other messengers to come from God to sustain and soothe. God's promise and the psalmist's delight in God's Law are the double ground of the twin petitions.

Then follow three verses which are discernibly connected, as expressing desires in regard to "the proud," the devout, and the psalmist himself. He prays that the first may be shamed—i.e., that their deceitful or causeless hostility may be balked—and, as in several other verses, contrasts his own peaceful absorption in the Law with their machinations. He repeats the prayer of v. 74 with a slight difference, asking that his deliverance may draw attention to him and that others may, from contemplating his security, come to know the worth of God's testimonies.

In v. 79b, the text reads "they shall know" (as the result of observing the psalmist), which the Hebrew margin needlessly alters into "those who know." For himself he prays that his heart may be sound, or thoroughly devoted to keep the Law, and then he is sure that nothing shall ever put him to shame. "Who is he who will harm you, if ye be zealous for that which is good?"

**119:81–88.** This section has more than usual continuity. The psalmist is persecuted, and in these eight verses pours out his heart to God. Taken as a whole, they make a lovely picture of patient endurance and submissive longing. Intense and protracted yearning for deliverance has wasted his very soul, but has not merged in impatience or unbelief, for he has "waited for thy word."

His eyes have ached with straining for the signs of approaching comfort, the coming of which he has not doubted, but the delay of which has tried his faith. This longing has been quickened by troubles, which have wrapped him round like pungent smoke wreaths eddying among the rafters, where disused wineskins hang and get blackened and wrinkled. So has it been with him, but through all, he has kept hold of God's statutes. So he plaintively reminds God of the brevity of his life, which has so short a tale of days that judgment on his persecutors must be swift, if it is to be of use.

Verses 85ff describe the busy hostility of his foes. It is truculently contrary to God's Law and therefore, as is implied, worthy of God's counterworking. Verse 85b is best taken as a further description of the "proud," which is spread before God as a reason for his judicial action.

| 904, 800 | 603 | 3940, 6013.115 | 6740 | | 3626, 2721 |
|---|---|---|---|---|---|
| prep, art, n fs | cj, pers pron | neg part, v Qal pf 1cs | n mp, ps 2ms | 88. | prep, n ms, ps 2ms |
| בָּאָרֶץ | וַאֲנִי | לֹא־עָזַבְתִּי | פִקֻּודֶיךָ | | כְּחַסְדְּךָ |
| vā'ārets | wa'ănî | lō'-'āzavtî | phiqquwdhêkhā | | kechasdekhā |
| on the earth | but I | I have not abandoned | your precepts | | according to your steadfast love |

| 2513.331 | 8490.125 | 5925 | 6552 | | 3937, 5986 | 3176 |
|---|---|---|---|---|---|---|
| v Piel impv 2ms, ps 1cs | cj, v Qal juss 1cs | *n fs* | n ms, ps 2ms | 89. | prep, n ms | pn |
| חַיֵּנִי | וְאֶשְׁמְרָה | עֵדוּת | פִּיךָ | | לְעוֹלָם | יְהוָה |
| chayyênî | we'eshmerāh | 'ēdhûth | pîkhā | | le'ôlām | yehwāh |
| revive me | that I may observe | the testimony of | your mouth | | unto eternity | O Yahweh |

| 1745 | 5507.255 | 904, 8452 | | 3937, 1810 | 1810 | 536 |
|---|---|---|---|---|---|---|
| n ms, ps 2ms | v Niphal ptc ms | prep, art, n md | 90. | prep, n ms | cj, n ms | n fs, ps 2ms |
| דְּבָרְךָ | נִצָּב | בַּשָּׁמָיִם | | לְדֹר | וָדֹר | אֱמוּנָתֶךָ |
| devārekhā | nitstsāv | bashshāmāyim | | ledhōr | wādhōr | 'ĕmûnāthekhā |
| your word | taking a stand | in the heavens | | unto generations | and generations | your faithfulness |

| 3679.313 | 800 | 6198.122 | | 3937, 5122 | 6198.116 | 3219 | 3706 |
|---|---|---|---|---|---|---|---|
| v Polel pf 2ms | n fs | cj, v Qal impf 3fs | 91. | prep, n mp, ps 2ms | v Qal pf 3cp | art, n ms | cj |
| כּוֹנַנְתָּ | אֶרֶץ | וַתַּעֲמֹד | | לְמִשְׁפָּטֶיךָ | עָמְדוּ | הַיּוֹם | כִּי |
| kônantā | 'erets | watta'ămōdh | | lemishpāṭêkhā | 'āmedhû | hayyôm | kî |
| You have established | the earth | and it stands | | at your judgment | they stand | today | because |

| 3725 | 5860 | | 4020 | 8784 | 8562 | 226 | 6.115 |
|---|---|---|---|---|---|---|---|
| art, n ms | n mp, ps 2ms | 92. | cj | n fs, ps 2ms | n mp, ps 1cs | adv | v Qal pf 1cs |
| הַכֹּל | עֲבָדֶיךָ | | לוּלֵי | תוֹרָתְךָ | שַׁעֲשֻׁעָי | אָז | אָבַדְתִּי |
| hakkōl | 'ăvādhêkhā | | lûlê | thôrāthekhā | sha'ăshu'āy | 'āz | 'āvadhtî |
| everything | your servants | | if not | your Law | my delight | then | I would have perished |

| 904, 6270 | | 3937, 5986 | 3940, 8319.125 | 6740 | 3706 | 904 |
|---|---|---|---|---|---|---|
| prep, n ms, ps 1cs | 93. | prep, n ms | neg part, v Qal impf 1cs | n mp, ps 2ms | cj | prep, ps 3mp |
| בְעָנְיִי | | לְעוֹלָם | לֹא־אֶשְׁכַּח | פִּקּוּדֶיךָ | כִּי | בָם |
| ve'āneyî | | le'ôlām | lō'-'eshkach | piqqûdhêkhā | kî | vām |
| in my affliction | | unto eternity | I will not forget | your precepts | because | by them |

| 2513.313 | | 3937, 603 | 3588.531 | 3706 | 6740 |
|---|---|---|---|---|---|
| v Piel pf 2ms, ps 1cs | 94. | prep, ps 2ms, pers pron | v Hiphil impv 2ms, ps 1cs | cj | n mp, ps 2ms |
| חִיִּיתָנִי | | לְךָ־אֲנִי | הוֹשִׁיעֵנִי | כִּי | פִקּוּדֶיךָ |
| chîyîthānî | | lekhā-'ănî | hôshî'ēnî | kî | phiqqûdhêkhā |
| You have preserved my life | | to You I | save me | because | your precepts |

| 1938.115 | | 3937 | 7245.316 | 7857 | 3937, 6.341 |
|---|---|---|---|---|---|
| v Qal pf 1cs | 95. | prep, ps 1cs | v Piel pf 3cp | n mp | prep, v Piel inf con, ps 1cs |
| דָרָשְׁתִּי | | לִי | קִוּוּ | רְשָׁעִים | לְאַבְּדֵנִי |
| dhārāshettî | | lî | qiwwû | reshā'îm | le'abbedhēnî |
| I have inquired about | | for me | they hope | the wicked | to destroy me |

| 5959 | 1032.725 | | 3937, 3725 | 8831 | 7495.115 | 7377 | 7622 |
|---|---|---|---|---|---|---|---|
| n fp, ps 2ms | v Hithpolel impf 1cs | 96. | prep, *adj* | n fs | v Qal pf 1cs | n ms | adj |
| עֵדֹתֶיךָ | אֶתְבּוֹנָן | | לְכָל | תִּכְלָה | רָאִיתִי | קֵץ | רְחָבָה |
| 'ēdhōthêkhā | 'ethbônān | | lekhol | tikhlāh | rā'îthî | qēts | rechāvāh |
| your testimonies | I comprehend | | to all | perfection | I have seen | a limit | broad |

| 4851 | 4108 | | 4242, 154.115 | 8784 | 3725, 3219 | 2026 | 7946 |
|---|---|---|---|---|---|---|---|
| n fs, ps 2ms | adv | 97. | intrg, v Qal pf 1cs | n fs, ps 2ms | *adj*, art, n ms | pers pron | n fs, ps 1cs |
| מִצְוָתֶךָ | מְאֹד | | מָה־אָהַבְתִּי | תוֹרָתֶךָ | כָּל־הַיּוֹם | הִיא | שִׂיחָתִי |
| mitswāthekhā | me'ōdh | | māh-'āhavtî | thôrāthekhā | kol-hayyôm | hî' | sîchāthî |
| your commandment | very | | how I love | your Law | all the day | it | my pondering |

**88. Quicken me after thy lovingkindness; so shall I keep the testimony of thy mouth:** ... In your kindness preserve my life, *Anchor* ... True to your faithful love, give me life, *JB* ... Give me life in your mercy; so that I may be ruled by the unchanging word of your mouth, *BB*.

**89. LAMEDH. For ever, O LORD, thy word is settled in heaven:** ... more stable than the heavens!, *Anchor* ... Your purposes stand in the Skies, *Fenton* ... word is set up in the heavens, *Young* ... the word thou hast spoken stands ever unchanged as heaven, *Knox*.

**90. Thy faithfulness is unto all generations: thou hast established the earth, and it abideth:** ... Thy promise endures for all time, *NEB* ... Your loyalty will go on and on; you made the earth, and it still stands, *NCV* ... and it stands firm, *NAB*.

**91. They continue this day according to thine ordinances: for all are thy servants:** ... They stand to this day, *KJVII* ... because all things serve you, *NCV* ... all creation is your servant, *JB*.

**92. Unless thy law had been my delights, I should then have perished in mine affliction:** ... I would have perished in my misery, *Beck* ... my troubles would have put an end to me, *BB*.

**93. I will never forget thy precepts: for with them thou hast quickened me:** ... forget thy laws, for they put new life into me, *Moffatt* ... through them you have given me life, *REB* ... by these you have kept me alive, *Anchor* ... thou didst keep me alive, *Goodspeed*.

**94. I am thine, save me; for I have sought thy precepts:** ... for I seek for Your Rules, *Fenton* ... for I have sought Your commandments, *KJVII*.

**95. The wicked have waited for me to destroy me: but I will consider thy testimonies:** ... I wait on thy will, *Knox* ... but I want to understand the truths You wrote, *Beck* ... but I will ponder your statutes, *NIV* ... but I will give thought to thy instruction, *NEB*.

**96. I have seen an end of all perfection: but thy commandment is exceeding broad:** ... To all perfection I see a limit; but your commands are boundless, *NIV* ... I see a limit to all things, but thy law has a mighty range, *Moffatt* ... I see that all things have an end, but your commandment has no limit, *REB* ... only thy law is wide beyond measure, *Knox*.

**97. MEM. O how love I thy law! it is my meditation all the day:** ... love Your teaching—I think about it all day long, *Beck* ... It is my study all day long, *NEB* ... I ponder it all day long, *JB* ... I give thought to it all the day, *BB*.

---

The antithesis in v. 86, between the "faithfulness" of the Law and the "lying" persecutors, is the ground of the prayer, "Help thou me." Even in extremest peril, when he was all but made away with, the psalmist still clung to God's precepts (v. 87), and therefore he is heartened to pray for reviving and to vow that then, bound by new chains of gratitude, he will, more than ever, observe God's testimonies. The measure of the new wine poured into the shriveled wineskin is nothing less than the measureless lovingkindness of God; and nothing but experience of his benefits melts to obedience.

**119:89–96.** The stability of nature witnesses to the steadfastness of the Word which sustains it. The universe began and continues, because God puts forth his will. The heavens with their pure depths would collapse, and all their stars would flicker into darkness, if that uttered will did not echo through their overwhelming spaces. The solid earth would not be solid, but for God's power immanent in it. Heaven and earth are thus his servants.

Verse 91a may possibly picture them as standing waiting "for thine ordinances," but the indefinite preposition is probably better regarded as equivalent to "in accordance with." The psalmist has reached the grand conceptions of the universal reign of God's Law and of the continuous forthputting of God's will as the sustaining energy of all things. He seeks to link himself to that great band of God's servants, to be in harmony with stars and storms, with earth and ocean, as their fellowservant; yet he feels that his relation to God's Law is closer than theirs, for he can delight in that which they unconsciously obey.

Such delight in God's uttered will changes affliction from a foe, threatening life, to a friend, ministering strength (v. 92). Nor does that Law when loved only avert destruction; it also increases vital power (v. 93) and reinvigorates the better self. There is a sense in which the Law can give life (Gal. 3:21), but it must be welcomed and enshrined in the heart, in order to do so.

The frequently recurring prayer for "salvation" has a double plea in v. 94. The soul that has yielded itself to God in joyful obedience thereby establishes a claim on Him. He cannot but protect his own possession. Ownership has its obligations, which He recognizes. The second plea is drawn from the psalmist's seeking after God's precepts, without which seeking there would be no reality in his profession of being God's. To seek them is the sure way to find both them and salva-

| | | | | |
|---|---|---|---|---|
| **4623, 342.152** | **2549.322** | **4851** | **3706** | **3937, 5986** |
| prep, v Qal act ptc mp, ps 1cs | v Piel impf 3fs, ps 1cs | n fp, ps 2ms | cj | prep, n ms |
| **98.** מֵאֹיְבַי | תְּחַכְּמֵנִי | מִצְוֹתֶךָ | כִּי | לְעוֹלָם |
| mē'ōyᵉvay | tᵉchakkᵉmēnî | mitswōthekhā | kî | lᵉʻôlām |
| than my enemies | they make me wiser | your commandments | because | unto eternity |

| | | | | |
|---|---|---|---|---|
| **2026, 3937** | | **4623, 3725, 4064.352** | **7959.515** | **3706** |
| pers pron, prep, ps 1cs | | prep, *adj*, v Piel ptc mp, ps 1cs | v Hiphil pf 1cs | cj |
| הִיא־לִי | **99.** | מִכָּל־מְלַמְּדַי | הִשְׂכַּלְתִּי | כִּי |
| hî'-lî | | mikkol-mᵉlammᵉdhay | hiskaltî | kî |
| they to me | | than all my teachers | I have more understanding | because |

| | | | | | | |
|---|---|---|---|---|---|---|
| **5959** | **7946** | **3937** | | **4623, 2292** | **1032.725** | **3706** |
| n fp, ps 2ms | n fs | prep, ps 1cs | | prep, n mp | v Hithpolel impf 1cs | cj |
| עֵדְוֹתֶיךָ | שִׂיחָה | לִי | **100.** | מִזְּקֵנִים | אֶתְבּוֹנָן | כִּי |
| ʻēdhᵉwōthêkhā | sîchāh | lî | | mizzᵉqēnîm | 'ethbônān | kî |
| your testimonies | pondering | to me | | than the elders | I have more discernment | because |

| | | | | | | | |
|---|---|---|---|---|---|---|---|
| **6740** | **5526.115** | | **4623, 3725, 758** | **7737** | **3727.115** | **7559** | **3937, 4775** |
| n mp, ps 2ms | v Qal pf 1cs | | prep, *adj*, n ms | n ms | v Qal pf 1cs | n fd, ps 1cs | prep, prep |
| פִקּוּדֶיךָ | נָצָרְתִּי | **101.** | מִכָּל־אֹרַח | רָע | כָּלָאתִי | רַגְלָי | לְמַעַן |
| phiqqûdhêkhā | nātsārᵉttî | | mikkol-'ōrach | rā' | kāli'thî | raghlāy | lᵉma'an |
| your precepts | I have kept | | from all pathways | evil | I have kept away | my feet | so that |

| | | | | | |
|---|---|---|---|---|---|
| **8490.125** | **1745** | | **4623, 5122** | **3940, 5681.115** | **3706, 887** |
| v Qal impf 1cs | n ms, ps 2ms | | prep, n mp, ps 2ms | neg part, v Qal pf 1cs | cj, pers pron |
| אֶשְׁמֹר | דְּבָרֶךָ | **102.** | מִמִּשְׁפָּטֶיךָ | לֹא־סָרְתִּי | כִּי־אַתָּה |
| 'eshmōr | dᵉvārekhā | | mimmishpāṭêkhā | lō'-sārᵉttî | kî-'attāh |
| I will observe | your word | | from your ordinances | I do not turn aside | because You |

| | | | | | |
|---|---|---|---|---|---|
| **3498.513** | | **4242, 4593.216** | **3937, 2541** | **577** | **4623, 1756** |
| v Hiphil pf 2ms, ps 1cs | | intrg, v Niphal pf 3cp | prep, n ms, ps 1cs | n fs, ps 2ms | prep, n ms |
| הוֹרֵתָנִי | **103.** | מַה־נִּמְלְצוּ | לְחִכִּי | אִמְרָתֶךָ | מִדְּבַשׁ |
| hôrēthānî | | mah-nimlᵉtsû | lᵉchikkî | 'imrāthekhā | middᵉvash |
| You have taught me | | how they are sweeter | to my palate | your word | than honey |

| | | | | | | | |
|---|---|---|---|---|---|---|---|
| **3937, 6552** | | **4623, 6740** | **1032.725** | **6142, 3772** | **7983.115** | **3725, 758** | **8632** |
| prep, n ms, ps 1cs | | prep, n mp, ps 2ms | v Hithpolel impf 1cs | prep, adv | v Qal pf 1cs | *adj, n ms* | n ms |
| לְפִי | **104.** | מִפִּקּוּדֶיךָ | אֶתְבּוֹנָן | עַל־כֵּן | שָׂנֵאתִי | כָּל־אֹרַח | שָׁקֶר |
| lᵉphî | | mippiqqûdhêkhā | 'ethbônān | 'al-kēn | sānē'thî | kol-'ōrach | shāqer |
| to my mouth | | from your precepts | I am discerning | therefore | I hate | all paths of | falsity |

| | | | | | | |
|---|---|---|---|---|---|---|
| | **5552, 3937, 7559** | **1745** | **214** | **3937, 5594** | | **8123.215** |
| | n ms, prep, n fs, ps 1cs | n ms, ps 2ms | cj, n ms | prep, n fs, ps 1cs | | v Niphal pf 1cs |
| **105.** | נֵר־לְרַגְלִי | דְבָרֶךָ | וְאוֹר | לִנְתִיבָתִי | **106.** | נִשְׁבַּעְתִּי |
| | nēr-lᵉraghlî | dhᵉvārekhā | wᵉ'ôr | linthîvāthî | | nishba'ttî |
| | a lamp for my feet | your word | and a light | for my path | | I have sworn |

**98. Thou through thy commandments hast made me wiser than mine enemies: for they are ever with me:** … because they are mine forever, *NCV* … Your commandment is with me all the time, *Good News.*

**99. I have more understanding than all my teachers: for thy testimonies are my meditation:** … for your instruction is my study, *REB* … when your decrees are my meditation, *NCB* … I have deeper insight than all my instructors, *Berkeley* … because I ponder your instructions, *JB.*

**100. I understand more than the ancients, because I keep thy precepts:** … the old men, because I keep Your commandments, *KJVII* … more understanding than the elders, *NIV* … the aged, *NRSV* … more discretion, *Goodspeed.*

**101. I have refrained my feet from every evil way, that I might keep thy word:** … I restrain my feet from every evil path, *Anchor* … because I guard Your Word, *Fenton* … I hold back my feet from every evil way,

*RSV* ... I set no foot on any evil path, *NEB* ... That I might observe thy word, *ASV.*

**102. I have not departed from thy judgments: for thou hast taught me:** ... departed from your laws, *NIV* ... I haven't walked away from your laws, *NCV* ... not turned aside from thine ordinances, *ASV.*

**103. How sweet are thy words unto my taste! yea, sweeter than honey to my mouth!:** ... How pleasant to my taste is what Thou hast said!, *Berkeley* ... How pleasant your promise to my palate, *JB* ... How sweet is thy promise in my mouth, *NEB* ... How smooth to my palate is thy speech, *Rotherham.*

**104. Through thy precepts I get understanding: therefore I hate every false way:** ... I gain discernment, *NAB* ... I acquire insight, *Anchor* ... that is why I hate all deception, *Beck.*

**105. NUN. Thy word is a lamp unto my feet, and a light unto my path:** ... lights my steps, and enlightens my paths, *Fenton* ... ever shining on my way, *BB.*

**106. I have sworn, and I will perform it, that I will keep thy righteous judgments:** ... I have taken an oath and confirmed it, *NIV* ... I have bound myself by oath and solemn vow to keep your just decrees, *REB* ... I resolve and swear to keep your just ordinances, *NAB* ... I will do what I have promised and obey your fair laws, *NCV.*

---

tion (v. 94). Whom God saves, enemies will vainly try to destroy, and while they lurk in waiting to spring on the psalmist, his eyes are directed, not towards them, but to God's testimonies.

To give heed to these is the sure way to escape snares (v. 95). Lifelong experience has taught the psalmist that there is a flaw in every human excellence, a limit soon reached and never passed to all that is noblest in man; but high above all achievements and stretching beyond present vision is the fair ideal bodied forth in the Law. Since it is God's commandment, it will not always be an unreached ideal, but may be indefinitely approximated to; and to contemplate it will be joy, when we learn that it is prophecy because it is commandment.

**119:97–104.** One thought pervades this section, that the Law is the fountain of sweetest wisdom. The rapture of love with which it opens is sustained throughout. The psalmist knows that he has not merely more wisdom of the same sort as his enemies, his teachers and the aged have, but wisdom of a better kind. His foes were wise in craft, and his teachers drew their instructions from earthly springs, and the elders had learned that bitter, worldly wisdom, which has been disillusioned of youth's unsuspectingness and dreams, without being thereby led to grasp that which is no illusion. But a heart which simply keeps to the Law reaches, in its simplicity, a higher truth than these know, and has instinctive discernment of good and evil. Worldly wisdom is transient.

"Whether there be knowledge, it shall be done away," but the wisdom that comes with the commandment is enduring as it (v. 98). Meditation must be accompanied with practice, in order to make the true wisdom one's own. The depths of the testimonies must be sounded by patient brooding on them, and then the knowledge thus won must be carried into act.

To do what we know is the sure way to know it better, and to know more (vv. 99f). And that positive obedience has to be accompanied by abstinence from evil ways; for in such a world as this "thou shalt not" is the necessary preliminary to "thou shalt."

The psalmist has a better teacher than those whom he has outgrown, even God himself, and his instruction has a graciously constraining power, which keeps its conscious scholars in the right path (v. 102). These thoughts draw another exclamation from the poet, who feels, as he reflects on his blessings, that the Law beloved ceases to be harsh and is delightsome as well as healthgiving. It is promise as well as Law, for God will help us to be what He commands us to be. They who love the lawgiver find sweetness in the law (v. 103). And this is the blessed effect of the wisdom which it gives, that it makes us quick to detect sophistries which tempt into forbidden paths and fills us with wholesome detestation of these (v. 104).

**119:105–112.** A lamp is for night; light shines in the day. The Word is both, to the psalmist. His antithesis may be equivalent to a comprehensive declaration that the Law is light of every sort, or it may intend to lay stress on the varying phases of experience and turn our thoughts to that Word which will gleam guidance in darkness and shine a better sun on bright hours.

The psalmist's choice, not merely the inherent power of the Law, is expressed in v. 105. He has taken it for his guide, or as v. 106 says, has sworn and kept his oath that he would observe the righteous decisions, which would point to his foot the true path.

The affliction bemoaned in v. 107 is probably the direct result of the conduct professed in v. 106.

| 7251.325 | 3937, 8490.141 | 5122 | 6928 | | 6257.215 |
|---|---|---|---|---|---|
| cj, v Piel impf 1cs | prep, v Qal inf con | *n mp* | n ms, ps 2ms | 107. | v Niphal pf 1cs |
| וָאֲקַיֵּמָה | לִשְׁמֹר | מִשְׁפְּטֵי | צִדְקֶךָ | | נַעֲנֵיתִי |
| wā'ăqayyēmāh | lishmōr | mishpeṭê | tsidhqekhā | | na'ănêthî |
| and I have confirmed | to observe | the ordinances of | your righteousness | | I am afflicted |

| 5912, 4108 | 3176 | 2513.331 | 3626, 1745 | | 5249 |
|---|---|---|---|---|---|
| adv, adv | pn | v Piel impv 2ms, ps 1cs | prep, n ms, ps 2ms | 108. | *n fp* |
| עַד־מְאֹד | יְהוָה | חַיֵּנִי | כִדְבָרֶךָ | | נִדְבוֹת |
| 'adh-me'ōdh | yehwāh | chayyēnî | khidhvārekhā | | nidhvôth |
| until very | O Yahweh | revive me | according to your word | | the freewill offerings of |

| 6552 | 7813.131, 5167 | 3176 | 5122 | 4064.331 |
|---|---|---|---|---|
| n ms, ps 1cs | v Qal impv 2ms, part | pn | cj, n mp, ps 2ms | v Piel impv 2ms, ps 1cs |
| פִי | רְצֵה־נָא | יְהוָה | וּמִשְׁפָּטֶיךָ | לַמְּדֵנִי |
| pî | retsēh-nā' | yehwāh | ûmishpāṭêkhā | lammedhēnî |
| my mouth | be pleased with please | O Yahweh | and your ordinances | teach me |

| | 5497 | 904, 3834 | 8878 | 8784 | 3940 | 8319.115 |
|---|---|---|---|---|---|---|
| 109. | n fs, ps 1cs | prep, n fs, ps 1cs | adv | cj, n fs, ps 2ms | neg part | v Qal pf 1cs |
| | נַפְשִׁי | בְכַפִּי | תָמִיד | וְתוֹרָתְךָ | לֹא | שָׁכָחְתִּי |
| | naphshî | vekhappî | thāmîdh | wethôrāthekhā | lō' | shākhāchăttî |
| | my life | in the palm of my hand | continually | and your Law | not | I forget |

| | 5598.116 | 7857 | 6583 | 3937 | 4623, 6740 | 3940 | 8912.115 |
|---|---|---|---|---|---|---|---|
| 110. | v Qal pf 3cp | n mp | n ms | prep, ps 1cs | cj, prep, n mp, ps 2ms | neg part | v Qal pf 1cs |
| | נָתְנוּ | רְשָׁעִים | פַּח | לִי | וּמִפִּקּוּדֶיךָ | לֹא | תָעִיתִי |
| | nāthenû | reshā'îm | pach | lî | ûmippiqqûdhêkhā | lō' | thā'îthî |
| | they put | the wicked | a snare | for me | but from your precepts | not | I will go astray |

| | 5336.115 | 5959 | 3937, 5986 | 3706, 8050 | 3949 |
|---|---|---|---|---|---|
| 111. | v Qal pf 1cs | n fp, ps 2ms | prep, n ms | cj, *n ms* | n ms, ps 1cs |
| | נָחַלְתִּי | עֵדְוֹתֶיךָ | לְעוֹלָם | כִּי־שְׂשׂוֹן | לִבִּי |
| | nāchaltî | 'ēdhewōthêkhā | le'ōlām | kî-sesôn | libbî |
| | I have taken possession of | your testimonies | unto eternity | because the joy of | my heart |

| 2065 | | 5371.115 | 3949 | 3937, 6449.141 | 2805 | 3937, 5986 | 6358 |
|---|---|---|---|---|---|---|---|
| pers pron | 112. | v Qal pf 1cs | n ms, ps 1cs | prep, v Qal inf con | n mp, ps 2ms | prep, n ms | adv |
| הֵמָּה | | נָטִיתִי | לִבִּי | לַעֲשׂוֹת | חֻקֶּיךָ | לְעוֹלָם | עֵקֶב |
| hēmmāh | | nāṭîthî | libbî | la'ăsôth | chuqqêkhā | le'ôlām | 'ēqev |
| they | | I have inclined | my heart | to do | your statutes | unto eternity | to the end |

| | 5783 | 7983.115 | 8784 | 154.115 | | 5848 | 4182 |
|---|---|---|---|---|---|---|---|
| 113. | adj | v Qal pf 1cs | cj, n fs, ps 2ms | v Qal pf 1cs | 114. | n ms, ps 1cs | cj, n ms, ps 1cs |
| | סֵעֲפִים | שָׂנֵאתִי | וְתוֹרָתְךָ | אָהָבְתִּי | | סִתְרִי | וּמָגִנִּי |
| | sē'ăphîm | sānē'thî | wethôrāthekhā | 'āhāvettî | | sithrî | ûmāghinî |
| | double-minded | I hate | but your Law | I love | | my Hiding Place | and my Shield |

**107. I am afflicted very much: quicken me, O LORD, according unto thy word:** ... I am cruelly afflicted; O LORD, revive me and make good thy word, *NEB* ... true to your promise, give me life, *JB* ... revive me as thou hast promised, *Moffatt.*

**108. Accept, I beseech thee, the freewill offerings of my mouth, O LORD, and teach me thy judgments:** ... Accept, LORD, the willing tribute of my lips, *REB* ... accept, LORD, the praise I gladly give, and teach me Your precepts, *Beck* ... teach me to do thy bidding, *Knox.*

**109. My soul is continually in my hand: yet do I not forget thy law:** ... My life is in my hand daily, *KJVII* ... my life is ever in danger, *Moffatt* ... My life is in your eternal hands, *Anchor* ... Though constantly I take my life in my hands, *NCB.*

**110. The wicked have laid a snare for me: yet I erred not from thy precepts:** ... Sinners have put a net to take me, *BB* ... from thy precepts I wandered not, *Young* ... I swerved not from Your rules, *Fenton* ... Yet have I not gone astray from thy precepts, *ASV* ... I haven't strayed from your orders, *NCV.*

**111. Thy testimonies have I taken as an heritage for ever: for they are the rejoicing of my heart:** ... Thy instruction is my everlasting inheritance, *NEB* ... Your decrees are my inheritance forever, *NAB* ... Truly they are my heart's joy, *Anchor.*

**112. I have inclined mine heart to perform thy statutes always, even unto the end:** ... My heart is ever ready to keep your rules, *BB* ... I have set my heart on practicing Thy statutes for ever, *Berkeley* ... I intend in my heart to fulfill your statutes always, *NCB* ... I am resolved to fulfill your statutes; they are a reward that never fails, *REB.*

**113. SAMEKH. I hate vain thoughts: but thy law do I love:** ... I hate disloyal people, but I love your teachings, *NCV* ... I hate a divided heart, *JB* ... hate them that are of a double mind, *ASV* ... Half-hearted ones do I hate, *Rotherham.*

**114. Thou art my hiding place and my shield: I hope in thy word:** ... Thou art my shelter and my shield, *Goodspeed* ... You are my Protector and my Suzerain, *Anchor* ... You are my shield of shelter, I trust on Your leading, *Fenton.*

---

The prayer for reviving, which means "deliverance from outward evils" rather than "spiritual quickening," is therefore presented with confidence and based upon the many promises in the Word of help to sufferers for righteousness. Whatever our afflictions, there is ease in telling God of them, and if our desires for his help are "according to thy word," they will be as willing to accept help to bear as help which removes the sorrow and thus will not be offered unanswered.

That cry for reviving is best understood as being "the free-will offerings" which the psalmist prays may be accepted. Happy in their afflictions are they whose chief desire even then is to learn more of God's statutes! They will find that their sorrows are their best teachers. If we wish most to make advances in his school, we shall not complain of the guides to whom He commits us.

Continual alarms and dangers tend to foster disregard of duty, as truly as does the opposite state of unbroken security. A man absorbed in keeping himself alive is apt to think he has no attention to spare for God's Law (v. 109), and one ringed about by traps is apt to take a circuit to avoid them, even at the cost of divergence from the path marked out by God (v. 110). But even in such circumstances, the psalmist did what all good men have to do, deliberately chose his portion and found God's Law better than any outward good, as being able to diffuse deep, sacred and perpetual joy through all his inner nature. The heart thus filled with serene gladness is thereby drawn to perform God's statutes with lifelong persistence, and the heart thus inclined to obedience has tapped the sources of equally enduring joy.

**119:113–120.** This section is mainly the expression of firm resolve to cleave to the Law. Continuity may be traced in it, since vv. 113ff breathe love and determination, which pass in vv. 116f into prayer, in view of the psalmist's weakness and the strength of temptation, while in vv. 118ff the fate of the despisers of the Law intensifies the psalmist's clinging grasp of awe-struck love. Hatred of "double-minded" who waver between God and idols and are weak accordingly rests upon, and in its turn increases, wholehearted adherence to the Law.

It is a tepid devotion to it which does not strongly recoil from lives that water down its precepts and try to walk on both sides of the way at once. Whoever has taken God for his defense can afford to bide God's time for fulfillment of his promises (v. 114). And the natural results of such love to, and waiting for, his word are resolved separation from the society of those whose lives are molded on opposite principles and the ordering of external relations in accordance with the supreme purpose of keeping the commandments of Him whom love and waiting claim as "my God" (v. 115). But resolves melt in the fire of temptation, and the psalmist knows life and himself too well to trust himself. So he betakes himself to prayer for God's upholding, without which he cannot live.

A hope built on God's promise has a claim on Him, and its being put to shame in disappointment would be dishonor to God (v. 116). The psalmist knows that his wavering will can only be fixed by God and that experience of his sustaining hand will make a stronger bond between God and him than anything besides.

The consciousness of salvation must precede steadfast regard to the precepts of the God who saves (v. 117). To stray from the Law is ruin, as is described in vv. 118f. They who wander are despised or made light of, "for their deceit is a lie"—i.e., the hopes and plans with which they deceive themselves are false. It is a gnarled way of saying that all godless life is a blunder as well as a

| 887 | 3937, 1745 | 3282.315 | | 5681.133, 4623 | 7778.552 | 5526.125 |
|---|---|---|---|---|---|---|
| pers pron | prep, n ms, ps 2ms | v Piel pf 1cs | 115. | v Qal impv 2mp, prep, ps 1cs | v Hiphil ptc mp | cj, v Qal juss 1cs |
| אַתָּה | לִדְבָרֶךָ | יִחָלְתִּי | | סוּרוּ־מִמֶּנִּי | מְרֵעִים | וְאֶצְּרָה |
| 'āttāh | lidhvārekhā | yichāletti | | sûrû-mimmenî | merē'îm | we'etstserāh |
| You | for your word | I wait | | turn aside from me | O evildoers | that I may keep |

| 4851 | 435 | | 5759.131 | 3626, 577 | 2513.125 |
|---|---|---|---|---|---|
| *n fp* | n mp, ps 1cs | 116. | v Qal impv 2ms | prep, n fs, ps 2ms | cj, v Qal juss 1cs |
| מִצְוֹת | אֱלֹהָי | | סָמְכֵנִי | כְאִמְרָתְךָ | וְאֶחְיֶה |
| mitswōth | 'ĕlōhāy | | sāmekhēnî | khe'imrāthekhā | we'echāyeh |
| the commandments of | my God | | sustain me | according to your word | that I may live |

| 414, 991.125 | 4623, 7888 | | 5777.131 | 3588.225 |
|---|---|---|---|---|
| cj, adv, v Qal juss 1cs, ps 1cs | prep, n ms, ps 1cs | 117. | v Qal impv 2ms, ps 1cs | cj, v Niphal juss 1cs |
| וְאַל־תְּבִישֵׁנִי | מִשִּׂבְרִי | | סְעָדֵנִי | וְאִוָּשֵׁעָה |
| we'al-tevîshēnî | missivrî | | se'ādhēnî | we'iwwāshē'āh |
| and do not let me be ashamed | from my expectation | | sustain me | that I may be saved |

| 8541.125 | 904, 2805 | 8878 | | 5733.113 |
|---|---|---|---|---|
| cj, v Qal juss 1cs | prep, n mp, ps 2ms | adv | 118. | v Qal pf 2ms |
| וְאֶשְׁעָה | בְחֻקֶּיךָ | תָמִיד | | סָלִיתָ |
| we'esh'āh | vechuqqêkhā | thāmîdh | | sālîthā |
| that I may have regard | with your statutes | continually | | You have disdain for |

| 3725, 8146.152 | 4623, 2805 | 3706, 8632 | 8988 | | 5698 |
|---|---|---|---|---|---|
| *adj*, v Qal act ptc mp | prep, n mp, ps 2ms | cj, n ms | n fs, ps 3mp | 119. | n mp |
| כָּל־שׁוֹגִים | מֵחֻקֶּיךָ | כִּי־שֶׁקֶר | תַּרְמִיתָם | | סִגִים |
| kol-shôghîm | mēchuqqêkhā | kî-sheqer | tarmîthām | | sighîm |
| all those who go astray | from your statutes | indeed vanity | their treachery | | dross |

| 8139.513 | 3725, 7857, 800 | 3937, 3772 | 154.115 | 5959 |
|---|---|---|---|---|
| v Hiphil pf 2ms | *adj*, *n mp*, n fs | prep, adv | v Qal pf 1cs | n fp, ps 2ms |
| הִשְׁבַּתָּ | כָל־רִשְׁעֵי־אָרֶץ | לָכֵן | אָהַבְתִּי | עֵדֹתֶיךָ |
| hishbattā | khol-rish'ê-ārets | lākhēn | 'āhavtî | 'ēdhōthêkhā |
| You cause to cease | all the wicked of the earth | therefore | I love | your testimonies |

| | 5763.111 | 4623, 6586 | 1340 | 4623, 5122 | 3486.115 |
|---|---|---|---|---|---|
| 120. | v Qal pf 3ms | prep, n ms, ps 2ms | n ms, ps 1cs | cj, prep, n mp, ps 2ms | v Qal pf 1cs |
| | סָמַר | מִפַּחְדְּךָ | בְשָׂרִי | וּמִמִּשְׁפָּטֶיךָ | יָרֵאתִי |
| | sāmar | mippachdekhā | vesārî | ûmimmishpātêkhā | yārē'thî |
| | it trembles | from the terror of You | my flesh | and of your judgments | I am afraid |

| | 6449.115 | 5122 | 6928 | 1118, 5299.523 |
|---|---|---|---|---|
| 121. | v Qal pf 1cs | n ms | cj, n ms | neg part, v Hiphil impf 2ms, ps 1cs |
| | עָשִׂיתִי | מִשְׁפָּט | וָצֶדֶק | בַּל־תַּנִּיחֵנִי |
| | 'āsîthî | mishpāt | wātsedheq | bal-tanîchēnî |
| | I have done | justice | and righteousness | do not leave me behind |

| 3937, 6456.152 | | 6386.131 | 5860 | 3937, 3005 |
|---|---|---|---|---|
| prep, v Qal act ptc mp, ps 1cs | 122. | v Qal impv 2ms | n ms, ps 2ms | prep, adj |
| לְעֹשְׁקָי | | עֲרֹב | עַבְדְּךָ | לְטוֹב |
| le'ōsheqāy | | 'ărōv | 'avdekhā | letôv |
| to my oppressors | | provide surety for | your servant | for good |

| 414, 6456.126 | 2170 | | 6084 | 3735.116 | 3937, 3568 |
|---|---|---|---|---|---|
| adv, v Qal juss 3mp, ps 1cs | n mp | 123. | n fd, ps 1cs | v Qal pf 3cp | prep, n fs, ps 2ms |
| אַל־יַעַשְׁקֻנִי | זֵדִים | | עֵינַי | כָּלוּ | לִישׁוּעָתֶךָ |
| 'al-ya'ashqunî | zēdhîm | | 'ênay | kālû | lîshû'āthekhā |
| do not let them oppress me | the insolent | | my eyes | they are failing | for your salvation |

**115. Depart from me, ye evildoers: for I will keep the commandments of my God:** ... Go away from me, you evildoers, *NRSV* ... I want to do what my God orders, *Beck*.

**116. Uphold me according unto thy word, that I may live:** ... sustain me according to your promise, *NIV* ... Sustain me as you have promised, *NAB* ... support me and I shall live, *JB*.

**and let me not be ashamed of my hope:** ... do not disappoint my hope, *REB* ... defeat not my trust, *Fenton* ... let me not be put to shame with my expectation!, *Berkeley* ... Don't let me be embarrassed because of my hopes, *NCV*.

**117. Hold thou me up, and I shall be safe: and I will have respect unto thy statutes continually:** ... let me delight for ever in thy will, *Moffatt* ... Strengthen me so I may be saved, *Beck* ... Strengthen me that I may be delivered, *Goodspeed* ... Sustain me, that I may see deliverance, *NEB*.

**118. Thou hast trodden down all them that err from thy statutes: for their deceit is falsehood:** ... rejected all those who wander, *NASB* ... hast made light of all them that err, *MAST* ... their whole talk is malice and lies, *REB* ... their cunning is in vain, *NRSV* ... because their idolatry is false, *Anchor*.

**119. Thou puttest away all the wicked of the earth like dross:** ... You throw away the wicked of the world like trash, *NCV* ... You drove all vile from the Land, *Fenton* ... earth like waste, *KJVII*.

**therefore I love thy testimonies:** ... I love thy decrees, *Goodspeed* ... I love thy instruction, *NEB* ... I give my love to your unchanging word, *BB*.

**120. My flesh trembleth for fear of thee; and I am afraid of thy judgments:** ... My flesh shudders in awe of Thee, *Berkeley* ... flesh shudders with dread of you, *NAB* ... My whole body trembles before you, *JB* ... I stand in awe of your laws, *NIV*.

**121. AYIN. I have done judgment and justice:** ... done justice and righteousness, *Rotherham* ... done what is fair and right, *NCV* ... All my conduct has been just and upright, *JB* ... Defend for me my right and my just cause, *Anchor*.

**leave me not to mine oppressors:** ... you will not give me into the hands of those who are working against me, *BB* ... never leave me at the mercy of my oppressors, *Knox* ... Leave me not to be oppressed, *Moffatt*.

**122. Be surety for thy servant for good: let not the proud oppress me:** ... Guarantee Your servant's welfare, *Beck* ... Pledge me thy word for good, *Goodspeed* ... do not let the godless oppress me, *NRSV* ... the proud press me down, *KJVII*.

**123. Mine eyes fail for thy salvation, and for the word of thy righteousness:** ... eyes fail for Your help, *Fenton* ... My sight grows dim with looking for thy deliverance, *NEB* ... for the saving justice you have promised, *JB* ... for the fulfilment of thy righteous promise, *RSV*.

---

sin and is fed with unrealizable promises. Dross is flung away when the metal is extracted. Slag from a furnace is hopelessly useless and this psalmist thinks that the wicked of the earth are "thrown as rubbish to the void." He is not contemplating a future life, but God's judgments as manifested here in providence, and his faith is assured that, even here, that process is visible.

Therefore, gazing upon the fate of evildoers, his flesh creeps (HED #5763) and every particular hair stands on end (as the word means). His dread is full of love, and love is full of dread. Profoundly are the two emotions yoked together in vv. 119b and 120b, "I love thy testimonies ... of thy judgments I am afraid."

**119:121–128.** The thought of evildoers tinges most of this section. It opens with a triplet of verses, occasioned by their oppressions of the psalmist, and closes with a triplet occasioned by their breaches of the Law. In the former, he is conscious that he has followed the "judgment" or Law of God and hence hopes that he will not be abandoned to his foes. The consciousness and the hope equally need limitation, to correspond with true estimates of ourselves and with facts; for there is no absolute fulfillment of the Law, and good men are often left to be footballs for bad ones. But in its depths, the confidence is true. Precisely because he has it, the psalmist prays that it may be vindicated by facts.

"Be surety for thy servant"—a profound image, drawn from legal procedure, in which one man becomes security for another and makes good his deficiencies. Thus, God will stand between the hunted man and his foes, undertaking for him. "Thou shalt answer, LORD, for me." How much the fulfillment in Christ has exceeded the desire of the psalmist! "The oppressors' wrong" had lasted long, and the singer's weary eyes had been strained in looking for the help which seemed to tarry (cf. v. 82), and that fainting gaze humbly appeals to God. Will He not end the wistful watching speedily?

Verses 124f are a pair, the psalmist's relation of servant being adduced in both as the ground of his prayer for teaching. But they differ, in that the former verse lays stress on the consonance of such

| 3937, 577 | 6928 | | 6449.131 | 6196, 5860 |
|---|---|---|---|---|
| cj, prep, *n fs* | n ms, ps 2ms | **124.** | v Qal impv 2ms | prep, n ms, ps 2ms |
| וּלְאִמְרַת | צִדְקֶךָ | | עֲשֵׂה | עִם־עַבְדְּךָ |
| ûlā'imrath | tsidhqekhā | | 'ăsēh | 'im-'avdekhā |
| and for the word of | your righteousness | | do | with your servant |

| 3626, 2721 | 2805 | 4064.331 | | 5860, 603 |
|---|---|---|---|---|
| prep, n ms, ps 2ms | cj, n mp, ps 2ms | v Piel impv 2ms, ps 1cs | **125.** | n ms, ps 2ms, pers pron |
| כְחַסְדֶּךָ | וְחֻקֶּיךָ | לַמְּדֵנִי | | עַבְדְּךָ־אָנִי |
| khechasdekhā | wechuqqêkhā | lammedhēnî | | 'avdekhā-'ānî |
| according to your steadfast love | and your statutes | teach me | | your servant I |

| 1032.531 | 3156.125 | 5959 | | 6496 | 3937, 6449.141 |
|---|---|---|---|---|---|
| v Hiphil impv 2ms, ps 1cs | cj, v Qal juss 1cs | n fp, ps 2ms | **126.** | n fs | prep, v Qal inf con |
| הֲבִינֵנִי | וְאֵדְעָה | עֵדֹתֶיךָ | | עֵת | לַעֲשׂוֹת |
| hevînēnî | we'ēdhe'āh | 'ēdhōthêkhā | | 'ēth | la'ăsôth |
| cause me to discern | that I may understand | your testimonies | | the time | to do |

| 3937, 3176 | 6815.516 | 8784 | | 6142, 3772 | 154.115 | 4851 |
|---|---|---|---|---|---|---|
| prep, pn | v Hiphil pf 3cp | n fs, ps 2ms | **127.** | prep, adv | v Qal pf 1cs | n fp, ps 2ms |
| לַיהוָה | הֵפֵרוּ | תּוֹרָתֶךָ | | עַל־כֵּן | אָהַבְתִּי | מִצְוֺתֶיךָ |
| layhwāh | hēphērû | tôrāthekhā | | 'al-kēn | 'āhavtî | mitswōthêkhā |
| for Yahweh | they have broken | your Law | | therefore | I love more | your commandments |

| 4623, 2174 | 4623, 6580 | | 6142, 3772 | 3725, 6740 | 3725 | 3595.315 |
|---|---|---|---|---|---|---|
| prep, n ms | cj, prep, n ms | **128.** | prep, adv | *adj, n mp* | n ms | v Piel pf 1cs |
| מִזָּהָב | וּמִפָּז | | עַל־כֵּן | כָּל־פִּקּוּדֵי | כֹּל | יִשָּׁרְתִּי |
| mizzāhāv | ûmippāz | | 'al-kēn | kol-piqqûdhê | khōl | yishshārettî |
| than gold | even than pure gold | | therefore | all the precepts of | everything | I make upright |

| 3725, 758 | 8632 | 7983.115 | | 6624 | 5959 | 6142, 3772 |
|---|---|---|---|---|---|---|
| *adj, n ms* | n ms | v Qal pf 1cs | **129.** | n fp | n fp, ps 2ms | prep, adv |
| כָּל־אֹרַח | שָׁקֶר | שָׂנֵאתִי | | פְּלָאוֹת | עֵדְוֺתֶיךָ | עַל־כֵּן |
| kol-'ōrach | sheqer | sānē'thî | | pelā'ôth | 'ēdhewōthêkhā | 'al-kēn |
| all the paths of | falsity | I hate | | extraordinary things | your testimonies | therefore |

| 5526.112 | 5497 | | 6860 | 1745 | 213.521 |
|---|---|---|---|---|---|
| v Qal pf 3fs, ps 3mp | n fs, ps 1cs | **130.** | *n ms* | n mp, ps 2ms | v Hiphil impf 3ms |
| נְצָרָתַם | נַפְשִׁי | | פֵּתַח | דְּבָרֶיךָ | יָאִיר |
| netsārātham | naphshî | | pēthach | devārêkhā | yā'îr |
| it will keep them | my soul | | the uncovering of | your words | it illuminates |

| 1032.551 | 6864 | | 6552, 6720.115 | 8079.125 | 3706 |
|---|---|---|---|---|---|
| v Hiphil ptc ms | n mp | **131.** | n ms, ps 1cs, v Qal pf 1cs | cj, v Qal impf 1cs | cj |
| מֵבִין | פְּתָיִים | | פִּי־פָעַרְתִּי | וָאֶשְׁאָפָה | כִּי |
| mēvîn | pethāyîm | | pî-phā'artî | wā'esh'āphāh | kî |
| giving discernment to | the simple | | my mouth I open wide | and I long for | indeed |

| 3937, 4851 | 3078.115 | | 6680.131, 420 | 2706.131 |
|---|---|---|---|---|
| prep, n fp, ps 2ms | v Qal pf 1cs | **132.** | v Qal impv 2ms, prep, ps 1cs | cj, v Qal impv 2ms, ps 1cs |
| לְמִצְוֺתֶיךָ | יָאָבְתִּי | | פְּנֵה־אֵלַי | וְחָנֵּנִי |
| lemitswōthêkhā | yā'āvettî | | peneh-'ēlay | wechānnēnî |
| for your commandments | I am desirous | | turn to me | and be gracious to me |

| 3626, 5122 | 3937, 154.152 | 8428 | | 6718 | 3679.531 |
|---|---|---|---|---|---|
| prep, n ms | prep, *v Qal act ptc mp* | n ms, ps 2ms | **133.** | n fp, ps 1cs | v Hiphil impv 2ms |
| כְּמִשְׁפָּט | לְאֹהֲבֵי | שְׁמֶךָ | | פְּעָמַי | הָכֵן |
| kemishpāṭ | le'ōhevê | shemekhā | | pe'āmay | hākhēn |
| according to the judgment | to those who love | your name | | my steps | establish |

**124. Deal with thy servant according unto thy mercy, and teach me thy statutes:** ... In your dealings with me, LORD, show your love, *REB* ... teach me your decrees, *NIV.*

**125. I am thy servant; give me understanding, that I may know thy testimonies:** ... wisdom, so that I may have knowledge of your unchanging word, *BB* ... give me insight, that I may know your stipulations, *Anchor* ... wisdom so I can understand your rules, *NCV* ... discernment that I may know your decrees, *NAB.*

**126. It is time for thee, LORD, to work: for they have made void thy law:** ... to act—they have violated Your teaching, *Beck* ... your law is being broken, *NIV* ... they have broken Your law, *KJVII* ... they have destroyed thy Law, *Geneva.*

**127. Therefore I love thy commandments above gold; yea, above fine gold:** ... Precious beyond gold or jewel I hold thy law, *Knox* ... purest gold, *JB* ... For this reason I have greater love for your teachings than for gold, *BB.*

**128. Therefore I esteem all thy precepts concerning all things to be right; and I hate every false way:** ... in all your precepts I go forward, *NAB* ... I direct my steps by all your precepts, *NRSV* ... I hate the paths of falsehood, *REB* ... hate all crooked paths, *Fenton.*

**129. PE. Thy testimonies are wonderful: therefore doth my soul keep them:** ... Wonderful are your instructions, *JB* ... Thy laws are a wondrous mystery, *Moffatt* ... Wonderful are your decrees, *NCB* ... therefore I obey them, *NIV* ... therefore I gladly keep it, *NEB.*

**130. The entrance of thy words giveth light:** ... Your word is a door that lets in light, *Beck* ... Your word is revealed, and all is light, *REB* ... The opening of Thy words, *MAST* ... The unfolding of Thy words, *NASB.*

**it giveth understanding unto the simple:** ... Instructing the simple, *Young* ... give the innocent insight, *Anchor* ... Giving understanding to the open-hearted, *Goodspeed* ... understanding even to the untaught, *NEB.*

**131. I opened my mouth, and panted: for I longed for thy commandments:** ... waiting with great desire for your teachings, *BB* ... I gasp with open mouth in my yearning for your commands, *NAB* ... I am open, eager, panting for thy commands, *Moffatt* ... panting eagerly for your commandments, *JB.*

**132. Look thou upon me, and be merciful unto me, as thou usest to do unto those that love thy name:** ... Turn to me and be gracious to me, *RSV* ... After Thy manner with those who love Thy name, *NASB* ... As is the right of those who love thy name, *Goodspeed* ... As Your custom is toward those who love Your name, *NKJV.*

**133. Order my steps in thy word:** ... Guide my steps as you promised, *NCV* ... Make my step firm according to thy promise, *NEB* ... Establish my steps in thy word, *Darby.*

---

instruction with God's lovingkindness, and the latter on its congruity with the psalmist's position and character as his servant. God's best gift is the knowledge of his will, which He surely will not withhold from spirits willing to serve, if they only knew how.

Verses 126ff are closely linked. The psalmist's personal wrongs melt into the wider thought of wickedness which does its best to make void that sovereign, steadfast Law. Delitzsch would render "It is time to work for Yahweh"; and the meaning thus obtained is a worthy one. But that given above is more in accordance with the context. It is bold—and would be audacious if a prayer did not underlie the statement—to undertake to determine when evil has reached such height as to demand God's punitive action. But, however slow we should be to prescribe to Him the when or the how of his intervention, we may learn from the psalmist's emphatic "therefores," which stand coordinately at the beginnings of vv. 127f, that the more men make void the Law, the more should God's servants prize it and the more should they bind its precepts on their moral judgment and heartily loathe all paths which, specious as they may be, are "paths of falsehood," although all the world may avow that they are true.

**119:129–136.** Devout souls do not take offense at the depths and difficulties of God's Word, but are thereby drawn to intenser contemplation of them. We weary of the trivial and obvious. That which tasks and outstrips our powers attracts. But the obscurity must not be arbitrary, but inherent, a clear obscure, like the depths of a pure sea. These wonderful testimonies give light because of their wonderfulness, and it is the simple heart—not the sharpened intellect—that penetrates furthest into them and finds light most surely (v. 130). Therefore, the psalmist longs for God's commandments, like a wild creature panting open-mouthed for water. He puts to shame our indifference. If his longing was not excessive, how defective is ours!

Verse 132, like v. 122, has no distinct allusion to the Law, although the word rendered "right" is that used in the Psalm for the Law considered as "judgments." The prayer is a bold one, pleading

| 904, 577 | 414, 8375.522, 904 | 3725, 201 | | 6540.131 |
|---|---|---|---|---|
| prep, n fs, ps 2ms | cj, adv, v Hiphil juss 3fs, prep, ps 1cs | *adj*, n ms | **134.** | v Qal impv 2ms, ps 1cs |
| בְּאִמְרָתֶךָ | וְאַל־תַּשְׁלֶט־בִּי | כָל־אָוֶן | | פְּדֵנִי |
| beʾimrāthekhā | weʾal-tashleṭ-bî | khol-ʾāwen | | pedhēnî |
| by your word | and do not let it gain power over me | all iniquity | | ransom me |

| 4623, 6480 | 119 | 8490.125 | 6740 | | 6686 |
|---|---|---|---|---|---|
| prep, *n ms* | n ms | cj, v Qal juss 1cs | n mp, ps 2ms | **135.** | n mp, ps 2mp |
| מֵעֹשֶׁק | אָדָם | וְאֶשְׁמְרָה | פִּקּוּדֶיךָ | | פָּנֶיךָ |
| mēʿōsheq | ʾādhām | weʾeshmerāh | piqqûdhêkhā | | pānêkhā |
| from the oppression of | men | that I may observe | your precepts | | your face |

| 213.531 | 904, 5860 | 4064.331 | 881, 2805 | | 6631, 4448 |
|---|---|---|---|---|---|
| v Hiphil impv 2ms | prep, n ms, ps 2ms | cj, v Piel impv 2ms, ps 1cs | do, n mp, ps 2ms | **136.** | *n mp*, n md |
| הָאֵר | בְּעַבְדֶּךָ | וְלַמְּדֵנִי | אֶת־חֻקֶּיךָ | | פַּלְגֵי־מַיִם |
| hāʾēr | beʿavdekhā | welammedhēnî | ʾeth-chuqqêkhā | | palghê-mayim |
| cause to shine | on your servant | and teach me | your statutes | | streams of water |

| 3495.116 | 6084 | 6142 | 3940, 8490.116 | 8784 | | 6926 | 887 |
|---|---|---|---|---|---|---|---|
| v Qal pf 3cp | n fd, ps 1cs | prep | neg part, v Qal pf 3cp | n fs, ps 2ms | **137.** | adj | pers pron |
| יָרְדוּ | עֵינָי | עַל | לֹא־שָׁמְרוּ | תוֹרָתֶךָ | | צַדִּיק | אַתָּה |
| yāredhû | ʿênāy | ʿal | lōʾ-shāmerû | thôrāthekhā | | tsaddîq | ʾattāh |
| they go down from | my eyes | because | they do not observe | your Law | | righteous | You |

| 3176 | 3596 | 5122 | | 6943.313 | 6928 |
|---|---|---|---|---|---|
| pn | cj, adj | n mp, ps 2ms | **138.** | v Piel pf 2ms | n ms |
| יְהוָה | וְיָשָׁר | מִשְׁפָּטֶיךָ | | צִוִּיתָ | צֶדֶק |
| yehwāh | weyāshār | mishpāṭêkhā | | tsiwwîthā | tsedheq |
| O Yahweh | and upright | your ordinances | | You have commanded | righteousness |

| 5959 | 536 | 4108 | | 7059.312 | 7352 | 3706, 8319.116 |
|---|---|---|---|---|---|---|
| n fp, ps 2ms | cj, n fs | adv | **139.** | v Piel pf 3fs, ps 1cs | n fs, ps 1cs | cj, v Qal pf 3cp |
| עֵדֹתֶיךָ | וֶאֱמוּנָה | מְאֹד | | צִמְּתַתְנִי | קִנְאָתִי | כִּי־שָׁכְחוּ |
| ʿēdhōthêkhā | weʾĕmûnāh | meʾōdh | | tsimmethathnî | qinʾāthî | kî-shākhechû |
| your testimonies | and truth | very | | it devastates me | my zeal | because they have forgotten |

| 1745 | 7141 | | 7170.157 | 577 | 4108 | 5860 |
|---|---|---|---|---|---|---|
| n mp, ps 2ms | n mp, ps 1cs | **140.** | v Qal pass ptc fs | n fs, ps 2ms | adv | cj, n ms, ps 2ms |
| דְבָרֶיךָ | צָרָי | | צְרוּפָה | אִמְרָתְךָ | מְאֹד | וְעַבְדְּךָ |
| dhevārêkhā | tsārāy | | tserûphāh | ʾimrāthekhā | meʾōdh | weʿavdekhā |
| your words | my adversaries | | refined | your word | very | and your servant |

| 154.111 | | 7087 | 609 | 995.255 | 6740 | 3940 | 8319.115 |
|---|---|---|---|---|---|---|---|
| v Qal pf 3ms, ps 3fs | **141.** | adj | pers pron | cj, v Niphal ptc ms | n mp, ps 2ms | neg part | v Qal pf 1cs |
| אֲהֵבָהּ | | צָעִיר | אָנֹכִי | וְנִבְזֶה | פִּקֻּדֶיךָ | לֹא | שָׁכָחְתִּי |
| ʾăhēvāhh | | tsāʿîr | ʾānōkhî | wenivzeh | piqqudhêkhā | lōʾ | shākhāchättî |
| he loves it | | small | I | and despised | your precepts | not | I forget |

| | 6930 | 6928 | 3937, 5986 | 8784 | 583 |
|---|---|---|---|---|---|
| **142.** | n fs, ps 2ms | adj | prep, n ms | cj, n fs, ps 2ms | n fs |
| | צִדְקָתְךָ | צֶדֶק | לְעוֹלָם | וְתוֹרָתְךָ | אֱמֶת |
| | tsidhqāthekhā | tsedheq | leʿôlām | wethôrāthekhā | ʾĕmeth |
| | your righteousness | righteous | unto eternity | and your Law | truth |

| | 7140, 4856 | 4834.116 | 4851 | 8562 |
|---|---|---|---|---|
| **143.** | n ms, cj, n ms | v Qal pf 3cp, ps 1cs | n fp, ps 2ms | n mp, ps 1cs |
| | צַר־וּמָצוֹק | מְצָאוּנִי | מִצְוֺתֶיךָ | שַׁעֲשֻׁעָי |
| | tsar-ûmātsôq | metsāʾûnî | mitswōthêkhā | shaʿăshuʿāy |
| | adversity and bondage | they have found me | your commandments | my delight |

**and let not any iniquity have dominion over me:** ... that no evil may triumph over me, *JB* ... let no wrong have the mastery over me, *REB* ... and do not let any iniquity rule over me, *KJVII* ... let no sin rule over me, *NIV.*

**134. Deliver me from the oppression of man: so will I keep thy precepts:** ... Redeem me from the oppression of man: So will I observe, *ASV* ... and I will follow the way You want me to live, *Beck.*

**135. Make thy face to shine upon thy servant; and teach me thy statutes:** ... Turn light on Your slave, and teach me Your Decrees, *Fenton* ... Smile on thy servant, teach thy laws to me, *Moffatt* ... Restore to thy servant the smile of thy living favour, *Knox.*

**136. Rivers of waters run down mine eyes, because they keep not thy law:** ... mine eyes stream with tears, *Moffatt* ... Tears run from my eyes like water brooks, *Berkeley* ... Mine eyes run down with streams of water, *Darby.*

**137. TSADE. Righteous art thou, O LORD, and upright are thy judgments:** ... and your judgments are right, *NRSV* ... You are just, O LORD, and your ordinance is right, *NAB* ... great is your righteousness, and upright are your decisions, *BB.*

**138. Thy testimonies that thou hast commanded are righteous and very faithful:** ... You impose uprightness as a witness to yourself, it is constancy itself, *JB* ... The rules you commanded are right and completely trustworthy, *NCV* ... When You gave Your truth, it was just and very dependable, *Beck* ... It is fixed firm and sure, *NEB.*

**139. My zeal hath consumed me, because mine enemies have forgotten thy words:** ... My anger was burning, for my foes neglected, *Fenton* ... My zeal wears me out, for my enemies ignore your words, *NIV* ... My zeal has eaten me up, *KJVII* ... My antagonists sought to annihilate me, *Anchor.*

**140. Thy word is very pure: therefore thy servant loveth it:** ... Thy word is tried to the uttermost, *MAST* ... Your promise is very sure, *NCB* ... Your promise has been well tested, and I love it, *REB* ... Shall not I, thy servant, love thy promises, tested and found true?, *Knox.*

**141. I am small and despised: yet do not I forget thy precepts:** ... I am insignificant and despised, *Berkeley* ... Though I am young and despised, *Anchor* ... and of no account; but I keep your orders in mind, *BB* ... despised and disinherited, I do not forget thy charge, *Knox.*

**142. Thy righteousness is an everlasting righteousness, and thy law is the truth:** ... Your goodness continues forever, and your teachings are true, *NCV* ... Your saving justice is for ever just, *JB* ... Thy justice is an everlasting justice, *NEB* ... your law is permanent, *NCB* ... your law is steadfast, *REB.*

**143. Trouble and anguish have taken hold on me: yet thy commandments are my delights:** ... Adversity and distress have found me, *Young* ... anguish have over-

---

what is justly due to the lovers of God's name. "God is not unrighteous to forget your work and labour of love, which ye have shown toward his name" (Heb. 6:10). One would have expected "Law" instead of "name" in the last word of the verse, and possibly the conception of Law may be, as it were, latent in "name," for the latter does carry in it imperative commandments and plain revelations of duty. God's name holds the Law in germ. The Law is but the expansion of the meaning of the Name.

"Word" (HED #577) in v. 133 (literally, "saying") must be taken in a widened sense, as including all God's revealed will. The only escape from the tyranny of sin is to have our steps established by God's Word, and his help is needed for such establishment. Rebellion against sin's dominion is already victory over it, if the rebel summons God's heavenly reinforcements to his help.

It is a high attainment to desire deliverance from men, chiefly in order to observe, unhindered, God's commandments (v. 134). And it is as high a desire to seek the light of God's face mainly as the means of seeing his will more clearly. The psalmist did not merely wish for outward prosperity or inward cheer and comfort, but that these might contribute to fulfilling his deepest wish of learning better what God would have him to do (v. 135). The moods of indignation (v. 53) and of hatred (vv. 104, 113, 128) have given place to softer emotions, as they ever should (v. 136). Tears and dewy pity should mingle with righteous anger, as when Jesus "looked round about on them with anger, being with the anger grieved at the hardening of their heart" (Mark 3:5).

**119:137–144.** The first word suggested to the psalmist under this letter is "righteous" (HED #6926). That august conception was grasped by devout Israelites with a tenacity and assumed a prominence in their thoughts unparalleled elsewhere. It is no mere yielding to the requirements of the acrostic scheme which sets that great word in four of the eight verses of this section (137f, 142f). Two thoughts are common to them all, that righteousness has its seat in the bosom of God and that the Law is

| | | | | | |
|---|---|---|---|---|---|
| **144.** | **6928** | **5959** | **3937, 5986** | **1032.531** | **2513.125** |
| | adj | n fp, ps 2ms | prep, n ms | v Hiphil impv 2ms, ps 1cs | cj, v Qal juss 1cs |
| | צֶדֶק | עֵדְוֹתֶיךָ | לְעוֹלָם | הֲבִינֵנִי | וְאֶחְיֶה |
| | tsedheq | ʽēdh$^{e}$wōthêkhā | l$^{e}$ʽôlām | h$^{e}$vînēnî | w$^{e}$'echăyeh |
| | righteous | your testimonies | unto eternity | cause me to discern | that I may live |

| | | | | | | |
|---|---|---|---|---|---|---|
| **145.** | **7410.115** | **904, 3725, 3949** | **6257.131** | **3176** | **2805** | **5526.125** |
| | v Qal pf 1cs | prep, *adj*, n ms | v Qal impv 2ms, ps 1cs | pn | n mp, ps 2ms | v Qal juss 1cs |
| | קָרָאתִי | בְכָל־לֵב | עֲנֵנִי | יְהוָה | חֻקֶּיךָ | אֶצֹּרָה |
| | qārā'thî | v$^{e}$khol-lēv | ʽănēnî | y$^{e}$hwāh | chuqqêkhā | 'etstsōrāh |
| | I cry out | with all the heart | answer me | O Yahweh | your statutes | let me keep |

| | | | | |
|---|---|---|---|---|
| **146.** | **7410.115** | **3588.531** | **8490.125** | **5959** |
| | v Qal pf 1cs, ps 2ms | v Hiphil impv 2ms, ps 1cs | cj, v Qal juss 1cs | n fp, ps 2ms |
| | קְרָאתִיךָ | הוֹשִׁיעֵנִי | וְאֶשְׁמְרָה | עֵדֹתֶיךָ |
| | qŏrā'thîkhā | hôshî'ēnî | w$^{e}$'eshm$^{e}$rāh | ʽēdhōthêkhā |
| | I have called to You | save me | that I may observe | your testimonies |

| | | | | | |
|---|---|---|---|---|---|
| **147.** | **7207.315** | **904, 5582** | **8209.325** | **3937, 1745** | **3282.315** |
| | v Piel pf 1cs | prep, art, n ms | cj, v Piel impf 1cs | prep, n mp, ps 2ms | v Piel pf 1cs |
| | קִדַּמְתִּי | בַנֶּשֶׁף | וָאֲשַׁוֵּעָה | לִדְבָרְךָ | יִחָלְתִּי |
| | qiddamtî | vannesheph | wā'ăshawwē'āh | lidhvārēkhā | yichāl$^{e}$ttî |
| | I go to meet | during the twilight | and I cry for help | for your words | I wait |

| | | | | | | | |
|---|---|---|---|---|---|---|---|
| **148.** | **7207.316** | **6084** | **847** | **3937, 7943.141** | **904, 577** | **149.** | **7249** |
| | v Piel pf 3cp | n fd, ps 1cs | n fp | prep, v Qal inf con | prep, n fs, ps 2ms | | n ms, ps 1cs |
| | קִדְּמוּ | עֵינַי | אַשְׁמֻרוֹת | לָשִׂיחַ | בְּאִמְרָתֶךָ | | קוֹלִי |
| | qidd$^{e}$mû | ʽênay | 'ashmurôth | lāsîach | b$^{e}$'imrāthekhā | | qôlî |
| | they go ahead | my eyes | the night watches | to ponder | on your word | | my voice |

| | | | |
|---|---|---|---|
| **8471.131** | **3626, 2721** | **3176** | **3626, 5122** |
| v Qal impv 2ms | prep, n ms, ps 2ms | pn | prep, n ms, ps 2ms |
| שִׁמְעָה | כְּחַסְדֶּךָ | יְהוָה | כְּמִשְׁפָּטֶךָ |
| shimʽāh | kh$^{e}$chas̱dekhā | y$^{e}$hwāh | k$^{e}$mishpāṯekhā |
| hear | according to your steadfast love | O Yahweh | according to your justice |

| | | | | |
|---|---|---|---|---|
| **2513.331** | **150.** | **7414.116** | **7579.152** | **2239** |
| v Piel impv 2ms, ps 1cs | | v Qal pf 3cp | *v Qal act ptc mp* | n fs |
| חַיֵּנִי | | קָרְבוּ | רֹדְפֵי | זִמָּה |
| chayyēnî | | qār$^{e}$vû | rōdh$^{e}$phê | zimmāh |
| revive me | | they draw near | the pursuers | a shameful deed |

| | | | | | |
|---|---|---|---|---|---|
| **4623, 8784** | **7651.116** | **151.** | **7427** | **887** | **3176** |
| prep, n fs, ps 2ms | v Qal pf 3cp | | adj | pers pron | pn |
| מִתּוֹרָתְךָ | רָחָקוּ | | קָרוֹב | אַתָּה | יְהוָה |
| mittôrāth$^{e}$khā | rāchāqû | | qārôv | 'attāh | y$^{e}$hwāh |
| away from your Law | they are far away | | near | You | O Yahweh |

taken me, *NKJV* ... I have met grief and woe, but I joy in Your Laws, *Fenton.*

**144. The righteousness of thy testimonies is everlasting: give me understanding, and I shall live:** ... Thy decrees are eternally right, *Goodspeed* ... Your decrees are righteous forever, *NRSV* ... Your decrees are forever just; give me discernment that I may live, *NAB* ... give me wisdom so that I may have life, *BB.*

**145. QOPH. I cried with my whole heart; hear me, O LORD: I will keep thy statutes:** ... Thy statutes will I observe, *Rotherham* ... called with my whole heart; answer me, *MAST* ... and I will obey your decrees, *NIV* ... I will keep Your laws, *Beck.*

**146. I cried unto thee; save me, and I shall keep thy testimonies:** ... deliver me, That I may keep thy decrees, *Goodspeed* ... that I may observe your decrees, *NRSV* ... that I may heed thy instruction, *NEB* ... I will keep your instructions, *JB.*

**147. I prevented the dawning of the morning, and cried:** ... I am up before the dawn to pray, *Moffatt* ... I rise before dawn and cry for help, *NIV* ... I looked toward you at dawn and cried, *Anchor* ... Before Dawn breaks I shout, *Fenton.*

**I hoped in thy word:** ... I wait for You to keep Your promise, *Beck* ... I wait for Thy words, *NASB* ... I am trusting in Thy promise, *Berkeley.*

**148. Mine eyes prevent the night watches, that I might meditate in thy word:** ... eyes anticipate the night-watches, *Darby* ... Through the night my eyes keep watch, to ponder thy sayings, *Knox* ... My eyes are awake through the night watches, *NKJV* ... My eyes greet the night watches in meditation on your promise, *NCB.*

**149. Hear my voice according unto thy lovingkindness:** ... Listen to me because of your love, *NCV* ... Hear my voice in thy steadfast love, *RSV* ... as thy love is unchanging, *NEB* ... In your faithful love, Yahweh, listen to my voice, *JB.*

**O Lord, quicken me according to thy judgment:** ... according to Your justice, LORD, give me a new life, *Beck* ... in your justice preserve my life, *NRSV* ... according to your ordinance give me life, *NAB.*

**150. They draw nigh that follow after mischief: they are far from thy law:** ... Those who devise wicked schemes are near, *NIV* ... those who follow after wickedness, *KJVII* ... My pursuers in their malice are close behind me, *REB* ... Pursuers of idols draw near, *Anchor.*

**151. Thou art near, O Lord; and all thy commandments are truth:** ... all Your Orders right, *Fenton.*

**152. Concerning thy testimonies, I have known of old that thou hast founded them for ever:** ... Long ago I learned from your rules that you made them to continue forever, *NCV* ... because you established them from eternity, *Anchor* ... Long ago I learned from the truths You wrote, *Beck* ... I have long seen that thy decrees are valid for all time, *Moffatt.*

---

a true transcript of that divine righteousness. These things being so, it follows that the Law is given to men in accordance with the divine "faithfulness"—i.e., in remembrance and discharge of the obligations which God has undertaken toward them.

Nor less certainly does it follow that that Law, which is the "eradiation" of God's righteousness, is eternal as its fontal source (vv. 142, 144). The beam must last as long as the sun. No doubt there are transient elements in the Law which the psalmist loved, but its essence is everlasting because its origin is God's everlasting righteousness. So absorbed is he in adoring contemplation of it that he even forgets to pray for help to keep it, and not until v. 144 does he ask for understanding that he may live. True life is in the knowledge of the Law by which God is known, as Jesus has taught us that to know the only true God is life eternal. A faint gleam of immortal hope perhaps shines in that prayer, for if the "testimonies" are forever, and the knowledge of them is life, it cannot be that they shall outlast the soul that knows and lives by them. One more characteristic of God's righteous testimonies is celebrated in v. 140, namely, that they have stood sharp tests and like metal in the furnace have not been dissolved but brightened by the heat.

They have been tested when the psalmist was afflicted and found them to hold true. The same fire tried him and them, and he does not glorify his own endurance, but the promise which enabled him to stand firm. The remaining verses of the section describe the psalmist's afflictions and clinging to the Law. Verse 139 recurs to his emotions on seeing men's neglect of it. "Zeal" (HED #7352) here takes the place of "grief" (v. 136) and of indignation and hatred. Friction against widespread godlessness generates a flame of zeal, as it should always do. "Small and despised" was Israel among the great powers of the ancient world, but he who meditates on the Law is armed against contempt and contented in insignificance (v. 141). "Distress and anguish" may surround him, but hidden springs of "delight" well up in the heart that cleaves to the Law, like outbursts of fresh water rising to the surface of a salt sea (v. 144).

**119:145–152.** The first two verses are a pair, in which former prayers for deliverance and vows of obedience are recalled and repeated. The tone of supplication prevails through the section. The cries now presented are no new things. The psalmist's habit has been prayer, wholehearted, continued, and accompanied with the resolve to keep by obedience and to observe with sharpened watchfulness the utterances of God's will. Another pair of verses follows (vv. 147f), which recall the singer's wakeful devotion. His voice rose to God before the dim morning broke, and his heart kept itself in submissive expectance. His eyes saw God's promises shining in the nightly darkness and making meditation better than sleep.

The petitions in v. 149 may be taken as based upon the preceding pairs. The psalmist's patient continuance gives him ground to expect an answer.

| 3725, 4851 | 583 | | 7208 | 3156.115 | 4623, 5959 | 3706 |
|---|---|---|---|---|---|---|
| cj, *adj*, n fp, ps 2ms | n fs | **152.** | n ms | v Qal pf 1cs | prep, n fp, ps 2ms | cj |
| וְכָל־מִצְוֺתֶיךָ | אֱמֶת | | קֶדֶם | יָדַעְתִּי | מֵעֵדֹתֶיךָ | כִּי |
| wekhol-mitswōthêkhā | 'ĕmeth | | qedhem | yādha'ttî | mē'ēdhōthêkhā | kî |
| and all your commandments | truth | | long ago | I have known | of your testimonies | that |

| 3937, 5986 | 3354.113 | | 7495.131, 6270 | 2603.131 |
|---|---|---|---|---|
| prep, n ms | v Qal pf 2ms, ps 3mp | **153.** | v Qal impv 2ms, n ms, ps 1cs | cj, v Qal impv 2ms, ps 1cs |
| לְעוֹלָם | יְסַדְתָּם | | רְאֵה־עָנְיִי | וְחַלְּצֵנִי |
| le'ôlām | yesadhtām | | re'ēh-'āneyî | wechalletsēnî |
| unto eternity | You founded them | | look on my affliction | and set me free |

| 3706, 8784 | 3940 | 8319.115 | | 7662.131 | 7663 | 1381.131 |
|---|---|---|---|---|---|---|
| cj, n fs, ps 2ms | neg part | v Qal pf 1cs | **154.** | v Qal impv 2ms | n ms, ps 1cs | cj, v Qal impv 2ms, ps 1cs |
| כִּי־תוֹרָתְךָ | לֹא | שָׁכָחְתִּי | | רִיבָה | רִיבִי | וּגְאָלֵנִי |
| kî-thôrāthekhā | lō' | shākhāchättî | | rîvāh | rîvî | ûghe'ālēnî |
| because your Law | not | I forget | | contend for | my case | and redeem me |

| 3937, 577 | 2513.331 | | 7632 | 4623, 7857 | 3568 | 3706, 2805 |
|---|---|---|---|---|---|---|
| prep, n fs, ps 2ms | v Piel impv 2ms, ps 1cs | **155.** | adj | prep, n mp | n fs | cj, n mp, ps 2ms |
| לְאִמְרָתְךָ | חַיֵּנִי | | רָחוֹק | מֵרְשָׁעִים | יְשׁוּעָה | כִּי־חֻקֶּיךָ |
| le'imrāthekhā | chayyēnî | | rāchôq | mēreshā'îm | yeshû'āh | kî-chuqqêkhā |
| with your word | revive me | | far | from the wicked | salvation | because your statutes |

| 3940 | 1938.116 | | 7641 | 7521 | 3176 | 3626, 5122 |
|---|---|---|---|---|---|---|
| neg part | v Qal pf 3cp | **156.** | n mp, ps 2ms | adj | pn | prep, n mp, ps 2ms |
| לֹא | דָרָשׁוּ | | רַחֲמֶיךָ | רַבִּים | יְהוָה | כְּמִשְׁפָּטֶיךָ |
| lō' | dhārāshû | | rachmêkhā | rabbîm | yehwāh | kemishpāṭêkhā |
| not | they seek | | your mercy | abundant | O Yahweh | according to your justice |

| 2513.331 | | 7521 | 7579.152 | 7141 |
|---|---|---|---|---|
| v Piel impv 2ms, ps 1cs | **157.** | adj | v Qal act ptc mp, ps 1cs | cj, n mp, ps 1cs |
| חַיֵּנִי | | רַבִּים | רֹדְפַי | וְצָרָי |
| chayyēnî | | rabbîm | rōdhephay | wetsārāy |
| revive me | | many | my pursuers | and my adversaries |

| 4623, 5959 | 3940 | 5371.115 | | 7495.115 | 931.152 |
|---|---|---|---|---|---|
| prep, n fp, ps 2ms | neg part | v Qal pf 1cs | **158.** | v Qal pf 1cs | v Qal act ptc mp |
| מֵעֵדְוֺתֶיךָ | לֹא | נָטִיתִי | | רָאִיתִי | בֹגְדִים |
| mē'ēdhewōthêkhā | lō' | nāṭîthî | | rā'îthî | vōghedhîm |
| away from your testimonies | not | I incline | | I have seen | the deceitful ones |

| 7248.725 | 866 | 577 | 3940 | 8490.116 | | 7495.131 |
|---|---|---|---|---|---|---|
| cj, v Hithpolel impf 1cs | cj | n fs, ps 2ms | neg part | v Qal pf 3cp | **159.** | v Qal impv 2ms |
| וָאֶתְקוֹטָטָה | אֲשֶׁר | אִמְרָתְךָ | לֹא | שָׁמָרוּ | | רְאֵה |
| wā'ethqôṭāṭāh | 'ăsher | 'imrāthekhā | lō' | shāmārû | | re'ēh |
| and I am disgusted | because | your word | not | they observe | | see |

| 3706, 6740 | 154.115 | 3176 | 3626, 2721 | 2513.331 |
|---|---|---|---|---|
| cj, n mp, ps 2ms | v Qal pf 1cs | pn | prep, n ms, ps 2ms | v Piel impv 2ms, ps 1cs |
| כִּי־פִקּוּדֶיךָ | אָהָבְתִּי | יְהוָה | כְּחַסְדְּךָ | חַיֵּנִי |
| kî-phiqqûdhêkhā | 'āhāvettî | yehwāh | kechasdekhā | chayyēnî |
| that your precepts | I love | O Yahweh | according to your steadfast love | revive me |

| | 7513, 1745 | 583 | 3937, 5986 | 3725, 5122 |
|---|---|---|---|---|
| **160.** | *n ms*, n ms, ps 2ms | n fs | cj, prep, n ms | *adj, n ms* |
| | רֹאשׁ־דְּבָרְךָ | אֱמֶת | וּלְעוֹלָם | כָּל־מִשְׁפַּט |
| | rō'sh-devārekhā | 'ĕmeth | ûlă'ôlām | kol-mishpaṭ |
| | the beginning of your word | truth | even unto eternity | all the ordinances of |

**153. RESH. Consider mine affliction, and deliver me: for I do not forget thy law:** ... Look at my suffering and rescue me, *JB* ... See in what trouble I am and set me free, *NEB* ... Look on my misery and rescue me, *NRSV.*

**154. Plead my cause, and deliver me: quicken me according to thy word:** ... Plead my cause and redeem me, *Rotherham* ... come to my help; give me life, as you have said, *BB* ... for the sake of your promise give me life, *NAB* ... revive me according to Thy word, *Berkeley.*

**155. Salvation is far from the wicked: for they seek not thy statutes:** ... Deliverance is far from the wicked, *Goodspeed* ... Keep distant from the wicked your salvation, *Anchor* ... for they do not seek out your decrees, *NIV.*

**156. Great are thy tender mercies, O LORD: quicken me according to thy judgments:** ... preserve my life according to your laws, *NIV* ... according to Your justice give me a new life, *Beck* ... revive me according to Thy ordinances, *Berkeley* ... true to your judgements, give me life, *JB.*

**157. Many are my persecutors and mine enemies; yet do I not decline from thy testimonies:** ... I never swerve from thy control, *Moffatt* ... I have not turned away from thy decrees, *Goodspeed* ... but I have not swerved from thy instruction, *NEB* ... I have not been turned away from your unchanging word, *BB.*

**158. I beheld the transgressors, and was grieved; because they kept not thy word:** ... I'm disgusted to see those who are unfaithful, *Beck* ... I saw the traitors and was grieved, *KJVII* ... I look at the faithless with disgust, *NRSV* ... because they kept not to your promise, *NCB.*

**159. Consider how I love thy precepts: quicken me, O LORD, according to thy lovingkindness:** ... witness the love I bear thy covenant, *Knox* ... Preserve my life according to thy steadfast love, *RSV* ... in your kindness give me life, *NAB* ... Grant me life, as thy love is unchanging, *NEB.*

**160. Thy word is true from the beginning: and every one of thy righteous judgments endureth for ever:** ... The sum of Thy word is truth, *Young* ... The content of your judgment is your justice, *Anchor* ... The entirety of Your word is truth, *NKJV* ... and all your just decrees are everlasting, *REB.*

---

But the true ground is God's character, as witnessed by his deeds of lovingkindness and his revelation of his "judgments" in the Law.

Another pair of verses follows (vv. 150f), in which the hostile nearness of the psalmist's foes, gathering round him with malignant purpose, is significantly contrasted, both with their remoteness in temper from the character enjoined in the Law and with the yet closer proximity of the assailed man's defender. He who has God near him and who realizes that his "commandments are truth" can look untrembling on mustering masses of enemies. This singer had learned that before danger threatened.

The last verse of the section breathes the same tone of long-continued and habitual acquaintance with God and his Law as the earlier pairs of verses do. The convictions of a lifetime were too deeply rooted to be disturbed by such a passing storm. There is, as it were, a calm smile of triumphant certitude in that "long ago." Experience teaches that the foundation, laid for trust as well as for conduct in the Law, is too stable to be moved and that we need not fear to build our all on it. Let us build rock on that rock and answer God's everlasting testimonies with our unwavering reliance and submission.

**119:153–160.** The prayer "revive me" (HED #2513) occurs thrice in this section. It is not a petition for spiritual quickening so much as for removal of calamities, which restrained free, joyous life. Its repetition accords with other characteristics of this section, which is markedly a cry from a burdened heart.

The psalmist is in affliction; he is, as it were, the defendant in a suit, a captive needing a strong avenger (v. 154), compassed about by a swarm of enemies (v. 157), forced to endure the sight of the faithless and to recoil from them (v. 158). His thoughts vibrate between his needs and God's compassions, between his own cleaving to the Law and its grand comprehensiveness and perpetuity. His prayer now is not for fuller knowledge of the Law, but for rescue from his troubles.

It is worthwhile to follow his swift turns of thought, which in their windings, are shaped by the double sense of need and of divine fullness. First come two plaintive cries for rescue, based in one case on his adherence to the Law, and in the other on God's promise. Then his eye turns on those who do not, like him, seek God's statutes, and these he pronounces, with solemn depth of insight, to be far from the salvation which he feels is his, because they have no desire to know God's will. That is a pregnant word.

Swiftly, he turns from these unhappy ones to gaze on the multitude of God's compassions, which hearten him to repeat his prayer for revival, according to God's "judgments"—i.e., his deci-

| 6928 | | 8015 | 7579.116 | 2703 | 4623, 1745 | 6585.111 |
|---|---|---|---|---|---|---|
| n ms, ps 2ms | | n mp | v Qal pf 3cp, ps 1cs | adv | cj, prep, n mp, ps 2ms | v Qal pf 3ms |
| צִדְקֶךָ | **161.** | שָׂרִים | רְדָפוּנִי | חִנָּם | וּמִדְּבָרֶיךָ | פָּחַד |
| tsidhqekhā | | sārîm | redhāphûnî | chinnām | ûmiddevārêkhā | pāchadh |
| your righteousness | | officials | they persecute me | without cause | but of your words | it trembles |

| 3949 | | 7919.151 | 609 | 6142, 577 | 3626, 4834.151 | 8395 |
|---|---|---|---|---|---|---|
| n ms, ps 1cs | | v Qal act ptc ms | pers pron | prep, n fs, ps 2ms | prep, v Qal act ptc ms | n ms |
| לִבִּי | **162.** | שָׂשׂ | אָנֹכִי | עַל־אִמְרָתֶךָ | כְּמוֹצֵא | שָׁלָל |
| libbî | | sās | 'ānōkhî | 'al-'imrāthekhā | kemôtsē' | shālāl |
| my heart | | rejoicing | I | concerning your word | like one who finds | booty |

| 7521 | | 8632 | 7983.115 | 8911.325 | 8784 | 154.115 | | 8124 |
|---|---|---|---|---|---|---|---|---|
| adj | | n ms | v Qal pf 1cs | cj, v Piel impf 1cs | n fs, ps 2ms | v Qal pf 1cs | | num |
| רָב | **163.** | שֶׁקֶר | שָׂנֵאתִי | וַאֲתַעֵבָה | תּוֹרָתְךָ | אָהָבְתִּי | **164.** | שֶׁבַע |
| rāv | | sheqer | sānē'thî | wa'ătha'ēvāh | tôrāthekhā | 'āhāvettî | | sheva' |
| abundant | | lies | I hate | yes I abhor | your Law | I love | | seven times |

| 904, 3219 | 2054.315 | 6142 | 5122 | 6928 | | 8361 |
|---|---|---|---|---|---|---|
| prep, art, n ms | v Piel pf 1cs, ps 2ms | prep | *n mp* | n ms, ps 2ms | | n ms |
| בַּיּוֹם | הִלַּלְתִּיךָ | עַל | מִשְׁפְּטֵי | צִדְקֶךָ | **165.** | שָׁלוֹם |
| bayyôm | hillaltîkhā | 'al | mishpetê | tsidhqekhā | | shālôm |
| in the day | I praise You | concerning | the ordinances of | your righteousness | | peace |

| 7521 | 3937, 154.152 | 8784 | 375, 3937 | 4520 | | 7887.315 |
|---|---|---|---|---|---|---|
| adj | prep, *v Qal act ptc mp* | n fs, ps 2ms | cj, *sub*, prep, ps 3mp | n ms | | v Piel pf 1cs |
| רָב | לְאֹהֲבֵי | תוֹרָתֶךָ | וְאֵין־לָמוֹ | מִכְשׁוֹל | **166.** | שִׂבַּרְתִּי |
| rāv | le'ōhevê | thôrāthekhā | we'ên-lāmô | mikhshôl | | sibbartî |
| abundant | to those who love | your Law | and there is not to them | stumbling | | I anticipate |

| 3937, 3568 | 3176 | 4851 | 6449.115 | | 8490.112 | 5497 |
|---|---|---|---|---|---|---|
| prep, n fs, ps 2ms | pn | cj, n fp, ps 2ms | v Qal pf 1cs | | v Qal impf 3fs | n fs, ps 1cs |
| לִישׁוּעָתְךָ | יְהוָה | וּמִצְוֹתֶיךָ | עָשִׂיתִי | **167.** | שָׁמְרָה | נַפְשִׁי |
| lîshû'āthekhā | yehwāh | ûmitswōthêkhā | 'āsîthî | | shāmerāh | naphshî |
| your salvation | O Yahweh | and your commandments | I do | | it protected | my soul |

| 5959 | 154.125 | 4108 | | 8490.115 | 6740 |
|---|---|---|---|---|---|
| n fp, ps 2ms | cj, v Qal impf 1cs, ps 3mp | adv | | v Qal pf 1cs | n mp, ps 2ms |
| עֵדֹתֶיךָ | וָאֹהֲבֵם | מְאֹד | **168.** | שָׁמַרְתִּי | פִקּוּדֶיךָ |
| 'ēdhōthêkhā | wā'ōhevēm | me'ōdh | | shāmartî | phiqqûdhêkhā |
| your testimonies | and I love them | very | | I observe | your precepts |

**161. SIN/SHIN. Princes have persecuted me without a cause: but my heart standeth in awe of thy word:** … Leaders attack me for no reason, *NCV* … it is your word that fills me with awe, *REB* … my heart trembles at your word, *NIV.*

**162. I rejoice at thy word, as one that findeth great spoil:** … I have joy in thy word, *Darby* … I rejoice at your promise, *NAB* … like a man who makes discovery of great wealth, *BB* … like one who finds a vast treasure, *JB* … as one who finds great beauty, *Berkeley.*

**163. I hate and abhor lying: but thy law do I love:** … Falsehood I hate and loathe, *Goodspeed* … I hate lying and am disgusted with it, *Beck* … ungodliness I hate and I abhor, *Moffatt.*

**164. Seven times a day do I praise thee because of thy righteous judgments:** … I thank you every day, *Fenton* … for the justice of thy decrees, *NEB* … for your righteous laws, *NIV.*

**165. Great peace have they which love thy law: and nothing shall offend them:** … Those who love your law have perfect security, *Good News* … Blessing in abundance have the lovers of thy law, *Rotherham* … and nothing will defeat them, *NCV* … they have no occasion of stumbling, *ASV.*

**166. LORD, I have hoped for thy salvation, and done thy commandments:** … I wait for you to save me, *Good News* … I hope for thy deliverance, *Moffatt* … and I do what You order, *Beck* … I have kept your teachings, *BB.*

**167. My soul hath kept thy testimonies; and I love them exceedingly:** ... I obey your statutes, for I love them greatly, *NIV* ... I keep thy decrees, And I love them dearly, *Goodspeed* ... I keep your decrees and love them deeply, *NCB* ... gladly I heed thy instruction and love it greatly, *NEB.*

**168. I have kept thy precepts and thy testimonies: for all my ways are before thee:** ... I obey your orders and rules, because you know everything I do, *NCV* ... for all my life lies open before you, *REB* ... you see everything I do, *Good News* ... living always as in thy sight, *Knox.*

**169. TAW. Let my cry come near before thee, O LORD: give me understanding according to thy word:** ... May my cry approach your presence, *JB* ... give me wisdom in keeping with your word, *BB* ... According to your word, give me insight, *Anchor* ... in keeping with your word, give me discernment, *NAB.*

---

sions contained in the Law. But, again, his critical position among enemies forces itself into remembrance, and he can only plead that, in spite of them, he has held fast by the Law and, when compelled to see apostates, has felt no temptation to join them, but a wholesome loathing of all departure from God's word. That loathing was the other side of his love. The more closely we cleave to God's precepts, the more shall we recoil from modes of thought and life which flout them.

Then the psalmist looks wistfully up once more, and asks that his love may receive what God's steadfast love emboldens it to look for as its result, namely, the reviving, which he thus once more craves. That love for the Law has led him into the depths of understanding God's Word, and so his lowly petitions swell into the declaration, which he has verified in life, that its sum total is truth and a perpetual possession for loving hearts, however ringed round by enemies and "weighed upon by sore distress."

**119:161–168.** The tone of this section is in striking contrast with that of the preceding. Here, with the exception of the first clause of the first verse, all is sunny, and the thunderclouds are hull down on the horizon. Joy, peace, and hope breathe through the song. Beautifully are reverential awe and exuberant gladness blended as contemporaneous results of listening to God's word. There is rapture in that awe; there is awe in that bounding gladness. To possess that Law is better than to win rich booty. The spoils of the conflict, which we wage with our own negligence or disobedience, are our best wealth. The familiar connection between love of the Law and hatred of lives which depart from it, and are therefore lies and built on lies, reappears, yet not as the ground of prayer for help, but as part of the blessed treasures which the psalmist is recounting.

His life is accompanied by music of perpetual praise. Seven times a day—i.e., unceasingly—his glad heart breaks into song, and the theme of his song is always God's righteous judgments. His own experience gives assurance of the universal truth that the love of God's Law secures peace, inasmuch as such love brings the heart into contact with absolute good, inasmuch as submission to God's will is always peace, inasmuch as the fountain of unrest is dried up, inasmuch as all outward things are allies of such a heart and serve the soul that serves God. Such love saves from falling over stumbling blocks, and enables a man "to walk firmly and safely on the clear path of duty."

Like the dying Jacob, such a man waits for God's salvation, patiently expecting that each day will bring its own form of help and deliverance, and his waiting is no idle anticipation, but full of strenuous obedience (v. 166) and of watchful observance, such as the eyes of a servant direct to his master (v. 167a). Love makes such a man keen to note the slightest indications of God's will and eager to obey them all (vv. 167b, 168a). All this joyous profession of the psalmist's happy experience he spreads humbly before God, appealing to Him whether it is true. He is not flaunting his self-righteousness in God's face, but gladly recounting to God's honor all the "spoil" that he has found, as he penetrated into the Law and it penetrated into his inmost being.

**119:169–176.** The threads that have run through the Psalm are knotted firmly together in this closing section, which falls into four pairs of verses. In the first, the manifold preceding petitions are concentrated into two for understanding and deliverance, the twin needs of man, of which the one covers the whole ground of inward illumination, and the other comprises all good for outward life, while both are in accordance with the large confidence warranted by God's faithful words.

Petition passes into praise. The psalmist instinctively obeys the command, "By prayer and supplication with thanksgiving let your requests be made known." His lips give forth not only shrill cries of need, but well up songs of thanks, and while a thousand mercies impel the sparkling flood of praise, the chief of these is God's teaching him his righteous statutes (vv. 171f).

| 5959 | 3706 | 3725, 1932 | 5224 | | 7414.122 | 7726 |
|---|---|---|---|---|---|---|
| cj, n fp, ps 2ms | cj | *adj*, n mp, ps 1cs | prep, ps 2ms | **169.** | v Qal juss 3fs | n fs, ps 1cs |
| וְעֵדֹתֶיךָ | כִּי | כָל־דְּרָכַי | נֶגְדֶּךָ | | תִּקְרַב | רִנָּתִי |
| weʻēdhōthêkhā | kî | khol-derākhay | neghdekhā | | tiqŏrav | rinnāthî |
| and your testimonies | because | all my ways | before You | | let it come near | my lamentation |

| 3937, 6686 | 3176 | 3626, 1745 | 1032.531 | | 971.122 |
|---|---|---|---|---|---|
| prep, n mp, ps 2ms | pn | prep, n ms, ps 2ms | v Hiphil impv 2ms, ps 1cs | **170.** | v Qal juss 3fs |
| לְפָנֶיךָ | יְהוָה | כִּדְבָרְךָ | הֲבִינֵנִי | | תָּבוֹא |
| lephānêkhā | yehwāh | kidhvārekhā | hevînēnî | | tāvô' |
| before You | O Yahweh | according to your word | cause me to discern | | may it come |

| 8798 | 3937, 6686 | 3626, 577 | 5522.531 |
|---|---|---|---|
| n fs, ps 1cs | prep, n mp, ps 2ms | prep, n fs, ps 2ms | v Hiphil impv 2ms, ps 1cs |
| תְּחִנָּתִי | לְפָנֶיךָ | כְּאִמְרָתְךָ | הַצִּילֵנִי |
| techinnāthî | lephānêkhā | ke'imrāthekhā | hatstsîlēnî |
| my supplication | before You | according to your word | rescue me |

| | 5218.527 | 8004 | 8747 | 3706 | 4064.323 | 2805 |
|---|---|---|---|---|---|---|
| **171.** | v Hiphil juss 3fp | n fd, ps 1cs | n fs | cj | v Piel impf 2ms, ps 1cs | n mp, ps 2ms |
| | תַּבַּעְנָה | שְׂפָתַי | תְּהִלָּה | כִּי | תְלַמְּדֵנִי | חֻקֶּיךָ |
| | tabbaʻānāh | sephāthay | tehillāh | kî | thelammedhēnî | chuqqêkhā |
| | they gush forth | my lips | praise | because | You teach me | your statutes |

| | 6257.122 | 4098 | 577 | 3706 | 3725, 4851 | 6928 |
|---|---|---|---|---|---|---|
| **172.** | v Qal juss 3fs | n fs, ps 1cs | n fs, ps 2ms | cj | *adj*, n fp, ps 2ms | adj |
| | תַּעַן | לְשׁוֹנִי | אִמְרָתֶךָ | כִּי | כָל־מִצְוֺתֶיךָ | צֶדֶק |
| | taʻan | leshônî | 'imrāthekhā | kî | khol-mitswōthêkhā | tsedheq |
| | let it reply | my tongue | your word | because | all your commandments | righteous |

| | 2030.122, 3135 | 3937, 6038.141 | 3706 | 6740 | 1013.115 |
|---|---|---|---|---|---|
| **173.** | v Qal juss 3fs, n fs, ps 2ms | prep, v Qal inf con, ps 1cs | cj | n mp, ps 2ms | v Qal pf 1cs |
| | תְּהִי־יָדְךָ | לְעָזְרֵנִי | כִּי | פִקּוּדֶיךָ | בָחָרְתִּי |
| | tehî-yādhekhā | leʻāzerēnî | kî | phiqqûdêkhā | vāchārettî |
| | may your hand be | to help me | because | your precepts | I have chosen |

| | 8703.115 | 3937, 3568 | 3176 | 8784 | 8562 | | 2513.122, 5497 |
|---|---|---|---|---|---|---|---|
| **174.** | v Qal pf 1cs | prep, n fs, ps 2ms | pn | cj, n fs, ps 2ms | n mp, ps 1cs | **175.** | v Qal juss 3fs, n fs, ps 1cs |
| | תָּאַבְתִּי | לִישׁוּעָתְךָ | יְהוָה | וְתוֹרָתְךָ | שַׁעֲשֻׁעָי | | תְּחִי־נַפְשִׁי |
| | tā'avtî | lîshûʻāthekhā | yehwāh | wethôrāthekhā | shaʻăshuʻāy | | techî-naphshî |
| | I long for | your salvation | O Yahweh | and your Law | my delight | | revive my soul |

| 2054.322 | 5122 | 6038.126 | | 8912.115 | 3626, 7902 |
|---|---|---|---|---|---|
| cj, v Piel juss 3fs, ps 2ms | cj, n ms, ps 2ms | v Qal juss 3mp, ps 1cs | **176.** | v Qal pf 1cs | prep, n ms |
| וּתְהַלְלֶךָּ | וּמִשְׁפָּטֶךָ | יַעֲזְרֻנִי | | תָּעִיתִי | כְּשֶׂה |
| ûthehalelekhā | ûmishpāṭekhā | yaʻăzrunî | | tāʻîthî | keseh |
| that it may praise You | and your ordinances | may they help me | | I go astray | like a sheep |

| 6.151 | 1272.331 | 5860 | 3706 | 4851 | 3940 | 8319.115 |
|---|---|---|---|---|---|---|
| v Qal act ptc ms | v Piel impv 2ms | n ms, ps 2ms | cj | n fp, ps 2ms | neg part | v Qal pf 1cs |
| אֹבֵד | בַּקֵּשׁ | עַבְדֶּךָ | כִּי | מִצְוֺתֶיךָ | לֹא | שָׁכָחְתִּי |
| 'ōvēdh | baqqēsh | ʻavdekhā | kî | mitswōthêkhā | lō' | shākhāchttî |
| lost | seek | your servant | because | your commandments | not | I forget |

| | 8302 | 4765 | | 420, 3176 | 904, 7150 | 3937 | 7410.115 |
|---|---|---|---|---|---|---|---|
| **120:t** | *n ms* | art, n fp | **1.** | prep, pn | prep, art, n fs | prep, ps 1cs | v Qal pf 1cs |
| | שִׁיר | הַמַּעֲלוֹת | | אֶל־יְהוָה | בַּצָּרָתָה | לִּי | קָרָאתִי |
| | shîr | hammaʻălôth | | 'el-yehwāh | batstsārāthāh | lî | qārā'thî |
| | a Song of | the Ascents | | to Yahweh | in the adversity | to me | I called |

**170. Let my supplication come before thee: deliver me according to thy word:** ... Let my prayer come to You, redeem me as You said, *Fenton* ... rescue me as You promised, *Beck* ... rescue me as you said you would, *LIVB* ... be true to thy promise and save me, *NEB.*

**171. My lips shall utter praise, when thou hast taught me thy statutes:** ... for you teach me your will, *JB* ... My lips bubble thanks, *Fenton* ... What praise shall burst from my lips, *Knox* ... Let your praise pour from my lips, *REB* ... for you teach me your decrees, *NIV.*

**172. My tongue shall speak of thy word: for all thy commandments are righteousness:** *BB* ... Let me sing about your promises, because all your commands are fair, *NCV* ... let the music of thy promises be on my tongue, *NEB.*

**173. Let thine hand help me; for I have chosen thy precepts:** ... Let Your hand become my help, *NKJV* ... because I have chosen the way You want me to live, *Beck.*

**174. I have longed for thy salvation, O LORD; and thy law is my delight:** .. I long for thy deliverance, *Goodspeed* ... longing for thy help, *Moffatt* ... I love your teachings, *NCV.*

**175. Let my soul live, and it shall praise thee; and let thy judgments help me:** ... Let me live to praise you, *REB* ... and may your laws sustain me, *NIV.*

**176. I have gone astray like a lost sheep:** ... If I should stray like a lost sheep, *Anchor* ... If I wander away like a lost sheep, *Beck.*

**seek thy servant; for I do not forget thy commandments:** ... seek out thy servant in his wanderings, *Moffatt* ... come and look for your servant, *JB* ... For Thy precepts I have not forgotten!, *Young* ... for I keep your teachings ever in mind, *BB.*

**120:t. A Song of degrees.**

---

In the next pair of verses, the emphasis lies, not on the prayer for help, so much as on its grounds in the psalmist's deliberate choice of God's precepts, his patient yearning for God's salvation, and his delight in the Law, all of which characteristics have been over and over again professed in the Psalm.

Here, once more, they are massed together, not in self-righteousness, but as making it incredible that, God being the faithful and merciful God which He is, his hand should hang idle when his servant cries for help (vv. 173f).

The final pair of verses sets forth the relations of the devout soul with God in their widest and most permanent forms. The true life of the soul must come from Him, the fountain of life. A soul thus made to live by communion with and derivation of life from God lives to praise, and all its motions are worship. To it the Law is no menace, nor unwelcome restriction, but a helper. Life drawn from God, turned to God in continual praise, and invigorated by unfailing helps ministered through his uttered will, is the only life worth living. It is granted to all who ask for it. But a lower, sadder note must ever mingle in our prayers. Aspiration and trust must be intertwined with consciousness of weakness and distrust of one's self. Only those who are ignorant of the steps of the soul's pilgrimage to God can wonder that the psalmist's last thoughts about himself blend confession of wandering like a straying sheep and profession of not forgetting God's commandments. Both phases of consciousness co-exist in the true servant of God, as, alas! both have grounds in his experience. But our sense of having wandered should ever be accompanied with the tender thought that the lost sheep is a sheep, beloved and sought for by the great shepherd, in whose search, not in our own docile following of his footsteps, lies our firmest hope. The psalmist prayed "Seek thy servant," for he knew how continually he would be tempted to stray. But we know better than he did how wonderfully the answer has surpassed his petition. "For the Son of Man is come to seek and to save that which was lost" (Luke 19:10).

***Psalm 120–134, The Psalms of Ascents.*** *These fifteen psalms form a short psalter within the Psalter, each having the same title (with a slight grammatical variation in Ps. 121). The meaning of the term "ascents" has been a matter of discussion throughout the years.*

*Another explanation fixes on the literal meaning of the word—i.e., "goings up"—and points to its use in the singular for the return from Babylon (Ezra 7:9), as supporting the view that these were psalms sung by the returning exiles. There is much in the group of songs to favor this view; but against it is the fact that Pss. 122 and 134 imply the existence of the Temple and the fully organized ceremonial worship.*

*A third solution is that the name refers to the structure of these psalms, which have a "step-like, progressive rhythm." This is Gesenius' explanation, adopted by Delitzsch. But the peculiar structure in question, although very obvious in several of these psalms, is scarcely perceptible in others, and is entirely absent from Ps. 132.*

| 6257.121 | | 3176 | 5522.531 | 5497 | 4623, 8004, 8632 |
|---|---|---|---|---|---|
| cj, v Qal impf 3ms, ps 1cs | 2. | pn | v Hiphil impv 2ms | n fs, ps 1cs | prep, *n fs*, n ms |
| וַיַּעֲנֵנִי | | יְהוָה | הַצִּילָה | נַפְשִׁי | מִשְּׂפַת־שֶׁקֶר |
| wayya'ănēnî | | yehwāh | hatstsîlāh | naphshî | missephath-sheqer |
| and He answered me | | O Yahweh | rescue | my soul | from the lips of lies |

| 4623, 4098 | 7711 | | 4242, 5598.121 | 3937 | 4242, 3362.521 |
|---|---|---|---|---|---|
| prep, *n fs* | n fs | 3. | intrg, v Qal impf 3ms | prep, ps 2fs | cj, intrg, v Hiphil impf 3ms |
| מִלָּשׁוֹן | רְמִיָּה | | מַה־יִּתֵּן | לָךְ | וּמַה־יֹּסִיף |
| millāshôn | remîyāh | | mah-yittēn | lekhā | ûmah-yōsîph |
| from the tongue of | deceit | | what will anyone give | to you | or what will anyone add |

| 3937 | 4098 | 7711 | | 2777 | 1399 | 8532.156 | 6196 | 1544 |
|---|---|---|---|---|---|---|---|---|
| prep, ps 2fs | *n fs* | n fs | 4. | *n mp* | n ms | v Qal pass ptc mp | prep | *n fp* |
| לָךְ | לָשׁוֹן | רְמִיָּה | | חִצֵּי | גִבּוֹר | שְׁנוּנִים | עִם | גַּחֲלֵי |
| lākh | lāshôn | remîyāh | | chitstsê | ghibbôr | shenûnîm | 'im | gachlê |
| to you | O tongue of | deceit | | the arrows of | the warrior | sharpened | with | the coals of |

| 7868 | | 187, 3937 | 3706, 1513.115 | 5084 | 8331.115 | 6196, 164 | 7223 |
|---|---|---|---|---|---|---|---|
| n mp | 5. | intrj, prep, ps 1cs | cj, v Qal pf 1cs | pn | v Qal pf 1cs | prep, *n mp* | pn |
| רְתָמִים | | אוֹיָה־לִי | כִּי־גַרְתִּי | מֶשֶׁךְ | שָׁכַנְתִּי | עִם־אָהֳלֵי | קֵדָר |
| rethāmîm | | 'ôyāh-lî | kî-ghartî | meshekh | shākhantî | 'im-'āhelê | qēdhār |
| broom trees | | woe to me | because I sojourn in | Meshech | I dwell | with the tents of | Kedar |

| | 7521 | 8331.112, 3937 | 5497 | 6196 | 7983.151 | 8361 | | 603, 8361 | 3706 |
|---|---|---|---|---|---|---|---|---|---|
| 6. | *adj* | v Qal pf 3fs, prep, ps 3fs | n fs, ps 1cs | prep | v Qal act ptc ms | n ms | 7. | pers pron, n ms | cj, cj |
| | רַבַּת | שָׁכְנָה־לָּהּ | נַפְשִׁי | עִם | שׂוֹנֵא | שָׁלוֹם | | אֲנִי־שָׁלוֹם | וְכִי |
| | rabbath | shākhenāh-lāhh | naphshî | 'im | sônē' | shālôm | | 'ănî-shālôm | wekhî |
| | much | it has dwelled to it | my soul | with | those who hate | peace | | I peace | but when |

| 1744.325 | 2065 | 3937, 4560 | | 8302 | 4765 | | 5558.125 | 6084 |
|---|---|---|---|---|---|---|---|---|
| v Piel impf 1cs | pers pron | prep, art, n fs | 121:t | n ms | prep, art, n fp | 1. | v Qal impf 1cs | n fd, ps 1cs |
| אֲדַבֵּר | הֵמָּה | לַמִּלְחָמָה | | שִׁיר | לַמַּעֲלוֹת | | אֶשָּׂא | עֵינַי |
| 'ădhabbēr | hēmmāh | lammilchāmāh | | shîr | lamma'ălôth | | 'essā' | 'ênay |
| I speak | they | for war | | a Song | of the Ascents | | I will lift up | my eyes |

**1. In my distress I cried unto the LORD, and he heard me:** … To Yahweh when I was besieged, I called and he answered me, *Anchor* … when I am in trouble I call, *JB* … and he answered me, *NEB*.

**2. Deliver my soul, O LORD, from lying lips, and from a deceitful tongue:** … rescue thou my soul, *Rotherham* … save me from liars and from those who plan evil, *NCV* … from rebellious tongue, *Fenton* … from treacherous tongue, *NAB*.

**3. What shall be given unto thee?:** … What punishment will he give you?, *BB* … What will he do to you, *NIV*.

**or what shall be done unto thee, thou false tongue?:** … What will he inflict on you, *NCB* … What in addition shall He do to you, *Berkeley*.

**4. Sharp arrows of the mighty, with coals of juniper:** … Only warrior's sharpened arrows and glowing coals of the broom shrub, *Beck* … and red-hot charcoal, *REB* … burning coals of broom-wood, *Darby* … with fiery coals of brushwood, *NAB*.

**5. Woe is me, that I sojourn in Mesech, that I dwell in the tents of Kedar!:** … that I am an alien in Meshech, *NRSV* … Sorrow is mine because I am strange in Meshech, *BB* … Hard is my lot, exiled in Meshech, *NEB* … How terrible it is for me to live in the land of Meshech, to live among the people of Kedar, *NCV*.

**6. My soul hath long dwelt with him that hateth peace:** … Too long have I been living where men hate peace, *Moffatt* … My soul has lived long enough with those who hate peace, *Berkeley*.

**7. I am for peace: but when I speak, they are for war:** … for peace I plead, and their cry is still for battle, *Knox* … when I speak they then prepare for War, *Fenton* … they are ready for war, *NCB* … they are all for war!, *JB*.

**121:t. A Song of degrees.**

**1. I will lift up mine eyes unto the hills, from whence cometh my help:** … where can I get help?, *Beck* … to the mountains; where is my help to come from?, *JB* … to the hills, to find deliverance, *Knox*.

*The remaining explanation of the title is that the "ascents" were those of the worshipers traveling to Jerusalem for the feasts.*

**120:1–2.** The verbs in v. 1 most naturally refer to former experiences of the power of prayer, which encourage renewed petition. Devout hearts argue that what Yahweh has done once He will do again. Since his mercy endures forever, He will not weary of bestowing, nor will former gifts exhaust his stores. Men say, "I have given so often that I can give no more"; God says, "I have given, therefore I will give."

The psalmist was not in need of defense against armed foes, but against false tongues. But it is not plain whether these were slanderous, flattering or untrustworthy in their promises of friendship. The allusions are too general to admit of certainty. At all events, he was surrounded by a choking atmosphere of falsehood, from which he longed to escape into purer air. To one who converses with God, there is nothing more appalling or more abhorrent than the flood of empty talk which drowns the world. If there was any specific foe in the psalmist's mind, he has not described him so as to enable us to identify him.

**120:3–4.** Verse 3 may be taken in several ways, according as "deceitful tongue" is taken as a vocative or as the nominative of the verb "give" and as that verb is taken in a good or a bad sense and as "thee" is taken to refer to the tongue or to some unnamed person. It is unnecessary to enter here on a discussion of the widely divergent explanations given. They fall principally into two classes. One takes the words "deceitful tongue" as vocative, and regards the question as meaning, "What retribution shall God give to thee, O deceitful tongue?" while the other takes it as asking what the tongue shall give unto an unnamed person designated by "thee." That person is by some considered to be the owner of the tongue, who is asked what profit his falsehood will be to him; while others suppose the "thee" to mean Yahweh, and the question to be like that of Job (10:3). Some take this view and paraphrase, "What increase of your riches can You expect that You permit the godless to oppress the righteous?" Grammatically, either class of explanation is warranted; and the reader's feeling of which is most appropriate must decide. The present writer inclines to the common interpretation, which takes v. 3 as addressed to the deceitful tongue, in the sense, "What punishment shall God inflict upon you?"

Verse 4 is the answer, describing the penal consequences of falsehood, as resembling the crimes which they avenge. Such a tongue is compared to sharp arrows and swords in Pss. 57:4; 44:3; etc. The punishment shall be like the crime. For the sentiment, compare Ps. 140:9f. It is not necessary to suppose that the "mighty" is God, although such a reference gives force to the words.

**120:5–6.** In the group of vv. 5ff, the psalmist bemoans his compulsory association with hostile companions and longs to be without contention. Meshech was the name of barbarous tribes who, in the times of Sargon and Sennacherib, inhabited the highlands to the east of Cilicia and in later days retreated northwards to the neighborhood of the Black Sea (Sayce, *Higher Criticism and Monuments*, p. 130). Kedar was one of the Bedouin tribes of the Arabian desert. The long distance between the localities occupied by these two tribes requires an allegorical explanation of their names. They stand as types of ruthless and oppressive foes. The psalmist's plaint struck on Cromwell's heart and is echoed, with another explanation of its meaning which he had, no doubt, learned from some Puritan minister: "I live, you know where, in Meshech, which they say signifies prolonging; in Kedar, which signifies blackness; yet the LORD forsaketh me not" (Carlyle, *Letters and Speeches*, 1:127: London, 1846). The peace-loving psalmist describes himself as stunned by the noise and quarrelsomeness of those around him. "I am peace" (cf. Ps. 109:4). But his gentlest word is like a spark on tinder. If he but speaks, they fly to their weapons and are ready without provocation to answer with blows.

**120:7.** So the Psalm ends as with a long-drawn sigh. It inverts the usual order of similar Psalms, in which the description of need is usually preceded by the cry for deliverance. It thus sets forth most pathetically the sense of discordance between a man and his environment, which urges the soul that feels it to seek a better home. So this is a true pilgrim Psalm.

***Psalm 121.*** *Verses 1f stand apart from the remainder, insofar as in them the psalmist speaks in the first person, while in the rest of the Psalm he is spoken to in the second. But this does not necessarily involve the supposition of an antiphonal song. The two first verses may have been sung by a single voice, and the assurances of the following ones by a chorus or second singer. But it is quite as likely that, as in other Psalms, the singer is in vv. 3–8 himself the speaker of the assurances which confirm his own faith.*

| | | | | | | | |
|---|---|---|---|---|---|---|---|
| **420, 2098** | **4623, 376** | **971.121** | **6039** | | **6039** | **4623, 6196** | **3176** |
| prep, art, n mp | prep, intrg | v Qal impf 3ms | n ms, ps 1cs | **2.** | n ms, ps 1cs | prep, prep | pn |
| אֶל־הֶהָרִים | מֵאַיִן | יָבֹא | עֶזְרִי | | עֶזְרִי | מֵעִם | יְהוָה |
| 'el-hehārîm | mē'ayin | yāvō' | 'ezrî | | 'ezrî | mē'im | y$^{e}$hwāh |
| to the mountains | from where | does it come | my help | | my help | from with | Yahweh |

| | | | | | | |
|---|---|---|---|---|---|---|
| **6449.151** | **8452** | **800** | | **414, 5598.121** | **3937, 4267.141** | **7559** |
| *v Qal act ptc ms* | n md | cj, n fs | **3.** | adv, v Qal juss 3ms | prep, v Qal inf con | n fs, ps 2ms |
| עֹשֵׂה | שָׁמַיִם | וָאָרֶץ | | אַל־יִתֵּן | לַמּוֹט | רַגְלֶךָ |
| 'ōsēh | shāmayim | wā'ārets | | 'al-yittēn | lammôṯ | ragh$^{e}$lekhā |
| the Maker of | the heavens | and the earth | | may He not allow | the faltering of | your foot |

| | | | | | | |
|---|---|---|---|---|---|---|
| **414, 5305.121** | **8490.151** | | **2079** | **3940, 5305.121** | **3940** | **3583.121** |
| adv, v Qal juss 3ms | v Qal act ptc ms, ps 2ms | **4.** | intrj | neg part, v Qal impf 3ms | cj, neg part | v Qal impf 3ms |
| אַל־יָנוּם | שֹׁמְרֶךָ | | הִנֵּה | לֹא־יָנוּם | וְלֹא | יִישָׁן |
| 'al-yānûm | shōm$^{e}$rekhā | | hinnēh | lō'-yānûm | w$^{e}$lō' | yîshān |
| my He not slumber | the One Who keeps you | | behold | not He slumbers | and not | He sleeps |

| | | | | | | |
|---|---|---|---|---|---|---|
| **8490.151** | **3547** | | **3176** | **8490.151** | **3176** | **7009** |
| *v Qal act ptc ms* | pn | **5.** | pn | v Qal act ptc ms, ps 2ms | pn | n ms, ps 2ms |
| שׁוֹמֵר | יִשְׂרָאֵל | | יְהוָה | שֹׁמְרֶךָ | יְהוָה | צִלְּךָ |
| shômēr | yisrā'ēl | | y$^{e}$hwāh | shōm$^{e}$rekhā | y$^{e}$hwāh | tsill$^{e}$khā |
| the One Who keeps | Israel | | O Yahweh | the One Who keeps you | Yahweh | your Shade |

| | | | | | | |
|---|---|---|---|---|---|---|
| **6142, 3135** | **3332** | | **3221** | **8507** | **3940, 5409.521** | **3507** |
| prep, *n fs* | n fs, ps 2ms | **6.** | adv | art, n ms | neg part, v Hiphil impf 3ms, ps 2ms | cj, n ms |
| עַל־יַד | יְמִינֶךָ | | יוֹמָם | הַשֶּׁמֶשׁ | לֹא־יַכֶּכָּה | וְיָרֵחַ |
| 'al-yadh | y$^{e}$mînekhā | | yômām | hashshemesh | lō'-yakkekkāh | w$^{e}$yārēach |
| on the hand of | your right side | | by day | the sun | it will not strike you down | nor the moon |

| | | | | | | |
|---|---|---|---|---|---|---|
| **904, 4050** | | **3176** | **8490.121** | **4623, 3725, 7737** | **8490.121** | **881, 5497** |
| prep, art, n ms | **7.** | pn | v Qal impf 3ms, ps 2ms | prep, *adj*, n ms | v Qal impf 3ms | do, n fs, ps 2ms |
| בַּלָּיְלָה | | יְהוָה | יִשְׁמָרְךָ | מִכָּל־רָע | יִשְׁמֹר | אֶת־נַפְשֶׁךָ |
| ballāy$^{e}$lāh | | y$^{e}$hwāh | yishmār$^{e}$khā | mikkol-rā' | yishmōr | 'eth-naphshekhā |
| by night | | Yahweh | He will keep you | from all evil | He will keep | your soul |

| | | | | | |
|---|---|---|---|---|---|
| | **3176** | **8490.121, 3428.141** | **971.141** | **4623, 6498** | **5912, 5986** |
| **8.** | pn | v Qal impf 3ms, v Qal inf con, ps 2ms | cj, v Qal inf con, ps 2ms | prep, adv | cj, adv, n ms |
| | יְהוָה | יִשְׁמָר־צֵאתְךָ | וּבוֹאֶךָ | מֵעַתָּה | וְעַד־עוֹלָם |
| | y$^{e}$hwāh | yishmār-tsē'th$^{e}$khā | ûvô'ekhā | mē'attāh | w$^{e}$'adh-'ôlām |
| | Yahweh | He will guard your going out | and your going in | from now | even until eternity |

**2. My help cometh from the LORD, which made heaven and earth:** ... My help comes only from the LORD, *REB* ... the Maker of heaven and earth, *NIV.*

**3. He will not suffer thy foot to be moved: he that keepeth thee will not slumber:** ... How could he let your foot stumble?, *NEB* ... not allow your foot to slip, *NASB* ... your guardian will not slumber, *Goodspeed.*

**4. Behold, he that keepeth Israel shall neither slumber nor sleep:** ... the guardian of Israel, *NAB* ... He who guards Israel never rests or sleeps, *NCV* ... the eyes of Israel's keeper will not be shut in sleep, *BB.*

**5. The LORD is thy keeper: the LORD is thy shade upon thy right hand:** ... Yahweh is your guardian, *JB* ... The LORD will guard, the LORD protect, will stand at your right hand, *Fenton* ... sheltering you upon the right, *Moffatt* ... your defence at your right hand, *NEB.*

**6. The sun shall not smite thee by day, nor the moon by night:** ... The sun's rays by day, the moon's by night, shall have no power to hurt thee, *Knox* ... You will not be touched by the sun in the day, *BB* ... The sun will not strike you during the day, *Beck.*

**7. The LORD shall preserve thee from all evil: he shall preserve thy soul:** ... will guard you against all harm, *REB* ... be watchful of your life, *Fenton* ... The LORD will protect you from all dangers, *NCV* ... will keep thee from all harm, He will keep thy life, *Rotherham.*

**121:1–2.** His first words describe the earnest look of longing. He will lift his eyes from all the coil of troubles and perils to the heights. To look beyond the low levels where we dwell to the unseen heights where we have our home is the condition of all noble living amid these lower ranges of engagement with the visible and transient.

"From where does my help come?" is a question which may be only put in order to make the assured answer more emphatic, but may also be an expression of momentary despondency. The loftier the ideal, the more needful, if it is ever to be reached, that our consciousness of its height and of our own feebleness should drive us to recognize our need of help in order to attain it.

Whoever has thus high longings sobered by lowly estimates of self is ready to receive the assurance of divine aid. That sense of impotence is the precursor of faith. We must distrust ourselves, if we are ever to confide in God. To know that we need his aid is a condition of obtaining it. Bewildered despondency asks, "From where does my help come?" and scans the low levels in vain. But the eye that is lifted to the hills is sure to see Him coming to succor, for that question on the lips of one whose looks are directed thither is a prayer, rather than a question, and the assistance he needs sets out toward him from the throne, like a sunbeam from the sun, as soon as he looks up to the light.

**121:3–4.** The particle of negation in v. 3 (HED #414) is not that used in v. 4 (HED #3940), but that which is employed in commands or wishes. The progress from subjective desire in v. 3 to objective certainty of divine help as expressed in v. 4 and the remainder of the Psalm is best exhibited if the verbs in the former verse are translated as expressions of wish—"May He not," etc. Whether the speaker is taken to be the psalmist or another makes little difference to the force of v. 3, which lays hold in supplication of the truth just uttered in v. 2 and thereby gains a more assured certainty that it is true, as the following verses go on to declare. It is no drop to a lower mood to pass from assertion of God's help to prayer for it. Rather, it is the natural progress of faith. Both clauses of v. 2 become especially significant if this is a song for pilgrims. Their daily march and their nightly encampment will then be placed under the care of Yahweh, Who will hold up their feet unwearied on the road and watch unslumbering over their repose. But such a reference is not necessary. The language is quite general. It covers the whole ground of toil and rest and prays for strength for the one and quiet security in the other.

**121:5.** The remainder of the Psalm expands the one thought of Yahweh the keeper, with sweet reiteration, and yet comprehensive variation. First, the thought of the last clause of the preceding verse is caught up again. Yahweh is the keeper of the community, over which He watches with unslumbering care. He keeps Israel, so long as Israel keeps his Law, for the word so frequently used here is the same as is continually employed for observance of the commandments. He had seemed to slumber while Israel was in exile and had been prayed to awake in many a cry from the captives. Now they have learned that He never slumbers: his power is unwearied, and needs no recuperation; his watchfulness is never at fault. But universal as is his care, it does not overlook the single defenseless suppliant. He is "thy keeper" and will stand at thy right hand, where helpers stand, to shield you from all dangers. Men lose sight of the individual in the multitude, and the wider their benevolence or beneficence, the less it takes account of units. But God loves all because He loves each, and the aggregate is kept because each member of it is. The light which floods the universe gently illumines every eye. The two conceptions of defense and impartation of power are smelted together in the pregnant phrase of v. 5b, "thy shade upon thy right hand."

**121:6–7.** The notion of shelter from evils predominates in the remainder of the Psalm. It is applied in v. 6 to possible perils from physical causes: the fierce sunlight beat down on the pilgrim band, and the moon was believed, and apparently with correctness, to shed malignant influences on sleepers. The same antithesis of day and night, work and rest, which is found in v. 3, appears again here. The promise is widened out in v. 7 so as to be all-inclusive. "All evil" will be averted from him who has Yahweh for his keeper; therefore, if any so-called evil comes, he may be sure that it is good with a veil on. We should apply the assurances of the Psalm to the interpretation of life, as well as take them for the antidote of fearful anticipations.

Equally comprehensive is the designation of that which is to be kept. It is "thy soul," the life or personal being. Whatever may be shorn away by the sharp shears of loss, that will be safe, and if it is, nothing else matters very much. The individual soul is of large account in God's sight: He keeps it as a deposit entrusted to Him by faith. Much may go, but

| 122:t | 8302 | 4765 | 3937, 1784 | 1. | 7975.115 | 904, 569.152 | 3937 | 1041 |
|---|---|---|---|---|---|---|---|---|
| | *n ms* | art, n fp | prep, pn | | v Qal pf 1cs | prep, v Qal act ptc mp | prep, ps 1cs | *n ms* |
| | שִׁיר | הַמַּעֲלוֹת | לְדָוִד | | שָׂמַחְתִּי | בְּאֹמְרִים | לִי | בֵּית |
| | shîr | hamma'ălôth | ledhāwidh | | sāmachtî | be'ōmerîm | lî | bêth |
| | a Song of | the Ascents | of David | | I was glad | when saying | to me | the Temple of |

| 3176 | 2050.120 | 2. | 6198.154 | 2030.116 | 7559 | 904, 8554 | 3503 |
|---|---|---|---|---|---|---|---|
| pn | v Qal juss 1cp | | v Qal act ptc fp | v Qal pf 3cp | n fd, ps 1cp | prep, n mp, ps 2fs | pn |
| יְהוָה | נֵלֵךְ | | עֹמְדוֹת | הָיוּ | רַגְלֵינוּ | בִּשְׁעָרַיִךְ | יְרוּשָׁלָםִ |
| yehwāh | nēlēkh | | 'ōmedhôth | hāyû | raghlênû | bish'ārayikh | yerûshālām |
| Yahweh | let us go to | | standing | they have been | our feet | in your gates | O Jerusalem |

| 3. | 3503 | 1161.157 | 3626, 6111 | 8054, 2357.412, 3937 | 3267 | 4. | 8054, 8427 |
|---|---|---|---|---|---|---|---|
| | pn | art, v Qal pass ptc fs | prep, n fs | rel part, v Pual pf 3fs, prep, ps 3fs | adv | | rel part, adv |
| | יְרוּשָׁלַם | הַבְּנוּיָה | כְּעִיר | שֶׁחֻבְּרָה־לָּהּ | יַחְדָּו | | שֶׁשָּׁם |
| | yerûshālam | habbenûyāh | ke'îr | shechubberāh-lāhh | yachdāw | | sheshshām |
| | Jerusalem | the one built | like a city | which it is joined to it | together | | which there |

| 6148.116 | 8101 | 8101, 3176 | 5925 | 3937, 3547 | 3937, 3142.541 | 3937, 8428 |
|---|---|---|---|---|---|---|
| v Qal pf 3cp | n mp | *n mp*, pn | *n fs* | prep, pn | prep, v Hiphil inf con | prep, *n ms* |
| עָלוּ | שְׁבָטִים | שִׁבְטֵי־יָהּ | עֵדוּת | לְיִשְׂרָאֵל | לְהֹדוֹת | לְשֵׁם |
| 'ālû | shevāṯîm | shivṯê-yāhh | 'ēdhûth | leyisrā'ēl | lehōdhôth | leshēm |
| they go up | tribes | the tribes of Yah | the testimony of | Israel | to praise | the name of |

| 3176 | 5. | 3706 | 8427 | 3553.116 | 3802 | 3937, 5122 | 3802 | 3937, 1041 |
|---|---|---|---|---|---|---|---|---|
| pn | | cj | adv | v Qal pf 3cp | n mp | prep, n ms | n mp | prep, *n ms* |
| יְהוָה | | כִּי | שָׁמָּה | יָשְׁבוּ | כִסְאוֹת | לְמִשְׁפָּט | כִּסְאוֹת | לְבֵית |
| yehwāh | | kî | shāmmāh | yāshevû | khis'ôth | lemishpāṯ | kis'ôth | levêth |
| Yahweh | | because | to there | they sit | thrones | for judgment | thrones | for the household of |

| 1784 | 6. | 8068.133 | 8361 | 3503 | 8347.126 | 154.152 |
|---|---|---|---|---|---|---|
| pn | | v Qal impv 2mp | *n ms* | pn | v Qal juss 3mp | v Qal act ptc mp, ps 2fs |
| דָּוִיד | | שַׁאֲלוּ | שְׁלוֹם | יְרוּשָׁלָםִ | יִשְׁלָיוּ | אֹהֲבָיִךְ |
| dāwîdh | | sha'ălû | shelôm | yerûshālām | yishlāyû | 'ōhevāyikh |
| David | | request | the peace of | Jerusalem | may they be at peace | those who love You |

**8. The LORD shall preserve thy going out and thy coming in from this time forth, and even for evermore:** ... The LORD will guard your coming and your going, *NAB* ... The LORD will keep your going out, *RSV* ... The LORD will shield your going out, *Berkeley.*

**122:t. A Song of degrees of David.**

**1. I was glad when they said unto me, Let us go into the house of the LORD:** ... 'Let's go to the Temple of the LORD,' *NCV* ... 'We will enter the house of Yahweh!', *Anchor* ... Unto the house of Yahweh let us go!, *Rotherham.*

**2. Our feet shall stand within thy gates, O Jerusalem:** ... Within thy gates, Jerusalem, our feet stand at last, *Knox* ... Our feet have been standing within your gates, *RSV* ... At last our feet are standing at your gates, *JB.*

**3. Jerusalem is builded as a city that is compact together:** ... you are like a town which is well joined together, *BB* ... that is now rebuilt, a city solid and unbroken, *Moffatt* ... built like a city that is all joined together as one, *KJVII* ... where people come together in unity, *NEB.*

**4. Whither the tribes go up, the tribes of the LORD:** ... To it the tribes go up, *NRSV.*

**unto the testimony of Israel, to give thanks unto the name of the LORD:** ... To witness to Israel, *Fenton* ... It is a decree for Israel, *Goodspeed* ... God ordered Israel to praise the LORD's name, *Beck* ... to praise the name of the LORD according to the statute given to Israel, *NIV.*

**5. For there are set thrones of judgment, the thrones of the house of David:** ... There the descendants of David set their thrones to judge, *NCV* ... there the thrones of justice were set, *REB* ... In it are set up judgment seats, *NCB* ... For there seats are placed for judging, *Berkeley.*

**6. Pray for the peace of Jerusalem: they shall prosper that love thee:** ... Pray for all that brings Jerusalem peace!, *Knox* ... May they pray for your peace, Jerusalem, *Anchor* ... prosperity for your homes!, *JB* ... At rest are those loving thee, *Young.*

**7. Peace be within thy walls, and prosperity within thy palaces:** ...

his hand closes round us when we commit ourselves into it, and none is able to pluck us thence.

**121:8.** In the final verse, the psalmist recurs to his favorite antithesis of external toil and repose in the home, the two halves of the pilgrim life for every man. In the first clause of the verse, he includes all varieties of circumstance, and in the second he looks on into a future of which he does not see the bounds and triumphs over all possible foes that may lurk in its dim recesses in the assurance that, however far it may extend and whatever strange conditions it may hide, the keeper will be there, and all will be well. Whether or not he looked to the last "going out," our exodus from earth (Luke 9:31; 2 Pet. 1:15) or to that abundant entrance (2 Pet. 1:11) into the true home which crowns the pilgrimage here, we cannot but read into his indefinite words their largest meaning and rejoice that we have One Who "is able to keep that which I have committed unto him against that day" (2 Tim. 2:12).

***Psalm 122.*** *The Psalm begins by recalling the joy with which the pilgrims began their march and in v. 2 rejoices in reaching the goal. Then, in vv. 3ff the psalmist paints the sight of the city which gladdened the gazers' eyes, remembers ancient glories when Jerusalem was the rallying-point for united worship and the seat of the Davidic monarchy, and finally pours out patriotic exhortations to love Jerusalem and prayers for her peace and prosperity. This seems the most natural construing of the Psalm. If, on the other hand, v. 2 refers to a past time, the poet, now again returning home or actually returned, remembers the whole pilgrimage from its beginning onward. This is possible, but the warmth of emotion in the exclamation in v. 3 is more appropriate to the moment of rapturous realization of a long-sought joy than to the paler remembrance of it.*

**122:1–2.** Taking, then, the former view of the verse, we have the beginning and end of the pilgrimage brought into juxtaposition in vv. 1 and 2. It was begun in joy and it ends in full attainment and a satisfied rapture, as the pilgrim finds the feet which have traversed many a weary mile planted at last within the city. How fading the annoyances of the road! Happy they whose life's path ends where the psalmist's did! The joy of fruition will surpass that of anticipation, and difficulties and dangers will be forgotten.

**122:3–5.** Verses 3ff give voice to the crowding thoughts and memories awakened by that moment of supreme joy, when dreams and hopes have become realities, and the pilgrim's happy eyes do actually see the city. It stands "built" (HED #1161), by which is best understood built anew, rising from the ruins of many years. It is "compact together," the former breaches in the walls and the melancholy gaps in the buildings being filled up. Others take the reference to be to the crowding of its houses, which its site, a narrow peninsula of rock with deep ravines on three sides, made necessary. But fair to his eyes as the Jerusalem of today looked, the poet-patriot sees more august forms rising behind it and recalls vanished glories when all the twelve tribes came up to worship, according to the commandment, and there was yet a king in Israel. The religious and civil life of the nation had their centers in the city, and Jerusalem had become the seat of worship because it was the seat of the monarchy. These days were past, but though few in number, the tribes still were going up, and the psalmist does not feel the sadness but the sanctity of the vanished past.

**122:6a.** Thus moved to the depths of his soul, he breaks forth into exhortation to his companion pilgrims to pray for the peace of the city. There is a play on the meaning of the name in v. 6a, for as the Tel-el Amarna tablets have told us, the name of the city of the priest-king was Uru Salim—the city of (the god of) peace. The prayer is that the nomen may become omen and that the hope that moved in the hearts that had so long ago and in the midst of wars given so fair a designation to their abode, may be fulfilled now at last. A similar play of words lies in the interchange of "peace" (HED #8361) and "prosper" (HED #8347), which are closely similar in sound in the Hebrew. So sure is the psalmist that God will favor Zion, that he assures his companions that individual well-being will be secured by loyal love to her. The motive appealed to may be so put as to be mere selfishness, although, if any man loved Zion not for Zion's sake but for his own, he could scarcely be deemed to love her at all. But rightly understood, the psalmist proclaims an everlasting truth, that the highest good is realized by sinking self in a passion of earnest love for and service to the city of God. Such love is in itself well-being, and while it may have no rewards appreciable by sense, it cannot fail of sharing in the good of Zion and the prosperity of God's chosen.

**122:6b–9.** The singer puts forth the prayers which he enjoins on others and rises high above all considerations of self. His desires are winged by two great motives—on the one hand, his self-oblivious wish for the good of those who are knit

| 7. | 2030.121, 8361<br>v Qal juss 3ms, n ms<br>יְהִי־שָׁלוֹם<br>yehî-shālôm<br>may peace be | 904, 2526<br>prep, n mp, ps 2fs<br>בְּחֵילֵךְ<br>bechêlēkh<br>inside your ramparts | 8358<br>n fs<br>שַׁלְוָה<br>shalwāh<br>ease | 904, 783<br>prep, n fp, ps 2fs<br>בְּאַרְמְנוֹתָיִךְ<br>be'armenôthāyikh<br>inside your citadels | 8. | 3937, 4775<br>prep, prep<br>לְמַעַן<br>lema'an<br>so that | 250<br>n mp, ps 1cs<br>אַחַי<br>'achay<br>my brothers |
|---|---|---|---|---|---|---|---|

| 7739<br>cj, n mp, ps 1cs<br>וְרֵעָי<br>were'āy<br>and my fellows | 1744.325, 5167<br>v Piel juss 1cs, part<br>אֲדַבְּרָה־נָּא<br>'ădhabberāh-nā'<br>let me say please | 8361<br>n ms<br>שָׁלוֹם<br>shālôm<br>peace | 904<br>prep, ps 2fs<br>בָּךְ<br>bākh<br>inside you | 9. | 3937, 4775<br>prep, prep<br>לְמַעַן<br>lema'an<br>so that | 1041, 3176<br>*n ms*, pn<br>בֵּית־יְהוָה<br>bêth-yehwāh<br>the Temple of Yahweh |
|---|---|---|---|---|---|---|

| 435<br>n mp, ps 1cp<br>אֱלֹהֵינוּ<br>'ělōhênû<br>our God | 1272.325<br>v Piel juss 1cs<br>אֲבַקְשָׁה<br>'ăvaqŏshāh<br>let me seek | 3005<br>adj<br>טוֹב<br>ṭôv<br>good | 3937<br>prep, ps 2fs<br>לָךְ<br>lākh<br>for you | 123:t | 8302<br>*n ms*<br>שִׁיר<br>shîr<br>a Song of | 4765<br>art, n fp<br>הַמַּעֲלוֹת<br>hamma'ălôth<br>the Ascents | 1. | 420<br>prep, ps 2ms<br>אֵלֶיךָ<br>'ēlêkhā<br>to You | 5558.115<br>v Qal pf 1cs<br>נָשָׂאתִי<br>nāsā'thî<br>I lift up |
|---|---|---|---|---|---|---|---|---|---|

| 881, 6084<br>do, n fd, ps 1cs<br>אֶת־עֵינַי<br>'eth-'ênay<br>my eyes | 3553.151<br>art, v Qal act ptc ms<br>הַיֹּשְׁבִי<br>hayyōshevî<br>the One Who sits | 904, 8452<br>prep, art, n md<br>בַּשָּׁמָיִם<br>bashshāmāyim<br>in the heavens | 2. | 2079<br>intrj<br>הִנֵּה<br>hinnēh<br>behold | 3626, 6084<br>prep, *n fd*<br>כְעֵינֵי<br>khe'ênê<br>like the eyes of | 5860<br>n mp<br>עֲבָדִים<br>'ăvādhîm<br>servants | 420, 3135<br>prep, *n fs*<br>אֶל־יַד<br>'el-yadh<br>to the hand of |
|---|---|---|---|---|---|---|---|

| 112<br>n mp, ps 3mp<br>אֲדוֹנֵיהֶם<br>'ădhônêhem<br>their master | 3626, 6084<br>prep, *n fd*<br>כְּעֵינֵי<br>ke'ênê<br>so the eyes of | 8569<br>n fs<br>שִׁפְחָה<br>shiphchāh<br>a female servant | 420, 3135<br>prep, *n fs*<br>אֶל־יַד<br>'el-yadh<br>to the hand of | 1435<br>n fs, ps 3fs<br>גְּבִרְתָּהּ<br>gevirtāhh<br>her mistress | 3772<br>adv<br>כֵּן<br>kēn<br>so | 6084<br>n fd, ps 1cp<br>עֵינֵינוּ<br>'ênênû<br>our eyes |
|---|---|---|---|---|---|---|

| 420, 3176<br>prep, pn<br>אֶל־יְהוָה<br>'el-yehwāh<br>to Yahweh | 435<br>n mp, ps 1cp<br>אֱלֹהֵינוּ<br>'ělōhênû<br>our God | 5912<br>adv<br>עַד<br>'adh<br>until | 8054, 2706.121<br>rel part, v Qal impf 3ms, ps 1cp<br>שֶׁיְּחָנֵּנוּ<br>shêyechānnēnû<br>that He is gracious to us | 3. | 2706.131<br>v Qal impv 2ms, ps 1cp<br>חָנֵּנוּ<br>chānnēnû<br>be gracious to us | 3176<br>pn<br>יְהוָה<br>yehwāh<br>O Yahweh |
|---|---|---|---|---|---|---|

| 2706.131<br>v Qal impv 2ms, ps 1cp<br>חָנֵּנוּ<br>chānnēnû<br>be gracious to us | 3706, 7521<br>cj, adj<br>כִּי־רַב<br>kî-rav<br>because great | 7881.119<br>v Qal pf 1cp<br>שָׂבַעְנוּ<br>sāva'ănû<br>we have been satiated with | 973<br>n ms<br>בוּז<br>vûz<br>contempt | 4. | 7521<br>adv<br>רַבַּת<br>rabbath<br>abundantly |
|---|---|---|---|---|---|

| 7881.112, 3937<br>v Qal pf 3fs, prep, ps 3fs<br>שָׂבְעָה־לָּהּ<br>sāve'āh-lāhh<br>it has been satiated to it | 5497<br>n fs, ps 1cp<br>נַפְשֵׁנוּ<br>naphshēnû<br>our soul | 4075<br>art, n ms<br>הַלַּעַג<br>halla'agh<br>the derision | 8077<br>art, adj<br>הַשַּׁאֲנַנִּים<br>hashsha'ănanîm<br>those at ease | 973<br>art, n ms<br>הַבּוּז<br>habbûz<br>the contempt | 3937, 1373, 3225<br>prep, *adj*, n fp<br>לְגַאֲ־יוֹנִם<br>legha'ă-yônim<br>of proud doves |
|---|---|---|---|---|---|

and security within your towers!, *RSV* ... prosperity in your buildings, *NCB* ... and undisturbed happiness in your palaces!, *Beck.*

**8. For my brethren and companions' sakes, I will now say, Peace be within thee:** ... Because of my relatives and friends, *NAB* ... Because of our friends and brothers, We pray that you now may have peace, *Fenton* ... 'Let Jerusalem have peace,' *NCV.*

**9. Because of the house of the LORD our God I will seek thy good:** ... for thy happiness I plead, *Knox* ... I shall pray for your wellbeing, *REB* ... I will seek your prosperity, *NIV.*

**123:t. A Song of degrees.**

**1. Unto thee lift I up mine eyes, O thou that dwellest in the heavens:** ... even to you whose seat is in the heavens, *BB* ... whose throne is in heaven, *NEB.*

**2. Behold, as the eyes of servants look unto the hand of their mas-**

**ters, and as the eyes of a maiden unto the hand of her mistress:** ... Slaves depend on their masters, and a female servant depends on her mistress, *NCV* ... as the handmaid's eyes are for her mistress' sign, *Fenton.*

**so our eyes wait upon the LORD our God, until that he have mercy upon us:** ... waiting for kindness from him, *NEB* ... till he takes pity on us, *Moffatt* ... Until He be gracious unto us, *MAST* ... Until that he shew us favour, *Rotherham.*

**3. Have mercy upon us, O LORD, have mercy upon us: for we are exceedingly filled with contempt:** ... Yahweh, have pity, for we have had our full share of scorn, *JB* ... show us favour, for we have suffered insult enough, *REB* ... we have had our fill of man's derision, *Knox* ... we have had more than enough of contempt, *Berkeley.*

**4. Our soul is exceedingly filled with the scorning of those that are at ease, and with the contempt of the proud:** ... For long enough have men of pride made sport of our soul, *BB* ... We've had our fill of being

---

to him by common faith and worship; on the other, his loving reverence for the sacred house of Yahweh. That house hallowed every stone in the city. To wish for the prosperity of Jerusalem, forgetting that the Temple was in it, would have been mere earthly patriotism, a very questionable virtue. To wish and struggle for the growth of an external organization called a church, disregarding the presence which gives it all its sanctity, is no uncommon fault in some who think that they are actuated by zeal for the LORD, when it is a much more earthly flame that burns in them.

***Psalm 123.*** *A sigh and an upward gaze and a sigh! No period is more appropriate, as that of this Psalm, than the early days after the return from exile, when the little community, which had come back with high hopes, found themselves a laughing-stock to their comfortable and malicious neighbors. The contrast of tone with the joy of the preceding Psalm is very striking. After the heights of devout gladness have been reached, it is still needful to come down to stern realities of struggle, and these can only be faced when the eye of patient dependence and hope is fixed on God.*

**123:1–2.** That attitude is the great lesson of this brief and perfect expression of wistful yet unfaltering trust joined with absolute submission. The upward look here is like, but also unlike, that in Ps. 121, in that this is less triumphant, though not less assured, and has an expression of lowly submission in the appealing gaze. Commentators quote illustrations of the silent observance of the master's look by his rows of slaves, but these are not needed to elucidate the vivid image. It tells its own story. Absolute submission to God's hand, whether it wields a rod or lavishes gifts or points to service, befits those whose highest honor is to be his slaves. They should stand where they can see Him, they should have their gaze fixed upon Him, and they should look with patient trust, as well as with eager willingness to start into activity when He indicates his commands.

**123:3–4.** The sigh for deliverance in the second half of the Psalm is no breach of that patient submission. Trust and resignation do not kill natural shrinking from contempt and scorn. It is enough that they turn shrinking into supplication and lamentations into appeals to God. He lets his servants make their moan to Him and tell how full their souls have long been of men's scorn. As a plea with Him, the psalmist urges the mockers' "ease." In their security and full-fed complacency, they laughed at the struggling band, as men gorged with material good ever do at enthusiasts, but it is better to be contemned for the difficulties which cleaving to the ruins of God's city brings, than to be the contemners in their selfish abundance. They are further designated as "haughty," by a word which the Hebrew margin reads as two words, meaning "proud ones of the oppressors," but this is unnecessary, and the text yields a good meaning as it stands, although the word employed is unusual.

**124:1–2.** The step-like structure is very obvious in this Psalm. But the repetitions are not mere artistic embellishments; they beautifully correspond to the feelings expressed. A heart running over with thankful surprise at its own new security and freedom cannot but reiterate the occasion of its joy. It is quite as much devotion as art which says twice over that Yahweh was on the singers' side, which twice recalls how nearly they had been submerged in the raging torrent and twice remembers their escape from the closely wrapping but miraculously broken snare. A suppliant is not guilty of vain repetitions although he asks often for the same blessing, and thanksgiving for answered petitions should be as persistent as the petitions were. That must be a shallow gratitude which can be all poured out at one gush.

| 124:t | 8302 | 4765 | 3937, 1784 | 1. | 4020 | 3176 | 8054, 2030.111 | 3937 |
|---|---|---|---|---|---|---|---|---|
| | *n ms* | art, n fp | prep, pn | | cj | pn | rel pron, v Qal pf 3ms | prep, ps 1cp |
| | שִׁיר | הַמַּעֲלוֹת | לְדָוִד | | לוּלֵי | יְהוָה | שֶׁהָיָה | לָנוּ |
| | shîr | hamma'ălôth | ledhāwidh | | lûlê | yehwāh | shehāyāh | lānû |
| | a Song of | the Ascents | of David | | if not | Yahweh | who he would be | for us |

| 569.121, 5167 | 3547 | 2. | 4020 | 3176 | 8054, 2030.111 | 3937 | 904, 7251.141 |
|---|---|---|---|---|---|---|---|
| v Qal juss 3ms, part | pn | | cj | pn | rel pron, v Qal pf 3ms | prep, ps 1cp | prep, v Qal inf con |
| יֹאמַר־נָא | יִשְׂרָאֵל | | לוּלֵי | יְהוָה | שֶׁהָיָה | לָנוּ | בְּקוּם |
| yō'mar-nā' | yisrā'ēl | | lûlê | yehwāh | shehāyāh | lānû | beqûm |
| let them say please | Israel | | if not | Yahweh | who he would be | for us | when rising up |

| 6142 | 119 | 3. | 232 | 2522 | 1142.116 | 904, 2835.141 |
|---|---|---|---|---|---|---|
| prep, ps 1cp | n ms | | adv | n mp | v Qal pf 3cp, ps 1cp | prep, v Qal inf con |
| עָלֵינוּ | אָדָם | | אֲזַי | חַיִּים | בְלָעוּנוּ | בַּחֲרוֹת |
| 'ālênû | 'ādhām | | 'ăzay | chayyîm | belā'ûnû | bachrôth |
| against us | men | | then | life | they would have swallowed us | when the burning of |

| 653 | 904 | 4. | 232 | 4448 | 8278.116 | 5337 |
|---|---|---|---|---|---|---|
| n ms, ps 3mp | prep, ps 1cp | | adv | art, n md | v Qal pf 3cp, ps 1cp | n fs |
| אַפָּם | בָּנוּ | | אֲזַי | הַמַּיִם | שְׁטָפוּנוּ | נַחְלָה |
| 'appām | bānû | | 'ăzay | hammayim | sheṭāphûnû | nachlāh |
| their anger | against us | | then | the waters | they would have washed us away | floods |

| 5882.111 | 6142, 5497 | 5. | 232 | 5882.111 | 6142, 5497 | 4448 |
|---|---|---|---|---|---|---|
| v Qal pf 3ms | prep, n fs, ps 1cp | | adv | v Qal pf 3ms | prep, n fs, ps 1cp | art, n md |
| עָבַר | עַל־נַפְשֵׁנוּ | | אֲזַי | עָבַר | עַל־נַפְשֵׁנוּ | הַמַּיִם |
| 'āvar | 'al-naphshēnû | | 'ăzay | 'āvar | 'al-naphshēnû | hammayim |
| they would have passed | over our soul | | then | it would have passed | over our soul | the waters |

| 2203 | 6. | 1313.155 | 3176 | 8054, 3940 | 5598.111 | 3073 |
|---|---|---|---|---|---|---|
| art, adj | | v Qal pass ptc ms | pn | rel pron, neg part | v Qal pf 3ms, ps 1cp | n ms |
| הַזֵּידוֹנִים | | בָּרוּךְ | יְהוָה | שֶׁלֹּא | נְתָנָנוּ | טֶרֶף |
| hazzêdhônîm | | bārûkh | yehwāh | shellō' | nethānānû | ṭereph |
| the raging | | blessed | Yahweh | Who not | He has handed us over | prey |

| 3937, 8514 | 7. | 5497 | 3626, 7109 | 4561.212 | 4623, 6583 | 3483.152 | 6583 |
|---|---|---|---|---|---|---|---|
| prep, n fp, ps 3mp | | n fs, ps 1cp | prep, n fs | v Niphal pf 3fs | prep, *n ms* | v Qal act ptc mp | art, n ms |
| לְשִׁנֵּיהֶם | | נַפְשֵׁנוּ | כְּצִפּוֹר | נִמְלְטָה | מִפַּח | יוֹקְשִׁים | הַפַּח |
| leshinnêhem | | naphshēnû | ketsippôr | nimleṭāh | mippach | yôqŏshîm | happach |
| for their teeth | | our life | like a bird | it escaped | from the snare of | the fowler | the snare |

| 8132.255 | 601 | 4561.219 | 8. | 6039 | 904, 8428 | 3176 |
|---|---|---|---|---|---|---|
| v Niphal ptc ms | cj, pers pron | v Niphal pf 1cp | | n ms, ps 1cp | prep, *n ms* | pn |
| נִשְׁבָּר | וַאֲנַחְנוּ | נִמְלָטְנוּ | | עֶזְרֵנוּ | בְּשֵׁם | יְהוָה |
| nishbār | wa'ănachnû | nimlāṭenû | | 'ezrēnû | beshēm | yehwāh |
| being broken | and we | we have escaped | | our help | in the name of | Yahweh |

| 6449.151 | 8452 | 800 | 125:t | 8302 | 4765 | 1. | 1019.152 |
|---|---|---|---|---|---|---|---|
| *v Qal act ptc ms* | n md | cj, n fs | | *n ms* | art, n fp | | art, v Qal act ptc mp |
| עֹשֵׂה | שָׁמַיִם | וָאָרֶץ | | שִׁיר | הַמַּעֲלוֹת | | הַבֹּטְחִים |
| 'ōsēh | shāmayim | wā'ārets | | shîr | hamma'ălôth | | habbōṭechîm |
| the Maker of | the heavens | and the earth | | a Song of | the Ascents | | those who trust |

| 904, 3176 | 3626, 2098, 6995 | 3940, 4267.221 | 3937, 5986 | 3553.121 | 2. | 3503 |
|---|---|---|---|---|---|---|
| prep, pn | prep, *n ms*, pn | neg part, v Niphal impf 3ms | prep, n ms | v Qal impf 3ms | | pn |
| בַּיהוָה | כְּהַר־צִיּוֹן | לֹא־יִמּוֹט | לְעוֹלָם | יֵשֵׁב | | יְרוּשָׁלַם |
| bayhwāh | kehar-tsîyôn | lō'-yimmôṭ | le'ôlām | yēshēv | | yerûshālām |
| in Yahweh | like Mount Zion | it does not totter | unto eternity | it sits | | **Jerusalem** |

mocked by those who are at ease, *Beck* ... We have endured much ridicule from the proud, much contempt from the arrogant, *NIV.*

**124:t. A Song of degrees of David.**

**1. If it had not been the LORD who was on our side, now may Israel say:** ... Had not the LORD been with us, let Israel say, *NAB* ... 'If it had not been the LORD who was for us,' *MAST* ... let Israel repeat it, *JB.*

**2. If it had not been the LORD who was on our side, when men rose up against us:** ... when people attacked us, *JB* ... when human foes assailed us, *Knox.*

**3. Then they had swallowed us up quick, when their wrath was kindled against us:** ... swallowed us up alive, *ASV* ... when their anger burned against us, *Berkeley* ... When their fury was inflamed against us, *NCB.*

**4. Then the waters had overwhelmed us, the stream had gone over our soul:** ... engulfed us like a torrent, sweeping over our neck, *Anchor* ... then the flood would have swept us away, *NRSV* ... Then the waters would have carried us away, *REB.*

**5. Then the proud waters had gone over our soul:** ... then over us would have gone the raging waters, *RSV* ... Then had gone over us The seething waters, *Goodspeed* ... Then the swollen waters, *NKJV.*

**6. Blessed be the LORD, who hath not given us as a prey to their teeth:** ... to be torn by their teeth, *NASB* ... to those ravening mouths!, *Knox.*

**7. Our soul is escaped as a bird out of the snare of the fowlers:** ... Like birds from trap he loosed our lives, *Fenton* ... We escaped like a bird from the hunters' trap, *Beck* ... Our soul has gone free like a bird out of the net, *BB.*

**the snare is broken, and we are escaped:** ... The trap broke, *NCV.*

**8. Our help is in the name of the LORD, who made heaven and earth:** ... Our help lies in the Eternal, *Moffatt* ... Who made the Skies and Earth, *Fenton* ... Maker of the heavens and earth!, *Young.*

**125:t. A Song of degrees.**

---

**124:3–5.** The psalmist's metaphors for Israel's danger are familiar ones. "They had swallowed us up quick" may refer to the open jaws of Sheol, as in other psalms, but more probably is simply a figure drawn from beasts of prey, as in v. 6. The other image of a torrent sweeping over the heads (or, as here, over the soul) recalls the contrast drawn by Isaiah between the gently flowing "waters of Siloam" and the devastating rush of the "river," symbolizing the King of Assyria, which like a torrent swollen by the rains suddenly rises and bears on its bosom to the sea the ruins of men's works and the corpses of the workers (Isa. 8:6f).

The word rendered "raging" (HED #2203) is a rare word, coming from a root meaning "to boil over" and may be used here in its literal sense, but it is more probably to be taken in its metaphorical meaning of "haughty" and applied rather to the persons signified by the waters than to the flood itself.

**124:6–8.** Verses 6f are an advance on the preceding, inasmuch as those described rather the imminence of danger, and these magnify the completeness of Yahweh's delivering mercy. The comparison of the soul to a bird is beautiful (Ps. 11:1). It hints at tremors and feebleness, at alternations of feeling like the flutter of some weak-winged songster, at the utter helplessness of the panting creature in the toils. One hand only could break the snare, and then the bruised wings were swiftly spread for flight once more and up into the blue went the ransomed joy with a song instead of harsh notes of alarm.

"Our soul is escaped." That is enough; we are out of the net. Whither the flight may be directed does not concern the singer in the first bliss of recovered freedom. All blessedness is contained in the one word "escaped," which therefore he reiterates and with which the song closes, but for that final ascription of the glory of the escape to the mighty name of Him who made heaven and earth.

***Psalm 125.*** *The references to the topography of Jerusalem in vv. 1f do not absolutely require, though they do recommend, the supposition that this Psalm completes a triad which covers the experience of the restored Israel from the time just prior to its deliverance up until the period of its return to Jerusalem. The strength of the city perched on its rocky peninsula and surrounded by guardian heights would be impressive.*

*In view of deliverance accomplished and of perils still to be faced, the psalmist sings this strong brief song of commendation of the excellence of trust, anticipates as already fulfilled the complete emancipation of the land from alien rule, and proclaims, partly in prayer and partly in prediction, the great law of retribution—certain blessedness for those who are good and destruction for the faithless.*

**125:1–2.** The first of the two grand images in vv. 1f sets forth the stability of those who trust in Yahweh. The psalmist pictures Mount Zion somewhat singularly as something that "cannot be removed," whereas the usual expression would be

| 2098 | 5623 | 3937 | 3176 | 5623 | 3937, 6194 | 4623, 6498 |
|---|---|---|---|---|---|---|
| n mp | adv | prep, ps 3fs | cj, pn | adv | prep, n ms, ps 3ms | prep, adv |
| הָרִים | סָבִיב | לָהּ | וַיהוָה | סָבִיב | לְעַמּוֹ | מֵעַתָּה |
| hārîm | sāvîv | lāhh | wayhwāh | sāvîv | l$^{e}$'ammô | mē'attāh |
| the mountains | all around | to her | and Yahweh | all around | to his people | from now |

| 5912, 5986 | | 3706 | 3940 | 5299.121 | 8101 | 7857 | 6142 | 1518 |
|---|---|---|---|---|---|---|---|---|
| cj, adv, n ms | 3. | cj | neg part | v Qal impf 3ms | *n ms* | art, n ms | prep | *n ms* |
| וְעַד־עוֹלָם | | כִּי | לֹא | יָנוּחַ | שֵׁבֶט | הָרֶשַׁע | עַל | גּוֹרַל |
| w$^{e}$'adh-'ôlām | | kî | lō' | yānûach | shēveṯ | hāresha' | 'al | gôral |
| even until eternity | | because | not | it will rest | the staff of | the wicked | on | the lot of |

| 6926 | 3937, 4775 | 3940, 8365.126 | 6926 | 904, 5983 | 3135 |
|---|---|---|---|---|---|
| art, n mp | prep, prep | neg part, v Qal impf 3mp | art, n mp | prep, n fs | n fd, ps 3mp |
| הַצַּדִּיקִים | לְמַעַן | לֹא־יִשְׁלְחוּ | הַצַּדִּיקִים | בְּעַוְלָתָה | יְדֵיהֶם |
| hatstsaddîqîm | l$^{e}$ma'an | lō'-yishl$^{e}$chû | hatstsaddîqîm | b$^{e}$'awlāthāh | y$^{e}$dhêhem |
| the righteous | so that | they will not put out | the righteous | on wrongdoing | their hands |

| | 3296.531 | 3176 | 3937, 3005 | 3937, 3596 | 904, 3949 |
|---|---|---|---|---|---|
| 4. | v Hiphil impv 2ms | pn | prep, art, n mp | cj, prep, n mp | prep, n mp, ps 3mp |
| | הֵיטִיבָה | יְהוָה | לַטּוֹבִים | וְלִישָׁרִים | בְּלִבּוֹתָם |
| | hêṭîvāh | y$^{e}$hwāh | laṭṭôvîm | w$^{e}$lîshārîm | b$^{e}$libbôthām |
| | cause to be good | O Yahweh | to the good | yes to the upright | in their hearts |

| | 5371.552 | 6366 | 2050.521 | 3176 | 881, 6713.152 |
|---|---|---|---|---|---|
| 5. | cj, art, v Hiphil ptc mp | adj, ps 3mp | v Hiphil impf 3ms, ps 3mp | pn | do, *v Qal act ptc mp* |
| | וְהַמַּטִּים | עֲקַלְקַלּוֹתָם | יוֹלִיכֵם | יְהוָה | אֶת־פֹּעֲלֵי |
| | w$^{e}$hammaṭṭîm | 'aqalqallôthām | yôlîkhēm | y$^{e}$hwāh | 'eth-pō'ălê |
| | and those who turn aside | their crooked | He will cause them to go | Yahweh | those who practice |

| 201 | 8361 | 6142, 3547 | | 8302 | 4765 | | 904, 8178.141 | 3176 |
|---|---|---|---|---|---|---|---|---|
| art, n ms | n ms | prep, pn | 126:t | *n ms* | art, n fp | 1. | prep, v Qal inf con | pn |
| הָאָוֶן | שָׁלוֹם | עַל־יִשְׂרָאֵל | | שִׁיר | הַמַּעֲלוֹת | | בְּשׁוּב | יְהוָה |
| hā'āwen | shālôm | 'al-yisrā'ēl | | shîr | hamma'ălôth | | b$^{e}$shûv | y$^{e}$hwāh |
| iniquity | peace | on Israel | | a Song of | the Ascents | | when turning | Yahweh |

**1. They that trust in the LORD shall be as mount Zion, which cannot be removed, but abideth for ever:** … Those who trust in the Lord are strong as mount Sion itself, that stands unmoved, *Knox* … it is not moved, it remains forever, *KJVII* … unshakeable, it stands for ever, *JB* … which is immovable; which forever stands, *NAB.*

**2. As the mountains are round about Jerusalem, so the LORD is round about his people from henceforth even for ever:** … surround Jerusalem, so the LORD surrounds his people, *NIV* … Even as the mountains encircle Jerusalem, So the LORD encircles his people, *Goodspeed.*

**3. For the rod of the wicked shall not rest upon the lot of the righteous:** … For the rod of sinners will not be resting on the heritage of the upright, *BB* … The wicked will not rule over those who do right, *NCV* … scepter of the wicked will not rest on the land allotted to the righteous, *Beck.*

**lest the righteous put forth their hands unto iniquity:** … so that the righteous shall not set their hands to injustice, *NEB* … That the righteous may not put forth their hands to do wrong, *NASB.*

**4. Do good, O LORD, unto those that be good, and to them that are upright in their hearts:** … to the sincere at heart, *JB* … whose hearts are right with the Lord, *LIVB.*

**5. As for such as turn aside unto their crooked ways, the LORD shall lead them forth with the workers of iniquity: but peace shall be upon Israel:** … those tottering for their devious ways—may Yahweh cause them to pass away with the evildoers, *Anchor* … as for the shifty and disloyal—may the Eternal scatter them, *Moffatt* … the LORD will lead away with evildoers, *NRSV.*

**126:t. A Song of degrees.**

**1. When the LORD turned again the captivity of Zion, we were like them that dream:** … When the LORD brought the prisoners back to Jerusalem, it seemed as if we were dreaming, *NCV* … restored the fortunes of Zion, *Beck* … When the LORD turned the tide of Zion's fortune, we were like men who had

"stands firm." But the former conveys still more forcibly the image and impression of calm, effortless immobility. Like some great animal couched at ease, the mountain lies there, in restful strength. Nothing can shake it, except one presence, before which the hills "skip like lambs" (Ps. 114:6). Thus quietly steadfast and lapped in repose, not to be disturbed by any external force, should they be who trust in Yahweh and shall be in the measure of their trust.

But trust could not bring such steadfastness, unless the other figure in v. 2 represented a fact. The steadfastness of the trustful soul is the consequence of the encircling defense of Yahweh's power. The mountain fortress is girdled by mountains; not, indeed, as if it was ringed about by an unbroken circle of manifestly higher peaks, but still Olivet rises above Zion on the east and a spur of higher ground runs out thence and overlooks it on the north, while the levels rise to the west, and the so-called Hill of Evil Counsel is on the south (where the United Nations building is humorously located today). They are not conspicuous summits, but they hide the city from those approaching, until their tops are reached. Perhaps the very inconspicuousness of these yet real defenses suggested to the poet the invisible protection which to eyes looked so poor, but was so valid. The hills of Bashan might look scornfully across Jordan to the humble heights around Jerusalem, but they were enough to guard the city. The psalmist uses no words of comparison, but lays his two facts side by side: the mountains around Jerusalem, Yahweh around his people. That circumvallation is their defense. They who have the everlasting hills for their bulwark need not trouble themselves to build a wall such as Babylon needed. Man's artifices for protection are impertinent when God flings his hand around his people. Zechariah, the prophet of the restoration, drew that conclusion from the same thought, when he declared that Jerusalem should be "inhabited as towns without walls," because Yahweh would be "unto her a wall of fire round about" (Zech. 2:4f).

**125:3–5a.** Verse 3 seems at first sight to be appended to the preceding in defiance of logical connection, for its "for" (HED #3706) would more naturally have been "therefore," since the deliverance of the land from foreign invaders is a consequence of Yahweh's protection. But the psalmist's faith is so strong that he regards that still further deliverance as already accomplished and adduces it as a confirmation of the fact that Yahweh ever guards his people. In the immediate historical reference, this verse points to a period when the lot of the righteous—i.e., the land of Israel—was, as it were, weighed down by the crushing scepter of some alien power that had long lain on it. But the psalmist is sure that that is not going to last, because his eyes are lifted to the hills from where his aid comes. With like tenacity and longsightedness, faith ever looks onward to the abolition of present evils, however stringent may be their grip and however heavy may be the scepter which evil in possession of the heritage of God wields. The rod of the oppressor shall be broken and one more proof given that they dwell safely who dwell encircled by God.

The domination of evil, if protracted too long, may tempt good men, who are righteous because they trust, to lose their faith and so to lose their righteousness, and make common cause with apparently triumphant iniquity. It needs divine wisdom to determine how long a trial must last in order that it may test faith, thereby strengthening it, and may not confound faith, thereby precipitating feeble souls into sin. He knows when to say it is enough.

So the Psalm ends with prayer and prediction, which both spring from the insight into Yahweh's purposes which trust gives. The singer asks that the good may receive good, in accordance with the law of retribution. The expressions describing these are very noticeable, especially when connected with the designation of the same persons in v. 1 as those who trust in Yahweh. Trust makes righteous and good and upright in heart. If these characteristics are to be distinguished, "righteous" may refer to action in conformity with the Law of God, good to the more gentle and beneficent virtues, and upright in heart to inward sincerity. Such persons will get "good" from Yahweh, the God of recompenses, and that good will be as various as their necessities and as wide as their capacities. But the righteous Protector of those who trust in Him is so, partly because He smites as well as blesses, and therefore the other half of the law of retribution comes into view, not as a petition, but as prediction. The psalmist uses a vivid image to describe half-hearted adherents to the people of Yahweh: literally, "they turn aside their crooked [ways]. Sometimes the torturous path points towards one direction, and then it swerves to almost the opposite. Those crooked, wandering ways, in which irresolute men, who do not clearly know whether they are for Yahweh or for the other side, live lives miserable from vacillation and can

| 881, 8285 | 6995 | 2030.119 | 3626, 2593.152 | | 226 | 4527.221 | 7926 |
|---|---|---|---|---|---|---|---|
| do, *n fs* | pn | v Qal pf 1cp | prep, v Qal act ptc mp | **2.** | adv | v Niphal impf 3ms | n ms |
| אֶת־שִׁיבַת | צִיּוֹן | הָיִינוּ | כְּחֹלְמִים | | אָז | יִמָּלֵא | שְׂחוֹק |
| 'eth-shîvath | tsîyôn | hāyînû | kechōlemîm | | 'āz | yimmālē' | sechôq |
| the captivity of | Zion | we were | like dreamers | | then | it was filled with | laughter |

| 6552 | 4098 | 7726 | 226 | 569.126 | 904, 1504 |
|---|---|---|---|---|---|
| n ms, ps 1cp | cj, n fs, ps 1cp | n fs | adv | v Qal impf 3mp | prep, art, n mp |
| פִּינוּ | וּלְשׁוֹנֵנוּ | רִנָּה | אָז | יֹאמְרוּ | בַגּוֹיִם |
| pînû | ûlāshônēnû | rinnāh | 'āz | yō'merû | vaggôyim |
| our mouth | and our tongue | shouts of joy | then | they said | among the nations |

| 1461.511 | 3176 | 3937, 6449.141 | 6196, 431 | | 1461.511 | 3176 |
|---|---|---|---|---|---|---|
| v Hiphil pf 3ms | pn | prep, v Qal inf con | prep, dem pron | **3.** | v Hiphil pf 3ms | pn |
| הִגְדִּיל | יְהוָה | לַעֲשׂוֹת | עִם־אֵלֶּה | | הִגְדִּיל | יְהוָה |
| highdîl | yehwāh | la'ăsôth | 'im-'ēlleh | | highdîl | yehwāh |
| He caused to be great | Yahweh | to do | with them | | He caused to be great | Yahweh |

| 3937, 6449.141 | 6196 | 2030.119 | 7976 | | 8178.131 | 3176 | 881, 8097 |
|---|---|---|---|---|---|---|---|
| prep, v Qal inf con | prep, ps 1cp | v Qal pf 1cp | adj | **4.** | v Qal impv 2ms | pn | do, n fs, ps 1cp |
| לַעֲשׂוֹת | עִמָּנוּ | הָיִינוּ | שְׂמֵחִים | | שׁוּבָה | יְהוָה | אֶת־שְׁבוּתֵנוּ |
| la'ăsôth | 'immānû | hāyînû | semēchîm | | shûvāh | yehwāh | 'eth-shevûthēnû |
| to do | with us | we are | glad | | turn back | O Yahweh | our captivity |

| 3626, 665 | 904, 5221 | | 2319.152 | 904, 1893 | 904, 7726 | 7403.126 |
|---|---|---|---|---|---|---|
| prep, n mp | prep, art, n ms | **5.** | art, v Qal act ptc mp | prep, n fs | prep, n fs | v Qal impf 3mp |
| כַּאֲפִיקִים | בַּנֶּגֶב | | הַזֹּרְעִים | בְּדִמְעָה | בְּרִנָּה | יִקְצֹרוּ |
| ka'ăphîqîm | banneghev | | hazzōre'îm | bedhim'āh | berinnāh | yiqōtsōrû |
| like the wadis | in the Negeb | | those who sow | with tears | with shouts of joy | they will reap |

| | 2050.142 | 2050.121 | 1098.142 | 5558.151 | 5083, 2320 |
|---|---|---|---|---|---|
| **6.** | v Qal inf abs | v Qal impf 3ms | cj, v Qal inf abs | v Qal act ptc ms | *n ms*, art, n ms |
| | הָלוֹךְ | יֵלֵךְ | וּבָכֹה | נֹשֵׂא | מֶשֶׁךְ־הַזָּרַע |
| | hālôkh | yēlēkh | ûvākhōh | nōsē' | meshekh-hazzāra' |
| | going forth | he will surely go forth | and weeping | carrying | a bag of the seed |

| 971.142, 971.121 | 904, 7726 | 5558.151 | 491 | | 8302 |
|---|---|---|---|---|---|
| v Qal inf abs, v Qal impf 3ms | prep, n fs | v Qal act ptc ms | n fp, ps 3ms | **127:t** | *n ms* |
| בֹּא־יָבוֹא | בְרִנָּה | נֹשֵׂא | אֲלֻמֹּתָיו | | שִׁיר |
| bō'-yāvô' | verinnāh | nōsē' | 'ălummōthâv | | shîr |
| he will surely come in | with a shout of joy | carrying | his sheaves | | a Song of |

found new health, *NEB* … like the sands of the sea, *Anchor.*

**2. Then was our mouth filled with laughter, and our tongue with singing:** … with ioy, *Geneva* … shouts of joy, *RSV* … with rejoicing, *NAB* … gave a glad cry, *BB.*

**then said they among the heathen:** … the nations, *BB.*

**The LORD hath done great things for them:** … What favour the Lord has shewn them!, *Knox.*

**3. The LORD hath done great things for us; whereof we are glad:** … we reioyce, *Geneva* … We are full of joy!, *Rotherham.*

**4. Turn again our captivity, O LORD:** … Restore our fortunes, O LORD, *NAB.*

**as the streams in the south:** … like the torrents in the southern deserts, *NCB* … like streams in the Negev, *NIV*… Like channels in the South, *Rotherham* … like the watercourses in the Negeb!, *RSV.*

**5. They that sow in tears shall reap in joy:** … with shouts of joy, *Moffatt* … Those who cry as they plant crops will sing at harvest time, *NCV*… shall reap with songs of joy, *NEB.*

**6. He that goeth forth and weepeth, bearing precious seed:** … Bearing seed enough to trail along, *Rotherham* … carrying your seed bag, *Beck.*

**shall doubtless come again with rejoicing:** … with songs of joy, *NIV* … with singing do reap, *Young.*

never lead to steadfastness or to any good. The psalmist has taken his side. He knows whom he is for, and he knows, too, that there is at bottom little to choose between the coward who would be in both camps and the open antagonist. Therefore, they shall share the same fate.

**125:5b.** Finally, the poet, stretching out his hands over all Israel as if blessing them like a priest, embraces all his hopes, petitions and wishes in the one prayer, "Peace shall be upon Israel." He means the true "Israel of God" (Gal. 6:16), upon whom the apostle, with a reminiscence possibly of this Psalm, invokes the like blessing and whom he defines in the same spirit as the psalmist does, as those who walk according to this rule, and not according to the crooked paths of their own devising.

***Psalm 126.*** *As in Ps. 85, the poet's perspective here comes in the midst of a partial restoration of Israel. In vv. 1ff, he rejoices over its happy beginning, while in vv. 4ff he prays for and confidently expects its triumphant completion. Manifestly, the circumstances fit the period to which most of these Psalms of Ascents are to be referred, namely, the dawn of the restoration from Babylon. Here the pressure of the difficulties and hostility which the returning exiles met is but slightly expressed. The throb of wondering gratitude is still felt, and although tears mingle with laughter and hard work which bears no immediate result has to be done, the singer's confidence is unfaltering.*

**126:1–3.** The mood of the first part of this little Psalm is momentary; but the steadfast toil amid discouragements, not uncheered by happy confidence, which is pictured in the second part, should be the permanent temper of those who have once tasted the brief emotion. The jubilant laughter and ringing cries with which the exiles streamed forth from bondage and made the desert echo as they marched witnessed to the nations that Yahweh had magnified his dealings with them. Their extorted acknowledgment is caught up triumphantly by the singer. He thanks the Gentiles for teaching him that word. There is a world of restrained feeling, all the more impressive for the simplicity of the expression, in that quiet "we are glad." When the heathen attested the reality of the deliverance, Israel became calmly conscious of it. These exclamations of envious onlookers sufficed to convince the returning exiles that it was no dream befooling them. Tumultuous feeling steadied itself into conscious joy. There is no need to say more. The night of weeping was past, and joy was their companion in the fresh morning light.

**126:4.** The metaphor in v. 4 brings before the imagination the dried torrent-beds in the arid Negeb, which runs out into the Arabian desert. Dreary and desolate as these dried wadies lie bleaching in the sunshine, so disconsolate and lonely had the land been without inhabitants. The psalmist would fain see, not the thin trickle of a streamlet, to which the returned captives might be compared, but a full, great rush of rejoicing fellow countrymen coming back, like the torrents that fill the silent watercourses with flashing life.

**126:5–6.** He prays, and he also prophesies. "They that sow in tears" are the pioneers of the return, to whom he belonged. Verses 6f merely expand the figure of v. 5 with the substitution of the image of a single husbandman for the less vivid, clear-cut plural. The expression rendered "handful of seed" means literally a "draught of seed"—the quantity taken out of the basket or cloth at one grasp, in order to be sown. It is difficult to convey the force of the infinitives in combination with participles and the finite verb in v. 6. But the first half of the verse seems to express repeated actions on the part of the husbandman, who often goes forth to sow and weeps as he goes, while the second half expresses the certainty of his glad coming in with his arms full of sheaves. The meaning of the figure needs no illustration. It gives assurances fitted to cause to toil in the face of dangers and in spite of a heavy heart, that no seed sown and watered with tears is lost; and further, that, although it often seems to be the law for earth that one soweth and another reapeth, in deepest truth "every man shall receive his own reward, according to his own labor" (1 Cor. 3:8). Whatever faith, toil and holy endeavor a man sows, trusting God to bless the springing of it, that he shall also reap. In the highest sense and in the last result, the prophet's great words are ever true: "They shall not plant, and another eat … for my chosen shall long enjoy the work of their hands" (Isa. 65:22).

***Psalm 127.*** *This pure expression of conscious dependence on God's blessing for all well-being may possibly have special reference to the Israel of the restoration. The instances of vain human effort and care would then have special force, when the ruins of many generations had to be rebuilt and the city to be guarded. But there is no need to seek for specific occasion, so general is this Psalm. It sings in a spirit of happy trust the commonplace of all*

| 4765 | 3937, 8406 | | 524, 3176 | 3940, 1161.121 | 1041 | 8175 | 6218.116 |
|---|---|---|---|---|---|---|---|
| art, n fp | prep, pn | | cj, pn | neg part, v Qal impf 3ms | n ms | n ms | v Qal pf 3cp |
| הַמַּעֲלוֹת | לִשְׁלֹמֹה | **1.** | אִם־יְהוָה | לֹא־יִבְנֶה | בַּיִת | שָׁוְא | עָמְלוּ |
| hamma'ălôth | lishelōmōh | | 'im-yehwāh | lō'-yivneh | vayith | shāwe' | 'āmelû |
| the Ascents | of Solomon | | if Yahweh | He does not build | a house | vanity | they labor |

| 1161.152 | 904 | 524, 3176 | 3940, 8490.121, 6111 | 8175 | 8613.111 |
|---|---|---|---|---|---|
| v Qal act ptc mp, ps 3ms | prep, ps 3ms | cj, pn | neg part, v Qal impf 3ms, n fs | n ms | v Qal pf 3ms |
| בּוֹנָיו | בּוֹ | אִם־יְהוָה | לֹא־יִשְׁמָר־עִיר | שָׁוְא | שָׁקַד |
| vônâv | bô | 'im-yehwāh | lō'-yishmār-'îr | shāwe' | shāqadh |
| its builders | on it | if Yahweh | He does not guard a city | vanity | he keeps the watch |

| 8490.151 | | 8175 | 3937 | 8326.552 | 7251.141 | 310.352, 3553.141 |
|---|---|---|---|---|---|---|
| v Qal act ptc ms | | n ms | prep, ps 2mp | *v Hiphil ptc mp* | v Qal inf con | *v Piel ptc mp*, v Qal inf con |
| שׁוֹמֵר | **2.** | שָׁוְא | לָכֶם | מַשְׁכִּימֵי | קוּם | מְאַחֲרֵי־שֶׁבֶת |
| shômēr | | shāwe' | lākhem | mashkîmê | qûm | me'achrê-sheveth |
| the keeper | | vanity | to you | those who rise early | rising | those who delay sitting |

| 404.152 | 4035 | 6325 | 3772 | 5598.121 | 3937, 3148 | 8524 | | 2079 |
|---|---|---|---|---|---|---|---|---|
| *v Qal act ptc mp* | *n ms* | art, n mp | adv | v Qal impf 3ms | prep, adj, ps 3ms | n fs | | intrj |
| אֹכְלֵי | לֶחֶם | הָעֲצָבִים | כֵּן | יִתֵּן | לִידִידוֹ | שֵׁנָא | **3.** | הִנֵּה |
| 'ōkhelê | lechem | hā'ătsāvîm | kēn | yittēn | lîdhîdhô | shēnā' | | hinnēh |
| those who eat | the bread of | the toiling | so | He gives | to his beloved | sleep | | behold |

| 5338 | 3176 | 1158 | 7964 | 6780 | 1027 | | 3626, 2777 |
|---|---|---|---|---|---|---|---|
| *n fs* | pn | n mp | n ms | *n ms* | art, n fs | | prep, n mp |
| נַחֲלַת | יְהוָה | בָּנִים | שָׂכָר | פְּרִי | הַבָּטֶן | **4.** | כְּחִצִּים |
| nachlath | yehwāh | bānîm | sākhār | perî | habbāṭen | | kechitstsîm |
| the inheritance of | Yahweh | sons | a reward | the fruit of | the womb | | like arrows |

| 904, 3135, 1399 | 3772 | 1158 | 5454 | | 869 | 1429 | 866 |
|---|---|---|---|---|---|---|---|
| prep, *n fs*, n ms | adv | *n mp* | art, n mp | | *n mp* | art, n ms | rel pron |
| בְּיַד־גִּבּוֹר | כֵּן | בְּנֵי | הַנְּעוּרִים | **5.** | אַשְׁרֵי | הַגֶּבֶר | אֲשֶׁר |
| beyadh-gibbôr | kēn | benê | hanne'ûrîm | | 'ashrê | haggever | 'ăsher |
| in the hand of a warrior | so | the sons of | the time of youth | | blessed | the man | who |

| 4527.311 | 881, 855 | 4623 | 3940, 991.126 | 3706, 1744.326 |
|---|---|---|---|---|
| v Piel pf 3ms | do, n fs, ps 3ms | prep, ps 3mp | neg part, v Qal impf 3mp | cj, v Piel impf 3mp |
| מִלֵּא | אֶת־אַשְׁפָּתוֹ | מֵהֶם | לֹא־יֵבֹשׁוּ | כִּי־יְדַבְּרוּ |
| millē' | 'eth-'ashpāthô | mēhem | lō'-yēvōshû | kî-yedhabberû |
| it is full | his quiver | of them | they will not be ashamed | when they speak |

| 882, 342.152 | 904, 8554 | | 8302 | 4765 | | 869 | 3725, 3486.152 |
|---|---|---|---|---|---|---|---|
| prep, v Qal act ptc mp | prep, art, n ms | | *n ms* | art, n fp | | *n mp* | *adj, v Qal act ptc mp* |
| אֶת־אוֹיְבִים | בַּשָּׁעַר | **128:t** | שִׁיר | הַמַּעֲלוֹת | **1.** | אַשְׁרֵי | כָּל־יְרֵא |
| 'eth-'ôyvîm | bashshā'ar | | shîr | hamma'ălôth | | 'ashrê | kol-yerē' |
| with enemies | in the gate | | a Song of | the Ascents | | blessed | all those who fear |

**bringing his sheaves with him:** … carrying bundles of grain, *NCV* … with the corded stems of grain in his arms, *BB.*

**127:t. A Song of degrees for Solomon.**

**1. Except the LORD build the house:** … the palace, *Anchor.*

**they labour in vain that build it:** … the builders' work is useless, *LIVB.*

**except the LORD keep the city:** … guards the city, *NKJV* … keeps watch over the city, *REB* … watch not the Tower, *Fenton.*

**the watchman waketh but in vain:** … stays awake in vain, *NKJV.*

**2. It is vain for you to rise up early, to sit up late:** … or put off your rest, *NAB* … and put off going to bed, sweating to make a living, *JB.*

**to eat the bread of sorrows:** … bread of toil, *MAST* … you that eat hard-earned bread, *NAB* … bread of griefs, *Young* … bread of idols, *Anchor.*

**for so he giveth his beloved sleep:** ... he supplies the need of those he loves, *REB* ... is it not in the hours of sleep that he blesses the men he loves?, *Knox.*

**3. Lo, children are an heritage of the LORD and the fruit of the womb is his reward:** ... See! Children are the LORD's estate, The body's sweetest fruits, *Fenton.*

**4. As arrows are in the hand of a mighty man:** ... a warrior, *NAB* ... a Giant's hand, *Fenton.*

**so are children of the youth:** ... who are born when he's young, *Beck.*

**5. Happy:** ... Blessed, *Geneva.*

**is the man that hath his quiver full of them: they shall not be ashamed:** ... How blest the man who has filled his quiver with them!, *Anchor* ... Happy is the man who has his bag full of arrows, *NCV.*

**but they shall speak with the enemies in the gate:** ... They will not be defeated when they fight their enemies at the city gate, *NCV* ... will not have to back down when confronted by an enemy in court, *REB* ... because they will drive the enemies from the gate, *Beck.*

---

*true religion, that God's blessing prospers all things and that effort is vain without it. There is no sweeter utterance of that truth anywhere, until we come to our Lord's parallel teaching, lovelier still than that of our Psalm, when He points us to the flowers of the field and the fowls of the air as our teachers of the joyous, fair lives that can be lived, when no burdensome care mars their beauty.*

**127:1.** In v. 1, the examples chosen by the singer are naturally connected. The house, when built, is one in the many that make the city. The owner's troubles are not over when it is built, since it has to be watched. It is as hard to keep as to acquire earthly goods. The psalmist uses the past tenses in describing the vanity of building and watching unblessed by God. They have built in vain and watched in vain. He, as it were, places us at the point of time when the failure is developed—the half-built house a ruin and the city sacked and in flames.

**127:2.** Verse 2 deals with domestic life within the built house and guarded city. It is vain to eke out the laborious day by beginning early and ending late. Long hours do not mean prosperous work. The evening meal may be put off until a late hour, and when the toil-worn man sits down to it, he may eat bread made bitter by labor. But all is in vain without God's blessing. The last clause of the verse must be taken as presenting a contrast to the futile labor reprehended in the former clauses. "So" (HED #3772) seems here to be equivalent to "even so," and the thought intended is probably that God's gift to his beloved secures to them the same result as is in effectually sought by godless struggles.

This is no preaching of laziness masquerading as religious trust. The psalmist insists on one side of the truth. Not work, but self-torturing care and work without seeking God's blessing are pronounced vanity.

**127:3–5.** The remainder of the Psalm dwells on one special instance of God's gifts, that of a numerous family, which in accordance with the Hebrew sentiment, is regarded as a special blessing. But the psalmist is carried beyond his immediate purpose of pointing out that this chief earthly blessing, as he and his contemporaries accounted it, is God's gift, and he lingers on the picture of a father surrounded in his old age by a band of stalwart sons born unto him in his vigorous youth, now able to surround him with a ring of strong protectors of his declining days.

In the clause, "They shall speak with the enemies in the gate," "They" probably refers to the whole band, the father in the midst and his sons about him. The gate was the place where justice was administered and where the chief place of concourse was located. It is, therefore, improbable that actual warfare is meant; rather, in the disputes which might arise with neighbors and in the interchange of city life, which would breed enmities enough, the man with his sons about him could hold his own. And such blessing is God's gift.

***Psalm 128.*** *The preceding Psalm traced all prosperity and domestic felicity to God's giving hand. It painted in its close the picture of a father surrounded by his sons able to defend him. This Psalm presents the same blessings as the result of a devout life, in which the fear of Yahweh leads to obedience and diligence in labor. It presents the inner side of domestic happiness. It thus doubly supplements the former, lest any should think that God's gift superseded man's work or that the only blessedness of fatherhood was that it supplied a corps of sturdy defenders. The first four verses describe the peaceful, happy life of the God-fearing man, and the last two invoke on him the blessing which alone makes such a life his. Blended with the sweet domesticity of the Psalm is glowing love for*

| 3176 | 2050.151 | 904, 1932 | | 3127 | 3834 | 3706 | 404.123 |
|---|---|---|---|---|---|---|---|
| pn | art, v Qal act ptc ms | prep, n mp, ps 3ms | | *n ms* | n fp, ps 2ms | cj | v Qal impf 2ms |
| יְהוָה | הַהֹלֵךְ | בִּדְרָכָיו | 2. | יְגִיעַ | כַּפֶּיךָ | כִּי | תֹאכֵל |
| yehwāh | hahōlēkh | bidhrākhâv | | yeghîa' | kappêkhā | kî | thō'khēl |
| Yahweh | and the ones walking | in his ways | | the labor of | your hands | indeed | you will eat |

| 869 | 3005 | 3937 | | 828 | 3626, 1655 | 6759.153 | 904, 3526 |
|---|---|---|---|---|---|---|---|
| n mp, ps 2ms | cj, adj | prep, ps 2ms | | n fs, ps 2ms | prep, n fs | v Qal act ptc fs | prep, *n fd* |
| אַשְׁרֶיךָ | וְטוֹב | לָךְ | 3. | אֶשְׁתְּךָ | כְּגֶפֶן | פֹּרִיָּה | בְּיַרְכְּתֵי |
| 'ashrêkhā | wetôv | lākh | | 'eshtekhā | keghephen | pōrîyāh | beyarkethê |
| your happiness | and good | to you | | your wife | like a vine | bearing fruit | in the remote parts of |

| 1041 | 1158 | 3626, 8691 | 2215 | 5623 | 3937, 8374 | | 2079 |
|---|---|---|---|---|---|---|---|
| n ms, ps 2ms | n mp, ps 2ms | prep, *n mp* | n mp | adv | prep, n ms, ps 2ms | | intrj |
| בֵּיתֶךָ | בָּנֶיךָ | כִּשְׁתִלֵי | זֵיתִים | סָבִיב | לְשֻׁלְחָנֶךָ | 4. | הִנֵּה |
| vêthekhā | bānêkhā | kishthilê | zêthîm | sāvîv | leshulchānekhā | | hinnēh |
| your house | your sons | like the cuttings of | olive trees | all around | your table | | behold |

| 3706, 3772 | 1313.421 | 1429 | 3486.151 | 3176 | | 1313.321 |
|---|---|---|---|---|---|---|
| cj, adv | v Pual impf 3ms | n ms | *v Qal act ptc ms* | pn | | v Piel juss 3ms, ps 2ms |
| כִּי־כֵן | יְבֹרַךְ | גָּבֶר | יְרֵא | יְהוָה | 5. | יְבָרֶכְךָ |
| khî-khēn | yevōrakh | gāver | yerē' | yehwāh | | yevārekhekhā |
| because thus | he will be blessed | the man | the one who fears | Yahweh | | may He bless you |

| 3176 | 4623, 6995 | 7495.131 | 904, 3008 | 3503 | 3725 | 3219 |
|---|---|---|---|---|---|---|
| pn | prep, pn | cj, v Qal impv 2ms | prep, *n ms* | pn | adj | *n mp* |
| יְהוָה | מִצִּיּוֹן | וּרְאֵה | בְּטוּב | יְרוּשָׁלָם | כֹּל | יְמֵי |
| yehwāh | mitstsîyôn | ûre'ēh | betûv | yerûshālām | kōl | yemê |
| Yahweh | from Zion | and look | on the good things of | Jerusalem | all | the days of |

| 2522 | | 7495.131, 1158 | 3937, 1158 | 8361 | 6142, 3547 | | 8302 |
|---|---|---|---|---|---|---|---|
| n mp, ps 2ms | | cj, v Qal impv 2ms, n mp | prep, n mp, ps 2ms | n ms | prep, pn | | *n ms* |
| חַיֶּיךָ | 6. | וּרְאֵה־בָנִים | לְבָנֶיךָ | שָׁלוֹם | עַל־יִשְׂרָאֵל | 129:t | שִׁיר |
| chayyêkhā | | ûre'ēh-vānîm | levānêkhā | shālôm | 'al-yisrā'ēl | | shîr |
| your life | | and see the sons | to your sons | peace | on Israel | | a Song of |

| 4765 | | 7521 | 7173.116 | 4623, 5454 | 569.121, 5167 | 3547 |
|---|---|---|---|---|---|---|
| art, n fp | | adj | v Qal pf 3cp, ps 1cs | prep, n mp, ps 1cs | v Qal juss 3ms, part | pn |
| הַמַּעֲלוֹת | 1. | רַבַּת | צְרָרוּנִי | מִנְּעוּרָי | יֹאמַר־נָא | יִשְׂרָאֵל |
| hamma'ălôth | | rabbath | tserārûnî | minne'ûray | yō'mar-nā' | yisrā'ēl |
| the Ascents | | abundantly | they have opposed me | from my youth | let them say please | Israel |

**128:t. A Song of degrees.**

**1. Blessed is every one that feareth the LORD:** ... Happy is the worshipper of the Lord, *BB* ... Blessings on all who reverence and trust the Lord, *LIVB* ... Happy is everyone who reveres the Eternal, *Moffatt* ... respect the LORD, *NCV.*

**that walketh in his ways:** ... who conform to his ways, *REB* ... and follow his paths!, *Knox* ... on all who obey him!, *LIVB* ... who live according to his will, *NEB.*

**2. For thou shalt eat the labour of thine hands:** ... You shall eat what your hands worked for, *Beck* ... Your own labours will yield you a living, *JB* ... You shall earn your daily bread, *Moffatt.*

**happy shalt thou be, and it shall be well with thee:** ... happy shall you be, and favored, *NAB.*

**3. Thy wife shall be as a fruitful vine by the sides of thine house:** ... In the very heart of you house, *NKJV* ... to decorate your home, *Fenton* ... in the recesses of your home, *NAB.*

**thy children like olive plants round about thy table:** ... your sons round your table will be like olive saplings, *REB* ... around about your board, *Fenton.*

**4. Behold, that thus shall the man be blessed that feareth the LORD:** ... See! this is the blessing of the worshipper of the Lord, *BB* ... thus shall the man be rewarded who reveres the LORD, *Berkeley.*

**5. The LORD shall bless thee out of Zion:** ... The LORD bless you from Zion, *NRSV.*

**and thou shalt see the good of Jerusalem all the days of thy life:** ... rejoice in the prosperity of Jerusalem, *REB* ... behold thou the welfare of Jerusalem, *Rotherham* ... you shall see Jerusalem flourish all your days, *Moffatt* ... share the prosperity of Jerusalem, *NEB.*

**6. Yea, thou shalt see thy children's children:** ... May you live to enjoy your grandchildren!, *LIVB* ... sons of thy sons!, *Young.*

**and peace upon Israel:** ... Prosperity on Israel!, *Rotherham* ... Peace to Israel!, *JB* ... peace resting upon Israel, *Knox.*

**129:t. A Song of degrees.**

**1. Many a time have they afflicted me from my youth:** ... have I been attacked, *REB* ... Grossly have they abused me, *Goodspeed* ... Cruelly have they harried me, *Moffatt* ... oppressed me, *NAB* ... attacked me, *NEB.*

---

*Zion. However blessed the home, it is not to weaken the sense of belonging to the nation.*

**128:1–2.** No purer, fairer idyll was ever penned than this miniature picture of a happy home life. But its calm, simple beauty has deep foundations. The poet sets forth the basis of all noble, tranquil life when he begins with the fear of Yahweh and then advances to practical conformity with his will, manifested by walking in the paths which He traces for men. Thence the transition is easy to the mention of diligent labor, and the singer is sure that such toil done on such principles and from such a motive cannot go unblessed. Outward prosperity does not follow good men's work so surely as the letter of the Psalm teaches, but the best fruits of such work are not those which can be stored in barns or enjoyed by sense; and the laborer who does his work "heartily, as to the LORD," will certainly reap a harvest in character, power and communion with God, whatever transitory gain may be attained or missed.

**128:3–4.** The sweet little sketch of a joyous home in v. 3 is touched with true grace and feeling. The wife is happy in her motherhood and ready, in the inner chambers (literally, "sides") of the house where she does her share of work, to welcome her husband returning from the field. The family gathers for the meal won and sweetened by his toil; the children are in vigorous health and growing up like young "layered" olive plants. It may be noted that this verse exhibits a home in the earlier stages of married life and reflects the happy hopes associated with youthful children, all still gathered under the father's roof; while in the latter part of the Psalm a later stage is in view, when the father sits as a spectator rather than a worker and sees children born to his children.

Verse 4 emphatically dwells once more on the foundation of all as laid in the fear of Yahweh. Happy a nation whose poets have such ideals and sing of such themes! How wide the gulf separating this "undisturbed song" of pure home joys from the foul ideals which baser songs try to adorn! Happy the man whose ambition is bounded by its limits and whose life is true to the kindred points of heaven and home! Israel first taught the world how sacred the family is, and Christianity recognizes "a church in the house" of every wedded pair whose love is hallowed by the fear of Yahweh.

**128:5–6.** In vv. 5f, petitions take the place of assurances, for the singer knows that none of the good which he has been promising will come without that blessing of which the preceding Psalm had spoken. All the beautiful and calm joys just described must flow from God and be communicated from that place which is the seat of his self-revelation. The word rendered above "mayest thou look" (HED #7495) is in the imperative form, which seems here to be intended to blend promise, wish and command. It is the duty of the happiest husband and father not to let himself be so absorbed in the sweets of home as to have his heart beat weakly for the public well-being. The subtle selfishness which is too commonly the accompaniment of such blessings is to be resisted. From his cheerful hearth, the eyes of a lover of Zion are to look out and be gladdened when they see prosperity smiling on Zion. Many a Christian is so happy in his household that his duties to the Church, the nation and the world are neglected. This ancient singer had a truer conception of the obligations flowing from personal and domestic blessings. He teaches us that it is not enough to "see thy children's children," unless we have eyes to look for the prosperity of Jerusalem and tongues which pray not only for those in our homes, but for "peace upon Israel."

***Psalm 129****. The point of view here is the same as in Ps. 124, with which the present Psalm has much similarity both in subject and in expression. It is a retrospect of Israel's past, in which the poet sees a uniform exemplification of two standing facts—sore affliction and wonderful deliverance. The bush burned without being consumed. "Cast down, but not destroyed," is the summary of the Church's history. No doubt the recent deliverance from captivity underlies this, as most of the Psalms*

| 2. | 7521 | 7173.116 | 4623, 5454 | 1612 | 3940, 3310.116 | 3937 |
|---|---|---|---|---|---|---|
| | adj | v Qal pf 3cp, ps 1cs | prep, n mp, ps 1cs | cj | neg part, v Qal pf 3cp | prep, ps 1cs |
| | רַבַּת | צְרָרוּנִי | מִנְּעוּרָי | גַּם | לֹא־יָכְלוּ | לִי |
| | rabbath | tserārûnî | minne'ûrāy | gam | lō'-yākhelû | lî |
| | abundantly | they have opposed me | from my youth | yet | they have not been able | against me |

| 3. | 6142, 1384 | 2896.116 | 2896.152 | 773.516 | 3937, 4778 | 4. | 3176 |
|---|---|---|---|---|---|---|---|
| | prep, n ms, ps 1cs | v Qal pf 3cp | v Qal act ptc mp | v Hiphil pf 3cp | prep, n fp, ps 3mp | | pn |
| | עַל־גַּבִּי | חָרְשׁוּ | חֹרְשִׁים | הֶאֱרִיכוּ | לְמַעֲנוֹתָם | | יְהוָה |
| | 'al-gabbî | chāreshû | chōreshîm | he'ĕrîkhû | lema'ănôthām | | yehwāh |
| | on my back | they plowed | the plowmen | they made long | their furrows | | Yahweh |

| 6926 | 7401.311 | 5895 | 7857 | 5. | 991.126 |
|---|---|---|---|---|---|
| adj | v Piel pf 3ms | *n ms* | n mp | | v Qal juss 3mp |
| צַדִּיק | קִצֵּץ | עֲבוֹת | רְשָׁעִים | | יֵבֹשׁוּ |
| tsaddîq | qitstsēts | 'ăvôth | reshā'îm | | yēvōshû |
| righteous | He has cut in pieces | the cords of | the wicked | | may they be ashamed |

| 5657.226 | 268 | 3725 | 7983.152 | 6995 | 6. | 2030.126 |
|---|---|---|---|---|---|---|
| cj, v Niphal juss 3mp | adv | adj | *v Qal act ptc mp* | pn | | v Qal juss 3mp |
| וְיִסֹּגוּ | אָחוֹר | כֹּל | שֹׂנְאֵי | צִיּוֹן | | יִהְיוּ |
| weyissōghû | 'āchôr | kōl | sōne'ê | tsîyôn | | yihyû |
| and may they be misdirected | backward | all | those who hate | Zion | | may they be |

| 3626, 2785 | 1437 | 8054, 7211 | 8418.111 | 3112.111 |
|---|---|---|---|---|
| prep, *n ms* | n mp | rel part, *n fs* | v Qal pf 3ms | v Qal pf 3ms |
| כַּחֲצִיר | גַּגּוֹת | שֶׁקַּדְמַת | שָׁלַף | יָבֵשׁ |
| kachtsîr | gaggôth | sheqqadhmath | shālaph | yāvēsh |
| like the grass of | the rooftops | which in the time before | someone draws out | it has dried up |

| 7. | 8054, 3940 | 4527.311 | 3834 | 7403.151 | 2786 | 6240.351 | 8. | 3940 |
|---|---|---|---|---|---|---|---|---|
| | rel part, neg part | v Piel pf 3ms | n fs, ps 3ms | v Qal act ptc ms | cj, n ms, ps 3ms | v Piel ptc ms | | cj, neg part |
| | שֶׁלֹּא | מִלֵּא | כַּפּוֹ | קוֹצֵר | וְחִצְנוֹ | מְעַמֵּר | | וְלֹא |
| | shellō' | millē' | khappô | qôtsēr | wechitsnô | me'ammēr | | welō' |
| | which not | it has filled | his hand | the harvester | or his bosom | the binder | | and not |

| 569.116 | 5882.152 | 1318, 3176 | 420 | 1313.319 | 881 |
|---|---|---|---|---|---|
| v Qal pf 3cp | art, v Qal act ptc mp | *n fs*, pn | prep, ps 2mp | v Piel pf 1cp | do, ps 2mp |
| אָמְרוּ | הָעֹבְרִים | בִּרְכַּת־יְהוָה | אֲלֵיכֶם | בֵּרַכְנוּ | אֶתְכֶם |
| 'āmerû | hā'ōverîm | birkath-yehwāh | 'ălêkhem | bērakhnû | 'ethkem |
| they said | those passing by | the blessing of Yahweh | to you | we bless | you |

**may Israel now say:** ... Israel is speaking, *LIVB.*

**2. Many a time have they afflicted me from my youth:** ... great have been my troubles, *BB* ... from my youth up, *MAST.*

**yet they have not prevailed against me:** ... but have never overpowered me, *Beck* ... never once outmatched me, *Knox* ... have not won over me, *KJVII.*

**3. The plowers plowed upon my back: they made long their furrows:** ... they scored my back with scourges, *REB* ... They cut deep wounds in my back and made it like a plowed field, *Good News.*

**4. The LORD is righteous:** ... the LORD is victorious, *REB* ... Yahweh the Just, *Anchor* ... the Eternal, he is just, *Moffatt.*

**he hath cut asunder the cords of the wicked:** ... cut me loose from the ropes of the wicked, *Beck* ... but Yahweh the upright has shattered the yoke of the wicked, *JB* ... cut the bonds of tyranny assunder, *Knox* ... He has cut the cords of the wicked in two, *KJVII.*

**5. Let them all be confounded and turned back that hate Zion:** ... be put to shame and turned backward!, *RSV* ... thrown back in confusion, *REB* ... turned back in disgrace, *Beck* ... retreat in humiliation, *Anchor.*

**6. Let them be as the grass upon the housetops:** ... like herbs growing on the housetops, *Beck* ... stalks on a house-top, *Knox.*

**which withereth afore it groweth up:** ... which is dry before it comes to full growth, *BB* ... dried up before it is cut, *JB* ... which withereth before it is plucked up, *Darby* ... which before the plucker's eyes withers away, *Anchor.*

**7. Wherewith the mower filleth not his hand:** ... no reaper can take a handful of it, *Beck* ... There is not enough of it to fill a hand, *NCV.*

**nor he that bindeth sheaves his bosom:** ... they do not make bands of it for the grain-stems, *BB* ... nor the binder's lap, *JB* ... or to make into a bundle to fill one's arms, *NCV.*

**8. Neither do they which go by say:** ... no passer-by will say, *JB.*

**The blessing of the LORD be upon you:** ... Give good thanks to the LORD, *Fenton.*

**we bless you in the name of the LORD:** ... we give you blessing in the name of the Lord, *BB* ... We bless you by the power of the LORD, *NCV.*

**130:t. A Song of degrees.**

**1. Out of the depths have I cried unto thee, O LORD:** ... O Lord, from the depths of despair I cry for your help, *LIVB.*

---

*of Ascents. The second part (vv. 5–8) blends confidence and wish, founded on the experience recorded in the first part, and prophesies and desires the overthrow of Israel's foes. The right use of retrospect is to make it the ground of hope. They who have passed unscathed through such afflictions may well be sure that any tomorrow shall be as the yesterdays were and that all future assaults will fail as all past ones have failed.*

**129:1–2.** The words which Israel is called upon to say twice with triumphant remembrance are the motto of the Church in all ages. Ever there is antagonism; never is there overthrow. Israel's "youth" was far back in the days of Egyptian bondage. Many an affliction has he since met, but he lives still, and his existence proves that "they have not prevailed against" him. Therefore, the backward look is gladsome, although it sees so many trials. Survived sorrows yield joy and hope, as gashes in trees exude precious gums.

**129:3–4.** Verse 3 expresses Israel's oppressions by a strong metaphor in which two figures are blended—a slave under the lash and a field furrowed by plowing. Cruel lords had laid on the whip, until the victim's back was scored with long wounds, straight and parallel, like the work of a plowman.

The divine deliverance follows in v. 4. The first words of the verse do not stand in the usual order, if rendered "Yahweh is righteous," and are probably to be taken as above; they relate a "righteous" standing in apposition to "Yahweh" and express the divine characteristic which guaranteed and, in due time, accomplished Israel's deliverance. God could not but be true to his covenant obligations. Therefore, He cut the "cords of the wicked." The figure is here changed to one occasioned by the former. Israel is now the draught ox harnessed to the plow, and thus both sides of his bondage are expressed—cruel treatment by the former figure, and hard toil by the latter. The same act which, in the parallel Ps. 124, is described as breaking the fowler's snare, is in view here; and the restoration from Babylon suits the circumstances completely.

**129:5–7.** The story of past futile attempts against Israel animates the confidence and vindicates the wish breathed in the latter half of the Psalm. To hate Zion, which Yahweh so manifestly loves and guards, must be suicidal. It is something far nobler than selfish vengeance which desires and foresees the certain failure of attempts against it. The psalmist is still under the influence of his earlier metaphor of the plowed field, but now has come to think of the harvest. The graphic image of the grass on flat housetops of clay, which springs quickly because it has no depth of earth, and withers as it springs, vividly describes the short-lived success and rapid extinction of plots against Zion and of the plotters.

The word rendered above "someone draws out" (HED #8418) is translated by some "shoots forth," and that meaning is defensible. Grass on the housetops would scarcely be worth plucking, (unless to replace with better) and the word is used elsewhere for unsheathing a sword. It may, therefore, be taken here to refer to the shooting out of the spikelets from their covering.

The psalmist dilates upon his metaphor in v. 7, which expresses the fruitlessness of assaults on God's chosen. No harvest is to be reaped from such sowing. The enemies may plot and toil, and before their plans have had time to bud, they are smitten into brown dust. When the contrivers come expecting success, there is nothing to mow or gather. They look for much and behold little. So it has been, so it shall be; so it should be, so may it be, wishes the psalmist. True hearts will say "Amen" to his aspiration.

**129:8.** Such reapers have no joy in harvest, and no man can invoke Yahweh's blessing on their bad work. Verse 8 brings up a lovely picture of a harvest field, where passers-by shout their good

| 904, 8428<br>prep, *n ms*<br>בְּשֵׁם<br>beshēm<br>in the name of | 3176<br>pn<br>יְהוָה<br>yehwāh<br>Yahweh | **130:t** | 8302<br>*n ms*<br>שִׁיר<br>shîr<br>a Song of | 4765<br>art, n fp<br>הַמַּעֲלוֹת<br>hamma'ălôth<br>the Ascents | **1.** | 4623, 4774<br>prep, n mp<br>מִמַּעֲמַקִּים<br>mimma'ămaqqîm<br>from the depths | 7410.115<br>v Qal pf 1cs, ps 2ms<br>קְרָאתִיךָ<br>qōrā'thîkhā<br>I have called to You |
|---|---|---|---|---|---|---|---|

| 3176<br>pn<br>יְהוָה<br>yehwāh<br>O Yahweh | **2.** | 112<br>n mp, ps 1cs<br>אֲדֹנָי<br>'ădhōnāy<br>O my Lord | 8471.131<br>v Qal impv 2ms<br>שִׁמְעָה<br>shim'āh<br>hear | 904, 7249<br>prep, n ms, ps 1cs<br>בְקוֹלִי<br>veqôlî<br>by my voice | 2030.127<br>v Qal impf 3fp<br>תִּהְיֶינָה<br>tihyênāh<br>let them be | 238<br>n fd, ps 2ms<br>אָזְנֶיךָ<br>'āzenêkhā<br>your ears | 7480<br>adj<br>קַשֻּׁבוֹת<br>qashshuvôth<br>attentive |
|---|---|---|---|---|---|---|---|

| 3937, 7249<br>prep, *n ms*<br>לְקוֹל<br>leqôl<br>to the voice of | 8800<br>n mp, ps 1cs<br>תַּחֲנוּנָי<br>tachnûnāy<br>my supplication | **3.** | 524, 5988<br>cj, n fp<br>אִם־עֲוֹנוֹת<br>'im-'ăwōnôth<br>if transgressions | 8490.123, 3176<br>v Qal impf 2ms, pn<br>תִּשְׁמָר־יָהּ<br>tishmār-yāhh<br>You observe Yah | 112<br>n mp, ps 1cs<br>אֲדֹנָי<br>'ădhōnāy<br>O my Lord | 4449<br>intrg<br>מִי<br>mî<br>who |
|---|---|---|---|---|---|---|

| 6198.121<br>v Qal impf 3ms<br>יַעֲמֹד<br>ya'ămōdh<br>he could stand | **4.** | 3706, 6196<br>cj, prep, ps 2ms<br>כִּי־עִמְּךָ<br>kî-'immekhā<br>rather with You | 5742<br>art, n fs<br>הַסְּלִיחָה<br>hasselîchāh<br>the forgiveness | 3937, 4775<br>prep, prep<br>לְמַעַן<br>lema'an<br>so that | 3486.223<br>v Niphal impf 2ms<br>תִּוָּרֵא<br>tiwwārē'<br>You are feared | **5.** | 7245.315<br>v Piel pf 1cs<br>קִוִּיתִי<br>qiwwîthî<br>I have hoped in |
|---|---|---|---|---|---|---|---|

| 3176<br>pn<br>יְהוָה<br>yehwāh<br>Yahweh | 7245.312<br>v Piel pf 3fs<br>קִוְּתָה<br>qiwwethāh<br>it hopes | 5497<br>n fs, ps 1cs<br>נַפְשִׁי<br>naphshî<br>my soul | 3937, 1745<br>cj, prep, n ms, ps 3ms<br>וְלִדְבָרוֹ<br>welidhvārô<br>and for his word | 3282.515<br>v Hiphil pf 1cs<br>הוֹחָלְתִּי<br>hôchālettî<br>I have waited more | **6.** | 5497<br>n fs, ps 1cs<br>נַפְשִׁי<br>naphshî<br>my soul | 3937, 112<br>prep, n mp, ps 1cs<br>לַאדֹנָי<br>la'dhōnāy<br>for the Lord |
|---|---|---|---|---|---|---|---|

| 4623, 8490.152<br>prep, v Qal act ptc mp<br>מִשֹּׁמְרִים<br>mishshōmerîm<br>than watchmen | 3937, 1269<br>prep, art, n ms<br>לַבֹּקֶר<br>labbōqer<br>for the morning | 8490.152<br>v Qal act ptc mp<br>שֹׁמְרִים<br>shōmerîm<br>watchmen | 3937, 1269<br>prep, art, n ms<br>לַבֹּקֶר<br>labbōqer<br>for the morning | **7.** | 3282.331<br>v Piel impv 2ms<br>יַחֵל<br>yachēl<br>wait | 3547<br>pn<br>יִשְׂרָאֵל<br>yisrā'ēl<br>O Israel |
|---|---|---|---|---|---|---|

| 420, 3176<br>prep, pn<br>אֶל־יְהוָה<br>'el-yehwāh<br>to Yahweh | 3706, 6196, 3176<br>cj, prep, pn<br>כִּי־עִם־יְהוָה<br>kî-'im-yehwāh<br>because with Yahweh | 2721<br>art, n ms<br>הַחֶסֶד<br>hachesedh<br>the steadfast love | 7528.542<br>cj, v Hiphil inf abs<br>וְהַרְבֵּה<br>weharbēh<br>and abundantly | 6196<br>prep, ps 3ms<br>עִמּוֹ<br>'immô<br>with Him | 6545<br>n fs<br>פְדוּת<br>phedhûth<br>redemption |
|---|---|---|---|---|---|

**2. Lord, hear my voice: let thine ears be attentive to the voice of my supplications:** … listen to my prayer for help, *NCV* … Pity me!, *Fenton* … Let your ears be attentive to my cry for mercy, *NIV* … let your ears be awake to the voice of my prayer, *BB*.

**3. If thou, LORD, shouldest mark iniquities, O Lord, who shall stand?:** … keep an account of sins, *REB* … LORD, if you punished people for all their sins, no one would be left, *NCV* … If you, O LORD, kept a record of sins, *NIV* … who could escape being condemned?, *Good News*.

**4. But there is forgiveness with thee, that thou mayest be feared:** … But thou hast pardon, that thou mayest be worshipped, *Moffatt* … And so You are loved, *Fenton* … that you may be revered, *NAB* … so you are repected, *NCV*.

**5. I wait for the LORD, my soul doth wait, and in his word do I hope:** … As dusk waits for the dawn, *Fenton* … my soul waits hoping for his promise, *Moffatt* … I rely, my whole being relies, Yahweh, on your promise, *JB* … My soul is in expectation, *Berkeley*.

**6. My soul waiteth for the Lord more than they that watch for the morning:** … more than the sentinels wait for the dawn, *NCB* … more eagerly than watchmen for the morning, *REB*.

**I say, more than they that watch for the morning:** … more than sentinels wait for the dawn, *NAB* … more than watchmen for daybreak, *JB*.

**7. Let Israel hope in the LORD:** … Oh Israel, look for the LORD, *NEB*.

wishes to the glad toilers and are answered by these with like salutations. It is doubtful whether v. 8c is spoken by the passers-by or is the reapers' responsive greeting. The latter explanation gives animation to the scene. But in any case, the verse suggests by contrast the gloomy silence of Israel's would-be destroyers, who find, as all who set themselves against Yahweh's purposes do find, that He blasts their plans with his bearth and makes their "harvest an heap in the day of grief and desperate sorrow" (Isa. 17:11).

***Psalm 130.*** *In a very emphatic sense, this is a Song of Ascents, for it climbs steadily from the abyss of penitence to the summits of hope. It falls into two divisions of four verses each, of which the former breathes the prayer of a soul penetrated by the consciousness of sin and the latter the peaceful expectance of one that has tasted God's forgiving mercy. These two parts are again divided into two groups of two verses, so that there are four stages in the psalmist's progress from the depths to the sunny heights.*

**130:1–2.** In the first group, we have the psalmist's cry. He has called and still calls. He reiterates in v. 2 the prayer that he had long offered and still presents. It is not only quotation, but is the cry of present need. What are these "depths" (HED #4774) from which his voice sounds, as that of a man fallen into a pit and sending up a faint call? The expression does not merely refer to his creatural lowliness or even to his troubles or even to his depression of spirit. There are deeper pits than these—those into which the spirit feels itself going down, sick and giddy, when it realizes its sinfulness. Unless a man has been down in that black abyss, he has scarcely cried to God as he should do.

**130:3–4.** Verses 3f are the second stage. A dark fear shadows the singer's soul and is swept away by a joyful assurance. The word rendered above "mark" (HED #8490) is literally "keep" or "watch," as in v. 6, and here seems to mean "to take account of" or "retain in remembrance," in order to punish. If God should take man's sin into account in his dispositions and dealings, "O LORD, who shall stand?" No man could sustain that righteous judgment. He must go down before it like a flimsy hut before a whirlwind or a weak enemy before a fierce charge. That thought comes to the psalmist like a blast of icy air from the north and threatens to chill his hope to death and to blow his cry back into his throat. But its very hypothetical form holds a negation concealed in it. Such an implied negative is needed in order to explain the "for" of v. 4. The singer springs, as it were, to that confidence by a rebound from the other darker thought.

The word rendered "forgiveness" (HED #5742) is a late form, being found only in two other late passages (Neh. 9:17; Dan. 9:9). It literally means "cutting off" and so suggests the merciful surgery by which the cancerous tumor is taken out of the soul. Such forgiveness is "with God," inherent in his nature. And that forgiveness lies at the root of true godliness.

**130:5–6.** The next stage in the ascent from the depths is in vv. 5f, which breathe peaceful, patient hope. It may be doubtful whether the psalmist means to represent that attitude of expectance as prior to and securing forgiveness or as consequent upon it. The latter seems the more probable. A soul which has received God's forgiveness is thereby led into tranquil, continuous, ever-rewarded waiting on Him, and hope of new gifts springs ever fresh in it. Such a soul sits quietly at his feet, trusting to his love and looking for light and all else needed to flow from Him. The singleness of the object of devout hope, the yearning which is not impatience, characterizing that hope at its noblest, are beautifully painted in the simile of the watchers for morning. As they who have outwatched the long night look eagerly to the flush that creeps up in the east, telling that their vigil is past and heralding the stir and life of a new day with its wakening birds and fresh morning airs, so this singer's eyes had turned to God and to Him only. Verse 6 does not absolutely require the supplement "hopes." It may read simply "my soul is toward Yahweh"; and that translation gives still more emphatically the notion of complete turning of the whole being to God. Consciousness of sin was as a dark night; forgiveness flushed the Eastern heaven with prophetic twilight. So the psalmist waits for the light, and his soul is one aspiration toward God.

**130:7–8.** In vv. 7f, the psalmist becomes an evangelist, inviting Israel to unite in his hope, that they may share in his pardon. In the depths, he was alone and felt as if the only beings in the universe were God and himself. The consciousness of sin isolates, and the sense of forgiveness unites. Whoever has known the truth that "with the LORD there is mercy" is impelled thereby to invite others to learn the same lesson in the same sweet way. The psalmist has a broad gospel to preach, the gen-

| | 2000 | 6540.121 | 881, 3547 | 4623, 3725 | 5988 | | 8302 |
|---|---|---|---|---|---|---|---|
| 8. | cj, pers pron | v Qal impf 3ms | do, pn | prep, adj | n fp, ps 3ms | 131:t | n ms |
| | וְהוּא | יִפְדֶּה | אֶת־יִשְׂרָאֵל | מִכֹּל | עֲוֺנֹתָיו | | שִׁיר |
| | wehû' | yiphdeh | 'eth-yisrā'ēl | mikkōl | 'ăwōnōthâv | | shîr |
| | and He | He will ransom | Israel | from all | its transgressions | | a Song of |

| 4765 | 3937, 1784 | | 3176 | 3940, 1391.111 | 3949 | 3940, 7597.116 | 6084 |
|---|---|---|---|---|---|---|---|
| art, n fp | prep, pn | 1. | pn | neg part, v Qal pf 3ms | n ms, ps 1cs | cj, neg part, v Qal pf 3cp | n fd, ps 1cs |
| הַמַּעֲלוֹת | לְדָוִד | | יְהוָה | לֹא־גָבַהּ | לִבִּי | וְלֹא־רָמוּ | עֵינַי |
| hamma'ălôth | ledhāwidh | | yehwāh | lō'-ghāvahh | libbî | welō'-rāmû | 'ênay |
| the Ascents | of David | | O Yahweh | it is not high | my heart | and they are not raised | my eyes |

| 3940, 2050.315 | 904, 1448 | 904, 6623.258 | 4623 | | 524, 3940 |
|---|---|---|---|---|---|
| cj, neg part, v Piel pf 1cs | prep, adj | cj, prep, v Niphal ptc fp | prep, ps 1cs | 2. | cj, neg part |
| וְלֹא־הִלַּכְתִּי | בִּגְדֹלוֹת | וּבְנִפְלָאוֹת | מִמֶּנִּי | | אִם־לֹא |
| welō'-hillakhtî | bighdhōlôth | ûveniphlā'ôth | mimmenî | | 'im-lō' |
| and I have not proceeded | with great things | or with extraordinary deeds | from me | | if not |

| 8187.315 | 1887.315 | 5497 | 3626, 1621.155 | 6142 | 525 |
|---|---|---|---|---|---|
| v Piel pf 1cs | cj, v Poel pf 1cs | n fs, ps 1cs | prep, v Qal pass ptc ms | prep | n fs, ps 3ms |
| שִׁוִּיתִי | וְדוֹמַמְתִּי | נַפְשִׁי | כְּגָמֻל | עֲלֵי | אִמּוֹ |
| shiwwîthî | wedhômamtî | naphshî | keghāmul | 'ălê | 'immô |
| I had set | and I was quieted | my soul | like a weaned child | on | his mother |

| 3626, 1621.155 | 6142 | 5497 | | 3282.331 | 3547 | 420, 3176 | 4623, 6498 |
|---|---|---|---|---|---|---|---|
| prep, art, v Qal pass ptc ms | prep, ps 1cs | n fs, ps 1cs | 3. | v Piel impv 2ms | pn | prep, pn | prep, adv |
| כַּגָּמֻל | עָלַי | נַפְשִׁי | | יַחֵל | יִשְׂרָאֵל | אֶל־יְהוָה | מֵעַתָּה |
| kaggāmul | 'ālay | naphshî | | yachēl | yisrā'ēl | 'el-yehwāh | mē'attāh |
| like a weaned child | on me | my soul | | wait | O Israel | to Yahweh | from now |

**for with the LORD there is mercy:** ... For in the LORD is love unfailing, *NEB* ... steadfast love, *RSV* ... because with Yahweh there is kindness, *Anchor* ... there is lovingkindness, *Berkeley.*

**and with him is plenteous redemption:** ... there is a wealth of saving power, *Moffatt* ... armloads of salvation, *LIVB* ... and great is his power to set men free, *NEB* ... and great is his power to deliver, *REB* ... abundant power to ransom, *Knox.*

**8. And he shall redeem Israel from all his iniquities:** ... and he will ransom Israel from all its sins, *JB* ... He alone will set Israel free from all their sins, *REB* ... For he will redeem Israel From all its guilt, *Goodspeed.*

**131:t. A Song of degrees of David.**

**1. LORD, my heart is not haughty:** ... My heart is not proud, *NAB*, *NIV* ... No; I submit myself, I account myself lowly, *NEB* ... LORD, I have given up my pride, *Good News.*

**nor mine eyes lofty:** ... I don't look down on others, *NCV* ... I do not set my sights too high, *JB* ... and turned away from my arrogance, *Good News* ... nor are my eyes disdainful, *Berkeley.*

**neither do I exercise myself in great matters, or in things too high for me:** ... I walk not in grandeur And great deeds not my own, *Fenton* ... I never meddle with high schemes, *Moffatt* ... things too sublime for me, *NCB* ... on marvels that are beyond my reach, *Knox.*

**2. Surely I have behaved and quieted myself:** ... Have I not compared, and kept silent my soul, *Young* ... Surely I have soothed and silenced my soul, *Rotherham* ... No, I've calmed down and silenced my ambitions, *Beck.*

**as a child that is weaned of his mother:** ... Like a weaned child rests against his mother, *NASB* ... like a little child in its mother's arms, *JB.*

**my soul is even as a weaned child:** ... Like a weaned child on its mother's lap, *NAB*, ... I am at peace, like a baby with its mother, *NCV* ... My spirit in me rests like a weaned child, *Beck.*

**3. Let Israel hope in the LORD:** ... Israel doth wait on Jehovah, *Young.*

**from henceforth and for ever:** ... From henceforth, and unto the age!, *Young* ... even to times age-abiding, *Rotherham* ... Let Israel hope in the LORD from this moment and forever, *KJVII.*

**132:t. A Song of degrees.**

**1. LORD, remember David, and all his afflictions:** ... Remember, O,

eralization of his own history. He had said in v. 4 that "with him is plenteous redemption" (literally, "the forgiveness," possibly meaning the needed forgiveness), and he thereby had animated his own hope. Now he repeats the form of expression, only that he substitutes for "forgiveness" the steadfast love which is its spring, and the redemption which is its result; these he presses upon his fellows as reasons and encouragements for their hope. It is "abundant redemption" (HED #7528), or "multiplied," as the word might be rendered. "Seventy times seven"— the perfect numbers seven and ten being multiplied together and their sum increased sevenfold—make a numerical symbol for the unfailing pardons which we are to bestow, and the sum of the divine pardon is surely greater than that of the human. God's forgiving grace is mightier than all sins and able to conquer them all.

"He shall redeem Israel from all his iniquities," not only from their consequences in punishment, but from their power, as well as from their guilt and their penalty. The psalmist means something a great deal deeper than deliverance from calamities which conscience declared to be the chastisement of sin. He speaks NT language. He was sure that God would redeem from all iniquity, but he lived in the twilight dawn and had to watch for the morning. The sun is risen for us, but the light is the same in quality, though more in degree: "Thou shalt call his name Jesus, for He shall save his people from their sins" (Matt. 1:21).

**131:1.** The haughtiness which the psalmist disclaims has its seat in the heart and its manifestation in supercilious glances. The lowly heart looks higher than the proud one does, for it lifts its eyes to the hills and fixes them on Yahweh as a slave on his lord. Lofty thoughts of self naturally breed ambitions which seek great spheres and would intermeddle with things above reach. The singer does not refer to questions beyond solution by human faculty, but to worldly ambitions aiming at prominence and position. He aims low, as far as earth is concerned, but he aims high, for his mark is in the heavens.

**131:2.** Shaking off such ambitions and loftiness of spirit, he has found repose, as all do who clear their hearts of that perilous stuff. But it is to be noted that the calm that he enjoys is the fruit of his own self control, by which his dominant self has smoothed and stilled the sensitive nature with its desires and passions. It is not the tranquility of a calm nature which speaks here, but that into which the speaker has entered, by vigorous mastery of disturbing elements. How hard the struggle had been, how much bitter crying and petulant resistance there had been before the calm was won, is told by the lovely image of the weaned child. While being weaned, it sobs and struggles, and all its little life is perturbed. So no man comes to have a quiet heart without much resolute self-suppression. But the figure tells of ultimate repose, even more plainly than of preceding struggle. For once the process is accomplished, the child nestles satisfied on the mother's warm bosom and wishes nothing more than to lie there. So the man who has manfully taken in hand his own weaker and more yearning nature and directed its desires away from earth by fixing them on God is freed from the misery of hot desire and passes into calm. He that ceases from his own works enters into rest. If a man thus compels his "soul" to cease its cravings for what earth can give, he will have to disregard its struggles and cries, but these will give place to quietness; and the fruition of the blessedness of setting all desires on God will be the best defense against the recurrence of longings once silenced.

**131:3.** The psalmist would have all Israel share in his quietness of heart and closes his tender snatch of song with a call to them to hope in Yahweh, whereby they, too, may enter into peace. The preceding Psalm ended with the same call, but there God's mercy in dealing with sin was principally in question, while here his sufficiency for all a soul's needs is implied. The one secret of forgiveness and deliverance from iniquity is also the secret of rest from tyrannous longings and disturbing desires. Hope in Yahweh brings pardon, purity and peace.

***Psalm 132.*** *Psalm 89 is often referred to as the "twin" of this Psalm. The Psalm is not divided into regular strophes. There is, however, a broad division into two parts, of which vv. 1–10 form the first, the pleading of Israel with Yahweh, and vv. 11–18 the second, the answer of Yahweh to Israel. The first part is further divided into two: vv. 1–5 setting forth David's vow and vv. 6–10, the congregation's glad summons to enter the completed sanctuary and its prayer for blessings on the worshiping nation with its priests and king. The second part is Yahweh's renewed promises, which take up and surpass the people's prayer. It is broken by a single verse (v. 13), which is an interjected utterance of Israel.*

**132:1–5.** David's earnest longing to find a fixed place for the Ark, his long-continued and

| 5912, 5986 | | 8302 | 4765 | | 2226.131, 3176 | 3937, 1784 | 881 |
|---|---|---|---|---|---|---|---|
| cj, adv, n ms | | *n ms* | art, n fp | | v Qal impv 2ms, pn | prep, pn | do |
| וְעַד־עוֹלָם | **132:t** | שִׁיר | הַמַּעֲלוֹת | **1.** | זְכוֹר־יְהוָה | לְדָוִד | אֵת |
| weʿadh-ʿôlām | | shîr | hammaʿălôth | | zekhôr-yehwāh | ledhāwidh | 'ēth |
| even until eternity | | a Song of | the Ascents | | remember O Yahweh | David | |

| 3725, 6257.441 | | 866 | 8123.211 | 3937, 3176 | 5265.111 | 3937, 47 |
|---|---|---|---|---|---|---|
| *adj*, v Pual inf con, ps 3ms | | rel part | v Niphal pf 3ms | prep, pn | v Qal pf 3ms | prep, *adj* |
| כָּל־עֻנּוֹתוֹ | **2.** | אֲשֶׁר | נִשְׁבַּע | לַיהוָה | נָדַר | לַאֲבִיר |
| kol-ʿunnôthô | | 'ăsher | nishbaʿ | layhwāh | nādhar | la'ăvîr |
| all his being afflicted | | when | he swore | to Yahweh | he vowed | to the Mighty One of |

| 3399 | | 524, 971.125 | 904, 164 | 1041 | 524, 6148.125 | 6142, 6446 | 3435 |
|---|---|---|---|---|---|---|---|
| pn | | cj, v Qal impf 1cs | prep, *n ms* | n ms, ps 1cs | cj, v Qal impf 1cs | prep, *n fs* | n mp, ps 1cs |
| יַעֲקֹב | **3.** | אִם־אָבֹא | בְּאֹהֶל | בֵּיתִי | אִם־אֶעֱלֶה | עַל־עֶרֶשׂ | יְצוּעָי |
| yaʿăqōv | | 'im-'āvō' | be'ōhel | bêthî | 'im-'eʿĕleh | ʿal-ʿeres | yetsûʿāy |
| Jacob | | if I enter | into the tent of | my house | if I go up | onto the bed of | my couch |

| | 524, 5598.125 | 8517 | 3937, 6084 | 3937, 6310 | 8900 | | 5912, 4834.125 | 4887 |
|---|---|---|---|---|---|---|---|---|
| | cj, v Qal impf 1cs | n fs | prep, n fd, ps 1cs | prep, n md, ps 1cs | n fs | | adv, v Qal impf 1cs | n ms |
| **4.** | אִם־אֶתֵּן | שְׁנַת | לְעֵינָי | לְעַפְעַפַּי | תְּנוּמָה | **5.** | עַד־אֶמְצָא | מָקוֹם |
| | 'im-'ettēn | shenath | leʿênāy | leʿaphʿappay | tenûmāh | | ʿadh-'emtsā' | māqôm |
| | if I allow | sleep | to my eyes | to my eyelids | slumber | | until I find | a place |

| 3937, 3176 | 5088 | 3937, 47 | 3399 | | 2079, 8471.119 | 904, 693 |
|---|---|---|---|---|---|---|
| prep, pn | n mp | prep, *adj* | pn | | intrj, v Qal pf 1cp, ps 3fs | prep, pn |
| לַיהוָה | מִשְׁכָּנוֹת | לַאֲבִיר | יַעֲקֹב | **6.** | הִנֵּה־שְׁמַעֲנוּהָ | בְאֶפְרָתָה |
| layhwāh | mishkānôth | la'ăvîr | yaʿăqōv | | hinnēh-shemaʿănûāh | ve'ephrāthāh |
| for Yahweh | a tabernacle | for the Mighty One of | Jacob | | behold we heard about it | in Ephrathah |

| 4834.116 | 904, 7899, 3404 | | 971.120 | 3937, 5088 | 8246.720 |
|---|---|---|---|---|---|
| v Qal pf 3cp, ps 3fs | prep, *n mp*, pn | | v Qal juss 1cp | prep, n mp, ps 3ms | v Hithpael juss 1cp |
| מְצָאנוּהָ | בִּשְׂדֵי־יָעַר | **7.** | נָבוֹאָה | לְמִשְׁכְּנוֹתָיו | נִשְׁתַּחֲוֶה |
| metsā'nûāh | bisdhê-yāʿar | | nāvô'āh | lemishkenôthâv | nishtachweh |
| we have found it | in the countryside of Jaar | | let us go | to his tabernacle | let us worship |

| 3937, 1986 | 7559 | | 7251.131 | 3176 | 3937, 4640 | 887 |
|---|---|---|---|---|---|---|
| prep, *n ms* | n fd, ps 3ms | | v Qal impv 2ms | pn | prep, n fs, ps 2ms | pers pron |
| לַהֲדֹם | רַגְלָיו | **8.** | קוּמָה | יְהוָה | לִמְנוּחָתֶךָ | אַתָּה |
| lahdhōm | raghlâv | | qûmāh | yehwāh | limnûchāthekhā | 'attāh |
| at the footstool of | his feet | | rise | O Yahweh | to your resting place | You |

| 751 | 6010 | | 3669 | 3980.126, 6928 |
|---|---|---|---|---|
| cj, *n ms* | n ms, ps 2ms | | n mp, ps 2ms | v Qal juss 3mp, n ms |
| וַאֲרוֹן | עֻזֶּךָ | **9.** | כֹּהֲנֶיךָ | יִלְבְּשׁוּ־צֶדֶק |
| wa'ărôn | ʿuzzekhā | | kōhenêkhā | yilbeshû-tsedheq |
| even the Ark of | your strength | | your priests | may they be clothed with righteousness |

| 2728 | 7728.326 | | 904, 5877 | 1784 | 5860 |
|---|---|---|---|---|---|
| cj, adj, ps 2ms | v Piel juss 3mp | | prep, prep | pn | n ms, ps 2ms |
| וַחֲסִידֶיךָ | יְרַנֵּנוּ | **10.** | בַּעֲבוּר | דָּוִד | עַבְדֶּךָ |
| wachsîdhêkhā | yerannēnû | | baʿăvûr | dāwidh | ʿavdekhā |
| and your godly ones | let them shout for joy | | on account of | David | your servant |

| 414, 8178.523 | 6686 | 5081 | | 7881.211, 3176 | 3937, 1784 |
|---|---|---|---|---|---|
| adv, v Hiphil juss 2ms | *n mp* | n ms, ps 2ms | | v Niphal pf 3ms, pn | prep, pn |
| אַל־תָּשֵׁב | פְּנֵי | מְשִׁיחֶךָ | **11.** | נִשְׁבַּע־יְהוָה | לְדָוִד |
| 'al-tāshēv | penê | meshîchekhā | | nishbaʿ-yehwāh | ledhāwidh |
| do not turn back | the face of | your anointed one | | Yahweh swore | to David |

LORD for David all his anxious care, *NAB* ... give thought to David, *BB* ... remember all his piety, *Moffatt* ... in the time of his adversity, *NEB* ... and all the hardships he endured, *NIV.*

**2. How he sware unto the LORD, and vowed unto the mighty God of Jacob:** ... the oath he swore to the Lord, the vow he made to the great God of Jacob, *Knox.*

**3. Surely I will not come into the tabernacle of my house:** ... tent of my house, *MAST, Young* ... I will not enter the house I live in, *NCB* ... I will not enter tent or house, *JB* ... the canopy in my house, *Anchor* ... Or go up to the comfort of my bed, *NKJV.*

**nor go up into my bed:** ... couch of my bed, *Young* ... couch where I sleep, *NAB* ... or climb up into the bed that is strewn for me, *Knox.*

**4. I will not give sleep to mine eyes:** ... or close my eyes, *NCV* ... will not allow myself to sleep, *JB.*

**or slumber to mine eyelids:** ... I will not shut my eyelids, *Moffatt* ... Nor to mine eye-lashes slumber, *Rotherham.*

**5. Until I find out a place for the LORD:** ... till I find some residence for the Eternal, *Moffatt* ... I couldn't rest, I couldn't sleep, thinking how I ought to build a permanent home for the Ark of the Lord, *LIVB.*

**an habitation for the mighty God of Jacob:** ... Tabernacles for the Mighty One of Jacob, *Young.*

**6. Lo, we heard of it at Ephratah:** ... We heard about the Ark in Bethlehem, *NCV* ... In Bethlehem we heard about the Covenant Box, *Good News.*

**we found it in the fields of the wood:** ... We found it in the fields of Jaar, *NASB* ... We found it at the Kiriath Jearim, *NCV* ... we came upon it in the region of Jaar, *NEB* ... we found it at Forest-Fields, *JB.*

**7. We will go into his tabernacles:** ... Let us go to His Tents, *Fenton.*

**we will worship at his footstool:** ... let us give worship at his feet, *BB.*

**8. Arise, O LORD, into thy rest:** ... unto Thy resting place, *MAST* ... Advance, O LORD, to your resting place, *NAB* ... Come, LORD, to Your resting place, *Beck*

**thou, and the ark of thy strength:** ... thou and thy mighty ark!, *Moffatt* ... Come to the Temple, LORD, with the Covenant Box, *Good News* ... You and your mighty chest, *Beck* ... and the ark which is shrine of thy glory!, *Knox.*

**9. Let thy priests be clothed with righteousness:** ... And Thy pious ones cry aloud, *Young* ... May your priests be clothed with justice, *NAB,* ... Your priests are robed in saving justice, *JB* ... Let thy priests go clad in the vesture of innocence, *Knox.*

**and let thy saints shout for joy:** ... let your faithful ones shout merrily for joy, *NAB* ... And let Thy godly ones sing for joy, *NASB* ... and let thy loyal servants shout for joy, *NEB* ... Thy men of lovingkindness, let them shout for joy!, *Rotherham.*

**10. For thy servant David's sake turn not away the face of thine anointed:** ... Your slave David leads,—from Your Anointed turn not, *Fenton* ... reject not thine own king, *Moffatt* ... reject not the plea of your anointed, *NCB.*

**11. The LORD hath sworn in truth unto David; he will not turn from it:** ... The Eternal swore an oath to

---

generous amassing of treasure for the purpose of building the Temple, are regarded as a plea with God. The solidarity of the family, which was so vividly realized in old times, reaches its highest expression in the thought that blessings to David's descendants are as if given to him, sleeping in the royal tomb. Beautifully and humbly, the singer, as representing the nation, has nothing to say of the toil of the actual builders. Not the hand which executes, but the heart and mind which conceived and cherished the plan, are its true author. The psalmist gives a poetic version of David's words in 2 Sam. 7:2. "See now, I dwell in an house of cedar, but the ark of God dwelleth within curtains" contains in germ all which the psalmist here draws out of it. He, the aged king, was almost ashamed of his own ease. God gave him rest from his enemies, but he will not "give sleep to his eyes" until he finds out a place for Yahweh. Wearied with a stormy life, he might well have left it to others to care for the work which the prophet had told him that he was not to be permitted to begin. But not so does a true man reason. Rather, he will consecrate to God his leisure and his old age and will rejoice to originate work which he cannot hope to see completed and even to gather materials which happier natures and times may turn to account. He will put his own comfort second, God's service first.

**132:6–10.** Verses 6–10 are the petitions grounded on the preceding plea, and asking that Yahweh would dwell in the sanctuary and bless the worshipers. Verse 6 offers great difficulties. It seems clear, however, that it and the next verse are to be taken as very closely connected (note the "we" and "us" occurring in them for the only time in the Psalm). They seem to describe continuous actions, of which the climax is entrance into the sanctuary. The first question as to v. 6 is what the "it" is, which

| 583<br>n fs<br>אֱמֶת<br>'ĕmeth<br>something reliability | 3940, 3553.121<br>neg part, v Qal impf 3ms<br>לֹא־יָשׁוּב<br>lō'-yāshûv<br>He will not return | 4623<br>prep, ps 3fs<br>מִמֶּנָּה<br>mimmennāh<br>from it | 4623, 6780<br>prep, *n ms*<br>מִפְּרִי<br>mippᵉrî<br>from the fruit of | 1027<br>n fs, ps 2ms<br>בִטְנְךָ<br>viṯnᵉkhā<br>your womb | 8308.125<br>v Qal impf 1cs<br>אָשִׁית<br>'āshîth<br>I will set |
|---|---|---|---|---|---|

| 3937, 3802, 3937<br>prep, n ms, prep, ps 2ms<br>לְכִסֵּא־לָךְ<br>lᵉkhissē'-lākh<br>to your throne | 12. | 524, 8490.126<br>cj, v Qal impf 3mp<br>אִם־יִשְׁמְרוּ<br>'im-yishmrû<br>if they observe | 1158<br>n mp, ps 2ms<br>בָנֶיךָ<br>vānêkhā<br>your sons | 1311<br>n fs, ps 1cs<br>בְּרִיתִי<br>bᵉrîthî<br>my Covenant | 5926<br>cj, n fp, ps 1cs<br>וְעֵדֹתִי<br>wᵉ'ēdhōthî<br>and my testimonies | 2181<br>rel part<br>זוֹ<br>zô<br>which |
|---|---|---|---|---|---|---|

| 4064.325<br>v Piel impf 1cs, ps 3mp<br>אֲלַמְּדֵם<br>'ălammᵉdhēm<br>I will teach them | 1612, 1158<br>cj, n mp, ps 3mp<br>גַּם־בְּנֵיהֶם<br>gam-bᵉnêhem<br>also their sons | 5912, 5911<br>prep, n ms<br>עֲדֵי־עַד<br>'ădhê-'adh<br>until everlasting | 3553.126<br>v Qal impf 3mp<br>יֵשְׁבוּ<br>yēshᵉvû<br>they will sit | 3937, 3802, 3937<br>prep, n ms, prep, ps 2ms<br>לְכִסֵּא־לָךְ<br>lᵉkhissē'-lākh<br>to your throne |
|---|---|---|---|---|

| 13. | 3706, 1013.111<br>cj, v Qal pf 3ms<br>כִּי־בָחַר<br>kî-vāchar<br>because He has chosen | 3176<br>pn<br>יְהוָה<br>yᵉhwāh<br>Yahweh | 904, 6995<br>prep, pn<br>בְּצִיּוֹן<br>bᵉtsîyôn<br>in Zion | 181.311<br>v Piel pf 3ms, ps 3fs<br>אִוָּהּ<br>'iwwāhh<br>He has desired it | 3937, 4319<br>prep, n ms<br>לְמוֹשָׁב<br>lᵉmôshāv<br>for a dwelling place | 3937<br>prep, ps 3ms<br>לוֹ<br>lô<br>to Him |
|---|---|---|---|---|---|---|

David, *Moffatt* … he will not swerve from it, *Anchor* … he will not turn from it: … from which he will not withdraw, *NAB* … A truth from which He will not turn back, *NASB*.

**Of the fruit of thy body will I set upon thy throne:** … Upon your Throne I will set one who from your body springs, *Fenton* … I will make one of your descendants rule as king after you, *NCV* … One of the sons of your body, *NRSV*.

**12. If thy children will keep my covenant:** … if thy sons hold fast to my covenant, *Knox*.

**and my testimony that I shall teach them:** … and the laws I teach them, *Moffatt* … and the statutes I teach them, *NIV*.

**their children shall also sit upon thy throne for evermore:** … their sons also for ever shall sit upon your throne, *RSV*.

**13. For the LORD hath chosen Zion:** … For the Lord's heart is on Zion, *BB*.

**he hath desired it for his habitation:** … He hath desired it for a seat to Himself, *Young* … wanting it for His home, *Beck*.

**14. This is my rest for ever, here will I dwell:** … This is My Home for ever, *Fenton*.

is spoken of in both clauses; and the most natural answer is the Ark, alluded to here by anticipation, though not mentioned until v. 8. The irregularity is slight and not unexampled. The interpretation of the verse mainly depends on the meaning of the two designations of locality.

Verse 7 must be taken as immediately connected with the preceding. If the same persons who found the Ark still speak, the "tabernacles" into which they encourage each other to enter must be the tent within which, as David said, it dwelt "in curtains," and the joyful utterance of an earlier age will then be quoted by the still happier generation who, at the moment while they sing, see the sacred symbol of the divine presence enshrined within the Holy Place of the Temple. At all events, the petitions which follow are most naturally regarded as chanted forth at that supreme moment, although it is possible that the same feeling of the solidity of the nation in all generations, which, as applied to the reigning family seen in v. 1, may account for the worshipers in the new Temple identifying themselves with the earlier ones who brought up the Ark to Zion. The Church remains the same, while its individual members change.

The first of the petitions is partly taken from the invocation in Num. 10:35, when "the Ark set forward"; but there it was a prayer for guidance on the march, and here, for Yahweh's continuance in his fixed abode. It had wandered far and long. It had been planted in Shiloh, but had deserted that sanctuary which He had once loved. It had tarried for a while at Mizpeh and at Bethel. It had been lost on the field of Aphek, been borne in triumph through Philistine cities and sent back thence **in ter-**

ror. It had lain for three months in the house of Obed-Edom, and for twenty years been hidden at Kirjath-Jearim. It had been set with glad acclaim in the Tabernacle provided by David, and now it stands in the Temple. There may it abide and go no more out! Solomon and Hiram and all their workmen may have done their best, and the result of their toils may stand gleaming in the sunlight in its fresh beauty; but something more is needed. Not until the Ark is in the shrine does the glory fill the house. The lesson is for all ages. Our organizations and works are incomplete without that quickening presence. It will surely be given if we desire it. When his Church prays, "Arise, O LORD, into thy rest; thou and the ark of thy strength," his answer is swift and sure, "Lo, I am with you always" (Matt. 28:20).

From this petition, all the others flow. If "the ark of thy strength" dwells with us, we too shall be strong and have that might for our inspiration as well as our shield.

The pure vestments of the priests were symbols of stainless character, befitting the ministers of a holy God. The psalmist prays that the symbol may truly represent the inner reality: "Let thy priests be clothed with righteousness." He distinguishes between priests and the mass of the people; but in the Church today, as indeed in the original constitution of Israel, all are priests and must be clothed in a righteousness which they receive from above. They do not weave that robe, but they must "put on" the garment which Christ gives them. Righteousness is no hazy, theological virtue, having little to do with everyday life and small resemblance to secular morality. To be good, gentle and just, self-forgetting and self-ruling, to practice the virtues which all men call "lovely and of good report" (Phil. 4:8), and to consecrate them all by reference to Him in whom they dwell united and complete, is to be righteous; that righteousness is the garb required of, and given by God to, all those who seek it and minister in his Temple.

Surely, if the saints dwell in the Temple, gladness will not fail them. True religion is joyful. If a man has only to lift his eyes to see the Ark, what but averted eyes should make him sad? True, there are enemies, but we are close to the fountain of strength. True, there are sins, but we can receive the garment of righteousness. True, there are needs, but the sacrifice whereof "the meek shall eat and be satisfied" (Ps. 22:26) is at hand. There is much unreached as yet, but there is a present God. So we may "walk all the day in the light of his countenance" (Ps. 89:15) and realize the truth of the paradox of always rejoicing, although sometimes we sorrow. The final petition is for the anointed king, that his prayers may be heard.

**132:11–12.** Such are the psalmist's petitions. The answers follow in the remainder of the Psalm, which as already noticed, is parted in two by an interjected verse (v. 13), breaking the continuity of the divine voice. The shape of the responses is determined by the form of the desires, and in every case the answer is larger than the prayer. The divine utterance begins with a parallel between the oath of David and that of God. David "sware unto the LORD" (v. 2). Yes, but "Yahweh has sworn to David" (cf. 2 Sam. 7:11). That is grander and deeper. With this may be connected the similar parallel in vv. 13 and 14 with v. 5. David had sought to "find an habitation" for Yahweh. But He himself had chosen his habitation long ago. He is throned there now, not because of David's choice or Solomon's work, but because his will had settled the place of his feet. These correspondences of expression point to the great truth that God is his own all-sufficient reason. He does not want to dwell with men by their importunity, but in the depths of his unchangeable love lies the reason why He abides with us who are unthankful.

The promise given in v. 12, which has respect to the closing petition of the preceding part, is substantially that contained in 2 Sam. 7. Similar references to that fundamental promise to David are found in Ps. 89, with which this Psalm is sometimes taken to be parallel; but that Psalm comes from a time when the faithful promise seemed to have failed forevermore and breathes a sadness which is alien to the spirit of this song.

**132:13.** Verse 13 appears to be spoken by the people. It breaks the stream of promises. God has been speaking, but now for a moment He is spoken of. His choice of Zion for his dwelling is the glad fact, which the congregation feels so borne in on its consciousness that it breaks forth into speech. The "for" at the beginning of the verse gives a striking sequence, assigning, as it does, the divine selection of Zion for his abode, as the reason for the establishment of the Davidic monarchy. If the throne was set up in Jerusalem, because God would dwell there, how solemn the obligation thereby laid on its occupant to rule as God's viceroy, and how secure each in turn might feel, if he discharged the obligations of his office, that God would grant to the kingdom an equal date with the duration of his own abode! Throne and Temple are indissolubly connected.

| | | | | | |
|---|---|---|---|---|---|
| **14.** | **2148, 4638** | **5912, 5911** | **6553, 3553.125** | **3706** | **181.315** |
| | dem pron, n fs, ps 1cs | prep, n ms | adv, v Qal impf 1cs | cj | v Piel pf 1cs, ps 3fs |
| | זֹאת־מְנוּחָתִי | עֲדֵי־עַד | פֹּה־אֵשֵׁב | כִּי | אִוִּתִיהָ |
| | zō'th-menûchāthî | 'ădhê-'adh | pōh-'ēshēv | kî | 'iwwithiāh |
| | this my resting place | until everlasting | here I will dwell | because | I have desired it |

| | | | | | | |
|---|---|---|---|---|---|---|
| **15.** | **6990** | **1313.342** | **1313.325** | **33** | **7881.525** | **4035** |
| | n fs, ps 3fs | v Piel inf abs | v Piel impf 1cs | adj | v Hiphil impf 1cs | n ms |
| | צֵידָהּ | בָּרֵךְ | אֲבָרֵךְ | אֶבְיוֹנֶיהָ | אַשְׂבִּיעַ | לָחֶם |
| | tsêdhāhh | bārēkh | 'ăvārēkh | 'evyônêāh | 'asbîa' | lāchem |
| | her provisions | blessing | I will greatly bless | her needy | I will satisfy with | bread |

| | | | | | |
|---|---|---|---|---|---|
| **16.** | **3669** | **3980.525** | **3589** | **2728** | **7728.342** |
| | cj, n mp, ps 3fs | v Hiphil impf 1cs | n ms | cj, n mp, ps 3fs | v Piel inf abs |
| | וְכֹהֲנֶיהָ | אַלְבִּישׁ | יֶשַׁע | וַחֲסִידֶיהָ | רַנֵּן |
| | wekhōhenêāh | 'albîsh | yesha' | wachsîdhêāh | rannēn |
| | and her priests | I will clothe with | salvation | and her godly ones | shouting for joy |

| | | | | | | |
|---|---|---|---|---|---|---|
| **7728.326** | **17.** | **8427** | **7048.525** | **7451** | **3937, 1784** | **6424.115** |
| v Piel impf 3mp | | adv | v Hiphil impf 1cs | n fs | prep, pn | v Qal pf 1cs |
| יְרַנֵּנוּ | | שָׁם | אַצְמִיחַ | קֶרֶן | לְדָוִד | עָרַכְתִּי |
| yerannēnû | | shām | 'atsmîach | qeren | ledhāwidh | 'ārakhtî |
| they will shout loudly for joy | | there | I will cause to sprout | a horn | to David | I will set in order |

| | | | | | | |
|---|---|---|---|---|---|---|
| **5552** | **3937, 5081** | **18.** | **342.152** | **3980.525** | **1350** | **6142** |
| n ms | prep, n ms, ps 1cs | | v Qal act ptc mp, ps 3ms | v Hiphil impf 1cs | n fs | cj, prep, ps 3ms |
| נֵר | לִמְשִׁיחִי | | אוֹיְבָיו | אַלְבִּישׁ | בֹּשֶׁת | וְעָלָיו |
| nēr | limshîchî | | 'ôyvâv | 'albîsh | bōsheth | we'ālâv |
| a lamp | for my anointed one | | his enemies | I will clothe with | shame | but upon him |

| | | | | | | | | |
|---|---|---|---|---|---|---|---|---|
| **6957.121** | **5325** | **133:t** | **8302** | **4765** | **3937, 1784** | **1.** | **2079** | **4242, 3005** |
| v Qal impf 3ms | n ms, ps 3ms | | *n ms* | art, n fp | prep, pn | | intrj | intrg, adj |
| יָצִיץ | נִזְרוֹ | | שִׁיר | הַמַּעֲלוֹת | לְדָוִד | | הִנֵּה | מַה־טּוֹב |
| yātsîts | nizrô | | shîr | hamma'ălôth | ledhāwidh | | hinnēh | mah-ttôv |
| it will blossom | his diadem | | a Song of | the Ascents | of David | | behold | how good |

| | | | | | | |
|---|---|---|---|---|---|---|
| **4242, 5456** | **3553.141** | **250** | **1612, 3266** | **2.** | **3626, 8467** | **3005** |
| cj, intrg, adj | v Qal inf con | n mp | cj, adv | | prep, art, n ms | art, adj |
| וּמַה־נָּעִים | שֶׁבֶת | אַחִים | גַּם־יָחַד | | כַּשֶּׁמֶן | הַטּוֹב |
| ûmah-nā'îm | sheveth | 'achîm | gam-yāchadh | | kashshemen | hattôv |
| and how pleasant | the dwelling of | brothers | also together | | like the olive oil | the virgin |

| | | | | | |
|---|---|---|---|---|---|
| **6142, 7513** | **3495.151** | **6142, 2291** | **2291, 172** | **8054, 3495.151** | **6142, 6552** |
| prep, art, n ms | v Qal act ptc ms | prep, art, n ms | *n ms*, pn | rel part, v Qal act ptc ms | prep, *n ms* |
| עַל־הָרֹאשׁ | יֹרֵד | עַל־הַזָּקָן | זְקַן־אַהֲרֹן | שֶׁיֹּרֵד | עַל־פִּי |
| 'al-hārō'sh | yōrēdh | 'al-hazzāqān | zeqan-'ahrōn | shêyōrēdh | 'al-pî |
| on the head | going down | on the beard | the beard of Aaron | which going down | onto the edge of |

**for I have desired it:** … Because I love, *Fenton* … for I prefer her, *NAB.*

**15. I will abundantly bless her provision:** … I shall generously bless her produce, *JB* … Her pilgrim's will I abundantly bless, *Anchor* … I will richly provide Zion with all she needs, *Good News* … I will greatly bless her hunting, *KJVII.*

**I will satisfy her poor with bread:** … I will give her needy bread in plenty, *MAST* … I will richly bless her destitute, *NEB.*

**16. I will also clothe her priests with salvation:** … Her Priests will clothe in safety, *Fenton* … I shall clothe her priests with victory, *REB.*

**and her saints shall shout aloud for joy:** … And her pious ones do sing aloud, *Young* … and those who worship me will really sing for joy, *NCV* … And her men of lovingkindness shall shout aloud for joy, *Rotherham.*

**17. There will I make the horn of David to bud:** … There I cause to spring up a horn for David, *Young* …

There will I make David's dynasty flourish, *Moffatt* ... I will provide my appointed one descendants to rule after him, *NCV* ... There will I renew the line of David's house, *NEB.*

**I have ordained a lamp for mine anointed:** ... and set my Messiah's light, *Fenton* ... and my chosen king shine prosperously, *Moffatt* ... I have made ready a light for my king, *BB.*

**18. His enemies will I clothe with shame:** ... his foes I shroud with dark disgrace, *Moffatt* ... I will cover his enemies with shame, *NCV* ... His enemies I will clothe with disgrace, *NRSV.*

**but upon himself shall his crown flourish:** ... but honour on him shine!, *Fenton* ... but his own crown shall sparkle, *Moffatt* ... but his kingdom will prosper and flourish, *Good News* ... But upon him his diadem shall shine, *Goodspeed.*

**133:t. A Song of degrees of David.**

**1. Behold, how good and how pleasant it is for brethren to dwell together in unity!:** ... How rare and lovely it is, this fellowship of those who meet together!, *Moffatt* ... for brothers to live harmoniously together!, *Berkeley* ... when brothers rest as friends, *Fenton* ... when God's people live together in peace!, *NCV.*

**2. It is like the precious ointment upon the head:** ... sweet as the sacred oil, *Moffatt* ... Gracious as balm poured, *Knox* ... It is like the oil of great price, *BB* ... It is like the fine oil, *Beck.*

**that ran down upon the beard, even Aaron's beard: that went**

---

**132:14–18.** With v. 14, the divine voice resumes and echoes the petitions of the earlier part. The psalmist asked God to arise into his rest, and He answers by granting the request with the added promise of perpetuity: "This is my rest for ever." He adds a promise which had not been asked—abundance for all, and bread to fill even the poor. The psalmist asked that the priests might be clothed in righteousness, and the answer promises robes of salvation, which is the perfecting and most glorious issue of righteousness. The psalmist asked that God's favored ones might utter shrill cries of joy, and God replies with an emphatic reduplication of the word, which implies the exuberance and continuance of the gladness. The psalmist asked for favor to the anointed, and God replies by expanded and magnificent promises. The "horn" is an emblem of power. It shall continually "sprout"—i.e., the might of the royal house shall continually increase. The "lamp for mine anointed" may be simply a metaphor for enduring prosperity and happiness, but many expositors take it to be a symbol of the continuance of the Davidic house, as in 1 Ki. 15:4, where the word employed is not the same as that used here, though closely connected with it. The promise of perpetuity to the house of David does not fit into the context as well as that of splendor and joy, and it has already been given in v. 12. Victory will attend the living representative of David, his foes being clothed by Yahweh with shame—being foiled in their hostile attempts—while their confusion is as a dark background, against which the radiance of his diadem sparkles the more brightly. These large promises are fulfilled in Jesus Christ, of the seed of David, and the Psalm is messianic, as presenting the ideal which it is sure shall be realized and which is realized in Him alone.

The divine promises teach the great truth that God abundantly answers our desires and puts to shame the poverty of our petitions by the wealth of his gifts. He is "able to do exceeding abundantly above all that we ask or think," for the measure of his doing is none other than "according to the power that worketh in us" (Eph. 3:20), and the measure of that power is none other than "the working of his mighty power, Which He wrought in Christ, when He raised Him from the dead, and set him at his own right hand in the heavenly places" (Eph. 1:19f).

**133:1.** The Psalm begins with "behold," as if the poet would summon others to look on the goodly spectacle which, in reality or in imagination, is spread before him. Israel is gathered together, and the sight is good, as securing substantial benefits and "pleasant," as being lovely. The original in v. 1b runs, "that brethren dwell also together." The "also" (HED #1612) suggests that, in addition to local union, there should be heart harmony, as befits brothers. The psalmist cares little for external unity, if the spirit of oneness does not animate the corporate whole.

**133:2.** Two metaphors set forth the same thought. In the first emblem, the consecrating oil, poured on Aaron's head, represents the gracious spirit of concord between brethren. The emblem is felicitous by reason of the preciousness, the fragrance and the manifold uses of oil; but these are only to be taken into account in a subordinate degree, if at all. The one point of comparison is the flow of the oil from the priestly head onto the beard and thence to the garments. It is doubtful whether v. 2d refers to the oil or to the beard of the high

| 4206 | | 3626, 3030, 2874 | 8054, 3495.151 | 6142, 2121 | 6995 | 3706 |
|---|---|---|---|---|---|---|
| n fp, ps 3ms | 3. | prep, *n ms*, pn | rel part, v Qal act ptc ms | prep, *n mp* | pn | cj |
| מִדּוֹתָיו | | כְּטַל־חֶרְמוֹן | שֶׁיֹּרֵד | עַל־הַרְרֵי | צִיּוֹן | כִּי |
| middôthâv | | k$^{e}$ṭal-chermôn | shêyōrēdh | 'al-har$^{e}$rê | tsîyôn | kî |
| his garments | | like the dew of Hermon | which going down | on the mountains of | Zion | because |

| 8427 | 6943.311 | 3176 | 881, 1318 | 2522 | 5912, 5986 | | 8302 |
|---|---|---|---|---|---|---|---|
| adv | v Piel pf 3ms | pn | do, art, n fs | n mp | prep, art, n ms | 134:t | *n ms* |
| שָׁם | צִוָּה | יְהוָה | אֶת־הַבְּרָכָה | חַיִּים | עַד־הָעוֹלָם | | שִׁיר |
| shām | tsiwwāh | y$^{e}$hwāh | 'eth-habb$^{e}$rākhāh | chayyîm | 'adh-hā'ôlām | | shîr |
| there | He has commanded | Yahweh | the blessing | life | until forever | | a Song of |

| 4765 | | 2079 | 1313.333 | 881, 3176 | 3725, 5860 | 3176 | 6198.152 |
|---|---|---|---|---|---|---|---|
| art, n fp | 1. | intrj | v Piel impv 2mp | do, pn | *adj, n mp* | pn | art, v Qal act ptc mp |
| הַמַּעֲלוֹת | | הִנֵּה | בָּרְכוּ | אֶת־יְהוָה | כָּל־עַבְדֵי | יְהוָה | הָעֹמְדִים |
| hamma'ălôth | | hinnēh | bār$^{e}$khû | 'eth-y$^{e}$hwāh | kol-'avdhê | y$^{e}$hwāh | hā'ōm$^{e}$dhîm |
| the Ascents | | behold | bless | Yahweh | all the servants of | Yahweh | those who stand |

| 904, 1041, 3176 | 904, 4050 | | 5558.133, 3135 | 7231 | 1313.333 |
|---|---|---|---|---|---|
| prep, *n ms*, pn | prep, art, n mp | 2. | v Qal impv 2mp, n fd, ps 2mp | n ms | cj, v Piel impv 2mp |
| בְּבֵית־יְהוָה | בַּלֵּילוֹת | | שְׂאוּ־יְדֵכֶם | קֹדֶשׁ | וּבָרְכוּ |
| b$^{e}$vêth-y$^{e}$hwāh | ballêlôth | | s$^{e}$'û-y$^{e}$dhēkhem | qōdhesh | ûvār$^{e}$khû |
| in the temple of Yahweh | by night | | lift up your hands | the holy place | and bless |

| 881, 3176 | | 1313.321 | 3176 | 4623, 6995 | 6449.151 | 8452 |
|---|---|---|---|---|---|---|
| do, pn | 3. | v Piel juss 3ms, ps 2ms | pn | prep, pn | *v Qal act ptc ms* | n md |
| אֶת־יְהוָה | | יְבָרֶכְךָ | יְהוָה | מִצִּיּוֹן | עֹשֵׂה | שָׁמַיִם |
| 'eth-y$^{e}$hwāh | | y$^{e}$vārekh$^{e}$khā | y$^{e}$hwāh | mitstsîyôn | 'ōsēh | shāmayim |
| Yahweh | | may He bless you | Yahweh | from Zion | the Maker of | the heavens |

| 800 | | 2054.333 | 3161 | 2054.333 | 881, 8428 | 3176 | 2054.333 |
|---|---|---|---|---|---|---|---|
| cj, n fs | 135:1 | v Piel impv 2mp | pn | v Piel impv 2mp | do, *n ms* | pn | v Piel impv 2mp |
| וָאָרֶץ | | הַלְלוּ | יָהּ | הַלְלוּ | אֶת־שֵׁם | יְהוָה | הַלְלוּ |
| wā'ārets | | hal$^{e}$lû | yāhh | hal$^{e}$lû | 'eth-shēm | y$^{e}$hwāh | hal$^{e}$lû |
| and the earth | | praise | Yah | praise | the name of | Yahweh | praise |

| 5860 | 3176 | | 8054, 6198.152 | 904, 1041 | 3176 | 904, 2793 |
|---|---|---|---|---|---|---|
| *n mp* | pn | 2. | rel part, v Qal act ptc mp | prep, *n ms* | pn | prep, *n fp* |
| עַבְדֵי | יְהוָה | | שֶׁעֹמְדִים | בְּבֵית | יְהוָה | בְּחַצְרוֹת |
| 'avdhê | y$^{e}$hwāh | | she'ōm$^{e}$dhîm | b$^{e}$vêth | y$^{e}$hwāh | b$^{e}$chatsrôth |
| the servants of | Yahweh | | who standing | in the Temple of | Yahweh | in the courts of |

**down to the skirts of his garments:** … flowing down over the collar of his garment, *Beck* … unto the opening of his robe, *Rotherham* … over the collar of his vestments, *REB, NEB* … That came down upon the skirt of his garments, *ASV.*

**3. As the dew of Hermon, and as the dew that descended upon the mountains of Zion:** … like the dew of Hermon and like the dew that came down on the mountains of Zion, *KJVII* … like the dew of Hermon coming down on Zion's mountians, *Beck.*

**for there the LORD commanded the blessing, even life for evermore:** … where the Lord grants benediction and life everlastingly, *Knox* … For there the LORD ordained his blessing, *NRSV* … the Lord gave orders for the blessing, *BB* … for there the Lord has pronounced his blessing, life forever, *NCB.*

**134:t. A Song of degrees.**

**1. Behold, bless ye the LORD, all ye servants of the LORD:** … Come, bless Yahweh, all the works of Yahweh, *Anchor.*

**which by night stand in the house of the LORD:** … wait on the Lord's house at midnight, *Knox* … who stand nightly, *Berkeley* … in the night seasons, *MAST* … who minister night after night in the house of the LORD, *REB.*

**2. Lift up your hands in the sanctuary, and bless the LORD:** … lift hands of prayer to the shrine, bless the Eternal!, *Moffatt* … raise your hands toward the holy place, *Beck* … Lift up your hand in holiness, *Rotherham* … Lift your hands in holiness and bless the Lord, *LIVB.*

**3. The LORD that made heaven and earth bless thee out of Zion:** ... Bless you from Zion!, *NKJV.*

**135:1. Praise ye the LORD:** ... Hallelujah!, *Goodspeed,* ... Give praise to THE LIFE, *Fenton.*

**Praise ye the name of the LORD:** ... Praise the Eternal's name, *Moffatt.*

**praise him, O ye servants of the LORD:** ... The LORD's servants give praise, *Fenton.*

**2. Ye that stand in the house of the LORD:** ... who minister in the house of the LORD, *REB* ... Who are standing in the house of Jehovah, *Young* ... you who stand in the LORD's Temple, *NCV.*

---

priest. The latter reference is preferred by many, but the former is more accordant with the parallelism and with the use of the phrase "flows down," which can scarcely be twice used in regard to oil and dew, the main subjects in the figures, and be taken in an entirely different reference in the intervening clause. The "opening" (literally, "mouth") of the robe is the upper edge or collar, the aperture through which the wearer's head was passed.

**133:3.** That brotherly unity is blessed, not only because it diffuses itself, and so blesses all in whose hearts it dwells, but also because it is the condition on which still higher gifts are spread among brethren by their brethren's mediation. God himself pours on men the sacred anointing of his divine Spirit and the dew of his quickening influences. When his servants are knit together, as they should be, they impart to one another the spiritual gifts received from above. When Christians are truly one as brethren, God's grace will fructify through each to all.

Verse 3b and c seem to assign the reason why the dew of Hermon will descend on Zion—why the blessings of brotherly concord should there especially be realized. God has appointed his blessing of life to be stored there; therefore, it becomes those who, dwelling there, receive that blessing, to be knit together in closest bonds and to impart to their brethren what they receive from the fountain of all good. That Zion should not be the home of concord, or that Jerusalem should not be the city of peace, contradicts both the name of the city and the priceless gift which Yahweh has placed there for all its citizens.

**134:1–2.** This Song closes the Psalms of Ascents after the manner of a blessing. It is evidently antiphonal, vv. 1f being a greeting, the givers of which are answered in v. 4 by a corresponding salutation from the receivers. The identity of the parties to the little dialogue is unclear. Some have thought of two companies of priestly watchers meeting as they went their rounds in the Temple; others, more probably, take vv. 1f to be addressed by the congregation to the priests, who had charge of the nightly service in the Temple, while v. 3 is the response of the latter, addressed to the speakers of vv. 1f. First Chronicles 9:33 informs us that there was such a nightly service (the nature of which is not known).

The designation "servants of the LORD" here denotes not the people, but the priests, for whose official ministrations "stand" is a common term. They are exhorted to fill the night with prayer as well as watchfulness, and to let their hearts go up in blessing to Yahweh. The voice of praise should echo through the silent night and float over the sleeping city. The congregation is about to leave the crowded courts at the close of a day of worship and now gives this parting salutation and charge to those who remain.

**134:3.** The answer in v. 3 is addressed to each individual of the congregation, "The LORD ... bless thee!" It invokes on each a share in the blessing which, according to the preceding Psalm, the LORD commanded in Zion. The watchers who remain in the sanctuary do not monopolize its blessings. These stream out by night, as by day, to all true hearts; they are guaranteed by the creative omnipotence of Yahweh, the thought of which recurs so often in these Psalms and may be due to the revulsion from idolatry consequent on the captivity and restoration.

***Psalm 135.*** *Like Pss. 97 and 98, this is a cento, or piece of mosaic work, apparently intended as a call to worship Yahweh in the Temple. His greatness, as manifested in nature and especially in his planting Israel in its inheritance, is set forth as the reason for praise; the contemptuous contrast of the nothingness of idols is repeated from Ps. 95 and followed, as there, by an exhortation to Israel to cleave to Him. This is not a song which gushed fresh from the singer's heart, but flowed with echoes of many strains which a devout and meditative soul had made its own. The flowers are arranged in a new bouquet, because the poet had long delighted in their fragrance. The ease with which he blends into a harmonious whole fragments from such diverse sources tells how familiar he was with these, and how well he loved them.*

**135:1–4.** Verses 1–4 are an invocation to praise Yahweh and largely consist of quotations or allusions. Thus Ps. 134:1 underlies vv. 1f. But here the reference to nightly praises is omitted, and

| 1041 | 435 | | 2054.333, 3161 | 3706, 3005 | 3176 | 2252.333 |
|---|---|---|---|---|---|---|
| *n ms* | n mp, ps 1cp | | v Piel impv 2mp, pn | cj, adj | pn | v Piel impv 2mp |
| בֵּית | אֱלֹהֵינוּ | **3.** | הַלְלוּ־יָהּ | כִּי־טוֹב | יְהוָה | זַמְּרוּ |
| bêth | 'ĕlōhênû | | hal$^{e}$lû-yāhh | kî-ṭôv | y$^{e}$hwāh | zamm$^{e}$rû |
| the Temple of | our God | | praise Yah | because good | Yahweh | sing praises |

| 3937, 8428 | 3706 | 5456 | | 3706, 3399 | 1013.111 | 3937 | 3161 | 3547 |
|---|---|---|---|---|---|---|---|---|
| prep, n ms, ps 3ms | cj | adj | | cj, pn | v Qal pf 3ms | prep, ps 3ms | pn | pn |
| לִשְׁמוֹ | כִּי | נָעִים | **4.** | כִּי־יַעֲקֹב | בָּחַר | לוֹ | יָהּ | יִשְׂרָאֵל |
| lishmô | kî | nā'îm | | kî-ya'ăqōv | bāchar | lô | yāhh | yisrā'ēl |
| to his name | because | lovely | | because Jacob | He has chosen | for himself | Yah | Israel |

| 3937, 5643 | | 3706 | 603 | 3156.115 | 3706, 1448 | 3176 | 112 |
|---|---|---|---|---|---|---|---|
| prep, n fs, ps 3ms | | cj | pers pron | v Qal pf 1cs | cj, adj | pn | cj, n mp, ps 1cp |
| לִסְגֻלָּתוֹ | **5.** | כִּי | אֲנִי | יָדַעְתִּי | כִּי־גָדוֹל | יְהוָה | וַאֲדֹנֵינוּ |
| lisghullāthô | | kî | 'ănî | yādha'ttî | kî-ghādhôl | y$^{e}$hwāh | wa'ădhōnênû |
| for his possession | | because | I | I know | that greater | Yahweh | and our Lord |

| 4623, 3725, 435 | | 3725 | 866, 2759.111 | 3176 | 6449.111 | 904, 8452 |
|---|---|---|---|---|---|---|
| prep, *adj*, n mp | | adj | rel part, v Qal pf 3ms | pn | v Qal pf 3ms | prep, art, n md |
| מִכָּל־אֱלֹהִים | **6.** | כֹּל | אֲשֶׁר־חָפֵץ | יְהוָה | עָשָׂה | בַּשָּׁמַיִם |
| mikkol-'ĕlōhîm | | kōl | 'ăsher-chāphēts | y$^{e}$hwāh | 'āsāh | bashshāmayim |
| than all gods | | all | that He is pleased with | Yahweh | He does | in the heavens |

| 904, 800 | 904, 3328 | 3725, 8745 | | 6148.551 | 5563 |
|---|---|---|---|---|---|
| cj, prep, art, n fs | prep, art, n mp | cj, *adj*, n fp | | *v Hiphil ptc ms* | n mp |
| וּבָאָרֶץ | בַּיַּמִּים | וְכָל־תְּהוֹמוֹת | **7.** | מַעֲלֶה | נְשִׂאִים |
| ûvā'ārets | bayyammîm | w$^{e}$khol-t$^{e}$hômôth | | ma'ăleh | n$^{e}$si'îm |
| and on the earth | in the seas | and all the deeps | | the One Who causes to go up | clouds |

| 4623, 7381 | 800 | 1326 | 3937, 4443 | 6449.111 | 3428.551, 7593 |
|---|---|---|---|---|---|
| prep, *n ms* | art, n fs | n mp | prep, art, n ms | v Qal pf 3ms | *v Hiphil ptc ms*, n fs |
| מִקְצֵה | הָאָרֶץ | בְּרָקִים | לַמָּטָר | עָשָׂה | מוֹצֵא־רוּחַ |
| miqōtsēh | hā'ārets | b$^{e}$rāqîm | lammāṯār | 'āsāh | môtsē'-rûach |
| from the end of | the earth | lightnings | for the rain | He makes | causing wind to go out |

| 4623, 212 | | 8054, 5409.511 | 1111 | 4875 | 4623, 119 | 5912, 966 |
|---|---|---|---|---|---|---|
| prep, n mp, ps 3ms | | rel part, v Hiphil pf 3ms | *n mp* | pn | prep, n ms | prep, n fs |
| מֵאוֹצְרוֹתָיו | **8.** | שֶׁהִכָּה | בְּכוֹרֵי | מִצְרָיִם | מֵאָדָם | עַד־בְּהֵמָה |
| mē'ôtsrôthâv | | shehikkāh | b$^{e}$khôrê | mitsrāyim | mē'ādhām | 'adh-b$^{e}$hēmāh |
| from his storehouses | | Who struck down | the firstborn of | Egypt | of man | unto cattle |

| | 8365.111 | 225 | 4295 | 904, 8761 | 4875 | 904, 6799 | 904, 3725, 5860 |
|---|---|---|---|---|---|---|---|
| | v Qal pf 3ms | n mp | cj, n mp | prep, sub, ps 2fs | pn | prep, pn | cj, prep, *adj*, n mp, ps 3ms |
| **9.** | שָׁלַח | אֹתוֹת | וּמֹפְתִים | בְּתוֹכֵכִי | מִצְרָיִם | בְּפַרְעֹה | וּבְכָל־עֲבָדָיו |
| | shālach | 'ōthôth | ûmōph$^{e}$thîm | b$^{e}$thôkhēkhî | mitsrāyim | b$^{e}$phar'ōh | ûv$^{e}$khol-'ăvādhâv |
| | He sent | signs | and wonders | in your midst | O Egypt | on Pharaoh | and on all his servants |

**in the courts of the house of our God:** … in the temple courts of our God, *REB* … in the courts where our God dwells, *Knox.*

**3. Praise the LORD; for the LORD is good:** … a Lord so gracious, *Knox.*

**sing praises unto his name:** … sing psalms to his name, *REB* … chant to his Name, *Anchor* … make melody to His name, *Berkeley.*

**for it is pleasant:** … For it is full of delight, *Rotherham, KJVII* … for he is gracious, *NRSV* … a name so well beloved, *Knox* … it brings joy, *JB* … for it is sweet!, *Berkeley.*

**4. For the LORD hath chosen Jacob unto himself:** … the Eternal has chosen Jacob to be his, *Moffatt* … The LORD has chosen the people of Jacob for himself, *NCV.*

**and Israel for his peculiar treasure:** … And Israel as his own treasure, *Goodspeed* … claimed Israel for his own?, *Knox* … and Israel for his property, *BB.*

**5. For I know that the LORD is great and that our Lord is above all gods:** ... Doubt it never, *Knox* ... As for me, I know that the LORD is great, *Berkeley* ... So I have learnt, *Fenton* ... and our Lord high over all gods, *Moffatt.*

**6. Whatsoever the LORD pleased:** ... the Lord accomplishes his will, *Knox* ... The LORD does anything He wants to do, *Beck.*

**that did he in heaven, and in earth:** ... in heaven and in earth, *Berkeley* ... throughout all of heaven and earth, *LIVB.*

**in the seas, and all deep places:** ... and all resounding deeps, *Rotherham* ... in the seas and the deep oceans, *NCV* ... in the sea, in the depths of ocean, *NEB* ... the seas and all abysses, *Moffatt.*

**7. He causeth the vapours to ascend from the ends of the earth:** ... Raising clouds from the ends of the earth, *Goodspeed* ... He bringeth vp the cloudes from the ends of the earth, *Geneva* ... Raises frogs from the bounds of the Earth, *Fenton.*

**he maketh lightnings for the rain:** ... rain-storm wedding to lightning-flash, *Knox* ... he opens rifts for the rain, *NEB.*

**he bringeth the wind out of his treasuries:** ... leads forth the wind from his storehouses, *Anchor* ... and he brings out the wind from his storeroom, *Good News.*

**8. Who smote the firstborn of Egypt:** ... He destroyed the firstborn sons in Egypt, *NCV* ... He cut off Mitzer's first-born of Man and of Beast, *Fenton* ... He put to death the first-fruits of Egypt, *BB.*

**both of man and beast:** ... man as well as beast, *Anchor* ... the firstborn of both people and animals, *NCV.*

**9. Who sent tokens and wonders into the midst of thee:** ... signs and wonders, *KJVII,* ... wonders and portents, *Goodspeed.*

**O Egypt, upon Pharaoh, and upon all his servants:** ... Pharaoh and all his subjects, *REB* ... against Pharaoh and all his officials, *JB.*

---

the summons is addressed not only to those who stand in the house of Yahweh, but to those who stand in its courts. That expansion may mean that the call to worship is here directed to the people as well as to the priests (so in v. 19).

Verse 3 closely resembles Ps. 147:1, but the question of priority may be left undecided. Since the act of praise is said to be "pleasant" in Ps. 147:1, it is best to refer the same word here to the same thing, and not, as some would do, to the name, or to take it as an epithet of Yahweh. To a loving soul, praise is a delight. The songs which are not winged by the singer's joy in singing will not rise high. True worship pours out its notes as birds do theirs—in order to express gladness which, unuttered, loads the heart.

Verse 4 somewhat passes beyond the bounds of the invocation proper and anticipates the subsequent part of the Psalm. Israel's prerogative is so great to this singer that it forces utterance at once, though out of season, as correct critics would say. But the throbs of a grateful heart are not always regular. It is impossible to keep the reasons for praise out of the summons to praise. Verse 4 joyfully and humbly accepts the wonderful title given in Deut. 7:6.

**135:5–7.** In vv. 5ff, God's majesty as set forth in nature is hymned. The psalmist says emphatically in v. 5, "I know," and implies the privilege which he shared, in common with his fellow Israelites (who appear in the "our" of the next clause), of knowing what the heathen did not know—how highly Yahweh was exalted above all their gods. Verse 6 is from Ps. 115:3, with the expansion of defining the all-inclusive sphere of God's sovereignty. Heaven, earth, seas and depths cover all space. The enumeration of the provinces of his dominion prepares for that of the phases of his power in nature, which is quoted with slight change from Jer. 10:13; 51:16. The mighty works of God call for praise: the mysterious might which gathers from some unknown region the filmy clouds which grow, no man knows how, in the clear blue; the power which weds in strange companionship the fire of the lightning flash and the torrents of rain; and the controlling hand which urges forth the invisible wind.

**135:8–14.** But while the psalmist looks on physical phenomena with a devout poet's eye, he turns from these to expatiate rather on what Yahweh has done for Israel. Psalmists are never weary of drawing confidence and courage for today from the deeds of the Exodus and the conquest. Verse 8 is copied from Exo. 13:15, and the whole section is saturated with phraseology drawn from Deuteronomy. Verse 13 is from Exo. 3:15, the narrative of the theophany at the bush. That name, proclaimed then as the basis of Moses' mission and Israel's hope, is now, after so many centuries and sorrows, the same, and it will endure forever. Verse 14 is from Deut. 32:36. Yahweh will right his people—deliver them from oppressors—which is the same thing as "repent himself concerning his servants," since his wrath was the reason of their sub-

| 10. | 8054, 5409.511<br>rel part, v Hiphil pf 3ms<br>שֶׁהִכָּה<br>shehikkāh<br>Who struck down | 1504<br>n mp<br>גּוֹיִם<br>gôyim<br>nations | 7521<br>adj<br>רַבִּים<br>rabbîm<br>many | 2103.111<br>cj, v Qal pf 3ms<br>וְהָרַג<br>wehāragh<br>and He killed | 4567<br>n mp<br>מְלָכִים<br>melākhîm<br>kings | 6335<br>adj<br>עֲצוּמִים<br>‘ătsûmîm<br>mighty | 11. | 3937, 5700<br>prep, pn<br>לְסִיחוֹן<br>lesîchôn<br>Sihon |
|---|---|---|---|---|---|---|---|---|

| 4567<br>*n ms*<br>מֶלֶךְ<br>melekh<br>the king of | 578<br>art, pn<br>הָאֱמֹרִי<br>hā’ĕmōrî<br>the Amorites | 3937, 5965<br>cj, prep, pn<br>וּלְעוֹג<br>ûlā‘ôgh<br>and Og | 4567<br>*n ms*<br>מֶלֶךְ<br>melekh<br>the king of | 1347<br>art, pn<br>הַבָּשָׁן<br>habbāshān<br>the Bashan | 3937, 3725<br>cj, prep, *n ms*<br>וּלְכֹל<br>ûlăkhōl<br>and the entirety of | 4608<br>*n fp*<br>מַמְלְכוֹת<br>mamlekhôth<br>the kingdoms of |
|---|---|---|---|---|---|---|

| 3791<br>pn<br>כְּנָעַן<br>kenā‘an<br>Canaan | 12. | 5598.111<br>cj, v Qal pf 3ms<br>וְנָתַן<br>wenāthan<br>and He gave | 800<br>n fs, ps 3mp<br>אַרְצָם<br>'artsām<br>their land | 5338<br>n fs<br>נַחֲלָה<br>nachlāh<br>an inheritance | 5338<br>n fs<br>נַחֲלָה<br>nachlāh<br>an inheritance | 3937, 3547<br>prep, pn<br>לְיִשְׂרָאֵל<br>leyisrā’ēl<br>to Israel | 6194<br>n ms, ps 3ms<br>עַמּוֹ<br>‘ammô<br>his people |
|---|---|---|---|---|---|---|---|

| 13. | 3176<br>pn<br>יְהוָה<br>yehwāh<br>O Yahweh | 8428<br>n ms, ps 2ms<br>שִׁמְךָ<br>shimkhā<br>your name | 3937, 5986<br>prep, n ms<br>לְעוֹלָם<br>le‘ôlām<br>unto eternity | 3176<br>pn<br>יְהוָה<br>yehwāh<br>O Yahweh | 2228<br>n ms, ps 2ms<br>זִכְרְךָ<br>zikhrekhā<br>the memory of You |
|---|---|---|---|---|---|

| 3937, 1810, 1810<br>prep, n ms, cj, n ms<br>לְדֹר־וָדֹר<br>ledhōr-wādhōr<br>to generations and generations | 14. | 3706, 1833.121<br>cj, v Qal impf 3ms<br>כִּי־יָדִין<br>kî-yādhîn<br>because He vindicates | 3176<br>pn<br>יְהוָה<br>yehwāh<br>Yahweh | 6194<br>n ms, ps 3ms<br>עַמּוֹ<br>‘ammô<br>his people |
|---|---|---|---|---|

| 6142, 5860<br>cj, prep, n mp, ps 3ms<br>וְעַל־עֲבָדָיו<br>we‘al-‘ăvādhâv<br>and on his servants | 5341.721<br>v Hithpael impf 3ms<br>יִתְנֶחָם<br>yithnechām<br>He has compassion | 15. | 6322<br>*n mp*<br>עֲצַבֵּי<br>‘ătsabbê<br>the idols of | 1504<br>art, n mp<br>הַגּוֹיִם<br>haggôyim<br>the nations | 3826B<br>n ms<br>כֶּסֶף<br>keseph<br>silver | 2174<br>cj, n ms<br>וְזָהָב<br>wezāhāv<br>and gold |
|---|---|---|---|---|---|---|

| 4801<br>*n ms*<br>מַעֲשֵׂה<br>ma‘ăsēh<br>the work of | 3135<br>*n fd*<br>יְדֵי<br>yedhê<br>the hands of | 119<br>n ms<br>אָדָם<br>'ādhām<br>a man | 16. | 6552, 3937<br>n ms, prep, ps 3mp<br>פֶּה־לָהֶם<br>peh-lāhem<br>a mouth to them | 3940<br>cj, neg part<br>וְלֹא<br>welō’<br>but not | 1744.326<br>v Piel impf 3mp<br>יְדַבֵּרוּ<br>yedhabbērû<br>they speak | 6084<br>n fd<br>עֵינַיִם<br>‘ênayim<br>eyes |
|---|---|---|---|---|---|---|---|

| 3937<br>prep, ps 3mp<br>לָהֶם<br>lāhem<br>to them | 3940<br>cj, neg part<br>וְלֹא<br>welō’<br>but not | 7495.126<br>v Qal impf 3mp<br>יִרְאוּ<br>yir’û<br>they see | 17. | 238<br>n fd<br>אָזְנַיִם<br>'āzenayim<br>ears | 3937<br>prep, ps 3mp<br>לָהֶם<br>lāhem<br>to them | 3940<br>cj, neg part<br>וְלֹא<br>welō’<br>but not | 237.526<br>v Hiphil impf 3mp<br>יַאֲזִינוּ<br>ya’ăzînû<br>they hear | 652<br>cj<br>אַף<br>'aph<br>also |
|---|---|---|---|---|---|---|---|---|

| 375, 3552, 7593<br>*sub, sub,* n fs<br>אֵין־יֶשׁ־רוּחַ<br>'ên-yesh-rûach<br>there is not breath | 904, 6552<br>prep, n ms, ps 3mp<br>בְּפִיהֶם<br>bephîhem<br>in their mouth | 18. | 3765<br>prep, ps 3mp<br>כְּמוֹהֶם<br>kemôhem<br>like them | 2030.126<br>v Qal impf 3mp<br>יִהְיוּ<br>yihyû<br>they are | 6449.152<br>v Qal act ptc mp, ps 3mp<br>עֹשֵׂיהֶם<br>‘ōsêhem<br>those who make them | 3725<br>n ms<br>כֹּל<br>kōl<br>everyone |
|---|---|---|---|---|---|---|

| 866, 1019.151<br>rel part, v Qal act ptc ms<br>אֲשֶׁר־בֹּטֵחַ<br>'ăsher-bōtēach<br>who trusting | 904<br>prep, ps 3mp<br>בָּהֶם<br>bāhem<br>in them | 19. | 1041<br>*n ms*<br>בֵּית<br>bêth<br>O household of | 3547<br>pn<br>יִשְׂרָאֵל<br>yisrā’ēl<br>Israel | 1313.333<br>v Piel impv 2mp<br>בָּרְכוּ<br>bārekhû<br>bless | 881, 3176<br>do, pn<br>אֶת־יְהוָה<br>'eth-yehwāh<br>Yahweh |
|---|---|---|---|---|---|---|

| 1041 | 172 | 1313.333 | 881, 3176 | 20. | 1041 | 4015 | 1313.333 |
|---|---|---|---|---|---|---|---|
| *n ms* | pn | v Piel impv 2mp | do, pn | | *n ms* | art, pn | v Piel impv 2mp |
| בֵּית | אַהֲרֹן | בָּרְכוּ | אֶת־יְהוָה | | בֵּית | הַלֵּוִי | בָּרְכוּ |
| bêth | 'ahrōn | bārᵉkhû | 'eth-yᵉhwāh | | bêth | hallēwî | bārᵉkhû |
| O household of | Aaron | bless | Yahweh | | O household of | Levi | bless |

**10. Who smote great nations:** ... who struck great nations, *KJVII* ... It was he who smote many nations, *Goodspeed.*

**and slew mighty kings:** ... and killed powerful kings, *Good News* ... and slew great kings, *NEB.*

**11. Sihon king of the Amorites, and Og king of Bashan, and all the kingdoms of Canaan:** ... And the Chiefs of Canan, *Fenton.*

**12. And gave their land for an heritage:** ... And he gave their land as a possession, *Goodspeed* ... and marked down their lands for a dwelling-place, *Knox* ... And he gave their land as patrimony, *Anchor* ... Then he gave their land as a gift, *NCV.*

**an heritage unto Israel his people:** ... a gift to his people, the Israelites, *NCV* ... a birthright to his people Israel, *JB.*

**13. Thy name, O LORD, endureth for ever:** ... age succeeds age, *Knox* ... Thy name is to the age, *Young* ... everlasting, *NASB.*

**and thy memorial, O LORD, throughout all generations:** ... thou art ever unforgotten, *Knox* ... thy remembrance is from generation to generation, *Geneva* ... Yahweh—your title is for all generations, *Anchor* ... your memory is fresh from age to age, *JB.*

**14. For the LORD will judge his people:** ... For Yahweh will vindicate his people, *Rotherham* ... the LORD will give his people justice, *Goodspeed, NEB* ... The Lord defends his people, *Knox, NAB* ... be pacified toward his seruants, *Geneva.*

**and he will repent himself concerning his servants:** ... takes pity on his servants, *Knox* ... And for His servants comforteth Himself, *Young* ... and have compassion on his servants, *NEB* ... Gives His servants gifts!, *Fenton.*

**15. The idols of the heathen are silver and gold:** ... The idols of the nations, *KJVII,* ... The gods of the nations are idols of silver and gold, *NEB.*

**the work of men's hands:** ... The product of men's hands, *Goodspeed* ... the work of human hands, *NCV.*

**16. They have mouths, but they speak not; eyes have they, but they see not;** ... They have mouths, but cannot speak, eyes, but they cannot see, *NIV* ... These have mouths but say nothing, have eyes but see nothing, *JB.*

**17. They have ears, but they hear not:** ... they have ears, but cannot hear, *NIV,* ... have ears but hear nothing, *JB.*

**neither is there any breath in their mouths:** ... Nose—there is no breath in their mouth!, *Young* ... there certainly is no breath in their mouth, *Berkeley.*

**18. They that make them are like unto them:** ... Their makers will end up like them, *JB.*

**so is every one that trusteth in them:** ... Yes, everyone who trusts in them, *NASB* ... everyone who relies on them, *JB* ... every one that confideth in them, *Darby.*

**19. Bless the LORD, O house of Israel: bless the LORD, O house of Aaron:** ... Family of Israel, praise the LORD. Family of Aaron, praise the LORD.

**20. Bless the LORD, O house of Levi:** ... Family of Levi, praise the LORD, *NCV* ... O Levi's family, bless the LORD!, *Beck.*

**ye that fear the LORD, bless the LORD:** ... You who revere the LORD, bless the LORD, *NASB* ... Bless the Eternal, ye his worshippers!, *Moffatt.*

jection to their foes. That judicial deliverance of Israel is at once the sign that his name, his revealed character, continues the same, unexhausted and unchanged forever, and the reason why the name shall continue as the object of perpetual adoration and trust.

**135:15–19.** Verses 15–19 are taken bodily from Ps. 115, to which the reader is referred. Slight abbreviations and one notable difference occur. In v. 17b, "Neither is there any breath in their mouths," takes the place of "Noses have they, but they smell not." The variation has arisen from the fact that the particle of strong affirmation "yea" is spelled like the noun "nose," and that the word for "breath" resembles the verb "smell." The psalmist plays upon his original, and by his variation makes the expression of the idols' lifelessness stronger.

**135:20–21.** The final summons to praise, with which the end of the Psalm returns to its beginning, is also molded on Ps. 115:9ff, with the addition of "the house of Levi" to the three groups mentioned there and the substitution of a call to "bless" for the original invitation to "trust." Verse 21 looks back to

| 881, 3176 | 3486.152 | 3176 | 1313.333 | 881, 3176 | | 1313.155 | 3176 |
|---|---|---|---|---|---|---|---|
| do, pn | *v Qal act ptc mp* | pn | v Piel impv 2mp | do, pn | **21.** | v Qal pass ptc ms | pn |
| אֶת־יְהוָה | יִרְאֵי | יְהוָה | בָּרְכוּ | אֶת־יְהוָה | | בָּרוּךְ | יְהוָה |
| 'eth-yᵉhwāh | yir'ê | yᵉhwāh | bārᵉkhû | 'eth-yᵉhwāh | | bārûkh | yᵉhwāh |
| Yahweh | those who fear | Yahweh | bless | Yahweh | | blessed | Yahweh |

| 4623, 6995 | 8331.151 | 3503 | 2054.333, 3161 | | 3142.533 | 3937, 3176 |
|---|---|---|---|---|---|---|
| prep, pn | v Qal act ptc ms | pn | v Piel impv 2mp, pn | **136:1** | v Hiphil impv 2mp | prep, pn |
| מִצִּיּוֹן | שֹׁכֵן | יְרוּשָׁלָם | הַלְלוּ־יָהּ | | הוֹדוּ | לַיהוָה |
| mitstsîyôn | shōkhēn | yᵉrûshālām | halᵉlû-yāhh | | hôdhû | layhwāh |
| from Zion | the One Who remains in | Jerusalem | praise Yah | | praise | Yahweh |

| 3706, 3005 | 3706 | 3937, 5986 | 2721 | | 3142.533 | 3937, 435 | 435 |
|---|---|---|---|---|---|---|---|
| cj, adj | cj | prep, n ms | n ms, ps 3ms | **2.** | v Hiphil impv 2mp | prep, *n mp* | art, n mp |
| כִּי־טוֹב | כִּי | לְעוֹלָם | חַסְדּוֹ | | הוֹדוּ | לֵאלֹהֵי | הָאֱלֹהִים |
| kî-ṯôv | kî | lᵉʻôlām | chas̱dô | | hôdhû | lē'lōhê | hā'ĕlōhîm |
| because good | because | unto eternity | his steadfast love | | praise | the God of | the gods |

| 3706 | 3937, 5986 | 2721 | | 3142.533 | 3937, 112 | 112 | 3706 |
|---|---|---|---|---|---|---|---|
| cj | prep, n ms | n ms, ps 3ms | **3.** | v Hiphil impv 2mp | prep, *n mp* | art, n mp | cj |
| כִּי | לְעוֹלָם | חַסְדּוֹ | | הוֹדוּ | לַאֲדֹנֵי | הָאֲדֹנִים | כִּי |
| kî | lᵉʻôlām | chas̱dô | | hôdhû | la'ădhōnê | hā'ădhōnîm | kî |
| because | unto eternity | his steadfast love | | praise | the Lord of | the lords | because |

| 3937, 5986 | 2721 | | 3937, 6449.151 | 6623.258 | 1448 |
|---|---|---|---|---|---|
| prep, n ms | n ms, ps 3ms | **4.** | prep, *v Qal act ptc ms* | v Niphal ptc fp | adj |
| לְעֹלָם | חַסְדּוֹ | | לְעֹשֵׂה | נִפְלָאוֹת | גְּדֹלוֹת |
| lᵉʻōlām | chas̱dô | | lᵉʻōsēh | niphlā'ôth | gᵉdhōlôth |
| to eternity | his steadfast love | | to the One Who does | extraordinary deeds | great |

| 3937, 940 | 3706 | 3937, 5986 | 2721 | | 3937, 6449.151 | 8452 |
|---|---|---|---|---|---|---|
| prep, n ms, ps 3ms | cj | prep, n ms | n ms, ps 3ms | **5.** | prep, *v Qal act ptc ms* | art, n md |
| לְבַדּוֹ | כִּי | לְעוֹלָם | חַסְדּוֹ | | לְעֹשֵׂה | הַשָּׁמַיִם |
| lᵉvaddô | kî | lᵉʻôlām | chas̱dô | | lᵉʻōsēh | hashshāmayim |
| by himself | because | unto eternity | his steadfast love | | to the Maker of | the heavens |

| 904, 8722 | 3706 | 3937, 5986 | 2721 | | 3937, 7847.151 | 800 |
|---|---|---|---|---|---|---|
| prep, n fs | cj | prep, n ms | n ms, ps 3ms | **6.** | prep, *v Qal act ptc ms* | art, n fs |
| בִּתְבוּנָה | כִּי | לְעוֹלָם | חַסְדּוֹ | | לְרֹקַע | הָאָרֶץ |
| bithᵉvûnāh | kî | lᵉʻôlām | chas̱dô | | lᵉrōqaʻ | hā'ārets |
| with skill | because | unto eternity | his steadfast love | | to the One Who spread out | the earth |

| 6142, 4448 | 3706 | 3937, 5986 | 2721 | | 3937, 6449.151 | 214 | 1448 |
|---|---|---|---|---|---|---|---|
| prep, art, n mp | cj | prep, n ms | n ms, ps 3ms | **7.** | prep, *v Qal act ptc ms* | n mp | adj |
| עַל־הַמָּיִם | כִּי | לְעוֹלָם | חַסְדּוֹ | | לְעֹשֵׂה | אוֹרִים | גְּדֹלִים |
| ʻal-hammāyim | kî | lᵉʻôlām | chas̱dô | | lᵉʻōsēh | 'ôrîm | gᵉdhōlîm |
| on the waters | because | unto eternity | his steadfast love | | to the Maker of | lights | great |

| 3706 | 3937, 5986 | 2721 | | 881, 8507 | 3937, 4617 | 904, 3219 | 3706 |
|---|---|---|---|---|---|---|---|
| cj | prep, n ms | n ms, ps 3ms | **8.** | do, art, n fs | prep, *n fs* | prep, art, n ms | cj |
| כִּי | לְעוֹלָם | חַסְדּוֹ | | אֶת־הַשֶּׁמֶשׁ | לְמֶמְשֶׁלֶת | בַּיּוֹם | כִּי |
| kî | lᵉʻôlām | chas̱dô | | 'eth-hashshemesh | lᵉmemsheleth | bayyôm | kî |
| because | unto eternity | his steadfast love | | the sun | for dominion | over the day | because |

| 3937, 5986 | 2721 | | 881, 3507 | 3676 | 3937, 4617 | 904, 4050 |
|---|---|---|---|---|---|---|
| prep, n ms | n ms, ps 3ms | **9.** | do, art, n ms | cj, n mp | prep, n fp | prep, art, n ms |
| לְעוֹלָם | חַסְדּוֹ | | אֶת־הַיָּרֵחַ | וְכוֹכָבִים | לְמֶמְשְׁלוֹת | בַּלָּיְלָה |
| lᵉʻôlām | chas̱dô | | 'eth-hayyārēach | wᵉkhôkhāvîm | lᵉmemshᵉlôth | ballāyᵉlāh |
| unto eternity | his steadfast love | | the moon | and the stars | for dominion | over the night |

**21. Blessed be the LORD out of Zion:** ... Praise be to the Lord out of Zion, *BB.*

**which dwelleth at Jerusalem:** ... Who inhabiteth Jerusalem, *Rotherham* ... Jerusalem's People praise THE LIFE, *Fenton* ... Blessed be He who lives in Jerusalem!, *Beck.*

**Praise ye the LORD:** ... Hallelujah, *MRB.*

**136:1. O give thanks unto the LORD; for he is good:** ... It is good to give thanks to the LORD, *NEB* ... Sing to the LORD who is good, *Fenton* ... O give praise to the Lord, *BB.*

**for his mercy endureth for ever:** ... For age-abiding is his lovingkindness, *Rotherham* ... for his love endures for ever, *REB, NEB* ... His love continues forever, *NCV* ... for His covenenat love is everlasting, *Berkeley.*

**2. O give thanks unto the God of gods: for his mercy endureth for ever:** ... Give thanks to the greatest of all gods, *Good News* ... Sing to the GOD of the Gods, *Fenton* ... O give praise to the God of gods, *BB.*

**3. O give thanks to the Lord of lords: for his mercy endureth for ever:** ... Give thanks to the mightiest of all lords, *Good News* ... Sing to the Prince of the Princes, *Fenton* ... O give praise to the Lord of lords, *BB.*

**4. To him who alone doeth great wonders: for his mercy endureth for ever:** ... who does great deeds as none else can, *Knox* ... who alone works great marvels, *REB* ... Only he can do great miracles, *NCV* ... He alone works wonders, *JB.*

**5. To him that by wisdom made the heavens: for his mercy endureth for ever:** ... by understanding, *MRB* ... with skill, *Goodspeed, NASB* ... With his wisdom he made the skies, *NCV* ... Who made the Skies with Skill, *Fenton.*

**6. To him that stretched out the earth above the waters: for his mercy endureth for ever:** ... who poised earth upon the floods, *Knox* ... He set the earth firm on the waters, *JB* ... To Him who laid out the earth above the waters, *NKJV.*

**7. To him that made great lights: for his mercy endureth for ever:** ... who made the great luminaries, *Knox* ... He made the sun and the moon, *NCV.*

**8. The sun to rule by day: for his mercy endureth for ever:** ... the sun to rule over the day, *NCB,* ... The Sun guiding by Day, *Fenton.*

**9. The moon and stars to rule by night: for his mercy endureth for ever:** ... to governe the night, *Geneva* ... to rule over the night, *NCB, RSV* ... To guide during night, *Fenton.*

**10. To him that smote Egypt in their firstborn: for his mercy endureth for ever:** ... He struck down the first-born of the Egyptians, *NEB* ... who struck Egypt through their firstborn, *NRSV* ... Who cut off tyrant's troops, *Fenton* ... To him who killed Egypt's firstborn, *Moffatt.*

---

the last verse of the preceding Psalm and significantly modifies it. There, as in Ps. 118, Yahweh's blessing comes out of Zion to his people. Here the people's blessing in return goes from Zion and rises to Yahweh. They gathered there for worship and dwelt with Him in his city and Temple. Swift interchange of the God-given blessing, which consists in mercies and gifts of gracious deliverance and of the human blessing, which consists in thanksgiving and praise, fills the hours of those who dwell with Yahweh, as guests in his house, and walk the streets of the city which He guards and inhabits.

***Psalm 136.*** *This Psalm is evidently intended for liturgical use. It contains reminiscences of many parts of Scripture and is especially based on the previous Psalm, which it follows closely in vv. 10–18, and quotes directly in vv. 19–22. Like Ps. 135, the addition in each verse of the refrain gives a noble swing and force to this exulting song.*

**136:1–9.** The Psalm opens with three groups of three verses, forming a general invocation to praise, colored by the phraseology of Deuteronomy. Verses 2a and 3a quote Deut. 10:17. The second and third triplets (vv. 4–9) celebrate Yahweh's creative power. "Doeth great wonders" (v. 4) is from Ps. 72:18. The thought of the divine wisdom as the creative agent occurs in Ps. 104:24 and attains noble expression in Prov. 3. In v. 6, the word rendered "spread" (HED #7847) is from the same root as that rendered "firmament" in Genesis. The office of the heavenly bodies to rule day and night is taken from Gen. 1. But the Psalm looks at the story of Creation from an original point of view, when it rolls out in chorus, after each stage of that work, that its motive lay in the eternal steadfast love of Yahweh. Creation is an act of divine love. That is the deepest truth concerning all things visible. They are the witnesses, as they are the result, of steadfast love which endures forever.

**136:10–22.** Verses 10–22 pass from world-wide manifestations of that creative steadfast love to those specially affecting Israel. If vv. 19–22 are left out of notice, there are three triplets in which the Exodus, desert life and conquest of Caanan are

| 3706 | 3937, 5986 | 2721 | | 3937, 5409.551 | 4875 |
|---|---|---|---|---|---|
| cj | prep, n ms | n ms, ps 3ms | 10. | prep, *v Hiphil ptc ms* | pn |
| כִּי | לְעוֹלָם | חַסְדּוֹ | | לְמַכֵּה | מִצְרַיִם |
| kî | le‘ôlām | chas̱dô | | lemakkēh | mitsrayim |
| because | unto eternity | his steadfast love | | to the One Who struck down | Egypt |

| 904, 1111 | 3706 | 3937, 5986 | 2721 | | 3428.521 | 3547 |
|---|---|---|---|---|---|---|
| prep, n mp, ps 3mp | cj | prep, n ms | n ms, ps 3ms | 11. | cj, v Hiphil impf 3ms | pn |
| בִּבְכוֹרֵיהֶם | כִּי | לְעוֹלָם | חַסְדּוֹ | | וַיּוֹצֵא | יִשְׂרָאֵל |
| bivkhôrêhem | kî | le‘ôlām | chas̱dô | | wayyôtsē’ | yisrā’ēl |
| on their firstborn | because | unto eternity | his steadfast love | | and He led out | Israel |

| 4623, 8761 | 3706 | 3937, 5986 | 2721 | | 904, 3135 | 2481 |
|---|---|---|---|---|---|---|
| prep, n ms, ps 3mp | cj | prep, n ms | n ms, ps 3ms | 12. | prep, n fs | adj |
| מִתּוֹכָם | כִּי | לְעוֹלָם | חַסְדּוֹ | | בְּיָד | חֲזָקָה |
| mittôkhām | kî | le‘ôlām | chas̱dô | | beyādh | chăzāqāh |
| from their midst | because | unto eternity | his steadfast love | | with a hand | strong |

| 904, 2307 | 5371.157 | 3706 | 3937, 5986 | 2721 |
|---|---|---|---|---|
| cj, prep, n fs | v Qal pass ptc fs | cj | prep, n ms | n ms, ps 3ms |
| וּבִזְרוֹעַ | נְטוּיָה | כִּי | לְעוֹלָם | חַסְדּוֹ |
| ûvizrôa‘ | netûyāh | kî | le‘ôlām | chas̱dô |
| and with an arm | extended | because | unto eternity | his steadfast love |

| | 3937, 1535.151 | 3328, 5675 | 3937, 1536 | 3706 | 3937, 5986 | 2721 |
|---|---|---|---|---|---|---|
| 13. | prep, *v Qal act ptc ms* | *n ms*, n ms | prep, n mp | cj | prep, n ms | n ms, ps 3ms |
| | לְגֹזֵר | יַם־סוּף | לִגְזָרִים | כִּי | לְעוֹלָם | חַסְדּוֹ |
| | leghōzēr | yam-s̱ûph | lighzārîm | kî | le‘ôlām | chas̱dô |
| | to the One Who clave | the Sea of Reeds | into pieces | because | unto eternity | his steadfast love |

| | 5882.511 | 3547 | 904, 8761 | 3706 | 3937, 5986 | 2721 |
|---|---|---|---|---|---|---|
| 14. | cj, v Hiphil pf 3ms | pn | prep, n ms, ps 3ms | cj | prep, n ms | n ms, ps 3ms |
| | וְהֶעֱבִיר | יִשְׂרָאֵל | בְּתוֹכוֹ | כִּי | לְעוֹלָם | חַסְדּוֹ |
| | wehe‘ĕvîr | yisrā’ēl | bethôkhô | kî | le‘ôlām | chas̱dô |
| | and He caused to pass over | Israel | in their midst | because | unto eternity | his steadfast love |

| | 5469.311 | 6799 | 2524 | 904, 3328, 5675 | 3706 | 3937, 5986 |
|---|---|---|---|---|---|---|
| 15. | cj, v Piel pf 3ms | pn | cj, n ms, ps 3ms | prep, *n ms*, n ms | cj | prep, n ms |
| | וְנִעֵר | פַּרְעֹה | וְחֵילוֹ | בְיַם־סוּף | כִּי | לְעוֹלָם |
| | weni‘ēr | pare‘ōh | wechêlô | veyam-s̱ûph | kî | le‘ôlām |
| | and He shook out | Pharaoh | and his army | into the Sea of Reeds | because | unto eternity |

| 2721 | | 3937, 2050.551 | 6194 | 904, 4198 | 3706 |
|---|---|---|---|---|---|
| n ms, ps 3ms | 16. | prep, v Hiphil ptc ms | n ms, ps 3ms | prep, art, n ms | cj |
| חַסְדּוֹ | | לְמוֹלִיךְ | עַמּוֹ | בַּמִּדְבָּר | כִּי |
| chas̱dô | | lemôlîkh | ‘ammô | bammidhbār | kî |
| his steadfast love | | to the One Who caused to go | his people | through the wilderness | because |

| 3937, 5986 | 2721 | | 3937, 5409.551 | 4567 | 1448 | 3706 |
|---|---|---|---|---|---|---|
| prep, n ms | n ms, ps 3ms | 17. | prep, *v Hiphil ptc ms* | n mp | adj | cj |
| לְעוֹלָם | חַסְדּוֹ | | לְמַכֵּה | מְלָכִים | גְּדֹלִים | כִּי |
| le‘ôlām | chas̱dô | | lemakkēh | melākhîm | gedhōlîm | kî |
| unto eternity | his steadfast love | | to the One Who struck down | kings | great | because |

| 3937, 5986 | 2721 | | 2103.121 | 4567 | 116 | 3706 | 3937, 5986 |
|---|---|---|---|---|---|---|---|
| prep, n ms | n ms, ps 3ms | 18. | cj, v Qal impf 3ms | n mp | n mp | cj | prep, n ms |
| לְעוֹלָם | חַסְדּוֹ | | וַיַּהֲרֹג | מְלָכִים | אַדִּירִים | כִּי | לְעוֹלָם |
| le‘ôlām | chas̱dô | | wayyahrōgh | melākhîm | ’addîrîm | kî | le‘ôlām |
| unto eternity | his steadfast love | | and He killed | kings | nobles | because | unto eternity |

| | 2721 | 19. 3937, 5700 | 4567 | 578 | 3706 | 3937, 5986 | 2721 |
|---|---|---|---|---|---|---|---|
| | n ms, ps 3ms | prep, pn | *n ms* | art, pn | cj | prep, n ms | n ms, ps 3ms |
| | חַסְדּוֹ | לְסִיחוֹן | מֶלֶךְ | הָאֱמֹרִי | כִּי | לְעוֹלָם | חַסְדּוֹ |
| | chasdô | lesîchôn | melekh | hā'ĕmōrî | kî | le'ôlām | chasdô |
| | his steadfast love | Sihon | the king of | the Amorites | because | unto eternity | his steadfast love |

| 20. 3937, 5965 | 4567 | 1347 | 3706 | 3937, 5986 | 2721 | 21. 5598.111 |
|---|---|---|---|---|---|---|
| cj, prep, pn | *n ms* | art, pn | cj | prep, n ms | n ms, ps 3ms | cj, v Qal pf 3ms |
| וּלְעוֹג | מֶלֶךְ | הַבָּשָׁן | כִּי | לְעוֹלָם | חַסְדּוֹ | וְנָתַן |
| ûlă'ôgh | melekh | habbāshān | kî | le'ôlām | chasdô | wenāthan |
| and Og | the king of | the Bashan | because | unto eternity | his steadfast love | and He gave |

| 800 | 3937, 5338 | 3706 | 3937, 5986 | 2721 | 22. 5338 |
|---|---|---|---|---|---|
| n fs, ps 3mp | prep, n fs | cj | prep, n ms | n ms, ps 3ms | n fs |
| אַרְצָם | לְנַחֲלָה | כִּי | לְעוֹלָם | חַסְדּוֹ | נַחֲלָה |
| 'artsām | lenachlāh | kî | le'ôlām | chasdô | nachlāh |
| their land | for an inheritance | because | unto eternity | his steadfast love | an inheritance |

**11. And brought out Israel from among them: for his mercy endureth for ever:** ... And led Israel from them, *Fenton.*

**12. With a strong hand:** ... with constraining power, *Knox* ... With a firm hand, *Rotherham* ... With mighty hand, *JB* ... a powerful hand, *Darby.*

**and with a stretched out arm: for his mercy endureth for ever:** ... his powerful arm, *Good News.*

**13. To him which divided the Red sea into parts: for his mercy endureth for ever:** ... To Him cutting the sea of Suph into parts, *Young* ... Eternal the mercy that divided the Red Sea in two, *Knox* ... into divisions, *Rotherham* ... To him who divided the Reed Sea in half, *Anchor.*

**14. And made Israel to pass through the midst of it: for his mercy endureth for ever:** ... And showed Israel through the middle of it, *Anchor.*

**15. But overthrew Pharaoh and his host in the Red sea: for his mercy endureth for ever:** ... But shook off Pharaoh and his host into the Reed Sea, *Anchor* ... And shook out Pharaoh and his force in the sea of Suph, *Young* ... And drowned Pharaoh and all his army, *JB* ... Pharoh's host caught in sea weeds, *Fenton*

**16. To him which led his people through the wilderness: for his mercy endureth for ever:** ... through the desert, *Rotherham, NCV, NIV* ... To him who marched his people across the desert, *Anchor* ... Marched His Race in the Waste, *Fenton.*

**17. To him which smote great kings: for his mercy endureth for ever:** ... He struck down great kings, *NEB.*

**18. And slew famous kings: for his mercy endureth for ever:** ... He doth slay honourable kings, *Young* ... He slew powerful kings, *REB* ... And slew haughty Kings, *Fenton* ... And put noble kings to death, *BB.*

**19. Sihon king of the Amorites: for his mercy endureth for ever:** ... As Shion king of the Amorites, *Geneva.*

**20. And Og the king of Bashan: for his mercy endureth for ever:** ... Og the king of Basan, *Knox.*

**21. And gave their land for an heritage: for his mercy endureth for ever:** ... as a possession, *Goodspeed* ... as their patrimony, *NEB* ... as a gift, *NCV* ... gave their land as a birthright, *JB.*

**22. Even an heritage unto Israel his servant: for his mercy endureth for ever:** ... a dwelling place for his servant Israel, *Knox.*

the themes: the first (vv. 10ff) recounting the departure; the second (vv. 13ff), the passage of the Red Sea; and the third (vv. 16ff), the guidance during the forty years and the victories over enemies. The whole is largely taken from the preceding Psalm and also has numerous allusions to other parts of Scripture. Verse 12a is found in Deut. 4:34.

The word for dividing the Red Sea (HED #1535) is peculiar. It means "to hew in pieces" or "in two" and is used for cutting in halves the child in Solomon's judgment (1 Ki. 3:25); while the word "parts" is a noun from the same root, and is found in Gen. 15:17 to describe the two portions into which Abraham divided the carcasses. Thus, as with a sword, Yahweh hewed the sea in two, and his people passed between the parts, as between the halves of the covenant sacrifice. In v. 15, the word describing Pharaoh's destruction (HED #5469) is taken from Exo. 14:27 and vividly describes it as a "shaking out," as one would shake vermin or filth from a robe.

| 3937, 3547 | 5860 | 3706 | 3937, 5986 | 2721 | | 8054, 904, 8586 |
|---|---|---|---|---|---|---|
| prep, pn | n ms, ps 3ms | cj | prep, n ms | n ms, ps 3ms | **23.** | rel part, prep, n ms, ps 1cp |
| לְיִשְׂרָאֵל | עַבְדּוֹ | כִּי | לְעוֹלָם | חַסְדּוֹ | | שֶׁבְּשִׁפְלֵנוּ |
| leyisrā'ēl | 'avdô | kî | le'ôlām | chasdô | | shebbeshiphlēnû |
| to Israel | his servant | because | unto eternity | his steadfast love | | Who in our abasement |

| 2226.111 | 3937 | 3706 | 3937, 5986 | 2721 | | 6811.121 |
|---|---|---|---|---|---|---|
| v Qal pf 3ms | prep, ps 1cp | cj | prep, n ms | n ms, ps 3ms | **24.** | cj, v Qal impf 3ms, ps 1cp |
| זָכַר | לָנוּ | כִּי | לְעוֹלָם | חַסְדּוֹ | | וַיִּפְרְקֵנוּ |
| zākhar | lānû | kî | le'ôlām | chasdô | | wayyiphreqēnû |
| He remembered | us | because | unto eternity | his steadfast love | | and He separated us |

| 4623, 7141 | 3706 | 3937, 5986 | 2721 | | 5598.151 | 4035 |
|---|---|---|---|---|---|---|
| prep, n mp, ps 1cp | cj | prep, n ms | n ms, ps 3ms | **25.** | v Qal act ptc ms | n ms |
| מִצָּרֵינוּ | כִּי | לְעוֹלָם | חַסְדּוֹ | | נֹתֵן | לֶחֶם |
| mitstsārênû | kî | le'ôlām | chasdô | | nōthēn | lechem |
| from our adversaries | because | unto eternity | his steadfast love | | the One Who gives | bread |

| 3937, 3725, 1340 | 3706 | 3937, 5986 | 2721 | | 3142.533 | 3937, 418 |
|---|---|---|---|---|---|---|
| prep, *adj*, n ms | cj | prep, n ms | n ms, ps 3ms | **26.** | v Hiphil impv 2mp | prep, *n ms* |
| לְכָל־בָּשָׂר | כִּי | לְעוֹלָם | חַסְדּוֹ | | הוֹדוּ | לְאֵל |
| lekhol-bāsār | kî | le'ôlām | chasdô | | hôdhû | le'ēl |
| to all flesh | because | unto eternity | his steadfast love | | praise | to the God of |

| 8452 | 3706 | 3937, 5986 | 2721 | | 6142 | 5282 | 928 | 8427 |
|---|---|---|---|---|---|---|---|---|
| art, n md | cj | prep, n ms | n ms, ps 3ms | **137:1** | prep | *n mp* | pn | adv |
| הַשָּׁמָיִם | כִּי | לְעוֹלָם | חַסְדּוֹ | | עַל | נַהֲרוֹת | בָּבֶל | שָׁם |
| hashshāmāyim | kî | le'ôlām | chasdô | | 'al | nahrôth | bāvel | shām |
| the heavens | because | unto eternity | his steadfast love | | beside | the rivers of | Babylon | there |

| 3553.119 | 1612, 1098.119 | 904, 2226.141 | 881, 6995 | | 6142, 6399 | 904, 8761 |
|---|---|---|---|---|---|---|
| v Qal pf 1cp | cj, v Qal pf 1cp | prep, v Qal inf con, ps 1cp | do, pn | **2.** | prep, n fp | prep, n ms, ps 3fs |
| יָשַׁבְנוּ | גַּם־בָּכִינוּ | בְּזָכְרֵנוּ | אֶת־צִיּוֹן | | עַל־עֲרָבִים | בְּתוֹכָהּ |
| yāshavnû | gam-bākhînû | bezākherēnû | 'eth-tsîyôn | | 'al-'ărāvîm | bethôkhāhh |
| we sat | also we wept | when our remembering | Zion | | on the poplars | in our midst |

| 8847.115 | 3780 | | 3706 | 8427 | 8068.116 | 8091.152 |
|---|---|---|---|---|---|---|
| v Qal pf 1cs | n mp, ps 1cp | **3.** | cj | adv | v Qal pf 3cp, ps 1cp | v Qal act ptc mp, ps 1cp |
| תָּלִינוּ | כִּנֹּרוֹתֵינוּ | | כִּי | שָׁם | שְׁאֵלוּנוּ | שׁוֹבֵינוּ |
| tālînû | kinnōrôthênû | | kî | shām | she'ēlûnû | shôvênû |
| we hung | our zithers | | because | there | they required of us | our captors |

| 1745, 8302 | 8767 | 7977 | 8301.133 | 3937 | 4623, 8302 | 6995 |
|---|---|---|---|---|---|---|
| *n mp*, n ms | cj, n mp, ps 1cp | n fs | v Qal impv 2mp | prep, ps 1cp | prep, *n ms* | pn |
| דִּבְרֵי־שִׁיר | וְתוֹלָלֵינוּ | שִׂמְחָה | שִׁירוּ | לָנוּ | מִשִּׁיר | צִיּוֹן |
| divrê-shîr | wethôlālênû | simchāh | shîrû | lānû | mishshîr | tsîyôn |
| the words of a song | and our tormentors | rejoicing | sing | for us | of a song of | Zion |

**23. Who remembered us in our low estate: for his mercy endureth for ever:** ... in our abasement, *Goodspeed* ... He remembered our utter weakness, *LIVB* ... in our abjection, *NAB* ... when we were in trouble, *NCV.*

**24. And hath redeemed us from our enemies: for his mercy endureth for ever:** ... And freed us with force from our adversaries, *Rotherham* ... from our oppressours, *Geneva* ... And has taken us out of the hands of our haters, *BB.*

**25. Who giveth food to all flesh: for his mercy endureth forever:** ... eternal the mercy that gives all living things their food, *Knox* ... He gives food to all mankind, *REB* ... He gives food to every living creature, *NCV* ... furnishes us all with food, *Moffatt.*

**26. O give thanks unto the God of heaven: for his mercy endureth for ever:** ... Prayse ye the God of heaven, *Geneva.*

**137:1. By the rivers of Babylon:** ... By the riuers of Babel we sate, *Geneva* ... By Babel's Rivers we sat down, *Fenton.*

**there we sat down, yea, we wept, when we remembered Zion:** ... loudly we wept, *Anchor* ... weeping at the memory of Zion, *BB.*

**2. We hanged our harps upon the willows in the midst thereof:** ... Willowtrees grow there, *Knox* ... we hung up our lyres, *REB* ... There on the poplars, *Moffatt* ... On the aspens of that land, *NAB, NCB.*

**3. For there they that carried us away captive required of us a song:** ... asked of us words of song, *Rotherham* ... asked of us the lyrics of our songs, *NCB* ... those who carried us off demanded music and singing, *NEB* ... For there our gaolers had asked us to sing them a song, *JB.*

**and they that wasted us required of us mirth:** ... And our spoilers—joy, *Young* ... We must make sport for our enemies, *Knox* ... and those who laid us in heaps demanded gladness, *KJVII* ... And our despoilers urged us to be joyous, *NAB* ... those who had harried us bade us be merry, *Moffatt.*

**saying, Sing us one of the songs of Zion:** ... Sing us a song about Jerusalem!, *NCV* ... Come sing us blithe a Song of Zion!, *Fenton.*

---

**136:23–26.** In the last verses, the singer comes to the Israel of the present. It, too, had experienced Yahweh's remembrance in its time of need and felt the merciful grasp of his hand plucking it, with loving violence, from the claws of the lion. The word for "low estate" (HED #8586) and that for "redeemed us from our enemies" (HED #6811) are only otherwise found in late writings—the former in Ecc. 10:6, and the latter in Lam. 5:8.

But the song will not close with reference only to Israel's blessings. He "giveth food to all flesh." The steadfast love which flashes forth even in destructive acts and is manifested especially in bringing Israel back from exile stretches as wide in its beneficence as it did in its first creative acts and sustains all flesh which it has made. Therefore, the final call to praise, which rounds off the Psalm by echoing its beginning, does not name Him by the name which implied Israel's special relation, but by that name which other peoples could and did address Him, "the God of heaven," from Whom all good comes down on all the earth.

***Psalm 137.*** *The captivity is past, as the tenses in vv. 1ff show and as is manifest from the very fact that its miseries have become themes for a Psalm. Grief must be somewhat removed before it can be sung. But the strains of triumph heard in other Psalms are wanting in this, which breathes passionate love for Jerusalem, tinged with sadness still.*

**137:1.** Nothing sweeter or sadder was ever written than that delicate, deeply felt picture of the exiles in the early verses of the Psalm. We see them sitting, as too heavy-hearted for activity and half noting, as adding to their grief, the unfamiliar landscape around them, with its innumerable canals, and the monotonous "willows" (rather, a species of poplar) stretching along their banks. How unlike this flat, tame fertility is to the dear homeland, with its hills and glens and rushing streams! The psalmist was probably a Temple singer, but he did not find solace even in the harp, his sole remaining joy. No doubt many of the exiles made themselves at home in captivity, but there were some more keenly sensitive or more devout, who found that it was better to remember Zion and weep than to enjoy Babylon. So they sat, like Michaelangelo's brooding figure of Jeremiah in the Sistine Chapel, silent, motionless, lost in bittersweet memories.

**137:2.** But there was another reason than their own sadness for hanging their idle harps upon the willows. Their coarse oppressors bade them sing to make mirth. They wished entertainment from the odd sounds of foreign music, or they were petulantly angry that such ignorant, dejected people should keep sullen faces, like unilluminated windows, when their masters were pleased to be merry. So like tipsy revellers, they called out "Sing!" The request drove the iron deeper into sad hearts, for it came from those who had made the misery. They had led away the captives, and now they bid them make sport.

**137:3.** The word rendered "captors" (HED #8091) is difficult. The translation adopted here is that of the Septuagint and others. It requires a slight alteration of reading. Some conjecture another alteration which gives "dancers" ("and of our dancers, festive glee"), while admitting that the other view is "somewhat more natural." The rude Babylonians did not care what kind of songs their slaves sang. Temple music would do as well as any other; but the devout psalmist and his fellows shrank from profaning the sacred songs that praised Yahweh by making them parts of a heathen banquet. Such sacrilege would have been like Belshazzar's using the temple vessels for his orgy. "Give not that which is holy

| 4. | 351 | 8301.120 | 881, 8302, 3176 | 6142 | 124 | 5424 | 5. | 524, 8319.125 |
|---|---|---|---|---|---|---|---|---|
| | intrg | v Qal impf 1cp | do, *n ms*, pn | prep | *n fs* | n ms | | cj, v Qal impf 1cs, ps 2fs |
| | אֵיךְ | נָשִׁיר | אֶת־שִׁיר־יְהוָה | עַל | אַדְמַת | נֵכָר | | אִם־אֶשְׁכָּחֵךְ |
| | 'êkh | nāshîr | 'eth-shîr-y$^{e}$hwāh | 'al | 'adhmath | nēkhār | | 'im-'eshkāchēkh |
| | how | will we sing | a song of Yahweh | on | the soil of | a foreign land | | if I forget you |

| 3503 | 8319.123 | 3332 | 6. | 1740.122, 4098 | 3937, 2541 | 524, 3940 |
|---|---|---|---|---|---|---|
| pn | v Qal juss 2ms | n fs, ps 1cs | | v Qal juss 3fs, n fs, ps 1cs | prep, n ms, ps 1cs | cj, neg part |
| יְרוּשָׁלָםִ | תִּשְׁכַּח | יְמִינִי | | תִּדְבַּק־לְשׁוֹנִי | לְחִכִּי | אִם־לֹא |
| y$^{e}$rûshālām | tishkach | y$^{e}$mînî | | tidhbaq-l$^{e}$shônî | l$^{e}$chikkî | 'im-lō' |
| O Jerusalem | may your forget | my right hand | | may my tongue cleave | to my palate | if not |

| 2226.125 | 524, 3940 | 6148.525 | 881, 3503 | 6142 | 7513 | 7977 |
|---|---|---|---|---|---|---|
| v Qal impf 1cs, ps 2fs | cj, neg part | v Hiphil impf 1cs | do, pn | prep | *n ms* | n fs, ps 1cs |
| אֶזְכְּרֵכִי | אִם־לֹא | אַעֲלֶה | אֶת־יְרוּשָׁלַםִ | עַל | רֹאשׁ | שִׂמְחָתִי |
| 'ezk$^{e}$rēkhî | 'im-lō' | 'a'ăleh | 'eth-y$^{e}$rûshālam | 'al | rō'sh | simchāthî |
| I remember you | if not | I cause to be high | Jerusalem | above | the top of | my joy |

| 7. | 2226.131 | 3176 | 3937, 1158 | 110 | 881 | 3219 | 3503 | 569.152 |
|---|---|---|---|---|---|---|---|---|
| | v Qal impv 2ms | pn | prep, *n mp* | pn | do | *n ms* | pn | art, v Qal act ptc mp |
| | זְכֹר | יְהוָה | לִבְנֵי | אֱדוֹם | אֵת | יוֹם | יְרוּשָׁלָםִ | הָאֹמְרִים |
| | z$^{e}$khōr | y$^{e}$hwāh | livnê | 'ĕdhôm | 'ēth | yôm | y$^{e}$rûshālām | hā'ōm$^{e}$rîm |
| | call to mind | O Yahweh | of the sons of | Edom | | the day of | Jerusalem | those saying |

| 6408.333 | 6408.333 | 5912 | 3356 | 904 | 8. | 1351, 928 |
|---|---|---|---|---|---|---|
| v Piel impv 2mp | v Piel impv 2mp | prep | art, n fs | prep, ps 3fs | | *n fs*, pn |
| עָרוּ | עָרוּ | עַד | הַיְסוֹד | בָּהּ | | בַּת־בָּבֶל |
| 'ārû | 'ārû | 'adh | haysôdh | bāhh | | bath-bāvel |
| raze | raze | unto | the foundation | under it | | O daughter of Babylon |

| 8161.157 | 869 | 8054, 8396.321, 3937 | 881, 1618 | 8054, 1621.114 |
|---|---|---|---|---|
| art, v Qal pass ptc fs | n mp | rel part, v Piel impf 3ms, prep, ps 2fs | do, n ms, ps 2fs | rel part, v Qal pf 2fs |
| הַשְּׁדוּדָה | אַשְׁרֵי | שֶׁיְשַׁלֶּם־לָךְ | אֶת־גְּמוּלֵךְ | שֶׁגָּמַלְתְּ |
| hashsh$^{e}$dhûdhāh | 'ashrê | shêshallem-lākh | 'eth-g$^{e}$mûlēkh | sheggāmalt |
| the devastated one | blessed | who requites to you | your recompense | what you did |

| 3937 | 9. | 869 | 8054, 270.121 | 5492.311 | 881, 5985 | 420, 5748 |
|---|---|---|---|---|---|---|
| prep, ps 1cp | | n mp | rel part, v Qal impf 3ms | cj, v Piel pf 3ms | do, n mp, ps 2fs | prep, art, n ms |
| לָנוּ | | אַשְׁרֵי | שֶׁיֹּאחֵז | וְנִפֵּץ | אֶת־עֹלָלַיִךְ | אֶל־הַסָּלַע |
| lānû | | 'ashrê | shêyō'chēz | w$^{e}$nippēts | 'eth-'ōlālayikh | 'el-hassāla' |
| to us | | blessed | who takes hold of | and he smashes | your small children | to the rock |

**4. How shall we sing the LORD's song in a strange land?:** ... in a foreign land?, *REB* ... upon alien soil?, *Anchor.*

**5. If I forget thee, O Jerusalem, let my right hand forget her cunning:** ... perish the skill of my right hand!, *Knox* ... may my right hand wither away, *REB* ... let my right hand forget its skill upon the harp, *LIVB* ... May I never be able to play the harp again, *Good News.*

**6. If I do not remember thee, let my tongue cleave to the roof of my mouth:** ... May my tongue cleave to my palate, *Goodspeed* ... May I never be able to sing again, *Good News.*

**if I prefer not Jerusalem above my chief joy:** ... dearer than heart's content!, *Knox* ... If I do not lift up Jerusalem above the head of mine own gladness, *Rotherham* ... If I do not raise you, O Jerusalem, Upon my head in celebration!, *Anchor* ... if I place not Jerusalem ahead of my joy, *NCB.*

**7. Remember, O LORD, the children of Edom in the day of Jerusalem:** ... Remember O LORD, what the Edomites did on the day Jerusalem fell, *NIV* ... O Lord, keep in mind against the children of Edom the day of Jerusalem, *BB.*

**who said, Rase it, rase it, even to the foundation thereof:** ... O'erthrow it, they cried, *Knox* ... Down with it, down with it, *REB*, *NEB* ... Make it bare! Make it bare, *KJVII* ... Let it be uncovered, uncovered even to its base, *BB.*

**8. O daughter of Babylon:** ... Babylon, pitiless queen, *Knox* ... People of Babylon, *NCV* ... O

unto dogs" (Matt. 7:6). And the singers were not influenced by superstition, but by reverence and by sadness, when they could not sing these songs in that strange land. No doubt it was a fact that the temple music fell into disuse during the Captivity. There are moods and scenes in which it is profanation to utter the deep music which may be sounding on perpetually in the heart. Songs unheard are sometimes not only sweetest, but the truest worship.

**137:4.** The psalmist's remembrances of Babylon are suddenly broken off. His heart burns as he broods on that past and then lifts his eyes to see how forlorn and forgotten Jerusalem stands, as if appealing to her sons for help. A rush of emotion sweeps over him, and he breaks into a passion of vowed loyalty to the mother city. He has Jerusalem written on his heart. It is noteworthy that her remembrance was the exiles' crown of sorrow; it now becomes the apex of the singer's joy. No private occasion for gladness so moves the depths of a soul, smitten with the noble and ennobling love of the city of God, as does its prosperity. Alas that the so-called citizens of the true city of God should have so tepid interest in its welfare and be so much more keenly touched by individual than by public prosperity or adversity! Alas that so often they should neither weep when they remember its bondage nor exult in its advancement!

**137:5.** Verse 5b is emphatic by its incompleteness. "Let my right hand forget!" It would be as impossibly unnatural for the poet to forget Jerusalem as for his hand to forget to move or cease to be conscious of its connection with his body.

**137:6.** Verse 6d reads literally, "Above the head of my joy," an expression which may either mean "the summit of my joy," i.e., "my greatest joy," or "the sum of my joy," i.e., "my whole joy." In either case, the well-being of Jerusalem is the psalmist's climax of gladness, and so utterly does he lose himself in the community founded by God, that all his springs of felicity are in her. He had chosen the better part. Unselfish gladness is the only lasting bliss, and only they drink of an unfailing river of pleasures whose chiefest delight lies in beholding and sharing in the rebuilding of God's city on earth.

**137:7–9.** The lightning flashes of the last part of the Psalm need little comment. The desire for the destruction of Zion's enemies, which they express, is not the highest mood of the loyal citizen of God's city and is to be fully recognized as not in accordance with Christian morality. But it has been most unfairly judged, as if it were nothing nobler than ferocious thirsting for vengeance. It is a great deal more. It is desire for retribution, heavy as the count of crimes which demands it is heavy. It is a solemn appeal to God to sweep away the enemies of Zion, who in hating her rebelled against Him.

First, the psalmist turns to the treacherous kinsmen of Israel, the Edomites, who had, as Obadiah says, "rejoiced over the children of Judah in the day of their destruction" (Obad. 12), and stimulated the work of razing the city. Then the singer turns to Babylon, and salutes her as already laid waste; for he is a seer as well as a singer, and is so sure of the judgment to be accomplished that it is as good as done.

The most repellent part of the imprecation, that which contemplates the dreadful destruction of tender infants, has its harshness somewhat softened by the fact that it is the echo of Isaiah's prophecy concerning Babylon (Isa. 13:1–18) and still further by the consideration that the purpose of the apparently barbarous cruelty was to make an end of a "seed of evildoers," whose continuance meant misery for wide lands.

Undoubtedly, the words are stern and the temper they embody is harsh discord when compared with the Christian spirit. But they are not the utterances of mere ferocious revenge. Rather, they proclaim God's judgments, not with the impassiveness, indeed, which best befits the executors of such terrible sentences, but still less with the malignant gratification of sanguinary vengeance which has been often attributed to them. Perhaps, if some of their modern critics had been under the yoke from which this psalmist has been delivered, they would have understood a little better how a good man of that age could rejoice that Babylon was fallen and all its race extirpated. Perhaps, it would do modern tenderheartedness no harm to have a little more iron infused into its gentleness and to lay to heart that the King of Peace must first be King of Righteousness, and that destruction of evil is the complement of preservation of good.

***Psalm 138.*** *This is the first of a group of eight Psalms attributed to David in the superscriptions. It precedes the closing hallelujah Psalms.*

*The structure of the Psalm is simple. It falls into three parts, of which the two former consist of three verses each, and the last, of two. In the first, the singer vows praise and recounts God's wondrous dealings with him (vv. 1ff); in the second, he looks out over all the earth in the confidence that these blessings, when known, will bring the world to worship (vv. 4ff); and in the third, he pleads for the completion to himself of mercies begun (vv. 7f).*

| 138:t | 3937, 1784 | 1. | 3142.525 | 904, 3725, 3949 | 5224 | 435 | 2252.325 |
|---|---|---|---|---|---|---|---|
| | prep, pn | | v Hiphil juss 1cs, ps 2ms | prep, *adj*, n ms, ps 1cs | prep | n mp | v Piel juss 1cs, ps 2ms |
| | לְדָוִד | | אוֹדְךָ | בְּכָל־לִבִּי | נֶגֶד | אֱלֹהִים | אֲזַמְּרֶךָּ |
| | lᵉdhāwidh | | 'ôdhkhā | vᵉkhol-libbî | neghedh | 'ĕlōhîm | 'ăzammᵉrekhā |
| | of David | | let me praise You | with all my heart | before | God | let me sing praises to You |

| 2. | 8246.725 | 420, 2033 | 7231 | 3142.525 | 881, 8428 |
|---|---|---|---|---|---|
| | v Hithpael juss 1cs | prep, *n ms* | n ms, ps 2ms | cj, v Hiphil juss 1cs | do, n ms, ps 2ms |
| | אֶשְׁתַּחֲוֶה | אֶל־הֵיכַל | קָדְשְׁךָ | וְאוֹדֶה | אֶת־שְׁמֶךָ |
| | 'eshtachweh | 'el-hêkhal | qodhshᵉkhā | wᵉ'ôdheh | 'eth-shᵉmekhā |
| | let me worship | at the temple of | your holy place | and let me praise | your name |

| 6142, 2721 | 6142, 583 | 3706, 1461.513 |
|---|---|---|
| prep, n ms, ps 2ms | cj, prep, n fs, ps 2ms | cj, v Hiphil pf 2ms |
| עַל־חַסְדְּךָ | וְעַל־אֲמִתֶּךָ | כִּי־הִגְדַּלְתָּ |
| 'al-chasdᵉkhā | wᵉ'al-'ămittekhā | kî-highdaltā |
| because of your steadfast love | and because of your faithfulness | because You have made great |

| 6142, 3725, 8428 | 577 | 3. | 904, 3219 | 7410.115 | 6257.123 |
|---|---|---|---|---|---|
| prep, *adj*, n ms, ps 2ms | n fs, ps 2ms | | prep, n ms | v Qal pf 1cs | cj, v Qal impf 2ms, ps 1cs |
| עַל־כָּל־שִׁמְךָ | אִמְרָתֶךָ | | בְּיוֹם | קָרָאתִי | וַתַּעֲנֵנִי |
| 'al-kol-shimkhā | 'imrāthekhā | | bᵉyôm | qārā'thî | watta'ănēnî |
| above all your name | your word | | on the day | I called | then You answered me |

| 7580.523 | 904, 5497 | 6010 | 4. | 3142.521 | 3176 |
|---|---|---|---|---|---|
| v Hiphil impf 2ms, ps 1cs | prep, n fs, ps 1cs | n ms | | v Hiphil juss 3mp, ps 2ms | pn |
| תַּרְהִבֵנִי | בְנַפְשִׁי | עֹז | | יוֹדוּךָ | יְהוָה |
| tarhivēnî | vᵉnaphshî | 'ōz | | yôdhûkhā | yᵉhwāh |
| You made me tenacious | in my soul | strength | | let them praise You | O Yahweh |

| 3725, 4567, 800 | 3706 | 8471.116 | 577, 6552 | 5. | 8301.126 |
|---|---|---|---|---|---|
| *adj*, *n mp*, n fs | cj | v Qal pf 3cp | *n mp*, n ms, ps 2ms | | cj, v Qal juss 3mp |
| כָּל־מַלְכֵי־אָרֶץ | כִּי | שָׁמְעוּ | אִמְרֵי־פִיךָ | | וְיָשִׁירוּ |
| kol-malkhê-'ārets | kî | shāmᵉ'û | 'imrê-phîkhā | | wᵉyāshîrû |
| all the kings of the earth | because | they heard | the words of your mouth | | and let them sing |

| 904, 1932 | 3176 | 3706 | 1448 | 3638 | 3176 | 6. | 3706, 7597.111 | 3176 |
|---|---|---|---|---|---|---|---|---|
| prep, *n mp* | pn | cj | adj | *n ms* | pn | | cj, v Qal pf 3ms | pn |
| בְּדַרְכֵי | יְהוָה | כִּי | גָדוֹל | כְּבוֹד | יְהוָה | | כִּי־רָם | יְהוָה |
| bᵉdharkhê | yᵉhwāh | kî | ghādhôl | kᵉvôdh | yᵉhwāh | | kî-rām | yᵉhwāh |
| in the ways of | Yahweh | because | great | the glory of | Yahweh | | because He is exalted | Yahweh |

Babylon, Babylon the destroyer, *NEB* … O! Babel's cruel daughter, *Fenton*.

**who art to be destroyed:** … you devastator, *Anchor* … doomed to destruction, *NIV*.

**happy shall he be, that rewardeth thee as thou hast served us:** … happy is he who repays you for what you did to us!, *REB* … Blessed be he who requites to you The treatment that you dealt out to us!, *Goodspeed*.

**9. Happy shall he be:** … How blessed will be the one, *NASB*.

**that taketh and dasheth thy little ones against the stones:** … O the happiness of him who doth seize, And hath dashed thy sucklings on the rock!, *Young* … And dash thy children against the crag, *Rotherham* … Happy is he who seizes your babes and dashes them against a rock, *REB* … They will grab your babies and throw them against the rocks, *NCV*.

**138:t. A Psalm of David.**

**1. I will praise thee with my whole heart:** … I confess Thee, *Young* … for listening to the prayer I uttered, *Knox* … I chant before You, GOD, *Fenton* … for you have heard the words of my mouth, *NCB*.

**before the gods will I sing praise unto thee:** … angels for my witnesses, *Knox* … Before the messengers of God, *Rotherham* … in the presence of the angels, *NAB* … I will make melody, *BB*.

**2. I will worship toward thy holy temple:** … I prostrate myself,

*Goodspeed* ... Bow in Your Holy Fane and give thanks to Your Power, *Fenton* ... I will bow down facing your holy Temple, *NCV* ... I bow before thy sacred shrine, *Moffatt.*

**and praise thy name for thy lovingkindness and for thy truth:** ... for your love and faithfulness, *REB* ... for Your truth's sake, *KJVII* ... for your love and loyalty, *NCV* ... because of Thy covenant love, *Berkeley.*

**for thou hast magnified thy word above all thy name:** ... For Thou hast made great Thy saying above all Thy name, *Young* ... thy own honour and thy pledged word thou hast vindicated for all the world to see, *Knox* ... you have exalted your promise above the heavens, *REB* ... your promises surpass even your fame, *JB.*

**3. In the day when I cried thou answeredst me:** ... When I called you granted me triumph, *Anchor* ... When I called, you answered me, *NAB.*

**and strengthenedst me with strength in my soul:** ... fill my heart with courage, *Knox* ... and made me bold and strong, *REB* ... you helped me storm with my ardor strong, *Anchor* ... make me bold and valiant-hearted, *NEB.*

**4. All the kings of the earth shall praise thee, O LORD:** ... all kings of earth confess Thee, *Young* ... All the kings of the earth shall celebrate thee, *Darby* ... When kings on earth hear of thy mind and methods, *Moffatt.*

**when they hear the words of thy mouth:** ... were not thy promises made in their hearing?, *Knox* ... when the words of your mouth come to their ears, *BB.*

**5. Yea, they shall sing in the ways of the LORD:** ... And they will sing of Yahweh's dominion, *Anchor* ... And sing the LORD on march who is the LIVING POWER!, *Fenton* ... they shall sing of the LORD's dealings, *Berkeley.*

**for great is the glory of the LORD:** ... For great is the honour of Jehovah, *Young* ... for great is the Eternal's sovereign might, *Moffatt.*

**6. Though the LORD be high:** ... The LORD is exalted, *REB* ... Though the LORD is supreme, *NCV* ... Sublime as he is, *JB.*

**yet hath he respect unto the lowly:** ... humble, *Knox* ... The LORD looks upon the high and the low, *Goodspeed* ... he takes care of those who are humble, *NCV* ... Yet He regards the lowly, *NASB.*

---

**138:1.** The first part is the outpouring of a thankful heart for a recent great blessing, which has been the fulfillment of a divine promise. So absorbed in his blessedness is the singer, that he neither names Yahweh as the object of his thanks, nor specifies what has set his heart vibrating. The great Giver and the great gift are magnified by being unspoken. To whom but Yahweh could the current of the psalmist's praise set? He feels that Yahweh's mercy to him requires him to become the herald of his name; therefore, he vows, in lofty consciousness of his mission, that he will ring out God's praises in the presence of false gods, whose worshipers have no such experience to loose their tongues. Dead gods have dumb devotees; the servants of the living Yahweh receive his acts of power, that they may proclaim his name.

**138:2–3.** The special occasion for this singer's praise has been some act, in which Yahweh's faithfulness was very conspicuously shown. "Thou hast magnified thy word above all thy name." If the history of David underlies the Psalm, it is most natural to interpret the "word" as that of the establishment of the monarchy. But the fulfillment, not the giving, of a promise is its magnifying, and hence one would incline to take the reference to be to the great manifestation of God's troth in restoring Israel to its land. In any case, the expression is peculiar and has induced many attempts at emendation.

In v. 3b, the psalmist uses a remarkable expression in saying that Yahweh had made him bold (HED #7580), or as the word is rendered, "You made me tenacious" by the context. The following words are a circumstantial or subsidiary clause and indicate how the consciousness of inbreathed strength welling up in his soul gave him lofty confidence to confront foes.

**138:4–6.** The second part (vv. 4ff) resembles many earlier Psalms in connecting the singer's deliverance with a worldwide manifestation of God's name. Such a consciousness of a vocation to be the world's evangelist is appropriate either to David or the collective Israel. Especially is it natural and, as a fact, occurs in post-exilic Psalms. Here "the words of thy mouth" are equivalent to the promise already spoken of, the fulfillment of which has shown that Yahweh "the High" has regard to the lowly, i.e., to the psalmist, and "the proud he knoweth," i.e., his oppressors, "afar off." He reads their characters thoroughly, without, as it were, needing to approach for minute study. The implication is that He will thwart their plans and judge the plotters. This great lesson of Yahweh's providence, care for the lowly and faithfulness to his word has exemplification in the psalmist's history; when it is known, the lofty ones of the earth shall learn the principles of Yahweh's ways and become lowly recipients of his favors and adoring singers of his great glory.

| 8587 | 7495.121 | 1393 | 4623, 4963 | 3156.121 | | 524, 2050.125 |
|---|---|---|---|---|---|---|
| cj, adj | v Qal impf 3ms | cj, adj | prep, n ms | v Qal impf 3ms | 7. | cj, v Qal impf 1cs |
| וְשָׁפָל | יִרְאֶה | וְגָבֹהַּ | מִמֶּרְחָק | יְיֵדָע | | אִם־אֵלֵךְ |
| w$^{e}$shāphāl | yir'eh | w$^{e}$ghāvōahh | mimmerchāq | y$^{e}$yēdhā' | | 'im-'ēlēkh |
| but the lowly | He sees | and the haughty | from a far distance | He knows | | if I walk |

| 904, 7419 | 7150 | 2513.323 | 6142 | 653 | 342.152 |
|---|---|---|---|---|---|
| prep, *n ms* | n fs | v Piel impf 2ms, ps 1cs | prep | *n ms* | v Qal act ptc mp, ps 1cs |
| בְּקֶרֶב | צָרָה | תְּחַיֵּנִי | עַל | אַף | אֹיְבַי |
| b$^{e}$qerev | tsārāh | t$^{e}$chayyēnî | 'al | 'aph | 'ōy$^{e}$vay |
| in the middle of | adversity | You will keep me alive | against | the anger of | my enemies |

| 8365.123 | 3135 | 3588.522 | 3332 | | 3176 | 1625.121 |
|---|---|---|---|---|---|---|
| v Qal impf 2ms | n fs, ps 2ms | cj, v Hiphil impf 3fs, ps 1cs | n fs, ps 2ms | 8. | pn | v Qal impf 3ms |
| תִּשְׁלַח | יָדֶךָ | וְתוֹשִׁיעֵנִי | יְמִינֶךָ | | יְהוָה | יִגְמֹר |
| tishlach | yādhekhā | w$^{e}$thôshî'ēnî | y$^{e}$mînekhā | | y$^{e}$hwāh | yighmōr |
| You stretch out | your hand | it saves me | your right hand | | Yahweh | He will accomplish |

| 1185 | 3176 | 2721 | 3937, 5986 | 4801 | 3135 | 414, 7791.123 |
|---|---|---|---|---|---|---|
| prep, ps 1cs | pn | n ms, ps 2ms | prep, n ms | *n mp* | n fd, ps 2ms | adv, v Qal juss 2ms |
| בַּעֲדִי | יְהוָה | חַסְדְּךָ | לְעוֹלָם | מַעֲשֵׂי | יָדֶיךָ | אַל־תֶּרֶף |
| ba'ădhî | y$^{e}$hwāh | chasd$^{e}$khā | l$^{e}$'ôlām | ma'ăsê | yādhêkhā | 'al-tereph |
| around me | Yahweh | your steadfast love | unto eternity | the works of | your hands | do not relax |

| | 3937, 5514.351 | 3937, 1784 | 4344 | | 3176 | 2811.113 | 3156.123 |
|---|---|---|---|---|---|---|---|
| 139:t | prep, art, v Piel ptc ms | prep, pn | n ms | 1. | pn | v Qal pf 2ms, ps 1cs | cj, v Qal impf 2ms |
| | לַמְנַצֵּחַ | לְדָוִד | מִזְמוֹר | | יְהוָה | חֲקַרְתַּנִי | וַתֵּדָע |
| | lam$^{e}$natstsēcha | l$^{e}$dhāwidh | mizmôr | | y$^{e}$hwāh | chăqartanî | wattēdhā' |
| | to the director | of David | a Psalm | | O Yahweh | You have investigated me | and You know |

| | 887 | 3156.113 | 3553.141 | 7251.141 | 1032.113 | 3937, 7740 |
|---|---|---|---|---|---|---|
| 2. | pers pron | v Qal pf 2ms | v Qal inf con, ps 1cs | cj, v Qal inf con, ps 1cs | v Qal pf 2ms | prep, n ms, ps 1cs |
| | אַתָּה | יָדַעְתָּ | שִׁבְתִּי | וְקוּמִי | בַּנְתָּה | לְרֵעִי |
| | 'attāh | yādha'āttā | shivtî | w$^{e}$qûmî | bantāh | l$^{e}$rē'î |
| | You | You know | my sitting | and my rising | You understand | my thoughts |

**but the proud he knoweth afar off:** … but he stays away from the proud, *NCV* … and from afar he humbles the proud, *NEB*.

**7. Though I walk in the midst of trouble:** … Though I am compassed about by trouble, *REB* … the midst of hostility, *Goodspeed* … In danger hold me up, if in my march I meet, *Fenton* … Though I must pass through the thick of trouble, *Moffatt*.

**thou wilt revive me:** … thou wilt give me life, *Rotherham* … you preserve my life, *REB* … you will keep me alive, *NCV*.

**thou shalt stretch forth thine hand against the wrath of mine enemies:** … it is thy power that confronts my enemies' malice, *Knox* … putting forth your power, *REB* … exerting thy power, *NEB*.

**and thy right hand shall save me:** … and give me victory with your right hand, *Anchor* … thy right hand delivers me, *RSV*.

**8. The LORD will perfect that which concerneth me:** … My purposes the Lord will yet speed, *Knox* … The LORD rewards me, *Goodspeed* … The LORD will fulfill his purpose for me, *NIV*, *RSV* … Yahweh will do all things for me, *JB*.

**thy mercy, O LORD, endureth for ever:** … Thy true love, O LORD, endures for ever, *NEB* … Thy lovingkindness, O Jehovah, endureth for ever, *ASV* … Thy covenant love is everlasting, *Berkeley*.

**forsake not the works of thine own hands:** … The works of Thy hands let not fall!, *Young* … the special work of your hands do not forsake!, *Anchor* … leave not thy work unfinished, *NEB* … don't drop the work You started, *Beck*.

**139:t. To the chief Musician, A Psalm of David.**

**1. O LORD, thou hast searched me, and known me:** … I lie open to thy scrutiny, *Knox* … thou hast searched me, and observed, *Rotherham* … You have probed me and you know me, *NAB* … searching out all my secrets, *BB*.

**2. Thou knowest my downsitting and mine uprising:** … Thou searchest out my path and my lying down,

The glowing vision is not yet fulfilled, but the singer was cherishing no illusions when he sang. It is true that the story of God's great manifestation of himself in Christ, in which He has magnified his Word above all his name, is one day to win the world. It is true that the revelation of a God Who regards the lowly is the conquering Gospel which shall bow all hearts.

**138:7–8.** In the third part (vv. 7f), the psalmist comes back to his own needs and takes to his heart the calming assurance born of his experience, that he bears a charmed life. He speaks the confidence which should strengthen every heart that rests on God. Such a one may be girdled about by troubles, but he will have an inner circle traced around him, within which no evil can venture. He may walk in the valley of the shadow of death unfearing, for God will hold his soul in life. Foes may pour out floods of enmity and wrath, but one strong hand will be stretched out against (or over) the wild deluge and will draw the trustful soul out of its rush on to the safe shore. So was the psalmist assured; so may and should those be who have yet greater wonders for which to thank Yahweh.

That last prayer of the Psalm blends very beautifully confidence and petition. Its central clause is the basis of both the confidence in its first clause and the petition in its last. Because Yahweh's steadfast love endures forever, every man on whom his shaping Spirit has begun to work, or his grace in any form to bestow its gifts, may be sure that no exhaustion or change of these is possible. God is not as the foolish towerbuilder, who began and was not able to finish. He never stops until He has completed his work, and nothing short of the entire conformity of a soul to his likeness and the filling of it with himself can be the termination of his loving purpose, or of his achieving grace. Therefore, the psalmist found it in his heart to pray that God would not abandon the works of his own hands. That prayer appeals to his faithfulness and to his honor. It sets forth the obligations under which God comes by what He has done. It is a prayer which goes straight to his heart, and they who offer it receive the old answer, "I will not leave thee, until I have done that which I have spoken to thee of" (Gen. 28:15).

***Psalm 139****. This is the noblest utterance in the Psalter of pure contemplative theism, animated and not crushed by the thought of God's omniscience and omnipresence. No less striking than the unequalled force and sublimity with which the Psalm hymns the majestic attributes of an all-filling, all-knowing, all-creating God is the firmness with which the singer's personal relation to that God is grasped. Only in the last verses is there reference to other men. In the earlier parts of the Psalm, there are but two beings in the universe—God and the psalmist.*

*The course of thought is plain. There are four strophes of six verses each: the first (vv. 1–6) magnifies God's omniscience; the second (vv. 7–12), his omnipresence; the third (vv. 13–18), his creative act, as the ground of the preceding attributes; and the fourth (vv. 19–24) recoils from men who rebel against such a God, and joyfully submits to the searching of his omniscient eye, and the guidance of his ever-present hand.*

**139:1**. The psalmist is so thoroughly possessed by the thought of his personal relation to God that his meditation spontaneously takes the form of address to Him. That form adds much to the impressiveness, but is not a rhetorical or poetic artifice. Rather, it is the shape in which such intense consciousness of God cannot but utter itself. How cold and abstract the awestruck sentences become if we substitute "he" for "thou," and "men" for "me"! The first overwhelming thought of God's relation to the individual soul is that He completely knows the whole man. "Omniscience" is a pompous word, which leaves us unaffected by either awe or conscience. But the psalmist's God was a God Who came into close touch with him, and the psalmist's religion translated the powerless generality of an attribute referring to the divine relation to the universe into a continually exercised power having reference to himself. He utters his reverent consciousness of it in v. 1 in a single clause and expands that verse in the succeeding ones. "Thou hast searched me" describes a process of minute investigation; "and known [me]," its result in complete knowledge.

**139:2–4.** That knowledge is then followed out in various directions and recognized as embracing the whole man in all his modes of action and repose, in all his inner and outward life. Verses 2 and 3 are substantially parallel. "Downsitting" and "uprising" correspond to "walking" and "lying down," and both antitheses express the contrast between action and rest. "My thought" in v. 2 corresponds to "my ways" in v. 3, the former referring to the inner life of thought, purpose and will and the latter, to the outward activities which carry these into effect. Verse 3 is a climax to v. 2, insofar as it

| | | | | | |
|---|---|---|---|---|---|
| 4623, 7632<br>prep, adv<br>מֵרָחוֹק<br>mērāchôq<br>from far away | **3.** | 758<br>n ms, ps 1cs<br>אָרְחִי<br>'ārechî<br>my path | 7541.141<br>cj, v Qal inf con, ps 1cs<br>וְרִבְעִי<br>weriv'î<br>and my lying down | 2306.313<br>v Piel pf 2ms<br>זֵרִיתָ<br>zērîthā<br>You scatter | 3725, 1932<br>cj, *adj*, n mp, ps 1cs<br>וְכָל־דְּרָכַי<br>wekhol-derākhay<br>and all my ways |

| | | | | | | | |
|---|---|---|---|---|---|---|---|
| 5725.513<br>v Hiphil pf 2ms<br>הִסְכַּנְתָּה<br>hiskantāh<br>You are accustomed to | **4.** | 3706<br>cj<br>כִּי<br>kî<br>because | 375<br>*sub*<br>אֵין<br>'ên<br>there is not | 4543<br>n fs<br>מִלָּה<br>millāh<br>a word | 904, 4098<br>prep, n fs, ps 1cs<br>בִּלְשׁוֹנִי<br>bilshônî<br>on my tongue | 2075<br>intrj<br>הֵן<br>hēn<br>behold | 3176<br>pn<br>יְהוָה<br>yehwāh<br>O Yahweh |

| | | | | | | | |
|---|---|---|---|---|---|---|---|
| 3156.113<br>v Qal pf 2ms<br>יָדַעְתָּ<br>yādha'ttā<br>You know | 3725<br>n ms, ps 3fs<br>כֻלָּהּ<br>khullāhh<br>its entirety | **5.** | 268<br>adv<br>אָחוֹר<br>'āchôr<br>behind | 7208<br>cj, adv<br>וָקֶדֶם<br>wāqedhem<br>and in front of | 6961.113<br>v Qal pf 2ms, ps 1cs<br>צַרְתָּנִי<br>tsartānî<br>You besiege | 8308.123<br>cj, v Qal impf 2ms<br>וַתָּשֶׁת<br>wattāsheth<br>and You place | 6142<br>prep, ps 1cs<br>עָלַי<br>'ālay<br>on me |

| | | | | | | | |
|---|---|---|---|---|---|---|---|
| 3834<br>n fs, ps 2ms<br>כַּפֶּכָה<br>kappekhāh<br>your hand | **6.** | 6627<br>adj<br>פְּלִאיָה<br>pil'îyāh<br>extraordinary | 1907<br>n fs<br>דַעַת<br>dha'ath<br>knowledge | 4623<br>prep, ps 1cs<br>מִמֶּנִּי<br>mimmenî<br>from me | 7891.212<br>v Niphal pf 3fs<br>נִשְׂגְּבָה<br>nisgevāh<br>it is high | 3940, 3310.125<br>neg part, v Qal impf 1cs<br>לֹא־אוּכַל<br>lō'-'ûkhal<br>I am not able | 3937<br>prep, ps 3fs<br>לָהּ<br>lāhh<br>about it |

| | | | | | | |
|---|---|---|---|---|---|---|
| **7.** | 590<br>intrg<br>אָנָה<br>'ānāh<br>where | 2050.125<br>v Qal impf 1cs<br>אֵלֵךְ<br>'ēlēkh<br>can I go | 4623, 7593<br>prep, n fs, ps 2ms<br>מֵרוּחֶךָ<br>mērûchekhā<br>away from your Spirit | 590<br>cj, intrg<br>וְאָנָה<br>we'ānāh<br>indeed where | 4623, 6552<br>prep, n mp, ps 2ms<br>מִפָּנֶיךָ<br>mippānêkhā<br>from before You | 1300.125<br>v Qal impf 1cs<br>אֶבְרָח<br>'evrāch<br>can I flee |

| | | | | | | | |
|---|---|---|---|---|---|---|---|
| **8.** | 524, 5753.125<br>cj, v Qal impf 1cs<br>אִם־אֶסַּק<br>'im-'essaq<br>if I ascend to | 8452<br>n md<br>שָׁמַיִם<br>shāmayim<br>the heavens | 8427<br>adv<br>שָׁם<br>shām<br>there | 887<br>pers pron<br>אָתָּה<br>'āttāh<br>You | 3440.523<br>cj, v Hiphil impf 1cs<br>וְאַצִּיעָה<br>we'atstsî'āh<br>or I make a bed | 8061<br>n fs<br>שְׁאוֹל<br>she'ôl<br>Sheol | 2079<br>intrj, ps 2ms<br>הִנֶּךָּ<br>hinnekhā<br>behold You |

| | | | | | |
|---|---|---|---|---|---|
| **9.** | 5558.125<br>v Qal juss 1cs<br>אֶשָּׂא<br>'essā'<br>let me bear | 3796, 8266<br>*n fd*, n ms<br>כַנְפֵי־שָׁחַר<br>khanphê-shāchar<br>the wings of the morning | 8331.125<br>v Qal juss 1cs<br>אֶשְׁכְּנָה<br>'eshkenāh<br>and let me stay | 904, 321<br>prep, *n fs*<br>בְּאַחֲרִית<br>be'achrîth<br>in the remote part of | 3328<br>n ms<br>יָם<br>yām<br>the Sea |

| | | | | | |
|---|---|---|---|---|---|
| **10.** | 1612, 8427<br>cj, adv<br>גַּם־שָׁם<br>gam-shām<br>also there | 3135<br>n fs, ps 2ms<br>יָדְךָ<br>yādhekhā<br>your hand | 5328.522<br>v Hiphil impf 3fs, ps 1cs<br>תַנְחֵנִי<br>thanchēnî<br>it will lead me | 270.122<br>cj, v Qal impf 3fs, ps 1cs<br>וְתֹאחֲזֵנִי<br>wethō'chăzēnî<br>and it will take hold of me | 3332<br>n fs, ps 2ms<br>יְמִינֶךָ<br>yemînekhā<br>your right hand |

*MRB* … You know me at rest and in action, *REB.*

**thou understandest my thought afar off:** … no movement of mine but thou art watching it, *Knox* … Thou hast given heed to my desire, from afar, *Rotherham* … You know my thoughts before I think them, *NCV* … you know every detail of my conduct, *JB.*

**3. Thou compassest my path and my lying down:** … My path and my couch Thou hast fanned, *Young* … Thou dost measure out my course and my camp, *Goodspeed* … Prepares my field and couch, *Fenton* … My journeys and my rest you scrutinize, *NAB.*

**and art acquainted with all my ways:** … and all my travels superintend, *Anchor* … You know thoroughly everything I do, *NCV* … I am scanned by thee, and all my life to thee lies open, *Moffatt.*

**4. For there is not a word in my tongue:** … even before I say a word, you already know it, *NCV.*

**but, lo, O Lord, thou knowest it altogether:** ... all my thought is known to thee; rearguard and vanguard, *Knox* ... which is not clear to you, O Lord, *BB.*

**5. Thou hast beset me behind and before:** ... Thou hast kept close guard before me and behind, *NEB.*

**and laid thine hand upon me:** ... and hast spread thy hand over me, *NEB.*

**6. Such knowledge is too wonderful for me:** ... Your knowledge is amazing to me, *NCV* ... Such knowledge is a wonder greater than my powers, *BB.*

**it is high, I cannot attain unto it:** ... It is too lofty; I am not equal to it, *Goodspeed* ... too towering, I cannot master it, *Anchor* ... it is more than I can understand, *NCV.*

**7. Whither shall I go from thy spirit?:** ... I walk by Your Spirit, *Fenton.*

**or whither shall I flee from thy presence?:** ... And whither from Thy face do I flee?, *Young* ... An led by Your mouth, *Fenton* ... Where can I flee from Your face?, *Beck.*

**8. If I ascend up into heaven, thou art there:** ... If I scale the heavens you are there, *JB* ... If I spread out hades as my couch, *Rotherham* ... You are there if I dive to the Grave!, *Fenton* ... if I sink to the nether world, *NAB* ... if I made the underworld my couch, *Berkeley.*

**if I make my bed in hell, behold, thou art there:** ... If I make my bed in Sheol, behold, thou art there, *ASV.*

**9. If I take the wings of the morning:** ... If I could wing my way eastwards, *Knox* ... Should I raise my wings in the Orient, *Anchor* ... If I take my flight to the frontiers of the morning, *NEB.*

**and dwell in the uttermost parts of the sea:** ... or find a a dwelling beyond the western sea, *Knox* ... Settle down in the region beyond the sea, *Rotherham* ... if I settle at the farthest limits of the sea, *NAB, NCB.*

**10. Even there shall thy hand lead me:** ... even there you would guide me, *NCV* ... thy hand even there would fall on me, *Moffatt.*

**and thy right hand shall hold me:** ... your right hand holding me fast, *REB* ... Thy right hand would take hold of me, *Berkeley* ... and your right hand will keep me, *BB.*

**11. If I say, Surely the darkness shall cover me:** ... Surely darkness bruiseth me, *Young* ... Or perhaps I would think to bury myself

---

ascribes a yet closer and more accurate knowledge to God. "And art acquainted" implies intimate and habitual knowledge. But thought and action are not the whole man. The power of speech, which the Psalter always treats as solemn and a special object of divine approval or condemnation, must also be taken into account. Verse 4 brings it, too, under God's cognizance. The meaning may either be that "there is no word on my tongue [which] thou dost not know altogether"; or, "the word is not yet in my tongue, [but] lo! Thou knowest," etc.

**139:5–6.** The thought that God knows him through and through blends in the singer's mind with the other, that God surrounds him on every side. Verse 5 thus anticipates the thought of the next strophe, but presents it rather as the basis of God's knowledge and as limiting man's freedom. But the psalmist does not feel that he is imprisoned, or that the hand laid on him is heavy. Rather, he rejoices in the defense of an encompassing God, Who shuts off evil from him, as well as shuts him in from self-willed and self-determined action; and he is glad to be held by a hand so gentle as well as strong. "Thou hast beset me" may either be a dread or a blessed thought. It may paralyze or stimulate. It should be the ally of conscience, and while it stirs to all noble deeds, should also emancipate from all slavish fear. An exclamation of reverent wonder and confession of the limitation of human comprehension closes the strophe.

**139:7–10.** Why should the thought that God is ever with the psalmist be put in the shape of vivid pictures of the impossibility of escape from Him? It is the sense of sin which leads men to hide from God, like Adam among the trees of the garden. The psalmist does not desire thus to flee, but he supposes the case, which would be only too common if men realized God's knowledge of all their ways. He imagines himself reaching the extremities of the universe in vain flight and stunned by finding God there. The utmost possible height is coupled with the utmost possible depth. Heaven and Sheol equally fail to give refuge from that moveless face, which confronts the fugitive in both and fills them as it fills all the intervening dim distances. The dawn flushes the east and swiftly passes on roseate wings to the farthest bounds of the Mediterranean, which, to the psalmist, represented the extreme west, a land of mystery. In both places and in all the broad lands between, the fugitive would find himself in the grasp of the same hand (cf. v. 5).

**139:11–12.** Darkness is the friend of fugitives from men, but is transparent to God. In v. 11, the language is somewhat obscure. The word rendered

| | | | | | |
|---|---|---|---|---|---|
| **11.** **569.125** cj, v Qal impf 1cs | **395, 2932** adv, n ms | **8220.121** v Qal impf 3ms, ps 1cs | **4050** cj, n ms | **214** n ms | **1185** prep, ps 1cs |
| וָאֹמַר | אַךְ־חֹשֶׁךְ | יְשׁוּפֵנִי | וְלַיְלָה | אוֹר | בַּעֲדֵנִי |
| wā'ōmar | 'akh-chōshekh | yeshûphēnî | welaylāh | 'ôr | ba'ădhēnî |
| when I say | only darkness | it crushes me | and night | light | around me |

| | | | | | |
|---|---|---|---|---|---|
| **12.** **1612, 2932** cj, n ms | **3940, 2931.521** neg part, v Hiphil impf 3ms | **4623** prep, ps 2ms | **4050** cj, n ms | **3626, 3219** prep, art, n ms | **213.521** v Hiphil impf 3ms |
| גַּם־חֹשֶׁךְ | לֹא־יַחְשִׁיךְ | מִמֶּךָּ | וְלַיְלָה | כַּיּוֹם | יָאִיר |
| gam-chōshekh | lō'-yachshîkh | mimmekhā | welaylāh | kayyôm | yā'îr |
| also darkness | it is not dark | from You | and night | like the day | it is light |

| | | | | | |
|---|---|---|---|---|---|
| **3626, 2934** prep, art, n fs | **3626, 218** prep, art, n fs | **13.** **3706, 887** cj, pers pron | **7353.113** v Qal pf 2ms | **3749** n fp, ps 1cs | **5718.123** v Qal impf 2ms, ps 1cs |
| כַּחֲשֵׁיכָה | כָּאוֹרָה | כִּי־אַתָּה | קָנִיתָ | כִלְיֹתָי | תְּסֻכֵּנִי |
| kacheshêkhāh | kā'ôrāh | kî-'attāh | qānîthā | khilyōthāy | tesukkēnî |
| like the darkness | so the light | because You | You created | my kidneys | You interwove me |

| | | | | | |
|---|---|---|---|---|---|
| **904, 1027** prep, *n fs* | **525** n fs, ps 1cs | **14.** **3142.525** v Hiphil juss 1cs, ps 2ms | **6142** prep | **3706** cj | **3486.258** v Niphal ptc fp |
| בְּבֶטֶן | אִמִּי | אוֹדְךָ | עַל | כִּי | נוֹרָאוֹת |
| beveten | 'immî | 'ôdhkhā | 'al | kî | nôrā'ôth |
| in the womb of | my mother | let me praise You | on account of | because | fearful deeds |

| | | | | | |
|---|---|---|---|---|---|
| **6640.215** v Niphal pf 1cs | **6623.256** v Niphal ptc mp | **4801** n mp, ps 2ms | **5497** cj, n fs, ps 1cs | **3156.153** v Qal act ptc fs | **4108** adv |
| נִפְלֵיתִי | נִפְלָאִים | מַעֲשֶׂיךָ | וְנַפְשִׁי | יֹדַעַת | מְאֹד |
| niphlêthî | niphlā'îm | ma'ăsêkhā | wenaphshî | yōdha'ath | me'ōdh |
| I am distinguished | extraordinary deeds | your works | and my soul | knowing | very |

| | | | | |
|---|---|---|---|---|
| **15.** **3940, 3701.211** neg part, v Niphal pf 3ms | **6344** n ms, ps 1cs | **4623** prep, ps 2ms | **866, 6449.415** rel part, v Pual pf 1cs | **904, 5848** prep, art, n ms |
| לֹא־נִכְחַד | עָצְמִי | מִמֶּךָּ | אֲשֶׁר־עֻשֵּׂיתִי | בַסֵּתֶר |
| lō'-nikhchadh | 'ātsemî | mimmekhā | 'ăsher-'ussêthî | vassēther |
| it was not hidden | my body | from You | when I was fashioned | in the secret place |

| | | | | | |
|---|---|---|---|---|---|
| **7844.415** v Pual pf 1cs | **904, 8809** prep, *adj* | **800** n fs | **16.** **1605** n ms, ps 1cs | **7495.116** v Qal pf 3cp | **6084** n fd, ps 2ms |
| רֻקַּמְתִּי | בְּתַחְתִּיּוֹת | אָרֶץ | גָּלְמִי | רָאוּ | עֵינֶיךָ |
| ruqqamtî | bethachtîyôth | 'ārets | gālemî | rā'û | 'ênêkhā |
| I was woven together | in the deepest parts of | the earth | my embryo | they saw | your eyes |

| | | | | | | |
|---|---|---|---|---|---|---|
| **6142, 5807** cj, prep, n ms, ps 2ms | **3725** adj, ps 3mp | **3918.226** v Niphal impf 3mp | **3219** n mp | **3443.416** v Pual pf 3cp | **3940** cj, neg part | **259** num |
| וְעַל־סִפְרְךָ | כֻּלָּם | יִכָּתֵבוּ | יָמִים | יֻצָּרוּ | וְלֹא | אֶחָד |
| we'al-siphrekhā | kullām | yikkāthēvû | yāmîm | yutstsārû | welō' | 'echādh |
| and on your scroll | all of them | they are written | days | they were fashioned | when not | one |

in darkness, *Knox* ... Even in the Darkness he observes me, *Anchor* ... Surely the darkness shall hide me, *NAB*.

**even the night shall be light about me:** ... Then night is light to me, *Young* ... Let the light around me turn into night, *NCV*.

**12. Yea, the darkness hideth not from thee:** ... darkness is not too dark for you, *REB* ... for even darkness does not hide from Thee, *Berkeley*.

**but the night shineth as the day:** ... night should surround me, friendlier than the day, *Knox* ... So Darkness and Light are the same!, *Fenton* ... the night is as bright as the day, *BB*.

**the darkness and the light are both alike to thee:** ... and night is as clear as the day, *JB*.

**13. For thou hast possessed my reins:** ... For thou didst create my vitals, *Goodspeed* ... You made my whole being, *NCV* ... My flesh was made by you, *BB*.

**thou hast covered me in my mother's womb:** ... you formed me in my mother's body, *NCV.*

**14. I will praise thee; for I am fearfully and wonderfully made:** ... because that with wonders I have been distinguished, *Young* ... because you are awesome, *Anchor.*

**marvellous are thy works; and that my soul knoweth right well:** ... marvelous is Thy workmanship, *Berkeley* ... My soul itself you have known of old, *Anchor* ... My soul also you knew full well, *NAB* ... My soul also you knew full well, *NCB* ... as my soul is well aware, *Berkeley.*

**15. My substance was not hid from thee:** ... and this mortal frame had no mysteries for thee, *Knox* ... My bones were not hidden from You, *KJVII* ... my body is no mystery to thee, *NEB* ... My limbs weren't hidden from You, *Beck.*

**when I was made in secret:** ... Since I was nipped off in the Secret Place, *Anchor* ... as I took shape in my mother's body, *NCV* ... and intricately fashioned in utter seclusion, *Berkeley* ... and skillfully woven as in an underground workshop, *Beck.*

**and curiously wrought in the lowest parts of the earth:** ... devise its pattern, there in the dark recesses of the earth, *Knox* ... And skillfully wrought in the depths of the earth, *NASB* ... and fashioned beneath in the earth, *Geneva* ... textured in the depths of the earth, *JB.*

**16. Thine eyes did see my substance:** ... Your eyes foresaw my deeds, *REB* ... Your eyes have seen my actions, *NCB* ... Thou didst see my limbs unformed in the womb, *NEB* ... Your eyes could see my embryo, *JB.*

**yet being unperfect:** ... Your eyes saw me, as I was evolving, *Fenton.*

**and in thy book all my members were written:** ... upon your scroll all of them were inscribed, *Anchor* ... All the days ordained for me were written in your book, *NIV* ... they were all prepared and written in Your scroll, *Beck.*

**which in continuance were fashioned:** ... Which day by day were fashioned, *MRB* ... my life was fashioned, *REB* ... The days that were ordained for me, *NASB.*

**when as yet there was none of them:** ... before it had come into being, *REB* ... my days were limited before one of them existed, *NAB* ... not one of them was late in growing, *NEB.*

---

"it crushes me" (HED #8220) is doubtful, as the Hebrew text reads "bruise," which is quite unsuitable here. There has probably been textual error, and the slight correction which yields the above sense is to be adopted, as by many moderns. The second clause of the verse carries on the supposition of the first and is not to be regarded, as in the KJV, as stating the result of the supposition, or, in grammatical language, the apodosis. That begins with v. 12 and is marked there, as in v. 10, by "even."

**139:13–14.** The third strophe (vv. 13–18) grounds the psalmist's relation to God on God's creative act. The mysteries of conception and birth naturally struck the imagination of nonscientific man and are to the psalmist the direct result of divine power. He touches them with poetic delicacy and devout awe, casting a veil of metaphor over the mystery and losing sight of human parents in the clear vision of the divine creator. There is room for his thought of the origin of the individual life behind modern knowledge of embryology. In v. 13, the word sometimes rendered "possessed" (HED # 7353) is better understood in this context as meaning "formed," and that rendered there "covered" (as in Ps. 140:7) here means "to plait or weave together" and picturesquely describes the interlacing bones and sinews, as in Job 10:11. But description passes into adoration in v. 14. Its language is somewhat obscure. The verb rendered "wondrously made" (HED #6640) probably means here "selected" or "distinguished" and represents man as the crowning work of the divine artificer. The psalmist cannot contemplate his own frame, God's workmanship, without breaking into thanks, nor without being touched with awe. Every man carries in his own body reasons enough for reverent gratitude.

**139:15–16.** The word for "substance" (HED #6344) in v. 15 is a collective noun and might be rendered "bony framework." The mysterious receptacle in which the unborn body takes shape and grows is delicately described as "secret" and likened to the hidden region of the underworld, where the dead are. The point of comparison is the mystery enwrapping both. The same comparison occurs in Job's pathetic words, "Naked came I out of my mother's womb, and naked shall I return thither" (Job 1:21). It is doubtful whether the word rendered "wrought like embroidery" refers to a pattern wrought by weaving or by needlework. The last clause of the verse is capable of two different meanings, according as the Hebrew text or margin is followed. This is one of a number of cases in which there is a doubt whether we should read "not" or "to him" (or "to it"). The Hebrew words having these meanings are each of two letters, the initial one being the same in both, and both words having the same sound.

| 904 | | 3937 | 4242, 3478.116 | 7740 | 418 | 4242 |
|---|---|---|---|---|---|---|
| prep, ps 3mp | **17.** | cj, prep, ps 1cs | intrg, v Qal pf 3cp | n mp, ps 2ms | n ms | intrg |
| בָּהֶם | | וְלִי | מַה־יָּקְרוּ | רֵעֶיךָ | אֵל | מַה |
| bāhem | | welî | mah-yāqōrû | rē'êkhā | 'ēl | meh |
| among them | | and to me | how precious are they | your thoughts | O God | how |

| 6343.116 | 7513 | | 5807.125 | 4623, 2437 | 7528.126 |
|---|---|---|---|---|---|
| v Qal pf 3cp | n mp, ps 3mp | **18.** | v Qal impf 1cs, ps 3mp | prep, n ms | v Qal impf 3mp |
| עָצְמוּ | רָאשֵׁיהֶם | | אֶסְפְּרֵם | מֵחוֹל | יִרְבּוּן |
| 'ātsemû | rā'shêhem | | 'esperēm | mēchôl | yirbûn |
| innumerable are they | their beginning | | I count them as more | than the sand | they are many |

| 7301.515 | 5968 | 6196 | | 524, 7272.123 | 438 | 7857 | 596 |
|---|---|---|---|---|---|---|---|
| v Hiphil pf 1cs | cj, adv, ps 1cs | prep, ps 2ms | **19.** | cj, v Qal impf 2ms | n ms | n ms | cj, *n mp* |
| הֱקִיצֹתִי | וְעוֹדִי | עִמָּךְ | | אִם־תִּקְטֹל | אֱלוֹהַּ | רָשָׁע | וְאַנְשֵׁי |
| hĕqîtsōthî | we'ôdhî | 'immākh | | 'im-tiqṭōl | 'ĕlôahh | rāshā' | we'anshê |
| I awake | and still I | with You | | if You kill | O God | the wicked | and O men of |

| 1879 | 5681.133 | 4623 | | 866 | 569.126 | 3937, 4343 | 5558.155 |
|---|---|---|---|---|---|---|---|
| n mp | v Qal impv 2mp | prep, ps 1cs | **20.** | rel pron | v Qal impf 3mp, ps 2ms | prep, n fs | v Qal pass ptc ms |
| דָמִים | סוּרוּ | מֶנִּי | | אֲשֶׁר | יֹאמְרֻךָ | לִמְזִמָּה | נָשֻׂא |
| dhāmîm | sûrû | menî | | 'ăsher | yō'merukhā | limzimmāh | nāsu' |
| bloodshed | go away | from me | | who | they say about You | for plots | those lifted up |

| 3937, 8175 | 6111 | | 1950B, 3940, 7983.352 | 3176 | 7983.125 |
|---|---|---|---|---|---|
| prep, art, n ms | n fp, ps 2ms | **21.** | intrg part, neg part, v Piel ptc mp, ps 2ms | pn | v Qal impf 1cs |
| לַשָּׁוְא | עָרֶיךָ | | הֲלוֹא־מְשַׂנְאֶיךָ | יְהוָה | אֶשְׂנָא |
| lashshāwe' | 'ārêkhā | | hălô'-mesan'êkhā | yehwāh | 'esnā' |
| for vanity | your cities | | do not those who hate You | O Yahweh | I hate |

| 904, 7251.752 | 7248.725 | | 8832 | 7985 |
|---|---|---|---|---|
| cj, prep, v Hithpolel ptc mp, ps 2ms | v Hithpolel impf 1cs | **22.** | *n fs* | n fs |
| וּבִתְקוֹמְמֶיךָ | אֶתְקוֹטָט | | תַּכְלִית | שִׂנְאָה |
| ûvithqômemêkhā | 'ethqôṭāṭ | | takhlîth | sin'āh |
| and on those who rise up against You | I am disgusted | | completion of | hatred |

| 7983.115 | 3937, 342.152 | 2030.116 | 3937 | | 2811.131 | 418 |
|---|---|---|---|---|---|---|
| v Qal pf 1cs, ps 3mp | prep, v Qal act ptc mp | v Qal pf 3cp | prep, ps 1cs | **23.** | v Qal impv 2ms, ps 1cs | n ms |
| שְׂנֵאתִים | לְאוֹיְבִים | הָיוּ | לִי | | חָקְרֵנִי | אֵל |
| senē'thîm | le'ôyvîm | hāyû | lî | | chāqŏrēnî | 'ēl |
| I hate them | for enemies | they are | to me | | investigate me | O God |

| 3156.131 | 3949 | 1010.131 | 3156.131 | 8040 |
|---|---|---|---|---|
| cj, v Qal impv 2ms | n ms, ps 1cs | v Qal impv 2ms, ps 1cs | cj, v Qal impv 2ms | n mp, ps 1cs |
| וְדַע | לְבָבִי | בְּחָנֵנִי | וְדַע | שַׂרְעַפָּי |
| wedha' | levāvî | bechānēnî | wedha' | sar'appāy |
| and know | my heart | examine me | and know | my disturbing thoughts |

**17. How precious also are thy thoughts unto me, O God!:** … A riddle, O my God, thy dealings with me, so vast their scope!, *Knox* … To me then, how precious have thy desires become, O GOD!, *Rotherham* … How weighty are your designs, *NAB* … How deep I find thy thoughts, O God, *NEB*.

**how great is the sum of them!:** … how vast in number they are!, *REB* … They are so many!, … how inexhaustible their themes!, *NEB*.

**18. If I should count them, they are more in number than the sand:** … If I made up their number, it would be more than the grains of sand, *BB*.

**when I awake, I am still with thee:** … I rouse myself—And am still with thee, *Rotherham* … to finish the count, my years must equal yours, *REB* … Were I to come to the end of them, my life-span must be like thine!, *Goodspeed* … May I rise and my continuance be with you!, *Anchor*.

**19. Surely thou wilt slay the wicked, O God:** ... slay the lawless one?, *Rotherham* ... God, I wish you would kill the wicked!, *NCV.*

**depart from me therefore, ye bloody men:** ... And the men of blood would depart from me, *Goodspeed* ... O men of idols, turn away from me!, *Anchor* ... then would bloodguilty men depart from me!, *Berkeley.*

**20. For they speak against thee wickedly:** ... Who exchange Thee for wickedness, *Young* ... Because they gaze upon every figurine, *Anchor* ... men who maliciously defy thee, *RSV* ... men who defy thee lawlessly, *Moffatt.*

**and thine enemies take thy name in vain:** ... and as your adversaries they rise in malice, *REB* ... your foes swear faithless oaths, *NCB* ... and rise in vicious rebellion against thee!, *NEB* ... and as Your enemies abuse You, *Beck.*

**21. Do not I hate them, O LORD, that hate thee?:** ... O LORD, how I hate those who hate you!, *Good News* ... LORD, shouldn't I hate those who hate You, *Beck.*

**and am not I grieved with those that rise up against thee?:** ... And with Thy withstanders grieve myself?, *Young* ... I loathe those who defy you, *REB* ... I am cut to the quick when they oppose thee, *NEB* ... and feel disgusted with those who attack You?, *Beck.*

**22. I hate them with perfect hatred:** ... With completenss of hatred, *Rotherham* ... with undying hatred, *REB* ... With the deadliest hatred, *Goodspeed* ... With a deadly hatred I hate them, *NCB.*

**I count them mine enemies:** ... they are my enemies, *NCV.*

**23. Search me, O God:** ... God, examine me, *NCV.*

**and know my heart:** ... and know my mind, *REB* ... let the secrets of my heart be uncovered, *BB.*

---

Confusion might easily therefore arise, and as a matter of fact, there are numerous cases in which the text has the one and the margin the other of these two words. Here, if we adhere to the text, we read the negative, and then the force of the clause is to declare emphatically that the "days" were written in God's book, and in a real sense "fashioned," when as yet they had not been recorded in earth's calendars. If, on the other hand, the marginal reading is preferred, a striking meaning is obtained: "And for it [i.e., for the birth of the shapeless mass] there was one among them [predestined in God's book]."

**139:17–18.** In vv. 17f, the poet gathers together and crowns all his previous contemplations by the consideration that this God, knowing him altogether, ever near him, and fashioner of his being, has great "thoughts" or purposes affecting him individually. That assurance makes omniscience and omnipresence joys and not terrors. The root meaning of the word rendered "precious" (HED #3478) is "weighty." The singer would weigh God's thoughts toward him, and finds that they weigh down his scales. He would number them and find that they pass his enumeration. It is the same truth of the transcendent greatness and graciousness of God's purposes as conveyed in Isaiah's, "as the heavens are higher than the earth, so are ... my thoughts than your thoughts" (Isa. 55:9). " I awake, and am still with thee" is an artless expression of the psalmist's blessedness in realizing God's continual nearness. He awakes from sleep and is conscious of glad wonder to find that, like a tender mother by her slumbering child, God has been watching over him and that all the blessed communion of past days abides as before.

**139:19.** The fiery hatred of evil and evil men which burns in the last strophe offends many and startles more. But while the vehement prayer that "Thou wilt slay the wicked" is not in a Christian tone, the recoil from those who could raise themselves against such a God is the necessary result of the psalmist's delight in Him. Attraction and repulsion are equal and contrary. The measure of our cleaving to that which is good and to Him Who is good settles the measure of our abhorrence of that which is evil. The abrupt passing from petition in v. 19a to command in 19b has been smoothed away by a slight alteration which reads, "And that men of blood would depart from me," but the variation in tense is more forcible and corresponds with the speaker's strong emotion. He cannot bear companionship with rebels against God. His indignation has no taint of personal feeling, but is pure zeal for God's honor.

**139:20.** Verse 20 presents difficulties. The word rendered "speak against" (HED #569) is peculiarly spelled, if this is its meaning, and its construction is anomalous. Therefore, the rendering should probably be as above. That meaning does not require a change of consonants, but only of vowel points.

**139:21–22.** The vindication of the psalmist's indignation lies in vv. 21f. That soul must glow with fervent love to God which feels wrong done to his majesty with as keen a pain as if it were itself struck. What God says to those who love Him, they

| 24. | 7495.131 | 524, 1932, 6326 | 904 | 5328.131 | 904, 1932 | 5986 |
|---|---|---|---|---|---|---|
| | cj, v Qal impv 2ms | cj, *n ms*, n ms | prep, ps 1cs | cj, v Qal impv 2ms, ps 1cs | prep, *n ms* | n ms |
| | וּרְאֵה | אִם־דֶּרֶךְ־עֹצֶב | בִּי | וּנְחֵנִי | בְּדֶרֶךְ | עוֹלָם |
| | ûre'ēh | 'im-derekh-'ōtsev | bî | ûnechēnî | bedherekh | 'ôlām |
| | and see | if a way of harm | in me | and lead me | in the way of | eternity |

| 140:t | 3937, 5514.351 | 4344 | 3937, 1784 | 1. | 2603.331 | 3176 | 4623, 119 | 7737 |
|---|---|---|---|---|---|---|---|---|
| | prep, art, v Piel ptc ms | n ms | prep, pn | | v Piel impv 2ms, ps 1cs | pn | prep, n ms | n ms |
| | לַמְנַצֵּחַ | מִזְמוֹר | לְדָוִד | | חַלְּצֵנִי | יְהוָה | מֵאָדָם | רָע |
| | lamnatstsēach | mizmôr | ledhāwidh | | challetsēnî | yehwāh | mē'ādhām | rā' |
| | to the director | a Psalm | of David | | separate me | O Yahweh | from men | evil |

| 4623, 382 | 2660 | 5526.123 | 2. | 866 | 2913.116 | 7750 |
|---|---|---|---|---|---|---|
| prep, *n ms* | n mp | v Qal impf 2ms, ps 1cs | | rel pron | v Qal pf 3cp | *n fp* |
| מֵאִישׁ | חֲמָסִים | תִּנְצְרֵנִי | | אֲשֶׁר | חָשְׁבוּ | רָעוֹת |
| mē'îsh | chămās̱îm | tintserēnî | | 'ăsher | chāshevû | rā'ôth |
| from men of | violent deeds | keep me | | who | they have devised | evil deeds |

| 904, 3949 | 3725, 3219 | 1513.126 | 4560 | 3. | 8532.116 | 4098 |
|---|---|---|---|---|---|---|
| prep, n ms | *adj*, n ms | v Qal impf 3mp | n fp | | v Qal pf 3cp | n fs, ps 3mp |
| בְּלֵב | כָּל־יוֹם | יָגוּרוּ | מִלְחָמוֹת | | שָׁנְנוּ | לְשׁוֹנָם |
| belēv | kol-yôm | yāghûrû | milchāmôth | | shānenû | leshônām |
| in the heart | all the day | they sojourned | wars | | they have sharpened | their tongue |

| 3765, 5357 | 2635 | 6141 | 8809 | 8004 | 5734 | 4. | 8490.131 | 3176 |
|---|---|---|---|---|---|---|---|---|
| prep, n ms | *n fs* | n ms | prep | n fd, ps 3mp | intrj | | v Qal impv 2ms, ps 1cs | pn |
| כְּמוֹ־נָחָשׁ | חֲמַת | עַכְשׁוּב | תַּחַת | שְׂפָתֵימוֹ | סֶלָה | | שָׁמְרֵנִי | יְהוָה |
| kemô-nāchāsh | chămath | 'akhshûv | tachath | sephāthêmô | s̱elāh | | shāmerēnî | yehwāh |
| like a serpent | the poison of | a viper | under | their lips | selah | | protect me | O Yahweh |

| 4623, 3135 | 7857 | 4623, 382 | 2660 | 5526.123 | 866 |
|---|---|---|---|---|---|
| prep, *n fd* | n ms | prep, *n ms* | n mp | v Qal impf 2ms, ps 1cs | rel pron |
| מִידֵי | רָשָׁע | מֵאִישׁ | חֲמָסִים | תִּנְצְרֵנִי | אֲשֶׁר |
| mîdhê | rāshā' | mē'îsh | chămās̱îm | tintserēnî | 'ăsher |
| from the hands of | the wicked | from men of | violent deeds | You keep me | who |

| 2913.116 | 3937, 1815.141 | 6718 | 5. | 3045.116, 1373 | 6583 | 3937 |
|---|---|---|---|---|---|---|
| v Qal pf 3cp | prep, v Qal inf con | n fp, ps 1cs | | v Qal pf 3cp, n mp | n ms | prep, ps 1cs |
| חָשְׁבוּ | לִדְחוֹת | פְּעָמָי | | טָמְנוּ־גֵאִים | פַּח | לִי |
| chāshevû | lidhchôth | pe'āmāy | | ṯāmenû-ghē'îm | pach | lî |
| they have plotted | to push | my feet | | the proud have hidden | a snare | for me |

| 2346 | 6816.116 | 7862 | 3937, 3135, 4724 | 4305 | 8308.116, 3937 |
|---|---|---|---|---|---|
| cj, n mp | v Qal pf 3cp | n fs | prep, *n fs*, n ms | n mp | v Qal pf 3cp, prep, ps 1cs |
| וַחֲבָלִים | פָּרְשׂוּ | רֶשֶׁת | לְיַד־מַעְגָּל | מֹקְשִׁים | שָׁתוּ־לִי |
| wachvālîm | pāresû | resheth | leyadh-ma'ggāl | mōqeshîm | shāthû-lî |
| and cords | they have spread out | a net | at the side of a worn path | snares | they have set for me |

**try me, and know my thoughts:** ... and observe my cares, *Rotherham* ... and understand my misgivings, *NEB* ... know my concerns, *JB* ... let my wandering thoughts be tested, *BB*.

**24. And see if there be any wicked way in me:** ... And see if there be any idol-way in me, *Rotherham* ... Watch lest I follow any path that grieves you, *REB* ... any hurtful way in me, *NASB* ... Make sure that I am not on my way to ruin, *JB*.

**and lead me in the way everlasting:** ... And lead me in a way age-during!, *Young* ... and lead me into the eternal dominion!, *Anchor*... And for ever lead me on Your road!, *Fenton* ... guide me in the ancient ways, *NEB*.

**140:t. To the chief Musician, A Psalm of David.**

**1. Deliver me, O LORD, from the evil man:** ... take me out of the power of the evil man, *BB* ... Rescue me, Lord, from human malice, *Knox*.

**preserve me from the violent man:** ... protect me from criminals, *Beck* ...

Preserve me from those who oppress, *Fenton* ... protect me from cruel people who make evil plans, *NCV.*

**2. Which imagine mischiefs in their heart:** ... who plan evil things in their minds, *NRSV* ... whose heart is bent on malice, *JB* ... whose heads are full of wicked schemes, *NEB.*

**continually are they gathered together for war:** ... and always stir up fighting, *Beck* ... and they are ever making ready causes of war, *BB.*

**3. They have sharpened their tongues like a serpent:** ... their tongues are barbed as a serpent's, *JB* ... They dart out their tongue like a snake, *Fenton.*

**adders' poison is under their lips:** ... their lips hide a viper's poison, *Beck* ... on their lips is spiders' poison, *NEB, REB* ... the venom of asps is under their lips, *NCB* ... Their words are like snake poison, *NCV.*

**Selah:** ... Music, *Beck* ... Pause, *JB.*

**4. Keep me, O LORD, from the hands of the wicked:** ... for they are designing my downfall, *BB* ... Guard me, LORD, from the clutches of the wicked, *REB* ... Keep me, O Yahweh, from the hands of the lawless one, *Rotherham.*

**preserve me from the violent man:** ... keep me safe from those who use violence, *REB* ... save me from outrageous men, *Moffatt.*

**who have purposed to overthrow my goings:** ... who are bent on making me stumble, *JB* ... who plan to thrust me out of the way, *NEB.*

**5. The proud have hid a snare for me:** ... Arrogant men have hidden a snare for me, *Beck* ... stretching nets in my way, *BB.*

**and cords; they have spread a net by the wayside:** ... and set traps for me along the path, *Beck* ... and with cords they have spread a net, *NRSV* ... And spread out their cord-woven nets, *Fenton* ... and lay snares for me along my path, *REB.*

**they have set gins for me. Selah:** ... to trap me as I pass, *JB.*

---

in their degree say to God: "He that toucheth you toucheth the apple of his eye" (Zech. 2:8). True, hate is not the Christian requital of hate, whether that is directed against God or God's servant. But there must be recoil, if there is any vigor of devotion; only pity and love must mingle with it, and the evil of hatred be overcome by their good.

**139:23.** Very beautifully does the lowly prayer for searching and guidance follow the psalmist's burst of fire. It is easier to glow with indignation against evildoers than to keep oneself from doing evil. Many secret sins may hide under a cloak of zeal for the LORD. So the psalmist prays that God would search him, not because he fancies that there is no lurking sin to be burned by the light of God's eye, like vermin that nestle and multiply under stones and shrivel when the sunbeams strike them, but because he dreads that there is and would have it cast out. The Psalm began by declaring that Yahweh had searched and known the singer, and it ends by asking for that searching knowledge.

**139:24.** It makes much difference, not indeed in the reality or completeness of God's knowledge of us, but in the good we derive from his knowledge, whether we welcome and submit to it, or try to close our trembling hearts that do not wish to be cleansed of their perilous contents from that loving and purging gaze. God will cleanse the evil which He sees, if we are willing that He should see it. Thoughts of the inner life and "ways" of the outer are equally to be submitted to Him.

***Psalm 140.*** *The arrangement is in four strophes of approximately equal length, the first and third of which consist of three verses of two clauses each, while the second (vv.4f) has two verses of three clauses each, and the fourth is abnormally elongated by having three clauses in v. 10. Selah again appears as dividing the strophes, but is omitted at the end of the fourth, to which a closing strophe of two verses is appended.*

**140:1–5.** The first two strophes (vv. 1ff and 4f) cover the same ground. Both set forth the psalmist's need and plead for deliverance. The first verse of the second strophe (v. 4) is almost identical with v. 1. Both paint the psalmist's enemies as evil and violent, plotting against him privily. The only difference in the two strophes is in the metaphors describing the foes and their devices and in the prominence given in the first to their slanderous and sharp tongues. The forms of their malice are like those in earlier Psalms. A characteristic of the Psalter is the prominence given to hostility which has but bitter speech for its weapon (Pss. 10:7; 58:4). The slanderer's tongue is sharp like a serpent's, with which the popular opinion supposed that the venom was injected. The particular kind of serpent meant in v. 3a is unclear, as the word is only found here.

**140:6–9.** The figures for hostility in the second strophe are the other equally familiar ones of setting snares and traps. The contrivers are here called "proud," since their hostility to God's servant implies haughty antagonism to God. But they are

| 5734 | | 569.115 | 3937, 3176 | 418 | 887 | 237.531 | 3176 | 7249 |
|---|---|---|---|---|---|---|---|---|
| intrj | 6. | v Qal pf 1cs | prep, pn | n ms, ps 1cs | pers pron | v Hiphil impv 2ms | pn | *n ms* |
| סֶלָה | | אָמַרְתִּי | לַיהוָה | אֵלִי | אָתָּה | הַאֲזִינָה | יְהוָה | קוֹל |
| selāh | | 'āmartî | layhwāh | 'ēlî | 'āttāh | ha'ăzînāh | yehwāh | qôl |
| selah | | I have said | to Yahweh | my God | You | listen to | O Yahweh | the voice of |

| 8800 | | 3176 | 112 | 6010 | 3568 | 5718.113 |
|---|---|---|---|---|---|---|
| n mp, ps 1cs | 7. | pn | n mp, ps 1cs | *n ms* | n fs, ps 1cs | v Qal pf 2ms |
| תַּחֲנוּנָי | | יֱהוִֹה | אֲדֹנָי | עֹז | יְשׁוּעָתִי | סַכֹּתָה |
| tachnûnāy | | yehōwih | 'ădhōnāy | 'ōz | yeshû'āthî | sakkōthāh |
| my supplication | | O Yahweh | my Lord | the strength of | my salvation | You have covered |

| 3937, 7513 | 904, 3219 | 5584 | | 414, 5598.123 | 3176 | 4112 | 7857 |
|---|---|---|---|---|---|---|---|
| prep, n ms, ps 1cs | prep, *n ms* | n ms | 8. | adv, v Qal juss 2ms | pn | *n mp* | n ms |
| לְרֹאשִׁי | בְּיוֹם | נָשֶׁק | | אַל־תִּתֵּן | יְהוָה | מַאֲוַיֵּי | רָשָׁע |
| lerō'shî | beyôm | nāsheq | | 'al-tittēn | yehwāh | ma'ăwayyê | rāshā' |
| my head | on the day of | battle | | do not allow | O Yahweh | the desires of | the wicked |

| 2247 | 414, 6572.523 | 7597.126 | 5734 | | 7513 | 5621.552 |
|---|---|---|---|---|---|---|
| n ms, ps 3ms | adv, v Hiphil juss 2ms | v Qal impf 3mp | intrj | 9. | n ms | v Hiphil ptc mp, ps 1cs |
| זְמָמוֹ | אַל־תָּפֵק | יָרוּמוּ | סֶלָה | | רֹאשׁ | מְסִבָּי |
| zemāmô | 'al-tāphēq | yārûmû | selāh | | rō'sh | mesibbāy |
| his plan | do not disperse | they raise | selah | | the head | those who surround me |

| 6219 | 8004 | 3803.326 | | 4267.526 | 6142 | 1544 | 904, 813 |
|---|---|---|---|---|---|---|---|
| *n ms* | n fd, ps 3mp | v Piel juss 3mp, ps 3mp | 10. | v Hiphil juss 3mp | prep, ps 3mp | n fp | prep, art, n fs |
| עֲמַל | שְׂפָתֵימוֹ | יְכַסּוּמוֹ | | יָמִיטוּ | עֲלֵיהֶם | גֶּחָלִים | בָּאֵשׁ |
| 'āmal | sephāthêmô | yekhassûmô | | yāmîṭû | 'ălêhem | gechālîm | bā'ēsh |
| the harm of | their lips | may they cover them | | may they totter | over them | coals | in the fire |

| 5489.521 | 904, 4254 | 1118, 7251.126 | | 382 | 4098 |
|---|---|---|---|---|---|
| v Hiphil juss 3ms, ps 3mp | prep, n fp | neg part, v Qal juss 3mp | 11. | *n ms* | n fs |
| יַפִּלֵם | בְּמַהֲמֹרוֹת | בַּל־יָקוּמוּ | | אִישׁ | לָשׁוֹן |
| yappilēm | bemahmōrôth | bal-yāqûmû | | 'îsh | lāshôn |
| may He cause them to fall | into pits | may they not rise | | men of | a tongue |

| 1118, 3679.221 | 904, 800 | 382, 2660 | 7737 | 6942.121 | 3937, 4215 |
|---|---|---|---|---|---|
| neg part, v Niphal juss 3ms | prep, art, n fs | *n ms*, n ms | n ms | v Qal juss 3ms, ps 3ms | prep, n fp |
| בַּל־יִכּוֹן | בָּאָרֶץ | אִישׁ־חָמָס | רָע | יְצוּדֶנּוּ | לְמַדְחֵפֹת |
| bal-yikkôn | bā'ārets | 'îsh-chāmās | rā' | yetsûdhennû | lemadhechēphōth |
| may they not be established | in the land | men of violence | evil | may it hunt him | with haste |

| | 3156.115 | 3706, 6449.121 | 3176 | 1833 | 6270 | 5122 |
|---|---|---|---|---|---|---|
| 12. | v Qal pf 1cs | cj, v Qal impf 3ms | pn | *n ms* | n ms | *n ms* |
| | יָדַעְתִּ | כִּי־יַעֲשֶׂה | יְהוָה | דִּין | עָנִי | מִשְׁפַּט |
| | yādha'ti | kî-ya'ăseh | yehwāh | dîn | 'ānî | mishpaṭ |
| | I know | that He executes | Yahweh | the vindication of | the afflicted | the judgment for |

**6. I said unto the LORD, Thou art my God: hear the voice of my supplications, O LORD:** … hear me pleading for mercy, *Beck* … Listen, Yahweh, to the sound of my prayer, *JB* … oh listen to my plea, *Moffatt.*

**7. O GOD the Lord, the strength of my salvation:** … mighty to save me, *Beck* … my strong deliverer, *NRSV.*

**thou hast covered my head in the day of battle:** … you shield my head when battle comes, *JB* … you are my helmet in the day of battle!, *NCB* … who screenest me against attack, *Moffatt.*

**8. Grant not, O LORD, the desires of the wicked:** … Frustrate, O LORD, their designs against me, *NEB.*

**further not his wicked device:** … do not further their evil plot, *NRSV* … do not grant the wicked their wishes, *JB.*

**lest they exalt themselves. Selah:** … or he may be uplifted in pride, *BB* … do not let their plans succeed, or they will become proud, *NIV* … lest they praise themselves, *KJVII.*

**9. As for the head of those that compass me about:** ... As for those who come round me, *BB* ... If any of those at my table rise against me, *NEB* ... You have covered my head in the fight, *Fenton* ... Those around me have planned trouble, *NCV.*

**let the mischief of their own lips cover them:** ... may their conspiracies engulf them, *REB* ... Let the heads of those who surround me be covered with the trouble their lips have caused, *NIV* ... Let their plots boomerang!, *LIVB* ... let their conspiracy prove its own undoing, *Knox.*

**10. Let burning coals fall upon them:** ... May red-hot embers rain down on them *JB* ... And rain burning coals upon them, *Fenton.*

**let them be cast into the fire:** ... may they be thrown into the fire, *NIV* ... into the Fire may he plunge them!, *Anchor.*

**into deep pits, that they rise not up again:** ... and when he casts them into the watery pit, *Beck* ... and into deep waters, *BB* ... Let them be flung into pits, no more to rise!, *NRSV.*

**11. Let not an evil speaker be established in the earth:** ... May the slanderer not stand in the land, *Beck* ... Let not a man of evil tongue be safe on earth, *BB* ... A man of wicked tongue shall not abide in the land, *NAB* ... For the backbiter shall not be established vpon the earth, *Geneva.*

**evil shall hunt the violent man to overthrow him:** ... and disaster pursue the criminal, blow after blow, *Beck* ... may evil hunt down violent men implacably, *JB* ... May disaster pursue the violent man with blow upon blow!, *Goodspeed* ... may violent men be hunted from one woe to another!, *Moffatt.*

**12. I know that the LORD will maintain the cause of the afflicted:** ... I know that the Lord renders justice to the afflicted, *NCB,* ... Let them know that the LORD will do right, *Fenton* ... They shall find the Eternal champions, *Moffatt.*

**and the right of the poor:** ... the rights of those who are troubled, *BB* ... justice to the downtrodden, *REB* ... rights of the forlorn and feeble, *Moffatt* ... right of the needy, *MAST* ... defend the needy in court, *NCV.*

---

not too proud to resort to tricks. Cunning and pride do not go well together, but they are united in these enemies, who spread a net "by the hand of the path."

In the third strophe, faith rouses itself to lay hold on God. The psalmist turns from contemplating what his foes are doing, to realize what Yahweh is to him and wants to do for him. Since He is the singer's God and protects him in all conflict, he finds it in his heart to ask confidently that the plots of the foe may be wrecked. Consciousness of danger drove the poet in the former strophes to prayer; Yahweh's character and loving relations to him draw him in this one.

"The day of battle" (v. 7) is literally "the day of armor"—when weapons clash and helmets are fitting wear. Then Yahweh will be as a headpiece to him, for He always gives the shape to his help which is required at the moment. The words in v. 8 for "desires" (HED #4112) and "plan" (HED # 2247) are found here only.

**140:10–12.** Verse 10 is very obscure. According to the Hebrew text, the first clause would have to be rendered, "Let burning coals fall upon them," but such a rendering is contrary to the usage of the language. The Hebrew margin, therefore, corrects into, "Let them [i.e., men indefinitely] cast down coals," but this is harsh, and the office is strange as one attributed to men. The emendation which finds favor with most modern interpretors substitutes for the inappropriate verb of the present text that which is used in precisely the same connection in Ps. 11:6, and gives the reading, "Let Him [i.e., Yahweh] rain coals on them." The following clause then swiftly adds another element of horror. Fire rains down from above; fire yawns below. They are beaten down by the burning storm, and they fall into a mass of flame.

The noun in v. 10c (HED #4254) is found only here and is by some rendered "pits," by others "floods" and by others is corrected into "nets." If "floods" is taken as the meaning, destruction by water is set by the side of that by fire, as if the antagonistic elements forgot their opposition and joined in strange amity to sweep the wicked from the earth. The terrible strophe ends with the assured declaration of the divinely appointed transience of the evildoers, especially of the slanderers against whom the psalmist took refuge in Yahweh. They shall be soon cut off, and the hunters (v. 5) shall become the hunted. "Evil"—the punishment of their evil deeds—shall dog their heels and with stroke after stroke chase them as dogs would follow vermin.

**140:13.** In v. 13, the poet comes back to brighter thoughts, and his words become limpid again with his change of mood. He knows as the result of meditation and experience that not only he, but all the afflicted and needy who are righteous and upright, have God on their side. He will stand by their side in their hour of distress; He will admit them to dwell by his side, in deep, still communion, made more real and sweet by the harassments of earth, which drive them for shelter and peace to his breast. That confi-

| 33 | | 395 | 6926 | 3142.526 | 3937, 8428 | 3553.126 | 3596 |
|---|---|---|---|---|---|---|---|
| n mp | | adv | n mp | v Hiphil impf 3mp | prep, n ms, ps 3ms | v Qal impf 3mp | n mp |
| אֶבְיוֹנִים | **13.** | אַךְ | צַדִּיקִים | יוֹדוּ | לִשְׁמֶךָ | יֵשְׁבוּ | יְשָׁרִים |
| 'evyōnîm | | 'akh | tsaddîqîm | yôdhû | lishmekhā | yēshevû | yeshārîm |
| the needy | | surely | the righteous | they will praise | your name | they will dwell in | the upright |

| 881, 6686 | | 4344 | 3937, 1784 | | 3176 | 7410.115 | 2456.131 | 3937 |
|---|---|---|---|---|---|---|---|---|
| do, n mp, ps 2ms | | n ms | prep, pn | | pn | v Qal pf 1cs, ps 2ms | v Qal impv 2ms | prep, ps 1cs |
| אֶת־פָּנֶיךָ | **141:t** | מִזְמוֹר | לְדָוִד | **1.** | יְהוָה | קְרָאתִיךָ | חוּשָׁה | לִי |
| 'eth-pānêkhā | | mizemôr | ledhāwidh | | yehwāh | qōrā'thîkhā | chûshāh | lî |
| your presence | | a Psalm | of David | | O Yahweh | I have called to You | hurry | to me |

| 237.531 | 7249 | 904, 7410.141, 3937 | | 3679.222 | 8940 | 7285 |
|---|---|---|---|---|---|---|
| v Hiphil impv 2ms | n ms, ps 1cs | prep, v Qal inf con, ps 1cs, prep, ps 2ms | | v Niphal juss 3fs | n fs, ps 1cs | n fs |
| הַאֲזִינָה | קוֹלִי | בְּקָרְאִי־לָךְ | **2.** | תִּכּוֹן | תְּפִלָּתִי | קְטֹרֶת |
| ha'ăzînāh | qôlî | beqāre'î-lākh | | tikkôn | tephillāthî | qŏtōreth |
| listen to | my voice | when my calling to You | | may it endure | my prayer | incense |

| 3937, 6686 | 5020 | 3834 | 4647, 6394 | | 8308.131 | 3176 |
|---|---|---|---|---|---|---|
| prep, n mp, ps 2ms | *n fs* | n fd, ps 1cs | *n fs*, n ms | | v Qal impv 2ms | pn |
| לְפָנֶיךָ | מַשְׂאַת | כַּפַּי | מִנְחַת־עָרֶב | **3.** | שִׁיתָה | יְהוָה |
| lephānêkhā | mas'ath | kappay | minchath-'ārev | | shîthāh | yehwāh |
| before You | the lifting of | my hands | a sacrifice of the evening | | station | O Yahweh |

| 8494 | 3937, 6552 | 5526.131 | 6142, 1858 | 8004 | | 414, 5371.523, 3949 |
|---|---|---|---|---|---|---|
| n fs | prep, n ms, ps 1cs | v Qal impv 2ms | prep, *n ms* | n fd, ps 1cs | | adv, v Hiphil juss 2ms, n ms, ps 1cs |
| שָׁמְרָה | לְפִי | נִצְּרָה | עַל־דַּל | שְׂפָתָי | **4.** | אַל־תַּט־לִבִּי |
| shāmerāh | lephî | nitstserāh | 'al-dal | sephāthāy | | 'al-taṭ-libbî |
| a guard | for my mouth | keep watch | over the door of | my lips | | do not incline my heart |

| 3937, 1745 | 7737 | 3937, 6177.741 | 6173 | 904, 7856 |
|---|---|---|---|---|
| prep, n ms | n ms | prep, v Hithpoel inf con | n fp | prep, n ms |
| לְדָבָר | רָע | לְהִתְעוֹלֵל | עֲלִלוֹת | בְּרֶשַׁע |
| ledhāvār | rā' | lehith'ôlēl | 'ălilôth | beresha' |
| to a matter | evil | to act wantonly | deeds | with wickedness |

| 881, 382 | 6713.152, 201 | 1118, 4033.125 | 904, 4664 |
|---|---|---|---|
| prep, n mp | *v Qal act ptc mp*, n ms | cj, neg part, v Qal impf 1cs | prep, n mp, ps 3mp |
| אֶת־אִישִׁים | פֹּעֲלֵי־אָוֶן | וּבַל־אֶלְחַם | בְּמַנְעַמֵּיהֶם |
| 'eth-'îshîm | pō'ălê-'āwen | ûval-'elcham | beman'ammêhem |
| with men | those who practice iniquity | for I will not eat | of their delicacies |

| | 2056.121, 6926 | 2721 | 3306.521 | 8467 | 7513 |
|---|---|---|---|---|---|
| | v Qal juss 3ms, ps 1cs, n ms | n ms | cj, v Hiphil juss 3ms, ps 1cs | *n ms* | n ms |
| **5.** | יֶהֶלְמֵנִי־צַדִּיק | חֶסֶד | וְיוֹכִיחֵנִי | שֶׁמֶן | רֹאשׁ |
| | yehelmēnî-tsaddîq | chesedh | weyôkhîchēnî | shemen | rō'sh |
| | let a righteous man strike me | kindness | and let him chastise | the oil of | the head |

| 414, 5285.521 | 7513 | 3706, 5968 | 8940 | 904, 7750 |
|---|---|---|---|---|
| adv, v Hiphil juss 3ms | n ms, ps 1cs | cj, adv | cj, n fs, ps 1cs | prep, n fp, ps 3mp |
| אַל־יָנִי | רֹאשִׁי | כִּי־עוֹד | וּתְפִלָּתִי | בְּרָעוֹתֵיהֶם |
| 'al-yānî | rō'shî | kî-'ôdh | ûthephillāthî | berā'ôthêhem |
| do not frustrate | my head | because still | and my prayer | against their evil |

| | 8447.216 | 904, 3135, 5748 | 8570.152 | 8471.116 |
|---|---|---|---|---|
| | v Niphal pf 3cp | prep, *n fd*, n ms | v Qal act ptc mp, ps 3mp | cj, v Qal pf 3cp |
| **6.** | נִשְׁמְטוּ | בִידֵי־סֶלַע | שֹׁפְטֵיהֶם | וְשָׁמְעוּ |
| | nishmeṭû | vîdhê-sela' | shōphetêhem | weshāme'û |
| | they will be thrown down | by the side of the rock | their judges | then they will hear |

righteous than to feast with the wicked. But while this is the bearing of the first part of the verse, the last clause is obscure. The psalmist's continuance in prayer against the wicked is not very obviously a reason for his accepting kindly rebuke, but no better explanation is proposed.

**141:6.** The darkness thickens in v. 6. The words indeed are all easily translatable, but what the whole sentence means or what an allusion to the destruction of some unnamed people's rulers has to do here or who they are who hear the psalmist's words are questions as yet unanswered. Those who take the revolt under Absalom to be the occasion of the Psalm find in the casting down of these judges an imaginative description of the destruction of the leaders of the revolt, who are supposed to be hurled down the rocks by the people whom they had misled; while the latter, having again come to their right mind, attend to David's word and find it pleasant and beneficent. But this explanation requires much supplementing of the language and does not touch the difficulty of bringing the verse into connection with the preceding.

**141:7.** Nor is the connection with what follows more clear. A various reading substitutes "their" for "our" in v. 7 and so makes the whole verse a description of the bones of the ill-fated "judges" lying in a litter at the base of the precipice. But, apparently, the reading is merely an attempt to explain the difficulty. Clearly enough, the verse gives an extraordinarily energetic and graphic picture of a widespread slaughter. But who the slain are, and what event or events in the history of Israel are imaginatively reproduced here, is quite unknown. All that is certain is the tremendous force of the representation and the desperate condition to which it witnesses. The point of the figure lies in the resemblance of the bones strewn at the mouth of sheol to broken clods turned up by a plow. "Sheol" (HED #8061) seems here to waver between the meanings of the unseen world of souls and the grave. The unburied bones of slaughtered saints lie "scattered," as unregarded as the lumps of soil behind the plowman.

**141:8–9.** In vv. 8ff, the familiar Psalm tone recurs, and the language clears itself. The stream has been foaming among rocks in a gorge, but it has emerged into sunlight and flows smoothly. Only the "but" (HED #3706) at the beginning of v. 8 is difficult, if taken to refer to the immediately preceding verses. Rather, it overleaps the obscure middle part of the Psalm and links on to the petitions of vv. 1–4. Patient, trustful expectance is the psalmist's temper, which gazes not interrogatively, but with longing which is sure of satisfaction, toward God from amidst the temptations or sorrows of earth. The reason for that fixed look of faith lies in the divine names, so rich in promise, which are here blended in an unusual combination. The devout heart pleads its own act of faith in conjunction with God's names and is sure that, since He is "O GOD the Lord," it cannot be vain to hide oneself in Him. Therefore, the singer prays for preservation from destruction. "Pour not out my soul" recalls Isa. 53:12, where the same vivid metaphor is used. The prayer of the earlier verses was for protection from temptation; here, circumstances have darkened, and the psalmist's life is in danger. Possibly, the "snares" and "gins" of v. 9 mean both temptations and perils.

**141:10.** The final petition in v. 10 is like many in earlier Psalms. It was a fundamental article of faith for all the psalmists that a great *lex talionis* was at work, by which every sin was avenged in kind; if one looks deeper than the outside of life, the faith is eternally warranted. For nothing is more certain than that, whomever else a man may harm by his sin, he harms himself most. Nets woven and spread for others may or may not ensnare them, but their meshes cling inextricably around the feet of their author, and their tightening folds will wrap him helpless, like a fly in a spider's web. The last clause presents some difficulties. The word rendered above "at the same time" (HED #3266) is literally "together," but seems to be used here, as in Ps. 4:8, with the meaning of "simultaneously." The two things are cotemporaneous—the enemies' ensnaring and the psalmist's escape.

***Psalm 142.*** *The superscription not only calls this a Psalm of David, but specifies the circumstances of its composition. It breathes the same spirit of mingled fear and faith which characterizes many earlier Psalms. This psalmist has as deep sorrows as his predecessors and as firm a grasp of Yahweh, his helper. His song runs naturally in well-worn channels and is nonetheless genuine and acceptable to God because it does. Trouble and lack of human sympathy or help have done their best work on him, since they have driven him to God's breast. He has cried in vain to man; now he has gathered himself up in a firm resolve to cast himself upon God. Men may take offense that they are only appealed to as a last resort, but God does not. The psalmist is too much in earnest to be content with unspoken prayers. His voice must help his*

| | 5030 | 3937, 1784 | | 904, 2030.141 | 904, 4792 | 8940 | 7249 | 420, 3176 |
|---|---|---|---|---|---|---|---|---|
| | n ms | prep, pn | | prep, v Qal inf con, ps 3ms | prep, art, n fs | n fs | n ms, ps 1cs | prep, pn |
| 142:t | מַשְׂכִּיל | לְדָוִד | 1. | בִּהְיוֹתוֹ | בַמְּעָרָה | תְפִלָּה | קוֹלִי | אֶל־יְהוָה |
| | maskîl | ledhāwidh | | bihyôthô | vamme'ārāh | thephillāh | qôlî | 'el-yehwāh |
| | a Maskil | of David | | when his entering | into the cave | a Prayer | my voice | to Yahweh |

| 2283.125 | 7249 | 420, 3176 | 2706.725 | | 8581.125 | 3937, 6686 |
|---|---|---|---|---|---|---|
| v Qal impf 1cs | n ms, ps 1cs | prep, pn | v Hithpael impf 1cs | | v Qal impf 1cs | prep, n mp, ps 3ms |
| אֶזְעָק | קוֹלִי | אֶל־יְהוָה | אֶתְחַנָּן | 2. | אֶשְׁפֹּךְ | לְפָנָיו |
| 'ez'āq | qôlî | 'el-yehwāh | 'ethchannān | | 'eshpōkh | lephānâv |
| I cry out | my voice | to Yahweh | I make supplication | | I pour out | before Him |

| 7945 | 7150 | 3937, 6686 | 5222.525 | | 904, 6063.741 | 6142 |
|---|---|---|---|---|---|---|
| n ms, ps 1cs | n fs, ps 1cs | prep, n mp, ps 3ms | v Hiphil impf 1cs | | prep, v Hithpael inf con | prep, ps 1cs |
| שִׂיחִי | צָרָתִי | לְפָנָיו | אַגִּיד | 3. | בְּהִתְעַטֵּף | עָלַי |
| sîchî | tsārāthî | lephānâv | 'aggîdh | | behith'aṯṯēph | 'ālay |
| my complaint | my adversity | before Him | I tell | | when fainting | on me |

| 7593 | 887 | 3156.113 | 5594 | 904, 758, 2182 | 2050.325 | 3045.116 |
|---|---|---|---|---|---|---|
| n fs, ps 1cs | cj, pers pron | v Qal pf 2ms | n fs, ps 1cs | prep, n ms, rel part | v Piel impf 1cs | v Qal pf 3cp |
| רוּחִי | וְאַתָּה | יָדַעְתָּ | נְתִיבָתִי | בְּאֹרַח־זוּ | אֲהַלֵּךְ | טָמְנוּ |
| rûchî | we'attāh | yādha'āttā | nethîvāthî | be'ōrach-zû | 'ăhallēkh | ṯāmenû |
| my spirit | then You | You know | my pathway | on this path | I walk | they have hidden |

| 6583 | 3937 | | 5202.531 | 3332 | 7495.131 | 375, 3937 |
|---|---|---|---|---|---|---|
| n ms | prep, ps 1cs | | v Hiphil impv 2ms | n fs | cj, v Qal impv 2ms | cj, *sub*, prep, ps 1cs |
| פַּח | לִי | 4. | הַבֵּיט | יָמִין | וּרְאֵה | וְאֵין־לִי |
| phach | lî | | habbēṯ | yāmîn | ûre'ēh | we'ên-lî |
| a snare | for me | | look down on | the right side | and see | for there is not to me |

| 5422.551 | 6.111 | 4642 | 4623 | 375 | 1938.151 |
|---|---|---|---|---|---|
| v Hiphil ptc ms | v Qal pf 3ms | n ms | prep, ps 1cs | *sub* | v Qal act ptc ms |
| מַכִּיר | אָבַד | מָנוֹס | מִמֶּנִּי | אֵין | דּוֹרֵשׁ |
| makkîr | 'āvadh | mānôs̱ | mimmenî | 'ên | dôrēsh |
| one who recognizes | it is lost | the stronghold | of me | there is not | one who searches |

| 3937, 5497 | | 2283.115 | 420 | 3176 | 569.115 | 887 | 4406 | 2610 |
|---|---|---|---|---|---|---|---|---|
| prep, n fs, ps 1cs | | v Qal pf 1cs | prep, ps 2ms | pn | v Qal pf 1cs | pers pron | n ms, ps 1cs | n ms, ps 1cs |
| לְנַפְשִׁי | 5. | זָעַקְתִּי | אֵלֶיךָ | יְהוָה | אָמַרְתִּי | אַתָּה | מַחְסִי | חֶלְקִי |
| lenaphshî | | zā'aqōttî | 'ēlêkhā | yehwāh | 'āmartî | 'attāh | machs̱î | chelqî |
| for my life | | I cried out | to You | O Yahweh | I said | You | my Refuge | my Portion |

| 904, 800 | 2522 | | 7477.531 | 420, 7726 | 3706, 1870.115 | 4108 |
|---|---|---|---|---|---|---|
| prep, *n fs* | art, n mp | | v Hiphil impv 2ms | prep, n fs, ps 1cs | cj, v Qal pf 1cs | adv |
| בְּאֶרֶץ | הַחַיִּים | 6. | הַקְשִׁיבָה | אֶל־רִנָּתִי | כִּי־דַלּוֹתִי | מְאֹד |
| be'erets | hachayyîm | | haqōshîvāh | 'el-rinnāthî | kî-dhallôthî | me'ōdh |
| in the land of | the living | | be attentive | to my lamentation | because I have become low | very |

**whilst that I withal escape:** ... while I go free, *BB* ... while I pass on my way, *JB* ... while I myself pass safely by, *Berkeley.*

**142:t. Maschil of David; A Prayer when he was in the cave.**

**1. I cried unto the LORD with my voice:** ... To Yahweh I cry out with my plea, *JB* ... I shout with my voice to the LORD, *Fenton.*

**with my voice unto the LORD did I make my supplication:** ... and plead with the LORD for mercy, *Beck* ... I plead aloud for mercy, *NEB* ... tell him of the affliction I endure, *Knox.*

**2. I poured out my complaint before him:** ... I put all my sorrows before him, *BB* ... I pour out before Him my thoughts, *Fenton* ... I will pour out my grief before Him, *Berkeley.*

**I showed before him my trouble:** ... and tell Him my trouble, *Beck* ... in his presence I unfold my troubles, *JB.*

**3. When my spirit was overwhelmed within me:** ... When my spirit is faint, *NRSV* ... My heart is ready to faint within me, *Knox*

**then thou knewest my path:** ... thou art there to watch over my steps, *NEB* ... it is you who know my way, *NIV.*

**In the way wherein I walked have they privily laid a snare for me:** ... nets have been secretly placed in the way in which I go, *BB* ... they have hidden a trap for me, *JB.*

**4. I looked on my right hand, and beheld:** ... Look on my right and see, *JB* ... I look to right and left, *Moffatt* ... I look to the right and I watch, *Berkeley.*

**but there was no man that would know me:** ... nobody's concerned about me, *Beck* ... I saw no man who was my friend, *BB* ... there is no one who takes notice of me, *NRSV* ... I find no friend by my side, *NEB.*

**refuge failed me:** ... My escape is cut off, *Beck* ... I had no safe place, *BB* ... To me chance of flying had failed, *Fenton* ... escape was lost to me, *KJVII.*

**no man cared for my soul:** ... no one cares whether I live or die, *JB* ... no one comes to rescue me, *NEB* ... no one seeks my welfare, *Berkeley.*

**5. I cried unto thee, O LORD:** ... Then, LORD, I shouted to You, *Fenton.*

**I said, Thou art my refuge and my portion in the land of the living:** ... You are my safe place, and my heritage in the land of the living, *BB* ... Thou art all I have in the land of the living, *NEB* ... My support in the land where we live, *Fenton.*

**6. Attend unto my cry:** ... Listen to me calling loud, *Beck* ... my cry of entreaty, *Berkeley* ... my cry, *NCV.*

**for I am brought very low:** ... for I am miserably weak, *JB* ... because I am helpless, *NCV* ... thou seest me all defenceless, *Knox.*

**deliver me from my persecutors:** ... Save me from those who harass me, *REB* ... rescue me from those who pursue me, *NIV.*

---

*thoughts. Wonderful is the power of articulate utterance in defining, and often in diminishing, sorrows. Put into words, many a burden shrinks. Speaking his grief, many a man is calmed and braced to endure. The complaint poured out before God ceases to flood the spirit; the straits told to Him begin to grip less tightly.*

**142:1–4.** Verse 1 resembles Ps. 77:1, and v. 3 has the same vivid expression for a spirit swathed in melancholy as Ps. 77:3. The outpouring of complaint is not meant to tell Yahweh what He does not know. It is for the complainer's relief, not for God's information. However a soul is wrapped in gloom, the thought that God knows the road which is so dark brings a little creeping beam into the blackness. In the strength of that conviction, the psalmist beseeches Yahweh to behold what He does behold. That is the paradox of faithful prayer, which asks for what it knows that it possesses and dares not ask unless it knew.

The form of the word rendered "look" (HED # 5202) is irregular, a hybrid; but when standing beside the following "see," it is best taken as an imperative of petition to Yahweh. The old versions render both words as first person singular, in which they are followed by several scholars. It is perhaps more natural that the psalmist should represent himself as looking around in vain for help than that he should ask God to look. As some have remarked, the copula before "There is none" in v. 4b favors this reading, as it is superfluous with an imperative. In either case, the focus of v. 4 is to set forth the suppliant's forlorn condition. The "right hand" is the place for a champion or helper, but this lonely sufferer's is unguarded, and there is none who knows him in the sense of recognizing him as one to be helped (Ruth 2:10, 19). Thus abandoned, friendless and solitary, confronted by foes, he looks about for some place to hide in; but that too has failed him (Job 11:20; Jer. 25:35; Amos 2:14). There is no man interested enough in him to make inquiry after his life. Whether he is alive or dead does not matter to anyone.

**142:5.** Thus, utterly naked of help, allies and earthly hiding place, what can a man do but fling himself into the arms of God? This one does so, as the rest of the Psalm tells. He had looked all around the horizon in vain for a safe cranny to creep into and escape. He was out in the open, without a bush or rock to hide behind, on all the dreary level. So he looks up, and suddenly there rises by his side an inexpungable fortress, as if a mountain sprang at once from the flat earth. "I said, Thou art my refuge!" Whoever says this has a shelter, someone to care for him, and the gloom begins to thin off from his soul. The psalmist is not only safe in consequence of his prayer, but rich; for the soul which, by strong resolve, even in the midst of straits, claims God as its portion will at once realize its portion in God.

**142:6–7.** The prayer for complete deliverance in vv. 6f passes into calmness, even while it contin-

| 5522.531 | 7579.152 | 3706 | 563.116 | 4623 |
|---|---|---|---|---|
| v Hiphil impv 2ms, ps 1cs | prep, v Qal act ptc mp, ps 1cs | cj | v Qal pf 3cp | prep, ps 1cs |
| הַצִּילֵנִי | מֵרֹדְפַי | כִּי | אָמְצוּ | מִמֶּנִּי |
| hatstsîlēnî | mērōdhephay | kî | 'āmetsû | mimmenî |
| rescue me | from my persecutors | because | they are stronger | than I |

| 7. | 3428.531 | 4623, 4674 | 5497 | 3937, 3142.541 | 881, 8428 | 904 |
|---|---|---|---|---|---|---|
| | v Hiphil impv 2ms | prep, n ms | n fs, ps 1cs | prep, v Hiphil inf con | do, n ms, ps 2ms | prep, ps 1cs |
| | הוֹצִיאָה | מִמַּסְגֵּר | נַפְשִׁי | לְהוֹדוֹת | אֶת־שְׁמֶךָ | בִּי |
| | hôtsî'āh | mimmasgēr | naphshî | lehôdhôth | 'eth-shemekhā | bî |
| | bring out | from prison | my life | for praising | your name | by me |

| 3932.526 | 6926 | 3706 | 1621.123 | 6142 | 143:t | 4344 | 3937, 1784 |
|---|---|---|---|---|---|---|---|
| v Hiphil impf 3mp | n mp | cj | v Qal impf 2ms | prep, ps 1cs | | n ms | prep, pn |
| יַכְתִּרוּ | צַדִּיקִים | כִּי | תִגְמֹל | עָלָי | | מִזְמוֹר | לְדָוִד |
| yakhtirû | tsaddîqîm | kî | thighmōl | 'ālāy | | mizmôr | ledhāwidh |
| they surround | the righteous | because | You will reward | concerning me | | a Psalm | of David |

| 1. | 3176 | 8471.131 | 8940 | 237.531 | 420, 8800 | 904, 536 |
|---|---|---|---|---|---|---|
| | pn | v Qal impv 2ms | n fs, ps 1cs | v Hiphil impv 2ms | prep, n mp, ps 1cs | prep, n fs, ps 2ms |
| | יְהוָה | שְׁמַע | תְּפִלָּתִי | הַאֲזִינָה | אֶל־תַּחֲנוּנַי | בֶּאֱמֻנָתְךָ |
| | yehwāh | shema' | tephillāthî | ha'ăzînāh | 'el-tachnûnay | be'ĕmunāthekhā |
| | O Yahweh | hear | my prayer | listen | to my supplication | by your faithfulness |

| 6257.131 | 904, 6930 | 2. | 414, 971.123 | 904, 5122 | 882, 5860 |
|---|---|---|---|---|---|
| v Qal impv 2ms, ps 1cs | prep, n fs, ps 2ms | | cj, adv, v Qal juss 2ms | prep, n ms | prep, n ms, ps 2ms |
| עֲנֵנִי | בְּצִדְקָתֶךָ | | וְאַל־תָּבוֹא | בְמִשְׁפָּט | אֶת־עַבְדֶּךָ |
| 'ănēnî | betsidhqāthekhā | | we'al-tāvô' | vemishpāṭ | 'eth-'avdekhā |
| answer me | in your righteousness | | and do not enter | into judgment | with your servant |

| 3706 | 3940, 6927.121 | 3937, 6686 | 3725, 2508 | 3. | 3706 | 7579.111 | 342.151 |
|---|---|---|---|---|---|---|---|
| cj | neg part, v Qal impf 3ms | prep, n mp, ps 2ms | *adj*, adj | | cj | v Qal pf 3ms | v Qal act ptc ms |
| כִּי | לֹא־יִצְדַּק | לְפָנֶיךָ | כָל־חָי | | כִּי | רָדַף | אוֹיֵב |
| kî | lō'-yitsdaq | lephānêkhā | khol-chāy | | kî | rādhaph | 'ôyēv |
| because | they are not righteous | before You | all living | | because | he pursued | an enemy |

| 5497 | 1850.311 | 3937, 800 | 2508 | 3553.511 | 904, 4423 |
|---|---|---|---|---|---|
| n fs, ps 1cs | v Piel pf 3ms | prep, art, n fs | n fs, ps 1cs | v Hiphil pf 3ms, ps 1cs | prep, n mp |
| נַפְשִׁי | דִּכָּא | לָאָרֶץ | חַיָּתִי | הוֹשִׁיבַנִי | בְמַחֲשַׁכִּים |
| naphshî | dikkā' | lā'ārets | chayyāthî | hôshîvanî | vemachshakkîm |
| my life | he crushed | to the ground | my life | He caused me to sit | in a dark place |

| 3626, 4322.152 | 5986 | 4. | 6063.722 | 6142 | 7593 | 904, 8761 |
|---|---|---|---|---|---|---|
| prep, *v Qal act ptc mp* | n ms | | cj, v Hithpael impf 3fs | prep, ps 1cs | n fs, ps 1cs | prep, n ms, ps 1cs |
| כְּמֵתֵי | עוֹלָם | | וַתִּתְעַטֵּף | עָלַי | רוּחִי | בְּתוֹכִי |
| kemēthê | 'ôlām | | wattith'aṭṭēph | 'ālay | rûchî | bethôkhî |
| like the dead of | eternity | | and it faints | on me | my spirit | within me |

| 8460.721 | 3949 | 5. | 2226.115 | 3219 | 4623, 7208 | 1965.115 | 904, 3725, 6713 |
|---|---|---|---|---|---|---|---|
| v Hithpoel impf 3ms | n ms, ps 1cs | | v Qal pf 1cs | n mp | prep, n ms | v Qal pf 1cs | prep, *adj*, n ms, ps 2ms |
| יִשְׁתּוֹמֵם | לִבִּי | | זָכַרְתִּי | יָמִים | מִקֶּדֶם | הָגִיתִי | בְכָל־פָּעֳלֶךָ |
| yishtômēm | libbî | | zākhartî | yāmîm | miqqedhem | hāghîthî | vekhol-pā'ălekhā |
| it is appalled | my heart | | I remember | days | of antiquity | I meditate | on all your doing |

| 904, 4801 | 3135 | 7943.325 | 6. | 6816.315 | 3135 | 420 | 5497 |
|---|---|---|---|---|---|---|---|
| prep, *n ms* | n fd, ps 2ms | v Polel impf 1cs | | v Piel pf 1cs | n fd, ps 1cs | prep, ps 2ms | n fs, ps 1cs |
| בְּמַעֲשֵׂה | יָדֶיךָ | אֲשׂוֹחֵחַ | | פֵּרַשְׂתִּי | יָדַי | אֵלֶיךָ | נַפְשִׁי |
| bema'ăsēh | yādhêkhā | 'ăsôchēach | | pērastî | yādhay | 'ēlêkhā | naphsh, |
| on the work of | your hands | I ponder | | I spread out | my hands | to You | my soul |

**for they are stronger than I:** ... because they are too strong for me, *NCV.*

**7. Bring my soul out of prison, that I may praise thy name:** ... Set me free from my prison, *NEB.*

**the righteous shall compass me about:** ... The righteous will crowd around me, *Beck* ... shall crown me with garlands, *NEB* ... The just shall gather around me, *NAB* ... for good men are waiting, *Moffatt.*

**for thou shalt deal bountifully with me:** ... for you have given me a full reward, *BB* ... because of your generosity to me, *JB* ... till thou deal kindly with me, *Moffatt* ... rejoicing to see they favour restored!, *Knox.*

**143:t. A Psalm of David.**

**1. Hear my prayer, O LORD, give ear to my supplications:** ... Listen, Lord, to my prayer; give my plea a hearing, *Knox* ... give ear, O El, to my plea for mercy, *Anchor* ... listen to my cry for mercy, *NCV* ... be true to thyself, and listen to my pleading, *NEB.*

**in thy faithfulness answer me:** ... come to my relief, *NIV* ... In thy fidelity answer me, *Goodspeed* ... In Your Justice give answer to me, *Fenton.*

**and in thy righteousness:** ... thou who lovest the right, *Knox* ... in your saving justice, *JB.*

**2. And enter not into judgment with thy servant:** ... But do not bring your servant into court, *Anchor* ... put not thy servant on his trial, *Moffatt* ... do not put your servant on trial, *JB.*

**for in thy sight shall no man living be justified:** ... in Your sight no one living is righteous, *NKJV...* before thee no living soul can be acquitted, *Moffatt* ... no one living can be found guiltless at your tribunal, *JB.*

**3. For the enemy hath persecuted my soul:** ... See how my enemies plot against my life, *Knox* ... My enemies are chasing me, *NCV* ... For the enemy has hunted after my soul, *Berkeley* ... The evil man has gone after my soul, *BB.*

**he hath smitten my life down to the ground:** ... He has crushed my life to the ground, *NKJV* ... how they have abased me in the dust, *Knox* ... ground my life into the nether world, *Anchor* ... has trampled my life to the ground, *Berkeley* ... has ground my living body under foot, *NEB.*

**he hath made me to dwell in darkness, as those that have been long dead:** ... like the ancient dead, *Rotherham* ... like the men of the eternal home, *Anchor* ... and left me to lie in darkness like those long dead, *REB.*

**4. Therefore is my spirit overwhelmed within me:** ... My spirits are crushed within me, *Knox* ... And my spirit in me is become feeble, *Young* ... And my spirit has become weak within me, *KJVII.*

**my heart within me is desolate:** ... my heart is cowed, *Knox* ... my heart has become weary within me, *KJVII* ... My heart is appalled within me, *NASB* ... I am afraid; my courage is gone, *NCV* ... And my heart in my breast is depressed, *Fenton.*

**5. I remember the days of old:** ... I have remembered the days of aforetime, *Rotherham* ... I call to mind times long past, *REB* ... I recall the days of old, *JB.*

---

ues fully conscious of peril and of the power of the pursuers. Such is the reward of invoking Yahweh's help. Agitation is soothed, and, even before any outward effect has been manifest, the peace of God begins to shed itself over heart and mind.

The suppliant still spreads his needs before God, is still conscious of much weakness, of strong persecutors, and feels that he is, as it were, in prison. But he has hold of God now, and so is sure of deliverance, and already begins to shape his lips for songs of praise and to anticipate the triumph which his experience will afford to those who are righteous, and so are his fellows. He was not, then, so utterly solitary as he had wailed that he was. There were some who would joy in his joy, even if they could not help his misery. But the soul that has to wade through deep waters has always to do it alone; for no human sympathy reaches to full knowledge of, or share in, even the best loved one's grief. We have companions in joy; sorrow we have to face by ourselves. Unless we have Jesus with us in the darkness, we have no one.

***Psalm 143.*** *The former half of this Psalm (vv. 1–6) is complaint; the latter (vv. 7–12), petition. It is clearly divided into two equal halves, as indicated by the selah, which is not found in books four and five, except here and in Ps. 140. Each part may again may be regarded as falling into two equal portions, so that the complaint branches out into a plaintive description of the psalmist's peril (vv. 1ff) and a melancholy disclosure of his feelings (vv. 4ff), while the prayer is similarly parted into cries for deliverance (vv. 7ff) and for inward enlightenment and help (vv. 10–12). We are not reading a logical treatise, however, but listening to the cry of a tried spirit, and so we need not wonder if the discernible sequence of thought is here and there broken.*

**143:1–6.** The psalmist knows that his affliction is deserved. His enemy could not have hunted and crushed him (v. 3) unless God had been thereby

| 3626, 800, 6107 | 3937 | 5734 | | 4257.341 | 6257.131 | 3176 |
|---|---|---|---|---|---|---|
| prep, n fs, adj | prep, ps 2ms | intrj | **7.** | v Piel inf con | v Qal impv 2ms, ps 1cs | pn |
| כְּאֶרֶץ־עֲיֵפָה | לְךָ | סֶלָה | | מַהֵר | עֲנֵנִי | יְהוָה |
| ke'erets-'ăyēphāh | lekhā | selāh | | mahēr | 'ănēnî | yehwāh |
| like a waterless territory | to You | selah | | acting quickly | answer me | O Yahweh |

| 3735.112 | 7593 | 414, 5846.523 | 6686 | 4623 |
|---|---|---|---|---|
| v Qal pf 3fs | n fs, ps 1cs | adv, v Hiphil juss 2ms | n mp, ps 2ms | prep, ps 1cs |
| כָּלְתָה | רוּחִי | אַל־תַּסְתֵּר | פָּנֶיךָ | מִמֶּנִּי |
| kālethāh | rûchî | 'al-tastēr | pānêkhā | mimmenî |
| it comes to an end | my spirit | do not hide | your face | from me |

| 5090.215 | 6196, 3495.152 | 988 | | 8471.531 |
|---|---|---|---|---|
| cj, v Niphal pf 1cs | prep, *v Qal act ptc mp* | n ms | **8.** | art, v Hiphil impv 2ms, ps 1cs |
| וְנִמְשַׁלְתִּי | עִם־יֹרְדֵי | בוֹר | | הַשְׁמִיעֵנִי |
| wenimshaltî | 'im-yōredhê | vôr | | hashmî'ênî |
| then I would become similar | with those going down to | the Pit | | cause me to hear |

| 904, 1269 | 2721 | 3706, 904 | 1019.115 | 3156.531 |
|---|---|---|---|---|
| prep, art, n ms | n ms, ps 2ms | cj, prep, ps 2ms | v Qal pf 1cs | v Hiphil impv 2ms, ps 1cs |
| בַבֹּקֶר | חַסְדֶּךָ | כִּי־בְךָ | בָטָחְתִּי | הוֹדִיעֵנִי |
| vabbōqer | chasdekhā | kî-vekhā | vātāchättî | hôdhî'ênî |
| in the morning | your steadfast love | because in You | I trust | cause me to know |

| 1932, 2182 | 2050.125 | 3706, 420 | 5558.115 | 5497 | | 5522.531 |
|---|---|---|---|---|---|---|
| n ms, rel part | v Qal impf 1cs | cj, prep, ps 2ms | v Qal pf 1cs | n fs, ps 1cs | **9.** | v Hiphil impv 2ms, ps 1cs |
| דֶּרֶךְ־זוּ | אֵלֵךְ | כִּי־אֵלֶיךָ | נָשָׂאתִי | נַפְשִׁי | | הַצִּילֵנִי |
| derekh-zû | 'ēlēkh | kî-'ēlêkhā | nāsā'thî | naphshî | | hatstsîlēnî |
| the way which | I should walk | because to You | I lift up | my soul | | rescue me |

**I meditate on all thy works:** … I think of all thou didst once, *Knox* … I have talked with myself of every deed of thine, *Rotherham* … I think over all you have done, *REB.*

**I muse on the work of thy hands:** … dwell on the proofs thou gavest of thy power, *Knox* … and consider what your hands have done, *NIV* … the wonders of your creation fill my mind, *REB* … I ponder the works of your hands, *JB.*

**6. I stretch forth my hands unto thee:** … I spread out my hands to You, *NKJV* … To thee I lift my outspread hands, *NEB* … My hands are stretched out to you, *BB.*

**my soul thirsteth after thee, as a thirsty land:** … My soul is as a weary land for Thee, *Young* … in the nether world my throat is parched with thirst for you, *Anchor* … I long for thee like a parched land, *Goodspeed* … My body to You, like earth's dust!, *Fenton.*

**Selah:** … Music, *Beck* … Pause, *JB.*

**7. Hear me speedily, O LORD:** … Answer me speedily, O LORD, *NKJV* … Answer me quickly, *NASB* … Make haste to answer me, O Jehovah, *ASV* … LORD, answer me soon, *REB.*

**my spirit faileth:** … My spirit hath been consumed, *Young* … my spirit is worn out, *JB* … for the strength of my spirit is gone, *BB* … my spirit wears out with longing, *Beck.*

**hide not thy face from me:** … Do no turn thy face away from me, *Knox* … Oh! hide not Your presence from me, *Fenton.*

**lest I be like unto them that go down into the pit:** … and leave me like one sunk in the abyss, *Knox* … I would resemble those who have descended the Pit, *Anchor* … or I will be like those who are dead, *NCV* … or I shall be like those who go down to the abyss, *REB.*

**8. Cause me to hear thy lovingkindness in the morning:** … Tell me in the morning about your love, *NCV* … Let me hear in the morning of thy steadfast love, *RSV* … Satisfy me with the dawn of thy love, *Moffatt* … Let me hear of Your mercy at dawn, *Fenton.*

**for in thee do I trust:** … For on You is my trust, *Fenton* … I have put my trust in thee, *NEB* … for in thee do I confide, *Darby.*

**cause me to know the way wherein I should walk:** … Show me the road which I must travel, *Anchor* … Show me the way I should go, *NIV.*

**for I lift up my soul unto thee:** … because my prayers go up to you, *NCV* … For unto thee I lift my desire, *Goodspeed.*

**9. Deliver me, O LORD, from mine enemies:** … Rescue me from my foes, Yahweh, *Anchor* … take me out of the hands of my haters, *BB.*

punishing him. His peril has forced home the penitent conviction of his sin, and therefore, he must first have matters set right between him and God by divine forgiveness.

His cry for help is not based upon any claims of his own, nor even on his extremity of need, but solely on God's character, and especially on the twin attributes of faithfulness and righteousness. By the latter is not meant the retributive righteousness which gives according to what is deserved, but that by which He maintains the order of salvation established by his holy love. The prayer anticipates John's declaration that God is "faithful and just to forgive us our sins" (1 John 1:9).

That answer in righteousness is just as eagerly desired as God's retributive judgment would be undesirable. "Enter not into judgment with thy servant" is not a prayer referring to a future appearance before the Judge of all, but the judgment deprecated is plainly the enmity of men, which, as the next verse complains, is crushing the psalmist's life out of him. His cry is for deliverance from it, but he feels that a more precious gift must precede outward deliverance, and God's forgiveness must first be sealed on his soul. The conviction that, when the light of God's face is turned on the purest life, it reveals dark stains which retributive justice cannot but condemn, is not, in the psalmist's mouth, a palliation of his guilt. Rather, it drives him to take his place among the multitude of offenders and, from that lowly position, to cry for pardon to the very Judge whose judgment he cannot meet. The blessedness of contrite trust is that it nestles the closer to God, the more it feels its unworthiness. The child hides its face on the mother's bosom when it has done wrong. God is our refuge from God. A little beam of light steals into the penitent's darkness, while he calls himself God's servant, and ventures to plead that relation, though he has done what was unworthy of it, as a reason for pardon.

The significant "for" (HED # 3706) beginning v. 3 shows that the enemy's acts were, to the contrite psalmist, those of God's stern justice. Verse 3a and b is molded on Ps. 7:5, and 3c is verbally identical with Lam. 3:6. "The dead of long ago" is by some rendered "dead forever"; but the translation adopted above adds force to the psalmist's sad description of himself by likening him to those forgotten ones way back in the mists of bygone ages.

In vv. 4ff, the record of the emotions caused by his peril follows. They begin with the natural gloom. As in Ps. 142:3 (with which this has many points of resemblance, possibly indicating identity of author), he describes his "spirit" as swathed in dark robes of melancholy. His heart, too, the center of personality, was stunned or benumbed, so that it almost ceased to beat. What should a "servant" of Yahweh's, brought to such a pass, do? If he is truly God's, he will do precisely what this man did. He will compel his thoughts to take another direction and call memory in to fight despair and feed hope. His own past and God's past are arguments enough to cheer the most gloomy sufferer.

"A sorrow's crown of sorrow" may be "remembering happier things," but the remembrance will be better used to discrown a sorrow which threatens to lord it over a life. Psalm 77:5f, 11f has shaped the expressions here. Both the contrast of present misery with past mercy and the assurances of present help given by that past mercy move the psalmist to appeal to God, stretching out his hands in entreaty. Psalm 63:1 echoes in v. 6b the pathos and beauty of which need no elucidation. The very cracks in parched ground are like mouths opened for the delaying rains; so also the singer's soul was gaping wide in trouble for God's coming, which would refresh and fertilize. Blessed is that weariness which is directed to Him; it ever brings the showers of grace for which it longs. The construction of v. 6b is doubtful, and the supplement "thirsteth" (KJV and RV) is possibly better than the "is" given above.

**143:7–9.** A glance at these three verses of petition as a whole brings out the sequence of the prayers and of their pleas. The deepest longing of the devout soul is for the shining of God's face, the consciousness of his loving regard, and that not only because it scatters fears and foes, but because it is good to bathe in that sunshine.

The next longing is for the dawning of a glad morning, which will bring to a waiting heart sweet whispers of God's steadfast love, as shown by outward deliverances. The night of fear has been dark and tearful, but joy comes with the morning. The next need is for guidance in the way in which a man should go, which here must be taken in the lower sense of practical direction, rather than in any higher meaning.

That higher meaning follows in vv. 10ff, but in v. 8, the suppliant asks to be shown the path by which he can secure deliverance from his foes. That deliverance is the last of his petitions. His pleas are beautiful as examples of the logic of supplication.

| 4623, 342.152 | 3176 | 420 | 3803.315 | | 4064.331 |
|---|---|---|---|---|---|
| prep, v Qal act ptc mp, ps 1cs | pn | prep, ps 2ms | v Piel pf 1cs | **10.** | v Piel impv 2ms, ps 1cs |
| מֵאֹיְבַי | יְהוָה | אֵלֶיךָ | כִסִּתִי | | לַמְּדֵנִי |
| mē'ōyevay | yehwāh | 'ēlêkhā | khissithî | | lammedhēnî |
| from my enemies | O Yahweh | to You | I have sought refuge | | teach me |

| 3937, 6449.141 | 7814 | 3706, 887 | 435 | 7593 | 3009B | 5328.523 |
|---|---|---|---|---|---|---|
| prep, v Qal inf con | n ms, ps 2ms | cj, pers pron | n mp, ps 1cs | n fs, ps 2ms | adj | v Hiphil impf 2ms, ps 1cs |
| לַעֲשׂוֹת | רְצוֹנֶךָ | כִּי־אַתָּה | אֱלוֹהָי | רוּחֲךָ | טוֹבָה | תַּנְחֵנִי |
| la'ăsôth | retsônekhā | kî-'attāh | 'ĕlôhāy | rûchăkhā | ṯôvāh | tanchēnî |
| to do | your will | because You | my God | your Spirit | good | You lead me |

| 904, 800 | 4473 | | 3937, 4775, 8428 | 3176 | 2513.323 |
|---|---|---|---|---|---|
| prep, *n fs* | n ms | **11.** | prep, prep, n ms, ps 2ms | pn | v Piel impf 2ms, ps 1cs |
| בְּאֶרֶץ | מִישׁוֹר | | לְמַעַן־שִׁמְךָ | יְהוָה | תְּחַיֵּנִי |
| be'erets | mîshôr | | lema'an-shimkhā | yehwāh | techayyēnî |
| in the land of | level ground | | because of your name | O Yahweh | keep me alive |

| 904, 6930 | 3428.523 | 4623, 7150 | 5497 | | 904, 2721 |
|---|---|---|---|---|---|
| prep, n fs, ps 2ms | v Hiphil impf 2ms | prep, n fs | n fs, ps 1cs | **12.** | cj, prep, n ms, ps 2ms |
| בְּצִדְקָתְךָ | תוֹצִיא | מִצָּרָה | נַפְשִׁי | | וּבְחַסְדְּךָ |
| betsidhqāthekhā | thôtsî' | mitstsārāh | naphshî | | ûvechasdekhā |
| by your righteousness | You lead | out of adversity | me life | | and by your faithfulness |

| 7059.523 | 342.152 | 6.513 | 3725, 7173.152 | 5497 | 3706 |
|---|---|---|---|---|---|
| v Hiphil impf 2ms | v Qal act ptc mp, ps 1cs | cj, v Hiphil pf 2ms | *adj, v Qal act ptc mp* | n fs, ps 1cs | cj |
| תַּצְמִית | אֹיְבָי | וְהַאֲבַדְתָּ | כָּל־צֹרְרֵי | נַפְשִׁי | כִּי |
| tatsmîth | 'ōyevāy | weha'ăvadhtā | kol-tsōrerê | naphshî | kî |
| You annihilate | my enemies | and You destroy | all the oppressors of | my life | because |

| 603 | 5860 | | 3937, 1784 | | 1313.155 | 3176 | 6962 | 4064.351 |
|---|---|---|---|---|---|---|---|---|
| pers pron | n ms, ps 2ms | **144:t** | prep, pn | **1.** | v Qal pass ptc ms | pn | n ms, ps 1cs | art, v Piel ptc ms |
| אֲנִי | עַבְדֶּךָ | | לְדָוִד | | בָּרוּךְ | יְהוָה | צוּרִי | הַמְלַמֵּד |
| 'ănî | 'avdekhā | | ledhāwidh | | bārûkh | yehwāh | tsûrî | hamlammēdh |
| I | your servant | | of David | | blessed | Yahweh | my Rock | the One Who teaches |

| 3135 | 3937, 7417 | 697 | 3937, 4560 | | 2721 | 4849 |
|---|---|---|---|---|---|---|
| n fd, ps 1cs | prep, art, n ms | n fp, ps 1cs | prep, art, n fs | **2.** | n ms, ps 1cs | cj, n fs, ps 1cs |
| יָדַי | לַקְרָב | אֶצְבְּעוֹתַי | לַמִּלְחָמָה | | חַסְדִּי | וּמְצוּדָתִי |
| yādhay | laqŏrāv | 'etsbe'ôthay | lammilchāmāh | | chasdî | ûmetsûdhāthî |
| my hands | for the battle | my fingers | for the war | | my steadfast Love | and my Fortress |

| 5021 | 6647.351 | 3937 | 4182 | 904 |
|---|---|---|---|---|
| n ms, ps 1cs | cj, v Piel ptc ms, ps 1cs | prep, ps 1cs | n ms, ps 1cs | cj, prep, ps 3ms |
| מִשְׂגַּבִּי | וּמְפַלְטִי | לִי | מָגִנִּי | וּבוֹ |
| misgabbî | ûmephaltî | lî | māghinî | ûvô |
| my Stronghold | and the One Who sets me free | to me | my Shield | and in Whom |

**I flee unto thee to hide me:** ... In You I take shelter, *NKJV* ... to thee I fly for refuge, *Knox* ... Unto thee have I come seeking refuge, *Rotherham* ... truly am I being submerged, *Anchor* ... I take refuge in Thee, *NASB*.

**10. Teach me to do thy will:** ... Teach me to do Thy good pleasure, *Young* ... Give me teaching so that I may do your pleasure, *BB*.

**for thou art my God:** ... because you are my God, *NCV*.

**thy spirit is good:** ... With your good spirit lead me, *Anchor* ... For Your spirit is pleasant, my God, *Fenton* ... in thy gracious kindness, *NEB*.

**lead me into the land of uprightness:** ... safe ground under my feet, *Knox* ... Wilt thou set me down to rest in a level, *Rotherham* ... Let thy good spirit guide me in a straight path, *Goodspeed* ... It can lead to the land that is safe, *Fenton* ... show me the level road, *NEB*.

**11. Quicken me, O LORD, for thy name's sake:** ... Revive me, O LORD, for Your name's sake!, *NKJV* ... For the honour of thy own name, *Knox* ... For the sake of Thy name, O Lord, revive me, *NASB*.

**for thy righteousness' sake bring my soul out of trouble:** ... In thy righteousness wilt thou bring forth, out of distress, my soul, *Rotherham* ... Save me from my troubles, *NCV* ... preserve my life!, *RSV* ... reduce my enemies to silence, *NEB*.

**12. And of thy mercy cut off mine enemies:** ... In your love defeat my enemies, *NCV* ... And in thy lovingkindness cut off mine enemies, *MRB* ... Cut off in Your mercy my foes, *Fenton*.

**and destroy all them that afflict my soul:** ... make an end of my cruel persecutors, *Knox* ... silence my enemies, *NIV* ... And destroy all who tortured my life, *Fenton*.

**for I am thy servant:** ... For I am Your slave, *Fenton*.

**144:t. A Psalm of David.**

**1. Blessed be the LORD my strength:** ... Blessed be the LORD my Rock, *NKJV*, *MRB* ... Blest be the Eternal One, my Strength, *Moffatt*.

**which teacheth my hands to war:** ... Who trains my hands for war, *NKJV* ... who makes these hands strong for battle, *Knox*.

**and my fingers to fight:** ... these fingers skilled in fight, *Knox* ... My fingers for battle, *Goodspeed*.

**2. My goodness, and my fortress:** ... My kind one, and my bulwark, *Young* ... my Crag, my Stronghold, *Moffatt* ... My hope, and my fortress, *Fenton*.

**my high tower, and my deliverer:** ... My stronghold and my deliverer, *NASB* ... my Fortalice and Deliverer, *Moffatt* ... My precipice, and my

---

He begins with his great need. His spirit faints, and he is on the edge of the black pit into which so much brightness and strength have gone down. The margin is slippery and crumbling; his feet are feeble. One helper alone can hold him up. But his own exceeding need is not all that he pleads. He urges his trust, his fixing of his desires, hopes and whole self, by a dead lift of faith on God. That is a reason for divine help. Anything is possible rather than that such hope should be disappointed. It cannot be that any man, who has fled for sanctuary to the asylum of God's heart, should be dragged thence and slain before the God whose altar he has vainly clasped.

**143:10–12.** The last part (vv. 10ff) puts foremost the prayer for conformity of will with God's, and although it closes with recurring prayer for outward deliverance, it breathes desires for more inward blessings. As in the preceding verses, there are in these closing ones many echoes of other Psalms. The sequence of petitions and pleas is instructive. To do, not merely to know, God's will is the condition of all blessedness and will be the deepest desire of every man who is truly God's servant. But that obedience of heart and hand must be taught by God, and He regards our taking Him for our God as establishing a claim on Him to give all illumination of heart and all bending of will and all skill of hand which are necessary to make us doers of his will. His teaching is no mere outward communication of knowledge, but an inbreathing of power to discern, and of disposition and ability to perform, what is his will. Verse 10b is best taken as a continuous sentence, embodying a prayer for guidance.

As this prayer is deep, so its plea is high. "For thy name's sake"—nothing can be pleaded of such force as that. God supremely desires the glory of his name, and for the sake of men whose blessedness depends on their knowing and loving it, He will do nothing that can dim its luster. His name is the record of his past acts, the disclosure of that in Him which is knowable. That name contains the principles of all his future acts. He will be what He has been. He will magnify his name, and the humblest, most tormented soul that can say, "Thou art my God," may be sure that divinely given life will throb in it, and that even its lowliness may contribute to the honor of the name.

The hunted psalmist must come back in the close of his Psalm to his actual circumstances, for earthly needs do clog the soul's wings. He unites righteousness and steadfast love as cooperating powers, as in v. 1 he had united faithfulness and righteousness. And as in the first verses, he had blended pleas drawn from God's character with those drawn from his relation to God, so he ends his petitions with pleading that he is God's servant and, as such, a fit object of God's protection.

**144:1–2.** Verses 1f are echoes of Ps. 18:2, 34, 46 with slight variations. The remarkable epithet "my steadfast love" (HED #2721) offends some critics, who emend so as to read "my stronghold"; but it has a parallel in Jon. 2:9 and is forcible as an emotional abbreviation of the fuller "God of my steadfast love" (Ps. 59:10). The original passage reads "people," which is the only appropriate word in this connection and should probably be read in v. 2c.

| 2725.115 | 7574.151 | 6194 | 8809 | | 3176 | 4242, 119 |
|---|---|---|---|---|---|---|
| v Qal pf 1cs | art, v Qal act ptc ms | n ms, ps 1cs | prep, ps 1cs | **3.** | pn | intrg, n ms |
| חָסִיתִי | הָרוֹדֵד | עַמִּי | תַחְתָּי | | יְהוָה | מָה־אָדָם |
| chās̱îthî | hārôdhēdh | ‘ammî | thachtāy | | yehwāh | māh-’ādhām |
| I have sought refuge | the One Who subdues | my people | under me | | O Yahweh | what humankind |

| 3156.123 | 1158, 596 | 2913.323 | | 119 | 3937, 1961 | 1880.111 |
|---|---|---|---|---|---|---|
| cj, v Qal impf 2ms, ps 3ms | *n ms*, n ms | cj, v Piel impf 2ms, ps 3ms | **4.** | n ms | prep, art, n ms | v Qal pf 3ms |
| וַתֵּדָעֵהוּ | בֶּן־אֱנוֹשׁ | וַתְּחַשְּׁבֵהוּ | | אָדָם | לַהֶבֶל | דָּמָה |
| wattēdhā‘ēhû | ben-’ĕnôsh | wattechashshevēhû | | ’ādhām | lahevel | dāmāh |
| that You know him | the son of a man | that You consider him | | a man | as a breath | he is like |

| 3219 | 3626, 7009 | 5882.151 | | 3176 | 5371.531, 8452 |
|---|---|---|---|---|---|
| n mp, ps 3ms | prep, n ms | v Qal act ptc ms | **5.** | pn | v Hiphil impv 2ms, n md, ps 2ms |
| יָמָיו | כְּצֵל | עוֹבֵר | | יְהוָה | הַט־שָׁמֶיךָ |
| yāmâv | ketsēl | ‘ôvēr | | yehwāh | haṭ-shāmêkhā |
| his days | like a shadow | passing on | | O Yahweh | cause your heavens to bend down |

| 3495.123 | 5236.131 | 904, 2098 | 6475.126 | | 1325.131 | 1326 |
|---|---|---|---|---|---|---|
| cj, v Qal impf 2ms | v Qal impv 2ms | prep, art, n mp | cj, v Qal juss 3mp | **6.** | v Qal impv 2ms | n ms |
| וְתֵרֵד | גַּע | בֶּהָרִים | וְיֶעֱשָׁנוּ | | בְּרוֹק | בָּרָק |
| wethērēdh | ga‘ | behārîm | weye‘ĕshānû | | berôq | bārāq |
| and come down | touch | on the mountains | that they may smoke | | flash | lightning |

| 6571.523 | 8365.131 | 2784 | 2072.123 |
|---|---|---|---|
| cj, v Hiphil impf 2ms, ps 3mp | v Qal impv 2ms | n mp, ps 2ms | cj, v Qal juss 2ms, ps 3mp |
| וּתְפִיצֵם | שְׁלַח | חִצֶּיךָ | וּתְהֻמֵּם |
| ûthephîtsēm | shelach | chitstsêkhā | ûthehummēm |
| and scatter them | send out | your arrows | that You may throw them into confusion |

| | 8365.131 | 3135 | 4623, 4953 | 6722.131 | 5522.531 |
|---|---|---|---|---|---|
| **7.** | v Qal impv 2ms | n fd, ps 2ms | prep, n ms | v Qal impv 2ms, ps 1cs | cj, v Hiphil impv 2ms, ps 1cs |
| | שְׁלַח | יָדֶיךָ | מִמָּרוֹם | פְּצֵנִי | וְהַצִּילֵנִי |
| | shelach | yādhêkhā | mimmārôm | petsēnî | wehatstsîlēnî |
| | stretch out | your hands | from on high | deliver me | yes rescue me |

| 4623, 4448 | 7521 | 4623, 3135 | 1158 | 5424 | | 866 | 6552 |
|---|---|---|---|---|---|---|---|
| prep, n md | adj | prep, *n fs* | *n mp* | n ms | **8.** | rel pron | n ms, ps 3mp |
| מִמַּיִם | רַבִּים | מִיַּד | בְּנֵי | נֵכָר | | אֲשֶׁר | פִּיהֶם |
| mimmayim | rabbîm | mîyadh | benê | nēkhār | | ’ăsher | pîhem |
| from the waters | many | from the hand of | the sons of | a foreign land | | who | their mouth |

| 1744.311, 8175 | 3332 | 3332 | 8632 | | 435 | 8302 | 2413 |
|---|---|---|---|---|---|---|---|
| v Piel pf 3ms, n ms | cj, n fs, ps 3mp | *n fs* | n ms | **9.** | n mp | n ms | adj |
| דִּבֶּר־שָׁוְא | וִימִינָם | יְמִין | שָׁקֶר | | אֱלֹהִים | שִׁיר | חָדָשׁ |
| dibber-shāwe’ | wîmînām | yemîn | shāqer | | ’ělōhîm | shîr | chādhāsh |
| it speaks vanity | and their right hand | the right hand of | lies | | O God | a song | new |

| 8301.125 | 3937 | 904, 5213 | 6452 | 2226.325, 3937 |
|---|---|---|---|---|
| v Qal juss 1cs | prep, ps 2ms | prep, *n ms* | num | v Piel juss 1cs, prep, ps 2ms |
| אָשִׁירָה | לָּךְ | בְּנֵבֶל | עָשׂוֹר | אֲזַמְּרָה־לָּךְ |
| ’āshîrāh | lākh | benēvel | ‘āsôr | ’ăzammerāh-lākh |
| let me sing | to You | with the harp of | ten | let me sing praises to You |

| | 5598.151 | 9009 | 3937, 4567 | 6722.151 | 881, 1784 | 5860 |
|---|---|---|---|---|---|---|
| **10.** | art, v Qal act ptc ms | n fs | prep, art, n mp | art v Qal act ptc ms | do, pn | n ms, ps 3ms |
| | הַנּוֹתֵן | תְּשׁוּעָה | לַמְּלָכִים | הַפּוֹצֶה | אֶת־דָּוִד | עַבְדּוֹ |
| | hannôthēn | teshû‘āh | lammelākhîm | happôtseh | ’eth-dāwidh | ‘avdô |
| | the One Who gives | deliverance | to the kings | the One Who delivers | David | his servant |

deliverer, *Goodspeed* ... My high hill of retreat, *Fenton.*

**my shield, and he in whom I trust:** ... who protects me and gives me confidence, *Knox* ... My buckler, and he in whom I have sought refuge, *Rotherham.*

**who subdueth my people under me:** ... who humbles my people under me, *KJVII* ... the Subduer of nations before me!, *Moffatt* ... Who to me brought my Tribe!, *Fenton* ... He makes my people obey me, *Beck.*

**3. LORD, what is man, that thou takest knowledge of him!:** ... LORD, what are human beings that you should care for them?, *REB* ... LORD, why should You teach man?, *Fenton.*

**or the son of man, that thou makest account of him!:** ... that You are mindful of him?, *NKJV* ... The son of a mortal, And yet thou hast taken account of him, *Rotherham* ... Or the son of man, that You think anything of him!, *KJVII* ... What are frail mortals that you should take thought for them?, *REB.*

**4. Man is like to vanity:** ... Man is like a breath, *NKJV* ... Man is no more than a puff of wind, *NEB.*

**his days are as a shadow that passeth away:** ... Like the wind he goes, *Knox* ... their days like a fleeting shadow, *REB* ... Whose days pass like a shade!, *Fenton.*

**5. Bow thy heavens, O LORD, and come down:** ... LORD, part the heavens and come down, *REB* ... LORD, bow the Skies and descend, *Fenton.*

**touch the mountains, and they shall smoke:** ... at thy touch, the mountains will be wreathed in smoke, *Knox* ... touch the mountains so that they pour forth smoke, *REB* ... Torch the hills and envelop in clouds, *Fenton.*

**6. Cast forth lightning, and scatter them:** ... Flash forth lightning, that thou mayest scatter them, *Rotherham* ... Send out Thine arrows and confuse them, *NASB* ... Flash forth lightning, and put them to flight, *NAB* ... With your storm-flames send them in flight, *BB.*

**shoot out thine arrows, and destroy them:** ... shoot thy arrows, and throw them into confusion!, *Knox* ... Send out thine arrows, and discomfit them, *MRB* ... and send your arrows humming, *REB.*

**7. Send thine hand from above:** ... Stretch out Your hand from above, *NKJV* ... Reach out your hands from on high, *REB.*

**rid me, and deliver me out of great waters:** ... Snatch me away and rescue me Out of mighty waters, *Rotherham* ... rescue me and deliver me from the many waters, *RSV* ... And pull from the powerful streams, *Fenton.*

**from the hand of strange children:** ... From the hand of foreigners, *NKJV* ... Out of the hand of strangers, *MRB.*

**8. Whose mouth speaketh vanity:** ... who make treacherous promises, *Knox* ... whose every word is worthless, *REB* ... Whose mouths swear false promises, *NAB.*

**and their right hand is a right hand of falsehood:** ... and lift their hands in perjury, *Knox.*

**9. I will sing a new song unto thee, O God:** ... I will make a new song to you, O God, *BB.*

**upon a psaltery and an instrument of ten strings will I sing praises unto thee:** ... On a harp of ten strings I will sing praises to You, *NKJV* ... psalms to the music of a ten-stringed harp, *REB* ... With the harp at the Tything will chant, *Fenton* ... I will chant your praise, *NAB* ... I will make melody to you on an instrument of ten cords, *BB.*

**10. It is he that giveth salvation unto kings:** ... Who is giving deliverance to kings, *Young* ... God who gave victory to kings, *REB.*

---

**144:3–4.** Psalm 8 supplies the original of vv. 3f, with a reminiscence of Ps. 39:5, and of Ps. 102:11, from which comes the pathetic image of the fleeting shadow. The link between this and the former extract seems to be the recognition of God's condescension in strengthening so weak and transient a creature for conflict and conquest.

**144:5–11.** The following prayer for further divine help in struggles is largely borrowed from the magnificent picture of a theophany in Ps. 18:9, 14ff. The energetic "flash lightning" is peculiar to this Psalm, but the imagery of judgment from the heavens is well attested in Scripture. The description of the enemies as "strange children" is like Ps. 18:44f. As in many other Psalms, the treachery of the foe is signalized. They break their oaths. The right hand which they had lifted in swearing is a lying hand. The vow of new praise recalls Pss. 33:2f; 96:1; 98:1. Verse 10 is a reproduction of Ps. 18:50. The mention of David's deliverance from the "hurtful sword" has apparently been the reason for the Septuagint referring the Psalm to the victory over Goliath—an impossible view. The new song is not sung here, but the Psalm drops from the level of praise to renew the petition for deliverance, in the manner of a refrain caught up in v. 11 from v. 7. This might make a well-rounded close and may have originally been the end of the Psalm.

| 4623, 2820<br>prep, n fs<br>מֵחֶרֶב<br>mēcherev<br>from the sword | 7737<br>adj<br>רָעָה<br>rā'āh<br>evil | 11. | 6722.131<br>v Qal impv 2ms, ps 1cs<br>פְּצֵנִי<br>petsēnî<br>deliver me | 5522.531<br>cj, v Hiphil impv 2ms, ps 1cs<br>וְהַצִּילֵנִי<br>wehatstsîlēnî<br>yes rescue me | 4623, 3135<br>prep, *n fs*<br>מִיַּד<br>mîyadh<br>from the hand of |
|---|---|---|---|---|---|

| 1158, 5424<br>*n mp*, n ms<br>בְּנֵי־נֵכָר<br>benê-nēkhār<br>sons of a foreign land | 866<br>rel pron<br>אֲשֶׁר<br>'ăsher<br>who | 6552<br>n ms, ps 3mp<br>פִּיהֶם<br>pîhem<br>their mouth | 1744.311, 8175<br>v Piel pf 3ms, n ms<br>דִּבֶּר־שָׁוְא<br>dibber-shāwe'<br>they speak vanity | 3332<br>cj, n fs, ps 3mp<br>וִימִינָם<br>wîmînām<br>and their right hand |
|---|---|---|---|---|

| 3332<br>*n fs*<br>יְמִין<br>yemîn<br>the right hand of | 8632<br>n ms<br>שָׁקֶר<br>shāqer<br>lies | 12. | 866<br>rel part<br>אֲשֶׁר<br>'ăsher<br>that | 1158<br>n mp, ps 1cp<br>בָּנֵינוּ<br>bānênû<br>our sons | 3626, 5379<br>prep, n mp<br>כִּנְטִעִים<br>kinṯi'îm<br>like plants | 1461.456<br>v Pual ptc mp<br>מְגֻדָּלִים<br>meghuddālîm<br>having grown | 904, 5454<br>prep, n mp, ps 3mp<br>בִּנְעוּרֵיהֶם<br>bin'ûrêhem<br>in their youth |
|---|---|---|---|---|---|---|---|

| 1351<br>n fp, ps 1cp<br>בְּנוֹתֵינוּ<br>benôthênû<br>our daughters | 3626, 2188<br>prep, n fp<br>כְּזָוִיֹּת<br>khezāwîyōth<br>like corners | 2497.458<br>v Pual ptc fp<br>מְחֻטָּבוֹת<br>mechuṯṯāvôth<br>squared | 8732<br>*n fs*<br>תַּבְנִית<br>tavnîth<br>the shape of | 2033<br>n ms<br>הֵיכָל<br>hêkhāl<br>a palace | 13. | 4330<br>n mp, ps 1cp<br>מְזָוֵינוּ<br>mezāwênû<br>our granaries | 4527.152<br>v Qal act ptc mp<br>מְלֵאִים<br>melē'îm<br>being full |
|---|---|---|---|---|---|---|---|

| 6572.552<br>v Hiphil ptc mp<br>מְפִיקִים<br>mephîqîm<br>disbursing | 4623, 2261<br>prep, n ms<br>מִזַּן<br>mizzan<br>from a granary | 420, 2261<br>prep, n ms<br>אֶל־זַן<br>'el-zan<br>to a granary | 6887<br>n fs, ps 1cp<br>צֹאונֵנוּ<br>tsō'wnēnû<br>our sheep | 509.554<br>v Hiphil ptc fp<br>מַאֲלִיפוֹת<br>ma'ălîphôth<br>producing thousands |
|---|---|---|---|---|

| 7525.458<br>v Pual ptc fp<br>מְרֻבָּבוֹת<br>merubbāvôth<br>becoming tens of thousands | 904, 2445<br>prep, n mp, ps 1cp<br>בְּחוּצוֹתֵינוּ<br>bechûtsôthênû<br>in our streets | 14. | 443<br>n mp, ps 1cp<br>אַלּוּפֵינוּ<br>'allûphênû<br>our cattle | 5628.456<br>v Pual ptc mp<br>מְסֻבָּלִים<br>mesubbālîm<br>having been carried |
|---|---|---|---|---|

| 375, 6806<br>*sub*, n ms<br>אֵין־פֶּרֶץ<br>'ên-perets<br>there is not breaking through | 375<br>cj, *sub*<br>וְאֵין<br>we'ên<br>and there is not | 3428.153<br>v Qal act ptc fs<br>יוֹצֵאת<br>yôtsē'th<br>going out | 375<br>cj, *sub*<br>וְאֵין<br>we'ên<br>and there is not | 6945<br>n fs<br>צְוָחָה<br>tsewāchāh<br>an outcry |
|---|---|---|---|---|

| 904, 7624<br>prep, n mp, ps 1cp<br>בִּרְחֹבֹתֵינוּ<br>birchōvōthênû<br>in our open plazas | 15. | 869<br>*n mp*<br>אַשְׁרֵי<br>'ashrê<br>blessed | 6194<br>art, n ms<br>הָעָם<br>hā'ām<br>the people | 8054, 3722<br>rel part, adv<br>שֶׁכָּכָה<br>shekkākhāh<br>who thus | 3937<br>prep, ps 3ms<br>לוֹ<br>lô<br>to them | 869<br>*n mp*<br>אַשְׁרֵי<br>'ashrê<br>blessed | 6194<br>art, n ms<br>הָעָם<br>hā'ām<br>the people |
|---|---|---|---|---|---|---|---|

**who delivereth David his servant from the hurtful sword:** ... Who delivers David His servant From the deadly sword, *NKJV* ... the God who has brought his servant David rescue. Save me from the cruel sword, *Knox* ... Who snatcheth away David his servant, from the calamitous' sword, *Rotherham.*

**11. Rid me, and deliver me from the hand of strange children:** ... Rescue me and deliver me from the hand of foreigners, *NKJV* ... Snatch me away and rescue me Out of the hand of the sons of the alien, *Rotherham* ... Out of the hand of strangers, *MRB.*

**whose mouth speaketh vanity:** ... who make treacherous promises, *Knox* ... whose every word is worthless, *REB* ... Whose mouths swear false promises, *NAB.*

**and their right hand is a right hand of falsehood:** ... and lift their hands in perjury, *Knox.*

**12. That our sons may be as plants grown up in their youth:** ... So may our sons grow to manhood, tall as the saplings, *Knox* ... Let our sons in their youth be as grown-up plants, *NASB* ... May our sons be straight and strong like saplings, *Moffatt* ... Our sons in their youth will be like thriving plants, *REB*.

**that our daughters may be as corner stones:** ... That our daughters may be as pillars, *NKJV* ... our daughters shapely as some column at the turn of a building, *Knox* ... our daughters like cornices carved in a palace!, *Moffatt* ... Our girls fruitful crops, building Homes, *Fenton*.

**polished after the similitude of a palace:** ... Sculptured in palace style, *NKJV* ... Polished—the likeness of a palace, *Young*.

**13. That our garners may be full:** ... That our barns may be full, *NKJV* ... Our garners are filled to overflowing, *Goodspeed*.

**affording all manner of store:** ... with every kind of provision, *REB* ... full of all good things, *BB*.

**that our sheep may bring forth thousands:** ... And our flocks bring forth thousands, *NASB* ... May our sheep in the field multiply in myriads!, *Moffatt*.

**and ten thousands in our streets:** ... And ten thousands in our fields, *NKJV* ... Ten thousands in our outplaces, *Young*.

**14. That our oxen may be strong to labour:** ... our oxen straining at the load, *Knox* ... Let our cattle bear, *NASB* ... the cattle in our fields will be fat and sleek, *REB* ... there is no miscarriage or untimely birth, *NEB*.

**that there be no breaking in, nor going out:** ... Without mishap and without loss, *NASB* ... May our rulers be strong, may nothing go wrong, *Moffatt* ... There will be no miscarriage or untimely birth, *REB* ... May there be no breach in the walls, no exile, *NAB*.

**that there be no complaining in our streets:** ... That there be no outcry in our streets, *NKJV* ... no lamenting in our streets, *Knox* ... And there is no crying in our broad places, *Young* ... no raids or retreats, no panic in our streets!, *Moffatt* ... There is no riot and no alarm, *Goodspeed*.

**15. Happy is that people, that is in such a case:** ... How happy the Race who are thus, *Fenton* ... Happy is the nation whose ways are so ordered, *BB*.

**yea, happy is that people, whose God is the LORD:** ... How happy the People whose God is THE LIFE, *Fenton*.

---

**144:12–14.** The substance of the description includes three things: a vigorous, growing population; agricultural prosperity; and freedom from invasion. The language is obscure, especially in v. 14, but the general meaning is plain. The characteristic Jewish blessing of numerous offspring is first touched on in two figures, of which the former is forcible and obvious, and the latter obscure. The comparison of the virgin daughters of Israel to "corner stones" is best understood by taking the word to mean "corner pillars," not necessarily caryatides, as is usually supposed—an architectural decoration unknown in the East. The points of comparison would then be slender uprightness and firm grace.

The description of a flourishing rural community is full of difficult words. "Streets" (HED #2445) literally means "places outside" and here, obviously, must refer to the open pastures without the city, in contrast to the "open spaces" within it, mentioned in the next verse. In that verse, almost every word is doubtful. That rendered "oxen" (HED #443) is masculine in form, but is generally taken as being applicable to both sexes and here used for the milky mothers of the herd. The word translated above "strong to labour" (HED #5268) means "laden," and if the accompanying noun is masculine, must mean "laden with the harvest sheaves"; but the parallel of the increasing flocks suggests the other rendering. The remainder of v. 14 would in form make a complete verse, yet it is possible that something has fallen out between the first clause and the two latter. These paint tranquil city life when enemies are far away.

**144:15.** The last verse sums up all the preceding picture of growth, prosperity and tranquillity and traces it to the guardian care and blessing of Yahweh. The psalmist may seem to have been setting too much store by outward prosperity. His last word not only points to the one source of it, but sets high above the material consequences of God's favor, joyous as these are, that favor itself, as the climax of human blessedness.

***Psalm 145.*** *This is an acrostic Psalm. Like several others of that kind, it is slightly irregular, one letter ("nun") being omitted. The omission is supplied in the Septuagint by an obviously spurious verse inserted between v. 13 and 14. Although the Psalm has no strophical divisions, it has distinct sequence of thought and celebrates the glories of Yahweh's character and deeds from a fourfold point of view. It sings of his greatness (vv. 1–6), goodness (vv. 7–10), kingdom (vv. 11ff) and the universality of his beneficence (vv. 14–21). It is largely colored by other Psalms and is unmistakably of late origin.*

| 8054, 3176 | 435 | | 8747 | 3937, 1784 | | 7597.325 | 435 | 4567 |
|---|---|---|---|---|---|---|---|---|
| rel part, pn | n mp, ps 3ms | | n fs | prep, pn | | v Polel impf 1cs, ps 2ms | n mp, ps 1cs | art, n ms |
| שֶׁיְהוָה | אֱלֹהָיו | 145:t | תְּהִלָּה | לְדָוִד | 1. | אֲרוֹמִמְךָ | אֱלוֹהַי | הַמֶּלֶךְ |
| sheyehwāh | 'ĕlōhâv | | tehillāh | ledhāwidh | | 'ărômimkhā | 'ĕlôhay | hammelekh |
| whom Yahweh | their God | | a Praise | of David | | I will exalt You | my God | the King |

| 1313.325 | 8428 | 3937, 5986 | 5911 | | 904, 3725, 3219 | 1313.325 |
|---|---|---|---|---|---|---|
| cj, v Piel impf 1cs | n ms, ps 2ms | prep, n ms | cj, n ms | | prep, *adj*, n ms | v Piel impf 1cs, ps 2ms |
| וַאֲבָרְכָה | שִׁמְךָ | לְעוֹלָם | וָעֶד | 2. | בְּכָל־יוֹם | אֲבָרְכֶךָּ |
| wa'ăvārekhāh | shimkhā | le'ôlām | wā'edh | | bekhol-yôm | 'ăvārekhekhā |
| and I will bless | your name | unto eternity | and everlasting | | in all the days | I will bless You |

| 2054.325 | 8428 | 3937, 5986 | 5911 | | 1448 | 3176 | 2054.455 |
|---|---|---|---|---|---|---|---|
| cj, v Piel impf 1cs | n ms, ps 2ms | prep, n ms | cj, n ms | | adj | pn | cj, v Pual ptc ms |
| וַאֲהַלְלָה | שִׁמְךָ | לְעוֹלָם | וָעֶד | 3. | גָּדוֹל | יְהוָה | וּמְהֻלָּל |
| wa'ăhalelāh | shimkhā | le'ôlām | wā'edh | | gādhôl | yehwāh | ûmehullāl |
| and I will praise | your name | unto eternity | and everlasting | | great | Yahweh | and praised |

| 4108 | 3937, 1449 | 375 | 2812 | | 1810 | 3937, 1810 | 8099.321 |
|---|---|---|---|---|---|---|---|
| adv | cj, prep, n fs, ps 3ms | *sub* | n ms | | n ms | prep, n ms | v Piel impf 3ms |
| מְאֹד | וְלִגְדֻלָּתוֹ | אֵין | חֵקֶר | 4. | דּוֹר | לְדוֹר | יְשַׁבַּח |
| me'ōdh | welighdhullāthô | 'ên | chēqer | | dôr | ledhôr | yeshabbach |
| very | and of his greatness | there is not | examination | | generation | to generation | they will glorify |

| 4801 | 1400 | 5222.526 | | 1996 | 3638 | 2003 |
|---|---|---|---|---|---|---|
| n mp, ps 2ms | cj, n fp, ps 2ms | v Hiphil impf 3mp | | *n ms* | *n ms* | n ms, ps 2ms |
| מַעֲשֶׂיךָ | וּגְבוּרֹתֶיךָ | יַגִּידוּ | 5. | הֲדַר | כְּבוֹד | הוֹדֶךָ |
| ma'ăsêkhā | ûghevûrōthêkhā | yaggîdhû | | hedhar | kevôdh | hôdhekhā |
| your works | and your might | they will tell | | the majesty of | the glory of | your splendor |

| 1745 | 6623.258 | 7945.125 | | 6020 |
|---|---|---|---|---|
| cj, *n mp* | v Niphal ptc fp, ps 2ms | v Qal juss 1cs | | cj, *n ms* |
| וְדִבְרֵי | נִפְלְאוֹתֶיךָ | אָשִׂיחָה | 6. | וֶעֱזוּז |
| wedhivrê | niphle'ôthêkhā | 'āsîchāh | | we'ĕzûz |
| and the matters of | your extraordinary deeds | may I ponder | | and the strength of |

| 3486.258 | 569.126 | 1449 | 5807.325 | | 2228 |
|---|---|---|---|---|---|
| v Niphal ptc fp, ps 2ms | v Qal impf 3mp | cj, n fp, ps 2ms | v Piel impf 1cs, ps 3fs | | *n ms* |
| נוֹרְאֹתֶיךָ | יֹאמֵרוּ | וּגְדוּלֹּתֶיךָ | אֲסַפְּרֶנָּה | 7. | זֵכֶר |
| nôr'ōthêkhā | yō'mērû | ûghedhûllōthêkhā | 'ăsapperennāh | | zēkher |
| your fearsome deeds | they will say | and your greatnesses | I will recount it | | the remembrance of |

| 7521, 3008 | 5218.526 | 6930 | 7728.326 |
|---|---|---|---|
| adj, n ms, ps 2ms | v Hiphil impf 3mp | cj, n fs, ps 2ms | v Piel impf 3mp |
| רַב־טוּבְךָ | יַבִּיעוּ | וְצִדְקָתְךָ | יְרַנֵּנוּ |
| rav-ṯûvkhā | yabbî'û | wetsidhqāthekhā | yerannēnû |
| your abundant goodness | they will bubble forth with | and your righteousness | they will shout for joy |

**145:t. David's Psalm of praise.**

**1. I will extol thee, my God, O king:** ... I shall praise you to the heights, God my King, *JB* ... I will exalt you, *NIV.*

**and I will bless thy name for ever and ever:** ... and extol your name for ever and ever, *NIV* ... to times age-abiding and beyond, *Rotherham.*

**2. Every day will I bless thee; and I will praise thy name for ever and ever:** ... Day after day I shall bless you, *JB.*

**3. Great is the LORD, and greatly to be praised:** ... The Lord is great; He deserves high praise, *Beck* ... and highly to be praised, *NCB* ... Great is the Eternal, loudly to be praised, *Moffatt* ... and most worthy of praise, *NIV* ... Can any praise be worthy of the Lord's majesty?, *Knox.*

**and his greatness is unsearchable:** ... his power may never be searched out, *BB.*

... his greatness is beyond all searching out, *REB* ... his greatness no one can fathom, *NIV* ... Since to his greatness there is no limit, *Anchor.*

**4. One generation shall praise thy works to another:** ... One generation will commend your works to the next, *REB* ... One generation shall laud thy works to another, *RSV* ... Parents will tell their children what you have done, *NCV.*

**and shall declare thy mighty acts:** ... and make clear the operation of your strength, *BB* ... and set forth Thy mighty acts, *Berkeley* ... and shall proclaim your exploits, *Anchor.*

**5. I will speak of the glorious honour of thy majesty:** ... dwelling on the glorious splendour of thy state, *Moffatt* ... On the glorious splendor of Thy majesty, *NASB* ... I will meditate on the glorious splendor of Your majesty, *NKJV.*

**and of thy wondrous works:** ... And of thy wondrous works, will I meditate, *MRB* ... and on the records of Thy wonders, *Berkeley* ... And I will think about your miracles, *NCV* ... about your wonders will I compose my songs, *Anchor.*

**6. And men shall speak of the might of thy terrible acts:** ... They discourse of the power of your terrible deeds and declare your greatness, *NCB* ... They will tell of the power of your awesome works, *NIV* ... They will tell about the amazing things you do, *NCV* ... Fearful are the tales they tell of thy power, proclaiming thy magnificence, *Knox.*

**and I will declare thy greatness:** ... I will recount it, *Berkeley* ... and I will proclaim your great deeds, *NIV* ... and I will tell how great you are, *NCV.*

**7. They shall abundantly utter the memory of thy great goodness:** ... They will bring out the memory of your great generosity, *JB* ... They shall utter the fame of Thy great goodness, *MAST* ... They will pour forth a recital of Thy great goodness, *Berkeley.*

**and shall sing of thy righteousness:** ... and joyfully acclaim your saving justice, *JB* ... And shall shout joyfully of Thy righteousness, *NASB* ... and will sing about your fairness, *NCV* ... and ring out your justice, *Anchor.*

---

*The first group of verses has two salient characteristics—the accumulation of epithets expressive of the more majestic aspects of Yahweh's self-revelation and the remarkable alternation of the psalmist's solo of song and the mighty chorus, which takes up the theme and sends a shout of praise echoing down the generations.*

**145:1–2.** The psalmist begins with his own tribute of praise, which he vows shall be perpetual. Verse 1 recalls Pss. 30:1 and 34:1. We "extol" God, when we recognize that He is King and worthily adore Him as such. A heart filled with joy in the thought of God would have no other occupation than the loved one of ringing out his name. The singer sets "for ever and ever" at the end of both v. 1 and 2, and while it is possible to give the expression a worthy meaning as simply equivalent to "continually," it is more in harmony with the exalted strain of the Psalm and the emphatic position of the words to hear in them an expression of the assurance which such delight in God and in the contemplation of Him naturally brings with it, that over communion so deep and blessed, death has no power. "Every day will I bless thee"—that is the happy vow of the devout heart. "And I will praise thy name for ever and ever"—that is the triumphant confidence that springs from the vow. The experiences of fellowship with God are prophets of their own immortality.

**145:3.** Verse 3a is from Ps. 48:1, and v. 3b is tinged by Isa. 40, but substitutes "greatness," the keynote of the first part of this Psalm, for "understanding." That note, having been thus struck, is taken up in vv. 4ff, which set forth various aspects of that greatness, as manifested in works which are successively described as "mighty" (HED #1448): instinct with conquering power such as a valiant hero wields; as, taken together, constituting the "splendor of the glory of thy majesty," the flashing brightness with which, when gathered in a radiant mass, they shine out, like a great globe of fire; as "wonders," not merely in the narrower sense of miracles, but as being productive of lowly astonishment in the thoughtful spectator; and as being "dread acts" such as fill the beholder with holy awe.

**145:4–6.** His passing and repassing from his own praise in vv. 1f, to that of successive generations in v. 4 and once more to his own in v. 5 and to that of others in v. 6 is remarkable. Does he conceive of himself as the chorus leader, teaching the ages his song? Or does he simply rejoice in the less lofty consciousness that his voice is not solitary? It is difficult to say, but this is clear, that the messianic hope of the world's being one day filled with the praises which were occasioned by God's manifestation in Israel burned in this singer's heart. He could not bear to sing alone, and his hymn would lack its highest note, if he did not believe that the world was

| | 2688 | 7631 | 3176 | 774 | 653 | 1462, 2721 | | 3005, 3176 |
|---|---|---|---|---|---|---|---|---|
| 8. | adj | cj, adj | pn | *adj* | n md | cj, *adj*, n ms | 9. | adj, pn |
| | חַנּוּן | וְרַחוּם | יְהוָה | אֶרֶךְ | אַפַּיִם | וּגְדָל־חָסֶד | | טוֹב־יְהוָה |
| | channûn | werachûm | yehwāh | 'erekh | 'appayim | ûghedhāl-chās̱edh | | ṯôv-yehwāh |
| | gracious | and merciful | Yahweh | long of | nostrils | and great in steadfast love | | good Yahweh |

| 3937, 3725 | 7641 | 6142, 3725, 4801 | | 3142.526 | 3176 |
|---|---|---|---|---|---|
| prep, art, n ms | cj, n mp, ps 3ms | prep, *n ms*, n mp, ps 3ms | 10. | v Hiphil impf 3mp, ps 2ms | pn |
| לַכֹּל | וְרַחֲמָיו | עַל־כָּל־מַעֲשָׂיו | | יוֹדוּךָ | יְהוָה |
| lakkōl | werachmâv | 'al-kol-ma'ăsâv | | yôdhûkhā | yehwāh |
| to everyone | and his mercies | on all his works | | they will praise You | O Yahweh |

| 3725, 4801 | 2728 | 1313.326 | | 3638 | 4577 |
|---|---|---|---|---|---|
| *adj*, n mp, ps 2ms | cj, n mp, ps 2ms | v Piel impf 3mp, ps 2ms | 11. | *n ms* | n fs, ps 2ms |
| כָּל־מַעֲשֶׂיךָ | וַחֲסִידֶיךָ | יְבָרְכוּכָה | | כְּבוֹד | מַלְכוּתְךָ |
| kol-ma'ăs̱êkhā | wachs̱îdhêkhā | yevārekhûkhāh | | kevôdh | malkhûthkhā |
| all your works | and your godly ones | they will bless You | | the glory of | your kingdom |

| 569.126 | 1400 | 1744.326 | | 3937, 3156.541 | 3937, 1158 | 119 |
|---|---|---|---|---|---|---|
| v Qal impf 3mp | cj, n fs, ps 2ms | v Piel impf 3mp | 12. | prep, v Hiphil inf con | prep, *n mp* | art, n ms |
| יֹאמֵרוּ | וּגְבוּרָתְךָ | יְדַבֵּרוּ | | לְהוֹדִיעַ | לִבְנֵי | הָאָדָם |
| yō'mērû | ûghevûrāthekhā | yedhabbērû | | lehôdhîa' | livnê | hā'ādhām |
| they will say | and your might | they speak | | to make known | to the children of | humankind |

| 1400 | 3638 | 1996 | 4577 | | 4577 | 4577 |
|---|---|---|---|---|---|---|
| n fp, ps 3ms | cj, *n ms* | *n ms* | n fs, ps 3ms | 13. | n fs, ps 2ms | *n fs* |
| גְּבוּרֹתָיו | וּכְבוֹד | הֲדַר | מַלְכוּתוֹ | | מַלְכוּתְךָ | מַלְכוּת |
| gevûrōthâv | ûkhevôdh | hedhar | malekhûthô | | malkhûthkhā | malkhûth |
| your might | and the glory of | the majesty of | his kingdom | | your kingdom | a kingdom of |

| 3725, 5986 | 4617 | 904, 3725, 1810 | 1810 |
|---|---|---|---|
| *adj*, n mp | cj, n fs, ps 2ms | prep, *adj*, n ms | cj, n ms |
| כָּל־עֹלָמִים | וּמֶמְשַׁלְתְּךָ | בְּכָל־דּוֹר | וָדֹר |
| kol-'ōlāmîm | ûmemsheltekhā | bekhol-dôr | wādhōr |
| all eternities | and your dominion | throughout all generations | and generations |

| | 5759.151 | 3176 | 3937, 3725, 5489.152 | 2296.151 |
|---|---|---|---|---|
| 14. | v Qal act ptc ms | pn | prep, *adj*, art, v Qal act ptc mp | cj, v Qal act ptc ms |
| | סוֹמֵךְ | יְהוָה | לְכָל־הַנֹּפְלִים | וְזוֹקֵף |
| | s̱ômēkh | yehwāh | lekhol-hannōphelîm | wezôqēph |
| | One Who supports | Yahweh | all those falling | and One Who raises up |

**8. The LORD is gracious, and full of compassion; slow to anger, and of great mercy:** … long-suffering and ever faithful, *REB* … slow to be angry, very kind, *Moffatt* … abounding in steadfast love, *RSV* … The LORD is kind and shows mercy, *NCV.*

**9. The LORD is good to all: and his tender mercies are over all his works:** … The LORD is good to everyone and shows compassion on everything He made, *Beck* … Yahweh is generous to all, his tenderness embraces all his creatures, *JB* … his compassion rests upon all his creatures, *REB* … he has compassion on all he has made, *NIV.*

**10. All thy works shall praise thee, O LORD:** … All your creatures shall thank you, Yahweh, *JB* … All thy works, O Yahweh, will give thanks unto thee, *Rotherham.*

**and thy saints shall bless thee:** … thy faithful followers shall bless thee, *Moffatt.*

**11. They shall speak of the glory of thy kingdom, and talk of thy power:** … and tell of your might, *JB* … and speak of your might, *NIV* … let them publish the glory of thy kingdom, and discourse of thy power, *Knox.*

**12. To make known to the sons of men his mighty acts:** … making known your mighty deeds to the children of Adam, *JB* … that they may make known to the children of men His feats of power, *Berkeley* … Then everyone will know the mighty things you do, *NCV.*

**and the glorious majesty of his kingdom:** … and the glorious splendor of your kingdom, *NIV* ... and the glorious spendor of thy kingdom, *RSV.*

**13. Thy kingdom is an everlasting kingdom:** ... Your kingship is a kingship for ever, *JB* ... Your kingdom will go on and on, *NCV* ... No age shall dawn but shall see thee reigning still, *Knox.*

**and thy dominion endureth throughout all generations:** ... and you will rule forever, *NCV* ... generations pass, and thy rule shall endure, *Knox.*

**14. The LORD upholdeth all that fall:** ... The LORD holds up all who are falling, *Beck* ... The Lord is the support of all who are crushed, *BB* ... Yahweh is trustworthy in all his words, and upright in all his deeds, *JB.*

**and raiseth up all those that be bowed down:** ... and the lifter up of all who are bent down, *BB* ... Yahweh supports all who stumble, *JB* ... And to raise all who are laid prostrate, *Rotherham* ... and straightens backs which are bent, *NEB.*

---

to catch up the song. In v. 5b, the phrase rendered above "thy wondrous works" is literally "words of his wonders," which some regard as being like the similar phrase in Ps. 65:3. But "words" may very well here retain its ordinary sense, and the poet represent himself as meditating on the records of God's acts in the past as well as gazing on those spread before his eyes in the present.

**145:7–10.** But greatness, majesty and splendor are not the divinest parts of the divine nature, as this singer had learned. These are but the fringes of the central glory. Therefore, the song rises from greatness to celebrate better things, the moral attributes of Yahweh. The psalmist has no more to say of himself, until the end of his Psalm. He gladly listens rather to the chorus of many voices which proclaims Yahweh's widespread goodness.

In v. 7, the two attributes that the whole OT regards as inseparable are the themes of the praise of men. Goodness and righteousness are not antithetical, but complementary, as green and red rays blend in white light. The exuberance of praise evoked by these attributes is strikingly represented by the two strong words describing it. The former, "abundantly utter" (HED #5218), or "well forth," compares its gush to the clear waters of a spring bursting up into sunlight, dancing and flashing, musical and living, and the latter (HED #7728) describes it as like the shrill cries of joy raised by a crowd on some festival, or such as the women trilled out when a bride was brought home.

Verse 8 rests upon Exo. 34:6 (cf. Ps. 103:8). It is difficult to draw a distinction between "gracious" and "full of compassion." Possibly, the former is the wider and expresses love in exercise toward the lowly in its most general aspect, while the latter specializes graciousness as it reveals itself to those afflicted with any evil. Being "slow to anger," Yahweh keeps back the wrath which is part of his perfection, and only gives it free course after long waiting and wooing. The contrast in v. 8b is not so much between anger and steadfast love, which to the psalmist are not opposed, as between the slowness with which the one is launched against a few offenders and the plenitude of the other.

That thought of abundant steadfast love is still further widened, in v. 9, to universality. God's goodness embraces all, and his compassions hover over all his works, as the broad wing and warm breast of the mother eagle protect her brood. Therefore, the psalmist hears a yet more multitudinous voice of praise from all creatures, since their very existence, and still more their various blessednesses, give witness to the all gladdening mercy which encompasses them. But creation's anthem is a song without words and needs to be made articulate by the conscious thanksgivings of those who, being blessed by possession of Yahweh's steadfast love, render blessing to Him with heart and lip.

**145:11–13.** The kingship of God was lightly touched in v. 1. It now becomes the psalmist's theme in vv. 11ff. It is for God's favored ones to speak, while creation can but be. It is for men who can recognize God's sovereign will as their law and know Him as Ruler, not only by power, but by goodness, to proclaim that kingdom which psalmists knew to be "righteousness, and peace, and joy" (Rom. 12:17).

The purpose for which God has lavished his favor on Israel is that they might be the heralds of his royalty to "the sons of men." The recipients of his grace should be the messengers of his grace. The aspects of that kingdom which fill the psalmist's thoughts in this part of his hymn correspond with that side of the divine nature celebrated in vv. 1–6—namely, the more majestic—while the graciousness magnified in vv. 7–10 is again the theme in the last portion (vv. 14–20).

An intentional parallelism between the first and third parts is suggested by the recurrence in v. 12 of part of the same heaped-together phrase which occurs in v. 5. There we read of "the glorious honor

| 3937, 3725, 3847.156 | | 6084, 3725 | 420 | 7887.326 | 887 |
|---|---|---|---|---|---|
| prep, *adj*, art, v Qal pass ptc mp | 15. | *n fd*, n ms | prep, ps 2ms | v Piel impf 3mp | cj, pers pron |
| לְכָל־הַכְּפוּפִים | | עֵינֵי־כֹל | אֵלֶיךָ | יְשַׂבֵּרוּ | וְאַתָּה |
| lekhol-hakkephûphîm | | 'ênê-khōl | 'ēlêkhā | yesabbērû | we'attāh |
| all those bowed down | | the eyes of everyone | to You | they will anticipate | and You |

| 5598.151, 3937 | 881, 406 | 904, 6496 | | 6858.151 | 881, 3135 |
|---|---|---|---|---|---|
| v Qal act ptc ms, prep, ps 3mp | do, n ms, ps 3mp | prep, n fs, ps 3ms | 16. | v Qal act ptc ms | do, n fs, ps 2ms |
| נֹתֵן־לָהֶם | אֶת־אָכְלָם | בְּעִתּוֹ | | פּוֹתֵחַ | אֶת־יָדֶךָ |
| nôthēn-lāhem | 'eth-'ākhelām | be'ittô | | pôthēach | 'eth-yādhekhā |
| One Who gives to them | their food | in its season | | One Who opens | your hand |

| 7881.551 | 3937, 3725, 2508 | 7814 | | 6926 | 3176 | 904, 3725, 1932 |
|---|---|---|---|---|---|---|
| cj, v Hiphil ptc ms | prep, *adj*, adj | n ms | 17. | adj | pn | prep, *adj*, n mp, ps 3ms |
| וּמַשְׂבִּיעַ | לְכָל־חַי | רָצוֹן | | צַדִּיק | יְהוָה | בְּכָל־דְּרָכָיו |
| ûmasbîa' | lekhol-chay | rātsôn | | tsaddîq | yehwāh | bekhol-derākhâv |
| and One Who satisfies | all the living | desire | | righteous | Yahweh | in all his ways |

| 2728 | 904, 3725, 4801 | | 7427 | 3176 | 3937, 3725, 7410.152 | 3937, 3725 |
|---|---|---|---|---|---|---|
| cj, adj | prep, *adj*, n mp, ps 3ms | 18. | adj | pn | prep, *adj*, v Qal act ptc mp, ps 3ms | prep, adj |
| וְחָסִיד | בְּכָל־מַעֲשָׂיו | | קָרוֹב | יְהוָה | לְכָל־קֹרְאָיו | לְכֹל |
| wechāsîdh | bekhol-ma'ăsâv | | qārôv | yehwāh | lekhol-qōre'âv | lekhōl |
| and steadfast | in all his works | | near | Yahweh | to all who call on Him | to all |

| 866 | 7410.126 | 904, 583 | | 7814, 3486.152 | 6449.121 |
|---|---|---|---|---|---|
| rel pron | v Qal impf 3mp, ps 3ms | prep, n fs | 19. | *n ms*, v Qal act ptc mp, ps 3ms | v Qal impf 3ms |
| אֲשֶׁר | יִקְרָאֻהוּ | בֶאֱמֶת | | רְצוֹן־יְרֵאָיו | יַעֲשֶׂה |
| 'ăsher | yiqōrā'uhû | ve'ĕmeth | | retsôn-yerē'âv | ya'ăseh |
| who | they call on Him | in truth | | the desire of those who fear Him | He will do |

| 881, 8210 | 8471.121 | 3588.521 | | 8490.151 | 3176 |
|---|---|---|---|---|---|
| cj, do, n fs, ps 3mp | v Qal impf 3ms | cj, v Hiphil impf 3ms, ps 3mp | 20. | *v Qal act ptc ms* | pn |
| וְאֶת־שַׁוְעָתָם | יִשְׁמַע | וְיוֹשִׁיעֵם | | שֹׁמֵר | יְהוָה |
| we'eth-shaw'āthām | yishma' | weyôshî'ēm | | shômēr | yehwāh |
| and their cry for help | He hears | and He saves them | | a Keeper | Yahweh |

**15. The eyes of all wait upon thee:** ... The eyes of all look hopefully to you, *NAB* ... All thy creatures look to thee, *Moffatt* ... The eyes of all look expectantly to You, *NKJV.*

**and thou givest them their meat in due season:** ... for Thou art ever giving them their food at the proper time, *Berkeley* ... and you give them their food at the proper time, *NIV.*

**16. Thou openest thine hand, and satisfiest the desire of every living thing:** ... they feast upon thy favour, *Moffatt* ... Thou art ever opening Thy hand to satisfy, *Berkeley* ... and fill with thy blessing all that lives, *Knox.*

**17. The LORD is righteous in all his ways, and holy in all his works:** ... The LORD is just in all His ways, and gracious in all His works, *Berkeley* ... and kind in all his doings, *RSV* ... unchanging in all that he does, *NEB.*

**18. The LORD is nigh unto all them that call upon him, to all that call upon him in truth:** ... even to all who give honour to him with true hearts, *BB* ... He is close to all who call upon him, all who call on him from the heart, *JB* ... who call to him in singleness of heart, *NEB.*

**19. He will fulfil the desire of them that fear him:** ... he satisfies his worshippers, *Moffatt* ... He fulfils their desire if only they fear him, *NEB.*

**he also will hear their cry, and will save them:** ... he hears and will help when they shout, *Fenton.*

**20. The LORD preserveth all them that love him:** ... The LORD protects all who love Him, *Beck* ... The Lord will keep all his worshippers from danger, *BB* ... Vigilantly the Lord watches over all that love him, *Knox.*

**but all the wicked will he destroy:** ... but He will destroy all the ungodly, *Berkeley* ... But all the lawless will he destroy, *Rotherham.*

**21. My mouth shall speak the praise of the LORD:** ... My lips shall pour out the Eternal's praise, *Moffatt* ... and all flesh shall bless his holy name, to everlasting eternity!, *Anchor.*

**and let all flesh bless his holy name for ever and ever:** ... Let every

of thy majesty" and here of "the glorious majesty of his kingdom"—expressions substantially identical in meaning. The very glory of the kingdom of Yahweh is a pledge that it is eternal. What corruption or decay could touch so radiant and mighty a throne? Israel's monarchy was a thing of the past, but as, "in the year that King Uzziah died," Isaiah saw the true King of Israel throned in the Temple, so the vanishing of the earthly head of the theocracy seems to have revealed with new clearness to devout men in Israel the perpetuity of the reign of Yahweh. Hence, the Psalms of the King are mostly post-exilic. It is blessed when the shattering of earthly goods or the withdrawal of human helpers and lovers makes more plain the unchanging friend and his abiding power to succor and suffice.

***145:14–20.*** *The last portion of the Psalm is marked by a frequent repetition of "all," which occurs eleven times in these verses. The singer seems to delight in the very sound of the word, which suggests to him boundless visions of the wide sweep of God's universal mercy and of the numberless crowd of dependents who wait on and are satisfied by Him. He passes far beyond national bounds.*

**145:14–16.** Verse 14 begins the grand catalog of universal blessings by an aspect of God's goodness. There is no man who is not often ready to fall and needing a strong hand to uphold him. The universality of man's weakness is pathetically testified by this verse. Those who are in the act of falling are upheld by Him, and those who have fallen are helped to regain their footing. Universal sustaining and restoring grace are his. The psalmist says nothing of the conditions on which that grace in its highest forms is exercised, but these are inherent in the nature of the case, for, if the falling man will not lay hold of the outstretched hand, down he must go. There would be no place for restoring help, if sustaining aid worked as universally as is proffered. The word for "raiseth" (HED #2296) in v. 14b occurs only here and in Ps. 146:8. Probably the author of both Psalms is one.

In vv. 15f, the universality of providence is set forth in language partly taken from Ps. 104:27f. The petitioners are all creatures. They mutely appeal to God with expectant eyes fixed on Him, like a dog looking for a crust from its master. He has but to "openest thine hand" and they are satisfied. The process is represented as easy and effortless.

Verse 16b has received different explanations. The word rendered "desire" (HED #7814) is often used for "favor"—i.e., God's—and is by some taken in that meaning here. Some translate "fillest everything that lives with goodwill." But seeing that the same word recurs in v. 19 in an obvious parallel with this verse and has there necessarily the meaning of desire, it is more natural to give it the same signification here. The clause then means that the opening of God's hand satisfies every creature, by giving it that which it desires in full enjoyment.

**145:17.** These common blessings of providence avail to interpret deeper mysteries. Since the world is full of happy creatures nourished by Him, it is a reasonable faith that his work is all of a piece, and that in all his dealings, the twin attributes of righteousness and steadfast love rule. There are enough plain tokens of God's character in plain things to make us sure that mysterious and apparently anomalous things have the same character regulating them. In v. 17b, the word rendered "steadfast" (HED #2728) is that usually employed of the objects of steadfast love, God's "favored ones." It is used of God only here and in Jer. 3:12 and must be taken in an active sense, as One who exercises steadfast love. The underlying principle of all his acts is love, says the psalmist, and there is no antagonism between that deepest motive and righteousness. The singer has indeed climbed to a sunlit height from which he sees far and can look down into the deep of the divine judgments and discern that they are a clear from the obscure.

**145:18–19.** He does not restrict this universal beneficence when he goes on to lay down conditions on which the reception of its highest forms depend. These conditions are not arbitrary, and within their limits, the same universality is displayed. The lower creation makes its mute appeal to God, but men have the prerogative and obligation of calling upon Him with real desire and trust. Such suppliants will universally be blessed with a nearness of God to them, better than his proximity through power, knowledge, or the lower manifestations of his steadfast love, to inferior creatures. Just as the fact of life brought with it certain wants, which God is bound to supply, since He gives it, so the fear and love of Him bring deeper needs, which He is still more (if that were possible) under pledge to satisfy. The creatures have their desires met. Those who fear Him will certainly have theirs, and that, not only insofar as they share physical life with worm and bee, whom their heavenly Father feeds, but insofar as their devotion sets in motion a new

| 881, 3725, 154.152 | 881 | 3725, 7857 | 8436.521 | | 8747 | 3176 |
|---|---|---|---|---|---|---|
| do, *adj*, v Qal act ptc mp, ps 3ms | cj, do | *adj*, art, n mp | v Hiphil impf 3ms | | *n fs* | pn |
| אֶת־כָּל־אֹהֲבָיו | וְאֵת | כָּל־הָרְשָׁעִים | יַשְׁמִיד | **21.** | תְּהִלַּת | יְהוָה |
| 'eth-kol-'ōhevâv | we'ēth | kol-hāreshā'îm | yashmîdh | | tehillath | yehwāh |
| all those who love Him | and | all the wicked | He will destroy | | the praise of | Yahweh |

| 1744.321, 6552 | 1313.321 | 3725, 1340 | 8428 | 7231 | 3937, 5986 |
|---|---|---|---|---|---|
| v Piel impf 3ms, n ms, ps 1cs | cj, v Piel impf 3ms | *adj*, n ms | *n ms* | n ms, ps 3ms | prep, n ms |
| יְדַבֶּר־פִּי | וִיבָרֵךְ | כָּל־בָּשָׂר | שֵׁם | קָדְשׁוֹ | לְעוֹלָם |
| yedhabber-pî | wîvārēkh | kl-bāsār | shēm | qādheshô | le'ôlām |
| my mouth will speak | and it will bless | all flesh | the name of | his holiness | unto eternity |

| 5911 | | 2054.333, 3161 | 2054.132 | 5497 | 881, 3176 | | 2054.325 |
|---|---|---|---|---|---|---|---|
| cj, n ms | | v Piel impv 2mp, pn | v Piel impv 2fs | n fs, ps 1cs | do, pn | | v Piel juss 1cs |
| וָעֶד | **146:1** | הַלְלוּ־יָהּ | הַלְלִי | נַפְשִׁי | אֶת־יְהוָה | **2.** | אֲהַלְלָה |
| wā'edh | | halelû-yāhh | halelî | naphshî | 'eth-yehwāh | | 'ăhalelāh |
| and everlasting | | praise Yah | praise | O my soul | Yahweh | | let me praise |

| 3176 | 904, 2522 | 2252.325 | 3937, 435 | 904, 5968 |
|---|---|---|---|---|
| pn | prep, n mp, ps 1cs | v Piel juss 1cs | prep, n mp, ps 1cs | prep, adv, ps 1cs |
| יְהוָה | בְּחַיָּי | אֲזַמְּרָה | לֵאלֹהַי | בְּעוֹדִי |
| yehwāh | bechayyāy | 'ăzammerāh | lē'lōhay | be'ôdhî |
| Yahweh | during my lifetime | let me sing praises | to my God | while my continuing |

| | 414, 1019.128 | 904, 5259 | 904, 1158, 119 | 8054, 375 | 3937 | 9009 |
|---|---|---|---|---|---|---|
| | adv, v Qal juss 2mp | prep, adj | prep, *n ms*, n ms | rel part, sub | prep, ps 3ms | n fs |
| **3.** | אַל־תִּבְטְחוּ | בִנְדִיבִים | בְּבֶן־אָדָם | שֶׁאֵין | לוֹ | תְשׁוּעָה |
| | 'al-tivtechû | vindhîvîm | beven-'ādhām | she'ên | lô | theshû'āh |
| | do not trust | in nobles | in the sons of man | whom there is not | to them | salvation |

| | 3428.122 | 7593 | 8178.121 | 3937, 124 | 904, 3219 | 2000 |
|---|---|---|---|---|---|---|
| | v Qal impf 3fs | n fs, ps 3ms | v Qal impf 3ms | prep, n fs, ps 3ms | prep, art, n ms | art, dem pron |
| **4.** | תֵּצֵא | רוּחוֹ | יָשֻׁב | לְאַדְמָתוֹ | בַּיּוֹם | הַהוּא |
| | tētsē' | rûchô | yāshuv | le'adhmāthô | bayyôm | hahû' |
| | it comes out | his spirit | he returns | to the ground | on the day | the that |

| 6.116 | 6491 | | 869 | 8054, 418 | 3399 | 904, 6039 | 7888 |
|---|---|---|---|---|---|---|---|
| v Qal pf 3cp | n fp, ps 3ms | | *n mp* | rel part, *n ms* | pn | prep, n ms, ps 3ms | n ms, ps 3ms |
| אָבְדוּ | עֶשְׁתֹּנֹתָיו | **5.** | אַשְׁרֵי | שֶׁאֵל | יַעֲקֹב | בְּעֶזְרוֹ | שִׂבְרוֹ |
| 'āvedhû | 'eshtōnōthâv | | 'ashrê | she'ēl | ya'ăqōv | be'ezrô | sivrô |
| they have perished | his thoughts | | blessed | whom the God of | Jacob | in his help | his hope |

creature praise his holy name for ever and ever, *NIV.*

**146:1. Praise ye the Lord. Praise the Lord, O my soul:** ... My whole being, praise the Lord, *NCV.*

**2. While I live will I praise the Lord:** ... I will praise the Lord as long as I live, *Berkeley.*

**I will sing praises unto my God while I have any being:** ... I will make melody to my God while I have by being, *BB* ... I sing praise to my God while I exist, *Young.*

**3. Put not your trust in princes, nor in the son of man, in whom there is no help:** ... Put not your trust in nobles, in a child of Adam, in whom is no salvation, *Berkeley* ... in mortal men, who cannot save, *NIV* ... he hath no deliverance, *Young* ... Do not ye trust in nobles, *Rotherham.*

**4. His breath goeth forth, he returneth to his earth:** ... His spirit departs, he returns to the earth, *NASB* ... When their spirit departs, they return to the ground, *NIV* ... His breath expires; he returns to the earth, *KJVII.*

**in that very day his thoughts perish:** ... on that very day their plans come to nothing, *NIV* ... In that very day his plans perish, *NKJV* ... all his designs will come to nothing, *Knox* ... and in that same hour all his thinking ends, *NEB.*

**5. Happy is he that hath the God of Jacob for his help:** ... Happy are those who are helped by the God of Jacob, *NCV.*

**whose hope is in the Lord his God:** ... Whose hope is on Yahweh his God, *Rotherham*

series of aspirations, longings and needs, which will certainly not be left unfulfilled.

Food is all the boon that the creatures crave, and they get it by an easy process. But man, especially man who fears and loves God, has deeper needs, sadder in one aspect, since they come from perils and ills from which he has to be saved, but more blessed in another, since every need is a door by which God can enter a soul. These more sacred necessities and more wistful longings are not to be satisfied by simply opening God's hand. More has to be done than that. For they can only be satisfied by the gift of himself, and men need much disciplining before they will receive Him into their hearts. They who love and fear Him will desire Him chiefly, and that desire can never be balked. There is a region, and only one, in which it is safe to set our hearts on unattained good. They who long for God will always have as much of God as they long for and are capable of receiving.

**145:20.** But notwithstanding the universality of the divine steadfast love, mankind still parts into two sections, one capable of receiving the highest gifts, one incapable, because of not desiring them. Therefore, the one light in its universal shining works two effects, being luster and life to such as welcome it, but darkness and death to those who turn from it. It is man's awful prerogative that he can distill poison out of the water of life and can make it impossible for himself to receive from tender, universal goodness anything but destruction.

**145:21.** The singer closes his song with the reiterated vow that his songs shall never close and, as in the earlier part of the Psalm, rejoices in the confidence that his single voice shall, like that of the herald angel at Bethlehem, be merged in the notes of "a multitude of the heavenly host praising God, and saying, Glory to God in the highest" (Luke 2:13f).

***Psalm 146–150.*** *The long-drawn music of the Psalter closes with five Hallelujah Psalms, in which, with constantly swelling diapason, all themes of praise are pealed forth, until the melodious thunder of the final Psalm, which calls on everything that has breath to praise Yahweh. Possibly, the number of these Psalms may have reference to the five books into which the Psalter is divided.*

***Psalm 146.*** *This is the first of the five. It is largely colored by earlier songs, but still throbs with fresh emotion. Its theme is the blessedness of trust in Yahweh, as shown by his character and works. It deals less with Israel's special prerogatives than its companions do, while it yet claims the universally beneficent ruler as Israel's God.*

**146:1–2.** The singer's full heart of thanksgiving must first pour itself out in vows of perpetual praise, before he begins to woo others to the trust which blesses him. Exhortations are impotent unless enforced by example. Verse 2 is borrowed with slight variation from Ps. 104:33.

**146:3–4.** This negative teaching, if it stood alone, would be a gospel of despair, the reduction of life to a torturing cheat, but taken as the prelude to the revelation of One Whom it is safe to trust, there is nothing sad in it. So the Psalm springs up at once from these thoughts of the helplessness of mortal man, to hymn the blessedness of trust set upon the undying God, like a song-bird from its lair in a graveyard, which pours its glad notes above the grassy mounds as it rises in spirals toward the blue and at each gives forth a more exultant burst of music.

**146:5.** The exclamation in v. 5 is the last of the twenty-five occurrences of "blessed" (HED #869) in the Psalter. Taken together, as any concordance will show, beginning with Ps. 1, they present a beautiful and comprehensive ideal of the devout life. The felicity of such a life is here gathered up into two comprehensive considerations, which supplement each other. It is blessed to have the God of Jacob on our side, but it is not enough for the heart to know that He bore a relation to another in the distant past or to a community in the present. There must be an individualizing bond between the soul and God, whereby the "God of Jacob" becomes the God Who belongs to the single devout man, and all the facts of whose protection in the past are renewed in the prosaic present. It is blessed to have Yahweh for one's "help," but that is only secured when, by the effort of one's own will, He is clasped as one's "hope." Such hope is blessed, for it will never be put to shame, or need to shift its anchorage. It brings into any life the all-sufficient help which is the ultimate source of all felicity and makes the hope that grasps it blessed, as the hand that holds some fragrant gum is perfumed by the touch.

**146:6–7.** But the psalmist passes swiftly from celebrating trust to magnify its object and sets forth, in an impressive series, the manifold perfections and acts which witness that Yahweh is worthy to be the sole confidence of men.

The nine divine acts, which invite to trust in Him, are divided into two parts, by a change in construction. There is, first, a series of participles

| 6142, 3176 | 435 | | 6449.151 | 8452 | 800 | 881, 3328 |
|---|---|---|---|---|---|---|
| prep, pn | n mp, ps 3ms | | v Qal act ptc ms | n md | cj, n fs | do, art, n ms |
| עַל־יְהוָה | אֱלֹהָיו | 6. | עֹשֶׂה | שָׁמַיִם | וָאָרֶץ | אֶת־הַיָּם |
| 'al-yᵉhwāh | 'ĕlōhâv | | 'ōseh | shāmayim | wā'ārets | 'eth-hayyām |
| on Yahweh | his God | | the Maker | the heavens | and the earth | the seas |

| 881, 3725, 866, 904 | 8490.151 | 583 | 3937, 5986 | | 6449.151 |
|---|---|---|---|---|---|
| cj, do, *adj*, rel part, prep, ps 3mp | art, v Qal act ptc ms | n fs | prep, n ms | | v Qal act ptc ms |
| וְאֶת־כָּל־אֲשֶׁר־בָּם | הַשֹּׁמֵר | אֱמֶת | לְעוֹלָם | 7. | עֹשֶׂה |
| wᵉ'eth-kol-'ăsher-bām | hashshōmēr | 'ĕmeth | lᵉ'ôlām | | 'ōseh |
| and all which in them | the Keeper | reliability | unto eternity | | One Who executes |

| 5122 | 3937, 6479.156 | 5598.151 | 4035 | 3937, 7744 | 3176 | 5609.551 |
|---|---|---|---|---|---|---|
| n ms | prep, art, v Qal pass ptc mp | v Qal act ptc ms | n ms | prep, art, adj | pn | v Hiphil ptc ms |
| מִשְׁפָּט | לָעֲשׁוּקִים | נֹתֵן | לֶחֶם | לָרְעֵבִים | יְהוָה | מַתִּיר |
| mishpāṭ | lā'ăshûqîm | nōthēn | lechem | lārᵉ'ēvîm | yᵉhwāh | mattîr |
| justice | for the oppressed | giving | food | to the hungry | Yahweh | One Who breaks free |

| 646.156 | | 3176 | 6741.151 | 5999 | 3176 | 2296.151 |
|---|---|---|---|---|---|---|
| v Qal pass ptc mp | | pn | v Qal act ptc ms | n mp | pn | v Qal act ptc ms |
| אֲסוּרִים | 8. | יְהוָה | פֹּקֵחַ | עִוְרִים | יְהוָה | זֹקֵף |
| 'ăsûrîm | | yᵉhwāh | pōqēach | 'iwrîm | yᵉhwāh | zōqēph |
| prisoners | | Yahweh | One Who opens | the blind | Yahweh | One Who lifts up |

| 3847.156 | 3176 | 154.151 | 6926 | | 3176 | 8490.151 |
|---|---|---|---|---|---|---|
| v Qal pass ptc mp | pn | v Qal act ptc ms | n mp | | pn | v Qal act ptc ms |
| כְּפוּפִים | יְהוָה | אֹהֵב | צַדִּיקִים | 9. | יְהוָה | שֹׁמֵר |
| kᵉphûphîm | yᵉhwāh | 'ōhēv | tsaddîqîm | | yᵉhwāh | shōmēr |
| those bowed down | Yahweh | One Who loves | the righteous | | Yahweh | One Who guards |

| 881, 1658 | 3605 | 496 | 5967.321 | 1932 | 7857 |
|---|---|---|---|---|---|
| do, n mp | n ms | cj, n fs | v Polel impf 3ms | cj, *n ms* | n mp |
| אֶת־גֵּרִים | יָתוֹם | וְאַלְמָנָה | יְעוֹדֵד | וְדֶרֶךְ | רְשָׁעִים |
| 'eth-gērîm | yāthôm | wᵉ'almānāh | yᵉ'ôdhēdh | wᵉdherekh | rᵉshā'îm |
| resident-aliens | orphans | and widows | He causes to continue | but the way of | the wicked |

| 6003.321 | | 4566.121 | 3176 | 3937, 5986 | 435 | 6995 | 3937, 1810 |
|---|---|---|---|---|---|---|---|
| v Piel impf 3ms | | v Qal impf 3ms | pn | prep, n ms | n mp, ps 2fs | pn | prep, n ms |
| יְעַוֵּת | 10. | יִמְלֹךְ | יְהוָה | לְעוֹלָם | אֱלֹהַיִךְ | צִיּוֹן | לְדֹר |
| yᵉ'awwēth | | yimlōkh | yᵉhwāh | lᵉ'ōlām | 'ĕlōhayikh | tsîyôn | lᵉdhōr |
| He makes crooked | | He reigns | Yahweh | unto eternity | your God | O Zion | unto generations |

**6. Which made heaven, and earth, the sea, and all that therein is:** … maker of heaven and earth and sea and all they contain, *Knox* .

**which keepeth truth for ever:** …who keeps faith for ever, *RSV.*

**7. Which executeth judgment for the oppressed:** … Who gives their rights to those who are crushed down, *BB* … who administers justice on behalf of the oppressed, *Berkeley* … He upholds the cause of the oppressed, *NIV* … who carries out judgment for the mistreated, *KJVII.*

**which giveth food to the hungry:** … who giveth bread to the hungry, *MAST.*

**The LORD looseth the prisoners:** … The LORD sets the prisoners free, *NRSV* … who brings release to the prisoner, *Knox.*

**8. The LORD openeth the eyes of the blind:** … The Lord gives sight to the blind, *NCB.*

**the LORD raiseth them that are bowed down:** … the Lord is the lifter up of those who are bent down, *BB* … The LORD lifts up people who are in trouble, *NCV* … the Lord, who comforts the burdened, *Knox.*

**the LORD loveth the righteous:** … the Lord is a lover of the upright, *BB* … The Lord loves the just, *NCB* … The Lord loves those who do right, *NCV.*

**9. The LORD preserveth the strangers:** … The Lord takes care of those who are in a strange land, *BB* … The LORD protects the immigrants, *Berkeley* … The Lord watches over the alien, *NIV.*

(vv. 6–7b) and then a string of brief sentences enumerating divine deeds (vv. 7c–9). No very clear difference in thought can be established as corresponding to this difference in form. The psalmist begins with God's omnipotence as manifested in creation. The first requisite for trust is assurance of power in the person trusted. The psalmist calls heaven and earth and sea, with all their inhabitants, as witnesses that Yahweh is not like the son of man, in whom there is no power to help.

But power may be whimsical, changeable, or may shroud its designs in mystery; therefore, if it is to be trusted, its purposes and methods must be so far known that a man may be able to reckon on it. Therefore, the Psalm adds unchangeable faithfulness to his power. But power, however faithful, is not yet worthy of trust, unless it works according to righteousness and has an arm that wars against wrong; therefore, to creative might and plighted troth the psalmist adds the exercise of judgment. Nor are these enough, for the conception which they embody may be that of a somewhat stern and repellent Being, who may be reverenced, but not approached with the warm heart of trust; therefore, the psalmist adds beneficence, which ministers their appropriate food to all desires, not only of the flesh, but of the spirit. The hungry hearts of men, who are all full of needs and longings, may turn to this mighty, faithful, righteous Yahweh and be sure that He never sends mouths, but He sends meat to fill them. All our various kinds of hunger are doors for God to come into our spirits.

**146:8a–8b.** The second series of sentences deals mainly with the divine beneficence in regard to man's miseries. The psalmist does not feel that the existence of these sad varieties of sorrow clouds his assurance in God's goodness. To him, they are occasions for the most heart-touching display of God's pitying, healing hand. If there is any difference between the two sets of clauses descriptive of God's acts, the latter bring into clearer light his personal agency in each case of suffering. This mighty, faithful, righteous, beneficent Yahweh, in all the majesty which that name suggests, comes down to the multitude of burdened ones and graciously deals with each, having in his heart the knowledge of, and in his hand the remedy for, all their ills. The greatness of his nature expressed by his name is vividly contrasted with the tenderness and lowliness of his working. Captives, blind persons and those bowed down by sorrows appeal to Him by their helplessness. His strong hand breaks the fetters, and his gentle touch opens without pain the closed eyes and quickens the paralyzed nerve to respond to the light. His firm, loving hold lifts to their feet and establishes the prostrate. All these classes of afflicted persons are meant to be regarded literally, but all may have a wider meaning and be intended to hint at spiritual bondage, blindness and abjectness.

**146:8c.** The next clause (v. 8c) seems to interrupt the representation of forms of affliction, but it comes in with great significance in the center of that sad catalog, for its presence here teaches that not merely affliction, whether physical or other, secures Yahweh's gracious help, but that there must be the yielding of heart to Him and the effort at conformity of life with his precepts and pattern, if his aid is to be reckoned on in men's sorrows. The prisoners will still languish in chains, the blind will grope in darkness, the bowed down will lie prone in the dust, unless they are righteous.

**146:9.** The series of afflictions which God alleviates is resumed in v. 9 with a pathetic triad—strangers, widows and fatherless. These are forlorn indeed, and the depth of their desolation is the measure of the divine compassion. The enumeration of Yahweh's acts, which make trust in God blessed in itself, and the sure way of securing help which is not vain, needs but one more touch for completion, and that is added in the solemn thought that He, by his providences and in the long run, turns aside (i.e., from its aim) the way of the wicked. That aspect of God's government is lightly handled in one clause as befits the purpose of the Psalm. But it could not be left out. A true likeness must have shadows. God were not a God for men to rely on, unless the trend of his reign was to crush evil and thwart the designs of sinners.

**146:10.** The blessedness of trust in Yahweh is gathered up into one great thought in the last verse of the Psalm. The sovereignty of God to all generations suggests the swift disappearance of earthly princes, referred to in v. 4. To trust in fleeting power is madness; to trust in the eternal King is wisdom and blessedness, and in some sense makes him who trusts a sharer in the eternity of the God in Whom is his hope, and from Whom is his help.

***Psalm 147.*** *The threefold call to praise Yahweh (vv. 1, 7, 12) divides this Psalm into three parts, the two former being closely connected, inasmuch as the first part is mainly occupied with celebrating God's mercy to the restored Israel, and the second takes a wider outlook, embracing his beneficence to all liv-*

| 1810 | 2054.333, 3161 | | 2054.333 | 3161 | 3706, 3005 | 2252.341 |
|---|---|---|---|---|---|---|
| cj, n ms | v Piel impv 2mp, pn | **147:1** | v Piel impv 2mp | pn | cj, adj | v Piel inf con |
| וָדֹר | הַלְלוּ־יָהּ | | הַלְלוּ | יָהּ | כִּי־טוֹב | זַמְּרָה |
| wādhōr | hal$^{e}$lû-yāhh | | hal$^{e}$lû | yāhh | kî-tôv | zamm$^{e}$rāh |
| and generations | praise Yah | | praise | Yah | because good | to sing praises to |

| 435 | 3706, 5456 | 5172 | 8747 | | 1161.151 | 3503 | 3176 |
|---|---|---|---|---|---|---|---|
| n mp, ps 1cp | cj, adj | adj | n fs | **2.** | v Qal act ptc ms | pn | pn |
| אֱלֹהֵינוּ | כִּי־נָעִים | נָאוָה | תְהִלָּה | | בּוֹנֵה | יְרוּשָׁלַם | יְהוָה |
| 'ĕlōhênû | kî-nā'îm | nā'wāh | th$^{e}$hillāh | | bônēh | y$^{e}$rûshālam | y$^{e}$hwāh |
| our God | because pleasant | proper | praise | | One Who builds | Jerusalem | Yahweh |

| 5258.256 | 3547 | 3788.321 | | 7784.151 | 3937, 8132.156 | 3949 |
|---|---|---|---|---|---|---|
| *v Niphal ptc mp* | pn | v Piel impf 3ms | **3.** | art, v Qal act ptc ms | prep, *v qal pass ptc mp* | n ms |
| נִדְחֵי | יִשְׂרָאֵל | יְכַנֵּס | | הָרֹפֵא | לִשְׁבוּרֵי | לֵב |
| nidh$^{e}$chê | yis$^{e}$rā'ēl | y$^{e}$khannēs | | hārōphē' | lishvûrê | lēv |
| the outcasts of | Israel | He gathers in | | the Healer | of those broken of | the heart |

| 2372.351 | 3937, 6329 | | 4630.151 | 4709 | 3937, 3676 | 3937, 3725 |
|---|---|---|---|---|---|---|
| cj, v Piel ptc ms | prep, n fp, ps 3mp | **4.** | v Qal act ptc ms | n ms | prep, art, n mp | prep, n ms, ps 3mp |
| וּמְחַבֵּשׁ | לְעַצְּבוֹתָם | | מוֹנֶה | מִסְפָּר | לַכּוֹכָבִים | לְכֻלָּם |
| ûm$^{e}$chabbēsh | l$^{e}$'atsts$^{e}$vôthām | | môneh | mispār | lakkôkhāvîm | l$^{e}$khullām |
| and One Who binds | their wounds | | One Who counts | a number | of the stars | to all of them |

| 8428 | 7410.121 | | 1448 | 112 | 7521, 3699 | 3937, 8722 | 375 |
|---|---|---|---|---|---|---|---|
| n mp | v Qal impf 3ms | **5.** | adj | n mp, ps 1cp | cj, *adj*, n ms | prep, n fs, ps 3ms | *sub* |
| שֵׁמוֹת | יִקְרָא | | גָּדוֹל | אֲדוֹנֵינוּ | וְרַב־כֹּחַ | לִתְבוּנָתוֹ | אֵין |
| shēmôth | yiqōrā' | | gādhôl | 'ădhônênû | w$^{e}$rav-kōach | lithvûnāthô | 'ên |
| names | He calls | | great | our Lord | and abundant in power | his ability | there is not |

| 4709 | | 5967.351 | 6262 | 3176 | 8584.551 | 7857 |
|---|---|---|---|---|---|---|
| n ms | **6.** | v Polel ptc ms | n mp | pn | v Hiphil ptc ms | n mp |
| מִסְפָּר | | מְעוֹדֵד | עֲנָוִים | יְהוָה | מַשְׁפִּיל | רְשָׁעִים |
| mispār | | m$^{e}$'ôdhēdh | 'ănāwîm | y$^{e}$hwāh | mashpîl | r$^{e}$shā'îm |
| a number | | One Who causes to continue | the lowly | Yahweh | One Who throws down | the wicked |

| 5912, 800 | | 6257.133 | 3937, 3176 | 904, 8756 | 2252.333 | 3937, 435 |
|---|---|---|---|---|---|---|
| prep, n fs | **7.** | v Qal impv 2mp | prep, pn | prep, n fs | v Piel impv 2mp | prep, n mp, ps 1cp |
| עֲדֵי־אָרֶץ | | עֱנוּ | לַיהוָה | בְּתוֹדָה | זַמְּרוּ | לֵאלֹהֵינוּ |
| 'ădhê-'ārets | | 'ĕnû | layhwāh | b$^{e}$thôdhāh | zamm$^{e}$rû | lē'lōhênû |
| to the ground | | sing | to Yahweh | with thanksgiving | sing praises | to our God |

**He relieveth the fatherless and widow:** ... the fatherless and the widow he sustains, *NCB* ... and sustains the fatherless and the widow, *NIV* ... The fatherless and widow He causeth to stand, *Young.*

**but the way of the wicked he turneth upside down:** ... but the way of the wicked doth he subvert, *Darby* ... He thwarts the way of the wicked, *NASB* ... but the way of the wicked he brings to ruin, *RSV.*

**10. The LORD shall reign for ever, even thy God, O Zion, unto all generations. Praise ye the LORD:** ... The LORD will be King forever. Jerusalem, your God is everlasting, *NCV.*

**147:1. Praise ye the LORD: for it is good to sing praises unto our God; for it is pleasant; and praise is comely:** ... It is good to sing hymns to our God, *Beck* ... it is good to make melody to our God, *BB* ... Praise ye Jah! for it is good. Sing Psalms of our God, *Darby* ... Praise the Lord, for he is good; sing praise to our God, for he is gracious, *NCB* ... for he is gracious, and a song of praise is fitting, *NRSV* ... it is fitting to praise him, *NAB* ... make melody to our God, for he is gracious, *Moffatt* ... for it is a delight; the song of praise is so befitting, *Berkeley.*

**2. The LORD doth build up Jerusalem:** ... The LORD builds up Jerusalem, *NRSV* ... The LORD rebuilds Jerusalem, *NCV* ... LORD, re-build Jerusalem, *Fenton.*

**he gathereth together the outcasts of Israel:** ... and gathering those of Israel who were driven away, *Beck* ... he makes all the outlaws of Israel come together, *BB* ... He gathereth together the dispersed of Israel, *MAST* ... he brings back the captured Israelites, *NCV.*

**3. He healeth the broken in heart:** ... He heals the brokenhearted, *NRSV* ... It is He who heals the brokenhearted, *Berkeley.*

**and bindeth up their wounds:** ... and bandages their wounds, *Beck* ... and puts oil on their wounds, *BB* ... and bandages their wounds, *NCV* ... And is binding up their griefs, *Young.*

**4. He telleth the number of the stars:** ... He determines the number of the stars, *NRSV* ... he counts out the number of the stars, *JB* ... He fixes the number of the stars, *Moffatt* ... He determines the number of the stars, *NIV.*

**he calleth them all by their names:** ... he giveth names to them all, *Darby* ... and assigns their names to them all, *Berkeley* ... and names them one and all, *NEB.*

**5. Great is our Lord, and of great power:** ... Our Lord is great and very strong, *Beck* ... Our LORD is great and mighty in strength, *Berkeley* ... Great is our Lord, and abundant in strength, *NASB* ... Great is our Lord, and of abounding strength, *Rotherham.*

**his understanding is infinite:** ... and there's no limit to what He knows, *Beck* ... there is no limit to his wisdom, *BB* ... his wisdom beyond all telling, *JB* ... His understanding is infinite, *MAST* ... And his knowledge cannot be expressed, *Rotherham*

**6. The LORD lifteth up the meek:** ... The LORD makes those who suffer happy again, *Beck* ... The Lord gives help to the poor in spirit, *BB* ... The LORD lifts up the downtrodden, *NRSV* ... The Eternal has relief for the afflicted, *Moffatt* ... The LORD defends the humble, *NCV.*

**he casteth the wicked down to the ground:** ... he sends sinners down in shame, *BB* ... and brings evildoers to the ground, *REB* ... and lays the wicked low in the dust, *Knox* ... Casting the lawless down to the earth, *Rotherham.*

**7. Sing unto the LORD with thanksgiving:** ... Sing praises to the LORD, *NCV* ... Strike up, then, in thanksgiving to the Lord, *Knox* ... Respond to Yahweh with thanksgiving, *Rotherham.*

**sing praise upon the harp unto our God:** ... make melody to our God on the lyre, *NRSV* ... make music to our God with the lyre, *Anchor.*

---

*ing things. Both of these points of view are repeated in the same order in the third part (vv. 12–20), which the Septuagint makes a separate Psalm. The allusions to Jerusalem as rebuilt, to the gathering of the scattered Israelites, and to the fortifications of the city naturally point to the period of the restoration. The emphasis placed on God's working in nature, in this and others of these closing Psalms, is probably in part a polemic against the idolatry, which Israel had learned to abhor through the punishment of losing the land blessing for seventy years. The two truths of God's special relation to his people and of his universal steadfast love are complementary not contradictory, despite views erroneously espoused at times by Jew and Gentile alike. This Psalm teaches a more excellent way.*

**147:1–6.** The main theme of vv. 1–6 is God's manifestation of transcendent power and incalculable wisdom, as well as infinite kindness, in building up the ruined Jerusalem and collecting into a happy band of citizens the lonely wanderers of Israel. For such blessings praise is due, and the Psalm summons all who share them to swell the song.

Verse 1 is somewhat differently construed by some, who would change one letter in the word rendered above "to harp," and making it an imperative, would refer "good" and "pleasant" to God, thus making the whole to read, "Praise Yahweh, for He is good; harp to our God, for He is pleasant: praise is comely." This change simplifies some points of construction, but labors under the objection that it is contrary to usage to apply the adjective "pleasant" to God, and the usual rendering is quite intelligible and appropriate. The reason for the fittingness and delightsomeness of praise is the great mercy shown to Israel in the restoration, which mercy is in the psalmist's thoughts throughout this part.

The psalmist has the same fondness for using participles as the author of the previous Psalm and begins vv. 2ff and 6 with them. Possibly, their use is intended to imply that the acts described by them are regarded as continuous, not merely done once for all. Yahweh is ever building up Jerusalem, and, in like manner, uninterruptedly energizing in providence and nature.

The collocation of divine acts in v. 2 bears upon the great theme that fills the singer's heart and lips. It is the outcasts of Israel of whom he thinks, while he sings of binding up the brokenhearted. It is they who are the "afflicted," helped up by that strong, gentle clasp, while their oppressors are the wicked, flung prone by the very wind of God's hand.

The beautiful and profound juxtaposition of gentle healing and omnipotence in vv. 3f is meant to signalize the work of restoring Israel as no less wondrous than that of marshaling the stars and to

| 904, 3780<br>prep, n ms<br>בְּכִנּוֹר<br>vekhinnôr<br>with the zither | 8. | 3803.351<br>art, v Piel ptc ms<br>הַמְכַסֶּה<br>hamkhasseh<br>the One Who covers | 8452<br>n md<br>שָׁמַיִם<br>shāmayim<br>the heavens | 904, 5854<br>prep, n mp<br>בְּעָבִים<br>be'āvîm<br>with clouds | 3679.551<br>art, v Hiphil ptc ms<br>הַמֵּכִין<br>hammēkhîn<br>the One Who prepares |
|---|---|---|---|---|---|

| 3937, 800<br>prep, art, n fs<br>לָאָרֶץ<br>lā'ārets<br>for the land | 4443<br>n ms<br>מָטָר<br>māṭār<br>rain | 7049.551<br>art, v Hiphil ptc ms<br>הַמַּצְמִיחַ<br>hammatsmîach<br>the One Who causes to sprout | 2098<br>n mp<br>הָרִים<br>hārîm<br>the mountains | 2785<br>n ms<br>חָצִיר<br>chātsîr<br>grass | 9. | 5598.151<br>v Qal act ptc ms<br>נוֹתֵן<br>nôthēn<br>One Who gives |
|---|---|---|---|---|---|---|

| 3937, 966<br>prep, n fs<br>לִבְהֵמָה<br>livhēmāh<br>to the beast | 4035<br>n ms, ps 3fs<br>לַחְמָהּ<br>lachmāhh<br>its food | 3937, 1158<br>prep, *n mp*<br>לִבְנֵי<br>livnê<br>to the young of | 6397<br>n ms<br>עֹרֵב<br>'ōrēv<br>ravens | 866<br>rel part<br>אֲשֶׁר<br>'ăsher<br>which | 7410.126<br>v Qal impf 3mp<br>יִקְרָאוּ<br>yiqōrā'û<br>they call | 10. | 3940<br>neg part<br>לֹא<br>lō'<br>not | 904, 1400<br>prep, *n fs*<br>בִּגְבוּרַת<br>vighvûrath<br>in the might of |
|---|---|---|---|---|---|---|---|---|

| 5670<br>art, n ms<br>הַסּוּס<br>hassûs<br>the horse | 2759.121<br>v Qal impf 3ms<br>יֶחְפָּץ<br>yechăppāts<br>He delights | 3940, 904, 8225<br>neg part, prep, *n fd*<br>לֹא־בְשׁוֹקֵי<br>lō'-veshôqê<br>not in the legs of | 382<br>art, n ms<br>הָאִישׁ<br>hā'îsh<br>the man | 7813.121<br>v Qal impf 3ms<br>יִרְצֶה<br>yirtseh<br>He is pleased | 11. | 7813.151<br>v Qal act ptc ms<br>רוֹצֶה<br>rôtseh<br>One Who is pleased with |
|---|---|---|---|---|---|---|

| 3176<br>pn<br>יְהוָה<br>yehwāh<br>Yahweh | 881, 3486.152<br>do, v Qal act ptc mp, ps 3ms<br>אֶת־יְרֵאָיו<br>'eth-yerē'âv<br>those who fear Him | 881, 3282.352<br>do, art, v Piel ptc mp<br>אֶת־הַמְיַחֲלִים<br>'eth-hamyachlîm<br>those who wait | 3937, 2721<br>prep, n ms, ps 3ms<br>לְחַסְדּוֹ<br>lechasdô<br>for his faithfulness | 12. | 8099.332<br>v Piel impv 2fs<br>שַׁבְּחִי<br>shabbechî<br>glorify |
|---|---|---|---|---|---|

| 3503<br>pn<br>יְרוּשָׁלַםִ<br>yerûshālam<br>O Jerusalem | 881, 3176<br>do, pn<br>אֶת־יְהוָה<br>'eth-yehwāh<br>Yahweh | 2054.132<br>v Piel impv 2fs<br>הַלְלִי<br>halelî<br>praise | 435<br>n mp, ps 2fs<br>אֱלֹהַיִךְ<br>'ělōhayikh<br>your God | 6995<br>pn<br>צִיּוֹן<br>tsîyôn<br>O Zion | 13. | 3706, 2480.311<br>cj, v Piel pf 3ms<br>כִּי־חִזַּק<br>kî-chizzaq<br>because He strengthens | 1308<br>*n mp*<br>בְּרִיחֵי<br>berîchê<br>the bars of |
|---|---|---|---|---|---|---|---|

| 8554<br>n mp, ps 2fs<br>שְׁעָרָיִךְ<br>she'ārāyikh<br>your gates | 1313.311<br>v Piel pf 3ms<br>בֵּרַךְ<br>bērakh<br>He blesses | 1158<br>n mp, ps 2fs<br>בָּנַיִךְ<br>bānayikh<br>your sons | 904, 7419<br>prep, n ms, ps 2fs<br>בְּקִרְבֵּךְ<br>beqirbēkh<br>in your midst | 14. | 7947.151, 1397<br>art, v Qal act ptc ms, n ms, ps 2fs<br>הַשָּׂם־גְּבוּלֵךְ<br>hassām-gevûlēkh<br>the One Who sets your borders | 8361<br>n ms<br>שָׁלוֹם<br>shālôm<br>peace |
|---|---|---|---|---|---|---|

**8. Who covereth the heaven with clouds:** … He veils the sky with clouds, *JB* … He fills the sky with clouds, *NCV.*

**who prepareth rain for the earth:** … and sends rain to the earth, *NCV.*

**who maketh grass to grow upon the mountains:** … who makes grass sprout on the mountains and herbs for the service of men, *NCB* … Who is causing grass to spring up on mountains, *Young* … he clothes the hills with grass, *NEB.*

**9. He giveth to the beast his food:** … Who giveth to the cattle their food, *Darby* … who gives wild animals their food, *Moffatt.*

**and to the young ravens which cry:** … that cry for it at eventide, *Moffatt* … and to the little birds that call, *NCV.*

**10. He delighteth not in the strength of the horse:** … In the strength of the steed he delights not, *NCB* … He cares not for the strength of the war-horse, *Moffatt* … Not the well-mounted warrior is his choice, *Knox.*

**he taketh not pleasure in the legs of a man:** … nor his pleasure in the speed of a runner, *NRSV* … no pleasure in human sturdiness, *JB* … nor is he pleased with the fleetness of men, *NCB* … not in man's thighs is he pleased, *Anchor.*

**11. The LORD taketh pleasure in them that fear him:** … The Lord takes pleasure in his worshippers, *BB* … the LORD takes satisfaction in those who revere Him, *Berkeley.*

**in those that hope in his mercy:** … who look for His grace, *Beck* … in those that hope in his loving-kindness, *Darby* ... in those who hope in his steadfast love, *NRSV* ... those who place their hope in His covenant love, *Berkeley* ... with those who rely on his strength, *Anchor.*

**12. Praise the LORD, O Jerusalem; praise thy God, O Zion:** ... Extol the LORD, O Jerusalem!, *Berkeley* ... Jerusalem, praise the LORD; Jerusalem, praise your God, *NCV.*

**13. For he hath strengthened the bars of thy gates:** ... He has made strong the iron bands of your doors, *BB* ... For he hath made the barres of the gates strong, *Geneva.*

**he hath blessed thy children within thee:** ... he has blessed your inhabitants, *REB* ... and has blessed your sons in your midst, *Berkeley.*

**14. He maketh peace in thy borders:** ... He grants peace within your borders, *NRSV* ... He it is that bolts thy gates fast, *Knox.*

---

hearten faith by pledging that incalculable power to perfect its restoring work. He who stands beside the sickbed of the brokenhearted, like a gentle physician with balm and bandage, and lays a tender hand on their wounds, is He who sets the stars in their places and tells them as a shepherd his flock or a commander his army. The psalmist borrows from Isa. 40:26–29, where several of his expressions occur. "Telleth the number of the stars" is scarcely equivalent to numbering them as they shine. It rather means determining how many of them there shall be. Calling them all by names (literally, "He calls names to them all") is not giving them designations, but summoning them as a captain reading the roster of his band. It may also imply full knowledge of each individual in their countless hosts.

Verse 5 is taken from the passage in Isaiah already referred to, with the change of "infinite" for "lacks might," a change which is suggested by the preceding reference to the number of the stars. These have a number, although it surpasses human arithmetic, but his wisdom is measureless. And all this magnificence of power, this minute particularizing knowledge, this abyss of wisdom, are guarantees for the healing of the broken-hearted. The thought goes further than Israel's deliverance from bondage. It has a strong voice of cheer for all sad hearts who will let Him probe their wounds that He may bind them up. The mighty God of creation is the tender God of providence and of redemption. Therefore, praise is comely, and fear and faltering are unbefitting.

**147:7–11.** The second part of the Psalm passes out from the special field of mercy to Israel and comes down from the glories of the heavens to magnify God's universal goodness manifested in physical changes by which lowly creatures are provided for. The point of time selected is that of the November rains.

The verbs in vv. 8f, 11 are again participles, expressive of continuous action. The yearly miracle which brings from some invisible storehouse the clouds to fill the sky and drop down fatness, the answer of the brown earth which mysteriously shoots forth the tender green spikelets away up on the mountain flanks, where no man has sown and no man will reap, the loving care which thereby provides food for the wild creatures, owned by no one, and answers the hoarse croak of the callow fledglings in the ravens' nests—these are manifestations of God's power and revelations of his character worthy to be woven into a hymn which celebrates his restoring grace and to be set beside the apocalypse of his greatness in the nightly heavens.

But what has v. 10 to do here? The connection of it is difficult to trace. Apparently, the psalmist would draw from the previous verses, which exhibit God's universal goodness and the creatures' dependence on Him, the lesson that reliance on one's own resources or might is sure to be smitten with confusion, while humble trust in God, which man alone of earth's creatures can exercise, is for him the condition of his receiving needed gifts. The beast gets its food, and it is enough that the young ravens should croak, but man has to "fear him" and to wait on his "steadfast love." Verse 10 is a reminiscence of Ps. 33:16f and v. 11 of the next verse of the same Psalm.

**147:12–13.** The third part (vv. 12–20) travels over substantially the same ground as the two former, beginning with the mercy shown to the restored Israel and passing on to wider manifestations of God's goodness. But there is a difference in this repeated setting forth of both these themes. The fortifications of Jerusalem are now complete, and their strength gives security to the people gathered into the city. Over all the land once devastated by war, peace broods, and the fields that lay desolate now have yielded harvest. The ancient promise (Ps. 81:16) has been fulfilled, its condition having been complied with, and Israel having hearkened to Yahweh. Protection, blessing, tranquillity and abundance are the results of obedience, God's gifts to them that fear Him. So it was in the psalmist's experience, and so, in higher form, it is still. These divine acts are continuous, and as long as there are

| 2561 | 2498 | 7881.521 | | 8365.151 | 577 | 800 |
|---|---|---|---|---|---|---|
| *n ms* | n fp | v Hiphil impf 3ms, ps 2fs | | art, v Qal act ptc ms | n fs, ps 3ms | n fs |
| חֵלֶב | חִטִּים | יַשְׂבִּיעֵךְ | **15.** | הַשֹּׁלֵחַ | אִמְרָתוֹ | אָרֶץ |
| chēlev | chittîm | yasbî'ēkh | | hashshōlēach | 'imrāthô | 'ārets |
| the fat of | wheat | He satisfies you with | | the One Who sends forth to | his word | the earth |

| 5912, 4259 | 7608.121 | 1745 | | 5598.151 | 8345 | 3626, 7055 |
|---|---|---|---|---|---|---|
| adv, n fs | v Qal impf 3ms | n ms, ps 3ms | | art, v Qal act ptc ms | n ms | prep, art, n ms |
| עַד־מְהֵרָה | יָרוּץ | דְּבָרוֹ | **16.** | הַנֹּתֵן | שֶׁלֶג | כַּצָּמֶר |
| 'adh-mehērāh | yārûts | devārô | | hannōthēn | shelegh | katstsāmer |
| until swiftness | it runs | his speaking | | the One Who gives | snow | like the wool |

| 3839 | 3626, 684 | 6582.321 | | 8390.551 | 7430 | 3626, 6846 |
|---|---|---|---|---|---|---|
| n ms | prep, art, n ms | v Piel impf 3ms | | v Hiphil ptc ms | n ms, ps 3ms | prep, n fp |
| כְּפוֹר | כָּאֵפֶר | יְפַזֵּר | **17.** | מַשְׁלִיךְ | קַרְחוֹ | כְפִתִּים |
| kephôr | kā'ēpher | yephazzēr | | mashlîkh | qarchô | khephittîm |
| a covering | like the ashes | He scatters | | One Who throws down | his frost | like morsels |

| 3937, 6686 | 7426 | 4449 | 6198.121 | | 8365.121 | 1745 | 4678.521 |
|---|---|---|---|---|---|---|---|
| prep, *n mp* | n fs, ps 3ms | intrg | v Qal impf 3ms | | v Qal impf 3ms | n ms, ps 3ms | cj, v Hiphil impf 3ms, ps 3mp |
| לִפְנֵי | קָרָתוֹ | מִי | יַעֲמֹד | **18.** | יִשְׁלַח | דְּבָרוֹ | וְיַמְסֵם |
| liphnê | qārāthô | mî | ya'ămōdh | | yishlach | devārô | weyamsēm |
| before | his cold | who | he can stand | | He sends out | his word | and it melts them |

| 5566.521 | 7593 | 5320.126, 4448 | | 5222.551 | 1745 | 3937, 3399 |
|---|---|---|---|---|---|---|
| v Hiphil impf 3ms | n fs, ps 3ms | v Qal impf 3mp, n mp | | v Hiphil ptc ms | n ms, ps 3ms | prep, pn |
| יַשֵּׁב | רוּחוֹ | יִזְּלוּ־מָיִם | **19.** | מַגִּיד | דְּבָרוֹ | לְיַעֲקֹב |
| yashshēv | rûchô | yizzelû-māyim | | maggîdh | devārô | leya'ăqōv |
| He causes to blow | his wind | the waters gush out | | One Who declares | his word | to Jacob |

| 2805 | 5122 | 3937, 3547 | | 3940 | 6449.111 | 3772 | 3937, 3725, 1504 |
|---|---|---|---|---|---|---|---|
| n mp, ps 3ms | cj, n mp, ps 3ms | prep, pn | | neg part | v Qal pf 3ms | adv | prep, *adj*, n ms |
| חֻקָּיו | וּמִשְׁפָּטָיו | לְיִשְׂרָאֵל | **20.** | לֹא | עָשָׂה | כֵן | לְכָל־גּוֹי |
| chuqqâv | ûmishpāṭâv | leyisrā'ēl | | lō' | 'āsāh | khēn | lekhol-gôy |
| his statutes | and his ordinances | to Israel | | not | He has done | so | to all the nations |

| 5122 | 1118, 3156.116 | 2054.333, 3161 | | 2054.333 | 3161 |
|---|---|---|---|---|---|
| cj, n mp | neg part, v Qal pf 3cp, ps 3mp | v Piel impv 2mp, pn | | v Piel impv 2mp | pn |
| וּמִשְׁפָּטִים | בַּל־יְדָעוּם | הַלְלוּ־יָהּ | **148:1** | הַלְלוּ | יָהּ |
| ûmishpāṭîm | bal-yedhā'ûm | halelû-yāhh | | halelû | yāhh |
| indeed ordinances | they do not know them | praise Yah | | praise | Yah |

**and filleth thee with the finest of the wheat:** … making your stores full of fat grain, *BB* … He giveth thee in plenty the fat of wheat, *MAST.*

**15. He sendeth forth his commandment upon earth:** … He sends His order throughout the earth, *Beck* … He sendeth forth his oracles to the earth, *Darby.*

**his word runneth very swiftly:** … and it quickly obeys him, *NCV.*

**16. He giveth snow like wool:** … he spreads the snow like flax, *JB* … He showers down snow, white as wool, *REB.*

**he scattereth the hoarfrost like ashes:** … He sends out ice-drops like dust, *BB* … He scatters the frost like ashes, *NKJV.*

**17. He casteth forth his ice like morsels:** … He hurls down hail like crumbs, *NRSV* … he sends ice-crytals like breadcrumbs, *JB* … He hurls down His ice in fragments, *Berkeley* … He hurls down his hail like pebbles, *NIV.*

**who can stand before his cold?:** … water is made hard by his cold, *BB* … who can withstand that cold?, *JB* … before his cold the water freeze, *NCB* … Who can withstand his icy blast?, *NIV* … No one can stand the cold he sends, *NCV.*

**18. He sendeth out his word, and melteth them:** … When he sends his word it thaws them, *JB* … He issues His order and makes them melt, *Berkeley.*

**he causeth his wind to blow, and the waters flow:** … when he makes his wind blow, the waters are unstopped, *JB* ... he lets his breeze blow and the waters run, *NCB* ... he stirs up his breezes, and the waters flow, *NIV.*

**19. He showeth his word unto Jacob:** ... He has proclaimed his word to Jacob, *NAB* ... He makes his purpose known to Jacob, *Moffatt* ... He has revealed his word to Jacob, *NIV.*

**his statutes and his judgments unto Israel:** ... His laws and decrees to Israel, *Beck* ... teaching Israel his laws and his decisions, *BB* ... his orders and his laws to Israel, *Moffatt.*

**20. He hath not dealt so with any nation:** ... He has not done these things for any other nation, *BB* ... he has not done this for other nations, *REB* ... He didn't do this for any other nation, *NCV.*

**and as for his judgments, they have not known them. Praise ye the LORD:** ... He hasn't taught them His decrees, *Beck* ... his ordinances he has not made known to them, *NAB* ... They don't know his laws, *NCV.*

**148:1. Praise ye the LORD. Praise ye the LORD from the heavens:** ... give him praise in the skies, *BB* ... Praise the LORD from the skies, *NCV.*

**praise him in the heights:** ... praise him in the heights above, *NIV* ... Praise him high above the earth, *NCV.*

---

men who trust, there will be a God who builds defenses around them, and satisfies them with good.

**147:14–15.** Again the psalmist turns to the realm of nature, but it is nature at a different season which now yields witness to God's universal power and care. The phenomena of a sharp winter were more striking to the psalmist than to us. But his poet's eye and his devout heart recognize even in the cold, before which his eastern makeup cowered shivering, the working of God's will. His "commandment" or word is personified, and compared to a swift-footed messenger. As ever, power over material things is attributed to the divine word, and as ever, in the biblical view of nature, all intermediate links are neglected, and the almighty cause at one end of the chain and the physical effect at the other are brought together. There is between these two clauses room enough for all that meteorology has to say.

**147:16–17.** The winter piece in vv. 16f dashes off the dreary scene with a few bold strokes. The air is full of flakes like floating wool, or the white mantle covers the ground like a cloth. Rime lies everywhere, as if ashes were powdered over trees and stones. Hailstones fall, as if He flung them down from above. They are like "morsels" of bread, a comparison which strikes us as violent, but which may possibly describe the more severe storms, in which flat pieces of ice fall. As by magic, all is changed when He again sends forth his word. It but needs that He should let a warm wind steal gently across the desolation, and every sealed and silent brook begins to trickle along its course. And will not He Who thus changes the face of the earth in like manner breathe upon frost bound lives and hearts, And every winter change in spring?

**147:18–20.** But the Psalm cannot end with contemplation of God's universal beneficence, however gracious that is. There is a higher mode of activity for his word than that exercised on material things. God sends his commandment forth, and earth unconsciously obeys, and all creatures, men included, are fed and blessed. But the noblest utterance of his word is in the shape of statutes and judgments, and these are Israel's prerogative. The psalmist is not rejoicing that other nations have not received these, but that Israel has. Its privilege is its responsibility. It has received them that it may obey them, and then that it may make them known. If the God who scatters lower blessings broadcast, not forgetting beasts and ravens, has restricted his highest gift to his people, the restriction is a clear call to them to spread the knowledge of the treasure entrusted to them. To glory in privilege is sin, to learn that it means responsibility is wisdom. The lesson is needed by those who today have been served as heirs to Israel's prerogative, forfeited by it because it clutched it for itself and forgot its obligation to carry it as widely as God had diffused his lower gifts.

***Psalm 148.*** *The mercy granted to Israel (v. 14) is, in the psalmist's estimation, worthy to call forth strains of praise from all creatures. It is the same conception as is found in several of the Psalms of the King (Pss. 93–100), but is here expressed with unparalleled magnificence and fervor. The same idea attains the climax of its representation in the mighty anthem from "every creature which is in heaven and on the earth, and under the earth, and such as are in the sea, and all that are in them," whom John heard saying, "Blessing and honor and glory, and power, be unto him that sitteth upon the throne, and unto the Lamb for ever and ever" (Rev. 5:13). The Psalm falls into two broad divisions, in the former of which heaven, and in the latter earth, are invoked to praise Yahweh.*

| 2054.333 | 881, 3176 | 4623, 8452 | 2054.333 | 904, 4953 |
|---|---|---|---|---|
| v Piel impv 2mp | do, pn | prep, art, n md | v Piel impv 2mp, ps 3ms | prep, art, n mp |
| הַלְלוּ | אֶת־יְהוָה | מִן־הַשָּׁמַיִם | הַלְלוּהוּ | בַּמְּרוֹמִים |
| hal$^e$lû | 'eth-y$^e$hwāh | min-hashshāmayim | hal$^e$lûhû | bamm$^e$rômîm |
| praise | Yahweh | from the heavens | praise Him | in the heights |

| 2. | 2054.333 | 3725, 4534 | 2054.333 | 3725, 6893 |
|---|---|---|---|---|
| | v Piel impv 2mp, ps 3ms | *adj*, n mp, ps 3ms | v Piel impv 2mp, ps 3ms | *adj*, n ms, ps 3ms |
| | הַלְלוּהוּ | כָּל־מַלְאָכָיו | הַלְלוּהוּ | כָּל־צְבָאוֹ |
| | hal$^e$lûhû | khol-mal'ākhâv | hal$^e$lûhû | kol-ts$^e$vā'ô |
| | praise Him | all his angels | praise Him | all his host |

| 3. | 2054.333 | 8507 | 3507 | 2054.333 | 3725, 3676 | 214 |
|---|---|---|---|---|---|---|
| | v Piel impv 2mp, ps 3ms | n ms | cj, n ms | v Piel impv 2mp, ps 3ms | *adj, n mp* | n ms |
| | הַלְלוּהוּ | שֶׁמֶשׁ | וְיָרֵחַ | הַלְלוּהוּ | כָּל־כּוֹכְבֵי | אוֹר |
| | hal$^e$lûhû | shemesh | w$^e$yārēach | hal$^e$lûhû | kāl-kôkh$^e$vê | 'ôr |
| | praise Him | O sun | and moon | praise Him | all the stars of | light |

| 4. | 2054.333 | 8452 | 8452 | 4448 | 866 | 4623, 6142 |
|---|---|---|---|---|---|---|
| | v Piel impv 2mp, ps 3ms | *n md* | art, n md | cj, art, n md | rel part | prep, prep |
| | הַלְלוּהוּ | שְׁמֵי | הַשָּׁמָיִם | וְהַמַּיִם | אֲשֶׁר | מֵעַל |
| | hal$^e$lûhû | sh$^e$mê | hashshāmāyim | w$^e$hammayim | 'ăsher | mē'al |
| | praise Him | the heavens of | the heavens | and the waters | which | from above |

| 8452 | 5. | 2054.326 | 881, 8428 | 3176 | 3706 | 2000 | 6943.311 |
|---|---|---|---|---|---|---|---|
| art, n md | | v Piel juss 3mp | do, *n ms* | pn | cj | pers pron | v Piel pf 3ms |
| הַשָּׁמָיִם | | יְהַלְלוּ | אֶת־שֵׁם | יְהוָה | כִּי | הוּא | צִוָּה |
| hashshāmāyim | | y$^e$hal$^e$lû | 'eth-shēm | y$^e$hwāh | kî | hû' | tsiwwāh |
| the heavens | | let them praise | the name of | Yahweh | because | He | He has commanded |

| 1282.216 | 6. | 6198.521 | 3937, 5911 | 3937, 5986 | 2805, 5598.111 |
|---|---|---|---|---|---|
| cj, v Niphal pf 3cp | | cj, v Hiphil impf 3ms, ps 3mp | prep, n ms | prep, n ms | n ms, v Qal pf 3ms |
| וְנִבְרָאוּ | | וַיַּעֲמִידֵם | לָעַד | לְעוֹלָם | חָק־נָתַן |
| w$^e$nivrā'û | | wayya'ămîdhēm | lā'adh | l$^e$'ôlām | chāq-nāthan |
| and they were created | | and He caused them to stand | unto eternity | unto eternity | He gave limits |

| 3940 | 5882.121 | 7. | 2054.333 | 881, 3176 | 4623, 800 | 8906 |
|---|---|---|---|---|---|---|
| cj, neg part | v Qal impf 3ms | | v Piel impv 2mp | do, pn | prep, art, n fs | n mp |
| וְלֹא | יַעֲבוֹר | | הַלְלוּ | אֶת־יְהוָה | מִן־הָאָרֶץ | תַּנִּינִים |
| w$^e$lō' | ya'ăvôr | | hal$^e$lû | 'eth-y$^e$hwāh | min-hā'ārets | tanînîm |
| and not | they passed by | | praise | Yahweh | from the earth | sea monsters |

| 3725, 8745 | 8. | 813 | 1287 | 8345 | 7290 | 7593 | 5788 | 6449.153 |
|---|---|---|---|---|---|---|---|---|
| cj, *adj*, n fp | | n fs | cj, n ms | n ms | cj, n ms | n fs | n fs | v Qal act ptc fs |
| וְכָל־תְּהֹמוֹת | | אֵשׁ | וּבָרָד | שֶׁלֶג | וְקִיטוֹר | רוּחַ | סְעָרָה | עֹשָׂה |
| w$^e$khol-t$^e$hōmôth | | 'ēsh | ûvārādh | shelegh | w$^e$qîtôr | rûach | s$^e$'ārāh | 'ōsāh |
| and all the deeps | | fire | and hail | snow | and thick smoke | wind | a storm | executing |

| 1745 | 9. | 2098 | 3725, 1421 | 6320 | 6780 | 3725, 753 | 10. | 2516 |
|---|---|---|---|---|---|---|---|---|
| n ms, ps 3ms | | art, n mp | cj, *adj*, n fp | *n ms* | n ms | cj, *adj*, n mp | | art, n fs |
| דְבָרוֹ | | הֶהָרִים | וְכָל־גְּבָעוֹת | עֵץ | פְּרִי | וְכָל־אֲרָזִים | | הַחַיָּה |
| dh$^e$vārô | | hehārîm | w$^e$khol-g$^e$vā'ôth | 'ēts | p$^e$rî | w$^e$khol-'ărāzîm | | hachayyāh |
| his word | | the mountains | and all the hills | trees with | fruit | and all the cedars | | the beasts |

| 3725, 966 | 7719 | 7109 | 3796 | 11. | 4567, 800 |
|---|---|---|---|---|---|
| cj, *adj*, n fs | n ms | cj, *n fs* | n fs | | *n mp*, n fs |
| וְכָל־בְּהֵמָה | רֶמֶשׂ | וְצִפּוֹר | כָּנָף | | מַלְכֵי־אֶרֶץ |
| w$^e$khol-b$^e$hēmāh | remes | w$^e$tsippôr | kānāph | | malkhê-'erets |
| and all the cattle | the creeping things | and the birds with | wings | | the kings of the earth |

**2. Praise ye him, all his angels:** ... give praise to him, all his armies, *BB* ... Praise him, all his messengers, *Rotherham* ... all his soldiers!, *Anchor.*

**praise ye him, all his hosts:** ... praise Him all His heavenly army!, *Beck* ... all his armie, *Geneva* ... all his heavenly hosts, *NIV* ... Praise him, all you armies of heaven, *NCV.*

**3. Praise ye him, sun and moon, praise him, all ye stars of light:** ... praise him, all you shining stars, *NCB* ... Praise Him, all you radiant stars!, *Berkeley.*

**4. Praise him, ye heavens of heavens: and ye waters that be above the heavens:** ... and you waters above the skies, *NIV* ... And ye waters that are above the heavens, *Rotherham.*

**5. Let them praise the name of the LORD: for he commanded, and they were created:** ... He ordered and they were created, *Beck* ... for he gave the order, and they were made, *BB* ... For His Order created, *Fenton.*

**6. He hath also stablished them for ever and ever: he hath made a decree which shall not pass:** ... He put them in their places forever, and gave a law that none can break, *Beck* ... he fixed their bounds, which cannot be passed, *NRSV* ... he gave them a duty which shall not pass away, *NCB.*

**7. Praise the LORD from the earth, ye dragons, and all deeps:** ... you sea monsters and all ocean depths, *Beck* ... you great sea-beasts, and deep places, *BB* ... ye depths of ocean and ye waterspouts, *Moffatt* ... you large sea animals and all the oceans, *NCV.*

**8. Fire, and hail; snow, and vapour:** ... snow and mists, *BB* ... snow and frost, *NRSV* ... lightning and hail and snow and ice, *Moffatt.*

**stormy wind fulfilling his word:** ... stormy wind doing what He tells you, *Beck* ... stormy wind fulfilling his command!, *NRSV* ... you windstorm carrying out His orders, *Berkeley* ... gales of wind obeying his voice, *NEB.*

**9. Mountains, and all hills; fruitful trees, and all cedars:** ... fruit-trees and all tree of the mountains, *BB* ... orchards and every cedar, *JB.*

**10. Beasts, and all cattle:** ... you wild beasts and all tame animals, *NCB.*

**creeping things, and flying fowl:** ... crawling things and winged birds, *Beck* ... insects and winged birds, *BB* ... reptiles and winged birds, *JB.*

**11. Kings of the earth, and all people:** ... kings of earth and all the nations, *Moffatt.*

**princes, and all judges of the earth:** ... princes and rulers of the earth!,

---

**148:1–4.** Verse 1 addresses generally the subsequently particularized heavenly beings. "From the heavens" and "in the heights," praise is to sound. The former phrase marks the place of origin and may imply the floating down to a listening earth of that ethereal music. The latter phrase thinks of all the dim distances as filled with it. The angels, as conscious beings, are the chorus leaders, and even to "principalities and powers in heavenly places," Israel's restoration reveals new phases of the "manifold wisdom of God" (Eph. 3:10).

The "host" (or hosts, according to the amended reading of the Hebrew margin) are here obviously angels, as required by the parallelism with v. 2a. The sun, moon and stars, of which the psalmist knows nothing except that they burn with light and roll in silence through the dark expanse, are bid to break the solemn stillness that fills the daily and nightly sky.

Finally, the singer passes in thought through the lower heavens, and would send his voice whither his eye cannot pierce, up into that mysterious watery abyss, which, according to ancient cosmography, had the firmament for its floor. It is absurd to look for astronomical accuracy in such poetry as this, but a singer, who knew no more about sun, moon and stars, and depths of space, than that they were all God's creatures and in their silence praised Him, knew and felt more of their true nature and charm than does he who knows everything about them except these facts.

**148:5–6.** Verses 5f assign the reason for the praise of the heavens—Yahweh's creative act, his sustaining power and his "Law," the utterance of his will to which they conform. Verse 6a emphatically asserts, by expressing the "He," which is in Hebrew usually included in the verb, that it is Yahweh and none other whose decrees never pass away.

The meaning of the close of v. 6b is doubtful, if the existing text is adhered to. It reads literally "and [it?] shall not pass." The unexpressed nominative is by some taken to be the before-mentioned "Law," and "pass" to mean "cease to be in force" or "be transgressed." Others take the singular verb as being used distributively, and so render "None of them transgresses." But a very slight alteration gives the plural verb, which makes all plain.

**148:7–10.** The summons to the earth begins with the lowest places, as that to the heavens did with the highest. The psalmist knows little of the uncouth forms that may wallow in ocean depths, but he is sure that they too, in their sunless abodes, can

| | | | | | |
|---|---|---|---|---|---|
| 3725, 3947 | 8015 | 3725, 8570.152 | 800 | | 1005 |
| cj, *adj*, n mp | n mp | cj, *adj*, v *Qal act ptc mp* | n fs | **12.** | n mp |
| וְכָל־לְאֻמִּים | שָׂרִים | וְכָל־שֹׁפְטֵי | אֶרֶץ | | בַּחוּרִים |
| wekhol-le'ummîm | sārîm | wekhol-shōphetê | 'ārets | | bachûrîm |
| and all the peoples | the officials | and all the judges of | the earth | | the young men |

| | | | | | | |
|---|---|---|---|---|---|---|
| 1612, 1359 | 2292 | 6196, 5470 | | 2054.326 | 881, 8428 | 3176 |
| cj, cj, n fp | n mp | prep, n mp | **13.** | v Piel juss 3mp | do, *n ms* | pn |
| וְגַם־בְּתוּלוֹת | זְקֵנִים | עִם־נְעָרִים | | יְהַלְלוּ | אֶת־שֵׁם | יְהוָה |
| wegham-bethûlôth | zeqēnîm | 'im-ne'ārîm | | yehalelû | 'eth-shēm | yehwāh |
| and also the young women | elders | with young people | | let them praise | the name of | Yahweh |

| | | | | | |
|---|---|---|---|---|---|
| 3706, 7891.255 | 8428 | 3937, 940 | 2003 | 6142, 800 | 8452 |
| cj, v Niphal ptc ms | n ms, ps 3ms | prep, n ms, ps 3ms | n ms, ps 3ms | prep, n fs | cj, n md |
| כִּי־נִשְׂגָּב | שְׁמוֹ | לְבַדּוֹ | הוֹדוֹ | עַל־אֶרֶץ | וְשָׁמָיִם |
| kî-nisgāv | shemô | levaddô | hôdhô | 'al-'erets | weshāmāyim |
| because exalted | his name | by himself | his majesty | above the earth | and the heavens |

| | | | | | | |
|---|---|---|---|---|---|---|
| | 7597.521 | 7451 | 3937, 6194 | 8747 | 3937, 3725, 2728 | 3937, 1158 |
| **14.** | cj, v Hiphil impf 3ms | n fs | prep, n ms, ps 3ms | n fs | prep, *adj*, n mp, ps 3ms | prep, *n mp* |
| | וַיָּרֶם | קֶרֶן | לְעַמּוֹ | תְּהִלָּה | לְכָל־חֲסִידָיו | לִבְנֵי |
| | wayyārem | qeren | le'ammô | tehillāh | lekhol-chăsîdhâv | livnê |
| | and He has exalted | a horn | to his people | praise | for all his godly ones | to the sons of |

| | | | | | | |
|---|---|---|---|---|---|---|
| 3547 | 6194, 7427 | 2054.333, 3161 | | 2054.333 | 3161 | 8301.133 |
| pn | *n ms*, adj, ps 3ms | v Piel impv 2mp, pn | **149:1** | v Piel impv 2mp | pn | v Qal impv 2mp |
| יִשְׂרָאֵל | עַם־קְרֹבוֹ | הַלְלוּ־יָהּ | | הַלְלוּ | יָהּ | שִׁירוּ |
| yisrā'ēl | 'am-qōrōvô | halelû-yāhh | | halelû | yāhh | shîrû |
| Israel | a people near Him | praise Yah | | praise | Yah | sing |

| | | | | | | | |
|---|---|---|---|---|---|---|---|
| 3937, 3176 | 8302 | 2413 | 8747 | 904, 7235 | 2728 | | 7975.121 |
| prep, pn | n ms | adj | n fs, ps 3ms | prep, *n ms* | n mp | **2.** | v Qal juss 3ms |
| לַיהוָה | שִׁיר | חָדָשׁ | תְּהִלָּתוֹ | בִּקְהַל | חֲסִידִים | | יִשְׂמַח |
| layhwāh | shîr | chādhāsh | tehillāthô | biqhal | chăsîdhîm | | yismach |
| to Yahweh | a song | new | his praise | in the assembly of | the godly ones | | may they be glad |

| | | | | |
|---|---|---|---|---|
| 3547 | 904, 6449.152 | 1158, 6995 | 1559.126 | 904, 4567 |
| pn | prep, v Qal act ptc mp, ps 3ms | *n mp*, pn | v Qal juss 3mp | prep, n ms, ps 3mp |
| יִשְׂרָאֵל | בְּעֹשָׂיו | בְּנֵי־צִיּוֹן | יָגִילוּ | בְּמַלְכָּם |
| yisrā'ēl | be'ōsâv | benê-tsîyôn | yāghîlû | vemalkām |
| Israel | in their Maker | the sons of Zion | let them rejoice | in their King |

*NRSV* ... kings of the earth and all nations, *JB* ... princes and all authorities, *Moffatt.*

**12. Both young men, and maidens; old men, and children:** ... young men and also girls, old men and boys, *Beck* ... Young men and virgins, *BB* ... old and young together!, *NRSV.*

**13. Let them praise the name of the LORD: for his name alone is excellent:** ... for his name alone is sublime, *JB* ... for his name alone is exalted, *NCB* ... for His name alone is supreme!, *Berkeley* ... For lofty is his Name alone, *Rotherham.*

**his glory is above the earth and heaven:** ... his splendour transcends earth and heaven, *JB* ... his majesty is above earth and heaven, *NCB* ... He is more wonderful than heaven and earth, *NCV.*

**14. He also exalteth the horn of his people, the praise of all his saints:** ... For he heightens the strength of his people, *JB* ... Be this his praise from all his faithful ones, *NAB* ... and he has raised his people to high honour, *Moffatt* ... God has given his people a king, He should be praised by all who belong to him, *NCV.*

**even of the children of Israel, a people near unto him. Praise ye the LORD:** ... something praise-worthy for those devoted to Him, *Beck* ... he should be praised by the Israelites, the people closest to his heart, *NCV.*

**149:1. Praise ye the LORD. Sing unto the LORD a new song:** ... Sing to Yahweh a song that is new, *Rotherham.*

praise Yahweh. From the ocean, the Psalm rises to the air, before it settles down on earth.

Verse 8 may refer to contemporaneous phenomena, and if so, describes a wild storm hurtling through the lower atmosphere. The verbal arrangement in v. 8a is that of inverted parallelism, in which "fire" corresponds to "smoke," and "hail" to "snow." Lightning and hail, which often occur together, are similarly connected in Ps. 18:12. But it is difficult to explain "snow and smoke," if regarded as accompaniments of the former pair—fire and hail. Rather, they seem to describe another set of meteorological phenomena, a winter storm, in which the air is thick with flakes as if charged with smoke, while the preceding words refer to a summer's thunderstorm. The resemblance to the two pictures in the preceding Psalm, one of the time of the latter rains and one of bitter winter weather, is noticeable. The storm wind, which drives all these formidable agents through the air, in its utmost fury is a servant. As in Ps. 107:25, it obeys God's command. The solid earth itself, as represented by its loftiest summits which pierce the air; vegetable life, as represented by the two classes of fruit-bearing and forest trees; animals in their orders, wild and domestic; the lowest worm that crawls and the light-winged bird that soars—these all have voices to praise God. The song has been steadily rising in the scale of being from inanimate to animated creatures, and last it summons man, in whom creation's praise becomes vocal and conscious.

**148:11–12.** All men, without distinction of rank, age or sex, have the same obligation and privilege of praise. Kings are most kingly when they cast their crowns before Him. Judges are wise when they sit as his vice regents. The buoyant vigor of youth is purest when used with remembrance of the Creator; the maiden's voice is never so sweet as in hymns to Yahweh. The memories and feebleness of age are hallowed and strengthened by recognition of the God Who can renew failing energy and soothe sad remembrances, and the child's opening powers are preserved from stain and distortion, by drawing near to Him in whose praise the extremes of life find common ground. The young man's strong bass, the maiden's clear alto, the old man's quavering notes, and the child's fresh treble, should blend in the song.

**148:13–14.** Verse 13 gives the reason for the praise of earth, but especially of man, with very significant difference from that assigned in vv. 5f. He has manifested himself to eyes that can see and has shown forth his transcendent majesty. Man's praise is to be based not only on the revelation of God in nature, but on that higher one in his dealings with men, and especially with Israel.

This chief reason for praise is assigned in v. 14 and indeed underlies the whole Psalm. "He also exalteth the horn of his people," delivering them from their humiliation and captivity, and setting them again in their land. Thereby, He has provided all his favored ones with occasion for praise. The condensed language of v. 14b is susceptible of different constructions and meanings. Some would understand the verb from 14a as repeated before "praise," and take the meaning to be "He exalts the praise [i.e., the glory] of his beloved," but it is improbable that praise here should mean anything but that rendered to God. The simplest explanation of the words is that they are in apposition to the preceding clause and declare that Yahweh, by "exalting a horn to his people," has given them a special occasion to praise Him. Israel is further designated as "a people near unto him." It is a nation of priests, having the privilege of access to his presence, and in the consciousness of this dignity "comes forward in this Psalm as the leader of all the creatures in their praise of God, and strikes up a hallelujah that is to be joined in by heaven and earth" (Delitzsch).

***Psalm 149.*** *In the preceding Psalm, Israel's restoration was connected with the recognition by all creatures, and especially by the kings of the earth and their people, of Yahweh's glory. This Psalm presents the converse thought, that the restored Israel becomes the executor of judgments on those who will not join in the praise which rings from Israel, that it may be caught up by all. The two Psalms are thus closely connected. The circumstances of the restoration accord with the tone of both, as of the other members of this closing group.*

**149:1–3.** Chiefly should God's praise sound out from "the congregation of saints," the long-scattered captives who owe it to his favor that they are a congregation once more. The jubilant psalmist delights in that name for Israel and uses it thrice in his song. He loves to set forth the various names, which each suggest some sweet strong thought of what God is to the nation and the nation to God—his favored ones, Israel, the children of Zion, his people, the afflicted. He heaps together synonyms expressive of rapturous joy—rejoice, be glad, exult. He calls for expressions of triumphant mirth in which limbs, instruments and

| 3. | 2054.326<br>v Piel juss 3mp<br>יְהַלְלוּ<br>yehalelû<br>let them praise | 8428<br>n ms, ps 3ms<br>שְׁמוֹ<br>shemô<br>his name | 904, 4369<br>prep, n ms<br>בְמָחוֹל<br>vemāchôl<br>with dancing | 904, 8929<br>prep, n ms<br>בְּתֹף<br>bethōph<br>with the timbrel | 3780<br>cj, n ms<br>וְכִנּוֹר<br>wekhinnôr<br>and the zither |
|---|---|---|---|---|---|

| 2252.326, 3937<br>v Piel juss 3mp, prep, ps 3ms<br>יְזַמְּרוּ־לוֹ<br>yezammerû-lô<br>let them sing praises to Him | 4. | 3706, 7813.151<br>cj, v Qal act ptc ms<br>כִּי־רוֹצֶה<br>kî-rôtseh<br>because pleased | 3176<br>pn<br>יְהוָה<br>yehwāh<br>Yahweh | 904, 6194<br>prep, n ms, ps 3ms<br>בְּעַמּוֹ<br>be'ammô<br>with his people | 6526.321<br>v Piel impf 3ms<br>יְפָאֵר<br>yephā'ēr<br>He exalts | 6262<br>n mp<br>עֲנָוִים<br>'ănāwîm<br>the lowly |
|---|---|---|---|---|---|---|

| 904, 3568<br>prep, n fs<br>בִּישׁוּעָה<br>bîshû'āh<br>with salvation | 5. | 6159.126<br>v Qal juss 3mp<br>יַעְלְזוּ<br>ya'ălzû<br>let them exult | 2728<br>n mp<br>חֲסִידִים<br>chăsîdhîm<br>the godly | 904, 3632<br>prep, n ms<br>בְּכָבוֹד<br>bekhāvôdh<br>in glory | 7728.326<br>v Piel juss 3mp<br>יְרַנְּנוּ<br>yerannenû<br>let them shout for joy | 6142, 5085<br>prep, n mp, ps 3mp<br>עַל־מִשְׁכְּבוֹתָם<br>'al-mishkevôthām<br>on their beds |
|---|---|---|---|---|---|---|

| 6. | 7604<br>*n mp*<br>רוֹמְמוֹת<br>rômemôth<br>the exaltations of | 418<br>n ms<br>אֵל<br>'ēl<br>God | 904, 1671<br>prep, n ms, ps 3mp<br>בִּגְרוֹנָם<br>bighrônām<br>in their throat | 2820<br>cj, *n fs*<br>וְחֶרֶב<br>wecherev<br>and a sword of | 6617<br>n mp<br>פִּיפִיּוֹת<br>pîphîyôth<br>double edges | 904, 3135<br>prep, n fs, ps 3mp<br>בְּיָדָם<br>beyādhām<br>in their hand |
|---|---|---|---|---|---|---|

| 7. | 3937, 6449.141<br>prep, v Qal inf con<br>לַעֲשׂוֹת<br>la'ăsôth<br>to execute | 5543<br>n fs<br>נְקָמָה<br>neqāmāh<br>vengeance | 904, 1504<br>prep, art, n mp<br>בַּגּוֹיִם<br>baggôyim<br>on the nations | 8762<br>n fp<br>תּוֹכֵחֹת<br>tôkhēchōth<br>chastisements | 904, 3947<br>prep, n fp<br>בַּלְאֻמִּים<br>bal'ummîm<br>on the peoples | 8. | 3937, 646.141<br>prep, v Qal inf con<br>לֶאְסֹר<br>le'ěsōr<br>to bind |
|---|---|---|---|---|---|---|---|

| 4567<br>n mp, ps 3mp<br>מַלְכֵיהֶם<br>malkhêhem<br>their kings | 904, 2288<br>prep, n mp<br>בְּזִקִּים<br>beziqqîm<br>with fetters | 3632.256<br>cj, v Niphal ptc mp, ps 3mp<br>וְנִכְבְּדֵיהֶם<br>wenikhbedhêhem<br>and their honored ones | 904, 3644<br>prep, *n mp*<br>בְּכַבְלֵי<br>bekhavlê<br>with fetter of | 1298<br>n ms<br>בַרְזֶל<br>varzel<br>iron | 9. | 3937, 6449.141<br>prep, v Qal inf con<br>לַעֲשׂוֹת<br>la'ăsôth<br>to execute |
|---|---|---|---|---|---|---|

| 904<br>prep, ps 3mp<br>בָּהֶם<br>bāhem<br>against them | 5122<br>n ms<br>מִשְׁפָּט<br>mishpāṭ<br>a judgment | 3918.155<br>v Qal pass ptc ms<br>כָּתוּב<br>kāthûv<br>written | 1994<br>n ms<br>הָדָר<br>hādhār<br>honor | 2000<br>dem pron<br>הוּא<br>hû'<br>this | 3937, 3725, 2728<br>prep, *adj*, n mp, ps 3ms<br>לְכָל־חֲסִידָיו<br>lekhol-chăsîdhâv<br>for all his godly ones | 2054.333, 3161<br>v Piel impv 2mp, pn<br>הַלְלוּ־יָהּ<br>halelû-yāhh<br>praise Yah |
|---|---|---|---|---|---|---|

**and his praise in the congregation of saints:** ... praising Him in the congregation of His devoted ones, *Beck* ... let his praise be in the meeting of his saints, *BB* ... his praise in the assembly of the faithful, *NRSV* ... where the faithful gather, let his praise be heard, *Knox.*

**2. Let Israel rejoice in him that made him:** ... Israel should be happy in Him who made them, *Beck* ... let Israel be joyful in their Maker, *Moffatt* ... Let Israel rejoice in his Supreme Maker, *Anchor.*

**let the children of Zion be joyful in their King:** ... let the children of Zion exult in their King, *Berkeley* ... let Sion's children keep holiday, *Knox.*

**3. Let them praise his name in the dance:** ... they shall dance in praise of his name, *JB* ... Let them praise his name in the festive dance, *NCB* ... Let them praise His name with processionals, *Berkeley.*

**let them sing praises unto him with the timbrel and harp:** ... and play on tambourine and lyre to Him, *Beck* ... let them make melody to him with instruments of brass and corded instruments of music, *BB.*

**4. For the LORD taketh pleasure in his people:** ... The LORD delights in His people, *Beck* ... For Yahweh loves his people, *JB* ... For the LORD accepts the service of his people, *REB.*

**he will beautify the meek with salvation:** ... He glorifies the humble with victory, *Beck* ... he gives the poor in spirit a crown of salvation, *BB* ... he adorns the lowly with victory, *NCB* ... He will beautify the afflicted ones with salvation, *NASB.*

**5. Let the saints be joyful in glory:** ... Let the godly exult in glory, *Darby* ... Let the faithful exult in glory, *NAB* ... Let the faithful exult over their triumph, *Moffatt* ... Let the godly rejoice in this honor, *Berkeley.*

**let them sing aloud upon their beds:** ... and shout happily on their beds, *Beck* ... let them sing for joy on their couches, *NRSV* ... let them shout for joy as they prostrate themselves, *REB* ... shouting joyfully in their great temple, *Moffatt* ... Let them sing for joy even in bed!, *NCV* ... let them shout for joy as they kneel before him, *NEB.*

**6. Let the high praises of God be in their mouth, and a twoedged sword in their hand:** ... Let the high praises of God be in their throats, *NRSV* ... praising God to the heights with their voices, *JB* ... God's praise upon their lips, and a sharp sword in their hands, *Moffatt* ... Let their throats voice hymns of adoration to God, *Berkeley* ... a double-edged sword in their hands, *NIV.*

**7. To execute vengeance upon the heathen:** ... to wreak vengeance on the nations, *JB* ... for vengeance upon pagans, *Moffatt* ... to bring retribution upon the nations, *Berkeley.*

**and punishments upon the people:** ... and correct the peoples, *Beck* ... and corrections among the people, *Geneva* ... And chastisements upon the peoples, *MAST.*

**8. To bind their kings with chains:** ... to load their kings with chains, *JB* ... to put their monarchs into chains, *Moffatt.*

**and their nobles with fetters of iron:** ... their rulers in bands of iron, *BB* ... their nobles into iron gyves, *Moffatt* ... and their nobles with iron handcuffs, *Berkeley.*

**9. To execute upon them the judgment written: this honour have all his saints. Praise ye the LORD:** ... to punish them as it is written. This is an honor which belongs to all His devoted ones, *Beck* ... to execute on them the judgement passed—to the honour of all his faithful, *JB* ... He is the glory of all His saints, Hallelujah, *MAST.*

---

voices unite. He would have the exuberant gladness well over into the hours of repose, and the night be made musical with ringing shouts of joy. Praise is better than sleep, and the beds which had often been privy to silent tears may well be witnesses of exultation that cannot be made silent (v. 5).

**149:4–5.** The psalmist touches very lightly on the reason for this outburst of praise, because he takes it for granted that so great and recent mercy needed little mention. One verse (v. 4) suffices to recall it. The very absorption of the heart in its bliss may make it silent about the bliss. The bride needs not to tell what makes her glad. Restored Israel requires little reminder of its occasion for joy. But the brief mention of it is very beautiful. It makes prominent, not so much the outward fact, as the divine pleasure in his people, of which the fact was effect and indication. Their affliction had been the token that God's complacency did not rest on them; their deliverance is the proof that the sunlight of his face shines on them once more. His chastisements rightly borne are ever precursors of deliverance, which adorns the meek afflicted, giving "beauty for ashes" (Isa. 61:3). The qualification for receiving Yahweh's help is meekness, and the effect of that help on the lowly soul is to deck it with strange loveliness. Therefore, God's favored ones may well exult in glory, on account of the glory with which they are invested by his salvation.

**149:6–8.** The stern close of the Psalm strikes a note which many ears feel to be discordant and which must be freely acknowledged to stand on the same lower level as the imprecatory Psalms, while even more distinctly than these, it is entirely free from any sentiment of personal vengeance. The picture of God's people going forth to battle, chanting his praises and swinging two-edged swords, may shock some, but it is not to be explained away as meaning the spiritual conquest of the world with spiritual weapons. The psalmist meant actual warfare and real iron fetters. But while the form of his anticipations belongs to the past and is entirely set aside by the better light of Christianity, their substance is true forever. Those who have been adorned with Yahweh's salvation have the subjugation of the world to God's rule committed to them. "The weapons of our warfare are not carnal" (2 Cor. 10:4). There are stronger fetters than those of iron, even "the cords of love" and "the bands of a man."

**149:9.** "The judgment written," which is to be executed by the militant Israel on the nations, does not seem to have reference either to the commandment to exterminate the Canaanites or to the punishments threatened in many places of Scripture. Verse 9b may be rendered, "Honor [or, majesty] is He to all his saints," in the sense that God manifests his majesty to them, or that He is the object of their honoring; but the usual rendering is more in accordance with the context and its high-strung martial ardor. "This"—namely, the whole of the crusade just described—is

| 150:1 | 2054.333 | 3161 | 2054.333, 418 | 904, 7231 | 2054.333 |
|---|---|---|---|---|---|
| | v Piel impv 2mp | pn | v Piel impv 2mp, n ms | prep, n ms, ps 3ms | v Piel impv 2mp, ps 3ms |
| | הַלְלוּ | יָהּ | הַלְלוּ־אֵל | בְּקָדְשׁוֹ | הַלְלוּהוּ |
| | hal$^{e}$lû | yāhh | hal$^{e}$lû-'ēl | b$^{e}$qādh$^{e}$shô | hal$^{e}$lûhû |
| | praise | Yah | praise God | in his holy place | praise Him |

| 904, 7842 | 6010 | 2. | 2054.333 | 904, 1400 |
|---|---|---|---|---|
| prep, *n ms* | n ms, ps 3ms | | v Piel impv 2mp, ps 3ms | prep, n fp, ps 3ms |
| בִּרְקִיעַ | עֻזּוֹ | | הַלְלוּהוּ | בִגְבוּרֹתָיו |
| birqîa' | 'uzzô | | hal$^{e}$lûhû | vighvûrōthâv |
| in the firmament of | his strength | | praise Him | because of his mighty deeds |

| 2054.333 | 3626, 7524 | 1465 | 3. | 2054.333 |
|---|---|---|---|---|
| v Piel impv 2mp, ps 3ms | prep, *n ms* | n ms, ps 3ms | | v Piel impv 2mp, ps 3ms |
| הַלְלוּהוּ | כְּרֹב | גֻּדְלוֹ | | הַלְלוּהוּ |
| hal$^{e}$lûhû | k$^{e}$rōv | gudh$^{e}$lô | | hal$^{e}$lûhû |
| praise Him | according to the abundance of | his majesty | | praise Him |

| 904, 8966 | 8223 | 2054.333 | 904, 5213 | 3780 |
|---|---|---|---|---|
| prep, *n ms* | n ms | v Piel impv 2mp, ps 3ms | prep, n ms | cj, n ms |
| בְּתֵקַע | שׁוֹפָר | הַלְלוּהוּ | בְּנֵבֶל | וְכִנּוֹר |
| b$^{e}$thēqa' | shôphār | hal$^{e}$lûhû | b$^{e}$nēvel | w$^{e}$khinnôr |
| with the blowing of | a ram's horn | praise Him | with the harp | and the zither |

| 4. | 2054.333 | 904, 8929 | 4369 | 2054.333 | 904, 4625 |
|---|---|---|---|---|---|
| | v Piel impv 2mp, ps 3ms | prep, n ms | cj, n ms | v Piel impv 2mp, ps 3ms | prep, n mp |
| | הַלְלוּהוּ | בְתֹף | וּמָחוֹל | הַלְלוּהוּ | בְּמִנִּים |
| | hal$^{e}$lûhû | v$^{e}$thōph | ûmāchôl | hal$^{e}$lûhû | b$^{e}$minîm |
| | praise Him | with the timbrel | and the round dance | praise Him | with the strings |

| 5966 | 5. | 2054.333 | 904, 7036, 8473 | 2054.333 |
|---|---|---|---|---|
| cj, n ms | | v Piel impv 2mp, ps 3ms | prep, *n mp*, n ms | v Piel impv 2mp, ps 3ms |
| וְעוּגָב | | הַלְלוּהוּ | בְצִלְצְלֵי־שָׁמַע | הַלְלוּהוּ |
| w$^{e}$'ûghāv | | hal$^{e}$lûhû | v$^{e}$tsilts$^{e}$lê-shāma' | hal$^{e}$lûhû |
| and the flute | | praise Him | with the cymbals of sound | praise Him |

| 904, 7036 | 8980 | 6. | 3725 | 5580 | 2054.322 | 3161 | 2054.333, 3161 |
|---|---|---|---|---|---|---|---|
| prep, *n mp* | n fs | | adj | art, n fs | v Piel juss 3fs | pn | v Piel impv 2mp, pn |
| בְּצִלְצְלֵי | תְרוּעָה | | כֹּל | הַנְּשָׁמָה | תְּהַלֵּל | יָהּ | הַלְלוּ־יָהּ |
| b$^{e}$tsilts$^{e}$lê | th$^{e}$rû'āh | | kōl | hann$^{e}$shāmāh | t$^{e}$hallēl | yāhh | hal$^{e}$lû-yāhh |
| with the cymbals of | shouting | | all | the breath | let it praise | Yah | praise Yah |

**150:1. Praise ye the LORD. Praise God in his sanctuary:** … Give praise to God in his holy place, *BB* … in his holy place, *NEB.*

**praise him in the firmament of his power:** … Praise Him for the sky spread out by His power, *Beck* … give him praise in the heaven of his power, *BB* … Praise Him for His mighty expanse, *NASB.*

**2. Praise him for his mighty acts:** … praise him for his acts of power, *REB* … Praise Him for His mighty deeds, *Berkeley.*

**praise him according to his excellent greatness:** … give him praise in the measure of his great strength, *BB* … according to the abundance of his greatness, *Darby* … praise him for his sovereign majesty, *NAB.*

**3. Praise him with the sound of the trumpet:** … Praise Him with a blast of a ram's horn, *Beck* … give him praise with corded instruments of music, *BB* … praise him with the fanfare of trumpet, *JB.*

**praise him with the psaltery and harp:** … praise him with lute and harp, *Darby* … praise him with harp and lyre, *JB* … praise him with harp and zither, *Knox.*

**4. Praise him with the timbrel and dance:** … praise him with tamborines and dancing, *REB* … Praise him with drum and with dance, *Fenton.*

**praise him with stringed instruments and organs:** … praise Him with string instruments and flutes, *Beck* … give him praise with horns and corded instruments, *BB* … praise him with strings and pipes, *JB* …

praise him with the music of string and of reed, *Knox.*

**5. Praise him upon the loud cymbals:** ... Praise him with clanging cymbals, *NRSV* ... cymbals of clear tone, *Rotherham.*

**praise him upon the high sounding cymbals:** ... praise Him with crashing cymbals!, *Beck* ... give him praise with the high-sounding brass, *BB* ... praise him with loud clashing cymbals!, *NRSV* ... praise him with triumphant cymbals, *JB.*

**6. Let every thing that hath breath praise the Lord:** ... Let everything that breathes praise the Lord!, *NRSV.*

**Praise ye the Lord:** ... Let the Lord be praised, *BB.*

---

laid upon all Yahweh's favored ones, by the fact of their participation in his salvation. They are redeemed from bondage that they may be God's warriors. The honor and obligation are universal.

***Psalm 150.*** *The noble close of the Psalter rings out one clear note of praise. Tears, groans, wailings for sin, meditations on the dark depths of providence, fainting faith and foiled aspirations all lead up to this. The Psalm is more than an artistic close of the Psalter; it is a description of the natural result of the devout life, and in its unclouded sunniness, as well as in its universality, it proclaims the certain end of the weary years for the individual and for the world. "Every thing that hath breath" shall yet praise the Lord. The Psalm is evidently meant for liturgical use, and one may imagine that each instrument began to take part in the concert as it was named, until at last all blended in a mighty torrent of praiseful sound, to which the whirling dancers kept time. It is a strange contrast to modern notions of sobriety in worship!*

**150:1.** The tenfold "Praise him" has been often noticed as symbolic of completeness, but has probably no special significance. In v. 1, the psalmist calls on earth and heaven to praise. The "sanctuary" (HED #7231) may, indeed, be either the Temple or the heavenly palace of Yahweh, but it is more probable that the invocation, like so many others of a similar kind, is addressed to men and angels, than that only angels are meant. They who stand in the earthly courts and they who circle the throne that is reared above the visible firmament are parts of a great whole, an antiphonal chorus. It becomes them to praise, for they each dwell in God's sanctuary.

**150:2.** The theme of praise is next touched in v. 2. "His mighty acts" might be rendered "his heroic [or, valiant] acts." The reference is to his deliverance of his people as a signal manifestation of prowess or conquering might. The tenderness which moved the power is not here in question, but the power cannot be worthily praised or understood, unless that divine pity and graciousness of which it is the instrument are apprehended. Mighty acts, unsoftened by loving impulse and gracious purpose, would evoke awe, but not thanks. No praise is adequate to the abundance of his greatness, yet He accepts such adoration as men can render.

**150:3–4.** The instruments named in vv. 3ff were not all used, so far as we know, in the temple service. There is possibly an intention to go beyond those recognized as sacred, in order to emphasize the universality of praise. The horn was the curved "shophar," blown by the priests; harp and psaltery were played by the Levites, timbrels were struck by women; and dancing, playing on stringed instruments and pipes and cymbals, were not reserved for the Levites. Consequently, the summons to praise God is addressed to priests, Levites, and people. In v. 4b, the word translated "organs" (HED #5966) is probably that used by shepherds, neither of which appear elsewhere as being employed in worship.

**150:5.** Too little is known of Jewish music to enable us to determine whether the epithets applied to cymbals refer to two different kinds. Probably, they do—the first being small and high-pitched, the second larger, like the similar instrument used in military music, and of a deep tone.

**150:6.** But the singer would fain hear a volume of sound which should drown all that sweet tumult which he has evoked; therefore, he calls on "every thing that hath breath" to use it in sending forth a thunder chorus of praise to Yahweh. The invocation bears the prophecy of its own fulfillment. These last strains of the long series of psalmists are as if that band of singers of Israel turned to the listening world, and gave into its keeping the harps which, under their own hands, had yielded such immortal music.

Few voices have obeyed the summons, and the vision of a world melodious with the praise of Yahweh and of Him alone appears to us, in our despondent moments, almost as far off as it was when the last psalmist ceased to sing. But his call is our confidence, and we know that the end of history shall be that to Him whose work is mightier than all the other mighty acts of Yahweh, "Every knee shall bow, and every tongue confess that Jesus Christ is Lord, to the glory of God the Father" (Phil. 2:11).

# PSALMS OVERVIEW

---

*Background*

*Outline*

*Summary*

---

# Overview

## BACKGROUND

The name of the Book of Psalms comes from the Greek word, psalmos (from the verb psallein, "to pluck a stringed instrument"), which is used to translate the Hebrew word mizmôr (HED #4344). This word, which means "song," appears in the titles of fifty-seven Psalms. In Rabbinic literature, the Book is referred to as the s̲ēpher tehillîm, the "Book of Praises." Although the word tehillîm occurs only in the title of Ps. 145, it appears many times in Psalms in various forms, speaking of the purpose of the Book. The designation "Psalter," another name for the Book, comes from the Greek word, psaltērion, which refers to a stringed instrument.

### Date and Author

The various Psalms were composed at different times throughout Israel's history for a wide variety of purposes. The Psalms do not contain references to their authors, except in some of their titles, and except for Ps. 72:20, which was possibly a later addition composed as a closing to a collection of Davidic Psalms. The titles list Moses, David, Asaph, the descendants of Korah, Solomon, Heman the Ezrahite and Ethan the Ezrahite as composers of most of the Psalms. (David is credited with seventy-three of the Psalms.)

The Psalms date from the time of Moses (ca. fourteenth century B.C.) up to the return from the Babylonian exile (ca. 500 B.C.). Psalm 90, the earliest Psalm, was written by Moses, and the latest Psalms (e.g., Pss. 102; 126; 137) reflect an exilic or post-exilic date. Some scholars attempt to date the Psalms as late as the Maccabean period, but such a late date is unlikely. The lack of understanding of the Septuagint translators (ca. 200 B.C.) concerning many Hebrew technical terms used in the Psalms indicates that the words were no longer in use at the time of translation. This would be unlikely if the Psalms were composed during the same period in which they were translated. Mitchell Dahood (AB, *Psalms I*, xxxii) argues against dating any of the Psalms to the Maccabean period on the grounds of their differences with the Qumran Hodayot. Furthermore, Ps. 79:3 is quoted in the apocryphal 1 Macc. 7:17 as Scripture. This Psalm likely would not have been held in such high regard if it had originated in the same period as the work quoting it. The arguments for a late date generally follow along the same lines as those denying Davidic authorship for most or all of the Psalms (see discussion below), and they are less than convincing. Thus, there is no reason to date any of the Psalms after 500 B.C., and the Book probably attained its final form by and large by the time of Ezra and Nehemiah (fifth century B.C.).

The most significant ambiguity surrounding authorship of the Psalms is interpreting the phrase ledāwid, "by David," which appears in several of the Psalm titles (e.g., Pss. 3–9; 11–32; 138–145). It could mean "by David," indicating Davidic authorship; it could be translated "to" or "for David," indicating that the Psalm was intended for David's use as part of the royal collection; or it could mean "concerning David," indicating that the Psalm was written about some aspect of his life. In several of the titles containing ledāwid (e.g., Pss. 3; 7; 18; 34; 51; 52; 54; 56; 57; 59; 60; 63; 117), historical information about the circumstances of David's life out of which the Psalm was composed is also given.

Although, in most cases, the preposition le (HED #3937) should be taken to indicate authorship, a position supported by the Septuagint and early church tradition, its presence in a Psalm title does not necessarily refer to authorship. Le in the title of Ps. 4, for example, is used in the expression, "for the director of music." Also, in the title of Ps. 92, le refers to the occasion on which the Psalm was to be used: "for the Sabbath day." The preposition's use with "the sons of Korah" (Ps. 47:t) is not an indication of authorship.

Otto Eissfeldt rejects Davidic authorship for most for the Psalms that list David as the author, arguing that later generations credited David with originating the organization of temple worship (cf. 1 Chr. 22:2; 2 Chr. 29:5) and thus of composing the Psalms (*The Old Testament: An Introduction*, 452). Some of the reasons many scholars reject Davidic authorship are that they reject the reliability of Psalm titles, that some of the Psalms attributed to David contain references to the king in the third person, that some speak of the Temple as having already been built, that some contain Aramaisms, and that David would not have had time to write poetry.

However, there is no convincing argument against Davidic authorship. The Psalm titles, although in many cases perhaps not original to the Psalms to which they are appended, are part of the canonical text (and thus historically considered by Jewish tradition and the Church to have the weight of Scripture; cf. 2 Tim. 3:16f), and they are ancient. The misapprehension of technical terms in some of the Psalm titles indicates that the words had been out of use for some time before the translation, and that the superscriptions are likely from the same time as the writing of the Psalms.

None of the other arguments for rejecting Davidic authorship is any more persuasive. It was common for writers of antiquity to refer to themselves in the third person. Examples of this are found in Xenophon's *Anabasis*, Julius Caesar's *Gallic Wars* and the OT (cf. Exo. 20:7, where God speaks the words "for the LORD will not hold guiltless"; Archer, *A Survey of Old Testament Introduction*, 488). The arguments based on references to the Temple in Davidic Psalms (e.g., Pss. 5; 28; 138) depend on an inappropriate, slavish understanding of the words used to describe the LORD's dwelling place. Furthermore, the presence of Aramaisms does not indicate a late date, as can be seen by the Aramaic influence on the Ugaritic literature of Ras Shamra, which dates to the time of Moses (Archer, 489). Finally, David's musical contributions are well-attested in Scripture (cf. 2 Sam. 23:1; Amos 6:5; 1 Chr. 16:4f).

The most important argument for accepting Davidic authorship is the belief of NT writers that the Psalms they quoted were written by David. Luke quotes the first two verses of Ps. 2 as part of a prayer of a gathering of Christians—including the apostles Peter and John—claiming that the words were spoken "by the Holy Spirit through the mouth of [God's] servant, our father David" (Acts 4:25f). On one occasion, in a discussion with a group of Pharisees, Jesus' argument rests on the Davidic authorship of Ps. 110:1 (Matt. 22:41–45). Thus, in the absence of irrefutable arguments for rejecting Davidic authorship, coupled with the biblical evidence, both in the Psalm titles and NT quotations, and the strong historical tradition in the Church of accepting his authorship, there is no compelling reason to reject David as the author of most of the Psalms.

Although it can be maintained that David authored the bulk of the Psalms, either accepting or rejecting Davidic authorship of those which bear his name will not greatly affect the interpretation of the Psalms. Peter Craigie, in most cases, does not interpret lᵉdāwid to indicate authorship; rather, he establishes authorship of a few of the Psalms on other grounds, while considering most of the Psalms to have anonymous authorship (WBC, p. 35).

Craigie's view does not cripple his interpretation of the Psalms, however. By and large, the Psalms are an expression of the human response to God's working in the world of his covenant people. They contain the heightened, poetic language of the heart and are intensely emotional. The feelings and reactions they reflect are shared by God's people of all ages; thus, the Psalms can be read and applied to a person's life today, regardless of what the reader believes as far as authorship.

## Compilation of the Psalter

The Book of Psalms is a divinely orchestrated compilation of individual Psalms and collections of Psalms into a rounded anthology of praise and supplication to God. The Psalms were certainly composed by a variety of authors who lived during widely different periods of Israel's history. Although they articulate the heart's cry of individuals, the Psalms were applied in ancient Israel, as today, on a wider scale for use in personal devotions as well as in public worship.

The process of compilation included gathering individual Psalms into small collections and eventually arranging these collections and adding additional Psalms to the Book. Clues to this process can be found in the Book itself. Most of the first seventy-two Psalms contain titles ascribing them to David. Psalm 72 ends with the statement, "This concludes the prayers of David son of Jesse," which probably concluded an early collection of Davidic Psalms. Other smaller collections can be discerned from their titles: the Psalms of the sons of Korah (Pss. 42; 44–49; 84; 85; 87; 88), the Psalms of Asaph (Pss. 73–83), the Songs of Ascents (Pss. 120–134), and the Hallelujah Psalms (Pss. 146–150). Although they lack titles, the Egyptian Hallels (Pss. 113–118) are similar in content.

# Overview

Psalms 42–83 are characterized by their use of "Elohim" in place of the divine name "Yahweh." Yahweh occurs 642 times outside the Elohistic Psalms and only 43 times within the collection; Elohim, 200 times in Pss. 42–83 and elsewhere 29 times (Eissfeldt, 449). Several Psalms which occur elsewhere are duplicated in this section (e.g., Ps. 14 is the same as Ps. 53; Ps. 40:14–18 corresponds to 70:2–6; Ps. 31:2ff to Ps. 71:1ff), indicating deliberate gathering and molding the Psalms into a new collection. In Ps. 14, the name Yahweh occurs four times, but is replaced by Elohim in Ps. 53 in three of these places. However, Elohim does not uniformly replace Yahweh. For example, Yahweh in Ps. 40:13 is replaced by Elohim in Ps. 70:1, while Elohim in Ps. 40:17 is replaced by Yahweh in 70:5.

The reluctance of the Jews to pronounce the name Yahweh, in an effort to avoid taking it in vain, may help explain the preference for the use of Elohim (although just how early this tendency began is not completely clear). Since the Psalms were used in public worship, the substitution of Elohim for Yahweh would make a substitution with Adonai unnecessary when singing praises to the LORD.

## Types of Psalms

Hermann Gunkel, in *Die Psalmen ubersetzt und erklart*, first applied form criticism to the study of the Psalms. Gunkel analyzed the content of the Psalms and attempted to categorize them according to the literary forms he discerned. Thus, the focus of interpretation shifted from attempting to uncover the historical situation out of which the Psalm was written to attempting to determine the Psalm's use in private devotions or public worship.

Gunkel identified five basic types of Psalms: hymns (e.g., Pss. 8; 19; 29; 33; 104; 105; 111; 113; 114; 117; 135; 136; 145–50), communal laments (e.g., Pss. 12; 44; 60; 74; 79; 80; 83; 85; 90; 126), royal Psalms (e.g., Pss. 2; 72; 110), individual laments (e.g., Pss. 3; 5; 7; 17; 25–27; 38; 39; 56; 62; 69; 88) and individual Psalms of thanksgiving (e.g., Pss. 30; 32; 34; 66; 116; 138). These categories focus on the Psalm as the prayer of an individual or the community and as a praise or a lament. Royal Psalms were used by the royal court.

Three other categories of Psalms should also be mentioned here. The royal Psalms are often referred to as messianic Psalms because they speak of the Messiah. Although the messianic import is not always obvious from the text of the Psalms themselves, many messianic Psalms are quoted by the NT writers as being prophetic of Jesus.

Psalm 22 is one of the most descriptive prophecies concerning Jesus' crucifixion. Such phrases as, "I am poured out like water," "All my bones are out of joint" (v. 14), and "My tongue cleaveth to my jaws" (v. 15) describe the tortures that our Savior endured. That this Psalm speaks of Jesus is attested by his quotation, while dying on the cross, of v. 1, "My God, my God, why hast thou forsaken me?" (Matt. 27:46). Psalm 110 is quoted by Jesus as referring to his own life (Matt. 22:44; cf. Acts 2:33ff; 5:30f; Rom. 8:34; Heb. 5:6; 6:20; 7:28; 10:13). Psalm 2 is another messianic Psalm. Paul quotes v. 7 as referring to Christ in the sermon recorded in Acts 13:33.

Although there is abundant evidence in NT quotations of the messianic reference of many Psalms, even some critics who hold a high view of Scripture deny that some of them refer to the Messiah. Craigie, for example, rejects the position that Ps. 2 refers to Jesus. He claims that it was originally meant for functions of the royal court, and even though the monarchy had already ended in Israel when the Psalter reached its final canonical state, Ps. 2 was still theologically significant to the nation. He writes, "Whereas in its original form, its theology pertained to the role of God in relation to the Davidic kings, that theology eventually blossomed into a fully messianic theology in one period of the history of the psalm's interpretation. The latter stage is not a new theology, but a growth and development from the initial nucleus" (WBC, pp. 40f). Thus, according to Craigie, Ps. 2 was not originally a messianic Psalm, but it "was a transformation being evident clearly in the NT" (p. 41). According to the theory this demonstrates a "later theological meaning."

Craigie's view unnecessarily weakens the prophetic import of the messianic Psalms. In trying to emphasize *sitz im leben* (the historical and cultural setting) of Ps. 2, he denies that it originally spoke of the coming of Christ. His attempt to apply the Psalm to Christ retrospectively does not do justice to the prophetic nature of the Psalm, nor to the power of the Holy Spirit when inspiring the writer.

It is true that Ps. 2 has its roots in history and speaks concerning Davidic kings. But it did not have its complete fulfillment until the advent of the consummate Davidic King, Jesus. Although the human author would not have completely understood his words when referring to his Lord, the divine Author was active during the writing process, moving him to write a more full prophecy than he could have composed without divine help. The Psalm had fulfillment in the earthly kings, but part of its fulfillment occurred in the life of Christ.

Another category of Psalm is the imprecatory Psalms (Pss. 12; 35; 52; 57–59; 69; 70; 83; 109; 137; 140). These are characterized by the psalmist expressing his desire for harm to come to his enemies. Some of the statements are quite harsh and appear vindictive, e.g., Ps. 137:8f, "O daughter of Babylon, who art to be destroyed; happy shall he be, that rewardeth thee as thou hast served us. Happy shall he be, that taketh and dasheth thy little ones against the stones." Some see these expressions as reflecting pre-Christian moral development; i.e., the psalmist is expressing his own desire for revenge on account of the harm done to him by his enemies.

However, this explanation is inadequate. The Book of Proverbs exhibits an ethic enjoining love for one's enemies that closely resembles the ethics put forth in the NT: "If thine enemy be hungry, give him bread to eat; and if he be thirsty, give him water to drink. For thou shalt heap coals of fire upon his head, and the LORD shall reward thee" (Prov. 25:21f; cf. Rom 12:20). Further, David, who wrote most of the imprecatory Psalms, showed a great degree of mercy toward his enemy Saul, refusing to harm God's anointed man because he regarded the Covenant as more important than his own distress.

Another consideration is the culpability of those who reject God's Covenant and harm his people. The LORD reserves the right to punish his enemies (Deut. 32:35). Wisdom is personified as laughing at the "fools" who reject the truth when they are caught in their own trap (Prov. 1:26f). "Therefore shall they eat of the fruit of their own way" (v. 31), and "Whoso diggeth a pit shall fall therein" (26:27; cf. Ps. 7:15f). Those who harm the LORD's people will be punished by him. Thus, the people of God can trust Him to vindicate them and save them from their distress. It is not their place to avenge their own injuries, but when the LORD avenges them, it is liberating—a liberation to be celebrated.

The third type of Psalm is the acrostic (Pss. 9; 10; 25; 34; 37; 111; 112; 119; 145). These are distinguished by their structure, in which the verses begin with a specific letter of the Hebrew alphabet, thus making an alphabetical acrostic. This was probably meant as a teaching device.

Psalm 119 is the most developed example of this form. Its structure consists of twenty-two stanzas of eight verses. Each verse in the stanza begins with the same letter. These letters progress from one stanza to the next from "aleph" through all the letters of the Hebrew alphabet to "taw" ("sin" and "shin" being seen as a single letter). The whole is a unified poem which praises the word of God and puts forth the benefits of following the LORD's commandments.

## Aspects of Hebrew Poetry

Unlike English poetry, the most significant characteristic of Hebrew poetry is not rhyme, nor does meter appear to be very significant. Although scholars have tried to discern a metrical scheme on the basis of both the number of accents in a line as well as the number of syllables, they have been unsuccessful. Petersen and Richards write, "In our judgment, however, no attempt, whether by ancient or modern scholars, to identify the presence of something like classic Greek metric forms in Hebrew poetry has proved successful" (*Interpreting Hebrew Poetry*, 39). This position was articulated long before by Delitzsch (*Commentary on the Psalms*, 28).

Hebrew poetry does, however, rely on rhythm, but a rhythm of thought more than one of meter. The basic unit is the line ("colon"). Most lines are more or less the same length, and they can be joined syntactically and semantically into larger combinations, most commonly pairs ("bicola") or triplets ("tricola"). This phenomenon is generally described as "parallelism."

There are three basic types of parallelism: antithetical, synonymous and synthetic. In antithetical parallelism, the second colon is contrasted semantically to the first, e.g., "For the LORD knoweth the way of the righteous: / but the way of the ungodly shall perish" (Ps. 1:6). In synonymous parallelism, the second line largely restates the first, e.g., "that walketh in the counsel of the ungodly / nor standeth in the way of sinners / nor sitteth in the seat of the scornful" (Ps. 1:1). In synthetic parallelism, the second line builds on the first, e.g., "He shall be like a tree planted by the rivers of water, / that bringeth forth his fruit in his season; / his leaf also shall not wither; / and whatsoever he doeth shall prosper" (Ps. 1:3).

A number of literary devices are also used in Hebrew poetry. The Psalms are full of heightened, terse language, containing vivid images and a full range of literary devices. David writes, using expressive language, that the LORD has heard his cry, "He brought me up also out of an horrible pit, out of the miry clay" (Ps. 40:2). His enemies are characterized as ones who prowl on the city walls day and night (55:10) and whose "tongue deviseth mischiefs; like a sharp razor" (52:2). After sinning with Bathsheba, he begs the LORD to cleanse him from sin, and he prays, "Let the bones you have crushed rejoice" (51:8, NIV). He encourages others to "taste and see that the LORD is good" (34:8). The LORD is so desirable that the psalmist thirsts for him like a deer panting for streams of water (42:1).

These images are brought to life more clearly with the use of rhetorical devices. Psalm 150 uses repetition to describe a great celebration of praise. The word "praise" begins every line of this short Psalm, which builds up in a crescendo to the exuberant "Let everything that hath breath praise the LORD." The entire Psalm is bracketed by the inclusio, "Praise the LORD." Such inclusios appear at the beginning and ending of a literary unit, marking it off as a unity.

Comparisons also abound in the Psalms. Similes are comparisons that contain such indicators as "like" (b$^{e}$, HED #904), "become like" (māshal, HED #5090) and "as" (ʻim, HED #6196). For example, the psalmist writes, "For my days are consumed like smoke" (Ps. 102:3). Metaphors are comparisons without indicators, as in "Their throat is an open sepulchre" (Ps. 5:9).

Various other literary devices are also used in the Psalms. Hyperbole is an exaggeration, e.g., "I will not be afraid of ten thousands of people, that have set themselves against me round about" (Ps. 3:6). Chiasmus is the inversion of elements in the second part of a literary unit which correspond to the first part. Thus a, b in the first line will be b, a in the second. This can be seen in Ps. 51:1; "Have mercy upon me, O God according to thy lovingkindness: / according unto the multitude of thy tender mercies blot out my transgressions."

## Problems of Translation

As in English, Hebrew poetry is more difficult to interpret than prose. Poetry is terse, the language is often metaphorical, and the syntax is often less straightforward. Determining the line structure can even be a problem as can be seen in the difference in line divisions between the *Biblia Hebraica Stuttgartensia* (BHS) and the *Biblia Hebraica Wurttembergensia* (BHK). These critical texts even differ on occasion as to whether a passage is poetry or prose (e.g., Isa. 4:2).

The development of the language through time also obscures our understanding. Hebrew underwent significant change during the interval between when the first Psalms were written and when they were fixed in their canonical form. This history can sometimes be discerned in the presence of ancient grammatical forms in the text as well as *matres lectionis*, a stage in the orthography of vowels which predated the Masoretic text. Occasionally, it is clear that the Masoretes were either at a loss to understand the text they received or that they misread the text.

*Hapax legomena*, words that occur only once in Scripture, abound in the Psalms, making interpretation even more difficult. Since words are defined by their use in literature, the lack of other biblical examples of a *hapax* makes determining its meaning difficult.

These problems can be overcome to a large degree by understanding the nature of the language. Since Hebrew is based by and large on a triliteral root system, (words are built on the foundation of a three-letter root, the basic meaning of the word being inherent in the root and other aspects of the word being indicated by affixes and vowels), the meaning of a *hapax* or other difficult word can often be determined by analyzing the root in terms of the word's context.

The parallelism of Hebrew poetry can also be used to unlock the meaning of an obscure word. Similarities in grammatical structure between parallel lines can be clues to the semantic parallels.

Thus, if a word in one line of synonymous parallelism is obscure, it can be assumed to be somewhat synonymous with its corresponding element in the parallel line.

Evidence from cognate languages can also be a clue to understanding obscure terms. For example, if Akkadian has a root analogous to that of an obscure biblical term, the use of the cognate root in Akkadian may be evidence for the word's use in the Bible.

Ugaritic, the Canaanite dialect of the tablets found at Ras Shamra, is valuable cognate evidence. The close relationship of Ugaritic to Biblical Hebrew and the early date of the tablets (ca. the time of Moses) make the Ugaritic evidence especially significant. Also, the poetry of the Ras Shamra tablets contains many idioms that are also found in the Psalms.

Mitchell Dahood, in his commentary for the *Anchor Bible*, undertook a thorough reading of the Psalms in light of the Ugaritic evidence. Although not all his suggestions should be accepted, as he himself admitted would be the case (*Psalms I*, xx), he does demonstrate the possibility of finding solutions to difficulties without resorting to textual emendation. Whether or not Dahood's solutions are valid, he does open the door to future answers to difficult problems.

It is commendable that Dahood avoids emending the text unnecessarily; in fact, he holds that only about half a dozen emendations are necessary. This is in contrast to others who emend the text at will. Douglass Stuart, for example, reconstructs the text, even in the absence of textual evidence that it is corrupt, when it does not match his notions of meter. He writes, "Textual emendation may be required, sometimes on a major scale.... [The translator] may find it necessary to improve upon the received text, with or without compelling evidence from the versions" (*Studies in Early Hebrew Meter*, 21). This demonstrates a low view of the biblical text, especially since scholars have not come to a consensus as to how to understand Hebrew meter.

## Technical Terms

Several obscure technical terms occur in the Psalms. The most common is s̲elāh (HED #5734), which occurs seventy-one times in the Psalms and three times in Habakkuk. It probably is derived from the verb s̲ālal (HED #5744), which means "to lift up," indicating a musical interlude or possibly an increase in volume. These possibilities are supported by a Greek manuscript that translates the word diapsalma. Jewish tradition interpreted the term as meaning "forever," indicating the place for a benediction. Another explanation is that it is a signal for worshipers to prostrate themselves before the LORD. A common understanding of the term is that it indicates a time of pausing and reflecting on the words just heard.

Other technical terms refer to the type of the Psalm. Mizmôr (HED #4344), used over fifty times in the Psalms, means "psalm." Shîr (HED #8302) indicates that the Psalm is a "song," maskîl (HED #5030) a teaching poem," tᵉphillāh (HED #8940), a "prayer," tᵉhillāh (HED #8747), a "song of praise" for the performance of some great deed. Shiggāyôn (HED #8150) and mikhtām (HED #4524) are obscure.

# Overview

## Outline

I. Book One 1–41
  A. Introduction 1–2
    1. The way of the righteous 1
    2. The reign of the anointed 2
  B. Davidic Psalms 3–41
    1. Fleeing from Absalom 3
    2. Sleeping in peace 4
    3. The wicked—their throat an open grave 5
    4. How long, O LORD, how long? 6
    5. Concerning Cush, a Benjamite 7
    6. How majestic his name 8
    7. The LORD, a refuge 9
    8. The fall of the wicked 10
    9. The LORD in his heavenly Temple 11
    10. The LORD, the Protector 12
    11. A cry for help 13
    12. The corruption of humanity 14
    13. The righteous not shaken 15
    14. Holy One not to see decay 16
    15. The apple of God's eye 17
    16. The salvation of the LORD 18
    17. The fear of the LORD 19
    18. May the LORD answer you 20
    19. The king rejoicing in the LORD 21
    20. My God, why have you forsaken me? 22
    21. The LORD is my shepherd 23
    22. The earth is the LORD's 24
    23. Remember not the sins of my youth 25
    24. Try me and know my mind 26
    25. That I may dwell in the house of the LORD 27
    26. The LORD a fortress 28
    27. Give glory to the LORD 29
    28. Joy comes in the morning 30
    29. Mercy in a time of distress 31
    30. Blessed is he whose sins are forgiven 32
    31. Contend for me, my God 33
    32. The LORD's love reaches to the heavens 34
    33. Contend for me, my God 35
    34. The LORD's love reaches to the heavens 36
    35. Do not envy sinners 37
    36. The LORD's arrows have pierced me 38
    37. My days but a handbreadth 39
    38. He lifted me out of the mire 40
    39. The LORD delivers from times of trouble 41
II. Book Two 42–72
  A. Of the sons of Korah 42
  B. Rescue me from wicked men 43

C. Of the sons of Korah 44–49
   1. A history of God's salvation 44
   2. A song for the king 45
   3. An ever present help in time of need 46
   4. Clap your hands all ye people 47
   5. Great is the LORD and worthy of praise 48
   6. Man does not live forever 49
D. A Psalm of Asaph 50
E. Davidic Psalms 51–65
   1. After adultery with Bathsheba 51
   2. The ruin of the wicked 52
   3. The fool says, "There is no God" 53
   4. Save me by your name 54
   5. God brings down the wicked 55
   6. When the Philistines seized David 56
   7. When David fled from Saul 57
   8. The righteous are still rewarded 58
   9. God is my fortress 59
   10. God in battle 60
   11. I long to dwell in God's tent 61
   12. God rewards according to deeds 62
   13. God's love better than life 63
   14. God shoots the enemies with arrows 64
   15. The provision of God 65
F. A Psalm of celebration 66
G. Davidic Psalms 67–70
   1. May all the peoples praise God 67
   2. Let God arise 68
   3. Rescue me from the mire 69
   4. God is my Helper and Deliverer 70
H. From birth I have relied on you 71
I. A Psalm of Solomon 72

III. Book Three 73–89
A. Psalms of Asaph 73–83
   1. God is good to Israel 73
   2. Why have you rejected us, O God? 74
   3. Give thanks to God 75
   4. God is a righteous Judge 76
   5. God leads his people like a shepherd 77
   6. Teaching of righteousness 78
   7. The destruction of Jerusalem 79
   8. Make your face shine upon us 80
   9. Sing to God for joy 81
   10. God is the Judge 82
   11. Entreating God to help 83
B. Psalms of the sons of Korah 84; 85
   1. My soul longs for the courts of the LORD 84
   2. Restore us again, O God 85
C. A Psalm of David 86

# Overview

8. Unless the LORD builds the house 127
9. Blessed are they who fear the LORD 128
10. Plowmen have plowed my back 129
11. From the depths I cry to the LORD 130
12. My heart is not proud 131
13. Do not reject your anointed one 132
14. How good is unity 133
15. May the LORD's servants praise him 134

G. Psalms of praise 135; 136
1. May the LORD's ministers praise Him 135
2. His love endures forever 136

H. Exiled to Babylon 137

I. Psalms of David 138–145
1. I will praise you with all my heart 138
2. LORD, You know me 139
3. Rescue me, O LORD 140
4. Do not let my heart be drawn to evil 141
5. Listen to my cry 142
6. I meditate on your works 143
7. What is man that You care for him? 144
8. I will exalt the LORD 145

J. Hallel Psalms 146–150
1. Praise the LORD, O my soul 146
2. How good it is to sing praises 147
3. Praise the LORD from the heavens 148
4. Sing unto the LORD a new song 149
5. Let everything that has breath 150

# Overview

## Summary

In its canonical form, the Book of Psalms is divided into five books (Pss. 1–41; 42–72; 73–89; 90–106; 107–150), each of which ends with a doxology. The doxologies may have been original to the Psalms in which they occur, but they may have been added as a conclusion to each of the books. There is ancient evidence that this division was intended to be analogous to the five Books of Moses (Midrash, Ps. 1:1).

The Masoretic text and the Septuagint differ as to the division of some of the Psalms, but both contain 150 Psalms, although the Septuagint has an additional apocryphal psalm at the end. Psalm 116 in the Masoretic text is broken into Pss. 114 and 115 in the Septuagint, and Ps. 147 is 146 and 147, while in the Septuagint, Ps. 9 combines the Masoretic Pss. 9 and 10, and 113 combines Pss. 115 and 116.

There was a purpose in the organization of the Psalms, although it is not always apparent. Psalms 1 and 2 form an introduction to the Psalter, and Ps. 150 provides a doxology to conclude the Book. Psalm 3 seems to be a morning Psalm, while Ps. 4 is an evening Psalm.

Psalms 3–41 are all ascribed by their titles to David, except for Pss. 10 and 33, which do not contain titles. However, Ps. 10 appears to be a continuation of the acrostic of Ps. 9, and Ps. 33 is similar to Ps. 32. Besides, there is some evidence of Davidic authorship of Ps. 33, as it has a title in the Septuagint ascribing it to David.

Psalm 42 begins what is often called the Elohistic Psalter, because the name "Elohim" occurs much more frequently than the divine name "Yahweh." This collection goes through Ps. 89, combining the second and third books of the Psalter. The second book (Pss. 42–72) is mostly a collection of Davidic Psalms, although Ps. 72 is ascribed to Solomon, and Pss. 42–49 are ascribed to the sons of Korah.

The Psalms of the third book (Pss. 73–89) are mostly ascribed to Asaph (Pss. 73–83). Psalms 84–88 are ascribed to the sons of Korah, except for Ps. 86, which is ascribed to David. Psalm 89, ascribed to Ethan the Ezrahite, concludes the book.

Book Four consists of Pss. 90–106, which are mostly "orphan Psalms"; i.e., they are not ascribed to any author. The group is largely made up of Psalms of ascension to the throne. Psalms 105 and 106 are historical Psalms, which recount God's past dealings with Israel.

The final book of the Psalms (Pss. 107–150) is made up mainly of Davidic Psalms and orphan Psalms. Psalms 113–118 are the Egyptian Hallel Psalms. Psalm 119 is an acrostic Psalm, which eulogizes God's Word.

Psalms 120–134 are the pilgrim Psalms, or the "Songs of Ascents." Each of these has a superscript that ties it to the collection. "Ascents" in these titles has been interpreted as "extolments," referring to the praise aspect of the Psalms (Dahood, AB, *Psalms III*, 193), but they are not all praise Psalms. Another explanation is that it refers to a step-like parallelism, but other Psalms outside this collection exhibit this structure, while some of the Songs of Ascents do not. The Psalms probably are connected with the pilgrimage of the exiles returning from Babylon. The word translated "ascents" could be related to 'ālāh (HED #6148), which means "to go up," in regard to pilgrimages (cf. Ps. 24:3; Isa. 2:3). The Psalms may have been sung by returning exiles or later pilgrims commemorating the event. A Jewish tradition claims that the fifteen Psalms of the collection correspond to the fifteen steps going up to the court of Israel from the court of the women in the Temple.

Psalm 137 is an imprecatory Psalm, which concerns the Exile. The next few Psalms (138–145) are attributed to David. And the last Psalms are known as the Hallel collection, because they are filled with praise to God. Psalm 150 serves as a doxology for the Psalter.

# APPENDICES

---

*Explanation of Grammar*

*Translations of the Various Versions*

*Books of the Old and New Testaments and the Apocrypha*

*How the Old Testament Came to Us*

*Manuscripts*

---

# Appendices

## APPENDIX A

### Explanation of Grammar

#### Explanation of Verb Stems

There are basically seven verb stems in the Hebrew language. Verbs are either active or passive, and they deal with past, present or future actions or conditions. The mood of the verb relates the general meaning, but context—the relationships of words within the literary unit—always determines the final meaning.

This volume uses a verb numbering system formatted to give (1) the word number; (2) the mood; (3) the tense; and (4) the person, gender and number. The first number is to the left of the decimal point, and the last three numbers are to the right of the decimal point. Following is a brief explanation of the numbers that occur to the right of the decimal point.

***Mood (first position)***

1. *Qal*—simple active verb stem. The Qal mood accounts for most of the verbs in the Old Testament. Qal usually indicates an action of the subject (*he told*). It can also indicate the state of the subject (*he was old*).

2. *Niphal*—the simple passive or reflexive counterpart of the Qal stem. Used passively, Niphal means the action of the verb is received by the subject (*he was told,* or, *it was told*). Although rare, Niphal is sometimes used reflexively, meaning that the subject performs the action of the verb upon himself or herself (*he realized*). The reflexive meaning is usually expressed using the Hithpael.

3. *Piel*—the intensive active or causative stem. The most common use of the Piel is as intensification of the action of the verb (*he often told,* or, *he fully explained*). It sometimes, however, is used in a causative sense like the Hiphil (*he caused to learn/he taught*).

4. *Pual*—the intensive passive counterpart of the Piel stem (*he was often told,* or, *he was completely informed,*or, *it was fully explained*).

5. *Hiphil*—the causative active counterpart of the Qal stem (*he caused to tell*). Sometimes it is used in a declarative sense (*he declared guilty*). Some Hiphil verbs are closer to the meaning of the simple active use of the Qal stem (*he destroyed*). Finally, some Hiphil verbs do not fit any of these categories, and they must be understood by their context.

6. *Hophal*—the causative passive counterpart of the Hiphil stem (*he was caused to tell*).

7. *Hithpael*—reflexive action (*he realized*). However, some Hithpael verbs are translated in a simple active sense like the Qal stem (*he prayed*), since the one performing the action is not transferring that action to anyone or anything else.

***Tense (second position)***

1. *Perfect.* The Hebrew perfect may be translated as a simple completed action (*he walked* to the store). It may also be translated as a *past perfect*, which is an action completed prior to a point of reference in past time (she gave money as *she had promised*). The perfect is translated in the present tense when the verb concerns the subject's attitude, experience, perception or

state of being (*you are old,* or, *I love you*). It may also represent action that is viewed as completed as soon as it was mentioned (*I anoint you* as king over Israel, 2 Ki. 9:3).

When this tense is used in promises, prophecies and threats, it commonly means that the action of the verb is certain and imminent (A star *will come* out of Jacob, Num. 24:17). Since this use is common in the prophetic writings, it is usually called the *prophetic perfect.* It is usually translated into English as either a present or future tense verb.

Finally, when the perfect occurs with the vav conjunctive prefixed, it is usually translated in the future tense (*I will lie down* with my fathers, Gen. 47:30).

2. *Imperfect.* This tense indicates an incomplete action or state. Perhaps the most common use of the imperfect is to describe a simple action in future time (*he will reign* over you). The imperfect is also used to express habitual or customary actions in the past, present or future (And so *he did* year by year, 1 Sam. 1:7; A son *honors* his father, Mal. 1:6; The LORD *will reign* forever and ever, Exo. 15:18). The imperfect frequently expresses contingency, and English modal auxiliaries such as *may, can, shall, might, could, should, would* and *perhaps* are used with the verb (Who is the LORD that I *should obey* his voice?, Exo. 5:2).

The modal use of the imperfect is common after the particles אֵיךְ (how) and אוּלַי (perhaps), and the interrogatives מָה (what), מִי (who) and לָמָּה (why). Two other uses of the imperfect are the *jussive* and *cohortative.*

The jussive expresses a desire for action from a third person subject (I pray *let* the king *remember* the LORD your God, 2 Sam. 14:11; *May* the LORD *lift up* his countenance unto you, Num. 6:26). The cohortative expresses the speaker's desire or intention to act, so it occurs only in the first person singular and plural (*let me pass* through the roadblock, *let us draw near* to God).

3. *Imperative.* This tense occurs only in the second person singular and plural. The main use of the imperative is in direct commands (*Separate yourself* from me, Gen. 13:9). The imperative can also grant permission (*Go up,* and *bury* your father, according as he made you swear, Gen. 50:6). It may also disclose a request (*Give* them, I pray, a talent of silver, 2 Ki. 5:22).

Imperatives may convey a wish (*May you be* the mother of thousands of millions, Gen. 24:60).

Imperatives are even used sarcastically (Come to Bethel and *transgress,* Amos 4:4).

Some uses of the imperative, however, do not carry the ordinary force of meaning. Sometimes it emphatically and vividly communicates a promise or prediction (And in the third year *sow* and *reap, plant* vineyards and *eat* the fruits thereof, 2 Ki. 19:29).

4. *Infinitive.* The infinitive occurs in either the absolute or the construct state. Infinitives express the idea of a verb, but they are not limited by person, gender and number.

The infinitive absolute is used in several ways. It most often stands before a finite verb of the same root to intensify the certainty or force of the verbal idea (You shall *surely* die, Gen. 2:17). It also functions as a verbal noun (*slaying* cattle and *killing* sheep, Isa. 22:13; It is not good *to eat* much honey, Prov. 25:27).

The infinitive absolute sometimes occurs after an imperative (Kill me *at once*, Num. 11:15; Listen *diligently* to me, Isa. 55:2). It may also occur after a verb to show continuance or repetition (*Keep on* hearing but do not understand, Isa. 6:9; and it went *here and there*, Gen. 8:7). Frequently, it is used in place of an imperative (*Remember[ing]* the Sabbath day, Exo. 20:8). Sometimes it is used in place of a finite verb (and he *made* him ruler over all the land of Egypt, Gen. 41:43).

The infinitive construct also has several uses. It may function as the object or subject of a sentence (I know not how *to go out* or *come in*, 1 Ki. 3:7; *to obey* is better than sacrifice, 1 Sam. 15:22). However, it most often occurs after the subject to express purpose (he turned aside *to see*, Exo. 3:4). The infinitive construct may also occur after a finite verb to express a gerundial meaning (The people sin against the LORD *by eating* blood, 1 Sam. 14:33). Moreover, it is frequently used in temporal clauses (*When you eat* from it, you shall surely die, Gen. 2:17).

5. *Participle*. This tense in the Hebrew does not indicate person, but it does indicate gender and number. It may be either masculine or feminine, and either singular or plural. Participles may also occur in either the active or passive voice. However, only the Qal stem has both active and passive participles. Verbal tense is not indicated by the Hebrew participle, so it must be inferred from the context, whether it is *past*, *present* or *future* tense. Uses of the participle include the following.

Since it is a verbal noun, a participle may indicate a continuous activity or state (I saw also the LORD *sitting* upon a throne, Isa. 6:1). Participles may also be used as attributive or predicative adjectives. As an attributive adjective, it follows the noun it modifies, and it agrees with the noun in gender, number and definiteness (blessed is *he who comes* in the name of the LORD, Ps. 118:26; the glory of the LORD was like a *devouring* fire, Exo. 24:17).

As a predicative adjective, the participle follows the noun it modifies and agrees with the noun in gender and number, but it never has the definite article (the man is *standing*, the women are *standing*). When the noun is indefinite, the participle may be attributive or predicative, so context must determine the correct translation. Participles are also used as substantives (one who climbs, *climber*; one who works, *worker*; one who loves, *lover*).

***Person, Gender, and Number (third position)***

*Person*—whether the verb is *first person* (I, we), *second person* (you) or *third person* (he, she, it, they).

*Gender*—whether the verb is *masculine, feminine* or *common*.

*Number*—whether the verb is *singular* or *plural* (Infinitives are only indicated as construct or absolute. Participles are indicated as active or passive, masculine or feminine and singular or plural).

## Verb Identification Chart

Following is the verb identification chart used in this volume, for the three digits following the decimal of every verb. This pattern follows the usual verb chart found in Hebrew grammars.

First numeral after decimal:

1. Qal
2. Niphal
3. Piel
4. Pual
5. Hiphil
6. Hophal
7. Hithpael

Second numeral after decimal:

1. Perfect
2. Imperfect
3. Imperative
4. Infinitive
5. Participle

Third numeral after decimal:

| | *Perfect* | *Imperfect* | *Imperative* | *Infinitive* | *Participle* |
|---|---|---|---|---|---|
| 1. | 3ms | 3ms | 2ms | construct | active ms |
| 2. | 3fs | 3fs | 2fs | absolute | active mp |
| 3. | 2ms | 2ms | 2mp | | active fs |
| 4. | 2fs | 2fs | 2fp | | active fp |
| 5. | 1cs | 1cs | | | passive ms |
| 6. | 3cp | 3mp | | | passive mp |
| 7. | 2mp | 3fp | | | passive fs |
| 8. | 2fp | 2mp | | | passive fp |
| 9. | 1cp | 2fp | | | |
| 0. | | 1cp | | | |

## Grammatical Abbreviations*:

abs=absolute; act=active; adj=adjective; adv=adverb; art=article; c=common (neither masculine, nor feminine); cj=conjunction; con=construct (genitival); dem pron=demonstrative pronoun; do=direct object; f=feminine; impf=imperfect; impv=imperative; inf=infinitive; intrg=interrogative; intrg part=interrogative particle; intrj=interjection; juss=jussive (optative); m=masculine; n=noun; neg part=negative particle; num=number; p=plural; part=particle; pass=passive; pers pron=personal pronoun; pf=perfect; pn=proper noun; prep=preposition; ps=pronominal suffix; ptc=participle; rel part=relative particle; rel pron=relative pronoun; s=singular; sub=substantive; v=verb; 1=1st person; 2=2nd person; 3=3rd person.

*construct relationships are shown by italicizing.

## APPENDIX B

### Translations of the Various Versions

In order to provide the reader with a sample representation of many versions of the Old Testament, the following versions are compared with the King James Version. These versions are used as much as needed to illustrate various shades of meaning and main differences among the translations. All of the material could not be included. Rather, the best representation of the thirty-three versions listed below has been used.

| **Abbreviation:** | **Translation:** |
|---|---|
| Anchor | Anchor Bible Commentaries |
| ASV | American Standard Version |
| BB | Dutton's Basic Bible |
| Beck | An American Translation |
| Berkeley | Berkeley's Version in Modern English |
| Darby | Darby's The Holy Scripture |
| Fenton | Fenton's Holy Bible |
| Geneva | Geneva Bible |
| Good News | Good News, The Bible in Today's English |
| Goodspeed | The Bible, An American Translation by Edgar Goodspeed |
| JB | The Jerusalem Bible |
| KJVII | King James Version II |
| Knox | The Holy Bible |
| LIVB | Living Bible |
| MAST | The Holy Scriptures According to the Masoretic Text |
| MLB | Modern Language Bible |
| Moffatt | A New Translation of the Bible |
| MRB | The Modern Readers Bible |
| NAB | New American Bible |
| NASB | New American Standard Bible |
| NCB | New Catholic Bible |
| NCV | New Century Version |
| NEB | New English Bible |
| NIV | New International Version |
| NKJV | New King James Version |
| NRSV | New Revised Standard Version |
| Phillips | The Old Testament in Modern English |
| REB | Revised English Bible |
| Rotherham | Rotherham's Emphasized Bible |
| RSV | Revised Standard Version |
| Torah | A New Translation of the Holy Scriptures According to the Traditional Hebrew Text |
| Tyndale | Tyndale's Old Testament |
| Young | Young's Literal Translation |

# APPENDIX C

## Books of the Old and New Testaments and the Apocrypha

### Old Testament

Genesis
Exodus
Leviticus
Numbers
Deuteronomy
Joshua
Judges
Ruth
1 Samuel
2 Samuel
1 Kings
2 Kings
1 Chronicles
2 Chronicles
Ezra
Nehemiah
Esther
Job
Psalms
Proverbs
Ecclesiastes
Song of Songs
Isaiah
Jeremiah
Lamentations
Ezekiel
Daniel
Hosea
Joel
Amos
Obadiah
Jonah
Micah
Nahum
Habakkuk
Zephaniah
Haggai
Zechariah
Malachi

### New Testament

Matthew
Mark
Luke
John
Acts
Romans
1 Corinthians
2 Corinthians
Galatians
Ephesians
Philippians
Colossians
1 Thessalonians
2 Thessalonians
1 Timothy
2 Timothy
Titus
Philemon
Hebrews
James
1 Peter
2 Peter
1 John
2 John
3 John
Jude
Revelation

### Books of the Apocrypha

1 & 2 Esdras
Tobit
Judith
Additions to Esther
Wisdom of Solomon
Ecclesiasticus of the Wisdom of Jesus Son of Sirach
Baruch
Prayer of Azariah and the Song of the Three Holy Children
Susanna
Bel and the Dragon
The Prayer of Manasses
Maccabees 1–4

## APPENDIX D

### How the Old Testament Came to Us

The Hebrew canon was written over a period of about 1000 years (1450–400 B.C.). These books were considered inspired and therefore canonical from the time they were written. The word *canon* means a "straight edge," "rod" or "ruler." It came to mean "the rule" or "the standard" of divine inspiration and authority. The only true test of canonicity is the testimony of God regarding the authority of his own Word.

Protestants and Jews have always agreed to a standard 39 books of the Old Testament as canonical, although the Jews have divided them differently to form 22, 24 or 36 books. The Roman Catholic Church, since the Council of Trent in A.D. 1546, also accepts seven books of the Apocrypha (Tobit, Judith, Wisdom, Ecclesiasticus, Baruch, 1 and 2 Maccabees, and some additions to the books of Esther and Daniel) as canonical.

We no longer have access to the infallible original manuscripts (called "the autographs") of the Hebrew Scriptures. The earliest manuscripts in some cases are a thousand years removed from the original writing. However, they constitute our primary authority as to the inspired Word of God, and all copies and orthodox translations are dependent upon the best and earliest Hebrew and Aramaic manuscripts. We must review all written evidence upon which our modern editions of the Hebrew Bible are based and have some knowledge of the wide range of evidence with which Old Testament textual criticism deals. Hebrew texts take priority in value, since God's revelation came first to Israel in the Hebrew tongue. Moreover, in the instances where very early manuscripts have been found, divine guidance is evident in the extreme accuracy of the copies.

Liberal scholars consider only the human side of the equation, thereby rejecting inspiration. From a nearly spiritually dead European church came the school of theology which developed a theory on the development of the Biblical text known as Documentary Hypothesis. Due, in particular, to the development of deistic philosophy and evolutionary science, the stage was set for literary and redaction criticism of the Bible and the rejection of the supernatural.

As a precursor, however, the humanistic philosophies developed during the Age of Enlightenment made their way into the churches of Europe, sadly producing a spiritual deadness. Consequently, every area of academics was affected, producing an antireligious stupefaction upon the milieu of the scholarly world.

With regard to the Pentateuch, the most famous of these theories is known as JEDP. Julius Wellhausen is perhaps the most famous proponent of this theory publishing his version in the 1800s.

The Documentary Hypothesis method of document analysis was used on the works of Homer, Horace and Shakespeare, as well as on works purported to have been written by them. However, it was eventually used only to attack the validity and reliability of the Bible. The "J" document is titled as such because of the use of *Yahweh* (sometimes called Jehovah), and the "E" document is titled as such because of the use of *Elohim* for God. Whether God's name or title is used, it is speculated, determines whether that section of the first Books of the Pentateuch is from the "J" or the "E" document. It is theorized that if the entire Pentateuch were written by one person, only one name would be used for God. The dozens of etymological unifying elements threaded throughout the Pentateuch are simply ignored. The "D" document is considered a *deuteronomic work*, and the "P" document is considered primarily a *priestly editorial*. Dates of these documents are set at 950 B.C. for J, 850 B.C. for E, 625 B.C. for D and 450 B.C. for P. The first five Books of the Bible, known for millennia as the Books of Moses, are viewed by JEDP theorists as four documents written over hundreds of years instead of one document written by Moses, as the Bible itself claims.

The major assumptions of the Documentary Hypothesis are (1) the guideline of divine names (Yahweh and Elohim) as evidence of diverse authorship; (2) the origin of J, E and P as separate documents, written at different periods of time; (3) the separate origin of E as distinct from J and compared prior to J; and (4) the origin of D in the reign of Josiah (621 B.C.). As referred to above, the essential purpose of the JEDP theory was to discount the miraculous and the prophetical. However, with the discovery of the Dead Sea Scrolls, this theory has been thoroughly disproven to the point that no Bible scholar who understands the Bible to be inspired can possibly subscribe to such a theory.

With regard to Isaiah, two or three separate writers are usually proposed; but theories range all the way up to nine. Once again, the so-called stylistic differences noted are merely a pretext for discounting the miraculous and the prophetical.

The Dead Sea Scrolls have clearly pointed to the unity of the Old Testament, particularly with regard to the Pentateuch and Isaiah. Moreover, the unity of each Book defends the miracles and prophecies of the Bible as genuine and thoroughly accurate.

## APPENDIX E

## Manuscripts

### The Masoretic Text

The Masoretic Text (MT) was developed A.D. 500–950, and it gave the final form to the Old Testament. It preserved in writing the oral tradition (*masorah*) concerning correct vowels and accents, and the number of occurrences of rare words of unusual spellings.

### Vowel Pointing of YHWH

Due to Jewish fears of bringing upon themselves possible retribution for breaking the third commandment, they began refusing to pronounce the divine name. This began in Nehemiah's time. It became the normal practice to substitute the title "Lord" (*adonai*) for the name Yahweh when reading aloud. The Masoretes, to indicate this replacement, inserted the vowels from *Adonai* under the consonants of YaHWeH, resulting in the word YeHoWaH, which came to be pronounced as *Jehovah*. Scholars of the Renaissance period misunderstood the purpose of this vowel pointing and began pronouncing the name as *Jehovah*, rather than pronouncing the name *Yahweh* or the title *Adonai*. This erroneous pronunciation became so common that many are still generally unwilling to accept the more correct pronunciation, Yahweh.

#### Qere Kethib

The terms are used to refer to textual variants that are understood, though not written. The word *qere* means "what is read," and the word *kethib* means "what is written." (Hence, "read for what is written.") One classic example of a *qere kethib* is mentioned in the preceding paragraph. Although the text has *written* Yahweh, Adonai is *read,* the hearers understanding what was meant by the reader. *Qere kethibs* were marginal notes written to the side of the manuscript.

#### The Masoretes

The Masoretes deserve much credit for their painstaking care in preserving the consonantal text that was entrusted to them. They devoted greater attention to accurately preserving the Hebrew Scriptures than has ever been given to any ancient literature in human history. They left the consonantal text exactly as it was given to them, refusing to make even the most obvious corrections. The work of the Masoretes has preserved for us a text which essentially duplicates the text considered authoritative at the time of Christ. Moreover, the Qumran evidence is that we have a Hebrew text with a true record of God's revelation.

### The Major Codices

1. British Museum Oriental 4445—a copy of the Pentateuch consonantal text (A.D. 850), vowel points added one century later, most of Genesis and Deuteronomy missing.

2. Codex Cairensus (C)—former prophets and latter prophets, copied by Aaron ben Asher (A.D. 895).

3. Leningrad MS—latter prophets (A.D. 916).

4. Leningrad MS B-19A—entire Old Testament, contains Ben Asher Masoretic Text (A.D. 1010), faithful copy of A.D. 980 MS (since lost), basis for Kittel's *Biblia Hebraica* (3rd edition and subsequent editions).

5. Samaritan Pentateuch—earliest MSS of this version is still in Nablus, withheld by Samaritan sectarians from publication, about 6,000 variants from MT (mostly spelling differences), contains biased sectarian insertions, no MS of the Samaritan Pentateuch known to be older than tenth century A.D.

6. Bologna Edition of the Psalter--A.D. 1477.

7. Soncino Edition of the Old Testament—(vowel-pointed) A.D. 1488.

8. Second Bomberg Edition of the Old Testament—(A.D. 1525–26) printed under the patronage of Daniel Bomberg, became basis for all modern editions up to 1929; contains text of Jacob ben Chayim, with Masorah and Rabbinical notes.

## The Qumran Manuscripts

The Qumran manuscripts, or Dead Sea Scrolls, were discovered in a series of caves near the canyon of Wadi Qumran, along the northwest coast of the Dead Sea.

Technical identification of these documents consists of: (1) a number specifying which of the caves was the scene of the discovery of the document, (2) an abbreviation of the name of the book itself and (3) a superscript letter indicating the order in which the manuscript came to light, as opposed to other copies of the same book.

Thus, the famous Dead Sea Scroll of Isaiah is labeled 1 QIsa, meaning that it was the first discovered, or most important, manuscript of Isaiah found in Cave 1 at Wadi Qumran. This particular discovery severely damaged any theories of multiple authorship. The following is a list of the most important finds at Wadi Qumran.

1. Dead Sea Scroll of Isaiah (1QIsa)—(150-100 B.C.) entire sixty-six chapters, same family of MS as MT.

2. Habakkuk Commentary (1QpHb)—(100-50 B.C.) chapters one and two only, with commentary notes between verses; commentary is usually concerned with how each verse is fulfilled in recent (Hasmonean) history and current events.

3. Hebrew University Isaiah Scroll (1QIsb)—(copied ca. 50 B.C.) substantial portions of chapters 41–66, closer to MT than 1QIsa is.

4. 1Q Leviticus fragments—(fourth or second century B.C.) a few verses each of chapters 19–22, written in paleo-Hebrew script.

5. 4Q Deuteronomy-B—32:41–43, written in hemistichs as poetry, not as prose, no date suggested.

6. 4Q Samuel-A—1 Samuel 1, 2, twenty-seven fragments (first century B.C.).

7. 4Q Samuel-B—1 Samuel 16, 19, 21, 23 (225 B.C. or earlier).

8. 4Q Jeremiah-A (no date suggested).

9. 4Q XII-A (XII signifies a MS of the minor prophets)—(third century B.C.) cursive script.

10. 4Q Qoha—(second century B.C.) cursive text of Ecclesiastes, derived from a source that is at least third century B.C. or earlier.

11. 4Q Exodus—a fragment of chapter 1.

12. 4Q Exodus—portions of chapters 7, 29, 30, 32 (and perhaps others), written in paleo-Hebrew script.

13. 4Q Numbers—written in square Hebrew with Samaritan type expansions (after 27:33 there is an insert derived from Deuteronomy 3:21).

14. 4Q Deuteronomy-A—chapter 32 (Song of Moses).

15. 11Q Psalms—a manuscript of Psalms from cave 11, copied in formal bookhand style of the Herodian period, the bottom third of each page has been lost, thirty-three Psalms are preserved with fragments containing portions of four others, Psalms represented are 93, 101–103, 105, 109, 118, 119, 121–130, 132–146, 148–150, and 151 from the LXX.

16. Nash Papyrus—(100–50 B.C.) contains the Decalogue and the Shema (Exo. 20:1–17 and Deut. 6:4–9), purchased by W. L. Nash from an Egyptian antique dealer.

### The Aramaic Targums

The word Targum means "interpretation," and these documents became necessary because the Hebrew people lost touch with their ancestral Hebrew during the Babylonian exile and Persian empire period. First there was a need for an interpreter in the synagogue services, and later the interpretations were written down. However, there is no evidence of a written Targum until about A.D. 200. Because their primary purpose was for interpretation, they have limited value for textual criticism. Following is a list of several targums:

1. The Targum of Onkelos on the Torah—(ca. third century A.D.) produced by Jewish scholars in Babylon. Traditionally assigned to a certain Onkelos, supposedly a native of Pontus. It is not quoted by extant Palestinian sources earlier than A.D. 1000.

2. The Targum of Jonathan ben Uzziel on the Prophets section (i.e., Joshua–Kings, Isaiah–Malachi)—(fourth century A.D.) composed in Babylonian circles. Far more free in its rendering of the Hebrew text than in Onkelos.

3. The Targum of Pseudo-Jonathan on the Torah—(ca. A.D. 650) a mixture of Onkelos and Midrashic materials.

4. The Jerusalem Targum on the Torah—(ca. A.D. 700).

### The Septuagint (LXX)

This is the Greek translation of the Hebrew Old Testament. It was translated for Greek-speaking Jews who knew no Hebrew. It is called the LXX because it was said to have been translated by seventy, or more accurately seventy-two, Jewish scholars. This was the common Bible of New Testament times, and it is quoted frequently in the New Testament. However, Matthew and the author of Hebrews follow a text that is closer to the MT. We must remember that the Septuagint is a translation of inspired Scripture, not the original or even a copy of the original. As such, it is subject to error as is any other translation.

It should also be noted, however, that the translators of the Septuagint were highly skilled to translate an accurate Greek Old Testament that could be depended upon by the New Testament writers for quotations and by early Christians for use. When all of the Greek manuscripts are compared with the Hebrew manuscripts, a rather high degree of textual certainty exists in spite of some difficulties.

# Bibliography


Aharoni, Yohanan. *The Archeology of the Land of Israel: From the Pre-historic Beginnings to the End of the First Temple Period.* trans. by Anson F. Rainey. Philadelphia: The Westminster Press, 1982.

Aharoni, Yohanan. *The Land of the Bible: A Historical Geography*, rev. Philadelphia: The Westminster Press, 1979.

Aharoni, Yohanan, Michael Avi-yonah, Anson F. Rainey, and Ze'ev Safrai. *The Macmillan Bible Atlas*, rev. 3rd ed. New York: Macmillan Publishing Co., 1993.

Allis, Oswald T. *The Old Testament: Its Claims and its Critics*. Philadelphia: Presbyterian and Reformed Publishing Company, 1972.

Amerding, Carl E. *The Old Testament and Criticism*. Grand Rapids, MI: William B. Eerdmans Publishing Company, 1984.

Archer, Gleason L. *Encyclopedia of Bible Difficulties*. Grand Rapids, MI: Zondervan Publishing House, 1982.

Archer, Gleason L. *A Survey of Old Testament Introduction*, rev. ed. Chicago: Moody Press, 1974.

Barker, Kenneth, Gen. ed., *The NIV Study Bible: New International Version*. Grand Rapids, MI: Zondervan Bible Publishers, 1985.

Beitzel, Barry J. *The Moody Atlas of Bible Lands*. Chicago: Moody Press, 1985.

Blaiklock, Edward M. and R. H. Harrison, eds., *The New International Dictionary of Biblical Archeology*. Grand Rapids, MI: Zondervan Publishing House, 1983.

Bromiley, Geoffrey W. ed., *The International Standard Bible Encyclopedia,* 4 vols. Grand Rapids, MI: William B. Eerdmans Publishing Company, 1979.

Brown, Francis, S.R. Driver, Charles A. Briggs. *The New Brown-Driver-Briggs-Gesenius Hebrew and English Lexicon*. Peabody, MA: Hendrickson Publishers, 1979.

Craigie, Peter C. *Ugarit and the Old Testament*. Grand Rapids, MI: William B. Eerdmans Publishing Company, 1985.

Davis, John D. *The Westminster Dictionary of the Bible*, rev. by Henry Snyder Gehman. Philadelphia: The Westminster Press, 1944.

Douglas, J. D., ed., *New Bible Dictionary*. Wheaton, IL: Tyndale House Publishers, Inc., 1962.

Eissfedlt, Otto. *The Old Testament, an Introduction*. Translated by Ackroyd. New York: Harper, 1965.

Even-Shoshan, Abraham, ed., *A New Concordance of the Old Testament Using the Hebrew and Aramaic Text*. Grand Rapids, MI: Baker Book House, 1990.

Finegan, Jack. *Light from the Ancient Past: The Archaeological Background of Judaism and Christianity*, 2nd ed. Princeton: Princeton University Press, 1959.

Freedman, David N. *Pottery, Poetry, and Prophecy.* Winona Lake, IN: Eisenbrauns, 1980.

Freedman, Noel David, ed., *The Anchor Bible Dictionary*, 6 vols. New York: Doubleday, 1992.

Gaebelein, Frank E., ed., *The Expositor's Bible Commentary*, 12 vols., John H. Sailhamer, Walter C. Kaiser, Jr., R. Laird Harris, Ronald B. Allen. Grand Rapids, MI: Zondervan Publishing House, 1990.

Gottwald, Norman K. *The Hebrew Bible—a Socio-Literary Introduction.* Philadelphia: Fortress Press, 1985.

Harris, R. Laird. *Inspiration and Canonicity of the Bible.* Grand Rapids, MI: Zondervan Publishing House, 1957.

Harris, R. Laird, Gleason L. Archer, Jr. and Bruce K. Waltke, eds., *Theological Wordbook of the Old Testament*, 2 Vols. Chicago: Moody Press, 1980.

Harrison, R. K., B. K. Waltke, D. Guthrie, G. D. Fee. *Biblical Criticism: Historical, Literary and Textual.* Grand Rapids, MI: Zondervan Publishing House, 1980.

Harrison, R. K. *Old Testament Times.* Grand Rapids, MI: William B. Eerdmans Publishing Company, 1970.

Holladay, William L. *A Concise Hebrew and Aramaic Lexicon of the Old Testament.* Grand Rapids, MI: William B. Eerdmans Publishing Company, 1971.

Horton, Stanley M., ed., *Systematic Theology.* Springfield, MO: Logion Press, 1994.

Humphreys, W. Lee. *Crisis and Story: An Introduction to the Old Testament.* Mountain View, CA: Mayfield Publishing Co., 1990.

Jennings, F.C. *Studies in Isaiah.* Neptune, NJ: Loizeaux Brothers, 1935, 1970.

Johns, Alger F. *A Short Grammar of Biblical Aramaic.* Berrien Springs, MI: Andrews University Press, 1963.

Kaiser, Walter C., Jr. *Toward an Old Testament Theology.* Grand Rapids, MI: Acadamie Books, 1978.

Kautzch, E. and A. E. Cowley, eds., *Gesenius' Hebrew Grammar.* Oxford: Clarendon Press, 1910.

Keil, C. F. and F. Delitzsch. *Commentary on the Old Testament*, trans. by James Martin. Peabody, MA: Hendrickson Publishers, 1989.

Keller, Werner. *The Bible as History*, 2nd rev. ed., trans. by William Neil and B. H. Rasmussen. New York: Bantam Books, 1982.

# Bibliography

Kelley, Page H. *Biblical Hebrew: An Introductory Grammar*. Grand Rapids, MI: William B. Eerdmans Publishing Company, 1992.

Kitchen, K. A. *The Bible in its World: The Bible and Archaeology Today*. Exeter: Paternoster Press, 1977.

Koehler, Ludwig and Walter Baumgartner. *The Hebrew and Aramaic Lexicon of the Old Testament*, 4 vols. Leiden, Netherlands: E. J. Brill, 1994.

Lasor, William Sanford, David Allan Hubbard, Frederic William Bush. *Old Testament Survey: The Message, Form, and Background of The Old Testament*. Grand Rapids, MI: William B. Eerdmans Publishing Company, 1992.

LaSor, William, David Allan Hubbard, and Frederic William Bush. *Old Testament Survey: The Message, Form, and Background of The Old Testament*. 2nd ed. Grand Rapids, MI: William B. Eerdmans Publishing Co., 1996.

Leupold, H. C. *Exposition of The Psalms*. Grand Rapids, MI: Baker Book House, 1969.

Lewis, C. S. *Reflections on the Psalms*. London: Geoffrey Bles, 1958.

Luckenbill, D. D. *Ancient Records of Assyria and Babylonia*, 2 vols. Chicago: The University of Chicago Press, 1926-1927.

MacLaren, Alexander. The Expositor's Bible: Psalms. New York: A. C. Armstrong & Son, 1890. [Adapted for the Psalms Commentary.]

Martens, Elmer A. *God's Design: A Focus on Old Testament Theology.* Grand Rapids, MI: Baker Book House, 1986.

Mays, James L. *Psalms*. (Interpretation). Louisville: John Knox Press, 1994.

Merrill, Eugene H. *An Historical Survey of the Old Testament*. Nutley, NJ: The Craig Press, 1966.

Miller, J. Maxwell and John H. Hayes. *A History of Ancient Israel and Judah*. Philadelphia: The Westminster Press, 1986.

Owens, John Joseph. *Analytical Key to the Old Testament*, 4 vols. Grand Rapids, MI: Baker Book House, 1990.

Payne, J. Barton. *The Theology of the Older Testament*. Grand Rapids, MI: Academie Books, 1962.

Petersen, David L., Kent Harold Richards. *Interpreting Hebrew Poetry*. Minneapolis: Fortress Press, 1992.

Pfeiffer, Charles F., ed., *Baker's Bible Atlas.* Grand Rapids, MI: Baker Book House, 1961.

Pfeiffer, Charles F. *Old Testament History*. Grand Rapids, MI: Baker Book House, 1987.

Pfeiffer, Charles F., Howard F. Vos, John Rea, eds., *Wycliffe Bible Encyclopedia*, 2 Vols. Chicago: Moody Press, 1975.

Pritchard, James B., ed., *The Ancient Near East: An Anthology of Texts and Pictures*, vol. 1. Princeton: Princeton University Press, 1973.

Purkiser, W. T., ed. *Exploring the Old Testament*. Kansas City, MO: Beacon Hill Press, 1955.

Rahlfs, Alfred, ed., *Septuaginta*. Stuttgart, Germany: Deutsche Bibelgesellschaft Stuttgart, 1935.

Rogerson, John and Philip Davies. *The Old Testament World*. Englewood Cliffs, NJ: Prentice-Hall, 1989.

Schoville, Keith N. *Biblical Archaeology in Focus*. Grand Rapids, MI: Baker Book House, 1982.

Schultz, Samuel J. *The Old Testament Speaks*. New York: Harper & Brothers, Publishers, 1960.

Seow, Choon Leong. *A Grammar for Biblical Hebrew*. Nashville, TN: Abingdon Press, 1987.

Shanks, Hershel, ed., Ancient Israel: *A Short History from Abraham to the Roman Destruction of the Temple*. Englewood Cliffs, NJ: Prentice-Hall, 1988.

Soulen, Richard N. *Handbook of Biblical Criticism*. Atlanta: John Knox Press, 1978.

Stuart, Douglas K. *Studies in early Hebrew meter*. Missoula, MT: Scholars Press, 1976.

Van Der Woude, A. S., ed., *The World of the Old Testament*, trans. by Sierd Woudstra. Grand Rapids, MI: William B. Eerdmans Publishing Company, 1989.

Waltke, Bruce K. and M. O'Connor. *An Introduction to Biblical Hebrew Syntax*. Winona Lake, IN: Eisenbrauns, 1990.

Watts, John D.W. *The Word Biblical Commentary on the Old Testament*, 34 vols. Waco, TX: Word Books, 1987.

Watts, J. Wash. *Old Testament Teaching*. Nashville, TN: Broadman Press, 1967.

White, Wilbert Webster. *Studies in Old Testament Characters*. New York: The Biblical Seminary in New York, 1931.